The People's Almanac

The People's
ALMANAC

By
DAVID WALLECHINSKY
and
IRVING WALLACE

"The exact contrary of what is generally believed is often the truth."

JEAN DE LA BRUYÈRE (1645–1696)

DOUBLEDAY & COMPANY, INC.
Garden City, New York

Library of Congress Cataloging in Publication Data
Main entry under title:

The people's almanac.

  Includes bibliographical references and index.
  I. Wallechinsky, David, 1948–   II. Wallace, Irving, 1916–
AG106.P46   031'.02
ISBN 0-385-04186-1 Trade
ISBN 0-385-04060-1 Paperbound
Library of Congress Catalog Card Number 75-2856

Associate Editor: CAROL ORSAG
Article Editors: ELIZEBETHE AND WALTER KEMPTHORNE
Assistant Editor: JOANNA BOUDREAUX
Editorial Aides: PATRICIA COPPING, DIANE BROWN
Art Editor: DAVID ROSE
Assistant Art Editor: MARGARET L. CARSON
Photograph Editor: GENOA CALDWELL

They Wrote the Original Material

When "The Eds." is used it means the material has been contributed by The Editors of the Almanac.

A.B.	Arthur Bloch	D.W.S.	Dody W. Smith
A.D.	Avram Davidson	D.X.B.	Dianne X. Brown
A.E.	Ann Elwood	E.A.G.	Elizabeth A. Gray
A.J.	Ann Jopling	E.J.G.	Ellen J. Greve
A.W.	Amy Wallace	E.K.	Elizebethe Kempthorne
B.B.	Brian Bland	E.K.S.	Ellen Kerrigan Smith
B.C.	Bill Carero	E.P.	Elizabeth Patelke
B.F.	Bruce Felton	E.R.	Eric Raimy
B.J.	Burr Jerger	E.Re.	Ed Rehmus
B.L.	Bryna Lawson	E.S.L.	Elizabeth S. Lamb
C.B.	Charles Bright	F.B.	Faubion Bowers
C.C.	Chet Cohen	F.C.	Flora Chavez
C.E.	Carol Easton	F.C.D.	Frederick C. Dyer
C.J.	Charlie Jones	F.D.	Frederick Drimmer
C.M.	Cynthia Marker	F.G.	Fred Gardner
C.O.	Carol Orsag	F.M.W.	Frank M. Woolley
C.S.	Carl Schroeder	G.F.	Gieda Fries
D.B.	Dennis Briskin	G.G.	George Gedon
D.C.	David Chesnick	G.T.	George Turner
D.E.	David Eide	H.B.	Herb Borock
D.H.	Dean Huggins	H.C.J.	Heber C. Jentzsch
D.J.	Dennis Jopling	H.E.	Harry Eisenberg
D.P.	Donald Pace	H.E.F.	Herbert E. French
D.Pe.	Doris Peters	H.E.N.	Harry E. Neal
D.P.P.	Daniel P. Perry	H.S.	Harry Squires
D.R.	Diana Robinson	I.S.	Isobel Silden
D.Ru.	Dahlia Rudavsky	I.W.	Irving Wallace
D.S.	Dee Seadler	J.A.	Jack Adler
D.W.	David Wallechinsky	J.B.	John Bronson

J.Be.	John Berger	N.N.	Nelda Neilson
J.B.C.	June Bundy Csida	N.O.	Norman Ober
J.C.	Jacqueline Cowan	P.A.	Paul August
J.Ca.	Jack Campbell	P.B.	Paul Bernstein
J.Ch.	Joe Chaikin	P.Ba.	Patty Barkley
J.Cs.	Joseph Csida	P.S.	Penny Smith
J.Cu.	John Curl	R.C.	Robin Chalek
J.D.	James Dawson	R.E.K.	Robert E. Kennedy
J.E.	James Eversole	R.H.	Robert Hendrickson
J.E.J.	James E. Jones	R.Ho.	Ruth Hoppin
J.F.	Jacques Freydont	R.H.C.	Ralph H. Clark
J.G.	John Galvani	R.K.	Robert Keane
J.L.	Jeanne Lance	R.M.	Ron Mendell
J.L.K.	Jerold L. Kellman	R.Me.	Robert Meyers
J.M.	John Moran	R.Mi.	Ralph Miller
J.M.N.	Joann M. Neath	R.Mo.	Ruth Moskovitz
J.O.	Judy Oringer	R.R.	Ron Rothbart
J.R.	Janet Reinka	R.Rh.	Rusty Rhodes
J.S.	Jack Scagnetti	R.S.	Roberta Satow
J.Sm.	Jennifer Small	R.T.	Richard Trubo
J.T.	John Tomlinson	R.W.	Robert Wennersten
J.Ta.	Judith Tannenbaum	R.Wo.	Richard Wormser
J.W.	Jurgen Wolff	R.W.G.	Roger W. Gale
J.Y.	Jordan Young	S.B.	Sid Blumenthal
K.C.	Karen Caviglia	S.D.P.	Susan D. Poole
L.A.W.	Leonard A. Weisenberg	S.H.Y.	Suzanne Helms-Yanok
L.S.	Lenny Siegel	S.L.W.G.	Stephen L. W. Greene
L.V.J.R.	La Vern J. Rippley	S.N.	Stuart Nixon
M.B.	Mike Baron	S.Sc.	Susan Schaffrath
M.C.	Marc Cadiot	S.Sp.	Sanford Spillman
M.D.	Michael Deasy	S.T.	Susann Tongas
M.G.	Myron Glaser	S.U.	Susan Ulbing
M.H.	Moss Hall	S.V.M.	Sondra Van Meter
M.Ho.	Mark Hoffman	S.W.	Shoshana Wechsler
M.J.M.	Mary J. MacKenzie	T.M.	Tom Mahoney
M.Le.	Michael Levitt	T.S.	Thomas Stuart
M.L.H.	Miriam Lee-Hutchins	W.F.R.	William F. Ryan
M.N.	Maxine Nunes	W.H.	William Hammons
M.S.	Michael Shedlin	W.K.	Walter Kempthorne
M.S.M.	Michael S. Medved	W.L.S.	William L. Siegel
M.T.	Michael Tracy	W.R.	William Rodger
N.B.	Newton Berry	W.W.C.	Walter W. Crites
N.H.M.	Nancy H. Medved	Y.S.R.	Y. S. Russell

They Wrote the Reprinted Material

When "rep." is found in the text, it means reprinted material. The following authors have been reprinted by permission of their publishers.

B.D.   Burke Davis. *Our Incredible Civil War*. New York, Holt, Rinehart and Winston, 1960.

B.H.   Bill Henderson. *The Publish It Yourself Handbook*. Yonkers, N.Y., Pushcart Book Press, 1973.

C.Y.R.   Carroll Y. Rich. *Journal of Popular Culture*. Bowling Green, O., Center for Popular Culture. Spring, 1973.

F.D.   Frederick Drimmer. *Very Special People*. New York, Amjon Publishers, Inc., 1973.

G.T.   George Turner. *George Turner's Book of Gun Fighters*. Amarillo, Tex., Baxter Lane Co., 1972.

H.A.S.   H. Allen Smith. (In: Durant, John, ed. *Yesterday in Sports*. New York, A. S. Barnes and Co., 1956.)

H.M.   Horace Miner. "Body Ritual Among the Nacirema." (In: *American Anthropologist*. June, 1956.)

I.W.   Irving Wallace. *The Fabulous Showman*. New York, Alfred A. Knopf, Inc., 1959.

I.W.   Irving Wallace. *The Nympho and Other Maniacs*. New York, Simon and Schuster, 1971.

J.Du.   John Durant. *Yesterday in Sports*. New York, A. S. Barnes and Co., 1956.

J.N.   Jawaharlal Nehru. *Glimpses of World History*. New York, The John Day Co., Inc., 1942.

L.W.E.   Lawrence W. Erven. *First Aid and Emergency Rescue*. Beverly Hills, Calif., Glencoe Press, 1970.

M.Gl.   Michael Glenn. (In: Agel, Jerome, ed. *Rough Times*. New York, Ballantine, 1973.)

M.M.W.   Margery Miller Welles. (In: Durant, John, ed. *Yesterday in Sports*. New York, A. S. Barnes and Co., 1956.)

N.C.S.   Nancy Caldwell Sorel. *Word People*. New York, American Heritage Press, 1970.

P.H.   Paul Hoch. *Rip Off the Big Game: The Exploitation of Sports by the Power Elite*. Garden City, N.Y., Doubleday & Co., 1972.

P.He.   Piet Hein. *Grooks*. Garden City, N.Y., Doubleday & Co., 1966.

R.H.   Robert Hendrickson. *Human Words*. Radnor, Pa., Chilton Book Co., 1972.

S.H.K.   Sarah H. Killikelly. *Curious Questions*. New York, David McKay Co., Inc., 1900.

T.A.   Tom Allen. *The Quest*. Radnor, Pa., Chilton Book Co., 1965.

T.Sz.   Thomas Szasz. *Ceremonial Chemistry: The Ritual Persecution of Drugs, Addicts, and Pushers*. Garden City, N.Y., Doubleday & Co., 1974.

W.C.V.   William C. Vergara. *Science in the World around Us*. New York, Harper & Row, 1973.

W.E.D.   Wilfred E. Dexter. *Marathi Folk Tales*. London, George G. Harrap & Co., 1938.

Contents

1. THE OTHER SIDE OF THE LOOKING GLASS   1
Predictions by Present-Day Psychics . . . Predictions by Psychics of the Past
. . . Predictions by Modern Scientists . . . Predictions by Others

2. PLUGGING IN AND SHEDDING LIGHT—SPECIAL ARTICLES   31
Snoopy: The Authorized Biography of a Great American by Charles M. Schulz
. . . P. T. Barnum Was Right by Edward A. Merlis . . . The Mafia—Menace
or Myth? by Hank Messick . . . The Men from Interpol by Vaughn Young
. . . On the Way to the 8-Hour Day—The Haymarket Affair by David Wallechinsky . . . Dr. Freud Visits America by Irving Wallace . . . Upton Sinclair
and the EPIC Campaign by Michael S. Medved . . . The Best from Books

3. U.S.A.—RED, WHITE, AND TRUE   76
What Do You Know about the U.S.? . . . Inside the Census Bureau . . . The
U.S. Patent System Today . . . Footnote People in U.S. History . . . What
about the Midnight Ride of William Dawes? . . . America's 1st Riot—the
Doctors' Mob of 1788 . . . Survivors of American History in Foreign Lands—The
Revolutionary War Tory Descendants in Nova Scotia; Confederate Descendants
in Mexico; Mormon Polygamists in Mexico . . . Survivors of American History
in the U.S.A.—The Hessians . . . The Zero Factor . . . Women Who Ran for
Vice-President of the U.S. . . . . Women Who Ran for President of the U.S.

4. U.S.A.—YEAR BY YEAR, 1770–1975   129

5. U.S.A.—THE PRESIDENCY   261
Full Profiles of Selected U.S. Presidents

6. THE ALMIGHTY DOLLAR   340
The Dollar Bill . . . The Great American Credit Card Factory . . . Unusual
Ways of Making a Living . . . Attic and Junkyard . . . Where to Buy a Hap-
piness Insurance Policy . . . The Origin of Famous American Trademarks and
Product Names . . . Let's Audit the IRS

7. WORLD NATIONS AND PEOPLE   360

8. WORLD HISTORY—UNSEALING THE TIME CAPSULE   483
Eyewitness Reports on Highlights of World History: Phoenicians Invent the
Modern Alphabet; The Age of Pericles; Socrates Condemned to Death; The
Ministry and Crucifixion of Jesus Christ; The Crusades; America Gets Its Name;
Luther Posts 95 Theses, Protestantism; Publication of the King James Version
of the Bible; Marx and Engels Write the *Communist Manifesto*; Darwin Pub-
lishes His *Origin of Species*; First Person on the Couch—the Beginning of

Psychoanalysis; Assassination at Sarajevo; Mao and the Long March; The Bomb and Hiroshima; Man First Walks on the Moon . . . Other Highlights in World History . . . Descendants of the *Bounty* Mutineers on Pitcairn Island . . . Footnote People in World History

9. DISASTERS AND VIOLENCE   543
Natural Disasters . . . Man-Made Disasters . . . Other Disasters: Natural and Man-Made . . . Extraordinary Murderers . . . Murder Will Out . . . Assassinations—Successful and Unsuccessful. . . The FBI's All-Time Ten Most Wanted Fugitives List

10. WAR   615
Famous Battles in History—Land, Sea, and Air . . . Weird Weapons of the American Military, from the U.S. Camel Corps to the U.S.S. *Dolphin* . . . Roll Call: A Who's Who of Military Brass . . . Court-Martials around the World . . . Small Incidents That Started Big Wars . . . An International Array of Spies . . . The 8-Eyed Spy: The Family That Gave You Pearl Harbor . . . Military Scrapbook

11. UNIVERSE—SPACED OUT   654
How High Is the Sky?—An Eyeful of Astronomical Facts and Figures: The Universe and the Solar System . . . The Astronomers . . . Travelers in Space . . . What's Out There? . . . Life on Other Planets: Another View . . . Message . . . The Science Fiction Observatory . . . An Earthy Look at the American Astronauts

12. DOWN TO EARTH   677
Some Firm Facts about Terra Firma . . . The Legend of Paper Plates . . . The 7 *Natural* Wonders of the World . . . Inside the Good Earth: What's Going On under Our Feet? . . . Animal Facts and Oddities . . . Unusual Animals

13. ON THE ROAD   700
A Unique Tour of Unusual Historical Sites in the U.S.A. . . . Sightseeing in Your Own Neighborhood . . . A Handy Dandy Traveler's Guide to Europe and Environs . . . The Auto Show, Come See: Bonnie and Clyde's Last Car; Adolf Hitler's Big Car; Everybody's '57 Chevy . . . The Continuing Search for: Atlantis; Noah's Ark; Camelot; the *Santa María*; El Dorado, the City of Gold . . . A Guide to Buried Treasure in the Continental U.S.

14. COMMUNICATIONS   746
In the Tower of Babel: Human Languages . . . Toward a Universal Language . . . Publish Your Own Book . . . Graffiti—the Handwriting on the Wall . . . Morse Code . . . Manual Alphabet . . . The Language of Flowers . . . Word Quiz . . . People Who Became Words . . . Words with Character . . . A List of Words Commonly Misspelled . . . Sexism in Language . . . The Wit of Wilson Mizner . . . You

15. THE MEDIA   775
Behind the Front Page in the U.S.A. . . . Behind the Front Page around the World . . . The Day Christ Edited a Newspaper . . . Advertising: Its Life

and Times . . . Advertising Wisdom . . . Must Be Unseen to Be Believed:
The Tachistoscope . . . A Newsletter on Newsletters . . . Tuning in on Tele-
vision: From 1925 to 1975 . . . Television around the World . . . A 6-year
Sampling of the Gallup Poll

16. THE ARTS—LIVELY AND OTHERWISE   830
The 25 All-Time Box Office Champion Films . . . Motion Picture Academy
Award-winning Films and Actors . . . The Super Difficult Filmlore Game by
Hank Grant . . . Stories behind Songs You Grew Up With . . . MUZAK-
MUZAKMUZAKMUZAK . . . Gallery of Painters and Their Paintings . . . She
Wrote It—He Got the Credit . . . Gallery of Great Performing and Creative
Artists: Actors and Actresses—Stage; Composers—Classical; Composers—Mod-
ern; Dancers; Moviemakers; Novelists; Playwrights; Poets; Sculptors; Singers—
Opera; Singers—Popular . . . Sideshow of Popular Offbeat Performing and Crea-
tive Artists

17. EUREKA!—SCIENCE AND TECHNOLOGY   908
Bolts from the Blue: Great Inventions in History . . . Better Mousetraps—and
Other Inventions: Extraordinary Stories Behind Ordinary Objects That Had
to Be Invented by Someone . . . Great Engineering Feats from Early Times
to the Present . . . Gallery of Famous and Infamous Scientists . . . Animals
Used for Laboratory Research in the U.S. in 1971–1973 . . . Can Man Change
the Climate? . . . How Do Computers Compute? . . . Leave On the Lights,
but Turn Off the Plutonium . . . Meet the Meter

18. THE FAMILY   939
The Story behind Mother's Day . . . Emergency Childbirth . . . What Hap-
pened to Children of Some Famous Parents? . . . A Riddle . . . Kitchen Helps
. . . A Guide to Kitchen Utensils . . . Recommended for the Family Reference
Shelf . . . Inside the IQ Test . . . Arthur Jensen—Right or Wrong? . . . Gather
Around for Some Teaching Stories

19. LOVE AND SEXUALITY   964
Uncensored Highlights in the History of Sex in the Last 500 Years . . . Dic-
tionary of Sex Related Terms . . . A Survey of Sex Surveys—1900–1975 . . .
Gallery of Important Persons in the History of Sex . . . Rape Control Fails to
Halt Increased Rape Rate . . . Famous Gays . . . The Birds and Bees—and
More

20. HEALTH AND WELL-BEING   1009
Some Favorite American Foods; Cocoa-Cola; Peanut Butter; Sugar; White Bread;
Eggs; Meat . . . "Behold, I Have Given You Every Herb Bearing Seed . . .":
Fruits of the Earth; Vegetables; Nuts; Grains; Legumes; Other Goodies . . . The
Story of Dairy Products . . . Guide to Nutrition . . . Three Kings of the
Kitchen . . . Leading Vegetarians . . . Juicy Moments in the History of Food
. . . The Body Owner's Manual by Dick Gregory . . . Cover Story . . . Body
Types . . . Homeopathy . . . The Bach Flower Remedies . . . How to Stay
Young by "Satchel" Paige . . . Self-Examination for Women . . . A Guide to
Shangri-La: The Leading Longevity Sites on Earth . . . Some Famous Alco-
holics . . . A Synoptic History of the Promotion and Prohibition of Drugs

21. HUMAN BEHAVIOR—AND DAILY LIFE   1085
     Studying the Strange People of Nacirema . . . Human Behavior Experiments . . .
     Seven Common Superstitions . . . Find Your Phobia . . . Teaching Stories on
     Human Behavior

22. HONORS   1098
     The Nobel Prize Awards . . . International Lenin Prize for Strengthening
     Peace Among Peoples . . . The International Jerusalem Prize . . . The Temple-
     ton Foundation Prize for Progress in Religion

23. ALL IN SPORT   1131
     What Was the Greatest Baseball Team in the Last Half Century? . . . The
     Little League World Series . . . The All-Time Heavyweight Championship
     of the World . . . The Super Fight: Muhammad Ali v. Rocky Marciano . . .
     The All-Time Middleweight Championship of the World . . . Your Form Sheet
     —The Greatest Horse Race of Modern Times . . . The World Cup . . . Big
     Moments in Sports History: The Great International Rifle Match; The Last
     Bareknuckle Prizefight; The All-Time Championship Bridge Match . . .
     Money and Sports: A History of the Marriage . . . The Crossword Puzzle
     . . . Sports Immortals: The Three-Foot-High Hitter; The Pedestrian; First
     to Swim the Channel; Cradle Genius with a Cue . . . A Gallery of Sports
     Greats: Auto Racing; Basketball; Golf; Hockey; Tennis; Track and Field . . .
     A Short Selection from the Baseball Hall of Fame . . . A Short Selection from
     the American Bowling Congress Hall of Fame . . . A Short Selection from
     the Women's International Bowling Congress Hall of Fame . . . A Short
     Selection from the College Football Hall of Fame . . . History of the Olympic
     Games . . . An Encyclopedia of Sports Oddities

24. LISTS—1 TO 10 (OR MORE)   1224
     20 Illegitimate Children . . . 20 Celebrities Who've Been Psychoanalyzed . . .
     The Most Loved Person in History . . . The Most Hated Person in History . . .
     The 9 Breeds of Dog That Bite the Most . . . Some Crime Statistics . . . 12
     People Who Disappeared and Were Never Found . . . Some Leading Best-
     Selling or Distributed Books . . . Most Common Last Names in U.S. . . . Some
     Most Married People in History . . . Famous Left-Handed People . . . 15 Re-
     nowned Redheads . . . 10 Largest Countries (by Area) . . . 10 Most Populous
     Countries, 1800 to 1975 . . . 15 Oldest Cities . . . 15 Most Populous Cities,
     1800 to 1975 . . . 10 Highest Cities . . . 10 Highest Buildings . . . 10 Countries
     with Highest and Lowest Life Expectancies . . . 10 Hottest Cities . . . 10 Cold-
     est Cities . . . 10 Longest Rivers . . . 10 Nations with Greatest and Least Per-
     centage of Population in Active Armed Forces . . . 13 Countries with Highest
     Birth Rates . . . 11 Countries with Highest Death Rates . . . What's in a Name?
     . . . The People Who Never Were—Yet Live Today: Superman; Wonder
     Woman; Sherlock Holmes; "Uncle" Scrooge McDuck; Tarzan; The Lone Ranger
     . . . Some 9-Day Wonders—on the 10th Day

25. THE PEOPLE'S DIRECTORY   1249

26. KEEPING THE FAITH: RELIGION 1262

Major World Religions . . . Prophets of the Word: Successful Preachers and Evangelists . . . Super Bible Statistics . . . Holy Places in the World . . . Modern Atheists/Agnostics of the Western World . . . A Ticket to the Oberammergau Passion Play . . . American Saints and Potential Saints . . . "In the Beginning . . .": Stories of Creation . . . The Golden Rule

27. PASSING ON—THE FINAL TRIP 1316

The Choice . . . Famous Last Words . . . Rest in Peace—A Collection of Bizarre Gravestone Epitaphs . . . Death: Do-It-Yourself . . . Good-bye, Cruel World, or: Notes on the Suicide Note . . . Where There's a Will (There's an Insight into the Deceased) . . . Afterlife and Reincarnation . . . Vampires

28. THE CURIOSITY SHOP 1340

The Most Odd, Unusual, Strange, Unique, Incredible, Amazing, Uncommon, Unheard of, Fantastic Facts in the World . . . The Almanac Anthology: Yes, Virginia, There Is a Santa Claus; Logan's Lament; The Most Beautiful Last Will and Testament Ever Written; The Best Tribute to Man's Best Friend

29. THE UNKNOWN AND MYSTERIOUS 1364

A Chronology of Mysterious Happenings in History . . . An Atlas to Enigmatic Lands . . . Queen Victoria's Saucerman . . . The Adventure—of Adventures . . . Psychic Phenomena . . . Tuning in on ESP . . . Astral Projection . . . How's Your Aura Today? . . . Spiritualism and Séances . . . Ghosts and Hauntings . . . Psychokinesis . . . Dowsing and Dowsers

30. SURVIVAL IN THE BELLY OF THE MONSTER 1399

The Man Who Survived the Belly of the Monster . . . Growing Food in the City . . . Trees Speak a Secret Language . . . Wilderness Survival . . . People's Psychiatry Sheet: Handling Psychiatric Emergencies . . . Your First-Aid Kit . . . Recharging Yourself through Meditation . . . The Wisdom of a Fox . . . A Psychological Tip . . . Calendars—1776 to 2000

31. UTOPIA 1418

Leading Theoretical Utopias throughout History . . . Attempted Utopias . . . Captain Mission's Unique Pirate Utopia . . . *The Almanac*'s Exclusive Symposium on Utopia

32. BY THE PEOPLE, FOR THE PEOPLE 1438

America Speaks . . . Invitation to the Reader

Index 1447

Hello People

"Another almanac?" you may ask.

Not quite. Not really. An almanac, yes, but not the kind that you've known all your life or that your ancestors grew up with.

In the past, an almanac was usually a book that contained a calendar, astrological and weather predictions, and agricultural data. In more modern times, an almanac became, as the dictionary defines it, "a publication containing statistical, tabular, and general information"; in short, an all-purpose reference book.

Since the 1st almanac was published in manuscript in the 12th century, there have been thousands of various almanacs throughout the world. The earliest in America was *An Almanak for the Year of Our Lord 1639, Calculated for New England* by William Pierce, published in Cambridge, Mass. Pierce, a shipmaster, hoped that the new almanac would attract settlers to the New World and give him more paying passengers for his ship. One of the most famous almanacs was *Poor Richard's Almanack* started by Benjamin Franklin in Philadelphia in 1732. He signed it with the name Richard Saunders and gave himself the title "Philom" (from philomath, a combination of philosopher plus mathematician). Another famous one was *The Old Farmer's Almanac* started by Robert B. Thomas in 1793, that gained renown for its meteorological predictions, sometimes as high as 87% accurate, convincing one town in India to name the editor its guru.

Gradually almanacs included general information, wisdom, and humor, and were forerunners of the modern-day, all-around miscellaneous reference books like *Whitaker's Almanack*, of England, and *The World Almanac*, of the U.S., both established in 1868.

So of almanacs there has been no end, each seeming to be similar to the other.

But *The People's Almanac* is something very different. It is a traditional almanac in the sense that it does make predictions (although on more than the weather) and it does provide general information (although not the usual facts). But where the familiar standard almanacs leave off and stop—well, that's where *The People's Almanac* begins.

We feel that adults, inundated and manipulated by special-interest propaganda and government double-talk in the guise of facts, are desperately searching for the truth and honesty in the information given them. We feel that young people are eager to learn about things that are relevant to their lives. We feel that most people suspect that there is more to a fact than meets the eye, and when possible we want to turn each fact around and show the world its backside.

The People's Almanac differs essentially from all other almanacs on the following points:

This is a reference book to be read for pleasure. This is an informative book that is meant to provide entertainment. This is a book in which to look up facts and also have fun.

This is a compendium that tries, when possible, to provide in-depth material on selective topics rather than endless, dry, bare-bones dates and figures on all subjects.

This is a volume that attempts to go beyond often repeated, unchallenged data and offer the behind-the-scenes, frequently omitted truths.

This is a manual that makes an effort to break a few molds, create original forms, and give you alternative information from what you've always accepted as complete.

This is a book with a bias for the little known and the curious—occasionally lifting a few historic rocks to see what crawls beneath, constantly trying to get past some traditional No Trespassing signs that have long hidden certain people and certain institutions.

In undertaking this new almanac, we knew that we had to sacrifice a small degree of comprehensiveness for detail. While we have tried to be thorough and far-ranging in our coverage of most things under the sun, we have deliberately chosen depth over breadth. We have purposely omitted retail figures on business, population of States, corn yields, lists of fraternities, common-stock dividends, hydroelectric plants, and similar data, in order to make room for a guide to existing Shangri-las where people live to the age of 100 or more, a revealing rundown of some last wills of celebrated personages, survival kits for those who live in the city or visit the wilderness, a gallery of fascinating footnote people who have been overlooked by history books.

We have thought it more important to know 10 times more about 10 artists or athletes than to know next to nothing about 100 of them.

"Another almanac?"

We think not; not at all. We have tried to write and compile an unusual reference tool, something unique, something different—not just for the sake of being different, but because we felt there was an information void to be filled.

We have not overlooked most standard subjects, but we have tried to take them one step further and in so doing we have tried to be innovative.

The world religions are here, but so are the world's leading atheists. The Motion Picture Academy Awards are here as well as the Nobel Prizes, but so are inside stories under the title "Behind the Awards." World nations are here, including "Who Rules," but so also is a section called "Who REALLY Rules." Highlights of history are here, but so are firsthand eyewitness reports of persons who actually attended or participated in those earthshaking events. Great moments in sports are here, but so also are computerized contests to find the greatest heavyweight boxer, baseball team, or racehorse of all time. Leading drugs from heroin to aspirin are here, but so also are the names of the leading alcoholics in history.

In this different kind of almanac, the useful and the unusual abound. Here is a tourist guide to unique sites in America, including the tomb of a traitor's left leg. Here, also, is a guide to places where fabulous buried treasures may be found. Here are countless famous and infamous people who have inhabited the earth, as well as a who's who of renowned beings who never lived, like Tarzan, "Uncle" Scrooge McDuck, Sherlock Holmes, including an exclusive biography of Snoopy by his creator. Here is a chronology of the greatest mysteries on earth that have baffled men and women for ages.

Above all, these pages are for people, regular and uncelebrated people, the people of planet earth, whom we wish to have participate in this project. Our ultimate aim is to make this a true almanac of the people, for the people, by the people. For too long, the majority of people have been muted, unheard, helpless, and we want to invite them to enter our pages in future editions. We want to hear from them—from you—to learn what is right and what is wrong about this book, and have you tell us what else you want to know about or you want others to know about. We want your own experiences, observations, special learning to be a part of all future versions of this book. Our invitation to have you join us is extended in our last chapter.

This book is the product of almost 200 staff members and free-lance writers, and for the best of it, credit is due to all who participated in its preparations. However, for the worst of it—inadvertent omissions, inaccuracies, errors—the undersigned who have created the volume accept the blame and tender sincere apologies and the promise to correct mistakes in future editions. Above all, our gratitude to thousands of authors of thousands of books who made this almanac possible. As Dr. Samuel Johnson once said, "The greatest part of a writer's time is spent in reading, in order to write: A man will turn over half a library to make one book." And this we have done.

Our credo throughout this project, 1st voiced by H. L. Mencken, has been a simple one. It is this: "I believe that it is better to tell the truth than a lie. I believe it is better to be free than a slave. And I believe it is better to know than to be ignorant."

We have spoken enough. From this point on, *The People's Almanac* will speak for itself.

Enjoy.

DAVID WALLECHINSKY
IRVING WALLACE

"The time has come," the Walrus said,
   "To talk of many things:
Of shoes—and ships—and sealing-wax—
   Of cabbages—and kings—
And why the sea is boiling hot—
   And whether pigs have wings."

Through the Looking-Glass
Lewis Carrol (Charles L. Dodgson)
1832–1898

1

The Other Side of the Looking Glass

Predictor: MALCOLM BESSENT

He is a young psychic who has trained at the College of Psychic Science in London.

Past Predictions: Wrong—In 1969, he predicted that Nixon would lose to Muskie in the 1972 elections. Muskie did not run as nominee, and Nixon was reelected. Bessent was wrong.

—In June, 1971, he predicted that the Greek military regime would be overthrown from within by the end of 1972. Bessent was wrong.

—He predicted that 1972–1973 would be a hard year for the U.S. It would, he said, begin with floods, which would be followed by social upheaval and political confusion from which a new political structure would arise. Although the U.S. had its troubles in those years, there were no floods of such proportion and the government structure stayed the same. Bessent was wrong.

Right—In December, 1969, Bessent predicted that De Gaulle would die within a year. De Gaulle died on November 10, 1970. Bessent was right.

—In the winter of 1969–1970, he predicted that there would be a change in the British Government the following summer. In June, 1970, Edward Heath became the new Prime Minister. Bessent was right.

—He predicted that Martin Luther King, Jr., would die an untimely death. Bessent was right.

—In 1969, he predicted that an American Indian leader would come into prominence by 1974 and unite the tribes. From this, he said, there might come a land settlement for the Indians. Though no one leader stands out, Indian activism in the early 1970s forced attention on Indian rights and brought about extensive land settlements. Bessent was right —to a degree.

—On December 19, 1969, he predicted that a Greek tanker, probably belonging to Onassis, would be involved in a disaster with international significance within 6 months' time. In February, 1970, an oil tanker owned by Onassis was wrecked off the coast of Nova Scotia. A resulting oil slick contaminated the beaches, bringing about the ire of ecologists everywhere. Bessent was right.

Future Predictions: For 1975–1980

—In a few years, New York will be uninhabitable. The water level will rise and eventually flood the city out of existence.

—By 1979, the U.S. will have a war with China.

Predictor: DAVID BUBAR

A Baptist minister as well as a psychic, David Bubar is the founder of the S.O.S. Foundation, a semireligious organization in Tennessee. He has made many radio and television appearances. In April, 1975, he was one of 10 men indicted for conspiracy in the bombing of a $10 million rubber plant in Shelton, Conn. Bubar had been psychic adviser to a leader of the alleged conspiracy.

Past Predictions: Wrong—In 1970, he predicted that in 1972 there would be 13 or 14 space units involved in headline activities. Some space exploration, he said, would be more adventurous than scientific. In actuality, there were only 2 major space launches in 1972. Bubar was wrong.

Right—On August 11, 1969, he predicted that Everett Dirksen, the Republican senator, would be dead within a month. Dirksen died on September 8 of that year. Bubar was right.

—He predicted that a major hurricane killing hundreds of people would hit the East Coast in the summer of 1969. Hurricane Camille, which hit Mississippi on August 17, killed 258 people. Bubar was partially right.

—Before George Wallace announced his candidacy, Bubar predicted that he would win the 1970 Alabama election for governor. Bubar was right.

Future Predictions: For 1975–1980
—During the last part of the 1970s, Americans will become involved in a mass physical-fitness program. Social drinking will virtually come to an end.
—At the end of the 1970s, many doctors will join ranks with faith healers.
—There will be mass murders, a kind of genocide, in South America.
—From 1979 to 1982, the U.S. Government will control the mental activities of Americans through a "mind-shaping" program. All people who do not follow the line of thinking advocated by the Government will be brought before "Thought Courts" and be subject to "modified thought," or brainwashing. All people in professions connected with mental health will come under civil service. Individual thought impressions will be filed like fingerprints with the Government.
For 1981–1990—Before 1985, all children will be tested for physical and psychological abilities. Their future lives will be programmed, through a computer, on the basis of the tests.
—Love, as we know it, will cease to exist.
—Intuition and clairvoyance will become more important, invading the private lives of Americans. Psychics will hold important government positions.
—The chemicals and antibiotics consumed by present-day peoples will cause generations of the 1980s to be grotesquely tall. This added height will weaken the personality and body.
—By the middle of the 1980s, Russians and Americans will try to colonize the moon. Rivalry between the 2 groups will result in lunar police actions.
—Space travel will be guided by invisible rays.
—Printing will be done electronically without ink, plates, and other equipment. More parts of newspapers and magazines will be 3-dimensional, somewhat like silent movies.
—A new, superior human species will be developed outside the female body.
—People will be able to transform thoughts into images on a televisionlike screen.
—The telephone will be used for thought transmission.
—A "Thought-Action-Deed" machine (TAD) will appear in 1986. Using the machine, scientists will be able to tune into past, present, or future events based on a computer analysis of the pattern of history. In 1996, TADs will be released for mass production. Before that, they will not be used by the public.
For 1991–2000—Privacy of thought will no longer exist.
—By 1996, most of the historical references in the Bible will have been proved true.
—American and Russian scientists will invent a device through which people can become invisible. It will look either like a flashlight or an aerosol can.

—People will be able to make their energy forces leave their bodies during sleep [astral projection] to go to other places to explore or conduct business.
—People will be able to project, from consciousness, images of what they want, and produce those images in reality through a thought process called "Electronic Substance."
—By the year 2000, a new spiritual leader will appear.

Predictor: CRISWELL
Criswell is a former teacher and mortician, now a newspaper man and newscaster, who says that his predictions are 86% accurate and claims to know the future through the year 1999.
Past Predictions: Wrong—All the following predictions were made in 1968:
—He foresaw a renewal of the Korean War by June, 1969. Criswell was wrong.
—He said that in October, 1969, a movie actor would be arrested for white slavery. The actor, Criswell predicted, would have kept 30 runaway girls in the basement of his Beverly Hills home. Criswell was wrong.
—He predicted that a woman would assassinate Castro on August 9, 1970. Criswell was wrong.
—By the early 1970s, Criswell predicted, "perversion" would become rampant in the U.S. By 1973, according to his prediction, completely homosexual cities would exist cheek-by-jowl with several major American metropolises, and the Supreme Court would uphold the right of these cities to exist. Criswell was wrong.
—He predicted that new islands would rise in the Pacific after the eruption of an underwater volcano in 1971. Criswell was wrong.
—He also predicted that by 1971 a male birth-control pill that would make a man sterile for 30 days would be put on the market. Criswell was wrong.
—In the spring of 1971, Criswell foresaw, Mao Tse-tung would die, and a Chinese Civil War would follow, after which China would be broken up into a group of small nations ruled by the military. Criswell was wrong.
—He foresaw a new head man for Russia by 1973; this leader would bring great changes, eventually leading Russia into the free enterprise system. Criswell was wrong.
—By 1973, Criswell predicted, blacks would take over Mississippi, under the leadership of a man named Sanders, and turn it into a model black State. Criswell was wrong.
—In the winter of 1974, Criswell said, 5,000 people in New Hampshire would die as the result of ice storms. Criswell was wrong.
Right—On March 10, 1963, on television, he predicted that President Kennedy would not run for reelection in 1964 because of something that would happen to him in the preceding November. Kennedy was shot and killed in November, 1963. Criswell was right.

—On December 31, 1965, he predicted, again on television, that Ronald Reagan would be the next governor of California. Criswell was right.

—On January 1, 1967, in his newspaper column, he predicted a one-week war in the Mid-East with Egypt and Russia against Israel. The Arab-Israeli 6-Day War broke out on June 5, 1967. Criswell was right.

—In the same column, he predicted the death of a blond sex symbol. Jayne Mansfield died that year. Criswell was right.

—On January 1, 1968, Criswell said that a black civil rights leader would be assassinated before October of that year. Martin Luther King, Jr., was shot on April 4, 1968. Criswell was right.

Future Predictions: For 1975–1980
—A woman physicist in Nebraska will discover antimagnetic forces that will make space travel without jet propulsion possible. This will happen in the late 1970s.

—From 1975 to 1978, the devil will rule the earth.

—In 1976, Canada, Mexico, and the U.S. will join a Common Market.

—Also in that year, tidal waves and earthquakes will devastate Hawaii.

—In March of 1976, the Government of the U.S. will give almost all of New Mexico back to the Indians.

—In 1977, the dairy industry in Wisconsin will end as a new disease kills all the cattle there.

—The year 1977 will be one of disaster. No rain will fall for 10 months. Tides will end. Ships will run aground. A "black death" will wipe out thousands of people. The availability of water from snow and ice will cause migrations of desperate people to the North and South Poles. After this drought, torrential rain will come, followed by floods. A woman in Pratt, Kans., will save the lives of 500 people and become a national heroine. The next 3 years will be peaceful as nations apply their energies to rebuilding.

—On August 27, 1977, Lago Maggiore in Switzerland will begin to boil as a volcano rises in its center.

—In 1978, Connecticut will lead a revolt against a Federal sales tax of 5% on food and rent.

—By 1979, mind control, using rays, will be applied to criminals.

—In 1978, Lake Michigan will be drained for land use.

—By 1980, do-it-yourself face lifts will be on the market.

—By the year 1980, New York City will be under water.

—From November 28 to December, 1980, Pennsylvanians will be afflicted by an outbreak of cannibalism caused by an experiment that goes awry.

—By 1980, all the mentally ill people in the U.S. will be sent to an Oregon mental hospital complex built by the Federal Government.

For 1981–1900—By 1981, birth-control substances will be in the water system, put there by the Federal Government. In order to conceive, people will have to get a pill from the Government.

—In 1981, Montana will become the penal State. All criminals given prison sentences will be sent there.

—On February 11, 1981, a foreign power will attempt to bomb the U.S. with atomic weapons. The attempt will fail, but 50 people in Vermont will be killed.

—By 1982, the practice of medicine will operate through automation to such a degree that an individual will be able to go through medical school in 6 months. All drug research will be under Federal control. Preventive medicine will dominate.

—In 1982, a dying planet named Bullanon will come so close to earth that it will affect earth's gravity, shifting the poles. This will cause the rising of a lost continent which will bridge West Africa and Southeast South America, and trigger earthquakes, the destruction of cities, eruption of volcanoes, storms, and tidal waves. It will also cause a 40-day snowstorm with ice, resulting in a "white death."

—Between February 11 and May 11, 1983, all the women in St. Louis will lose their hair. It will grow back only after a period of panic which will produce divorces, murder, lawsuits, suicides, and massacres, mainly of hairdressers.

—By 1983, all divorces will come under Federal law and be handled in Reno, Nev.

—In 1985, a Caucasian woman, called the Lady of Light, will become leader, 1st of the Orient, then of the world. Under her leadership, men will become slaves and women will hold the power. War will end; the world will become a near-paradise. Her end will come after she is raped in Africa, then dies in childbirth.

—In 1985, polygamy will become legal in North Dakota.

—Also in that year, Texas will split into 3 States.

—From May 11, 1988, to March 30, 1989, the Aphrodisiacal Era will flourish. Clouds of aphrofragrance will float over the U.S. An aphrodisiac will also be put in water and heating systems. Sexual craziness will overcome the populace. Sex will be performed in the streets of Hollywood, and Florida will become a huge nudist camp. The Secretary of State will be caught in acts of perversion. The invention of an antidote will end the era.

—The year 1988 will see records of visits to earth by beings from other planets.

—On October 18, 1988, a meteor will hit London, almost destroying the city.

—On June 9, 1989, Denver will be wiped out by a "pressure" from outer space, which will turn solids to a jellylike mass.

—In the 1980s, Mexico City will sink into the lake bed upon which it is built. All its people will be evacuated.

—In the 1980s, all reading material will be printed on plastic.

—In the 1980s, all disease will be virtually eradicated by an artificially induced fever.

—In the 1980s, all pollution problems will be solved.

—During the decade, the seat of the Government of the U.S. will be switched to caverns under Wichita, Kans., and the surrounding area.

—On March 10, in the Convention Center on the Strip in Las Vegas, Nev., the 1st Interplanetary Convention will be held. The participants will come from Mars, Venus, Neptune, and the moon, as well as the U.S.

For 1991–2000—In the 1990s, man's thoughts and morals will be controlled from without.

—Space flight to Venus, Mars, and Neptune will be a reality.

—Buses will be driven by atomic power.

—There will be no spectator sports, no cities, little crime, almost no disease.

—People will buy goods at a mono-market.

—By 1995, nudity will be common, houses will have transparent walls, and power will come from solar energy.

—Also by 1995, most people will take food in concentrated form and be known as "Pill Takers." The "Pill Takers" will be in rivalry with the old-fashioned "Bulk Takers," who still eat food as we know it now.

—The world will come to an end on August 18, 1999. A black rainbow (a magnetic disturbance in the atmosphere caused by gravitational pulls in the universe) will draw the oxygen from the earth. Earth will leave its orbit and race to the sun. The only earth people left will be colonists on 200 space stations.

Predictor: JOSEPH DELOUISE

A hairdresser who never finished the 8th grade, DeLouise has made predictions, particularly those concerning disasters, over radio and television and in the newspapers. He uses a crystal ball to focus his energy.

Past Predictions: Wrong—No record.

Right—On November 25, 1967, he predicted the collapse of a bridge. On December 16, 1967, the Silver Bridge across the Ohio River at Point Pleasant, W.Va., collapsed. Forty-six people were killed. DeLouise was right.

—On January 8, 1968, he predicted that in the near future there would be no major riots but there would be an insurrection. On April 7, 1968, Governor Samuel H. Shapiro of Illinois called a civil disturbance in Chicago an "insur-

rection." Five thousand Federal troops were flown in. DeLouise was right.

—On January 8, 1969, he predicted that Ho Chi Minh would soon die. Ho Chi Minh died in 1969. DeLouise was right.

—In 1968, he predicted that the U.S. and Russia would suffer disasters in space exploration. On June 30, 1971, 3 Russian cosmonauts died during their return to earth during a 23-day space flight. American astronauts had touble on the *Apollo 13* space flight; no one died, however. DeLouise was right—more or less.

—On December 14, 1968, he predicted a wreck involving 2 trains on the Illinois Central tracks in the Midwest. A little over a month later, 2 trains crashed near Manteno, 45 mi. south of Chicago, on the Illinois Central tracks. DeLouise was right.

—On December 15, 1968, he predicted a tragedy involving water around the Kennedys. Later he "saw" a woman drowning. On July 13, 1969, Mary Jo Kopechne was killed at Chappaquiddick. Senator Edward Kennedy was involved. DeLouise was right.

—On May 21, 1969, he predicted a jet plane crash near Indianapolis. He said that the number 330 would be important, but wasn't sure how, and that 79 persons would be killed. On September 10, 1969, at 3:30 P.M., an Allegheny Airlines DC-9 collided with a private plane near Indianapolis. The crew of 4 and 79 passengers were killed. DeLouise was right about everything but the number of deaths.

—In mid-August, 1969, he predicted that the police would make great strides in solving the Sharon Tate murders on September 14–15. DeLouise was right.

Future Predictions: For 1975–1980

—By 1980, an economic panic will take place in which thousands of people will lose businesses and homes.

No Dates Given—The Caribbean will be a hotbed of revolution. During the unrest, pirates will capture a large ship.

—After a revolution, Japan will merge with China.

—Detroit will be the capital of a smaller nation, which will be a police state.

—Human beings will win the battle against air pollution.

—Marriage will become a business arrangement.

—Artificial insemination will be common.

—Queen Elizabeth will be the last monarch of England. That country will no longer be able to support a government figure with no real function.

Predictor: JEANE DIXON

This businesswoman and author, based in Washington, D.C., is the best known of the modern psychics. She employs a crystal ball, but depends mainly on visions sent her by the Lord. Also, she receives premonitions in dreams. She claims the future has been shown to her until the year 2037.

Past Predictions: Wrong—She predicted that Jawaharlal Nehru would not last more than 5 to 7 years as Prime Minister of India. He lasted 14 years, until his death in 1964. She was wrong.

Right—She personally told President Franklin D. Roosevelt that he had only a few months to live. He died shortly thereafter. Dixon was right.

—She personally warned actress Carole Lombard not to take an airplane flight that she had scheduled. Lombard took the flight and died when the plane crashed. Dixon was right.

—She predicted that President Harry Truman, an underdog, would be reelected over Thomas Dewey in 1948. Truman won an upset victory at the polls. Dixon was right.

—Before the 1953 Kentucky Derby, she predicted that the unbeaten *Native Dancer* would be beaten but finish 2nd. *Native Dancer* was beaten by *Dark Star* and did finish 2nd. Dixon was right.

—She foresaw Russia as being the 1st nation to put a satellite into orbit. In 1957, Russia placed the 1st Sputnik into orbit. Dixon was right.

—She predicted that UN Secretary Dag Hammarskjöld would die in an airplane crash. He was killed in an airplane crash in 1961. Dixon was right.

—In 1952, in a magazine, she predicted that a youngish Democrat would become President in 1960, and he would die or be assassinated in office. John F. Kennedy became President in 1960, and was assassinated in 1963. Dixon was right.

—She twice predicted that Senator Robert Kennedy would be "assassinated in California in June" of 1968. He was assassinated in California in June of that year. Dixon was right.

Future Predictions: For 1975–1980
—She foresees, for 1976, a "drastic change in the Government of the U.S. This Government will be committed to partial disarmament and appeasement."

—In 1978, the U.S. will suffer an economic depression brought on by "social and political giveaways and internal subversion."

—In 1979, Israel will "be attacked by its neighbors." Russia will be deeply involved in the Middle East.

—There will be a major earthquake in the Middle East, which will inspire the enemies of Israel to invade it. This will result in an 8-year war.

For 1981–1990—The U.S. will have its 1st woman President.

—A comet will collide with the earth, causing huge tidal waves and mighty earthquakes.

—In 1988, at the end of the long Israel-Arab war, "the Russians and their satellite armies will move into the area and occupy the lands of all the participants." Bloodshed will continue for 7 more years. The U.S. will be "too weakened economically and militarily" to intervene.

For 1991–2000—In 1995, the U.S., with England, France, Germany, Japan as allies, will set up headquarters in Rome to begin the counteroffensive against Russia in the Middle East. A great allied leader will emerge in Rome.

—In 1999, the U.S. and its allies will be at war with Russia and its satellites. Russian missiles "will rain down a nuclear holocaust" on U.S. "coastal cities, both east and west." Russian missiles launched fom the Carpathians will devastate the cities of Europe. Then, there will occur "a phenomenon" similar to "the stand of Moses at the Red Sea in Israel's early history." The Russians will find "the intervention of God" superior to their armies.

—The following year, 2000, Russian forces in Israel will be surrounded and destroyed by the U.S. and its allies based in Rome. Israel will be saved. Peace will come. "The leader in Rome will be hailed as a savior, ruler, and great conquering hero."

—This leader in Rome, "born in 1962 and now growing up somewhere in the Arab world," will prove to be a "false prophet of evil."

—Jesus Christ will be seen "bodily in the Holy Land," and all Jews will proclaim Him the true Messiah.

—With the advent of the year 2000, China will emerge as the greatest industrial power on earth. Within 5 years, China will conquer all of Asia and move into the Middle East. The U.S. and its allies will engage China in a nuclear war. The resultant "nuclear blasts, radiation, firestorms, followed by pestilence" will cost China millions of lives. China will go down in defeat.

Predictor: IRENE HUGHES
She probably inherited her psychic ability from her mother, a Cherokee woman, who read the future in coffee grounds. Her spirit guide, a Japanese, 1st contacted her in 1961. Since then, many of her predictions have come through him. Formerly a secretary and reporter, Irene Hughes gives private consultations, lectures, makes predictions in a weekly newspaper column, and writes an astrology column. The Psychical Research Foundation in Durham, N.C., has tested her for psychic abilities.

Past Predictions: Wrong—In April, 1968, she predicted that the Vietnam War would come to an end in the spring of 1969. Hughes was wrong.

—At the same time, she predicted that a major war involving the Middle East would break out late in 1969. There was no such war. Hughes was wrong.

—She also predicted a war in the U.S. in 1969. A token attack would emanate from Mexico, hit Florida and Texas, and wind up in Washington, D.C. The war would also affect the Middle East, Australia, Alaska, and Greenland. Of all the nations taking part, China would seem to be the winner, though the victory would not be clear-cut. Hughes was wrong.

—In late October, 1968, she predicted that the Pope would allow Catholics to take the birth-control pill and would also allow priests to marry and remain priests. Though some priests have been allowed to marry and act as lay priests, her prediction has not come true. Hughes was wrong.

Right—In her diary, she wrote that President Kennedy would be assassinated and that more than one rifle would be involved. Hughes was right. (She also wrote that the assassination would involve a conspiracy to be revealed 25 years later.)

—She "saw" 3 men dying in a space ship. On January 27, 1967, 3 men died in a fire in an Apollo capsule. Hughes was right.

—Six weeks before it happened, she predicted the death of Robert Kennedy by a bullet in the head. Hughes was right.

—On June 9, 1969, she broadcast a prediction about Ted Kennedy over a Canadian radio station: "He will be involved in an auto accident on or near the water. His companion will be fatally injured, but he may not be injured." On July 18, Ted Kennedy drove his car off a bridge into a tidal pool on Chappaquiddick Island. Mary Jo Kopechne, who was with him, did not survive. Hughes was right.

—On April 8, 1970, she dreamed that the astronauts aboard Apollo 13 would become ill, that there would be a short in an electrical wire, and that there would be an oil leak. She also dreamed that Apollo 13 would reach the moon, be unable to land, and return to earth. On April 11, Apollo 13 was launched. An oxygen tank exploded, and the astronauts were forced to return to earth without landing on the moon. Except for a few technical details, Hughes was right.

Future Predictions: For 1975–1980
—Throughout the late 1970s and on into the 1980s, cures will be discovered for older diseases like arthritis, multiple sclerosis, and epilepsy. However, new diseases will crop up.

For 1981–1990—By 1982, the U.S. will have a new monetary system. Eventually, nations will reach an agreement leading to a world monetary system in which a kind of credit card will be used instead of money all over the world.

—A neo-Nazi group with some Hitlerian ideas will take over Germany, both East and West. This group will fight a war which will extend from Europe to the U.S.

For 1991–2000—In February of 1993, an all-out nuclear war will begin. However, the war will not completely destroy the world.

—By 2026, the U.S. Constitution will no longer exist. The U.S. will be under a new kind of governmental rule. People will be very happy, freer than today, and full of good will toward their fellow humans.

Predictor: ANN JENSEN
A prominent seer in Dallas, Tex., who has made her forecasts while using a crystal ball or while hypnotized and in a trance.

Past Predictions: Wrong—No record.

Right—In 1970, she predicted for the years immediately ahead: "It will be a very trying time in the White House. It will need a steady hand and a steadier brain. This will come some time before 1976." The trying time in the White House came in 1973–1974. Jensen was right.

Future Predictions: For 1975–1980
—No world wars.

—The assassination in the U.S. of an important, beloved figure, but not the President.

—By 1976, the U.S. stock market will fall to a point close to the low reached during the 1929 Wall Street crash.

—In 1975 science will produce compounds for treatment of those "who have ruined their minds with drugs."

—All fighting will cease in Vietnam by 1980.

For 1981–1990—Again, no world wars.

—No catastrophic natural disasters anywhere. California will not suffer a major earthquake and fall into the ocean.

—There will be greater cooperation between the U.S. and U.S.S.R. There will be a worldwide move to make "rules for peace."

—Mount Pelée "will act up," but not seriously.

For 1991–2000—"I see a woman at the head of a world government." The world government will be set up on an island, although its headquarters will shift from one country to another.

—Man-made islands will be built in space. "Our grandchildren will land there."

—A planet will be found "that is very beautiful." This planet will have "trees, water, vegetation, strange fruits, and vegetables. There will be a form of life—animal life."

—There will be "calamities" during man's further exploration of space.

—Again, on earth, no major wars, but there will be uprisings in the Far East.

—Also, in the Far East, there will be terrible epidemics, involving cholera and malaria, with countless people dying in the streets. Nations with good sanitation standards will be safe.

—There will be discoveries of life-giving plants. Longevity of human beings will be extended. There will be a means of a "visionary communication without mechanisms."

—In some parts of the world there may be a return to the barter system for commodity exchange.

Predictor: OLOF JONSSON

A Swedish psychic known for his amazing extrasensory abilities, Olof Jonsson has solved murders and communicated through ESP with Apollo astronaut Edgar Mitchell while Mitchell was on his way to the moon.

Past Predictions: Wrong—In 1970, Jonsson predicted a terrible catastrophe in southern Europe that would take many lives. This would occur, he said, in 1971 or 1972. There was no catastrophe of that magnitude. Jonsson was wrong.

—Also in 1970, he predicted that China would become far more active in the Asian War in 1971–1972 causing bad feelings toward China in the U.S. and Soviet Union. Actually, relations between China and the U.S. improved in 1972. Jonsson was wrong.

—At the same time, he predicted Communist-inspired riots would take place in West Germany, with Berlin as the focal point. Jonsson was wrong.

—He predicted that Princess Margaret and Anthony Armstrong-Jones would get a divorce in 1971. Jonsson was wrong.

—He predicted that Muskie, rather than Nixon, would win the 1972 election for President. Jonsson was wrong.

Right—He predicted a new war in the Middle East, with the Arab States uniting against Israel, sometime in late 1971 or in 1972. This war would be, he said, more serious than the 1967 6-Day War and Russia would demand that the U.S. withdraw support from Israel or risk a serious confrontation. All of this happened, including the threat, in 1973. Jonsson was right—except for his timing.

—For 1971, he predicted a major government scandal involving high-level officials, who would be exposed for mismanagement and personal appropriation of government funds. The Watergate scandal did not occur until the election year of 1972. Jonsson was right—except for his timing.

—In January, 1970, he predicted that Nasser would die. Nasser did die, on September 28, 1970. Jonsson was right.

—In January, 1970, he predicted a fire in Chicago by the end of the month. In January, a fire in the Chicago Hilton killed 2 people. Jonsson was right.

—In 1970, he predicted that De Gaulle would die within a year. De Gaulle died on November 9, 1970. Jonsson was right.

—In 1970, he predicted that 1972 would be a crisis year in relations between Russia and the U.S. and that an American statesman would, through high-level talks, cause cracks in the Iron Curtain. This would be followed by a period of relative harmony between the governments of the U.S. and Russia. In May, 1972, Nixon visited Russia for a week of talks with Kremlin leaders which resulted in an important arms pact between the 2 nations. Jonsson was right.

Future Predictions: For 1975–1980

—By 1980, the internal combustion engine will be outlawed in all major American cities.

For 1981–1990—All major cities will ban private cars. Only medical and law enforcement personnel will be allowed to use cars, and those will be compact and electrically powered.

For 1991–2000—Because of drastic natural changes in the earth, climate will change dramatically in several parts of the world.

—There will be no more automobiles.

—We will no longer be dependent on plants and animals for food and energy. Instead, we will get food and energy directly from the sun.

Predictor: BILL LINN

Besides being a medium, Bill Linn is a Manhattan businessman who specializes in sales promotion.

Past Predictions: Wrong—In 1970, he predicted that large areas of land would arise in the Atlantic Ocean and near Hawaii. Linn was wrong.

Right—He predicted that President John F. Kennedy would be killed. Linn was right.

—He predicted that Robert Kennedy would be assassinated. Linn was right.

—When Nixon lost the governorship of California in 1962, Linn predicted that Nixon would be President. Linn was right.

—Before the beginning of the Vietnam War, he predicted that there would be trouble in that area. Linn was right.

Future Predictions: For 1975–1980

—A committee rather than a President and Cabinet will run the country. Representatives of labor unions will have tremendous power. They will dictate how people will live and on what terms.

—By 1980, China, Russia, and the U.S. will be the only majors powers. Smaller countries will combine money and manpower and brains to challenge the big 3.

Predictor: RICHARD McCLINTIC

He is a middle-aged blue-collar worker who has had extrasensory experiences all his life. At various times, he has seen ghosts, left his body (astral projection), and foreseen the future. He even claims the ability to look through walls. Hans Holzer, a writer and researcher in the field of parapsychology, is the agent through which McClintic relays his predictions of future events. McClintic does not want to take advantage of his psychic ability and wishes to keep a low profile as an amateur medium.

Past Predictions: Wrong—He predicted that men would 1st land on the moon in 1973. It was July 20, 1969, when this momentous event actually occurred. McClintic was wrong.

—In 1968, he predicted that Senator Ted Kennedy would run for President in 1972. McClintic was wrong.

—In 1968, he predicted that an American atomic-powered submarine would be lost in deep waters. At least 110 men would die. McClintic was wrong.

—On October 10, 1968, he predicted that Arabs would make bold statements about wanting to buy material to make atomic bombs within a year. McClintic was wrong.

—On September 20, 1968, he predicted that Mao Tse-tung would die by 1971 and that the Chinese army would rule China. McClintic was wrong.

Right—On August 7, 1968, he predicted that Jacqueline Kennedy would marry again. She married Onassis on October 20, 1968. McClintic was right.

—On the same date, he predicted a train crash in a State with a name beginning with the letter "O." On August 14, a Penn Central train containing 150 mm howitzer shells and fuses derailed near Urbana, O., forcing the evacuation of 3,500 people. McClintic was right.

—Early in August, 1968, he made a number of predictions about the coming elections: that Humphrey would win the Democratic nomination; that there would be trouble at the Chicago Convention, including a walkout; and that Nixon would win the election. McClintic was right.

—In 1968, he predicted more student protests at colleges, strikes by high school teachers, and strikes by students. McClintic was right.

—In 1968, he predicted that Dubcek of Czechoslovakia would be hounded from his leadership position in that Communist country within 2 years. McClintic was right.

—In 1968, he predicted that Egypt's Nasser would call another Arab council within a few months to get more money from oil-producing countries to use against Israel. McClintic was right.

—On November 11, 1968, he predicted more fighting in Vietnam and invasions of Laos and other South Asian countries. McClintic was right.

—In September, 1968, he predicted bomb scares in stores in some larger cities, including New York. In actuality, there were bomb explosions in some leading New York department stores. McClintic was right.

—In 1968, unlike many psychics, he predicted no atomic war for the next 3 to 4 years. McClintic was right.

—In 1968, he predicted that China and Russia would have no full-scale war but that fights would break out on the Russo-Chinese border. McClintic was right.

—On August 8, 1968, he said, "I don't think General Dwight D. Eisenhower will be alive a year from now." Former President Eisenhower died on March 28, 1969. McClintic was right.

—On January 16, 1969, he predicted that members of the Egyptian military would plot against Nasser. McClintic was right.

—On January 18, 1969, he predicted that 1969 would see riots of radical students in Japan. McClintic was right.

—On November 11, 1968, he predicted another earthquake in Iran and Turkey. In March, 1970, 1,086 people lost their lives in an earthquake in Turkey; in April, 1972, another earthquake hit Iran, killing over 5,000 people. McClintic was right.

—He predicted that Barbra Streisand would win a movie Oscar. She did, in 1970. McClintic was right.

—On January 16, 1969, he predicted that Prime Minister Wilson would be forced out of office. In 1970, Conservative Edward Heath became Prime Minister, replacing Wilson. McClintic was right.

Future Predictions: No Dates Given

—A new cure for blood diseases will be discovered.

—An atomic-energy-powered engine will be invented.

—A new laser gun will be able to kill people and destroy huge tanks.

—Scientists will invent a new weapon that will make air or space blow up without shelling. This will work on the same principle as the atomic bomb, but it will work across distances.

—A machine to speed up nature's processes of healing will cure people faster than any present method.

—People will be grown, or at least "started" in gardens like nurseries. This will take place at least 500 years from now.

—New ways of keeping people from aging and of leaving earth will be discovered.

—There will be devices to reverse gravity and to read people's thoughts.

Predictor: ETHEL JOHNSON MEYERS

A trained singer who performed in vaudeville, Ethel Meyers did not discover her psychic abilities until late in life. She was contemplating suicide after the death of her husband when he materialized before her and talked her out of it. Her talents are many: She helps people find missing objects, gives readings, and is both a trance medium and clairvoyant. The Edgar Cayce Foundation and the American Society for Psychic Research have tested her for mediumship.

Past Predictions: Wrong—In 1970, she predicted free travel from Iron Curtain countries to other parts of Europe and to the U.S. Meyers was wrong.

—Also in 1970, she predicted that Mao Tsetung would be dead within 3 years. Meyers was wrong.

Right—In 1970, she predicted an open war in the Middle East by the end of the decade. The Yom Kippur War broke out in 1973. Meyers was right.

Future Predictions: For 1975–1980

—The Russians will "level off," making a kind of peace with the U.S. in a common stand against Red China.

—In the late 1970s or early 1980s, the Red Chinese will use atomic bombs on the U.S. The bombs will do damage, but major cities will be protected by sophisticated detection devices.

No Dates Given—Under a new powerful President, entirely new methods of bringing together ideas on how to run the country will be in operation.

—Pollution will come to an end.

—Many earthquakes and famines will plague the earth.

—Small wars will keep the population in check.

—People will use food and herbs, rather than drugs, for healing.

—There will be no sinkings of major cities.

—The U.S. and Russia will not engage in an atomic war.

—Sometime around 2000 or 2500, the earth will turn and "go to the opposite pole," causing great changes in climate. Melting snow and ice will cause great floods.

Predictor: DR. N

A prominent physician and psychiatrist, Dr. N does not want his identity revealed when he gives predictions.

Past Predictions: Wrong—Dr. N predicted a Red Chinese bombing attack on San Francisco to take place on December 29, 1970. He later changed the date to 1972. Dr. N was wrong.

—In 1970, he predicted that the U.S. and China would be at war by 1971, by 1972 at the latest. During this war, he said, the West Coast States would be rendered uninhabitable by radioactive fallout from "water blasts," most of the rest of the country would be destroyed, and 190 million Chinese would be killed. Dr. N was wrong.

—Also in 1970, he predicted that, in 1971 or 1972, a Dr. Martin would discover a cure for cancer. Dr. N was wrong.

—At the same time, he predicted that, by 1973, there would be a sharp rise in temperature. Dr. N was wrong.

Right—The morning of the Apollo 13 space launching in April, 1970, he predicted that "It

may just get back if they can get the electricity and oxygen to hold out." The trouble he foresaw did occur. Dr. N was right.

Future Predictions: For 1975–1980

—In 1980, Spain, Africa, and Israel will have far more power than they do now.

—After a war in 1979, cancer research will be of paramount importance.

For 1981–1990—The next President will die in office after serving for 12 years.

—By 1986, one of every 3 children will be deformed in some way by radiation. Because of this, the Government will mount a huge research program in genetics and embryology.

—By 1987, clinics will test people for cancer every 6 months. They will use a cold sore virus to induce a lesion, which will be tested with a serum to see if any cancerous sores are present.

Predictor: JOHN REEVES

A former schoolteacher, John Reeves has a Bachelor of Arts degree with a major in English Literature and did some graduate work in English and Library Science at Columbia University. He calls himself a "semiprofessional" psychic.

Past Predictions: Wrong—In 1970, he predicted that there would soon be detention camps for rioters. Reeves was wrong.

Right—On August 8, 1964, he predicted that Eastern Airlines would, in a short time, merge with another airline. There *was* such a merger with Mackey Airlines. Reeves was right.

—On August 16, 1964, he predicted that President Johnson would not complete his term or would choose not to run again. He also foresaw Johnson's heart disease. Reeves was right.

—In November, 1964, he saw De Gaulle "stepping down." De Gaulle did so, in 1969. Reeves was right.

—In 1970, he predicted that the Vietnam War would drag on. It did. Reeves was right.

—Also in 1970, he predicted that trade relations between China and the U.S. would be established within 16 months. In February of 1972, Nixon visited China; trade relations were established shortly thereafter. Reeves was right.

—In 1970, he predicted that Nixon would be reelected in 1972. Reeves was right.

Future Predictions: For 1975–1980

—Russia and the U.S. will remain as leading world powers.

—A breakthrough in developing a cure for cancer will occur in 1977–1978. However, there will be no actual cure available until sometime between 1986 and 1991.

—By 1980, the area between Baja California and California will separate, making Baja an island. Five or 6 new islands will rise in the Caribbean.

For 1981–1990—A cure for cancer will be discovered.

For 1991–2000—By 2000, the racial problem will be resolved through intermarriage.

Predictor: SHAWN ROBBINS
She is a young, middle-class woman who has had psychic experiences all her life. Attractive and beautifully dressed, she does not fit the stereotype of a medium as an old crone hunched over a crystal ball. But then, neither do her colleagues.
Past Predictions: Wrong—(All made in 1970)
—In 1970, she predicted that Yugoslavia would make headlines sometime in the coming year. Nothing special happened in 1971 in that country. Robbins was wrong.
—She predicted that a replacement for present birth-control methods would be discovered by Dutch doctors or a foreign-born doctor in the U.S. Robbins was wrong.
—She predicted that in August–September, 1973, researchers would discover a new, safer birth-control substance in liquid form. Robbins was wrong.
—She predicted that bad weather in California in 1973—floods and other disasters—would cause houses to start sinking into the ocean. Robbins was wrong.
—She predicted that in 1973, or the early part of 1974, tremors in the mountains around San Francisco would cause openings in the ground. Robbins was wrong.
—She predicted a flood for New Hampshire in 1973. Robbins was wrong.
Right—She predicted that a country with a name beginning with "I" would suffer terrible earth disasters, such as earthquakes and landslides. She also predicted that a landslide would kill hundreds of people in Turkey and Iran. Both predictions were for 1970. In 1972, an earthquake in Iran took 5,000 lives. Robbins was right—except for her timing.
—In 1970, she predicted that the U.S. would become involved in trouble in the Middle East by 1974. As a result, she said, oil supplies to the U.S. would be cut off. Robbins was right.
Future Predictions: For 1975–1980
—In 1975–1976, the U.S. and Russia will become bitter enemies over a war in the Middle East involving an Arab country other than Egypt.
—In 1975, "something big," perhaps a flood, will occur in inland California.
—Within this time, an earthquake will cause great damage someplace within 300 mi. of New York City.
—From 1975 on, pollution will be the major health concern.
—In 1975, a doctor with a name like Frazer or Azur with a white crew cut will find a way to perform heart transplants, using cold, without danger of rejection.

—In 1977, cancer will be controlled by "R waves," or "radium waves."
—Between 1977 and 1981, China and the U.S. will be at war. During this war, which China will lose, China will be bombed. Russia will also fight China, but not as an ally of the U.S.
—A new leader in Russia in 1980 will encourage good relations between that country and the U.S.
—Sometime between 1978 and the 1980s, there will be a change in the Government of the U.S. A new legislative branch will be added and merged with those that now exist.
For 1981–1990—The Russian Government will change in 1981.
—On November 12, 22, or 25, 1989, the U.S. will officially declare war. The wife of the President then in office will die during the 2nd year of his term.
—In 1990, China will be a major world power, and a war will begin which involves her.
—By 1990, there will be more talk about life on other planets—plant life or life which is just starting now.

Predictor: ALAN VAUGHAN
Graduated from University of Akron. Former science editor in New York. Now editor of *Psychic* magazine in San Francisco, Calif.
Past Predictions: Wrong—In November, 1973, he predicted that President Nixon would become ill in December, 1973, and be temporarily replaced in the Presidency by another. He was wrong.
—In November, 1973, he predicted that Arab nations would resume sending oil to the U.S. in January, 1974. He was wrong.
Right—In May, 1968, in a letter sent to the Central Premonitions Registry, N.Y., he predicted that Senator Robert Kennedy would be assassinated within 2 months. Senator Kennedy was shot and killed on June 5, 1968. Vaughan was right.
—In 1970, he predicted that a madman would attack Pope Paul VI. In November, 1970, a deranged would-be assassin tried to kill the Pope. Vaughan was right.
—In November, 1968, he filed the following prediction with the Central Premonitions Registry, N.Y.: "Richard M. Nixon's Administration will follow a pattern similar to that of Ulysses S. Grant. Enormous scandals in the Nixon Administration will come to light." In 1973–1974, the Watergate scandals engulfed the Nixon Administration. Vaughan was right.
—He predicted Aristotle Onassis would die in an accident in 1975, and Jacqueline Kennedy Onassis would survive and thus be widowed a 2nd time. Vaughan was partially right.
Future Predictions: For 1975–1980
—Senator Edward Kennedy will be elected President of the U.S. in 1976.

—There will be no presidential election in 1980 because a constitutional convention will change the presidential 4-year term to a single term of 5 or 6 years.

—The water level around New York will rise gradually until New York is uninhabitable.

—A new form of rocket propulsion will be introduced, increasing the speed of spaceships 10 to 100 times. It will take only one month to reach Mars.

For 1981–1990—In 1981, the U.S. will go to war with China.

For 1991–2000—A major new religion, one combining the elements of Christianity with those of other religions, will catch on. In some way this religion will have the "sun" involved in it.

—A great war will be fought on the "plains of Palestine." Israel will be neither obliterated nor diminished.

Predictor: BERKELEY PSYCHIC INSTITUTE
At this school for psychic readings located in Berkeley, Calif., 7 experienced psychics—Lewis Bostwick, Michael Symonds, Sue Viera, Carol Irvine, Connie Westberg, Ken Burke, Cynthia Lester—gathered in January, 1974, to tape their group predictions exclusively for *The People's Almanac*.

Past Predictions: Wrong—Never worked together before as a group. *Right*—Never worked together before as a group.

Future Predictions: For 1975–1980

—Egypt will start trying to expand her borders.

—In the U.S., an association of natural therapists will be founded, its organization consisting of well-trained psychics, humanistic psychologists, and similar healers.

—In 1976, the President of Mexico, along with 2 of his Ministers and members of his family, will be assassinated, "with the Government being fully overthrown."

—Late in 1976 or in 1977, there will be revolutions in India. New Dehli will suffer famine or natural disaster, "a lot of people dying."

—"On May 26, 1977, there will be the start of a short war in the area of Labrador, between Greenland and Russia, over fishing rights. Nuclear torpedoes will be used."

—"In November, 1977, extensive flooding in the coastal area of Virginia, in the U.S., with 200 people killed."

—Before or during 1978, Israel will get the atom bomb. Australia will also get the bomb and become a world power.

—Russia and Germany will have a conflict in 1978 "involving several smaller countries." The Government of Russia will change in that time.

—During February or the 1st 2 weeks in March, 1978, the Prime Minister of Japan will be assassinated.

—In 1978, there will be a major earthquake in Northern California and parts of Oregon.

—During 1978, China will instigate an internal uprising inside Afghanistan.

—"In 1978 or 1979, a scientist in China or Russia will discover some new way of using the atom to produce energy. A major breakthrough. It will be kept secret because the person who discovers it wasn't supposed to be working on it—he was doing something he wasn't supposed to do."

—Around 1978 or 1979, an avatar will appear —not from India, maybe a Slovak—who will operate on a psychic level, and some time later will manifest himself as God.

—In 1980, "there will be a breaking up of icebergs around the North Pole. Scientists will get together in a submarine to go into waters they hadn't gone into before. They will be looking for Atlantis again. They will find machines, data, far below the surface and frozen in ice. They will find a time capsule, and maybe materials from other worlds that started things on earth. One object that the scientists will also discover—it will scare them away from this area—is a huge ball, part of it protruding, from which radiates tremendous energy."

For 1981–1990—"In 1981, there will be a U.S. Supreme Court Justice appointed who will eventually go on to become Vice-President of the U.S. He might have a double last name or a name with 'Van' in it."

—A.E. & I.W.

PREDICTIONS BY PSYCHICS OF THE PAST

Predictor: GREAT PYRAMID OF CHEOPS
Some pyramidologists claim that the Great Pyramid, 2600 B.C., could actually be used for predicting the future, each year corresponding to one "pyramid inch" along its various passageways and corridors.

Past Predictions:—Mid-September, 1936, as a crucial date for U.S. and Britain which would undergo constitutional crises. The Pyramid was wrong.

—Second Coming and Day of Judgment at 1st interpreted for 1881, then 1936, then 1953. The Pyramid was wrong.

—Between 1936 and 1953 a new and enlarged Israel to emerge. The Pyramid was right.

—W.W. I to break out in 1914 and last until 1918. The Pyramid was right.

Future Predictions:

—Period of "Reconstruction" toward lasting

peace, which may contain some wars along the way from 1953 until 2001.
—Beginning in 2001, the "Builders' Rest," a new stage for mankind, based on world peace and perhaps a theocratic world-state.

Predictor: THE BIBLE—NEW TESTAMENT
Believed to have been written between 60 and 120 A.D.
Future Predictions:
—Portents of the coming end of the world:

> JESUS: "Ye shall hear of wars and rumors of wars . . . the sun shall be darkened, and the moon shall not give her light, and the stars shall fall from heaven, and the powers of the heavens shall be shaken" (Matt. 24:6–30).

—End of the world:

> PETER: "The heavens shall pass away with a great noise, and the elements shall melt with fervent heat, the earth also and the worlds that are therein shall be burned up" (II Pet. 3:10).
> PAUL: "The Lord himself will descend from heaven with a cry of command, with the archangel's call, and with the sound of the trumpet of God. The dead in Christ will rise 1st; then we who remain alive shall be caught up together with them in the clouds to meet the Lord in the air; and so we shall always be with the Lord.
> "We shall not sleep, we shall all be changed, in a moment in the wink of an eye, at the last trumpet. For the trumpet shall sound and the dead will be raised imperishable, and we shall be changed" (I Thess. 4:16–17).

Predictor: MALACHY O'MORGAIN
1094–1148. Considered Ireland's greatest prophet. Archbishop of Armagh, Bishop of Down, and Papal Legate to Ireland. Later canonized. The famous "Malachy Papal Prophecies" attributed to him.
Past Predictions: Forecast of each Pope from 1143 up to and beyond our times. Examples:
De Ruro Albo: Adrian IV (1153–1159), an Englishman born at St. Albans.
Signum Ostiense: Alexander IV (1254–1261), Cardinal of Ostia.
Aquila Rapax: "Rapacious Eagle" was Pius VII (1800–1823), victim of Napoleon rather than rapacious himself.
De Balneis Etruria: Gregory XVI (1831–1846) before his election served at Balnea in Etruria.
Religio Depopulatea: "Christianity laid waste" applied to Benedict XV (1914–1922) during W.W. I's havoc.
Pastor Angelicus: Pius XII (1939–1958), an

avid follower of St. Thomas Aquinas, the Angelic Doctor.
Pastor et Nauta: John XXIII (1958–1963) as "shepherd and navigator" of the Ecumenical Council.
Flos Florum: Paul VI (1963–   ), whose coat of arms is *flos florum*, a floral design.
Future Predictions:
Only 4 more Popes may be expected, and then there will be none. The last 4:
De Medietate Lunae: "From the half-moon"—perhaps from the Middle East. Signaled by persecutions of the Church. Will fall victim to his enemies.
De Labore Solis: "From the toil of the sun"—as Gregory XVIII, he will be a lull in the midst of persecution.
Gloria Olivae: "Glory of the olive"—as Leo XIV, he will unite humanity under Christianity in one last brilliant explosion.
Petrus Romanus: "Peter of Rome"—last of the Popes of Rome. He will preside over the destruction of Rome and the End of the Age.
—If each Pope's reign averages 10 years, the last would end in 2013.

Predictor: URSULA SONTHIEL (MOTHER SHIPTON)
1488–1561. Long, crooked nose, goggling eyes, misshapen body made this English psychic look like the proverbial crone. Inherited powers to raise storms, kill or heal, to command men and animals, to foresee the future. Cardinal Wolsey threatened to burn her at the stake. "If this burn, so shall I," she retorted, throwing her kerchief into her blazing fireplace. It did not burn. Neither was she sent to the stake.
Past Predictions:
—*To Lord Percy:* "Show your horse in the quicke, and you shall doe well, but your body will be buried in Yorke pavement and your head shall be stolen from the barre and carried into France." He was beheaded, and his head carried to France.
—*Most famous prophecies attributed to her:*

> Carriages without horses shall go,
> And accidents fill the world with woe.
>   (Automobile)
> Around the earth thoughts shall fly
> In the twinkling of an eye; (Telegraph, telephone)
> The world upside down shall be,
> And gold be found at the foot of a tree.
>   (Too general for authentication)
> Through hills man shall ride,
> And no horse be at his side. (Railroad)
> Under water men shall walk,
> Shall ride, shall sleep, shall talk. (Submarine)
> In the air men shall be seen
> In white, in black, in green; (Airplane)

Iron in the water shall float,
As easily as a wooden boat. (Steamship)
Gold shall be found and shown
In a land that's not now known. (South
   Africa, U.S.)
Fire and waters shall wonders do,
England shall at last admit a foe. (Eng-
   land to be conquered. Unfulfilled as yet)
The World to an end shall come
   in Eighteen hundred and eighty-one.
   (She was wrong)

It has been claimed by some that Charles Hindley, noted English editor of the mid-19th century, was the real author of the poem. Even admitting this, it would have been an admirable feat to predict its many inventions even at that late time. But about the following prediction of Mother Shipton's, there can be no dispute over its authenticity:
Future Predictions:
"Then shall come the Son of Man, having a fierce beast in his arms, which kingdom lies in the Land of the Moon, which is dreadful throughout the whole world; with a number of people shall he pass many waters and shall come to the land of the Lyon (Lion); look for help of the Beast of his country, and an Eagle shall destroy castles of the Thames, and there shall be a battle among many kingdoms . . . and therewith shall be crowned the Son of Man, and the 4th year shall be many battles for the faith and the Son of Man, with the Eagles shall be preferred, and there shall be peace over the world, and there shall be plenty of fruit, and then shall he go to the land of the Cross." Interpretation: The "Land of the Moon" indicates an Arab invasion. The Eagle may refer to the U.S. as the standard-bearer of Christianity in a religious war that shall last 4 years. Christianity to be victorious, after conquering the Holy Land ("Land of the Cross").

Predictor: MICHEL DE NOSTREDAME, known as Nostradamus
1503–1566. French physician, astrologer, clairvoyant. Acclaimed even today as one of the foremost seers in the history of the world. Appointed by Charles IX "physician in ordinary" at the French court.
Past Predictions:—In 1555, his 1st volume of *Centuries*, which contained 354 quatrains, included a verse that would bring him fame 4 years later:

The young lion shall overcome the old one
In martial field by a single duel.
In a golden cage he shall put out his eye,
Two wounds from one, then shall die he a
   cruel death.

In 1559 Henry II, the Old Lion, had his golden helmet accidentally pierced with a splinter from a wooden lance in tournament with a knight calling himself the Young Lion. It put out his eye and penetrated his brain.

—The Great Fire of London in 1666:

The blood of the just shall be dry in London.
Burnt by the fire of 3 times 20 and 6.
The ancient dame shall fall from her high
   place,
Of the same sect many shall be killed.

The Virgin's statue atop St. Paul's did indeed fall.

—Louis XV's spendthrift ways would lead to the monarchy's collapse:

He who succeeds to the Grand Monarch dead,
Will lead an evil and illicit life,
By his neglectful habit, he will entrust
   the management to others,
So that at last the Salic law will fall.

—The French Revolution, including France's financial collapse:

Despite the king, the coin shall be
   brought lower,
The people shall rise against their king,
Peace being made, holy laws made worse,
Paris was never in such great disorder.

—Deaths of Louis XVI, Marie Antoinette, and Reign of Terror:

The Assembly will condemn the king taken,
And the queen taken by jurors sworn by lot;
They will deny life to the dauphin,
And the prostitute at the fort will partake
   the same fate.

—The rise of the earlier "rejected" Queen Elizabeth over the cruel Mary Tudor, traitorous Mary Queen of Scots, her glory, and her death at 70 in 1603:

The rejected one shall at last reach
   the throne,
Her enemies found to have been traitors.
More than ever shall her period be
   triumphant,
At 70 she shall assuredly go to her
   death in the 3rd year of the century.

—Of Napoleon, born on Corsica, he predicted:

An emperor will be born near Italy,
Who will be sold to the Empire at a very
   dear price,
One will say from the men he rallies
   round him,
That he is less prince than butcher.

—Of Napoleon's downfall and exile to Elba, his escape, and his final defeat at Waterloo by the British where his men, like bees, yielded up their blood ("liquor"), though he himself escaped death:

The captive prince, conquered, to Elba,
He will pass the Gulf of Genoa by sea to
    Marseilles,
He is completely conquered by a great effort
    of foreign forces,
Though he escapes the fire, the bees yield
    liquor by the barrel.

—W.W. I is predicted astrologically for 1914:

The regions subject to Libra [Austria
    and the Balkan]
Will make the world tremble by great war,
Blood, fire there will be
When Mercury, Mars, Jupiter are in France.

—The Russian Revolution is foreseen when the Czar was killed and Lenin took his place:

The Slavic people in a warlike hour
Will be so highly lifted up by their ideals,
That they will change a prince,
And bring forth a person of lowly birth
    to rule.

—The weakness of the League of Nations results in W.W. II:

By the Germans and neighboring countries,
There will be wars because of grievances,
The faults of Geneva
Will be laid bare.

—Hitler himself is named, according to some interpreters, by popular anagram fashion of Nostradamus' day, as well as the dictator's vexatious rule over his ally, Italy:

Liberty shall not be recovered,
A black, fierce, villainous, evil man shall
    occupy it,
When the ties of his alliance are wrought.
Venice shall be vexed by Hister.

Future Predictions:
—Revolution shall come, the result of the troops of a great nation scattered abroad:

Through the abundance of the army scattered,
High will be low, low will be high,
Too great a faith, lives lost in jesting,
To die by thirst through abundance of want.

—Yet Communism shall not be the victor:

The philosophy of life according to
    Thomas More,
Will be unsuccessful, and will give way
    to another much more seductive,
In the land of cold winds is where it will
    first fail,
Because of the deeds and language of one
    more attractive.

—The Soviet Union and the U.S. shall join forces to oppose a new tyrant:

One day the 2 great masters shall be
    friends,
Their great powers shall be increased,
The new land shall be in a flourishing
    condition,
The numbers shall be told to the Bloody
    Person.

—The new tyrant shall be a militant Arab leader:

Out of the country of greater Arabia,
Shall be born a strong master of Mohammedan
    law,
Who shall vex Spain and conquer Granada,
And by sea shall come to the Italian nation.

—And Arab-Western forces will meet in conflict:

In the fields of Media, Arabia, and Armenia
Two great armies shall meet thrice,
Near the shore of Araxes, the people
Of great Suleiman shall fall down.

—As a result of the U.S.-U.S.S.R. alliance, China will feel betrayed and ally herself with the Arab powers:

When those of the Arctic pole shall be
    united together,
There shall be in the East great fear and
    trembling,
One shall be newly elected that shall bear
    the brunt,
Rhodes, Constantinople shall be dyed with
    barbarian blood.

—An Arab-Chinese invasion:

The African heart will come from the Orient,
To vex the head of Italy and the heirs of
    Romulus,
Accompanied by the Libyan fleet,
Malta will tremble, the neighboring isles
    will be empty.

—And on into France:

The Oriental will leave his seat,
He will pass the Apennine Mountains to
    see France,
He will pierce through the sky, the
    waters, and the snow,
And he will strike everyone with his rod.

—The invasion, having swept through the Balkans, will enter Germany and France:

In the Danube and Rhine shall come to drink
The great Camel, and shall not repent,
The Rhone shall tremble and more those of
    Loire,
And near the Alps the Cock shall ruin them.

—In spite of this temporary rear-guard victory by the French:

The Arab Prince Mars, Sun, Venus, Leo,
The rule of the Church will succumb by sea,
Towards Persia nearly a million men,
The true serpent will invade Byzantium
  and Egypt.

—Guided missiles are forecast:

After great trouble for humanity, a greater
  one is prepared,
The Great Mover renews the ages,
Rain, blood, milk, famine, steel and
  plague,
In the heavens fire seen, a long spark running.

—Nuclear bombing will light the heavens with the blinding brilliance of 2 suns, and the Pope himself shall flee:

The great star will burn for 7 days,
The cloud will cause 2 suns to appear,
The big mastiff will howl all night,
When the great Pontiff will change country.

—The Arabs and Chinese will finally be driven off by a German:

A Germanic heart will be born of
  Trojan blood,
Who will attain to a very high degree of
  power,
He will drive out the foreign Arabian people,
Restoring the Church to its pristine
  preeminence.

—Then, in Nostradamus' only dated quatrain, he stated that in July, 1999, this new leader will wage terrible war against the foe:

In the year 1999 and 7 months,
From the skies shall come an alarmingly
  powerful king,
To raise again the great King of Jacquerie,
Before and after, Mars shall reign at will.

—War continues until the old century is about to expire, when, between November 23 and December 21, 1999, the fabled Battle of Armageddon takes place:

When a fish pond that was a meadow
  shall be moved,
Sagittarius being in the ascendant,
Plague, Famine, Death by the military hand,
The Century approaches renewal.

—With victory, the world enters upon an Age of Peace. Not until the 7th millennium will the destruction of the earth occur:

The year of the great 7th number
  accomplished,
There shall be seen the sports of the
  ghostly sacrifices,
Not far from the great age of the millennium,

That the buried shall come out of their
  graves.
Twenty years of the reign of the moon
  having passed,
Seven thousand years shall another hold
  his monarchy,
When the sun shall resume his days past,
Then is fulfilled and ends my prophecy.

Predictor: Coinneach (Kenneth) Odhar (The Brahan Seer)
Scottish seer of the time of Charles II (1630–1685)—noted for "2nd sight" by staring into round blue stone with hole in center. Countess of Seaforth put him to death, thrusting his head into barrel of boiling tar, for predicting infidelity of her husband. Most famous prophecy: "Doom of the Seaforths."
Past Predictions:—"Doom of the Seaforths": Saw "far into the future" when last of line would be "both deaf and dumb." (The last, Francis Humbertson Mackenzie, became deaf after attack of scarlet fever; later, also dumb.)
"He himself shall sink into the grave, and the remnant of his possessions shall be inherited by a white-hooded lassie from the East." (Lord Seaforth's eldest daughter, Lady Hood, returned from the East to bury her father, white-coiffed in the mourning fashion of the time.)
"As a sign by which it may be known that these things are coming to pass, there shall be 4 great lairds in the days of the last deaf and dumb Seaforth—Gairloch, Chisholm, Grant, and Ramsey, of whom one shall be bucktoothed, another harclipped, another half-witted, and the 4th a stammerer." (Of the 4 Scottish lairds who were his neighbors, Sir Hector Mackenzie of Gairlock was bucktoothed, Chisholm of Chisholm was harelipped, Grant of Grant was half-witted, and MacLeod of Ramsey stammered.)
Future Predictions:
—Warns of the doom of the entire country of Scotland when "a dun hornless cow will appear in Minich and will make a bellow which will knock the 6 chimneys off Gairloch House." The "cow" interpreted as a submarine; the "bellow" as a powerful detonation, perhaps from a fleet of submarines based in Holy Loch nearby.
—Then, "the whole country will become so utterly desolate and depopulated that the crow of a cock shall not be heard."
—". . . after which deer and other wild animals shall be exterminated by horrid black rain." "Horrid black rain" in reference to radiation fallout. In Coinneach's day, Gairloch House was wattled, thatched with turf, having no chimneys. Today it does indeed have 6 chimneys.

Predictor: Baron de Novaye
Occultist of the late 19th century, who recorded prophecies of others as well.

Past Predictions:—The period 1928–1938 to be a disastrous one of wars and massacres. De Novaye was wrong.
—The period 1942–1954 to be peaceful years. De Novaye was wrong.
—1900–1912 to be a socialistic-revolutionary period. De Novaye was right.
—1914–1924 to be an imperial patriotic period including a Great War. De Novaye was right.
—1956–1969 to be another socialist-revolutionary period. De Novaye was right.
Future Predictions:
—1973–1983 to be another imperial-patriotic period filled with small wars.
—1985–1998 to be a period of great war, violence, then restoration.
—2004–2016 to usher in a peaceful period for all nations.

Predictor: LEO TOLSTOI
1828–1910. Russian novelist and writer on religion, ethics. Just before death, in trancelike state, he made the following prophecy:
Past Predictions:—"I see floating upon the sea of human fate the huge silhouette of a nude woman. Nations rush madly after her. In her hair—an ornament of diamonds and rubies—is engraved her name: 'Commercialism.'"
"Commercialism" interpreted as "Materialism."
—"And behold, she has 3 gigantic arms with 3 torches of universal corruption in her hands. The 1st torch represents war. The 2nd torch bears the flame of bigotry and hypocrisy. The 3rd torch is that of law, that dangerous foundation of all unauthentic traditions." Law interpreted as a device to justify false ethics.
—"The great conflagration will start about 1912, set by the torch of the 1st arm in the countries of southeastern Europe." The assassination of Archduke Ferdinand in the Balkans in 1914 ushered in W.W. I.
—"But, about the year 1915 a strange figure from the North—a new Napoleon—enters the stage of the bloody drama. He is a man of little militaristic training, a writer or journalist, but in his grasp most of Europe will remain until 1925." Nikolai Lenin, revolutionary writer, threatened to spread Communism over all Europe until his death in 1924.
—"The end of the great calamity will mark a new political era. The world will form a federation of the United States of Nations. There will remain only 4 great giants—the Anglo-Saxons, the Latins, the Slavs, and the Mongolians." League of Nations and power blocs: U.S. and Britain, Russians (Slavs), Chinese (Mongolians), but Latin power bloc as yet unfulfilled.
—"After the year 1925 I see a change in religious sentiments. The 2nd torch has brought about the fall of the Church. The ethical idea

has almost vanished." Present worldwide moral decay, beginning with hedonism of the Twenties.
Future Predictions:
—"But, the great reformer arises. He will clear the world of the relics of monotheism and lay the cornerstone of the temple of pantheism. I see the peaceful beginning of an ethical era. The man determined to this mission is a Mongolian Slav. He is already walking the earth." The reformer has not yet appeared. If so, he must be over 60 now. It is getting late for the fulfillment of the prophecy.
—"In place of the polygamy and monogamy of today, there will be poetagamy—a relation of the sexes based fundamentally upon poetic conceptions of life." Trend of youth toward expression of sexual freedom in poetic rather than hypocritical manner.
—"And I see the nations growing wiser and realizing that the alluring woman of their destinies is after all nothing but an illusion. There will be a time when the world will have no use for armies, hypocritical religions, and degenerate art."

Predictor: HELENA P. BLAVATSKY
Russian seer, 1831–1891, whose prophetic powers she attributed to her learning from the "Mahatmas of India, Masters of Wisdom."
Past Predictions:—"Between this time [1886] and 1897 there will be a large rent made in the veil of nature . . ." Taking this to mean new scientific discoveries, such as the discovery of the X ray in 1895 making possible further work with the atom, it was correct.
Future Predictions:
—"We are at the close of the cycle of 5,000 years of the present Aryan Kaliyuga or dark age. This will be succeeded by an age of light."
—A new messenger of the spirit to be sent to the Western nations. He is to appear by 1975.
—Regarding the U.S., ". . . even now under our very eyes, the new Race or Races are preparing to be formed, and that is in America that the transformation will take place, and has already silently commenced." This race, if that is the proper word, will be altered in mentality and physique, and move toward a more perfect spiritual existence.

Predictor: COUNT LOUIS HAMON (Cheiro)
1866–1936. Brilliant and charming bon vivant whose consultations were sought by the wealthy and famous.
Past Predictions:—A year or 2 before each occurred, he foretold: the Boer War, death of Queen Victoria, assassination of King Umberto of Italy, and the day, month, and year of the death of King Edward VII.

—W.W. I to break out in midsummer, 1914, and end in November, 1918.

—Downfall of the Czar, and massacre of him and all his immediate family.

—Of the then Prince of Wales, later to be Edward VIII: "It is within the bounds of possibility . . . that he will in the end fall victim to a devastating love affair. If he does, I predict that the Prince will give up everything, even the chance of being crowned, rather than lose the object of his affection." Edward VIII did indeed give up his throne "for the woman I love," Wallis Simpson, and became the Duke of Windsor.

—For the years 1926–1930, he predicted that adverse conditions would strike almost every country and that unemployment would rise to the highest known level. Although failing to give the exact year, he foresaw the stock market crash of 1929 that heralded the Great Depression.

—India would gain her freedom, but "religious warfare will rend that country from end to end, until it becomes equally divided between Mohammedans and the followers of Buddha." India received her independence in 1947, and divided itself into Hindu India and Moslem Pakistan.

—Spain would have a dictator. Franco became dictator of Spain.

—Palestine would be returned to the Jews and be called Israel. In 1948, Israel proclaimed her independence.

Future Predictions:

—"Communism will spread like an infective fever through all the countries."

—"Russia will become the most dreaded power in the history of modern civilization."

—A dictator for France and "a new form of government for the time being will save France."

—"The U.S. is predestined to have dominion of the air" (control of outer space).

—China and Japan to unite and "will control that part of the globe."

—Armageddon to start in the area of Palestine (Israel).

Predictor: NICHOLAS K. ROERICH
Artist, scholar, archaeologist, explorer of the 1930s who, on a 5-year expedition to the East, recorded the following predictions of Tibetan Lamas.

Past Predictions:—"The year 1936 appears as truly momentous for human fate." There have been other recent years of much greater importance, such as 1939, 1941, 1945. Roerich was wrong.

—June 11, 1936, to be a date of great significance. The Soviet Union on that date submitted for discussion to its people a new constitution. Roerich was right.

Future Predictions:

—"First will begin an unprecedented war of all nations. Afterward brother shall rise against brother. Oceans of blood shall flow. They shall forget the meaning of the word Teacher. But, then shall the Teachers appear and in all corners of the world shall be heard the true teaching. To this word of truth shall the people be drawn, but those who are filled with darkness and ignorance shall set obstacles. As a diamond, glows the light on the tower of the Lord of Shambhala. (Interpreted as the great spiritual kingdom, according to the Lamas.) One stone in his ring is worth more than all the world's treasures. Even those who by accident help the Teachings of Shambhala will receive in return a hundredfold. Already many warriors of the teaching of truth are reincarnated. Only a few years shall elapse before everyone shall hear the mighty steps of the Lord of the New Era. And one can already perceive unusual manifestations and encounter unusual people. Already they open the gates of knowledge, and ripened fruits are falling from the trees.

"The banner of Shambhala shall encircle the central lands of the Blessed One. Those who accept him shall rejoice. And those who deny him shall tremble. . . . The denier shall be given over to justice and shall be forgotten. And the warriors shall march under the banner of Maitreya [the coming spiritual king of the world]."

Predictor: EDGAR CAYCE
1877–1945. Edgar Cayce, the "prophets' prophet," was born on a western Kentucky farm. Though he never finished school, he was able to absorb the contents of books just by sleeping on them. He made his living as a professional photographer. Most of his visions and extrasensory experiences occurred while he was hypnotized. Famous for his miraculous medical diagnoses, he ostensibly was responsible for the cures of many people on whom doctors had given up. Before he died, he predicted a catastrophic earthquake, which would cause California to break away from the mainland and sink into the Pacific. He neglected to give a date for this event. In the 1960s, a group of seers got together and came up with April, 1969, as the time the earthquake would occur. When April rolled around, believers in Cayce's prediction—and there were many—fled the State in fear. Though the earthquake didn't happen, many people still believe it will occur, but at a later date.

Past Predictions:—In 1943, he predicted that in the 25 years following, China would become more democratic and would have more Christian leaders. Cayce was wrong.

—On June 28, 1940, he predicted the Poseidia (Atlantis) would rise again, sometime in 1968 or 1969, around the Bahamas, southwest of Bimini. Cayce was wrong.

—Also in 1940, he predicted that shortly thereafter shifting of the poles would cause temperatures to rise in frigid and semitropical zones. Cayce was wrong. (However, the waters of the Atlantic are warming up because of the decrease in the thickness of the polar ice cap.)

—Seven months before it happened, he predicted the collapse of the stock market which was instrumental in causing the 1929 Depression. Cayce was right.

—He foresaw W.W. II as a world catastrophe which would kill millions. Cayce was right.

—He said that Roosevelt would die before the end of the war. Cayce was right.

—Fifteen years before it happened, he predicted that the Jews would proclaim the State of Israel. Cayce was right.

—In 1932, he predicted earth changes that would produce disasters like the Alaska earthquake of 1964, the eruptions of Mount Etna in 1960 and 1971, the 1968 and 1970 floods in India, the 1968 earthquake in Iran that killed over 11,000 people, and the 1970 earthquake in Peru that killed over 66,000 people. Though he did not pinpoint places and dates, Cayce was generally right.

—In 1932, Cayce predicted that Norfolk, Va., would be the chief port on the East Coast of the U.S. In 1957, this came true. Cayce was right.

—He foresaw that a vast new temple containing records from antiquity would be discovered in Egypt in 1964. Cayce was right.

Future Predictions:

—Europe will disappear "in the twinkling of an eye."

—Cayce will return to earth as world liberator in 1998, then will again be reborn in 2100.

—In 1998, New York City will be destroyed.

—The poles will shift, starting in 1998.

—Alabama will be partially under water.

—Peace will come to the world in 1998.

—L.A.W.

PREDICTIONS BY MODERN SCIENTISTS

Predictor: DANIEL BELL

Daniel Bell, a sociology professor at Harvard University, heads the Commission on the Year 2000—a group of researchers, government officials, and professors organized by the American Academy of Arts and Sciences. He is the author of *The Post-Industrial Society; The End of Ideology; Work and Its Discontents.*

Past Predictions: No record.

Future Predictions: For 2000

—Supersonic transport will make the world "smaller."

—The physical environment will still be livable though there will be less privacy and many problems will exist.

—The society of the year 2000 will be more fragile, with greater hostility and polarization.

—The world will generally be in a postindustrial state with:

 • A services, rather than a goods, economy.

 • Accessible central knowledge used for innovation and policy formation.

 • Power residing in intellectual institutions, like universities, rather than in industry.

 • Greater individual autonomy.

 • A more hedonistic culture distrustful of the achievement-oriented technological world.

Predictor: JAMES BONNER

James Bonner is a professor of biology at the California Institute of Technology. With Ruchih Huang, he succeeded in setting up a test-tube chromosome system to synthesize RNA. He has been somewhat criticized for tampering with life processes and in retaliation

tells of a lady in Pasadena who argued that if God had expected men to fly in jets, he would have had the Wright brothers invent them.

Past Predictions: Wrong—With other scientists, he predicted a 2%–4% yearly increase in agricultural productivity as reasonable in 1957. Ten years later, he himself admitted that yields in developing countries had risen only 8% in an entire decade, or less than 1% per year. He attributed this disappointing increase to American investments in slow-payoff technology in developing countries, and to lack of training and education in those same countries. Though he believes that sending grain to developing countries discourages initiative, he feels that massive aid is still the only way to combat poverty.

Future Predictions: For 1975–1980

—By 1980, the world will consist of 2 cultures—the permanently poor and the permanently rich. While technology will increase wealth exponentially in rich countries, the reverse will be true in poor ones. If we are not careful, eventually we will start looking at the inhabitants of poor countries as another species and find a rationalization for getting rid of them.

—By 1980, the U.S. will have about 1,700,000 engineers and scientists in the working population.

—Men will be able to direct the growth of human organs; in other words, we might be able to grow new arms, hearts, or livers by genetic means. Bonner says, "Maybe you will go to the doctor and he will say, 'Well, I think your heart isn't so good now. Maybe we had

better start growing you a new one. In another 2 or 3 years, it will be grown up, and we can plumb it in.' "
—The brain code will be broken.
For 1991–2000—Population will double in the 25 years from 1967 to 1992.
—Unless developing countries are given massive aid, the population in them will rise 1% a year faster than the rate of production. Famine will become more widespread, impeding industrial development.
—In 2000, there will be about 3,300,000 working engineers and scientists in the U.S., but we will need 3 times that.
No Dates Given—The time will come when we won't work at all because of automation.
—We will be able to make gargantuan holes in deserts to create lakes, and we will use the dirt removed to build mountains.
—Self-contained cities will be possible.
—Someday it may be possible to replace, through synthesis of brain neurons, the 100,000 neurons in the brain that die every day. The new cells will have to be trained, because they will have no memory.
—It will be possible in the near future to develop a superspecies of human being through cloning (i.e., manipulation of body cells to produce individuals identical to the cell donor).

Predictor: D. G. BRENNAN
A mathematician and expert on national security problems, D. G. Brennan is a member of the Hudson Institute, which does research into problems of the future, and is editor of the international journal *Arms Control and Disarmament Annual Review.*
Past Predictions: Wrong—He himself says that had he been asked, in 1958, which Buck Rogers weapons would be most impossible to produce, he would have chosen the disintegrator ray gun. Invention of the laser that year made such a weapon possible.
Future Predictions: For 1975–2018
—Computers as sophisticated as the human brain will be small enough to be carried in a shoe box.
—The laser will be used for target illumination and tracking, target destruction, radar, and communication. An infrared laser using holographic techniques will provide 3-dimensional spatial information.
—Aircraft capable of orbital speeds will be possible.
—Hurricanes will be controllable and will be employed as weapons against the enemy; however, by the time that happens, vessels may be fast enough to outrun them.
—Submarines will be capable of going to depths of 20,000' or more. There will be deepwater fortifications, fences, and weapons centers.

—It will be literally possible to put an intercontinental ballistic missile down a smokestack from a range of 6,000 mi.
—A back-carried antigravity belt may be used to lift individual soldiers.
—We may make war by using only automated or remote-controlled mechanisms and no people, particularly in outer space.

Predictor: ARTHUR C. CLARKE
A prolific writer of science fiction, Arthur C. Clarke is also the originator of communication satellites, for which he was awarded a Franklin Institute Gold Medal. He was formerly Chairman of the British Interplanetary Society. One of his books served as the basis for the movie *2001.*
Past Predictions: Right—In 1945, Clarke predicted the use of satellites for communication. About 15 years later, the 1st such satellite was launched. In 1947, he predicted that the 1st moon rocket would be launched in 1959. It was.
Future Predictions: For 1991–2000
—A road sign of the future is likely to read "No wheeled vehicles on this highway." Cars without wheels will float on air, bringing about the passing of the wheel.
—Television from satellites will bring to underdeveloped countries advice on agriculture, birth control, and other educational topics. (Possible now.)
—Air-conditioned settlements on the moon will be situated under domes or below ground to avoid solar radiation. Food will be grown in air-conditioned domes, and building materials will be mined from the moon itself.
No Dates Given—Video-telephones will make possible business lunches with "the 2 halves of the table 10,000 mi. apart." They might also be used to show new designs to the consumer, allowing selection to be made in the home.
—Centralization of work in cities will become obsolete with improved electronic communications.
—It will be possible to radio or cable a letter anywhere in the world in less than a day with privacy assured because of "robot handling at all stages of the operation."
—Physical and chemical sieves may enable us to tap the minerals in the ocean. (A cubic mile of sea water might contain as much as 25 tons of gold.)
—"The 1st intelligent computer will be the last machine man will need to make—and quite possibly the last that he'll be permitted to make."
—People of the future may live on food made from the protein in oil. Three percent of the world's oil production could feed everyone.

—It will probably be possible to observe the past and the future through telepathy.

—We might be able to increase the intelligence of our domestic animals.

—All of the following might be possible: robots, death rays, transmutation, artificial life, immortality, invisibility, levitation, teleportation, and communication with the dead.

Predictor: CHARLES DeCARLO
A Ph.D. in mathematics, Charles DeCarlo is director of automation research at International Business Machines Corporation.

Past Predictions: No record.

Future Predictions: No Dates Given
—Due to laser holography, "total" sensory information will be available eventually, through the use of a small portable unit. Thus, if an individual wants to learn about almost anything at all, he will be able to push a button to call up the simulated presence of experts on that subject.

—A common language, probably some form of English, will be developed.

—Computers may become self-repairing. They may be capable of working directly with the physical environment (e.g., robots) and of imitating the behavior of other machines or people.

—Computers will become smaller, yet will hold far more information and achieve greater speed in performing logical functions. This will be a real advantage for prosthetic medicine (in artificial limbs, for instance) and education.

—Development of such computers and systems will affect the world as follows:

1) Because enormous banks of data will permit examination and monitoring of activities everywhere, the value of national and international secrecy will be diminished. Nations will share what they know.

2) Atomic warfare will be internationally controlled. Search-and-destroy tactics will be so efficient that movements of large-scale armies will be impossible. It will become more and more apparent that no one "wins" a war. Defense strategies will become more important.

3) International banking and finance will be even more influential in foreign-policy formation. Businesses in various countries will get together to establish common methods of production and distribution.

4) The world's scientific and educational communities will share computer programs and methods, cooperating in research and development, environmental control, food production, space exploration, and the eradication of disease.

5) The spread of materialistic science and the desire of people throughout the world for a better standard of living will decrease the importance of ideological differences. People will pay more attention to "what works."

6) The developed nations will increase their lead in science and technology, and the gap between them and the less developed nations will widen.

7) The "computer revolution" will cause governments at 1st to exert more centralized control, but this will eventually be offset by rising educational levels and mobility of populations.

Predictor: PAUL EHRLICH
An expert on population and ecology with somewhat gloomy predictions, Paul Ehrlich is a professor of biology at Stanford and coauthor of *The Population Bomb and How to Be a Survivor.* He calls for stringent controls on population growth, "redevelopment" of technologically developed nations, and other measures to avert worldwide ecological disaster.

Note: Ehrlich's predictions are given in the form of somewhat extravagant scenarios which tell what would happen *if* man doesn't do something to prevent disaster. Therefore, they are not absolute predictions.

Past Predictions: Wrong—In 1964, he said that the Indian vasectomy program was going to fail because of the beliefs of the populace and technical problems. The progam is not an entire failure.

—In 1969, he claimed that it was "ignorant and irresponsible" to expect increased food production from underwater farming. In 1970, food production increased in Asia because of marine agriculture.

—In 1972, he said that 1973 smog disasters in Los Angeles and New York would leave 200,000 dead. He painted a picture of hundreds of people dying without medical help in hospitals, while others watched on their television screens. It would be announced, he said, that Americans born since 1946 (when DDT came into wide use) had a life expectancy of 49 years. Neither event has happened, though smog and DDT remain real dangers.

—In 1972, he said that by 1973 even industrialists from companies like Union Oil would be concerned over the reduction in bird populations because of DDT. Insects and rodents would increase in number at frightening rates. In actual fact, the Environmental Protection Agency announced an almost complete ban on the use of DDT, which became effective on December 31, 1972.

—In 1972, he predicted that water rationing would occur in nearly 2,000 municipalities in 1974 and that hepatitis and epidemic dysentery rates would go up 500%. Neither event took place.

—In 1972, he said that, because of a shift of the jet stream caused by air pollution, a per-

manent drought would occur in the Midwest, turning it into a desert. In reaction, the economy would start to fail. This has not happened.
—In 1972, he said that Congress would pass a Population Control Bill which would authorize an increase in money spent for family planning and would stipulate that all American aid to overpopulated countries would be required to consist partly of assistance in birth control. As a result, underdeveloped countries would try to get the UN to condemn the U.S. as a "genetic aggressor." An Indian Ambassador to the UN would point out that the U.S., with 6% of the people in the world, consumes 50% of its raw materials and that the average American family dog gets fed more animal protein in a week than the average Indian gets in a month. Such a bill has not passed.
Right Somewhat—In 1972, he said that the whaling industry would be close to failure in 1973. In truth, the whaling industry isn't dead, but there is real concern that overkill will indeed cause extinction of certain species of whale.
Future Predictions: For 1975–1980
—In 1975, it may become apparent that a few types of phytoplankton are becoming resistant to chlorinated hydrocarbons. This will vitally affect the ecology of the ocean.
—By 1975, most ocean fishes that return to fresh water to breed (e.g., salmon) will be extinct because of pollution of breeding streams.
—In 1976, a Russian insecticide called "Thanodrin" will be banned in Russia because of its effects on the environment.
—In 1977, the annual fish yield per capita will be less than ½ that in 1967. Fifty million people a year will starve.
—In 1977, solar radiation will be so reduced by air pollution that the world's vegetation will be seriously damaged.
—In 1978, Russia will supply underdeveloped countries with Thanodrin in return for trade and military concessions. Soon insect strains resistant to it will appear, and the environment will be in deep trouble. Reactions against the Russian action will be violent.
—In 1979, new diatom forms will appear in the sea; these will kill off sea life, and within the year the sea may be dead. Japan and China will face mass starvation. Both countries will blame Russia for this (because of the Thanodrin disaster, which would be partially responsible), will demand food from her without success, then will invade her.
For 2800—The population of the earth will be housed in an apartment house 2,000-stories high, which will cover the entire planet.

Predictor: GERALD FEINBERG
A professor of physics at Columbia University, Gerald Feinberg is deeply concerned with the future of the planet. In the next 50 years, he believes, people will for the 1st time make decisions that will cause a radical change in human life. In order to facilitate this, he wants to begin the "Prometheus Project," an international movement through which experts of all kinds will suggest such decisions, which would then be accepted or rejected through a poll of the general populace.
Past Predictions: No record.
Future Predictions: No Dates Given
—It will be possible to tinker with the brain— to make the human memory more reliable and accessible at the expense, say, of breadth in sensory responses.
—Intelligent machines will probably be able to provide enough goods so that all people can live decently.
—Life may be so extended that travel to the stars will be feasible. Tachyon beams may be used for information transfer between stars. (Tachyons are hypothetical particles that move faster than the speed of light.) It may even be possible to use tachyons to "transfer" people, atom by atom, to some other place in space.
—Humans will be able to reach new levels of consciousness, to control creative processes, to perceive logic in a direct way (as we now perceive color, for instance).
—It may be possible to bring about a collective consciousness, a merging of all human minds into one, and then link this up with extraterrestrial consciousness.

Predictor: ORVILLE FREEMAN
Orville Freeman was Secretary of Agriculture during the Kennedy and Johnson Administrations and is now president of Business International Corporation. He believes that if the human race does not develop plans for land use, the world may become even more divided into have and have-not nations, where the haves try to protect themselves from the have-nots with arms and tariffs, as hostility arises. Eventually, he feels, the hostility would end in desperate aggression toward the haves by the have-nots. He is also strongly in favor of alternatives to big cities, such as town-country communities.
Past Predictions: No record.
Future Predictions: No Dates Given
—Space satellites 200 or more miles above the surface of the earth will analyze weather, differences in soil, crops and forests, and spot crop damage.
—It will be possible to speed or retard ripening of crops for market reasons through the use of artificial light and growth-regulating chemicals.
—Bugs, drought, and disease will be kept in check by biological control (e.g., sterilization of insects by radiation), specific insecticides, and weather control. The dozen or so insects

that cause half the world's crop losses will be totally eradicated.

—It will be possible to breed plants and trees unaffected by plant diseases.

—Weeds will be controlled by harmless chemicals that keep seeds from germinating.

—Nuclear heat-tapping of deep snow and glacier ice will provide new water supplies.

By 2000—Soil throughout the world will have been inventoried. Crops will be grown on the soils best suited for them, or soils will be chemically modified for the optimum output.

—Agricultural products will be grown and distributed in accordance with plans made by a sophisticated computer system.

—Unproductive hillsides will be treated to shed rainfall so that this water may be delivered to reservoirs. The surfaces of water bodies will be chemically treated to eliminate water loss by evaporation.

—Irrigation will be completely automated and controlled by computers.

—Livestock will be kept in environmentally controlled shelters, will grow to market size on ⅓ less feed and in ⅓ less time.

—Cornstalks will grow multiple ears; cotton bolls will be clustered on the tops of plants for ease of picking.

—Crops will grow faster and plants will be genetically redesigned so that all their leaves are exposed to sunlight and so that they can live on much less water.

—Farming will be done by computers and computer-controlled machines, but farms will still be family-owned and operated.

Predictor: THEODORE J. GORDON
Theodore Gordon is president of the Futures Group, a private research organization, and was formerly director of Space Stations and Planetary Systems at McDonnell Douglas as well as senior research fellow for the Institute for the Future. He is co-developer of the "cross impact matrix analysis" forecasting technique. Like many modern scientists, his concerns range beyond his field: He is a social analyst of everything from drugs to religion.
Past Predictions: No record.
Future Predictions: For 1981–1990
—Inexpensive nonnarcotic drugs which produce changes in personality as well as sensation may be used in established churches for religious ceremonies.
For 1991–2000—The average man will live to be 100.
No Dates Given—Genetic manipulation will enable man to produce tiny research scientists with IQs of 200 or humble servants or special athletes.
—It will be possible perhaps to provide self-contained life support systems for astronauts, including conversion of body wastes through an artificial kidney built into a spaceship.

Sleep could be electronically induced to lower the metabolism rate.

—It might be possible to make a huge "hollow earth" world from an asteroid, with a mirror placed at an opening in one end to concentrate light, which could be turned on and off as the asteroid's interior inhabitants wished.

Predictor: E. S. E. HAFEZ
An internationally respected biologist, Dr. Hafez is affiliated with Washington State University. He once asked a colleague in Germany to send him 100 head of prize sheep. The sheep arrived, airmail, in a box that could be held in one hand. In the box was a female rabbit, in whose uterus were implanted 100 sheep embryos. These were removed and put into the uteri of 100 ewes, and a few months later, 100 lambs were born.
Past Predictions: No record.
Future Predictions: For 1981–1990
—A woman will be able to walk into a kind of "store" where frozen human embryos are sold in packets, and select a baby with specific physical, mental, and emotional attributes. Then, she will be able to have the embryo implanted in her uterus by her doctor and in 9 months will give birth to a baby. It will be possible for such embryos to be guaranteed free of genetic defects.

Predictor: OLAF HELMER
Dr. Helmer is a founding member of the Institute for the Future in Connecticut and, with others, the developer of Delphi, a method of predicting the future by making use of the intuitive guesses of many experts. A mathematician and philosopher, he says, "We must cease to be mere spectators in our own ongoing history and participate with determination in molding the future."
Past Predictions: No record.
Future Predictions: For 2000
—The world population will be over 5 billion, but the rate of increase will be decreasing because of more efficient methods of population control.
—The World Gross Product will be from 3 to 4 times what it is today. This means that the per capita Gross Product will be double or triple present levels.
—People will live in urban complexes, and life will be automated, with central data banks, a credit-card economy, and portable video-telephones.
—Personality-changing drugs will be used as alcohol is today.
—Plastic and electronic replacements for human organs will extend life.
—A permanent colony will exist on the moon.
—Men will have landed on Mars.
—*Possible, but less probable:*
 • Weather will be controlled.

• Large-scale ocean mining will be in progress.
• Artificial life will have been created.
• There will be immunization against all germ-caused diseases.
• Machines will work as collaborators with scientists and engineers.
—*Even less probable:*
• We will be farming the ocean.
• Highway transportation will be fully automated.
• Men-machine symbiosis will exist.
• We may have learned to control hereditary defects in man; to control the aging process; to cause artificial growth of new organs.
• Drugs to raise intelligence levels may be available.
• We may be mining the moon; have established a permanent base on Mars; have landed on Jupiter's moons.

Predictor: ERICH JANTSCH
Originally Dr. Jantsch, an Austrian, was an astronomer. His increasing concern with possibilities of what might happen in the future led him in the mid-1960s to study forecasting techniques. He is critical of those who believe that forecasting—or science—can be neutral, and he has sympathy with young revolutionaries who want the role of science to be reevaluated. He fears for the ecological future of the world.
Past Predictions: No record.
Future Predictions: For 1981–1990
—The gap between the rich and poor is growing. If we don't do something about it, by 1985 we will be unable to visit developing countries for fear of our lives. The Western countries, Jantsch believes, must halt their economic growth and effect an equitable distribution of goods throughout the world. The alternative is an eventual worldwide class war. He envisions a nightmare of hungry Asians ravaging American and European cities.
For 1991–2000—The maximum amount of food we can hope to get from agriculture will sustain us until about 1990, or possibly 2000. After that time, many will starve. It's already too late for us to do much about it even with population controls.
No Dates Given—If the rest of the world starts using pesticides, the planet's ecological balance will be seriously affected.

Predictor: HERMAN KAHN
A 300-lb. economist whose iconoclastic ideas often shock the academic community, Herman Kahn is co-founder and director of the Hudson Institute at Harmon-on-Hudson, N.Y., where with his colleagues he develops scenarios of the future. He believes the world is changing so fast that it is almost impossible to predict the future accurately; accordingly, he creates triple scenarios which include predictions on the high,

medium, and low sides of optimism. He also believes that the only feasible way to solve the problem of poverty is to make rich countries richer; the resulting gap between rich and poor might be greater, but the poor would still be a lot less poor.
Past Predictions: Wrong (Somewhat)—In 1960, in his book *On Thermonuclear War*, Kahn said that at least 200 well-aimed 20-megaton bombs would be needed to knock out the 53 main urban areas in the U.S. At the time, the U.S.S.R. did not have the nuclear capacity to do this. If such an attack had been possible, "only" about 70 million people would have been killed and only about half the U.S. wealth would have been destroyed. If food stocks had been prepared for 4 years beforehand and fallout shelters were common, most of the 120 million people in the rural areas would have survived the fallout. Fifteen years after, the wealth and some of the population of the U.S. would have been restored. This optimistic prediction is, of course, impossible to evaluate, because the war did not happen. However, it is no longer valid because a much heavier attack by the Russians is now feasible.
Right—In *Foreign Affairs* in 1968, Kahn predicted that the U.S. would not soon be out of Vietnam and that neither the Government of the U.S. nor that of South Vietnam would collapse.
Future Predictions: For 1975–1980
—Under certain conditions an economic depression could begin in the mid-1970s. If so, by the late 1970s the U.S. dollar will be worth a great deal less and inflation will increase. Polarization of the political left and right will occur. Bonn will devalue the mark. At this point the President of the U.S. will probably turn to the Board of Governors of the International Monetary Fund to solve the problem, but it will be too late, and his action will cause a run on the dollar. In response, the President will have to make the dollar incontrovertible, England will do the same with the pound sterling, and a panic will then ensue. In the end, there will be a worldwide depression, in which governments will fall and people may starve.
For 1985—Over 70 problems of various kinds may cause a technological crisis.
For 2000—Kahn divides the world into 5 categories:

Category of Nation	Annual per capita average in Gross National Product
Preindustrial	Less than $200
Traditional	$200–400
Industrial	$600–1,500
Highly Industrial	$1,500–4,000
Postindustrial	More than $4,000

Kahn predicts that by the year 2000, if conditions continue to follow present trends, the U.S. GNP per head will rise from the 1965

level of $3,557 to $10,160, while India's will
rise from $99 to $270. About ⅜ of the world's
population will be above the $600 per capita
line, and the *average* of those over $600 will
be almost $4,000, but those below the line
will average only a little over $300.

The U.S. and the U.S.S.R. will still be
superpowers so far as Gross National Product;
the next 8 intermediate powers, with half the
GNP, will be Japan, West Germany, France,
China, the United Kingdom, India, Italy, and
Canada. The next 120 powers on the list will
have ⅔ the GNP of the intermediate powers.
In short, gaps will still exist, but people will be
generally richer, with the Gross World Product
up from $2.1 trillion in 1965 to $10.9 trillion
(in 1965 U.S. dollars). The per capita GWP
will increase from half to 4 times that of 1965,
depending on world conditions, with the shift
in favor of the developing nations. Most nations will go up a notch or 2 on Kahn's 5-
category ladder.

—In the year 2000, the population of the
world will be about 6.4 billion, slightly more
than 2 times the 1965 population. Africa and
South America will have the greatest growth
rates, but nearly 60% of the world's peoples
will still be Asian.

—In the year 2000, people will throw out inexpensive appliances rather than repair them
because repair and maintenance costs will have
risen so much. Complete modular replacement
units may be widely available.

—Productivity per capita will rise, providing
more leisure. By 2000, the U.S. may have a
population of 318 million, of which 38% may
be unemployed, while, under optimal conditions, one family in 12 will have an income of
over $50,000 a year. (Now only one family in
several hundred earns that much.) Over 25%
of all families will have incomes above $25,000
a year.

—It is possible that many people will be kept
in a permanently drugged state and adapted to
a specific ecology to which they will be assigned
by some computerized calculation. The central
government may be faced with such overwhelming immediate problems that it may not
be able to see the forest for the trees. To many
problems there may be no solutions which do
not reject modern technology or condemn billions of surplus humans to death or deprivation. (This is one of Kahn's pessimistic scenarios.)

—Technology will have made possible multiple
application of the laser, new power sources, new
airborne and submarine vehicles, 3-dimensional
photography, and human hibernation for medical purposes.

—Cultures will become increasingly sensate,
humanistic, and hedonistic.

—Increased literacy and education will encourage the formation of elite groups according
to individual merit rather than material factors
such as money.

Predictor: DESMOND KING-HELE
A leading authority on earth satellites,
Desmond King-Hele is deputy chief scientific
officer of the Royal Aircraft Establishment in
England. He graduated from Trinity College,
Cambridge, with 1st-class honors in mathematics in 1948. A fellow of the Royal Society
and of the Institute of Mathematics and Its
Applications, he is also a member of the International Academy of Astronautics and of
the Council of World Bureaus of Satellite
Geodesy. He is the author of several books on
satellites.

Past Predictions: No record.
Future Predictions: For 1981–1990
—If overuse of antibiotics continues, by 1980
germs may have a virulence that would have
taken 1,000 years to develop under natural
conditions.

—The moon will be the main sphere of operations in space.

—Accurate working models for computer
weather forecasting will determine the effects
of removing Arctic ice and damming the Bering
Strait.

—Scientists will have found out more about
sleep, and ways will be available whereby
people can get along on less sleep.

—By 1980, people's real earnings will increase
by 20%.

For 1991–2000—Slave robots are likely to
appear. It also may be possible to devise a
way for a disembodied brain to be kept alive
so that it can give instruction to a robot
which will act as its body.

—Three-dimensional color television, with
smell, touch, and taste added, may be available by the 1990s.

—We will be sensible enough to reduce birth
rates so that the world population in 2000
will be only 6 billion. It will be possible to
feed these billions through an increased yield
per acre, fish farming, and other means.

—By 2000, air travel will be 15 times faster
than in 1970, delivering passengers anywhere
in the world within 2 hours of takeoff. Trains
may be replaced with continuous teleporters
with individual "cabins" which are gradually
speeded up, traveleators, or horizontal escala-
tors.

—Men may land on Mars before the end of
the century.

—Adhesive tape will be strong enough to take
care of all household repairs, and shoes will
last a human lifetime.

—Watches will be accurate within ⅕ of a
second a year.

—There will be more efficient methods of

treating cancer, heart attacks, strokes, malnutrition, rheumatism, and the common cold, though these diseases will not necessarily be eradicated.

—By 2000, it might be possible to inject new knowledge into the brain, and rudimentary brain-computer links are likely to have been devised.

No Dates Given—A natural catastrophe—such as a change in the sun's radiation or a collision of the earth with an asteroid—is possible.

—A radio "transceiver," as small as a wristwatch, will be used as a miniature portable telephone.

—In new cities, transportation will be provided by small publicly-owned electric cars, into which the driver can insert a coin for use for a certain number of miles. Roads will be devised which will control the speed of traffic so that the driver will not have to "drive" but will, instead, be on automatic pilot.

—Other transportation will be provided by pneumatic trains blown along transparent tubes by compressed air, by monorails, by hover-trains, by rocket trains.

—Lunar bases will be used as research centers, and as resorts where those with physical difficulties can feel well again because of the low gravity.

—In orbits near earth, large manned space stations, used as staging posts for moon journeys, will shine at night. Smaller satellites will give minute details about weather.

—It may be possible to use huge mirrors on satellites to concentrate heat and disperse clouds at selected places; to run a huge double pipe from Britain to the Sahara, in order to exchange desert heat for cool English air; to equalize the distribution of sunlight and rain over all latitudes between 30° south and 60° north.

—Antigravity devices may become available.

—Time travel will be impossible; a time traveler from the future could tell us what we're about to do next, whereupon we'd be able to do something else, which contradicts logic.

Predictor: JOHN MCHALE
John McHale is an artist, designer, ecologist, sociologist, and scientist. Formerly executive director of the World Resources Inventory at Southern Illinois University, he is an active member of the Continuing Committee of the World Future Research Congress and has written books about the future.
Past Predictions: Wrong—No record.
Right—He predicted personal computers would one day be available. McHale was right.
—He once said computers would be able to

learn from experience on nontrivial tasks. McHale was right.
Future Predictions: For 1975–1980
—It will be possible to put information into computers with handwritten manuscript.
—A flat-screen wall television will be developed, as will experimental digital television.
For 1981–1990—It will be possible to put information into a computer by talking into it.
—Three-dimensional television will be developed.
—The telephone network will be fully digitalized.
For 1991–2000—Home video-computers will become available.
No Dates Given—Art will tend to become more a part of the environment and less value will be placed on permanence (in life, as well as in art).

Predictor: MARGARET MEAD
A highly respected anthropologist, Margaret Mead has often spoken up on aspects of popular culture. She is curator emeritus of ethnology at The American Museum of Natural History, and past president of both the American Anthropological Association and the World Federation for Mental Health. At 23, she spent 9 months on a field trip to Samoa, and after that returned repeatedly to the Pacific to study island cultures. Dr. Mead is the author of several classics in anthropology—*Coming of Age in Samoa, New Lives for Old, Male and Female.* In her column for *Redbook* magazine, she has commented on the world scene.
Past Predictions: No record.
Future Predictions: To 1998
—If man has not found ways to deal with environmental problems such as water and air pollution by 1998, it will be too late. "The future is not determined and it lies in our own hands."
No Dates Given—In recent years, we have gone from a postfigurative culture, in which the young learn from the old, to a cofigurative culture, in which children and adults learn from their peers. The culture in which the young live is so different that the old can give them little guidance in how to deal with it. The young take for granted satellites, war, computers, pollution, the idea of population control. No longer bound by the linear sequences of the printed media, they learn from television where they see killing and other events as they happen in 3-dimensional "reality." They make few distinctions between friend and foe, peacetime and wartime, "my" group and "their" group, according to Dr. Mead. The older generation is similarly isolated and knows more about change than any other generation. In the future, we will prob-

ably live in a prefigurative culture in which the old learn from the young. We must, Dr. Mead says, discover prefigurative ways of teaching and learning that will keep the future open, so that children will learn how to learn and discover the value of commitment, rather than be told what to learn or be committed to. In addition, elders will need the experiential knowledge of the young as a basis on which to make plans. The young must be allowed to participate directly and ask the questions; however, there must exist enough trust between generations so that the old will be allowed to work on the answers.

Predictor: ITHIEL DE SOLA POOL
A professor of political science at Massachusetts Institute of Technology, Pool is the author of several books—*Symbols of Democracy; American Business and Public Policy; The People Look at Educational Television; Candidates, Issues, and Strategies.*
Past Predictions: No record.
Future Predictions: No Dates Given—Information technology will make possible indices of everything—e.g., public happiness according to race, sex, and age; reports of levels of public knowledge; statistics on traffic delays. Such computerized data systems will raise the issue of invasion of privacy.
—Knowledge of the human brain—cognition, memory, ability to make associations, categorization—will increase. Educational technology will be extremely sophisticated.
—Computers will be built that will be capable of formulating grammatical sentences in answer to verbal questions and of translating from one language into another.
—It will be possible to determine specifically the effects of the family, genetic inheritance, and parental treatment on the individual child.
—People will be even more uninhibited than today and will talk openly about their feelings.
—Nations will regulate their economic condition, making conscious choices concerning growth, consumption, and leisure.
—The economic gap between developed and undeveloped nations will narrow.
—Nationalism will be less important.
—Sophisticated information systems will make it possible for diplomats to experiment on-line with alternate strategies by means of simulation models of international systems.

Predictor: ROBERT PREHOLDA
Dr. Preholda is an expert in biological technology.
Past Predictions: No record.
Future Predictions: For 1981–1990
—Antiaging pills that cost no more than 30¢ a day will be available. Composed of antioxidants, such as vitamin E, these will neutralize "free radical" molecules that multiply and at-

tack stable molecules in the body. The effect on society and human life will be tremendous.
No Dates Given—Cloning (asexual reproduction) will be possible. It will be accomplished by stimulating a random cell of a person's body so that it develops into a complete "identical twin." Through one method, the nucleus would be removed from a woman's ovum and replaced with a nucleus from a body cell of another person. This altered ovum, now containing genetic DNA not from the woman but from the other person, would be stimulated into dividing, then would be raised in a "host" other mother or "test tube" environment. The resulting embryonic individual might then be used as a source of cellular replacement for the original "twin."

Predictor: ROGER REVELLE
Dr. Revelle is dean of research at the University of California.
Past Predictions: No record.
Future Predictions: For 1975–2018
—By chemically modifying energy transfer between the ocean and the atmosphere, hurricanes and other violent storms may be forestalled. Reflecting materials might be spread over parts of the oceans where hurricanes begin in order to stop the overheating of water near the surface which creates them. (This might decrease rainfall over land areas, however.) The same process might be used over ice- and snow-covered land areas, using nonreflecting materials, to increase solar heating.
—Weather will be predicted through satellite sensors and networks of ocean buoys.
—At the beginning of the 21st century, it may be possible to increase the harvest of ocean fish and other animals to 4 times the amount taken in 1968—from 50 million tons to 200 million tons. This, however, would depend on advances in ocean technology—and an increased harvest of small fish and "krill" (large planktonic crustacea).
—Junk dumped on the continental shelves could form a shelter for sea life and kelp, causing yields of food from the sea.
—Ocean farming will greatly increase, particularly in places near the shore and in estuaries. These areas would be made more productive by "fertilizing" them with nutrients. By changing circulation patterns and plankton production, fish yield would be increased.
—Oil and other commodities could travel through the oceans in giant plastic bladders towed by submarines, or be transported in transoceanic pipelines.
—An international system for keeping track of missile-launching submarines may be established. It could consist of a network of underwater sound devices, possibly combined with lasers.
—Worldwide navigational systems using satel-

lites and ground-based radio stations would allow a ship anywhere to locate itself accurately and quickly.

—Waste from nuclear plants on the shore might keep a wide ribbon of water heated to comfortable levels for swimming and other recreation the year round.

—Underwater parks and marine wilderness areas are likely to be established.

—It will be possible to "wrinkle" the shore line by building peninsulas, bars, and islands and dredging estuaries and bays (which might disturb the ecological balance of the ocean). Such wrinkling would increase the amount of coastline available for recreation.

—Before the turn of the 21st century, a recreational submarine, capable of submerging to depths of several miles, may be available for about $5,000.

Predictor: JEAN ROSTAND
A world-renowned biologist, Rostand has received numerous awards and prizes for research into such areas as parthenogenesis, malformation in growth and structure of organisms, amphibian genetics, and cryogenics. He has written over 3 dozen scientific books and 16 short books on life and philosophy. He is round-faced, with a walrus mustache and a twinkle in his eye.
Past Predictions: No record.
Future Predictions: Dates Not Specified—Science will someday be able to preserve people after death.

—Brain transplants will probably never be possible.

—Parthenogenesis, reproduction through development of an unfertilized gamete, will someday be possible, so that we will be able to have as many exact copies of an exceptional individual as we want.

—Science will be able to reprogram gametes by changing the composition of the nucleic acids that determine heredity, thus modifying an embryo at its start.

—Animals might be "humanized." For instance, human bone marrow could be transplanted into apes so that they would produce human blood. Human hormones could be introduced into an ape to increase its intelligence. Treatments could be performed on ape embryos to increase the number of cortical cells in the brain, and thus increase intelligence.

—It is possible that human beings will be able to create life artificially, though not in the near future. Rostand says, "By manufacturing that humble assimilating and self-reproducing particle, by causing life to be born, for the 2nd time, of something other than itself, man will have closed the great mysterious cycle. A product of life, he will have in turn become a producer of life."

—Through chemicals, such things as fatigue, anxiety, and grief will be alleviated, and pleasurable emotion will be available on demand. Control of feelings, opinions and ideas will be possible, as will the replacement of memories.

Predictor: LLOYD V. STOVER
Stover is senior research scientist at the University of Miami Institute of Marine Science.
Past Predictions: Wrong—In 1970, Stover predicted that by the mid-1970s Surface Effect Ships (SES), like hovercraft, would be providing transportation systems for commuters, using waterways near cities like Washington, D.C.
Future Predictions: For 1975–1980
—Along the coasts, people might be enjoying themselves in boats propelled by water jets and in small submarines.

—Through international agreement in the United Nations, a seabed registry will be established which will regulate ocean exploration and development beyond national boundaries.

—With diver assistance, the U.S. Navy expects to be able to salvage large objects (e.g., submarines) from depths as great as 850'.

—Stable ocean platforms will be used as large sea-station systems for airports, shipping terminals, resorts, and perhaps oil refineries. To reach shore, operators will use VTOL (Vertical Take Off and Landing) and STOL (Short Take Off and Landing) vehicles, hydrofoils, Surface Effect Ships, and conventional surface ships.

—Large moving laboratories will be operating at depths as great as 6,000'. These will contain excursion modules which can leave the mother lab and go down 4,000' deeper.

—Mobile mining systems may mine minerals from shallow parts of the ocean.

—The fishing industry will be back in operation at greater capacity than before. Large submersible systems will process, in the ocean, plants and animals for food.

—Offshore petroleum will supply 33% of U.S. needs.

—A giant undersea exploratory operation along ocean ridges, extending from Iceland through the Atlantic and around the Cape of Good Hope into the Indian Ocean, will provide information which will aid in evaluation of undersea resources.

—The nations of the world will cooperate in planning for the use of resources in order to control pollution and improve the environment.
For 1981–1990—Large oceangoing SES vehicles might provide transportation over the world's oceans.

—A World Weather Watch will change local weather, tame hurricanes, and possibly cause artificial upswellings in the ocean in order to bring up nutrients from the bottom, which will increase the number of fish.

—The ocean will supply the world with significant amounts of power, water, food, and drugs.
—By 1990, large commercial submersible vehicles will be in operation, and submerged ports to handle them will be under study.
—Surveys to great depths will be conducted in order to determine possible uses of calcium carbonate, silicon dioxide, and the red clays found there.
For 1991–2000—Large undersea stations supported by nuclear power and used for research will be possible at depths greater than 10,000′.

—By 1995, complete underwater resorts will have been built.
—Scientists will be seriously considering mobile floating cities, which by 2000 will have been built in prototype. These would be used for space launchings, for plants for processing food from the sea, and for special research.
—By 2000, the world demand for food from the sea will reach 350 billion lbs. (In 1970, it was 123 billion lbs.)
—The ocean could be considered as a major source of food, power, fresh water, and other resources.

—A.E.

PREDICTIONS BY OTHERS

Predictor: KENNETH E. BOULDING
Kenneth E. Boulding, a professor of economics at the University of Colorado, is the author of several books, including *The Meaning of the Twentieth Century, The Prospering of Truth,* and *Peace and the War Industry.*
Past Predictions: No record.
Future Predictions: For 1975–2020
—The short-term economic outlook for the world is bleak. Depletion of fossil fuel reserves will cause great calamities especially in the poorer nations, where economic growth proceeds at a snail's pace—or not at all. The U.S., however, will not experience radical changes, although inflation will continue to worsen. An overhauling of the tax structure will be called for, in which the rich and the middle class are expected to assume a larger share of the tax burden than they do now.
For 2120—Within 150 years from now, mankind will have devised solutions to the problems that threaten to overwhelm the world. Productivity will be increased, shortages will be eliminated, and wealth will be distributed fairly. Moreover, the fuel shortage will have been solved.

Predictor: MCGEORGE BUNDY
McGeorge Bundy served as special assistant for national security affairs under Presidents John F. Kennedy and Lyndon B. Johnson. A political scientist by profession, he is currently president of the Ford Foundation.
Past Predictions: No record.
Future Predictions: For 1979–1991
—Bad harvests for 3 years running produce the Great Famines of 1979–1981. Food shortages in the U.S. spark the worst riots in the nation's history, and similar shortages in France cause equally devastating civil violence there. Some 65 million people throughout the world die. The immediate crisis ends with bountiful grain harvests in 1982 and 1983.
For 1984—A succession of sudden and entirely unexpected nuclear explosions ravages an American city. The U.S. Nuclear Uses Technology Reaction Analysis Team (NUTRAT) determines at once, through quick but thorough analysis of scientific data involved, that the blast is the doing of Communist China. The President of the U.S. thereupon authorizes an identical missile-launched attack upon a large Chinese city. Peking, assuming that the American attack is a cover for what is actually Soviet aggression, responds in kind against a Russian city to complete the triangle. As it turns out, China was not the original belligerent, and the President of the U.S. offers reparations. Peace is restored among the 3 nations. The 3 cities, where 10 million people have died, are rebuilt, never again to be known by their original names. (Instead, they are renamed "Remembrance"—each in the language of the country in which it is located.) It city was done by 2 terrorists—who commit suicide—working in tandem with 2 American is discovered that the bombing of the American nuclear energy companies and 2 small totalitarian countries bent on destroying the U.S.
For 1988—Seventy nations, including the 30 most highly populated, sign the Population Protocols of 1988, under which they agree to stabilize their populations at specific levels. China and India each pledge to hold their population steady at 1.2 billion. Brazil's level of stabilization will be 400 million. Brazil, incidentally, has emerged as the most powerful country in Latin America.
For 1989—On October 24—United Nations Day—the Great Covenant of Survival is signed in New York City. Its guiding principle is capsulized in the Preamble: "To do all that must be done for our survival—and to do nothing more." For the 1st time in history, the nations of the world are able to establish guidelines that effectively insure peace, and end threats to their own survival—without sacrificing their own sovereignty or national identity.
For 2024—A World Conference on Under-

employment and Inflation has been established as a 1st step in dealing with an international underemployment rate of 12% and a monthly inflation rate of 3%.

Predictor: YEHEZKEL DROR

Yehezkel Dror, the distinguished Israeli political scientist, teaches at the Hebrew University of Jerusalem and is a former member of the Rand Corporation, in Santa Monica, Calif. His most recent book is *Crazy States*.

Past Predictions: No record.

Future Predictions: No Dates Given

—Dror believes that the phenomenon of nations' and political action groups' "going crazy," as Nazi Germany did in the 1930s and the Christian Crusaders did in the Middle Ages, will become increasingly more common in the future. He suggests several possible scenarios:

—In the U.S., a wave of civil violence aimed at schools, public facilities, government officials, municipal transportation systems, and prominent industrialists throws the population into chaos. The Government's ability to control the unrest deteriorates to the point of quavering helplessness while the population is dangerously polarized into 2 groups—one which advocates all-out violence, and one which promotes absolute pacifism. In the meantime, a presidential candidate emerges who vows to clean up the bureaucratic hodgepodge and get the country back on its feet. He is charismatic and convincing, and he is elected. The new President uses Soviet belligerence in the Middle East as an excuse to suppress civil liberties in the U.S. and set up martial law. Dissent is suppressed, minorities are oppressed, and stepping up the country's nuclear 1st-strike capability is given top priority. The nation, now a totalitarian State, is seized by a collective mania for wiping communism off the face of the earth.

—A Sukarno-like military dictator assumes power in Indonesia and infuses the population with a passion for territorial expansion in the Far East. The armed forces are beefed up enormously, an atomic weapons development program is established, and the leader tightens his already viselike grip on what is an all but omnipotent political machine. There is Indonesian terrorist infiltration into bordering nations, and Indonesia's bellicosity is supported by the Soviet Union. The nation threatens to conquer all of the East Indies—including Malaysia, Singapore, New Guinea, and the Philippines—and makes inroads into Australia.

—Chaotic economic and political conditions give rise to a general strike in France, and an atmosphere of violence and terror. From it all, a political junta consisting of generals and high-ranking civil servants takes over and restores order through sheer physical force. France

pursues an aggressive, almost hostile foreign policy aimed at destroying the European Common Market, isolating the U.S. from Europe, and establishing a United Europe with France as the dominant power.

—A resurgence of Mexican nationalism and anti-U.S. feeling culminates in Mexican demands that the U.S. return California and Texas to Mexico. The sentiment spreads quickly through Latin America, fueled in part by a series of incidents in which Mexican-Americans are injured. There is widespread terrorist activity in the U.S.

—State power in the oil-rich nation of Kuwait is seized by a band of Islamic religious zealots who seek world domination. Important policy decisions are made by a small coterie of power-holders during drug-induced trances. Kuwait's income from oil increases, and the Government uses its vast revenues to strengthen its army, steal weapons secrets from other countries, and build up a nuclear capability and a missile arsenal.

Predictor: EMMET JOHN HUGHES

Emmet John Hughes, who is currently a political science professor at Rutgers University and a columnist for *Newsweek*, spent 20 years as a foreign correspondent for *Time-Life* and was a speech writer for President Eisenhower. He predicts dramatic changes in the world map over the course of the next few decades.

Past Predictions: Right—In 1974, Hughes said that the Sino-Soviet conflict would never explode into total war; that Great Britain would not throw in its lot with the U.S., but instead, would ally itself more closely with France, West Germany, and Italy; and that the Communist satellite nations of Eastern Europe would not rise up in rebellion against the Soviet Union. To date, these prophecies have been borne out.

Future Predictions: For 2024

—In Asia, the 2 Vietnams will be united under a Communist regime, as will North and South Korea. Conversely, India's insuperable top-heaviness will eventually fragment that nation into several parts. Mainland China, of course, will engulf Taiwan, and then direct its quest for new conquests southward.

—Economic necessity will override patriotism and cause the nations of Western Europe to band together—if not under a single government, then certainly in a close politico-economic alliance.

—Quebec will secede from Canada and form an independent republic. The 3 prairie provinces—Alberta, Saskatchewan, and Manitoba—will likewise secede and become part of the U.S.

Predictor: HERBERT A. OTTO

Herbert A. Otto is a psychologist who has

written extensively on male-female relationships.
Past Predictions: No record.
Future Predictions: No Dates Given
—Changes in society now taking place—such as increasing employment for women and greater equality between the sexes—will liberate women from the conscious feelings of worthlessness that hold them back. Male-female relationships will become more intimate, less superficial, and more egalitarian.
—Increasingly, women will be initiating relationships, rather than consistently allowing the man to make the 1st move.
—Marriage—as well as erotic friendships and sexual liaisons—between members of contrasting races and religions will take place with greater frequency, and will be more accepted than it is today.

—There will be a proliferation of alternatives to the mom-and-pop approach to raising children, including single parents, communes, multiple parents, and family clusters. The participation of the father in the delivery of his child will be taken for granted. Children will be treated with greater respect and given more autonomy.
—Sex will be seen less and less as a male-oriented activity in which the woman remains essentially passive; rather, it will be viewed as an activity in which both sexes play an equal role, and are equally entitled to the pleasures it offers.
—Variant sexual preferences, including homosexuality, will be tolerated and respected universally.

—B.F.

2

Plugging In and Shedding Light—
Special Articles

Snoopy: The Authorized Biography of a Great American

By Charles M. Schulz

It is difficult to write an accurate biography of Snoopy because many of his recollections seem to be marred by fanciful dreams. We are led to believe that he was very active in W.W. I and that he was actually the victim of the accurate gunfire of Baron von Richthofen on sev-

eral dramatic occasions. Military records are vague about these encounters.

One thing is sure, however. He was born at the Daisy Hill Puppy Farm. His father's occupation was probably much like that of other beagles. He chased his quota of rabbits and retired early. We know little about his mother, although at one time we almost discovered her whereabouts when Snoopy set off to find her. The high point of that journey was the supposed sighting of his mother and his rushing across a field toward a farmyard shouting, "Mom! Mom! Mom!" only to be brought up short when he discovered that it wasn't his mom. He had been deceived by the fact, on his own admission, that to him all beagles look alike.

We are not sure how many brothers and sisters Snoopy has, but we do know that one brother lives in Washington and the other in Texas. One sister lives in St. Louis, one in Hollywood, and one in Kansas. A family reunion was arranged at one time, but it turned out to be rather a letdown. To quote Snoopy, "The anticipation far exceeded the actual event." When he was asked to describe what went on at the reunion, he said that none of them spoke the same language. The years had turned them into strangers. His advice from Lucy, when he felt guilty about being disappointed in the reunion, was simply not to feel guilty about it. "Just because you are related to people," she said, "doesn't mean you have to like them."

Snoopy's memories of the Daisy Hill Puppy Farm seem to be mostly good ones. We are told that he used, especially, to enjoy the beautiful summer evenings. One thing he described was how they sat around and sang, while someone strummed a banjo, although, upon being pressed for details, he admitted that perhaps no one actually played the banjo, and they didn't really sing, but what happened was they merely howled a lot. Snoopy has revisited his birthplace several times, but on his last trip, he was horrified to discover that the Daisy Hill Puppy Farm no longer exists. It has been replaced by a multistoried parking lot. Upon seeing this monstrosity, he cried out, "You stupid people, you're parking on my memories."

His career as a W.W. I flying ace has been replaced with that of a barnstormer. He is also well into a career as a novelist and has had a fair amount of success with the publication of a stirring drama called It Was a Dark and Stormy Night. He almost gained immortality as a baseball player when he had the opportunity to become the 1st player to tie Babe Ruth's home-run record of 714 home runs. Unfortunately, in his last time to bat, in the last game of the season, Charlie Brown got picked off 2nd, thus ending the game, and Snoopy was beaten out by Hank Aaron.

There are many dreams left, and dreams of the future are just as good as dreams of the past. Lying on top of a doghouse enables one, also, to look upward. This is the advantage that he has over the rest of us.

The Author: Creator of the most widely circulated and most widely read comic strip in the world, Peanuts, Charles M. Schulz has fathered such memorable characters as Charlie Brown, Lucy, and Snoopy.

P. T. Barnum Was Right

By Edward A. Merlis

Advertising which is informative, imaginative, tasteful, and appealing is the cornerstone of a healthy, free-market economy. But advertising which deceives and misleads, advertising which manipulates the vulnerable psyches of young children, advertising which absorbs enormous human and material resources in wasteful and spurious product differentiation, advertising which becomes a weapon for the preservation of concentrated economic power and inefficiency—that is advertising which cheats the consumer, saps the perfecting fires of true competition, and subjects our children to an onslaught of distorted, shallow values.

Unfortunately, the latter is more often the case than the former. The advertiser starts his intrusion into our lives while we are at a tender age. With the advent of television, and associated increases in income, the youth market expanded. And as the child is weaned from the bottle, he is introduced to the wonderful world of television advertising. Each year, our average child watches 25,000 commercials—220 minutes of such intellectual stimulation each week. Is it any wonder that 8- and 10-year-olds are cynical and skeptical?

No rational parent would allow a door-to-door salesman to peddle to his children, yet our children are subjected to an unrestricted assault upon their sensibilities by TV advertisers. During a sample week in 1969, according to testimony delivered to a U.S. Senate Subcommittee, CBS broadcast 72 minutes of commercials on a single Saturday morning. As Mother and Dad slept late, their 20th-century babysitter succeeded in exposing the little tykes to 130 individual sales pitches, 63 of which were for toys. Is it any wonder that upon awakening, Mom and Dad are routinely harangued by the toy makers' surrogate salespeople, the tiny tots of America?

Throughout the country, research organizations are dedicated to finding out how to sell products to parents through children. Motivational research houses experiment with children, seeking to find the way to the child's brain and on to the parent's pocketbook. This is the stuff upon which our free enterprise system thrives.

Fortunately, the unceasing prodding of pressure groups has succeeded in wearing down the resiliency of resistance groups. Today, the parents and educators have convinced the broadcasters that they can no longer continue their subterfuge unabated. The broadcasters' code of ethics has reduced the number of minutes of "nonprogram" (read that as "commercial") material in kiddie TV.

The lessons of childhood linger. If for no other reason, that is the objective and motive of the pitchman. In spite of new math, we do old math. In spite of Mali and Upper Volta, we call it French Equatorial Africa. In spite of reason, we buy Kellogg's Rice Krispies. Yes, even we rational and intelligent adults prove P. T. Barnum's axiom—"There's a sucker born every minute"—daily. Why else would the $20+ billion a year advertising industry survive? Advertisers have thoroughly researched human behavior and their findings would make Pavlov's dog and Skinner's pigeons small potatoes in the academic world. Observe some commercials and you will see certain repetitive patterns.

Many advertisements in the broadcast media, particularly television, can be divided into 4 parts. These might be denoted as: 1. the problem; 2. the solution; 3. the consumption; and 4. the resolution. Whether the advertiser is pushing pills, peanuts, or pens, he will often return to the basic 4. It's surprising how much can be condensed into a 30-second spot.

The "problem" is usually one with which we are all familiar—bad breath, unstartable cars, headaches. No matter what the "problem," the set designer or makeup man has succeeded in making a bad situation look worse. The young man with the bad breath is ugly; the unstartable car is old and dirty; the young mother with a tension headache, perhaps from watching too many commercials or thinking about her children's watching them, looks haggard and twice her age.

Next, our friends in the advertising community present us with "the solution." Whether it is a breath mint, an automobile battery, or a headache remedy, the genius of Madison Avenue combines with the skill of Broadway to present an image of the product which, upon rational analysis, is staggeringly ludicrous. Even

a flash cube has been advertised as if it were the 8th wonder of the world. Which isn't so bad, until you realize that the public goes for it.

Next, our public disposition to being "turned on" is released by our benevolent advertising junkie. The act of "consumption" is presented with an almost reverent awe. The actors in our 30-second playlet are euphoric as they chew the breath mint, they dance ecstatically as they install the automobile battery, and they exalt the virtues of the wonder-drug aspirin. To some extent, our vicarious fascination with the bizarre has resulted in our becoming addicted to the inane. The advertiser knows of this fascination, for as the actor turns on, few of us tune out.

We have now arrived at the denouement. Phase 4 of this well-prepared and structured seduction, the "resolution" of the problem, is a relatively easy scene to produce. The homely young man who has consumed the breath mint walks off into the setting sun with his girl—his acne gone, his hair now combed, and his clothing stylish and neat. That old heap destined for the junk yard now starts with a feather touch; its convertible top is down, it has a fresh coat of paint, and an attractive blonde sits next to the driver as he motors off into the setting sun. Our besieged mother of 3 has found her headache relieved by the wonders of science. Suddenly 10 years younger, she smiles approvingly as her hyperactive 4-year-old stops punching the crying 2-year-old, the one with the oatmeal in his hair. She walks off with her mud-stained 6-year-old—into the setting sun, of course.

The repetitive pattern contained in most advertising promises instant gratification through the tasting, swallowing, touching, hearing, and even simulated smelling of an extraordinary variety of material goods. No wonder critics have laid at advertising's doorstep blame for the erosion of our traditional value system, based primarily upon intrinsic rewards for effort, discipline, and responsibility. Thanks to our pals in the advertising business, we are all now equally subjected to the whims and whinings of the commodity pushers and junkies. Maybe that is why our values have changed.

Dr. Natalie Shainess, a noted psychiatrist, has suggested that advertising, not only broadcast commercials, is damaging to society. You don't have to be a Freudian analyst to understand her theory and see its application to many of the advertisements to which we are daily subjected. Dr. Shainess suggests 4 negative aspects are prevalent in advertising today. She says:

1) Advertising is a powerful educational force, counteracting certain aspects of formal education through an appeal to illogic and irrationality.

2) Advertising, as it now exists, weakens character structure through appeal to selfishness and self-centeredness.

3) Advertising fosters greediness, discontent, and the wrong kind of competitiveness between people—that is, not the competition for excellence, but of things; it fosters self-esteem based on consumerism, and human worth is equated with brand names and conspicuous consumption.

4) It is hurtful to human relationships. The growth of selling through sexism and sexual exploitation is one important growing failure in man-woman relationships. It is one of the reasons why the woman over 45 is considered worthless, and tossed on the social dump heap.

Pick up any newsweekly or sit down to an evening of television and you will see Dr. Shainess's hypothesis borne out. The claim that propelled a toilet paper brand to previously untold market shares—"Please don't squeeze the Charmin"—best typifies Dr. Shainess's 1st point concerning appeals to irrationality. And as meaningless as the claim might be, the ultimate absurdity is that the American people have fallen for it.

Appeals to selfishness, Dr. Shainess's 2nd point, are exemplified in advertisements for houses and condominiums. However, consumer product manufacturers who like to think of themselves as luxury-oriented or trend-setters more often than not will use this approach. Who will ever forget the pitch in the Chivas Regal advertisements urging the buyer to save the Chivas for himself? For instance, the entire copy of one Chivas advertisement read, "When serving Chivas Regal, do you suddenly become exceedingly generous with your ice cubes?"

Dr. Shainess suggests that a 3rd antisocial aspect of advertising is the popularizing of negative character traits. This is particularly disturbing since it has most often been used as the foundation of advertising addressed to children. How often have our children been urged, "Be the 1st on your block . . ." or "Don't tell your friends . . ."? Appeals do not stop as we mature; as adults, advertisers continue to appeal to our less virtuous characteristics.

Lastly, and perhaps the most easily demonstrated aspect of Dr. Shainess's theory, is the negative attitude toward women which pervades much of contemporary advertising. Airline commercials are not alone in this area. A Sero King coat advertisement, for the Warwick model, best illustrates this feature common to much of contemporary advertising. The copy reads, in part, "If more girls treated men as considerately as an alpaca-lined wool coat, such as the Warwick, there'd be fewer bachelors."

Talk about mindless simplification of complex interpersonal relationships!

Dr. Erich Fromm, the noted social commentator, 2nds Dr. Shainess's hypothesis about sex in advertising. Upon viewing a National Airlines commercial, with the entreaty "Fly me" uttered by an attractive young stewardess, Dr. Fromm was asked how he would analyze it. He replied, "Well, by a slight change of letters. And I think that is its meaning. And that is not even so unconscious. One doesn't even need a specialist in symbolic language for that. But it is just an attempt to shift the argument completely from the value of an airline to a sexual allusion."

In further support for her contention about the treatment of women in advertising, Dr. Shainess brought to the attention of a congressional committee the ultimate irony in 20th-century America—the feminine spray deodorant. It is most fitting that the crowning achievement in advertising belongs to the cosmetic industry, which is the primary bastion of unprincipled tactics. Dr. Shainess has explained to the Senate Small Business Committee that this wonder of modern science, the feminine spray deodorant, is nothing but a useless "remedy" for a nonexistent medical problem. To add injury to insult, there is considerable evidence that adverse reactions are caused by the product. Just think of it. Advertisers have tried to convince women that they have an antisocial problem which can only be cured with their product; however, in reality, there is no problem other than the one which the use of the product creates. If Madison Avenue runs true to form, we will probably see, in the not too distant future, a product on the market which treats adverse reactions brought on by the use of feminine spray deodorants.

In April, 1973, CBS News, in a most heretical but heroic program entitled "You and the Commercial," broadcast the most eloquent statement on the manipulative aspects of advertising. The accuracy of the program was clearly demonstrated when the fulsome kingpins of unfairness and deception, the advertising industry, attacked the program as being unfair and deceptive. The commentary of Dr. Erich Fromm particularly raised the hackles of the admen. In noting the use of fear as an important selling tool, Dr. Fromm said: "This is very apparent in all the deodorant ads; fear of body odor and all that. But in a more subtle way, the general fear of not being loved and then to be able, by some product, to be loved. That's a subtle fear pervading most people, and the ads speculate on that and show, in more or less drastic ways, here are the things which will make you loved. All that is sought to [play on] these unconscious fears."

Dr. Fromm quickly cut through the illusionary devices of the advertisers, and came up with a comment on the junkie syndrome so prevalent in much of advertising today. He said, "The 2nd thing which struck me was the concept of the miracle. The miracle drugs. Something, some type of miracle, will happen with the consumption of the product."

Conspicuous consumption did not evade Dr. Fromm's perceptive eye either. He noted, "The general theme is: Love is dependent on a gadget. And this is a very potent theme in our whole modern life: the expectation that not human power, human effort, not being, but gadgets create the good life and that there is no limit to what a gadget can do."

Dr. Fromm also noted Dr. Shainess's 1st and 3rd guideposts in these comments. "I would say that our ads, by and large, tend to misinform the reader and not to make him think rationally, but irrationally. . . . Advertising tends to make a person greedy, to create the man who wants more and more instead of trying to be more and more. Thinking—rational thinking, critical thinking, independent thinking—is undermined."

The U.S., as both an exporter of material goods and culture, has other developing countries to look to in order to see the microcosm of advertising's negative social value repeating itself. In September, 1974, Nippon Cultural Broadcasting, Inc., published a report entitled,

New Directions in Japanese Consumerism. In analyzing Japanese society in the postwar period, the report suggested that during the '60s, Japan went through "the era of desire for possessions." The report states: ". . . from the viewpoint of industry, this period was an age of mass production, consumption, distribution, and communication. Through mass media advertising, especially the power of TV and the adoption of American marketing strategies, manufacturers conducted widescale sales campaigns to combat competition, endeavoring to occupy the largest share in the market. During this period, consumers never doubted the advertisers' claims."

So what is the citizen-consumer to do? He is bombarded at every flip of the magazine page, at every turn of the TV dial. Can he be proud that we now export our form of mental gangrape to the people of other countries? Advertising is a science, designed to attack people's weak spots in order to sell a product. Wolfbane may have been the antidote for vampires and wolfmen, but it appears that only knowledge and awareness are the antidotes for our 20th-century monster, advertising.

The Author: Edward A. Merlis works for the U.S. Senate Commerce Committee, and devotes much of his time to advertising legislation.

The Mafia—Menace or Myth?

By Hank Messick

A Federal Bureau of Investigation report dated December 1, 1966, listed "50 known members of La Cosa Nostra" in the 4 New England States comprising the Boston Division: Massachusetts, Maine, New Hampshire, and Rhode Island.

Of these 50, 39 were said to be under the command of Raymond L. S. Patriarca, described by the FBI report as "the policymaker, judge, and overlord of organized crime in this area." Thirteen of Patriarca's men were located in Providence, 25 in Boston, and one in Portland. Eleven others in Worcester and Springfield were said to be under another Capo.

Yet some months after this report was written, the Attorney General of Massachusetts, one Elliot L. Richardson, estimated that there were, "5,000 members of organized crime in Massachusetts" alone.

Nevertheless, the FBI went right on assuming that Patriarca and his handful of men controlled organized crime in all New England (outside Worcester and Springfield, of course). This amounted to the tail wagging the dog on

a big scale and was absurd on its face. Ethnic gangs abounded in Boston where gang warfare was as violent as in Chicago in the days of Al Capone. You don't have gang wars in a city tightly controlled by an "overlord." And in Boston the Mafia was a dying organization composed of elderly officers and very few privates.

Back when the century was young and thousands of Italian immigrants were pouring into the Boston area, the Mafia attained a certain importance. The organization preyed, as always, on the frightened and ignorant immigrants, selecting from their ranks certain ones to serve the bosses as enforcers. During the national vendetta since known as the Maranzano-Masseria War of the early '30s, a Boston man, Gaspare Messina, became provisional Capo di Capi Re of the Mafia. He called a "Grand Council" meeting in Boston in a futile effort to end the vendetta which was hurting business. Shortly thereafter, Charles "Lucky" Luciano, with help from Meyer Lansky, "Americanized" the Mafia and found an uneasy place for it within the developing "Combination."

With the passage of time, things changed even in Boston. As 1st-generation Americans learned their way around, the 2nd-generation Americans grew into adulthood and the social and economic conditions that had made the Mafia possible ceased to exist. The ritual mumbo jumbo of Black Hands and blood oaths no longer impressed anyone. Young men saw no need to take orders from old men in a land where the freest of enterprise was encouraged. It became impossible to maintain an army of killers under a semimilitary discipline. By the '60s the Mafia was living on its reputation.

Such men as Patriarca tried to overcome the lack of soldiers by following the tradition of the old city-states of Italy—the hiring of mercenaries.

FBI wiretaps on Mafia telephones revealed discussions that went on for years about the need to have some punk "hit." The bosses just couldn't get anyone to do the job, and they weren't about to undertake such adventures in their prosperous old age. When circumstance demanded a death, however, a mercenary such as Joe "the Animal" Barboza was employed. He killed for cash, or for favors, but with Barboza it was strictly a business proposition. Unlike the traditional Mafia killer he was bound to his employer by no bond of brotherhood, no code of *omerta*, no sense of loyalty or even respect. Upon being rewarded with a personal interview with Patriarca, Barboza had eyes only for the Capo's diamond ring. He told his friends later he was preoccupied with the thought of biting off Patriarca's finger to get the ring.

No Godfather figure was Patriarca insofar as Barboza was concerned. He killed for the Capo when it seemed to his advantage to do so, and, later, when the situation changed, he testified against him. Patriarca went to prison as a result of that testimony.

Yet the FBI, brought belatedly into the battle against organized crime after denying its existence for decades, clung to the notion that 39 Mafia members controlled crime in New England. On the national level, the same blind approach was used, and everything that conflicted with the theory was ignored. In Boston and across the country, the press and the public cooperated. The Mafia was built up to Super Menace status, and the real leaders of crime were bypassed unless they happened to have Italian names. The public ate it up. Where crime was concerned it didn't know the difference between fact and fiction, and really didn't care. A romantic novel such as *The Godfather*, to use Mario Puzo's description, shaped public opinion far more effectively than a hundred factual books.

The idea that organized crime could be blamed on one ethnic or national group is, of course, absurd. It smacks of fascism. If one can ascribe all evil to one race, it can also attribute all that is noble to another, a master race. And if the Mafia is so powerful, and so dangerous, how can so many write so freely about it?

In fact, the Mafia is and has often been a handy whipping boy, a scapegoat. The 1st Mafia hysteria in this country began in 1890 in New Orleans where 2 Sicilian factions were enjoying a typical vendetta for control of the docks. The Irish police chief took sides and branded the opposing "family" as the Mafia. When the chief offered to testify on behalf of his friends in a murder case, he, too, was killed. Officials blamed "the Mafia" and indicted 19 members of the rival group. The trial jury acquitted the defendants. Enraged, some of the city's leading citizens led a lynch mob to the jail where the prisoners were executed with rope and gun. The leading citizens were highly praised for this murderous stunt, but Italy broke diplomatic relations with the U.S. over the incident. Eventually, to avoid an investigation, the U.S. apologized and made reparation, but writers have been hailing the affair ever since as the beginning of the Mafia menace in this country.

To understand the peculiar status of the Mafia's image today, it is necessary to define organized crime. In the absence of a better one, this writer will quote his own:

"Organized crime is a continuing conspiracy to gain money and power without regard for law by utilizing economic and physical force, public and private corruption, in an extension of the free-enterprise system."

To link organized crime and the free-enterprise system may shock some, but, after all, the goal of the gangster and the legitimate businessman is basically the same: to make as many fast bucks as possible. The gangster is simply more free with his enterprise than the businessman. And in a society where material wealth has assumed an almost theological aura, the gray area between the legitimate and the illicit narrows daily until it is sometimes impossible to say where one ends and the other begins.

The real executives of organized crime, the men who have made crime the biggest business in the country, were happy enough to let the Mafia take the heat. Much the same thing happened earlier when bank robbers such as John Dillinger and Alvin Karpis got the headlines while Lansky and Luciano built a national crime syndicate. Law-enforcement officials went along with the FBI's version of events because, one, they didn't know any better, and, 2, it was nice to have things made so simple. Law enforcement remains about 20 years behind in weapons, techniques, and intelligence anyway, and the things Joe Valachi described were comfortably outdated.

All the propaganda notwithstanding, the Mafia remains a dying institution and sooner or later will have to be abandoned as the old boys die off. Organized crime, on the other hand, is flourishing as never before. The war on crime, begun by Robert F. Kennedy, faltered badly under President Johnson and ground to a halt under Richard M. Nixon. With the heat off,

even the Mafia is no longer needed. Crime will continue to prosper until, as the President's Commission on Law Enforcement put it in 1967, there is a change in "the hearts and minds of men."

Such a change isn't going to happen tomorrow.

The Author: A onetime college professor and investigative newspaper reporter, Hank Messick's recent published books include *John Edgar Hoover, The Private Lives of Public Enemies,* and *The Beauties and the Beasts.*

The Men from Interpol

By Vaughn Young

Formed in 1924, the International Criminal Police Organization has come to be known best by its cable designation, "Interpol." With its world headquarters in St. Coud, a Paris suburb, Interpol is, to the casual observer, an admirable effort: cooperation among the police of various nations to apprehend criminals, control drug traffic across international borders, and similar activities. To the surprise of many, however, Interpol is a *private* organization to which law enforcement agencies of over 100 nations belong and pay annual dues. Its position and growth have stemmed entirely from the support of these police around the world, whence comes the mistaken belief that Interpol is a legally constituted international agency.

Throughout its history, Interpol has worked only with the national police force of each country. In the U.S., which officially has no national police force, Interpol is funded, staffed, and housed by the Treasury Department, across the street from the White House. With a direct hookup to the computerized National Crime Information Center (NCIC) run by the FBI and direct contact to State and local police, over 100 Interpol nations have access to U.S. files and records denied the American citizen.

With the growing amount of information being collected and kept by government agencies, such unregulated access to confidential files and records by a private organization serving 100 foreign police groups has disturbed a number of citizens. Any police state, or private group via their police, can obtain information on American citizens, businesses, clubs, diplomats and tourists, immigrants, suspected agents, without regard to validity, relevance, truth, or source. In turn, a foreign agency could even *plant* information in U.S. Government files, a possibility even more frightening due to its counterintelligence aspect.

When Interpol was 1st established in 1924, Vienna was chosen as its "permanent" home by fixing in the constitution that the head of the Austrian federal police would automatically lead the organization from the capital of that nation. In short, whoever ran the Austrian police ran Interpol, which Hitler would quickly recognize.

The Nazis strongly supported the organization and encouraged its expansion. By 1937, Interpol officials elected Nazi General Kurt Daluege, destined to be executed in 1946 for war crimes, as their vice-president. At the same time, J. Edgar Hoover, director of the FBI, was expressing interest and corresponding directly with Interpol's secretary general, Oscar Dressler. In 1937, H. Drane Lester, assistant director of the FBI, attended the Interpol congress in London and recommended to Hoover that the U.S. formally join.

Undaunted by growing Nazi participation, U.S. Attorney General Homer Cummings recommended to the Congress, a mere 2 weeks after Hitler's take-over of Austria and Interpol, that the U.S. formally join the group "as advocated by Director Hoover." Since Secretary of State Cordell Hull had no objection to the membership "from the point of view of our international relations," Congress voted the money and as of June 8, 1938, the U.S. was officially a member of Interpol. The U.S. was a member of a Nazi-run organization for only $1,500 annual dues.

With Hitler now in full command in Germany, the 1939 Interpol conference was scheduled for Berlin under the patronage of the Reichsführer, the SS, and Chief of the German Police Heinrich Himmler. For over a month, the U.S. State Department debated about whether or not to attend this Nazi conference. On August 11—3 weeks before W.W. II began—it declined to accept the invitation it had been sent.

Reinhard Heydrich, appointed to head the Nazi SS, became Interpol's new president, announcing that "Under its new German leadership [Interpol will] be a real center of criminal police." On December 8, 1941, Berlin was named as Interpol's new home and the move was made. Sharing a villa in Wannsee, a wealthy suburb of Berlin, with the Gestapo, Interpol was placed under Heydrich's *Sicherheitdienst* (SD) or Security Police. Also working in the SD at the time was a young SS officer (#337259), commissioned on July 1, 1939, by the name of Paul Dickopf. After the war, Dickopf was to reemerge and become Interpol's president from 1968 to 1972.

In June, 1942, Heydrich was assassinated. For 6 months, the Gestapo (and Interpol) lacked a leader. Himmler finally chose Ernst Kaltenbrunner, who had been working in Austria, to succeed Heydrich. With the Gestapo and the SS as his primary concern, Kaltenbrunner finally turned his attention to Interpol and wrote all member nations on July 28, 1943, in words to be echoed at St. Cloud 20 and 30 years later, that he would "continue the strictly nonpolitical character" of the police organization. Meanwhile, the ovens of Dachau, Buchenwald, and Treblinka burned into the night. And with them, the worth of Interpol's word.

As the 3rd Reich fell apart, so did Interpol. In the Reich's final days, a drama unfolded that was to be one of Interpol's unsolved mysteries and possibly a key to its postwar behavior. Interpol's files, nurtured for 6 years by the Nazis, were a prize for any would-be dictator. Culled from European police dossiers with the Nazi penchant for blackmail, one can imagine what they contained: the names of thieves, assassins, informers, forgers, and counterfeiters, as well as information on political leaders, businessmen, and citizens in general. The files were in Wannsee when the Allies began to close in on Berlin. Interpol has insisted that they were destroyed in the bombings. But one official tells a different, albeit odd, story.

Harry Soderman, a Swedish policeman, had worked with Interpol since its inception in 1924 and was one of 2 men responsible for its reemergence in 1946. In his book, *Policeman's Lot*, he offered some interesting insights, including information on what may have actually happened to the files in 1945. According to Soderman:

> . . . Carlos Zindel, who headed the Prussian and later the German Criminal Investigation Department (CID) . . . left Berlin just before the collapse of the 3rd

Reich and headed for the south in his car, which was filled to the brim with the documents of the Commission. When he reported to French headquarters in Stuttgart to give himself up, he was badly treated, kicked out, and told to return in the afternoon. His dignity mortally injured, he went to a park and swallowed a capsule of potassium cyanide.

As a neutral country, Switzerland was being used by the Odessa as a major collection and jumping-off point for Nazis fleeing with money, documents, and their lives. Zindel, apparently, was heading there. Armed with papers that would have allowed him passage clear to Zurich, Zindel found his way blocked. As a colonel in the SS working under Kaltenbrunner, he knew that the Allies would be interested in him, so he took the only alternative, leaving the files in French hands. The next year, Interpol was established in Paris with strong backing by the French police.

In 1946, Soderman worked with Florent E. Louwage of the Belgian Political Police, who was also a member of Interpol's executive staff under Kaltenbrunner and the only one to have escaped "untainted," according to the Swedish policeman, to keep Interpol alive. Using the Belgian embassies, Louwage sent out invitations to former member countries to meet in Brussels "to constitute the International Criminal Police Commission, choose its headquarters, and appoint new directors."

The U.S. State Department, upon receiving the invitation, telegraphed Brussels on May 15 that a decision to attend was "in abeyance pending advice Justice Department," and asked for more information. Two days later, Brussels replied that Norton R. Telford, later to become an Interpol delegate on J. Edgar Hoover's behalf, had visited "interested Belgian police . . . and is believed to have reported fully results to FBI Washington." Nothing was said about Interpol's Nazi history.

On May 21, 1946, Tom Clark, U.S. Attorney General, recommended to the State Department "that no representative of the Government of the U.S. be designated to attend this meeting." The State Department complied, unknowingly opening the way for Hoover. Two days after the State Department notified the Belgian Embassy that it would not be sending a representative to the conference, J. Edgar Hoover was elected vice-president of Interpol in Brussels. Hoover had just bluffed the State Department and established a foothold in Europe.

For a few brief months in 1946, Interpol had 2 presidents. But on October 16, Ernst Kaltenbrunner quickly relinquished his position when he wound up at the end of an executioner's rope in Nuremberg Prison, leaving Louwage to carry on the tradition as Interpol's sole president. Elected at the same meeting as Hoover, Louwage was to lead Interpol for the next 10 years. Jean Nepote, later to become Interpol's powerful secretary general in 1963, joined Louwage from the French Sûreté. During the war, Nepote had worked in the Nazi-supported Vichy Government and from 1968 to 1972 he would work with former SS officer Dickopf.

As vice-president, Hoover supported Interpol's growth. But in 1950, the relationship came to an abrupt end. Czechoslovakia, one of the Communist members, used the Interpol network to track down refugees fleeing that country. Hoover, to say the least, was not amused. He told Paris—Interpol's new headquarters—that he was pulling the FBI out. Louwage, knowing that U.S. support was ultimately vital for Interpol's growth, flew to Washington to ask the FBI director to reconsider. Hoover, however, had made up his mind. Reluctantly, Louwage returned to Paris and the membership was informed on November 26, 1950, that Hoover had resigned as vice-president for "special reasons."

For 8 long years, Interpol returned to the image of a European police force. But in 1958, another friend was found to bolster its tarnished image. Hoover had been convinced by Treasury Department officials to relinquish the membership that he still held and to allow its transfer. Although the bill for U.S. membership had jumped from $1,500 to $25,000, Congress approved the move and the Treasury Department was now a member of Interpol.

Since the war, Interpol has puzzled those not acquainted with its history, and Louwage's, by politely but firmly refusing to aid in the search for wanted Nazi war criminals. Citing Article 3 of its constitution, Interpol has insisted that Nazi war criminals are beyond its "jurisdiction." The matter came to a head in 1961 with the capture and trial of Adolf Eichmann, who had sat in Interpol's offices 19 years earlier toasting the Führer.

The World Jewish Congress, meeting in Geneva that same year, took notice of Interpol's refusal. Charging that such an attitude gave "an unexpected sense of safety" to other Nazis in hiding, the WJC did not accept Interpol's view that the murder of 6 million Jews was beyond its jurisdiction. Interpol, however, refused to listen. Instead, it began to concentrate on the worldwide drug traffic, still its favorite program today. Backed by the U.S. Treasury Department, Interpol no sooner attacked the movement of heroin and opium than the problem turned into an epidemic. Each new program touted to combat the illicit traffic was

followed by an increase in drugs from Europe and the Far East. Interpol's ineffectiveness was becoming painfully apparent.

By 1968, the Nazi issue had quieted sufficiently to allow the election of Paul Dickopf as president. Besides working in Heydrich's SD, where Interpol was located during the war, Dickopf had helped to reestablish the police in postwar Germany, achieving a senior position for himself in the *Bundeskriminalamt*. During his 4-year reign, the organization achieved a momentary state of financial affluence. When Dickopf stepped down in 1972, Interpol owned a new 8-story building in St. Cloud, a radio station, over 100 acres of French land, and had nearly 2 billion Swiss francs in the bank, due, in part, to large contributions by 3 member countries during his tenure: Venezuela, Brazil, and Switzerland, where, coincidentally, the Nazi Odessa brotherhood is very much alive.

At the White House, in 1969, events were transpiring that would reach across the ocean 5 years later. The image of fair and efficient law enforcement, carefully nurtured since Heydrich, was about to fall away. Eugene Rossides, as Interpol's boss in the Treasury Department, moved up the international ladder to follow in Hoover's footsteps. Elected to serve with Dickopf as a vice-president, Rossides was also busy in the U.S. Treasury giving a job to a young man by the name of G. Gordon Liddy. While Rossides got out before the Watergate scandal hit, Edward L. Morgan didn't make it. Coming from the White House, where he worked as a deputy counsel under John Ehrlichman, Morgan was appointed the Assistant Secretary of the Treasury for Enforcement and took command of Interpol activity there in 1970. By October, 1973, he was elected to Interpol's powerful Executive Committee.

As information poured out during the Watergate investigations, Morgan's name came up. Apparently, Morgan had gone to the IRS, on Ehrlichman's orders, to check the tax returns of former Presidents "for guidance" in preparing Nixon's. Then, in 1969, he reportedly signed and backdated a deed for Nixon which turned over the President's papers to the National Archives as a $500,000 tax write-off. When the matter hit the press in January, 1974, Morgan quickly resigned.

Before Interpol could catch its breath, events in Europe continued to force its actual operations into the open. A revolution in Portugal revealed atrocities being committed by the politically controlled—and dreaded—state police department that had been trained by the Nazis. Col. Fernando D. da Silva Pais, their director general, was also the head of the Portuguese Interpol bureau.

In Belfast, Interpol admitted that it had been working with NATO officials to compile information on terrorists, in violation on Article 3 several times over. It was also discovered that, in 1969, Interpol was reported at a Bermuda airport helping that government find "undesirables" arriving for an International Black Power Conference so they could be sent home immediately on the next plane. Yet, when asked to help track Palestinian terrorists, especially after the Munich massacre and numerous skyjackings, Interpol refused, citing Article 3 again.

By the time Interpol met in Cannes, France, for its 1974 conference, criticism was coming from within Interpol's own ranks. (One official has estimated that over 90% of police inquiries between nations are now made directly, not through Interpol, due to the growing lack of confidence in the organization.) After Dick-

opf's SS history was exposed, Interpol officials were kept busy trying to prevent matters from getting completely out of hand. But it was too late. As one correspondent put it, Interpol is "far from being the slick and sophisticated organization of popular mythology."

With the romantic tales of "the man from Interpol" gone, what was left was a most unpleasant picture: an organization that was steeped in Nazism, one wracked with political and financial turmoil, unable to make any dent in the rising crime rate, and one which arbitrarily selected the terrorists that would receive its attention. As a cynic put it, "They just haven't been the same since *der Führer* died."

The Author: Vaughn Young has been published in numerous periodicals. In recent months, he has investigated Interpol in depth, and is still continuing his researches.

On the Way to the 8-Hour Day—The Haymarket Affair

By David Wallechinsky

Today most people take it for granted that a work week is 8 hours a day, 5 days a week, but it was not always so. As late as 1886, most laborers worked a 10-hour day, 6 days a week. Most transportation workers put in at least 84 hours a week, and New York City bakers worked up to 120 hours a week.

The struggle for an 8-hour day led to one of the most dramatic events in U.S. history—the incident that has come to be known as the Haymarket Affair.

In 1884, a weak labor organization, the Federation of Organized Trades and Labor Unions of the U.S. and Canada, resolved to make May 1, 1886, the target date for a movement to win the 8-hour day. As that date approached, the federation had all but faded away, but their idea caught on, and in Chicago, which was a hotbed of worker organizing, the month of April saw huge rallies in support of the 8-hour day, despite unanimous opposition from the Chicago daily newspapers and all business leaders.

On April 30, the railroad and gas company employees, the iron mill workers, the meatpackers, and the plumbers all went on strike. The next day, May 1, 30,000 workers struck and joined in peaceful parades and demonstrations. Sunday, May 2, was quiet.

But on Monday there were strike rallies throughout the city. One such gathering, of the Lumber Shovers Union, attracted 6,000 strikers, including several hundred workers from the nearby McCormick Harvester factory, which had been run by scabs since February

16 when its regular employees had been locked out over a dispute about unionization.

The main speaker at the rally was August Spies, a noted Chicago social-revolutionary. Many in the crowd objected to his being allowed to speak because he was a "socialist," but the secretary of the union spoke on his behalf and satisfied the crowd by saying that Spies had been "sent by the Central Labor Union."

Spies avoided revolutionary propaganda and spoke mainly about shorter hours, urging the workers to stand together or be defeated. Shortly before he concluded his speech, the bell at the McCormick factory 3 or 4 blocks away rang and 500 members of Spies's audience—those who were McCormick strikers—broke away and ran toward the factory. With stones and sticks they attacked the exiting scabs and drove them back into the factory. Soon 200 police with clubs and revolvers arrived to supplement the permanent police force which the city had graciously supplied to the owners to protect the factory. Shooting broke out and when the battle ended, one striker had been shot to death, 5 or 6 were seriously wounded, and 6 policemen were injured, although none had been shot.

Spies, who had urged the McCormick strikers to stay at the rally, was horrified at the sight of the blood of fellow workers splattered on the streets of Chicago and immediately ran off a poster ("To arms, we call you, to arms!") printed in English and German, which was distributed at labor meetings that night.

The Chicago papers put the blame for the violence on the anarchists and a "liquor-crazed mob." But the workers thought otherwise and Tuesday morning found them in an ugly mood. There were clashes all day including another bloody battle at the McCormick plant.

That night there were several meetings scheduled, but the biggest one was expected to be the demonstration against police brutality to be held in Haymarket Square.

Only 1,200 to 1,300 persons showed up, so the rally was moved to a truck wagon in front of the Crane Brothers' factory nearby. The 1st speaker was Spies, who gave a relatively mild 20-minute speech in which he attacked the "capitalistic" press "for misrepresenting the cause of labor." He blamed the employers and the police for the violence: "McCormick is the man who created the row Monday, and he must be held responsible for the murder of our brothers." (Cries of "Hang him!") "Don't make any threats, they are of no avail. Whenever you get ready to do something, do it and don't make any threats beforehand."

At 9 P.M., the 2nd speaker, Albert Parsons, mounted the truck. Parsons, a noted anarchist leader, was born in Alabama and served in the Confederate Army. He then alienated his distinguished family by marrying a Mexican-Indian woman named Lucy Gonzales and becoming involved in radical causes.

This evening, sensitive to the volatile atmosphere, he was less incendiary than usual, choosing to speak on the general state of labor. Filling his speech with lots of statistics, he pointed out that the worker received only 15¢ out of every dollar, while the rest went to the capitalists.

The last speaker was Samuel Fielden, a 40-year-old teamster who had immigrated from England. His main theme was a statement that had been made by Congressman Foran of Ohio that the workingman could expect no relief or aid from legislation. After 10 minutes, a cold wind and rain convinced ¾ of the crowd not to wait for the end of Fielden's speech.

At 10:20 he began, "In conclusion . . ." and then, to everyone's amazement, 180 police appeared in formation, led by Captains Bonfield and Ward. A short interchange took place.

Ward: "In the name of the people of the State of Illinois, I command this meeting immediately and peaceably to disperse."

Fielden: "We are peaceable."

He, Spies, and others began to descend from the truck wagon. Without warning, a dynamite bomb flew through the air, hit the ground, and exploded in front of the police. The police re-formed and opened fire. There was a feeble response from the crowd, which quickly dispersed.

One policeman, Mathias J. Degan, died immediately and 6 others died in the hospital. Over 70 law officers were injured. The civilian casualties were 2 dead and an estimated 60 injured.

The public was shocked by the affair, and the nation's press almost universally condemned radicals, anarchists, socialists, and aliens, particularly Germans. On May 5, *The New York Times* declared that the anarchists were guilty of the bomb throwing. Within 2 days the police, under the command of the infamous Captain Michael J. Schaack, raided 50 supposed "hangouts" of anarchists and socialists and arrested or questioned over 200 people.

Chief of Police Ebersold, speaking 3 years later, said, "Schaack wanted to keep things stirring. He wanted bombs to be found here, there, everywhere. . . . Now here is something the public does not know. After we got the anarchist societies broken up, Schaack wanted to send out men to organize new societies right away. . . . He wanted to keep the pot boiling, keep himself prominent before the public."

The police were more concerned with getting evidence against those arrested than in finding the bomb-thrower. They offered money and jobs to those who would be witnesses for the State. The atmosphere in Chicago was so hostile to radicals that the color red, symbolic of revolution, was cut out of street advertisements.

A grand jury of businessmen indicted 31 persons, but they concentrated their prosecution on 9 men: August Spies, Albert Parsons, Samuel Fielden, Michael Schwab, Adolph Fischer, George Engel, Oscar Neebe, Louis Lingg, who was accused of having made the Haymarket bomb, and Rudolph Schnaubelt, who was accused of having thrown it. They were charged with: 1. being accessories before the fact to the murder of Mathias J. Degan by means of a bomb; 2. murder by pistol shots; 3. accessories to one another in the murder of Degan; 4. general conspiracy to murder. The remaining 22 never came to trial. Several purchased immunity by becoming witnesses for the State. Most were released on $400 bail.

But when the trial opened on June 21, only 7 defendants were in court. Parsons and Schnaubelt were missing. Schnaubelt presumably spent the rest of his life in Europe, but he was never officially located.

At 2:30 P.M. on the 21st, Parsons, who had been hiding in Waukesha, Wis., walked into the courtroom and sat down with the other defendants. His friend William Holmes said,

"When I heard that he [Parsons] had gone to Chicago to stand trial, I hastened . . . to the jail. I said to him, 'Do you know what you have done?' and he said, 'Yes, thoroughly. I never expect while I live to be a free man again. They will kill me, but I could not bear to be at liberty, knowing that my comrades were here and were to suffer for something of which they were as innocent as I. . . .' "

Judge Joseph Eaton Gary refused to let the Chicago 8 be tried separately. A special bailiff, Henry L. Ryce, was appointed to find potential jurors. Ryce was blunt about where his sentiments lay: "I am managing this case, and know what I am about. Those fellows are going to be hanged as certain as death. I am calling such men as the defendants will have to challenge peremptorily and [so] waste their time and challenges. Then they will have to take such men as the prosecution wants."

With the help of Judge Gary, Ryce's strategy worked perfectly. Gary refused to disqualify one potential juror who was a friend of one of the dead policemen and another who admitted not only to being prejudiced against all anarchists, but to being a relative of one of the dead policemen. The defense was forced to use up its challenges on these and other unacceptable potential jurors.

The final jury consisted of 12 white males, only one of whom was foreign-born. (Five of the defendants had been born in Germany and one in England.) Seven jurors were white-collar workers, one an employer of labor, one a commercial agent, and 2 were businessmen. There were no industrial workers.

The prosecution case was flimsy, to say the least, particularly since they had no evidence that any of the defendants had actually thrown the bomb. In fact, to this day, it is not known who the bomb-thrower was. The prosecution claimed it was Rudolph Schnaubelt and the labor supporters said it was a police provocateur. There is no substantial evidence to support either theory or any other theory for that matter.

So the prosecution relied on the conspiracy charge, despite the fact that most of the accused hadn't even known each other before the trial. The State felt that their most effective tactic was to attack the political ideals of the anarchists, so they centered on the hypothesis that a "general conspiracy" had existed in Cook County for several years which planned to overthrow the Government and destroy the "legal authorities of the State and county. . . ."

Following the logic of the prosecution, it was necessary only to prove that the defendants supported anarchism to justify convicting them. This was easily done since all of them readily admitted it.

The jury spent 3 hours discussing the case —⅔ of the time devoted to Oscar Neebe against whom no real evidence had been presented.

On the morning of Friday, August 20, the jury gave its verdict—all Guilty. Neebe was sentenced to 15 years in prison, the rest were sentenced to be hanged.

Immediately after the verdict was read, the defendants were led back to jail. Fielden could not walk without support, Neebe was crushed. Outside the courthouse a crowd of over 1,000 was ecstatic and let out 3 cheers for the jury. The citizens of Chicago were relieved, and throughout the nation newspapers gushed with pride that justice had been done.

In October, Judge Gary denied defense arguments for a new trial and the court, following custom, asked the defendants if there were reasons why sentence should not be pronounced. Indeed there were, and for 3 days the 8 anarchists spoke about their lives, their beliefs, and what they thought of the trial and the evidence that had been presented. For 3 days, from October 7 to 9, the accused became the accusers.

Spies was the 1st. Born in Central Germany in 1855, he moved to the U.S. after his father died. He settled in Chicago where he learned about socialism and ran for office several times before becoming editor of the Arbeiter-Zeitung, a leading anarchist newspaper.

". . . if you think that by hanging us you can stamp out the labor movement—the movement from which the downtrodden millions who toil and live in want and misery—the wage slaves—expect salvation—if this is your opinion, then hang us! Here you will tread upon a spark, but there and there, and behind you and in front of you, and everywhere, flames will blaze up. It is a subterranean fire. You cannot put it out."

In response to the accusation that the Arbeiter-Zeitung had advocated violence, and that this alone was reason enough for them to be hung, Spies responded, "Let me read to you an editorial which appeared in the Fond du Lac Commonwealth, in October, 1886, a Republican paper. If I am not mistaken, the court is Republican too.

" 'To arms, Republicans . . . Every Republican in Wisconsin should go armed to the polls on next Election Day. The grain stacks, houses, and barns of active Democrats should be burned; their children burned and their wives outraged, that they may understand that the Republican party is the one which is bound to rule, and the one which they should vote for, or keep their vile carcasses away from the polls. If they persist in going to the polls . . . meet them on the road, in the bush, on the hill, or anywhere, and shoot everyone of these base cowards and agitators. If they are too strong in any locality, and succeed in putting their opposition votes into the ballot box, break open the box and tear in shreds their discord-breathing ballots.'

"What does your honor say to these utterances of a 'law and order' organ—a Republican organ?"

After speaking at great length, Spies concluded with, "I say, if death is the penalty for proclaiming the truth, then I will proudly and defiantly pay the costly price! Call your hangman! Truth crucified in Socrates, in Christ, in Giordano Bruno, in Huss, Galileo, still lives —they and others whose numbers are legion have preceded us on this path. We are ready to follow!"

Michael Schwab, born in 1853, had come to Chicago from Bavaria when he was 26. Like Spies, he took the opportunity to explain his doctrines and, like Spies, he used the words communism, socialism, and anarchism as if they meant the same thing—a naïve misconception which was exposed years later during the Russian Revolution when Lenin and Trotsky killed or imprisoned every active anarchist their special police could get their hands on.

The 3rd defendant to speak was 36-year-old Oscar Neebe, of German descent, but born in New York City. A quiet, simple man, he was not a revolutionary and he knew little about anarchism and socialism.

"Before the 4th of May I committed some other crimes. My business [yeast-peddling] brought me in connection with the bakers. I saw that the bakers in this city were treated like dogs . . . I said to myself: 'These men have to be organized, in organization there is strength.' And I helped organize them. That is a great crime. The men are now working, instead of 14 and 16 hours, 10 hours a day . . . And I committed a greater crime than that . . . I saw in the morning when I drove away with my team that the beer brewers of the city of Chicago went to work at 4 o'clock in the morning. They came home at 7 and 8 o'clock at night. They never saw their families, they never saw their children by daylight . . . I went to work and organized them."

". . . hang me, too; for I think it is more honorable to die suddenly than to be killed by inches. I have a family and children; and if they know their father is dead, they will bury him. They can go to the grave, and kneel down by the side of it; but they can't go to the penitentiary and see their father, who was convicted for a crime that he hasn't had anything to do with. That is all I have got to say, your honor, I am sorry not to be hung with the rest of the men."

Twenty-eight-year-old Adolph Fischer was born in Bremen and arrived in the U.S.

when he was 15. He had become interested in socialism in Germany as a result of an instructor's attack against it.

"I protest against my being sentenced to death because I have committed no crime. I was tried . . . for murder, and I was convicted of anarchy. I protest against being sentenced to death, because I have not been found guilty of murder. However, if I am to die on account of being an anarchist . . . I will not remonstrate."

The 5th to speak was 22-year-old Louis Lingg. Lingg was the only one of the 8 defendants who was actively a violent revolutionary. He made bombs and he was not ashamed to admit it. Born in Mannheim, Germany, his father died when Louis was 7. He was apprenticed to a carpenter, traveled to Switzerland, and then came to the U.S. to avoid military service. He addressed the court in German.

"I do not recognize your law, jumbled together as it is by the nobodies of bygone centuries, and I do not recognize the decision of the court . . . I repeat that I am the enemy of the order of today, and I repeat that, with all my powers, so long as breath remains in me, I shall combat it . . . You laugh. Perhaps you think, *you'll* throw no more bombs; but let me assure you that I die happy on the gallows, so confident am I that the hundreds and thousands to whom I have spoken will remember my words, and when you shall have hanged us, then, mark my words, they will do the bomb throwing! In this hope do I say to you: 'I despise you. I despise your order; your laws, your force-propped authority! *Hang me for it!*'"

George Engel, 50 years old, had come to the U.S. in 1873.

"We see from the history of this country that the 1st Colonists won their liberty through force, that through force slavery was abolished, and just as the man who agitated against slavery in this country had to ascend the gallows, so also must we.

"I hate and combat, not the individual capitalist, but the system that gives him those privileges."

Samuel Fielden, spoke at great length about his life, beliefs, and his innocence of any wrongdoing.

Next to speak was Albert Parsons, and speak he did, for 2 hours on October 8 and 6 hours the next day. An excellent orator, he took this opportunity of his last public appearance to tell the history of the working classes in the U.S. He freely admitted his support for the use of dynamite because, "today dynamite comes as the emancipator of man from the domination and enslavement of his fellow men. . . . It is democratic; it makes everybody equal. . . . Now I speak plainly. Does it follow, because I hold these views, that I committed or had anything to do with the commission of that act at the Haymarket?"

The last speaker was Judge Gary. "In substance and effect it is that the defendant Neebe be imprisoned in the State Penitentiary at Joliet at hard labor for the term of 15 years. And that each of the other defendants, between the hours of 10 o'clock in the forenoon and 2 o'clock in the afternoon of the 3rd day of December next, in the manner provided by the statute of this State, be hung by the neck until he is dead. Remove the prisoners."

The verdict was appealed to the State Supreme Court and then to the U.S. Supreme Court which, on November 2, 1887, upheld the lower court decision. The execution date was reset for November 11 and the only hope left for the condemned men was an appeal to the governor to commute their sentences. Fortunately, public opinion had changed considerably in the 1½ years since the bomb had exploded.

People of all classes now spoke out in favor of the "anarchists," and the cause had even spread to France and England. In London on October 14, a large mass meeting was addressed by a diverse set of speakers including socialist William Morris, anarchist-philosopher Peter Kropotkin, playwright George Bernard Shaw, and theosophist Annie Besant.

Attempts were made to convince the prisoners to submit written pleas for mercy, but only Fielden, Schwab, and Spies would do it.

On November 6, Lingg's cell was searched and 4 small bombs were discovered. Although the explosives were only large enough for self-destruction, the discovery brought about an increased fear of an anarchist revolt and damaged the movement to obtain clemency for the prisoners. Lingg claimed to have never seen the bombs before and there was much speculation that they had been planted by the prison guards.

On November 8, Governor Oglesby received petitions with 200,000 signatures urging him to spare the lives of the condemned anarchists. All day he met with prominent people who were supporters of commutation, including members of the State legislature and Samuel Gompers, president of the American Federation of Labor.

The next day it was announced that Judge Gary and Prosecuting Attorney Grinnell had petitioned the governor to commute the sentences of Fielden and Schwab. Oglesby met with more prominent citizens and also was read a letter from Parsons which said that he had been found guilty of murder simply because he had attended the Haymarket meeting. This being the case, Parsons requested a re-

prieve so that his wife and children, who had also been at the meeting, could be indicted, convicted, and put to death together with him. When he heard this, Governor Oglesby exclaimed, "My God, this is terrible."

Shortly before 9, on the morning of November 10, Louis Lingg placed a small bomb in his mouth and blew off the bottom half of his face. He died 6½ hours later. At 7 P.M., Governor Oglesby announced that he would commute to life imprisonment the sentences of Fielden and Schwab, but that Spies, Parsons, Engel, and Fischer would die on schedule the next day.

November 11, 1887

The night before the execution, before going to sleep at 2 A.M., Albert Parsons chilled the prison guards with a moving rendition of "Annie Laurie." The condemned men were completely composed and their jailers were much disturbed and impressed.

At 11:30 A.M., the 4 anarchists were taken from their cells, cloaked in white muslin shrouds, and led, handcuffed, to the scaffold. Two hundred people watched as the nooses were placed around their necks. Fischer helped to adjust his. Spies complained that his noose was too tight and smiled a thank-you when it was loosened.

The nervous silence which covered the room was shattered suddenly as Spies's voice boomed out from beneath the hood which covered his head:

"There will come a time when our silence will be more powerful than the voices you strangle today!"

Fischer: "Hurrah for anarchy!"

Engel: "Hurrah for anarchy!"

Fischer: "This is the happiest moment of my life!"

Parsons: "Will I be allowed to speak, O men of America? Let me speak, Sheriff Matson! Let the voice of the people be heard!"

At that moment, the trap was sprung.

The Funeral

On Sunday, November 13, Chicago saw one of the largest funerals in its history. Mayor Roche ordered that no banners, flags, or arms be displayed, no music be played other than dirges, and that there be no demonstration or speeches.

At least 6,000 people marched behind the 5 coffins while 250,000 people lined the route. Only one banner was carried—an American flag proudly held by a Civil War veteran. Over 10,000 persons observed the simple burial at Waldheim Cemetery.

The final chapter in the story of the Haymarket Affair came in 1893 when Illinois' new governor John P. Altgeld severely damaged his career by pardoning Fielden, Neebe, and Schwab. What hurt his career was not that he pardoned the men, but the reason for which he pardoned them. Altgeld, after studying the case carefully, declared that the anarchists should be freed because they were innocent, as were the 5 who lay in their graves at Waldheim. He said that the jury had been packed, and he personally attacked Judge Gary for having been prejudicial.

Altgeld was viciously condemned by most major newspapers and he was even hung in effigy. But he refused to respond to any of the criticism.

"Remember this about any slander," he said to a friend, "Denial only emphasizes, and gives added importance to falsehood. Let it alone and it will die for want of nourishment."

The Author: David Wallechinsky has recently had 2 books published, *Chico's Organic Gardening and Natural Living* and *Laughing Gas.*

Dr. Freud Visits America

By Irving Wallace

One of the little known facts in the life of one of the historic movers and shakers of the 20th century is that Dr. Sigmund Freud spent one month in the U.S. during August and September of 1909, the year in which William Howard Taft became President.

In 1909, Dr. Freud was 53 years old and the new mental treatment that he had developed, which he named "psychoanalysis," was 14 years old. Dr. Freud had already published numerous papers and a half dozen books, but they were not widely read. One of the most important, *The Interpretation of Dreams*, brought out in late 1899, had sold only 600 copies in 8 years and earned him $250. However, Dr. Freud and his theory were making headway in Europe. He had formed a Psychological Wednesday Society in Vienna in 1902—later the Vienna Psychoanalytical Society—which attracted followers who met with him weekly in his waiting room. Also, he had a crowded appointment calendar of patients, mostly neurotics from Eastern Europe.

Yet, in the U.S., Dr. Freud was almost unknown. He had gained only a handful of American disciples. One of these was Dr. Abraham A. Brill, who had come to see the master in Vienna and had been converted. Another, who had never set eyes on Freud, was Dr. Granville Stanley Hall, president of Clark University in Worcester, Mass. And it was Dr. Hall who would be instrumental in bringing Dr. Sigmund Freud to the country that in future years would be the heartland of psychiatry.

Clark University, a small private coeducational school (today the enrollment is 2,700 students), was about to observe its 20th anniversary in 1909. To celebrate the occasion, President Hall decided to invite Dr. Sigmund Freud to give a series of lectures on the origin and growth of psychoanalysis, in July, before a conclave of psychologists. Dr. Freud declined this 1st invitation. He was solidly booked with patients for July and felt that he was "not rich enough" to cancel out 3 weeks of therapy. "America should bring in money, not cost money," he said.

However, President Hall of Clark University would not be denied. Shortly after, he extended a 2nd invitation to Dr. Freud, stating that the celebration had been rescheduled for early September, and offering Freud 3,000 marks—$714.60—for 5 lectures devoted to his new discoveries about sex and dreams. This time Dr. Freud accepted.

Dr. Freud requested one of his closest disciples, Dr. Sandor Ferenczi, of Budapest, Hungary, to accompany him. Ferenczi was delighted, and immediately began to study English and to bury himself in travel books about the U.S. Meanwhile, Freud learned that another recent disciple, Dr. Carl Gustav Jung, assistant director of the Burghoelzli Clinic in Zürich, had also been invited to Clark University. Freud lost no time in asking Jung to travel with him also.

Freud faced the trip to a distant, alien land with mingled anticipation and misgivings. He was pleased at the opportunity to introduce his ideas to the U.S. firsthand. At the same time, he was worried about the discomforts of the journey and over the reception he might receive in America. He refused to read any books about the U.S. He told Ferenczi, "The thought of America does not seem to matter to me, but I am looking forward very much to our journey together. It is a good illustration to the profound words in the *Magic Flute*: 'I can't compel you to love.'"

Freud told intimates that all he wanted to see in the U.S. was a collection of Cyprian antiquities in a New York museum and the Niagara Falls. Concerning Freud's seeming lack of enthusiasm, Dr. Ernest Jones—his leading British disciple and later his biographer, who planned to join the master in the U.S.—remarked: "I think there was some suppression of the earlier elation lest it lead to some apprehensiveness about his task. He pretended it was not really important. He did not prepare anything for his lectures, saying he would do that on the ship."

After insuring his life for 20,000 marks—$4,764—Freud took a train to Bremen to join Jung and Ferenczi the day before boarding their ship. Hosting a farewell lunch, Freud ordered wine. Jung, a teetotaler, didn't want wine, but at Freud's insistence he agreed to have some. Curiously, after Jung capitulated and drank, Freud fainted.

The following day, the pioneer psychiatric trio boarded the German liner *George Washington*. Freud, who alone insisted he never got seasick, enjoyed the smooth but foggy voyage. The first 3 days at sea, Freud kept a diary, then abandoned it to write pages of letters to his wife. "During the voyage," reported Jones, "the 3 companions analyzed each other's dreams—the 1st example of group analysis—and Jung told me afterwards that Freud's dreams seemed to be mostly concerned with cares for the future of his family and of his work." A high spot of the crossing was the day Freud learned that his cabin steward was reading one of his books.

The Lloyd liner docked in New York Harbor on August 27, 1909. Only his American disciple, Brill, and several curious reporters were on hand to greet Freud.

Just one New York newspaper bothered to note the arrival of "Professor Freud of Vienna." Freud and his companions had checked into the Hotel Manhattan where the rate was $2.50 per night. Their 1st day in America's largest city was a busy one. After calling upon his brother-in-law, Eli Bernays, and meeting with an old friend, Freud was ready for sight-seeing. With Brill as their guide, the trio drove through Central Park, Chinatown, the Jewish ghetto. In the afternoon, they relaxed at Coney Island. Freud, his mind still on his beloved Vienna, called Coney Island "a magnified Prater."

The following day, with Brill again leading the way, the threesome went to the Metropolitan Museum, where Freud satisfied his desire to see the great collection of Cyprian antiquities. After that, the group went on a tour of Columbia University.

The 3rd day, Freud's British disciple, Dr. Ernest Jones, came down from Canada to join them. As Jones recalled it: "We all dined together in Hammerstein's Roof Garden [where "Shine on Harvest Moon" by Norworth and Bayes and "Take Me Out to the Ball Game" by Von Tilzer were still reigning hits], afterwards going on to a cinema to see one of the primitive films of those days with plenty of wild chasing. Ferenczi in his boyish way was

very excited at it, but Freud was only quietly amused; it was the 1st film they had seen." While there is no record of the American movie Freud viewed that evening, it could have been either *The Count of Monte Cristo* starring Hobart Bosworth, or more likely, since it contained "wild chasing," a Western film shot in New Jersey starring Al Christie, both big hits in New York at the time.

By the 4th day in the U.S.—more museums in the morning—Freud was beginning to grumble. Suffering a prostatic condition, he complained about the lack of urinals, telling Jones, "They escort you along miles of corridors and ultimately you are taken to the very basement where a marble palace awaits you, just in time." Another grumble was the richness of American food, and Freud determined to diet for 24 hours.

After a week in the U.S., some of it spent preparing his 1st of 5 lectures, Freud and company traveled by sea from New York to New Haven, Conn., and then by train to Boston, and finally they continued on to their destination, Worcester, Mass., seat of Clark University.

The party was welcomed by their host, G. Stanley Hall, the college president, who had reserved rooms for them in the local Standish Hotel. Freud was quite taken by Hall, later writing a friend: "It is one of the pleasantest phantasies to imagine that somewhere far off, without one's having a glimmering of it, there are decent people finding their way into our thoughts and efforts, who after all suddenly make their appearance. That is what happened to me with Stanley Hall. Who could have known that over there in America, only an hour away from Boston, there was a respectable old gentleman waiting impatiently for the next number of the *Jahrbuch*, reading and understanding it all, and who would then, as he expressed it himself, 'ring the bells for us'?"

When Freud learned that President Hall had introduced psychoanalysis into the university curriculum, and that members of the faculty had read his books and were discussing them with their students, Freud was astonished. He called Hall a "kingmaker," and was pleased the instructors were so unexpectedly free of "prudery."

At last the lectures began. Jung had suggested the subject be dreams. Jones advised against it, feeling the subject too specialized. Freud finally "agreed that Americans might regard the subject of dreams as not 'practical' enough, if not actually frivolous." He decided to concentrate on discussing the birth and growth of psychoanalysis.

During 5 days in September of 1909, addressing himself to a gathering of psychologists at Clark University, Dr. Sigmund Freud delivered his 5 lectures. Except for the 1st lecture, each talk was prepared during a stroll on campus with Ferenczi a half hour before Freud faced his audience. Freud spoke without a single written note, addressing his listeners in German in a conversational tone of voice.

Years later he would remember his feelings as he entered to begin his opening lecture: "As I stepped onto the platform at Worcester to deliver my 'Five Lectures Upon Psychoanalysis,' it seemed like the realization of some incredible daydream: Psychoanalysis was no longer a product of delusion—it had become a valuable part of reality." With each lecture, Freud gained confidence, still recalling 15 years later, "In Europe I felt like an outcast, here I saw myself received by the best men as their equal."

Among those who came to hear and meet Freud was Dr. James J. Putnam, professor of neurology at Harvard University. Earlier, Putnam had put down psychoanalysis as "immoral." But Freud's lectures turned him into a vocal defender and advocate of the new therapy.

Many members of the audience wanted to hear more from Freud about sex. One lady made this desire known. Jones translated her request into German, and then he relayed Freud's reply to the lady saying that, as to sex, Freud "is not to be driven *to* the subject any more than *away* from it."

Yet, Freud did discuss sex, and when the dean of the University of Toronto read the lectures, he announced: "An ordinary reader would gather that Freud advocates free love, removal of all restraints, and a relapse into savagery."

Also, Freud's remarks on and off the platform provoked misunderstandings that generated controversy. Among other things, Freud was accused of advocating parricide, and of predicting that Negroes would eventually control the U.S. The parricide rumor grew out of a joke. President Hall had asked Freud's advice on what could be done for a sick male friend whose problem was an overly strict father, and Freud had replied, "Why, kill his father." The prediction about Negroes dominating the U.S. had also been a joke. Freud had told his follower Marie Bonaparte that in a few thousand years the white race might be extinct, to be replaced by the black race, and then he added lightly, "America is already threatened by the black race. And it serves her right. A country without even wild strawberries!"

It was at Clark University, one morning during breakfast, that Freud confided to Jung how much he was disconcerted by American women, admitting they gave him erotic dreams. "I haven't been able to sleep since I came to America," said Freud. "I continue to dream of prostitutes."

"Well, why don't you do something about it?" asked Jung.

Freud shrank back in horror. "But I'm a married man!" he exclaimed.

During his time in the U.S., Freud got a bad impression of American women and American sexual life. Years later he spoke his mind to an American caller: "You have a real rule of women in America. Your young men go to college with girls, fall in love and marry at an age when girls are usually much more mature than the men. They lead the men around by the nose, make fools of them, and the result is matriarchy. That is why marriage is so unsuccessful in America—that is why your divorce rate is so high. Your average American man approaches marriage without any experience at all. You wouldn't expect a person to step up to an orchestra and play 1st fiddle without some training. . . . In Europe, things are different. Men take the lead. That is as it should be. . . . [Equality in marriage] is a practical impossibility. There must be inequality, and the superiority of the man is the lesser of 2 evils." Freud made only one favorable observation about the American woman: "She hasn't got the European woman's constant fear of seduction."

The climactic moment of Freud's visit to the U.S. occurred during the last day at Clark University. He was awarded an honorary doctorate. He was deeply moved, and his words of thanks began, "This is the 1st official recognition of our endeavors." It was, in fact, the only academic recognition Freud would receive in his lifetime.

There was one other high point. Freud was brought together with the great American philosopher, William James, who was suffering a fatal illness and would be dead within a year. The 2 giants took a stroll together, discussed in German Freud's lectures which James had followed. As they parted, James, despite his puritanical upbringing, said to Freud, "The future of psychology belongs to your work." James's fortitude remained indelible in Freud's memory, and he wrote later, "I have always wished that I might be as fearless as he was in the face of approaching death."

Freud spent 8 more days in the U.S., and most of it was downhill. He was in constant pain not only from his prostatic condition but also from intestinal disorders, which he blamed on American cooking. He felt that his hosts were not sympathetic enough toward his illness. He disliked not being understood when he spoke in German, resented the lack of Old World manners, disapproved of the inhibitions and prudery he perceived in most Americans.

Forever after, Freud rarely had a kind word for the U.S. He told Jones, "America is a mistake; a gigantic mistake, it is true, but none the less a mistake." He told Hanns Sachs, who later taught psychology in Harvard Medical School, "America is the most grandiose experiment the world has seen, but, I am afraid, it is not going to be a success."

Nevertheless, in 1909, despite his feelings about the U.S. and its people, despite his weariness and sickness, he decided to continue with his sight-seeing tour. He finally set eyes on Niagara Falls, which he told Jones he "found even grander and larger" than he had expected. Unfortunately, one incident marred this visit. As Freud waited to enter the Cave of the Winds, a guide pushed other tourists back and beckoned Freud, explaining to the tourists, "Let the old fellow go 1st." The 53-year-old Freud, who was age-conscious, fumed at the remark. But his good humor was briefly restored when he was allowed to set foot on Canadian soil. After that, he wound up his American visit by spending his last few days at a new American friend's cabin near Lake Placid, N.Y., where Jung enlivened the evenings by singing German songs.

On September 21, 1909, Freud sailed out of New York Harbor on the *Kaiser Wilhelm der Grosse,* never to return to the U.S.

However, he did not forget Clark University or G. Stanley Hall, its president. Freud maintained a sporadic correspondence with Hall—and this correspondence illuminated a personal scandal in Freud's life—but not until 60 years later.

The 1st hint of trouble appeared in a letter Freud wrote to Hall in November, 1913: "The only unfavorable developments within the psychoanalytical movement concern personal relationships. Jung, with whom I shared my visit to you at that time, is no longer my friend, and our collaboration is approaching complete dissolution."

Jung split from Freud completely, because he felt Freud placed too much emphasis on the role sex played in life energy. Speaking of Freud's theories, Jung said, "The brain is viewed as an appendage of the genital glands." What Freud had to say about Jung was not fully known until 1969, when 13 long-lost letters Freud had written to G. Stanley Hall were discovered in the basement of the Clark University library. In one of these letters to Hall, Freud dwelt angrily on Jung's motives for leaving him: "If the real facts were more familiar to you, you would very likely not have thought that there was again a case where a father did not let his sons develop, but you would have seen that the sons wished to eliminate their father, as in ancient times."

Exposure of this letter by Clark University did not sit well with John M. Billinsky, a psychologist and professor at nearby Andover Newton Theological School. Billinsky, who had studied under Jung in Zürich a dozen years earlier, determined to let the world know more of the reasons behind Jung's defection from Freud. And so, in January, 1970, Billinsky made public a private fact that Jung had told him about Freud.

It seems that in 1907, Jung was a houseguest of Freud's in Vienna. Also under the same roof lived Freud's wife, Martha, their children, and Freud's sister-in-law, Minna Bernays, who was part of the family for 40 years. Minna, the robust, younger sister of Freud's wife, one day spilled out her big secret to Jung. "From her," Jung had told Billinsky, "I learned that Freud was in love with her and that their relationship was indeed very intimate." Upset by Freud's hidden life, his lack of openness, Jung confronted the master. He suggested to Freud that he be analyzed by someone else, and Jung offered himself as the analyst. Irked, Freud flatly rejected the suggestion. "It was my knowledge of Freud's triangle," said Jung, "that became a very important factor in my break. And then I could not accept Freud's authority above the truth. This led to further problems . . ."

Fortunately, neither Freud nor Hall was alive in 1970 to see what the visit to America wrought.

Hall had died in 1924 at the age of 80. And Freud, after being rescued from the Nazi invaders of Austria and spirited off to England, had died in London in 1939.

Freud died still believing, as he had once remarked, that tobacco was the only excuse for Columbus' great mistake in discovering America. Yet, ironically, it was to be the U.S., not Austria, not Germany, that would become the world center of psychoanalysis and the one nation above all others to immortalize the genius of Freud, "the great liberator who freed the human mind from medieval bondage."

The Author: Novelist and biographer Irving Wallace's international best sellers have included *The Fan Club, The Word, The Man.*

Upton Sinclair and the EPIC Campaign

By Michael S. Medved

On a mild summer evening in 1933, the well-known writer Upton Sinclair attended a dinner party at a small hotel by the beach at Santa Monica, Calif. During the course of the meal his friends suggested to him a plan that led to "one of the great adventures of his life." They urged Sinclair to change his registration immediately from the Socialist to the Democratic party and to seek the Democratic nomination for governor of California in 1934. Sinclair was the author of 47 volumes, most of them novels exposing the corruption of the capitalist system, and he had been a Socialist all his life. On 5 previous occasions he had allowed his name to be used as the Socialist party candidate for various offices, but he had never campaigned actively and never received more than a tiny percentage of the vote. But now, at the height of the Depression, with 28% of the California population either unemployed or the dependents of the unemployed, Sinclair's friends were convinced that he could capture the Democratic nomination, and then go on to win the governorship. Without committing himself one way or the other, Sinclair went home to think it over.

A few days later he took a walk from his home to the Beverly Hills City Hall, and quietly reregistered as a Democrat. He then prepared for the coming campaign in a characteristic manner: He sat down and wrote another book. The product of his labors—*I, Governor of California and How I Ended Poverty: A True Story of the Future*—described in advance Sinclair's successful campaign, his triumphant administration, and the beginning of a new social order in California. The key element in the story was "Governor" Sinclair's EPIC plan—for END POVERTY IN CALIFORNIA. Under EPIC, the State would acquire unused land and idle factories and put the unemployed to work raising food and manufacturing products for their own use. For the 1st time, America would see a system of production for use, rather than production for profit. The workers in the State land colonies and the State-owned factories would be paid in special scrip currency, which could be used to purchase any items from other elements in the EPIC system. When other workers saw the spirit of cooperation, ideal working conditions, and generous salaries that typified EPIC, they would leave their jobs and come to work for the State, and so the capitalist system would slowly collapse as the people took control of their own lives. Sinclair concludes his book with a description of his last acts as governor:

> The Governor made a last speech over the radio saying that he had caused a careful investigation to be made throughout the State of California and that the only poor person he had been able to find was a religious hermit who lived in a cave. Therefore he considered his job done, and he purposed to go home and write a novel.

Sinclair published the book himself, and within 2 weeks his 1st edition of 10,000 copies had been sold out. By the end of 1934, more than 250,000 copies of *I, Governor* had been distributed—making it by far the best-selling book in California history to that time. After reading Sinclair's manifesto, thousands of people across the State began following his organizational blueprint to the letter. EPIC Clubs were organized in over 1,000 different locations across the State, appealing largely to the unemployed, who had time on their hands. A weekly newspaper was printed—*The EPIC News*—and distributed to nearly a million homes. To run with Sinclair, EPIC candidates were chosen for other State offices and for key seats in the State legislature.

As might be expected, the regular Democrats did not look kindly on these interlopers in their midst. With his sharp, pointed nose, his thick spectacles, his shrill voice, and his prim professorial air, Sinclair did not exactly fit their idea of a political heavyweight. Moreover, he had been associated over the years with dozens of causes, ranging from vegetarianism to mental telepathy, and it was easy to discredit him as a kindly crackpot. With 8 regular Democrats in the race against him, it seemed certain that one of them would win enough votes to beat Sinclair.

But on Primary Day, the EPIC forces won an astounding victory. Not only did Sinclair win the Democratic nomination by a huge margin, but he actually polled more votes than all of his 8 rivals combined. His primary vote was the largest ever received by a Democratic gubernatorial candidate. EPIC's candidate for lieutenant governor, Sheridan Downey, also won the nomination, thus giving rise to the popular description of the new Democratic ticket as "Uppie and Downey." Many EPIC candidates also proved successful in State legislative races; in Southern California, 23 out of 26 EPIC State assembly candidates won nomination.

The leaders of business and industry could no longer afford to ignore Sinclair. The Republican incumbent was so reactionary that many GOP voters had already defected to the 3rd-party "Progressive" candidacy of Raymond L. Haight, and it looked as if the Democrat Sinclair had the best chance for victory. The Chamber of Commerce executives did not look forward to the prospect of watching Mr. Upton Sinclair try his EPIC experiments on *their* State, so they resolved to do something to stop him.

The result was the most expensive statewide campaign in American history up to that time, and in California, no campaign down to this day has spent more than the estimated $10 million the Republicans spent to beat Sinclair.

Every big business in the State did its part in the effort to stop EPIC. Led by the Hearst newspapers, the press mounted a campaign against Sinclair which shocked even some anti-Sinclair forces with its viciousness and one-sidedness. No major newspaper in the State dared to support the Democratic nominee, and his speeches and press releases were consistently ignored. Editorial cartoons showed Sinclair as a devil, with drooling lips and pointed fingernails, attacking the sanctity of marriage; or as a would-be dictator riding alongside Hitler and Mussolini. In his 47 books, Sinclair had attacked many of the most beloved American institutions—including the DAR and the Boy Scouts and these attacks were naturally turned against him now. The *Los Angeles Times* ran a front-page box every day, under the heading "Upton Sinclair on . . ." which featured out of context quotes from Sinclair's writing, designed to depict the Democratic candidate as a menace to goodness and respectability. In their efforts to "prove" that Sinclair was an advocate of "free love," the *Times* quoted one of his fictional characters as if that character were Sinclair himself, even when in the context of the novel, it was clear that the author disapproved of this individual and his views.

The most devastating charges against Sinclair concerned his 1918 book *The Profits of Religion*, in which the author had asserted that every organized church was a "mighty fortress of graft" and had gone on to expose the inner workings of church establishments. Catholics, in particular, were deeply offended, especially since Sinclair's views were presented in the most damaging possible light, and the EPIC crusader's claim that he was only "exposing hypocrisy, which Jesus Christ himself had done many times," carried little weight with orthodox believers.

The motion picture industry also came to play a leading role in the effort to smear Sinclair. Louis B. Mayer, the head of MGM, happened to be statewide chairman of the Republican party, and he put his studio to work producing a series of "newsreels" concerning the campaign, which theater owners were required to show along with their features. One of these newsreels featured an interviewer going around the State, asking people whom they would vote for. First he came to a little old lady, sitting and knitting in her rocking chair, in front of a white frame house. "Who are you voting for, Mother?" the reporter asked. "I am voting for the Republican, Frank Merriam."

"Why, Mother?"

"Because this little home may not be much, but it is all I have in this world. I love my home and I want to protect it."

Next, the reporter approached a seedy-looking man in a soiled overcoat and unkempt whiskers. In answer to the question, the stranger responded:

"I am voting for Seen-clair."

"Why?"

"His system vorked vell in Russia, so vy can't it vork here?"

In yet another "newsreel," a whole army of hobos and tramps were shown jumping off a freight train, and celebrating their arrival in California. When asked by the ubiquitous interviewer why they had come to California, the bums declared that "Sinclair says he'll take the property of working people and give it to us."

On 2,000 Republican billboards across the State, appeared the words: "If I am elected governor, half the unemployed in the country will hop the 1st freight to California. —Upton Sinclair." When a friend of Sinclair's asked one lady if she really believed that Sinclair wanted that to happen, she answered "Of course. You can see for yourself he's put his billboards up all over town and signed his name to it."

Last, but not least, were the anti-Sinclair leaflets. One of these, which received wide circulation in the last weeks of the campaign, described Sinclair under the following subheadings: "Sinclair, the dynamiter of all churches and christian institutions," "Sinclair, the Communist Agitator," and, most nefarious of all, "Sinclair's attack on the P.T.A."

Despite these assaults it was generally believed that Sinclair could still win if the national Administration of President Franklin Roosevelt would come out strongly in his favor before Election Day. But Roosevelt, always suspicious of those to his left, kept his enthusiasm for EPIC well under control. As the campaign progressed and the Administration stuck to its position of strict neutrality Sinclair's claims that he was only trying to bring California "its share of the New Deal" began to lose credibility.

On Election Day, Sinclair and EPIC were soundly beaten, and "solid citizens" across the State breathed a sigh of relief. Sinclair drew 37% of the vote while the Republican, Merriam, polled less than 49%, with the balance going to 3rd party moderate Raymond Haight. After his defeat, Sinclair observed bitterly: "I have written too many books to be a politician. If we had had a better candidate we might have won."

Yet it is impossible to write off the EPIC campaign as a complete failure. The Democratic party in California had taken a definite turn to the left, and in future years, many party leaders were drawn from the ranks of onetime EPIC volunteers. Sinclair's running mate, Sheridan Downey, was elected to the Senate in 1938, where he served until replaced by Richard Nixon in 1950. It was another EPIC veteran, Culbert Olson of Los Angeles, who in 1938—4 years after Sinclair's defeat—was elected the 1st Democratic governor of California in the 20th century. It is interesting to note that many of Olson's "radical" reforms were ultimately blocked by the conservative forces in the State legislature.

The Author: An authority on the American Presidency, Yale graduate Michael S. Medved has been a speechwriter for a number of prominent politicians.

The Best from Books

A Review of Recent Books—Letting Them Speak for Themselves

KARL MARX: HIS LIFE AND THOUGHT. By David McLellan, New York: Harper & Row, 1974.

About the book: Half the world's population lives under political systems that claim their inspiration from Karl Marx. For someone so influential, it is surprising that so little has been known of his private life and that his ideas were so misunderstood. McLellan's balanced and comprehensive biography presents for the 1st time a full picture of Marx.

From the book: Here is Karl Marx's own account of himself as he gave it playing the Victorian parlor game of "Confessions."

Marx's Confession
Your favorite virtue
  Simplicity
Your favorite virtue in man
  Strength
Your favorite virtue in woman
  Weakness
Your chief characteristic
  Singleness of purpose
Your idea of happiness
  To fight
Your idea of misery
  Submission
The vice you excuse most
  Gullibility
The vice you detest most
  Servility
Your aversion
  Martin Tupper (*Victorian popular writer*)
Favorite occupation
  Bookworming
Favorite poet
  Shakespeare, Aeschylus, Goethe
Favorite prose-writer
  Diderot
Favorite hero
  Spartacus, Kepler
Favorite heroine
  Gretchen
Favorite flower
  Daphne
Favorite color
  Red
Favorite name
  Laura, Jenny

Favorite dish
  Fish
Favorite maxim
  Nihil humani a me alienum puto ("I consider that nothing human is alien to me.")
Favorite motto
  De omnibus dubitandum ("You must have doubts about everything.")

THE ILLUSTRATED BOOK OF WORLD RECORDS. By Bill Adler. New York: Grosset and Dunlap, 1974.

About the book: According to Adler, "Nothing is more exciting than reading about someone or something that is the fastest, the tallest, the biggest, the tiniest, or the 1st." And that's what he has written, a juvenile version of the *Guinness Book of Records*, which stands on its own and will prove entertaining and educational for parents as well as their children.

From the book: Most people need to sleep every night. One person holds the record for the most hours without sleep. How long did she stay awake?

In 1968, Mrs. Bertha Van Der Merwe went without sleep for 282 hours and 55 minutes. Mrs. Van Der Merwe was being watched by doctors in Cape Town, South Africa, as part of a medical experiment to see how long a person could actually stay awake.

The dog is man's best friend. Which dog lived the longest?

A Labrador gun dog lived with his master in England for 27 years and 3 months.

Has a cat ever lived that long?

A woman in England had a tabby that was 36 years old. His name was Puss.

Which country has the most neighbors on its borders?

Russia has 12—Norway, Finland, Poland, Hungary, Romania, Turkey, Iran, China, North Korea, Afghanistan, Mongolia, and Czechoslovakia.

When were pretzels invented?

In 610 A.D. monks in southern France shaped strips of dough to look like a little child's arms folded in prayer.

When were pizzas 1st made?

More than 2,000 years ago, when Roman soldiers added olive oil and cheese to Jewish matzos. Pizzas were 1st made in America about 45 years ago. Today pizzas are among our favorite foods, and there are more than 30,000 pizzerias in the U.S.

FAREWELL AMERICA. By "James Hepburn." Vaduz, Liechtenstein: Frontiers Co., 1968.

About the book: Who really killed John F. Kennedy? This heavily researched report, prepared by the British Secret Service and published under the pseudonym "James Hepburn," is one of the few books which is not allowed to pass through the U.S. Customs. Much of this book is devoted to background, telling us who liked Kennedy, who disliked him, and who detested him. One whole chapter is devoted to excerpts from Kennedy's speeches during his last year as President. There is a long chapter on the history of the oil industry, with specific emphasis placed on Texas and Louisiana oilmen whose independent status made them more vulnerable to Kennedy's economic policies than the well-rooted wealth of the Rockefellers and other Northern oil powers. The authors estimate that the assassination and its cover-up cost between $5–10 million and that this money was raised by at least 100 people contributing from $10,000 to $50,000 each.

From the book: The attack was to be carried out by a team of 10 men, including 4 gunmen, each seconded by an assistant who would be responsible for their protection, evacuation, and radio liaison, and who would retrieve the shells. The 9th man would serve as a central radio operator, and the 10th was to create a last-minute diversion to enable the gunmen to get into position. . . .

A few minutes before the arrival of the motorcade, a man wearing green army fatigues had a sudden fit of epilepsy in Elm Street. The attack lasted less than a minute and was over as suddenly as it had begun, but it drew the attention of the people standing around him. The police took the "epileptic" away. . . .

In 30 years on the job, J. Edgar Hoover has developed an intelligence system which nothing—no racket, and certainly no conspiracy—can escape. Through its extensive network of informers, the FBI knows everything worth knowing that goes on in the U.S., even in areas that lie outside its legal jurisdiction. (After the assassination, the FBI submitted 25,000 investigative reports. It went so far as to describe the dreams of some of the witnesses.) The Dallas conspiracy was born and took root in places where the FBI was well represented. Its informers included former FBI agent James Rowley, chief of the Secret Service, Dallas

District Attorney Henry Wade, CIA agent Guy Bannister, also a member of the Minutemen, and Lee Harvey Oswald. H. L. Hunt used former FBI agents as bodyguards, and Dallas police chief Curry was in contact with several FBI men and was under surveillance by the FBI, which had no fewer than 75 agents in Dallas.

By mid-October, Hoover had been informed of the existence of a plot and was familiar with many of the details. The FBI often launches an investigation on the strength of a rumor, and the information it received that fall from Boston, Chicago, and Dallas was based on far more than hearsay. These reports were checked out and verified. The week before the President's departure for Texas, Hoover knew exactly what was going to happen. Why did the FBI fail to intervene?

It is true that the FBI bore no responsibility for the security of the President. It is also true that every year dozens of investigations are made of threats against the life of the President. Moreover, the FBI is an investigative agency, not a national police force. Nevertheless, a section of the FBI Manual issued to each agent stipulates that:

"Any information indicating the possibility of an attempt against the person or safety of the President, members of the immediate family of the President, the President-Elect or the Vice-President must be referred immediately by the most expeditious means of communication to the nearest office of the U.S. Secret Service." . . .

The regulations, however, were ignored.

Hoover, "the man who is almost a legend" (in the words of Rep. Gerald Ford) would probably not have agreed to cooperate with the Committee, but he did absolutely nothing to stop it. He may not have approved of the assassination, but he didn't disapprove of it either. Hoover preferred to stay out of other people's fights, especially when they involved business circles over which he exercised little control. Faced with a choice between his professional duty and his abhorrence of everything that President Kennedy represented, he chose the latter alternative. He also hoped that the affair would tarnish the reputation of the CIA and shatter his Attorney General.

After the assassination, the FBI pulled out its files and submitted its report. It laid the blame and designated the culprits. Texas got back at Hoover by declaring, on January 24, 1964, that Lee Oswald had been on the FBI payroll as an informer since 1962. Neither the FBI nor the CIA were ever called upon to clear themselves. The assassination was bigger than both of them.

THE WOMAN'S BIBLE. By Elizabeth Cady Stanton and the Revising Committee. 4759 15th

Ave. N.E., Seattle, Wash.. Seattle Task Force on Women and Religion, 1974.

About the book: First released in 1895, this feminist commentary on the Old and New Testaments attacks the way that women are portrayed in the Holy Book. When some women denounced her book, Stanton wrote that "the only difference between us is, we say that these degrading ideas of woman emanated from the brain of man, while the church says that they came from God."

From the book: Here are excerpts from "Comments on Genesis" (3:1–24—wherein Eve eats the Forbidden Fruit):

Reading this narrative carefully, it is amazing that any set of men ever claimed that the dogma of the inferiority of woman is here set forth. The conduct of Eve from the beginning to the end is so superior to that of Adam. The command not to eat of the fruit of the tree of Knowledge was given to the man alone before woman was formed (Gen. 2:17). Therefore the injunction was not brought to Eve with the impressive solemnity of a Divine Voice, but whispered to her by her husband and equal. It was a serpent supernaturally endowed, a seraphim as Scott and other commentators have claimed, who talked with Eve, and whose words might reasonably seem superior to the secondhand story of her companion —nor does the woman yield up at once . . .

Then the woman fearless of death if she can gain wisdom takes of the Fruit, and all this time Adam standing beside her interposes no word of objection. "Her husband with her" are the words of v. 6. Had he been the representative of the divinely appointed head in married life, he assuredly would have taken upon himself the burden of the discussion with the serpent, but no, he is silent in this crisis of their fate. Having had the command from God himself he interposes no word of warning or remonstrance, but takes the fruit from the hand of his wife without a protest. It takes 6 verses to describe the "fall" of woman; the fall of man is contemptuously dismissed in a line and a half.

The subsequent conduct of Adam was to the last degree dastardly. When the awful time of reckoning comes, and the Jehovah God appears to demand why his command has been disobeyed, Adam endeavors to shield himself behind the gentle being he has declared to be so dear. "The woman thou gavest to be with me, she gave me and I did eat," he whines—trying to shield himself at his wife's expense! Again we are amazed that upon such a story men have built up a theory of their superiority!

THE LAST WEST. By Russell McKee. New York: Crowell, 1974.

About the book: This is a lively history of one of the most ignored parts of the U.S.: the Great Plains. Starting with the land, the author moves on to the peopling of the Plains: the Indians, the Spanish conquistadores, the French trappers and traders and the English explorers. Emphasis is placed on some of the unusual and forgotten personalities who were part of the transition from wilderness to civilization. A good book for people who are used to relating to the area as something to be passed through on the way to somewhere else.

From the book: Though only sketchy accounts of [Etienne de] Bourgmond remain, and almost no accounts of some of the others, he at least led a full life. Born of an old Norman family, son of a renowned physician, young Bourgmond entered French military service, was soon shipped to America, and in the spring of 1706 found himself an ensign commanding the tiny garrison at Fort Detroit, now Detroit, Mich. One night soon after he arrived, a large and determined force of Fox Indians attacked the post. After an all-night battle, Bourgmond and his 15-man army succeeded in driving off the attackers. The residents of the village were pleased by the courage the little garrison had shown, and generous in their praise. The settlement's most luscious member, Madame Tichenet, was especially generous to the gallant young commander. The pair eloped from her bedchamber to join a colony of deserters tenting through the summer on the shore of Lake Erie. Monsieur Tichenet, understandably annoyed, raised a posse of 50 men and marched off to capture the fugitives. The battle was brief and all the renegades were hauled back to Detroit. Despite the obvious evidence of desertion and wife theft, Bourgmond was acquitted by the court at Fort Detroit. His judges also saw fit to reinstate him in the army and soon after rewarded him with a promotion. As French officers, they recognized merit when they saw it.

His next amorous encounter was with an Indian girl named La Chenette, and she led him to still another Indian charmer who has remained nameless, but who proved so fascinating that Bourgmond again deserted, this time for the land of the Missouri River, where he set up housekeeping and lived with his new mate from 1712 to 1719.

It was during this period that he began to change from a simple frontier rogue to a political power among the Indians of the eastern plains border. As his prestige increased, his sway with the Missouri Indians soon built a bastion of French influence against the Spanish further west. There seemed to grow from Bourgmond an element of trust that the Indians found easy to accept. One story that has survived tells of Bourgmond going alone and unarmed to an Indian village where a French trapper had been murdered. Bourgmond called for a public trial of the killer. It was held on the spot, and the murderer was sentenced by his people to die. Before Bourgmond left the village, the condemned man had been executed by his own brother.

THE VERSE BY THE SIDE OF THE ROAD: THE STORY OF THE BURMA-SHAVE SIGNS AND JINGLES. By Frank Rowsome, Jr., drawings by Carl Rose. Brattleboro, Vt.: Stephen Greene Press, 1965.

About the book: The history of an American tradition—the Burma-Shave roadside ad campaign, which began in 1927. The book's best feature is a complete listing of 600 Burma-Shave jingles that lined America's highways. Very enjoyable reading.

From the book:

1930   DOES YOUR HUSBAND
      MISBEHAVE
      GRUNT AND GRUMBLE
      RANT AND RAVE
      SHOOT THE BRUTE SOME
      BURMA-SHAVE

1930   HINKY DINKY
      PARLEY VOO
      CHEER UP FACE
      THE WAR IS THROUGH
      BURMA-SHAVE

1933   HE PLAYED
      A SAX
      BUT HIS WHISKERS SCRATCHED
      HAD NO B.O.
      SO SHE LET HIM GO
      BURMA-SHAVE

1934   COLLEGE BOYS!
      YOUR COURAGE MUSTER
      SHAVE OFF
      THAT FUZZY
      COOKIE DUSTER
      BURMA-SHAVE

1935   HIS FACE WAS SMOOTH
      AND COOL AS ICE
      AND OH LOUISE!
      HE SMELLED
      SO NICE
      BURMA-SHAVE

1935   YOU KNOW
      YOUR ONIONS
      LETTUCE SUPPOSE
      THIS BEETS 'EM ALL
      DON'T TURNIP YOUR NOSE
      BURMA-SHAVE

1936   COOTIES LOVE
      BEWHISKERED PLACES

      CUTIES LOVE THE
      SMOOTHEST FACES
      SHAVED BY
      BURMA-SHAVE

1938   DON'T TAKE
      A CURVE
      AT 60 PER
      WE HATE TO LOSE
      A CUSTOMER
      BURMA-SHAVE

1939   PAST
      SCHOOLHOUSES
      TAKE IT SLOW
      LET THE LITTLE
      SHAVERS GROW
      BURMA-SHAVE

1940   DON'T STICK
      YOUR ELBOW
      OUT SO FAR
      IT MIGHT GO HOME
      IN ANOTHER CAR
      BURMA-SHAVE

1940   SHE KISSED
      THE HAIRBRUSH
      BY MISTAKE
      SHE THOUGHT IT WAS
      HER HUSBAND JAKE
      BURMA-SHAVE

1942   PA ACTED
      SO TICKLED
      MA THOT
      HE WAS PICKLED
      HE'D JUST TRIED
      BURMA-SHAVE

1947   THAT SHE
      COULD COOK
      HE HAD HIS DOUBTS
      UNTIL SHE CREAMED
      HIS BRISTLE SPROUTS WITH
      BURMA-SHAVE

1950   THE WHALE
      PUT JONAH
      DOWN THE HATCH
      BUT COUGHED HIM UP
      BECAUSE HE SCRATCHED
      BURMA-SHAVE

1951   I KNOW
      HE'S A WOLF
      SAID RIDING HOOD
      BUT GRANDMA DEAR,
      HE SMELLS SO GOOD
      BURMA-SHAVE

1959   SAID FARMER BROWN
      WHO'S BALD
      ON TOP
      WISH I COULD

ROTATE THE CROP
BURMA-SHAVE

THE ARAB MIND. By Raphael Patai. New
York: Charles Scribner's Sons, 1973.

About the book: With the emergence of the
Arab countries into positions of world power,
this anthropologist's study of the traditions
of Arab society takes on timeliness and importance. The book offers an insight into Arab
social, political, and cultural behavior.

From the book: In traditional Arab society,
a man and his wife would never dream of walking together in the street, side by side, let
alone arm in arm or hand in hand. Such behavior would be considered an indecent public
display of intimacy whose proper place is at
home, in the privacy of the bedroom. Even at
home in the presence of children, siblings, or
parents, the contact between husband and wife
evinces the same restraint. This is carried so far
that it is considered utterly bad form for a man
to inquire about the well-being of a friend's
wife. The very word for "wife" (*zawja*) in
Arabic is felt to be too indelicate to use, because of its sexual connotations (it is derived
from the verb meaning to couple), and is replaced by various euphemistic expressions or cir-
cumlocutions, such as *imrā'ati* or *maddamti*
("my lady"); *haram* ("woman," "that which
is forbidden," and "that which is sanctified");
umm Hasan ("mother of Hasan," if Hasan
is the name of the 1st-born son); *bint 'ammī*
("my cousin," used by the husband even if the
wife is not a cousin); *yakhtī* ("O, my sister");
or *yā bint al-nās* ("O, daughter of people"). . . .
The taboo on homosexuality is not so strong
as it was in America in the 1950s . . . and the
active homosexual role in particular is thought
of by the Arab students as compatible with
virile masculinity. In this respect, the Arab attitude coincides with that of the Turks, among
whom the performance of the active homosexual act is considered as an assertion of one's aggressive masculine superiority, while the acceptance of the role of the passive homosexual is
considered extremely degrading and shameful
because it casts the man or youth into a sub-
missive, feminine role.
In most parts of the Arab world, homosexual
activity or any indication of homosexual leanings, as with all other expressions of sexuality, is
never given any publicity. These are private
affairs and remain in private, especially since
homosexual relations are forbidden in the Koran. Popular opinion, however, takes no stand
against them, and despite the warnings of the
Muslim schools of jurisprudence, the practice
seems to be common to this day. Only in outlying areas, such as the Siwa Oasis in the
Western Desert of Egypt, has homosexuality
come out into the open with the sheikhs and
the well-to-do men lending their sons to each
other. It is interesting that even in a place like
Siwa where homosexuality is the rule and practiced completely in the open, the passive partner in the relationship is derided as a woman.

CYCLES: THE MYSTERIOUS FORCES THAT
TRIGGER EVENTS. By Edward R. Dewey with
Og Mandino. New York: Hawthorn Books,
1971.

About the book: A fascinating study of cycles,
a new science dealing with the behavior of
events recurring at reasonably regular intervals
throughout the universe. This science may ultimately enable people to predict, scientifically
and accurately, the events of tomorrow. Our
excerpt discusses the emotional ups and downs
of human beings.

From the book: Some years ago a scientific
study of these emotional fluctuations in male
human beings was conducted by Professor
Rex Hersey of the University of Pennsylvania.
His conclusion was that although the emotional
cycles of individual men vary with the individual from 16 days to 63 days, the average
length for men is about 5 weeks. This is the
typical length of time it takes for a normal man
to move from one period of elation down the
scale to a feeling of worry (the most destructive emotion, according to Hersey) and back
up again to the next period of elation. , . .
To simplify and portray the fluctuating
moods of his subjects, Professor Hersey constructed a scale of emotions to which he applied
numerical values. Happiness and elation received the highest value, plus 6; worry was assigned the lowest value, minus 6.
Each day for 13 weeks the subjects were
briefly interviewed 4 times and given a "mood
rating" for that day, ranging from plus 6 to
minus 6. . . .
The major surprise to Hersey was that although different individuals had different cycle
lengths, they were always fairly constant for
that individual. If one worker had an average
mood cycle of 5 weeks, it was almost never
less than 4 weeks, almost never more than
6. . . .
Obviously it would be of great help to you if
you knew your "high" and "low" periods—and
this can be quite easily learned, with a minimum of time. Begin by preparing a simple
chart similar to the one shown. . . .
This is a simplified version of the graph used
by Professor Hersey but it is sufficient to chart
your own emotional cycle. Every evening take
a few moments and review your general mood
of the day. Then place a dot in the box which
you believe most aptly defines your state of

mind. Connect the dots with a straight line as time goes on.

Soon a pattern will emerge. This is your natural mood rhythm and in most cases it will continue. After a few months you will know, with amazing accuracy, when your next "high" is due and when you should prepare for your next "low." As I mentioned earlier, this cycle will normally not vary by more than one week either way. With this knowledge, this ability to at least partially "see into your future," you will be able to adjust your behavior to suit your mood. When you are going through your high period of elation, you will think twice before making rash promises, impossible commitments, or misguided installment purchases. You will also be able to live through your low periods of sadness and depression because you will know that these too will pass, within a few days. A greater knowledge of cycles, as you can see, will help you to change what can be changed and prepare for what cannot.

THE PARADISE PROGRAM. By Anthony Haden-Guest. New York: William Morrow and Co., 1973.

About the book: A kinky personal investigation by an English author of some remarkable offbeat business empires. Haden-Guest guides the reader into the dizzying worlds of Edgar Rice Burroughs, Inc., Reader's Digest, Hilton Hotels, Coca-Cola. Most memorable of all, in Elk Grove, Ill., a suburb of Chicago, he found a stone slab announcing the entrance to Hamburger University, one of the most unique colleges in the world and the training ground for those who wish to open a McDonald's Hamburger franchise.

From the book: Hamburger University is not the playful whim of a very rich company. It offers a training course for new batches of managerial talent. They will have paid $100,-000/$125,000 for a franchise, depending on the trimmings, and the course is free. McDonald's

	Month										
		1	2	3	4	5	6	7	8	9	10
Elated	+3										
Happy	+2										
Pleasant feeling	+1										
Neutral	0										
Unpleasant feeling	-1										
Disgusted; sad	-2										
Worried; depressed	-3										

Set up graph for 30 days

A Grid for Recording Your Emotions

isn't the only fast-food chain to offer some of the trappings of the groves of Academe (there is also a Dunkin' Donuts University in Quincy, Mass.) but it is, indisputably, the fanciest. The end product is a Diploma in Hamburgerology, with a Minor in French Fries. There have been 130 classes, and there are upwards of 5,000 Bachelors of Hamburgerology. It is a handsome diploma, with black Gothic lettering, signed by Ray Kroc (Chairman) and Fred Turner (President), and there is no reason to suppose that the BHs find it a comical document. Rather it is, in the best academic traditions, jocular-solemn.

Classes can vary from 10 to 40. The franchisees tend to be in their middling 30s, and competent. Not just anybody can get a franchise. Despite the costs, and despite the 11.5%

of monthly sales that the franchisee pays to McDonald's, a strictly average McDonald's operator should make profits of 50, 60, 70 thousand dollars a year.

THE MAKING OF A MODEL CITIZEN IN COMMUNIST CHINA. By Charles Price Ridley, Paul M. B. Godwin, and Dennis J. Doolin. Stanford, Calif.: The Hoover Institution Press, 1971.

About the book: By analyzing elementary school readers, the authors show how the Chinese Government uses the educational system to help mold what they consider to be model citizens. They stress cleanliness, bravery, patriotism, personal sacrifice, and unquestioning loyalty to Chairman Mao, the Party, and the

Government. Included are 200 pages of excerpts from the readers.

From the book: Selections from Volume 1 of the Readers (grade one):

Thirty, Study Hard. Chairman Mao loves us. Chairman Mao tells us to study hard and advance upwards every day. We must be obedient to the words of Chairman Mao and be good children of Chairman Mao.

Thirty-eight, On Duty for the Day. Today we are on duty. After school is out, we sweep the classroom. Some of us sprinkle water, some of us sweep, some of us clean the blackboard, and some of us wipe the desks and chairs. After we finish sweeping, the classroom is very clean, and in our hearts we are very happy.

Forty-two, I Will Love to Wear My Jacket. Hsiao-chu's mother sewed a jacket for her. Hsiao-chu began to sing happily:

Mother sewed a jacket for me,
A thousand stitches, 10 thousand stitches, she sewed fine.
How hard my mother worked to sew my clothes,
I will love to wear my jacket.

Her mother said: "Well sung! Hsiao-chu, I ask you, who planted the cotton? Who wove the cloth?"

Hsiao-chu said: "The cotton was grown by us peasants, and the cloth was woven by the workers."

Her mother said: "That's right! See, how many people must labor to make a piece of clothes! How could we help but love the clothes we wear?"

(Why should we love our clothes?)

THE LAST MEN OF THE REVOLUTION. By Rev. E. B. Hillard. Barre, Mass.: Barre Pub., 1968.

About the book: Ever wondered about those grand old survivors, the final handful of Revolutionary War soldiers who lingered on into the 19th century? This book tells it all, zeroing in on 7 men still alive in 1864, the year the Reverend Hillard arranged a personal interview with each one. Hillard gives an account of these talks, plus detailed biographical sketches, "views" of all the homes he visited, and adds a "photo gallery" of the ancient 7. The Reverend Hillard was, incidentally, Archibald MacLeish's grandfather, and a "controversial figure in his own day."

From the book: The 1st in order visited was SAMUEL DOWNING, and the sketch of his life shall introduce the series.

Mr. Downing lives in the town of Edinburgh, Saratoga County, N.Y. *Edinburgh, N.Y., had a population of 1,479 in 1860. By contrast, Saratoga Springs, the largest town in the county, had 7,496 at the same time.*

To reach his home, you proceed to Saratoga,

and thence by stage some 20 mi. to the village of Luzerne, on the upper Hudson.

On entering the yard I at once recognized him from his photograph, and addressing myself to him, said, "Well, Mr. Downing, you and the bees seem very good friends." (There was barely room for him between the 2 hives, and the swarms were working busily on both sides of him.) "Yes," he replied, "they don't hurt me and I don't hurt them." On telling him that I had come a long way to see an old soldier of the Revolution, he invited me to walk into the house, himself leading the way. . . . Seated, in the house, and my errand made known to him, he entered upon the story of his life, which I will give as nearly as possible in the old man's own words.

"Well, the war broke out. Mr. Aiken was a militia captain; and they used to be in his shop talking about it. I had ears, and I had *eyes* in them days. They was enlisting 3 years men and for-the-war men. I heard say that Hopkinton was the enlisting place. One day aunt said she was going a-visiting. So I said to myself, 'That's right, Aunty; you go, and I'll go too.' So they went out, and I waited till dinner time, when I thought nobody would see me, and then I started.

"The 1st duty I ever did was to guard wagons from Exeter to Springfield. We played the British a trick; I can remember what I said as well as can be. We all started off on a run, and as I couldn't see anything, I said, 'I don't see what the devil we're running after or running away from, for I can't see anything.' One of the officers behind me said, 'Run, you little dog, or I'll spontoon you.' SPONTOON: "A *species of half-pike or halberd carried by infantry officers in the 18th century (from about 1740)*" (Oxford English Dictionary). 'Well, I answered, 'I guess I can run as fast as you can and as far.' "

HOW TO USE COLOR TO SELL. By Eric P. Danger. Boston: Cahners, 1969.

About the book: This book is primarily for those with something to sell, but is fascinating in general from the point of view of color-psychology and manipulation. The author treats "color strategy" in general, and specific products.

From the book: What is color? Color is a physical phenomenon, but from a sales point of view color is people. People decide which colors will sell and people decide whether they will pass over a product because they do not like its color. The reason why color commands such importance in the sales picture is that it appeals to the emotions, not to reason. And the appeal is largely subconscious. A baby responds to color long before it recognizes shape or form, and this awareness remains throughout life. Almost everyone is attracted by color; those who are not can be disregarded in this context.

Customers who like red are extrovert.
Customers who prefer yellow have an intellectual bent.
Customers with a fondness for blue-green are discriminating.
People who buy blue have close control of their emotions.
Orange clients are convivial.
Purple purchasers are artistic.
Disciplined customers go for maroon.

The average consumer is basically fearful of making a decision for herself (or himself) and she will seek guidance from what is going on around her; from what Mrs. Jones up the road is doing; from what she sees advertised or recommended in the press; and from various other influences, all of which are cumulative. As Mrs. Jones up the road is doing exactly the same thing, they tend to follow the same path because they are influenced by the same pressures.

This is not to say that every consumer will choose exactly the same thing. Life would be much simpler if they did—although, by the same token, the penalty of failure on the part of the manufacturer would be greater. Some people have a preference for one color and others have a preference for another, but likes and dislikes tend to move in the same direction. A woman who liked red, for example, would tend to purchase an orange-red rather than a rose-red if the trend was moving that way, but she might not purchase an orange-yellow.

MASTERS OF MAGIC. By Lace Kendall. Philadelphia: Macrae Smith Co., 1966.

About the book: Not only the famous Harry Houdini, but many of the other great stage magicians are covered in this book. The lives of the magicians, and the secrets of their art, are revealed.
From the book: The group tensed as the Frenchman handed a cavalry pistol to the marabout and spoke to him with the aid of an interpreter.

"Aim directly at me. Then you shall see what kind of sorcerers we have in France." He walked off 15 paces and turned. Behind him a newly whitewashed wall glittered, making his figure stand out in black relief.

The marabout raised the pistol, triumph already showing in his eyes. On the faces of the Arab spectators there was both fear and awe. No man, not even the clever Robert-Houdin about whom they had heard so much since he had come to show his tricks in Algeria, could withstand a lead bullet. True, the chiefs who had watched him perform in the great theater in Algiers had reported that he was a miracle man, but he had performed then on a stage. Here in the open the watchers had seen the lead bullet with their own eyes and looked closely as he had placed it in the pistol and wadded it down.

The sound of the pistol cracked the silence. A horse nearby gave a snort of fear. A wandering goat racketed away in flight. The suave Frenchman stood perfectly calm, untouched. He stretched his lips to expose his teeth. There between his teeth was the bullet!

"Allah!" the marabout cried, and the pistol fell from his shaking hands. The other Arabs ran forward murmuring, "Djenoum!"—demon.

Robert-Houdin shook his head, smiled, and handed the marked bullet to the foremost leader for his inspection. "No, not a demon. Only a magician. I make no claim to supernatural powers." He glanced toward the wincing marabout. "As some conjurers do." He removed another pistol from the hip pocket of his coat and turned to face the whitewashed wall. "Now, if you will, please watch the wall."

He fired. A red splotch appeared on the masonry; blood dripping and running downward in the sunlight.

The marabout recovered his nerve enough to scoff. "It is red wine only."

"Go dip your finger in it," Robert-Houdin said. "You will find it is real enough."

The native magician ran forward, tested the blood with his finger, and raised it to his mouth. More shaken than ever, he turned and hurried away. The others crowded around Robert-Houdin, bowing in respect.

IN THIS CORNER. By Peter Heller. New York: Simon and Schuster, 1973.

About the book: The unvarnished stories of 40 world boxing champions still alive in 1973—Jack Dempsey, Mickey Walker, Pete Herman, Gunboat Smith, Fidel LaBarba, Jack Sharkey, Rocky Graziano, Jake LaMotta, Carmen Basilio, Joe Louis, Willie Pep, Floyd Patterson, Archie Moore, and others. Each tells of his championship, his career, his life, his greatest fights, his controversies, and the behind-the-scenes dealings. Illustrated with photos of the champions.
From the book: JACK DEMPSEY—He couldn't come out, 4th round. It's a great feeling. You've worked for something, thought about something all your life, and you win the title. I don't think I slept all night. As a matter of fact, I remember this very well. I went to bed and tried to sleep and couldn't sleep. I had a dream that I got knocked out, and I couldn't believe it. I said there's something wrong someplace, so I'm going to go out and went down in front of the hotel. I said, "Give me a paper, kid." I said, "Who won the fight?" The kid

looked at me and said, "Aren't you Jack Dempsey?" I said, "Yeah." He said, "You damn fool, you did! Don't you know?" So then I went back to bed and went to sleep.

BATTLING BATTALINO—Well, anyway, I went along, went to New York and had my hands operated on. I got as heavy as 155 lbs. I got fat as a pig. Gradually, I kept taking long hikes and I got to taper down. Start to go to the gym, work out. I was world champion. I fought one guy, Lew Massey from Philadelphia, I had an infected finger. If I didn't fight him it was going to cost me money for paying doctor bills, training, and whatnot. I had to pay it all myself. Boboo Hoff was a big racketeer in those days in Philly, so he paid all my bills, paid my training expense, transportation from Hartford to Philly. He was the promoter. He didn't want me to call off the fight. They had a full house. By having a full house, he paid all the expenses and everything and made money himself. He paid everything, and I got $3,500, damn good money in those days during the heart of the Depression, 1930. They would throw me in against anybody. I didn't give a damn who it was, big guys, little guys. I was like a bull. So finally that year I made out my taxes. I made $72,000 in 1930.

CARMEN BASILIO—Everybody's personality is different, how they feel about getting hit. You have to know that when you're fighting good fighters you're going to get hit. The greatest fighters in the world get hit. The classiest boxers in the world get hit with punches. The thing is, if you start developing a fear, then you're going to have to quit fighting.

OLD AGE, THE LAST SEGREGATION. By Claire Townsend, Project Director of Ralph Nader's Study Group Report on Nursing Homes. New York: Bantam Books, 1971.

About the book: A Nader Task Force gives the Nader Treatment to conditions in America's public and private nursing homes.

From the book: Drug companies frequently carry out experimental research on nursing home patients. One woman's report of an experiment involving her mother is a striking example of abuses that can occur. The case is unusual only in that the patient's family made exhaustive inquiries following her death and found that no one—not the Government, or the attending physician, or the home—had been adequately protecting the patient.

According to a Food and Drug Administration report made at the family's insistence after the death of the patient, the G. D. Searle & Company had gained FDA permission to test "Anavar," a drug supposed to increase appetite and retard bone deterioration. The drug was already approved for use in doses of 2.5 milligrams 2 to 4 times a day for no more than 3 months. Searle wanted to test its usage over a long period of time at doses of 10 milligrams once a day.

Although the woman's daughter had expressly told the attending physician not to allow her mother to be given experimental drugs, the nursing home and the attending physician approved her, among others, for the experiment.

After taking the drug for about 6 months, the patient became critically ill. Medical diagnoses never confirmed the cause of illness. No move was ever made to find out whether the experimental drug had caused or contributed to the illness, and the drug continued to be given.

Two months later, the woman died. Both the home and the coroner who filled out the death certificate refused to tell the family exactly how or why the woman died. The home has refused to release the woman's medical records to her family.

The family did obtain a record of the drugs given and discovered the patient had been taking an experimental drug. When they demanded to know why they had not been consulted, the home produced a "consent" document marked with the patient's X. Although the patient had been judged senile by her doctor, who recommended that she live in an institution, the home maintained and the FDA concurred that the "consent" of a person medically diagnosed as senile was sufficient.

THE WORLD THROUGH BLUNTED SIGHT. By Patrick Trevor-Roper. New York: Bobbs-Merrill Co., 1970.

About the book: That visual abnormalities have affected the work of many of the most renowned artists is not a new concept. Nor is it surprising to hear it said that this or that artist was depressed, in love, or heartbroken, when he painted a particular picture. But seldom does one hear about the effect which visual problems—myopia, hypermetropia, color-blindness, etc.—can have upon the psychological makeup of the individual.

This book uses the subjective world of the artist to illustrate this theme.

From the book: The classical instance of an artist whose characteristic style has been attributed to an astigmatic eye is El Greco, for in nearly all his paintings there is a vertical elongation, but on a slightly oblique axis, so that all his characters seem to be in danger of sliding off the bottom righthand corner of the picture. It is interesting to discover how constant, both in degree and meridian, these distortions are when we neutralize them by photographing his paintings through an 1·0D astigmatic lens along an opposite meridian (15° off the horizontal). If one looks at the portrait of the Cardinal Inquisitor Nino de Guevara (which has an incidental ophthalmological interest, in that the cardinal is wearing a pair of archetypal spectacles, fastened with a cord behind the ears in the Chinese fashion), and then at the neutralized rendering of the same painting, one can see that the latter has indeed restored more normal proportions and removed the rather disquieting mal-equilibrium of the cardinal, who had seemed to be slipping off his chair.

BIRTHRIGHT OF MAN. By Jeanne Hersch, ed. New York: Unipub Inc., 1969.

About the book: To mark the 20th anniversary of the Universal Declaration of Human Rights, the General Conference of UNESCO decided to publish a collection of quotations from a wide variety of traditions and periods which illustrate how human beings everywhere and always have claimed their rights as humans.
From the book: One should allow everything to run its course without check or restriction. Let the ear hear what it likes, let the eye see what it likes; let the nose smell what it likes, let the mouth say what it likes; let the body enjoy what it likes and let the mind think what it likes.
> Lieh-tzu, Taoist school, 4th to 3rd century
> B.C., China

For I mean not that other men be eased, and ye burdened: But by an equality, that now at this time your abundance may be a supply for their want, that their abundance also may be a supply for your want: that there may be equality: As it is written, He that had gathered much had nothing over; and he that had gathered little had no lack.
> New Testament, St. Paul, Second Epistle to
> the Corinthians, 8

Take any parliamentary country, from America to Switzerland, from France to England, Norway and so forth—in these countries the actual work of the State is done behind the scenes, being carried on by the departments, the chancelleries and the General Staffs. Parliament itself is given up to talk, for the sole purpose of fooling the "common people" . . .
> Lenin, *The State and Revolution,* 1917

When the waters rise the fish eat the ants; when the waters recede the ants eat the fish.
> Khmer proverb, Cambodia

OUR BODIES, OURSELVES. By the Boston Women's Health Book Collective. New York: Simon and Schuster, 1973.

About the book: A book by and for women which covers such subjects as sexuality, anatomy, rape, health, nutrition, and emotions. Women are encouraged to acquire knowledge and gain control of their own lives. There is a lot of practical information about abortion, birth control, and other topics which is illustrated with numerous 1st-person accounts of personal experiences.
From the book: What to expect from your doctor:
1. An accurate diagnosis of your condition, healthy or otherwise, at your request.
2. Results and meaning of any tests or examinations performed by him or by others at his direction, as soon as they are available.
3. Indications for treatment, varieties, and alternatives, pros and cons of particular treatments in the opinion of other experts, as well as the doctor's own preference and the reasons for it.
4. Answers to your questions about any examination or procedure he may perform, in advance of or at any time during the performance of it. Stopping any examination or procedure at any moment, at your request.
5. Complete information about purpose, content, and known effects of all drugs prescribed or administered, including possible risks, side-effects, and contra-indications, especially of any combination of drugs.
6. Willingness to accept and wait for a 2nd medical opinion before performing any elective surgery which involves alteration or removal of any organ or body part.
7. Answers to your questions about your body or your general physical health and functioning, in addition to any particular condition. Or, encouragement to seek these answers from another source.

INTEGRAL YOGA HATHA. By Yogiraj Sri Swami Satchidananda. New York: Holt, Rinehart and Winston, 1970.

About the book: This is by far the clearest introduction to basic yoga techniques which is available in book form. It is extensively illustrated with pictures of lovable Swami Satchidananda demonstrating basic, intermediate, and advanced poses.
From the book: Om Shanthi. Shanthi. Shanthi.
Uddhiyāna Bandha or the Stomach Lift
TECHNIQUE: Stand with the feet apart. Bend slightly forward, placing the hands on the corresponding knees. Empty the lungs by a deep expiration. Contract the front muscles of the abdomen and draw it in, forming a hollow. Do not inhale while this lift is being maintained. Before the breath can force its way back, release the abdomen and inhale slowly. This makes one round of Uddhiyāna. You may do this while sitting in Padmāsana, also (lotus pose).
CAUTION: Uddhiyāna should not be held beyond one's capacity. The moment you find that you cannot hold the breath *out* comfortably,

release the muscles slowly to bring the abdomen back to the normal position. Uddhiyāna is to be avoided in cases of circulatory disturbances and serious abdominal troubles.

TIME: Repeat this pose from 3 to 7 times, retaining the lift from 5 to 30 seconds each time.

BENEFITS: This is a fine exercise for the abdomen. It tones the nerves of the solar plexus. It relieves constipation, indigestion, and liver troubles; reduces abdominal fat; and strengthens flabby stomachs.

NOTE: The ancient treastises on Yoga claim that by the regular practice of Uddhiyāna, death can be conquered. This much is certain: It bestows youth and vitality. Uddhiyāna Bandha has been added to this 1st section on Cultural Poses because, among all the Bandhas, it is considered easy enough to be practiced by everyone.

Lokaa Samastaa Shukino Bhavanthu. May the entire world be happy.

Jai Shree Sat Guru Maharaj Ki!
OM TAT SAT

PATTERNLESS FASHIONS. By Diehl Lewis and May Loh. Washington, D.C.: Acropolis Books, 1973.

About the book: This book is designed to liberate the novice or the professional from being dependent on making clothes from standard patterns. The methods illustrated allow for the creation of more economical and better fitting garments. Over 80 formulas are presented for designing all types of clothing from evening dresses to hot pants, men's bathrobes to children's sunsuits.

From the book: The technique described in this book is really a very simple one—even for the beginner. First, it involves the construction of front and back torsos using your 25 measurements and 9 basic formulas. These torsos are then used to make any fashions you may choose, simply by drawing the torsos on your fabric with tailors chalk and making the necessary style changes described in the book.

How to take measurements accurately

The person to be measured should stand straight in a natural posture and the measurer should measure step-by-step with a tape measure. Start taking measurements from the front side of the body. In taking measurements, it is important to make note of such shapes as a high waist, round or square shoulders, or one shoulder lower than the other. A string should be tied around the thinnest part of the torso which will usually be the waist circumference. The string should not be tied too high or too low, but right at the waistline.

Circle skirt

This skirt has big waves downward, and a gentle sloping line. Fold the material in a square 1st, then fold again into a triangle. Move down from the point of the triangle until you are able to measure the amount figures in the formula across the pattern. The formula for drafting a circle skirt is:

Waist measurement divided by 6=amount to measure across the pattern.

In our drawing the waist measurement is 28″ divided by 6=4⅝″. Move down from the triangle point until you can make a line across the pattern equal to 7″. Draw a line with a curved ruler. This is the waistline. Measure down from the waistline for the skirt measurement in several places so hem will be even. Always make the hem in a circle skirt 1½″ wide.

A GOOD COOK . . . TEN TALENTS. By Dr. Frank J. Hurd and Rosaline Hurd. Chisholm, Minn. (privately printed), 1968. Available from: Dr. and Mrs. Hurd, Box 86, A-Route 1, Chisholm, Minn. 55719.

About the book: A natural foods cookbook and nutrition manual. Mrs. Hurd includes her award-winning meal from the "Mrs. America Contest," as well as a large number of delicious and unusual hints and recipes. Beautiful color photographs.

From the book: Let the table be made inviting and attractive, as it is supplied with the good things which God has so bountifully bestowed.

Fanny Salad
(Fruit doll)

½ pear   1 banana
½ peach   berries
soy cream   pieces of apple

Arrange fruit on individual salad plates using:

Head—Pear half small end down
Body—Peach half rounded side up
Arms—Banana sliced in half
Skirt—Triangular mound of berries
Hair—Berries set in soy whipped cream
Eyes—2 blueberries
Mouth—Piece of red apple
Feet—2 dabs of soy cream

Communion Wafers
(150 people)

2 cups sifted 100%   ⅜ cup oil (6 tbs.)
whole wheat flour   ½ cup pure water
½ tsp. salt

Sift flour with salt again. Blend oil and cold water. Pour over flour and mix into soft ball. Knead a few minutes. Roll out very thin. Mark off with a dull knife into 1″ squares. Bake in moderate oven till golden brown.

TRIPPING IN AMERICA. By Bill Thomas. Radnor, Pa.: Chilton Books, 1974.

About the book: Many vacationing tourists are tired of going to the same places and doing the same things as everyone else. If sterile, packaged tours leave you unsatisfied, why not see what the U.S. really has to offer by visiting some of these unusual events and colorful places.

From the book:

National Coon Dog Cemetery—Cherokee, Ala.

The Annual Ice Worm Festival—Cordova, Alaska, early February

Floatdown and World Inner Tube Race—Yuma, Ariz., late June or early July

Wild Turkey Calling Contest—Yellville, Ark., autumn

Mission Bay Sand Castle Contest—San Diego, Calif., July

Arapaho Glacier Hike—Boulder, Colo., 2nd Sunday in August

Nut Museum—Old Lyme, Conn. (admission—one nut, regardless of variety)

Swamp Cabbage Festival—LaBelle, Fla., February

Moonshine Museum—Dawsonville, Ga.

Crystal Ice Cave—American Falls, Ida.

Hobo Convention—Britt, Ia., August or September

House of Telephones—Coffeyville, Kans.

National Dump Week—Kennebunkport, Me., July

Eastern Experimental Aircraft Show—Frederick, Md., autumn.

National Mushroom Hunt—Boyne City, Mich., spring

Tobacco Spitting Championships—Raleigh, Miss., August

National Basque Festival—Elko, Nev., 1st weekend in July

Museum of Immigration—Statue of Liberty, N.Y.C.

National Hollerin' Contest—Spivey's Corner, N.C., June

The Circleville Pumpkin Show—Circleville, O.

The Cowboy Hall of Fame—Old Chisolm Trail, Okla.

Watermelon Seed Spitting Contest—Paul's Valley, Okla., July

Rooster Crowing Contest—Rogue River, Ore., last Saturday in June

Country Music Hall of Fame—Nashville, Tenn.

Zoo for Near Extinct Animals—Brownsville, Tex.

Dowsers Convention—Danville, Vt., autumn

Great Dismal Swamp—South of Portsmouth, Va.

Mountain Climbing School—Moose, Wyo., mid-June to mid-September.

And many more.

THE BEAUTIES & THE BEASTS: THE MOB IN SHOW BUSINESS. By Hank Messick. New York: David McKay Co., Inc., 1973.

About the book: THE BEAUTIES & THE BEASTS explores the interrelationships of organized crime with such show business personalities as Marilyn Monroe, Jean Harlow, Fanny Brice, Jill St. John, George Raft, Joe E. Lewis, and Frank Sinatra. Crime reporter Hank Messick probes Jean Harlow's involvement in a murder and its subsequent cover-up; the Mob's high-level contacts with some of the major studios and banks; Bugsy Siegel's attempt to sell Mussolini the secret of the atomic bomb, and organized crime's abortive attempt to use Robert Kennedy's association with Marilyn Monroe, and Marilyn's suicidal tendencies, for blackmail.

From the book: When Humphrey Bogart died of cancer in 1957, Frank Sinatra attempted to take over "Bogie's" image as the leader of Hollywood's middle-aged delinquents. Bogart had done what came naturally, but Sinatra seemed to be playing a part—a part dictated by a need to cultivate an ego that would conceal a basic insecurity. To fight with reporters, consort with gangsters, curry favor with the politically powerful, and throw money around as if it was meaningless—all was part of the pattern. Bogart was an admirer of Franklin Roosevelt, a cynic about Douglas MacArthur, in both cases as a matter of principle. Sinatra supported men in power; their politics were immaterial. His passion was aroused only when his vanity was hurt, and the price of his friendship was "respect."

Although not a member of "the clan," Marilyn Monroe had an enduring friendship with Sinatra which lasted from her early days in films until the time of her death and he was one of the few to whom she confided the then well-kept secret of her romance with Robert Kennedy.

While one can wonder if Kennedy knew that Marilyn and Sinatra were still friends, there can be no doubt that he was completely unaware that she had told Sinatra about their affair. For Kennedy knew in the early summer of 1962 that Sinatra hated his very guts. And he knew also that Sinatra's gangster associates would do anything to destroy him. The Kennedy-ordered investigation even then under way into the true ownership of Las Vegas casinos and the distribution of the "off the top" skim threatened to undermine the entire structure of organized crime.

THE BOOK OF SURVIVAL: EVERYMAN'S GUIDE TO STAYING ALIVE AND HANDLING EMERGENCIES IN THE CITY, THE SUBURBS, AND THE WILD LANDS BEYOND. By Anthony Greenbank. New York: Harper & Row, 1967.

About the book: What to do when: drowning, attacked, stranded, frostbitten, burned, charged by a bull, caught in a crowd, etc. A little chilling for coffee-table reading, but perhaps, as the author points out, "Instead of being mesmerized with fright, you are more likely to be ready and braced in a sudden crisis after reading this book than before."

From the book: WOMAN BEING FOLLOWED—At sign of persistent footsteps behind . . . 1. WALK FASTER. If footsteps still follow, 2. RUN. If footsteps follow running, 3. SCREAM. If attacked give your resistance everything. Screaming is often sufficient deterrent. But if not, fight like hell. The object is to stay alive, so don't use half measures. Think ahead when followed and choose some weapon to have in hand if grabbed, from whole arsenal you carry —from high heels to hat pins.

    a. Umbrella stabbed forward.
    b. Comb with teeth dragged across underneath nose.
    c. Matchbox held protruding from thumb side of fist—struck hard on assailant's temples.
    d. Nail file/hairpins/safety pins/fingernails/ballpoint pens/hairbrush handle— all useful jabbers and gougers.
    e. Key ring held in palm with keys sticking through slits between fingers.
    f. Face powder blown or hair spray sprayed into attacker's eyes.
    g. Coins slipped between fingers of clenched fist in advance.
    h. Handbag with hand and wrist slipped through strap ready to swing as a club or wield stiletto heel like a battle-axe.

If approached suddenly by man, and no time for running—TALK. And in meantime prepare defense as above (looping hand through handbag strap, etc.).

THE COUNTRY MUSIC ENCYCLOPEDIA. By Melvin Shestack. New York: Crowell, 1974.

About the book: Lots of friendly personal biographies and photos of stars and important figures in the world of country music. There are also discographies for all the artists included, as well as a listing of country radio stations and the words and music of a sampling of country favorites.

From the book: COUNTRY MUSIC HALL OF FAME

Every year a nominating committee selects from 10 to 20 candidates for the Country Music Hall of Fame. An electorate of 250 industry leaders (artists, executives, journalists, producers, etc.) then chooses one of the nominees as the new Hall of Fame member. The members are memorialized on bronze plaques, which are on public display at the Country Music Foundation's Hall of Fame in Nashville, Tenn.:

Fred Rose (songwriter and publisher)	1961
Jimmie Rodgers	1961
Hank Williams	1961
Roy Acuff	1962
Tex Ritter	1964
Ernest Tubb	1965
James Denny (executive)	1966
Eddy Arnold	1966
George D. Hay (executive)	1966
Uncle Dave Macon	1966
Jim Reeves	1967
J. L. (Joe) Frank (executive)	1967
Red Foley	1967
Steven C. Sholes (executive)	1967
Bob Wills	1968
Gene Autry	1969
Original Carter Family (Maybelle, A.P., and Sara)	1970
Bill Monroe	1970
Art Satherley (executive)	1971
Jimmy Davis	1972
Patsy Cline	1973
Chet Atkins	1973

Williams, Hank
Born: September 15, 1923, Georgiana, Ala.
Died: January 1, 1953, West Virginia
Married: w. Audrey Shepard (divorced) (s. Randall Hank: d. Lycrecia Ann); w. Billie Jean Jones

Hank Williams, an extraordinary artist, died on January 1, 1953, of "too much living, too much sorrow, too much love, too much drink and drugs." He couldn't read or write music, but his 125 compositions include many classics of popular music. He was the 1st country musician and writer whose songs were eagerly grabbed by pop singers. The 20 years since his death haven't diminished his stature. Millions of his albums are still sold, and millions more will be sold.

Hank Williams was born in a 2-room log cabin to the poverty-stricken family of a shell-shocked veteran of W.W. I. When he was 7, his mother gave him a $3.50 guitar. His music lessons came from a black street singer who taught him while Hank shined shoes or sold peanuts on Montgomery street corners. When he was 12, he won a songwriting contest with "WPA Blues." With the $15 prize he decided to form a band, the Drifting Cowboys. (He had always dreamed, he said, of becoming a cowboy.) At 17, he tried rodeoing in Texas and was thrown from a horse, and back trouble plagued him all his life. He joined a medicine show, selling and singing, and met Audrey Shepard. After a stormy courtship, he married "Miss Audrey." Meanwhile, his reputation was growing. Ernest Tubb heard him and tried to get Grand Ole Opry to sign him on, but Williams' reputation as a "womanizing, hard-drinking wild man" preceded him, and Opry officials felt he'd be trouble. *Louisiana Hayride* had no such reservations and Hank joined the show.

INVENTIONS NECESSITY IS NOT THE MOTHER OF. By Stacy V. Jones. New York: Quadrangle, 1973.

About the book: The range of inventions which have been patented in the U.S. since 1790 is truly extraordinary. Stacy Jones, the patent columnist for *The New York Times*, has presented over 300 of the most unusual ones with accompanying illustrations. Here you will learn about a golf ball that sends out a smoke signal when it lands to help its owner locate it, an alarm clock that squirts the sleeper in the face, a parakeet diaper, a cigarette pack that starts coughing loudly when someone picks it up, and many other inventions you never realized that you needed.

From the book: Inventors have produced many aids to feminine beautification. A striking example, patented by Martin Goetze of Berlin, Germany, in 1896 is a device for producing dimples. The instrument looks like a brace and bit. The knob or bit—which is to be made of ivory, marble, celluloid, or India rubber—is pressed on the site selected for the dimple and a massaging cylinder revolves around it as the handle is turned.

Perhaps to avoid complaints from the children, Clair R. Weaver and Mary A. Weaver of Long Beach, Calif., devised a pie cutting guide that assures everybody an equal share. Mom can place over the pie a metal pattern with slots for 4, 5, or 6 equal slices. Then, as shown in the 1963 patent, all she need do is run a knife blade through the channels.

Medical science has surely progressed since 1854, but at least 2 inventions recorded in that year are still of interest. One is the trap for removing tapeworms from the stomach and intestines patented by Alpheus Myers, M.D., who practiced in Logansport, Ind. Dr. Meyers described his invention as a trap that is baited, attached to a string, and swallowed by the patient after a fast of suitable duration to make the worm hungry.

As the patent explains, the worm seizes the bait and its head is caught in the trap, which is then withdrawn from the patient's stomach by the string which has been left hanging from his mouth, dragging after it the whole length of the worm.

The trap consists of a cylinder of gold, platinum, or other metal, about ¾″ long and ¼″ in diameter. The bait may be "any nutritious substance." When the worm sticks its head in through a hole, it releases a spring and is caught behind the head. Dr. Myers cautions that the spring must be only strong enough to hold the worm and not strong enough to cut its head off.

GREG BRIGHT'S MAZE BOOK. By Greg Bright. London: Latimer New Dimensions, Ltd., 1973.

About the book: An excellent collection of 32 unusual mazes with photos of a mile-long maze dug by the author in a field in Pilton, England.

From the book: I suggest that the best way to follow the paths is with the aid of a matchstick. The reader will probably get the most out of a maze by treating his journey as if he were walking it refraining from jumping back to the start and from one point to another, and from trying with his eyes to work the route back from the end.

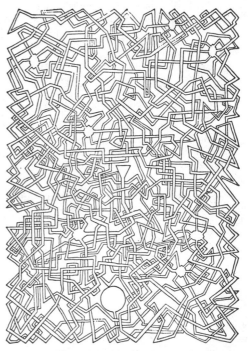

From the triangle in the center, to the large circle below.

THE SCHOOL THAT I'D LIKE. By Edward Blishen, ed. Baltimore, Md.: Penguin Books, 1969.

About the book: With all the controversy about what should and shouldn't be taught in school and all the discussion about education reform, it is easy to forget the opinions and feelings of those who are most affected—the students. In December, 1967, the *London Observer* ran a competition for school children to describe "The School That I'd Like."

From the book: "I don't think I would get on very well in my ideal school because I am too used to being told what to do."—Frances, 15.

"The music department would be in the shape of a violincello, the music books kept in the thinner part of the building, and the remainder of the rooms having instruments which people could learn."—Sally, 14.

"Youths from 12 to 18 years of age are the most rawly aware, most dissatisfied and most rebellious age group in society. As soon as such and such an activity is compulsory, it becomes an unattractive thing to do. If every school activity is optional, even the boy who always 'hated' sport will go to a games lesson 'just to see what it's like,' and probably attend again when he finds that it's fun even when one does badly, as long as one takes everything in good heart.

"The staff would have to be ready to accept almost anything, from watching a boy read a German novel throughout French lessons for a week, to giving incessant homework to a girl who has nothing to do at home. Even the most rebellious pupils would be found to be quite quiet and well-behaved, simply because they feel that they could escape at any moment should they wish it. There is no feeling of being fenced in, which can send the delicate and developing emotions of a teenager into frantic tempers and tension."—Vanessa, 17

PHOTOANALYSIS: HOW TO INTERPRET THE HIDDEN PSYCHOLOGICAL MEANING OF PERSONAL AND PUBLIC PHOTOS. By Dr. Robert U. Akeret, edited by Thomas Humber. New York: Peter H. Wyden, 1973.

About the book: A fascinating manual on how to analyze photographs from the family album or newspaper to discover the relationships between the people that may not have been obvious. Included are many photographs with analyses made on poses, smiles, hand gestures, groupings, distances between people, and how they relate to the camera. Snapshots will never be the same after reading this.

From the book: Here is an analysis made on a photograph: Like most people, you probably see a father, his son, and his daughter. Given the background and their informal dress, you guess they are on a vacation in the country. They seem cozy, affectionate. They stand close together, and the father warmly and protectively has his arms around the children. They are all relaxed, casual. . . . This seemingly innocent, everyday photograph—certainly it was casually taken—is packed with meaning, some of it disturbing and mystifying. There is an element here that shouldn't be, something unusual and out of character with the other elements. . . . The daughter is tilting her head slightly toward her father, indicating a closeness with and an affection for him. But she is having trouble making the contact. There is an obstruction, something preventing her from getting closer. If you look closely you will see it is her brother's fist. His arm is extended straight and stiff behind his father's back, and his fist pushes against his sister's neck.

When I 1st saw this photo, I asked the daughter, now in her 30s, if she and her brother had fought. They had, constantly, for many years, but she could not understand how I knew, since she had never mentioned it.

"It's all there in the photo," I said. As we talked further about her relationship with her brother, she realized that the fist in the photo was symbolic of their battles, and of the anger and resentment her brother had expressed toward her since her birth, when she displaced him as the only child. As he used the straight arm and fist in the photo to keep her away from her father, the brother often used the same technique to keep her away from him. He would infuriate her by teasing, and then hold her off so she couldn't move in close to retaliate.

MAKE YOUR OWN MUSICAL INSTRUMENTS. By Muriel Mandell and Robert E. Wood. New York: Sterling Publishing Co., 1972.

About the book: For children, this book provides simple-to-follow directions for making musical instruments out of materials you can find around the house. Included are flower-pot bells, lamb-chop-bone rattles, wire-hanger harps and 100 other ingenious instruments.

From the book: Here are directions for making a bone rattle: The Indians made dance rattles from buffalo and deer claws and hoofs. But the round bones of lamb chops make an effective bone rattle and can be put together with few tools.

You'll need from 4 to 6 of these little bones; each shoulder chop has only one. Clean off the meat thoroughly and dig out the marrow from the center. Soak the bones in hot water and detergent to get rid of all the grease. Then dry them out in the sun. Usually the bones have a handsome ivory look and need no further decoration. If they are discolored or if you prefer a highly colored rattle, you can paint each bone a different bright color.

With their ready-made center holes, the bones are easy to attach to a ring made from a wire hanger. Unwind the ends of the hanger so that you have a long length of wire. Break off a 10″ or 12″ piece by bending the wire back and forth at the same spot until it snaps. Don't touch the broken ends for a few seconds —they will be hot from the friction. Then thread the bones on. Wind the ends of the wire around each other, with the help of pliers if necessary, and make a short handle. Wrap any sharp points with colorful tape.

Hold the rattle by its taped ends and shake away. Try shaking it slowly side to side for a "change of pace." You can make the rattle louder by mounting it on a wooden base. Sand down and shellac a slab of scrap wood. Wedge a nail through the 2 wire-bound ends and hammer it to the wood.

Pop top castanets: For dancing fun, soda pop bottle tops make fine castanets. Each castanet requires a narrow strip of heavy cardboard about 6″ long, some thin string or yarn and 2 bottle tops. Plan to make 2 castanets at a time.

Drill or punch a tiny hole through the center of each of the bottle tops. Then make similar holes 1″ from each end of the cardboard.

Place each bottle top, face down, over a cardboard hole. Push string through the holes, with the help of a needle if necessary. Draw the ends of each string together and knot them so that the bottle top is attached tightly.

Center the cardboard in your palm with your thumb and one finger on the bottle caps. When you bring your fingers together the 2 caps strike one another and you are ready to tap out a Spanish dance. To make the castanets more colorful, crayon both sides or paste bits of foil or construction paper on the cardboard.

THE SCIENCE AND PRACTICE OF IRIDOLOGY. By Bernard Jensen, D.C., N.D. Escondido, Calif.: Bernard Jensen Products, Publishing Div., 1952.

About the book: "Iridology" is the science of diagnosing illness within an organism through markings and signs (color, density, etc.) in the iris of the eye. It is not a widely accepted science, nor do its adherents declare it to be the last word in medical diagnosis. However, many claims are made in this book—including many case histories, wherein Dr. Jensen claims to have successfully diagnosed and cured patients for whom more traditional medical practitioners had given up hope.

From the book: As you look at the different lesions or markings, bear in mind that each of them has its own story. The amount of pathology in the organ can be determined by the degree of discoloration and the size of the lesion in the particular area with which you are dealing. The amount of repair work to be done can be judged by the stage of inflammation and how the rest of the body will respond to help that particular organ get well. . . . If we find that the organ we are working on has poor density and is in a very heavy toxic condition, and that the intestinal tract is quite toxic, you can readily see the many complications preventing the body from becoming well. Like the chain and its weakest link, it can be no stronger than its weakest organ. From the iris analysis standpoint we are most interested in discovering which are the weak organs we have to take care of and which are those that have the greatest amount of encumbrance to overcome. The strong organs can take care of themselves.

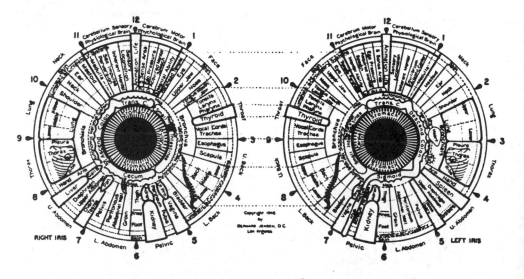

Iridology Chart developed by Dr. Bernard Jensen

TIRED DRAGONS: ADAPTING CHURCH ARCHI-
TECTURE TO CHANGING NEEDS. By Edwin C.
Lynn. Boston: Beacon Press, 1972.

About the book: An architect and minister
considers how church buildings, many originally
constructed as static monuments, can be transformed into living environments to serve community needs for space where people can gather
for entertainment, lectures, and educational
classes, as well as for worship.

From the book: The railroads are an example
of a large national institution that did not alter
its patterns and cooperate within itself or with
others and was almost forced to extinction.
Many churches operate much like the railroads.
Other churches are seen as insidious rivals;
pennies are looked upon as dollars; minor expenses are regarded as major catastrophes; buildings are seen as valuable baggage that must be
protected with every possible safeguard. The
churches should consider that all these security
methods have not protected the railroads
from continued decline.

In the context of order, pews have taken on a
theological importance. Their symmetry symbolizes the desired order—not the extreme
social order of the pew renters and purchasers of
colonial times but the order of religious tradition. However, to sit securely in the pews,
smugly oblivious with present changes is inconsistent with a revitalized, meaningful religious
belief. Architects have created fancy building
shapes and spectacular roof structures, clergymen have inspired changing worship forms.
Nevertheless, congregations have refused to
change their attitudes, and their immobile seats
confirm their rigidity. The obstacles are difficult to overcome. Until the rigid pew structure
is changed, the church will not substantially
alter its present course. The pews are where the
people are, and unless they are willing to alter
their patterns, there is little hope for the tired
dragons. This does not mean that by destroying
all pews we would have a revitalized church; it
only means as long as pews are worshiped, there
is little hope for a relevant church.

HISTORY WAS BURIED: GREAT DISCOVERIES IN
ARCHAEOLOGY. By Margaret Wheeler, ed.
New York: Hart, 1967.

About the book: This fascinating and very
readable book assembles the writings of some of
the foremost archaeologists of all times on their
most famous discoveries. Included is the un-
covering of treasure ships, royal tombs, the
Dead Sea Scrolls, prehistoric caves with ancient drawings on the walls, and many more.
The author precedes each story with a synopsis
of the events that led up to the discovery, the
conditions under which the dig was organized,
and a statement as to why the find is important.

From the book: [The British Egyptologist
Howard Carter tells of one of the most spectacular archaeological discoveries of modern times
—the discovery of the tomb of a young Egyptian Pharaoh, Tutankhamen, who ruled Egypt
for a few years beginning in 1357 B.C.:]
Slowly, desperately slowly it seemed to us as
we watched, the remains of passage debris that
encumbered the lower part of the doorway
were removed, until at last we had the whole
door clear before us. The decisive moment had
arrived. With trembling hands I made a tiny
breach in the upper left-hand corner. Darkness
and blank space, as far as an iron testing-rod
could reach, showed that whatever lay beyond
was empty and not filled like the passage we
had just cleared. Candle tests were applied as
a precaution against possible foul gases, and
then, widening the hole a little, I inserted the
candle and peered in. . . . At 1st I could see
nothing, the hot air escaping from the chamber causing the candle flame to flicker, but
presently, as my eyes grew accustomed to the
light, details of the room within emerged slowly
from the mist, strange animals, statues, and
gold—everywhere the glint of gold. . . . I suppose most excavators would confess to a feeling
of awe—embarrassment almost—when they
break into a chamber closed and sealed by pious hands so many centuries ago. For the moment, time as a factor in human life has lost
its meaning. Three thousand, 4 thousand years
maybe, have passed and gone since human feet
last trod the floor on which you stand, and yet,
as you note the signs of recent life around you
—the half-filled bowl of mortar for the door,
the blackened lamp, the fingermark upon the
freshly painted surface, the farewell garland
dropped upon the threshold—you feel it might
have been but yesterday. The very air you
breathe, unchanged throughout the centuries,
you share with those who laid the mummy to
its rest. Time is annihilated by little intimate
details such as these, and you feel an intruder.
That is perhaps the 1st and dominant sensation,
but others follow thick and fast—the exhilaration of discovery, the fever of suspense, the almost overmastering impulse, born of curiosity,
to break down seals and lift the lids of boxes,
the thought—pure joy to the investigator—
that you are about to add a page to history, or
solve some problem of research, the strained
expectancy—why not confess it?—of the treas-
ure-seeker.

"WHERE DID I COME FROM?": THE FACTS OF
LIFE WITHOUT ANY NONSENSE AND WITH
ILLUSTRATIONS. By Peter Mayle, illustrated
by Arthur Robins. Secaucus, N.J.: Paul Walter Lyle Stuart Inc., 1973.

About the book: A uniquely funny and
straightforward "facts of life" book, featuring

the differences between men and women, orgasm, conception, and birth. As much fun for parents as for kids. The illustrations are great.

From the book: MAKING LOVE—This is a very nice feeling for both the man and the woman. He likes being inside her, and she likes him being inside her. It's called making love, because it all starts with the man and the woman loving each other. It's a difficult feeling to describe, but if you can imagine a gentle tingly sort of tickle that starts in your stomach and spreads all over, that will give you some idea of what it's like. And as you know, when you're feeling tickly you wriggle about a bit. It's just the same here, except it's a special kind of wriggling. It's easier to understand when you realize that the parts that tickle most are the man's penis and the woman's vagina. So most of the wriggling happens down there. The man pushes his penis up and down inside the woman's vagina, so that both the tickly parts are being rubbed against each other. It's like scratching an itch, but a lot nicer. This usually starts slowly, and gets quicker and quicker as the tickly feeling gets stronger and stronger.

Why does the tickling stop? Now you may be thinking: If it's so nice, why don't people do it all the time? There are 2 reasons. First, it's very tiring. More than playing football, or running, or skipping, or climbing trees or almost anything. Good as it is, you just can't do it all day long. And the 2nd reason is that something really wonderful happens which puts an end to the tickly feeling, and at the same time starts the making of the baby. When the man and the woman have been wriggling so hard you think they're both going to pop, they nearly do just that. All the rubbing up and down that's been going on ends in a tremendous big lovely shiver for both of them. (Again, it's not easy to tell you what this feels like. But you know how it is when you have a tickle in your nose for a long time, and then you have a really big sneeze? It's a little like that.) At the same time, a spurt of quite thick, sticky stuff comes from the end of the man's penis, and this goes into the woman's vagina.

FORT DIX STOCKADE: OUR PRISON CAMP NEXT DOOR. By Joan Crowell. New York: Links Books, 1974.

About the book: On June 5, 1969, 250 men imprisoned in the military stockade at Fort Dix, most of them for being Absent Without Leave, rioted to let the public know about the tortures, brutality, and barbarous conditions under which they were condemned to live. When the author, a writer and a mother of 5, investigated and reported the atrocities she discovered, she was ignored by the media which, to this day, have failed to give attention to the circum-

stances of the riot. The book is a chilling investigation of the conditions that caused the riot, the details of the riot itself, and the stories of the young men each of whom faced court-martial sentences of up to 50 years.

From the book: Neither the conditions at Fort Dix nor at the Presidio are rare instances of psychopathology in the military penal system. In this country and overseas the Pentagon supervises 138 Army, Air Force, Navy, and Marine brigs and stockades with an overflow population of 15,000 prisoners. Most prisoners it must be remembered, are only guilty of the heinous crime of being AWOL; half of these prisoners are simply awaiting trial.

From these establishments comes an endless stream of grotesque reports: of the homosexual at the brig on Treasure Island, San Francisco, who was forced to suck on a flashlight for the amusement of the Marine Guards; of the Army officers at Fort Riley, Kans., who panicked when they discovered one of their soldiers was only 12 years old and "hid" him for 3 months in solitary confinement; of the Marines forced to strip to the waist and roll in fresh feces; of the inmate in the Great Lakes Naval Training Center brig who was punished by wrapping his throat in a wet towel, clamping a bucket over his head and making him smoke cigarettes under it until he passed out; of the 300 suicide "gestures" at Fort Dix in one year, and of the soldiers at Fort Dix who were sprayed with water and then pushed into wintry weather, naked, for varying lengths of time (one of them for 3 hours); of Fort Dix soldiers seeking conscientious-objector status discharges who were imprisoned "for their own protection" in a special cell with known homosexuals; of the Fort Leonard Wood inmate whose body was covered with gray paint and who was made to stand at attention until the paint was dry; of the Marines at Treasure Island who, according to reports from different bases, were made to do such strenuous exercises right after eating that they threw up, after which the guards pushed their faces in the vomit and made them roll in it or (in 2 instances reported) made them eat it.

ADVENTURES IN LIVING PLANTS. By Edwin B. Kurtz, Jr., and Chris Allen. Tucson, Ariz.: Univ. of Ariz. Press, 1965.

About the book: A grammar school biology textbook, this book takes an unusual approach to its subject. The format is a trip through plant cells, fibers, roots, etc. It has delightful illustrations, and includes the usual experiments for children to do.

From the book: Are you ready? Let's visit the green cells in the leaves of grass in your front yard. Take my hand! Now, swallow the pill. There goes mine. And now yours. Don't be frightened. I've made this trip many times. Just hold on to my hand so we won't get lost! Since we were standing on your front yard on some grass, we won't have any trouble finding some grass cells to ... go ... in ... too ... oo ...o...

Ah, here we are now. You are now one millionth as tall as you were a few seconds ago! Didn't hurt a bit, did it? This wide flat thing we are standing on is a grass leaf. Watch out! You almost fell in one of those big holes in the leaf surface! Molecules of gases go in and out of the leaf through those holes. The holes are called stomates. See that swarm of small flealike bodies coming out of that stomate? They are molecules of oxygen and water coming out of the leaf. But let's not bother with them. We came here to see some cells! Be careful now, and hold my hand. We are going to slide down the side of one of these large holes. Then we will be inside the leaf where the cells are. Hold on. Here we go!

I forgot to ask you if you can swim. Glad to see that you can, because the water gets rather deep at times inside the leaf. Each cell has a coating of water over it, and it may get over our heads as we walk along the surface of the cells. See how bright it is inside the leaf? We can see our way easily because sunlight shines through the leaf. But be careful where you walk! You may slide over the edge of the cell we're standing on and get hurt from the fall! Because you are reduced in size, a fall off this cell would be like falling off a tall building!

NATURAL HAIR CARE COMIX & STORIES. By Mary Lee and Suzanne Perelman, illustrated by W. M. Johnson. San Francisco: Straight Arrow Books, 1973.

About the book: How to care for your hair without harming it, told in cartoon form. Discusses hair brushing, shampooing, nutrition, cutting, baldness, hair treatments, and how hair grows. Appealing illustrations, easy to read.
From the book: Natural hair care is neither mysterious nor complex, and relates to everyone ... all the little hairs in the world. We want you to be aware of the ways you can restore the damage already done to your hair, naturally, as well as to stimulate its growth and keep it in its natural condition.

Don't lend your brush. Not even to your best friend, not even to your mother. Dandruff, ringworm, and your own personal bacteria are easily passed along on your brush. And for heaven's and your own sake, don't lend it to your cat or dog. Enuf said.

Beware, "organic," "natural," and/or "herbal" products have become subject to Mad. Avenue style big business. Don't insult your hair with a so-called "sham" poo, obviously labeled and marketed for the advertiser's

conception of what "young moderns want to buy."

Take home message: your hair is unlike any other; let it be. There is a tribe of people out there, voicing the complaint that, geez, if I let my hair dry naturally, it will turn all weird or frizzy or something. BAH, HUMBUG! Your hair may look more appealing if it is dried in the following manner: When it is still wet, use a towel to dry it to remove excess water. This by no means implies that you should furiously rub a towel all over the rest of your head as well. If your hair is long, bend forward from the waist, then stand up quickly. Repeat this until your hair is full of air . . . when it dries, thorough brushing with our old friend rosemary oil will help eliminate your particular hair problem, e.g., frizziness or static.

THE CURVE OF BINDING ENERGY. By John McPhee. New York: Farrar, Straus and Giroux, 1974.

About the book: McPhee, a *New Yorker* author, has written an enthralling biography of Theodore B. Taylor, the incredibly inventive nuclear physicist. Taylor designed the smallest and lightest nuclear bomb ever made, as well as the largest-yield fission bomb ever exploded. Working in secrecy, backed by the U.S. Government, he made the spaceship *Orion*, the size of a 16-story building. Powered by 2,000 atomic bombs, exploding one at a time, *Orion* was intended to move very rapidly to Mars, Jupiter, Saturn, Pluto, but the Limited Nuclear Test Ban Treaty of 1963 shelved the project. As to any individual, anywhere, having the capability to make a private atomic bomb, both McPhee and Taylor seem convinced it is possible.

From the book: Just how few people could achieve the fabrication of an atomic bomb on their own is a question on which opinion divides, but there are physicists with experience in the weapons field who believe that the job could be done by one person, working alone, with nuclear material stolen from private industry.

The Los Alamos Primer, which contains the mathematical fundamentals of fission bombs, was declassified in 1964 and is now available from the Atomic Energy Commission for $2.06 a copy. For $4, a book titled *Manhattan District History, Project Y, the Los Alamos Project* can be bought from the Office of Technical Services of the U.S. Dept. of Commerce. Written in 1946 and 1947, this was the supersecret technical description of the problems that came up during the building of the 1st atomic bombs. The book was declassified in 1961. On its inside front cover is a legal notice that says, in part, "Neither the U.S., nor the Commission, nor any person acting on behalf of the

Commission . . . assumes any liabilities with respect to use of, or from damages resulting from the use of, any information, apparatus, method, or process disclosed in this report."

Taylor to McPhee: In England, about 5 years ago, somebody—it was a hoax—*advertised* U-235 for sale. He got plenty of takers. For the making of a bomb, more than enough information is in the public domain already.

SUPERPOWER. By Robert Hargreaves. New York: St. Martin's Press, 1973.

About the book: British journalist Robert Hargreaves traveled over 150,000 mi. in the U.S. in 4 years while working as a correspondent for the British television network ITN. In 600 pages he presents the diversity of life in the U.S.: the rich, the poor, the cities, the farms, religions, advertising, Henry Kissinger, organized crime, and much more. It is fascinating and illuminating to see a visitor's view of what we Americans take for granted.

From the book: Nearly 90 years ago, Lord Bryce said of New York that it is "a European city, but of no particular country," and ever since New York has been the most racially mixed of any city in the world, a modern Babel that has more German-speakers than Cologne, more Jews than Jerusalem, more Irish than Cork, more Italians than Venice—and now, more Puerto Ricans than San Juan. Even today, over 3 million of the city's present population of 7.8 million were either themselves foreign-born or had at least one foreign-born parent.

What has gone wrong with New York? Why do more and more of its people speak as though their city is doomed and on its way to becoming ungovernable? A modern Voltaire could continue almost endlessly about the miseries of life in New York today. More murders take place there now than ever before, well over 30 a week; in fact, New York has as many murders every 10 days as all England suffers in a year, and mugging has become an ever-present problem—over 78,000 such crimes in 1972, which actually represents an *improvement* over previous years. That year, in a case chillingly reminiscent of the murder of Kitty Genovese 8 years earlier, Dr. Wolfgang Friedmann, a distinguished professor of international law, was murdered in broad daylight, 3 blocks away from Columbia University, where he had just finished a day's teaching. As he lay bleeding to death on the sidewalk, passers-by ignored his cries for help, and for some time no one even thought of calling the police. "The jungle could not be more unfeeling towards its creatures," said *The New York Times* in a bitter editorial on the killing—a comment which led to a vehement reply from a local resident, who pointed out that the area was so noisy no one farther than 10' away could possibly have heard a strangled cry for help. Later that same year there was a spate of armed holdups of teachers in their classrooms before the very eyes of their pupils. "Walk behind your desk and sit down," one holdup man had said. "There are a lot of children in your class. If you move, I'll blow your brains out."

Every week the city tows away 2,000 illegally parked cars from Manhattan alone, and its traffic jams can be so bad its traffic commissioner once remarked, "to get to the West Side, you have to be born there."

LIVE LONGER NOW. By Jon N. Leonard, J. L. Hofer, and N. Pritikin. New York: Grosset and Dunlap, 1974.

About the book: After 3 years of intensive research by 15 members of the Longevity Foundation, a new 2100 *Program* of diet and exercise was developed. Three members of the foundation—representing biology, psychology, business—have outlined it all in this simple and useful book. To add years to the human lifespan, the researchers concluded that with a proper diet and exercise program, human beings could add many healthy years to their lives and avoid the destructiveness of heart attacks, liver ailments, and other diseases. They've advocated only one exercise in their entire program, and that exercise is based on a concept called "roving."

From the book: Roving is a combination of walking and running with you in the pilot's seat. You decide if and when to run or whether merely to walk. Roving is the most natural of all exercises and has an extremely high-conditioning potential.

The key idea in roving is to set yourself a distance goal of so many miles. Then 4 or 5 times each week you set out to walk (or run if you prefer) that distance. Enjoy yourself as you go. Go different places on different days if you like. Change the scenery whenever you want to.

The central principle in roving is to cover a lot of ground, but to do it in your own good time. Roving can fit easily into the life of the average man or woman because it is so flexible. The working person can arrange to walk all or a part of the way to work each day. . . .

Roving can start off as walking by itself, with no running at all. It may remain that way indefinitely. If it is at all possible, you should arrange your roving so that you can run during a rove whenever you feel like it. Physically it is beneficial, and it is very good emotionally to let a walking rove turn into a run then back into a walk, whenever you feel the urge. And you will feel the urge, once you have done it a few times. It is your million years of heredity coming into play that brings upon you a strong urge to lean forward and jog or run in the middle of a rove. If you have arranged things so that you can satisfy this urge without feeling foolish, it will be of great benefit to you. . . .

That is all there is to roving. Set your distance. Travel that distance on foot 4 or 5 times each week. Go for distance, not time. Allow yourself to satisfy the urge to run.

ENCYCLOPEDIA OF THE UNEXPLAINED: MAGIC, OCCULTISM AND PARAPSYCHOLOGY. By Richard Cavendish, ed. New York: McGraw-Hill, 1974.

About the book: Concise, interesting, and well-illustrated articles on a wide range of subjects, including ESP, witchcraft, alchemy, drugs, dreams, the Loch Ness Monster and the Abominable Snowman, numerology, the I Ching, UFOs, Flat Earthers and Hollow Earthers, astrology and Yoga.

From the book: [On PHYSICAL POWERS:] It would appear that it is possible for the law of gravitation to be suspended, as in the case of levitation, where a person is seen to rise in the air and float above the level of the ground. . . . The case of St. Joseph of Copertino (d. 1663) is the best authenticated in Christian literature. Like many others to whom extraordinary powers suddenly descended, he lived a life of rigid austerity, eating food which he 1st used to sprinkle with a bitter powder in order to render it unpalatable, so much so that when a brother monk once tasted it he was ill for 3 days. He scourged himself with a barbed whip till the blood flowed down his back. One day while he was praying, his body left the ground and remained floating in the air. From then on his levitations increased. Once, when moved to ecstasy, he rose to the high altar and then to the pulpit ledge 15' above the ground. If restrained, he would bear the others up with him. In the open air he would float to the level of the treetops, and if he alighted on one of the thinner branches at the top, it did not even bend under his weight. His levitations were witnessed by a host of eminent persons, kings, prelates, and professors, including the philosopher Leibniz. The Protestant Duke of Brunswick was so overwhelmed by the miracle he witnessed that he became a convert to Roman Catholicism.

[Here is a sample biography:] Joseph-Antoine Boullan (1824–1893). A French magician and defrocked Roman Catholic priest who in 1875 announced that he was a reincarnation of John the Baptist and appointed himself head of the Work of Mercy, which had been founded by the Norman wonder-worker Pierre Vintras. Boullan believed that the path to salvation lay through sexual intercourse with archangels and other celestial beings. He was attacked by a group of rival magicians who, it was claimed, eventually murdered him by magic.

THE NEW AGE BABY NAME BOOK. By Sue Browder. New York: Warner Paperback Library, 1974.

About the book: If you are trying to decide what to name your new baby and you are tired of common names like John, Mary, Susan, and Bill, this is the book for you. Included are over 3,000 unusual names from all over the world as well as astrological names, flower names, and ethnic versions of English names, such as the Polish name Melcia instead of Amelia. There is also a chapter on how to create a name.

From the book:

GIRLS

Ajuji (ah-JOO-jee) The Hausa of Africa always give this name to the surviving child of a woman whose children have always died. According to the tradition, when the baby is born, the grandparents take the child out to the refuse heap or the juji, and pretend to throw it away. After this gesture to the demons, the mother rushes out and reclaims the child.

Melantha "Black Flower." The name probably comes from the deep purple lily which once grew along Mediterranean shores.

Yonina (yoh-NEE-nuh) Hebrew for "dove." Variants include Yona, Yonit, Yonita, Jona, Jonina, and Jonati. Yona is often used as a boy's name.

BOYS

Blair "Child of the fields." Earth name for boys born under the earth signs of the zodiac: Capricorn, the Goat, Taurus, the Bull, and Virgo, the Virgin. An astrologer may advise such an earth name if a child's horoscope contains too many metal or water influences, since earth controls metal and destroys water. The name, then, is thought to restore the balance of the basic elements in the child's horoscope so the universal order will work smoothly throughout his life.

Radomil (RAH-doh-mil) "Love of peace." Popular in Czechoslovakia.

Tunu (TOO-noo) Miwok Indian name which means "deer thinking about going to eat wild onions."

THE AMERICAN CONNECTION: PROFITEERING AND POLITICKING IN THE "ETHICAL" DRUG INDUSTRY. By John Pekkanen. Chicago: Follet, 1973.

About the book: There is in this country a vast "gray market" of drug abuse made up of average people addicted to prescription drugs. Pekkanen's book details how the big drug companies, with their enormous advertising budgets and a core of Washington lobbyists, join forces with druggist and doctor to keep the American public well supplied with amphetamines, barbiturates, and tranquilizers.

From the book: Contrary to their accepted image and contrary to what the public rightfully expects, doctors often know very little about the drugs they are prescribing. . . . So who does the doctor rely on? He relies to some extent on what his colleagues tell him, on articles in medical journals when he gets time to read them, on the Physician's Desk Reference, which lists current drugs and their indications, but in which the information is written by the drug companies. But most of all, if we are to believe the doctors themselves, he relies on the detail men, those ambassadors of good will from the drug industry who sell their drugs to doctors door-to-door like Fuller sells brushes. In an AMA-sponsored study in the 1950s taken in Fond du Lac, Wis., it was disclosed that 68% of the doctors there were dependent on detail men for their drug information. Here is how one detail man describes his job. . . . He complains that his fellow detail men have little if any background in the field; "English and education majors most of them," he says. He points to some of the sale projections on the computer readout. "Look at those numbers go up. It's selling, just selling," he says. . . .

"I'd say," he continues, "the average salary for a detail man where I work is about $15,000 and if you've been there a while about $20,000. But you've also got a company car and a great medical plan. But of course this doesn't include the deals you can make." The deals? "A lot of us started out in this business as idealists. I thought I was going to serve humanity by learning about medicine and getting it to people. Well, that doesn't last long. You're corrupted by the system very quickly, by the drugstores and by the doctors. The druggists are after you all the time to see what you can give them. They want your samples so they can sell them at retail and it's all profit for them. I've given a druggist a big supply of free samples and then made a $10,000 sale to him. We both come out ahead."

THE HERO IN AMERICA: A CHRONICLE OF HERO-WORSHIP. By Dixon Wecter. New York: Charles Scribner's Sons, 1972.

About the book: What made Daniel Boone, Davy Crockett, Abe Lincoln, Buffalo Bill, and General Grant household words? Dixon Wecter tells all about the lives (and, moreover, the myths surrounding those lives) of America's "great men." The style of this thick volume is at the same time one of warmth and irony.

From the book: The ageing Boone—so crippled by rheumatism that his wife had to go hunting with him to hold his gun—fared less well at home. Bankrupt in Kentucky, he moved on to Missouri, impelled by hope and restlessness, rather than by the legendary sense of claustrophobia. To the last, he protested that he loved friends and neighbors. Congress was slow in confirming his title to a Spanish land grant, and even his countrymen began to forget the man whose fame overseas grew mightily. Chester Harding, who traveled 100 mi. to paint the old man shortly before Boone's death in 1820, reported: "I found that the nearer I got to his dwelling, the less was known of him. When within 2 mi. of his house, I asked a man to tell me where Colonel Boone lived. He said he did not know any such man. 'Why, yes, you do,' said his wife. 'It is that white-headed old man who lives on the bottom, near the river. . . .' I found the object of my search engaged in cooking his dinner. He was laying in his bunk near the fire, and had a long strip of venison wound around his ramrod, and was busy turning it before a brisk blaze, and using salt and pepper to season his meat. I at once told him the object of my visit. I found that he hardly knew what I meant. I explained the matter to him, and he agreed to sit. He was 90 years old, and rather infirm."

When it was broadcast that Daniel Boone had died, the world remembered. In his honor the legislature of Missouri adjourned, and his funeral was the largest the West had ever known. Boone was buried in the cherrywood coffin which he had kept under his bed for many years, in the manner of John Donne.

Meanwhile the lore of Boone was built by the passing years. Stories were told of how he nearly shot his future wife, by mistake, on a panther hunt at night; how he owned a cow, Old Spot, who learned to give Indian alarms, and was wounded in the siege of Boonesborough, where the good Lord had miraculously sent a heavy rain to put out the burning stockade; how Boone ran backwards in his tracks and swung on grapevines for intervals of many yards, to baffle the redskins; how he led a party to rescue young Jemima Boone and her playmates from Indian kidnappers. In 1818 Boone was amused by the story, published in the East and abroad, that he had been found dead, kneeling by a stump, rifle in hand, and a deer dead some hundred yards away.

LIVING MY LIFE. By Emma Goldman. New York: Dover, 1970.

About the book: An eloquent and moving autobiography by Emma Goldman, the famed anarchist and feminist of the late 1800s and early 1900s. Her fiery rendering of her personal and political life and the flavor of the times makes this an irresistible memoir. As relevant today as she ever was, Emma speaks from her heart about the struggle of a vibrant individual to be free in society, and to create a free society.

From the book: The applause had barely died away when an elderly woman rose belligerently. "Mr. Chairman," she demanded, "does Miss Goldman believe in God or does she not?" She was followed by another. "Does the speaker favor killing off all rulers?" Then a small, emaciated man jumped to his feet and in a thin voice cried: "Miss Goldman! You're a believer in free love, aren't you? Now, wouldn't your system result in houses of prostitution at every lamppost?"

"I shall have to answer these people straight from the shoulder," I remarked to the minister. "So be it," he replied.

"Ladies and gentlemen," I began, "I came here to avoid as much as possible treading on your corns. I had intended to deal only with the basic issue of economics that dictates our lives from the cradle to the grave, regardless of our religion or moral beliefs. I see now that it was a mistake. If one enters a battle, he cannot be squeamish about a few corns. Here, then, are my answers: I do not believe in God, because I believe in man. Whatever his mistakes, man has for thousands of years past been working to undo the botched job your God has made." The house went frantic. "Blasphemy! Heretic! Sinner!" the women screamed. "Stop her! Throw her out!"

When order was restored, I continued: "As to killing rulers, it depends entirely on the position of the ruler. If it is the Russian Czar, I most certainly believe in dispatching him to where he belongs. If the ruler is as ineffectual as an American President, it is hardly worth the effort. There are, however, some potentates I would kill by any and all means at my disposal. They are Ignorance, Superstition, and Bigotry—the most sinister and tyrannical rulers on earth. As for the gentleman who asked if free love would not build more houses of prostitution, my answer is: They will all be empty if the men of the future look like him."

There was instant pandemonium. In vain the chairman pounded for order. People jumped up on benches, waved their hats, shouted, and would not leave the church until the lights were turned out.

OVER THE COUNTER AND ON THE SHELF: COUNTRY STOREKEEPING IN AMERICA. 1620–1920. By Laurence A. Johnson, edited by Marcia Ray. Rutland, Vt.: Charles E. Tuttle Co., 1970.

About the book: The American country store was a hodgepodge of merchandise, from groceries, drugs, and hardware to the whiskey sold in the back room. Merchandising has changed since the days of the open cracker barrel, but the general store is remembered as a pleasant and important part of America's past.

From the book: The storekeeper himself was a man of consequence, his opinions respected, if not always agreed with. Though he often lacked formal education, he was almost always exceptionally well informed. As postmaster he kept up with the times through the periodicals and newspapers that passed through the office. Yearly buying trips to Philadelphia, New York, Boston, or New Orleans introduced him to a wider world. Slack time in winter could be improved by reading and meditating on the books he carried in stock. Not at all unusual was the book selection of a merchant in a small Missouri town in 1829, who advertised volumes by Josephus, Byron, Shakespeare, Cervantes, Scott, Fielding, Herodotus, Hume, Smollett, Milton, Defoe, Homer, and Bunyan. No wonder, in an age of flowery harangue, the storekeeper was capable of Fourth of July speeches full of classical reference, and holiday toasts 2nd to none. In his political beliefs, he seldom hesitated to stand up and be counted.

With the years, the general health of the public became even more precarious if one can judge from the amount of patent medicines sold by peddlers and through general stores. In June, 1841, *The New York Tribune* printed a testimonial from Jane Bemee of Utica, N.Y., a young woman of 32, who, in the 2 years she had been bedridden with a disease that was "eating away her face," had consumed: 14 bottles of Phoenix Bitters, 20 Boxes of Life Pills, 100 boxes of Brandreth's Life Pills, 3 bottles of Phelps Arcanum, 4 Bottles of Smith's Anti-Mercurial Syrup, 5 Bottles of Swaims's Panacea, 3 Bottles of Indian Panacea, $6 worth of Conway's Boston Medicine, a large quantity of Fowler's Solution of Arsenic, and different preparations of mercury prepared by doctors. Blissfully, she concluded her testimonial, which was witnessed and corroborated by a justice of the peace at Utica—"I am satisfied that my life has been preserved and my health entirely restored by the blessing of God and the use of Bristol's Fluid Extract of Sarsaparilla."

Benjamin T. Babbitt was the 1st of the soap manufacturers to put soap in a wrapper and sell it as a "bar." Up to that time, in 1851, soap had been made in loaves for the grocer to slice off and weigh, much as he did cheese. Babbitt was also the 1st to give his wrappers a trade-in value and put a premium offer on the wrappers. This innovation grew out of necessity, for people did not take readily to packaged soap. It seemed to lose its identity in its new wrapping, even though the name and trademark appeared on it. The premium offer changed all this, and as his sales spurted, other soap merchants quickly followed suit.

THE LIFE CYCLE BOOK OF CATS. By Ronald Ridout and Michael Holt, illustrated by Tony Payne. New York: Grosset & Dunlap, 1974.

About the book: This beautifully illustrated book for 8- to 12-year-olds describes the evolution and history of the cat family, mating, reproduction, and kitten care. A wonderful way for youngsters to learn about the "facts of life" in relation to their pets.

From the book: THE GROWING FETUS—It is an average of 63 days from the time the eggs are fertilized to the time the kittens are born. By comparison, some butterfly eggs in hot countries turn into caterpillars in 5 or 6 days. A hen's eggs take about 21 days to turn into chicks. The human egg will take about 280 days to turn into a baby. But though length of time varies from creature to creature, all embryos look somewhat alike after about a quarter of the time has passed. Scientists believe that this is evidence of evolution—an indication that higher animals have developed from lower ones. In the end, of course, embryos grow into completely different creatures.

THE BIRTH—As the 63 days near an end, the mother cat becomes interested in snug corners. She is looking for a quiet place to have her kittens. It is usually well away from activity in a dark place, and here she makes her nest. She also becomes restless, meows a great deal, and demands a lot of attention. Then she will disappear altogether into her nest for a long spell.

When a kitten is ready to be born, the mother cat contracts her stomach muscles and squeezes. She does this several times, pushing the unborn baby down the uterus toward the enlarged vagina. Presently the head of the kitten appears through the vagina and a moment later the whole kitten appears. Each kitten is born one at a time in this way. The average number of kittens in a litter is 4, and there may be 20 minutes to an hour between each birth.

AFTER THE BIRTH—Usually the kitten is born in a sac of tissue, called the placenta, in which it "floated" inside its mother. The mother cat cuts this with her teeth and then licks the kittens clean. The mother cat licks the newborn kitten vigorously, not just to clean it, but also to stimulate the nervous system.

At birth the kitten is still attached to its mother by the umbilical cord. When the mother cat licks the kitten, this cord is found, severed with her teeth, and swallowed along with the placenta.

CHINESE EROTIC ART. By Michel Beurdeley, Kristofer Schipper, Chang Fu-Jui, and Jacques Pimpaneau. Rutland, Vt.: Charles E. Tuttle Co., 1969.

About the book: A large and somewhat expensive collection of the art of love in China as described by Chinese authors, particularly those of the late Ming Period. The luscious illustrations are from paintings of the great masters of the early 16th century, and also included are love poems, excerpts from erotic novels, Taoism and sexuality, foot fetishism, and more.

From the book: [On FOOT FETISHISM] —The term "Golden Lotus" was reserved for the smallest foot, 7.5 centimeters (3″) at the most. If it was 10 centimeters (4″) it could only be a "Silver Lotus." The "Iron Lotus" is scarcely worthy of mention.

More than any other thing Chinese women feared criticism made without their knowledge about their feet, should they not conform to established criteria. The greatest humiliation was if a young husband expressed disapproval on his wedding night. The young woman would never dare to show her face in public again. Insults such as "Demon with large feet," "Goose foot," and so on, would be poured on the head of the hapless girl. What man in his senses would marry such a girl: "Her figure is all right, but her huge feet are ridiculous. . . ."

The foot is a pretext for endless play between lovers. A small foot appearing below a skirt doubles a woman's charm and exalts her femininity. In bed, slipping out from under the blankets, it increases a man's ardor. What voluptuousness to be kicked by a woman in pretended anger, or to touch the foot surreptitiously and to rub it with one's palm! These are the delights of amorous lovers, to which the sexual scent brings an extra spice— "the scent of the odorous bed," as Fang Hsün notes.

To the initiate or aesthete the sight of a woman washing her feet is so charged with poetry that it is like the sudden blossoming of flowers in a garden. It is also very pleasant to watch her fastening on her shoes, cleaning them, trying them on, undoing the laces, or playing with a balloon with the tips of her foot under the flowering trees.

GATES OF HORN AND IVORY. By Brian Hill, ed. New York: Taplinger, 1968.

About the book: An anthology of dreams of well-known persons including Nebuchadnezzar, Abraham Lincoln, Charles Dickens, Carl Gustav Jung, Mary Baker Eddy, and Oscar Wilde. There is also a chapterful of dreams from fictional works. The range of dreams is from sad to funny, beautiful to grotesque, and prophetic to fantastic.

From the book: PLEASE LEAVE YOUR LEGS
The most extraordinary dream I ever had was one in which I fancied that, as I was going into a theater, the cloak-room attendant

stopped me in the lobby and insisted on my leaving my legs behind me.

I was not surprised; indeed, my acquaintanceship with theater harpies would prevent my feeling any surprise at such a demand, even in my waking moments; but I was, I must honestly confess, considerably annoyed. It was not the payment of the cloak-room fee that I so much minded—I offered to give that to the man then and there. It was the parting with my legs that I objected to.

I said I had never heard of such a rule being attempted to be put in force at any respectable theater before, and that I considered it a most absurd and vexatious regulation. I also said I should write to *The Times* about it.

The man replied that he was very sorry, but that those were his instructions. People complained that they could not get to and from their seats comfortably, because other people's legs were always in the way; and it had, therefore, been decided that, in future, everyone should leave their legs outside.

It seemed to me that the management, in making this order, had clearly gone beyond their usual right; and, under ordinary circumstances, I should have disputed it. Being present, however, more in the character of a guest than in that of a patron, I hardly liked to make a disturbance; and so I sat down and meekly prepared to comply with the demand.

I had never before known that the human leg did unscrew. I had always thought it was a fixture. But the man showed me how to undo them, and I found that they came off quite easily.

The discovery did not surprise me any more than the original request that I should take them off had done. Nothing does surprise one in a dream. . . .

I dreamt that the ticket the man gave me for my legs was No. 19, and I was worried all through the performance for fear No. 61 should get hold of them, and leave me his instead. Mine are rather a fine pair of legs, and I am, I confess, a little proud of them—at all events, I prefer them to anybody else's. Besides, number 61's might be a skinny pair, and not fit me.

It quite spoilt my evening fretting about this.

Jerome K. Jerome, 1859–1927

3

U.S.A.—Red, White, and True

What Do You Know about the U.S.?

QUESTIONS

1. What is the one spot in the U.S. where you could stand in 4 States at one time?
2. How many States are there in the U.S.? Too easy? Well, try it.
3. Which of these cities—New York, Chicago, Phoenix, Miami—has the highest average temperature in July?
4. Which is farther west—Pensacola, Fla., or Washington Island, Wis.?
5. Which is farther west—Los Angeles, Calif., or Reno, Nev.?
6. Can you name the dozen States commonly considered to comprise the Midwest?
7. Which 3 of these States were named after real persons—California, Florida, Georgia, Minnesota, Delaware, Texas, Louisiana, Oklahoma?
8. Can you match each State with its correct State motto?

Indiana	"With God, all things are possible"
Montana	"Equal Rights"
New Hampshire	"Gold and Silver"
Ohio	"The Crossroads of America"
Wyoming	"Live free or die"

9. Can you identify the 2 States that have no counties?
10. The 1st coeducational college in the U.S. was founded in Ohio. Can you name this school?
11. What cities in Michigan are impossible to leave on the ground without going through another city?
12. Name the 2 States that are touched by 8 other States.
13. In the State of Washington may be found the single largest concrete structure ever made by man. It was built in 1942 at a cost of $200 million. It weighs 3 times as much as the pyramid of Cheops in Egypt. The con-crete that went into it could build a highway encircling the whole U.S.A., and the population of the entire county would fit inside it. What is it?
14. Can you pair up the correct State with its State flower?

Alabama	Rose
Hawaii	Violet
Illinois	Camellia
New York	Violet
Oklahoma	Hibiscus
Rhode Island	Mistletoe

15. Part or all of what 3 states can be reached by land only if you leave the U.S.?
16. Can you name the State which has the largest man-made harbor in the country, and 2 cities named Ono and Igo?
17. What American river did Charles Dickens describe as "a slimy monster hideous to behold"?
18. Of what State is it said—it would be the biggest State in the union if it were ironed out flat?
19. Can you give the number of States in the U.S. that are named after Presidents?
20. How many State capitals are named after Presidents?
21. Which was the 1st of the original 13 States to ratify the new Constitution?
22. Here is the city—can you name the State that belongs to it?

What Cheer	Missouri
Peculiar	Iowa
Napoleon	Arkansas
Monte Cristo	Hawaii
Winooski	Mississippi
Volcano	South Dakota
Rugby	Vermont
Kosciusko	Pennsylvania
Le Beau	Tennessee
King of Prussia	Washington

23. What year was Alaska admitted to the Union?
24. Who named New York "the Empire State"?
25. Have diamonds ever been mined in any State of the U.S.?
26. In what State did Adolf Hitler once own 8,960 acres of land?
27. Of the 5 Great Lakes, only one is located entirely inside the U.S. Can you name the one?
28. What State is populated with the most people per square mile?
29. To what State do Basques come from northern Spain to work as sheepherders?
30. What State was an independent republic for 14 years before it joined the Union?
31. What percentage of Utah's population is Mormon?
32. If the U.S. Federal Government took over welfare payments, what 3 States would get 51% of all the money?
33. In recent years there have been proposals to create a new State to be called Columbia or Lincoln out of parts of 3 existing neighboring States. Can you name the 3 States?
34. The region of what State was called by such names as Cibola, Quivira, Panuco, New Philippines before it got its present-day name?
35. In 1861, a convention was held to form the new State of Kanawha. The following year, at another convention, the new State was given its present-day name. Do you know the name?

ANSWERS

1. The one place in the U.S. where you could stand in 4 States at the same time is that point formed by the junction of Utah, Colorado, Arizona, and New Mexico.
2. If you think there are 50 States in the U.S., you are wrong. There are only 46 States. The other 4 are not officially States but Commonwealths. The 4 Commonwealths are Kentucky, Massachusetts, Pennsylvania, and Virginia. According to George W. Stimpson, "The 2 words have about the same meaning, but *commonwealth* originally connoted more of self-government than state."
3. Phoenix averages 94° to 96° Fahrenheit in July, and is easily the most consistently hot city. Next comes Miami. New York and Chicago are last.
4. Pensacola, Fla., is farther west.
5. Reno, Nev., is farther west.
6. The Midwest or Middle West or Central States of the U.S. are commonly considered to be the following: Minnesota, Wisconsin, Illinois, Indiana, Iowa, Missouri, Kansas, Nebraska, South Dakota, North Dakota, Michigan, Ohio.

7. Delaware, Louisiana, and Georgia were named after real people. Delaware derived its name from Lord De La Warre, 1st governor of the Virginia Company. Louisiana was named after King Louis XIV of France. Georgia was named for King George II of England.
8. The 5 States with their correct State mottoes are:

Indiana	"The Crossroads of America"
Montana	"Gold and Silver"
New Hampshire	"Live free or die"
Ohio	"With God, all things are possible"
Wyoming	"Equal Rights"

9. There are no counties in either Louisiana or Alaska. What other States call counties are called parishes in Louisiana and divisions in Alaska.
10. The 1st coeducational college in the U.S. was Oberlin College, founded in Oberlin, O., in 1833.
11. Hamtramck, an independent community of 27,245 and almost entirely Polish, is surrounded by Detroit. Also, Centerline is completely surrounded by the city of Warren, and Lathrup Village is completely surrounded by the city of Southfield.
12. Eight different States touch both Tennessee and Missouri.
13. The Grand Coulee Dam, near Spokane, Wash., is the single largest concrete structure ever made by man. It is 4,300' long, 550' high, and the water has a drop of 330', twice that of Niagara Falls.
14. The correct State flower with its State:

Alabama	Camellia
Hawaii	Hibiscus
Illinois	Violet
New York	Rose
Oklahoma	Mistletoe
Rhode Island	Violet

15. First, Minnesota. A northern portion of Minnesota is isolated from the rest of the State by the Lake of the Woods, which borders it on the north, east, and south—with Canada's Province of Manitoba on the west side. As a result, this section of Minnesota cannot be reached from the U.S. by land. Second, the new State of Alaska is separated from the State of Washington by Canada's British Columbia. Third, Point Roberts, off the State of Washington, can only be reached by traveling through British Columbia.
16. California, of course. The harbor is the Port of Los Angeles.
17. The Mississippi River.
18. Idaho.
19. Just one State in the U.S. was named after a President. This is the State of Washington. As new States were admitted to the Union, efforts were constantly made to name one or

another after Jackson, Jefferson, Washington, but for a half century, these efforts failed. Finally, in 1853, the formation of a new territory came before the House of Representatives. It was to be named the Territory of Columbia. Rep. Richard H. Stanton, of Kentucky, rose to say that "we never yet have dignified a Territory with the name of Washington" and said that he would like to see "at some future day, a sovereign State bearing the name of the Father of His Country. I therefore move to strike out the word Columbia, wherever it occurs in the bill, and to insert in lieu thereof the word Washington." The amendment was approved and the bill passed. Washington became the 42nd State on November 11, 1889.

20. Four State capitals are named after Presidents of the U.S. They are: Jackson, Miss.; Jefferson City, Mo.; Lincoln, Nebr.; Madison, Wis.

21. On December 7, 1787, Delaware became the 1st State to ratify the Constitution.

22. Here are the cities and the States in which they may be found:

What Cheer	Iowa
Peculiar	Missouri
Napoleon	Arkansas
Monte Cristo	Washington
Winooski	Vermont
Volcano	Hawaii
Rugby	Tennessee
Kosciusko	Mississippi
Le Beau	South Dakota
King of Prussia	Pennsylvania

23. Alaska became the 49th State on January 3, 1959.

24. President George Washington, in discussing the original 13 States, referred to New York as "the seat of Empire." Thereafter, it was known as "the Empire State."

25. Diamonds are mined in Arkansas.

26. In 1942, it was discovered that the German Führer, Adolf Hitler, then at war with the U.S., actually owned 8,960 acres of valuable land in Colorado. The Mayor of Kit Carson, Colo., revealed that Hitler had inherited the grazing land from relatives in Germany. The spread, 4 mi. from the small city of Kit Carson, was used by neighboring ranchers for grazing cattle.

27. Lake Michigan, alone among the Great Lakes, is entirely in the U.S.

28. New Jersey has the greatest population density in the U.S. It has an average of 953 people crowded into every square mile.

29. The Basques tend sheep in Idaho.

30. Vermont was a republic before it became a State. The governor of New Hampshire gave out land grants to settlers of the Vermont area, and the area was called New Hampshire Grants. In 1777, to protect themselves against New York, which considered their land grants invalid, the settlers of New Hampshire Grants held a convention and established "a true and independent State." They named their republic New Connecticut. Later, the name was changed to Vert-Mont, French for "Green Mountain." This became Vermont by 1791 when the State joined the Union.

31. Seventy percent of Utah's population is Mormon.

32. New York, Massachusetts, and California are the leading welfare States in the Union.

33. It has been proposed that eastern Washington, all of Idaho, and western Montana be combined into a new State.

34. Southern Texas had a variety of names on Spanish maps before it was named after an Indian greeting that sounded like "Teckas."

35. When West Virginians broke away from Virginia, after Virginia had joined the Confederacy, they decided to call their new State Kanawha, from the Indian name of a river in the area. Later, by a vote, they called their new State West Virginia.

—The Eds.

Inside the Census Bureau: 1, 2, 3, 4 . . . and Counting . . .

How did it all begin? One of the earliest census reports was made in Babylonia in 3800 B.C. Revenues there were dependent upon the proper determination of who should pay taxes. In Egypt, for the next 1,300 years, population counts were also made. During the rule of Ramses II (1292–1225 B.C.), complete registration of heads of households and their families took place in order to divide the land for cultivation, to tax, and to provide manpower for public works projects. With the coming of the Roman in the 1st century B.C., the Egyptian census was taken over by an appointed "censor," who chiefly handled the official registration of all citizens. The biblical phrase of Luke 2:1, "all the world should be taxed . . ." referred to the Hebrew practice of returning to one's legal residence to be counted for purposes of taxation.

In England, William the Conqueror began that country's exposure to the census with the *Domesday Book*, which was compiled in 1085–1086. Every landowner was called in to a hearing to answer, under oath, a long series of questions to identify his holdings. In the 15th to 17th centuries, the Tudor kings added a new reason for counting the people: to provide a ready pool for army replacements during the continuous fighting in western Europe.

A Parliamentary bill to authorize a regular

census met defeat in 1753. Its opponents felt that the information gathered publicly would reveal the country's weaknesses to its enemies. In 1800, another measure was offered and this time it passed, setting up the 1st general enumeration for Great Britain. The change in attitude was partially credited to the theories proposed by Malthus in 1798, in which he questioned the assumption that a country should encourage population growth. The Census Act of 1800 echoed the point that, in times where subsistence was a prime problem for the State to consider, ". . . it is surely important to know the demand for which we are to supply."

The 1st U.S. Census, that of 1790, was undertaken for the same general purpose: to provide guidelines whereby the Government could meet the specific needs of the community. The specific reason for this census was political—to apportion representation for the States in the Congress. The 18 counts made in the "o" years since have been used to solve problems where meaningful statistics are of importance.

Who said Go? Article I, Section 2, of the Constitution authorized the census. Representation in Congress, it said, shall be at the rate of at least one member for each State, and the number shall not exceed one for each 30,000 citizens. Further, the enumeration shall be taken in 1790 and each 10 years thereafter. Today, with membership in the House of Representatives set at 435 and frozen there, each congressman represents an average of 465,000 constituents.

What's the tab for the job? The 1st census of 1790 was relatively simple and inexpensive. The findings, published in one volume of 56 pages, cost about $44,000, or just over a penny for each person counted. By comparison, the census of 1970 cost $247,653,000, was put out in 15,000 separate publications totaling 200,000 pages, and cost about $1.22 per head. Special recounts: For disgruntled towns who feel they've been shorted and thereby cheated of a greater share of tax revenues to be allocated, the Bureau does the work over. The cost: From $20 to count 100 people, to $14,200 for 40,000. But it will recount any disputed census for anybody—for a price.

What else goes on? Francis Walker, director of the 1880 census, began the 1st extensive expansion into activities other than a simple head count. Walker accumulated statistics on population characteristics such as general health, overall literacy, and the level of employment.

Within 10 years, a crisis occurred. Walker's department was unable to process the vast quantities of raw data using the manual bookkeeping and accounting techniques then available. He arranged for a contest to be staged, to produce a machine that would handle tabulations mechanically. The competition was won, hands-down, by Herman Hollerith, a young Census Office engineer, who transformed the punch-card information system used by Jacquard loom-weavers into a workable electric tabulating machine. From that date on, keeping up with the work coming in became a simple problem of improving the equipment.

Hollerith's influence still continues. In 1896 he organized the Tabulating Machine Company, and it later became a founding pillar for the International Business Machines combine. IBM computers today are responsible for processing Census Bureau data.

Besides its well-known "o" census, taken every 10 years, the Bureau conducts over 100 lesser polls, at weekly, monthly, biyearly, and other intervals as necessary. In 1975 a Congress-approved survey—to take the U.S.'s mid-decade pulse—will occur, covering a sample 1 million households and costing $45 million. In years ending with "2" and "7," there are extensive surveys on transportation. In the "3" and "8" years, the emphasis is on data to assist in economic planning. In the "4" and "9" years, the major analyses for agriculture are made. Much of the information comes from U.S. businesses, big and little, since these, too, are required by law to answer the questions of the Census Bureau.

Nearly all of the Government's statistics (98%) come from the Census Bureau's work, regardless of what agency releases them. The raw data is digested and spewed out in thousands of ways: new unemployment rates for the month, cost-of-living changes, industrial production summaries, housing "starts," meat prices, man-in-the-street reaction to Government policies. It's all constantly derived from the enumerator's busy pencil.

Who does the work? For the 1790 census, 650 U.S. marshals were used. Today, the "o" census is handled by 4,400 Census Bureau employees assisted by 160,000 part-time workers. In the 1970 census, the field work was eased by sending out the basic forms in the mails. Some 41,200,000 households received the questionnaires, and an amazing 87% sent the marked forms back. This huge response permitted the Bureau's workers to concentrate on the people who either gave partial answers or none at all.

Who's that knocking at my door? Under Section 5, Title 13, of the U.S. Code, the Secretary of Commerce has the authority to make up the schedules with the questions that gather in the statistics. The Code sets a fine of up to $100 or 60 days in jail for anyone over 18 who refuses to answer or willfully neglects to give information for the census. The penalties are raised to $500 and a year in jail for anyone who knowingly gives a false reply. Rarely are these punishments invoked, however. In 1960 only 2 cases were taken to court for imposition of nominal fines.

The citizen must answer 7 basic questions:

Name and address

Age

Sex

Race

Relationship to head of household

Marital status

Visitors in the home when census is taken

In the 1970 census, the largest number of questions that anyone had to answer was 20, all dealing with the types of housing in which the citizen was living (number of rooms, type of plumbing, etc.). There were 50 other questions, posed to specific individuals according to a random sampling plan. Another question— "What is your social security number?"—had been considered for the 1970 census but was dropped because of objections that its inclusion would allow information on other records to be found and added to the census data. Opponents of the question claimed that it violated the confidentiality of the census and bordered on "invasion of privacy" of the individual.

Who's that knocking at my door—again? Ranking high in importance, for its immediate effect on Government policy, is the Bureau's mini-census called the "Current Population Survey." It is scheduled for the 19th day of the month, year around, to gather statistics on unemployment. Budget billions are spent—or not spent—depending on whether the unemployment rate goes up or down, from month to month.

The "CPS" is carried out by sampling techniques. A 52,500-household sample (about 105,000 people) is drawn from the 1,913 "primary sampling units," or PSUs, into which the entire U.S. has been divided. The PSUs are further split into 357 "strata sets," where each set has traits that are as alike as possible (same geographic area, same % of nonwhite, etc.).

A total of 449 sample areas is then chosen, automatically including each of the 107 largest metropolitan areas. From the 449, the Bureau selects, at random, smaller units called the ED, for "enumeration district." These EDs are of a size just large enough to be handled by a single census taker. To assure that the EDs represent the PSU as a whole, they are picked from a master ED list where the arrangement is set up geographically. For that final reduction to limit the sample size to the 52,500 figure, approximately 6 households in each ED are chosen. The monthly information is collected by about 1,000 interviewers.

How do I become a statistic? Census forms are designed so that the marked answers, recorded as blackened dots, can be optically scanned by FOSDIC—short for Film Optical Sensing Device for Input to Computers. FOSDIC "reads" the dot patterns made by the citizen or with the enumerator's help, and translates them into input data for the computers. The computers, in turn, digest, compile, summarize, and direct the output figures into "slave" high-speed equipment that prints out the final summaries, in sequential page-and-column format, ready for the Government Printing Office to publish.

Census Bureau headquarters are at Suitland, Md. The data-processing offices here are connected by tie lines to the clerical and paper-processing center at Jacksonville, Ind. Scattered around the U.S. are 12 regional offices. The department normally carries about 4,400 employees, hiring its thousands of part-time helpers as the workload peaks. Among its many slogans to pep up morale: "We can't know where we're going if we don't know where we're at."

Who counted the whole bag? The 50 States are divided into thousands of EDs, the "enumeration districts," varying in size from a few city blocks to an area as large as a county. The criterion: A unit must be covered by a single census taker in the time allotted. The schedules mailed out for the 1970 census were all coded for the "ED" number, and further identified by tract, ward, block, and street address. To insure that each address was covered once— and only once—the Bureau's geography division updated over 25,000 maps, where possible, to record changes in city and county growth patterns. Because of funding limitations, they concentrated on the 100,000 square mi. in the urban areas where over 53% of the people live.

1, 2, , 4 . . . Where were you, Mabel, on Census Day? The Bureau reported that the 1970 census, taken as authorized on April 1, missed about 5,300,000 people. Although ⅔ of these were white, the economic and political impact fell more heavily on the blacks where an omission of 1.88 million equaled 7.7% of the total black population, who roughly equal the entire citizenry of Canada. Chicanos were also among the missing, by comparable percentages.

Economically, the lower count meant less money would be available from Federal programs to help the poor. Funding is parceled out according to head count: Less People=Less Funding. Politically, representation suffered: Less People=Less Representation. The inner cities generally lost a voice or 2 in Government. Some black and Chicano leaders disputed the reported Census release on the minority percentage "not counted," claiming it may actually be as great as 15%.

The "short count" is due to many factors. The census enumerator is reluctant to enter the inner city, particularly at night, when the chances of being mugged, robbed, or raped (most interviewers are female) are greatest. The easiest people to overlook are the "floaters," with no permanent address. Others may have a regular "pad," but, like the swinging bachelor, be visiting elsewhere at the time. Some deliberately will disappear, or not answer the door, fearful that the information given out may get them in trouble with housing regulations or the law.

Census Man, tell me, Who has the bread? The richest 5% in the U.S. own 14% of the country's assets. In total income, U.S. workers earned over $1,000,000,000,000 in 1972, or about $5,000 apiece for each of roughly 200 million people. About 5,000 had a net worth of $10 million or more. In liquid assets (cash and other assests easily convertible to cash), ½ of the U.S. had less than $800 to call their own. And one person out of 6 had no liquid assets at all.

The poverty level for nonfarm families was $4,275 for a family of 4. For those living on farms, who could add to their subsistence with home-grown food, the level dropped to $3,643. There were 27,125,000 who qualified as "living in a state of poverty" in 1970. Nearly 8 million were black, and just over 2 million were of Spanish origin. The totals were wildly disproportionate to the ethnic percentage in the total U.S. population. The black poor are poorer than the white poor, by an average of $300 less annually.

Senior citizens, too, are hungry. The 1970 census showed that 48.5% of all 65-and-uppers, not living with their families, were classed as "poverty stricken." For the entire senior-citizen group, representing 10% of the U.S., the median income was a bare $5,053, most of it coming from Social Security payments.

Where did all the bread go? In 1970, the Census reported, the U.S. consumer spent a total of $615,800,000,000. For the median income of about $10,000 it was apportioned as follows:

$2,330	Food, beverages, and tobacco
1,480	Housing
1,390	Household expenses
1,260	Transportation
1,010	Clothing
770	Medical bills
630	Recreation
580	Personal business matters
160	Personal care
390	All other
$10,000	

How do I fit in? The "average" U.S. family profile, from the 1970 census:

White
Husband 44, wife 41
Schooling: high school graduate+0.2 years of college
2.35 children
Owned home of 5.3 rooms, worth about $17,000, in suburbs
Husband held various occupations
Income: $9,867

Black
Husband 41, wife almost 39
Schooling: through the 11th grade
3 children, eldest almost 17
Occupied rental in center of large city
Husband a mechanic, truck driver, or waiter
Income: $6,280

Blacks owned 163,073 businesses, mostly of the Ma-and-Pa variety. Average income: $7,000, a very poor return when the total hours of business were considered. Comparison of incomes showed that 85% came from salaries for both white and black. Whites, however, derived the remainder from dividends and interest primarily, while blacks obtained theirs from some form of public assistance. In 1971, over 5 million black families were on welfare.

The extremes
Poorest U.S. County: Tunica, Miss.
Income per capita: $1,145
Richest U.S. County: Fairfield, Conn.
Income per capita: $4,676

Transportation Note: In 1970, 59,722,550 out of 76,852,389 workers reported that they used the car to drive to work. Only 9 million shared a ride. On weekdays, there are over 50 million cars being driven with one person—the driver—in them. . . .

Has the Vanishing Indian vanished? The Bureau figures on the American Indian show a total of 763,594 in 1970. Over 340,000 now live in a metropolitan area, and 60 major cities have at least 1,000 each. The Indian's life expectancy has risen to 46, which is still 23 years below the national average. Their suicide rate is twice the average. Nearly ⅓ now marry non-Indian mates, the greatest ethnic line crossing of all minorities. But in procreation, the Indian is in 1st place—and in no danger of vanishing.

Who sees the Census files? By Federal law, the personal information collected by the Bureau cannot be divulged to any individual or organization. But, as a part of an anonymous group characteristic, your personal habits, traits, or life-style work their way into the public domain.

There is one exception to this rule. The Personal Census Branch will give you—and you only—what information it may have, from previous censuses, on when and where you were born if you are in need of some type of birth certificate. The facility at Pittsburg, Kans., will furnish a suitable document ($5 charge) giving this information.

—W.K.

The U.S. Patent System Today

"Every man, woman, and child is a potential inventor," says Isaac Fleischman, longtime public information officer for the U.S. Patent Office, "and 90% of them have tried to invent something. Most think about it a week or so and then let go, but a surprisingly large number take the idea to a patent lawyer or engineer and, if not discouraged, start on the path to a patent."

The majority run out of internal steam and their fires of genius flicker out. A goodly number talk it over with their friends, or with a lawyer, engineer, or teacher, and then give up: "You know, I might have done something with my idea for an automatic toast freshener, but . . ." However, over 100,000 patent applications are filed each year, and in 1973 54,960 U.S. citizens were granted patents, which is one patent per 3,790 persons. Oddly enough, Delaware led on a per capita basis with one patent per 1,052 persons. California had the most: 7,603, which comes to one patent for every 2,668 residents of the State. Foreigners obtained 23,344 U.S. patents. The grand total for 1973 was 78,304 patents granted.

You are probably reading this because: (1) you are interested in getting a patent—or trademark; (2) you wonder how good the U.S. patent system is; or (3) you want a general understanding suitable to an educated citizen. We'll focus on how to get a patent and answer the other questions in passing.

Is it a patent you want? First, are you talking about a patent, a trademark, or a copyright? Since 1870 (and 1939 for prints and labels) *all copyright* matters go to the Library of Congress. For patents, design patents, plant patents, and trademarks you go to the U.S. Patent Office.

What's a patent? A *patent* is a grant issued by the U.S. Government giving an inventor the right to exclude all others from making, using, or selling his invention within the U.S., its territories and possessions. It runs for 17 years (except for design patents, which run for 3½, 7, or 14 years) and it cannot be extended except by special act of Congress—a very rare occurrence.

A *design patent* covers any "new, original, and ornamental design for an article of manufacture." It protects only the appearance of an article, not its structure or utilitarian features. Design patents can be obtained for 3½ years (fee is $10), 7 years ($20), and 14 years ($30); the applicant has the choice of period of time.

A *plant patent* covers the invention of, or lucky discovery of, any *asexually* reproduced and distinct and new variety of plant, including cultivated sports, mutants, hybrids, and newly found seedlings, other than a tuber-propagated plant or a plant found in an uncultivated state. (Asexually means reproduced by means other than seeds, such as by the rootings of cuttings, by layering, budding, grafting, and inarching.) Incidentally, Plant Patent No. 3546 was issued on May 7, 1974, for a hybrid floribunda rose named the "Pat Nixon"—invented by Maire-Louis Meilland of Cap d'Antibes, France. Plant patents run for 17 years.

A *trademark* is a word, name, symbol, or device, or any combination used to identify a manufacturer's or merchant's goods. For example, "Vaseline." (Some years ago the lawyers for Vaseline wrote the author of this article to protest his use of vaseline instead of Vaseline in *Executive's Guide to Effective Speaking and Writing*. He's glad now to show them he learned his lesson.) A trademark registration is good for 20 years. Unlike the patent, a trademark can be renewed for terms of 20 years as many times as the applicant desires and for as long as the mark is in use in commerce.

A *trade name* simply identifies a business, partnership, company, or organization and can NOT under present law be registered. Note the distinction: A trademark identifies a product; a trade name identifies a producer. Interestingly enough, titles of books cannot be copyrighted or registered as trademarks. Could you put out a book titled *The People's Almanac?* There's nothing in the patent, trademark, or copyright laws to prohibit it. However, you could run afoul of the Common Law Tort of "unfair competition," because when a person or company has built up the reputation of a name or title, others can be restrained from unfairly taking advantage of it.

Can you patent an idea? No. Ideas are unpatentable. Once you've revealed an idea, it becomes public property.

Will the Patent Office prosecute for you? No. Neither the Patent Office nor any other branch of the U.S. Government will prosecute anyone who "steals" your patent or infringes on it. You have to bring civil suit to have the infringer cease and desist or to pay you damages.

If you want a patent . . . The procedures for obtaining a patent are simple—in principle. Anyone except an employee of the Patent Office can make his own application with a *filing* fee of $65; if the patent is granted, there is an *issue* fee of $100; and *printing charges,* currently around $70, make for a grand total of $235. (The fee for design patents was given earlier.)

For a trademark, the procedures are parallel, except that the fees are $35 for the *registration,* and the applicant must show that the mark is being used in commerce. For a patent you must NOT have sold or published the details more than a year before the date of filing; for a trademark you must already have had it in use. There are about 35,000 applications for trademarks a year in the U.S.

You may apply for your own patent, but most people find it better to obtain professional assistance. The Patent Office will provide you—free—with a listing of registered attorneys in your geographical area. (This is excerpted from its directory which covers the whole U.S. and sells for $3.25.) A majority of the patent lawyers also have engineering degrees and most of the agents who make the searches of past patents are engineers or engineering students.

After almost 180 years of experience, the collective wisdom of the U.S. Patent Office recommends:

1. Make sure your invention has something others don't and be sure it is salable.

2. Have a trustworthy witness date and sign a drawing or description of your invention and keep careful records of the steps taken and their dates. Write the Commissioner of Patents, Washington, D.C. 20231, for a copy of the free brochure on the Disclosure Document Program.

3. Search all the patents already issued in the area of your invention. It costs less to make a search than to try for a patent; if your invention is already patented, you save the cost of filing. One of the existing patents may have a better way of doing what you propose—or be more salable. And, seeing what's in the other patents will give you ideas for preparing your own patent application.

4. Study the results of the search. Does your invention really have something new and different? Assuming you got the patent and built your device, would people buy it? Or can they get the equivalent, or better, for less money elsewhere?

5. Prepare and file the patent application. Here, as we said, you need professional advice and representation. But it's still up to you to ensure the application represents what you have in mind.

6. The Patent Officer Examiner will probably find one or more of your claims unpatentable because of prior patents or publications. Keep your representative informed and answer any rejections within the time allowed. Keep at it until you get the patent or the rejection marked "final." (There are appeal procedures, but we'll leave them to the specialists.)

How long will the patent take? Then what? The process will take about 2 years. Then you are on your own as far as marketing the invention goes. If some patent-promotion organizations approach you, check them out with your Better Business Bureau or your State Bureau or Office of Commerce and Industry. The Patent Office has *no* authority to review or report on such organizations. (There are plenty of shady outfits that look to make money off *you,* not your invention.)

You can obtain marketing information and assistance from banks, chambers of commerce, trade associations, and from the district offices of the U.S. Chamber of Commerce or of the Small Business Administration.

The one thing the Patent Office can do—which can be valuable—is to publish at your expense (currently $3.00) a notice in the *Official Gazette* (a weekly of the Patent Office available by subscription from the Superintendent of Documents, U.S. Government Printing Office) that your patent is available for licensing or sale. It can be read by potentially interested parties throughout the world.

"Patent Pending" must not be faked. The words "Patent Pending" on an invention or design, or "Trademark Applied For" on a mark, have no legal standing. They are just notices to others that you are *trying* to get a patent or trademark. The U.S. Patent Office has no authority or means of extending any protection in advance of a patent. A person who thinks he can scare infringers away by simply printing "Patent Pending" or "Applied For"—but doesn't actually apply for the patent or trademark—can get himself in trouble. Falsely using "Patent Pending" is against the law and punishable by fine.

Why the U.S. Patent System? The U.S. Patent System is designed to help the individual invent and market useful things and at the same time avoid the development of "patent monopolies." If there's no money or benefits from invention, people won't make the effort; on the other hand, if the patents are too restrictive or last too long, the spread of inventions is limited or the products made too costly to many in society. *Patent protection* versus *antitrust* will always be a fighting issue. In general, the worth of the U.S. patent system lies in the 3 types of benefits it provides:

* It stimulates the inventor to make the invention.
* It helps the inventor, or his assignees, to develop and market the invention, thereby providing the public with the use of the invention.
* It encourages the inventor to make his invention known to others. He knows it is protected by law and so he doesn't have to maintain secrecy about it. Moreover, by publishing the patent in the *Official Gazette* and making copies of the patent available to the public at 50¢ each, the Patent Office facilitates the dissemination of new ideas, designs, technology, and plants for use by others.

How good is the U.S. Patent System? You'll

see or hear reports like: "More than 70% of the patents litigated in the courts of appeals are held invalid, while less than 20% are ruled valid and infringed." Or: "The best system is in Sweden . . . you are granted a leave of absence from your job . . . and the Government pays your regular salary plus extra money to construct your model . . . and at the end of 2 years if your invention is successful, you can sell it . . . if not you keep the salary and funding and return to your job."

Of course, no system as complex as one required for inventions in a modern technological society as large as the U.S. can be perfect. And legislation is pending in the U.S. Congress for an overhaul of the U.S. patent system. However, each "problem" of today was the "solution" to a problem of the past, and the U.S. system grew out of efforts to avoid the patents-by-whim-or-favor of the kings—and dictators— of other countries.

There are different ways of treating the statistics, but a 5-year study (1968–1972) of patent litigations indicates that less than 1% of patents were actually challenged in the courts, and of those so challenged less than 1% were found invalid. And that's out of 70,000 patents granted a year!

With regard to Sweden, the description given above is not accurate. Sweden does have a *Stiftellsen för Teknisk Utveckling* (STU), or Board for Technical Development, which can grant "reasonable," i.e., small, amounts of money to a company or individual inventor to help in the development of "promising" and "feasible" ideas. The funds are not linked to the salary of the inventor or his job. He or the company concerned has to put money into the project, too.

There are as many patent systems as there are countries. For instance, Great Britain and the U.S. have *examining* systems; that is, the patent is checked out before issuance. France has a *registration* system: The patent is accepted and published, and then the fights over it begin. Countries that do not have antitrust laws or traditions of free enterprise naturally do things quite differently from countries like the U.S.

As our society changes, our patent system will have to change. The history of science and technology (and of art and literature) has shown that you can NOT legislate easily *for* creativity, but you can easily legislate *against* it. In the words of Abraham Lincoln, the U.S. system seeks to "add the fuel of interest to the fire of genius." Of course, the balance between too much protection and not enough will constantly shift: The patent examiners, like the courts, will "follow the headlines" and will tend to move faster on some types of applications and more slowly on others. Collectivists will

want more government controls; individualists will want fewer. Congress will tilt now one way and now the other. But until the nature of man and our society changes more basically, the U.S. patent system will serve the goals of society by helping the individual serve society in ways that also reward him for his own ingenuity and industry.

Some Key Dates of the American Patent System

—1641. First patent on North American continent: to Samuel Winslow by Massachusetts General Court for method of making salt.

—1787. U.S. Constitution gives Congress power to legislate for patents and copyrights.

—1790. President Washington signs 1st patent bill into law which is soon followed by 1st copyright law. Authority lodged in a Board which is located in Dept. of State. On July 31 1st U.S. patent is granted Samuel Hopkins.

—1836. Establishes Patent Office as separate entity, still lodged in Dept. of State, but headed by a Commissioner of Patents.

—1842. Designs made patentable.

—1849. Patent Office transferred to newly created Dept. of the Interior.

—1859. Copyright matters transferred from Dept. of State to Dept. of the Interior, and Patent Office adds a "Librarian of Copyrights" to its staff.

—1870. First law regarding trademarks but only in regard to other nations and Indian tribes. Copyright matters transferred to Librarian of Congress.

—1887. U.S. joins International Convention for the Protection of Industrial Property (patents and trademarks). Member governments give to other nationals what they give to own citizens.

—1905. Trademark laws applied to interstate commerce. This made them useful in U.S. and gave them real importance they have today.

—1922. Patent Office transferred to Dept. of Commerce by Executive Order.

—1930. Plants become patentable. In 1931 Henry F. Bosenberg obtains Plant Patent No. 1 for "a climbing rose . . ."

—1939. Registration of copyrights for prints and labels transferred to Library of Congress, ending all connection of Patent Office with copyright matters.

—1952. All patent laws of and since 1870 codified in one act with many changes and with revisions to clarify language.

—1967. Patent Office begins move to present quarters in Crystal Plaza, a complex on U.S. Highway 1, between Washington, D.C., and Alexandria, Va.

—1970. Senate ratifies Convention establishing the World Intellectual Property Organization (WIPO) and the revision of the Paris Convention for the Protection of Industrial Property.

For Further Information about U.S. Patents

* Order from Superintendent of Documents, U.S. Government Printing Office, Washington, D.C. 20402.

° Request from Office of Information, U.S. Patent Office, Washington, D.C. 20231. No charge.

GENERAL INFORMATION

* *The Story of the United States Patent Office*, 1972, 41 pages, 35¢. Excellent little summary; all the history most people want to know.

* *Commissioner of Patents Annual Report.* Review of the fiscal year (July 1–June 30), recently running about 40 pages and about 50¢. Covers changes in law and procedures and all statistics you want.

* *Patents: Spur to American Progress*, 1969, 49 pages, 35¢. A bit of the hard sell from the establishment view, but well done, readable, superb coverage, and an excellent bibliography.

HOW TO GET A PATENT

* *General Information Concerning Patents*, 1973, 43 pages, 45¢. Includes sample forms, definitions of terms, advice on each step to take, and enough about infringements and interferences.

* *For Inventors: Patents & Inventions: An Information Aid.*, Rev. 1974, 22 pages, 40¢. Discusses the "Six Steps" an inventor must or should take, and tells what to do after as well as before getting a patent.

° *Q&A About Patents: Answers to Questions Frequently Asked About Patents*, 1974, 15-page pamphlet, no price given. Handy, but no replacement of above materials. Includes locations of the 22 libraries that have printed copies of U.S. patents and of U.S. Department of Commerce Field Offices.

° *Q&A About Plant Patents: Answers to Questions Frequently Asked About Plant Patents*, 1970, 9 pages, no price given. Twenty-two questions on plant patents within the system outlined in the above booklets.

HOW TO GET A TRADEMARK

* *General Information Concerning Trademarks*, 1974, 28 pages, 50¢. Definitions, laws, rules, explanations, and examples of forms to be used.

° *Q&A About Trademarks: Answers to Questions Frequently Asked About Trademarks*, 1971. 5 pages, no price given. Twenty-six questions and answers. Also illustrations of well-known marks.

HOW TO GET A PATENT LAWYER OR AGENT

* *Attorneys and Agents Registered to Practice Before the U.S. Patent Office*—1974, $3.25. (As noted earlier, for a listing in your geographical area, contact the Patent Office for the excerpt at no charge.)

—F.C.D.

Footnote People in U.S. History

American men and women, with unique backgrounds and achievements, who deserve better than to be buried in the footnotes of history and in the pages of specialized biography.

DELIA BACON (1811–1859). *Originator of Shakespeare-Bacon theory.*

In 1852, a strange, frail, possessed New England lady, who had dabbled in teaching, writing, lecturing, jolted literary circles with the announcement that William Shakespeare had not written the classical plays attributed to him. These plays had actually been written, the lady insisted, by a group of English scholars— a secret Elizabethan club—whose ranks included Sir Francis Bacon, Sir Walter Raleigh, and Edmund Spenser. The originator of this sensational theory was 41-year-old Delia Bacon, of Hartford, Conn., the spinstress daughter of impoverished missionary parents and no relative to Queen Elizabeth's favorite adviser.

Delia Bacon was the 1st Baconian, the founder of the Shakespeare-Bacon movement, and her theory kicked off a controversy that has already lasted a century. Miss Bacon argued that William Shakespeare was no more than "a vulgar, illiterate . . . deerpoacher" and "Lord Leicester's stableboy." His name had been used merely as a front by a school of brilliant writers who wished to promote radical political philosophies without revealing their true identities.

Not only had *Hamlet, Macbeth, Othello* been penned by Sir Francis Bacon and company, but their advanced political propaganda had been concealed in the dramas by a clever system of ciphers. As to proof, Delia Bacon offered, beyond her unshakable intuition, evidence that she had deciphered the plays. If more proof were needed, she said, it could be found inside Shakespeare's grave at Stratford-on-Avon. There, moldering beside the Bard's body, were the documents that would tell the entire world the truth. If she could reach England, open the crypt, her theory would be fully vindicated.

Within a year, Miss Bacon was on her way to England, backed by Ralph Waldo Emerson, who had been converted to her theory and who considered her, with Walt Whitman, "the sole producers that America has yielded in 10 years." Emerson's support encouraged *Putnam's Magazine* to give Miss Bacon a series of assignments reporting upon her researches.

Until she had made her startling announcement, Delia Bacon had been a nonentity. She was one of 6 children, born in a Tallmadge, O., log cabin in 1811. Her father, the Rev. David Bacon, went broke, moved his brood to Hartford, Conn., and died when Delia was 6. She attended a famous private school run by Catharine Beecher, sister of Henry Ward Beecher, until she was 15. Later, with an older sister, she tried to set up a private school of her own. For 4 years, in Connecticut, New Jersey, and New York, she tried and each time failed, mainly because she lacked sufficient funds and because she was plagued by ill health.

At 20, she published a book of short stories, at 28 a play. Meanwhile, she began lecturing before women's groups on literature. Slight and graceful of presence, highly enthusiastic about her subjects, she managed sufficient speaking engagements to support herself. During this period she became involved in a disastrous love affair with one Rev. Alexander MacWhorter, which led to his almost being defrocked and to her total disillusionment with men. Apparently, she had to take it out on some man, and so she took it out on William Shakespeare. For it was at this time, continuing her researches, that she became convinced Shakespeare was a hoax and a fraud. At once, in a burst of energy, she delved deeper into the plays, fending off all family resistance and ridicule, until she became a fanatic on her thesis.

Moving about New England, peddling her Shakespeare-Bacon convictions, she stumbled upon the much respected sage of Concord, Ralph Waldo Emerson, who was at once charmed and impressed. By 1853, armed with Emerson's encouragement and his letters of introduction, Delia Bacon sailed for England.

In London, however, dizzied by the nearness of the 17th century, Delia gradually began to abandon scholarship for intuitive rhapsodies. This change in attitude filled her few backers with concern. Emerson had given her a warm letter to Thomas Carlyle, author of *The French Revolution*, and he had welcomed her as a friend, prepared to assist her in every way. When Carlyle suggested Delia consult original Shakespearean sources, she hedged. Annoyed, Carlyle dropped her.

Shortly thereafter, *Putnam's Magazine* dropped her too. After publishing one of her pieces, they rejected the rest, presumably because the articles were devoid of authentic research. Delia's disregard for facts, her growing monomania, finally alienated even the faithful Emerson.

Without funds or supporters, Delia dwelt on in an unheated room, in the home of a Stratford shoemaker, often not knowing where her next meal would come from, feverishly bent to her new task of putting her Shakespeare-Bacon theory to paper. She worked so hard, with so little nourishment, that finally, in the summer of 1855, she fell seriously ill. Her doctor, who happened also to be the Mayor of Stratford, wrote posthaste to the American consulate in Liverpool asking "advice or suggestions" about this ailing, destitute American lady. "She is in a very excited and unsatisfactory state, especially mentally," wrote the doctor, "and I think there is much reason to fear that she will become decidedly insane."

The American consul in Liverpool, at the time, was none other than Nathaniel Hawthorne who, at 52, already had *The Scarlet Letter* behind him. Promptly, Hawthorne thanked the Stratford physician for his "kind attention to my countrywoman" and authorized full care for the patient.

Briefly, Delia rallied. She had completed the writing of her book, *The Philosophy of the Plays of Shakespeare Unfolded*. She needed a publisher. Again, Hawthorne came to her rescue. He did not approve of her theory, but he felt it deserved a public hearing. He penned a foreword to her manuscript and, after she had alienated one English publisher, he found another, Groombridge and Sons, to bring it out.

While waiting for its publication, Delia became more and more obsessed with the idea of opening Shakespeare's tomb. Sometimes, at night, lantern in hand, she entered the Stratford church, and for hours stood bemused before the altar. Beneath the church floor, before the altar, the key to the enigma lay in a wooden coffin. He had rested there since 1616, with the following warning, possibly written by himself, engraved on the slab above—

Good frend for Iesvs sake forbeare,
To digg the dvst encloased heare!
Blest be ye man yt spares thes stones,
And curst be he yt moves my bones.

Nevertheless, Delia persisted. The vicar of the Stratford church wavered, actually considered permitting her to open the grave. Then, suddenly, ill again, Delia backed down. She withdrew her request. As Hawthorne later wrote: "A doubt stole into her mind whether she might not have mistaken the depository and mode of concealment of those historic treasures. And after once admitting the doubt, she was afraid to hazard the shock of uplifting the stone and finding nothing. She examined the surface of the gravestone, and endeavored, without stirring it, to estimate whether it were of such thickness as to be capable of containing the archives of the Elizabethan club. She went over anew the proofs, the clues, the enigmas, the pregnant sentences, which she had discovered in Bacon's letters and elsewhere, and now was frightened to perceive that they did not point so definitely to Shakespeare's tomb as she had heretofore supposed."

Her quest ended, she had to talk to someone. There was no one. Hawthorne had left England. Her brother in Hartford—who had written Hawthorne, "in my opinion her mind has been verging on insanity for the last 6 years"—begged her to come home. She refused, writing, "I do not want to come back to America. I can not come."

As she fought to hold on to reality, she awaited the publication of her book. The 682-page volume appeared in April, 1857. It established the battle lines for the modern-day Shakespeare-Bacon controversy. It alleged that Shakespeare was ignorant and unlettered, that he lacked the knowledge of sports, law, court usages displayed in the plays, that lines in the dramas themselves paralleled the authorship of Spenser, Oxford, and others. Few read the book. According to the Dictionary of American Biography, "Hawthorne in later years averred that he had met one man who had read it through; there is no record of another." Although Mark Twain and Ignatius Donnelly were later to be impressed by it—and in the years to follow Walt Whitman, Henry James, Sigmund Freud would subscribe to her theory—most of the critics and public at the time the book appeared heaped ridicule upon it. Delia's mind was already unhinged. Now she completely lost her reason.

She was placed in a private asylum at Henley-in-Arden, 8 mi. from Stratford. In 1858, a young nephew, returning from China, picked her up and took her home to Hartford. There, a year later, she died, "clearly and calmly trusting in Christ," as her brother recorded, "and thankful to escape from tribulation and enter into rest."

—I.W.

AMELIA BLOOMER (1818–1894). *Promoter of bloomers.*

Although she had persuaded her husband to omit the word "obey" from their marriage vows, Amelia Jenks Bloomer was no 19th-century Women's Liberationist. She would not sign the Declaration of Independence for Women that was drawn up right in her own town of Seneca Falls, N.Y., and her real concern was temperance, not feminism. She contributed articles (signed "Gloriana" or "Eugene") on morality, alcoholism, and other social issues to the *Free Soil Union* and the *Seneca County Courier*, but her enterprising spirit was not satisfied, and she resolved to start her own magazine.

The Lily was officially the house organ of the Seneca Falls Ladies' Temperance Society, but to all intents and purposes it was the personal mouthpiece for the crusading opinions of its petite and rather pretty editor. "A simple young thing with no education for business, in no way fitted for such work," Amelia Bloomer described herself to a subscriber. Nevertheless, she established her pressroom in the room adjoining the post office (she was also deputy postmaster), wrote copy, read proof, edited, contracted for the printing, and by herself wrapped and mailed all the copies that her public had subscribed to at 50¢ a year. It was the 1st women's magazine in America.

In spite of these innovations, Mrs. Bloomer's neighbors were hardly prepared for her sudden appearance on the town's main thoroughfare with her skirt apparently shrunk all the way up to her knees and the lower half of her legs enveloped in a kind of Turkish trouser. In truth, credit for inventing this scandalous attire must go to the wealthy abolitionist Gerrit Smith, whose fashionable daughter, Mrs. Elizabeth Smith Miller, 1st wore it. Amelia Bloomer was merely joining the reaction against the voluminous hoopskirts that fashion decreed for every lady. The hoops could be propelled through doorways only with difficulty, and they were especially ill-suited to the unpaved streets of small-town America. After *The Lily* took up the cause of dress reform and even included patterns for the new costume, Gerrit Smith's invention became permanently associated with the name of the magazine's editor.

Mrs. Bloomer and her disciples were soon swept up in a tremendous hubbub, for the new fashion was as feverishly discussed as the Fugitive Slave Law or abolition. A large Boston daily wrote glowingly in its society section of a bride attired "in the poetry and bloom of a Bloomer costume . . . of elegant white satin," and the *Brooklyn Eagle* raved about "a young lady, apparently in the bloom of her teens, and beautiful as a bouquet of roses . . . her limbs, which appeared symmetrical as the chiseled pedestals of a sculptured Venus, encased in a pair of yellow pantaloons." But *Godey's Lady's Book* disapproved, and Gordon Bennett's *New York Herald* was vehemently opposed: ". . . the attempt to introduce pantaloons . . . will not succeed. Those who have tried it, will very likely soon end their career in the lunatic asylum, or, perchance, in the State prison."

The raging battle produced side skirmishes hardly less interesting. A certain reverend of Easthampton, Mass., forbade 2 Bloomer girls to enter his church, threatening them with excommunication and causing periodicals on both sides of the issue to temporarily unite in denouncing him for such an unwarranted assumption of holy authority. Another and more famous divine, Dr. DeWitt Talmage, cited Moses as an early opponent of Bloomerism ("A woman shall not wear anything that pertains to a man . . ." Deut. 22:5), but Mrs. Bloomer countered with Genesis, which, she pointed out, makes no distinction between the fig leaves of Adam and Eve.

The fashion crossed the Atlantic when a small band of proselytizing Bloomer girls invaded England. A "London Bloomer Committee" was formed and almost immediately issued a handbill announcing that "a public lecture relating to the same will be delivered at the Royal Soho Theatre on October 6. The ladies of the committee will themselves appear in full Bloomer costume, and the mothers and daughters of England are cordially invited to attend." That winter "A Grand Bloomer Ball" was held in the elegant Hanover Square Rooms, and although it was attended by youthful members of both Houses of Parliament as well as Guards, officers, dandies, writers, painters, actors, and barristers (among others), too few of the bloomer-clad ladies present were exactly "respectable," and the bloomer lost face accordingly.

The general mockery that 1st greeted the bloomer never abated, and although the feminists continued to wear the bloomer for a few years, even they gave it up in time. Feeling martyred in Seneca Falls, Amelia and her husband moved west, where the fame (but not the ridicule) had preceded her. They settled happily in Council Bluffs, Ia., where Mrs. Bloomer continued to wear the costume for a few more years. She gave it up when the Union cause superseded feminism and dress reform in her heart. The guns at Ford Sumter were hardly silent before she had organized the Soldiers' Aid Society; it met in her home to stitch the large silk flag which Company B of the 4th Iowa Volunteer Infantry eventually received from her hands. "You are now going forth to sustain and defend the Constitution," emoted Mrs. Bloomer at the presentation, "against an unjust and monstrous rebellion, fomented and carried on by wicked and ambitious men who have for their object the overthrow of the best Government the world has ever seen." A local reporter, recording the scene, noted that among the volunteers "many a brawny breast heaved, and tears trickled down many a manly face."

Amelia Bloomer had won them at last!

—N.C.S. rep.

NELLIE BLY (1867–1922). *Pioneer newspaperwoman.*

It wasn't her real name, of course. But in the heyday of yellow journalism and the penny press—when an American newspaper publisher could plausibly promote war between his country and Spain to boost circulation—a girl reporter needed a good, catchy nom de plume.

The future "Queen of the Sob Sisters" was born Elizabeth Cochrane in a small Pennsylvania mill town, and came to Pittsburgh as a teen-ager wanting to be a writer. She sprang from obscurity with a stinging rebuke to an editorial in the *Pittsburgh Dispatch* titled, "What Girls Are Good For." In spite of themselves, the editors were impressed by the girl's spirit. They offered her a job.

Fine, she said, and proposed a series of articles on divorce as her 1st contribution. The editors, for all their external toughness, were conventional Victorians. They doubted that this innocent child could write with the maturity and tact such a delicate subject demanded. But under the by-line "Nellie Bly" she turned out stories spiced with the personal tales she heard from the older women she shared living quarters with in the boardinghouse district. Her writing rang true. It was sharp and controversial. Best of all, it sold newspapers.

Nellie's 1st effort was followed by exposés of conditions in Pittsburgh's slums, its sweatshops, and its jails. Under pressure from advertisers the *Dispatch* encouraged Nellie to take a vacation. She went to Mexico. Soon the young muckraker was pouring forth lurid stories of decadence, debaucheries, and official corruption South of the Border. The Mexican authorities asked her to leave. She did, but managed to get a suitcase full of notes out with her, explaining to railroad agents that it contained ladies "unmentionables."

Pittsburgh was now too tame for Nell. She went to New York where she promised Joseph Pulitzer a scoop on conditions at the city's insane asylum on Blackwell's Island if he would put her on the staff of the *New York World*. Soon she was practicing wild shrieks and facial grimaces in front of her mirror. She showed up without identification at a local rooming house, threw a fit at mealtime and was on her way to Bellevue within 24 hours. She returned from Blackwell's Island 10 days later with stories of "a human rat hole," of brutal nurses, inedible food, and stifling sanitary conditions. Her stories electrified the nation, empaneled a grand jury, and brought considerable reform. They also made Nellie Bly a celebrity.

Next she went underground as an immigrant girl and came up with an exposé of fraudulent employment agencies. Nellie framed herself on a theft charge and landed in prison. The result was another scoop for the *World*, this time with tales of indignities, leering jailhouse guards, and a Tammany henchman who offered to buy her freedom. Her revelations forced the segregation of male and female prisoners and placed police matrons in charge of frisking the ladies.

Once she threw herself off a Hudson River ferry to test the efficiency of its rescue crew. Another time she posed as the wife of a patent medicine manufacturer and obtained the services of Albany's chief briber to kill a bill that would ruin her husband's business. She missed their final payoff meeting to hurry back to New York and write the story that would lead to the man's indictment.

The *World* protected Nellie's identity so that she could pursue her stories anonymously. New York speculated wildly on the person or persons behind the by-line. Many believed Nellie Bly to be a team of brilliant male reporters. It was more plausible than the truth. The real Nellie, deceptively demure and diminutive with sad gray eyes, was not yet 22.

She now was ready for the capstone of her career. In response to the popularity of Jules Verne's novel, *Around the World in Eighty Days*, Nellie proposed to outdo the fictional Phileas Fogg and circumnavigate the globe in less than 80 days. Pulitzer liked the idea, but wanted to send a man. "If you do," she warned, "I'll leave at the same time and race against him." Pulitzer relented.

Fitted out in plaid ulster and cape, wearing a 2-peaked Sherlock Holmes cap, and clutching a leather gripsack with all her travel needs, she set out from New York on November 14, 1889. She crossed the Atlantic and stopped to interview Verne in France. From there her itinerary included the Suez, Ismailia, Calcutta, Singapore, Yokohama, then across the Pacific to San Francisco and a breakneck race across the continent. The readers of the *World* eagerly followed her course. Pulitzer sponsored a lottery based on her time of arrival.

When she roared into Jersey City, factory whistles blew, cannons roared, flags flew, and a massive parade started down Broadway. Nell appeared to a crowd of jubilant New Yorkers with a monkey she had acquired in Hong Kong perched on her shoulder. Her total elapsed time: 72 days, 6 hours, 10 minutes, and 11 seconds.

Although she continued to write tearjerkers about poor working girls and abandoned children, the remainder of her career was sheer anticlimax. At 28, she married a 72-year-old millionaire hardware manufacturer. When he died, she tried to run the business but ended up in bankruptcy court complaining that unscrupulous employees had bilked the company out of more than $2 million.

She was in Europe at the outbreak of W.W. I. For a time she supplied International News Service with dispatches from the Austrian Front. After the war she was hired by the *New York Journal*, but her style of writing was then sadly out of date.

She died of pneumonia at 55. Her obituaries, small and little noticed, played on all the inside pages.

—D.P.P.

Charles E. Bolton (1835?–1899?). *Stagecoach robber.*

> I've labored long and hard for bread—
> For honor and for riches—
> But on my corns too long you've tred,
> You fine haired sons of bitches.
> Black Bart, the P o8

This bit of doggerel was written by one of America's more colorful poets and was found in an empty express box following the robbery of a California stagecoach in 1877.

Black Bart was but one of the many stagecoach robbers who operated in California during the more than 50 years that State depended upon the horse-drawn coaches for communication between its scattered outposts. The railroads had not yet crossed the continent.

On August 3, 1877, the stage traveling from Fort Ross to Russian River was stopped by a lone man who wore a long linen duster and whose face was concealed by a flour sack with cut-out eyeholes. He pointed a rifle at the drivers and, in a "deep and hollow" voice, told them to throw down the express box. Later the box was recovered with the above verse written on the back of a waybill. Missing were $300 in coin and a check for $305.52 on the Grangers' Bank of San Francisco. Written at the bottom of the waybill was the following: "Driver, give my respect to our friend, the other driver, but I really had a notion to hang my old disguise hat on his weather eye. Respectfully, B.B."

This was the 1st robbery to be ascribed to Black Bart, and he was not heard from again for about a year. He stopped the stage from Quincy to Oroville on July 25, 1878, and demanded the Wells-Fargo box. This time he netted $379 in coin, a diamond ring said to be worth $200, and a silver watch valued at $25. As before, he also robbed the mail. Next day the box was recovered and in it was another verse signed by "Black Bart the P o8."

Here I lay me down to sleep
To wait the coming morrow,
Perhaps success, perhaps defeat
And everlasting sorrow.
[repeat here the 1st poem]
Yet come what will, I'll try it once,
My condition can't be worse
And if there's money in that box
Tis munny in my purse.

Each line of the verse was written as though in a different hand. Wells, Fargo & Co. put up a reward of $800 for his capture.

Black Bart's robberies were unusual in that there never was any bloodshed. He just took the strongbox, removed what he wanted, left his message in the box and then vanished.

His last holdup was in late 1883 on the line from Sonora to Milton, near Copperopolis. The strongbox was more secure than most and Black Bart cut his hand working on the lock. Finally opening it, he found $4,800 in cash. At this moment a rider arrived and the driver, borrowing the newcomer's gun, fired at the highwayman. Black Bart scooped up the money and rode away, leaving behind his bloodstained handkerchief, which bore the laundry mark "F.O.X.7."

After checking with 91 laundries, detectives were rewarded with the real name of Black Bart. He was Charles E. Bolton, a fine-looking old gentleman with a white moustache, gold-headed cane and dapper clothes. When asked if he were Black Bart he replied, "Sir, I am a gentleman." As questioning persisted, he confessed that he was indeed "the P o8."

Bolton was born in Jefferson County, N.Y., and came west at the age of 10. "I never robbed a passenger or ill-treated a human being," he told them. He was convicted and given a long term at San Quentin, but was released about 4 years later for exceptional behavior. After that, nothing is known of his life.

—G.T. rep.

"Diamond Jim" BRADY (1856–1917).
Millionaire and gourmand.

James Buchanan "Diamond Jim" Brady, Gilded Age personality and the all-time U.S. eating champion, was born of Irish working-class parents in New York's Lower West Side. As a boy he got a job as a baggage-handler at a local railroad station and after a few years won the chance to represent a major railroad-equipment firm as a salesman. Jim's selling ability was extraordinary, and by putting together a succession of multimillion-dollar railroad deals, he amassed a substantial fortune. Jim went on to use his wealth for a record-breaking display of public vulgarity that has never been challenged.

At 1st Jim's passion for fine clothes and ex-pensive jewelry was merely a sound business investment for an ambitious young salesman. "If you're going to make money, you have to look like money," he declared. Accordingly, he acquired a wardrobe of 200 custom-made suits and some 50 glossy silk hats. He further adorned himself with a collection of personal evening jewelry with a net worth conservatively estimated at $2 million. For a single set of shirt studs, vest studs, and cuff links, Jim paid $87,315. His diamond rings were the biggest even seen in New York, and among his 30-odd celebrated timepieces was a single watch that was appraised at $17,500 after his death. Brady was never embarrassed, no matter how gaudy his display of glitter and gilt, and he gloried in his nickname "Diamond Jim." "Them as has 'em wears 'em," he told the world.

Brady lavished diamonds on his personal accessories as well as his wardrobe: He was fond of taking the air in Central Park on one of his 12 gold-plated bicycles with diamonds and rubies embedded in the handlebars. To one of the women in his life, the buxom, 200-lb. singer-actress Lillian Russell, Brady presented a special gilt bicycle with mother-of-pearl handlebars and emeralds and sapphires mounted on the spokes of each wheel. Miss Russell made use of this famous machine every Sunday, when she appeared for photographers in her white serge cycling suit topped with a Tyrolean hat.

But despite his occasional interest in the fair sex, the reigning passion of Diamond Jim's life was always food. It was in this area that Brady's achievements reached truly heroic proportions, and that he made his most lasting contribution to American history and folklore.

A typical day would begin with a hearty breakfast of hominy, eggs, corn bread, muffins, flapjacks, chops, fried potatoes, a beefsteak, and a full gallon of orange juice. (This "golden nectar" was Jim's favorite beverage—in all his eating escapades he never touched a drop of liquor.)

At 11:30 in the morning, Diamond Jim customarily enjoyed a before-lunch snack: 2 to 3 dozen clams and oysters.

He lunched at 12:30, consuming additional clams and oysters, a brace of boiled lobsters, 3 deviled crabs, a joint of beef, and several kinds of pie.

Afternoon tea included a platter of seafood washed down with another Brady favorite—lemon soda.

After that, Jim saved his appetite until evening and what was always the major meal of his day. Dinner was often taken at Charles Rector's—an exclusive Broadway establishment where the proprietor boasted that Brady was the "best 25 customers" he had.

Dinner generally began with 2 to 3 dozen Lynnhaven oysters—selected especially for

Brady by Maryland dealers. Crabs followed— 6 of them—and then at least 2 bowls full of green turtle soup.

So much for appetizers. Jim's main courses included: 6 or 7 lobsters, 2 whole canvasback ducks, 2 portions of terrapin (turtle meat), a sirloin steak, vegetables, and an entire platter of pastries for dessert. Additional beakers of orange juice further tested Jim's capacity. As an after-dinner treat, he customarily downed a 2-lb. box of candy.

Small wonder that crowds used to gather around the Brady table to cheer him on his progress and to make bets on whether or not he'd drop dead before dessert.

But in addition to quantity, the quality of his consumption was important to Big Jim. Once, when visiting Boston, he sampled the product of a modest local manufacturer of chocolates. "Best goddamned candy I ever ate," announced Brady, as he polished off a 5-lb. box of assorted chocolate creams, French bonbons, and glazed walnuts. When he wanted to order several hundred additional boxes of the candy to send to his various friends and acquaintances, he was told that the merchandise was in short supply. "Hell," said Brady, taking out his checkbook, "tell them to build a candy foundry with twice their capacity. Here's the money." He proceeded to write out an advance of $150,000 to be taken out in trade.

On another occasion, Brady was dining at Rector's when a member of his party began talking rapturously about the splendors of *filet de sole Marguery*—as prepared only at the Café Marguery in Paris from a secret recipe.

This new dish immediately became an obsession with Big Jim, and he refused to rest until he could enjoy the fabled fish on a regular basis in New York. He threatened to take his business elsewhere unless Charles Rector was able to come up with the secret recipe.

The next day, Rector's son George was pulled out of Cornell and prepared for a difficult undercover mission. Under an assumed name, young Rector began by washing pots at the Café Marguery, and slowly worked his way up to the position of apprentice chef. After months spent under the watchful eyes of his masters, Rector was finally admitted into the inner circle which knew the secrets of the special sole and its priceless sauce. After more than 2 years in Paris, he was able to sail for New York with the knowledge demanded by Diamond Jim.

Brady was at the dock to meet young Rector when he arrived. "Have you got the sauce?" Diamond Jim bellowed while the vessel was still out in the river. That night, Jim fully indulged himself after his long wait, finishing 9 portions of the sole and sopping up the last bit of sauce with a piece of bread held between 2 bejeweled fingers. When he went back to the kitchen to congratulate the chef, he said he guessed that "If you poured some of the sauce over a Turkish towel, I believe I could eat all of it."

For years, Diamond Jim went on defying the dire predictions of medical experts, until he finally developed serious stomach trouble at the age of 56. His career as a fabled eater was over, but he lived on for 5 more years until his death at the Shelburne Hotel in Atlantic City in 1917. A postmortem on his body performed at Johns Hopkins Hospital in Baltimore showed that his stomach had been expanded to a size 6 times larger than normal. Jim left much of his fortune to the James Brady Urological Clinic which he had established at Johns Hopkins.

—M.S.M.

ANTHONY COMSTOCK (1844–1915). *American censor.*

A veteran of the Civil War, a stalwart of the YMCA, he embarked on a lifetime crusade to remove all that was "lewd and lascivious" from art and literature. Born on a 160-acre farm in Connecticut, he was of Puritan ancestry. His mother died when he was 10, and he determined to dedicate his life to pursuits that would honor her memory. At 18, remorseful at having got drunk for the 1st and the last time in his life, he broke into the local liquor store, opened the spigots on the kegs, and let the liquor pour out on the floor. With Demon Rum out of the way, pornography was his next target. At 24, learning that a friend had been "led astray and corrupted and diseased" by an erotic book, Comstock determined to avenge this wrong. In so doing, he found his lifelong vocation. Until then, he had worked at a variety of clerking jobs. Now he became a full-time censor.

Comstock established the New York Society for the Suppression of Vice in 1873. Later, he became an official agent of the U.S. Post Office. He alone was responsible for obtaining the stronger laws that barred obscenity from the mails. As a result, publishers were forced to convert explicit language in their books into euphemisms—"pregnant" fell from their pages to be replaced by "enceinte."

Among the books Comstock successfully had banned or destroyed were *Fanny Hill, The Lustful Turk, Peep Behind the Curtains of a Female Seminary, A Night in a Moorish Harem, Love on the Sly.* Despite rising opposition— "Jesus was never moved from the path of duty, however hard, by public opinion," said Comstock—he was responsible for the censorship of 500,000 reproductions of drawings or paintings, among them the innocent candy-box nude,

September Morn by Paul Chabas. Comstock's idea of what was wrong in art was simple. As he told a reporter: "Anything which tends to destroy the dignity of womanhood or to display the female form in an irreverent manner is immoral. No one reveres the female form more than I do. In my opinion there is nothing else in the world so beautiful as the form of a beautiful maiden woman—nothing. But the place for a woman's body to be—denuded—is in the privacy of her own apartments with the blinds down."

His censorship was indiscriminate. His 5'10", 210-lb. blunderbuss presence, his muttonchop whiskers and black frock coat (Bible in its pocket) could be seen everywhere, as he flayed out, smashing the good along with the bad. He was instrumental in getting Margaret Sanger's books on birth control banned in New York. He had the Dept. of the Interior fire Walt Whitman for *Leaves of Grass*. He had 3,000 persons arrested for obscenity. They ranged from Victoria Woodhull, female candidate for President, to Margaret Sanger's husband, who was charged with selling his wife's books. Only 10% of these victims were eventually convicted. Proudly, he took credit for hounding 16 persons to their deaths, some through fear, others from suicide, all sacrificed to his fanatical puritanism.

In 1913, he told the *New York Evening World:* "In the 41 years I have been here I have convicted persons enough to fill a passenger train of 61 coaches, 60 coaches containing 60 passengers and the 61st almost full. I have destroyed 160 tons of obscene literature."

One of the few times that he met his match was when he tried to remove George Bernard Shaw's play, *Mrs. Warren's Profession*, from the stage. Enraged, Shaw thundered back: "Comstockery is the world's standing joke at the expense of the U.S. It confirms the deep-seated conviction of the Old World that America is a provincial place, a 2nd rate country town."

Comstock's only relaxations were his wife and his hobbies. He had married Margaret Hamilton, daughter of a Presbyterian elder, when he was 27. His senior by 10 years, she weighed 82 lbs., always wore black, rarely ever spoke a word. He had one child by Margaret, a daughter Lillie, who died at 6 months. He and his wife then adopted a newborn girl, Adele, who turned out to be retarded, although he never admitted this fact. (After his death, 40-year-old Adele was confined to an institution.) His other loves were his collections of postage stamps and Japanese vases.

In 1915, President Woodrow Wilson appointed Comstock U.S. delegate to the International Purity Congress meeting at the San Francisco Exposition. At the convention, he weakened himself by "overdoing," contracted pneumonia, returned home, and died. He was buried in Brooklyn's Evergreen Cemetery. His tombstone bore the epitaph: "In memory of a fearless witness."

But columnist Heywood Broun wrote a less sentimental obituary: "Anthony Comstock may have been entirely correct in his assumption that the division of living creatures into male and female was a vulgar mistake, but a conspiracy of silence about the matter will hardly alter the facts."

—I.W.

ENOCH CROSBY (1750–1835). *American spy.*

When James Fenimore-Cooper, aged 30, moved to Scarsdale, N.Y., in 1819, to occupy himself as a gentleman farmer, he had no thought of becoming a writer. He was independently wealthy, he had a whaling boat, he had a family of 5, he had an aversion for New England (he liked to call Plymouth Rock the Blarney Rock), and that seemed enough occupation for one man. But one evening, when his wife lay abed with a minor ailment, and he read aloud to her from a particularly sticky English novel of the period, he was suddenly brushed by the Muse. In a fit of exasperation, he cast the novel aside and exclaimed, "I could write you a better book than that myself!" His wife displayed doubt, and thus goaded, Cooper retired to his desk. In November, 1820, the finished product, published at his own expense, appeared without by-line. It was called, *Precaution*. It dealt with the landed gentry of England, and it was abominable. He had not yet proved his boast, but soon he would.

Before he had published his 1st novel, Cooper had read it aloud to an old friend of his father's, the venerable John Jay, who resided in sprawling Bedford House, situated across the rolling Westchester Hills in Katonah, N.Y. It was Jay's disapproval of *Precaution*, and his suggestion for a 2nd novel, that finally made Cooper a successful author.

At 75, John Jay had behind him an illustrious career, and he enjoyed reliving it for the attentive Cooper. Many evenings, in 1820, the aged patriot would suck at his long pipe and remember his experiences, in his 20s, as one of the 56 delegates to the 1st Continental Congress. He would recollect, too, how he had supported the Declaration of Independence at the next Congress in 1776. His wealth of memory was limitless. He had been the new republic's minister to Spain, he had been its Secretary of Foreign Affairs, and, once, he had been burned in effigy for a treaty with England that opened the Mississippi River to British commerce. After 6 years as chief justice of the Supreme Court, and 6 more as governor of New York, he had retired to Bedford House to develop new varieties of melon.

But Jay's most fascinating reminiscences, for

the budding author, concerned his role in America's 1st system of espionage. During the Revolutionary War, George Washington had allocated $17,000 for secret service work. A Committee of Safety, with John Jay as one of its leaders, employed spies and informers. Many of these, operating in Westchester County, a neutral territory, posed as Tory sympathizers to obtain information from the British, and passed their findings along by means of cipher, invisible ink, and the hanging of clothes from wash lines.

Of the many spies who served the struggling American cause, one in particular had fascinated John Jay. It was this brave man's story that John Jay told to James Fenimore Cooper as a possible basis for a novel. During the critical years of the war, Jay recollected, this man had wandered about Westchester County posing as a shoemaker and a peddler. He had pretended that he was a Tory in support of the British. His family and his friends had despised him for his beliefs and work, and several times the Yankees had almost caught and hung him. Yet, secretly, he had been in the service of General George Washington, sending regular reports to the American Army on the names and activities of English supporters and the disposition of Redcoat troops. When the war ended, his true role had been revealed to a few, and Congress had voted him a special bonus. The last he had refused. He had acted, he said, out of patriotism, and freedom was payment enough.

Cooper was deeply impressed by Jay's story. The patriotism of the little-known spy appealed to him. Cooper tracked the subject further. He invited to his home elderly neighbors, in the country, who had known the Revolutionary War and the spy in question. When Cooper had what he wanted, he sat down and wrote *The Spy: A Tale of the Neutral Ground.* He wrote it, he said, "because I was told I could not write a grave tale; so to prove that the world did not know me, I wrote one so grave nobody could read it." He wrote it rapidly, finishing 60 pages in a few days, and he had his publisher set it up in type as he wrote. After the 1st volume, he lost confidence, and hesitated about continuing the story. But belated reviews from England, lauding his 1st novel, gave him encouragement. He went on. Then his publisher worried that he was running too long and that the project might prove unprofitable. To reassure him, Cooper concluded the last chapter, and permitted it to be set in type, before he attempted the chapters preceding it.

The Spy appeared in December, 1821. It related the life of a lowly peddler of laces named Harvey Birch, who was thought to be a British agent, but was secretly in the service of a Mr. Harper, actually George Washington in disguise.

The Spy was an immediate success. Not only was it read throughout America and England, but it was translated into French, Spanish, German, Italian, and Russian. At a time when Yankee authorship was regarded with condescension, it was hailed as "the 1st living American novel." Its acclaim and sales convinced James Fenimore Cooper that he was an author and encouraged him to produce *The Last of the Mohicans* and *The Deerslayer.*

There was enormous public curiosity about the origin of *The Spy.* Beyond admitting that he had 1st heard the basis of the story from John Jay, and that it was true, Cooper said nothing. Who, then, was really Harvey Birch? Perhaps Cooper knew, but did not choose to tell. Or perhaps he did not know at all, since Jay may have related the spy's exploits without revealing his name, as Cooper several times insisted. Nevertheless, public curiosity was soon to be satisfied. Just 6 years after publication of *The Spy,* the name of the real Harvey Birch was revealed. He was Enoch Crosby, and he still lived, in retirement, on a farm in Carmel, N.Y., aged 77.

The 1st disclosure of the real Harvey Birch occurred in 1827 when old Enoch Crosby was brought to New York to stand as witness in a real estate lawsuit. Upon entering the courtroom, in City Hall, he was recognized, he said, "by an old gentleman, who, not having heard of him for a number of years, supposed (like Jay and Cooper), that Crosby had been, long since, numbered with the dead. After such mutual greetings as are usual on similar occasions, Crosby's old acquaintance turned to the court, and introduced his friend as 'the original Harvey Birch of Mr. Cooper's Spy.'" This meeting, and revelation, was accorded wide publicity in the press. It encouraged the shrewd proprietor of the Lafayette Theatre, who was producing a dramatized version of *The Spy,* to invite the original to see himself on the stage. Crosby attended, sat in a special box, and was introduced to the packed house as "the real spy." He was given a great ovation.

Apparently, the elderly gentleman continued to be treated as a celebrity in New York. For, when he returned to his farm, he wrote a letter to the *Journal of Commerce.* It was published on December 21, 1827, and it read, "Messrs. Editors, It would be an unsatisfactory restraint of my feelings, should I not express my gratitude to the citizens of New-York, for their kind attention to me during my late visit to the city, and particularly to the managers of the theatre, who politely invited me to witness the play called The Spy. I was much gratified with the performance."

Thus, in 1827, the real Harvey Birch was known to the inhabitants of New York. Four years later, he was known throughout the nation. In 1831, a 216-page nonfiction book appeared entitled, *The Spy Unmasked; or, Memoirs of Enoch Crosby, Alias Harvey Birch, The Hero of Mr. Cooper's Tale of the Neutral Ground: Being an authentic account of the secret services which he rendered his country during the Revolutionary War. (Taken from his own lips, in short-hand.) Comprising many interesting facts and anecdotes, never before published. By H. L. Barnum."* The slender volume included a dedication to James F. Cooper, Esq., whose "pen 1st immortalized the subject of the following Memoir," and an autographed engraving of the prototype—big eyes and hooked nose appended to the face of a beaver, with forehead and chin receding briskly from the nose—captioned with the legend, "the true Harvey Birch, Hero of The Spy."

The author of this documentation, the enterprising H. L. Barnum, explained in his preface how he had authenticated the model for *The Spy.* "A gentleman of good standing and respectability," he wrote, "who has filled honorable official stations in the county of Westchester, and who has long enjoyed the friendship and confidence of Mr. Cooper, informed the writer of this article, on the authority of Mr. Cooper himself, that the outline of the character of Harvey Birch, was actually sketched from that of Enoch Crosby; but filled up, partly from imagination, and partly from similar features in the lives of 2 or 3 others, who were also engaged in secret services, during the Revolutionary War. But Mr. Cooper had frequently assured our informant, that, though he had borrowed incidents from the lives of others to complete the portrait, yet Enoch Crosby was certainly the original which he had in his 'mind's eye.'"

Mr. Cooper neither affirmed nor denied this added disclosure. But readers of *The Spy,* in Cooper's lifetime, and critics and biographers since, were almost unanimous in accepting the identification of the prototype. When Enoch Crosby, who did not read fiction in his latter years, was finally persuaded to glance at *The Spy,* he agreed that many incidents in the novel "resembled his own life."

Enoch Crosby was born in Harwich, Mass. His family moved to a farm in Carmel, N.Y., and his father's poverty forced him to leave home to learn a trade. When he departed, with a haversack of clothes, Bible, and a few shillings, his mother wept, but soon he was established as an apprentice cordwainer, and then a shoemaker, in Danbury, Conn. In 1775, he heard the news of the battle of Lexington. He was a lean, muscular 6-footer of 25 years, and anxious to avenge the depredations committed by the Redcoats.

He enlisted in the Continental Army. From New York, with 3,000 other rebels, he was sent on foot and by boat to Lake Champlain in Canada. To the tune of "Yankee Doodle Dandy," he helped in the siege of Fort St. Johns and in the taking of Montreal. Much of the campaign was fought in bitter winter weather, and after several forays Crosby returned to his headquarters ill and underweight. His superior told him he looked more "like a scarecrow than a soldier fit for duty." Crosby replied, with some spirit, that "if I was not able to fight, I might at least frighten the enemy, as he thought I looked like a scarecrow." When his enlistment period expired, shortly after, he made his way back to Danbury to resume the less exacting profession of shoemaker again.

This interlude did not last long. The Declaration of Independence was signed. Crosby chafed for action. In the autumn of 1776, he took up his old musket and headed toward the American lines. Then occurred the accidental meeting that changed the course of his life. "It was towards the close of a warm day," wrote H. L. Barnum, "that he reached a wild and romantic ravine, in the county of Westchester. Here he fell in with a gentleman, who appeared to be traveling in the same direction, and with whom he soon entered into familiar conversation. Among other questions, the stranger inquired, if Crosby was going 'down below?'—to which he readily answered in the affirmative. The interrogator appeared pleased with this reply, and let fall some expressions which plainly indicated that he had 'mistaken his man,' supposing Crosby to be a Loyalist, on his way to join the British army." Crosby kept up his pretense of being pro-British, and was invited to the Tory gentleman's house. There he met many persons who, while pretending to be loyal to the American Revolution, were actually working for England. At the 1st opportunity, Crosby hurried off to the home of a man named Young whom he knew to be a supporter of the Colonial cause. Crosby spilled out his story, and was escorted by his contact to White Plains.

In White Plains resided the 4 patriots who made up George Washington's secret service—the Committee of Safety—under John Jay. Crosby told his story. To test it, Jay dispatched a company of mounted Rangers to hunt down the Tory gentleman and his friends. The hunt was successful and Crosby was congratulated. He was also asked to serve the Revolution in a new capacity. "It is your intention again to serve your country as a private in the ranks," said Jay. "But you must now be convinced that much greater services may be rendered by pursuing a different, though certainly not less hazardous course. The greatest danger which now threatens this country, is from her internal foes." Crosby understood at once. "It is indeed a hazardous part you would have me play. I must become a spy." Jay hastened to reassure him. "In appearance only. Our bleeding country requires such service at this momentous crisis." Crosby's decision was immediate. "I will be that man. I have counted the cost, and am aware of the danger. I know that I must be content to endure reproach, obloquy, and detestation; to cover my poor doting parents with shame and misery, and incur the hatred of those I dearest love. Perhaps to suffer an ignominious death, and leave a name of infamy behind. I know it all, and yet I will not shrink from the task."

When Enoch Crosby left White Plains, he left as The Spy. His musket was discarded. Instead, he carried a peddler's pack containing the tools of a shoemaker. In the lining of his vest was a signed pass, revealing his true identity and loyalty. "It must never be exhibited," he had been warned, "save in the last extremity." He went on the road as a pro-British cobbler. His secret assignment was to expose 5th columnists and to send back reports on the activities of British forces.

His success was remarkable. One night, seeking lodging in a farmhouse, he was admitted by a woman who wanted her son to have new shoes before he joined the British army. Crosby indicated that he was sympathetic to the Crown. He was shown the hideout, in a cave concealed by hay, of 50 Loyalists. While his hostess slept, Crosby stole off to White Plains, reported to John Jay, and returned to his lodgings before dawn. The next evening, while Crosby and the Loyalists held a meeting, the American Rangers struck. All hands were captured, Crosby among them. While being marched to a prison, Crosby was recognized by a childhood tutor who "started with terror and astonishment, on beholding his favorite pupil, the son of his dearest friend, manacled like a felon, and dragged to prison, with a gang of unprincipled wretches, under the ignominious charge of treason to their country." A few days later Crosby had his next assignment and an opportunity to escape. He went out a prison window, and into a swamp, while 4 musket shots were conveniently fired over his head. Harvey Birch, under the same circumstances, evaded "50 pistols."

Soon, Enoch Crosby, posing as one John Smith, "a faithful friend to His Majesty," was manufacturing shoes at a farm 12 mi. beyond the Hudson River and volunteering to join 30 neighbors who were going over to the British. A note was sent posthaste to John Jay. It was acknowledged by the trusty Rangers, who made captive the 30 and Crosby again. Returned to his stone prison, Crosby was rescued by a serving maid named Charity. She drugged the captain of the Rangers, took his keys, intoxicated the prison guard with brandy, opened the cell, and freed Crosby.

After that, as Crosby recollected, he was "hunted like a beast of the forest by one party—suspected and avoided by the other" so that "he felt himself, at times, an outcast in the world—a houseless wanderer, without a country or a home!" Only once, in all his adventures, when trapped by Americans in a tavern, was he forced to display his pass from John Jay. Meanwhile, the British had become suspicious. They realized that wherever the wandering shoemaker appeared, the Rangers followed soon after. Crosby hid out in the Highlands with a brother-in-law who knew of his activity. Someone fired a shot at Crosby through a window. Thereafter, he slept with a loaded musket in his bed. Days later, a gang of assassins broke into the house in search of the spy. One, a "large hideous looking fellow," rushed the awakened Crosby, firing at him and missing. Crosby leaped to his feet, floored his attacker with a punch, before being beaten insensible by 3 others. Crosby's life was saved when neighbors, aroused by the commotion, chased the gang away. James Fenimore Cooper employed this incident when he had Harvey Birch assaulted by a gang known as the Skinners.

Crosby now sought the comparative safety of the Continental Army, where he served as an officer under Lafayette. With the successful end of the Revolution, he retired to his father's farm in Carmel, N.Y. He married twice, had 4 children, and for 28 years served as justice of the peace in the township of Southeast. He had received $250 as his military mustering-out pay. In 1794, at the instigation of John Jay, he was offered a special bonus for his undercover work. He declined the gift, stating, "It was not for gold that I served my country." His simple patriotism, as much as his courage, stimulated Cooper in the creation of the 1st great adventure novel written by an American author.

—I.W.

John F. "Honey Fitz" Fitzgerald (1863–1951). *Political boss.*

One of the most colorful politicians of modern times, founder of an American political dynasty, Fitzgerald was born in Boston's North End, the son of Irish immigrants. Like many other Irish Americans of his generation, he grew up in a red brick tenement and received much of his education in the streets.

In the Boston of the 1880s the Irish may have constituted a majority of the city's population, but they remained largely under the thumb of the Yankee aristocracy. Fitzgerald's 1st step in politics was to prove himself a "regular fellow" to his Irish neighbors in the North End. He became active in the Ancient

Order of Hibernians, the St. Alphonsus Association, the Knights of St. Rose, the Neptune Associates, the Catholic Union of Boston, and dozens of other religious and fraternal organizations.

All this sociability paid off in 1892 when young Fitzgerald, who had been earning his living in the insurance business, got himself elected to the Boston Common Council. He now set out to consolidate his position and establish himself as boss of the North End. In a shabby upstairs office, he set up the "Jefferson Club," where anyone with a problem was free to drop in at any time. He kept an indexed card file of everyone in his district who needed a job. At Thanksgiving and Christmas he was on hand with food baskets that contained, among other things, a festive turkey. No wedding took place in the North End without a prominently displayed gift from Johnny Fitzgerald. Each morning he scanned the death notices in the papers, and he never missed a wake.

Before long, Fitzgerald was ready to announce his candidacy for the Massachusetts State Senate. In the course of his campaign, the flattering phrase "Dear old North End" tripped so easily and so frequently from Fitzgerald's tongue that his North End supporters became known as "Dearos." To his opponents, the talkative young politico was known as "Fitzblarney."

On Election Day, the Dearos came through and sent their man to the State Senate. In his new position, Fitzgerald distinguished himself primarily by sponsoring Columbus Day as a State holiday in order to please the thousands of Italian immigrants who were then arriving in Boston. He also used his State House connections to place a horde of relatives and supporters in comfortable state jobs.

This record of accomplishment was more than enough to please the Dearos. In 1894, they sent their favorite to the U.S. Congress. Fitzgerald served in Washington for an undistinguished 3 terms.

Meanwhile, the Yankee establishment in Boston quaked at the prospect of John Fitzgerald and his Dearos moving into city hall, and in the mayoral election of 1905, they united behind a Republican blue blood to stop him. This well-meaning Harvard man, Louis Frothingham, had nearly all of Boston's "respectable" element behind him, but once on the streets, he never knew what hit him. For weeks, Fitzgerald made 10 speeches every night, denouncing his opponents as anti-Catholic, anti-Irish, and un-American. He toured the wards in a large red car, followed by flying squads of what the reporters described as "Napoleon's Lancers."

The result was predictable enough—Johnny

Fitzgerald and his Dearos marched into city hall with the zeal of an occupying army. The new mayor made spectacular changes in the way the city was governed. A saloonkeeper replaced a physician on the Board of Health. Another saloonkeeper became superintendent of public buildings. A whitewasher, the superintendent of sewers, and a bartender who had been expelled from the legislature, the superintendent of streets. For deserving Dearos, Fitzgerald created new positions such as city dermatologist. Civil service was easily circumvented by the invention of novel job categories—rubber boot repairers, tea warmers, tree climbers, wipers, watchmen to watch other watchmen.

Fitzgerald made no apologies for the graft in his administration, and as a result he was thrown out of office by a "good government" coalition in 1907. The Republicans kept their pledge to "clean up the mess in City Hall," but after 2 years of this antiseptic government, the voters became so bored that they longed for the return of the colorful Fitzgerald.

Fitzgerald's opponent in the next round was New England's wealthiest banker, another Harvard blue blood named James Jackson Storrow. Storrow spent over half a million dollars on his own campaign, but Fitzgerald turned even this fact to his advantage. The slogan "Manhood against Money" was used beneath a touchingly domestic photograph of Fitzgerald and his brood. The most dramatic event of the campaign occurred during a huge rally one warm Saturday night in "the dear old North End." Fitzgerald had hired a brass band for the occasion and had instructed them to play "The Star-Spangled Banner" and "The Wearing of the Green" when he walked onto the platform. Both songs were concluded, however, before Johnny Fitzgerald had finished with his handshaking, and so the bandleader struck up "Sweet Adeline," a popular favorite of the day. With his face beaming, Fitzgerald came up to the edge of the platform and sang the song solo, then led the crowd in the chorus. At that moment, the "Honey Fitz" legend was born. "Sweet Adeline" and the "honey-sweet voice" in which Fitzgerald sang it became his trademarks, and at every public occasion he was obliged to sing the song at least once.

Needless to say, Fitzgerald won the election and served a final term as mayor of Boston. For a while, Honey Fitz toyed with the idea of running for reelection, but he was rudely shouldered aside by the brash young upstart, James Michael Curley, boss of the South Side. In order to attack Fitzgerald, Curley announced a series of "educational" lectures contrasting famous characters in history with John F. Fitzgerald. His 1st lecture, given at Dorchester High School, was on "Graft in Ancient Times v. Graft in Modern Times" and featured a comparison between the Rome of the Decadent Ancients and the Boston of the Dearos. The title of the next lecture—"Great Lovers: from Cleopatra to Tootles"—alluded to the unsubstantiated rumors of a romance between Mayor Fitzgerald and a blond cigarette girl named Tootles Ryan. Before Curley could deliver this knockout blow, Honey Fitz withdrew as a candidate.

In the years that followed, Fitzgerald ran for various public offices (including that of U.S. senator), but he never won an election again.

While Fitzgerald was still riding high, he formed a temporary alliance with Patrick "P.J." Kennedy, a genial saloonkeeper and political rival. The alliance was solidified when Kennedy's ambitious son, Joseph, married Fitzgerald's beautiful daughter, Rose. This marriage combining 2 of the great families of old-time Boston machine politics, produced 3 notable brothers—John F., Robert, and Edward ("Teddy") Kennedy—who have put their marks on American history.

Fitzgerald spent much of his time in his declining years watching the progress of his grandson and namesake, John Fitzgerald Kennedy. When in 1948 the young man decided to run for Congress from his grandfather's old district, Honey Fitz was overjoyed. Grandson and grandfather spent hours together laying plans and recalling political sagas of the past. Young Kennedy was swept into office, and at the victory celebration Honey Fitz, aged 85, danced an Irish jig on a tabletop, sang "Sweet Adeline" in a quavering voice, and predicted for all to hear that his grandson would become President of the U.S. Unfortunately, the old man did not live to see his prediction come true. He died in 1951, 9 years before his grandson was elected President. But John F. Kennedy did not forget the old man. When he entered the White House, he renamed the presidential yacht *The Honey Fitz* in honor of his remarkable grandfather.

—M.S.M.

MARY "Mother Jones" HARRIS (1830–1930). *Labor organizer.*

Born in Cork, Ireland, Mary Harris was the daughter of Richard and Helen Harris, who emigrated to Canada. Although her school years were spent in Toronto, where her father's work as a railway construction laborer had taken the family, she was proud when she became an American.

As a young woman, Mary alternated between teaching and dressmaking. Teaching led her to Memphis, Tenn., where she married a member of the Iron Holders' Union, a man named Jones, who then lured her to Chicago, where the great Chicago Fire in 1871 destroyed all of her possessions, as well as the dressmaking establishment she had built up with a partner. There, she had worked on the wardrobes of wealthy families. But her destiny was interwoven with the fabric of national history. Patterns of wealth and power, poverty and helplessness, took shape as America changed from a land of farms to a modern industrial country. Unskilled native and immigrant laborers, and their wives and children, bore the heaviest burden of progress. In this period, from about 1870 to 1920, Mary Jones roamed up and down the land, agitating, organizing, preaching a gospel of justice and dignity for the working man wherever these were sadly lacking.

To railroad workers in Pittsburgh, as well as to coal miners in West Virginia, Pennsylvania, and Colorado, she was a familiar sight as she went about organizing local unions and walkouts, educating and aiding the workers. Cotton mill workers in the North and in the South, streetcar and garment strikers in New York City, steel and copper workers, all came within the orbit of her concern. Wherever depressed conditions were found, or there was a struggle to better such conditions, she appeared. But for the most part, Mother Jones put her heart and soul into the plight of the coal miners. Working as a paid organizer for the United Mine Workers, she was a prime mover in the unionization of coal workers in West Virginia. In Colorado to investigate conditions caused by the Colorado Fuel and Iron Co., a Rockefeller subsidiary, she went to coal camps disguised as a peddler. As she put it: "I then got myself an old calico dress, a sunbonnet, some pins and needles, elastic and tape and such sundries, and went down to the southern coal fields of the Colorado Fuel and Iron Co."

She soon discovered that a feudal system existed in which there was company ownership of whole towns—including their schools, churches, and newspapers—and the prevalence of such questionable practices as payment of wages in scrip instead of cash. The miners wanted an 8-hour day plus other reforms. Under militia control, strikers suffered atrocities, deportations, and even murder. The bitter struggle flared again some years later, accompanied by more violence. Mother Jones was shocked by the Ludlow Massacre of April 20, 1914, in which 20 persons died. Some of these victims, who had been living in a miners' tent colony, were mere children. Mother Jones related this story to audiences across the country.

During the Ludlow strike, Mother Jones was pulled off a train by guardsmen and then held incommunicado for 9 weeks. She headed right back to the scene of danger as soon as she was released, a move which ended with her illegal arrest and imprisonment. Of this, she said: "I was put in the cellar under the courthouse. It was a cold, terrible place, without heat, damp and dark. I slept in my clothes by day, and at night I fought great sewer rats with a beer bottle." There she languished for 26 days. But this time the miners won better conditions, although collective bargaining was still not achieved.

In Arnot, Pa., this redoubtable senior citizen attracted national attention when she led a march of women who, armed with brooms and mops, sent strikebreakers fleeing in all directions. These women stood guard at the mines day and night, to see that no scabs went in. Under one arm, each carried a broom or a mop. In the other arm, each cradled a baby wrapped in little blankets. The heroism of their mothers, inspired by Mother Jones, ensured these babies a better future. This thought must have offered some consolation to Mother Jones, who had lost her own 4 small children in the yellow fever epidemic which swept Memphis, Tenn., in 1867. The epidemic had also claimed the life of her husband.

Mother Jones worked in Alabama textile mills to see whether the gruesome tales of child labor were true. She saw 6-year-olds, who looked gaunt and aged, working 8-hour shifts for 10¢ a day, and 4-year-olds who had been brought in to help the older children without pay. In a factory in Tuscaloosa, run entirely by child labor, she saw the fragile bodies of 6- and 7-year-old children crawling inside and under dangerous machinery, oiling and cleaning. Many times a hand was crushed or a finger was snapped off. Sometimes these children fell asleep and then cold water was dashed in their faces.

Mother Jones boarded with a family in Selma. Their 11-year-old daughter, who worked in the mill, died when her hair got caught in some machinery and her scalp was torn off. On Sunday, the day before the accident, the youngster had been invited to go on an outing with a group of mill children. She had refused, saying, "I'm so tired. I just want to sleep forever."

Mother Jones moved on to Kensington, Pa., where textile workers, including 10,000 children, were on strike. Maimed children filed into Union Headquarters, some with hands or thumbs missing, or finger off at a knuckle. With their parents' consent, Mother Jones gathered an army of about 75 boys and girls to importune President Theodore Roosevelt in person about passing a law to prohibit their exploitation. Each child took a knife and fork, a tin cup and a plate, in a knapsack. They carried banners, and for a band, had a drum and fife. In a holiday mood, this children's crusade set out from Philadelphia, passed through New Jersey and moved on to New York. Farmers gave them food. People gave them clothes and money. Trainmen gave them free rides. Mass meetings on the horrors of child labor were held in cities along the way. Mother Jones spoke at a rally opposite the campus of Princeton University. She persuaded the mayor of New York to let them enter the city. At Coney Island, the owner of a wild animal show invited her to speak. She put the children in empty cages and they clung to the iron bars while she talked to the crowd about their servitude.

They marched on to Oyster Bay, the home of President Roosevelt. He refused to see them. Meanwhile, the strike of the textile workers in Kensington had been lost, and the children went back to work. But not for long. Aroused public opinion led the Pennsylvania legislature to pass a new child labor law, and this one was enforced. Children by the thousands returned home from the mills, and additional thousands were kept out of factories until they were 14.

As *The New York Times* editorialized when Mother Jones died November 30, 1930, at the age of 100, "Her special faculty was the arrangement of pageants of poverty, processions of the ill-used." Mother Jones was a centenarian Joan of Arc, a saint with whom she has often been compared.

—R.Ho.

"Wild Bill" HICKOK (1837–1876). *Legendary western lawman.*

He was born James Butler Hickok on a farm in La Salle County, Ill. After distinguished service as an Indian scout for the Army, he turned up at Fort Riley, Kans., where he was appointed a U.S. deputy marshal in 1866. His major responsibility was rounding up army deserters and horse thieves, but the record of his service is not clear. In August, 1869, Wild Bill was elected sheriff of Ellis County, Kans., and he soon developed the reputation of being one of the best gunmen—and most colorful characters—in all of Kansas Territory.

Bill's physical appearance contributed significantly to his fame. While most of his fellow lawmen favored rough-and-ready dress, Wild Bill was a notorious dandy. He was fond of elegantly tailored European-style suits with fancy satin lapels, and liked to show off his collection of colorful silk ties. Along with 2 6-guns he carried on his hips, he also sported a knife thrust into a bright red sash. His most striking feature was his hair. This he wore below shoulder length, carefully formed into little ringlets that were kept in place by the use of fragrant hair oil. His long, drooping moustache was waxed, and it twirled up at the ends.

As early as 1866, Wild Bill boasted to a reporter that he had personally killed "considerably over 100 men" (not counting Indians, of course) and as sheriff of Ellis County,

Hickok had a chance to improve upon his record. Once, in Solomon, Kans., a pair of murderers fled from him—one running up the street and the other running down the street in the opposite direction. Wild Bill fired at the 2 men simultaneously and killed them both. During a visit to Topeka in 1870, Wild Bill boasted so loud and so long about his abilities with a 6-gun, that no less a man than Buffalo Bill Cody decided to put him to the test. Cody threw his hat into the air, taunting his rival to hit it more than once. Wild Bill drew his 6-gun and, before the hat hit the ground, had shot a row of evenly spaced holes along the edge of the brim.

In 1871, Wild Bill arrived in Abilene, one of the most celebrated cow towns in American history. This was the peak year for Abilene. More than 600,000 cattle would pass through its yards on the way to eastern markets, and all summer long, hundreds of cowboys, weary from months on the trail would squander a full year's wages in the brothels, saloons, gambling houses, and other amusements to be found in the bustling little metropolis. Wild Bill, already a legendary figure, was appointed marshal of Abilene and ordered to "clean up" the town. But even though Wild Bill continued to indulge in brawls and gunfights, he found it easier to accept protection money from pimps and gamblers than to interfere in their business. Wild Bill had originally come to Abilene to earn his living playing cards at the Alamo saloon. After he was appointed marshal, he continued this activity at the Alamo most afternoons, and could be found in the town's red light district nearly every night.

While the "respectable elements" in Abilene complained about their marshal's behavior, Bill continued to pose as a defender of righteousness. But finally, he overplayed his hand. On the night of October 5, 1871, a bunch of drunken cowboys were hurrahing the town of Abilene in their time-honored fashion—forcing clothing merchants to outfit poorly clad strangers, obliging passersby to stand drinks for all regulars. Wild Bill left the poker table at the Alamo long enough to ask the drunks to quiet down. No sooner had the marshal returned to the saloon and picked up his cards, than he heard someone fire a shot. He ran out into the darkness and killed a harmless Texan named Phil Coe, and then, hearing someone running up behind him, he turned around in time to plug his own deputy, one Mike Williams. For the good citizens of Abilene, this incident was the last straw. Wild Bill was relieved of official duties a few weeks later and forced to leave town.

Lacking the capital needed to pursue his career as a professional gambler, he decided to trade on his notoriety. He joined the Wild West Show organized by his old friend Buffalo Bill Cody. Before long, however, Wild Bill found this work not only tiresome but degrading, and he quit the show to strike out on his own. In June, 1876, a Kansas newspaper reported a story just in from Fort Laramie, Wyo. The great Wild Bill Hickok had been "arrested on several occasions as a vagrant, having no visible means of support."

Later that same month, Bill came riding into Deadwood, S. Dak., accompanied by Calamity Jane, the notorious alcoholic Amazon of Western legend. It is possible that Calamity was Wild Bill's mistress, but considering contemporary descriptions of her mannish body and strikingly homely face, it seems more likely that they were only trail companions. In any event, while Calamity settled down to her customary full-time drinking, Bill established himself at the poker table in "Saloon Number 10" along the main street. On the afternoon of August 2, 1876, a young man named Jack McCall came into the saloon and interrupted Wild Bill's card game by shooting him in the back of the head. The bullet passed straight through Bill's brain, exited from his cheek, and struck the left forearm of one Captain Massey, a river boat pilot who had been sitting across the table from Bill. Wild Bill held onto his cards as he died. He had 2 pairs, aces and 8s, a combination known ever since as "the dead man's hand."

—M.S.M.

BURTON HOLMES (1870–1958). *World traveler.*

He drove the 1st motorcar in Denmark, and peddled the 1st bicycle ever seen on the island of Corsica. He took the 1st motion pictures inside China and Japan, and rode the trans-Siberian railroad across Russia while they were still laying the track.

For more than 60 years, the brisk little man with the impeccable Van Dyke turned up in some of the oddest places. He was in Rheims for the world's 1st aviation meet. He was in Athens when the 1st modern Olympic games were held in 1896. When the 1st war films were taken (an insurrection in the Philippines, 1899), Holmes was holding the camera. He was also on the scene, cranking his Kodak, during the last great eruption of Mount Vesuvius. And the opening of Yellowstone Park? Queen Victoria's Jubilee? Haile Selassie's coronation? Holmes was always there.

He gave the language a new word: travelogue. In 56 summers abroad he crossed the Atlantic Ocean 30 times, the Pacific 20, and circumnavigated the globe 6 times gathering material for his films and lecture shows.

His grandfather made a bundle introducing

the sturdy settlers of early Chicago to the delights of French foods and fine wines. Father didn't do badly either. He loaned George Pullman the capital he needed to convert day coaches to sleeping cars. So, by the time Burton came along, he enjoyed the financial wherewithal to indulge his every fancy.

And Burton fancied cameras. He lugged his 1st clumsy box model abroad at 16 to see Europe with his grandmother. He was never good for the sedentary life thereafter. The next year he and Grandma saw California, Cuba, and Europe again. When the Chicago Camera Club, of which he was secretary, needed to boost its treasury, Burton agreed to show travel slides and give a running commentary. He took in $350 for the Camera Club the 1st night and went into business for himself soon afterward.

One of the most remarkable one-man shows in entertainment history had begun. Before it was over, he would earn more than $5 million.

Holmes improved on black-and-white "magic lantern" slides by using glass slides he had hand painted by local artisans while visiting Japan. He was one of the 1st to show movies commercially. He interspersed his travel lectures with jerky, 25-second reels of "The Omaha Fire Department Responds to an Alarm," or "A Police Parade in Chicago," or "Neapolitans Eating Spaghetti." Later he would use talkies, technicolor, radio, and in 1944 television.

For more than a half century he was a man in almost constant motion. He kayaked in the Klondike, rode rickshaws in Rangoon and ponies across the Peloponnesus. He told an interviewer in 1939 his travel expenses averaged 50¢ a day.

In spite of it all, Holmes considered himself a conventional sightseer. "Let others blaze the trails," he once said, "I'm just a Cook's tourist, a little ahead of the crowds, but not too far."

He was a trifle eccentric. From the Far East he brought a fortune in Buddhas, temple bells, and altar pieces to turn his Manhattan penthouse into a splendiferous oriental shrine. He called it "Nirvana." Visitors would likely as not find their host knocking about Nirvana casually garbed in pith helmet and cape, or Arab burnoose, a Japanese kimono, or Korean yangban. Five years before Pearl Harbor, he sold Nirvana for $2 million to Robert ("Believe It or Not") Ripley. He moved to Hollywood where he made travelogues under contract for MGM and Paramount.

Holmes avoided politics, but was known to hold that return to the gold standard would be the salvation of the Western world. He could also get exercised over Prohibition which he considered an affront to civilized living.

His travelogues always focused on what was pleasant and comfortable, studiously avoiding controversy and the uglier side of foreign lands. He filmed bullfights in Mexico but never showed the kill. He declined to show European scenes during W.W. II, saying: "I don't think my public would be interested. There's too much rubble and misery over there now. I'll wait until it's tourist time again."

For all his wanderings abroad, he always recommended seeing America 1st, and was particularly enthusiastic about Monticello, West Point, and the pueblo cities of the American Southwest. But when pressed, he would allow that the island of Bali is "one quaint spot where you can really get away from it all." He was less discriminating when choosing a honeymoon retreat. Holmes and his bride went to Atlantic City.

Summing up a lifetime of passenger tickets, steamer trunks, and unfamiliar surroundings he said: "The traveler possesses the world more completely than those who own vast properties. Owners become slaves of what they own. Travelers possess—and pass on to possess in other lands—all that appeals to them, for as long as they like. Then they pass on to fresh fields and let the owners stay behind and pay the taxes."

Advanced age slowed the ubiquitous Holmes, but not much. He continued active travels and lecture tours until he was 78. He was senior adviser to Burton Holmes Travelogues for another 8 years. Two years after full retirement he was dead. His remains were cremated, at his request, and stored in his favorite Siamese urn. Once, while contemplating what lay beyond the grave, Holmes radiated on the potentials for returning with the ultimate travelogue. "How I could pack them in with that one!" he cried.

Before her death in 1968, Margaret Oliver Holmes completed the enormous task of organizing her husband's library. Today the entire Holmes Collection—photographs, films, books, and memorabilia—can be seen at the offices of Burton Holmes, Inc., located at 8853 Sunset Blvd., Hollywood, Calif. The company, under the direction of Robert M. Mallett and Robert R. Hollingsworth, was incorporated in 1954 "to carry on the work Burton Holmes had started—bringing the world to audiences everywhere."

—D.P.P.

Joe Knowles (18??–1942). *Naturalist.*

Unsuccessful as a portrait painter, Joe Knowles captured the imagination of the country when he ventured out into the forest undressed, unarmed, and unaided to demonstrate that civilized man had not grown too soft to cope with nature. Not much is known about Joe prior to 1913 when he confided one of his dreams to a newspaper reporter. "I dreamt I was lost in the woods, alone and naked, with no hope ever of getting out." Joe then transformed his dream into reality—with the help of the Hearst newspapers—and thereby created a front-page story that held the nation spellbound.

The Hearst papers actually passed up an opportunity to sponsor Joe's 1st sensational adventure. Knowles initially suggested his "Man Against Nature" experiment to Hearst's *Boston American* but was rejected; the reasons behind the rejection are still unclear. As a result, Knowles took his idea to the *American*'s somewhat moribund competitor, the *Boston Post*. Seeking to reestablish its slumping circulation, the *Post* snatched the chance to launch what it called a test of 20th-century man's ability to combat nature in the raw.

On August 4, 1913, Joe Knowles—attired only in a breechclout—plunged into the wilderness of northern Maine, and for the next 61 days New England, New York, and every other area served by the *Post*'s special syndication followed the exploits of this atavistic adventurer. Displaying a definite gift for showmanship, Joe left birchbark messages at intervals timed to keep readers fascinated.

The *Post*'s circulation figures more than doubled as Joe's terse notes revealed that he lived on roots and berries and made sandals out of bark. Later he caught and cooked some trout, then killed a deer with his hands and made moccasins from the hide; he even snagged a bear in a crude pit he dug with his hands. City dwellers could barely wait for the next installment to read of Joe's exploits.

Knowles got word, however, that the game wardens were not as entranced with his activities as were the newspaper readers. Killing animals without a license was still against the law whether you did it with a gun or with your hands. Pursued by the wardens, Joe crossed into Canada, where he faced no further harassment. Again came the notes left in forked saplings for the reporters who were covering the story. Later on, Joe started leaving charcoal sketches and even a painting that he apparently did to fill idle hours.

On October 10, Joe Knowles came back to civilization looking healthy, tanned, and none the worse for his 2-month sojourn in the woods. He had seemingly surmounted all the rigors of nature; now, however, he would have to contend with the deceits of man.

The *Boston American* released a story— "complete exposé" the paper called it—claiming that Joe Knowles was not the Nature Man he and the *Boston Post* had portrayed him to be. Instead, the whole adventure had been rigged, and Joe had spent 2 very comfortable months in an abandoned logging camp enjoying nearly all the comforts of home. Although the *American* killed the story when faced with a court injunction brought by the *Post*, an early edition carrying the exposé reached well into New England. Charges and countercharges shook Boston and the countryside, and Joe Knowles's reputation as "a naked man against the tooth and claw of nature" was tainted with the scent of fraud.

The one unquestioned triumph of Joe Knowles's adventure—the enormous circulation boost given to the *Boston Post*—was not lost upon the Hearst newspaper management, despite the attempts of Hearst's *Boston American* to discredit the whole affair. The following year (1914), the *San Francisco Examiner*—another Hearst newspaper—sponsored a west-coast version of what Joe had done in the Maine woods. The *Examiner* employed 2 academicians to verify Joe's primitive life-style as he plunged into the Siskiyou Mountains of Oregon for 60 days. He took no clothing, food, weapons, or any other vestige of civilization; the Nature Man was back at it again.

It was July 20, 1914, when Joe set off on his 2nd great adventure. Western newspaper readers found themselves as entranced as their counterparts in New England had been. Again, Joe's messages—picked up by the professors in remote areas of the mountains—testified to his living on fish and small game as well as to his plans to capture and kill a deer. Joe dominated the headlines for a week, until his bad luck caught up with him again.

On July 28, W.W. I began when an Austrian prince was assassinated in the tiny country of Serbia. As the Russian army mobilized, the Germans declared war, and the French and British decided to oppose the powers of Central Europe, the headlines were given over to these earthshaking events. The story of Joe Knowles was pushed to the back pages. Since there seemed little point in persisting in an adventure that thrived on the manna of newspaper sales, Joe returned from his retreat in the Siskiyou Mountains.

There was to be one more stunt, however, before Joe Knowles would hang up his breechclout. Hearst was not discouraged when the war ruined his fine gambit of sensational journalism—far from it. He was convinced that Joe could work wonders for newspaper circulation, and he sent Knowles to New York in 1916 for another atavistic attempt.

A new wrinkle was added this time. A female counterpart, also nude (they were the Dawn Man and the Dawn Woman), would enter the woods at the same time but in a different location. They were not to make contact with each other in the woods. Joe trained the Dawn Woman in basic woodcraft and survival techniques prior to their great adventure, but she could manage to last only 7 days by herself in the wilds of Essex County, N.Y. Since all the publicity had centered on the fact that this was a Nature Couple, when the Dawn Woman gave up Joe saw no point in persisting. He, too, came out of the woods.

Joe Knowles, his wilderness adventures over, returned to his paintings and etchings. Living in a remote area along the Pacific Coast in Washington, he refused to answer letters about his experiments in atavism. As a result, the man who had captured headlines and thrilled millions faded quickly from public attention and died quite forgotten on October 21, 1942.
—J.L.K.

CARRY NATION (1846–1911). *Militant temperance leader.*

Carry Nation, the saloon-smashing Amazon at the turn of the century, was born in Kentucky. She was well equipped by Providence for the career of destruction to which the Lord summoned her: She stood nearly 6′ tall and weighed more than 175 lbs.

Carry learned from personal experience that whiskey could destroy a man's life. After marrying a physician at the age of 21, she watched helplessly while her husband drank himself to death within 2 years.

By the time she remarried in 1879, Carry had determined to devote her life to a crusade against alcohol. Her new husband, David Nation, was an itinerant preacher and lawyer who wandered with his new wife from town to town in the Midwest. When they settled in Medicine Lodge, Kans., Carry was elected county chairman of the Women's Christian Temperance Union.

At this point in history, Kansas was technically a "dry" State, but the law was generally disregarded and saloons flourished in every city and town. Carry Nation was naturally disgusted at such hypocrisy and she wrote passionate letters of protest to the governor, the attorney general, the sheriff of Barber County, and to various local newspapers. When she received not a single response, she decided to take matters into her own hands. After a period of prayer and divination, she heard a voice from above, which she later described in her autobiography. "Take something in your hands," she was told, "and throw at those places and smash them!"

Carry knew how to follow orders. The next day—June 5, 1900—singing hymns and full of holy fire, she picked up a collection of bricks and stones from her backyard and wrapped them in old newspapers. Then she hitched up the buggy and drove to the town of Kiowa, nearly 20 mi. away.

As she walked into one of the town's saloons,

the men at the bar turned in amazement to see this 54-year-old woman, dressed in black, invading their all-male inner sanctum.

"Men," Carry announced, "I have come to save you from a drunkard's fate!" Without further ado, she began heaving her stones with stunning accuracy. Within minutes, every bottle in the place had been smashed, not to mention the mirror behind the bar and both of the front windows.

Carry resolved to move on to bigger and better things, and turned her sights to "the murder mills of the metropolis of Wichita." Her 1st target was the most elegant bar in all of Kansas, located in the basement of the Hotel Carey. This establishment featured a huge, $1,500 plate-glass mirror, surrounded by hundreds of sparkling electric lights. There was also a popular painting ("for men only") entitled *Cleopatra at the Bath.* When Carry Nation beheld this lewd work of art she stopped dead in her tracks. She reflected—so she wrote later—that woman is stripped of everything by the saloons. Her husband is torn from her. She is robbed of her sons. Then they take away her clothes and her dignity. Trembling with rage, Carry approached the bartender.

"Young man," she demanded, "what are you doing in this hellhole?"

"I'm sorry, madam," he answered, "but we do not serve ladies."

"Serve *me?*" screamed Carry. "Do you think I'd drink your hellish poison?" She waved a furious finger at Cleopatra. "Take that filthy thing down and close this murder mill!"

When her request was ignored, Carry set to work. A barrage of rocks shattered the immense mirror and tore the offending canvas. "Glory to God!" she shouted, "Peace on earth, good will to men!"

Terrified, the drinkers and bartender managed to escape through the rear doorway as Carry began overturning tables and slashing chairs. She sent row upon row of bottles crashing to the floor. When Detective Massey of the Wichita Police arrived on the scene, she had lifted one of the finest and biggest brass cuspidors (spittoons) in Kansas to the top of the cherrywood bar and was beating it furiously.

"Madam," said the officer, "I must arrest you for defacing property."

"Defacing?" she screamed. "I am defacing nothing! I am destroying!"

In the trial that followed, many Kansas citizens rallied to Carry Nation's defense. After all, the establishments she had dismantled were supposed to be illegal under Kansas law. When the charges against her were finally dropped, Carry had won a moral victory as well as a good deal of national publicity.

In the next year alone, Carry launched

more than 20 successful raids and became the most notorious female in the U.S. The mere mention of her name was enough to strike terror in a saloonkeeper's heart and when she arrived in a town the taverns would either close down for the day or hire a special detachment of armed guards. As her rampage continued, Carry perfected her technique. She began to use metal hatchets in her work of destruction and these hatchets soon became her trademark. She was arrested more than 30 times for her escapades, and she paid her fines with proceeds from the sale of souvenir hatchets inscribed with her name. During some of her raids, this motherly woman accomplished prodigious feats of strength: She tore icebox doors clean off their hinges, and once ripped a huge cash register off its moorings on a bar, hoisted it over her head, and sent it sailing halfway across the room. On one occasion, a courageous barkeep attempted to defend his premises at gunpoint. Carry, undaunted, swung at his head with her hatchet and the foolhardy male dropped his weapon and ran.

As her notoriety grew, Carry took to the lecture circuit, speaking across the U.S. on the vices of alcohol. She even began publication of a weekly newspaper, *The Hatchet.* Women throughout the country were inspired by Carry's example, and saloon-smashers sprang up in many cities. Few, however, could rival Carry in terms of devastating effectiveness.

When she was 63 years old, she undertook one of her most ambitious raids in Washington, D.C., wreaking havoc in the famous barroom of the Union depot with the aid of 3 hatchets named "Faith, Hope, and Charity."

Carry's last raid took place in Butte, Mont., in 1910. A few months later she collapsed while speaking against saloons and saloon-keepers in Eureka Spring, Ark., and died in Evergreen Hospital, Leavenworth, Kans., on June 9, 1911.

—M.S.M.

CHARLES H. PARKHURST (1842–1933).
Clergyman and reformer.

A seemingly mild-mannered and scholarly Presbyterian clergyman, Charles Parkhurst shocked New York City in the 1890s when he launched a spirited crusade against police corruption, political connections with the underworld, and all forms of urban vice. Born in Framingham, Mass., Parkhurst lived the simple life of a farmboy until he displayed unusual scholarly ability. He was graduated from Amherst College in 1866 after having been rejected for service during the Civil War due to his severe nearsightedness. Following a trip to Germany to study theology, Parkhurst returned to teach Greek and Latin in Massachu-

setts high schools, but at the urging of an Amherst professor Parkhurst entered the ministry in 1874.

After preaching for 6 years at the Congregational Church in Lenox, Mass., Parkhurst was appointed pastor of the Madison Square Presbyterian Church in New York City. He preached his 1st sermon there in 1880, but it is fair to say that he created few waves and attracted little attention until February 14, 1892, when he delivered a blistering jeremiad directed at Tammany Hall and the entire New York municipal administration.

"They are a lying, perjured, rum-soaked, and libidinous lot," he roared to his congregation and to the reporter from the *New York World* who had received a tip that an extraordinary sermon would be delivered there that morning. The next day, the *World* published much of the sermon, and readers were astonished to find that a Presbyterian minister was charging the police department with protecting and profiting from the city's prostitutes, gamblers, and racketeers. Parkhurst was quoted: ". . . while we fight iniquity they shield or patronize it; while we try to convert criminals they manufacture them."

His attack swept the city with excitement, but Reverend Parkhurst soon found himself on the defensive rather than the offensive. The politicians, of course, denounced him and denied his charges, and most of the press took the side of the politicos. All demanded proof to substantiate the accusations. Called before the grand jury 9 days after his sermon, Parkhurst was humiliated when he could offer nothing that would stand up in a court of law to corroborate his charges. Tammany Hall sighed with relief as the grand jury criticized Parkhurst for making unfounded statements and thereby undermining the trust the citizens of New York had in their governmental officials.

Dr. Parkhurst, however, had lost only the opening skirmish; he was resolved to win the war. Since he knew that no one in official capacity would do anything to substantiate the facts regarding police corruption, he made up his mind that he himself would go underground to visit the saloons, gambling dens, and houses of prostitution; he would garner the evidence required to transform his general accusations into indictable charges.

To look at him, one could never imagine Reverend Parkhurst in any setting other than a schoolhouse or a church. His serious but myopic eyes stared out from behind his steel-rimmed spectacles. He habitually wore sober clerical clothing (including a black waistcoat and clerical collar); but with the help of a private detective, Parkhurst developed a sufficient disguise that let him enter all the places he had condemned in sermons but had never known firsthand.

The private detective who accompanied Parkhurst on his rounds later wrote: "Dr. Parkhurst was a very hard man to satisfy. 'Show me something worse,' was his constant cry. He really went at his slumming work as if his heart was in his tour." Brothels and saloons were the primary targets. Although Parkhurst did not object to saloons—in fact, he opposed Prohibition 30 years later—he was an ardent foe of these establishments' paying protection money to the police in order to violate the excise laws and, more importantly, the law forbidding their doing business on Sundays.

The same was true of his attitude toward houses of prostitution. He did not object so much to the houses themselves as he did to the police's collecting payoffs from them. It was well understood in New York that no prostitutes would be in business long if they did not pay the police. His visits to the whorehouses were, of course, what really captured the public's attention when the story of Dr. Parkhurst's crusade finally was published in the newspapers. He became the butt of a ribald song when it was known that he had witnessed a game of leapfrog involving the girls and the private detective who guided him on his slumming tour. Sung to the tune of the then-popular "Ta-ra-ra-Boom-de-ay," it went: "Dr. Parkhurst on the floor/Playing leapfrog with a whore,/Ta-ra-ra-Boom-de-ay/Ta-ra-ra-Boom-de-ay."

On Sunday, March 13, 1892, Dr. Parkhurst preached his 2nd sermon on vice and the protection it received from the New York municipal administration. This time, however—in contrast to his sermon of February 14—he used affidavits from private detectives as evidence for his charges. He accused the police of being accomplices of the lawbreakers, and he defied Tammany Hall to dispute the particulars, which he could now document from his personal experience of the preceding weeks.

The 2nd sermon shocked the city even more than had Parkhurst's initial charges. Many people thought that the preacher was merely seeking publicity, and others who did not question the sincerity of his motives did question his choice of tactics; they thought it unseemly that a man of the cloth should enter such dens of iniquity, no matter how much good might come of it. Nevertheless, Parkhurst slowly convinced both the public and the state legislature that some drastic reform measures had to be taken. As a result of his efforts, the legislature sent the Lexow Committee to investigate municipal corruption. The investigation, of course, revealed an extraordinary amount of corruption. Fourteen police officers were indicted or dismissed between 1892 and 1895, and a reform ticket defeated the Tammany Hall candidates at the next municipal election.

The reform bubble soon burst, however. Most of the police officials who had lost their jobs were restored to duty, and the Tammany Hall mayoral candidate was victorious in 1897, prompting a torchlight parade of snake-dancing men and women chanting, "Well, well, well, Reform has gone to hell!" Dr. Parkhurst continued to speak out against corruption, but he was never again in the forefront of civic affairs.

Charles Parkhurst retired as a preacher in 1918, and in 1927—at age 85—he married for the 2nd time. His 1st wife had been a pupil of his at a Massachusetts high school; his 2nd was his secretary. On his 90th birthday Parkhurst appealed for the overthrow of the "New Tammany," which he felt was as corrupt as his foe in the 1890s. Less than 2 years later, while walking in his sleep, Parkhurst plunged 16' from his bedroom window to the sidewalk below and died.

—J.L.K.

GEORGE WASHINGTON PLUNKITT (1842–1924). *Politician.*

Plunkitt, the son of poor Irish immigrants, was born in a rundown section of New York that was sometimes known as "Nigger Hill." He quit school at the age of 11 and went to work in a butcher shop. By the time he cast his 1st vote at the age of 21, young George had already decided that politics was his true vocation, and with his considerable cunning and charm he quickly worked his way into the Democratic hierarchy of New York's Tammany Society organization (later known as Tammany Hall).

In this era, the Tammany machine maintained firm control over New York politics, and Plunkitt was elected to a long succession of public offices as a reward for his loyalty to the organization. In 1870, through a strange combination of circumstances, he was simultaneously an assemblyman, an alderman, a police magistrate, and county supervisor, and he drew 3 salaries at once—a record still unequaled in New York politics. Plunkitt's political connections helped him amass a considerable fortune and when he died in 1924 at the age of 82, his 60 years of service to Tammany Hall had made him a millionaire.

Despite this illustrious career, Plunkitt is remembered today for his words rather than his deeds. In 1905, he took time from his busy schedule to talk with a reporter named William L. Riordon. The result was a series of celebrated interviews called "Very Plain Talks on Very Practical Politics." Most of these interviews were conducted at Plunkitt's "office": Graziano's shoeshine stand in the basement of the old county courthouse. Today, in an era in which politicians are not always completely candid, Plunkitt's straight talk about American politics is particularly refreshing. For example—

Honest Graft and Dishonest Graft

"Everybody is talkin' these days about Tammany men growin' rich on graft, but nobody thinks of drawin' the distinction between honest graft and dishonest graft. There's all the difference in the world between the 2. Yes, many of our men have grown rich in politics. I have myself. I've made a big fortune out of the game, and I'm gettin' richer every day, but I've not gone in for dishonest graft —blackmailin' gamblers, saloonkeepers, disorderly people, etc.—and neither has any of the men who have made big fortunes in politics.

"There's an honest graft, and I'm an example of how it works.

"Just let me explain by examples. My party's in power in the city, and it's goin' to undertake a lot of public improvements. Well, I'm tipped off, say, that they're going to lay out a new park at a certain place.

"I see my opportunity and I take it. I go to that place and I buy up all the land I can in the neighborhood. Then the board of this or that makes its plan public, and there is a rush to get my land, which nobody cared for before.

"Ain't it perfectly honest to charge a good price and make a profit on my investment and foresight? Of course it is. It's just like lookin' ahead in Wall Street or in the coffee or cotton market. It's honest graft, and I'm lookin' for it every day in the year. I will tell you frankly that I've got a good lot of it, too.

"For instance, the city is repavin' a street and have several hundred thousand old granite blocks to sell. I am on hand to buy, and I know just what they are worth.

"How? Never mind that. I had a sort of monopoly on this business for a while, but once a newspaper tried to do me. It got some outside men to come over from Brooklyn and New Jersey to bid against me.

"Was I done? Not much. I went to each of the men and said: 'How many of these 250,000 stones do you want?' One said 20,000 and another 15,-000, and the other wanted 10,000. I said: 'All right, let me bid for the lot, and I'll give each of you all you want for nothing.'

"They agreed, of course. Then the auctioneer yelled: 'How much am I bid for these 250,000 fine pavin' stones?'

" 'Two dollars and fifty cents,' says I.

" 'Two dollars and fifty cents!' screamed the auctioneer. 'Oh, that's a joke! Give me a real bid.'

"He found the bid was real enough. My rivals stood silent. I got the lot for $2.50 and gave them their share. That's how the attempt to do Plunkitt ended, and that's how all such attempts end."

Bosses Preserve the Nation

"Look at the bosses of Tammany Hall in the last 20 years. What magnificent men! To them New York City owes pretty much all it is today. John Kelly, Richard Croker, and Charles F. Murphy— what names in American history compares with them, except Washington and Lincoln?"

On the Use of Money in Politics

"The civil service gang is always howlin' about candidates and officeholders puttin' up money for campaigns and about corporations chippin' in. They might as well howl about givin' contributions to churches. A political organization has to have money for its business as well as a church, and who has more right to put up than the men who get the good things that are goin'? Take, for instance, a great political concern like Tammany Hall. It does missionary work like a church, it's got big expenses and it's got to be supported by the faithful. If a corporation sends in a check to help the good work of the Tammany Society, why shouldn't we take it like other missionary societies? Of course, the day may come when we'll reject the money of the rich as tainted, but it hadn't come when I left Tammany Hall at 11:25 A.M. today."

Epitaph

"Now, in conclusion, I want to say that I don't own a dishonest dollar. If my worst enemy was given the job of writin' my epitaph when I'm gone, he couldn't do more than write:

" 'George W. Plunkitt. He Seen His Opportunities, and He Took 'Em.' "

—M.S.M.

POCAHONTAS (1595?–1617). *Indian princess and British lady.*

What can you say about a 22-year-old Indian princess who died over 3½ centuries ago?

Reams. Volumes. Plays, poems, novels, stories, paintings, children's books, chronicles seemingly without end have immortalized Pocahontas, daughter of Powhatan. Ever since the 1st English Colonists planted their crops (along with the seeds of the Revolution) at Jamestown, Va., the tale of Pocahontas and Capt. John Smith has been told, retold, embellished, and perpetuated. Her name has been bestowed upon ships, monuments, coal mines, towns, counties, and business firms. More than 3½ centuries after her death, Pocahontas' memory is green as ever—dearer to Americans, it would seem, than apple pie—held up to each new generation of schoolchildren as an example of self-sacrifice, romance, and brotherhood. No character in our history has been more idealized than Pocahontas, yet the John Smith incident is only the tip of the iceberg; the remainder of her life —her marriage, her religious conversion, her son, her travels, her celebrity—is even more fantastic. Since her death in 1617, the truth about Pocahontas has been distorted by literature, obscured by legend, neglected by all but a few scholars and historians.

For openers, Pocahontas wasn't even her real name. It was a nickname meaning "playful one," bestowed by her father. Her tribal name was Matoaka. Neither was Powhatan her father's rightful name; he was born Wahunsonacock, and became known as Powhatan only when he became chief of a village by that name.

We know that the 1st English settlement in America was established when "3 floating islands," as the Indians reported it, brought the Colonists to Jamestown in 1607. We also know that Capt. John Smith was among them. We have only Smith's word, however, for his dramatic capture and subsequent rescue from hostile Indians by the 12-year-old Pocahontas who (he said) rushed to his side and laid her head upon his as the executioners stood over him, clubs upraised. Smith's account has been the center of an unresolved controversy for centuries. All we really know of his relationship with Pocahontas is that he enjoyed her company at Jamestown, where she is said to have entertained the Colonists by cartwheeling around the fort in the nude. In 1609, shortly before the severe winter brought the settlers to such desperate straits that one man ate his wife, Smith returned to England.

Pocahontas may or may not have missed him, may even have thought him dead, but she did not pine away. A few months later she met and married an Indian named Kocoum. The next 2 years of her life are a mystery, as is the fate of Kocoum—but in December of 1612, she was kidnaped by Capt. Samuel Argall, a British sea captain, and held hostage against the return of some English prisoners and ammunition being held by Powhatan. The chief eventually capitulated to Argall's demands, but negotiations dragged on for months, during which Pocahontas was confined, 1st on Argall's ship, then at Jamestown. Although a prisoner, she was treated as befitted a princess. During the period of her captivity, 2 encounters drastically changed the course of her life. The 1st was with Christianity, to which she was introduced by the fort's missionary. The 2nd was with John Rolfe, another Englishman, who made her his wife, a mother, and the toast of London's high society.

Rolfe was a kind but coldly pious widower, and the very idea of marriage to a heathen Indian was no simple matter for him and his conscience. In a lengthy letter asking Sir Thomas Dale, deputy governor of Virginia, to approve the marriage, Rolfe bared his soul and his trepidations. The union, he claimed, would be "for the good of the plantation, the honor of our country, for the glory of God, for mine own salvation, and for the converting to the true knowledge of God and Jesus Christ an unbelieving creature, namely Pocahontas, to whom my heart and best thoughts are and have been a long time so entangled and enthralled in so intricate a labyrinth, that I was even awearied to unwind myself thereout . . ." He acknowledged that his beloved was "one whose education hath been rude, her manners barbarous, her generation cursed, and so discrepant in all nutriture [background] from myself." Anticipating that "the vulgar sort" might mistake his love for mere sexual desire, Rolfe added that if this were the case, he "might satisfy such desire . . . with Christians more pleasing to the eye." It was not his wish, he said, "to gorge myself with incontinency" but, according to God's wish, to convert the girl. The wordy harangue made its point. The wedding of John Rolfe and Pocahontas, now known by her Christian baptismal name of Rebecca, took place in April, 1614, with the blessing of not only the governor, but of Powhatan and his tribe, as well. It was probably more than coincidental that the period immediately following the marriage was one of unprecedented peace between the settlers and the Indians.

Two years later, Governor Dale took Mr. and Mrs. Rolfe and their infant son to England on a sort of promotional junket, to publicize the success of Jamestown. Pocahontas, "child of the forest," was suddenly thrust into London's high society. She attended a performance at the Globe Theatre of Shakespeare's The Tempest—just weeks after the death of its author. She was presented at the court of King James I to the King and his consort, Queen Anne. She was received and entertained royally by the bishop of London. She was visited by a drunken Ben Jonson, who seemed unimpressed at the time but referred to her 10 years later in one of his more forgettable plays. Wherever she went, she was as exotic a sensation as a visitor from a flying saucer would be today. Her conduct was irreproachable, and she is said to have conducted herself at all times like the daughter of a king.

It may have been culture shock or simply a virus, but in the epicenter of civilization, Pocahontas' health began to fail. She was relocated on an estate in the country, where she was visited by Capt. John Smith. That meeting has been the subject of endless speculation, but remains shrouded in Smith's ambiguous accounting of it. He left her feeling guilty for having betrayed their friendship and, perhaps, her love. They never met again.

In 1617, John Rolfe was appointed secretary of the Virginia Colony. For reasons that at least appear obvious, Pocahontas was reluctant to leave London, where she had been the object of such flattering attention. Nevertheless, in March, the family boarded a ship commanded by the same Captain Argall who had once tricked Pocahontas into captivity. But while the ship was still anchored in the Thames, Pocahontas became ill and died—some say of smallpox, others, more romantically, say of a broken heart and the English climate. She was buried on March 21, 1617, in an unmarked grave on a bank of the Thames.

John Rolfe returned to Virginia, married again, and was killed 4 years later by Indians led by Pocahontas' uncle. Powhatan survived his daughter by only a year. But Thomas, Pocahontas' son, grew up in England, raised by his uncle, and returned to the U.S. as an adult. His descendants are said to have included the Virginia Jeffersons, Lees, Randolphs, Marshalls, and millions of other Americans who claim to have traced their ancestry back to Pocahontas. For all these claims to be genuine, Thomas Rolfe would have had to be the most prolific of men.

If there had never been a Pocahontas, Americans would probably have invented her; yet much of the literature that perpetuates her memory is sentimental, inaccurate, embarrassingly dreadful stuff. In *Beautiful Legend of the Amorous Indian*, published in 1918, the playwright gives Powhatan's wife the line (referring to her senile mother-in-law): "When she talks in that old manner it nearly drives me crazy." Henry Wadsworth Longfellow never produced any Pocahontas poems, but many of his imitators did, using his monotonous "By the-shores-of-Gitchee-Gumee" meter. In an eloquent essay entitled "The Mother of Us All: Pocahontas," Phillip Young refers to this genre of godawful Pocahontas poems as "the curse of Hiawatha."

Some of the better-grade efforts by Carl Sandburg, Vachel Lindsay, and Hart Crane present Pocahontas as a kind of American fertility goddess; in their work, says Young, "an image of the beautiful Indian girl is set in perpetual motion, and comes cartwheeling through our veins and down our generations." Many have speculated but none can say precisely what element of her story touches a nerve in our national psyche. Perhaps there are, as some contend, heavy, hidden, symbolic meanings. On the other hand, our enshrinement of her as our 1st authentic native American folk heroine may simply be our way of acknowledging—belatedly—that Mrs. John Rolfe, née Matoaka, had class.

—C.E.

SEQUOYAH (c. 1770–1843). *Inventor of an alphabet.*

While living in the Cherokee territory of Tennessee, young Sequoyah and his companions would argue as to whether the mysterious power of "the talking leaf" was a gift from the Great Spirit to the white man, or the white man's own discovery.

Sequoyah's companions had seen white men with books and had seen them write messages on paper. They were convinced that this form of communication was just another of those blessings that the Great Spirit had seen fit to bestow upon the white man but not upon the red. But Sequoyah strenuously maintained the opposite: that the Great Spirit had had nothing to do with it; and that the white man had himself invented "the talking leaf." It was an argument that remained fixed in his mind and continued to haunt him with its possibilities.

Sequoyah was born about 1770, most probably the son of a white trader named Nathaniel Gist. Nobody dwelt much on these matters of little significance. The important facts were that his mother was a member of the family of the Emperor Moytoy and the legendary warrior-king Oconostota; that Sequoyah was born in the Indian village of Taskigi (later Tuskegee), just 5 mi. from the sacred town of Echota; and that he was a Cherokee. He became a craftsman in silverwork, an accomplished storyteller, and a happy participant in the Green Corn Dances, footraces, and ball games. And, along with his entire tribe, he was illiterate.

Sequoyah's life might have continued without incident had not a hunting accident left him partially crippled. As a result, he had more leisure and more opportunity to ponder the idea that the red man also might come to possess the secret of "the talking leaf." He began to wander off into the woods and spend hours there alone, avoiding everyone, playing like a child with pieces of wood or making odd little marks with one stone on another. His wife and friends offered no encouragement, or even sympathy, for they were convinced that he was either going mad or in communication with the spirits. Months became years, and lack of sympathy became ridicule and contempt. But Sequoyah was obsessed with his dream.

At 1st, Sequoyah tried to give every word a separate character, but eventually he realized the futility of such an approach and settled on assigning a character to each sound. When his friends and neighbors talked, he no longer heard what they said but listened to the sounds, trying to separate them and trying to identify any new sound that he might theretofore have missed. What he eventually achieved was not so much an alphabet as a syllabary—86 characters representing all the sounds of spoken Cherokee—which when combined produced a written language of remarkable simplicity and effectiveness. It had taken 12 years.

There are many stories of how Sequoyah presented his "alphabet" to his doubting people and overcame their reluctance to try it. According to one legend, there was actually a great demonstration before the chiefs during which his little daughter read aloud what the chiefs had privately told him to write on a paper and thus in a single moment amazed and convinced everyone. So beautifully simple and precise was Sequoyah's alphabet that it could be learned in a few days. Moreover, whoever learned, taught; until suddenly a most remarkable thing had happened. Within a matter of months, a population that had been almost entirely illiterate suddenly became almost entirely literate! And the lame little man who had been ridiculed by his people was now respected, revered, regarded as almost superhuman and a great benefactor.

In 1828, Sequoyah was named one of a delegation of Arkansas Cherokees that went to Washington to attempt to settle with the Federal Government all the unfulfilled promises of all previous treaties. Sequoyah's fame preceded him, and he was the subject of much attention in the capital. Charles Bird King asked him to sit for a portrait, and many newspapermen requested interviews. Jeremiah Evarts asked him why and how he had invented the alphabet and later wrote this account of Sequoyah's answer:

> He had observed, that many things were found out by men, and known in the world, but that this knowledge escaped and was lost, for want of some way to preserve it. He had also observed white people write things on paper, and he had seen books; and he knew that what was written down remained and was not forgotten. He had attempted, therefore, to fix certain marks for sounds, and thought that if he could make certain things fast on paper, it would be like catching a wild animal and taming it.

The result of the Washington visit was that the Cherokees agreed to yet another treaty by which they exchanged their lands in Arkansas for new and more extensive ones in what is now Oklahoma. Most of the Cherokees were still clinging desperately to their ancestral territories in Tennessee and Alabama, but the Arkansas band, to which Sequoyah now belonged, once again uprooted itself and moved westward to Oklahoma. Sequoyah, now in his 60s, built himself a new cabin with his own hands, tended his little farm, and at intervals traveled up through the woods to the salt springs. There he would live for days or weeks at a time filling his kettles, tending his fires, scooping out the salt and, Thoreau-like, pausing in his work to talk to anyone who—out of curiosity to see and speak with the now-famous Cherokee philosopher—sought him out there.

But the Great Spirit did not allow Sequoyah to end his life in the tranquility of the forest around Lee's Creek. The Federal Government, which had for so long coveted the Cherokees' ancestral land in Tennessee and Alabama, contracted a treaty of removal, and well-armed soldiers drove some 17,000 Cherokees from their homes. The long trek westward began, months of suffering ensued, and some 4,000 Cherokees died before the great mass of them began to arrive in the Oklahoma territory in the spring of 1839. Problems arose immediately. The new arrivals greatly outnumbered the already established inhabitants; there were profound conflicts over the land, over the makeup of the local government, over everything. Sequoyah, foreseeing an irreparable breach, brought his influence to bear on the side of reason and necessity. At a meeting of the tribe, an act of union was adopted, and the Cherokees of Alabama, Tennessee, Arkansas, and Oklahoma joined together to become the Cherokee Nation.

But even then Sequoyah could not rest. According to tradition, a band of Cherokees had migrated west of the Mississippi at just about the time that Sequoyah was born. Where were they now, these lost Cherokees who did not know of his alphabet or the new Nation? Sequoyah, now aged, set off with a party of 9 horsemen and headed south. Legend has it that before he died, somewhere deep in Mexico, he did find the lost Cherokees. Not long afterward that genus of California redwoods that included the largest trees in the world was named "sequoia" after the only man in history to conceive and perfect in its entirety an alphabet or syllabary.

—N.C.S. rep.

BELLE STARR (1848–1889).
Legendary western heroine.

Horse thief, cattle rustler, suspected robber of stagecoaches, perennial concubine, and protector of desperate criminals, she was born Myra Belle Shirley in Carthage, Mo. As with most of the legendary figures of the Old West, the facts known about her life are few, though fictionalized accounts of her activities could fill several volumes.

Young Myra Belle 1st became involved in questionable activity while still in her early teens through her brother, Ed Shirley, who was a member of the infamous Cole Younger-Jesse James gang in Missouri. During the Civil War, the members of this lively group were able to indulge their taste for violence as "Confederate Partisans," participating in such escapades as the raid on Lawrence, Kans., in 1863, during which 182 citizens of this town were murdered. When the War ended, however, these high-spirited young people were unable to adjust to a country at peace. In February, 1866, the James gang pulled off its 1st bank robbery in Liberty, Mo., and this was to be followed by a long and notorious series of robberies and murders.

But now young Myra Belle decided to part from her brother and the James boys. She made her way south and west until she reached the vicinity of Dallas, Tex. There she set up a "ranch" of dubious reputation. In 1868, when Cole Younger was forced to flee from the law, he came to Myra Belle for refuge. She had recently turned 20, and apparently Younger was struck by the way in which his old friend's kid sister had developed since their earlier days in Missouri. At any rate, Myra Belle was soon the mother of Cole Younger's illegitimate child, a daughter she named Pearl.

In 1870, Jim Reed, another member of the James gang, followed in Younger's footsteps, going underground for several months at Myra Belle's. The result was another illegitimate child, this time a boy she named Ed.

Between lovers, Myra Belle supported herself through various activities including horse stealing, cattle rustling, and (it was rumored) occasional ventures into prostitution. As far as robberies were concerned, it is thought that Myra Belle organized these forays but that she seldom participated personally, although she was an excellent horsewoman.

In the 1870s, as local authorities began to lose patience with Myra Belle and her various enterprises, she found it advisable to relocate in a remote section of Oklahoma along the Canadian River. For nostalgic reasons, Myra Belle named this place "Younger's Bend," in honor of her 1st great passion. After entertaining a series of outlaw lovers including Jack Spaniard, Jim July, Jim French, and John Middleton, she began to develop an interest in native Americans. She lived several years with a handsome brave named Blue Duck and then finally married a Cherokee named Sam S. Starr. Though this union was predictably short-lived, Myra Belle permanently adopted the name "Belle Starr," the name under which she has come down through history.

In 1881, Jesse James himself turned to Belle Starr for help, and she was delighted to provide a hideout for the leader of her old associates. Poor Jesse should have remained with Belle, because shortly after he returned to Missouri he was shot in the back by "that dirty little coward" Robert Ford.

A few years later, Belle Starr was to meet a similar fate—she was shot in the back and killed near Eufaula, Okla., on February 3, 1889, at the age of 41. A neighbor, Edgar Watson, was accused of the murder, but charges against him were eventually dropped.

It was generally believed that Belle Starr was slain by her own son, 18-year-old Ed Reed, with whom she had been having incestuous relations. He was angry with his mother, according to the story, because she had whipped him after he rode her favorite horse without her permission.

Whatever the actual circumstances of her death, her friends and children provided Belle Starr with a touching tombstone. Underneath a primitive carving of her horse, a bell, and a star, they placed the following lines—

Shed not for her the bitter tear
Nor give the heart to vain regret
'Tis but the casket that lies here
The gem that filled it sparkles yet.

—M.S.M.

CHARLES S. STRATTON (1838–1883).
General Tom Thumb.

Charles was the 3rd child of Sherwood and Cynthia Stratton, a couple of normal size and modest means who lived in Bridgeport, Conn. At birth, he weighed over 9 lbs., and for the 1st 6 months of his life, his growth was normal. But at the age of 5 years, his height and weight remained what they had been at 6 months: 25"; 15 lbs., 2 oz.

His fateful meeting with showman Phineas T. Barnum came about when he was nearly 6. Barnum thought him "the smallest child I ever saw that could walk alone . . . a perfectly formed, bright-eyed little fellow, with light hair and ruddy cheeks, and he enjoyed the best of health. He was exceedingly bashful but after some coaxing he was induced to talk with me."

Bashfulness was never a problem for Barnum, who hired the boy on a short-term basis (what if he started growing?) for the munificent sum of $3 a week, travel expenses, and room and board. He whisked the boy and his mother off to New York, where he billed his new attraction as "General Tom Thumb, a dwarf of 11 years of age, just arrived from England." Mrs. Stratton and her son were installed in the converted billiard parlor where Barnum's wife and 3 daughters lived, while Barnum concocted an image and an act to hype The General. After a week of rehearsing, Tom Thumb made his debut in the lecture hall of Barnum's Museum. "Good evening, ladies and gentlemen," he began. "I am only a Thumb, but a good hand in a general way at amusing you, for though a mite, I am mighty. . . . In short, don't make much of me, for making more would be making me less. Though I grow in your favor, no taller I'd be."

After some banter with Barnum, he cavorted about the stage in a variety of costumes: as Cupid, in flesh-colored tights, carrying a bow and a quiver of arrows; as a Revolutionary War soldier, waving a 10″ sword and singing "Yankee Doodle Dandy"; as the biblical David, in a mock fight against 2 giants provided by Barnum; as a seminude gladiator, a bell-bottomed sailor, Napoleon Bonaparte in full regalia.

Tom Thumb proved to be a "natural" as a performer, and became an overnight sensation in New York and other U.S. cities. In 1844, Barnum raised his salary to $50 a week and took him, with much fanfare, to London, where he performed "songs, dances and imitations" at the Princess' Theater to overflow crowds. He was acclaimed and petted by aristocrats and commoners alike, and gave a command performance at Buckingham Palace for the young Queen Victoria and her court; again, he was a tremendous hit. A return engagement took place for the benefit of the 3-year-old Prince of Wales. "The Prince is taller than I am," observed Tom Thumb, "but I feel as big as anybody." With that, he became the rage of London.

The next stop was Paris, where the exploitation of The General reached its frenzied peak, culminating in 3 audiences with King Louis-Philippe. The French press had a field day. A café was named after Tom Thumb; snuffboxes bore his picture on their lids, and his statue graced hundreds of shop windows. He inspired poems and lithographs, and was elected an honorary member of the French Dramatic Society. His 2 shows a day at the Salle Musard were sold out months in advance.

In Spain, Tom Thumb attended bullfights with Queen Isabella. In Belgium, he was entertained by King Leopold. After 3 years as the toast of the Continent, the midget (Barnum erred when he called him a dwarf) returned to America having become, in Barnum's words, "an educated, accomplished little man."

At 23, The General had grown to 35″, 52 lbs. With a more equitable share of the profits (in his lifetime, 20 million people paid to see him), he retired to enjoy the pleasures of his miniature billiard table and his yacht. Then he met Lavinia Warren, Barnum's newest midget attraction. Lavinia was 20 years old, 32″ tall and weighed 29 lbs. At 1st sight, Tom Thumb fell head-over-his-little-heels in love. Their wedding, which took place on February 10, 1863, was attended by thousands of people, including governors, congressmen, and millionaires, and thousands more sent gifts. The newlyweds were received at the White House, where President Lincoln observed, apropos of their respective heights, "God likes to do funny things; here you have the long and the short of it."

The couple lived happily in The General's Bridgeport home for 20 years. Tom Thumb grew portly; he also grew extravagant. He owned a sailing sloop, pedigreed horses, and a carriage and driver. He was a 32nd Degree Mason and a Knight Templar. When he died (of apoplexy) at the age of 45, more than 10,000 persons attended his funeral. A life-sized granite statue of himself, which he had commissioned, was placed atop his grave in Bridgeport. Lavinia married again, but when she died in 1919, at the age of 78, she was buried beside Tom Thumb; the words on her headstone read simply, "His Wife."

—C.E.

TECUMSEH (1768–1813).
Indian leader.

Tecumseh, one of the greatest leaders of the Indian struggle against the encroachments of white civilization, was born in a Shawnee village in the Ohio wilderness. When Tecumseh was still a boy, his father, a Shawnee war chief, was brutally murdered by white frontiersmen who had crossed onto Indian land in violation of a recent treaty. After this tragedy, Tecumseh resolved to become a warrior like his father and to be "a fire spreading over the hill and valley, consuming the race of dark souls."

At the age of 15, Tecumseh joined a band of Shawnees who were determined to stop the white invasion of their lands by intercepting settlers' flatboats as they came down the Ohio River from Pennsylvania. In time, Tecumseh became the leader of his own band of marauding warriors. For a while, these Indian raids were so effective that river traffic virtually ceased.

In 1796, at the age of 28, Tecumseh met a beautiful blond girl named Rebecca Galloway, the daughter of a pioneer farmer. A close relationship was formed between the Indian leader and this frontier family, and Rebecca taught Tecumseh to speak English fluently and read to him from the Bible, Shakespeare, and history books. Tecumseh was fascinated; he wanted to learn even more about white civilization and in time asked the girl's father if he could marry her. Mr. Galloway respected Tecumseh and left the decision up to his daughter. Rebecca said she would marry Tecumseh if he would give up his Indian traditions and live with her as a white man. Tecumseh pondered the decision for a month, and finally he told Rebecca that he could never abandon his people. With that, he bade good-bye to his white friends, and thereafter Tecumseh never took a wife, either Indian or white.

In 1805, Tecumseh allied himself with his younger brother Tenskwautawa, who had become known as "the Shawnee Prophet." For years the Prophet had lived like many other Indians on the frontier. He was a depraved and idle drunkard. Then, during a frightening and mysterious epidemic among the Shawnees, Tecumseh's brother was overcome with a sense of his own wickedness and fell into a trance in which he met the Indian Master of Life. He soon began to preach to his Indian brothers about the evils of alcohol, and as he continued to commune with the Master of Life his message evolved into a fully developed religious creed. This creed called for a return to ancient traditions, a rejection of all aspects of the "depraved" white civilization, and an end to intertribal warfare so that a united resistance would challenge the advancing Americans.

This emotional appeal spread quickly across the old Northwest Territory, and Tecumseh and Tenskwautawa built a village in which there was a large wooden meeting house to accommodate the converts who joined them from every tribe. In an attempt to destroy the Prophet's influence, Gen. William Henry Harrison, the governor of the Indiana Territory, wrote to a group of Indians that Tenskwautawa was not a real prophet unless he could "cause the sun to stand still or the rivers cease to flow." This challenge backfired, because Tenskwautawa soon learned of an impending eclipse of the sun and assembled a huge crowd of natives to watch his God-given magic on that day. After the Prophet darkened the sun, he then successfully called upon the Master of Life to bring back the sunlight.

News of this miracle electrified tribes as far away as Minnesota, where entire bands pledged complete loyalty to Tecumseh and his brother. In August, 1809, Tecumseh and his brother set off to meet with Governor Harrison. In a tense confrontation in front of the governor's mansion, Tecumseh told the general: "You try to prevent the Indians from doing what we, their leaders, wish them to do —unite and consider their land the common property. . . . I am a Shawnee. My forefathers were warriors. Their son is a warrior. . . . I have made myself what I am. And I would that I could make the red people as great as the conceptions of my mind, when I think of the Great Spirit that rules over all. I would not come to Governor Harrison to ask him to tear the treaty. But I would say to him, Brother, you have liberty to return to your own country."

When Harrison asked Tecumseh to have faith in the protections provided by the treaty, the chief answered, "How can we have confidence in the white people? When Jesus Christ came upon the earth you killed Him, and nailed Him to a cross."

Displeased by this response, Harrison resolved to crush Tecumseh and the Prophet.

In the fall of 1811, while Tecumseh was traveling across the South attempting to rally the southern tribes to his cause, Harrison struck against the Prophet's town. After an intense fight, he was able to disperse the Indians and burn the village. This was the celebrated battle of Tippecanoe, in which white casualties were actually twice as high as those suffered by the Indians. Nevertheless, this "great victory" helped decide the election in 1840. Harrison successfully exploited the nickname "Old Tippecanoe" during his campaign.

When Tecumseh returned and heard about the disaster, he was furious with his brother for having failed to prevent the battle. Tecumseh knew that his Indian confederation still required several years of preparation before it could fight the white man effectively.

Yet events on the world scene worked against Tecumseh's plans when the U.S. and England drifted into the War of 1812. Tecumseh's Indian confederation, caught between these 2 opposing powers, was forced to take sides and it was clear that the Americans posed the greater long-range threat to Indian lands. Wearing only a breechclout and moccasins, Tecumseh spoke before tribal councils throughout the South and Midwest, rallying support for his cause.

On the Canadian side of the Detroit River, Tecumseh soon had an army of nearly 3,000 men, which helped support a small British garrison at Fort Malden. The British commander, Isaac Brock, was a brilliant general who established a relationship of mutual respect and affection with Tecumseh. The 2 men worked together so effectively that though outnumbered, they were able to force the surrender of the major American army forces that had been dispatched to invade Canada. Because of his success in battle, Tecumseh was made a brigadier general—certainly one of the most unconventional officers ever to serve the British Crown.

In 1813, following the death of General Brock and the American naval victory in the Battle of Lake Erie, the initiative in the war passed to the Americans. The new British commander, Henry Procter, insisted on retreating before the American advance, despite Tecumseh's objections.

Finally, Tecumseh forced Procter to make a stand on the Thames River, and because of Procter's feeble leadership, the Shawnee himself took command of the British troops in addition to his own Indian forces. On the night of October 4, Tecumseh sat by a campfire and told some of his closest Indian lieutenants, "Brother warriors, we are about to enter an engagement from which I shall not return. My body will remain on the field of battle."

During the battle the next day, Tecumseh was not only conspicuous among his Indian followers, but he raised the morale of the British officers as well. "He yelled like a tiger," according to one eyewitness, and offered an inviting target to the attacking Americans. Tecumseh was killed in the midst of the fighting, and the dream of an Indian Confederation died with him.

The battle was a decisive victory for the Americans. The honor of slaying the great Indian leader had gone to Col. Richard Mentor Johnson of Kentucky. This distinction was enough to elect him to the U.S. Senate several years later, and it also earned Johnson a place as Van Buren's Vice-President in 1836.

Tecumseh's Indian followers looked for his body after the fighting, but they looked in vain. It had disappeared. According to one dismaying report, he was flayed and his skin made into souvenir razor strops—by the same white men who had offered him a more "civilized" way of life.

—M.S.M.

Clement L. Vallandigham
(1820–1871). *Politician, dissenter, exile.*

Everybody who goes to school reads "The Man without a Country," a short story written in 1863 by Edward Everett Hale, a Boston Unitarian minister and member of a famous New England family. Millions of copies have been sold of the moving account of the life and death of a prisoner condemned to lonely exile aboard ship because he cursed the U.S. and said he wished never again to hear the name of his country.

Forgotten is the fact that the story's central fictional figure was based on an original person and the story grew out of actual events. "No court-martial can ever have had the right to fix such a penalty," wrote Carl Van Doren. But President Lincoln gave a troublesome Civil War politician a similar sentence.

He was Clement Laird Vallandigham, a handsome, eloquent, enigmatic, vain lawyer. On the eve of the Civil War, he was 40 years old and represented the 3rd Ohio District in Congress. He had been born there but his family was from Virginia. His wife was the daughter of a Maryland planter and he had many ties with the South. He was a Peace Democrat. He believed that States had a right to secede.

Vallandigham called Lincoln "a despot" and became the spokesman in Congress for the Copperheads, a derogatory term applied to Northerners who opposed the war. Resolutions demanding Vallandigham's expulsion from Congress failed, but in 1862 the Ohio Legislature added strongly Republican Warren County to Vallandigham's district and he was defeated for reelection.

He returned to Ohio in the spring of 1863 and sought the Democratic nomination for governor. "The war is a bloody and costly failure," the bearded man argued sonorously. "The dead, the dead, the numerous dead; think of Fredericksburg. Let us make peace. Let the armies fraternize and go home." With this sort of talk, Union enlistments declined.

To combat it, the commander of the Dept. of Ohio, Maj. Gen. Ambrose Everett Burnside, who had been defeated at Fredericksburg, issued General Order No. 38. This said "all persons . . . who commit acts for the benefit of the enemies of our country will be tried as spies or traitors, and, if convicted, will suffer death." It also warned: "The habit of declaring sympathy for the enemy will not be allowed in this department. Persons committing such offenses will be arrested, with a view to being tried as above stated, or sent beyond our lines into the lines of their friends."

Vallandigham defied the order and publicly tore up a copy. "I have the most supreme contempt for General Order No. 38," he shouted at a May 1 meeting at Mount Vernon, O. "I have the most supreme contempt for King Lincoln. Come up, united and hurl the tyrant from his throne. The men in power are attempting to establish a despotism." And in answering a question, he may have said: "Hang the U.S., I hope the day will come when I will never hear the name."

Two captains in civilian clothes were in the crowd taking notes for Burnside. At 3 A.M. on May 5, Vallandigham was arrested at his home in Dayton by soldiers. He was brought before a military commission on charges of "publicly expressing, in violation of General Order No. 38 . . . his sympathies for those in arms against the Government of the U.S. . . . with the object and purpose of weakening the power of the Government in its efforts to suppress an unlawful rebellion."

After hearing evidence for 2 days, the commission found Vallandigham Guilty and sentenced him to "close confinement" for the duration of the war. In a decision later upheld by the Supreme Court, Federal Judge Humphrey H. Leavitt refused a writ of *habeas corpus*. Burnside approved the sentence and designated Fort Warren, in Boston harbor, as the place of confinement.

A great uproar followed. Vallandigham argued that he was a martyr for liberty and free speech. President Lincoln was asked both to free Vallandigham and to remove Burnside. In response to the charge that Vallandigham was being prosecuted because he was a Democrat, Lincoln pointed out that General Burnside and Judge

Leavitt were also Democrats. "Must I shoot a simple-minded soldier boy who deserts, while I must not touch a hair of a wily agitator who induces him to desert?" asked Lincoln. "I think that in such a case to silence the agitator and save the boy is not only constitutional, but withal, a great mercy."

Confining Vallandigham anywhere in the North, however, was not likely to silence him. Lincoln found the answer in the line of General Order No. 38 that promised deportation of enemy sympathizers "into the lines of their friends." On May 19, he changed Vallandigham's sentence to banishment to the Confederacy.

Under a flag of truce, the Ohioan was delivered to a surprised Confederate outpost in Tennessee on May 25, 1863. The next day Gen. Braxton Bragg, the Confederate commander, gave him a passport to travel "as any citizen of the Confederacy" but on May 31 this was picked up and Vallandigham became "a prisoner on parole."

The Confederates didn't know what to do with Vallandigham and gladly allowed him to depart for Canada. He left Wilmington, N.C., on June 17 on a blockade runner for Bermuda, and sailed from there to Halifax. He reached Niagara Falls on July 15, announced that his "convictions as to war and peace" were unchanged and accepted the Democratic nomination for governor of Ohio voted him by the party convention while he was in the Confederacy. In order to be closer to the campaign, he moved to Windsor, opposite Detroit.

With the idea of helping defeat Vallandigham in the election in October, Hale conceived "The Man without a Country" and James T. Fields, editor of *The Atlantic Monthly* agreed to publish it before the election, but the story arrived too late. Vallandigham was defeated by a margin of 101,000 votes and the story appeared in the December *Atlantic*.

Six months later, he donned a false moustache, took a night ferry to Detroit, and returned to Ohio. This was reported to Lincoln but the war was going so well for the North by then that the President ignored the Ohioan. In 1868, Vallandigham sought his party's nomination for U.S. senator, but the Democrats gave it to another. He was nominated for his old 3rd District seat in Congress, but was beaten and returned to the practice of law.

A gambler named Thomas Myers was attacked by 5 intruders on Christmas Eve in 1870 as he played faro above a saloon in Hamilton, O. Myers drew a pistol and fired several shots. When the smoke cleared, he lay dead. One of the intruders, Thomas McGehan, was arrested and charged with murder. He retained Vallandigham, who, because of local feeling, obtained a change of venue to Lebanon, O. When the case came to trial, McGehan contended that he did not have a pistol the night Myers was killed. As part of his defense, Vallandigham bought a pistol and fired it several times through muslin to study the powder marks. They returned to the Lebanon House on the evening of June 16, 1871.

"A man could easily shoot himself as Myers was shot," argued Vallandigham and pulled the pistol from his pocket to demonstrate. He had forgotten that there were bullets in it. One crashed into his stomach.

Some of the jurors rushed in Vallandigham's room. A mistrial was declared. After 2 later trials, McGehan was freed. Vallandigham did not live to see his client exonerated. In the final anticlimax of his life, he died the morning after his accident, just short of his 51st birthday.

"The Man without a Country" established Hale as a writer. Ticknor and Fields of Boston 1st published it in book form in 1865. Many new editions followed. Hale's passionate tale lives on. It is included in countless anthologies, in many languages, in Pitman and Gregg shorthand, and in Braille. It has been dramatized and made into a motion picture. It went to 25 million readers during the Korean War when a Sunday newspaper supplement and 2 magazines reprinted it. Hale lived to write a foreword for a special Spanish-American War Edition and collected royalties on perhaps a million copies before his death at 87 in 1909. These royalties enabled him to maintain a salty independence. When he became chaplain of the U.S. Senate late in life, a visitor asked him if he prayed for the senators. "No," answered Hale. "I look at the senators and pray for the country!"

—T.M.

MASON WEEMS (1760–1825).
Clergyman, author, bookseller.

That George Washington zealously felled a cherry tree at the tender age of 6 is American history. What most Americans don't know is that this touching portrait of American honesty is the product of Mason Locke "Parson" Weems's lively pen. The cherry tree escapade is but one of the tales in Weems's *Life of George Washington; with Curious Anecdotes, Equally Honorable to Himself, and Exemplary to His Young Countrymen,* a largely fictitious, or at least lavishly embellished, account of our 1st President's life and times. To say that the good parson had a flair for exaggeration would surely be an understatement, but what he did have was an eye for what the reading public thrived on, and what would sell a book. This is not to say that Reverend Weems was deceitful, only that the extreme vivacity of his character was easily translated to the printed page.

Born in Maryland in 1760, Weems was the youngest of 19 children. He studied medicine, then took up theology, and in 1784, he and another were the 1st Americans to be ordained in the Church of England after the American Revolution.

For 8 or 9 years, Weems preached with a passion in small Maryland churches, using a fiery style that appealed to the emotions. Not wholly satisfied with this life, he took up the printing and selling of religious works, and from there came into the employ of the pioneer Philadelphia publisher, Matthew Carey.

Weems reveled in his new trade as a traveling bookseller, which he was to continue for the rest of his life. He wrote quite a number of "improvement books" with such titles as *Hymen's Recruiting Sargeant, or, the New Matrimonial Tat-too for Old Bachelors—The Philanthropist; or a Good Twenty-Five Cents Worth of Political Love-Powder—God's Revenge against Dueling—God's Revenge against Gambling—God's Revenge against Adultery—The Immortal Mentor; or Man's Unerring Guide to a Healthy, Wealthy and Happy Life.* The virtues of the last were attested to by George Washington himself, who wrote that he had "perused it with singular satisfaction" and found it "invaluable." Although Weems boasted that he had preached for Washington at Mount Vernon, in truth they had never met.

In 1795, Weems married, and he and his wife Fanny had 12 children. He loved her very much, but was to spend a great deal of time away from home, so devoted was he to his task of spreading the Lord's word.

His favorite (and also best-selling) item was the Bible, in his words, "smooth, fair and spotless as a young Bride." He wrote of his work in New York, "I have been soliciting Purchasers of the Bible the whole day long, and have not been able to find *one!!!* The town is deluged with Bibles and Deism."

In his bookselling, he was known for his outrageous behavior and racy remarks. In Fredericksburg, he preached from the text, "We are fearfully and wonderfully made," then ended his sermon, saying, "I must stop; for should I go on, some young ladies present would not sleep *a wink* tonight." In selling his *Drunkard's Looking Glass,* he would appear at the door of a tavern in a drunken and haggard state, appearing to be "A little on the Staggers or so." When he had got the attention of the clientele, he would begin to offer forth his pamphlets. He said they sold "like hotcakes." Weems was not all-out in favor of prohibition, only of moderation.

He was also an excellent fiddler, and he played to please his customers. All in all, his behavior was considered scandalous by many, not the least of whom was his employer, Carey. They argued constantly for the 30 years of their partnership, and both being of excitable temperaments, their correspondence was vitriolic in the extreme. Despite their feuding, Weems was simply invaluable as a salesman. He wrote to Carey: "God knows there is nothing I dread so as dead stock, dull sales, back loads, and blank looks. But the Joy of my soul is quick and clean sales—Heavy pockets, and light hearts."

Next to the beloved Bible, his *Life of Washington* was the best seller. It was published in 1800, and was so immensely popular that before 1850, 59 editions were published. The frontispiece (by Weems) bore the inscription:

Go thy way old George. Die when thou wilt,
We shall not look upon thy like again.

(It was altered accordingly when Washington died 6 months later.)

Here is the historic anecdote: "When George was about 6 years old, he was made the wealthy owner of a hatchet! of which, like most little boys, he was immoderately fond; and was constantly going about chopping every thing which came in his way. One day, in the garden, where he often amused himself by hacking his mother's pea-sticks, he unluckily tried the edge of his hatchet on the body of a beautiful young English cherry tree, which he barked so terribly, that I don't believe the tree ever got the better of it. The next morning, the old gentleman, finding out what had befallen his tree, which, by the by, was a great favourite, came into the house; and with much warmth asked for the mischievous author, declaring at the same time, that he would not have taken 5 guineas for his tree. Nobody would tell him anything about it. Presently George and his hatchet made their appearance. 'George,' said his father, 'do you know who killed that beautiful little cherry tree yonder in the garden?'

"This was a tough question; and George staggered under it for a moment; but quickly recovered himself; and looking at his father, with the sweet face of youth brightened with the inexpressible charm of all-conquering truth, he bravely cried out, 'I can't tell a lie, Pa; you know I can't tell a lie. I did cut it with my hatchet.'—Run to my arms, you dearest boy, cried his father in transports, run to my arms; glad am I, George, that you killed my tree, for you have paid me for it a thousand fold. Such an act of heroism in my son is worth more than a thousand trees, though blossomed with silver and their fruits of purest gold."

Parson Weems's devotion was no less than his eloquence, and he toiled mightily and ceaselessly. He said to Carey: "I wish you to remember that the family Bible is my favorite book and I hope to die selling it." He had his wish, and in 1825 he died in harness, on the road, in South Carolina.

—A.W.

What about the Midnight Ride of William Dawes?

Listen, my children, and you shall hear
Of the midnight ride of Paul Revere,
On the eighteenth of April, in seventy-five;
Hardly a man is now alive
Who remembers that famous day and year.

Certainly, in January, 1861, when Henry Wadsworth Longfellow sat down to write the 1st of 14 stanzas of a poem he would call "Paul Revere's Ride" he was one of the men alive who *failed* to remember that famous day and year. Ignoring the facts or unaware of them, Longfellow created a poem filled, as one historian noted, with "bemused inaccuracies," and in so doing invented a new hero who was given all credit for a daring deed, to the complete neglect of the real hero, who was ever after ignored by American history.

In Longfellow's fanciful poem, complete credit was given to young, Boston-born Paul Revere for alerting the American Colonists to the coming of the British troops and thereby sparking the Revolutionary War at Lexington. This was an utter corruption of truth, and Longfellow's myth has persisted to the very present.

Actually, on that fateful day in April of '75, 2 young men were sent out on steeds to alert the American rebels between Boston and Lexington; one was, indeed, Revere, and the other was a callow cordwainer and carpenter named William Dawes, a daring hothead. In truth, it was Dawes who rode 1st, rode longest, and who did the whole job right. Revere, on the other hand, got sidetracked and was finally captured by the British near the end of his ride. To begin at the beginning of the real event . . .

It was the spring of 1775 and British imperial troops were pouring into Boston. Revolutionary violence was mounting daily, and the militant American Sons of Liberty made steady preparations for a civil war. The Colonials stored arms at Concord, drilled, and readied themselves for the inevitable.

The imperial army would certainly not watch passively while the insurrection grew and men were armed: The radicals thought that it would move to seize the weapons cache. Thirty Sons of Liberty were detailed to keep a constant watch on British troop activities. The commander of the Colonial forces, Dr. Joseph Warren, tagged 2 experienced couriers, Paul Revere and William Dawes, as his special messengers. Revere, a silversmith, and Dawes, a shoemaker, were a good team.

On April 15, the Saturday before Easter, Warren received a midnight report of British troop movements: A regiment of light infantry and one of grenadiers had been relieved of drill and guard duties. Furthermore, the Royal Fleet had launched all its small boats and floated them astern in long lines. An amphibious operation was forming and that meant a movement against Concord.

Warren sent Paul Revere to Lexington to warn Sam Adams, the old firebrand whose inflammatory pamphlets, speeches, and demonstrations had placed him atop His Majesty's wanted list, and his wealthy friend, John Hancock. The 2 leaders, upon hearing of the movement, summoned the Committees of Safety and Supply to discuss countermeasures. The committees decided to raise a "home guard" artillery battery, to hide their reserve weapons, and to distribute some of their ammunition and provisions among the insurrectionary forces. The American Army was called upon to gather at Concord on the 19th of April to receive the provisions, including 10 hogsheads of rum.

On the way back from Lexington, Revere stopped and told Colonel Conant of the Charlestown minutemen that the Redcoats would be coming his way. Conant wanted to know how he would be alerted when the troops were coming. Revere pointed across the Charles River toward the steeple of Christ's Church. "Two lanterns if they really come across the river," he said. "But they may be faking an amphibious movement. One lantern means they're marching overland through Cambridge." Conant agreed.

On Tuesday, April 18, a Redcoat sergeant-major became unaccountably impatient over a Colonial gunsmith's slowness in fixing his firelock. Also, a stableboy overheard 2 British grenadiers griping about an upcoming night march. Warren listened keenly to these and other bits of scuttlebutt, and he knew that the crisis was very near. In the evening, the government barracks were unusually active, and Warren's most valuable spy now confirmed his suspicion: The order to move on Concord had been given. The man-of-war *Somerset* was moving down the river as if to protect the ferry, and Warren surmised that the army would cross the water.

Warren summoned Billy Dawes and sent him

along the land route to spread the word. The young shoemaker moped by the assembling imperial troops, his horse ambling slowly, and then he spurred his mount furiously toward Roxbury. When he approached the picket line, Dawes again slowed and mixed with a group of farmers as they passed through the checkpoint.

A guard eyed the courier suspiciously and began to ask piercing questions about his identification papers. Just as things were looking bad for Dawes, a sentry with whom he had drunk many ales and beers walked up and advised the hostile guard to forget his interrogation. This man, he explained, was just a typical, good-natured Colonial bumpkin, quite harmless. The bumpkin was allowed to pass, and soon he was galloping through Cambridge yelling, "The British are coming!"

It was late in the evening when Warren got hold of Paul Revere. Warren dispatched him by the water route, which he would be traveling barely ahead of the government troops. Revere, in turn, recruited an old coconspirator, John Pulling, to give the signal at the steeple. Pulling then enlisted the Christ's Church sexton, Robert Newman, to do the actual signaling, while he watched for Redcoats in the street below.

Two lights beamed briefly from the church tower, and across the river Conant spotted them. The Royal army saw them too, and troops ran to the church to deal harshly with the culprit. Finding the church empty, they marched off to the sexton's house and arrested him. Interrogating Newman, they obtained Pulling's name and troops were sent to seize him. Fortunately, he had hidden for the night. In the morning, he and his family slipped aboard a boat which was delivering beer to the Royal fleet, and they escaped into the rebel countryside.

When Revere arrived at the docks, he found that his boatmen friends, Josh Bentley and Tom Richardson, had forgotten to bring said oars. One of the conspirators remembered that a girl friend lived nearby: He called at her window and asked for some material. She obligingly removed her petticoat and threw it to him.

The boat, now equipped with the petticoat, delivered Revere safely to the Charlestown shore, where Conant and Richard Devens waited for a full report. After receiving his information, Devens warned Revere that there were already Royal detachments between him and Lexington. Conant added that he had sent his own riders toward Lexington, but none were as respected and resourceful as Revere and Dawes. Revere decided to continue on his own mission and asked for a horse. Devens soon fetched Deacon Larkin's horse, *Brown Beauty*. Devens assumed that the Deacon would

be glad to sacrifice his property for the Cause. Revere was off, galloping in bright moonlight.

When the silversmith reached Lexington, he found Adams and Hancock in the company of Hancock's fiancée, Dolly Quincy, and her chaperone, Aunt Lydia. Hancock was in a combative and flamboyant mood. Hearing of the approach of the Royal army, he picked up a musket and prepared to stand his ground against the might of the empire. Sam Adams patiently told him to put down the gun and take a more prudent course.

Lexington was awakening to the electrifying news Revere had yelled as he thundered into town. Lights were going on and the church bell began to peal frantically. Then the drum was pounded in the town common. Armed men gathered, rubbing their eyes. It was midnight, and in the midst of the turmoil, the excitement, and the terrible fear, Billy Dawes rode in on his horse, bone tired. He had come by land.

Revere suggested that they continue on to Concord to warn the patriots there, and Dawes nodded and climbed wearily back into the saddle. Dr. Sam Prescott, who had been visiting a woman in Lexington, joined them, and the 3 riders pounded away toward Concord. They took turns riding off the road to warn farmhouses along the way. As Revere rode on one of these side missions, he was apprehended by 2 government officers. "Lobsterbacks!" Revere yelled to his friends. "Help! Only 2 of them! Hurry!"

But when Prescott reached the spot, 2 more officers were there. Dawes was still far away, and Revere frantically warned him away. "Back to Lexington, Billy!" Dawes fell off his horse but managed to remount and escape. Revere and Prescott rode toward a wooded area but 6 more troopers cut them off. Prescott swerved and jumped the fence and was soon back on the road toward Concord, but Revere was captured.

Dawes returned to Lexington, where the action was, having made the longest ride of the long night. When the British major heard shots, Revere haughtily warned him that the Revolutionary forces in Lexington were cutting His Majesty's army to pieces. The Major quickly released his prisoner and led his detachment to the rear.

Decades later, Henry Longfellow would wander around the scenes of all this Revolutionary excitement and thrill to the memory of "the midnight ride of Paul Revere." After all, Revere became famous for his silverware, and Longfellow had certainly seen the glittering stuff in the best houses in Boston. But nobody ever bragged because they had a pair of shoes made by Billy Dawes, no matter how good a cobbler he was.

—C.J.

America's 1st Riot—the Doctors' Mob of 1788

"In a spirit of medical humor," one chronicler of the period wrote, a medical student, John Hicks, Jr., picked up the arm of a corpse he had just dissected and pointed it at the youngsters peering in through the window. "This is your mother's hand!" he shouted. "I just dug it up! Watch out or I'll smack you with it!"

The children scattered into the dark, but one frightened boy took Hicks at his word. By a strange coincidence his mother *had* died recently. The boy repeated Hicks's threat to his father, who gathered some friends and hurried toward the local cemetery. There, by another strange coincidence, he found his wife's grave quite empty indeed. Whoever had robbed it hadn't even bothered to refill the hole. The exposed coffin was broken apart, and the enraged spouse vowed to make someone pay for its desecration. He led his friends through the streets of lower Manhattan, others joining them, and a mob of hundreds soon stormed toward the New York Hospital and its unsuspecting staff. The mob had heard too many stories about young interns, stealing bodies from private cemeteries and now they had "proof." The "Doctors' Mob" of April 13–15, 1788, America's 1st riot, had begun.

Soon the frenzied mob reached what are now Worth and Duane streets where the hospital was located. Men with brickbats and torches encircled the large building, blocking exits and screaming for all the doctors to come out. They howled for blood and might have lynched the entire staff if the doctors hadn't escaped out rear windows. With no time to spare, those doctors on duty—with one exception—slipped past the mob.

The hospital was empty now, except for Dr. Wright Post and 3 students who had stayed to protect the valuable anatomical specimens —to no avail. After the unthinking rioters had spent themselves, the inside of the hospital was bare and broken. Glass was strewn about the floor; surgical instruments were bent beyond recognition; the collection of important anatomical specimens was ruined, and Dr. Post and the 3 students had been put in the city jail by the sheriff in order to protect them. They were joined there later by the professor of anatomy, Dr. Richard Bayley.

The mob had understood nothing in its path and everything was destroyed, but despite the ruins at its feet, its appetite for vengeance wasn't sated. Out the mob flowed into the city, searching for doctors. A number of strange incidents occurred. At the home of Sir John Temple the rioters stopped and entered for apparently no reason at all. Temple wasn't a doctor, but the mob completely destroyed his house, almost leveling the building, without ever realizing that "Sir John" did not mean "surgeon." Luckily, no one was killed, but a few narrowly escaped with their lives. Hicks had taken refuge in the home of a prominent physician. The crowd entered the house looking for him. It was Hicks's good luck that they looked no farther than the attic, for when he had seen the mob coming he had hidden behind the chimney on the roof of the house next door.

Only by early morning did the mob seem to have expended its hate. Meanwhile Gov. George Clinton had called out the militia and many city doctors had left town. Clinton and Mayor James Duane were quite sure that they had the situation well under control. When the riot began again at daybreak, the 2 officials were dumbfounded.

The mob had increased substantially and was hurrying toward Columbia College. There they attacked the building, looking for more anatomical specimens. Curious onlookers were assaulted. Alexander Hamilton faced the rioters and tried to persuade them to go home. That evening, in front of the city jail, it became apparent that the mob could not be dispersed without resorting to force. John Jay, soon to become Chief Justice of the Supreme Court, was knocked unconscious by a rock. Another onlooker, Baron Friedrich von Steuben, a hero of the American Revolution, pleaded with Governor Clinton not to order his troops to fire. Many would be killed, he insisted—try to curb the mob with words, not bullets. Yet, even as Steuben spoke, the rioters surged forward and the baron got hit on the head with a brick.

The baron quickly changed his mind. "Fire, Clinton, fire!" he shouted, and the governor gave the order.

The militiamen fired, and felled 20 men. Eight rioters were killed. Many more were seriously wounded. Not till morning was the "Doctors' Mob" finished, and doctors could tend the injured rioters.

No one ever identified the corpse that had incited the "Doctors' Mob," and the husband who avenged the desecration of his wife's grave remains anonymous to this day. The riot was completely in vain. Although New York's legislature soon passed a law authorizing the dissection of the bodies of persons executed for burglary, arson, and murder, it was a long time before body snatchers stopped escorting their night's work from Long Island to Manhattan via ferry, purchasing tickets for "drunken friends," who more than repaid their kindness at $100 a body. The era of the "resurrectionists" or grave robbers lasted until almost the middle of the 19th century and spawned such characters as the infamous Englishman William Burke, who killed—by "burking" or smothering his victims—in order to supply the demands of the anatomists.

The "Doctors' Mob" was not nearly so violent as the mob uprisings that were to follow in its wake. Nor was the cause of the uprising more unjust than most—many riots in the 1st half of the 19th century were directed against newly arrived immigrants, and often were led by groups not too long here themselves. On the other hand, the "Doctors' Mob" did not arise out of real grievances like the Bread Riot in 1857 and the labor troubles throughout 1877, when economic conditions forced people into the streets to demand food and work. Only one other uprising seems quite as senseless as the "Doctors' Mob"—the riot in 1849 when English actor W. C. Macready was driven from the stage of the Astor Place Opera House, and eventually from the country, by a mob that gathered in response to the anti-English demagoguery of American actor Edwin Forrest. But few accurate comparisons can be made among these disturbances. The "Doctors' Mob" is similar to most mob uprisings in America, or anywhere else, only in that it destroyed much and accomplished little, especially for the people involved.

—R.H.

Survivors of American History in Foreign Lands

Throughout the course of American history there have been political, regional, religious groups who have suffered defeat or persecution, yet were determined not to abandon their beliefs or old way of life. These people sought a better future than the one that awaited them in the U.S. They felt that by escaping the boundaries of their homeland they could find freedom and perhaps perpetuate their past traditions and customs in a foreign land. This is a brief record of some Americans who fled the traumas of U.S. history, and settled in another land. This is also a record of what happened to their children's children, their successors and descendants living in today's world. In short, the history book comes alive in the following accounts of these touchingly human expatriates.

The Revolutionary War Tory Descendants in Nova Scotia

On a chill autumn day in 1783, 1,500 men and women stood on the decks of the British ships anchored in the Bay of Fundy off Nova Scotia. They looked at the coastline—the site for the new town they would call Digby—with both apprehension and determination. They had chosen life in a new country and that life included allegiance to the British Crown rather than allegiance to the infant United States of America. Behind them lay landholdings, mercantile fortunes, and positions of authority, all confiscated by American Revolutionary forces either during or immediately following the bloody war years.

Tories in the Colonies had ranged in social rank from farmers to merchants to lawyers to office-holders appointed by the Crown. Their motives for remaining loyal varied as much as their stations in life. Colonial governors and other officials were, of course, anxious to hold on to the influence and remuneration that came along with their appointments. Farmers and landholders, too, were loathe to relinquish the material benefits that came to them under British rule. Royal land grants had brought enormous wealth to such families as the Penns in Pennsylvania, the Calverts in Maryland, the Pepperells in New England, the Johnsons in New York, and Lord Fairfax in Virginia. Merchants had little to gain by severing connections with the British for a nation still caught up in its birth pangs and not yet affluent enough to replace the loss of trade with the home country. Clergymen of the Episcopal Church were also largely in the Tory camp, as were lawyers, whose income derived chiefly from Crown fees.

When the Continental Congress, on November 27, 1777, recommended to the States that they seize Loyalist property, sell it, and use the proceeds to finance the War, Loyalists had reacted bitterly to the loss of their holdings and became even more staunch supporters of King George. There was, too, the strong pull of tradition, and many who had nothing to lose in terms of worldly goods found it impossible to turn against their homeland. Among the Dutch, Scotch, Irish, and Germans who had emigrated to America, there also were many who chose not to cast their lot with the revolutionaries.

From the beginning, those with Loyalist sentiments were subjected to confiscation of personal property, public harassment, tar-and-feathering, and imprisonment. Because of this, Tories began leaving the Colonies as early as 1776, when over 1,000 fled Boston with the British. Another 9,000 left New York City and a like number departed from Charleston, S.C., when those cities were evacuated by British troops. All told, about 100,000 eventually left, to be scattered around Great Britain, Canada, Florida, and the British West Indies.

When peace was negotiated in 1783, the British attempted to assure the Loyalists that they would be compensated for their losses. But all that the Continental Congress included in the treaty was an "earnest recommendation" that the States recompense the Loyalists, a provision that was almost totally ignored.

The British Government itself undertook to reimburse its loyal subjects to some degree, and set up a commission to receive claims. Although some £8 million in claims was filed, actually only about £3 million was awarded. Relocation of the Loyalists, however, was carried out on a large scale, and land grants were freely given to make immigration easier. Not all Tories took advantage of this, some preferring to remain in their familiar homes and adjust themselves to the new Government. Many returned to England, where Colonial officers were generally given jobs or put on pension, but few were happy in exile. These exiles eventually found ways of picking up their lives again in America.

Far more successful was the movement of Tories to Canada. Here, in Nova Scotia, New Brunswick, Upper Canada, and Ontario, the British Government made farsighted arrangements to assist them. To heads of families, it granted 500 acres of land, with 300 acres allotted to single men; each township was awarded 2,000 acres for the support of religion and 1,000 acres for schools; rations, fuel, clothing, and other assistance were freely given for a period of years after settlement. Under this program, more than 3 million acres of land were handed over to the United Empire Loyalists, as they were called, and about $9 million was spent on their relocation.

The Digby settlers' experience was a typical one following the end of the American Revolution. Arriving in early winter made theirs a hard task. Unable to put up shelters before the cold weather set in, many passed that 1st winter aboard ships commanded by the Hon. Robert Digby, anchored close to shore. Digby had commanded the British fleet off New York during the Revolution and had a special interest in the relocation of those who had provided hospitality and support to British troops during the fighting. He now made every effort to ease the lot of the new settlers. Food, however, was in short supply, and they quickly learned to rely heavily on the herring caught in the harbor, a meal that became so monotonous that some, in jest, referred to it as "Digby chicken," a

name that persists today for herring from the Fundy shore area.

In April, 1783, another group of Loyalists packed all its possessions, including a large number of slaves, aboard 18 ships and sailed from New York to Port Roseway, Nova Scotia. These Loyalists laid out a city complete with 5 streets, while their black retainers felled trees and built houses. Soon the city was populated by 5,000 Tories and 1,000 slaves. One rich Loyalist, Stephen Shakespeare, had 20 slaves; another Loyalist, Charles Oliver Bruff, a goldsmith, owned 15 slaves. Four other families had 9 slaves each. After a number of years, these slaves were freed. Under Colonel Burch, they formed their own neighboring community of Burchtown, today called Birchtown. One of their black leaders, a mulatto schoolteacher named Colonel Stephen Black, once entertained Prince William Henry, a future King of England.

But initially, the settlers faced hard times. Conditions in Halifax were especially bad, and hundreds of settlers lived in tents on the Common or in cellars and attics, eating anything they could find. The dog and cat population of Halifax was decimated as the town's human population increased. As one disillusioned newcomer wrote as late as 1784: "We have nothing but his Majesty's rotten pork and unbaked flour to subsist on. It is the most inhospitable clime that ever mortal set foot on."

These displaced Loyalists played a crucial part in the building of modern Canada. Out of the Nova Scotia contingent have come such figures as Joseph Howe, the reformer, who was born in Halifax in 1804, the son of refugee John Howe. Even today, the Howe name is prominent in Halifax. Thomas Chandler Haliburton (1796–1865) emerged from Windsor to become a satirist of international fame, and this family, too, remains quite active in Nova Scotian affairs and politics. And Samuel Cunard (1787–1865), founder of the Cunard North Star Steamship Line, was born in Halifax to a Dutch Quaker family who fled Pennsylvania to escape the Revolution. The ancestors of Cyrus Eaton, chairman of the board emeritus of the Chesapeake & Ohio Railway in 1974, were engaged in the shipping industry between Halifax and Havana in the early 1800s.

Today, descendants of those 1st settlers carry on the fishing industry established by their forebears, as well as the pulpwood and lumber industries that came later. Their scallop fleet is the largest in the world. Still prominent in the little town of Digby (population 2,363)— named for the man who supported its 1st wooden church with £100 sterling and gave it a bell brought from England, and who dug the well that provided most of Digby's fresh water supply—are families whose names have roots in New York, New Jersey, and Massachusetts. From New Jersey came one John Edison, who moved on to Ontario in 1810. From there, his grandson, Samuel Edison, moved back to the State of Ohio, where Thomas Alva, his 3rd child, was born. Thus one branch of the Loyalist refugees completed its cycle of immigration.

—S.D.P. & E.K.

For further reading: Bird, Will R. *This is Nova Scotia.* Toronto, McGraw-Hill Ryerson, 1950. An excellent guide for the off-the-beaten-path traveler who wants to visit Tory enclaves in Nova Scotia today.

Confederate Descendants in Mexico

After the Civil War, the men and women who left the defeated Confederate States and set out for Mexico and South America were journeying toward a dream. For the soldiers of the losing army, it was a dream of battles; for the civilians, who had seen their gracious antebellum way of life destroyed, it was a dream of reestablishing that graciousness. For both, it was also an escape from the repressive measures of the victors.

Some of these expatriates traveled to Brazil, and their descendants are to be found to this day in the communities of Santarém, near Belterra, and Villa Americana, in the State of São Paulo. Others went to Venezuela. But Mexico proved by far the most enticing destination, as it seemed to offer a nearly perfect site for relocation. What drew the exiles to Mexico? Geographical proximity was by no means the only consideration. The current political situation in Mexico invited their immigration, and one of their staunchest Confederate compatriots was deeply involved with the colonization movement sponsored by Maximilian and Napoleon III. Napoleon had seized control of the country in 1863 and placed it under the rule of his Habsburg relative, Maximilian. Then, in 1865, an appeal for settlers was made by Maximilian's protégé Matthew Fontaine Maury, an internationally respected oceanographer who was revered in his native Virginia as a Civil War leader. Commodore Maury had spent long months in England seeking tangible aid for the Confederate cause during the war, and his word was enough to inspire confidence in any colonizing venture. The colonization boom now took on real impetus.

There had been an earlier scheme fostered by Dr. William M. Gwin, who had visualized a grand colony of ex-Confederates in the province of Sonora, in the northwest district of Mexico. Napoleon had approved Gwin's plan, knowing that an exploitation of the metals in that region would yield France an appreciable return on her investment. However, Gwin's grandiose ideas and his desire for personal glory had antagonized Maximilian, and nothing came of the plan.

With Maury, it was different. He had known Maximilian when the latter was archduke of Austria and in command of the Austrian navy in 1854; the 2 seafarers had much in common and understood each other well. It was natural that Maximilian should turn to his old friend to head colonization from the States. Their effort got under way formally on September 5, 1865, when Maximilian set aside a tract of 500,000 acres for the new immigrants. The little community of Carlota offered a man with a family 640 acres, at $1 an acre, plus a lot in town. The land was given with a certificate that it was free from mortgage. In addition, it was exempt from taxes the 1st year. For those who had lost everything in the Civil War, the Mexican Government was willing to provide transportation to Mexico and arrange for the colonist's trip to the undeveloped parts of the public domain set aside for this type of immigrant.

Maximilian's offer was, needless to say, attractive to the civilians anxious to flee the ruthless reconstruction going on in their beloved South under the direction of Northern occupation forces. Even those Confederate soldiers—among them Generals Kirby-Smith, Magruder, Shelby, Slaughter, Walker, and Hindman—who went to Mexico in search of new battles in the service of either Juárez, the leader of the rebel forces, or Maximilian and his Imperialist forces, were soon drawn to colonization when they found little welcome from these opposing armies. True, some of the disillusioned returned to Texas, but more stayed on in Mexico to take advantage of the land offers being made under Maury's direction as commissioner of immigration and colonization.

By January of 1866, some 260 immigrants had landed in Campeche and Tampico. During the spring, their numbers swelled, with many colonists having to sail from the States under pretext of heading for Havana. The U.S. Government was arresting Maury's agents when they could be found, in an attempt to end the Southerners' exodus to Mexico. In all, about 2,500 Confederates eventually settled in Mexico in an attempt to perpetuate their past way of life. The largest settlement of these self-exiled Southerners was in and around the town of Carlota, located some 70 mi. west of the port of Vera Cruz, where several hundred colonists banded together.

Unfortunately, Maury's advertisements and promises were more enticing to the indigent who were escaping fear and future poverty, than to those with remnants of personal wealth. He found his office overrun with penniless immigrants, and these people soon became a burden either to their friends who were already in the country or to the Government. For those who hoped to establish plantations run by slave labor, like those they had known at home before the War, it came as a shock to learn that slavery had been outlawed in Mexico for years. The land area set aside to be given without cost proved to be inadequate for the numbers appearing daily, and Maury had difficulty in obtaining enough free or cheap land to satisfy their demands. It was a time of disillusionment and a period of real hardship for the Confederates with their dreams. Private land companies stepped in, hoping to make exorbitant profits, and colonization efforts began to founder in the chaos of disorganization. As word of true conditions seeped back to the States, departures slackened considerably and finally came to a halt. Maury, who wrote his wife that he "despaired of ever seeing his 'New Virginia' firmly established" in Mexico, abandoned his office and fled to England, leaving his "New Virginia" settlers to shift for themselves.

In the years immediately following Maury's departure, the Mexican revolutionists were able to overthrow the French, and in the turmoil of that time, no accurate statistics were kept of the stranded Confederates. A few stayed on, married into Mexican families, and were absorbed into the Mexican culture (names like Obregón and Alire in modern Mexico have their origin in the O'Briens and O'Learys from Confederate States). But the Confederate colonies themselves were plundered and burned by the triumphant Juárista forces, and the colonists were driven out of Mexico. "Today few traces of the Mexican exodus exist below the border or above it," wrote Andrew Rolle in *The Lost Cause*. "Carlota and the other Confederate towns have disappeared. . . . Because they did not cling together in tight enclaves, the Confederates made little impression on the country's history or its population pattern. Rather, the exodus is striking for its futility, the delusion of its participants, and the inevitability of its failure. The colonists went to Mexico at the wrong time, with the wrong attitudes, and chose the wrong occupations. It was a spontaneous, informal exodus, without proper organization and with few goals. Yet, even if all this had been otherwise . . . the exodus would still have failed. Colonists could not, indeed would not, in most cases, have stayed abroad permanently."

Within 2 years of the end of the Civil War, a great majority of the Confederates-in-exile had pulled up stakes and headed north out of Mexico back to Texas. Many settled in the Lone Star State. The rest returned to the depleted South they had earlier left with so much

hope, ready now to join in the job of reconstruction.

—S.D.P.

For further reading: Rolle, Andrew F. *The Lost Cause: The Confederate Exodus to Mexico.* Norman, Okla.: Univ. of Okla. Press (c. 1965). A thorough account of Confederates-in-exile.

Mormon Polygamists in Mexico

The Mormons—members of the Church of Jesus Christ of Latter-Day Saints—had either fled or been violently expelled from New York State, Missouri, Ohio and Illinois. But once they had made the incredibly difficult traverse from eastern Nebraska to the Great Salt Lake, they thought themselves safe. Not so. Congress passed 3 laws forbidding polygamy, a practice which was sacred to the Mormons, though only a small percentage of them could afford to indulge in it.

The 1st 2 laws, the Morrill Act of 1862 and the Poland Bill of 1874 were not very strong; in general, they left enforcement and punishment to local officers and juries, which meant, in effect, that Mormons judged other Mormons for being good Mormons. But the 1882 Edmunds Act had gnawing, tearing teeth. For every day that a Mormon man cohabited with more than one wife, he could be imprisoned for 5 years and fined $500.

The Edmunds Act was probably unconstitutional, interfering as it did with the right to worship guaranteed by the 1st Amendment, but the times were Victorian, and Utah—the Mormons called it Deseret—was not a State. Nor were the other western territories as yet except for Nevada, where the Mormon population was also large enough to merit political consideration. Every State has 2 senators, and the loss of 2 votes in the Senate is important to politicians today. When the Senate was ¾ its present size, those 2 votes mattered even more.

Since 1875, Mormon missionaries had been considering the possibility of seeking freedom from persecution by moving to Mexico. As harassment grew worse, Church leaders studied the reports on Mexico with mounting interest, and finally in March, 1885, 25 families headed south for the Border. The following months the number swelled, until 350 Saints were camped south of the Border while their leaders negotiated to buy Mexican land. Finally about 150,-000 acres in the Piedras Verdes Valley, a little more than 100 mi. south of Columbus, N. Mex., were turned over to the Mormons and they had their new home.

Many of the Mexican-based Saints thought that some day their *colonias* would become the true center of the whole Church, and toward this end they began to work their valley with vigor. And how they worked! They not only tilled and tended fields, built dams for irrigation, tanned leather for shoes, but they produced kiln-hardened brick so they could have the sort of houses they were used to—narrow 2-story-plus-attic affairs like the ones that gave the Mormon towns in Arizona and New Mexico a New England look. Not for them the simple, single-story adobe structures of northern Mexico and the southwestern U.S.; there was something immoral, perhaps, in living in a house whose bricks were merely sunbaked.

An error in surveying forced the Mormons to abandon their 1st towns and move to rockier and steeper country. They went through the whole process all over again, this time adding a flour mill. Now they shipped flour and lumber and saddles and boots to the Border for cash sale.

Porfirio Díaz, President of Mexico, had been in office since 1877 and would continue to rule—if not as President, then by controlling whomever he had made President—until 1910. Díaz believed not only in foreign capital but in foreign ways, whether European or American, and he admired the Mormons' Yankee-type industry. But under Díaz more and more land passed into the hands of a few *hacendados,* landowners who were frequently not even Mexican citizens. Publisher William Randolph Hearst owned enough Mexican land to make San Simeon seem the size of a weekend camp.

In 1910, the Mexican peasants, who had become mere slaves or *peons,* began to rebel. Francisco Madero, the liberal son of a rich liquor distilling family, headed a revolution. Díaz was overthrown, sent into exile, and civil war engulfed all Mexico. The Mormon settlers, against the advice of church leaders in both Utah and Mexico City, were inclined to side with the conservatives rather than remain neutral. They had done well under Díaz, and the Mormon philosophy of hard work and hard ambition and hard land titles did not agree with the Maderista-Mexican policy of *ejidal.* Under this policy, a man and his family were given what land they needed, rather than what they could acquire.

Furthermore, the rebels, poorly financed and coming mostly from poor backgrounds, had to seize what they needed in order to conduct their war. Pancho Villa, it is true, issued money in large quantities—he had it printed for him by the American Banknote Company in the U.S.—but there were no assets to back up this paper money. Mormon cattle, Mormon food, Mormon fodder were seized by the revolutionaries, and even if they were paid for in Villista money, the Mormons resented the loss of their goods.

They complained to the local judge, who deputized 4 Mormons to go and arrest a local Mexican who was looting on his own account, rather than from patriotism. This man, Sosa by name, resisted arrest and the Mormons shot him dead. They were promptly thrown into jail, along with 4 freebooting looters, and there was talk of lynching the Mormons until Raul Madero, the local general's brother, came into town and released them.

Shortly after, the local general told Mormon stake president Junius Romney that the Mormons must hand over the large supply of weapons and ammunition they had been storing in case of trouble. Romney stalled. Despite the fact that flatcar-mounted artillery was trained on Colonía Dublan, he went into council with his people and decided to turn over some, but not all and certainly not the best of their guns to the rebels. In this way, he tried to gain time to get the multiple wives of each family, the women and children of the *colonías,* out of Mexico.

This was in July of 1912. The Mormon women, like refugees in every war, were ill-prepared for a hasty departure. They took with them what they valued most, which was not necessarily the things most needed on a trip across the Chihuahuan desert, or even on a journey by train. They arrived in El Paso thirsty, hungry, and poorly clad.

Ironically, the Mormon Church petitioned the U.S. Government to aid these refugees. The Government issued tents and food and offered to provide train tickets for any of the Mexican Mormons who had friends or relatives they could join. But they had been in Mexico for 24 years, ties were broken, and few of the women had a place to go.

Meanwhile, the Mormon men in the *colonías* were not having it easy. The rebel looting—or requisitioning—was still going on, and the Mormons were not mountain men or cowboys —they were men who missed family life. This may have been a governing factor in their decision, under Junius Romney, to get out of Mexico. They made this drastic decision despite the advice of Bishop Joseph Bentley in Mexico, and that of A. W. Ivins, the church elder Salt Lake City had sent down to El Paso to supervise the relocation of the refugees. Ivins scattered them across Arizona and New Mexico, and some he sent back to Utah.

Once back in the U.S., the colonists did not find life easy. It is painful for men who have owned their own farms and businesses to work as hired hands. Three weeks after the male refugees had arrived in New Mexico on their way to El Paso, a band of 35—including both sexes and all ages—decided to return to Colonía Juárez. Others drifted after them, and by 1917 the Mormon *colonías* were again populated. There were still requisitioning raids, but the Mormons found they could live with them. Not a single case of rape was ever recorded, by the way.

Then, in 1916, came Pancho Villa's raid on Columbus, N. Mex., in which 20 Americans were killed. Brig. Gen. John J. "Black Jack" Pershing was ordered to enter Mexico and get Villa dead or alive. But Villa was too elusive to be caught. Pershing, because he paid in good American dollars for supplies, found the Saints so receptive to his troops that when the U.S. finally gave up and called him back across the Border, the Mormons might well have predicted Mexican reprisal. This did occur when General Salazar rode into Colonia Juárez and told the Saints that all their able-bodied men would either join his Mexican army or be shot. He added that they would not only have to fight against the Mexican Federalistas, but also against the U.S. troops in reprisal for Pershing's interference in Mexican matters.

Bishop Bentley, who had succeeded Junius Romney as stake president, thought over General Salazar's demands and then he made a short speech. Mormons, he said, were peaceful men, who devoted their lives to working and to educating their children. They did not wage war. If Salazar wanted to shoot them for that, let him do so. Bentley was a small man, and quite possibly his spunk tickled Salazar's Mexican sense of humor. At any rate, the last great threat against the *colonistas* had been avoided.

There were further minor troubles—the windup of the revolution, the depression in the U.S., which deprived the Mexican Mormon polygamists of their markets, and so on—but the *colonías* have persisted. Today both Mormon boys and girls are usually sent back to the States for college. Brigham Young University and the University of Utah are, of course, favored. But now some of the youngsters complete their education in other States, or even in Mexico City. All are bilingual.

Several of the descendants of the hegira to Mexico have made international names for themselves in the arts and sciences. One, George Romney, was governor of Michigan, and he was considered as a possible Republican candidate for President, despite the fact that he was born in Mexico.

—R.Wo.

Survivors of American History in the U.S.A.

The Hessians

Unlike those who flocked to the New World around 1750 to escape religious discrimination, the Germans who came to America during the Revolutionary War were mercenaries, hired by England's King George III.

Because many British openly sympathized with the American rebels, deploring the tactics of a government that would take up arms against brothers and cousins, George III was hard put to round up a decent-sized army. Forced to turn to other sources for hired help, he signed a contract in 1775 with the Landgrave Frederick of Hesse-Cassel that would supply Britain with 22,000 soldiers. Six German principalities furnished Britain with troops, but since half came from Hesse-Cassel, all were called Hessians. By 1777, of the 21,000 British troops in America, 15,000 were Hessians.

Since the principality of Hesse-Cassel was poverty-stricken, the Landgrave greedily seized the opportunity to make money, filling the ranks with peasants. No one in the lower classes was immune from recruitment, and many a hapless lad was carried off by press gangs. Discipline was of the harshest kind; the officers were martinets, demanding instant obedience, floggings among the rank and file were common, and desertion was punishable by death. Recruits were subjected to endless close-order drills, and even when they rode in the flatboats as assault troops, they were forced to stand at rigid attention, with arms sloped, in tight ranks, like puppets.

They were outfitted smartly in blue uniforms with turned-back tails and the tall metal caps resembling a bishop's miter. And the Jaegers, the elite sharpshooters recruited from the German forests, wore green uniforms with scarlet cuffs and carried short rifles. But smartly dressed or not, they were Hessians, a name synonymous with brutality.

Because of their brutality, the Colonists called them the "Huns from Hell." Since most of the Hessians had known nothing but dire poverty, they saw no reason for not taking what they wanted from the neat homes and flourishing farms. Few understood English, so they made no distinction between Whig and Tory, looting and despoiling all that stood in their path.

Though they fought side by side with the British, the Hessians were not comrades-in-arms. The British took an immediate dislike to these heavy-going, hard-drinking foreigners whose guttural language fell harshly on English ears. So many brawls erupted between the 2 that they had to be kept separate when not in battle. And many British went over to the rebel side, so outraged were they by these Huns from Hell.

It was during the summer of 1776, however, that a one-man crusade got under way. Christopher Ludwick, a German-born Philadelphia baker, had Washington's blessing to pose as a rebel deserter, infiltrate the British lines at Staten Island, and persuade the Hessians stationed there to desert. This tall, erect man established an immediate rapport with the Hessians. He talked of the lush farmlands in Pennsylvania that could be had for the asking, filling the Hessians' minds with visions of wealth. In Pennsylvania, he assured them, they could speak their own tongue, work their own farms, and the Pennsylvania Dutch girls were buxom and willing. Ludwick's plan worked. Hundreds of Hessians slipped away by night, with Ludwick accompanying them. Many did indeed escape to Pennsylvania where they turned to the nonaggressive life of farming. And later on, at Ludwick's suggestion, many captured Germans were sent to Pennsylvania to become useful citizens of this new country.

The loss of a few hundred Hessians, however, was negligible, for on July 12, 1776, Admiral Richard Howe arrived in New York harbor with 150 ships and a reported 15,000 reinforcements for his brother, Gen. William Howe. And on August 1, another 40 ships dropped anchor with 3,000 more troops to join those already stationed on Staten Island, that stronghold of Tories. Such a gathering of might made it obvious that George Washington's days were numbered in New York.

The Battle of Long Island ensued on August 22 and lasted 7 days. The British and Hessians were victorious, and a British officer wrote: "Rejoice, my friend, that we have given the Rebels a damned crush. . . . The Hessians and our brave Highlanders gave no quarter, and it was a fine sight to see with what alacrity they dispatched the Rebels with their bayonets after we had them surrounded. . . ."

Washington suffered another crushing defeat at the Battle of Fort Washington, that supposedly impregnable fortress on the Hudson opposite the Palisades, at the hands of the Hessians under the command of Gen. Wilhelm von Knyphausen, known to his tablemates as the man who buttered his bread with his thumb. At least 2,500 Americans were taken prisoner, and tormented after being forced to strip by their German captors, until some disgusted British officers put a stop to it. The incident prompted the famed British orator, Edmund Burke, to say in Parliament that "This sort of glory, won by German mercenaries against free-born English subjects has no charms for me."

Thus began Washington's humiliating retreat south across the Jersey flats. He arrived on the Pennsylvania side of the Delaware on December 8 with only 3,000 men, many of them dispirited and broken, and most of them without shoes and coats.

While Washington waited with his shivering, ragged troops, Col. Gottlieb Rall, commandant of 1,400 Hessians in the sleepy village of Trenton, across the river, kept his troops busy with endless, comic-opera parades. Rall was a boisterous, party-loving drunk who enjoyed music. Each day he got his musicians out to lead a parade through Trenton, with his troops following in close order drill. He turned a deaf ear, however, to Col. Carl von Donop's advice to fortify the town against attack from those "country clowns," as Rall called them; their activities across the river could hardly be ignored. But Rall had beaten them at Fort Washington and felt nothing but contempt for them.

Washington chose Christmas for the attack on Trenton. He knew that for a good Hessian, Christmas is the season for orgies. He could count on finding a drunken, groggy garrison. Late in the afternoon of Christmas day, the troops began to move down the riverbank, their bare feet swathed in gunnysack, and waited in shivering silence for the early fall of darkness.

Meanwhile, the Hessians were celebrating the Yuletide with considerable abandon, gathered around gaily decorated evergreen trees —the 1st Christmas trees seen in America— as was the custom in Germany, quaffing a liquor called applejack. Colonel Rall spent most of the night playing cards at a party at Postmaster Abraham Hunt's house. A Tory farmer delivered a note warning of the rebel attack, but was refused admittance by Hunt's butler. When the butler gave Rall the note, Rall, too intent on his cards and his applejack, and not too familiar with the English language, stared bleary-eyed at the note and then shoved it into his pocket unread.

The patriots surprised the Hessians about 7 A.M. on December 26. Rall, still groggy, was roused by an aide who left immediately to try and organize the still drunken troops. When Rall emerged onto the street, hung over, half dressed, but with broadsword in hand, he tried vainly to rally his men. Those who weren't mowed down by the bullets flying through the streets fled in panic, stumbling over the white, frozen snow away from the awful onslaught. Christmas ended in disaster for many Hessians in 1776.

Rall sustained 3 gunshot wounds, the last one mortal, and he was carried into the Presbyterian Church where he was laid out in a pew. When the note he had ignored fell out of his pocket, and was handed to him by an aide, he groaned with remorse. For a game of cards and a night of drinking, Rall paid dearly with the loss of Trenton and with his life. Nearly 1,000 Hessians were taken prisoner, 40 were killed or wounded, and 6 cannon and more than 100 muskets were confiscated. Two Americans were killed, 3 wounded.

The victory at Trenton renewed confidence in the hearts of the patriots. Hungry, exhausted soldiers who had thought seriously of deserting before Trenton, now stayed around, curious to see what would happen. Many other young men flocked in from the surrounding countryside to enlist. Trenton had saved the day.

In the late spring of '77, far north of Trenton, an army of 9,000 moved down the sparkling blue waters of Lake Champlain. The British general, John Burgoyne, was on the 1st leg of his campaign to invade North America from Canada. An impressive sight, Burgoyne's flotilla of 3 large vessels, 20 gunboats, 200 flat-bottomed bateaux and canoes covered a mile of the lake. The sound of music from both German and British regiments echoed gaily across the shimmering waters. Of the 9,000 soldiers, more than half —about 5,000—were Hessians. Burgoyne's 2nd in command was the chubby, earnest-looking General Baron Friedrich von Riedesel. Only 39, but highly regarded by his British peers, Von Riedesel was not only an excellent battle officer, but he directed all the building of bridges and roads between Ticonderoga and Saratoga, an almost insurmountable feat through the mosquito-infested wilderness. He was no armchair general, and fought bravely with his men at Saratoga before Burgoyne's surrender.

His wife, Baroness Fredrika von Riedesel, a petite, vivacious woman, was probably one of the most remarkable women of the Revolutionary War. To be with her husband, she had traveled all the way from Quebec to Ticonderoga by various means—canoe, calash (a 2-wheeled cart) and gunboat—with her 3 little girls, all under 6, 3 servants and her husband's British aide, a Lieutenant Willoe. They spent one night on a wild island to escape the fury of a storm on Lake Champlain, unaware until the next day that it was called Isle aux Sonnettes, or Rattlesnake Island. At Fort Edward, she ran a well-ordered household, tutored her little girls, dressed for dinner and dined on bear's paws, a rare delicacy. But when Burgoyne's army retreated after the battles of Saratoga, she took refuge in the cellar of an abandoned farmhouse with wounded soldiers, women and children. Appalled by the stench from human defecation because people were afraid to venture out, the baroness, who had been reared in the protective atmosphere afforded by the German aristocracy, organized a clean-up squad, fed the soldiers broth, comforted the children, and by her own cheerful

presence was "commanding general" in her own sphere. The Riedesels spent 6 years in America, some of that time near Charlottesville, where they became friends of Thomas Jefferson. The baron and his wife both published books about their experiences in America when they returned to Germany.

The 5-month period between June and October of 1777 was to thin out Riedesel's army due to the shattering defeat at Bennington, wholesale desertion, and the battles of Saratoga. (Of the 336 Hessian officers who started out at Quebec, only 20 or so were left at Saratoga.)

The Battle of Bennington was one of Burgoyne's many mistakes. At his headquarters in Fort Edward, he learned that the little village of Bennington in the Hampshire Grants— overflowing with provisions—was guarded by only a handful of patriots. On August 11 he sent out a diversionary force, led by the young, stout, blond Colonel Baume, who spoke no English, with 500 Hessians and about 100 Indians to "take" Bennington.

Baume had no way of knowing that the men drifting into his encampment were crack riflemen, part of Col. John Stark's New Hampshire Militia, and not Loyalist sympathizers. He couldn't understand this strange language anyway. But the message was undeniably clear when, too late, Baume realized he was surrounded. Stark attacked Baume with all the precision of a jungle cat, in an ever-closing circle that contracted like an iron fist. The well-disciplined Hessians fought manfully, but were ultimately slaughtered in fierce hand-to-hand combat. The clumsy, overburdened Hessians were no match for Stark's tough, forest-trained men. The note Baume hastily scribbled in German for a runner to take back to Fort Edward brought reinforcements, under command of Col. Heinrich Breymann, but it was too late. Hessian casualties were heavy; 300 dead or wounded, 700 taken prisoner from both Baume's and Breymann's troops. When darkness fell, those Hessians who got away crept back through the woods to Fort Edward, leaving their cannon, ammunition, baggage wagons, and dead and wounded behind them. Many of them deserted.

On October 9, during the height of the 2nd battle of Saratoga, the lean, "emotionless" Breymann suddenly went berserk and started slashing at his own men with his broadsword, screaming in German, until one of his officers sent a bullet into his brain. It was at the Breymann Redoubt, too, that a Hessian soldier changed the course of Benedict Arnold's life. Arnold—clearly the hero of Saratoga because of the wound that left him unable to walk without aid of a cane—was never again to take up arms for his country as the brilliant battle officer that he was. Instead he was made commander of Philadelphia where he met his future wife, the beautiful Peggy Shippen. The daughter of a Tory judge, she was instrumental in Arnold's ultimate treason. But at the Breymann Redoubt on October 9, when one of Arnold's men raised his rifle to shoot the Hessian who had wounded his general, Arnold stopped him with, "For God's sake! Don't kill him; he's only doing his duty."

Although the Hessians fought in every major battle from Ticonderoga to Yorktown, Congress passed a resolution in July, 1776, which offered tracts of land to Hessians who would desert and settle in America. It isn't certain how many accepted this calculated offer, but by 1782, the estimated number of Hessians who had fought on American soil alongside the British was 29,867. About 7,555 of these were killed in action, or died from wounds or disease. Another 5,000 remained in America, settling down here as new citizens.

—E.J.G.

The Zero Factor

Since 1840, no U.S. President elected in a year ending in a zero has left the White House alive. This chilling and bizarre coincidence has become known as the zero factor.

In 1840, William Henry Harrison was elected President. He promptly caught a cold that developed into pneumonia, and he died only one month after his Inauguration.

The victor in the 1860 presidential election was an Illinois lawyer named Abraham Lincoln. He was reelected in 1864, while the country was embroiled in the War between the States. Five days after the South surrendered, while the President was attending the theater in Washington, actor John Wilkes Booth shot him in the back of the head. The next morning Mr. Lincoln died, the 2nd victim of the zero factor. Booth had fled the theater after the shooting, but 12 days later, he was cornered in a barn near the town of Bowling Green, Va. There he was either shot to death or he committed suicide.

James A. Garfield was elected President in 1880. On July 2, 1881, Mr. Garfield was shot by Charles J. Guiteau, who had applied unsuccessfully for the post of U.S. Consul in Paris. Mr. Garfield died in the resort town of Elberon, N.J., on September 19, 1881. He had been in office slightly more than 6 months. Guiteau was arrested, tried, and hanged in Washington on June 30, 1882.

The victorious presidential candidate in 1900 was William McKinley. At the Pan-American Exposition in Buffalo, N.Y., on September 6, 1901, President McKinley was fired upon by an anarchist named Leon Czolgosz. As the President was being taken away in an ambulance, he said weakly, "Let no one hurt him." McKinley died in a hospital in Buffalo on September 14, 1901. Czolgosz was tried, found Guilty, and executed in an Auburn, N.Y., prison on October 29, 1901.

The winner in the 1920 presidential race was Warren G. Harding. While on a speaking tour in the West, he was suddenly taken ill and he died in San Francisco on August 2, 1923. Over 50 years have now passed, and during that time there has been much speculation about the cause of Harding's death.

The next presidential election that took place in a year ending in a zero was that of 1940. The victor was Franklin D. Roosevelt, who was elected for his 3rd consecutive time. He won again in 1944, the only U.S. President in history to be elected to 4 terms. On April 12, 1945, while he was working at his desk in the Summer White House in Warm Springs, Ga., Mr. Roosevelt collapsed. A few hours later, he was dead.

As the 1960 presidential campaign got under way, those persons who had either thrown their hats into the ring or who were prominently mentioned as probable candidates were contacted by letter in order to get their reactions to the zero factor.

Sen. John F. Kennedy's reply is an interesting footnote to history, especially coming from a man who made his mark as a student of history as well as a statesman:

> "The historical curiosity . . . ," he wrote, "is indeed, thought-provoking: 'Since 1840 every man who has entered the White House in a year ending with a zero has not lived to leave the White House alive.' . . . As to 'what effect, if any, this will have on your future presidential aspirations,' I feel that the future will have to necessarily answer this for itself—both as to my aspirations and my fate should I have the privilege of occupying the White House.
>
> "On face value, I daresay, should anyone take this phenomenon to heart . . . anyone, that is, who aspires to change his address to 1600 Pennsylvania Ave.

. . . that most probably the landlord would be left with a 'For Rent' sign hanging on the gate-house door."

The original of this letter has been donated to the Library of Presidential Papers by Rep. Seymour Halpern (Dem.-N.Y.), who acquired it through a dealer. The library, a private, nonprofit institution, was opened in New York in 1967.

The assassination of President Kennedy on November 22, 1963, shocked the world. A relatively young, dynamic, brilliant world leader had been cut down during his most vigorous years. His supposed assassin, Lee Harvey Oswald, was killed 2 days later in Dallas, Tex. With Kennedy's death in office, the zero factor had again surfaced.

Only Thomas Jefferson, elected in 1800,

and James Monroe, elected in 1820, escaped the zero factor. And Zachary Taylor was the solitary President to die in office without benefit of the zero factor. He was elected in 1848 —but note: He died in 1850.

Astrologers theorize that the zero factor is in some way connected with the conjunction of Jupiter and Saturn. Jupiter orbits the sun approximately every 12 years and Saturn in approximately 28, and they meet every 20 years on the same degree of the zodiac. Astrological theory is that whenever a President is elected to office under the Jupiter/Saturn conjunction, he will die in office.

In any event, since 1840 the zero factor has repeatedly spelled tragedy for American Presidents. Will it again bring a tragedy in 1980? Only time will tell.

—H.S.

Women Who Ran for Vice-President of the U.S.

1892—Mary L. Stowe shared the ticket with Victoria Woodhull.

1924—Marie Caroline Brehm, Calif., ran with Herman P. Faris, Mo., Prohibition party, winning 56,289 votes against Coolidge.

1948—Grace Carlson, Minn., ran with Farrell Dobbs, N.Y., Socialist Workers & Militant Workers parties, winning 13,613 votes against Truman.

1952—Charlotte A. Bass, N.Y., ran with Vincent W. Hallinan, Calif., Progressive & American Labor parties, winning 140,023 votes. Myra Tanner Weiss, N.Y., ran with Farrell Dobbs, N.Y., Socialist Workers & Militant Workers parties, winning 10,306 votes against Eisenhower.

1956—Georgia Cozzini, Wis., ran with Eric Haas, N.Y., Socialist Labor party, winning

44,450 votes. Myra Tanner Weiss, N.Y., ran with Farrell Dobbs, N.Y., Socialist Workers & Militant Workers parties, winning 7,797 votes. Ann Marie Yezo, N.J., ran with Henry B. Krajewski, N.J., American Third party, winning 1,892 votes against Eisenhower.

1960—Georgia Cozzini, Wis., ran with Eric Haas, N.Y., Socialist Labor party, winning 46,478 votes. Myra Tanner Weiss, N.Y., ran with Farrell Dobbs, N.Y., Socialist Workers party, winning 39,541 votes against Kennedy.

1972—Genevieve Gunderson, Minn., ran with Louis Fisher, Ill., Socialist Labor party, winning 53,831 votes against Nixon. Toni Nathan ran with Dr. John Hospers as the Libertarian Party candidate for Vice-President, winning one vote in the Electoral College.

—I.W.

Women Who Ran for President of the United States

YEAR	CANDIDATE	POLITICAL PARTY	PLATFORM	VOTES RECEIVED	TOTAL VOTES CAST	ELECTION WINNER	COMMENT
1872	Victoria C. Woodhull	Equal Rights party	The 34-year-old onetime spiritualist, Wall Street broker, and publisher advocated free love, short skirts, birth control, vegetarianism, end of the death penalty, magnetic healing, easier divorce laws, an excess profits tax, world government.	A "few thousand popular votes"	6,431,086	Ulysses S. Grant, Republican	Woodhull spent Election Day in New York City jail.
1884	Belva Ann Lockwood	National Equal Rights party	The 54-year-old teacher and lawyer advocated political and economic equality for women. "Is not Victoria Empress of India?" she asked. "Is not history full of precedents of women rulers?" She was the 1st woman lawyer to argue a case before the U.S. Supreme Court.	4,149 (In Pa., pollsters threw out all her ballots.)	10,095,701	Grover Cleveland, Democrat	Susan B. Anthony disavowed her, supported James G. Blaine.
1888	Belva Ann Lockwood	National Equal Rights party	Advocated women's rights, international disarmament.	Not recorded	11,388,037	Benjamin Harrison, Republican	After defeat, she drafted suffrage amendments for 3 States.
1892	Victoria C. Woodhull Martin	Women's Suffrage party and Humanitarian party	Advocated stirpiculture (the science of breeding human beings), health tribunals, free courts of justice for the poor, analysis of impure foods, anthropologists in police departments, revenue and tariff reforms, woman suffrage.	Not recorded (Some of her votes were thrown out in New York City.)	12,049,519	Grover Cleveland, Democrat	Woodhull died in England, June 10, 1927, in her 90th year.
1940	Anna Milburn	National Greenback party		Less than 2,600	49,897,781	Franklin D. Roosevelt, Democrat	
1952	Ellen L. Jensen	Washington Peace party		Less than 8,500	61,714,924	Dwight D. Eisenhower, Republican	
1964	Yette Bronstein	Best party		Not recorded	70,440,367	Lyndon B. Johnson, Democrat	
1968	Charlene Mitchell	Communist party		1,075	73,211,562	Richard M. Nixon, Republican	
1972	Linda Jenness	Socialist Workers party	Advocated abortion, day-care centers, a 30-hour work week, 100% tax on polluting industries, employee control of factories.	65,290	76,384,509	Richard M. Nixon, Republican	

4

U.S.A.—Year by Year

1770

—U.S. population—2,205,000.
—The art of tarring and feathering was invented, supposedly in the Salem, Mass., witch country. A basic recipe was provided for the neophyte cook:

First, strip a Person naked, then heat the Tar untill it is thin, & pour it upon the naked Flesh, or rub it over with a Tar brush. . . . After which, sprinkle decently upon the Tar, whilst it is yet warm, as many Feathers as will stick to it. Then hold a lighted Candle to the Feathers, & try to set it all on Fire; if it will burn so much the better. But as the experiment is often made in cold Weather, it will not then succeed—take also an Halter, & put it round the Person's Neck, & then cart him the Rounds.

Jan. 11 Benjamin Franklin shipped a new delicacy from London to Philadelphia-friend John Bartram. It was America's 1st consignment of rhubarb. (See: Bartram in Gallery of Famous and Infamous Scientists, Chap. 17.)
Feb. 22 Storm warning. Christopher Snyder, an 11-year-old Boston boy, participating in a mob attack on the home of Ebenezer Richardson, was shot dead, thereby becoming the Revolution's 1st martyr. Richardson had objected to actions taken against a friend, who had defied a merchants' ban on importing. Convicted of murder, Richardson served 2 years in prison.
Mar. 5 The confrontation called the "Boston Massacre" began around 9 P.M. on a clear, cold night. Faced by an unruly crowd of 50 jeering, taunting waterfront toughs—throwing snowballs and chunks of ice—the British sentry on duty called for help. Eight soldiers responded, headed by Capt. Thomas Preston. Twenty minutes later, the affair was over. Three of the mob had been killed: Samuel Gray, James Caldwell, and the giant mulatto, Crispus Attucks, the 1st man of Negro blood to die in the fight for freedom. Two others, Sam Maverick and Patrick Carr, were carried away, to succumb to their wounds later.

But was it really a "massacre"? And an early example of "police brutality"? Yes, cried firebrand Sam Adams, who turned the word "massacre," with all its vivid images, into a verbal bellows with which to fan the flickering flame of revolt. No, decided the jury which tried the captain and 8 of his men on charges of murder.

John Adams, Sam's fair-minded cousin, assisted by Josiah Quincy, coolly directed the defense. Preston and 6 other defendants were acquitted. Two were found guilty, but on the lesser charge of manslaughter. They were branded on the thumb and dismissed from the army.

Adams' defense hinged on whether or not Preston, goaded by taunt and threats, had given the order to fire. He denied it, and eyewitness testimony supported him. British army records show that he had actually tried to pacify the mob but failed. Ignoring him, the crowd rushed the soldiers, striking at their muskets with sticks and hefty clubs. They taunted his men, said Preston, shouting: "Come on, you rascals, you bloody backs, you lobster scoundrels, fire if you dare, God damn you, fire and be damned, we know you dare not."

While Preston stood in front of his squad, to prevent their firing, one member of the mob struck a heavy blow at a soldier. Some accounts say this was Attucks, who had led the crowd from a gathering at Faneuil Hall where a gentleman in a "red cloak and red wig" had harangued them into action. Attucks or not, the blow set off the fight. In the confusion that followed, 6 or 7 other soldiers also fired at their tormentors, in the belief Preston had given a command. Not so, said Preston. Many in the mob had been calling out "Fire! Fire!" and it was these shouts which had touched off the muskets.

The word "massacre" served Sam Adams's needs perfectly. It implied that scores of brave patriot bodies lay crumpled in virgin snow, staining it red with blood. His close friend, Paul Revere, quickly put out an engraving of the action that depicted the British as the villains. In Boston, the alarm bells tolled constantly. By night, marchers carried pictures of the 5 victims through the streets and emitted groans, to show the suffering of the newly departed.

Sam Adams did not allow the incident to fade into oblivion. He reminded his fellow Bostonians that the dogs of the town had been seen "greedily licking human BLOOD in Kingstreet." In 1772, Joseph Warren took up the Cause, reminding the people that the hated British had "promiscuously scattered death amidst the innocent inhabitants of a populous city."

1771

—£8,921 in customs duties was collected at Boston. In this year, and the 2 to follow, the town imported a total of nearly 500,000 lbs. of tea.

—A Philadelphia theatrical group produced a play titled *The Rising Glory of America*.

—Benjamin Franklin started to write his *Autobiography*. His purpose was to acquaint his son, William, now the New Jersey governor, with his family background. Franklin's famous work combined remarks on literary affairs, religion, and utilitarian philosophy, with colorful comments on his life in Boston, Philadelphia, and London.

—Philadelphians ridiculed the use of a new device—the umbrella—to ward off sunburn. Effeminate, said the newspapers. The doctors were all for it, however. Good for preventing vertigo, epilepsy, sore eyes, fevers, and other ailments.

—Genealogy in America began. Ebenezer Watson published a 24-page pamphlet on the Stebbins family of Hartford, Conn. It gave births, marriages, and deaths from 1707 to 1771 for the Samuel and Hannah Stebbins ancestors.

Mar. 15 The *Virginia Gazette* recorded the marriage of William Carter, 23, and Mrs. Sarah Ellyson, widow of Gerald, aged 85. The former Mrs. Ellyson, it said, was "a sprightly old Tit, with three Thousand Pounds Fortune." Recording a bride's worth was common practice in the Colonies.

May 16 Some North Carolinians calling themselves the "Regulators" protested to the royal governor, William Tryon, about discrimination in new laws and lack of representation for western counties. A battle at Alamance Creek followed, between Tryon's 1,200 soldiers and 2,000 Regulators, the latter mostly without weapons. Tryon's forces won, and tried 13 men for treason. Seven were executed.

Aug. 22 The Widow Bignall placed an advertisement in the Massachusetts *Spy*. The notice informed seekers of the bizarre that a 22"-high dwarf could be seen at her Boston home near Hancock's wharf. Admission: 1 shilling. The exhibition of this 53-year-old man was the 1st such event in the Colonies.

Dec. 31 American imports from England totaled more than £4,200,000 for the year.

1772

May Settlers in the North Carolina and Tennessee mountains organized the 1st civil government set up by a community of American-born free men. By terms of a treaty made at Fort Stanwix in 1768, the Indian confederation called the 6 Nations had agreed to cede all land between the Ohio and Tennessee rivers. Living outside of Colony boundaries, the settlers in this area were allowed by the British to band together for mutual protection. They drew up a written agreement called the "Articles of the Watauga Association." An elected assembly of 13 chose a ruling committee of 5.

June 9–10 The British revenue cutter *Gaspee* was lured into shallow water in Narragansett Bay, R.I., while in pursuit of a suspected smuggler. This ship was highly unpopular with the local citizenry, nearly all of whom dabbled in smuggling. It was boarded and captured by prominent citizens from Providence, including John Brown, founder of the university that bears his name. The *Gaspee* was then burned.

The incident placed Governor Wanton in an untenable position. Since Rhode Island elected its own governor, Wanton had to enforce the King's Regulations *without* offending the people who had put him in office. He solved his dilemma by offering £200 reward for identification of the guilty parties, who were subject to immediate removal to England for trial. As expected, no one came forward with the names. They were kept secret from the British until after the outbreak of hostilities in 1775.

Sept. 26 New Jersey legislators passed a bill to forbid the practice of medicine without a license. Effective for a trial 5-year period, the new law excepted those who pulled teeth, drew blood, or gave free medical advice.

Dec. 22 Moravian missionaries began construction of the 1st schoolhouse west of the Allegheny Mountains, at Schoenbrunn, Pa.

1773

—Women's fashion note. A diarist commented sadly about the adoption of the corset stay, complaining that these objects ". . . are produced upwards so high that we can have scarcely any view at all of the Ladies' Snowy Bosoms."

—Harvard College announced that students would no longer be listed in its catalog in order of social prominence.

—First successful electrocution done by Benjamin Franklin. Writing to French friends, he described killing numerous chickens, a 10-lb. turkey, and a small lamb with an electrical current he had generated, using 6 Leyden jars.

—Phillis Wheatley's *Poems on Various Subjects* was published. She was the slave of Boston merchant John Wheatley, who was impressed by her talent and encouraged her to write.

Jan. 12 The 1st public museum was organized in Charleston, S.C.

May 10 The British Parliament passed the Tea Act to prevent the British East India Company from going bankrupt. This act authorized the company to sell, through its own consignees in the Colonies, a huge tea surplus (a supply ample for 7 years at the current rate of consumption) without payment of duty charges. Established tea merchants objected bitterly, since the Act meant the East India Company could undersell them.

Oct. 12 The State of Virginia opened its "Publick Hospital for Persons of Insane and Disordered Minds." Its 1st patient: Zachariah Mallory.

Dec. 16 The Boston Tea Party. This incident was staged to prevent the East India Company's duty-free tea from reaching the Colonial market, *not* because of the tea tax, a minor irritation that brought only £300 ($750 today) into the King's coffers annually. Resentment this day had been further increased by news of Governor Hutchinson's decision to commission 2 of his sons as East India Company consignees.

December 16 was cold and rainy. In the back room of a newspaper print shop, the Sons of Liberty met in protest, and built their courage slowly with the contents of a huge punch bowl containing rum, arrack, applejack. By nightfall they had decided to act. With some men disguised as Mohawk Indians, and others donning ragged clothing, they smeared grease and lampblack on their faces. Led by Lendall Pitts, son of a wealthy merchant, the men divided into 3 parties of 50 each, boarded the 3 tea ships in the harbor, and emptied 342 chests of tea into the water.

It is not known for sure who the 150 Tea Party members were because the printer who had the only complete list of participating rebels ordered it destroyed when he died in 1803. However, industrious 19th-century historians managed to draw up a list of 110 men, ranging in age from 14 to 57 who allegedly took part in the Tea Party. The most notable names on the list were Paul Revere and Dr. Thomas Young, who was John Adams's family physician.

Note for tea fanciers: The tea dumped was of Ceylon and Darjeeling blends.

The very same tea, from the very same shipper who suffered its loss in 1773, is being sold today, exported from England to the U.S. You can buy an 8-oz. tin, labeled *Boston Harbour Tea, 1773–1774, From the Original Shippers, Davison Newman & Co. Ltd. of London,* for $2.95. The back of the tin carries this lament: "This Tea is from the same London blending House which in the Year of Our Lord 1773 had the Misfortune to suffer a Grievous Wrong in that certain Persons did Place a quantity of its Finest Produce in Boston Harbour."

1774

—Goethe's *Werther,* written while he was on the verge of suicide, swept the Colonies in this year. It provoked unparalleled interest, possibly because it was so widely condemned. The book, Goethe's 1st popular success, had been cited as the reason for suicides among young European romantics, who identified with its morbid theme.

Jan. Virginia's governor, the Earl of Dunsmore, appropriated Indian lands in Pennsylvania, forcing the Shawnees and the Ottawas into a confrontation. The subsequent 10-month struggle ended in British victory and a concession from the 2 tribes which allowed peaceful access to, and use of, the Ohio River for settlers.

Mar. 31 The 1st of the political bills which would be called the "Intolerable Acts" by the Colonists was passed. In reprisal for the tea destroyed in Boston harbor, the harbor was closed to all shipping until monetary restitution was made.

June 2 A new Quartering Act was authorized, calling for billeting of troops in private homes. Another "Intolerable" imposition by the Crown, one which led directly to Article III of the Constitution's Bill of Rights.

Aug. 6 Ann Lee, with 8 companions, landed in New York City. Founder of the Shakers in America, Mother Lee voiced a conscientious objection to the War of Independence, refusing to help the Cause. The pacifist group was accused of treason in 1776 and jailed in Albany without a formal trial. They were not freed until December, 1780, over 4 years later.

Sept. 5–Oct. 26 The 1st Continental Congress was held at Philadelphia. All 13 Colonies except Georgia were represented.

Dec. 14 The shot "heard round the world" was fired—at Fort William and Mary, N.H., not at Lexington/Concord. Learning that General Gage was about to strengthen the small garrison in Portsmouth, Sam Adams dispatched Paul Revere. It was Revere's lesser-known "midnight ride," and possibly his most important contribution. He warned John Sullivan, a local militia captain who later rose to the rank of major general under Washington, of Gage's intent to protect his powder and ammunition supplies. Gage's military strategy was sound: The Colonists were desperately short of military supplies everywhere.

Sullivan's small group, hastily assembled from the local militia, surrounded the fort and demanded its capitulation. The commander, Captain Corcoran, refused and opened fire. After a decent interval, during which no one was hit or otherwise hurt on either side, Corcoran gave up. Sullivan gleefully seized almost 100 kegs of gunpowder and transported his booty up the river to Durham, where it was hidden. Some of the powder eventually found its way into the muskets at Bunker Hill, at a time when the need was critical.

1775

—Baltimore, Md., appointed a woman, Mary Katherine Goddard, to the office of postmaster.

Jan. 1 Of 37 newspapers now being published, 23 were of the patriot persuasion, 7 were loyalist, and 7 were neutral. One, the *New York Weekly Mercury*, had something for everyone: a patriot edition in Newark, N.J., and a loyalist version in New York City. The average weekly circulation for all papers: 3,500.

Jan. 11 Francis Salvador was the 1st Jew to be elected to public office. His term of office was brief. On July 31, he also became the 1st Jew to die for U.S. Independence.

Mar. 6 Masonic Lodge 441, operating under the Irish Constitution, initiated a Negro member. The man, Prince Hall, formed African Lodge 1 in July. It was not recognized by American Masons.

Mar. 23 Virginia's 2nd revolutionary convention was being held in Richmond's St. John's Episcopal Church, and proposals were being made for a peaceful settlement between the Colonies and England. On the 3rd day, one

impatient delegate, Patrick Henry, known as the Virginia Demosthenes by admirers, decided he'd had enough of this compromise talk. He rose to his feet and offered a resolution: Since war was inevitable, the Virginia militia must be armed for defense. With growing passion he concluded his speech—

> Is life so dear, or peace so sweet, as to be purchased at the price of chains and slavery? Forbid it, Almighty God. I know not what course others may take, but as for me, give me liberty or give me death!

Patrick Henry's eloquence carried the day. His resolution to arm the militia was adopted unanimously.

Apr. 14 The 1st Abolition Society was organized in Philadelphia, Pa.

Apr. 19 Milestone Battle: Lexington/Concord. British losses: 73 killed, 200 wounded or missing. Rebel losses: 49 dead, 46 wounded. Also lost: Paul Revere's horse, commandeered into British army service after Revere was captured. Released, Revere walked home.

May 10 It was Benedict Arnold, *not* Ethan Allen, who 1st conceived the attack on Fort Ticonderoga that took place this day. Told by Colonal Sam Parsons that the line at Cambridge had needed cannon, Arnold remembered some artillery pieces he'd seen at the New York fort. He estimated the quantity at about 80 heavy cannon, 20 brass guns, and 12 mortars. In Boston, he submitted a plan to the Committee on Safety which, reluctant to move armed forces into an area outside their jurisdiction, hastily sent it on to their New York counterparts.

Dr. Joseph Warren, however, was unable to wait. He persuaded the Massachusetts group to reconsider, and they then granted Arnold a colonel's commission, authorizing 400 men for the raid. Arnold, who left promptly to recruit his force, soon learned that Parsons, mulling over their talk, had gone to citizens in Connecticut with a similar proposal. They, too, had issued a commission: to Ethan Allen and the vigilante group (outlawed by New York for its subversive activities) he called his "Green Mountain Boys."

In a panic over the news, Arnold left his men far behind and galloped north in Allen's wake. At Castleton, N.Y., 20 mi. from the fort, he found them enjoying a pre-fight, Saturday-night drinking bout of rum and cider. Arnold challenged Allen's command. The huge outlaw guffawed, but he agreed that the arrogant Arnold could accompany him—provided Arnold gave no orders.

At 3 A.M., the 2 men co-stormed the fort, each one striving to be the 1st through the gate. Except for the startled sentry, who fled after his musket misfired, everyone else was sound asleep inside—49 men (many of them old and sick), with 24 members of their families.

Aroused by shrieks of "No quarter! No quarter!" Lieutenant Feltham, the dilapidated fort's 2nd-in-command, hurriedly awoke, grabbed his breeches, and met the boisterous attackers head-on as they stumbled up the stairs to his bedroom. The mountain men fell silent. With great presence of mind, Feltham coolly asked for their credentials. Colonel Arnold stepped forward, holding his paper from Massachusetts, and genteelly asked Feltham to give up. Allen was more forceful. Waving his drawn sword menacingly over the lieutenant's head, he demanded immediate surrender, without any shots being fired, or he'd kill every man, woman, and child there.

Feltham could not comply. Surrendering was the right of Captain Delaplace, the fort commander who—unknown to both Arnold and Allen—was still struggling into his uniform.

Delaplace, years later, still did not know to whom he should have turned over his sword. The "Who's in command here?" controversy went on for weeks. Arnold finally quit the service in disgust, with the official decision yet to be made. Ethan Allen, in his autobiography written 4 years after, carefully avoided any suggestion that Benedict Arnold had even been at the fort.

His account, rife with error and false recollection, included his famous request to surrender "In the name of the Great Jehovah and the Continental Congress." The Tories pointed out that Ethan Allen had had no commission from either of these sources.

Allen's men, interviewed about this request later, could recall only that Allen's actual words were both profane and unprintable. Lieutenant Feltham, in his official report to superiors, recouched it as a demand for "immediate possession of the fort and all the effects of George, the 3rd."

The Continental Congress, embarrassed at not being told of the raid beforehand, gave serious thought to handing back the fort, since open revolt was in the planning stages as yet.

Ironic postscript: The captured cannon had to be left where they were. No transport capable of handling such heavy objects was available to haul them out.

May 20 The Mecklenburg Declaration of Independence was allegedly approved. North Carolina, whose State seal and flag carry this date, has celebrated the day as a State holiday.

June 7 Landmark Day. From this day forward, the "United Colonies" would be called the "United States."

June 15 Congress selected George Washington to be military commander in chief. The choice was basically political: a Virginian, to gain support of the Southern Colonies.

June 17 Milestone Battle: Bunker Hill. General Israel Putnam's decision to dig in on Breed's Hill, where the battle actually took place, probably forced the British attack. Breed's Hill, although lower in elevation than Bunker Hill, commanded the sea approach to Boston harbor, an intolerable situation for a military commander to accept.

Credit for the famous war cry, "Don't fire till you see the whites of their eyes!" is usually given to the American colonel William Prescott. But he did not originate the phrase.

Pietro Duodo, Venetian Ambassador to France in the 17th century, wrote of a new cavalry charge called the "pistolade." The horsemen, he wrote, withheld the use of pistols or sword "until they could see the whites of their eyes." In 1745, Prince Charles of Prussia is believed to have said to his officers, "Silent, till you see the whites of their eyes." A decade later, during the Prussian attack on the Austrians at Prague, Frederick the Great gave his soldiers a general order, "By push of bayonets; no firing until you see the whites of their eyes."

The Battle for "Bunker" Hill lasted 90 minutes. Proportionately, for the total number of men engaged, the British army casualties were the heaviest in its history: 1,054 out of 2,400, almost 50%.

June 22 The 2nd Continental Congress issued its 1st money, paper currency with a face value of $3 million.

June 25 In a letter from Boston, British general John Burgoyne, writing after the battle of Bunker Hill, where he commanded artillery, said: "The British Empire in America is overturned. If the confederacy of this continent is general as I am now to believe, & you determine to subdue it by arms, such a pittance of troops as Great Britain & Ireland can supply will only serve to protract the war." His letter was *not* brought to the attention of George III by its recipient.

June 25 A nervous New York City staged 2 official welcoming parades: one for the new commander in chief, General Washington, the other for Royal Governor Tryon. The small town of 20,000 had only one street, Broadway, long enough for a line of march. To keep the celebrators from meeting, Washington's welcoming affair was assigned the upper half, Tryon's the downtown half of Broadway. Tryon, told of the dilemma while still aboard his ship in the harbor, agreed to postpone his landing by 4 hours, to avoid an embarrassing meeting in midtown Manhattan.

July 3 General Washington took formal command of the Continental Army. Traditionally, the ceremony occurred under a large elm near Mason and Garden streets in Cambridge, Mass.

No contemporary documents exist to support the story. The fabled elm died in 1923, and an examination of its growth rings gave it an age of just over 2 centuries. A cutting, taken before its death, was planted near the original site in Boston.

July Washington's siege of Boston began. By Sunday, March 17, 1776, General Howe and over 7,000 of his men had pulled back to the safety of British ships in Boston harbor, abandoning the town.

July 25 Dr. Benjamin Church was appointed surgeon general. In October, Church was tried by court-martial, with General Washington presiding at the trial. The charge: "Criminal correspondence with the enemy." He was sentenced to life imprisonment, but allowed to remain free for reasons of health.

July 26 The U.S. Post Office was established by the 2nd Continental Congress. Its 1st Postmaster: Benjamin Franklin.

Fall Folks of Tar River, N.C., changed its name to "Washington," to honor the new leader.

Sept. Pierre Augustin Caron de Beaumarchais, French dramatist and secret agent, returned to France after an undercover reconnaissance. He advised King Louis XVI to assist the Colonists, and reported they could well be the means for bringing civil war to England, France's eternal enemy.

Nov. 10 The 1st day of existence for the U.S. Marines. "Semper Fidelis"—"Always Faithful."

Nov. 29 Congress established the Committee on Secret Correspondence, the forerunner of the Department of State. Members: John Dickinson, John Jay, Benjamin Franklin, Thomas Johnson. Purpose: to sound out European powers on their feelings toward the Colonies, for possible military and economic aid.

Dec. 3 The 1st official American flag was raised aboard Commodore Esek Hopkins' flagship, the *Alfred*. The flag had 13 red and white stripes, plus the crosses of St. George and St. Andrew.

Dec. 31 On this day, most enlistments in the Continental Army expired. Of the 16,770 who had been in service in the year that Washington assumed the command, 3,100 had already gone home prior to the end of their 12 months' term, or were otherwise unfit for active duty. By January 10, 1776, the ranks had swelled slightly due to 5,582 new arrivals.

—The Committees of Safety, with the authorization of the Continental Congress, seized property owned by British sympathizers including the 6-million-acre Fairfax estate in Virginia, the 300 sq. mi. Philips estate in New York, and the domain of Sir William Pepperell which stretched along 30 mi. of Maine coastline.

1776

—Barmaid Betsy Flanagan mixed the 1st cocktail at Elmsford, N.Y. When a drunk waved at the tail feathers pinned to the wall behind the bar and asked for a glassful of "those cocktails," she refilled his last order and stuck in one of the feathers.

Jan. An ex-corsetmaker and onetime bankrupt, Thomas Paine, came to the U.S. with a letter of recommendation, written in guarded terms, by Benjamin Franklin. Paine quickly found a more receptive niche as a journalist with something to say. His *Common Sense*, a fervent cry for independence, sold over 100,000 in 3 months, at the rate of one copy for every 20 people in the Colonies at the time.

Feb. Silas Deane utilized invisible ink for the 1st time to convey secret messages between France and the U.S. Using a tannic acid solution, he wrote between the lines of a routine message. A ferrous sulfate bath would combine iron with the tannic acid to form an easily-read dark compound.

June 27 The 1st American army execution in time of war: Thomas Hickey, in New York town. The charge: plotting to kidnap General Washington and deliver him to Lord Howe. A total of 20,000, including all the men in Washington's 4 brigades stationed at New York, turned out to view the spectacle, which was held near the Bowery.

July 2 Women's suffrage vote. By constitutional statute, New Jersey gave "all inhabitants" of adult age, with a net worth of £50 and residing in their county for 12 months, the right to vote in the general election. In 1790, after 14 years, someone realized it meant both men *and* women. The law was legal until November 16, 1807, when the General Assembly passed new laws, limiting the vote to "free, white males."

July 4 Congress adopted the Declaration of Independence. England virtually ignored it, with only a 6-line mention in the *London Morning Post*, below a theatrical notice.

Virginian Richard Henry Lee made the 1st move for independence on June 6. He voiced a formal demand for a complete break with England, startling both himself and his fellow delegates. The motion was at 1st tabled, but gained support rapidly. By the next Tuesday, June 11, a 5-man committee (John Adams, Thomas Jefferson, Benjamin Franklin, Roger Sherman, Robert Livingston) had been named to produce the rough draft of a written declaration. When Jefferson got the committee's assignment, he protested, saying the work should have been given to a senior member such as John Adams. Adams demurred. "You write," he said bluntly, "10 times better than I do." It was true. Jefferson's talent for the adeptly-turned, gracious phrase was well-known.

The committee edited their 1st draft heavily. During congressional debate, further changes were made. Jefferson gave his colleagues a total of 20 clauses of flowing rhetoric that had to be cut, deleted, or modified to reflect the common mind of Congress. Clause 20, dealing with slavery, was left out entirely. Politically, it was too dangerous. Many Colonists, including members of Congress, still supported the practice.

Comparison of Jefferson's original wording with the edited version that finally was approved shows the manuscript changes that took place.

When in the course of human events it becomes
       one   dissolve the political
necessary for ~~a~~ people to ~~advance from that~~
bonds which have connected them with another,
~~subordination in which they have hitherto~~
and to
~~remained, & to~~ assume among the powers of the
        separate and equal
earth the ~~equal & independent~~ station to which
the laws of nature & of nature's god entitle them,
a decent respect to the opinions of mankind
requires that they should declare the causes
         the separation.
which impel them to ~~the change~~. We hold these
        self-evident
truths to be ~~sacred & undeniable~~ . . .

"Self-evident" was Franklin's choice, reasoning that one hyphenated word was better than 3 others.

Jefferson denied the draft had drawn upon any other source. But subconsciously, it may have done so. He greatly admired the principles expressed in John Locke's *Second Treatise of Government* (1690).

Following approval on July 4, the document went to John Dunlap, a printer, to run off broadsides. The Dunlap manuscript was lost; the holograph copy in the National Archives was made *before* the loss, but it is not the original.

Aware of the document's historical importance, Congress voted to have it "engrossed on parchment," by Timothy Matlack, a penman. The actual signing of the parchment was on August 2, when most of the 56 men were present. Several, for various reasons, signed later. The last to sign, Thomas McKean of Delaware, had left, after July 2, to join General Washington and did not realize, until 1781, that his signature was not on the historic document. He was allowed, after special authorization, to affix his signature then.

A $2,500 reward was offered by England to learn the names of the signatories, and the Crown declared the act of signing to be high treason, punishable by death. For that reason, all names were kept secret for almost a year.

The hanging threat grimly amused Benjamin Harrison, who had read the draft aloud during debate. A heavy man, he told a fellow signer, Elbridge Gerry, who was both small and frail, that ". . . when the hanging comes . . . it will be over with me in a minute, but you will be kicking the air for an hour after I'm gone."

Aug. 27 Milestone Battle: Long Island, N.Y. U.S. General Israel Putnam was defeated.
Sept. 22 Nathan Hale was hung.

> He behaved with great composure and resolution, saying he thought it the duty of every good officer to obey any orders given him by his Commander-in-Chief, and desired the spectators to be at all times prepared to meet death in whatever shape it might appear.
> —Journal entry, Sept. 22,
> Lieut. Frederick MacKenzie,
> British army, New York

Dec. 5 The oldest Greek-letter society, Phi Beta Kappa, was founded at the College of William & Mary, Williamsburg, Va. Charter members: 50. High scholastic achievement soon became a hallmark for admission.
Dec. 19 First appearance of *The Crisis* by Thomas Paine, with its famous opening, "These are the times that try men's souls . . ."
Dec. 26 Milestone Battle: Trenton. Col. Johann Rall, the Hessian commander, liked both his beer and a good game of cards. A Tory, learning of Washington's plan to cross the Delaware, sent a note to Rall. Intent on the hand he'd been dealt, card-playing Rall stuffed the message into his pocket without reading it. This card game left him unprepared for the fight that cost him his life and gave Washington a much-needed victory.

1777

—Cold-cut nails appeared. Thought of by Jeremiah Wilkinson of Cumberland, R.I., he used pieces of a discarded chest lock, headed up in a blacksmith vise.

Jan. 3 Milestone Battle: Princeton. With his final fight, lasting a half-hour, Washington concluded a campaign which Frederick the Great called one of the greatest.
June 14 The birthday of the "Stars and Stripes" as the official flag of the U.S.
July 2 Vermont became the 1st State to abolish slavery.

Summer Reflecting European sympathies, the Marquis de Lafayette and Baron Jean de Kalb arrived to join Washington's army. The marquis was 19. The baron, 61.

Aug. 6 The bloody Battle of Oriskany. Great losses were suffered by both the Americans and their opponents, the Indians of the Iroquois Confederacy. For the 1st time since it was formed, the Confederacy split into civil war with some tribes supporting the British and some the Americans. Their united front was gone forever.

Aug. 27 The Charge of the American Light Brigade. William Alexander, Earl of Stirling, was not really an earl. The House of Lords had denied his claim to an extinct Scottish title. But in the hills of New Jersey, his home before joining Washington as a major general, his neighbors accepted him as Lord Stirling, a genuine nobleman.

Although Stirling had been a miserable failure at the art of making money, verging continually on bankruptcy, his military genius was never in doubt. Outnumbered by odds of 6 to 1 in the battle of Long Island, Stirling's gallant but hopeless counterattack—personally leading Smallwood's Marylanders against Cornwallis —prompted Washington's agonized exclamation, "Good God, what brave men must I lose this day!" Only 9 men escaped in the charge. Stirling himself was captured, but released later.

A monument in Prospect Park, Brooklyn, carries the inscription:

> In honor of Maryland's 400 who on this battlefield . . . saved the American Army.

Stirling's decision to attack at Long Island preserved the integrity of Washington's command. It led the way for a successful evacuation, a feat which, in the opinion of British military historian Trevelyan, was "a master stroke . . . by which Washington saved his army and his country."

Oct. 17 Milestone Battle: Saratoga. To the strains of "Yankee Doodle" on one side and the "Grenadiers' March" on the other, Gen. John Burgoyne surrendered to General Gates. An adjutant had asked Gentleman Johnny if he saw the U.S. party coming, and the general replied, "Yes, I have seen them too long."

Oct./Nov. The culmination of the Conway Cabal, a plot to remove Washington as commander in chief after defeats at Brandywine and Germantown. Gen. Thomas Conway had supposedly criticized Washington severely in a letter to Gen. Horatio Gates. James Wilkinson, on Gates's staff, leaked a demeaning passage— allegedly taken from the letter—to Lord Stirling, who relayed it: "Heaven has been determined to save your country, or a weak general and bad counselors would have ruined it."

However, the much-quoted comment, intended as a wedge to drive Washington out and replace him with Gates, was never written by Conway.

Dec. 25 Washington wintered at Valley Forge, the nadir of the Revolution. The Christmas Day menu:

> Soggy fire-cake (bread baked over the fire)
> Carrion beef (as available)
> Creek water on-the-rocks.

1778

—According to Thomas Jefferson, "30,000 slaves escaped from Virginia in the year of 1778."

Jan. 5 David Bushnell tested the 1st naval contact mine. He combined a gunlock, acting as a contact fuse, with a keg of gunpowder. Several hundred of these "mines" were set afloat amid the drifting ice in the Delaware River at Philadelphia. The kegs were seen, and the English ships commenced fire. For days after, they fired at anything afloat, inspiring the ballad, "The Battle of the Kegs," by New Jersey congressman Francis Hopkinson. One quatrain which appealed to most described Lord Howe's love life:

> Sir William, he, as snug as flea
> Lay all this time a-snoring;
> Nor dreamed of harm, as he lay warm
> In bed with Mrs. Loring.

Feb. 6 France signed a treaty with the U.S. It brought the benefits of economic and military assistance, which the U.S. badly needed. This treaty was the 1st and only military alliance made by the U.S. until April 4, 1949, when the North Atlantic Treaty Organization (NATO) was created.

Mar. 11 Said the *Pennsylvania Ledger*, commenting on John Hancock's vanity and love of display:

> John Hancock of Boston appears in public with all the state and pageantry of an Oriental prince; he rides in an elegant chariot . . . attended by 4 servants dressed in superb livery, mounted on fine horses richly caparisoned; and escorted by 50 horsemen with drawn sabers, the one half of which precedes and the other follow his carriage.

May 18 Sir William Howe, resigning his command because his request for reinforcements had been ignored, was given a farewell party called the "Meschianza." The pageant, which recreated a tournament in the Middle Ages, included: decorated barges, heralds and trumpeters, a jousting field, and the Knights of the Blended Rose. The costumes used over £50,000 worth of silks, paid for by rich junior officers. Capt. John André was the designer. (He was to be hung as a spy in October, 1780.)

June The U.S. Secret Service was organized. Director: Aaron Burr.

June 28 In later years, she remarried and friends knew her as Molly McKolly. But American folklore calls her "Molly Pitcher," for her alleged efforts to provide thirsty cannoneers with water during the Battle of Monmouth, N.J., fought on this day. The official records list 59 British and 40 American deaths from a common enemy: sunstroke. The temperature soared over 100°.

July 3–4 Col. John Butler, leading 400 Tories, and Iroquois chieftain Joseph Brant, with 500 of his warriors, swept into Wyoming Valley, Pa. They massacred some 360 settlers, taking over 200 scalps.

Sept. 17 The 1st Indian peace treaty was signed, at Fort Pitt. Signing for the Delawares: Captains Pipe, John Kill Buck, and White Eyes.

Dec. 29 The British invaded the deep South, capturing Savannah, Ga.

1779

—American quarter-horse racing began in Virginia.

Jan. 9 Opening night at the John Street Theater, New York City. Publicity carried the notice that parts would be played "by young ladies . . . who never appeared on any stage before."

June Spain formally declared war on England, persuaded by France's promise to assist it in recovering the Floridas and Gibraltar. The promise was not kept.

June 24 On this day, marked by a total eclipse, George Rogers Clark set out to capture the Illinois country. Exactly 8 months later, his band of 127 men, including 50 Frenchmen picked up along the way, entered Vincennes. They came in with "colors flying and drums brassed," waving some 20 flags stitched for them by the women of Kaskaskia. The grand entry was meant to give the impression of a much larger force.

July 15 Milestone Battle: Stony Point, N.Y. General Wayne's "Mad Anthony" sobriquet was given to him for his "crazy" orders that were enforced:

1. empty muskets, shouldered, with fixed bayonets.
2. penalty for removing muskets from the shoulder, or firing them: death, at the hands of the nearest officer.
3. absolute silence until the assault.
4. then, all men to shout "The fort's our own!"
5. white slips of paper to be stuck in each soldier's headdress, for identification.

Aug. 14 Britain won the battle for ship's masts, in Penobscot Bay, Me. It was common practice for the Admiralty to keep a 3-year supply of masts on hand, soaking in navy-yard mast-ponds. But the supply was being cut off, partly by U.S. capture of the British mast ships, which were especially designed to carry the long timbers.

A Tory settlement was established to protect the shipments, at Castine, Me. Commodore Saltonstall, with 3 ships carrying 300 guns, was sent to attack it. Col. Paul Revere accompanied him, commanding an artillery unit.

Upon his arrival, Saltonstall began daily councils of war, planning the attack. They turned into debating societies. As opposition, they faced a British commander with a small land force and a navy of only 3 ships with 30 guns. Badly outclassed, he would have surrendered if asked.

Saltonstall wasted 47 days in minor skirmishes, enough time for Adm. Sir George Collier to arrive in a 64-gun man-o'-war along with 6 support ships. In the disaster that followed, Saltonstall lost his 3 ships and 500 men, fleeing in panic. The survivors drifted back to the U.S. for weeks. For his inept performance he was dismissed from the service. Revere himself lost his commission and was convicted of negligence in a 1st trial, but later cleared in a 2nd. The engagement was ranked as the worst fiasco of the Revolution.

—W.K.

Sept. 23 "Sir, I have not yet begun to fight." (John Paul Jones, replying to Captain Pearson of the *Serapis*, when Pearson demanded he surrender the sinking *Bon Homme Richard*.)

Jones won the celebrated Revolutionary War sea battle off Scarborough, England, boarding the *Serapis* after a 3½-hour struggle by moonlight, the casualties so great on each side that neither captain ever issued a complete casualty list. The intrepid seaman came to be regarded as America's greatest naval hero and founder of the American naval tradition, but his genius wasn't much appreciated in his own time.

The naval hero's real name was John Paul, not John Paul Jones. Born near Kirkcudbright, Scotland, John Paul went to sea when only 12, serving as 1st mate aboard a slaver and even having some experience ashore as an actor before receiving his 1st command in 1770. It was then that his troubles began. A ship's carpenter he had had flogged for laziness died, this resulting in a murder charge. Released on bail, John Paul purchased a ship in the West Indies in order to hunt for evidence proving his innocence, but in 1773 killed the ringleader of a mutinous crew. To avoid trial he fled to America and changed his name to John Paul Jones, receiving a commission as a senior lieutenant in the new Continental navy under this name in 1775. His naval genius soon resulted in a promotion to captain and command of the new *Ranger*, whose daring raids off England were climaxed with the capture of the British warship *Drake*, the 1st ever to surrender to an American vessel. But political machinations, which plagued him and obscured his fame all his life, forced Jones to relinquish command of *Ranger*, and it was on the old rebuilt merchantman named *Bon Homme Richard* in honor of Benjamin Franklin and his *Poor Richard's Almanack* that he fought his most famous battle. It is little known that Jones became a rear admiral in the Russian navy after the Revolutionary War. Here again political intrigue and scandal prevented his recognition, his victories against the Turks credited to others and his name dishonored when he was falsely accused of a criminal assault on a young girl.

John Paul Jones died in Paris in 1792 when only 55, a broken and embittered man. Buried in an unmarked grave in the St. Louis cemetery for Protestants, it was more than a century before his remains were brought back to America to be enshrined in a crypt in the naval chapel at Annapolis.

—R.H. rep.

Oct. 9   Count Casimir Pulaski was killed in a cavalry charge as he headed his Pulaski Legion during the battle to retake Savannah.
Dec. 1   U.S. monetary woes increased. Since January, when the ratio of paper currency ("Continentals") to coin was 8 to 1, the ratio had skyrocketed to 40 to 1.

1780

—U.S. population—2,781,000.
May 29   The term "Tarleton's quarter" entered the English language when this British colonel, ignoring the white flag of surrender at the battle of Waxhaws, shot, bayoneted, or sabered 113 Virginians fatally, and left an additional 150 wounded to die where they lay.
Aug. 17   Milestone Battle: Camden, S.C. A U.S. disaster. The militiamen fled in wild panic, suffering over 1,000 in casualties. Their leader, Gen. Horatio Gates, outdistanced them, covering 180 mi. in 3 days. Said Alexander Hamilton: "Was there ever such an instance of a General running away . . . from his whole army?"

Tories snickered over one explanation: Gates may have had diarrhea. Baron de Kalb was killed in the fight.
Sept. 21   Benedict Arnold offered to exchange West Point for £20,000 and a major general's commission in the British army. He met Maj. John André aboard the *Vulture* in the Hudson River. Unaccountably, a U.S. soldier along the river bank fired without orders on the ship, and the British captain weighed anchor. His hasty action left André stranded and forced him to make his way back to New York City by land. Caught carrying top secret papers and wearing civilian clothing, Andre was hung a week later.
Oct. 6   Henry Laurens was imprisoned in the Tower of London, the 1st American ever to be jailed there. He had sailed for Holland to serve as U.S. minister, but was captured off Newfoundland and charged with high treason. Laurens was required to pay for his room, board, and his guard's salary until his release on December 31, 1781. He was exchanged for Lord Cornwallis.
Nov.   A 3-day horse-racing meet was held at Hempstead Plains, Long Island. It featured a "Ladies Subscription" special and, in one race, women riders.
Dec. 1   A Boston naval board of inquiry looked into the mental behavior of Capt. Pierre Landais, master of the U.S. Navy frigate *Alliance*. In a situation that closely paralleled the plot of Herman Wouk's best seller *The Caine Mutiny*, the ship's officers "mutinied," relieving Landais of command while on the high seas. Acting with great caution, they carefully wrote down every move they made, after electing a reluctant Lieutenant Degge to take command. Behaving like a "Captain Queeg" prototype, Landais gave irrational commands, talked to himself, and eventually took to his bed, feigning illness. He was partially acquitted by the military court, but still cashiered. Degge fared little better. This hapless officer escaped the death penalty by a split verdict, but also was dismissed.

1781

—Negro Quork Walker won his freedom in Massachusetts, basing his plea on a simple statement of fact: the State constitution said, "All men are born free and equal."
Jan. 17   Milestone Battle: Cowpens. Brig. Gen. Daniel Morgan, fighting his rheumatism along with Tarleton's feared Legionnaires, set a trap. The site he chose was shaped like a cattle chute, and he counted upon his undependable militia—they would flee before the British straight toward the "bullpen." The

plan worked. The retreating militia drew the British into range of the encircling Continental infantry, upon whom Morgan *could* depend, and he executed that professional soldier's dream: successful, sequential attacks on an enemy's front, flanks, and rear.

Jan. 30 The Articles of Confederation were adopted.

Feb. 30 Adm. Sir George Rodney seized the island of St. Eustatius, a West Indies center of the contraband trade. Over £3 million in booty was taken, together with numerous blockade-running ships. But Rodney's preoccupation with St. Eustatius allowed the French admiral De Grasse to reach Martinique safely with 20 ships loaded with troops and munitions for the U.S. war effort. In an ironic twist of fate, Rodney's 24 shiploads of loot were nearly all recaptured later by coastal privateers.

Mar. A new snowfall left 8″ on the ground. During this record-cold winter, the Hudson River froze solid, and foot traffic crossed at King's Ferry. The British brought supplies to Staten Island by horse and sleigh.

May 12 In South Carolina, Rebecca Motte urged the patriots to shoot flaming arrows into her home because the British were using it as a fort.

June 4 Twenty-six-year-old Virginia militia captain Jack Jouett was visiting his family at their inn, the Cuckoo Tavern, 35 mi. east of Charlottesville, when 250 Redcoats led by Col. Banastre Tarleton arrived for a rest. Pretending to be asleep, Jouett eavesdropped on the soldiers and learned of their plans to capture Thomas Jefferson and disperse the Virginia General Assembly. Jouett slipped away and set out on horseback to warn Jefferson at Monticello, 40 mi. away. Riding all night, Jouett arrived at dawn and woke Jefferson and the leaders of the Assembly, some of whom were guests at Monticello. Jefferson breakfasted at leisure, spent 2 hours picking out his most important papers, and then fled to the safety of a neighbor's estate some miles away.

Sept. 8 Milestone Battle: Eutaw Springs. During a 10-month Carolinas campaign, Gen. Nathanael Greene had waged a hit-and-run action unique in military annals: He lost *all* 4 major battles, including Eutaw Springs, but won the war, inflicting heavier losses than he took. The British retreated after every encounter.

Sept. 26 The siege at Yorktown began. Twenty-four days later, Cornwallis surrendered, allegedly to the tune of "The World Turned Upside Down." General O'Hara, acting on behalf of Cornwallis, wanted to turn over his sword to the French general, Count "Popa" de Rochambeau (the French army and navy allied with Washington totaled over 30,-000, 3 times the U.S. forces). The count declined, saying the honor belonged to Washington.

Oct. Six prisoners on the prison ship *Jersey*, anchored in New York's East River, tried to escape. Five died at once. The 6th scrambled back on the ship to hide, and lived to tell of the horrors on board the rotting, demasted hulk. In the 3½ years to follow, over 11,000 seamen died on the *Jersey*. With over 1,100 jammed below decks at all times, dysentery, smallpox, and other virulent diseases took such a nightly toll that the sentry's morning greeting became a routine "Rebels, turn out your dead!"

Oct. 20 Christopher Ludwick baked and delivered 12,000 loaves of his bread to Cornwallis' troops in accordance with Washington's magnanimous order. The baker-general—appointed in 1777—produced bread so tasty that at the war's end he received a certificate attesting to his patriotism. Following the Hessian defeat at Trenton, Ludwick suggested that the captured Germans, once converted, would "be as good Whigs as any of us." Washington concurred, and put Ludwick in charge of them. The genial baker took 948 wide-eyed Hessians on a beer-and-cake odyssey around Pennsylvania. Many, it's said, left the British for good after their mouth-watering indoctrination tour.

Oct. 22 Lafayette, borrowing a phrase used by French classical drama, wrote to Monsieur de Maurepas: "The play, sir, is over . . . the 5th act has come to an end."

Dec. The Rev. Sam Peters published his *General History of Connecticut*. His effort gained him a reputation as a teller of tall tales. Said he about a caterpillar invasion along the Connecticut River: They advanced in a phalanx 3 mi. wide and 2 in length, eating everything green in sight for 100 mi. They were over 2″ long, with white, thorny bodies, and red throats. Peters mixed actual happenings, wild tirades, and improbable fantasies so thoroughly that many people actually believed that a 4-mi. march of bullfrogs through Windham in 1758 really took place.

1782

Mar. 4 The British Parliament called for the end of the war and the recognition of the Colonies' independence.

Apr. 12 The Battle of the Saints. British Admiral Rodney defeated French Admiral De Grasse in a massive, classic attack, staged in the island group named after the Saints, between Guadeloupe and Dominica. Rodney split the French line, capturing De Grasse himself. It shook U.S. morale.

May A 22-year-old woman named Deborah

Sampson, disguised as a man, began 17 months' service in the 4th Massachusetts Regiment of the Continental Army under the name of Robert Shurtleff. After the war she married, had 3 children, and in 1802 became the 1st female lecturer in the U.S.

June 20 The Great Seal of the U.S. became official. Its designer, William Barton, chose the eagle—the symbol of Imperial Rome—as the new nation's emblem, rejecting such suggestions as the wild turkey and the dove. Other seal symbolisms: a 13-star crown, representing a new constellation in the galaxy of nations; a 13-tiered pyramid (with room to add more), the tiers signifying permanence. Lesser known are 2 Latin mottoes on the reverse side. These are based on Vergil's *Aeneid* (ix 625) and the *Eclogues* (iv 5–7) passages.

Aug. 7 George Washington established the order of the Purple Heart as an honor badge for enlisted men. The 1st, and only, 3 men to receive it in the Revolution: Sgts. Daniel Bissell, William Brown, Elijah Churchill.

Nov. 10 George Rogers Clark, commanding 1,100 mounted riflemen, routed Shawnee Indians at Chillicothe, O. It was the last land battle of the Revolution on U.S. soil.

1783

—Noah Webster published his *American Spelling Book*. Estimated sales in the next 100 years: 70 million. It Americanized English for such words as *colour* and *labour* by dropping the "u's."

Mar. 12–15 The "Newburgh Addresses" urged Continental officers to revolt against a "country that tramples on your rights. . . ." Exerting his great personal influence, Washington convinced military leaders to reject the anonymous sedition. Later, Major John Armstrong, Jr., was identified as the author.

Apr. 26 About 7,000 Tories sailed from New York, the last of nearly 100,000 Loyalists who voluntarily left the U.S. Their destination: Nova Scotia and other foreign lands.

May 30 The *Pennsylvania Evening Post* became the 1st newspaper to be published daily.

Sept. Yale reported the highest enrollment of any U.S. college: 270.

Sept. 3 A Day of Peace. The final treaty was signed in Paris. Its terms: Britain kept Gibraltar. France was given Tobago and Senegal. Spain got the Floridas. The U.S. got all land east of the Mississippi, south of Canada, and north of the Floridas. Negotiated by Benjamin Franklin, John Adams, and John Jay, the treaty has been called the greatest diplomatic feat in U.S. history.

1784

—Deer hunting by night was abolished in the Carolinas. Farmers complained bitterly that cows and horses were being shot by mistake.

—British painter Robert Edge Pine returned to Philadelphia with a cast of his *Venus de Medici*. The Quaker city was shocked to see the bare facts in public.

—Pope Pius VI appointed the Rev. John Carroll, of Baltimore, to be his apostolic emissary in the U.S. Catholic affairs were formerly handled from London.

Jan. 7 David Landreth founded the 1st U.S. seed supply firm, on High Street, in Philadelphia. All seeds had previously been shipped from Europe. His firm merged with Robert Buist and Company 40 years later.

Feb. 22 The trade with China opened. The 360-ton *Empress of China* sailed with a cargo of ginseng for Canton. The herb cargo, on which the owners made $30,727 with an investment of $120,000, was eagerly sought by the Chinese as a "virility" restorative.

June 23 America's 1st teen-age balloonist soloed on this sunny Wednesday. He was 13-year-old Edward Warren of Baltimore, who went aloft in a 35'-diameter silk balloon that carried a cylindrical iron stove beneath it, to heat the confined air. The balloon craze that swept this decade began on the Champ de Mars, in Paris, on August 27, 1783. Ben Franklin was among the spectators who watched the 1st untethered and manned ascent. Some 16 months later, he also posted the 1st air mail letter carried by balloon from Dover to Calais on January 7, 1785. The 2 balloonists on this flight, Jean Pierre Blanchard and Dr. John Jeffries, had problems. Plagued by loss of lift, they 1st jettisoned everything removable, including their clothes, and then urinated as well, to prevent a forced landing in the English Channel. The nude gentlemen were received by the French with a great display of *savoir faire*.

Aug. 23 Settlers organized the independent State of Franklin, the 1st American State west of the Alleghenies. Headed by Gov. John Sevier, Franklin existed for about 4 years, but Congress steadfastly refused to recognize it.

1785

—The New England custom of bundling began to disappear, due to severe criticism from bluenose reformers. However, this practice, which allowed courting couples to occupy the same bed—if fully clothed and separated by a "bundling board"—persisted in western Pennsylvania until the 1840s.

—A Federal land law put up for sale government holdings in lots of 640 acres. Although the price was only $1 per acre, this was too much for common people and the land was grabbed up by speculators who made huge profits by subdividing the land and reselling it.

May 20 By congressional authority, Section 16 in each township of the Western Reserve in the Great Lakes region was set aside to support public schools. This was the 1st Federal land grant that subsidized education.

May 23 Ben Franklin, annoyed at having to carry 2 sets of eyeglasses, invented bifocals. He made a pair of glasses whose lenses had separate areas to correct near and far vision. The idea did not impress the visually limited. An ordinary set of spectacles—with just the standard type of lens—cost $100, the equivalent of 15 months' pay for a soldier in Washington's army.

July 6 Thomas Jefferson proposed the monetary decimal system to Congress. Crediting the original idea to Gouverneur Morris, Jefferson suggested 4 coins: the $10 gold piece, the silver dollar, the silver dime, and the copper penny. Jefferson had also considered 3 other coins: a silver half-dollar, "one of the value of ⅖ . . . equal to the Spanish pistereen, and one of the value of 5 coppers . . . equal to the Spanish halfbit,"—which became the modern half-dollar, the quarter, and the nickel.

Oct. 1 John MacPherson published Philadelphia's 1st city directory. It contained the names and residences of 6,250 citizens, 686 of whom had ordered a copy.

1786

—The Tammany Society was incorporated in New York City. Named after the Delaware chief Tamanend, it was divided into 13 tribes that symbolized the 13 Colonies. Initially formed for social and patriotic reasons, the society shifted over into the political area, achieving its greatest notoriety during the reign of "Boss" Tweed at Tammany Hall.

Jan. 26 Mallet-and-chisel work on cemetery headstones reached a new high in detailing the demise of the deceased:

> In Memory of Mr. Elijah Bardwell who died Janry 26th 1786 in ye 27th Year of his Age having but a few days surviv'd ye fatal Night when he was flung from his Horse & drawn by ye Stirrup 26 rods along ye path as appear'd by ye place where his hat was found & where he had

Spent ye whole following severe cold night treading ye Snow in a small circle.

May 31 The Typographical Society (membership: 26) went on strike to support brother workers who refused to have their wages cut to less than $6/wk. The strikers won.

June 8 Commercial ice cream was advertised for sale in New York. The man responsible for bringing so much joy to the U.S.: Mr. Hall, of 76 Chatham Street.

1787

Jan. 25 Daniel Shays and 800 (some say 2,000) Massachusetts farmers attacked the Springfield arsenal to seize arms. Faced with high taxes—shifted onto landowners by commercial interests—farmers were unable to meet mortgage payments or obtain survival loans at less than 20–40% interest. Continuing evictions, imprisonment for debts, and an inability to get redress in the courts forced an insurrection. Shays's desperate action, taking the law into his own hands, threw a scare into provincials who had opposed a strong, centralized republic, and it encouraged Massachusetts to ratify the Federal Constitution. George Washington, writing to James Madison: "If there exists not a power to check them, what security has a man for life, liberty or property?" Thomas Jefferson thought differently: "A little revolution now and then is a good thing; the tree of liberty must be refreshed from time to time with the blood of patriots and tyrants."

May 14 The Constitutional Convention opened in Philadelphia. The delegates were mostly wealthy men of property. Tom Paine and Thomas Jefferson were in Europe. Sam Adams was not one of the chosen. Patrick Henry, though elected, refused to attend because he "smelt a rat." For 4 weeks, the Virginia Resolves, 15 in all, were debated and amended. Should a lower house be elected by the people? Should the upper be chosen by State legislatures? Could a one-house legislative body like Pennsylvania's be used? Equal representation posed a problem. Could small States be protected against the depredations of the large? It took Roger Sherman's immense talents to devise the compromise: proportional representation in the House, and one representative per State in the Senate (later revised to 2).

And what about the Presidency? Should it be a 3-man troika, with one man elected from the North, one from the South, and a 3rd from the Middle States? A one-man Presidency, snorted Randolph, would be the "foetus of Monarchy." Even Franklin had doubts, saying that some future leader, presiding alone, might prove corrupt.

The delegates cast 60 ballots while threshing out presidential selection. The original term of office was set at 6, then 11, 15, 7, and finally 4 years. On September 8, they gave 23 resolves to the Committee of Style, which cut these to 7. "We the People of the United States . . ." they began (giving anonymous status to those States that might elect to remain *outside* the Union), are establishing this Constitution to secure ". . . the Blessings of Liberty . . ."

There were 39 out of 55 delegates on hand to sign on September 17. Franklin, aged 81 and infirm, had to be helped to do so, as tears streamed down his lined cheeks. Three other men refused: Randolph, Mason, and Gerry. They later published their objections, provoking from the trio of Hamilton, Madison, and John Jay an eloquent, ringing defense: 85 separate essays called *The Federalist* papers, which were signed commonly as "Publius."

Sept. 30 Nomination for the Sailing Hall of Fame: the 212-ton *Columbia*. In company with the sloop *Washington*, the ship left Boston for British Columbia, to trade with the Indians. Capt. Robert Gray started as the *Washington*'s master, swapped commands at Vancouver, and went on around the world in the *Columbia* by way of China, a 1st for U.S. ships.

1788

—Nicholas Pike published a new arithmetic book, titled *A New and Complete System*. It became the standard schoolboy's text.

Spring Flame from a church candle set a destructive fire in old New Orleans that wiped out 19 blocks and 856 homes—most of the town. Architectural styles brought over from France and Spain were abandoned, and the city took on a new look, with a greater use of brick in place of wood.

June 21 By a vote of 57 to 47, New Hampshire became the 9th State to ratify the Constitution, the last approval needed to put it into effect. Due to its centralism and its "strong tendency to aristocracy," the Constitution met stiff opposition in many Colonies. Rhode Island and North Carolina rejected it outright. In Virginia, the vote was 89–79 for approval, in New York, 30–27, and in Massachusetts, 187–168.

1789

—Alexander Hamilton's fiscal policies as Secretary of the Treasury derived from his political beliefs:

All communities divide . . . into the few and the many. The 1st are the rich and well-born; the other the mass of the people . . . turbulent and changing, they seldom judge or determine right. Give therefore to the 1st class, a distinct, permanent share in the Government.

Choose this "governing class," he said, from the old families, the financiers, the merchants, and keep their loyalty with policies that favor their interests.

—*Figure*, the stallion owned by Thomas Justin Morgan of Springfield, Mass., was born in this year, beginning the lineology of the Morgan horse in the U.S. Standing only 14 hands high and weighing less than 1,000 lbs., the horse became famous for his feats of strength. In log-pulling contests, he moved loads the other entries could not budge.

A dark red bay with black points, *Figure* had a compact body, small, delicate ears, a long, thick mane, and an even disposition, traits passed on to the breed today. The Morgan was truly the "people's horse" for all-around performance, whether winning a quarter-mile race, working in a wagon team, or carrying the children to school.

Brought to Randolph, Vt., as a 2-year-old, *Figure* won a reputation that lasted over 25 years. Before his death at 30 (a very old age for horses), he had sired hundreds of stallions and brood mares. His great-grandson *Ethan Allen* won honors in 1850 as the "World's Fastest Trotting Stallion." The champion pacing horse *Dan Patch* had strong Morgan lines in his pedigree. Vermont's famous Civil War cavalry was mounted exclusively on Morgans. Gen. George Custer's *Comanche* was also Morgan-bred.

Although *Figure*'s own ancestors are unknown, they probably were English—the thoroughbred *True Briton* is one claimant as sire. The Morgan's clean lines are a balanced blend of the English thoroughbred and the Arabian.

Jan. 21 The 1st novel published in the U.S. —*The Power of Sympathy*—dealt with the subject of sex. Author William Hill Brown's plot included an impending incestuous marriage, mistress peccadilloes, and successful seduction. For extra value, Brown added one death from shock and 2 by suicide. It was an epistolary romance.

Feb. 4 The Electoral College named Washington as President. He left Mount Vernon with mixed emotions. "My movement to the chair of Government will be accompanied by feelings not unlike those of a culprit who is going to the place of his execution."

Apr. 23 Moving Day for Martha. The Washingtons moved into the 1st presidential home, at ⚹1 Cherry Street, New York City. It was at the intersection of Cherry and Franklin, now Franklin Square.

Apr. 30 The 1st Cabinet was selected. Members: Thomas Jefferson (Va.), Secretary of State; Edmund Randolph (Va.), Attorney General; Henry Knox (Mass.), Secretary of War; Samuel Osgood (Mass.), Postmaster General; Alexander Hamilton (N.Y.), Secretary of the Treasury. Politically balanced: 2 Southerners, 2 Northerners, and one from the Middle.

Sept. 13 The 1st loan was made, to the U.S. To pay the salaries of the President and the members of Congress, Hamilton negotiated for $191,608.81 from the Bank of New York and the Bank of North America. Called the "Temporary Loan of 1789," and due by February 17, 1790 (at 6% interest), the transaction was illegal.

—W.K.

1790

—U.S. Population—3,929,214. (The 1st U.S. Census, completed August 1, revealed that Virginia was the most populous State at 747,-610. Philadelphia was the largest city at 42,444.)

Jan. 14 Alexander Hamilton, the new nation's Secretary of the Treasury, submitted to Congress a national fiscal program recommending that the Federal Government be responsible for the entire national debt, and assume most of the debt incurred by the States during the Revolution. Southern congressmen agreed to vote for the Assumption Bill if northern congressmen would vote for a southern site for the Federal capital. The bill was passed and 10 years later the capital was moved from Philadelphia to the banks of the Potomac.

Apr. 17 Benjamin Franklin died in Philadelphia at 84. Half the population of Philadelphia attended his funeral—an estimated 20,000 people. He was widely known at home and abroad as a distinguished statesman, scientist, and philosopher. Four of the key documents of his time bore Franklin's signature: The Declaration of Independence, Constitution of the U.S., Treaty of Alliance with France, and Treaty of Peace with Great Britain. In 1789 George Washington wrote to Franklin: "If to be venerated for benevolence; if to be admired for talents; if to be esteemed for patriotism; if to be beloved for philanthropy, can gratify the human mind, you must have the pleasing consolation that you have not lived in vain."

May 31 President Washington signed the U.S. copyright act.

July Four Carmelite nuns founded Mount Carmel, at Port Tobacco, Charles County, Md.; the 1st convent of religious women established in what had been the original 13 Colonies. The convent throve until 1891, when the nuns were transferred to Baltimore. The buildings had almost disappeared by 1935, the year a group of interested citizens launched a restoration campaign. Two surviving buildings were restored and a new chapel built. Now public pilgrimages are made year around.

Dec. First U.S. patent went to Samuel Hopkins of Vermont for new method of making crude and commercial carbonate of potassium, used in glassmaking.

1791

—When Philadelphia carpenters went on strike, they formed a cooperative and offered their services for 25% less than their employers had charged.

—Jeremy Belknap, Boston clergyman, founded the Massachusetts Historical Society for the purpose of collecting important historical documents.

Mar. First Internal Revenue law passed by Congress.

Mar. 4 Vermont admitted to the Union, becoming the 14th State.

Dec. 15 The Bill of Rights became a part of the Constitution. Developed from ideas set forth in the Bible and in ancient Greek and Roman civilizations, the 1st 10 Amendments guaranteed basic freedoms and rights to the people.

1792

—U.S. mail service from the district of Maine to Virginia provided 3 deliveries a week in winter and 2 a week in summer. Although there were 6,000–7,000 mi. of post roads, the western limits of service were Pittsburgh and Albany. By 1799, the total miles of post roads had doubled and service to the west was considerably extended.

—The U.S. Mint was established in Philadelphia, using the decimal system of coins in which 10¢ equal one dime and 10 dimes $1. The U.S. silver dollar, patterned after the Spanish milled dollar, wasn't issued until 1794.

June 1 Kentucky became the 15th State.

—George Washington was chosen unanimously for 2nd term as President—this time by the electors from 15 States.

1793

—The French Revolution began when Washington had been in office only a short time. When news came that the French King had been guillotined, there were wild demonstrations and parades in the U.S. In Boston, Royal Exchange Alley was renamed Equality Lane, and in New York, radicals forced the city to change King Street to Liberty Street. President Washington denounced such activities, and declared official neutrality.

—George Washington officiated at the cornerstone-setting of the U.S. Capitol, an occasion which featured the Masonic rites. The trowel he used was later used by the Grand Master of Masons at cornerstone-laying ceremonies for the Washington Monument, July 4, 1848.

Mar. 14 Eli Whitney obtained a patent for the cotton gin which he invented while employed as a tutor at "Mulberry Grove," the plantation of Mrs. Nathanael Greene, in Georgia. Southern plantation owners reaped enormous profits as a result of his invention, but Whitney received so little that he had to return to the North and find another means of making a living. He invented machinery whereby unskilled men could make interchangeable parts for muskets. Ultimately his method of manufacture resulted in mass production and assembly lines.

Apr. Citizen Genêt was the 1st foreigner to be granted political asylum in the U.S. He had received a warm popular welcome upon his arrival as Minister from France, but Washington and Jefferson objected to his organizing anti-British and anti-Spanish projects on American soil and demanded his recall. France complied, ordering him returned under arrest. Since his party, the Girondists, had fallen in France, Genêt's return meant the guillotine. Consequently, Washington allowed him to remain in America, refusing demands for his extradition. He married Governor Clinton's daughter and became a country gentleman.

July Jefferson resigned as Secretary of State because he believed Washington to be partial to the Federalists and to Hamilton's opinions on foreign affairs. Washington appointed in his place Edmund Randolph, whom a kinsman, John Randolph, compared to "the chameleon on the aspen, always trembling, always changing." Edmund did ultimately resign in disgrace when evidence seemed to show that, although officially he professed approval of Washington's policy, he secretly worked against it. This ended Washington's attempt to govern with a bipartisan Cabinet.

Aug. The yellow fever epidemic in Philadelphia, the largest city in the U.S., was listed in current record books as a major disaster.

1794

—*Charlotte Temple*, a sentimental "seduction" novel by Susanna Rowson, achieved wide popularity in America after having been unsuccessful in England. It has been continuously in print since its original publication date.

—Whiskey Rebellion in western Pennsylvania. The frontier farmers objected to a tax on whiskey when whiskey itself was their medium of exchange. The cost of sending grain to eastern markets was more than the grain would bring, so they converted it to whiskey which could be easily stored, transported, and traded. Tax collectors were tarred and feathered or met with shotguns. One farmer and his neighbor welcomed excise officers with generous servings of Jamaica ginger laced with whiskey. The genial hosts remained hospitable until the officers passed out, then slipped off and hid the still. President Washington ordered Federal troops to put down the "acts" that he said amounted to treason. With General "Light-Horse Harry" Lee in command, the army restored order. Some of the leaders were arrested and taken to Philadelphia for trial. Only 2 were convicted and they were pardoned by the President. The new Government had proved to the nation that it could enforce laws enacted by Congress.

—The 1st independent Methodist Church for Negroes was established at Philadelphia. Its founder, Richard Allen, a former slave, became bishop of the African Methodist Episcopal Church in 1816.

Mar. 27 An act of Congress marked the founding of the U.S. Navy. After the Revolution (circa 1785) the Navy declined to virtual nonexistence. It had to be re-established to protect neutral American ships from being plundered.

Aug. 20 Gen. Anthony Wayne decisively defeated the Indians at the battle of Fallen Timbers. A strict disciplinarian, Wayne had trained his troops for 2 years in the tactics of forest warfare before launching his successful campaign which, followed by the Treaty of Greenville in 1795, opened up most of what is now Ohio for settlement. Thus Indian resistance was broken, and the fighting—at least for a time—came to an end.

1795

—Two major books were published: 1. In Paris, part 2 of Thomas Paine's treatise *The Age of*

Reason. As a result, Paine was called that "dirty little atheist," although actually he was a deist. 2. In the U.S., Philip Freneau's *Poems Written Between the Years 1768 and 1794*. Called "that rascal Freneau" by Washington for his pro-Jefferson leanings, Freneau was variously a seaman, postal employee, translator, editor, as well as the 1st competent poet in the Colonies.
—America's 1st mass murderers, Wiley and Micajah Harpe, began a 4-year spree in which they ranged across the present States of Tennessee, Kentucky, southern Illinois, and Mississippi, accompanied by their 3 wives (Micajah had 2), butchering between 30 and 40 people. According to tradition, when Micajah was captured for the last time in late summer of 1799, his head was severed by the husband of his final victim. Still breathing at the start of his own execution, Micajah looked his executioner in the eye and said, "You are a God Damned rough butcher, but cut on and be damned." Wiley was hung 5 years later when he was recognized while trying to collect a bounty for having killed a fellow outlaw.
—Daniel Boone, aided by "buffalo streets" and Indian trails, created the Wilderness Road. This famous route led the way westward for many future settlers. Boone was captured by the Indians several times but always managed to escape. Less fortunate was his oldest son whom the Indians tortured and killed. Boone's wife and daughter Jemima, were the 1st white women to see the part of Kentucky around Boonesborough. Settling down to a quiet, peaceful life did not appeal to Boone. "Too many people! Too crowded! Too crowded! I want more elbow room." He spent his last years in Missouri hunting and trapping. After a short illness, he died at age 86.
—The 1st circus arrived in the U.S. Rickett's Circus, an equestrian troupe from England, performed before delighted audiences in New York.
—Seven literary periodicals were launched in this one year. And another 50 or more sprang up before 1800. Of the total, 3 survived to celebrate a 2nd anniversary of their natal day.

1796

June 1 Tennessee became the 16th State to join the Union.
Sept. 17 Before he left office, George Washington issued a "Farewell Address" to the American people, but he did not deliver it orally. Instead, it was published in the *Philadelphia American Advertiser*. A long-established custom still observed in the Senate and House of Representatives today is to convene on Washington's Birthday for an oral reading, by one of their members, of the famous address. In it Washington said: "My 1st wish is to see this plague of mankind—war—banished from the earth."

1797

—In retirement, General Washington dined well. One of his favorite dinner menus: cream of peanut soup; Smithfield ham with oyster sauce; mashed sweet potatoes with coconut; string beans with mushrooms; Southern spoon bread; Virginia whiskey cake. Wife Martha had the recipe for the Virginia whiskey cake:

> To make a great cake
> Take 40 eggs and divide the whites from the yolks and beat them to a froth then work 4 lbs. of butter to a cream and put the whites of eggs to it a spoon full at a time till it is well worked then put in the youlks [sic] of eggs and 5 lbs. of flower [sic] and 5 lbs. of fruit. 2 hours will bake it add to it half an ounce of mace and nutmeg half a pint of wine and some fresh brandy.
> This was wrote [sic] by Martha Curtis
>   for her Grandmama.

—At a meeting of the American Philosophical Society, Benjamin Rush argued that black skin color was a disease like leprosy. His main evidence was a Virginia slave, Henry Moss, whose skin lightened after he moved to the North.
Mar. 4 John Adams was inaugurated as 2nd President. He was the 1st Chief Executive to live in the White House. Vigorous in demanding American independence, he nevertheless managed to preserve neutrality. Adams lived longer than any other President—91 years.
May 31 The XYZ affair: President Adams sent Charles Pinckney, John Marshall, and Elbridge Gerry to negotiate a treaty with France. The 3-man commission was met by 3 "go-betweens" of the French Government, who demanded a loan and bribes before their leaders would begin talks. Incensed and insulted, the Americans broke off negotiations and returned home. When Adams reported the matter to Congress, he did not name the agents (Hottinguer, Bellamy, and Hauteval) but referred to them as X, Y, and Z. The incident gave rise to the slogan, "Millions for defense, but not one cent for tribute," which was 1st used by Robert Goodloe Harper as a toast at a banquet in Philadelphia on June 18, 1798.
Oct. A reoccurrence of yellow fever drove many wealthy Philadelphians out of the city and allowed tavern keeper Israel Israel, a champion of the poor, to be elected to the State

legislature. Horrified, the State senate declared the election illegal on the grounds that a large number of Israel's supporters had not taken an oath of allegiance. The new election on February 22 found Israel the loser.

1798

—*Alcuin: A Dialogue* by Charles Brockden Brown is said to be the 1st sustained and earnest argument for the rights of women to appear in this country.
—After the failure of the French mission, fear of war with France prompted Congress to pass measures to strengthen national defense. George Washington was called from retirement to serve as commander in chief; existing treaties with France were repealed, and 2 years of undeclared war with France began.
—The Alien and Sedition Act was passed by Congress. This gave the President power to imprison or deport any foreigner believed to be dangerous to the U.S., and made it a crime to attack the Government with "false, scandalous, or malicious" statements or writings.
—The Kentucky and Virginia resolutions, drawn up by Madison and Jefferson, declared the Alien and Sedition Act contrary to the Constitution in that it interfered with the powers of the States. From these resolutions grew the doctrines of States' rights.
Mar. 9 George Balfour was appointed 1st surgeon in the Navy.
Apr. 20 "Hail Columbia," the patriotic song written by Joseph Hopkinson, was published in *Porcupine's Gazette*. It was introduced to audiences by actor Gilbert Fox as a patriotic spur when war with France appeared inevitable.
Apr. 30 The Navy Dept. established.
July 9 U.S.S. *Delaware* captured French ship *Croyable*. Capt. Stephen Decatur, Sr., sighted 4 French schooners while cruising off the Atlantic Coast. Pretending to be anxious to avoid them he turned away and one schooner gave chase. Decatur let it approach, then suddenly turned to give battle. The Frenchman, discovering he was facing a warship, attempted to escape. A few rounds from the *Delaware's* guns forced him to surrender. The privateer *Croyable* was taken into Philadelphia and renamed the U.S.S. *Retaliation*.

1799

—Congress suspended all trade with France and her colonies. The frigate *Constellation* captured French *Insurgente*.
Mar. President Adams appointed William

Varns Murray as the new Minister to France. The latter headed the peace commission which ended hostilities with France.
Oct. 30 William Barch became the 1st navy chaplain.
Dec. 14 George Washington died of a severe throat infection, following a cold caught while riding around his farm in the rain and snow. An Alexandria, Va., newspaper published in its entirety the report submitted by the attending physicians.
—D.W.S.

1800

—U.S. population—5,308,483. Almost ⅕th of this—896,849—consisted of slaves.

—To the memory of the man, 1st in war, 1st in peace, and 1st in the hearts of his countrymen.
        —Henry "Light-Horse Harry" Lee
        in his eulogy on Washington

—Jeffersonian Republicans (present-day Democrats) successfully challenged the single-party Government of the Federalists in a bitterly fought campaign between Jefferson and Federalist John Adams. It was the 1st election to employ name-calling—Adams was called a madman, warmonger, spendthrift; Jefferson was characterized as a radical revolutionary just waiting to set up a military dictatorship, and to confiscate all Bibles and replace them with his own version thereof.
—Hamilton admitted paying blackmail money to hush up "an amorous connection" with a certain Mrs. Reynolds while he was Secretary of the Treasury under Washington.
—Clergyman-bookseller Mason Locke ("Parson") Weems's popular *Life of Washington*, the source of numerous fabricated legends believed by many to this day, was published. (See also: Footnote People in U.S. History, Chap. 3.)
—The "Johnny Appleseed" legend became one of the few folk tales based on fact. "Johnny's" real name was John Chapman, and for over 50 years he wandered up and down the Ohio Valley distributing not only appleseeds, but Swedenborgian religious tracts. Chapman was also a frontier Paul Revere, galloping through frontier settlements warning them of Indian attacks during the War of 1812.
—There was a new frontier fad—growing long thumbnails for gouging out an opponent's eye. This sadistic idea was imported from England.
Apr. 24 The Library of Congress was established. Jefferson donated his own private library as its initial collection.

June Washington, D.C., became the nation's new capital. Earlier it had been New York and Philadelphia. John Adams, the 1st President to live in the White House, moved into it November 17. The White House, which stood on a desolate bog, had no bathrooms, and water had to be carried by hand a distance of 5 city blocks. For want of space, Abigail Adams hung her laundry in the East Room.

July 8 The 1st cowpox vaccination in the U.S. was performed by Harvard professor of medicine, Dr. Benjamin Waterhouse, upon his own son, Daniel. This vaccination was to prevent smallpox.

1801

—The 1st undeclared U.S. war. Conflict with the North African port city of Tripoli began when the Pasha of Tripolitania cut down the flagpole at the U.S. Consulate, after the U.S. refused to pay tribute to pirates along the Barbary Coast. Later, on the night of February 16, 1804, Lieut. Stephen Decatur and his daredevil crew slipped aboard the captured American ship *Philadelphia* as it lay docked in Tripoli harbor, knifed the guards, set the ship afire by using gunpowder, and rowed safely away. Finally, in 1805, the U.S. consul in Tunis, William Eaton, collected a rabble army in Egypt—consisting of 38 Greeks, 300 Arabs, a dethroned pasha, and 7 marines under Lieut. Preston N. O'Bannon—and marched 600 mi. across the desert to attack Tripoli from the rear. The phrase "To the shores of Tripoli" in the U.S. Marines' hymn refers to this incident.

—Josiah Bent of Milton, Mass., introduced hard water crackers in New England, where they enjoyed widespread popularity.

Jan. 20 John Marshall was appointed chief justice of the Supreme Court. This tall, lanky Virginian, raised on the frontier, made decisions establishing the right of the Federal courts to annul as unconstitutional laws passed by Congress (*Marbury* v. *Madison*), and to annul a State law because it conflicted with a Federal one (*McCulloch* v. *Maryland*).

Feb. 17 Thomas Jefferson became the 1st President to be elected by the House of Representatives. This came about as a result of the 1st and only tie in a presidential election. Jefferson and Aaron Burr both received 73 electoral votes, which threw the election into the House. Here Hamilton came out strongly against Burr, calling him "a cold-blooded Cataline" and "a profligate; a voluptuary . . . without doubt insolvent." (Thus began the feud that resulted in the famous Burr-Hamilton duel 3 years later.) Six days of balloting and 36 ballots later, Jefferson was elected 3rd President of the U.S.

Mar. 4 Jefferson became the 1st President inaugurated in Washington, D.C. In his Inaugural Address he called for:

> . . . a wise and frugal Government which shall restrain men from injuring one another . . . and shall not take from the mouth of labor the bread it has earned. . . .

It was here that Jefferson coined the expression "entangling alliances," words commonly attributed to Washington:

> Peace, commence, and honest friendship with all nations—entangling alliances with none.

—Jefferson abolished social affairs at the White House. He received callers in his working clothes: a tattered brown coat, corduroy breeches, wool (not silk) hose, and down-at-the-heels carpet slippers. Most sophisticated and versatile of the Presidents, he invented both a plow and a swivel chair, sorted mammoth bones on the White House floor, edited his own version of the Bible, played the fiddle, and designed Monticello ("Little Mountain").

1802

—The 1st real hotel was built in America—the Union Hotel in Saratoga, N.Y.—by Gideon Putnam. While there had been many taverns and inns previously, this was the 1st hostelry used primarily for lodging instead of entertainment.

—A famous navigation guide was published, the *New American Practical Navigator*, written by Nathaniel Bowditch. A school dropout at age 10, Bowditch went to sea 12 years later, pursuing his interest in navigation. During 5 long voyages he found and corrected over 8,000 errors in Moore's *Practical Navigator*. Bowditch was the 1st to compute longitudes with a sextant by measuring angular distances between fixed stars and the moon. His guide has been continually issued by the U.S. Hydrographic Office since 1867.

—The banjo clock was designed by Simon Willard, the well-known clockmaker of Roxbury, Mass. It was a wall-hung clock.

Mar. 16 A U.S. military academy was established by act of Congress at West Point, N.Y. Originally this was the Revolutionary fortress that Benedict Arnold attempted to sell to the British in his famous act of treason.

1803

—John Randolph of Virginia, Jefferson's leader in the House of Representatives, set tongues to wagging with his announcement that he had fathered an illegitimate child. This was all the more unusual because of Randolph's unique personality. His beardless face and shrill soprano voice, the result of a childhood disease, brought unending taunts which had forced him into numerous duels. Unmatched for his cutting remarks, he once shot back at someone who had ridiculed him on his so-called lack of virility: "You pride yourself upon an animal faculty in respect to which the Negro is your equal and the jackass infinitely your superior!" It was he who characterized Edward Livingstone, his political enemy thus: "He shines and stinks like rotten mackerel by moonlight!"
—Many flinched again when Tom Paine spent 2 weeks at the White House at the invitation of President Jefferson. Most had forgotten the service this old hero of the Revolution had rendered his country by writing *Common Sense* and *The American Crisis*. Ever since he had taken part in the French Revolution and had written what many considered an atheistic tract, *The Age of Reason*, he had been persona non grata in America. And now that atheist, that drunkard, that unwashed revolutionary was actually dining in the White House!
—The 1st tax-supported public library was founded in Salisbury, Conn., the gift of Caleb Bingham, Boston publisher.
—Ezekial Case started glove manufacturing in Gloversville, N.Y., which inevitably became famous as a glove-making center.
—Sign of the times: Immigration into the U.S. increased so rapidly that Britain decreed that her ships crossing to America must allow 43' of space for each passenger—there were fears that if the crowding continued, bunks would soon have to be stood on end!
Apr. John James Audubon, famous ornithologist-to-be, arrived from France, and almost immediately began banding phoebes, the 1st time this had been done in the U.S. for scientific reasons. Later he operated a general store in Louisville, Ky. Had this store not gone bankrupt in 1819, Audubon might never have traveled down the Mississippi, painting wild birds en route.
Apr. 30 President Jefferson "breaks the law." Jefferson purchased the Louisiana Territory from Napoleon. Since the Constitution did not specifically give the President authorization to buy land, Jefferson was at 1st reluctant to

finalize the purchase. Thus the largest real estate deal in U.S. history—one doubling the size of the country—almost went down the drain. Jefferson's practical mind prevailed, however, and he bought over 800,000 sq. mi. for a mere $15 million!

1804

—Andrew Jackson, a young frontier lawyer, built a small 3-room cabin in the Tennessee wilderness for his wife Rachel, little realizing that it would eventually become the "Hermitage," a national shrine.
—Although seldom credited with it, Oliver Evans actually built the 1st "automobile." The famous Philadelphia inventor constructed a 5-hp steam engine for dredging the harbor area between the city docks. This engine propelled a scow used for that purpose. The 15½ ton, 30' boat was put on wheels and driven 1½ mi. from its construction shed down Center Street to the docks, where its drive belt was shifted from land wheels to paddle wheels before the scow entered the river. Thus it was actually the 1st "automobile." Evans bet any comers $3,000 that he could build a steam-driven land vehicle that would beat any horse. But, like many prophets, he was ahead of his time. No one took him up on his offer, and interest in the idea died.
—The schooner *Reynard* brought the 1st shipment of bananas from Latin America to New York.
—An unusual "Coonskin Library" was started in Marietta, O. Settlers along the Ohio River exchanged and bartered coonskins, much in demand back East, for books from Boston merchants.
—Two patents were granted for "galluses"— otherwise known as "suspenders"—in the same year. This dual patent reflects the longing for security of the man who today wears both suspenders and a belt.

> —In all your intercourse with the natives, treat them in the most friendly and conciliatory manner which their own conduct will admit; allay all jealousies as to the object of your journey, satisfy them of its innocence . . . of our wish to be neighborly, friendly, and useful to them.
> —Jefferson's instructions to Lewis

May 14 The Lewis and Clark expedition set out from St. Louis to explore the Louisiana Territory. Captain Meriwether Lewis, Jefferson's personal secretary, and William Clark were to explore 8,000 mi. along the Missouri and Columbia rivers as far as the Pacific, returning in 1806.

July 11 Alexander Hamilton was killed in a duel with Vice-President Aaron Burr on the banks of the Hudson at Weehawken, N.J. At the 2nd's command of "Present," Burr immediately fired, and Hamilton fell forward discharging his pistol into the air. Many claimed Hamilton had purposely aimed high. A coroner's jury demanded the Vice-President's arrest, but Burr fled to Georgia and South Carolina where he made a 400-mi. trip through the swamps in a canoe. Meanwhile, insulting poems appeared:

Oh Burr, oh Burr, what hast thou done,
Thou hast shooted dead great Hamilton!
You hid among a bunch of thistle
And shooted him dead with a great hoss pistol!

The former 1st Secretary of the Treasury left behind 7 children and $55,000 in debts.

1805

—Brother, our seats were once large and yours were small. You have now become a great people, and we have scarcely a place left to spread our blankets. You have got our country but are not satisfied; you want to force your religion upon us. . . . We also have a religion which was given to our forefathers and has been handed down from father to son. . . . It teaches us to be thankful for all the favors we receive, to love each other, and be united. . . .
— Red Jacket's address
to a missionary

—Author Hugh Henry Brackenridge issued a lesson for the times when, in his *Modern Chivalry*, he pinpointed the evil of ambition, which he called "the poison of public virtue":

. . . The 1st lesson I would give to a son of mine would be to have nothing to do with public business, but as a duty to his country. . . . They should be warned of flatterers, whose object is not to serve them but themselves. The demagogue in a democracy and the courtier in a monarchy are identical. . . .

July 8 Bill Richmond, a Negro, became the 1st American to win distinction in a prize fight. Richmond, the son of a slave owned by a Reverend Clayton, knocked out Jack Holmes, alias Tom Tough, in the 26th round at Cricklewood Green, England.

1806

—Noah Webster's *Compendious Dictionary of the English Language* was published. Noah was often confused with Daniel Webster, but the 2 were not related. Many words in Webster's Dictionary—such as "lengthy," "sot," "spry," "belittle," and "caucus"—were condemned as being nothing more than vulgar New Englandisms.

—The 1st industry-wide strike occurred when 200 Philadelphia shoemakers walked off the job and issued a nationwide strike order. At issue were wages, but leaders of the strike were indicted for criminal conspiracy, and the infant union was ordered disbanded. The shoemakers then established a cooperative shoe warehouse.

—Up-and-coming frontier lawyer Andrew Jackson shot and killed Charles Dickinson in a Kentucky backwoods duel. Jackson suffered several broken ribs. Throughout his political career, he would be attacked for his many dueling bouts. At his death, Jackson carried one bullet lodged in his chest near his heart, and another in a bone in his left arm.

—Newport, R.I., became the 1st American city to have its streets illuminated by gas lights. It was the brainchild of David Melville, who installed these lights along Pelham Street. Unfortunately, due to legal complications, the project had to be abandoned.

—Aaron Burr was again in the news. But this time Burr was charged with treason, after being dropped as a vice-presidential candidate, for trying to set up a separate nation on land owned by the U.S. and Spain.

Nov. 15 Zebulon Pike sighted the Colorado peak that now bears his name during an expedition in the southwest. He did not climb it, however.

1807

—The A. B. Lindsley comedy, *Love and Friendship, or Yankee Notions,* opened on the New York stage where it was an immediate success. Hero Dick Dashaway was the 1st satiric characterization of the foppish college stereotype.

—In Connecticut, Seth Thomas and Eli Terry began manufacture of clocks with interchangeable parts.

—Robert Fulton's steamboat *Clermont* made its 1st run, crossing the Hudson River from

New York to New Jersey. Later it traveled up the Hudson from New York to Albany, making the trip in about 30 hours at 5 mph. Contrary to popular opinion, Fulton did not invent the steamboat. Instead, he was the 1st to make it a commercial success. Fulton also proposed that torpedoes be used as the major defense weapon for U.S. ports, but Jefferson was afraid of gambling the defense of the nation upon a single weapon. However, Jefferson did encourage Fulton to continue his research on the submarine.

1808

—John Elihu Hall founded the *American Law Journal* in Baltimore, probably the earliest legal periodical in the U.S. Unusual was the fact that Hall himself was not an attorney; instead, he was a professor of rhetoric at the University of Maryland.

Jan. 1 The African slave trade was prohibited by Congress. Nevertheless an illicit trade continued so that between 1808 and the start of the Civil War an estimated 250,000 slaves were imported.

Oct. 30 When the schooner *Betty*, commanded by Benjamin Ireson, arrived at Marblehead, Mass., Ireson was accused of sailing away from a sinking ship because he feared for his own safety. Marblehead citizens tarred and feathered Ireson and rode him out of town. Later, the poet John Greenleaf Whittier dramatized the event in his poem "Skipper Ireson's Ride."

Nov. James Madison, the 4th President of the U.S., was elected.

1809

—The 1st American humorous book of note, *History of New York* by Washington Irving, was published. European critics raved over the book, the 1st American work to impress the Old World. A best seller, it was a satirical history of old Dutch New Amsterdam. Irving wrote it under the Dutch pseudonym, "Diedrich Knickerbocker."

For what is a history, but a kind of Newgate calendar, a register of the crimes and miseries that man has inflicted on his fellowman? It is a huge libel on human nature, to which we industriously add page after page, volume after volume, as if we were holding up a monument to the honor, rather than the in-

famy of our species. . . . What are the great events that constitute a glorious era?—The fall of empires—the desolation of happy countries—splendid cities smoking in their ruins—the proudest works of art tumbled in the dust—the shrieks and groans of whole nations ascending unto heaven!
—Washington Irving, in his *History of New York*

—A new medicine was placed on the market: "Hamilton's Essense and Extract of Mustard: for Rheumatism, Gout, Palsy, Swelling, Numbness, Etc."

—John Stevens's steamboat *Phoenix* completed the 1st successful sea voyage from New York to Philadelphia. Stevens, a well-known inventor, had earlier designed the screw propeller in 1802 and had influenced the writing of the 1st Federal patent laws.

—Abel Stowel of Massachusetts designed and manufactured the 1st screw-cutting machine in the U.S.

Mar. 4 Madison was sworn in as 4th President of the U.S., while Jefferson quietly retired to his beloved Monticello. Jefferson would die there on July 4, 1826, in virtual poverty, his home and all its furnishings sold to satisfy creditors.

June 8 Tom Paine, whose pamphlets had inspired the Revolutionary spirit of Americans 35 years earlier, died in obscurity while living at 59 Grove Street in New York. Only 6 people followed his casket to its grave.

Oct. 31 Sign of the times: A Northerner, George Hicks of Brooklyn, ran an ad in the *New York Post* offering a reward of $25 for the return of a runaway slave: "Negro woman named Charity and her female child . . . 25 years of age, 5′ high, of a yellowish complexion . . . has lost the use of one of her fingers, occasioned by a fellon [sic], took with her several suits of clothes."

Nov. 1 A New York exhibit opened featuring a "Grand Panorama," a view of New York and the surrounding area "as seen from an eminence in the neighborhood of the Park." Cost of admission was 50¢ with a lifetime ticket available for $2.

—L.A.W.

1810

—U.S. population—7,239,881. (The 3rd U.S. census listed: 1,211,364 slaves; 186,746 free Negroes; and 60,000 immigrants.)

—Between 1810 and 1830, 2 million people left the eastern States for the West.

—Tecumseh (spelled variously Tecumtha, Tecumthe, and Tikamthi) was the Indian chief of the Shawnees who, with his brother Tenskwatawa (The Prophet), tried to unite the Indians in the western part of the U.S. against the whites. In 1810 he told the President's messenger:

> These lands are ours. No one has a right to remove us, because we were the 1st owners. The Great Spirit above has appointed this place for us, on which to light our fires, and we will remain. As to boundaries, the Great Spirit knows no boundaries, nor will His red children acknowledge any.

(See also: Tecumseh in Footnote People in U.S. History, Chap. 3.)

—There were 366 newspapers in the U.S.
—Greek Revival Architecture had caught on in the U.S. The pillared, templelike buildings were usually painted white, causing James Fenimore Cooper to remark that the homes "looked like 'mushroom temples' lined along the Hudson River marring the landscape with their whiteness."
Apr. 16 Congress voted to reduce the size of both the Army and the Navy.
Summer The French seized, and sold, U.S. merchantmen in the Bay of Naples.
June 23 John Jacob Astor, a German immigrant who eventually became the richest man in America, organized the Pacific Fur Company. Astor's fortune was made in the fur trade and from shrewd real estate investments.
July 12 The trial of journeymen cordwainers began in New York City. They had conspired to raise wages by calling a strike. Union members lost the case and were fined $1 each.
Aug. 30 In Boston, forts were repaired and strengthened and a new one was built.
Dec. 15–Jan. 1815 The Hartford Convention was called by the dissident Federalist group. Delegates from Massachusetts, Connecticut, Rhode Island, 2 New Hampshire counties and one Vermont county, met in Hartford, Conn. Their grievances included government placement of regular army officers—illegally—in command of local militia; discrimination against New England commerce; the neglect of the coastline defense (which was left to the States because the Government was concentrating its forces on Canada and the lakes). Other accusations included Federal weakening of the commercial regions by admitting Western States; governmental insistence on following party lines; and pitting States against each other. Though many at the convention called for secession, the moderates prevailed and instead produced these proposals:

1. Nullification of the conscript act
2. Arrangement for part of national taxes

from the States to go for defense of those States paying said taxes
3. Provision for sending troops for defense from one New England State to another
4. Amendments to the Constitution:
   a. Abolition of the ⅗ rule
   b. No new States except by a ⅔ vote in Congress
   c. Except in case of invasion, declaration of war to require a ⅔ vote
   d. Naturalized persons not to be eligible for civil office, House or Senate
   e. No 2nd term for President, nor should a President come from the same State twice in succession
5. If peace not concluded, or the above provisions not met, or the defense of
6. the New England States continued to be neglected, a new convention should be called.

1811

—Construction began on the Cumberland Road, now U.S. 40, providing an important aid to westward expansion.
—Josiah Quincy of Massachusetts, during a debate on the Louisiana Purchase, told members of the House of Representatives that if the bill passed, it would be the dissolution of the Union.
—Congressional elections were won by the War Hawks, who favored expansion and the conquest of Canada. They also protested the impressment of U.S. citizens and other British outrages.
Apr. 12 The 1st permanent Pacific Northwest Colony was founded at Cape Disappointment in the present State of Washington.
May 1 An American sailor was removed from an American vessel off Sandy Hook and taken aboard the frigate *Guerrière* by the British.
May 16 The U.S. frigate *President*, in searching for the *Guerrière*, mistakenly disabled the British sloop *Little Belt*, causing 32 British casualties. The U.S. offered to compensate for the loss in November on condition that the British revoke Orders in Council, which prohibited trade with ports closed to British ships.
Nov. 7 Prophetstown, Ind., where the Tippecanoe and Wabash rivers meet, was the scene of the Battle of Tippecanoe when about 1,000 Indians attacked William Henry Harrison's camp before dawn. The Shawnee Indians were led by Tenskwatawa.
Dec. 9 Speaking to the House of Representatives, Felix Grundy of Tennessee called for war rather than submit to England's impressment of

seamen. Grundy, whose brothers had been killed by the Indians, felt the Indian massacres were encouraged by the British. Therefore, he called for removal of the British from the American Continent.

Arguing against war was John Randolph of Virginia. Randolph admonished Grundy for his assumption that the British had put the Indians up to the Battle of Tippecanoe, and he questioned Grundy's motives. Randolph maintained that acquisition of Canada and not maritime security was the real reason that Grundy favored war. He argued that America and England had a common ancestral bond; that the British shared religion and language with the Americans; and even America's legal system owed its being to England.

Eloquent though Randolph was in the cause of peace, many doubted his concern for the country except as it would affect Virginia. Whittier later wrote of Randolph:

> Too honest or too proud to feign
> A love he never cherished,
> Beyond Virginia's border line
> His patriotism perished.

Dec. 16 An earthquake in the Ohio-Mississippi valleys caused death and destruction, and the earth's surface rose or sank 5′ to 25′ over an area of 30,000 sq. mi.

1 8 1 2

—Antiwar Federalists gained strength in Congress.
—The 1st life insurance company was formed in the U.S., in Philadelphia.
Apr. 30 Louisiana was admitted as the 18th State with a constitution allowing slavery.
May 11 England's Prime Minister, Spencer Perceval, who had decided to repeal the Orders in Council, was assassinated before he had actually revoked the orders. Delay in finding his successor pushed the revocation date to June 16. News of the revocation arrived in the U.S. 57 days later, on August 12.
June 18 Congress declared war against England. The Federalists and others were opposed but they were outvoted 79–49 in the House and 19–13 in the Senate.
June 26 A Day of Fast was proclaimed by the governor of Massachusetts as a protest against the war.
July 28 Amos A. Evans, navy surgeon aboard the frigate *Constitution*, commented in his journal that Boston bookstores have "plenty of sermons in pamphlet form and pieces against 'Madison's ruinous war.'" Evans questioned:

Will the U.S. receive any assistance from the Eastern States in the prosecution of the present war? Judging from the present symptoms, I fear not. Good God! Is it possible that the people of the U.S. enjoying the blessings of freedom under the only republican government on earth have not virtue enough to support it!

July 29 Just 41 days after war was declared, word of the war arrived in England.
Aug. 18 Accounts of the Kentucky Volunteers and Regulars, commanded by Gen. James Winchester, 1812–1813, were kept by several men and published in 1854 by Elias Darnell. One such account says that the volunteers received 2 months' advance pay, but wanted an additional $16 due them in lieu of clothing. The men were given a choice of forgetting about the $16 or going home. Six chose to go home and were drummed out of camp. The journal continues with stories of accidental shootings; of farms in Fort Wayne, Ind., destroyed by Pottowatomies; and of commanding officers ready to surrender, whose commands were taken from them by their lieutenants.
Aug. 19 Amos A. Evans's journal this date: "Wednesday 2 P.M. discovered a large sail leeward, at 4 P.M. discovered it was a large frigate. When we were within 2 to 2½ mi. she hoisted English colors and fired a gun." Evans described the battle, listed the dead and wounded, and continued, "After she struck, Capt. J. R. Dacres, Esq., came on board and informed us it was His Britannick Majesty's ship, *La Guerrière*." The ship was too dangerous to board, Evans said, and the night was spent getting the men and the crew onto the *Constitution*.

The *Guerrière* had mounted 49 guns and carried about 260–300 men, according to Evans's report. He described Captain Dacres as a young man of 24, agreeable and pleasant, and noted that the English crew "behaved very nobly and fought like heroes." Evans's report indicated that from "firing of 1st gun to close of action was one hour, 10 min." The *Guerrière* had 15 dead, 62 wounded. The *Constitution* suffered 7 deaths, 7 wounded, and had "4 or 5 others not too disabled to come to quarters."
Fall Trade with the enemy in some New England States, as well as in New York, Pennsylvania, and others, was business as usual from the time the war began. Licenses to get through blockades were openly sold by brokers in New York City, Philadelphia, and Boston. American captains in collusion with the British provided the enemy with supplies, and earned money themselves, by pretending to be captured in the blockades.
Nov. 23 "Captain John" of the Kentucks bragged about taking the scalp of Pottowatomie

chief Wynemack, breaking his knife in the process.

Dec. 10   Kentuckians made shoes out of green hides. Many didn't have shoes or clothing to keep them from freezing.

Dec. 16   Volunteers threatened to leave in 2 days if flour did not arrive. On the 18th, 300 head of hogs arrived and the men were temporarily pacified. Flour arrived 8 days later.

1813

—During Americanization of the French game "hazards" by a wealthy New Orleans playboy named de Marigny, the game became "Crapaud," later shortened to "craps." "Johnny Crapaud" was a common term for Louisiana Creoles.

Jan.   Battle at the River Raisin. The almost starved U.S. troops under General Winchester took Frenchtown when the inhabitants begged for protection from the British and the Indians. The Kentucks gorged themselves and enjoyed the comforts of the village after 5 months in the wilderness. Most of Winchester's army was within the sturdy 8' fence surrounding the village, but Winchester—anxious to get away from his discontented troops—stayed at a house about a quarter mile from the village. Some of the regulars also stayed outside the general camp.

Jan. 22   The British attacked and captured Winchester, who was forced to witness atrocities committed by the Indians. General Winchester surrendered his troops, much to their dismay, but word was received that the British Colonel Procter had threatened to "let loose" the Indians on the troops if Winchester did not do so. Further, Procter was said to have guaranteed Winchester's men protection from the Indians. The wounded were to be taken care of, the dead collected and buried, and private property respected. However, Procter, fearing American reinforcements were on their way, moved out of Raisin River hurriedly, leaving only a handful of British and the Indians in charge. Once the British had gone, Indians raided the camp and massacred the wounded. Tecumseh, upon hearing of the barbarism at Raisin River, was enraged. He blamed Procter for the massacre and said, "I conquer to save, and you [Procter] to murder."

Some of the American prisoners in charge of the wounded, and the wounded who were able to march, were "adopted" by the Indians in place of sons lost in battle. Later these captives told of the "adoption" ceremony, their ordeals as prisoners, and of offers from Detroit citizens to "buy" them, which the Indians refused, preferring to keep their "Yankees" for the cooking chores and hard labor. One cap-

tive said that after the Indians finished the stores purchased in Detroit, they ate fragments of dog or horsemeat, not caring whether the animal had been killed that day or whether it had died of unknown causes 7 or 8 days prior. Intelligence gleaned from the Indians indicated that 2,500 Indians and 1,000 British had engaged in the January 22nd battle. Historians have estimated 500 British and 600 Indians were involved in the battle. The American forces numbered about 1,000.

Apr. 15   U.S. occupied west Florida.

Apr. 27   The destruction of York (Toronto) during the U.S. effort to take Lake Ontario gave the British their excuse for the later burning of Washington.

June 1   "Don't give up the ship" were the dying words of 32-year old Capt. James Lawrence when the British frigate *Shannon* disabled the U.S. frigate *Chesapeake* and captured its crew off Boston's shore.

It is uncertain whether the words were actually spoken by Lawrence or if they were coined by Benjamin Russell, editor of the *Boston Centinel*. At any rate, the phrase became popular and some ladies of Presque Isle presented 27-year-old Lieut. Oliver Hazard Perry, (called "Commodore" because of his responsibility for a fleet of 9 ships) with a flag bearing that inscription for his flagship, the *Lawrence*. During the battle, Perry transferred from the *Lawrence* when it was disabled and took the flag with him aboard the *Niagara*. The young naval officer then captured an entire British fleet, the 1st time the Americans had accomplished such a feat. "Don't give up the ship" became an even more popular slogan after this decisive naval battle.

Sept. 10   Lieut. Oliver Hazard Perry sent a terse, often quoted message to Gen. William Henry Harrison after the successful Battle of Lake Erie: "We have met the enemy and they are ours." As a result of this American naval victory, the British vacated Detroit.

Oct. 5   General Harrison defeated British general Procter at the Battle of the Thames in Canada. Tecumseh was killed in this battle, thus ending the Indian confederation in the Northwest. The British thereby lost an important ally.

1814

—The 1st cotton cloth was manufactured by power machinery in Waltham, Mass.

—Secretary of War James Monroe proposed a draft or generous bounties to raise a regular army of about 100,000. Congress did nothing.

—Education at Harvard cost approximately $300 per year. Classes were given 5 days a week from 6 A.M. to 4 P.M. Harvard president John Thornton Kirkland encouraged social life and contributed to the beginnings of some of Harvard's clubs, among them the Hasty Pudding club.

Jan. 3 England's proposal for peace negotiations reached Washington.

Jan. 18–Feb. 8 The Senate confirmed 5 peace commissioners: John Quincy Adams, Henry Clay, James A. Bayard, Albert Gallatin, and Jonathan Russell.

May 27 Creek chief William Weatherford (Red Eagle) surrendered to Gen. Andrew Jackson after the Battle of Horse Shoe Bend. This broke the power of the Creeks as a nation.

> I am in your power; do with me as you please. I am a soldier, I have done the white people all the harm I could. I have fought them and fought them bravely. If I had an army, I would yet fight, and contend to the last.

Aug. 8 Peace negotiations began in Ghent, Belgium.

Aug. 9 The Creeks, through a treaty, gave most of their lands to the U.S., ending Indian occupation of south and west Alabama.

Aug. 23 As the British prepared to invade Washington, D.C., Dolley Madison wrote her sister indicating the President had departed the day before after instructing her to be ready to leave the White House at a moment's notice. Dolley told of "watching with unwearied anxiety" for the return of her husband. Later in the day, when the battle at nearby Bladensburg was won by the British, Dolley fled. She took with her the White House silver plate, a portrait of Washington, some official papers, and her parrot.

British accounts the next day told of a table spread for 40 guests, complete with several wines, joints of various sorts, and "all other requisites for an elegant and substantial repast . . . in a state which indicated that they had been lately and precipitately abandoned." Dolley Madison's fame as a hostess deserves to be legendary if, indeed, during the 48 hours everyone was either leaving Washington or bracing for attack, she blithely went on preparing dinner for 40.

Aug. 24 The British set the White House, Capitol, and Navy Yard afire. Adm. George Cockburn supervised demolition of the office of the *National Intelligencer*, telling his men to "destroy all the 'C's' so they can't abuse my name."

Dec. 24 Treaty of Ghent signed. One provision concerned the return of slaves under the classification of property. The British protested this stipulation and it wasn't until 1824

that a price was set for those slaves who had been freed due to the war. Another article related to the Indians and guaranteed them the same status and territory they held in 1811. Though the U.S. signed treaties with the Indians after British withdrawal, it never returned their lands to them.

Considering the comings and goings of the inexperienced militiamen, it is a wonder that the American troops had any success at all— 398,000 militiamen served for less than 6 months, while some served for a period of hours. When these men left after their term of service, they usually took home supplies, adding to the already critical materials shortage. The U.S. cost for the War of 1812 was $105 million. And at the war's end, 25,975 British troops were still in Canada.

1815

Jan. Three messages were en route to Washington:
1. news of peace
2. word of the Battle of New Orleans
3. message of the Hartford Convention

Jan. Congress authorized the President to put State troops into national service.

Jan. 8 At the Battle of New Orleans, there were 2,000 British casualties. News of peace had not yet reached the States.

Mar. 3 War was declared by Congress on Algiers. The Dey of Algiers had been demanding tribute and taking American prisoners.

Mar. 4 James Madison in his Inaugural Address said, ". . . always remember that an armed and trained militia is the firmest bulwark of republics. . . ." This was a departure from his sentiments during the Virginia Convention of 1787, when he had called a standing army "one of the greatest mischiefs that can possibly happen."

July 3 Treaty with Algiers. Americans were returned without ransom, and tribute payments were no longer demanded.

1816

—A congressional committee reported that of 100,000 industrial workers producing $2,430,-000 worth of goods a year, almost 2 out of 3 were women and girls.

—The 2nd Bank of the U.S. was chartered.

—New horse-racing mile record set at 1:47 by *Timoleon*.

Jan. 1 Public debt stood at $127,335,000, amounting to about $15 per person.

June The 1st gas company was established

in Baltimore, Md., to provide coal gas for lighting city streets.

Dec. 11 Indiana was admitted as a State.

1817

—Machine-made paper was produced by Thomas Gilpin near Wilmington, Del., making available custom-made paper.

—The New York legislature authorized building of the Erie Canal from Albany to Buffalo.

—William Read, a black boy, blew up a ship in Boston harbor when he couldn't take part in Election Day festivities.

—Cup plates were in vogue and continued to be fashionable until just prior to the Civil War, when it was no longer fashionable to drink from saucers.

Jan. 22 The House of Representatives debated over privateering by American ships. This was being practiced against the lawful commerce of Spain and her colonies, which the *United States Gazette* said "has been known and connived by the Government."

Jan. 23 The *United States Gazette* of Philadelphia reported that fire broke out in a Pennsylvania poorhouse when an old woman threw the contents of her tobacco pipe into a spitting box.

May 21 A letter was presented to the legislature of the State of New York signed by Peter Dodge, Seth Y. Wilson, and Joseph Hodgson from Watervliet, dated March 20, 1817, in defense of Shakers. This stemmed from charges leveled by Eunice Chapman, a nonbeliever, whose husband James had left her and taken their children to live with the Society.

The letter pointed out that married couples who joined the Shakers could remain married and bring up their children without control of the Society; that parents and other relatives could visit loved ones if they conducted themselves civilly; that married men without their wives were rarely accepted into the Society, and then only with their wives' consent.

The apologists for the Society indicated the couple had had difficulties before the husband attempted to join the Society and the Shakers had tried to reconcile them. They disputed charges of hiding children by saying that in the past 3 weeks 20 children had been urged on them and they had reluctantly accepted 3 only because the children would have died of starvation if they hadn't. They said that the Chapman children were brought to them when James left his wife and refused to leave the children in her care. They further noted that James was "pacifick" when in their Society, but Eunice was abusive in conduct and conversation. Further, they invited examination of their Society and questioned the State legislature whether abstinence from sexual cohabitation for conscience's sake was sufficient cause for divorce.

Aug. Gloucester's magistrate, Lonso Nash, saw a sea serpent off the coast of Gloucester, and 10 others testified to having seen it also. The sea serpent was dark in color and 80' or 90' long; its body was the size of a half barrel; and its tongue resembled a harpoon. Witnesses estimated that the beast swam between 12 and 14 mph and said that it had sunk into the water like a rock, rather than swimming downwards.

Dec. 2 President James Monroe in his message to Congress told of purchases made from Indian tribes that included land in Ohio, Indiana, and Michigan. An exchange was made with the Cherokee for lands beyond the Mississippi and for lands in the States of North Carolina, Georgia, and Tennessee. Alabama territory was also expected to be acquired.

1818

—First mention of bowling pins occurred in Washington Irving's tale "Rip Van Winkle."

Mar. The newspapers *Union, United States Gazette,* and *True American for the Country* stated Gen. Andrew Jackson had ordered all friendly Indians to join him immediately or they would be treated as hostiles. Inspector General Davis from Washington said it was the intention of the Government to occupy Florida immediately.

Dec. 3 Illinois was admitted as the 21st State of the Union.

1819

—Financial panic. State banks closed and the Bank of the U.S. received much western property. Immigration was down and continued low for the next 10 years.

—Thomas Jefferson, after years of work and maneuvering, established the University of Virginia. The Virginia legislature had provided a $15,000 endowment in 1818. The university made chapel attendance voluntary. It had been mandatory in other American colleges.

—Massachusetts' deaf, dumb, and blind were boarded in an asylum in Hartford, Conn.

—New Yorkers Ezra Daggett and Thomas Kensett began a fish-canning business.

—A reward of 6¢ was offered in the *New York Evening Post* for a 19-year-old apprentice blacksmith who was either "lost, stolen, or strayed."

Feb. Spain signed the Adams-Onis treaty ceding Florida to the U.S., in return for a $5 million credit on its debt to this nation.

Mar. 2 First immigration law passed which included a numerical tally of immigrants, thus making statistics on immigration available.

Dec. 14 Alabama, with a population of 128,000, became the 22nd State. Slavery was permitted.

—J.M.N.

1820

—U.S. population—9,638,453.
—New York City's population had swelled to 123,000.
—Pennsylvania and Massachusetts permitted all who paid State or county taxes to vote.

> . . . is there a single line in the Old or New Testament either censuring or forbidding it [slavery]? I answer without hesitation, no. But there are hundreds speaking of and recognizing it. . . . Hagar, from whom millions sprang, was an African slave, brought out of Egypt by Abraham, the father of the faithful and the beloved servant of the Most High; and he had besides, 318 male slaves.
>
> —Rep. Charles Pinckney
> of South Carolina, one of the framers
> of the Constitution

—Trade between the U.S. and England was now flourishing. Lord Liverpool told England's House of Lords that whoever wishes prosperity to England must also wish it to the U.S.

Jan. 5 Rachel Konkapot, a 26-year-old Indian woman, gave birth to a daughter 2 hours after being shot through the thigh bone. Rachel had been returning to New York with her husband and other members of the Stockbridge tribe who were dissatisfied with the tribe's new home in Indiana. Rachel's child survived, but Rachel lingered for 2 months and died. In February, the Licking County Court of Common Pleas at Newark indicted 2 white men, J. M'Lean and James Hughes, for Rachel's murder. Rachel, a Christian, called for forgiveness for her murderers before she died.

Mar. 3 The Missouri Compromise passed, prohibiting slavery north of the 36°37′ line except in Missouri. Maine entered the Union as a free State, but Arkansas would enter as a slave State in 1836.

Mar. 21 Connecticut's *Hartford Courant* was among several newspapers to print a Black List of those members of Congress from free States who had voted for the Missouri Compromise, or had vacated their seats during the time of the final vote.

April. 24 The Land Act of 1820 abolished sale of land on credit but reduced the minimum price for public land to $1.25 per acre (minimum purchase, 80 acres). The previous 1804 Land Act called for a $1.64 minimum charge per acre (minimum purchase, 160 acres). While the reduction was considerable, settlers during this period still could not afford the new terms and it was the speculators who benefited from this act.

May 12 A letter from Turk's Island, from "Capt." Sebor to his former owner, is the 1st information from "people of color" who had left on the ship *Elizabeth* to establish a settlement in Africa. Sebor reported that the ship had arrived at the Sherbo River on March 19 but that "landing" passengers and cargo had taken until April 6, as the settlement, Campellar, was 25 mi. inland. He added that there had been little sickness among the new settlers and he foresaw no problems with the climate or the natives.

1821

—Debate in the New York Constitutional Convention centered on voting rights. Judge James Kent, chief of the New York Supreme Court, held that universal suffrage would not be good for the State. Kent argued that men who worked on the road or served in the militia should not be given the vote because, he felt, they did not have the same fidelity to the State, nor did they care as much about Government as the landowners. Kent's fear was that the manufacturers and their workers would descend on the polls and offset the interests of the farmers.

Until this time in New York, farmers, or those with at least $250 in land, excluding debts, had the right to elect State senators and the governor. The assembly of the State was elected by landholders having land worth $50 or more, and by persons renting tenements with an annual tax value of $5.

Nathan Sandford, a farmer, argued for universal suffrage, calling attention to the success universal suffrage had in other States and the benefits derived from town meetings, where those governed had a voice in their government. Stipulations for voting recommended by Sandford included: 1) that the voter must be a citizen; 2) that a person performing some service could vote as long as he continued to contribute this particular service; and 3) that a 6-month residency be required.

Result: suffrage was extended, the property qualification dropped.

—Massachusetts established the 1st high school in the country. The previous year, Boston's 1st mayor, Josiah Quincy, had called for equal education for the poor. By 1827 Massachusetts had made a high school mandatory in every town of 500 families or more.

—Emma Hart Willard opened the Troy Female Seminary, the 1st institution in the U.S. to offer a high school education for girls.

—The Kentucky legislature abolished imprisonment for debt. In the next 27 years, 8 other States would follow Kentucky's lead.

—Dept. of Overseers of the Poor in Boston published these statistics for the almshouse population: 78 sick persons; 77 children; 9 maniacs and idiots; 155 unclassified (mostly old people). A house of industry was established as a separate institution from the almshouse to provide employment for those poor who were able to work. However this did not eliminate the almshouse as a catchall institution, especially for indigent children.

Feb. The *New York Daily Advertiser* took the honorable Mr. Clay to task for his conflicting objectives: He favored the advancement of freedom in South America, while proposing an extension of slavery in his own country.

Mar. 4 Since Inauguration Day fell on a Sunday, James Monroe—a good Episcopalian—chose Monday, March 5, to be sworn into office. He thus set a precedent.

June 17 Lightning tore through a house in King George County, Va., killing 62-year-old Charles Massey, Sr., and 3-year-old Alexander Kosckiusko Mason. Mrs. Massey, lying asleep beside her husband, was not hurt. Both victims had been sleeping on feather beds and had not been in contact with any other substance. Since feathers are a nonconductor of electricity, the mystery of how they could be struck was never solved.

Aug. Reports from New Orleans told of sudden deaths from yellow fever. Travelers stopping to drink grog at 11 A.M. were dead by 4 P.M. the same day.

Sept. Fear of the fever drove over 200 people out of Charleston in one 24-hour period. Twelve to 15 people died daily. In some homes entire families lay dead or dying. The mayor recommended that all who could, leave the city immediately. Business was suspended, with banks open only 2 hours a day.

1822

—Murder conviction statistics for Virginia slaves between 1780 and 1864:

Of the master	56
Of the mistress	11
Of the overseer	11
Of other whites	120
Of free Negroes	7
Of slaves	85
Children killed by their mothers	12
Victim not described	60
TOTAL	362

May–June Denmark Vesey was a 55-year-old slave. Vesey's original name, Telemaque, was shortened to Telmak, then became Denmark. Having won a lottery of $1,500 when he was 33, Vesey had spent $600 of it to purchase his freedom, after which he worked as a carpenter.

With the help of Peter Poyas and other blacks, Vesey plotted an insurrection of slaves in the Charleston area. His plan, aimed at annihilating the whites in Charleston, received support from blacks within a 70- to 80-mi. radius of this city. Peter Poyas warned their recruits not to mention insurrection plans to those who "receive presents of old coats from their masters, or they'll betray us." Poyas was right.

The insurrection was scheduled for the 2nd Sunday in July. In late May, a slave informed his master of the plans. Poyas and another leader were arrested but insisted the charge was preposterous. When a 3rd slave, hearing he was also a suspect, went voluntarily to his accusers, the whites were reassured and freed all 3 men. But yet another slave, hearing that the date had been changed to Sunday, June 16, passed this news on to his master. On checking the streets Saturday night, whites found black sentinels on guard and arrests were made. One hundred thirty-one blacks were arrested, 43 banished, and 35 hanged, among them, Vesey and Poyas.

Following the abortive insurrection and subsequent trial, South Carolina passed a Negro seaman's act. This permitted removal of Negroes, or persons of color, from vessels upon their entry into South Carolina ports. That the blacks, employed as cooks, stewards, or mariners, were free mattered not at all. Blacks were jailed until their ship was ready to sail. Costs of detention had to be paid by the ship's master. Failure to pay these costs made the captain liable for a $1,000 fine or 2 months' imprisonment. In addition, the blacks involved were sold as slaves.

Not long after this law was passed, over 41 ships in the harbor had their black cooks and sailors seized. An entire crew from a British ship was taken. A test case challenging the arrest produced the ruling that the arrests had been made in accordance with the law of 1822. The case was appealed, and this time drew a divided verdict.

American captains complained to Congress, British captains to George Canning, Under

Secretary for Foreign Affairs. He in turn demanded action from the U.S. Secretary of State, John Quincy Adams. Adams assured the British that an end would be put to this practice, yet it continued. The law of 1822 remained on the books until the Civil War.

One result of this controversy was the idea that the slavery problem could be resolved by sending blacks back to Africa. As early as 1776, funds had been collected for a colony there, but not much was done until 1817, when the American Colonization Society was founded. It purchased land near present-day Monrovia, capital of Liberia. The motivation behind the society's purchase was not humanitarian.

Several States had passed resolutions supporting such colonization. Ohio called for emancipation of all slaves, and recommended that children of slaves be freed at 21, provided they agreed to move to a black colony. Delaware called for all free Negroes and mulattoes to be removed from the U.S. New Jersey recommended that her sister States join her in fostering emancipation coupled with colonization.

The Colonization Society's agent, Jehudi Ashmun, along with his wife and 37 other blacks, sailed from Baltimore for Liberia in the brig *Strong* to join a group already settled there. When Ashmun arrived, he found that about 40 of the original settlers had died of fever, and those still living were ill. Of the 2 whites sent to help establish the colony, one was dead, the other had deserted. To make matters even more desperate, jungle natives planned to attack the settlement. Shortly before the attack, both the delicate Ashmun and his wife became ill, and Mrs. Ashmun died. Ashmun, grieving but determined, took command of his pathetic army —27 able men, one small cannon and such obsolete weapons as pikes and muskets—and on November 11, repulsed 2 attacks made by a force of over 800 natives. Only 4 of Ashmun's men were killed and 4 more were injured.

Ashmun assumed leadership of the colony, only to be replaced by a white doctor named Ayres, sent by the Society. Ayres, however, came down with fever and soon returned to the U.S. Ashmun began to teach his colonists to farm—all the while hoping that his colony would prove an alternative to slavery in America. But 6 years later, realizing he hadn't long to live, he had to return to the U.S. A few days after his arrival in New Haven, he died at the age of 35.

1823

Dec. 2 In his annual message to Congress, President Monroe outlined a policy on foreign

intervention. It wasn't until 30 years later that this document became known as the Monroe Doctrine. John Quincy Adams, then Secretary of State, is credited with having created this policy. An entry in his diary for November 7, 1823, tells of a meeting with Calhoun and Southard on the subject of British proposals to join them in issuing a warning to the Holy Alliance (Russia, Austria, Spain, and France) against aggression in the Americas.

It was Adams's suggestion that the U.S. decline Great Britain's invitation and issue its own warning. Adams felt that while the U.S. had no intention of seizing Texas or Cuba, the people there might find it more beneficial to unite with the U.S., than with England or any other European nation.

Russia had made overtures for negotiations with the U.S. concerning their mutual northwest coastal interests. Spain at this time was not felt to be a threat. It was the moment to initiate a tough policy. Though the Europeans were not happy with that policy, they were in no situation to oppose it.

1824

—Lafayette returned to the U.S. briefly. While here he visited the 81-year-old Jefferson at Monticello.

—Weavers in Pawtucket, R.I., went on strike against increased hours and lower wages. This was the 1st recorded strike involving women workers.

Mar. 2 Interstate commerce came under Federal control as a result of the steamboat case, *Gibbons* v. *Ogden*.

Apr. 17 The 54°40′ parallel was agreed on as the dividing line separating Russian and U.S. claims in the Pacific northwest.

May 7 Mexico designated Texas as one of its provinces.

June Estimated number of Indians in the U.S. and its territories: 471,417.

July 19 Agustín de Iturbide, Mexican soldier and, later, Emperor—who forced the Spanish Government to capitulate in 1821, thus assuring Mexican independence—was captured and shot upon his return to Mexico this year. Iturbide had become Emperor after the Treaty of Córdoba, but was later deposed. He had abdicated and gone into exile, but made the mistake of returning to his homeland in 1824.

1825

—The working class began organizing and agitating for its children's education. Free schools for children of poor parents were considered offensive because of their obvious separation of rich and poor, calling attention to the inability of the working class to pay for its children's education.

—Glassworks at Sandwich, Mass., made glass cheaper and more standardized through the pressing process.

—Six hundred carpenters in Boston struck for a 10-hour day.

—Travel in America was aided by the publication of *The American Traveller*, Daniel Hewett's guide for stagecoach travelers.

Stagecoach travel was rough going. Journeys sometimes began as early as 3 A.M., but the sturdy fare at most taverns compensated for the tiresome journey. Stagecoach drivers in the U.S. didn't accept tips, but sometimes indulged in "shouldering," picking up unscheduled fares and pocketing the money. Passengers often invited the drivers to drink with them, and more often than not, the drivers accepted. Tipsy drivers, and those who couldn't resist a race, were 2 hazards travelers had to face. Often however, stage drivers were friendly and popular with the people along their routes. One driver in Massachusetts was delegated by the ladies on his route to pick out their bonnets. He was glad to oblige, seeing to it that he never purchased 2 alike. Other drivers carried messages, letters, packages and engaged in shopping for people along their routes, until the practice was so abused that it had to be ended.

—By 1825 turnpikes and canals brought cities closer together. Boston was within 2 days of New York City; New York City to Philadelphia took 11 hours; and the distance between Pittsburgh and Washington could be covered in 15 hours.

Feb. 12 Creek Indians vowed after "deep and solemn reflection" and with "one voice" not to sell one foot of their land to the Government. Several chiefs and leaders of the Creeks, however, entered into a treaty with the Government selling almost all the Creek territory within the State of Georgia and some land west of the Mississippi for $400,000.

The spurious treaty was rushed to Washington over the objection of the local Indian agent. Creek justice demanded that the traitors be punished and in May, 3 signers of the treaty, McIntosh, Tustunugge, and Hawkins, were executed. The State of Georgia was uneasy, fearing an Indian uprising. Governor Troup of Georgia rushed news of the executions to Washington, and President Adams, in an effort to get the whole truth, sent a special agent to gather facts.

Adams, convinced that 50% or more of the Creeks were not in favor of the treaty of February 12, and that they would not leave their homes unless force was used, called the chiefs to Washington. A new treaty was drafted. This one gave less land to the Federal Government, and it also allowed the Indians to remain until January, 1827.

July William H. Ashley organized the Trappers' Rendezvous in the Coche Valley north of Salt Lake. Trappers and Indians from all over the Rockies gathered to exchange their furs for goods from the East and lots of whiskey. Then they partied for 6 weeks, drinking, gambling, playing cards, swapping stories, and fornicating. Ashley departed for St. Louis with $60,000 worth of furs.

Oct. 26 Erie Canal officially opened. Freight was moved from New York City to Buffalo via the Canal for 4¢ a ton per mi.

1826

—Maryland decreed that public office could be held by a Jew. Previously a belief in Christianity was required of office holders.

Jan. An influenza epidemic hit the South, New York, and New England.

Feb. In a letter to Madison, Thomas Jefferson proposed selling some of his property through a lottery. Prior to the Revolution this was the practice, but in 1826 it required approval of the legislature. Jefferson's financial situation was precarious. In 1823 his debts totaled over $40,-000, while his farms brought in a mere $10,-000 yearly. Besides being the patriarch of a large clan, Jefferson entertained constantly at Monticello, and the cost of maintaining a county gentleman's life-style was becoming unsupportable.

Shortly after his letter to Madison, a lottery bill was passed, but by that time news of Jefferson's financial straits had spread throughout the country, and people began sending gifts of money to their former President. Over $16,000 was raised in the 3 cities of New York, Philadelphia, and Baltimore alone. Jefferson called this a pure and unsolicited offering of love, adding, "I have spent 3 times as much money and given my whole life to my countrymen and now they nobly come forward, in the only way they can, to repay me and save an old servant from being turned like a dog out of doors."

Apr. 8 Henry Clay and John Randolph fought a duel in Virginia. Neither was injured. Randolph had accused Clay of being corrupt.

July 4 At 12:50 P.M. on this 50th anniversary of the signing of the Declaration of Independence, Thomas Jefferson died. Hours later another signer, former President John Adams, died at his Quincy, Mass., home. Now only one of the document's signers, Charles Carroll, remained alive.

1827

—The 1st railroad in the U.S. was built in Qumcy, Mass.
—Writer Sarah J. (Buell) Hale promoted the idea of Thanksgiving as a national holiday in her publication, *Ladies Magazine*. She was founder and editor of this, the 1st woman's magazine.
—Following an unsuccessful carpenter's strike, unionists in Philadelphia formed the Mechanics' Union of Trade Associations, made up of delegates from all labor organizations in the city. Their constitution pledged to establish a just balance of power both mental, moral, political, and scientific, between all the various classes and individuals which constitute society at large. The next 6 years saw the beginning of 68 labor newspapers and 61 workingmen's parties.
Feb. 2 Final authority was given to the President to call out the militia.
May 18 Josiah Warren opened the 1st "Time Store" on the corner of 5th and Elm streets in Cincinnati. Dissatisfied with normal commerce in which money was paid for goods purchased and on which merchants made large profits, Warren decided to open a general store in which payment was made through labor exchange. For example: If a customer bought 10 lbs. of flour and it took Warren 5 minutes to pour the flour and wrap it, then the customer paid the same price for the flour that Warren had paid. Instead of adding a profit to the price, Warren charged the customer 5 minutes of work, perhaps helping to build a shelf or repairing Mrs. Warren's shoe. Time Stores were extremely popular for a while, but they never caught on nationally.
July Sectional differences again came to the fore when the Pennsylvania Society for the Promotion of Manufacturers and the Mechanic Arts called for States to send delegates to a convention in Harrisburg. It was attended by 100 delegates from 13 of the 24 States. The northern manufacturing States wanted higher tariffs; the South vigorously opposed this because they depended on foreign markets for their farm products. The South accused the North of taxing them to increase northern riches. Dr. Thomas Cooper, President of South Carolina College, said, ". . . what use is this unequal alliance by which the South has always been the loser and the North always the gainer? Is it worth our while to continue this union of States where the North demands to be our master?"
July 23 Swimming was taught at the 1st U.S. swimming school, in Boston. John Quincy Adams was one of the prominent people who attended the school.

1828

—Webster's *American Dictionary of the English Language* was published. Noah Webster, called the "father of his country's language," was born on an 80-acre farm west of Hartford, Conn. He graduated from Yale shortly after the Revolutionary War and soon declared his own revolution against the English in both language and the field of education. As a teacher, he found himself having to use books that had been written and published in England. For Americans to be truly independent, Webster reasoned, they must read *American* books.
Webster set about simplifying spelling for Americans with his *American Spelling Book* and later labored 20 years compiling his dictionary, which he wrote in longhand. This prolific writer was also a lawyer, historian, and publisher and the man responsible for America's copyright laws.
—The Democratic party was formed, advocating Jeffersonian principles (i.e., equality, and the end of special privilege). Ironically, the new party's 1st President was Andrew Jackson, a man whom Jefferson had called "dangerous" and "unfit for the Presidency."
—Popular sentiment and Oliver Wendell Holmes's poem "Old Ironsides," saved the U.S.S. *Constitution* from being scrapped. The famed battleship was rebuilt in 1833 and is today berthed in Boston Harbor.
May A tariff, called the "tariff of abominations" by the South, was passed. Some southerners continued to call for secession while others called for temperate opposition.
July 15 The *Cherokee Phoenix*, the 1st Indian newspaper in the country, expressed the attitude of the tribes toward leaving their lands: ". . . coercion alone will remove them to the western country allotted for the Indians."

1829

—President Andrew Jackson surrounded himself with a group of unofficial advisers who became known as his "Kitchen Cabinet." Jackson was accused of giving jobs to his royal supporters at the cost of throwing out dedicated office-holders. Jackson supporters claimed those replaced were careless and inefficient, having grown old in their jobs. Actually during his 1st year in office, Jackson's Administration replaced only 9% of the office-holders.

Public officials in high office were one thing, but when it was reported that 300 postmasters had been replaced, a mighty hue and cry arose. The local postmaster, after all, was a man everyone knew. Further, it was said, those postmasters who had lost their jobs had lost them simply because they voted for Adams. Not so! declared administration spokesmen, who insisted that the postal system needed updating —and officials who executed the laws echoed this sentiment, pointing out that in the 40 years since Washington's Administration, the number of post offices had grown from 75 to 7,600.

Postage for a single letter now ran from 6¢ to 25¢, depending on the distance it traveled. There had been laxity in enforcing the postage rates and Jackson's Administration sought to remedy this. It was a tremendous job. In some places, especially big cities like New York, lines of people were kept waiting while every item of mail was opened before a clerk to determine correct postal charges. A proposal for establishment of a private carrier between Boston and Baltimore was made by indignant citizens who were angered over these long lines at the post office and by the Government's enforcement of postal rates.

—David Walker, a free Negro living in Boston, outraged Southern whites when he wrote:

Let 12 good black men get armed for battle and they will kill and put to flight 50 whites. . . . Kill or be killed. Had you rather not be killed than be a slave to a tyrant who takes the life of your wife and children? Look upon your wife and children and mother and answer God Almighty, and believe this that it is no more harm to kill a man who is trying to kill you than to take a drink of water when you are thirsty.

Walker was arrested in Richmond, Va., and never seen again.

—*Encyclopaedia Americana*, the 1st American encylopedia, was published in Philadelphia.

—The Mormon Church was founded in New York and Joseph Smith published his *Book of Mormon*.

—Increased immigration from Catholic countries fostered anti-Catholic sentiment. Anti-Catholic literature and Protestant sermons added to the agitation.

Mar. 2 The 1st U.S. school for the blind was founded in Boston, Mass., by John Dix Fisher. It was called the New England Asylum for the Blind.

Apr. 6 Mexico's revolutionary government forbade further colonization of Texas by Americans and abolished slavery.

Aug. 25 President Jackson offered to purchase Texas from Mexico, but his offer was turned down.

Oct. Two young mechanics established *The Workingman's Advocate*. The 2 editors commented that something was radically wrong with a country when one part of its society lived in idleness and luxury, a 2nd segment was engaged in worthless employments, and the 3rd and largest part of its society suffered from deprivations caused by the other 2, and existed in an ignorance caused by poverty.

—"Workies," members of workingmen's parties, agitated for the rights of laborers. They particularly objected to imprisonment of debtors and the militia system, which required all males to receive military training 3 times a year. Those who didn't report were fined $12 or jailed. The wealthy could easily afford the $12 fine, but workers could not.

—J.M.N.

1830

—U.S. population—12,866,020. The 1st census to exceed 10 million, and the 1st to list the deaf, dumb, and blind separately.

—Sam Patch became the sensation of the country by making daring leaps from bridges and into waterfalls. His 1st success was a 90' jump from the Patterson, N.J., bridge into the Passaic River. Next he leaped into Niagara Falls from Goat Island, a distance more than half the height of the Falls. His last leap in New York State—which ended in his death—was into Genesee Falls.

—First covered wagons made it all the way to the foot of the Rockies, led by Jedediah Strong Smith and William Sublette. Smith was typical of the so-called Mountain Men who were at home in the wilderness passes of the high ranges. It was Smith who would discover famous South Pass through the Rockies, and who accumulated a distinguished number of 1sts: 1st American to discover the Great Basin, 1st to cross the high Sierras into California, and 1st to travel the entire Pacific Coast from Southern California to northern Oregon.

—First bars of soap of a standard weight and individually wrapped were processed by Jessie Oakley, Newburgh, N.Y. Before this, soap had been sent to grocers in large blocks, from which pieces were cut as they were sold.

—Forerunner of Rube Goldberg, John Nepomuk Maelzel returned from Europe with his exhibition of useless inventions. An automatic trumpeter, speaking dolls, tiny mechanical birds that flew out of boxes, an exhibit entitled "Conflagration of Moscow," and a mechanical chess player were just a few. Later, author Edgar Allan Poe played detective and exposed the chess player as a hoax. (See also: Maelzel in Footnote People in World History, Chap. 8.) —The only Cabinet meeting ever called to discuss a woman's virtue. When Peggy O'Neale Timberlake, an innkeeper's daughter of much beauty and boldness, married Secretary of War John Eaton, tongues wagged and other Washington wives would not entertain her because of her "reputation." President Jackson, still bitter about the gossip that had sent his wife Rachel to her grave, called a Cabinet session to discuss Mrs. Eaton's morals. After declaring her innocent, he angrily replaced his entire Cabinet.

Apr. 13 Defying Southern States' rights and South Carolina's bold nullification of Federal laws, President Andrew Jackson threw down the gauntlet at a Democratic banquet. Raising his glass and looking squarely at his Vice-President, John C. Calhoun, chief proponent of nullification attempts, Jackson proposed a toast in a commanding voice: "Our Union: It must be preserved!" While everyone stood and drank, Calhoun's hand was shaking so much that the golden wine ran down the sides of his glass. But then he took up the challenge and offered the next toast: "The Union, next to our liberty, most dear!"

May 28 President Jackson signed the Indian Removal Act, requiring eastern Indians to be resettled west of the Mississippi. Historians coined the phrase "The Trail of Tears" to describe the forced treks in which thousands died. But Jackson felt differently: "Rightly considered, the policy of the general Government toward the red man is not only liberal but generous."

Sept. 15 The 1st national Negro convention was held at Bethel Church, Philadelphia, Pa., to better the condition of American blacks.

Sept. 18 Get-a-horse department: A racehorse finished 1st in a race with "Tom Thumb," the 1st locomotive built in America. Tom pulled 40 passengers along a 9-mi. track, but it just wasn't enough. His boiler sprung a leak and he couldn't stay the course.

Dec. First American book on birth control was published—Robert Dale Owen's *Moral Physiology.* Although "respectable" publications refused to advertise it, 25,000 copies were sold.

1831

—The term "Old Glory" was coined by New England seaman William Driver. Before setting sail for Asia, he saluted the flag as it was un-furled, saying: "I name thee Old Glory!" The term was not popularized until the Union troops used it in the Civil War.

—A practical reaper was invented by Cyrus McCormick. Contrary to popular opinion, McCormick's was not the 1st. Earlier models had been made by Jeremiah Bailey, in 1822, and by Obed Hussey in 1830.

—The electric bell was accidentally invented by Joseph Henry. In attempting to magnetize iron at a distance, he used a magnet which vibrated the armature of an intensity battery, causing a bell to ring at the other end of a mile of copper wire.

Jan. 1 William Lloyd Garrison published the 1st number of the *Liberator,* a militant abolitionist newspaper, in Boston. The editorial in this issue concluded:

> On this subject, I do not wish to think, or speak, or write with moderation. . . . I will not equivocate—I will not excuse —I will not retreat a single inch—AND I WILL BE HEARD.

The Georgia Senate offered $5,000 reward for his apprehension and conviction in Georgia. Earlier Garrison had called the Constitution "an agreement with hell" because it sanctioned slavery.

Mar. 19 First bank robbery in the U.S. The City Bank of New York was opened with duplicate keys and robbed of $245,000. Edward Smith was later convicted and sentenced to 5 years at Sing Sing.

July 4 Dr. Samuel Francis Smith, Baptist minister, 1st introduced the song "America" in services at Park Street Church, Boston. He had composed it in half an hour, taking the tune from a German songbook, completely unaware that the melody was the same as that of "God Save the King," the British national anthem.

Aug. Southampton Insurrection. Nat Turner, a Negro preacher in Virginia, led a slave insurrection in which 54 whites were killed. During the manhunt which followed, at least 100 blacks were killed. Twenty-eight blacks were later convicted and 20, including Turner, were hanged. Said Nat Turner in his oral confession:

> . . . And on May 12, 1828, I heard a loud noise in the heavens, and the Spirit instantly appeared to me and said the Serpent was loosened, and Christ had laid down the yoke He had borne for the sins of men, and that I should take it on and fight against the Serpent, for the time was fast approaching when the 1st should be last and the last should be 1st. . . .

1832

—Johann Kaspar Spurzheim of Vienna introduced phrenology in Boston. Phrenology, which swept the country, determined a man's intellect and character from the shape of his cranium and the "bumps on his head." Many notables, such as Daniel Webster and Andrew Jackson, actively endorsed the new "science."

—*Atkinson's Casket* recommended calisthenics for young city women, to prevent physical deterioration. Muscular development of the back was especially stressed, through use of swinging-type exercises. This was typical of the fears-of-the-time about big-city unhealthiness as opposed to farm-life wholesomeness.

Apr. 1 Robert the Hermit died near Seekonk, Mass. A black slave born at Princeton, N.J., he became one of the most famous hermits in the U.S. He had obtained his freedom early, but later was cheated out of it. Shipped to a foreign slave market, he escaped and returned to America. His 1st wife was torn from him, while his 2nd rejected him. Embittered, he withdrew from society to his lonely hermitage.

Apr. 6 The Black Hawk War began when Sac chief Black Hawk recrossed the Mississippi River to plant corn in the tribe's old fields in Illinois. White settlers panicked, killing a Sac holding a truce flag, whereupon the enraged Black Hawk killed the settlers. The war ended in August with the massacre of the tribe by Illinois militia under General Atkinson. Old men, women, children were all slaughtered despite a truce flag and pleas for mercy. Two future Civil War opponents took part in this shameful affair—Capt. Abraham Lincoln and Lieut. Jefferson Davis.

June 28 The 1st cholera epidemic in the U.S. broke out in New York City and spread throughout the country: 2,251 died in New York; 6,000 in New Orleans, where corpses weighted down with stones were thrown into the river. The epidemic swept through the Plains Indians in the 1840s reducing their numbers until they could not defend themselves against encroaching whites. Historians cite this as one reason the major Indian wars did not start until the 1860s.

July Andrew Jackson vetoed the bill to recharter the Bank of the U.S., stating:

> It is to be regretted that the rich and powerful too often bend the acts of government to their selfish purposes. . . . When the laws undertake . . . to make the rich richer and the potent more powerful, the humble members of society, the farmers, mechanics, and laborers, who have neither the time nor the means of securing like favors to themselves, have a right to complain of the injustice of their government.

Nov. 14 First horse-drawn streetcar made its appearance in New York on lower 4th Avenue. Designed and constructed by John Stephenson, it was called the "John Mason" and accommodated 30 passengers,. The fare was 12½¢.

Dec. 28 First Vice-President to resign. John C. Calhoun did so after being elected a senator from South Carolina, in order to carry on the fight for slavery and States' rights. Calhoun never did get along very well with his superior, President Jackson, a strong Union man.

1833

—Dept. of bloopers: Horatio Greenough was commissioned to sculpt a colossal marble statue of George Washington, then discovered it weighed so much the floor of the Capitol could not hold it. Placed outdoors, it began to deteriorate from the weather. Finally it was moved into the Smithsonian. Purists condemned the work as obscene since Washington was only half-draped in the classical style.

—First U.S. appearance of Irish actor Tyrone Power, who was noted for playing comic Irish roles. His great-grandson of the same name was the famous matinee idol of the 1930s and 1940s.

—George Fibbleton invented a shaving machine for use in his New York barber shop. Although he passed himself off as "Ex-Barber to His Majesty, the King of England," his machine was a flop, shaving off more of the skin than the beard.

—Samuel Colt perfected the 1st handgun with a revolving barrel—the legendary 6-shooter. Colt adopted the mass production ideas of Eli Whitney, using interchangeable parts and an assembly line in his plant at Patterson, N.J. The Colt's rapid fire and handy size made it indispensable for western horsemen and was a major factor in government victories over the Indians.

—The *Ann McKim* was launched at Baltimore. First of the clipper ships, it was designed for speed rather than for carrying bulky cargo in trade with California and the Orient. Clipper ships were faster than steamships until after the Civil War.

Mar. 2 President Jackson was authorized by Congress to use the Army and Navy to collect tariff in South Carolina. The Force Bill was the result of South Carolina's Ordinance of Nullification the previous November 24, making null and void the existing tariff laws of the U.S. An extreme application of the principle of States' rights, it was the brainchild of Jackson's own Vice-President, John C. Calhoun. Jackson was prepared to call out 35,000 troops and lead them himself against his native State. As a 1st step, he announced, he would try Calhoun for treason and, if convicted, "hang him as high as Haman." When Calhoun heard this he trembled and turned pale. Confrontation was avoided when, on March 15, South Carolina revoked its Ordinance of Nullification. Still, years later, Jackson said that he had only 2 regrets in his life—that he had been unable to: 1) shoot Henry Clay (for slurs made against Mrs. Jackson), and 2) hang John C. Calhoun.

April 24 A patent for the 1st soda fountain was granted to Jacob Ebert of Cadiz, O., and George Dulty of Wheeling, W.Va.

Oct. 1 President Jackson had to remove 2 Secretaries of the Treasury before finding one to carry out his order to withdraw government deposits from the Bank of the U.S., thereby killing the bank, which he opposed as a tool of vested interests.

Dec. 3 The 1st coeducational college in the U.S. was founded at Oberlin, O. Oberlin College opened with 44 students—29 men and 15 women. Later it was also the 1st college to advocate the abolition of slavery and to accept black men and women on equal terms with whites.

1834

—The 1st national union of unions was formed —the National Trades' Union, which claimed a membership of 300,000.

—"Zip Coon" was 1st played in New York by Bob Farrell, who composed it. Later the title was changed to "Turkey in the Straw," and it became a popular fiddle tune.

—*A Narrative of the Life of David Crockett* was published. Ostensibly an autobiography, the book contained tales, tall stories, and yarns which augmented the myth of the great hunter, Indian fighter, and congressman. Ironically, the book was meant to answer an earlier account which pictured the frontiersman as "fresh from the backwoods, half-horse, half-alligator, a little touched with snapping turtle."

Mar. First censure of a President by the Senate. After Jackson killed the Bank of the U.S., more and more people saw him as a despot: He was called "King Andrew the 1st," "Destroyer of Our Liberties," and "Tyrant." Senate censure charged that he had "assumed upon himself authority and power not conferred by the Constitution and laws." Later, Sen. Thomas Hart Benton of Missouri, who had become Jackson's devoted follower after trying to kill him in a free-for-all, finally succeeded in getting the censure erased in 1837, when a black line was drawn around the resolution and the word "expunged" written across it.

Oct. Proslavery rioting swept Philadelphia— 4 homes in the black community were destroyed.

1835

—Sign of the times: Growth of the temperance movement was signaled by an address by the Rev. Charles Giles in which he thundered that "500,000 drunkards are now living in our blessed America, all moving onward to the dreadful verge. What a scene of immolation!"

—Down in Texas, Col. James Bowie invented the famed "bowie knife." Legend has it variously that he got the idea from Mexicans who had been using it; that in a battle with a Mexican, his sword broke off some 20" from the hilt; and that he made it out of a file. In any case, it was shorter than a regular sword, which made for easier handling, but longer than a knife. The "bowie knife" had but a single edge and a curved point. Bowie knives were also called "Arkansas toothpicks."

—Almost 30,000 spectators were drawn to a footrace at Union Course, Long Island. A $1,000 prize was offered to any who could run the 10-mi. course in less than an hour. Henry Stannard was the winner, covering the 1st and last miles in 5:36 and 5:54, and the entire course in 59:44.

—One of the largest protests in the history of the young nation took place when 27,000 people gathered in New York City's Hall Park to demonstrate against the conviction of 25 union tailors on a charge of "conspiracy."

Jan. It was the only time in our history that the U.S. was free from debt. And President Jackson commented: "Let us commemorate the payment of the public debt as an event that gives us increased power as a nation and reflects luster on our Federal Union." The national debt in 1976 was estimated to be 605 billion, 900 million dollars.

Jan. 30 First attempt on the life of a U.S. President occurred. President Jackson was fired on twice by Richard Lawrence, who brandished a pair of dueling pistols while attending the funeral of Warren Ransom Davis. Both pistols misfired. Lawrence was later judged to be insane.

July 8 The Liberty Bell cracked as it tolled the death of Chief Justice John Marshall.

Oct. 21 William Lloyd Garrison, abolitionist editor of the *Liberator*, was mobbed and almost lynched by some 200 Boston proslavers who were enraged by his speech claiming "that all men are created equal. . . ." For his own safety, he was lodged in the Leverett Street Jail for the night.

Nov. 23 Henry Burden of Troy, N.Y., developed the 1st machine for manufacturing horseshoes, later making nearly all the horseshoes used by the Union cavalry during the Civil War.

1836

—Maria Monk published her scandalous book entitled *Awful Disclosure of Maria Monk, as Exhibited in a Narrative of Her Suffering during a Residence of Five Years as a Novice, and Two Years as a Black Nun, in the Hotel Dieu Nunnery at Montreal.* Although the public eagerly swallowed her "disclosures," the book later proved to be an anti-Catholic hoax.

—The Rev. Thomas P. Hunt started a children's temperance crusade. Working through Sunday Schools, Hunt enlisted children to distribute pledge cards to drinkers in the community.

—Washington Monument was begun by Robert Mills, the noted government architect who was also responsible for designing the Treasury, Post Office, and Patent Office buildings in Washington. The Washington Monument was unique in its classic simplicity at a time when ornamentation was becoming more pronounced.

—Ernestine L. Rose, an early feminist, requested the New York State legislature to give married women the right to hold property in their own names.

Feb. 23–Mar. 6

I am besieged by a thousand or more of the Mexicans under Santa Anna. I have sustained a continued bombardment for 24 hours and have not lost a man. The enemy have demanded a surrender . . . I have answered the summons with a cannon shot, and our flag still waves proudly from the walls.

—W. Barret Travis,
commander at the Alamo

Mar. 6 Three thousand Mexican troops under Santa Anna stormed the Alamo, a fortified mission in San Antonio, Tex. It was defended by 182 Texans, and Tennessean Davy Crockett, under command of Cols. William B. Travis and James Bowie. Contrary to opinion, Crockett led only a small force of Tennessee sharpshooters, no more than 6 or 7. Within an hour the garrison was overpowered and every man killed. All the dead bodies were then stripped, thrown into a pile in the courtyard, and burned. The only survivors were the wife of Lieutenant Dickinson, her baby daughter, a Negro slave, and several Mexican women.

Little-known facts about the Battle of the Alamo: Santa Anna's "troops" included boys 13 and 14 from a nearby military academy. "Alamo" is the Spanish word for the cottonwood tree, many of which grew on the mission grounds. The Texans' War for Independence has been cited by some historians as U.S. aggression, since Texas was rightfully a Mexican province, but in the popular mind of the time it was seen as a revolt against Mexican injustice. "Remember the Alamo," one of our earliest war cries, was 1st used by Americans 6 weeks later at the victorious Battle of San Jacinto.

May 31 John Jacob Astor, fur trader and millionaire, opened the Astor Hotel in New York, forerunner of the fabulous Waldorf-Astoria.

July 4 Narcissa Prentiss Whitman and Eliza Hart Spalding became the 1st women to journey clear across the continent. They accompanied their husbands, Dr. Marcus Whitman and the Rev. Henry H. Spalding, who set up a mission near present Walla Walla, Wash.

Dec. 7 Martin Van Buren, the "Little Magician" and political boss of New York, was elected President as the handpicked successor to Andy Jackson. For the 1st time the Senate had to choose a Vice-President, since none of the 4 vice-presidential candidates received a majority. It chose Richard M. Johnson. This action would not be repeated until the Congress affirmed Gerald Ford as successor to Spiro Agnew. "Little Van" began the 10-hour day on Federal public works. His enemies said he was so vain that he wore out the carpet in front of his mirror.

1837

—P. T. Barnum, fabulous showman, sold a credulous public his 1st successful hoax: Joice Heth, a 46-lb., 161-year-old ex-slave, who allegedly was the midwife who brought George Washington into the world. Over 10,000 New Yorkers jammed into Niblo's Garden to catch a glimpse of the "wonder." After her death, an

autopsy revealed that she was no more than 80.
—The American Peace Society condemned all
wars, defensive as well as offensive. Its founder,
William Ladd, called for a Congress of Nations
and a world court of arbitration. Later, author
James Russell Lowell summed up the Society's
philosophy in his *Bigelow Papers:*

> Ez fer war, I call it murder,—
>   There you hev it plain an' flat;
> I don't want to go no furder
>   Than my Testyment fer that. . . .

—Sign of the times: Washington Irving coined
a new phrase in his book *The Creole Village*
when he referred to "The Almighty Dollar,
that great object of universal devotion throughout the land." Irving felt Americans were concerned only with the material goods that "Almighty Dollar" would purchase.
—The Forty Thieves, the Roach Guards, the
Plug Uglies, the Shirt Tales, and the Dead
Rabbits were predominantly Irish gangs which
flourished in the Five Points area of New York
City, bounded by Broadway, Canal Street, the
Bowery, and Park Row.
—Robert Montgomery Bird was responsible
for an Indian stereotype which lasted for generations—that of the unwashed dirty heathen
who is a vicious animal. Bird's popular novel of
the frontier, *Nick of the Woods*, presented the
Indian as a savage beast that it was necessary to
exterminate. Because of American acceptance
of this attitude, the book has gone through
more than 25 editions in this country.
Feb. The Flour Riot of 1837 broke out when
the crowd attending a "bread, meat, rent, and
fuel" meeting in Chatham Square, N.Y., drove
the police and mayor to cover and stormed a
flour warehouse.
Mar. First major depression in the U.S. Stock
prices broke on Wall Street, plunging the nation into the deep depression now known as
the Panic of 1837. George Templeton Strong's
diary revealed its extent:

> April 19 . . . State of things in Wall
> Street worse than ever. The whole city is
> going to the devil in a pecunia point of
> view.
> May 2 . . . Matters worse and worse . . .
> everyone discouraged; prospect of univer-
> sal ruin. . . . Workmen thrown out of
> employ by the hundred daily.
> May 5 . . . Something like 20 failures
> yesterday! . . .
> May 10 . . . The Bank of America, Mer-
> chants, and Manhattan which had re-
> solved to try and hold out a little longer,
> have closed. Immense crowd and excite-
> ment in Wall St. . . .

Nov. 7 Abolitionist Elijah P. Lovejoy was
killed by a proslavery mob at Alton, Ill. Earlier,
Reverend Lovejoy, as editor of the *Alton Observer*, had run an abolitionist editorial stating:

> Abolitionists, therefore, hold American
> slavery to be a wrong, a legalized system
> of inconceivable injustice, and a SIN . . .
> against God . . .

Lovejoy was cornered in his newspaper office by
an angry law-and-order "posse" that shot him
5 times, dumped his printing press into the
river, and set fire to the building. The next
day, proslavers lined the streets and cheered as
his mutilated corpse was dragged through the
town.
Nov. After 2 years of raising money at small
meetings, parlor gatherings, and sewing circles,
Mary Lyon was able to open the 1st women's
college—Mount Holyoke.

1838

> This people have much idle time on their
> hands, which we feel anxious to have em-
> ployed to some valuable end. It is a most
> difficult task to teach industry to an idle
> people. But it is necessary to the promo-
> tion of their Christianity.
>   —A. Bishop, missionary in Hawaii

—The "Underground Railroad" was in full
swing. The Railroad provided escape routes for
Southern slaves to the Northern States and
then on to Canada. Fourteen Northern States
set up operations. It was most active in the
Western Reserve of northern Ohio, starting
there as early as 1790. Contrary to general
opinion, the Railroad actually had little effect,
since only 500 to 1,000 slaves fled North each
year. One slave, Henry Brown, escaped from
Richmond to Philadelphia in a box labeled,
"This side up with care." If discovered, any
alleged runaway could be seized and shackled,
denied a trial by jury, prevented from testifying or summoning witnesses, and shipped South
to his master regardless of when he had escaped.
James Hamlet, a free black living in New
York, was apprehended where he worked by a
Federal officer and was returned to Baltimore
in chains.
—Artist Thomas Cole complained of American
anticultural attitudes: "I am out of place . . .
there are few persons of real taste; and no
opportunity for the true artist to develop his
powers. The tide of utility sets against the fine
arts."
—Rolling hoops became a new fad among the

young ladies on the Washington Parade Ground in New York City.

—Quack medicines became popular. In the *New York Herald*'s advertising columns, which ran 130", 54" were devoted to quack remedies.

1839

The far-reaching, the boundless future will be the era of American greatness. In its magnificent domain of space and time, the nation of many nations is destined to manifest to mankind the excellence of divine principles; to establish on earth the noblest temple ever dedicated. . . .
—John L. O'Sullivan, in the
*United States Magazine and
Democratic Review*

—The *Amistad* incident occurred. Slaves being transported from Havana to Cuban sugar plantations aboard the Spanish vessel *Amistad*, mutinied. Managing to free themselves of their chains and arming themselves with machetes intended for sugarcane cutting, they seized the ship. But the Spanish navigators tricked the slaves, and instead of taking them back to Africa they put in at Montauk Point, Long Island. The slaves were later freed by the U.S. Supreme Court, almost precipitating an international crisis between the U.S. and Spain.

—Charles Goodyear 1st vulcanized rubber successfully, making rubber nonsticky and solid at high temperatures. The discovery was an accident—Goodyear happened to drop rubber mixed with sulfur upon a hot stove and vulcanization took place. While his discovery later brought fortunes to others, he himself died a poor man because of the many infringements upon his patent.

—The 1st woman horse thief in the U.S. published her confessions. Josephine Amelia Perkins, born and raised in England, stole her 1st horse from her own father for her elopement. Eventually she came to America completely broke, and continued her career of horse-stealing. She herself admitted to being "4 times detected, twice pardoned on account of my sex, once for reasons of supposed insanity, and the 4th and last time, convicted and sentenced to 2 years imprisonment in Madison County jail, Kentucky."

Mar. 3 The *New York Mirror* printed the following program for a dinner conversation: "When you are seated next to a lady, you should be only polite during the 1st course; you may be gallant in the 2nd; but you must not be tender till the dessert."
—L.A.W.

1840

—U.S. population—17,069,453. So said the 6th national census.

—The expansion of the railroads (there were 2,818 mi. of rails by 1840), the production of farm machinery, pistols, stoves, clocks, sewing machines, and the development of the iron industry evoked this remark from Henry David Thoreau: "How little do the most wonderful inventions of modern times detain us. They insult nature. Every machine or particular application seems a slight outrage against universal laws. How many fine inventions are there which do not clutter the ground. . . ."

—Immigration figures soared to 1,750,000 by 1840, and would reach 2,500,000 by the end of the decade. "Runners," themselves immigrants at one time, took advantage of the new arrivals by steering them to 2nd-rate boardinghouses and hotels, and conning them into trips West that promised 1st class passage when actually the worst possible accommodations were provided. Eventually, knowledge of this treatment made immigrants reluctant to leave their port of immigration, thus overcrowding these port cities.

—Methods of travel diversified and developed. Besides wagon trains on land, rafts, pirogues (40′ canoes costing $10 to $20), keelboats, and bateaus were in use on the waterways but the increased traffic of the steamboat, with its more comfortable passage, saw the decline of the smaller boats.

—The American Society of Dental Surgeons was established and the College of Dental Surgery was founded in Baltimore.

—Potawatomie Indians in Indiana were moved west.

—Pennsylvania boasted 608 mi. of canals. A trip on the Pennsylvania Canal covering a distance of 394 mi. required "only" 4 days.

—John W. Draper, physicist and astronomer, took the 1st photograph of the moon. Draper was also the 1st to produce a photograph of a person with eyes open.

—*Two Years before the Mast* was published. Its author, Richard Henry Dana, was admitted to the Massachusetts bar the same year. Dana's book was based on his experiences as a common sailor during a voyage to California.

Jan. 8 The House passed a resolution refusing to accept resolutions or petitions concerning the abolishment of slavery.

Mar. 31 Ten-hour day established for Federal employees.

July Samuel Cunard, a Canadian, aided by the British Government, established the 1st transatlantic steamship line. Its 1st ship left Liverpool on July 4 and arrived in Boston on July 19.

1841

—First wagon train arrived in California.
—"Rock oil," skimmed from Pennsylvania streams, was used in patent medicines.
—George Ripley, a bespectacled Unitarian clergyman, and his wife, Sophia, founded the Brook Farm Institute of Agriculture and Education. This was an anticapitalist, cooperative community, situated on 192 acres in West Roxbury, Mass., and its purpose was "to substitute brotherly cooperation for selfish competition; to prevent anxiety in men by competent supplying in them of necessary wants."
Twenty-four shares of membership stock were sold at $500 a share. Male members, wearing smocks, labored 60 hours a week at farming. Female members, wearing shortened skirts, toiled at housework and teaching. Destined to become the most prominent member of the short-lived commune was 37-year-old Nathaniel Hawthorne, who produced *The Scarlet Letter* in 1850. Hawthorne quit after one year; Brook Farm gave up after 5 years. Emerson praised the experiment as utopian. Thoreau disagreed, stating, "I'd rather keep bachelor's hall in hell than go to board in heaven if that place is heaven."
Mar. A shy, consumptive, 39-year-old spinster teacher, Dorothea Dix, entered the East Cambridge, Mass., House of Correction to conduct a Sunday school class for the inmates. When Miss Dix emerged from the House of Correction, shocked and shaken by what she had witnessed, she was a changed woman. The harrowing experience started her on a crusade that would last 4 decades and reform the treatment of the mentally ill and insane in the U.S. and England.
In that time, it was believed that the insane were born defective, were depraved, were hopeless, and therefore should be treated as animals. There were few insane asylums. Inmates were often kept in the worst parts of jails, prisons, almshouses. More often than not they were chained and whipped. Dorothea Dix set out to improve those conditions radically.
After a 2-year investigation, Miss Dix addressed a Memorial to the Massachusetts legislature: "I shall be obliged to speak with great plainness, and to reveal many things revolting to the taste, and from which woman's nature shrinks with peculiar sensitiveness. I proceed, gentlemen, briefly to call your attention to the present state of insane persons within this Commonwealth, in cages, closets, cellars, stalls,

pens—chained naked, beaten with rods, and lashed into obedience." The Memorial created a sensation. Her credibility was questioned by 2 Massachusetts newspapers, but her testimony was supported by several respected, influential men. Soon, the legislators sought to provide better treatment and clean rooms in hospitals for the insane.
Vigorously, Dix carried her crusade across the nation, traveling 10,000 mi. in 3 years, visiting 18 prisons, 30 jails, 500 almshouses, speaking before a dozen State legislatures. Everywhere she went, she succeeded in reforming conditions, so that the insane were housed in better quarters and treated more humanely. Dix then sailed to England and Europe, exposed the horrors there, and won additional drastic reforms.
With the outbreak of the Civil War, she volunteered to serve as a nurse, but instead was appointed Superintendent of Women Nurses for the Union, the 1st person ever to serve in that capacity. At war's end she resumed her crusade, which was halted only by her death at the age of 80.
Apr. 4 President William Henry Harrison died after a mere 30 days in office.
Apr. 10 Horace Greeley established the *New York Tribune* with a $1,000 backing. Greeley differed from his contemporary publishers in that he believed that advertisements and police reports disgraced newspapers.
June 12 An act calling for a fiscal bank of the U.S. was introduced in the Senate. It was later passed by both Houses, but was vetoed by President Tyler. Tyler's entire Cabinet, with the exception of Secretary of State Daniel Webster, resigned in protest over the veto.
June 27 Five shipwrecked Japanese were rescued by an American vessel. Four were put ashore at Honolulu but one boy, Manjiro Nakahma, was not. He later became the 1st Japanese immigrant in the U.S. Nakahma eventually returned to Japan where he was interpreter for Matthew Perry in 1854.
Aug. 9 Steamship *Erie* burned on Lake Erie, killing 175.
Sept. Alfred Niger, a black barber and abolitionist from Providence, was nominated as treasurer of the Rhode Island Suffrage Association, a group of disenfranchised workmen. Niger's nomination was defeated but the association found itself with an added issue. Debate raged over confining the voting in the convention to the whites. A lawyer, Thomas Dorr, and a grocer, Benjamin Arnold, supported black suffrage, but the issue was defeated by a 46–18 vote.
Dorr became the leader in the rebellion against the Rhode Island constitution, which was actually the Royal Charter of 1663. This outdated charter, which allowed suffrage only

to property owners and their oldest sons, disenfranchised half the white male population at that time.

1842

—A landmark decision upholding workers' rights to organize was handed down by Chief Justice Shaw in the case of *Massachusetts Commonwealth* v. *Hunt*. Most State laws deemed it a conspiracy for men to join together for the purpose of securing wage increases and regulating the terms of the employment. Seven years earlier, workmen in New York were indicted for this reason. The New York judge hearing this case had ruled that the workmen had no right to demand wage increases that would cause the price of consumer goods to be raised.
—Connecticut established the 1st public education system in the U.S.
—John C. Frémont headed an expedition to the Rocky Mountains. Kit Carson was his guide.
—Charles Dickens visited America and traveled to Toledo and Sandusky, O., where he encountered "corduroy roads" which he described as being constructed by ". . . throwing trunks of trees into a marsh and leaving them to settle. . . ."
—First artificial fertilizer was produced commercially.
—"Vote yourself a farm" was the slogan of the National Reform Association which advocated giving 160 acres to anyone who wanted them. The Association's founder, George Henry Evans, had this to say about banks:

> Is not this fact enough to alarm the American people? A *bank* in the heart of the Republic with its branches, scattered over the Union; wielding $200 million of capital; owning an immense amount of real property; holding at its command a 100,000 debtors; buying up our newspapers, entering the field of politics; attempting to make Presidents and Vice-Presidents for the country.

Jan. A Rochester, N.Y., medical student, William E. Clarke, used ether as an anesthetic during a tooth extraction performed by Dr. Elijah Pope.
Mar. 3 First Massachusetts child labor law, limiting the workday to 10 hours for children under 12 in manufacturing establishments, was signed into law, but it did not prove effective.
Apr. Thomas Dorr was nominated for governor by the People's party of Rhode Island while the incumbent, Samuel W. King was chosen by the Freeman's party. Dorr, in May,

unsuccessfully attempted to capture the Providence Armory.

In the fall, a new Constitution was adopted which found support among some of Dorr's former followers. This new Constitution granted the vote to those born in the U.S. who could pay the $1 poll tax or who owned at least $134 in real estate. Aliens and naturalized citizens could vote after living in the State for 2 years. Dorrites called this Constitution the Algerine Constitution after the Dey of Algiers, a tyrant.

After this Constitution was ratified, Dorr and some of his followers were arrested. Dorr was found guilty of high treason in 1844 and sentenced to solitary confinement and hard labor for life. The sentence was unpopular and Dorr was released a year later. His civil rights were restored in 1851, and 3 years after that the court judgment against him was dropped.

1843

—Congress appropriated $30,000 for an experimental telegraph line from Washington to Baltimore.
Jan. 1 Total school expenses for the city of Chicago for the year ending January 1, 1834, were $3,874.34.
Feb. 4 John Quincy Adams, who was returned to Congress after his term as President, in a speech to the House of Representatives said: "If slavery must go by blood and war, let war come."
Feb. 28 Salary of special or traveling post-office agents was limited to $1,000 a year by amendment in the Senate. An allowance of $2 per day for traveling expenses was also accorded them.
Mar. Marcus Whitman, 40-year-old doctor and missionary, who had moved to Oregon country in 1836, returned East to report to his church and to seek answers to rumors that the Oregon country would be abandoned. Secretary of State Webster—who years before had asked, "What do we want with . . . this region of savages and wild beasts, of deserts and shifting sand and whirlwinds of dust, of cactus and prairie dogs?"—was not encouraging. President Tyler, however, assured Whitman that the territory, which encompassed land from Mexican California to Alaska, would not be abandoned.
Mar. A Troy, O., man was fined $10 for kissing a married lady.
Mar. 10 The Virginia Court of Appeals, contrary to other recent decisions, ruled that aliens could lawfully enlist in the Army.
Apr. 5 *Chicago Express* carried an ad for "operations on teeth done in superior style

. . . causing the least possible pain." A footnote to the ad indicated that advice was given gratis.

May 29 Another Frémont expedition. This expedition was to Oregon, but it also provided corrections of errors concerning the geography of California.

Aug. Wisconsin Territory had 12 newspapers.

Oct. 11 The *Chicago Democrat* complained about the inexcusable state of affairs caused by the mail contractors.

Nov. A gentleman from Abbeville, S.C., refused a challenge to a duel, and was given a barbecue by his approving neighbors.

Nov. "What next?" was the comment in the *Chicago Democrat* on the news report that Rochester, N.Y., journeymen coopers resolved not to make any more flour barrels for less than 15¢ apiece.

1844

—Political cry, "Fifty-four Forty or Fight!" was adopted by supporters of Polk. The slogan sprang from the desire to claim western territory which had been jointly held by Spain, Russia, and England. In 1819, Spain indicated it wouldn't claim anything north of California; in 1824 Russia agreed to stay north of the 54°40' parallel. The U.S. and Great Britain had agreed to share rights within those 2 boundaries, since this land was earlier thought to be almost worthless. Both nations had the right to hunt and settle the territory until a later agreement could be reached.

—New York got a police department, but no uniforms.

—Cassius Marcellus Clay, the abolitionists' sometimes embarrassing ally, published his opinions on slavery. Clay had once been introduced to an audience of blacks in Philadelphia as, "Cassius Clay—Liberator, though he has a white skin he has a very black heart." Clay's constant companions were 2 pistols and a bowie knife which, along with his fists, he seemed to use regularly.

In 1845, Clay's enemies forced him to move his press from Lexington, Ky., to Cincinnati but Clay continued his publication there and in Louisville. Though Clay initially opposed the annexation of Texas on grounds that it might become a slave State, he later served as a captain in the Mexican War. During the 1860s Clay was minister to Russia and served in the Civil War as a major general of volunteers. At the age of 84, he married a 15-year-old girl who soon left him. It is said that while he was on his deathbed, he used his pistol to shoot flies off his bedroom wall.

—First private bathtub appeared in a New York hotel but a year later bathtubs were still prohibited in Boston except when prescribed by a physician.

Jan. 15 University of Notre Dame chartered.

Feb. 28 President Tyler, with a group of distinguished guests, boarded the steam frigate, U.S.S. *Princeton,* for an outing on the Potomac which was to demonstrate the ship and its tremendous gun, the Peacemaker. The gun could hurl a 212-lb. shot 3 mi.

Among those on board was Abel P. Upshur, Secretary of State, who had been secretly carrying on negotiations concerning the annexation of Texas. The gun misfired and exploded, killing Upshur and 7 others.

Apr. 12 Texas Annexation Treaty signed, providing for the admission of Texas as a State in 1845.

Apr. 27 Van Buren and Clay expressed opposition to the annexation of Texas until Mexican consent could be obtained.

May 3 Heavy fighting broke out when several thousand anti-Catholic "Native Americans" tried to hold a street meeting in the heavily Irish Kensington district of Philadelphia. On May 8, a primarily Protestant mob set fire to churches, houses, the schoolhouse, and the rectory in the Catholic neighborhood. Finally, the cavalry arrived, dispersed the mob, and declared martial law. On July 4, the final battle, complete with cannons on both sides, took place between the Nativists and the U.S. Army. The Army won. Total casualties in 2 months: 30 dead, 150 wounded, 220 families burned out.

May 24 First message ever sent by telegraph, the message going from Washington to Baltimore. Samuel Finley Breese Morse, inventor of the telegraph, was an artist and apparently a good one during his 1st 50 years of life. While working on his invention, he supported himself with income derived from teaching art students at New York University. They, along with his fellow professors and friends, thought him a bit deranged because of his preoccupation with the telegraphic system used in Europe to relay messages great distances.

June 7 Joseph Smith, founder of Mormonism, had made romantic overtures to the wife of a Canadian convert named William Law. Incensed, Law quit the Latter-day Saints and brought out one issue of the *Nauvoo Expositor* in which he attacked the practice of Mormon polygamy. Law's lead article explained: "We are earnestly seeking to explode the vicious principles of Joseph Smith, and those who practice the same abominations and whoredoms."

Smith, accompanied by the Nauvoo city marshal, proceeded to destroy Law's printing

In 1909, on his only visit to the U.S., Dr. Sigmund Freud, who found that American women gave him erotic dreams, sat for a picture on the campus of Clark University with his disciples.

Front row, L to R: Freud, G. Stanley Hall, Carl G. Jung; Back row, L to R: A. A. Brill, Ernest Jones, Sandor Ferenczi. (See: Chap. 2) *Clark University*.

"Because we live in the suburbs we don't eat too much Chinese food. It's not available in the supermarkets, so on Saturdays we eat hot dogs."

"My dad thinks it's a good idea to take all the leaves off the tree and rake up the yard. I think he's crazy." From: *Suburbia* by Bill Owens. San Francisco, Straight Arrow, 1972. (For more Best of Books, See: Chap. 2)

A famous actress and movie star.

A renowned painter (L).

The leader of a nation.

A well-known actress and movie star.

A glamorous actress and movie star.

Mayor of a major U.S. city.

How many of these childhood photographs of famous people can you identify? Turn page upside down.

Mayor Richard Daley

Elizabeth Taylor

Marilyn Monroe

Fidel Castro

Pablo Picasso

Marlene Dietrich

From: *As They Were* by Tuli Kupferberg and Sylvia Topp. New York, Links, 1973. (For more Best of Books, See: Chap. 2)

"Diamond Jim" Brady, the financier, was one of the greatest eaters in American history. A typical Brady dinner consisted of 30 oysters, 6 crabs, green turtle soup, 6 lobsters, 2 whole ducks, turtle meat, sirloin steak, vegetables, quarts of orange juice, an entire platter of pastries, and a 2-lb. box of candy. (See: Chap. 3) *Brown Brothers.*

Tom Thumb, 25"-tall son of a New England carpenter whom showman P. T. Barnum made famous. Shown here while in England, he is impersonating Napoleon. Married for 20 years, Tom Thumb became a wealthy Mason, owned a sailing sloop, pedigreed horses, a carriage. (See: Chap. 3) *Alice Curtis Desmond Collection, Barnum Museum.*

Sequoyah   (See: Ch. 3)
Drawing by Edward Sorel

Amelia Jenks Bloomer   (See: Ch. 3)
Drawing by Edward Sorel

Victoria Woodhull, who had been a spiritualist, Wall Street broker, newspaper publisher, ran against Ulysses S. Grant for President of the U.S. in 1872. Her platform advocated free love, birth control, easier divorce laws, an excess profit tax, better public housing. (See: Chap. 3) *Culver Pictures, Inc.*

The most famous of the early female investigative reporters, Nellie Bly, exposed American slums, sweatshops, jails, insane asylums. In 1889, age 22, she decided to beat Phileas Fogg's record of going around the world in 80 days. She did it in 72 days and became a celebrity. (See: Chap. 3) *Brown Brothers.*

Of labor organizer Mother Jones (c), 1830-1930, folksinger John Farrance recalled, "I saw her one time in Monongahela. Two company thugs grabbed [her] horse by the bridle and told her to turn around and get back down the road. She wore a gingham apron, and she reached under it and pulled out a .38 Special pistol and told them to turn her horse loose, and they sure did." (See: Chap. 3) *Brown Brothers.*

press. Charged by the governor of Illinois with inciting a riot, Smith started to flee, changed his mind, and went to jail.

June 27 Confined to a spacious upstairs cell of the Carthage, Ill., jail, Joseph Smith was drinking wine with his brother and some friends in the late afternoon when he heard an angry mob approaching. Arming himself with a 6-chambered revolver that had been smuggled to him, Smith waited. Part of the mob forced his cell door, and emptied their weapons into Smith's brother and friends. Smith, throwing down his revolver, leaped for the window ledge. Bullets from the court below and from inside the cell struck him. Groaning, "Oh Lord, my God," Smith pitched over and plummeted 2 stories to the ground below. Some accounts say he was killed by his fall. Others claim he survived it only to be propped up in a sitting position and dispatched by a firing squad of 4. The Mormon prophet was dead, but in less than 2 months there would be a new prophet, a 43-year-old onetime carpenter and house painter from Vermont named Brigham Young.

1845

—The Baptists split over the slavery issue. Antislavery Baptists did not permit a slaveholder to be a missionary. The Southern Baptist Convention came about as a result.

—A postal act in 1845 reduced postage to 5¢ per half ounce for a 300-mi. delivery.

Jan. 23 Uniform Election Day for presidential elections was set by law.

Mar. 4 President James K. Polk said in his Inaugural Address: "Melancholy is the condition of that people whose government can be sustained only by a system which periodically transfers large amounts from the labor of the many to the coffers of the few."

Mar. 28 The Mexican Government broke off diplomatic relations with the U.S.

June 4 Hatch's sowing machine was demonstrated. This invention sowed wheat, oats, and other grasses.

July John L. O'Sullivan, editor of *U.S. Magazine and Democratic Revue* espoused the divine right, or "manifest destiny," of the U.S. to occupy and govern the whole North American continent. The term quickly became popular.

July 4 Delegates to the 1st National Convention of the Native American party met in Philadelphia to take political action against "the danger of foreign influence," otherwise known as immigrants.

Dec. 29 Texas was admitted as the 28th State; it was also the 15th slave State.

1846

—A former alcoholic turned temperance lecturer, John Bartholomew Gough began a campaign for a prohibition amendment.

Feb. 4 Under pressure from the governor of Illinois, who wanted to avoid a violent confrontation, the 1st contingent of Mormons left Illinois, crossing the frozen Mississippi River for the Iowa side, the preliminary step in their migration west to the Salt Lake Basin.

Mar. Gen. Zachary Taylor was ordered to advance and occupy positions on or near the Rio Grande in mid-January; however, Taylor was delayed by rains and mud and arrived in March. Mexico refused to honor the boundary claimed by the State of Texas, formerly the Mexican province of Texas. For almost a month the Mexicans and Americans played cat-and-mouse, with the Mexicans ordering the Americans to retreat but not attempting to enforce this demand.

Apr. 24 Polk notified Britain that the U.S. was terminating the 1827 agreement concerning the Oregon Territory.

Apr. 25 Word arrived in General Taylor's camp that the Mexicans had crossed the Rio Grande. The next day a guide informed Taylor that the dragoons sent to verify the crossing had been killed, wounded or taken prisoner. This report proved false. However, on the 26th, Taylor sent a report to Washington indicating hostilities had commenced.

Apr. 30–May 8 The Mexican Army crossed the Rio Grande. Fort Texas was placed under siege and the 1st important battle, the Battle of Palo Alto, was fought.

May 12

> We can easily defeat the armies of Mexico, slaughter them by thousands, and pursue them perhaps to their capital; we can conquer and "annex" their territory; but what then? . . . Is not Life miserable enough, comes not death soon enough, without resort to the hideous enginery of War?
>
> People of the U.S.! Your Rulers are precipitating you into a fathomless abyss of crime and calamity!. Why sleep you thoughtless on its verge, as though this was not your business. . . .
> —Horace Greeley, editorial in the *New York Tribune*

May 13 President Polk told Congress, Mexico had "invaded our territory and shed American blood on American soil." Congress declared war and appropriated an initial $10 million.

June 15 The Oregon Treaty was signed. The U.S. compromised, accepting the 49th parallel —instead of 54°40'—for a common border.

June 19 A New York Knickerbocker baseball player, Davis by name, was fined 6¢ for swearing at the umpire. The umpire happened to be Alexander J. Cartwright, a bewhiskered surveyor, who had originated modern baseball 2 years earlier.

Gen. Abner Doubleday, a West Pointer who became a Union hero in the Civil War, was said to have invented baseball at Cooperstown, N.Y., in 1839. This is a myth. No one invented baseball. The game evolved naturally from an imported English sport called "Rounders." As for Doubleday's developing modern game, this claim was promoted by a relative. Doubleday neither played anything resembling baseball nor did he write a word about it in his long literary career. The real founder was Cartwright, who sketched the 1st diamond, laid out the 1st rules, and assembled the 1st team.

July 20 The party headed by George Donner, an elderly, well-to-do Illinois farmer, and the equally wealthy James Frazier Reed decided to separate its 20 wagons from the rest of the wagon train heading over the regular route west. Lansford W. Hastings, explorer, wagon-train guide, author, and promoter, had suggested in a letter sent to emigrants at the Sweetwater encampment that they take a new route, 350 to 400 mi. shorter. Hastings assured them that he would guide them over this new trail after meeting them at Fort Bridger.

Hastings, however, upon getting together a train of 66 wagons, had left the fort before the Donner party arrived. Having missed their guide, the Donner party went on alone. Trapped in the Sierras by early snows at the end of October, the Donners, Reeds, and others in their group were forced to kill their cattle for food. Snow, freezing weather, and lack of wood for fires added to their hardships. After the hides of the cattle and oxen had been devoured, the survivors faced a decision: It was cannibalism or perish.

Lewis Keseberg, who was accused of committing 6 murders in order to feast off the flesh of his victims, discussed his cannibalism 3 decades later:

I cannot describe the unutterable repugnance with which I tasted the 1st mouthful of flesh. There is an instinct in our nature that revolts at the thought of touching, much less eating, a corpse. It makes my blood curdle to think of it! It has been told that I boasted of my shame—said that I enjoyed this horrid food, and that I remarked human flesh was more palatable than California beef. This is a falsehood. . . . This food was never otherwise than loathesome, insipid, and disgusting.

Keseberg claimed he had been trapped in a cabin with 5 companions who had died naturally. To survive, he was forced to carve them up, boil them, eat them. He said, "A man, before he judges me, should be placed in a similar situation."

The struggle of the Donner party ended in April, 1847, when 47 survivors of the original party of 82 finally reached California.

July 23 Protesting slavery as well as his country's involvement in the Mexican War, Henry David Thoreau refused to pay his $1 poll tax and was casually arrested by his friend, the Concord, Mass., constable, and put in jail. Three years later, in "Resistance to Civil Government," a lecture reprinted in a periodical called *Aesthetic Papers*, Thoreau recalled his incarceration:

"I have paid no poll-tax for 6 years. I was put into a jail once on this account, for one night; and, as I stood considering the walls of solid stone, 2' or 3' thick, the door of wood and iron, a foot thick, and the iron grating which strained the light, I could not help being struck with the foolishness of that institution which treated me as if I were mere flesh and blood and bones, to be locked up. . . . I saw that, if there was a wall of stone between me and my townsmen, there was a still more difficult one to climb or break through, before they could get to be as free as I was. . . .

"I could not but smile to see how industriously they locked the door on my meditations, which followed them out again without let or hindrance, and *they* were really all that was dangerous. As they could not reach me, they had resolved to punish my body; just as boys, if they cannot come at some person against whom they have a spite, will abuse his dog. I saw that the State was half-witted, that it was timid as a lone woman with her silver spoons; and that it did not know its friends from its foes, and I lost all my remaining respect for it, and pitied it."

It was said that Ralph Waldo Emerson visited Thoreau in jail. Emerson asked, "Henry, why are you here?" Thoreau replied, "Waldo, why are you not here?" Beautiful, but the exchange took place later and involved different words.

That night a relative, possibly an aunt, came by the jail and paid Thoreau's poll tax for him. When he woke in the morning, Thoreau was told he could leave. When he objected to this, the constable threatened to use force to remove him. So, "as mad as the devil," Thoreau left the jail, had a shoe mended in town, attended a huckleberry party, and returned to Walden Pond. His account of this experience was later read by Leo Tolstoi, and then by the young Mohandas K. Gandhi and it persuaded them to advocate civil disobedience.

Dec. 8 In his 2nd annual message to Congress, President Polk declared: "The war [with Mexico] will continue to be prosecuted with vigor as the best means of securing peace."

1847

—California was claimed by the U.S. through Frémont, the Navy, and 100 dragoons. This had long been an American goal.

Feb. 22 Gen. Zachary Taylor, old Rough and Ready, was ordered to stay in a defensive position in Monterrey, Mexico. Taylor regarded the decision as political because there was talk of him being a presidential contender. He decided to disobey orders. Pitting his 5,500 U.S. soldiers against Mexican general Santa Anna's 20,000 troopers, Taylor won the hard-fought battle of Buena Vista, bringing the war in the north of Mexico to an end.

Out of this decisive battle grew a legend. Capt. Braxton Bragg, a North Carolinian who had graduated from West Point, was suffering severe losses at his artillery battery. Bragg reported to Taylor, "General, I shall have to fall back with my battery or lose it." To which Taylor replied, "A little more grape, Captain Bragg." This legendary exchange was denied by all who were on hand at the time. According to L. B. Mizner, Taylor's interpreter who overheard the conversation, "when Bragg reported he would have to fall back or lose his battery, Taylor replied, 'Captain Bragg, it is better to lose a battery than a battle.'" Taylor went on to become U.S. President; Bragg went on to become a Confederate general who was promoted to serve as Jefferson Davis's military adviser.

July 1 The U.S. post office issued an adhesive 5¢ stamp bearing Franklin's image and a 10¢ stamp with Washington's image. Prior to this issue, postage was paid in cash and was indicated on the envelope in writing or by stamp. Mail cost 5¢ per ounce to send. When a user had only a 10¢ stamp, and his letter weighed an ounce or less, he cut the stamp in half.

Sept. American forces took Mexico City.

Oct. 1 Massachusetts astronomer, schoolteacher, librarian, Maria Mitchell, discovered a comet. She was awarded a gold medal for her discovery by the King of Denmark. Later Miss Mitchell was made a professor of astronomy at Vassar. Her special studies concerned sunspots, nebulae, and satellites. She was the idol of many women of that period and the 1st woman to be elected to the American Academy of Arts and Sciences.

1848

—Harvard president Edward Everett replied to protests over admission of a Negro: "If this boy passes the examination he will be admitted; and if the white students choose to withdraw, all the income of the college will be devoted to his education."

—Lincoln's views on the Mexican War expressed to his law partner, W. H. Herndon: ". . . the war was unnecessarily and unconstitutionally commenced by the President." And to the Rev. J. M. Peck: "It is a fact that the U.S. Army in marching to the Rio Grande, marched into a peaceful Mexican settlement and frightened the inhabitants away from their homes and their growing crops."

—Many enlisted men were shocked at the way the American soldiers treated Mexican peasants. Horrified by American desecration of Catholic churches in Mexico, some enlisted men, mostly Irish-Catholic immigrants, followed the lead of Sgt. John Riley of the 5th U.S. Infantry and joined the Mexican Army, forming a battalion called *Los Patricios* (for St. Patrick). They fought in several battles and were finally annihilated at the Battle of Churubusco when their ammunition ran out.

—The Free Soil party was organized which urged prohibition of slavery in new territories.

—Interest in spiritualism grew in the U.S., inspired by the experiences of 2 sisters, Margaret and Katherine Fox, of Hydesville, N.Y., who heard mysterious rappings at night "as though someone was knocking on the floor and moving chairs." The sisters regarded these rappings as communications from the spirit world. A gathering of medical men in Buffalo, N.Y., disagreed, insisting the rappings came from the sisters themselves when they cracked their knee joints. Despite this dissent, the Fox sisters were in demand everywhere, and audiences at their séances included such notables as James Fenimore Cooper, William Cullen Bryant, and Horace Greeley.

—San Francisco's population was about 800, but within 2 years the number would jump to over 30,000.

Jan. 24 John Sutter's sawmill partner, James Marshall, thought by some to be a bit peculiar, approached Sutter nervously with news of the discovery of gold grains. The grains, found at Sutter's Coloma mill, had been compared by Marshall with a $5 half eagle gold piece. Marshall was sure about his discovery and wanted no one but Sutter to know. Sutter was skeptical at 1st, but checked an article on gold in an encyclopedia and then told Marshall he believed that the grains might possibly be the finest kind of gold.

Feb. 2 The Treaty of Guadalupe Hidalgo was signed, ending the war with Mexico.

Mar. 1 The College of Villanova was chartered in Pennsylvania.

May Ten men, representing the 6 leading New York newspapers, were brought together in an office of the *New York Sun* by 57-year-old David Hale, editor of the *Journal of Commerce*. Hale told his colleagues that it had become too difficult and too expensive for them to gather national and international news individually. One publisher alone, the upstart Scotsman, James Gordon Bennett, used newsboats, railroads, a private pony express, and even carrier pigeons for a pigeon post, to collect his news. Samuel F. B. Morse's new telegraph was still in its infancy, with only a single wire available to all New York papers. Hale suggested a "union of the foremost New York newspapers, each contributing its share to a general fund which could be used in a concerted effort to provide readers with wider coverage of all important world events." After much debate, the 10 men finally agreed to form a union of newspapers that would gather and share news. It was decided the organization would be called the Associated Press.

June 27 A Broadway theater bill announced a steam-powered "extensive apparatus for the perfect ventilation of the entire building." This air-conditioning machinery was patented by J. E. Coffee.

July First woman's rights convention was held at Seneca Falls, N.Y. Organizers of the convention were Elizabeth Cady Stanton and Lucretia Mott. The Seneca Falls Declaration of Sentiments and Resolutions drawn up at the convention declared that woman was man's equal, advocated suffrage for women, and called attention to other inequities and limitations imposed upon women. Of the 260 women and 40 men who attended the convention, only one, Charlotte Woodward, lived to see women vote.

1849

—New York State granted married women equal property rights with men.

—Elizabeth Blackwell, onetime resident of New York, was the 1st woman doctor to practice medicine in the U.S.

—One thousand sixty-six vagrancy arrests of children between the ages of 6 and 16 were reported in Boston this year.

Mar. 3 A 6th Cabinet post—that of Secretary

of Home Dept., later called Dept. of the Interior—was created. The Home Dept. included the Office of Census, Office of Indian Affairs, General Land Office, and Pensions Office.

Mar. 3 Minnesota was established as a Territory with slavery prohibited.

Mar. 4 David Rice Atchison served as President of the U.S. for this one day. President Polk's term had expired, but because it was a Sunday, President-elect Zachary Taylor chose to be inaugurated the following day, a Monday. Since the nation could not be leaderless for even 24 hours, the next in line of succession, the President *pro tempore* of the Senate, Senator Atchison, took over the office. When asked what he did during his time as President, Atchison said that because he had been exhausted by his work in Congress he slept soundly all through his term as Chief Executive.

June 15 James Polk died at the age of 53.

Sept.–Oct. Californians, tired of waiting for a congressional decision, decided on their own to prohibit slavery in their territory.

—J.M.N.

1850

—U.S. population—23,191,876. Two million people lived west of the Mississippi River. In the next 50 years, the population of the U.S. more than tripled.

—Nathaniel Hawthorne completed *The Scarlet Letter*. The book later was condemned by the Rev. A. C. Coxe, a popular clergyman of the time, as "a brokerage of lust."

—Utah was established as a territory with the option to decide for itself whether to be slave or free upon its admission as a State. Brigham Young was named the 1st governor of the Utah Territory.

—The U.S. Navy and the Merchant Marine outlawed flogging.

—By the end of 1850 an estimated 20,000 blacks had escaped to the North via the Underground Railroad.

Jan. Henry Clay, former senator and presidential candidate, returned to the Senate with resolutions for a compromise between the North and South. These resolutions later became the foundation for the Compromise of 1850, adopted in August of that year.

Feb. 12 Messrs. Henry Clay, Sam Houston, Daniel Webster, and others sent a letter to Dr. Dods, author and lecturer on electrical psychology, asking him to speak in Washington on spiritual manifestations.

Mar. 4 John C. Calhoun, frail and near death, mustered the strength to attend a Senate session where his colleague from Virginia, James Mason, read Calhoun's final formal speech.

Calhoun called for decisive action to stop the agitation against slavery so that the South would not be forced to secede. Calhoun said the goal of democracy was equity and that 51% of the people do not have a moral right to coerce the other 49%.

Aug. Compromise of 1850 adopted which provided for California's admittance as a free State, but did not forbid slavery in other territory. The Compromise further forbade selling slaves brought into the District of Columbia, and called for stricter laws to ensure return of runaway slaves to their masters.

Sept. 9 California was admitted as a free State.

Sept. 11 Jenny Lind—the illegitimate Swedish Nightingale whose voice had been praised by Chopin, Wagner, Mendelssohn but criticized by Carlyle, Hawthorne, Walt Whitman—made her long-awaited U.S. debut at Castle Garden in New York City, under the auspices of showman Phineas T. Barnum.

Barnum had signed the 29-year-old soprano to appear in 150 concerts for $150,000, plus salaries for her maid, valet, secretary, and a friend. Barnum gave her debut the biggest promotional buildup in American history to date. Four days before Jenny Lind's opening night, Barnum auctioned off 3,000 tickets, the 1st going to the proprietor of a hat store for $225.

At curtain time, 5,000 people—⅞ of them male—filled the Garden, having paid $17,864 for the privilege. Backed by a 60-piece orchestra, Jenny Lind began with "Casta Diva" from Bellini's *Norma*. As number succeeded number, the Garden became a growing madhouse of enthusiasm. The next morning, the *New York Tribune* spoke for the majority of critics: "Jenny Lind's 1st concert is over, and all doubts are at an end. She is the greatest singer we have ever heard. . . ."

1851

—Daniel Webster was nominated for President by the American party (nicknamed the Know-Nothings) at their national convention in Trenton. The party's nickname was derived from its members' negative answers to questions about their secret party policies. Know-Nothings were anti-Catholic, anti-immigrant.

—A quarter of a million Irish came to the U.S. this year. Twenty thousand French arrived also, adding to the 54,000 French already residing in the U.S. prior to 1851.

—The Young Men's Christian Association opened its 1st American chapter in Boston.

—Isaac Singer patented an improved sewing machine.

Feb. 18 A runaway slave called Shadrach, actually Frederick Jenkins, was rescued from court custody by a Boston mob, and 2 powerful blacks spirited him off to the safety of Canada.

June 2 Maine reinforced its 1846 law prohibiting the manufacture and sale of alcoholic beverages.

Sept. 18 *The New York Times* began publication. The paper sold for 1¢ per copy.

1852

—Massachusetts workers struggled for a 10-hour day. The workday in the 1850s ran from 8 hours in some few places to as much as 14 and 15 hours. By 1853 many employers had made a concession to the 11-hour day.

Mar. 20 *Uncle Tom's Cabin* by Harriet Beecher Stowe was published in Boston in 2 volumes with a 1st printing of 5,000 copies which sold out within a week. In 8 weeks, 50,000 copies had been sold, and in 20 weeks, 100,000. In a year sales reached 300,000 and in 16 months, one million. The novel provoked a wave of hatred against slavery, as well as the publication of 30 books defending slavery.

Mrs. Stowe, daughter of a Congregational pastor in Connecticut, the 6th of 11 children, was the wife of an erudite clergyman and the mother of 7 children. Her husband had interested her in the slavery question, and once she had visited slaves on a Kentucky plantation. She got her idea for *Uncle Tom's Cabin* after reading a 76-page autobiographical pamphlet by a real-life Maryland slave named Josiah Henson, who had escaped to Canada. After her novel's success, Mrs. Stowe gave another version of its inspiration. When a visitor asked to shake hands with the woman who'd written the immortal book, Mrs. Stowe stated she hadn't written it. "God wrote it," she said. "I merely wrote his dictation." The book contributed to the bloody conflict between the North and South. When Mrs. Stowe called on President Lincoln at the White House a decade later, he greeted her with the question, "Is this the little woman whose book made such a great war?"

Nov. 21 The 1st of 32 earthquake shocks in California was felt. They continued into the spring of 1853. Little attention was paid to these shocks, as they occurred in the southern part of the State, but they were blamed for the disappearance of the waters of New River and Big Lagoon, which were replaced by "volumes of sulfurous and effervescent sulfur."

Dec. 23 The 1st train west of the Mississippi traveled its route from St. Louis to Cheltenham Mo.—a distance of 5 mi. It was no big deal, but it got people excited that maybe someday the country could be crossed by train.

Dec. 29 Emma Snodgrass, referred to by East Coast newspapers as "the girl who has recently been visiting parts of New England in pants" was "again" arrested in Boston on a charge of vagrancy. Since Emma was regularly employed as a clerk, and paid her bills, the vagrancy charge didn't hold. She was released after the judge had given her some "wholesome advice about her eccentricities," to which she "responded with becoming grace and promised reformation." The next day, however, Emma was back on the street in her "male attire."

1853

—East Coast newspapers carried a lot of European news but often shrugged off the news coming from the West as unimportant.

—At least $65 million worth of gold was taken from California mines this year.

—Governor Lane of New Mexico seized a portion of Mexican territory on his own responsibility.

—New York police were required to wear a uniform consisting of a blue cap bearing the officer's number, and a blue, swallowtail coat with brass buttons, and gray trousers.

—First newspaper story on baseball was written by Sen. William Cauldwell, owner and publisher of the *New York Mercury*.

—The U.S. *Review* said that soon machinery would perform all work via direction of automata. The only tasks left for humans, it claimed, would be to make love, study, and be happy.

—The Crystal Palace was built in New York City to house the 1853 Exhibition.

—A number of universities were chartered across the country including Willamette University in Salem, Oreg., and Illinois Wesleyan in Bloomington, Ill. (both founded earlier under Methodist auspices). Washington University in St. Louis, Mo., was chartered as Eliot Seminary; Louisiana State University was chartered in Alexandria, La.; Ohio Wesleyan Female College (later combined with Ohio Wesleyan University) in Delaware, O.; and Loyola College in Baltimore, Md.

Jan. 27 A black man appeared at an antislavery rally in Boston. He said he was a fugitive and asked for funds to free his wife and 2 children. Parker Pillsbury of the convention told him antislavery people refused to buy slaves and referred the man to the editors of the *New York Journal of Commerce*. Spectators at the antislavery convention, however, contributed between $10 and $12 each.

Jan. 27 Mr. Venable presented an amendment in the House of Representatives for a $5,000 appropriation to finish the statue of General Jackson in Lafayette Square, Washington, D.C. One of the distinguishing features of the work

is the way the horse's reared legs are placed dead center. It was done by Clark Mills whose later creations proved more anatomically convincing.

Mar. 3 Funds for the transcontinental railroad survey were authorized by Congress. The sum of $150,000 was appropriated and the survey was to be done by the War Dept.

Apr. Dispatch from the *St. Louis Intelligencer* indicated 900 passengers on 2 boats had passed through St. Louis in one day, carrying folks heading West. These 900 were soon followed by many more immigrants who had recently arrived at New York ports.

June 8 Steamer *El Dorado* arrived in New York from Aspinwall (now Colón, Panama) with mail and $1 million in gold dust.

1854

—William Lloyd Garrison, founder of the New England Anti-Slavery Society, parent organization for other antislavery groups, publicly burned the Constitution at an open air meeting of Abolitionists in Framingham, Mass.

—Com. Matthew Galbraith Perry returned to Japan for a 3rd time, but now he was welcomed. Japan had opened its doors to America. A tipsy Japanese official at a celebration proclaimed, "Nippon and America, all the same heart."

—German immigration to the U.S. in 1854 provided 215,000 of the 400,000 immigrants arriving this year.

—The American party (Know-Nothings) reached its zenith as thousands of additional immigrants reached America's shores.

—A petition containing 15,000 signatures asking the Senate to establish a commission to investigate occult phenomena got a negative response.

—Prejudice was not confined to the North and South. As 13,000 Orientals reached California, Congress was asked by the California legislature to put a tax on all Chinese immigrants.

Jan. 23 Stephen Douglas introduced the Kansas-Nebraska Act which violated terms of the Missouri Compromise, making Independent Democrats move toward a new political party.

Feb. 4 The name for this new party was suggested by Alvan Bovay, a Ripon, Wis., attorney, who in a letter to Horace Greeley, *New York Tribune* editor, proposed that the editor help slavery opponents organize a new party under the name of Republican, a name Bovay had suggested previously.

June 2 Anthony Burns, a fugitive slave, was sent back South from Boston. Streets were lined with troops and policemen and it was estimated that the U.S. Government cost of returning Mr.

Burns was $100,000. Burns later was sold to people in Boston who wanted to see him freed.

1855

—Abraham Lincoln wrote to his friend James Speed:

> Our progress in degeneracy appears to me to be pretty rapid. As a nation, we began by declaring that "all men are created equal." We now practically read it "all men are created equal except Negroes." When the Know-Nothings get control, it will read "all men are created equal except Negroes and foreigners and Catholics." When it comes to this I should prefer emigrating to some country where they make no pretense of loving liberty— to Russia, for instance, where despotism can be taken pure and without the base alloy of hypocrisy.

—Sarah Hale, advocate of higher education for women and editor of *Godey's Lady's Book*, which influenced the manners and morals of the day, launched a campaign against the use of the word "female," in connection with women in public activity.
—Henry Wadsworth Longfellow's *The Song of Hiawatha* was published.
Jan. 1 The 1st oil business was formed by 2 New York City law partners, Jonathan J. Eveleth and George H. Bissell. Yale professor and chemist-toxicologist Benjamin Silliman discovered 8 products which could be extracted from the oil by commercial processes, thus making an oil business feasible, and the Pennsylvania Rock Oil Co. began obtaining oil from a spring in Venango County, Pa.
Mar. 30 Proslavery forces won the election in the Kansas Territory after bitter fighting between antislavery Free-Soilers and proslavery Border Ruffians, both of whom had moved to Kansas, just for the election.
Apr. 1 A judge commented in a *New York Herald* article that various crimes could be assigned to ethnic groups. Murders, riots, and violent assaults, said this judge, were the work of Irishmen. Daring burglaries and highway robberies he assigned to Englishmen, while petty thefts and larcenies were attributed to the Germans. Skillful forgeries and obtaining goods under false pretenses were designated as strictly American offenses.

1856

May 14 James King, owner of the *San Francisco Daily Evening Bulletin*, was killed by a rival newspaper owner. Confidence in local authority was low and a vigilante group snatched the assassin from the sheriff. The vigilantes tried, convicted, and executed King's murderer. Vigilante committees continued to spring up in the lawless California territory.
May 19 Sen. Charles Sumner, of Massachusetts, rose in the Senate to speak out against the proslavery people. In his speech, Sumner attacked old Senator Butler, of South Carolina, stating that Butler had taken "the harlot, Slavery" for his "mistress."
May 22 Senator Butler's nephew, Congressman Preston Brooks, also from South Carolina, burst into the Senate Chamber in search of Senator Sumner, the man who had insulted his uncle. Sighting Sumner at his desk, busily writing, Congressman Brooks charged at him, beating him over the head with the heavy cane he was carrying. Sumner, his legs caught under the desk, tried to rise, but finally crumpled to the Senate floor from the steady rain of blows, tearing his desk loose as he fell. Brooks continued to strike at Sumner's head until his cane broke. Two Georgia senators who were standing nearby watched the attempted murder, merely laughing at the assault.

Senator Sumner survived, but his injuries disabled him for 3 years and left him almost blind in one eye. Meanwhile, Southern supporters deluged Congressman Brooks with gifts of more canes and even a few whips to use on other abolitionists.
May 25 Free-Soilers, led by John Brown, killed 5 sleeping proslavers in a village on the Pottowatomie River.

1857

—The 1st patent was granted for a postmarking and stamp-canceling machine.
—German immigration for 1857 was 119,000.
—First baseball convention was held, which set a 9-inning game and established a rule that an interrupted game called after 5 innings was legal.
Mar. 6 The incendiary decision on the *Dred Scott* v. *Sanford* case was finally handed down by the U.S. Supreme Court, Chief Justice Roger B. Taney presiding.

Just who was Dred Scott and what was his historic case all about? Scott was a black man born a slave in 1795 on a plantation in Southampton County, Va. Later he was taken to St. Louis by his master, Capt. Peter Blow. According to historians, Scott himself was an illiterate, dim-witted, undependable person, who by chance became a pawn in the national slavery controversy.

During his lifetime, Dred Scott was the chattel of at least a half dozen slave owners. The last of these legal owners, finding him incompetent, let him drift off on his own. Unable to hold a job, Scott turned to Henry Blow, son of his 1st master, for support. Henry Blow, a wealthy man who had made his fortune in Missouri lead mines, gave Scott his support. He also decided to give him something else—freedom. To this end, Blow went to court in Missouri, and the marathon Dred Scott case was under way.

Blow's argument was that Dred Scott had lived for 4 years on the free soil of Wisconsin and Illinois, and therefore was automatically a free man despite his return to a slave State like Missouri. The original case, oddly titled *Scott, A Man of Color* v. *Emerson*, dragged through the courts for 7 years. At one point a lower court gave Scott his freedom, but in 1852 the Missouri Supreme Court reversed the lower court's decision and made Scott a slave once more.

With righteous anger, Henry Blow got Dred Scott's case appealed to the Supreme Court. At 1st the Supreme Court wanted to dispose of this hot potato by letting the lower court judgment stand, but public pressure had turned the case into a constitutional crisis. The question was raised: Could slavery be introduced into new States?

After sitting on the case for over a year, the 9 Supreme Court justices—Taney and 4 associate justices were from the South (although only one of them, Justice Campbell, supported the Confederacy 4 years later)—handed down their decision: 7–2 against Dred Scott and against freedom. Chief Justice Taney declared that the Declaration of Independence was never intended to include Negroes. In the Supreme Court's opinion: Dred Scott was not a citizen of the U.S. and had no right to sue in Federal court; residence in a free territory did not make him free; the Missouri Compromise which made the area north of 36°30′ free was unconstitutional. In short, the Court denied Congress the right to exclude slavery from new territories, and insisted that slaves did not own their own bodies but were someone else's private property. The decision not only made it clear there would be no peaceful solution to the slave problem, but it accelerated the coming of the Civil War.

And Dred Scott? Henry Blow got legal title to him, and then freed Scott and his family. Dred Scott went to work as a porter in the Barnum Hotel in St. Louis, basking in the attention and notoriety he received. A year later he was dead. Henry Blow paid for his funeral expenses.

Aug. 24 A financial panic erupted, which was blamed on the failure of the New York City branch of the Ohio Life Insurance Co., a collapse which was in turn blamed on over-speculation in railroads and real estate. Banks crashed and almost 5,000 businesses failed. The Panic of 1857 brought unemployment to the cities. Rural areas went back to using the barter system for the exchange of goods.

Sept. 8–11 Captain Fancher, en route to California from Arkansas with 30 wagons filled with 137 emigrants, reached Utah. A small minority of his party were rowdies who taunted and threatened the countryside Mormons. While camping in an 8-mi.-long valley known as Mountain Meadows, the Fancher party was attacked by 54 whites and 300 Indians. The whites, conferring under a flag of truce with the Fancher group, persuaded them to lay down their arms, assuring them of safe passage back to Cedar City. The offer was accepted—and all the adult emigrants were ruthlessly slaughtered. The attackers spared 17 children. One Mormon leader was briefly excommunicated for his role in the massacre, and another, John D. Lee, was tried and executed, but not until 1877, some 20 years later.

1858

—In White County, Tenn., a slave owner sued the members of a mob who had lynched one of his slaves.

—Indians from the Dakota territories were induced to sell their land and move to a reservation.

—George Mortimer Pullman, a 27-year-old cabinetmaker, began work on his idea to provide better sleeping accommodations on trains. The 1st 2 sleeping cars, with upper berths hinged at the side and supported by 2 jointed arms, were built in Chicago. Unable to sell these models, Pullman became a shopkeeper in a Colorado mining town. In 1863, Pullman returned to Chicago and invested his entire $20,000 savings in a 3rd model of his sleeping car, which he built with the help of a friend. This was a super luxury model called the Pioneer. When it was ready to test, it seemed to be a white elephant. Too large to pass under bridges or through stations, the Pioneer was put to rest on a siding.

Two years later, after President Lincoln's assassination, every State offered its finest railroad cars to join his funeral train. The State of Illinois, where the dead President had practiced law and entered politics, wished to be represented by the best car possible. Then someone remembered George Pullman's oversized Pioneer sleeping car. It was brought into service, as railroad stations were quickly torn down and bridges raised to accommodate it.

Attached to the funeral train, the Pioneer and its comforts were praised by General Grant and other dignitaries. At once, other railroad lines began rebuilding their stations and bridges to make way for it. George Pullman's moment had come. He formed the Pullman Palace Car Co. in partnership with millionaire Andrew Carnegie, and soon was a millionaire himself. In 3 decades, Pullman's gouging tactics—which included forcing his employees to live in a city called Pullman—and his antilabor practices earned him the reputation of being one of the most heartless capitalists of his century.

—"Pike's Peak or Bust" became the cry of gold seekers heading for what today is Denver, Colo.

—U.S. marshals seized the "yacht" *Wanderer*. Its captain was arrested for bringing 300 naked Africans to Brunswick, Ga. Later reports indicated "270 of the wild Africans from the *Wanderer* were working on a South Carolina plantation."

—In New Orleans, where many immigrants chose to disembark because of less stringent observation by immigration officials, 3,414 cases of yellow fever were reported during the recent season. Of these, 2,643 were cured and 771 died. Reports of the day broke down the cases according to nationalities.

—Reports from Arizona gold mines indicated miners earned between $4 and $150 per day. Silver mine discoveries were contained in the same dispatch.

July 3 Brigham Young was interviewed by a *New York Times* reporter who described Young as not so much wise and profound as shrewd and cunning, and as a man who didn't like to have his word questioned. The Mormons, according to this same reporter, were kind, yet inhospitable to Gentiles; protective and fanatic about their religion, yet honest and truthful where religion was not concerned. Young scoffed at the idea that the Mormon practice of polygamy generated much of the ill will directed toward the Mormons, countering that Mormons treated their women like human beings, unlike Easterners who treated them like "w —— s."

Aug. 22 Overland mail communications were interrupted by Indians.

Sept. 1 Success of the 1st transatlantic telegraph was celebrated in New York City with services, speeches, a fireworks display, and a torchlight parade of firemen.

Sept. 1 Disguised, armed parties gained admittance to a quarantine establishment at Staten Island. Patients were dragged from their beds, their mattresses piled up and burned. *The New York Times* criticized the governor, mayor, and superintendent of police for making merry while gangs of desperadoes were letting loose smallpox and yellow fever patients, and burning buildings. The newspaper asked why no arrests were made, no militia ordered out, and no rewards offered for the capture of these culprits.

Sept. 5 Catherine Gruk was admitted to a hospital in New York City with a case of yellow fever, her infection blamed on contact with garments that had been strewn about during the September 1 havoc. The Board of Health finally acted and arrests were made. The police superintendent was suspended.

Dec. The overland mail's assistant superintendent Davis informed a Dallas newspaper that the El Paso route was one of the worst owing to "depredations" by Comanches and Apaches.

Dec. 18 At an antislavery convention, Lucretia Mott proposed opening public schools to black children on equal terms, as was the practice in most New England towns.

1859

—Harriet Beecher Stowe accepted an invitation to dine at the Atlantic Club on the stipulation that no wine be served.

—Ad in a Richmond, Va., paper offered $25,000 for the heads of a number of Northerners. The *Richmond Enquirer* recommended establishing a strict surveillance over Northern visitors and the Virginians who dealt or associated with them.

—Oregon was admitted as a free State.

—The slave market reports indicated that up to $2,000 was being paid for "prime field hands."

July 25 At a town meeting in St. Joseph, Mo., a resolution was introduced: that the new free State paper, the *Free Democrat*, was a nuisance and its editor, Mr. Grant, should leave town immediately. The resolution was voted down by a large majority.

Sept. 26 Overland mail arrived in St. Louis from San Francisco in 24 days.

Oct. 16 Backed by money received from abolitionists in Canada and New England, John Brown led a raiding party of 16 white men and 5 Negroes in an attack on the Federal arsenal at Harpers Ferry, Va. Brown's long-range motive in seizing the arsenal was to set up a republic of fugitive and freed slaves in the Appalachians, and then to declare war on the slave States of the South.

During his raid, Brown killed the town mayor, took 60 hostages, and held off the local militia. When the U.S. Marines, commanded by Col. Robert E. Lee, arrived 2 days later, Brown and his party, along with their hostages, found refuge in a locomotive roundhouse. Brown and his men battered holes through the brick wall of the roundhouse to fire their rifles through, and began to fight. One of the hostages said later: "Brown was the coolest and firmest man I ever saw defying danger and death. With one son dead by his side, and another shot through, he felt the pulse of his dying son with one hand and held his rifle with the other, and commanded his men with the utmost composure, encouraging them to be firm and sell their lives dearly as they could."

By nightfall, with 10 of his men dead and Brown himself wounded, Brown was taken prisoner.

Oct. 17 Dispatches arrived at Baltimore telling how 250 whites and a gang of Negroes had taken possession of the arsenal. Another report told of a stampede of Negroes from Maryland and yet another said the streets were filled with insurgents who were plundering the town. Still another report was that the town was in the possession of Negroes who were arresting citizens and throwing them into prison. One account placed the number of insurrectionists at between 500 and 700, including both whites and blacks.

Oct. 18 The President, through the mayor of Washington, ordered a detachment of volunteer militia sent to Harpers Ferry.

Oct. 31 Refusing to plead insanity as a defense for his actions at Harpers Ferry, John Brown went on trial. He was found guilty of treason, criminal conspiracy, murder, and was sentenced to be hanged. Important people around the U.S. voiced shock at Brown's extremism. Almost alone, Ralph Waldo Emerson hailed Brown as "that new saint" who "will make the gallows glorious like the Cross."

Nov. Newspaper reports alleged Buchanan's Cabinet knew about Brown's plan as early as August 20.

Dec. 2 John Brown was hanged.

Dec. 13 Henry Clay said he was confident the election of a Republican President meant the end of the Union.

—J.M.N.

1 8 6 0

—U.S. population—31,443,321. Center: somewhere near Chillicothe, O. New York City became the largest Irish city in the world with 203,740 Irish-born out of a total population of 805,651.

—Erastus and Irwin Beadle published a series of novelettes about pioneer life, the Revolutionary War, Indians, and Mexico. Bound in yellowish-orange paper, the Beadle Dime Novel Library offered 386 titles to start, each title enjoying sales of up to 80,000 copies. The books were eagerly sought by young soldiers desperate for escape reading. The Beadles' formula for success: Assign writers to hack out cliffhangers starring heroes such as Kit Carson, Calamity Jane, and "Deadwood Dick." By the end of the Civil War, total sales were over 4 million.

Apr. Baseball's ritual for relieving spectator fatigue—the "7th-inning stretch"—was commonly adopted. The custom had superstitious origins. It was thought to bring good luck to the home team, since "7" was a winning number at dice.

Apr. 3 The Pony Express began fast overland mail service, operating between St. Joseph, Mo., and Sacramento, Calif. It offered 8–10-day delivery, with an "emergency" time of 7 days, 7 hours. Riders changed horses at 153 stations, spaced from 7 to 20 mi. apart. The route followed the old emigrant trail to the Platte River, through South Pass to Fort Bridger in Wyoming, then south around the lower end of the Great Salt Lake to Carson City, Nev., and through Donner Pass to Sacramento. Financially, the service was a failure and ended with the arrival of the transcontinental telegraph 18 months later.

Dec. 20 South Carolina, voting 169–0, seceded from the Union.

1 8 6 1

—The *Chicago Times* stated its credo: "It is a newspaper's duty to print the news, and raise hell."

Jan. 9 The *Star of the West*, a merchant steamer carrying Union recruits to reinforce Major Anderson at Fort Sumter, was fired on. Anderson, cut off by land by South Carolina's secession 2 weeks earlier, had moved his 75 men out to the red brick fortress in Charleston harbor. Rebel Charles Haynesworth, a Citadel cadet, fired a handgun at the ship, shooting the 1st shot of the Civil War. In a later volley, a cannonball was put across the *Star*'s bow, alerting the Southern militiamen at Sullivan Island's Fort Moultrie. They hit the unarmed vessel twice before it turned about and fled.

Apr. 12 At 4:30 A.M., following a one-hour ultimatum, Confederate batteries fired on Union forces in Fort Sumter. Edmund Ruffin, a fiery Virginia secessionist, is often credited with firing the 1st shot. Despite this legend, the signal shot probably came from Capt. George James's post at Fort Johnson. Ruffin fired from the battery on Cummings Point, and the sequence of firing orders called for this battery to fire after James's.

Anderson's 84 men in Fort Sumter rotated in firing the fort's 48 guns, assisted by 43 workmen. Their heaviest-caliber weapon—the barbette—had to be abandoned after Confederates tore down a house on Sullivan's Island to reveal a secret battery that enfiladed the barbettes.

Sumter's garrison ignored the initial hail of cannonballs and shells until after breakfast, a repast that took several hours and produced a silence that thoroughly baffled the Rebels. Capt. Abner Doubleday then fired the Union's 1st defensive shot, aiming at Cummings Point.

Brought under attack from 4 directions—Fort Moultrie, Fort Johnson, Cummings Point, and a floating battery—Major Anderson surrendered after 34 hours of bombardment in which over 4,000 projectiles were fired. No one was killed, and only a few were injured, by falling bricks.

In the pomp-and-circumstance surrender ceremony, a 50-gun salute was delivered. On the 50th reloading, a spark accidentally touched off a premature explosion, killing Daniel Hough. His was the 1st death of the war. The hot embers fell on the cartridges stacked below, exploding these as well, injuring 5 other men.

Sumter would have fallen anyway, having nothing to eat except salt pork. But Southern politicians, fearful that the new Confederacy would splinter "unless you sprinkle blood in the face of the people," ordered that 1st shot to be fired.

July 18 Much of Washington society turned out for a trip to Bull Run, Va., to watch the Federal troops crush the Rebels. But confusion was the order of the day. In the general fight that followed, as many as 12,000 soldiers could be seen wandering about aimlessly in the smoke of battle. In the ensuing Union rout, a panicked mix of wagon and carriage, of soldier and civilian, retreated back to the capital.

The news of Union defeat came to the Rev. Henry Cox of Illinois while he was preaching. He closed the service with "Brethren, we'd better adjourn this camp-meeting and go home and drill."

Aug. 5 Congress enacted the 1st income tax law. The sum of $20 million was to be raised by a levy on real estate and on personal earnings. The latter rate: 3% on income of over $800 a year.

1862

—A 23-year-old enterpreneur invested $4,000 of his life savings in an oil refining venture. His name: John D. Rockefeller.
—The Morrill Land Grant Act gave each State 30,000 acres per congressman to be used to create colleges of agriculture and mechanical arts. Sixty-nine land-grant colleges were established on 13 million acres.
—Mathew Brady began to photograph the Civil War. Wealthy before it began, Brady ruined himself financially, spending $100,000 of his own funds for the effort. He followed the armies in a cumbersome, black wagon he named the "What-is-it," because this question was continually asked by curious soldiers. Many of his most striking photographs were made by riding to the battle scene with the wagons sent to collect the dead and wounded.

Brady and his assistants used large box cameras mounted on tripods. For processing, his wet-glass, collodion-coated plates required immersion in one chemical bath, after exposure, followed by immediate transfer to the developing solution.

Feb. 10 "Gen. Tom Thumb," P. T. Barnum's 2'5" midget, married Mercy Lavinia Warren Bump at Grace Church, New York City. It was the 1st marriage for both. (See also: Tom Thumb in Footnote People in U.S. History, Chap. 3.)

Mar. 9 Two armored warships, the *Monitor* and the C.S.S. *Virginia* (formerly known as the Union's *Merrimac*), fought to a draw off Hampton Roads, Va. The designer of the *Monitor*, a Swedish immigrant named John Ericsson, 1st submitted his unusual design to the Navy Dept. in 1861. He was told to "take it home and worship it," because the idea was like nothing that had ever been seen before. Wiser heads prevailed, and a $275,000 contract was awarded to build the armor-plated raft. A sum of $5,000 was paid to Theodore Timby, who held a patent on a fast-revolving gun turret that Ericsson incorporated for the ship. There were at least 40 other design features that were patentable.

Crew members on the *Virginia*, returning to finish off the grounded *Minnesota*, had found what they took to be a "floating water tank" alongside. When the "tank" ran up the Union flag, the *Virginia* fired a full broadside at the strange object. Most of the shots missed the target entirely, but a few struck its flat deck, skipping off in a shower of sparks. The *Monitor*'s circular turret then spun around, bringing twin guns to bear. A shot hit the *Virginia*'s iron-plated side so hard that over 100 sailors standing behind it were knocked flat, their ears and noses bleeding profusely from the concussion.

The 2 vessels slugged it out for 4 hours without a winner being declared.

The 2 ironclads met again on April 11, but no action occurred. They both had orders to stand clear of each other, and to shoot only if fired upon. Neither the Union nor the Confederacy wanted to risk the loss of its only ironclad a 2nd time.

The *Virginia* was scuttled by its crew in May, 1862. The *Monitor*, caught by a hurricane off the Carolina coast on December 31, 1862, went to the bottom with all hands. In July of 1974, a team of divers finally located the sunken *Monitor*, lying upside down in 220' of water about 15 mi. SW of Cape Hatteras, N.C., but it was not raised.

Apr. 6–7 Milestone Battle: Shiloh, Tenn. Of

the 77,000 men who took part on both sides, over 60,000 were raw recruits who had to be shown how to use their rifles. Said one Union private, detailed to instruct his comrades on the line of battle: "It's just like shooting squirrels, only these squirrels have guns . . ."

The inexperienced troops took heavy losses on the 1st day, with ⅓ of Grant's command put out of action, and the rest demoralized. Asked if he planned to retreat, Grant replied, "No! I propose to attack at dawn and whip them." He did, breaking down the back door into the Confederacy.

Apr. 12 The Great Locomotive Chase. Striving to cut the rail line to Chattanooga, Tenn., James J. Andrews and his 21 cohorts stole the *General* and 3 freight cars at Marietta, Ga. Caught near Ringgold, Andrews and 7 of his men were hung. The others were imprisoned.

May 20 Lincoln signed the Homestead Act, giving a settler title to 160 acres provided he worked this public-domain land for 5 years. By 1890, 375,000 homesteaders received 48 million acres. However, most of the land went to railroad companies who acquired 20-million acres.

June 1 Robert E. Lee was appointed as Commander-in-Chief of the Confederate armies.

July Union general Daniel Butterfield improvised a new "Lights Out" bugle call: "Taps." Unhappy with the harsh sound of the official call, he whistled a new melody for his bugler.

July 12 Congress authorized the "Medal of Honor" for enlisted men who distinguished themselves in battle. The same legislation ordered 2,000 medals struck, and the U.S.'s highest award for valor nearly began as a Good Conduct Medal: In June, 1863, Secretary Stanton OK'd awards to every member of the 27th Maine regiment who reenlisted, a total of about 300 men.

Sept. 17 Milestone Battle: Antietam. In Frederick, Md., 2 Union soldiers on leave picked up a few cigars inside a paper wrapping. The "paper" proved to be a copy of Lee's orders for the Maryland campaign. So much artillery fire was concentrated at Antietam, in the woods near Dunker church, that the metal fragments embedded in the trees completely ruined a sawmill years later. Burnside's losses of 12,000 were partly caused by his determination to cross Antietam creek by a stone bridge that now bears his name. The narrow, 3-arch bridge, covered by Confederate guns in the heights just beyond, was taken only after 2 regiments had been mowed down in charges. Burnside could have crossed the creek elsewhere—it was shallow enough to wade in many places.

Sept. 22 Lincoln read the Emancipation Proclamation to his Cabinet. At Seward's advice, he delayed news of his decision until after a big Union victory. Antietam had occurred on September 16–17—Lincoln released the Proclamation on January 1, a full 100 days later. He had deliberately refrained from such an action when the war began, to avoid angering border States which still practiced slavery. His primary interest was in preserving the Union, not in freeing the slaves: "If I could save the Union without freeing *any* slave, I would do it; and if I could save it by freeing *all* the slaves, I would do it; and if I could do it by freeing some and leaving others alone, I would also do that." The Proclamation gave 3,063,392 slaves their technical freedom.

Nov. 4 Dr. Richard J. Gatling patented the revolving 6-barrel machine gun. Lincoln ignored its military potential for the Union Army due to political considerations: The doctor was rumored to be a Copperhead, a member of a secret society with Confederate sympathies.

Dec. 13 Milestone Battle: Fredericksburg, Va. In one of only 3 major battles fought over open ground (Gettysburg and Antietam were the other 2), Burnside sent 113,000 in 6 frontal assaults against a strongly-fortified Confederate Army on Marye's Heights. Said Robert E. Lee, watching the fighting from the Heights: "It is well that war is so terrible, or we should grow too fond of it." But down on the field, eyewitness Randolph Shotwell (a prophetic name) recorded a different view:

> Eleven hundred dead bodies . . . in every conceivable posture . . . some on their backs . . . here one without a head— there one without legs . . . everywhere horrible expressions . . . fear, rage, agony, madness . . . lying in pools of blood . . . lying with heads half buried in mud . . .

Dec. 17 Grant, from his Holly Springs, Miss., headquarters, issued General Order ✕11:

> The Jews, as a class violating every regulation of trade established by the Treasury Department and also department orders, are hereby expelled from the department within 24 hours from the receipt of this order.

Probably aimed at the peddlers and speculators who plagued his camps, the "Jew Order" was interpreted as a religious slur and it followed him for years. The order was immediately rescinded by Lincoln.

1863

—Ebenezer Butterick invented the paper dress pattern.

Mar. 2 Congress authorized a track width of 4'8½" as the standard for the Union Pacific R.R. This gauge became the accepted width for most of the world's railroads. Notable exceptions: Spain, Russia.

May 2 Milestone Battle: Chancellorsville. Lee won his greatest victory and lost his greatest general, "Stonewall Jackson," shot in the dark by the 33rd North Carolinians. Jackson had many strange dietary beliefs. He continually sucked lemons as a palliative for his "dyspepsia," and often supped on a simple meal of raspberries and milk. After being wounded—this cost him an arm—Jackson began to recover, but had a servant apply cold towels to relieve his persistent "dyspepsia." The moist packs encouraged both pleurisy and pneumonia, which led to his death.

July 3–4 Milestone Battle: Gettysburg, Pa. Confederate General Pickett's charge, in which he lost almost half of his 15,000 men, was largely the result of a terrible tactical error. Lee, believing the Union Army's center on Cemetery Ridge was weak, had ordered a frontal assault. Lee guessed wrong. The Union commander, Hancock, had 80 cannon and 9,000 men, well entrenched there, plus the advantage of holding higher ground. In the ensuing slaughter, 21 Union and Confederate generals were killed or wounded.

The attack began slowly, with Pickett's 3 brigades halting on the gently-sloping terrain which led down from Seminary Ridge, to assemble in parade formation. On a one-mile advance across the open field to Cemetery Ridge, Pickett's ranks were steadily decimated by rifle and artillery fire. Only a few hundred ever went the full distance up the reverse slope to reach the Union line, and they were promptly killed or captured. General Longstreet, Lee's corps commander, had told him the attack was impossible to carry out, but Longstreet was overruled. The magnificent but futile infantry charge helped to fill 17 mi. of ambulance wagons in Lee's retreat into Virginia the next day. His casualties: over 28,000.

The Gettysburg battle took place by accident. Most of Pettigrew's North Carolina brigade was marching barefoot, its shoes long since worn out. On June 30, the *Gettysburg Compiler* had blithely carried an advertisement for men's fine calf boots, Wellingtons, brogans, and other footgear. Pettigrew was ordered on a 9-mi. forced march from Cashtown to seize the shoes. The Confederate presence drew Union eyes, followed by Union skirmishers, and the inevitable full contact. Neither Lee nor Meade wanted a confrontation at Gettysburg. Meade had chosen a site near Pipe Creek. Lee preferred Harrisburg, 30 mi. away.

July 11–14 The working-class Irish of New York City touched off 4 days of riots that left hundreds dead and caused property damage of several million dollars. The conscription act, passed March 3, made money the key to exemption: For $300, a man could be passed over on a specific quota call, or he could evade the war entirely by buying a substitute who enlisted for 3 years in his place. For the Irish, to whom $300 was nearly a year's wages, neither alternative was feasible. Infuriated, they burned 2 provost-marshal offices, the Colored Orphan Asylum at 5th Avenue and 44th Street, and an entire block on Broadway. Their anger escalated into a race riot against the "nigger" they believed to be responsible for the war.

It is estimated that as many as 50,000 people took part in the fighting. The rioters injured 50 policemen—3 of whom died—and they killed 18 others, mostly blacks. Police retaliation, utilizing soldiers hastily brought in, accounted for an additional 1,200 deaths while quelling the disturbance.

In the 4 national drafts held in 1863–1864, some 776,829 names were called. Of these, 200,921 men evaded the draft by buying substitutes, and another 400,723 either paid $300 to be passed over, or were declared physically unfit for service. Voluntary enlistments, for which a bounty was paid, reduced the State draft quotas further. The 4 calls netted only 46,347 draftees, or 6% of the total draft pool.

Aug. 21 A band of gunmen, led by William C. Quantrill, known as the "Bloodiest Man in American History," invaded Lawrence, Kans., killing every man in town and burning 185 buildings despite the fact that they encountered no resistance. Quantrill's gang included Frank and Jesse James and Cole Younger and his brothers.

Sept. 20 Milestone Battle: Chickamauga, Ga. Major Bond, serving on Rosecrans's staff, wrote the garbled command order sent to General Woods that created a Union disaster. Rosecrans, riding down his division lines confronting the Confederate forces under General Bragg, noticed one regiment slightly out of position. He snapped an order to Bond: "Tell General Woods to close that gap." Bond hastily complied:

> To General Woods—
> The general commanding directs that you close up on Reynolds as fast as possible, and support him.
>
> > Bond

The order dumfounded Woods. On his left flank, General Brannan's troops were properly in line. And General Reynolds's men were in line on Brannan's left. To "close up" meant, in strict military parlance (and Woods was a West Point graduate), to eliminate any gap in a battle line. To "support" meant to take up a position behind the line, ready to advance if ordered. Bond—a non-West-Pointer—did not understand the technical distinction.

Faced with 2 orders that contradicted each other, Woods elected to support Reynolds. He pulled his troops *out* of the line of battle and marched them to the rear of General Reynolds. Within minutes, the skirmishers under command of General Longstreet, directly facing Woods's previous position, became aware of the error.

The astounded Longstreet took immediate steps. He hurled 30,000 through the gap in the Union line created by Bond's order. Only General Thomas was able to hold his position, earning the name by which he is remembered: the Rock of Chickamauga. His resistance blunted Longstreet's advance long enough to thwart total Union collapse.

—W.K.

Nov. 19   Edward Everett dedicated the Gettysburg cemetery. Also speaking: Abraham Lincoln, who was expected to say a few words.

Mr. Lincoln was suffering from a fresh case of smallpox when he delivered the most famous speech in American history. It was not diagnosed until he had made his brief appearance and rode back to Washington from Gettysburg. It was a mild case, as it happened, but the President fell ill on the train journey, and lay with a wet cloth across his brow, seeking relief.

The Address accumulated legends from the start, many of them false, like the tale that Lincoln wrote his speech on an envelope as he jostled along the rails to Gettysburg.

Lincoln wrote at least one page of the 1st draft of the speech in Washington, on White House stationery, on November 17, 1863. He added the final 9½ lines, in pencil, when he went to his bedroom in the Gettysburg home of David Wills the following evening.

On the morning of the Address, November 19, Lincoln wrote a new draft, copying the 1st, and making a few changes. There were 239 words in the 1st and 269 in the 2nd draft.

Lincoln left the Wills house for the ceremonies at 10 A.M., riding horseback in a military parade. He sat on a crowded platform facing an audience of some 15,000, a bit restless, companions noted, as Everett intoned a 2-hour oration. The President wore glasses when he rose, his little speech in hand. He glanced at the paper but once or twice and was on his feet less than 3 minutes, delivering the 10 chiseled sentences in his high, squeaky voice.

The Address began to acquire value in the marketplace early in 1864. At the request of Everett, who was prompted by Mrs. Hamilton Fish of New York, Lincoln made a copy of the speech and sent it to the Metropolitan Fair in New York, to be sold for charity. Lincoln inserted 2 words which every newspaper had quoted him as using, but which were not in the original draft: "under God." It is uncertain whether Lincoln actually spoke those words.

Lincoln later made 2 more such copies for the historian George Bancroft, to be sold at a Baltimore fair. The 1st of these copies was not auctioned because the President failed to sign it. The 2nd received some editing by Lincoln, who changed the punctuation slightly, and at one point omitted the word "here."

Of these 5 known copies, experts report, 3 have been sold commercially several times, for a total of $605,000, an average rate of about $2,225 per word, said to be the highest price ever brought by written words.

—B.D. rep.

Dec.   Edward Everett Hale's "The Man without a Country," appeared in the *Atlantic Monthly*. His inspiration: "Copperhead" Clement Laird Vallandigham, who violated General Burnside's order about declaring public sympathy for the South. After a trial, Lincoln sentenced Vallandigham to exile from the Union —and had him sent to the Confederacy. (See also: Vallandigham in Footnote People in U.S. History, Chap. 3.)

Dec. 1   Samuel Goodale, of Ohio, patented the stereopticon. His device, operated by hand, made multiple use of the magic lantern, projecting a combination of images onto a wall or screen. It introduced the 1st of the "peepshow" offerings.

1864

—The motto "In God We Trust" appeared on the 2¢ coin.

Mar. 10   Ulysses S. Grant assumed command of the Union Army.

Apr. 12   Gen. Nathan Forrest annihilated the garrison at Fort Pillow, Tenn., and set off atrocity charges that resulted in a congressional investigation. The fort was manned by 500 soldiers, half of them Negro. Forrest's cavalry— actually infantrymen who rode to their battles and dismounted to fight—were accused of killing the blacks after they had surrendered.

In his report, Forrest wrote, in his unique phonetic spelling, "We bust the fort at ninerclock and scatered the niggers. The men is still a killanem in the woods. . . ." A millionaire slave-trader and cotton planter before earning his reputation as one of the greatest soldiers of the War, Forrest traditionally gave his foe an ultimatum: Surrender unconditionally, or face being given no quarter. This practice served him badly in the Fort Pillow incident.

His most famous saying, "git thar fustest with the mostest min," exaggerates his quaint phraseology. He actually spoke and wrote clearly and graphically most of the time. But, as in his scrawled reply to the soldier who asked a 3rd time for leave, his King's English was not formally spelled: "I tole you twist, godammit know."

July 4 A Federal immigrant-labor act was passed. The law guaranteed newcomers a 12-month contract and encouraged immigration.

July 30 Milestone Battle: Petersburg, Va. Burnside's Pennsylvania regiment of coal miners dug a 586' tunnel beneath the Rebel lines at Elliott's Salient. The blasting of the tunnel, which had been packed with 8,000 lbs. of gunpowder, killed the entire 300-man garrison in the fort above. It created a crater 170' long, 80' wide, and 30' deep. The Union's black division led by General Ledlie rushed into the crater area and then halted, uncertain what to do next. While thousands of men milled around like cattle, the Rebels returned and began to fire down into the massed troops. The fiasco cost Burnside 4,000 men and his corps command.

Aug. 5 Milestone Battle: Mobile Bay, Ala. Adm. David Farragut—shouting "Damn the torpedoes! Go ahead!"—led an attack to seal off Mobile. The "torpedoes" were what now are called mines—floating casks of gunpowder with contact fuses. They were anchored in a line across the bay's entrance. A narrow passage, unmined, was left by Mobile's defenders, to permit the blockade runners to enter.

Farragut's attack force consisted of 4 ironclads, 7 wooden sloops-of-war, and 7 gunboats. To each sloop, he lashed a gunboat in tandem. The lead ironclad, *Tecumseh*, hit a "torpedo" and sank. The ship following, the *Brooklyn*, halted and began to reverse. Farragut, seeing that the *Brooklyn*'s retreat imperiled the entire line, gave his famous order, and his flagship, *Hartford*, pulled out and bypassed the *Brooklyn*. For whatever reason, the remaining "torpedoes" failed to explode, and Farragut sailed in to defeat the waiting Confederate fleet.

Nov. 8 Lincoln was reelected. Defeated Democratic candidate General McClellan received only 21 electoral votes.

Nov. 15 General Sherman left, after burning Atlanta, for his 300-mi. march to the sea. His orders:

A 7 A.M. start, 15 mi. daily.
4 columns on 4 parallel roads.
Liberal foraging.
Loading of forage as wagons moved.
Devastate where opposed.

His army cut a swath 40 to 60 mi. wide, losing only 764 men out of 62,000.

1865

—The potato chip was introduced to the U.S. by a Negro chef.
—The U.S. Post Office guaranteed free mail delivery to all cities with a minimum population of 50,000.

—William Sheppard produced soap in liquid form. He added 100 lbs. of ammonia to one lb. of regular soap, and thinned the mixture with water until it had the consistency of molasses.

—The Union Stockyards opened in Chicago. Within 10 years, the city became the world's leading meat-packing center.

Apr. A newspaper-publishing breakthrough. William Bullock produced the revolutionary printing press which utilized a continuous roll of newsprint rather than precut sheets. His automatically-fed press printed on both sides of the paper and cut the printed sheets at the proper interval. The initial model was capable of putting out 15,000 sheets per hour.

Apr. 9 General Lee surrendered to General Grant during a cordial meeting and ceremony at Appomattox Court House in Virginia. With this act there was no longer any doubt that the balance of power had shifted from the Southern plantation owners to the Northern industrialists. However, within a few years they would join forces against their common enemies, the workers and small farmers.

Apr. 11 Lincoln, Mrs. Lincoln, Col. Ward H. Lamon, a lawyer and presidential aide, and 2 other friends, were spending the evening in conversation, when Lincoln suddenly began to discuss his dreams. "I had one the other night which has haunted me ever since," he said. Mrs. Lincoln pressed him to repeat the dream. With an air of sadness, Lincoln began to recount it:

"About 10 days ago I retired very late. I had been up waiting for important dispatches from the front. I could not have been long in bed when I fell into a slumber, for I was weary. I soon began to dream. There seemed to be a deathlike stillness about me. Then I heard subdued sobs, as if a number of people were weeping. I thought I left my bed and wandered downstairs. There the silence was broken by some pitiful sobbing, but the mourners were invisible. I went from room to room; no living person was in sight, but the same mournful sounds of distress met me as I passed along. It was light in all the rooms; every object was familiar to me; but where were all the people who were grieving as if their hearts would break? I was puzzled and alarmed. What could be the meaning of all this? Determined to find the cause of a state of things so mysterious and shocking, I kept on until I arrived at the East Room, which I entered. There I met with a sickening surprise. Before me was a catafalque, on which rested a corpse wrapped in funeral vestments. Around it were stationed soldiers who were acting as guards; and there was a throng of people, some gazing mournfully upon the corpse, whose face was covered, others weeping pitifully. 'Who is dead in the White House?' I demanded of one of the soldiers. 'The President,' was his answer; 'he was killed by an assassin!' Then came a loud burst of grief from the crowd, which awoke me from my dream. I slept no more that night; and although it was only a dream, I have been strangely annoyed by it ever since."

"That is horrid!" exclaimed Mrs. Lincoln. "I wish you had not told it. I'm glad I don't believe in dreams, or I should be in terror from this time forth."

"Well, it is only a dream, Mary. Let us say no more about it, and try to forget it."

Later that night, alone, Colonel Lamon wrote a record of the conversation.

Apr. 14 Washington, D.C., was celebrating the end of the war this Good Friday. President Lincoln's schedule for the day was full: work in the office until 8; breakfast; receive business callers; meet with the Cabinet at 11; lunch; interviews in the office; a brief drive with Mrs. Lincoln; meet with Illinois friends; visit the War Department; in evening, attend a play at Ford's Theatre.

At the end of the grueling day, Lincoln considered not going to the theater. But then, aware that Mrs. Lincoln had invited General and Mrs. Grant to be their guests—and their attendance had been announced in the press—Lincoln decided to attend after all.

In his theater box that night, Lincoln and his party sat watching a 14-year-old English play, *Our Country Cousin*, starring Laura Keene. A member of the audience, Julia A. Shephard, later reported the events occurring shortly before 7:30 P.M.: "The President is in yonder upper right-hand private box so handsomely decked with silken flags festooned over a picture of George Washington. The young and lovely daughter of Senator Harris is the only one of his party we see as the flags hide the rest. But we know Father Abraham is there like a Father watching what interests his children. The American cousin has just been making love to a young lady who says she'll never marry but for love but when her mother and herself find out that he has lost his property they retreat in disgust at the left hand of the stage while the American cousin goes out at the right. We are waiting for the next scene."

The next scene took place not onstage but in the presidential box itself. Unnoticed by others, a man had slipped into the hallway behind the presidential box. He peered through a peephole he had secretly drilled that morning in the rear door opening into the box. He opened the door, stepped inside, raised his brass derringer pistol 5′ from Lincoln's head—and fired.

Just offstage, an actor, W. J. Ferguson, heard the shot and looked up. He saw "Mr. Lincoln lean back in his rocking chair, his head coming to rest against the wall which stood between him and the audience."

Slashing at another occupant of the box with a knife, the assassin, John Wilkes Booth, leaped to the stage (breaking a shinbone), dashed off into an alley, mounted a bay horse, and rode away.

Five seconds before 7:22 in the morning, Lincoln's heart stopped beating. Someone said, "Let us pray." Mrs. Lincoln cried out, "Oh my God, and I have given my husband to die!" Secretary of War Edwin Stanton said quietly, "Now he belongs to the ages."

Nov. 10 Capt. Henry Wirz, notorious commandant of the Andersonville, Ga., prisoner-of-war camp—and the only officer from this camp to be tried—was hanged for war crimes. His trial, held in Washington from August 23 to November 4, produced 2,000 pages of testimony, with the Government presenting only a part of its evidence.

Wirz was accused of establishing imaginary "dead lines"—often known only to the guards—and ordering prisoners found within them to be shot on sight (300 deaths), of sending vicious bloodhounds after escaped prisoners (50 deaths), of experimenting with deadly vaccine injections (200 deaths, 100 cases of paralysis). Because of an intensely aroused public, Wirz was brought North in disguise and under heavy guard.

In 1905, a sympathetic Southern group placed a monument to honor his memory in a deliberately chosen location: overlooking the 12,884 graves marking the former stockade.

Nov. 18 Mark Twain's "The Jumping Frog of Calaveras County" appeared in the very last issue of Henry Clapp's *The Saturday Press*. Hitherto unknown, Twain became an instant success. He had left San Francisco for the gold-mining country to avoid the San Francisco police—they were unhappy with his biting one-word epithets which ranged from "lazy" to "brutal." In the camps, he ran across a humorous incident and recorded it in his notebook:

Coleman with his jumping frog—bet stranger $50—stranger had no frog, and C. got him one—in the meantime stranger filled C's frog full of shot and he couldn't jump. The stranger's frog won.

Twain told the tale to Artemus Ward, who suggested that Twain put it down on paper and send it to Ward's publisher. Although the publisher needed extra material to fill out a thin book, he rejected the story. As an afterthought, it was sent on to editor Clapp, who accepted the piece as a funeral present for his dying literary journal, a gift which launched Twain's literary career.

Dec. 24 A new social organization appeared in Giles County, Tenn. Its name was carefully derived: "Kyklos," from the Greek word for circle, and "Klan," to reflect the Scotch-Irish nature of the community. Later, the members simplified this name to one which was an attention-getter: Ku Klux Klan. The KKK's notoriety as a white supremacy group did not come about until after the Negro was granted the right to vote. The 1st Grand Wizard: Gen. Nathan Forrest. Included in the Klan's Constitution were declarations that it was to be guided by the ideals of chivalry, mercy, humanity, and patriotism.

Dec. 26 James Nason, of Franklin, Mass., came out with a new device for brewing coffee: the percolator.

1866

—Dr. James Marion Sims, practicing at Woman's Hospital, New York City, performed the 1st artificial insemination on a female patient.
—Tammany Hall's boss, William Marcy Tweed, "bought" the State legislative assembly. Tweed's organization, using bribery and fraud, garnered illegal sums that may have amounted to $200 million in the next 6 years.
—The 1st big cattle drive took place as cowboys drove 260,000 head from Texas to Kansas, Missouri, and Iowa. In the next 20 years, between 4 and 8 million cattle were driven north. This practice was hotly opposed by Indians and farmers who lived en route, and many battles took place.
Apr. 9 Congress passed the Civil Rights Act over President Johnson's veto. Excluding the Indian, it made citizens of all native-born Americans.
May In Memphis, 46 ex-slaves were murdered in one month.
May 16 The nickel was authorized. Except for the years 1942 to 1946, its composition has always been 75% copper, 25% nickel.

1867

—Abilene, Kans., prospered as a result of J. G. McCoy's decision to establish a cattle yard there. McCoy saw the town's advantage: It was a gathering point from which Texas beef, driven north on the cattle trails, could be shipped by railroad to stockyards in meat-packing Chicago.
—"Ragged Dick" became the new American folk hero. Dick's neurotic "father," Horatio Alger, Jr., who had become a minister after an abortive fling in Paris, based the *Ragged Dick Series* on his experiences as chaplain for the Newsboy's Lodging House in Manhattan. Invariably, Alger wrote of newsboys or bootblacks

who, through virtuous effort, achieved the twin goals of riches and success. Although his "Horatio Alger" hero was perpetuated in some 120 books for boys, Alger had really wanted to write books for adults.
—A real-life financial success was Jay Gould who, at the age of 32, made a name for himself on Wall Street by printing and selling counterfeit stock in the Erie Railroad. When his fraud was discovered, Gould and his partner, Jim Fisk, slipped away to New Jersey with $6 million in cash.
Mar. 30 Alaska natives learned that 2 foreign countries had bought and sold their entire property without consulting them. Secretary of State Seward, paying slightly less than 2¢ per acre, had purchased Alaska from the Russians. Total price: $7,200,000.

"Seward's Folly," as his purchase was called, had its beginnings in the late evening hours of March 29. The Secretary was called upon at home by the Russian Minister, Baron de Stoekl, who relayed the news that Czar Alexander II was willing to sell his North American territory. Seward, who had been playing whist, began negotiations immediately, going down to his office to reopen it just before midnight. The treaty of cession was finished at 4 A.M.

The Senate ratified Seward's treaty in June. But the House did not authorize money for the purchase until July 27—it was reluctant to ease its drive for more economy in Government after the huge expenditures during the war.

The exact amount of money involved was shrouded in secrecy. Charges of bribery and secret deals were leveled, some accusers claiming that $5 million had been agreed upon and an additional $2,200,000 was unaccountably missing. Another theory: The Russians were being secretly reimbursed with some of the money for Russian fleet expenses during an 1863 demonstration of friendship in U.S. ports. These appearances, at New York and San Francisco, had been tacit warnings to England and France not to recognize the Confederacy, an action they had been considering.

The Alaska transaction was handled by the Riggs National Bank. In 1911, a memorandum was reportedly written by Franklin Lane, President Wilson's Secretary of the Interior, who claimed he had been a party to the deal in his youth while working in the Riggs bank. Lane said he had been handed 2 U.S. Treasury warrants: the 1st for $1,400,000, to purchase Alaska, and the 2nd for $5,800,000 to pay for the Russian fleet expenses.

No evidence to support the 2-warrant theory has ever been found. The warrant of record, said to be the original warrant, is dated July 29, 1868, for the amount of $7,200,000 payable to Edward de Stoekl.
Oct. In the next 8 months, railroad supplier

Bill Cody killed 4,300 buffalo, earning for himself the name "Buffalo Bill."

1868

—Charles Fleischmann of Cincinnati, O., introduced an exciting new product for the housewife: compressed fresh yeast.

Feb. 24 The House of Representatives voted to impeach President Johnson. Angered by Johnson's policies for the defeated South, House radical leaders passed laws that included the controversial Tenure of Office Act, a bill which forbade Johnson to dismiss Cabinet members without congressional approval. He promptly fired Secretary Stanton, who defied him with an office sit-in. Thaddeus Stevens, the radicals' leader, accepted the challenge and drew up 11 charges for impeachment. They were all politically motivated and, although titled "high crimes and misdemeanors," were of a trivial, vindictive nature.

In the Senate hearing, staged as a trial with Chief Justice Salmon P. Chase presiding, 8 of the charges were speedily voted down. On the 2nd, 3rd, and 11th charges, accusing Johnson of violating the Tenure of Office Act, the Senate voted 35–19 for conviction, one vote short of the constitutionally-required ⅔ needed for removal from office.

The trial lasted 11½ weeks. Some witnesses for Johnson were kept out of court, others were offered bribes. Benjamin Wade, the President *pro tempore* of the Senate and 1st in line to succeed Johnson if the President were convicted was allowed to vote as a member of the Senate jury. Wade was so sure that the President would be removed that he had already chosen the men he wanted in his Cabinet.

The Tenure of Office Act was declared unconstitutional in 1926 by the Supreme Court. But it was too late to save the political careers of 7 Republican senators who followed their consciences and voted for acquittal: Grimes (Ia.), Trumbull (Ill.), Ross (Kans.), Van Winkle (W.Va.), Fessenden (Me.), Fowler (Tenn.), and Henderson (Mo.).

Mar 21 "Sorosis," the 1st professional club for women, was founded in New York City by English-born journalist Jane Cunningham "Jennie June" Croly. Later she helped to found the Federation of Women's Clubs.

June 23 A new machine called the "typewriter" was assigned patent #79265. Conceived by Christopher Latham Sholes in 1867, the design resembled a miniature piano with 2 rows of black walnut keys. Its letters, painted on the keys in white, were all capitals, and there were other keys for numbers 2 through 9, plus a comma and a period. Sholes coined

the name for the invention. To test the "typewriter" for efficiency, his friend, Charles Weller, created the sentence, "Now is the time for all good men to come to the aid of the country."

1869

—H. J. Heinz organized a food-packing company to market the 1st of his "57" varieties: horseradish.

Jan. Comanche Chief Toch-a-way met Gen. Philip Sheridan at Fort Cobb, Mo. To the Indian's initial greeting of friendship, "Me good Indian," Sheridan is reported to have replied, "The only good Indian is a dead Indian."

Feb. 6 *Harper's Weekly* published a new cartoon version of "Uncle Sam." He now had chin whiskers.

May 10 At Promontory Point, Utah, a silver sledge slammed a golden spike into a railroad tie, completing the transcontinental railroad. Built in just over 3 years, by 20,000 workmen, it had 1,775 mi. of track. The railroad's promoters had been given 23 million acres of land and $64 million in loans as an incentive.

May 24 One-armed, 110-lb. John Wesley Powell set out to map the last unsurveyed and unexplored frontier in the U.S.: the Grand Canyon of the Colorado. His party of 10 men left Green River City in 4 customized boats, strengthened to withstand the river's treacherous rapids: the *Emma Dean*, named for the cousin he married, the *Maid of the Canyon*, *Kitty Clyde's Sister*, and *No Name*. Two weeks later, he lost *No Name* in an accident and continued with 3 boats. Frank Goodman, the English adventurer who joined the party on a whim, changed his mind and left in the early stages of the expedition. Three others (Billy Dean and 2 brothers—O. G. and Seneca Howlands) decided to climb out by a side canyon at Separation Rapid. They were met by a band of Shivwits Indians and killed. Powell abandoned their boat, the *Emma Dean*. At the junction of the Virgin River, Powell greeted the 3 Mormons who had been sent by Brigham Young to watch for him, and he considered his epic journey over. Four of his party, still enthused with the adventure, continued on: 2 (Sumner and Bradley) stopped at Fort Yuma, Ariz., and the others (Hawkins and Hall) took the last boat all the way to salt water at the Gulf of California. Three times during the 101-day trip through 1,000 mi. of torrents and rapids Powell was erroneously reported as having been killed.

Sept. 6 A fire broke out in the only shaft of the Avondale Mine in Luzerne County, Pa., and 175 men died because the mine owners had not constructed a safety exit. John Siney of the Workingmen's Benevolent Association spoke to friends and relatives at the mine gate: "Men, if you must die with your boots on, die for your families, your homes, your country, but do no longer consent to die like rats in a trap for those who have no more interest in you than in the pick you dig with."

Sept. 24 Black Friday in Wall Street. James Fisk and Jay Gould plotted to corner the gold market. They hoped to buy all the $15 million of gold then in circulation and thus drive up its price. The conspiracy failed when President Grant ordered additional government gold sold by the U.S. Treasury in the open market. However, Gould's Administration spies (including Grant's brother-in-law) leaked news of Grant's decision, and Gould was still able to clear a profit of $11 million.

—W.K.

1870

—U.S. population—38,558,371.
—Between 1870 and 1880, 3 million immigrants came to the U.S.
—Between 1870 and 1880, one million buffalo were slaughtered annually.
—A total of 300,000 nonfarm workers belonged to 33 labor unions.
—Approximately 72,000 church congregations were reported in existence.
—John D. Rockefeller and his associates founded the Standard Oil Company of Ohio. It was capitalized at $1 million.

Feb. The Beach pneumatic subway system was unveiled in New York City. The brainchild of Alfred Ely Beach, the tiny system consisted of a round tube, 9' in diameter and 312' long, running beneath the center of Broadway. Its only car carried 22 passengers and was powered by air—a giant blower propelled the vehicle to the end of the line, and then "drew" it back to the beginning when a wire, tripped by the car, reversed the huge fan. Top speed: about 10 mph.

Beach's idea was not just a whim. By 1870, New York City had become jammed with over 700,000 people. The surface streets were so choked with horse-drawn vehicles that traffic was brought to a standstill. Beach—even then well-known as the inventor of the pneumatic tube, the cable railway, and the hydraulic tunneling bore—actually proposed to extend his line from the initial station, near the Manhattan end of the Brooklyn Bridge, to Central Park, nearly 5 mi. away. He claimed his system would handle 20,000 passengers daily at speeds up to 60 mph, and could be built for $5 million.

The corrupt politicians at Tammany Hall had given Beach permission to build only a small pneumatic mail tube, to test his system's practicality for New York's needs. Knowing that his new system could break Boss Tweed's monopoly on surface transportation, Beach kept the work on his gigantic underground "mailing tube" a complete secret. Work went on stealthily, for 58 nights, with the dirt being hauled off in bags by wagons with wheels muffled to insure silence. His men came and went like thieves.

During the subway's debut, astonished New Yorkers visited a waiting room that was furnished with elegant paintings, frescoed walls, a grand piano, and a water fountain. Over 400,000 rode in its tiny car during the next 12 months, earning Beach well over $100,000. Although defeated eventually in his grandiose pneumatic scheme, Alfred Beach is given credit as the father of the present 726 mi. New York City subway system.

Feb. 25 Mississippi sent a new senator to the U.S. Congress. He was Senator Hiram R. Revels, the 1st black man ever to sit in the Senate.

May 30 The 1st "Force Act" was passed by Congress in order to prevent violations of the 14th and 15th Amendments. It established Federal supervision of elections, proscribed State officials' employment of race as a discriminatory franchise test, and prohibited the use of force, bribery, or threat during Federal elections.

July 16

> Look at me, I am poor and naked, but I am the Chief of the Nation. We do not want riches, we do not seek riches, but we want our children properly trained and brought up. Our riches will do us no good; we cannot take away into the other world anything we have.
> —Red Cloud, chief of the largest tribe of the Teton Sioux nation

Dec. For the 1st time in U.S. history, a State governor was impeached and found guilty. The unpopular Gov. William W. Holden was found guilty of high crimes and misdemeanors by the North Carolina State legislature and removed from office.

Dec. 28 Boss Tweed was forced to resign as New York commissioner of public works. During his 20-year career in city and State politics, which included a stint as State senator and one as chairman of the New York board of supervisors, Tweed gained control of New York City Democratic politics and became chief of the Tammany Hall machine. He and his cronies embezzled possibly as much as $200 million from various public projects until their operations were exposed by *Harper's Weekly*. Tweed was charged with felonious misappropriation of public funds and brought to trial, but the jury failed to reach a verdict. After a 2nd trial, he was found guilty and imprisoned in the Ludlow Street jail in New York City. He served a one-year sentence, was released, and then was arrested once more on new charges. In December, 1875, he escaped to Cuba and took a steamer from there to Spain, where he was identified through a Thomas Nast caricature of him in an old *Harper's* magazine. He was extradited to the U.S., where he died in New York's Ludlow Street prison 2 years later.

1871

—A Vermont tanner invented a process of tanning buffalo hide, which made it commercially usable. In 1872, the slaughter began. With government approval, marksmen and skinners moved in, and by 1878 the great southern buffalo herd, estimated at 10 million head, had been wiped out. Then the hunters moved north and slaughtered another 5 million. The hunters often moved onto Indian land. If the Indians objected and drove the hunters out, the Army would come in and destroy all of the Indians' possessions, forcing them to surrender or face the elements, without homes, horses, food, or tools. Between 1860 and 1889, the number of Great Plains buffalo was reduced from 50 million to 551.
—Walt Whitman's *Democratic Vistas* was published.
—John Pierpont Morgan established the New York concern of Drexel, Morgan and Company. In 1895, it became J. P. Morgan and Company. Meanwhile Morgan had had his hand in railroads, banking, shipping, steel, coal, utilities, and insurance as well. After the turn of the century, he founded the U.S. Steel Corporation, the 1st $1 billion corporation in the world. It controlled 70% of the nation's iron and steel business.
—P. T. Barnum opened his circus in Brooklyn, billing it as "The Greatest Show on Earth."
Jan. Virginia Woodhull presented a petition to Congress demanding enfranchisement of women under the 14th Amendment. Her presentation brought her considerable public acclaim, but the petition was denied.
Feb. 28 The 2nd "Force Act" was passed by Congress, providing that State and congressional elections be brought under control of Federal supervisors.
Mar. Smith College for women opened.
Mar. 3 An act was passed changing the status

of Indian tribes and nations from that of independent powers with whom the Government must contract by treaty, to that of dependents, to be governed by legislation or executive order.
Apr. 20 President Grant signed into law a 3rd "Force Act," also known as the Ku Klux Klan Act. It gave the President military powers, which included suspension of *habeas corpus* in order to stamp out terrorism.
May 11–12 Suffragist anniversary celebrated in New York's Apollo Hall. Virginia Woodhull spoke of "The New Rebellion":

> If the very next Congress refuses women all the legitimate results of citizenship, we shall proceed to call another convention expressly to frame a new constitution and erect a new Government. . . . We mean treason! . . . We are plotting Revolution! We will overthrow this bogus republic and plant a Government of righteousness in its stead!

Oct. 8–9 A fire which started in a stable on Chicago's west side rampaged through the city, destroying $200 million worth of property and leaving it in total ruin. Over 90,000 people were homeless and 3 died. The original draft of Lincoln's Emancipation Proclamation was consumed by these flames. (See also: Man-Made Disasters, Chap. 9.) The same night of the Chicago fire, the logging town of Peshtigo, Wis., caught fire, killing about 1,150 persons.
Oct. 9 Mormon leader Brigham Young appeared in court to face charges of practicing polygamy and committing murder.
Oct. 24 Anti-Chinese riots raged through the pueblo of Los Angeles. When an interclan dispute—a struggle between 2 rival tongs over possession of a slave woman—erupted into street fighting, Chinatown's Nigger Alley residents barricaded themselves behind their doors for 2 days while revolvers blazed and bombs exploded in the streets. Large, uneasy crowds gathered at the edges of the Chinese neighborhoods, afraid that the fighting might spread into the rest of the town. The town marshal was called in. When a deputized bystander was caught in the crossfire and killed, hundreds of armed white citizens rushed into Nigger Alley seeking revenge. Twenty-three Chinese men were lynched by the rampaging mobs. One riot spectator, P. S. Dorney, wrote: "The mob was in a state of frenzy over the famine of rope. 'Rope, more rope!' was hoarsely howled upon all sides. and—let humanity blush—a woman, a married one, and a mother, rushed to appease the human tigers with her clothesline." An elderly Chinese doctor pleaded for his life in English and Spanish, offering his executors a bribe of $15,000 if they would spare him. The doctor was hung on the makeshift gallows

and the crowd made away with his money. A valuable diamond ring he wore on his index finger was also found missing—along with his finger. When the violence spree ended, 30 Chinese had been hanged, shot, or stabbed to death, and countless others were wounded. A large part of Nigger Alley was gutted as the result of arson.

1872

—There are thousands on thousands in New York who have no assignable home and flit from attic to attic and cellar to cellar; there are other thousands more or less connected with criminal enterprises, and still other tens of thousands, poor, hard-pressed, and depending for daily bread on the day's earnings, swarming in tenement houses, who behold the gilded rewards of toil all about them but are never permitted to touch them.

—Charles Loring Brace,
social reformer

—Montgomery Ward began its mail-order business.

—S.W.
Sept. In New York and Philadelphia men were seen harnessed to carts and trolleys, pulling them along streets. In Boston a great fire wiped out the downtown area with a loss of over $80 million. In cities across the country, homes went without heat, garbage went uncollected . . . public transportation ceased, deliveries halted . . . stores closed, unemployment soared. .

The Great Epizootic of 1872 had struck and America was without the power it needed to function—most power at the time being horse power.

An epizootic is a disease prevalent in one kind of animal and in this case an unknown equine virus had been imported via Canada. The disease hit in epidemic proportions, claiming almost a quarter of the nation's horses—some 4 million in all before it ran its course. As a result, America suffered a shock that helped bring on the Panic of 1873.

From the time the Great Epizootic struck in late September until the day the last horse died, 19th-century medical science was unable to provide veterinarians with any method to stem the disease. The doctors were powerless against the deadly virus which strangely enough, seemed to strike hardest at horses stabled in the urban areas. Within a month, 200 horses a day were dying in New York City, and metropolitan newspapers devoted their front pages to the Great Epizootic. New York was virtually shut down, transportation and deliveries almost at a standstill, unemployed transit workers pulling trolleys down the street. Belmont Park and other racetracks closed their gates, and one great American thoroughbred, *Pocahontas*, fell to the disease.

In Buffalo, Rochester, and Syracuse, the situation was just as bad and soon outbreaks were reported in southern cities, including New Orleans, Atlanta, and Savannah. Some southern cities escaped without much damage, but in Washington, D.C., all mail service had to be discontinued and street railways were closed down.

Yet in no city were the results worse than in Boston. On November 9, a fire broke out in the downtown section and few horses were available to move fire-fighting equipment to the scene, over ⅔ of them being dead or incapacitated by the disease. Oxen were used in place of horses and the 1st steam-powered fire engine was tried in this fire, but they were employed too late to be of any real use. The fire had a good start and raged for 3 days, resulting in the destruction of 600 buildings, property damage of more than $75 million.

The Boston fire scared people, and scientists were urged to work even harder to find the cause of the Great Epizootic. But the virus was never isolated. The disease continued taking its toll until well into December, when really cold weather set in and suddenly ended its ravages. Only later did scientists learn that cold weather had killed the mosquitos that transmitted the deadly virus.

—R.H.
Nov. 5 U. S. Grant was reelected President over his opponent Horace Greeley. Susan B. Anthony and other suffragettes were arrested for attempting to vote in Rochester, N.Y.

1873

—The National Granger movement, responding to the farmers' plight of small profits and high costs, listed some 800,000 members in 4 States.

—John Henry, a black railroad worker whose almost mythical strength made him a legend in his lifetime, died while working on the construction of the Big Bend Tunnel in West Virginia. A symbol to his fellow workers of the supremacy of man over machine, he probably was the inspiration for a ballad that gained quick popularity throughout the country.

—President White of Cornell University refused to allow his college's football squad to travel to Cleveland for a game against Michigan. Said President White: "I will not permit

30 men to travel 400 mi. to agitate a bag of wind."

Jan. 17 Four hundred Federal troops were routed by Modoc Indians in the lava beds of Northern California. During the Civil War, white settlers had poured into the Tule Lake area, occupying the lands of the Modoc tribe. The Modocs put up continued resistance. A government attempt to move them into the southern Oregon Klamath reservation was unsuccessful. The tribal members, denied promised food and tools, were facing starvation and they refused to be exiled from their old hunting grounds. They foiled an ambush set by the U.S. 1st Cavalry and moved into their old volcanic sanctuary in the California lava beds. In this eerie setting of volcanic cones and subterranean caves, they carved out a stronghold and waged a successful guerrilla war for several months against State and Federal troops.

On Good Friday, U.S. General Canby led a group of Federal commissioners to the lava beds to urge immediate surrender. "The Modoc law is dead; the white man's law rules the country now; only one law lives at a time," one commissioner announced, after he had passed out cigars. Captain Jack, the chief of the Modoc tribe, responded with a bullet through Canby's chest. Two months later, Captain Jack was tried and hung for the General's murder. The Modoc chief's mummified body turned up on the East Coast as a carnival exhibit. By July, Federal troops finally defeated the Modocs and the survivors were exiled to Indian Territory. In 1909, the Government allowed the 50 remaining Modocs to return to an Oregon reservation.

May 7 U.S. Marines landed in Panama to protect American lives and property.

Sept. 18 The Panic of 1873. Unbridled railroad speculation, combined with overextended credit, had severely weakened the U.S. financial structure. When the leading American banking company, managed by government agent Jay Cooke, suddenly declared bankruptcy, the stock market plummeted. The New York Stock Exchange closed its doors by the end of the month. That year alone, 5,183 businesses worth a total of over $200 million failed. The nation suffered a heavy depression that lasted until 1877. Throughout industry, wages were cut by more than 25%, and approximately one million industrial workers were left unemployed.

Dec. 7 A race riot broke out in Vicksburg, Miss., leaving 75 blacks dead.

Dec. 12 A procession of the unemployed marched through Chicago.

1874

—The worst grasshopper plague in U.S. history scourged the Great Plains from the Dakotas to northern Texas.

—The discovery of gold brought thousands of gold seekers into the Black Hills reservation in the Dakota Territory.

—The Woman's Christian Temperance Union was founded. The 1st president had been an active member of the Civil War Sanitary Commission.

Jan. 13 Police attacked a meeting of unemployed workmen in Tompkins Square in New York City. Hundreds were injured.

Feb. 13 American troops landed in Honolulu, Hawaii, to protect the King.

Mar. 11 Sen. Charles Sumner of Massachusetts, prominent abolitionist and fiery leader of the radical Republican forces in the Congress, died. Frederick Douglass was present at his deathbed. From 1870 until his death, Sumner had tried without success to pass legislation to desegregate the public schools.

July 1 Headline in the *Philadelphia Inquirer:* "A MYSTERY." The story: "On Wednesday last, Charley Brewster Ross, aged 4 years and his brother, aged 6, sons of Christian K. Ross, were playing in a lane in the rear of their residence, Germantown, when a wagon containing 2 men drove up, and at their invitation the children got in for the purpose of taking a ride. The vehicle was driven off and the oldest boy was . . . put out of the carriage, but Charley, the youngest, is still missing. The former states that he had been given some money by one of the men to buy shooting crackers, and that he started for the store for that purpose, but when he returned, the carriage and his little brother were missing."

The abduction of Charley Ross was America's 1st major kidnapping for ransom. The 2 kidnappers asked $20,000. Ross's fairly wealthy father, determined not "to compound a felony," refused to pay it. P. T. Barnum came forward, offering to pay the ransom if he could exhibit Charley Ross once the boy was released. Barnum's offer was ignored. Later, the elder Ross tried to negotiate with the kidnappers through classified ads, but following police advice, he continued to withhold the ransom. The kidnappers were trapped during a robbery and were both shot to death. Little Charley Ross was never found.

Aug. 21 The highest paid preacher in America, the Rev. Henry Ward Beecher, pastor of the wealthy Plymouth Church in Brooklyn, was sued by newspaper editor Theodore Tilton for

$100,000 for alienation of his wife's affections. Tilton claimed that his young wife, Elizabeth, grieving over the death of their son, had gone to her pastor's house for consolation and there "she had surrendered her body to him in sexual embrace; that she had repeated such an act on the following Saturday evening at her own residence . . . that she had consequently upon those 2 occasions repeated such acts at various times, at his residence and at hers, and at other places . . ."

On trial, the Reverend Beecher admitted platonic friendship, denied adultery. After a 112-day trial, the jury balloted 52 times and then gave up (with a vote of 9 to 3 for Beecher). The hung jury saved Beecher and restored him to his worshipful flock, although the Louisville Courier-Journal branded him "a dunghill covered with flowers."

Nov. 7 The Republican party elephant was born—in a Thomas Nast cartoon in Harper's Weekly attacking a possible 3rd term for Republican President U.S. Grant.

1875

—The Molly Maguires, a secret terrorist organization developed by the Irish miners of the Pennsylvania anthracite coal mines to fight the mine operators, was infiltrated and exposed by a Pinkerton spy in the pay of the coal companies. Charged with blackmail and making threats on the lives of mine bosses and officials, 19 Molly Maguires were found guilty and hung, while an additional number were imprisoned. The organization, in existence since 1854, was effectively destroyed.

Mar. 1 A bill written by Charles Sumner, the last civil rights law of the Reconstruction Era, was passed. Its intent was to accord to all citizens the full and equal use and enjoyment of public accommodations and places of public amusement. Violators of the anti-segregation ruling, including officers of the courts and jurors, were subject to heavy fines and imprisonment.

May 5 The nation reeled at the exposure of yet another public scandal when the Whiskey Ring was uncovered and brought to public attention. An association of distillers and Federal officials had been defrauding the Government of a large slice of the tax revenue, part of which was used to bribe other public officials and finance lobbying activity. A number of Grant appointees were indicted, including the President's secretary.

May 17 The running of the 1st Kentucky Derby. The race was created by Col. M. Lewis Clark, of Louisville, Ky., who 3 years earlier had been impressed by watching the Epsom Downs Derby in England. With a group of friends, Clark acquired a parcel of land in Kentucky from the Churchill brothers, laid out a track, constructed a grandstand. He named his creation Churchill Downs.

The initial Kentucky Derby had a fast track, 15 entries, and a purse of $2,850. The favorite was H. Price McGrath's entry of stretch-runner Chesapeake and sprinter Aristides. The strategy was for Aristides to set the pace for a mile, and then let Chesapeake come on in a closing rush to win. With the drop of the flag, the 1½-mi. race was under way. As the horses came into the backstretch, Aristides led, followed by Ten Broeck and Volcano, with Chesapeake right behind. Entering the stretch, Chesapeake was given the signal to go. He failed to go. Owner McGrath, dismayed, waved frantically to Jockey Lewis aboard Aristides to make the run for the roses himself. Under a strong ride, Aristides drove to the finish line, clinging to the lead, to win by a nose.

1876

—Mark Twain's The Adventures of Tom Sawyer was published, sold by subscription, and became a best seller. It was banned by the Denver Public Library.

—Baseball's National League was founded. Before the organization of the National League, amateur games were riddled with extralegal practices such as bribery and betting. The creation of professional teams, subject to one set of enforceable rules, resulted from the foundation of the League.

—The annual Republican National Convention was held. Frederick Douglass addressed the assembled party members:

What does it amount to if the black man, after having been made free by the letter of your law . . . is to be subject to the slaveholder's shotgun? . . . The question now is, do you mean to make good to us the promises in your Constitution?

Feb. 14 Alexander Graham Bell patented the telephone.

Mar. 2 The Judiciary Committee of the U.S. House of Representatives recommended the impeachment of Secretary of War William W. Belknap on 5 charges, one of which read that Belknap did "willfully, corruptly, and unlawfully take and receive from one Caleb P. Marsh the sum of $1,500, in consideration that he would continue to permit one John S. Evans to maintain a trading establishment at Fort Sill, a military post of the U.S. . . ." The House voted to send articles of impeachment to the

Senate. Although Belknap had already resigned his office, the Senate tried him and found him Not Guilty.

May The nation celebrated its Centennial Anniversary with a $10 million International Exhibition held in Philadelphia. The fairgrounds covered 236 acres and contained hundreds of exhibits dedicated to American social, industrial and cultural progress. On the opening day, President Grant and his invited guest, Dom Pedro, the Emperor of Brazil, the 1st major foreign potentate ever to visit the U.S., promenaded to the grandstand to the strains of the "Grand Centennial March," composed especially for the occasion by Richard Wagner. One thousand singers chanted John Greenleaf Whittier's "Centennial Hymn." At the start of the welcoming speech to Dom Pedro, 5 women, including Susan B. Anthony, rushed to the speaker's podium and presented a declaration of women's rights, completely disrupting the proceedings.

June 25 The 2nd Sioux War was sparked by a gold rush into Dakota territories, as well as the extension of the route of the Northern Railroad. The Secretary of War had warned of serious trouble if nothing were done "legally" to obtain possession of the Dakotas "for the white miners who have been strongly attracted there by reports of the precious metal."

The President sent in troops led by 36-year-old Gen. George A. Custer—he had been a Brigadier General at the age of 23, despite the fact that he had been last in his class at West Point—to search out and destroy the local Sioux, who were led by Sitting Bull and Crazy Horse. On the afternoon of this day, in a ravine of the Little Big Horn River in Montana, General Custer and his 5 companies of the U.S. 7th Cavalry were ambushed by Sitting Bull's 3,500 Sioux and Cheyenne braves. In a fierce 3-hour battle, Custer and his 266 officers, enlisted men, and guides were wiped out.

Sitting Bull later recalled Custer's death: "Where the last stand was made, the Long Hair stood like a sheaf of corn with all the ears fallen around him." Custer's corpse was later found stripped naked, a bullet through his brain, another through his chest. The only living thing to survive the massacre was Capt. Myles Keogh's horse, *Comanche*, who, despite 7 bullet wounds, reached the age of 28. (The oldest horse in today's U.S. Army is *Black Jack*, who was 28 in 1975 and who was the riderless horse in the funerals of President Hoover, General MacArthur, President Kennedy.) *Comanche*'s mounted body may be seen in the Kansas State University Museum, in Lawrence, Kans.

One of the legends of American history is that not one human being survived Custer's Last Stand. Yet for Custer's 266 presumed dead—there were only 260 bodies. What happened to the other 6? The bodies of these 6—3 lieutenants, 2 enlisted men, one doctor—were never found nor were the men heard of again. They were listed as missing in action. In his study of Little Big Horn, the historian Charles Kuhlman reported the end of the massacre:

> At last the [soldiers'] shots ceased to come from behind the dead horses. The Indians near them ran forward, shouting to those farther back that all the soldiers were dead. To their surprise, 6 men jumped up and ran away toward the river, getting over the cutbank before any of them could be killed. Both Wooden Leg and Kate Bighead saw these men run away, but the ridge shut them from sight of the former at once and he saw nothing further of them . . . Kate Bighead could see them until they disappeared in the smoke and dust with hundreds of Cheyennes and Sioux after them, but she did not see what became of them.

Years later, the Indians reported the rumor that these 6 had killed themselves to avoid capture. Army historians speculated that they were probably captured by the Indians and tortured to death. The Army wrote them off as being among Custer's 266 killed in the Last Stand.

But the mystery remains. Besides Custer, 266 men—but only 260 bodies. And the remaining 6 bodies never discovered. Suicides? Tortured to death? Maybe—yet, the surrounding area was combed clean for months and years after, and not a trace of an additional corpse, skeleton, or grave was ever found.

Oct. 31 The victorious Sioux, led by Sitting Bull and Crazy Horse, were finally defeated and forced to surrender.

1877

—The largest puffball mushroom ever recorded was discovered in a New York pasture. At a distance it was mistaken for a sheep.

Jan. 4 Cornelius Vanderbilt died, having made a $100-million fortune in his lifetime. The wily captain of industry began his career as a captain of a ferryboat, then went on to make $10 million in the steamboat industry during the Civil War. After the war, he increased his profits with railroad investments. Vanderbilt provided the capital to build the New York Central Railroad, which opened in 1873 with the 1st train route between New

York and Chicago. He also financed the 1st female-managed stock brokerage firm in history, the Wall Street concern of Woodhull and Claflin. Vanderbilt met the young Victoria Woodhull and her sister Tennie shortly after their arrival in New York, and he helped them capture the public's eye, supplying them with capital and inside market tips. Woodhull and her associates used the profits to publish an anti-capitalist "free love" news weekly, and to launch an anarcho-feminist presidential campaign. Vanderbilt, his wife later apologized, had a strange sense of humor and was a great admirer of spunk.

Feb. 27 The Electoral Commission announced Rutherford Hayes as the winner of the Hayes-Tilden presidential contest.

Apr. 10 President Hayes began withdrawal of Federal troops from the occupied South, signaling the end of the Reconstruction Period.

July 16 What became the 1st American general strike started in the little railroad town of Martinsburg, W.Va. The Baltimore and Ohio Railroad announced a 10% wage cut, the 2nd in 8 months and the 4th such reduction since 1870. Railroad workers countered the measure by blocking the passage of trains through Martinsburg pending rescinding of the order. Local police were called in to disperse the strikers but were forced to withdraw. Railroad officials requested that the governor of the State send in State militia. The Berkeley Light Guards were ordered to the occupied station, but as most of them were railroaders, they joined with the crowd of strikers instead of dispersing them. A new shipment of State militia was rebuffed.

When news of the success at Martinsburg was circulated, the shutdown rapidly spread to all other divisions of the B. and O. In response, President Hayes ordered 300 troops to suppress what his Secretary of War was publicly labeling "an insurrection." Local people—working men as well as the unemployed—came to the aid of the strikers. The Pennsylvania Railroad ordered a doubleheader (a speedup) and resistance increased. In Pittsburgh, 26 strikers were killed and an angry mob retaliated by tearing up railroad tracks and burning down machine shops and the Union depot. Police stood by as hundreds of people broke into the idle freight cars in the yards and distributed their contents to the crowd. Nine workers were killed in further rioting in Martinsburg. The general strike spread through Chicago, New York, and St. Louis, where the employees of a beef cannery joined the railroaders. Then workers in steel foundries, flour mills, bagging companies, sugar refineries, chemical and lead works also joined in. In many cases, workers resumed production for themselves and distributed the goods they produced.

The Great Upheaval was finally put down by the use of military force. Wage concessions were won in a number of cases. The vast, spontaneous, and cooperative effort was the 1st occurrence of worker occupation of businesses and blue-collar self-management in the U.S.

1878

—Edison took out a patent on the phonograph.

—A new vehicle, called "Wheels," appeared in the streets of America. It consisted of a large wheel in front and a small wheel in back, and had a connecting bar and pad upon which the rider could seat himself while he pedaled precariously forward. This was the forerunner of the modern bicycle.

Jan. 3 Dennis Kearney led a procession of the unemployed to city hall in San Francisco to demand work or bread.

1879

—The 1st telephone line connecting 2 American cities went up, and thereafter Boston and Lowell, Mass., were in communication.

—A reporter cornered William H. Vanderbilt, head of the New York Central Railroad, demanding an interview and stating that the public was waiting for one. Vanderbilt brushed past him, snapping the immortal words, "The public be damned!"

—In his 2nd effort to establish a low-priced shopping center, Frank W. Woolworth finally succeeded with a flourishing 5-and-10-cent store in Lancaster, Pa.

—S.W.

1880

—U.S. population—50,155,783.

—Between 1880 and 1890, 5,246,613 immigrants entered the U.S.

—There is no such thing in America as an independent press, unless it is in the small towns . . . The business of the New York journalist is to destroy the truth, to lie outright, to pervert, to vilify, to fawn at the feet of Mammon, and to sell his race and his country for his daily bread. . . . We are the tools and vassals of rich men behind the scenes. We are the jumping jacks; they pull the strings and we dance. Our talents, our

possibilities and our lives are all the property of other men. We are intellectual
prostitutes.

—John Swinton, labor editor
& journalist

—Two popular books published: *Ben-Hur* by
Lew Wallace, governor of New Mexico Territory, and *Five Little Peppers and How They
Grew* by Margaret Sidney, pseudonym for
Harriet Mulford Stone Lothrop. Both sold over
500,000 copies in the 1st decade after publication.
Nov. 8 Sarah Bernhardt made her U.S. stage
debut in 4 plays, one of them *La Dame aux
Camélias*, at Booth's Theater, N.Y. The greatest actress of her time, the Divine Sarah made
2 more acting trips to the U.S., the last in
1915, when she was 70 and had suffered the
amputation of one leg.
Nov. 17 Unlimited immigration of Chinese
to U.S. ended because of tensions created in
West by cheap coolie labor. A treaty was signed
in Peking in which the U.S. promised not to
ban Chinese but to "regulate, limit, or suspend" their entry to the Land of the Free.

1 8 8 1

—Tennessee enacted 1st Jim Crow law segregating railroad coaches—this provided for "separate but equal" 1st-class coaches for blacks
instead of no 1st class for blacks at all.

Whoever controls the volume of money
in any country is master of all its legislation and commerce.

—President Garfield

—Clara Barton, 8 years after her return to
U.S. from Europe, founded the American National Red Cross in Washington, D.C., and
was its president for the next 23 years.
—Helen Hunt Jackson, later renowned for
her novel *Ramona*, foreshadowed Dr. Spock
with publication of a handbook entitled, *The
Training of Children*.
July 2 President Garfield was shot by Charles
Guiteau, a disgruntled office-seeker, in a Washington, D.C., railroad station.
July 19 After the Canadian Government refused to provide them with a reservation, Sitting Bull and the Sioux Indians returned to the
U.S. The U.S. Army had promised to pardon
Sitting Bull if he returned, but instead they
held him in a military prison for 2 years.
Aug. 31 Richard D. Sears won the 1st men's
singles tennis championship under auspices of
the newly created U.S. Lawn Tennis Association.

Sept. 5

The interests, commercial and political, of the U.S., on this continent, transcend in extent and importance those of
any other power.

—Secretary of State James Blaine

Sept. 19 After clinging to life for 2½ months,
President Garfield died. He was succeeded by
Vice-President Chester A. Arthur the following
day.

1 8 8 2

—"Opening" of Korea.
—*Pace* v. *Alabama*—Supreme Court ruled that
an Alabama law providing severer punishment
for illegal interracial sexual intercourse than for
illegal sexual intercourse in which both parties
were of the same race did not violate the equal
protection clause of the 14th Amendment.
Jan. 2 Through legal chicanery, Samuel C. T.
Dodd, attorney for John D. Rockefeller, circumvented current anti-monopoly laws by creating the Standard Oil Trust, a powerful car-
tel.
Jan. 3 Under the auspices of Richard D'Oyly
Carte, producer of the Gilbert and Sullivan
comic operettas, 28-year-old Oscar Wilde,
playwright, poet, wit, set foot on American
soil, having sailed from Liverpool for a coast-to-
coast lecture tour. "Have you anything to declare?" asked the customs inspector. "Nothing," said Wilde, "nothing but my genius."
The lecture tour grossed £4,000, of which
Wilde got £1,200. Ready to board his Cunard
ship for England 12 months later, Wilde was
asked his opinion of the average American.
The average American? "For him Art has no
marvel, and Beauty no meaning, and the Past
no message."
Apr. 3 Bank robber Jesse James was shot and
killed by a member of his own gang at St.
Joseph, Mo.
May 6 Congress passed the Chinese Exclusion
Act, suspending entry into U.S. of all Chinese
laborers for 10 years. The next year Chinese
immigration plummeted by ⅘, down to a mere
8,000.
Sept. 4 Edison switched on 1st commercial
electric lights in New York Central Station.

1 8 8 3

—The *Ladies' Home Journal* magazine was
founded.
—Joseph Pulitzer bought the *New York World*
from Jay Gould, converted it into a successful

2¢ mass newspaper through sensationalism and comic strips. Circulation soared from 20,000 to 250,000 in 4 years. Nine years after Pulitzer's death in 1911, 38-year-old Herbert Bayard Swope became the paper's crusading editor. The new *World* gave the public Rollin Kirby, H. T. Webster, Walter Lippmann, Heywood Broun, F.P.A., Dorothy Parker, Frank Sullivan.

> —I regard my employees as I do a machine, to be used to my advantage, and when they are old and of no further use, I cast them into the street.
> —Manufacturer to Samuel Gompers

—U.S. businessmen began maneuvering for open access to a free market in the Congo.
—Hiram S. Maxim, a 43-year-old American, successfully demonstrated his invention of a single-barreled gun that automatically loaded, fired, ejected cartridges by means of recoil force. This was the prototype of the modern-day machine gun. Maxim later moved to England, where he was knighted.
Mar. 3 Since the U.S. had dropped to 12th among world sea powers, Congress voted funds for the building of 3 new cruisers, the 1st warships built since the Civil War.
Mar. 24 The 1st telephone line connected New York and Chicago.
June 24 Umpire Richard Higham was expelled from the National Baseball League for dishonesty. He was the only umpire ever thrown out of the major leagues.
Nov. 3 The U.S. Supreme Court ruled that Indians are by birth aliens and dependents.
Nov. 26 Isabella Baumfree, who also called herself Sojourner Truth, died. She was an illiterate slave who was freed and became a powerfully effective speaker for obstetrics and woman's rights.

May 14. A new political party, the Anti-Monopoly Organization of the U.S., was formed in Chicago. Its convention nominated Benjamin F. Butler, of Massachusetts, to be its standard-bearer for President. Two weeks later, the National Convention of the Greenback party also nominated Butler for President. Pudgy, cross-eyed Butler had been a Union general in the Civil War and military governor of New Orleans after the war. He was known as Beast Butler for his uncavalier attitude toward Southern womanhood. When the ladies of New Orleans insulted Northern soldiers, Butler announced that each female offender should "be treated as a woman of the town plying her vocation." This stopped the verbal insults, but the angered Southern belles turned their backs on Butler whenever they saw him, which provoked his memorable remark: "These women know which end of them looks best."
May 16 The 10th Kentucky Derby, at Churchill Downs in Louisville, Ky., was won by a black jockey, Isaac Murphy, astride the horse *Buchanan*. The winning stake was $3,990. In all, during 23 years of riding, Murphy won 3 Kentucky Derbies and 4 American Derbies. In 1956, he was elected to the Jockey's Hall of Fame and is enshrined at Pimlico in Maryland.
Oct. 28 The cornerstone of the Statue of Liberty was laid. The Statue itself was unveiled by President Grover Cleveland on Bedloe's Island (now Liberty Island) in Upper New York Bay 2 years later. The 152', 225-ton copper statue, a centennial gift from France to the U.S., was not actually a representation of Liberty but a likeness of the face of French sculptor Frédéric Auguste Bartholdi's mother, as she appeared in her younger years. Today, one million sightseers visit the Lady—and the $2.5 million American Museum of Immigration at the base of the statue—annually.

1884

1885

—In Alabama it became unlawful for black and white convicts to be chained together or confined in the same cell.
—In northern and eastern Montana, Granville Stuart led the deadliest vigilante movement in U.S. history. Thirty-five accused horse and cattle thieves were killed.
—*The Adventures of Huckleberry Finn* by Mark Twain was published. Said Lionel Trilling in 1965: "One might say of *Huckleberry Finn* that it is totally available to a man all through his life. It's a book that one can read at the age of 10 or even at 80; one can read and reread it from that time on, and always find something new in it."

May 14 Apaches on the San Carlos, Ariz., Reservation protested U.S. Government regulations against wife-beating and making *tiswin* (corn liquor). Fearing reprisals, Geronimo convinced 38 warriors, 8 boys old enough to fight, and 100 women and children to escape with him to the Sierra Madres in Mexico. In March, 1886, they negotiated an agreement whereby they would be sent to Florida for 2 years. That night, a Swiss-American gunrunner smuggled liquor to the Apaches and convinced many of them that they would be killed if they surrendered. Eighteen warriors and 19 women and children fled.

For 5 months, Geronimo and the Chiricahuas eluded 5,000 U.S. Army troops and 500 Indian scouts under the command of the ambitious Gen. Nelson A. Miles, who ordered the construction of an elaborate network of heliograph stations to track the Indians with morse code.

Summer Sitting Bull toured with Buffalo Bill's Wild West Show. He gave away most of his money to hungry boys who followed the show. He said to Annie Oakley: "The white man knows how to make everything, but he does not know how to distribute it."

Summer The Knights of Labor won a strike against Jay Gould. It was Gould who used illegal Erie Railroad stock to defraud Com. Cornelius Vanderbilt, and who then escaped with $6 million to New Jersey. Later, Gould bribed the New York legislature to legalize the Erie stock. With $23 million profit, Gould bought New York City's elevated railroad, Union Pacific Railroad, and Western Union. It was also Gould who bribed the brother-in-law of President Grant to serve as his White House spy. When Gould got inside information that the nation's gold reserve would be frozen, he bought up $47 million of free gold, drove the greenback price up from $132 to $162.50 for $100 worth of gold, and thus made himself a tidy profit. But in the strike against him, he was defeated by the Knights of Labor, whose prestige and membership promptly soared:

1884   71,326 members
1885   111,395 members
1886   729,677 members

The leaders of the Knights of Labor opposed strikes and revolution; they favored voting and the creation of producers' cooperatives. However, the Chicago Central Labor Union recommended to its locals that "the workers arm in answer to the employment of Pinkertons, police, and militia by their employers."

July 23 Ulysses S. Grant died of cancer at 63. Lying in state in New York City Hall, his body was viewed by a seemingly endless line of mourners who filed past for 96 consecutive hours. He was laid to rest in the landmark now known as Grant's Tomb on Riverside Drive. A vine plucked from Napoleon's tomb at St. Helena was planted beside the ex-President's grave.

1886

—"I can hire one half the working class to kill the other half."—Jay Gould, before the strike on his southwestern system.

Mar. 6 A strike broke out against Jay Gould's southwestern railroad system when a worker was fired for attending a union meeting. Despite opposition from the Knights of Labor, the strike was joined by shopmen, switchmen, trackmen, telegraph operators, firemen, and miners. Shops were occupied. The authorities countered with court injunctions, arrest warrants, and strikebreakers. The workers sabotaged the engines to prevent strikebreakers from running them. The railroad owners brought in the militia and hired vigilantes to run the engines.

On April 9, in St. Louis, deputies fired into a crowd of striking railroad workers, killing 9 and wounding many. The Knights of Labor tried to restrain the enraged crowd, who burned shops, the railroad yards, and the depot. The governor sent in 700 militia and put the city under military law.

May 1 First day of a general strike for an 8-hour day.

> We mean to make things over
>   We're tired of toil for nought
> But bare enough to live on; never
>   An hour for thought.
> We want to feel the sunshine, we
>   Want to smell the flowers
> We're sure that God has willed it
>   And we mean to have 8 hours.
> We're summoning our forces from
>   Shipyard, shop and mill,
> Eight hours for work, 8 hours for rest,
>   Eight hours for what we will!

The Jewish workers, who did not read the English papers and who had no papers of their own, knew nothing about the general movement for an 8-hour day. . . . One day, it was a Saturday, rumors spread that a "meeting" would be held. No one knew who spread the rumor. My mother brought the news from the butcher shop. The meeting was to be held at De Koven Street Hall, but when I arrived there I found the owner of the hall quarreling with some workers and insisting that no one had engaged the hall. Nickels were quickly gathered among those present and paid to the owner, who opened the hall to us.

Some 500 or 600 tailors and contractors filled the hall quickly. No one could be discovered who would claim to have called the meeting. No one acted as chairman or secretary. All talked at once, until it became noticeable that Wolf the buttonholemaker talked the loudest, and then all calmed down. . . . At last A. Solomon, one of the operators, shouted that all should stop work the following day. There were loud protests. The meeting lasted till 1 A.M.

No vote was taken and no resolutions were passed. But on the following day,

which was Sunday, nobody appeared at work. For 6 weeks no one worked. There were no strikebreakers, and meetings were held daily in the same fashion as the 1st one. Then we discovered that there was a labor movement. . . .
—A. Bisno, New York City

—Over 340,000 people participated in the 8-hour demonstrations, 190,000 by striking. Of these, 200,000 won shorter hours, some of them before May 1.

—At 1st, the 2 most influential labor groups opposed the 8-hour movement. The leaders of the Knights of Labor opposed a general strike because they feared it would lead to armed revolution, while the anarchists argued that it was a compromise with the wage system. But the movement caught the workers' imagination, and they hurried to join the Knights of Labor who, horrified by the militance of the new members, refused to approve the creation of new locals. Terence Powderly, the head of the Knights of Labor, ordered the membership not to strike and suggested instead that members write short essays on the question of an 8-hour day.

May 4 Haymarket Square bombing in Chicago. (See: On the Way to the 8-Hour Day—the Haymarket Affair, Chap. 2.)

June 2 Grover Cleveland, the 2nd bachelor to be elected President (the other was James Buchanan), succumbed to matrimony and became the 1st Chief Executive to be married in the White House. In the Blue Room, he was wedded to his ward, the daughter of his deceased onetime law partner, 21-year-old Frances Folsom. Cleveland was 27 years older than his bride. The marriage lasted 22 years, until his death at the age of 71. The Clevelands had 5 children. Mrs. Cleveland lived to the age of 83, dying in 1947.

July 23 The expression "to pull a Brodie" or "to do a Brodie"—meaning to attempt a dangerous stunt—was born when a 23-year-old New York saloonkeeper, Steve Brodie, jumped off the Brooklyn Bridge 135' into the East River below to win a $200 wager. Many believed that Brodie did not actually leap but pushed a dummy off the bridge instead. *The New York Times* supported Brodie's claim, however, reporting that a friend in a rowboat fished him out of the water. And the police arrested him for perpetrating this suicidal stunt.

Later, heavyweight champion Jim Corbett's father met Brodie and said, "So you're the fellow who jumped over the Brooklyn Bridge." "No," said Brodie," "I jumped *off* it." "Oh," exclaimed the elder Corbett with disgust, "I thought you jumped *over* it. Any damn fool could jump off it."

Sept. 4 Geronimo agreed, for the last time, to quit the warpath. He and his fellow Chiricahuas were shipped to Fort Marion, Fla., where they found many other Apaches dying from the unaccustomed humidity. At least 100 died of consumption. The children were separated from their parents and sent to the Indian school in Carlisle, Pa., where more than 50 died. Some Apaches were eventually allowed to return to the San Carlos Reservation, but the people of Arizona refused to accept Geronimo and the Chiricahuas. When the Kiowas and Comanches learned of the plight of their old Apache enemies, they offered them part of their reservation and, in 1894, surviving exiles moved to Fort Sill, Okla., where Geronimo died on February 17, 1909.

1887

—U.S. Government claimed rights to Pearl Harbor, leasing it as a coaling and repair station from Hawaii.

—Passage of the Dawes Allotment Act required all Indian reservations to be subdivided into individual plots of land of 160 to 320 acres. "Surplus" land was bought by the Government and opened to white settlers. For the Sisseton Sioux tribe of South Dakota, the Dawes Act meant that their 918,000-acre reservation was reduced to 308,000 acres.

June 7 War booty of the Union Army, consisting of captured Confederate flags, was ordered returned to the South by President Cleveland.

1888

—Edward Bellamy's provocative socialist-utopian novel, *Looking Backward*, was published. It sold only 35,000 copies the 1st year, but by 1890 over 200,000 copies had been sold. The slender, diffident, 38-year-old Bellamy, son of a Baptist minister, spent most of his life in Chicopee Falls, Mass. After being admitted to the bar, he gave up law for writing.

He never improved upon his 3rd book, *Looking Backward*, which predicted a cooperative commonwealth in the U.S., music transmitted over telephone wires, and delivery of goods by city-wide pneumatic-tube systems. His book gave birth to the Nationalist party, which promoted his theories. He died of tuberculosis at 48, leaving a wife, a small daughter, and a 13-year-old son.

—A simple box camera and roll of film taking round pictures was produced by George Eastman, of Rochester, N.Y., enabling photography to be enjoyed by ordinary people and enabling

Mr. Eastman to become very wealthy and very philanthropic.

June 3 On page 4, column 4, of the *San Francisco Examiner*, there appeared a 13-stanza poem signed E.L.T. entitled, *Casey at the Bat, A Ballad of the Republic, Sung in the Year 1888*. Thousands welcomed its 1st appearance right down to the final explosive verse:

> Oh, somewhere in this favored land
>   the sun is shining bright;
> The band is playing somewhere,
>   and somewhere hearts are light,
> And somewhere men are laughing,
>   and somewhere children shout;
> But there is no joy in Mudville—
>   mighty Casey has struck out.

This ode to Humpty Dumpty's fall was penned by Ernest Lawrence Thayer, heir to the American Woolen Mills, who studied philosophy at Harvard under William James and was editor of the Harvard *Lampoon*, with young William Randolph Hearst as the magazine's business manager. When young Hearst's father had him take over the *San Francisco Examiner*, Hearst induced Thayer to come aboard and write a humor column. Thus, *Casey* was spawned. Thayer got $5 for the poem.

The poem became a classic 2 months later when William De Wolf Hopper, a comedian and singer, was doing a comic opera at Wallack's Theatre on Broadway. On the fateful night, the management had invited baseball players from the New York Giants and Pop Anson's Chicago White Stockings to attend as front-row guests. While searching for material the players could relate to, Hopper was given the clipping of *Casey at the Bat* by a novelist friend. Hopper thundered forth the poem in 6 minutes, and the reading created a sensation. Thereafter, Hopper delivered the poem 10,000 times in public, and was always remembered for it as well as for the fact that Hedda Hopper, the actress and movie columnist, was his 5th wife.

selected Herschberger of Chicago at fullback in 1898, and a year later broke the big-college hold on the All-American selections by admitting Seneca of Carlisle as halfback.

Mar. 16 A major conflict among U.S., British, and German war ships anchored off the Samoan Islands was averted when a hurricane destroyed all but one vessel. A tripartite agreement proclaimed the islands neutral territory, and this lasted until 1899.

Apr. 22 President Harrison opened a portion of Oklahoma to white settlement.

May 31 An abandoned reservoir broke, flooding the city of Johnstown, Pa., and killing about 3,000 people. Some said that the flood was caused by excessive lumbering which had denuded the surrounding hills and changed the natural drainage. (See also: Man-Made Disasters, Chap. 9.)

Aug. 3 The Sioux signed away 9 million acres to the U.S. Government for use by the railroad and for land speculators to sell to white immigrants. For years, the U.S. Government had wanted the land, but they had wanted to avoid breaking a treaty to get it. The agreement was finally achieved by holding a secret meeting with several Sioux leaders and not informing Sitting Bull.

Nov. 2–11 North and South Dakota, Montana, and Washington became States.

Nov. 14 The *New York World* started reporter Nellie Bly on a journey around the world to beat the record set by Jules Verne's fictional Phileas Fogg in *Around the World in Eighty Days*. Bly detoured only once, to confront Verne in Amiens, France. She told him she'd beat Fogg's record. Verne was politely doubtful. He was wrong. Nellie Bly completed her circuit of the earth in 72 days, 6 hours, 11 minutes, 14 seconds, lowering Fogg's record by 8 days. When she was 28, she married a 72-year-old millionaire named Robert L. Seaman, and upon his death inherited his manufacturing empire. Later, her companies went into bankruptcy. (See also: Bly in Footnote People in U.S. History, Chap. 3.)

—D.W. & I.W

1889

—The 1st All-American football team was picked by Walter Camp. It resembled an All-Ivy League team. The 11 who made it: Ends —Stagg (Yale) and Cumnock (Harvard); tackles—Gill (Yale) and Cowan (Princeton); guards—Heffelfinger (Yale) and Cranston (Harvard); center—George (Princeton); quarterback—Poe (Princeton); halfbacks—Channing (Princeton) and Lee (Harvard); fullback—Ames (Princeton). It was not until 10 years later that the Eastern monopoly on All-American teams was broken when Camp

1890

—U.S. population—62,622,250.

—*Black Beauty, His Grooms and Companions* by Anna Sewell was published in Boston by the American Humane Education Society, as a paper-bound tract against cruelty to animals. It sold for 20¢.

—Despite the fact that vigilantism was illegal, 4 ex-vigilantes, including Leland Stanford, served in the U.S. Senate.

—The Sherman Anti-Trust Act introduced in

Congress by Sen. John Sherman, O., was passed with almost no dissent. It was intended to combat the monopolistic greed of big businessmen. However, it was 1st used successfully not against the corporations, but against Eugene Debs and the American Railway Union in 1894–1895.
—The governor of New York, Theodore Roosevelt, labeled Leo Tolstoi a "sexual and moral pervert," during the controversy sparked by the U.S. Post Office's banning of Tolstoi's *The Kreutzer Sonata.*
—The U.S. Government made an official declaration that the western frontier was now closed.

June 1 Facts learned from the census: The richest 1% of the population received more income than the poorest 50%. One-half of the national income was enjoyed by 1/8 of the families, and of the 12 million families in the U.S., 5½ million had no property.

Occupation

	Agriculture, hunting, fishing	Domestic, personal service	Manufacturing	Trade & transportation	Profession
Blacks	57%	31%	6%	5%	1%
Native Whites	47%	12%	19%	16%	6%
Foreign-Born Whites	26%	27%	31%	14%	2%

July 3–10 Wyoming became a State after vowing, "We will stay out of the Union 100 years rather than come in without woman suffrage." Idaho was also admitted to the Union.
July 16 Newspapers in New York City announced the end of a 2-month strike by cloakmakers, much to the surprise of the cloakmakers, who had not yet been consulted by their leaders. A mass meeting was held at which the terms of the agreement were explained to the cloakmakers who rejected it by a vote of 1,536 to 20. In his book *Memoirs of a Cloakmaker,* A. Rosenberg described the dramatic scene that followed.

The enthusiasm was indescribable. Men and women jumped on the tables. Their voices could be heard 10 blocks away. After the audience cooled off a little, the chairman of the meeting declared that though everybody voted for the continuation of the strike, the thing most needed was money and that was lacking, and he would advise the people to reconsider their decision. But he had hardly concluded his sentence, when one of the people walked up to the chairman's table and taking off a ring from his finger

handed it over to the chairman with the request to sell it or pawn it and give the money to the strikers. In less time than it takes to tell it, the chairman's table became covered with rings, watches, earrings, brooches, and other pieces of jewelry. All were shouting that these offerings be sold and the strike go on. He who witnessed this scene will never forget it. Many cried. Others yelled and argued. The entire meeting gave the impression of an immense cauldron.

The strike was won 9 days later.

Aug.

There are 3 great crops raised in Nebraska. One is a crop of corn, one a crop of freight rates, and one a crop of interest. One is produced by farmers who by sweat and toil farm the land. The other 2 are produced by men who sit in their offices and behind their bank counters and farm the farmers.

—Farm Editor

Aug. 6 The 1st man in history to die in an electric chair was put to death on this day. He was William Kemmler, alias John Hart, who was electrocuted in the new death chamber of Auburn Prison in Auburn, N.Y. Earlier, Kemmler had run off with Matilda Ziegler, wife of another man. Tiring of her, he killed her with an axe in March, 1889, in Buffalo, N.Y. He was convicted of 1st-degree murder, and sentenced to die in the newly installed electric chair, invented by Dr. Alphonse D. Rockwell. The chair had replaced hanging in New York as of January 1, 1889. A reporter for the *New York World* witnessed this landmark in human progress:

The 1st execution by electricity has been a horror. . . . The doctors say the victim did not suffer. Only his Maker knows if that be true. To the eye, it looked as though he were in a convulsive agony.

The current had been passing through his body for 15 seconds when the electrode at the head was removed. Suddenly, the breast heaved. There was a straining at the straps which bound him, a purplish foam covered the lips and was spattered over the leather headband.

The man was alive. Warden, physicians, everybody, lost their wits. There was a startled cry for the current to be turned on again. . . . The rigor of death came on the instant. An odor of burning flesh and singed hair filled the room. For a moment, a blue flame played about the base of the victim's spine. . . . This time the electricity flowed 4 minutes.

Kimmler was dead. Part of his brain had been baked hard. Some of the blood in his head had been turned into charcoal.

At last, capital punishment had been made civilized.

Sept. Indians from many reservations gathered at Walker Lake in Nevada to see Wovoka, the Paiute Messiah. He said that the whites had treated Christ so badly the 1st time that this time He was returning as an Indian. Wovoka promised that the next spring, when the grass was knee-high, the earth would be covered with new soil and all whites would be buried. Those Indians who danced the Ghost Dance would be saved and they would be rewarded with the return of the buffalo, wild horses, and the ghosts of all dead Indians. News of the Ghost Dance spread quickly and by mid-November Ghost Dancing on the Sioux reservations prevailed over almost all activities. Although the dance was purely Christian, many whites were afraid and the Indian Bureau prepared a list of "fomentors of disturbances." Because Sitting Bull's name appeared on the list, he was blamed for everything.

Dec. 15 Forty-three Indian police surrounded Sitting Bull's log cabin with the intention of arresting him. One hundred and seventy Ghost Dancers appeared to protect Sitting Bull. Catch the Bear pulled out a rifle and shot arresting officer Lieut. Bull Head in the side. Sgt. Red Tomahawk then shot Sitting Bull through the head and killed him. The fighting was stopped by the arrival of the U.S. Cavalry. So prevalent was the belief that Ghost Dancing would cause the white man to disappear by spring that the Sioux did not retaliate after the murder of Sitting Bull.

Dec. 29 The massacre at Wounded Knee Creek. Three hundred and fifty Indians (120 men and 230 women and children) being held prisoner by the U.S. Cavalry's 7th Regiment were being disarmed in the morning snow when a hidden rifle was discovered. Shooting broke out, and within minutes, half the Indians were dead or dying. Many crawled away to die alone, and 51 survivors were taken away. The soldiers suffered 24 dead and 39 wounded, most of them struck by their own bullets or shrapnel.

1891

—The National Colored Farmer's Alliance had 1,300,000 members.
—Georgia became the 1st State to segregate passengers on streetcars.
—The 1st interracial boxing match of signifi-

cance, between Peter Jackson, the champion of Australia, and James J. Corbett, ended in a draw after 61 rounds.
—Basketball was invented by Dr. James A. Naismith, physical education instructor at the YMCA Training College in Springfield, Mass. Recalled Dr. Naismith in 1937: "We decided that there should be a game that could be played indoors in the evening and during the winter seasons. . . . Football was rough because you had to allow the defense to tackle because the offense ran with the ball. Accordingly, if the offense didn't have an opportunity to run with the ball, there would be no necessity for tackling and we would thus eliminate roughness. This is the fundamental principle of basketball." Dr. Naismith's original game used 7 men on each side and 2 peach baskets. By 1906, the modern hoop was in use. Of Dr. Naismith's 13 basic rules, 12 are still in effect for high school and college games.

Mar. 4 The International Copyright Act, halting the piracy of British, Belgian, French, Swiss books by U.S. publishers, was passed by Congress.

Mar. 15 A mob in New Orleans broke open a prison and murdered 11 Sicilians accused of being Mafia members.

July 5 Mine operators in Briceville, Tenn., brought in 40 convicts to work a mine that was being struck by miners who had refused to sign a contract which required that they be paid in scrip redeemable only at the company store. The convicts tore down the miners' houses and built a stockade for themselves.

At midnight on July 15, 300 armed miners overwhelmed the convicts and marched convicts, guards, and mine officials to the depot, where they put them on the train to Knoxville. The next day, the governor, accompanied by 125 militiamen, personally led the convicts back to the mine. Miners from other counties began arriving and, on July 20, 2,000 armed miners easily persuaded the militia, guards, and convicts to accompany them to the depot and return to Knoxville. The governor then sent 600 militiamen to Anderson County and a truce was called so that a special session of the Tennessee legislature could meet to repeal the convict lease law. When the legislators failed to do this, the miners appealed to the courts, who also did nothing, so the miners returned to a policy of direct action.

Between October 31 and November 2, the miners ousted several hundred convicts from 3 mines and burned the stockades to the ground. The miners won their demands, but in mid-December the governor sent the convicts back and built "Fort Anderson," a permanent military camp with 175 guards, trenches, and a Gatling gun.

Nov. 29 A gridiron tradition began with the 1st Army-Navy football game. Played at West Point, N.Y., the Navy crushed the Army, 24–0.

1892

—Ward McAllister coined the expression, "The 400," meaning the social elite. This was inspired by the fact that New York's Astor Hotel ballroom held only 400 persons at one time.

—One hundred and sixty blacks were reported lynched. Over 1,400 had been lynched since 1882.

—World bantamweight boxing champion George Dixon refused to fight in the New Orleans Olympic Club unless the proprietors set aside 700 seats for blacks. It was the 1st time that black spectators were allowed in the club.

Jan. 1 Ellis Island was opened to screen all immigrants. Twenty million immigrants went through it in 62 years before it was closed down in 1954.

June 11 A striking miner was fired on by guards at the Frisco Mill in Coeur d'Alene, Ida. The miners surrounded the mill, which was being run by strikebreakers, and a battle raged. The miners loaded a car with gunpowder and sent it down the hill with a short fuse, demolishing the old mill. There were no injuries, but the strikebreakers surrendered. The miners then peaceably occupied other mills and plants in the area. The sheriff and marshal, having been elected by the miners, refused to act against them. Martial law was declared, but the militia was unable to control the situation, so Federal troops were sent in and the striking miners were imprisoned in stockade enclosures surrounded by barbed wire. The Government indicted 480 men, but none were convicted.

July 2 Henry Clay Frick, the manager of Andrew Carnegie's steelworks in Homestead, Pa., laid off the entire work force of 3,800 workers because they insisted on negotiating a new contract as union members instead of as individuals. In preparation for the strike, Frick had stepped up production and constructed a 12'-high fence, topped with barbed wire, around the entire plant. The fence was 3 mi. long. He also sent for 300 Pinkerton guards. At this time, the Pinkerton Agency employed 2,000 active agents and had 30,000 reserves, which was more than the standing Army of the U.S.

At 3 A.M. on July 6, strike supporters in Pittsburgh spotted the Pinkertons on a barge headed for Homestead. At 4 A.M., a mounted sentry burst into Homestead shouting, "The Pinkertons are coming." Ten thousand workers, their families and supporters raced to the landing armed with sticks, stones, nail-studded clubs, and hundreds of rifles and guns. The Pinkertons, armed with Winchester repeaters, tried to land and shooting started. All day the Pinkertons were kept under heavy attack and prevented from landing. At the end of the day, the Pinkertons mutinied and surrendered to the workers, who forced them to run a bloody gauntlet in which all were injured. Forty strikers had been shot and 9 were killed. Twenty Pinkertons had been shot and 7 died.

On July 12, Governor Pattison sent in 8,000 state militiamen armed with Springfield 45s and Gatling guns. They were welcomed by the strikers and the soldiers fraternized with the people of Homestead until they were forbidden to do so by General Snowden. Said Snowden: "Pennsylvanians can hardly appreciate the actual communism of these people. They believe the works are theirs quite as much as Carnegie's."

Strikebreakers were brought in to run the works, but they often deserted. In Cincinnati, 56 men who were told that they were being hired to work at one mill were actually put on a train to Homestead. When they discovered their true destination, 35 battled their way out of the train. The rest were held prisoner inside the mill and forced to work. Over 160 strikers were arrested, including the leaders, who were charged with murder. All were acquitted, and then recharged, this time for treason. No Pittsburgh jury found a single striker guilty, but the strikers' money was eventually depleted from paying legal fees and posting bail and when it ran out, the leaders were still in jail. On November 18, the unskilled workers asked to be released from the strike pledge and the strike ended 2 days later with the men returning as individuals, not as a union.

July 4 The 1st nominating convention of the People's party, or Populists, nominated for President, James Baird Weaver, a Union general from Iowa, and for Vice-President, James C. Field, a Confederate general from Virginia. A single banner across the stage said, "We Do Not Ask for Sympathy or Pity: We Ask for Justice." Most Populists were farmers and workers.

Aug. 15 When 100 miners marched on the convicts' quarters at the Oliver Springs mine in Anderson County, Tenn., the guards opened fire, wounding several. Miners poured into the area, marched on the stockade, disarmed the guards, burned the blockhouse, and returned the guards and convicts to Knoxville. Then they laid siege to Fort Anderson until an army of 500 soldiers arrived. The miners were arrested and locked up in railroad cars, a schoolhouse, and a Methodist church, but nearly all were eventually acquitted by local juries. The militia crushed the revolt, but the convict lease system was discredited and soon abolished.

Sept. 7 After decades of bareknuckled fighting, the 1st heavyweight championship in which the contestants wore padded gloves was staged in New Orleans, La., with James J. Corbett knocking out the heretofore invincible John L. Sullivan in the 21st round.

Oct. 12 The dedication of grounds at the World's Columbian Exposition in Chicago, a super world's fair to celebrate the 400th anniversary of the discovery of America. The fairgrounds sprawled over 686 acres, and the event cost $28 million. Over 21 million visitors came to the fair, wandering through the modernistic Transportation Building designed by Dankmar Adler and Louis Sullivan, enjoying the 27 colossal sculptures created by Daniel Chester French, listening to the popular "After the Ball Is Over" and to the martial music of John Philip Sousa's band, attending the races to see jockey Ed "Snapper" Garrison make another Garrison Finish, watching the world's 1st national fly-casting tournament, and observing the antics of Little Egypt doing the hootchy-kootchy, strongman Earl Sandow lifting weights, Swami Vivikenanda preaching purity and love.

—In Georgia, Populist gubernatorial candidate Tom Watson said to poor blacks and poor whites:

> Now the People's party says to these 2 men, you are kept apart that you may be separately fleeced of your earnings. You are made to hate each other because upon that hatred is rested the keystone of the arch of financial despotism which enslaves you both.

When H. S. Doyle, a black preacher who had been campaigning for Watson, was threatened with lynching, 2,000 armed white farmers guarded him for 2 nights.

—During the election campaign in Georgia, white Democrats murdered 15 Negroes. They also stuffed ballot boxes extensively—in Augusta, the total vote was twice the number of registered voters.

Nov. 8 The Populists elected governors in Colorado, Kansas, North Dakota, and Wyoming. They also elected 2 senators, 11 House members, and sent 354 representatives to 19 State legislatures.

Nov. 8 In New Orleans, 20,000 workers, white, black, skilled, unskilled, industrial, and clerical, went on general strike demanding union recognition and closed shops. When the militia was called in, the unions backed down and the strike ended.

1893

—*The Strange Case of Dr. Jekyll and Mr. Hyde* by Robert Louis Stevenson was published in the U.S.

—U.S. Government moved to oust Great Britain from Nicaragua in order to build a canal.

—Metropolitan business interests, flour millers, and meat-packers supported U.S. diplomatic and naval intervention against a Brazilian revolt whose leaders opposed a recent trade agreement with the U.S.

Jan. 4 Three years after the Mormon Church gave up polygamy, President Benjamin Harrison offered amnesty to all polygamists in jail if they promised to end their plural marriages and remain monogamous thereafter.

Jan. 16 In Hawaii, pro-American interests, with the aid of U.S. naval forces and a contingent of marines, staged a successful coup against Queen Liliuokalani. When Cleveland became President, he sent John Blount of Georgia to investigate the situation in Hawaii and study the possibilities for annexation. Blount reported that the mass of natives opposed the new Government, so Cleveland demanded restoration of the Queen. Pro-annexation leaders in the U.S. rejected this, so Cleveland withdrew his demand, and the coup leaders who had hoped for annexation, settled for creation of the Republic of Hawaii in 1894 with Sanford B. Dole as President.

Jan. 23 Eleonora Duse, the great Italian actress and mistress of author D'Annunzio, made her U.S. debut on Broadway in *La Dame aux Camélias*.

Apr. Henry Ford displayed his 1st Ford car powered by a gasoline engine, and successfully road tested it.

June 9 Another Ford in the news. Ford's Theatre building, Washington, D.C., where Lincoln was shot, collapsed, killing 22.

June 2 The American Railway Union was founded in Chicago. Dues were $1 a year, and anyone employed by the railroads was eligible including miners and longshoremen. This did not apply to Negroes, who were excluded from membership regardless of their occupation.

1894

—William Hope Harvey, lawyer, speculator, money crank, published a 152-page 25¢ book entitled *Coin's Financial School*. This book, *Review of Reviews* editorialized, will "sway public opinion from the Alleghenies to the

Pacific and from the Great Lakes to the Gulf of Mexico."

It did. It sold 300,000 copies in a year, with later sales totaling 2 million. Through use of a character named Professor Coin—who is shown teaching bankers and merchants at his fictitious financial school why silver was as important as gold, and how silver and gold could remain at a fixed ratio to each other—Harvey converted William Jennings Bryan. Thereafter, Bryan ran for President as a free-silver advocate against McKinley, and lost. Author Harvey, himself, was the Liberty party candidate for President in 1932. He died in 1936.

—One hundred thirty-five blacks were lynched.

—Hugh Duffy, of the Boston National League baseball club, set an all-time single-season major league batting average, hitting .438. He won the batting championship twice.

Apr. 21 Approximately 125,000 miners from Tacoma, Wash., to Birmingham, Ala., to Springhill, Nova Scotia, joined a strike called by the 20,000-member United Mine Workers. This left no more than 24,000 bituminous miners still at work. At 1st, the strike was peaceful as strikers marched with brass bands to nonstriking mines. But when the mine operators tried to reopen with strikebreakers, violence erupted. Freight trains were captured and derailed, and bridges were burned. In Pennsylvania, strikers were shot dead. In Spring Valley and La Salle, Ill., strike leaders who had been arrested were liberated from jail by their fellow workers.

Coal shortages appeared in many parts of the country, and trains, Missouri River steamers, and St. Louis flour mills were forced to burn wood. But the strike was ultimately defeated because it did not become universal and because increased coal production in the anthracite fields of Pennsylvania and Virginia kept the nation's businesses going long enough to force the miners and their families to the brink of starvation.

May 1 Coxey's Army marched on Washington, D.C. In fall, 1893, in Massillon, O., Jacob Sechler Coxey, a Theosophist, Populist, horse-breeder, and owner of a sandstone quarry, announced a march on Washington by the unemployed. At 1st, the press treated it as a joke, but by spring of 1894, 20,000 "Coxeyites" were Washington-bound by a dozen routes. Hordes of laughing and singing tramps with no supplies begged their way across the West and Midwest where they were fed and encouraged to go on by sympathetic farmers. But the people of the East were more hostile, and most of the "army" fell away, leaving only 600 to march through Washington, D.C., to the Capitol where mounted police barred their way. Coxey was arrested for walking on the grass, jailed, and not allowed to speak.

May 10 The railroad strike of 1894 began. Pullman, Ill., the home of the Pullman Palace Car Co., was a company town all the way. Everything—the land, the houses, the stores, the churches—was owned by George Pullman. Even the sewage from the workers' homes was pumped to Pullman's stock farm. Rent was deducted from the workers' paychecks:

> One man has a paycheck in his possession of 2¢ after paying rent. . . . He has it framed.
>
> —Minister of the Pullman Methodist-Episcopal Church

This day, May 10, the Pullman workers went on strike. A month later, they appealed for aid to the 1st convention of the newly formed American Railway Union, whose president was Eugene V. Debs. When Pullman refused to arbitrate, the convention voted unanimously to boycott Pullman cars.

On June 26, switchmen in Chicago refused to man the switches for Pullman cars and were instantly fired. The boycott began and 2 days later 4 or 5 Chicago railroads were stopped with 18,000 men on strike. Soon the only line running out of Chicago was the Great Northern which carried no Pullman cars. The struggle quickly extended to 27 States and Territories, and 260,000 railroad workers joined the strike. *The New York Times* of June 29 called it "the greatest battle between labor and capital that has ever been inaugurated in the U.S." On June 30, the Trades and Labor Assembly in Chicago pledged its 150,000 members in support of the strike, but Debs considered a general strike to be too extreme.

The railroad owners were also active, and the leaders of 26 Chicago railroads organized the General Managers' Association to plan strategy in support of Pullman. Their major tactic was to persuade the Federal courts to issue an anti-strike injunction which they knew would be ignored. This gave them the excuse to call in Federal troops. It is worth noting that U.S. Attorney General Richard Olney, who had been a railroad lawyer for 35 years, was on the Board of Directors of one of the railroads being boycotted.

Despite the protests of Illinois governor Altgeld, the city of Chicago was occupied by 14,000 armed troops (6,000 Federal troops, 5,000 deputy U.S. marshals, and 3,000 police) under the command of Gen. Nelson A. Miles. With the arrival of Federal troops, the peaceful mood of the strike gave way to violence. On July 5, crowds overturned boxcars, threw switches, and changed signal lights. Seven structures at the World's Columbian Exposition were destroyed by fire. On July 4, a railroad agent on the Illinois Central shot 2 members of a crowd, and the crowed burned the yard. Action spread to other lines and, at night, 700 cars were destroyed at the Panhandle yards in South Chicago.

President Grover Cleveland, without consulting the Populist governor of the State, sent 5 companies of U.S. troops to Trinidad, Colo., to combat a large crowd which had captured and disarmed 42 deputy marshals. In Raton, N. Mex., the railroad strikers gained the support of the sheriff and 300 striking coal miners. When a U.S. marshal and his deputies entered Raton, the hotel workers quit rather than serve them. In Los Angeles, 5 companies of State militia declared themselves in sympathy with the strike, which was broken there only by putting a detachment of troops on each train. In Sacramento, Calif., many of the militiamen deserted or refused to fire on the strikers, and 542 Federal troops were finally called in to clear the railroad tracks with fixed bayonets. In Hammond, Ind., large crowds ranged over the tracks, attacking strikebreakers and derailing trains. They also seized the telegraph office to prevent an appeal for the militia. On July 8, State militia and Federal troops cleared the tracks by firing indiscriminately into the crowd.

By the end of the strike, 34 strikers had been killed, including 13 in Chicago, and Federal or State troops had been called out in Illinois, Indiana, Nebraska, Iowa, Oklahoma, Colorado, and California.

Back in Chicago, where workers passionately supported the strike, newsboys dropped newspapers which opposed the Pullman boycott into the sewers. The working class pushed the union leaders toward a general strike, and on July 7, the Building and Trades Council, representing 25,000 workers, gave Pullman until July 10 to accept arbitration. This delay proved fatal. On July 10, Debs and the other leaders of the American Railway Union were arrested for conspiracy, and their offices were ransacked by U.S. marshals in a raid that the Dept. of Justice later admitted was illegal. By this time, the military was in control, and the blockade out of Chicago was broken. The leaders of the American Federation of Labor refused to endorse a general strike and instead pledged $1,000 to Debs's legal defense fund. The strike ended.

Even as George Pullman announced that the main issue had been "the principle that a man should have the right to manage his own property," the working class was trying to determine why their strike had failed. It had failed for 3 primary reasons:

1) Their leadership had been too centralized. When Debs and the other ARU leaders were jailed, the organization of the strike fell apart completely.

2) The ARU, despite its slogan of "One Union for All Workers," excluded Negroes. When the strike was called, blacks gladly worked as strikebreakers.

3) Debs and the ARU leadership were addicted to orderly, legal tactics. Debs had said that he preferred to end the strike rather than let it develop into a revolution. Consequently, when Federal troops were called out, the workers found themselves unprepared and ill-equipped to fight back.

June 13 W. E. B. DuBois became the 1st black person to receive a Ph.D. from Harvard.

1895

—American men got a new pin-up queen, the Gibson Girl, drawn by Charles Dana Gibson for major magazines.

—It had been 30 years since the U.S. had been at war and many Americans were itching for action. Theodore Roosevelt was among those who desired a war with England over a boundary dispute between Venezuela and British Guiana. But calmer heads prevailed—for a few years. In the words of William James: "It is instructive to find how near the surface in all of us the old fighting spirit lies and how slight an appeal will wake it up."

—During a 2-month stay in Denver, Colo., faith healer Francis Schlatter treated 2,000 to 3,000 persons daily. As they passed by him single file, he silently took each person's right hand and prayed softly for a few seconds. In appearance, Schlatter resembled Jesus Christ. He walked the countryside barefoot and penniless and sometimes fasted for 40 to 60 days. While in one place he would be worshiped by throngs of people, in another he would be imprisoned for vagrancy or locked up as a lunatic. He appears to have died in 1896.

Sept. 9 The American Bowling Congress was organized in Beethoven Hall, N.Y., to restore respectability to the sport and popularize it.

Oct. A 24-year-old novelist named Stephen Crane published an enduring book, *The Red Badge of Courage.*

1896

—The prototype of modern-day comic strips, "The Yellow Kid," by R. F. Outcault, made its appearance in the *New York World.* There was one major innovation—the dialogue was printed on the yellow shirt of the kid inside the frame instead of being a caption on the outside.

—Ragtime, a blending of West African rhythm and European musical form was born in the Midwest. Its popularity had begun to decline by 1910, but it saw a revival in 1974, due to recordings made by Joshua Rifkin, and the musical score for the movie, *The Sting*. (See: Scott Joplin in Gallery of Great Performing and Creative Artists, Chap. 16.)

May 18 The U.S. Supreme Court, in *Plessy* v. *Ferguson*, upheld Louisiana's Jim Crow Car Law and the conviction of Homer Plessy, a New Orleans Negro who had attempted to ride in a white railroad car. The High Court justices ruled that the 14th Amendment had "been intended to abolish distinction based on color, or to enforce social as distinguished from political . . . equality." This decision found segregation of blacks and whites acceptable as long as both races received equal facilities. In short, separate but equal. It was not until 1954–1955 that the Warren Supreme Court reversed this ruling, stating that in public education, separate was unequal.

Aug. 12 Gold was discovered in Klondike Creek, Yukon Territory, in Northwest Canada. It took 10 months for the news to sweep the U.S., and then 30,000 gold seekers rushed to the area.

Nov. 2 William McKinley defeated William Jennings Bryan in the election for President of the U.S. McKinley won—and the people lost.

Election night at midnight:
Boy Bryan's defeat.
Defeat of the western silver.
Defeat of the wheat.
Victory of the Letterflies
And plutocrats in miles
With dollar signs upon their coats,
Diamond watchchains on their vests
And spats on their feet.
Victory of the custodians,
Plymouth Rock,
And all that in-bread landlord stock.
Victory of the neat.
Defeat of the aspen groves of Colorado Valleys,
The blue bells of the Rockies,
And blue bonnets of old Texas,
By the Pittsburgh alleys.
Defeat of alfalfa and the Mariposa lily.
Defeat of the Pacific and the long Mississippi.
Defeat of the young by the old and silly.
Defeat of tornadoes by the poison vats supreme.
Defeat of my boyhood, defeat of my dream.
                              Vachel Lindsay

(See also: U.S. Presidents, Chap. 5, for details of McKinley's victory.)

1897

—One hundred twenty-three Negroes lynched.

Mar. 2 As one of his last acts in office, President Cleveland vetoed a bill that would have required all immigrants to take literacy tests.

1898

—The U.S. Government annexed Hawaii because it was considered vital to Asian trade and because the Navy desired it as a station to block foreign invasion.

Mr. President, we want those islands. We want them because they are the stepping way across the sea. . . . Necessary to our safety, they are necessary to our commerce."
—Sen. Henry M. Teller (Rep.-Colo.)

Feb. 15 At 9:40 in the evening, the 6,000-ton U.S. battleship *Maine*, moored in Havana harbor, commanded by 53-year-old Civil War veteran Capt. Charles D. Sigsbee, suddenly blew up and sank to the bottom of the sea. Two of the 26 officers and 250 out of the 329 sailors and marines aboard, were immediately killed by explosion, fire, or drowning. Of the 103 rescued, 8 died of injuries.

The *Maine* had come to Spain's colony of Cuba on a supposed goodwill tour, but actually was sent to protect American property during a period of revolution. The Spanish Government had clearly resented this show of marine muscle. The question to this day remains: What caused the explosion? A Spanish Board of Investigation, although not allowed by the U.S. to visit the wreckage, called it accidental, blaming it on spontaneous combustion. The U.S. Naval Board of Inquiry blamed it on a Spanish mine. William Randolph Hearst's *New York Journal*, alone, had the answer and bannerlined it on February 17.

1st HEADLINE: DESTRUCTION OF THE WAR SHIP *MAINE* WAS THE WORK OF AN ENEMY.
2nd HEADLINE: ASSISTANT SECRETARY ROOSEVELT CONVINCED THE EXPLOSION OF THE WAR SHIP WAS NOT AN ACCIDENT.
3rd HEADLINE: THE JOURNAL OFFERS $50,000 REWARD FOR THE CONVICTION OF THE CRIMINALS

WHO SENT 258 AMERICAN SAILORS TO THEIR DEATH. NAVAL OFFICERS UNANIMOUS THAT THE SHIP WAS DESTROYED ON PURPOSE.

In a Broadway bar, an unknown man lifted his drink and intoned to the other patrons, "Gentlemen, remember the *Maine!*" At once, Hearst and the Yellow Press had their battle cry.

Feb. 25 Assistant Secretary of the Navy Theodore Roosevelt ordered the U.S. Pacific fleet, under Com. George Dewey, to the Spanish-ruled Philippine Islands.

Apr. 11 President McKinley was against a war with Spain. But politicians and the press-manipulated public wanted war. At last, McKinley gave in, asked Congress to support an ultimatum that Spain clear out of Cuba and allow Cuba to be independent. Nine days after Congress passed such a resolution, McKinley signed it, and then broke off all diplomatic relations with Spain.

Apr. 22 U.S. blockaded all Cuban ports, captured a Spanish ship, *Buena Ventura*. Also, the Volunteer Army Act was passed, allowing the 1st Volunteer Cavalry, the colorful "Rough Riders," to be formed under the leadership of Col. Leonard Wood and Lieut. Col. Theodore Roosevelt, who had resigned from the Navy Dept.

Apr. 24 Spain refused to buckle under to the ultimatum that it give Cuba independence. Instead, Spain declared war on the U.S. At once, the U.S. declared war right back—but made its declaration retroactive to April 21.

What about this war? At the time, Henry Watterson wrote in his *Louisville Courier-Journal*: "Whether the war be long or short, it is a war into which this nation will go with a fervor, with a power, with a unanimity that would make it invincible if it were repelling not only the encroachments of Spain, but the assaults of every monarch of Europe who profanes the name of divinity in the cause of kingcraft. . . . This is the right of our might; that is the sign in which we conquer."

From the cooler perspective of time, historian Stewart H. Holbrook reassessed the U.S. role in this war: "History has listed but few cases of plainer military aggression, and even fewer where the aggressor has labored under so profound a conviction of righteousness. We simply had to protect the honest and noble Cubans from their oppressors, and to make certain that all the Cuban virgins, who were said to be many and pretty, remained intact."

May 1 Com. George Dewey, on his flagship *Olympia*, approached the Spanish fleet in Manila Bay. Dewey wrote later: "At 5:40, when we were within 5,000 yards [of the Span-

ish], I turned to Captain [Charles] Gridley and said, 'You may fire when you are ready, Gridley.'" The result? A tier of 5 headlines in the *St. Louis Globe-Democrat* proclaimed it:

DEWEY'S VICTORY. NOT A SERIOUS CASUALTY SUSTAINED IN DESTROYING SPANISH FLEET. AMERICANS CONTROL MANILA BAY AND CAN TAKE THE CITY AT ANY TIME. COMMODORE REPORTS TO WASHINGTON AND IS MADE AN ACTING ADMIRAL. SPANISH LOST ELEVEN SHIPS AND 150 MEN KILLED AND 250 WOUNDED.

The U.S. lost no men, suffered 7 or 8 wounded . . . Keeping Cool Note: In the middle of the showdown sea battle, at 7:30 in the morning, Dewey briefly pulled back his ships to give his crews a quiet breakfast, and then returned to the engagement.

June 19 The U.S.S. *Charleston* moved in on the Spanish island of Guam in the Pacific and unloaded a cannon shot. The Spanish commander replied with a message apologizing for not returning the salute, explaining he had no ammunition. It turned out he had not been informed of the Spanish-American War. The next day, informed, he surrendered Guam.

June 22 U.S. general William Rufus Shafter, the 63-year-old walrus-moustached, 310-lb. veteran who had been wounded in the Civil War, led the 24th Infantry (the Army's best black regiment in the Indian wars) in the landing at Daiquiri, east of Santiago, with 20,000 men to begin the ground war.

Shafter had 2 problems. One was his army, the other his press relations. As strong as the U.S. Navy was, so was the Army weak. President McKinley called for 200,000 volunteers to supplement the regular Army. In truth, there was almost no regular Army. There were only 67,000 rifles, many with obsolete percussion locks, to go against Spain's modern German Mausers. Boxcars of Army food were lost somewhere between Washington, D.C., and Florida. "And, of course," wrote Holbrook, "the usual scandals over government contracts rose high, higher than the stench of rotten beef which had laid a thousand American soldiers low to every one hit by a Spanish bullet." Then there was the press corps. Richard Harding Davis, dean of correspondents, asked for special treatment for the press, and Shafter refused. "From that moment," Davis wrote later, "pencils began to be sharpened for General Shafter."

While the high command in Washington fouled things up, the Yellow Press, led by Hearst and Pulitzer, blamed Shafter for every blunder, and screamed for his removal. Day after day, in the U.S. press, Shafter was described "as a profane, cowardly, and incompetent soldier, a monstrosity of flabby flesh" who was stalling the ground war, despite the successes of "those brilliant and magnificent officers, Fighting Joe Wheeler and Rough-Riding Teddy Roosevelt." What was the truth?

June 24 Against orders, Gen. Joe Wheeler jumped into the 1st land battle against the Spanish. He impulsively attacked Las Guasimas. His men were slaughtered, he was driven back, until Gen. Henry W. Lawton and his foot cavalry came to the rescue and saved the day. It was in this battle that General Wheeler, who had gained fame as a Confederate leader in the Civil War, forgot he was fighting the Spaniards and, in a moment of nostalgia, shouted to his men, "Come on, boys! We've got the damn Yankees on the run!"

July 1 Lieut. Col. Theodore Roosevelt and his Rough Riders (former cowboys, college men, sons of the prominent, armed with the latest carbines), who rarely followed orders, charged up Kettle Hill toward San Juan Hill. Since the Rough Riders had no horses to ride, they ran and climbed up the Hill. Dominating the scene were Roosevelt's big hat, big grin, and big press following. Roosevelt took the Hill—and his 1st big step toward the Presidency.

July 17 The truth was that despite the foul-ups of Wheeler and Roosevelt, General Shafter took Santiago this day. Reported Holbrook: "Shafter moved an army of 20,000 men a distance of 1,500 mi. by water, landed on an enemy shore in open boats—after making a feint at landing elsewhere; in 10 days drove the enemy back to his last line of entrenchment in front of Santiago, and in 15 days more, compelled surrender of the city and an army of 24,000, an army larger than his own."

Aug. 12 Manila fell to U.S. troops, as Spain signed an armistice, and gave up rule of the Philippines.

Nov. 10 Following a Democratic party election victory, white supremacists in Wilmington, N.C., invaded the Negro district, burned down the houses, killed and injured many people, and chased the remaining Negroes out of town.

Dec. 10 The Spanish-American War formally ended with the signing of a treaty in Paris. Spain gave Cuba freedom, ceded Guam and Puerto Rico to the U.S., and turned over the Phillippines and 2 outlying islands to the U.S. in return for $20,100,000 to cover damages to Spanish property.

1899

—To the people of Puerto Rico, the results of the Spanish-American War seemed to be a bad joke. For the 1st time in 400 years, the people of the island were free of Spanish rule. For 7 months they enjoyed the fruits of their revolution—self-government. Then suddenly, without any discussions with the Puerto Ricans, the U.S. military moved in, occupied the island, and established U.S. rule, which persists to this day.

Jan. 15 The San Francisco Examiner published a protest poem, "The Man with the Hoe," which caused a sensation. Written by Edwin Markham, a schoolteacher, the poem protested the exploitation of labor and had been inspired by a Millet painting of a work-worn French peasant.

Feb. 4 A Filipino people's revolt, headed by General Emilio Aguinaldo, ignited against the 70,000 U.S. occupation forces. Since the U.S. would not give the Philippines independence, the guerrillas fought for 3 years, costing "the U.S. more men and money than did the Spanish-American War itself." Aguinaldo was captured, and the main Filipino insurrection put down. For almost a half century, the U.S. controlled the Philippines, treating the natives as nationals and not as citizens of the U.S., not allowing them citizenship unless they served in the U.S. Army. Finally, on July 4, 1946, the Philippines won its independence from the U.S. Government, if not from U.S. economic control.

Spring The $250,000 mill of the Bunker Hill Co. was destroyed by miners using dynamite. The Populist governor of Idaho, Frank Steunenberg, asked President McKinley for troops and declared Shoshone County in a state of "insurrection and rebellion." In an attempt to divert the anger of the miners, McKinley sent Negro soldiers from Brownsville, Tex., who, under orders from white officers, rounded up the miners and put them in bullpens. But the miners continued to feel betrayed by Steunenberg, who left office in a far more prosperous condition than he had entered it, and became a sheep-rancher and businessman. On December 3, 1905, he opened the gate of his home in Caldwell, Ida., and was blown to pieces by a bomb attached to the gate.

—D.W. & I.W.

1900

—U.S. population—75,994,575.
—Between 1890 and 1900, 3,688,000 immigrants entered the U.S.

—If bad institutions and bad men be got rid of only by killing, then the killing must be done.
—William Randolph Hearst

—Dwight F. Davis offered the Davis Cup to start an annual tennis competition between the U.S. and England, later opening up the matches to most nations.

Jan. 20 G. H. White, a black congressman from North Carolina, introduced a bill to make lynching of an American a Federal crime. The bill died in committee. One hundred and five blacks were lynched this same year.

Jan. 25 Congressman-elect Brigham H. Roberts, of Utah, was unseated by the House of Representatives, voting 268–50, because he had 3 wives and numerous offspring.

Mar. 18 John Luther Jones, veteran engineer of the Chicago and New Orleans Limited, stayed at the throttle despite the certainty of a wreck, in an effort to slow down his hurtling express and protect as many lives as possible. He died in the crash, but lived on in the folk ballad, "Casey Jones."

July 5 At the Democratic National Convention in Kansas City, Mo., war hero Adm. George Dewey tried to wrest the presidential nomination from William Jennings Bryan. But Dewey had married a Catholic woman, and this troubled the public and scuttled his chances.

Aug. In a "Gentleman's Agreement" between Japan and the U.S., Japan agreed to limit emigration of laborers to the U.S. by refusing to issue passports.

Nov. The 1st American automobile show was held in Madison Square Garden in New York. Nineteen makes of gasoline vehicles, 7 steamers, 6 electrics and 2 hybrids were among the 51 exhibitions at the show. Laid out in the Garden was a circular track ⅛ mi. long and 20' wide. Skilled automobileers competed in contests of starting, stopping, turning, and driving between obstacles. There were 13,824 of these strange vehicles registered in the U.S.

Nov. 8 Theodore Dreiser's 1st novel, *Sister Carrie*, a realistic book, was published by Doubleday & Company, in a nervous 1st printing of 1,000 copies. Worried about the immorality of the tale, and suffering public pressure, the publisher pulled the book off the stands. Morbidly depressed, Dreiser was unable to write another novel for over a decade.

1901

—Progressive Republican, Robert LaFollette, took office as governor of Wisconsin, putting into effect the "Wisconsin Idea" which served as a model of "progressive government." This provided for a direct primary in 1903, a railroad commission in 1905, opposed political bosses, and instituted tax reform.

—*The Octopus*, the 1st volume of a proposed 3-volume epic by Frank Norris, was published. The book depicted the struggle between the Southern Pacific Railroad and the wheat farmers in California.

Mar. 2 The Army Appropriation Bill was passed by Congress. Included in the Bill was the Platt Amendment, a provision which facilitated U.S. withdrawal from Cuba and gave the U.S. a quasi-protectorate over it. Cuba agreed to: (1) never enter into any treaty with any foreign power impairing Cuban independence; (2) authorize the U.S. to preserve Cuban independence and maintain law and order; (3) sell or lease the U.S. such lands as were necessary for naval or coaling stations. On June 12 Cuba added these provisions to its constitution; the U.S. withdrew from Cuba on May 12, 1902; and in May, 1903, the Platt Amendment was added to a U.S.-Cuban treaty.

Mar. 23 Emilio Aguinaldo, leader of the Filipino rebels was captured. At the outbreak of the Spanish-American War the U.S. had returned Aguinaldo to the Philippines to direct the native uprisings against the Spanish. In 1899 when the Filipinos learned the U.S. did not intend to give them their independence, Aguinaldo led an armed revolt against U.S. rule. An American force of 70,000 was sent to ·suppress the "insurrection." Despite the loss of their leader, the Filipinos continued the guerrilla warfare until mid-1902.

Sept. 6 President McKinley was shot in Buffalo, N.Y., by Leon Czolgosz, an American-born anarchist. McKinley died on September 14 at the age of 58. McKinley's assassination led to political tests of immigrants in order to bar anarchists. After McKinley's death William Randolph Hearst was hung in effigy, his life was threatened, and his newspapers were burned and banned at libraries and clubs due to his vicious attacks on the deceased President. (See also: Assassinations, Chap. 9.)

Sept. 14 Theodore Roosevelt, the 26th President, took his oath of office.

Oct. Admission of the 5 Civilized Tribes—the Choctaw, Cherokee, Seminole, Chickasaw, and Creek—to U.S. citizenship. Forced to move from the Southeast to the Indian Territory, now Oklahoma, the 5 Civilized Tribes were pledged everlasting possession of their communally-owned domain and authority for their tribal governments. In the name of "land allotment" and liquidation, the U.S. Government through the Bureau of Indian Affairs succeeded in passing 14.5 million acres of the Indian's 16 million acres into the hands of the whites, and through successive acts of Congress it abolished tribal courts and tribal taxes, and forbade tribal legislatures to remain in session more than 30 days per year.

1902

—Theodore Roosevelt created his trust-busting image when he had Attorney General Knox file suit against Northern Securities, a railroad holding company, and against the beef trust of Chicago. Both suits were upheld by the U.S. Supreme Court under the Sherman Anti-Trust Act.

May 12 An anthracite coal strike was called by the United Mine Workers when mine owners declined to arbitrate their demands for union recognition, an increase in wages and an 8-hour day. Under pressure from President Roosevelt, who threatened to use the Army to run the mines as receivers, thus dispossessing the operators, the owners agreed to arbitrate. Roosevelt appointed a commission to mediate the settlement. The strike ended October 21, with a 10% wage increase promised in 1903. Union recognition did not come until 1916. The average annual wage of miners was $250 at this time.

June 2 Oregon adopted the general initiative and referendum, by which people can initiate legislation and override legislative rulings. Oregon was the 1st State to put through this reform in an attempt to control machine rule of State government.

Sept. 2 In Dahomey, the most successful black musical both artistically and financially up to this time, opened in Boston to fantastic reviews. The musical with lyrics and book by Paul Lawrence Dunbar and music by Will Marion Cook was to run for 3 years.

Oct. With the publication of "Tweed Days in St. Louis" by C. H. Wetmore and Lincoln Steffens in *McClure's Magazine*, the era of the muckrakers had begun. "Muckracker" was a term that Theodore Roosevelt would coin in 1906 to describe the literature of exposure.

Nov. The 1st part of Ida Tarbell's exposé of the Standard Oil Company was published in *McClure's*. The writer spent 5 years investigating and researching her series, "The History of Standard Oil Company," which appeared in *McClure's* from 1902 to 1904. One reviewer called it, "a fearless unmasking of moral criminality masquerading under the robes of respectability and Christianity."

1903

—The publication of *Souls of Black Folks* by W. E. B. DuBois heralded a new approach to social reform for black Americans—an approach of patriotic, nonviolent activism. DuBois attacked Booker T. Washington's ideas of work and money, his lack of emphasis on dignity and manhood, and his failure to oppose discrimination. The book met with strong opposition from the conservative voices of both the North and the South. "This book is dangerous for the Negro to read, for it will only excite discontent and fill his imagination with things that do not exist, or things that should not bear upon his mind," said the *Banner* in Nashville. "The problem of the 20th C. is the color line," countered DuBois.

—Dr. Helen Bradford published "The Mental Traits of Sex." After testing the physical co-ordination, sense of pitch, perception of light, and memory of 25 college-educated men and women, Dr. Bradford found small differences between the sexes.

—The National Women's Trade Union League was formed to combat conditions that included low wages for women and exclusion from the unions. Women's wages averaged ⅓ as much as union men.

Aug. 1 Fifty-two days after leaving San Francisco, a Packard car arrived in New York, the 1st transcontinental automobile trip.

Oct. 1–13 In baseball's 1st annual World Series, Boston of the American League defeated Pittsburgh of the National League 5 games to 3 to become the World Champions.

Nov. 3 Under the instigation of the foreign promoter of the Panama Company, and with the approval of the Roosevelt Administration, native groups from Panama revolted against Colombia. Shortly before, Colombia had rejected an agreement with the U.S. regarding the Panama Canal. On November 6, the U.S. Government recognized the Republic of Panama.

1904

—Kentucky passed a school segregation law. In *Berea College* v. *The Commonwealth of Kentucky*, Berea College, an integrated school, challenged the law. However the Court of Appeals, and later, in 1908, the U.S. Supreme Court, upheld the law reflecting the courts' hands-off policy on segregation.

—Edwin S. Porter's *The Great Train Robbery*, the 1st well-known American film with a story line, was released to exhibitors. The 14-minute, single-reel film was also featured at the opening of the 1st modern movie theater in 1905 in Pittsburgh. Porter, working in the Edison laboratory, discovered the principle of editing. By piecing together films from the stockroom he had 1st made *The Life of an American Fireman*, which was released in 1903 to a limited audience.

May 5 Cy Young of the Boston Americans pitched the 1st perfect major league game.
—Angered by the abusive Ban Johnson, President of the American League, Giant manager John McGraw called off the World Series. He refused to allow his Giants to meet Boston.
Sept. 28 "You can't do that on 5th Avenue," exclaimed the police officer who arrested a woman for smoking a cigarette while riding in an open automobile in New York City.

1905

—The slum population in New York exceeded the population ratio in Bombay, reaching a density ratio of 1,000 persons an acre in some areas.
—The Supreme Court in a 5–4 decision declared unconstitutional a New York law which provided that no bakery could employ anyone more than 60 hours per week or 10 hours per day. The court invalidated the New York law, ruling that it interfered with freedom of contract protected by the 14th Amendment.
—Bob Marshall, a black athlete from the University of Minnesota, was selected for the All-American Football team.
—The Japanese and Korean Exclusion League was organized on the West Coast, where there was growing anti-Japanese antagonism and a fear of Japan as a military power. The Hearst newspapers helped foment this feeling by labeling the Japanese "the yellow peril."
—Comedians Fatty Arbuckle and Harry Bulgar, and actor John Mason sang the praises of Murad cigarettes, the 1st entertainers to give cigarette testimonials in advertisements.
Apr.

> Sensible and responsible women do not want to vote. The relative positions to be assumed by man and women in the working out of our civilization were assigned long ago by a higher intelligence than ours.
>
> —Grover Cleveland in
> *Ladies' Home Journal*

June The "fastest long-distance train in the world," Pennsylvania Railroad's 18-hour train between New York and Chicago, was inaugurated on June 11. New York Central Railroad began its 18-hour service one week later with the "20th Century Limited." Within a week both trains had had wrecks, leaving 19 dead.
June 27 "One Big Union for All" was the goal of the 200 delegates composed of radical labor leaders and Socialists who gathered in Chicago in June, 1905, for the formation of the Industrial Workers of the World (also known as IWW or the Wobblies). Representing

the Western Federation of Miners were Charles Moyer and Big Bill Haywood ("Fellow workers, this is the Continental Congress of the working class. The aims and objects of this organization shall be to put the working class in possession of economic power . . . without regard to the capitalist masters.") and Mother Jones, 75-year-old veteran of miners' strikes who organized the "women's armies" ("Pray for the dead, but fight like hell for the living."). (See also: Mother Jones in Footnote People in U.S. History, Chap. 3.) Eugene Debs, American Socialist party standard-bearer and Daniel DeLeon ("The Pope") of the Socialist Labor party were prominent Socialist leaders, along with Father Thomas Haggerty, Marxist ex-priest and editor of the *Voice of Labor*.

Repudiating the craft elitism of the American Federation of Labor (AFL), the IWW opened its membership to any wage earner regardless of occupation, race, creed, or sex. Initiation fees and dues were low. The IWW was united in its opposition to the AFL and capitalism, declaring that "The working class and the employing class have nothing in common." However, its members were divided on tactics. The Socialists called for political action ("every class struggle is a political struggle") while radicals called for direct action such as strikes and sabotage.

1906

—Upton Sinclair's exposé of the Chicago Stockyards, *The Jungle*, was published. Sinclair went to Chicago and lived in Packingtown for 7 weeks. A best seller in the U.S. and England, *The Jungle* has been translated into 17 languages. By describing in nauseating detail the squalid conditions of laborers and how diseased cattle were sold as clean meat, Sinclair, who claimed he had aimed at the public's heart, had by accident hit it in the stomach. As a result of Sinclair's exposé, President Roosevelt appointed a commission to investigate the meat industry. Their findings corroborated Sinclair's accusations. As a direct result, in June Congress passed the Pure Food and Drug Act which forbade manufacture, etc., of adulterated or mislabeled food and drugs, and the Meat Inspection Act which provided for enforcement of sanitary regulations in the meat-packing industry.
—Typhoid Mary was found working as a cook under an assumed name. Eight years earlier she had been discovered to be a carrier of typhoid fever although in good health herself. She was confined by health authorities until her death in 1929 since it was impossible to change her carrier state.

—George Bernard Shaw was well represented in New York with 6 of his plays performed during the theater season: *Caesar and Cleopatra, Arms and the Man, Man and Superman, John Bull's Other Island, Major Barbara,* and *Mrs. Warren's Profession.* The latter was raided by the police and closed after one performance on grounds of obscenity.

Apr. 18 The most damaging earthquake in U.S. history devastated San Francisco. For 192 mi., from Point Arena to the Pajaro Valley in Monterey, the land shifted 16′ to the north. The quake lasted for 47 seconds, buildings collapsed, fires broke out, and underground water mains were destroyed. Among the thousands caught in the disaster was the great tenor, Enrico Caruso, who vowed he would never return to a city "where disorders like that are permitted." When the last fire was put out, 400 people had died, 4 sq. mi. had burned and $500 million worth of damage had been done. The Japanese Government headed the list of contributors of funds for the victims of the quake.

Sept. 22 An anti-Negro riot in Atlanta, Ga., left 10 blacks and 2 whites dead and over 70 wounded. The militia was called out to bring order. Two days later the riot spread to the middle-class black suburb of Brownsville, where the homes of innocent blacks were looted and property was destroyed by the county police and bands of armed white citizens who joined them.

Oct. U.S. troops took over the Cuban Government for 13 days and restored order after a revolt erupted over an election dispute. U.S. intervention was requested by Tomás Estrada Palma, 1st President of Cuba.

Oct. 11 The San Francisco school board ordered the segregation of all Japanese, Chinese, and Korean children. Strong anti-Japanese feeling permeated the city from organized labor to the press. On March 13, 1907, under pressure from the President, San Francisco rescinded this action, and Japan agreed to enforce their "Gentleman's Agreement" by stopping the emigration of laborers.

Dec. 5 The Rev. Algernon S. Crapsey, Episcopal clergyman and rector of St. Andrew's Church, Rochester, N.Y., was found guilty of heresy and deposed from the ministry in a trial that began on April 18 before an ecclesiastical court. The trial drew attention both in Europe and the U.S. A highly respected and much loved minister, Crapsey had become a "rationalist" and preached against the divinity of Christ. In his autobiography, *The Last of the Heretics,* published in 1924, he explained:

> . . . I have a religion and if asked to give it a name I should say I am a Pantheistic Humanist, and if one were to ask, "What is a Pantheistic Humanist?" I should say one who believes in the divinity of a telegraph pole.

1907

—In his 7th annual message to Congress, President Theodore Roosevelt said:

> We are prone to speak of the resources of this country as inexhaustible; this is not so. The mineral wealth of the country, the coal, iron, oil, gas and the like, does not reproduce itself, and therefore is certain to be exhausted ultimately; and wastefulness in dealing with it today means that our descendants will feel the exhaustion a generation or 2 before they otherwise would.

During his Presidency 148 million acres were set aside as national forest lands and more than 80 million acres of mineral lands were withdrawn from public sale.

—The *San Francisco Chronicle* printed the 1st daily comic strip, H. C. (Bud) Fisher's "Mr. Mutt," later called "Mutt and Jeff."

Jan. 22 The debut of *Salome,* the controversial opera by Richard Strauss taken from the play by Oscar Wilde, aroused a storm of protest at the Metropolitan Opera House in New York City. Citing the perverse passion of Salome for the head of John the Baptist, critics labeled the opera "morbid" and "immoral." The reviewer for the *New York Tribune* wrote, "Many voices were hushed as the crowd passed out into the night, many faces were white . . . many women were silent and men spoke as if a bad dream were upon them." It was 21 years before the opera was performed again at the Metropolitan.

Mar. 21 U.S. Marines landed in Honduras to protect American lives—and capital investments in banana plantations—from the dangers of revolution.

Aug. The death of former Idaho governor Frank Steunenberg by an assassin's bomb began the Haywood case, one of the most renowned trials in American labor history. Steunenberg, a "friend of miners" when elected in 1896 and reelected in 1898, earned the wrath of the miners when he called in troops during the miners' strike in Coeur d'Alene in 1899. Local police arrested Harry Orchard and turned him over to James McParland, Pinkerton special investigator. No friend of unions, McParland earned a reputation as a strikebreaker during the Molly Maguires' conspiracy in Pennsylvania in the 1880s. Under McParland's investigation, Orchard not only admitted his guilt but also confessed that he had been a tool of the Western Federation of Miners "inner circle."

On February 17, 1906, Big Bill Haywood, secretary of the WFM; Charles Moyer, president of the WFM; and George Pettibone, a blacklisted miner, were arrested without warrant and extradicted to Idaho. Taken from their homes in Denver, Colo., during the middle of the night, the 3 men were transported to Boise, Ida., and put in cells in the death house. It was 18 months before Haywood, the 1st to be tried, was vindicated. Under the brilliant defense of Clarence Darrow, who gave an 11-hour summation, Big Bill was acquitted in August, 1907. (In attendance at the opening of the trial on June 24 was actress Ethel Barrymore, who had come to town for a one-night stand in her hit *Captain Jinks of the Horse Marines*. She commented most favorably on the jury, "the most wonderful looking men I've ever seen . . . the bluest eyes used to looking great distances.")

In spite of President Roosevelt's unprecedented comment that the 3 union officials were "undesirable citizens," throughout the ordeal Haywood received unanimous support from the IWW, WFM, Socialist party, Socialist Labor party, and the AFL, in a rare show of solidarity.
Oct. Overspeculating by "reckless operators" —plus a money shortage caused by the Russian-Japanese War, the rebuilding of San Francisco, railroad expansion and the general growth of the economy—created a panic situation in 1907. Rumors spread like wildfire and people began to withdraw their deposits from any bank or trust company that was suspected of being in danger. The Knickerbocker Trust Company, with $67 million in deposits and 18,000 depositors, was the largest trust company to fail. President Roosevelt, who by his own admission was bored by economics, was off shooting bear in Louisiana. That left financier J. Pierpont Morgan, whose enormous interests would suffer greatly from a depression or panic, to salvage the rapidly deteriorating New York financial world. Morgan locked the leading bank presidents in the East Room of his new marble library, forcing them to come up with a solution. By pumping millions into failing trust companies, they were able to stem the tide. Morgan rescued the stockmarket when his U.S. Steel Corporation purchased Tennessee Coal and Iron (TC&I) for $25 million. A grateful President Roosevelt rewarded him by granting U.S. Steel Corporation immunity from prosecution under the Sherman Anti-Trust Act.
Nov. 16 Oklahoma was admitted to the U.S. as the 46th State. It was formerly 2 separate Territories—the Territory of Oklahoma, and Indian Territory, the land given to the 5 Civilized Tribes. The Indians and some non-Indians voted to have the Indian Territory admitted as the separate State of Sequoyah, but President Roosevelt and Congress recommended joint statehood. The population was 1,414,000. The State constitution included prohibition of liquor.
Dec. 16 Sixteen battleships ("The Great White Fleet") set sail for an around-the-world cruise. President Roosevelt wanted to impress the Japanese, as well as display American Naval strength. The Rev. Robert MacArthur of Calvary Baptist Church, New York, expressed the feeling of many Americans:

> The departure of the fleet was momentus. It drove me to prayer. I could see in it America's assertion of her right to control the Pacific in the interest of civilization and humanity.

The fleet returned one year and 68 days later.

1908

—In his autobiography, *A Mind That Found Itself*, Clifford W. Beers described the brutalities of attendants toward inmates in mental institutions. In spite of the harsh treatment he had received as a mental patient, Beers recovered and went on to establish the National Committee for Mental Health.
—The Supreme Court inhibited the growth and limited the effectiveness of unions by its rulings in 2 cases that came before it. In *Loewe* v. *Lawler*, the Supreme Court declared the 1902 boycott by the United Hatters of America against D. H. Loewe and Co. of Danbury, Conn., a violation of the Sherman Anti-Trust Act. The Sherman Anti-Trust Act, passed in 1890 to regulate trusts and monopolies, was being applied to unions for the 2nd time. If the use of the boycott was an illegal restraint of trade, any act to raise wages, shorten hours or improve conditions, might be declared unlawful. In *Adair* v. *U.S.*, the Supreme Court invalidated the Erdman Act of 1898, which had said railroads engaged in interstate commerce could not prevent workers from joining a union by making it a condition of employment (the "yellow-dog" contract). The Court called the act a violation of freedom of contract as guaranteed by the 5th Amendment.
—A ray of hope came to the working woman and ultimately to the working man in the Supreme Court's decision in *Muller* v. *Oregon*. The Supreme Court for the 1st time acknowledged the need for facts, not just legal arguments, to establish the reasonableness of social legislation. Louis Brandeis, chief counsel for the State of Oregon, used sociology rather than a legalist approach to prove the reasonableness of Oregon's law to restrict the hours that a woman could work.

—Most popular song of the year: "Take Me Out to the Ball Game."

Feb. Angered by the slights of the conservative National Academy of Arts, artists Robert Henri, Ernest Lawson, Maurice Pendergast, Arthur Davie, and former newspaper illustrators George Luks, John Sloan, William Glackens, and Everett Shinn arranged for their own show, the Exhibition of the 8. The critics were disturbed by the realist subject matter of their paintings and called them the "apostles of ugliness," labeling the group "the Ash Can School." The cityscapes, portraits and slices of life portrayed by the artists were considered "too frank and vulgar," and caused one critic to comment, "Is it fine art to exhibit our sores?" Although the 8 never exhibited as a unit again, Henri established his own art school in 1909 and held a 2nd exhibition of 200 artists in 1910, which included examples by the original 8 as well as his students.

Aug. 14–15 Some 4,200 militia men were called in when a race riot erupted in Springfield, Ill. The riot started when a white woman claimed she had been raped by George Richardson, a black man. Richardson was removed from the town for his own protection. Meanwhile a mob gathered and began to destroy black homes. After 2 days of rioting, 2,000 blacks had left the city, 2 had been lynched, 6 others killed, and over 70 blacks and whites wounded. The alleged riot leaders escaped punishment despite arrests and indictments. Before a special grand jury, the woman later admitted that a white man, whom she refused to identify, had raped her.

Dec. 26 Jack Johnson, a black boxer from Galveston, Tex., knocked out Canadian Tommy Burns for the heavyweight championship of the world. White promoters searched for a "Great White Hope" to defeat the new champion. In 1915, Johnson was defeated by Jess Willard. Hounded by racial tension and accusations of violating the Mann Act, Johnson, it was rumored, threw the fight. Johnson's ring career lasted over 30 years, with 7 losses in 112 fights.

1909

—Henry Ford presented his "universal" car, the Model T. The Ford Motor Company, like other automobile companies, had been making expensive luxury cars priced as high as $2,800. In 1906, Ford experimented with the Model N, which sold for $600. Then came Models R and S, and—finally—the incomparable Model T. Priced at $850 originally, by 1924 the "T" was available to all at $290. Henry Ford, for better or worse, had put the nation on wheels.

Apr. 7 Explorers Robert Peary and Matthew Henson—and 4 Eskimos—discovered the North Pole. Henson, Peary's black assistant on all his Arctic expeditions after 1891, spoke the language of the Eskimos, acted as trader and hunter, built the sledges and trained the dog teams. On their return, Peary discovered that Dr. Frederick Cook claimed he had reached the Pole a year earlier. The dispute over the authenticity of Cook's v. Peary's claim was finally resolved in December, 1909, in an official report by the University of Copenhagen. After reviewing Cook's data, the Committee members concluded that his observations proved nothing and called the case "shameless." Peary received his just reward, although the moment of glory had passed.

May 22 President Taft opened 700,000 acres of government land in Washington, Montana, and Idaho for settlers.

May 31–June 1 Prompted by the race riot in Springfield in 1908, a biracial group of concerned citizens organized the National Negro Conference in New York City. Participants included members of W. E. B. DuBois's Niagara Movement, prominent religious leaders, and such humanitarians as Jane Addams, and William Dean Howells. The participants decided to incorporate as the National Association for the Advancement of Colored People (NAACP). W. E. B. DuBois was the editor of the Association's magazine, *Crisis*. The organization demanded equal civil, political, and educational rights, and enforcement of the 14th and 15th Amendments.

Nov. 18 When reports were received that Zelaya, dictator of Nicaragua, had executed 500 revolutionaries, including 2 Americans, U.S. troops and warships were sent to Nicaragua. The troops supported the revolutionaries and hostilities ended on December 18.

—M.L.H.

1910

—U.S. population—91,972,266.

—An obscure British music-hall performer with a French kick toured the U.S. with a pantomime troupe, and appeared in a vaudeville act billed as "Karno's Wow Wows." His name: Charlie Chaplin.

—Mrs. Carrie Jacobs Bond wrote the words and music for "A Perfect Day." Self-taught, she turned out over 175 other songs including the wedding favorite, "I Love You Truly."

—Dr. George McCoy and Dr. Charles Chapin identified a new, strictly American disease: *Bacterium tularense* ("tularemia"), occurring in ground squirrels of Tulare County, Calif.

Apr. 19 Halley's Comet flashed across the horizon, making its 1st visit since 1759. Many people fearfully awaited Doomsday, the moment when the earth passed through its tail, staying home with their families. The next appearance: 9:30 P.M. Greenwich Mean Time, February 9, 1986.

June 25 The Mann Act was passed, making it illegal to transport women across State lines, or bring them into the U.S., for immoral purposes. The going price: $200 minimum, escalating to $2,000 for prime specimens to add to the world's oldest profession. The "white slavery" law crimped business in New Orleans, which published an annual guidebook to its houses of ill repute. Red light districts in 30 other cities were closed up.

Sept. 1 Nan Aspinwall left San Francisco on horseback, headed for New York City. She arrived 10 months later, after meandering over 4,500 mi.

1911

—Republican rebels bolted the party and formed the National Progressive Republican League, with Robert "Fighting Bob" La Follette as their leader. The Progressive party's platform included abolition of monopolies, endorsement of collective bargaining by unions, and public control and conservation of natural resources.

Mar. 8 New York City police introduced a new prosecutor's tool: latent-fingerprint evidence, to prove Caesar "Charley Crispi" Cella's presence during a burglary. He was convicted.

Mar. 25 175 Jewish and Italian immigrant women were killed in a fire at the Triangle Shirtwaist Co. in New York.

Fall Edward Hines painted white lines by hand on River Road near Trenton, Mich., to indicate traffic lanes.

1912

—Research began at Yale on a mysterious group of substances that affect body health. Professor Elmer McCollum announced that 2 organic compounds called "vitamin A" and "vitamin B" were needed to prevent dietary deficiencies.

Jan. Twenty-five thousand textile workers of 14 nationalities went on strike against the American Woolen Co., of Lawrence, Mass. When money and food became dangerously scarce, IWW organizers arranged to have the children of Lawrence sent to other cities to be housed and fed by supporters there. On February 10, the 1st 119 children were sent to New

York where they were met by a crowd of 5,000. Public opinion swayed heavily to the side of the strikers and on February 4, police in Lawrence tried to stop a group of children from boarding a train to Philadelphia by attacking the children and their parents with clubs. By March 12, so much hostility was directed at the American Woolen Co. that the firm gave in and agreed to a wage hike.

Feb. 24 Rough Rider Theodore Roosevelt reentered politics with the flamboyant phrase echoed by politicians ever since: "My hat is in the ring." As the "Bull Moose" party candidate for President, he drew enough votes away from William Howard Taft to ensure Woodrow Wilson's election.

Apr. 14–15 On its maiden voyage, the unsinkable *Titanic* struck an iceberg and sank, carrying 1,500—including many prominent Americans—to their deaths. The disaster initiated new Federal orders that steamships must carry lifeboats sufficient in number to hold all passengers and crew. An "iceberg patrol" was also begun.

1913

—"The masters of Government of the U.S. are the combined capitalists and manufacturers."—President Woodrow Wilson

Feb. 17 The 69th Regiment Armory in New York City offered an exhibition of the latest avant-garde, post-Impressionist works in U.S. and European art. Hung among the Gauguins and the Picassos was the hit of the show: *Nude Descending a Staircase*, by Marcel Duchamp. Few visitors could understand Duchamp's cubist painting, which projected the idea of continuous action by depicting a series of overlapping figure outlines.

Mar. 23 Easter Sunday Disaster in Middle America. The 1st of a series of death-dealing tornadoes and floods hit Nebraska, Iowa, Illinois, Indiana, and Ohio. In Dayton, O., the hardest hit, a swollen Miami River inundated downtown business areas to a depth of 12'. Flood damages of over $100 million were reported, with more than 3,000 believed dead.

Summer Henry Ford, adapting the conveyer-belt system in use by the meat-packing industry, began to assemble 1,000 "Model T" automobiles daily, on a continuous-production line in Detroit.

Oct. 10 President Wilson, pressing an electric button at the White House, blew up the Gamboa Dike. With its destruction in the Isthmus of Panama, passage by ship through the new ocean-to-ocean Canal became possible.

Nov. 1 Upset on the Gridiron. Unknown

Notre Dame jumped into national prominence by defeating mighty Army, using a new technique: Wait for the brawny forward line to charge—and then throw the football over their heads, to a downfield receiver. The "forward pass" gave small schools an incentive to take on the larger, more powerful teams, and greatly helped to popularize the game.

Dec. 23 The Carter-Owen bill established the Federal Reserve System, dividing the U.S. into 12 districts. The crowning effort of Wilson's domestic legislation, it was achieved in the face of public and private abuse from the "Money Trust," the big banks who had placed a strangle-hold on the nation's currency and credit system.

1914

—Edgar Rice Burroughs conceived a new folk hero for the world: *Tarzan of the Apes.* The tree-swinging British lord starred in 25 books which were translated into 56 languages.

—Thirty-five thousand workers were killed in accidents on the job and 700,000 were injured.

Apr. 20 On Easter night, coal miners striking against John D. Rockefeller's Colorado Fuel & Iron Co. in Ludlow, Colo., were attacked by company guards and National Guardsmen who set fire to the tent camp they had been living in since they had been evicted from their company-owned homes. Among those killed were 11 children and a pregnant woman. By the time the strike, or the Ludlow War as it was called, was over, 74 people had died.

Apr. 21 Awakened abruptly at 2:30 A.M. by the telephoned news that Mexico's President Huerta had arrested American sailors at Tampico, President Wilson issued orders for Admiral Mayo, anchored off Vera Cruz: "Take Vera Cruz at once." The landing party of sailors and marines captured the port, with U.S. losses of 4 dead and 20 wounded. Mexican casualties were in the hundreds.

Later in the morning, Wilson sent for his chief usher, shook an angry finger at him, and gave emphatic orders that he was never again to be awakened for a telephone call in the middle of the night. No man, he said, can make a clear decision when startled out of a sound sleep.

Wilson's selection of Vera Cruz as the target rather than Tampico, was influenced by the knowledge that a German freighter was unloading munitions there, possibly for anti-U.S. use. On the 24th of April, 3,400 U.S. reinforcements left Galveston, Tex., for Vera Cruz and the occupation closed off Huerta's only source of ready cash—from the custom

house there. By July he was forced to flee from the country, after which Wilson withdrew the U.S. forces.

June 28 Archduke Franz Ferdinand was assassinated in Sarajevo, beginning W.W. I. Of greater interest to the U.S. in some newspaper headlines: Suffragettes had marched on Washington.

July 4 Negro Jack Johnson successfully defended his heavyweight boxing championship against Jim Jeffries. Congress immediately enacted Federal statutes, valid for decades to come, which forbade interstate transportation of prizefight film. Its reasoning: Such films were Evil. If they showed a black man winning against a white, it could incite race riots.

Aug. 5 Cleveland, O., motorists obeyed signals from the 1st traffic light in the U.S., installed at Euclid Avenue and East 105th Street. Besides the red and green lights, mounted on cross arms, 15' above the ground, the device had a loud buzzer: 2 buzzes directed the traffic on Euclid to "Go," and one buzz meant "Go" on 105th.

Aug. 19 Elmer Rice utilized a new plot technique called "the flashback" in his play *On Trial.* It widened story possibilities for the infant cinema industry, just then relocating in Hollywood, Calif., where the "independents" had fled. The future film capital was fortuitously located just over 100 mi. from the Mexican border. Film crews could continue to work in Mexico should the Motion Picture Patents Company win its legal fight to put unlicensed independents out of business in the U.S.

Sept. 14 *The New York Times* published the erroneous news that 72,000 Russians, traveling via the Arctic port of Archangel, had reached the French lines on the Western Front. Almost complete censorship of battle news by the warring powers led to eager acceptance by the U.S. citizen of all such rumors in the 1st months of the war. The U.S. newspapers also carried many "eyewitness" stories of alleged atrocities committed by Germans.

Dec. 8 Irving Berlin's 1st musical, *Watch Your Step,* opened on Broadway.

1915

—The taxicab appeared. For a short ride, drivers charged a nickel, or a "jitney," and the word became a synonym for the vehicle.

Jan. 25 Alexander Graham Bell, speaking into a New York City telephone which was an exact copy of his 1876 invention, said to his assistant, Dr. Thomas A. Watson: "Mr. Watson, come here, I want you." Watson, in his reply, said it would probably take him 4 days by fast train. He was then in San Francisco, helping to inaugurate the U.S. transcontinental telephone service.

May 7 The *Lusitania* was torpedoed by a German submarine, the *Unterseeboot 20*, off the Irish coast. (See: Man-Made Disasters, Chap. 9.)

Nov. Poet, songwriter, and labor leader Joe Hill was executed in Utah despite the pleas of President Wilson, the Swedish Government, and thousands of others. He had been convicted of murdering an ex-policeman. His last words were "Don't mourn for me—organize!"

Dec. 4 Henry Ford's chartered "Peace Ship," *Oscar II*, sailed from Hoboken, N.J. Ford had seen a newspaper account that reported the senseless death, within a 24-hour period, of 20,000 soldiers in the trenches. They had been slaughtered ". . . without shifting the position of the armies." Sickened, he publicly avowed to spend half of his fortune if it would cut the war by a single day. His impulsive statement attracted the attention of the pacifist group which included welfare workers Jane Addams and Mme. Rosika Schwimmer. Mme. Schwimmer had just returned from Europe with a "little black bag" bulging with statements allegedly made to the pacifist group by foreign ministers of the warring powers. She convinced Ford that he could personally mediate and stop the war.

Sailing aboard the ship: 54 newspaper and magazine correspondents, some 60 peace delegates, 3 men from the newsreels, and Ford's personal staff of 20.

After 2 days at sea, the reporters organized their own group, called "The Friendly Sons of St. Vitus," with a motto, "Skoal!," and club headquarters were located in the ship's bar. Their daily dispatches from this "wet" pressroom noted that fighting had broken out among the pacifists as well. Six days after leaving Hoboken, magazine publisher Samuel McClure read to those aboard President Wilson's speech on preparedness, delivered to Congress on December 10. The next morning, the pacifists' Committee on Resolution offered a declaration for signatures, flatly rejecting Wilson's pleas. McClure and others, objecting vociferously, refused to sign. The correspondents promptly sent stories to their papers of "mutiny aboard *Oscar II*," and the British went so far as to send out a party of marines to check on the uprising.

The ship docked at Christiania, Norway, on December 19. Ford, ill and homesick, left secretly for the U.S. on Christmas Eve, remarking that he had not seen much peace during the crossing, and he had learned only that "Russia is going to be a great market for tractors." His departure crippled the mission. Some delegates quit at once. A few others continued to tour through the neutral countries in 1916, giving speeches intended to end the war. The Peace Expedition, ridiculed on all sides, hamstrung other pacifist causes in the U.S.

1916

—John Dewey introduced the progressive educational theory that subject material should be tailored to fit the child's needs, and not vice versa.

Jan. 28 Louis Dembitz Brandeis was nominated to be an associate justice of the U.S. Supreme Court. A Jew, his appointment was contested bitterly by some who felt that his "Oriental" mind could not function effectively in a legal system based on Occidental principles.

Mar. 9 Mexican revolutionary Pancho Villa, riding with 1,500 men, crossed the U.S. border to attack Columbus, N. Mex. He killed 9 civilians and 8 men from the nearby camp of the U.S. 13th cavalry. The troopers then engaged in a running fight with the Mexicans, killing 50 on the U.S. side of the border, and 70 more during a 15-mi. penetration into Mexico. The U.S. recognized that Venustiano Carranza, the Mexican President it had helped to gain power, would voice loud regrets about Villa's murderous raid, but would do nothing. Wilson therefore sent 6,000 soldiers, led by Brig. Gen. John "Black Jack" Pershing, to capture and bring back this bandit for trial. Despite a 300-mi. search—which lacked air support—Pershing was unable to find Villa, who had split up his main forces and dispatched them, piecemeal, into the wild mountains of northern Mexico.

In June, a Mexican army column clashed with part of Pershing's detachment near Carrizal, claiming that his invasion represented a hostile act. They captured 23 U.S. soldiers. When the men, primarily black troopers, were set free at the International Bridge in El Paso, in July, they were greeted with blankets. These were needed to cover their embarrassment—and their nudity. The bandits had appropriated their uniforms. General Pershing was not ordered out of Mexico until February 5, 1917.

July 18 *The Official Gazette*, of London, published the names of 80 U.S. firms and individuals suspected of trading with Germany. This blacklisting, legal under Britain's trading-with-the-enemy act, prevented the firms from doing business with the neutral countries as well.

July 22 At a pro-war "preparedness parade" in San Francisco, a bomb exploded near a saloon wall on Steuart near Market St. Ten people were killed and 40 injured. Labor leader Thomas J. Mooney and shoe-worker Warren K. Billings were convicted of murder. Although the 2 key witnesses against them later admitted to having perjured themselves, Mooney and Billings stayed in jail until 1939 when they were pardoned by New Deal governor Culbert L. Olson of California.

Oct. 7 With cool German arrogance, the U-53, under command of *Kapitan-Leutnant* Hans Rose, entered Newport harbor, R.I., and calmly requested a berth assignment. After inviting U.S. officers to visit his ship, and carefully observing neutrality regulations while in port, Rose left. Once outside the 3-mi. limit, he again began to sink Allied shipping.

1917

—The Columbia School of Journalism submitted its 1st list of candidates for the Pulitzer Prize, to the Columbia College trustees. On the list and an eventual winner for 1917: Herbert Bayard Swope, for his war reporting in Germany as a foreign correspondent for the *New York World*.

Mar. 1 The Associated Press published the full text of the "Zimmermann Note," sent from Berlin to the German Ambassador in Mexico. It informed him that unrestricted submarine warfare would begin on February 1, although Germany would continue efforts to keep the U.S. neutral, and proposed a full alliance with Mexico. President Carranza was to be encouraged to woo Japan away from the Allies, perhaps with Hawaii as the reward if she were to attack the U.S.

The U.S. State Department, baffled beyond belief, spent days trying to determine whether the original German text in one section was a hoax. It read:

Einverstandnis unsurerseits dass Mexico *in* Texas, New Mexico, Arizona *früher verlorenes Geibiet zurück erobert.*

The words promised Mexico a full recovery of its lost territory in the States mentioned.

Apr. 4 Republican senator George W. Norris of Nebraska, who ultimately represented his State in Congress for 39 years, delivered an indignant speech opposing a declaration of war:

There are a great many American citizens who feel that we owe it as a duty to humanity to take part in this war. . . . This has brought us to the present moment, when Congress, urged by the Presi-

dent and backed by the artificial sentiment, is about to declare war and engulf our country in the greatest holocaust that the world has ever known.

In showing the position of the bondholder and the stockholder, I desire to read an extract from a letter written by a member of the N.Y. Stock Exchange to his customers. This writer says:

"Regarding the war as inevitable, Wall Street believes that it would be preferable to this uncertainty about the actual date of commencement. Canada and Japan are at war, and are more prosperous than ever before. The popular view is that stocks would have a quick, clear, sharp reaction immediately upon outbreak of hostilities, and that then they would enjoy an old-fashioned bull market such as followed the outbreak of war with Spain in 1898. . . . If the U.S. does not go to war, it is nevertheless good opinion that the preparedness program will compensate in good measure for the loss of the stimulus of actual war!"

. . . Here we have the cold-blooded proposition that war brings prosperity to that class of people who are within the viewpoint of the writer. . . .

To whom does war bring prosperity? Not to the soldier who for the munificent compensation of $16 per month shoulders his musket and goes into the trench, there to shed his blood and to die if necessary; not to the broken-hearted widow who waits for the return of the mangled body of her husband; not to the mother who weeps at the death of her brave boy; not to the little children who shiver with cold; not to the babe who suffers from hunger; not to the millions of mothers and daughters who carry broken hearts to their graves. War brings no prosperity to the great mass of common and patriotic citizens. It increases the cost of living of those who toil and those who already must strain every effort to keep soul and body together. War brings prosperity to the stock gambler on Wall Street—to those who are already in possession of more wealth than can be realized or enjoyed. . . .

We are taking a step today that is fraught with untold danger. We are going into war upon the command of gold. . . . By our act we will make millions of our countrymen suffer, and the consequences of it may well be that millions of our brethren must shed their life-blood, millions of broken-hearted women must weep, millions of children must suffer, and millions of babes must die from hunger, and all because we want to preserve the commercial right of American citizens to deliver munitions of war to belligerent nations.

Apr. 6 The U.S. declared war against Germany. It became the 13th country to fight the Central Powers. Six senators and 50 congressmen voted against the declaration.

May 18 Proclamation Day. President Wilson, following Secretary of War Baker's advice, issued a formal proclamation to announce universal conscription. This affected 10 million men between the ages of 21 and 30. The wording was shrewdly chosen to infuse the nation with a maximum upsurge of patriotic spirit, to ready it for a great adventure, a joyous pilgrimage—and some heroic sacrifices.

June 15 Congress passed the Espionage Act, providing a $10,000 fine and 20 years in prison for anyone who encouraged disloyalty or interfered with the draft. Over 1,500 were eventually arrested and charged with its violation. Among them: Eugene V. Debs, Socialist party candidate for President, who threatened that his followers would refuse to support the war, and Victor Berger, the 1st Socialist ever elected to Congress. Rose Pastor Stokes received a 10-year sentence for writing a letter to the *Kansas City Star* in which she said, "No government which is for the profiteers can also be for the people, and I am for the people while the Government is for the profiteers."

July 20 Lottery Day. Secretary of War Newton Baker, reaching into a large glass bowl, withdrew ✕258, the number of the 1st man to be called up in each draft office. His group continued to draw, one by one, the 10,500 black capsules with their numbered slips inside for the next 16 hours, to determine the order of the draft, and the 2,702,687 men finally sworn into the Army.

1918

Jan. 8 President Wilson's idealized proposals for future peace, the "Fourteen Points," were delivered to Congress. The credit for the itemized approach belonged to his press agent, George Creel, head of the Committee of Public Information. Creel's man in St. Petersburg, Russia, Edgar Sisson, had cabled that Wilson's long speeches describing his war aims and peace proposals were too difficult to translate into a form easily understood by the German and the Russian commoner. Before any attempts were made to reach these people with propaganda leaflets, Sisson suggested that the facts for these leaflets be reduced to a simple placard-type style. Wilson, apprised by Creel of Sisson's advice, grasped its logic immediately and followed the suggestion.

Clemenceau, the French Prime Minister, was not impressed by the proposals. Noting that Wilson had listed 14 points, he said: "Even God Almighty has only 10!"

Mar. 20 An Executive Order recognized the rights of men who objected to war service on grounds other than religious. Pvt. Richard Stierheim benefited: A 3-time deserter sentenced to be shot, because he refused to kill while serving in France, he so distinguished himself under enemy fire by saving wounded men that Wilson canceled the death sentence and restored him to noncombatant duty.

Mar. 31 The nation's clocks were set ahead one hour, marking the start of Daylight Saving Time.

June 6–25 Milestone Battle: Belleau Wood. U.S. Marines, with army elements joining them, fought a bitter one-week battle for one sq. mi. of forest and lost 55% of their effective strength. Their victory, well-publicized in the U.S., earned the Marine Corps much praise from the people, and decades of rancor from the Army, which felt slighted from nonrecognition. The ill-feeling persisted through Generals Eisenhower and MacArthur in W.W. II, who both commented about the battle.

July 8–Aug. 6 Milestone Battle: the Aisne-Marne Offensive. In a 4-week-long counterattack, 250,000 U.S. troops drove the Germans back to the Vesle, marking the turning point for the Allies in the war.

Aug. 8 Grover Cleveland Bergdoll did not report to his local draft board. The war's most infamous draft dodger was not caught until January 7, 1920, although he had been living in Hagerstown, Md., under various assumed names. Sentenced to 5 years in prison, he somehow secured permission to retrieve a gold cache of $105,000 he claimed to have buried, convinced his military escort to travel to the reported hiding place via his Philadelphia home and evaded them there, to effect a permanent disappearance.

Aug. 10 General Pershing was given Allied consent for his independent command of the American Expeditionary Force—the AEF—in France.

Sept. 26–Nov. 11 Milestone Battle: Meuse-Argonne. In a massive drive, 1,200,000 U.S. troops—the largest number committed to the attack in army history—surged forward in the St. Mihiel sector in the 1st American offensive. Their objective: to cut the Sedan-Mezieres railroad which supplied the entire German army opposing them. The Germans reeled under the blow, all along the Hindenburg Line, and went into a general retreat that continued until the Armistice on November 11. The AEF lost 120,-000 in casualties in this drive.

Sept. 28 The 4th and last Liberty Loan Drive began. Aided by prominent entertainers such as Douglas Fairbanks, over $18 billion in Liberty Bonds was sold to over ½ of the adult population. In other home-front mobilization to "do your bit," home gardens and wheatless-meatless days were promoted.

Oct. 1 The death rate in the influenza epidemic hit a peak of 202 deaths daily. In the poorer sections of the cities, the dead lay unburied for days because of coffin shortages. Nearly ¼ of the U.S. was sick, and almost 500,000 died in 46 States before the disease had run its course in early 1919. Approximately 130,000 cases raged through 20 army camps, killing about half as many as died in combat in France. War plants shut down and panic spread from coast to coast, with citizens scanning the long lists of the dead in the newspapers, published side-by-side with rules for preventative hygiene.

1919

Jan. 29 The Secretary of State announced the ratification of the 18th Amendment to the Constitution: the Prohibition Amendment. Liquor was legally outlawed for all U.S. citizens.

Feb. In bitter cold weather just south of the Arctic Circle, 3 U.S. battalions, attached to British command, suffered 400 casualties fighting the Bolsheviki at Archangel. Some 10,000 others were in action in Siberia as far East as Vladivostok, the Pacific terminus for the Trans-Siberian Railroad.

Apr. 28 Leslie Irving successfully jumped using the new Army Air Corps parachute at McCook Field, Dayton, O. The experimental design called for the rip cord to be pulled after falling free of the airplane.

Sept. 22 Three hundred and fifty thousand steelworkers struck, followed by 400,000 miners 40 days later. Union demands among the 4 million who walked off the job during the year: Reduce the average work week of 68.7 hours, and increase the "inhuman" pay. Big Steel broke numerous strikes with the aid of the military.

Nov. 7 Department of Justice agents, under orders from Attorney General A. Mitchell Palmer, raided leftist headquarters in more than a dozen cities. About 2,000 people in New York alone were arrested.

Nov. 19 The Senate failed to ratify the Treaty of Versailles, voting 55 to 39—9 votes short of the required ⅔ majority. Wilson's opposition had come from many sides. Some were the hard-line imperialists who wanted the U.S. free to expand. Others, like Sens. Hiram Johnson and William Borah, were isolationists who wanted no international entanglements. But Wilson's main enemies were the Republican party leaders, and chiefly Sen. Henry Cabot Lodge, chairman of the powerful Foreign Relations Committee. To lend his support, Lodge wanted 14 amendments plus other changes inserted, to "Americanize" the treaty.

A Wilson-Lodge feud began, and neither man would give in. Wilson, in September, had decided to go on a national tour, to take his case to the people. On September 25, he delivered his 40th speech, in Pueblo, Colo., and that night collapsed from a stroke. After his recovery in November, he still maintained that none of the Republican changes were acceptable to him. His refusal to compromise cost him the necessary Republican votes needed for ratification.

Dec. 11 Enterprise, Ala., farmers dedicated a monument to the Boll Weevil. The insect's devastation of the cotton crop had forced them to diversify, and their income now tripled that of the best cotton years.

—W.K.

1920

—U.S. population—105,710,620. For the 1st time in U.S. history the farm population stood below 50% of the total. It was, in fact, less than 30%.

—F. Scott Fitzgerald published his 1st novel, *This Side of Paradise*. It was a tremendous financial success.

—Chicago Underworld leader Johnny Torio hired a new bodyguard from Brooklyn—Al Brown. In the next 12 years, with Brown gaining control of the Underworld, Chicago experienced 629 unsolved gang murders, not to mention 5,000 non-gang killings. Al Brown became quite famous under his real name—Alphonse Capone.

Jan. 2 Government agents in 33 cities made simultaneous assaults on members of the IWW and the Communist party. In Boston, 500 men and women were arrested, shackled, and driven through the streets. Nationwide, 556 aliens were deported because of their political beliefs.

Jan. 16 The 18th Amendment prohibiting the manufacture, sale or transportation of intoxicating liquors went into effect at midnight. Prior to the Federal amendment, 32 States had already passed liquor prohibition laws beginning with Maine in 1851. Soon after the Amendment passed, Daniel C. Roper of the Internal Revenue Service commented that he expected a few problems of enforcement but eventually the nation would not know alcohol. As for home brew, it was too much trouble for uncertain results according to Dr. A. B. Adams, chief chemist of the Treasury Bureau.

—Harry M. Daugherty, Ohio politician, commenting on the upcoming presidential nominating convention:

> The convention will be deadlocked, and after the other candidates have gone their limit, some 12 or 15 men, worn out and bleary-eyed for lack of sleep, will sit down about 2 o'clock in the morning around a table in a smoke-filled room in some hotel and decide the nomination. When that time comes, Harding will be selected.

—Alice Roosevelt Longworth, daughter of President Theodore Roosevelt and wife of the Speaker of the House, recalled that "Harding was not a bad man, he was just a slob."

Aug. 18 Tennessee became the 36th State to ratify the Woman's Suffrage Amendment to the U.S. Constitution. The deciding vote was cast by 24-year-old Harry Burns, the youngest member of the Tennessee House of Representatives. His mother had written to him, "I've been watching to see how you stood but have noticed nothing yet. Don't forget to be a good boy and help Mrs. Catt [President of the National American Woman Suffrage Association] put 'Rat' in Ratification." The law went into effect on August 26, 1920.

Sept. 28 Professional baseball had been regarded as one of the most honest of professional sports until it suffered the Black Sox scandal, the worst scandal in baseball history. In Chicago, a grand jury brought indictments against 8 players of the Chicago team for "throwing" the 1919 World Series baseball games between the Chicago White Sox and the Cincinnati Reds. The trial, held in late July, ended in a verdict of Not Guilty. However, the 8 players were forbidden to return to big league baseball.

Nov. 20 Tucson, Ariz., inaugurated the 1st municipal airport in the U.S.

1921

What is the finest game? Business. The soundest science? Business. The fullest education? Business. The fairest opportunity? Business. The cleanest philanthropy? Business. The sanest religion? Business.

—Edward E. Purinton, *Independent*

—Black leader Marcus Garvey announced organization of the Empire of Africa and appointed himself Provisional President. Garvey insisted that it was futile to expect justice for the black man in the U.S. and that the only hope for American Negroes was to leave America and organize an empire of their own in Africa. Garvey attracted at least half a million followers and is credited with leading the 1st and only real mass exodus of Negroes in the history of the U.S. to date.

Apr. Professor Albert Einstein, lecturing at Columbia University on the theory of relativity, introduced "time" as the 4th dimension.

Apr. 11 The sale of cigarettes to adults became legal in Iowa.

July 2 The Jack Dempsey-Georges Carpentier heavyweight championship fight, the 1st prizefight with a million-dollar gate, was held at Jersey City. Dempsey won by a knockout in the 4th round.

Oct. 5 The 1st radio broadcast of play-by-play action of World Series baseball games was done by radio station WJZ, Newark, N.J.

Dec. Short skirts were high fashion and also the object of many jokes. One that was widely reprinted went:

Policeman: "Lost yer mammy, 'ave yer? Why didn't yer keep hold of her skirt?"
Little Alfred: "I cou-cou-couldn't reach it."

1922

Mar. Daily broadcasting of music and news, as well as Sunday sermons, were scheduled in New York City. Crystal headphone receiving sets were selling rapidly.

Apr. 15 Sen. John B. Kenrick of Wyoming introduced a resolution that called upon Secretary of the Interior Albert B. Fall to explain if, and why, the Teapot Dome oil lands in Wyoming—which had been set aside by the Senate for the use of the Navy—were being leased secretly to the Mammoth Oil Company, which was controlled by Harry F. Sinclair. This was the 1st formal action of the investigation leading to the revelation of the Teapot Dome scandals.

May 30 The Lincoln Memorial was dedicated in Washington, D.C., before a crowd of 100,000 people. Artists and critics called the Memorial the most beautiful edifice in America.

Dec. 1 "The greatest archeological discovery of all time," the finding of the tomb of the Egyptian King Tutankhamen (14th century B.C.) was made by Lord Carnarvon and his American assistant, Howard Carter. As the men crawled into the tomb's dark passageways illuminated by a single candle, they perceived "colossal gilt couches," statues and alabaster vases over 3,000 years old. King Tut's Tomb would become headline news in the U.S.

1923

—President Warren G. Harding, lamenting because his friends had been indicted and he was legally unable to save them from jail, said: "My God, this is a hell of a job! I have no trouble with my enemies. But my damn friends, they're the ones that keep me walking the floor nights."

—Henry R. Luce and Briton Hadden founded *Time*, a cleverly written, weekly news-review magazine.

June 11 Tommy Milton of St. Paul, Minn., won the 500-mi. Indianapolis race, averaging 91.4 mph. He collected the $35,000 1st-place money.

Oct. Governor Walton of Oklahoma attempted to use the force of his office to fight the Ku Klux Klan, which he said had been responsible for 2,500 floggings in one year. However, the Oklahoma legislators opposed him, passed a bill of impeachment and suspended him as governor. The Oklahoma Supreme Court upheld the suspension and he was removed from office.

Oct. 25 The Senate subcommittee to investigate Teapot Dome oil leases met for the 1st time. Chairman Sen. Thomas J. Walsh of Montana had been studying the case for some 18 months and during that time public interest had subsided, but it revived quickly as the investigation got under way.

Nov. 6 A patent was issued to Col. Jacob Schick for the 1st electric shaver.

1924

Feb. 12 George Gershwin's *Rhapsody in Blue*, a new kind of symphonic jazz, was performed for the 1st time, with Gershwin as piano soloist and the Paul Whiteman orchestra accompanying.

Mar. 18 The worst U.S. tornado to date obliterated 35 towns in Indiana, Illinois, Tennessee, Kentucky, and Missouri. Eight hundred persons were killed, 3,000 were injured, and 15,000 were left homeless.

May Congress decreed that admissions of immigrants were to be on a quota basis, 2% of the number of persons of foreign birth residing in the U.S. in 1890. The discriminatory bill reduced the number allowed to approximately 150,000 immigrants per year.

May As 13-year-old Bobby Franks, son of millionaire Jacob Franks, a retired pawnbroker and real estate investor, was walking home from school he was kidnapped. Before ransom could be delivered, the boy was killed and thrown in a culvert. Clues led to Nathan Leopold, Jr., and Richard Loeb, son of Albert H. Loeb, vice-president of Sears, Roebuck and Co. Both young men confessed to killing Bobby Franks for "the thrill of it." Each was sentenced to life imprisonment for murder and 99 years for kidnapping.

Aug. 23 Mrs. Miriam A. (Ma) Ferguson won the Democratic nomination for governor of Texas by more than 80,000 votes. She then went on to become one of 2 women elected governor of a State in 1924.

1925

—While the U.S. Army had 9,500 men still assigned to horse-drawn cavalry units, Brig. Gen. William "Billy" Mitchell vigorously proposed establishment of a modern military air service. Because he refused to keep quiet on this issue, despite demotion in rank and assignment to a remote Texas post, he faced a court-martial for insubordination. Mitchell was found Guilty and suspended from rank, command and duty and pay for 5 years. (See also: Court-Martials, Chap. 10.)

Feb. According to the U.S. Attorney General, approximately 332 foreign vessels were engaged in organized liquor smuggling. Most of the large foreign vessels lay 3 mi. or more out at sea waiting for smaller boats to ferry the liquor ashore to U.S. bootleggers.

July Earlier in the year, Tennessee legislators had voted it unlawful for a teacher in a State-supported school "to teach any theory that denies the story of the divine creation of man as taught in the Bible, and to teach instead that man has descended from a lower order of animals." John Scopes, a high school teacher in Dayton, decided to test the law. In late July, Scopes was convicted of violating the Tennessee law and fined $100.

Sept. Henry Ford announced that his cars, previously all black, would now be offered in "deep channel green" and "rich Windsor maroon" as well as black.

Oct. A torrent of migrants poured into Florida during early fall, seeking to buy a plot of ground. Arriving by touring car, train, steamship, and afoot, tourists and fortune seekers camped along the 300-mi. route from Jacksonville to Miami and also along Florida's west coast. Most of the 20 million lots offered for sale had been put on the market in 1924–1925.

1926

—The 1st woman to swim the English Channel was 19-year-old Gertrude Ederle of New York. It took her 14 hours and 31 minutes. (See: Ederle in Some 9-Day Wonders, Chap. 24.)
—The widespread depression in the auto industry led Henry Ford to introduce the 8-hour day, and the 5-day week. American industrial leaders were shocked, but the AFL welcomed this as a means of checking overproduction and reducing unemployment.
—The National Broadcasting Company was organized as the 1st nationwide radio broadcasting network.
—Popular songs for the year included "Bye Bye Blackbird," "The Desert Song," "The Blue Room," and "When Day Is Done."
Nov. 9 Rear Adm. Richard E. Byrd and Floyd Bennett made the 1st successful flight over the North Pole.

1927

—A major bill before Congress was one authorizing government funds for building a huge dam, to be known as the Boulder Canyon Project, on the Colorado River to provide for flood control, irrigation, and electrical power. This bill, introduced by California Senator Hiram Johnson, was vigorously opposed by the State of Arizona. The issue set off a historic 28½-hour filibuster and the bill was defeated.
—The motion picture industry was revolutionized this year by the production of the 1st important all-talking motion picture, *The Jazz Singer*, starring Al Jolson.
—The Academy of Motion Picture Arts and Sciences was established. Two years later it would begin to present annual awards, the "Oscars," for outstanding achievements in the art of the motion picture.
Apr. "Hello, General, you're looking fine. I see you have your glasses on." This comment was provoked by television's 1st successful transmission—the image of Gen. J. J. Carty, vice-president of American Telephone and Telegraph. He was in Washington, D.C., and the receiving set was located in the Bell Telephone Laboratories in Manhattan. Because early television equipment was bulky and expensive, it was to be decades before TV would become commonplace in the home.
May 21 Lindbergh reached Paris! The 25-year-old aviator landed his *Spirit of St. Louis* in Paris 33 hours and 29 minutes after taking off from Roosevelt Field, Long Island, N.Y.

During the 3600-mi. flight he averaged 107½ mph. Upon emerging from his airplane, the tousle-haired Lindbergh laconically remarked: "Well, here we are. I am very happy."
Novelist F. Scott Fitzgerald said this of Charles Lindbergh:

> In the spring of '27 something bright and alien flashed across the sky. A young Minnesotan who seemed to have nothing to do with his generation did a heroic thing, and for a moment people set down their glasses in country clubs and speakeasies and thought of their old best dreams.

June 30 In the fiscal year ending on this date the income of some 6,300,000 American farmers averaged only $548. For many, their financial situation was so hopeless they sold their farms and farm tenancy became widespread.
July 29 Bellevue Hospital in New York City installed the 1st electric respirator, later called the iron lung.
Aug. 23 Anarchists Nicola Sacco and Bartolomeo Vanzetti, convicted of killing 2 men in a payroll robbery, were executed after having spent 7 years in prison while controversy over their innocence or guilt stirred the U.S. and Europe. Both men were supported in their plea for justice by such prominent persons as Albert Einstein, Mrs. Louis Brandeis, wife of Supreme Court justice Brandeis, Anatole France, and Isadora Duncan. Demonstrations and strikes had taken place in Belgrade, Buenos Aires, Cairo, Havana, Melbourne, Moscow, and Warsaw. After the executions, 250,000 people in Boston participated in a silent protest march; and in Paris, fighting with police broke out when 150,000 demonstrated in front of the U.S. Embassy. Shortly before the 2 men were executed, Vanzetti gave this statement:

> I would not wish to a dog or to a snake, to the most low and misfortunate creature of the earth—I would not wish to any of them what I have had to suffer for things that I am not guilty of. But my conviction is that I have suffered for things I am guilty of. I am suffering because I am a radical and indeed I am a radical; I have suffered because I was an Italian, and indeed I am Italian . . . but I am so convinced to be right that if you could execute me 2 times, and if I could be reborn 2 other times, I would live again to do what I have done already.

Vanzetti's last letter was to become required reading in many colleges:

> If it had not been for these things, I might have lived out my life talking at

street corners to scorning men. I might have died, unmarked, unknown, a failure. This is our career and our triumph. Never in our full life could we hope to do such work for tolerance, for justice, for man's understanding of man as now we do by accident. Our words—our lives —our pains—nothing! The taking of our lives—lives of a good shoemaker and a poor fish peddlar—all! That last moment belongs to us—that agony is our triumph.

In his book *Tragedy in Dedham*, Francis Russell presents strong evidence that Sacco was, in fact, guilty but that Vanzetti's only crime was knowledge of Sacco's guilt.

Sept. 22 More than 150,000 boxing fans jammed into Soldiers Field in Chicago to see Gene Tunney defend his Heavyweight Championship against ex-Champ Jack Dempsey. Then in the 7th round, in the words of Tunney himself, "With all his speed and accuracy, Dempsey hit me flush on the jaw, the button. I was knocked dizzy." In fact, Tunney slumped to the canvas, unconscious. Above him, Dempsey hovered, waiting to smash Tunney if he got up. But the referee, following a special Illinois law, refused to start counting until Dempsey retired to a neutral corner. The 4 seconds which intervened were all that Tunney needed. He regained consciousness at the count of 2. "What a surprise! I had 8 seconds in which to get up. . . . I thought—what now? I'd take the full count, of course. Nobody but a fool fails to do that." Tunney regained control of the fight and won a 10-round decision—10 people died of heart attacks listening to Graham McNamee describe the fight and the Long Count over the radio.

Sept. 30 Babe Ruth hit his 60th home run in the 8th inning in a New York game against Washington. Baseball pitchers dared not walk Ruth because he was followed in the batting order by another consistent hitter, Louis Gehrig.

Dec. 27 *Show Boat*, a new kind of musical comedy, opened in New York City. It was based on Edna Ferber's novel; music and lyrics were by Oscar Hammerstein II and Jerome Kern.

1928

—The Kellogg-Briand Treaty (the Pact of Paris) by which 62 nations, including Germany, Italy, and Japan, renounced war "as an instrument of national policy" was signed in Paris.

—Walt Disney released his 1st Mickey Mouse cartoon entitled *Plane Crazy*. During the same year he also produced *Steamboat Willie*, the 1st animated cartoon to use sound.

May Alphonse Capone, once Chicago's Number 1 Underworld leader, was picked up by Philadelphia police as he came out of a movie theater. The next day he was indicted by a Grand Jury for carrying concealed weapons, tried and sentenced and placed in jail. Philadelphia and Chicago officials were convinced that Capone was using prison as a refuge.

May 25 Amelia Earhart, the 1st woman to fly the Atlantic, took off from Boston with 2 passengers in her airplane *Friendship*.

July 10 George Eastman at Rochester, N.Y., showed a group of viewers the 1st color motion pictures ever exhibited. Film subjects included flowers, butterflies, peacocks, goldfish, and pretty girls.

1929

—The South was the scene of much labor discontent. Southern textile manufacturers had erected mills there, thus making use of the large supply of nonunion labor. In addition, northern textile manufacturers were attracted to the South by special tax exemptions, abundant water power and lenient laws whereby the 72-hour workweek was not unusual, and women and children worked nights. Union organizers urged textile workers to strike for the 40-hour week and for a $20 per week minimum wage. At Gastonia, N.C., numerous clashes occurred between militant union organizations, the local companies, and local police. Several were killed and the guilty were sentenced to the State's prison. One striking southern textile worker remarked: "I ain't a-feared of Hell. I've spent 20 summers in the mills."

—*Middletown*, by Robert S. and Helen Lynd of Columbia University, surveyed the town of Muncie, Ind., and substantiated the tendencies toward conformity in U.S. society.

—The 1st American experiment in the creation of a garden community was attempted in Radburn, N.J. Homes, parks, schools, playgrounds, safe walks without traffic crossings were set amid natural surroundings for the health, safety, and aesthetic pleasure of the residents.

Feb. 14 Fourteen members of Bugs Moran's North Siders were shot to death in a warehouse on Clark Street in Chicago on orders from Al Capone in what became known as the St. Valentine's Day Massacre.

Sept. A study revealed that 60% of U.S. citizens had annual incomes of less than $2,000, which was estimated as the bare minimum to supply the basic necessities of life.

Oct. 24   On Wall Street, the N.Y. Stock Exchange recorded some unusually large sales of Kennecott Copper and General Motors stock. Brokers asked why, talked to their clients, and by 11 A.M. stock prices had plunged dramatically, reflecting a sellers' panic. Shortly after 12 noon, 5 of New York's leading bankers met with Thomas W. Lamont of J. P. Morgan & Co. and raised a $240 million emergency fund to steady the market. The effect was temporarily encouraging, yet doubt and fear continued to pervade the market, and panic took over within a few days. Stocks dropped $40, $50, and even $60 per share on Tuesday the 29th. Prices continued to drop thereafter.

Dec.   When President Hoover was inaugurated in March, 1929, the future had appeared bright for a prosperous America. By December of this same year, businessmen and farmers were facing the most difficult crisis in U.S. business history.

—S.V.M.

1930

—U.S. population—123,203,000.
—During the 1930s, 528,000 immigrants entered the U.S., the lowest number since the 1830s.
—*The Strange Death of President Harding* was a best seller. This book implied that Harding's wife poisoned him because of his numerous infidelities.
—The Nobel Prize in literature was awarded to Sinclair Lewis for his novel *Babbitt*. He was the 1st American to receive the prize.

Mar. 6   Demonstrations by unemployed workers demanding unemployment insurance took place in virtually every major city in the country. Police attacked a crowd of 35,000 in New York City and 10,000 people engaged in a melee with police in Cleveland. On the same day, Republican congressman Hamilton Fish, with the support of the American Federation of Labor, introduced a measure in Congress that would create a committee to investigate radical activities. This was the beginning of the House Un-American Activities Committee.

Mar. 13   The planet of Pluto was identified by a photograph made at Lowell Observatory in Flagstaff, Ariz. This confirmed the calculations made by Harvard professor Percival Lowell in 1914.

Dec. 11   Albert Einstein arrived in the U.S. from Germany. His wife sent a note to reporters, who had frightened the Professor with their aggressive behavior: "Professor Einstein is no eccentric. He is not absentminded. He dislikes dirt and confusion. Politically we are socialists."

1931

—A film, *I Am a Fugitive from a Chain Gang*, starring Paul Muni and based on a true account, caused such an uproar that many of the abuses of the chain-gang prison system were ended.

—A group of writers, including Theodore Dreiser and John Dos Passos, went to Harlan County (popularly known as "Bloody Harlan"), Ky., to investigate a miners' strike. These authors were indicted for criminal syndicalism to overthrow the Government.

Mar. 3   Herbert Hoover signed an act making "The Star-Spangled Banner" the national anthem.

Mar. 25   Nine black youths seized near Scottsboro, Ala., were charged with rape. The case of the "Scottsboro Boys" aroused worldwide concern. The defendants were released and vindicated after years of confinement. The case established the right of blacks to serve on juries.

1932

—The number of unemployed reached 13 million and wages were 60% less than in 1929.
—Edwin H. Land invented the 1st polaroid glass.
—"Brother, Can You Spare a Dime?" was a popular song.
—The Nevada legislature limited persons to 3 divorces in one lifetime.

Mar. 1   Charles Lindbergh, Jr., was kidnapped. His body was found 2 months later on the Lindbergh estate, while 5,000 Federal agents under direct order of the President were scouring the country for him. A typical reaction to the murder was that of the New York *Daily News:*

> Christ died, according to the Bible, to atone for the sins of the world. . . . Is it possible that this little boy is destined to play some such role in the history of the U.S.? . . . If that comes to pass, this child will not have been taken in vain.

Mar. 7   Three thousand people marched on Ford's River Rouge factory asking for jobs. Police fired on the demonstrators at point-blank range with pistols and a machine gun. Four died—all were Communists. On March 12, over 30,000 people attended the funeral of the slain marchers in Detroit. The "Internationale" was played as the 4 were laid to rest in a common grave.

May 14 "We Want Beer" marches were held in many cities to protest Prohibition. In Detroit, 15,000 marched, including 172 labor unions.

July 2 Franklin Delano Roosevelt, the Democratic candidate for President, pledged a "New Deal" for Americans.

July 28 After camping in tar-paper shacks for 2 months near the U.S. Capitol, thousands of veterans demanding a bonus were attacked by police and U.S. Army units commanded by Gen. Douglas MacArthur. Two members of the Bonus Army were killed.

Sept. 12 A large crowd of the unemployed in Toledo, O., near starvation after county authorities cut off relief, marched on grocery stores and seized food.

Oct. 3 One hundred and sixty-four students of the Kincaid, Ill., high school walked out on strike after they discovered that the school board bought coal from a company employing scab labor.

Nov. 8 Franklin D. Roosevelt, was elected President.

1933

—Sixty-seven thousand homeless children were reported to be wandering the streets of New York City.

—Walt Disney won an Academy Award for his cartoon *The Three Little Pigs*.

—In Roosevelt's 1st 100 days in office numerous Federal agencies were created to deal with the pervasive crisis. Three years later, at the New York State Democratic convention, FDR said:

> In the spring of 1933, we faced a crisis. . . . We were against revolution. And, therefore, we waged war against those conditions which make revolution— against the inequities and resentments that breed them.

Jan. 30 President von Hindenburg of Germany appointed Adolf Hitler Chancellor. On Hitler's 44th birthday, April 20, millions of Germans paraded to the Nazi song "When Blood Flows from Our Knives."

May 18 The Tennessee Valley Authority, the 1st publicly owned and socially responsible corporation in America, was established.

Dec. 5 Prohibition was repealed.

1934

—The Catholic League of Decency was founded to proscribe movies that would be offensive to Catholic audiences.

—Nevada, Utah, and California were shaken by earthquakes. The only fatality was a woman who died of fright.

Jan. 1 Dr. Edward Townsend, a 66-year-old Long Beach, Calif., physician, announced his Old Age Revolving Pensions Plan, which would establish a decent pension for retired citizens. He proposed his scheme after he found 3 elderly women rummaging through the garbage in his alley. Thousands of old folks joined Townsend Clubs and the *Townsend National Weekly* had a circulation of 200,000. This movement spurred the enactment of Social Security by Congress the following year. Interviewed many years later, Townsend stated:

> I suppose I have always been more or less socialistically inclined. I believe we ought to plan as a nation for all the things we need. I suppose that taking care of people runs against the American grain—against the feeling that everyone ought to hustle for himself. But there comes a time when people can't hustle any more. I believe that we owe a decent living to the older people. After all, they built our country and made it what it is.

May 23–24 The Battle of Toledo occurred. Thousands of workers trying to prevent scabs from breaking their strike against the Electric Auto-Lite Company in Toledo, O., were assaulted by police and the National Guard. Two workers were killed but the strike won basic collective-bargaining rights for the strikers.

July 16 A general strike took place in San Francisco after police attempted to suppress a longshoremen's strike. The week before the general strike, 2 workers were shot dead in the street by police.

July 20 A city-wide teamsters' strike in Minneapolis reached a head as police attacked a group of strikers, killing 2. Eric Sevareid, who left school to cover the strike for the *Minneapolis Star*, described the incident bluntly: "They had been shot while trying to run out of the ambush."

July 22 John Dillinger, termed "Public Enemy Number One" for robbing banks, was shot and killed by Melvin Purvis of the FBI, while he was leaving a movie theater in Chicago.

1935

—The largest salary earned during the year was that of William Randolph Hearst; the 2nd largest was Mae West's.

—Sinclair Lewis's *It Can't Happen Here*, a novel about the coming of Fascism to America, was a best seller. Lewis's Fascist leader was Berzelius "Buzz" Windrip, the "Professional Common Man." The embodiment of American democracy (ultimately defeated in the book) was Doremus Jessup, editor of a small-town Vermont newspaper. "In the humorous, friendly, happy-go-lucky land of Mark Twain," wrote Lewis, "Doremus saw the homicidal maniacs having just as good a time as they had had in central Europe."

July 6 The Wagner Act, guaranteeing the worker's right to collective bargaining, became law.

Sept. 8 Huey Long, the dictatorial, populist governor of Louisiana, was assassinated in the marble corridor of the State capitol. Long's most memorable statement was: "If Fascism came to America it would be on a program of Americanism." (See also: Assassinations, Chap. 9.)

Sept. 24 Joe Louis knocked out former heavyweight champion Max Baer. Thousands of blacks listening to the fight on the radio poured into the streets in spontaneous celebration. Richard Wright, writing in *New Masses* magazine, described the scene he witnessed on Chicago's South Side: "It was a feeling of unity, of oneness . . . a fluid mass of joy. . . . Here's the real dynamite that Joe Louis uncovered."

Oct. 10 George Gershwin's *Porgy and Bess* opened in New York.

Oct. 18 The American Federation of Labor refused to recognize industrial unions as an appropriate form of labor organization. John L. Lewis, president of the United Mine Workers, left the AFL after landing a powerful right cross on the jaw of William Hutcheson, president of the Carpenters and an opponent of industrial unionism. He struck his blow in full view of all attending the AFL convention. In less than a month's time, the Committee for Industrial Organization (CIO) was formed with Lewis at its head.

1936

—The runaway best seller of the year was Margaret Mitchell's *Gone With the Wind*, which in 6 months surpassed the sales of the previous best seller in American history, *Uncle Tom's Cabin*.

—Charles Chaplin's *Modern Times* was released.

Feb. 17 Fourteen thousand Goodyear rubber workers staged a sit-down strike in Akron, O., demanding recognition of their CIO union. The tactic was suggested by a Hungarian rubber worker who had read about its use in Europe.

Summer Jesse Owens, a black, won 4 gold

medals in track events at the Olympics in Berlin. Hitler had expected these games to be a showcase that would prove the superiority of the Aryan race and the Nazi system.

June 27 Franklin Roosevelt, nominated again as the Democratic presidential candidate, said in his acceptance speech:

> Concentration of economic power in all-embracing corporations . . . represents private enterprise become a kind of private government which is a power unto itself—a regimentation of other people's money and other people's lives.

July 17 Fascist forces led by Gen. Francisco Franco started the Spanish Civil War in an attempt to overthrow the republican Government. Franco was aided by German bombers and Italian troops.

Nov. 3 FDR won the election, defeating Republican Alf Landon. Roosevelt carried every State except Maine and Vermont. Above 80% of the press opposed his reelection as President.

Dec. 30 Auto workers in Flint, Mich., organized a sit-down strike that spread through the General Motors factories across the country. Production ground to a halt and the most decisive labor struggle of the decade began.

1937

—The U.S. Government estimated that nearly a half million workers took part in sit-down strikes from September, 1936, to May, 1937.

—Howard Hughes established a transcontinental flight record.

—The Golden Gate Bridge was dedicated in San Francisco.

—Mayor Fiorello LaGuardia of New York City told the American Jewish Congress that he wished he had a "chamber of horrors" at the coming World's Fair in which to exhibit a figure of Hitler, who was "menacing world peace." Secretary of State Cordell Hull sent the German Ambassador in Washington, D.C., a note of apology for LaGuardia's intemperate remark.

—The Abraham Lincoln Brigade, composed of about 3,000 Americans, was formed to fight Fascism in Spain. Ernest Hemingway, in his essay "On the American Dead in Spain," wrote:

> Just as the earth can never die, neither will those who have ever been free return to slavery. The peasants who work the earth where our dead lie know what these dead died for. There was time during the war for them to learn these things, and there is forever for them to remember them in.

Feb. 11 General Motors capitulated to workers' demands and recognized the United Auto

Workers. This occurred after a 44-day occupation of GM factories, violent clashes between police and strikers, and the stationing or machine-gun nests in Flint, Mich., streets by the National Guard.

Mar. All of Chrysler's Detroit plants were closed by sit-downs. When police officials indicated that they might forcibly expel the strikers, 150,000 workers rallied in downtown Detroit. In April, Walter P. Chrysler signed an agreement recognizing the union.

Apr. 12 The 1st nation-wide student strike against war took place in the U.S. Students took a vow against participation in any war.

May 30 Workers striking Republic Steel in Chicago were parading with their families toward the Republic factory when without provocation the police attacked them. Ten were killed and hundreds were wounded. This incident has become known as the Memorial Day Massacre.

Nov. 27 *Pins and Needles,* a musical comedy produced by local garment workers, was a hit on Broadway, breaking box-office records. Its catchiest song was "Sing Me a Song of Social Significance."

1938

—Richard Whitney, former president of the New York Stock Exchange and a partner in J. P. Morgan and Company, was sentenced to Sing Sing Prison for grand larceny.

—The top moneymaking movie of the year was Walt Disney's *Snow White and the Seven Dwarfs.*

Apr. 12 New York became the 1st State in which marriage license applicants were required to take a medical test for syphilis.

July 17 Douglas G. Corrigan, unable to obtain a flight exit to Europe, took off anyway and landed in Dublin, Ireland. He claimed he was heading for California and thereafter was called "Wrong-Way Corrigan." (See: Corrigan in Some 9-Day Wonders, Chap. 24.)

Sept. 30 The Munich Pact, which effectively turned over Czechoslovakia to Nazi Germany, was signed by Great Britain, France, Italy, and Germany. Later, a Gallup poll showed that most Americans approved of this act of appeasement.

1939

—FDR became the 1st President to appear on television, as he opened the World's Fair in New York. However, only NBC's experimental channel carried the telecast.

—John Steinbeck's *The Grapes of Wrath* was published.

—Ten million people were unemployed despite all of the efforts of the New Deal.

—The LaFollette Civil Liberties Committee of the U.S. Senate issued its report, after 4 years of investigation, on corporate interference with the rights of labor. The committee revealed that in 1936 alone, American corporations spent at least $80 million on labor spies, anti-union agents, and provocateurs. Millions more were spent to outfit armed private police forces. The committee concluded: "The subjugation on one group of citizens to the economic interest of another by the use of armed forces saps the very foundation of democracy."

—The Nobel Prize in physics was awarded to Ernest O. Lawrence for the discovery and development of the cyclotron. Lawrence's invention enabled scientists to split the atom, a crucial step in the production of a nuclear reaction.

Jan. 7 Tom Mooney, a labor leader serving time for a crime he claimed he did not commit, was pardoned by the governor of California after 23 years of imprisonment.

Feb. 27 The sit-down strike was declared to be illegal by the U.S. Supreme Court.

Apr. 9 Marian Anderson, the black contralto, was denied use of Constitution Hall by the Daughters of the American Revolution. Eleanor Roosevelt greeted her instead at the Lincoln Memorial, where 75,000 people had assembled to hear her sing.

Aug. Henry Ford was decorated with the Grand Cross of the German Eagle by the Nazi regime.

Sept. The American Psychological Association, meeting in convention, put the question of Hitler's sanity on the agenda.

Sept. 1 German armies invaded Poland. Two days later Great Britain and France declared war.

Oct. Charles E. Lindbergh received a medal from Hitler. At the time, Lindbergh blamed the potential war with the U.S. on "the British, the Jews, and the Roosevelt Administration."

—S.B.

1940

—U.S. population—131,669,275.

Feb. 29 Hattie McDaniel won the "Best Supporting Actress" award for her mammy role in *Gone With the Wind,* the 1st black ever to win an Oscar.

Apr. 20 Dr. Ladislaus Morton demonstrated a new research tool in Philadelphia, Pa.: the electron microscope. Invented by Dr. Vladimir Zworkin, the original model was 10' high, weighed over 1,000 lbs., and gave a magnification of 100,000 diameters.

May 15 British Prime Minister Winston Churchill, smarting over serious Royal Navy losses in the war, wrote to President Roosevelt, asking for U.S. aid. In negotiations ending on September 3, the U.S. delivered 50 overage destroyers, receiving in exchange 99-year leases on 8 military bases in Newfoundland and the West Indies.

May 15 Nylons were placed on public sale throughout the country. In New York, the 72,000-pair allotment was sold out in 8 hours. Limit: 2 pairs per customer. Du Pont's initial production could satisfy only a fraction of the prewar demand for women's silk stockings, estimated at 6 million pairs in the U.S. The synthetic replacement for silk was invented by Dr. Wallace Carothers in 1937 as patent ✕2071250.

June 28 The Smith Act was passed, requiring aliens to be fingerprinted and outlawing organizations which advocated the overthrow of the U.S. Government. Five million registered. The Act was the 1st to condone and support "guilt by association."

July 18 Igor Ivan Sikorsky flew the VS-300 helicopter successfully for 15 minutes at Stratford, Conn. His radical new concept for aircraft was powered by a single main rotor with 3 auxiliary tailrotors.

Aug. The Republican presidential candidate, Wendell L. Willkie, addressed 200,000 at Elwood, Ind., the largest number ever to gather for a political rally. Unknown 6 months before, he captured a record 22 million votes in November, but it was not enough to defeat Roosevelt's 3rd-term bid. An appealing speaker, he might have won but for his indecisive barnstorming. He attacked—and supported—Roosevelt's anti-Hitler position. He attacked Roosevelt's "New Deal" program—but supported its major reforms.

Sept. 9 W.E.B. Du Bois's autobiographical *Dusk of Dawn* was published. Rejected by blacks for accepting racial segregation and by whites for his Marxist philosophies, Du Bois was grudgingly given credit by the NAACP for being the creator of a black "intelligentsia."

Oct. Mrs. Thomas Solomon "Grandma" Moses held her 1st art show at the Galerie St. Étienne, exhibiting 35 of her New England "primitives." Using Sears, Roebuck paint and scraps of threshing canvas from her farm, the 80-ish gray-haired widow displayed scenes of carefully stippled, speckled Green Mountains farm life—taken from around her familiar Eagle Bridge, N.Y., home—in old mirror frames found in her attic.

Nov. 21 John L. Lewis, outspoken labor chief of the Congress of Industrial Organization— the CIO—carried out his threat to resign if Roosevelt were elected.

Dec. President Franklin Delano Roosevelt, returned to office for an unprecedented 3rd term, called upon the U.S. to become the "great arsenal of democracy" in the fight against Hitlerism.

1941

Jan. 7 The Office of Production Management was created to oversee U.S. defense programs. Named as joint directors: William S. Knudson (for Management) and Sidney Hillman (for Labor).

Jan. 13 Roosevelt addressed a joint session of the 77th Congress. He appealed for its support to defend the Four Essential Freedoms: Freedom of Speech, Freedom of Religion, Freedom from Want, Freedom from Fear.

Mar. 11 Lend-Lease Bill ✕1776 was signed into law. It provided $50 billion in arms, services, and supplies for the Axis's enemies. Britain, nearly bankrupt after draining its Treasury of cash for war supplies, advised the U.S. of its financial situation through a letter from Churchill. Roosevelt learned of an 1892 Statute which gave the Secretary of War the right to lease, for a 5-year period, any army property that was not needed for public use. Further research showed that this leasing actually had been done in the past, setting a legal precedent. The President applied the hoary statute to aid Britain. Three months later, he extended the credit plan to include Russia, attacked by Hitler on June 22 in one of *der Führer's* most colossal blunders.

Mar. 27 The U.S. Joint Chiefs of Staff, meeting with their British counterparts, agreed that, if the U.S. became militarily involved with both Germany and Japan, the best strategy was to make a concentrated effort to beat the European Axis powers 1st. Their reasoning: Germany's war potential was greater and her superior technology could at any moment produce some secret weapon that might tip the scales in her favor.

Apr. 11 The Office of Price Administration —the OPA—headed by Leon Henderson, was established. The OPA "czar" was given full authority to set production priorities, to fix maximum price schedules, to punish—by withholding materials—plants which refused to cooperate, and to set up rationing programs. On December 27, the OPA announced the 1st item to be rationed: rubber tires.

Summer In an action to back up his policies, President Roosevelt "froze" all German and Italian assets, all assets belonging to European countries already invaded or occupied, and all assets owned by the Japanese. He also prohibited, by embargo, all shipments of gasoline or scrap iron to Japan.

Aug. 3 President Roosevelt, leaving Washington for an announced "fishing trip" off Martha's Vineyard, Mass., continued on to Placentia Bay, Newfoundland, for the Atlantic Conference with Winston Churchill. The Atlantic Charter, drawn up there by the U.S. and Britain, in its 8 articles laid out the common war aims of the 2 countries. The U.S., technically still a neutral, agreed to join in "the final destruction of the Nazi tyranny." Taking note of Japan's menacing southward movement in the Pacific to establish the "Greater East Asia Co-Prosperity Sphere," FDR reassured the British leader: "Leave that to me. I think I can baby them along for 3 months."

Dec. 7 Admiral Nagumo's strike force of 6 carriers, supported by battleships and cruisers, attacked a U.S. fleet of 94 ships at Pearl Harbor, Hawaii. The 2-hour surprise blow by 368 bombers and fighters, flying in 2 waves from a fleet position 275 mi. north of Oahu, heavily damaged or sank 19 ships including all U.S. battleships except the *Pennsylvania*, then in drydock. The Japanese lost only 19 planes. U.S. casualties: 3,457 soldiers, sailors, and civilians, and property damage into the millions. Full details of actual U.S. losses were kept secret for a year.

The idea for the surprise strike originated with the Japanese commander in chief Admiral Yamamoto, who assembled the force at Tankan Bay, a remote corner of the Kurile Islands. He recalled a similar British success against the Italians at Taranto in November, 1940, and decided to work out a Japanese version during a war games session in Tokyo in September, 1941. His plan was approved on November 5. Commanded by Admiral Nagumo, the 1st Air Fleet, preceded by an advance probe of 28 submarines, left the Kuriles on November 26, subject to an instant recall if detected. Its orders: Proceed slowly east, into the North Pacific, and await orders to attack, or to return. This depended on whether or not U.S. negotiations had reached a satisfactory solution.

At Pearl Harbor, the positions of the 8 battleships, anchored in tandem, and of many other ships there had been accurately plotted by Japanese spies and sympathizers. (See: The 8-Eyed Spy, Chap. 10.) One-third of the U.S. naval officers were on shore leave. Only ¼ of the antiaircraft guns were manned. Military planes on Oahu were parked in clusters, wing tip to wing tip, to reduce the problem of impending sabotage, and their pilots were off duty, subject to a 4-hour call.

In 1940, U.S. cipher experts, using cryptographic techniques called "Magic," had broken the Japanese secret diplomatic codes. During November, 1941, Washington officials monitored the fast-breaking crisis. On Saturday, December 6, an intercept of a message being sent in 14 parts was made. Thirteen parts were received, with the 14th yet to come. The transmission, from Tokyo to the 2 Japanese envoys in Washington, D.C., summarized the negotiations to date and rejected—as envoy Kurusu had said his Government would—the U.S. note of November 26, calling for Japanese withdrawals in China and other treaty stipulations. Roosevelt, when notified, reportedly exclaimed to Naval Chief of Operations Adm. Harold Stark, "This means war!" By 8 A.M., part 14 had been received and completely decoded.

At Fort Myers, Va., just outside Washington, Gen. George Marshall's subordinates, cognizant of his strict orders not to bother him during off-duty hours, decided to inform him *after* he had finished his regular horseback ride on Sunday morning and had arrived at post headquarters. Belatedly shown the message, Marshall immediately realized that the command—for the envoys to submit an official reply to the U.S. note at precisely 1 P.M.—was of great significance. Later, he would know why: The time would soon be 7:55 A.M. in Honolulu, the moment when Nagumo's bombers arrived over Pearl Harbor.

Marshall bypassed his telephone "scrambler" to the Hawaiian commanders, possibly from fear that somehow the Japanese might unscramble the call. Instead, he ordered a telegram, encoded, to be sent. By chance, or unfortunate circumstance, the War Department radio had been unable to contact the Hawaiian department that morning. Faced with a decision, Washington message center chief, Colonel French, elected to use commercial facilities. He transmitted by Western Union to San Francisco, then by commercial overseas radio to Honolulu.

Marshall's urgent message was filed in Washington at one minute past noon. It reached RCA's Honolulu office at 1:33 P.M., Washington time (7:33 A.M., Honolulu time). The office manager, aware that the hour was slightly early to begin the daily teletype service to army headquarters at Fort Shafter, sent the critical warning out by motorcycle messenger. The boy was leisurely making his way along when the 1st wave of planes swept around Diamond Head.

In 8 official investigations, scapegoats were sought upon whom to fix the top blame for the humiliating defeat. Roosevelt himself was accused of deliberately ignoring all final warnings and permitting the attack, to jolt the American people into outraged support of his plans to lead the country into war. His statement that, if war was to come, it had to result from an initial blow by Japan, was pointed to by his critics. General Marshall, as Chief of Staff, was charged with running a "one-man shop," where vital command decisions in the War Department were shelved during his off-duty hours. The Hawaiian Department military commanders, Gen. Walter Short and Adm. Husband Kimmel, were called to account by a special commission, set up by Roosevelt. This civilian committee quickly declared both men "in dereliction of duty," but the Army and Navy, 3 years later, jointly decided there were insufficient grounds for court-martial. Both men were denied trials, for political reasons, although they repeatedly asked for the chance to clear their names. Kimmel, after his retirement from the Navy, repeated the charge that the crucial information had been deliberately held back until after the attack had occurred.

1942

Feb. 10 The world's fastest ocean liner, France's *Normandie*, was gutted by fire and capsized at her New York pier. The cause was never discovered.

Feb. 19 President Roosevelt signed into law Executive Order No. 9066 which allowed the military to move 112,000 Japanese-Americans from their homes on the West Coast to concentration camps inland. Apparently, the U.S. Government hoped to use them as bargaining items to regain American POWs after the war, because the Government arranged to have 2,000 Japanese living in Peru rounded up and incarcerated in the camps as well.

Mar. 17 Obeying a direct order from President Roosevelt, Gen. Douglas MacArthur left the hopeless fight on Bataan, traveling by submarine from the Philippines to Australia. He assumed command of the Southwest Pacific forces.

Apr. 10 The Bataan Death March began. Japanese soldiers forced 10,000 U.S. prisoners-of-war and about 45,000 Filipino Scouts to undergo a forced march of 120 mi. to San Fernando, in Pampanga Province. All sick and wounded prisoners who were unable to walk any further at the end of each day were shot, stabbed, or buried alive. Held to one meal of rice per day and denied any fresh water, over 5,200 Americans and uncounted thousands of the Filipinos died in the 6-day-long atrocity. In their 1st 2 months of stockade life, another 2,200 U.S. and 27,000 Filipinos succumbed to maltreatment, malnutrition, and cold-blooded murder.

Apr. 18 In the 1st U.S. offensive strike against the Japanese, Col. James Doolittle's carrier-based flyers bombed Tokyo on a one-way trip. They continued past Japan, bailing out over or crashing in mainland China.

May 3–8 Milestone Battle: Coral Sea. In a showdown fought exclusively by carrier-based aircraft—the surface ships never fired upon, or saw, each other, with 180 mi. between them—the U.S. fleet under Adm. Frank Fletcher disrupted Japanese High Command plans to expand the war into a land invasion of Australia.

In the initial phase, Fletcher struck at an auxiliary force of invasion transports escorted by the light carrier *Shoho*. He sank the *Shoho*, depriving the troop ships of their vital air cover, and Japanese Vice Admiral Inouye, dismayed with the carrier's loss, ordered them to turn around. But Fletcher's commitment gave away his position to the Japanese main fleet, headed by the carriers *Zuikaku* and *Shokaku* with heavy cruisers in support. Helpless because of having no time to rearm his planes for adequate defense or a fresh attack, Fletcher was fortunately aided by bad weather that hid his carriers *Yorktown* and *Lexington* from the 29 bombers sent to find them. The heavy rain did not prevent Fletcher—who had spotted the approaching bombers by radar—from sending fighters up to shoot down nearly all of the enemy planes.

On May 8, the decisive air battle was fought. Fletcher lost 33 planes, the Japanese 43. His slight margin of victory was more than overshadowed by disaster on the surface: The *Lexington* was badly damaged by torpedo and bomb hits. Within an hour after the fight ended, the carrier had to be scuttled.

May 4 The last of 67 escort vessels, built under a "crash" 2-month program, was delivered, and the 2nd "60 vessels in 60 days" effort began. The armed ships were urgently needed to protect Atlantic shipping from the U-boat menace.

May 15 Gasoline rationing was put into effect. Allocation: 3 gallons per week, to cover ordinary driving demands.

June 3–6 Milestone Battle: Midway. In a major sea battle which utilized Midway Island as an additional "unsinkable carrier," the U.S. stopped Admiral Yamamoto's thrust into the Central Pacific. He lost major units of his fleet, including 4 carriers, 2 cruisers, and 11 other vessels. The carnage so sickened him that he kept to his quarters during the retreat into Japanese home waters.

July 25 Beleaguered by cries from both Russia and U.S. left-wing elements for a "2nd front, now," Roosevelt and Churchill executed "Operation Torch." This plan called for an invasion of French North Africa, and then using it for a jump-off stage into Sicily and Italy.

Aug. 7 Milestone Battle: Guadalcanal. In 6 months of savage jungle fighting on the 2,500-

sq.-mi. island, General Vandegrift's 16,000 Marines, supported by army elements, forced veteran Japanese ground troops to retreat. The general began the vicious campaign under a severe handicap. On August 9, a heavily-supported Japanese force of cruisers and destroyers, well experienced in night maneuvering, with darkness and stormy weather to help them, surprised Admiral Turner's task force off Savo Island, sinking 3 heavy cruisers and the Australian cruiser *Canberra*. The Japanese commander did not follow up his opportunity to close in and attack the U.S. transports which were still being unloaded for the marine landing. The naval defeat did, however, force Admiral Fletcher to withdraw, after suffering heavy plane losses, a retreat that left the marines without air cover. They held, nevertheless, and improved their beachhead until they had captured nearby Henderson Field as well. Once the airfield was secured, they thereafter provided their own air cover with great tactical effect, driving the Japanese into final evacuation of Guadalcanal 6 months later.

In other naval fighting, the U.S. nearly lost its carrier capability in the Pacific. The *Wasp* was sunk. In October, the *Hornet* was lost. With extensive damage also to the *Enterprise* and *Saratoga*, putting them out of battle readiness, Adm. William Halsey appealed to Washington for help, having no other carriers under his command. Prime Minister Churchill came to his aid in December by temporarily reassigning the British carrier *Victorious* for Halsey's use.

All through September and October, the Japanese discharged men and supplies to reinforce their land forces on Guadalcanal. Running by night with such fast and nearly regular schedules that U.S. forces dubbed them "the Tokyo Express," the Japanese troop transports slipped into "the Slot"—a central channel through the Solomons—slowed briefly to allow the troops to scramble ashore at the closest approach to Guadalcanal, and then sped on, hurrying to be beyond range of air attack before daylight.

Nov. 28 Fire, touched off by a busboy's match, swept through the artificial palm-tree decorations in Boston's Coconut Grove nightclub. The subsequent holocaust killed 491, including many servicemen who were celebrating before being shipped overseas.

1943

—A new form of mold, discovered on a cantaloupe in an Illinois market, yielded nearly 10 times the amount of penicillin as previous sources. It was quickly placed into mass production to alleviate the critical shortage of the antibiotic.

—MacArthur's "leapfrog" strategy went into effect. Jointly credited to the general and to Adm. Theodore Wilkinson, the plan called for the bypass of strongly-fortified enemy bases, moving around them to establish new U.S. bases closer to the Japanese homeland. The enemy bases were then to be sealed off from fresh supplies by U.S. air and sea power until they capitulated.

Jan. 14 Roosevelt met with Churchill at Casablanca, North Africa, to plan future strategy. One major decision and possibly a mistake: "Unconditional surrender" was demanded from all enemies. The no-compromise demand may have helped Hitler to persuade his troops to fight on to the end.

Jan. 22 Milestone Battle: Anzio. The amphibious landing, intended as a flanking operation for the 5th Army which was then stalled in its advance 60 mi. away, was accomplished with few casualties. But 6th Corps commander, General Lucas, had been given orders *not* to advance from his beachhead *if* it meant his troops could be cut off. His decision was to secure and consolidate his beachhead position 1st, strengthening his supply lines before moving out. He lost the element of surprise. German Field Marshal Kesselring immediately rushed up 2 full divisions to contain the invasion. Dug into the high ground of the surrounding Alban Hills, they stopped the American advance until the Cassino breakthrough in May, 3½ months later.

June 5–8 A minor fight between sailors and Mexican *pachucos* wearing zoot suits led to the Los Angeles Zoot Suit riots in which uniformed sailors, marines, and soldiers rampaged through downtown Los Angeles, beating 1st zoot-suiters and then anyone with dark skin, including Filipinos and blacks. The police stood by and then moved in and arrested the victims. The City Council adopted a resolution declaring that the wearing of zoot suits was a misdemeanor and the rioting did not end until military authorities declared Los Angeles off limits.

June 10 W-2 Day. The Withholding Tax Act was signed. Following a Treasury suggestion, and listening to intensive lobbying from Beardsley Ruml, chairman of the Federal Reserve Bank of New York, Congress provided for the "pay-as-you-go" tax. The law leveled out tax collections and drastically reduced the total number of tax-delinquent bills in 1944.

June 20 In the white section of Detroit, rumors spread quickly that a Negro had raped and killed a white woman and thrown her baby into the river. In the black section of Detroit, rumors spread that a white man had killed a

Negro woman and her baby. Actually, no one had been killed or injured—yet. Only the integrated neighborhoods remained free from rioting that left 25 blacks and 9 whites dead.

July 24 Air attacks on Hamburg, Germany, conducted jointly by the Royal Air Force and the U.S. 8th Air Force, and delivered in 4 massive raids ending on August 3, destroyed over 75% of the city, killing 43,000 people and injuring as many more. In the 2nd raid, the mixture of incendiary and high-explosive bombs was so intense that a new phenomenon called the "fire storm" was born. The numerous searing fires from the bombs created an air column 2½ mi. high and nearly 2 mi. in diameter, so hot that it sucked in cooler air at ground level, producing tornado-like winds which spread the fires with uncontrollable speed.

These raids and other operations by the British, Canadian, and American air crews (7 for RAF, 10 for U.S. bombers), eventually cost almost 160,000 Allied flyers their lives during the war.

July 25 Benito *Il Duce* Mussolini "resigned." Weary of military disasters and acutely aware that mainland Italy would soon be conquered by the Allies, the Fascist Grand Council convened for the 1st time since 1939. The session was set for Saturday, July 24. One week earlier, General Ambrosio, accompanying Mussolini to an urgent meeting with Hitler near Rimini, had urged *Il Duce* to tell the German leader that Italy would not continue the war. Mussolini, either from sheer fright or stubbornness, had kept silent. Ambrosio and his fellow generals then realized they could no longer depend on Mussolini's leadership, and the Grand Council meeting was used to issue an ultimatum: Bring the King out of his current obscurity to lead the demoralized armed forces, and then form a new national Government. King Victor Emmanuel III was willing to resume Italy's leadership.

Mussolini listened to the proposal of his chief opponent, Count Dino Grandi, former Ambassador to Great Britain, and a man of strong will who had deplored the war privately. But Mussolini could not be swayed. Instead, he mouthed meaningless words about intensifying his own control. The discussion, at times emotional, continued until 2 A.M., with Mussolini's son-in-law, Count Ciano, supporting Grandi. Then, the Council took a vote, and it was 19 to 7 in favor of Grandi's motion to restore the King. Mussolini promptly declared the meeting to be at an end, and the men present left in silence. As a precaution against being arrested by Mussolini's personal bodyguard during the rest of the night, they all slept away from their homes.

On Sunday, July 25, Mussolini went to see the King. He found, everywhere, *carabinieri*

brought in as reinforcements. King Victor Emmanuel III, wearing his marshal's uniform, came to meet him. For the 1st time, *Il Duce* learned that Marshal Pierot Badoglio had already replaced him as the head of the military Government. The now ex-dictator was taken into "protective" custody, and spirited away in an ambulance, heavily guarded by 6 policemen carrying machine guns. Within 48 hours, Benito Mussolini was interned on the island of Ponza, thus ending his 21 years of one-man rule in Italy.

Aug. With Italy facing collapse, Germany rushed in strong reinforcements. The Italians' bargaining, to get terms better than "unconditional surrender," delayed the final agreements with the Allies long enough for the German High Command to establish strong defense positions.

Sept. 12 In a daring landing by glider in the mountains of central Italy, Col. Otto Skorzeny and 90 men rescued Mussolini from the hotel to which he had been moved, and flew him to Munich. The former dictator was declared by Hitler the new head of a puppet Fascist Government: the Republic of Salò. Near the 1st of October, Mussolini was taken to his "seat of Government" on Lake Garda, to begin his "Hundred Days" of rule. Here, with his mistress Clara Petacci, he was closely watched by German guards and German doctors, carefully chosen.

1944

—Kathleen Winsor's *Forever Amber* was published. Its generous supply of sex passages helped to sell over one million copies and brought charges of obscenity and indecency from its critics.

—Faced with serious shortages, the book publishers turned to a "new" old idea: soft covers or "paperbacks." There was an overwhelming demand for them.

May 3 An eye bank was established by New York Hospital and 19 other local hospitals followed suit. Corneal transplants were stored to be used to cure certain types of blindness.

June 6 D-Day in Europe. In the 1st 48 hours, over 156,000 Allied soldiers were landed on the Normandy beaches or parachuted behind the German lines. Just over ½ (53%) were British and Canadian. The original plan called for 3 divisions to make the assault. Field Marshal Bernard Montgomery recommended 5, and 6 were finally used: the U.S. 1st, 4th, and 29th divisions, assigned to "Omaha" and "Utah" beaches; the British 3rd and 50th divisions, plus the Canadian 3rd, coming ashore on "Gold," "Sword," and "Juno."

Realizing that it would take 15 weeks to build up a force equal to the number the Germans already had in readiness in France and Belgium, General Eisenhower approved a massive bombing proposal. It called for the destruction of railroad marshaling yards, major rail and road junctions, and every repair shop of importance between Normandy and the Rhine. Without transportation, movement of the German troops to repulse the invasion would be extremely limited. The campaign succeeded. Field Marshal Erwin Rommel's defense plan required at least 48 troop trains daily to assemble the reserves he would need to throw back the assault; he was able to muster only 6.

The Germans were aware that the invasion was imminent. A Frenchman who was also a double agent working for the Germans had already passed on the starting signal. In the British Broadcasting Company's regular messages of coded instructions for the French underground, Paul Verlaine's poetic line about autumn—*Les sanglots longs des violons de l'automne* ("The long sobs of the violins of autumn")—was to be sent out on the 1st, 2nd, 15th, or 16th day of the month. Its release was the directive to listen continuously for the 2nd half of the signal—*Blessent mon coeur d'une langueur monotone* ("Wound my heart with a monotonous languor")—which would indicate invasion within 48 hours. At 9:15 P.M. on June 5, the German 15th Army intelligence officers intercepted the Verlaine "heart" signal 4 times within the hour, and dutifully notified their superiors. Rommel ignored the report, preferring to believe that the attempt would not be possible because of the foul weather over the Channel. He left for a brief visit to Germany. Field Marshal von Rundstedt likewise refused to accept the intelligence message, saying that such a decision was impossible from a tactician of Eisenhower's caliber.

In an internal dispute on command, both Rommel and Von Rundstedt had demanded sole control over the 6 armored divisions kept in reserve for the Normandy sector. The argument was carried up to Hitler, who gave 3 to Rommel but placed the remaining 3 under new orders, to be used only by *his* direct command. The orders never came, and Rommel lost the immediate use of uncommitted troops which might have stopped the invasion. He did succeed in surprising the Allied forces with a secret weapon never seen before: tiny, 26"-high tanks called "Goliaths." The tracked vehicles carried 200 lbs. of explosives and were directed by remote control at the Allied tanks.

Despite extraordinary precautions to keep the operational plan for D-Day a secret, at least 10,000 people knew fragments of it. The British War Office furnished over 170 million maps for personnel who were to take part, using every small print shop in the British Isles. The individual map units were parcelled out in small segments to different printers, so that no one man could draw any significant conclusions. The maps for the invasion sectors were complete to the last detail, but false coordinates and proper names were substituted. The real identities were given out to the men only after their ships had left the English harbors.

June 13 Hitler's assault on English soil using unmanned missiles began. The flying bomb, or "doodle-bug," as it was soon named, flew at about 400 mph, was powered by a loud jet engine, and carried about a ton of high explosive. Its guidance system was primitive. When the propeller had revolved a rotary distance approximately equal to the distance between the launching sites, in the Pas de Calais area of France, and London, the missile's controls were tipped forward. This cut off the engine, making the missile dive and destruct. The cutoff could—and often did—occur prematurely along the general route, and a regular path through Sussex and Kent gained the unwanted reputation of being "Bomb Alley."

The Germans launched some 9,000 missiles. Only about 25% managed to penetrate London's defenses, but these killed over 6,000 people and destroyed 750,000 dwellings. The attacks continued through September 5, when the launching regiment was forced to abandon the launching sites or face capture by advancing Allied soldiers.

On this same date in June, trials on the more advanced V-2 long-range rockets were held at Peenemünde, on the Baltic. British plans to capture an actual rocket for technical evaluation were unexpectedly assisted by the Germans themselves. A German glider-bomb operator, experienced in directing glider bombs against shipping from an aircraft, was brought in to fire a V-2, to see if the new weapon could be adapted for glider-bomb use. In his astonishment at seeing the awesome 12-ton rocket blast off, his hand froze to the control lever, guiding the missile left, and the missile obediently continued to veer left—flying into Sweden. Its remains were quickly recovered for the British.

June 22 The Serviceman's Readjustment Act was signed. The law, known also as "the GI Bill of Rights," provided extensive educational and vocational benefits for the returning veterans.

July 19–21 President Roosevelt was nominated at the Democratic National Convention in Chicago, Ill., to run for a 4th term as President. He dropped left-winger Henry Wallace and chose a haberdasher-turned-senator from Missouri, Harry S (no middle name, no period) Truman.

July 20 The plot to assassinate Hitler in his

map room at Rastenburg, East Prussia, failed. (See also: Assassinations, Chap. 9.)

July 25 Gen. George S. Patton's 3rd Army broke through the German defenses at Saint-Lô, beginning its sweep across France.

Aug. 25 General von Choltitz, the German military governor of Paris, surrendered the city to General Leclerc, leader of the French 2nd Armored Division. Von Choltitz did so against Hitler's fanatic order to defend the city at all cost. With only a few antiaircraft batteries and a regiment of low-grade men, mostly unfit for general combat duty, the military governor faced annihilation by the well-armed French resistance. He made a secret pact with Resistance leaders to take no action against them, if they would help him to maintain some degree of order until Allied forces arrived. His action prevented widespread destruction of the French capital.

Oct. 25 Milestone Battle: Leyte Gulf. In the largest naval battle ever fought, Admiral Toyada committed a 75-ship fleet to drive back MacArthur's bid to recapture the Philippines. His plan, based on trick and surprise, had fatal flaws. He split his fleet into 3 divisions, and sent Admiral Nichimura through Surigao Strait to attack the amphibious forces of Admiral Kinkaid. Nichimura was met by every ship the U.S. could muster and suffered a crushing defeat in a Strait night battle. Adm. Jesse Oldendorf added to Nichimura's embarrassment by "crossing the T," the classic naval maneuver in which maximum broadside firepower is brought to bear by steaming rapidly *across* the enemy's approaching formation.

Toyada lost 24 major ships—⅓ of his total fleet. For the U.S., it was revenge for Pearl Harbor: 5 of the battleships hit at Hawaii took part in the action at Surigao Strait.

Dec. 16 Milestone Battle: Ardennes. In an attempt to repeat his successful drive of May, 1940, Von Rundstedt tried to split the Allied armies with a Panzer thrust aimed at Antwerp. The idea was Hitler's, a mistake that cost 120,000 men and took away the remaining reserves needed to stop future Allied progress. Von Rundstedt objected to the wild plan, but found himself hamstrung: His personal copy of the planned operation bore the notation, "Not to be altered," in Hitler's own handwriting.

The area chosen for the counterattack, the Ardennes Forest of Luxembourg, was thickly wooded and thinly defended by the green troops of the 106th U.S. Division, as yet unseasoned in battle. Because of the sector's quiet nature, it was also used for additional training of troops recently arrived from the U.S. and as a rest area for battle veterans temporarily withdrawn from the front lines.

The central assault, by Von Manteuffel's 5th Panzer Army, created the "Bulge" in the opposing lines by which the German counterattack became commonly known. Von Manteuffel's initial advance toward Bastogne was stalled by a number of small firefights and roadblocks. He elected, in a tactical error, to bypass Bastogne. Within the week he realized that the Belgian town was the key point, the hub of the regional road system he needed to bring up his supplies. His subsequent order, to take the town, came too late. By then, 18,000 men of the 101st "Screaming Eagles" Airborne Division had been moved in. These U.S. troops were completely surrounded at one critical stage. Given an ultimatum to surrender, General McAuliffe's reported reply was "Nuts."

1945

Jan. 25 Grand Rapids, Mich., became the 1st U.S. city to add fluoride to a municipal water supply, for prevention of tooth decay.

Apr. Admiral Nimitz announced the existence of a suicidal branch of the Japanese air force: the Kamikaze Corps. Navy use of shells with proximity fuses had virtually stopped hits by conventional bombing methods, and the Japanese had enlisted pilots who, willing to die for Emperor Hirohito, crashed their explosive-laden planes into their targets. Radio Tokyo gave out the names of the latest "hero gods" daily. In the battle for Okinawa, 7 U.S. aircraft carriers were badly hit by kamikaze pilots.

Apr. 15 The horror of the Nazi concentration camps came to the world's eye as Allied troops pushed deeper into the Fatherland. In the most notorious—Treblinka, Auschwitz, and Dachau—over 6 million men, women, and children, particularly Jews and Poles, were gassed or otherwise murdered. Unrepentant Dr. Gustav Schuebbe, head of the Nazi Annihilation Institute at Kiev, admitted that he, personally, had killed 21,000 inmates in the 9 months he had "processed" his human material. Said Dr. Schuebbe:

> I still maintain that, just as one prunes a tree—by removing old, undesirable branches in the spring—so for its own interest a certain hygienical supervision of the body of a people is necessary from time to time.

Apr. 30 The leader of the 3rd Reich, Adolf Hitler, committed suicide in an underground bunker in Berlin. Dying with him: Eva Braun, his longtime mistress and wife of one day.

May A poll conducted by the University of Denver, Colo., asking adult civilians if they thought the U.S. would be involved in another war within 25 years, produced a 36% "Yes" response.

May 5 Mrs. Elsie Mitchell and 5 neighborhood children were killed during an outing in the Gearhart Mountains 65 mi. east-northeast of Klamath Falls, Oreg., when a strange object which they had chanced upon in the forest exploded. The object turned out to be a Japanese balloon bomb, one of 285 which found their way to American soil between November, 1944 and April, 1945. The Japanese had floated over 9,000 of the balloons toward North America, but malfunctioning of the ballast-control mechanism doomed the attack to failure. Mrs. Mitchell and the children were the only W.W. II victims to die on the U.S. mainland.

May 7 Germany surrendered. Signing for Germany at Rheims: Col. Gen. Alfred Jodl, Chief of Staff. He was subsequently jailed, tried at Nuremberg, and hung as a war criminal.

June 26 The Charter for the United Nations was written in San Francisco, Calif., with delegates from 50 nations in attendance. Selected as the UN Secretary General for the conference: Alger Hiss.

Aug. 6 The atomic bomb was dropped on Hiroshima, Japan. Weighing a respectable 400 lbs., it had a destructive power exceeding that of 20,000 tons of TNT. The air detonation killed over 100,000 including the entire 2nd Japanese Army and leveled 4 sq. mi. In a 2nd drop at Nagasaki, 3 days later, following Russia's declaration of war on Japan, 36,000 more were killed.

Through the Potsdam Declaration on July 26, Truman, Churchill, and Chiang Kai-shek of China issued a joint statement calling for Japan to surrender unconditionally or face complete destruction. Japan had already, on June 22, held a meeting of its Supreme Council and Emperor Hirohito had ordered that steps be taken to secure a negotiated peace. To speed up the progress, the Russians were asked to inquire about deletion of the "unconditional" clause announced at Potsdam. Russian Foreign Minister Molotov gave no reply to the Japanese, but did inform Truman of the inquiry. The President allowed the unconditional surrender demand to stand.

Still believing that negotiations were possible, the Japanese voted to wait, pending further diplomatic maneuvers. In a release to the world press, the Japanese translator used the English word "ignore" in describing the attitude of Japan, and this was viewed by U.S. leaders as a Japanese expression of contempt for the U.S.

Truman gave the order for the Hiroshima drop. Even then, the Japanese did not answer. On August 8, the Japanese Ambassador in Moscow was called before Molotov. The shocked Ambassador learned that Russian troops were immediately taking over Manchuria. After the 2nd atomic strike at Nagasaki, the following day, the Japanese Government waited no longer. It offered to surrender.

Aug. 25 Capt. John M. Birch, Baptist missionary and army intelligence expert, was killed by Chinese communists in northern Anhwei Province. The 1st victim of the "Cold War with Communism," he became the hero of Robert H. W. Welch, Jr., who founded the John Birch Society in his honor.

Sept. Hideki Tojo, Japanese general and Prime Minister, attempted suicide. After his recovery, he and 5 other former ministers of the Japanese Cabinet were tried for war crimes, found guilty, and executed. In lesser trials, 720 officers and civilians were executed, primarily for torture and murder of prisoners. Nearly 3,500 others served prison terms.

Sept. The Surplus Property Board, custodian of war supplies no longer needed, announced the availability of 10 million lbs. of contraceptive jelly. It had $90 billion in other leftovers to be placed on sale in the civilian market.

Sept. 2 Japan formally surrendered in a ceremony aboard the U.S.S. *Missouri* in Tokyo Bay. General MacArthur, as the Allied Supreme Commander, was assigned the task of occupying Japan and rehabilitating the Japanese. He disbanded the secret police, purged the hardcore militarists from the civil service, broke up the cartels (or *zaibatsu*), and redistributed almost 5 million acres of land to the peasants. Politically, he set up a new democratic government guided by a liberal constitution. Women were allowed to vote and workers were encouraged to form trade unions. General MacArthur's civilian achievements in his role as administrator for a vanquished nation of 83 million overshadowed his most impressive feats as a military leader.

Nov. 20 The trials in Nuremberg, Germany, for war crimes, began. The Charter for the International Military Tribunal required 2 days to read in 4 languages. (See also: Highlights of World History, Chap. 8.)

New milestones for international law were set. Blind obedience to superiors was declared to be no defense. Entire organizations such as the SS were found guilty collectively. This plugged loopholes that had permitted 890 out of 896 to go free in W.W. I war crimes trials.

Dec. 14 John D. Rockefeller, Jr., donated $8½ million for purchase of land along New York City's East River, to erect the permanent headquarters of the United Nations.

1946

—Calculation by computer began, at the University of Pennsylvania. Designed by J. Presper, Jr., and John Mauchly, the ENIAC (Electronic

Numerical Integrator and Computer) used 18,000 vacuum tubes in its system, with components spread around a 30′×50′ room.

Jan. 10 The United Nations held its 1st session in London. After that meeting, it moved to Lake Success, N.Y., and then on to its permanent skyscraper home at East 43rd Street, New York City, in 1952.

Mar. Winston Churchill, speaking at Westminster College, Fulton, Mo., coined the most famous propaganda phrase of the Cold War: "From Stettin in the Baltic to Trieste in the Adriatic, an iron curtain has descended across the Continent."

July 7 The Roman Catholic Church canonized Mother Francis Xavier Cabrini. The founder of the Missionary Sisters of the Sacred Heart of Jesus was the 1st American to be elevated to this rank. Her feast day: December 22.

Aug. 1 The Atomic Energy Commission was created to promote peaceful application of atomic power.

Oct. 9 The Simmons Company of Petersburg, Va., offered an "electronic" blanket for sale. Cost to sleep the electric way: $39.50 each.

Nov. 12 The Exchange National Bank of Chicago offered a new service, called "Autobank." Motorists could drive directly to one of 10 windows where tellers sat behind bulletproof glass. They used slide-out drawers to handle transactions.

1947

—Financier Bernard Baruch named the power struggle taking place between the East and West when he said: "We are in the midst of a cold war."

Mar. 22 President Truman signed Executive Order 9835. It called for a loyalty investigation of all Federal employees. Of 3 million, 308 were fired as "security risks." Only one was arrested on spying charges: Judith Coplon. She was convicted twice, but released because of illegal FBI telephone taps.

The House Committee on Un-American Activities collected a file with over one million names of known or suspected Communists, "fellow travelers," "dupes," and "bleeding-heart liberals."

May 11 B. F. Goodrich Tire Company of Akron, O., announced production of the tubeless tire, designed to seal itself if punctured. The company ran road tests in Indiana, Ohio, West Virginia, and Kentucky, before making them available nationally.

Oct. 14 Air Force Captain Charles Yeager, flying the Bell X-1, exceeded the speed of sound to become the world's 1st supersonic flyer.

Oct. 29 Conducting experiments on the control of weather, the General Electric Company used dry ice to "seed" cumulus clouds at Concord, N.H. It produced rain.

1948

Mar. 8 The U.S. Supreme Court abolished religion in the public schoolroom, declaring it to be a violation of the 1st Amendment.

Apr. 3 The Foreign Assistance Act was passed. Popularly called the Marshall Plan—named after Secretary of State George Marshall, who 1st proposed the aid in a 1947 speech at a Harvard College Commencement—the law initiated a program that eventually was funded with over $100 billion.

May The U.S. formally recognized the new republic of Israel, homeland for thousands of European and Asiatic Jews.

June 21 Columbia Records introduced the 33⅓-rpm, "long-playing" record at the Waldorf-Astoria Hotel in New York. Each side played for 23 minutes, compared to 4 minutes for the standard 78-rpm record.

June 24 The U.S.S.R.'s Joseph Stalin set up blockades on all road and rail approaches to the noncommunist areas of Berlin. With his military squeeze, he hoped to force out the Allies and take over the entire city for East Germany. The U.S. and British air forces organized an extensive air lift, using transport planes to supply 100% of West Berlin's needs. In 321 days, until the blockade ended in May, 1949, they brought in over 2½ million tons of cargo, and took out the city's exports.

Nov. 3 Making the century's worst political prediction, the *Chicago Tribune* prematurely "elected" Thomas Dewey to the Presidency with its morning-after headline. Dewey's "give 'em hell" opponent, Harry S Truman, scored a stunning upset due to voter acceptance of his "Fair Deal" program.

Dec. Pumpkin Patch Day in Maryland. Leading 2 men from the House Un-American Activities Committee into his pumpkin field, Whittaker Chambers produced the film evidence, concealed inside a pumpkin, which documented a communist conspiracy in Washington. Chambers later swore that his "rather romantic communist" friend, Alger Hiss, had given him the State Dept. documents which were photographed on the film. Hiss denied it under oath and claimed he had been framed. The jury believed Chambers and sent Hiss to prison for perjury, indirectly labeling him a spy for the U.S.S.R. The man who forced the confrontation between Hiss and Chambers, leading to the perjury charge: Richard M. Nixon.

Dec. 24 A solar heating system developed by Dr. Maria Telkes was incorporated into a house built in Dover, Mass.

1949

—Mrs. Iva Ikuko Toguri D'Aquino was convicted of treason. U.S.-born Mrs. D'Aquino—better known as "Tokyo Rose," for her propaganda broadcasts from Japan to U.S. troops in the South Pacific—received a 10-year sentence and a $10,000 fine. Her 65-minute show, heard at 8 P.M. daily all over the Pacific theater, mixed war news, good dance music, chitchat, and other entertainment. It was extremely popular due to its nonpropaganda segments.
—French fashion produced a new type of bathing suit for women: the "bikini."
Jan. 7 Drs. Daniel Pease and Richard Baker announced their success in photographing the gene during experiments at the University of Southern California. The tissue sections they used were magnified by 120,000 diameters.
Apr. 4 The U.S. signed the North Atlantic Treaty Organization—or NATO—pact. It pledged to join Canada and 10 West European countries in mutual resistance of armed attack on any member nation.
Apr. 20 Cortisone was discovered. Its most immediate use: for relief of rheumatoid arthritis.
Oct. 21 Judge Harold Medina sentenced 11 top U.S. Communists to terms of up to 5 years in prison and fined them $10,000.

—W.K.

1950

—U.S. population—150,697,361.
—Between 1950 and 1960, 2,515,000 immigrants entered the U.S.
—*The New York Times* reported from Hollywood:

> Fear that a motion picture dealing with the life and exploits of Hiawatha might be regarded as Communist propaganda has caused Monogram Studio to shelve such a project. It was Hiawatha's efforts as a peacemaker among the warring Indian tribes of his day, which brought about the federation of 5 nations, that gave Monogram particular concern, according to a studio spokesman. These, it was decided, might cause the picture to be regarded as a message for peace and therefore helpful to present Communist designs.

—The *Los Angeles Times* editorially advised its readers what to do if approached by a petitioner for peace: "Don't punch him in the nose. Reds are used to that. Get his name and address and phone the FBI."
—A short circuit in the New York City subways caused 1,000 passengers to stampede, believing that W.W. III had started. Many shrieked: "War! The Russians!"
—Sen. Joseph McCarthy, speaking before the Women's Republican Club in Wheeling, W.Va., stated: "I have here in my hand a list of 205—a list of names that were known to the Secretary of State as being members of the Communist party and who nevertheless are still working and shaping the policy in the State Dept." The next day McCarthy charged that there were "57 card-carrying members of the Communist party" in the State Dept.; he wired President Truman demanding action. McCarthy latched onto the issue of communism after discarding proposals advocating the St. Lawrence Seaway and old-age pensions as too mundane to attract the attention of Wisconsin voters. The notion of a crusade against Communists originated with the FBI. The FBI leaked a 100-page document to a Pentagon intelligence officer with instructions for him to pass it on to the Jewish American League Against Communism. The League sifted through a roster of potential anticommunist campaigners and offered the document to McCarthy. Father Edmund A. Walsh, vice-president of Georgetown University and author of an anticommunist volume, *Total Power*, urged McCarthy to take up the struggle. Roy Cohn, McCarthy's top assistant, said: "Joe McCarthy bought communism in much the same way as other people purchase a new automobile."
May A Special Senate Committee to Investigate Organized Crime in Interstate Commerce, chaired by Sen. Estes Kefauver, conducted the 1st televised congressional hearings. The nation was held spellbound by the parade of witnesses and the continuous revelations. Young and Rubicam, a big advertising firm, took out full-page ads in New York newspapers reading:

> Out of many pictures has come a broader picture of the sordid intermingling of crime and politics, of dishonor in public life. And suddenly millions of Americans are asking: What's happened to our ideals of right and wrong? What's happened to our principles of honesty in government? What's happened to public and private standards of morality? Then they ask the most important question of all: How can we stop what's going on? Is there anything we can do about it?

June 9 The 1st 2 members of the Hollywood 10—a group of movie writers and directors who refused to answer the questions of the House Un-American Activities Committee—began their prison terms.

June 25 War began between the Democratic People's Republic of Korea and South Korea. Sir John Pratt, former adviser in Far Eastern Affairs for the British Government and head of the Far Eastern Section of the British Ministry of Information, stated:

> The fighting that broke out at dawn on June 25 saved Syngman Rhee [the South Korean dictator] from ruin and gave President Truman the pretext he required for seizing Formosa. No one who studies the evidence . . . can doubt that the Korean War began with an attack upon North Korea launched by Syngman Rhee with the support of his friends in the American Military Advisory Group.

June 27 The United Nations Security Council adopted a U.S. resolution approving armed intervention on the side of the South Koreans. The Soviet delegation to the UN was absent from this session.

July 1 U.S. ground forces landed in Korea.

Sept. 23 The McCarran Internal Security Act was passed by Congress. The Act provided for a Subversive Activities Control Board to register members of groups the Attorney General determined to be a "Communist-action or Communist-front." The Act also included a provision establishing "emergency" concentration camps; the sponsor of this section of the law was Sen. Hubert Humphrey.

Oct. 7 U.S. forces invaded the Democratic People's Republic of Korea by crossing the 38th parallel.

Nov. 20 American troops reached the Chinese border. Chou En-lai stated that the Chinese people would not "supinely tolerate seeing their neighbors being savagely invaded by imperialists."

Nov. 29 The Chinese threw 850,000 "volunteers" into Korea against 700,000 South Korean, U.S. and UN forces, and the "police action" escalated.

1951

—Approximately 3 million Koreans were dead after one year of war. American casualties totaled about 15,000 dead and 75,000 wounded.

—Popular songs included "Hello, Young Lovers" and "Getting to Know You," from the Rodgers and Hammerstein score for *The King and I*, the Broadway smash of the season.

—Mickey Spillane's *One Lonely Night* sold 3 million copies. In it, the hero, Mike Hammer, gloats: "I killed more people tonight than I have fingers on my hands. I shot them in cold blood and enjoyed every minute of it. . . . They were Commies, Lee. They were red sons-of-bitches who should have died long ago. . . . They never thought that there were people like me in this country. They figured us all to be soft as horse manure and just as stupid."

—The American Committee for Cultural Freedom was founded by James Burnham, James T. Farrell, Arthur M. Schlesinger, Jr., Sidney Hook, and others to "counteract the influence of mendacious communist propaganda." Annual forums were held on topics like "The Ex-Communist: His Role in a Democracy" and ideas like "the end of ideology" were approvingly discussed. The ACCF was an affiliate of the international Congress for Cultural Freedom, which was funded by the CIA.

Feb. 5 General Grow, the U.S. military attaché in Moscow, wrote in his diary: "War! As soon as possible! Now! We need a voice to lead us without equivocation: Communism must be destroyed!" Grow's diary was made public in late 1951. Six months later he was court-martialed for failure to safeguard secret military information.

Feb. 26 The 22nd Amendment to the Constitution was adopted. It stipulated that no person could be elected to the Presidency for more than 2 terms.

Apr. 5 Julius and Ethel Rosenberg were sentenced to die in the electric chair for stealing atomic-bomb secrets. The main prosecution exhibits were 2 Jell-O box halves for spy-to-spy identification, photostats of New Mexico hotel registration cards signed "Harry Gold" (a key prosecution witness, later revealed to be a mythomaniac), and sketches of the atomic bomb made by David Greenglass, who flunked most of his academic courses in high school and was Ethel Rosenberg's younger brother. Dr. J. Robert Oppenheimer, the foremost U.S. scientific authority on atomic weapons stated in January, 1951: ". . . there were no 'unpublished secrets concerning atomic weapons, and no 'secret laws of nature' available to only a few." Judge Irving Kaufman said in his judgment of the Rosenbergs: "I consider your crime worse than murder." He accused the couple of causing "the communist aggression in Korea."

Apr. 11 Gen. Douglas MacArthur, commander in chief of the American Army in Korea, was dismissed from his post by President Truman for publicly challenging the policies of his civilian superiors. MacArthur had advocated the American bombing of China and an invasion of the Chinese mainland. His slogan was: "There is no substitute for victory!" MacArthur was greeted at home with tumultuous ticker-tape parades and addressed a reverent congressional audience, after which he gradually faded from public view.

Nov. W.E.B. Du Bois, one of the greatest black scholars of the century, after being handcuffed, fingerprinted, and searched for concealed weapons, was brought to trial for not registering as a subversive. He was acquitted. Du Bois said: "A great silence has fallen on the real soul of this nation."

Dec. 17 A delegation of black Americans, led by Paul Robeson and William L. Patterson, presented a petition to the UN which charged the U.S. Government with a policy of genocide against its black citizens.

1952

—A campaign of harassment by the FBI and the Internal Revenue Service against Charlie Chaplin, instigated because of his heretical political opinions, drove the filmmaker into exile. Chaplin stated:

> America is so terribly grim in spite of all that material prosperity. They no longer know how to weep. Compassion and the old neighborliness have gone, people stand by and do nothing when friends and neighbors are attacked, libeled and ruined. The worst thing is what it has done to the children. They are being taught to admire and emulate stool pigeons, to betray and to hate, and all in a sickening atmosphere of religious hypocrisy.

Jan. General Van Fleet, the commander of U.S. troops in Korea, said: "Korea has been a blessing. There had to be a Korea here or some place in the world."

Sept. 23 Richard M. Nixon, the Republican vice-presidential candidate, went on nationwide television to explain an $18,000 private slush fund set up for him by a group of millionaire backers. Nixon described his childhood ("Most of my early life was spent in a family grocery store."), his war experience, and his battle against communism. He claimed that the slush fund was for "necessary political expenses" and "exposing communism." He asserted about his wife: "I should say this—that Pat doesn't have a mink coat. But she does have a respectable Republican cloth coat." He then added that he had received another gift, "a little cocker spaniel dog in a crate that [was] sent all the way from Texas. Black and white spotted. And our little girl—Trisha, the 6-year-old—named it Checkers. And you know, the kids love the dog, and I just want to say this right now, that regardless of what they say about it, we're gonna keep it!" The next day Dwight Eisenhower embraced Nixon and assured him that he would remain on the GOP

ticket. "You're my boy!" said Ike. Addressing a cheering crowd, Eisenhower said about his running mate: "He is . . . completely vindicated as a man of honor." Some time later, at a New York advertising men's luncheon, Nixon reflected: "No TV performance takes such careful preparation as an off-the-cuff talk."

Nov. 4 Dwight D. Eisenhower was elected President over the Democratic candidate, Adlai E. Stevenson.

1953

—Charles E. Wilson, president of General Motors, was appointed Secretary of Defense by President Eisenhower. Wilson did not want to sell his GM stock, which he was required by law to do if he was to assume the high government post. "I thought what was good for the country was good for General Motors, and vice versa," he said.

Mar. 9 Stalin's funeral.

May 22 President Eisenhower signed a bill surrendering Federal ownership of $80 billion of offshore oil and gas reserves to the oil corporations. The Supreme Court had earlier ruled that this oil was the property of the whole nation. A former U.S. Solicitor General called the episode "the largest wholesale looting of national assets in history."

June 19 Julius and Ethel Rosenberg died in the electric chair. The Rosenbergs' petition to the White House for executive clemency said: "We are innocent. This is the whole truth. To forsake this truth is to pay too high a price even for the priceless gift of life—for life thus purchased we could not live out in dignity and self-respect."

Jean-Paul Sartre wrote in an open letter to Americans:

> The atomic secret is the fruit of your sick imaginations: Science develops everywhere at the same rhythm, and the manufacture of bombs is a mere matter of industrial capacities. You have quite simply tried to halt the progress of science by human sacrifice—we are here getting to the point: Your country is sick with fear. . . . If we can have some hope, it is because your country gave birth to this man and this woman whom you have killed.

July 26 Fidel Castro led an attack on the Moncada barracks in Cuba in an attempt to overthrow the Batista dictatorship. Castro was jailed but he proclaimed at his trial: "History will absolve me!"

July 27 An armistice ending the Korean War

was signed. U.S. casualties in the war totaled 165,485: 54,246 were killed, 103,284 were wounded, and 7,955 were reported missing in action.

Aug. 19 The popularly elected Prime Minister of Iran, Dr. Mohammed Mossadegh, whose Government had nationalized the country's oil, was overthrown in a coup initiated by the CIA. The chief CIA man in the operation, Kermit Roosevelt, later became a vice-president of Gulf Oil, which had greatly profited from the changed Iranian political situation.

Oct. 6 Casey Stengel's New York Yankees beat the Brooklyn Dodgers 4 games to 2 to win their 5th straight world series championship.

1954

—Henry David Thoreau's *Walden* was banned from U.S. Information Service libraries and categorized "downright socialistic."

—*I Love Lucy*, starring Lucille Ball as a comical housewife and Desi Arnaz as her Cuban bandleader husband, was the most popular television show.

Feb. 2 The 1st hydrogen bomb explosion was announced by President Eisenhower.

—"The bomb's brilliant gleam reminds me of the brilliant gleam Beacon Wax gives to floors. It's a science marvel!" read an ad in the *Pittsburgh Press*.

Mar. 1 Five congressmen were shot on the floor of the House of Representatives by Puerto Rican nationalists seeking the independence of their country.

Apr. 22 The Army-McCarthy hearings began. Sen. Joseph McCarthy had charged that the Secretary of the Army was interfering with McCarthy's investigation of communists in the Army; the Army had countercharged that McCarthy had sought favors for an aide who was in the service. The daily hearings became the most dramatic TV show of the decade. After 36 days of bitter wrangling and 2 million words of testimony, McCarthy was totally discredited. Shortly after, the U.S. Senate, which set out to censure him, merely "condemned" him by a vote of 67–22.

May 8 The French garrison at Dien Bien Phu fell to the popular insurgent forces, the Viet Minh, led by Ho Chi Minh. Vice-President Nixon urged direct American intervention.

May 17 The Supreme Court ruled unanimously in *Brown* v. *The Board of Education of Topeka* that segregated education was illegal. Chief Justice Earl Warren: "We conclude that in the field of public education the doctrine of 'separate but equal' has no place. Separate education facilities are inherently unequal."

May 24 The Supreme Court upheld the constitutionality of the Internal Security Act, thus making membership in the Communist party sufficient grounds for the deportation of aliens.

June 18 A right-wing coup in Guatemala, financed by the CIA, overthrew the popularly elected Government of Jacobo Arbenz, which had nationalized the property of the United Fruit Company. Secretary of State John Foster Dulles's law firm had written the United Fruit contracts with Guatemala in the '30s; Assistant Secretary of State for Inter-American Affairs, John Moors Cabot, was a major United Fruit shareholder; CIA director Allen Dulles had been president of United Fruit; and Allen Dulles's predecessor as CIA director, Gen. Walter Bedell Smith, became a United Fruit vice-president in 1955.

1955

—Bishop Fulton Sheen said: "The communist loves nothing better than to be arrested. But he is not like the martyr for the faith. St. Joan of Arc did not like being tied to a stake; a communist does."

—An animal hospital in Massachusetts fired a direct descendant of Nathan Hale because she invoked the 5th Amendment rather than sign a loyalty oath.

—Harvey Matusow, a frequent witness testifying against leftists before the House Un-American Activities Committee, announced that he had done it for the money and that he had consistently lied.

—Bill Haley's "Rock Around the Clock" was the music for the film *Blackboard Jungle*, about juvenile delinquents. This was a major factor in stimulating the popularity of rock 'n' roll.

Jan. 1 American aid to South Vietnam, amounting to $216 million in 1955, began.

Aug. 28 Emmett Till, a black 14-year-old, was kidnapped by 2 white men from his uncle's home in LeFlore County, Miss. It had been rumored that the youngster had "whistled at a white woman." Four days later, Emmett Till's body, tied in barbed wire, was recovered from the Tallahatchie River. An all-white, all-male jury acquitted the 2 men accused of the crime.

Oct. 4 The Brooklyn Dodgers finally defeated the New York Yankees in the World Series.

Dec. Mrs. Rosa Parks, a black woman coming home from work, refused to give up her seat on a Montgomery, Ala., city bus to a white man; she was arrested. Two days later the Montgomery bus boycott began, forcing the desegregation of public transportation facilities. The boycott was led by the Rev. Dr. Martin Luther King, Jr., who had arrived in Montgomery a few months earlier. Dr. King advocated nonviolent, direct action instead of a purely legal strategy of filing law suits.

Dec. 5 The American Federation of Labor and the Congress of Industrial Organizations merged, with George Meany presiding as president.

1956

—Grace Metalious' novel, *Peyton Place*, about sexual intrigue in a small town, became a best seller.

—Elvis Presley's songs "Hound Dog" and "Don't Be Cruel" were the hits of the year.

—Allen Ginsberg's book of poetry, *Howl*, was published. Ginsberg wrote: "I have seen the best minds of my generation destroyed by madness."

Aug. 1 A polio vaccine developed by Dr. Jonas Salk was made available on a mass basis.

—President Eisenhower said: "We've done some damn good things—in the economy, especially, and overseas too—Iran and Guatemala. . . ."

Nov. 6 Eisenhower defeated Adlai E. Stevenson in the presidential election.

1957

—Sen. John F. Kennedy was awarded a Pulitzer Prize for his book *Profiles in Courage*.

—Jack Kerouac's *On the Road* was published. "Beat" literature signified a conscious withdrawal from the American cultural consensus.

—Dr. Martin Luther King, Jr., organized the Southern Christian Leadership Conference.

—An Academy Award for the best screenplay of the year was given to "Robert Rich," author of *The Brave One*. "Rich" failed to claim his Oscar. "Rich" was actually a blacklisted member of the Hollywood 10, Dalton Trumbo.

—The Senate's McClellan Committee investigated the corrupt practices of union officials, principally those of the Teamsters union. The chief majority counsel of the committee was Robert Kennedy.

May 2 Sen. Joseph McCarthy, who had gone badly downhill after his condemnation by the Senate, died in the Bethesda Naval Hospital, Md., of cirrhosis of the liver brought on by acute alcoholism.

Sept. 18 The Ethical Practices Committee of the AFL-CIO charged that Teamster leader James Hoffa maintained criminals in the union hierarchy. It ordered the Teamsters to expel Hoffa or leave the federation. On December 6, the AFL-CIO expelled the Teamsters.

Sept. 24 One thousand army paratroopers were dispatched to Central High School, Little Rock, Ark., to permit 9 black students to attend the previously all-white school.

Oct. 4 The Soviet Union launched the 1st man-made satellite, *Sputnik I*.

1958

—Vladimir Nabokov's *Lolita* was a best seller.

May 1 Four pacifists attempting to sail into the atomic bomb testing area in the Pacific Ocean to protest the tests were seized in their ship, the *Golden Rule*, by the Coast Guard.

July 10 The heaviest human being of all time, Robert Earl Hughes, died at Bremen, Ind., at the age of 32. His greatest weight was 1,067 lbs. His coffin was the size of a piano case and had to be lowered into the grave by a crane.

Sept. 22 Sherman Adams, an assistant to President Eisenhower, resigned because he had accepted a freezer from Boston industrialist Bernard Goldfine.

1959

Jan. 1 Fidel Castro, at the head of a guerrilla army, marched triumphantly into Havana. The Cuban Revolution had succeeded.

Jan. 3 Alaska became the 49th State.

Apr. 9 The 1st 7 astronauts were selected.

June 8 The Supreme Court upheld the right of Congress and individual States to investigate communism.

June 11 The Postmaster General banned D. H. Lawrence's *Lady Chatterley's Lover* from the mails.

July 15 The United Steelworkers union began a nationwide strike, which ended when the President invoked the Taft-Hartley Act, forcing the strikers back to work.

Aug. 3 Vice-President Nixon debated Soviet Premier Nikita Khrushchev in the model kitchen of an American exhibition in Moscow.

Aug. 21 Hawaii was proclaimed the 50th State.

Sept. 15 Premier Khrushchev began an official visit to the U.S. He admired American hot dogs and was severely disappointed when he was told he could not visit Disneyland because of security considerations.

Fall The 1st New Left journal, *Studies On the Left*, began publication.

—Clark Kerr, the chancellor of the University of California, stated: "The employers will love this generation. They aren't going to press many grievances. They are going to be easy to handle. There aren't going to be any riots."

—S.B.

1960

—U.S. population—179,323,175. In the 1960s, 3,321,677 persons immigrated to the U.S.
—Entrepreneur Del Webb opened Sun City, a 30,000-acre town for people over 52 outside Phoenix, and sold 272 homes the 1st weekend. By 1970 there were dozens of such "retirement villages" across the country.
—The crime rate more than doubled in the '60s, from 1,126 major felonies per 100,000 people in 1960 to 2,747 per 100,000 in 1969 (violent crime up 126%, property crime up 146%). Local, State, and Federal expenditures for police increased even faster, from $2.03 billion in 1960 to $5.08 billion in 1969. The cost of the whole criminal justice system went up from $3.349 billion in 1960 to $8.571 billion in 1969, or from under $19 to over $42 per person.
—Following a press investigation, a House subcommittee reported that 207 disk jockeys in 42 cities had received over $260,000 in payments ("payola") to play records on the air. A New York grand jury indicted 11 disk jockeys for commercial bribery, including Allen Freed, the self-proclaimed inventor of the term "rock 'n' roll," after 23 record companies admitted payments. In August, Congress passed legislation setting high fines for those involved with payola and fixing quiz shows.
Jan. 15 The U.S. and Japan signed a mutual cooperation and security treaty in Washington with provisions for U.S. defense of Japan, U.S. military bases in Japan, and "economic collaboration." Leftist opposition to the treaty in Japan was so vocal that the Japanese Government had to ask President Eisenhower to cancel his trip there in June after Ike's press secretary, surrounded by 6,000 demonstrators, had to be rescued from his car by helicopter. The treaty was ratified by the Japanese Diet and U.S. Senate, June 22 and 23.
Feb. 1 Black students sat down at the Charlotte, N.C., Woolworth's lunch counter in protest to the "local custom" of serving blacks only if they stood. In response, 8 lunch counters in Charlotte closed. This began the "sit-in" movement which spread to 15 cities in 5 Southern States by the end of the month. The campaign was marked by fights between blacks and whites in many areas, $1 cups of coffee, 1,000 blacks arrested by mid-March, black students and faculty expelled from black colleges, and finally on March 21, the 1st integration of lunch counters in San Antonio, Tex. While the "sit-ins" began spontaneously, on April 8 the Student Non-violent Co-ordinating

Committee (SNCC) was established to guide antisegregation efforts. A nationwide boycott of Woolworth & Kress Co. protested company policy of letting local managers decide whom to serve. By August 1, lunch counters had integrated in 15 cities, and on October 17, 4 national chain stores capitulated and announced the integration of 150 stores in 112 cities.

In September 1961, the Southern Regional Council reported that the sit-in movement had involved 70,000 participants in 100 cities in 20 States, resulted in 3,600 arrests, 187 students plus 58 faculty expelled from colleges, and succeeded in integrating one or more eating facilities in 108 cities.
May 2 Caryl Chessman was executed at San Quentin prison, Calif., despite worldwide protests. Chessman had been convicted on 17 counts of robbery, kidnapping, and attempted rape in 1948. Since then he had taught himself law, received 8 stays of execution and written 4 books—*Cell 2455 Death Row*, sold 500,000 copies in the U.S. and was translated worldwide. Albert Schweitzer, Pablo Casals, and Aldous Huxley were among thousands that sent personal appeals for his life.
May 5 A U.S. U-2 reconnaissance plane was shot down over central U.S.S.R. The incident led to the collapse of the May 16 Eisenhower-Khrushchev Paris summit when the U.S. did not apologize, though Eisenhower did announce discontinuing such flights. On May 11, Eisenhower called espionage "a distasteful but vital necessity" caused by the U.S.S.R.'s "fetish of secrecy and concealment." On May 24, the U.S. launched the Midas I satellite, 1st of a series which replaced the U-2 in military reconnaissance.

U-2 pilot Gary Powers was sentenced by the U.S.S.R. August 19 to 10 years in prison, but was released during February, 1961, in exchange for a Russian spy.
May 9 The Federal Drug Administration approved the 1st public sale of contraceptive pills, Enovid, at $10–$11 for a month's supply.
May 10 U.S. atomic submarine *Triton* surfaced after 1st underwater circumnavigation of the globe: 30,708 mi. in 84 days.
Sept. 26–Oct. 17 Four TV debates between Republican and Democratic presidential candidates Richard Nixon and John Kennedy were seen by 8 million Americans. The candidates spent most of the time debating the U.S.'s commitment to defend Quemoy and Matsu, islands just offshore China, and neither clearly won. Political commentators agree, however, that the debates gave Kennedy his slim election victory (0.1%), since he came off at least as knowledgeable and articulate as Nixon, offsetting Nixon's claim to superior experience, and because Kennedy was the more appealing

TV personality, due in part to Nixon's poor makeup job in the 1st debate.

1961

Jan. 3 The U.S. broke diplomatic relations with Cuba after Cuba demanded the U.S. reduce its embassy staff to 11, claiming 80% of the staff were FBI and Pentagon spies. Two weeks later the U.S. forbade its citizens to travel to Cuba.

Feb. 7 Twenty-nine major electrical firms, including General Electric and Westinghouse and 44 of their executives, were convicted of rigging bids and fixing prices in the sale of $1.75 billion of heavy electrical equipment per year. The corporations were fined $1,787,000 and GE was successfully sued for almost $8 million by the Federal Government and New York State. Seven of the executives got 30-day jail terms, 23 received suspended sentences. Sentencing Judge Garvey said the defendants had, "flagrantly mocked the image of that economic system of free enterprise which we profess . . . and destroyed the model we offer today as a free world alternative to state control and eventual dictatorship."

Mar. 1 By Executive Order, President Kennedy created the Peace Corps, sending American volunteers to meet "urgent needs for skilled manpower" in underdeveloped countries and to "live at the same level as the citizens of the countries they are sent to." Over 1,000 were on the job in the West Indies and Africa by September when Congress appropriated $40 million for the program.

Apr. 12 The U.S.S.R. put the 1st man in space, Yuri Gagarin—one orbit, 108 minutes.

Apr. 17 In an attempt to "liberate" Cuba, 1,500 Cuban refugees landed at the Bay of Pigs. All were killed or captured by the Cuban armed forces within 3 days. They had been trained and armed in Guatemala by the CIA since May, 1960; but, as Secretary of State Rusk testified, all U.S. agencies involved had unanimously recommended the attack. In December, 1962, Cuba released 1,113 invaders and 922 of their relatives in exchange for $53 million in medical supplies and baby food.

May In a speech to the National Association of Broadcasters, Federal Communications Committee chairman Newton Minow called TV "a vast wasteland" and threatened not to renew licenses unless there was more programing in the public interest. "I do not think the public taste is as low as some of you appear to believe."

May 1 A National Airlines plane bound for Miami was "hijacked" to Havana by an armed passenger. On September 5, President Kennedy signed a bill making hijacking a Federal crime punishable by prison or death.

May 4 Thirteen "Freedom Riders" left Washington, D.C., for New Orleans to test the desegregation of public facilities along the way. Between May 15 and 20 the Freedom Riders, now 2 buses strong, were attacked in 3 cities in Alabama. One bus was firebombed in Anniston, the other was met in Birmingham by 40 "toughs" who beat the passengers with pipes for 10 minutes before police came. Continuing to Montgomery, the Riders were attacked by a mob of 1,000. A police commissioner watching from across the street said, "We have no intention of standing guard for a bunch of troublemakers coming into our city." That day President Kennedy dispatched 350 Federal marshals to protect the Riders as interstate travelers. On May 21, the National Guard was called in when a black church meeting was besieged by 1,000 whites. On May 23, 2 buses of Riders accompanied by marshals resumed their trip to Jackson, Miss., where all 27 were arrested for entering a "white" washroom and failure to obey officers.

The Freedom Ride movement grew with "Freedom Flights" and "Freedom Trains," and by the end of June, 163 Freedom Riders had been convicted in Jackson.

Summer The Berlin crisis. Soviet Premier Khrushchev gave Western powers an ultimatum: to sign a German peace treaty by the end of the year or else the U.S.S.R. would sign a separate treaty with East Germany not recognizing Western occupation of West Berlin. The U.S., France, and Britain reaffirmed their determination to stay in Berlin as both sides built up their armed forces. The U.S.S.R. backed down on the treaty, but on August 13 East Germany began to build the Berlin Wall, closing access from East to West Berlin and blocking the path of refugees to the West.

Oct. 2 Roger Maris of the New York Yankees hit his 61st home run in the 162nd and last game of the season, breaking Babe Ruth's 154-game 1927 record.

Nov. 13 Pablo Casals gave a recital at the White House at the special request of the President, highlighting Kennedy's efforts to promote government patronage of the arts. Previously cellist Casals had refused to play in the U.S. because of U.S. aid to Spain.

Nov. 16 The New York Metropolitan Museum of Art paid a record $2.3 million for Rembrandt's *Aristotle Contemplating the Bust of Homer.*

Dec. 11 The 1st 2 U.S. military companies arrived in South Vietnam, including 32 helicopters and 4,000 men. They were assigned to Vietnamese units, but remained under U.S. order to fire only if fired on. In October and November the U.S. had accelerated its military aid to South Vietnam, on October 29 President Kennedy wrote South Vietnamese President Diem, "The U.S. is determined to help Vietnam preserve its independence, protect its people against communist assassins and build a better life."

Dec. 12–16 In Montgomery, Ala., 737 were arrested in a march on city hall protesting the trials of 11 Freedom Riders. Black groups organized a boycott of the city's white merchants. On December 18, the city and black groups reached a "peace agreement" in which public facilities were desegregated and charges reduced in return for ending the protests and boycott.

1962

—Rachel Carson's exposé of the widespread damage to all life caused by pesticides in her best-selling book *Silent Spring* heralded an increasing concern with ecology and the risks of destruction inherent in man's technological progress.

Jan. 26 Orson Welles's *Citizen Kane* (U.S. 1941) was voted the best movie ever made in a poll of 70 film critics from 11 countries.

Feb. 8 The U.S. established the Military Assistance Command (MAC) in South Vietnam. At this time, 5,000 U.S. troops were in Vietnam with the official purpose of providing training and technical assistance. On March 9, the Pentagon admitted U.S. pilots were flying combat missions in Vietnam.

Feb. 20 Lieut. Col. John Glenn orbited the earth 3 times in space capsule Friendship 7, becoming the 1st American in orbit. Television beamed his flight to 135 million viewers.

Apr. 11 U.S. Steel and 5 other major steel companies announced a 3½% ($6 a ton) steel price raise. This increase evoked the anger of President Kennedy: "The American people will find it hard, as I do, to accept a situation in which a tiny handful of steel executives, whose pursuit of private power and profit exceeds their sense of public responsibility, can show such utter contempt for the interest of 185 million Americans." On April 13, the Defense Dept. awarded a $5 million contract to a small steel company that had not raised prices. On April 14, the big steel companies backed down.

Apr. 20 The segregationist New Orleans Citizens Council initiated a plan to give free one-way transportation to blacks wishing to move to northern cities. By October 7, 96 persons had taken the "reverse freedom rides."

Apr. 25 The U.S. resumed nuclear tests in the atmosphere over the South Pacific in response to the Russian breach of a 4-year unofficial test moratorium the previous fall. The U.S. exploded 36 nuclear bombs through November 4.

May 12 *The New York Times* reported:

> U.S. aid to South Vietnam reached a peak and will start to level off, Robert S. McNamara, Defense Secretary disclosed today. Before departing for Washington Mr. McNamara said he doubted whether U.S. military personnel assigned to South Vietnam would be increased above the present strength. After 48 hours in South Vietnam Mr. McNamara was tremendously encouraged by developments. . . . "I found nothing but progress and hope for the future," he said.

May 12–15 The U.S. sent 1,500 troops to Thailand in order to force the pro-communist Pathet Lao to stop the offensive in Laos and negotiate. The 3 rival Laotian factions began negotiations May 16 and agreed to a cease-fire and coalition Government June 11. On July 23, 14 nations, including the U.S., Russia, China, and North and South Vietnam, signed a pact in Geneva guaranteeing the freedom and neutrality of Laos. By April, 1963, however, there was civil war in Laos again.

June 25 The Supreme Court barred the use of a 22-word "nondenominational" prayer in New York State schools on the basis of the 1st Amendment, separating church and state. Justice Douglas condemned the conduct of school prayers as "a public official on the public payroll performing a religious exercise in a governmental institution" before "a 'captive' audience."

July 18 The 1st privately owned satellite, Telstar (AT&T), relayed TV programs across the Atlantic.

Aug. One of the attractions of the Seattle World's Fair in Washington was a 25,000-lb. cake baked by Van de Kamp's Holland Dutch Bakers.

Aug. 5 Marilyn Monroe found dead of a barbiturate overdose in her Los Angeles home, officially suicide. "MM" was the world film "sex goddess" and was rumored to have been the mistress of Attorney General Robert Kennedy.

Oct. 1 By Federal court order, veteran James Meredith became the 1st black student at the University of Mississippi. Before his admission, Governor Barnett of Mississippi declared that State schools were not answerable to the Federal Government and that public officials would be willing to go to jail for the cause of segregation. He ordered the arrest of Federal officials who tried to enforce the court order. The State legislature appointed Barnett special registrar to deny Meredith admission. Four times Meredith failed to register, blocked twice by Governor Barnett personally, the 3rd time by the lieutenant governor and 20 State troopers, the 4th by a crowd of 2,500 whites. He succeeded the 5th time, escorted by several hundred U.S. marshals. This provoked a riot of 2,500 white students—leaving 2 dead and 375 injured, including 166 marshals—which was finally quelled by 3,000 Federal troops and National Guard.

Oct. 23 The U.S. blockaded Cuba after announcing that it had photographs of Cuban-Russian missile bases capable of sending nuclear bombs 1,000 mi. into the U.S. The U.S. threatened to invade Cuba if the bases were not dismantled and Russia threatened nuclear war. On October 27 Russia offered to trade the loss of Cuban missile bases for the withdrawal of American missiles from Turkey. The U.S. refused. On October 28 Russia agreed to withdraw the missiles and dismantle the bases. On November 8 the Pentagon announced that the bases had been dismantled and on November 20 the U.S. ended its naval blockade.

Dec. 8 Typographers struck all 9 major New York City newspapers, leaving 5,700,000 subscribers without their daily journals until April 1, 1963. St. Louis and Cleveland newspaper workers also struck.

1963

Jan. 14 George Wallace, sworn in as governor of Alabama, pledged, "segregation now, segregation tomorrow and segregation forever."

Mar 20 The 1st large "Pop art" exhibition opened at the Guggenheim Museum in New York, featuring such artists as Andy Warhol, Robert Rauschenberg, and Jasper Johns.

Spring Civil rights campaigns throughout the South started with a voter registration drive in Greenwood, Miss., and segregation protests in Birmingham, Ala., in April; continued in May, in Birmingham, and 3 North Carolina cities, Jackson, Nashville, and Atlanta; and spread in June to 6 major cities outside the South as well as 12 more in the South. Most of the protests were against segregation, but job discrimination and police brutality were often issues as well. Several thousand blacks and their white supporters were arrested.

From May 2 to 7 in Birmingham, 2,543 demonstrators were arrested, prompting Governor Wallace to say he was "beginning to tire of agitators, integrationists and others who seek to destroy law and order in Alabama." On May 9, black leaders and the Birmingham Chamber of Commerce reached an agreement to desegregate public facilities in 90 days, hire blacks as clerks and salesmen in 60 days, and release demonstrators without bail in return

for an end to the protests. Still, on May 11, 2 bombings of black organizers' homes provoked a riot of 2,500 blacks which ended with State troopers clubbing any blacks they could catch. In Cambridge, Md., the National Guard enforced martial law from June 14 to July 11 after several shooting incidents. In Detroit peaceful antidiscrimination march of 125,000 was held with the support of the mayor and governor.

June 9 *Cleopatra*, the most expensive movie ever made ($40 million) with the highest paid star, Elizabeth Taylor ($1.725 million+10% of the gross over $7.5 million), opened in New York. Though critical and public reception was lukewarm, enough people paid at least $4 so that Warner Bros. could later claim that it had made money on the film *after* it had sold the TV rights for a substantial amount.

June 12 Medgar Evers, Mississippi civil rights leader, was shot in the back and killed late at night.

June 17–19 A U.S.S.R. woman astronaut, Valentina Tereshkova, orbited the earth 45 times. The U.S. still has not put a woman in space.

Aug. 5 The U.S., the U.S.S.R., and Britain signed a treaty in Moscow banning nuclear tests in the atmosphere, outer space, and underwater. Later, 113 other nations cosigned, but not France or China.

Aug. 28 Over 200,000 blacks and whites marched for civil rights in Washington and 10 black leaders met with President Kennedy. In his keynote speech at the Lincoln Memorial, Dr. Martin Luther King, Jr., proclaimed, "Now is the time to rise from the dark and desolate valley of segregation to the sunlit path of racial justice. . . . There will be neither rest nor tranquility in America until the Negro is granted his citizenship rights. . . . No, we are not satisfied and we will not be satisfied until justice rolls down like water and righteousness like a mighty stream."

Aug. 3 A 24-hour "hot line" was installed between Washington and Moscow to insure emergency consultation which could prevent "accidental" nuclear war.

Sept. Schools peacefully integrated throughout the South, except in Alabama where President Kennedy ordered the National Guard to keep schools open after Governor Wallace sent State troopers to close them.

Sept. 15 A black church in Birmingham, Ala., was bombed, killing 4 girls. Two more blacks died in the riots that followed.

Oct. 2 Chief of Staff Taylor and Defense Secretary McNamara returned from South Vietnam and "reported in their judgment that the major part of the U.S. military task can be completed by the end of 1965," as the U.S. stepped up military aid. At the same time, the

U.S. had cut off economic aid to South Vietnam due to its government's repression of Buddhists. On November 1, South Vietnamese President Diem, whom Secretary of State Rusk once called the "Churchill of Asia," was killed in a military coup which had U.S. approval.

Nov. 19 Cambodia renounced U.S. foreign aid (it had received $365 million) and asked U.S. troops to leave. "By this measure we will be poorer but more independent."

Nov. 22 President Kennedy was assassinated in a Dallas motorcade; Lyndon Johnson became the 36th President of the U.S. (See: Assassinations, Chap. 9.)

1964

—An English rock group, The Beatles, became so popular that the media coined the term "Beatlemania." In 2 U.S. tours during the spring, the Beatles made $1 million and their screaming teen-age fans often had to be restrained by police. They had 8 gold records for the year. In their 9 years together The Beatles recorded the following albums:

The Beatles: The Early Years	1962
(reissue of the Hamburg tracks)	
Please Please Me	1963
With the Beatles	1963
A Hard Day's Night	1963
Beatles for Sale	1964
Help!	1965
Rubber Soul	1965
Revolver	1966
Sgt. Pepper's Lonely Hearts	1967
Club Band	
Magical Mystery Tour	1967
(plus: Hello Good-bye;	
Strawberry Fields Forever;	
Penny Lane; Baby, You're	
a Rich Man Now; All You	
Need Is Love)	
The Beatles (The Double	1968
White Album)	
Abbey Road	1969
Let It Be	1970

—American folk singer Bob Dylan also skyrocketed in popularity in '64 with songs protesting the conditions and hypocrisy of American society.

Jan. 9–12 Nineteen Panamanians and 4 U.S. soldiers died in fighting which started when Panamanian students protested U.S. students' raising the U.S. flag alone over their school. On January 10, Panama broke relations with the U.S., accusing the U.S. of "an unprovoked attack" on its citizens and demanding a complete revision of the 1903 treaty ceding the Canal and Canal Zone to the U.S. On April 4, Panama resumed relations on U.S. terms.

Jan. 16 Ex-hog-cutter Antonio De Angelis, accused of perpetrating the greatest swindle in history, was arrested and held on bail of $46,500,000, also a record. De Angelis was convicted of making a profit of $175 million by substituting sea water for salad oil.

Jan. 23 Ratification of the 24th Amendment to the Constitution barring a poll tax in Federal elections. Five Southern States still had a poll tax, and 2, Texas and Virginia, passed laws for "dual elections" retaining the poll tax on the State and local levels.

Jan. 27 U.S. Defense Secretary McNamara remarked:

> The survival of an independent government in South Vietnam is so important to the security of all Southeast Asia and to the free world that I can conceive of no alternative other than to take all necessary measures within our capability to prevent a Communist victory.

Feb. 3 Over 464,000 students were absent from New York City schools in a one-day protest to de facto segregation. The boycott was repeated on March 16. On June 15, New York came out with a desegregation plan acceptable to black groups. Similar boycotts were held in Chicago, Boston, Cincinnati, and Cleveland.

Feb. 7 In a nationwide Gallup Poll, 63% said they prayed frequently, 6% not at all, and 48% said they attended church regularly, 20% not at all.

Feb. 17 The Supreme Court ruled that U.S. congressional district apportionment had to follow the "one-man, one-vote" principle as nearly as possible. Thirty-seven States had over 100,000 vote differences in districts, and these variations had often been manipulated to underrepresent minority groups and city-dwellers in general. On June 15, the Supreme Court also ruled that *both* houses of State legislatures had to be apportioned by population.

Mar. Sen. Ernest Gruening (Dem.-Alaska) registered the 1st congressional opposition to the Vietnam War, calling it a "wanton and bloody stalemate." Sen. Wayne Morse (Dem.-Oreg.) concurred.

Mar. 27 One of the worst earthquakes in modern history (8.4 on the Richter scale) struck Alaska, leveling downtown Anchorage and leaving 117 dead plus $750 million damage.

July 2 President Johnson signed the most comprehensive civil rights act in U.S. history. It integrated public accommodations (hotels, restaurants, gas stations, recreational facilities) and prohibited job discrimination by both employers and labor unions with over 25 employees or members on the basis of sex, religion, or race. It also had voting, education, and Federal funding provisions, and simplified legal complaint procedures. Civil rights groups immediately began testing the new law and were generally successful. One exception was in Atlanta, where restauranteur Lester Maddox chased away blacks with a pistol and sold ax handles to white patrons, starting a political career which made him governor of Georgia in 1966.

July and Aug. The "long, hot summer" was marked by riots, 1st in New York City, then Rochester, then Philadelphia, Chicago, and 3 New Jersey cities, where looting blacks rampaged through their ghettos. In New York City, for instance, the riot was triggered July 18 when an off-duty policeman shot a black youth. In the riot that followed, one more black died, 114 were injured (including 35 police), 185 were arrested, and 112 businesses were damaged before the police regained control of the streets.

Aug. 2 The U.S. Government announced that a U.S. destroyer had been attacked by North Vietnamese PT boats in the Gulf of Tonkin 30 mi. off North Vietnam. On August 4–5, the U.S. unleashed 64 bombers on North Vietnam in "reprisal raids." Later disclosures showed that the U.S. had provoked the "attack" by accompanying South Vietnamese boats shelling North Vietnam within 10 mi. offshore, and that the sunken PT boats may not have fired a single shot while chasing the destroyer out to sea. Nonetheless, on August 7 Congress passed the Gulf of Tonkin Resolution, empowering the President to take military action in response to aggression against U.S. forces and to support our allies in Southeast Asia on request. This became the substitute Declaration of War used to justify the constitutionality of all further U.S. actions in Southeast Asia.

Oct. 14 The Rev. Martin Luther King, Jr., received the Nobel Peace Prize for his leadership in the civil rights movement and his advocacy of nonviolence.

Oct. 16 China exploded an A-bomb and became the 5th nuclear power.

Nov. 3 President Johnson led the Democrats to their easiest win since 1936 with a landslide (61%) victory over Republican Barry Goldwater. Johnson managed to brand Goldwater as an extreme conservative and as "trigger-happy" in Vietnam, making himself the sensible, progressive "peace" candidate.

Dec. 4 Most students at the University of California's Berkeley campus "struck" (stopped attending classes) after 796 students had been arrested in a sit-in at the administration building. This was part of the Free Speech Movement (FSM) to stop the administration's monitoring of political activity on campus and generally to reduce arbitrary authority over students' lives. With the support of the faculty, students attained a "free speech area" and the chancellor resigned, but 293 students

were convicted in the following spring for the sit-in. The FSM heralded a movement of student activism directed at college authorities across the nation.

1965

Feb. 7–8 The U.S. bombed North Vietnam in retaliation for a National Liberation Front (NLF) attack on U.S. ground troops in South Vietnam. On February 11, the U.S. announced a general policy of bombing North Vietnam to punish "aggression" against South Vietnam. Said President Johnson: "The people of South Vietnam have chosen to resist this threat. At their request the U.S. has taken its place beside them in this struggle."

Feb. 21 Malcolm X, leading spokesman among "black nationalists," was shot and killed while speaking in New York City. (See also: Assassinations, Chap. 9.)

Mar. 2 One hundred and sixty U.S. planes bombed North Vietnam.

Mar. 8–9 The 1st U.S. combat troops (3,500 Marines) landed at Da Nang.

Mar. On March 7, black marchers leaving Selma, Ala., for the State capital at Montgomery were attacked by 200 State police with tear gas, nightsticks, and whips. For over a month, blacks in Selma had been trying to register to vote with little success. Over 2,000 had been arrested in demonstrations and on registration lines. President Johnson met with Governor Wallace in hopes of improving the situation. Wallace, however, considered marches (and black votes) "a threat" and later accused the Federal judge who approved a new Selma-Montgomery march of "prostituting our law in favor of mob rule while hypocritically wearing the robes." Wallace refused to provide protection for the 2nd march, claiming that he didn't have enough police and that mobilizing the National Guard was too expensive; so President Johnson sent 3,000 federalized National Guardsmen and military police. The 5-day Selma to Montgomery march began March 21 and over 25,000 attended the final rally at the State capital. That day, a white woman driving a black passenger was killed by 4 Ku Klux Klan members outside Montgomery.

Apr. 28 The U.S. sent 405 marines to the Dominican Republic in the midst of a rebellion, presumably to protect and evacuate American citizens. By May 5, there were 20,000 marines occupying much of the Dominican capital with a new purpose: "to help prevent another communist state in this hemisphere." Later, the Government admitted that they hadn't had any proof that leftists were taking over the rebellion, but that the threat of their doing so existed. U.S. forces remained in the Dominican

Republic for several months and fought some small engagements with the rebels (20 U.S. dead).

May 15 A "teach-in" opposing the Vietnam War was broadcast to over 100 colleges.

June 8 The U.S. announced that its ground troops in Vietnam would engage in direct combat if requested by the South Vietnamese army. On June 28, U.S. forces began their 1st full-scale combat offensive.

June 11–15 Chicago police arrested 526 anti-segregation demonstrators acting in response to the rehiring of the school superintendent. Protests continued through July 26, when Dr. Martin Luther King, Jr., led a march of 20,000 to City Hall, the 42nd such march in 47 days.

July 27 President Johnson signed the law requiring cigarette packages and ads to be printed with health warnings.

July 28 President Johnson announced that there were 125,000 U.S. troops in South Vietnam and that draft calls would be doubled; he asked the UN to help negotiate peace.

Aug. 11–16 A rebellion broke out in the black Watts section of Los Angeles involving at least 10,000 blacks who burned and looted a 500-square-block area. Fifteen thousand police and National Guardsmen were brought in to control the situation. Thirty-four persons were killed, including 28 blacks; over 3,900 were arrested; and over 200 business establishments were totally destroyed.

Oct. 15 Anti-Vietnam War rallies were held in 4 U.S. cities, the largest (10,000) in New York and Berkeley. In New York, police made the 1st arrest under a new Federal draft-card-burning law. In Berkeley, marchers were blocked from entering Oakland by police, then attacked by the Hell's Angels motorcycle gang. When the Angels threatened to attack the next peace march, poet Allen Ginsberg and some friends went to the home of Angels president Sonny Barger to discuss the situation and share some LSD with Barger and his friends. By dawn the 2 groups had chanted together. The day before the march the Angels called a press conference and distributed a news release: "Although we have stated our intention to counter-demonstrate at this despicable un-American activity, we believe that in the interest of public safety and the protection of the good name of Oakland, we would not justify the VDC (Vietnam Day Committee) by our presence . . . because our patriotic concern for what these people are doing to a great nation may provoke us into violent acts." The march was peaceful.

Nov. Through *Look* magazine, the American people learned that the U.S. had rejected secret peace talks with North Vietnam arranged by UN Secretary General U Thant in September, 1964.

Nov. 9–10 A "powder cascade" from a major electrical installation caused a "great blackout" from Pennsylvania to southern Canada, affecting over 30 million people and stranding some 800,000 in New York City subways.

Dec. 15 At its Biennial Convention, the AFL-CIO declared "unstinting support" for "measures the Administration might deem necessary to halt Communist aggression and secure a just and lasting peace" in Vietnam.

1966

—Use of consciousness-altering drugs, particularly marijuana and LSD, gained national attention. In May, LSD was the object of Senate hearings and a Federal prohibition. In September, Dr. Timothy Leary, an early LSD researcher and later a proselytizer of its use, founded the League for Spiritual Discovery, trying unsuccessfully to legalize LSD and marijuana as religious sacraments. While accurate estimates on LSD use do not exist, Federal authorities put marijuana users at over 8 million by 1970.

—In 1966, a record 52,500 Americans died and 9 million were injured in traffic accidents. Ralph Nader, a young lawyer who published *Unsafe at Any Speed* late in 1965, was a leader in the fight for new safety regulations. General Motors hired investigators who questioned over 50 of Nader's friends and neighbors about his personal life in an effort to discredit him, but this served only to embarrass GM during Senate hearings.

Jan. 10 The Georgia legislature refused to seat Julian Bond, 25-year-old black pacifist and member of SNCC, for opposing U.S. Vietnam policy and expressing sympathy with draft resisters. He was reelected and on December 5, the Supreme Court unanimously ruled he must be seated since expressing his political views was his constitutional right.

Jan. 13 President Johnson nominated Dr. Robert Weaver to become the 1st black Cabinet member in U.S. history. Weaver, a Harvard graduate and head of the Housing and Home Finance Agency since 1961, became Secretary of the new Department of Housing and Urban Development (HUD) when confirmed by the Senate January 17.

Apr. 19 Bill Russell was named coach of the Boston Celtics, becoming the 1st black coach of a major pro team. He led the Celtics to an NBA championship in 1967.

May Congressional opposition to the Vietnam War intensified as Senator Fulbright charged that the U.S. was "succumbing to the arrogance of power." President Johnson's 1st response was subdued, "not arrogance but agony"; but after another wave of antiwar protests, he called war critics "Nervous Nellies" and added, "If America's commitment is dishonored in Vietnam, it is dishonored in 40 other alliances we have made." Meanwhile, titular Republican leader Goldwater asked Fulbright to resign as chairman of the Foreign Relations Committee for giving "aid and comfort to the enemy."

May 16 Stokely Carmichael was elected chairman of SNCC, beginning a shift from civil rights to "Black Power" in the black movement. The idea was for blacks to organize blacks into their own political groups—"to ask Negroes to get in the Democratic party is like asking Jews to join the Nazi party" (Carmichael)—and for whites to organize whites against racism if they wished. In July, CORE also endorsed "Black Power" and "self-defense," but the NAACP and the SCLC (Martin Luther King's group) rejected "Black Power" as a separatist movement.

June The U.S. escalated the Vietnam War by bombing Hanoi for the 1st time, bombing rail lines up to the Chinese border, and declaring that U.S. planes would pursue North Vietnamese planes into China. President Johnson said: "We must continue to raise the price of aggression at its source." Meanwhile, some students refused college degrees in protest to the war and 6,400 people, including 3,938 college faculty members, paid for a 3-page antiwar ad in *The New York Times*.

June 6 James Meredith, who had integrated the University of Mississippi, began a march around Mississippi to encourage the State's 450,000 unregistered blacks to use their voting right. He was ambushed and shot. Though Meredith said later he would never "knowingly expose" himself unarmed again in Mississippi, his march was taken up by SNCC, SCLC, and other groups. Attacked several times, the march was completed June 26 with a 15,000-person rally in Jackson at which Meredith, Carmichael, and Dr. Martin Luther King, Jr., shared the podium.

July Nine blacks died in riots in Cleveland, Chicago, and Brooklyn. There were also smaller riots in 5 other large cities.

July 7 Despite his conviction for taking $250,000 in union funds and his status on bail pending appeal, Jimmy Hoffa was reelected to a 5-year term as Teamsters President by acclamation.

July 10 Dr. Martin Luther King, Jr., kicked off his campaign to make Chicago an "open city" by ending job and housing discrimination with a 40,000-person rally. On August 5, after 4,000 whites attacked 600 black marchers and he himself was injured, King said he had "never seen such hate—not in Mississippi or Alabama —as I see here in Chicago." On August 26, civil rights groups reached a 10-point accord with city government, church leaders, and the

Real Estate Board for "open occupancy" in Chicago neighborhoods. More militant blacks considered the August 26 agreement a "sellout," and on September 3 CORE led a march into Cicero, Ill., that was attacked by teen-age gangs despite National Guard protection.

July 14 Richard Speck, an itinerant worker, bound and killed, one-by-one, 8 student nurses in their Chicago dormitory room.

Aug. 1 Charles Whitman, Boy Scout leader and ex-marine, terrorized students, teachers, passersby, at the University of Texas in Austin. Located at the top of the clocktower for 80 minutes, he shot 44 people, killing 14, before he himself was killed. Earlier in the day he had killed his wife and his mother.

Aug. 5 Beatle John Lennon said The Beatles were more popular than Jesus, leading many U.S. radio stations to take Beatles' songs off the air.

Sept. U.S. troops in Vietnam reached 300,000 and suffered a record 970 casualties, 145 dead, in one week. The Treasury Dept. reported the Vietnam War was now costing the U.S. $1.2 billion a month.

—The National Guard was called out during black riots in Dayton and San Francisco. In Atlanta, disturbances led to the arrest of Chairman Carmichael of SNCC for "inciting to riot." In Grenada, Miss., 200 whites beat with pipes, chains, and ax handles 30 black students and parents integrating the high school.

Sept. 16 The Metropolitan Opera opened the world's largest opera house—$45 million, 3,788 seats—in New York's Lincoln Center.

1967

—The Pentagon announced that 5,008 Americans died in Vietnam in 1966. U.S. troop strength stood at 380,000.

Jan. 10 Black congressman Adam Clayton Powell was barred from taking his seat in the House and stripped of his chairmanship of the Education and Labor Committee because he supposedly misused congressional travel funds and was under indictment for contempt-of-court in New York. On March 1, the House voted to exclude Powell, the 1st time in 46 years it had taken such action. Powell called it "lynching Northern style." On April 11, Powell won a special election in his Harlem district by almost 7 to 1 despite his remaining in the Bahamas to avoid arrest. Powell finally got his seat back, without seniority, January, 1969, after winning another election.

Feb. Opposition to the Vietnam War broadened as civil rights leader Dr. Martin Luther King, Jr., spoke against it, Women's Strike for Peace demonstrated at the Pentagon, 5,000 scientists petitioned for a bombing halt, University of Wisconsin students forced Dow Chemical recruiters off campus, and Sen. Robert Kennedy proposed the U.S. halt bombing and negotiate troop withdrawal.

Feb. 10 Ratification of 25th Amendment. It empowered the President to nominate a new Vice-President subject to the approval of Congress in case of a vacancy in that office and provided that the Vice-President would become acting President when the President suffered a disability.

Feb. 20 The National Gallery of Art paid a record $5–$6 million for a Da Vinci portrait, *Ginevra dei Benci.*

Mar. 13 Confirming a *Ramparts* magazine exposé, the National Student Association admitted it had received over $3 million from the CIA through dummy foundations. A series of subsequent disclosures revealed that 30 organizations in education, labor, law, journalism, and religion had received secret CIA funding.

Apr. 15 The largest antiwar demonstration to date—100,000 by police estimates, 400,000 according to its organizers—took place in New York City while 50,000 rallied in San Francisco. On April 4, Martin Luther King had proposed that the civil rights and antiwar movements merge and counseled in favor of draft evasion. He called the U.S. Government "the greatest purveyor of violence in the world."

Apr. 22 The 1.6 million member United Auto Workers voted to leave the AFL-CIO, criticizing its lack of organizing effort and democratic leadership.

Apr. 28 Heavyweight champion Muhammad Ali was arrested for refusing induction into the Army after having been denied conscientious objector status. Boxing authorities immediately stripped him of his title.

May 13 Demonstrators 70,000 strong marched "supporting our men in Vietnam" in New York City.

June 5 A Chicano group led by Reis Tijerina seized the county courthouse in Tierra Amarilla, N. Mex., and freed 11 prisoners as part of a movement claiming land granted their ancestors by Spain. Tijerina was arrested for kidnapping and assault, but he was acquitted after presenting his own defense in court. Later he served over 2 years in prison for burning a U.S. Forest Service sign.

June 23 The Senate voted to censure Sen. Thomas Dodd (Dem.-Conn.) for paying personal debts with campaign contributions; unlike Powell, Dodd kept his seat and his chairmanship.

Summer Tens of thousands of young people converged on the San Francisco Haight-Ashbury district for the "Summer of Love," with similar migrations to the East Village, New York City, and other centers of "hip culture." The "hippies" or "flower children" set them-

selves apart by dropping out of straight society and turning on to communal living, free love, marijuana, LSD, heavily amplified music, and spiritualism. This generally horrified their elders.

July 12–17 The Newark Riot, covering 10 sq. mi., left 26 dead (24 black), over 1,500 injured and 1,397 arrested. It started when police beat a black man after a traffic arrest. It ended with what even the New Jersey governor's Select Commission called "excessive and unjustified force" as police and National Guardsmen vandalized black businesses and indiscriminately shot at blacks. Meanwhile, the House refused to consider a $4 million bill for rat control in urban slums.

July 23–30 The Detroit Riot left 43 dead (36 black), over 2,000 injured, 5,000 arrested, 1,700 stores looted by whites as well as blacks, and 5,000 homeless from 1,442 fires. It started when police arrested 73 blacks in a raid on an after-hours club and ended with the 1st use of Federal troops to quell a civil disturbance in 25 years.

—There were riots or disturbances in 127 cities over the summer. Among the largest of the others were New York (2 dead), Milwaukee (4 dead), Cambridge, Md. (SNCC chairman "Rap" Brown arrested for inciting to riot), Minneapolis (National Guard called out), and Chicago (2 dead).

Aug. 31–Sept. 4 Over 2,000 delegates from 200 black, student, labor, war, and leftist organizations attended the "New Politics" convention in Chicago. The convention's platform called for "revolutionary change" and "open draft resistance."

Sept. 30 President Johnson signed a record $70 billion defense appropriation including $20 billion for direct support of the Vietnam War.

Oct. 2 Thurgood Marshall was sworn in as the 1st black Supreme Court justice.

Oct. 15 Florence Beaumont, a 56-year-old housewife from La Puente, Calif., burned herself to death in front of the Los Angeles Federal Building in protest against U.S. fighting in Vietnam. She was one of 7 Americans to choose self-immolation as a means of protest.

Oct. 21 Fifty thousand to 150,000 people marched to the Pentagon and 647 were arrested in the antiwar demonstration immortalized by Norman Mailer in *Armies of the Night.* Folk singer Joan Baez was among 125 arrested in a sit-in at the Oakland Draft Induction Center. Other antiwar demonstrations were held in Los Angeles, Chicago, Philadelphia, and on many college campuses.

Nov. 7 Selective Service chief General Hershey announced that college students arrested in antiwar demonstrations would lose their draft deferments.

Dec. Reports by the Census on "Social and

Economic Conditions of Negroes" showed that 41% of nonwhite families made less than $3,-300 a year (compared to 12% of white families), 7.3% of nonwhites were unemployed (3.4% white), and 29% lived in substandard housing (8% white). Another report revealed that 83% of black students still attended all-black schools in 11 Southern States.

1968

—In 1967, 9,419 Americans died in Vietnam, more than in all previous years combined. U.S. troop strength reached 486,000. On January 5, the U.S. lost its 10,000th plane over Vietnam.

Jan. 14 The Green Bay Packers (NFL) beat the Oakland Raiders (AFL) 33–14 in the 2nd Super Bowl game.

Jan. 23 The U.S. intelligence ship *Pueblo* with 83 crew members was captured by North Korea somewhere just inside or outside North Korean waters. *Pueblo* crew members signed admission of "aggression" during captivity, but claimed later they were coerced. On December 22, North Korea released the *Pueblo* crew after a strange ceremony in which U.S. General Woodward signed a statement of apology and verbally repudiated it at the same time.

Jan. 30 The NLF and North Vietnam launched the "Tet Offensive" against all major cities in South Vietnam, including an attack on the U.S. Embassy in Saigon. While U.S. troops drove them out and General Westmoreland called it a "go-for-broke effort" that failed, the Tet Offensive shattered any belief in an approaching U.S. military victory in Vietnam among most politicians and the public.

Feb. 8 Alabama Governor Wallace announced he would run for President on the newly formed American Independent party ticket, declaring he would keep peace in the streets with "30,000 troops with 2'-long bayonets" if necessary and repeal "so-called civil rights laws."

Mar. 3 FBI director J. Edgar Hoover issued a memo to FBI offices concerning the goals of a "Counter-intelligence Program" against "Black Nationalist-Hate Groups":

> 1. Prevent the coalition of militant black nationalist groups. In unity there is strength; a truism that is no less valid for its triteness. An effective *coalition* of black nationalist groups might be the 1st step toward a real "Mau Mau" in America, the beginning of a true black revolution.

> 2. Prevent the *rise of a "messiah"* who could unify, and electrify the militant black nationalist movement. Malcolm X

might have been such a "messiah"; he is the martyr of the movement today. . . . King could be a very real contender for this position should he abandon his supposed "obedience" to "white, liberal doctrines" (nonviolence) and embrace black nationalism. . . .

Mar. 16 U.S. soldiers lined up between 300 and 500 old men, women, and children in a ditch in the Vietnamese village of My Lai and shot them. This massacre was covered up by the Army until November, 1969. On August 8–10, the U.S. killed 72 Vietnamese civilians in an "accidental" attack on a friendly Mekong Delta village. Estimates of the number of civilians killed in the Vietnamese conflict, mostly by U.S. ground fire and bombing of "free fire zones," generally exceed one million.

Mar. 31 President Johnson announced he would not seek reelection as President. This came after Sen. Eugene McCarthy's strong showing as a peace candidate in Democratic primaries, Sen. Robert Kennedy's decision to enter the Democratic race, and Johnson's own Tet-engendered doubts about his Vietnam policy. Johnson also ordered a halt to U.S. bombing of most of North Vietnam, excluding its southern 170 mi., and called for negotiations. On April 3, North Vietnam agreed to direct talks with the U.S. which began May 10 in Paris.

Apr. 4 Civil rights leader Dr. Martin Luther King was assassinated in Memphis while supporting a civil sanitation workers' strike. His death led to riots in 125 cities with 46 deaths, 21,270 arrests, and 55,000 Federal troops and National Guard used in riot control, the biggest in Washington, D.C., Chicago, Baltimore, and Kansas City. Although escaped convict James Earl Ray was convicted of murdering Dr. King, there is still widespread doubt about his guilt.

Apr. 23–24 Students at Columbia University seized 5 buildings in protest against Columbia's plan to build a new gymnasium in an adjacent ghetto area and to the university's connections with the Pentagon-sponsored Institute of Defense Analysis. Duke, Oregon, and several other large universities also had student protests against their administrations' policies during the spring.

June 5 Sen. Robert Kennedy was assassinated in Los Angeles. Kennedy had just won the California primary making him the front-runner for the Democratic presidential nomination. (See also: Assassinations, Chap. 9.)

June 14 Dr. Benjamin Spock, the Rev. William Sloane Coffin of Yale, and 2 others were convicted for counseling and aiding draft evasion. The Rev. Daniel J. Berrigan was convicted twice, April 16 with 3 others for pouring lamb's blood on draft files and October 16 with 8 others for burning draft files.

June 19 President Johnson signed a bill giving over $400 million in Federal aid to law enforcement and allowing police considerable freedom to wiretap and eavesdrop.

June 29 The U.S. death toll in Vietnam had already reached 9,557, more than in all of 1967.

July 23–24 A riot in Cleveland was sparked by a gun battle between police and a black nationalist group. Altogether, 11 people, including 3 police, died as a result of the shootout.

July 29 Pope Paul issued an encyclical reaffirming the Church's opposition to all forms of birth control except the rhythm system. A survey 2 months later showed about ½ of U.S. Catholic priests rejected the Pope's birth-control stand.

Aug. 25–29 The old line Democratic party leadership railroaded the presidential nomination of Vice-President Hubert Humphrey at the party convention in Chicago. Meanwhile, some 5,000 young people, ranging from supporters of peace candidate Senator McCarthy to "Yippies," were unable to get into the convention and engaged in street fighting with the police, who, in the words of even Vice-Presidential nominee Senator Muskie, "overreacted" in their clubbing of demonstrators and some TV reporters. The turmoil, seen by 50–80 million on the tube, probably cost Humphrey the election.

Sept. 8 Black Panther party leader Huey Newton was convicted of manslaughter for allegedly killing a policeman in a shoot-out, beginning a nationwide campaign to "Free Huey." The BPP, an armed revolutionary socialist organization founded October, 1966, was becoming a leading black political group with its 10-point program for self-determination in the ghettos and its tactics of following police to prevent police harassment and brutality toward blacks. By 1970 more than 25 Black Panthers had been killed, mostly by police and police agents.

Sept. 9 New York City teachers struck after 19 teachers who protested the new school policies of decentralization and community control were dismissed. The strike lasted until November 19 and kept over one million students out of school. In December, New York high school students "rampaged" several schools in protest to lengthened school days and canceled vacations imposed to make up for time lost.

Oct. 31 President Johnson announced a complete halt in U.S. bombing of North Vietnam and the expansion of the Paris peace talks to include the National Liberation Front and the U.S.-backed South Vietnamese Government.

The South Vietnamese Government did not agree to negotiate, however, until November 26, and 4-way talks did not begin until 1969 because of disagreement over the shape of the conference table.

Nov. 6 Students at San Francisco State College began a student strike demanding a 3rd World Studies department and an open admissions policy. San Francisco State closed November 19 after daily confrontations between police and students, but was reopened December 2 by new college president Hayakawa. The level of violence cooled after Hayakawa ordered that the school close early for Christmas vacation, thus avoiding the spectacle of high school students joining the battles when their vacation began the next day. The strike lasted 5 months.

Nov. 14 "National Turn in Your Draft Card Day" featured draft card burning at many campuses and rallies in several cities.

Dec. 14 The U.S. Vietnam death toll passed 30,000. U.S. forces in Vietnam were about at their peak of 550,000 men.

—J.Ch.

1969

—Sixty-five airplanes were hijacked.

Jan. 20 Richard Milhous Nixon was sworn in as the nation's 37th President. Thousands attended the ceremony, including demonstrators protesting the inauguration.

Mar. The U.S. Air Force began 14 months of secret bombings of Cambodia, a recognized neutral country. The request for the bombings by President Nixon bypassed the chain of command.

Apr. 10 A police assault forced students out of University Hall, at Harvard University. A mass strike began there against Harvard's intimate ties to the national security and military apparatus.

May Assistant Attorney General Richard Kleindienst called for the repression of "ideological criminals." He said about the student and antiwar movements: "When you see an epidemic like this cropping up all over the country—the same kind of people saying the same kinds of things—you begin to get the picture that it is a national subversive activity." Five years later, on May 16, 1974, Kleindienst became the 1st Attorney General in American history to plead Guilty to a crime. For having testified dishonestly during his Senate confirmation, he was sentenced to one month in jail and fined $100, both suspended, which drew much fire from proponents of equal justice for all citizens.

May 15 Supreme Court justice Abe Fortas resigned after *Life* magazine revealed that he had received a $20,000 fee from the foundation of Louis Wolfson, a man convicted of selling unregistered securities.

July 18 Sen. Edward Kennedy drove his car off a bridge on Chappaquiddick Island, off Martha's Vineyard, Mass. His companion, 28-year-old secretary Mary Jo Kopechne, was killed. Kennedy reported the accident the next morning.

July 20 Astronaut Neil Armstrong was the 1st human to walk on the moon. He said: "That's one small step for man, one giant leap for mankind." President Nixon announced that this was the greatest event since the Creation.

Aug. 16 About half a million people gathered on a 600-acre farm near Woodstock, N.Y., to hear rock music for 4 days. *The New York Times* editorialized: "The dreams of marijuana and rock music that drew 300,000 fans and hippies to the Catskills had little more sanity than the impulses that drive the lemmings to march to their deaths in the sea. They ended in a nightmare of mud and stagnation that paralyzed Sullivan County for a whole weekend. What kind of culture is it that can produce so colossal a mess."

Oct. 15 Millions of Americans demonstrated in their towns and cities against the Vietnam War. Vice-President Spiro Agnew said that the Vietnam Moratorium Day was "encouraged by an effete corps of snobs who characterized themselves as intellectuals."

Nov. 15 Over 250,000 people gathered in Washington to protest the war in Vietnam. While demonstrators marched past the White House, President Nixon entertained himself and close friend Charles "Bebe" Rebozo before a color television watching a football game.

About 10,000 marchers, gathered at the Justice Department building to protest government prosecution of antiwar dissenters, were dispersed by tear gas. Martha Mitchell, the wife of Attorney General John Mitchell, commented: "It looked like the Russian Revolution."

Nov. 16 The 1st reports of the My Lai massacre were published.

Nov. 20 Eighty-nine American Indians occupied Alcatraz Island in San Francisco Bay. The move signaled a coming together of many normally divided tribes.

Dec. 4 Chicago Black Panther leader Fred Hampton was shot to death by police while he lay asleep in his bed. The chief of security of the Chicago Panthers was actually a police agent acting under the direction of the FBI. The FBI had, in early 1968, initiated a program of disruption and provocation against black groups, and the Panthers in particular. The program, called "Cointelpro" (counter intelligence program), was secretly ordered by FBI Director J. Edgar Hoover, and operated out of at least 41 field offices across the nation.

1970

—U.S. population—203,211,926.

Jan. 5 Joseph "Jock" Jablonski, the defeated reform candidate for president of the United Mine Workers union, and his wife and daughter were found murdered in their home in Clarksville, Pa. W. A. "Tony" Boyle, the UMW president and Jablonski's opponent, was convicted 4 years later of ordering the assassination.

Feb. 20 The Chicago Seven—Abbie Hoffman, Jerry Rubin, Tom Hayden, Rennie Davis, David Dellinger, Lee Weiner, and John Froines—were convicted of a conspiracy to cross State lines and instigate a riot at the Democratic Convention of 1968. Tom Hayden stated: "We were invented. We were chosen by the Government to serve as scapegoats for all that they wanted to prevent happening in the 1970s." Black Panther leader Bobby Seale, a defendant in the case, was silenced in November, 1968, after being bound with chains and gagged in the courtroom. Judge Julius Hoffman, justifying this measure, said: "I would tell you, sir, that the U.S. District Judge who practiced law in the courts of the U.S. and sat on State and Federal benches for 50 years has to sit here, sir, and have a defendant call him a pig? Listen to him now." William Kunstler, the attorney for the defense, replied: "Your Honor, we cannot hear him because of the binding and gag on him." In time, all of the charges and contempt citations against the defendants were dropped by higher courts.

Apr. 30 American troops began what President Nixon called an "incursion" into Cambodia.

May 4 National Guardsmen killed 4 students at Kent State University in Ohio after a campus protest against the Cambodian invasion. President Nixon called antiwar college students "bums."

May 5 A nationwide student strike, supported on the majority of campuses in the country, protested the extension of the war and the killing of students at Kent State.

May 14 Two black students at Jackson State College, in Mississippi, were killed by police firing on a dormitory.

June 27 Henry Kissinger approved the expenditure of millions of dollars for clandestine CIA action in Chile aimed at preventing the election and inauguration of Marxist Salvador Allende as President. After Allende's ascension to power, Kissinger authorized funds to "destabilize" the democratically-elected socialist Government. Kissinger stated on this date, in a secret meeting of the 40 Committee, the overseer of the CIA: "I don't see why we need to stand by and watch a country go communist due to the irresponsibility of its own people."

July 23 President Nixon approved a plan for coordinating all domestic intelligence into one superagency. The plan's architect, Tom Charles Huston, a White House aide, informed Nixon that the plan had aspects that were "clearly illegal."

1971

Early Feb. Tape-recording equipment was installed in the Oval Office of the White House, the President's Executive Office Building office across the street, the Cabinet Room, and the Lincoln Sitting Room. The tape system was not revealed to those having conversations with President Nixon.

Mar. 23 President Nixon raised milk price supports. The dairy industry subsequently contributed $2 million to his reelection campaign.

Apr. 30 Two thousand Vietnam veterans, members of Vietnam Veterans Against the War, rallied in Washington to protest the war. Many of them threw their combat medals on the steps of the Capitol.

May 3 Antiwar demonstrators engaged in civil disobedience in Washington. Police arrested 12,000 people at random. All of the arrests were overturned by a court ruling that they were unconstitutional.

June 13 *The New York Times* began publishing the Pentagon Papers, a government history of the Vietnam War, which revealed that the American public had been consistently lied to.

President Nixon authorized the establishment of a "special investigations unit," later known as the Plumbers, to "stop security leaks and to investigate other sensitive matters."

June 28 Daniel Ellsberg, a former Deputy Secretary of Defense, confessed that he had leaked the Pentagon Papers because he had become convinced of the Vietnam War's immorality.

June 30 The 26th Amendment, giving 18-year-olds the right to vote, took effect.

Aug. 16 White House counsel John Dean prepared a memo, "Dealing with our Political Enemies," suggesting ways "we can use the available Federal machinery to screw our political enemies." An "Enemies List" was subsequently drawn up by White House aides.

Sept. Donald Segretti was employed by the Committee for the Reelection of the President (CREEP) to infiltrate the campaigns of Democratic candidates and disrupt them.

Sept. 3 The Plumbers burglarized the office of Daniel Ellsberg's psychiatrist. The CIA assisted the leader of the group—ex-CIA agent, E. Howard Hunt—by providing him with a red wig, a special camera, and a "speech-altering device."

Sept. 13 Fifteen hundred armed police killed 31 prisoners and 9 hostages while retaking control of Attica State Prison in New York State. The prisoners had held the prison for 4 days and pressed their grievances. A State-appointed commission, the McKay Commission, placed responsibility for the tragedy on Gov. Nelson Rockefeller (who refused to go to the prison), prison officials, and conditions within the prison system.

Dec. 29 Daniel Ellsberg and a co-worker at the Rand Institute, Anthony Russo, were indicted for espionage and conspiracy.

1972

Feb. 1 A wildcat strike began at the Lordstown, O., General Motors plant against speed-up and arbitrary management rules. The workers' average age was 24. This signaled the discontent of the younger generation with labor conditions.

Feb. 20–27 President Nixon visited the People's Republic of China, ending 23 years of pretense that the whole of China began and ended with the Chiang Kai-shek regime in Formosa.

Feb. 29 Newspaper columnist Jack Anderson disclosed a memo of the International Telephone and Telegraph Corporation's Washington lobbyist, Dita Beard, which connected ITT's funding of part of the Republican National Convention with a Justice Department settlement of an antitrust suit favorable to ITT.

Apr. 10 Financier Robert Vesco, under investigation by the Securities and Exchange Commission for fraud, contributed $200,000 in cash to CREEP fund-raiser, Maurice Stans.

May 9 President Nixon ordered the harbor of Haiphong mined, and authorized massive bombing raids over North Vietnam.

May 15 Gov. George Wallace, campaigning for President in Laurel, Md., was shot by Arthur Bremer. Wallace, paralyzed from the waist down and forced to withdraw from the presidential race, later expressed his belief that the attempted assassination may have been a Plumbers-type operation. (See also: Assassinations, Chap. 9.)

June 17 Five men, on another Plumbers' operation, were apprehended burglarizing the Democratic National Committee's headquarters in the Watergate building complex.

July 12 George McGovern won the Democratic nomination for President. The next day, he named Thomas Eagleton as his vice-presidential running mate. It was revealed later in the month that Eagleton had undergone shock therapy for recurrent depression. After declaring his "1,000%" support for Eagleton, McGovern requested, and received, his resignation from the ticket.

Oct. 10 The *Washington Post*, in articles by reporters Carl Bernstein and Bob Woodward, uncovered a massive effort on the part of CREEP to disrupt the Democratic campaign.

Oct. 26 Henry Kissinger announced that "peace is at hand" in Vietnam, and that the war would be over within 60 days.

Nov. 7 Richard Nixon and Spiro Agnew were reelected with 61% of the popular vote.

Dec. 18 President Nixon ordered the bombing of Hanoi and Haiphong. There was widespread destruction of civilian areas. Bach Mai hospital was destroyed in the raids. The reason for the bombings was unconnected to the willingness of the North Vietnamese to sign an agreement. President Thieu of South Vietnam had threatened to sabotage any agreement, and in order to placate him Kissinger and Nixon sent the B-52s to bomb North Vietnam, including many heavily populated areas. Kissinger, in a National Security Council meeting, called this a "brutal ending" but a necessary one to win Thieu's acquiescence.

1973

Early Jan. President Nixon, in an interview, said that the average American was like "a child in the family."

Jan. The Miners for Democracy ticket, headed by rank-and-file miner Arnold Miller, was elected to the top posts in the United Mine Workers union, ending a long reign of corruption.

Jan. 28 The U.S. and the North Vietnamese signed a treaty ending direct American military intervention in Vietnam. The U.S. continued to fund the Saigon dictatorship, which held at least 200,000 political prisoners in jail.

Feb. 27 The American Indian Movement occupied the trading post and church at Wounded Knee, S.D., the site of the 1890 massacre of Sioux Indians by the U.S. Army cavalry, to draw attention to the grievances of the American Indians.

Mar. 19 James McCord, a defendant in the Watergate break-in case, wrote a letter to Judge John Sirica charging that perjury had been committed at the trial, that high Administration officials were involved in pressuring defendants to maintain silence and plead Guilty.

Mar. 21 President Nixon ordered the payment of $75,000 in hush money to defendant E.

Howard Hunt. The next day Nixon told John Mitchell: "I don't give a shit what happens. I want you all to stonewall it, let them plead the 5th Amendment, cover-up or anything else, if it'll save it—save the plan. . . ."

Apr. 12 CREEP deputy director Jeb Magruder confessed his perjury to prosecutors of the Watergate case.

Apr. 17 Presidential news secretary Ron Ziegler declared all previous statements about Watergate "inoperative."

Apr. 30 H. R. Haldeman and John Ehrlichman, President Nixon's top 2 assistants, resigned. Nixon fired John Dean. Nixon said that he, personally, accepted the responsibility for Watergate, "but not the blame."

May 11 Judge Matthew Byrne dismissed all charges in the Pentagon Papers case, against Daniel Ellsberg and Anthony Russo, because of government misconduct.

May 17 The televised Senate hearings into Watergate began. Sen. Sam Ervin, the committee chairman, quoted during the hearings: "O what a tangled web we weave, when 1st we practice to deceive!"

July 16 White House aide Alexander Butterfield inadvertently revealed to Senate Watergate investigators that President Nixon maintained a secret tape-recording system.

Sept. 11 The elected Marxist Government of Salvador Allende was overthrown by a military junta in Chile. Allende died defending the presidential palace.

Oct. 6 War erupted in the Middle East between Israel and Syria and Egypt.

Oct. 10 Spiro Agnew pleaded *nolo contendere* (no contest) to a charge of evading income tax. U.S. attorneys had uncovered alleged kickbacks to Agnew, from Baltimore County contractors, while he was Baltimore County executive, governor of Maryland, and Vice-President. Agnew is said to have received the graft in unmarked envelopes. He resigned as Vice-President.

Oct. 12 Nixon nominated House minority leader Gerald Ford as Vice-President. Ford stated: "I'm a Ford not a Lincoln."

Oct. 17 Arab nations began an oil embargo against the U.S. in an attempt to raise prices and alter U.S. support of Israel.

Oct. 20 The "Saturday Night Massacre" occurred. President Nixon ordered Attorney General Richardson to fire special prosecutor Archibald Cox because Cox sought key White House tapes. Richardson refused and resigned. Deputy Attorney General Ruckelshaus also refused and was fired. Nixon's Chief of Staff, Gen. Alexander Haig, told Ruckelshaus: "You have received an order from your Commander-in-Chief." Robert Bork, the Solicitor General, was then named Acting Attorney General and he fired Cox and abolished the special prosecutor's office under Nixon's direction.

Oct. 23 Nixon reversed himself because of intense public pressure, and offered to release the tapes Cox sought and to maintain the special prosecutor's office.

Nov. 17 Richard Nixon declared: "I'm not a crook."

Dec. 8 Nixon revealed that he paid less than $1,000 in taxes in 1970 and 1971.

Dec. 31 In separate incidents, 31-year-old Roy Buck and 67-year-old Willie Camber were killed by robbers, bringing the total number of murders in Detroit during 1973 to 746. Mayor Terry Troutt of nearby Romulus, Mich., complained that Detroit murderers were using his city as a dumping grounds. He asked murderers with a body on their hands to "leave it where you got it."

—S.B.

1974

Jan. The price of sugar began to climb. It was to go up 400% in the next 12 months.

Jan. The Federal Energy Administration printed 4.8 billion gas-rationing coupons at a cost of $11 million. They went unused and cost $11,000 a month to store.

Jan. 11 A tour of the U.S. figured heavily in the plans of Sue and Colin Rosenkowitz, of Cape Town, South Africa, after Mrs. Rosenkowitz gave birth to the 1st sextuplets to survive in modern times. The proud parents were promised $750,000 in advertising tie-ups for spending a year in the U.S. displaying their 3 girls and 3 boys. Little more than a year later, on January 13, 1975, the 40-year-old father would tell the press: "I'm very, very disappointed and am struggling to support my family. We've had nothing but promises. Had the trip to America taken place, it would have changed the whole picture."

Feb. Motorists waited hours to buy gasoline as the oil embargo and the big oil corporations' policies limited the supply. Truck drivers, protesting the rise in gasoline and diesel fuel prices and purchasing limits, staged stoppages on major interstate highways.

Feb. Paul Castellano and 3 business associates discovered a telephone bug and a television camera secretly installed in their office. When FBI agents, angered at having been cut off, learned that the bug had been removed and the camera destroyed, they arrested the 4 men on charges of conspiracy and theft of government property.

Feb. 5 Patricia Hearst, of the Hearst newspaper family, was "kidnapped" by the Symbionese Liberation Army in Berkeley, Calif. The SLA was led by Donald "Field Marshal Cinque" De Freeze, an escaped convict and onetime informer for the Los Angeles police. When the ransom, a multimillion-dollar food program for the poor, was not expedited speedily by publisher Randolph Hearst, Patty declared that she had changed her name to Tania and joined the SLA. In July, the bulk of the SLA membership—6 people—were killed by the police. The climactic shoot-out was televised live statewide in California. Patty/Tania was not among the SLA dead.

Mar. 7 Commenting on the SLA's ransom demand of free food for the poor, California's Gov. Ronald Reagan said, "It's just too bad we can't have an epidemic of botulism."

Apr. 3 The Internal Revenue Service stated that Nixon owed $432,787 in back taxes, and interest penalties totaling $33,000.

Apr. 8 Hank Aaron hit his 715th home run, breaking Babe Ruth's 47-year-old record.

Apr. 30 President Nixon released an edited version of the transcripts of White House conversations concerning Watergate. It became an instant best seller.

May 2 The Maryland Court of Appeals disbarred Spiro Agnew and called him "morally obtuse."

May 9 The House Judiciary Committee began formal hearings on the impeachment of Richard Nixon.

June 30 The mother of Martin Luther King, Jr., was shot to death while she played the organ in church.

July 15 Sarasota, Fla., TV commentator Chris Chubbuck finished reading the news to her audience and then said, "And now, in keeping with Channel 40's policy of always bringing you the latest in blood and guts, in living color, you're about to see another 1st—an attempted suicide." She then shot herself in the head and later died in a hospital.

July 24 The Supreme Court ruled unanimously that President Nixon had no right to withhold evidence in a criminal case, and ordered him to release 64 tapes to the Watergate special prosecutor.

July 27 The Judiciary Committee voted 27-to-11 to recommend to the full House of Representatives that President Richard Nixon be impeached for criminal acts committed while covering up the Watergate break-in and for obstructing the subsequent investigation. The Articles of Impeachment stated: ". . . Richard Nixon has acted in a manner contrary to his trust as President and subversive of Constitutional Government, to the great prejudice of law and justice and to the manifest injury of the people of the U.S."

Aug. 5 Nixon released a transcript that revealed that he had approved the cover-up only 6 days after the Watergate break-in.

Aug. 8 Richard Milhous Nixon resigned as President of the U.S.

Aug. 9 In a farewell speech to the White House staff, Nixon stated that he wished he were a rich man; that a biography would never be written about his saintly mother; and that the nation needed more plumbers (and carpenters). "Au revoir," he said. Gerald Ford became President.

Sept. 8 President Ford granted Richard Nixon a "full, free and absolute pardon" for any crimes he may have committed.

Oct. 26–27 The largest cash theft in U.S. history occurred in Chicago when burglars removed $4.3 million from the vault of Purolator Security, an armored-car and guard-service company. The loot weighed 700 lbs.

Oct. 29 In Africa, Muhammad Ali regained his heavyweight championship by KO'ing George Foreman in the 8th round. Draft-refuser Ali was invited to the White House by President Ford. New York City declared a Muhammad Ali Day.

Nov. 5 Citizens in Rush Springs, Okla., voted to outlaw dancing in public.

Dec. 5 The movie system of rating pictures was endorsed when a Federal court in Chicago threw out a $7 million law suit filed by Paul Bernstein. When the film *Papillon* opened in March, it was rated PG—preteen-agers might attend with parental guidance. Bernstein took his 3 daughters, aged 7, 11, 14, to the movie, was shocked by its violence, claimed he had been misled, and filed the 1st suit in the 6-year history of the rating system against the Motion Picture Association of America. The judge ruled: "Plaintiff was accurately put on notice that he should exercise caution in letting children view this movie and he failed to do so."

Dec. 9 Johnson Van Dyke Grigsby, 89, was released from Indiana State Prison after serving a world-record 66 years for stabbing a man to death at a poker game in 1908.

Dec. 19 Former New York Governor Nelson Rockefeller was sworn in as Vice-President of the U.S. Rockefeller was appointed VP by Gerald Ford who had been appointed VP by Richard Nixon whose election in 1972 proved to be the result of illegal campaign tactics.

Dec. 31 Glen Bladen, 23, shot to death in a Chicago alley, became the city's 968th homicide victim of the year. There were over 20,-000 murders in the nation as a whole.

1975

Jan. 1 After a 13-week trial in Washington, D.C., a jury found 4 major Nixon Administration officials guilty in the Watergate cover-up case. Mr. Nixon's 2 closest aides, H. R. Haldeman and John D. Ehrlichman, as well as former Attorney General John N. Mitchell and assistant Robert C. Mardian, were the defendants found Guilty. All 4 said they would appeal. Mr. Nixon, in seclusion at his 5-acre "St. Helena" in California, said he was "deeply anguished" by what Watergate had done to these men and their families.

Jan. 3 The U.S. Army announced that its course on human sexuality—the 1st such initiated in military history—was a huge success. At Brooke Army Medical Center in San Antonio, Tex., 270 soldiers completed the course, taught à la Masters-and-Johnson by a major and his wife.

Jan. 4 Unemployment in the U.S. reached 6.5 million, the highest number in 13 years.

Jan. 5 After intense bidding by 23 baseball clubs, Jim "Catfish" Hunter signed a new 5-year contract with the New York Yankees for $3.75 million. Formerly the ace pitcher for the World Series champion Oakland Athletics, Hunter had been declared a free agent after team-owner Charles O. Finley defaulted on Hunter's contract. Hunter, a North Carolina boy, claimed "we'd had better offers but New York was closer to home and they played on regular grass."

Jan. 9 Rabbi Baruch M. Korff, a Nixon defender and his unofficial spokesman, visited the former President on his 62nd birthday and found him too thin—"his bones are sticking out." Korff indignantly announced that the Government in Washington was "illegally" holding some of Nixon's prized personal effects —among them his favorite fountain pen, his cartoon collection, his elephant collection, and Julie Nixon Eisenhower's wedding dress.

Jan. 16 In a landmark decision, the U.S. District Court in Washington, D.C., awarded $12 million in damages for false arrest and infringement of rights to 1,200 protestors who had been jailed in the May Day antiwar demonstration of 1971. Each of the 1,200 protestors was expected to receive an average sum of $10,000. The successful suit had been filed by the ACLU against the District of Columbia. It was, the *Los Angeles Times* reported, "probably the largest amount ever awarded in a civil suit in which no large corporations were involved . . . It was also the 1st time damages have been awarded to persons who cited violation of their rights under the U.S. Constitution—in this case the 1st and 8th amendments—rather than citing civil rights legislation."

Jan. The Vinnell Corporation of Los Angeles received a $77 million U.S. Dept. of Defense contract to train Saudi Arabian troops to protect their oil fields. It was the 1st time that a private American company had been given Government authorization to train a foreign army.

Apr. 12 On the eve of the take-over of all Cambodia by the Communist Khmer Rouge insurgents, the official U.S. presence in that nation came to an end. Four Marine helicopters landed in the capital city of Phnom Penh and evacuated 276 persons—a handful of Cambodians and the rest Americans—including U.S. Ambassador John Gunther Dean and 50 members of his Embassy staff, as well as 40 journalists (3 newsmen chose to remain behind).

Apr. 19 The U.S. began its official Bicentennial celebration with reenactments of the battles of Lexington and Concord. Over 160,000 people showed up, including 20,000 demonstrators who booed President Ford's portrayal of the U.S. as a military power which "stands in the front lines of the free world."

Apr. 30 An emergency helicopter evacuation removed the last 1,000 Americans from South Vietnam, ending over 2 decades of U.S. military involvement. A few hours later, the South Vietnamese Government surrendered, and soldiers representing the Communist-led Provisional Revolutionary Government occupied Saigon, renaming it Ho Chi Minh City. The war cost the U.S. 56,555 lives, 303,654 wounded, and, in the last 14 years alone, $141 billion. The total Vietnamese fatalities came to over 1,250,000. Advisers, bombers, napalm, antipersonnel weapons, laser-guided "smart bombs," automated battlefields, free fire zones, body counts—finished at last—at least in Vietnam.

May 1 After 25 years on the Government payroll, Smokey the Bear retired from public service. Bear and his mate, Goldie, moved to Carson National Forest in his native New Mexico and turned over their responsibilities to their 6-year-old adopted son.

May 5 Bishop Frederick Freking issued personal interdicts to farm woman Mary Ann Van Hoof and 6 of her followers in Necedah, Wis. Interdict is a rarely used Catholic punishment which excludes the accused from all sacraments except confession. Mary Ann Van Hoof claimed that the Virgin Mary had been appearing before her in visions since 1949. Crowds of up to 100,000 had converged on Necedah to join in vigils with Van Hoof.

—D.W. & I.W.

5

U.S.A.—the Presidency

First 1st President JOHN HANSON

Born: April 14, 1721, at Mulberry Grove, Charles County, Md.

Died: November 27, 1783, in his sleep, at Oxen Hills, Md.

Career: Educated in England, master of the 1,000-acre family plantation. Elected to the Maryland House of Delegates at 36; served there for 24 years. Elected as Maryland representative to the Continental Congress in 1781.

His Person: Plump, long nose, amused mouth, double chin. His portrait, as painted by Charles Willson Peale, hangs in Independence National Historical Park, Philadelphia, Pa.

Election: In 1781, while General Washington was still fighting the last battles of the Revolution, the 13 Colonies joined together in a loose union under the Articles of Confederation. After the British surrender at Yorktown, this new confederation needed a leader. In order to placate public opinion in Maryland (Maryland had been the last State to join this union), in November, 1781, the Continental Congress elected John Hanson "President of the United States in Congress Assembled." George Washington wrote and congratulated Hanson on his "appointment to fill the most important Seat in the United States."

Term of Office: Hanson's powers were limited; he was little more than a chairman of the Continental Congress. After serving as President for one year, he resigned the job because of ill health. His presidential successors were Elias Boudinot, Thomas Mifflin, Richard Henry Lee, Nathan Gorham, Arthur St. Clair, Cyrus Griffin, before President George Washington came along.

Little-Known Facts: In 1973, the Maryland legislature passed a bill that declared April 14 of every year as John Hanson Day. The John Hanson Society also got U.S. 50 in Maryland named "The John Hanson Highway."

Quote about Him:
"It's about time due recognition was given to John Hanson and the role he played in the founding of his country. His energy, drive and devotion helped hold this country together."
—Gov. Marvin Mandel of Maryland

1st President GEORGE WASHINGTON

(See: Full Profile)

2nd President JOHN ADAMS

Born: October 30, 1735, in Braintree (later Quincy), Mass.

Died: July 4, 1826, at his Braintree home. This day was the 50th anniversary of the Declaration of Independence for which Adams was largely responsible. By remarkable coincidence, Adams's old friend and colleague, Thomas Jefferson, died on the same day. Adams lived 90 years, 247 days—longer than any other President.

Career: Harvard graduate, schoolteacher, Boston lawyer, revolutionary essayist and pamphleteer, member of Massachusetts legislature, delegate to Continental Congress, envoy to France and Holland, Minister to Great Britain, 1st Vice-President of the U.S.

Personal Life: At 29 he married a brilliant, independent-minded parson's daughter named Abigail Smith. Abigail was one of the best educated women of her time, and she and her intellectual husband enjoyed 54 years of a marriage that can only be described as a "love feast." Their passionate letters to one another helped make up for long absences while John was away on government business. His opponents criticized Adams for listening to his wife's political advice, and derisively dubbed Abigail "Mrs. President."

His Person: Only 5'7" tall, with a round face, puckered lips, and heavy, curved brows. His corpulence earned him the title "His Rotundity."

Election: As Vice-President, Adams was the Federalist party's heir apparent when Washington retired in 1796, but in the Electoral College he won only a narrow 71 to 68 victory over Republican Thomas Jefferson. Four years later, when Adams ran for reelection, Jefferson beat him in another close race.

Term of Office: March 4, 1797–March 4, 1801 (4 years).

Little-Known Facts: Adams was the 1st President to occupy the White House, and when he and his family moved in, the building was still unfinished. The walls were so wet that 7 cords of wood had to be burned in order to dry them out. Showing her practical nature, Abigail used the unfinished East Room as a place to dry the family's wash.

Quotes from Adams:
"Here lies John Adams, who took upon himself the responsibility of peace with France in the year 1800."—His suggested epitaph for himself

"Let the human mind loose. It must be loosed; it will be loose. Superstition and despotism cannot confine it."

"I do not say when I became a politician, for that I never was."

Quotes about Him:
"He is distrustful, obstinate, excessively vain, and takes no counsel from anyone."—Thomas Jefferson

"He is as disinterested as the being who made him."—Thomas Jefferson

3rd President THOMAS JEFFERSON

Born: April 13, 1743, in Albemarle County, Va.

Died: July 4, 1826—the 50th anniversary of American independence—at his hilltop Virginia home, Monticello.

Career: Prosperous Colonial lawyer, member of Virginia House of Burgesses at 26, author of the Declaration of Independence at 33, governor of Virginia, Minister to France, Secretary of State under Washington, defeated presidential candidate (1796), and Vice-President. A planter and an amateur scientist all his life.

Personal Life: As a young man, he attempted to seduce the wife of one of his friends and pursued an unhappy infatuation with another Virginia belle before his attentions settled on a young widow named Martha Skelton. His 10

years of marriage were happy ones, but Martha died at 33. Jefferson honored his promise to her never to remarry, but while serving as Minister to France he became romantically involved with Mrs. Maria Cosway, a famous beauty. He also developed an attachment to Sally Hemings, one of his teen-age slaves. Some, if not all, of Sally's 5 children were probably fathered by Jefferson.

His Person: Known as "Long Tom," Jefferson was 6'2½" tall, with a pinkish, freckled complexion, carrot-red hair, and hazel eyes. As President, he scandalized the British Ambassador with his informal dress (a worn brown coat and carpet slippers without heels). He suffered most of his life from migraine headaches.

Elections: In the "Revolution of 1800," running as the candidate of "equal rights and civil liberties," Jefferson unseated President John Adams, 73 electoral votes to 65. Running for reelection in 1804, the popular Jefferson had an easier time of it, beating Federalist Gen. Charles C. Pinckney 162 electoral votes to 14.

Term of Office: March 4, 1801–March 4, 1809 (8 years).

Little-Known Facts: Jefferson bathed his feet in cold water every morning in the belief that this kept off colds. During his 8 years in the White House he ran up a personal wine bill of $10,835. He kept a pet mockingbird in his study in Washington. He taught the bird to sit on his shoulder, and even to peck its food from its master's own lips. Jefferson's many noteworthy inventions included: the revolving chair, a pedometer, a revolving music stand, a letter-copying press and a hemp machine.

Quotes from Jefferson:
"Science is my passion, politics my duty."

"I view great cities as pestilential to the morals, the health and the liberties of man."

"A little rebellion now and then is a good thing, and as necessary in the political world as storms in the physical."

Quotes about Him:
"He was a mixture of profound and sagacious observation, with strong prejudices and irritated passions."—John Quincy Adams

"The principles of Jefferson are the axioms of a free society."—Abraham Lincoln

4th President JAMES MADISON

Born: March 16, 1751, at Port Conway, Va.

Died: June 28, 1836, at Montpelier, the Virginia estate that had been his home for 85 years.

Career: Princeton graduate, revolutionary activist, but too frail to enlist in the Continental Army. Elected to Virginia legislature at 25, delegate to Continental Congress, leading figure at Constitutional Convention ("Father of the Constitution"), coauthor of *The Federalist* papers, member of House of Representatives, organizer of Democratic-Republican party, Secretary of State under Thomas Jefferson.

Personal Life: A lonely bachelor till age 43, when Sen. Aaron Burr introduced him to a merry widow named Dolley Todd. The lively and popular Dolley often overshadowed her soft-spoken husband. Their marriage was childless.

His Person: Madison was 5'4" tall and weighed under 100 lbs. Washington Irving described him as "a withered little apple-john." His popular nickname, "Jemmy," emphasized both his small stature and his boyish subservience to his friend Jefferson.

Elections: As Jefferson's personal choice and the candidate of the Democratic-Republicans, Madison rolled to easy victory in 1808 over the declining Federalists and their candidate, C. C. Pinckney: 122 electoral votes to 47. Four years later, however, Madison's controversial decision to enter the War of 1812 had breathed new life into the Federalist party, and DeWitt Clinton, with Federalist support, drew 89 votes to Madison's 128. A switch of one hotly contested State (Pennsylvania) would have defeated Madison.

Term of Office: March 4, 1809–March 4, 1817 (8 years).

Little-Known Facts: Both of Madison's Vice-Presidents died in office. Madison was the only President to face enemy gunfire while in office. With the British invading Washington, "Jemmy" personally took command of an artillery battery, but after a while, when he saw how things were going, he got back into his carriage and hurried off in the other direction.

Quote from Madison:
"I flung forward the flag of the country, sure that the people would press onward and defend it."—Explaining his decision to enter War of 1812

Quote about Him:
"Our President, though a man of amiable manners and great talents, has not I fear those commanding talents which are necessary to control those about him."—John Calhoun

5th President   JAMES MONROE

Born: April 28, 1758, in Westmoreland County, Va.

Died: July 4, 1831, in New York City.

Career: College dropout, volunteer in the Revolutionary Army, rising to the rank of major. Student of law (under Thomas Jefferson). Virginia assemblyman, U.S. senator, Ambassador to France, governor of Virginia, Secretary of State *and* Secretary of War (serving simultaneously during the War of 1812).

Personal Life: At 28, Monroe married the beautiful daughter of a wealthy New York merchant. In personal matters, he was often dominated by his wife and his 2 elegant daughters, who put on aristocratic airs and were known as notorious snobs. They spent Monroe's money so freely that he was in serious financial difficulty when he died.

His Person: A 6-footer with a broad chest, a finely sculptured nose, and gentle blue-gray eyes, Monroe was said to bear a striking resemblance to George Washington.

Elections: By 1816, the Federalist party was in a state of collapse and, as the candidate of the Democratic-Republicans, Monroe swept to an easy electoral victory—183 to 34—over Rufus King. When he ran for reelection in 1820, he was virtually unopposed, and carried the Electoral College 231 to 1. Because of the absence of heated 2-party competition, Monroe's terms were characterized as "The Era of Good Feelings."

Term of Office: March 4, 1817–March 4, 1825 (8 years).

Little-Known Facts: During the Revolution, Monroe served as aide to General Stirling, a notorious alcoholic. Legend has it that the General taught his young aide how to drink, and all his life Monroe was known as a serious (but never a problem) drinker.

Quotes from Monroe:
"There is every reason to believe that our system will soon attain the highest degree of perfection of which human institutions are capable."—1820.

"The American continents . . . are henceforth not to be considered as subjects for future colonization by any European powers."—The Monroe Doctrine, 1823

Quote about Him:
"His virtue was not in flying high but in walking orderly, his talents were exercised not in grandeur but in mediocrity."—Arthur Styron, Monroe biographer

6th President   JOHN QUINCY ADAMS

Born: July 11, 1767, at Braintree (now Quincy), Mass.

Died: February 23, 1848, in Washington. After leaving the White House, Adams served as a congressman for 18 years, and he was at his desk in the House of Representatives when he suffered a fatal stroke.

Career: Aide and companion to his father, John Adams; Harvard graduate; Boston lawyer; diplomatic representative to Holland, Prussia, and Russia; U.S. senator; Minister to England; Secretary of State under Monroe; and the actual author of "The Monroe Doctrine."

Personal Life: At 30, he married the beautiful daughter of an American diplomat in London; the marriage lasted more than 50 years, despite major difficulties. His wife wrote: "As it regards women, the Adams family are one and all peculiarly harsh and severe in their characters. There seems to exist no sympathy, no tenderness for the weakness of the sex." Adams's oldest son was a would-be poet who suffered hallucinations and committed suicide at age 28.

His Person: Only 5'7" tall, with a plump body, shiny bald head, and white sideburns. His eyes were red and watery, and they bothered him constantly but he went without spectacles all his life. He was notoriously careless about clothes and wore the same hat for 10 years.

Election: In the electoral free-for-all of 1824, Adams finished 2nd, behind Gen. Andrew Jackson, but since none of the 4 candidates had a majority, the choice was thrown to the House of Representatives. There, speaker Henry Clay swung the election to Adams. When Adams appointed Clay as Secretary of State, the Jackson forces cried "corrupt bargain"—a charge that doomed Adams's bid for reelection in 1828.

Term of Office: March 4, 1825–March 4, 1829 (4 years).

Little-Known Facts: In 1832, Adams published a 108-page book of his poetry. He was the only President who was a published poet. Every warm morning at 5 A.M., President Adams would slip down to the Potomac River for a quick dip in the buff. Once a lady reporter, Anne Royall, surprised him during his swim, sat down on his clothes and refused to go away until he had given her an interview he had been trying to avoid.

Quote from Adams:
"I am a man of reserved, cold and forbidding manners."

Quote about Him:
"Of all the men whom it was ever my lot to accost and to waste civilities upon, he was the most doggedly and systematically repulsive. With a vinegar aspect, cotton in his leathern ears and hatred in his heart, he sat . . . like a bulldog among spaniels."—W. H. Lyttleton

7th President ANDREW JACKSON

Born: March 15, 1767, in the frontier region known as "The Waxhaws" along the border between North and South Carolina. Both States claim the honor of being Andrew Jackson's birthplace.

Died: June 8, 1845, in his plantation home "The Hermitage" near Nashville, Tenn.

Career: Volunteer in Revolutionary forces at age 14, gambler, cockfighting enthusiast, lawyer, public prosecutor in Tennessee Territory,

member of House of Representatives, U.S. senator, superior court judge, speculator in land, slaves, and race horses, "major general of volunteers" in the War of 1812, and hero of the Battle of New Orleans. Defeated presidential candidate in bitterly contested election of 1824.

Personal Life: Jackson married Rachel Donelson before her divorce from a previous husband had come through officially. This led to charges of immorality, and Jackson fought numerous duels to defend his wife's honor. During Jackson's presidential campaigns, Rachel was deeply depressed by the hysterical charges concerning their marriage; she suffered a nervous breakdown and died shortly before Jackson entered the White House.

His Person: Height 6'1"; 140 lbs.; long, thin face, blue eyes, bushy gray hair.

Elections: As the candidate of the frontier and "the common man," Jackson swept to easy victory over President J. Q. Adams in 1828. The margin in popular votes was 647,286 to 508,064; in the Electoral College, Jackson won 178 to 83. In 1832, Henry Clay opposed Jackson and tried to make an issue of the President's "war" against the Bank of the U.S., but most people supported the stand of the popular "Old Hickory." Jackson won with 55% of the popular vote, and 219 electoral votes to Clay's 49.

Term of Office: March 4, 1829, to March 4, 1837 (8 years).

Little-Known Facts: While Jackson was President, an operation was performed to remove a bullet that had been lodged in his arm during a brawl 20 years before. The 1st attempt on the life of a President was made in 1835 by an insane housepainter who believed he was the rightful heir to the English throne. He fired 2 pistols at Jackson from a distance of only 6', but both guns misfired. Jackson was unhurt.

Quote from Jackson:
"I have only 2 regrets: that I have not shot Henry Clay or hanged John C. Calhoun."—1837

Quote about Him:
"I feel much alarmed at the prospect of seeing General Jackson President. He is one of the most unfit men I know for such a place."—Thomas Jefferson, 1824

8th President MARTIN VAN BUREN

Born: December 5, 1782, in the sleepy Dutch village of Kinderhook, N.Y.

Died: July 24, 1862, at his 200-acre estate "Lindenwald" near Kinderhook.

Career: Helper in his father's tavern, lawyer, county judge, State senator, organizer of "Albany Regency"—one of the 1st political machines in American history. U.S. senator at 38, governor of New York, Secretary of State, Minister to England, and Vice-President under Jackson. After leaving the White House, Van Buren tried unsuccessfully for the Democratic presidential nomination in 1844; 4 years later, as the candidate of the "Free Soil" party, he drew only 10% of the vote.

Personal Life: Van Buren married a plain Dutch homebody who bore him 4 sons, but his political pursuits were always more important to him than his marriage. His wife died when he was 36, and Van Buren never remarried. In his autobiography, he included not even a single mention of his wife of 12 years.

His Person: Height 5'6"; slender, erect, and always dressed at the height of fashion. He had a high forehead, blue eyes, and curly red sideburns.

Election: As Jackson's heir apparent in 1836, Vice-President Van Buren had an easy time defeating his 4 different Whig opponents. Van Buren won 170 electoral votes, while his nearest rival polled 73. By the time Van Buren tried for reelection 4 years later, his popularity had been destroyed by the Depression of 1837, and he was swept from office by William Henry Harrison.

Term of Office: March 4, 1837–March 4, 1841 (4 years).

Little-Known Facts: No one in American history won so many colorful nicknames as Van Buren. To his friends, he was always "Matty Van," "Old Kinderhook," or "The Little Magician." Other titles included "The American Talleyrand," "The Red Fox of Kinderhook," or "Petticoat Pet" (an allusion to his dandylike dress). His Whig opponents blamed Van Buren for the Depression by branding him "Martin Van Ruin."

Quote from Van Buren:
"As to the Presidency, the 2 happiest days of my life were those of my entrance upon the office and my surrender of it."

Quotes about Him:
"He rowed to his object with muffled oars."
—John Randolph
"He is not of the race of the lion or of the tiger; he belongs to the lower order—the fox."
—John Calhoun

9th President

WILLIAM HENRY HARRISON

Born: February 9, 1773, Berkeley Plantation, Va.

Died: April 4, 1841, of pneumonia, in the White House. He was the 1st President to die in office.

Career: Son of the governor of Virginia,

medical school dropout, U.S. Army Indian fighter, governor of Indiana Territory, leading expert in cheating Indians out of their land. Victor over Indians at Battle of Tippecanoe, major general in War of 1812, member of the House, U.S. senator. Harrison's high living on his 3,000-acre Ohio estate left him deeply in debt, and he served as Minister to Colombia and clerk of the court of Hamilton County (2 highly lucrative positions) in hopes of paying off his debts. These positions were the only public posts he had held when he was called to the Presidency.

Personal Life: At 23, Captain Harrison eloped with the daughter of a prominent frontier judge. Over the years, she bore him 10 children and developed into a stolid matron who took little interest in her husband's career.

His Person: He was 5'8" tall, with a long thin face, gray hair, pointed nose. Harrison was 68 when he became President, the oldest man ever to be sworn into office.

Election: After a strong showing as one of the 4 Whig candidates in 1836, Harrison had the support of a united party in 1840. He said nothing on the issues, and was portrayed as a simple man of the frontier who was happiest sipping hard cider in his log cabin. It was alleged that President Van Buren, on the other hand, was a foppish dandy who lived in "Oriental splendor." On Election Day, the "hard cider candidate" won 53% of the popular vote, and a 234 to 60 landslide in the Electoral College.

Term of Office: March 4, 1841–April 4, 1841, (31 days). Harrison caught cold while delivering a 2-hour inaugural address in the freezing rain. He was seriously ill during much of his brief term, and made not a single major decision as President.

Little-Known Facts: Harrison produced more grandchildren (48) and great-grandchildren (106) than any other President. One of his grandchildren, Benjamin Harrison, became the 23rd President of the U.S.

Quote from Harrison:
"I am the clerk of the Court of Common Pleas of Hamilton County at your service. . . . Some folks are silly enough to have formed a plan to make a President of the U.S. out of this Clerk and Clod Hopper."

Quote about Him:
"Let Van from his cooler of silver drink wine
   And lounge on his cushioned settee;
Our man on his buckeye bench can recline
   Content with hard cider is he!"
     —Whig campaign song

10th President   JOHN TYLER

Born: March 29, 1790, Charles City County, Va.

Died: January 18, 1862, in Richmond, Va.

Career: Studied law under Edmund Randolph (former U.S. Attorney General), admitted to bar at 19, elected to Virginia House of Delegates at 21, while his father served as governor. U.S. House of Representatives, governor of Virginia, U.S. senator.

Personal Life: After 29 years of marriage and 8 children, Tyler's wife, Letitia, died in the White House. The 52-year-old widower-President lost little time in developing new interests: Before his term was over, he had married Julia Gardiner, 23, a Washington belle with a spectacular hourglass figure. Julia bore him 7 more children, the last one when Tyler was 70.

His Person: An even 6' tall, with long limbs and a narrow chest, light brown hair and blue eyes. He had high cheekbones and a long, high-bridged nose. An accomplished violinist, and a lover of fine wines and poetry.

Election: In 1840, Tyler was named as the running mate for Gen. William Henry ("Old Tippecanoe") Harrison. In November, the Whig ticket of "Tippecanoe and Tyler Too" swept to landslide victory.

Term of Office: April 6, 1841–March 4, 1845 (3 years, 333 days). Tyler was the 1st Vice-President to take office as President on the death of his predecessor. He vetoed 9 bills during his term—more than any previous one-term President, giving rise to the nickname "Old Veto."

Little-Known Facts: Tyler was the 1st President to be the subject of a serious impeachment attempt. On January 10, 1843, the House turned down a resolution of impeachment, which charged Tyler with gross usurpation of power. The final vote was 127 to 83.

Quotes about Him:

"Tyler is a political sectarian of the slave-driving, Virginian, Jeffersonian school, principled against all improvement, with all the interests and passions and vices of slavery rooted in his moral and political constitution."—John Quincy Adams

He looked somewhat worn and anxious, and well he might be, being at war with everybody."—Charles Dickens

bid for the vice-presidential nomination in 1840.

Personal Life: During 25 years of marriage, Sarah Childress Polk devoted all her energies to working at her husband's side. The Polks never had children. In the White House, Sarah served as Polk's personal secretary and they worked together 12 to 14 hours a day. A devout Presbyterian, Sarah banned all drinking and dancing at the White House. Polk's last words were addressed to her: "I love you, Sarah, for all eternity, I love you."

His Person: About 5'8" tall, slight build; his clothes always seemed too large for him. Cold gray eyes, grim mouth. A compulsive worker with no sense of humor.

Election: In 1844, former President Andrew Jackson personally engineered the nomination of the dark horse, Polk, over a number of better-known candidates. In the general election, the popular vote was 1,338,464 for Democrat Polk, with 1,300,097 for his Whig opponent, Henry Clay. The Electoral College margin was 170 to 105. The major issue of the campaign was expansionism—Polk came out strongly for a U.S. takeover of Texas and Oregon. During his Presidency, he managed to fulfill his key campaign promises.

Term of Office: March 4, 1845–March 4, 1849. Polk was so exhausted by his 4-year ordeal that he died just 3 months after leaving office.

Little-Known Facts: At the inaugural ball, in deference to Mrs. Polk's religious convictions, dancing and music were halted when the Polks entered, then resumed 2 hours later after they had left.

Quote from Polk:

"I prefer to supervise the whole operations of the Government myself rather than entrust the public business to subordinates and this makes my duties very great."

Quote about Him:

"Polk's mind was rigid, narrow, obstinate, far from 1st-rate. . . . But he knew how to get things done, which is the 1st necessity of Government, and he knew what he wanted done, which is the 2nd."—Historian Bernard De Voto

11th President JAMES KNOX POLK

Born: November 2, 1795, in Mecklenburg County, N.C.

Died: June 15, 1849, at his home near Nashville, Tenn. The cause of death was officially listed as "diarrhea."

Career: Son of a prominent planter, Tennessee lawyer, State legislator at 27, follower of Andrew Jackson, congressman, speaker of the House, governor of Tennessee, defeated in a

12th President ZACHARY TAYLOR

Born: November 24, 1784, Orange County, Va. He was a 2nd cousin of President James Madison.

Died: July 9, 1850, in Washington. During 4th of July ceremonies at the partially completed Washington Monument, President Taylor sat for several hours under the blazing summer sun. When he returned to the White

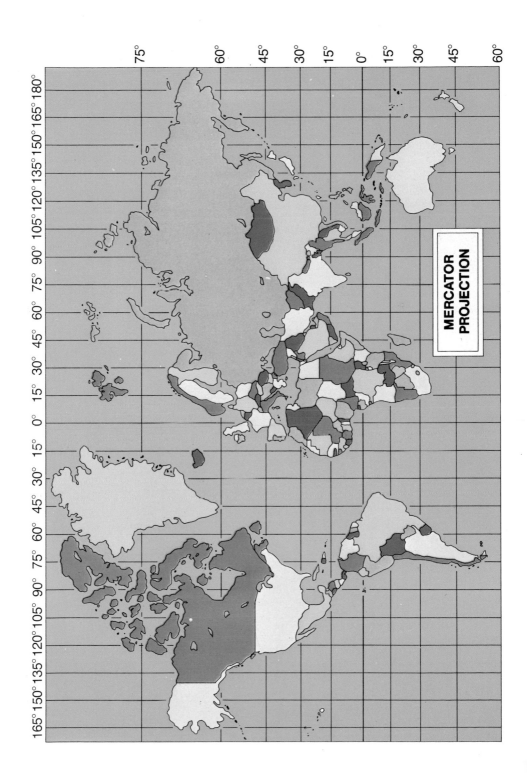

MERCATOR PROJECTION

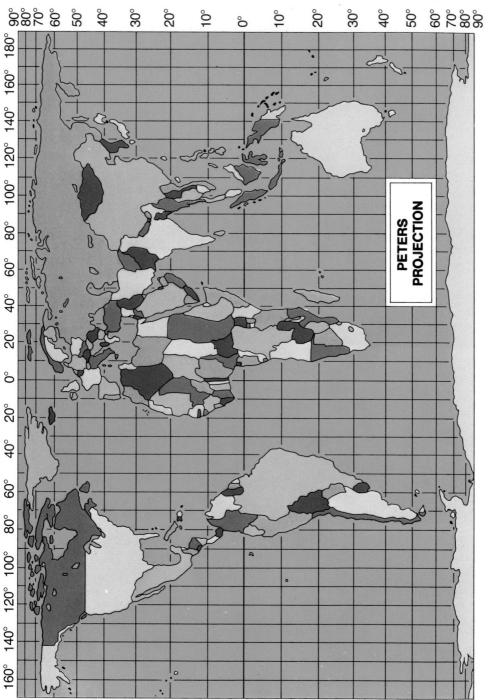

PETERS
PROJECTION

Peters Projection

That map on the wall is not a hangover from the era of colonial domination. If it's a Mercator projection, as most maps are, it gives the following picture:

Two-thirds of the land surface seems to lie north of the equator.

Europe is in the very center of it.

The Soviet Union appears to be at least twice the size of Africa, whereas, in fact, Africa is [about 35%] larger.

Gerardus Mercator (Latinized version of Gerhard Kremer), who produced the map some 400 years ago, really wasn't a colonialist. He merely wanted to produce a map that could be used by seamen to navigate around the world, and in this he succeeded admirably.

But the fact is that Kremer's projection has been in constant use ever since, contributing a major distortion to mankind's ideas of what the world really looks like.

Answer to Distortions

For some years, this has annoyed Arno Peters, a 56-year-old German historian. In Bonn recently, he unveiled his answer to Mercator's distortions. It's called the Peters projection, or the orthogonal map of the world. And it will take a bit of getting used to.

To start with, Peters put the equator where it belongs—exactly in the middle of his map. His 2nd major task was to represent every country on the earth in its exact size and, as closely as possible, its real shape.

One major handicap was that he insisted on using the conventional, rectangular-shaped map. And he had the built-in obstacle of the mathematical impossibility of projecting a globe onto a 2-dimensional surface.

The result is a compromise, but Peters insists it is the most honest projection of the world yet devised.

Particularly in the case of Europe—which appears as a tiny blurb on his map—he has stuck to Mercator's shapes of countries, thus distorting actuality.

Other map makers have tried to improve upon Mercator, with limited success. The elliptical map was closer to reality, but the public never accepted it because it looked like a collection of pieces of a peeled orange.

"We live in a 4-cornered world," Peters says. "The television tube we sit in front of is perhaps the best symbol of it."

Peters claims his map is absolutely accurate on areas, and 50% more accurate on land shapes than the Mercator projection.

"Eurocentrism" Attacked

Peters's new orthogonal map exemplifies his political concern with what he calls "Eurocentrism" to the detriment of the rest of the world. He recognizes that, from the earliest map makers on, all put their own countries as the center of the universe as it was then known.

In the late 20th century, he suggests that it is time to change this. He doesn't want to abolish Mercator altogether—Kremer's projection is still the best for sailors.

His new projection is not likely to find favor everywhere, least of all in the Soviet Union, which appears most squashed together of all countries on his map. But he points out his map gives a much better picture of the relative size and juxtaposition of the Soviet Union and its arch rival, China.

"It makes it easy to see why the Russians are so nervous about the Chinese," he adds.

—Joe Alex Morris. Copyright, *Los Angeles Times*. Reprinted with permission of *Los Angeles Times/Washington Post* News Service

Despite Erasmus' tongue-in-cheek remark, in 1508, that "the moon is made of green cheese," we today know firsthand exactly what it is made of and looks like. For the 59% of the moon visible to earthlings has been mapped by astronomers. And a dozen U.S. astronauts traveled a quarter of a million miles through space to reach the moon, spent 160 hours walking or driving 60 miles on its surface. These humans found that the moon, possessing ⅙ the gravity of earth, has no climate: It has no water, no wind, no weather. The lunar surface consists largely of ancient boulders, meteorite craters, thick dusty soil. Volcanic lava deposits and basalt rock (some 4 billion years old) abound. The lunar canyons bear a mad mixture of names ranging from Galileo and Gagarin to Jules Verne and Marie Sklodowska Curie.

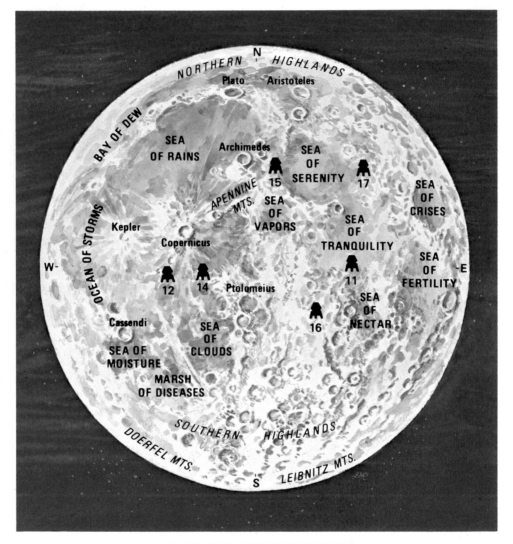

ABOVE: THE MEN ON THE MOON
The Landing Sites of the U.S. Apollo Space Program

APOLLO 11 — 1969
Where: Sea of Tranquility
Stay: 21 hrs., 36 min.

APOLLO 12 — 1969
Where: Ocean of Storms
Stay: 31 hrs., 31 min.

APOLLO 14 — 1971
Where: Fra Mauro
Stay: 33 hrs., 31 min.

APOLLO 15 — 1971
Where: Hadley Rille
Stay: 66 hrs., 55 min.

APOLLO 16 — 1972
Where: Descartes
Stay: 71 hrs., 2 min.

APOLLO 17 — 1972
Where: Sea of Serenity
Stay: 75 hrs.

House, he cooled off by consuming huge quantities of iced milk and cherries. His doctor pleaded with him to stop, but Taylor went right on eating. That night he was stricken with violent cramps and died 5 days later.

Career: Little education, commissioned army lieutenant at 23, career officer, Indian fighter, promoted to brigadier general. Leading commander in Mexican War, he emerged as a national hero.

Personal Life: Margaret Taylor stoically endured the hardships of an army wife: long separations from her husband, constant moving from place to place, even the death of her 2 youngest children during a malaria epidemic. As First Lady, she was a semi-invalid who refused to attend public functions and remained secluded in her quarters, shivering by the fire.

His Person: Stocky build; 5'8" and 170 lbs.; large head; unusually short legs. Noted for the sloppiness of his military dress, his colorful cursing, and his habit of chewing tobacco. His troops nicknamed him "Old Rough and Ready."

Election: In 1848, the Whigs nominated Taylor for President—despite the fact that the general despised politics and politicians and had never cast a vote in a presidential election in his life. In the campaign, Taylor said nothing, and relied on the split in Democratic ranks to elect him. The "Free Soil" candidate, former President Martin Van Buren, took enough votes away from Democrat Lewis Cass to send Taylor to the White House as a minority President. Taylor won only 47% of the popular vote, but his Electoral College margin was 163 to 127.

Term of Office: March 4, 1849–July 9, 1850 (1 year, 127 days). He was the 2nd President to die in office.

Little-Known Facts: Taylor was several days late in officially acknowledging his presidential nomination, because he had refused to pay 10¢ postage due on his formal letter of notification.

Quotes from Taylor:

"I am a Whig, but not an ultra-Whig."

"The idea that I should become President seems to me too visionary to require a serious answer. It has never entered my head, nor is it likely to enter the head of any sane person."

Quote about Him:

"His nomination is a plot to deprive me of his society and to shorten his life by unnecessary care and responsibility."—Mrs. Zachary Taylor

13th President MILLARD FILLMORE

Born: January 7, 1800, in a log cabin at Locke (today Summerhill), N.Y.

Died: March 8, 1874, in his home in Buffalo, N.Y. His last words, as he accepted a spoonful of soup from the doctor at his bedside: "The nourishment is palatable."

Career: Apprenticed to a wool-carder at 14, began his formal education at 19, clerk in a law office, practicing attorney, elected to State assembly, U.S. House of Representatives (chairman of Ways and Means Committee). Defeated candidate for governor of New York, elected State comptroller, Vice-President of U.S.

Personal Life: As a young man, Fillmore fell in love with his schoolmistress, Abigail Powers, an accomplished scholar and musician. Their courtship lasted 7 years, with the marriage postponed until Fillmore had established a prosperous law practice. Abigail died the year Fillmore left the White House, ending an unusually happy marriage. Five years later, at age 58, Fillmore married a wealthy widow.

His Person: About 5'9" tall, well-developed chest, deep voice, blue eyes. Noted for his handsome features and dignified bearing.

Election: In 1848, the Whigs nominated Fillmore for the Vice-Presidency in an effort to balance the ticket. After winning a close election, and the sudden death of President Taylor, Fillmore found himself in the White House.

Term of Office: July 9, 1850–March 4, 1853 (2 years, 238 days).

Little-Known Facts: One of the heated controversies during Fillmore's term concerned the guano reserves off the coast of Peru. This seafowl excrement, which could be converted into valuable fertilizer, was a bone of contention between American businessmen and the Peruvian Government. Fillmore intervened in the dispute and negotiated a special treaty.

Quote from Fillmore:

"Where is the true-hearted American whose cheek does not tingle with shame to see our highest and most courted foreign missions filled by men of foreign birth to the exclusion of the native-born?"—During his unsuccessful "Know Nothing" campaign for the Presidency, 1856

Quote about Him:

"Whether to the nation or to the State, no service can or ever will be rendered by a more able or a more faithful public servant."—John Quincy Adams

14th President FRANKLIN PIERCE

Born: November 23, 1804, Hillsboro, N.H.

Died: October 8, 1869, Concord, N.H. The cause of death is officially listed as "stomach inflammation" but it was well known that alcoholism had undermined his health during his last years.

Career: Son of a New Hampshire governor, prosperous lawyer, State legislator at 25, member of U.S. House of Representatives, youngest U.S. senator at 33. After one Senate term, he returned to private law practice, until he won appointment as a brigadier general in the Mexican War.

Personal Life: At 30, Congressman Pierce married the well-born Jane Appleton, a high-strung religious fanatic. Jane always hated politics, and after all of their 3 sons had died, the marriage disintegrated. In the White House, Jane wore black every day and spent much of her time writing notes to one of her dead sons. After Jane herself died in 1863, Pierce gave up his lifelong fight against alcoholism and abandoned himself to his drinking.

His Person: Height 5'10", with wavy black hair, penetrating gray eyes, and a fine physique. Known as "Handsome Frank." He was vain and a colorful dresser.

Election: After 48 deadlocked ballots at their convention in 1852, the Democrats startled the nation by nominating the unknown Pierce as a "compromise" choice for President. As Sen. Stephen Douglas quipped: "Hereafter, no private citizen is safe." Pierce swept to victory in November over the dying Whig party and its candidate, Gen. Winfield Scott. Pierce carried 27 of 31 States, for an Electoral College margin of 254–42—though he won only 51% of the popular vote.

Term of Office: March 4, 1853–March 4, 1857 (4 years).

Little-Known Facts: During the campaign of 1852, the Whigs charged that Pierce—"the hero of many a well fought *bottle*"—had been a coward during the Mexican War. The truth was that as Pierce rode to the front in his 1st and only major engagement, his horse, startled by exploding shells, tossed him forward so that the pommel of his saddle was driven sharply into his groin. Pierce fainted; the horse fell, broke its leg, and tore Pierce's knee.

Quote from Pierce:
"You have summoned me in my weakness. You must sustain me by your strength."—Inaugural Address

Quotes about Him:
"Whoever may be elected, we cannot get a poorer cuss than now disgraces the Presidential Chair!"—B. B. French, Pierce's former Secretary

"Frank, I pity you—indeed I do, from the bottom of my heart!"—Nathanial Hawthorne

15th President   JAMES BUCHANAN

Born: April 23, 1791, Cove Gap, Pa.
Died: June 1, 1868, at his mansion "Wheatland" near Lancaster, Pa.

Career: Graduate of Dickinson College, prosperous lawyer, member of the Pennsylvania State legislature, congressman, Ambassador to Russia, senator, Secretary of State, Ambassador to Britain. Three times (1844, 1848, and 1852) Buchanan tried unsuccessfully for the Democratic presidential nomination.

Personal Life: When Buchanan was 28, his fiancée committed suicide following a lover's quarrel. This experience scarred him permanently, and though he enjoyed the company of beautiful women, he never married. For many years his niece, Miss Harriet Lane—a statuesque blonde with violet eyes—lived with him and acted as his official hostess.

His Person: Heavyset, nearly 6' tall. His sight was uneven (one eye nearsighted and the other farsighted) so he always held his head at a tilt, cocked down and to one side.

Election: On his 4th try, at age 65, Buchanan finally won the Democratic presidential nomination. His chief opponent in the general election of 1856 was the candidate of the newly organized Republican party, John C. Frémont. Former President Millard Fillmore was the candidate of the anti-Catholic, anti-immigrant "Know Nothing" party. Buchanan won only a minority of the popular vote (45% —to 33% for Frémont and 22% for Fillmore), but in the Electoral College he triumphed over his 2 opponents—174 to their 114 and 8 respectively.

Term of Office: March 4, 1857–March 4, 1861 (4 years). Buchanan's obvious pro-Southern bias in the bitter conflicts over slavery extension made him unpopular, and he did not try for reelection.

Little-Known Facts: Buchanan's niece and hostess, the stunning Harriet Lane, was more popular than her President-uncle. The well-known song "Listen to the Mocking Bird" was one of dozens of popular entertainments dedicated to her.

Quotes from Buchanan:
"There are portions of the Union in which if you emancipate your slaves they will become your masters. Is there any man who would for a moment indulge the horrible idea of abolishing slavery by the massacre of the chivalrous race of men in the south?"

"Whatever the result may be, I shall carry to my grave the consciousness that I at least meant well for my country."

Quote about Him:
"By half measures, evasions and stealthy approaches, by all the arts of weakness, he had gained the Presidency at just the moment when a man of all but superhuman vision and strength was needed."—Historian Allan Nevins

16th President ABRAHAM LINCOLN

(See: Full Profile)

17th President ANDREW JOHNSON

Born: December 29, 1808, Raleigh, N.C.

Died: July 31, 1875, Carter's Station, Tenn., not far from his longtime home in Greeneville.

Career: Apprenticed to a tailor at age 12, ran away, worked at transient jobs, opened a tailor shop in Greeneville, active in local debating society, elected alderman, mayor, and to the Tennessee State legislature. U.S. congressman at 35, governor of Tennessee, U.S. senator. Only Southern senator to remain loyal to the Union during the Civil War; served as military governor after Union troops took over his State. Six years after he left the White House, Tennessee sent him back to Washington as a U.S. senator.

Personal Life: Married at 18; his wife taught him to read and write. (Johnson had never spent a day in school.) Of his 5 children, 2 sons were alcoholics. Deep religious convictions held his marriage together during difficult times.

His Person: Stocky, 5'10" tall, powerful build, unruly hair, heavy brows, grim mouth. His short temper was legendary.

Election: In 1864, the Republicans placed Johnson on the ticket as Lincoln's running mate in order to appeal to the broadest possible range of opinion—Johnson was a Democrat, and a pro-Union Southerner. After Lincoln's assassination, Republican leaders were startled to find this "stranger in their midst" President of the U.S.

Term of Office: April 15, 1865–March 4, 1869 (3 years, 324 days). Johnson's single-minded opposition to Negro rights and congressional efforts at Reconstruction led the House of Representatives to vote a Resolution of Impeachment, by the lopsided margin of 126 to 47. In the Senate trial that followed, Johnson avoided removal from office by only one vote, with a majority of the senators (35 of 54) actually voting for conviction.

Little-Known Facts: Johnson was always proud of his skill as a tailor. During most of his life he made his own clothes, and while governor of Tennessee he complimented the governor of Kentucky by making a suit for him.

Quotes from Johnson:

"Of all the dangers which our nation has yet encountered, none are equal to those which must result from success of the current effort to Africanize the southern half of the country."—Commenting on proposals to grant blacks the right to vote

"Let them impeach and be damned!"

Quote about Him:

"He is surrounded, hampered, tangled in the meshes of his own wickedness. Unfortunate, unhappy man, behold your doom!"—Congressman Thaddeus Stevens, during Impeachment proceedings

18th President

ULYSSES SIMPSON GRANT

Born: April 27, 1822, Point Pleasant, Ohio.

Died: July 23, 1885, Mount McGregor resort, N.Y., ending his battle with throat cancer.

Career: Sent to West Point by his father against his will, graduated near bottom of his class, army commission, career officer, but forced to resign because of heavy drinking. After unsuccessful farming and real estate ventures, Grant (age 38) returned home for a job as clerk in his father's store. The Civil War rescued him from his cycle of failure, as he won a commission as colonel of volunteers. Due to a combination of luck and military genius, he rose through the ranks to the position of general in chief of all Union armies. After his service in the White House, Grant incurred a debt of $16 million in a disastrous venture on Wall Street, and wrote his best-selling *Memoirs* in an effort to restore his family's fortunes.

Personal Life: A devoted family man, Grant was deeply dependent on his plump wife, Julia. His favorite among his 5 children was Nellie, a celebrated beauty who enjoyed a spectacular White House wedding at age 17.

His Person: Exactly 5'8½" tall, always walked in a slouch, rough reddish beard, clear blue eyes. By the time he reached 40 his drinking problems were under control; as President he would turn down his glass at White House dinners when waiters came around offering wine. Smoked 20 cigars every day.

Elections: In 1868, America's greatest war hero easily defeated Democrat Horatio Seymour, 214 electoral votes to 80. Grant was helped by the newly enfranchised black voters of the South. Four years later, despite scandals in his Administration and a split in Republican ranks, Grant won an even bigger landslide, beating Horace Greeley by 750,000 votes. Greeley won only 66 electoral votes, and he died in humiliation before they could be officially cast.

Term of Office: March 4, 1869–March 4, 1877 (8 years). Grant's try for a 3rd term in

1880 was blocked by the Republican convention.

Little-Known Facts: During the Civil War, Grant would often breakfast on a cucumber soaked in vinegar. If he ate meat at all, it had to be cooked black; he detested the sight of blood, and a serving of rare meat was enough to make him queasy.

Quote from Grant:
"The art of war is simple enough. Find out where your enemy is. Get at him as soon as you can. Strike at him as hard as you can, and keep moving on."

Quotes about Him:
"He combined great gifts with great mediocrity."—Woodrow Wilson
"I cannot spare this man; he fights."—Abraham Lincoln

19th President

RUTHERFORD BIRCHARD HAYES

Born: October 4, 1822, Delaware, Ohio.
Died: January 17, 1893, at his home in Fremont, Ohio.
Career: Harvard Law School, prosperous attorney, Cincinnati city solicitor, major of volunteers at outbreak of Civil War, promoted to major general, elected to U.S. Congress, governor of Ohio. Noted as a competent but colorless reformer.
Personal Life: Hayes's adolescence was marked by a passionate attachment to his older sister—a beautiful, high-strung woman who later spent time in an insane asylum. When he was 30, he escaped from her domination by marrying Lucy Webb, 21. Lucy bore Hayes 7 sons. As First Lady she was noted for her intelligence, energy, and her ban on all alcoholic beverages in the White House, giving rise to the popular nickname "Lemonade Lucy."
His Person: Described as "one of the most mediocre-looking men ever to run for President," he was 5'8" tall, with a sandy red "rat's nest" beard, large nose, blue eyes.
Election: As the Republican nominee in 1876, Hayes ran 250,000 votes behind Democrat Samuel Tilden, but the count in the Electoral College was disputed. In the most controversial electoral decision in American history, Hayes was awarded all of the 19 contested electors at the last minute—giving him a razor-thin 185–184 "victory."
Term of Office: March 4, 1877–March 4, 1881 (4 years).
Little-Known Facts: In the White House, Hayes and Lucy held morning prayer readings every day after breakfast. For intimate family

entertainment, the favorite presidential diversion was old-fashioned Sunday night hymn-singing. Cabinet members, congressmen, and Vice-President Wheeler often participated.

Quote from Hayes:
"Nobody ever left the Presidency with less regret, less disappointment, fewer heartburnings, or any general content with the result of his term (in his own heart, I mean) than I do."

Quotes about Him:
"He is a 3rd rate nonentity, whose only recommendation is that he is obnoxious to no one."—Henry Adams
"Hayes is a modest man, but a very able one."—Senator John Sherman

20th President

JAMES ABRAM GARFIELD

Born: November 19, 1831, Orange, Ohio.
Died: September 19, 1881, Elberon, N.J. The President had been shot 2½ months before, and in the last stages of his long struggle for life he asked that he be moved from Washington to enjoy the sea air of the New Jersey resort.
Career: Williams College (graduated 1st in his class), professor of Latin and Greek at Ohio's Hiram College, lay minister and evangelist, State senator, general in the Civil War, 8 terms in U.S. House of Representatives.
Personal Life: Garfield's wife Lucretia shared his passion for classical literature and his commitment to the Disciples of Christ—a devout sect opposed to both war and slavery. A scholarly woman most often described as plain, Lucretia personally instructed her children in Latin and designed the family mansion. The Garfields enjoyed a stable, satisfying marriage, despite the constant presence of Garfield's mother. She accompanied them everywhere—even to the White House.
His Person: An even 6' tall, broad shoulders, athletic build. Bright blue eyes, ruddy complexion, brown hair going gray at the temples.
Election: As the compromise choice of the Republican convention, Garfield faced Democrat Winfield Hancock—a 250-lb. Civil War hero—in the election of 1880. The popular vote was remarkably close—4,454,416 for Garfield, to Hancock's 4,444,952. Garfield's 214 to 155 margin in the Electoral College was more decisive.
Term of Office: March 4, 1881–September 19, 1881 (199 days). Garfield was the 2nd President to die from an assassin's bullet.
Little-Known Facts: Garfield was the 1st President who was left-handed. Garfield may have had a premonition of his own death. Two

days before he was shot he sent for Robert Lincoln, the son of the late President, and asked him to recount all his memories of the assassination of his famous father. Lincoln talked for more than an hour while the President listened intently.

Quote from Garfield:
"My God! What is there in this place that a man should ever want to get into it?"

Quote about Him:
"How could anybody be so cold-hearted as to want to kill my baby?"—Garfield's mother

21st President   CHESTER ALAN ARTHUR

Born: October 5, 1830. Two towns in Vermont claim the honor of being his birthplace. His political opponents insisted that Arthur had actually been born in Canada, and some recent historians agree with them.

Died: November 18, 1886, New York City.

Career: A Phi Beta Kappa and graduate of Union College, schoolteacher in Vermont, law student, New York lawyer active in Republican politics. Appointed New York "engineer in chief" and kept New York troops supplied during Civil War. Chairman of the Republican State Executive Committee, collector of the port of New York.

Personal Life: At 29, Arthur married the socially prominent Nell Herndon. Nell's main interest outside her family was singing in New York's Mendelssohn Glee Club. When she died of pneumonia at 42, Arthur was inconsolable. He gave orders that her room should remain forever untouched.

His Person: He was 6'2" tall, with reddish-brown hair, gray moustache and side-whiskers. Considered a handsome man and an elegant dresser. A lover of fine wines and good living, he usually spent 2 to 3 hours at the dinner table.

Election: Though he had never run for public office before, Arthur was nominated for Vice-President in 1880 in order to placate New York boss Roscoe Conkling. Many reform-minded Republicans, disgusted at his choice, wanted to devise some means of voting for Garfield without voting for Arthur.

Term of Office: September 19, 1881–March 4, 1885 (3 years, 166 days). Arthur succeeded to the Presidency on the death of President Garfield. In 1884, he tried for a term in his own right, but the Republican convention failed to nominate him.

Little-Known Facts: Arthur was appalled at the hodgepodge of furniture in the White House that greeted him when he became President. He refused to move in until 24 wagonloads of furniture (some of it priceless) had

been auctioned off and the entire mansion redone in late Victorian style.

Quote from Arthur:
"The Office of Vice-President is a greater honor than I ever dreamed of attaining."

Quotes about Him:
"Chet Arthur, President of the U.S.! Good God!"—A New York political associate

"I can hardly imagine how he could have done better."—Henry Ward Beecher

22nd and 24th President

GROVER CLEVELAND

Born: March 18, 1837, Caldwell, N.J. Son of a Presbyterian minister.

Died: June 24, 1908, at his home in Princeton, N.J. His last words: "I have tried so hard to do right."

Career: Clerk in a law office, attorney in Buffalo, N.Y., active in Democratic politics, appointed district attorney, elected sheriff of Erie County, resumed private law practice for 7 years. Elected mayor of Buffalo, governor of New York, and President of the U.S. all within the space of 3½ years.

Personal Life: Cleveland entered the White House as a bachelor, but he had enjoyed an involvement back in Buffalo that had culminated in the birth of an illegitimate child. During his 2nd year as President, Cleveland married a beautiful 21-year-old named Frances Folsom. Frances was the daughter of Cleveland's late law partner, and "Uncle Cleve" had been her legal guardian since she was 11. The marriage produced 5 children, and frequent (but unsubstantiated) rumors that "the Beast of Buffalo" beat his lovely wife.

His Person: At 5'11" and 260 lbs., he was a corpulent figure, with a short, bull neck constantly bulging out of stiff collars. High-pitched voice, gray eyes, huge walrus moustache. His favorite dish was corned beef and cabbage.

Elections: In the election of 1884, Cleveland beat Republican James G. Blaine by one of the narrowest popular margins in American history: 4,879,507 to 4,850,293. The count in the Electoral College was 219 to 182. A switch of just 528 votes in one crucial State (New York) would have thrown the election to Blaine. Four years later, against the Republican nominee Benjamin Harrison, President Cleveland faced another close race, but this time the pendulum swung against him and he lost. In 1892, after 4 years of "retirement," Cleveland made a comeback in his rematch with Harrison. He won 5,555,426 votes to Harrison's 5,182,690. The Electoral College margin was 277 to 145. James B. Weaver, candidate of the radical Populist party, polled more than one million votes, while carrying 4 States worth 22 electors.

Terms of Office: March 4, 1885–March 4, 1889, *and* March 4, 1893–March 4, 1897 (8 years).

Little-Known Facts: In 1893, a cancerous growth was discovered on the roof of Cleveland's mouth, and most of the President's upper left jaw was removed. This major surgery was a closely guarded secret—Cleveland feared that worries over his health might make a gloomy economic situation (the "Depression" of '93) even worse. The surgery proved successful and Cleveland was provided with an artificial jaw of vulcanized rubber. The facts of the case did not come out until 1917.

Quote from Cleveland:
"I am honest and sincere in my desire to do well, but the question is whether I know enough to accomplish what I desire."

Quotes about Him:
"Backbone! He has so much of it, it makes him stick out in front!"—Samuel Tilden

"I feel that the vast business interests of the country will be safe in your hands."—Jay Gould

23rd President   BENJAMIN HARRISON

Born: August 20, 1833, North Bend, Ohio, on the estate of his grandfather, Gen. (and later President) William Henry Harrison.

Died: March 13, 1901, Indianapolis, Ind.

Career: Graduate of Miami University (Ohio), young lawyer in Indianapolis, active in Republican politics, elected reporter of the State supreme court, commissioned as 2nd lieutenant at outbreak of Civil War, used political influence to rise to rank of general (despite lackluster battlefield record). Twice defeated as candidate for governor of Indiana, elected to U.S. Senate, but defeated in his 1st reelection bid (1886).

Personal Life: While in college, Harrison fell in love with the daughter of one of his professors, and married her when he was only 20. The new couple shared a deep commitment to the Presbyterian Church; for years, Harrison taught a men's Bible class and served as superintendent of a Sunday school. Caroline Harrison died after a long illness during her husband's last months in the White House. Three years later, the former President married his wife's niece, a young widow who had lived with the family for several years. His 3 children were so disturbed at this match that they refused to attend the wedding.

His Person: Height 5'6"; squat, stocky frame, blond-graying hair, reddish beard, blue eyes. Cold and humorless. His only self-indulgence: his love for fine cigars.

Election: In 1888, James Blaine, the leading Republican candidate, broke a convention deadlock by announcing his surprising support for Harrison. In the election that followed, Harrison benefited from Republican trickery and vote-buying to defeat President Grover Cleveland. Cleveland actually won more popular votes (5,540,309 to 5,444,337) but Harrison carried the key States of New York and Indiana and with them the Electoral College, 233–168. Four years later, when Harrison tried for reelection, Cleveland came back to beat him.

Term of Office: March 4, 1889–March 4, 1893 (4 years).

Little-Known Facts: In 1891, the Edison company installed electricity in the White House for the 1st time. The Harrisons, however, were so fearful of the new device that they refused to touch the switches. Often, they slept with all the lights burning.

Quote from Harrison:
"When I came into power, I found that the party managers had taken it all to themselves. I could not name my own Cabinet. They had sold out every place to pay the election expenses."

Quote about Him:
"He is a cold-blooded, narrow-minded, prejudiced, obstinate, timid old psalm-singing Indianapolis politician."—Theodore Roosevelt

25th President   WILLIAM McKINLEY

Born: January 29, 1843, Niles, Ohio.

Died: September 14, 1901, in Buffalo, N.Y., 8 days after he was shot by a young anarchist, Leon Czolgosz.

Career: Postal clerk, schoolteacher, volunteer in the Civil War, rose from private to major, returned to Ohio and studied law, elected prosecuting attorney of Stark County, U.S. House of Representatives (6 terms), governor of Ohio.

Personal Life: After 4 years of marriage, McKinley's wife Ida suffered a breakdown following the death of their 2 infant daughters. She never recovered, and spent the rest of her life as a tormented epileptic at the borders of sanity. Even McKinley's opponents were amazed at his devotion to her. Protocol was often violated at formal dinners to permit McKinley to sit next to his wife in case of one of her frequent seizures. Even at the moment of his own assassination, his wife's health was foremost in his mind. "My wife," he gasped, "be careful how you tell her—oh, be careful!"

His Person: Only 5'6" tall, stout, dignified bearing, beak nose, known for his spotless white vest which he changed several times a day. Wore a red carnation in his buttonhole at all times.

Elections: As 1st-ballot nominee of the Republican party, McKinley faced the radical "Boy Orator" William Jennings Bryan in the election of 1896. Despite a strong campaign by Bryan, business interests united behind McKinley, and helped him win a popular margin of 51.7%. In the Electoral College, McKinley beat Bryan 271–176. Four years later, the same 2 candidates faced each other, with Bryan sharply critical of McKinley's "imperialist" policy following the Spanish American War. The majority of Americans stood by their expansionist President—7,219,525 to Bryan's 6,358,737. The count in the Electoral College was a decisive 292–155.

Term of Office: March 4, 1897–September 14, 1901 (4 years, 194 days).

Little-Known Facts: McKinley smoked so heavily that his doctors ordered him to stop. Whenever photographers were present he self-consciously put cigars aside. "The children of America must not see their President smoking," he said.

Quote from McKinley:
"I am a tariff man, standing on a tariff platform."

Quotes about Him:
"That kind, gentle, fatherly way of Mr. McKinley's made all comers feel that he was their friend, but left doubt in their minds as to the substantial result they had come to accomplish."—Ike Hoover, White House usher
"I love McKinley! He is the best man I ever knew."—Mark Hanna, his campaign manager

26th President THEODORE ROOSEVELT

Born: October 27, 1858, New York, N.Y.
Died: January 6, 1919, at his home Sagamore Hill, Long Island, N.Y.
Career: Harvard graduate, a Phi Beta Kappa, studied law at Columbia, elected to New York legislature at 23, reputation as outspoken reformer, defeated candidate for mayor of New York, professional writer (historical and autobiographical volumes), appointed to National Civil Service Commission, New York police commissioner, Assistant Secretary of the Navy. At outbreak of Spanish-American War, he resigned to organize "Rough Riders" volunteer regiment, hero of Battle of San Juan Hill, elected governor of New York after the war.
Personal Life: At 22, married his college sweetheart. An idyllic marriage for 3 years. Then she died in childbirth, on the same day that Roosevelt's mother died. To lift his spirits TR worked as a cowboy on a ranch in Dakota Territory. Six years later, he married an old

friend of his sister's. Their relationship was a jovial friendship rather than a passionate romance. TR adored his 6 children; his greatest joy was leading them in games and camping expeditions.

His Person: An even 5'10", brown hair, heavy moustache, pince-nez with thick lenses. Unusually high-pitched voice. Generally gritted his teeth when smiling.

Elections: In 1900, Boss Platt of New York was anxious to get rid of the State's new reform governor, so he arranged to "kick Roosevelt upstairs" as the Republican nominee for Vice-President. A year later, following McKinley's assassination, conservatives were appalled to find "that damned cowboy" as President. In 1904, President Roosevelt was so popular that he had no trouble winning the election in his own right. Against Democrat Alton Parker, he won 57% of the popular vote, and swept every State outside the South for a 336–140 Electoral College margin.

Term of Office: September 14, 1901–March 4, 1909 (7 years, 172 days). In 1912, 4 years after leaving the White House, Roosevelt made an unsuccessful bid for the Presidency as the candidate of the "radical" Progressive party.

Little-Known Facts: According to White House usher Ike Hoover, President Roosevelt used to get up from his desk after a busy day, sneak out the back door and run several times around the Washington Monument to work off excess energy. Roosevelt personally originated such familiar phrases as "lunatic fringe," "muckrakers," and "my hat is in the ring."

Quotes from Roosevelt:
"Stand the gaff, play fair; be a good man to camp out with."
"No President has ever enjoyed himself as much as I."

Quotes about Him:
"When Theodore attends a wedding he wants to be the bride and when he attends a funeral he wants to be the corpse."—A relative
"To President Roosevelt we ascribe that quality that medieval theology ascribed to God —he was pure act."—Henry Adams

27th President

WILLIAM HOWARD TAFT

Born: September 15, 1857, Cincinnati, Ohio.
Died: March 8, 1930, Washington, D.C.
Career: Son of former U.S. Attorney General, Yale graduate, prosecuting attorney in Cincinnati, superior court judge, U.S. solicitor general, Federal district judge, governor general of the Philippines, Secretary of War under Roosevelt. After his term in the White House, Taft served as a law professor at Yale, and then as chief justice of the Supreme Court.

Personal Life: Taft's lifelong ambition was to serve on the Supreme Court, and he had little interest in electoral politics. It was his imperious wife Nellie who forced him, against his better judgment, to accept the presidential nomination in 1908. Nellie was unable to enjoy the years in the White House, however; she suffered a severe stroke in 1909. During her slow recovery, the President lovingly taught her to speak again.

His Person: At 5'11", he weighed 220 lbs. when he graduated from Yale, and 325 lbs. when he became President. Frequently compared to a bison or a battleship. Famous smile beneath blond walrus moustache; his deep laugh called "the most effective chuckle in the history of politics."

Election: As the handpicked successor of the popular Theodore Roosevelt, Taft had little trouble winning nomination and election in 1908. He beat Democrat William Jennings Bryan 321 electoral votes to 162. Four years later, when he tried for reelection, Taft finished 3rd behind both Democrat Woodrow Wilson and the "Bullmoose" Progressive, his old friend Theodore Roosevelt.

Term of Office: March 4, 1909–March 4, 1913 (4 years).

Little-Known Facts: When Taft moved into the White House a special bathtub had to be built to accommodate him: It was large enough to hold 4 ordinary men. On several occasions while President, Taft fell asleep in public.

Quote from Taft:
"Politics, when I am in it, makes me sick."

Quotes about Him:
"It's very difficult for me to understand how a man who is so good as Chief Justice could have been so bad as President."—Justice Louis Brandeis

"Taft meant well, but he meant well feebly." —Theodore Roosevelt

28th President WOODROW WILSON

Born: December 28, 1856, Staunton, Va.

Died: February 3, 1924, Washington, D.C. He had been in poor health and partially paralyzed since suffering a stroke while President in 1919.

Career: Graduate of Princeton and University of Virginia Law School. Bored with law practice, he did graduate work in political science at Johns Hopkins, won Ph.D. in 1885. Teaching positions at Bryn Mawr, Wesleyan, and Princeton, named president of Princeton at 46, noted for his educational reforms, mentioned as possible presidential candidate as early as 1906. Elected governor of New Jersey, 1910; 2 years later won Democratic presidential nomination.

Personal Life: His devotion to his 1st wife was passionate and obsessive; when she died in the White House in 1914, he sat beside her body for 2 full days and came close to a nervous breakdown. In order to restore the President's balance, friends helped to engineer a meeting between Wilson and a beautiful Washington widow, Edith Galt. They were married in 1915—despite fears that their romance might hurt Wilson's chances for reelection. Wilson had 3 daughters from his 1st marriage; he generally preferred the company of "clever" women to that of men.

His Person: Tall, lean, with sparse iron-gray hair, blue eyes hidden behind glittering rimless glasses. Square, heavy jaw, arched eyebrows. Thought of himself as unattractive. Strong tenor voice.

Elections: As the Democratic candidate in 1912, Wilson's victory was assured by the split in Republican ranks. Though he polled only 42% of the popular vote, it was enough to beat the Progressive candidate Theodore Roosevelt (27½%) and the incumbent Republican William Howard Taft (23%). The count in the Electoral College was 435–88–8. Four years later, with the Republicans once again united, Wilson faced a more difficult race against Charles E. Hughes. In the popular vote, Wilson topped Hughes 49%–46%, but a switch of some 2,000 votes in California would have made Hughes President. (The Electoral College tally was 277–254.) The theme of Wilson's reelection victory was the slogan, "He Kept Us Out of War." Just one month after his 2nd inauguration, this "Peace President" led the U.S. into W.W. I.

Term of Office: March 4, 1913–March 4, 1921 (8 years).

Little-Known Facts: In 1915, a typographical error in the *Washington Post* made President Wilson the object of lewd laughter. Describing an evening at the theater, enhanced by the presence of Wilson and his new fiancée, a reporter wrote that instead of watching the performance "the President spent most of his time entertaining Mrs. Galt." "Entertaining" came out "entering" in the newspaper's earliest edition.

Quotes from Wilson:
"It is only by working with an energy which is almost superhuman and looks to uninterested spectators like insanity that we can accomplish anything worth the achievement."

"Segregation is not humiliating but a benefit, and ought to be so regarded by you gentlemen." —To black leaders, November, 1913

"Why has Jesus Christ so far not succeeded in inducing the world to follow his teachings? . . . I am proposing a practical scheme to carry out His aims."—1919

"I believe in Divine Providence. If I did not I would go crazy."—1919

Quotes about Him:

"He had to hold the reins and do the driving alone; it was the only kind of leadership he knew."—Arthur Link, Wilson's biographer

"He is an utterly selfish and cold-blooded politician always."—Theodore Roosevelt

The Other 28th President

EDITH BOLLING WILSON

(See: Full Profile)

29th President

WARREN GAMALIEL HARDING

Born: November 2, 1865, in the village of Corsica (later Blooming Grove), Ohio.

Died: August 2, 1923, in San Francisco. His sudden death, in the middle of a presidential goodwill tour, led to speculation that he had been poisoned by his wife in order to avoid disgrace (and probable impeachment) as the corruption in his Administration became known. Mrs. Harding refused to permit an autopsy on her husband's body.

Career: Schoolteacher, insurance salesman, organizer of the town band, small-town newspaper publisher, State senator, lieutenant governor, U.S. senator.

Personal Life: At 25, Harding married Florence DeWolfe, a divorcée 5 years his senior and the daughter of the town's richest banker. A cold, imperious woman, Florence was known to Harding and all his friends as "The Duchess." Over a period of 15 years, Harding conducted a passionate affair with the wife of a good friend; later, as senator and President, he became secretly involved with a gorgeous blonde in her 20s, Nan Britton, who bore him an illegitimate daughter.

His Person: A well-built 6-footer with white hair, blue eyes, and a smooth, dark complexion, Harding had the face and bearing of a matinee idol. Persistent rumors in his hometown alleged that the Harding family was "tainted" by Negro blood.

Election: In 1920, when the Republican convention deadlocked, a group of party bosses assembled in the original "smoke-filled room" to pick Harding—a little-known senator from Ohio—as their candidate. In November, public disgust with Woodrow Wilson and the Democrats gave Harding the greatest landslide in history to that time. He won more than 60% of the popular vote, and swamped Democrat James M. Cox in the Electoral College—404-127. Nearly one million Americans voted for the Socialist candidate, Eugene Debs, who was then serving time in Federal prison.

Term of Office: March 4, 1921–August 2, 1923 (2 years, 151 days).

Little-Known Facts: Despite his surface calm, Harding suffered serious breakdowns in time of stress. He was only 22 when he suffered his 1st nervous breakdown and went off to a sanitarium for several weeks. This was the 1st of 5 such episodes over the next 12 years.

Quotes from Harding:

"I am not fit for this office and never should have been here."

"American business is not a monster, but an expression of God-given impulse to create, and the savior of our happiness."

Quote about Him:

"If you were a girl, Warren, you'd be in the family way all the time. You can't say No."—Harding's father

30th President CALVIN COOLIDGE

Born: July 4, 1872, Plymouth, Vt. Only President born on 4th of July.

Died: January 5, 1933, at his home in Northampton, Mass.

Career: Amherst graduate, Northampton lawyer, elected to Northampton Common Council, city solicitor, State representative, mayor, State senator, lieutenant governor. Elected governor of Massachusetts in 1918; won national reputation by breaking the Boston police strike.

Personal Life: Warm, well-educated Grace Goodhue had many suitors, but Coolidge won her because "he outsat everybody else." They were married when he was 33 and she was 26. From the beginning, it was an austere marriage: no dinner guests, no parties, no discussion of his work. ("He did not trust my education," Grace Coolidge recalled.) They had 2 sons, John and Calvin, Jr.

His Person: Exactly 5'10", reddish hair, pale, freckled complexion, blue eyes, thin nose and lips. He spoke in a high-pitched twang, and his main characteristic—holding his tongue—earned him the epithet "Silent Cal."

Elections: Named as Harding's running mate in 1920, took over the White House after the President's sudden death 2 years later. In 1924, the campaign slogan "Keep Cool and Keep Coolidge" won him a term in his own right, with a landslide of 15,725,016 against 8,386,704 for Democrat John W. Davis, and 4,832,532 for Progressive candidate "Battling Bob" La Follette. The electoral count was 382–136–13.

Term of Office: August 3, 1923–March 4, 1929 (5 years, 215 days).

Little-Known Facts: He had a distant Indian

ancestor. His stinginess provoked the White House chef to quit. He examined all his wife's bills to be sure she wasn't overspending.

Quotes from Coolidge:

"The business of America is business."

"If you don't say anything, you won't be called on to repeat it."

Quotes about Him:

"He was weaned on a pickle."—Alice Roosevelt Longworth

"He was an economic fatalist with a God-given inertia. He knew nothing and refused to learn."—William Allen White

31st President

HERBERT CLARK HOOVER

Born: August 10, 1874, West Branch, Ia.

Died: October 20, 1964, New York, N.Y.

Career: Graduate of Stanford University, worked for 20 years as a mining engineer, building up an international business empire and personal fortune of $4 million. During W.W. I, he coordinated worldwide efforts to provide relief for starving civilians, served as American Food Administrator. In Cabinet under Harding and Coolidge as "Secretary of Commerce and Assistant Secretary of everything else." During W.W. II, long after his term as President, Hoover once more headed humanitarian relief efforts. He also chaired government reorganization commissions for Truman and Eisenhower.

Personal Life: At 24, he married Lou Henry, a Stanford co-ed who shared his interest in minerals. (Later they collaborated on a published translation of an ancient treatise on metals.) Lou followed "Bert" on his travels even after their 2 sons were born. By the time Herbert, Jr., was 4, he had circled the globe 3 times.

His Person: He was 5'11", with broad shoulders, round face, hazel eyes, ruddy complexion, straight hair parted near center. A deeply religious Quaker. A stickler for detail and a compulsive worker.

Election: In his 1st try for elective office, Secretary of Commerce Hoover won the Presidency in 1928. He beat Democrat Al Smith by nearly 6½ million votes, and had 444 electoral votes to Smith's 87.

Term of Office: March 4, 1929–March 4, 1933 (4 years). The stock market collapsed just 8 months after he took office, and Hoover was crushed in his bid for reelection.

Little-Known Facts: During the Depression, Hoover lent his name not only to the shantytowns that sprang up everywhere ("Hoovervilles") but to "Hoover blankets" (old newspapers wrapped around the body for warmth), "Hoover wagons" (broken-down automobiles hauled by mules), and "Hoover flags" (empty pockets turned inside out).

Quotes from Hoover:

"Prosperity cannot be restored by raids upon the public treasury."

"The sole function of Government is to bring about a condition of affairs favorable to the beneficial development of private enterprise."

Quotes about Him:

"A private meeting with Hoover is like sitting in a bath of ink."—Secretary of State Henry Stimson

"He seems to me to be close to death. He has the look of being done, but still of going on and on, driven by some damned duty."—Raymond Moley, 1932

32nd President

FRANKLIN DELANO ROOSEVELT

(See: Full Profile)

33rd President   HARRY S TRUMAN

(See: Full Profile)

34th President

DWIGHT DAVID EISENHOWER

Born: October 14, 1890, in Denison, Tex. Before his 1st birthday the family moved to Abilene, Kans., and that is where "Ike" grew up.

Died: March 28, 1969, at Walter Reed Hospital in Washington, following his 7th heart attack.

Career: West Point graduate (65th in class of 165); 1st lieutenant, rising in the ranks to assistant to Chief of Staff George Marshall, and eventually supreme commander of Allied armies in Europe in W.W. II. After the war, he served briefly as president of Columbia University.

Personal Life: At 25, he married a vivacious young small-town belle, Mamie Doud. Over the next 20 years the Eisenhowers lived in 30 different homes as Ike pursued his military career. During W.W. II, it was rumored that the general had an affair with Kay Summersby, the pretty WAC officer who was his driver and personal assistant, but the evidence is sketchy. She died at age 64 in 1975 without confirming the story.

His Person: Ike was 5'10½" tall, and kept his weight at around 170. He had blue eyes and a fair, ruddy complexion—as a boy he had been nicknamed "Swede" by friends.

Elections: As the major military hero of W.W. II, Ike was the most popular man in America, and both parties wanted him as their presidential candidate. After winning the Republican nomination in 1952, he swept to an easy victory over Adlai Stevenson—442 electoral votes to 89. In 1956, in a rematch with Stevenson, Ike widened his margin, winning nearly 58% of the vote, and an electoral victory of 457 to 73.

Term of Office: January 20, 1953–January 20, 1961 (8 years).

Little-Known Facts: At West Point, Ike played left halfback on the football team. In one game, he seriously wrenched his knee while tackling the famous Jim Thorpe. Ike's favorite dessert was prune whip. Eisenhower used to practice his putts on the White House lawn. When squirrels interfered with his golfing concentration, the President had them box-trapped and removed.

Quotes from Eisenhower:
"I can think of nothing more boring, for the American public, than to have to sit in their living rooms for a whole half an hour looking at my face on their television screens."

"You know, once in a while I get to the point, with everybody staring at me, where I want to go back indoors and pull down the curtains."

Quotes about Him:
"The trouble with Eisenhower is he's just a coward. He hasn't got any backbone at all."—Harry Truman

"Remember, folks, Eisenhower is a great man. A vote for Eisenhower is a vote for what's good in America."—Richard Nixon

35th President

JOHN FITZGERALD KENNEDY

(See: Full Profile)

36th President

LYNDON BAINES JOHNSON

Born: August 27, 1908, in the vicinity of Johnson City, Tex.

Died: January 22, 1973, at the LBJ Ranch, the 360-acre retreat not far from his birthplace.

Career: Graduate of Southwest Texas State College, teacher of public speaking at a Houston high school, volunteer in local congressional campaign, appointed congressman's secretary, appointed Texas director of the Na-

tional Youth Administration, elected to House of Representatives, unsuccessful candidate for U.S. Senate, volunteer navy officer during W.W. II, elected U.S. senator by questionable 87-vote margin, chosen Senate Democratic leader at age 44—and in his freshman term.

Personal Life: At age 26, he met Claudia "Lady Bird" Taylor, the shy, intelligent daughter of a well-to-do merchant. LBJ proposed to her on the 1st date and 2 months later they were married. While Lyndon concentrated on politics, Lady Bird supervised every aspect of home life, and used her inheritance and her sharp business sense to build up a multimillion-dollar communications empire. Johnson was always proud of his 2 daughters, though he was unable to spend much time with them when they were growing up. In 1968 he announced: "I'm the luckiest man alive. None of my girls drinks or smokes or takes dope and they both married fine men."

His Person: An imposing 6'3", massive bone structure, slightly paunchy in middle age. Long nose, enormous fleshy ears, and leathery skin. Liked to relax every day with Cutty Sark Scotch stirred into watery highballs. Smoked 3 packs of cigarettes a day, then quit after suffering a severe heart attack at age 47. Boundless energy; as President, he worked every day from 6:30 A.M. till one or 2 the next morning, with a brief break for a nap after lunch.

Elections: In 1960, he was John Kennedy's chief rival for the Democratic nomination, and Kennedy named Johnson as his running mate in a bid for party unity. In the year following Kennedy's assassination, LBJ managed to push most of the stalled "New Frontier" legislation through Congress, and became a heavy favorite to win a term in his own right in 1964. His success was virtually assured when the Republicans nominated outspoken conservative Barry Goldwater. In the campaign, Johnson billed himself as the peace candidate and repeatedly promised "no wider war" in Vietnam. The result was a landslide with LBJ winning an all-time record of 61.1% of the popular vote. He also carried 44 States, for a total of 486 electoral votes, to Goldwater's 52.

Term of Office: November 22, 1963–January 20, 1969 (5 years, 59 days). Johnson unexpectedly withdrew from the presidential race in 1968 amid heated controversy concerning his Vietnam policy.

Little-Known Facts: After he became President, LBJ briefly considered firing FBI Director J. Edgar Hoover, but eventually changed his mind. "I'd rather have him inside the tent pissing out, than outside pissing in," the President reasoned. Once, as Johnson prepared to leave an airport after a speech, an army staff sergeant noticed that the President was heading for the wrong helicopter. He came up to LBJ, pointing: "Mr. President, *that* is your helicopter over there." Johnson threw one of his huge arms over the sergeant's shoulders and smiled: "Son, they are *all* my helicopters."

Quotes from Johnson:

"Never trust a man whose eyes are too close to his nose."

"I wake up at 5 A.M. some mornings and hear the planes coming in at National Airport and I think they are bombing me."

"Just like the Alamo, somebody damn well needed to go to their aid. Well, by God, I'm going to Vietnam's aid."

"If we quit Vietnam, tomorrow we'll be fighting in Hawaii, and next week we'll have to fight in San Francisco."

"I can't trust anybody! What are you trying to do to me? Everybody is trying to cut me down, destroy me!"—To an aide, 1967

Quotes about Him:

"When all the returns are in, perhaps President Johnson will have to settle for being recognized as the greatest American President for the poor and for the Negroes, but that, as I see it, is a very great honor indeed."—Ralph Ellison

"He doesn't like cold intellectuals around him. He wants people who will cry when an old lady falls down in the street."—Jack Valenti

"Can it be that this President, so competent and masterful and overwhelming, is plagued and eaten and driven to immoderation by some inward insecurity?"—John Osborne

37th President

RICHARD MILHOUS NIXON

(See: Full Profile)

38th President

GERALD RUDOLPH FORD, JR.

(See: Full Profile)

—M.S.M.

Full Profiles of Selected U.S. Presidents

1st President GEORGE WASHINGTON

VITAL STATISTICS

Born: February 22, 1732, on his family's modest estate in Westmoreland County, Va. His birthplace was destroyed by fire in 1779, and no records describing the house have survived. Nevertheless, in 1932 Washington enthusiasts erected a building on the site, based on designs of well-known homes of the period. This Washington birthplace "shrine" is currently administered by the National Park Service. Located in Wakefield, Va., it is open to the public daily. Admission: $1.

Died: December 14, 1799, at his longtime home, Mount Vernon, Va. Two days earlier, Washington, who was nearly 68, made his normal circuit of the farms that he owned, riding 15 mi. through hail and snow. He awoke that night with a chill. Though scarcely able to speak and breathing with difficulty, he would not let his wife get up to call a servant, for fear that she might catch cold. He had contracted pneumonia, and his condition was soon worsened by the attending physicians, who bled him according to the practice of the time. Just moments before his death, he put the fingers of his left hand on his right wrist to count his pulse, his lips moving. It is reported that his last words were: "'Tis well." Washington is buried on the grounds of Mount Vernon. This estate, which has been carefully preserved, is each year visited by more tourists than any other presidential home. It is located off State highway 235, overlooking the Potomac River. Admission: $1.25.

BEFORE THE PRESIDENCY

Career: As a younger son in a land-poor family, Washington had to work hard to win his position as a Virginia gentleman. His education was sketchy—he was the only one of the 1st 6 Presidents who never attended college—and the only subjects he pursued in depth were mathematics and surveying. When he was 11 his father died, and at 14 Washington wanted to run away to sea, but his mother prevented him. The dominant figure in his adolescence was his older half-brother, Lawrence, who had advanced the family fortunes by marrying into the wealthy Fairfax family. When Washington was 17, Lawrence got him a job as a surveyor for the Fairfaxes. For $7 a day, the young man endured severe hardships while mapping out new lands on the frontier. With this experience behind him, the 21-year-old Washington was named as a special messenger to carry an ultimatum from the governor of Virginia to French outposts far to the west. On this dramatic mission, Washington handled himself with dignity and resourcefulness, and his published account of his adventures won him a favorable reputation. In 1753, with Virginia threatened by a conflict with France, Washington was commissioned a lieutenant colonel of the militia. Dreaming of conquest and glory, he marched out with a tiny force and rashly attacked a French scouting party—in one of the key incidents that provoked the French and Indian War. His blunders, however, were soon forgotten after he showed great courage at the battle known as "Braddock's Defeat," in which Washington's leadership was largely responsible for allowing ⅓ of the British-American troops to escape with their lives. At 23, he was promoted to full colonel and placed in command of all Virginia forces in the war. For 3 years he conducted a dogged and skillful defense of the Virginia frontier against sporadic attacks by the French and their Indian allies. This was the sum of his military experience before he was named commander-in-chief of the Revolutionary armies some 18 years later.

Resigning his commission in 1758, Washington was elected to the Virginia House of Burgesses on his 3rd try. He served diligently for 15 years, but without particular distinction. Most of his attention was centered on the administration of his plantation, Mount Vernon, which he had inherited after his half-brother Lawrence died of tuberculosis.

In 1774 Washington was chosen as one of the 7 Virginia representatives to the 1st Continental Congress in Philadelphia. By the time the 2nd Congress convened in May, 1775, the Revolutionary fighting was already under way. With thousands of unorganized troops camped near Boston, the representatives pondered the choice of a commander-in-chief. For political reasons, it was considered necessary to appoint a Virginian: With all the fighting centered in Massachusetts, special care had to be taken in order to insure full southern support for the cause. Not only did Washington meet the geographical qualification, but he had a quiet, soldierly bearing, a reputation for dependability, and few political enemies. On June 16, Congress selected him as supreme commander. Washington protested that he was unqualified, citing his lack of military experience, but a few days later he was in full uniform and on his way to Boston.

Personal Life: A romantic and emotional young man, Washington loved to dance and craved the company of attractive women. He was socially handicapped, however, by his shyness and his modest financial resources. By the time he was 25 he had fallen painfully in love several times, and on at least 2 occasions his proposals of marriage had been rejected.

The young soldier's deepest affections were reserved for a married lady. Through his brother Lawrence, Washington became friendly with the brilliant Fairfax family, and spent many evenings playing cards, dancing, or acting in amateur theatricals with the elegant Sally Fairfax. Two years older than Washington, the slim and sophisticated Sally was the daughter-in-law of his former employer and the wife of his good friend. She was also a notorious flirt, and may not have realized how deeply she had smitten the awkward and impressionable Washington. Nonetheless, Washington's devotion to her was enough to scandalize some of the Fairfax relatives. One of them wrote to the young officer in camp that fighting the enemy was "a nobler prospect than reflections of hours past that ought to be banished from your thoughts." Washington's many letters to Sally leave no doubt as to the depth of his passion —and frustration—in this impossible love. Even after his engagement to another, he wrote to her pledging his devotion and declaring: "Misconstrue not my meaning; doubt it not, nor expose it. The world has no business to know the object of my love declared in this manner to you, when I want to conceal it." Three months later, Washington married Martha Custis, a short, plump, amiable woman, who at the death of her 1st husband had become the richest widow in Virginia. No one ever assumed that her marriage to Washington was a love match: George was anxious for money and social prestige, while Martha needed an administrator for her vast estates and a guardian for her 2 children. It soon became clear that she had made a wise decision in choosing Washington. A 1st-rate administrator and a skillful businessman, he steadily expanded her already sizable holdings. An estimated net worth of $530,000 at his death marked them as one of the wealthiest couples in America. Over the years, it appears that George and Martha developed a genuine, if not passionate, attachment to one another. Many of the details of their relationship remain in doubt, since Martha burned all their correspondence after Washington's death. Though they never had children, Washington proved an overly indulgent stepfather to Martha's offspring from her previous marriage. When her son Jacky died at age 27, leaving behind children of his own, George and Martha formally adopted 2 of his youngsters.

At Mount Vernon, the Washingtons offered generous but down-to-earth hospitality. Martha, who could barely read and write, was known as a homebody. She took a special interest in cooking and often appeared with a ring of kitchen keys tied at her wide waist. When she became First Lady, her receptions were considered somewhat stiff and old-fashioned. All presidential entertainments ended promptly at 9 P.M., when George and Martha went to bed. Martha survived her husband by 2½ years.

The year before he died, Washington wrote a final letter to Sally Fairfax, the love of his youth, who was a destitute widow of 68 living in London. In it, Washington told her that not all the glories of the Revolution, not even the splendors of the Presidency, had "been able to eradicate from my mind those happy moments, the happiest of my life, which I have enjoyed in your company."

On the Way to the White House: Some military historians assert that Washington was a battlefield genius who deserves to rank with Napoleon and Alexander the Great; many others see him as a fumbling beginner who succeeded in the Revolution only through the utter incompetence of his British opponents. But whatever his skills as a battlefield commander, there can be little question of his overall effectiveness as a war leader. He worked with skill, determination, and unbelievable patience to organize and inspire the American Army, and despite numerous defeats he kept that Army in the field. A skilled propagandist, he helped swing public opinion to the patriot cause. Though he often talked of his wish to retire to Mount Vernon, he moved swiftly and subtly to squelch a conspiracy of senior officers that attempted to replace him as commander-in-chief. In 1781, at the time of the final American victory, Washington's personal prestige was so overwhelming that he was already widely hailed as "the father of his country."

After the war, his desire to spend his days quietly at Mount Vernon was probably sincere, but he was soon drawn back into public life despite his protests. As commander-in-chief, he had struggled for 8 long years to work with a quarreling and ineffective Continental Congress and had become deeply convinced of the need for a stronger national Government. In 1787, when a Constitutional Convention assembled to bring about that change, Washington's presence was needed to legitimize that gathering. On his arrival at Philadelphia, Washington was unanimously elected president of the convention, and his dignity and restraint in the chair kept the often stormy meetings from falling apart. When his colleagues at the Constitutional Convention created the office of President of the U.S., they did so with Washington specifically in mind.

His Person: Washington's commanding appearance always inspired trust and admiration from those around him; as much as any other President, he had the elusive quality of charisma. When he was 27, a fellow member of the Virginia House of Burgesses described him as "straight as an Indian, measuring 6'2" in his stockings and weighing 175 lbs." This estimate may have been conservative: After Washington's death, his private secretary claimed that he measured the body and found it to be 6'3½" tall. Whatever his actual height, Wash-

ington was always considered a giant, and his body remained sinewy and strong, never exceeding 200 lbs. in weight. His massive frame supported enormous hands that required specially-made gloves and feet that called for size 13 boots. His cool, steady, blue-gray eyes, recalling in Emerson's phrase, "an ox gazing out of a pasture," furthered the impression of massive strength. An attack of smallpox when he was 18 had left his skin pockmarked, but it also left him immune to the disease that later ravaged his Continental Army. By age 57, Washington had lost nearly all his teeth, and he began a long and frustrating search for a pair of dentures that would fit him properly. The wooden and ivory false teeth that he finally selected were so unsatisfactory that he kept his lips tightly compressed during his later years, and his jaw developed that awkward, unnatural set that appears in most of his portraits. His dentures also left Washington with such deeply sunken cheeks that Gilbert Stuart, when painting his most famous likeness of the great man, stuffed his subject's cheeks with cotton; a close examination of this portrait reveals the artificial bulge. The natural color of Washington's hair was sandy brown, but he wore it powdered white and further obscured under a fashionable white wig. In 1760, Capt. George Mercer noted that in conversation Washington "looks you full in the face, is deliberate, deferential and engaging. His movements and gestures are graceful, his walk majestic, and he is a splendid horseman." But beneath this cool and polished exterior, Washington hid a furious temper. On one occasion as commander-in-chief, he became so exasperated at the quarreling of drunken soldiers in front of his headquarters, that he forgot the dignity of a general, rushed out, and knocked several of the brawlers cold with his own massive fists. When provoked, the "father of our country" could let loose a torrent of curses that would make even a modern President blush. Washington's private secretary once commented that the most dreaded experience in his life was hearing the general swear.

PRESIDENCY

Election: February 4, 1789 . . .
After 11 of the 13 States had ratified the new Constitution, the Electoral College was assembled as quickly as possible, and on February 4, 1789, Washington, as expected, was elected unanimously—the only President to receive that honor. The only disagreement involved the race for Vice-President, which was won by John Adams of Massachusetts against token opposition.

First Term: April 30, 1789 . . .
Washington's inauguration had to be postponed until Congress had time to assemble in New York, the capital city, and as the day

drew near, the joyous mood of the citizens began to approach hysteria. When Washington finally appeared on the morning of the ceremony, crossing New York harbor in a ceremonial barge, the town's citizens and thousands of visitors cheered wildly and tirelessly. The general looked majestic, calm, and tall, dressed in brown broadcloth and white silk stockings, with his dress sword at his side. His suit had been made in America—a gesture intended to boost New England's infant textile industry.

The oath of office was administered on the balcony of the Senate Chamber at Federal Hall by Robert Livingston, chancellor of New York State. According to one newspaper account, the new President repeated the oath with such "devout fervency" that many members of the huge crowd were in tears. After he had finished, Washington bowed to kiss the Bible. Then Chancellor Livingston said, "It is done," and shouted out, "Long live George Washington, President of the U.S.!" The crowd repeated the cry, as cannonfire and bell-ringing rolled out across the city.

Election: 1792 . . . Washington was in poor health and desperately wanted to retire after his 1st term, but political leaders of every faction united in begging him to stay on. The newly forged union of the States was still fragile, and it was widely believed that without Washington as a unifying symbol, the Government would break apart in partisan and sectional bitterness. Jefferson and Hamilton, though they agreed on little else, both considered Washington's reelection a national necessity. Even Vice-President Adams, who was eaten with envy and in line for the top office himself, privately conceded that Washington had to be drafted again. Under these circumstances, the President could hardly refuse to subject himself to a 2nd term, though, as he expected, that term was characterized by mounting partisan frenzy and vicious personal attacks against the Chief Executive. On February 13, 1793, Congress officially tabulated the votes of the election of 1792 and found, to the surprise of absolutely no one, that Washington had once more been unanimously elected.

Second Term: March 4, 1793 . . .
The seat of Government had been moved from New York to Philadelphia in 1790, and Washington took his 2nd oath of office in the Senate Chamber of Philadelphia's Federal Hall. His inaugural address—only 135 words—was the shortest in history.

During Washington's 2 terms a total of 409 bills were passed by Congress, 2 of which were vetoed by the President. The 1st veto in U.S. history (April, 1792) concerned a bill reapportioning the House of Representatives according to the 1790 census. Washington vetoed the measure on constitutional grounds: He believed that it provided for a greater number of representatives than were permitted by the Constitution. A majority of the House actually voted to override the President on this issue, but supporters of the bill fell short of the necessary ⅔. The 2nd veto in our history involved a congressional attempt to trim defense spending. Congress had voted to reduce the number of cavalry units in the Army, but Washington insisted that such a move would dangerously weaken U.S. military strength. He was able to persuade a majority of congressmen to support his position and to sustain his veto.

His 7 Years, 308 days as President

PRO

With his enormous prestige as a leader and his considerable political skill, Washington managed to keep 13 quarreling States together for 8 difficult years. During most of his 2 terms, he managed to work successfully with representatives of every political faction. Placing himself deliberately above party and sectional divisions, he focused the aspirations of all citizens on the office of the President. In his key role as the setter of precedent, he managed to strike the perfect balance: He was neither a dictator, nor a cipher, but the strong republican leader that the times—and constitutional balance—demanded.

CON

Washington was unduly obsessed with presidential prerogatives and the dignity of his office; his insistence on bowing rather than shaking hands with his visitors is only one example of his pompous, aristocratic approach to the office.

PRO

Although he carefully weighed advice from all his advisers, Washington wisely followed Alexander Hamilton's economic policies, thereby establishing the U.S. Government as a going concern. Under Washington, financial chaos gave way to a thriving, national economy that ultimately benefited all citizens and strengthened the nation as a whole.

CON

The Hamiltonian policies favored by Washington emphasized special benefits for the rich and well-born, while ordinary farmers and artisans were left to fend for themselves. While Washington made a great show of impartiality at his frequently bitter Cabinet meetings, he almost always sided with the devious Hamilton, a special favorite adopted by Washington as a sort of foster son.

PRO

When the farmers of western Pennsylvania took up arms to protest the Federal excise tax in the Whiskey Rebellion, Washington moved effectively to establish the authority of the new Government. His swift and decisive action prevented the uprising from growing to dangerous proportions. His eventual amnesty for all leaders of the rebellion prevented the incident from leaving lasting scars.

CON

Washington's handling of the Whiskey Rebellion was a gross overreaction. His mobilization of an elaborate army of 15,000 men to subdue a mere handful of frontier rioters was an unnecessary show of force that reflects the basically authoritarian side of Washington's nature. The image of Washington and Hamilton, marching personally at the head of this huge army in their glorious effort to quell the hapless Whiskey Boys is ludicrous, to say the least.

PRO

Washington's policy of neutrality in the conflict that was emerging between England and revolutionary France was exactly what was called for under the circumstances. While hotheads demanded American moves in favor of France and against the hated mother country, Washington successfully avoided a war that would probably have meant the end of the independent republic. In negotiating a treaty with England, Washington won some significant concessions that helped protect Americans on the frontier from attack by the Indians and the British.

CON

"Jay's Treaty," Washington's opponents asserted, was little more than a thinly disguised sellout to Great Britain. Not only did Washington fail to lend support to the new republican forces in France, but gradually allowed U.S. policy to drift in a pro-British direction. In his horror at the people's revolution in France, he showed his lack of sympathy for true revolutionary principles and his conservative, oligarchical preferences.

AFTER THE PRESIDENCY

In 1797, at age 65, Washington attended the inauguration of his successor, John Adams, and then at long last retired to Mount Vernon. His peace lasted for only a year, however. In the summer of 1798, as war with France threatened, President Adams asked General Washington to take over once more as commander-in-chief of the American armies. Washington accepted, but fortunately the war was averted and he never had to assume active duty. At Mount Vernon, Washington genuinely enjoyed the routine of plantation life. Like many of the Virginia founding fathers, he deplored slavery even while he owned hundreds of slaves, but unlike many of the others, Washington did something to limit his hypocrisy. He made it a policy never to sell one of his slaves to another master, and so always had on hand far more blacks than were needed to do the work at Mount Vernon. In his will, Washington provided that all of his 300 slaves—not just special favorites—should be permanently freed. In 1799, the aging Washington jokingly assured

his friends that he would not die until he had ushered in the new century. On December 14 he passed away, just 18 days too early to keep his promise.

PSYCHOHISTORY

Mary Washington, hardly the perfect American mother depicted in schoolboy biographies, was a bad-tempered shrew who largely succeeded in her efforts to make George's young life miserable. All of her children got away from her as soon as they could, and George was no exception. As her son advanced in the world, she openly resented his success, claiming that he thoughtlessly neglected her. She refused to participate in any ceremony honoring him (including his inauguration as President) and deprecated his achievements. Emerging from this background, it is not surprising that Washington fell head-over-heels for a succession of young ladies, in hopes of winning the love and admiration he had been denied at home. Frustrated in love, and particularly in his hopeless passion for Sally Fairfax, Washington was similarly disappointed in the early stages of his military career. His father had died when George was a boy, and it was only natural that the shy, socially insecure youth should turn to warfare as a means of establishing his own manhood. But his 1st combat experience, when he was 22, was an ill-managed fiasco for which young Colonel Washington was held personally responsible. It may be assumed that all of these youthful disasters contributed to the celebrated patience and perseverance that were among Washington's most notable features in later life. He had learned that the only way to cope successfully with his environment was to gain rigid command of his own passionate nature. Even as a schoolboy, Washington had begun his lifelong drive for self-mastery, as he laboriously copied over more than 100 rules of "proper behavior for a *Gentleman*"—including admonitions not to pick teeth at the table or to stand too close to other people during conversation "for fear of bedewing their faces with spittle." Few observers noting Washington's glacial calm later in life would have suspected that it was the product of a conscious effort; hence their surprise at his occasional outbursts of temper. Yet the painter Gilbert Stuart, who spent countless hours with Washington while executing his numerous portraits, detected the emotional nature that lay behind the dignified façade. "All his features were indicative of the most ungovernable passions," Stuart wrote, "and had he been born in the forests, it is my opinion that he would have been the fiercest man among the savage tribes." It was Washington's willful mastery of that savage temperament, and his ability to cope with hardship and defeat, that gave him his remarkable power as a leader of men.

LITTLE-KNOWN FACTS

—Washington's experiences as a young man made it seem unlikely that he would ever live long enough to achieve greatness. He suffered from malaria, smallpox, pleurisy, and dysentery, all before he was 30. On his way back from the famous expedition to the French Fort le Boeuf, he fell off his raft in an icy river and nearly drowned. Later in the same trip he was shot at (and missed) by an Indian standing less than 50′ away. In Braddock's Defeat in 1755, 4 bullets punctured Washington's coat and 2 horses were shot out from under him, but the young officer somehow emerged unscathed.

—In 1755, in the midst of an election campaign for seats in the Virginia assembly, 23-year-old Colonel Washington said something insulting to a hot-tempered little fellow named Payne, who promptly knocked him down with a hickory stick. Soldiers rushed up to avenge Washington, who got to his feet just in time to tell them that he could take care of himself, thank you. The next day he wrote Payne a letter requesting an interview at a tavern. When Payne arrived, he naturally expected a demand for an apology and a challenge to a duel. Instead, Washington apologized for the insult that had provoked the blow, hoped that Payne was satisfied, and then generously offered his hand.

—Admiring biographers make much of the fact that Washington turned down a salary from the Continental Congress and asked instead that he be paid only for his expenses as commander-in-chief. As it turns out, the general made a sound financial decision. If he had accepted the salary ($500 a month) he would have received a total of $48,000 for his service. As it was, his expense account during 8 years of war came to $447,220, according to the smallest estimate. Included in this total were sums for a new carriage, expensive saddles, and imported wines for his headquarters.

—When the capital was moved from New York to Philadelphia, Washington, who had been disappointed in the food that he had been eating as President, brought his black slave Hercules from Mount Vernon to serve as cook. Pennsylvania law provided that slaves be given their freedom after 6 months' residence in the State. To avoid the possibility of losing the services of his master chef, Washington would send Hercules back to Mount Vernon just before the 6 months were up. Then, several weeks later, he would have him returned to the capital. Hercules, who soon won a reputation in Philadelphia as a flashy and colorful dresser, was much too smart to stand this arrangement for long. One night before the end of Washington's term he disappeared and much to the President's disappointment was never heard from again.

—One of the most seriously misleading of the Washington legends is the story of the pious general kneeling in prayer in the snow at Valley Forge. Not only is there no evidence to support this tale, but Washington was notorious in his parish church for his refusal to kneel at any of the customary moments in the Episcopal service. As his minister declared disapprovingly after the President's death, "Washington was a Deist." Although Martha was a devout churchwoman, George never shared her enthusiasm. On communion Sundays he always walked out before taking the eucharist, leaving Martha to participate in the service alone.

—Like many another farmer, Washington looked on with amused interest at the mating habits of his domestic animals. One creature in particular delighted him: a prize jackass, presented to him by the King of Spain and named by Washington *Royal Gift*. In a letter to Lafayette, Washington commented, "The Jack I have already received from Spain in appearance is fine, but his late Royal master, tho' past his grand climacteric, cannot be less moved by female allurements than he is; or when prompted can proceed with more deliberation and majestic solemnity to the matter of procreation." In a similar vein, Washington later wrote to a neighbor who patronized the Mount Vernon stud farm: "Particular attention should be paid to the mares which your servant brought, and when my Jack is in humour, they shall derive all the benefits of his labor, for labor it appears to be.

Quotes from Washington:

"I long ago despaired of any other reward for my services than the satisfaction arising from a consciousness of doing my duty, and from the esteem of my friends."

"I have heard the bullets whistle, and, believe me, there is something charming in the sound."—1754

"I am embarked on a wide ocean, boundless in its prospect and in which, perhaps, no safe harbor is to be found."—1775, shortly after his appointment as commander-in-chief

"My movements to the chair of Government will be accompanied by feelings not unlike those of a culprit who is going to the place of his execution."—1789

"How pitiful in the eyes of reason is that false ambition which desolates the world with fire and sword for the purposes of conquest and fame, when compared to the milder virtues of making our neighbors and our fellow men as happy as their frail conditions and perishable natures permit them to be."—1794

Quotes about Him:

"He is next only to the divinity."—Lord Byron

"As to you, sir, treacherous in private friendship and a hypocrite in public life, the world will be puzzled to decide whether you are an apostate or an imposter, whether you have abandoned good principles, or whether you ever had any."—Thomas Paine

"Never had I beheld so superb a man!"—Lafayette

"He is too illiterate, unread, unlearned for his station and reputation."—John Adams

"His mind was slow in operation but sure in conclusion. . . . Hearing all suggestions, he selected whatever was best, but was slow in readjustment."—Thomas Jefferson

"He has a dignity which forbids familiarity, mixed with an easy affability which creates love and reverence."—Abigail Adams

"I have been told that he preserves in battle the character of humanity which makes him so dear to his soldiers in camp."—Marquis de Barbe-Marbois, French staff officer

"Washington is the last person you'd ever suspect of having been a young man."—Samuel Eliot Morison

"A life without a stain, a fame without a flaw."—William Makepeace Thackeray

"He had no nakedness, but was born with clothes on, and his hair powdered, and made a stately bow on his 1st appearance in the world."—Nathaniel Hawthorne

"Washington was the one truly 'indispensable man.' With his towering prestige, unfaltering leadership, and sterling character, he was perhaps the only man in the history of the presidency bigger than the Government itself. . . . Although his every move could be deemed a potential precedent binding generations unborn, his foot did not slip once. He made no major mistakes—something that cannot be said of any of his successors. . . . If we must rank Presidents, Washington, in my judgment, deserves the place at the very top."—Historian Thomas A. Bailey, in *Presidential Greatness,* 1966

"He is the purest figure in history."—Gladstone

16th President   ABRAHAM LINCOLN

VITAL STATISTICS

Born: February 12, 1809, in a log cabin on Sinking Spring Farm, near Hodgenville, Ky. His birthplace has been enclosed in a marble memorial building and is open to the public. Admission: free. A more worthy object for a Lincoln pilgrimage—and perhaps the most interesting of the many shrines and historic sites dedicated to Lincoln's memory—is his home at 430 South 8th Street, in Springfield, Ill. The only house that Lincoln ever owned (the family lived there from 1844 to 1860), it is filled with authentic furniture and other memorabilia. Open to the public daily except Thanksgiving, Christmas, and New Year's Day. Admission: free.

Died: April 15, 1865, the morning after he was shot in the head while attending a play at Ford's Theatre in Washington, D.C. Lincoln was 56 years old. He was the 1st of 4 American Presidents to be assassinated. He was buried in Oak Ridge Cemetery in Springfield, where his body remains at rest, despite the efforts of a pair of thieves to break into the tomb in 1876, steal Lincoln's remains, and hold them for $200,000 ransom. The plot was uncovered by a Pinkerton detective, and the grave robbers were caught red-handed, tried, and sentenced to a year in prison.

BEFORE THE PRESIDENCY

Career: The son of a poor frontier farmer, Lincoln moved with his family from Kentucky to Indiana to Illinois. After several years working as an itinerant laborer, he moved on his own to the village of New Salem, Ill., where he got a job as clerk in the general store. Though he had attended school for a total of less than one year, Lincoln was passionately interested in politics, and made speeches on political subjects to anyone who would listen. In 1832, after he had been in New Salem less than a year, Lincoln decided to run for the State legislature. He was 23 years old, and from this time until his death—with the single exception of a 5-year period during which discouraging political prospects forced him into the full-time practice of law—Lincoln was busy as an office seeker or an officeholder. In April of 1832, Lincoln decided to help his campaign by volunteering to fight Indians in the Black Hawk War. Though he was elected captain of a company of local volunteers, he never saw battle and the voters in his district were unimpressed: Lincoln finished 8th in a field of 13 candidates. Nevertheless, his political prominence helped win him a job as postmaster, and then as deputy county surveyor, and in 1834, Lincoln was elected to the legislature on his 2nd try. During his 4 terms in the Illinois assembly, Lincoln emerged as the Whig floor leader and a skillful and hardworking party organizer. In 1846 he was rewarded with the Whig nomination for Congress, under the condition that he step aside after a single term to make way for other deserving party workers. In Washington, Congressman Lincoln introduced a major bill that would have abolished slavery in the District of

Columbia, and gained some national attention for his spirited opposition to the "immoral and unnecessary" Mexican War. This stand cost him his popularity at home, and though he campaigned vigorously for Zachary Taylor and the Whig ticket in 1848, he was denied the political plum that he desired: appointment as commissioner of the General Land Office. Bitterly disappointed, Lincoln retired to private law practice back home in Illinois. A remarkable courtroom performer with a knack for swaying juries, Lincoln used his legal talents in behalf of some major corporate clients (like the Illinois Central Railroad) as well as in a variety of criminal cases. Though in nominal retirement, Lincoln remained in the thick of behind-the-scenes political activity. As his law partner William Herndon later observed: "It was in the world of politics that he lived. Politics were his life, newspapers his food, and his great ambition his motive power."

Personal Life: Young Lincoln was often uneasy around women, but he was never embarrassed about sex. In the all-male world of frontier politics he had a reputation for salty humor, and he once made a special point of asking a New Salem neighbor for permission to watch his stud bull in action. By the time the young legislator had settled permanently in Springfield, the new State capital, he had already been disappointed in his courtship of a well-to-do girl named Mary Owens and he may have also experienced other romantic involvements, though historical evidence remains unclear. Finally, at the age of 31 he met Mary Todd, the plump, pretty, sophisticated daughter of one of the leading families of Kentucky. Miss Todd, a brilliant conversationalist and a notorious flirt, was staying in Springfield with her sister, who had married the son of the Illinois governor. Deeply interested in politics, Mary entertained a host of suitors from the political world, apparently including Stephen A. Douglas, later senator from Illinois and Lincoln's arch-rival. She and Lincoln soon became engaged, though Lincoln broke off this 1st engagement because of his fears that he would not be able to earn enough money to support a wife. Amid considerable emotional turmoil, Lincoln's health began to suffer and he attended to his legislative duties with less enthusiasm than usual. His depression ended when he and Mary were married after all on November 4, 1842. In less than a year, their 1st son was born and 3 more boys had arrived by 1853. The demands placed upon a typical 19th-century wife and mother often proved too much for Mary Lincoln's high-strung personality—on those occasions she exploded in violent bursts of temper (once chasing Lincoln from the house with a butcher knife) and suffered from migraine headaches. The main source of the diffi-

culty between Lincoln and his wife seems to have been the many hours he spent away from home in pursuit of his political goals. Despite such difficulties, the marriage survived. According to James Gourley, the Lincolns' back-door neighbor in Springfield for many years, "Whenever Mrs. L got the devil in her, Lincoln would pick up one of his children and walk off—would laugh at her—pay no earthly attention to her when in that wild furious condition." Mary's burdens were only intensified when her 2nd son, Edward, died at the age of 4. Her greatest suffering, however, did not come until after Lincoln had entered the White House. Mary, who attempted to dazzle the capital city, was widely criticized for her expensive clothing and lavish entertainments in the midst of the Civil War. She was also accused of being a Confederate spy, since she had a brother, 3 half-brothers, and 3 brothers-in-law serving in Confederate uniform. When her 3rd son, Willie, died in 1862 her sanity was seriously compromised. She began reporting nightly "visitations" from her 2 dead sons. She ran up a debt of $27,000 for new clothes without telling her husband, buying more than 300 pairs of gloves in just 4 months. Most embarrassing of all, she berated the President in public for his alleged "attentions" to other women. Generally, Lincoln sighed and tried to soothe her, calling her "Mother"; for years they had been held together by their doting, indulgent attitude toward their children. After the assassination, Mary was hysterical for months and finally her son Robert asked for a hearing to determine her sanity. In 1875, she was formally committed to an institution for the insane. She was released after 4 months, and died in 1882 at the age of 63. Only one of Lincoln's 4 sons survived adolescence: Robert Todd Lincoln, who served as Secretary of War under President Garfield.

On the Way to the White House: In 1854, Illinois senator Stephen Douglas pushed his controversial Kansas-Nebraska bill through Congress. In effect, this legislation allowed slavery in newly opened territories, and public opinion in the North was outraged. This agitation, which was particularly strong in Douglas's home State of Illinois, left Lincoln, with his long-standing hostility to slavery, in an excellent position to make a political comeback. He was quickly returned to the Illinois State legislature as an outspoken opponent of the expansion of slavery, and in 1855 he was narrowly defeated as a candidate for the U.S. Senate. Lincoln remained loyal to his old party ties down to the last moment, but as the Whigs collapsed as an effective political party, Lincoln threw in his lot with the newly emerging antislavery Republicans. In 1858, the Republicans named Lincoln as their nominee for the Senate to oppose Stephen Douglas. Because of Douglas's prominence (he was universally recognized as the front-runner for the Democratic presidential nomination in 1860) this Senate contest received intensive national publicity. Lincoln was ready to make the most of his opportunity—he challenged his well-known opponent to a series of debates, and the 2 men met 7 times in various Illinois towns. In these justly celebrated debates, they spoke (without a microphone, of course) to crowds of up to 15,000 and explored the issues with a depth and seriousness unknown in any of our modern televised "debates." Douglas, an aggressive, pugnacious battler who at 5'4" was widely known as "The Little Giant" or "The Steam Engine in Britches," was perhaps a better platform orator than Lincoln, though Lincoln, with his rare gift for reasoning with an audience and his ability to explain even complex questions in simple, logical terms, was able to demolish the arguments of his opponent. Central to Lincoln's position was the contention that slavery was not only unjust, but a threat to free workers; if allowed to spread unchecked, it might reduce all laborers, white as well as black, to a state of virtual slavery. Lincoln's solution was to leave slavery alone where it already existed (while hoping that it would ultimately disappear) but to move decisively to prevent its spread into any unsettled (or previously free) territories. In the final balloting, Lincoln actually outpolled Douglas, though the Democrats had gerrymandered the State legislative districts so skillfully that "The Little Giant" was nonetheless returned to the Senate. Though exhausted from his campaign, and disappointed at the outcome, Lincoln emerged from his defeat with political prospects brighter than ever. His battle with Douglas had made him a national hero to antislavery forces. While publicly denying that he was qualified for the Presidency, Lincoln departed on an extended speaking tour of the Midwest and Northeast, designed to advertise his "availability." As the Republican convention of 1860 approached, party leaders in ever-increasing numbers began taking a serious look at "Honest Abe" of Illinois. As Republican chieftain Jesse Fell saw the situation in 1858: "What the Republican party wants, to insure success in 1860, is a man of popular origin, of acknowledged ability, committed against slavery aggressions, who has no record to defend, and no radicalism of an offensive character." Abraham Lincoln fit the bill perfectly.

His Person: "If any personal description of me is thought desirable," wrote Lincoln in 1860, "it may be said I am, in height, 6'4", nearly; lean in flesh, weighing on an average 180 lbs.; dark complexion, with coarse black hair and gray eyes." It might be added that his nose was prominent and slightly askew, his heavy eyebrows overhung deep eye-caverns in which his eyes—sometimes dreamy, sometimes penetrating—were set. His cheekbones were high, his mouth wide, his lips thick. On the right cheek a solitary mole stood out. His skin was wrinkled and dry, giving him a leathery, weather-beaten look. He had projecting—some said flapping—ears. His remarkable face never failed to make a powerful impression. As a London *Times* correspondent observed: "It would not be possible for the most indifferent observer to pass him in the street without notice." According to contemporaries, photographs were totally incapable of capturing the animation and power in his face. Because of the primitive techniques of the time, Lincoln was forced to pose rigidly before the camera, which gave him an awkward, ungainly appearance. Physically, Lincoln remained until the end of his life a remarkably strong man—even at 50, he was powerful enough to lift a long-handled axe with one hand and hold it straight out in front of him at the level of his shoulders. A young man who was hired to give Lincoln a bath and rubdown before his debate with Douglas in Galesburg, Ill., described the 49-year-old senatorial candidate as "the most powerful man I ever saw." Clean-shaven until his 51st year, Lincoln began to grow a beard shortly after his election to the Presidency at the suggestion of an 11-year-old girl who told him that with whiskers he would "look a great deal better for your face is so thin." Lincoln never used alcohol or tobacco, and though fond of telling lengthy anecdotes featuring barnyard humor, he always avoided profanity; during Lincoln's Presidency the strongest expletive used in the White House was "By Jingo!" Despite movie and TV portrayals that offer us a Lincoln with a resonant bass voice, the actual historical Lincoln spoke in a piercing, high-pitched tenor; his shrill voice carried for many hundred yards and was considered perfect for the open-air stump-speaking of the day.

PRESIDENCY

Nomination: May 16, 1860 . . .

As the Republican national convention assembled in Chicago, the likely presidential nominee was William H. Seward, the senator from New York. For more than a quarter of a century Seward had been the universally acknowledged leader of national Free-Soil forces, but his opposition to slavery was considered too radical for him to carry the key "doubtful" States of Pennsylvania, New Jersey, Indiana, and Illinois. During the opening days of the convention, worried party leaders searched desperately for a more moderate alternative to head off the Seward bandwagon. Lincoln, who had won solid favorite-son support from Illinois, was one of several possibilities. His cause was helped enormously by the fact that the convention was held in his home State. His managers were able to pack the galleries with leather-lunged Lincoln supporters, using forged convention passes and other dubious means, while nearly a thousand Seward supporters were shut out of the hall. On the 1st ballot, Seward polled 173 delegate votes (far short of the 233 needed to nominate) with Lincoln making a surprisingly strong showing with 102 votes. On the 2nd ballot, with most of the anti-Seward forces rallying to his banner, Lincoln drew even with the New Yorker, and on the 3rd ballot, amid hysterical cheering from the galleries, "Honest Old Abe" was nominated. One of the key factors in his success was the willingness of his managers to negotiate deals with rival leaders in the moderate wing of the party. Lincoln had sent a telegram to his headquarters, ordering "Make no contracts that will bind me," but his campaign manager swept it aside with a curt "Lincoln ain't here and don't know what we have to meet!"

Along with receiving the Republican nomination, Lincoln entered the general election battle with one of the most successful publicity devices in the history of American politics—the image of being the hardfisted rail-splitter. At a Republican meeting in Illinois, Lincoln's cousin John Hanks had appeared with 2 fence rails labeled "Two Rails from a lot made by Abraham Lincoln and John Hanks in the Sangamon Bottom in the year 1830." With his usual candor, Lincoln confessed that he had no idea whether he'd split these particular rails, but he was sure he had actually split rails every bit as good. The time soon came when Lincoln's son Tad would say: "Everybody in this world knows Pa used to split rails."

Election: November 6, 1860 . . .

Even before the general election campaign was fairly under way, Lincoln's victory was a foregone conclusion. The Democratic party was hopelessly split. When Northern Democrats persisted in their intention to nominate Stephen Douglas, the Southern proslavery wing of the party, which distrusted Douglas because of his equivocal position, pulled out to nominate their own candidate: Vice-President John C. Breckinridge of Kentucky. The situation was further complicated by the presence of a 4th party—the Constitutional Unionists, represented by a distinguished ticket featuring John Bell of Tennessee and Edward Everett of Massachusetts. The Bell campaign was a last forlorn attempt to breath new life into the remnants of the old Whig party, and to avoid civil war by a renewed drive for sectional compromise. Except for the nervous border States, which seemed to have the most to lose from sectional conflict, the Constitutional Union party attracted little support. Throughout the campaign, Southerners announced that if Lincoln were elected they would secede from the Union, even while their continued support for Breckinridge made Lincoln's victory inevitable.

The final outcome of this 4-way contest offered few surprises. Lincoln won with only 39.8% of the vote (1,865,593), but carried all 18 of the Northern States for an electoral vote of 180, a comfortable majority.

Douglas finished 2nd in the popular balloting with 29.5% (1,382,713) but despite his vigorous campaign, he carried only Missouri and 3 out of 7 New Jersey electors, for a total of 12 electoral votes.

Breckinridge swept the Solid South for 72 electoral votes, but won only 18% of the popular vote; Bell carried Tennessee, Kentucky, and Virginia for a total of 39 electoral votes, and only 12.6% of the national popular ballots.

As soon as Lincoln was formally elected, the South began to make good on its promises to secede, as South Carolina led the other Southern States out of the Union.

First Term: March 4, 1861 . . .

The mood of the capital was tense as Lincoln was sworn in by Chief Justice Roger B. Taney. Seven Southern States had already seceded from the Union and for the 1st time the new President's military escort was used as much for protection as for show. In his inaugural address, Lincoln assured the Southerners: "The Government will not assail you. You have no conflict without being yourselves the aggressors." Within 5 weeks, he had expertly manipulated the situation of South Carolina's Fort Sumter so as to trap the Confederacy into firing the 1st shots of the Civil War. Northern public opinion, which had been bitterly divided before the attack on Sumter, was immediately crystallized behind Lincoln's "War for the Union."

Reelection: As the election of 1864 approached, Lincoln, like most other political experts, considered his chances for reelection to be slim indeed. The North was weary of the bloodiest war in American history, and Radicals in Lincoln's own party were impatient with the President's moderate approach to the abolition of slavery. For several months, Radical leaders talked of dumping Lincoln from the ticket and replacing him with Secretary of the Treasury Salmon P. Chase, but using his control of Federal patronage, Lincoln moved swiftly and ruthlessly to crush the threatened revolt. Nevertheless, a number of antislavery activists left the Republican ranks to nominate Gen. John C. Frémont as a 3rd party candidate. As the election approached, Lincoln's agents met with Frémont and his supporters and an agreement was reached: The President would support a constitutional amendment ending slavery in all States forever (a position that Lincoln seemed willing to take anyway), if Frémont would withdraw from the race.

This still left the Democrats to deal with in the final elections in the fall. In nominating Gen. George B. McClellan (a former commander of the Union armies who had been removed by Lincoln) the Democrats achieved the best of both worlds: a war hero as presidential candidate along with a peace-at-any-price platform. The key factor in the contest was the shifting tide of war. By November, 1864, the Confederacy was already in its death throes and the Union forces scored impressive victories. Nevertheless, Lincoln wasn't going to take any chances. He personally coined that redoubtable political slogan "Don't swap horses while crossing a stream" and issued orders to his generals to send major detachments of troops home to vote, thereby protecting slim Republican margins in several key States.

Lincoln swamped McClellan in the Electoral College 212 to 21, but the popular vote was much closer with 2,206,938 for Lincoln and 1,803,787 for McClellan.

Second Term: March 4, 1865 . . .

Lincoln was sworn in by the newly appointed Chief Justice Salmon P. Chase—the same man who had briefly opposed Lincoln's renomination. Despite wartime security measures, the atmosphere was optimistic, almost festive, with the long sectional struggle drawing to a close. At the inaugural ball Mrs. Lincoln horrified observers with her white silk-and-lace dress complete with headdress, an ensemble that cost the then unheard-of sum of $2,000. In his inaugural address Lincoln invited the Southerners to rejoin the Union and pledged a policy of "malice toward none, and charity for all." Six weeks later the war was over and Lincoln was dead.

Assassination: April 14, 1865 . . .

Initially John Wilkes Booth, a well-known actor and Confederate sympathizer who was plagued with guilt feelings for not having fought in the war, had organized a conspiracy to kidnap President Lincoln. The idea was to hold Lincoln captive until the Northern Government agreed to recognize the Confederacy, but after Lee's surrender at Appomattox the focus of the plot was shifted to murder. While Booth shot Lincoln in the back of the head during a performance at Ford's Theatre (where Lincoln had gone to help celebrate the end of the War) Booth's cohort Lewis Powell savagely attacked Secretary of State Seward, stabbing him severely while Seward lay in bed recovering from a carriage accident. Another conspirator was supposed to kill Vice-President Johnson, but he lost his nerve at the last moment. Booth was injured during his escape, and was soon intercepted by Federal troops. As he was dragged, mortally wounded, from a burning barn in Virginia, his last words were, "Useless! Useless!"

The significance of the fact that Lincoln was shot on Good Friday was not lost on his religious contemporaries, who immediately began the Lincoln-Christ comparisons that have continued down to this day.

His 4 Years, 42 Days as President

PRO

In the critical period between his election as President and the attack on Fort Sumter, while lesser men desperately sought a compromise, Lincoln had the strength to say No. He refused to abandon the Republican platform or to retreat from his own stubborn opposition to the extension of slavery. While even antislavery "Radicals" like Seward talked of a plan that would allow slavery to spread to the unsettled areas of the Southwest, Lincoln had the moral vision to see that the time for compromise had passed.

CON

The proposed Crittenden Compromise would have at least postponed—and might have altogether avoided—the Civil War, and its failure was due primarily to Lincoln's stubborn inflexibility. His refusal to retreat was motivated as much by personal pride and concern for the survival of his party as by moral imperatives, and this refusal led to a war that cost 600,000 American lives. Despite his self-serving attempts to place all blame for the war on Southern shoulders, Lincoln himself must share the responsibility for bringing on the cataclysmic conflict.

PRO

As a war leader, Lincoln exercised the most effective and inspiring presidential leadership in our history. His strength, vision and consummate political skill steered a bitterly divided country successfully through the bloodiest war in its history. He dramatically expanded the powers of the Presidency to meet the needs of the moment. He showed a better grasp of overall strategy than any of his generals, and he had the courage to replace one general after another until he found the men he wanted. In dealing with Northern public opinion and the threat of European intervention on behalf of the Confederacy, Lincoln's moves were strong, decisive, and unerring.

CON

No President, either before or after, has shown so callous a disregard for civil liberties as Abraham Lincoln. He suspended the writ of habeas corpus and ordered the arbitrary arrest of more than 15,000 Northern civilians, often with little or no cause. In ordering the arrest of Congressman Clement Vallandigham, an antiwar Democrat, Lincoln perpetrated one of the most infamous acts of political repression in American history. Lincoln himself admitted that he would "follow forms of law *as far as convenient.*"

PRO

In steering a middle course between antislavery Radicals and Northern Conservatives on his handling of Southern slavery, Lincoln held the country together and managed to preserve the Union. He wisely ignored Radical demands for immediate emancipation, and thereby kept the key border States in the Union; if those States had joined the Confederacy, the South might very well have won the war. Lincoln's Emancipation Proclamation in 1862, was a perfectly timed, brilliantly conceived political masterstroke that helped to rally the Northern people and to prevent European recognition of the Confederacy. Though the celebrated Proclamation actually freed few slaves, Lincoln deserves his title of "Great Emancipator" for his support for the 13th Amendment, which abolished slavery forever throughout the U.S.; he had already successfully steered the amendment through Congress by the time he died. Though preserving the Union always remained his primary goal, Lincoln never lost sight of his secondary desire to end a slave system which he had always opposed as a grave moral wrong.

CON

Lincoln's 1st actions relating to slavery were his moves to countermand the orders of 2 abolitionist generals who had freed slaves in some Union-occupied territory; Lincoln considered public opinion in the wavering border States to be more important than the continued enslavement of several hundred thousand human beings! Never a believer in true racial equality, Lincoln moved to free the slaves only after the overwhelming majority of his party had demanded it. Unlike the so-called "Radical" Republicans, Lincoln never considered the possibility that the freed Negroes might some day function as full-fledged American citizens; Lincoln favored colonization in Central America as the "final solution" to the Negro problem.

PRO

Lincoln was more than a great President; he was a great man. He was not corrupted by power, he was deepened and saddened by it. He never lost sight of the human consequences of his actions. His utter lack of personal malice toward even his most bitter opponents is unique in the annals of political history. He demonstrated time and again the qualities of patience, forbearance, and understanding, while his enormous intellectual power enabled him to inspire the nation with the most sublime prose ever written or spoken by an American President. Lincoln was probably the most accessible of all our Chief Executives, and spent hours each day meeting with ordinary citizens in what he called "his public opinion baths." His moderate and sensible plans for Reconstruction, protecting the rights of both blacks and whites in the South, might have avoided much of the bitterness and suffering of the postwar era; it was a supreme tragedy for the nation that Lincoln did not live to carry them out.

CON

Though it is easy to recognize qualities of greatness in Lincoln the man, this says nothing for Lincoln the politician who time and again chose expediency over principle. Nor does it atone for his record as a sloppy administrator, who was often unable to manage either Congress or his own Cabinet. It was only Lincoln's timely assassination that assured his place in history; he has been deified because of the tragic nature of his death, rather than for the accomplishments of his life. If he had lived to carry out his plans for Reconstruction, his name would be obscured today by the same cloud of partisan bickering that has blighted the memory of his successor, Andrew Johnson.

PSYCHOHISTORY

Lincoln began life with a strong sense of his own inferiority. His mother, Nancy Hanks Lincoln, was an illegitimate child, and young Lincoln was painfully aware of the fact. This circumstance, combined with the bitter poverty of his own youth, produced a desperate desire to excel, to win what Lincoln called "the race of life." When the young man found out that he could often outtalk and outthink even well-educated aristocrats, this desire became a burning passion. His friend and law partner Herndon aptly described Lincoln as "a man totally swallowed up in his ambitions." Yet even in his vigorous pursuit of political success, Lincoln's personal impulses remained unfailingly generous, decent, and human. As a young man, he was considered "soft" and sentimental by frontier standards; on one notable occasion he risked a punishing brawl when he stopped a gang of boys who were torturing a tortoise with burning sticks. It is likely that the hard-boiled Thomas Lincoln felt some contempt for his oldest son's love for storytelling, poetry, and books, and it is certain that there was lasting bad blood between the 2 men. In 1851 when his father lay dying, Lincoln refused a request that he come to the sickbed, and also failed to attend the funeral. This isolation from those closest to him —begun with the death of Lincoln's mother when the boy was only 9—became a lifelong habit. In later life, Lincoln's extended periods of unbroken silence, and his recurrent melancholy, often drove his wife Mary to the point of fury. As Lincoln's friend and campaign manager David Davis observed: "I knew the man so well; he was the most reticent, secretive man I ever saw or expect to see." Finally, it must be said that a seemingly endless succession of personal tragedies gave Lincoln a deep sense of mortality and the ultimate futility of all human effort. At the age of 3½, young Abe watched his baby brother die; when he was 9 his mother passed away; when he was 18 his sister died. As a husband and father, Lincoln had to cope with his wife's near-insanity and the death of 2 of his sons. When his son Willie died at the age of 11 in 1862, the President wept uncontrollably. It is small wonder that he was haunted by visions in the last years of his life. "I have all my life been a fatalist," Lincoln wrote. "What is to be will be, or rather, I have found all my life as Hamlet says, 'There is a divinity that shapes our ends, Rough hew them how we will.' "

LITTLE-KNOWN FACTS

—Lincoln was never associated with any organized church, and as a young man in New Salem he had a reputation as an outspoken nonbeliever. Having read Thomas Paine, he liked to argue with friends against the tenets of conventional religion. In his 1846 congressional campaign, Lincoln's unorthodox position became a campaign issue, and he offered the only public statement of his career on his religious convictions:

That I am not a member of any Christian Church, is true; but I have never denied the truth of the Scriptures; and I have never spoken with intentional disrespect of religion in general or of any denomination of Christians in particular.

—In 1842, Lincoln accepted a challenge to a duel from James Shields, the Democratic State auditor. Shields was furious over a satiric letter in a local paper. Actually, the letter had been written by Lincoln's fiancée, Mary Todd, but Lincoln willingly took responsibility. Since he was given the choice of weapons, Lincoln, with typical cunning, selected broadswords—with his 6'4" frame and his enormous arms, Lincoln had an insurmountable advantage over his diminutive opponent when it came to dueling with swords. Shields wisely decided to make up his differences with Lincoln and the scheduled duel failed to take place.
—Lincoln was the only President ever to obtain a patent. In 1849 he invented a complicated device for lifting ships over dangerous shoals by means of "buoyant air chambers." Much to Lincoln's disappointment, U.S. Patent No. 6,469 was never put into practical use.
—The clutter in Lincoln's law office was notorious, and a continual source of irritation to his partner, William Herndon. On his desk,

Lincoln kept one envelope marked "When you can't find it anywhere else, look into this."
—Lincoln was the 1st major leader in our history to favor extending the vote to women. In 1836—a full 12 years before the 1st woman's rights convention had even convened—State legislator Lincoln gave an Illinois paper a statement endorsing "female suffrage."
—In 1858, Lincoln was so concerned that the text of his "House divided" speech be reported accurately, that even after he had given a copy of the address to reporters, he insisted on going to the newspaper office himself and proofreading the galleys.
—When an 1860 campaign document boasted that the self-educated Lincoln spent his spare time reading Plutarch, Honest Abe sat down immediately to validate the claim by reading the Lives for the 1st time.
—It is well known that Lincoln used to pace the White House long past midnight during the years of the Civil War; what is less celebrated is his habit of imposing his insomnia on his overworked aides. Often, he would keep his young personal secretary, John Hay, awake, listening to the funny stories that Lincoln loved to tell. ("Without these stories I would die," he once said.) On one occasion, according to Hay, "he read Shakespeare to me, the end of Henry VIII and the beginning of Richard III, till my heavy eyelids caught his considerate notice and he sent me to bed."
—Frederick Douglass, the celebrated black abolitionist and former slave, was invited by Lincoln to the inaugural reception in 1865, but when Douglass tried to enter, policemen manhandled him and forced him back out. Making his way in again, he managed to catch Lincoln's eye. "Here comes my friend Douglass," the President exclaimed, and, leaving his circle of guests, he took Douglass by the hand and began to chat with him.
—After the death of his son Willie, Lincoln was persuaded by his wife to participate in several séances held in the White House. The President was deeply interested in psychic phenomena and wanted to communicate with his dead son. Once Lincoln reported that he had attended a séance in which a piano was raised and moved around the room. It was the professional opinion of the mediums who had worked with him that Lincoln was definitely the possessor of extraordinary psychic powers.
—Once, shortly before his election to the Presidency, Lincoln reported that he was startled by a vision. As he lay down to rest, weary over a hard day of politics, he caught a glimpse of his face in a mirror—and was startled to see a double image of himself. The 2nd image in the mirror was pale, "like a dead man's." After a few days, when the same pair of images reappeared, he discussed the phenomenon with his

wife. She interpreted it to mean that Lincoln would be elected to 2 terms as President, but that he would die during his 2nd term.

—Lincoln took his dreams seriously. On one occasion he wrote to his wife to be watchful with their son Tad because Lincoln had experienced an "unpleasant" dream. On the day of his assassination, April 14, 1865, he was so troubled by a dream that he actually discussed it at a Cabinet meeting. He told his colleagues that he had seen himself sailing "in an indescribable vessel and moving rapidly toward an indistinct shore." Even more explicit was a dream that he discussed just a week before he was shot. In his dream, Lincoln awoke, and walked through the silent White House, following the sound of sobbing. When he came to the East Room, he saw a catafalque draped in black. "Who is dead?" Lincoln asked. A military guard replied that it was the President.

Quotes from Lincoln:

"I am rather inclined to silence and whether that be wise or not it is at least more unusual now-a-days to find a man who can hold his tongue than to find one who cannot."

"If slavery is not wrong, nothing is wrong."

"To sin by silence when they should protest makes cowards of men."

"The dogmas of the quiet past are inadequate to the stormy present. The occasion is piled high with difficulty, and we must rise with the occasion. As our case is new, so we must think anew and and act anew. We must disenthrall ourselves, and then we shall save our country."

"My policy is to have no policy."

"The pilots on our Western rivers steer from point to point as they call it—setting the course of the boat no farther than they can see—and that is all I propose to myself. . . . I am not going to cross 'Big Muddy' until I reach it."

"Republicans are for both the man and the dollar, but in case of conflict the man before the dollar."

"Men moving only in an official circle are apt to become merely official—not to say arbitrary—in their ideas, and are apter and apter with each passing day to forget that they only hold power in a representative capacity."

"I claim not to have controlled events, but confess plainly that events have controlled me."

"Public opinion in this country is everything."

"Men are not flattered by being shown that there has been a difference of purpose between the Almighty and them."

"Fellow Citizens, I presume you all know who I am. I am humble Abraham Lincoln. My politics are short and sweet like the old woman's dance. I am in favour of a national bank. I am in favour of the internal improvement system and a high protective tariff. If elected, I shall be thankful; if not, it will be all the same."—Lincoln's 1st campaign speech, New Salem, 1832

My childhood's home I see again
  And sadden with the view;
And still, as memory crowds my brain,
  There's pleasure in it too.
O Memory! Thou midway world
  Twixt earth and paradise,
Where things decayed and loved ones lost
  In dreamy shadows rise,
And, freed from all that's earthly vile,
  Seem hallowed, pure, and bright,
Like scenes in some enchanted isle
  All bathed in liquid light.
    —Poem by Lincoln, 1844, after
     revisiting, for the 1st and only
     time, the Indiana scenes of his
     boyhood

"A universal feeling, whether well or ill formed, cannot be safely disregarded."—1854

"As a nation, we began by declaring that 'all men are created equal.' We now practically read it 'All men are created equal, except Negroes.' When the Know-Nothings get control, it will read, 'all men are created equal, except Negroes, and foreigners, and Catholics.' When it comes to this I should prefer emigrating to some other country where they make no pretense of loving liberty—to Russia, for instance, where despotism can be taken pure, without the base alloy of hypocrisy."—1855

"I protest, now and forever, against that counterfeit logic which presumes because I do not want a Negro woman for a slave I do necessarily want her for a wife. My understanding is that I do not have to have her for either."—Debate with Douglas, 1858

"As I would not be a slave, so I would not be a master. This expresses my idea of democracy. Whatever differs from this, to the extent of the difference, is no democracy."—1858

"Fellow Citizens, we cannot escape history. We of this Congress and this administration will be remembered in spite of ourselves. The fiery trial through which we pass will light us down, in honor or dishonor, to the latest generation."—Message to Congress, 1861

"For my own part, I consider the 1st necessity that is upon us, is of proving that popular Government is not an absurdity."—1861

"My paramount object in this struggle is to save the Union, and it is not either to save or destroy slavery. If I could save the Union without freeing any slave I would do it, if I could save it by freeing all the slaves I would do it; and if I could save it by freeing some and leaving others alone I would also do that."—Summer, 1862

"Among free men there can be no successful appeal from the ballot to the bullet; and those who take such appeal are sure to lose their cause and pay the costs."—1863

"Fondly we do hope—fervently do we pray —that this mighty scourge of war speedily pass away."—2nd inaugural address, 1865

Quotes about Him:

"If you heard him fellin' trees in a clearin' you would say that there was 3 men at work by the way the trees fell."—Dennis Hanks, Lincoln's cousin

"He worked for me, but was always reading and thinking. I used to get mad at him for it. I say he was awful lazy. He would laugh and talk, crack jokes and tell stories all the time. He said to me that his father taught him to work but he never taught him to love it."— John Romaine

"He always told only enough of his plans and purposes to induce the belief that he had communicated all; yet he reserved enough to have communicated nothing."—Leonard Swett, Lincoln's friend and one of his campaign managers

"Anyone who thinks Lincoln calmly gathered his robes about him, waiting for the people to call him, has a very erroneous knowledge of Lincoln. He was always calculating and planning ahead."—William Herndon, Lincoln's law partner

"We know Old Abe does not look very handsome, but if all the ugly men in the U.S. vote for him, he will surely be elected."—Republican campaign propaganda, 1860

"Can you Republicans deny that this day and this hour your candidate, Abraham Lincoln, is the agent and attorney of the Illinois Central Railroad, making stump speeches on its money? Can you deny that he received from the company a single fee of $5,000 for procuring a decree releasing its property from taxation in McLean County, thus taking the side of the company against the people whose votes he is now seeking?"—Stephen A. Douglas, October 5, 1858

"He is a huckster in politics; a 1st-rate 2nd-rate man."—Abolitionist Wendell Phillips

"His was the greatest character since Christ." —Lincoln's personal secretary, John Hay

"My father's life was of a kind which gave me but little opportunity to learn the details of his early career. During my childhood and early youth he was almost constantly away from home, attending courts or making political speeches."—Robert Todd Lincoln

"Do you mean to say that she saw the President alone? Do you know that I never allow the President to see any woman alone?"— Mary Todd Lincoln, 1865

"In Washington the most striking thing is the absence of personal loyalty to the President. It does not exist. He has no admirers, no enthusiastic supporters, none to bet on his head."—Richard Henry Dana, 1862

"Our country owes all her troubles to him, and God simply made me the instrument of His punishment."—John Wilkes Booth

"Keenly aware of his role as the exemplar of the self-made man, he played the part with an intense and poignant consistency that gives his performance the quality of high art. The 1st author of the Lincoln legend and the greatest of the Lincoln dramatists was Lincoln himself." —Historian Richard Hofstadter

LINCOLN THE COMMUNIST

All political parties have claimed Lincoln as their property, and the American Communist party has been no exception. During the '30s and '40s the CP began holding Lincoln-Lenin rallies in February. This policy may not seem so absurd when one considers some of Lincoln's actual public statements:

"The strongest bond of human sympathy, outside of the family relation, should be one uniting all working people, of all nations, and tongues, and kindreds."

"Inasmuch as good things are produced by labor, it follows that all such things of right belong to those whose labor has produced them. But it has so happened, in all ages of the world, that some have labored and others have without labor enjoyed a large proportion of the fruits. This is wrong and should not continue. To secure to each laborer the whole product of his labor, or as nearly as possible, is a worthy object of any good government."

"Labor is prior to, and independent of, capital. Capital is only the fruit of labor and could never have existed if labor had not 1st existed."

"The legitimate object of government is to do for a community of people, whatever they need to have done, but cannot do for themselves in their separate and individual capacities."

WAS LINCOLN A RACIST?

"You and we are different races. We have between us a broader difference than exists between almost any other 2 races. Even when you cease to be slaves, you are yet far removed from being placed on an equality with the white race. You are cut off from many of the advantages which the other race enjoys. It is better for us both to be separated."—Abraham

Lincoln, during a meeting with free Negro leaders, at the White House, August, 1862

"I will say then that I am not, nor ever have been in favor of bringing about in any way the social and political equality of the white and black races—that I am not nor ever have been in favor of making voters or jurors of Negroes, nor of qualifying them to hold office, nor to intermarry with white people; and I will say in addition to this that there is a physical difference between the white and black races which I believe will forever forbid the 2 races living together on terms of social or political equality. And inasmuch as they cannot so live, while they do remain together there must be the position of superior and inferior, and I as much as any other man am in favor of having the superior position assigned to the white race. I say upon this occasion that I do not perceive that because the white man is to have the superior position that the Negro should be denied everything.

". . . Notwithstanding all this, there is no reason in the world why the Negro is not entitled to all the natural rights enumerated in the Declaration of Independence—the right to life, liberty and the pursuit of happiness. I hold that he is as much entitled to these as the white man. I agree with Judge Douglas he is not my equal in many respects—certainly not in color, perhaps not in moral or intellectual endowment. But in the right to eat the bread, without leave of anybody else, which his own hand earns, he is my equal, and the equal of Judge Douglas, and the equal of every living man."—Abraham Lincoln, debating with Douglas in Illinois, 1858

"In all my interviews with Mr. Lincoln I was impressed with his entire freedom from popular prejudice against the colored race. He was the 1st great man that I talked with in the U.S. freely, who in no single instance reminded me of the difference between himself and myself, of the difference of color, and I thought that all the more remarkable because he came from a State where there were black laws."—Frederick Douglass, radical black abolitionist and former slave

—M.S.M.

The Other 28th President

EDITH BOLLING WILSON

The likelihood of a woman's becoming President of the U.S. in the near future is discussed more and more frequently these days. In an almost forgotten episode in the recent past, a woman who opposed the campaign for female suffrage was hailed by newspapers in this nation and abroad as "Presidentress of the U.S." She was Edith Bolling Galt Wilson, Woodrow Wilson's 2nd wife, who was virtual head of Government during his prolonged illness.

The Bollings were direct descendants of the Indian princess Pocahontas. Reduced to poverty in the aftermath of the Civil War, the onetime prosperous planter William Bolling took his wife, Sallie White Bolling, to Wytheville, Va. Here Edith was born October 15, 1872, the 7th of 9 children. Her father, a judge in the circuit court, had a modest income which permitted schooling for her brothers, but Edith was tutored in reading, writing, arithmetic, and French by her father and grandmother. Until she was nearly 13 years old, Edith was never outside the poor rural town the Bollings lived in. Eventually she was sent to boarding school, where she received 2 years of formal education.

Edith's 1st husband was wealthy businessman Norman Galt, who owned an exclusive jewelry store in Washington, D.C. When he died, she ran the store successfully herself for a time. Childless, she became the guardian of a teen-aged girl named Altrude Gordon, who later was engaged to White House physician Dr. Cary Grayson. Miss Gordon and her fiancé asked Edith to befriend Helen Bone, a young cousin of the President. Through Helen, Edith met Woodrow Wilson, who was then a widower. Much to the dismay of Col. Edward House, the President's close adviser, Wilson soon married Edith Galt, who replaced the colonel as Wilson's confidante.

On the evening of September 25, 1919, in the midst of a triumphant speaking tour to rally support for the League of Nations, President Wilson collapsed and was rushed back to the White House. On October 2, he suffered a paralytic stroke and was totally incapacitated until mid-November. During the next few months, he slowly regained a tenuous hold on the responsibilities of the presidential office. In this interim, his wife embarked on the strange interlude known as "Mrs. Wilson's Stewardship," the words she preferred to use in describing her role. Some historians believe her stewardship lasted 17 months, until the end of Wilson's 2nd term.

A unique configuration of circumstances led Edith Wilson to become "Acting President," as some called her. She was strongly influenced by Dr. F. X. Dercum, who implored her to take over, stressing that her husband's life depended upon her. He explained that the President had a blood clot in his brain. The clot would dissolve and he would probably recover —if he was spared the chore of making decisions and he was shielded from all disturbing problems. Resignation was no answer, Dr. Dercum warned. His will to live would be gone, and the ratification of the peace treaty would be endangered, along with the League of Nations, the cause that meant the most to him. Dr. Grayson, Wilson's personal physician and friend, concurred in this opinion. Both doctors agreed that the elevation of Vice-President Thomas Riley Marshall to head of state would be calamitous. Marshall, the logical stand-in for Wilson by virtue of official rank, was a happy-go-lucky chap whose affability and entertaining speeches endeared him to everyone. It was he who coined the phrase, "What this country needs is a good 5¢ cigar." However, at the prospect of assuming the Presidency, he simply dissolved. On one occasion, when he was reminded that he might have to take over Woodrow Wilson's job, he buried his head in his hands and could not speak. Another time, when he was asked what he would do if he became President, he blurted out, "I can't even think about it."

Secretary of State Robert Lansing was not much better suited temperamentally to fill the role of chief of state. Nor did he know as much about foreign policy as Edith Wilson, who had been Wilson's confidante. In fact, all Lansing knew about Wilson's policies was what he read in the newspapers. For that matter, Marshall knew little more. Marshall sidestepped Cabinet meetings, quipping that if he couldn't have the $75,000 a year that went along with the President's job, he wasn't going to do any of his work.

Lone wolf Wilson had one alter ego on whom he relied—his wife, Edith. He told her everything, and she helped him make all his decisions. When he weighed the alternatives to acceptance of William Jennings Bryan's letter of resignation, Edith tipped the scales, urging him to replace Bryan. Bryan, who was Secretary of State before Lansing, was a dedicated pacifist. His opposition to preparedness for war Edith considered dangerous. Wilson deferred to Edith's opinion.

Edith had sat in on all of Wilson's private conferences. She was the *only* person who knew the secret code by which he communicated with Colonel House and his emissaries in Europe. Wilson had taught her the code in February of 1915, and from then on he wrote his top-secret communications in longhand for Edith to encode in her own writing. Edith also decoded incoming messages during those 4½ years. Not another soul knew the mind of Wilson and the nuances of his foreign policy the way that Edith Bolling Wilson did. Thus she was eminently suited to the awesome cares thrust upon her by destiny.

Edith stood guard over her critically ill husband, warding off Cabinet members and other officials who "had to see the President." Joseph Tumulty, Wilson's loyal secretary, wore a hangdog expression, for he was shunted aside. Now and then Edith would disappear into the sickroom, carefully closing the door behind her, to relay a message from some official. Emerging, she would report that "the President says . . ." Edith screened all problems that would ordinarily reach the President, and for a few minutes each day she consulted with her husband, whose mind was lucid despite his physical condition. But it was Edith who decided which matters should be brought to his attention. She conferred with officials, giving advice; when 2 department secretaries resigned, she selected men to replace them.

All papers, letters, and documents from the Cabinet and Congress went to Edith. She guided Wilson's hand as he signed congressional bills. Senators who knew his handwriting suspected Edith of forgery. Sometimes Edith related the President's wishes on memorandums received. Her big round handwriting would circle the margin of a letter written by a senator. Eyebrows were raised as a senator or Cabinet member viewed her childish writing, and balefully turned the paper this way and that to decipher the weaving message.

Congress viewed her activities with a good deal of consternation. Sen. Albert Fall of New Mexico almost became violent. He pounded on the table and thundered, "We have a petticoat Government! Mrs. Wilson is President!" An avalanche of newspaper criticism of her "regency" disheartened her, and some of the White House servants, alluding to her ancestry, resented "being forced to work for an Indian."

As for the country's domestic affairs, it must be admitted that a number of "housekeeping chores" had to go by the board. A mining strike awaited the setting up of a commission to resolve it. Vacancies on a few commissions went unfilled temporarily. But then, Vice-President Marshall had refused to do "any of the President's work." At least Edith, although swamped by the demands of national leadership, was trying.

As to foreign affairs, one crucial time, Wilson did not heed her advice. When she asked him to consent to Senator Lodge's stipulations on U.S. entry into the League of Nations, Wilson said No. Because Wilson refused to compromise, the Senate voted to keep the U.S. out of the League. Edith's political acumen might have changed the course of history here.

Edith Wilson's initiative and determination won praise as well as castigation. The London *Daily Mail* reported that Mrs. Wilson was proving to be a perfectly capable "President." A member of the opposition party, a Republican journalist named Dolly Gann, exulted over the fact that a woman in the White House knew how to take over and act when necessary for the good of her country.

Wilson recovered and completed his term. Had it not been for Edith, he could long since have been removed from office for inability to perform his duties as President, and Thomas Marshall, who liked being Vice-President because he had "no responsibilities," would have succeeded to the highest office in the land. Edith Wilson never wavered in her loyalty to her husband, the 28th President of the U.S. After his death, she maintained her interest in the League of Nations and international cooperation, the cause in which he had so firmly believed.

There is no chance today of having another Edith Wilson acting as an American "Presidentress." The 25th Amendment, ratified February 10, 1967, clearly defines what happens in case the President is incapable of governing. The 1st official female President will have to be duly elected.

—R.Ho.

32nd President

FRANKLIN DELANO ROOSEVELT

VITAL STATISTICS

Born: January 30, 1882, at Hyde Park, N.Y. His gracious Hudson River valley birthplace is usually described as an "estate," but FDR himself preferred to think of it as a "farm." Visitors to the 187-acre site, now a historic landmark, can decide for themselves which title is more accurate. Hyde Park is located on U.S. 9, 4 mi. north of Poughkeepsie. Admission: 50¢.

Died: April 12, 1945, in the "Little White House" at Warm Springs, Ga. The President had gone to Warm Springs to rest (under doctor's orders) and to prepare for the upcoming organizational meeting of the UN. On the morning of April 12, he donned a Harvard crimson tie and his familiar black navy cape and went into the living room of his cottage to pose for a portrait. The artist worked quietly at her easel and Roosevelt glanced through a sheaf of papers, while the servants laid out lunch dishes on a nearby table. Suddenly, the President raised a hand to his forehead and said softly: "I have a terrific headache." Then he slumped back in his chair, unconscious. Three hours later, he was dead of a cerebral hemorrhage. Roosevelt, who was 63, was buried in his garden at Hyde Park.

BEFORE THE PRESIDENCY

Career: No American President came from a more patrician background than Franklin Roosevelt. His mother's family claimed that they could trace their genealogy all the way back to William the Conqueror. Between them, the Roosevelts and the Delanos boasted no fewer than 12 Mayflower ancestors. As a boy, Franklin was educated by private tutors and he toured Europe 8 times before he was 16. At the proper time he attended Groton School (where 90% of the students were from Social Register families) and Harvard. Roosevelt was a mediocre student (maintaining a "gentlemanly" "C" average at Harvard) but a notable social success. His 5th cousin, Theodore Roosevelt, was then serving as President, and Franklin enjoyed a good deal of reflected glory. In his junior year, he was elected editor of the Harvard *Crimson* and wrote ringing editorials urging the football team to victory and lamenting the decline in school spirit. After graduation, he attended Columbia Law School, but was thoroughly bored by his studies there. He flunked several courses and dropped out before winning his degree, but he absorbed enough information to pass a bar·examination anyway and take his place in a fashionable New York law firm. When Roosevelt was 28, the Democratic leaders in his home district became interested in the handsome young lawyer with the famous last name. Only one Democrat had carried the district since 1856, and now the party needed a State senate candidate. The main qualification was that the nominee be wealthy enough to pay his own expenses in a hopeless cause. Roosevelt agreed to run, and then startled his neighbors with a flamboyant, person-to-person campaign in a red touring car. He won an upset victory, took his seat in Albany, and immediately identified himself with genteel reform elements. Though admirers have cited FDR's "courage" in defying the statewide Democratic machine, he was actually doing exactly what his overwhelmingly Republican constituents expected of him. In 1912, State senator Roosevelt was an early supporter of Woodrow Wilson's presidential bid, and when Wilson was elected, he was rewarded with a post in the new Administration. Roosevelt was appointed Assistant Secretary of the Navy—a position that his cousin Teddy had made famous some 15 years before. In the Navy Dept., FDR proved himself a skillful and aggressive administrator, with a knack for personal publicity. With the coming of W.W. I, the Assistant Secretary, long an advocate of increased naval power, gained stature as a prophet. In 1920, the 38-year-old Roosevelt was nominated by his party for the Vice-Presidency, in the hope that his famous name would attract Progressive Republicans to the Democratic ticket. Though Roosevelt and his running mate were crushed under the Harding landslide, FDR gained a reputation as a tireless and popular campaigner, and after the election his political prospects seemed brighter than ever.

All of that came to an end in August, 1921, while FDR was vacationing at his family's summer home at Campobello, in New Brunswick, Canada. While yachting with his sons, Roosevelt stopped to put out a forest fire on a small island, then refreshed himself with a swim in the icy waters of the bay. He suffered severe body shock, and that evening was overcome by a stab of pain and a chill. The next morning his legs failed him when he tried to stand up, and within 24 hours he was paralyzed from the waist down. He had contracted poliomyelitis, but it was more than a week before the doctors diagnosed his condition correctly. By that time, Roosevelt, aged 39, had been permanently crippled: He would never regain the use of his legs.

Personal Life: Though he was considered a devastatingly handsome young man, Roosevelt showed no interest in women until his junior year at Harvard, when he fell in love with his 4th cousin, Eleanor Roosevelt. Eleanor was shy, plain, and insecure; an orphan; and the product of an unhappy childhood. What it was about her that attracted the dashing and fun-loving FDR remains a mystery, since Mrs. Roosevelt, in later life, destroyed his early letters to her. It may have been that Franklin was impressed by his cousin's brilliant mind, or by her social concern: Eleanor spent her free time as a volunteer in a Manhattan settlement house. It is also possible that he was swayed by her close connection to the family's most famous member: Eleanor was the daughter of Teddy Roosevelt's younger brother, and Uncle Ted appeared personally at the brilliant society wedding in 1905 to give away the bride.

Despite this auspicious beginning, the 23-year-old FDR and his 20-year-old wife ran into difficulties almost immediately. The 1st problem was Franklin's mother, an intelligent, strong-willed widow who wasn't about to give up her hold on her only child. She had moved to Boston to be close to Franklin during his years at Harvard, and now she insisted on setting up house with the young couple. She easily dominated the unassuming Eleanor and made all crucial decisions concerning the Roosevelt home.

There were also deeper tensions in the marriage: Family papers, made public for the 1st time in 1971, show that Eleanor always considered sex an ordeal, while Franklin had an unusually vigorous sexual appetite. In the early years of the marriage, FDR usually got his way, but in 1916, after the birth of her 6th child, Eleanor put her foot down. During the 29 years of marriage that remained to them, the Roosevelts never slept together again. They maintained separate bedrooms and in the White House actually took over different wings of the mansion.

Not surprisingly, FDR looked for consolation outside his marriage. His 1st and most serious affair involved Lucy Mercer, his wife's beautiful and sophisticated social secretary. By the time Eleanor discovered a batch of love letters and found out about the affair, Franklin and Lucy were deeply in love. There was talk of a divorce and remarriage, but Roosevelt's mother squelched all such plans by threatening to cut off her boy's generous financial allowance. Franklin was forced to give up Lucy Mercer, but his interest in her continued from a distance for the rest of his life.

In a sense, Roosevelt's paralysis probably strengthened his bond with Eleanor, but their relationship was one of mutual respect and dependence rather than personal intimacy. Medical reports prove that FDR's sexual prowess was unimpaired by polio, and rumors continued to link him with other women. Wartime gossip centered on a supposed romantic involvement between the President and the glamorous young Princess Martha of Norway. Then in 1973, FDR's son Elliott published a book in which he declared that Missy LeHand, his father's tall, slim, gray-eyed private secretary, was Roosevelt's mistress for 20 years. Elliott also asserts that Eleanor not only knew about the relationship, but approved of it—allowing Missy and Franklin to occupy adjoining bedrooms.

Though some Roosevelt intimates have doubted the accuracy of this account, there can be no question that as the years went by, Eleanor became more and more her own woman. In the White House, she was without a doubt the most active and most controversial First Lady in American history. She wrote a daily newspaper column, held regular press conferences, chaired public works committees, and earned the nickname "Public Energy Number One." She also made countless far-flung inspection tours for her husband and filed the reports of her travels, in writing, in a small basket by FDR's bed. Roosevelt called her his "eyes and ears," and would often answer department heads by saying, "Yes, but, my missus tells me . . ." He was obviously proud of his brilliant wife, and she was no doubt devoted to him. The public knew nothing of the persistent problems in their marriage.

In 1944, Missy LeHand died of a stroke, and in his loneliness FDR turned once again to Lucy Mercer, now an aging but attractive widow. On several occasions, he risked exposure to spend time with her; he once ordered an unscheduled stop on a presidential train so that he could spend half a day at Lucy's New Jersey home. Privileged observers noted a romantic, somewhat melancholy aspect in this "lonely hearts" relationship. Lucy was with

Roosevelt in Warm Springs on the day that he died, but after his collapse she left hurriedly, before Eleanor and the press had arrived on the scene.

On the Way to the White House: In the 1920s, FDR set out with unshakable confidence to prove to himself and his family that he need not live as an invalid. He worked tirelessly at a series of special exercises for his paralyzed legs, traveled to Georgia for water therapy, and accustomed himself to wheelchairs, or to crawling on his hands from room to room. Eventually, his condition improved enough so that he was able to "walk," using a cane, 8-lb. leg braces, and the supporting arm of one of his sons. This was an important triumph for FDR, because it allowed him to resume his political career: He could take the necessary steps from his chair to a speaker's platform, then lock his braces and hold the podium for support. At the 1924 Democratic convention, Roosevelt's appearance electrified the delegates, as he made a stirring speech nominating Al Smith for President. It seemed that FDR's handicap only served to increase his political appeal. As historian Paul Conkin has written: "Polio made the aristocratic Roosevelt into an underdog. For him it replaced the log cabin." In 1928, when Al Smith finally won the Democratic presidential nomination, he asked Roosevelt to run for governor of New York in order to lend strength to the ticket. Smith assured the hesitant FDR that the duties of the governorship need not interfere with continued therapy for his legs. "Don't hand me that baloney!" laughed Roosevelt, but he decided to make the race anyway. In the campaign that followed, Smith lost the State to Hoover by 100,000 votes, but the popular Roosevelt was elected governor by a narrow margin. With the coming of the Depression, Roosevelt used his office to win relief for the hungry and unemployed in his State. In 1930, he ran for reelection as governor and won by the biggest margin in the history of New York State up to that time. Despite lingering doubts concerning his physical incapacity, he automatically emerged as a leading contender for the Democratic presidential nomination in 1932.

His Person: FDR was 6'2" tall and weighed about 190 lbs. Woodrow Wilson once described him as "the handsomest young giant I have ever seen." Roosevelt was always broad-shouldered, but after he lost the use of his legs he built up his arms and chest to prodigious strength. "Maybe my legs aren't so good," he once said, "but look at those shoulders! Jack Dempsey would be green with envy." While recovering from polio, he used to wrestle with his young sons on the floor, 2 at a time. Roosevelt had a high forehead, a roman nose, and was almost always smiling. Political opponents cited his unfailing optimism, good humor, and charm as evidence of a shallow, flabby nature. Roosevelt could even make light of his own affliction. During one of her visits to the White House, Madame Chiang Kai-shek thoughtlessly told the President not to stand up as she rose to leave the room. "My dear child," laughed Roosevelt, tossing his head back in a characteristic gesture, "I couldn't stand up if I had to!" Visitors to Washington social functions, no matter how large, could always find the President by following the sound of his booming laughter. Roosevelt was a steady, but never a problem, drinker, who generally enjoyed 2 or 3 cocktails a night. He was also a heavy smoker, and consumed 30 cigarettes a day despite doctor's orders to cut down. His long-stemmed cigarette holder, tilting upward from his toothy grin, became a Roosevelt trademark. Another trademark, the flowing black navy cape, had a practical justification: Aides found it extremely awkward to help the crippled President in and out of overcoats, and the cape greatly simplified matters. FDR's mellow, resonant voice, often described as "the best radio voice in the world," became a key political asset.

PRESIDENCY

Election: June 27, 1932 . . .

As the Democratic convention assembled in Chicago, the delegates knew that the man they chose would be the next President. The "Hoover Depression" had made a Democratic victory a virtual certainty. FDR had won an impressive string of primary victories, but had lost California to "Cactus Jack" Garner of Texas and had lost Massachusetts to his old friend Al Smith. On the 1st ballot, Roosevelt had more than half the delegate votes, but he fell short of the 2/3 necessary for nomination. As the convention completed its 3rd ballot, it seemed that the opposition candidates might have enough strength to create a long-term deadlock. In desperation, an agreement was reached: Garner, who was speaker of the House, would get the vice-presidential nod in exchange for releasing his delegates to Roosevelt. On the 4th ballot, FDR and Garner were duly nominated, and the confident Democrats moved on to the general election. As Sen. W. G. McAdoo told Roosevelt: "Now all you have to do is stay alive until the election."

November 8, 1932 . . .

The final election returns offered few surprises. Roosevelt polled 22,809,638 votes to 15,758,901 for Herbert Hoover, the Republican incumbent. Roosevelt carried 42 of the 48 States and buried Hoover in the Electoral College, 472 to 59. Much of Roosevelt's campaign rhetoric was naïve and misleading; he promised, for instance, to *cut* Federal spending at the same time he would increase relief. Nevertheless, the personality of the genial New Yorker seemed to catch on with the voters, as did his promise of a "new deal for the American people."

First Term: March 4, 1933 . . .

Roosevelt was sworn in by Chief Justice Hughes at the east portico of the Capitol. With the nation near panic as the economic crisis worsened, the new President assured his countrymen:

"This great nation will endure as it has endured, will revive and will prosper. So, 1st of all, let me assert my firm belief that the only thing we have to fear is fear itself—nameless, unreasoning, unjustified terror, which paralyzes needed efforts to convert retreat into advance."

Within 100 days, Congress had approved all key aspects of Roosevelt's sweeping legislative program, setting up a host of new Federal agencies and providing changes in nearly every aspect of American life.

Reelection: November 3, 1936 . . .

The Republicans had hysterically denounced nearly all of Roosevelt's reforms, and in the '36 campaign they launched a noble crusade to "save America from Socialism." Their presidential candidate was a genial but colorless conservative named Alf Landon, who was dubbed by his supporters "the Kansas Coolidge." Another Landon nickname, "the Kansas Sunflower," led to a popular Democratic bumper sticker which read: "Sunflowers Wilt in November." This proved an accurate prediction, as Roosevelt and Garner rolled up one of the greatest landslides in American history, carrying every State in the union except Maine and Vermont. The final electoral tally was 523 to 8. The popular vote saw a record plurality of nearly 11 million.

Third Term: November 5, 1940 . . .

For months, Roosevelt refused to say whether or not he would break tradition and run for a 3rd term, but his hesitation prevented any other Democrat from emerging as a strong contender. When the President finally announced that he would accept a "draft," many Democrats were unhappy, but they had little choice but to nominate him. The vice-presidential nomination was another matter: Roosevelt wanted to replace the retiring Vice-President Garner with the Secretary of Agriculture, the radical Henry Wallace. The convention seemed to favor a more conservative choice, and it was only the surprise appearance of Eleanor Roosevelt, making a forceful speech in behalf of her husband's choice, that secured the nomination for Wallace.

The Republicans entered the campaign with a new issue: the claim that Roosevelt's aid to Great Britain in the struggle with Hitler would lead the U.S. into an unnecessary war. Their candidate, however, agreed with Roosevelt on most key policy questions. Wendell Willkie was a political amateur who had used a strong grassroots organization to "steal" the Republican nomination from party professionals. Adding insult to injury was the fact that Willkie had been a Democrat all his life—and had actually contributed $150 to Roosevelt's campaign in 1932. Willkie was a corporation lawyer and his business interests were soon threatened by the New Deal and he began criticizing the Administration. In the campaign of 1940, he stumped the country with extraordinary vigor, pushing himself until his speaking voice grew hoarse and raspy. Wherever possible, the Republicans emphasized the 3rd term issue. "No Man Is Good 3 Times," proclaimed one of their slogans, while the Democrats answered: "Better a 3rd Termer Than a 3rd Rater."

The election returns showed that Roosevelt's popularity had slipped significantly (Willkie won 45% of the vote), but "the Champ" still won by a comfortable margin. Roosevelt outpolled Willkie, 27,241,939 to 22,327,276. Willkie carried 10 States (most of them in the Midwest) for 82 electoral votes to Roosevelt's 449.

Fourth Term: November 7, 1944 . . .

With the U.S. in the middle of the war, Roosevelt was not about to retire; though his health had deteriorated, he was determined to see the war through to its conclusion and play the leading role in forging international peace. His renomination by his party was, of course, a foregone conclusion, but once again the vice-presidential slot was a subject of controversy. Conservatives were intent on dumping Vice-President Wallace from the ticket, and in order to avoid a convention floor fight, FDR personally selected a compromise candidate—a little-known senator from Missouri named Harry S Truman.

The Republicans, behind Gov. Thomas E. Dewey of New York, waged a particularly bitter and personal campaign, charging that "communist influences" had taken over the Administration and whispering about the President's failing health. Stung by these charges, Roosevelt was determined to show some of his old mettle. In October, he greeted more than 3 million New Yorkers, campaigning in an open car in a blinding rain. In the end, the Republicans were unable to shake Roosevelt's image as a war leader of international stature. Dewey was beaten by 3½ million votes and lost the Electoral College, 432 to 99.

January 20, 1945 . . .

Roosevelt took the oath of office for the 4th time in an austere, sparsely attended ceremony on the south portico of the White House. A light snow had fallen the night before and the thermometer registered only one degree above freezing; nevertheless, the President appeared bareheaded and without an overcoat to deliver a 6-minute address.

Two weeks later he traveled 14,000 mi. to confer with Churchill and Stalin at Yalta. When he spoke to Congress after his return, he did so from a sitting position—the 1st time he had delivered a major speech without standing up. "I hope that you will pardon me for the unusual posture of sitting down," he said. "It makes it a lot easier for me not having to carry about 10 lbs. of steel around on the bottom of my legs." It was also the 1st time the President had ever referred to his braces in public.

Five weeks later, Roosevelt was dead.

Vetoes: Roosevelt dominated Congress more completely than any other President in history, and he used his veto power with unparalleled zest. His 635 vetoes set an all-time record. Only 9 of his vetoes were overridden by Congress. Old New Dealers tell the story that Roosevelt used to ask his aides to find something he could veto in order to remind Congress not to get "uppity."

His 12 Years, 39 Days as President

PRO

Roosevelt restored the confidence of the people in their Government at a time when that confidence was failing. He not only promised "Action, and action now . . ."—but he kept that promise. It was only through his leadership that a disastrous social upheaval was avoided in the Depression-torn U.S. Responding to the worst domestic crisis in our history, FDR's magnificent buoyancy, self-assurance, and political skill gave the U.S. a new sense of purpose and direction.

CON

Roosevelt's enemies considered him a power-mad demagogue who expanded the powers of the Presidency to dictatorial proportions. His infamous "court-packing" plan—which would have allowed him to appoint new justices and to remake the Supreme Court according to his will—showed his basic contempt for constitutional processes. In violating the unwritten law against a 3rd term, he set a dangerous precedent of interminable one-man rule. In response to the excesses of the Roosevelt era, the nation wisely adopted the 23rd Amendment to the Constitution—limiting all future Presidents to 2 terms only.

PRO

With its free-wheeling, experimental approach to America's problems, the New Deal provided jobs and relief for millions of hungry Americans. For the 1st time, Government recognized its responsibility for the economic well-being of ordinary citizens. While the captains of industry howled, FDR began dismantling the mighty fortress of special privilege that had been built up over the course of a century. The Wagner

Act guaranteed labor's right to organize, while other New Deal programs such as Social Security, the Tennessee Valley Authority, and the Works Progress Administration, provided lasting benefits for the country and its citizens. The New Deal put an end to the bad old days of *laissez-faire* capitalism, and moved the nation toward a more healthy and rational economic structure.

CON

After promising the voters that he would "balance the budget," FDR launched happily into an irresponsible spending spree, the likes of which had never before been seen in American history. His massive give-away program encouraged the masses to develop "their wishbones more than their backbones." The effects of this paternalistic policy are still felt today, with a massive, all-powerful government bureaucracy overshadowing the life of the individual. The New Deal panaceas were not only costly, they were ineffective in combating the Depression. It was only the beginning of wartime production that returned prosperity to a nation dangerously weakened by 6 years of Roosevelt's ill-considered social experiments.

PRO

In an era of rampant isolationism, Roosevelt worked effectively to make his countrymen aware of their international responsibilities. His "Good Neighbor Policy" in Latin America was an unqualified success, restoring friendly relations after a generation of high-handed U.S. imperialism. He ordered diplomatic recognition of the Soviet Union, after 16 years of blind hostility to the Communist regime. Against fierce domestic opposition, he provided crucial aid to Britain in her lonely fight against Hitler in 1940 and 1941. Without this support, England might well have succumbed to the Nazi onslaught.

CON

Roosevelt became aware of the Fascist menace too late to take effective action to stop it, and even then he failed to take the necessary steps to prepare the U.S. for war. He did nothing to prevent the appeasement of Hitler at Munich or elsewhere. During the Spanish Civil War he supported the embargo of arms to Spanish Loyalists—thereby assuring success to the pro-Fascist Franco forces. The Japanese surprise attack on Pearl Harbor was the product of either gross incompetence on the part of the Commander-in-chief or a deliberate willingness to sacrifice American lives to political expediency. It has often been suggested that the President knew a Japanese attack was coming—and welcomed it, as a means of easing himself out of the controversial decision to lead the nation to war.

PRO

Roosevelt's contributions to the Allied victory were enormous. He personally kept the alliance together through difficult times, and his eloquence and determination inspired millions of people throughout the world. As Commander-in-chief, he chose an unusually gifted group of men for the top military positions, and then backed them up effectively. FDR showed great vision, though he angered Churchill, with his insistence that a permanent postwar peace required the breakup of the old colonial empires. The United Nations—established by Roosevelt over the doubts of other world leaders and political opponents—is a permanent legacy of his wartime leadership. Roosevelt was determined to pursue friendly relations with the Soviet Union after the war, and if he had lived the "Cold War" might have been avoided.

CON

During the war, FDR did absolutely nothing to rescue the doomed Jews of Europe—even after he learned that millions of them were being slaughtered by the Nazis. At home, he approved the unconstitutional and inhuman internment of more than 100,000 Japanese Americans in the infamous "relocation camps." Throughout the war, Roosevelt was naïvely confident that our Soviet "allies" would keep their promises, and at the Yalta conference he personally sanctioned Stalin's takeover of most of Eastern Europe. By the time of the Yalta meeting, Roosevelt's health was so bad that his performance was impaired: His mind wandered, and he found it hard to concentrate on the business at hand. With his doctor, Roosevelt conspired to keep his failing health a secret from the American public—so as not to jeopardize his chances for a 4th term. Even Vice-President Truman was left in the dark, and Roosevelt did nothing to prepare his successor for the enormous responsibilities of the wartime Presidency.

PSYCHOHISTORY

At Hyde Park, Roosevelt enjoyed an unusually happy and secure childhood. He had his own pony at age 4; his own 21′ sailboat at age 16. An only child, he called his mother "Sallie" and his father "Popsie" and absorbed all their attention. His father, a wealthy financier and country squire, was 54 when Franklin was born, and naturally he adored the boy. Father and son rode horses, hunted, swam, sailed boats together, and every day they walked into town to get the mail. By the time he went away to school, Franklin was used to being the center of attention, and even with his own wife and children, FDR was always something of the bright, favored child who could do no wrong. He was used to having his own way, and whether it was a mistress, a 3rd term, or a reconstituted Supreme Court, he never questioned his right to get what he wanted. At every level, Roosevelt was filled with confidence that he could personally overcome any obstacle. In a strange way his experience with polio only intensified this sense of personal invulnerability. "If you have spent 2 years in bed trying to wiggle your big toe," he said, "then anything else seems easy." In other words, since he had experienced physical paralysis and gone on to success, he could undertake anything and emerge, in the end, triumphant. As historian Richard Hofstadter has written, the essence of the New Deal was "Roosevelt's confidence that even when he was operating in unfamiliar territory he could do no wrong, commit no serious mistakes." How else can you explain a man who sincerely expected that his own personal charm would be enough to persuade Joseph Stalin to make key postwar concessions? There is a legend, fostered by Roosevelt admirers, that FDR used the years of his convalescence for wide-range reading on economic theory, and that out of this intellectual ferment came a new commitment to social change. While this was hardly the case (Roosevelt was never a very serious reader), it does seem probable that his sympathies, as well as his self-confidence, were deepened by his affliction. Once, while lecturing in Akron, Ohio, Eleanor Roosevelt received a cruel written question from a member of the audience: "Do you think your husband's illness has affected his mentality?" Eleanor paused for a moment and then replied: "I am glad that question was asked. The answer is Yes. Anyone who has gone through great suffering is bound to have a greater sympathy and understanding of the problems of mankind." The audience rose in a standing ovation.

LITTLE-KNOWN FACTS

—At her wedding, the orphaned Eleanor Roosevelt was given away by her uncle, President Theodore Roosevelt. After the ceremonies, reporters asked the President what he thought of his niece's marriage to her young 4th cousin, Franklin. "It is a good thing to keep the name in the family," TR observed.

—Model shipbuilding and stamp collecting were FDR's favorite hobbies. At his death, the sale of his personal stamp collection brought in more than $200,000.

—Mark Twain was Roosevelt's favorite writer, and FDR is reputed to have taken the term "New Deal" from a chapter in *A Connecticut Yankee at King Arthur's Court.* Roosevelt once wrote: "If people like my choice of words and my oratorical style, it is largely due to my constant study of Twain's works."

—While recovering from polio, FDR worked at various projects. He spent some time writing a movie script based on the history of the ship *Old Ironsides,* but he never succeeded in selling this product to Hollywood. He also invested money in several novel schemes, including a proposed intercity dirigible freight line.

—Eleanor was often idiosyncratic in her supervision of the White House menus. Particularly fond of sweetbreads, she once ordered that they be served 6 times in a single week. This was too much for FDR, who sent his wife a note reading: "I am getting to the point where my stomach rebels, and this does not help my relations with foreign powers. I bit 2 of them today."

—The Roosevelts hosted the 1st visit of a reigning British monarch to the U.S. George VI and his wife Elizabeth spent a day and a night at the White House, and were introduced to that great American food, hot dogs, for the 1st time.

—Roosevelt not only appointed the 1st woman Cabinet member (Secretary of Labor Frances Perkins) but the 1st woman to represent the U.S. as Ambassador to a foreign country. Shortly after taking the oath of office for the 1st time, he named Ruth Bryan Owens, daughter of the late Democratic war-horse, William Jennings Bryan, as Minister to Denmark.

—During the war years, FDR's travel plans were kept secret for security reasons. It was during this period that the President's dog, Fala, won the nickname "the informer." That famous Scottish terrier insisted on being taken for a walk at every stop on a train trip, and the sight of him, accompanied by weary Secret Service agents, was a tip-off to reporters that the President was on board.

—Informal Sunday night dinners became a White House tradition during the Roosevelt Administrations. Invitations went out only to personal friends and special guests, and Eleanor would preside over the gatherings, standing at the end of the table and scrambling eggs personally in a silver chafing dish. On other occasions, Eleanor would use the dinner table as a forum for her political ideas, often arguing with her husband. "Mother, can't you see you are giving Father indigestion?" asked daughter Anna after one exhausting diatribe.

—Speaking in Cleveland during his campaign for a 3rd term, FDR assured his audience that "when the next 4 years are over, there will be another President." There were loud shouts of "No!" from the crowd, but FDR thrust his mouth close to the microphone and went right on talking so that the shouts which suggested that he be elected permanently would not be heard over the radio.

Quotes from Roosevelt:

"A conservative is a man with 2 perfectly good legs, who, however, has never learned to walk."

"I have no expectation of making a hit every time I come to bat. What I seek is the highest possible batting average."

"The test of our progress is not whether we add more to the abundance of those who have much; it is whether we provide enough for those who have little."

"These unhappy times call for plans that build from the bottom up and not from the top down, that put their faith once more in the forgotten man at the bottom of the economic pyramid."—1932

"One thing is sure. We have to do something. We have to do the best we know how at the moment. If it doesn't turn out right, we can modify it as we go along."—1933

"These economic royalists complain that we seek to overthrow the institutions of America. What they really complain of is that we seek to take away their power. These economic royalists are unanimous in their hate for me—and I welcome their hatred."—1936

"There is a mysterious cycle in human events. To some generations much is given. Of other generations much is expected. This generation of Americans has a rendezvous with destiny. . . . We are fighting to save a great and precious form of government for ourselves and for the world."—June 27, 1936, acceptance speech, Democratic convention

"I want to go back to Hyde Park. I want to take care of my trees. I want to make the farm pay. I want to finish my little house on the hill."—1939

Quotes about Him:

"Dear Mr. President: This is just to tell you that everything is all right now. The man you sent found our house all right, and we went down to the bank with him and the mortgage can go on for a while longer. You remember I wrote you about losing the furniture too. Well, your man got it back for us. I never heard of a President like you."—Letter to the White House, summer, 1933

"Meeting him is like opening a bottle of champagne."—Winston Churchill

"He is a pleasant man, who, without any important qualifications for the office, would very much like to be President. . . . Here is a man who has made a good governor, who might make a good Cabinet officer, but who simply does not measure up to the tremendous demands of the office of President."—Walter Lippmann, 1932

"One thing is sure—that the idea people get from his charming manner—that he is soft or flabby in disposition and character—is far from true. When he wants something a lot, he can be formidable; when crossed, he is hard, stubborn, resourceful, relentless."—Presidential aide Raymond Moley

"The country is being run by a group of college professors. This Brain Trust is endeavoring to force socialism upon the American people."—Sen. Henry D. Hatfield of West Virginia

"He might have been happier with a wife who was completely uncritical. That I was never able to be. Nevertheless I think I sometimes acted as a spur. I was one of those who served his purposes."—Eleanor Roosevelt, 1945

33rd President HARRY S TRUMAN

VITAL STATISTICS

Born: May 8, 1884, in Lamar, Mo. In 1957, his birthplace was purchased by the United Auto Workers and presented to the State of Missouri as a historic site. Located at 1009 Truman Street (U.S. 71), it is open to the public daily except Mondays. Admission: free.

Died: December 26, 1972, at the age of 88. For 22 days at Kansas City's Research Hospital Truman had been stubbornly holding on to life, until he lost consciousness for the last time on Christmas Day. Doctors described the cause of death as "organic failures causing a collapse of the cardiovascular system." Truman was buried in Independence, Mo., the town that had been his home for more than 70 years. Originally, he had approved plans by the U.S. Army for an elaborate State funeral. "A damn fine show. I just hate that I'm not going to be around to see it." His widow, however, insisted on a quick and simple ceremony. Truman was laid to rest in the courtyard of the Harry S Truman Library, near a stand of pin oaks, flowering cherry, and hawthorn trees. This library, housing millions of papers from his Presidency, also includes a museum and a replica of his White House office. It is open to the public daily. Admission: 50¢.

BEFORE THE PRESIDENCY

Career: The son of a prosperous farmer and mule trader, Truman's main interest as a boy was piano playing, and he seriously considered a career as a professional musician. He also loved to read and by age 14 had finished all the books in the Independence library. College was out of the question, however, since business reverses and bad investments had wiped out the family savings by the time Harry graduated from high school. Truman remains the only President of the 20th century who never attended college. Starting at age 17, Harry worked at a long series of menial jobs: timekeeper for a railroad construction gang, mailroom clerk for the *Kansas City Star*, a bookkeeper in a Kansas City bank, and so forth. Most of his energy and earnings, however, were devoted to helping his parents build up a new family farm. At age 33, he was still living at home and had failed to distinguish himself in any way, when he decided to volunteer to fight in W.W. I. His Army comrades seemed to discern leadership qualities in this "regular fella" and gifted poker player and they elected him as one of their officers. By the time his unit arrived in France, Truman was "Captain Harry" of Battery D, 129th Field Artillery. In the service that followed, he proved himself a competent and courageous commander, who came close to being killed so often that his men began to think he had some special protection. "Captain Harry" eventually received such a glowing recommendation from his superior that it was returned with the notation, "There isn't anybody that good."

Back in Independence after the war, Truman was a local hero with a new sense of self-confidence. He decided to go into business and, with one of his war buddies, he opened a haberdashery in Kansas City. At 1st, they prospered, but after 2 years business slumped and the store had to close. Too proud to declare bankruptcy, Truman promised to pay off all his debts. It was in this context that he turned to politics for the 1st time. His father had been a minor official in the local Democratic party, and during the war Truman became friendly with Mike Pendergast, the nephew of the notorious "Big Tom" Pendergast, reigning boss of Kansas City Democrats. The Pendergasts proved only too glad to sponsor this well-spoken newcomer with the distinguished war record, and in 1922 Truman was elected judge of the eastern district of Jackson County—an administrative and not a judicial position. In this capacity—and later as presiding judge for all of Jackson County—Truman saved the taxpayers thousands of dollars, serving with determination, efficiency, and scrupulous honesty, rare qualities in the Pendergast machine. Naturally, "Big Tom" was somewhat hesitant about promoting this incorruptible lieutenant, but in 1934, when 3 other candidates declined to make the race for U.S. Senate, Pendergast reluctantly turned to Truman. In the primary, Truman narrowly beat out the candidate of the rival bosses from St. Louis, and he was elected to the Senate in November.

Personal Life: In his later years, Truman told the story of his courtship and marriage in the simplest possible terms. At Sunday school at age 6 he met Bess Wallace, "a beautiful little girl with golden curls. I was smitten at once and still am." Nevertheless, he waited 29 years before he married her. In contrast to the bespectacled and bookish Truman, Bess was a willowy, popular, and athletic girl who won a local shot-put and basketball championship and had a reputation as the only girl in Independence who could whistle through her teeth. She came from one of the town's leading families (her father had been mayor) and her relatives always looked down on Truman and continued to do so even after he entered the White House. During the long difficult years when Truman was attempting to make his way in the world, Bess had many suitors, but she waited for Harry. After they were finally married (Bess was 34; Harry 35) the new couple moved in with the bride's mother and grandmother in the big Victorian Wallace home on North Delaware Street. Conscious of his wife's superior social standing, Truman always referred to her as "the Boss"—even in public. He deferred to her in many personal and political decisions, and as senator, when the Trumans found it difficult to make ends meet on their $10,000-a-year salary, Harry put Bess on the payroll as his secretary. As First Lady, Bess tried to keep out of the limelight as much as possible and so projected a drab public image, especially in comparison with her superactive predecessor, Eleanor Roosevelt. Congressman Adam Clayton Powell even went so far as to call Bess Truman "the Last Lady of the Land." The Trumans' only child, Margaret, was even more controversial. She attempted to launch herself on a career as a concert singer while her father was President, but she generally received scathing reviews. One such notice so infuriated Truman that he personally wrote to the music critic of the *Washington Post*: "I have just read your lousy review. . . . I have never met you, but if I do you'll need a new nose and plenty of beefsteak and perhaps a supporter below. Westbrook Pegler, a guttersnipe, is a gentleman compared to you." While some observers considered such words demeaning of presidential dignity, many Americans appreciated Truman's fierce devotion to his family, and this warm family feeling proved a definite asset in the campaign of 1948. In retirement, at the age of 75, Truman looked back on his career and observed: "Three things can ruin a man—money, power, and women. I never had any money, I never wanted power, and the only woman in my life is up at the house right now."

On the Way to the White House: During his 1st term in Washington, Senator Truman earned the respect and affection of other members of the Senate "club," but won few headlines. In 1940, he faced an uphill battle for re-election. The Pendergast machine was in ruins ("Big Tom" had been jailed for tax evasion in 1939) and Truman faced a primary challenge from a popular Democratic governor. President Roosevelt favored Truman's opponent and urged the senator to drop out of the race and accept an appointment to the Interstate Commerce Commission. Truman refused, and sitting behind the steering wheel of his own car, he began a tireless tour of Missouri, meeting the voters where they lived and worked. Truman won by a narrow margin, and he returned to

Washington with a new issue. During his campaign tour, he had been struck by the waste and inefficiency in the army bases and munitions plants that he had visited. Truman made an angry speech to call attention to the situation, and the Senate decided to placate its "uppity" member by naming him as chairman of the committee to "investigate" the situation. No one expected that in a matter of months, the senator from Missouri would turn up unbelievable tales of governmental stupidity and corruption. When the U.S. entered W.W. II, these revelations assumed new importance, and the Truman committee became front-page news. Demonstrating consummate political skill, Truman kept his committee at work on an efficient and bipartisan basis and made a series of common-sense recommendations that were generally adopted. It is estimated that his efforts saved taxpayers more than $15 *billion* during the war years. In 1944, a poll of Washington newspaper correspondents named Truman as 2nd only to President Roosevelt in his contribution to the U.S. war effort.

As a leader of national stature, Truman agreed to make the nominating speech for one of the rival candidates for the Democratic vice-presidential nomination in 1944. When he was told that President Roosevelt wanted Truman himself to accept that nomination as a compromise candidate, Harry shot back: "Tell him to go to hell. I'm for Jimmy Byrnes." At a convention hotel room, however, a prominent group of Democratic kingmakers sat down to twist Truman's arm. In the middle of their harangue, the President called. FDR always spoke loudly over the phone and the Democratic national chairman, Robert Hannegan, held the receiver so the others could hear.

"Bob," the President said, "have you got that fellow lined up yet?"

"No, Mr. President," Hannegan replied. "He is the contrariest Missouri mule I've ever dealt with."

"Well, you tell him that if he wants to break up the Democratic party in the middle of a war, that's his responsibility."

Hannegan hung up the phone and turned to Truman. "Now what do you say?"

"My God," Truman mumbled.

The next day, the man from Missouri was nominated for Vice-President, and the ticket of Roosevelt-Truman swept to victory in the November elections.

His Person: After he became President, commentators habitually referred to Truman as a "little man"; actually, he was 5′9″ tall and weighed 167 lbs. He had steel-gray hair and light hazel eyes. Since the age of 8, Truman had been virtually blind without his thick, rimless glasses. His weak eyes, in fact, had blocked his youthful desire to enroll at West

Point. "Haberdasher Harry" was always fond of bright-colored bow-ties and the loud sport shirts that he wore when relaxing were widely considered too "undignified" for a President. Truman's favorite form of exercise was walking; early each morning he got up and circled the White House at such a brisk pace that reporters and Secret Service men found it difficult to keep up with him. These walks continued during Truman's retirement, even as the former President approached 85 and was forced to use a cane. Though Truman's fiery temper was well-publicized, he was invariably open and friendly in his relations with aides and the press, and he refused to hold grudges. During the 1946 congressional campaign, he had called union leader Al Whitney, "un-American" and "an enemy of the people," and Whitney shot back with a much-publicized comment: "You can't make a President out of a ribbon clerk." When Whitney came to the White House some months after this exchange of insults, he had to walk twice around the building before working up the nerve to go in. Truman, however, greeted him without bitterness. "It's good to see you, Al. You look wonderful," he said. "Let's not waste time discussing the past. Let's just agree we both received bad advice."

Truman's preference for "earthy" language was of course legendary. He once offended a friend of his wife's at a Washington horticulture show by referring repeatedly to the "good manure" that must have been used to nurture the blossoms. "Bess, couldn't you get the President to say 'fertilizer'?" the woman complained. Replied the First Lady: "Heavens, no. It took me 25 years to get him to say 'manure.'"

PRESIDENCY

April 12, 1945 . . .

After spending the day presiding over the Senate, the Vice-President strolled over to Speaker Sam Rayburn's celebrated "Board of Education" to relax with a Bourbon highball. As he walked in at 5:10, Rayburn gave him the message to go over to the White House immediately. Truman's face turned white. "Holy General Jackson!" he said, and made it to the White House by 5:25. He was immediately directed to Mrs. Roosevelt's private study. "Harry," Eleanor said without hesitation, "the President is dead." For a moment, Truman was too stunned to speak. He finally managed to choke out, "Is there anything I can do for you? Eleanor replied, "Is there anything we can do for you? For you are the one in trouble now."

An hour and a half later, Truman took the oath of office in the Cabinet room of the White House. He was so nervous that the words wouldn't come to him, so he took a slip of paper from his pocket with the oath written on it and held it on top of his Bible. Then his voice began to function and he read the words firmly.

The next day he told reporters: "Boys, if you ever pray, pray for me now."

Nomination: July 15, 1948 . . . As the Democratic convention assembled in Philadelphia, most delegates agreed that the President faced a hopeless fight in his drive to win the election in his own right. In his 1st 3 years in office, he had presided over the difficult economic conversion from war to peace and the beginnings of a frustrating "Cold War." In the midterm elections, the Republicans asked the country "Had Enough?" and the answer was a resounding "Yes," as the GOP gained control of both houses of Congress for the 1st time since 1930. In the face of such overwhelming popular sentiment, one Democratic senator, J. William Fulbright of Arkansas, even suggested that the President resign.

Truman not only ignored such proposals, but pushed ahead with plans for the campaign of '48. Democratic chieftains searched desperately for a more popular alternative, and for a while there was widespread talk about a movement to draft Gen. Dwight D. Eisenhower for the nomination. Eisenhower, however, soon declared himself unavailable and the Democrats had to settle for Truman. "We're Just Mild About Harry," declared numerous signs at the national convention.

Truman's situation was made even more difficult by the breakup of the old New Deal coalition. Many liberal intellectuals disagreed with the President's anti-Communist stance and insisted that the Soviet Union was actually a peace-loving nation, forced into hostility by the American policy of "containment." Led by former Vice-President Henry A. Wallace, they organized the Progressive party to block Truman's reelection. Wallace, with his impressive credentials and personal following, actually believed that he could win, and most commentators agreed that the left-wing Progressives would draw at least 5 million votes from the Democratic ticket.

The final nail on Truman's "political coffin" was the mass defection of the Southern Democrats. When the convention adopted a platform plank endorsing Truman's strong civil rights program, the Southerners bolted, and organized their own "State's Rights" or "Dixiecrat" party. Their candidate was Gov. Strom Thurmond of South Carolina, who waged a regional campaign with strong appeal to Southern anti-Negro sentiment.

At 2 in the morning, Truman appeared before the convention to make a fighting acceptance speech. In an effort to rally disheartened delegates he promised that he and

Sen. Alben Barkley (his chosen running mate) would "win this election and make these Republicans like it—don't you forget that." As one commentator observed, he was the only man in the country who actually believed he could win.

Election: For the 2nd time, the Republicans nominated Gov. Thomas E. Dewey of New York. As his running mate, they chose Earl Warren, the popular and progressive governor of California. Though Dewey's slick appearance counted against him in some quarters ("How," asked Alice Roosevelt Longworth, "can you vote for a man who looks like the bridegroom on a wedding cake?"), the divisions in the Democratic party and the obvious conservative trend of the electorate seemed to assure his victory. Rather than jeopardize a "sure thing" with an issues-oriented campaign, Dewey decided to concentrate on windy platitudes about "national unity," and his speeches bored both the press and the public. Aboard his train, the "Victory Special," Dewey spent most of his time trying to look like a statesman, while his well-financed campaign rolled at a smooth and leisurely pace toward November.

Truman, on the other hand, plunged into his "hopeless" struggle with gusto. His whistle-stop campaign brought him to nearly 400 cities and small towns, where he had a chance to meet the people and tear into the record of the "do-nothing Republican Congress." In stop after stop, he introduced his wife and daughter and then minced no words in a series of blistering speeches that delighted his audiences: "That notorious do-nothing Republican 80th Congress has stuck a pitchfork in the farmer's back. . . . These Republican gluttons of privilege want a return of the Wall Street dictatorship. Your typical Republican reactionary is a very shrewd man with a calculating machine where his heart ought to be. . . . The Republicans tell me they stand for unity. As Al Smith used to say, 'That's a lot of hooey,' And if that rhymes with anything, it's not my fault. . . ."

As Truman "poured it on," he was often interrupted by shouts of "Give 'em hell, Harry!" The reporters who traveled with the President noted the large and enthusiastic crowds that greeted him everywhere, but they assumed that this only reflected people's inevitable interest in seeing a sitting President, and the confident predictions of a Dewey landslide never wavered. Under these circumstances, few Americans were willing to contribute to Truman's campaign. His efforts were so woefully underfinanced that he was regularly cut off the radio in midspeech for nonpayment, and once in Oklahoma City his staff had to take up a collection to get his train out of the station. Such difficulties only served to endear the underdog Truman to the electorate. As one ordinary

voter from Ohio put it: "I kept reading about that Dewey fellow, and the more I read the more he reminded me of one of those slick ads trying to get money out of my pocket. Now Harry Truman, running around and yipping and falling all over his feet—I had the feeling he could understand the kind of fixes I get into. . . ."

November 2, 1948 . . .

On election night, Truman was ahead from the beginning, but many commentators refused to believe it. A heavy vote for Henry Wallace in New York had thrown that State to Dewey, while Thurmond had carried 4 States in the Deep South. How could a Democratic candidate possibly win, while losing both New York *and* the Solid South? Harry Truman showed them how. He swept the big cities, the West, and the farm belt, including many traditionally Republican States, for 303 electoral votes to Dewey's 189. The popular totals were 24,179,345 for Truman, and 21,991,291 for Dewey. Strom Thurmond won 1,176,125 votes and 39 electoral votes (Alabama, Mississippi, South Carolina, and Louisiana). Henry Wallace and his Progressives, who had been badly hurt by the prominence of Communist party members in their campaign organization, drew only 1,157,326 votes (half of them in New York)—a far weaker showing than expected. In explaining the upset of "President Dewey," observers pointed to the extraordinarily low turnout; many voters, bored by a campaign that appeared to be over before it even started, simply stayed home on Election Day.

On its front page of November 3, the *Washington Post* advertised a banquet for the President, during which "political reporters and editors, including our own, along with pollsters, radio commentators, and columnists" would be treated to "breast of tough old crow, en glacé." If Truman came, he would eat "turkey."

January 20, 1949 . . .

Truman was sworn into office by Chief Justice Fred M. Vinson on the east portico of the Capitol. Certain of Dewey's victory, the Republican Congress had made an unusually generous allowance for inauguration ceremonies, so Truman was treated to one of the most elaborate public celebrations in inaugural history. Over a million persons in Washington watched a 3-hour parade, while 700 airplanes roared overhead.

Vetoes: Faced with a Republican Congress for several years of his term, Truman was forced into extensive use of his veto power; of all American Presidents, only FDR and Cleveland used that power more often. Among the 250 bills vetoed by the President were the antilabor Taft-Hartley Act, the highly repressive McCarran "Internal Security" Act, and a bill extending anti-Semitic and anti-Catholic immigration quotas. All of these measures were passed over Truman's veto. A total of 12 of the President's vetoes were overridden by Congress.

His 7 Years, 283 Days as President

PRO

Truman was right in his decision to use the atom bomb to end W.W. II. In August, 1945, the Japanese were still fighting with suicidal determination. Military experts agree that an invasion of the Japanese home islands would have cost far more lives—both American and Japanese—than the bombing of Hiroshima. Truman's 1st responsibility was to end the war as quickly as possible and to stop the daily battlefield slaughter. In accepting that responsibility, he actually saved hundreds of thousands of lives.

CON

No practical military considerations can possibly justify an immoral act such as using an atomic weapon on a populous city. Truman should have tried harder to warn the Japanese of the terrible potential of our new weapon and to negotiate a surrender. Even if you assume that the bombing of Hiroshima was inevitable, the subsequent attack on Nagasaki was totally unnecessary.

PRO

Truman deserves praise for his insistence—over the objections of allies and domestic political opponents—that the Nazi war criminals be tried at Nuremberg. He would not allow the German slaughter of 6 million Jews to be dismissed as "typical wartime atrocities." "Now nobody can say that it never happened, because the thing is on the record," the President said. Truman also proved himself a humanitarian in his concern for the survivors of the Nazi holocaust. Despite warnings from State Department "experts," he personally intervened to help establish the State of Israel, and he granted U.S. recognition only 11 minutes after Israel officially declared its independence.

CON

The State Department was right, and Truman was wrong: By adopting a pro-Israel stance, the President permanently compromised U.S. interests in the oil-rich Arab states.

PRO

The greatest accomplishment of Truman's Presidency was keeping the peace in Europe. He effectively countered Stalinist expansionism while steering clear of W.W. III. The Marshall Plan, called by Churchill "the most unsordid act in all history," provided generous aid to war-ravaged European nations for feeding hungry millions and rebuilding their shattered economies. "Point Four" committed the U.S. for the 1st time to sharing our wealth and technology with underdeveloped nations. With the Berlin airlift, Truman effectively sidestepped a Russian invitation to begin a shooting war, and in organizing NATO he provided for an effective and concerted defense in case of Russian attack. Perhaps most impressive of all, Truman skillfully engineered solid, bipartisan support for all of these major foreign-policy achievements, winning approval from an often reluctant Republican Congress.

CON

The "Cold War" which Truman launched was costly and unnecessary. It is possible that the Soviet Union had only peaceful intentions after W.W. II, but that they were alarmed by the aggressive American initiatives and forced to take defensive action. The Soviet "conquest" of Eastern Europe which so concerned Truman and other anti-Communists represented little more than Russia's assumption of her legitimate sphere of influence.

PRO

Truman's sweeping "Fair Deal" program was one of the most visionary and progressive legislative packages ever presented by an American President. Not only did he call for a national health insurance program, increased aid to the elderly, more Federal housing, and aid to education, but he pushed for the 1st major civil rights bill since Reconstruction. Truman also fought against congressional attempts to give special tax breaks to the corporations and the rich. In domestic policy, the President was a tireless spokesman for ordinary Americans, and for once, black Americans were not excluded.

CON

Most of Truman's domestic reforms never got off the ground. Of all his major programs, only the housing construction bills won approval by Congress. Truman was sincerely dedicated to progressive ideas but he lacked Roosevelt's skill in mobilizing popular support for his proposals.

PRO

The world was lucky indeed that Harry Truman was America's President during the Korean conflict. Another President—Johnson or Nixon, for example—would have almost certainly followed the advice of General-in-Chief Douglas MacArthur and authorized the invasion of mainland China, thereby plunging the world into an unprecedented holocaust. When MacArthur continued to talk of military action against China, Truman had the courage to fire him—the most controversial decision of his Presidency. Americans of the 1970s should remember that Korea, unlike Vietnam, had not been the scene of a people's guerrilla movement: The act that provoked American intervention was an outright invasion from North Korea. At stake in repelling this aggression were not only the interests of the U.S., but the integrity of the United Nations, which had voted to take immediate defensive action.

CON

Truman certainly deserves credit for restraining the irresponsible demagogue MacArthur, but he must also accept blame for committing the U.S. to an unnecessary war in the 1st place. Korea was actually outside the vital "defense perimeters" recommended by the military, and Truman's hasty decision to intervene was a costly mistake. Still worse, Truman accepted MacArthur's assurances that the Chinese would never intervene, and thus permitted the general to push the war to the Chinese border. The result was the commitment of hundreds of thousands of Chinese troops to a tragic war which Americans could not possibly win, and in which even a "victory" would have been meaningless. Over 50,000 Americans died in vain.

PRO

As much as any man, Truman fought to stop the anti-Communist hysteria that began poisoning American life during his Presidency. In sharp contrast to his successor, Dwight D. Eisenhower, Truman spoke out courageously against McCarthyism. "All this howl about organizations a fellow belongs to gives me a pain in the neck," he told the country, and then, later: "The House Un-American Activities Committee is the most un-American activity in the whole Government." Truman vetoed repressive "anti-Red" legislation and attempted to return the country to common sense, but he was outshouted by the McCarthys, the McCarrans, and the Nixons. Standing up for civil liberties and common decency in the face of mounting pressure, he left office in a howl of public protest.

CON

Truman himself gave an early and unwitting boost to McCarthyism by authorizing "loyalty boards" to investigate Federal employees. When Republicans claimed that these investigations were only a "whitewash," it was already too late to stop the drift toward paranoia and repression. Public confidence in Government was further shaken by revelations that some of Truman's friends and associates had engaged in shoddy influence-peddling schemes. As the Republicans shook their heads over "Korea, Communism, and Corruption," Truman returned to Missouri under a thick, dark cloud.

AFTER THE PRESIDENCY

In January, 1953, a reporter asked Truman to name the 1st thing he had done after returning to the white frame house in Independence. The former President thought for a moment, then replied: "I took the suitcases up to the attic."

In retirement, Truman read extensively, answered mail, and worked on his memoirs. He also enjoyed talking with neighbors and old friends and could often be seen eating lunch at drugstore lunch counters. He seemed to enjoy his quiet home life with Bess, and for the 1st time they were free of his mother-in-law (who died in 1952), an impossible old woman who had publicly predicted that Harry would lose to Dewey in 1948.

Truman's main interest was in the construction and organization of the Truman Library, which was formally dedicated in 1957. Even into his late 70s, Truman took particular pleasure in addressing assemblies of schoolchildren at the library and delivering homespun lectures about American history and the founding fathers. The old man also found time to campaign actively for Democratic candidates. In the presidential election of 1960, Truman worked particularly hard to insure the defeat of his old enemy, Richard Nixon.

At his 80th birthday, Truman told reporters: "Remember me as I was, not as I am," and in his later years he deteriorated noticeably. Nevertheless, he continued to dismiss all suggestions that he had been a great President. On May 6, 1971, he refused to accept the Congressional Medal of Honor, which Congress had planned to present to him on his 87th birthday. "I do not consider that I have done anything which should be the reason for any award, congressional or otherwise," he wrote.

PSYCHOHISTORY

Harry's father, John Anderson ("Peanuts") Truman, was a warmhearted, 2-fisted, emotional little man who was willing to defend his family or his honor on any occasion. Young Harry admired him, but with his slight build and his breakable glasses, the boy was forced to turn away from most fights. Harry was a "mama's boy," who spent most of his time at home, reading books, playing the piano, or taking care of his little sister. Truman compensated for this boyhood weakness in several ways. First, he chose—and then won—the boyish, athletic, and socially prominent Bess Wallace as his wife—a solid, protective woman always known to him as "the Boss." Even more importantly, Harry, at 17, deliberately turned away from bookish pursuits to prove himself in the world of "hard knocks." His 1st chance came in W.W. I, when he faced battlefield danger on many occasions and mastered his sometimes insubordinate troops with colorful curses that "took the skin off their ears." Harry, the underrated Mama's boy, was showing the world that he could be as tough as his popular old man, and the combative, "regular guy," straight-from-the-shoulder style became a permanent part of Truman's makeup. When Roosevelt died suddenly in 1945, Truman confronted a psychological situation that was in many ways familiar to him: He had to prove to a doubting world that he was capable of filling the shoes of an awesome father figure. Needless to say, Truman rose to the challenge and worked hard to carve out a distinctive and independent reputation for himself. His greatest fear was always indecision, uncertainty, and weakness; Harry would never be a "mama's boy" again. Historians agree that the worst moments of his Presidency stem from this need for instant decision in complex matters and an unfortunate tendency of shooting from the hip. With rare self-awareness, Truman himself offered an important clue to his personality. Speaking to a group of schoolchildren at the Truman Library, he was asked by one skinny 12-year-old: "Mr. President, was you popular when you was a boy?"

"Why no," Truman answered. "I was never popular. The popular boys were the ones who were good at games and had big, tight fists. I was never like that. Without my glasses I was blind as a bat, and to tell the truth, I was kind of a sissy. If there was any danger of getting into a fight, I always ran. I guess that's why I'm here today."

LITTLE-KNOWN FACTS

—The "S" in Harry S Truman is not an abbreviation—it is Truman's complete middle name. His parents could not agree on whether to honor his father's father, Anderson Shippe Truman, or his mother's father, Solomon Young, and so the noncommittal initial was accepted as a compromise.

—Truman's mother, the daughter of an old-line Confederate family, had been briefly locked up in a Federal "internment camp" during the Civil War and she never quite forgave either President Lincoln or the U.S. Government. Many years later, when she came to visit her son in the White House and was offered accommodations in a particularly historic room, she said she would rather sleep on the floor "than spend the night in the Lincoln bed." At the age of 92, back in Independence, Mrs. Truman broke her hip when she tripped in her kitchen and the President flew out to see her. Looking up at him from her bed of pain as he walked into the room she said: "I don't want any smart cracks out of you. I saw your picture in the paper last week putting a wreath at the Lincoln Memorial."

—Many Americans have heard about the sign Truman kept on his White House desk, with its famous inscription: "The Buck Stops Here." Less well-known is the motto that graced his desk when he was a senator. A quotation from fellow-Missourian Mark Twain, it read: "Always do right. This will gratify some people and astonish the rest."

—Truman had been President for less than 2 days when he phoned an Administration official to inform him of a presidential appointment. The official wanted to know if the President had made the appointment before he died. "No," Truman snapped, "he made it just now."

—In March, 1947, while visiting Mexico City, Truman made an unscheduled stop at Chapultepec Castle, where 100 years before American troops had stormed the heights. Supposedly the only Mexicans alive after the assault were 6 teen-age cadets—but they committed suicide rather than surrender. Against the hysterical warnings of his aides and protocol experts, the President of the U.S. went to the monument to *Los Niños Héroes*, placed a wreath on it, and bowed his head in tribute. The cadets in the color guard burst into tears. Later, it was said that nothing in the history of the 2 countries has ever done more to cement their relationship. Reflecting on the incident in his retirement, Truman recalled that he had been told that his "pro-Mexican" gesture would alienate the State of Texas. "I said, 'What the hell. Any Texan that's damn fool enough to be put out when a President of the U.S. pays tribute to a bunch of brave kids, I don't need their support.' So I went out there, and I put a wreath on that monument, and it seemed to work out all right."

—In 1956, the former President traveled to England, where he received an honorary degree from Oxford. The Latin citation praised him as the "truest of allies," but addressed the man from Missouri as "Harricum Truman." Student cheers of "Give 'em hell, Harricum!" followed the ceremony.

—While Truman was campaigning for John Kennedy in 1960, the Associated Press reported that in one of his speeches he had said that "anyone who voted for Nixon and Lodge ought to go to hell" and that Nixon "never told the truth in his life." Later, Truman denied having made the 1st statement, but added "they can't challenge the 2nd."

Quotes from Truman:

"In the middle of the speech, some big voice up in the corner hollered out, 'Give 'em hell, Harry!' Well, I never gave anybody hell—I just told the truth on these fellows and they thought it was hell."

"I learned that a leader is a man who has the ability to get other people to do what they don't want to do, and like it."

"Being a President is like riding a tiger. A man has to keep on riding or be swallowed. The fantastically crowded months of 1945 taught me that a President either is constantly on top of events, or, if he hesitates, events will soon be on top of him. I never felt that I could let up for a moment."

"You know, right here is where I've always wanted to be, and the only place I've ever wanted to be. The Senate—that's just my speed and style."—April, 1945

"Bess and Margaret went to Mo. at 7:30 EDT, 6:30 God's time. I sure hated to see them go. Came back to the great white jail and read the papers, some history, and then wrote this. It is hot and humid and lonely. Why in hell does anybody want to be a head of state? Damned if I know."—Memo to himself, summer, 1945

"The Presidency is an all day and nearly an all night job. Just between you and me and the gatepost, I like it."—To an audience of Masons, October, 1945

"All the President is, is a glorified public relations man who spends his time flattering, kissing, and kicking people to get them to do what they are supposed to do anyway."—A letter to his sister, 1947

"Slanders, lies, character assassination—these things are a threat to every single citizen everywhere in this country. When even one American—who has done nothing wrong—is forced by fear to shut his mind and close his mouth—then all Americans are in peril. It is the job of all of us—of every American who loves his country and his freedom—to rise up and put a stop to this terrible business."—Speech to American Legion, 1951

"I fired MacArthur because he wouldn't respect the authority of the President. I didn't fire him because he was a dumb son of a bitch, although he was, but that's not against the law for generals. If it was, half to three-quarters of them would be in jail."—1961

"There is an epitaph in Boot Hill Cemetery in Arizona which reads: 'Here lies Jack Williams. He done his damnedest! What more can a person do?' Well, that's all I could do. I did my damnedest, and that's all there is to it."—1964

Quotes about Him:

"He didn't put on airs."—Bess Truman

"I must confess, sir. . . . I loathed your taking the place of Franklin Roosevelt. I misjudged you badly. Since that time, you, more than any other man, have saved Western Civilization."—Winston Churchill

"Mr. Truman is not performing, and gives no evidence of his ability to perform, the function of the Commander-in-chief. At the very center of the Truman Administration there is a vacuum of responsibility and authority."—Walter Lippman, 1946

"I had talked with Mr. Truman for only a few minutes when I began to realize that the man had a real grasp of the situation. What a surprise and relief this was! He knew the facts and the sequence of events and he had a keen understanding of what they meant."—W. Averell Harriman, U.S. Ambassador to Russia

"To err is Truman."—Republican slogan

"At this writing, the President's influence is weaker than any President's has been in modern history."—Arthur Krock, *The New York Times*, April, 1948

"I don't care how the thing is explained. It defies all common sense to send that roughneck ward politician back to the White House."—Sen. Robert Taft on the election of 1948

"Mr. Truman, Dean Acheson and other Administration officials for political purposes *covered up* this Communist conspiracy and attempted to halt its exposure."—Richard M. Nixon, 1952

"Truman was the last authentic American, with all the characteristic faults and virtues of the breed, to occupy the White House, and I doubt very much if there will ever be another."—Malcolm Muggeridge

"I have read over and over again that he was an *ordinary* man. . . . I consider him one of the most extraordinary human beings who ever lived."—Dean Acheson

GHOSTS IN THE WHITE HOUSE?

A letter from Truman to his daughter in 1946 . . .

"I told your mother a 'hant' story which you'd better hear her read to you. This old place cracks and pops all night long and you can imagine that old Jackson or Andy Johnson or some other ghost is walking. Why they'd want to come back I could never understand. It's a nice prison but a prison nevertheless. No man in his right mind would want to come here of his own accord.

"Now about those ghosts. I'm sure they're here and I'm not half so alarmed at meeting up with any of them as I am at having to meet the live nuts I have to see every day. I am sure old Andy could give me some good advice and probably teach me some good swear words to use on Molotov and De Gaulle. And I am sure old Grover Cleveland could tell me some choice remarks to make to some political leaders. So I won't lock my doors or bar them either if any of the old coots in the pictures out in the hall want to come out of their frames for a friendly chat."

35th President

JOHN FITZGERALD KENNEDY

VITAL STATISTICS

Born: May 29, 1917, in Brookline, Mass. Brookline is an unpretentious suburb of Boston, and the gray frame house in which he spent his childhood was located in a middle-class neighborhood. The fabulous wealth for which his family is celebrated came only in later years. Kennedy was the 1st President born in the 20th century.

Died: November 22, 1963, in Dallas, Tex., from bullet wounds in the neck and head. Kennedy was riding in a downtown motorcade when he was cut down by a sniper. The identity of the sniper—and other details of the assassination—are still a matter of controversy. (See also: Assassinations, Chap. 9.) Kennedy, who was 46, lived a shorter life than any other President. He was buried in Arlington National Cemetery, beneath a memorial "eternal flame." As E. B. White observed: "He died of exposure, but in a way that he would have settled for—in the line of duty, and with his friends and enemies all around, supporting him and shooting at him."

BEFORE THE PRESIDENCY

Career: On both sides, Kennedy's grandfathers were leading Democratic ward bosses in an age when a handful of Irish "pols" ruled Boston. His father, however, sought power in a different way. By age 25, Joe Kennedy had gained control of a bank in East Boston, and with subsequent investments in real estate, Hollywood, and the stock market, he built a financial empire worth $250 million. Naturally, he sent his children to the best schools, and young "Jack," the 2nd oldest, prepared for college at Choate School in Connecticut. Kennedy had a difficult time at prep school, and his housemaster wrote home: "He is casual and disorderly in almost all of his organization projects. Jack studies at the last minute, keeps appointments late, has little sense of material values, and can seldom locate his possessions." Though his popularity with his classmates won him election as "most likely to succeed," Kennedy graduated in the bottom half of his class. In the choice of a college, Jack was naturally anxious to avoid direct competition with his brilliantly successful older brother, Joe, Jr., so he steered clear of Harvard and enrolled instead at Princeton University. After 2 months, however, an attack of jaundice forced him to drop out of school and return home. By the time he was ready to start again the next year (1936), he had given in to the urgings of his family and agreed to join his brother at Harvard. As a student, Kennedy maintained a "C" average during his 1st 2 years, and devoted much of his time to athletics, until he seriously injured his back playing football. Jack took off the 2nd semester of his junior year to travel through Europe. His father was then serving as U.S. Ambassador to Great Britain (a reward for his generous support of FDR), and so young Kennedy was admitted to high-level

political and diplomatic circles. Back at Harvard, he used this experience in his senior thesis —a study of England's complacency on the eve of W.W. II. Not only did this thesis win a *magna cum laude* from the political science department, but rewritten and retitled *Why England Slept*, it was published and became a best seller. Though Kennedy began to lean toward a writing career, he studied briefly at Stanford's Graduate School of Business after his graduation from Harvard. In October, 1941, as the U.S. moved close to war, Kennedy dropped everything to accept a commission in the Navy. On a summer night in the South Pacific in 1943, Lieutenant Kennedy was in command of PT-109 when it was rammed and sunk by a Japanese destroyer. He was thrown against the wall of the cockpit, severely aggravating the old football injury to his back, but he still managed to marshal the 10 surviving members of his crew and swim with them to a nearby island. One of the men was too badly injured to swim, so Kennedy took the man's life preserver in his teeth and, for several hours, towed his wounded shipmate through the dark water. For his heroism, Kennedy won the Navy Medal and the Purple Heart, and he was sent back to a navy hospital in the U.S. for treatment of malaria and complications concerning his back. It was while he was still hospitalized that Jack learned that his older brother Joe had been killed while flying a dangerous mission over Europe. This in effect settled Jack's career plans—though he got a job as a reporter for the Hearst newspapers and continued to talk about a writing career, his family now demanded that he go into politics. As his father recalled years later: "I told him Joe was dead and it was his responsibility to run for Congress. He didn't want to. But I told him he had to." The Cambridge district, which the family selected as a target, was one in which John "Honey Fitz" Fitzgerald—Jack's grandfather and a former mayor of Boston— still had a considerable following. An energetic, well-organized campaign, with the emphasis on the young candidate's distinguished war record, brought Kennedy an easy victory. In January of 1947 he entered Congress, and impressed one of his new colleagues as a "29-year-old kid who looked 19 and showed up for House debates in khaki pants with his shirttail out." This didn't seem to bother Jack's constituents, who twice reelected him by lopsided margins. In 1952, Congressman Kennedy felt ready to challenge the State's incumbent Republican senator, Henry Cabot Lodge. In the battle which followed, Kennedy dazzled the voters with the most intensive and professional campaign in Massachusetts history. Papa Joe not only provided generous financing for these efforts, but came through with a timely "business loan" of

$500,000 to the failing *Boston Post*, and that normally Republican paper soon came out strongly for Kennedy. In November, Eisenhower swept the State by 200,000 votes, but Kennedy managed to buck the Republican tide and beat Lodge by 70,000. At the age of 35, Jack moved up to the U.S. Senate.

Personal Life: During Kennedy's years in the House of Representatives, he won national publicity as "Washington's Gay Young Bachelor"; but when he began to entertain higher ambitions, it seemed time to put an end to all that. In 1952, he met Jacqueline Bouvier, the daughter of a socially prominent New York stockbroker and a former "Deb Queen of the Year." The 23-year-old Jackie, who had studied at Vassar and the Sorbonne, was working as an "Inquiring Camera Girl" for a Washington newspaper. She was obviously fascinated by publicity and power, and some Washington friends tried several times to introduce her to Kennedy before they were finally brought together at a small dinner party. As Jack later recalled: "I reached across the asparagus and asked her for a date." The courtship that followed was frequently interrupted by Jack's trips to Massachusetts to campaign for the Senate. Nevertheless, he managed to keep in touch with Jackie. As she remembered it: "He was not the candy-and-flowers type, so every now and then he'd give me a book. He gave me *The Raven*, which is the life of Sam Houston, and also *Pilgrim's Way* by John Buchan." (Jackie's favorite reading, however, was Marcel Proust's *Remembrance of Things Past*.) Kennedy and Jacqueline were married in a brilliant society wedding in Newport, R.I., in 1953, when Jack was 36, and Jackie 24. During their 10 years together, they seldom expressed their affection in public, but Kennedy was obviously proud of his brilliant and stylish wife. On one occasion, he showed off her knowledge of antiquity by taking out a book on Greek civilization and quizzing her in front of their friends for half an hour. As President, he was delighted with the attention that she received everywhere, and on a trip to Europe he once introduced himself as "the man who accompanied Jackie Kennedy to Paris." Over the course of the marriage, Jackie was pregnant 5 times; but she suffered 2 miscarriages and her last child, Patrick, died when he was 2 days old. Kennedy had never been particularly fond of children before his marriage, and once, when the 4-year-old daughter of a friend recoiled rather than kiss him, the father quipped: "I don't think she quite caught that strong quality of love of children—so much of the candidate's makeup—which has made him so dear to the hearts of all mothers." Nevertheless, when he had children of his own, Kennedy

was a doting father, and his favorite hours of the day as President were the occasions when Caroline and John-John were allowed to run wild in his office. Kennedy also delighted in touring toy stores with his children and running up bills for hundreds of dollars.

When Kennedy was elected President, one of his top aides privately predicted, "This Administration is going to do for sex what the last one did for golf." Naturally, there was constant gossip concerning the handsome young President's extramarital adventures. The most persistent rumors centered on movie stars Marilyn Monroe and Angie Dickinson—Ms. Dickinson was a friend of the Kennedy family. Though it is certainly true that Kennedy maintained his eye for beautiful women, the stories of passionate love affairs are outlandish and unsubstantiated. The evidence suggests that he always considered women a pleasant diversion, but that in his later years he hardly had time for them. Moreover, he was much too careful a politician to risk exposure with a public that was already suspicious.

His days as "Washington's Gay Young Bachelor," however, were another matter. Kennedy dated a dazzling succession of debutantes and Hollywood starlets, and no one claims that his interests were exclusively platonic. During his Senate campaign in '52, his Republican opponents got hold of a snapshot showing the young congressman reclining on a Florida beach beside a nude and spectacularly buxom girl. His worried aides brought the photo to Kennedy's attention and the candidate studied it for a moment with obvious interest. Finally, he smiled in recollection: "Yes, I remember her. She was *great*."

On the Way to the White House: Kennedy never entirely gave up on his ambitions as a writer, and a successful book played a key role in his march to the Presidency. In 1954, the condition of his back had deteriorated to such an extent that he couldn't walk without crutches, so he submitted to a painful and potentially dangerous spinal fusion operation. At 1st, the surgery was unsuccessful and for several days the 37-year-old senator lay close to death, and only after a 2nd operation did Kennedy begin to recover. During the long months when he was unable to leave his bed at his father's Palm Beach home, Kennedy read extensively and began working on a book describing past U.S. senators who had bravely defied public opinion. Under the title *Profiles in Courage*, this book caused a mild sensation when it was published in '56—it went on to become a best seller and to win the Pulitzer Prize. Because of this book, Kennedy's name was inevitably associated with the idea of political courage—even though the bedridden senator had been conveniently absent during the stormy Senate debates on Joseph McCarthy's censure, and had even refused to declare himself on the issue. In the Democratic convention of 1956, Kennedy was widely respected as a young leader of national stature, and he made a strong bid for the vice-presidential nomination. When Adlai Stevenson told the delegates to make their own choice for the 2nd spot on the ticket, Kennedy was neck and neck with Sen. Estes Kefauver, until Kefauver finally won on the 3rd ballot. A graceful concession speech, however, meant that Jack's political prospects were brighter than ever. With their eyes on the 1960 presidential nomination, the Kennedys worked Jack's bid for reelection to the Senate in 1958; a landslide victory there could give Jack's national ambitions a powerful boost. Kennedy campaigned night and day to build up his vote, even though victory was assured from the very beginning. In November, he won with a staggering majority of 875,000—an all-time record for the State of Massachusetts.

His Person: John Kennedy was 6'1" tall, and he kept his weight at a slender 175. He had cool gray eyes and light brown hair—several shades lighter than it usually appeared in photographs. He was noted for his elegant and expensive wardrobe, and always took great care with his clothing. He changed his clothes from the skin out at least twice each day, and often wore as many as 4 different shirts in a single day. He particularly disliked button-down collars, and ordered the members of his staff to stop wearing them. He also disliked hats—convinced that they made him look silly. This created a problem with the hat industry when Kennedy was President—the public was so impressed with their hatless President that sales had dropped off sharply. Yet he continued to ignore pleas that he allow himself to be photographed in some fedora. This continued to his dying day, when he went through the Texas ritual of being presented a cowboy hat in Fort Worth, yet steadfastly refused to put it on, despite the wishes of 2,000 Texans.

Kennedy's enthusiastic pursuit of physical fitness was well known. Despite his bad back, he enjoyed touch football, golf, and sailing; and he also exercised every day in his bedroom, in the White House gym, or even on the floor of his jet plane. At one point, he became so annoyed with the "flabbiness" of his staff, that he asked them to lose 5 lbs. each. Kennedy himself was little interested in food—he was strictly a "meat and potatoes man" who, according to a close friend, "always ate as if somebody were about to grab his plate." Kennedy was a modest drinker—occasionally he would enjoy a daiquiri or a bloody Mary, but seldom more than one in an evening. All his life, he disliked people who put their hands on him, and despised the habits of old-time politicians who tried to throw friendly arms over his shoulders. Though he learned to shake hands with the public like any other politician, he was distinctly uncomfortable with handshakes that lasted more than a second.

Kennedy enjoyed going to the movies, and his favorites were Westerns and Civil War pictures. If a film did not meet with his approval, however, he was reluctant to waste his time with it: He would tell his companions, "Let's haul it out of here," and expect them to leave the theater with him. His ability as a speedreader amazed his colleagues; he could read close to 2,000 words per minute with 95% comprehension. Every morning he would read 4 newspapers in the course of 15 minutes, and then be prepared to discuss in detail any of the articles in each of them. He was impatient with people who digested material at a slower rate, and would sometimes tell them: "I asked you to read it—not to memorize it."

Everyone who met Jack Kennedy came away impressed by his sense of humor. He particularly enjoyed laughing at himself. Once, during the early stages of his campaign for the Presidency, he told a private gathering in Washington: "I have just received the following telegram from my generous daddy. It says, 'Dear Jack: Don't buy a single vote more than necessary. I'll be damned if I'm going to pay for a landslide.' " His humor also had a sadistic edge and he delighted in embarrassing his friends and his staff. When his brother paid his daily visit to the presidential office, for instance, Kennedy would often call in his aide Kenny O'Donnell and say: "Now—tell Bobby why you think that idea of his is terrible."

At work or at play, Kennedy had to win, and his temper occasionally flared up at touch football partners who put out less than the maximum effort. Once, during the Bay of Pigs crisis, he tried to relax by playing checkers with his old friend Undersecretary of the Navy "Red" Fay. When it became clear that Fay was winning their 1st game, JFK deliberately upset the board. "One of those unfortunate incidents of life, Redhead," he smiled. "We'll never really know if the Undersecretary was going to outmaneuver the Commander-in-chief strategically."

PRESIDENCY

Nomination: The main obstacle standing between Kennedy and the Democratic presidential nomination in 1960 was the belief that no Catholic could possibly be elected. Kennedy sought to overcome this religious prejudice by entering—and winning—a string of State party primaries. With his generously financed, brilliantly organized campaigns, and his fresh and youthful appeal, Kennedy easily outdistanced all his rivals. The decisive blow came in West

Virginia—a State that was 95% Protestant—where Kennedy beat Sen. Hubert Humphrey so badly that Humphrey was forced to withdraw from the race.

July 11, 1960 . . .

As the Democratic convention convened in Los Angeles, Kennedy had emerged as the clear choice of the Northern, liberal wing of his party and appeared close to a 1st ballot victory. His chief convention rival was Senate majority leader Lyndon Johnson, who had the support of the South and the party's more conservative elements. At the last minute, an unexpected development jeopardized Kennedy's almost certain nomination: A strong drive to "draft" Adlai Stevenson for a 3rd try as Democratic standard-bearer began to drain liberal strength from Kennedy. Sen. Eugene McCarthy of Minnesota gave an impassioned nominating speech for Stevenson, and in the convention's longest and most emotional floor demonstration, delegates and the public showed their support for the Illinois leader. In the face of all this, Stevenson's repeated assurances that he was not a candidate began to lose credibility. Nevertheless, Kennedy's support remained surprisingly firm, and when the 1st roll call reached Wyoming, everyone at the convention knew that those 15 votes would put JFK over the top. As the convention paused in silence for a moment, the candidate's brother Teddy, in the middle of the Wyoming delegation, urged its members to use their votes to name a President. When the chairman of the delegation announced that all 15 votes went to the Kennedy column, the convention went wild as JFK was nominated on the 1st ballot. The next day, in a bid for party unity and Southern support, Kennedy asked that Lyndon Johnson be named as his running mate. Despite complaints from organized labor and Stevensonian liberals, this choice was finally accepted by the convention.

On Friday afternoon of convention week, in the shadows of the setting sun, Kennedy appeared before 80,000 people in the Los Angeles Coliseum to deliver his acceptance speech. There he sounded the keynote for his campaign and his Presidency:

I stand tonight facing west on what was once the last frontier. From the lands that stretch 3,000 mi. behind me, the pioneers of old gave up their safety, their comfort and sometimes their lives to build a new world here in the West. . . .

Today some would say that those struggles are all over, that all the horizons have been explored, that all the battles have been won, that there is no longer an American frontier. But the problems are not all solved and the battles are not all won, and we stand today on the edge of a new frontier—the frontier of the 1960s. . . . Beyond that frontier are unchartered areas of science and space, unsolved problems of peace and war, unconquered pockets of ignorance and prejudice, unanswered questions of poverty and surplus.

It would be easier to shrink back from that frontier, to look to the safe mediocrity of the past. . . . But I believe the times demand invention, innovation, imagination, decision. I am asking each of you to be new pioneers on that new frontier.

Election: To oppose Kennedy and Johnson, the Republicans chose Vice-President Richard Nixon and Ambassador to the UN Henry Cabot Lodge—the same man Kennedy had beaten in a Massachusetts Senate race 8 years before. In their campaign, Nixon and Lodge attempted to identify themselves with the popular Eisenhower, and to raise public doubts concerning Kennedy's maturity. Their national slogan *"Experience Counts"* seemed to ignore the fact that Kennedy and Nixon had been 1st elected to Congress in the same year (1946), or that Nixon was only 4 years older than the 43-year-old JFK.

An unspoken issue throughout the campaign was the widespread fear that a Catholic President would allow his policies to be dictated by the Vatican. Kennedy decided to confront this issue head on in a dramatic speech to a gathering of Protestant ministers in Houston. "Because I am a Catholic, and no Catholic has ever been elected President, it is apparently necessary for me to state once again—not what kind of church I believe in, for that should be important only to me, but what kind of America I believe in. I believe in an America where separation of Church and State is absolute—where no Catholic prelate would tell the President (should he be a Catholic) how to act and no Protestant minister would tell his parishioners for whom to vote." In the final analysis, Kennedy's religion may have won him as many votes among his fellow Catholics as it cost him in the rest of the population.

Easily the most celebrated moment of the campaign came in September, when Nixon and Kennedy met for the 1st of their 4 televised debates before a national audience estimated at 70 million. Most commentators expected that Nixon, with his reputation as a seasoned and effective TV performer, would demolish the inexperienced Kennedy. But the moment the 2 faces appeared on the screen, the entire election seemed to swing in Kennedy's direction. Nixon made the mistake of using dark-toned "lazy shave" face powder, and poor lighting threw deep shadows around his eyes. As historian

Roger Butterfield expressed it, "He looked for all the world like a man with shaving and perspiration problems, glumly waiting for the commercial to tell him how not to offend." Kennedy, on the other hand, seemed cool and confident, in total command of the facts and the situation. After the 1st debate, the charge that JFK was too "young and inexperienced" for the Presidency seemed to lose most of its potency.

Compared to these image differences, disagreements on the issues seemed unimportant. In fact, many liberals considered the candidates so similar to one another that Kennedy partisan Arthur Schlesinger felt called upon to write a book called *Kennedy or Nixon: Does It Make Any Difference?*

In a bizarre sidelight to the campaign, strong differences did develop. For many months, Vice-President Nixon had been secretly urging an exile invasion of Cuba, and he was delighted when the CIA decided to go ahead with plans for the mission. Then, in the campaign, Kennedy came out publicly for the same proposal. Nixon was enraged; he felt that revealing his backing for the project would blow its cover. Facing what he considered "probably the most difficult decision of the campaign," Nixon decided: "There was only one thing I could do. The covert operation had to be protected at all costs. I must not even suggest by implication that the U.S. was rendering aid to rebel forces in and out of Cuba. In fact, I must go to the other extreme: I must attack the Kennedy proposal to provide such aid as wrong and irresponsible because it would violate our treaty commitments."

In other words, Nixon came out strongly against Nixon's plan.

November 8, 1960 . . .

On Election Day, Kennedy won with one of the shakiest mandates in American history. He polled 34,227,096 votes to Nixon's 34,108,-546—a margin of only 49.9% to 49.6%. Most of the States had actually voted against Kennedy, as had majorities of whites, college graduates, high-income people, women, Protestants, farmers, senior citizens, and business and professional people. In the Electoral College, with the help of Lyndon Johnson's strong appeal to the Solid South and some disputed votes from Mayor Daley's Chicago, Kennedy won by the more comfortable margin of 303 to 219.

January 20, 1961 . . .

On Inauguration Day, Washington was blanketed by an unexpected snowstorm as temperatures plunged to 20° above zero. The city was plagued by traffic jams, and the spectators who gathered to watch the inaugural ceremonies stamped their feet, slapped their arms, and blew into cupped hands to keep warm.

At Kennedy's request, the aged poet Robert Frost made a special appearance on the inaugural platform. He read a poem which he had written in honor of the occasion:

Summoning artists to participate
In the august occasions of the state
Seems something artists ought to celebrate . . .
A golden age of poetry and power
Of which this noonday's the beginning hour.

In the blinding winter sunlight, the old man had difficulty reading his text; he eventually gave up his effort, and recited instead a poem he knew by heart.

As Kennedy stood up to take the oath of office from Chief Justice Earl Warren, he stunned the freezing crowd by stripping off his overcoat. His address, considered one of the most eloquent inaugurals in American history, contained more than a dozen ringing phrases which have since become shopworn political cliches. His most famous line had originally read: "Ask not what your country will do for you, but what you will do for your country." At the last moment, he had scratched out the words "will" on his text and replaced them by "can."

At the inaugural ball, Jack and Jackie dazzled the crowds. According to one of the new President's close friends, JFK "saw the whole thing and adored it . . . you knew this was one of his great moments, you could tell. Here was the reigning prince, and he was loving it."

Vetoes: In his brief term, JFK vetoed only 21 bills—a smaller number than any President since Harding. None of his vetoes were overridden by Congress.

His 2 Years, 306 Days as President

PRO

Though the disastrous Bay of Pigs invasion had been planned and orchestrated by the previous Administration, Kennedy took full responsibility for the fiasco—and learned never to trust military "experts" again. In the Cuban missile crisis of '62, Kennedy ignored his military advisers and took a cool and moderate course—which prevented the outbreak of nuclear war, and brought about America's greatest cold war victory. In his handling of the Laos situation, Kennedy also moved the world closer to peace by accepting a neutralist Government and avoiding a U.S. commitment to an Asian land war. His success in negotiating a test ban treaty ended the threat of atmospheric fallout, and was the 1st step toward international disarmament. Under Kennedy, the U.S. began to acknowledge its obligations to underdeveloped nations. The Peace Corps won worldwide praise, and JFK's generous "Alliance for Progress" made him a hero throughout Latin America.

CON

In foreign policy, Kennedy lurched unsteadily from one crisis to another—it was his apparent ineptitude in the handling of the Bay of Pigs invasion that encouraged the Soviets to test his resolution by moving missiles to Cuba. In calling out American reserves to reenforce Berlin, Kennedy grossly overreacted to a Soviet threat, and his inflated, warlike rhetoric consistently aggravated cold war tensions. The big increases in military spending under Kennedy offer another example of dangerous saber-rattling, and provoked similar increases by the U.S.S.R. In committing the U.S. to the much-publicized "space race" with the Russians, Kennedy began a pointless competition which cost the American people some $50 billion.

PRO

Kennedy championed a progressive and enlightened domestic program, including Medicare, aid to education, tax reform, and a strong new civil rights bill. In his successful effort to force the big steel companies to retract their announced price hike, Kennedy worked effectively to curb inflation, and showed that a strong President can overcome corporate power. Under Kennedy, unemployment declined and America prospered.

CON

Kennedy's handling of Congress was dismal and inept, and *none* of the major domestic proposals of his much-heralded "New Frontier" were enacted into law. As Senate minority leader Everett Dirksen aptly commented, a Kennedy legislative recommendation had "about as much impact as a snowflake on the bosom of the Potomac." In the 1st 2 years of his Administration, Kennedy was often tardy and reluctant in his commitment to equal rights for black Americans. As a candidate, he announced that a President could end discrimination in Federal housing "with the stroke of a pen"; as President, it took him 22 months to pick up that pen.

PRO

Kennedy brought new style, vigor, and intelligence to the Presidency; during his Administration, the American people were fascinated by the 1st family as never before. Kennedy's youthful leadership awakened the so-called "silent generation" from the long sleep of the Eisenhower years, and Americans developed a new commitment to the welfare of their country. In the White House, Kennedy entertained Nobel Prize winners, listened to classical music and Shakespeare, took an active interest in Washington architecture, and generally gave American cultural life an important boost.

CON

Kennedy's "Camelot" was all glitter and no substance. It is true that JFK inspired a generation of Americans and raised them to a pitch of high excitement, but his promises were never followed by performance. The tense, crisis atmosphere of the Kennedy years produced no significant progress for the American people. It was this gap between rhetoric and reality that caused much of the frustration and bitterness that came back to plague the nation in the late '60s.

PRO

At the time of his death, Kennedy was just shifting his gears as President. All observers agree that his commitment to black Americans had deepened significantly in the last year of his life. On a host of other issues, Kennedy was preparing to move forward, preparing to take on the big oil companies and other corporations on issues like tax reform and public welfare. His plan was to take his case to the people in a vigorous reelection campaign, and to sweep into office with him a more progressive and flexible Congress. He had also told his aides that as soon as possible after the election, he intended to terminate the American commitment to the faltering government in South Vietnam. If Kennedy had lived, the U.S. would have avoided the Vietnam War and entered a new era of social progress.

CON

Kennedy's fascination with "counter insurgency" broadened U.S. commitments in Southeast Asia. Kennedy would have probably made the same mistakes that Johnson did. There is no reason to believe that his death had any major effect on the overall sweep of American history.

PSYCHOHISTORY

Jack Kennedy was a weak and sickly boy who was plagued by a host of childhood diseases. According to his brother Robert, "When we were growing up together, we used to laugh about the great risk a mosquito took in biting Jack—with some of his blood the mosquito was almost sure to die." As in the case of Theodore Roosevelt, this boyhood weakness was later reflected in a desperate emphasis on physical fitness and competition. This tendency was encouraged by Jack's father, who taught his sons that 2nd-best was unacceptable. On one occasion, Joe Kennedy went so far as to send 2 of his children away from the dinner table because they had "goofed off" and lost a sailing race that day. "I can feel Pappy's eyes on the back of my neck," Kennedy told a friend when he was trying to decide about entering politics, and Papa Joe was always the driving force behind Jack's career. Even as President, Jack called his father at least once a day. The other dominant figure in Kennedy's life was his older brother, Joe, Jr. "Joe was the star of our family," Jack once said. "He did everything better than the rest of us." In the family structure, with Joe 2 years older than Jack, and then 5 girls before Bobby and Teddy, it was only natural that the 2 oldest boys should struggle for the leading position. They used to fight so fiercely at home that the younger children would run upstairs and hide, while the muscular Joe pounded away at his slender brother. The father insisted that no one interfere with these sometimes bloody struggles: Jack had to learn to fend for himself. Once, when the 2 boys were riding bicycles at each other they both refused to turn aside: Joe was unhurt, but Jack required 28 stitches. Though the brothers were friends at Harvard, and often ate together, the competition continued. Joe was in the habit of moving in on Jack's dates, with the kind words: "Get lost, baby brother." In later years, in the space race, in politics, and a dozen other areas, Kennedy stridently declared that 2nd-best was unacceptable. In taking this position, he was unconsciously recalling his own painful position as "2nd-best" in the Kennedy family. When his brother Joe was killed during the war, Jack was left to compete with a ghost. No matter how tough or successful he might seem, he could never fill his dead brother's shoes, and so he had to continue his struggle for the top. If Jack ever forgot about his own basic inadequacy, his mourning father was there to remind him. In 1957, when Jack was a U.S. senator and already widely discussed as a presidential possibility, a reporter went to Florida to talk with Joseph P. Kennedy, Sr. As he was asked about his children, Kennedy happily ran down the list, obviously proud of their achievements. Then the reporter noted that Joe, Jr., had been left out, and asked Kennedy to comment on his eldest. The father's reaction "was a terrible thing to see. He sat there at the table weeping, unable to speak or to control himself for almost 5 minutes. It seemed to the rest of us like an hour. Finally, he pulled himself together and wiped his eyes but still he couldn't talk. He gestured toward his wife and said, 'She can tell you about him. I can't.'"

LITTLE-KNOWN FACTS

—Kennedy was never particularly religious, but he made an effort to attend confession regularly. As President, he was always worried that a priest might recognize the famous voice and then someday reveal the contents of the confession. In order to avoid recognition, Kennedy would drive to church with a group of Catholic Secret Service men, and then find an inconspicuous place in the middle of their line as they lined up for confession. On one occasion, this subterfuge proved such a miserable failure that the moment he stepped into the booth, the priest said: "Good evening, Mr. President." Kennedy replied, "Good evening, Father," and then walked out immediately.

—Kennedy was notoriously careless about money. He never carried cash with him, and was always "borrowing" from friends—for restaurant checks, cab fares, or even the collection plate at church. Occasionally, even his closest friends became irritated with the fact that the wealthy Kennedy made no effort to pay them back.

—Sen. Barry Goldwater is a 1st-rate photographer, and he once took a picture of President Kennedy and sent it to him for an autograph. The picture came back with this inscription:

> For Barry Goldwater, whom I urge to follow the career for which he has shown so much talent—photography. From his friend, John Kennedy.

—In his home State, Kennedy's name had acquired such magic by the late 1950s, that another John F. Kennedy—a stockroom worker at a razor factory—got himself elected as treasurer of Massachusetts simply by putting his name on the ballot. In 1958, his total campaign expenses were $150—most of it for an election night victory party. Treasurer Kennedy drove around the State in a chauffeur-driven limousine and appointed many of his relatives to State positions.

—Kennedy usually swam twice a day during his Presidency, in a White House pool which he ordered heated to 90°. On the wall facing the pool, Kennedy had an artist paint a floor to ceiling mural of a typical Massachusetts waterfront, complete with launches at anchor, Cape Cod houses, and trees.

—According to the polls, Kennedy's highest rating as President came right after the Bay of Pigs fiasco, as the American people rallied to support their President in difficult times, and 82% expressed approval of his handling of the job. No one was more amazed at this development than Kennedy. "My God," he said, "it's as bad as Eisenhower. The worse I do the more popular I get."

—In the fall of '63, Kennedy appeared at a Boston dinner honoring his brother Teddy— the newly elected junior senator from Massachusetts. In the course of his speech, the President joked about his own upcoming reelection bid in 1964. "My last campaign may be coming up very shortly," he said, "but Teddy is around, and therefore these dinners can go on indefinitely."

Quotes from Kennedy:

"Sure it's a big job, but I don't know anyone who can do it better than I can."

"Those who make peaceful revolution impossible, make violent revolution inevitable."

"I had announced earlier this year that if successful I would not consider campaign contributions as a substitute for experience in appointing Ambassadors. Ever since I made that statement I have not received one single cent from my father."—1960

"The political campaign won't tire me, for I have an advantage. I can be myself."—Spring, 1960

"The New Frontier of which I speak is not a set of promises—it is a set of challenges. It sums up not what I intend to offer the American people, but what I intend to ask of them."—Acceptance speech, July, 1960

"Let us never negotiate out of fear, but let us never fear to negotiate."—Inaugural address, 1961

"If a free society cannot help the many who are poor, it cannot save the few who are rich."—Inaugural address, 1961

"All my life I've known better than to depend on the experts. How could I have been so stupid, to let them go ahead?"—On the Bay of Pigs, April, 1961

"When we got into office, the thing that surprised me most was to find that things were just as bad as we'd been saying they were."—May, 1961

"There is a limitation upon the ability of the U.S. to solve these problems . . . there are greater limitations upon our ability to bring about a favorable result than I had imagined. . . . It is much easier to make the speeches than it is finally to make the judgments. . . ."—TV interview, 1962

Quotes about Him:
"What future historians may well note 1st about JFK is what they note 1st about the Roman Emperor Trajan—that he presided at the high-water mark of empire."—Richard Boeth, *Newsweek,* 1973

"Jack did like to have little things done for him without hearing about the problems and the difficulties."—Kenneth O'Donnell

"John Kennedy was a happy man, and those who knew him well will always remember him that way."—Paul "Red" Fay

"After long experience in sizing up people, I definitely know you have the goods and you can go a long way. Now aren't you foolish not to get all there is out of what God has given you. . . ."—Joseph P. Kennedy, in a letter to his 14-year-old son

"My son was rocked to political lullabies."—Rose Kennedy

"It is true that we have a President with a face. And it is the face of a potential hero. But he embodies nothing, he personifies nothing, he is power, rather a quizzical power, without light or principle. . . . He learned too much and too early that victory goes to the discreet, that one does not speak one's opinion, that ideally one does not even develop one's opinion."—Norman Mailer, 1963

"It is a good thing to have a brave man as our President in times as tough as these are."—Ernest Hemingway

"I feel that I would hesitate to place the difficult decisions that the next President will have to make with someone who understands what courage is and admires it, but has not quite the independence to have it."—Eleanor Roosevelt

"He seems to combine the best qualities of Elvis Presley and Franklin D. Roosevelt."—An anonymous Southern senator, 1960

"What a joy that literacy is no longer prima-facie evidence of treason, that syntax is no longer subversive at the White House."—John Steinbeck

"You certainly can't say that the people of Dallas haven't given you a nice welcome."—Mrs. John Connally, November 22, 1963

"Now I think that I should have known that he was magic all along. I did know it—but I should have guessed that it would be too much to ask to grow old with him and see our children grow up together. . . . So now he is a legend when he would have preferred to be a man."—Jacqueline Kennedy, 1964

—M.S.M.

37th President

RICHARD MILHOUS NIXON

VITAL STATISTICS

Born: January 9, 1913, in the small frame house adjoining his father's lemon grove in Yorba Linda, Calif. He was named after King Richard the Lion-Hearted—3 of Hannah Nixon's 5 sons were named after English kings. When he was growing up, the nickname "Dick" was never used; as his mother recalled, "I always called him Richard, and he always called me Mother."

BEFORE THE PRESIDENCY

Career: When Richard was 9, his parents gave up citrus farming and moved to nearby Whittier, a small Quaker community 15 mi. east of Los Angeles. Hannah Nixon's family, the Milhouses, were well established in Whittier, and they helped their unlucky son-in-law set up a small gas station-grocery. As a teenager, Richard spent much of his time working in that store. He got up every day at 4 A.M. to drive the family's truck into Los Angeles to pick up a load of vegetables. He would then wash them off and carefully set up a display, before putting in his full day at school. Every afternoon, he worked several more hours at the store, then studied alone in his room until midnight. Thanks to his iron self-discipline, he did well in school and won a local reputation as an intellectual. Nevertheless, he had to give up his dreams of going to Harvard because his parents continued to demand his help in the store. After graduation from high school, Richard won a scholarship to Whittier College—a scholarship that had been established by his grandfather specifically for members of the family. Richard continued his grueling routine and high academic achievement, also developing his skills as a championship debater. He was never popular with his classmates, but he won the election for student body president by promising to allow dancing on campus. Actually, Richard himself seldom attended dances, but he convinced the administration that it was better to have dances under campus control, rather than let students seek their entertainment in the sinful atmosphere of nearby Los Angeles. Graduating 2nd in his class at Whittier, Nixon won a scholarship to the recently established Duke University Law School in Durham, N.C. There, his long hours of uninterrupted study in the library won him the nickname "Iron Butt." Other classmates addressed him as "Gloomy Gus." After finishing 3rd in his law school class of 26, Nixon applied for jobs with New York law firms, but he was turned down. He also tried for a position with the FBI (the director of the FBI, J. Edgar Hoover, was one of his personal heroes), but the bureau never responded to Nixon's application. Sorely disappointed, Richard returned to Whittier and got a job with the law firm of Wingert and Bewley—his grandfather had known Mr. Bewley's grandfather years before. In Nixon's very 1st case as a trial lawyer in 1937, 10 days after he had been admitted to the California Bar, he represented a Los Angeles woman to execute a judgment in recovering a bad debt. During this case, Nixon was accused by the judge of unethical behavior, threatened with disbarment, and was also sued by his client for mishandling her case. (Bewley settled with the client by giving her $4,000.) With a salary of $250 a month, the young lawyer was naturally anxious to improve his financial position. He organized a company called Citra-Frost, but despite 18 months of intensive effort by Nixon, the company's plan to market frozen orange juice in plastic bags did not work. Nixon's law partner, Thomas Bewley, was city attorney of Whittier, and he appointed his young colleague to the post of assistant city attorney. However, this job hardly provided the excitement that Richard was looking for. Shortly after Pearl Harbor, Nixon went to Washington for a job with the tire-rationing department of the Office of Price Administration. As a Quaker, he was exempt from service in the armed forces during the war, but after 6 months in Washington, he decided to abandon the pacifist dictates of his religion and enlisted in the Navy. Assigned to the South Pacific, Lieutenant Nixon divided his time between building jungle airstrips and playing poker. On the island on which he was stationed, he built a little shack with a makeshift bar, stocked with liquor he managed to requisition. Officers and men flocked to this gambling resort, and found "Nick" Nixon ready to play for high stakes. By the time his tour of duty was over, Nixon's poker skills had netted him more than $10,000!

In 1946, with Nixon back in the U.S. working as a navy lawyer, 100 wealthy Republicans placed the following ad in Whittier area newspapers:

WANTED: Congressman candidate with no previous political experience to defeat a man who has represented the district in the House for 10 years. Any young man resident of district, preferably a veteran, fair education, may apply for the job. . . .

The initial response to the ad was poor, and someone suggested Nixon. After he was contacted, the 33-year-old attorney jumped at the chance. After some hesitation, the Republican leaders agreed to sponsor him. As one of them put it: "He was the best of a bad lot." Nixon made his 1st campaign appearances dressed in his navy uniform, and attacked his opponent, incumbent Congressman Jerry Voorhis, as a "friend of the communists." To "prove" his charges, Nixon repeatedly associated the name of his opponent with the CIO's Political Action Committee (PAC). Actually, the communist-dominated *California* PAC bitterly opposed Voorhis—the congressman was a member of the House Un-American Activities Committee and a dedicated anticommunist. But the modern *national* PAC had endorsed Voorhis—thereby confusing everyone and making Nixon's charges believable. The turning point in the campaign was the birth of Nixon's daughter Tricia. Voorhis made it a policy to send out a special pamphlet on infant care to all new parents in his district. On the cover of the pamphlet for Nixon the congressman added a friendly personal note: "Congratulations. I look forward to meeting you soon in public." Nixon seized on this message, read it to his audiences at every speech, and claimed that it committed Voorhis to a series of public debates. Finally, Voorhis felt compelled to accept, and in 5 debates, Nixon's aggressive rhetoric made mincemeat of his mild-mannered opponent. Nixon accused Congressman Voorhis of being "a lip service American, who is fronting for un-American elements, wittingly or otherwise." Three days before the election, he charged that Voorhis had "consistently voted the Moscow-PAC-Henry Wallace line in Congress."

On Election Day, Nixon was helped by a nationwide Republican trend, and he swamped his opponent, 65,586 to 49,994. Across the country, dozens of politicians—including Joe McCarthy of Wisconsin—carefully noted Nixon's effective and pioneering use of charges of "communist influence" to destroy a political opponent.

In the 80th Congress, Nixon was naturally assigned to the House Un-American Activities Committee, and he was soon leading a crusade for tough new "antisubversive" legislation. His major proposal—introduced as the Mundt-Nixon bill—was so repressive that even Nixon's fellow Republican Thomas Dewey condemned it as an attempt "to beat down ideas with clubs." Though Congress refused to pass this legislation, the well-publicized debate helped to establish Nixon—still in his freshman term—as the nation's leading Red-baiter. He solidified this reputation with his leadership in the celebrated Hiss case. When a former communist (and probable psychotic) named Whittaker Chambers appeared before the Un-American Activities Committee to accuse former State Department official Alger Hiss of communist involvement, Nixon was at 1st the only one to believe the charges. In the months that followed, he pursued the case with such energy, persistence, and clever manipulation of the evidence and the press that Hiss was publicly discredited and Nixon's name became a household word. (Eventually, enough evidence was gathered to send Hiss to prison, though the facts of his case continue to be the subject of heated controversy.) By 1948, as he faced re-election back in Whittier, Nixon had emerged as a local hero and was nominated by *both* the Republicans and the Democrats in the primaries. In 1950, this popular young congressman was ready to move on to better things, and he announced his candidacy for the U.S. Senate. His opponent was Congresswoman Helen Gahagan Douglas, a liberal and a former Hollywood actress, who was immediately dubbed "The Pink Lady" by Nixon. One piece of "hard-hitting" Nixon campaign literature was addressed directly to Mrs. Douglas: "You, *and you can't deny it,* have earned the praise of communist and pro-communist newspapers for opposing the very things Nixon has stood for." The most widely circulated leaflet of the campaign was the infamous "Pink Sheet," printed on pink paper and distributed to over 500,000 California voters. The leaflet stated that on 354 separate occasions Nixon's opponent had voted the same way as a "notorious communist-line congressman" from New York. The sheet failed to report that on hundreds of other issues, Mrs. Douglas had disagreed with the congressman in question, or that even Nixon himself, on 112 different occasions, had voted with this same "notorious" left-winger. It was in honor of his campaign tactics in this election that a small Southern California paper, the *Independent Review*, 1st used the label "Tricky Dick" above Nixon's picture. The nickname seemed so appropriate that it was soon widely used. Nevertheless, Nixon won a handsome victory over his Democratic opponent—crushing Helen Douglas by a margin of nearly 700,000 votes.

As the Senate's youngest member (he was 38) Nixon spent most of his time supporting General MacArthur in his call for "victory" in Korea, and Generalissimo Chiang Kai-shek in his pleas for "liberation" of the Chinese mainland. Nixon also found his way onto Joe McCarthy's Government Operations Committee and worked closely with the Wisconsin senator in exposing communist subversion. In his spare time, Nixon kept a close eye on the developing battle for the 1952 presidential nomination. The liberal-moderate wing of the Republican party was working hard to assure the nomination of General Dwight Eisenhower and to block the selection of arch-conservative Robert Taft. Though Nixon was ideologically much closer to Taft, the moderate leaders correctly guessed that the California senator would put personal advantage ahead of principle. New York Governor Thomas E. Dewey, who was spearheading the Eisenhower drive, told Nixon in secret that if Ike were nominated, Nixon would be his most likely choice as a running mate. Inspired by that prospect, Nixon did everything he could to undercut Taft's candidacy, telling his conservative audiences that even though Taft would make a "fine President," he couldn't possibly be elected. At the Republican convention, Nixon performed further services to the Eisenhower cause by skillfully undermining the favorite-son candidacy of his fellow Californian, Governor Earl Warren. When Eisenhower finally won the nomination, he was persuaded to follow through on Dewey's earlier promise to Nixon. Many delegates still had their doubts about "Tricky Dick," but they did not have the energy to act on them. As one Republican recalled: "We took Dick Nixon not because he was right wing or left wing—but because he came from California and we were tired."

After the convention, the campaign got off to a hopeful start, with Ike and Dick hitting hard with charges of Democratic corruption. But in mid-September, the press began carrying stories that Nixon himself had benefited from a secret fund raised in his behalf by a small group of California businessmen. Immediately, politicians of both parties demanded that Nixon resign from the ticket. Eisenhower refused to commit himself one way or another. Nixon began cracking under the pressure. In a famous phone conversation, he shouted at Eisenhower: "General —there comes a time when you have to piss or get off the pot!" When Ike still refused to speak out, it became clear that he was all too willing to abandon his tarnished running mate. In a last ditch effort to save himself, Nixon persuaded the Republican National Committee to buy $75,000 worth of television time so that he could explain his $18,000 fund. The speech that followed—broadcast live immediately after the top-rated Milton Berle show—was a political classic. In it, Nixon claimed:

> Not one cent of the $18,000 or any other money of that type ever went to my personal use. Every penny of it was used to pay for political expenses that I did not think should be charged to the taxpayers of the U.S.

What Nixon forgot to mention was that it would have been *illegal* for him to have charged such expenses to the taxpayer—which was precisely why the Nixon fund was a closely guarded secret. The candidate used it to finance personal politicking that other senators were forced to pay for out of their salaries. The speech climaxed on a personal note:

> One other thing I probably should tell you, because if I don't they'll probably be saying this about me too. We did get something, a gift, after the election. A man down in Texas heard Pat on the radio mention the fact that our 2 youngsters would like to have a dog. And, believe it or not, the day before we left on this campaign trip we got a message from Union Station in Baltimore saying they had a package for us. We went down to get it. You know what it was? It was a little cocker spaniel dog in a crate that he sent all the way from Texas. Black and white spotted. And our little girl Tricia, the 6-year-old, named it Checkers. And you know, the kids love the dog, and I just want to say this right now, that regardless of what they say about it, we're gonna keep it.

As Nixon went on to conclude the speech, he still had a few sentences to go when the red light flashed on signifying he was off the air. "I'm terribly sorry I ran over," he said to his aide William Rogers. "I loused it up, and I'm sorry." He thanked the technicians in the studio, then he gathered the notes from his desk, stacked them neatly, and threw them on the floor. "Dick, you did a terrific job," beamed his campaign manager Murray Chotiner, patting him on the back. "No, it was a flop," Nixon insisted. "I couldn't get off in time." When he reached the dressing room, Nixon turned away from his friends and let loose the bitter tears he had been holding back.

Nevertheless, the public response to the speech was highly favorable, and though Eisenhower appeared to have been disgusted by Nixon's performance, he was forced to keep the young Californian on the ticket. Greeting Nixon in Wheeling, W.Va., Eisenhower told him "You're my boy," and the team of Ike and

Dick went on to a landslide victory in November.

Personal Life: As he was growing up, Richard expressed little enthusiasm for the company of women. As one classmate recalled: "Oh, he used to dislike us girls so! He would make horrible faces at us. As a debater, his main theme in grammar school and the 1st years of high school was why he hated girls." This situation improved only slightly with time. As Nixon's mother recalled: "Richard was not much of a mixer in college, either. He never had any special buddy, and on the dates that he had during his college years he talked not of romance but about such things as what might have happened to the world if Persia had conquered the Greeks." The one girl who managed to arouse Richard's interest was Ola-Florence Welch, the daughter of the Whittier police chief. They met while acting together in a high school play and dated each other for 6 years. Most of their friends expected them to get married, but Nixon's stormy temper eventually caused problems in their relationship. On one occasion, he took Ola-Florence to a prom, but they began arguing on the dance floor and Dick simply walked out on her. She had to phone her parents to come and pick her up. After Richard went away to Duke's School of Law, Ola-Florence began seeing another boy—Gail Jobe, the man she eventually married. Nevertheless, Nixon still considered her "my girl," and when he came home during one vacation he called Ola and demanded that she see him immediately. That was impossible as Gail Jobe was sitting in Ola's living room at the moment Dick called. But Nixon wouldn't take no for an answer. "Ola, I'm coming over," he said. When she still refused, he "went through the roof." "Don't worry," he told her, "you'll never hear from me again." Despite this promise, he continued writing letters to Ola-Florence for several months. As she remembers them, "his letters were well-written and informative. Nothing mushy. He always kept himself in check." Meanwhile, Nixon concentrated on his law school studies and took little interest in social life, though he occasionally attended dances "stag."

In 1938 Nixon was back in Whittier and beginning his legal career when a friend told him about a gorgeous redhead who had recently arrived in town. Pat Ryan had been hired to teach typing and shorthand at the local high school. Her real name was Thelma Catherine Ryan, but her father, an Irish miner in Ely, Nev., had been so thrilled by the fact that his daughter had been born the day before St. Patrick's day that he called her "St. Patrick's Babe in the Morn." Eventually this was shortened to Pat. As a girl, Pat spent most of her time nursing her mother, who died of cancer when Pat was 13, and her father, who died 4 years later. Pat managed to finish high school, then went to New York and worked as a secretary and X-ray technician. Eventually, she saved enough money to enroll at the University of Southern California. In order to support herself, she worked in a department store and as a Hollywood extra. After graduation came the teaching job at Whittier. She joined an amateur theater group to make new friends, and one night at rehearsal in walked Richard Nixon. He had come there specifically to meet Pat, but he accepted a part in the play as a crusading district attorney—the 2nd romantic lead. After rehearsal, Nixon drew Pat aside and following a brief conversation he asked her to marry him. She stared at him and blinked her eyes. "I thought he was nuts," she later recalled. In the months that followed, Nixon pursued Pat with the same dogged persistence he later used on Alger Hiss. Pat was one of the most popular young women in Whittier, and she dated all of the town's most eligible bachelors. As she remembered it, Nixon "would drive me to meet other beaux, and wait around to take me home." After 2 full years of this, Pat finally capitulated. They were married in an ornate hotel in Riverside, Calif., when Pat was 28 and Richard was 27. Shortly thereafter, they moved into their 1st home—a small apartment over a garage.

One of the ties that held their marriage together over the years was their common attitude toward work. As Pat once told a reporter: "I had to work. I haven't just sat back and thought of myself or what I wanted to do. I've kept working. I don't have time to worry about who I admire or who I identify with. I've never had it easy. I'm not like all you—all those people who had it easy." Pat had mixed feelings about her husband's political career. On the one hand, she provided the strength that allowed him to go on. Just 3 minutes before he went on the air with his "Checkers" speech, Nixon turned to Pat and said: "I can't go through with this." She reassured him, and sat next to him as he delivered the address. On the other hand, Pat was continually urging Nixon to retire from politics. On 2 separate occasions she forced him to make written promises that he would quit. Both times Nixon broke his promises. In 1962, when he surprised her at a small dinner party with an announcement that he would run for governor of California, Pat "chewed him out" with such noisy vehemence that the evening was spoiled for everyone. Nevertheless, she followed her husband in all his political adventures and campaigned tirelessly on his behalf. Once, when she was asked if she weren't bored by the same tedious rally day after day, she answered: "I'm always interested in the rallies, they're so different. Some are outside; some are inside. Some have old people; some have young people."

When Pat was 34, her daughter Tricia was born, and 2 years later came Julie. Needless to say, Nixon had little time to spend with his daughters. Just before Tricia's wedding, he told newsmen: "I was out making a political speech the day she was born. . . . I wasn't around much while she grew up. For the rest of the time, up to the present time, it seems I've always been saying good-bye—good-bye to her at airports."

During Nixon's White House years Pat spent much of her time alone. She and her husband often ate their meals in different parts of the mansion. The First Lady's own staff was frequently indignant at the way the President ignored her during public appearances, and no one could overlook the many weekends he spent at the Bahamas or Camp David with his friend Bebe Rebozo—leaving Pat behind in Washington.

When asked about Nixon's career, Pat once commented: "The only thing I could do was help him, but it was not a life I would have chosen." Later, when a reporter suggested that she had had a good life, Pat raised her eyebrows and shot back, "I just don't tell all."

On the Way to the White House: Nixon proved himself to be an unusually active Vice-President. With Ike intent on remaining above politics, it was up to the Vice-President to serve as the Republicans' politician-in-chief. Nixon also sat in on Cabinet meetings, though he usually listened in silence while others conducted the business of Government. At one Cabinet meeting Nixon surprised his colleagues by pulling a mechanical drummer out of his pocket. He quickly wound up the toy, set it down on the long table, and let it march around for a few moments as the most powerful men in America looked on in stunned silence. Finally, Nixon got to the moral of his demonstration: "We've got to drum up support for Republican candidates."

In 1956, when Ike ran for reelection, he wanted to drop Nixon from the national ticket. He called the Vice-President in for a tense Oval Office meeting, and offered Nixon any post in the Cabinet (except Secretary of State) if he would voluntarily step down. Nixon refused, and with his strong support from conservatives and Republican professionals, Ike could not have purged him without a fight. The general reluctantly accepted Nixon as his running mate once again, but he continued to snub the Vice-President both socially and politically. Nixon was considered so unimportant in the White House scheme of things that there were parts of the building that he had never even seen until President Lyndon Johnson invited him there one day and took him around. Not even Eisenhower's heart attack and stroke—which brought Nixon so close to the Presidency—could persuade Ike to take his Vice-President seriously. In 1960, Ike was asked at a press conference, "What major decisions of your Administration has the Vice-President participated in?" Ike's flip response was: "If you give me a week, I might think of one."

By the beginning of 1959, it was clear that despite Eisenhower's distaste for him, Nixon would be virtually unopposed in his bid for the Republican presidential nomination in 1960. Looking ahead to a hard fight against the Democrats, Nixon was eager to enhance his reputation as a major statesman so he and his staff came up with the idea of taking a trip to the Soviet Union. When this plan was discussed with officials in the State Dept., their enthusiasm was well under control. Nixon insisted, however, and he was finally granted permission to make the trip so long as it was clearly understood that the purpose of the visit was purely "ceremonial." Nixon's chief responsibility in Russia was to open a U.S. exhibition in a Moscow park. But while touring the grounds of the exhibit (including an American model kitchen) Nixon couldn't resist the opportunity to join Soviet Premier Khrushchev in a shouting match in front of the television cameras and the world press. Naturally, the subject was the relative strength of the U.S. v. the U.S.S.R. "Now we were going at it toe-to-toe," Nixon later recalled in his book *Six Crises.* "To some, it may have looked as though we had both lost our tempers." He was right—that was exactly how it looked. "But," Nixon insisted, "exactly the opposite was true. I had full and complete control of my temper and was aware of it. I knew the value of keeping cool in a crisis." Nonetheless, it was Khrushchev who got off the best lines of the day. He told Nixon: "You don't know anything about communism —except fear." Throwing an arm over a nearby smiling worker, Khrushchev asked, "Does this man look like a slave laborer?" Despite the contents of the "kitchen debate," the American press felt obliged to report a Nixon "victory"—after all, the Vice-President was representing the U.S. Soon after Nixon came home, his poll ratings soared, and he entered the campaign as the heavy favorite against Sen. John Kennedy.

Nixon's inept campaigning, however, soon managed to turn the tide. As one of his aides confessed after Nixon's defeat: "Dick didn't lose this election. Dick blew this election." One of his problems was physical. While getting out of his car, Nixon had banged his knee so hard against the door that he had to be hospitalized in the middle of the campaign. When he managed to crack the same kneecap again, in

exactly the same way, one of the reporters assigned to him could no longer hold back. "My God, he's trying to kill himself," he said. This 2nd injury came on the very morning of Nixon's 1st "Great Debate" with Kennedy. One of the reasons that Nixon looked drawn and haggard on the broadcast that evening was that his bad knee gave him almost constant pain. The debate itself—which he had agreed to in the foolhardy belief that he could humiliate Kennedy—was Nixon's biggest setback. His campaign never fully recovered its momentum, and Nixon, in Murray Kempton's words, ended his election drive "wandering limply and wetly about the American heartland begging votes on the excuse that he had been too poor to have a pony when he was a boy." Nevertheless, the final result was so tantalizingly close that Nixon tortured himself with the thought that any one of his minor mistakes might have meant the crucial difference between victory and defeat.

Most observers agree that if Nixon had simply "retired" from politics after 1960, the Republicans would have gladly given him a 2nd try for the Presidency 4 years later. But Nixon was still smarting from the 1st defeat of his political career, and he felt the need to prove himself a winner. He entered the race for the California governorship in 1962 against the incumbent, Pat Brown. Almost from the beginning, Nixon's campaign seemed to go badly, and he predicted to friends that he would lose. One issue that counted heavily against him was "The Hughes Loan"—a secret loan of $200,-000 from billionaire Howard Hughes to Nixon's brother Donald. Questions about this twisted deal seemed to confront Nixon wherever he went. In San Francisco's Chinatown, he nearly exploded when he opened a fortune cookie in a public ceremony only to find the message "What About the Hughes Loan?" The cookie had been placed there by political prankster Dick Tuck. More seriously damaging to his cause was the common impression that Nixon was interested in the California governorship only as a steppingstone to the White House. Nixon himself furthered that impression with a well-publicized slip in the last days of the campaign, describing himself as a candidate for "governor of the U.S." On Election Day, Brown easily defeated Nixon with a comfortable margin of 350,000 votes. All night, Nixon watched the returns with bitterness and refused to concede defeat. The next morning, he was still watching—with glassy eyes—the numbers on his television screen. His press secretary, Herb Klein, told him that the reporters downstairs were demanding a statement. "Screw them," Nixon replied, and he sent Klein down to make a statement in his place. Klein was in the middle of that presentation, in front of television cameras of all major networks, when he was suddenly interrupted by a commotion behind him. Nixon—still unshaven, and wearing his soiled and rumpled clothes—had unexpectedly walked into the room. He proceeded to offer the press a tirade that has been aptly described as "a nervous breakdown in public." His jerky, convulsive gestures and nervous giggles furthered the impression that here was a man who had been pushed to the outer fringes of sanity. Among Nixon's statements on that memorable day:

> Now that all the members of the press are so delighted that I have lost . . . I believe Governor Brown has a heart, even though he believes that I do not. . . . I did not win. I have no hard feelings against anybody, against any opponent and least of all the people of California. . . . And as I leave the press, all I can say is this: For 16 years, ever since the Hiss case, you've had a lot of fun—a lot of fun—that you've had an opportunity to attack me . . . Just think about how much you're going to be missing: You won't have Nixon to kick around any more, because, gentlemen, this is my last press conference."

The political obituaries that appeared across the country following this remarkable performance proved entirely premature. By 1964, Nixon was back on the campaign trail, stumping tirelessly for Republican candidates even in the midst of the Goldwater debacle. Two years later, he continued his nonstop campaigning and received a good deal of the credit for Republican congressional gains. In between elections, Nixon worked for a Wall Street law firm at a salary of $200,000 a year. Nixon told reporters that he enjoyed living in New York because it was "a fast track." He added, "Any person tends to vegetate unless he is moving on a fast track." By 1968 Nixon's own fast track, along with the gratitude of Republican regulars throughout the country, brought him into contention once again as a leading candidate for the presidential nomination.

His Person: Nixon is 5′11″ tall with brown eyes and dark hair. He has no illusions about his own attractiveness. "This is the face I've got," he once said. "I've got to accept it as it is." During the 1960 campaign, he refused to view tapes of his debates with Kennedy because he couldn't stand the way he looked on TV. Nixon's heavy growth of beard has always been notorious, and during campaign tours he had to shave at least 2 or 3 times every day in order to keep himself presentable. When he was 3 years old, Nixon was seriously injured when he fell from a carriage, and his head was cut under its wheels. He still bears a long scar on the side of his head but the scar is carefully hidden by his hair. This accident—which nearly killed him—left him permanently subject to motion sickness. Nixon has also had problems with hay fever all his life.

As a boy, Nixon wore a tie and jacket to school, and his classmates often made fun of his solemn formality. An item in his Whittier High School newspaper declared: "Nothing is funnier than to call Richard Nixon 'Nicky' and watch him bristle. I did it once and he was too surprised to speak, if you can imagine Nixon inarticulate." This stiff, unyielding sense of personal "dignity" has been a permanent feature of the Nixon personality. During the White House years, when an old friend and business associate from Florida, Hoke T. Maroon, addressed Nixon as "Dick," the President shot back: "Don't you dare call me 'Dick.' I am the President of the U.S. When you speak to me you call me 'Mr. President.'" Nixon always appeared to be more comfortable in his 3-button business suits than in casual wear. While relaxing in the sun at Key Biscayne or San Clemente, he was often dressed primly in a sports jacket. During his solitary walks along the beach, he generally wore his black dress shoes. After he became President, his wardrobe became more stylish, and he began sporting gold cufflinks emblazoned with the presidential eagle.

Nixon has always had a difficult time coordinating his body. Childhood acquaintances agree that he had "2 left feet." Because the Whittier College football team was short on players, Richard was allowed to participate—but he warmed the bench for 4 years. Whenever he was put into the game, as one teammate recalls, everyone "knew a 5-yard penalty was coming up. Richard had such determination to win that he would rush ahead before the play started. I knew he'd be offside just about every play." Nixon's habit in later years of clumsily banging into car doors led to the serious knee injury that slowed down his campaign for the Presidency in 1960. As President, his coordination problems continued to surprise observers. At one press conference, he raised his hands, beckoning the reporters in the room to stand up, while telling them, "would you please be seated." As he was delivering a major speech, he once pointed to the audience and said "I," then pointed back at himself and said, "you." Nixon was often so tense that when someone touched him lightly on the arm, he would jump as though struck by a blow.

Nixon has never taken much of an interest in sleeping or eating. In *Six Crises*, he boasts continually of his ability to function even after a long succession of sleepless nights. At meals, he is generally preoccupied. Among his favorite culinary delights are spaghetti, cottage cheese, and meat loaf. His favorite form of relaxation is sitting for hours in silent communion with his good friend, Florida banker Bebe Rebozo. It was Rebozo's function—at the White House or at Nixon's vacation retreats—to enforce the long silences that the President so much enjoyed. On one occasion, another Florida businessman joined Rebozo and the President for a cruise on Bebe's luxurious houseboat. This 3rd party became concerned when Nixon "lapsed into silence," and he attempted to dispel the gloomy atmosphere with small talk. Rebozo cut him off immediately with a firm, "Shhh!" In a shocked whisper, Bebe added, "He's meditating." That was the last word spoken on the trip.

PRESIDENCY

Nominaton: As Murray Chotiner, Nixon's former campaign manager, so eloquently put it: "It was clear that Dick was going to be the party nominee in 1968. He had more brownie points than anyone." Some 20 years of active campaigning on behalf of Republican candidates in thousands of cities and towns across the country had made Richard Nixon the favorite of the old-guard professionals who ran the party. His policies were so ambiguous that they offended almost no one. Nixon was, of course, a past master of the art of making a "strong statement" while committing himself to nothing. His pronouncements of the Vietnam War were a case in point:

> Never has so much military, economic, and diplomatic power been used as ineffectively as in Vietnam. And if after all of this time and all of this sacrifice and all of this support there is still no end in sight, then I say the time has come for the American people to turn to new leadership—not tied to the policies and mistakes of the past. I pledge to you: We will have an honorable end to the war in Vietnam."

Brilliantly designed to attract both the advocates of escalation and the partisans of peace, such statements naturally pleased the victory-hungry Republican leaders. Of course, there were still lingering doubts about Nixon's personality, but the press began commenting incessantly and favorably on the "New Nixon." Gone was the ruthless partisan of the past. In his place stood a mellow, elder statesman, who impressed the nation with the calm wisdom of his foreign policy articles in *Reader's Digest.*

If Nixon could prove himself in the primaries and overcome his loser's image, the nomination would be his for the asking. His chief opponent in the early stages of the campaign was Michigan Governor George Romney, champion of the party's moderate-liberal wing. Romney soon

managed to take himself out of contention when he told an interviewer that he had been formerly "brainwashed" on the Vietnam War. Romney convinced many Americans that he didn't have a brain worth washing. Facing certain defeat at Nixon's hands in the New Hampshire primary, Romney withdrew from the race. In the remaining primaries, no other Republican was willing to challenge Nixon's lavishly financed campaign. As the Whittier Wonder sailed smoothly toward the convention in Miami, it appeared all but certain that he would stage "the greatest comeback since the Resurrection of Jesus."

August 5, 1968 . . .

As the convention assembled, the liberal Nelson Rockefeller and the reactionary Ronald Reagan tried desperately to chip enough delegates away from Nixon's "centrist" candidacy to prevent his nomination on the 1st ballot. Reagan appeared to be making some headway among Southern delegates formally committed to Nixon, until Nixon promised Sen. J. Strom Thurmond of South Carolina and other influential Southerners that he would choose a conservative as his running mate. By the time the balloting had begun, it was clear to everyone that Nixon had the nomination sewn up. The Republican delegates seemed ready to agree with the sentiments of Maryland Governor Spiro T. Agnew, who had placed Nixon's name in nomination: "When a nation is in crisis and history speaks firmly to that nation, it needs a man to match the time. You don't create such a man; you don't discover such a man—you recognize such a man."

The only excitement remaining at the convention was Nixon's choice of a running mate. In making that decision, the candidate told his advisers that he wanted to avoid a "super star" who might outshine him in the campaign ahead. In selecting Spiro Agnew, Nixon succeeded beyond his wildest dreams. Press and public alike were aghast at the choice of the little-known and inexperienced Maryland governor. Agnew's only claim to fame was a headline-making tirade—directed at representatives of the Baltimore black community—in which he lambasted the "ready-mix, instantaneous, circuit-riding, Hanoi-visiting, caterwauling, riot-inciting, burn-America-down type of leaders." Even Agnew seemed surprised that Nixon had selected him. "I stand here with a deep sense of the improbability of this moment," he said when he formally accepted the nomination for the Vice-Presidency.

In the face of widespread criticism, Nixon eloquently defended his choice of Agnew. "There is a mysticism about men," he said. "There is a quiet confidence. You look a man in the eye and you know he's got it. . . ."

Brains. This guy has got it. If he doesn't, Nixon has made a bum choice."

Election: Nixon started off with a huge lead over his Democratic opponent, Vice-President Hubert Humphrey. The Democrats were deeply divided over the Vietnam War. Humphrey was closely associated with the unpopular Johnson Administration, and his nomination had been tarnished by the bloody televised riots at the Democratic convention in Chicago. Barring some disaster, Nixon was a sure winner, and the Republican leaders decided that the best way to avoid that disaster was to keep Nixon away from the people.

One "secret weapon" in the Republican arsenal was former President Eisenhower's undiminished popularity. Throughout the campaign, the general lay close to death at Walter Reed hospital. Remembering his days on the Whittier College football team (or perhaps his viewing of *Knute Rockne, All American,* starring Ronald Reagan as "the Gipper"), Nixon told the Republicans at the convention: "Let's win this one for Ike!" As if this weren't enough, Murray Chotiner insisted that cameras be brought into Ike's hospital room in order to film an endorsement of Nixon. The resulting footage horrified even Nixon's own staff. Ike, dressed in pajamas, was obviously a dying man, and he lay there with a microphone hanging limply from his neck. "No," said Nixon media wizard Harry Treleaven, "that's one thing I'm not going to do. I'm not going to make a commercial out of that." "If you can't get 5, how about at least one minute?" pleaded Chotiner. In the end, the Nixon staff found a clever compromise as Nixon's son-in-law-to-be, David Eisenhower, read his grandfather's endorsement to the cameras.

Despite his best efforts to avoid the issue for the duration of the campaign, Nixon was forced to elaborate on his previous platitudes concerning the Vietnam War. He told the nation that he had a "secret plan" to end the war but said that he could not divulge its contents for fear of compromising President Johnson's negotiating position. The transparent hypocrisy of this position—combined with Agnew's controversial use of phrases such as "Fat Jap," "Polack," and "If you've seen one slum you've seen them all"—began to create serious doubts about the Nixon-Agnew ticket. Meanwhile, millions of Peace Democrats, faced with the real possibility that Nixon might actually become President of the U.S., began streaming reluctantly back to the Humphrey column as the election went down to the wire.

November 5, 1968 . . .

In the end, Richard Nixon, despite the most expensive campaign in U.S. history, came within a hairbreadth of blowing his "sure-thing" election. He actually polled 2½ million *fewer* votes

than he had drawn in his losing effort in 1960. His overall percentage of the popular vote—43.4—was lower than that of any winning candidate since 1912. His victory was made possible only by the presence in the race of Alabama's George Wallace—the "American Independent" candidate, whose law-and-order campaign drew nearly 10 million votes—or 13.5% of the total. Wallace won enough normally Democratic, blue-collar votes in key industrial States like Illinois and Ohio to swing those States to Nixon—and with them the election. Nixon won 301 electoral votes to Humphrey's 191. But the difference in the popular vote was only 510,000—or 0.7%. Wallace carried the States of the deepest South—Alabama, Arkansas, Georgia, Louisiana, and Mississippi—for a total of 46 electoral votes. The morning after the election, when Nixon appeared before his supporters and the press to claim victory, he received a unique gift from his daughter Julie: a needlepoint replica of the presidential seal.

Term of Office: January 20, 1969 . . .

The 56-year-old Nixon was sworn into office by Chief Justice Earl Warren at ceremonies on the east plaza of the Capitol. His inaugural address was distinguished chiefly by its haunting reminders of John Kennedy's inaugural address in 1961. Among the most striking parallels (Nixon's words in italics):

Let the word go forth, to friend and foe alike . . .
Let this message be heard, by strong and weak alike . . .
Let every nation know . . .
Let all nations know . . .
To those nations who would make themselves our adversary, we offer not a pledge but a request: that both sides begin anew the quest for peace . . .
Those who would be our adversaries, we invite to a peaceful competition . . .
We dare not tempt them with weakness, for only when our arms are strong beyond doubt can we be certain beyond doubt that they will never be employed . . .
But to all those who would be tempted by weakness, let us leave no doubt that we will be as strong as we need to be, for as long as we need to be . . .
We observe not a victory of party, but a celebration of freedom . . .
In the orderly transfer of power, we celebrate the unity that keeps us free . . .

At one of the inaugural balls that evening, Nixon forgot to introduce the First Lady and broke a tradition as old as the ball itself. At the next ball, he 1st introduced his daughters, his son-in-law David Eisenhower, and then he finally remembered his wife. "I just assumed that everybody knew the lady I was with," he said. Later, as he was about to step into his limousine to go to the next ball, Nixon had to be reminded by an aide that he had left Pat back at the ballroom, standing by herself. He sent a Secret Service man back to fetch her.

As he moved into the White House the next day, Nixon ordered a crew of wreckers into the Oval Office to destroy any trace of his predecessor, Lyndon Johnson. Furniture, portraits, bookshelves, rocking chairs, even utilitarian news tickers, television sets, and a console of telephones were carted away and consigned to oblivion. The rug was stripped from the floor and the paint from the walls. This was Nixon's way of announcing to all those around him that a bright, new day had dawned in the White House.

Reelection: The full story behind Nixon's victory in 1972 may never be known. The former leaders of the Committee to Reelect the President (CREEP) have proved somewhat reluctant to reveal the full extent of their criminal activities. This much is already clear: Nixon raised and spent more money than any candidate in history—including millions of dollars of illegal corporate contributions; every arm of Government was politicized to an unprecedented degree in order to insure his re-election; a massive campaign of sabotage and espionage helped to divide and discredit the President's opponents. Though the Watergate transcripts later showed that Nixon was passionately concerned with every trivial detail of his own campaign, he pretended at the time that he was too busy attending to "great issues" to bother himself with politics. On October 26, the President's envoy Henry Kissinger announced that "peace was at hand" in the Vietnam negotiations. It was, of course, "purest coincidence" that this announcement came less than 2 weeks before the elections. Unfortunately, Kissinger's optimism proved "premature." Only a month after the votes were counted, the Administration leveled wide areas in Vietnam and slaughtered thousands of civilians in one of the most intensive bombings in human history.

Meanwhile, the Democrats' intraparty difficulties played directly into Nixon's hands. After an unusually bitter preconvention fight, the party nominated Sen. George McGovern of South Dakota—an outspoken antiwar liberal who had alienated many party regulars and labor leaders. McGovern selected as his running mate young Sen. Thomas Eagleton of Missouri, but shortly after the convention adjourned it was learned that Eagleton had a history of psychiatric problems. After telling the press and public that he stood behind Eagleton "1,000%" McGovern proceeded to force

his running mate from the ticket. He thereby convinced many voters that he was just as slippery as Tricky Dick, and he added the appearance of political duplicity to an image already badly tarnished by charges of radicalism. As the campaign neared its climax, McGovern concentrated his fire on the mounting evidence of corruption in the Nixon Administration. His charges were, however, generally dismissed as political propaganda.

November 7, 1972 . . .

The American people voted overwhelmingly for "4 More Years" of the Nixon-Agnew leadership. Nixon's 60.7% of the popular vote was the highest percentage ever bestowed on a Republican candidate. Only 3 men in presidential history had won landslides of comparable proportions—Franklin Roosevelt, Lyndon Johnson, and Warren G. Harding. McGovern managed to carry Massachusetts and the District of Columbia for a total of 17 electoral votes. Nixon won the rest of the Union, for an electoral tally of 521.

January 20, 1973 . . .

Nixon was sworn in for a 2nd term by Chief Justice Warren Burger. In his inaugural address, he once more echoed his old rival Kennedy: "Let each of us ask, not just what will Government do for me—but what can I do for myself." Nixon included one particularly inspiring note in his speech: "Let us again learn to debate our differences with civility and decency, and let each of us reach out for that precious quality Government cannot provide—a new level of respect for the rights of one another."

In the most expensive and elaborate inaugural festivities on record—a series of parades, concerts, balls, and receptions costing $4 million—the President's supporters celebrated "4 More Years" of the Nixon-Agnew team.

Ultimately, they got only 10 more months of Agnew—and 20 more months of Nixon.

His 5 Years, 201 Days as President

PRO

The Nixon years marked a key turning point in U.S. foreign policy. Under the President's able leadership, the U.S. began to move away from its costly and unfortunate role as "policeman of the world." The dangers and hysteria of the cold war subsided as Nixon moved toward a more reasonable relationship with Russia. For the 1st time since 1950, America opened its eyes to China and established a promising dialogue with Peking. Having inherited the war in Vietnam from his predecessor, Nixon managed to bring home the American troops and POWs and won, at long last, peace with honor. In the Middle East, Nixonian diplomacy brought about a cease-fire and negotiations between Arabs and Israelis, and the best chance for a peaceful settlement in Israel's 25-year history. By the time Nixon left office, he had moved the world a giant step closer to his dream of a "new generation of peace." None of the scandals of his Administration can obscure the glow of this monumental achievement.

CON

Nixon's celebrated "detente" with Russia was more cosmetic than substantive—none of the key issues between the 2 superpowers were resolved, and Nixon failed in his drive for meaningful arms control agreements. The new policy toward China was inevitable, considering China's internal development and growing differences with the U.S.S.R. Nixon simply benefited from an inexorable trend in world affairs. In Vietnam, he willfully continued a tragic war for 4 unnecessary years, at a cost of thousands of lives and billions of dollars. When direct U.S. involvement was finally terminated, Nixon accepted the same settlement that war critics had been urging for years. His endless talk of peace with honor was only a sham. His invasion of Cambodia, his lies to the public and the Congress, his genocidal Christmas bombing of Vietnam in 1973 were all a tragic waste. Despite the intensive Nixon-Kissinger public relations efforts, the ruthless U.S. position in the India-Pakistan dispute, the threat of renewed fighting in the Middle East, the continuing bloodshed in Vietnam, and the CIA intervention in Chile, show that American policy is just as immoral—and the world situation is just as dangerous—as it has ever been.

PRO

On the domestic scene, Nixon established a revenue-sharing program that restored a measure of balance to the State-Federal relationship. He set up the Council on Environmental Quality to give recognition to the problems of pollution and consumption. He ended the peacetime draft and helped to restore peace to the nation's campuses. He cut back on many of the wasteful programs of LBJ's "Great Society" that had been squandering the taxpayer's money.

CON

Nixon's funding cutbacks crippled dozens of necessary programs providing health care, education and job training services, as the Government adopted a policy of "benign neglect" toward the nation's poor. Meanwhile, Nixon urged increased Federal spending for ill-considered military-industrial boondoggles like the ABM and SST. On the environment, he always put the interests of big corporations (like the oil companies, auto makers and lumber barons) ahead of the needs of the people. Most serious of all, his totally inept handling of the economy produced the most serious domestic crisis since the Great Depression—as inflation soared to unheard of levels and the country skidded in and out of "Nixon reces-

sions." While corporate profits reached all-time highs, the Administration could offer the average citizen only 4 phases of economic waffling. By the time Nixon left office, all of America's most serious domestic problems had been notably aggravated.

PRO

Nixon made it clear that Administration policy would not be affected by demonstrations in the streets. His firmness helped put an end to a dangerous cycle of ghetto and campus unrest.

CON

Nixon's "law and order" Administration gave America the most lawless Government in its history. The criminal activity started at the very top of the ticket. Even leaving Watergate aside, Nixon was clearly guilty of tax fraud in cheating the IRS out of the tidy sum of $500,000. He also contributed $17 million in public funds to the improvement of his own resort homes. Meanwhile, Vice-President Spiro Agnew preferred more traditional forms of graft as he accepted thousands of dollars in bribes and payoffs. With these examples to inspire them, it is hardly surprising that Nixon appointees in every branch of Government (including Cabinet members who have pleaded guilty to or been indicted and convicted of Watergate-related crimes) disgraced themselves and abused the public trust. No one in America has done as much as Nixon to secure Washington's reputation as "The Crime Capital of the World."

PRO

In perpetrating the Watergate affair, Richard Nixon inadvertently performed his greatest service to his country. Thanks to Nixon, the people received an invaluable education concerning their constitutional rights, the criminal justice system, the importance of a free press, and the hypocrisy of many of their leaders. During the Nixon Administration, Congress began to reassert its authority after a long period of dormancy, and the dangerous growth in presidential power was at last arrested. At the very end of his Presidency, Nixon fulfilled his promise to unite the country as never before—with Americans of every political persuasion joining forces to demand his impeachment or resignation.

CON

It is hard to decide which is more amazing in Nixon's handling of Watergate—the President's immorality or his incompetence. Nixon will not only be remembered as the greatest liar in American history, he may also be remembered as the most inept administrator. The antics of Nixon and his palace guard would be simply laughable except that they came so close to achieving their objectives. His efforts to subvert the rights of citizens, spy on his opponents, smear his "enemies," intimidate the press, defy the courts, diminish Congress, and manipulate the FBI, CIA, and IRS all proved—at least partially—temporarily successful. As historian Henry Steele Commager put it: "Other things being equal, we haven't had a *bad* President before now. Mr. Nixon is the 1st dangerous and wicked President."

RESIGNATION

July 24, 1974 . . .
The Supreme Court ruled unanimously that Nixon had no right to withhold evidence in criminal proceedings and ordered him to turn over 64 previously unreleased White House tapes.

July 27, 1974 . . .
The House Judiciary Committee voted 27 to 11 to recommend the impeachment of Richard Nixon. Even Nixon himself conceded that passage of an Impeachment Resolution by the full House was a "foregone conclusion."

August 5, 1974 . . .
The President released to the public transcripts of 3 of the tapes the Supreme Court had ordered him to turn over. The tapes revealed that Nixon personally ordered a cover-up of the facts of Watergate within 6 days of the break-in at Democratic national headquarters. The transcripts proved that Nixon had been lying consistently to the public—and to members of his own family and staff—for more than 2 years.

August 8, 1974 . . .
Faced with the absolute certainty of impeachment and conviction, and pressed hard by members of his own party, Nixon decided to abandon his intention of "stonewalling it" for a few more months. In a dramatic speech to the nation, he announced his intention to resign the Presidency—the 1st President in history to resign his office. In his speech, Nixon explained the situation with his usual candor and sincerity: "I have concluded that because of the Watergate matter I *might* not have the support of the Congress that I would consider necessary. . . . I would say only that if some of my judgments were wrong, and some *were* wrong, they were made in what I believed at the time to be the best interest of the nation."

In anticipation of Nixon's resignation, the Dow-Jones averages shot up more than 27 points—in Wall Street's 3rd largest rally of the year. By appropriate coincidence, August 8 has gone down in history not only as the day Nixon announced his resignation, but as the day that Napoleon Bonaparte sailed for St. Helena in 1815 to spend the rest of his life in exile.

AFTER THE PRESIDENCY

After a tear-soaked farewell to his staff in the East Room of the White House ("Only if you've been in the deepest valley can you ever know how magnificent it is to be on the highest mountain."), Nixon boarded an army helicopter and raised his arms one last time in his familiar V-for-victory gesture. Nixon was air-borne somewhere above the middle of the country when Gerald Ford officially took the oath of office as Nixon's successor. The former President did not listen to the proceedings. He and Pat rode in silence—and in separate compartments—on their way "home" to San Clemente.

In the early weeks of his retirement, Nixon's health began to deteriorate—which, of course, made it impossible for him to honor any of the court subpoenas that required his testimony. Meanwhile, Nixon planned to write his memoirs—for which he was to receive an advance estimated at $2 to $3 million. As incredible as it may seem, an aide disclosed that in this project, Nixon would follow the format established in *Plain Speaking,* a best-selling book about Harry Truman.

Just one month after Nixon's resignation, his handpicked successor, Gerald Ford, granted the former President a "full, complete, and absolute pardon" for any crimes he had committed—thereby shielding Nixon from prosecution. In accepting the pardon, Nixon issued a statement that touched a new note of humility: "I was wrong in not acting more decisively and more forthrightly in dealing with Watergate. . . . I know that many fairminded people believe that my motivation and actions in the Watergate affair were intentionally self-serving and illegal."

PSYCHOHISTORY

Richard's father, Frank Nixon, was a bitter, violent, and unpleasant man who was disliked by most of his Whittier neighbors. He would often chase customers out of the family store with his noisy bad-tempered arguments on political subjects. Having failed at nearly everything he tried—as a carpenter, lemon rancher, trolley operator, and service station manager—he often took out his frustrations on his 5 sons. It is reported that Richard, the 2nd oldest, submitted to these beatings "without a whimper." During his early years, the boy's only shelter in his unhappy and poverty-ridden home was his mother—a woman described by all who knew her as "a Quaker saint." She responded to her grim life and her difficult marriage with quiet resignation and iron self-control. "I have never heard her complain," her minister remembered. "I have never heard her criticize anyone." Young Richard wanted to achieve the same kind of self-control, and his rhetoric throughout his political career has emphasized the virtues of discipline, self-mastery, and "keeping cool." "The best test of a man," he once said, "is not how well he does the things he likes, but how well he does the things he doesn't like." The fact that Richard could never fully conquer himself and live up to his mother's teachings was a source of a most painful sense of self-hate and worthlessness. His violent temper—identified in his mind with a hated father figure—was one aspect of his own personality that he could never accept. Accordingly, whenever Nixon began losing control, he had to assure himself—and everyone else—that he was actually keeping cool. Note, for instance, his fervent denials in *Six Crises* that he ever lost his temper at Khrushchev or Kennedy. Also note his insistence at his "Last Press Conference" that "I do not say this in any bitterness . . ." when everyone in the country could see how bitter he was. Nixon, in short, was still trying desperately to be the kind of person who would please his mother—but knew, subconsciously at least, that he was bound to fail. His only resolution for this conflict was to talk like Hannah—mouthing platitudes about peace, gentleness, and restraint—even while he acted like Frank—bitterly and violently battling the enemies he saw everywhere.

When Richard was 3 years old, he nearly died after cracking his skull in a fall from a carriage. When he was 4, he contracted pneumonia and once more lay close to death. Then, just before he reached adolescence, 2 of his brothers died—the oldest, Harold, after a long bout with tuberculosis, and the youngest, Arthur, as an unexpected victim of tubercular meningitis. These experiences only deepened Richard's sense of guilt and unworthiness. His older brother had been his main competitor for his mother's love and attention, and now, with that rival gone, Richard felt responsible for his death. Hannah Nixon herself sensed the pattern clearly. "I think that Richard may have felt a kind of guilt," she wrote, "that Harold and Arthur were dead and he was alive." The only way to overcome that guilt was to succeed—to prove to everyone that he *deserved* to survive, to remain alive while 2 idealized brothers had departed. In the words of political scientist James David Barber: "His political life —which is nearly his whole life—is a punishing one. At most he derives from it a grim satisfaction in endurance. . . . Nixon exerts extraordinary energies on a life which brings him back extraordinary hardships."

But those hardships were necessary if Nixon was to keep his balance. Unless his successes were tempered by failure and humiliation, he lived in unbearable tension—the tension of a man who feels that things are going "too well" and believes that he is winning triumphs that he doesn't deserve. In 1952, after his nomination for the Vice-Presidency at the age of 39, he left himself politically vulnerable by continuing to accept money from the "Nixon fund." In 1960, when he was running well ahead of Kennedy in the polls, he invited disaster by agreeing to televised debates. In 1972, while winning one of history's greatest landslides, he provided for his own undoing by his incredible mishandling of Watergate. Along with his fierce desire to win respect, to prove his strength at the expense of his enemies came a desperate need to expose himself, to demonstrate his own unworthiness, to show the world that beneath the carefully composed mask of cool professionalism and self control stood a vulnerable, painfully human man, as petty and bitter as Frank Nixon. How else can one explain Nixon's incredible "Last Press Conference"—an orgy of self-exposure and public humiliation? How else can one explain his careful commitment to putting on tape even those private conversations that he knew would discredit him?

Nixon's entire career was built around what he calls "the exquisite agony" of crisis. Time and again, he deliberately placed himself in high-risk situations—the Hiss case, the "Checkers" speech, the dangerous visit to Caracas as Vice-President, the debates with Kennedy, the California governor's race—yet each time he managed to survive and went away with deeper suspicions about his own unworthiness. From the beginning, he seemed to sense that he would ultimately fail. Most comfortable playing the role of a pious martyr—a role echoing his "saintly" mother—Nixon found politics, from the beginning, ideally suited to his psyche's needs. It permitted him the "exquisite agony" of destroying himself in public, while blaming the entire process on his invisible "enemies." As Hannah Nixon recalled, while her son was serving as Vice-President: "I've often wished that Richard and his brothers had not been burdened with the hardships they had to endure as boys; they should have had more fun."

LITTLE-KNOWN FACTS

—Nixon's mother once told the public about Richard's celebrated talents. "He was the best potato masher one could wish for," she recalled. "Even in these days, when I am visiting Richard and Pat in Washington, or when they visit me, he will take over the potato mashing. My feeling is that he actually enjoys it."

—When Nixon became Vice-President, his mother hung a huge, transparent, 3-dimensional color photograph of Richard in her stairwell. When she pressed a special button, the image lit up.

—At Whittier College, the annual bonfire was a point of class pride. Each year the fire was fueled with scrap wood topped by an outhouse. The competition was to see which senior chairman could top the pile of debris with the largest outhouse—a 2-holer, say, or even a 3. Young Nixon scored an immense and well remembered triumph when his diligence turned up a 4-holer! As writer Garry Wills suggests: "Picture the systematic intensity that went into this achievement."

—After his "Checkers" speech Nixon received

a congratulatory phone call from Hollywood producer Darryl Zanuck. "The most tremendous performance I've ever seen," Zanuck told him.

—Despite its spectacular success as a political device, Nixon was always sensitive to teasing about his "Checkers" speech. During one campaign appearance in 1952, a young man in the audience shouted up at Nixon: "Tell us a dog story, Dick!" The candidate lost control of himself almost completely. "When we're elected," he shouted back, "we'll take care of people like you!" Then Nixon turned to the Secret Service men in the hall and told them, "OK, boys, throw him out!"

—In 1954, while serving as Vice-President, Nixon found time to travel to Whittier College to deliver a commencement address. Feelings were so divided on Nixon's old campus that 2 reception lines had to be set up by the college administration. Those who wanted to greet the Vice-President stood in one, while those who desired to avoid that honor stood in the other.

—Occasionally, Nixon found it necessary to lash out physically at hecklers. During his trip to Peru as Vice-President, a man in the crowd spat on him. "As I saw his legs go by," Nixon remembers, "at least I had the satisfaction of planting a healthy kick on his shins. . . . Nothing I did all day made me feel better."

—One of Nixon's more fanciful campaign proposals in 1960 was a pledge that, if elected, he would send ex-Presidents Hoover, Truman, and Eisenhower to "visit Eastern Europe and organize Freedom's underground against communism there."

—During one of his 1960 debates with Kennedy, Nixon demanded that his opponent "apologize" for the salty language being used by former President Harry Truman in Truman's vigorous anti-Nixon campaign. As Nixon pointed out to the television audience: "I can only say that I am very proud that President Eisenhower restored dignity and decency, and frankly, good language to the conduct of the Presidency. And I can only hope—should I win this election—that I would approach President Eisenhower in maintaining the dignity of the office." Kennedy's reaction was off-camera laughter. A few minutes later, the debate over, Nixon retired to his dressing room and exploded in front of reporters. "That fucking bastard," he said, "he—he wasn't supposed to use notes!"

—At the close of a business trip to Finland in 1965, Richard Nixon, then in private law practice, impulsively took a 20-hour train ride to Moscow. At 11 o'clock at night, he knocked on Khrushchev's door. Khrushchev was not at home. Nixon had to satisfy himself with a deputy director of Moscow State University and a policeman who happened to be near Nixon on the street, both of whom he tried to debate. In 1967, for no apparent reason, he went to Moscow once again, visiting Sokolniki Park, the site of his famous "kitchen debate" with Khrushchev 8 years before. Once more Khrushchev himself was unavailable, and Nixon had to entertain himself by debating with passersby.

—Nixon was the only President in American history who managed to visit all 50 States while in office.

—During his campaign for Republican candidates in 1970, Nixon was riding in a motorcade in St. Petersburg, Fla., when a motorcycle policeman was thrown from his vehicle and severely injured. The President rushed up to the suffering policeman and expressed his sympathies. The officer replied pathetically that he was sorry the motorcade had been delayed. Then there were some moments of embarrassing silence, until Nixon blurted out: "Well—do you like the work?"

—During the last day of his visit to China in 1972, Nixon was escorted by a weary Chou En-lai through an exhibition of export merchandise in Shanghai. The President stopped for a moment and peered through a magnifying glass at a tiny seed of ivory on which was engraved Mao Tse-tung's "Ode to the Plum Blossom." With a sigh of admiration, Nixon informed the world of something it had little suspected. "Art is my weakness," he said.

—Nixon's favorite President was—of all people —Democrat Woodrow Wilson. Psychologists might point out that Wilson's martyrdom would naturally appeal to Nixon's own well-developed martyr complex. Moreover, Nixon obviously envied Wilson's intellectual credentials. "I think he was our greatest President of this century," Nixon once said. "You'll notice too that he was the best educated." When he moved into the White House, Nixon ordered that LBJ's desk be removed and had it replaced by the old, half-forgotten desk that had been used by President Wilson.

Quotes from Nixon:

"You don't win campaigns with a diet of dishwater and milk toast."

"I believe in the battle, whether it's the battle of the campaign or the battle of this office, which is a continuing battle. It's always there wherever I go. I, perhaps, carry it more than others because that's my way."

"Anybody in politics must have a great competitive instinct. He must want to win. He must not like to lose, but above anything else, he must have the ability to come back, to keep fighting more and more strongly when it seems that the odds are greatest. That's the world of sports. That's the world of politics. I guess you could say that's life itself."

"The word politics causes some people lots of trouble. Let us be very clear—politics is not a dirty word."

"People go through that psychological bit nowadays. They think they should always be reevaluating themselves. I fight the battles as they come along. That sort of juvenile self-analysis is something I've never done."

"Those who have known great crisis . . . can never become adjusted to a more leisurely and orderly pace. They have drunk too deeply of the stuff which really makes life exciting and worth living to be satisfied with the froth."

"I won my share of scholarships, and of speaking and debating prizes in school, but not because I was smarter but because I worked longer and harder than some of my more gifted colleagues."

"Frankly, most people are mentally and physically lazy. They believe you can get places by luck alone. They fail to do the hard grinding work required to get all the facts before reaching a decision."

"Your mind must always go, even while you're shaking hands and going through all the maneuvers. I developed the ability long ago to do one thing while thinking about another."

"Once you're in the stream of history you can't get out."

"There is one thing solid and fundamental in politics: the law of change. What's up today is down tomorrow."

"It doesn't come natural to me to be a buddy-buddy boy. . . . I can't really let my hair down with anyone. No, not really with anyone, not even with my own family."

"I'm introvert in an extrovert profession."

"If ever the time comes when the Republican party and the others are looking for an outwardly warm, easygoing gregarious type, then they will not want the sort of man I am."

"I would have made a good pope."

"There is nothing more wearing than to suppress the natural impulse to meet a crisis head on, using every possible resource to achieve victory."

"You know very well that whether you are on page one or page 30 depends on whether they fear you. It is just as simple as that."

"One vote is worth a hundred obscene slogans."

"You've got to have something where it doesn't appear that I am doing this in, you know, just in a—saying to hell with the Congress and to hell with the people, we are not going to tell you anything because of executive privilege. That they don't understand. But if you say, 'No, we are willing to cooperate,' and you've made a complete statement, but make it very incomplete. See, that is what I mean."

"I never in my life wanted to be left behind."

"If the dry rot of corruption and communism, which has eaten deep into our body politic during the past 7 years, can only be chopped out with a hatchet—then let's call for a hatchet."—1952

"Ninety-six percent of 6,926 communists, fellow travelers, sex perverts, people with criminal records, dope addicts, drunks and other security risks removed under the Eisenhower security program were hired by the Truman Administration."—1954

"I have never had much sympathy for the point of view 'It isn't whether you win or lose that counts, but how you play the game.' How you play the game does count. But one must put top consideration on the will, the desire, and the determination to win."—1960

"Whenever any mother or father talks to his child, I hope he can look at the man in the White House, and whatever he may think of his politics, he will say, 'Well, there is a man who maintains the kind of standards personally I would want my child to follow.'"—Debate with Kennedy, 1960

"I believe that I spent too much time in the last campaign on substance and too little time on appearance; I paid too much attention to what I was going to say and too little to how I would look."—1961

"What few disappointments have been my lot in the world of politics are as nothing compared to the mountain-top experiences which have been mine."—1962

"From considerable experience in observing witnesses on the stand, I had learned that those who are lying or trying to cover up something generally make a common mistake—they tend to overreact, to overstate their case. . . ."—Six Crises, 1962

"There is no substitute for victory in South Vietnam."—1964

"Out here in this dreary, difficult war, I think history will record that this may have been one of America's finest hours."—On Vietnam, 1964

"I'm known as an activist and an organizer, but some people have said I'm sort of an egghead in the Republican party. I don't write as well as Stevenson, but I work at it. If I had my druthers, I'd like to write 2 or 3 books a year, go to one of the fine schools—Oxford, for instance—just teach, read, and write. I'd like to do that better than what I'm doing now."—1966

"All right. They still call me 'Tricky Dick.' It's a brutal thing to fight. The carefully cultivated impression is that Nixon is devious. I can overcome this impression in one way only: by absolute candor."—1968

"Nobody is a friend of ours. Let's face it." —September 15, 1972

"We are all in it together. This is war. We take a few shots and it will be over. We will give them a few shots and it will be over. Don't worry. I wouldn't want to be on the other side right now. Would you?"—September 15, 1972

"How much of a crisis? It will be—I am thinking in terms of—the point is, everything is a crisis. (Expletive deleted) it is a terrible lousy thing."—March 13, 1973

"I'm putting him up. The only thing I would say is that—to him—I would say that as President's Counsel (unintelligible) executive (unintelligible) and all that—(expletive deleted) I wouldn't even (unintelligible)."—April, 1973

"I don't know. Am I seeing something (unintelligible) that really isn't (unintelligible) or am I?"—April 14, 1973

"We can't get the President involved in this. His people, that is one thing. We don't want to cover up, but there are ways."—April 14, 1973

"I have a quality which I guess I must have inherited from my Midwestern mother and father, which is that the tougher it gets, the cooler I get."—1974

"I made my mistakes, but in all my years of public life I have never profited, *never* profited from public service. I have earned every cent. And in all of my years of public life I have never obstructed justice. And I think too that I could say that in my years of public life that I welcome this kind of examination because people have got to know whether or not their President is a crook. Well, I am not a crook." —1974

"If I were basically a liberal by the standards of the press, if I had bugged out on Vietnam, which was what they wanted, Watergate would have been a blip."—May, 1974

"Always give your best. Never get discouraged. Never be petty. Always remember: Others may hate you. Those who hate you don't win unless you hate them. And then you destroy yourself."—Farewell speech to White House staff, August 9, 1974

"You know, I always wondered about that taping equipment, but I'm damn glad we have it, aren't you?"—Nixon to Haldemann, April 25, 1973

Quote about Him:

"Nixonland is a land of slander and scare, of lay innuendo, of a poison pen and the anonymous telephone call, and hustling, pushing, and shoving—the land of smash and grab and anything to win."—Adlai E. Stevenson, 1952

"Dick was always reserved. He was the studious one of the bunch, always doing more reading while the rest of us were out having more fun."—Donald Nixon

"Nixon went into politics the way other young men home from the war went into construction, or merchandising, or whatever—for lack of anything better to do. . . . The fact is that as a candidate for office, Nixon has

consistently been a thoroughly 2nd-rate politician, because he was made, not born."—Stewart Alsop

"The man who uncovered Alger Hiss is in California to do the same housecleaning here. Help Richard Nixon get rid of the Jew-Communists."—Gerald L. K. Smith, February 27, 1950

"I'd love to see Ike's face when he finds out that Tricky Dick, his partner in the fight against Democratic corruption, has been on the take for the last 2 years. . . . This should blow that moralizing, unscrupulous, double-dealing son-of-a-bitch right out of the water." —*New York Post* editor James Wechsler, September 18, 1952

"There is built into Nixon an automatic response mechanism triggered by opposition. Offer him the element of competition, tempt him with a fight, hint that someone might want to deprive him of some prize, and a tiger emerges from the camouflage he normally shows the world."—Leonard Lurie

"Let's show them, Daddy—let's run!"— Tricia Nixon, 1967

"People seldom dictate to Richard."—Hannah Nixon

"He is the kind of politician who would cut down a redwood tree, then mount the stump and make a speech for conservation."—Adlai E. Stevenson

"Nixon is a shifty-eyed goddamn liar, and people know it. He's one of the few in the history of this country to run for high office talking out of both sides of his mouth at the same time and lying out of both sides."—Harry S Truman, 1961

"I once read that Lincoln had worse critics. He was big enough not to let it bother him. That's the way my husband is."—Pat Nixon

"He's probably the most informed President there's ever been. I really can't understand how people can call him isolated. He's aware of everything that's going on."—John Mitchell

"While he is likely to maintain a serious, almost brooding countenance in the company of 3 or 4 persons, he lights up like a Christmas tree when confronted with a crowd. He genuinely likes people."—William Rogers

"There are very few of the human juices in Nixon. You like him. You admire him. But not because you feel that he loves you. . . . I mean, I always knew that in a showdown, if my friendship with Nixon were embarrassing to him, that he'd just let me go."—Ralph de Toledano

"I think basically he is shy, and like a lot of shy people he appears not to be warm."—Rose Mary Woods

"One has the uneasy feeling that he is always on the verge of pronouncing himself the victim of some clandestine plot."—Arthur Schlesinger, 1968

"Let me say with absolute candor that I think he is the most civil man I ever worked for. He really does have some sense of your own feelings."—Daniel P. Moynihan

"The President *is* the Government."—John Ehrlichman

"There were days when the entire White House seemed to be in the grip of a morbid obsession, not unlike the mood aboard the *Pequod* when Ahab was at the helm."—Dan Rather

"He has never cared about money in his whole life. . . . In that innocent mind of his, he left his tax work for others to do because he was working on world problems."—Bebe Rebozo

"The great division in retrospective appraisal of Nixon will be between those who regard this as the most inept of presidential performances, and those who will regard it as the most vicious."—Richard E. Neustadt

"That man is not fit to be President."—Henry Kissinger, 1968

"Dick's a team man."—Gerald Ford

"I don't think the son-of-a-bitch knows the difference between telling the truth and lying." —Harry S Truman

"He has no taste."—John Kennedy

"I just knew in my heart that it was not right for Dick Nixon to ever be President of this country."—Lyndon B. Johnson, 1964

"THE CHILD IS FATHER OF THE MAN . . ."

"No, he has always been exactly the same. I never knew a person to change so little. . . . As you know, most boys go through a mischievous period. Well, none of these things happened to Richard. He was thoughtful and serious."— Hannah Nixon

"Dick always planned things out. He didn't do things accidentally. . . . Once, when he had just about as much of me as he could take, he cut loose and kept at it for a half to ¾ of an hour. He went back a year or 2, listing things I had done. He didn't leave out a thing. I was only 8, and he was 10, but I've had a lot of respect ever since for the way he can keep things in his mind."—Donald Nixon

"Each morning, he would take great pains in brushing his teeth, was careful to gargle, and asked me to smell his breath to make sure he would not offend anyone on the school bus." —Hannah Nixon

"Mother, I want to be an old-fashioned lawyer—an honest lawyer who can't be bought by crooks."—Richard Nixon, age 12

"He was so good it kind of disturbed me. He had this ability to kind of slide around an argument, instead of meeting it head on, and he

could take any side of a debate."—Mrs. Norma Vincent, his high school debate coach

"Dick was a marvelous actor—quick, perceptive, responsive, industrious. . . . I honestly believe that if he had made the stage his career instead of studying law, he would have developed into a top-notch leading man."—Ola-Florence Welch, Nixon's college sweetheart

"I taught him how to cry, in a play by John Drinkwater called *Bird in Hand*. He tried conscientiously at rehearsals, and he'd get a pretty good lump in his throat and that was all. But on the evenings of the performance tears just ran right out of his eyes. It was beautifully done, those tears."—Dr. Albert Upton, his Whittier College drama coach

"Dick had 2 left feet. He couldn't coordinate. But boy, was he an inspiration. That's why the coach let him hang around, I guess. He was one of those inspirational guys."—A member of the Whittier College football team

"I would put him down as the man least likely to succeed in politics."—A Whittier College classmate

—M.S.M. & N.H.M.

38th President

GERALD RUDOLPH FORD, JR.

VITAL STATISTICS

Born: July 14, 1913, in Omaha, Nebr. His name at birth was Leslie Lynch King, Jr.— he was the son of Dorothy Gardner King and Leslie King, a western wool dealer. When the boy was 2 years old, his parents were divorced, and his mother took him with her back to her family's home in Grand Rapids, Mich. Shortly thereafter, she married a paint salesman named Gerald Rudolph Ford. Ford agreed to adopt young Leslie as his own son, and the boy's name was changed to Gerald R. Ford, Jr. As he was growing up, he was known neither as Gerald nor Leslie—everyone called him Junior, or "Junie" for short. The facts about his birth and adoption were kept secret from Junior until he was 16, and his younger half-brothers didn't learn the truth until later—when they stumbled onto the formal adoption papers one day while rummaging through the attic. Ford saw his real father only twice—once while he was in high school in Grand Rapids, and once as a law student at Yale. Both visits were brief and unfriendly, and Ford had no intention of following up his father's pleas for further contacts. It is believed that Leslie L. King, Sr.— father of the future President—died some time in the 1940s, but the details are uncertain.

Career: At South High School in Grand Rapids, Ford's main interest was football: He was the star center on a team that won the State championship in his senior year. Though he showed little interest in student politics, he received a free trip to Washington as the winner of a movie theater's promotional contest for "the most popular high school senior." After graduation, Jerry's football coach arranged a scholarship for him at the University of Michigan. Ford maintained a "B" average in his course work, but he continued to focus most of his energies on football. In his senior year, he was named Michigan's Most Valuable Player, and selected as the All-Conference Center. Two professional football teams (the Green Bay Packers and the Detroit Lions) made offers to Ford after his graduation, but he turned them down to accept a job as assistant football coach at Yale. After working 2½ years to prove his skills to the Yale athletic establishment (he also coached freshman boxing), Ford approached the dean of Yale Law School and asked for permission to take some classes there. The law school agreed to admit Ford on a trial basis, but he did well enough in his studies to be allowed to continue. He took a light course load because he continued to be preoccupied with his coaching duties, and he didn't graduate until January, 1941, at the age of 27½. At that point he returned to his proud family in Grand Rapids and set himself up in the practice of law, but his career was interrupted a few months later by U.S. entry into W.W. II. Ford enlisted in the Navy, where he was originally assigned to a physical training program and given responsibility for whipping new recruits into shape as quickly as possible. Later, the navy brass agreed to give Ford the battle assignment that he wanted, and in the South Pacific he won commendation from his superiors as a loyal and dependable "team player." Captain Harry Sears stated for the Navy's records that Ford ". . . was at his best in situations dealing directly with people because he commanded the respect of all with whom he came in contact."

Discharged from the Navy in 1946 with the rank of lieutenant commander, Ford returned to Grand Rapids and resumed his legal career. In his spare time, he was active in veteran's groups and took a mild interest in politics—his stepfather was serving as chairman of the County Republican Committee. In 1948, the "Reform" faction in local Republican politics was looking for a candidate to oppose the incumbent U.S. congressman—a mossback isolationist who was associated with the corrupt McKay machine. Though Ford's only prior political experience was a brief stint as a volunteer in the Willkie-for-President crusade in 1940, he seemed to be a logical man for the job: His reputation as a past football hero and his war record gave him stature in the community, and his "internationalism" (he was a supporter of the UN and the Marshall Plan) offered a strong contrast to the old-fashioned ways of the incumbent, Barney Jonkman. The Republican primary was all-important (no Democrat had won in the Grand Rapids district since 1910) and Ford campaigned tirelessly, pitching hay with farmers in order to get the chance to talk with them and meeting city voters at shopping centers and picnics. Confident of victory, Jonkman scornfully refused his young opponent's challenge to public debate, thereby handing Ford a key issue. In the primary, the 35-year-old Ford won by a vote of 23,632 to 14,341, and went on to easy victory over the Democrats in November.

Personal Life: Despite his popularity in high school and college, Ford did not lead a particularly active social life. As one of his best friends recalls: "I don't know more than 5 girls Jerry dated. He just didn't have the money or the time. Compared to the average college guy—a date every weekend—hell, he just didn't do that." Shortly after he arrived at Yale in 1935, Ford started dating an elegant beauty named Phyllis Brown—a student at Connecticut College (then Connecticut College for Women) and later a New York fashion model. They saw each other on a steady-date basis for 4½ years, and Ford even took Phyllis home with him to meet his family. "I almost married that girl," he recalls, but for some reason the relationship broke up before Jerry graduated from law school. His next serious involvement did not come until after the war, when Ford was 34. In the autumn of 1947, he decided to contact an old acquaintance in Grand Rapids, Betty Bloomer, who had just won a divorce decree from her husband of 5 years. Betty, who was 30, was serving as fashion coordinator at a local department store. She had worked several years as a model, but her main interest had always been dance. For 2 years she had studied in New York with the famous Martha Graham, before her worried parents persuaded her to return to Grand Rapids and "settle down." Then came her marriage to William Warren, a traveling salesman—a marriage, Betty says, "I could just as well have skipped." There were no children, and the divorce was uncontested. When Ford called her shortly after the decree was finalized, Betty remembers that he insisted that she see him that same evening. "So we went around the corner to a small bar that we knew, sat in a booth, and talked for quite a while. There were many dates later that were not quite so spur-of-the-moment, you know, but so far as I was concerned, that 1st date was it!" Jerry proposed in February of '48, but the wedding was delayed for political reasons: Ford did not want his marriage to a divorcée and a former dancer to jeopardize his chances in the hotly contested Republican primary during his 1st race for Congress. The wedding finally took place on October 15, 1948—after the primary but before the general election. The day after the ceremony, the newlyweds left for a brief honeymoon: Ford took his bride to a University of Michigan football game. Then, after one night in a Detroit hotel, they returned to Grand Rapids so that Jerry could resume his campaigning.

In the years of marriage that followed, Betty kept house and raised their 4 children while Jerry concentrated on his political career. He accepted as many as 200 speaking engagements a year, which meant that he often came home—if at all—only after his family was in bed. Betty's attempts to get Jerry to help around their suburban Washington home generally ended in disaster. "He hangs the screen doors upside down," she reports. "When I said, 'Jerry, you've done it all wrong,' he said, 'OK, if you don't like the way I did it, hire somebody.' I got the message right there. Don't ask him to do anything around the house." In 1965, Betty's domestic responsibilities—including exhausting service as a cub-scout den mother—proved too much for her. She began complaining of a pinched nerve in her neck, which left her in almost constant pain. Doctors reported that many of her symptoms were psychosomatic, and she soon began psychotherapy. After that, Betty depended on tranquilizers—she has admitted to taking them at least once every day. In order to help Betty "gear down," Ford himself submitted to 3 consultations with her psychiatrist. He finally promised his wife that he would retire from politics after 1976—but then came his appointment as Vice-President and his elevation to the Presidency. These events ended Ford's retirement plans, and even after his wife's breast cancer surgery in the fall of 1974, he denied any intention of scaling down his political activities. Nevertheless, Betty describes him as a "good husband" by Washington standards, and proudly tells reporters that even after 25 years of marriage, she and Jerry still "go to bed together."

On the Way to the White House: After his 1st election to Congress in 1948, Ford was re-elected by the voters of his district 12 times in a row—each time with more than 60% of the vote. On 2 separate occasions, Michigan Republican leaders urged Ford to try for a seat in the U. S. Senate, but the congressman liked his job and worked hard to advance himself in the hierarchy of the House of Representatives. He 1st won a name for himself with his meticulous

attention to the details of military budgets, and soon earned a reputation as an armed forces "expert" and friend of the Pentagon. This endeared him to the House establishment, and he received a series of choice committee assignments. He was also active in the "Chowder and Marching Society," a jolly group of young Republicans, including that rising congressman from California, Richard M. Nixon. By the mid-1960s, many of the members of this group had become dissatisfied with the aging Republican leader of the House, Charles Halleck of Indiana. The "Young Turks" insisted that their party needed more aggressive and up-to-date leadership, and eventually they settled on Ford as their candidate to challenge Halleck. The congressman from Michigan had the right combination of politics (staunchly conservative), physical appearance (youthful), and personality (inoffensive) to appeal to his fellow Republicans in the House. In January, 1965, on a vote of 73 to 67, they elected Ford as the new minority leader.

During the 9 years he served in that role, Ford won many friends among his colleagues but few headlines from the national press. Among the highlights of his House leadership were his impassioned pleas for escalation in Vietnam (Why, he asked, are we "pulling our punches"? He urged the Johnson Administration to "unleash devastating air and sea power.") Another was his unsuccessful "crusade" to impeach liberal Supreme Court Justice William O. Douglas. It was widely reported in Washington that Ford actually launched his attack on Douglas as a favor to his old friend, President Richard Nixon. In fact, on every major issue before Congress, Ford proved himself one of the President's most loyal and outspoken supporters. In October, 1973, after Vice-President Spiro Agnew had resigned amid charges of accepting illegal payoffs, it came as no surprise that Nixon nominated Ford to be the new Vice-President. Ford's popularity on Capitol Hill assured congressional approval of his nomination; after 2 months of hearings and investigations, and despite grumbling by liberals and civil rights groups, Ford was confirmed with only minor opposition.

December 6, 1973 . . .

At 6:10 P.M., in the chamber of the House of Representatives, Ford raised his right hand and took the oath of office as Vice-President. He fluffed his lines when he came to the words "I will well and faithfully discharge . . ." Chief Justice Warren Burger had to repeat the words, and on his 2nd try, Ford mastered the phrase. After the ceremonies, reporters asked Ford what had been going through his mind during the historic moments while he was taking the oath. "I was trying to remember my lines," answered the new Vice-President. "I guess I blew them once, though."

Ford's 1st pledge as Vice-President was not made to the American people—it was made to Nixon. "Mr. President," he said, "you have my support and my loyalty."

In order to fulfill that pledge, Ford traveled more than 100,000 mi. and made more than 500 appearances over the next 8 months, stubbornly defending the Nixon record on Watergate. In one particularly aggressive speech, he declared that "a coalition of groups like the AFL-CIO, Americans for Democratic Action, and other powerful pressure organizations is waging a massive propaganda campaign against the President of the U.S. And make no mistake about it—it is an all-out attack. Their aim is total victory. . . . If they can crush the President and his philosophy, they are convinced they can then dominate the Congress and, through it, the nation." In the same address, he cited the "mountainous achievements" of the Nixon Administration, and dismissed Watergate as "a tragic but grotesque sideshow."

His Person: Ford is more than 6' tall, and he maintains the sharp, erect bearing and broad shoulders of a former athlete. Even at 61, he keeps his weight at 203—only 4 lbs. over his football-playing weight of 40 years ago. He has deep blue eyes and thinning, graying, blond hair. His nose, according to a veteran Grand Rapids reporter, was "obviously damaged on the football field." His admirers claim there is a close physical resemblance between Ford and George Washington.

In order to keep in shape, Ford swims twice daily for 20 minutes at a time and plays occasional rounds of golf (scoring as low as 86). He limits lunch to a salad, or to cottage cheese smothered with ketchup—the same lunch that Richard Nixon enjoyed during his years as Vice-President. Ford also has a passion for raw onions—which makes after-lunch conferences uncomfortable, even for some of his closest associates. His favorite dessert is pecan ice cream with fresh peach slices—but he indulges himself only occasionally. For years, Ford relaxed every evening with 2 or 3 dry martinis, with a pair of olives in each, but since he has become President he has tried to cut down to 1 or 2 martinis a day. He also enjoys Bourbon and water, and often smokes Edgeworth or Sir Walter Raleigh pipe tobacco.

Ford has been described as a happy extrovert who likes people enormously. As Vice-President, he tried to memorize the 1st names of all 60 Secret Service agents assigned to him—but he did not quite succeed. Since his youth, he has always been the center of attention from the moment he walks into a room. According to an aide, in "a one-to-one situation he will charm you right out of your socks."

Ford freely admits that he almost never reads books, but he finds time on Monday nights and Sunday afternoons to watch professional football games on TV. On these treasured occasions, he sits glued to the screen, calling plays out loud and exulting when the teams follow his suggestions. As a congressman, he also enjoyed watching his sons play football for their high school teams—even though on several occasions they seriously injured themselves. Picking up the paper every morning at 6 A.M., Ford generally turns straight to the sports section.

Friends have always been amazed at Jerry's stamina—he can often manage his grueling schedule on just 4 hours' sleep. No matter how trying his day has been, his wife reports that Ford has little difficulty falling asleep. "He hits the pillow and bang—he's asleep." During his service as Vice-President, however, Betty awoke one night to hear her husband talking in his sleep. "He kept saying, 'Thank you, thank you, thank you.' He was in a receiving line."

PRESIDENCY

August 8, 1974 . . .

Faced with incontrovertible evidence that he had obstructed justice and blocked proper investigation of the Watergate break-in, Richard Nixon looked ahead to certain impeachment by the House and conviction by the Senate. After more than 2 years of controversy, he decided at long last to resign the Presidency.

In an evening speech to the nation, Nixon pointedly reminded the people that even though he was personally stepping down, power would be passed to his handpicked successor: "In turning over direction of the Government to Vice-President Ford, I know, as I told the nation when I nominated him for that office 10 months ago, that the leadership of America will be in good hands."

Just one month later, Ford justified Nixon's confidence by granting the former President a "full, complete, and absolute pardon" for all crimes that he might have committed as Chief Executive.

August 9, 1974 . . .

At noon, Ford and his wife walked into the packed East Room of the White House amid thunderous applause. "Mr. Vice-President," intoned Chief Justice Warren Burger, "are you prepared to take the oath of office as President of the U.S.?" "I am, sir," Ford replied. Even before the chief justice asked him to do so, Ford raised his right hand, placing his left on a Bible held by his wife. It was opened to Proverbs 3:5-6—a passage Ford says every night as a prayer: "Trust in the Lord with all thine heart; and lean not unto thine own understanding/ In all thy ways acknowledge Him, and He shall direct thy paths." After repeating the oath of office, Ford turned and kissed his wife on both cheeks, as the audience rose to its feet in applause.

In the brief inaugural address that followed, Ford told the nation: "As we bind up the internal wounds of Watergate, more painful and more poisonous than those of foreign wars, let us restore the golden rule to our political process, and let brotherly love purge our hearts of suspicion and hate."

Within 3 months, Ford was hitting the campaign trail in an all-out effort to discredit his opposition. He told the people that the Democrats in Congress were to blame for the nation's disastrous rate of inflation, and warned that the election of more Democrats would "jeopardize world peace."

PSYCHOHISTORY

Ford was 3 years old when his mother remarried, and he must have been at least vaguely aware of the sudden adjustment to a new home and a new father. It is only natural that this experience might leave a nagging sense of insecurity, and this insecurity would have been heightened by his mother's treatment of this "scandal" in her past. She refused to tell her growing son the truth about his early life, and pretended that Gerald Ford, Sr., was his real father. Young Jerry's confusion and sensibility on this point was seemingly reflected in later years—when he himself finally married at age 35, he chose a woman, who, like his mother, had been previously married and divorced. Yet in all accounts of his life released before he became Vice-President, Ford carefully blocked any mention of the divorce of either his mother or his wife. He himself 1st learned the facts when he was 16—at a most sensitive point in his adolescence. In that same year came his frightening confrontation with his real father. One afternoon, while he was working at Skougi's restaurant across the street from South High School, Jerry noticed a man at the candy counter who was staring at him. "He stood there for a long time—he was a stranger—and finally he walked across to me and said, 'Leslie, I'm your father.' I was a little startled to be addressed as Leslie." As they ate lunch together, the older man told his son time and again, "Your name is not Ford!" Naturally, Jerry showed considerable relief when the interview was over, and the stranger shook hands, said good-bye, and left town. The entire experience only served to strengthen the boy's suspicion that he was somehow different—different from his 3 half-brothers, different from the other young people in his high school. This suspicion probably gave birth to Jerry's need to make himself as normal, as average as possible. He was unwilling to stand out in any way. Even on the football field, he played center—not the backfield. He wanted a position where he could submerge himself in the team personality, and function in near anonymity as part of a well-integrated unit. This role assured Ford's success in football, and the same tendency has been carried over into every phase of his career. It was his well-deserved reputation as an unassertive "team player" that won him advancement in the House of Representatives, and led to his selection as Vice-President. As journalist Larry L. King observes: "He is so average one almost suspects it to be deliberate." Ford's old friend, Grand Rapids reporter Bud Vestal, talks of Ford's conscious resolve to "outdumb" his opponents rather than "outsmarting" them, and many of those who know him well assert that Ford's image as a bumbling, slow-witted, good-natured jock is only a pose. If so, it is a pose that not only hides the driving ambition that has sustained him through 25 years of exhausting effort in politics, but also conceals the painful sensitivity of a boy who was once unsure about his father and apparently embarrassed by his adoption.

LITTLE-KNOWN FACTS

—During the 1930s, a group of young socialists was going around Grand Rapids painting slogans on the walls of public buildings. Football hero Jerry Ford soon emerged as the leader of a group of South High School athletes dedicated to putting a stop to such un-American activities. In one after-dark expedition, they caught the "Reds" at work, ordered them to stop, and then poured the paint over their heads.

—Ford is our only President who has worked as a professional male model. In 1939, while he was coaching football and studying law at Yale, Ford's girl friend, Phyllis Brown, persuaded him to invest some money in a New York modeling agency. Later, Ford joined Phyllis and a Look magazine photographer on an expedition to model winter sports clothing at a ski resort in Vermont. Look used 21 pictures of Ford and Phyllis in a feature article on a weekend in the life of "the beautiful people."

—On the day of his wedding, Ford was so nervous that it is reported that he appeared at the ceremony wearing one brown and one black shoe.

—As the congressman from Grand Rapids, Ford kept a Polaroid camera permanently mounted on a tripod in his office. Whenever visitors from "back home" appeared in Washington, they had their pictures taken with the smiling congressman. If Ford himself wasn't there, the guests were photographed while sitting at his impressive desk.

—It was Congressman Gerald Ford—not Richard Nixon or Attorney General John Mitchell—who was originally responsible for bringing Watergate "mastermind" Gordon Liddy to Washington. Ford had met Liddy on a campaign tour in upstate New York in '68, and agreed to help the former FBI agent get a job in the new Republican Administration. Ford wrote a letter on Liddy's behalf, and then followed it up with timely phone calls to Treasury Dept. officials. Finally, thanks to Ford's help, Liddy was appointed to the anticrime division of the Treasury Dept. More than 4 years later, after Liddy's leading role in the Watergate break-in had been made public, Ford commented: "I didn't pay any attention to Liddy. . . . He was just one of the many persons I tried to help get jobs at the time."

Quotes from Ford:

"When a man is asked to make a speech, the 1st thing he has to decide is what to say."

"If Lincoln were alive today he would be spinning in his grave."

"I must have centered the ball 500,000 times in high school and college."

"If we give up in South Vietnam, it would give up Southeast Asia, and our defense lines would be driven back to the Hawaiian Islands." —1965

"Personally, I am glad that thousands of fine young Americans can spend this Saturday afternoon knocking each other down in a spirit of clean sportsmanship and keen competition."—1966

"I personally believe that the communist powers of the world implacably seek the downfall of the Free World nations—chiefly, the U.S."—1968

"The election of Richard Nixon . . . would mean that laws already on the books would be enforced. Criminals and crime bosses would come under massive attack led by a Republican President and a Republican Attorney General." —1968

"I believe President Nixon—like Abraham Lincoln—is a man uniquely suited to serve our nation in a time of crisis."—February 10, 1969

"Thanks to my football experience, I know the value of team play. It is, I believe, one of the most important lessons to be learned and practiced in our lives."—1969

"I only wish that I could take the entire U.S. into the locker room at half time. I would simply say that we must look not at the points we have lost but at the points we can gain. We have a winner. Americans are winners."—Speech to football awards dinner, 1973

"I would say I am a moderate on domestic issues, a conservative in fiscal affairs, and a dyed-in-the-wool internationalist in foreign affairs."—1973

"I'm a Ford, not a Lincoln. My addresses will never be as eloquent."—1973

"Truth is the glue that holds governments together. Compromise is the oil that makes governments go."—1973

"You can literally move mountains, mine the oceans, master the energy of the sun, and climb the highest peak of all—world peace. It won't be easy. But the achievements of the Tinley Park Titans weren't won easily either."—Speech to Tinley Park High School, Ill., 1974

"It's the quality of the ordinary, the straight, the square, that accounts for the great stability and success of our nation. It's a quality to be proud of."—1974

"I am the 1st eagle scout Vice-President of the U.S.!"—1974

Quotes about Him:

"I got the impression of a fellow with the mind of a child in a man's body, a big St. Bernard."—Virginia Berry, one of Ford's high school classmates

"He played too much football with his helmet off."—Lyndon Johnson

"Mediocre is a word people in Grand Rapids often used to describe him, as though that would be the best kind of official to have."—Peter Rand

"Gerald Ford is one of the relatively few living Americans who not only admires Richard Nixon but actually *likes* him."—Larry L. King

"I cannot dislike him personally—he's cordial and gracious. But he's consistently wrong and consistency is a virtue of small minds. He's never proposed a constructive solution to anything."—Congressman Robert F. Drinan

"He doesn't have the intellect and magnificence of Adlai Stevenson, the flourish of John Kennedy, or the fire of Spiro Agnew—but he tends to be more believable and sincere than Richard Nixon."—Michael Doyle, editor of a volume of Ford's speeches

"Jerry's the only man I ever knew who can't walk and chew gum at the same time."—Lyndon Johnson

"Jerry doesn't really have a 1st-class mind. But, then, neither did Eisenhower."—Anonymous member of Ford's staff

"Ford isn't a bad man, but he's dumb—dumb. He shouldn't be dumb either. He went to school just like everybody else."—Rev. Duncan Littlefair, Grand Rapids

"He has a slow mind, but he has backbone."—Congressman Barber Conable

"He's a go-getter. When he skis, he skis hard. When he's with the family, he's with the family hard. He goes at everything 100%."—Ford's son, Michael

"I'm for women's lib, but I don't mind walking 3 paces behind Jerry."—Betty Ford

"He's not stupid, he's not dumb. He's ignorant. . . . If Jerry saw a hungry child, he would give the kid his lunch. But he can't see that voting against the school lunch program is depriving millions of kids of food."—A. Robert Kleiner, early Ford supporter

"You couldn't do as well as Jerry has done without being bright."—John Milinowski, former Ford aide

"He's not dumb. . . . He's a very solid, straightforward, decent sort of bird of moderate ability."—Yale Law Professor Eugene Rostow

"I wish I'd married a plumber. At least he'd be home by 5 o'clock."—Betty Ford

"The common idea that he's just like the guy next door—good-natured, well-adjusted and easygoing—is obviously absurd. The guy next door doesn't spend 16 hours a day and 25 years of his life in a nonstop quest for votes, power, and admiration. Like most politicians, Ford is a driven man."—Michael S. Medved

"I can't possibly believe Jerry's a dumb-dumb. He couldn't possibly have been reelected from the district all these years. . . . How many really intelligent Presidents have we had? I think a President has to be able to think like the people think."—Betty Ford

"Poor, dull Jerry."—Alice Roosevelt Longworth

—M.S.M.

6

The Almighty Dollar

The Dollar Bill

The $1 bill—people will pray for it, work for it, lie and cheat for it, but few ever take a good look at it.

It is a piece of paper measuring 2⅝" by 6⅛" with a thickness of .0043". The composition of the paper and ink is a state secret. New notes will stack 233 to an inch, if not compressed, and 490 notes weigh a lb. Every thousand notes cost the Government $8.02 to print. At the same time, over 2 billion bills are in circulation, each with an average life span of 18 months.

The word "dollar," which appears on both sides of the bill, is a variation of the German word *Taler*, the name of a silver piece that was 1st coined in 1518 and, under Charles V, Emperor of Germany, King of Spain, and ruler of Spanish America, became the chief coin of Europe and the New World.

The dollar bill is a relatively recent innovation in American currency. Before 1862 only dollar coins were issued. At the time of the signing of the Constitution, the people had little faith in paper currency due to the constant depreciation of paper money during the Colonial period. As a result, the new Government decided to mint only coins. A paper currency of sorts was issued during this early period of American history, but it was in the form of interest-bearing bank notes used to finance urgent undertakings such as the War of 1812.

In 1862, in the midst of the Civil War, Congress decided to print the 1st noninterest-bearing paper currency, which became known as "greenbacks" or "legal tenders."

The dollar, as we know it today, is a Federal Reserve note. It is issued by the 12 Federal Reserve banks scattered across the U.S. under the auspices of the national Government which prints the bills. Unlike previous notes that were redeemable for gold or silver, the Federal Reserve notes are guaranteed only by a pledge of collateral such as government securities or special drawing-right certificates.

—S.L.W.G.

THE SHRINKING VALUE OF THE DOLLAR

The average retail cost of certain foods in selected years, 1890-1975 (to the nearest cent)

	5 lb. flour	1 lb. round steak	1 qt. milk	10 lb. potatoes
1890	.15	.12	.07	.16
1910	.18	.17	.08	.17
1930	.23	.43	.14	.36
1950	.49	.94	.21	.46
1970	.59	1.30	.33	.90
1975	.98	1.89	.45	.99

SOURCE:

United States Bureau of the Census. *Historical Statistics of the United States from Colonial Times to 1957.* (Washington, D.C., 1960). p. 128.

United States Bureau of the Census. *Statistical Abstract of the United States, 1972.* 93rd edition (Washington, D.C., 1972). p. 353.

The People's Almanac's personal survey, January, 1975.

Abolitionist John Brown in 1859, the year that he led a raiding party in an attack on the Federal arsenal at Harpers Ferry, Va. Captured and hanged, he was condemned by the nation's leaders, but it wasn't long before Brown was known as a folk hero and a martyr to the cause of equal rights. (See: Chap. 4) *Library of Congress.*

On July 7, 1865—over 2 months after Lincoln's assassin, John Wilkes Booth, was killed in a Virginia barn—Booth's 4 fellow conspirators were hanged. Being prepared for hanging in a Washington, D.C., jail yard are: (L to R) Mrs. Mary Surratt, who ran the boardinghouse where Booth and his conspirators met; David Herold, Booth's aide; Lewis Paine, a Confederate deserter; George Atzerodt, a Confederate spy. (See: Chap. 4) *Library of Congress.*

Missouri-born Jesse James turned outlaw in 1866, and for 10 years he and his gang robbed stagecoaches, trains, banks, plundering and killing. In the 1870s, James (extreme L) proudly showed off his gang to a photographer he had summoned to their Missouri cave hideout. (See: Chap. 4) *Time, Inc.*

Tatanka Iyotanka or Sitting Buffalo Bull, best known as Sitting Bull. A military leader, noted orator, and elder statesman. In 1886, he told Annie Oakley that "the white man knows how to make everything, but he does not know how to distribute it." (See: Chap. 4) *Smithsonian Institution, National Archives.*

In spring, 1894, Ohio horse breeder Jacob S. Coxey led an army of unemployed in a march on Washington, D.C. His aide, Grand Marshal Carl Browne, a California poet, can be seen here on his stallion. At the capital, Coxey was arrested without being allowed to speak. (See: Chap. 4) *Library of Congress.*

James Naismith, the father of basketball, seen here with the original equipment, a peach basket and a ball. In 1892 he wrote a list of 13 rules, 12 of which are still in use for high school and college games. (See: Chap. 4) *U.P.I.*

Oscar Wilde, Dublin-born poet, playwright, wit, whose reputation was based on such works as *The Importance of Being Earnest* and *The Picture of Dorian Gray.* In 1895, after a trial for homosexual offenses, Wilde was sent to prison for 2 years. (See: Chaps. 4, 14) *George Eastman House Collection.*

Reverend Martin Luther King, Jr., being hustled into police headquarters while under arrest in Montgomery, Ala., on September 3, 1958. (See: Chap. 4) *Charles Moore from Black Star.*

Abraham Lincoln was clean-shaven until his 51st year when an 11-year-old girl told him that with whiskers he would "look a great deal better for your face is so thin." (See: Chap. 5) *Sophia Smith Collection, Smith College.*

The Great American Credit Card Factory

Over 300 million credit cards are in use in the U.S. For those consumers who qualify, "charge it" can pay for everything from a vacuum cleaner, television set, or tuxedo to tooth extractions, taxi rides, and psychiatric care. This convenient system allows consumers to buy more goods and services than ever before. However, it has also brought financial disaster to many Americans. In 1971 approximately a quarter of a million Americans declared personal bankruptcy. According to a 1972 report issued by the National Business Council for Consumer Affairs, total outstanding consumer credit for 1971 was $137 billion and ". . . from a national perspective, delinquent debts amount to approximately $2.4 billion on nearly 4.4 million late-paying or nonpaying accounts."

Consumer education and national legislation are both necessary in order to deal with the complex problems of the credit-card industry. We need a better understanding of today's credit world and a look at the new system for the future—namely, "electronic money transfer," which will make cash, checks, and even credit cards obsolete.

WHY USE CREDIT CARDS?

A report issued by the National Business Council for Consumer Affairs states that ". . . credit enables individuals to make purchases, benefit immediately from their utility, and pay for them over a period of time." The American consumer explains that he uses credit cards, "because it's safer than carrying cash," "to buy what I have always dreamed of," and "to make traveling more convenient." He also gains the psychological "prestige" from carrying a wallet loaded with credit cards, his proof that he qualifies as a good financial risk.

Surveys have shown that consumers spend 23% more when they are able to use credit cards than they do when paying cash. The psychology behind this spending pattern has not gone unnoticed, as credit-card issuers continue to expand their operations and increase their profits. The growth of the industry is remarkable, considering the fact that credit cards are "relatively" new.

HISTORY

1887 The term "credit card" was 1st used by Edward Bellamy, a lawyer and author, in his book *Looking Backward: 2000–1887*. Bellamy foresaw a society in which each citizen was the holder of a yearly credit card, issued by the Government, which paid for all necessary goods and services. The dollar amount on the face of the card equaled each citizen's "share of the annual product of the nation." When a purchase was made, the cost of the item was "pricked" out of tiers of squares on the credit card. There was no need for cash or monthly bills since the transaction was really between the consumer and the Government.

1900 Several hotels issued credit cards to their most prestigious customers.

1914 Department stores and chains of gasoline stations entered the picture.

1947 Railroad and airline companies issued credit cards.

1950 Diners Club introduced a "new" kind of credit card. Instead of directly providing specific goods and services, Diners Club acted as a "middleman" who paid for all charges made in restaurants belonging to Diners Club. The plan soon grew to cover general travel and entertainment expenses.

1951 Today's most popular card, the bank card, was initiated by the Franklin National Bank of Franklin Square, New York.

1958 Bank of America and the Chase Manhattan Bank of New York began issuance of bank credit cards.

COST: NOTHING IS REALLY FREE

As Americans continue to charge billions of dollars on credit cards, credit-card issuers are counting their profits and projecting future increases. With over 81 million consumers on "extended rotating credit," it is necessary to look at the cost of the credit card.

First, the "free cards," which are received without charge to consumers who meet qualification standards. These cards are issued by department stores, airlines, oil companies, and banks. Free cards grant a 25–30-day "grace period" after receipt of bill for customers to pay without finance charges. After the grace period, interest accumulates usually at the rate of 1½% per month, or 18% a year (on balances under $500). By paying interest, consumers are allowed to take advantage of what credit-card advertising calls "extended payment."

Second are the travel and entertainment cards (American Express, Carte Blanche, Diners Club). These do not usually offer the option of extending payment on a revolving account in return for interest on the unpaid balance. Instead they charge a fixed initiation fee, usually $20, before cards are issued. This fee is intended to cover paper work, and in the case of American Express, it also includes a subscription to *Travel and Leisure* magazine.

In addition, banks also profit from "discounting income" from the merchants who use their credit-card services. For example: Joe cannot afford to extend credit to the customers of his general store. He contacts a bank and arranges for the bank to sponsor the credit plan. Joe then puts the bank's decal on the window of his store, after paying an initiation fee, renting an imprinter (machine used to print charge slips), and agreeing to keep a "demand deposit account" with the bank. When Joe turns over the customer charge slips to the bank, he does not get "face value" for them. Instead, he receives the amount left after discounting by the bank at rates of between 2.5% and 7%. Although Joe benefits because his money is not tied up in credit transactions, he may have to "hike up" the selling price of his goods to cover what he must pay the bank.

PROFITS: ON THE INCREASE

Compare the percent of interest on your savings account with the 18% annual interest fees on revolving charge accounts, and you will begin to see where the profits lie. Although bank credit cards entered the picture late in the game and were sponsored only locally until 1965, they now have become the most popular type of credit card. In 1972 BankAmericard and Master Charge claimed approximately 30 million cards *each*. Al Griffin, author of *The Credit Jungle*, states that in California alone, "Bank of America nets $1 million a month from its BankAmericard operations."

In *The Cashless Society*, author Robert Hendrickson says that over 40 million consumers probably hold 2 or more oil company cards, and airlines have issued approximately 5 million cards. According to Hendrickson, "In 1969, more than 3 million American Express cardholders charged about $1.8 billion worth of goods and services, 2 million Diners Club cardholders charged about $1 billion worth and 650,000 Carte Blanche cardholders charged about $200 million worth."

KNOW YOUR RIGHTS

Credit-card holders are not liable for more than $50 charged on lost or stolen cards. In addition to this financial protection, Congress passed the Fair Credit Reporting Act in 1971 "to protect consumers against the circulation of inaccurate or obsolete information, and to insure that consumer reporting agencies exercise their responsibilities in a manner that is fair and equitable to consumers."

A leaflet published by the Federal Trade Commission states: "Under this law you can take steps to protect yourself if you have been denied credit, insurance, or employment, or if you believe you have difficulties because of a consumer report on you."

For detailed information, write the Federal Trade Commission in Washington, D.C., or contact the regional office nearest you.

NEED HELP? COUNSELING IS AVAILABLE

Approximately 150 consumer credit counseling services exist in the U.S. These nonprofit, community service agencies offer counseling, usually free, for consumers with debt problems.

A working example in Los Angeles: The bulletin distributed by Consumer Credit Counselors of Los Angeles reads, "To help people help themselves solve their debt problems." How it works: Client contacts counseling service and is sent a questionnaire on which client lists all income and debts. Upon receipt of the completed questionnaire, an appointment is made with a counselor. Counselor aids client in analyzing the problem, helps client make a budget for monthly living expenses, and determines what amount of income is available to pay existing bills. The counselor then contacts all of the client's creditors and arranges for "an agreeable and feasible plan for debt payment." Client can then choose to handle distribution of the funds or can have the counseling service do it. There is a small fee for postage, record keeping, and check processing if client requests the counseling service to pay the bills. But, if the client chooses to handle these personally, there is "no charge for the actual counseling or for the advice and recommendations given."

For nearest Consumer Credit Counselors office contact:

National Foundation for Consumer Credit, Inc.
Federal Bar Building West
1819 H Street, N.W.
Washington, D.C. 20006

Remember: Declaration of personal bankruptcy remains on your credit records for 14 years.

WHERE TO WRITE FOR CONSUMER EDUCATION MATERIALS

National Consumer Finance Association
1000 16th Street, N.W.
Washington, D.C. 20036

Council of Better Business Bureaus, Inc.
Education Division
230 Park Avenue
New York, N.Y. 10017

National Foundation for Consumer Credit, Inc.
Federal Bar Building West
1819 H Street, N.W.
Washington, D.C. 20006

Council for Family Financial Education
1110 Fidler Lane, Suite 1616
Twin Towers
Silver Spring, Md. 20910

ELECTRONIC MONEY TRANSFER:
A FUTURE REALITY?

Cash payments have been replaced by credit cards and payment by check. However, the paper work involved in the processing of checks is costly, running the banking industry billions of dollars a year. Elimination of this expense depends on elimination of the check and the credit card. Before such a drastic change can occur, a new system of money transfer is needed to replace the old one. Electronic money transfer is the answer, and it is now being developed. It is a system totally run by computer. In it each individual is the holder of a single national credit card which can provide him with all necessary goods and services. The desirability of this method is highly controversial, due particularly to the computer and the "controls" it will bring.

Dependence upon the computer is already evident in our credit-card society. Computer banks record and evaluate a consumer's past credit history, his current credit status and "capability" to pay, and even his character. In the U.S. there are over 2,500 credit bureaus. Somewhere in the records of these bureaus there is a file on every American who has applied for credit. In his book, *Credit Cardsmanship*, Martin J. Meyer states that the information contained in the files "is sometimes so private that the FBI is now buying 25,000 credit reports a year." Meyer also points out that there is no legislation to prevent computer "linkups" and that "already 25 States exchange computerized tax data with the Internal Revenue Service."

"Invasion of privacy" complaints have been voiced due to the massive amounts of information being recorded on computers. Former Senator Sam J. Ervin, Jr. (Dem.-N.C.), has said that existing computer files in Washington are leading the country toward a "police state." Ralph Nader says, "Invisible changes are taking place everywhere. We feel them every minute of every day and they are having cataclysmic overtones as to how we operate this society. This is leading to a significant kind of tyranny. The key democratic principle of man's control over his life is being abused. Unless we do something about it, we're suddenly going to wake up a nation of slaves."

Are Americans en route to the system of electronic money transfer? The Federal Reserve Board says that credit cards are "a step toward . . . electronic money transfer" and "an interim and useful phase in the evolution of . . . the checkless society."

—C.O.

FOR FURTHER READING

Meyer, Martin J. *Credit Cardsmanship*. New York, Farnsworth Publishing Co., Inc., 1971. An in-depth probe into a cashless system versus a cash and credit economy:

Hendrickson, Robert. *The Cashless Society*. New York, Dodd, Mead & Co., 1972. A detailed look at how to play the credit-card game—how you can make money, save money, or lose it.

Unusual Ways of Making a Living

"Blessed is he who has found his work."
—Thomas Carlyle

Doctor, lawyer, or Indian chief? There are alternative ways to earn the daily bread. Writing "shepherd" in the occupation blank on your income tax form may seem silly, but one Colorado woman does just that. Whether you're a young graduate in search of fame and fortune, a wealthy executive in search of a new life-style, or simply someone in search of a little extra cash and fun, this sampler of unusual occupations is guaranteed to kindle your imagination.

Clown: Want to run away and join the circus? Ringling Brothers Barnum and Bailey circus conducts a yearly clown training school in Venice, Fla. Approximately 30 students are picked from 300 hopefuls; not everyone graduates, but those who make it get a 2-year contract starting at $200 per week. "Clowns are the pegs to hang the circus on," said P. T. Barnum. A former actor and present clown trainee says, "The clown is pure—pure pathos, pure slapstick. It's the essence of drama."

Chimney Sweep: Sweeps are respected professionals in Europe, with an official uniform—black funeral suits, top hats, and turban—that reflects the romantic image of the trade. Sweden's sweeps (both men and women) must serve a 2-year apprenticeship before being licensed to practice. The occupation is almost nonexistent in the U.S., but one Southern California sweep, formerly in the beauty supply business, charges $25 per 1½-to-2-hour cleaning job and plans eventually to have sweeps all over Los Angeles working for him. "Chimneys in Southern California are terribly neglected," he says. "There are just no sweeps to clean them."

Shepherd: The 23-year-old daughter of a wealthy California family works 18 hours a day, accompanied only by her horse, dog, and 30-

30 rifle, tending sheep in the Colorado high country. Her main duty is moving the herd of 2,300 sheep to new pasture daily, but she also doubles as veterinarian, treating the sheep for maggots and mending wounds. At night she sleeps under the stars, armed with a rifle to guard against coyotes and bears. It's lonely, tiring work, but she wouldn't trade it for any office job. "There aren't all the little hassles," she says. "Being alone lets you get your thinking together." She also says that women shepherds are in demand. "Other ranchers have asked me to work for them. There's not much muscle involved in this business, and ranchers seem to realize gals are more reliable or conscientious. A lot of the old sheepherders are retiring and no one seems to want this job."

Forest Fire Lookout: Author Jack Kerouac did this. It's the perfect job for solitary types with no fear of heights and the ideal opportunity to write the great American novel. The job consists of manning a tower in a national park or forest preserve and watching for signs of fire. It can be lonely work; for years the Forest service sought newlywed couples for this job. Pay is based on civil service wage levels (starting around $6,000) and includes generous health benefits. Contact the U.S. Forest Service in Washington, D.C., to apply.

Moonshiner: "Moonshining," says one Georgia old-timer, "has just plain gone to hell." The independent moonshiner has been largely replaced by syndicated crime operations, but some mountaineers still take pride in the old art, and a small segment of the population still has a taste for the original white lightning. "They grow up with it and it's just in their blood," says one moonshiner. He's retired now, and admits times are hard for the old-time moonshiner. But he also observed that the modern organized-crime moonshiners "don't know the 1st thing about making good liquor."

Christmas Tree Farmer: It's Christmas year-round for one Southern California family. Parents, kids, and grandparents work all year preparing trees for holiday sales. The project started as a sideline to asparagus farming and grew into 3 tree farms. The family claims profits are relatively small, but "families are fragmented today and we wanted something that we could all do together, outdoors."

Street Vendor: Every American city has street peddlers, ranging from old men selling frankfurters to young blue-jean-clad craftsmen selling macramé belts. The range of profits and products is enormous; one California pretzel salesman averages $10 per day, while a leather-goods salesman only one block away averages $250 per weekend. Peddling is ideal for struggling artists and craftsmen. A Berkeley jewelry-maker enthused, "I should have done this years ago.

I don't have to give half the profits to some big business store just for selling my stuff. I work when I want and sell when I want, and I'm never bored out here." All vendors must be licensed, so call the local license bureau before setting up business.

Beetleboarder: Here's extra income for Volkswagen "beetle" owners. Beetleboards of America, based in Los Angeles, pays VW owners $20 per month to allow their cars to be repainted with graphics advertising stereos, soft drinks, blue jeans, and beer. In keeping with VW's image, advertising is geared toward the youth market, and prospective beetleboarders are interviewed to match the driver to the product. A blue-jean advertiser prefers long-haired drivers, while a beer company prefers athletic, clean-cut young men. College students, especially favored as beetleboarders, can save toward tuition just by driving to campus.

Carnival Barker: Hustlers of all types can find their life's calling or an exciting summer job working as a carny. The job offers good pay (commission averaging $250 per week in lucrative locales), travel, and excitement. Long hours —often an 18-hour shift—are standard, and strong vocal cords are a must. It's also necessary to learn carnival language: A barker is a carny, a customer is a mark, a booth or concession is a joint, cheap prizes are slum. To apply, go to the nearest State or county fair when it opens and speak with the joint-owners. Tell them you want to be a "1st-of-May" (carny for short-term or new employee).

Card Dealer: If you like to play cards, are manually dexterous, and hate working a 9-to-5 day, you have the qualifications for a casino card dealer. Contrary to the stereotyped shady gambler myth, casinos prefer to hire responsible people, train them carefully, and pay them middle-class incomes. Gambling is a business, and dealers are business representatives. One ex-bank teller started dealing blackjack as the result of a Las Vegas vacation. "Dealing," she says, "is like bank work. You handle money and you're on your feet all day. But the pay is better, the atmosphere is exciting, and the hours are flexible." Where to apply? Las Vegas. Or Reno. Or anywhere else that gambling is legal.

Belly Dancer: Good exercise, good pay, flexible hours, and it's art too. Legitimate belly dancing is not just go-go dancing. It's an art, but because it has sexual overtones, it's a money-making art. Restaurants and clubs pay $5 to $15 per hour, depending on the dancer's expertise. One California sociology student took several belly-dance classes and now works her way through school by moonlighting in a San Francisco restaurant. She dances only 20 minutes out of each hour, spends the rest of the time studying. "It started as just a job," she says, "but I like it so much that I'm thinking of changing my major to dance."

Male Escort: A happily married father of 3 regularly dates strange women and his wife doesn't object. He's the owner and sole employee of the Bucks County Male Escort Service in Pennsylvania, and for an hourly fee plus date expenses, he'll act as male companion for an evening. Female escorts have been around a long time, but this Pennsylvanian feels there's a growing demand for male escorts. He stresses that safety and companionship rather than sex are the services he provides. "Many women don't want dates. They want to feel independent. But they also need an escort, either to talk to, or just to help them get around safely and conveniently. This is where I'm of service."

Finder: An Oklahoma City man makes a living finding unusual things for people—like a pair of fleas dressed as bride and groom, a baseball signed by Jim Thorpe in 1933, and a client's missing brother. Finders Keepers, Inc., was started by an ex-advertising agency employee who discovered he had a knack for finding odd props for TV commercials. "I have always been able to locate the rare and unusual with an uncanny facility," he says. "Suddenly it dawned on me that I could capitalize on my ability." Finders Keepers will look for anything, provided it's legal. The company's manager boasts a high success rate; however, he's still looking for an electric clock motor that runs backward.

Fantasy Broker: A postal clerk wants to be a stand-up comedian for one night. A businessman wants to drive a freight train across a western State. A psychiatrist wants 20 dates on 20 weekends with 20 girls from 20 different countries. How do they do it? They see a fantasy broker whose business is making dreams come true. Originally pioneered in Chicago by an advertising executive, fantasy firms in several cities now do a booming business, charging from $150 to thousands to turn dreams into reality. Fantasy Fulfillment Institute in Washington, D.C., did $2,500 worth of business as a result of an ad that read:

> You can do anything you want . . . drive a formula race car, ride a camel down Pennsylvania Avenue at 3 P.M., live in a ghost town, float down the Potomac on a magnificent barge with one hundred slaves, or kiss a buffalo.

Fantasy Fulfillment's manager, an ex-insurance salesman, sees a big future in fantasy. "Why not? Look at all the money people spend on cars that make them brutally handsome, aftershaves that make them karate experts, clothes that make them girlish and thin. Why not cut out the middleman and sell directly to the buyer—original fantasies in the factory cartons?"

Some jobs are unusual because of who's doing them. Female pilots and male airline stewards were once a rarity, but as sex roles change, even the most sex-biased occupations change. Spain recently admitted its 1st professional lady bullfighter (a blonde) into the bullfighters' union. In 1972, the Jewish synod ordained the world's 1st woman rabbi. And one of America's most traditional types—the solitary truck-driving man—may soon be an endangered species; there are now over a thousand husband-and-wife trucking teams rolling down the nation's highways.

Still thinking doctor, lawyer, or Indian chief? If you're dissatisfied with your work—if you're sweating through school or bored with your 9-to-5 desk job—then maybe it's time to think butcher, baker, or candlestick maker instead. It's never too late to earn big money and be the envy of your friends. You might have more fun, too.

—S.U.

Attic and Junkyard

The California gold mines may have played out, and pirate loot has vanished, but more treasure hunting goes on today than ever before.

Modern fortune seekers do their seeking in attics, under porches of old houses (antique bottles are sometimes found there), at flea markets, charity bazaars, antique shops, junkshops, house-wreckers' lots, country auctions.

The current collecting boom has made superstars out of a lot of very ordinary things—or seemingly ordinary, anyway. Things like political campaign buttons, Shirley Temple dolls, *carte-de-visite* photos, jail padlocks, railroad spikes, 1st-edition novels, even lengths of old barbed wire. Believe it or not, all are collectibles sought by avid collectors and dealers prepared to pay the top dollar for wanted specimens. Those are the 2 key words in this kind of treasure trek: "wanted specimens." Not every campaign button, not every 1st edition, not "every" anything is valuable. Only a precious few. But they can be precious indeed.

The following is a brief checklist of items in various hobby fields that are worth looking for. Where they might turn up is anybody's guess. A sheaf of Ben Franklin documents—official records kept by Franklin when Postmaster General—was discovered in the binding of an old book. The binder had stuck them there, eons ago, to stiffen the covers. The last printed copy in private hands of the Declaration of Independence was found in 1968 in the cellar of a

Philadelphia bookshop, where it had remained hidden 50 years or more. It was then sold for $404,000. One of the world's scarcest stamps, a Hawaiian "missionary," turned up under a hunk of peeling wallpaper. Any place old things are stored or sold is worth rummaging through. But do keep in mind that condition is all-important in fixing value. Collectors are a fussy lot. A stamp that brings $500 in pristine shape may sell for $250 if at all worn or smudged. A book with a page missing is just about worthless, unless very rare. So take a good look. Be sure your bargain is a bargain indeed, and won't end up as a white elephant.

Banks. All old mechanical banks are worth big premiums. Minimum value for a pre-W.W. I bank in good condition, not badly scratched or dented, is $50. They go all the way up to $3,000. The $3,000 plum is called "Shoot the Chute." Other valuable banks (over $1,000) are Turtle, Giant, Girl Skipping Rope, Bank Teller, Bowling Alley, Cat Jumping for Mouse, and many more. Mechanical banks were made of heavy cast iron. A penny or some other coin was placed in a holder and a spring fired it into the bank, which could be a whale's mouth, the trunk of a tree, or a baseball catcher's mitt. Mechanical banks were 1st made around 1870. Their heyday was 1890 to 1910. After 1920 some of the old designs were reproduced. Because of collector interest, reproductions are still made today. Naturally these are worth comparatively little. "Still" banks—those that do not move—nearly always bring less than mechanicals, except for early "personality" banks (Mickey Mouse, Popeye, and other comic and film characters).

Coins. Ancient coins need not be gold or silver to have substantial value. Most Imperial Roman bronzes, those struck by the Emperors, are worth under $20, but there are exceptions. A bronze sestertius struck by Claudius (41–54 A.D.) with the figure of Liberty on the reverse and inscribed *Libertas Avqvsta S.C.*, brings up to $250. A sestertius of Titus (79–81 A.D.) with standing portrait of the god Aeternitas on the reverse, inscribed *Aeternit Avq S.C.*, is worth $600.

Prices of ancient silver coins can go very high. A silver stater from the city of Metapontum (550–480 B.C.) is worth $1,000. An ear of barley is pictured on the obverse. A tetradrachm (4-drachm piece) from Catania (461–430 B.C.) is priced at $3,000. One side carries a portrait of Apollo, the other a charioteer in a quadriga or 4-horse carriage.

Are worthwhile coins still found in pocket change? No more "oldies" are in circulation, but "goodies" occasionally turn up. Most recent rarity was the 1972 double-die Lincoln cent, which looks like a double exposure. Its value is

around $110 uncirculated. A double-die variety occurred on the 1955 Lincoln cent, too. It's worth $385 uncirculated; even an ordinary specimen with the luster gone brings $160. (In numismatic jargon, "uncirculated" doesn't stand for "never circulated." It means the coin is just as bright and fresh *as if* it hadn't been circulated.)

Catalogs. Until the early 1960s nobody but a few specialists showed the least interest in vintage mail-order catalogs. Then the reprint publishers started coming out with facsimiles, and a funny thing happened. People bought the reprints and it kindled a desire to own the real McCoy—which must prove there's a collector hidden deep in most of us.

The 1st mail-order catalog was put out by Montgomery Ward of Chicago in 1874. Don't even try looking for a copy of that one; they just aren't around. But if your grandmother was the sort who saved things, your attic might yield one of the following: Sears, Roebuck 1908 (approximate value $4), 1910 ($15), 1916 ($50), 1948 ($7), and Montgomery Ward 1925 ($25). Much sought after are the catalogs of Johnson Smith, a Racine, Wisc., novelty firm that sold exploding cigars, smoke bombs, and rubber rats to millions of kids in the 1920s and '30s. Its catalogs of that era are worth $5–$15. Copies with covers missing, pages stained or other defects bring about half the usual prices.

Also available, and more valuable on the whole, are early trade catalogs, issued by manufacturers and shopkeepers. These date back as far as the 1700s and are strongly in demand. Not only hobbyists but libraries collect them. Any pre-1900 trade catalog has value. Best are the earliest ones, and those with illustrations. Some to watch for are: Harris' catalog of Copper Weather-Vanes, 1860; New Haven Clock Co., 1860; Hasse's Music Boxes, 1894–1895.

Posters. Remember old theater posters? They stood out on the street, in big glass frames, picturing scenes or stars from the theater's current movie. Showhouses discarded them by the ton. Today, movie buffs pay up to $75 for some. A 39" by 30" full-color poster of Hoot Gibson riding a bucking bronco is in the $50–$75 category. It dates from 1935. A poster advertising *Reckless* with Jean Harlow is worth $55. Humphrey Bogart posters are all highly collectible. A 35 by 14 incher for *All Through the Night* commands $20–$25.

W.W. I was the 1st "poster war." Brightly colored lithographs went up all over the U.S., seeking not only volunteers but buyers for bonds, books for camp libraries and so on. All original W.W. I posters have become valuable, some more than others. "PRO PATRIA! JOIN ARMY FOR PERIOD OF WAR," 40" by 26", is worth $20. A $75 value is placed on a poster bearing the slogan "AMERICA'S ANSWER

TO THE KAISER," 45" by 36". "BOOKS WANTED FOR OUR MEN IN CAMP AND OVER THERE," 38" by 25", retails for $30. One of the most valuable, worth $150, is a small poster titled "SAVE FOOD," which measures 20" by 13".

Scrapbooks. There was a time, not so long ago, when scrapbook-keeping was a favorite hobby. Nobody seems to keep them anymore, but collectors avidly buy old scrapbooks. As with most collectibles the older the better, but content is important, too. Scrapbooks loaded with snapshots of aunts and uncles don't arouse much enthusiasm. But those containing postcards, advertising cards, newspaper and magazine clippings always bring good prices. A well-filled scrapbook from the early 1900s can sell for $50 to $75—higher if any of its contents are valuable in themselves.

Political Ephemera. Did you wonder, back in '72, if McGovern-Eagleton buttons would ever be collectors' items? There was good cause to wonder, as collecting campaign buttons and other political memorabilia has become a popular hobby. On top of the heap is the 1920 Cox/Roosevelt button. That was FDR, 2nd on the ticket, running for Vice-President and losing. A button collector will pay $350 or more for it. Other rare and valuable buttons, in the $75–$100 category, are the 1924 Davis/Bryan, 1928 Smith/Robinson, 1928 Hoover/Curtis. Celluloid buttons came along in 1896, the year McKinley defeated Bryan (but the Bryan buttons are worth twice as much as McKinley's). What about Lincoln? In Lincoln's day, ribbons and fancy brooches were the thing. Several Lincoln ribbons were made, and now are worth $150 to $250. Some fairly recent buttons have value: $15 and up for 1948 Truman/Barkley, $20 for Dewey/Bricker. So far, post-1948 specimens aren't drawing much interest. The "Come Home America" McGovern/Eagletons are now selling at $2.50. Many bogus McGovern/Eagleton buttons exist.

Stamps. In 1878, a 13-year-old boy made the biggest, most publicized hobby "find" of all time. L. Vernon Vaughn was rummaging through old correspondence in his parents' attic when he discovered the only known specimen of the British Guiana one-pence of 1856. Though he got only a few cents for it, that stamp is now worth more than a quarter-million dollars. It was last sold in 1970, for $280,000 and is now owned by a wealthy investor from Wilkes-Barre, Pa. During the 1920s a rumor circulated that a 2nd copy had turned up, but nothing more was heard of it. It's very likely that one, or more, could exist. Originally the stamp must have been printed on a sheet, with a number of impressions to the sheet.

Comic Books. If you were a kid back in the '30s, one of the biggest events of your life was publication of volume one, number one of *Action Comics.* It hit the stands in 1938 and within a few days was sold out, bought up by crowds of eager readers. The 1st comic of its kind, it was packed with slambang adventure stories. Everybody's superhero, Superman, made his debut in *Action Comics.* There he was on the cover of the 1st issue, hoisting a car over his head like a toy, while bystanders stood about struck with awe. Inside was the story of how he got that way. Thousands of copies of *Action Comics* were sold, at 10¢ a toss, but only 9 are known to be in existence today. The remainder fell victim, like many another collectible, to heavy handling and spring cleaning. Those 9 are valued at around $2,000 each. The most recent sale was for $1,801.26. A 10th could be lurking somewhere, in a box of junk that never got discarded, or in the back of an old high school locker.

Buckets. Remember "The Old Oaken Bucket?" It might not have been your song, but antique farm equipment is worth money, oaken or otherwise. There are 2 kinds of antique wooden farm buckets: (a) carved out by hand from a tree section, and (b) made of wooden rails or slats held together by metal hoops. The 1st is much more valuable. Determining the age of carved buckets is very tough, as there's no "style" and there are no identifying marks. But any scooped-out bucket has to be at least 150 years old. That was the way early settlers made buckets and other farming gear. Later, professionally crafted items were available, but some diehards continued making their own in the old-fashioned way. As collectors' items they can fetch up to $100. The hooped variety brings $10–$30. That's still not bad, considering that some specimens can be found along roadsides and in ditches, there for the taking.

Folk Art. In the later 1700s and through most of the 1800s, before photography put them out of business, folk painters roamed America. Itinerants working from donkey carts and knapsacks, they went from door to door offering to paint portraits. Most folk artists had no art training of any kind. They rose from the ranks of house painters, sign painters, and general handymen. But some had real talent and versatility. And they worked everywhere. Average cost for group portraits (all members of a family, plus dogs and cats) was $3 to $25. These were full-sized canvases. Small portraits and miniatures on ivory or wood sold for as little as 25¢.

Large and small, these items followed a pretty standard route. For one or 2 generations they hung proudly on the owner's wall. Then, when the age of photography came along, photos of current family members went up on the walls, sending these old oils to the attic. At that time nobody gave a moment's thought to the possibility of their having any value—and they hadn't. But as they sat in those attics, folk art gradually got discovered. Even the gawkiest, most 2-dimensional canvases have enflamed the passions of art lovers. Folk portraits aren't yet on the Rembrandt level, but they can bring thousands of dollars in the salesrooms. Works by known artists who signed their canvases are especially sought. The "old masters" of American folk art are: Winthrop Chandler; Erastus Field; William Prior; John Brewster; James Sanford Ellsworth; and the celebrated Ammi Phillips.

If any of your distant ancestors had their portraits painted, and the portraits are now in your attic, you might own something valuable.

Disney Items. In 1928 the 1st animated cartoon with a sound track was produced. Called *Steamboat Willie*, it put both its creator (Walt Disney) and star (Mickey Mouse) on the road to fame and fortune. Mickey took the country by storm, not only in movie theaters but in variety stores, drugstores, and everywhere else. Products of all sorts sported his name and likeness: tea services, toothbrushes, jewelry sets, sterling silver tableware, dolls, handbags, wind-up toys, books, comics, schoolbags, pencils, pens, sweat shirts, beany caps. And wristwatches. The acknowledged king of nostalgia is the original "1st edition" of Ingersoll's Mickey Mouse watch, made in 1932. It's been advertised for as much as $750. But this isn't the only valuable Mickey Mouse watch. Any specimen from the '30s in good working order brings a minimum of $100. Early Donald Duck watches have sold as high as $350; so have Big Bad Wolf watches (another Disney character). The Big Bad Wolf watch sold originally at $3.50, in 1937. It, too, was made by Ingersoll.

Books. Probably the best opportunities for making attic and junkyard finds lie with old, scarce, and rare books. Because they were originally cheap, these ended up in the hands of average, ordinary folk, who never realized they could be worth anything. Book rarities look like nothing special. They're no older, or larger, or handsomer than other volumes. They're printed on no better paper. So they can easily be overlooked—even by the pros. A copy of one of the most valuable American 1st editions, a little pamphlet titled *Tamerlane* by Edgar Allan Poe, was found in a "slush box" outside a bookshop, mixed in with back-date magazines, reprints and textbooks. It might have been handled by hundreds of browsers who failed to take note of it. But when a bibliophile (book collector) finally happened by, he knew what to do. He took the item inside and sold it to the bookshop's proprietor, for a handsome sum.

One of the 11 known copies of the *Bay Psalm Book*, the 1st book printed in America, turned up unexpectedly in Ireland in the 1930s. Even a Gutenberg Bible, which doesn't look very ordinary, was once stumbled upon. A German peasant family of the 1800s was using leaves from a damaged copy as wrapping paper. Each morning, as the children of the house went off to school, they wrapped their primers in Gutenberg Bible leaves. Today, single leaves from this most famous of all books sell for $5,000.

First editions of most "collected" authors are worth a premium. F. Scott Fitzgerald's *The Beautiful and the Damned*, published in 1922, brings $60 in the 1st edition. William Faulkner's *The Wild Palms*, 1939, is worth $45. Other collectible 1st editions are:

—Theodore Dreiser's *Sister Carrie*, New York, 1900, $350
—Max Beerbohm's *Zuleika Dobson; or An Oxford Love Story*, London, 1911, $90
—Rudyard Kipling's *France at War*, London, 1915, $35
—T. E. Lawrence's (Lawrence of Arabia) *Seven Pillars of Wisdom*, London, 1926, privately printed for the author, $6,500
—Jack London's *The Cruise of the Dazzler*, London, 1906, $325
—Norman Mailer's *The Naked and the Dead*, New York, 1948, $50
—George Orwell's *1984*, New York, 1949, $20

Not every 1st edition becomes valuable, even if the book gets to be a best seller. Differences in value depend on edition size and collector demand. But it's always the 1st edition that collectors want, not a reissue, a 2nd printing, or (worse than poison) a book club edition. Many 1st editions state the fact that they are 1st editions, on the reverse side of the title page. Others can sometimes be identified by matching the title page date with the copyright date; if they jibe, the book is likely a 1st edition.

Not only novels and poetry are sought. Many nonfiction works have value. Here, collectors aren't so much interested in the authors, so it's not necessary to seek out famous names. Instead, look for early works on popular topics. Chess, ballooning, football, astronomy are a few of many. Remember that book collectors want pioneer works in their fields, no matter how unelaborate or unauthoritative. Just what is and isn't "pioneer" has to be measured according to the subject's age. A book on radio electronics from 1918 would qualify; so would any circa 1900 work on "horseless carriages."

Avon Bottles. If you said Yes when the Avon lady called, you might now have yourself a valuable bottle. Over the years Avon has packaged its products in some highly decorative bottles, and they've become favorites of bottle buffs. The older ones are usually worth more, but many Avons from as recently as the '60s are sought after. The bottle for Blossom Cologne, 1936, is worth $85. Bubble Bath, 1949, $18 to $20. Other prices include: Wassail Bowl, 1969, $8; Cologne Gem set, 1967, $5.50; Lady Belle Styrofoam Bell, 1966, $59.50. The later bottles are considered collectible only when full and in the original box.

Clocks. The old clock on the wall—or in the secondhand shop—can be worth big money. Wall clocks made by American factories in the 19th century weren't very pretty, but collectors like them just the same. "Banjo" models, made in the shape of banjos, bring up to $5,000. That's the value placed on a Simon Willard "banjo" from about 1805, 40¾" high, with a gilded eagle on top. Other prices include: $1,500 for a Sawin & Dyar of about 1822 with brass side arms, roman numerals, and painted glass front panels; $1,800 for a Curtis & Dunning circa 1815, 51" high, with the glass painted.

Black clocks are worth money, too. Not nearly as much, but a lot more than Sears, Roebuck charged for them in the 1890s. Black clocks were mantel or shelf models, with black iron or imitation marble cases. Everybody, even their most avid admirers, agree black clocks are ugly. But the prices aren't—$50 to $100 for specimens in good working condition and with all the original caseparts.

Locks. All locks made before 1900 have value to collectors, if the original key is present and the lock is in working order. Most in demand are unusual or bizarre specimens: very large padlocks and those with decorative shapes. They can bring as much as $600—for Madrid-made "inquisition locks" of the 16th century. Keys can be valuable even without locks; ornamental French and Italian keys of the 1700s and 1800s fetch up to $40.

Autographs. Batches of old papers sometimes contain celebrity autographs. Look closely at any early legal document. It might be signed by a State governor, Cabinet member, even a President. Before their White House days, most of our Presidents served in posts that required them to sign documents. These aren't worth as much as documents signed as President, but definitely have value. Any Washington document commands a minimum of $500, and with any luck will bring $1,000 or more. Many documents signed by Washington as President were also signed by Jefferson as Secretary of State, a double treat for the autophile.

The sort of Washington document that gets pulled from boxes of family records is unimposing at 1st glance—so unimposing that generations of the family will have failed to notice the signature. Washington was not only President of the U.S. but president of the "Society of the Cincinnati," and inked numerous documents in that capacity.

Toys. In the Gay Nineties, many a child thrilled to find a cast-iron fire engine, drawn by cast-iron horses and manned by cast-iron firemen, under the Christmas tree. As toy making evolved, stamped tin replaced cast iron; then plastic replaced tin. Collectors now prize those cast irons as highly as did the original owners. A horse-reel wagon, which carried the hose spool, made by Wilkins around 1880, sells for $250–$300. Carpenter's steam fire engine of the same date is worth $225 to $275. In the same price category is a wagon marked "Fire Patrol," packed with firemen riding to the blaze site, offered by Wilkins around 1900.

Prints. Prints used to be called "art for the poor"—imitation pictures for people who couldn't afford oil paintings. But those executed by certain Old Masters and popular modern artists are for the poor no more. Recent auction-sale prices have included $4,250 for Piranesi's *View of the Interior of the So-Called Temple of Neptune at Paestum,* an etching; $20,000 for Mantegna's *Bacchanale with Silenus* (engraving); and $55,000 for Rembrandt's portrait of an elderly goldsmith named Jan Lutma, an etching and drypoint. Among modern artists, engravings by Joan Miró sell mainly in the $600–$3,000 range. Many of Picasso's are in that neighborhood, but some go much higher.

The lithography firm of Currier & Ives was in business from 1835 to 1906, in the lower Manhattan area of New York City. It published prints of every description: portraits of George Washington, views of steamships cruising the Mississippi, hunting scenes, skaters on a frozen Central Park lake, Barnum's American Museum the day after it burned down.

There's a mystique about Currier & Ives, and 2 mistaken schools of thought about the value of their prints. Some people believe all are worthless, as they were printed in such large numbers; others think the name "Currier & Ives" on a print guarantees a big sale price, regardless of subject. Some of the firm's output is rare; but many of its prints can be had for less than $10. The subject matter counts: Most of the cheaper specimens are just portraits and religious scenes. But size also is important. C & I used 3 standard sizes for its prints: 7¾" by 13", 13" by 20", and 20" by 27", not including margins. Though some of the smaller-sized works are valuable, nearly all of the largest prints are worth $1,000 and more.

Among the most valuable are:

—*Trout Fishing on Chateaugay Lake,* 1856, $1,250
—*Grand Match for the Base-Ball Championship,* 1862, $3,750
—*Clipper Ship 'Hurricane',* 1852, $3,750
—*The Express Train,* 1859, $2,600
—*Happy Family—Ruffed Grouse and Young,* 1866, $4,600

If you find any of the items herein described, or any other collectibles, you'll want to: (a) have them appraised to learn their up-to-the-minute market value, and (b) locate a buyer who'll pay a fair price for them. Many people go to museums with their discoveries, but few museums are equipped or willing to make appraisals. They may give an opinion on whether or not an item is genuine, but not an estimate of value. Instead they refer such inquiries to dealers, with the warning that the appraisal will cost money. This is true. "Appraisal" means the dealer studies the material and gives a written report on what it is and what it's worth. For this service the owner pays a fee, which varies according to the amount of work involved. Appraisals can be made on single items or entire collections. The alternative to paying for an appraisal is simply to present the item(s) for sale and ask for an offer. Don't, unless desperate, accept the 1st offer, but get a few competitive offers. Try, when possible, to sell to a specialist. If you have dolls, sell to a doll specialist; if you have porcelain, sell to a porcelain specialist. Because he has more outlets for his material—more customers waiting—a specialist will pay higher prices.

There are 2 *important points to keep in mind when selling.*

First, condition greatly affects price. A stamp that would sell for $100 if perfect might bring only $40 or $50 with a missing perforation. A coin whose design has been rubbed nearly smooth is worth less than 10% of a fine specimen. Books with pages missing are almost impossible to sell.

Second, if you sell to a dealer, the dealer's margin of profit will always be figured into the price. In the antiques business, a markup of 100% is normal. Therefore, a $15 offer for an item that sells at retail for $30 is fair; or $50 for an item that sells at $100.

The following dealers may be able to help in evaluating and/or purchasing your "finds." *Always write 1st* before sending anything. Give a full description and enclose a good clear photo. If the dealer asks to see the item(s), wrap securely and send insured. Enclose return postage with the shipment.

Phonograph Records (Old)
Old Barn Record Service
   P.O. Box 269
   Penngrove, Calif.   94951
Mr. Records
   P.O. Box 2071
   Union, N.J.   07083
Arnold's Archives
   1106 Eastwood, S.E.
   East Grand Rapids, Mich.   49506

Indian Relics
H. M. Worcester
   2204 Sacramento Street
   Berkeley, Calif.   94702
C. Secrist
   Deerfield, Mo.   64741

Glass and China
Wheat & Chaff Antiques
   P.O. Box 456
   Contoocook, N.Y.   03229
Ruth S. Wurzburger
   2253 Rogene Drive
   Baltimore, Md.   21209
Henry C. Johnson, Jr.
   1325 North Flores Street
   San Antonio, Tex.   78212

Dolls
Shirley Bertrand
   50 Willow Trail
   Wheeling, Ill.   60090
Mrs. James Shearer
   2901 Tremont Drive
   Louisville, Ky.   40205
Grace Ochsner's Doll House
   Niota, Ill.   62358

Banks (Mechanical)
F. H. Griffith
   P.O. Box 10644
   Pittsburgh, Pa.   15235
Scofield's
   P.O. Box 3443
   Tequesta, Fla.   33458
Sidney Partridge
   Marlborough, N.H.   03455

Clocks and Watches
D. D. Way
   11 Eastwood Court
   Oakland, Calif.   94611
Joseph Finelli—"Clocks & Things"
   209 Columbus Avenue
   New York, N.Y.   10024
"Mr. Barny"
   1145 Second Avenue
   New York, N.Y.   10021

Nostalgia
Second Childhood
   283 Bleecker Street
   New York, N.Y.   10014

Autographs, Documents, Manuscripts
Conway Barker
   P.O. Box 35
   LaMarque, Tex.   77568
Paul C. Richards
   49 Village Drive
   Bridgewater, Mass.   02324
Goodspeed's
   18 Beacon Street
   Boston, Mass.   02108

Coins
Lyle Clark
  2433 El Cajon
  San Diego, Calif.   92104
Carter's of San Diego
  419 Broadway
  San Diego, Calif.   92101
Crystal Coin Shop
  349–351 Main Street
  Wakefield, Mass.   01880
Coast Coin Company
  1313 25th Avenue
  Gulfport, Miss.   39501

Tools and Gadgets
Sidney Strange Antiques for Men
  855 2nd Avenue
  New York, N.Y.   10021

Books
Peter Decker
  45 West 57th Street
  New York, N.Y.   10019
Heritage Bookshop
  6707 Hollywood Boulevard
  Los Angeles, Calif.   90028
George S. MacManus Bookshop
  1317 Irving Street
  Philadelphia, Pa.   19107

Currier & Ives Prints
Jacques Schurre
  280 9th Avenue
  New York, N.Y.   10001
Katherine Ebert
  P.O. Box 234
  Wellesley Hills, Mass.   02181

Jewelry (Old)
Amco Jewelry Company
  Houston Citizens Bank Building
  1010 Jefferson Street
  Houston, Tex.   77002
Edward Wilson
  1802 Chestnut Street
  Philadelphia, Pa.   19103

Comic Books
Claude Held
  P.O. Box 140
  Buffalo, N.Y.   14225
The Book Sail
  106 West Lincoln Avenue
  Anaheim, Calif.   92805

Maps
J. N. Bartfield
  45 West 57th Street
  New York, N.Y.   10019
Cape Cod Books
  East Orleans, Mass.   02643

Furniture (Antique)
Abe Kessler Antiques
  533 3rd Avenue
  New York, N.Y.   10016
Shreve, Crump & Low
  Boylston at Arlington Street
  Boston, Mass.   02116
Evelyn Anderson Galleries
  Westgate Shopping Center
  Nashville, Tenn.   37205

Paintings
Graham Galleries
  1014 Madison Avenue
  New York, N.Y.   10019
David David, Inc.
  260 South 18th Street
  Philadelphia, Pa.   19103

Silverware
Greenblatt Antiques
  800 South Long Beach Avenue
  Freeport, N.Y.   11520
James Robinson
  12 East 57th Street
  New York, N.Y.   10022

Art (Folk)
Jerome Blum
  Ross Hill Road
  Lisbon, Conn.   06351
John Gordon
  313 West 57th Street
  New York, N.Y.   10019

Baseball Cards
First George Company
  305 Northview Avenue
  West Columbia, S.C.   29169

Firearms
Robert Abels
  P.O. Box 428
  Hopewell Junction, N.Y.   12533
N. Flayderman & Company
  5 Squash Hollow Road
  New Milford, Conn.   06776

Campaign Buttons
Donald Ackerman
  400 East 55th Street
  New York, N.Y.   10022

Stamps
Ideal Stamp Company
  48 West 48th Street
  New York, N.Y.   10036
Earl P. L. Apfelbaum
  1420 Walnut Street
  Philadelphia, Pa.   19102
Garcelon Stamp Co.
  Calais, Me.   04619

A REGISTER OF COLLECTORS' MAGAZINES

The following magazines and newspapers are published for hobbyists. In addition to articles and photos they contain many ads, which serve as a pricing guide to various antiques and collectibles.

Collector's News
  P.O. Box 156
  Grundy Center, Ia. 50638
Hobbies
  1006 South Michigan Avenue
  Chicago, Ill. 60605
Antiques
  551 5th Avenue
  New York, N.Y. 10017

Collector's Weekly
  P.O. Box 1119
  Kermit, Tex. 79745
The Antiques Journal
  P.O. Box 88128
  Dunwoody, Ga. 30338
The Antique Trader
  P.O. Box 1050
  Dubuque, Ia. 52001
Flea Market Quarterly
  P.O. Box 243
  Bend, Oreg. 97701
The Spinning Wheel
  Hanover, Pa. 17331
Tri-State Trader
  P.O. Box 90
  Knightstown, Ind. 46148

—W.R.

Where to Buy a Happiness Insurance Policy

Lloyd's of London, the world-famous insurance association, has insured everything from the 1st airplane and *zaftig* [pleasingly plump] Hollywood sex symbols to John Glenn as America's 1st astronaut, but wrote only marine insurance at its inception. Lloyd's takes its name from a coffeehouse operated by Edward Lloyd, the earliest record of whom is in 1688 and who died in 1713. For travelers, Lloyd served as a sort of one-man tourist bureau and there is even evidence that he would fix the press gang who shanghaied men into the naval service—for a price.

Virtually nothing else is known about the elusive enterprising Lloyd except that businessmen willing to insure against sea risks congregated at his coffeehouse on Lombard Street and issued marine policies to shipowners. Here *Lloyd's List*, a paper devoted to shipping news, was published in 1734, making it the oldest London newspaper excepting the London *Gazette*. By 1760 the precursor of *Lloyd's Register of Shipping* had been printed and only 15 years later the phrase A-1 was used in its pages to denote the highest class of ship, novelist Charles Dickens 1st applying A-1 to people and things in 1837.

Lloyd's, now international in scope, eventually moved to the Royal Exchange and finally to its present $15-million palace on Lime Street. It adopted its name legally when incorporated a century ago, not long before writing the 1st burglary insurance (1889). Lloyd's also wrote the 1st policy covering loss of profits resulting from fire and pioneered in automobile and workman's compensation insurance.

The corporation can issue anything but long-term life insurance. Rather than an insurance company, it is a corporate group of some 300 syndicates composed of about 5,500 strictly supervised individual underwriters, each of whom must deposit large sums—about $35,000 —as security against default on the risks each accepts. Lloyd's name has been adopted by several foreign shipping companies having no connection with it. Although the group did not write the 1st marine policy—this dating back to a Florentine policy issued in 1501—its name is synonymous with marine insurance and Lloyd's has long pioneered in setting maritime standards and safety measures. Lloyd's prime concern is still shipping insurance and it boasts that its agents watch every mile of seacoast throughout the world.

Three million dollars daily in premiums is taken in by Lloyd's, an underwriter of the 1880s named Cuthbert Bean having been mainly responsible for the group pioneering beyond marine insurance. Some interesting Lloyd's policies and losses in its risky history include:

. . . a $100,000 "love insurance" policy that provided payment if a certain photographer's model married (she did, but after the policy expired).

. . . a "happiness policy" that insured against "worry lines" developing on a model's face.

. . . losses paid of $3,019,400 after the Lutine Bell rang over the rostrum announcing the *Titanic* disaster; more than $5.6 million on the *Andrea Doria*; $1,463,400 on the San Francisco earthquake; $110 million on Hurricane Carol in 1954.

. . . $22,400 worth of protection ($74 premium) against "death caused by accident" in the form of a falling *sputnik*.

. . . policies insuring against the chances of having twins, one's golf opponent making a hole in one, war and peace, rained-out church socials, and losing one's lover.

. . . Betty Grable's legs insured for $250,000; Jimmy Durante's nose, $140,000; a corporation executive's brain for an undisclosed amount; flamenco dancer José Greco's special trousers insured against splitting at $980 a pair; Fred Astaire's legs for $650,000; Zorina's toes at $25,000 per; Abbott and Costello insured for $250,000 against disagreement over a 5-year period; actress Julie Bishop, $25,000 against her gaining 4″ around the hips or waist over a 7-year period; and a $250,000 policy on the 42″ bust of an unnamed English actress.

. . . risks turned down include a policy insuring the back teeth of an acrobat, who hung from them in her act, and the request by a European gentleman to insure his daughter's virginity.
—R.H. rep.

The Origin of Famous American Trademarks and Product Names

ARM & HAMMER BAKING SODA   The muscular arm and raised hammer represent Vulcan, Roman mythological god of fire and metalworking, and was once the symbol of the Vulcan Spice Mill in Brooklyn, N.Y. James A. Church, owner of the firm, took the symbol with him when he shut down the mill in 1867 and went into business with his father, a baking soda manufacturer. Shortly afterwards, the "power" behind Vulcan's arm and hammer became the trademark of Church's baking soda, which had the "force" to make bread dough rise.

AUNT JEMIMA PANCAKE MIX   Newspaperman Chris L. Rutt produced the 1st self-rising pancake mix in 1889 in St. Joseph, Mo. The vaudeville team of Baker and Farrell, who sang a catchy tune called "Aunt Jemima," provided the advertising gimmick. Impressed with the song's popularity, Rutt adopted its title for his pancake mix. He sold out to Davis Milling Company who, in 1893, hired a black cook, Nancy Green, to appear as "Aunt Jemima" at the World's Columbian Exposition in Chicago.

AVON   In 1886, door-to-door book salesman, D. H. McConnell was handing out free perfume to American housewives before attempting to sell his books. Fewer and fewer doors were slammed in his face, and finally the perfume was in such demand that McConnell rented an office in New York City and started the California Perfume Company. On the firm's 50th anniversary, he changed its name to Avon because of his admiration for Shakespeare and Stratford-on-Avon.

BAKER'S CHOCOLATE   The trademark was derived from a portrait of "La Belle Chocolatière," which currently hangs in the Dresden Gallery in Germany. In 1745, an Austrian prince entered a chocolate shop in Vienna where he met and fell in love with Anna Baltauf, a waitress and the daughter of an impoverished knight. They were married and, as a wedding gift, the prince hired Jean Étienne Liotard, a famous Swiss artist, to do a portrait of Anna—dressed in her waitress outfit. The romantic tale was heard by Walter Baker, American chocolate manufacturer, who in 1825 packaged his breakfast cocoa with a label bearing the silhouette of the Austrian girl.

BIRDS EYE   Adventurer, explorer, and inventor, Clarence Birdseye went to Labrador in 1916 on a wildlife expedition for the U.S. He, his wife, and their child lived mainly on a diet of fish and meat. Since fresh vegetables were available only when the supply ship arrived, Birdseye preserved them in barrels full of freezing water. His experiments with fish and meat, as well as vegetables, earned him the title of "Father of Frozen Food." Back in the U.S., Birdseye started a frozen foods company and in 1929 sold out to the Postum Company (forerunner of General Foods Corporation). The Birdseye name was retained in the trademark, although it was split into 2 words. Clarence did not complain as the new spelling was identical to the old family name and reminded him of the heroic origin of his surname. According to Birdseye, one of his ancestors saved the life of an English Queen by shooting an arrow directly through the eye of an attacking hawk. For his valiant deed, the ancestor was christened, "Birds Eye."

CAMEL CIGARETTES   (Warning: The Surgeon General Has Determined That Cigarette Smoking Is Dangerous to Your Health.)   Richard Joshua Reynolds, founder of the R. J. Reynolds Tobacco Company in Winston, N.C., introduced Camel cigarettes to the American public in 1913. The camel symbol was chosen because the cigarette was made from Turkish tobaccos and, supposedly, had an "exotic" flavor. When "Old Joe," a camel traveling with the Barnum and Bailey circus, came to town, Reynolds dispatched an employee to get a picture of the dromedary for an advertising campaign. Old Joe refused to play "model," tossed his head and tail about, and made threatening advances on the cameraman. The resulting "indignant" snapshot has been reproduced on billions of packages of Camel cigarettes. The slogan for Camels supposedly came from a conversation between a hobo and a sign painter employed by the Reynolds Company. After bumming a cigarette from the painter, the hobo spoke the well-known words, "I'd walk a mile for a Camel."

CHEVROLET   In the early 1900s, 2 race car drivers, Louis Chevrolet and William C. Durant, met on a racetrack in Michigan. French driver Chevrolet was also a car designer and American driver Durant was an executive of the Buick car plant in Flint, Mich. The cars designed by Chevrolet were large and costly, but Durant modified them into smaller, less expensive models. He kept the name, "Chevrolet," because it "had a musical sound and the romance of foreign origin." The rectangle-superimposed-upon-a-parallelogram trademark designed for Chevrolet cars was discovered by Durant while he traveled in France. He was attracted by the pattern which appeared in the wallpaper of a hotel room and ripped off a sample to take back to the U.S.

COCA-COLA   The 1st batch of Coca-Cola was mixed in 1886 in a 3-legged iron pot in the backyard of John S. Pemberton, a Confederate veteran who opened a drugstore in Atlanta after the Civil War. His friend and bookkeeper, F. M. Robinson, named the drink after its 2 main ingredients: coca, the dried leaves of a South American shrub, and cola, an extract of the kola nut. When Pemberton died in 1888, ownership of the soft drink was sold for $2,300. The American public coined the nickname "Coke," much to the dismay of company executives. Advertising insisted: "Ask for Coca-Cola by its full name; nicknames encourage substitution." However, customers continued to order "Coke" and it was finally registered as a legal trademark (Supreme Court decision, 1920). Today Coca-Cola is not only America's most popular soft drink, but it is widely sold throughout the world. The syrup from which it is made remains a company secret.

GILLETTE   "Father of the Safety Razor" was King C. Gillette. At age 21, he was a traveling salesman who longed to be a successful inventor. A friend, William Painter (inventor of the disposable bottle cap), said to Gillette, "King, you are always inventing something. Why don't you concentrate on just one thing—something like the Crown Cork—that people use once and throw away?" Gillette became obsessed with inventing a disposable item, and in 1895 his search ended. He described the historic occasion: "As I stood there with the razor in my hand, my eyes resting on it as lightly as a bird settling down on its nest, the Gillette razor was born—more with the rapidity of a dream than by a process of reasoning. In that moment I saw it all: the way the blade could be held in a holder; the idea of sharpening the 2 opposite edges on the thin piece of steel; the clamping plates for the blade, with a handle halfway between the 2 edges of the blade."

GREYHOUND BUS   In 1914, Carl Eric Wickman, a miner, was trying to sell the Hupmobile, a 7-passenger auto, to citizens of the Mesabi Iron Ore Range in Minnesota. A failure as a salesman, Wickman used the Hupmobile to open a bus line, carrying passengers between the towns of Hibbing and Alice, a 2-mi. journey. The bus was so popular that Wickman bought more autos and added 3 extra seats to each one. The long, sleek appearance of the "expanded" buses plus their gray color caused someone to remark that they looked "just like greyhounds streaking by." From then on, Wickman used the slogan, "Ride the Greyhounds."

HEINZ 57 VARIETIES   In 1860, Henry J. Heinz, age 16, was selling homegrown vegetables to Pittsburgh grocers. In 1869, he and a friend, L. C. Noble, went into business and marketed their 1st product—horseradish. The company went bankrupt, but Heinz started a new company in 1876, F. and J. Heinz. One of this firm's 1st products was ketchup. The inspiration for the "Heinz 57 Varieties" trademark came to Heinz one day as he rode an elevated train in New York City. He noticed an advertisement which promoted "21 styles" of a brand of shoes. He later said, "It set me to thinking. I said to myself, 'We do not have styles of products, but we do have varieties of products.'" Although Heinz had well over 57 products, he liked the sound of that particular number, especially the 7 because of the "psychological influence of that figure and of its alluring significance to people of all ages."

IVORY SOAP   The "floating" quality of the pure new "White Soap" developed by Procter & Gamble in 1878 was an accident. An employee at the firm's plant in Cincinnati left the soap vats churning one day while he took a lunch break. After this batch of soap was shipped out to market, the public began to place orders for the "soap that will float." The floating ability was due to the lengthy beating, which whipped extra air into the soap liquid. Harley Procter, sales manager of the company, thought the revolutionary product needed a new name. One Sunday morning while in church, he listened to the minister read from the scriptures: "All thy garments smell of myrrh, and aloes, and cassia, out of the ivory palaces, whereby they have made thee glad." Overnight, the "White Soap" became "Ivory Soap." To add validity to the soap's "purity" claim, Procter sent samples of the soap to chemistry professors for scientific analysis. The verdict: "99 and 44/100% pure."

KODAK   George Eastman, inventor of the Kodak camera, once said, "A trademark should be short, vigorous, incapable of being misspelled to an extent that will destroy its identity; and —in order to satisfy trademark laws—it must mean nothing." Eastman liked the letter "K" —a "strong, incisive sort of letter." Thus, he decided that "K" would be the 1st letter of the camera trademark. He then shuffled vowels and consonants around until he came up with a proper sounding name, "Kodak."

LIFE SAVERS   Cleveland chocolate manufacturer Clarence A. Crane introduced Life Savers to aid low chocolate sales in the hot summer months. The white circular mints were made on a pill machine by a pharmaceutical manufacturer and were advertised as "Crane's Peppermint Life Savers—5¢—For That Stormy Breath." In 1913, a New York advertising salesman, Edward J. Noble, tried to persuade Crane to enlarge the Life Saver business, believing that it could be "pyramided into a fortune." Crane refused, instead selling all rights to his mint candies to Noble for $2,900. Noble's sales motto was: "Put Life Savers near the cash register. Then be sure every customer gets a nickel with his change and see what happens." Life Saver's hole in the middle is patented as "Nothing enclosed by a circle."

MAXWELL HOUSE COFFEE   The ambitions of a Kentucky traveling salesman, Joel Cheek, plus the spontaneous comments of President Theodore Roosevelt, guaranteed the success of Maxwell House coffee. In 1874, Cheek developed a new coffee blend and was selling it to the eminent Maxwell House hotel in Nashville, Tenn. Popularity of the coffee at the hotel's restaurant led to its brand name. Years later, Theodore Roosevelt tasted the coffee while staying at "The Hermitage" (the old home of Andrew Jackson). When asked if he would like another cup of Maxwell House coffee, he replied, "Will I have another? Delighted! It's good to the last drop."

MORTON SALT   Joy Morton founded the Morton Salt Company in 1910, but his son, Sterling, chose the umbrella girl trademark and the slogan, "When It Rains It Pours." The younger Morton rejected the 1st 12 trademarks suggested by an advertising agency, and 3 "on the bench" sketches were presented to him. As he said, "I was immediately struck with one. It showed a little girl with an umbrella over her head, rain falling, a package of salt under her arm tilted backward with spout open and salt running out. Perhaps the fact that my daughter, Suzette, was occupying a lot of my time and attention at that period had something to do with my interest. But, anyway, it struck me that here was the whole story in a picture—that the message that the salt would run in damp weather was made beautifully evident." The appearance of the Morton Salt girl has changed over the years. She has progressed from a curly-

headed blonde, to a brunette, and finally back to a blonde with a Dutch bob.

DR. SCHOLL'S FOOT AIDS   The motto of Dr. Scholl was, "Early to bed, early to rise, work like hell and advertise." Former shoemaker and shoe salesman, William Scholl graduated in 1904 from medical school in Illinois and patented his 1st arch support. A firm believer in the power of advertising, Scholl held walking contests throughout the country and sold "pedometers" for calculating distances walked. Also, he held a "Cinderella Foot Contest" in which he measured foot imbalance on a machine called a Pedo-Graph. An award was then given for the "most perfect foot." "Foot doctor to the world," Dr. Scholl has eased millions of tired, aching feet. His corn, callus, and bunion pads, sold in blue and yellow packages, are famous worldwide.

SCOTCH TAPE   In 1925, Detroit's car manufacturers were looking for an effective masking tape to use when painting 2-tone automobiles. The Minnesota Mining and Manufacturing Company (3M) developed a tape that successfully enabled the manufacturers to get a clean, sharp edge where the 2 colors met. However, producing the tape was costly and a 3M employee cut down the amount of adhesive on the tape—not putting it in the center of the strip. The new tape did not stick, and car painters cried to company salesmen: "Take this tape back to those Scotch bosses of yours and tell them to put adhesive all over the tape. . . ." The missing adhesive was again applied, but the name "Scotch" tape remained.

SMITH BROTHERS COUGH DROPS   William and Andrew Smith (known as "Trade" and "Mark") were the sons of a carpenter, James Smith, who migrated from Quebec in 1847 and became a restaurant owner in Poughkeepsie, N.Y. A customer at the Smith's Dining Saloon gave the elder Smith a "secret" formula for cough candy. The Smiths mixed batches of the remedy on the kitchen stove and advertised the cough drops as a cure for all "afflicted with hoarseness, coughs or colds." When their father died in 1886, William and Andrew continued the business, but their success inspired a bevy of impostors—Schmitt Brothers, Smythe Sisters, and even other Smith Brothers. In need of an identifying trademark, they had their pictures put on the glass bowls which held the drops and on the envelopes in which the drops were packaged. The picture of the 2 bearded brothers became an American institution.

"Shorts"

BABY RUTH   The candy bar was named after the oldest daughter of President Grover Cleveland, and not after baseball's Babe Ruth.
BARBIE DOLL   The teen-age fashion model

was the idea of Ruth Handler, executive of Mattel, Inc., after she noticed that her daughter, "Barbie," preferred "older-looking" dolls to baby dolls.

B.V.D. UNDERWEAR Although consumers have come up with many hilarious, oftentimes embarrassing, meanings for the BVD letters appearing on men's underwear, the label actually derives from the initials of the men who in 1876 originated the brand under their company's name, Bradley, Voorhees and Day.

CAMPBELL'S SOUP TWINS The "mischievous, roly-poly, fun-loving" twins who sing the praises of Campbell's soup were originally sketched by Grace Gebbie Drayton (of Philadelphia). In 1904 she was handing out prototypes of the twins as party favors to her friends.

DUBBLE BUBBLE GUM It used to be called "Blibber Blubber."

FULLER BRUSH MAN Alfred C. Fuller, founder of the Fuller Brush Company, came to the U.S. from Nova Scotia in 1903 at the age of 18 with $375 in his pocket. In 1905 he began

making brushes in the basement of his sister's house and sold them door-to-door for 50¢ apiece. He died, aged 88, in 1973.

KLEENEX The "pop-up" tissues were 1st used in W.W. I as a mask filter.

LOLLIPOPS In the early 1900s, George Smith, employed by a Connecticut candy manufacturer, "put together the candy and the stick" and called it *Lolly Pop*, the name of one of the era's most famous race horses.

NOXZEMA The cream was sold as "Dr. Bunting's Sunburn Remedy," until someone discovered that it "knocks eczema."

SCRABBLE An unemployed architect, Alfred Mosher Butts, invented the word game in 1931, and he called it "Scrabble" to reflect the "digging" for letters involved, a key part of game strategy.

TOOTSIE ROLL Austrian candy manufacturer, Leo Hirshfield, named his chewy, chocolate rolls after a former girl friend, "Tootsie."

—C.O.

Let's Audit the IRS

Each year the Internal Revenue Service audits some 2½ million Americans. Through the use of computers and over 45,000 employees, the IRS seeks to find someone cheating on his income tax. Yet since the inception of the IRS in 1913, the IRS itself has never been audited. In 1921 a law was enacted by Congress to audit several government agencies including the IRS, but the IRS has steadfastly refused to be included. One wonders in this era of Watergate, and political and governmental upheaval, what freedom may be denied the American taxpayer by the IRS.

In 1912—on March 16 to be exact—Congress was discussing the impending bill to extend the "special excise tax now levied with respect to doing business by corporations to persons, and to provide revenue for the Government." Some of the Congress seriously debated the issue. Congressman Hull, who was for the measure, spoke of the then current system: "That system, unequal as it is indefensible, is the mightiest engine of oppression imposed upon an honest yeomanry since the feudal ages." He could well be speaking of the system today. He said further: "This system places a high premium on wealth and a severe penalty on poverty."

The major portion of the taxes in America comes from the person who is earning $3,000 to $25,000 a year. Regardless of what the IRS would like the public to believe, it has always been and always will be the small wage earner who bears the heaviest burden of taxation. The passing of the income tax law, which became

the 16th Amendment to the Constitution, squeaked by close to Christmas when few congressmen were there to oppose its passage. Some of today's "tax rebels" still oppose the amendment on the grounds that Ohio, which signed the bill, was not at that time a legally recognized State. The charge is a valid one.

The bill's passage certainly was not the mandate of the people, as they would have voted it down. The final decision for such a bill lay not with the Congress but with the Supreme Court, thus taking away the possibility for removal of the bill. Judge Walter Clark, chief justice of the Supreme Court of North Carolina, spoke out in 1906 on the actions of the U.S. Supreme Court in making acts of Congress unconstitutional. "A more complete denial of popular control of this Government could not have been conceived than the placing of such unreviewable power in the hands of men not elected by the people and holding office for life. . . . If 5 lawyers can negate the will of 100 million men, then the art of Government is reduced to the selection of those 5 lawyers."

With this rather strange legislation, the IRS was born. Unwanted, perhaps unneeded, and certainly undesired by the liberals as well as the conservatives, it came into being. The Church of Scientology's publication *Freedom* reported recently: "The IRS has nearly 70,000 employees and a budget in the vicinity of $1 billion. Approximately ⅔ of the IRS' manpower (nearly half of the entire Treasury Dept.) and ¾ of the IRS budget ($750 million) are poured into auditing, investigating, and policing the individual taxpayer, yet all this money and manpower yields only 3% of the total revenue collected by the IRS." In reviewing the IRS statistics, much does come to view of their heretofore secret operations. For every $50,000 that the small businessman earns, the IRS spends over 200 hours auditing his books. Yet for every $50,000 that the corporate giant earns, the IRS spends a scant 30 minutes auditing its books. Proportionally speaking, while the little businessman's books are scrutinized in every detail, the corporate giant's are given but a cursory glance.

The IRS operates on manuals and policies that are unavailable to the public. The index to the manual alone is over 1,000 pages, the manual itself has some 40,000 pages, and settlements vary from agent to agent, from city to city and State to State. One can imagine how much the IRS employees absorb of this mountain of data, especially in the Taxpayer Assistance programs where they are trained for an average of 2 weeks (it was one week until 1972). They would have to read some 4,000 pages a day of highly technical materials to be fully informed. To avoid all this they operate under fluid policy called "guidelines." These guidelines are determined by a private, not a governmental, organization called Commerce Clearing House.

The American people were incensed when the news of Watergate broke. Yet in 1968, testimony before the Senate Judiciary Committee on Administrative Practice and Procedure revealed that the IRS has defied court orders, picked locks, stolen records, threatened reputable people, illegally tapped telephones, and opened and read the personal mail of taxpayers. The IRS has denied these accusations yet its manuals are full of such titles as "9141-The Intelligence Mission; 9141.2-Methods to Achieve Intelligence Mission; 9383.5-Electronic or Mechanical Eavesdropping; 9444-Arrests without Warrants; 9452-Searches without Warrants; and 9774.1-Handbook for Special Agents."

Mr. Johnny Walters, a recent commissioner of the IRS and a man who was quick to affirm that he had nothing to do with President Nixon's use of the IRS for political purposes, told the Senate Hearings in 1971 ". . . I think that all taxpayers and taxpayers' representatives should be treated equally and fairly. . . ." That was in 1971; today there are over 30,000 rulings annually that are kept confidential. Thus certain firms are getting tax breaks that their competitors are not.

In addition, the IRS continues to deny that it has a quota system. Yet testimony before subcommittee hearings on the IRS has shown "close to one million seizures in 1973 or 7 for each minute of each working day." Further, Vincent L. Connery, national president of the National Association of Internal Revenue Employees, said on April 10, 1974: "Hardly a week passes that we do not receive a letter from a revenue officer somewhere in the country complaining about his unmanageable inventory and the pressure-cooker environment created by assigning to him more than he could ever possibly work."

As to the integrity of the IRS in keeping the laws of the country such as the Freedom of Information Act, subcommittee staff director for the Committee on Government William G. Phillips had this to say: "The policies of the Internal Revenue Service in Freedom of Information matters has almost become a national scandal."

Another agency that has tried to encourage some sort of ethical conduct in the IRS is the General Accounting Office (GAO). Robert F. Keller, Deputy Controller General of the U.S. stated: "The Internal Revenue Service is a problem of long standing, Mr. Chairman. GAO's review efforts at the Internal Revenue Service have been materially hampered, and in some cases terminated, because of the continued refusal by IRS to grant GAO access to records necessary to make an effective review of IRS operations and activities. Without access to necessary records GAO cannot effectively evaluate the IRS administration of operations involving billions of dollars in annual gross revenue collections [about $192 billion in fiscal 1971] and millions in appropriated funds [about $978 million in fiscal year 1971]."

Ideally a citizen should consider a government agency one of "us" or "our agency." Most Americans consider the IRS one of "them."

Campus Studies Institute put out a study in 1974 titled "The $44,000 Ripoff Method." It offered an interesting view of the aged and their Social Security "benefits":

"Take $468 a year from the average wage earner and make his employer match it, for a total of $936 taken from each worker. (If the employer did not pay the matching money, he could pay the worker instead.)

"At this rate, the average worker puts in a total of $34,532 over a period of 37 years. If the $936 per year were deposited in a savings account at 5% simple interest, it would grow to more than $66,000 by age 65.

"Now at the age of 65, the average married worker gets $223 per month and has about 101 months left to live. That means he gets back a little over $22,000 from his $66,000, or about ⅓ of what it cost him.

"But that's not all. For every $2 the over-65 worker earns, $1 is deducted from his Social Security benefits. On top of that, he must continue to pay Social Security and income taxes. This means up to ⅔ of his income may go to taxes."

The aged have long been a victim of the IRS. In the April 15, 1970, hearing conducted by the Senate Special Committee on Aging the subject of income tax overpayments by the elderly contained variously supported assertions by a variety of witnesses that as many as 50% of the aged taxpayers overpay on their taxes. Unfortunately the IRS system is geared toward what it considers the underpaying taxpayer rather than those who overpay.

In addition, the elderly have to contend with an increasingly complex tax form. As if this were not enough, they must do so with physical, mental, and academic limitations that may be substantial. Since decreasing vision, hearing, physical mobility, and the process of aging are not allowed for by the IRS, many of the aged will continue to overpay.

Churches have come under the attack of the IRS for some time. In 1969 the IRS established the SSS (Special Services Section). The IRS admonished its members not to attack too strong an organization. Just the ones that would not attract national attention. Some of those attacked were churches, the Boy Scouts, and other nonprofit groups. The SSS achieved a great deal of notoriety during the Watergate hearings. The IRS, fearing public censure of its activities, disbanded the group "officially." However, recent subcommittee hearings indicate it may still be in operation. The SSS gathered information on some 16,000 entities including intellectuals, artists, activists, and opinion leaders of American society. Some of these were on President Nixon's famed "Enemies List." Unfortunately, most of the information has not been released, not even to Congress. Much of this evidence, which is in the hands of the FBI, proves that the IRS has used the material to harass these carefully selected people greatly. National statistics showing IRS audit rates indicate an average of 14% audited in the general "enemies" earning range. However, the SSS list rate was as high as 28%. A double figure. Yet the IRS declared it was not inflicting undue harassment. A recent investigation into the IRS dated December 20, 1973, states: "The Collection Division does not appear to have made an inordinate effort to collect small amounts of tax as it presumably would do if it wished to harass the individuals in question." The report goes on to show that the Collection Division brought in only $100,000 in over 3 years of operation. With 16,000 entries in its files, collections averaged $6.20 per person or corporation. Not political? Tom Huston's White House Memorandum dated September 21, 1970, to H. R. Haldeman, indicated the use to which the SSS could be put. "What we cannot do in a courtroom via criminal prosecutions to curtail the activities of some of these groups, IRS could do by administrative action. Moreover, valuable intelligence-type information could be turned up by IRS as a result of their field audits."

An Internal Revenue Dispatch from the Regional Commissioner, North-Atlantic regions, to All Directors and dated December 18, 1972, spoke gleefully of the SSS as a weapon. "Although some of the files are top secret, Special Services Staff members with this clearance can extract data of this nature if needed. [Signed: John J. Flynn]" Some of the groups to be investigated were ". . . Nonviolent groups who by alleged peaceful demonstrations oftentimes deliberately initiate violence and destruction. . . . Those who organize and attend rock festivals. . . ." Further Flynn stated: "The magnitude and potential of this facility is unlimited." (We have not heard the last of this sprightly little crew.)

One church—the Church of Scientology—took on the IRS by sending out surveys to other churches to find out whether they were being harassed, and the reply list grew alarmingly. Dr. Billy James Hargis, founder of Christian Crusade, had his tax-exempt status revoked in 1966 on grounds that the Crusade supported the Becker Amendment (prayer and Bible reading in the schools). He appealed and the judge ruled against the IRS for unlawful discrimination and harassment. Said Hargis in an interview for *Freedom:* "We feel that the IRS has become the executioner for the Administration in power. In my opinion, the IRS represents a greater threat to freedom under law, because of its coercive power, than any agency of the Government, and the Congress should certainly reassess its activities." Other churches experiencing IRS harassment include the Mormon Church and its welfare programs. If the IRS destroyed the Mormon's $75 million in welfare assistance it would cost the American taxpayers more than $500 million a year, as the program makes workers out of the recipients and thus they become productive members of society. The Catholic Church is losing a school a day. It is not allowed to take deductions for its parochial schools under the IRS determination that there are already plenty of public schools—the latter, incidentally, show a decline in teaching competence as compared to private schools. This loss of private schools could cost the U.S. billions of dollars. Yet the IRS has given tax-exempt status to the American Nazi party.

The entire SSS operation could have cost in the neighborhood of several millions of dollars. The IRS spent millions of dollars in collecting piddling sums from "tax protestors" who refused to pay their phone tax because of the Vietnam War. Most of the accounts amounted to $10 or less. One protester owed $2 and 2 agents were sent out to collect the $2 or impound his car. He had no money and the car in front of his house was towed away. The car was not his. It cost the real owner $78 to retrieve it, with no IRS apology for the error forthcoming.

In order to watch the taxpayer more closely, the IRS will expend vast sums of the taxpayer's own monies. The actual amount of monies spent is hard to come by, as the IRS does not release this information readily. However, take a look at *The Electronic Invasion* by Robert W. Brown, published by Hayden (an electronics publishing house). According to this book, the IRS spent $43,876 with Fargo Company for recorders and intelligence kits between 1962 and 1964. It also spent $85,780 with Kel Company (an electronics firm) for "equipment of undetermined nature."

If you are wondering whether the IRS may be wasting all this money by using amateur "plumbers" for their annual operations on the unsuspecting taxpayer, rest assured that they will use only the most competent talent. The Intelligence Manual, under "272.3-Recording and Listening Devices," states: "The installation and operation of these devices require a high degree of skill and experience to produce the best results. When authorized to use them it is generally the practice to utilize the services of a specialist from within the Intelligence Division or from other Treasury enforcement agencies. Arrangements for the service of these specialists can be made through the Chief, Intelligence Division, and the Assistant Regional Commissioner (Intelligence)."

The Omnibus laws of 1968 set up fairly strict guidelines for bugging American homes. Basically such activity has to be cleared through the Attorney General. However, the IRS has more power than the FBI according to "272.3."

The Intelligence Manual, under the title: "*Overhearing or recording non-telephone conversations*" (dated 12-12-73), states rather plainly the absolute power the IRS has over other agencies. "The use of eavesdropping devices to overhear or record any non-telephone conversation without the consent of all parties to the conversation, but with the consent of at least one, must be approved in writing by the Attorney General or his designee: *except for emergency situations when an official designated by the Commissioner may grant prior approval.*"

Some taxpayers would rather die than give up all their monies to the IRS. The IRS has provisions for this kind of taxpayer too. Under "Use of Firearms by Special Agents (c) Firing a weapon should be with the intent of rendering the person at whom the weapon is fired incapable of continuing the activity which prompted the agent to shoot." The type of ammunition is also described: "The standard service ammunition for Intelligence will be the .38 special caliber, 110 grain jacketed hollow point." This type of bullet can blow an awfully big hole in any kind of taxpayer. In the event a special agent has to board a plane, how does he get by all that electronic stuff without being detected? This is merely alluded to in the Intelligence Manual. "9382.35-Carrying Firearms on Commercial Airplanes. . . . If, however, his mission would be compromised by disclosure of his identity, the armed employee will act with utmost discretion in maintaining complete concealment of the weapons he is carrying. This will prevent air carrier employees from taking drastic emergency action which they might properly consider necessary should they detect a weapon on a passenger whose authority to carry arms was not known to them."

So what can be done with this monstrous inequity of the IRS? First of all the taxpayer should be able to fight the IRS legally and handily. In order to do this:

1. If approached by an IRS agent, get a trustworthy friend to witness everything that transpires.

2. Use a tape recorder to record all that the IRS agent says wherever you talk to him.

3. When notified by the IRS that you have a deficit, demand to know the exact part of the IRS manual he is operating under in your case, and have him send you a copy under the Freedom of Information Act.

4. Insist that the IRS fully identify all the documents they have in their possession that indicate that you may owe them any additional monies. They must give the names, dates, and numbers of the receipts. You are innocent until proven guilty. The IRS works on the reverse assumption.

5. Form groups that can protect their members with legal representation. These can be supported through membership dues, so that illegal actions of the IRS can be challenged in the courts.

6. Demand on a State and Federal level that all tax offices be elective offices. Get your congressman to support you and your community's interests.

7. Do not settle easily. If you are going through the illegal appellate system of the IRS, keep appealing and so reduce the amount demanded by the IRS (they'll bargain). If you have to pay, pay under protest and in writing, keeping a copy of your protest. If a decision in your favor is then made on a case you can demand a refund later. Above all, do not break the existent laws. However, do stand up for your constitutional rights.

—H.C.J.

$1,000,000,000.00

Q. How long would it take to spend $1 billion?

A. If you had spent $1,000 a day, every day since Christ was born, you would not yet have spent $1 billion.

7

World Nations and People

AFGHANISTAN

Location—Where Central Asia, India, and Iran meet. Along the northern border lies the Soviet Union, to the west is Iran, and to the south and east is Pakistan. Afghanistan has a short border on the northeast with China.

How Created—Afghanistan was formed during the 18th and 19th centuries out of the efforts of Britain and Czarist Russia to create a buffer zone between their empires in the subcontinent and Central Asia. Several Khans of the region were involved at the same time in attempting to form an effective unity out of the 15 different ethnic groups in the area. It was 1880 before the British finally found a Khan they could work with and depend upon, and who was able to hold the region together without direct intervention of British troops. By 1901, at this Khan's death, the present borders of the state were largely settled.

Size—251,823 sq. mi. (652,221 sq. km.), about the size of Texas.

Population—Over 18 million: Pathans (Pushtuns, Pakhtuns), 58.7%; Tadzhik, 28.7%; Uzbek, 5.3%; Hazara, 2.7%; others, 4.6%. 99% Muslim.

Who Rules—The military clique that overthrew the monarchy in 1973 declared a republic, suspended the 1965 constitution and the landlord-dominated legislature. The leader of the coup, a former Prime Minister of the country, set up a republican government, but not a democracy. There are no legal political parties.

Who REALLY Rules—The leader of the 1973 coup, Lt. Gen. Sardar Muhammad Daud, has become President of Afghanistan. He is a brother-in-law and cousin of the deposed King, and was forced out as Prime Minister a decade before the coup. The royal family has been ousted from power, but by a faction of the same ruling elite. The Pathan ruling class is still the ruling class. The military faction is very sympathetic to the Soviet Union, from which it gets military aid, but is not controlled by its northern neighbor. Most powerful in terms of day-to-day control of the impoverished masses of Afghanistan are the religious clerics. They act as legal arbiters and teachers in the villages, and wield great moral authority among the villagers.

NOTES

The 70% of the population that lives in villages scattered through the mountain or desert countryside is too remote from urban centers to have much part in the urban economy. Their social structures are basically feudal or tribal. The merchant class of the cities is largely involved in agricultural trade, including export of agricultural goods. There is little industry. Landlords, supported by the religious clerics, form the ruling class of the country.

In the past 2 decades, Afghanistan has received a total of $1.5 billion in military and economic aid from the Soviet Union; $425 million from the U.S.; and $72 million from China.

Afghanistan is known for its high-quality hashish, particularly in Mazar-e-Shariff and Kandaar.

—J.G.

ALBANIA

NITTY GRITTY

Location—On the west coast of the Balkan peninsula, bordered by Yugoslavia on the north and east, by Greece on the southeast, and by the Adriatic and Ionian seas on the west.

How Created—Slavic invasions following the 5th century drove the ancient Illyrians (the Albanians' ancestors) southward from the large portion of Yugoslavia they had inhabited. They then settled in the largely mountainous region which is their present home. Independence was achieved following W.W. I.

Size—11,100 sq. mi. (28,748 sq. km.).

Population—2,400,000: Albanian, 95.2%; Greek, 2.4%; Gypsy, Macedonian, Romanian, and others, 2.4%. 69% Muslim, 21% Greek Orthodox, 10% Roman Catholic.

Who Rules—The People's Assembly, which is elected every 4 years and meets twice a year.

Who REALLY Rules—The leadership of the Albania Worker's party controls the entire functions of government. It is the only political party. Enver Hoxha, a former French teacher who led the National Liberation Movement in W.W. II, has been the guiding force since independence.

NOTES

The Shkumbi River forms a boundary between the 2 main racial groups of Albanian peoples—the Ghegs in the north and the Tosks in the south. The Ghegs are a superstitious and predatory clan; stern, hardy, and fierce, they live a pastoral life in the largely barren land of their region. The Tosks are a lively, friendly people, more advanced than their neighbors to the north; their land is more fertile and they are better equipped to pursue their agricultural and industrial labors. As they are isolated mountain dwellers, the 2 groups have a tendency to feud among themselves and with each other.

Albania sponsored the General Assembly resolution that secured recognition of Communist China as the sole representative of China in the United Nations in 1971.

The largest number of Albanians that live outside their country are concentrated in the Kossovo and Macedonia regions of Yugoslavia. Massachusetts has the largest population of Albanian immigrants in the U.S.

—J.Y.

ALGERIA

NITTY GRITTY

Location—North Africa, fanning out from the Mediterranean in the north to the Sahara in the south where it borders Niger and Mali. Tunisia and Libya are on the east; Morocco, Mauritania, and Spanish Sahara on the west.

How Created—Algiers was one of the North African Barbary States which, throughout the 17th and early 18th centuries, thrived on piracy. In 1830, the French subjugated the coastal cities and over the next 70 years conquered the interior and established the present-day boundaries. There was resistance to the French from the outset. The final drive for independence, led by the National Liberation Front (FLN), culminated in the French pullout in 1962.

Size—896,588 sq. mi. (2,332,164 sq. km.). Three times the size of Texas.

Population—Over 16 million: Arab, 80.4%; Berber, 18.7%; French and others, 0.9%. 98% Muslim.

Who Rules—The National Revolutionary Council headed by the President, and the National Assembly, which has been suspended since 1965.

Who REALLY Rules—The National Liberation Front is the only recognized political party. Its members nominate all candidates for the National Assembly, who are then "elected."

NOTES

The great Catholic theologian, St. Augustine, was an Algerian, born in Tagaste (now Souk-Ahras) in 354 A.D. Following his conversion to Christianity in Italy, he returned to Algeria and became Bishop of Hippo (south of present-day Bône), an office he held from 395 A.D. until his death in 430 A.D.

Another great Algerian was the Nobel Prize author Albert Camus. Born in Mondovi (now Drean) in 1913, he was educated at the University of Algiers and lived in his homeland until 1940, when he moved to Paris.

When France took Algiers in 1830, the immediate pretext for the conquest was an incident in which the Algerian ruler, Dey Hussein struck French Consul Deval with his fly whisk during an argument.

Prior to independence, Algeria was regarded as an integral part of metropolitan France. Nearly a million Frenchmen made their homes in Algeria. Five thousand Europeans owned ⅓ of the arable land.

Today, in the official propaganda a great deal of lip service is paid to the principles of socialism. In actuality, the economy is run partly along socialist and partly along capitalist lines. The following groups exist, although there is a marked tendency to play down social distinctions:

Bourgeoisie—They operate the many successful smaller enterprises in the cities. The Government has set no ceiling on how much they can earn but the members of the bourgeoisie are very discreet as to how they spend their wealth. They tend to keep a low profile. They also prefer a vacation abroad to flaunting their money at home.

Bureaucrats—There is a considerable bureaucracy, but the Government has set a limit on the income of officials. They can earn no more than 5 times the pay of a factory worker.

City Workers—Whether employed privately or by the Government, they are protected by an extensive system of social insurance. There has been a significant migration to the cities in the past 40 years, with more people moving in than the cities can absorb. The result has been that about ⅓ of the labor force is unemployed.

Peasants—Onetime French holdings have been confiscated by the Government and turned into collectives. The workers are entitled to a percentage of the profits of their farms. The vast majority of farms are privately run; half of them consist of holdings smaller than 12 acres.

Desert nomads—They live pretty much as they always have, although the Government has been attempting to provide permanent settlements for some of them.

—H.E.

AMERICAN TELEPHONE
& TELEGRAPH

NITTY GRITTY

Location—Headquarters at 195 Broadway, New York City, N.Y. 10007.

How Created—Alexander Graham Bell spilled acid on himself and, without thinking, picked up the gadget in front of him, yelling, "Mr. Watson, come here; I want you."

That 1st telephone conversation came a week after Bell had been granted a patent for his invention in 1876. As Bell worked on his invention, he interested 2 wealthy men, Thomas Sanders and G. G. Hubbard, in his progress. These 3 formed the basis of the American Telephone & Telegraph Company.

The original patent ran out in 1894, but any struggling competitor who challenged Bell found himself involved in costly harassment suits, or the price of his service drastically undercut by Bell.

But AT&T did not become the power it is today until it became highly centralized. In the early 20th century, AT&T officials spread the rumor that the company was faltering. Panicky investors sold their stock in the companies under contract to AT&T. AT&T bought up the stock and established nationwide control.

Size—AT&T is the biggest monopoly in the world. It holds assets of over $60 billion, which is more than the combined Gross National Products of every country in Africa. Only 7 countries, including the U.S., have GNPs larger than the assets of AT&T. Net income in 1973 was $2.993 billion.

Population—Over 1 million employees (1973: 1,023,000): white, 87%; although of the management population, 96% is white.

Who Rules—A 19-member board of directors, 18 of whom are white and 18 of whom are male.

Who REALLY Rules—The Executive Policy Committee.

NOTES

AT&T produces and services communications equipment. The Bell System handles 80% of the nation's telephones, plus hookups for the rest. Bell telephones in service totaled 110 million in 1973. The Bell System handles 432 million messages per business day.

The U.S. Government is the largest user of Bell System's communications services. This includes the Autovon network, which interconnects all the U.S. military installations around the world and is the most complicated and expensive of all phone hookups.

AT&T owns outright Western Electric, which itself is the 10th largest manufacturer in the U.S. Western Electric is employed by the Government to make war missiles.

AT&T is the nation's 6th largest war contractor.

The Equal Employment Opportunity Commission has stated that AT&T is "without doubt the largest oppressor of women workers in the U.S." Customers dealing with the phone company usually speak to a woman because AT&T assumes that women are more pleasant and charming than men. Service representatives (mostly women) are regularly monitored as they talk to customers to make sure they do their job by the book.

A practice currently common in industry is the "speed-up," wherein workers are forced to do more work at a faster rate. Here is how the phone company describes a speed-up: "Now, instead of simplifying jobs, we seek to enlarge them. Instead of fragmenting assignments, we seek to enhance their challenge."

AT&T keeps a private dossier on every stockholder with a significant share of stock.

—D.E. & M.S.

ANGOLA

NITTY GRITTY

Location—Southwestern Africa; to the north is Zaire and to the east is Zambia. Namibia is to the south and to the west is the South Atlantic.

How Created—Angola's boundaries were formed by the Berlin West Africa Congress (1884–1885), in which France, Germany, and Portugal won recognition of their colonies. In 1974, after 13 years of guerrilla warfare, Angola gained a promise of independence from

Portugal. Official independence day is set for November 11, 1975.

Size—481,351 sq. mi. (1,246,700 sq. km.), 14 times bigger than Portugal—its former colonial master.

Population—5.8 million: Bantu, 91.5%; European, 6%; mixed, 2.5%. Of the African population, 33% are members of the Ovimbundu tribe, 25% Bakongo, 25% Kimbundu, 8% Chokewe. 50% of the population follows tribal religions, 38% Roman Catholicism, 12% Protestantism.

Who Rules—Theoretically, an interim government of whites and liberation groups pledged to a "one-person one-vote" election to form a constituent assembly, which will then draw up a new constitution.

Who REALLY Rules—The liberation parties are the only groups allowed to present candidates for election. They are the Popular Movement for the Liberation of Angola, the National Front for the Liberation of Angola, and the National Union for Total Independence of Angola.

NOTES

At least 95% of the people are illiterate. Only 35,000 blacks out of a total of over 5 million were ever able to reach the *assimilado* status legally offered. To become an *assimilado*, a black would have to apply to a tribunal and prove that he was a Christian, could read and write Portuguese, had a steady income, and would give up pagan for European customs.

"Angola" might appear to be a Portuguese name. Not so. The name actually derives from that of the old native King *N'gola*, who led one of the proud kingdoms which throve in western Africa before the immigration of the Europeans. Once the Europeans arrived, Angola quickly became known as the "Mother of Brazil," because it was the homeland of most of the blacks who were packed off to work on plantations in Brazil. Angola became one of the chief sources of slaves for the New World.

North of Angola is the tiny oil-rich enclave of Cabinda, which is also a former Portuguese colony. The new leaders of Angola want Cabinda to be ruled as part of Angola, but many people in Cabinda prefer independence. This issue, among others, has led to violence between revolutionary groups in the area.

—M.D.

ARGENTINA

NITTY GRITTY

Location—Occupies southeastern South America, between the Andes Mountains and the Atlantic. Neighbors are Bolivia and Paraguay to the north, Chile to the west, Uruguay to the east, and Brazil to the northeast.

How Created—The 1st Spanish settlement at the site of Buenos Aires was made in 1516. Soon wiped out by Indians, it was refounded in 1580, and grew rapidly in trade relations with Europe. The Spanish Government in Lima, disturbed at the independence and power of Buenos Aires, established a separate viceroyalty there in 1776 to control the area, which also included Bolivia, Uruguay, and Paraguay. In 1810 independence was achieved through the efforts of José de San Martín, but was not solidified until 1816, due to the reluctance of some provinces to be ruled by Buenos Aires.

Size—1,072,763 sq. mi. (2,778,456 sq. km.), 2nd largest country in Latin America (after Brazil) and 8th largest in the world.

Population—27,800,000: European, 97% (Italian: 50%, Spanish, English, French, German accounting for most of the remainder); 3% is Arab, Indian, and mestizo. 95% Roman Catholic.

Who Rules—Argentina is a federal republic with a constitution somewhat similar to that of the U.S., which served as its model. Presidents are elected to 6-year terms by the Electoral College, and there is a National Congress composed of a Senate and Chamber of Deputies.

Who REALLY Rules—Three major groups: 1. the military, who have ruled the country at various times, most recently from 1955 to 1973; 2. the principal industrialists and beef producers, who control much of Argentina's wealth; 3. the supporters of the late President Juan Domingo Perón, who are split into many factions ranging from his conservative 3rd wife Isabel Martínez de Perón, to the Montoneros, a Perónist youth movement which has declared war on the Government.

NOTES

One of Argentina's greatest heroines is Eva Perón. Illegitimate child of a farm laborer and a coachman's daughter, Eva was born in 1919 in a small pampas village 150 mi. west of Buenos Aires. At 15 she ran off to Buenos Aires to enter show business. Eventually, as "Señorita Radio," a broadcaster, she became widely known. She met Juan Perón in 1944 in connection with a radio interview, and they were married soon after.

Through her charitable works and projects, and with the aid of her particular kind of charismatic appeal, she soon won the adoration of Argentina's poor. Through the Eva Perón Foundation, a blanket charitable organization developed and run by her personally, she dispensed money and gifts of food and clothing to the needy. She became affectionately known as "Evita" (Little Eva), and wielded considerable power in the country.

When only 29, she was suddenly stricken with cancer. Despite her increasingly serious state of health, she continued to conduct her public life as normally as possible for the next 4 years. Perón wanted her to run as his Vice-President in the 1951 presidential election, but she was not well enough. On July 16, 1952, at the age of 33, she died.

Her body lay in state for 2 weeks, and 8 people were trampled to death in the frenzied crowds that flocked to her funeral. Perón arranged for her body to be embalmed and preserved forever, and planned an enormous mausoleum for her. However, when he was overthrown in 1955, he had to leave the body behind him in Argentina. The body disappeared for some time, and there are 2 versions of what happened to it. According to the generally accepted version, Eva Perón was buried in a Milan, Italy, cemetery under a false name, and it was several years before Perón learned about this. According to a little-known version—told to the *Almanac* by a biographer and friend of Perón's—the embalmed corpse of Eva was sent to Perón in Spain, where he lived in exile. There, as he dined nightly with his living wife, Isabel, his deceased wife, Eva, was also in attendance. When Perón returned to power in Argentina, Eva's body followed him, arriving just before his own death in 1974.

The burst of kidnap activity that preceded and accompanied the reappearance of Perón on the Argentine political scene resulted in 500 kidnappings (150 of them involving foreign businessmen or diplomats) by late 1973. Enormous ransoms of over $1 million were demanded in several cases, the record being the $14.2 million paid by Exxon for the release of American executive Victor Samuelson in April, 1974. Concerned for their own safety, over half of the 6,000-member American community in Argentina had left the country by early 1974.

Buenos Aires, the capital, is considered by many to be one of the most civilized and cosmopolitan cities in the world. It resembles Paris, with its many parks, diagonal boulevards, tree-lined streets, and gray mansard roofs. Its restaurants, in a country where many people have customarily eaten steak for both lunch and dinner, are excellent, and there are theaters, art galleries, and museums to rival anything in London or New York.

On the other hand, present-day life on the Falkland Islands off Argentina's southern tip remains much as it was in the 19th century, when the islands were 1st populated by British, largely Scottish, sheepherders.

—E.P.

AUSTRALIA

NITTY GRITTY

Location—Southeast of Asia between the Pacific and Indian oceans.

How Created—The oldest continent, but last to be discovered by Europeans. Claimed for Britain in 1770, colonization began in 1788 with English convicts (25% female). The Commonwealth includes the entire continent plus Tasmania, an island off the southeast coast of the mainland. The various colonies were federated in 1901. (Has some small island dependencies, 2.5 million sq. mi. in Antarctica, and retains advisory interest in Papua New Guinea, a self-administering former trust territory.)

Size—Mainland: 2,941,526 sq. mi.; Tasmania: 26,383 sq. mi. Total: 2,967,909 sq. mi. (7,686,849 sq. km.), almost equal to the conterminous States of the U.S.

Population—13,800,000: British, 95.6%; Italian, 1.3%; Greek, 0.9%; other, 2.2% including 50,000 fullblooded Aborigines. 31.2% Church of England, 27% Roman Catholic, 8.6% Methodist, 8.1% Presbyterian, 11.3% other Christian, 13.8% non-Christian or non-religious.

Who Rules—A Federal Parliament consisting of a 125-member House of Representatives and a 60-member Senate. A Cabinet is formed from the majority party with one minister serving as Prime Minister. The Queen's representative, the governor-general, has largely ceremonial duties.

Who REALLY Rules—Trade unions and foreign investors wield much power. British, American, and Japanese interests have considerable economic ownership and control. Foreign money is behind: 88% of auto manufacture and assembly (primarily GM); 80% of all oil and mineral operations; 72% of nonferrous metal processing; 75% of the drug and toiletry industry.

NOTES

So vast are the west-central desert lands that accurate aerial maps have been made only in the last 12 years, and in 1973 there was still no airline that would fly over the Gibson desert. There are miles of surfing beach, and divers love the Great Barrier Reef, 1,250 mi. long, which is located off the northeast coast, the greatest continuous coral formation in the world. Unfortunately, the Reef has been disappearing and is considered to be an endangered environment.

Australia's isolation has preserved some of the world's most unusual animal life, including the wombat, dingo (Australian dog), platypus, wallaby, koala, kangaroo (from the size of a hare to 6' tall), the giant earthworm (10' long), and the emu.

Australia, with 163 million sheep, leads the world in wool production, supplying ⅓ of the world's total need. One worker in 5 is employed by the Government.

The stereotype of the friendly Aussie with a love of beer, gambling, and sports is, to a large degree, accurate.

One visitor credits the Aussie reputation for being happy in part to the lotteries: "If a man has a bet going, he won't commit suicide because he has a chance of winning." Aussies spend $2 billion a year on gambling, ⅔ of it legally, but a great portion on the outlawed coin-toss game "2-up." And if happiness equals beer drinking, the Aussies must be approaching nirvana. A 1974 government report says the Australians are downing 100 gallons of beer per person annually, one of the world's highest marks. Most Aussies spend one or 2 evenings a week at the pub.

Aussies are extremely upset over French testing of nuclear devices in the atmosphere above the Pacific. Fallout has occurred over a widespread area of Australia. Protests range from formal government objections to individuals parachuting into the test zones.

Voting is compulsory, and few risk the $4 fine for abstaining.

The constitution is silent on civil rights. Special authority is needed in many areas for picketing, parading, or outdoor meetings.

—B.B.

AUSTRIA

NITTY GRITTY

Location—In the heart of Central Europe, landlocked Austria is bounded by West Germany and Czechoslovakia on the north, Hungary on the east, Yugoslavia and Italy on the south, and Switzerland and Liechtenstein on the west.

How Created—The name Österreich means the "Eastern Empire," that is, the territory which came into Charlemagne's conglomerate in 788 A.D. After the ascension of the Hapsburgs to the throne in 1273, Austria expanded its borders by successful wars and even more successful political marriages, and by 1700 Austria was unquestionably one of Europe's great powers. Then in the 18th century, Austria gradually lost power to Prussia. The current state of Austria owes its basic size and governmental structure to the Treaty of Saint-Germain in 1919 which ended W.W. I. Annexed by Germany in 1938, Austria was liberated by

U.S. and Soviet troops in 1945 and then occupied by the Allied powers until 1955, when it again became independent.

Size—32,375 sq. mi. (83,850 sq. km.), slightly smaller than Maine.

Population—7,600,000: Austrian, 98.6%; German, 0.6%; Italian, Hungarian, and others, 0.8%. Over 90% Roman Catholic.

Who Rules—The President is elected for a 6-year term. He shares power with a 2-house legislature. The 183 members of the National Council are popularly elected to 4-year terms. The 54 members of the Federal Council are chosen by the 9 state assemblies.

Who REALLY Rules—The most powerful person is the Chancellor, who is appointed by the President. Generally the Chancellor is chosen because he is the head of the ruling party. The vast majority of private enterprise is financed or owned by West Germans.

NOTES

Tourism is the most important source of revenue. Over one million visitors spend their vacations in Austria each year, and without this currency input, Austria's economy would suffer greatly from large trade deficits—especially with West Germany.

The Austrian roster of heroes is crowded with cultural figures; political and military heroes are conspicuous by their absence. Native composers Haydn, Mozart, and Schubert are considered worthy of admiration and emulation.

The beautiful blue Danube was only a figment of Johann Strauss's imagination. The Danube is brown and highly polluted now, just as it was when Strauss wrote the song.

The coffee house, the favorite Viennese institution and a way of life, was an unexpected dividend resulting from the 1683 victory over the Turks. When the Turks retreated from the walls of Vienna, they left behind sacks of coffee.

—L.V.J.R. & J.T.

BANGLADESH

NITTY GRITTY

Location—Bangladesh, or "Bengal Nation," is located at the eastern edge of Asia's Indian subcontinent, on the delta and alluvial plain of the Padma (Ganges-Brahmaputra) River. It is surrounded by India on the west, north, and south, Burma on the southeast, and the Bay of Bengal on the south.

How Created—Somewhere around the 5th century B.C., Aryan people, originally from Central Asia, migrated to Bengal and intermixed with its aboriginal inhabitants. The area came under Buddhist influence in the 3rd century B.C., remaining so until the 12th century A.D., when Hindus achieved dominance. In the 13th and 14th centuries Muslim Turks and Afghans ruled Bengal. Finally, the Mogul empire united the entire subcontinent, including Bengal, in the 16th century.

The British East India Company established the 1st European settlement in Bengal in 1633. By the end of the 17th century, with Mogul influence in Bengal declining, the Nawab of Bengal (a local prince within the Mogul empire) made a fortune selling land to the British.

In 1756 the French encouraged the Nawab of Bengal to drive out the British. With French help, the Bengalis seized Fort William, the East India Company's Calcutta outpost. The Nawab imprisoned the English under harsh conditions in what came to be known as the "Black Hole of Calcutta."

The East India Company mounted a counterattack in 1757, under the command of Lord Robert Clive. He fought off the French and defeated the Bengalis at the Battle of Plassey. Upon entering Dacca, the Bengali capital, in 1757, he said, "This city is as extensive, populous, and rich as the city of London."

Following an anticolonial uprising throughout India in 1857, the East India Company turned its Indian territories directly over to the British Crown in 1858.

In 1947 the British granted independence to India and Pakistan. Pakistan, the Muslim state, included the eastern half of Bengal plus a few adjacent districts from Assam and the western part of Punjab, as well as other far west provinces. The 2 sections of Pakistan were divided by over 1,000 mi. of Indian territory.

Though Bengalis formed a majority of Pakistan's population, West Pakistanis ran the government and West Pakistan businessmen gained control of East Bengal's industry.

In 1970 the Awami League, which campaigned for Bengali autonomy, won all but 2 seats in the East Pakistan delegation to the national assembly. Though the Awami League did not run candidates in the West, the East's population edge gave it a majority. Realizing that Awami League rule meant division of Pakistan for all purposes other than defense and foreign affairs, General Yahya Khan delayed the March, 1971, opening of the national assembly. Bengal rose in anger, but the Awami League leadership refused to declare independence.

On March 25, 1971, the Federal Pakistani Army "intervened" to restore order in East Pakistan. They arrested the Awami League's leader, Sheikh Mujibur Rahman. In the ensuing months the Army killed tens or hundreds of thousands of Bengalis, raped and looted, and drove millions of Bengalis from their homes (many to refugee camps in India). India stepped in, recognized an Awami League government in exile and supported Bengali guerrillas. In December, the Indian Army invaded East Bengal while the Indian Navy and Air Force blockaded the ports. Isolated Pakistani troops in Dacca surrendered on December 16, 1971. Indian troops withdrew, leaving the new nation of Bangladesh under Awami League rule.

Size—55,126 sq. mi. (142,776 sq. km.).

Population—80 million: Bengali, 98.4%; Urdu, Hindu, and others, 1.6%. 80% Muslim, 18% Hindu.

Who Rules—A 315-member elected parliament, a President, and a Prime Minister.

Who REALLY Rules—The Awami League —barely—with much "advice" given by the World Bank. In January, 1975, the parliament outlawed all political parties except the Awami League.

NOTES

Today, with the Awami League unable to govern adequately, the underground movements are growing and attempting to unite. During the Pakistani occupation all groups armed themselves. Though Awami League leader Mujibur asked his people to turn in their arms, the underground opposition remains well armed.

Some of the various hill tribes of the Chittagong Hills, near the Burmese border, seek regional autonomy—a "Bangladesh within Bangladesh." And some of the anti-Indian left-wing parties advocate a united, independent Bengal, including Calcutta and the rest of Indian West Bengal.

Decaying public order led Mujibur to promulgate laws in 1974 allowing unlimited detention of government opponents. Under martial law he banned public meetings and authorized warrantless arrests. His government has seized editions of the leading opposition newspaper, and in June, 1974, he even arrested Maulana Bhashani, the 90-year-old opposition leader, who defied Mujibur's restrictions by calling for one more mass demonstration.

—L.S.

BANKAMERICA
CORPORATION

NITTY GRITTY

Location—Headquarters are in the Bank of America Center in San Francisco. The principal offices of the Bank of America are in San Francisco and Los Angeles. FinanceAmerica's executive offices are in Allentown, Pa. Milan is the headquarters for Banca D'America D'Italia.

How Created—Amadeo Peter Giannini opened the Bank of Italy in San Francisco in 1904. In 1909 the State of California passed a law permitting branch banking outside a bank's home city. Giannini began buying other banks, and by 1918 had 24 branches throughout the State. On November 30, 1930, Giannini consolidated his Bank of Italy with the Bank of California of America to form the Bank of America National Trust & Savings Association. In 1928 he had set up a holding company—TransAmerica Corporation—to own his bank's stock and to acquire banks and other investments outside California.

By 1948 TransAmerica controlled 645 bank offices in Arizona, California, Nevada, Oregon, and Washington, as well as insurance companies, finance companies, real estate operations, and business services. TransAmerica was forced to sell its Bank of America stock between 1937 and 1952.

Meanwhile Bank of America continued to grow. In May, 1966, the bank announced a licensing plan to develop BankAmericard into a national all-purpose credit card. BankAmerica Corporation was organized as a holding company on October 7, 1968, to acquire the stock of Bank of America, which it did on March 31, 1969. On January 1, 1974, the new holding company acquired GAC Finance, Inc., the finance, loan, and insurance business of the former GAC Corporation. In August, 1974, GAC Finance, Inc., was renamed FinanceAmerica Corporation.

Size—The corporation's subsidiary, Bank of America National Trust & Savings Association, has over 1,000 branches in California and over 100 branches in 47 countries in Europe, the Middle East, Africa, Asia, and Latin America. It is the world's largest commercial bank company. Another subsidiary, FinanceAmerica Corporation, has 442 offices in 41 States and Canada. Banca D'America D'Italia, 90% owned by the Bank of America, has 86 branches in Italy. Over 10,500 bank outlets in the U.S. and over 25,000 worldwide participate in the corporation's National BankAmericard, Inc.

Population—Work force (BankAmerica, 1973): 56,250; work force (FinanceAmerica, 1972): 2,724.

Who Rules—A 16-member board of directors.

Who REALLY Rules—Policy decisions are made by Chairman Chauncey J. Medberry, President and Chief Executive Officer Aldin Winship (Tom) Clausen, Vice-Chairman Clarence Herman Baumhefner, and the chairman of the General Trust Committee, Samuel B. Stewart.

NOTES

During the Depression, Bank of America held the largest share of California farm debt mortgages, equipment loans, and advances on crops. Using the bank's power to acquire property when customers defaulted on their loans, the bank's subsidiary, California Lands, became one of the State's largest landowners in the 1930s. By 1940 California Lands grew 60 crops on over 2,600 farms consisting of over 600,000 acres. The bank then sold these lands to integrated agribusiness companies. These companies have interlocking directorates with oil companies, railroads, and banks, including the Bank of America. Through these interlocking boards of directors, the agribusiness companies and the banks control California's economy and government.

Giannini was responsible for introducing H. J. Kaiser to President Franklin D. Roosevelt. The new President was eager to help Kaiser since Kaiser sat on the bank's board of directors and Giannini was one of the few bankers to contribute to Roosevelt's election. Roosevelt returned the favor by giving Kaiser Industries contracts for building 35% of the country's ship tonnage during W.W. II. Kaiser had never built a ship before. In California during the war, the bank opened branches at Japanese-American detention centers, so the internees could deposit with the bank any of their possessions that had not been confiscated by the Government.

When asked why they had burned the Bank of America's Isla Vista branch in 1970, one student replied: "Well, it was there . . . the biggest capitalist establishment thing around."

—II.B.

BELGIUM

NITTY GRITTY

Location—Northwestern Europe between France (to the southwest) and the Netherlands (to the northeast). The North Sea is to the north; Luxembourg and West Germany are south and east.

How Created—The Belgae were a Celtic tribe conquered by Julius Caesar. The country was ruled by various European powers until 1815, when it was united with the Netherlands by the Congress of Vienna. In 1830 the Belgians revolted against the Dutch and invited a German Prince, Leopold of Saxe-Coburg, to be their King. The Treaty of Versailles, after W.W. I, added another 400 sq. mi. in the east.

Size—11,781 sq. mi., (30,514 sq. km.), slightly larger than Maryland.

Population—Over 11 million: Belgian, 95.1%; Italian, 2.2%; French, Dutch, Polish, and others, 2.7%. 93.2% Roman Catholic.

Who Rules—Parliamentary democracy under a constitutional monarchy. The King, Baudouin I (born September 7, 1930, crowned July 17, 1951), is chief of state. Government is headed by the Prime Minister and Cabinet. Parliament consists of the Senate and Chamber of Representatives.

Who REALLY Rules—All postwar governments have been formed by one or more of 3 major parties: Catholics, Socialists, and Liberals (actually a conservative party).

NOTES

The main issue in Belgium is language and culture: French v. Dutch. The country has been divided into 2 regions since 1932: Dutch-speaking Flanders in the north, French-speaking Wallonia in the south, with the capital, Brussels, a French-speaking island in a Dutch sea.

It rains in Belgium about 300 days per year.

The Belgians are Europe's worst drivers. Even the French say so. There has been driver licensing only since 1968 and only for new drivers.

The Belgians don't go to war. The wars come to them. With no natural frontiers the wars of Europe have been fought here. The Battle of Waterloo (1815) was fought a few miles outside of Brussels and the Battle of the Bulge, the last German offensive of W.W. II, was fought in the Ardennes Forest in the southeast. The British have gone to war at least once in each of the last 7 centuries, usually to keep the French from controlling the Low Countries. The French have fought to keep a buffer between themselves and the Germans.

—D.B.

BHUTAN

NITTY GRITTY

Location—In the eastern Himalayan mountains between China and India, bordered by Tibet on the north, India's Assam-Bengal plain on the south, Sikkim on the west, and Assam on the south and east.

How Created—Knowledge of Bhutan's early history is meager, and research has always been made even more difficult due to the country's long isolation, which ended only recently. Early in the 17th century a Tibetan refugee established himself as monarch and set up an enduring administrative system; this event is generally accepted as Bhutan's birth as a separate nation. Until quite recently the borders were not usually clearly defined and were generally disputed by Bhutan's neighbors.

Size—18,000 sq. mi. (47,000 sq. km.), a little larger than Switzerland.

Population—1,150,000: Tibetan (Bhutias), 51.5%; Gurung, 17.6%; Assamese, 14.7%; Toba, 4.4%; other, 11.8%. 75% Buddhist, 25% Hindu.

Who Rules—Bhutan is a monarchy ruled by a King. An advisory council appointed by the King and an assembly, the Tsongdu, ¾ of which is chosen by the villages and ¼ by the King, assist the King in enacting legislation.

Who REALLY Rules—Because of Bhutan's strategic location between India and China in an area vital to India's defense, the King's authority in domestic affairs is overshadowed in other respects by India's influence, which decides matters pertaining to defense and foreign policy.

NOTES

Once a feudal kingdom isolated from the rest of the world by steaming jungles in the south and snow-covered mountains in the north, Bhutan is finally opening up to contact with the "civilized" world.

—R.E.K.

BOLIVIA

NITTY GRITTY

Location—A landlocked country astride the Andes in western South America. Neighbors are: Brazil on the north and east, Paraguay and Argentina to the south, and Chile and Peru to the west.

How Created—Originally part of the Incan Empire, Bolivia was known as Upper Peru during Spanish colonial times. Since receiving independence from Spain in 1825, Bolivia has, through a series of wars, treaties, and land grabs, been deprived of nearly half the territory it originally claimed. This includes Pacific seaports taken by Chile.

Size—425,165 sq. mi. (1,098,561 sq. km.), the 5th largest country in South America.

Population—5.6 million: Quechua Indian, 37.1%; Bolivian (Spanish ancestry), 35.7%; Aymará Indian, 23.7%; other Indians, 3.5%. 72% Roman Catholic.

Who Rules—Technically a republic with nearly universal suffrage, Bolivia's last popular election occurred in 1966. The country has a long history of political difficulties, having experienced close to 200 changes of government in the 150 years since independence. Bolivia today is ruled by a right-wing military junta, which ousted a left-wing general in 1971.

Who REALLY Rules—The U.S. Government, in conjunction with the tiny oligarchy that runs Bolivia. The President, Colonel Banzer, has strong ties to the U.S. He trained in the School of the Americas and in the U.S., and also had a stint as military attaché in Washington, D.C. Bolivia has been a major recipient of U.S. foreign economic assistance ($500 million since 1952), and the U.S. is presently the biggest foreign investor in Bolivia's economy.

NOTES

La Paz is the highest capital city in the world, with its airport at 13,358'.

The Aymará Indians (who live in both Bolivia and Peru) are responsible for the development of the potato, and cultivate over 110 varieties.

The Peace Corps was ousted by Bolivia in 1970, allegedly for subversive activity, including aiding Bolivian guerrillas and sterilizing Indian women without their permission.

A Bolivian hero is Ernesto "Che" Guevara, guerrilla leader born in Argentina in 1928. He traveled widely in Latin America, and witnessed the CIA-sponsored coup in Guatemala in 1954. He met Fidel and Raul Castro in Mexico City in 1955, and soon went with them to Cuba, to help lead the revolution there in 1959. He resigned his cabinet post in the Cuban Government in 1965, and turned his energies toward Bolivia as a strategically located country ready for revolution. After a year of guerrilla activity in that country, he and a small band of men were captured by a Green Beret-organized unit of the Bolivian army. To avoid a trial and the accompanying international attention it would focus on the guerrillas' activities, Che Guevara was executed on October 9, 1967, and his body secretly disposed of.

—E.P.

BRAZIL

NITTY GRITTY

Location—Brazil occupies central and eastern South America, with borders on all South American countries except Chile and Ecuador.

How Created—First "discovered" by Pedro Alvares Cabral in 1500, the territory was claimed for Portugal because it lay on the eastern or Portuguese side of the line dividing Spanish and Portuguese colonies in the New World. (This line was established by the 1494 Treaty of Tordesillas, which was intended to prevent bickering between the 2 countries involved.) Brazil remained Portugal's colony for 3 centuries until, in 1807, the royal court of Portugal fled to Brazil to escape Napoleon.

Brazil briefly acquired the same status as Portugal, but the presence of the royal family hindered revolts for independence such as were occurring in other South American (Spanish) colonies. With the overthrow of Napoleon, the royal family returned to Portugal, leaving Dom Pedro, the King's son, as regent in Brazil. In defiance of his family's wishes, Dom Pedro separated Brazil from Portugal, and the country became an independent monarchy in 1822. Dom Pedro's son, Pedro II, ruled Brazil until 1889, when he was forced to abdicate. Brazil became a republic in 1891.

Size—3,286,488 sq. mi. (8,512,004 sq. km.), largest country in South America and 6th largest country in the world.

Population—Over 108 million. Brazil accounts for half of the total population of South America. European, 62% (mostly Portuguese, but also Spanish, Italian, and German in significant numbers); black, 11%; mixed white/Indian/black, 27% but also including a large Japanese colony. These official figures belie the fact that almost no group has maintained complete racial purity.

Who Rules—Theoretically a federal republic with a bicameral legislature elected by all adult literates. However, a 1964 military coup with U.S. assistance ousted President João Goulart, a leftist, and instituted effective military rule. The last 4 Presidents have been generals.

Who REALLY Rules—Military men and technocrats currently run Brazil, with considerable U.S. and other foreign assistance. The Brazilian Congress exists but is powerless; its teeth were pulled by the 1969 constitution, which gave most of Congress's powers to the executive branch. The U.S. has considerable investments in Brazil, and maintains a large military mission there. Some 100,000 of Brazil's police have received assistance from a U.S.-operated "public safety" program, and at least 344 of the top military officers have trained in Washington's International Policy Academy.

NOTES

While Brazil's booming economy has brought great wealth to the country as a whole and to certain groups in particular, not all Brazilians have benefited. It is estimated that as much as 60% of the population is basically unaffected by this new wealth. In the drought-ridden northeast, Brazil's poorest area, the standard of living has in some cases actually been reduced. The Government has stated its preference for increasing the country's income 1st, and redistributing the wealth later.

Censorship exists on every level. Some publications have a resident censor; others self-censor their material or submit it to a board. Song lyrics are censored, and the tunes themselves are scrutinized for double meanings or subversive connotation. Many foreign films do not pass the censor, but Brazilians interested in such forbidden films as *A Clockwork Orange* and *Last Tango in Paris* have organized short jaunts to neighboring Uruguay.

Brazil has officially opposed population control, fearing that it will hinder economic development. Abortions are strictly outlawed, but even so there are 1.5 million illegal abortions performed yearly.

Brazil's irresponsibility toward its Indian population has aroused protest both from the Church and civic groups at home, and from concerned groups abroad. Reports of deliberately spread disease, massacres, and callous neglect have filtered out from the interior. Some observers believe that an unofficial policy of genocide has been adopted in order to clear the way for settlement of the area.

The Brazilian National Indian Foundation confirmed that it had found a tribe of blue-eyed, brown-haired, bearded Indians. The tribe numbers about 100 members, and lives in a remote Amazon area.

The Carnival in Rio lasts from the Saturday before Ash Wednesday until Wednesday evening. It is a time of massive exuberance and colorful display of costumes and dancing. All businesses, shops, and offices shut down, and no one seems to go to bed. The streets are jammed for 4 days with dancing, singing people, and there are competitions among various clubs for the best samba dances.

Emperor Dom Pedro II was morally opposed to slavery, but for political reasons he favored a gradual rather than immediate abolition. While he was on a trip to Europe in 1888, his daughter Isabel freed all the slaves without compensation to their owners. This caused the conservative landowners to drop their support of Dom Pedro and the monarchy was easily deposed in 1889. Dom Pedro went to France, where he died 2 years later.

—E.P.

BULGARIA

NITTY GRITTY

Location—Southeastern Europe, in the eastern corner of the Balkan Peninsula. Bordered by Romania to the north, most of the northern boundary defined by the course of the Danube River. Bordered by the Black Sea to the east, by Greece and Turkey to the south, and by Yugoslavia to the west.

How Created—Thrace, as Bulgaria was known in ancient times, was 1st conquered by Alexander the Great in the 4th century B.C., then by the Romans in 46 A.D. Roman rule lasted 500 years and was followed by a massive invasion of Slavs, who completely absorbed the Thracians. The next invaders were the Bulgars, a warlike and nomadic tribe from the central Asian steppes, who were also absorbed by the more numerous Slavs and left behind little of note but their name. In both the 9th and 13th centuries Bulgaria possessed a large southeastern European empire, but by 1397 the Ottoman Turks had seized complete control of the area. Bulgaria suffered under Turkish rule for 500 years. It was finally liberated by Czarist Russia and granted full national independence in 1878.

Size—43,000 sq. mi. (111,000 sq. km.), roughly the size of Ohio.

Population—8,850,000: Bulgarian, 87.9%; Turkish, 9.5%; Gypsy, 1.8%; Armenian, Macedonian, and others, 0.8%.

Who Rules—According to the constitution of May, 1971, "all power resides in the working people of town and country." Chief legislative body is the National Assembly. The State Council is the executive power, and its President is also Premier. The Council of Ministers administrates the government.

Who REALLY Rules—The Politburo of the Bulgarian Communist party. Bulgaria is the most loyal and orthodox of all Soviet satellites, and its policies copy those of the U.S.S.R. in nearly every respect.

NOTES

The growth rate of Bulgaria's economy in postwar years has been and remains one of the world's highest. Whereas before W.W. II most people were peasant farmers, now 30% work in industry and only 35% work the land. Rapid urbanization has brought half of the people to the cities, where factories are located.

Bulgaria is a Soviet-style police state which discourages deviant political belief and "bourgeois" personal mannerisms by its relentless propaganda, its alert secret police, and its disciplined mass organizations (unions, guilds, youth groups, farm brigades, etc.) to which citizens are encouraged to belong. Freedom of the press and of expression is unknown, nor has it ever been known in Bulgaria in its Western form. Travel outside Bulgaria is restricted to party elite.

In recent years Bulgarian leaders have shown concern over the restlessness of young people, who are attracted to Western bourgeois styles, and over the disquiet of the rigidly controlled artists and writers.

Spartacus, leader of the most famous slave revolt in ancient Rome, was born in the territory that is now Bulgaria.

Bulgaria is known for its excellent cigarettes, which compare favorably with Western cigarettes.

—R.Mi.

BURMA

NITTY GRITTY

Location—Burma is situated in Southeast Asia, along the valleys of the Irrawaddy, Sittang, and Salween rivers, and along the west coast of the northern Malayan peninsula. It is bounded by Bangladesh and India on the west, China on the north and east, Laos and Thailand on the east, and the Andaman Sea and Bay of Bengal on the southwest.

How Created—The inhabitants of Burma migrated south from Tibet and Yunnan (China) over a period of many centuries. The dominant ethnic Burmese arrived in the Irrawaddy Valley about the 9th century. In 1054 King Anawrahta unified Burma into one empire, building a magnificent capital at Pagan and inaugurating a golden age. His Pagan dynasty lasted until 1287, when Mongol Kublai Khan conquered the country.

During the 17th century Portuguese, Dutch, and English traders temporarily established settlements, but the inhabitants drove them out. In 1823–1826, in 1852, and in 1885 the British fought 3 wars against the Burmese, conquering the entire country by January 1, 1886. The British ruled Burma as part of India until 1937, when they separated it and established limited self-government.

In 1942 Japan conquered Burma, installing a puppet regime of Burmese nationalists. By 1944 the nationalists had turned against the Japanese, helping the British and Americans drive them out.

The Anti-Fascist Organization (later the Anti-Fascist Peoples Freedom League, or AFPFL), which led the anti-Japanese fight, pressed for independence and the British complied in 1948.

Size—261,789 sq. mi. (678,034 sq. km.), almost the size of Texas.

Population—30 million: Burmese, 71.5%; Karen, 8.4%; Shan, 6.5%; Chin, 2%; Mon, 1.9%; Kachin, 1.5%; Chinese, 1.4%; Tamil, 0.8%; Koyak, 0.5%; other, 5.5%. 85% Buddhist, 14% Animist, 1% Christian and others.

Who Rules—The Revolutionary Council of military leaders and the ruling Burmese Socialist Program party.

Who REALLY Rules—The military bureaucrats control the economy as well as politics and international affairs. When, in 1974, pop-

ular elections ran against the military's candidates, it overrode the public.

NOTES

Though the ethnic Burmese dominate the lowlands, the Union of Burma has no unified national character. The various tribes and nations that inhabit the mountains and border regions have never been fully governed by either the British or the Burmese. Many cannot be distinguished from people living across the borders.

Due to Britain's efforts to promote the cultivation of the lower delta lands for wet rice farming, Burma became the largest exporter of rice in the world. However, after W.W. II, as part of the economy's general decline, rice production fell sharply. Today, Burma still produces less rice than before the war.

Tattooing is considered an art form in Burma. In precolonial times (and, to a lesser extent, today) many males at the age of puberty had their body from the navel to the kneecaps completely covered with religious and mystical designs.

The violence and cruelty of the Burmese Kings is legendary, but perhaps slightly exaggerated. For instance, King Thisithu Dhamana reportedly sought to increase his power through an elixir made out of 6,000 human hearts. The last Burmese King, mounting the throne in 1878, tried to eliminate all possible contenders by executing his 80 half brothers and sisters.

Hundreds, maybe even thousands, of Kuomintang troops left over from the Chinese Civil War still operate in northern Burma. They run a protection racket for the opium trade, carry out intelligence missions within China, and occasionally fight Burmese troops.

Herbert Hoover, former U.S. President, called the Burmese "the only genuinely happy people in all of Asia."

—L.S. & S.L.W.G.

BURUNDI

NITTY GRITTY

Location—A landlocked nation in Central Africa; to the north, Rwanda; to the east and southeast, Tanzania; to the west, Lake Tanganyika and Zaire.

How Created—see Rwanda.

Size—10,759 sq. mi. (27,865 sq. km.).

Population—4 million: Hutu, 86%; Tutsi, 13%; Twa Pygmies, 1%. 51% Roman Catholic, 45% Animist, 4% Protestant, 1% Muslim.

Who Rules—The President and the Political Bureau of the Unity and National Progress party (UPRONA).

Who REALLY Rules—UPRONA is the only political party. Burundi receives aid from China, Belgium, the UN, the U.S., the Common Market, France, and West Germany.

NOTES

The tribal wars in Burundi, Hutu against Tutsi, have, in the past 3 years, reached alarming proportions. In 1972, the Government of Burundi, led by the Watutsi extremist Michel Micombero, conducted an orderly, systematic, methodical massacre of the Hutu elite, wiping out almost all of the Hutu who might offer resistance to the Tutsi Government. A "list" of educated, wealthy, or government-employed Hutu citizens served as a guideline for the Micombero government assassins, who killed 100,000 Hutu in the 1st 6 weeks of their slaughter. The Hutus have now been effectively reduced to 2nd-class citizens and are excluded from the army, the civil service, the university and secondary schools.

The Mwami (Tutsi King) of Burundi, at the time of independence, was Mwambutsa IV, an intelligent, fair-minded, and easygoing man. He did what he could for peace and equality in Burundi, but his efforts finally collapsed in 1966 when he was deposed by his son, Crown Prince Charles, who declared himself Mwami Ntare V. Mwambutsa went into exile; 3 months later, he was joined by his son, now dethroned by his Premier, Michel Micombero. Together they lived, father and son, both mwamis-in-exile, in luxury and comfort, in Mwambutsa's elegant and fashionable Geneva home. In 1972 Ntare, promised a safe-conduct pass by Micombero, visited his homeland. He was executed.

Fifty-one percent of the population is 14 years old or younger.

—R.C.

CAMBODIA

NITTY GRITTY

Location—In the large, fertile basin of the lower Mekong River in Southeast Asia. Cambodia is bordered by South Vietnam to the east, the Gulf of Siam to the southwest, Thailand to the northwest, and Laos to the north.

How Created—One of the oldest kingdoms in Southeast Asia. Descended from Funan, which some historians believe was founded prior to the 1st century A.D. At that time, Funan's power extended over much of present-day Thailand, Laos, and Malaysia.

For much of its history, Cambodia has been subject to the intense pressures of her 2 neighbors, Thailand and Vietnam. Both have established protectorates over Cambodia at various times.

When the French seized Cambodia in the 19th century, they established the present boundaries, most of which consist of low mountain ranges.

However, boundary disputes continue to occur. For instance, Thailand and Cambodia battled each other for most of the 1960s over possession of a temple. This dispute was finally settled in favor of Cambodia by the World Court, but Thailand declared it was only a temporary solution.

Size—69,898 sq. mi. (181,035 sq. km.), about the size of Missouri.

Population—7.5 million: Khmer, 85%; Vietnamese, 7%; Chinese, 6%; Cham, 1%; hill tribes and others, 1%. 75% Buddhist, 1% Muslim (the Chams), 1% Christian.

Who Rules—In March, 1970, the right wing overthrew chief of state King Norodom Sihanouk with the aid of CIA-trained Khmer Serei troops and perhaps the CIA itself. The right, under Lon Nol, established the Khmer Republic. Sihanouk, who had been traveling abroad, joined with the Khmer Rouge guerrilla movement to form the Royal Government of the National Union of Cambodia (known by its French acronym, GRUNK).

In April, 1975, the Khmer Rouge defeated the troops of Lon Nol and took control of Cambodia.

Who REALLY Rules—GRUNK projects a democratic image, but it is at least influenced by its chief foreign supporters, China and North Vietnam.

NOTES

Following national independence Sihanouk attempted to steer a course of international neutrality, condemning violations of Cambodian territory by all parties, including the U.S., South Vietnam, and the Vietnamese communists. In 1969 the U.S. military, under orders from President Richard Nixon and his adviser Henry Kissinger, began a major bombing campaign in eastern Cambodia which was kept secret from the U.S. Congress and the people. Following the March, 1970, coup, the U.S. and South Vietnam mounted a massive invasion across Cambodia's border, officially aimed at communist "sanctuaries."

The invasion actually fed the Cambodian civil war. Sources on all sides predicted the Republic would fall when the U.S. Congress halted American bombing in Cambodia in August, 1973, but the Lon Nol regime remained in power in the urban areas for another 20 months.

The Prince—or *Samdech*—Norodom Sihanouk, a questionable hero to outsiders, still commands a following within Cambodia. Chosen

King by the French at age 19 in 1941, he crusaded for independence. In 1955 he gave the throne to his father, but continued in government. In 1960, when his father died, he again became chief of state, but he retained his nonroyal title. While balancing domestic political forces and foreign influences, he worked as a movie actor and developed a reputation as a dilettante.

He is currently a figurehead leader, and he has relatively little influence within GRUNK.

Cambodians, or Khmers, constitute 85% of the population. For the most part, they are rice farmers scattered about the countryside in small villages. The few who are not farmers earn their livelihood by working for the Government or the Buddhist Church.

Until the Khmer Rouge take-over, the Chinese were the most powerful ethnic minority. Thanks to the policies of the French during the colonial period, the approximately 400,000 Chinese held a virtual stranglehold on the Cambodian economy.

The Chams, the descendants of the former kingdom of Champa, now number 100,000. Most are Muslims and speak a Malayo-Polynesian language, but are regarded as full citizens of Cambodia. They work primarily as lumberjacks, cattle herders, and fishermen.

—L.S. & S.L.W.G.

CAMEROON

NITTY GRITTY

Location—In West Central Africa, with a 125-mi. coastline on the Gulf of Guinea. The northern tip of the country touches Lake Chad; to the west, Nigeria; to the east, Central African Republic and Chad; to the south and east, Congo; to the south, Rio Muni and Gabon.

How Created—The original colony was established by the Germans in 1884, through treaties with tribal chiefs. A W.W. I League of Nations Mandate put 80% of the country under French control, 20% under British control. The present Cameroon is a federation of French Cameroon with the south region of British Cameroon.

Size—183,568 sq. mi. (475,441 sq. km.).

Population—6,300,000: more than 100 different ethnic groups; Bamileks, 26%; Fulani, 6%; Bassa, 3.5%; Bulu and Tanga, 3%; Eton, 2.5%; Ewondo, 2%; Bamoun, 1.5%; others, 55.5%. 53% Animist, 20% Roman Catholic, 15% Protestant and other Christian, 12% Muslim.

Who Rules—The National Assembly has 120 members, serving 5-year terms. The President and Vice-President, elected for 5-year terms, must, by law, come from different provinces. The Cameroon Government provides for the preservation of traditional chiefdoms, and local power is still in the hands of traditional elders. National elections are held with universal adult suffrage.

Who REALLY Rules—For funds to support industry and development programs, Cameroon must rely upon France, the World Bank, the U.S., and the Netherlands. An international consortium has built an aluminum smelting plant, and millions of U.S. dollars have been put into the Alucam industrial complex.

NOTES

The name "Cameroon" comes from the Portuguese word *cameroes*, the word for the delicious edible prawns found in the waters of Cameroon's Wouri River.

Debundscha, the wettest place in Africa, has a yearly rainfall of over 400". The southern part of the country is grassy plain and humid rain forest, where the red-purple orchid *lissochilus* grows to 15'. The center of the country is dry savanna, and the north is semi-arid desert.

Dwindling tribes of Pygmies live in the remote forests, and still communicate with one another through a highly advanced language of drumming on logs.

Tribal women in Cameroon are uneducated, and considered "merchandise" in the Arab-dominated tribes. The "bride price" is still included in the legal marriage certificate; widows must be bought back by their families, or inherited by their husband's kin. The Government is trying to institute changes in the attitude toward women through legislation.

The slums of Cameroon's cities stretch out for miles, row upon row of one-room cement-block houses, projects built hastily to meet the growing need for cheap housing created by the migration of rural tribespeople coming to the cities. Seeking work they rarely find, newcomers to the city add to the housing shortage and acute unemployment; masses of Cameroon's citizens live in idle poverty in the nation's cities.

—R.C.

CANADA

NITTY GRITTY

Location—Canada forms the northern half of the North American continent, stretching from the Atlantic to the Pacific; flanked by huge islands on either coast, and sharing a 3,897-mi. southern border with the U.S. Canada also shares a border with the U.S. in Alaska.

How Created—The St. Lawrence River valley was the 1st part of the area to be explored by Europeans. Through the efforts of Samuel de Champlain the 1st permanent settlement in Canada was founded in 1608 at Quebec on the banks of the great river.

The word "Canada" probably comes from the Iroquois Indian word *Kanata* or *Kanada*, meaning "a group of huts." The French had a more grandiose name for the colony: New France. Voltaire was not deceived: "A few acres of snow!" he called it derisively.

In 1760, by which time there were 60,000 French settlers in the St. Lawrence valley area, Britain conquered Canada. The new leaders were content to leave the French undisturbed, preoccupied as they were with the rebellious Colonies to the south. During the American Revolution, 40,000 to 60,000 Loyalists moved to Canada, especially to the upper St. Lawrence region (Ontario), confirming British control. Thereafter, the independent nation of Canada evolved as the result of a mostly peaceful, evolutionary process of political integration. In 1867, the British Parliament passed the British North America Act, providing that "the Provinces of Canada [Quebec, Ontario], Nova Scotia and New Brunswick shall form one Dominion under the name of Canada." Other British North American territories were included as provinces in the Dominion later: Manitoba (1870), British Columbia (1871), Prince Edward Island (1873), Alberta and Saskatchewan (1905), Newfoundland (1949).

By 1931, when the British passed the Statute of Westminster, Canada was an independent nation, a voluntary partner in the Commonwealth of Nations.

Size—3,851,809 sq. mi. (9,976,139 sq. km.), second largest nation in the world. A country so vast that air-mapping still discovers "new" northern frontiers.

Population—23 million: British descent, 44%; French, 27%; other Europeans, 24%; Asian, Indian, Eskimo, and others, 5%. 45.7% Roman Catholic, 20.1% United Church of Canada (Methodists, Congregationalists, Presbyterians), 13.2% Anglican Church of Canada, 4.5% Presbyterian, 3.6% Lutheran, 3.3% Baptist, 9.6% others.

Who Rules—Head of state: Queen Elizabeth II. (She told a Toronto audience on June 23, 1973, "I want the crown to be seen as a symbol. . . ." This is a statement of the reality of the situation.) The Queen is represented by Jules Léger, governor-general, who took office in January, 1974, appointed by the Prime Minister, who is the head of the government. There is also a Parliament consisting of a Senate and a House of Commons.

Who REALLY Rules—A hot question in Canadian politics. Warnings have been sounded since the mid-'50s that the real power is vested in American corporations. There is no doubt of Canadian dependence on American markets and capital. American investment fueled the boom in the Canadian economy after W.W. II. The "branch plants" of American companies proliferated. In 1973, the U.S. took 68% of Canadian exports, and supplied 71% of imports.

NOTES

Because of forbidding geography and weather, most of Canada is sparsely populated. More than ⅔ of the population lives within 100 mi. of the U.S. border and 90% lives within 200 mi. The 40% of Canada's land mass lying above the 60th parallel is the most sparsely settled land on earth after Antarctica.

There are 16,000 Eskimos in the Arctic and sub-Arctic regions. Once nomadic, with strong family ties, they are dependent now on trading posts. Initial contact with white traders brought severe health problems for the Eskimos. In the early 1950s, ⅓ of the Eskimo population was in tuberculosis sanitariums.

Canada has immense and varied resources. It is a major producer of barley (2nd among world producers, 1972), oats (2nd in the world, 1972), and wheat. Its mineral resources made it the world's premier producer of both nickel and asbestos (1971), and 3rd in production of gold (1971). Canada's forest reserves have made it the world's leading producer of newsprint.

As recently as 1970, the Canadian Career Directory had 3,268 listings of jobs open to men, with 1,244 open to women. Sex-based wage differences are also common.

French Canadians in Quebec have felt threatened by assimilation since the British conquest 200 years ago. During the "Quiet Revolution" of the 1960s Quebec was transformed from a rural, agrarian, strongly traditional society to a modern, urbanized state. The *Front de Liberation Québec* responded with terrorist activities and urged French Canadians to demand independence. French Canadian Prime Minister Pierre Trudeau lashed back with severely repressive police actions. But it was not just a political movement. It was a social revolution, caused by industrialization and the impact of mass communication, especially television. This social revolution:

> . . . has led to a transformation in the image of a good life and the good society that most French Canadians hold. Instead of a vision of self-sufficing farm families linked together by parish institutions, asking only that the state protect them from outside influences, there has been substituted a basically urban

model: one that resembles substantially that held by North Americans from Texas to Toronto. . . .

F. Scott and M. Oliver, eds. *Quebec States Her Case*, Toronto, 1964.
—R.K.

CENTRAL AFRICAN REPUBLIC

NITTY GRITTY

Location—In Central Africa, landlocked. To the north, Chad; to the northeast, the Sudan; to the south, Zaire and Congo; to the west, Cameroon.

How Created—The borders of the Central African Republic were originally the arbitrary lines which defined the French colony of Ubangi-Shari, explored in 1900 by Emil Gentil.

Size—240,377 sq. mi. (622,557 sq. km.). Slightly smaller than Texas.

Population—1.7 million: 80 different ethnic groups including the Banda, Baya-Mandjia, and various Ubangi tribes. 60% Animist, 20% Roman Catholic, 15% other Christian, 5% Muslim.

Who Rules—The military, under the leadership of Gen. Jean-Bedel Bokassa, Premier and President for Life of the Central African Republic.

Who REALLY Rules—The Central African Republic is dependent upon France for her market: France buys 50% of CAR's exports, and supplies the nation with 58% of her imports. Treaties of financial and technical aid with France keep CAR afloat. In 1965 CAR began to accept loans from China and other communist countries.

NOTES

The people of the Central African Republic have been slow to develop political awareness, and slow to become educated in the ways of the "modern" world. They are still very much involved in the traditional animist rites practiced by their ancestors—cults, fetishes, ancestor worship, and sacrificial ceremony survive in some places. In 1955 John Gunther commented, "This territory is an anthropologist's paradise."

"Ubangi lips" are made by inserting wooden or ivory disks beneath the lower lip, stretching the lip to hold larger and larger disks (up to 8" platters). Originally, Ubangi women were disfigured in this way in order to discourage Arab slave traders from hauling them off. The distended, distorted lip grew to be considered a mark of beauty among Ubangi women, outliv-

ing the slave trade by nearly 100 years; the custom is finally dying out now.

Lush forests are full of rare birds and wild animals, butterflies, and flowers, some of which are found nowhere else on earth.
—R.C.

CHAD

NITTY GRITTY

Location—Landlocked in North Central Africa, bounded on the north by Libya; on the east by the Sudan; on the south by the Central African Republic; and on the west by Cameroon, Nigeria, and Niger.

How Created—Britain and France demarcated their respective spheres of influence in the area in 1899, resulting in Chad's becoming a French colony once its people were subdued.

Size—489,750 sq. mi. (1,268,460 sq. km.).

Population—4.2 million: Sudanese Arab, 29.9%; Bagirmi, Sara, and Kreish, 24.6%; Teda, 7.5%; Mbum, 7.1%; Maba and Masalit, 6.7%; Tama, 6.3%; Mubi and Sokoro, 4.5%; Kanuri, 2.6%; Dagu, 2.4%; Hausa, 2.2%; Masa and Musgu, 2.2%; Kotoko, 2.2%; others, 1.8%. 41% Muslim, 30% Animist, 29% Christian.

Who Rules—A 9-member Supreme Military Council which took power following a coup on April 13, 1975.

Who REALLY Rules—The military is definitely in control. France continues to pour millions of francs into the country for economic development and maintains a garrison of military officer "advisers" at Ndjamena.

NOTES

A 1952 *New York Times* article explains another root cause of Chad's poverty apart from the paucity of natural advantages and the advance of the Sahara Desert: "French penetration was accompanied by highly uneconomic methods of colonization. . . . France simply assumed title to all the land and then proceeded to portion vast tracts of it out on a concession basis to large monopolistic companies. . . . These companies depleted all the human and natural resources that they could easily get their hands on and returned virtually nothing to the economy of the country."

Over 100 different dialects are spoken in Chad and this reflects some of the diversity and potential tension which has permeated the nation since its independence. The greatest rift lies between Muslim northerners and black southerners. Northerners claim that shortly after Charles de Gaulle granted Chad independence, this pastoral country was taken over by the southerners, who helped their own kind, e.g.: 95% of the southern children have been sent to school versus 5% of the northern children. Overall, only 35% of the school-age population actually attends school.

Leader of the Muslims, Dr. Abbe Siddik, a European-trained surgeon and former Minister of Éducation, claims that France has continued to rule Chad even after Chad's independence and that Chad remains "underdeveloped and overcolonized." This dissatisfaction led to the eruption of guerrilla groups along the Libyan and Sudanese borders: the Front de la Libération Nationale de Tchad (Frolinat) and the smaller Front National Tchadien (FNT). They aim to overthrow the Government, reduce French influence, and tie in with the Arab states of the north.

To put down the Muslim insurgents, the Chad Government called in 2,500 French Foreign Legionnaires. France pulled half of them out eventually but the rest stayed on as "advisers" more or less integrated into the Chad army.

Among the Sara tribe, the most important person in the village is the veteran who served in the French army. With his pension, his galvanized steel roof and modern latrine, and his ability to schedule himself according to Western time frames, he has become a model his fellows try to emulate.

—M.D.

CHILE

NITTY GRITTY

Location—Southwest coast of South America. Neighbors are: Peru to the north, Argentina and Bolivia to the east. Chile also includes in its territory several islands, notably Easter Island (Isla de Pascua) 2,400 mi. out in the Pacific, the Juan Fernández or "Robinson Crusoe" Islands, and the large archipelago at the southern tip of the continent.

How Created—The original inhabitants, fierce Araucanian Indians, successfully resisted Spanish incursions until 1540, when Pedro de Valdivia managed to found several cities including Santiago, Concepción, and Valdivia. Isolated during most of the colonial period by distance and the tremendous barrier of the Andes, Chile eagerly declared its independence from Spain in 1810, when the Spanish King was ousted by Napoleon. Independence, however, was not really achieved until 1818, through the combined efforts of Bernardo O'Higgins and José de San Martín.

The War of the Pacific (1879–1883) established Chile's claim to the nitrate-rich Atacama Desert on the border between Peru and Chile. The boundaries of Peru, Chile, and Bolivia (which at that time had a Pacific seacoast) had never been defined, and with the discovery of nitrates in the region, Chile moved to claim the area for its own. War ensued; Bolivia dropped out quickly, but Peru fought on, until Chile occupied Lima, annexed Bolivia's seacoast, and forced Peru to cede its southern provinces.

Size—292,257 sq. mi. (756,946 sq. km.). A distinctively shaped country, 2,650 mi. long but nowhere wider than 250 mi. Chile also claims 483,000 sq. mi. of Antarctica, which is disputed by Great Britain.

Population—Over 10 million: mestizo, 66%; Spanish, 25%; Araucanian Indian, 5%; others, 4%. 89% Roman Catholic.

Who Rules—For many years a republic with President and bicameral legislature elected by a highly politicized population, Chile is now ruled by a military junta which seized power in a bloody coup on September 11, 1973, in which the democratically elected Marxist President, Salvador Allende, was assassinated. It was revealed a year later that the U.S., through its CIA, helped finance the growing protests against Allende.

Who REALLY Rules—The military is in control, backed by and working with a wealthy elite having interests in industry, commerce, and finance. Only the rich are content with the current situation.

NOTES

Chile's largest single export is copper. The country's 3 major mines—Chuquicamata, El Teniente, and El Salvador—are estimated to contain about 40% of the world's total supply of copper. Chuquicamata itself is the biggest copper mine in the world, with reserves to last 100 years at present production rates. Dependence on one major export has hurt Chile. During the Allende years the country suffered a severe economic blockade, initiated and controlled largely by the U.S. Most international lending organizations and private banks withheld credits, at the insistence of the U.S. With limited alternative sources of national income, Chile could not buy the machinery, foodstuffs, and transportation equipment that it needed. The Allende Government received the blame for the inflation (about 300% for the 12-month period ending in June, 1973), the shortages of basic foods such as flour and oil, and the lack of spare parts, but actually the U.S. is heavily implicated in Chile's economic chaos. (Since the military took power, inflation has worsened and is headed toward 600%.) The military junta has received worldwide criticism for its continuing policy of torture, imprisonment without trial, and vengeful execution of Chileans who supported President Allende. In an attempt to counter this criticism, the junta hired the U.S. advertising firm of J. Walter Thompson, but the contract was terminated after one month because the firm received threats of violence against several of its overseas offices.

Chile's great length and range of latitudes make for tremendous diversity and variety in geography, climate, and scenery. From the Atacama Desert in the north, one of the world's driest, most desolate regions, where no rain has fallen in 400 years in some areas, to the far south, reminiscent of Norway with its fjords, glaciers, and mountain lakes, the country displays incredible beauty. A final touch is the Andes Mountains, which are almost never out of sight.

—E.P.

CHINA

NITTY GRITTY

Location—Largest Asian country, running 3,000 mi. from Mongolia and Soviet Siberia in the north to the south where it borders the South China Sea, North Vietnam, Laos, Burma, India, Bhutan, Sikkim, Nepal, and Pakistan; and 3,000 mi. from Afghanistan and the U.S.S.R. in the west to the Yellow and East China seas in the east.

How Created—Spanning 4,000 years of history, China has the longest continuous tradition of national identity, historically consisting of 2 distinct regions: China proper, with an inner core of Han Chinese settlement, culture, and political administration; and an outer ring of buffer territories, originally inhabited by non-Han peoples, but controlled by China proper.

European powers forced China to establish fixed boundaries in the 19th century, to China's disadvantage. Since the 1949 Revolution, China has reestablished authority over former outlying territories, sparking current border disputes with India and the U.S.S.R.

Size—3,691,500 sq. mi. (9,560,900 sq. km.). Slightly larger than the U.S.

Population—Over 900 million: Han, 94%; 53 other groups including Chuang, Uighur, Hui, Yi, Tibetan, and Miao, 6%. Religion is discouraged by the Government, but Confucianism, Buddhism, Taoism, and Islam still have a strong influence.

Who Rules—People's Congress of 3,040 members elected for 4-year terms: Provinces elect one deputy for each 800,000 inhabitants; municipalities one for every 100,000; ethnic minorities have 150 deputies; armed forces 120; overseas Chinese 30. Congress elects

Chairman and Vice-Chairman of country; but no elections since 1964, no convention since 1965, and no head of state since Liu Shao-ch'i was deposed in 1968.

Executive is the State Council, which controls the state through various ministries.

Who REALLY Rules—Struggling factions within the Chinese Communist party, particularly the faction headed by Premier Chou En-lai and other military leaders and elder statesmen.

The party selects the people's deputies, although the people do not ordinarily know who their deputies are, and the deputies may not represent the interests of the people. According to Chairman Mao, the political system of China is that of a people's democratic dictatorship. Although the constitution declares that the Government is responsible to the democratically constituted National People's Congress, in actuality the Government's policies are all decided by the party.

NOTES

Inflation does not exist in China. In fact, the prices of some foods actually decrease consistently.

The Chinese character differs from the Western and even some other Eastern characters in 3 major ways. First, the Chinese see the universe and its parts as a single whole versus the European schizophrenia which sees everything as either spiritual or physical. Second, the Chinese have always believed in the importance of social cohesion versus the strong individualism of the West. Third, unlike Europe, the U.S., and Japan, the Chinese have relied on civil versus military conquest. China has surely engaged in wars; but she has depended more often upon diplomacy and the obvious superiority of her culture to win her influence and friends among nations. The Chinese have historically esteemed the status of scholar, farmer, artisan, and merchant, in that order. Capitalist mercantilism has always been held lower in importance than knowledge and agriculture, almost the reverse of values in the U.S.

Antiquated agriculture accounts for 80% of China's output. Although the U.S. and China are about equal in area, China has less land (11% presently) suitable for cultivation to feed a population 4 times larger.

Chairman Mao has said that when "city and countryside are one, and no distinction exists between manual and intellectual labor, between urban workers and rural workers," China will have the basis for a truly utopian, egalitarian society. Consequently, since 1968, the Government has forced nearly half of the graduates of metropolitan middle schools, over 30 million youths, to the farm's to live with, teach, and learn from peasants. But the peasants don't like the extra mouths to feed. And many young graduates don't like the bleak future of farm life, so many escape with forged identities. But the Government continues the policy because it relieves the cities of the pressures of population and political dissent.

Chinese family structure has also changed from the original Confucian idea in which the father-guardian controlled the family's production, income, and expenses as well as all authority. Today each adult member of the family is theoretically given equal status. The communist revolution saw the old family system as a bulwark for private wealth, so the new regime pushed to transform the family from a hierarchy to a democracy in which children and women have the right to speak, make decisions, and even criticize.

The marriage law of 1950 advocates equality between men and women and abolishes family-arranged marriages while guaranteeing divorce. Day-care centers, canteens, and homes for the aged have been widely established, enabling women to participate in the productive, political, and scientific work of the country. Nearly half of the labor force of the agricultural communes is composed of women. Moreover, the very collectivization of land has deprived the male of opportunities to use land ownership for oppressing and exploiting women. Nevertheless, while wages and educational opportunities for women generally equal or exceed those for men, some inequalities that favor men still exist in agricultural communes, higher education, and in the upper echelons of the Communist party and People's Army. Men dominate leadership roles in the People's Republic because few older women escaped the pre-1949 oppression and because revolutionary and party committees are only partly made up of workers. Army members and political cadres, already reflecting the sexual bias of the older era, make up an entrenched and large part of many committees.

China tried the lawyer system in its courts from 1954 to 1957, but decided to let the individual be self-represented or be represented by a friend. "The procedures are so simple, they don't have all the technical procedures we do here," writes an American lawyer who recently visited Red China. Minor crimes are judged by people elected from the neighborhood block or village, major ones by regular courts. While the death penalty exists on the books for such crimes as murder, rape, sabotage, and crimes against the state, only one death sentence has been carried out in 13 years. A person sentenced to death is given 2 years to rehabilitate himself, after which the sentence is reviewed.

The Chinese don't have the concept of tort law that the Americans have. "How does one judge how much pain is worth?" the Chinese will ask. In an accident case, for example, the one responsible would be required to bring meals or cook for the victim and/or his family until the victim recovers.

In late 1973, 300 workers were charged with "aggravated hooliganism" and "anarcho-syndicalist deviationism" because they believed that factory committees should be controlled by the workers and not by the Communist party.

MINORITY REGIONS

Though they originally were comprised of non-Han Chinese, Manchuria, Inner Mongolia, Sinkiang, and Tibet have at various times formed the outer or buffer zone to China proper. Today, in order to restore China's traditional influence to actual political boundaries, the Red Chinese have taken over the outlying areas and set them up as autonomous regions. While it hasn't forced Chinese culture upon these areas, with the exception of Tibet, Peking has gerrymandered these regions' boundaries so they include at least half Han Chinese.

Tibet—An autonomous region with 1.3 million people, Tibert covers about 13% of the Chinese land area. As the highest and largest plateau on earth, the Tibetan highlands are the source of many of Asia's great rivers such as the Yangtze, Mekong, and Indus. The people are primarily farmers and nomadic herdsmen.

Before the Chinese take-over, Tibet was led by a holy man and king, the Dalai Lama. Both he and the Panchen Erdeni, another civil-religious leader, were generally confirmed by the Chinese Emperor. All the land was owned by less than 3% of the population: the noble families, feudal lords, and Buddhist monasteries. The remaining 90% were serfs; 5% were slaves. Nearly ⅓ of the male population at any one time were monks, most of whom had quasi-serf status.

After their successful revolution at home, the Chinese communists defeated the small Tibetan army in an effort to bring Tibet back into the fold. As a result, in 1957, the Dalai Lama agreed to come under the Chinese umbrella so long as the political structure and religious culture remained intact and the Chinese army remained outside. For their part, the Tibetan leaders promised to reform serfdom gradually. But the reform didn't come quickly enough for the Chinese, who finally invaded Tibet and took outright control in 1959. The Chinese freed the serfs and, with the exception of a few showplaces, converted the monasteries into granaries, barracks, prisons, and offices.

Today the Chinese army remains in Tibet as

an obvious military presence and as a service for the agriculture and grazing economy. The Peking Government has poured more capital and development projects into Tibet than its small population and economic return warrant in comparison with other provinces. Roads have been built to Lhasa and small-scale industries begun in the other small urban areas. Although all this effort helps secure China's border with India, pockets of resistance against the Chinese overlords still exist in Tibet's isolated upland valleys.

Inner Mongolia—North of the Great Wall is the sparsely populated, semiarid homeland of the nomadic groups who often surged southward across the steppe to invade the prosperous cities and fertile farmlands of old China proper. Today this homeland forms the autonomous regions of Inner Mongolia and Ningsia Hui.

The Mongol population, which now numbers only slightly over 2 million, is far outnumbered by the Han Chinese in the region. Since only a few Mongols can still depend solely upon the nomadic existence of animal husbandry for their livelihood, most also grow crops in settlements centering in a few irrigated river valleys and oases. Still others have been absorbed into the urban life of larger settlements, and a few still take up hunting and trapping to supplement their incomes. Most Mongolians believe in the Tibetan brand of Buddhism.

The Han Chinese of the region are concentrated in a narrow band just north of the Great Wall. They populate the numerous state farms Peking has established to supplement the animal husbandry industry and ensure ethnic Chinese dominion.

Sinkiang—is a vast autonomous region of deserts and high mountains, lightly populated—only 8 million—and largely undeveloped: an area well suited for China's nuclear and missile testings. Because it occupies a pivotal position in Central Asia, sharing an 1,800-mi. border with Russia, the Chinese have always tried historically to prevent the area from falling into hostile hands by controlling key caravan routes which still crisscross Sinkiang.

Uighuirs, a Turkic people, live in the oases of the region's desert, the Tarim Basin. Over the centuries they have built intricate systems of canals and dug wells to supply water for fields growing grains, fruit, vegetables, and cotton. Kazakh, Mongol, and Kirghiz nomads herd sheep, cattle, and horses to graze the rather dry grasslands of northern Sinkiang. Oil has been discovered here, however, so factories producing iron, steel, cement, farm machinery, fertilizers, and textiles have been opened

mostly in and around the chief city and capital of Urumchi.

During the '60s, Peking sent massive numbers of Han Chinese into the Production and Construction Corps, a paramilitary organization under the army, to develop Sinkiang. The corps was assigned land reclamation and water conservancy projects.

Kwangsi Chuang—The Chuangs, with 6.6 million people at the time of the last (1953) census, are China's largest minority group. Over 90% of them live in the Kwangsi Chuang Autonomous Region, where they comprise about ¼ of its total population. Because the region borders Indochina, the Chuangs and Han who are here share many of the cultural and economic traits found in the peoples of Vietnam and Cambodia: Most of the Chuangs depend upon rice cultivation for sustenance; in religion, they are animists, worshiping their ancestor spirits in particular.

—M.D.

COLOMBIA

NITTY GRITTY

Location—Northwest South America. Its neighbors are Brazil, Venezuela, Peru, Ecuador on the continent, and Panama in Central America.

How Created—Originally part of the viceroyalty of New Granada (along with present-day Peru and Ecuador), Colombia won its independence from Spain in 1819, through the efforts of Simón Bolívar. The loss of Panama occurred in 1903, when the U.S. and Colombia could not agree on terms for the construction and maintenance of a Central American shipping canal and the U.S. seized the area.

Size—439,737 sq. mi. (1,138,914 sq. km.).

Population—24 million: mestizo, 50%; mulatto, 25%; European, 20%; African, 4%; Indian, 1%. Mostly Roman Catholic with some Protestants and Jews.

Who Rules—A federal republic with separate executive, judicial, and legislative branches.

Who REALLY Rules—Often pointed out as a model Latin American republic capable of handling its own political problems, Colombia is actually run by an elite handful of politicians and businessmen who are members of its 2 political parties. The U.S. has large investments in petroleum, cattle, mining, sugar, and bananas. Colombia has received over $1 billion in U.S. economic assistance since 1961, so the U.S. is definitely a power in the country. U.S. investors include W. R. Grace & Company, ITT, IBM, Standard Oil of California, Phillips Petroleum, Dow Chemical, and Ralston Purina.

NOTES

Coffee is the principal crop and main export—67% in 1973. Colombia provides over 90% of the world's emeralds. Control over the emerald mines has recently been taken away from the local prospectors and traders, who have run the business for 50 years, and will be offered to a foreign company in an attempt to reduce the smuggling that erodes the government's profits.

The year 1948 marked the beginning of a decade of civil war which followed the assassination of populist leader Jorge Eliécer Gaitán. Two hundred and fifty thousand died during "La Violencia," as this period is known. It was particularly prevalent in the countryside, where villages that had been traditionally liberal or conservative were wiped out by invaders from the other party. The country was ruled by dictators until 1957, when the military ousted Gen. Rojas Pinilla and proposed a compromise solution—a 16-year period of constitutionally ordered alternation of parties in both elective and appointed offices, including the Presidency. By then, much of the rural violence had degenerated into banditry and unprovoked attacks, and a strong governmental effort was made to clear out isolated pockets of violence.

Colombia is the source of 80% of the counterfeit dollars passed in the U.S.—$1.3 million since 1967. It is not against the law to counterfeit U.S. dollars in Colombia.

—E.P.

CONGO

NITTY GRITTY

Location—In West Africa, on the equator, with a 100-mi. southwest coastline on the Atlantic Ocean. To the west, Gabon and Cameroon; to the north, the Central African Republic; to the east, Zaire.

How Created—Its modern-day borders outlined by the explorer Francesco de Brazza, it became part of French Equatorial Africa in 1910, under the name "Moyen Congo."

Size—132,000 sq. mi. (342,000 sq. km.).

Population—Over one million: Kongo, 45%; Teke, 20%; Bangi, 16%; Gabonese Bantu, 15%; others, 4%. 45% Animist, 40% Catholic, 15% Protestant.

Who Rules—The military, under Maj. Gen. Marien Ngouabi, head of state. The National Council of the Revolution holds legislative power. Since the coup of 1968, there is one political party, the National Revolutionary Movement.

Who REALLY Rules—The People's Republic of the Congo is a member of the European Economic Community, and receives a good deal of foreign aid from France. Communist China also pours a lot of money into the country.

NOTES

The name of the country has been a point of confusion for some time. In 1884 it was dubbed "Moyen Congo" by the French, after the Congo River which borders it. In 1960, when Moyen Congo got its independence, it did a strange thing: It took the very same name that its neighbor, the former Belgian Congo, had taken not 2 months earlier, on the occasion of *its* independence. The name, "Republique du Congo," serving 2 countries at once, led to the use of each nation's capital to distinguish them. The former Belgian Congo became Congo Republic (Kinsasha), and the former Moyen Congo became Congo Republic (Brazzaville). Now, the former has changed its name to Zaire, and the latter has become the People's Republic of the Congo.

—R.C.

COSTA RICA

NITTY GRITTY

Location—Central America. Nicaragua is to the north, Panama to the southeast. The Caribbean is to the east, the Pacific Ocean to the west.

How Created—Columbus touched the Caribbean shore of Costa Rica in 1502, on his 4th and last voyage to the New World. Food was scarce and the Spanish experienced considerable harassment from a number of fierce Indian tribes. No serious settlement occurred until the mid-16th century, and then only in the form of small farms. No large Indian population existed to act as slave labor for large plantations, and the area remained poor and isolated from the centers of Spanish administration. When the Central American countries declared their independence from Spain in 1821, Costa Rica joined them in the Central American republic. The republic collapsed in 1838, and Costa Rica became independent.

Size—19,650 sq. mi. (50,900 sq. km.).

Population—2 million: white (mostly Spanish), 80%; mestizo, 17%; Jamaican blacks, 2%; Chibcha Indians, 1%.

Who Rules—A republic with a President and unicameral legislature elected every 4 years. Costa Rica has had an orderly change of government in every election since 1948, when the current constitution was adopted. Costa Rica is considered one of the most honestly and democratically run countries in Latin America today, and a great friend of the U.S.

Who REALLY Rules—In the past, the foreign-owned banana exporters, such as United Brands (formerly United Fruit) and Standard Brands (a subsidiary of Castle & Cooke), in addition to the coffee exporters, have been a force in the country. However, in the 1970s, racketeers and capitalists speculating in Costa Rican land and resort facilities have become increasingly important. Robert Vesco, U.S. financier who is wanted in the U.S. and Europe on swindling and bribery charges, is the most flamboyant example of the group. His $3.5 million "loan" to then-President Figueres, plus the $10 million he holds in Costa Rican bonds, seems to have secured him against extradition to the U.S. Public outcry over Vesco's close ties to Figueres, and over his vast investment in Costa Rica's economy, has focused public attention on a growing problem.

NOTES

Costa Ricans have in the past generally extended a warm welcome to any and all foreign capital. Now, however, new public awareness of the extent of such investments may change the pattern for the future. The proposed Alcoa Aluminum processing plant has been the cause of some student protests.

Costa Rica's European life-style, Hispanic culture, and relaxed, tolerant attitudes have caused many North Americans to make the country their home. The Government welcomes most such foreigners, and has established procedures for granting them visas and citizenship. They are required to have some independent income, and may not take away jobs from Costa Ricans.

Costa Rica has accepted large numbers of refugees from a variety of sources. Chileans leaving the socialist Government of Salvador Allende went to Costa Rica, and after the military coup that overthrew Allende in 1973, his supporters also fled to Costa Rica.

Voting is compulsory for all citizens over 18. Failure to vote is punished by increasingly stiff fines. Women 1st voted in 1949.

—E.P.

CUBA

NITTY GRITTY

Location—Cuba lies on the north edge of the Caribbean, 90 mi. south of Key West, Fla. It is the most westerly of the West Indies.

How Created—Columbus discovered Cuba on October 28, 1492, on his 1st trip to the New World. In colonial times Cuba followed the usual pattern of the West Indies—the search for mineral wealth, decimation of the native population (of one million Ciboney Indians living on Cuba when Columbus arrived, virtually all were dead by 1600), importation of black slaves, exploitation of land and resources, raids by pirates.

On July 15, 1895, a rebel junta-in-exile in New York proclaimed Cuba a republic. The Spanish-American War followed, and Spain was forced to withdraw from Cuba. The U.S. established a military occupation government, which on May 20, 1902, relinquished power to an elected Cuban Government, headed by Tomás Estrada Palma. However, Cuba remained a trusteeship of the U.S. for 20 years, experiencing corresponding interference in Cuban affairs by the U.S.

Size—44,218 sq. mi. (114,524 sq. km.), including the Isle of Youth (Isle of Pines).

Population—9.3 million: European (mostly Spanish), 73%; mulatto, 15%; black, 12%. Also a sprinkling of Orientals. Mostly Roman Catholic.

Who Rules—A Council of Ministers.

Who REALLY Rules—Prime Minister Fidel Castro and other leaders of the Communist party. On the local level neighborhood organizations distribute various goods, provide services, and promote education and involvement on a personal level. "Popular tribunals" composed of neighbors and residents of a small local area have the power to sentence local offenders.

NOTES

Sugar was and is the backbone of Cuba's economy. Sugar and sugar products such as rum still earn over 80% of the country's foreign exchange, and Cuba is usually the world's biggest producer and exporter of sugar.

Son of a well-to-do sugar planter and a servant (whom his father later married after the death of his 1st wife), Fidel Castro was born in 1926. Educated as a child by the Jesuits and the Christian Brothers, he received his advanced education at the Colegio Belén in Havana. At the university, he 1st began to develop a political outlook. He was associated with a number of political groups, and also went to the Dominican Republic and Colombia to protest. In 1948 he married Mirtha Díaz Balart, of a conservative family. His own leanings toward the left led him to work with the Ortodoxo party, which opposed Batista. He was a member of the assembly, but after the Batista coup of 1952 he turned from the traditional political structure to armed opposition. In 1956 he led a small band of exiled students and professionals from Mexico to the Sierra Maestra mountains in Cuba. From then until

1959 he was continuously engaged in guerrilla warfare with the Government. He is a man of great personal charm and energy, and a charismatic leader who has the support of nearly all Cubans. People may complain of the bureaucracy or the red tape, but Castro himself receives no blame. A big man, over 6' tall, he has a commanding physical presence, and is renowned for his speechmaking ability, sometimes speaking for 8 hours nonstop.

In 1964, with the U.S. in the lead, the OAS (Organization of American States) voted political and commercial sanctions against Cuba. No hemispheric countries were to conduct any trade or other relations with Cuba. For many years the U.S. had supplied 90% of Cuba's imports; after the blockade, Cuba turned to the Soviet Union and Eastern European countries to buy goods. When the nation of Bangladesh was formed in 1971–1972 and starvation and malnutrition were widespread, the U.S. Government refused to send aid until Bangladesh agreed not to trade with Cuba.

—E.P.

CZECHOSLOVAKIA

NITTY GRITTY

Location—In the "heart of Europe" according to traditional descriptions; is roughly midway between Spain and Moscow, and between Britain and Greece. A landlocked country bordered by Germany, Austria, Hungary, Poland, and the U.S.S.R.

How Created—In the 6th century the westernmost of migrating Slavic tribes settled in the present area (a large plateau region with mountains on 3 sides); they became split into 2 peoples, Czechs and Slovaks, when the eastern half (Slovakia) was occupied in the 10th century by Hungarians (who stayed until 1918).

Size—49,373 sq. mi. (127,876 sq. km.), about the size of New York State.

Population—15 million: Czech, 65.1%; Slovak, 29.2%; Magyar, 4%; German, Polish, Ukrainian, Ruthenian, and others, 1.7%. 50% Roman Catholic, 7% Czechoslovak Church, 3% Lutheran.

Who Rules—Cabinet and Federal Assembly drawn from Communist, Socialist, and Catholic parties. Also 2 state governments, one for the Czech region and one for Slovakia, empowered to decide on all matters except foreign affairs, national economy and defense, and international trade.

Who REALLY Rules—A 3-part coalition: the Soviet Union (through its secret police, embassy, and army), Gustav Husak (moderate head of the Czechoslovak Communist party),

and some hardline Czechoslovak communists (the liberal ones were all purged by the Russians in 1969–1970).

NOTES

Czechs and Slovaks present a contrast, the latter tending to be more fiery and hence more willing to use arms to defend the country. Czechs tend to be more intellectual and fatalistic; they love debate and analysis, and much prefer to use words to arms as political weapons. Because of the simple origins of the country's leaders, the central role of culture, and the practical experience of vital democracy between the 2 World Wars, a "democratic mentality" pervades the people (especially the Czechs)—they utilize all opportunities, are effective organizers, and show a willingness to compromise. They try to look critically at every ruler's statements, and consider each action according to its human consequences. Comparing Czechoslovak students to American and West European students he had visited, Stephen Spender remarked:

> Their Western student colleagues lay stress on *aims and objectives*, whereas the Czechs tend to emphasize *the means* which should be used to achieve them. They have had bitter experience [the 1950s Stalinism] of how human and lofty ends can be [negated] by inhuman means. They understand the process by which a revolution may turn into the very things Western students are rebelling against: centralized authoritarian government, bureaucracy, censorship, boredom. [Thus] the Czechs give not only a feeling of here and now but also of having lived through terrible realities.

A very different side of their character is shown by their spokesman, the fictional Schweik, who humorously outwits a superior force by appearing to be too dumb to carry out his commands (or he carries them out to absurd extremes). This habit developed when the Czechs were still under Austrian rule (before 1918) and had to fight in the Emperor's army, though desiring his defeat and the end of Austrian domination. Jaroslav Hašek began writing his stories, *The Good Soldier: Schweik*, in 1920, and Czechs have imitated his pranks as their fallback strategy ever since.

—P.B.

DAHOMEY

NITTY GRITTY

Location—In the "hump" of West Africa, with a 70-mi. coastline along the Gulf of

Guinea. To the north, Niger; to the west, Togo; to the east, Nigeria; to the northwest, Upper Volta.

How Created—The ancient Kingdom of Dahomey was already centuries old when the Portuguese landed there in the 16th century. Today's borders are the result of late-19th-century rivalry between Britain and France.

Size—43,483 sq. mi. (112,620 sq. km.).

Population—3 million: Fon, 32.1%; Adja, 8.3%; Bariba, 6.6%; Yoruba, 6%; Aizo, 3.5%; Somba, 3.4%; Fulani, 2.6%; over 35 other groups, 37.5%. 64.8% Animist, 13.6% Muslim, 12.3% Roman Catholic, 2.5% Protestant, 6.8% other.

Who Rules—Political activity is banned and the constitution has been suspended ever since the military came to power.

Who REALLY Rules—France. Dahomey lacks the resources to build an independent and modern nation. France picks up the tab on road building, education, and communications, providing a subsidy to support the national development program and to help balance the budget. France buys about 75% of Dahomey's exports.

NOTES

The name Dahomey ("Dan-ho-mey") means "on the belly of Dan." Dan was a haughty native chieftain who threatened to eat King Ouegbadja of Abomey with the words, "You'll soon be building on my stomach." Ouegbadja, with a touch of irony perhaps, had Dan killed, devoured him himself, and built a palace upon his remains.

King Gezo (1818–1858), "the Redeemer of the Dahomeyan Empire," was a Fon warrior who, with 18,000 Amazons, fought the Yorubas and freed his countrymen from these harsh overlords. A harsh man himself, Gezo's palace walls were made of human skulls; nonetheless, he ended a cruel tradition by requesting that his family and retainers not be sacrificed upon his death and buried with him. He signed a treaty with France in 1851, but war between the 2 nations broke out 7 years later, at the end of Gezo's rule.

Scarification is still practiced in Dahomey. Young girls receive 12 sets of deep cuts which leave scars bearing ritual significance. Many of the cuts are intended to augment the sexual act. Among the standard cuts are parallel lines near the temples which become livid and pulsate when a woman falls in love, and numerous sets of scars to be caressed in sexual play, including 3 on the neck, several at the base of the spine, and 81 cuts on each inner thigh, called *zido*, or "push me" cuts.

—R.C.

DENMARK

NITTY GRITTY

Location—The southernmost of the Scandinavian countries, Denmark consists of the Jutland peninsula, 500 islands between the North Sea and the Baltic Sea, the 17 Faeroe Islands in the northern Atlantic Ocean, and Greenland (See: Greenland). Denmark proper is bordered on the south by West Germany.

How Created—From the 8th through the 11th centuries, the Vikings made Denmark a major power in Europe. During the 17th century, wars with Sweden resulted in the rollback of Denmark's eastern border to its current position. In the early 19th century, Denmark was forced to cede Norway to Sweden. In 1864, war with Prussia and Austria resulted in Denmark's loss of over ⅓ of her southern territory, but in 1920, Denmark recovered through a plebiscite a major portion of this territory.

Size—16,629 sq. mi. (43,069 sq. km.).

Population—5.1 million: almost 100% Scandinavian. 95% Lutheran.

Who Rules—Denmark is a constitutional monarchy ruled by Queen Margrethe II. The Parliament is unicameral and consists of 179 members who are elected at least every 4 years.

Who REALLY Rules—Denmark seems to be ruled by its elected representatives. There is no great individual personal wealth in Denmark. In the 1973 Parliamentary elections, ⅓ of the seats were won by parties which had never held seats before.

NOTES

In 1940, Nazi troops invaded Denmark and occupied that nation for 5 years. Danish citizens displayed exceptional bravery during the Nazi occupation. Danish Jews were protected from the Nazis and helped to escape from German-occupied territory. In 1944, Danish workers called a general strike and refused to be coerced into returning to work by Nazi ultimatums. It was not until after the Germans eased restrictions on Danish citizens that Danish workers returned to their jobs.

Denmark has pioneered in the field of socialized medicine. All students under the age of 16 get free medical and dental care. Medical payments for people over 16 are based upon earnings with the State absorbing remaining costs.

—M.G.

DOMINICAN REPUBLIC

NITTY GRITTY

Location—The Dominican Republic occupies the eastern ⅔ of Hispaniola, a Caribbean island lying between Cuba and Puerto Rico. (Haiti occupies the western end of the island.) Florida is 600 mi. to the northwest; Colombia and Venezuela lie 310 mi. to the south.

How Created—Columbus discovered the island in 1492, naming it "La Isla Española," later corrupted to Hispaniola. Although important in the settling of Spanish America, Santo Domingo (as the colony was called at that time) went into a steady decline after the mid-16th century, as many settlers soon emigrated to the continent. Santo Domingo proclaimed its independence November 30, 1821, but Haitian troops almost immediately invaded the colony. Santo Domingo was under a harsh and humiliating Haitian rule from 1822 until February 27, 1844, when Dominican patriots Juan Pablo Duarte, Ramón Mella and Francisco del Rosario Sánchez led the fight for independence. Although Dominicans celebrate February 27 as their Independence Day, over a century of foreign intervention, occupation, and attempted annexation have followed.

Size—18,816 sq. mi. (48,733 sq. km.).

Population—4.6 million: mulatto, 73%; white, 16%; black, 11%. 95% Roman Catholic, 2% Protestant, 3% Jewish and others.

Who Rules—In theory, a republic with a 1966 constitution providing for a President and bicameral legislature to be elected every 4 years. In fact, since independence, the Dominican Republic has been ruled by a succession of dictators. Latest is President Joaquín Balaguer, reelected to his 3rd term in May, 1974, in an election boycotted by half the electorate, protesting election fraud.

Who REALLY Rules—The U.S., both historically and through its present investment interests, has played a dominant role in Dominican affairs. Twice, from 1916–1924 and 1965–1966, the U.S. Marines have occupied the Republic. The Trujillo regime, while initially favored by the U.S., soon lost its popularity when the dictator began to compete with U.S. business interests through his own vast empire. (The Trujillo family is estimated to have controlled over ⅔ of the entire Dominican economy.) After Trujillo's assassination in 1961, a struggle for power began between those whom Trujillo had raised to prominence and the traditional elite. A 3rd group, composed of workers and peasants, managed to elect left-progressive Juan Bosch to the Presidency in 1962. The military deposed him in 1963, but in 1965 other, younger military officers attempted to reinstate him. The U.S. Marines landed, aiding the forces opposed to Bosch. New elections were engineered, resulting in the Presidency of Balaguer, who has managed to continue in office with massive U.S. aid and approval. (For a time after 1965, the U.S. paid the salaries of those on Dominican government payrolls.)

NOTES

U.S. business interests are very prominent: Falconbridge Nickel, a Canadian-based, U.S.-operated mining concern, has opened a $200 million mining/refining complex; Shell Oil is building a $30 million oil refinery; and Gulf & Western has extensive interests in sugar and tourism. In addition, the Dominican Government has established 4 "free zones" where U.S. firms may operate free of taxes for up to 20 years, while they exploit the $2 daily wage and the absence of unions. The country's official unemployment rate is around 30%, not including the cyclical unemployment or underemployment of the 80% of the work force engaged in the sugar industry.

Santo Domingo, capital of the Dominican Republic, boasts an impressive series of 1sts: Oldest city in the Western Hemisphere, it has the oldest cathedral, and its university was authorized in 1538, 13 years before that of Lima or Mexico City. The remains of Christopher Columbus lie in the cathedral. Santo Domingo also had the 1st mint and the 1st hospital in the New World.

There is a small group of English-speaking blacks living at Samaná, in the northeastern part of the island. They escaped from slavery in the U.S., and were settled there by the Dominican Government in 1824. For nearly 100 years they lived in near-total isolation. They still speak the English of the antebellum Deep South.

—E.P.

ECUADOR

NITTY GRITTY

Location—Ecuador lies on the equator (from which it derives its name) on the Pacific coast of South America. Its neighbors are Colombia to the north and Peru to the south and east. The Galápagos Islands, 600 mi. out in the Pacific Ocean, also belong to Ecuador.

How Created—Originally the northern part of the Incan Empire which extended south from Ecuador into Chile, the country was briefly part of the federation of Gran Colombia, whose freedom was achieved by Simón Bolívar in the early 19th century. Ecuador withdrew from the federation in 1830, and, through a series of border disputes with Peru, has lost nearly half of the original territory claimed by it.

Size—109,483 sq. mi. (283,561 sq. km.), about the size of Colorado.

Population—6.8 million: Indian, 40%; mestizo, 40%; black, 10%; European, 10% (mostly of Spanish descent). 44% Roman Catholic.

Who Rules—In form a classical republic, Ecuador has had a 150-year history of dictators, coups, countercoups, assassinations, and military rulers. Between 1931 and 1940 there were 12 different Presidents. The Government is currently headed by Gen. Guillermo Rodriguez Lara, who in 1972 ousted the elected President José María Velasco Ibarra, and canceled the upcoming elections.

Who REALLY Rules—Ecuador is in the hands of the country's very small Liberal/Conservative oligarchy, who control the land and the commerce in conjunction with U.S. business interests such as Texaco and Gulf. The military has long been a major political force: At present they control the Government, and have earmarked much of Ecuador's oil revenue for defense spending.

NOTES

The vast majority of the Indians live in the Sierra highlands and work the plantations, legally free but virtually in peonage to the hacienda owners due to debt. They are not paid cash but are permitted to use the master's land, and subsist outside the economy on less than 1,000 calories daily. Many speak Quechua, not Spanish, and most are denied the right to vote because they are illiterate. Even more primitive and isolated groups of Indians inhabit the Amazon jungle areas to the east of the Andes.

Quito, the capital city, with its red tile roofs, winding streets, and whitewashed buildings, is a perfect example of Spanish colonial architecture. It is the "City of Eternal Spring," almost on the equator but 9,000' above sea level.

The giant tortoises of the Galápagos Islands (*galápagos* is the Spanish word for the turtles) are the world's oldest living animals. They weigh 400 lbs., are 4' long, and may be 300–400 years old. Many other unique species are also found on these islands, described by Herman Melville as "5-and-20 heaps of cinders . . . magnified into mountains."

Ecuador's fishing grounds are guarded against U.S. poaching by American-made equipment which has been loaned or leased to the Ecuadorean navy.

—E.P.

EGYPT

NITTY GRITTY

Location—Egypt is in the northeast corner of the continent of Africa, bordered on the west by Libya, on the south by the Sudan, on the east by the Red Sea, the Gulf of Aqaba, and Israel. Its northern boundary is the Mediterranean shore.

How Created—Egypt has been defined for centuries by the Nile River. Its present shape and existence were affected by British occupation of Egypt in the 19th and 20th centuries, but certainly not created by the British. At present, large parts of the Sinai peninsula are under Israeli occupation as a result of the 1967 war.

Size—386,900 sq. mi. (1,002,000 sq. km.).

Population—38 million: Arab, 99.6%. 92.9% Muslim, 6.7% Christian, 0.4% other.

Who Rules—The President, currently chosen by the National Assembly and confirmed by plebiscite. The legislature, or National Assembly, has 350 members elected by universal suffrage and 10 who can be appointed by the President.

Who REALLY Rules—The Arab Socialist Union, Egypt's only political party. It is devoted to pan-Arabism and controls all seats in the National Assembly. The President heads and effectively controls the party. The political bureaucrats of the ASU are not responsible to an electorate.

NOTES

Egypt goes back 6,000 years—the longest history of any Western civilization, with the possible exception of Mesopotamia. The Pharaohs fused Egypt into one nation in 3200 B.C. and it continued to be ruled by a succession of dynasties until Alexander the Great conquered it in 332 B.C. This began wave after wave of outside conquerors who ruled the land: Romans, Persians, Islam-bearing Arabs, Turks—they all came and conquered. Then came Napoleon in 1798, whose conquest introduced the Western powers to the game.

The British and the Turks drove out the French in 1801–1805 and put up Mohammed Ali, Albanian by birth, who ruled as the 1st of the Khedive monarchy. After the opening of the Suez Canal in 1869, the British took greater interest and watched over the area with imperial-eagle eyes. When nationalist politics became too hot for her interests in 1882, Britain deposed the Egyptian leader, Ahmed Arabi, and took more control of the Government, finally making Egypt a protectorate in

1914. After independence in 1936, Britain stayed on as steward over the Suez Canal.

In 1948–1949 the Egyptian monarchy and other Arab states made war on the newly created state of Israel, but Israel defeated them. In 1952 the military overthrew the monarchy and Gamal Abdul Nasser became Egypt's leader. Nasser then set about to end British control of Egypt by forcing Britain to withdraw its troops from Egyptian territory and by nationalizing the Suez Canal.

When Egypt barred Israel from using the Canal, Israel, supported by France and Britain, invaded Egypt. But the Suez War was a failure for the invading forces, because the U.S. refused to support them and insisted that they withdraw. For Egypt, it meant the end of British domination and the opportunity to move out on an independent nationalist course under Nasser's leadership.

Subsequent wars have broken out between Egypt and Israel in 1967, during which Egypt lost Sinai and the Gaza Strip, and again in 1973.

The Suez Canal—the "richest ditch on earth"—connects the Mediterranean and Red seas. It cuts 103 mi. across the Suez isthmus. Both the isthmus and the Canal link Europe and Asia and because of this the area continues to be a world hot spot. It was built by the French and opened after 10 years' work in 1869. Giuseppe Verdi wrote *Aida* to celebrate the event. The British at 1st tried to block its building but once it was built they saw the Canal as a vital link to the Empire's interest in India, and so Prime Minister Benjamin Disraeli bought 43% of the Canal company's stock from the Egyptian monarch. The French-Anglo combine, Société Universelle du Canal Maritime de Suez, continued to own the Canal until Egypt nationalized it in 1956. Before the Canal was closed because of 2 recent Arab-Israeli wars, it had more than 10,000 ships pass through every year, more than twice that of the Panama Canal, many carrying oil from Saudi Arabia. The Suez Canal was reopened June 5, 1975.

It is difficult to do justice to the wonders of Egypt. Mediterranean beaches and elaborate tourist hotels in Cairo and elsewhere are touted by tourist agencies, but there is much more. The pyramids and the sphinx are surrounded by tourist trappings, yet must be seen. Particularly in early evening as one enters Cairo on the road from Alexandria, the looming dark massiveness of the pyramids is spectacular. The National Museum contains many wonders, including the treasures of the tomb of Tutankhamen. At Luxor and Karnak there are fabled ruins of ancient Egypt. However, the relics of the Islamic age should not be overlooked, especially in Cairo. Travel is restricted to cities and archaeological sites, so it is not possible to see the fellaheen (peasants) and come to understand them—except from train windows. For real mirages, the drive from Alexandria to Cairo is unsurpassed.

—M.D. & J.G.

EL SALVADOR

NITTY GRITTY

Location—Central America. Neighbors are: Honduras (north and northeast) and Guatemala (northwest). The Pacific Ocean is on the southwest.

How Created—An extensive Indian civilization had existed in the area since 3000 B.C. When Pedro de Alvarado invaded El Salvador in 1524, he was met by stiff Indian resistance. In 1525 he succeeded in conquering the Indians and he established San Salvador in 1528. During colonial times, the area was administered by the captaincy-general of Guatemala, but remained isolated and poor. Along with the other Central American Spanish possessions, El Salvador declared its independence from Spain in 1821. However, a Mexican attempt to absorb all the Central American states resulted in a unique request—El Salvador became the only Latin American country to request U.S. statehood. On November 22, 1822, the El Salvadorean Congress formally declared itself a State of the Union in an Act of Annexation. The U.S. Congress rejected the move, the Mexican Government fell, and El Salvador joined its neighbors in establishing the United Provinces of Central America. In 1838 the union collapsed, and El Salvador became an independent, sovereign state.

Size—8,260 sq. mi. (21,393 sq. km.).

Population—4 million: mestizo, 89%; Indian, 10%; white, 1%. 75% Roman Catholic.

Who Rules—El Salvador is a republic with a 1962 constitution, which provides for a President and bicameral legislature.

Who REALLY Rules—Since the 1940s the military, in conjunction with the PNC (Party of National Reconciliation), has been in effective control of the Government. Backbone of the PNC is the "14 families" who control most of the wealth and power of El Salvador. Conservative, they seek to maintain the status quo, and vigorously resist any social, political, or economic reform.

NOTES

Although called the Soccer War, the World Soccer Cup competition was only a spark to the long-smoldering tensions between El Salvador and Honduras that erupted into a 5-day war in 1969. Large-scale migration from crowded El Salvador to relatively empty Honduras, plus economic discrimination against Honduras via the Central American Common Market (CACM), were important contributing factors. At least 2,000 died on both sides, and the economies of both countries are still feeling the effects.

Leftist guerrilla groups continue to operate in El Salvador, despite government efforts to suppress them. Shortly after his inauguration, President Arturo Molina carried out a "purge" of the National University in San Salvador, claiming that it had "fallen into the hands of communists." The rector and the governing council of the university were arrested, along with about 50 students. Thirty-seven foreign professors were asked to leave the country. The university has long been a leftist intellectual center.

—E.P.

ETHIOPIA

NITTY GRITTY

Location—Near the extreme eastern bulge of Central Africa. The Sudan forms its western boundary, the Red Sea its northern, and Kenya its southern boundary. To its east are the Somali Republic and the French Territory of the Afars and the Issas.

How Created—As the ancient Abyssinian Empire, Ethiopia dates from biblical times. The recent monarchy traced its origin to the Queen of Sheba and King Solomon. Conquered by Italy in 1936 and liberated 5 years later, Ethiopia added the former colony of Eritrea in 1952 and made it a province in 1962.

Size—471,800 sq. mi. (1,221,900 sq. km.), about as big as France and Spain combined.

Population—27 million: Galla, 33%; Amhara, 25%; Tigre, 12%; Walamo, 8%; Somali, 6%; Gurage, 4%; Afar-Saho, 3%; Sidamo, 3%; other, 6%. 55% Coptic Christian, 35% Muslim, 10% Animist.

Who Rules—The Provisional Military Administrative Council which deposed Emperor Haile Selassie in 1974.

Who REALLY Rules—The military is supported by student groups and sometimes by the Coptic Church.

NOTES

Enter Ethiopia and you enter the Middle Ages—at least until very recently. Known to his subjects as the "Lion of Judah," "King of Kings," and the "Elect of God," its Emperor was one of the world's only living examples of an absolute monarch. Ethiopia's society was a classic feudal state with the royal family, feudal lords, and the Church controlling the land and life of the people. The Amharas, the

landowning, aristocratic class, collected 90% of their tenants' harvest. In Hararge, Ethiopia's largest province, 75% of the land was owned by 1% of the people. In March, 1975, the military Government announced the nationalization of all rural land, and banned the use of hired labor.

Haile Selassie tried to lead his subjects to a limited form of democracy and agrarian reform, but it was cosmetic rhetoric. After all, such a move ran against the interests of his own class. Reform came too slowly for the military, students, and professionals, who at 1st struck for higher wages but eventually toppled the monarchy. (Among striking groups were the capital's 50,000 prostitutes. As guardians of the people's "happiness and well-being," they demanded a minimum fee of $10.)

During the spring and summer of 1974, the military jailed some of the biggest landowners, bureaucrats, and imperial aides in a fairly bloodless coup and dragged the "King of Kings" out of his Jubilee Palace in a blue VW police car amid students' shouts of "Thief, thief." He was, evidently, no longer the "Elect of God."

The Coptic Church has kept Christianity alive in a sea of pagan and Muslim hostility for over 1,500 years. The institution has changed little in that time, gathering both power and land. It obliges the people to fast 180 days of the year and commemorates so many saints' days that between feasting and fasting very little work gets done. This is particularly true in the rural areas, where it wields its greatest power.

Eritrea

Location—Ethiopian province along the Red Sea.

Size—45,400 sq. mi. (117,600 sq. km.).

Population—2 million of mixed Arab-black stock.

NOTES

During the 19th century, the Amharas conquered adjoining Muslim lands and imposed their language and government. Part of Eritrea, the Roman name for the land around the Red Sea, has been under intermittent Ethiopian control. This part was the Kingdom of Tigre in the central mountains. Tigre is part of the Ethiopian plateau and its people are Christian. Because they have participated in Ethiopian culture for over 1,000 years, most Tigreans believe Eritrea is a lost province of Ethiopia. However, that part of Eritrea right along the Red Sea, in the north and west of the province, has been traditionally Muslim. These people have fought any union with Ethiopia and want Eritrea to be an independent state. After

W.W. II, however, the UN decided Eritrea should federate with Ethiopia: Eritrea would handle local affairs while Ethiopia would handle external ones like defense and foreign affairs. In 1962 Ethiopia canceled Eritrea's autonomy and made her a province. Eritreans meanwhile, having enjoyed greater political freedoms under British and Italian colonial rule, weren't about to be returned to the Middle Ages. So separatists formed the ELF, the Eritrean Liberation Front, made up of both Christians and Muslims. Over a decade of guerrilla fighting exploded into major battles in early 1975, resulting in over 6,000 deaths. The fighting continues.

—R.C.

EXXON

NITTY GRITTY

Location—Headquarters at 1251 Avenue of the Americas in New York City.

How Created—Exxon is a direct descendant of the Standard Oil Company of Ohio, the corporation John D. Rockefeller started in 1870, 5 years after he began refining oil in Cleveland. By 1878 Standard Oil, in collusion with other Rockefeller companies, controlled about 85% of the country's oil industry. They achieved this control by monopolizing almost every transportation facility in the oil regions of the country. In 1881 Rockefeller formed the Standard Oil Trust to own the stock of Standard Oil's various companies, but the courts ordered the trust dissolved in 1892 as the result of a suit filed by the State of Ohio. In 1899 Rockefeller created the Standard Oil Company of New Jersey as the holding company for all the separate units which the Standard Oil Trust had been forced to yield up. By 1907 the new company controlled 67 companies in all phases of the oil industry. The Supreme Court found the new trust to be in violation of the Sherman Anti-Trust Act and ordered it broken up in 1911. Today 3 of the "7 sisters"—the world's largest oil companies—are products of that split: Exxon, Standard Oil of California (Chevron), and Mobil Oil. Another, Standard Oil of Indiana (American Oil), ranks a close 8th.

Size—The world's largest industrial corporation, Exxon operates in over 100 noncommunist countries throughout the world. Its principal properties in the western hemisphere are in Texas, Louisiana, and Illinois, but it also has major production facilities in the Canadian provinces of British Columbia and the Northwest Territories, and in Venezuela and Colombia. In the eastern hemisphere Exxon owns 200 million acres (much of it in deep water) in 37 countries, and in 1973 it acquired interest in another 95 million acres including property in Egypt, France, Guinea-Bissau, Indonesia, Mali, Mauritania, Niger, Norway, Portugal, South Vietnam, and Spain. The company and its subsidiaries have 69 refineries in 37 countries on 6 continents, and its products travel the 7 seas in over 200 company-owned tankers and more than 140 chartered tankers.

Population—145,000 employees.

Who Rules—Day-to-day policy decisions are made by officers who are elected by a 16-member all-male board of directors that includes 10 officers. The directors are elected by 722,549 stockholders owning 223,867,276 shares.

Who REALLY Rules—Ownership of the company is usually thought to be concentrated in the Rockefeller family. However, since ownership figures are not public, the current Rockefeller percentage is not available. Exxon directors sit on the boards of the 4 largest New York banks, including David Rockefeller's Chase Manhattan Bank. Since the banks' trust departments own large blocks of stock, Exxon management helps decide the policy of the stockholders who determine Exxon policy.

NOTES

Exxon operates 1,240 Signal Gas stations on the West Coast of the U.S.; it purchased them from Standard Oil of California in 1967. In the past the company's brand names have included Esso, Enco, Enjay, and Humble. Exxon also makes Atlas Bucron tires.

Tax laws have made it profitable for Exxon to charge artificially high prices for crude oil. The oil depletion allowance has permitted Exxon to subtract from its gross income before taxes an amount equal to 22% of its total revenues from crude oil production, up to 50% of the firm's net pretax income. The company thus has had an incentive to charge high crude prices and, since crude prices are a cost to the company's refineries, thereby reduce their refinery profits. Exxon benefits because the depletion allowance reduces the tax on crude oil profits, and the artificially low refinery profits result in lower taxes on refinery operations. Since Exxon consolidates the finances of its production and refinery operations, its low refinery profits actually help the company make more money than if the refinery profits were normal (and higher), and the crude profits were normal (and lower). However, independent refineries that have no crude production of their own are hurt by Exxon's high crude prices. The independents have not been able to take advantage of the oil depletion allowance because they have no crude production. Exxon can thus force the independents out of business by raising its crude prices high enough to make the independents' refinery operations unprofitable.

—H.B.

FINLAND

NITTY GRITTY

Location—Part of the Scandinavian peninsula. Norway borders the north; the Soviet Union the east; Sweden and the Gulf of Bothnia on the west and the Gulf of Finland on the south.

How Created—Settled 5,000 years ago by peoples who came from Russia, Scandinavia, and Central Europe. They were divided into 3 groups which are still the main ethnic divisions: the Tavastians who entered by way of the Gulf of Finland; the Karelians who came from the southeast; and the Nordics who occupied the coast and the archipelagoes. Glacial movement was important in the creation of Finland and the country is still scattered with glacial debris. Finland lost 1/10 of its land to the U.S.S.R. following a war in 1939–1940.

Size—130,129 sq. mi. (337,032 sq. km.), about the size of New England, New Jersey, and New York combined.

Population—4,900,000: Finnish, 92.4%; Swedish, 7.4%; Russian and others, 0.2%. 92.5% Lutheran.

Who Rules—The legislative powers rest in a Parliament of 200 members elected every 4 years. Representation of each party is determined by the proportion of total votes' cast in these regular elections. The President is elected for 6 years. He appoints a Council of State (Cabinet) which is responsible to the Parliament. Finland is divided into 12 counties under the supervision of governors appointed by the President. The counties are further subdivided into rural and urban districts. A Chancellor of Justice is the highest judicial authority and there is a Supreme Court which appoints the circuit judges together with 4 Courts of Appeal.

Who REALLY Rules—A coalition of several political parties with much care taken not to offend the Soviet Union too much. Per capita, Finland has more consumer cooperatives than any other country in the world. Forestry is the most important natural resource and 62.7% of the forest area is owned by private farmers; the State owns 28% and private companies own 7.1%. The remaining 2.2% is owned by communes.

NOTES

Finland has 55,000 lakes. Approximately 72% of the country is covered with forests and

Finland is the world's foremost producer of plywood, the 2nd largest producer of paper products, and the 3rd of paper pulp.

—E.K.S.

FRANCE

NITTY GRITTY

Location—In Western Europe, bordered on the northwest by La Manche (the English Channel), on the north by Belgium and Luxembourg, on the east by West Germany, Switzerland, Italy, and Monaco, on the south by Spain, Andorra, and the Mediterranean, and on the west by the Atlantic Ocean.

How Created—In 52 B.C. Julius Caesar defeated Vercingetorix, the Gallic ruler, and Gaul became Roman. Less than 2 centuries later, the 1st major invasions reached the Rhine. The invaders called themselves Franks.

Roman Gaul fell in 273 A.D. and Northern Gaul became the Land of the Franks.

By the 5th century, the map of present-day France was practically drawn. The barbarians divided the territory among themselves against a Gallic-Roman background: Franks in the north, Burgundians in the east, Visigoths in the south. They made war frequently among themselves.

The Britons who were chased out of Great Britain by the Angles and the Saxons formed Brittany in the west.

In 800 A.D. Emperor Charlemagne created a single European state whose capital was Aix-la-Chapelle (today, Aachen in Germany). After his death in 814 his sons split up the Empire: In the east, Louis the German created Germania; in the center, Lothaire took over Lotharingia (with Burgundy, Alsace, Lorraine, Luxembourg, and what is Belgium today); in the west, Charles the Bald took over Western Francia.

In 911, after a century of savage incursions, the Vikings (Normans or "North Men") gained control of Normandy (from which they conquered England in 1066). In exchange, they agreed to become French.

In 987, the divided Frankish leaders in the west at last elected a King, Hugues Capet. Hugues Capet is considered to be France's 1st King. The Capetian family and then the Bourbons ruled France, directly or indirectly, until the Revolution of 1789 and even after that date. (There was a royal restoration in 1815, after Napoleon the 1st, which lasted until 1848 and Napoleon III.)

Size—212,742 sq. mi. (551,000 sq. km.).

Population—53 million: French, 85.8%; Alsatian and Lorrainer, 2.7%; Breton, 2.4%; Italian, 2.2%; other, 6.9%. 88% Roman

Catholic, 1.5% Protestant, 1.1% Jewish, 1% Muslim, 8.4% other or no religion.

Who Rules—A presidential régime, set up by De Gaulle after his return to power (1958–1969). Successors: Pompidou (1969–1974), and Giscard d'Estaing (1974–   ). There are 2 Chambers (Chamber of Deputies and the Senate) which have relatively limited powers. Giscard d'Estaing represents the modern European liberal wing of the Right, of which Pompidou and De Gaulle were the traditionalist, nationalist representatives.

Who REALLY Rules—The country is run by the large capitalist companies on the one hand (many of which are multinationals and have supported Giscard d'Estaing officially), and by a technocratic planning administration on the other hand. This double, contradictory direction allows French capitalism to apply one of its most significant theories: to be capitalist for the profits and socialist for the losses. (The State rarely lets the important businesses "fall"; it intervenes because of employment or for prestige, as in the case of the supersonic "Concorde.")

The key Ministers and important officials graduate from the École Nationale d'Administration (ENA), a supertechnocratic school. Upon graduation ENA students divide up into those who back the régime in power, and those who want to "change life" (slogan of the Socialist party whose Brain Trust also comes out of the ENA). People talk about "Enarchie"; they watch to see who will become the next president of the school's Alumni Association in order to learn whether or not France will become socialist.

NOTES

In May, 1968, a group of students at the University of Nanterre (Paris) rebelled against the educational system. They paralyzed the university and started to build another one in its place, a free university. This spontaneous movement shut down France for a month while solidarity grew between the people and the students being attacked by the police. Barricades were set up in the Latin Quarter; there was a general strike and the prevailing powers were forced to retreat. De Gaulle resigned some time later. The explosion of new ideas of May, 1968, is conditioning French political life today (i.e. giving the vote to 18-year-olds, an abortion law, workers' self-management, etc.). The conflict concerning the LIP watch factory (1973–1974) can be explained by May, 1968: Without respecting the union leadership, the employees seized the factory which was close to going bankrupt, continued production, sold stock, negotiated directly with the financiers

and the Government, and the business got going again.

Almost 50% of the French voted for a socialist President in 1974. The Government of Giscard d'Estaing felt the reality of its near defeat (0.8%) and quickly set up a legislative system which applied a number of measures that the socialists were asking for. They:
—gave 18-year-olds the right to vote
—offered free contraception
—legalized abortion
—passed reform laws concerning women
—liberalized the state-monopolized radio-television media

At the same time, the Government announced it was going to:

—end official telephone wiretaps
—stop censoring the news and stop seizure of newspapers
—permit associations to be formed and meetings to be held freely
—stop keeping files on people (There are files kept on 8 million people in France; the "Jewish File" of the Gestapo still exists.)

But the French are still waiting for:

—the end of "arrest on sight." A person can be arrested for 24 hours (or more if it is for state security) without having the right to let anyone know about it.
—the end of "preventative" detention (being put in prison before being sentenced or even tried).
—the end of police corruption. Identification cards are not mandatory, but if a person does not have one he or she can be arrested for "verification."
—the end of secret house searches without a search warrant.
—the end of secret judicial orders.

They are also waiting for humane, democratic legislation of the habeas corpus type, that is in the interest of the 3 million foreigners (800,000 Algerians, 700,000 Portuguese, plus Spanish, Yugoslavians, Moroccans, Senegalese, Turks, etc.) who make the French factories operate.

—M.C.

GENERAL ELECTRIC

NITTY GRITTY

Location—Headquarters at 570 Lexington Avenue, New York, N.Y. 10022, and in Schenectady, N.Y.

How Created—GE was incorporated in 1892, combining Thomas Edison's company with other electrical firms. The rest of GE's history consists of worldwide expansion—the acquisition of countless foreign and domestic manufacturing corporations, electronic services, broadcasting stations, etc.

Size—GE has 215 manufacturing plants in the U.S., 80 manufacturing plants in 20 other countries, and more than 100 laboratories throughout the world.

Population—390,000 employees.

Who Rules—GE is a highly decentralized company with over 300 operating departments and service components. Each of these departments is run as if it were a separate company, but the departments are organized into 10 operating groups with about 60 managers who oversee the performance of the departments. Overall company policy is determined by the corporate executive officers who are elected by a 19-member board of directors that includes the 4 top officers and the chairmen or presidents of 13 major corporations and banks. The board of directors is elected by 530,000 stockholders owning 182,147,498 shares.

Who REALLY Rules—The Chase Manhattan Bank owns the largest share of GE stock and voting rights (8.2%, $425 million worth). The Morgan Guaranty Trust owns the 2nd largest share ($325 million worth).

NOTES

Women at GE generally hold the most boring and repetitious jobs, as well as the lowest paying. Of the 105 top executives in the company, none are women.

Over $1 billion in tax dollars goes to GE each year for military and related work. The company makes excessive profits on this aspect of production, often 50–100% above the average profits for domestic consumer production. For the Indochina war GE produced major components of the F-4 Phantom fighter-bomber, including the J-79 jet engines, the 20-mm Vulcan cannon, a TV display panel for guiding Walleye "smart" bombs, automatic fire control systems, and electronic countermeasures. The company also produced electronic countermeasures for B-52 and F-105 bombers, an aircraft mini-gun and other aircraft armaments, and components for the "people-sniffer" chemical sensor.

—M.S. & H.B.

GENERAL MOTORS

NITTY GRITTY

Location—Headquarters in Detroit, Mich., where it has 9 plants. It has 10 plants in Flint, Mich.

How Created—William C. Durant, who had headed the nation's top carriage and wagon-making firm before the rise of the motorcar,

formed GM as a holding company in 1908, to purchase the stock of his Buick Motor Company. In the next 2 years GM bought out 25 separate companies, including Cadillac, Olds, and Oakland, which later became Pontiac. Following a period of financial difficulties, during which Durant temporarily lost control of the corporation, Durant changed GM into an operating company and sought financing from the Du Pont family and its corporations.

Though GM's early history was characterized by consolidation, it also "spun off" other major manufacturers. In 1917 GM president Charles Nash rambled off to form his own company, and in 1920 GM vice-president Walter Chrysler quit the company, and eventually formed the Chrysler Corporation.

Size—The world's 2nd largest industrial corporation, GM maintains operations in 30 countries, but is centered and headquartered in the U.S., where it has 100 plants in 67 cities.

Population—810,920 employees.

Who Rules—GM's day-to-day major policy decisions are made by its officers, who are elected by a 24-member board of directors, which includes 6 present officers and 3 past officers. The directors are elected by 1,283,260 stockholders owning 285,730,153 shares.

Who REALLY Rules—Major differences between management, the directors, and larger stockholders never occur, so it is difficult to determine real control. Residual power, however, lies with the big stockholders. Institutions, such as bank trust departments, own large blocks of stock, as do members and associates of the Du Pont family.

In 1972 GM refused to turn over a list of its large stockholders to a Senate subcommittee, so there is no public information on the size of institutional or Du Pont stockholdings. But presently 9 members of the board of directors are also directors of commercial banks.

NOTES

In GM's early years the corporation refused to recognize its employees' right to unionize. The UAW won recognition from GM only after the bloody, 44-day Flint, Mich., sitdown strike of 1937.

During W.W. II GM converted its assembly lines to war production, not only in the U.S., but in (and for) Nazi Germany as well! After the war GM had the nerve to sue the U.S. Government for wartime damages to its German facilities.

GM destroyed most of the nation's urban rail transit during the 1930s, 1940s, and early 1950s, by buying and then dismantling over 100 electric railway (streetcar) systems in 45 cities, including New York, Los Angeles, and

Philadelphia. GM converted all these systems to bus lines.

In 1965 a lawyer named Ralph Nader challenged the safety of GM's Corvair. GM not only denied Nader's charges, but it hired a private detective to "dig up dirt" on Nader's personal life. The ensuing scandal propelled Nader into his present position as America's leading "consumer advocate."

—H.B. & L.S.

GERMANY

NITTY GRITTY

Location—In the heart of North Central Europe. Before the division into East and West in 1945, Germany shared borders with Denmark, Holland, Belgium, Luxembourg, France, Switzerland, Austria, Czechoslovakia, Poland, and Russia.

How Created—Native tribes wandered largely at will between 400 and 800 A.D., until Charlemagne unified several tribes with his own Franks. This federation eventually came to be known as the Holy Roman Empire of the German Nation, the First Reich. For the next thousand years, Germanic peoples were organized in kingdoms and duchies loosely controlled by an Emperor, most notably those from the Hapsburg dynasty. Between 1740 and 1790 the state of Prussia grew phenomenally under King Frederick II. When Napoleon dissolved the Holy Roman Empire in 1806, the 2 German-speaking states of Prussia and Austria vied for control of the remaining states. Under the skillful leadership of its Chancellor, Otto von Bismarck, Prussia decisively won the allegiance of member German states when it defeated France in the war of 1870–1871. The Second German Reich was proclaimed in 1871 with the Germanic competitor state of Austria excluded from the union. The Second Reich lasted until 1918, when Germany was defeated in W.W. I. Hitler founded the Third Reich in 1933, claiming it too would last 1,000 years, but it collapsed in 1945.

When Hitler committed suicide on April 30, 1945, the victorious W.W. II Allies occupied Germany according to plans largely determined at the February, 1945, conference at Yalta and reaffirmed at the Potsdam meeting the following July.

The Federal Republic of Germany (West Germany) was proclaimed in May, 1949, from the lands occupied by France, Britain, and the U.S. Full independence was granted by the Allies in 1955.

In retaliation to the establishment of West Germany, the Soviet Union allowed its sector of Germany to call itself the German Democratic Republic in October, 1949. Five years later, in 1954, the Soviet Union issued a proclamation constituting East Germany a sovereign republic.

East Germany

Size—41,748 sq. mi. (108,178 sq. km.), somewhat larger than Ohio.

Population—17,900,000: German, 98.5%; Sorb, 1.5%. 81% Protestant, 12% Roman Catholic, 7% other.

Who Rules—The *Volkskammer* or People's Chamber which is unicameral. It has 434 members elected by universal suffrage for 4-year terms. In addition, there are 66 nonvoting representatives from East Berlin. The Chamber elects the Council of State, the Council of Ministers, the National Defense Council, and the judges of the Supreme Court.

The Council of State consists of a chairman, 6 deputy chairmen, 16 members, and a secretary. It has the authority to issue decrees and decisions which have the force of law and it may interpret laws.

Who REALLY Rules—The East German Communist party, known as the *Sozialistische Einheits Partei* (the Socialist Unity Party). Behind the scenes, but not very far behind them, is the Government of the Soviet Union. There are "free" elections but generally only one candidate on the ballot. Second parties are not permitted. Occasionally party candidates have competition from same-party candidates and therefore inefficient and ineffectual party functionaries *can* be removed from office.

West Germany

Size—96,094 sq. mi. (248,882 sq. km.), about the size of Oregon.

Population—62 million: German, 98.7%; Italian, 0.4%; others, 0.9%. There are 2 million foreign workers, primarily from Greece, Turkey, Italy, and Yugoslavia. 49% Protestant, 44.6% Roman Catholic, 6.4% other.

Who Rules—The Federal Parliament which is bicameral, consisting of the Federal Diet (*Bundestag*) and the Federal Council (*Bundesrat*). Members of the Diet are elected for a 4-year term; members of the Council are deputies of the governments in their respective states (*Länder*). The office of the President is insignificant compared to that of Chancellor, who is chosen by members of the majority party in the Federal Diet.

The equivalent of the U.S. Supreme Court is broken down into a series of supreme courts for different case categories, e.g. for constitutional and jurisdictional questions, the court is in Karlsruhe; for labor problems, in Kassel; for fiscal matters, in Munich.

Who REALLY Rules—Since the departure of Konrad Adenauer, the 1st and continuous Chancellor of the Federal Republic of Germany from its inception in 1949 to 1963, a coalition of forces has controlled Germany. During the Adenauer period it was indeed Chancellor Adenauer who ruled. The Germans have always liked strong, personal, authoritarian rulers and Adenauer was such a man. Since then, the coalition has wielded power. Big business and finance are strong partners in the coalition. Labor unions are relatively weak and undemanding.

Agriculture is a larger partner in the coalition than the principle of one-man one-vote would call for, but the Germans tolerate this in part because they subconsciously think back to the post-W.W. II days when there was nothing to eat. A great many Germans are overweight—indicating perhaps that big appetites permit the small agricultural minority to rule.

NOTES

No other country in the world has harbored such thorough militarism nor fielded such splendid armies (except perhaps France under Napoleon) nor won such sweeping military campaigns. Nor has any other country ever suffered such total defeat. Germany lost both of the world's 2 global wars—but unlike the majority of her conquerors, it arose each time mightier after defeat than before, reconquering economically the countries which it could not defeat militarily.

Germany has a special banking arm of the Government which enforces a policy of "Equalization of burdens." Accordingly, if someone had his house destroyed during the war he was entitled to credit for rebuilding. Those whose structures were spared had to pay a special "tax" to establish capital for those who needed to rebuild.

The 1st interstate highway system in the world was the German *Autobahn*, a 4-lane roadway system started by Hitler in the mid-1930s as a work relief program for the jobless. Its ostensible purpose was a public motorized-traffic network, but its real purpose was the rapid movement of arms and armies. The Pennsylvania Turnpike planners studied the *Autobahn* before introducing the same type of highway system in the U.S.

In 1933 there were 530,000 Jews in Germany. In 1946 the figure stood at 180,000 of which the great majority have since emigrated so that there are at most 30,000 left in Germany today, largely in Berlin.

—L.V.J.R.

GHANA

NITTY GRITTY

Location—In the "hump" of West Africa, with a 300-mi. southern coastline along the Gulf of Guinea. To the north, Upper Volta; to the east, Togo; to the west, Upper Volta and Ivory Coast.

How Created—Borders are arbitrary, resulting from a long series of battles among kingdoms, colonists, and natives. Prior to independence, Ghana was the British colony of Gold Coast.

Size—92,100 sq. mi. (238,539 sq. km.).

Population—10 million: Akan, 44.1%; Mossi-Dagomba, 15.9%; Ewe, 13%; Ga-Adangme, 8.3%; Guima, 3.5%; Yoruba, 1.6%; 70 other tribes, 13.6%. 38.2% Animist, 29% Protestant, 13.8% Roman Catholic, 12% Muslim, 7% other religion or no religion.

Who Rules—The military. Ghana's republican constitution has been "temporarily suspended."

Who REALLY Rules—Cocoa. Struggling to get out of a deep national debt, Ghana has borrowed considerable amounts of money, mostly interest-free, from the U.S., Britain, France, and other Western nations, and has relied on technical and financial assistance from the U.S.S.R., China, and East European countries, in an effort to establish an independent economy based on modern industries. So far, it has been unable to build up a sound economy, and remains indebted to foreign governments. Meanwhile, the economy is based on the cocoa crop, all of which is purchased by the Ghana Cocoa Marketing Board, whose sales offices are based in London.

NOTES

The name "Ghana" was adopted by nationalists in the 1950s, in the hopes of emulating the wealth and splendor of the ancient Black Kingdom of Ghana, which flourished from the 5th to the 12th century. The original empire was reputedly a place of scholarship and learning, rich, pompous, and ceremonious, stretching from Timbuktu to Bamako.

Cocoa, the nation's only important crop, is not a native of Ghana. The 1st cocoa pod was imported by an African blacksmith in 1879. For a time there was only one cocoa tree in all of Ghana. It grew and multiplied, and gave birth to the world's largest center of cocoa farming.

Ghanaian society is matriarchal and matrilineal. Women have been the workers by tradition, while men have engaged in politics and war, music and the arts. Now both men and women work as teachers, office workers, doctors, lawyers, creative artists, and government officials, with almost no sex discrimination in jobs.

"Market women" control the country's produce trade. The women travel to market at dawn, via "mammy wagons," small trucks with seats. Men may ride only after all the women have been seated. In Accra the women have their own Marketing Board in a modern government building.

At marriage a Ghanaian woman receives a sum of money from her husband; it is hers to invest or spend as she sees fit, accounting to no one. She handles her own finances and is responsible for her own wealth.

Tribal power passes through the mother's line, a son inheriting from his mother's brother.

No whites may own land in Ghana and settlements by Europeans are forbidden.

—R.C.

GREAT BRITAIN

NITTY GRITTY

Location—An island off the northwest coast of Europe, consisting of England, Scotland, and Wales. Also the Channel Islands in the south, the Orkney and Shetland Islands in the north, and the Isle of Man in the west.

How Created—Originally inhabited by Celts, Britain was invaded by the Romans in 55 B.C. and eventually made a Roman province. When the Romans withdrew in 442 A.D., the island was besieged by various invaders and settlers including the Jutes, the Saxons, and the Angles (whose gods Twi, Woden, Thunor, and Frigg have survived to this day as Tuesday, Wednesday, Thursday, and Friday). In 1066 England succumbed to the Norman Conquest and thereafter the British stopped being invaded and began invading. The independent kingdom of Wales was conquered in 1282 and fighting between England and Scotland was settled in 1707 when the 2 nations united to form Great Britain.

Size—88,764 sq. mi. (229,899 sq. km.).

Population—55,500,000: (including No. Ireland) English, 81.5%; Scottish, 9.6%; Irish, 2.4%; Welsh, 1.9%; Ulster, 1.8%; other, 2.8%. 50% Church of England, 10.9% Roman Catholic, 2.7% Muslim, 2.2% Church of Scotland, 1.2% Methodist, 0.8% Jewish, 0.5% Baptist, 0.3% Congregationalist, 33.4% no religion, other religion, or not stated.

Who Rules—Great Britain is a constitutional monarchy. The Crown rules symbolically while the power lies in Parliament and the Cabinet headed by the Prime Minister.

Who REALLY Rules—American and British corporations exert great influence on the Government. For example, in spite of protests at home and abroad, Britain sold aircraft and arms to South Africa to "protect it from Communism." Obviously, the arms are to be used to protect the white minority from the black majority. American corporations like Ford and Esso Europe receive great privileges such as tax exemptions. Americans working for American institutions including American schools are tax exempt for the 1st 2 years. If they leave England at the end of 2 years, they have lived tax free, both in England and in the U.S.

Polls indicate that only 10% of the people feel the Government is the real power; 66% think it is the unions. However, a wide gap usually exists between the union leaders and the workers.

NOTES

The English national character is dualistic: One aspect is conservative, the other extroverted. The pub is a fine example of the conservative aspect of English character. The pub, unlike the bar in the U.S., is a focal point for the "locals." One goes to the pub for the same reasons one used to go to church: for fellowship and spiritual enlightenment. There is nothing flashy or plastic about most pubs. Many look like one's living room, full of plush, soft chairs, couches, a fireplace, and bright lights. The pubs keep respectable hours, too—open from 10 A.M. to 2 P.M. and 5 P.M. to 10 P.M.; Friday and Saturday nights they stay open until 11 P.M. There are no all-night or 3 A.M. public bars. When the pubs close everyone goes home. The pub represents pleasure with control and in good taste.

This control is exemplified in English humor. Most Americans find nothing funny in English comedy shows, since English humor is word oriented while American humor is more action oriented.

The same control that is found in English pubs and humor is also found in the English pace of living. Where else does one stand in line quietly for the bus or the taxi?

Tea drinking is another expression of the English spirit of control and patience. Only barbarians drink tea by placing a tea bag in a cup of hot water. There is a whole ritual to tea drinking in England: The water must be boiling rapidly, the teapot warm, the tea loose, then steeped at least 5 minutes in a teapot covered by a tea cosy. Then and only then does one pour the tea into a cup and drink it. Not only old ladies in lace with Pekingese on their laps drink tea, but a whole nation of workers, entrepreneurs, and aristocrats have tea for breakfast, lunch, and, of course, all activity stops in the afternoon for the customary tea break.

However, there is another side to the English character—the bizarre, the audacious, and the innovative. It was not the U.S. but conservative England that produced the Beatles with their long hair and sounds that have influenced a decade of rock musicians and adolescents. Out of a very straight middle-class family comes the androgynous Mick Jagger of the Rolling Stones whose very existence violates the rigid sexual stereotypes of Western culture.

The English are innovators and experimenters in many areas: A. S. Neill's *Summerhill* has become the model for progressive education. R. D. Laing, psychiatry's antipsychiatrist, claims that it is not the individual who is insane but his society, which constantly categorizes him and forces him to fit into abstract norms. It was in England that Marx wrote *Das Kapital* which so traumatized Western civilization and radicalized Eastern ones. Perhaps because of Marx's ever-present presence (he is buried in Highgate Cemetery in London), England was one of the 1st countries to have socialized medicine and welfare benefits for all.

The final reflection of this dualism was the British Empire. These well-controlled, patient, slow-moving people conquered and ruled ¾ of the world.

The English policemen (or "bobbies" as they have also been called) are almost never armed. Even during large demonstrations, they are expected to use their minds, not a lethal weapon, to keep order.

England's greatest export for the past 400 years has been its culture. The 1st disseminators of English culture were the explorers and settlers to the New World, later the colonizers and rulers of the Empire. Today the English language is spoken throughout the world: in Europe, in the Americas, in Africa, and in Asia.

Besides its language, England has exported its religion, its morality, and its Government and laws. The U.S. is basically a white, Anglo, Protestant nation in its attitude, no matter what other races, nationalities, and religions exist there. Every nationality and race that has come to America ultimately uses English as its main language; even the Indians have had to adopt English as their 1st language. American education today still reflects this cultural bias. Although in the last 15 years, inroads have been made by other racial and national groups, especially those in urban areas, too much of American education still emphasizes white-Anglo history, literature, and culture. All American Presidents with the exception of Kennedy, who was a Catholic, have been male, white, and Protestant. The English Puritans

are called the Founding Fathers, although the Spanish, the French, and certainly the Indians, were in the U.S. ahead of them. The Puritan ethic of hard work and restricted pleasure is still strong, especially in middle America. The Government and laws of the U.S. are basically modeled after those of England. Perhaps that is why the 13 Colonies broke away from England: No one was going to deny an Englishman his independence, not even another Englishman.

In other English colonies which later formed the Empire, the English took up "the white man's burden" of superimposing their morally superior culture and religion upon the "natives." This often resulted in the natives, those who wanted to get ahead, becoming more English than the English themselves. Today in countries like Kenya, Jamaica, even India, one can see the effects of English rule. The ruling class and the middle class still copy the English in dress, in forms of education, in law and government, and in the military and police forces.

The Empire is now dead; the Commonwealth members are quite independent, but the cultural effects of English rule will be felt for a long time.

Wales is poorer and more agricultural than England and, because the Welsh have their own language, they do not feel themselves nationally or culturally to be a part of the English people. Although they have the same legal rights as Englishmen, they are struggling to maintain their national identity by practicing Welsh customs, by speaking Welsh, and by securing more power in Parliament.

The Scots too seem to have received the bad part of the bargain when they dissolved their Parliament and joined England. In the late 1960s and early 1970s, a deteriorating economic situation led large numbers of young Scotsmen to join the army in order to make a living, only to find themselves shipped across the North Channel to fight the Irish on behalf of the English.

One group of people has generally been excluded from mainstream British society— the 1.5 million dark-skinned immigrants who have entered the country in recent years: the West Indians, Pakistanis, and others, who drive buses, sweep floors, and work in the factories.

The English, especially the working class and the lower middle class, see the immigrants as a threat to their jobs. The colonial attitude of white supremacy is also still flourishing, and Third World people are known as "wogs," equivalent to the use of "gooks" or "niggers" in the U.S.

In comparison to her American sisters, the Englishwoman, in general, is not so well educated or so well off socially or economically. Most English girls do not go on to university or even to a 2-year polytechnical school. They get married, and/or work in shops, offices, factories, or at crafts for low wages. The true symbol for English womanhood is the Queen. Queen Elizabeth II has all the social prestige, but no political or economic power. Above all, she accepts her role as natural.

—G.F.

GREECE

NITTY GRITTY

Location—A jagged, mountainous peninsula jutting into the Mediterranean Sea and including virtually all of the island groups in the surrounding waters. Its neighbors are: to the northwest, Albania; to the north, Yugoslavia and Bulgaria, and it is separated from Turkey in the northeast by the River Evros.

How Created—The boundaries have been basically the same since ancient times with alterations occurring according to the empire currently in power. More recent additions are: Thessaly, added in 1881; Macedonia, Crete, Epirus, and part of Thrace after the Balkan Wars in 1913; and the Dodecanese Islands, ceded by Italy in 1946.

Size—50,944 sq. mi. (131,944 sq. km.).

Population—over 9 million: Greek, 94.9%; Macedonian, 1.8%; Turkish, 1.4%; Albanian, 0.6%; Aromanian, 0.6%; other, 0.7%. 96.8% Greek Orthodox, 1.3% Muslim, 1.9% other.

Who Rules—In July, 1974, the government-led plot to overthrow President Makarios of Cyprus and unite the island with Greece failed. This was followed by the dissolution of the Greek military cabinet and Constantinos Caramanlis, a former premier, was asked to return to Greece from a self-imposed exile and form a civilian government. He is once again Premier Caramanlis, having won election in November, 1974.

Who REALLY Rules—The Greeks have changed the rules of the game and at present it is difficult to discern who has exactly what sphere of influence. U.S. involvement (CIA, Pentagon) has fallen into much disfavor since the U.S. Government gave tacit approval to the colonels. At this time it is also difficult to say just how much power the military will wield since it was they who called Caramanlis back to office. There is a good chance they are pulling some strings in the background.

NOTES

Greece's rate of inflation is 33.4%—higher than any other country in Europe.

It was only with worldwide acceptance of the Jules Dassin film *Never on Sunday*, starring Melina Mercouri and Dassin, that educated Greeks permitted themselves the luxury and enjoyment of listening to and dancing to the Bouzouki music of movie fame. Before that time it was frowned upon by upper- and middle-class Greeks as something best left to those lower-class creatures.

The ancient Greek word for "private citizen"—i.e. someone not involved in public affairs—is *idiotis*, which means roughly the same as "idiot" in English and French.

Corporate investment in Greece has been tremendous, but at the present time it looks like American investors will not be so favored and Greece will turn more and more to the European market. The U.S.'s main interest in Greece has been bases for the 6th Fleet, but the development of the new Government may put an end to U.S. existence in the area.

In 1972 the Crocker Bank led a 10-bank consortium to lend the Bank of Greece $70 million. At the same time, the U.S. sold Greece $400 million in arms. France also sold the military Government $800 million worth of guided missile patrol boats, 125 tanks, and 40 Mirage supersonic fighter bombers. Though the Government could not afford it, on July 4, Greek armed forces were granted permission to borrow money from Greek banks to buy this equipment which would strengthen "military preparedness." It does in fact seem that the U.S. was, in part, giving the military Government the money to purchase the arms that the U.S. was offering, filtered through the Bank of Greece.

—S.T.

GUATEMALA

NITTY GRITTY

Location—Northernmost country in Central America. Mexico is on the north and west. Belize, the Caribbean, and El Salvador to the east. The Pacific Ocean is to the south.

How Created—The area was conquered in 1524 by Pedro de Alvarado operating out of Mexico. In colonial times, the whole of Central America was administered through the Captaincy-General of Guatemala, located in Antigua. When Central America declared its independence from Spain in 1821, Guatemala was the only Central American province to become a part of Mexico. With the collapse of the Mexican Empire in 1823, Guatemala joined its neighbors in forming the United Provinces of Central America. Because of bickering and rivalries both within and between countries, this too collapsed, and in 1838 Guatemala became an independent nation.

Size—42,042 sq. mi. (108,889 sq. km.).

Population—5,900,000: Mayan Indian, 54%;

Ladino (mestizos and acculturated Indians), 42%; Spanish and German, 4%. Over 90% Roman Catholic.

Who Rules—In theory a republic with a President and unicameral legislature, Guatemala's history since independence has been a series of dictators, coups, and political repression. The current President, Gen. Kjell Laugerud García, came to the office through a fraudulent election, in which his moderate leftist opponent actually outpolled him 2–1.

Who REALLY Rules—The U.S.-trained military is at present the dominant force in Guatemalan politics.

Guatemala's military has the support and backing of the country's small elite, who actually control most of the wealth and power. Only 2.2% of the population own 70% of the arable land, mostly in the form of huge plantations of coffee and bananas, and vast cattle ranches.

NOTES

The Mayan Indians, whose territory eventually covered 125,000 sq. mi., 1st appeared in Guatemala several centuries B.C. The 1st centuries A.D. saw the development of the Mayan civilization into one of the most advanced in the New World. Especially adept in the study of mathematics and astronomy, the Mayas worked out a complex calendar, the orbits of the sun and the moon, and had developed the concept of zero. In addition, they were master builders, and left several cities which, even by today's standards, are considered big. For reasons no longer known, the great population centers in the northern Guatemalan jungles were abandoned by 1200 A.D. Most of the Indians moved north to the Yucatán Peninsula in Mexico, where they again built cities and temples. The structures they abandoned in Guatemala soon were overgrown by the jungle, and were not rediscovered until 1848. Although the Mayas employed a hieroglyphic system of writing, all attempts to decipher it have failed thus far. Until it is understood, much about the Mayas must remain a mystery.

Since 1950, over 2,000 Guatemalan military personnel have trained at the U.S. Army School of the Americas in Panama; 300 Guatemalan police have received training through the U.S. Public Safety Assistance Program. AID money has been used to purchase police equipment including paddy wagons and weapons, and the U.S. military mission in Guatemala advises the Government on counterinsurgency techniques for dealing with the country's guerrilla groups.

In late 1970 the Government imposed a national state of siege, which was in force for nearly a year. During that time, many student leaders and left-wing intellectuals disappeared, all political meetings or demonstrations were forbidden, and police could make searches and arrests without warrants. Thousands of persons were arrested, and many hundreds died or "disappeared" during the year. Some Guatemalans estimate that 13,000 died between 1966 and 1972—casualties in Guatemala's virtual civil war. U.S. diplomats stationed there have received a 15% "hardship allowance" since 1970.

—E.P.

GUINEA

NITTY GRITTY

Location—In West Africa, with a western coastline along the Atlantic Ocean; to the north, Guinea-Bissau, Senegal, Mali Republic; to the east, Ivory Coast; to the south, Liberia and Sierra Leone.

How Created—In the late 19th century Guinea's borders were agreed upon by the French colonists and the British who occupied Sierra Leone; later, the borders between Portuguese Guinea and Liberia were established.

Size—94,925 sq. mi. (245,857 sq. km.).

Population—4,350,000: Fulani, 40.3%; Mandingo, 25.8%; Susu, 11%; Kisi, 6.5%; Kpelle, 4.8%; Dyalonke, 3.2%; Loma and Banda, 3.2%; other, 5.2%. 62% Muslim, 35% Animist, 3% Christian and others.

Who Rules—President elected by direct universal suffrage to a 7-year term. Currently, President Ahmed Sékou Touré. National Assembly has 75 members; all belong to the Parti Démocratique de Guinée.

Who REALLY Rules—Touré's independence slogan is famous: "We prefer poverty in freedom to riches in slavery." It seems to be true, too. This impoverished nation has held on to its independence remarkably well. When relations were suspended with France, Guinea accepted economic and technical assistance from the U.S.S.R., but repudiated "foreign communism": Touré, an African Marxist, would not allow Guinea to become a satellite nation. At the present, aid is accepted, with no strings attached, from the U.S., the U.S.S.R., and China, and from several other Western capitalist countries.

NOTES

The people of Guinea have by far the shortest life expectancy of any nation in the world—27 years.

The Fouta Djallon region is composed of high plateaus and mountains, waterfalls and rapids; the Sudan region has arid plains and savannah, with elephants, antelope, and buffalo; the forest region is dense and lush, with monkeys, panthers, and many other wild animals; the coast region is swampy and full of tiny islands, with crocodiles and hippopotami in the jungle rivers.

Independence—October 2, 1958. When Guinea voted massively against De Gaulle's proposed constitution, the French withdrew from the former territory overnight. Not only did all French aid cease immediately, but within days, all French administrators, technicians, doctors, officers, teachers, and judges disappeared. They took all their records, unhooked the electricity and telephones in the government offices, and even removed the furniture and file cabinets. Guinean leaders moved into offices without a scrap of paper in them and had to rebuild the country's records from scratch, establishing a new bureaucracy upon no foundations at all.

—R.C.

HAITI

NITTY GRITTY

Location—Haiti occupies the western ⅓ of Hispaniola, a Caribbean island 550 mi. southeast of Florida, 50 mi. east of Cuba. The Dominican Republic occupies the eastern part of the island.

How Created—The island was discovered by Christopher Columbus on December 6, 1492. He named the island La Isla Española (later corrupted to Hispaniola) and left his brother Bartholomew there in 1493 to explore and settle the island. The entire island was at 1st claimed by Spain, but the French encroached on the western part. Louis XIV gave this to the French West Indies Company in 1664, and by the Treaty of Ryswick (1697), Spain officially ceded the western ⅓ to France. Now called Saint-Domingue (the Spanish part was known as Santo Domingo), the colony soon became one of the world's richest, far more prosperous than its neighbor. However, the slave revolt of 1791, led by freed slave Toussaint L'Ouverture, and partially inspired by the French and American Revolutions, gave control of the entire island to the slaves by 1804. On January 1, 1804, Saint-Domingue was proclaimed an independent republic, taking the name of Haiti (an Indian word meaning land of mountains). With the final ouster of Haitian forces from Santo Domingo in 1844, the boundary still current between the 2 countries was established.

Size—10,714 sq. mi. (27,750 sq. km.).

Population—5.3 million: black, 95%; mulatto, 5%, with a sprinkling of whites. 66%

Roman Catholic, 10% Protestant, 24% native beliefs and others.

Who Rules—In name only, the country is governed under a 1964 Constitution. Actually, since its independence in 1804, Haiti has been run by a succession of dictators, except for the period 1915–1934, when the U.S. Marines invaded and occupied the country. François ("Papa Doc") Duvalier, President-for-Life from 1957–1971, was notorious for his repressive measures and for the *Tontons Macoutes* ("bogeymen" in Creole), his private militia, who did his dirty work. Current President-for-Life is Jean-Claude ("Baby Doc") Duvalier, 23-year-old son of François.

Who REALLY Rules—Although named to the Presidency-for-Life by his father, Jean-Claude shared the power with his sisters and particularly with his mother during the 1st few years of his rule. However, increasingly self-confident and secure, he has squelched power moves on the part of family and advisers, and is now acknowledged to be firmly in control of Haiti. Still one of the most repressive regimes in the Western Hemisphere, there is no press or political freedom, opposition parties are banned, and graft and corruption abound. Jean-Claude has nonetheless achieved a slightly more relaxed climate, thus luring investors and tourists to desperately poor Haiti.

The French, after virtually ignoring their onetime colony for 150 years, are starting to invest, while the U.S., concerned about retaining U.S. control in the Caribbean, is also investing in Haiti.

NOTES

The U.S. baseball industry exploits cheap Haitian labor for sewing the leather covers on the baseballs. All U.S. baseballs are now produced in Haiti.

Quickie divorces and the export of blood plasma have both come under scrutiny. The divorce business, booming since Mexico ceased to offer divorces in 1971, is criticized as drawing the wrong kind of tourists, and the blood plasma export is considered rank exploitation of poor Haitians, who receive $4 and a bottle of soda pop for 1½ pints of blood.

Haitian refugees, who have been arriving on U.S. and Bahamian shores in leaking boats, are posing a problem for the Immigration and Naturalization Service. Claiming to be political refugees fleeing the repressive Haitian regime, they seek asylum in the U.S. The INS, insisting that this is merely a pretext to enter the U.S., calls them *economic* refugees who are taking jobs away from Americans. However, since the U.S. is simultaneously welcoming planeloads of Cuban economic refugees, moves to deport the Haitians strike many as hypocritical.

Toussaint L'Ouverture (also spelled Louverture), was a freed man who, born into slavery in 1743, had received an education from his master. Able and intelligent, he had long been concerned over the plight of black slaves. He had early gained some influence in the slave community through his knowledge of herbs —some blacks believed him associated with the gods. When the Revolution broke out, he 1st aided his master's family to escape to the U.S., then organized an army of some 4,000 blacks and joined the revolt. He was a brilliant military strategist who easily gained prominence in the struggles that followed. However, the expedition sent by Napoleon to reconquer the colony succeeded in tricking him—he arrived nearly alone at a meeting, was captured, bound, and shipped to France. There he died in jail of combined neglect and abuse at the hands of his jailers, on April 7, 1803.

—E.P.

HONDURAS

NITTY GRITTY

Location—Central America. To the west are Guatemala and El Salvador. To the south, Nicaragua. The Caribbean is on the north and east.

How Created—Columbus touched the eastern tip of Honduras in 1502, and named the area "Honduras" meaning "depths" in Spanish, possibly in reference to the deep coastal waters. The 1st settlement occurred in 1524, and in 1539 the area became part of the Captaincy-General of Guatemala. The rich silver mines of Honduras attracted Spanish adventurers, and both the mines and the Indians (about 500,000 at the time of the conquest, descendants of the Mayas) were ruthlessly exploited. In 1821 Honduras, along with the other Central American Spanish possessions, declared its independence from Spain. In 1823 Honduras joined the Central American federation of republics, which was dissolved in 1838, due to both internal and external factionalism. Honduras has been independent since 1838, but has had persistent border problems with El Salvador, which flared into war in 1969.

Size—43,277 sq. mi. (112,088 sq. km.), about the size of Ohio.

Population—3 million: mestizo, 90%; Indian, 6%; white and black, 4%. 71% Roman Catholic, 2% Protestant, 27% other.

Who Rules—In theory, a republic with a President and unicameral legislature elected every 6 years. However, constitutional succession is rarely achieved.

Who REALLY Rules—The Supreme Council of the Armed Forces. Since 1821 there have been over 120 presidential changes, mostly at the instigation of the military.

The U.S. is Honduras' biggest foreign investor (United Brands, formerly United Fruit), and has an active AID program there. AID loans have been for roads, education, agricultural development, and technical assistance. The USIS (U.S. Information Service) administers a cultural and educational exchange program.

NOTES

United Brands is the largest landholder in Honduras, controlling about 200,000 acres that it leases or owns outright. Much controversy has in the past centered around the company's political and economic power in Honduras as well as in other Central American banana-exporting countries. Today, the banana workers form an elite within the Honduran labor force. Earning as much as 1000% more than a comparable employee *not* employed by United Brands, and living in a comfortable company town with health care and schooling provided, the workers resist the sale or nationalization of their employer's holdings. In April, 1975, President Lopez Arellano was removed from office when it was revealed that he had accepted a $1.25 million bribe from United Brands.

Historical border differences between Honduras and El Salvador resulted in the "Soccer War" in 1969. The tense nationalism accompanying the World Soccer Cup competition did not cause the war but, combined with the presence of some 300,000 illegal Salvadorean immigrants, added fuel to the long-standing rivalry between the 2 countries. In the 5-day war, at least 2,000 died on both sides, and commercial and diplomatic ties have not been restored.

In 1971 a U.S.-Honduras source of disagreement for over a century was resolved by the return of the Swan Islands to Honduras. Claimed by the U.S. under the Guano Islands Act of 1863, the islands were occupied by a variety of U.S. installations, including a weather station and CIA radio station which broadcast to Cuba and Latin America in the early 1960s.

—E.P.

HONG KONG

NITTY GRITTY

Location—Hong Kong is an enclave on the coast of Kwangtung, a southern province of China. Urban Hong Kong is about 90 mi. southeast of the Chinese city of Canton.

How Created—England seized the island of Hong Kong from China in 1841 during the

1st Opium War. Following the 2nd Opium
War (1860), during which British forces
sacked the Chinese capital of Peking, the Chinese Imperial Government ceded the Kowloon
peninsula and nearby Stonecutters Island to the
British Crown Colony of Hong Kong. After
Japan defeated China in the Sino-Japanese War
of 1894-1895, England joined other European
powers in grabbing new Chinese concessions.
In 1898 England signed a 99-year lease with
the Imperial Government, under which the
"New Territories," 355 sq. mi. of islands and
mainland adjacent to Kowloon, would be governed as part of Hong Kong. To take control
of the New Territories, the British defeated
armed Chinese peasants in 1899.

Size—404 sq. mi. (1,046 sq. km.).

Population—4,500,000: Cantonese (including Tanka), 81.2%; Hoklo, 8.1%; Hakka,
3.3%; Sze Yap, 3%; Shanghai and Mandarin,
2.8%; English, 1%; other, 0.6%. Mostly Buddhist and Taoist.

Who Rules—Hong Kong is ruled by a governor appointed by the British Crown. There is a
legislative council, headed by the governor, but
it only advises and has no real power.

Who REALLY Rules—The colonial administration shares power with the wealthier
members of Hong Kong's integrated (English-
Chinese) business community.

NOTES

Hong Kong suffers from police corruption,
heavy crime, widespread heroin addiction (an
estimated 300,000 in 1973), gang warfare,
huge slums, and incredibly poor working conditions. Half the colony's workers work 10-hour
days; 60% of all male workers work a 7-day
week.

The main business of Hong Kong has always
been trade. During its initial colonization, the
main product was opium; then the port became a debarkation point for "coolie" labor.
Today Hong Kong is among the world's top 20
trading nations, exporting some 65% of its
domestic product. One quarter of Hong Kong's
exports are 1st imported from Communist
China.

When communist forces drove Kuomintang
troops ("Nationalist Chinese") from the mainland in 1949, business groups from Canton
and Shanghai transferred their investments to
Hong Kong. Hong Kong's industrialization is
largely a product of this shift.

Hong Kong was a popular "R&R" (Rest and
Recuperation, also known as Rape and Run)
spot for American GIs and sailors during the
Indochina Wars. In 1968 some 220,000 Amer-
ican troops spent their leaves in Hong Kong.
—L.S.

HUNGARY

NITTY GRITTY

Location—A landlocked country in Central
Europe, occupying the center of the Middle
Danube Basin. It is bordered on the west by
Austria, on the north by Czechoslovakia, on
the northeast by the Ukrainian Republic of the
U.S.S.R., on the east by Romania and on the
south by Yugoslavia.

How Created—Nomadic tribes took occupation of the Carpathian Basin at the end of the
9th century. The Treaty of Trianon in 1920
legalized the annexation of territories of what
are today Slovakia, Carpathian Ukraine, Transylvania, etc., by neighboring nations to form
the modern boundaries. After German and Soviet occupation in W.W. II, a new peace
treaty restored the Trianon frontiers, with a
small alteration in favor of Czechoslovakia.

Size—35,919 sq. mi. (93,030 sq. km.). The
present country occupies only the central portion (about 30%) of the original territory.

Population—10,700,000: Magyar, 98.2%;
German, 0.5%; Slovak, 0.3%; Gypsy, 0.3%;
Croatian, 0.3%; other, 0.4%. 55% Roman
Catholic, 25% Lutheran and Calvinist, 1%
Jewish.

Who Rules—The National Assembly with
349 members elected for 4-year terms. They
elect a Presidential Council which serves as a
collective Head of State. The National Assembly also elects the Supreme Court.

Who REALLY Rules—The Hungarian Socialist Worker's party, a Soviet-manipulated
puppet regime based on a platform of
Marxism-Leninism, directs, guides and coordinates all activities of the State. It has a membership of 600,000.

NOTES

The key event of recent Hungarian history
is, without question, the nationwide uprising of
1956 in which the people of Hungary demanded worker management of factories, a
government consisting of representatives of
the trade unions and the youth, withdrawal of
all Russian troops, and numerous other radical
changes. This was too much for the Soviet
Government in Moscow who sent in 6,000
tanks and tens of thousands of troops to put
down the revolution and reestablish their own
brand of communism. Two hundred thousand
Hungarians fled their homeland.

Since that time, the Soviet-approved Hungarian Government has gone to great lengths to
please the people on a material level. Rather
than institute a super-repressive regime, they
have chosen to allow more private property,
more "verbal" criticism of the bureaucracy,

and they have even allowed Hungarians to travel abroad freely. However, there are still 100,000 Soviet troops stationed inside Hungarian borders.

—J.Y. & D.W.

INDIA

NITTY GRITTY

Location—India makes up the bulk of the Indian subcontinent in South Asia. It is bounded by Pakistan on the west, China, Nepal, and Bhutan on the north, and Burma on the east. In the southeast, India surrounds Bangladesh on 3 sides. It faces the Arabian Sea on the southwest, and the Bay of Bengal on the southeast, and juts south into the Indian Ocean. The Andaman and Nicobar islands, an Indian territory, form an arc between Burma's Irrawaddy Delta and the Indonesian island of Sumatra.

How Created—Between 2000 and 1000 B.C. successive waves of Aryans migrated to India from Central Asia. The Aryans drove many of the original Dravidian inhabitants farther south on the Indian peninsula, but the 2 groups intermixed, creating the fundamentals of Hindu culture.

From 711 to 1526 various Muslim armies —Arabs, Turks, Afghans, and Moguls—conquered northern India from the west. Early Muslim invaders sought to impose Muslim religion and culture upon India, and they were partially successful. The Moguls (*Mogul* comes from the Arab word for Mongol), who seized power in 1526, synthesized Muslim and Indian culture, creating a new age of cultural achievement.

The last major Mogul Emperor was Aurangzeb (1659–1707). He repressed Indian (Hindu) culture and invaded independent Muslim and Hindu kingdoms and tribal territories in southern India. He was the only Indian ruler ever to govern—though not too effectively—the entire subcontinent. Aurangzeb's intolerance and expansionism stimulated rebellions throughout India. Following his death, the Mogul Empire disintegrated into a number of independent and semi-independent states.

In 1756 the *Nawab* (Mogul Prince) of Bengal sided with the French in the 7 Years' War (known as the French and Indian War in North America). Initially the Bengalis defeated the British and imprisoned them, but the British East India Company retaliated, defeating the Bengalis at the Battle of Plassey in 1757. In the next 3 years the British defeated French forces, driving the French from all but a few insignificant Indian outposts. By the early 19th century the British controlled all of India, either ruling states directly or dominating princely protectorates. During the 19th century the British conquered Burma and Nepal, incorporating them for a time into India.

In 1885, 68 Hindus and 2 Muslims met to form the Indian National Congress (Congress for short), the major vehicle of the Indian independence movement. As Hindu culture revived at the end of the 19th century, the Congress became the voice of the nationalist Hindu community.

The post W.W. I period saw a change in the class nature of the nationalist movement. Mahatma Gandhi attracted Indians of all classes to the Congress, and in 1919, 1920–1922, and 1930–1932 he organized strikes, boycotts of British goods, and a variety of other nonviolent actions to protest British rule. For a time he even won the cooperation of the Muslim League which had been organized in 1906. Whenever the people resorted to violence or began to turn their energies toward class conflict, Gandhi and the upper-class-led Congress called off their passive resistance campaigns.

When W.W. II broke out the Congress declared that it would oppose Indian participation in the war without complete, immediate independence. Congress planned an antiwar campaign of civil disobedience, but the British arrested its leaders before the campaign started.

At the end of W.W. II, Labor won control of the British Government and prepared to make India independent. India was prepared economically, since its war production had wiped out its debt to Great Britain. But there was one major problem: communal conflict.

While Congress leaders languished in jail, the Muslim League consolidated its strength. Under Mohammed Ali Jinnah, the League had finally become a mass movement, appealing to all classes of Muslims. Provincial self-government had shown the League how difficult coexistence with the Congress would be in an independent nation with a Hindu majority. So in 1940 the Muslim League adopted a resolution calling for partition of India into separate Muslim and Hindu zones.

Eventually the British agreed to form Muslim Pakistan from the eastern half of Bengal and a few districts from Assam on the east; and from Sind, the North-West Frontier Province, and the western half of Punjab on the west. Several far-western princely and tribal states elected to join Pakistan as well. Britain granted independence to both India and Pakistan on August 15, 1947.

The disposition of 3 princely states created a major problem at partition. Junagadh and Hyderabad were predominantly Hindu states ruled by Muslims who wished to associate with

Pakistan. Kashmir was a predominantly Muslim state with a Hindu ruler who wished to join India.

Though the *Nawab* of Junagadh chose to join Pakistan upon independence, riots by Hindus—who made up 80% of the population—drove him out of power. Indian troops occupied the state and staged a plebiscite which confirmed Indian rule.

Hyderabad was a more difficult matter. Ruled by a Muslim *Nizam*, Hyderabad had 2 million Muslims and 13 million Hindus. The city of Hyderabad was India's 4th largest city and the center of India's Muslim cultural heritage. It covered a huge area in the middle of the Indian peninsula. The *Nizam* refused to join India, and he even sought the assistance of the UN but Hindu rebels and an Indian economic blockade undermined his rule, and eventually the Indian Army seized the province, killing thousands of Muslims.

Meanwhile, the Maharajah of Kashmir joined his state, which bordered both India and West Pakistan, to India. When Muslims rebelled, the Indian Army intervened. Muslim tribesmen from West Pakistan then intervened on the other side, but the Pakistani Government did not commit regular troops. The U.S. eventually established a cease-fire, with Kashmir and adjacent Jammu divided between Pakistan and India.

By the time India became a republic in 1950, it had generally established its current boundaries. In the 1960s it annexed remaining French and Portuguese enclaves and in 1974 it took over the Himalayan kingdom of Sikkim.

Size—1,261,810 sq. mi. (3,268,900 sq. km.).

Population—Over 600,000,000: (by language) Hindi, 30.4%; Telegu, 8.6%; Bengali, 7.7%; Marathi, 7.6%; Tamil, 7%; Urdu, 5.3%; Gujarati, 4.6%; Kannada, 4%; Malayalam, 3.9%; Bihari, 3.8%; Oriya, 3.6%; Rajasthani, 3.4%; Punjabi, 2.5%; Assamese, 1.5%; Santali, 0.7%; other, 5.4%. Religion: 82.7% Hindu, 11.2% Muslim, 2.6% Christian, 1.9% Sikh, 0.7% Buddhist, 0.5% Jain, 0.4% other.

Who Rules—India is a federation of 22 states and 9 union territories. The Central Government operates the union territories, while the states normally govern themselves. However, the Central Government has the power to suspend state governments and impose "presidential rule." India's chief of state is the President, elected by an electoral college consisting of elected members of the Federal Parliament and state assemblies.

The Federal Parliament has 2 houses. The upper house, the Council of States, has limited powers. The lower house, the House of the People, is similar to the British House of Commons. Seventy-five seats in the House of the

People are reserved for "former" untouchables. Thirty-seven are reserved for the tribespeople.

Following independence the Congress party dominated virtually all of the state legislatures, but gradually it has lost its grip, facing defeat in 1967 at the hands of ethnic or leftist united fronts in key provinces. When these governments have not governed according to the Central Government's standards, the Federal Government has imposed presidential rule.

Who REALLY Rules—Congress, since its formation, has been the organ of upper-class and middle-class Indian nationalists, including British-trained administrators. It remains dominated by these groups.

Though the Congress under Jawaharlal Nehru sought to develop India as an economically independent nation, it was unwilling to threaten the position of the upper classes. Instead of taxing agriculture and professional income, the Government borrowed money from abroad.

Western creditors, notably the U.S., the U.K., West Germany, and the World Bank, dominate India's economic planning—especially in agriculture—through the Aid-India Consortium, which they and other public creditors established in 1958.

The Soviet Union, also a major creditor, attempts to counterbalance Western influence by subsidizing India's oil industry and industrial sector. Furthermore, Russian military support for India (against Pakistan) has also given the Russians sizable influence over Indian foreign policy.

NOTES

Hindu culture is based upon the caste system, a hierarchical division of society into a multitude of hereditary groups for social, economic, and religious purposes. People work with, live adjacent to, marry, and worship with members of the same caste. Violators are punished by *panchayati* (councils), which exist at local levels for each caste.

Originally there were 4 castes: *brahmans*—the priests; *kshatriyas*—nobles and warriors (forerunners of modern *rajputs*); *vaisyas*—traders; and *sudras*—serfs. Over the centuries these 4 basic castes split into more than 3,000 separate subdivisions, based usually on occupation and geography. The caste system rigidified over a period of time, and it remains intact in most of rural India. The higher castes, which are of purer Aryan descent, dominate politics and business in rural areas.

Below the castes are 80 million casteless people, known as "untouchables." Though the Indian Constitution outlaws "untouchability" and discrimination against former untouchables, these people live in enforced poverty in most Indian villages. They may not dress well; they must live in inferior, segregated housing; and according to tradition they may not even worship in Hindu temples. There are even castelike subdivisions among untouchables.

In 1972 militant untouchables formed the *Dalit* (Oppressed) Panthers (after the American Black Panthers) to demand social and economic equality.

Tribal groups, some still relatively primitive, face similar discrimination. These 40 million people are primarily descendants of pre-Dravidian Indians.

The status of Indian women is paradoxical. On the one hand, India has only 932 women for every 1,000 men because of the tradition of female infanticide; on the other hand, the Prime Minister is a woman. Fifteen percent of the Congress Party's political candidates are women and 20% of the nation's doctors are women. Peasant women often dominate movements for food distribution and social change and even Muslim women are beginning to campaign for equal rights.

Hindus, who make up over 80% of the population, follow a religious tradition that confounds foreigners concerned about India's perennial food shortages. Hindus do not eat meat. (This is the origin of the term "sacred cow.")

Since independence, American aid agencies, the World Bank, and other Western governments have promoted the modernization of Indian agriculture, encouraging the use of machines, fertilizers, pesticides, and hybrid grains. Because larger farmers could more easily adopt these more efficient methods, this "Green Revolution" in farming methods has accentuated the differences between rich and poor farmers, allowing large farms to grow even larger.

India has 15 main languages, most of which derive from Sanskrit (the ancient Brahman language), as well as 1,652 separate dialects.

In 1967 peasants in the Naxalbari region of West Bengal seized the land and killed the landlords. The movement, known as the Naxalite movement, spread to other areas of India. Though sometimes the name Naxalite is used to describe any land-seizing peasant movement, the Naxalites became a political party: the Communist party (Marxist-Leninist). The Government stifled the Naxalite movement and some 18,000 are now in prison.

India currently has as many as 40,000 political prisoners, including the 18,000 Naxalites, some of whom were imprisoned without trial. The non-Naxalite left wing in West Bengal charged the Congress with rigging elections in 1972, following earlier left-wing electoral victories which had been negated by presidential rule. The Congress Government responded to strikes there by arresting thousands, evicting workers from their homes, and forcing unions from their offices and plants.

In 1974, when India's railroad workers planned a strike, the Federal Government quickly arrested 20,000 leaders and workers.

Modern India's greatest hero is Mohandas K. Gandhi, better known as Mahatma (Great Soul). Gandhi, a lawyer who renounced material wealth, 1st developed a reputation as leader of the Indian community in South Africa. When he returned to India in 1914 he attracted the Hindu lower classes to the nationalist movement.

Gandhi was a nationalist, not a social revolutionary. He organized boycotts, strikes, and hunger strikes to attack British rule nonviolently, but he never organized such campaigns to alter India's class or caste structure. He sympathized with the untouchables, calling them *harijans* (people of God), but he advocated only that they be allowed into the lower castes. He did not advocate abolition of the caste system. His program for land reform was weak as well: He urged landlords to donate ⅙ of their lands to the poor.

Gandhi's nonviolence was courageous, but somewhat inconsistent. He supported the British during W.W. I, but he advocated passive resistance to Hitler and Japan during W.W. II.

India has come a long way since the nonviolent teachings of Mahatma Gandhi. In 1974 it startled the world by testing its 1st nuclear weapon.

MINORITY REGIONS

Most of India's states and territories are populated by minority racial, ethnic, or linguistic groups. The following 4 have especially tenuous links to the Federal regime:

1) *Nagaland.* Nagaland is an Indian state in eastern India. On the Burmese border, it actually lies east of Bangladesh. It is populated by 516,000 Naga tribespeople, ⅔ of whom are Christians, mostly Baptists. When American evangelist Billy Graham visited Nagaland in 1973, he drew over 100,000 people.

Nagaland was not included in Britain's Indian Independence Act, but India asserted authority in 1947. The Nagas never agreed to join India, and they have been fighting for independence ever since. China and Pakistan have both reportedly supplied the Nagas with arms. To mute the Naga independence movement, India made Nagaland a self-governing state in 1963, but it restricted access by foreigners, including missionaries.

2) *Mizoram.* Mizoram is a union territory not too far from Nagaland. It is sandwiched between Burma and Bangladesh. Eighty percent of its 400,000 Mizo people are Christians.

Forty-four percent of the people are literate, a remarkable number for hill tribes.

The Mizos have been in rebellion against Indian rule since 1966. They are allied with the Nagas and the Razakars, non-Bengali Muslims from Bangladesh.

3) *Sikkim.* The ancient Himalayan kingdom of Sikkim is a vertical country. There are 20 peaks over 20,000' high, but by far the most spectacular is Kanchenjunga, on the Sikkim-Nepal border. This peak is 28,208' high, the 3rd highest in the world. In deference to the ancient belief that a great god resides there, those who have climbed the mountain recently have stopped a few feet short of the very top.

The valley below the sheer, cloud-topped cliffs is a lush forest of flowers: hibiscus, bougainvillaea, ferns, to mention a few. Orchids, of which there are 600 kinds, are so common that they are often used as cow fodder.

In 1974 Sikkim became an Indian-associated state. The Buddhist *Chogyal* (King) had asked for help from Indian police in 1973, after Sikkim's Hindu majority rioted, protesting the *Chogyal's* rule. India sent police, restored order, appointed a new Government, and made concessions to the rebels. In 1974–1975 the Indian police deposed the *Chogyal,* annexing Sikkim as India's 22nd state. Until then, one dynasty had ruled Sikkim since the 14th century. India's action brought protests from 2 other Himalayan nations, Nepal and China.

The majority of Sikkim's 220,000 people are Hindu Gorkhalis (Nepalese), who have immigrated in the past 100 years. Other major groups are the indigenous Lepchas and the Bhutias, originally from Tibet.

4) *Andaman and Nicobar Islands.* The Andaman Islands and the Nicobar Islands consist of 204 and 19 islands respectively, in an arc between Burma's Irrawaddy Delta and the Indonesian island of Sumatra. They are populated by 115,000 Indians, including many refugees, and an unknown number of Negrito aborigines. For many years the Andamans served as a penal colony for British India. These 2 island groups were the only sections of India occupied by the Japanese during W.W. II. They are governed as a union territory.

—L.S.

INDONESIA

NITTY GRITTY

Location—A huge chain of 13,677 islands (6,044 inhabited) situated along the equator between mainland Southeast Asia and Australia. The only land borders are with Malaysia on the island of Borneo, with Australia's possession on the island of New Guinea, and with Portugal's colony on the island of Timor.

How Created—Humans 1st inhabited the East Indies some 500,000 years ago. The 1st known civilization began about 2,000 years ago when Hindu traders 1st came to the islands for their spices. Various Hindu and Buddhist kingdoms dominated the islands for the next 1,400 years, establishing many of Indonesia's current cultural traditions.

Before the advent of Dutch colonial rule, which lasted from the early 17th century to just after W.W. II, the many people of Indonesia were split into small political groupings. Notable exceptions were the 2 early empires, Srivijaya (c. 700–c. 1200) and Majapahit (1293–c. 1520), which controlled large parts of the islands of Java and Sumatra, the Malay peninsula, and other scattered islands. However, at no time prior to the arrival of the Dutch did any one kingdom control all of the islands that today constitute the state of Indonesia. The Dutch created a system of provincial administration for Indonesia, centering power in the city of Batavia (present-day Djakarta) on the most heavily populated island, Java.

As the Japanese left, the Preparatory Committee for Indonesian Independence, led by Sukarno and Mohammad Hatta, declared independence (August 17, 1945). However, the Dutch, aided at 1st by the British, sought to reassert control. Fighting broke out, and the fledgling UN formed a commission to settle the dispute. Finally, the Dutch agreed to transfer sovereignty in December, 1949. In 1950 the United States of Indonesia transformed itself into the unitary Republic of Indonesia.

Originally the Dutch did not agree to allow West Irian (the western half of New Guinea island) to be part of Indonesia, but the UN turned the territory over to Indonesia in 1963. Since independence, several revolts have occurred outside of Java to secure more local autonomy, but none have been successful.

Size—782,663 sq. mi. (2,027,087 sq. km.).

Population—135 million: Javanese, 45.4%; Sundanese, 13.6%; Modurese, 6.6%; Riau, 5.2%; Minangkabau, 3.8%; Buginese, 2.8%; Batak, 2.3%; Chinese, 2.3%; Balinese, 1.9%; Achinese, 1.5%; more than 300 other ethnic groups, 14.6%. 89% Muslim, 5% Protestant, 2% Roman Catholic, 1% Hindu, 3% other.

Who Rules—Indonesia calls itself a democracy based on the 5 Pillars (*Pantja Sila*) state ideology: belief in the one, supreme God; just and civilized humanity; unity of Indonesia; democracy which is guided by the inner wisdom in the unanimity arising out of deliberations amongst representatives; and social justice for the whole of the people of Indonesia.

The President is elected by the People's Consultative Assembly, a 920-member body which meets every 5 years to determine broad lines of policy for the Government.

Who REALLY Rules—The Indonesian armed forces, whose strength is estimated at 350,000. The Army acquired its initial training from the Japanese during W.W. II, and emerged as a potent political force during the struggle for independence with the Dutch after the war.

President Sukarno was the country's primary political force for Indonesia's 1st 17 years of independence. He could usually easily enforce his rule over most elements of the society, including the Indonesian Communist party (PKI), various Muslim groups, and trade unions. With the armed forces, however, Sukarno had to coax rather than demand.

In 1965, an attempted coup d'état by pro-communist members of the Army gave General Suharto an excuse to rid his organization of what he considered "undesirable" elements. A year later, Suharto was named Army Chief of Staff. He marshaled the conservatives and together they assassinated an estimated 300,000 to one million Indonesians suspected of pro-communist leanings. In February, 1967, Sukarno was forced into retirement—he died in 1970—and Suharto became the Head of Government.

An international consortium of Indonesia's creditors oversees and influences Indonesia's economic policies. The Inter-Governmental Group on Indonesia (IGGI) consists of the world's major capitalist nations plus international financial institutions such as the World Bank, the International Monetary Fund, and the Asian Development Bank. (The Soviet Union, which lent vast sums to Indonesia before the 1965 coup, is still a major creditor, but it does not participate in IGGI.) Working through the International Monetary Fund, IGGI has made Indonesia a "debt slave." Rather than encourage debt repayment and independence, IGGI delays due dates for repayment or approves new loans on the condition that Indonesia adopt its recommended economic policies.

A powerful U.S.-trained group of planners formulate economic policy. Called the "Berkeley Mafia," because so many had studied on that particular campus of the University of California, their power depends also upon retaining the good will of the military. The group receives support from the Ford Foundation as well.

NOTES

Indonesia was not a significant military theater during W.W. II, but it was the richest prize of the Asian war and its possession a major cause of the U.S.-Japan conflict. According to Foreign Relations of the United States, published by the U.S. Department of State, American leaders decided to fight Japan (before the Pearl Harbor attack) when it became clear the Japanese would seize the Netherlands East Indies and restrict American access to the islands' vast natural resources—including oil, tin, and natural rubber.

Following Indonesian independence the nation's natural wealth continued to influence U.S. policy in Southeast Asia. In defending American support for the French War to reimpose colonial rule in Indochina, President Dwight Eisenhower said that American financial aid to the French was the "cheapest way . . . to get certain things we need from the riches of the Indonesian territory."

The Javanese dominate most spheres of Indonesian life. They not only control the Government and military but also the economy since the majority of the country's agricultural products are produced on Java.

Nine years after the military coup and anti-communist campaign, the Indonesian régime still holds some 70,000 political prisoners, most of whom have never received a trial.

Michael Rockefeller, son of the U.S. Vice-President, Nelson Rockefeller, disappeared near Agats, on the coast of West Irian, in 1961. He was there to collect primitive carvings for a New York museum. Since young Rockefeller was never seen again, and since some Irianese are cannibals, it has been speculated that he may have been eaten.

In 1971 the military commander of West Irian promised that there would be no more naked people there by 1973. He was wrong.

Teeth filing is practiced on many children in Bali. The rationale is that small teeth will ensure entry to heaven after death. People with unfiled teeth might be considered demons with great fangs and be barred from entering.

The batik method of printing cloth originated in Indonesia.

In 1883 the volcano of Krakatoa exploded, killing 35,000 people with its tidal waves and sending ashes and smoke around the globe. Krakatoa is west of Java in the Sunda Strait, but when Hollywood producers made their Cinerama epic about the explosion, they titled it Krakatoa, East of Java because it sounded more exotic.

Indonesia has probably never known a more brilliant orator than the charismatic former President, Sukarno. Here is a sampling of his thoughts:

On the east and west: "To me, both the Declaration of Independence and the Communist Manifesto contain undying truths, but the West doesn't permit a middle road. They manipulate you so you're no longer able to stay independent. To President Roosevelt's 4 freedoms I add a 5th: the freedom to be free! The West keeps threatening, 'Do you want to be dominated by the communists?' We answer, 'No . . . but neither do we want to be dominated by you!' At least Russia and China don't call us names when we smile sweetly at America. A nation engaged in surviving must take help from all sides, accept whatever is useful and throw away the rest."

On American aid: "Americans are under the impression they're saying to us, 'Here, poor, dear, poverty-stricken brother . . . have some money . . . here, poor, little underdeveloped Indonesia, we are going to give aid because we love Indonesia.' This is hypocrisy. America tolerates underdeveloped Asian countries for 2 reasons. One, we're a good market. We pay back with interest. And 2, she worries we'll turn communist. She tries to buy our loyalties. She gives bounty and plenty only because she's afraid. Then, if we don't act the way she wants, she yanks back her credit and warns, 'No more unless you behave yourself!' Manuel Quezon of the Philippines once said, 'It is better to go to hell without America than to go to heaven with her!' "

—S.L.W.G. & L.S.

INTERNATIONAL BUSINESS MACHINES (IBM)

NITTY GRITTY

Location—The company's headquarters are on Old Orchard Road in Armonk, N.Y. 10504, and its plants and laboratories are concentrated in the upstate New York cities of East Fishkill, Endicott, Kingston, Mohansic, Oswego, Poughkeepsie, and Rochester.

How Created—Charles R. Flint incorporated IBM's predecessor, the Computing-Tabulating-Recording Company, on June 16, 1911. C-T-R acquired the International Business Machines Corporation, on February 14, 1924, and assumed the name of that company. In July, 1933, IBM bought Electronic Typewriters, Inc., and 2 years later produced its 1st electric typewriter. The company established the IBM World Trade Corporation on January 1, 1950, to manage the firm's foreign business. On February 28, 1964, IBM acquired Science Research Associates, Inc., a producer of educational and testing materials.

Size—IBM markets its products in over 100 countries. The company's plants and laboratories in the U.S. cover 27.8 million sq. ft. in 25 cities, 9 of which are in New York State. Overseas, the company's manufacturing and development facilities take up 11.5 million sq. ft., including 23 manufacturing plants in Argentina, Brazil, Canada, Colombia, France, India, Italy, Japan, Mexico, The Netherlands, Sweden, the United Kingdom, and West Germany.

Population—274,108 employees. Around 94% of the domestic professional employees and 96% of the managers are white. Men have 92% of the professional jobs.

Who Rules—IBM's day-to-day major policy decisions are made by a 3-man corporate office which is elected by a 24-member board of directors. The directors are elected by 574,887 stockholders owning 146,712,688 shares.

Who REALLY Rules—IBM is so large that it is hard to tell whether the company rules, or is ruled by, the bankers, ex-government officials, and leaders of financial institutions who sit on its board of directors. The banks control large blocks of stock, and the board includes 8 directors of 5 of the 6 largest New York banks. In 1974 the board of directors also included a former U.S. Attorney General, a former Undersecretary of State, a former Deputy Secretary of Defense, a former Secretary of the Air Force, a former governor of Pennsylvania, a former chairman of the New York Stock Exchange, a former chairman of the Federal Reserve Board, and a current member of the Federal Reserve Bank of Boston.

NOTES

IBM sells and leases data processing machines and systems, electric typewriters, input word processing equipment, educational and testing materials, and related supplies and services. IBM has produced about 70% of the computers in the world and over 90% of the electric typewriters in the U.S. The company is so much bigger than its competitors that the computer industry used to be described as IBM and the 7 dwarfs.

T. J. Watson, Sr., IBM's 1st president, insisted upon a rah-rah atmosphere at IBM, particularly at sales meetings. Watson chose "Think" as the company slogan, and IBM gatherings included company fight songs. One song was about Watson:

> Our voices swell in admiration;
> Of T. J. Watson proudly sing;
> He'll ever be our inspiration,
> To him our voices loudly ring.

The company's most famous song was its rally song, "Ever Onward."

> There's a feeling ev'rywhere of bigger things
>   in store,
> Of new horizons coming into view.
> Our aim is clear,
> To make each year exceed the one before,

Staying in the lead in ev'rything we do.
The will to win is built right in,
It will not be denied,
And we will go ahead we know by working
    side by side.
Ever Onward, Ever Onward,
That's the spirit that has brought us fame.
We're big but bigger we will be,
We can't fail for all can see
That to serve humanity has been our aim.
Our products now are known in ev'ry zone,
Our reputation sparkles like a gem.
We've fought our way thru and new
Fields we're sure to conquer too.
Ever Onward, Ever Onward,
We're bound for the top to never fall.
Right here and now we thankfully
Pledge sincerest loyalty
To the corporation that's the best of all.
Our leaders we revere and while we're here
Let's show the world just what we think of
    them!
So let us sing men, sing men,
Once or twice then sing again,
Ever Onward, Ever Onward.

In 1937 T. J. Watson, Sr., received the Order of Merit of the German Eagle with Star from Adolf Hitler for "foreign nationals who have made themselves deserving of the German Reich."

—H.B.

INTERNATIONAL TELEPHONE
& TELEGRAPH (ITT)

NITTY GRITTY

Location—ITT's world headquarters are located at 320 Park Ave., New York, N.Y. 10022, and its European headquarters are in Brussels. ITT Continental Baking has its own headquarters on 25 acres in Rye, N.Y. Hartford Fire Insurance Company's home office is in Hartford, Conn.

How Created—On June 16, 1920, Sosthenes and Herman Behn incorporated ITT as a holding company to own the Puerto Rico Telephone Company, the Cuban Telephone Company, and ½ of the Cuban American Telephone and Telegraph Company. Sosthenes Behn chose the name International Telephone & Telegraph so investors would confuse his company with the long-established American Telephone & Telegraph. To add to the confusion, on September 30, 1925, AT&T sold its foreign manufacturing subsidiary International Western Electric, which had facilities in 11 countries, to ITT. The subsidiary, which ITT renamed ITT Standard Electric Corporation,

transformed ITT overnight from an operator of Caribbean telephone utilities into a major international manufacturer of telecommunication equipment and systems. ITT later acquired the telecommunication manufacturing companies of another 11 countries. During and after W.W. II, ITT was forced to sell 3 telephone operating companies and 7 manufacturing companies, while 3 other telephone operating companies were expropriated.

Harold Sydney Geneen joined the company as its top officer in 1959, and in the next 15 years presided over the acquisition of 250 other companies. In the process, ITT's sales increased from $534 million in 1958 to over $10 billion in 1973, and income after taxes rose from $18 million to $528 million.

Size—ITT's major manufacturing and consumer service facilities include 27 locations in 18 States and Puerto Rico, and 23 locations in 15 foreign countries. Its manufacturing facilities in the U.S. and Canada occupy 29 million sq. ft., and its manufacturing plants in 22 other foreign countries cover 59,100,000 sq. ft., most which is in Western Europe. The company's hotels and motor inns are in 150 cities in the U.S. and Canada, and in 22 other foreign countries. ITT operates 420 urban and airport parking facilities, including those at airports in Paris and 16 major U.S. cities. The company has cables under the seas and satellites above the earth, which provide telecommunication services between the U.S., its possessions, the United Kingdom, the Philippines, Latin America, and the Caribbean; also these provide international telephone service for Puerto Rico, the Virgin Islands, Bolivia, Indonesia, and Panama. ITT has food plants in 7 States and operates 42 bakeries in 19 States, the District of Columbia, the Bahamas, and Mexico. The company has finance operations in 333 offices in 24 States and Puerto Rico, and sells insurance in the U.S., Puerto Rico, the Virgin Islands, Canada, and many other foreign countries. It owns, leases, and has cutting rights on over 2 million acres of timberlands in British Columbia, and owns 68,000 acres in Flagler County, Fla., where ITT plans to build a new city with a population that will reach 600,000 by the year 2000.

Population—438,000 employees.

Who Rules—ITT's top management consists of 20 executives who work in the company's New York headquarters. The 2 top men are Chairman Harold Sydney Geneen and Vice Chairman, President, and Chief Operating Officer Francis J. Dunleavy. The officers are elected by an 18-member board of directors that includes 8 officers. The directors are elected by 157,390 stockholders owning 94,536,884 shares.

Who REALLY Rules—Although ITT is an

international company, U.S. laws forbid aliens from owning more than 25% of the company. As of February 28, 1974, 17% of ITT's stock was held by non-U.S. citizens. Although the company refused to make public a list of its largest stockholders, large blocs of ITT stock, like that of most major corporations, are held by banks and brokers.

NOTE

ITT Sheraton owns, leases, and manages 55 hotels in the U.S. containing 27,894 rooms, and 28 foreign hotels containing 14,037 rooms. Sheraton also grants franchises for 216 U.S. hotels with 35,636 rooms and 14 foreign hotels with 2,527 rooms.

ITT Continental Bakeries bakes and sells bread, snacks, cakes, and other bakery items under the brand names Daffodil Farms, Home Pride, Hostess, Profile, and Wonder Bread. It also manufactures and sells potato chips, corn chips, and Morton frozen food. ITT Gwaltney, Inc., produces fresh and processed pork products, including Genuine Smithfield Hams. O. M. Scott & Sons sells lawn seed, fertilizer, weed and insect controls, and other lawn care products. Hartford Life Insurance sells fire, marine, casualty, life, and accident and health insurance, annuity contracts, and surety bonds.

ITT Rayonier produces chemical cellulose, wood pulp, lumber, and treated wood products.

Airport Parking Company of America manages parking facilities at airports, downtown lots and garages, hospitals, and stadiums in the U.S. and Europe.

Howard W. Sams Company provides reference services, magazines and books, including Bobbs-Merrill books.

In 1973 ITT and Transcontinental Gas and Pipeline began a joint venture, U.S. Transmission System, which plans to provide private line communications service in a 200-mi.-wide corridor from New York to Houston.

For the Indochina War ITT developed and produced electronic countermeasures for B-52 bombers, navigation systems for laser guided bombs dropped by F-4 and F-105 bombers, and ground surveillance radar and gunfire control for the Army's automated battlefield. The company operates the Western Test Range and Space and Missile Center at Vandenberg Air Force Base, and operates and maintains the Distant Early Warning System and the Ballistic Missile Early Warning System.

In 1969 after ITT acquired Canteen Corporation, Grinnell Corporation, and Hartford Fire Insurance, the U.S. Justice Dept. filed suits against ITT charging that the mergers were in violation of the antitrust laws. From August, 1970, a month before the Grinnell trial began, to April, 1971, when President

Richard Nixon's aides began searching for a 1972 convention site, ITT officials tried to persuade the Government to drop the antitrust suits. During that time ITT chairman Geneen, vice-president William Merriam, director Felix Rohatyn, and lobbyist Dita Beard met with Vice-President Agnew, presidential assistants Ehrlichman, Colson, Peterson, and Krogh, Cabinet Secretaries Connally and Stans, Justice Dept. officials Mitchell, Kleindienst, and McLaren, and the President's military aide, Colonel Hughes. In May or June, 1971, ITT offered the Nixon Administration $400,000 to finance the Republican national convention in San Diego. In a memo made public the following February by columnist Jack Anderson, lobbyist Dita Beard said that only President Nixon, Attorney General John Mitchell, Bob Haldeman, and California's Lieut. Gov. Edward Reinecke knew of the $400,000 offer. Then on July 31, 1971, the Justice Dept. and ITT announced a consent decree whereby ITT would keep Hartford, but dispose of Canteen, parts of Grinnell, and Avis, Levitt & Sons, and some life insurance companies. On August 5, 1971, ITT made a $100,000 payment as the 1st part of its $400,000 commitment. The antitrust settlement was advantageous to ITT, since the companies it disposed of were losing money, while Hartford was its biggest profit maker. In 1973, Avis and Levitt lost money equal to 1% of ITT's income, while Hartford made 24% of ITT's profits. When Jack Anderson disclosed the Dita Beard memo, ITT shredded documents that discussed the antitrust settlement and the convention offer.

In columnist Jack Anderson's words, "ITT operates its own worldwide foreign policy unit, foreign intelligence machinery, counterintelligence apparatus, communications network, classification system, and airliner fleet." The most recent and blatant example of this power was reflected in ITT's relations with Chile. In 1970 ITT's board of directors concluded that Salvador Allende would be elected President of Chile. Allende was campaigning on a platform calling for the expropriation of American businesses, including ITT. ITT tried to get the CIA to support Allende's right-wing opponent with ITT funds and offered to pay the CIA $1 million to prevent the Chilean Congress from confirming Allende after he was elected. In October, 1971, after Allende nationalized ITT's 70% interest in the Chilean Telephone Company (Chiltelco), ITT proposed an 18-point action plan to the U.S. Government to strangle Chile's economy, create panic among its population, and cause social disorder, so the Chilean armed forces would overthrow Allende. Three months later President Nixon created a special inter-agency group to implement ITT's proposal, and the National Security Council's 40 Committee approved a plan to overthrow Allende. ITT directors John A. McCone, former head of the CIA, and Eugene R. Black, former head of the World Bank, were instrumental in getting the U.S. to approve ITT's plan. Funding for the covert actions was channeled through the CIA, and the World Bank was one of the 1st financial institutions to cut off credit to Chile.

—H.B.

IRAN

NITTY GRITTY

Location—Iran is located in Southwest Asia, stretching from the Caspian Sea to the Arabian Sea. On the west it is bordered by Turkey and Iraq, on the north by the Soviet Union and the Caspian. Afghanistan and Pakistan form its eastern boundaries. The Gulfs of Persia and Oman lie to the south.

How Created—Iran is the historical Persia. Its borders have been determined by centuries of empire building and dissolution. At the end of W.W. II for example, the northwest portion attempted to gain independence when the Azerbaidis and Kurds declared independent republics. But the Iranian Government, with the aid of the Allies (the British and Americans), forced Soviet troops to withdraw from Iran and forcefully suppressed the secessions. A secessionist movement now exists in Baluchistan, in the southeast. Iran keeps its territory by force, as many of the national minorities have little commitment to the Iranian entity.

Size—The total area is 636,296 sq. mi. (1,648,000 sq. km.), slightly larger than Alaska.

Population—34 million: Indo-European, 66%; Turk, 25%; Kurd, 5%; Lur, Semitic Arab and others, 4%. 96.2% Muslim (mostly Shi'a), 0.9% Christian, 0.2% Jewish, 0.1% Zoroastrian, 2.6% other.

Who Rules—The Shah, as an absolute monarch, though he has a powerless National Assembly.

Who REALLY Rules—The Shah and his clique, in close alliance with international capitalist interests and Western Governments, especially the U.S. The Shah's relation to the U.S. is not one of a satellite, but is one of a junior partner. He may have begun in 1953 as very dependent on the U.S., but now it is a question of mutuality of interest.

NOTES

Oil is the essential ingredient of Iran's economy. Without it, Iran would never have been able to undertake its development programs of the last 20 years, nor could it have attracted the interest and capital of the industrial powers. Iran is 2nd only to Saudi Arabia in oil production in the Gulf.

Agri-business interests from California's Imperial Valley participate in Iran in the production of products such as asparagus and strawberries for European and Japanese markets. The list of U.S. corporations is lengthy, including Dow Chemical, John Deere, Transworld Agriculture Development, Bank of America.

The Shah's claim to the Iranian throne is not based upon a long and unbroken dynasty, as his publicity often implies. In fact, the Pahlavi dynasty is very recent. At the end of W.W. I, Britain attempted to make Iran into a virtual protectorate through the proposed Anglo-Persian Treaty of 1919. That effort failed, but in 1921 the British backed a coup by a journalist. The military support for that coup was provided by a colonel in the Cossack Brigade, Reza Khan, the son of a peasant. After the coup, the most important problem for the new Government was assertion of control over the provinces. The Army under the effective command of Reza Khan accomplished this goal. By 1925, rebellious areas had been subdued. In the interim, Reza Khan had been named Prime Minister in 1923, and by 1925 became the reigning Shah. His predecessor (who lived in Europe) was formally deposed by the Parliament. The new Shah took the name Pahlavi for his dynasty-to-be, and designated his son Mohammad Reza as the crown prince. Crown Prince Mohammad Reza became Shah in 1941, and still rules Iran.

The turning point in modern Iranian history was the 2-year struggle over the nationalization of Iran's oil. Nationalist groups in Iran had gained strength enough by 1951 to gain control of the Majlis (Parliament), and force the appointment of the leader of the National Front, Mohammad Mossadeq, as Prime Minister. Upon assuming office, Mossadeq nationalized Iran's oil. Since it was necessary for Iran to import many vital goods, Britain responded with an economic boycott. The U.S. was slow to support Britain, until its own objective was met: the elimination of preferential British treatment in Iran and an "open door" for U.S. participation in Iran's oil resources. The U.S. succeeded in its aims, since Britain was forced to turn to the U.S. for assistance in negotiating with Mossadeq. Then the U.S. realized that Mossadeq and Iran were capable of exploiting the oil resources without U.S. participation. At that point, the Americans turned to the Shah, the leader of the antinationalist forces in Iran. With direct CIA aid, a military coup ousted the nationalists and restored the Shah in August, 1953.

In the 1950s Iran's annual military budget was roughly $10 million a year; in the 1960s it increased to around $150 million a year. After 1968, however, Iran's annual military expenditures soared dramatically to its current $2 billion a year level. According to U.S. Dept of Defense figures, Iran accounts for almost ½ ($3.8 billion) of current foreign orders for U.S.-made military equipment.

The Shah's military buildup is aimed at giving him the role of guardian of the Gulf. In practice, this has meant that in 1971 Iran seized the island of Abu Musa and the islands of Big and Little Tunb near the strategic mouth of the Gulf, the Strait of Hormuz. These islands were seized from the United Arab Emirates, since the Shah doubted their ability to keep the islands secure, and wanted control of the Gulf in his own hands. In 1972, the Shah seized the island of Um al-Ghanam in the same region from Oman. In late 1972 Iran sent helicopters and commando units to Oman to aid the British and their puppet Sultan in the province of Dhofar in the war there against the rebellion of the Popular Front for the Liberation of Oman. Iran's intelligence service is aiding Pakistan and North Yemen in intelligence work. Finally, the Shah gave aid to Kurdish rebels in the north of Iraq. When the Shah withdrew aid to the Kurds in 1974, the rebellion collapsed.

The ruling clique depends on the secret police, SAVAK, to repress antigovernment activity. During the 1960s the U.S. spent $1.7 million on a Police Assistance Program to Iran. SAVAK has at least 60,000 agents.

—J.G.

IRAQ

NITTY GRITTY

Location—At the eastern end of the Levant, stretching from the mountains of Turkey in the north to the Persian Gulf in the southeast, Iraq is bordered on the east by Iran and shares borders in the desert to the west with Syria and Jordan. Saudi Arabia lies to the south and Kuwait is to the southeast.

How Created—Iraq is the Mesopotamia of Western literature. It is dependent upon 2 great rivers, the Tigris and the Euphrates, which create livable country out of the desert, but these interior rivers could not establish borders for Iraq. Sumeria, Assyria, Babylonia, the Persian Empires, the Arab Empire, and the Turkish Empires have all chopped the area at will. The present borders are the creation of European imperialist intervention, mainly British and French. These countries drew their own borders after W.W. I, with the rubber stamp approval of their League of Nations. As a result, Kuwait is separate from Iraq, the Mosul region is part of Iraq rather than of Syria, and the desert has boundaries drawn through it.

Size—168,927 sq. mi. (437,522 sq. km.), larger than California.

Population—Over 10 million: Arab, 77.8%; Kurd, 17.9%; Persian, 1.2%; Turkmen, 1.2%; Assyrian, 0.5%; other, 1.4%. 95% Muslim, 4% Christian.

Who Rules—The Arab Baath Socialist party in alliance with the Iraq Communist party through a National Front. The Kurdish Democratic party has been invited to join the Front, but has mainly refused to join. The President of the Republic has extensive powers, and is appointed by the Revolutionary Command Council. The National Assembly is controlled by the National Front. In the Kurdish autonomous region, a separate executive and legislative Government exists, but has limited independence from the Central Government. Various regional assemblies and popular organizations exist in the Arab sections of the country and have roles within the governmental structure, but are dominated by the Baath party.

Who REALLY Rules—Real power is in the hands of a clique within the Baath party, made up of civilians and military officers, but dominated by the civilians. It has been able to beat back challenges from other military cliques, including challenges from the governing clique itself. The Government and party machinery, and perhaps more significantly the military, are now fully in the hands of this group, which is based largely at Tikrit, a small city northwest of Baghdad. The Tikriti clan and its associates have controlled the Baath party for over a decade, mainly through Tikriti military officers.

The Soviet Union and its allies strongly support the Iraqi Government, but have no effective control over the country. Because of these ties to the Soviet Union, the Baath party had admitted the Communist party into the National Front, though little power has passed into the hands of the CP.

NOTES

Male domination is almost total on all levels from the Government to the family.

The Sunni Arab population of central and northwest Iraq, with extensions in Basra and some other southern urban areas, has long been the base of power in Arab Iraq. The majority Shiite Arab population is powerless; it is an impoverished, often landless, agricultural population found both in the rural southern areas and, increasingly, among the underemployed and unemployed urban poor.

Oil production is the key element in the

Iraqi economy. In 1972 Iraq nationalized the bulk of Western oil interests, and further smaller nationalizations now give the Iraqi Government control of over 90% of the oil production from Iraqi fields. Many experts feel that Iraq's total reserves may prove 2nd only to those of Saudi Arabia.

The name "Iraq" means "well-rooted country," an allusion to the area's long history. It is said that it was here that Adam and Eve lived in the Garden of Eden, that Nebuchadnezzar ruled, and that Hammurabi established the 1st written code of law.

—J.G.

IRELAND

NITTY GRITTY

Location—An island to the west of Great Britain separated by the North Channel, St. George's Channel, and the Irish Sea.

How Created—Ireland is an island with natural boundaries, but it is divided into the Republic of Ireland (Eire) and Northern Ireland. Northern Ireland is bounded on the north by the Atlantic, on the east by the North Channel and Irish Sea, and on the south and west by Eire. The island is divided into the 26 counties of the Republic and 6 counties of Northern Ireland.

Irish Republic

Size—27,136 sq. mi. (68,893 sq. km.), slightly larger than Virginia.

Population—Over 3 million: Irish, 97.5%; English, 1.6%; other, 0.9%. 94.9% Roman Catholic, 3.7% Church of Ireland (Episcopalian), 0.7% Presbyterian, 0.2% Methodist, 0.1% Jewish, 0.4% other.

Who Rules—President elected for 7 years by direct vote of the entire electorate. He appoints the Prime Minister and other Cabinet members. The national Parliament has 2 houses—the Dáil Cireann or House of Representatives, and the Seanad Eireann or Senate. The Dáil is composed of 144 members elected by adult suffrage and the Seanad has 60 members of whom 11 are appointed by the Prime Minister, 6 are elected by the 2 universities, and 43 are elected by the Dáil, the county and county borough councils. The Dáil must stand for reelection within 5 years.

Who REALLY Rules—The President of the Republic is not a strong executive, but rather a figurehead like the Queen of England. He appoints the Prime Minister but only after nominations from the Dáil. The Roman Catholic Church is extremely powerful in Eire. A reflection of this is that the constitution invokes "the Name of the Most Holy Trinity" and speaks of "all our obligations to our Divine Lord, Jesus Christ. . . ." The constitution recognizes freedom of religion but also recognizes the special position of the Catholic Church. The strong influence of the Church can be seen in the government ban on divorce and prohibition of remarriage of persons divorced elsewhere.

Northern Ireland

Size—5,452 sq. mi. (14,121 sq. km.).

Population—1,500,000: almost 100% Irish except for British troops and other English. 34.9% Roman Catholic, 29% Presbyterian, 24.2% Church of Ireland, 5% Methodist, 6.9% other.

Who Rules—By provision of the Ireland Act of 1920, Northern Ireland has its own Parliament which is composed of the governor, the Senate, and the House of Commons. The governor is appointed by the British Monarch for a 6-year term, and he represents the Crown. The Senate has 24 members elected by the House of Commons, and 2 members who are government officials. The House of Commons has 52 members elected by universal suffrage (over 18). Northern Ireland also has representatives in the House of Commons at Westminster in London.

Who REALLY Rules—Although Northern Ireland has a Parliament, a wide range of legislative and fiscal powers are reserved to the Parliament of the United Kingdom—those relating to foreign policy, trade, war, armed forces, and most matters of taxation. Most important, the British can suspend the Government of Northern Ireland, as they did in 1972.

NOTES

In a 1959 study comparing Irish and Italian schizophrenics, Marvin Opler found that the Irish were more repressed, more passive, and significantly more guilty and concerned with sin than the Italians.

For centuries Protestants have been the educated, property-holding, politically dominant group in Ireland, while the Catholics, despite their numerical majority, have been the predominantly landless, illiterate, and politically impotent group. The Protestants have been the absentee landlords while the Catholics have been the peasants; the Protestants have been the bankers and industrialists, while the Catholics have been the workers; the Protestants have been the creditors—while the Catholics have been the debtors.

In 1155 the King of England was given title to Ireland by the Pope. Things were relatively quiet until Henry VIII converted to Protestantism and the Catholic Irish felt that he was a traitor to the Pope and therefore had forfeited his right to rule Ireland. When Henry VIII's daughter, Elizabeth, became Queen in 1558, the political situation worsened because, from the Irish standpoint, Elizabeth was not Queen since the Church did not recognize her father's divorce from his 1st wife and, hence, his marriage to Elizabeth's mother. Thus, the religious conflict was inextricably connected to the question of political legitimacy. In 1609, James I established a colony of Scots and northern English in Ulster, in an attempt to create a power base for English rule. The Irish Protestants who now dominate Northern Ireland are the descendants of those passionately British settlers. The Protestant domination and introduction of English law in Ireland drove the Irish to revolt in 1641. When Cromwell took over control of England after the Puritan Revolution, he came to Ireland to colonize it and to destroy the hold of Catholicism. The Catholics were ordered to give up Catholicism or lose their land and be exiled. This became the root of the link between religion and economic position in Ireland. In 1688 Catholic Ireland and France supported James II in his unsuccessful fight to maintain the English Crown. When James was defeated, the British passed the "penal code" which banished the clergy, forbade the Catholics from voting and sitting in Parliament, and forbade Catholic schools. Nor could Catholics be attorneys or constables or buy or inherit land from Protestants. In 1916, and later in 1919–1921, the Irish Nationalist party fought a war of independence against Britain which resulted in the division of Ireland into the Irish Free State and Northern Ireland. The Irish Free State was granted dominion status in 1922. When the IFS was born, the world looked to Ireland to see if the Protestant minority in the south would be discriminated against after so many generations of Protestant domination and oppression. Interestingly enough, the Catholics did not confiscate Protestant property or make violent attacks on remaining Protestants. In fact, Protestants in the south still remain in their traditional position of dominance in banking, industry, and land ownership.

—R.S.

ISRAEL

NITTY GRITTY

Location—At the eastern end of the Mediterranean. It is bordered on the west by the Mediterranean Sea, on the north by Lebanon, on the east by Syria and Jordan, and on the southwest by Egypt.

How Created—The original Jewish State in Palestine was destroyed by the Romans in 70

A.D. "Israel" came to mean the Jewish people: Palestine was the place to which "Israel" sought to return. In the 19th century the view began to evolve that the Jews all over the world were the fragments of a nation which must once again be united.

During the last decade of the 19th century, a Hungarian Jew named Theodore Herzl became obsessed with the concept of creating a homeland for the Jewish people. Herzl, a journalist, called upon and wrote letters to influential men in Europe trying to convince them of the importance of the Jews' returning to Zion (the promised land). In 1897, Herzl called the 1st World Zionist Council at Basel, Switzerland, and Zionist organizations were set up in countries where there was a large Jewish population. By 1905, the Zionist movement was split over where the Jews should seek to establish their homeland. Herzl and his followers wanted to accept the British offer of space in Uganda, East Africa. Russian Jews insisted that the Jewish State be located in Palestine. Herzl lost, and Uganda was rejected. In 1917, Great Britain, through the person of Arthur James Balfour, its Foreign Minister, promised to help establish a national home for the Jewish people in Palestine. Following W.W. I, England assumed control of Palestine, and Jewish immigration to that area increased rapidly. The Zionists, citing Foreign Minister Balfour's promise, which was now called the Balfour Declaration, demanded the immediate formation of a Jewish State in Palestine. But the British policy was to try to reconcile the 2 nationalisms which now focused on Palestine: the nationalism of the Jews, and the nationalism of the Arabs.

After W.W. II ended, and the Nazi extermination camps had captured newspaper headlines, world opinion began to favor a Jewish takeover in Palestine. Palestinian Jews had long been preparing the implementation of the Jewish State, and in 1949 the State of Israel came into being. War with the Arabs broke out immediately, and has continued intermittently up to the present.

Size—7,992 sq. mi. (20,700 sq. km.), about the size of Massachusetts.

Population—3,500,000: Jewish, 85%; Arab, 15%. 85.3% Jewish, 10.9% Muslim, 2.5% Christian, 1.3% Druzean and other.

Who Rules—Israel is a parliamentary democracy with a unicameral (one house) Parliament led by a Prime Minister who represents the majority party. Local communities are governed by locally elected councils.

Who REALLY Rules—Because of Israel's almost constant conflict with surrounding Arab States, the military in Israel has amassed a considerable amount of political power. The Government is also greatly influenced by its financial supporters—in particular the U.S.

NOTES

Israel is the only nation where children teach the mother tongue to their mothers. The national language of Hebrew had not been widely used for almost 2,000 years when independence was declared in 1948 and most of the adults spoke Yiddish, a mishmash language made up of words from various other languages including Russian, German, Polish, and Hebrew. So children learned Hebrew in school and taught their parents.

By 1960, over one million immigrants had arrived in Israel since statehood was declared. Of that number 431,000 came from Europe (beginning with 100,000 refugees from German concentration camps), and about 500,000 came from Asia and North Africa. Thirteen thousand Jews came from North and South America. Every Jew admitted to Israel becomes a citizen with the right to vote upon entry. Non-Jews, once admitted, must wait 3 years for citizenship.

—M.G.

ITALY

NITTY GRITTY

Location—Described as a "boot kicking a 3-cornered hat," Italy is comprised of a 700-mi.-long peninsula (the boot) extending southeast from continental Europe into the heart of the Mediterranean; 2 large islands, Sardinia and Sicily (the hat); and numerous small islands. The Alps separate northern Italy from France, Switzerland, Austria, and Yugoslavia.

How Created—Italy was proclaimed a nation on March 17, 1861, after a long struggle for unity. Although her ancient history shows there were inhabitants before 1500 B.C., the geographic entity of Italy had never been successfully united. Greek, Carthaginian, and Etruscan civilizations existed there even before the rise of Rome, but they were continually at war among themselves and with tribes of Gauls and Celts from the north. Even under the rule of the Roman Empire the provinces were not completely subjugated.

Size—116,314 sq. mi. (310,258 sq. km.), about the size of Florida and Georgia combined.

Population—56,500,000: Italian, 98.1%; Romansh, 0.7%; Austrian, 0.4%; other, 0.8%. 98.8% Roman Catholic.

Who Rules—A parliamentary republic with 2 houses: a Senate and Chamber of Deputies. The President, a figurehead, is elected every 7 years. He nominates the Premier who, in turn, selects the Council of Ministers (Cabinet) from among members of Parliament. Both houses are elected by popular vote for a maximum of 5 years.

A separate judiciary branch, based largely on Roman law, has partial judicial review of legislation. A Constitutional Court is roughly equivalent but not as strong as the U.S. Supreme Court. The highly centralized Government appoints executives for the 93 provinces and 20 regions which have limited governing powers.

Who REALLY Rules—The Premier and his Cabinet, the top vote-getters from major parties, plan policy and make major decisions. Neither the Government nor the bureaucracy has efficient means of gathering and assessing information so the decision makers rely on data and ideas furnished by pressure groups. Often, major industrialists furnish the economic reports which are the basis for major economic policy decisions.

NOTES

In 1969, Italian multimillionaire Michele Sindona bought from the Vatican the controlling interest in Società Generale Immobiliare, a giant real estate and construction conglomerate whose best known property is Washington's Watergate development.

While it lasts, Venice is the most unique, if not the most beautiful city in Europe. It changes moods at each hour of the day as the shifting sun is reflected by the canals onto ocher, sienna, and cream-colored stucco buildings. The water, the light, the absence of autos, make Venice dreamlike. The bonus is that it also happens to be a treasure trove of art and architecture. The Government, industry, and groups of Venice-lovers have been battling for years over plans to save the city from ruin as salt air, pollution from nearby factories, and sinking foundations erode the Queen of the Adriatic.

Built on both banks of the Arno River, Florence is a city for walkers and culture buffs. Its galleries and churches make it the art-lover's dream; one-way streets and parking shortages make it the driver's nightmare. Once the heart of the Renaissance, the center city looks more like the 15th than the 20th century. Admirers of Michelangelo, Da Vinci, Raphael, and Botticelli jam the museums, bargain hunters crowd the arcaded straw market and the workshops of the leather artisans. Few think to go out to the magnificent villas with formal gardens that dot the surrounding Tuscan countryside. Not a very big city, but one that takes days to explore.

Rome stuns the visitor; the scale is awesome but there is a Rome for everyone. Rome of the

Empire, Rome of the Church, the Capital, the center of fashion, the center of the Baroque. Its holy places attract the pilgrim, its antiquities lure the scholar. The Colosseum by moonlight is a cliché, but a good one if you are not accosted or mugged. Cafés of the fashionable Via Veneto provide a genteel setting for Rome's aristocracy in the morning, a gawker's paradise for tourists in the afternoon, and a human circus by night for the jet-setters and double-gaited swingers who hang on. In and around the Forum stand buildings from the time of Christ; not far away is Europe's oldest Jewish ghetto. Rome's fountains alone would make a city famous but there are also over 50 major churches, palaces, and museums. An author once said, "The problem isn't getting to Rome but getting away from it."

In a 13th-century version of germ warfare, the Florentines besieged the city of Siena by catapulting excrement and dead, decaying donkeys over the city walls to start a plague.

Peasants and the Exodus: Upward mobility is difficult in Italy's rigidly stratified social structure. The peasant in the south who wants to better himself must distinguish himself in school, move to a northern industrial town, or leave to seek his fortune in another European nation or the U.S. Between 1954 and 1969 the number of agricultural workers dropped by half as peasants abandoned the south for opportunities in the north and abroad. Those remaining are primarily small farmers who are hesitant to form cooperatives and so have little bargaining power in marketing their crops. They make up the poorest 35% of the population and earn less than ¼ of the national income.

Factory Workers: Largely immigrants from the south, this group has increased in number rapidly since W.W. II. The peasant-turned-factory-worker used to consult his local priest on political questions. Once in the north he finds the Communist party responsive to his needs for employment, friends, and a place to live. The Communist party becomes the shelter for this rural immigrant, who works through his union.

Service Employees: Second to industrial workers in number, they include bureaucrats, clerical workers, and military personnel. The heavily bureaucratic Government has created many of these jobs to forestall heavy unemployment. An Italian official estimates that there may be 55,000 semiautonomous government agencies.

Aristocracy, Industrialists, Professionals: The aristocracy is respected socially but does not constitute a power group politically or economically. Even at the time of national unification, the nobility did not form a barrier to the advance of republican government. The edu-

cated and professional class is well respected and assured of a living standard comparable to other Western European nations.

Only 20% of national government income comes from direct taxes, while 80% is from excise and turnover taxes included in products' selling prices. The major tax burden is on the consumer. There are taxes on wine, on staples like wheat, a 60% tax on sugar, and a 70% tax on salt. Lately, in an effort to curb inflation, property taxes were raised by $80 per room.

"I hate city Italians; they wear ugly neckties."—D. H. Lawrence.

—D.J. & A.J.

IVORY COAST

NITTY GRITTY

Location—In the southern part of West Africa, it is bounded on the south by Liberia and Guinea, on the north by Mali and Upper Volta, on the east by Ghana, and on the south by the Gulf of Guinea.

How Created—The borders evolved from the arbitrary lines drawn in 1904 within the West African territory grabbed by the French.

Size—127,483 sq. mi. (319,822 sq. km.).

Population—5,800,000: Baule, 23.2%; Bete, 17.6%; Senuto, 15.2%; Malinke, 11.4%; Dan and Guro, 9.8%; Lobi, 5.8%; Lagoon, 5.2%; Ngere, 4.5%; Bakwe, 4.5%; over 50 other groups, 2.8%. 65% Animist, 23% Muslim, 12% Christian.

Who Rules—Republican constitution. Full executive power is held by President Félix Houphouet-Boigny, founder and party leader of the interterritorial RDA (Rassemblement Démocratique Africain).

The Legislative Assembly has 70 members, all of whom belong to the Parti Démocratique de Côte d'Ivoire (territorial section of the RDA). Citizens of European descent (1/300 of the national population) hold ¼ of Assembly seats.

Who REALLY Rules—Foreign industrialized nations. France, the old colonial power, is still very much the principal economic and financial controller, but her importance is diminishing in favor of the U.S., whose interests are manifested in major banks, insurance companies, and industrial development. Other investors: West Germany, the Netherlands, Britain, Israel, Italy.

NOTES

The name "Ivory Coast" was given to the country hundreds of years ago by elephant hunters. Their method was to encircle whole herds of elephants with fire, and, after all the elephants had been killed, to harvest the bodies for the tusks.

Rural Life—Most of Ivory Coast's black natives live in small villages or in tribal communities, working in the forests, farms, mines, and factories. Local customs and traditional ways of life prevail. Political power at the local level is held by tribal chiefs and kings, who can often influence national decisions. Women in the tribes maintain traditional roles according to local custom. In most places, weaving is strictly a male occupation, while the women make pottery.

The Exodus—Through radio and newspapers villagers learn about the cities, where a worker can earn 20 to 30 times a country laborer's salary. Ivory Coast is plagued by thinning rural populations as villagers (mostly men and youths) flock to the cities.

City Life—Distribution of wealth in Ivory Coast is highly unbalanced. In Abidjan, the fashionable Baie de Cocody is inhabited by rich Africans and affluent foreigners. They live in tall, white skyscrapers or luxurious villas on the water. The fun-loving Ivorian elite (businessmen, professionals, plantation owners) share a swinging night life with the European immigrants, in nightclubs and jazz cellars, casinos, cinemas; they shop in expensive boutiques, work in modern office buildings, drive European sports cars on Abidjan's new 6-lane highway.

The poor of Abidjan live in the Treichville district across the bay. They are mostly black natives from the rural villages, living in crowded, small city huts. They work in the factories and fisheries, or sell their wares in the steaming, "quaint" marketplace. Night life is singing and dancing by firelight.

Women have difficulty getting work in the cities. Of all registered job applicants, 81% are men, 19% women. Of all job holders, only 2% are women.

Among the foreign companies doing business in the Ivory Coast are: Development and Research Corporation (U.S.—completing a deepwater port in San Pedro); Kaiser Engineering and Construction (U.S.—hydroelectric dam in Kossou); Pickands Mather and Company (U.S.—mining iron ore in Bongolo); Union Carbide (U.S.—dry-cell battery factory); Renault (France—car assembly in Abidjan); Esso, Shell, Erap (U.S.—off-shore drilling for oil).

Serving as an Ivorian senator in Paris in the 1950s, Victor Biaka-Bodo returned to his native land to do some electioneering. He traveled into the bush to acquaint himself with his fellow countrymen, and disappeared soon afterward. In 1953, an official court declared that Biaka-Bodo had been eaten by his constituents.

—R.C.

JAMAICA

NITTY GRITTY

Location—An island in the central Caribbean, 500 mi. south of Miami, 90 mi. south of Cuba.

How Created—Part of an ancient mountain chain. Original settlers were the Arawak Indians, later completely wiped out by the Spanish who came to the island searching for gold not long after it was discovered by Columbus. The Spanish were driven out by the British in 1655 after a series of battles in the mid-17th century.

Size—4,244 sq. mi. (10,991 sq. km.), about the size of Connecticut.

Population—Over 2 million: African, 76.8%; Afro-European, 14.6%; European, 0.8%; Chinese, 0.6%; other, 7.2%. 19.8% Anglican, 19% Baptist, 11.9% Church of God, 7.2% Roman Catholic, 6.7% Methodist, 5.1% Presbyterian, 17% no religion, 13.3% other.

Who Rules—The island operates under a British-type parliamentary system with a 2-chamber legislature. There are 60 elected members in the House, and 21 members in the Senate, 13 of whom are appointed by the governor-general on the advice of the Prime Minister, while the remaining 8 are appointed on the advice of the leader of the opposition.

Who REALLY Rules—The major aluminum producers, who own and operate Jamaica's rich bauxite mines, including Alcan, Kaiser Aluminum, Alcoa, Reynolds, Revere, and Anaconda. Also the United Brands Company, which, although it no longer directly owns Jamaican banana plantations, buys in quantity from the island's growers, thus controlling prices and production.

NOTES

Jamaica's economy is in some trouble. Tourism has decreased, and prices for many food exports have stayed relatively low, while the prices for imported manufactured goods, oil, and foodstuffs, have soared.

With more than 90% of the population of African or mixed descent, the social divisions tend to follow economic rather than color lines. Although some status attaches to being lighter than average in skin color, the dual standards that exist in wages, public services, work facilities, personal relationships and criminal justice are leveled mainly at the poorer sectors. The middle class is small, and the vast bulk of the population is poor. There is a minimum 25% unemployment rate. There is vast urban poverty, and the cities are ringed with slums. "Scuffling" (local term for scrounging) a living is an accepted way of life among the poor, who rely on their extensive family connections to get by. The rural poor frequently have a little plot of land, possibly shared with another family or relations, which may provide a subsistence living or a small income.

The Rastafarian sect is a uniquely Jamaican group of black nationalists, who desire a return to Africa and who refuse to involve themselves with Jamaican society. They will not beg, preferring to be self-employed or unemployed rather than take charity from Jamaicans. They never cut their hair, but twist it into long hanks. They have believed in the divinity of Haile Selassie of Ethiopia, from whose title—Ras Tafari—comes their name. Many smoke *ganja* (marijuana) for religious purposes.

Marijuana is Jamaica's 3rd largest export, after bauxite and bananas. Plots of it are cultivated in the mountains by whole villages, but it also grows wild all over the island. Cutbacks in Mexican exports have increased Jamaica's production.

—E.P.

JAPAN

NITTY GRITTY

Location—Japan (*Nippon* or *Nihon*) is an island chain of about 500 islands that forms an arc along the coast of East Asia. The southern end of Japan is 125 mi. from the southern tip of Korea. Japan's northernmost island is less than 30 mi. south of the island of Sakhalin, now part of the Soviet Union.

How Created—Official legends of Imperial Japan claimed that Jimmu Tenno, a descendant of the Sun Goddess, established the Japanese nation in 660 B.C. Nevertheless, his supposed descendants, members of the House of Yamato, unified the islands in about 200 A.D. The current Emperor, Hirohito, descends directly from that dynasty.

In 1192 a *shogun* (military governor) seized power from the Yamato dynasty, establishing a feudal system which lasted for nearly 700 years. Japan was able to avoid conquest by Mongol Emperor Kublai Khan in the 13th century when a typhoon destroyed his armada.

In 1542 the 1st European traders, who were Portuguese, landed in Japan. To prevent European domination in 1637 the Tokugawa Shogunate barred trade and contact with the outside world.

But the long, isolated regime of the Tokugawas could not withstand the European onslaught, and exposure to modern civilization stimulated a social revolution in Japan. In

1867–1868, Mutsohito, a member of the House of Yamato, regained power as Emperor, and assumed the name of "Meiji" (meaning "enlightened government"). In 1871 he abolished Japan's feudal system. In 1889 he and his supporters created a modern constitutional government.

The early rule of Meiji, known as the Meiji Restoration, marked the birth of the modern Japanese nation.

In 1894–1895 Japan defeated China in the Sino-Japanese War, annexing Formosa (Taiwan), the Pescadores Islands, and the Liaotung peninsula in southern Manchuria.

In 1904–1905 Japan defeated Russia in the Russo-Japanese War, stimulating a near-revolution in Czarist Russia and winning Teddy Roosevelt the Nobel Peace Prize. Japan annexed half the island of Sakhalin, on its northern border, and won control over Russian concessions in China.

In 1910 Japan annexed Korea and in 1931 it seized Manchuria from China, establishing the puppet state of Manchukuo. Throughout the 1930s Japan waged an undeclared war against China, seizing much of the Chinese coast, but never winning control over the interior.

In 1940 Japan joined the Axis alliance of Nazi Germany and Fascist Italy. While Germany occupied France, Japan moved into French Indochina.

At its peak, the Japanese Empire included the Philippines, the Dutch East Indies, Indochina, Malaya, Burma, Thailand (as a collaborator), and a number of Pacific islands. In 1944 the U.S., allied with England, Australia, and indigenous Asian liberation movements, began to drive the Japanese back. As a result of losing W.W. II, Japan lost all of its recently acquired possessions and kept only the home islands.

Size—143,818 sq. mi. (372,488 sq. km.).

Population—112 million: Japanese, 99.4%; Korean, 0.5%; Chinese, Ainu, and others, 0.1%. Over 80% of the people are Buddhist, over 80% are Shintoist, and most are both. Less than 1% are Christian.

Who Rules—Japan is a constitutional monarchy, headed by Emperor Hirohito since 1926. Hirohito renounced his divinity following W.W. II.

Under the supervision of American occupation forces, the Japanese adopted their current constitution in 1947. Japan has a bicameral, parliamentary form of government. The House of Representatives, the 491-member lower house of the Diet, has the power to overrule the 252-member House of Councillors.

Who REALLY Rules—Since it was formed from smaller parties in the mid-'50s, the Liberal Democratic party (LDP) has governed

Japan. Changes of government have been the result of disputes within the party.

Despite its name, the LDP is basically conservative and is the political voice of Japanese business. Big-businessmen openly dominate the Government through the party and through a network of advisory boards from the lowest bureaucratic level to the Cabinet.

The business community itself is dominated by *Zaikai*, a financial elite that dominates both business and politics. The *Zaikai* works through the elite *Sanken* (Industrial Problems Study Council) and the broader *Keidanren* (Federation of Economic Organizations).

The "Prime Minister" of the *Zaikai* is Kazutaka Kikawada, the chairman of *Sanken* and the Japanese Committee for Economic Development and the president of Tokyo Electric Power, the world's largest power company.

The Japanese tradition of loyalty goes beyond nation (Emperor) and family: It also includes employers. Japanese corporations maintain a paternal system of industrial relations. They provide company dormitories for unmarried employees, and sometimes they provide housing projects for families. Workers at many companies sing company hymns in unison ("Grow, Matsushita, Grow, Grow, Grow") before beginning work each day.

Women in Japanese culture have been traditionally subservient to men. Before W.W. II, women had no property rights. Most married Japanese women still call their husbands *shujin* (master) and young girls still attend bridal schools to learn wifely skills.

Though traditionally Japanese marriages have been arranged by families, "love matches" now make up 63% of all marriages.

In 1945 the Soviet Union, having defeated Nazi Germany, prepared to enter the Pacific war. Before the Soviets could commit many troops to the Asian theater, the U.S. had dropped atomic bombs on the Japanese cities of Hiroshima and Nagasaki, destroying those cities and hastening Japanese surrender. The atomic bombs essentially kept the Soviets out of Japan and established American postwar military superiority over the Soviet Union.

NOTES

American troops occupied Japan following the war, not returning sovereignty until 1952. The peace treaty which reestablished Japanese sovereignty did not call for the removal of American troops, however. Instead, the 2 governments negotiated a mutual security pact, known as "Ampo," providing for U.S. bases in Japan. Despite anti-"Ampo" demonstrations, the 2 governments renewed the treaty in 1960, and since 1970 they have agreed to let the 1960 treaty remain in force. Under the terms of "Ampo," the U.S. has had as many as 186,000 troops in Japan (in 1953, at the conclusion of the Korean War). Today the U.S. has 18,000 troops in Japan (not including Okinawa), but no ground combat forces.

Rapid industrial development in Japan's small area has brought severe environmental problems, including air and water pollution, urban congestion, and housing shortages. Unlike other nations', Japan's environmental movement has been led by the poor. When, in the late '50s, several people died from eating mercury-polluted fish, 1,500 fishermen invaded the polluting factory. Poor people have led fights to halt industrial expansion, and popular movements have opposed the use of nuclear energy (the Japanese, at least, remember Hiroshima).

—L.S.

Okinawa Islands

NITTY GRITTY

Location—The Okinawa island chain, known in Western writings as the Ryukyu island chain, consists of 143 separate islands, but the term usually refers to the 73 islands which were under American administration until 1972. The entire chain stretches some 700 mi. between Taiwan and the Japanese island of Kyushu, but the U.S. governed only the southern half after 1952. Okinawa Island, at the northern end of the former American territory, is the main island.

How Created—In the past several hundred years the Kingdom of Okinawa has been under Chinese or Japanese domination many times.

During the 1870s the Japanese Meiji regime took control of the Okinawa archipelago, making it a prefecture of Japan. After W.W. II the U.S. military governed the islands. Then, in the 1960s, the Okinawans and the Japanese Government pressed for reversion of the territory to Japan. In 1968 the U.S. returned a few islands and in 1972 it returned the rest, including the Daito Islands. Although Okinawans and the Japanese left supported reversion, they opposed the terms of the agreement, which allowed U.S. military bases to remain.

Size—922 sq. mi. (2,389 sq. km.) total land area. U.S. bases cover about 12% of the land.

Population—1 million: primarily Japanese, with some Americans.

Who Rules—In 1968 the Okinawans elected their 1st chief executive. Neither the chief executive nor the elected legislature has ever had full governing power. In 1972 power passed to the Japanese national Government.

Who REALLY Rules—Though the Japanese Government now governs Okinawa, the U.S. military remains influential.

Near the end of W.W. II Japan's retreating armed forces made Okinawa a major base. In early 1945 U.S. forces invaded, setting off W.W. II's last major battle. Approximately 12,500 American troops, 65,000 Japanese troops, and 110,000 Okinawan civilians died in the fighting, which devastated the islands.

The U.S. now maintains 88 bases, with 40,000 air, land, and sea forces on the Okinawa chain. These include huge logistics facilities, a jungle warfare school, and a Voice of America transmitter (to be phased out).

The U.S. used Okinawa as a base to support its minor intervention in the Chinese civil war. During the Korean War U.S. planes flew bombing missions from Okinawa. Also, Okinawa was a major transshipment point for the Indochina War.

In 1970 American and Japanese business began to build major aluminum and oil refineries on Okinawa, thus avoiding the legal environmental restrictions of the Japanese main islands.

Commodore Perry captured an ancient Okinawan bell during one of his visits. It now rings out the score at Army-Navy football games.

—L.S.

JORDAN

NITTY GRITTY

Location—In Southwest Asia, Jordan is bordered on the west by Israel, stretching to the Gulf of Aqaba on the southwest. On the south and east lies Saudi Arabia, except for a short stretch of border with Iraq. Syria lies to the north.

How Created—In the wake of W.W. I, Colonial Secretary Winston Churchill was concerned that Britain maintain close control of the strategically important region east of the Jordan River. Thus the territory of Transjordan came to be separated from the rest of Palestine and Syria. The Amir Abdullah was installed as surrogate ruler for the British. After the 1949 Arab-Israeli War, Abdullah unilaterally annexed the west bank of the Jordan River and proclaimed the Kingdom of Jordan. Israel conquered the west bank in 1967, and though Jordan still claims the area, Palestinians reject such claims.

Size—36,909 sq. mi. (95,594 sq. km.), about the size of Indiana.

Population—2,750,000: Arab, with a smattering of others. 93.6% Sunni Muslim, 6% Christian.

Who Rules—The King, Hussein, grandson of King Abdullah. He has the trappings of a government around him, but the style tends to be personal.

Who REALLY Rules—Hussein and his top military officers rule internally, but are kept in power by the U.S. Personal devotion of the bedouins to Hussein is essential to his ability to control the Army, and he keeps their loyalty by providing benefits to tribal leaders.

NOTES

In the 1967 Arab-Israeli War, Jordan witnessed the loss of Jerusalem and the entire west bank to Israel. In the aftermath of that defeat, the Palestinian Resistance began to take the lead from the defeated Arab Governments in the fight against Israel and for Palestinian national rights. Hussein was clearly one of the main agents in the denial of those rights to the Palestinians, so the Resistance moved to gain control of Jordan. This challenge resulted in a full-scale war (a civil war) in Jordan, in which Hussein and his bedouin Army defeated the Palestinian Resistance with U.S. weapons and support. Hussein in the process napalmed and strafed Palestinian refugee camps, killing and maiming thousands of civilians. Since that time, the King has been an object of increasing hatred among large numbers of Palestinians living in Jordan. He has responded with a continuing heavy policing of Palestinian camps in an extremely repressive atmosphere.

—J.G.

KENYA

NITTY GRITTY

Location—On the equator in East Africa. North are the Sudan and Ethiopia; east are the Somali Republic and the Indian Ocean; south is Tanzania; and west is Uganda.

How Created—Carved from British East Africa in 1963; became a republic the following year.

Size—224,960 sq. mi. (582,646 sq. km.), a bit larger than France.

Population—12.8 million: Kikuyu, 20.1%; Luo, 13.9%; Luhya, 13.3%; Kamba, 10.9%; Gusii, 6.4%; Meru, 5.1%; 65 other African tribes, 18.4%; Asian and Arab, 1.5%; European and other, 0.4%. 45% Animist, 36% Protestant, 21.8% Roman Catholic, 3.8% Muslim and Hindu.

Who Rules—The constitution provides for a chief executive who is President and a legislature, a one-house National Assembly of 158 elected members who then choose 12 additional members.

Who REALLY Rules—President Jomo Kenyatta led the former British colony to independence with the slogan *"Harambee"*—Swahili for "Let's all pull together." But in most ways it has been Kenyatta who has personally pulled Kenya together during the past formative decade.

NOTES

Half of the population is less than 16 years old.

Women figure strongly in Kenya's politics. Bantu women generally have been freer than their Muslim counterparts. And though the African males "believe" in polygamy, it's actually on the decline. Marriages are not prepackaged and a woman can refuse a suitor. Nevertheless, women still hold a lower status than men. The Kikuyus not only practice female circumcision, but defend and extol it as a way of binding the tribe together.

Among the Kikuyu the more ornaments a man can carry on his ears—earrings, bells, others' cars—the more his community will respect him. But if he loses an earlobe, he loses face as well.

In 1904 the British passed a law barring all nonwhites from owning or managing land in the highlands. By the end of the year 220,000 acres had been transferred to 342 Europeans. Eventually the one million Kikuyus were squeezed into an area 1/10 the size of that owned by 1,000 whites. The Kikuyus reacted by forming the Kenya African Union with Jomo Kenyatta as its head. An extremist group—the Mau Mau—later spun off from the KAU and began a guerrilla war against all non-African domination. Mau Mau members were bound to each other by secret oaths and mystic ritual and swore to rid Kenya of white domination by using terrorism. Their terror tactics became a rampage. All members participated in the killing of a European, an Asian, or a white-oriented African to share the common guilt and hide individual responsibility. The brutal Mau Mau uprising, which produced white retaliation that was just as brutal, lasted from 1952 to 1959. Its outcome was greater black participation in government, eventual general elections which frustrated European hopes for a white supremacist state, and final independence from Britain under Jomo Kenyatta in 1963.

—M.D.

KOREA

NITTY GRITTY

Location—Korea is a peninsula on the East Asian mainland, directly west of Japan. Most of its northern border, along the Yalu River, fronts China, but it also touches a small section of the Soviet Union near Vladivostok, on the Pacific coast. The Sea of Japan lies to the east; the Yellow Sea to the west.

How Created—Throughout Korean history the Chinese have often maintained control over Korea. In 1637 the Chinese Manchu rulers assumed loose authority, not renouncing it until defeated by Japan in the Sino-Japanese War (1894–1895).

Following the Russo-Japanese War (1904–1905), Japan made Korea a virtual protectorate. In 1910 Japan formally annexed Korea, ruling it until the end of W.W. II.

Under the Potsdam agreement, the Soviet Union occupied the northern half of the country in 1945 while the U.S. took over the southern half. Following W.W. II, left-wing Korean nationalists established the People's Republic of Korea, which was recognized by the U.S.S.R. The U.S., however, 1st acknowledged Japanese rule (even rearming Japanese, who had been disarmed by the Koreans, to put down independence demonstrations), and then —in 1948—staged elections to establish the anticommunist Republic of Korea.

Supporters of the People's Republic (later the Democratic People's Republic) in 1948 began a guerrilla campaign in the south to unify the country under northern leadership. The U.S. supervised the suppression of this movement, but the guerrilla war continued until the June 25, 1950, outbreak of conventional hostilities between the 2 Korean Governments, which did not end until 1953.

North Korea

Size—46,800 sq. mi. (121,200 sq. km.).

Population—15 million: almost 100% Korean. The traditional religions are Buddhism, Confucianism, Shamanism, and Ch'ŏrdogyoisin, but glorification of Kim Il Sung seems to be the official religion.

Who Rules—The national Supreme People's Assembly and local People's Assemblies. Legislators are elected from the Workers (Communist) party. The Premier, Kim Il Sung, is also General Secretary of the Workers party.

Who REALLY Rules—It is difficult to determine to what degree power is shared within North Korea's communist leadership, since North Korean publications credit Kim Il Sung with everything good that is done, everything wise that is said. There have been factions within the Workers party supporting both China and the U.S.S.R. in the Sino-Soviet split, but North Korea has managed to remain neutral.

South Korea

Size—38,022 sq. mi. (98,477 sq. km.).

Population—35 million: almost 100% Korean with a few Chinese and others. Buddhist, 12.2%, Confucian, 10.9%, Protestant, 10%, Roman Catholic, 2.2%, Ch'ŏrdogyoist, 2%, Wonbulgyoist, 2%.

Who Rules—In 1960 student-led protests brought down the dictatorial regime of the Republic of Korea's 1st President, Syngman Rhee. The democratic regime that followed did not last long. In 1961 Gen. Park Chung Hee (also spelled Pak Jung Hi) seized power. His U.S. supporters insisted on civilian government, so he staged elections to make himself President. In 1972 he declared martial law and forced the adoption of a new constitution continuing his rule.

Who REALLY Rules—Park's rule is enforced by the Korean Central Intelligence Agency (KCIA), but the military is supreme. Dissatisfied military leaders forced Park to dismiss the KCIA director in 1973.

The Park regime, both militarily and economically, is dependent upon external support. The U.S. and Japan, with the assistance of the International Monetary Fund, control the economy, while the U.S. actually has operational control of the military. The U.S. probably could replace Park, and it may be unhappy with his despotism, but it has no desirable alternative.

NOTES

Supporters of each side claim the other started the Korean War, and their claims are virtually impossible to prove. Regardless, both governments considered themselves lawful governments of all Korea. North Korean troops seemed better prepared. They poured across the 38th parallel, nearly driving the South Korean Government (which had already been weakened by guerrilla fighting) into the sea.

The U.S. got United Nations' sanction—a Security Council resolution, in Soviet absence—to intervene. It landed troops and began a heavy bombing campaign. The U.S. drove North Korean military forces back to the Chinese border. At that point Chinese "volunteer" troops intervened in support of the North Koreans, fighting the U.S. back down to the 38th parallel. After long truce negotiations, the 2 sides agreed to an armistice in 1953.

The U.S. spent as much as $80 billion on the Korean conflict, losing 54,246 men. The war was more costly for the Koreans, especially in the north. U.S. bombers destroyed virtually every building in the Democratic People's Republic.

Kim Il Sung was an important independence leader, and he has led North Korea since independence. But the government campaign to glorify his thoughts and actions is incredible. His name is always preceded with titles such as "Beloved and Respected Leader, Comrade" and his pictures (and statues) are posted prominently throughout North Korea, and may even be found at the bottom of soup dishes.

South Korea's armed forces, now numbering over 630,000 men, have been subsidized by the U.S. since their inception, for a total of $5 billion in loans and grants. The U.S. currently has 42,000 troops stationed in Korea.

Under martial law President Park has outlawed all opposition to the Government. Under his emergency decrees, suspected critics can be arrested without warrants and imprisoned without trial.

The Korean CIA has a network which not only spies on the activities of people within South Korea, but keeps tab on Koreans abroad. In 1973 it kidnapped Kim Dae Jung, Park's 1971 presidential opponent, while Kim was in Japan, and then smuggled him into Korea.

In late 1973 large student demonstrations and a national petition with hundreds of thousands of signatures called for democracy. Park's regime responded with repression, arresting hundreds of students, journalists, churchmen, and others.

Anticommunist evangelical Protestants, including the Reverend Sun Myung Moon's *Genri Undo* sect, are important backers of the Park regime. They have been subsidized by the ROK Government and right-wing U.S. evangelical organizations. The U.S. based Campus Crusade for Christ staged its "Explo '74" evangelical student congress in South Korea, drawing several hundred thousand believers.

—L.S.

LAOS

NITTY GRITTY

Location—A landlocked nation in Southeast Asia, surrounded by Thailand, Burma, China, Vietnam, and Cambodia.

How Created—The Kingdom of Laos, originally Lane Xang (Land of a Million Elephants), was formed in the 14th century. Wars with neighboring peoples frequently altered its borders. In the early 19th century, the Kingdom of Siam (Thailand) established control over Laos, but the French seized it from the Thai in 1893. France made Laos part of its Union of Indochina and established the kingdom's current borders. In 1946 some Laotian leaders unsuccessfully declared independence but the French did not grant even limited independence until 1949.

Size—91,400 sq. mi. (236,800 sq. km.).

Population—3.2 million: Lao, 62.2%; Thai, 5.4%; Khmu, 5.4%; Phouteng, 5.4%; Miao, 3.2%; Sui including Alak, 3.2%; Loven,

3.2%; others and unknown, 12%. Mostly Buddhist and Animist.

Who Rules—Laos is a constitutional monarchy. Since September, 1973, it has been governed by a coalition of the leftist Pathet Lao and the rightist, pro-American factions that previously ran the Royal Lao Government. Before the cease-fire each group governed the zone it militarily controlled. A 13-man Cabinet, headed by pro-Western "neutralist" Prince Souvanna Phouma (Prime Minister), governs the country, but the 42-member Joint Political Consultative Council, headed by the Pathet Lao's Prince Souphanouvong, has an equal voice in setting policy.

"Pathet Lao" is the informal, historical name for the Lao Patriotic Front, the Neo Lao Hak Xat.

Who REALLY Rules—The Pathet Lao is the dominant force in Laos.

NOTES

Before extensive American bombing, 85% of the population were subsistence (rice) farmers, and many other rural tribesmen cultivated opium, which was the country's primary export.

Meo hill people cultivated the precious poppy on their mountaintops and trekked to the regional centers to sell their crop. In exchange, they accepted only silver or gold, which they wore proudly around their necks in the form of necklaces.

Opium dens can be found in all major towns. Marijuana is sold openly in most markets, but Coca-Cola and Pepsi-Cola are not sold in Laos.

A loophole in an American-Laos trade agreement allowed many Lao to import deluxe Mercedes-Benz automobiles at a fraction of their cost under the heading of "agricultural equipment."

As short a time ago as the 1950s, any Lao woman seen wearing shoes was considered a harlot.

When the Japanese invaded Indochina during W.W. II, they bypassed Laos until 1945, just before their defeat. When the Japanese left, a group of Lao leaders declared independence, but the French returned. In 1949 the French granted Laos "independence within the French Union," but this dissatisfied left-leaning leaders, who formed the Pathet Lao and fought in alliance with the Vietnamese Viet Minh against the French.

The Geneva accords of 1954 were to have neutralized Laos and to have integrated the Pathet Lao into the Royal Government, but the Pathet Lao did too well in elections. The CIA backed a right-wing military coup, leading to new outbreaks of fighting between the Pathet Lao and the right.

In 1962 another Geneva agreement set up a coalition government between rightists, neutralists, and the Pathet Lao. The CIA, however, organized its mercenary Meo army, and, as the right wing assumed control over the major cities, fighting broke out again.

In 1964 the U.S. began bombing Laos. U.S. planes bombed the Ho Chi Minh Trail in southern Laos and Pathet Lao-held areas in northern Laos. Through early 1973, the U.S. dropped over 2 million tons of bombs on Laos, destroying nearly all visible villages in Pathet Lao areas and forcing the people to live in caves or flee to Royal Government zones.

In 1971 South Vietnamese forces invaded southern Laos to halt the flow of supplies to Communist forces in South Vietnam and Cambodia, but North Vietnamese troops drove them back. In early 1973 representatives of the Pathet Lao and the Royal Lao Government agreed upon a cease-fire and the removal of all foreign troops from Laos. The U.S. has reduced its presence, but most observers believe that the North Vietnamese are maintaining units along the Ho Chi Minh Trail.

U.S. involvement in Laos was so cruel and coldhearted that it made the authoritarian Pathet Lao communists look good by comparison.

—L.S. & S.L.W.G.

LEBANON

NITTY GRITTY

Location—A strip of land along the east shore of the Mediterranean, bordered on the north and east by Syria, and on the south by Israel.

How Created—Lebanon historically was part of Syria, but in the 19th century France forced the Ottoman Empire to make Lebanon a separate administrative district. After the destruction of the Ottoman Empire during W.W. I, France obtained control over both Lebanon and Syria but as separate territories despite a decision by Lebanese leaders in 1920 that Lebanon should be merged again into an independent Syria. France administered Lebanon until independence in 1945.

Size—3,950 sq. mi. (10,230 sq. km.).

Population—3.3 million: Arab, 92.9%; Armenian, 4.6%; Kurd, 0.7%; Jewish, 0.4%; Greek, Turkish, and others, 1.4%. 30% Maronite Catholic, 20% Sunni Muslim, 19% Shiite Muslim, 10% Greek Orthodox, 6% Druzean, 15% other.

Who Rules—Members of Parliament are elected along religious lines. The Parliament then selects the President, who must be a Maronite Catholic. The Prime Minister must be a Sunni Muslim and the President of the Chamber of Deputies must be a Shiite Muslim.

Who REALLY Rules—Foreign (mainly U.S.) capitalists and their dependent domestic bourgeoisie in alliance with the semifeudal landlords. Coinciding with and indistinguishable from this alliance are the major religious leaders, Christian, Muslim, and Druze.

NOTES

There is strong opposition from student groups in the country to the existing directions of Lebanese policy. Lengthy student strikes in 1973 and 1974 closed the American University of Beirut and other schools for stretches of several months at a time. Lack of official Lebanese support for the Palestinians has been a major part of this protest. Israeli bombings of Palestinian refugee camps in Lebanon and Israeli raids at the Beirut airport as well as in apartment buildings in the center of the city have produced no reaction from the Lebanese Government except for the repression of the Palestinian guerrillas. This response, coupled with extreme inflation and high unemployment, is causing some factions to question the entire Lebanese political system.

Not until 1969 were left-of-center parties, with alternative socioeconomic platforms, legalized. However, the electoral laws discriminate against such parties as the voter must vote in his or her birthplace, not in the place of residence or employment.

—J.G.

LESOTHO

NITTY GRITTY

Location—Medallion-shaped country in Africa's southeast corner, totally surrounded by the Republic of South Africa.

How Created—Former British Protectorate of Basutoland, became an independent constitutional monarchy in 1966.

Size—11,720 sq. mi. (30,355 sq. km.).

Population—1,250,000: Sotho and Nguni, 99.7%; European, mixed, and Asian, 0.3%. 38.7% Roman Catholic, 24.3% Lesotho Evangelical, 18.2% Animist, 10.4% Anglican, 8.4% other.

Who Rules—King is head of state; Prime Minister heads the Government. Two-house Parliament makes the laws, theoretically.

Who REALLY Rules—When it appeared that he was going to lose the nation's 1st elec-

tion, Prime Minister Leabua Jonathan invalidated the election and suspended the constitution and Parliament. The Government of South Africa wields a strong influence.

NOTES

This small mountainous kingdom is what remains of a larger refuge to which the Basotho people were driven by tribal wars and the deprivations caused by South African Boers. It has remained an independent enclave primarily because of the genius of one man, King Moshoeshoe I. His Basotho soldiers ambushed vengeance-seeking British soldiers on Berea Mountain by leaving a large herd of cattle as decoys for the greedy foreigners. Though he won the battle, Moshoeshoe ordered a local missionary to write the British governor in South Africa what has been called "the most politic document that has ever been penned in South Africa." He wrote: "Your Excellency— This day you have fought against my people and taken much cattle. I entreat peace from you—you have shown your power—let it be enough, I pray you. I will try all I can to keep my people in order for the future. Your humble servant, Moshoeshoe." The British were satisfied.

Eighty percent of Lesotho is meadows and pastureland.

About 60% of Lesotho's working-age males are employed in the mines and farms of South Africa.

—M.D.

LIBERIA

NITTY GRITTY

Location—In the "hump" of West Africa, with a 300-mi. southern coast along the Atlantic Ocean. To the north, Guinea; to the northwest, Sierra Leone; to the east, Ivory Coast.

How Created—The land was purchased from tribal chiefs in 1822 by the American Colonization Society as a place to settle freed American slaves. (The price included a box of beads, 3 pairs of shoes, a box of soap, one barrel of rum, and 12 spoons.) Liberia became a "voluntary haven" for slaves from the U.S., the West Indies, and those freed from ships at sea. By 1865, around 14,000 former American slaves, and 6,000 from elsewhere, had settled the land.

Size—43,000 sq. mi. (111,400 sq. km.).

Population—1,750,000: Kpell, 20.8%; Bassa, 16.3%; Gio, 8.2%; Kru, 8%; Grebo, 7.6%; Mano, 7.1%; Americo-Liberians, 3%; other,

29%. 90% Animist, 7% Christian, 3% Muslim.

Who Rules—President and Vice-President directly elected by universal suffrage; 8-year initial term, 4-year terms if reelected. Senate: 2 senators from each of the 9 counties; 6-year terms. House: one representative for every 10,000 voters; 4-year terms.

Who REALLY Rules—Since the 1959 defense pact, Liberia has agreed to consult the U.S. in the event of aggression and the U.S. has provided economic aid and military assistance. The U.S. built Monrovia's airport as a military base during W.W. II, and the Port of Monrovia after the war. The Liberian Frontier Force (the Army) is trained by Americans.

The U.S. now controls all of Liberia's major industry; the basis of the Liberian economy is an American-owned rubber plantation; one of Liberia's 1st 2 banks was owned by First National City Bank of New York.

Still, Liberia has on occasion voted against the U.S. in the UN.

NOTES

Americanization of Liberia is extreme. The nation's capital is named for James Monroe, the founding fathers were from the U.S., the official language is English, the Government and constitution were patterned after the U.S. system, the Liberian dollar is at par with and interchangeable with the U.S. dollar, the Liberian flag is red, white, and blue (one star, 11 stripes), and the Liberian police uniforms are like those worn by New York City police.

The road system is extremely poor. Going into the Hinterland (as the interior is called) is difficult except for the industrialized areas. The back country, inhabited solely by aborigines, is virtually unexplored and completely undeveloped. The trip into the Hinterland can be made by "ankle express"—in a hammock carried by porters. Even in Monrovia there were no roads until 1916, when an American diplomat received an automobile by mistake and, in order to have the use of it, was obliged to build the nation's 1st road.

Social Structure—Americo-Liberians: the English-speaking descendants of U.S. slaves who have been settling in Liberia since the founding of the colony. They are a well-defined ruling class including intellectuals, professionals, government officials, and—until 1931—slave traders. Afro-Liberians: This 97% of the population has been oppressed and exploited by the Americo-Liberian blacks since the latter's arrival. The Afro-Liberians are farmers, fishermen, mine workers, or house servants for the elite.

—R.C.

LIBYA

NITTY GRITTY

Location—On the north coast of Africa, between the Mediterranean on the north and Niger and Chad on the south, between Tunisia and Algeria on the west and Egypt and Sudan on the east.

How Created—Once a territory of Turkey, then Italy, modern Libya was formed by the UN in 1949 by uniting Tripolitania, Cyrenaica, and Fezzan.

Size—681,200 sq. mi. (1,764,240 sq. km.).

Population—2.3 million: Arab-Berber, 96.9%; Italian and other, 3.1%. 97.2% Muslim, 2.4% Christian, 0.4% Jewish and other.

Who Rules—A 12-man military junta, called the Revolutionary Command Council, headed by Chairman and President Col. Muammar el-Qaddafi. The 2,000 Soviet-like "popular committees" have local authority in villages, factories, and universities.

Who REALLY Rules—Colonel Qaddafi and the 22,000-man Army that backs him. No political parties are allowed. The national parliament remains dissolved. Local officials are appointed.

NOTES

An officer of the Revolutionary Command Council has complained, "Our peasants need water, but every time we dig for water, we find oil." With production at about 3 million barrels daily, oil provides an annual income of over $4 billion. Because of its low sulphur content, as well as the country's nearness to Europe, Libyan oil has been especially prized.

The Islamic *Shari'a* law is the law of this Muslim land. A thief can suffer loss of his hand, although the amputation is now done by a doctor in a hospital and under anesthesia. Alcohol is banned. There is, however, a black market for liquor run by diplomats and visiting Arabs. Colonel Qaddafi has stated that alcohol should be banned throughout the "entire world on order of the UN." There are dress regulations. Police have been known to splash red paint on the legs of women wearing skirts deemed too short. Long-haired males have been given haircuts. Use of makeup and jewelry is restricted. There is a shortage of women's hairdressers as, according to Islamic law, it is "forbidden for a man to touch a woman's hair."

The Qaddafi record includes:
—Backing of an attempt on the life of King Hassan of Morocco.
—Responsibility for the success of a countercoup by Sudan's General Nimeiry in 1971, by forcing down the BOAC jetliner carrying leftist

coup leaders and turning them over to Nimeiry to be executed.

—Financial backing of Palestinian al-Fatah guerrillas, totaling $50 million annually. He also gave a special bonus of $5 million to the Black September terror group following the 1972 Munich Olympics massacre of Israeli athletes.

—Promising financial support to those black African nations that would break ties with Israel, and threatening those that would not. All but 4 agreed to do so.

—Providing arms and money to the Irish Republican Army, apparently as a vendetta against Britain for its role in the creation of Israel.

—Providing loans to American Black Muslims.

　　　　　　　　　　　　　　　　—H.E.

MALAGASY REPUBLIC

(MADAGASCAR)

NITTY GRITTY

Location—An island in the Indian Ocean 240 mi. off the southeast coast of Africa. Its western coast helps form the Mozambique Channel.

How Created—Believed to be a part of the submerged continent of Gondwana.

Size—226,444 sq. mi. (586,486 sq. km.), it is the 4th largest island in the world.

Population—8 million: Merina, 26.1%; Betsimisaraka, 14.9%; Betsileo, 12%; Tsimikety, 7.2%; Sakalava, 5.9%; Antandroy, 5.3%; other Malagasy groups, 27.2%; French, Comoran Islanders, East Indians, and Chinese, 1.4%. 50% Animist, 25% Roman Catholic, 20% Protestant, 5% Muslim.

Who Rules—In 1972 Maj. Gen. Gabriel Ramanantsoa closed both houses of the legislature and established a Cabinet of 4 army officers and 6 civilians. Under police supervision a referendum was held, and the military rule was approved for 5 years—until 1977.

Who REALLY Rules—Malagasy is a member of the French Community, and France spends about $40 million annually on Malagasy public works, communications, schools, hospitals, housing, etc. The country is also dependent upon France as its best customer. An international consortium has plans to build cement, plate glass and rubber factories, and a huge shipyard and dry dock.

NOTES

The name "Madagascar" means "the land at the end of the earth." The original inhabitants of the island probably came from Indonesia 2,000 years ago, most likely in a single voyage.

The main ethnic groups and the English translations of their names are: the Merina (the Elevated People), the Betsimisaraka (the Inseparable Multitude), the Betsileo (the Invincible Multitude), the Tsimikety (Those Who Do Not Cut Their Hair), the Sakalava (People of the Long Valley), the Antandroy (People of the Thorn Bush), the Tanala (People of the Forest), the Bara (a name of unknown origin), the Antaimoro (People of the Banks), the Antanosy (People of the Island), the Sihanaka (People of the Lake), the Mahafaly (the Joyful People), the Antaifosy (People of the Sand), the Bezanozano (Those with Many-Braided Hair), the Antakarana (People of the Rocks), and the Betanimena (People of the Red Soil).

Rice is the most important crop, but the island produces ⅔ of the world's supply of vanilla.

　　　　　　　　　　　　　　—D.W. & R.C.

MALAWI

NITTY GRITTY

Location—In East Africa; to the east, Lake Malawi (Lake Nyasa); to the east, south and west, Mozambique; to the west, Zambia; to the north, Tanzania.

How Created—Originally the British protectorate of Nyasaland, its borders were arbitrarily set by the British. It was explored by David Livingstone, and developed under a charter given to Cecil Rhodes in 1884.

Size—45,747 sq. mi. (118,484 sq. km.), about the size of Pennsylvania.

Population—Over 5 million: African (Chewa, Nyanja, Lomwe, Yao, Tumbuka, Sena, Tonga, Ngoni, and Ngonde), 99.4%; Asian, European, and other, 0.6%. 30% Animist, 23% Presbyterian, 20% Muslim, 18% Roman Catholic, 9% other Protestant.

Who Rules—Dr. H. (Hastings) Kamuza Banda has been declared "President for life." He is the sole head of state. The 55-member National Assembly is the single legislative body, with 50 of its members elected by universal adult suffrage, and 5 nominated by the President.

Who REALLY Rules—Malawi is extremely poor and needs all the help it can get. A member of the Commonwealth of Nations, it accepts aid from many Westerns nations, on a policy of "discretionary nonalignment." Aid and investments come from Denmark, West Germany, France, Britain, the U.S., Portugal, and some communist countries too. Malawi also relies on South Africa and Rhodesia for access to the sea, and has been strongly criticized for its increasing dependence on trade with South Africa. Malawi is the only African nation with full diplomatic relations with South Africa; other black radical leaders have expressed their anger at this to Banda, who replies that it has increased Malawi's trade, attracted South African tourists, drawn $25 million in aid from South Africa as well as South African private investments, and assured work for more Malawi migrant workers in South Africa. Banda claims, "I would do business with the devil himself to further the interests of the people of my country."

NOTES

Banda's policy of accepting aid and doing trade with any willing party has drawn criticism, but it has also worked wonders for Malawi's struggling economy. In order to do this, he has exercised unchallenged and unchecked authority. In the late 1960s he threw the Peace Corps out. Later he forbade Malawi women to wear skirts above the knee and altered the judicial system, declaring himself President for life. Banda has also allowed his youth group to practice religious discrimination—even violence—against the Jehovah's Witnesses. In July, 1973, he deported the foreign press corps.

—R.C.

MALAYSIA

NITTY GRITTY

Location—Malaysia is located at the southeastern tip of Asia. The 11 states of West Malaysia occupy the southern 400 mi. of the Malay peninsula. The 2 states of East Malaysia, 400 mi. across the South China Sea, follow the northwestern coast of the island of Kalimantan (Borneo), shared with Indonesia.

How Created—By the early 1900s, the British had gained control of Malaya and North Borneo through conquest and deals made with the Sultans. In 1948 they combined the 11 states of Malaya into the Federation of Malaya and in 1957 they granted formal independence.

Under British auspices the Federation of Malaya, together with the Crown Colonies of North Borneo, Sarawak, and Singapore, and the protectorate of Brunei, planned to form the new Federation of Malaysia in 1963. Brunei backed out before federation, and Singapore pulled out in 1965.

Size—128,553 sq. mi. (332,952 sq. km.): West Malaysia (the former Federation of Malaya), 50,915 sq. mi., and East Malaysia (Sabah and Sarawak), 77,638 sq. mi.

Population—11,750,000: West Malaysia—Malay, 50.6%; Chinese, 36.3%; Indian and Pakistani, 11%; other, 2.1%. (Malays are Muslim, Chinese are Buddhist, Confucian, and Taoist, and Indians are Hindu and Muslim.) Sabah—Kadazan, 29.8%; Chinese, 21.9%; Bajau, 11.7%; Murut, 4.4%; European, 0.4%; other indigenous, 18.1%; other, 13.7%. 37.9% Muslim, 16.6% Christian, 45.5% Animist and other. Sarawak—Chinese, 33.1%; Iban, 28.6%; Malay, 18.2%; Land Dayak, 8.4%; Melanau, 5.7%; European, 0.2%; other, 5.8%. 23.4% Muslim, 15.8% Christian, 60.8% Animist and other.

Who Rules—Malaysia is a constitutional monarchy, with an elective monarch. The *Yang di-Pertuan Agong*, or head of state, is elected by the hereditary rulers (most are Sultans) of 9 states. The 4 former Crown Colonies—Sabah, Sarawak, Penang, and Malacca—are headed by appointed governors.

Malaysia's political system is modeled after Britain's. The upper house, the Senate, is both elective and appointive. The powerful lower house, the House of Representatives, is fully elective.

Who REALLY Rules—Britain carefully orchestrated Malaysia's independence and development because it has a strong economic interest there. Malayan tin and rubber exports have been a major source of British income for decades. Now American business interests are moving in. Foreigners reportedly control 70% of Malaysia's investment.

With the growth of American investment, American foundations have stepped in to train and advise young leaders, scholars, and officials. The Agricultural Development Council, the Asia Foundation, and a number of American universities have replaced the British as Malaysia's mentors.

NOTES

Most of the Chinese were brought to Malaysia by the British in the 19th century to work the tin mines. Today half are self-employed; most of the rest are skilled. With foreign firms, they dominate Malaysia's economy.

The British brought in the Indians during the 19th century, to work on rubber plantations. Sixty percent still live and work under harsh conditions on the plantations.

The Ibans or Sea Dayaks are the legendary headhunters of Borneo. They are a proud and independent people who like to adorn their bodies with tattoos and distend their earlobes 6" or more with iron rings. They are quite fond of the water, sometimes spending most of their day squatting in the rivers conversing with each other. In olden times, they settled disputes by declaring the man who could remain submerged under water the longest by holding his breath as the winner.

English words borrowed from the Malay language include bamboo, bantam, and orangutan.

The left hand in Malaya, as in many Muslim countries, is considered "dirty" since it is used to perform all "unclean" bodily functions. Consequently, the Malays make sure never to touch food or another person with the left hand.

The Government, while appearing liberal, practices press censorship and occasionally imprisons left-wing opponents without trial under the Internal Security Act. In 1972 some 1,700 people were in jail under this act.

The Philippines claim Sabah, which was once ruled by the Sultan of Sulu (a nearby Philippines island). The 2 countries nearly went to war over this claim in the 1960s. Meanwhile, the Chief Minister of Sabah has reportedly been supporting Muslim secessionists in the southern Philippines.

The largest flower in the world, the Rafflesia, which reaches a diameter of up to 36", and a weight of up to 15 lbs., grows on mountain slopes in Borneo.

After W.W. II, the Malayan Communist party initiated a bloody revolution which continues today. The fact that the party is predominantly Chinese and Peking-oriented has led many Malays to question the loyalties of all Chinese. In 1969 riots broke out between the 2 ethnic groups. One hundred and sixty-three people were killed and over 4,000 were arrested.

—L.S. & S.L.W.G.

MALI

Location—Landlocked in West Africa. To the northeast, Algeria; to the east, Niger; to the west, Mauritania and Senegal; to the southwest, Guinea; to the southeast, Upper Volta; and to the south, Ivory Coast.

How Created—Borders were established by the conquering French, and subsequently altered many times for political reasons. Originally called French Sudan.

Size—478,822 sq. mi. (1,240,142 sq. km.).

Population—5.7 million: Mandé (Bamabara, Malinké, Sarakollé), 50%; Peul, 17.2%; Voltaic, 12.2%; Songhai, 5.6%; Tuareg and Moors, 4.6%; other, 10.4%. 65% Muslim, 30% Animist, 1.6% Christian, 3.4% other.

Who Rules—The military; President of the National Liberation Committee is the nation's leader, Lieut. Moussa Traore.

Who REALLY Rules—Mali is trying to establish a capitalist system of free enterprise, which requires a good deal of foreign invest-

ment. Rather than depend upon any one nation, Mali, which is considered a radical independent state, remains neutral in world affairs and manages to carry on diplomatic relations with around 40 different countries. Mali's budget is well balanced, and her development programs are financed by aid from France, the U.S., West Germany, the U.S.S.R., East Europe, and China.

NOTES

Mali has 3 geographical zones. The Saharan is desert, where wild long-maned sheep and cheetahs live. The Sahelian is scrub savanna, with gazelle, ostrich, red monkey, lion, leopard, fox, and hyena. The Sudanic is the plains region, rich farmland with lush vegetation, including the famed baobab tree; animals there include guinea hen, buffalo, elephant.

A national hero is Mansa Musa, Emperor of ancient Mali (1307–1332), who conquered Timbuktu. On his pilgrimage to Mecca, Mansa Musa took 80 camels, 500 slaves, and 5,500 men. Along the way he handed out money to the poor, dispensing over 50,000 ounces of gold by the time he was through. He returned from Mecca with tutors, scholars, and philosophers, and made Timbuktu a center of medieval learning.

Timbuktu, once Musa's capital, has been reduced to a sleepy, dusty town of 5,000, which now does little more than attract a few tourists.

—R.C.

MAURITANIA

Location—In northwestern Africa, with a 375-mi. western coastline on the Atlantic Ocean; to the northwest, Spanish Sahara; to the south, Senegal; to the east and south, Mali; to the northeast, Algeria.

How Created—The borders of Mauritania, an ancient kingdom, were never really clearly defined until 1904, when it became a French territory.

Size—398,000 sq. mi. (1,030,700 sq. km.).

Population—1.5 million: Arab, 80.3%; Fulani, 13.8%; Soninke, 3.3%; Zenaga, 1.3%; Wolof, Malinke, and other, 1.3%. 95% Muslim.

Who Rules—The President is elected to a 5-year term by direct vote; the 40-member Assembly is also elected to 5-year terms; the current President, Moktar Ould Daddah, is also the secretary-general of the Parti de Regroupement Mauritanien, to which all members of the Assembly belong.

Who REALLY Rules—Mauritania's economic independence will depend upon the success of her iron ore and copper mines, which are being developed by France, Britain, Germany, and Italy. The country has very few educated people, and few experienced administrators, and must rely upon foreign technicians and administrators to organize the nation's industry and big business. Most of these administrators are French.

France has, over the years, lent much in the way of technical and financial assistance to her former colony. At times French armed forces have been called upon to help Mauritanian police keep the peace.

NOTES

The majority of Mauritanians are Maures (after whom the country is named), or, in English, Moors. They are Arab nomads who live in the desert, following the rains with their cattle, sheep, goats, and camels. Cattle are an important status symbol, a sign of wealth and power. In the north are the Tuareg "blue men," so called because of the blue dye of their robes which rubs off and impregnates their skin, tinting it blue. The Tuareg men are very proud and dignified, gracious to guests, fierce with enemies. An old Tuareg proverb advises: "Kiss the hand you cannot sever."

Racial discrimination in Mauritania has posed a serious problem for the blacks, who do not have equal social status with the Maures. Clashes have arisen over the compulsory teaching of Arabic in the public schools, and violence has erupted because of job discrimination. In 1966, President Daddah officially forbade any talk of the race problem.

Women in Mauritania receive the treatment which is customary for Arab women—they are considered the property of their husbands. Even the Tuareg women, who are unveiled, are otherwise bound to their traditional roles. The Tuareg men like their women fat, and stuff them with macaroni and bread to keep them that way.

In the early 1970s the desert began to "move" southward. Drought turned Mauritania into an emergency disaster area. Famine grew severe, and foreign aid was finally enlisted. Money came from the UN Food and Agricultural Organization, from the U.S. Agency for International Development (which pledged $24 million for the purchase and transport of 56,000 tons of food grain), and from Canada, the European Common Market nations, and many others. Independently, the Catholic Relief Service and the Church World Service organizations, and Jesse Jackson's African Relief Fund, have tried to get food to the disaster area, which includes Mauritania and 6 other African nations.

Despite all efforts, thousands are dying of starvation, and thousands more will suffer the aftereffects of malnutrition—physical underdevelopment and mental retardation. With the drought over, it will take 3–4 years for a tribe to rebuild its livestock herds, and it will be many years before Mauritania is back to normal.

—R.C.

MEXICO

NITTY GRITTY

Location—The north and widest end of the Central American isthmus. Neighbors are: the U.S. to the north; Guatemala and British Honduras to the southeast; Gulf of Mexico to the east; Pacific Ocean to the west and south.

How Created—At the time of the Spanish conquest, Mexico was home to 700 tribal groups, speaking over 100 different languages and dialects. The center of Aztec power lay in Tenochtitlán, now occupied by Mexico City. Exploration and conquest began in 1517, directed from Cuba by Spanish governor Diego Velásquez. The 3rd and definitive expedition to Mexico, under the leadership of the Spanish adventurer Hernán Cortés, arrived in the Yucatán peninsula in 1519. Moving north along the coast, Cortés founded Veracruz. Then, playing upon existing dissension within the Aztec Empire, he captured and destroyed Tenochtitlán and executed the Aztec chiefs.

Dominated for 3 centuries by Spain in its political, religious, cultural, and economic spheres, Mexico at last gained its freedom in 1821 following 10 years of agitation and guerrilla warfare by the peasants. Not until the Creoles joined the movement, under the leadership of Augustín de Iturbide, was independence achieved, on September 27, 1821. Iturbide seized power in 1822, proclaiming himself Emperor Agustín I, but the empire lasted less than a year. The entire monarchical system was overthrown, and Mexico sought a republican form of government.

Size—761,600 sq. mi. (1,972,547 sq. km.).

Population—59 million: mestizo, 55%; Indian, 29%; white, 15%; other, 1%. 96.2% Roman Catholic, 1.8% Protestant, 2% other religion or none.

Who Rules—Mexico is a Federal republic with a President and bicameral legislature. The chief executive is strong, with considerable power centralized in his office. The President's term lasts 6 years, and he cannot be reelected.

Who REALLY Rules—The U.S. exercises considerable direct influence in Mexican affairs. In addition to having extensive financial investments in Mexico, the U.S. is very interested in seeing a stable, cooperative, and noncommunist neighbor. Problems regarding the shared border have generally been resolved in favor of the U.S.

Most power within Mexico resides in the group of industrialists and businessmen who control the principal means of wealth: commerce, banking, manufacturing. The dominant political party, the PRI (Institutional Revolutionary party), once the champion of revolutionary aims, has become institutionalized over the years. It is increasingly influenced by conservative elements: those opposing further land reform or restructuring of the society.

NOTES

Father Miguel Hidalgo y Costilla (1753–1811), parish priest of a village 100 mi. northwest of Mexico City, was known for his scholarship and good works. He taught his Indian parishioners to raise silkworms, and established a tannery, a brickyard, and a pottery works. In addition he read widely and was much influenced by French philosophy and the French Revolution. Discovering that nearby Creoles were plotting a revolt, he actively participated. When the Spanish authorities discovered his plot, Father Hidalgo moved quickly to arm his parishioners. With some 55,000 men, under the banner of the Lady of Guadalupe, on September 16, 1810, they began a march on the nearby cities, ravaging and killing as they went. In Guadalajara, Father Hidalgo received the title of Serene Highness. However, driven out by Spanish troops, and having lost most of his army due to desertion or death, Father Hidalgo was captured by trickery in March, 1811. Tried and convicted by a military court, he died before a firing squad on July 10, 1811. September 16, the day the uprising began, is celebrated as Mexico's Independence Day, although true independence was not achieved until 1821, 11 years after Hidalgo's revolt.

With the recognition by the U.S. of Texas in 1836, considerable bad feeling developed between the U.S. and Mexico. In 1845, Texas was annexed outright, and the U.S. also had its eye on California and the rest of the Southwest. U.S. offers to buy the area were rejected by the Mexicans, still outraged at the annexation of Texas. The U.S., fearing British intervention in the situation, cast aside diplomacy and sent forces into the debated area. To the Mexicans, this constituted an invasion, and so they attacked, whereupon the U.S. Congress declared war in 1846.

The Mexicans, crippled by poor arms and internal divisions, could not fend off the invaders, and by late 1847 the Mexican Government conceded victory, establishing a peace commission. The Treaty of Guadalupe Hidalgo (February 2, 1848) gave Mexico $15 million, but cost it about half of its national domain—Texas, Nevada, Utah, Arizona, New Mexico, California, and part of Colorado. The loss hurt Mexico economically, and an enduring resentment of the U.S. may be traced to this.

Emiliano Zapata (1883–1919), a Mexican revolutionist of Indian birth who was born in poverty, 1st found work as a stable hand on a large hacienda. Legend has it that he was radicalized through reflecting on the difference between his own dirt-floored hovel and the clean, tiled stables assigned to his master's horses. In 1911, Zapata eagerly joined the revolution proclaimed by Francisco Madero, and began a rebellion of his own. However, he did not support President Madero, whose agrarian reform program was too moderate. He led his forces against local landholders, burning their haciendas during the counterrevolution of Huerta, and, with Pancho Villa, continued to support measures more radical than those proposed by President Venustiano Carranza. He was assassinated on April 10, 1919, after Carranza put a price on his head. He is now recognized as the great champion of agrarian reform, and his name has been inscribed in gold in the Chamber of Deputies.

On October 2, 1968, 10 days before the Olympics began in Mexico City, soldiers opened fire on a student rally at the Plaza of Three Cultures, killing hundreds of people. The total number of dead has never been determined. Early in 1975, several leftover skeletons were discovered in the basement of a nearby housing project.

The flood of Mexican laborers illegally crossing the border into the U.S. may continue to cause considerable friction between the countries if the worldwide economic situation worsens. Jobs for unskilled labor are already in short supply, and the Mexicans, who will work for very low wages, are considered unfair competition. U.S. Immigration Service officers apprehended over 600,000 illegal immigrants in 1973.

The U.S. Justice Dept. operates a Border Patrol Academy in Port Isabel, Tex., whose program includes Spanish lessons and training in self-defense and the use of firearms. The patrol's main job is to prevent illegal aliens from entering the U.S. The U.S. Bureau of Customs has instituted a computerized data bank system on known or suspected smugglers. Since 1970 this system, known as CADPIN (Customs Automatic Data Processing Intelligence Network), has been in operation at border checkpoints and at major U.S. international airports. The system is also linked to the computerized crime files of the FBI. In addition, electronic sensors which detect body heat—developed for use in the Vietnam War—are now being used to detect hidden Mexicans.

Domestically, Mexico may be headed for a crisis. President Luis Echeverría, elected as a moderate, has been unable to please either the left or the right. Guerrilla groups of the left have stepped up their activities, particularly in the region of Guadalajara. Bombings, kidnappings of prominent Mexicans and foreigners, and shoot-outs with government forces have increased. In April, 1974, some 50 suspects were arrested and 12 killed in an acknowledged "war" on Mexico's urban guerrillas. Caches of arms and Mexican Army uniforms have been found. Members of the conservative right, who are frequently the kidnap targets, feel that Echeverría is not handling the situation forcefully enough. In addition, Echeverría's occasional mention of agrarian or tax reform does not sit well with the wealthy elite. Inflation of over 20% in 1973 has not helped to ease the national situation—the poor are still the hardest hit.

—E.P.

MONGOLIA

NITTY GRITTY

Location—A landlocked, oval-shaped country in the middle of East Asia isolated between the Soviet Union to the north and the People's Republic of China to the south.

How Created—Early in the 13th century after the nomadic tribes roaming the area united to form a feudal state, the borders as they are now began to assume roughly their present shape. Genghis Khan's rule established Mongolian autonomy soon after and although expansion nearly equal to the Eurasian communist land mass today followed his conquests, only a territory approximately the same as the present area was considered to be Mongolia. The boundaries established coincide with a plateau that averages 5,000′ in altitude.

Size—604,000 sq. mi. (1,565,000 sq. km.), about the same area as Western Europe.

Population—1,650,000: Khalka, 75.3%; Kayakh, 5.2%; Durbet, 2.9%; Buryat, 2.5%; Bayat, 2.1%; Russian, 1.8%; Dariganga, 1.7%; Uryankhai, 1.3%; Dzakhchin, 1.3%; other, 5.9%. All religion is discouraged by the Government, but the influence of Tibetan Buddhism is still strong.

Who Rules—The 1960 constitution describes Mongolia as a socialist state. There is only one political party, the Mongolian People's Revolutionary party, and it governs through a Parliament and Council of Ministers. The party has nearly 60,000 members

and it is 2nd only to the Soviet Union's in experience with socialist administration.

Who REALLY Rules—Although Mongolia is its own boss, the Soviet Union, which was instrumental in establishing the country as a socialist state in 1921, wields tremendous influence in Mongolian affairs because of the vast amount of economic, technological, and military assistance it has continuously poured into the country.

NOTES

Except for the capital, Ulan Bator, and a couple of industrialized cities, Mongolia has changed very little since the days of Genghis Khan 700 years ago. Although the Gobi Desert accounts for 25% of the country, natural scenery also includes snow-capped mountains, forests, countless acres of grazing land, and deep valleys. It is said that at night 3 times the number of stars observed elsewhere can be seen in the clear, cold sky.

The Mongols never overwhelmed their opponents by sheer numbers as the romantic legends frequently maintain. At the peak it is estimated their armies probably never exceeded 250,000. The real truth is that they were all elite, thoroughly disciplined, practically born in the saddle, and capable of incredible feats of endurance ranging from living endless days on horseback while surviving off the surrounding countryside to covering tremendously long distances in a short time. Another important factor is their unification at a time when the surrounding long-established societies were declining. Although they were primitive, they were also technologically superior: Centuries before, their tribal ancestors had begun using iron stirrups for warfare, making it possible for men on horseback to stand and shoot arrows at their enemies while riding. This innovation appears simple by modern standards but its development greatly changed the tactical balance, favoring the Mongol rider over the ordinary fighting man he generally encountered during the Mongolian quest for empire.

—R.E.K.

MOROCCO

NITTY GRITTY

Location—A 900-mi.-long, narrow land at Africa's northwest corner, wedged between Algeria to the east and south, the Atlantic to the west, and the Mediterranean to the north. It is south of the Strait of Gibraltar and Spain. Morocco also shares a southern border with Spanish Sahara.

How Created—By the union of the Spanish and French protectorates with the international zone of Tangier in 1956; in 1969 the Spanish enclave of Ifni was added.

Size—177,117 sq. mi. (458,730 sq. km.).

Population—18 million: Arab, 68.5%; Berber, 30%; French, Spanish, Jewish, and other, 1.5%. 99.1% Muslim.

Who Rules—There is a semblance of a constitutional monarchy headed by King Hassan II. There is a unicameral Parliament of 240 members but only 90 are directly elected.

Who REALLY Rules—The King, who doubles as the religious leader of the country's Muslim majority, is traditionally assisted by a strongman from the military.

NOTES

The city of Casablanca, where the Humphrey Bogart film *Casablanca* has never been allowed to be shown, boasts the largest and most spectacular brothel in the world—Bousbir.

Morocco is that part of Africa which is closest to Europe. The Atlas Mountains separate the country from Saharan Africa to the south and Arab Africa to the east. Consequently Morocco looks as much across the Gibraltar Strait to Christian Spain as to the Arab East. The stamp of Spain is unmistakable: Parts of Marrakesh look like its sister city Seville.

Westerners and Arabs alike know Moorish history blended generously with myth from the *Arabian Nights*. One well-known figure from these stories is Harun el Rashid, who poisoned the 1st Sultan—founder of the Moroccan Empire in 788—by sending him a fragrant but deadly perfume. Yet the most fiendish character of all was Sultan Moulay Ismail, a contemporary of Louis XIV, one of whose daughters the Sultan wanted to marry. In building his new capital near Fez he wanted to outdo Versailles. The new stables were 3 mi. long and lodged 1,200 horses. If slaves did not work on the project industriously, he had them cemented into the walls. Of his several hundred thousand slaves, 25,000 were captured Christians. His courtiers had to catch his saliva before it reached the ground whenever he spat and preserve his excrement to give out as tokens of his love for ladies in the harem. Although he is said to have killed 36,000 people with his own hand, Moulay was also a devout and accomplished theologian, who tried to convert England's James II to Islam.

A group that is largely resented is the Moroccan bureaucracy, which requires continual palm-greasing in order for anything to function. Economic enterprises are expected to pay various sorts of protection money. Jewish enterprises find it convenient to operate under Muslim "umbrellas." At the head of the bureaucracy is the King. The turnover is very high as civil

servants are made to realize that they have not earned their positions but hold them only because of the King's favor. Hassan once remarked in an interview: "If one day all my ministers resigned, I would say to my chauffeur, be minister." The prevalent attitude in the bureaucracy seems to be: Get yours while you can.

More and more, women are lifting their veils in defiance of Muslim custom and romantic love is gaining ground. Polygamy is now too expensive except for the wealthiest of pashas, so wealthier families are now insisting on marriage contracts to protect the interests of their daughters. More and more girls go to school, attend movies alone, and join feminist groups in the cities. Still, the price for liberation is high: Muslim men still look with deep suspicion—for "suspicion" read "fear"—upon the liberated Moroccan woman.

—M.D. & H.E.

MOZAMBIQUE

NITTY GRITTY

Location—Runs along the southeast African coast, sharing borders with Tanzania in the north, with Malawi, Zambia, and Rhodesia to the west, and with the Republic of South Africa and Swaziland in the southwest. To the east is the Indian Ocean.

How Created—The British and Portuguese arbitrarily set the frontiers of their spheres of influence here in 1891. After W.W. I, Mozambique got the Kionga triangle from German Tanganyika.

Size—303,075 sq. mi. (784,961 sq. km.).

Population—9 million: African (mostly Bantu), 97.8%; white, 1.5%; other, 0.7%. 69.6% Animist, 15.3% Christian, 12.5% Muslim, 2.6% other.

Who Rules—Marxist Front for the Liberation of Mozambique (FRELIMO).

Who REALLY Rules—FRELIMO, which is expected to align itself with China, has squelched all attempts to form an opposition party.

NOTES

The coast of Mozambique was Portugal's logical choice for a halfway point for her fleets trading with India, because Mozambique had citrus fruits (introduced earlier by the Arabs), which would treat crews' scurvy. The coast protected ships from winter monsoons and its ports had the gold the Arabs had been extracting from Rhodesia. But as Portugal's trading empire declined so did Mozambique's value to it. In the early 1900s Portugal offered its colony to Britain for £3 million. Evidently Britain did not need it. With the rise of black African nationalism, the U.S.-educated Dr. Eduardo Mondlane founded the Mozambique Liberation Front or FRELIMO. He was later assassinated at his home in Dar es Salaam in 1969. In 1974 Portugal announced its decision to grant Mozambique full independence the following year. White settlers tried to sabotage the process by staging a coup in Lourenco Marques. The Portuguese Army did not support the whites, however, and the aborted coup led only to violence, bloodshed, and a backlash against the whites that sent many scurrying across the borders to the white-dominated countries of Rhodesia and South Africa.

Between 1971 and 1974, 865 black political prisoners died in Portuguese secret jails.

The new black administration evidently believes Mozambique should be a multi-racial society and many whites have decided to stay. "There is a place for everybody in Mozambique," the Premier said shortly after the formation of the interim government.

"We're not fighting the color of whites; we are fighting against their laws. . . ."—Raimundo Dalepa, FRELIMO guerilla, described by villagers as a black James Bond.

—M.D.

NEPAL

NITTY GRITTY

Location—"A yam between 2 boulders," Nepal is landlocked between India and China in the central Himalayas, the world's highest mountain range.

How Created—Nepal was founded in 1769 as a kingdom consisting of 46 previously sovereign principalities.

Size—54,362 sq. mi. (140,798 sq. km.), about the size of Wisconsin.

Population—12,750,000: Nepali (Gurkha, Khāsi, and others), 51.1%; Tharu, 13.8%; Bihari, 10.7%; Tamang, 6.1%; Newar, 4.8%; Magar, 3.3%; Kiranti, 2.9%; other, 7.3%. 90% Hindu, 9% Buddhist, 1% other.

Who Rules—The King, currently Birendra Bir Bikram Shah Dev, rules with the help of members selected by him from Parliament. Parliament cannot question the conduct of the King and the King can overrule Parliament on any issue. King Birendra studied under Dr. Henry Kissinger at Harvard.

Who REALLY Rules—India has in the past exerted tremendous cultural and political influence over Nepal. India's cultural ties with Nepal's Hindu population are centuries old. During the past decade, however, Nepal has managed to free itself somewhat from India's orbit and has initiated trade agreements with China, and receives aid from both the U.S. and the U.S.S.R.

NOTES

In 1951 a revolution headed by the Nepali Congress took place and a Government was set up wherein a constitutional monarch led an elected Congress. A democratic constitution was put into effect in 1959 which resulted in the election of a socialist-inclined Government. Twenty months later, a land-reform program being considered by the new Government inspired the King to dismiss the Parliament, suspend the constitution, outlaw political parties, and assume full control of Nepal. After outlawing political parties, which had grown almost too numerous to count, the King instituted a system of "village council democracy" which essentially has allowed traditional rural power elements, such as landlords and moneylenders, to retain local power.

Among the many attractions which lure visitors to Nepal (the number of tourists quadrupled between 1966 and 1971) are the massive Himalaya Mountains, including Mount Everest, the highest mountain on earth; Lumbini, the birthplace of Buddha; and Government-approved hashish stores.

—M.G.

THE NETHERLANDS

NITTY GRITTY

Location—Northwestern Europe along the estuaries of the Rhine, Meuse, and Schelde rivers. Borders with Germany on the east, Belgium on the south, and the North Sea on the west and north.

How Created—The Low Countries—Holland, Belgium, and Flanders—were a Germanic fragment of the Middle Kingdom formed after the death of Charlemagne in 814. They were passed among the European powers—Burgundy, Spain, and France—until 1815, when the Congress of Vienna created the Kingdom of The Netherlands. Modern Netherlands was formed when the Belgians revolted in 1830 and formed a separate state.

Size—15,892 sq. mi. (41,160 sq. km.).

Population—13,750,000: Dutch, 98.4%; German, Belgian, and other, 1.6%. 40.4% Roman Catholic, 28.3% Dutch Reformed, 18.3% no religion, 9.3% Reformed Church, 0.6% Lutheran, 3.1% other.

Who Rules—The Netherlands is a hereditary constitutional monarchy led by Queen Juliana. The head of Government is the Prime Minister, who presides over The Netherlands' 2-house legislature.

Who REALLY Rules—The Netherlands is

one of the best-functioning democracies in the world, but business interests still wield a disproportionate amount of power.

No Dutch boy ever used his finger to plug a leaky dike. The story is a creation of the 19th-century American writer Mary Mapes Dodge, and is unknown to Dutch schoolchildren. Nonetheless, the Dutch are willing to go along with the joke and have built a statue honoring this nonexistent hero at Spaarndam, near Haarlem.

When asked what professions they admired most, the Dutch put university professors at the top. Directors of large corporations ranked well behind physicians, judges, city mayors, and engineers.

More books are published per capita in The Netherlands than anywhere else. The Dutch also have more bicycles per capita than anyone else.

In The Netherlands, television is Government-subsidized. Owners of television sets (about 73% of all Dutch homes include at least one TV) pay about $20 a year for a television "license." The Government-owned Netherlands Broadcasting Foundation is responsible for filling up 40% of TV transmitting time. The remaining time is allocated to broadcasting organizations. Any group wishing to become a broadcasting organization must conform to certain standards; its broadcasts must meet with the cultural, religious, or spiritual needs of the Dutch people, and the organization must have at least 100,000 members paying for radio and/or television licenses. Organizations that conform to cultural standards but do not meet the membership requirements may be granted provisional broadcasting licenses provided they have at least 15,000 listener (radio) or 10,000 viewer (TV) members. Commercials were introduced on Dutch TV in 1965. These are broadcast as blocks of advertising spots before and after the newscasts. Advertising time is sold by a corporation set up by the Government. The proceeds are used to help finance the programs of the broadcasting societies and to compensate the press for loss of advertising revenue caused by the introduction of radio and television advertising.

The Kabouters, cousins of the hippies, are young people who have set up self-governing communities ("states within the State") in order to organize and propagate their political ideas. The Kabouters are opposed to contamination of food products, and water and air pollution. They are nonviolent. The Kabouters' housing plans call for relief of the housing shortage by allowing homeless people to occupy abandoned buildings. The Kabouters' Orange Free State has its own ministry and Parliament, its own currency and press, and a national anthem called "The Owl Was in the Elms." In 1970, 5 Kabouters were elected to seats on the Amsterdam municipal council, 2 on both the municipal councils of The Hague and Leeuwarden, and one each on the councils of Arnhem, Leyden, and Alkmaar.

Sixty percent of the Dutch population lives behind dikes, on reclaimed land with an elevation below sea level.

—M.G. & D.B.

NEW ZEALAND

Location—1,200 mi. east of the southeast coast of Australia in the South Pacific.

How Created—The 2 major and several minor islands comprising New Zealand are the crests of a giant and unstable earth fold. The main islands are geologically quite young. The Maoris (Polynesians) arrived around 800 A.D. Dutch explorer Abel Janszoon Tasman named the country in 1642 (New Sealand). British settlement began soon after Captain Cook charted the islands in 1769–1770. Given self-government in 1852, dominion status in 1907; achieved autonomy gradually, but this was formally granted in 1931 by the Statute of Westminster, adopted in New Zealand in 1947.

Size—New Zealand proper consists of North Island (44,281 sq. mi.), South Island (58,093 sq. mi.), Stewart Island (670 sq. mi.), Chatham Island (372 sq. mi.), and many minor outlying islands. Total sq. mileage 103,736 (268,676 sq. km.). New Zealand also administers the Cook Islands, the Tokelaus, and the Ross Dependency in Antarctica (160,000 sq. mi.).

Population—Over 3 million: European (mostly British), 90.6%; Maori, 7.5%; Pacific Islanders, 1.9%. 33.7% Church of England, 21.8% Presbyterian, 15.9% Roman Catholic, 7% Methodist, 1.7% Baptist, 19.7% other religions or no religion.

Who Rules—A unicameral Parliament of 80 European and 4 Maori members. A Cabinet is formed from the majority party with one minister serving as Prime Minister. Election is for 3 years by popular vote.

Who REALLY Rules—Trade unionism is powerful. There are heavy foreign investments, but strong regulations against a foreign company's having a large degree of ownership. New Zealand's economy is extremely dependent on specialized products (wool, lamb, mutton, butter, timber), on the disposal of these products overseas, and on the maritime commerce involved.

NOTES

Some 70% of the occupied land in New Zealand (45% of the total area) is directly devoted to supporting livestock. New Zealand has 60 million sheep and 2 million cows, mostly Jerseys.

New Zealanders have nicknamed themselves "Kiwis" after the flightless bird of their land. They are a friendly people, in love with their beautiful country.

The Kiwis are very angry over French testing of nuclear devices in the Pacific atmosphere. New Zealand got an injunction against the tests from the World Court, which the French ignored. Public protests are supported by the Government and one Kiwi frigate sailed near the test area carrying a cabinet minister. New Zealand is hoping the World Court will condemn the tests with a formal decision.

New Zealand is becoming more industrial to lessen its dependency on agriculture. The potential hydroelectric power is there, but many Kiwis are conscious of potential environmental harm. In 1971, 250,000 persons signed a protest halting a planned dam on Lake Manapouri.

In 1893 New Zealand became the 1st country to give women the right to vote.
—B.B.

NICARAGUA

NITTY GRITTY

Location—Central America. Honduras is to the north, and Costa Rica to the south. The Caribbean is to the east, the Pacific Ocean to the west.

How Created—Gil González de Ávila was the 1st Spaniard to reach Nicaragua, in 1522. The Spanish easily conquered the indigenous Indians with little bloodshed, taking from them their few gold possessions, and converting them to Christianity. In 1838 Nicaragua proclaimed its independence, with most of its present territory. Final boundary lines with Honduras and Costa Rica remained unsettled for a number of years.

Size—49,759 sq. mi. (128,875 sq. km.).

Population—2,350,000: mestizo, 70%; European (mostly Spanish), 17%; black, 9%; Indian, 4%. 83.1% Roman Catholic, 3.3% Protestant, 13.6% other.

Who Rules—In theory, Nicaragua is a republic with a 1950 constitution providing for a President and bicameral legislature. In reality, Nicaragua has been governed since the 1930s by the Somoza family or its representatives. Three members of the Somoza family have been President in the 20th century, and a great-grandfather of the current President held the office briefly in 1893 before being overthrown in a military coup. President today is Anastasio Somoza Debayle, who was 1st elected in 1967. Since he was constitutionally unable to succeed himself, he stepped down in 1972, handing the Government to a 3-man junta. Meanwhile, a constituent assembly drafted a new constitution which enabled Somoza to be reelected in 1974. However, the catastrophic earthquake that destroyed Managua on Christmas Eve, 1972, gave Somoza an excuse to step in and reassume control of the country. He named himself chairman of the National Emergency Committee, and functioned as President. President Somoza is a West Point graduate.

Who REALLY Rules—The Somoza family, backed by Nicaragua's top industrialists and merchants, have almost total control of the country. In addition, there is a long history of both direct and indirect U.S. intervention in Nicaraguan affairs. The U.S. supplies Nicaragua with considerable military assistance, and Nicaragua was the Central American jumping-off point for the CIA-sponsored Bay of Pigs invasion of Cuba.

In addition to their political power, the Somozas control a vast fortune, estimated to be worth at least $150 million. They have interests in coffee, rice, beer, cattle and meat packing, banking and hotels, television and newspapers. They also control the country's only cement factory, its only roofing outfit, the national airlines, and the country's only shipping line, plus 20–25% of Nicaragua's arable land. Somoza has been accused of profiteering off the Managua earthquake by raising prices of vital commodities such as cement. One Nicaraguan official claimed the country is run as a "kleptocracy."

NOTES

Lake Nicaragua, in southwest Nicaragua, is the largest freshwater lake in Central America. Once an arm of the sea, it is now home to the world's only freshwater sharks, who managed to adapt when the area was cut off from salt water.

The earthquake in Managua on December 23, 1972, killed about 10,000 people and injured 15,000.
—E.P.

NIGER

NITTY GRITTY

Location—Landlocked, to the northwest of the center of Africa. To the east, Chad; to the northeast, Libya; northwest, Algeria; west, Mali and Upper Volta; to the south, Dahomey and Nigeria.

How Created—The boundaries are artificial, enclosing an area explored by the French and established as a military district for the purpose of unifying France's West African and Central African territories.

Size—458,075 sq. mi. (1,186,408 sq. km.).

Population—4.6 million: Hausa, 53.7%; Zerma-Songhai, 23.6%; Fulani, 10.6%; Beriberi-Manga, 9.1%; Tuareg and others, 3%. 85% Muslim, 14.5% Animist, 0.5% Christian.

Who Rules—The President is elected to a 5-year term, as are the 50 members of the legislative Assembly. A ⅔ majority in the Assembly on a motion of censure will dissolve the Assembly and force the Government to resign. The Parti Progressiste Nigerien is the only legally constituted political party.

Who REALLY Rules—Niger, a very poor nation with a totally inadequate transportation system for the export of goods, must rely on foreign assistance for survival. As a member of the Conseil de l'Entente, Niger receives financial aid and has about 250,000 teachers and technicians from France. Roads are being built at the expense of France, Canada, the U.S., and the UN.

NOTES

The educated elite in Niger is very small. Ninety-five percent of the population consists of subsistence farmers, stock-raisers, and is extremely poor. Three quarters of the country receives too little rain to support agriculture, and there are many poverty-stricken citizens with no source of income whatsoever.

Traditional hostility between the nomads and the farmers has been somewhat eased by the solidarity which arose as a result of a 5-year drought. The Government established a National Solidarity Fund, to which the people, poor themselves, managed to contribute around $2 million yearly to aid those of their fellow countrymen who were in greater need.

—R.C.

NIGERIA

NITTY GRITTY

Location—On the southern side of the West African bulge, with a 680-mi. southern coast along the Gulf of Guinea; to the north, Niger; to the northeast, Lake Chad; to the east, Cameroon; to the west, Dahomey.

How Created—The British began at the coast, through successive annexations inland, and combined a Crown Colony and 2 protectorates into one possession.

Size—356,699 sq. mi. (923,773 sq. km.).

Population—63.5 million: Hausa, 21.4%; Ibo, 17.9%; Yoruba, 17.8%; Fulani, 10.3%; Tiv, 5.6%; Kanuri, 4.9%; Ibibio, 4.7%; Edo, 3.6%; 200 other groups and unknown, 13.8%. 47% Muslim, 35% Christian, 18% Animist.

Who Rules—The military, under the leadership of Maj. Gen. Yakubu Gowon, and the Supreme Military Council.

Who REALLY Rules—The old colonial power, Great Britain, is still a close partner, and remains the main customer for Nigerian exports and the chief supplier of imported goods. Following the Nigerian "civil war" in 1967, the Soviet Union, which had provided strong support for the Federal Government, emerged a powerful ally, with a good hold on Nigeria's rich oil fields. British, American, and French banks help support the Nigerian economy.

NOTES

The 1st Nigerian slaves were sent to Haiti by the British captain Sir John Hawkins in 1562. Nearly 10 million slaves were eventually exported from Nigeria. Most of these were Ibos captured by the coastal Ijaw chiefs conducting inland raids. King Akitoye signed a slavery-abolition agreement in 1852, and when King Pepple was caught still in business 2 years later he was deposed and exiled. King Jaja was deported to England for slaving as late as 1887.

Old Nigerian saying: "Nigeria is a place where the best is impossible but where the worst never happens."

Chief Obafemi Awolowa: "West and east Nigeria are as different as Ireland from Germany. The north is as different from either as China."

In 1966 thousands of Ibos were killed by Hausas and over one million Ibos were driven from the northern region.

On May 30, 1967, Lieut. Col. Odumegwu Ojukwu, an Ibo, took control of the eastern region and declared it the Independent Republic of Biafra. The Federal Republic of Nigeria, aided by the United Arab Republic, Britain, Czechoslovakia, and the U.S.S.R., fought to keep the region. The Biafran rebels had the support of Portugal, France, and Israel. Foreign interest in the war was due to the fantastic oil wealth of the seceding region. Most of the non-Ibo tribes of the eastern region did not want to secede, and most of the Ibos themselves did not want to secede either, but the rebellious soldiers led by Ojukwu insisted on trying to break away from the federation, taking all the wealth of the eastern region with them. The people of the eastern region were trapped and at the mercy of the

Ibo leaders, who treated them ruthlessly. When the federation set up a blockade to stop weapons from reaching the Biafrans, the International Red Cross offered to cross the blockade to bring first aid and food supplies to starving and wounded eastern region people. Ojukwu refused all aid, letting his people starve to death, in what many observers believed to be the most horrendous piece of propaganda ever employed—drumming up sympathy and support by allowing thousands of people to starve.

On January 12, 1970, the Biafran leaders surrendered and Ojukwu went into exile in the Ivory Coast.

Nigeria is the world's largest producer of palm kernels and palm oil, the world's largest exporter of peanuts, and a major supplier of cocoa, cotton, bananas, hides and skins, rubber, coffee, and ginger.

The women of the south control the markets and are a powerful political force. Women's trade cooperatives occupy modern office buildings in the large cities. Women own factories, are business executives, judges, doctors, educators. They are considered some of the most advanced women in Africa. The women of the north, however, are typically Muslim—uneducated, hardly exposed to "modern" ways. They rarely appear in public, and when they do are always completely covered to the eyes. The women of the northern Muslim tribes are the only adults in Nigeria who cannot vote.

—R.C.

NIPPON STEEL

NITTY GRITTY

Location—Nippon Steel's headquarters are in Tokyo. It has offices in Düsseldorf, Los Angeles, New York, Sydney, and Singapore.

How Created—For 20 years Fuji Iron & Steel dominated the steel industry in northern Japan and Yawata Iron & Steel dominated the industry in southern Japan. Then, in October, 1969, the Japanese Fair Trade Commission approved merger of the 2 companies into Nippon Steel, with the provision that the new company give its competitors some plant equipment and technical know-how, and divest itself of a tin plate subsidiary. Nippon Steel began on April 1, 1970.

Size—Nippon Steel is the world's largest steel company. It operates 11 principal plants throughout Japan and sells its products throughout the world.

Population—96,841 employees.

Who Rules—Nippon Steel's overall policy is set by Chairman Yoshihiro Inayama and President Tomisaburo Hirai. The top executive positions are divided equally between former executives of the Yawata and Fuji steel companies. These executives are elected by a board of directors that includes the officers.

Who REALLY Rules—Monetary institutions and corporations own almost all of Nippon Steel's stock, just as they own most of the stock of Japan's 1,700 other publicly held companies.

The Industrial Bank of Japan is Nippon Steel's largest stockholder and largest lender, while Nippon Steel is the 2nd largest stockholder of the Industrial Bank of Japan. The Fuyo Group is Nippon Steel's 2nd largest lender and, through its Fuji Bank, is Nippon Steel's 3rd largest stockholder, while Nippon Steel is Fuji Bank's largest stockholder.

Although little of Nippon Steel's stock is held by individual citizens, the company must answer to these few shareholders at 2 meetings each year. These meetings usually last less than 20 minutes because paid management supporters, called *sokaiya*, surround the speaker's podium, protect management from verbal abuse, drown out criticism, and help management ram through their proposals.

NOTES

Former Chairman of the Board Shigeo Nagano is one of Japan's foremost industrial and business leaders. He is counselor to the Japan Development Bank and the Bank of Japan, adviser to the Ministry of International Trade & Industry, councillor in the Ministry of Foreign Affairs, vice-president of the Pacific Basin Economic Council, chairman of the Prime Minister's Council for Foreign Economic Aid, president of the Japan and Tokyo Chambers of Commerce and Industry, and honorary president of the Japan Iron and Steel Foundation.

Chairman of the Board Yoshihiro once said, "Steel is the State."

—H.B.

NORWAY

NITTY GRITTY

Location—Norway consists of the western and northernmost parts of the Scandinavian peninsula. It is bordered on the east by the U.S.S.R., Finland, and Sweden; on the south by the North Sea; and on the west and north by the Norwegian Sea and the Arctic Ocean. One third of Norway lies north of the Arctic Circle.

How Created—Norway has been inhabited for thousands of years, but not until the early centuries of the Christian era can tribes and individuals be identified by name by modern historians. The Norse Vikings emerged as an identifiable group in the 8th century when they began their raids on Britain. The raids of the Vikings brought to previously isolated Norway both wealth and an exposure to cultures more civilized than its own. In the 10th century, a Viking king named Harald Fairhair (Harald I) united Norway. In the 14th century Norway, Sweden, and Denmark were united under Queen Margrethe of Denmark. From the 15th to 18th centuries Norway was ruled by Danish governors. Denmark sided with France during the Napoleonic Wars and when Napoleon was defeated in 1814, Denmark was forced by European powers to cede Norway to Sweden. A Norwegian constitution was drawn up in 1814 which, as amended, is still in use today. In 1905 Norway won its independence from Sweden.

Size—125,051 sq. mi. (323,883 sq. km.).

Population—Over 4 million: Norwegian, 97.7%; Lapp, 0.6%; other, 1.7%. 96.3% Evangelical Lutheran, 1% Pentecostal, 2.7% other.

Who Rules—Norway is a constitutional monarchy led by King Olav V. The head of Government is a Prime Minister, who is chosen from the unicameral (one-house) legislature. After election, the legislature divides into 2 sections, one 3 times larger than the other. Bills are introduced in the larger section and on being passed are sent to the smaller one. If the 2 disagree, a joint session is held with a ⅔ majority required for a decision.

Who REALLY Rules—Norway is governed by its elected representatives.

NOTES

The Vikings occasionally colonized the countries they invaded. The Isle of Man, located off the coast of England, was settled by Norse Vikings whose kingdom lasted there until the early 15th century, when the island voluntarily submitted to Henry IV of England. In the late 9th century, the Vikings colonized Iceland. These settlers developed a code of laws, a Parliament of sorts, and a court with powers to pass judgment and legislate laws. In the late 10th century, Erik the Red, a Norse Viking, discovered Greenland, and his discovery led to the establishment of a Viking colony on Greenland from which Viking explorers journeyed farther west. It was from the Greenland settlement that Leif Erikson sailed when he discovered Vinland (North America).

The sun never sets in northern Norway from May 12 to August 1, and even in Oslo the nights are not really dark from the last days of April to the middle of August. The nights, however, are correspondingly long and the dark winter of the north and even to some degree that of the south have a psychologically depressing effect.

—M.G.

PAKISTAN

NITTY GRITTY

Location—In South Asia, the southern border of Pakistan is the Arabian Sea. On the west lies Iran. Afghanistan is to the northwest and north, with China on the northeast. To the east is India and the disputed state of Jammu and Kashmir.

How Created—British colonial rule over the subcontinent ended in 1947 with the proclamation of 2 independent States, Pakistan and India. Pakistan was constituted from several provinces in which the majority population was Muslim. The decision was determined by a plebiscite in each province. As a result, Pakistan's territory was not contiguous, since the provinces of Punjab, Sind, Baluchistan, and North West Frontier (the present provinces of Pakistan) were divided by 1,000 mi. of India from East Bengal (now Bangladesh). Kashmir, with a Muslim majority, is still occupied by India.

In 1971, East Bengal declared independence from West Pakistan after denial of autonomy had become intolerable. The central Government in West Pakistan sent in troops to control East Bengal, but India intervened, defeated the Pakistani Army, and promoted the declaration of an independent Bangladesh.

Size—307,374 sq. mi. (796,095 sq. km.).

Population—65 million: Punjabi, 66.4%; Sindhi, 12.6%; Pashto, 8.5%; Urdu, 7.6%; Baluchi, 2.5%; Brahui, 0.9%; Gujarati, 0.6%; other, 0.9%. 97.2% Muslim, 1.4% Christian, 1.4% Hindu.

Who Rules—Pakistan has a parliamentary system. Regional governments exist in each province, but the central Government has taken direct control of the regions of Baluchistan and North West Frontier, negating the results of elections there.

Who REALLY Rules—The emerging Punjabi bourgeoisie in conjunction with the older elites: the government bureaucracy, the military, and the monopolist capitalists. But all these elites are strongly tied to the U.S., and such heavy dependence gives the U.S. Government a significant say in Pakistan's policies and economic development, as it has had since 1951.

NOTES

In 1951, the U.S. began to give military and economic aid to Pakistan and a mutual defense agreement was signed in 1954. The Pakistani military ousted the elected Government in 1958, and Gen. Mohammad Ayub Khan became dictator. By 1969, the U.S. had given between $1.5 and $2 billion to the Pakistani military.

When Ayub Khan took power he set out to unify the military, the bureaucracy, the industrialists, and some landlords. The U.S. provided aid and advisers for the new economic development and by 1969, $3 billion in economic aid, mainly loans, had been given. Pakistan was mortgaged to the U.S. The condition attached to this "aid" was that private enterprise be encouraged. Experts from Harvard University's Development Advisory Service poured in to direct the new development. The result of Pakistan's "decade of development" was control of the national economy by 20 to 25 families. These families monopolized 80% of banking, 70% of insurance, and 66% of industry by 1968.

Pakistan is faced with a continuing problem of nationalities, even after the secession of the Bengalis in 1971. In Baluchistan, Sind, and North West Frontier the repression—social and economic, as well as political—of the various minority nationalities has created movements for equality and social change that sometimes take on a secessionist thrust.

—J.G.

PANAMA

NITTY GRITTY

Location—Southernmost country in Central America. Colombia is to the east, Costa Rica to the west. The Caribbean Sea is north, the Pacific Ocean south.

How Created—Panama's 1st inhabitants were Indians. Rodrigo de Bastidas discovered the area for Spain in 1501. Panama is the site of Vasco Núñez de Balboa's 1st view of the Pacific Ocean. From 1542–1717, Panama was part of the viceroyalty of Lima, but then joined the new viceroyalty of New Granada (Colombia). Panama continued as part of Colombia after that country's independence in 1821, but its own independence was increasingly an issue. There were 53 rebellions against Colombia between 1846–1903. In 1903, the U.S. seized Panama in order to assure U.S. control of a Panamanian canal route. Panama became a U.S. protectorate, granting the Canal Zone to the U.S. in perpetuity, plus the right to interfere in Panamanian political affairs if they threatened the smooth operation of the Canal.

Size—29,783 sq. mi. (77,138 sq. km.), including the Canal Zone, which has an area of 553 sq. mi.

Population—1.6 million: mulatto, 72%; African, 14%; European, 12%; Indian and other, 2%. 91.5% Roman Catholic, 6% Protestant, 2.5% none.

Who Rules—According to the 1946 constitution, Panama is to elect its President and legislature every 4 years. However, Gen. Omar Torrijos, head of the National Guard (Panama has no Army), took power in a coup in 1968, suspending the National Assembly. The figurehead President is Demetrio Lakas.

Who REALLY Rules—The dominant force in Panama is the U.S., which has complete sovereignty in the Canal Zone and corresponding power in Panama itself. The U.S. provides Panama's only foreign military assistance, and the Canal Zone is headquarters of the U.S. Southern Command. U.S. per capita foreign aid to Panama is higher than to any other country receiving U.S. economic assistance.

NOTES

The Panama Canal remains an impressive engineering feat. Instead of the 7,000-mi. journey around Cape Horn, there is a 50-mi. passage through the Canal linking the Atlantic and Pacific oceans.

From Colonial times, there had been recurring interest in a transisthmian canal. Sites in both Nicaragua and Panama were contemplated and by 1901 the U.S. had decided on a Nicaraguan route as the more practical. However, the French, who had begun work on a Panamanian canal in 1881 (under the direction of Ferdinand de Lesseps, who also built the Suez Canal), offered to sell their rights to the U.S. for $40 million. The French effort had failed, due to disease, corruption, and high costs, and was bankrupt. The U.S. agreed to the purchase, provided that Colombia would also agree, since Panama still belonged to Colombia.

The Colombian Senate, however, refused to ratify the agreement, and President Theodore Roosevelt, unwilling to wait, encouraged Panamanian revolt for independence. In addition, U.S. Naval Forces prevented Colombian ships from landing troops in Panama to quell the uprising. On November 18, 1903, Panama, now a U.S. protectorate, signed a canal agreement with the U.S. Colombia's resultant bitterness over the high-handed U.S. intervention marred relations between the countries for some time.

The Canal was formally opened July 12, 1920, though it had been in limited use since 1914. Average passage time is about 8 hours, and control of the ship is handed over to special canal pilots.

The continued existence of the Canal Zone as a U.S. enclave in the heart of a foreign country is an increasingly hot political issue, both in Panama and in the U.S. General Torrijos insists that the U.S. presence will not be tolerated much longer by Panamanians. U.S. defenders of the status quo believe that the Canal is vital to U.S. defense, and that the Panamanians are not competent to operate the Canal. Sen. Strom Thurmond, who introduced a sense-of-the-Senate resolution opposing return of the Canal, stated, "We bought it; we paid for it; it is ours."

A further thorn, not only for Panama but for all of Latin America, is the U.S. Army-operated School of the Americas. Through this institution, the U.S. Army provides military training to Latin American armed forces personnel. Twenty-nine thousand officers and enlisted men have graduated from its program since the school was established in 1949, having learned combat methods and counterinsurgency tactics. Many members of the military governments in various Latin American countries today were trained at this school, including General Torrijos himself.

The San Blas Islands, an archipelago of 360 islands off Panama's Caribbean coast, is home to the Cuna Indians, whose culture and handicrafts are distinct from anything else found in Panama. Their culture, which may predate the Christian era, provides for communal ownership of the islands. However, the coconut groves, which bring their only source of income, are owned and worked individually. Coconuts are the local currency, and are traded for any needs supplied from the mainland. Their customs forbid intermarriage with outsiders—in fact, strangers are not allowed to spend the night on the islands. The women wear the family wealth in the form of heavy gold jewelry.

The women of San Blas are also well known for their creative needlework panels, known as *molas*. The *mola* is approximately 16" by 24", rectangular in shape, and worked in "reverse appliqué." In this technique, multiple layers of brightly colored cloth are cut away and the edges turned under and stitched to form a fabric "sculpture." The panels are worn in matching sets to form the front and back of a blouse. Increasing foreign interest in the *mola* as an art form has sent the prices up and, in some cases, the quality down. The introduction of sewing machines on the islands may further endanger the quality of the *molas*, and tourists are rushing to buy them before the craft disappears.

—E.P.

PAPUA NEW GUINEA

NITTY GRITTY

Location—Papua New Guinea consists of the eastern half of the Southwest Pacific island of New Guinea, plus a number of smaller islands off its east coast. It is just east of Indonesia, a few hundred miles north of Australia, and 2° south of the equator.

How Created—Great Britain declared Papua, the southeastern quarter of New Guinea island, a protectorate in 1884. In the same year Germany established a protectorate in the northeastern quarter of the island. Australia assumed control of Papua in 1906, and during W.W. I the Australian military occupied the German section. Since 1949 Australia has governed the 2 territories together. Formal independence is expected to be declared by 1976.

Size—180,530 sq. mi. (467,573 sq. km.).

Population—2,850,000: mostly Melanesian and Pygmoid (Negrito), with some Australians and others. New Guinea is 35.4% Roman Catholic, 34.8% Lutheran, 7% Animist, 5.5% Methodist, 4% World's Evangelical Alliance, 3.1% Seventh-Day Adventist, 10.2% other.

Who Rules—Michael Somare is the independent nation's 1st Prime Minister, heading a coalition Cabinet approved by both Australia and the native Parliament.

Who REALLY Rules—The national Government's authority is small in remote areas, where tribal groups still have a great deal of autonomy.

As the new Government asserts its power, it is constrained by Australia's External Affairs Ministry, which annually supplies a massive dose of aid.

NOTES

Fearing the ill effects of gambling on uneducated natives, Australian colonial authorities outlawed all card playing.

Papua New Guinea has no tradition of social, political, or economic unity, other than the fact that Australia has declared it a political entity. There are several nascent secession movements.

The nation's people speak 700 distinct languages, chiefly Melanesian and Papuan in origin.

Some tribes have a reputation for practicing headhunting and cannibalism.

In 1972 an international corporate venture, headed by Australia Conzinc Rio Tinto (a subsidiary of Britain's Rio Tinto Zinc) and the Bank of America, began mining copper from the Panguna mine on the island of Bougainville, one of the richest copper deposits in the world. At 1st, many of the 80,000 people living on the 3,880-sq.-mi. island objected, but Australian police drove them from the mine site and the Bougainville Copper Company (the joint venture) hired an anthropologist to handle relations with the islanders.

In 1973, the 1st full year of operation, the company earned amazing profits of $236 million on sales of $372 million. Though the Government of Papua New Guinea received, as its share, $42 million, it wants a larger share of the profits. Meanwhile, residents of Bougainville want more of the government share spent on them and less on their mainland brethren. In May, 1975, 1,000 workers occupied the copper mine for 2 days before being driven out by police.

—L.S.

PARAGUAY

NITTY GRITTY

Location—One of the 2 landlocked South American countries, located in central South America. Neighbors are Brazil to the northeast, Bolivia to the northwest, and Argentina to the south and southwest.

How Created—Early Spanish gold seekers used the extensive Paraguayan river system as an easy gateway to the riches of the Incan Empire, which lay on Paraguay's western edge. Lacking in mineral wealth, Paraguay was settled by farmers rather than exploited by treasure hunters, and generally ignored by the Spanish Government. Independence occurred in 1811, after Paraguay refused a joint independence with Argentina in 1810. Paraguay's territory was increased by 20,000 sq. mi. in the Chaco War (1932–1935).

Size—157,047 sq. mi. (406,752 sq. km.).

Population—2,850,000: mestizo, 74%; white, 21%; Amerindian, 3%; black, 1%; other, 1%. 95.1% Roman Catholic.

Who Rules—In theory a republic with a President and bicameral legislature elected every 5 years. Current head of state is Gen. Alfredo Stroessner, who had himself elected President in 1954 after a coup, and who has been "reelected" 3 times since. Recently he has permitted token political activity, and has run opposite sure losers in the presidential campaigns. In the 1973 election, 25% of the voters cast blank ballots or did not go to the polls at all, in protest. His 20-year-old dictatorship is the most enduring in South America.

Who REALLY Rules—Paraguay has been called Stroessner's "private estate." He controls the country, in conjunction with a select group of foreign businessmen, upper-level military,

and landed wealth (11 huge farms cover 35% of eastern Paraguay). He rules the country virtually unchallenged; every 90 days the puppet legislature automatically renews the state-of-siege law which gives him the right to jail anyone, anytime, without a trial. (There are believed to be over 100 political prisoners in Paraguayan jails who have been held for as long as 10 years without trial.)

NOTES

Paraguay has fought 2 catastrophic wars with its neighbors:

War of the Triple Alliance (1865–1870): Fought with Brazil, Uruguay, and Argentina over Brazilian intervention in Uruguay. One of the bloodiest wars ever fought in the western hemisphere, it resulted in the death of over half of Paraguay's population of one million and the complete disruption of the social, political, and economic life of the country. The country was bankrupt and starving, even the generals were barefoot, and ⅔ of the young men were dead. After the war there were 190,-000 adult women to only 29,000 adult men, and this hastened the racial and cultural mixture that is one of the distinctive features of present-day Paraguay. Polygamy was legalized for a while in order to increase the population as quickly as possible.

Chaco War (1932–1935): After a series of skirmishes with Bolivia over rights to the Chaco region of western Paraguay, war was declared in 1932. Paraguayans considered it a defense of their homeland and, armed only with machetes in some cases, managed to drive the Bolivians back to the Andes. The total dead of both sides was 135,000.

Paraguay, because of its unguarded borders and central location, has been considered a key link in the heroin traffic between Europe and the U.S. Recently, a CIA report linked President Stroessner to the smuggling, claiming that he turned a blind eye toward smuggling by his generals.

Argentina is Paraguay's best customer and largest single investor. The Casados, an Argentine family, own an estate of 5 million acres, about the size of Belgium.

Paraguay is the only country in the world with 2 different faces to its flag: One side has the treasury seal, the other has the national coat of arms.

—E.P.

PERU

NITTY GRITTY

Location—West coast of South America. Neighbors are: Ecuador and Colombia to the north; Brazil and Bolivia to the east; Chile to the south.

How Created—Originally the center of the Incan Empire, which stretched along the coast from Colombia to southern Chile, and then the seat of Spanish power in colonial South America, Peru achieved independence in 1824. Border disputes with Chile over Peru's southern deserts led to loss of territory in the War of the Pacific (1879–1883). In 1942 Peru gained half of the territory of Ecuador, including oil-rich Amazon lands.

Size—496,225 sq. mi. (1,285,216 sq. km.).

Population—Over 15 million: Indian (mainly Quechua and Aymará), 46%; mestizo, 43%; Caucasian (mostly Spanish), 10%; Chinese and black, 1%. 99.3% Roman Catholic.

Who Rules—Peru is technically a republic, whose 1933 constitution provides for a President and bicameral legislature. At present, the Government is in the hands of a military junta, which took power in 1968 following disenchantment with the civilian Government's inability to handle a nationalization crisis.

Who REALLY Rules—Until recently, 3 foreign companies (Cerro Corporation, International Petroleum, and W. R. Grace & Co.) in conjunction with a tiny elite (the "40 families") held virtually all the power in Peru. Since the military take-over of 1968, all 3 of these companies have been nationalized, and the traditional oligarchy, while still present in the life of the country, holds 2nd place to the military.

NOTES

San Marcos University in Lima is one of the oldest universities in the western hemisphere. It was founded in 1551, 85 years before Harvard University.

The Central Railroad, built by the American Henry Meiggs, is the world's highest standard-gauge railway. It rises from sea level to 16,000' in the space of only 85 mi. One of its stations, at 15,693', is the highest in the world.

The military junta wants to build a society that is, in its words, "neither communistic nor capitalistic," and believes that by using military leadership and organization, this goal can be accomplished.

In industry, the Government is promoting the policy of *propiedad social*, or social property. Under this system, the owners of a company would be those who work in it, with the workers or their delegates responsible for all major decisions.

Despite the many changes, old Peru is very much in evidence. Most Indians still work very hard for very little, scratching at the land with the same types of tools they have used for cen-turies. Their diet is poor, their health neglected. Rural Indians, living in isolated Andean hamlets, may not always know what kind of Government they have, or have any feeling for Peru as a nation.

In recent years Peru has become the world's leading fishing country, surpassing Japan in fish meal exports. However, a 1971 change in the temperature and direction of the cold Humboldt current, plus serious overfishing of anchovies (the source of most fish meal), drastically reduced Peru's fish meal exports.

—E.P.

PHILIPPINES

NITTY GRITTY

Location—"Pearl of the Eastern Sea," a chain of 7,100 islands 500 mi. off the coast of Southeast Asia; directly east of Vietnam, south of Taiwan.

How Created—The Philippines as a nation is the creation of Spanish colonial conquest. It is named after King Philip II of Spain. In 1898 Spain passed the title to the U.S., which granted formal independence in 1946.

Size—115,830 sq. mi. (300,000 sq. km.).

Population—43 million: Cebuano, 24.1%; Tagalog, 21%; Ilocano, 11.7%; Hiligaynon (Illongo), 10.4%; Bicolano, 7.8%; Pampanga, 3.2%; other, 21.8%. 83.8% Roman Catholic, 5.2% Aglipayan, 4.9% Muslim, 2.9% Protestant, 3.2% other.

Who Rules—Before September, 1972, the Republic of the Philippines was governed according to a constitution modeled after the American one. On September 22, 1972, President Ferdinand Marcos declared martial law, dissolved the Congress, and imprisoned the opposition (Liberal party) leadership. Soon after, he staged public meetings as part of a plebiscite to adopt a new constitution under which he would retain the powers of President and Premier indefinitely. Marcos prefers to call his Government "authoritarian" rather than "a dictatorship."

Who REALLY Rules—Marcos, his wealthy cronies, the military, and the Philippine Constabulary exercise day-to-day power, but they could not do it without the support of the U.S. The U.S. Government props up the Philippine economy with economic aid, and it maintains the Marcos regime by training and supplying the military and police.

NOTES

Filipinos, led by the worker-peasant *Katipunan*, rebelled against Spain in 1896 and drove the Spanish from most of the archipelago. They declared independence on June

12, 1898, and laid siege to Manila during the Spanish-American War (1898), U.S. Admiral Dewey, supposedly in alliance with the rebels, destroyed the Spanish fleet in Manila Bay.

However, instead of turning Manila over to the Filipino rebels, the U.S. "bought" the Philippines from Spain for $20 million, as part of the Spanish-American peace treaty. The Americans won the support of the upper classes, as well as some middle-class reformers, and sought to impose control militarily. Thus began America's "1st Vietnam." One hundred and twenty-six thousand American troops, schooled in Indian fighting, defeated the rebels in major encounters, forced Filipinos into "relocation" camps, and killed perhaps as many as 600,000 people. In 1901 American troops captured the Filipino President, Gen. Emilio Aguinaldo. The following year U.S. President Theodore Roosevelt declared the war over, but it continued for many years.

Japanese troops invaded the Philippines on December 8, 1941, the day after Pearl Harbor; an American-run Army—80% Filipino—unsuccessfully resisted. During the Japanese occupation (1942–1945), the communist-led *Hukbalahap* (the Huks) guerrillas fought the Japanese. At the end of W.W. II, the U.S. granted the Philippines formal independence (July 4, 1946). The Huks agreed to participate in American-organized elections, but finding neocolonialism no less desirable than colonialism, they took up arms again. At one point the Huks nearly seized power, but, aided by the CIA's Col. Edward Lansdale, pro-American Filipinos destroyed Huk power by 1953.

Rebellion broke out again in the late 1960s. The Maoist New People's Army began guerrilla warfare in remote areas of the north, and Moro secessionists took control of large areas on the southern islands. The Government responded by napalming rebel-held areas. With the imposition of martial law, both struggles intensified, but the Marcos regime does not face imminent collapse.

An estimated 40% of Filipino physicians are practicing abroad, most in the U.S.

Eighty-five percent of Philippine TV is American programming.

—L.S.

POLAND

NITTY GRITTY

Location—In Eastern Europe, bounded on the north by over 300 mi. of Baltic seacoast, on the west by East Germany, the east by the Soviet Union, and the south by Czechoslovakia.

How Created—Tribes known as the Western Slavs settled in the fertile river valleys of present-day Poland before Christ. In 966 A.D., the Slavs converted to Roman Catholicism and the Polish state was officially born. The spirit of Polish nationalism grew strong enough to survive a 125-year period when Poland did not exist because Prussia, Russia, and Austria had divided the country among themselves. An independent Poland returned to the map following W.W. I.

Size—120,725 sq. mi. (312,677 sq. km.), almost the size of New Mexico.

Population—34,500,000: Polish, 98.5%; Ukrainian, 0.6%; Byelorussian, 0.5%; other, 0.4%. 90% Roman Catholic, 10% none or other.

Who Rules—There is a unicameral legislature, the Sjem, and 3 political parties—the Polish United Workers' party (the Communist party), United Peasants' party, and Democratic party. People's councils, elected at the commune, district, and province levels, are the local governments.

Who REALLY Rules—Political power is concentrated in the Politburo of the Communist party. Foreign policy is made in consultation with the U.S.S.R. and all important decisions are affected by the knowledge that any attempt to drift away from the Eastern bloc would trigger a Soviet military invasion such as the one that restored Czechoslovakia to the Russian sphere in 1969. Although they have no power to rule, the industrial workers of Poland's major cities have brought down governments by strikes and rioting (1956 and 1970). The country's only mass organization not controlled by the Communist party, the Catholic Church, allows the party to monopolize political power, but competes with it for control over the beliefs and attitudes of the people.

NOTES

A Catholic country ruled according to the tenets of materialistic, atheistic Marxism—here is the great Polish paradox from which innumerable incongruities flow. To take just one: The Poles have the only communist army with chaplains. As might be expected, Church-state relations have not always been pleasant. When the communists came to power at the close of W.W. II, thousands of priests were imprisoned. Following their release, the party sought to eliminate the competing ideological leadership of the Church by less extreme methods. In 1963, for example, the régime sought to ban the annual pilgrimage to Jasna Gora, holiest of Polish shrines, by creating a false smallpox scare. When the Church celebrated the millennium of Polish Catholicism in 1966, the State tried a subtler method to discourage attendance—for the duration of the weekend observance, state-controlled television aired John Wayne and Marilyn Monroe movies, soccer games, and other favorite programs.

In a communist state with a centrally planned economy, the only business is supposed to be Government-owned, but this is not entirely true of Poland. About 85% of the farms remain in private hands, the drive to collectivize agriculture having been abandoned in the face of fierce peasant resistance. Another anomaly is the existence of thousands of private retail shops, artisan workshops, and other small private businesses.

A poll of youths, taken after 2 decades of communist rule, showed that their heroes were, in order: John Kennedy, Yuri Gagarin, Charles de Gaulle, Pope John XXIII, and Karl Marx.

In one recent year, 59% of medical school graduates were women, as were 50% of graduates in the pure sciences.

When Hitler's armies seized Warsaw in 1939 they erected a brick wall around ¼ of the city, creating a ghetto for 500,000 Jews. Food rations were gradually reduced to the starvation point. A railroad line was run into the ghetto and the residents were removed to be exterminated at Treblinka and other death camps. The population had fallen to 70,000 when the Jews obtained arms from the Polish underground in 1943 and fought back for almost one month until their inevitable defeat. Before the war, 2.7 million Jews lived in Poland. (Some historians believe that in the Middle Ages, 80% of the world's Jews lived there.) In 1968 an "anti-Zionist" drive sent many of the few remaining Jews to Israel and other countries. By the mid-1970s only 10,000 Jews, mostly older people, remained in Poland.

—E.R.

PORTUGAL

NITTY GRITTY

Location—On the western coast of the Iberian peninsula in southwest Europe, mainland Portugal is bounded on the north and east by Spain and on the south and west by the Atlantic Ocean. Metropolitan Portugal includes the Azores (9 islands 740 mi. west of Portugal) and the archipelago of Madeira (600 mi. to the southwest).

How Created—By the 12th century the Moors controlled all of what is now Portugal except for a small area in the north. In 1139, Affonso, son of Henry of Burgundy, defeated the Moors in Santarém and declared himself King of Portugal.

In 1147 Lisbon was taken from the Moors and in 1249 the Portuguese drove them from the Algarve. The boundaries of continental Portugal have remained virtually unchanged since, and, except for a 60-year period from 1580–1640 when Spain ruled the country, it has been an independent nation.

Size—35,383 sq. mi. (91,641 sq. km.), about the size of Indiana.

Population—10 million: Portuguese, 99.7%. 98.4% Roman Catholic.

Who Rules—On April 25, 1974, a group called the Movement of Armed Forces overthrew the right-wing dictatorship of Premier Marcello Caetano in an almost bloodless coup d'état. In 1975, Portugal's 1st elections in 50 years resulted in a victory for the Socialists and Popular Democrats.

Who REALLY Rules—The military is still in power. Until the coup the Government represented the interests of the "10 families" who are in control of interlocking cartels and conglomerates, and of various international corporations such as Shell Oil, which has interests in Angola.

NOTES

The majority of the population are peasants. In the north, the land is usually divided into small family farms of about 2 acres each. This is not enough to support the owners and many of them are forced to seek work in the cities or to emigrate. In the south and central portions, peasants usually farm large estates for absentee landlords. Portugal's primary exports are cork (half of the world's cork is produced in Portugal), wines (port and Madeira are the best known), and olive oil.

Since 1960 one of the other main exports has been cheap labor. Because of economic conditions and required military service in the colonial wars in Africa, the country has lost a great deal of its young, working population to France, West Germany, Brazil, and Canada. Paris has the largest Portuguese population of any city in the world outside of Lisbon. Remittances sent home by Portuguese workers abroad have amounted to approximately $1 billion.

Salazar, Portugal's dictator for 40 years, suffered a stroke in 1968. Marcello Caetano was appointed Premier, but no one dared to inform Salazar, during the 2 following years he remained alive, that he had been replaced.

The resolution which gave all literate women the vote in 1968, concluded that "it has been verified that women are more conservative than men and much more afraid of adventure and chance."

—M.N.

PUERTO RICO

Location—A Caribbean island about 885 mi. southeast of Miami, Fla., and 540 mi. north of the Venezuelan coast of South America.

How Created—The 1st European to visit the island was Columbus, who touched land there on November 19, 1493, and gave it the name San Juan Bautista. Ponce de León founded the 1st Spanish settlement on the island's *puerto rico*, or rich port, in 1506. Gradually, the island took the name Puerto Rico, while the major settlement was called San Juan. Some 30,000 indigenous Arawak Indians were eliminated by the late 16th century through disease, slavery, and wars. After much agitation for independence or autonomy, the Spanish granted permission for an elected Puerto Rican legislature, although Spain reserved the right to appoint the governor, who had real power. Self-government lasted less than a year. In the course of the Spanish-American War (1898) American troops landed on Puerto Rico, and the Treaty of Paris obliged Spain to cede Puerto Rico, Guam, and the Philippines to the U.S. (Cuba was placed in a U.S. trusteeship.) After 2 years of U.S. occupation and military Government, a civil Government was established in 1900, but with the U.S. appointing the governor, upper house, and judiciary. Puerto Rico's eventual official status as either State or independent country was not defined.

Size—3,435 sq. mi. (8,897 sq. km.), including dependencies.

Population—2,800,000: mixed, 60%; black, 20%; white, 20%. 88% Roman Catholic. In addition, about 1,700,000 Puerto Ricans live in the U.S. at any one time.

Who Rules—An outright U.S. colony from 1898 to 1952, Puerto Rico is now an "Associated Free State," with the right to elect the governor, senate, and house of representatives, much on the model of U.S. mainland States. Puerto Ricans have been U.S. citizens since 1917. Although obliged to serve in the U.S. military, Puerto Ricans may not vote in the national elections which determine U.S. military policy, unless they happen to be living on the mainland.

Who REALLY Rules—The U.S. Aside from immense U.S. military installations, including the 72nd Bomb Wing of SAC, the Antilles Command of the U.S. Army, and one of the largest U.S. Navy bases in the world, Puerto Rico's tax-exempt status has resulted in rampant exploitation of the island's human and natural resources. Under an economic development program known as Operation Bootstrap, investors pay *no taxes* to either the U.S. or Puerto Rico. Consequently, many companies operate branch plants there which produce articles for export only.

NOTES

Although the soil in Puerto Rico is rich, very little of it is being used to grow food for domestic use. Pinto beans, which are a staple in the diet of rural Puerto Ricans, are imported from Stockton, Calif.

The island's social structure, once the traditional model of a society with a tiny elite and vast peasant class, is changing rapidly under the onslaught of Americanization. Not only has the immense amount of foreign investment affected some living standards, but the 2-way flow of Puerto Ricans between the mainland and the island has exposed thousands, directly or indirectly, to U.S. life-styles and consumerism. Returning Puerto Ricans import the American emphasis on material gain and competitiveness, shaking the traditional Hispanic-Caribbean culture. A proliferation of cars and televisions—bought on credit—are evidence of the new middle class who want what they see abroad or hear of from tourists.

The use of the island of Culebra for U.S. Navy target practice was halted only in 1974 by order of the U.S. Congress. The 800 inhabitants of Culebra complained for years of the danger of duds or misdirected shells, and of the noise and the restrictions they had to suffer.

When Castro took power in Cuba, American gangsters moved their casinos, hotels, nightclubs, and prostitutes to Puerto Rico.

—E.P.

RHODESIA (ZIMBABWE)

NITTY GRITTY

Location—Landlocked in southeastern Africa; to its northwest is Zambia, to the north and east Mozambique, to the south the Republic of South Africa, and to the southwest is Botswana.

How Created—Formerly Southern Rhodesia and a member of the Federation of Rhodesia and Nyasaland until 1963 when it became a self-governing British Protectorate. In 1965 Rhodesia unilaterally declared independence from Britain, but has gone unrecognized by the official world community.

Size—150,820 sq. mi. (390,622 sq. km.).

Population—Over 6 million: Bantu, 94.9%; European, 4.5%; other, 0.6%. 80% Animist, 11% Christian, 9% none and other.

Who Rules—Technically still a British colony. Head of state is a President appointed by the elected Prime Minister who heads the Government. Laws are made by the racially apportioned Parliament: a 50-white and 16-black House of Assembly, and a 23-member Senate. A 25-member Council of Chiefs acts as spokesman for the black population.

Who REALLY Rules—The constitutionally-guaranteed white minority.

NOTES

It is said that Rhodesia was the ancient land of Ophir and the site of King Solomon's mines. Whether or not this is true, her mines have brought riches to more than one King or adventurer. One of them gave his name to the country. Cecil Rhodes, the giver of scholarships to British and American boys and the organizer of the British South Africa Company, by wile, purchase, and conquest extracted the land from the Mashona and Matabele tribes and brought in British settlers to people it. Not since the sale of Manhattan have natives been bilked out of such valuable real estate.

In 1964 Britain granted full independence to the 2 northern territories of the former federation of Rhodesia and Nyasaland, but withheld it from (Southern) Rhodesia until blacks were represented in the Government. Rather than lose control to the vast majority, the white Rhodesian Government declared itself independent from Britain. Despite worldwide sanctions, Rhodesians voted for a constitutional republic perpetuating white rule. Eligible to vote in that election: 82,583 whites; 6,634 blacks.

Until recently, it was quite common to see signs such as the following in parks and public places: "Cyclists, dogs and Africans not allowed." Today Rhodesia is still an absolutely racially segregated state.

The African nationalist name for the country is Zimbabwe. There are 3 different African parties which have been engaging in guerrilla warfare against the Rhodesian armed forces in the Zambezi valley.

Your Servant & You, a government publication addressed to the housewife, says as much about the Rhodesian view of women as of black Africans: "The African has dignity. Do not allow your small children to give cheeky orders to a grown-up, or to speak or act rudely to him. . . . His women are his inferiors, and it is asking for trouble for a woman to scold a native loudly or, above all, to strike him. . . . Be as modest before him as before any man of your own race. Respect his ideas about women. You may think him a savage—and in many cases his moral outlook has little in common with ours—but he never allows even a small native girl to appear naked before a man or boy, so your little girl should not do this . . . you must never leave your daughter with an African male, nor allow her to wander alone in sparsely populated areas. Make your own beds, wash your own underclothing, and do not expect your houseboy to wash stained linen. It outrages his sense of what is proper."

Fifty percent of the population is less than 16 years old.

—M.D.

ROMANIA

NITTY GRITTY

Location—Southeastern Europe, in the Balkan peninsula, straddling the Carpathian Alps. Shares a 900-mi. border with the U.S.S.R. Also bordered by Hungary, Yugoslavia, Bulgaria, and the Black Sea; the southern boundary mostly follows the course of the Danube River.

How Created—Known in ancient times as Dacia, it was a province of the Roman Empire (106–271 A.D.). Withdrawal of Roman legions led to nearly 1,000 years of barbarian invasions by tribes pouring out of the Mongolian steppes. It was part of the Turkish Empire for the next 500 years. With the waning of Turkish power in the 19th century, the 2 "Old Principalities"—Moldavia and Wallachia—were united and granted limited autonomy (1859), then full independence following the Treaty of Berlin (1878). The historically disputed territory of Transylvania was annexed in 1918 due to the collapse of the Austro-Hungarian Empire in W.W. I.

Size—91,699 sq. mi. (237,500 sq. km.), roughly the size of Oregon.

Population—21,500,000: Romanian, 87.7%; Hungarian, 8.5%; German, 2%; other, 1.8%. 80% Romanian Orthodox, 10% Greek Catholic (uniate), 9% Roman Catholic, 1% Jewish and other.

Who Rules—The "supreme organ of State power" and "sole legislative body" of the Romanian Socialist Republic is the Grand National Assembly. Members chosen from the ranks of the GNA comprise the State Council, the true center of power, whose president is also Chief of State. This post has been occupied since 1965 by Nicolae Ceausescu (chow-SHESS-koo). Day-to-day administration is carried out by the Council of Ministers, which supervises the activities of the People's Councils. Participation in the power structure is limited to members of the Romanian Communist party.

Who REALLY Rules—Ceausescu (who is also General Secretary of the RCP) and his trusted inner circle of advisers. The Soviet

Union exercises a degree of influence that is major but nowadays mainly diplomatic, though members of the Soviet secret police are known to operate inside the country alongside their Romanian counterparts.

NOTES

Article 28 of the Constitution of the Romanian Socialist Republic reads: "The freedom of speech, press, assembly, meetings, and demonstrations is guaranteed to the citizens of the RSR." Article 29 reads: "The freedom of speech, press, assembly, meetings, and demonstrations must not be used for purposes which are contrary to the socialist system and the interests of those who work." A major job of the secret police is to prevent the violation of Article 29.

In the middle 1960s Romania was pressured by the Soviet Union and other members of COMECON, the Russian version of the Common Market, to forego industrializing and concentrate on producing only grain and oil. Romania refused, saying that it was unwilling to become merely "the gas station and grocery store" of Eastern Europe.

Dracula—For Westerners this is by far the most famous figure associated with Romania. The 1897 novel by Irishman Bram Stoker, plus countless movies based on it, have familiarized the world with the sinister vampire Count Dracula. In fact, the historical model for this villain—the Wallachian (not Transylvanian, as in the novel) Prince Vlad Tepes, or Vlad the Impaler—was a cruel and ingenious psychopath of such monstrous proportions that beside him the famous character of Stoker's novel is a mere pussycat. (See: Vampires, Chap. 27.) Because of the worldwide Dracula craze, the Romanian Government is currently restoring Castle Dracula as a tourist attraction.

Vampirism—True vampire bats do not exist in Europe at all, but only in South America. However, the ancient Romanian peasant belief in the *moroi*, the undead, and in the *strigoi*, demon birds of the night, is still alive. The Eastern Orthodox Church, to which most Romanians, or at least their pre-communist elders, belong, preaches that a body bound by a curse will not be received by the ground. This may be the source of belief in the undead.

Mud-bathing—Perhaps nowhere else in the world is this ancient health practice indulged in so widely and by all strata of the populace. It is said to be good for nearly everything that ails you, and Romanians congregate in large numbers at mud-bath spas, where they coat their bodies in mud and bake in the sun.

Gypsies—Possibly the largest contingent of Eastern European gypsies—or *Rom*, as they call themselves—live in Romania. As the smallest and most visibly different minority in the area, they have historically suffered merciless persecution. Up until the 19th century they were considered slaves in law and fact, though at the same time their music and their practice of the occult arts have become a distinctive part of Romanian peasant culture. The present Government is forcing them to abandon their nomadic ways and settle down.

Both the pride and the long-suffering resignation of the Romanian people can be seen in their proverbial sayings:
"There is no more bitter fruit than foreigners in one's land."
"Justice is as the rulers make it."
"Kiss the hand you cannot bite."
"A sword won't cut a lowered head."
"Many dogs will eat a lone wolf."
"The water flows, but the stones remain."
—R.Mi.

RWANDA

NITTY GRITTY

Location—In East Africa, 100 mi. south of the equator. To the north, Uganda; to the east, Tanzania; to the south, Burundi; to the west, Zaire and Lake Kivu.

How Created—The combined areas of Rwanda and Burundi are isolated from the world by volcanic mountains, swampy jungles, marshes, lowland lakes, and the Kagera River. These natural borders defined the ancient Tutsi-Hutu Kingdom which, at some unknown point in history, broke up into the 2 separate kingdoms of Ruanda and Burundi, under 2 different Tutsi Kings.

Size—10,169 sq. mi. (26,338 sq. km.).

Population—Over 4 million: Hutu, 90%; Tutsi, 9%; Twa (Pygmy) 1%. 45% Animist, 45% Roman Catholic, 9% Protestant, 1% Muslim.

Who Rules—The President of Rwanda is the militant Hutu, Maj. Gen. Juvenal Habyalimana. He seized power in a bloodless coup d'état in July, 1973.

Who REALLY Rules—The Belgians had supported the Hutus from the beginning, even when the Tutsi were in control of Rwanda. After the massacres of both Hutu and Tutsi tribesmen, amounting in some cases to genocide, the Belgian Government cut back some of the $4.5 million it had been sending Rwanda yearly. However, aid has not stopped altogether, and the country is kept out of total bankruptcy by the U.S., the European Common Market, France, West Germany, and the UN. One-half of Rwanda's export industry is in coffee and the U.S. buys almost all of it.

NOTES

Batutsi (members of the Tutsi tribe; a single tribesman is called a Watutsi): These people are extraordinarily tall (many over 6'6" in height), slim, and very handsome. Four hundred years of absolute rule (in an 18-generation dynasty) has made them proud, sophisticated, and not particularly strong-looking. They are, however, arrogant and powerful warriors.

The Batutsi have always been seminomadic cattlemen. At home they are exotic, aristocratic, and elegant; they are extremely graceful, and their facial features are delicate. The women bind the heads of infant females to accentuate the elongation of their heads.

Bahutu (members of the Hutu tribe): Peasant farmers, indigenous to the region, these tribespeople have for centuries been oppressed by the Batutsi. The Bahutu are, by comparison, short and coarse-featured and unsophisticated. They are a Bantu people.

Batwa: Pygmies of the Twa tribe, they are dying out in Africa. They have always inhabited dense tropical forests, hunting and finding nuts and berries to live on.

The deep and abiding hatred which has grown between the Bahutu and Batutsi over the centuries has, in the last 2 decades, erupted continually into massacres, tribal wars, and genocide. The recent wars began in 1959, when the Bahutu finally rebelled against the Tutsi tribe. Encouraged and armed by the Belgians, the Bahutu had the advantage in numbers as well as in weaponry. They slaughtered their former overlords, who fought back with bows and arrows, knives and swords. Five thousand Batutsi were killed and hundreds of thousands wounded; finally they fled—150,000, plus the Mwami (King) Kigeri V, to Uganda, Tanzania, Burundi, and Zaire.

With independence in 1962, the Tutsi monarchy was officially abolished; the Batutsi did not give up, though. Armed at the borders for an invasion, the Batutsi attacked and murdered the Bahutu in the night, bands of them running into the country after dark, ravaging and torturing the Hutu villagers. These Tutsi bands were called *inyenzi*, the Swahili word for cockroach. Finally, in 1963, the *inyenzi* staged a full-force attack, invading from 3 borders and engaging in bloody battle with the Hutus. The Hutus, still more powerful in numbers and machinery, massacred thousands of the invading Batutsi. Encouraged by their easy victory over the people who had oppressed them for centuries, the Bahutu went on to perform a systematic mass murder—actually genocide—against the Batutsi.

The surviving Batutsi went into exile again, and the Mwami set up a government-in-exile outside Rwanda. Ten years later, in 1973, militant Bahutus, not content with the Batutsi suppression, forced private employers to dismiss Batutsi employees, and forced Batutsi students to quit the University of Rwanda (the 175 Tutsis made up half of the school's total enrollment). A fresh massacre took the lives of 750 to 3,000 Batutsis.

Meanwhile, thousands of exiled Batutsis are encamped along the borders of their homeland. They are being armed and trained in guerrilla warfare by the communist Chinese, and the young Batutsis are pursuing their educations abroad, preparing themselves for leadership, in the hope of reclaiming Rwanda as a Tutsi Kingdom.

The Royal Ballet: For centuries, the sons and protégés of chieftains and notables of the Tutsi aristocracy have been trained to fill the posts of the elite court dancers. All 6'6" to 7' tall, the dancers are magnificently trained, and learn to control the very details of facial expression as part of their graceful, acrobatic dance. One popular dancer in the 1950s was Butera who was famous for his stature—7'5" and 300 lbs.—and so well-loved for his high jumping that his portrait appeared for a time on local banknotes.

R.C.

SAFEWAY STORES

NITTY GRITTY

Location—Headquarters at 4th and Jackson streets, Oakland, Calif. 94604.

How Created—Safeway Stores was incorporated in 1914 to operate a chain of grocery stores in Southern California. When it merged with Skagg's grocery stores on March 26, 1926, Safeway had 332 stores and Skagg's operated almost as many in Northern California, the Rocky Mountain States, and the Pacific Northwest. In 1931 the MacMarr grocery chain was merged into Safeway, and in 1934 MacMarr's president, Lingan A. Warren, became president of Safeway.

By 1955 Warren's policies of pushing Safeway brands and meeting any competitor's price, no matter how low, produced inadequate profits as far as some stockholders were concerned. Charles E. Merrill, who had got Warren his job 20 years before, owned the largest block of stock (6%), and he forced Warren to retire. The board of directors then chose Merrill's son-in-law, Robert A. Magowan, as Safeway's president and chairman. Magowan reversed Warren's pricing and buying policies, and decentralized Safeway's operations. He also acquired a number of companies, including the purchase in September, 1962, of John Gardner,

Ltd. (Super Markets), and Prideaux, Ltd. (London). In November, 1968, Safeway began a joint venture with Holly Farms Poultry Industries, Inc., to locate ready-to-eat, take-home chicken stores on Safeway parking lots.

Size—Safeway is the world's largest chain of retail food stores, operating over 2,300 retail food stores, grocery warehouses, and distribution centers in the U.S., Canada, Australia, England, Scotland, and West Germany. In the U.S., the company has over 1,970 stores in 27 States and the District of Columbia, with most stores west of the Mississippi River. In Canada the company has over 270 stores in the provinces of Alberta, British Columbia, Manitoba, Ontario, and Saskatchewan.

Population—117,221 employees.

Who Rules—Each of the company's stores is run as if it were a separate business. The individual retail stores are organized into 26 retail divisions with each division responsible for about 100 stores. Overall company policy is set by the chairman of the executive committee, the chairman of the board and the president. The officers are elected by a 13-member board of directors that includes 7 officers. The directors are elected by 62,767 stockholders owning 25,797,229 shares.

Who REALLY Rules—Safeway's 30 largest stockholders owned 33.5% of the company's shares in 1971. The 7 largest New York banks had 17.8% of the shares, with Chase Manhattan Bank holding 10.5%.

NOTES

Safeway owns 2,100 tractor-trailers, 38 free-standing warehouses, 25 distribution warehouses, 19 fluid milk plants, 16 produce packaging plants, 16 bakeries, 16 ice cream plants, 12 meat cutting and aging plants, 6 egg candling plants, 4 soft drink bottling plants, 3 meat processing plants, 3 coffee roasting plants, 2 jam and jelly plants, an edible oil refinery, a soap plant, and a dressing and salad oil plant.

When Lingan Warren headed Safeway the company was literally run by the book—a set of more than 50 black loose-leaf manuals, which set forth in meticulous detail company policy on every conceivable management problem, including such things as warnings to butchers to wash their hands, comb their hair, and shave. Under Warren, division managers could not communicate directly with each other. Instead they had to send all messages through Warren.

As the largest chain of retail food stores, Safeway has been a target of the United Farm Workers' efforts to get retailers to stock only UFW-picked grapes and lettuce. Safeway has consistently bought non-UFW grapes and let-

tuce in defiance of the union. The UFW initiated a consumers' boycott against Safeway in support of the union's attempt to organize agricultural workers in California. The boycott lowered Safeway's sales and threatened the jobs of the company's employees, who are represented by the Retail Clerk's union. In exchange for AFL-CIO's support of the grape and lettuce boycott, the UFW stopped their store-wide campaign against Safeway.

—H.B.

SAUDI ARABIA

NITTY GRITTY

Location—The Arabian peninsula. Almost the entire interior of the peninsula and the eastern Red Sea coast, but with a shorter coastline on the Persian Gulf. Its northwestern borders are with Jordan, Iraq, and Kuwait. Its western boundary is the Red Sea. On the south lie North Yemen and South Yemen, while Oman is to the east. Its northeastern borders are with the United Arab Emirates, Qatar, and the Persian Gulf.

How Created—By W.W. I, a conservative Islamic religious movement, Wahhabism, led by the Saudi tribe, had succeeded in uniting large sections of the peninsula. Eventually, the Saudis conquered Britain's old allies, the Hashemites, who controlled the Hejaz (the strip along the Red Sea which is the holiest territory in Islam), and by 1926 the Saudis had united most of the peninsula, though the British kept them out of a number of small coastal areas and British-controlled Oman and Yemen.

Size—865,000 sq. mi. (2,240,000 sq. km.).

Population—About 8 million: Almost 100% Arab and Sunni Muslim.

Who Rules—Saudi Arabia is an absolute monarchy, with no constitution. The Koran and Wahhabi religious law are the only existent forms of legislation. All jurisprudence is religious.

Who REALLY Rules—The Saudi Royal Family is supported by the religious establishment, headed by the al-Shaykh family. The U.S. Government provides the military aid and training needed for the severe internal repression that exists and the U.S. oil corporations provide the needed revenue.

NOTES

In Saudi Arabia are Mecca and Medina, cities sacred to the world of Islam. Five times every day Muslims around the world bow toward Mecca and every year over 500,000 foreign pilgrims come to the Great Mosque and the *Kaaba* with its sacred black rock. But these sites are accessible only to Muslims, and Saudi Arabia as a whole is not open to tourists.

As one of the 2 most important members of the Organization of Petroleum Exporting Countries (OPEC), the Saudi state has emerged from its formerly dependent status to become a major force within the capitalist world economy. Its new-found strength derives directly from the fact that it sits atop approximately 28% of the world's recoverable oil reserves, from which the Royal Family realizes an annual income of over $20 billion.

Although the people of Saudi Arabia have no civil rights, some relaxation has occurred since 1970. The religious police can no longer enter private homes to enforce Wahhabi religious and moral laws, though they still enforce them in public places. There are still prohibitions against smoking, music, and liquor. Mandatory veils for women and mosque attendance requirements remain unchanged.

—J.G.

SENEGAL

NITTY GRITTY

Location—In the "hump" of West Africa, with a western coastline along the Atlantic Ocean; to the north, Mauritania; to the east, Mali Republic; to the south, Guinea-Bissau and Guinea; Gambia cuts into the south of Senegal.

How Created—Senegal is the oldest of the French West African colonies. The borders were created arbitrarily.

Size—78,684 sq. mi. (203,793 sq. km.).

Population—4,350,000: Wolof, 35.5%; Serer, 19.1%; Tukulor, 13.6%; Fulani, 7.4%; Dyola, 6.9%; Malinke, 5.3%; other, 12.2%. 89.7% Muslim, 5.7% Christian, 2.6% no religion, 2% Animist.

Who Rules—President has full executive power; 100-member Legislative Assembly, elected by universal suffrage to 5-year terms.

Who REALLY Rules—France supplies Senegal with technical and financial aid, and maintains military bases in the country. Senegal maintains cordial relations with the U.S., U.S.S.R., Israel, and the Arab states.

NOTES

The 1st black slaves to come to the New World and Europe were probably the 12 young Negroes sold by an Arab chieftain in 1441 to 2 Portuguese captains at Cap Blanc, Senegal.

Senegal, being the 1st of France's African colonies, had the 1st university, the 1st museum, and the 1st cathedral in West Africa. The elite of Senegal are so luxury-loving that

the Government has had to curb their spending by placing a ceiling-price to be legally spent on weddings ($60), baptisms ($40), and circumcision ceremonies ($20).

In the spring of 1965, the 1st World Festival of Negro Arts was held in the capital of Dakar. American representatives included Duke Ellington, Langston Hughes, and Josephine Baker.

About ¾ of Senegal's people remain in the country, uneducated, without modern conveniences or political awareness. They live according to the ancient customs of their tribes, little affected by the modernization which prevails in Dakar.

Eighty percent of Senegal's economy relies upon the peanut industry.

—R.C.

SIERRA LEONE

NITTY GRITTY

Location—In the "hump" of West Africa, with a 210-mi. west and southwest coastline along the Atlantic Ocean. To the north, northeast, and east is Guinea; to the southeast, Liberia.

How Created—The British Crown Colony of Sierra Leone was purchased by abolitionists from King Niambana in 1788 as a settlement for runaway slaves who had escaped to London, and blacks discharged from the British armed forces. The Colony combined with the mainland Protectorate in 1896 to make the present-day boundaries.

Size—27,925 sq. mi. (72,325 sq. km.).

Population—2,850,000: Mende, 30.9%; Temne, 29.8%; Limba, 8.4%; Kono, 4.8%; Koranko 3.7%; Sherbro, 3.4%; Loko, Kissi, Creole and other, 19%. 66% Animist, 28% Muslim, 6% Christian.

Who Rules—President elected to a 5-year term by universal suffrage. Unicameral legislative house—62 elected representatives, 12 indirectly elected paramount chiefs. Only one party ran candidates in the 1973 elections.

Who REALLY Rules—The Republic of Sierra Leone is an independent nation within the British Commonwealth. The Queen is represented by the governor-general of Sierra Leone.

NOTES

The Colony—The inhabitants of the original Crown Colony are called "Creoles." There are less than 45,000 of these descendants of former slaves. They make up the aristocracy: an educated, sophisticated group of lawyers, doctors, clergymen, and politicians. They center around the capital city, Freetown, a sleepy Victorian city with few modern buildings.

The Protectorate—The indigenous tribes who live in what was the British Protectorate of Sierra Leone make up the nation's large lower class. They hold low-paying jobs in the mines, railroads, and waterfronts. In 1956 they revolted against the strict class distinction. Gaining political awareness, they are moving toward political equality with the Creoles.

Sierra Leone supplies ¼ of the world's diamonds. In 1945 the 3rd largest diamond in the world was found in the Woxie River.

—R.C.

SIKKIM (see: INDIA)

SINGAPORE

NITTY GRITTY

Location—An island and scattered islets at the southern tip of the Malay peninsula in Southeast Asia. The main island is separated from the mainland by the narrow Strait of Johore which is bridged in one location by a 4-lane causeway.

How Created—It is believed that an important trading center existed on the island sometime before the 13th century. However, when Sir Thomas Stamford Raffles stopped there in 1819, the island was an almost uninhabited swamp.

Raffles, concerned about the lack of a British port between India and China and aware of Singapore's strategic location on the Strait of Malacca, through which all sea trade between those 2 countries passed, immediately began to develop the island. Control of Singapore later went to the East India Company and eventually, in 1867, to the British Government.

In 1959 the British granted Singapore internal self-government, and in 1963 the island helped form the Federation of Malaysia. Racial and commercial hostility between Singaporeans and other Malaysians made this marriage unworkable, so Singapore seceded, by mutual agreement, in 1965. The separation was not marked by much acrimony, but there have been disputes over the "property settlement." In the early 1970s the 2 nations were still dividing joint institutions, such as their joint airline and shared stock market.

Size—226 sq. mi. (586 sq. km.).

Population—2,250,000: Chinese, 76.2%; Malay, 15%; Indian, 7%; other, 1.8%. Most major religions are represented.

Who Rules—Singapore has one legislative body—its 65-member Parliament. The Parliament elects the President, who in turn appoints the Prime Minister. There are no local governments.

Who REALLY Rules—Since achieving independence in 1959, Singapore's politics have been dominated by Lee Kuan Yew, a Cambridge-educated lawyer. Though not a military man, Yew has the reputation of being a "strongman." His Government jails many of its opponents and it has shut down critical newspapers, including the *Singapore Herald* in 1971.

NOTES

In addition to repressing political opponents, Lee Kuan Yew represses any cultural phenomena he associates with the drug trade. Long hair on males is essentially illegal, and airport guards confiscate passports until long-haired travelers get haircuts.

Singapore's main business has traditionally been trade. It is the world's 3rd busiest port with a ship arriving or departing every 15 minutes.

—S.L.W.G. & L.S.

SOMALIA (SOMALI REPUBLIC)

NITTY GRITTY

Location—At the "Horn of Africa," the continent's easternmost point; north is the Gulf of Aden; east and south, the Indian Ocean; west, Kenya, Ethiopia, and the French Territory of the Afars and the Issas.

How Created—Somalia (Italian Somaliland) and British Somaliland joined in 1960 to form the Somali Republic. Its frontiers, however, are artificial and nomadic Somalis spread out to all neighboring countries.

Size—246,154 sq. mi. (637,541 sq. km.), slightly smaller than Texas.

Population—3,200,000: Somali, 76%; Sab, 19%; Bantu, 3.6%; Arab, 1.1%; other, 0.3%. Predominantly Sunni Muslim.

Who Rules—As a constitutional republic, Somali has a one-house legislature, the National Assembly. Both constitution and assembly are presently suspended.

Who REALLY Rules—The Supreme Revolutionary Council, which took power in 1969, dissolved the legislature, and rules in its place by decree through a strongman head. The régime pledges to erase the "inefficiency, graft, and injustice of the past."

NOTES

The Ancient Egyptians thought Somali was the Land of Punt or "God's Land." The ancients also thought it to be the home of myrrh and incense and called it Regio Aromatica. Perhaps the aromas attract locusts, for Somali was also considered to be the home of the locust which plagued Egypt in the days before the Exodus.

Seventy-five percent of the people graze herds totaling 1.4 million cattle, 2 million camels, 2.3 million sheep, and 4.1 million goats.

The capital, Mogadiscio, is also spelled Mukdisha, Magadisho, Mukdishu, Mogadisho, Mogadaxo, and Mogadischo. It is reputed to be the place Mussolini sent Italians he really wanted to be rid of.

—M.D.

SOUTH AFRICA

NITTY GRITTY

Location—Southern tip of Africa, between the Atlantic on the west and the Indian Ocean on the east. North are Namibia (South-West Africa), Botswana, and Rhodesia; to the east are Swaziland and Mozambique. Inside lies the independent kingdom of Lesotho.

How Created—Formerly the Union of South Africa. Withdrew from the British Commonwealth in 1961 to become a republic.

Size—471,445 sq. mi. (1,221,037 sq. km.), twice the size of Texas.

Population—24,500,000: Bantu, 70.2%, in-including Zulu, 18.8%; Xhosa, 18.3%; Tswana, 8%; Sepedi, 7.5% and Seshoeshoe, 6.8%; white, 17.5%; colored (mixed white and African or Malay), 9.4%; Asian, 2.9%. 14.5% Bantu Christian, 14.3% Nederduits Gereformeerde (Dutch Reformed), 10.7% Methodist, 8.8% Anglican, 6.7% Roman Catholic, 18.4% other Christian, 22.5% no religion or unknown, 4.1% other.

Who Rules—State President serves as Head of State but the Prime Minister heads the Government and has the greater power. Parliament makes laws. Senate: 44 members elected by the Provinces and 10 appointed by the State President; House of Assembly: 160 elected by South Africa and 6 by South-West Africa (Namibia).

Who REALLY Rules—The white minority—in the general sense. Only whites can vote or run for office in parliamentary elections. But in the particular sense: (1) *Afrikaner nationalists*, embodied in the Dutch Reformed Church and the *Broederbond*, a white-supremacist secret society with tentacles into the highest levels of government; and (2) the *Chamber of Mines*, the gold-diamond-uranium monopolies (e.g. Anglo-American, Kennecott, etc.), in very tight with the Gov-

ernment and the English-speaking financial interests.

NOTES

South Africa's main wealth lies below the soil in the form of gold, diamonds, and uranium. South Africa is practically one big gold mine, and the world's largest gold mine, located here, happens to be the world's largest uranium field as well. South Africa produces 60%–70% of the world's gold supply through vast holding companies which have nearly semi-official government status. They are: the Gold Mining Group, Consolidated Gold, Central Mining, Anglo-Transvaal (Kennecott), and the Anglo-American Corp. The mines of the Rand, that ridge of gold which runs through the country, are quite deep—up to 9,000' deep—and therefore dangerous. Whites will not work them. So, in a large way, the whole South African economy depends upon the black labor which can be induced or forced literally to "go under."

One of gold mining's by-products is uranium. Uranium oxide comes from the slime left over once the gold ore is extracted. This uranium is owned by the Government, which markets it but sends a good portion of the proceeds back to the mining companies.

South Africa also has a cheap supply of coal as well as important deposits of iron, manganese, tin, copper, tungsten, chrome, and nickel. All this mineral wealth has spurred rapid industrialization—steel mills, auto plants, shipyards, and the accompanying commercial enterprises. Manufacturing-finance is now the biggest sector of the South African economy: 21% of gross domestic production, nearly as much as agriculture and mining combined.

About 87% of South Africa is reserved for Europeans while the remaining 13% is reserved for blacks. Two-thirds of the black population live on agricultural compounds or urban locations in bondage to the whites. The English-speaking whites control industry and commerce and so form the top of the social pyramid. Afrikaners (descendants of Dutch, German, and French settlers), as farmers, professionals, and civil servants, form the middle of the pyramid—the poorer white class. The huge base of the pyramid is formed by native blacks and colored who hold up the whole structure and are kept there by "apartheid."

The goals of apartheid are: (1) to prevent blacks from "swamping" the white minority, (2) to let each racial group develop itself separately, and (3) to halt the detribalization of blacks. These goals are accomplished by imposing: (a) separate and unequal education, (b) job restrictions, (c) restrictions on mobility and residence, and (d) restrictions on political movements and open protest. The Government implements apartheid by requiring any black or colored person to carry a number of passes and identifications. Without the required certificate, one can be arrested and thrown in jail without further charges or trial. Any native or group of natives can be transported to another residence or job on purely administrative orders. And, of course, interracial marriages are absolutely banned.

Most Afrikaners are strict Calvinists by way of one of the 3 branches of the Dutch Reformed Church. Like Catholicism in medieval Spain, the Church here dominates the state by preaching that all power comes from God and races must be separate. Its rationale: Blacks are considered "Sons of Ham" and thus cursed to be "hewers of wood and drawers of water."

—M.D.

SOVIET UNION (U.S.S.R.)

NITTY GRITTY

Location—Northern Eurasia from the Baltic to the Pacific. To the west are Romania, Hungary, Czechoslovakia, Poland, Finland, and Norway; to the north is the Arctic Ocean; to the east is the Pacific and its various north Asian seas; to the south are Korea, China, Mongolia, Afghanistan, Iran, and Turkey; about ¼ lies in eastern Europe, ¾ in northern Asia.

How Created—Greater Russia grew up from the duchies around Moscow and Kiev and pushed to the Volga Steppe and Caspian Sea during the 16th century under Ivan the Great and his son. Siberia was gradually added during the 17th century. In 1639 Russians reached the Pacific and in 1689 fixed their boundaries with China at the Amur River. Peter the Great opened up a window onto the Baltic in the 18th century. Russia expanded into its present frontiers by annexing or conquering the following nations which are presently socialist republics within the Soviet Union:

Nation/Republic
Ukraine: 47,000,000; added mostly during the 18th century; part sliced from Poland after W.W. II.
Belorussia: 9,000,000; 18th-century addition.
Georgia: 4,700,000; 18th-century addition.
Lithuania: 3,100,000; 18th-century conquest, part after W.W. II.
Moldavia: 3,600,000; part of Russia at various times.
Kazakh: 13,000,000; by conquest of Nicholas I, early 19th century.
Kirghiz: 2,900,000; 19th-century addition.
Tadzhik: 2,900,000; 19th-century addition under Nicholas I.

Armenia: 2,500,000; finally subdued in mid-19th century.
Azerbaijan: 5,100,000; 19th-century addition.
Uzbek: 12,000,000; Alexander II added in the 19th century.
Turkmen: 2,200,000; late 19th-century addition under Alexander III.
Latvia: 2,400,000; handed to Russia by Hitler in the German-Soviet Non-Aggression Pact; retained after the war.
Estonia: 1,400,000; another Non-Aggression Pact casualty though Peter the Great had controlled it earlier.

Size—8,650,000 sq. mi. (22,400,000 sq. km.). Area-wise Russia is the world's largest country covering ⅙ of its land surface.

Population—255 million: Russian, 50%; Ukrainian, 16.9%; Uzbek, 4%; Belorussian, 4%; Kazakh, 2%; Azerbaijanian, 2%; Armenian, 1.5%; Georgian, 1.4%; Moldavian, 1.2%; Lithuanian, 1.2%; 160 other ethnic groups, 12.8%. Most people belong to no organized religion, but there are 13% Russian Orthodox, 13% Muslim, 12% Roman Catholic, 1% Jewish, 0.8% Russian Baptist Union.

Who Rules—The U.S.S.R. Federal constitution provides for legislative and executive branches. One house of the legislature, or Supreme Soviet, is composed of representatives elected from the 15 Union republics (25 from each), the 20 autonomous republics (11 each), the 8 autonomous regions (5 each), and the 10 national districts (one each). These deputies, running on either the Communist party ticket or as a nonparty member, comprise the Council ("Soviet") of Nationalities. The 2nd house—the Council of the Union—is composed of one deputy for each 300,000 of the population. Both houses usually meet twice per year during the 4-year term. The 37-member Presidium is chosen by the Supreme Soviet from among its members; the chairman is the titular head of state, or President. The Council of Ministers, which includes the Premier and his deputies, is also appointed by the Supreme Soviet. Its chairman is the Premier.

Who REALLY Rules—The Communist party, whose membership is rigidly controlled through a strict indoctrination program that admits only a carefully-chosen few. Party membership (a necessity for political advancement): about 9% of total population. The party elects the Central Committee which, in turn, names the Politburo members who determine U.S.S.R. policy. The Committee also elects the Secretariat, or executive, body. The First Secretary, or chairman, of the Central Committee is the U.S.S.R.'s political leader, overseeing the corporate-manager types who maintain control. At times the party secretary has also been the Premier, e.g. Nikita Khrushchev. But whether or not he heads the Government, the head of the party is in control of the U.S.S.R.

NOTES

Despite government claims to the contrary, the Soviet Union still has class distinctions. How the Soviet citizen lives today is determined by his position in a 3-tier hierarchy: a privileged upper class; the urban, educated mid-class; and the blue-collar farmer class. In a society without private property or inherited private wealth and without great income disparities, the basis of "class" is power and status.

The upper class: 600,000 power-elite bureaucrats, ⅓ party members, who run the Government and society. Its nucleus is the Politburo-Secretariat surrounded by several hundred thousand technocrats, engineers, and lawyers. Most come from peasant origins and have less education than the recently-graduated specialists.

The mid-class: These are the specialists and professionals required to run a modern, urban society at the behest of the power elite. Most of these 2 million are university or technical school graduates and their numbers are growing daily. To this class also belong the prestige elite: the writers, artists, senior professors, and scientists whose individual talents rather than managerial positions give them their status.

The lowest class: manual workers and farmers—the proletariat for whom the Revolution was carried out and in whose name the party rules. Include here the office workers and simple artisans.

The Communist party is organized according to Lenin's principle of "democratic centralism." In theory, the leading units of the party up to the highest are elected democratically. The party rank and file choose delegates to local conferences who in turn meet to elect delegates to the next highest level until the national Party Congress is elected. The Party Congress usually meets every 5 years to elect a Central Committee which exercises legislative authority in the party between congresses. This Central Committee in turn elects a Political Bureau (Politburo) and a secretariat to conduct the party's daily work. In practice, however, power flows in the opposite direction. Delegates are preselected from the top and voted for automatically by the units below. The Politburo selects candidates for the Central Committee, not the other way around. In U.S. political jargon, this makes for a system of self-perpetuating bossism. Since any person who wants a party career must be approved by the person above him, loyalty to the boss is guaranteed by self-interest. The overriding requirement for party discipline naturally overrules any opportunity for open debate or dissension.

About ⅘ of Soviet women between 20 and 25 now work full time and enjoy equal status with men in the labor force. Women comprise more than half the country's doctors, economists, and teachers and about ⅓ of its engineers, lawyers, and judges. From 1959 to 1965 the number of full-time housewives dropped by half. But sexual equality has not worked its way into the home yet since the Soviet male does not keep house or rear children. Consequently the working woman is still a half-time housewife. Without many of the Western appliances, she spends 35–40 hours a week on domestic duties in addition to her outside work, while her husband spends no more than 20 hours.

Nor are women equal to men politically. Though comprising more than half the adult population, women form no more than ⅓ of the party membership. Only 6 sit as full members of the Central Committee and none at all sit on the Politburo.

Early Russia was converted by Greek Orthodoxy. When Ivan III married Sophia, the niece of the last Byzantine Emperor, the Russian monarchy then became the standard-bearer for the Orthodox Church. Because of this tie to the czarist regime and its opposition to the theoretic grounds for materialism, the communists shut the Church down when they took power. But to get more popular support during W.W. II, Stalin made peace with the Church and allowed it and other religions to flourish on a limited basis. Judaism did not fare as well, however, and because of recent persecution, 6 to 10 times as many Jews are trying to emigrate today as did 5 years ago. Although they are well-educated and fill the professional ranks, they have a double burden to bear: They are officially suspect as "rootless cosmopolitans" insufficiently loyal to the Soviet state, and also as supporters of Israel. Traditional domestic anti-Semitism has now been fortified by Soviet foreign policy interests in the Middle East.

The party's treatment of writers led to a protest movement in 1966 which grew out of the trial and conviction of 2 young writers, Andrei Sinyavski and Yuli Daniel. The protest demanded a "return to the socialist legality"—the right to speak, write, and publish freely, and the abolition of illegal trials, censorship, and religious persecution.

Scientists and academics have also mounted protests for greater information, expression, travel, and human rights, but few of these have been imprisoned or exiled because the Government views their services as indispensable to the society.

Because of the repression, writers, scientists, and other dissenters have resorted to an underground press or *samizdat* which mimeos and circulates banned manuscripts. These have been primarily novels, plays, letters from prison camps, protests against unfair trials and imprisonments, petitions to the UN on behalf of human rights, open letters to the régime, and chronicles of illegal party or government actions against human rights. (For further information, see *Samizdat: Voices of the Soviet Opposition* edited by George Saunders, distributed by Pathfinder Press, 410 West Street, New York, N.Y. 10014.)

Though Russia did not start industrializing until the late 19th century—and then, the communists insist, only on a minor scale—her industrial production is 2nd only to the U.S. It consists mainly of oil, steel, electricity, cement, pig iron, and other heavy industrials as well as foodstuffs and textiles. Much of this heavy industry goes into the production of armaments, especially missiles and warships. As in the U.S., defense and exportation of arms are big business, important economically as well as strategically.

—M.D.

SPAIN

NITTY GRITTY

Location—In southwest Europe, forming more than ⅘ of the Iberian peninsula. It is bounded to the northeast by France and Andorra, to the west by Portugal and the Atlantic Ocean. To the east is the Mediterranean and, 20 mi. to the south across the Strait of Gibraltar, Africa.

How Created—Settled gradually by successive migrations of Celts, Iberians, Phoenicians, Greeks, and Carthaginians; it took the Romans to unify the peninsula, ca. 218 B.C. By 1492 the kingdoms of Aragón and Castile were united through the marriage of Ferdinand and Isabella; the kingdom of Granada was then released by the Moors to Spain.

Though the Pyrénées Mountains form a natural border with France, it was only in the 17th century that Spain relinquished territories in southern France (and in the Low Countries). Portugal, part of which was a gift from King León of Castile to Count Henri of Burgundy, proclaimed itself an independent state in 1140.

Size—195,985 sq. mi. (504,750 sq. km.).

Population—35,600,000: Spanish, 72.8%; Catalan, 16.4%; Galician, 8.2%; Basque, 2.3%; other, 0.3%. 97.5% Roman Catholic.

Who Rules—Constitutionally, Spain is a monarchy, at present without a monarch. Legislation is initiated by the Council of Ministers,

and General Franco, as Head of State, has the power of veto.

Who REALLY Rules—Generalissimo Francisco Franco, who has ruled Spain since 1939, has other titles: Commander-in-Chief of the Armed Forces and leader of the "National Movement." Franco rules Spain not through a monolithic power machine, but through the skillful balancing and suppressing of forces which include the following:
—The Falange—extreme right. Now divided and discredited, but still the only legal political organization in Spain. The Falange's power was eclipsed in the '60s by . . .
—Opus Dei, a Catholic lay organization whose influence has now slightly declined.
—Monarchists, in a position of expectant semi-legality.
—Christian Democrats (has both Conservative and Radical branches).
—Socialists, communists, and anarchists (underground).

In 1973 Franco relinquished the post of Prime Minister to the ultraconservative Adm. Luis Carrero Blanco who was subsequently blown to bits later that year (the Basque separatist association took credit for the assassination). Instead, Señor Arias Navarro was sworn into this 2nd-in-line office in January, 1974.

NOTES

The Spanish Civil War was the result of a revolt by Army officers led by Franco (the Nationalists) against the Popular Front Government (the Republicans). The one thing common to all factions—republicans, monarchists, liberals, conservatives, radicals, fascists, socialists, the Church, anarchists, the military, communists, peasants, and regionalists alike—was a stubborn refusal to compromise. The reforms undertaken or attempted by successive governments of the Republic were, in the last analysis, always too little for the left and too much for the right to accept. Enormous pressures from all sides led inevitably to the outbreak of the Civil War in July, 1936. One million people are said to have died in that war. (See: Attempted Utopias, Chap. 31.)

Traditionally an agricultural country, food products continue to represent half or more of the total value of Spanish exports, especially olives and olive oil, citrus fruits, cereals, grapes, wine and sherry. However, tourism has rapidly become a major source of income as Spanish resorts have become increasingly popular with foreigners, due, it seems, to Spain's relatively cheap prices. In 1974 over 30 million tourists visited Spain.

—J.O.

SRI LANKA (CEYLON)

Location—A pear-shaped island situated in the Indian Ocean 20 mi. southeast of India. The Sinhalese name, Sri Lanka, means, "the resplendent land" or "Holy Ceylon."

How Created—Ceylon has been inhabited since the Stone Age, and some claim that Ceylon is the cradle of civilization. Migratory tribes from northern India came to settle under the 1st Sinhalese dynasty, founded in 543 B.C. under Bengali prince Vijaya, whose capital at Anuradhapurs lasted a thousand years. Ceylon was a British colony from 1798 to 1948, when it finally gained independence.

Size—25,332 sq. mi. (65,610 sq. km.).

Population—14 million: Lowland Sinhalese, 42.8%; Kandyan Sinhalese, 29.1%; Ceylonese Tamil, 11.1%; Indian Tamil, 9.4%; Ceylonese Moor, 6.5%; other, 0.1%. 67.4% Buddhist, 17.6% Hindu, 7.7% Christian, 7.2% Muslim, 0.1% other.

Who Rules—Ceylon is a self-governing member of the British Commonwealth. Its Government is modeled after the British Parliament with a Prime Minister and Cabinet. The British Monarch is represented by a Ceylon governor general, who acts in only an advisory capacity.

Who REALLY Rules—Currently in power: the Sri Lanka Freedom party (SLFP) headed by Mrs. Sirimavo Bandaranaike, widow of the former Prime Minister who was assassinated in 1959. The SLFP is aligned with the pro-Moscow Communist party and the Lanka Sama Samaj party (LSSP), a supposedly Trotskyist organization.

Although seemingly leftist, the Sri Lanka coalition is as bourgeois as its predecessors, the United National party (UNP). The UNP was hastily formed by the Sinhalese just before independence, to guard against a "power vacuum." They were defeated by the SLFP in 1956. The SLFP is pro-Sinhalese, anti-Tamil, as demonstrated in such measures as the Public Security Act (an antiworking class bill), its suppression or indifference to labor strikes, and its brutal repression of the JVP (Juanta Vimukhti Peramuna or People's Liberation Front) uprising of April, 1971. In the JVP uprising, a protest against the Bandaranaike Government, over 15,000 people were killed, most of them youths, many after having been taken into custody. People were made to dig their own graves, lined up and shot, others were hung by their feet and tortured. The atrocities were committed openly in order to terrorize the people. Britain, the U.S., the U.S.S.R., India, Pakistan, East and West Germany, Yugoslavia, and Egypt supplied weapons to help squash the revolt.

The Ceylonese are family-oriented and marriages are arranged by parental preferences. Until the past few decades, men and women wore only white, but due to modern influences, colorful saris have replaced traditional wear. In fact, it is not uncommon to see Buddhist monks in chauffeur-driven limousines amid bullock carts and dirt roads. The fact that many Buddhist monks are rich landowners, and that the temples themselves are often the center for political intrigue, corruption, and anti-Tamil racism, leaves many with a more than cynical attitude about the religion. Buddhism is widely recognized as a steppingstone to a scholarship, an export permit, or a local job.

Ceylon is swarming with animals: elephants, buffaloes, bears, leopards, monkeys, elks, deer, and 400 species of birds, 40 of which are peculiar to Ceylon.

—J.Sm.

SUDAN

Location—Northeast Africa; running along its east are the Red Sea and Ethiopia; along the west are Libya, Chad, and the Central African Republic; north is Egypt; south are Zaire, Uganda, and Kenya.

How Created—The Sudan did not exist as a single territory until 1821, when the forces of Mohammed Ali, viceroy of Egypt under the Turks, conquered the area (excepting Darfur) and added it to the Ottoman Empire. Later, British control and influence prevented Egypt from annexing its southern neighbor, though the 2—Britain and Egypt—ruled the Sudan jointly. Following W.W. II, it was agreed that the Sudan should become independent, and a Parliament was elected. Independence was proclaimed on January 1, 1956.

Size—967,491 sq. mi. (2,505,805 sq. km.).

Population—18,000,000: Arab, 48.7%; Dinka, 11.5%; Nubian, 8.1%; Beja, 6.4%; Nuer, 5%; Azande, 2.7%; Bari, 2.6%; For, 2.2%; Koalib, 1.9%; other, 10.9%. 72% Muslim, 27% Animist, 1% Christian.

Who Rules—Executive is the President, theoretically limited by an interim constitution and constituent assembly but these are currently suspended.

Who REALLY Rules—President Gaafer al-Nimeiry, who seized power in a military coup in 1969 and dissolved the legislative body, the constituent assembly. Political parties are banned except for the Nasser-style Sudanese

Socialist Union created by Nimeiry. The general serves as both its chairman and secretary-general. The opposition, though driven underground, is still felt. General Nimeiry received his Master's degree in military science at the U.S. Command and General Staff College at Fort Leavenworth, Kans., in 1966.

NOTES

Sudan is a country of 2 distinct cultures and many subcultures. The 6 northern provinces, containing ¾ of the population, are inhabited by Arabic-speaking Muslims, while the population of the 3 southern ones consists of darker, nilotic blacks who are animist (believing that all living things and natural phenomena have souls), with a Muslim/Christian minority. Throughout the existence of the Sudan, it has been the northerners, unified by language and religion, who have dominated the country, while in the south, suspicion of the north has been the only unifying factor.

The 16-year-long Sudanese civil war, which was not ended until March, 1972, represented opposition to a policy of Arabization and Islamization which was being forced on the south. Although little reported in the West, this was one of the greatest wars of this century in terms of death toll. This war, between the Arabized Muslim north and the animist and Christian south, took over 500,000 lives, mostly southern, representing ⅛ of that region's populace. Another 500,000 or more southerners fled their homes, going either into the bush or into refugee camps in neighboring black African countries. Following the 1972 Addis Ababa agreement, mediated by Ethiopia's Emperor Haile Selassic and providing for southern autonomy, Anya Nya guerrillas, the backbone of southern resistance, were absorbed into the Sudanese Army and police.

While some 90% of the population is illiterate, for women this figure rises to 98%. Women are generally regarded as emancipated politically (they have the vote) but not socially. Women rarely enter public places unescorted. A riot occurred in Khartoum when a young woman appeared in a miniskirt.

In Khartoum, the streets are laid out in the pattern of the British flag.

The extreme northwestern part of the country, an area of over 50,000 sq. mi., is virtually uninhabited.

A national hero is Mohammed Ahmed ibn Abdullah, known as the Mahdi. A religious mystic, Mohammed Ahmed in 1881 proclaimed himself the expected Mahdi (a Muslim messiah) and announced a *Jihad* (holy war) to drive out the Turko-Egyptian occupiers of the country. His dervish forces, armed only with spears, swords, and knives, in 3 years captured 21,000 rifles while killing or capturing 20,000 Turkish and Egyptian soldiers. In 1885, Khartoum, defended by British General Charles "Chinese" Gordon fell. (The British had occupied Egypt in 1882.) Five months later the Mahdi died of typhus. The Mahdist state remained independent until reconquered in 1898 by British and Egyptians led by Gen. Horatio Kitchener, who was served by a young officer named Winston Churchill.

Sudan is the world's leading supplier of gum arabic with 50,000 tons (80% of the world's supply) exported each year.

—H.E.

SWEDEN

NITTY GRITTY

Location—Sweden covers the eastern part of the Scandinavian peninsula. It shares borders with Norway on the west and northwest and Finland on the northeast.

How Created—The entire Scandinavian peninsula was carved out by Ice Age glaciers. The southern regions of the peninsula did not become habitable until about 10,000 B.C. In the 14th century, Norway, Sweden, and Denmark were united under the Danish Queen Margrethe to combat a Germanic alliance. Sweden did not reestablish its independence until the 16th century.

Size—173,649 sq. mi. (449,750 sq. km.).

Population—Over 8,100,000: Swedish, 94.1%; Finnish, 2.4%; Yugoslavian, 0.5%; Danish, 0.4%; Norwegian, 0.3%; German, 0.2%; Greek, 0.2%; Italian, 0.1%; other, 1.8%. Almost 90% Lutheran; 10% Baptist, Pentecostal, and other.

Who Rules—Sweden, like Denmark and Norway, is a constitutional monarchy. King Carl XVI Gustaf, who was born in 1946, became the world's youngest reigning monarch when he succeeded to the throne in 1973. The head of government is a Prime Minister, who is the majority party leader of the Riksdag (Parliament), which consists of a single chamber of 349 members elected for 3 years.

Who REALLY Rules—The Swedish King is almost wholly without power. The Social Democrat party has been in power for over 40 years and is responsible for most of Sweden's social welfare legislation.

NOTES

One-third of the Swedish budget is spent on social welfare. This money is spent for such programs as free college tuition for all Swedes, free child delivery, annual allowances to the mother until the child reaches the age of 16, rent rebates for large families, special pensions for needy persons, and retirement and health care benefits. Personal income tax rates vary from around 50% to 80%.

Although Sweden has a socialist Government, 90% of industry is privately owned and strikes are occurring more frequently as workers become disenchanted with the leadership of their unions.

During the Viking Age, Sweden made raids into Russia and joined with Danish and Norwegian Vikings to plunder Europe. It is interesting to note the name "Russia" derives from "Rus," the name Slavic peoples gave to the Vikings.

—M.G.

SWITZERLAND

NITTY GRITTY

Location—Landlocked in the center of Western Europe. Bordered by France, Western Germany, Austria, Liechtenstein, and Italy.

How Created—Present political boundaries stem from 700 years of economic, military, and political treaties signed between Swiss states, or *cantons*. First mutual assistance pact dates from 1291 when 3 *cantons* combined to defend against attacks from Hapsburg Austria. Switzerland now comprises 22 *cantons*, the last 3 having joined the Swiss Confederation in 1815.

Size—15,941 sq. mi. (41,288 sq. km.). More than twice the size of New Jersey.

Population—Over 6,500,000: German, 64.9%; French, 18.1%; Italian, 11.9%; Romansch, 0.8%; other, 4.3%. 49.4% Roman Catholic, 47.7% Protestant, 0.3% Jewish, 2.6% other.

Who Rules—The Swiss have long prided themselves on their experience with a constitutional, federal, democratic form of government. Universal suffrage—women received the vote only in 1972—elects members to a 2-house legislature every 4 years. National Council has 44 members, two from each *canton*; National Assembly has 200 members. Both houses elect Federal Chancellor; Chancellor's Council is composed of 7 members from various political parties, the Federal Tribunal, and in times of crisis the Federal General. The latter directs Switzerland's 400,000 person reservist Army. There is no standing Army.

Who REALLY Rules—Three political parties voicing the attitudes of their respective followers have distinct advantages. The Radicals, the Social Democrats, and the Conservative and Christian Social party habitually control 75% of the seats in the Federal Assembly. Consequently they select the administrative, legislative, and judicial branches of government. It is customary for 2 members of each party to occupy 6 of the 7 seats in the Chancellor's Council.

NOTES

The Swiss like to cite the Treaty of Westphalia (1648) as the beginnings of their present commitment to neutrality. However, between 1663 and 1789 Switzerland supplied mercenary soldiers to all countries in Europe but especially to the French. The famed Swiss Guard was the finest physical and ornamental defense between the French kings and their peoples. Today the Swiss Guard at the Vatican is the last vestige of an age when Switzerland was the broker for mercenary soldiers.

The official Swiss policy of neutrality, which has enabled Switzerland to avoid the dreadful experiences of both world wars, encourages the image of the removed and distant Swiss. Switzerland is not a member of the United Nations, NATO, or the Common Market. Although neutrality may explain the apparent indifference of the Swiss to the plight of her continental neighbors, it has also made Switzerland a haven for international organizations and *émigré* intellectuals. After W.W. I the League of Nations made Geneva its headquarters; today the European branch of the UN is located in Geneva. The International Red Cross—founded by a Swiss—and many UN agencies such as UNICEF and UNESCO are based in Geneva. The dissident writer Aleksandr Solzhenitsyn is only the most recent "man without a country" who has lived in Switzerland. During W.W. II, many European intellectuals, such as Thomas Mann, found asylum in Switzerland. Long before Mann, however, many European thinkers gravitated to Switzerland's uncomplicated distance from the vortex of European power struggles. Hermann Hesse, Friedrich Nietzsche, and Jacob Burckhardt lived in undisturbed tranquility in Switzerland as did Voltaire and Edward Gibbon.

—J.T.

SYRIA

NITTY GRITTY

Location—The eastern shore of the Mediterranean forms part of the western boundary of Syria, with Turkey forming its northern boundary. Iraq is to the east, with Jordan on the south, and Israel and Lebanon on the west.

How Created—The present Republic of Syria was carved out of Greater Syria by Britain and France in the wake of the conquest of the Ottoman Empire during W.W. I. Syrian and other Arab nationalists declared independence for the whole region in 1919, but the European powers (through the League of Nations) thwarted independence and occupied all of Syria, creating several states out of Greater Syria—Lebanon, Palestine, Transjordan, and Syria—and eventually ceding some of the northern parts of Syria to Turkey and part of the east to Iraq.

Size—71,498 sq. mi. (185,180 sq. km.).

Population—Over 7 million: Arab, 87.9%; Kurdish, 6.3%; American, 2.8%; Jewish, 0.7%; Turkmen, 0.6%; Circassian, 0.5%; Assyrian, 0.3%; other, 0.9%. 87.7% Muslim (mostly Sunnis), 12% Christian, 0.3% other.

Who Rules—An elected President, with a partially elected and partially appointed People's Assembly (legislature). Candidates are selected by the National Progressive Front, though independents may stand for election.

Who REALLY Rules—The Baath party, at present dominated by a small group of military men who in fact are attempting to broaden the base of their power outside the party.

NOTES

Syrian nationalists were a major force in the Arab nationalist movement and the Arab Army that won independence from the Ottomans in W.W. I, but they were then faced with years of struggle against the French armed occupation until France withdrew in 1946 after De Gaulle viciously bombed Damascus.

Syria's defeat at the hands of Israel in 1948–1949 caused such unrest in Syria that military dictators came to power for the next 5 years. Civilian government had returned by 1956, but the defeat suffered at that time and an unrelated plot to install a pro-Western government in Syria at the same time led to Syria's unhappy union with Egypt and Nasser in the United Arab Republic. The U.A.R. had failed by 1961 and in its aftermath the nationalist Baath party finally attained power, and gradually moved further to the left. The disastrous 1967 war with Israel, in which Syria lost the Golan Heights, undermined that leftist trend and allowed the present régime to come to power.

By 1973, the Syrian Government was pushing the other Arab governments to take action on Israel's continued occupation of territories seized in 1967, as well as urging that some effort again be made to resolve the Palestine question. President Hafez Assad, of Syria, eventually found acceptance of his efforts to build a united front with Egypt and Saudi Arabia. The result was the October, 1973, war with Israel. Though militarily not a victory for Syria, enough success was achieved politically so that the Syrian ruling group has been able to consolidate its internal position and begin to force some Israeli withdrawal.

—J.G.

TAIWAN

(REPUBLIC OF CHINA)

NITTY GRITTY

Location—A leaf-shaped island less than 100 mi. from the coast of southern China at a point where the East and South China seas and the western Pacific Ocean come together. The Republic of China also includes many smaller islands such as the Penghus (Pescadores), between Taiwan and mainland China; Kinmen (Quemoy), adjacent to the Chinese coast at Hsia-men (Amoy); and Matsu, near the coast at Foochow.

How Created—Aborigines similar to certain tribes found in the Philippines were the original inhabitants. Chinese began migrating to the island as early as the 6th century A.D., but large-scale migration did not occur until the 17th century, when Chinese came from the nearby coastal provinces of Fukien and Kwangtung.

In 1895, as part of the settlement of the Sino-Japanese War, the Manchus ceded Taiwan to Japan, which ruled the island through W.W. II.

The Kuomintang (KMT, or Nationalist Chinese) received the Japanese surrender of Taiwan. The KMT-appointed governor ruled so ruthlessly that the native Taiwanese rebelled spontaneously in 1947, taking control of the island but pledging support to the national (not provincial) KMT Government. The KMT dispatched 10,000 troops from the mainland to put down the revolt. They did, and in the process killed at least 10,000 people. In the next few years, refugees from all over China, fleeing the advancing communist armies, arrived on Taiwan. In December, 1949, the KMT National Government moved itself and most of its remaining army to Taiwan.

Size—13,892 sq. mi. (35,981 sq. km.).

Population—16 million: pre-W.W. II Chinese, 81%; post-W.W. II Chinese, 18%; Aborigine, 1%. 95% Buddhist and Taoist, 5% Christian and some Muslim.

Who Rules—A National Assembly of delegates elected at the county level elects a President who is assisted by a Cabinet in running the country. Since the Assembly theoretically represents all of China, new national elections supposedly cannot be held until the KMT recovers the mainland. The current Assembly is the same one that fled in 1949, with 2 changes. First, over half the members have died. Second, in 1972 the Government staged new elections (ostensibly for Taiwan province), adding 53 new members to the body which once had almost 3,000. The Legislative Yuan, Taiwan's congress, and the Control Yuan, which is supposed to monitor efficiency and honesty in government, are theoretically elective. The legislative Yuan shrank from 760 members in 1949 to 435 members in 1972, including 180 over 70 years old. In 1972 elections added 36 new members.

Who REALLY Rules—Generalissimo Chiang Kai-shek (born 1887) had been head of the Kuomintang since 1927 and Taiwan's only President until his death in April, 1975. In 1972 he appointed his son, Chiang Ching-kuo, Prime Minister. Following his father's death Premier Chiang was also appointed Chairman of the KMT.

NOTES

Taiwan has formally been under martial law since the KMT exodus. Criticism of the Government, sympathy or communism, and discussion of Taiwanese independence are prohibited. Military courts try political crimes. There are an estimated 4,000 political prisoners. Strikes are illegal.

Taiwan's peasants are better off than peasants in most other Third World capitalist countries. The transplanted KMT had no vested interest in maintaining the Taiwanese landlord class, and it needed popular support somewhere, so it introduced an exhaustive land reform program in the early '50s. All 800,000 farm households on Taiwan work their own land. Farms, which cannot be larger than 7.5 acres, average 2.2 acres.

The People's Republic of China has never mounted an invasion to regain control of Taiwan (both the communists and the KMT consider Taiwan a province of China), but in 1954-1955 and 1958 it applied military pressure to Taiwan-held islands along the mainland coast. In 1954 the communists seized the distant Tachen islands. The U.S., however, backed Taiwan's claim to Kinmen (Quemoy) and Matsu with the 7th fleet and increased military aid, signing a mutual security pact.

Since 1949 the U.S. has supplied Taiwan with well over $3 billion in military aid, including the training of over 24,000 military personnel. Currently the U.S. has 4,500 troops stationed on Taiwan.

—L.S.

TANZANIA

NITTY GRITTY

Location—Where Stanley met Livingstone; East Africa, just south of the equator; with Uganda and Kenya to the north; the Indian Ocean to the east; Mozambique, Malawi, and Zambia to the south; Zaire, Burundi, and Rwanda to the west.

How Created—From the union of the (British) Trust Territory of Tanganyika and the Protectorate of Zanzibar (the 2 small islands of Pemba and Zanzibar in the Indian Ocean 22 mi. from the Tanzanian mainland).

Size—364,945 sq. mi. (945,203 sq. km.).

Population—15 million: Sukuma, 12.6%; Makonde, 4%; Chagga, 3.6%; Haya, 3.4%; Nyamwezi, 3.4%; over 120 other African groups, 70.1%; Asian, 0.7%; Arab, 0.7%; other, 1.4%. 34.6% Animist, 30.6% Christian, 30.5% Muslim, 4.3% other religion or no religion.

Who Rules—*Executive*: President and 2 Vice-Presidents whom the President appoints from elected members of the National Assembly. The 1st Vice-President is also the President of Zanzibar. *Legislature*: The National Assembly of 204 members—107 elected by universal suffrage on the mainland; 10 nominated by the President; 15 nominated by national organizations; 20 are regional commissioners; 20 are of the Zanzibar Revolutionary Council; and 20 are nominated by the President and (Zanzibari) 1st Vice-President.

Who REALLY Rules—Presently governed under an interim constitution which incorporated the constitution of the Tanganyika African Nation Union party of President Julius Nyerere, the TANU. Tanzania is essentially a one-party state: The TANU under Julius Nyerere rules on the mainland while the Afro-Shirazi party, the ASP, rules on Zanzibar.

NOTES

Tanzania may well be one of the 1st places humans ever put down roots. At the famous Olduvai Gorge in 1959, British anthropologist Louis S. B. Leakey discovered Homo Zinjanthropus, a human fossil over 1,500,000 years old.

In more recent times, the Arabs set out to control the East African coast from their island colony of Zanzibar in the 8th century. From here they managed successful slave trading until the Age of Imperialism when Queen Victoria supposedly gave Tanganyika to her cousin Kaiser Wilhelm as a birthday present because he had complained she had 2 African snow-capped mountains. So Victoria kept Mount Kenya and gave him Kilimanjaro, and the surrounding area became German East Africa. But after W.W. I Germany was forced to give her protectorate back to the British, who changed its name to Tanganyika and expelled German settlers.

Mount Kilimanjaro, the "Shining Mountain," stands over 19,000', nearly on top of the equator, but it is perennially capped with snow. Myths say the mountain arose from lumps of earth dropped by a young boy fleeing an evil spirit. To many East Africans, the mountain is the very soul of the country. It gives life by plucking clouds out of the sky for rain and sending waters to gardens and lakes below.

The Masai tribe are probably the best cattlemen in the world, roaming over 25,000 sq. mi. with at least 500,000 cattle and as many sheep and goats. Their vitality is often traced to their diet—milk and blood drawn directly from living cows. They don't like schooling, look down on neighboring tribes, and seldom hire out their own labor to others.

Zanzibar's local courts and laws are more puritanical and fascist than those of the mainland. The wearing of miniskirts, long hair, tight trousers, or wigs is punishable by floggings.

Zanzibar is practically the world's sole producer of cloves.

—M.D.

THAILAND

NITTY GRITTY

Location—Located in Southeast Asia, with a shape like the head of an elephant. The skull, including the Chao Phraya River Valley and part of the Mekong Valley, is circled by Laos on the north and east, Cambodia on the southeast, and Burma on the west. The trunk, the Malayan peninsula, is bordered by Malaysia on the south, with the Gulf of Siam to the east, and the Andaman Sea to the west.

How Created—Prior to the arrival of the European colonizing forces in the 19th century, Thailand's borders were only vaguely defined. The power of the central Government was felt primarily in the capital city and its immediate environs; provincial areas enjoyed a great deal of autonomy as long as they met their tax obligations. From time to time, Thailand established protectorates over other states, such as Laos and Cambodia.

The European powers took advantage of this fluid situation and, one by one, seized these outlying provinces and kingdoms. France took Laos and Cambodia; England acquired the northern Malay states. All together, Thailand was stripped of over ⅓ of her territory. As a result, the Thai Government finally realized the importance of delineated borders and took steps to create a more centralized provincial administration.

Size—198,455 sq. mi. (514,000 sq. km.).

Population—Over 41 million: Thai, 74.5%; Chinese, 17.7%; Malay, 2.9%; Khmer, 1.3%; Soai (Kui), 1.3%; Karen, 0.4%; Indian and Pakistani, 0.4%; other, 1.5%. 93.6% Bud-

dhist, 3.9% Muslim, 0.6% Christian, 1.9% other.

Who Rules—Thailand is a constitutional monarchy in the process of forming a new constitution. King Bhumipol Adulyadej is a noted jazz clarinetist. In February, 1975, Seni Pramoj was elected Prime Minister.

Who REALLY Rules—Before October, 1973, a corrupt group of military leaders, supported by the U.S., held absolute rule. This military group had close ties to the Chinese-dominated commercial community. A popular movement, spearheaded by students, overthrew the military régime, but it succeeded only because certain army leaders were unwilling to put down the revolt. Consequently, the current Government walks a tightrope trying to balance these various forces: the military, the business community, the students, a growing labor movement, and the governments of the U.S., Vietnam, and Cambodia.

NOTES

Bangkok is considered the sex capital of Asia. Hundreds of inexpensive massage parlors, short-term motel rooms, and secret pornographic movie houses cater to the desires of Thais and foreigners, especially the growing number of Japanese businessmen.

Every Thai male at an early age is expected to don the saffron robe and enter a Buddhist monastery. Each morning, the Buddhist monks roam the streets to beg for their day's food, which they must consume before 12 noon. They are not allowed to eat anything else the rest of the day.

The movie *The King and I* and the book upon which it is based are banned in Thailand. The story is a distorted version of the life of King Rama IV, who reigned from 1851 to 1868.

The Bridge over the River Kwai is located in northwestern Thailand near the Burmese border. This infamous structure, built with the lives of prisoners-of-war during W.W. II, was a vital link between Thailand and Burma for the Japanese.

Thailand's professional "Foot Boxers" are the world's most accomplished martial artists. Repeatedly they have defeated Chinese Kung Fu experts in staged combat.

Thais have never paid much attention to family names. In fact, not until 1916 did the King require all Thais to adopt family names, which are patrilineal.

The Thais have developed elaborate methods for avoiding conflict. For instance, the ubiquitous smile is a convenient device for masking true emotions. If a Thai wants to express his anger with someone, he will usually do so through a 3rd person who will pass the infor-

mation on, thus avoiding a face-to-face confrontation.

Thailand, a member of SEATO, was an
important ally of the U.S. throughout the Indochina War. The U.S. had as many as
50,000 airmen at once at 8 major Thai bases
to support its air war in Laos, Cambodia, and
both Vietnams. Furthermore, the U.S. Central
Intelligence Agency hired and trained some
12,000 Thai irregulars to fight in Laos, and
U.S. scientists used Thailand as a laboratory to
test out communications and surveillance
equipment for Indochina.

Traditionally peasants have owned their
land, but land shortages, the introduction of
money, technology, and government agents
have created a growing class of landless farmers.

Today there are 3 active communist guerrilla
fronts in Thailand: Ethnic Chinese and Malay
Muslims operate in south Thailand, as well as
in northern Malaya; Meo tribespeople fight in
the north; and Thai-Lao insurgents are based
in the northeast. The 3 fronts have a unified
command, and they receive at least moral support from China, from which their radio station broadcasts.

Elements of Chiang Kai-shek's Army who
fled China in 1949 still live in northern Thailand where they cultivate opium with the support of the Thai Government which reportedly
realizes large sums of money from the venture.
— L.S. & S.L.W.G.

TOGO

NITTY GRITTY

Location—In the "hump" of West Africa,
with a short southern coastline on the Gulf of
Guinea. To the west, Ghana; to the north,
Upper Volta; to the east, Dahomey.

How Created—By a League of Nations mandate at the end of·W.W. I. The former German Colony of Togoland was divided between
France and England. Today's Republic of
Togo is the French (eastern) half; the British
(western) half has been incorporated into
Ghana.

Size—21,926 sq. mi. (56,785 sq. km.).

Population—2,200,000: Ewe, 20.8%; Kabre,
13.9%; Watyi, 11.9%; Noudeba, 6%; Mine,
5.8%; Kotokoli, 5.1%; Moba, 4.8%; other,
31.7%. 56.1% Animist, 17.7% Roman Catholic, 8.8% Muslim, 6.5% Protestant, 10.9%
other.

Who Rules—The military. Self-declared
President is Lieut. Col. Étienne Eyadéma, who
took over in 1967, and intends to stay in
power "indefinitely."

Who REALLY Rules—France is the chief

economic support. Having balanced off a trade
deficit of $11 million at the time of independ-
ence, France is continuing, along with the
U.S. and West Germany, to supply Togo with
foreign aid.

NOTES

The Togolese people have the dubious honor
of being one of the few modern nations to be
ruled by an assassin. President Eyadéma claims
to have fired the shots that killed Togo's 1st
President, Sylvanus Olympio, in 1963.

Angry efforts toward tribal unification occupy the Ewe leaders. Arbitrarily divided 3
ways at the end of W.W. I, the Ewes found
themselves scattered among British Togoland
(170,000), Gold Coast (which later became
Ghana—250,000) and French Togoland
(200,000). With the incorporation of British
Togoland into Ghana, the French Togolese
Ewes stepped up their efforts toward complete
tribal unity. Nkrumah tried to incorporate
Togo into Ghana, but Togolese leaders
resisted. The result was the termination of relations between the 2 countries; the borders
remain closed today, and the Ewes continue to
fight to become one people again.
— R.C.

TRINIDAD AND TOBAGO

NITTY GRITTY

Location—A 2-island nation in the West
Indies, lying 7 mi. off the northeast coast of
Venezuela. Trinidad is the most southerly of
the Lesser Antilles. Tiny Tobago lies 20 mi. off
the northeast corner of Trinidad.

How Created—Columbus discovered Trinidad on July 31, 1498, on his 3rd voyage. After
the French and Haitian revolutions, many
French planters fled to Trinidad with their
slaves. Great Britain captured the island from
the Spanish in 1797, and it became an official
British colony in 1802 (Treaty of Amiens).
Tobago, although discovered by Columbus,
was not claimed for Spain. James I claimed it
for Great Britain in 1608, but the island
changed hands many times among the Dutch,
French, Spanish, and British, until it finally
was ceded to Britain in 1814. Tobago's economic problems, including its extremely small
size, falling world prices for sugar, and labor
shortage after the abolition of slavery, obliged
it to join with Trinidad as a single colony in
1889. The 2-island nation has been independent since 1962.

Size—The 2 islands together total 1,980 sq.
mi. (5,128 sq. km.); Trinidad: 1,864; Tobago:
116.

Population—1,200,000: black, 40%; East

Indian, 40%; mixed, 16%; white, 2%; Chinese, 1%; other, 1.1%. 36.2% Roman Catholic, 23% Hindu, 21.1% Anglican, 6% Muslim, 3.9% Presbyterian, 9.8% other. The 1970 census revealed that Trinidad has more East Indians than blacks, but the Negro-controlled government changed the figures before releasing them.

Who Rules—The islands form an independent nation within the British Commonwealth. Currently operating under a 1961 Constitution which provides for a ministerial-type system, the Government is considering a new constitution establishing a republican form of government.

Who REALLY Rules—Although no longer a Crown Colony, the islands still recognize the Queen as head of state, and Britain maintains a governor-general in Port-of-Spain. Foreign interests, particularly the U.S., control the oil and sugar industries, and hence the economic and political life of the nation.

NOTES

Increasing racial and labor unrest has marred Trinidad and Tobago's relative stability. Black power groups have become active, and a guerrilla group, the National Union of Freedom Fighters (NUFF) maintains a running battle with the Government. Although the incumbent People's National Movement is largely black, the guerrillas (also black) insist that the real power is in the hands of the white foreign investors who control the principal sources of national wealth—oil, insurance, banking, natural gas, sugar. Bank holdups and raids on police stations for arms have become common. In addition, East Indians complain of job discrimination, believing that government and private hiring policies favor blacks.

The economy is dominated by petroleum, which accounts for 80% of all exports. Considerable oil is also imported, to be refined in Trinidad's vast refinery complex. Amoco, Tesoro, Shell, and Texaco dominate the oil industry along with British Petroleum.

Pitch Lake, near La Brea on Trinidad, is 105 acres of warm gray tar, the result of an oil seepage. Trinidad exports the natural asphalt formed there without visibly depleting the supply. Visitors can walk on the yielding surface of the lake—an eerie experience as it gives slightly beneath one's feet.

Angostura Bitters, one of Trinidad's most famous exports, has been produced by the same family since its invention in 1824. The secret recipe, known to only 4 people, was for years relayed orally. At last written out for safety's sake, the sheet was torn in 2 and the halves placed in separate banks. The 4 who share the secret never travel together in the same conveyance, and only they may enter the secret room where the formula is mixed once a week. The U.S. imports half of all the Bitters produced.

—E.P.

TUNISIA

NITTY GRITTY

Location—Northernmost tip of Africa. Bounded by the Mediterranean on the east and north, Libya on the southeast, Algeria on the west.

How Created—The site of ancient Carthage. In 1574 the Ottoman Turks conquered Tunisia and went on to establish its present-day boundaries. Following the establishment of a French protectorate in 1881, a Tunisian independence movement gradually arose. On June 3, 1955, French and Tunisian negotiators agreed on independence for the nation. A treaty was signed with France and independence was declared on March 20, 1956.

Size—63,378 sq. mi. (164,150 sq. km.).

Population—6,300,000: Arab, 94%; Berber, 1.5%; French, 1.5%; Jewish, 1.3%; Italian, 0.8%; other, 0.9%. Almost 100% Muslim.

Who Rules—In theory, Tunisia is a constitutional democracy. There is an elected National Assembly and President.

Who REALLY Rules—As the head of state, the Government, the country's only party, and its armed forces, Habib Bourguiba's power goes beyond his role as President. He has been Tunisia's only head since it became a republic and the only Arab President outside Lebanon without a military background. His despotism, however, could be termed benevolent; it has enhanced independent personal freedom and the status of women. President Bourguiba is not in good health and a successor is not in sight. In the event of his death, a power struggle could destroy Tunisian stability.

NOTES

Following the Roman conquest of Carthage, Tunisia became the Roman province of Africa—a name that spread to the rest of the continent. It was regarded as the granary of the empire. During their 400-year stay, the Romans built 180 cities in Tunisia.

President Bourguiba, though himself a Muslim (married to a Frenchwoman), has shown little patience for those Islamic traditions which he believes hinder progress. As a result, Tunisia is one of the few Muslim countries where women can divorce their husbands. Bourguiba has urged women to discard the veil and take a greater part in community affairs. In 1960 polygamy was banned, although older husbands were allowed to keep their wives. Contraceptives are free with newspapers carrying reports of How, When, and Where each type is to be used. Abortions are legal for mothers of more than 5 children.

On the outskirts of Sfax, on the central coast, is the Forest of the Olive Trees, containing 8 million of them, on 1,500,000 acres of land. Tunisia is the world's 2nd largest exporter of olive oil.

—H.E. & M.D.

TURKEY

NITTY GRITTY

Location—In Asia Minor and southeast Europe. Asiatic Turkey composes 97% of the total Turkish land area. In Asia, Turkey shares borders with Syria, Iraq, Iran, and the Soviet Union; in Europe, with Bulgaria and Greece. The Black Sea is to its north, the Mediterranean Sea to the south.

How Created—Turkey is one of the oldest inhabited areas in the world, and has a recorded history that stretches back centuries before the birth of Christ. The 1st real traces of modern Turkey appeared in the 13th century with the birth of the Turkish Ottoman Empire. At its height, the Ottoman Empire stretched from the Persian Gulf to the border of Poland, and from the Caspian Sea to Algeria. Ottoman power began to decline in the 17th century. A series of wars in the 18th and 19th centuries so weakened the Turkish Empire that by the early part of the 20th century Europeans had taken to calling it the "sick man of Europe." In 1909, a revolt by young liberals established a constitutional régime in Turkey.

Size—301,380 sq. mi. (780,576 sq. km.).

Population—40 million: (by mother tongue) Turkish, 90.2%; Kurdish, 6.9%; Arabic, 1.2%; Circassian, Greek, and others, 1.7%. 99.2% Muslim (mostly Sunni).

Who Rules—The Turkish Republic has a President and a Prime Minister who leads a bicameral (2-house) legislature whose members are elected by a popular vote. Women were given the right to vote and run for office in 1934.

Who REALLY Rules—Turkey is a Muslim country, and in spite of administrators' attempts to modernize Turkey by getting rid of some of the older Muslim traditions, the religion maintains an effective hold on Turkish society.

NOTES

In recent years Turkey has been at odds with Greece over the island of Cyprus and war broke out between Turkey and Greece over this issue in 1974 when Turkey successfully occupied much Cypriot territory.

In 1974, despite the objections of the U.S. Government, Turkey resumed growing opium, from which heroin is derived. Another sore point between Turkey and the U.S. is the presence of several thousand U.S. military personnel within Turkish borders. At times this has been the cause of widespread demonstrations. At one point, the entire population of Istanbul was confined to their homes while the Government searched door-to-door for dissidents.

Whirling dervishes dance to abandon themselves to God's love and free themselves from earthly bondage. Specific rules govern every move in the dervishes' dance. The ritual begins with prayers and meditation. Then flutes play an introductory melody which symbolizes man's desire for mystic union, and the dance begins. Each dance consists of 3 stages; the 1st is the knowledge of God; the 2nd, the seeing of God; and the 3rd, union with God. The conical hat the dervish wears represents a tombstone, the dervish's jacket represents the grave, and the dervish's skirt is the funeral shroud. As the dervishes dance they remove their jackets to show they are shedding earthly ties and escaping from their graves. As they whirl, the dervishes raise their right hands in prayer and extend their left hands toward the floor. The meaning of these gestures is "what we receive from God, we give to man; we ourselves possess nothing." Their whirling symbolizes the rotation of the universe in the presence of God.

—M.G.

UGANDA

NITTY GRITTY

Location—Landlocked on the equator in east-central Africa. Bordered on the north by the Sudan, east by Kenya, south by Tanzania with which it shares Lake Victoria, southwest by Rwanda, and on the west by Zaire.

How Created—This former East African Protectorate of Britain became a fully independent member of the Commonwealth in 1962 by the union of the kingdoms of Buganda (largest and most important), Toro, Ankole, and Bunyoro. Its emergence as a republic in 1967 abolished the traditional kingdoms.

Size—91,452 sq. mi. (236,860 sq. km.).

Population—11,500,000: Bantu, including Baganda, Iteso, Banyankore, and Basoga, ca. 93.5%; non-Ugandan Africans, 5.7%; Asian and European, less than 1%. 60% Christian, 33% Animist, 5% Muslim.

Who Rules—The President, together with the lawmaking National Assembly in which he serves with 91 other elected members.

Who REALLY Rules—The President, Maj. Gen. Idi Amin, whose military coup overthrew the former President while he was abroad.

NOTES

"I had travelled through tropical forests in Cuba and India, and had often before admired their enchanting yet sinister luxuriance. But the forests of Uganda, for magnificence, for profusion of brilliant life and awful fecundity of the natural processes eclipsed all previous impressions. One becomes the spectator of an intense convulsion of life and death."—Winston Churchill, 1908.

Most Ugandans are peasant farmers but they are very prosperous, especially in the south where fertile, picturesque farms give Uganda its name "Pearl of East Africa."

Lake Victoria is larger than West Virginia, beautiful and inviting, but impossible to swim in. It is full of crocodiles and hippos, and its islands are infested with the tsetse fly.

Trade and commerce, until recently, were carried on by the Asians—mostly Indians—who made up Uganda's rather aloof and insular middle class. Because God "told him so" in a dream, strongman General Amin made war on the Asians; he gave them 90 days to leave the country or find themselves "sitting on the fire." His campaign expelled or scared most of them out, leaving a vacuum in the mercantile trades.

"Idi Amin Dada . . . has established a sinister state that would startle fiction writers. Dissidents, real or potential, are dragged screaming from bar or café by gun-toting young men in dark glasses; bodies of well-known former citizens are washed up on the shores of otherwise picturesque lakes; swaggering glazed-eyed soldiers waylay and molest tourists and travelers in the bush . . . and the jails are witnesses to unmitigated brutality." —Christopher Munnion, British journalist who reported from Uganda before being jailed and expelled in September, 1972.

—M.D.

UNILEVER GROUP

NITTY GRITTY

Location—Unilever Group and Unilever, Ltd., have headquarters in Unilever House in London. Unilever N.V. has headquarters in Rotterdam. In the U.S., Lever Brothers' headquarters are at 390 Park Avenue, New York, N.Y. 10022, while Thomas J. Lipton, Inc., is at 800 Sylvian Avenue, Englewood Cliffs, N.J. 07632.

How Created—The result of the 1930 merger of Britain's Lever Brothers and Holland's Margarine Union. Lever Brothers, Ltd., was formed June 21, 1894, to manufacture soaps. N.V. Margarine Unie was formed November 9, 1927, to manufacture edible fats, and it bought Anton Jurgens' Vereenigde Fabrieken N.V. from the Jurgens family and Van den Bergh's Fabrieken N.V. from the Van den Bergh family. Lever Brothers and Margarine Union decided to merge their companies because both used the same raw materials and were expanding into each other's marketing areas.

Size—The world's largest manufacturer of consumer packaged goods, Unilever manufactures and markets its products in 70 countries on 6 continents.

Population—353,000 employees.

Who Rules—Unilever's overall management is the responsibility of a 3-man special committee, which directs the coordination of major corporate policy, controls capital investment, and makes top executive assignments. The British and Dutch companies have identical 24-member boards of directors, and every director is also a Unilever executive who oversees the operations of one of the company's geographical regions or product lines. The directors are elected by 93,728 stockholders owning 183,067,262 ordinary shares of Unilever, Ltd., 1,307 stockholders owning preference shares of Unilever, Ltd., and an unknown number of shareholders owning Unilever N.V. preference shares and 32,008,250 Unilever N.V. ordinary shares.

Who REALLY Rules—In 1969, 18% of Unilever's ordinary shares were held by the Leverhulme Trust, whose beneficiaries are Lord Leverhulme and a Unilever subsidiary. Corporations held 48% of the ordinary shares, and individuals the remaining 34%. As in the case of U.S. corporations, Unilever's major stockholders include banks.

NOTES

Unilever manufactures and sells a wide variety of products, mostly for home consumption. Its products are organized into 9 major product groupings: animal feeds; chemicals; detergents; edible fats and dairy products; convenience foods; meat and fish; paper, printing, packaging, and plastics; toiletries; and transportation.

Unilever's U.S. subsidiaries are Lever Brothers Co. and Thomas J. Lipton, Inc., which together accounted for 9% of the company's sales and 6% of its profits in 1973. Lipton produces 70% of the dried soup sold in the

U.S. (one brand name is Cup-a-Soup) and 50% of the tea bags.

Unilever has 20% of the detergent market in all major industrialized countries and over 60% of the European frozen food market (brand names Birds Eye in Britain and Iglo in the rest of Europe). It is the world's largest ice cream maker and the world's 2nd largest tea supplier. The company owns A & W Food Service of Canada, Ltd., and operates 86 Nordsee Quick Fish Restaurants in Austria, Germany, and Holland.

Among Unilever's many brand names are Good Humor ice cream; Imperial and Promise margarine; Spray 'n Vac rug cleaner; All and Wisk detergents; Knox gelatine; Aim, Close-up, and Pepsodent toothpaste; and Caress, Dove, Lifebuoy, and Lux soap. Unilever is concentrating on the expansion of its operations in the food business, but continues to expand in other areas as well. In 1973 it bought chocolate producers in Holland and Ireland, ice cream makers in Brazil, Ireland, and Spain, and yogurt companies in Belgium and France. Its subsidiary UAC International bought 2 motor vehicle distributorships, an engineering company, and a building supplies company, all in Britain.

—H.B.

UNION OF SOVIET
SOCIALIST REPUBLICS
(See: SOVIET UNION)

UNITED STATES OF AMERICA

NITTY GRITTY

Location—The central ⅓ of North America, bordered by the Pacific Ocean, Canada, the Atlantic Ocean, the Gulf of Mexico, Baja California, and Mexico. The State of Alaska is on the northwest tip of the continent, with Canada to its east. The State of Hawaii lies in the mid-Pacific.

How Created—The land claimed by the original 13 States was added to as follows (See: Chap. 3 for details):

1803—The Louisiana Territory purchased from France for $15 million plus over $8 million in interest payments. This acquisition almost doubled the size of the U.S.

1819—Florida and adjacent lands bought from Spain for $5 million.

1845—The Republic of Texas was annexed.

1846—The Oregon Territory was acquired by treaty with Great Britain.

1848—Much of the Southwest was acquired as a result of the Mexican War.

1853—More land in the Southwest claimed from Mexico (the Gadsden Purchase).

1867—Alaska bought from Russia for $7,200,000.

1898—Republic of Hawaii annexed.

1968—Mexico exchanged the northern half of Cordova Island for Chamizol Island in the Rio Grande River near El Paso, Tex.

Size—3,615,122 sq. mi. (9,363,123 sq. km.).

Population—212 million: white (a mixture of over 40 ethnic groups), 87.5%; black, 11.1%; Indian, 0.4%; Japanese, 0.3%; Chinese, 0.2%; Filipino, 0.2%; other, 0.3%. 35% Protestant, 24% Roman Catholic, 3% Jewish, 38% other or no religion.

Who Rules—A President (usually elected), a 2-house legislature (Senate and House of Representatives), and a 9-man Supreme Court, appointed by the President with the approval of the Senate. There are also State, county, and city governments, but most of their laws can be voided by the Federal Government.

Who REALLY Rules—There are many forces at work in U.S. society, but the most powerful by far are the interlocking directorates of the major banks, corporations, and insurance companies, with the backing of the leaders of the military: In the words of former President Dwight Eisenhower, "the military-industrial complex."

NOTES (See: Chaps. 3, 4, 5.)

—D.W.

UPPER VOLTA

NITTY GRITTY

Location—In West Africa; to the northwest, Mali; to the northeast, Niger; to the south, Dahomey, Togo, Ghana, and Ivory Coast.

How Created—The borders of Upper Volta were reshuffled in 1947 by the French, in an effort to reunite the Mossi tribes and to weaken the RDA, the Black Nationalist party.

Size—105,792 sq. mi. (274,000 sq. km.).

Population—5,800,000: Mossi, 48%; Fulani, 10.4%; Lobi, 7%; Malinke, 6.9%; Bobo, 6.7%; Senufo, 5.5%; Grunshi, 5.3%; Bisansi, 4.7%; Gurma, 4.5%; other, 1%. 75% Animist, 20% Muslim, 5% Roman Catholic.

Who Rules—After a military takeover in 1966, Gen. Sangoule Lamizana was elected President. A 1970 constitution provides for a republican form of government.

Who REALLY Rules—France, through the Fund for Aid and Cooperation, supplies Upper Volta with economic aid, technical assistance, and supports national development programs. France has at times paid higher than world-market prices for Upper Volta's exports in order to balance the trade deficit. No country, not even France, may maintain military bases in Upper Volta.

NOTES

Some 98% of the population is involved with agriculture and livestock, 97% is illiterate, and almost 100% is suffering from the effects of a severe drought.

Maurice Yameogo, the 1st President of Upper Volta (1960), was an irresponsible and incompetent ruler. He banned the opposition party, jailed its leaders, and introduced austerity programs which severely cut the wages of civil servants. Meanwhile, he had divorced his 1st wife to marry "Miss Ivory Coast 1965," and had gone off to Brazil on an expensive honeymoon. He lived extravagantly and enjoyed his luxury until 1966, when angry union leaders rallied the people to demonstrations outside the palace, demanding Yameogo's resignation and asking for a military takeover. Yameogo also asked the military to take the country off his hands, which it did, and subsequently the military fined Yameogo $200,000 and sentenced him to 5 years' hard labor for having embezzled $3 million during his Presidency. He was reprieved in 1970.

—R.C.

URUGUAY

NITTY GRITTY

Location—Situated on the Atlantic Ocean in southeastern South America. Neighbors are: Brazil on the northeast; Argentina on the west.

How Created—The original inhabitants, the warlike and cannibalistic Charrua Indians, successfully fended off any attempts at settlement of the area. The Spanish viceregal Government at Buenos Aires at last managed to establish a settlement at Montevideo in 1723, and for the following century, Uruguay was essentially an Argentine colony. In 1828 the English, fearing Brazilian penetration southward would threaten their interests in Argentina, created the independent republic of Uruguay to act as a buffer zone.

Size—68,536 sq. mi. (177,508 sq. km.).

Population—Over 3 million: European origin and native born, 87.5%; Italian, 2.6%; mulatto, 1.7%; Jewish, 1.4%; Galician, 1.2%; Brazilian, 0.9%; Spanish, 0.9%; black, 0.3%; other, 3.5%. About 90% Roman Catholic with some Jews and Protestants.

Who Rules—In 1973 Juan María Bordaberry, elected President of Uruguay the preceding year, was obliged by the armed forces to accept a co-dictatorship with the military leaders.

Who REALLY Rules—Although Uruguay's military has traditionally stayed out of politics, the generals are now in control of the country. Most observers believe the change is due to Bordaberry's use of the Army rather than the national police to suppress the Tupamaros, Uruguay's urban guerrilla movement. Members of the armed forces made thus aware of the Tupamaros' political aims, and also convinced of their own political importance in crushing the guerrillas, demanded a role in the Government. For a brief time it seemed that the military might go the way of Peru's leftist junta, but Uruguay's generals closed Congress, muzzled the press, outlawed the Communist and Socialist parties, and disbanded the large national labor union.

NOTES

The name "Uruguay" derives from an Indian word meaning "River of Painted Birds."

A nation of immigrants, Uruguay's population is one of the most racially, ethnically, and culturally homogeneous on the continent. Most Uruguayans are of Spanish or Italian descent, speaking Spanish with an Italian lilt, and maintaining Hispanic and southern European values.

Dueling is still legal in Uruguay under certain circumstances. In 1972, 2 generals, both defeated presidential candidates, acquitted themselves with honor in a duel on an airfield near Montevideo.

The Tupamaros, Uruguay's urban guerrilla group, have apparently been crushed for the time being. President Bordaberry, who campaigned on a strong antiterrorist platform, finally had to call in the armed forces to deal with the Tupamaros. Among Latin American guerrilla groups, they were the best organized and equipped, and captured the imagination of many with a spectacular series of kidnappings, bank robberies, and prison breaks. In 1972, 14 Tupas escaped from prison through a 200' tunnel between the prison hospital and a sewer outside. The year before, a group had escaped from the same prison in a tunnel 120' long.

Many members of the Tupamaros were middle- or upper-middle-class students and professionals: teachers, doctors, lawyers, engineers. They had dozens of underground hideouts, and safe-houses in the suburbs and the countryside, including medical and dental facilities, emergency hospitals with all the latest equipment, and a complete laboratory for counterfeiting every conceivable kind of document. Taking their name from the great Inca leader Tupac Amaru, who made a last stand against the

Spaniards in 1780, they made efficient, highly-organized raids on banks, and kidnapped foreign and national officials with seeming impunity.

The military, using highly repressive tactics including torture of captured Tupamaros, was able to bring guerrilla activity to a stop, and for this claimed a place in the Government. However, in mid-1974 the guerrilla group was once again operating, although on a smaller scale than before. With most of their top leaders captured and awaiting death or imprisonment in 1975, it is unclear when or whether the Tupamaros will again be a force in the country.

—E.P.

VENEZUELA

NITTY GRITTY

Location—North coast of South America, with a 1,750-mi. Caribbean and Atlantic coastline and Brazil, Colombia, and Guyana as neighbors.

How Created—Originally part of the Spanish viceroyalty of New Granada (which also included Peru, Ecuador, and Colombia), Venezuela was freed from Spanish rule by Simón Bolívar in 1818. Venezuela, Ecuador, and Colombia temporarily joined together under the title of Republic of Gran Colombia, but Venezuela seceded in 1830, proclaiming itself an independent republic.

Size—355,759 sq. mi. (921,417 sq. km.).

Population—12,400,000: mestizo, 70%; white, 20%; black, 8%; Indian, 2%. 93.4% Roman Catholic.

Who Rules—After 150 years of dictatorships, both military and civilian, Venezuela is developing some forms of representative government. All citizens over 18 vote every 5 years, selecting at one time a new, bicameral legislature and one-term President, who may not succeed himself for 10 years. There are no by- or mid-elections. There is a large number of political parties, including the communists who were banned from political activity between 1962–1969.

Who REALLY Rules—The big oil companies—Exxon, Shell, and Gulf—have long held considerable political and economic influence in Venezuela, and have engineered favors for the country in return for liberal oil-exploiting terms. However, the international energy crisis has given Venezuela much greater leverage in dealing with foreign investors, and in February, 1975, the President of Venezuela announced the gradual nationalization of the oil industry. Venezuela has been the recipient of a great deal of U.S. Government and private aid and investment, and close economic ties will continue.

NOTES

Venezuela's high per capita income conceals great disparities in actual income among different sectors of the population. Caracas has been made a showplace of handsome modern highrises and intricate superhighways, but the hillsides surrounding the city are thick with "ranchos," or shanty huts, in which it is estimated live one million of the city's inhabitants.

A scant 3% of the population holds 90% of the land.

Angel Falls, at 3,212′ the world's highest, is 15 times the height of Niagara Falls. It was discovered by U.S. aviator Jimmy Angel, who requested that his ashes be scattered there after his death.

The half of the country south of the Orinoco River contains only 4% of the population.

—E.P.

VIETNAM

NITTY GRITTY

Location—Vietnam follows the eastern coast of the Indochina peninsula, in Southeast Asia. It is bounded by China on the north, Cambodia and Laos on the west, and the South China Sea on the east and south. The country is divided into North Vietnam and South Vietnam near the 17th parallel (lat. 17° N.).

How Created—The Vietnamese migrated to the Red River Valley (now in North Vietnam) from Southern China during the 3rd century B.C. China conquered the area a century later. Once they had thrown out the Chinese in 939 A.D., the Vietnamese expanded southward to form the general boundaries of modern Vietnam, but various factions frequently carved the nation into smaller states. Vietnam was last reunified during the 19th century by the French who, in 1899, grouped Vietnam with Laos and Cambodia to form the Indochinese Union.

The Japanese occupied Indochina during W.W. II, using it to stage attacks throughout Southeast Asia. When the Japanese surrendered in August, 1945, the Viet Minh anti-guerrilla movement declared Vietnamese independence. The French, however, were unwilling to accept Vietnamese independence. With the aid of British and Nationalist Chinese troops, they reasserted colonial rule. The French and their Vietnamese supporters (with American financial support) fought the communist-led Viet Minh until 1954, when they signed a peace agreement in Geneva.

The Geneva accords of 1954 divided Vietnam into 2 temporary zones. The Viet Minh established the Democratic Republic of Vietnam in the north. Ngo Dinh Diem, an anticommunist Catholic, with American backing, established the Saigon-based Republic of Vietnam in the south. The peace agreement, which neither the U.S. nor the Diem régime signed, called for reunification elections within 2 years. Diem refused and established a dictatorial régime in the southern zone.

Vietnamese in the south took up arms against Diem, forming the National Liberation Front (NLF) in 1960. As the struggle escalated, the North Vietnamese Government sent supplies, irregular troops, and eventually regular troops to fight with the NLF in the south. The U.S. backed Diem and his successors with training, advice, and supplies at 1st, then with some 550,000 American troops and history's heaviest bombing campaign. America's most sophisticated bombers saturated NLF-controlled areas in South Vietnam and transportation routes throughout Laos and North Vietnam and eventually hit the industrial center of North Vietnam. On April 30, 1975, the Saigon Government finally surrendered to the NLF's Provisional Revolutionary Government.

North Vietnam

Size—63,360 sq. mi. (164,102 sq. km.).

Population—Over 25 million: Vietnamese (Kinh), 85.2%; Tay, 3.2%; Muong, 2.6%; Tai, 2.4%; Nung, 2%; other, 4.6%. Predominantly Buddhist.

Who Rules—An elective National Assembly, which in turn elects an executive body, the Standing Committee. People's Councils, elected at provincial, district, and village levels, choose administrative committees to handle local issues.

Who REALLY Rules—The politburo of the communist *Lao Dong* (Workers') party. Since the death of national President and party head Ho Chi Minh in 1969, party leadership has been collective. Both China and the Soviet Union have influence over North Vietnam, but the Vietnamese have refused to take sides in the Sino-Soviet split.

South Vietnam

Size—66,263 sq. mi. (171,621 sq. km.).

Population—21 million: Vietnamese, 89%; Chinese, 5.6%; Montagnard, 2.9%; Khmer, 2.4%; Cham, 0.1%. Mostly Animist and Buddhist with large Cao Dai and Roman Catholic minorities.

Who Rules—The Revolutionary Government, which is ostensibly a coalition of intellectual, religious, labor, women's, and peasant groups.

Who REALLY Rules—The Revolutionary Government is clearly communist-led, but it tries to maintain the image of a united front. It is probably dominated by the North Vietnamese Lao Dong party, since it has relied upon North Vietnam for 2 decades for external communications, food, and military support (troops and supplies).

NOTES

Most of North Vietnam's people are collectivized peasants. Since most men serve for a period in the regular armed forces, women have surmounted many traditional prejudices. They are armed as members of the militia, they do heavy labor, and they are active in the professions.

Though the majority of the South Vietnamese are still peasants, the war drove many into urban areas. Some American professors considered this "forced urbanization" to be a "modernizing influence," but the cities became filled with slums, unemployment, crime, corruption, and vice. A few military officers, businessmen, and others who did not allow their moral scruples to interfere with making a profit benefited from the war, but their wealth contrasted sharply with the visible urban poverty.

—L.S.

YEMEN

NITTY GRITTY

Location—In the south of the Arabian peninsula, bordered by the Red Sea, Saudi Arabia, Oman, and the Arabian Sea.

How Created—For centuries Yemen was under the rule of the religious leader of the Zeidi Muslim sect (a Shia sect). The territory of Yemen was defined historically in rough terms by its fertile regions, but its borders varied over the centuries. It is the most fertile and most densely populated area in the Arabian peninsula. The division of the country into 2 states began with the British invasion of Aden in the south. In 1839 the British seized that port, and gradually pried many local sheikhs in what is now South Yemen away from allegiance to the Zeidi leader in the north. After British withdrawal from the south in 1967, that area became a separate state. Parts of North Yemen bordering Saudi Arabia had been taken by Saudi Arabia in the 1930s, and the border with Saudi Arabia in the desert region of the northeast is not defined. In 1972, a unity accord was signed between the 2 Yemens in which they set forth practical steps directed toward the unification of Yemen. However, this process is moving slowly.

Northern Yemen (Sana)

Size—77,200 sq. mi. (200,000 sq. km.).
Population—Over 6 million: Almost 100% Arab and Muslim (Zeidi and Sunni).
Who Rules—A clique of young army officers took power in June, 1974.
Who REALLY Rules—A Revolutionary Command Council has been set up, dominated by the army officers, who are heavily dependent on Saudi Arabia for financial aid. The membership of the Council consists primarily of members of the Zeidi sect. Only one Sunni is represented on the Council.

Southern Yemen (Aden)

Size—111,074 sq. mi. (287,682 sq. km.).
Population—1,600,000: Mostly Arab and Muslim with some Indian, Somali, Christian, Hindu, and others.
Who Rules—A 3-person presidential council with a ministerial form of government. On the regional and local levels, locally selected committees direct the activities of the various agricultural and fishing cooperatives.
Who REALLY Rules—The Central Committee of the Marxist-Leninist National Liberation Front. Most of the top government people are members of the 30-person Central Committee. South Yemen is economically in a very dire situation, since no development took place under British rule. The Soviet Union, China, and Iraq give aid, but the Front has kept this aid balanced in such a way that no one of these states exercises control over South Yemen.

Aida Yafe'i, the only woman who is a full member of the Central Committee of the Front and also on the 5-person Secretariat that directs the daily business of the Front, has described the situation of women: "Here, too frequently, the progressiveness of some men in the Front stops at their doorsteps. They still consider women as property. We don't blame men personally for this. We recognize it as an illness that pervades the whole society."

NOTES

The economy of Northern Yemen is one of the poorest in the Middle East. Exports stand at 6% of imports. All industrial and most consumer products have to be imported.
Exports include mocha coffee (the name comes from the port of Al-Mukha), which is one of the most prized coffees in the West. There is a growing export business in *gat*, the leaves of an evergreen shrub, which produce a mild narcotic effect when chewed.

Yemen was under a theocratic régime for centuries, as the Zeidi Imam (religious leader) and his tribes dominated the rest of the population, and kept the country in an incredibly underdeveloped state. In 1962, nationalist elements in the military overthrew the Imam, but civil war ensued that lasted for 6 years. Saudi Arabia came to the aid of the Imam, in an effort to prevent the growth of a republic of any kind in the peninsula, and especially one that was linked to Egypt and Nasser. Egypt came to the aid of the new Government, and introduced its own troops into the country. The civil war continued for several years, ending finally in 1967 when Egypt agreed to withdraw its troops after its defeat at the hands of Israel and in return for Saudi financial aid in recouping from that defeat.

—J.G.

YUGOSLAVIA

NITTY GRITTY

Location—In southeastern Europe; shares its borders with 7 countries: northern Italy on the west, Austria and Hungary on the north, Romania and Bulgaria on the east, Greece and Albania on the south. To the southwest is the Adriatic Sea.
How Created—In the 6th and 7th centuries several Slavic tribes migrated, some southward and some westward, over the Carpathians into the area between the Danube and the Adriatic. It was not until 1918 that the various nationalities united to form an independent state, at that time called the Kingdom of Serbs, Croats, and Slovenes.
Size—98,766 sq. mi. (255,804 sq. km.), roughly the size of Wyoming.
Population—21,700,000: Serb, 42.1%; Croat 23.1%; Slovene, 8.6%; Macedonian, 5.6%; Muslim, 5.2%; Albanian, 4.9%; 16 other groups, 10.5%. 42% Serbian Orthodox, 25% Roman Catholic, 10% Muslim.
Who Rules—The President, a collective Presidency, a Premier, a Parliament (the Federal Assembly), and a Cabinet (the Executive Council). The position of President has been changing due to the problem of President Tito's succession. The policy is to try to create the conditions for collective leadership after Tito's death. The 1971 constitution established a 22-person collective Presidency, while at the same time reelecting Tito President for 5 years.
Who REALLY Rules—Tito, with the other leaders of the League of Communists as his lieutenants, has (since successfully leading the Partisan forces during W.W. II) held ultimate power, whatever the political form. As head of

the party, the Government and the Socialist Alliance (the only other legal political party), and as a charismatic national hero who is never directly criticized but plays the role of critic of the bureaucracy in favor of the people (à la Mao), Tito has enjoyed a kind of autocratic reign, though sharing his power with his comrades-at-arms, the ruling clique of the party.

NOTES

Josip Broz, who became secretary-general of the Yugoslav Communist party in 1937, rose, during W.W. II, from relative obscurity to international fame as "Marshal Tito," leader of the aggressive resistance group, the Partisans. The group, ill-clad and undernourished, fought against tremendous odds; Tito himself was wounded and narrowly escaped capture. At the war's end he was both a military hero and leader of the antifascist political alliance, AVNOJ.

With a large enough personal following to withstand the machinations of Stalin, who tried to have him ousted, Tito emerged as unquestioned leader of his country. At first, Tito-worship followed the pattern of Stalin-worship in the U.S.S.R., but this was toned down a bit due to the break with Stalin and criticism of the "cult of the individual" as it applied to Stalinism. Still, wherever he went in public, Tito was greeted with cheers and the chant, "Tito is ours, we are Tito's." His trivial acts have been chronicled in the newspapers and made to seem significant. Yet, in the course of the spectacle of his rule Tito has played many roles: benevolent father of his peoples; stern, scolding uncle; critic of bureaucracy; simple man of the soil; world traveler; comrade-in-arms of W.W. II days; dignified head of state in his Rolls-Royce; and finally resplendent military leader on his white charger.

The supposed absence of class conflict in Yugoslavia has been contradicted by over 2,000 strikes since 1958, the number of strikers increasing each year. Now the ideologists are beside themselves trying to explain why the workers are "striking against themselves." Since all these strikes have been illegal, i.e. "wildcats," and therefore difficult to control, there have been recent proposals to have the Communist party-run unions organize and lead them.

—R.R.

ZAIRE

NITTY GRITTY

Location—In south-central Africa; west is the Congo; north the Central African Republic and the Sudan; east Uganda, Rwanda, Burundi, and Tanzania; southeast is Zambia; and southwest is Angola. Zaire puts out a skinny leg to the Atlantic where it has a 20-mi. coastline.

How Created—Former Belgian Congo whose frontiers emerged from the consent of the neighboring colonial powers of Britain, France, and Portugal. Won freedom from Belgium in 1960, temporarily lost Katanga Province, but was reunited with it in 1964.

Size—905,365 sq. mi. (2,344,885 sq. km.), 77 times the size of its former colonial master and equal to that 3rd of the U.S. which is east of the Mississippi.

Population—25 million: Luba, 17.7%; Mongo (including Totela), 16.9%; Kongo, 12.1%; Rwanda, 10%; about 200 other groups, 43.2%. 50% Animist, 50% Christian.

Who Rules—The current President, Mobuto Sese Seko, is Head of State and Government by way of coup d'état in 1965. The 1967 constitution theoretically provides for a 420-member National Assembly.

Who REALLY Rules—Head of State and Government does pretty much what he wants while the National Assembly nods. The remnants of the old mining companies, now somewhat controlled by the Government, still wield some power.

NOTES

Although at the time of independence the Congo's living standard was the highest in black Africa, the Belgian rule had been essentially paternalistic. Colonial monopolies raped the country of its mineral wealth while plantation owners raped the native populace to obtain a labor force. The old régime had not given any administrative responsibility to the natives and there was no secondary education until the '50s. Consequently, with the Belgians' sudden departure in 1960, the Congo was left in the lurch.

Internal strife followed independence. The provinces of Kasai, Kivu, and Katanga, on whose mineral deposits the rest of the country depended economically, all broke away. The country more or less pulled itself back together again in 1964. In 1965, after some minor rebellions, Col. Joseph D. Mobuto (now Mobuto Sese Seko), a tough, Israeli-trained paratrooper, regained control and established a strong central Government. In 1970 he was elected as the only candidate to a 7-year term as President. He has since set about getting cash for industrial development from Western countries but at the same time expelling foreigners and Africanizing all culture. He has banned neckties and Christian names and has changed the date of the celebration of Christmas.

Leyland Motors, Fiat, and Peugeot have auto assembly plants here and GM and Ford may soon follow.

Zaire has huge mineral wealth. It is the world's 5th largest producer of copper which constitutes ⅔ of its exports. It also produces most of the world's industrial diamonds and smaller amounts of gold, cassiterite, manganese, zinc, cobalt, and silver. Its uranium, one of the only known sources during W.W. II, made possible the world's 1st atomic bomb.

A national hero is Patrice Lumumba, the fiery 1st Prime Minister of Zaire. He was deposed in 1960 and captured while trying to flee to Kinu Province. He was then turned over to his archenemy, Moishe Tshombe of Katanga Province, who had him assassinated.

—M.D.

ZAMBIA

NITTY GRITTY

Location—South-central Africa; to the northwest, Zaire; to the northeast, Tanzania; to the east, Malawi; southeast, Mozambique; to the south, Rhodesia and Botswana; to the west, Angola.

How Created—Part of the empire built by Cecil Rhodes, Northern Rhodesia became a British protectorate in 1924. In 1953 the area was made part of the Federation of Rhodesia and Nyasaland, but extensive agitation led to its independence on October 24, 1964, at which time Northern Rhodesia became the Republic of Zambia. The people preferred to have their country named after the Zambesi River rather than the detested colonialist Cecil Rhodes.

Size—290,586 sq. mi. (752,614 sq. km.).

Population—4,850,000: African (mostly Bantu tribes), 98.5%; European, 1.1%; other, 0.4%. Mostly Animist but with over 15% Christian and some Hindus and Muslims.

Who Rules—President Kenneth Kaunda, elected by universal adult suffrage; the legislative assembly has 105 members, 100 elected by universal suffrage and 5 nominated by the President.

Who REALLY Rules—Kaunda has arranged for the gradual national takeover of foreign-owned copper-mining companies and foreign oil production companies. Zambia has nationalized billion-dollar industries—causing disputes with Britain and other foreign investors, which often had to be settled by 3rd parties and UN teams—in a determined effort to gain economic independence. Millions of dol-lars in aid come from Britain and other Western nations; a $10-million loan from Peking is being added to the contributions of Peking engineers who are building highways and bridges for Zambia.

NOTES

The 1st self-governing legislative elections were held in January of 1964. Ninety-five percent of the population voted. Some walked as far as 20 mi. in the rain to reach the polls. A thumb dipped in red ink prevented people from voting twice; the people voted by symbol for the parties of their choice (lion, corncob, or hoe). Kenneth Kaunda's "hoe party" was victorious, and, when he became President in October, he was firm. He told a group of labor leaders, "This Government is strong and here to stay. I do not want to hear any more nonsense from anyone."

David Livingstone, the Scottish missionary and explorer, went to Zambia more than a century ago, and was horrified at the slaving he witnessed; blacks were terrorized, their families broken up, as they were led off by the Arabs to be sold. Livingstone, who immediately vowed to end the trade where he could, tried to replace the slave trade with general commerce in Africa. He spent his last days in Zambian country. When no one had heard much from him in about a year, the *New York Herald* dispatched a reporter, whose assignment was simply to find Livingstone. The reporter, Henry Morton Stanley, succeeded, finally coming upon the missing missionary at Lake Tanganyika where Stanley greeted him with the words, "Dr. Livingstone, I presume?" He was the last white man to speak with Livingstone, who died at the age of 60, on May 1, 1873, of malaria, following an 8-month trek through disease-infested swamps. His chief bearer, Susi, insisted that the doctor be buried in England. His body was dried out for 2 weeks, then embalmed in brandy and salt. The bearers had the body shipped to Westminster, after they had carried it to the sea—the trip to the African coast, which now takes 24 hours on an American-built highway, took them 9 months.

On the 100th anniversary of Livingstone's death, President Kaunda led 1,000 Zambians to Cipundu (where Livingstone had died) to pay tribute to the Scotsman. Kaunda said at that time, "What dominated Livingstone's life was his sense of mission as a servant of the people of Africa. He did not see himself a leader in any sense at all."

—R.C.

ZIMBABWE (See: RHODESIA)

Nations Smaller Than Baltimore

A listing of nations with populations smaller than the city of Baltimore, Md.

Afars and the Issas, French Territory of the

Size—8,880 sq. mi. (23,000 sq. km.). *Population*—180,000.

A desert land of nomads and traders located on the east coast of Africa where the Gulf of Aden meets the Red Sea, the territory has no rivers except after rain. About 85% of the people belong to the Issa (Somali) or Afar (Danakil) tribes, both of which are Muslim and have a caste system. Men treat women as property. The neighboring Republic of Somalia is constantly striving for a "Greater Somalia" —trying to annex territories, to unite the peoples of the Somali races.

Andorra

Size—179 sq. mi. (464 sq. km.). *Population*—25,000.

Surrounded by the peaks of the Pyrénées between France and Spain, Andorra is alleged to have been created by Charlemagne as a buffer state against the advancing Muslims. Andorra's citizens are very conservative and devoutly Catholic. They suffer no income tax, and postal service is free thanks to the booming business of selling stamps to tourists and collectors. Smuggling abounds on all levels, much as if it were a national sport. Andorra is governed by an elected General Council which meets in secret twice a year. The real rulers, however, are the President of France and the Spanish bishop of Urgel, who have shared joint suzerainty (a kind of feudal control) over Andorra since 1278. The French get paid $180 and the bishop gets $6.87 a year.

Antigua (See: Leeward Islands)

Bahamas

Size—5,382 sq. mi. (13,939 sq. km.). *Population*—215,000.

The Bahamas are a chain of nearly 700 islands (30 are inhabited) in the northern Caribbean Sea. Between 1492 and 1508 Spanish raiders enslaved about 40,000 native Indians and shipped them to Haiti to work in the mines; by 1530 the Bahamas were uninhabited. The islands became a nesting place for Blackbeard and other pirates, but by the early 18th century the pirates had been driven out by the English Navy whose motto was "Expel the pirates and restore commerce." A member of the British Commonwealth, the Bahamas

gained full independence in July, 1973. The current Prime Minister and most of the Parliament are black, as are 85% of the people. Tourism is the major industry.

Bahrain

Size—256 sq. mi. (662 sq. km.). *Population*—230,000.

An archipelago of 33 islands in the Persian (Arabian) Gulf, Bahrain is strictly ruled by the Al-Khalifa family who ousted the Persians in 1783. The British assumed control officially in 1861 and took advantage of the strategic location by setting up their Gulf headquarters in Bahrain. In 1971 Bahrain became an independent state, but the people, 96% of whom are Muslim, are still ruled by the Al-Khalifas. The main exports are oil and other petroleum products.

Barbados

Size—166 sq. mi. (430 sq. km.). *Population*—275,000.

The easternmost Caribbean island, Barbados was under uninterrupted British control from 1627 until its independence in 1966. In fact, British influence over the island is still considerable as evidenced by the continuing presence of a British governor-general. Barbados is a classic case of a one-crop economy. In 1970, sugar provided about 80% of the island's foreign exchange and the foreign-owned sugar companies wield much social, economic, and political power. About 89% of the population is black.

Belize (formerly British Honduras)

Size—8,866 sq. mi. (22,963 sq. km.). *Population*—140,000.

Occupying the southeast corner of the Yucatán peninsula in Central America, Belize is the site of several Mayan ceremonial cities which were abandoned for unknown reasons centuries before the arrival of Europeans. The British took formal possession of the area in 1862 and, although the colony is now internally self-governing, Britain still retains control of defense and foreign affairs and receives half of all exports. The colony has been promised independence, but increasing border problems with Guatemala have caused a delay. Belizeans fear that to receive independence without settling the border dispute will invite Guatemalan occupation.

Bermuda

Size—21 sq. mi. (54 sq. km.). *Population*—57,000.

A British colony, Bermuda is a cluster of over 300 small coral islands in the Northwest Atlantic, less than 600 mi. from Cape Hatteras, N.C. Local sentiment favoring independence is growing most insistent. In late 1972, the police commissioner was murdered and on March 10, 1973, the British-appointed governor, Sir Richard Sharples, was assassinated. Though no one has been charged with the assassination, some whites believe that black nationalist groups may be involved. Approximately 60% of the population is black. Bermuda's year-round spring climate has made it a favorite tourist spot. The islands have also attracted U.S. air and naval bases.

Botswana

Size—222,000 sq. mi. (569,797 sq. km.). *Population*—690,000.

A landlocked country in southern Africa, Botswana was known as the British Protectorate of Bechuanaland until it was granted independence as a republic within the Commonwealth in 1966. One of Africa's poorest nations, Botswana is linked, if not indentured, to South Africa. When at home and not in South Africa, 90% of the labor force works on small cattle and dairy farms. But about 25% of the working population comprises Botswana's most important export—manpower for South African mines.

British Honduras (See: Belize)

Brunei

Size—2,226 sq. mi. (5,765 sq. km.). *Population*—150,000.

Brunei is a sultanate consisting of 2 enclaves on the northern coast of Kalimantan (Borneo). Over half the population is Malaysian and most are Muslims. Britain controls Brunei's foreign affairs and other foreign powers control its economy, which is based on oil. Since 1929 a subsidiary of Royal Dutch Shell has pumped oil from the Seria oil field and a joint venture involving a U.S. firm, Shell, and Japan's Mitsubishi is now developing a project to export liquified natural gas.

Cabinda (See: Angola)

Cape Verde Islands

Size—1,557 sq. mi. (4,033 sq. km.). *Population*—275,000.

The Cape Verde Islands are an archipelago of 10 islands and 5 islets west of Senegal in the Northeast Atlantic Ocean. Most of the population is of mixed African and Portuguese descent. African influence can be seen in the use of calabashes, the mortar and pestle, the practice of carrying loads on the head, the use of drums, and the existence of polygamy. Portuguese influence is evident in cropping techniques, terraced gardens, mode of dress, the use of the grinder, methods of house building, and the use of bagpipes and triangles in music. About 99% of the people are Roman Catholic.

Ceuta and Melilla

Size—12.5 sq. mi. (32 sq. km.). *Population*—180,000.

These Spanish-controlled enclaves are on the north coast of Morocco. Ceuta is opposite Gibraltar and Melilla is 200 mi. to the east. They are considered private paradises by the Spanish who have settled there, or who use the 2 cities as vacation homelands. There is almost one car for every family in both places. The towns are filled with yacht clubs and cafés; life is easygoing, relaxed, and entertaining. Both are free ports, and right now Spain is building them up as tourist havens.

Comoro Islands

Size—864 sq. mi. (2,236 sq. km.). *Population*—300,000.

This small group of islands is located about halfway between Madagascar and the southeastern coast of Africa. In December, 1974, the predominantly Muslim inhabitants of the islands voted to break away from France and become an independent nation. The President, Ahmed Abdallah, boasts that he is unable to read or write. However, this has not prevented him from becoming known as one of the 10 richest men in the Indian Ocean area.

Cook Islands

Size—92.5 sq. mi. (241 sq. km.). *Population*—24,000. About 12,000 Cook Islanders live in New Zealand.

The Cook Islands are widely scattered in an area east of Samoa and Tonga, about 1,700 mi. northeast of New Zealand, to which they are tied as a "freely associated state." In July, 1974, Premier Albert Henry called for a referendum on independence and said he would ask New Zealand to allow the Cook Islands to conduct its own foreign affairs. The New Zealand Government said it would not object to these developments. There is little likelihood that political independence would lessen the Cook Islands' economic dependence on New Zealand.

Cyprus

Size—3,572 sq. mi. (9,251 sq. km.). *Population*—680,000.

The 3rd largest island in the Mediterranean, Cyprus is located in that sea's extreme eastern corner, south of Turkey and west of Syria. This strategic location has made Cyprus a prime target for every European and Asian invader since the Egyptians. Cyprus gained independence from Britain in 1960 and has been trying to steady itself between the Greek majority (77%) and Turkish minority (18%) ever since. The latest clash occurred in July, 1974, when the Cypriot National Guard, led by army officers from Greece, took over the Government in an attempt to force union with Greece. Turkish forces invaded Cyprus and widespread fighting broke out. By the end of the year, Turkey controlled the northern 40% of Cyprus which was well on the road to becoming a partitioned island.

Diego Garcia

Size—11 sq. mi. (28.5 sq. km.). Population—In 1974 there were 150 American military communications personnel based on the island, and the Navy had plans to raise that to 279 communications and 195 support personnel. In addition, 800 Seabees (naval construction) personnel were temporarily stationed there.

The largest island in the Chagos archipelago, in the center of the Indian Ocean, Diego Garcia is officially a British Colony, part of the British Indian Ocean Territories. However, in 1966 the British signed an agreement with the U.S. allowing American military use of the Chagos group for 50 years. The Navy plans to expand their Diego Garcia facility into a major refueling spot for U.S. ships, including aircraft carriers and submarines. This plan has alarmed congressional doves and brought protests from the Governments of India, Sri Lanka, Malaysia, Australia, New Zealand, and the Malagasy Republic.

Dominica (See: Windward Islands)

Equatorial Guinea

Size—10,830 sq. mi. (28,051 sq. km.). Population—310,000.

Equatorial Guinea is made up of a mainland region, Rio Muni, which is just above the equator along the Gulf of Guinea, on the west coast of Africa; a main island region, the volcanic Fernando Po; and 4 smaller islands. Since receiving their independence from Spain in 1968, the people of Equatorial Guinea have been ruled by a dictator, Francisco Macias Nguema. Relations with Spain have been strained, but Spain is still the main supplier and the main customer. In Rio Muni, 75% of the population are Fangs; on Fernando Po, the Ibos predominate. Most of the people are Catholic.

Fiji

Size—7,055 sq. mi. (18,274 sq. km.). Population—575,000.

Fiji is a group of 844 islands in the Southwest Pacific, about 1,500 mi. east of Australia and 1,200 mi. north of New Zealand. Fijian chiefs ceded the islands to Britain in 1874 and 96 years later to the day, the British granted political independence. Native Melanesians, who make up 43% of the population, are guaranteed land rights by the Fijian constitution, but Indians, who were originally brought to Fiji as indentured sugarcane-field workers and now constitute 51% of the population, must rent their land. Another 4% of the inhabitants are European, part-European, and Chinese. They hold the political balance of power as well as most of the professional and administrative jobs. Their income levels are roughly twice those of Fijians and Indians.

French Guiana

Size—34,700 sq. mi. (90,000 sq. km.). Population—52,000.

On the northeast coast of South America, Guiana is an underpopulated jungle (90% of the land is tropical rain forest) whose chief claim to fame is Devil's Island, 6 mi. offshore. It was to this island that Alfred Dreyfus was unjustly condemned for supposed treason in 1895. So many criminals and political prisoners died either on the island or in one of the many penal colonies on the mainland that French Guiana was known as the "dry guillotine." Today Guiana is overly dependent on France and the presence of a satellite-launching post has given great control over the colony to the French military and Federal bureaucracy.

Gabon

Size—103,347 sq. mi. (267,667 sq. km.). Population—525,000.

Straddling the equator on Africa's west coast, Gabon was carved from French Equatorial Africa in 1960 and given its independence. However, Frenchmen still control the economy, the schools, and some say the Government. Nevertheless, the current administration is seeking investments from other Western countries to trade off French economic domination for a many-headed one. At least 80% of the people still hunt, fish, and grow their own food. In 1970 the Salvation Army and Jehovah's Witnesses were officially banned from the country. It was in Gabon that Albert Schweitzer set up a hospital for lepers.

The Gambia

Size—4,003 sq. mi. (10,368 sq. km.). Population—400,000.

Gambia is a sliver of a country on Africa's northwest coast. Gambia, which gained independence in 1965, was Great Britain's 1st African colony when it was "purchased" in 1588 as a corridor along the river best suited for getting into West Africa. Since the French had arrived there earlier, Gambia was a gate that failed to give the British access to the French-controlled backcountry. Later in the colonial period, human beings became the area's chief export commodity. Today peanuts represent 95% of Gambia's exports and the economy has been further improved by an influx of Scandinavian winter vacationers. Gambia added "The" to its name in order to distinguish it further from Zambia.

Gibraltar

Size—2.25 sq. mi. (5.8 sq. km.). Population—30,000.
Gibraltar is a rocky, steep-sided peninsula connected to Spain by a sandy isthmus. It has been a British Colony since 1713, but Spain has been appealing to the UN and fighting for decolonization since 1964. In ancient times the rock was known as one of the Pillars of Hercules which marked the limits of the known world. (The other pillar was on the African coast.) Gibraltar has the only colony of monkeys living wild in Europe. They live all over the rock and are a main tourist attraction.

Gilbert and Ellice Islands

Size—376 sq. mi. (974 sq. km.). Population—60,000.
Scattered over one million sq. mi. of ocean, most of these islands are small coral atolls about 2,000 mi. southwest of Hawaii. They have been a British Colony since 1892, but independence is likely in a few years. The Gilbertese, who are Micronesian, are notorious for their fierce opposition to foreigners. The Ellice Islanders, who are Polynesian, were more passive and found their population cut from 20,000 to 3,000 after foreigners began visiting their islands regularly in the 1st half of the 19th century. In recent years the Ellice Islanders have protested unequal access to government programs and have threatened to separate from the Gilberts.

Greenland

Size—840,000 sq. mi. (2,175,600 sq. km.). Ice-free: 131,900 sq. mi. (341,700 sq. km.). Population—50,000.
The world's largest island (Australia is considered a continent, not an island), most of Greenland lies within the Arctic Circle off the extreme northeast coast of North America. The people of Greenland, most of whom are Eskimos, are ruled by the Danish Government.

Nearly all of the administrators and businessmen are Danes, as are 80% of the teachers. Most Greenlanders survive much the same way as their Eskimo and Norse ancestors did: raising livestock, hunting and fishing. But more and more they are living in modern, multistory apartment houses, working in modern fish-processing plants, and watching cable TV or contributing to the province's rising alcoholism and birth rate.

Grenada

Size—133 sq. mi. (344 sq. km.) Population—110,000.
Tourists cavorting on the beaches of this Caribbean Island (the southernmost of the Windward Islands in the West Indies) have little awareness that many natives think of Grenada as a "little Haiti" ruled by a Prime Minister seeking all power and control through his armed secret police and paid informers. On the day of Grenada's independence from Britain on February 7, 1974, Prime Minister Eric M. Gairy held a cocktail reception at the Holiday Inn, a popular hangout for his régime. As he spoke, 60 of his secret police (recruited from the notorious Mongoose Gang of hardened criminals) were rounding up middle-class opposition leaders. Said Prime Minister Gairy, "We are the most progressive country in the world and I am one of the most dynamic leaders in the Caribbean. . . . Lots of people have tried to get rid of me, and they are lying in the cemetery." Grenada is the world's largest producer of nutmegs.

Guadeloupe

Size—687 sq. mi. (1,780 sq. km.). Population—350,000.
Two main islands and several smaller islands between the British Leewards and Windwards in the eastern Caribbean, Guadeloupe became a French Overseas Department in 1946, theoretically equal in political status to mainland French departments. Once hailed as a daring and liberal move, the Overseas Department status of Guadeloupe has come under criticism from islanders who maintain that they are still considered 2nd-class citizens. Economic troubles and racial unrest have been dealt with only gingerly by France. When Algerian independence was achieved, many of the officers most involved in the North African repression were then transferred to the French West Indies, another cause for complaint.

Guam

Size—210 sq. mi. (554 sq. km.). Population—115,000, including over 30,000 U.S. military personnel and dependents.
Located east of the Asian continent, Guam

is about 1,550 mi. from Tokyo and Manila. Off the edge of Guam is the Marianas Trench, the deepest known point on earth (38,198'). The southernmost of the Mariana Islands, Guam is the most distant of all U.S. colonies, being over 5,000 mi. from San Francisco. Well known as a launching pad for B-52 raids in Indochina, the U.S. military remains the mainstay of the economy. The admiral in charge still refers to himself as the "mayor of Guam" since the Navy and Air Force own over ⅓ of the island. Tourist promoters and speculators control most of what the military does not. Guamanians are American "citizens" but cannot vote in U.S. presidential elections. Men on the island must register for the draft and, on a per capita basis, Guamanians had more of their men killed in Vietnam than any U.S. State. In 1973 the UN General Assembly called on the U.S. to hold a free election on Guam to allow the people of the island to choose their own future.

Guinea-Bissau

Size—13,948 sq. mi. (36,125 sq. km.). Population—500,000.

After 5 centuries of Portuguese rule, this nation, on the coast of West Africa, ended an 11-year-war by having its independence "granted" by Portugal in 1974. According to Gil Fernandes, a leader of the ruling Parti Africano da Independencia da Guinee e Cabo Verde, "We are avoiding having the elite doing everything; the masses will. We think we can do it in Guinea. We can make the so-called elites go into the fields and plow for a while. Maybe it would be better for them than sitting at a desk. When you switch roles, you learn the value of the work someone else is doing."

Guyana

Size—83,000 sq. mi. (214,970 sq. km.). Population—850,000.

Located on the northeast coast of South America, Guyana was known as British Guiana until it received independence in 1966. The population is 51% East Indian, 30.7% African, 11.4% mixed, 4.4% Amerindian and 2.5% Portuguese, Chinese, and others. Considerable friction has developed between blacks and East Indians. For example, the Administration of Prime Minister Forbes Burnham, a black, has stressed cooperatives in all economic sectors, but East Indians, who are frequently self-employed, do not feel they need this sort of assistance. The blacks, who have a lower birth rate, are slowly being outnumbered. A powerful force in Guyana are the foreign corporations which own and operate the country's major industries, bauxite and sugar. However,

Burnham is moving toward nationalization and hopes to establish closer ties to Africa and other Caribbean producers of bauxite.

Iceland

Size—39,768 sq. mi. (103,000 sq. km.). Population—225,000.

A large island in the North Atlantic Ocean, Iceland—now a republic with a President and a Prime Minister—was originally settled by Irish hermits in the 9th century. They were followed by peoples of Nordic origin, mostly Norwegians, with a blending of Celtic blood that resulted from raids along the Irish coast. Most of the people live in concrete houses because every plank of lumber has to be imported. Buildings are heated by water from volcanic springs. Volcanic eruptions occur every 5 or 6 years and ⅓ of the total output of lava on the earth since 1500 A.D. has come from Icelandic volcanoes.

Kuwait

Size—6,880 sq. mi. (17,818 sq. km.). Population—920,000.

Located along the northwest coast of the Persian Gulf, Kuwait contains 15–20% of the world's oil reserves. This has made the Sheikh very, very wealthy and has allowed the royal family to set up the most complete welfare state in any capitalistic country. However, conditions are not that good for the 80% of the labor force who are not Kuwaiti. This includes Indian and Pakistani clerks, Iraqi, Saudi Arabian and Iranian laborers, and Palestinian professionals and workers, none of whom are allowed to vote or own property. Kuwaiti women suffer the same discrimination.

Leeward Islands

Size—349 sq. mi. (904 sq. km.). Population—145,000.

The northern arc of the Lesser Antilles in the eastern Caribbean, the Leewards include St. Christopher (also known as St. Kitts), Nevis, Anguilla, Antigua, Barbuda, Redonda, and Montserrat. Generally without industry or even incentives for industry, the islands remain poor and largely depend on Britain to maintain their economies. Increased tourist trade is a possible solution, but many blacks feel that more foreign investment in tourist-oriented projects would mean further repression. In 1967 the 6,000 people of Anguilla declared independence, but the Republic of Anguilla ended in 1969 when British soldiers landed on the island.

Liechtenstein

Size—61.78 sq. mi. (160.01 sq. km.). Population—24,000.

Nestled in Central Europe between Austria and Switzerland, Liechtenstein was established in its present form in 1719 when the territory was purchased by the princely House of Liechtenstein. Liechtenstein distinguishes itself by being the only independent country outside the Arab world in which women are not allowed to vote or to participate in public affairs. This tradition was broken once in 1968 when women were allowed to vote along with the men in a consultative poll to determine if women should be allowed to vote in national elections. The proposal was rejected.

Luxembourg

Size—999 sq. mi. (2,586 sq. km.). *Population*—350,000.

Located in northwestern Europe between France, Belgium, and Germany, Luxembourg was passed around among various European powers until it was granted autonomy by the Congress of Vienna in 1815. It was overrun and annexed by Germany during W.W. II and after the war it renounced its neutrality by joining NATO. The national motto is *Mir woelle bleiwe wat mir sin*—"We want to remain what we are." A strong small-town atmosphere is maintained throughout the country as a matter of government policy. There are more Luxembourgers in Chicago than in Luxembourg City.

Macao (Macau)

Size—6 sq. mi. (15.51 sq. km.). *Population*—295,000.

Macao (Ao-Men to the Chinese) is situated at the mouth of southern China's Pearl (Canton) River, about 17 mi. west of Hong Kong. Famous as a gambling resort, Macao attracts almost 2 million people annually, mostly from Hong Kong. Theoretically governed by a Portuguese governor, the people of Macao and the Government of China consider Macao a part of China to be returned in the near future. At the present time, however, China prefers to use Macao as an outlet for its exports to noncommunist nations. So real authority is exercised by the Chinese Chamber of Commerce, led by Chinese business leaders who negotiated an agreement with the Portuguese following a series of riots by pro-Peking youths in 1967.

Maldives

Size—115 sq. mi. (298 sq. km.). *Population*—130,000.

A chain of at least 1,087 coral islands 400 mi. southwest of India's southern tip, Maldives became a republic in 1968 after being ruled by sultans for centuries. However, the present

President had been Prime Minister under the last Sultan and political and economic power is still concentrated among a few families. A Muslim country, legal punishments include lashings with a leather strap for adultery and banishment to uninhabited islands for theft. There are no banks, no bars, and no taxes. There is, however, malaria which has kept away all but a few foreigners.

Malta

Size—122 sq. mi. (316 sq. km.). *Population*—325,000.

Malta's strategic location in the central Mediterranean Sea has caused it to be occupied by various foreign powers for over 35 centuries. The Phoenicians were 1st, followed by the Greeks, the Carthaginians, the Romans, the Arabs, the French, and, finally, the British, who annexed Malta in 1814. In December, 1974, Malta became a republic. According to tradition, St. Paul was shipwrecked on Malta in 58 A.D. and personally converted the islanders to Christianity. The Catholic Church is still a major force, especially on the local level where priests maintain influence over townspeople and villagers. The Maltese Labor party is anticlerical and in 1969 many priests warned their parishioners that their crops would die if they voted for the Labor party.

Martinique

Size—431 sq. mi. (1,116 sq. km.). *Population*—360,000.

One of the Windward Islands in the Caribbean, Martinique was continuously involved in the conflict between France and Britain, participating in some 20 wars in its history. Martinique has also suffered some sort of natural disaster on the average of every 4½ years. Hurricanes and earthquakes are not uncommon, but the most dramatic catastrophe was the May, 1902, explosion of Mount Pelée, the island's active volcano. Ash and lava buried the city of St. Pierre, killing nearly all 30,000 inhabitants. One of the few who survived was a prisoner who was protected by the thick walls of his cell. Martinique is an Overseas Department of France, theoretically equal with Departments in France, but many islanders believe that the French Government is unwilling or unable to deal with the problems of poverty and unemployment.

Mauritius

Size—720 sq. mi. (1,865 sq. km.). *Population*—900,000.

An island about 500 mi. east of Madagascar in the Indian Ocean, Mauritius has a mixed population of Hindus, Muslims, Catholics, and

Chinese. The economy is dependent on sugar which provides 89% of the exports and 62% of the jobs. Since independence in 1968, the nation has been wracked with problems. The defeat of malaria in the 1940s led to a population boom, and increased unemployment. A strong 3rd-world-oriented labor movement was squashed in 1972 and its leaders were imprisoned. Mauritius was the home of the extinct dodo, a flightless bird which was destroyed by European sailors and their domestic animals.

Melilla (See: Ceuta and Melilla)

Micronesia

Size—717 sq. mi. (1,857 sq. km.). *Population*—115,000.

The Mariana, Caroline, and Marshall Island chains, 2,300 islands scattered across 3 million sq. mi. of ocean, lie in the western Pacific Ocean, north of the equator, east of the Philippines, and west of the international dateline. The islands were conquered by Spain, sold to Germany, ceded to Japan by the League of Nations, and ceded to the U.S. after W.W. II. Although ultimate authority over Micronesia is theoretically in the hands of the Trusteeship Council of the UN, the islands are actually ruled by the U.S. Dept. of Interior with much help from the U.S. Dept. of Defense, which considers them vital to national defense. There has been a growing movement for independence among Micronesians, but the U.S. Government has tried to avoid the issue. According to Walter Hickel's memoirs, several members of the Nixon Cabinet proposed a settlement of the Micronesia status question in 1970, but were vetoed by Henry Kissinger, who said, "There are only 90,000 people out there, so who gives a damn?" On the northern Mariana Islands there is a movement to obtain commonwealth status, such as that of Puerto Rico. However, this would violate the UN Trust. Also, there is some question as to whether the U.S. Congress would vote its approval.

Monaco

Size—370 acres, to be expanded to 447 acres by filling in a small portion of the Mediterranean Sea. 0.73 sq. mi. (1.89 sq. km.). *Population*—26,000.

Situated on the French Riviera, 5 mi. from the Italian border, Monaco is the site of the famous Monte Carlo Casino. Although the French Government wields much power in Monaco, the official ruler is Prince Rainier of the Grimaldi family which was awarded the territory in 1297 by the Holy Roman Emperor. Over half the population is more than 44 years old.

Montserrat (See: Leeward Islands)

Namibia (formerly South-West Africa)

Size—318,261 sq. mi. (824,296 sq. km.). *Population*—800,000.

South African forces conquered the German colony of South-West Africa in 1915 and, under the Treaty of Versailles, the territory was given over to South Africa as a mandate. In 1969, despite objections from the UN, South Africa incorporated the area as a colony. Since then South Africa has ignored international pressure including condemnation by the World Court and a Security Council endorsement of independence for Namibia. Namibia has great potential wealth including one of the world's richest offshore diamond beds. The South African rock lobster, which costs a fortune in American restaurants, is caught off the coast of Namibia. The U.S. buys a large portion of the lobster catch, and the U.S. also buys most of Namibia's karakul pelts (the skins of newborn lambs—so-called Persian lamb).

Nauru

Size—8 sq. mi. (21 sq. km.). *Population*—8,000.

An oval island in the Central Pacific, just south of the equator and about 1,300 mi. northeast of Australia, Nauru is composed largely of phosphate-rich guano or, as it is better known, bird droppings. This unusual resource has provided Nauruans with one of the highest per capita incomes in the world and has allowed them to build a 51-story skyscraper in Melbourne, the Australian city's tallest building. They also own a 1st-class-only airline and a large and growing shipping line. The only problem is that by 1990 Nauru will be an empty hulk and uninhabitable. But the people of Nauru have several options open to them including buying another island.

Netherlands Antilles

Size—371 sq. mi. (861 sq. km.). *Population*—240,000.

The Netherlands Antilles are 5½ Caribbean islands (half of one island belongs to France) in 2 distinct groups. The ABC islands (Aruba, Bonaire, Curaçao) lie just off the Venezuelan coast. The Netherlands Leeward Islands (Saba, St. Eustatius, and the southern part of St. Maarten) lie about 550 mi. northeast of the ABCs. The economy of the entire area is based on the oil refineries of Aruba and Curaçao. Thirty to 40% of the population is directly involved in the oil industry. In May, 1969, a general strike in Curaçao, protesting automation and working conditions, turned into a riot and caused the downfall of the Government. St. Eustatius was almost totally destroyed by the British in 1780 in revenge for the island's trade ties with Americans during the American Revolution.

New Caledonia

Size—7,374 sq. mi. (19,099 sq. km.). *Population*—130,000.

The 1st missionaries and French colonists who came to this island group situated east of Australia were killed and eaten. The French later used the islands as a penal colony for French prisoners who at one time numbered up to 40,000. The French Government is still in charge, although the nickel companies are quite powerful. With the exceptionally high number of Europeans in the colony (42% of the population) and a fairly large number of imported laborers (8%), the New Caledonians themselves have little real power and anti-government rioting has developed in reaction to economic woes. At one point there were as many as 5,000 Vietnamese in New Caledonia, but most were sent home after the French claimed a "communist bridgehead" was being established.

New Hebrides

Size—5,700 sq. mi. (14,763 sq. km.). *Population*—90,000.

The New Hebrides are a double chain of about 80 islands 500 mi. west of Fiji and 250 mi. northeast of New Caledonia in the southwestern Pacific. Since 1906 the area has been ruled jointly by the British and the French. The New Hebrideans have to contend with 2 police forces, 2 sets of laws, 2 banking and currency systems, 2 sets of schools, and 2 chief colonial officials. In addition, they have no citizenship or civil rights. Strong support for independence is now being pushed by the National party and by the Presbyterian Church. Britain would support the independence movement, but does not want to anger France which wants to maintain permanent control.

Oman

Size—82,000 sq. mi. (212,400 sq. km.). *Population*—800,000.

Oman, a sultanate in southeastern Arabia, has the dubious distinction of being one of the most repressive nations in the world. Until 1970 it was ruled by Said bin Taimur who banned alcohol, tobacco, drums, movies, and travel. Without his permission, no one could build a new house, repair an old one, or cultivate new land. In 1970 he was overthrown by his son Qabus bin Said who has made slight changes. However, he is basically a puppet controlled by the British who also control the military. Most of the western province of Dhofar is now controlled by a liberation movement and fighting continues in the interior.

Pacific Islands, Miscellaneous

Under British control:
Line Islands, straddling the equator about 1,400 mi. from Hawaii. These islands are uninhabited except for Christmas Island. Between 1958 and 1962 the U.S. and Britain detonated a number of nuclear bombs at Christmas Island.

Phoenix Islands, a series of tiny uninhabited coral atolls about 2,000 mi. south of Honolulu. Two of them, Canton and Enderbury are jointly administered by the U.S. and Britain.

Under Chilean control:
Easter Island, located 2,300 mi. off the coast of Chile, is the easternmost island in Polynesia. It is the site of the famous "Moai" statues.

Under Japanese control:
Bonin (includes Chichi-shima), Volcano (includes Iwo Jima), and Marcus islands. Settled by American sailors in the 19th century but colonized by the Japanese in 1875, the Bonins are inhabited by Westernized families with names like Savory and Washington, and by Japanese families. Occupied by the U.S. at the end of W.W. II, the islands were returned to Japan in 1968. They are administered by the Prefecture of Tokyo.

Under New Zealand control:
Tokelau Islands, located northeast of the Samoas. There are about 1,600 people living in 4 main island groups.
Niue Island, located just east of Tonga. There are about 5,500 inhabitants.

Under U.S. control:
The U.S. is colonial landlord of over 2,300 islands in the Pacific, excluding Hawaii. These islands form a series of stepping-stones that span the entire Pacific to within 400 mi. of Indonesia and the Philippines. The major islands are Guam, Micronesia (officially known as the Trust Territory of the Pacific Islands), and American Samoa. There are also a number of other islands including:
Midway Islands, actually a western extension of Hawaii, are inhabited only by the U.S. Navy and gooney birds.
Wake Island, located 2,000 mi. west of Hawaii, is actually part of Micronesia but is now run by the Air Force. Until recently a major refueling stop for trans-Pacific flights, the island is now being used for a series of missile tests.
Johnston Island, located about 800 mi. from

Honolulu, is an Air-Force-controlled depot for nerve gas and hydrogen bombs. It was formerly an H-bomb launching site and retains a capability for rapidly restarting atmospheric nuclear tests.

Canton and Enderbury islands in the Phoenix Island group are jointly administered with the British. Canton is a missile-tracking base for the Air Force.

Howland, Jarvis, and Baker islands, uninhabited since W.W. II, are located south of Honolulu.

Palmyra and Kingman Reef are the northernmost islands in the British-controlled Line Islands group. They are uninhabited even by the U.S. military.

Polynesia, French

Size—1,544 sq. mi. (3,999 sq. km.). *Population*—150,000.

These 130 islands in the south-central Pacific Ocean were violently annexed by the French in the 1840s despite fierce opposition from the people and British threats of war. The islands are still ruled from Paris with an iron hand. The steadily growing independence movement has been focusing its attention on damage done by the continuing H-bomb tests. Many of the islands close to the test area in Mururoa have been closed to outsiders including relatives of the inhabitants. Polynesia is famous as a tourist spot, but the biggest industry is the bomb and there is widespread fear that when the tests end, the economy will collapse.

Qatar

Size—4,400 sq. mi. (11,400 sq. km.). *Population*—170,000.

Qatar is an oil-rich peninsula extending 90 mi. into the Persian Gulf from the Arabian peninsula. It is ruled by Sheikh Khalifa bin Hamad al-Thani and the other male members of the extended al-Thani family. Qatar, which achieved independence from Britain in 1971, is a religiously-oriented state like Saudi Arabia and the school curricula reflect this orientation. Arabic language and religious education (Islamic) combine to account for up to 50% (and at least ⅓) of class time at all levels through secondary school.

Réunion

Size—970 sq. mi. (2,512 sq. km.). *Population*—475,000.

An island in the Indian Ocean, about 450 mi. east of Madagascar, Réunion is an Overseas Department of France. Because 70% of the total cultivated land consists of sugarcane plantations, a few European plantation owners control the island, which is overcrowded and filled with disease. Malnutrition is common among the poor and alcoholism, venereal disease, tuberculosis, and asthma are widespread. In recent years, DDT spraying has eliminated malaria.

Saint Christopher—Nevis—Anguilla (See: Leeward Islands)

Saint Lucia (See: Windward Islands)

Saint Vincent (See: Windward Islands)

Samoa

Western Samoa: *Size*—1,097 sq. mi. (2,841 sq. km.). *Population*—180,000. American Samoa: *Size*—76 sq. mi. (197 sq. km.). *Population*—30,000. There are also at least 20,000 American Samoans living in California and Hawaii.

These 15 islands in the South Pacific, 2,300 mi. southwest of Honolulu, Hawaii, were probably the cradle of Polynesian civilization. It was from here that the other islands, including Hawaii, were settled. Samoa 1st came under foreign sway in the 1860s. As a result of Germany's defeat in W.W. I, the western part of Samoa became a League of Nations mandate under New Zealand's control and in 1962 it became independent although New Zealand continued to supply financial support. Eastern Samoa came under U.S. control in 1899. Since then, the U.S. has refused to consider granting independence, preferring to maintain power through a paternalistic U.S.-appointed governor. Samoan society is organized around the village, which is a group of related households or extended families headed by a chief, whose title is inherited.

San Marino

Size—23.5 sq. mi. (61 sq. km.). *Population*—21,500.

The oldest republic in the world, San Marino is situated on the slopes and summit of Mount Titano in north-central Italy. Tourism and postage stamps provide 80% of the Gross National Product. Whenever the nation needs money, it prints a new stamp for philatelists. San Marino receives $1 million a year from Italy in return for an agreement not to run a gambling casino, TV or radio stations, duty-free shops, or sell imported cigarettes. San Marino has always taken risks to help the oppressed—hiding the Duke of Urbino from the Borgias, hiding Giuseppe Garibaldi from Austria in 1849 and then helping him escape to America. In 1921, it hid refugees from Mussolini, and in 1938 fugitives from Nazi-conquered Austria. It offered help to Jews persecuted by Hitler and became a haven for Italian partisans near the end of W.W. II.

São Tomé and Príncipe

Size—372 sq. mi. (964 sq. km.). *Population*—69,000.

This archipelago about 125 mi. off the west coast of Africa in the Gulf of Guinea was 1st colonized by the Portuguese in 1471. Slavery was abolished in 1869, but the abolition of slavery actually worsened the status of blacks. As a slave, the native was bought like a head of cattle or any other possession, but, since he represented a certain investment of capital, his owner treated him in such a way that he kept in good health. As a wage laborer, the native was no longer purchased. Instead he was hired by the Government and if he became sick, he was simply fired and replaced. The main product of São Tomé and Príncipe is cocoa. Over 500 years of Portuguese rule ended when independence was declared on July 12, 1975.

Seychelles

Size—107 sq. mi. (278 sq. km.). *Population*—60,000.

Mostly used as a resting place for pirates until the mid-18th century, these 85 islands in the Indian Ocean, 1,000 mi. east of Kenya, were captured by the British in 1794. The Seychelles are still a British Colony. Some of the most exotic flora and fauna in the world exist there. Ian Fleming, author of the James Bond novels, used to tell his friends: "Get there before the American millionaires take over." British land developers seem to have taken his advice, having recently built modern hotels and golf courses in the Seychelles. Meanwhile, poverty is widespread due to a high birth rate and a lack of employment.

Solomon Islands, British

Size—11,500 sq mi. (29,785 sq. km.). *Population*—180,000.

The Solomons are a double chain of islands in the Southwest Pacific off the coast of New Guinea. Over 60 languages and dialects are spoken although there is a relative homogeneity in culture and political systems. A powerful influence are the Australian traders and Japanese businessmen who buy over 50% of the island's agricultural exports. The 1st missionaries and capitalists who arrived in the mid-19th century were all killed.

South-West Africa (See: Namibia)

Spanish Sahara

Size—102,703 sq. mi. (266,000 sq. km.). *Population*—77,000.

Spanish Sahara is an overseas province of Spain on the western edge of North Africa. Half of the inhabitants are nomads who enter with their flocks from Mauritania after the rainy season. The Governments of Morocco and Mauritania covet the area because it is rich in iron and phosphate so, in 1966, the UN General Assembly asked for a referendum to let the people of the province decide whether or not to remain under Spanish rule. Spain ignored the request and the Saharans did not protest because Spanish rule means health facilities, schools, and jobs. The referendum was not asked for again.

Surinam (formerly Dutch Guiana)

Size—63,251 sq. mi. (163,820 sq. km.). *Population*—475,000.

Surinam is located on the northeast coast of South America. By the Treaty of Breda (1667) the Dutch obtained possession of Surinam and gave the British permanent possession of New Amsterdam (New York). The area was originally populated by Arawak and Carib Indians who still make up 2.7% of the population. When the Dutch came, they imported African slaves to do the work, but the Africans escaped into the jungle. Their descendants, known as "Bush Negroes" are 10.2% of the population. Next the Dutch brought in indentured servants from India (36.9%) and Indonesia (15.3%). Most of the remainder of the inhabitants today are Creoles (30.7%). There is also a smattering of Chinese and even a few leftover Dutch. Surinam is the world's 2nd largest supplier of bauxite and about 80% of its production goes to the U.S. U.S. interests, principally Alcoa, control the entire industry.

Swaziland

Size—6,704 sq. mi. (17,384 sq. km.). *Population*—500,000.

A small, oval-shaped land in Africa's southeastern corner, Swaziland gained independence from Britain in 1968. In 1973, King Sobhuza II, who has been head of the Swazi nation since 1921, scrapped the British-style constitution and decided to rule without one. Swaziland is almost entirely surrounded by South Africa and the Royal Swazi Hotel Casino makes a lot of money from staid South African white men who have to cross the border to gamble and cavort with black women. Families in Swaziland are extended. Upon marriage, for example, a new bride receives a child from someone in her husband's family. The bride assumes all parental responsibilities for the child in order to prepare her for having her own, at which time she gives back the surrogate child.

Timor, Portuguese

Size—5,763 sq. mi. (14,925 sq. km.). *Population*—650,000.

The island of Timor in the Malay archipelago, 360 mi. northwest of Australia, is divided between Indonesia and Portugal. Portuguese Timor includes the eastern half of the island, an enclave on the northern coast of Indonesian Timor known as Ocussi-Ambeno, and 2 smaller islands. Since the 1974 coup in Portugal, the political future of Timor has been uncertain. Those who are politically aware favor either union with Indonesia, or independence. However, large sections of the inland population remain unaffected by government policy, or the modern economy, except when the Portuguese come around to collect taxes.

Tonga

Size—269 sq. mi. (696 sq. km.). *Population*—100,000.

Named the Friendly Islands by Capt. James Cook, Tonga consists of 150 islands in the South Pacific east of Fiji. Tonga is a monarchy which became independent on June 4, 1970. Although oil exploration and encouragement of tourism may bring changes, the economy is now based almost entirely on agriculture. When a Tongan male reaches the age of 16 he is entitled to 8¼ acres of land for cultivation. A group of Southern California businessmen has claimed ownership of a coral reef in what Tonga considers its territorial waters. They have announced that the reef is now the "Republic of Minerva."

United Arab Emirates (formerly Trucial States)

Size—32,300 sq. mi. (83,650 sq. km.). *Population*—275,000.

Along the Persian Gulf and the Gulf of Oman are 7 tiny sheikhdoms, Abu Dhabi, Dubai, Sharjah, Ras al-Khaimah, Fujairah, Umm al-Qaiwain, and Ajman, which joined together in 1971–1972 to form the United Arab Emirates. Oil is the source of the comparatively great wealth of the UAE, although smuggling is quite important in Dubai. Over $250 million in goods enters Dubai, but there is no record of how much is reexported or where it goes. The large population of foreign nationals (over 50% of the total UAE population) has few rights and constitutes a badly exploited and discontent work force. It consists, for the most part, of men without families.

U.S. Trust Territory of the Pacific Islands (See: Micronesia)

Vatican City

Size—109 acres or 0.16 sq. mi. (0.4 sq. km.), plus 13 buildings outside the papal boundaries, in Rome. *Population*—less than 1,000.

The State of Vatican City is in the heart of Rome, near the west bank of the Tiber River. It is a center of Catholic pilgrimage and Italian tourism. In 1870 the papal domain was annexed by the new Kingdom of Italy. The Popes refused to accept the annexation, convinced that they needed a physical domain to assure the independent exercise of their spiritual power. Finally, in 1929, Pope Pius XI recognized the Italian State as the legal embodiment of the Italian people, and in return was accorded his 109 acres. Vatican City's railroad line is the shortest in the world, 300 yards.

Virgin Islands

American Virgins: *Size*—133 sq. mi. (344 sq. km.). *Population*—80,000. British Virgins: *Size*—59 sq. mi. (153 sq. km.). *Population*—12,000.

The Virgins are a group of almost 100 islands east of Puerto Rico, between the Caribbean and the Atlantic. There are 7 main islands, 3 U.S. (St. Croix, St. Thomas, St. John) and 4 British (Tortola, Virgin Gorda, Anegad, Jost Van Dyke). The American Virgins were purchased from Denmark in 1917 for $25 million for use as a naval base when the U.S. feared that the Germans might seize them and then move on to the Panama Canal. The British Virgins fell into English hands in 1666 when British buccaneers drove out the Dutch and claimed the islands for Charles II. Tourism, the mainstay of the economy, experienced a serious decline following a series of slayings and crimes in 1973 and 1974 that appeared to be racially motivated. However, the industry seems to have recovered. "Crucians" (or Cruzans), native-born blacks, are a minority numbering about 25%. "Down-islanders," English-speaking blacks from other Caribbean islands, number about 33%. Forty percent of the population are Spanish-speaking, mainly from Puerto Rico. A tiny number of "continentals," U.S. whites, generally dominate the economy. American Virgin Islanders are U.S. citizens, but they are not allowed to vote in national elections and they have no representative in Congress.

Western Samoa (See: Samoa)

Windward Islands

Size—1,292 sq. mi. (3,346 sq. km.). *Population*—300,000.

Forming the southern arc of the Lesser Antilles in the easternmost Caribbean, the British-controlled Windwards include the major islands of Dominica, St. Lucia, and St. Vincent. In the 1830s, St. Vincent, Grenada, Barbados, Tobago, and St. Lucia joined together in the Windward Islands Colony. Barbados left in 1885, and Tobago became attached to Trinidad in 1889. In 1940, Dominica joined the Colony, but the Colony was finally dissolved on January 1, 1960, and the 4 islands became 4 separate colonies. In 1974, Grenada declared its independence. Like most of the Caribbean, the Windwards offer sun, beaches, and a more relaxed pace of life. The islands export lime products, sugar, cacao, and spices. St. Vincent has a virtual monopoly on arrowroot, producing about 98% of the total world supply. In late 1974, members of a group called Dreads terrorized white settlers, and the Government responded with a law allowing a person to kill suspected Dreads if they appeared in one's home.

—The Eds. (Pacific Islands by R.W.G.)

8

World History—
Unsealing the Time Capsule

Eyewitness Reports on Highlights of World History

PHOENICIANS INVENT THE MODERN ALPHABET

WHEN: About 1000 B.C.

HOW: Most letters in our English alphabet are simplifications of what were ancient drawings of animals or objects. A capital *Q*, for instance, represents a monkey. *Ch*, from the word for "fence," became *H*. An *M* was 1st an owl and later meant "water."

But let's go back to the beginning—or as close to it as we can get. Historians generally agree that our alphabet descended from ancient Egyptian hieroglyphics, meaning "sacred writings," because they were 1st recorded by priests more than 5,000 years ago. Hieroglyphics were simple pictures carved in stone or inscribed on papyrus. A small circle with a dot in its center stood for "sun." A figure showing 2 arms, one holding a shield and the other a spear, meant "battle."

As new words came into the vocabulary, new picture symbols were created, until finally the "writing" of some documents became more complicated than a wiring diagram for a modern computer. So the Egyptians began to combine certain pictures to represent *sounds* instead of the objects pictured. For example, orally the Egyptian word meaning "lapis lazuli" was *khesteb*. There was no picture of a *khesteb*, but there was a symbol called *khesf*, meaning "to stop," and a picture of a *teb*, or "pig." Thus a combined drawing of a man holding a pig by the tail meant *khesteb* or "lapis lazuli."

Centuries after Egypt's decline, explorers who discovered hieroglyphic carvings in Egypt were mystified as to their meanings until 1799, when an officer in Napoleon's Army near the Egyptian village of Rosetta discovered a smooth, thick, black stone covered with carvings divided into 3 separate sections. One section was a historical account in Greek; the other 2 were in hieroglyphics and demotics (simplified hieroglyphics). The Greek account said that it was exactly the same as the Egyptian, and this now enabled scholars to decipher the mysterious ancient carvings.

One great difficulty with picture writing was that different "readers" might make wrong interpretations of what they saw. An old story tells how Darius the Great, King of the Persians, led an army against Scythian forces north of the Black Sea about 512 B.C. As the armies neared one another, an emissary from the enemy brought Darius a message. Instead of pictures carved in stone, the enemy commander had sent Darius the real things—a mouse, a frog, a bird, and some arrows.

Darius summoned his officers. "We've won," he said. "These arrows mean the enemy will lay down his weapons. The mouse and frog mean he will give us his land and water. And the bird means that his armies will fly from our victorious legions!"

That night the Scythians swooped down and conquered the Persians. Said the Scythian general: "My message was clear. It said that unless you could turn yourselves into birds and fly away, or into mice and burrow under the ground, or into frogs and hide in the swamps, you would never escape death from our arrows."

By 1000 B.C., picture writing had become too cumbersome for daily use, especially for those in business. And business was brisk not only for local merchants, but for those dealing in exports and imports among the nations bordering the Mediterranean Sea. The most active among the seagoing traders were Semitic groups called Phoenicians, or Canaanites, who came from the lands we now know as Lebanon and Syria. They were literate and creative, and traded both goods and knowledge with their customers, particularly the Greeks.

The animals, objects, and sounds represented by the Egyptian hieroglyphs did not satisfy the needs of the Phoenicians for record-keeping, sales contracts, receipts, and other business documents. Accordingly, they conceived the idea of using symbols that would mean *only* sounds that could be combined to make words.

For example, the Semitic word *aleph*, meaning "ox," was recorded as a simple outline of an ox's head. But instead of using the sketch to mean "ox," the Phoenicians chose to make it represent *only* the sound of the 1st letter of the word *aleph*, or A. The word *beth*, meaning "house," was to lose that meaning and instead represent the sound of B, the 1st letter of the word.

Other words the Phoenicians transformed from pictorial to alphabetical symbols are:

The Word	The Sound	Pictorial Meaning
Gimel (or Gamal)	G	Camel
Daleth	D	Door
He	H	Window
Vau	V	Hook (or nail)
Zayin	Z	Balance scale
Cheth	Ch	Fence
Teth	Th	Ball of string
Yod	Y	Hand
Kaph	K	Palm of hand
Lamed	L	Whip (rod of authority)
Mem	M	Waters
Nun	N	Fish
Sameth	S	Post
'Ayin	A (short)	Eye
Pe	P	Mouth
Tsade	Ts	Fishpole
Qoph	Q	Ape
Resh	R	Head
Shin	Sh	Teeth
Tau	T	Mark (or cross)

With the 1st 2 words, *aleph* and *beth*, this arrangement provided 22 symbols representing 22 different sounds. None represented vowels except for the short A and possibly Y.

The Greeks adopted the Phoenician alphabet and found it more efficient and useful than the ancient picture system, but the Greeks needed vowels in their vocabulary, so they made a few changes and additions. They kept 19 of the Phoenician letters and added vowels and other characters to make an alphabet totaling 24 letters. Among the changes, the Phoenician *aleph*

became the Greek *alpha*, and *beth* became the Greek *beta*—and it is from combining these 2 Greek terms that we get our word *alphabet*.

Historians agree that the Greek alphabet came to the Romans perhaps by way of the mysterious Etruscans, and that the Romans also made a few changes which resulted in a 23-letter alphabet: A B C G D E F H I K L M N O P Q R S T V Y X Z. During the conquests of the Caesars the Roman alphabet and language—Latin—spread to other nations. In England, however, Norman scribes found a need for a new letter, W. It is said that they added 1st the letter U and then formed a "double U" (UU) or doubled the letter V (VV), which had been used as a U.

Not until the 15th century was the 26th letter added to the alphabet. The I, when used at the beginning of certain words, carried the sound *dz*, and gradually developed into our letter *J*.

EYEWITNESS REPORT: Herodotus, the Greek historian, said, "The Phoenicians introduced into Greece the knowledge of letters, of which, as it seems to me, the Greeks had heretofore been ignorant."

Pliny the Elder, Roman statesman and author, made some interesting observations: "I have always been of the opinion that letters were of Assyrian origin, but other writers, Gellius, for instance, suppose that they were invented in Egypt by Mercury; others, again, will have it that they were discovered by the Syrians; and that Cadmus brought from Phoenicia 16 letters into Greece. To these, Palamedes, it is said, at the time of the Trojan War, added these 4, Th, X, Ph and Ch. Simonides, the lyric poet, afterwards added a like number, Z, E [long], Ps, and O [long]; the sounds denoted by all of which are now received into our alphabet.

"Aristotle, on the other hand, is rather of the opinion that there were originally 18 letters, A B G D E Z I K C M N O P R S T U Ph, and that 2, Th namely, and Ch, were introduced by Epicharmus and not by Palamedes. Aristides says that a certain person of the name of Menos, in Egypt, invented letters 15 years before the reign of Phoroneus, the most ancient of all the kings of Greece, and this he attempts to prove by the monuments there. On the other hand, Epigenes, a writer of very great authority, informs us that the Babylonians have a series of observations on the stars for a period of 720,000 years, inscribed on baked bricks. Berosus and Critodemus, who make the period the shortest, give it as 490,000 years. From this statement it would appear that letters have been in use from all eternity. The Pelasgi were the 1st to introduce them into Latium. [Latium was an ancient country in central Italy.]"

Dr. Isaac Taylor, Canon of York, famed scholar and author of a 2-volume work, *The History of the Alphabet* (1899), wrote: "It is only by means of the potent simplicity of the alphabet that the art of writing can be brought within general reach. The familiar instances of Egypt, Assyria and China are sufficient to prove that without the alphabet . . . science and religion necessarily tend to remain the exclusive property of a sacerdotal caste; any diffused and extended national culture becomes impossible, religion degenerates into magic, the chasm which separates the rulers and the ruled grows greater and more impassable, and the very art of writing, instead of being the most effective of all the means of progress, becomes one of the most powerful of the instruments by which the masses of mankind can be held enslaved."

FROM ART TO ALPHABET

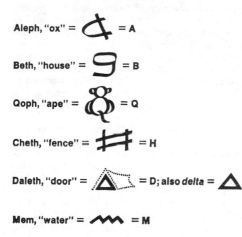

Aleph, "ox" =   = A

Beth, "house" =   = B

Qoph, "ape" =   = Q

Cheth, "fence" =   = H

Daleth, "door" =   = D; also *delta* =

Mem, "water" =   = M

Hieroglyph for "owl" =   = M

—H.E.N.

THE AGE OF PERICLES

WHEN: 457 B.C.–430 B.C.

HOW: Pericles was the political leader of Athens during the great age of Athenian imperialism. Although his name is often associated with the form of government known as democracy, the system he presided over was hardly the "rule of the people," as the name implies. Only Athenian citizens—less than a quarter of the adult population—had political rights. Women, slaves, and foreigners were not citizens; and Pericles himself passed a measure limiting citizenship to those whose parents were *both* Athenian. Even among the citizens

there were severe class divisions based on property and revenues. Only the wealthiest could hold high office. Unpropertied citizens were eligible only to vote and to sit on juries.

Pericles was of noble birth. His mother was a niece of Cleisthenes, a former ruler who had helped formulate the Athenian constitution; his father, Xanthippus, was a successful general. Even as a young man Pericles was known for an aloof, reserved manner and a subtle oratorical style. He made it a rule never to be seen at dinners or informal social situations because, as Plutarch observed, "These friendly meetings are very quick to defeat any assumed superiority, and in intimate familiarity an exterior of gravity is hard to maintain. . . . Pericles, to avoid any feeling of commonness or satiety on the part of the people, presented himself at intervals only, not speaking to every business, nor at all times coming into the assembly, but reserving himself for great occasions."

Like many a ruling-class politician, Pericles found it expedient to assume the role of a reformer. According to Plutarch, "He took his side not with the rich and few, but with the many and poor, contrary to his natural bent, which was far from democratical; but most likely fearing he might fall under suspicion of aiming at arbitrary power, and seeing Cimon (the leader he sought to replace) on the side of the aristocracy . . . he joined the party of the people, with a view at once both to secure himself and procure means against Cimon."

Pericles' political career began shortly after the Persian wars—in which Persia's attempts to conquer Greece were rebuffed under the leadership of Athens (Sparta had declined to help the other city states). Ultimate power was in the hands of the Council of Areopagus, whose members came only from the wealthiest social strata. The chief of state was Cimon, the general who had led the fight against Persia. His foreign policy was to share control of Greece with Sparta: Athens as mistress of the sea, Sparta as mistress of the mainland. Cimon went so far as to lead an expeditionary force to Messenia to help the Spartans put down a slave revolt. This act enraged the poor of Athens—who had counted on getting some political power after their years of service in the war against Persia. Under the leadership of Ephialtes, an authentic democrat, and Pericles, the opposition party stripped the Council of Areopagus of its key powers and arranged the banishment of Cimon. Shortly thereafter, Ephialtes was mysteriously murdered. One contemporary historian, Idomenus, charged Pericles with doing in his rival. The more widely accepted view was that the Athenian aristocracy, finding Pericles more acceptable, killed his "ally."

Under Pericles, Athens became the most

powerful and influential of the Greek city-states. Her leadership was exercised through the Delian League, ostensibly a confederation of equals but in fact an apparatus through which Athens extracted tributes and support. A period of great cultural accomplishment followed: Aeschylus, Sophocles, and Euripides brought tragic drama to its height; the Parthenon and other magnificent public buildings were constructed; mathematics, astronomy, and medicine flourished; and a key political reform—payment for public service—was instituted. But imperialism and its concomitant, slavery, were undermining the strength of Athenian society, and even the great cultural achievements of the Periclean age can be viewed as responses to the cancer of the slave economy.

Athens had achieved military supremacy in the Mediterranean because her advanced technology, notably the development of iron tools, gave her the largest ships and the best weapons. Machines for pressing olives for oil and for crushing silver ore led to exportable surpluses. Athenian pottery, wines, and armaments were also in demand wherever her ships entered port. Because exporting manufactured goods was so profitable, there was pressure to increase production. Small factories were organized, with labor divided among several workers. Whereas one craftsman used to make pots, start to finish, in a factory one man would fire the kiln, another throw the pot, another paint it, and so on. His work divided into simpler steps, the master craftsman was replaceable by slaves. Factories employing 15 or more men became common in the age of Pericles. In the mines the numbers ran up to 1,000. One effect of reliance on slave labor was to inhibit invention. It became cheaper to use 3 or 4 slaves for a heavy task than to design and build a machine to do it. And the existence of slave labor not only determined the income to be derived from manual work, but the social status of it. Labor became despised.

Competing against slave labor, the resident aliens sank to the status Aristotle later called "limited slavery." As for the poorer citizens, they used their voting power to pressure Pericles into establishing a kind of welfare system. Many of his key "democratic" reforms, such as payment for jury duty, were attempts to maintain the unpropertied citizens in a slightly privileged status.

By 430 B.C., the last year of Pericles' reign, some 20,000 citizens (between ⅓ and ½ the whole citizenry) were being supported at public expense. The money came in part from the other Greek city-states, and from further colonial expansion. As a result of this situation, the political spokesmen of the poorer citizens became the leading advocates of Athenian imperialism. They supported Pericles in a policy of confrontation with Sparta, a policy that made the Peloponnesian War—and the decline of Athenian power—inevitable.

Plutarch pointed out the connection between Pericles' expansionist foreign policy and his "Great Society" achievements at home:

"He sent a thousand [Athenians] into the Chersonese as planters, to share the land among them by lot, and 500 more into the isle of Naxos, and half that number to Andros, a thousand into Thrace to dwell among the Bisaltae, and others into Italy. . . . And this he did to ease and discharge the city of an idle and, by reason of their idleness, a busy meddling crowd of people; and at the same time to meet the necessities and restore the fortunes of the poor townsmen, and to intimidate also, and check their allies from attempting any change, by posting such garrisons, as it were, in the midst of them.

"That which gave most pleasure and ornament to the city of Athens, and the greatest admiration and even astonishment to all strangers, and that which now is Greece's only evidence that the power she boasts of and her ancient wealth are no romance or idle story, was his construction of the public and sacred buildings. Yet this was that of all his actions in the government which his enemies most looked askance upon and cavilled at in the popular assemblies, crying out how that the commonwealth of Athens had lost its reputation and was ill-spoken of abroad for removing the common treasure of the Greeks from the isle of Delos into their own custody; and how that their fairest excuse for doing so, namely that they secure it in a safe place, this Pericles had made unavailable, and how that 'Greece cannot but resent it as an insufferable affront and consider herself to be tyrannized over openly, when she sees the treasure, which was contributed by her upon a necessity for the war, wantonly lavished out by us upon our city, to gild her all over, and to adorn and set her forth, as it were some vain woman, hung round with precious stones and figures and temples, which cost a world of money.'

"Pericles, on the other hand, informed the people that they were in no way obliged to give any account of those moneys to their allies, so long as they maintained their defence, and kept off the barbarians from attacking them."

The intellectual legacy of the age of Pericles was as pseudo-democratic as its politics. The principal themes were that Athens was superior to the rest of Greece (and the world) and should be regarded as the "school of Hellas"; that slaves were inferior beings to freemen, and women inferior to men; and that "moderation in all things," particularly social action, was the highest good.

EYEWITNESS REPORT: In 431 B.C. Pericles delivered a famous funeral oration in honor of the Athenians who had died fighting Sparta during the 1st year of the Peloponnesian War. The version of Athenian democracy he presents is quoted by Thucydides:

"Our ancestors . . . are worthy of our praises; and still more so are our fathers. For they enlarged the ancestral patrimony by the empire which we hold today and delivered it, not without labor, into the hands of our own generation; while it is we ourselves, those of us who are now in middle life, who consolidated our power throughout the greater part of the empire and secured the city's complete independence both in war and peace. . . .

"Our government is not copied from those of our neighbors; we are an example to them rather than they to us. Our constitution is named a democracy, because it is in the hands not of the few but of the many. But our laws secure equal justice for all in their private disputes, and our public opinion welcomes and honors talent in every branch of achievement, not for any sectional reason but on grounds of excellence alone. . . . Open and friendly in our private intercourse, in our public acts we keep strictly within the control of law. We acknowledge the restraint of reverence; we are obedient to whomsoever is set in authority, and to the laws, more especially to those which offer protection to the oppressed and those unwritten ordinances whose transgression brings shame.

"Yet ours is no workaday city only. No other provides so many recreations for the spirit—contests and sacrifices all the year round, and beauty in our public buildings to cheer the heart and delight the eye day by day. Moreover, the city is so large and powerful that all the wealth of all the world flows in to her, so that our own Attic products seem no more homelike to us than the fruits of the labors of other nations. . . .

"We are lovers of beauty without extravagance, and lovers of wisdom without unmanliness. Wealth to us is not mere material for vainglory but an opportunity for achievement. In doing good we are the exact opposite of the rest of mankind. We secure our friends not by accepting favors but by doing them. And so we are naturally more firm in our attachments; for we are anxious, as creditors, to cement by kind offices our relation toward our friends. If they do not respond with warmth, it is because they feel that their services will not be given spontaneously but only as the repayment of a debt. We are alone among mankind in doing men benefits, not on calculations of self-interest, but in the fearless confidence of freedom.

"Our pioneers have forced a way into every sea and every land, establishing among all mankind, in punishment or beneficence, external memorials of their settlement. . . . Such were the men who lie here and such the city that inspired them. We survivors may pray to be spared their bitter hour, but must disdain to meet the foe with a spirit less triumphant. Let us draw strength not merely from twice-told arguments—how fair and noble a thing it is to show courage in battle—but from the busy spectacle of our great city's life as we have it before us day by day, falling in love with her as we see her, and remembering that all this greatness she owes to men with the fighter's daring, the wise man's understanding of his duty, and the good man's self-discipline in its performance. . . ."

—F.G.

SOCRATES CONDEMNED TO DEATH

WHEN: 399 B.C.

HOW: Socrates was, said the Delphic Oracle, the wisest man in Greece. He was probably more, probably the greatest philosopher of the ancient world. He never wrote a word about his life or ideas. They were all written down for him by his student Plato, who was 2nd only to the master in wisdom, and by Xenophon.

Socrates was born around 469 B.C., the son of a sculptor and a midwife. He served in the Athenian Army and fought in 3 campaigns. A marble bust of him may still be seen in the Louvre. He was repulsively ugly. "But does the outer man represent the man within?" asked W. Somerset Maugham. "The face of a scholar or saint may well mask a vulgar and trivial soul. Socrates with his flattened nose and protruding eyes, his thick lips and unwieldy belly, looked like Silenus, and yet was full of admirable temperance and wisdom."

He was married to sharp-tongued Xanthippe, who constantly bawled him out for neglecting his family. He had little vanity, except to consider losing weight by dancing. He enjoyed drinking. He disliked possessions, liked human company. He disliked travel and work, liked reading and teaching. He went about barefooted, wearing the same shabby robe over and over.

He was a gadfly who taught in the marketplace, although he may have also had a school. He instilled learning in others not by lecturing but by questioning, by artfully cross-examining his followers. Typically: "Tell me, Euthydemus, have you ever gone to Delphi? . . . Did you observe what is written on the temple wall—Know thyself? . . . And did you take no thought of that inscription, or did you attend to it, and try to examine yourself, and ascertain what sort of character you are?"

He was irreligious. He was full of doubts about the physical sciences. He was against democracy as well as tyranny. He believed a nation should be governed by those who had ability and knowledge, not by men chosen in a popularity contest. He preferred his austere civilized living, whatever its shortcomings, to returning to Nature. He believed in logic, which leads to truth, which in turn provides man with moral and ethical systems. When Socrates argued, said Will Durant, "that the good is not good because the gods approve of it, but that the gods approve of it because it is good," he was proposing "a philosophical revolution," insisting goodness was not theological or abstract, but rather earthly and practical.

His influence in his own time and on future ages was profound. His teaching, wrote Durant, with its "emphasis on conscience as above the law, became one of the cardinal tenets of Christianity. Through his pupils, the many suggestions of his thought became the substance of all the major philosophies of the next 2 centuries."

When Athens lost the Peloponnesian War, conservative Athenians sought a scapegoat. They had long resented Socrates for implanting among the young impiety as well as skepticism of traditional institutions and family importance. They determined to rid themselves of him. Since under Athenian law any citizen could accuse a neighbor of a crime and bring him to trial before the Court of Heliasts, 3 of Socrates' enemies determined to do this. His accusers were Meletus, Lycon, and Anytus, whose son was one of Socrates' pupils. The indictment read: "Socrates is guilty of not believing in the gods in which the city believes, and of introducing other new divinities. He is also guilty of corrupting the young. The penalty proposed is death."

Socrates was tried by a jury of 501 male citizens, all over the age of 30. There were no lawyers. The accusers rose, one after the other, and addressed themselves to the jury in time limited by a water clock. Then, Socrates rose in his own defense. "At the age of more than 70 years, I am now for the 1st time appearing before a court of justice, so that I am an utter stranger to the manner of speaking here." As he went on, he said, "If I am corrupting some of the young men, and have corrupted others, surely some of those who are now grown up, and have come to know that when young they received bad advice from me, ought now to appear in court to accuse me and have me punished." M. I. Finley wrote that, on the whole, "Socrates gave a bumbling performance.

He was no orator but an arguer and conversationalist."

At last, the jurors voted. Each one dropped his ballot into an urn. The final vote stood: Guilty—281, Not Guilty—220. Now the jury had to fix the punishment. Meletus repeated his demand for the death penalty. Socrates countered with the suggestion that as a penalty he be voted one of the highest honors in the gift of the state, namely, maintenance at public expense in the Prytaneum for the rest of his life. Infuriated by this mockery, the jury overwhelmingly voted the death penalty, 361–140. Socrates was sentenced to die a month later by drinking a cup of hemlock.

EYEWITNESS REPORT: Among those with Socrates in his last hours—spent inside the Greek prison at Phlius, 60 mi. west of Athens—was Phaedo, a onetime slave freed by Socrates' friends and a student of the master. Phaedo dictated to Plato the scene that followed upon the jailer's approaching Socrates with the cup of hemlock:

"Socrates then said: 'You, my good friend, who are experienced in such matters, shall give me directions as to how I am to proceed.'

" 'You have only to walk about until your legs are heavy, and then lie down, and the poison will act.'

"As he said this, he gave the cup to Socrates, who, in the easiest and gentlest manner, without the least fear or change of color or feature, looking the man straight in the eye, as was his manner, took the cup and said: 'What do you say about making a libation out of this cup to any god? May I, or not?'

" 'We only prepare, Socrates, just so much as we deem enough.'

" 'I understand. Yet I may and must pray to the gods to prosper my journey from this world to the other. May this, then, which is my prayer, be granted to me!'

"Then holding the cup to his lips, quite readily and cheerfully, he drank off the poison.

"Until this point most of us had been able to control our sorrow. But now, when we saw him drinking and saw, too, that he had finished the draught, we could no longer control ourselves. In spite of myself my tears began to flow quickly. . . .

"Socrates alone retained his calm spirit. 'What is this strange outcry?' he asked. 'I sent the women away mainly that they might not offend in this way, for I have been told that a man should die in peace. Be quiet, then, and have patience. . . .'

"He walked about until, as he said, his legs began to fail. Then he lay on his back, according to the directions. The man who had given him the poison now and then looked at his feet and legs. After a while he pressed his foot hard and asked him if he could feel. Socrates replied: 'No.' Then his leg, and so on upward and upward, showing us that Socrates was cold and stiff. Then he said: 'When the poison reaches his heart, that will be the end.'

"Socrates was beginning to grow cold about the groin, when he uncovered his face, for he had covered himself up, and said (they were his last words): 'Crito, I owe a cock to Asclepsius. Will you remember to pay the debt?'

"'The debt shall be paid,' said Crito. 'Is there anything else?'

"There was no answer to this question. But in a minute or 2, a movement was heard. The attendants uncovered him. His mouth was set. Crito closed his eyes and mouth."

—I.W.

THE MINISTRY AND CRUCIFIXION OF JESUS CHRIST

WHEN: 27–30 A.D.

HOW: Revolutionary, religious fanatic, or messiah? Each of these terms has been applied through the centuries to Jesus of Nazareth, a man who, in the short space of 3 years—some authorities make it even less—created such religious turmoil that it cost him his life and, indeed, changed history.

No reliable information can be found on his infancy, adolescence, or early adulthood, although the date 4 B.C. has been accepted as the year of his birth. Even this is confusing, due to calendar rearrangement at a later date.

Jesus wrote nothing during his lifetime that has survived, and we are forced to rely mainly on the Gospels of Matthew, Mark, Luke, and John, all written down some years after the turmoil had subsided, about 65 to 125 A.D. These, unfortunately, cannot be considered strictly biographical in content, since their message became more important than the man to the writers. And there is some evidence that they took their lead from the subject himself, who, in one passage from the Gospel of Mark (8:30), admonishes his disciples to "tell no man of me." This would seem to imply that Jesus was more interested in creating a spiritual image than a physical one.

Like many other Jews in the area, Jesus came under the influence of John the Baptist, a wild-eyed ascetic who roamed the shores of Galilee and the banks of the Jordan River, preaching impending judgment and the need to repent before Judgment Day came.

In the year 28 A.D., Jesus left the quiet life of Nazareth and joined the multitudes that had gathered at the River Jordan to see John the Baptist. Jesus received the baptism of John and when he came out of the water had a profound religious experience in which he heard a voice from Heaven proclaim him to be the Son of God (Mark 1:9–11).

There followed 40 days and 40 nights of wandering and fasting in the desert, during which time Jesus was sorely tempted by Satan and resisted (Luke 4:1–13). When he returned from this ordeal he began to teach in earnest.

Eventually John the Baptist ran afoul of the authorities, namely King Herod, and was imprisoned and killed. Jesus stepped into the void, but where John had preached a future of fire and brimstone, Jesus took a softer line, emphasizing gentleness and a gracious, merciful God. Once or twice, however, he seems to have accepted everlasting hell for nonbelievers, but these examples are rare. He took his teachings out of the wilderness, and into the synagogues and city streets. He had a magnetism that drew people to him, and he taught in parables—simple stories in which it was almost impossible to miss the point.

Jesus differed from John the Baptist in yet another way. While John had lived the life of an ascetic, surviving mostly on dried locusts and honey and wearing animal skins, Jesus was gregarious and readily joined groups on all social levels. Indeed, his 1st miracle was performed at a wedding party, where the host had run out of wine. Jesus said, "Fill the jars with water" (John 2:3–10), and when the water was sampled, the host was astounded to discover that it was wine. Jesus was not adverse to joining rich men in banquets or to seeking out the company of "publicans and sinners," but he was more oriented to the poor and the humble, and he built his plans on them.

The people flocked to him. His message was simple; his delivery, direct. He fast became an unsettling element in society. It must be understood that the atmosphere in Jerusalem was already volatile. The Jews had been prepared for a coming of some sort, but they were not ready for Jesus. The Romans, who were in fact a Government of occupation, were uneasy because of the increasing instability of the populace.

While the Romans were not generally considered to be oppressive occupiers, there were, nevertheless, 2 widely diverse systems in opposition to each other. For the Romans, the State was the primary consideration, while for the Jews, God and the spiritual aspects of life were more important. Moreover, the Jews were fragmented into secular groups of varying degrees of orthodoxy. In short, the scene was chaotic.

Jesus was at 1st looked upon more as a political messiah than a spiritual one. The crowds hailed him as "King of Israel" and thought that he had been sent to overthrow the Romans and make Judea supreme. This view changed, however, when he began to tamper with some of the Judaic law and openly attacked the Pharisees, who were this law's defenders. Then he became more and more convinced that he was indeed the Messiah, and when he openly proclaimed this, his doom was sealed.

As his reputation as a healer and miracle worker spread, the apprehension of his adversaries increased. Turning water into wine was one thing, but raising Lazarus from the dead was something else. It soon became evident to both the Romans and the Sanhedrin, the highest ecclesiastical council of the Jews, that this man was going to have to be dealt with. "If we let him go on thus, everyone will believe in him, and the Romans will come and destroy both our holy places and our nation" (John 11:48). And the high priest Caiaphas went on, "You know nothing at all. You do not understand that it is expedient for you that one man should die for the people, and that the whole nation should not perish" (John 11:49–53). From that time on, the Sanhedrin worked on ways to put an end to Jesus legally.

During February, 30 A.D., notice was given that anyone knowing the whereabouts of Jesus should notify the authorities so that he might be apprehended, but he remained secluded, having decided that the Passover period would be more appropriate for the end that he knew was in store for him. A week before Passover, Jesus began his return to Jerusalem, and on the way, his path led to the summit of the Mount of Olives. He was joined by a multitude of pilgrims who escorted him in a solemn procession, expecting that he would intervene in their behalf politically.

When he reached the city, he spent several days teaching and healing in the temple, but was not arrested immediately because the authorities wanted to avoid a major incident. Instead, they plotted ways to take him quietly. It was at this point that Judas Iscariot offered his services for "30 pieces of silver."

Jesus and his apostles met to celebrate the Seder, or Passover Supper, at the house of a friend in Jerusalem. He was aware that one of the disciples present had betrayed him and openly accused Judas during the course of the evening. He was apparently reconciled to what he knew was to take place, but was anxious that it happen according to his schedule. When the supper was over, he and his followers went outside the city to the Garden of Gethsemane, where they hid in order to avoid immediate arrest. But a detachment of temple guards found them, and when Judas identified Jesus by kissing him on the cheek, Jesus was arrested and taken back to the city for trial.

It was still dark when Jesus was taken before Caiaphas. The Jews were so anxious to get the trial under way that they had already heard witnesses against Jesus, and when Caiaphas asked him, "Are you the Messiah, the Son of God?" Jesus is said to have answered, "I am He." That was just about all they needed. They met again in the morning and delivered a verdict that found Jesus guilty of blasphemy—at that time, a capital crime.

There was a hitch, however. The pronouncement of a capital sentence was not within the authority of the Sanhedrin, since the Roman procurator, Pontius Pilate, was the highest authority in the city. Pilate had the reputation of being a hard man, but he was not convinced that what Jesus had done warranted so severe a sentence, and was not anxious to see the sentence carried out. But the Sanhedrin brought political pressure to bear, and in the end Pilate turned Jesus over to his persecutors, saying, "I find in him no fault at all."

EYEWITNESS REPORT: As was the custom, these state executions were open to the public. Countless numbers of people were on hand for this one, but very little was written as a 1st-person account, so we must again return to the Gospels—this time to John, who was, it has been said, a witness to the spectacle.

"Then Pilate therefore took Jesus, and scourged Him. And the soldiers plaited a crown of thorns, and put it on His head, and arrayed Him in a purple garment; and they came unto Him, and said, Hail, King of the Jews!

"And Pilate went out again, and saith unto them, Behold, I bring Him out to you, that ye may know that I find no crime in Him. Jesus therefore came out, wearing the crown of thorns and the purple robe, and Pilate saith to them, Behold, the man! When therefore the chief priests and officers saw Him, they cried out, saying Crucify Him, crucify Him. . . .

"They took Jesus therefore: and He went out, bearing the Cross Himself, unto the place called the Place of a Skull, which is called in Hebrew, Golgotha: where they crucified Him, and with Him, 2 others, on either side one, and Jesus in the midst. And Pilate wrote a title also, and put it on the Cross. And there was written, JESUS OF NAZARETH, THE KING OF THE JEWS.

"The soldiers therefore when they had crucified Jesus, took His garments and made them in 4 parts, to every soldier a part; and also the coat: now the coat was without seams, woven from the top throughout. They therefore said, one to another, let us not rend it, but cast lots for it, whose it shall be: that the Scripture might be fulfilled, which saith, They parted my garments among them. And then upon my vesture did they cast lots. These things therefore the soldiers did.

"After this, Jesus, knowing that all things are now finished, that the Scripture might be accomplished, saith, I thirst. There was set there a vessel full of vinegar: so they put a sponge full of vinegar upon hyssop, and brought it to His mouth. When Jesus therefore had received the vinegar, He said, 'It is finished': and He bowed His head, and gave up His spirit."

—J.Ca.

THE CRUSADES

WHEN: 1095–1272

HOW: Many devout Christians believed that the world would come to a sudden end just 1,000 years after Christ. The word millennium means a thousand years. It comes from 2 Latin words: *mille* meaning thousand, and *annus*, year. As the end of the world was expected then, the millennium came to mean a sudden change to a better world. There was great misery then in Europe, and this prospect of the "millennium" brought relief to many a weary person. Many sold up their lands and journeyed to Palestine to be present in their Holy Land when the end of the world came.

But the end of the world did not come, and the thousands of Pilgrims who had journeyed to Jerusalem were ill-treated and harassed by the Turks. They returned to Europe full of anger and humiliation, and spread the story of their sufferings in the Holy Land. One famous pilgrim especially, Peter the Hermit, went about, staff in hand, preaching to the people to rescue their Holy City Jerusalem from the Muslims. Indignation and enthusiasm grew in Christendom, and, seeing this, the Pope decided to lead the movement.

About this time had come an appeal from Constantinople for help against the infidel. All Christendom, both Roman and Greek, now seemed to be ranged against the oncoming Turks. In 1095, a great Church council decided to proclaim a holy war against the Muslims for the recovery of the Holy City of Jerusalem. Thus began the Crusades—the fight of Christendom against Islam, of the Cross against the Crescent.

The rising power of the Seljuk Turks frightened Europe, and especially the Constantinople Government, which was directly threatened. Stories of the ill-treatment of Christian pilgrims to Jerusalem and Palestine by the Turks excited the people of Europe and filled them with anger. So a "holy war" was declared, and the Pope and the Church called upon all the Christian peoples of Europe to march to the rescue of the Holy City.

Thus began the Crusades in 1095 A.D., and for more than 150 years the struggle continued between Christianity and Islam. There was almost a continuous state of war, and wave after wave of Christian Crusaders came to fight and mostly to die in the Holy Land. This long warfare yielded no substantial results to the Crusaders. For a short while, Jerusalem was in their hands, but later it went back to the Turks, and there it remained. The chief result of the Crusades was to bring death and misery to millions of Christians and Muslims and again to soak Asia Minor and Palestine with human blood. In Europe the Crusades increased the idea of "Christendom"—the world of Christianity, as opposed to all non-Christians. Europe had a common idea and purpose—the recovery of the Holy Land from the so-called infidel. This common purpose filled people with enthusiasm, and many a man left home and property for the sake of the great cause. Many went with noble motives. Many were attracted by the promise of the Pope that those who went would have their sins forgiven. There were other reasons also for the Crusades. Rome wanted once and for all to become the boss of Constantinople. Remember that the Constantinople Church was different from that of Rome. It called itself the Orthodox Church and it disliked the Roman Church intensely and considered the Pope an upstart. The Pope wanted to put an end to this conceit of Constantinople and to bring it within his fold. Under the cloak of a holy war against the infidel Turk, he wanted to obtain what he had long desired. That is the way of politicians and those who consider themselves statesmen! It is well to remember this conflict between Rome and Constantinople, as it continually crops up during the Crusades.

Another reason for the Crusades was a commercial one. The business people, especially of the growing ports of Venice and Genoa, wanted them because their trade was suffering. The Seljuk Turks had closed many of their trade routes to the East.

The common people, of course, knew nothing about these reasons. No one told them. Politicians usually hide their real reasons and talk pompously of religion and justice and truth and the like. It was so at the time of the Crusades. It is so still. People are taken in then; and still the great majority of people are taken in by the soft talk of politicians.

So large numbers gathered for the Crusades. Among them were good and earnest people; but there were also many who were far from good who were attracted by the hope of plunder. It was a strange collection of pious and religious men and the riffraff of the population, who were capable of every kind of crime. Indeed, these Crusaders, or many of them, going out to serve in what was to them a noble cause, committed the vilest and most disgusting of crimes. Many were so busy with plundering and misbehaving on the way that they never reached anywhere near Palestine. Some took to massacring Jews on the way; some even massacred their brother Christians.

Fed up with their misbehavior, sometimes the peasantry of the Christian countries they passed through rose and attacked them, killing many and driving the others away.

The Crusaders at last managed to reach Palestine under a Norman, Godfrey of Bouillon. Jerusalem fell to them and then the "carnage lasted for a week." There was a terrible massacre. A French eyewitness of this says that "under the portico of the mosque the blood was knee deep and reached the horses' bridles." Godfrey became King of Jerusalem.

Seventy years later, Jerusalem was retaken from the Christians by Saladin, the Sultan of Egypt. This excited the people of Europe again and several Crusades followed. This time the Kings and Emperors of Europe came in person, but they had little success. They quarreled among themselves for precedence and were jealous of each other. It is a dismal story of ghastly and cruel war and petty intrigue and sordid crime. But sometimes the better side of human nature prevailed over this horror, and incidents took place when enemies behaved with courtesy and chivalry to each other. Among the foreign kings in Palestine was Richard of England, Coeur de Lion, the Lion-Hearted, noted for his physical strength and courage. Saladin was also a great fighter, and famous for his chivalry. Even the Crusaders who fought Saladin came to appreciate this chivalry of his. There is a story that once Richard was very ill and was suffering from the heat. Saladin, hearing of this, arranged to send him fresh snow and ice from the mountains. Ice could not be made artificially then by freezing water, as we do now. So natural snow and ice from the mountains had to be taken by swift messengers. . . .

One batch of Crusaders went to Constantinople and took possession of it. They drove out the Greek Emperor of the Eastern Empire and established a Latin kingdom and the Roman Church. Terrible massacres also took place in Constantinople and the city itself was partly burned by the Crusaders. But this Latin kingdom did not last long. The Greeks of the Eastern Empire, weak as they were, came back and drove away the Latins after a little over 50 years. The Eastern Empire of Constantinople continued for another 200 years, till 1453, when the Turks finally put an end to it.

This capture of Constantinople by the Crusaders brings out the desire of the Roman Church and the Pope to extend their influence there. Although the Greeks of this city had, in a moment of panic, appealed to Rome for help against the Turks, they helped the Crusaders little, and disliked them greatly.

The most terrible of these Crusades was what is called the Children's Crusade. Large numbers of young boys, chiefly French and some from Germany, in their excitement left their homes and decided to go to Palestine. Many of them died on the way, many were lost. Most of them reached Marseilles, and there these poor children were tricked and their enthusiasm was taken advantage of by scoundrels. Under the pretext of taking them to the Holy Land, slave traders took them on their ships, carried them to Egypt, and sold them into slavery.

Richard of England on his way back from Palestine was captured by his enemies in eastern Europe and a very heavy ransom had to be paid for his release. A King of France was captured in Palestine itself, and had to be ransomed. An Emperor of the Holy Roman Empire, Frederick Barbarossa, was drowned in a river in Palestine. Meanwhile, as time went on, all the glamour went out of these Crusades. People got fed up with them. Jerusalem remained in Muslim hands, but the Kings and people of Europe were no longer interested in wasting more lives and treasure for its recovery. Since then for nearly 700 years, Jerusalem continued to be under the Muslims. It was only recently, during the Great War in 1918, that it was taken from the Turks by an English general.

—J.N. rep.

EYEWITNESS REPORT: During the 1st Crusade, while the Christians laid siege to the Turkish city of Antioch before proceeding to Jerusalem, a wealthy soldier and nobleman named Count Stephen of Blois (who later deserted, and eventually was killed in battle) wrote the following to his wife, Adele, in a letter dated March 29, 1099:

"We found the city of Antioch very extensive, fortified with the greatest strength and almost impossible to be taken. In addition, more than 5,000 bold Turkish soldiers had entered the city, not counting the Saracens, Publicans, Arabs, Turcopolitans, Syrians, Armenians, and other different races of whom an infinite multitude had gathered together there. In fighting against these enemies of God and of us we have, by God's grace, endured many sufferings and innumerable hardships up to the present time. Many also have already exhausted all their means in this most holy enterprise. Very many of our Franks, indeed, would have met a bodily death from starvation, if the mercy of God and our money had not come to their rescue. Lying before the city of Antioch indeed, throughout the whole winter we suffered for our Lord Christ from excessive cold and enormous torrents of rain. What some say about the impossibility of bearing the heat of the sun in Syria is untrue, for the winter there is very similar to our winter in the West.

"I delight to tell you, dearest, what happened to us during Lent. . . . The city of Antioch is about 5 leagues distant from the sea. For this purpose they sent the excellent Bohemond and Raymond, Count of St. Gilles, to the sea with only 60 horsemen, in order that they might bring mariners to aid in this work. When, however, they were returning to us with these mariners, the Turks collected an army, fell suddenly upon our 2 leaders and forced them to a perilous flight. In that unexpected flight we lost more than 500 of our foot-soldiers—to the glory of God. Of our horsemen, however, we lost only 2, for certain. Our men, full of fury at these most evil tidings, prepared to die for Christ and, deeply grieved for their brethren, rushed upon the wicked Turks. They, enemies of God and us, hastily fled before us and attempted to enter the city. But by God's grace the affair turned out very differently; for, when they tried to cross a bridge built over the great river Moscholum, we followed them as closely as possible, killed many before they reached the bridge, forced many into the river, all of whom were killed, and we also slew many upon the bridge and very many at the narrow entrance to the gate. I am telling you the truth, my beloved, and you may be assured that in this battle we killed 30 emirs, that is, princes, and 300 other Turkish nobles, not counting the remaining Turks and pagans. Indeed the number of Turks and Saracens killed is reckoned at 1,230, but of ours we did not lose a single man."

AMERICA GETS ITS NAME

WHEN: 1507
HOW: Since Christopher Columbus was the most publicized of the several candidates believed to have discovered the New World, it would seem logical for the land to be called Columbiana. Instead, because of an error made by a mapmaker, and because Columbus refused to believe he had found an unknown continent, the New World was named America.

Columbus refused to take credit for discovery of a new continent. To the day of his death, in 1506, he persisted in the belief that he had landed on an unexplored eastern part of Asia. Meanwhile, Amerigo Vespucci—he later took the Latin name Americus Vespucius—a Florentine merchant and astronomer turned adventurer and navigator, made 4 voyages to the western hemisphere, the 1st a private Spanish expedition in 1497, the others in 1499, 1500, and 1503. Vespucci's voyages were to the land now designated as South America, and he was the 1st to perceive that this was a land unknown to Europeans and he therefore suggested it be called Mundus Novus—New World.

Vespucci never once suggested the New World be named for him. That came about through an unusual chain of circumstances. While abroad, Vespucci wrote numerous letters about what he saw to friends. Apparently, an unsavory author got hold of some of these letters, rewrote and sensationalized them, and published them as Four Voyages, attributing them to Vespucci. The published letters have since been proved to be forgeries. However, 2 authentic letters written by Vespucci—one to his patron, the notorious Italian nobleman Lorenzo de' Medici, the other to an old schoolmate, Piero Sodorini—were located by scholars in Florence during the 1700s.

But it was one of the counterfeit letters that inspired the baptizing of the New World. This letter was published by the Academy of the Vosges in Lorraine during April, 1507. It was read by a young German cartographer, Professor Martin Waldseemüller, who was working at the academy with 4 other scholars, preparing an updated version of Ptolemy's Geography. Waldseemüller, impressed by the so-called Vespucci letter describing the New World, included it in his book, Cosmographiae introductio. In his Latin text, Waldseemüller also wrote the following: "But now, since these parts have been more extensively explored, and another 4th part has been discovered by Americus Vespucius (as will appear from what follows); I see no reason why it should not be called Amerigo, after Americus, the discoverer, or indeed America, since both Europe and Asia have a feminine form of name from the names of women." The map of the New World was published separately, and what is now Brazil was then boldly named "America."

In later writings and maps, more aware of the role Columbus played, Waldseemüller dropped "America" and renamed it "the Land Unknown," crediting Columbus with its discovery. By then his book had gone into many editions. His 1st suggestion that the new land be named after Amerigo or Americus had caught on, and soon Mercator had made it official by calling the entire western hemisphere "America." But Vespucci had died in Seville in 1512, at the age of 61, unaware of his accidental immortality.

In the years since, Vespucci has been accused of fraud and of usurping credit from Columbus. In fact, essayist Ralph Waldo Emerson wrote: "Strange that broad America must wear the name of a thief! Amerigo Vespucci, the pickle-dealer at Seville, who went out in 1499, a subaltern with Hojeda, and whose highest naval rank was boatswain's mate, in an expedition that never sailed, managed in this lying world to supplant Columbus, and baptize half the earth with his own dishonest name."

But Vespucci did sail on his 1499 expedition, made no effort to give half the earth his name, and had nothing but praise and friendship for Columbus, who in turn considered him "a very worthy man."

EYEWITNESS REPORT: Here is what Vespucci saw of the New World named after him, as written in an authentic letter to Lorenzo de' Medici in 1502: "We sailed on the wind within a half a point of southwest [of Cape Verde], so that in 64 days we arrived at a new land which, for many reasons that are enumerated in what follows, we observed to be a continent. . . . We found the whole land inhabited by people entirely naked. . . . For 27 days I ate and slept among them, and what I learned about them is as follows:

"Having no laws and no religious faith, they live according to nature. They understand nothing of the immortality of the soul. There is no possession of private property among them, for everything is in common. They have no boundaries of kingdom or province. They have no king, nor do they obey anyone. Each one is his own master. There is no administration of justice, which is unnecessary to them, because in their code no one rules. They live in communal dwellings, built in the fashion of very large cabins. . . . They sleep in nets woven out of cotton, going to bed in mid-air with no other coverture. They eat squatting upon the ground. Their food is very good; an endless quantity of fish; a great abundance of sour cherries, shrimps, oysters, lobsters, crabs, and many other products of the sea. The meat which they eat most usually is what one may call human flesh à la mode. When they can get it, they eat other meat . . . the country is a very thick jungle full of ferocious wild beasts. . . .

"Their marriages are not with one woman only, but they mate with whom they desire and without much ceremony. I know a man who had 10 women. . . . They are also a warlike people . . . they use bows and arrows, darts, and stones. They use no shields for the body, but go into battle naked. . . .

"That which makes me more astonished at their wars and cruelty was that I could not understand from them why they made war upon each other, considering that they held no private property or sovereignty of empire and kingdoms and did not know any such thing as lust for possession, that is, pillaging or a desire to rule, which appear to me to be the causes of wars and of every disorderly act."

—I.W.

LUTHER POSTS 95 THESES, PROTESTANTISM

WHEN: October 31, 1517
HOW: In itself, his posting of the theses meant little. After all, the castle church door

in Wittenberg served as a kind of bulletin board, and all he meant to do was to call for a debate on a matter of some theological importance. "Those who cannot be present and discuss the subject orally are asked to do so by letter," Martin Luther appended to his 95 theses. Indeed, the whole matter seemed rather academic, a dispute within the Roman Catholic family that would be resolved in the traditional manner: The Church hierarchy would either ignore Luther or execute him as a heretic. There were precedents for either course of action, and certainly the behavior of some obscure Augustinian monk in Germany was not about to ruffle the equanimity of the mighty Leo X, Pope of the Roman Catholic Church.

For, despite challenges from such individuals as John Wycliffe and John Huss, and from such diverse political and intellectual trends as nationalism and neoclassicism, the Roman Catholic Church entered the 16th century as a "catholic" church—the single most powerful unifying force in Western culture. There can be no doubt, however, that Europe was a fertile seedbed for revolt; in addition to the challenges to Church orthodoxy posed by the religious dissenters, there was tremendous social and economic unrest as the feudal order decayed and a capitalist and urbanized society began to replace it. Luther would tap these feelings of discontent—quite unknowingly, a great portion of the time—in launching what the world would later call the Reformation.

Martin Luther was, in fact, a reformer; he was not a revolutionary. He was an insider, a member of the establishment, who for personal and psychological reasons—as well as out of concern for his fellow Christians—could not remain silent in the face of what he considered to be gross impiety on the part of the Roman Catholic Church. It was the meshing of Luther's own theological position with the Church's inability to curb its worst practices that created the schism in Christian ranks between Protestant and Catholic.

Luther abandoned his intention of pursuing a legal career and turned instead to the Church. He became an Augustinian monk, and in 1512 was appointed a professor of biblical studies at the University of Wittenberg. Driven by a profound fear of his own damnation and by a deep concern for the fate of his parishioners (he was also parish priest for the town of Wittenberg), Luther immersed himself in the Scriptures. He had to find exactly what it was that God demanded in return for His saving grace. Did He expect people never to sin? That, of course, had not been possible since Adam fell from Eden. No loving God could expect the impossible from corrupt humanity.

Was God satisfied with the confessions, good

works, and other acts of atonement prescribed by the Catholic Church? As a novice at the Augustinian monastery in Erfurt, Luther had exasperated his confessor, reciting the most trivial wrongdoings in sessions that could last up to 6 hours. Finally, Luther became convinced that no person could remember all his sins, much less atone for them via good works and confession. The problem, therefore, was to reconcile the notion of a loving God with the concept of divine justice. How was a human being—unable to escape his sinful nature and unable to alter his inherent corruption—to win God's mercy and salvation?

"The just shall live by faith." These words from St. Paul's Epistle to the Romans were quite literally the answer to Martin Luther's prayers. "All at once I began to understand the justice of God as that by which the just live by the gift of God, which is faith: that passive righteousness with which the merciful God endures us in the form of faith, thus justifying, rendering us just. . . . At this I experienced such relief and easement, as if I were reborn and had entered through open gates into paradise itself."

God saves not those who do good works but those who believe in Him and in His saving grace. That is all He expects from corrupt humanity. Therefore, the Roman Catholic Church's emphasis on holy relics, contributions, and all sorts of other vehicles to assure one's salvation was not only useless, but also deceitful in that it prevented people from recognizing what God truly required of them for salvation.

Thus, the stage was set for revolt when the Dominican friar Tetzel launched the great indulgence campaign throughout Germany to raise money for the rebuilding of St. Peter's basilica in Rome. Tetzel promised the indulgence purchaser just about anything and everything, but the main thrust of his pitch was that a contribution to this holy cause could free souls from purgatory and win forgiveness for transgressions committed by the indulgence buyer.

Luther's 95 theses were merely his reasons for opposing the overblown claims for indulgences, claims which could not be reconciled to his belief that man is saved by faith alone. Posting his theses on the castle church door, Luther never expected the explosion that soon followed. To his amazement, he was flooded with letters of praise from all over Europe where the theses had been printed and disseminated; in Germany, Luther became something of a folk hero. He had intended his theses only as a theological challenge, but they had become a revolutionary document. His call for a debate turned on a question of religious orthodoxy turned overnight into a movement destined to take the meaning of the word "catholic" out of the Roman Church.

Emboldened by his support from the German people and nobility, Luther refused to recant. Three years after posting his theses, he burned—in public—the codex of the canon law, thereby excommunicating the Church before he himself was excommunicated. Pope Leo, no longer willing to consider this contrary monk as merely a nuisance, directed the Holy Roman Emperor Charles V to execute the heretic. The Emperor ordered Luther to appear at the Diet of Worms in 1521, thereby creating one of the truly dramatic moments in the history of Western civilization.

"I neither can nor will recant anything, since it is neither right nor safe to act against conscience. Here I take my stand. I cannot do otherwise. So help me God." With that, Martin Luther left the assembly hall to face arrest and probable execution. Instead, however, he was captured by knights sympathetic to the new theology and anxious to diminish both the power of the Emperor and the taxes of the Church. During his year in hiding at a castle in Wartburg, Luther began his translation of the Bible into German and the codification of his beliefs into what would become the Lutheran religion.

When he emerged from his protective custody, Luther was the acknowledged leader of the Reformation. The protester was no longer an insider, but rather the spiritual head of a new Church that recognized only 2 sacraments: baptism and communion. He married, raised 6 children, and tried to direct the struggling Protestant movement. At Luther's death in 1546, however, the outcome of what had started with his 95 theses was still very much in doubt.

EYEWITNESS REPORT: The following is a letter written by Martin Luther and addressed to Pope Leo X. It is dated September 6, 1520.

"Among those monstrous evils of this age with which I have now for 3 years been waging war, I am sometimes compelled to look to you and to call you to mind, most blessed Father Leo. . . . I find that blame is cast upon me, and that . . . in my rashness I am judged to have spared not even your person.

"Now, to confess the truth openly, I am conscious that, whenever I have had to mention your person, I have said nothing of you but what was honorable and good. . . . I have indeed inveighed sharply against impious doctrines, and I have not been slack to censure my adversaries on account, not of their bad morals, but of their impiety. . . . Accursed is the man who does the work of the Lord deceitfully. . . .

"Your see, however, which is called the Court of Rome, and which neither you nor any

man can deny to be more corrupt than any
Babylon or Sodom, and quite, as I believe, of a
lost, desperate, and hopeless impiety, this I
have verily abominated, and have felt indignant that the people of Christ should be
cheated under your name and the pretext of
the Church of Rome; and so I have resisted,
and will resist, as long as the spirit of faith
shall live in me. . . . For many years now,
nothing else has overflowed from Rome into
the world—as you are not ignorant—than the
laying waste of goods, of bodies, and of souls,
and the worst examples of all the worst things.
These things are clearer than light to all men;
and the Church of Rome, formerly the most
holy of all Churches, has become the most
lawless den of thieves, the most shameless of
all brothels, the very kingdom of sin, death,
and hell; so that not even antichrist, if he were
to come, could devise any addition to its
wickedness. . . .

"Under the influence of these feelings, I
have always grieved that you, most excellent
Leo, who were worthy of a better age, have
been made pontiff in this. For the Roman
Court is not worthy of you and those like you,
but of Satan himself, who in truth is more the
ruler in that Babylon than you are. . . .

"Is it not true that there is nothing under
the vast heavens more corrupt, more pestilential, more hateful, than the Court of Rome?
She incomparably surpasses the impiety of the
Turks, so that in very truth she, who was formerly the gate of heaven, is now a sort of open
mouth of hell, and such a mouth as, under the
urgent wrath of God, cannot be blocked up;
one course alone being left to us wretched
men: to call back and save some few, if we
can, from that Roman gulf.

"Behold Leo, my father, with what purpose
and on what principle it is that I have stormed
against that seat of pestilence. I am so far from
having felt any rage against your person that I
even hoped to gain favor with you and to aid
you in your welfare by striking actively and
vigorously at that your prison, nay your hell.
For whatever the efforts of all minds can con-
trive against the confusion of that impious
Court will be advantageous to you and to your
welfare, and to many others with you. Those
who do harm to her are doing your office;
those who in every way abhor her are glorifying
Christ; in short, those are Christians who are
not Romans."

—J.L.K.

PUBLICATION OF THE KING JAMES VERSION OF THE BIBLE

WHEN: 1611
HOW: The King James Version of the Bible
was called by Thomas Babington Macaulay "a

book which if everything else in our language
should perish, would alone suffice to show the
whole extent of its beauty and power."

King James himself, however, had very little
to do with the translation that bears his name.

Translation of the Bible into English had
been going on since the 14th century. The 1st
was completed in 1380 and named for John
Wycliffe. It was taken from the Vulgate, itself a
Latin translation of the Hebrew and Greek
sources. William Tyndale made a translation
of the New Testament, based on Latin, Greek,
and German versions, in 1525. Miles Coverdale brought out the 1st complete English
Bible in 1535–1536, based largely on Tyndale. The Great Bible of 1539–1541 was
Coverdale's revision of his earlier translation.
The Geneva Bible of 1560 had a Calvinist
leaning. The Bishops' Bible of 1568 was basically a revision of the Great Bible. And English Catholics relied on the Rheims-Douay
Bible of 1582 (N.T.) and 1610 (O.T.).

The very notion of translating the Bible out
of its original tongues was a controversial one.
Tyndale himself had to flee England because
of his work and was burned to death in Belgium in 1536. Major doctrinal questions were
involved: Should average citizens have the
right to read the Bible in their own language
in their homes, or should the Bible be read
only in the original by churchmen? Was the
Bible a Catholic document or a Protestant
one? What *was* the Word of God?

These great religious questions still raged
when James VI of Scotland ascended the English throne in 1603, upon the death of Queen
Elizabeth. James had ruled in Scotland for 36
years, having been put on that throne at the
age of one, upon the abdication of his mother,
Mary, Queen of Scots. As a boy he had been
scholarly, and had actually translated some
Psalms. As a man he was a strong ruler, but
given to craft and trickery. His personal life,
however, was held in some doubt. When he assumed the English throne at the age of 37, it
was commonly said that King Elizabeth had
been succeeded by Queen James.

Shortly after Elizabeth's death on March 24,
1603, James was accepted as the new monarch
by custom, although he had not yet been
confirmed by Parliament. England, and particularly London, was in the grips of the plague,
and, allegedly to avoid the Black Death, James
and his retinue began a series of lengthy—and
expensive—"progresses" around his new realm.
While James indulged himself in feasts, hunting, and watching theatrical performances,
major questions of state went unresolved. Perhaps because he would have to meet with the
Parliament in a few months to ask for more
money, and so (in the view of Christopher Anderson) wanted at least to show his good inten-

tions, James stopped at Hampton Court in early 1604 "for the hearing, and for the determining, [of] things pretending to be amiss in the Church."

At that conference, held January 14, 16, and 18, the suggestion was made by the Puritan scholar from Oxford, John Rainolds, that another English translation of the Bible ought to be made. Opposition was immediately voiced by the Bishop of London, Richard Bancroft, who complained, "If every man's humor were followed, there would be no end of translating."

Nevertheless, James liked the idea. Geddes MacGregor thinks that James may have seen a new English translation as his own personal monument, much as Versailles was the monument of Louis XIV. Perhaps the production of a new Bible translation would act as a safety valve for seething religious turmoil. And James was well known to be in disapproval of the Geneva Bible, which, in a marginal note, questioned the divine right of Kings.

According to an account written by the King's chaplain Patrick Galloway (and corrected in the King's own handwriting), James then ordered "that a translation be made of the whole Bible, *as consonant as can be to the original Hebrew and Greek*; and this be set and printed, *without marginal notes*, and only [exclusively] to be used in all Churches of England in time of divine service."

On July 22, 1604, King James and Bishop Bancroft worked out a set of 14 instructions to the translators, which were circulated among them 9 days later, on July 31. The instructions were designed to ensure that, despite the variety of views among the translators, the forthcoming work would be a Protestant Bible; that it would be largely a revision of the popular Bishops' Bible; that Bible names be "retained as near as may be" to the original; and that when the translators had completed work on their assigned sections, they should "all meet together, confer what they have done, and agree for their part what shall stand." This last instruction is the reason why the King James Version is often referred to as the most successful work ever done by a committee.

James appointed 54 scholars to perform the task, although only 47 actually worked on it. The men were divided into 6 companies, 2 of which were to meet at Oxford, 2 at Cambridge, and 2 at Westminster. The translators were a diverse group. It included professors, preachers, linguists, Bible scholars. One was expert in 15 languages, including Arabic, Persian, and Aramaic. Another had tutored Queen Elizabeth in Greek. Yet another had been able to read the Bible in Hebrew at the age of 6. One was a refugee from Belgium. Another, a drunkard. One, dying from tuberculosis, translated

on his deathbed. One more, a widower who died during the project, left behind 11 destitute children.

The years between 1604 and 1607 were apparently spent by the scholars in private study of their assigned sections. From 1607 to 1609 they worked together at their respective places. Then a group of 12 (2 from each of the 6 companies) met at the Stationers' Hall in London to smooth out the translation, before Dr. Miles Smith, a butcher's son who had graduated from Oxford at 19, did the final rewrite with Bishop Thomas Bilson overseeing him. The King's Printer, Robert Barker, who had exclusive rights to the sale of the work, then spent nearly 1½ years printing the new translation.

"THE HOLY BIBLE, Conteyning the Old Testament and the New" bears a publication date of 1611, appearing just 5 years before Shakespeare's death. Because the work was regarded as a revision of the Bishops' Bible, it was not licensed at the Stationers' Company (as all new books were required to be). For this reason no more specific publication date is available than that printed on the title page.

The translation is dedicated to King James, which accounts for its popular title. It is also often referred to as the Authorized Version of the Bible, although there is no available proof that it ever was authorized by either King James or Parliament (the specific evidence, beyond the fact that James endorsed the idea of the translation, may have been destroyed with other records in a 17th-century fire).

Who paid for the work on the King James Version of the Bible? Not King James. On July 31, 1604, he sent a message to all English churchmen, saying that he was unable to pay the translators, and asking that any available Church positions be offered to them. As far as is known, none ever was.

In 1651 a London lawyer, William Ball, indicated for apparently the 1st time that indeed Robert Barker, the King's Printer, had paid £3,500 to the translators. Modern scholars accept this figure, although there is some disagreement as to whether Barker began paying this money in 1607 to all the translators, or in 1609 and only to the 12 revisers plus Smith and Bilson.

It is thought that perhaps as many as 20,000 copies of the 1,500-page work were printed, each of which sold for about 30 shillings. The King James Version of 1611 is often jocularly referred to as the "He" or "She" Bible, because of the misprinting of the word "she" in the Book of Ruth.

EYEWITNESS REPORT: In this letter, dated July 22, 1604, King James wrote to Bishop Bancroft, and asked him to write to all of England's churchmen, requesting that they make paying positions available to the otherwise financially unrewarded translators. In a part of the letter not reprinted here, James also asked that the churchmen be on the lookout for people who were expert in foreign languages, in case their aid might eventually be needed.

"Right trusty and well beloved, we greet you well. Whereas we have appointed certain learned men, to the number of 4 and 50, for the translating of the Bible, and that in this number, divers of them have either no ecclesiastical preferment at all, or else so very small, as the same is far unmeet for men of their deserts, and yet we in ourself in any convenient time cannot well remedy it, therefore we do hereby require you, that presently you write in our name as well to the archbishop of York, as to the rest of the bishops of the province of Cant.[erbury] signifying unto them, that we do will, and straitly charge every one of them . . . that (all excuses set apart) when any prebend or parsonage . . . shall next upon any occasion happen to be void . . . we may commend for the same some such of the learned men, as we shall think fit to be preferred unto it. . . . Given unto our signet at our palace of West.[minster] the 2 and 20th of July, in the 2nd year of our reign of England, France, and Ireland, and of Scotland xxxvii."

—R.Me.

Marx and Engels Write the *Communist Manifesto*

WHEN: 1848

HOW: In the 1840s, all Europe seemed to be in a state of unrest. England's trade unions were strong and dissatisfied. German workers were turning into socialist activists. The Parisian working class was angry and restless. It was a world waiting for Karl Marx.

Descended on both sides from a long line of rabbis, Karl Marx was the son of a successful attorney. By 1842 he was already intensely political and had established in Cologne, Germany, a magazine called *Neue Rheinische Zeitung*, for which he wrote brilliant articles. One of these articles encouraged citizens to resist, with arms, tax collections by the Government. Unhappy about this, the Government arrested and tried him. His speech in his own defense was so effective that he was acquitted, and he went on to write more articles against the Government in his magazine, which was finally suppressed. Marx issued a last edition in red ink and went to Paris.

Paris was thick with intellectuals—social theorists, especially—and Marx met most of them, men like the poet Heinrich Heine and the socialist Pierre Joseph Proudhon. Marx read again the histories of France, Germany,

and the U.S., and he studied the works of Machiavelli, Rousseau, Montesquieu, and Ricardo. However, it was Hegel that influenced him most, and Marx applied to his own ideas the Hegelian dialectic that everything contains the germ of change from which emerges thesis and antithesis, which in turn create synthesis. Later, Marx's son-in-law said of him, "He never saw a thing-by-itself, out of touch with its setting; but contemplated it as part of a complicated and mobile world of things. His aim was to expand all the life of this world of things in its manifold and incessantly varying action and reaction." Marx did not buy all of Hegel's ideas. He particularly didn't believe in the Hegelian Absolute, which, according to Hegel, directed the progress of man. Marx thought that economics, not a spiritual Absolute, caused human movements.

In 1844, Marx met Friedrich Engels, who was to become his lifelong disciple. Engels, the son of a German cotton manufacturer, was an economics student making a study of the British working class. In his research, he ran across an article by Marx and immediately decided to get in touch with him. The 2 hit it off. The man Engels met was an unusual-looking character, who was later described by Otto Ruhle: "A thick crop of black hair, a huge round beard . . . and an overcoat buttoned awry; yet he appeared like one endowed with the right . . . to command respect. . . . His movements were awkward, yet bold and self-confident."

Marx had belonged for some time to the League of the Just, a group of German refugees who had faced political persecution. At the 1st congress of this group, held in London in 1847, Marx and Engels got partial control, and it became the International Communist League. Needless to say, it had a Marxist viewpoint. In order to clarify what this "Marxist viewpoint" was, Marx and Engels wrote a document that was to influence millions all over the world—the *Communist Manifesto*. It was published in 1848 in London as the *Manifest der Kommunistischen Partei*, a pamphlet of only 40 pages. In it, Marx expounded his ideas, beginning with a brilliant appraisal of socioeconomic conditions in Europe from the time of ancient slave civilizations. It is all the same, he said—there is always a ruling class and a subject class, the haves and have-nots, the upper and lower crust. Their names may change, but always it seems that one group owns the means of production and the other does the work. He predicted that when the forces of production cannot be utilized fully because of capitalistic private ownership, then the working classes will come to power. In the *Manifesto*, Marx and Engels called on the working classes to take such power, and they advocated "forcible overthrow of all existing social conditions." Marx softened this 25 years later by saying that England and the U.S. were countries "in which the workers may hope to secure their ends by peaceful means."

The *Manifesto* was not immediately successful. (However, by 1964, more than 1,000 editions in more than 100 languages had appeared; more than 14 million copies had been sold.) In that same year, 1848, revolution broke out in Paris, then in Germany. People were too busy manning the barricades to read inflammatory literature. It looked as though Marx's revolution was happening. Then gold was discovered in California, and the world got richer. With better economic conditions, uprisings stopped. Marx thought it was all over. Thrown out of Paris, Marx went to London with his wife, the daughter of an aristocrat, and his children. He lived there the rest of his life in near poverty. If it had not been for Engels, who continually sent him money, he might have starved to death. In 1851, he got work writing articles for the *New York Tribune*, but it didn't pay much, and when the Civil War broke out, the job ended. Marx spent most of his time in the reading room of the British Museum, a drafty, gloomy place, where he read voraciously.

In 1864 Marx became influential in the International Workingmen's Association, which was founded in London. His ideas gradually became central to the organization, but were challenged by Bakunin, the revolutionary anarchist. Split by conflicting ideas, the historical group collapsed, to rise again later as the 2nd International. By January, 1867, Marx finished writing *Das Kapital*, his masterwork, in which he defined capitalism as the discrepancy between the value that labor produces and the value it gets back in wages. It was so difficult to read that even the Russian censor passed it, although he thought it might be subversive, saying, "It is unlikely to find many readers among the general public." Translated into a dozen languages, it has become a bible for socialists everywhere. Marx didn't make much money from it. He said to his son-in-law, "*Kapital* will not even pay for the cigars I smoked writing it."

If you read about Marx, you will find 2 people—an arrogant, sarcastic, dogmatic demagogue (a reputation he gained by crushing those who disagreed with him), and a kindly, loving, honest family man. Perhaps both estimates of him are somewhat true. He *was* romantic and loving with his family. On Sundays, they went on long hikes, sometimes stopping for cheese, bread, and ginger beer at an inn somewhere, reading the papers on the grass. Marx would make up stories about a character named Hans Rockle, a happy-go-lucky magician who was a lot like Marx himself. Sometimes he would quote Dante or Shakespeare or sing German folk songs. Heine called Marx "the tenderest, gentlest man I have ever known." It was said that the children on the London streets named him "Daddy Marx." He was fond of playing out sea battles in a tub of water, setting whole fleets of paper ships on fire, to amuse children. Though his general health was good, he, like Job, was plagued with boils. When writing *Das Kapital*, he wrote Engels, "to finish I must at least be able to *sit down*. I hope the bourgeoisie will remember my carbuncles."

And he was poor. On Easter, 1852, one of his children died, and he had no money for a coffin. His wife wrote, "A French refugee gave me £2. With this sum I was able to buy the coffin in which my poor Francisca now lies at peace. She had no cradle when she came into the world and for a long time it was difficult to find a box for her last resting place." In 1881, his beloved wife, with whom he was always romantically in love, died. Engels remarked, "Marx is dead, too." Two years later, he was. At the funeral, Engels said, "Before all else, Marx was a revolutionist. Few men ever fought with such passion." And it was true, in spite of the fact that Marx, who fought for the worker, had never worked physically a day in his life, and in spite of the fact that, though he was a revolutionist, he had never manned a barricade.

EYEWITNESS REPORT: From the *Communist Manifesto*: "A spectre is haunting Europe—the spectre of communism. All the powers of old Europe have entered into a holy alliance to exorcise this spectre: Pope and Czar, Metternich and Guizot, French Radicals and German police-spies.

"Where is the party in opposition that has not been decried as communistic by its opponents in power? Where is the opposition that has not hurled back the branding reproach of communism, against the more advanced opposition parties, as well as against its reactionary adversaries?

"Two things result from this fact:

"I. Communism is already acknowledged by all European powers to be itself a power.

"II. It is high time that Communists should openly, in the face of the whole world, publish their views, their aims, their tendencies, and meet this nursery tale of the spectre of communism with a manifesto of the party itself. . . .

"The history of all hitherto existing society is the history of class struggles.

"Freeman and slave, patrician and plebian, lord and serf, guild-master and journeyman, in a word, oppressor and oppressed, stood in constant opposition to one another, carried on an uninterrupted, now hidden now open fight, a fight that each time ended, either in a revolutionary reconstitution of society at large, or in the common ruin of the contending classes. . . .

"The Communists disdain to conceal their views and aims. They openly declare that their ends can be attained only by the forcible overthrow of all existing social conditions. Let the ruling classes tremble at a Communist revolution. The proletarians have nothing to lose but their chains. They have a world to win. 'Working men of all countries, unite.' "

—A.E.

DARWIN PUBLISHES HIS *Origin of Species*

WHEN: 1859

HOW: Charles Darwin's father, a 350-lb. jolly gentleman, said of his son that he "cared for nothing but shooting, dogs, and rat-catching." Like many famous men, Charles as a child showed little promise of future greatness. He was lazy, and he was a poor student.

However, he did like to collect things—bugs, shells, coins, and so on. His father's comment on this was that Charles would "mess up the house with his everlasting rubbish."

When Charles was 16, his father decided to make a doctor out of him and sent him off to Edinburgh University. Charles could not bear to watch operations, but he stayed in Edinburgh for 2 years anyway because he was afraid to admit this to his father. When the truth came out, he was sent to Cambridge to become a parson. He later said of his college career, "During the 3 years I spent at Cambridge, my time was wasted as far as the academic studies were concerned." He fell into bad company, "including some dissipated, low-minded young men. I know I ought to feel ashamed of days and evenings thus spent."

Perhaps Charles would have become a rather incompetent preacher with a mild interest in nature, had not one of his teachers, Professor J. S. Barlow, recommended him for an unpaid job on HMS *Beagle*, which was bound for South America for a 2-year scientific expedition. (It lasted 5 years.)

Even then, he almost didn't get to go. His father thought it would contribute little to his work as a preacher, and the ship's captain didn't like the shape of Charles's snub nose, saying that it indicated the young man lacked energy and determination. Eventually, Charles obtained the consent of both, and he was off.

During the voyage on the *Beagle*, Charles made the observations that later led him to formulate his theory of natural selection. He kept a diary in which he noted his wonder at "the rondure of the world and the mysteries of its teeming life"—as well as detailed notes on the fossils, plants, and animals that he collected. Every place the *Beagle* stopped, he went exploring, then took what he had found back to his laboratory, where he put the data together.

The sailors called him "the Flycatcher." The captain, even though he still disliked Darwin, named places after him, including the Darwin Mountains and Darwin Sound in Tierra del Fuego.

All along, Darwin was noticing patterns. In the Galápagos Islands, there were 14 different species of finchlike birds with different-sized bills. There was a resemblance, too, between the species on the South American mainland and this island. And mice on one slope of the Andes were different from those on the other. He later wrote, "It was evident that such facts as these, as well as many others, could only be explained on the supposition that species gradually become modified, and the subject haunted me."

After the *Beagle* returned to England, Darwin got his notes into shape for publication as the *Journal of Researches into the Natural History and Geology of the Countries Visited During the Voyage of HMS Beagle Around the World*. The book gained Darwin immediate status among men of science, and his father gave approval to his career as a naturalist.

In 1837, he started his 1st notebook, and by the end of 1838, he had formulated his theory of natural selection, and only had to prove it. In brief, his theory said:

1. Animals reproduce in much greater numbers than can be supported by the environment.

2. Great numbers, those that are least fit, die in the struggle for existence. The fittest are naturally selected to survive. (Later, Herbert Spencer named the process "survival of the fittest.")

3. Variations in structure are inherited. He believed that the environment could modify the individual organism and that the modification would reach the germ plasm and be passed on to the next generation.

Other scientists before him had come close to his theory, especially Lamarck, who missed the concept of natural selection since he was inclined to jump to conclusions. (He wrongly believed that the horns of bulls developed from their habit of butting their heads.)

A meticulous researcher, Darwin talked to breeders of domestic animals to find out how they produced animals with desired characteristics. He also collected piles of other data to support his theory.

In 1842, Darwin wrote a short paper on the theory of natural selection—35 penciled sheets. Two years later, he expanded this to 230 pages, which he put in an envelope and gave to his wife to keep for publication in the event that he should die. He said, "At last gleams of light have come and I am almost convinced (contrary to the opinion I started with) that the Species are not (it is like confessing a murder) immutable."

He then narrowed his research down to one species—the barnacle.

In 1858, he received a disturbing letter from a friend, Alfred Russel Wallace, who lived in the Malay archipelago. With the letter was a manuscript, "On the Tendencies of Varieties to Part Indefinitely from the Original Type." It was an explanation of the theory of natural selection, partly derived from material in Darwin's *Journal*, and Wallace wanted Darwin to look it over and present it to other scientists. Darwin didn't know what to do. He said, "I would far rather burn my whole book than that Wallace or any other man should think that I behaved in a paltry spirit."

An admirable compromise was reached. A short abstract of Darwin's theory was read along with Wallace's manuscript at a meeting of the Linnaean Society. Wallace later said, "The one great result which I claim for my paper of 1858 is that it compelled Darwin to write and publish his *Origin of Species* without further delay."

By November, 1859, Darwin's book—*On the Origin of Species, by Means of Natural Selection, or the Preservation of Favored Races in the Struggle for Life*—was published. The publisher had been wary of the manuscript and had suggested that Darwin rewrite it, confining it to pigeons, because "everybody is interested in pigeons." (Naturally, Darwin had said No.) On the 1st day of publication, the entire print run of 1,250 copies sold out at 15 shillings each. The book quickly became a great— if controversial—classic in scientific literature.

Many scientists opposed it. Herschel, the astronomer, called the theory the "law of higgledy-piggledy." Sedgwick, a geologist, wrote to Darwin, "I have read your book with more pain than pleasure. Parts of it I laughed at until my sides were almost sore; other parts I read with absolute sorrow."

However, there were many scientists who were for Darwin. One was Thomas Huxley, who said he was "sharpening his claws and beak in readiness" and was "prepared to go to the stake" to defend Darwin. He also called himself "Darwin's bulldog."

The Church was against the book. It contradicted the 1st chapter of Genesis, and, by implication, said that man had an ancestor in common with the ape, which people immediately misinterpreted to mean that man was descended from the monkeys. The theory soon became known as Darwin's "monkey theory."

Samuel Wilberforce, Bishop of Oxford, called *Origin of Species* an "utterly rotten fabric of guess and speculation." A meeting was held in a library—so crowded with people that some were sitting on the window ledges— where Wilberforce spoke against the theory, using information from Richard Owens, Superintendent of Natural History at the British Museum. Wilberforce, nicknamed "Soapy Sam," made an eloquent speech. Then he turned to Huxley, who had come to the meeting, and said, "Is it on your grandfather's or your grandmother's side that the ape ancestry came in?" People laughed. Then Huxley gave his answer: "I asserted, and I repeat, that a man has no reason to be ashamed of having an ape for an ancestor. If there were an ancestor whom I should feel shame in recalling, it would be a man of restless and versatile intellect, who, not content with success in his own sphere of activity, plunges into scientific questions with which he has no real acquaintance, only to obscure them by aimless rhetoric and distract the attention of his hearers from the point at issue by digressions and appeal to religious prejudice." Pandemonium followed, during which there were fistfights and a lady fainted. The furor continued right through the Scopes trial in Tennessee 43 years after Darwin died.

Some used Darwin's theory for their own ends. Language experts said the fittest words survive. In Nazi Germany, it was used to justify the extermination of the Jews.

The man around whom the furor raged was a gentle, sickly, kindly person, with blue eyes, a balding head, and a long, shaggy beard. He was modest to a fault, once saying about himself, "I have no great quickness or apprehension of wit." He had 10 children, whom he loved dearly. He liked to read Mark Twain and Lewis Carroll and said that all novels should have a happy ending.

He listened to the criticisms, evaluated them, and revised his work in light of his evaluations. He said, "If I am wrong, the sooner I am knocked on the head and annihilated, so much the better."

He wrote several other books, including *The Descent of Man*. On April 15, 1882, he died; he was buried in Westminster Abbey next to Newton.

EYEWITNESS REPORT: From *Origin of Species*: "It is interesting to contemplate a tangled bank, clothed with many plants of many kinds, with birds singing on the bushes, with various insects flitting about, and with worms crawling through the damp earth, and to reflect that these elaborately constructed forms, so different from each other, and dependent upon each other in so complex a manner, have all been produced by laws acting around us. These laws, taken in the largest sense, being Growth with Reproduction; Inheritance which is almost implied by reproduction; Variability from the indirect and direct action of the conditions of life, and from use and disuse: a Ratio of Increase so high as to lead to a Struggle for Life, and as a consequence to Natural Selection, entailing divergence of Character and the Extinction of less-improved forms. Thus, from the war of nature, from famine and death, the most exalted object which we are capable of conceiving, namely, the production of the higher animals, directly follows. There is grandeur in this view of life, with its several powers, having been originally breathed by the Creator into a few forms or into one; and that, whilst this planet has gone cycling on according to the fixed law of gravity, from so simple a beginning endless forms most beautiful and wonderful have been, and are being evolved."

—A.E.

First Person on the Couch—the Beginning of Psychoanalysis

WHEN: 1880–1882

HOW: It was not until 17 years after her death that the real identity of Anna O., the 1st person to be psychoanalyzed, was revealed to the world at large. Until then, it was a well-kept secret, and few people knew that the subject of the 1st psychoanalytic case history later became a prominent person in her own right. Her analyst was not Sigmund Freud, but a friend of his, Dr. Josef Breuer, a charming Viennese physician famous for his almost magical diagnostic skill and sympathetic bedside manner.

Late in December, 1880, Breuer was called to the apartment of a well-to-do family. There were 2 sick people in that apartment—a father dying of a tubercular lung abscess and a daughter who had, her mother said, a troublesome cough. It was the 21-year-old daughter that Breuer came to see.

The patient was lying in bed. Her dark eyes were glazed, almost unseeing. Almost immediately, Dr. Breuer saw that a cough was only one of her many symptoms. Her right arm and both legs were gripped in a paralysis for which neurologists had found no cause. She was mute. She had headaches. Her vision was poor. Often, she lay sleepless until the sun came up.

Breuer recognized a classic case of hysteria, a mysterious malady which had interested him for some time. In those days (and sometimes in these), doctors often thought that women with the disease were faking it to get attention. Breuer did not agree. He saw the disease as real, though inexplicable. Many cases of hysteria had been temporarily cured by hypnotic suggestion. Since the young patient was in a trancelike state anyway, Breuer decided to try hypnosis with her.

After she was "under," Breuer asked whether anything was bothering her. She shook her head in answer. He asked again. This time she spoke, but all that came from her mouth was incomprehensible gibberish. For some reason, Breuer decided not to make any hypnotic suggestions, as was the usual practice, but to return the following night and hypnotize her again.

When he did, he asked once more whether anything was bothering her. This time she answered, "Jamais acht nobody bella mio please lieboehn nuit," a meaningless sentence in 4 languages—French, German, English, and Italian. What was going on in the girl's head? It was as though she had 2 minds—one that was in control when she was awake and another that spoke when she was hypnotized. Breuer decided that the key to her illness lay in what that 2nd mind might say, not in hypnotic suggestion, and he embarked on what she later called "the talking cure." For the next year and a half, the doctor and patient together explored that other mind, her unconscious, in the 1st documented case of psychoanalysis.

Almost every evening, Breuer came to see the young patient, whom he later called Anna O. (a pseudonym to protect her identity). While she was in a hypnotic state, she would tell him a story from what she called her "private theater." The story was usually sad, somewhat like one of Andersen's fairy tales, and almost always involved a sick father who was being saved by a young girl's devoted care, a reflection of her feelings while nursing her own sick father. In telling the story, she was able to express her hidden emotions, and usually was calm the next day. If she did not get a chance to tell her story, she was likely to be moody or violent.

The treatment continued. There was a great setback when her father died. For 3 days after that, Anna could not speak at all. Then she told Breuer that she could not recognize faces until she had done "recognizing work." To figure out who family members or friends were, she had to note separately each feature—long, dark hair or a certain facial shape—then assume it was so-and-so, who had those features. Everyone except Breuer looked like a wax figure to her. It was like a nightmare, but so were many of her hallucinations. In the terrifying world of her unconscious, there were snakes, death's heads, and other horrors. She and Breuer discovered that when they were able to identify the incidents in her life during which the hallucinations had 1st appeared and to link them to her physical symptoms, the hallucinations and physical symptoms both disappeared.

In every case, there were complexes of incidents, each of which had to be brought from the unconscious to the conscious level. Most had 1st occurred during her father's illness. For instance, one night she had been sitting by her father's bedside and had fallen asleep, her arm hanging over the back of her chair. When she woke, she saw a snake about to attack her father. She could not move her arm because, held in an awkward position, her arm had gone numb. Looking down, she saw each finger as a little black snake and each fingernail as a death's head. When she tried to pray, all she could remember was a nursery rhyme in English, "All the King's horses and all the King's men couldn't put Humpty Dumpty together again." This incident had frightened Anna so much that she had buried it deep in her unconscious mind, and her arm had become paralyzed. However, once she remembered what had happened and talked about it with Dr. Breuer, she stopped seeing snakes and death's heads and could move her arm again.

At last, in June of 1882, Anna seemed cured. The treatment over, she and Breuer said goodbye, supposedly for the last time. However, a day later, Breuer was called again to the apartment. When he arrived, Anna's mother told him the girl was suffering from cramps. It was more than cramps. When Breuer entered Anna's room, he heard her saying, "Now Dr. Breuer's baby is coming." She was acting out childbirth. Shocked by this openly sexual display that involved him, Breuer hypnotized Anna and told her that the incident was imaginary. He made it a point never to see her again.

It was probably because of this final incident that Breuer waited for a long time before publishing anything about the case and did not carry his study of hysteria much further. Later he heard that Anna, treated by another doctor, had become a morphine addict and had been committed to a sanitarium.

If Breuer had not told his friend Sigmund Freud about the case, Freud might not have come up with the great theories which revolutionized concepts of the human mind. But Breuer did tell him. At 1st Freud was only mildly curious because his professional interests lay elsewhere. By 1886, however, women suffering from hysteria comprised a large part of his medical practice. Conventional methods of treatment were not too successful. He remembered the case of Anna O., and he tried Breuer's "talking cure" on one of his patients. Freudian analysis was born.

It was Breuer who 1st identified the unconscious mind, the mind that held thoughts "not admissible to consciousness," thoughts so terrible they could not be allowed to surface. It was he who saw that bringing these ideas to light could cure the symptoms of hysteria. But it was Freud who developed these rudimentary ideas into a theory. It was Freud who saw the

elements of sexuality that lay behind much mental illness. (He always felt that Breuer had made a mistake in not facing the sexuality in the case of Anna O.) It was Freud who saw that the patient "transferred" her love-hate feelings to the analyst. It was, finally, Freud who fathered psychoanalysis.

Anna O. was, in reality, Bertha Pappenheim—a writer, feminist, and crusader against white slavery who devoted her life to helping others. The time between her treatment by Breuer and the beginnings of her career is largely a blank.

When she was 29, she became interested in helping the Jews left homeless by the pogroms of Eastern Europe. She was then living in Frankfurt, Germany, with her mother. Soon she was running an orphanage for Jewish children and had formed a local and a national organization for Jewish women volunteer workers.

At the time, there was extensive white slave trafficking in poor Jewish girls from the ghettos. When Bertha Pappenheim discovered this, she began a one-woman campaign against it—writing pamphlets, giving lectures, and starting a home for delinquent and feeble-minded young women.

Through it all, she found time to write—stories for children (much like those from her "private theater"), plays, and translations of feminist literature.

In spite of all she did for others, she was lonely. She enjoyed few real friendships and, as far as we know, no lovers at all. Once she wrote in a letter, "I have often thought that if one had nothing to love, to hate something is a good substitute."

On May 28, 1936, she died, an old woman in her 70s, bravely making jokes about how the color of some yellow roses matched her complexion.

Years later, Dr. Ernest Jones revealed the link between Anna O. and Bertha Pappenheim in a biography of Freud.

Questions remain. What caused Bertha Pappenheim's illness? Since several of her relatives had been mentally ill, can it be said that she was genetically predisposed to it? What would she have become if she had been able to continue treatment? Would she still have followed a career of helping others or would she have become a happier, but less socially productive, wife and mother?

EYEWITNESS REPORT: While treating Anna O., Breuer kept notes which he later wrote up for publication:

". . . I undertook her treatment, and I at once recognized the seriousness of the psychical disturbance with which I had to deal. Two entirely different states of consciousness were present which alternated very frequently and without warning and which became more and more differentiated in the course of her illness.

In one of these states she recognized her surroundings; she was melancholy and anxious, but relatively normal. In the other state, she hallucinated and was 'naughty'—that is to say, she was abusive, used to throw cushions at people . . . tore the buttons off her clothes and linen. . . .

"While she was in the country, when I was unable to pay her daily visits, the situation developed as follows. I used to visit her in the evening, when I knew I would find her in hypnosis, and I then relieved her of the whole stock of imaginative products she had accumulated since my last visit. It was essential that this should be effected immediately if good results were to follow. When this was done, she became perfectly calm, and the next day would be agreeable, easy to manage, and even cheerful; but on the 2nd day she would be increasingly moody, contrary and unpleasant, and this would become still more marked on the 3rd day. When she was like this, it was not easy to get her to talk, even in her hypnosis. She aptly described this procedure, speaking seriously, as a 'talking cure,' while she referred to it jokingly as 'chimney sweeping.' . . .

"She derived much benefit from a Newfoundland dog which was given to her and of which she was passionately fond. On one occasion, though, her pet made an attack on a cat, and it was splendid to see the way in which the frail girl seized a whip in her left hand and beat off the huge beast with it to rescue his victim. Later, she looked after some poor, sick people, and this helped her greatly. . . .

"She was markedly intelligent, with an astonishingly quick grasp of things and penetrating intuition. . . . She had great poetic and imaginative gifts, which were under the control of a sharp and critical common sense. . . . Her willpower was energetic, tenacious, and persistent; sometimes it reached the pitch of an obstinacy which only gave way out of kindness and regard for other people. . . ."

—A.E.

ASSASSINATION AT SARAJEVO

WHEN: 1914
HOW: The news that the Austrian Archduke Francis Ferdinand was coming to Bosnia didn't take long to reach the Green Garland, a restaurant in Belgrade, through a student grapevine. At the Green Garland, 300 students, mostly politicals, met daily, talking mainly of how to get back territory, including Bosnia, that Austria had recently annexed. Three Bosnian-Serb high school students—Cabrinovic, Grabez, and Gavrilo Princip—were intensely interested in the royal visit. They had been planning to kill an Austrian, but were not sure whom, and now a victim far more important than they had hoped for was about to present himself. As they plotted, they were overheard by an officer of Serbian Military Intelligence, Capt. Vogislav Tankosic. He, in turn, told his superior, Col. Dragutin Dimitrijevic, who, in addition to his job in Intelligence, was the head of the Black Hand, a Serbian terrorist organization whose goal was to get back Serbian land which had been seized by other nations. Dimitrijevic was known in the Black Hand as "Apis." His colleagues disagreed about his personality—one described him as a "primitive savage," another as a "genuine patriot." Apis told Tankosic to bring the 3 students to him with the idea that he could aid them in creating a disturbance in Sarajevo, a Bosnian town that the archduke was going to visit. This would create political embarrassments and might help the Black Hand to get into a more favorable position with the Serbian Government.

The 3 students, mere teen-agers, were brought into a dark, candlelit room where Apis sat behind a table that held a skull, a pistol, a bomb, and a vial marked "poison." He made the 3 put their hands on the skull and repeat the Black Hand oath: "By the sun which warms me, by the earth which feeds me, by God, by the blood of my ancestors, by my honor and my life, I swear fidelity to the cause of Serbian nationalism, and to sacrifice my life for it." Apis gave them each a pistol and a grenade. Later they also acquired 6 bombs, 4 Browning revolvers, and some doses of cyanide with which to commit suicide if they were caught. They were sneaked across the border to Sarajevo, where they were hidden at the house of a member of the Black Hand, Danilo Ilic. Ilic was told to get more assassins and train them.

News of the plot reached the Austrian Government, but it reached the wrong man—a confidant of the Emperor, Dr. von Bilinski, who didn't like the archduke. When he told General Potiorek about the danger, he was reminded that civilians shouldn't interfere in military matters. The general decided not to send troops to the town, because he was afraid that the Emperor would be angry if he did. The Emperor, the archduke's uncle, disapproved of the archduke's marriage to a mere countess, Sophie Chotek, and didn't want any pomp and ceremony to accompany their visit. He had already declared the marriage morganatic and had disinherited the couple's children.

The archduke, his wife, and their entourage left Vienna on a Tuesday and spent 4 days at a small village not far from Sarajevo. One of his men urged him to go back to Vienna, because he had heard rumors of assassination plots. The group was nervous. A court photographer carrying a long flashlight hid in the bushes and tried to snap pictures of the archduke and his wife as they passed. He was arrested. The archduke decided not to cancel his visit to Sarajevo, to which he went by railway. He was met at the station and got into the 2nd car, a dark green open one, of a parade going into the city. The archduchess wore a white dress and a big hat; the archduke wore a costume comprised of a light blue tunic and black pants with a cocked hat decorated with ostrich plumes. It was like a comic opera—at 1st. They waved to the crowds, who replied with "Zivio!" Among the crowd were 120 policemen.

Also in the crowd were 7 potential assassins, including the 3 students. Though they had been drilled in shooting and throwing bombs, no one had warned them about the hazards of shooting through crowds at a moving target. One of them was standing too near a policeman to risk shooting. Another was pinned in by the crowd. A 3rd took pity on Sophie. A 4th lost his nerve. The 5th, Cabrinovic, managed to knock the detonator from a bomb against a water hydrant and throw it at one of the cars. Here stories of what happened differ. One account says that it fell under the wheels of the 3rd car because Cabrinovic's throw was poor; another says that the bomb landed on the hood of the archduke's car and the archduke knocked it off, whereupon it rolled under the wheels of the 3rd car. Whichever is true, the bomb exploded and wounded an army officer. Cabrinovic swallowed his cyanide, but it did not work, so he jumped into the river and was caught. Princip heard the bomb explode. Thinking the plot had succeeded, he went to a café and celebrated by spending his last coin on a cup of coffee. By now, the procession had reached the Town Hall. Furious, the archduke said Sarajevo should be punished and that he would not proceed with the planned ceremonies and parade through town. He would instead go to the hospital to see the injured officer. Everyone climbed back into the cars. Count Harnack, an aide, jumped on the footboard of the archduke's car to guard him. "Don't make a fool of yourself," shouted Francis Ferdinand. The drivers of the cars didn't know about the change in plans. The 1st car, carrying the chief of police, drove along the Appel-Quai and turned off into a narrow street. The soldier driving the archduke's car followed. But it was not the way to the hospital. Told of this, the driver started backing out onto the quay, where, by sheer coincidence, Princip was drinking his coffee. Princip looked up to see the archduke, immediately pulled out his revolver, walked over to the car, and shot the archduke in the neck. He then pointed the gun at General Potiorek. As Sophie rose in her seat, someone tried to grab Princip's arm and this spoiled his aim. The bullet intended for the general hit Sophie. She died almost at once. "Sophie, don't die. Live for the children," cried Francis Ferdinand. Fifteen minutes later, he, too, was dead. Princip swallowed his cyanide, but it only made him sick. Francis Joseph buried his nephew and Sophie very casually and marked Sophie's grave with 2 white gloves, the symbol of her position as lady-in-waiting.

It should have ended with a series of apologies. It didn't. Germany and Russia got involved in the argument between Serbia and Austria over the affair. Then France got into it, and Britain. W.W. I had started. Just 4½ years later, 20 million people were dead. Of the 25 conspirators brought to trial in Sarajevo, 9 were acquitted and 16 were found guilty, among them the 3 students (including Princip), who were sentenced to 20 years in prison. All 3 were dead within 4 years. Apis was later sentenced to death.

Today, on that very spot in Sarajevo where Princip stood to carry out the assassination his footprints are marked in the pavement, and on that street the Gavrilo Princip Museum has been built to honor him.

EYEWITNESS REPORT: Borijove Jevtic was arrested, too, and later described the crime in an article printed in the *New York World:* "A tiny clipping from a newspaper, mailed without comment from a secret band of terrorists in Zagreb, capital of Croatia, to their comrades in Belgrade, was the torch which set the world afire with war in 1914. That paper wrecked old, proud empires. It gave birth to new, free nations.

"I was one of the members of the terrorist band in Belgrade which received it.

"The little clipping declared that the Austrian Archduke Francis Ferdinand would visit Sarajevo, the capital of Bosnia, June 28, to direct army maneuvers in the neighboring mountains.

"It reached our meeting place, the café called Zeata Moruna [Green Garland] one night in the latter part of April, 1914. . . . The men who were terrorists in 1914 embraced all classes. Most of them were students. Youth is the time for the philosophy of action. There were also teachers, tradesmen, and peasants; artisans and even men of the upper classes were ardent patriots. They were dissimilar in everything except hatred of the oppressor.

"Such were the men into whose hands the tiny bit of newsprint was sent by friends in Bosnia that April night in Belgrade. At a small table in a very humble café, beneath a flickering gas jet we sat and read it. . . . our decision was taken almost immediately. Death to the tyrant!"

He goes on to describe the aftermath of the assassination. "The officers seized Princip. They beat him over the head with the flat of their swords. They knocked him down, they kicked him, scraped the skin from his neck with the edges of their swords, tortured him, all but killed him. . . . I was placed in the cell next to Princip. . . .

"Awakened in the middle of the night and told that he was to be carried off to another prison, Princip made an appeal to the prison governor: 'There is no need to carry me to another prison. My life is already ebbing away. I suggest that you nail me to a cross and burn me alive. My flaming body will be a torch to light my people on their path to freedom.' "

—A.E.

MAO AND THE LONG MARCH

WHEN: 1934
HOW: The war between Chiang Kai-shek's Kuomintang and the peasant Red Army had been going on in China since 1928. The Red Army was an army of volunteers with strict discipline yet egalitarian brotherhood between the men and officers. Foremost among its leaders were Chang Kuo-t'ao and Mao Tse-tung, old friends since student days in Peking and co-founders of the Chinese Communist party at Shanghai. Their goals were extreme: to confiscate landlords' estates and distribute the land among the poor peasants, to establish socialist leadership over the means of production, and to correct the inequality then existing in China. Chinese soldiers before them had had a reputation for cruelty. There was even a proverb about it: "Good iron doesn't become a nail, nor does a good man become a soldier." Mao changed that. His soldiers, unlike those before, treated the people well. There was even a song about it:

1. Replace doors when you leave a house. 2. Return and roll up the straw matting. 3. Be courteous and polite to the people and help them. 4. Return all borrowed articles. 5. Replace all damaged articles. 6. Be honest in all transactions with the peasants. 7. Pay for all articles purchased. 8. Be sanitary; establish latrines at a safe distance from people's houses.

Beginning in 1930, concerned about the burgeoning Red Army, Chiang Kai-shek went into all-out war, but kept losing battles. The Red Army was winning by practicing its tactical slogans: "When the enemy advances, we retreat. When the enemy halts and encamps, we trouble him. When the enemy seeks to avoid battle, we attack. Whenever the enemy retreats, we pursue."

Then Chiang began to use new methods suggested by his Prussian advisers. He built a series of forts, extended highways, and began to encircle the Red Army. The Red Army was getting German advice, too—theirs from Gen. Li Teh ("Otto") who had been smuggled in by the Comintern, the Soviet-dominated Communist International. Mao and other Red leaders had been winning battles by operating from the countryside and avoiding the cities. Against the advice of Mao and his men, Li Teh committed about 180,000 men to great battles planned to hold towns and cities. They were badly defeated. After 7 years of fighting and winning, the Red Army found itself encircled; the only choices were surrender or withdrawal. In a bold stroke, Mao decided to withdraw the 90,000 men that were left to his command.

On October 16, 1934, Mao and his army began what later became known as *Liang Wan Wu-Ch'ien-Li Ch'ang Ch'eng*—the Long March of 25,000 *li*. It began in Fukien and ended at the end of the road near the Gobi Desert—a distance of about 6,000 mi. Not since Xenophon was there such a magnificent and morally triumphant retreat. It was a road marked by battle, privation, death, and faith. Thousands died.

The Red Army started by breaking through the lines and moving into Kweichow, where they captured the governor's headquarters. Here, in a politburo conference, Mao was made chairman of the party. It was fairly easy for the Army to cross the upper Yangtze, the "Gold Sand" River, but from there they went into the wild mountains of West Yünnan, where a treacherous river ran through gorges thousands of feet deep. All the bridge crossings were occupied by enemy troops. All the ferryboats were drawn to the opposite bank. Chiang figured he had won. All he had to do was finish off the Red Army, caught in the defiles of the mountains. He forgot to consider their desperation and resourcefulness. A Red commando force, after marching 85 mi. through the mountains in 24 hours, captured a Nationalist group at a ferry crossing. Then they dressed in the enemy uniforms and persuaded the troops on the other bank to send over the ferryboats. In the dark, they crossed the river, took a fort, and secured a route to the west.

But there was another river to cross, the Tatu, in western Szechwan. Mao knew it was imperative that the Red Army beat Chiang to the river. In order to do so, the Army entered a dangerous piece of land dominated by aborigines, the Lolos, who hated the Chinese. There were 2 kinds of Lolos—Black and White. The Reds approached the Black Lolos, telling them that they were Red Chinese, enemies of the White Chinese (the Nationalists), and therefore friends of the Black Lolos. Through a Red commander who knew the Lolo language, an agreement with the Black Lolos was reached, and the Red Army was able to take the short-cut through their territory. They crossed the bridge at the Tatu 1st. If they had not, they would likely have been forced into the mountains of Tibet to die in the snow. Ahead of them were mountains, the Great Snowy Mountains of Szechwan, and more mountains after that. Mao said later, "On Pao-tung Kand peak alone, one army lost ⅔ of its transport animals. Hundreds fell down and never got up again." The men and women on the march did not do much better. In July, they reached eastern Tibet, where they met the 4th Front Red Army led by Chang Kuo-t'ao. Here Chang Kuo-t'ao and Mao locked horns in a battle for supremacy, a battle that was interrupted by the advance of Chiang Kai-shek's forces and the rising of a river, which divided the 2 armies physically. For weeks after that, Mao's Army advanced through gloomy forests, jungles, treacherous marshlands, and mountain passes, constantly threatened by natives who hated them. "To get one sheep," Mao later reflected, "cost the life of one comrade."

By September, they were deep in the nearly uninhabited Great Grasslands. It rained almost all the time, and they had to pick their way, guided by captured natives, along narrow footholds. Many people were lost as they foundered in the wet grass or disappeared in the swamps. There was nothing to eat but wild vegetables and herbs. At night they tied bushes together to make rude shelters. And in spite of the rain, there was no safe water, so that sometimes they had to drink their own urine. By the time they came into the Kansu Plain, there were only 7,000 of them left. After resting for a while, they broke through Muslim cavalry and joined the local Red forces in northern Shensi. It was October 25, 1935. The Long March was over.

Of the 368 days in the journey, 235 were spent in marches by day and 18 in marches by night. The Army had averaged a skirmish with the enemy a day and had spent 15 days in major battles. They had crossed 24 rivers and 18 mountain ranges, 5 of which were always snow-covered. In Peking, an entire floor of the Revolutionary Museum is devoted to the Long March. On a huge map, colored lights trace each stage of the march, while a guide retells the story.

EYEWITNESS REPORT: According to Chou En-lai: "For us, the darkest time in history was during our Long March, 24 years ago—especially when we crossed the Great Grasslands near Tibet. Our condition was desperate. We not only had nothing to eat, we had nothing to drink. Yet we survived and won victory."

According to Mao Tse-tung's poem: "The Red Army, never fearing the challenging Long March,/Looked lightly on the many peaks and rivers,/Wu Meng's range rose, lowered, rippled,/And green-tiered were the rounded steps of Wu Meng./Warm-beating the Gold Sand River's waves against the rocks,/and cold the iron chain spans of Tatu bridge./A thousand joyous *li* of freshening snow on Min Shan,/And then, the last pass vanquished, the Armies smiled."

—A.E.

THE BOMB AND HIROSHIMA

WHEN: 1945
HOW: The dropping of "Little Boy," scientists' nickname for the 9,000-lb., 10'-long, 28"-round uranium bomb encasing the equivalent of 20,000 tons of TNT, which had been achieved at a cost of $2 billion over a 2½-year period, was the most controversial decision ever made in military history. The atom bomb—so called because it involves splitting an atomic nucleus by bombarding it with neutrons, which sets off a chain reaction of fission that releases enormous quantities of energy, infinitesimal matter bursting into infinite power—fell on Hiroshima on August 6, 1945. Immediately it turned Japan's 8th major city, with a population of 300,000, into what one writer called "the world's largest guinea pig." No warning had been given, other than the half-million leaflets that had shimmered down from the skies like so much confetti 2 days earlier. These warned, "Your city will be obliterated unless your Government surrenders."

Already by the summer of 1945 Japan's great urban centers of Tokyo-Yokohama and Osaka-Kobe had endured "conventional" destruction by saturation and carpet bombings to an unimaginable degree. B-29s fire-bombed these cities daily—weather permitting—and had incinerated 100 sq. mi. of habitation, gutted or razed 2 million buildings, devastated and rendered homeless 13 million people. In one massive, all-night raid by 1,000 planes, 74,000 people were killed or wounded. Hiroshima, however, a city of minor military significance and until then quite undamaged (the Japanese conjectured that Americans were saving it as a residential sector, if and when they won the war), was wiped from the map by one plane discharging a single bomb.

That morning of August 6, a B-29 Superfortress from the 509th Composite Group of the 20th Air Force, the *Enola Gay*—so-named for the mother of the young Southern pilot who commanded the plane, Paul Tibbets, Jr.—set off from the tiny Pacific atoll of Tinian, which had been captured from the Japanese a year earlier. Flying at a speed of 285 mph and a height of 32,000′, its target was Aioi Bridge in the heart of downtown Hiroshima. The bomb, inscribed with nasty remarks about the Emperor, exploded in the air 660 yards above the ground and only 300 yards off its target.

There was a *pika*, a blinding flash of pink, blue, red, or yellow light—none of the survivors ever agreed on the color—brighter than 1,000 suns but coming from a fireball only 110 yards in diameter. In that split second the hypocenter or point of impact reached a heat of 300,000° C. Within a 1,000-yard radius granite buildings melted, steel and stone bridges burned and so did the river below them, roof tiles boiled, and people evaporated, leaving their shadows "photographed" like X-ray negatives on walls and pavements.

In a matter of seconds, 4 sq. mi. of central Hiroshima was flattened into extinction. Every clock and watch stopped at exactly the same time: 8:15. Because of ionization, the choking air filled with a sickish sweet "electric smell." The bright blue, sunlit sky turned darkly yellow, and a churning cloud of smoke spurted upward for 50,000′. From a distance it looked like a gigantic mushroom, but to the escaping *Enola Gay* the shape was more that of a grotesque question mark. Capt. Robert Lewis, the co-pilot, exclaimed as he saw it roiling in the air, "My God, what have we done?" The cloud rose so high its heat condensed water vapor. In minutes "black rain," sticky, pebble-sized drops of wet radioactive dust dripped down over Hiroshima, staining the skin of the survivors with red blotches.

Within an hour or so, 100,000 Japanese had died outright. So did 22 American men and women, who were prisoners of war. A 23rd, a young soldier surviving the explosion, was dragged from the rubble of the detention camp and slaughtered by angry Japanese. The population still able to walk wandered about the smoking ruins in a bewildered daze, unable to find their loved ones, incapable of orienting themselves, as all landmarks had vanished. Amazingly, the survivors felt little pain. It was as if the greater terror of the unknown canceled the lesser horror of suffering. Most of the walking wounded were naked, their clothes having been burned or blown off, but among the sizzled bodies it was impossible to tell men from women. Those who had been wearing white were less scarred than others, since dark colors absorbed, rather than deflected, thermonuclear light. Friends did not recognize each other, because some had lost their faces. Others had "imprints" of their nose or ears outlined on their cheeks. Those who reached out to help the more severely disabled drew back their hands only to find they were holding gobbets of charred flesh. Wounds smoked when dipped in water.

In time, another 100,000 Japanese would slowly die from thermal burns and radiation sickness. This, one of the most horrifying side effects of atomic bombing, manifested and continues to manifest itself capriciously—sooner or later—among persons badly injured and whose keloid scars have healed, as well as among others who apparently had originally escaped unharmed. The symptoms, erratic and sudden as they may be, are unmistakable—loss of hair, sudden and immobilizing weakness, vomiting, diarrhea, fever on the coldest days, chills at the height of summer, boils, blood spots under the skin, and a massive drop in white corpuscle blood count. Most terrible to the people of Hiroshima was the biological aftereffect: An extraordinary number of birth defects and genetic mutations were found in infants born to mothers who lived through the bombing. For the 1st time in history, as one correspondent wrote, not only had innocent people been killed, but the as-yet-unborn were maimed.

Although it was Americans who dropped it, the atom bomb was the product of many men past and present pooling knowledge from all over the world. From Roentgen's 1895 discovery of the negative electricity of X rays, the Curies' discovery of radium, and Einstein's 1905 discovery that matter and energy are one, to Rutherford's establishing in England how radioactivity works and the "look" of an atom, history steadily delivered piece after piece of the atomic bomb's jigsaw puzzle. In the 1920s and 1930s, the Japanese physicist Shimizu and his counterpart in the U.S.S.R., Kapitka, shared information with the Italian Fermi, who produced the 1st chain reaction in uranium; with the German Hahn, who uncovered nuclear fission; with the Danish Bohr, who produced "heavy water" as a booster to radioactivity and thereby speeded "the chain reaction in natural uranium under slow neutron bombardment"; and with the American Lawrence, who separated isotopes in thermal diffusion. Fascism in Europe drove many of the most distinguished atomic scientists in the world to America, and it was here that the know-how, means, method, and money all crystallized the reality. It began in October, 1938, when Einstein wrote to President Roosevelt about the possibility of creating a fission bomb of superlatively destructive power. "This requires action," Roosevelt said to an aide.

The theory behind the possibility turned from probability into likelihood. After the establishment of the super-secret Manhattan Project at Los Alamos, N. Mex., in 1943, where a team of foreign and American scientists worked with breathtaking speed and cooperation, the implications of the future began to rise like unwelcome specters. Niels Bohr, the Nobel Prize winner and one of the brightest luminaries working at Los Alamos, worried as early as February, 1944, about the political implications of the bomb and the tensions it would create between the superpowers, Russia and America. "A weapon of unparalleled power is being created. Unless, indeed, some international agreement about the control of the use of the new active materials (uranium, plutonium, etc.) can be obtained, any temporary advantage, however great, may be outweighed by a perpetual menace to human society," he wrote to both Churchill, who said, "I do not agree," and to Roosevelt, who answered, "The suggestion is not accepted."

Meanwhile, Klaus Fuchs, another German refugee at Los Alamos, convinced that no one country, however benevolent, should be the sole possessor of the means of destroying the entire earth, passed the bomb's secrets to the Russians. In April, 1945, Einstein himself had 2nd thoughts about what he had started. Again he wrote to Roosevelt, asking for extreme caution in the use of the bomb, but Roosevelt died and the letter lay on his desk. By June, 1945, the German James Franck, the Hungarian Leo Szilard, and 57 other top-ranking scientists petitioned from New Mexico that "if the U.S. releases this means of indiscriminate destruction upon mankind, she will sacrifice public support throughout the world and precipitate the race for armaments." Robert Oppenheimer, in charge of the Manhattan Project's scientists, said, "When you see something that is technically sweet, you go ahead and do it." His co-worker Arthur Compton, on the other hand, wanted a nonmilitary demonstration to "warn" and "impress" the Japanese before actually using the bomb.

The Government in Washington argued back and forth. Secretary of War Stimson and some of the members of the Joint Chiefs of Staff insisted that it would save 100,000 American lives and that dropping it by surprise on a "combined military and residential target would produce maximum psychological shock." (These were the same reasons Hitler had given for the attack on Rotterdam.) General Marshall wanted the Soviets to join the war against Japan and to save the bomb for use at some possible future date against the Soviets. General Eisenhower felt that the Japanese were already beaten, that acceptable warfare could finish off the job and bring about surrender. He said, in short, that the bomb was completely unnecessary and would rouse world condemnation.

Throughout the discussions and disputations, as Compton would later say, "It seemed a foregone conclusion that the bomb would be used." The final decision was up to President Truman. When John Toland, author of *The Rising Sun*, asked him if he had done any soul-searching before deciding, Truman replied, "Hell, no. I made it like that," and he snapped his fingers in the air. To Truman the bomb was just "another powerful weapon in the arsenal of righteousness." On July 24, 1945, from Potsdam, he ordered the bomb sent to the Air Force. On July 16 it was in Tinian. On the 27th the Japanese were informed for the 1st time of the Potsdam ultimatum threatening "utter devastation" or "unconditional surrender." In any event, the Japanese were already suing for peace through the Russians, who were not yet at war with them. Still, the bomb fell, ushering in a new era in troubled world history.

A-bombs, H-bombs, and all their thermonuclear relatives are today commonplace in our lives, if not in our consciences. The U.S., U.S.S.R., China, France, and India detonate versions of them in varying degrees of megatonnage and magnitude without constraint. England, Canada, and Japan use atomic reactors for civilian purposes while knowing that these facilities can be converted to the manufacture of atomic warheads and armaments on short notice. The bomb's secret, once the most closely guarded piece of military intelligence in the war, is now in the open. Anyone with a high school knowledge of physics and a basement laboratory can easily construct his own simplified, do-it-yourself atomic weapon. Internationally, though, it is claimed that another 12 aboveground explosions—tests or actual use—will irreversibly poison the earth's atmosphere. The hands of the "Doomsday Clock" that appears on the cover of the *Bulletin of Atomic Scientists*, founded after W.W. II by the men who made the 1st bomb, now stand at 3 minutes to midnight.

EYEWITNESS REPORT: Dr. Michihiko Hachiya, director of the Hiroshima Communications Hospital, was wounded in the bombing of Hiroshima while at his home 1,700 meters from the hypocenter at Aioi Bridge. His hospital was 200 meters away, and closer to the center of destruction. Eighty of Hiroshima's 190 doctors were killed in the bombing, and Hachiya was the only one to keep a day-by-day record of his experiences from August 6 to September 30, 1945. This document, unique in the annals of atom bomb literature for its 1st-hand, technical, and perceptive information, was 1st serialized in a small medical magazine for circulation among doctors and staff tending postal, telegraph, and telephone employees of the Communications Ministry. In 1955 the manuscript was translated and published in America under the title *Hiroshima Diary, The Journal of a Japanese Physician*. Below are excerpts from Hachiya's entries for that 1st day: "We stood in the street, uncertain and afraid, until a house across from us began to sway and then with a rending motion fell almost at our feet. Our own house began to sway, and in a minute it, too, collapsed in a cloud of dust. Other buildings caved in or toppled. Fires sprang up and whipped by a vicious wind began to spread.

"It finally dawned on us that we could not stay there in the street, so we turned our steps towards the hospital. Our home was gone; we were wounded and needed treatment; and after all, it was my duty to be with my staff. This latter was an irrational thought—what good could I be to anyone, hurt as I was.

"We started out, but after 20 or 30 steps I had to stop. My breath became short, my heart pounded, and my legs gave way under me. An overpowering thirst seized me and I begged Yaeko-san [his wife] to find me some water. But there was no water to be found. . . .

"I was still naked, and although I did not feel the least bit of shame, I was disturbed to realize that modesty had deserted me. . . .

"I paused to rest. Gradually things around me came into focus. There were the shadowy forms of people, some of whom looked like walking ghosts. Others moved as though in pain, like scarecrows, their arms held out from their bodies with forearms and hands dangling. These people puzzled me until I suddenly realized that they had been burned and were holding their arms out to prevent the painful friction of raw surfaces rubbing together. A naked woman carrying a naked baby came into view. I averted my gaze. Perhaps they had been in the bath. But then I saw a naked man, and it occurred to me that, like myself, some strange thing had deprived them of their clothes. An old woman lay near me with an expression of suffering on her face; but she made no sound. Indeed one thing was common to everyone I saw—complete silence. . . .

"The streets were deserted except for the dead. Some looked as if they had been frozen by death while in the full action of flight; others lay sprawled as though some giant had flung them to their death from a great height.

"Hiroshima was no longer a city, but a burnt-over prairie. To the east and to the west everything was flattened. The distant mountains seemed nearer than I could ever remember. How small Hiroshima was with its houses gone. . . .

"Between the Red Cross Hospital and the center of the city I saw nothing that wasn't burned to a crisp. Streetcars were standing and inside were dozens of bodies, blackened beyond recognition. I saw fire reservoirs filled to the brim with dead people who looked as though they had been boiled alive. In one reservoir I saw one man, horribly burned, crouching beside another man who was dead. He was drinking blood-stained water out of the reservoir. In one reservoir there were so many dead people there wasn't enough room for them to fall over. They must have died sitting in the water. . . .

"What a weak and fragile thing man is before the forces of destruction. After the *pika* the entire population had been reduced to a common level of physical and mental weakness. Those who were able walked silently towards the suburbs and distant hills, their spirits broken, their initiative gone. When asked whence they had come, they pointed to the city and said, 'That way'; and when asked where they were going, pointed away from the city and said, 'This way.' They were so broken and confused that they behaved like automatons. . . .

"A spiritless people had forsaken a destroyed city; the way and the means were of no importance. Some had followed the railways, some as if by instinct had chosen footpaths and paddy fields, whereas others found themselves shuffling along dry river beds. Each to his separate course for no better reason than the presence of another in the lead.

"As the day ended I might as well have been suspended in time, for we had no clocks and no calendars."

—F.B.

MAN FIRST WALKS ON THE MOON

WHEN: 1969

HOW: It began at 9:32 A.M., Eastern Daylight Time, on July 16, 1969, when 3 astronauts—Neil Armstrong, Michael Collins, and Edwin Aldrin—lifted off from Launch Complex 39 in *Apollo II*, powered by a 364'-tall Saturn V rocket. They were on their way to the moon, where man would set foot for the 1st time. After a temporary parking period 115 mi. above the earth to check instruments, the spacecraft started on its journey, traveling at a speed of 24,300 mph. When they were 34 hours into the flight, the astronauts began broadcasting to the world a live color television special of what they were doing. Over 500 million people were watching. The 3 said they were impressed by the sight of the earth receding, and Aldrin added, "The view is out of this world."

As they neared the moon's surface, the propulsion system was fired; engine burn brought the spacecraft's velocity down from 6,500 mph to 3,700 mph and put it into an elliptical orbit around the moon. It was 1:22 P.M., Eastern Daylight Time, July 19. They had traveled 244,930 mi. in a little over 3 days. They went twice around the moon, then reignited the propulsion system to put the craft into a

President Calvin Coolidge campaigning for election in 1924. To win the farm vote, Coolidge posed as a farmer in Vermont, slipping into clean overalls but not bothering to change his dressy, polished shoes. His presidential touring car can be seen waiting behind him on the roadside. (See: Chap. 5) *U.P.I.*

The Chicago *Tribune* has recorded many scoops, but the editors blew it when, in a burst of exuberance, they prematurely declared Thomas Dewey the winner of the 1948 presidential race. The real winner, Harry S Truman, didn't let them forget their mistake. (See: Chaps. 5, 15) *U.P.I.*

President Richard Nixon (R) and friends C. G. Rebozo (C) and Robert Abplanalp (L) eyed photographers as the trio took off in Rebozo's houseboat *Cocolobo III* at Key Biscayne, Fla., on November 3, 1973. (See: Chap. 5) *U.P.I.*

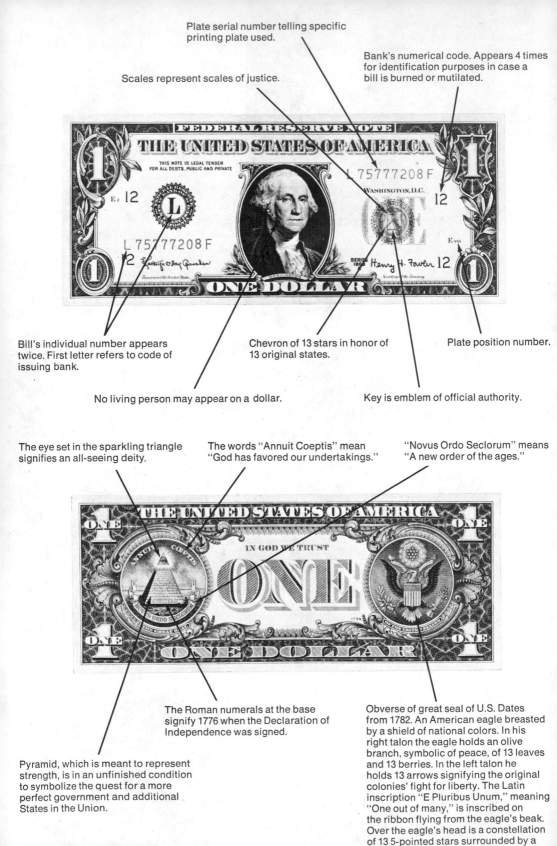

Plate serial number telling specific printing plate used.

Scales represent scales of justice.

Bank's numerical code. Appears 4 times for identification purposes in case a bill is burned or mutilated.

Bill's individual number appears twice. First letter refers to code of issuing bank.

Chevron of 13 stars in honor of 13 original states.

Plate position number.

No living person may appear on a dollar.

Key is emblem of official authority.

The eye set in the sparkling triangle signifies an all-seeing deity.

The words "Annuit Coeptis" mean "God has favored our undertakings."

"Novus Ordo Seclorum" means "A new order of the ages."

The Roman numerals at the base signify 1776 when the Declaration of Independence was signed.

Obverse of great seal of U.S. Dates from 1782. An American eagle breasted by a shield of national colors. In his right talon the eagle holds an olive branch, symbolic of peace, of 13 leaves and 13 berries. In the left talon he holds 13 arrows signifying the original colonies' fight for liberty. The Latin inscription "E Pluribus Unum," meaning "One out of many," is inscribed on the ribbon flying from the eagle's beak. Over the eagle's head is a constellation of 13 5-pointed stars surrounded by a wreath of clouds.

Pyramid, which is meant to represent strength, is in an unfinished condition to symbolize the quest for a more perfect government and additional States in the Union.

THE ALMIGHTY DOLLAR (See Ch. 6)

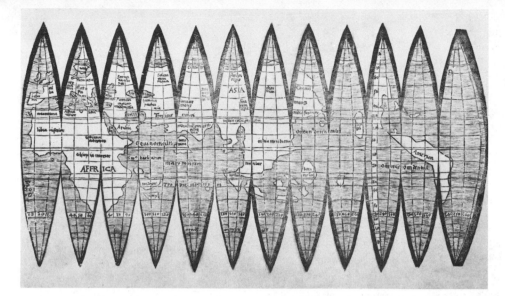

In 1507, a young geographer, Martin Wald-seemüller, prepared this map of the world—designed to be pasted around a ball—which was the 1st to use the name "America." The new continent, seen at the far right, was mistakenly named after Amerigo Vespucci instead of Christopher Columbus. (See: Chap. 8) *James Ford Bell Collection, University of Minnesota.*

Simón Bolívar, a Venezuelan, enjoyed 200 mistresses and fought an equal number of battles from 1813 to 1826 to liberate Venezuela, Colombia, Ecuador, Peru, Bolivia, Panama. (See: Chap. 8) *Library of Congress.*

Lorenzo da Ponte, an Italian ghetto Jew, wrote the libretti for Wolfgang Mozart's 3 greatest operas. He was a celebrated roué, who wound up running grocery stores in New York City and Sunbury, Pa. He died at the age of 89 in 1838. (See: Chap. 8) *Library of Congress.*

The Wall of the Communards in the Cemetery of Père-Lachaise in Paris. Most historians tried to erase from the pages of history the days of the 1871 Paris Commune, when 20,000 of the workers who controlled Paris were executed by the Army, but like the figures on the wall, the memory of the communards has never faded completely. (See: Chap 8) *Sylvia Wallace.*

This photo of German soldiers herding Polish Jews in Warsaw was taken from an SS commander's report to his superior officer. It was used at the Nuremberg War Crimes Trial as evidence of Nazi terrorism in Poland. (See: Chap. 8) *U.P.I.*

roughly circular orbit between 62 mi. and 75 mi. above the surface. Armstrong said, "It looks very much like the pictures but like the difference between watching a real football game and one on TV. There's no substitute for actually being here." While the *Apollo* was on the far side of the moon, they undocked the *Eagle*, the Lunar Module, from the *Columbia*, the Command Module. Armstrong and Aldrin, who would walk on the moon while Collins piloted the *Columbia*, crawled through the pressurized tunnel between the 2 modules and opened connective hatches to enter the *Eagle*. When they came around to the near side of the moon, NASA experts in Houston asked via radio, "How does it look?" "*Eagle* has wings," answered Armstrong. The Lunar Module was free from the *Columbia*.

The *Eagle* went into an extremely elliptical orbit, with a perilune of about 50,000' above the surface. From that near point, it began to sink downward until it was about 7,600' above the surface and 26,000' away from the planned touchdown point in the Sea of Tranquility northwest of Moltke Crater. When still about 500' up, Armstrong and Aldrin looked down at the moon's surface to decide on the best place to land. Shortly after, the 2 took over the controls, running the *Eagle* on semiautomatic. Then, because a program alarm showed the onboard computer to be overloaded, the astronauts, with the help of Houston, brought the *Eagle* down with instruments and visual landmarks. It was a tense moment, and the *Eagle* was heading toward a rocky crater, a poor place to land. Armstrong burned the engines for another 70 seconds in order to reach another landing site about 4 mi. away. Aldrin, in the last moments, said, "Forward, forward, good. Forty feet. Picking up some dust. . . . Drifting to the right. . . . Contact light. OK. Engine stop!" They had landed. Armstrong looked down, he said later, to see a sheet of moon dirt being blown by the rocket exhaust. He shut off the engine and reported, "Tranquility base here. The *Eagle* has landed." He seemed to be calm. However, his heart was beating at 156 beats per minute, twice its usual rate. It was 4:17:41 P.M., Eastern Daylight Time, July 20, 1969.

The 2 were supposed to spend 8 hours checking the *Eagle* out, eating, and resting, but they were anxious to leave the *Eagle* and explore the moon, certainly too excited to rest, so Houston agreed that they could skip the rest period. It took them 3 hours to put on their equipment, including the awkward life-support-system backpacks. It was 6½ hours after landing before they had depressurized the cabin and were ready to open the hatch. Slowly Armstrong went down the 9-rung ladder.

When he reached the 2nd rung, he let down a television camera. On home viewing screens all over earth the image of his heavy-booted foot appeared. Then his foot—encased in a size 9½ B boot—landed on the surface. It was 10:56:20 P.M. He stopped to say his now famous words, "That's one small step for a man, one giant leap for mankind."

He began describing the material on which he was walking: "The surface appears to be very, very fine-grain, like a powder. . . . I can kick it loosely with my toes. Like powdered charcoal. I can see footprints of my boots in the small, fine particles. . . . No trouble to walk around." Aldrin, who had stayed in the capsule, said "Is it OK to come out?" and received permission to do so. "I want to back up and partly close the hatches, making sure to lock it on my way out," he said. "Good thought," answered Armstrong. "That's our home for the next couple of hours. We want to take care of it," said Aldrin. The 2 men bounded with a "kangaroo hop," finding it far easier to maneuver than experts had predicted.

Armstrong showed viewers the plaque that he placed at the landing site: "Here men from the planet earth 1st set foot upon the moon July, 1969 A.D. We came in peace for all mankind."

It was signed by the astronauts and by President Richard Nixon. The 2 put up a metallic American flag, which would never wave on the windless moon.

During the next 2½ hours, Armstrong and Aldrin checked the *Eagle* for landing damage, studied the depressions made by its footpads, practiced running and walking, and collected data. Armstrong picked up about 50 lbs. of rock and soil samples which were put 1st into sealed bags, then into aluminum boxes. Later, a NASA official was to say that they were "worth more than all the gold in Fort Knox." The rocks were amazingly old, some dated before any that had ever been found on earth. The men set up 3 instrument systems: a solar wind composition detector, a seismic detector, and a laser reflector. Armstrong tried to take some core samples of subsurface materials but had trouble: "I could get the 1st coring device down about the 1st 2" without much of a problem and then I would pound it in about as hard as I could do it. The 2nd one took 2 hands on the hammer, and I was putting pretty good dents in the top of the extension rod. And it just wouldn't go much more than—I think the total depth might have been about 8" or 9". But even there, it . . . didn't seem to want to stand up straight, and it would dig some sort of a hole, but it wouldn't just penetrate in a way that would support it . . . if that makes any sense at all. It didn't really to me." They talked about the craters, their footprints, which went only ⅛" deep, and the tiny glass balls in the soil that made it slippery.

After the 2½ hours were up, they returned to the module. Their visit to the moon was over. Behind them, they left "junk"—cameras, backpacks, tools, and some footprints that would probably, in that airless place, remain forever. It had been a strange adventure, described almost prosaically by the 2 awed men—the triumph of technology and the fulfillment of a dream that was as old as mankind.

EYEWITNESS REPORT: Once they landed on the moon, Armstrong and Aldrin gazed out at the satellite on which they would soon walk and then they radioed earth a description of what they saw: "[There is a] level plain cratered with a fairly large number of craters of the 5-to-50 variety. And some ridges, small, 20' to 30' high, I would guess. And literally thousands of little one- and 2' craters around the area. We see angular blocks out several hundred feet in front of us that are probably 2' in size and have angular edges. There is a hill in view just about on the ground track ahead of us. Difficult to estimate, but might be half a mile or a mile. . . .

"I'd say the color of the local surface is very comparable to that we observed from orbit at this sun angle—about 10° sun angle or that nature. It's pretty much without color. It's gray and it's very white as you look into the zero phase line. And it's considerably darker gray, more like an ashen gray, as you look out 90° to the sun. Some of the surface rocks in close here that have been fractured or disturbed by the rocket engine plume are coated with this light gray on the outside. But where they've been broken, they display a dark, very dark, gray interior and it looks like it could be country basalt."

—A.E.

Other Highlights in World History

THE FIRST TRUE HUMANS EMERGE IN AFRICA AND THE EAST INDIES

The creatures came down from the trees and ventured out on the plains. At 1st moving on all fours, they learned to walk and run on 2 legs, which enabled them to carry weapons. They discovered fire, learned to cook. As their vocal apparatus developed, they started to talk. As they spoke, their brains developed. They became human beings. All we know about them is based on findings of fossilized bone and excrement, ashes, tools.

1792–1750 B.C. HAMMURABI WRITES HIS CODE OF LAWS

The 6th and best-known King of the 1st Amorite Dynasty of Babylon, Hammurabi gained immortality by introducing a legal code of 282 case laws. These laws dealt with matters such as commerce, marriage, theft, slavery, debts.

1250 B.C. EXODUS FROM EGYPT AND 10 COMMANDMENTS

Moses led 600,000 enslaved Hebrews out of Egypt—through the Red Sea, which parted for them—to safety. Climbing Mount Sinai, Moses received the 10 Commandments from God. The 1st was, "You shall have no other gods before me." The 10th was, "You shall not covet your neighbor's house; you shall not covet your neighbor's wife. . . ."

C. 1210–1200 B.C. THE TROJAN WAR

According to Greek poet Homer's *Iliad*, Paris, son of the King of Troy, abducted Helen, wife of a Greek King. This led to a bloody 10-year conflict between the Greeks and Trojans, the 1st clash between the Occident and the Orient. The Greeks duped the Trojans into admitting a huge wooden horse into their city. Greek warriors were hidden inside the horse, and Troy fell.

355–323 B.C. ALEXANDER THE GREAT CONQUERS THE WORLD

Raised by his mother, educated by Aristotle, the young Alexander seized control of Macedonia after his father had been assassinated. At the head of 30,000 soldiers, Alexander conquered the Persian Empire. He went on to conquer India only to die of malaria in Babylon.

73 B.C. THE SPARTACUS SLAVE REVOLT

Spartacus was a Roman slave being trained as a gladiator. Leading a slave rebellion, Spartacus and 78 others escaped. Soon the slave army swelled to 120,000 men. For 3 years they fought and defeated Roman legions. Finally, the armies of Crassus and Pompey combined to crush the rebels.

800 A.D. CHARLEMAGNE CROWNED EMPEROR
OF THE HOLY ROMAN EMPIRE

The greatest of medieval Kings, Charlemagne of Frankland, conquered and converted to Christianity territory that is now France, Belgium, The Netherlands, Germany, Austria, Switzerland, northern Italy, Poland, Hungary, Yugoslavia. For defending the life and papacy of Pope Leo III, Charlemagne was proclaimed head of the Holy Roman Empire.

1215 KING JOHN SIGNS THE MAGNA CARTA

When 40 English barons, angry at King John for usurping their rights and privileges, prepared to dethrone their monarch, John compromised. He met with them in a meadow at Runnymede and signed a charter, the Magna Carta, which would eventually serve as the blueprint for English common law.

1231 THE BEGINNING OF THE INQUISITION

The Inquisition was the procedure initiated by the Catholic Church to suppress heresy. In secret proceedings, anyone found to be a heretic was turned over to secular officials to be burned. This medieval Inquisition, covering mainly northern Italy and southern France, was followed by the even more barbaric Spanish Inquisition of 1483, in which 2,000 persons were burned at the stake.

1256 THE INVENTION OF GUNPOWDER

While an explosive powder was invented by the Chinese in the 10th century, the modern version was invented by an English Franciscan monk, philosopher, and experimenter named Roger Bacon. Bacon's formula for gunpowder: "41.2% of saltpeter and 29.4% each of carbon and sulphur." Gunpowder and the gun were mated in 1325.

1272 MARCO POLO GOES TO CATHAY

A 13th-century Venetian merchant, traveler, storyteller, Marco Polo was the 1st outside traveler to cross the entire continent of Asia. He twice visited Cathay—the Tartar name for China—and was received by Kublai Khan, Emperor of the Tartars. Polo gave the West its 1st picture of life in medieval China. Later, while a prisoner of war, he wrote *The Travels of Marco Polo*.

1381 THE PEASANTS' REVOLT

English clergyman John Ball preached social equality and was jailed. Then an ex-soldier, Wat Tyler, led 20,000 dissatisfied peasants against London. The 14-year-old King Richard II gave in and introduced reforms. The short revolt ended when the lord mayor of London stabbed Tyler to death, and clergyman Ball was hanged. All of the rights granted the peasants were revoked by Parliament.

1428 JOAN OF ARC DEFENDS FRANCE

King Charles II controlled southern France, and his abbreviated kingdom was threatened by the English siege of Orléans. A 17-year-old farmer's daughter, Jeanne d'Arc, heard God's voice tell her to save the King. She went to Charles II, who made her head of his Army and sent her against the English at Orléans. She won. Later, captured by the enemy, she was tried, condemned, and burned at the stake. In 1920, the martyred Joan was made a saint of the Catholic Church.

1455 THE INVENTION OF PRINTING:
THE GUTENBERG BIBLE

Mark Twain once called printing "the incomparably greatest event in the history of the world." Johann Gutenberg, of Mainz, Germany, may have introduced modern mass printing by his invention of movable type. Thirty documents exist proving there was a Gutenberg, but only 3 indicate he was a printer. Gutenberg launched the printing of the famous 42-line Bible associated with his name, but his financial backer, Johann Fust, and another printer, Peter Schoeffer, probably produced the greater part of the historic Bible.

1492 COLUMBUS DISCOVERS AMERICA

At 2 A.M. on October 12, a sailor on board the ship *Pinta* sighted a distant limestone cliff in the moonlight. For 88 weary men in 3 little ships who had been sailing for 9 weeks in search of the western coast of Asia under the command of a visionary, charismatic captain named Christopher Columbus, the sight was welcomed as a deliverance. At dawn, Columbus put ashore in full regalia and with banners flying to claim this land (actually, a minor island in the Bahamas) in the name of the King and Queen of Spain. Members of his crew, who had been talking of mutiny for several days, now fell at his feet and begged for forgiveness. But was Columbus the real discoverer of America? According to Norse sagas, Leif the Lucky, son of Erik (Leif Erikson) was blown off course on a voyage from Greenland and drifted to North America around the year 1000. Yet the accounts in Viking sagas are both contradictory and inconclusive.

1543 COPERNICUS LEADS AN ASTRONOMICAL REVOLUTION

Using the naked eye, following the pinpricks of light in the night sky, Nicholas Copernicus, born in Poland 19 years before the discovery of America, put forth the radical theory that the earth revolves around the sun, not the sun around the earth. He overturned Ptolemy's entrenched theories and laid the groundwork for today's astronomy.

1684 ISAAC NEWTON FINDS GRAVITY

It was on the family farm in England that Newton saw the famous apple fall, but actually he had been working on theories about gravity earlier. He was a genius who also determined properties of light, invented the reflecting telescope, developed fundamental laws of motion, created the calculus. After publishing his theory of gravity, he did little scientific work. Instead, he went into politics and was appointed director of the mint.

1783–1830 BOLÍVAR AND SOUTH AMERICAN FREEDOM

In Rome, 22-year-old Simón Bolívar vowed to free his native Venezuela and other colonies in South America from Spanish rule. Eventually, he led armies that liberated Venezuela, Colombia, Ecuador, Bolivia (named after him), and Panama. He fought 200 battles, and enjoyed 200 mistresses. He died at 47 of tuberculosis.

1789 FALL OF THE BASTILLE—FRENCH REVOLUTION

In Paris, the Bastille was King Louis XVI's prison for aristocrats. When the King refused to give the people representative government, 5,000 to 8,000 people looted an armory and marched on the Bastille. They overwhelmed the prison, found a mere 7 prisoners inside—4 forgers, 2 madmen, and an Irish lord who had been incarcerated 30 years for debts—and freed them. The King's only diary entry for that date was, "Nothing." But it *was* something—it led to the French Revolution, which lasted 10 years. Although this revolution spawned the dictatorship of Napoleon Bonaparte and a return to monarchy with Louis XVII, it finally led to a system of political liberty and human rights.

1792 THE BATTLE FOR WOMEN'S RIGHTS BEGINS

Mary Wollstonecraft, an English governess, published her book, *A Vindication of the Rights of Women*, demanding that women receive an education and have a voice in govern-ment. It was the 1st feminist manifesto. She was also the mother of Mary Shelley.

1812 NAPOLEON'S RETREAT FROM RUSSIA

Interested in personal power and in expansion of his French empire, Napoleon invaded Czarist Russia, reaching Moscow. The Russians constantly retreated to let time, topography, and climate collaborate with them in defeating Napoleon. Fleeing from Moscow and Russia in a bitter winter, Napoleon's army of 500,000 men was reduced to 20,000 survivors. As a result, France's imperial system and empire disintegrated, and Napoleon soon vanished from the world scene.

1821 CHAMPOLLION AND THE ROSETTA STONE

The mysterious stone was discovered by a French engineering officer near Rashid, or Rosetta, in Egypt in 1799, when Jean-François Champollion was only a 9-year-old boy in France. Resembling a tabletop, the slab of black basalt bore an indecipherable inscription. At 13, Champollion was studying Arabic, Chaldean, Coptic, Chinese, and obscure languages like Zend, Pahlavi, Parsi, and at 17 he was an eminent Egyptologist. Champollion turned his attention to the Rosetta Stone, which had been moved to London after Napoleon's defeat. Using his knowledge of dead languages, Champollion deciphered the writing on the stone—a decree of the Egyptian priesthood in 196 B.C.—and unlocked the door to the glorious past of ancient Egypt.

1871 THE PARIS COMMUNE

After France's defeat in the Franco-Prussian War, the nation was split into 2 factions. There was the new republic and regular army under Thiers at Versailles; and there was the Commune de Paris composed of working people and the National Guard. The Commune, which controlled Paris, abolished military conscription, separated State from Church, reduced salaries of public officials to that of skilled workmen, planned the transfer of abandoned factories to workers' associations, brought women into government. On May 21, the Versailles army entered Paris, executed 20,000 Communards, arrested 36,000 citizens, jailed and deported 15,000.

1905 EINSTEIN FORMULATES THEORY OF RELATIVITY

A 26-year-old unknown, Einstein, working in a Swiss patent office, published a paper, "Special Theory of Relativity." Einstein's relativity theories stated that light did not follow some of Newton's fundamental laws of motion, that nothing can move faster than the speed of light, that mass and energy and space and time are related far more than had been thought. The basic principles of his theory led to the electron microscope, television, the electric eye —and the atom bomb.

1917 THE RUSSIAN REVOLUTION

The Russian uprising began not with a grand political design but with millions of empty stomachs, as well as the Czar's oppression and the strain of the nation's participation in W.W. I. In March, 150,000 soldiers in Petrograd joined rebellious workers and took control of that city. Soon the Czar abdicated. In October, after Lenin returned to Russia from Europe and Trotsky came back from America, the minority Bolsheviks began to assume power. A temporary moderate Government—set up by Kerensky—was routed, and the Bolshevik party established a new Soviet Government and introduced a program of "state communism."

1933 THE REICHSTAG FIRE—AND EMERGENCE OF HITLER

Just before a crucial election to confirm Adolf Hitler as chancellor of Germany, the Reichstag (German Parliament Building) was gutted by fire. The Nazis blamed it on a young Dutch arsonist who they claimed was part of a German Communist party plot to take over the nation. Later evidence indicated the Nazis had started the blaze themselves. The Reichstag fire produced an all-powerful Hitler, and because of him, the end of the Weimar constitution, of all political opposition, of all civil liberties, and it led to the savage persecution of Jews and the catastrophe of W.W. II.

1942–1943 STALINGRAD: HITLER AGAINST THE RUSSIANS

Operation Barbarossa was the code name of Hitler's invasion of Russia. The German attack covered 1,500 mi. from the Black Sea to the Arctic. Initially, the Wehrmacht scored spectacular victories. But gradually, German supply lines and troop movements were hampered by rains, cold, snow. German troops reached Stalingrad, and there Russia girded for the showdown. For weeks the battle raged in the streets. Then the Russian armies succeeded in a pincer movement that cut off 250,000 German troops. The encircled Germans wanted to break out and regroup with relief units. Hitler would not have it. On January 30, the battered, starving Germans surrendered en masse.

1944 D-DAY

Cloaked in secrecy, Operation Overlord, the cross-Channel invasion of Hitler's Europe from England by Allied forces, was begun on June 6, 1944. Five French beaches were the spearheads of the invasion, protected by the largest airborne attack in history (900 planes, 100 gliders, 183,000 paratroopers). Landing craft disgorged wave upon wave of Allied soldiers. On bloody Omaha Beach 2,500 men were reported killed, wounded, or missing—but the invasion succeeded, and Hitler's 3rd Reich was doomed.

1945 THE FOUNDING OF THE UNITED NATIONS

Forty-six nations sent 300 delegates to San Francisco to form a world body that would "save succeeding generations from the scourge of war." After 9 weeks of intensive work, the Charter of the United Nations was completed on June 25, 1945. The UN was housed in New York, with a General Assembly that "recommends" and a Security Council (grown from 9 original members to 27 today) that gives the big powers permanent seats and a veto.

1945–46 THE NUREMBERG WAR CRIMES TRIAL

The U.S., Great Britain, France, the Soviet Union, represented by 8 judges, sat on the Nuremberg International Military Tribunal in southern Germany. The trial concerned crimes against humanity committed by Nazi leaders in Germany after 1939. Of the 22 Nazis tried for torture, deportation, persecution, murder, mass extermination (such as the killing of 6 million Jews), 19 were found guilty while 3 were acquitted. Twelve received death sentences, 3 got life imprisonment, 4 were given lesser prison terms.

1957 "SPUTNIK": THE BEGINNING OF THE SPACE AGE

On October 5, the Soviet Union rocketed an artificial satellite into space. The satellite, *Sputnik* ("traveling companion"), was the size of a beach ball (23″ in diameter), possessed 4 folded antennas and an interior transmitter that sent back signals on 2 standard radio frequencies. *Sputnik* also carried scientific instruments. It orbited the earth for 15 weeks before falling back through the atmosphere and burning up. *Sputnik* inaugurated a new age in history—the space age.

Dr. Christiaan Barnard, the 44-year-old son of a minister, and a team of 30 associates performed the 1st human heart transplant at the Groote Schuur Hospital in Capetown, South Africa. The recipient was Louis Washkansky, a 55-year-old wholesale grocer, who had suffered progressive heart failure. The donor was Denise Ann Darvall, a 25-year-old automobile accident victim. The surgery took 5 hours. Said Dr. Barnard: "My moment of truth—the moment when the enormity of it all really hit me—was just after I had taken out Washkansky's heart. I looked down and saw this empty space. . . ." Washkansky died 18 days after the heart transplant, his new heart still strong, but his body the victim of pneumonia.

—The Eds.

Descendants of the *Bounty* Mutineers on Pitcairn Island

For nearly 2 centuries descendants of the famous *Bounty* mutineers have labored for their existence on an isolated pinhead of volcanic rock in the southeastern Pacific Ocean—Pitcairn Island. Fletcher Christian selected this remote, inaccessible spot as a safe hiding place from the British search parties which were sure to be sent out when news of the mutiny reached England.

On April 28, 1789, the day of the mutiny, H.M.S. *Bounty* was returning homeward after having been in Tahiti almost 6 months. (The mission there was to obtain plantings of the breadfruit tree for West Indies plantation owners seeking a cheap food supply for their native workers.) Some say that the *Bounty* crew became homesick for the good life they had enjoyed in Tahiti and found Captain Bligh's discipline increasingly intolerable. In any case, Christian and his fellow mutineers cast Bligh and 18 loyal crew members adrift in a small boat. Their journey in the overcrowded boat and their eventual return to England is a well-known story of survival against incredible odds.

As for the mutineers, Christian sailed the *Bounty* to Tahiti, where 16 of the men chose to stay. But Christian, together with 8 other mutineers, 6 Tahitian men, and 12 women, sailed the *Bounty* to Pitcairn. They ran her onto the rocks, stripped her of all usable material, and then on January 23, 1790, they burned her.

The marooned little group began what Fletcher Christian envisioned as an idyllic, peaceful existence—an island utopia. However, problems plagued the group almost immediately, owing in part to the unequal proportion of men to women. Within 4 years, 5 of the mutineers were dead, including Fletcher Christian, as were all of the Tahitian men. Edward Young, who died of asthma in 1800, was the 1st to die of natural causes. Only 10 years after the landing, John Adams (alias Alexander Smith) was the sole surviving male, with 11 women and 23 children.

"I had a dream," Adams related, "that changed my whole life. There seemed to be standing beside me an angel who spoke to me, warning me of my past life, and then he called me to repent and go down and teach the children in the way of the Christian's Bible." Whereupon Adams, together with Fletcher's oldest son, searched through Christian's sea chest and found the Bible and prayer book Fletcher's mother had given him years before. These became texts in the school Adams started. Hence, under the benevolent guidance of a penitent mutineer, the settlement began to develop into a peaceful society.

The outside world 1st learned of its existence in 1808 when Capt. Mayhew Folger aboard the American ship *Topaze* sighted the island and stopped to look for seals. To his great amazement, a small boat paddled out from the island and 3 young men hailed him "in perfect English," requesting him to land there as they had a white man ashore. Captain Folger reported his find, but the discovery of Fletcher Christian's hideaway made no impression on an England preoccupied with the Napoleonic Wars. It was 7 more years before 2 British naval ships discovered the island quite by accident, and again their astounded captains were met by English-speaking young men.

Mutineer John Adams assumed he would be returned to England under arrest, and in fact indicated a longing to return to his native land despite charges pending against him. His wife, daughter, and members of the community pleaded with him not to leave. Captain Pipon of the *Taugas* wrote: "To have forced him away in opposition to their joint and earnest entreaties would have been an outrage on humanity." Adams, then, remained at Pitcairn, dying there in 1829 at the age of 62.

Now more in touch with the world, Pitcairners made 2 attempts (in the 1800s) to secure their future against the threats of drought and the fear of overpopulation of their island. They emigrated once to Tahiti, then to Norfolk Island. Both times, after bitter trials, a number of them returned to Pitcairn. They organized a system of government and the entire colony embraced the Seventh-Day Adventist faith. Today the Seventh-Day Adventist Church is the only one on Pitcairn.

Early visitors reported the Pitcairn community as being devout, hospitable, self-supporting, and contented. Homes and furniture were crude but adequate. For clothing, the women employed the ancient Polynesian craft of making *tapa*, a kind of paper cloth. It was slow, laborious work, but the garments produced were comfortable and modest. The women also knew how to prepare ample meals from the food sources available on the island. The predominantly vegetable and fruit diet included meat and fish once or twice a week. The community lived as one big family, increasing its population by the enforced choice of cousin spouses. It should be noted that after generations of inbreeding, there are no apparent degenerative conditions and no diseases endemic to the island. On the contrary, recent visitors describe Pitcairners as basically healthy, strong, and alert individuals. Their population has declined from a high of over 200 in 1937 to fewer than 70 in 1974. Only 6 family names are now represented on the island, 3 of which perpetuate the surnames of mutineers—Christian, Young, and McCoy.

Despite many modern conveniences, people live there today much in the same way as did their forefathers. Their *tapa* clothing has been replaced by Western-style dress, much of it cast-offs from passing ships. They have a few motorbikes and Mini-moke cars for getting about and there are motors for the longboats. But the hazards of launch and landing still require the supreme skill of seafaring men. Longboats have always been, and are today, the only method by which anything or anybody enters or leaves the island. There are still days and weeks of guessing when the next ship will call.

It is not easy to arrange a visit to Pitcairn. Would-be tourists wishing to stay more than 24 hours must have approval from the island council and from the British governor in Auckland, New Zealand. Even if approval is granted, it takes months to process. Ian M. Ball, an Australian-born newspaper correspondent, succeeded in obtaining permission for a visit in 1972. In his book *Pitcairn: Children of Mutiny*, there are some observations on the lifestyle of "what is probably our planet's most remote inhabited island."

Ball wrote, "The social life revolves around one thing: food." He counted 42 different dishes on the table at a birthday party he attended soon after his arrival. It was the 1st of about a dozen feasts to which the Balls and their 3 children were invited during their month-long stay. There was goat meat and

chicken; canned bully beef and tongue imported from New Zealand; and cold canned spaghetti, set out on the buffet table, label and all. Dishes of pickfish, an island product, appeared side by side with cans of sardines from Portugal. Side dishes included Irish potatoes, sweet potatoes, string beans, peas, cabbage, pickled onions, stewed tomatoes, boiled carrots, bananas, baked pumpkin, and baked beans. A variety of salads, all with the same dressing, were flanked by bread and biscuits, home-baked in stone ovens. And then there were the desserts, all placed on the table along with the 1st course—pumpkin pies baked in square pans made by the menfolk from flattened-out tin containers, fruit gelatins, and assorted cakes, buns, and cookies. Fresh fruit was missing, probably because it is too common in daily life to be used on festive occasions. Also missing were dairy products. Pitcairners have no taste for cheese and milk. Water is their favorite drink.

The party guests, well scrubbed and neatly dressed, ranged in age from 11 months to 80 years. They chatted excitedly with relatives they had been with most of the day. Talk was primarily about food. The host called for silence, then intoned a solemn blessing. After a hearty "Amen" from everyone in the room, the host yelled, "Now get tah it! Make sure yawley get enough!"

Pitcairn's post office, courthouse, church, and small dispensary are grouped together on the public square. Also in the square are the only 2 pieces of *Bounty* memorabilia on public display: the *Bounty*'s 12' stern anchor and the "*Bounty* Bible." Actually it is not the ship's Bible but the one Christian's mother gave him, and the same one John Adams retrieved from Christian's sea chest. It is the most revered relic on the island.

The ship's bell in the square has always been the basic means of communication on the island. Over the years, the bell code has remained the same:

Five bells:	"Sail Ho!"
Four bells:	Public share out of goods received from passing ships.
Three bells:	Public work, in lieu of income tax, for all able-bodied men between 15 and 65.
Two bells:	Village meeting.
One bell:	Religious services.

The children are taught that they must never, never in play ring the main bell or the relay bell. Ian Ball noted that "the relay bell today has a deep hole dug beneath it, the remedy the islanders adopted when one toddler could not be cured of reaching for the rope, clanging the bell a confusing number of times, and putting the community on false alert."

When the bell sounds 5 times, there is great excitement in the village. The men scurry to the longboats, taking with them their supply of handcarved curios, baskets woven by their women, postage stamps, and fresh fruits to sell on the visiting ship. Pitcairn postage stamps, incidentally, are popular with dealers and collectors throughout the world. Five bells may also mean that medical aid is near, if the ship has a doctor aboard. There has never been a doctor on the island. In the past, if home remedies failed, the patient died. Now the island has a ham radio operated by Tom Christian, 6th-generation descendant of Fletcher, and emergency aid can be summoned if a ship is near enough to answer a call. In recent years the Seventh-Day Adventist Church has required the pastor assigned there to have a wife who is a registered nurse.

According to Ian Ball, the present pastor of the island feels that most members of his congregation regard their origins as "dishonorable history." There is no folk culture and little thought is given to the past. When asked for their own interpretation of why their forefathers mutinied, men of some standing in the community answered:

—"Oh, it was the row over the coconuts. . . ."

—"It was all in that Charles Laughton film. It was the cruelty of Bligh. . . . I would've done the same thing as Fletcher did. . . . But that's not to say we have any grudge against Bligh."

—"No one here really has strong feelings about it."

Fletcher Christian's hopes for an island utopia never materialized. The Pitcairners continue to face daily hardships and an uncertain future—the uncertainty compounded by France's recent nuclear tests 500 mi. away.

Despite many and constant threats to the continued existence of their community, old residents prefer to remain on Pitcairn. The young, however, seem to be succumbing more and more to the lure of the outside world and talk with eagerness of a 3rd and perhaps final evacuation.

—D.W.S.

Footnote People in World History

A collection of persons, from past to present, in various fields of human endeavor, whose fascinating achievements or colorful careers have gained them small renown, but whose personal lives have been overlooked or forgotten by historians and biographers.

JOAN ANGLICUS (818–855). *Pope of Rome.*

"Our Father which art in heaven, Hallowed be thy name. Thy kingdom come. Thy will be done in earth, as it is in heaven. Give us this day our daily Florus . . ." Pope Joan Anglicus (Her alleged Lord's Prayer substituted the name of Florus, her private chamberlain and lover.)

The Vatican has many secrets. Perhaps its most carefully guarded one throughout history is this: that for 2 years, 5 months, and 4 days, between 853 and 855 A.D., the Pope was a woman.

Somewhere between Pope Leo IV (847–855) and Pope Benedict III (855–858), Joan, in the lifelong guise of a man, rose to the highest seat in the Roman Catholic Church. She ruled almost 2½ years, and would have ruled longer except that her true gender was exposed after a love affair that resulted in her giving birth to a boy during a public ceremony.

For 3 centuries, the Catholic Church has attempted to dismiss her as a myth, although over 150 Church historians between the 13th and 17th centuries acknowledged her short reign.

Born in Britain in 818, she went to school in Cologne, where she fell in love with a young Benedictine monk named Felda. She disguised herself as a man in order to accompany him to Athens. When he died several years later, Joan went to Rome to enter the priesthood. Because of her scholarship, she won a university chair as a professor of science. From there, it was a short step to the Vatican, where Joan—called John of England—became notary of the Curia.

She lectured and gave sermons constantly, and her popularity grew. Her rise in the hierarchy of the Vatican was rapid. In 853, after Pope Leo IV's probable actual death (changed to 855 by Church apologists), a new Pontiff was sought. As Emmanuel Royadis wrote in his romanticized biography, *Papissa Joanna*, published in 1886: "They praised the virtue and unselfishness of Father John, insisting that as he had neither nephews to advance nor a harem to keep up he was most likely to spend the revenue of St. Peter's among the poor. The struggle lasted for 4 whole hours. . . . All at once she heard the great cry of her supporters mount up into the sky, hailing the new Pontiff John VIII. . . . The new Pope trembled with joy as she drew the purple robe about her shoulders and put on the slippers bearing the Cross."

For writing this account of Pope Joan, author Royadis was excommunicated by the Catholic Church. When critics disparaged Royadis' biography as being largely fabrication, he published a stream of indignant pamphlets, insisting, "Every sentence in my book . . . is based upon the testimony of contemporary authors."

During Pope Joan's reign, she introduced Ember Days and consecrated King Louis II of France. According to Royadis, she also "ordained 14 bishops, built 5 churches, added a new article to the Creed, wrote 3 books against the iconoclasts. . . ."

Things were going well enough for Joan until, in the 2nd year of her reign, she fell in love with her private chamberlain, a blond youth of 20 named Florus. They became lovers, and to her horror, Joan found herself pregnant. She hoped to escape the Vatican for a period, to bear the child in secrecy and be rid of it, but circumstances kept her confined.

Then, one day during a ceremonial procession from St. Peter's to the Lateran Palace, while she rode on horseback, she suffered the pangs of premature childbirth. The procession was halted. She was lifted from her horse, and fell to the street, and before the eyes of an astounded mob "a premature infant was produced from among the voluminous folds of the papal vestments."

The crowd, upon realizing that it was not a miracle but in fact a deception, became enraged. Joan was tied to the tail of her horse, dragged through the streets of Rome and back to the spot where she had been exposed; there she was stoned to death.

Pope Joan was buried in the midst of this avenue. Her son survived and later grew up to become the Bishop of Ostia. Florus retired to a monastery.

The attempts to discredit Joan's very existence have been many and vigorous. And yet, even today the Popes avoid the road where Joan gave birth to the child in angry deference to this example of a woman's struggle in a man's world.

—A.W. & I.W.

WILLIAM BECKFORD (1759–1844). *Eccentric builder.*

William Beckford was the most eccentric builder who ever lived. A pampered child of the 18th century, he was a prolific author, a pianist of great promise, and a brilliant linguist; but history remembers him best for his wildly bizarre tastes in architecture, and the equally extravagant fashion in which he satisfied them.

He was born in London in 1759, the son of a wealthy and influential landowner with espe-

cially extensive holdings in the West Indies. When his father died, 10-year-old William inherited those estates, as well as £1 million and the Beckford family estate—Fonthill—in Wiltshire. The Earl of Chatham was entrusted with the boy's raising, and young William learned to play the piano from Mozart. He was well-schooled in languages, including Arabic and Persian; and he traveled widely through Europe, educated entirely by private tutors, for his mother did not believe in formal education.

At the age of 20, he found himself in Venice enjoying the favors of an aged paramour who had previously been the mistress of Casanova. He later married a lady of title and fathered 4 children, but was accused widely of homosexuality. One rumor—which he never tried to quash—had him sodomizing a young friend in the village of Powderham.

For all the philandering he did in his 20s, Beckford was quite productive, writing 10 or 11 books (2 under the improbable pseudonyms of Lady Harriet Marlowe and Jacquetta Agneta Mariana Jenks). His literary output included *Vathek*, an oriental romance that has come to be considered a masterpiece of Gothic literature. (Its protagonist is a caliph who builds 5 palaces, each one devoted to one of the 5 senses.) He wrote the novel in French and then had it translated into English. He also dabbled in literary criticism, offering a collection of rather unconventional marginal scribblings entitled *Fruits of Conceit and Flowers of Nonsense* to a less than enthusiastic public.

It was in 1790 that young Beckford took over the managing of his own business affairs, and returned to Fonthill bent on living the life of a gentleman of leisure. He had picked up some knowledge of architecture during his travels abroad, and was determined to build himself a new home of epic proportions. More than merely a home, it would be a monument to himself; even as he had once told Lady Craven in the tones of a biblical patriarch, "I grow rich and mean to build towers."

The 1st step was the building of a wall around the construction site to keep out the curious. Beckford commissioned the noted architect James Wyatt to design the wall, and when it was completed it measured 12' high and 7 mi. around. With work on the tower itself ready to begin, Beckford rounded up some 500 workers—hiring many of them away from projects they were already working on by offering generous wages.

Beckford, who all his life had acted on impulse, often at great expense, now showed all the signs of the classic obsessive-compulsive personality, insisting that work continue around the clock, even under inclement conditions and poor lighting—even when lighting was virtually nonexistent. The site continually buzzed with activity, and even at midnight—with a torrential rain falling and an impenetrable fog obscuring the trees—onlookers and casual passersby could see a steady procession of workers, lighting their way with torches, working on the scaffolds. The workers and those who lived nearby were all convinced that Beckford was mad.

He was so obsessed with speed that the workers had to slap the wood-and-concrete tower together haphazardly and with no thought at all to its strength or safety. Dubbed Fonthill Abbey, the cathedral-like structure rose 300′ into the air from an impossibly narrow foundation, like a candied apple balanced on a stick; and even before the final touches had been put on this colossal architectural outrage, a mild breeze snapped it in 2 like a piece of balsa wood, and it came crashing to the ground.

Beckford surveyed the damage—briefly—and then issued an order: "Build me a new tower—at once!" The original foundation was too narrow and that was why the tower had collapsed in the 1st place, but it would simply have to do: Beckford would not wait for a new one to be built. He paid over a quarter of a million pounds to have stone added to the wood and cement, and his workers moved faster than ever. By December 20, 1800, Beckford had his tower.

Beckford's housewarming party was as bizarre as his new home itself. Beckford supervised the hanging of several thousand colored lanterns in the dense undergrowth that separated the abbey from his ancestral estate nearby, where his most distinguished guests at the party had been staying after arriving from the Continent. They included Admiral Nelson and Sir William Hamilton, and when they arrived at the abbey with their host, they were struck dumb by the opulence and vastness of it all. Rich tapestries hung on the walls, plush purple curtains draped the windows, and the house was furnished with inlaid ebony furniture.

They were greeted by a brass band playing "Rule Britannia," and soldiers from Beckford's "private army," whom he had hired solely for decorative purposes. The guests feasted at a 50′ table and were thrilled beyond words, albeit a bit disappointed. Beckford, it seems, had promised them "a few comfortable days of repose—uncontaminated by the sight and prattle of drawing-room parasites"; yet when they arrived, they found that quite a few other guests had been invited.

The sumptuous meal that was served that evening had to be cooked at the old family estate and carried over to the abbey, where the kitchen had not yet been built. But on Christmas Eve, Beckford decreed that the morrow's meal would be cooked at the abbey. This meant that a kitchen would have to be built literally overnight. Again, his builders worked through the night at breakneck pace, skimping on materials here, cutting corners there and producing by daybreak a kitchen—of sorts. It was functional, fully equipped, and appeared at 1st glance to be solid enough; but of course, it was of the flimsiest construction. Later that day, as Beckford and his guests dined on an excellent meal, the 1st ever cooked at the abbey, they were distracted by a thundering crash. Predictably, the heat of the cooking fires had been more than the still-damp mortar and cement could bear, and the kitchen had collapsed. Beckford was informed of the mishap and, without so much as rising from his chair, he directed his servant to see that a new kitchen be built at once. He then returned to his food, as if he had been interrupted by nothing more disturbing than some spilled wine.

Shortly thereafter, Beckford took up full-time residence in the abbey, moving into one of its 18 tiny, badly ventilated rooms. He was waited upon by an army of servants, which included a Spanish dwarf in livery who received guests.

As the years wore on, Beckford's fortune dwindled and his income disappeared altogether. Growing bored with the abbey, he sold it for £350,000 to a munitions dealer, John Farquhar; he then moved to Bath, building himself a 130′ tower there. Beckford was phobic about 2 things—mirrors and women—and, as at Fonthill, he built niches into the corridors for his maids to hide in when their master passed nearby. Comfortably ensconced at his new estate, he laughed quietly to himself when he heard that Fonthill Abbey was completely destroyed by a strong gale. He lived out his years complacently at Bath, and died in 1844 at the age of 84.

—B.F.

LOUIS BRAILLE (1809–1852). *Inventor and teacher.*

He was the son of a harness maker of the village of Coupvray outside Paris. At the age of 3, while playing in his father's workshop, he drove an awl into his left eye, and in the course of a few weeks went blind in both eyes. Napoleon's reforms had not extended to the weak or handicapped, and a blind child was usually either trained as a professional beggar or set to shoveling coal in a factory. Simon René Braille, however, was determined that his son should suffer no such fate. Louis attended the village school until he was 10. Then his father drove him to Paris and entered him in the Institution Nationale des Jeunes Aveugles.

The Institution had in its library at that time exactly 3 books, each of which were divided into 20 parts weighing some 20 lbs. each. The contents of these volumes were engraved in large embossed letters, and from these Louis learned to read. He was an exceptionally able student, both in his academic work and at the piano and organ, and before very long he was helping to teach the younger children.

In the same year that Louis Braille entered the Institution, a certain Charles Barbier, an artillery captain in Louis XVIII's Army, reported to the Academy of Sciences on his invention of "night writing"—a system of dots and dashes in relief on thin cardboard by which sentinels, using predetermined combinations, could send messages to each other at night. When Barbier later brought his work to the Institution, young Braille set about to improve it. Working silently in bed at night with his board, stylus, and reams of soft paper, he tried and discarded this method and that until finally he hit upon a system of writing using only dots. He discovered that a simple key pattern of 2 dots across and 3 dots down—6 altogether—had quite a number of possible variations. Using this pattern as his "cell," Braille gradually devised 63 separate combinations representing all the letters in the French alphabet (w was added later at the request of an Englishman), accents, punctuation marks, and mathematical signs.

Dr. Pignier, director of the Institution and Braille's sympathetic supporter, adopted his method almost immediately, and for a few happy years Braille saw his system flourish there while he himself taught, attended courses at the Collège de France, served as organist at Notre Dame des Champs, and by applying his system to musical notation, began to compose. His musical talents were immediately recognized; he gave a concert that was acclaimed by many of the foremost musicians of his day, and he began to frequent the many musical salons of the French capital. But government bureaucracy prevented his system from being officially adopted at the Institution, and when Pignier left, his successor insisted that the teachers return to the officially approved embossed letters. Braille's method went underground: The students continued to learn and use it, but surreptitiously, and they were punished if caught.

There exists a very romantic story of how the French Government finally realized the superiority of the Braille method over all other reading systems for the blind. Supposedly, a lovely, young, and very talented blind girl, Thérèse von Kleinert, to whom Braille had taught the organ and his reading method, performed at the fashionable salon of a wealthy Parisian lady before many of the intellectuals of the day. After the applause, she informed her audience that the person they should be honoring was a man named Louis Braille, who had developed the system that enabled her to copy out her many musical scores and to read and write. She noted sadly that Braille was dying of tuberculosis unheralded and unrecognized. According to the story, Thérèse's disclosure turned the tables, and Braille's system was very soon adopted all over France.

—N.C.S. rep.

DEACON WILLIAM BRODIE (1741–1788).
Prototype for Dr. Jekyll and Mr. Hyde.

The real-life figure who inspired the fictional Dr. Jekyll and Mr. Hyde was an Edinburgh cabinetmaker and deacon named William Brodie. He was born in 1741. He died by hanging in 1788, after having made elaborate preparations to have his "corpse" secretly revived by a French doctor. Between reaching maturity and his death, William Brodie lived an incredible double life, by day a prosperous businessman and respected city official, by night the masked leader of a notorious gang.

In 1885, when the ailing Robert Louis Stevenson locked himself in his study for 3 days to write *The Strange Case of Dr. Jekyll and Mr. Hyde*, he used William Brodie for his model. All his life, Stevenson had had an obsession about Brodie. Raised in Edinburgh, where a street is named after Brodie, reared in a nursery that was furnished with a handmade antique cabinet produced by Brodie, Stevenson was steeped in the 2-faced gent's background.

At the age of 15, Stevenson wrote a melodrama called *Deacon Brodie, or The Double Life*. Later he rewrote the play in collaboration with W. E. Henley, and it was a moderate success in London, New York, Philadelphia. In it, foreshadowing Jekyll and Hyde, Stevenson has Deacon Brodie remark, "If we were as good as we seem, what would the world be? The city has its vizard on, and we, at night, are our naked selves." Later in the play Brodie reflects, "Shall a man not have half a life of his own? Not 8 hours of 24? Eight shall he have. Only the stars to see me, I'm a man once more till morning." However, Stevenson was not satisfied that he had made the best use of Brodie. In 1885, his wife woke him from a horrible nightmare. He had been dreaming the 1st transformation scene of Jekyll and Hyde. At once, basing his plot on the dream, he created his modern masterpiece. But the character itself, confirmed by Mrs. E. Blantyre Simpson, a friend of Stevenson's, was rooted in Brodie. Even William Roughead, the great Scottish crime authority, agreed that "there can be little doubt that Stevenson's subconscious was influenced by his old acquaintance with Deacon

Brodie. For years he had been writing and re-writing plays about that admirable double-dealer, whose character supplies so striking an example of the individuality of man's nature and the alternation of good and evil."

William Brodie, well-educated, a member of Edinburgh's leading club, entered his father's prosperous woodworking business and became a deacon or headman of the Incorporation of Wright, a trade union of woodworkers. He also gained a seat in the town council. Since he obtained most of the municipal contracts, his business prospered. When he was 41, his father died, and he inherited £10,000 and a fashionable house in High Street. "A great man in his day was the Deacon," Stevenson wrote later. "Well seen in good society, crafty with his hands as a cabinetmaker, and one who could sing a song with taste. Many a citizen was proud to welcome the Deacon to supper, and dismissed him with regret at a timeous hour, who would have been vastly disconcerted had he known how soon, and in what guise, his visitor returned."

The complete picture of respectability in the daytime, Deacon Brodie became transformed by night. In Stevenson's story, Dr. Jekyll, born to money and commanding respect, a man of learning and taste, found he had a 2nd nature, "a certain impatient gaiety of disposition" and in trying to satisfy that nature he was "often plunged into a kind of wonder at my vicarious depravity." But where Dr. Jekyll tried to separate the 2 sides to his nature with a potion of powder and red liquid, Deacon Brodie needed no more than a few beers to give way to his 2nd self. With nightfall, Brodie shunned his society friends and neighbors, and kept company with thieves in low dives. He gambled with loaded dice, outwitted cardsharps at their own games, hid vicious gamecocks in his backyard, and, besides his own family, secretly maintained 2 mistresses and their families. His gambling losses, and the expenses involved in running 3 households, forced Brodie to search for another means of obtaining spare cash.

It was the custom of the period for shopkeepers to hang keys to their establishments inside their front doors. Brodie, using a wad of putty he had concealed in his hand, would take quick impressions of these keys while his friends were occupied elsewhere. Soon, a series of daring burglaries had the city in an uproar. At 1st, Brodie worked alone. Twice he was almost trapped. Once, Stevenson recalls, "A friend of Brodie's had told him of a projected visit to the country, and afterwards, detained by some affairs, put it off and stayed the night in town. The good man had lain some time awake; it was far on in the small hours; when suddenly there came a creak, a jar, a faint light. Softly he clambered out of bed and up to

a false window which looked upon another room, and there, by the glimmer of a thieves' lantern, was his good friend the Deacon in a mask." The friend was too confused ever to repeat what he had seen. On another occasion, a wealthy widow fell suddenly ill and, for the 1st time, decided not to attend church services. From her bed she saw a masked bandit enter her house, use her keys to open her desk, and then sneak off. As he left, his face disguised by his crepe mask, she thought, "That is Deacon Brodie." But the idea was too absurd, and so she kept it to herself.

In July, 1786, tired of small pickings, Brodie decided to go after bigger hauls. He organized a gang of 3, all ex-convicts. Swiftly they cleaned out a goldsmith's shop and a tobacconist's. Brodie had been remodeling a jewelry shop by day; he suggested it be robbed by night. The night of the theft he was winning a fortune at cards, and failed to keep his date. The gang, leaderless, raided the jewelry store and came away with £350 in stolen goods. Brodie promptly inveigled his followers into a card game, and won all their loot away from them.

Where Dr. Jekyll, in fiction, clubbed a man to death, the good deacon confined his crimes to robbery, though he was later charged with murder. Where Dr. Jekyll maintained a midtown mansion for his public person and a small room in Soho for his alter ego, Deacon Brodie maintained his house in High Street for his daylight activities and 2 apartments elsewhere in Edinburgh for his evening amours and adventures. Where Dr. Jekyll dressed in black for his nightly excursions, Deacon Brodie daringly wore all white until his final crime, when he dressed himself all in black, sporting also a cocked hat and 2 pistols.

The final crime took place on a windy March evening in 1788. With special police patrolling Edinburgh, Brodie and Company prepared for their boldest robbery yet. There were thousands of pounds in the Edinburgh Excise Office. Like Mr. Hyde, who always "had a song upon his lips" after a crime, Brodie also liked a merry tune. Over his tankard he sang "The Rogue's March" from *The Beggar's Opera*, and slipped out of his house early in order to be finished with the Excise Office before the watchman came on at 10 o'clock. Brodie and his 2 helpers, all masked, entered the government building, leaving their 4th member—supplied with an ivory whistle—as lookout. At 8:30 the whistle blasted frantically. A government solicitor, who had forgotten some papers in the Excise Office, was returning. In a frenzy, Deacon Brodie fled, leaving the others behind to escape as best they could.

The next morning the Government offered £150 and a full pardon to any member of the gang who turned stool pigeon. One member, angry at having been deserted, went to the police. Hastily, Brodie left Edinburgh. A King's Messenger was dispatched to hunt him down. Twice, in London, Brodie barely evaded the detective. Next, the fugitive boarded a small sailing vessel bound for the Continent. Later, fellow passengers saw posters with his picture, and reported to the police that he had crossed the Channel. Brodie was found hiding in a cupboard in Amsterdam.

He went on trial August 27, 1788. Since felony trials could not be adjourned, Brodie literally stood at the bar, and the jury sat without a break, for 21 consecutive hours. He was found guilty, and sentenced to hang.

In his cell, he was chained to the floor. On his last morning he heartily ate a beefsteak and went cheerfully to the gallows. He was positive he would cheat death. He had slid a silver tube into his throat to prevent suffocation, had bribed the hangman to keep the rope short in order not to break his neck, and had hired a French surgeon to revive him. After he dropped, and was cut down, his friends threw him into a cart and drove furiously to the surgeon, who bled him but was unable to bring him back to life. There is still a legend in Scotland that he did survive, and was seen strolling in Paris years later. But his grave can be found behind the Chapel of Ease in Edinburgh, and in the Court of Justice stand his lantern and his sets of false keys. No, Deacon Brodie was not revived—until Robert Louis Stevenson was awakened from a nightmare.

—I.W.

CINQUE (1813?–1880). *African mutineer.*

Even after his death in 1974 Donald David DeFreeze, the Symbionese Liberation Army leader who adopted the name General Field Marshal Cinque, remains a mysterious figure unknown really to his own family. More is known about the man from whom the terrorist group's leader took his name, a slave who led a mutiny aboard a slave ship and attempted to sail the vessel back to Africa, becoming a cause célèbre in the process.

The 1st Cinque commanded even more newspaper headlines than DeFreeze did 135 years later. Born the son of a minor chief in what is now the republic of Sierra Leone on the west coast of Africa, he was more properly called *Sing-Gbe* in his tribal Mendi language. Cinque he was to be called by the press, though, and Cinque he remains to history.

In the spring of 1839 Cinque was seized by black slave traders while walking in the bush, and eventually he was sold to a Portuguese dealer for shipment to Cuba. On this 1st voyage he had little chance to escape, the slaves being chained leg to leg in the cramped slave decks of the *Tecora*. It took all his strength and courage to survive the 3-month voyage what with men, women, and children dying in their chains all around him, his captors force-feeding them like geese for the market, whipping them into submission, and rubbing vinegar and gunpowder in their wounds to prevent infection.

On landing in Havana, Cinque and 52 others were purchased by 2 Cubans named José Ruiz and Pedro Montez for what averaged out at less than $10 apiece. Packed aboard the schooner *Amistad*, unshackled now, the slaves were to be shipped to another Cuban port, farther east. But the *Amistad* never reached her destination, for Cinque persuaded his fellow captives to mutiny. They must have been much impressed by their leader, who even in the patronizing words of a contemporary newspaper reporter seems a rather heroic figure. "He is about 5'8" in height, 25 or 26 years of age, of erect figure, well built and very active," the reporter wrote later. "He is said to be a match for any 2 men aboard the schooner. His countenance, for a native African, is unusually intelligent, evincing uncommon decision and coolness, with a composure characteristic of true courage. . . . He expects to be executed, but nevertheless manifests a sang-froid worthy of a stoic under similar circumstances."

Cinque's voice certainly inspired his band, too, for in the words of abolitionist Lewis Tappan, he was "a powerful natural orator, and one born to sway the minds of his fellowmen." In any event, on the 4th night out, the other slaves followed Cinque on deck, where all the crew but the helmsman were sleeping.

Seizing the sailors' 2'-long cane knives, the mutineers quickly took charge, Cinque himself killing the captain and the cruel ship's cook. No one else was harmed, and the crew was put over the side in boats, except for Montez and Ruiz. They were kept to sail the schooner back to Africa.

Wearing a snuff box attached to a string tied around his neck as insignia of his rank, Captain Cinque assumed command of the ship. His crew was decked out in whatever finery could be found aboard. Using sign language, he ordered Montez and Ruiz to sail southeast for Sierra Leone, spelling each other at the wheel. But his former masters tricked him, edging the ship a bit north or west every night. After about 50 days, the *Amistad* wound up in New York waters off Montauk Point. Cinque and his men landed, purchasing supplies with gold they'd found aboard, a slave who had learned a few words of English in Africa doing the bartering, but soon an American coastal survey brig sighted the *Amistad*, her "bottoms and sides . . . covered with barnacles and sea-grass, while her rigging and sails presented an appearance of the *Flying Dutchman*, after her fabled cruise." When the Americans boarded, Cinque dove overboard, evading his pursuers for almost an hour before they caught him. The *Amistad* was then turned over to the U.S. marshal in New London, where Cinque and his men were charged with murder and piracy.

There followed one of the most sensational trials of the century, a trial that many historians believe was a cause of the Civil War. A committee of abolitionists defended the slave mutineers and their case finally reached the Supreme Court in February, 1841, ex-President John Quincy Adams arguing their case eloquently. The court ruled that since Cinque and his men were not Spanish slaves or subjects they must "be declared free, and be dismissed from the custody of the Court, and go without delay."

Afterward, Cinque and the mutineers toured the North to raise money for their return trip. The tour was a great success critically and financially. Wrote a *New York Sun* reporter of Cinque: "His eye can exhibit every vanity of thought, from the cool contempt of a haughty chieftain to the high resolve which would be sustained through martyrdom. . . . Many white men might take a lesson in dignity and forbearance from the African chieftain." More than enough money was raised to enable the band of blacks to charter the brig *Gentlemen* and sail for Sierra Leone on December 2, 1841.

Cinque later became an interpreter at a Christian mission in Sierra Leone. But he never really regretted his action aboard the *Amistad*. One time he was asked if he had it to do all over, wouldn't he pray for the captain and cook of the ship instead of killing them. "Yes," Cinque replied, "I would pray for 'em—and kill 'em, too." He died in 1880, when about 67 years old.

—R.H.

JOHN CLELAND (1709–1789). *British author.*

He gained immortality for creation of a single book, *Fanny Hill, or the Memoirs of a Woman of Pleasure*, which censor Anthony Comstock would later call "the most obscene book ever written." Thought to have been the son of a Scottish tax commissioner named William Cleland (a roisterer who served as a prototype for Joseph Addison's fictional Will Honeycomb), John Cleland was educated at Westminster School in 1722. He became the British consul in Smyrna, and in 1736 worked for the East India Company in Bombay. After quarreling with his employer, Cleland lost his job and returned to London impoverished.

Failing to support himself with his pen, he wound up in debtors' prison.

While incarcerated, he was approached by a 28-year-old printer, Ralph Griffiths, who offered to bail him out of jail if he would write a licentious novel. Cleland agreed, and the result was the overtly sexual (30 acts of copulation and perversion), euphemistic (not one 4-letter word), and scandalous *Fanny Hill*, the story of the acrobatic bedroom experiences of a 15-year-old orphan lass, which appeared in 2 volumes in 1750. The novel earned its printer £10,000 (about $25,000 today) and its author a mere 20 guineas (about $50). The book also earned a bookseller, Drybutter, punishment in the pillory for having "altered the language of the book for the worse after it had been favorably noticed in the *Monthly Review*." Cleland himself escaped punishment when Lord Granville, a president of the Privy Council, intervened on his behalf and even got him a pension of £100 a year in return for the promise that he would write no more dirty books.

Actually, Cleland had written 2 dirty books, for his *Memoirs of a Coxcomb* had followed *Fanny Hill* by a year. But Cleland desisted from any further indulgence in pornography. He wrote political pieces for newspapers, signing them "A Briton" or "Modestus." He wrote several dramatic plays, one entitled *Timbo-Chiqui, or the American Savage, a Dramatic Entertainment in .Three Acts*. After leaving England to make his home in France, he devoted himself entirely to writing benumbing books on philology. Among his better-known language pamphlets and books, one dealt with Sanskrit, another with ancient Celtic.

The Gentleman's Magazine, February, 1789, listed obituaries of personages who had just died, among them, "In Petty, France, aged 80, John Cleland, esq. . . . In conversation he was very pleasant and anecdotal, understanding most of the living languages, and speaking them all very fluently. As a writer, he shewed himself best in novels, song writing, and the lighter species of authorship; but when he touched politics . . . he was soporific." Cleland's *Fanny Hill* remained the major underground classic of erotic literature for over 2 centuries, until it was published openly by the New York firm of G. P. Putnam's Sons in 1963. Putnam's was taken to trial, won, lost an intermediate appeal, and in 1964 won again in New York's Court of Appeals, 4 votes to 3. *Fanny Hill* was free at last.

—I.W.

ROBERT COATES (1772–1848). *British actor.*

One of the worst actors in legitimate stage history was an Englishman named Robert Coates, who had been born in the West Indies.

Coates, nicknamed Romeo because of his passionate desire to act, and Diamond for his originality in attire, became stagestruck in puberty. In 1809 he invaded—perhaps assaulted would be the more accurate word—the London theater. Often referred to as the Gifted Amateur, Coates devoted a long and riotous life to proving he was another Garrick. That he was not, but in his own way he was certainly as entertaining. He liked to play Shakespeare, and he designed his own costumes for *Hamlet* and *Macbeth*—as Romeo he appeared in white feathered hat, spangled cloak, and pantaloons. He wore these same costumes in public. Before appearing in a Shakespearean play, he would rewrite it to suit his talents. "I think I have improved upon it," he told his shocked friends. In *Romeo and Juliet* he improved the ending by trying to pry open Juliet's tomb with a crowbar. If he particularly enjoyed playing a scene, he would repeat the same scene 3 times in one evening as his audiences sat stupefied.

Coates was probably the most inept working actor in the history of the British theater. Yet he tirelessly tramped up and down the British Isles declaiming from the boards. Year after year he was met with derision, catcalls, hilarity, but he persisted. At a performance in Richmond, several spectators were so shaken by laughter that a physician had to be summoned to attend them.

When theater managers, fearing audience violence, barred him from their stages, he bribed them to let him appear. When fellow thespians, fearing bodily injury, refused to act beside him, he provided guards to reassure them. Eventually, by sheer persistence and by the audacity of his mediocrity, he became a legendary figure decked out in furs, jewels, and Hessian boots. He starred in London's leading theaters and gave command performances before royalty. Nothing, it seemed, not criticism, not ridicule, not threats of lynching, could remove him from his place before the footlights. Only death, it was agreed, might silence him and save the English stage. But he would not die. In his 74th year, reduced in circumstances but spouting and gesturing still, he was as active as ever. But the year following, on an afternoon in 1848, a carriage ran him down, and he died. Although English drama survived his passing, its comedy would never be the same again.

—I.W.

ÉMILE COUÉ (1857–1926). *French healer.*

"Every day, in every way, I am getting better and better."
"Every day, in every way, I am getting better and better."
"Every day, in every way, I am getting better and better."

Sound like a primitive Dale Carnegie? Or perhaps the moral of a story designed to enrich the young?

In fact, it is neither: It is the chant of the devotees of Émile Coué, whose unusual method of cure was sweeping the nation in the 1920s. The idea is this: By persistently applying "autosuggestion"—that is, by insisting to yourself that you are in fact "getting better and better"—you will talk yourself right out of your illness.

Émile Coué, described as "the little dried-up Frenchman from Nancy," was also considered to be kindly, forceful yet dignified, "sometimes firm, sometimes gently bantering." He developed his ideas when, working as an apothecary, he observed his patients receiving from certain drugs beneficial effects that could not be ascribed to the medicines. This led him to believe that it was the power of "imagination" that effected the cure.

Coué did not venture a theoretical explanation to his patients—he let his results speak for themselves. In the 1st exercise, the patient was instructed to clasp his hands together and think "I cannot open them." The patient, finding his hands firmly melded, was then ordered to think, "I can open them," and they inevitably unclasped.

From there it was a short step to the crux of the cure—"*Tous les jours, à tous points de vue, je vais de mieux en mieux*"—to be repeated 20 times in a row, twice a day.

Coué recorded cured cases of heart trouble, ulcers, bronchitis, sores, clubfeet, inflammation, nerves, etc. From his records: "Mme. M——, aged 43, Rue d'Amance, 2, Malzeville, comes at the end of 1916 for violent pains in the head from which she has suffered all her life. After a few visits they vanished completely. Two months afterward she realized that she was also cured of a prolapse of the uterus which she had not mentioned to me and of which she was not thinking when she made her autosuggestion. (This result is due to the words 'in every way' contained in the formula used morning and evening.)"

Coué started a free clinic in Nancy, and then in New York he organized and staffed another, eventually leaving for a lecture tour of the Midwest. He was so popular that even the largest lecture halls could not contain the enthusiastic crowds, thronging to see the master himself repeat the famous words.

The story is told of the bowlegged man who repeated the formula too often and became knock-kneed; but for all the jesting, many will agree that getting better is as simple as wanting to be better with the help of M. Coué's little ditty.

—A.W.

ALEISTER CROWLEY (1875–1947). *Occultist.*

Aleister Crowley was perhaps the greatest master of the occult to live and practice in the past century.

Crowley was born in Leamington, England. His life, says his literary executor, John Symonds, was "a series of ecstasies, abominations, and bizarreries." After being thrown out of Cambridge, Crowley gave himself more fully to writing. During his career he was the author of 45 books of poetry, 3 books of erotica, 15 or more books on the occult and religion, as well as an autobiography.

One of Aleister Crowley's most absorbing literary legacies is a little book, now extremely rare, called *The Yi King*, "A new translation of the Book of Changes" by The Master Therion. Of course, The Master Therion was Crowley himself, and his *Yi King* is what today is known as the *I-Ching*. Crowley also published a limited edition of this in London in 1909, when he was 34, and at the time he called it *Liber Trigrammaton*, "The Book of the Trigrams of the permutations of the Tao with the Yin and the Yang."

Crowley not only translated and wrote his version of the *I-Ching*, but he passionately believed in its predictions. Throughout his life, he practiced what he preached in the *Book of Changes*. John Symonds cites countless occasions when the master consulted his *I-Ching*. Two examples:

Crowley wanted to establish an occult center. "Where should they go to do the Great Work? The *Yi King*, that ancient Chinese book of oracles, was consulted. Should they go to Algeria, Or the Italian lakes? How about Spain? Naples or Sicily? The answer of the hexagram was indecisive. . . .

"On the 1st of March, 1920, at half past 5 in the afternoon, he again consulted the Chinese oracle. Where should he start the Great Work? For nothing but the universal acceptance of the Law of Thelema as the sole and sufficient basis of conduct could save the world. He must found a community, the archetype of all future communities, whose only code of convention will be the one law of Do what thou wilt.

"Shall I spend April and June in or near Marseilles?

"Fire of Water. No.

"Capri? Earth of Air. No.

"Cefalu? Earth of Lingam. This couldn't be better.

"The Chinese oracle had spoken and Crowley made a very emphatic note in his diary that it was solely on this answer from the *Yi King* hexagram that he went to Cefalu [a fishing village on the northern shore of Sicily]."

In 1923, the dictator Mussolini ordered Crowley expelled from Sicily. "This was a stab in the back indeed. Was his life's work ruined? He must consult the *Yi King*. What course should he adopt? . . . The Chinese sticks were laid out on the table. What was the general symbol for the present situation? Hexagram XLVII. Constraint. And what was the best course of action to adopt? Prepare to move. Be steady. Prepare to reconstruct. Seek relief from friends. Accept substantial assistance. Turn the situation to advantage by increasing sympathizers. There should be an unexpectedly large number of such ready to help us.'

"Should they make a direct protest to the Minister of the Interior? If so, what should they say? The Chinese oracle was unfailing. Thwan. Yes. They should state their case systematically. Press the matter. Beware of divided counsels. Retire in order to advance. Refute all falsehoods about themselves. Make it clear that they represent a widespread and important movement.

"Should they make an appeal to their national Ambassadors in Rome? Yes, but don't expect much result.

"Meanwhile where should The Beast go? The Oracle told him to cross the water. Africa would be very favorable. What part of Africa? The coast or some well-watered spot, but isolated, difficult of access, and where there is indifference to public affairs."

And so, following the advice of his *Yi King*, Crowley moved to a suburb of Tunis.

But Crowley was far more than a writer and a delver into the *I-Ching*.

He was also, incredibly, a mountaineer. He climbed Mount Popocatapetl in Mexico, and made the 1st assault on K2 in the Himalayas, reaching the 20,000' level. In 1905, he was a leader of the expedition that tried to climb Kanchenjunga in Tibet, an effort that ended in the death of 5 men. Crowley was forever traveling. At 30, he went from India to Burma, and then hiked through a great part of China. Later, he turned up in Greenwich Village to paint dwarfs, tattooed ladies, and black women, and to lecture in New York.

He hated Christianity, and founded his own religion. He believed in "the worship of the sun and of man's organ of creation, and of sexual union as the highest form of religious &M secration." He founded the Abbey of Thélèma in Sicily, and with his women and followers practiced pagan and sexual rites. In Italy and France, he performed black magic masses and conducted sexual orgies, and for this activity he was expelled from both countries.

His followers considered him the Messiah. Crowley's creed expounded the following com-

Footnote People in World History **527**

mandments: "Do what thou wilt shall be the whole of the law. . . . Every man and every woman is a star. . . . The only sin is restriction."

Crowley was into drugs, ultimately on heroin. His 1st 2 wives wound up in insane asylums. Of his dozens of mistresses, 5 committed suicide. The British press reviled him as "The Beast" and "The Wickedest Man in the World!" His admirers worshiped him as a mystical genius. He died on December 1, 1947, at the age of 74, in Brighton, England, where he was cremated.

—I.W.

LORENZO DA PONTE (1749–1838). *Italian librettist.*

It takes a great libretto to make a great opera, but, ironically, few persons have gained fame writing operatic libretti. In producing his 3 greatest operas—*The Marriage of Figaro, Don Giovanni,* and *Così Fan Tutte*—Wolfgang Amadeus Mozart collaborated with the most talented librettist of his time, Lorenzo da Ponte. Oddly, he was a "facile, mediocre poet," according to his biographer April Fitz-Lyon, and a "very inexperienced dramatist." It boggles the mind to realize that he is the man who, "above all others, succeeded in providing Mozart with the perfect framework for his music." And yet Da Ponte's libretti were but one of his accomplishments: He was, at various times, a Catholic priest, a poet, a scholar, a storekeeper, and one of the most colorful roués who ever lived. But Da Ponte died in obscurity and even the whereabouts of his bones is unknown. Surely history owes him more.

He was born Emmanuele Conigliano in the Jewish ghetto of Ceneda, Italy, in 1749. However, his father, a tanner, was converted to Catholicism along with his 4 sons in 1763. The old man thought it fitting to rename his boys after the bishop who baptized them all—Msgr. Lorenzo da Ponte—and while 3 of them took only the cleric's surname, young Emmanuele became his namesake.

Fourteen years old and full of mischief, Lorenzo was enrolled in the seminary in Ceneda immediately, the pleased bishop paying the bill. As far as the boy was concerned, the priesthood seemed as good a line of work as any other, and he prepared his lessons diligently, showing a particular talent for writing in both Latin and Italian.

Ordained in 1771, he was appointed to the chair of rhetoric at the seminary of Portoguaro. His colleagues were angered by this quick promotion, which seemed to them to be eminently unfair. They'd doubtless have been even angrier had they known that he was not the very model of ecclesiastical decorum he let on

to be: Whenever he could, he would slip out of the seminary and off to Venice, where he dallied with Angela Ticpolo, a down-and-out young woman from a once wealthy Venetian family.

In 1773, Father da Ponte left the school altogether and moved to Venice, where he was free from the celibacy vow and no longer had to endure the jealous taunts of his rivals on the faculty. Angela, a penniless shrew, made life difficult for Da Ponte. She was amorous, but petulant; generous, but jealous. And when she suspected her lover of being unfaithful, she threw a bottle of ink in his face and cut off all his hair. For Da Ponte, life in the city seemed to be an unbroken string of robberies and swindlings—even Angela's brother had extorted money from him—it was the proverbial last straw. He gathered his belongings and left.

From Venice, he went to the seminary of Treviso, where he taught for 2 years until he was expelled for writing heretical poems. From Treviso he moved to Padua, living on bread and olives for 6 weeks and supporting himself by hustling checker games in cafés. From there it was back to Venice, where he took up with Angioletta Bellaudi, a married woman who had been peddling her favors since early adolescence. Pregnant by Da Ponte, she went into labor on a sidewalk, where Da Ponte delivered the child. Adding outrage to outrage, the priest and his current mistress opened a brothel, where the cassock-garbed father provided violin background music. Having sired 3 illegitimate children and making, as far as the authorities could see, a general nuisance of himself, he was banned from the city.

For 2 years, Da Ponte knocked about Europe—mostly in Germany—supporting himself through writing. He was continually being bilked and cheated, and he dallied with the ladies, discarding one conquest after another like so many squeezed lemons. (On one occasion he painted himself into a corner by being too attentive to a woman *and* her 2 daughters.)

Da Ponte settled in Vienna, where he became Poet of the Italian Theatre under the patronage of Emperor Joseph II, writing libretti for the operas of obscure Italian composers. It was there, in 1783, that he met Mozart and the 2 decided to collaborate on an operatic version of Beaumarchais's play, *The Marriage of Figaro.* They finished the work in 6 weeks and it was an immediate sensation throughout Austria.

In 1787, Da Ponte wrote 3 libretti for 3 different composers in 9 weeks, working 12 hours a day and fortifying himself with tokay, snuff, and the attentions of the nubile 16-year-old daughter of his landlady. Mozart's *Don Giovanni* was one of these operas—Da Ponte's libretto was partly autobiographical—and it had its premiere in Prague in 1788, followed by *Così Fan Tutte* the following year.

When Joseph II died, Da Ponte lost his meal ticket and he was out of a job. He went to Trieste and there, at the age of 43, "an age at which respectable married men take mistresses, and disreputable adventurers think about marriage," he fell in love with an Englishwoman, Nancy Grahl. They settled in London, where Da Ponte wrote operatic libretti as Poet to the Italian Opera in the Drury Lane Theatre. He was in England 12 years, and during that time he did the libretti for 5 now forgotten operas. In the same period, he traveled to Italy once to recruit singers, opened a printing shop, helped promote a piano factory, established an Italian bookshop, wrote and published several scandalous—and quite obscene—broadsides against his enemies, was arrested 30 times, and went bankrupt.

Disconsolate and deeply in debt, he decided that England had nothing more to offer him and so he, Nancy, and their 5 children set sail for America. In New York, he opened a grocery store and then moved to Elizabeth, N.J., where he deplored the fact that he was now writing "bills for sausages and dried prunes," for carpenters and draymen, when once he had written operatic libretti for Kings.

His grocery business was doomed to failure because the softhearted Da Ponte allowed his customers infinite credit, finally accepting "lame horses, broken carts . . . old shoes . . . rancid butter" in payment for goods. In 1807, he returned to New York, where he gave Italian lessons. He met the poet Clement Clarke Moore in New York (author of "A Visit from St. Nicholas"), and together they founded the Manhattan Academy for Young Gentlemen, dedicated to the moral uplifting of its students. Da Ponte left New York for greener pastures, in Sunbury, Pa., where he ran a small general store. He went bankrupt once again and moved to Philadelphia, this time operating a millinery shop and a delivery service which he called "L. de Ponty's Wagon."

But he missed New York, and in the spring of 1819, at the age of 70, he returned. He lectured on Italian culture, taught Italian, wrote poetry, translated Byron into Italian, published his memoirs, opened a bookstore. In 1825, he became the 1st professor of Italian literature at Columbia College.

At the age of 84, Da Ponte financed and built New York's 1st opera house, at the corner of Church and Leonard streets in lower Manhattan. The project was immensely rewarding to him, but it drained him financially and physically. On August 17, 1838, at the age of 89, Da Ponte died. Although he had converted to Anglicanism, he was buried in a Catholic cemetery. The cemetery was moved long ago, and no one today has the slightest idea where Da Ponte's headstone or his bones might be.

—B.F.

DON MANUEL DE GODOY (1767–1851).
Royal favorite.

He may have been the most inept statesman Europe has ever known. But then, his power over Spanish affairs—which was near total at the time of Napoleon—was derived more from his performances in the Queen's bedchamber than from any achievements military or diplomatic.

Godoy was just a muscular country boy when he came to Madrid in 1784. Assigned to the royal bodyguard at 17, Manuel cut a striking figure in the cocked hat and sword of the cavalryman. He was tall and uncommonly well put together, with creamy pink skin and dark, almond-shaped eyes.

Soon he was involved in a dozen dalliances with ladies of the court. In time, he was noticed by Maria Luisa of Parma, a notorious sensualist in her own right. She was also the wife of the next King of Spain.

Maria Luisa was remarkably unattractive: Sixteen years older than Godoy, she had beady eyes, a sallow complexion, and a tight, bitter mouth full of false teeth. Her appearance hadn't stopped her from acquiring an impressive number of lovers, even before she met Godoy. Afterward, though he would be the love of her life, she went right on enjoying the attentions of others as well. Everyone at the Spanish court knew all the lusty details. Everyone, that is, except her husband. By the time he became Carlos IV, his wife was already firmly under Godoy's spell.

With the Queen's patronage, the young officer was promoted a rank a month until, at 21, he was head of all Spanish armed forces. A local wag set a dog loose in the streets of Madrid with a collar note that read: "I belong to Godoy, I fear nothing." When the joker could not be found, the dog was put in jail instead.

Carlos IV did not have the stomach for leadership. He grew up thinking he would never have to lead. But when his older brother was ruled out of succession because he was an imbecile, the crown fell, by default, to Carlos, who was only half an imbecile. Not only did he never suspect the relationship between his wife and Godoy, but he was as fond of the handsome young cavalier as she was.

Don Manuel was a coolly confident man of the flesh, cast among a warbling brood of royal cretins whose swollen bodies and shrunken souls are forever preserved in Goya's devastating portraits.

At 25, Godoy was made Prime Minister. He quickly antagonized Louis XVI of France. Then when the Bastille fell, Godoy sought to appease the new French Republic and bargained for the return of Bourbon rule. The revolutionists were outraged when he suggested they restore the monarchy and go set up a republic, if they liked, on the island of San Domingo. By way of reply, they cut off Louis's head.

Aroused by such treatment of a King—and a Bourbon at that—Spain went to war to stomp out French radicalism once and for all. Within months, French troops had crossed the Pyrenees. Godoy quickly sued for peace and began currying favor with Napoleon, hoping to make a powerful ally out of his late enemy. His efforts won Spain 12 years of war with England and the annihilation of Spanish naval power at Trafalgar.

Meanwhile, Godoy had acquired a full-time mistress and a wife, in addition to keeping up his amour with the Queen. Now a dissolute 36, the Prime Minister was "a big, sturdy, coarse man, with a bright red complexion and a heavy, sleepy, sensual look," according to one observer.

In 1801, he collaborated with Napoleon in the invasion of Portugal. While Godoy was reveling in the subjugation of his neighbor, French troops marched into Spain and forced the abdication of Carlos IV. Godoy was nearly torn to shreds by an angry mob, then was summoned to Bayonne by Napoleon along with the deposed Carlos IV and Maria Luisa. Napoleon received the trio graciously and ordered them into exile. They retired to Rome, taking along Godoy's entourage of wife, mistresses, and children. While the Napoleonic Wars raged, and new crown heads came and went in Spain, the pitiful little group spun out their years in Italy.

In 1819, both Carlos and Maria Luisa died. The Little Corporal was gone now too. Godoy's entourage deserted him and he was left alone. Many years later, the new Spanish monarch, Queen Isabella—who was almost certainly Godoy's granddaughter—restored some of his titles. But he was still a man without a country.

Now, stooped and gray-whiskered, he moved to Paris, where he was often seen in later years playing with French children in the Tuileries. He died at 84, utterly forgotten in a strange land.

—D.P.P.

DANIEL DUNGLAS HOME (1833–1886).
Notable British psychic.

A luminous vapor gathered above the table, and, as they watched, slowly formed itself into a

child's hand. . . . The room shook; the crystal pendants of the chandelier clashed together; the Empress's lace handkerchief climbed into space . . . an accordion held by Napoleon played melodious airs; and the table itself became light or heavy at command.

This peculiar occurrence at the court of Napoleon III, in 1857, was a routine event for those who frequented the parlors where Daniel Dunglas Home, medium, held his séances.

Born in Scotland, Daniel Home was raised in Connecticut by an aunt. He suffered from tuberculosis and was of a delicate constitution. At a very early age, Daniel gave evidence that he was not an average child. When he was 13, he had his 1st vision—a dead friend appeared before him, and shortly thereafter, he also saw his dead mother. By the time he was 17, furniture was moving unexpectedly around his aunt's house, and strange rapping sounds were often to be heard. In exasperation, his aunt threw him out of the house when he was 18.

Then began for Daniel a lifetime of exotic travels, aristocratic supporters, costly gifts, public outrage and scandal, and most of all, a series of perhaps the most extraordinary séances the world had seen.

The general format was this: In a well-lit room (Home despised the abundant imposters who plied their trade in the dark), Home would sit with a circle of about 8 eager persons, almost always members of the upper class. Home would enter a trancelike state, and the denizens of the spirit world would take over. Cool breezes would be felt, furniture would bump and shake, rapping sounds would be heard, spirit hands gloved in silk would materialize (sometimes those of a dead relation of someone in the room), and objects floated about independently or were borne by the disembodied hands, musical instruments (accordions were favored) were played by the spirit hands, and questions were answered by rappings. Sometimes there were spirit voices, and even inspirational sermons.

Home, a young man of charming appearance and ill health (his health never ceased to trouble him), would not accept money for his work and was much offended by such an offer. However, he was very fond of jewelry, furs, and other gifts, which he always accepted. Moreover, he accepted more than graciously the lodgings he was given at the houses of well-to-do and socially elite persons. He was said to be quite affable company, his presence entertaining his host, and as Home was a much coveted guest, he added to the host's prestige. "Nature had, in short, formed him to be the perfect houseguest." Home's successes included New England, England, Italy, France, and Russia. Not only aristocrats, but artists as well, became devotees of Home's abilities, most notably the poetess Elizabeth Barrett Browning. Her husband, poet Robert Browning, violently despised Home and his spirit friends, and he even went so far as to write the poem *Mr. Sludge, The Medium* to disparage him. Home had one difficult year when the spirits abandoned him because they found his behavior a bit too dissolute. (He became a Roman Catholic during this period.) The spirits returned a year later on a given date, as they had promised.

In 1858, when Home married a young Russian girl, his friend Alexandre Dumas, père, was his best man. Sasha, his bride, did not know of his abilities and at 1st was somewhat disconcerted to find spirits materializing in their bedroom, but soon she too became an avid devotee of spiritualism. She bore him a son, Gricha, and died at an early age. He wrote his autobiography soon after her death, and then, deciding to study sculpture, he went to Rome, where he was promptly excommunicated as a sorcerer.

More adventures followed, including a messy legal case with an elderly widow who adopted him. At this time, he became a very close friend of a Lord Adare, who took scrupulous note of his activities and wrote a book about him, observing at length such feats as levitation and the handling of hot coals and fire. Adare writes of a séance in the late 1860s—"We heard Home go into the next room, heard the window thrown up, and presently Home appeared standing upright outside over a window; he opened the window and walked in quite coolly." What is notable here is that the windows were on the 3rd floor, 60′ to 70′ above the ground, and there was no balcony.

Near the end of his life, Home who had remarried, devoted his time to writing and traveling, giving occasional séances for friends, including Mark Twain. He died in France at the age of 53.

Although countless skeptics attempted to discredit Home's feats as charlatanry, none ever succeeded in the slightest degree, and today D. D. Home is considered one of history's greatest mediums.

—A.W.

SIR JEFFERY HUDSON (1619–1682).
English midget gallant.

Barely 19″ tall at the age of 30, Jeffery Hudson was one of the most remarkable men of his time, as well as one of the smallest. He gained fame in the 17th century as a confidant of royalty, soldier of fortune, and political prisoner. When he died in 1682, at the age of 63, he was as well-known throughout England for his reputedly radical politics as he was for his size.

One could hardly say that smallness of stature ran in Hudson's family. He was born to normal-sized parents in Oakham, Rutlandshire, in 1619, and his brothers and sisters all grew to normal height. As a youngster his diminutiveness was often used by pranksters. Once, some neighborhood jokers stole an old woman's cat—named Rutterkin—killed and skinned it, and dressed young Jeffery in the pelt. That afternoon, just after the unsuspecting widow served lunch to some guests, the boy padded out of his hiding place into the drawing room, and one of the women asked if Rutterkin would like a bit.

"Rutterkin can help himself when he is hungry," Jeffery answered glibly. The ladies panicked and ranted hysterically at their hostess and the entire party was thrown into an uproar.

Jeffery's father was in the employ of the Duke of Buckingham, and when the boy was 8, he was presented to the Duke and Duchess, who took him into the royal household. He was treated with great honor there and attended by servants. When Charles I of England and his Queen Henrietta Maria came to visit the ducal estate in Burleigh-on-the-Hill, Jeffery surprised—and amused—them by emerging chicklike from a cold baked pie served at dinner. Presenting the boy thus had been the brainchild of the fun-loving Duchess, who offered Jeffery as a gift to the Queen. Maria was delighted and flattered by the gift, and eagerly accepted the child into her service.

In the royal palace, Jeffery was endlessly pampered and doted upon and he performed frequently in court entertainments. In one, William Evans, the court giant, who was well over 7′ tall, pulled a large loaf of bread out of one pocket and Jeffery out of another. He then pretended to eat the 2 together, as a sandwich.

But despite the royal favors he enjoyed, the normal requirements of everyday living created problems for Jeffery because of his small size, and sometimes threatened his life. Once, while washing his face and hands, he nearly drowned in the washbasin. On another occasion, a strong wind would have swept him to a watery death in the Thames had he not grabbed hold of a shrub.

Not that his diminutiveness was without its rewards. A journalist of the day wrote that the ladies at court were quite fond of the midget child: "He could make married Men Cuckolds, without making them jealous, and mothers of Maids, without letting the World know they had any Gallants."

In 1630, when he was only 11, Jeffery was dispatched by Queen Henrietta Maria to France to bring back a French midwife. The French Queen, Marie de' Medici, was greatly impressed by the maturity, the savoir faire, and the worldliness of this supremely precocious youngster, bestowing great riches upon him and upon the Queen of England, her daughter. On the way back to England, however, Jeffery's ship was waylaid by pirates and he was taken captive. After a brief internment, he escaped and returned to England, altogether surprised to find that he had lost no favor at court or among the masses despite his delay in completing his mission.

Jeffery was steadfastly loyal to the Queen, defending her against political enemies, and following her to Paris when she expatriated herself there in 1644. While in the French capital, he fell into a dispute with Mr. Crofts—the younger brother of a British lord in attendance upon Queen Henrietta Maria—and challenged him to a duel. Crofts accepted and appeared at the appointed place armed to the teeth—with a squirt gun. Jeffery was enraged at the insult, and rechallenged Crofts to a legitimate duel with real guns. On a tree-shaded sward not far from the palace of the Duke of Nevers, where the Queen was lodged, Jeffery shot his foe dead.

Dueling, particularly when it ended fatally, was outlawed in France, and Jeffery was imprisoned. However, a beguiling letter on his behalf written by Queen Henrietta Maria herself to the authorities had him freed and on his way home to England, banished forever from France.

The details of the last 38 years of Jeffery's life are vague and clouded with rumor and supposition. During the English civil war he served with distinction in the King's Cavalry as a captain of the horse guards. In 1649, he was taken captive by Turkish pirates and sold into slavery, where he was abused and reviled. It was during this confinement that he mysteriously doubled in height to 3'9". Jeffery was eventually ransomed and he returned once again to England, where he lived on the favors of the Duke of Buckingham. He gained notoriety when he was arrested, in 1679, for his involvement in Titus Oates's Popish Plot. He was imprisoned in the Gate House at Westminster for 3 years, released in 1682, and died soon after at the age of 63.

—B.F.

WILLIAM HENRY IRELAND (1777–1835). *English forger.*

William Shakespeare wrote 37 plays in his lifetime. Not one, or even a fragment of one, written in his hand survived him. Even Shakespeare's signature was scarce. The 3 existing on the 3 sheets of his will became national treasures. Not a shred of correspondence from Shakespeare to a publisher, producer, patron, fellow writer actor, or friend existed. And documents concerning Shakespeare—not by him but about him—were extremely rare. There

were documents to be seen on his marriage, the baptism of his 2 daughters and son, the death of his son at age 11, his performance as an actor in court, the purchase of his large house, and a few others relating to real estate investments. But there was not a single document giving evidence of Shakespeare's activities between 1585 and 1592, among the peak years of his career. The lack of documentation by and about Shakespeare was a loss to humanity and scholarship.

William Ireland's claim to fame—or notoriety—was that he tried to make up this loss. When he was 17 and 18 years old, Ireland stunned and thrilled the world by bringing forth a mass of papers, written by or about Shakespeare, that he had found. For 2 years, an excited world paid homage to these priceless papers and to young Ireland himself.

There was only one problem, as it turned out: The bonds, deeds, leases, letters, plays written by Shakespeare had been written not by the Bard but by the precocious Ireland himself. The forgeries were among the most daring and successful in the history of literature.

Young Ireland's father, Samuel Ireland, was a well-known London engraver, as well as a dealer in rare books and antiques. The boy grew up among the musty treasures of the past. One day, finding in his father's collection an ancient volume bearing the crest of the royal family's library, William Ireland prankishly penned a dedication on the flyleaf from the author to the long-dead Queen Elizabeth. William was shaken when his father unquestioningly accepted the fake inscription as genuine. With that success, William learned two things: that he possessed a natural gift for forgery, and that it was possible to deceive an expert totally.

A combination of 3 events turned the boy to Shakespeare. A visit to Stratford-on-Avon proved inspirational. There, too, he learned of the severe shortage of original Shakespeare papers. Finally, brief employment as a conveyancer's clerk allowed him to handle early documents, which provided him with the models for the undertaking that was stirring in his head.

One day, Ireland located a rent roll from the Elizabethan period. It had a blank parchment sheet. Next, he diluted bookbinding fluid to approximate a well-faded brown ink. Then, from a printed book, he traced Shakespeare's signature until he was able to write it freehand. Finally, he created a 16th-century property lease and at the bottom, with a flourish, he signed it, "Wm. Shakespeare." He hurried to his father with the lease, and breathlessly told how he had obtained it. He explained that he had "made an acquaintance at a coffeehouse with a gentleman of fortune, who was from my conversation given to understand that I had a great predilection for everything like antiquity, he had in consequence requested that I would pay him a visit; stating at the same time that he had many old papers which had descended to him from his ancestors." Ireland visited the wealthy gentleman's apartment, and examining bundles of aged papers, "I discovered to my utter astonishment, the deed between our Bard and Michael Fraser, bearing the signature of Shakespeare." The gentleman then offered this document to Ireland, and any others by Shakespeare that might be found, on the condition that the owner's name be kept anonymous, for the gentleman "did not think fit to subject himself to the impertinent questions" that might follow.

The dazed elder Ireland studied the lease, checked the ancient paper, cracked old seals, faded ink, the signature itself, and authenticated the find. Immediately, he sent word of it to the nation's scholars and press.

Meanwhile, son William began producing a steady stream of 16th-century licenses, notes, receipts, deeds, snippets of verse, contracts with actors—all in Shakespeare's handwriting and all gifts of the mysterious wealthy gentleman.

Early in 1796, Samuel Ireland collected his son's discoveries and published them as *Miscellaneous Papers and Legal Instruments under the Hand and Seal of William Shakespeare*.

The Irelands were soon celebrities. Young William was advancing his own prestige, but he also wanted to do something for his idol. He wanted to show that the great poet was a recognized man of social consequence even in his own day. So William fabricated correspondence between Shakespeare and the Earl of Southampton, forging the poet's letters with his right hand and the nobleman's replies with his left. Going one better, he "discovered" several chatty exchanges between Shakespeare and Queen Elizabeth. And to refute lingering suspicions that the great playwright had been a Catholic, William conveniently found a 300-word "Profession of Protestant Faith," proving the great man a good Anglican after all. A learned clergyman who read the statement declared: "We have many fine passages in our Church Service and our litany abounds in beauty, but here, Sir, is a man who outdistances us all."

Stirred by such praise, Ireland went on to discover the complete manuscript of *King Lear* and portions of the original *Hamlet*. He also came up with a love letter from Shakespeare to Anne Hathaway, and a lock of Shakespeare's hair.

By now Samuel Ireland was charging admission to the public to inspect the evidence on display in his house. William Pitt, Edmund Burke, and the Prince of Wales were among those who came away deeply moved. James Boswell knelt before the fakes and cried: "I now kiss the invaluable relics of our Bard, and thank God I have lived to see them."

William was now 18, and ready for the big move. He announced that, through his gentleman friend, he could lay his hands on a complete, unpublished, unproduced Shakespeare play. Remembering an oil painting in his father's study showing the Saxon princess Rowena giving wine to Vortigern, William said the play *Vortigern* was a tragedy set in Romanized Britain. Now William had to stall an anxious public 2 months while he brought forth *Vortigern* a scene at a time.

While the world waited for the climactic discovery, there were those who had run out of patience for what they perceived to be a hoax. Three eminent Shakespearean scholars suspected forgery, but only one of them prepared to speak out. The vocal one was Edmund Malone, who was readying to expose Ireland's finds in his work *An Inquiry into the Authenticity of Certain Papers Attributed to Shakespeare, Queen Elizabeth, and Henry, Earl of Southampton*. Word of this book, which would not appear until later in 1796, was already spreading through London.

By now Ireland had delivered the complete play. Every theater manager in London was clamoring for Shakespeare's lost masterpiece. Richard Brinsley Sheridan acquired it with a down payment of £300 and a promise of half the profits to the Irelands. Sheridan objected only to the length of the play. As young Ireland confessed later: "Being under the age of 18 when I wrote the play of *Vortigern*, the following fact will not appear singular. I was really so unacquainted with the proper length of a drama as to be compelled to count the number of lines in one of Shakespeare's plays, and on that standard to frame *Vortigern*; and the play I had chosen happened to be so uncommonly long, mine consequently became so: when completed it contained, to the best of my recollection, 2,800 lines and upwards."

Meanwhile, the production proceeded. The great John Philip Kemble was selected to play the lead. Henry James Pye, the Poet Laureate of England, was commissioned to write a suitable prologue. More than 2,000 persons bought tickets for opening night, April 2, 1796, at Drury Lane. Hundreds more crashed the gate and crowded the pit.

Ireland always insisted that *Vortigern* went well for 2 acts, and came apart in the 3rd act. Doubters in the audience, influenced by the scholar Malone, let their hostility be known only when the actors onstage became their allies. For the actors in the cast sensed what most politicians and literary critics had missed: The clumsy dialogue put in their mouths could never have been written by the same man who penned the most enduring words in the English language. They became saboteurs. When one actor was supposed to call the trumpets of war to "Bellow on," he pronounced the line in falsetto, leaving the audience gasping with laughter. Another actor was "slain" in stage battle, but fell where the drop curtain left the lower half of his body sticking out onstage. He groaned audibly under the weight of the heavy curtain roller. Eventually the "dead man" pulled himself free and crawled into the wings.

The actor playing Vortigern gave a speech containing the line: "And when this solemn mockery is over." He gave the phrase such meaningful emphasis that the audience understood immediately. When the guffaws died down, he did not go on but repeated, "And when this solemn mockery is over . . ." William Ireland had already slipped out of the theater, seeing what was coming.

When the final curtain fell that night, it ended the 1st and last performance of *Vortigern*. Before that night, young Ireland had dreamt of glory. As he would write: "Had the play of *Vortigern* succeeded with the public, and the manuscript been acknowledged as genuine, it was my intention to have completed a series of plays from the reign of William the Conqueror to that of Queen Elizabeth; that is to say, I should have planned a drama on every reign the subject of which had not been treated of by Shakespeare."

But hoax was in the air, and William Ireland's grand scheme was dead. Everyone, it seemed, blamed his father, the elder Ireland, for having committed the hoax, unable to believe one as young as William could have done it successfully. Loyal friends begged young William to exonerate his father by revealing the name of the wealthy gentleman who had provided the Shakespearean papers. Since the wealthy gentleman was nonexistent, in a final effort to clear his father's name, William Ireland confessed his entire forgery late in 1796 in a book entitled *An Authentic Account of the Shakespearean Manuscripts*. But even this confession did not fully absolve his father, who died in 1800 still professing his innocence.

William Ireland lived another 40 years. In 1805, he confessed his forgery a 2nd time in a more detailed book, *Confessions of William Henry Ireland*. He continued to write under several names, producing a string of forgettable novels, collections of verse—and even a factual catalogue of Shakespeare's works, from which the title *Vortigern* was missing.

—D.P.P. & I.W.

DIDIUS JULIANUS (132–193).
Roman Emperor.

On the morning of March 28, 193 A.D., 300 members of the Roman Praetorian Guard (the private bodyguard of the Caesars numbering 12,000 in all) invaded the Emperor's palace—which they were supposed to protect—and hunted down their ruler, an honest and earthy disciplinarian named Pertinax. Members of the guard had long smarted under Emperor Pertinax's stringent rule, and now they had determined to get rid of him. They did not have to search long. Pertinax came forward to meet them, fearlessly reproaching the would-be assassins. Momentarily, they were immobilized and shamed. Suddenly, one guard broke from the rest, plunged forward, and ran his sword through Pertinax, and others joined in to decapitate him. The deed was done.

What followed next remains one of the more incredible episodes in the annals of history.

The brutal act of assassination left the throne of Rome vacant. The throne was an important one. For the man who sat on this throne ruled not only Italy but 150 million people scattered from the Rhine east to the Euphrates and west to the Thames, and thus in effect held sway over most of the known civilized world of the period.

Having eliminated their Emperor, members of the Praetorian Guard had to find someone to replace him. The scepter was offered to several senators. They refused it. Pertinax had been popular, and government officials as well as the populace were angered by the murder. The senators suspected the throne might become a hot seat.

Then an anonymous soldier, inspired, suggested that the guard give the job to the Roman citizen who paid the highest price for it. At once, other members of the guard suggested a public auction. Herodianus, the 3rd-century historian, tells us that a soldier with a loud voice immediately scrambled up the embankments surrounding the city and rushed along the ramparts bellowing, "The Empire is for auction! The Empire is for auction!"

This remarkable news was relayed to 61-year-old Didius Julianus, the wealthiest senator in Rome, as he sat at dinner with his wife Marilina Scantilla and his daughter Didia Clara. Milan-born Julianus, characterized by Edward Gibbon as "a vain old man," had made his fortune in the merchant marine. Now, convinced by his family and slaves that the purple mantle might fit neatly into his wardrobe, he hurried to the camp where the soldiers were impatiently waiting to get their auction under way.

Besides Didius Julianus, the only other bidder was Sulpicianus, father-in-law of the murdered Pertinax, who made the 1st offer. Immediately, Julianus countered, and soon the bidding became intense. According to historian Dio Cassius, "Guards kept reporting to Julianus, 'Sulpicianus offers so much; now how much will you add to that?' And again to Sulpicianus, 'Julianus offers so much, how much will you raise it?'" At last, Sulpicianus made his final bid, offering the guard 240 million sesterces, or the equivalent of $800 to each of the 12,000 soldiers of the guard. Instantly, Julianus made his winning bid "with a great shout, indicating the amount likewise on his fingers." This bid was 300 million sesterces or $1,000 to each soldier of the guard. In a moment, the Roman Empire was going, going, gone.

The 1st act of the new ruler, that very night, was to assemble the hostile Senate. As Dio Cassius, who was present, reports it, Julianus sat down comfortably in the traditional Emperor's chair of the Senate and delivered to his recent pro-Pertinax peers the following address:

"Perceiving, O venerable fathers, that the throne is vacant, I must tell you that I think nobody more worthy to fill it than myself. I shall not take up much of your time by praising myself, or putting you in mind of my virtues, for I believe none of you are ignorant of them.

"I am persuaded you all know me very well, so without giving you further trouble, I beg to inform you that the Army has thought proper to choose me Emperor, and I come hither that you may confirm their choice."

The embittered Senate, intimidated by the proximity of the armed Praetorian guardsmen, promptly confirmed Didius Julianus as Emperor of Rome.

Protected from the enraged and stone-throwing citizenry by the phalanx of his private bodyguard, Emperor Julianus was led to his new home, the royal palace. "A magnificent feast was prepared by his order," wrote Gibbon, "and he amused himself till a very late hour, with dice, and the performances of Pylades, a celebrated dancer. Yet it was observed that, after the crowd of flatterers dispersed, and left him to darkness, solitude, and terrible reflection, he passed a sleepless night; revolving most probably in his mind his own rash folly, the fate of his virtuous predecessor, and the doubtful and dangerous tenure of an empire, which had not been acquired by merit, but purchased by money."

But although Didius Julianus was suffering 2nd thoughts in the dark night, he did not know that his fate was already being decided.

A group of rebellious citizens of Rome had already dispatched messengers to the combat units of the Roman legions in far corners of the Empire. In the outposts in Britain, Syria, Pannonia, and Dalmatia, powerful Roman generals received the news of the infamous auction. Only one, Septimius Severus, a cruel, handsome ex-lawyer who'd been raised in Africa, acted. In his Pannonian camp, he offered his soldiers a bonus of $2,000 each if they would agree to leave their stations on the Danube (near the present site of Vienna) and march on Rome at once.

As the money-hungry troops of Septimius Severus started toward Rome, Julianus read the messengers' daily reports of their crossing of the Alps and their rapid approach. Local affairs no longer interested Julianus. He rejected the suggestion of a gold statue of himself and chose instead one made of brass. He appointed his son-in-law governor of Rome. He issued an order to massacre the vacillating Senate, but then revoked it. He fretted and worried.

He expected other Roman cities to resist Severus. They did not. He expected Ravenna to fight. It surrendered. Feverishly, he spent money on new fortifications, and drilled his unhappy guard. He attempted to prepare elephants for defense, hoping to terrify the northern troops. But the elephants, previously used only for parades, were too flabby, and there were very few riders skilled enough to remain seated upon them.

Grasping last straws, Julianus secretly sent private assassins to cut down Severus. This was impossible. The general marched with a personal bodyguard of 600. In desperation, Julianus sent a messenger to offer Severus half the Empire, and to kill him if he refused. Severus replied that he would rather have Julianus for an enemy than a colleague, and promptly executed the messenger. At wit's end, Julianus sent a group of priests and vestal virgins to block Severus. This failing, Julianus concentrated on magic rites and sacrifices.

The march of 800 mi. made by Severus was a thing of military wonder. Striding at the head of his men, clad in full armor, he rarely paused for food or rest, but pushed his warriors 20 mi. a day. They reached Rome on their 40th day, June 2, 193 A.D., and violated all tradition by entering the capital in battle dress.

Didius Julianus was found trembling in his palace. A dozen ordinary soldiers led him to the baths of his apartment, as he cried out, "What harm have I done? Have I put anybody to death?" In his baths, they beheaded him. Didius Julianus had bought an Empire for 66 days. It had been a bad bargain.

—I.W.

JOHANN NEPOMUK MAELZEL (1772–1838).
Austrian impresario.

In his prime, Johann Nepomuk Maelzel was known on both sides of the Atlantic as inventor, showman, and charlatan extraordinaire. But he began his professional life modestly enough, as a music teacher in Vienna in 1792. Uninspired by his work, Maelzel spent his spare hours building outlandish musical contraptions which were a showcase for his mechanical talents and his passion for the absurd. The most elaborate of them was the panharmonicon—an interconnected assortment of wind instruments through which a bellows blew, with the notes controlled by a revolving brass cylinder fitted with pins. Several years later, the inventor befriended Ludwig van Beethoven and talked the great composer into creating a composition especially for this "mechanical orchestra." Then Maelzel proposed they tour the Continent together, putting the machine through its paces in the great concert halls of Europe.

It was a grandiose plan that might have worked. Beethoven liked the idea and composed *Wellington's Victory* (or the *Battle Symphony*) for the panharmonicon, a piece of questionable quality commemorating the Duke of Wellington's victory over Napoleon at the Battle of Vitoria, Spain, in June, 1813. After a few initial performances, however, the composer accused his partner of trying to cheat him. He withdrew the piece—which is still played today by human orchestras—and Maelzel's plans foundered.

Maelzel was to have far greater success with an automatic chess player intriguingly known as the Turk. Even today, he is remembered more for the Turk, in fact, than for his collaboration with Beethoven or for the "Maelzel metronome," which unjustly bears his name.

For, just as Maelzel was not the inventor of the metronome—he merely added some refinements to what was essentially Stockel's creation—he did not invent the Turk either. Its real progenitor was Baron Wolfgang von Kempelen, an engineer in the employ of the Empress Maria Theresa of Hungary. When Von Kempelen died in 1805, Maelzel swiftly descended on the Baron's son like a bird of prey, offering to take the Turk off his hands.

In 1809, Napoleon himself locked horns with the machine and was beaten handily. (Not only was he beaten, but the machine mechanically chastised the Emperor by sweeping all the pieces off the board when Napoleon tried to "test" it by playing a false move.) The Emperor's stepson, Eugene de Beauharnais, was endlessly intrigued by the Turk and offered to purchase it from Maelzel for 30,000 francs. Maelzel accepted the offer, but with an eye to buying the Turk back eventually. By 1817, he had scraped up enough money to make a down payment on the Turk, agreeing to pay out the balance over the next few years. The terms were easy, but the inventor had trouble keeping up with the installments. Rather than relinquish the machine because of defaulted payments, he sealed it carefully into a packing crate, gathered his belongings, slipped unobtrusively out of Vienna in the night, and eventually took passage on a ship bound for America. The year was 1825.

His 1st stateside appearance with the Turk was on April 13, 1826, at New York's National Hotel. Maelzel's twice-daily performances consistently drew standing-room-only crowds. What they saw, when the curtains lifted, was this:

An imposing if expressionless Turk—carved of wood, of course—turbaned, robed, and bedecked with jewels. He was seated erectly behind a 2½' high wooden chest, a chess board carved into its top. When the audience had seen its fill of the Turk's outer self, Maelzel proceeded to open a series of doors in the wooden chest to expose the machine's mechanical innards, a whirring mass of cogs, wheels, metal cylinders, and brass fittings.

Closing the door and cranking the contraption up, he asked for a volunteer from the audience to challenge the Turk. Several spectators raised their hands; one man came forth. The Turk had white and played 1st, as it always did. Maelzel threw a switch, and the cogs and wheels ground noisily into motion. The long arm of the Turk creaked woodenly toward the king's pawn, made the opening move, and then returned to rest on a pillow atop the wooden chest as his opponent prepared to respond. Within a half hour the game was over. The Turk had won.

The audience was agog. "Nothing of a similar nature has ever been seen in this city that will bear the slightest comparison with it," wrote the *New York Evening Post*, and they were right: The Turk *was* unique. However, he wasn't all machine.

Although most spectators swallowed Maelzel's act whole, marveling at the wonder of a chess-playing machine, little did they know that the impressive machinery which Maelzel had so cavalierly displayed to his public was merely a front for an agile young assistant tucked neatly inside. The internal structure of the wooden chest allowed the assistant to move from one compartment to another rather quickly on a series of casters and skate boards, and with Maelzel opening only one door at a time, it wasn't difficult at all to escape detection.

During those 1st New York shows, it was a young woman who pulled the strings. A petite and rather attractive Parisienne—with whom Maelzel was forced to make do until William Schlumberger, a European chess bum he had recruited in Paris, could arrive in New York—the woman was a chess neophyte; but a crash course in strategy and technique enabled her to win most of her matches. Nevertheless, a nervous Maelzel, deciding that the risk of losing was too great, announced midway through his New York engagement that the Turk would no longer play full games against challengers. They took too long, he said, and those in the audience who were not confirmed chess buffs would surely lose interest. Instead, the Turk would play only end games.

Maelzel then had his young assistant memorize a large repertoire of end-game situations, as well as all the possible moves which could develop—a substantial achievement in itself, and one that assured the automaton of a perfect record, provided that he always have the 1st move. In the meantime, the impresario waited anxiously for Schlumberger to arrive.

He had good reason to be anxious. Competent chess players were stepping forth by the dozen to challenge the Turk to full games, which they felt were the only real test of his credentials. If Maelzel felt that a full game would not be a profitable drawing card, they said, they would be happy to play the Turk privately. Maelzel eluded them as best he could, offering lame excuses and making himself generally inaccessible while he waited for Schlumberger to bail him out.

Maelzel closed his New York show and moved on to Boston, thrilling the crowds at Concert Hall and deeply impressing master showman P. T. Barnum. But he still felt the Turk's supremacy was shaky at best. Toward the end of his tour, Schlumberger arrived, and Maelzel breathed easily.

On a swing through Baltimore in May, 1827, Maelzel's cover was blown. Two boys, looking in on the concert hall from a rooftop next door, spotted Schlumberger emerging from the chest after the show. Maelzel flatly denied the accusations that ran the following day on the front page of the *Baltimore Gazette*, but he put the Turk in cold storage temporarily and took the summer off, hoping that the story would blow over by the fall. In the meantime, several competitors appeared. They may have been inferior to the original, but they seriously undermined Maelzel's claim to uniqueness. Some, like the "American Chess Player," promoted by entrepreneur John Scudder, he attempted to buy out. Others he discredited publicly as weak imitations.

In the early 1830s, Maelzel plied the New York-Boston-Philadelphia-Baltimore-Richmond circuit. He still drew audiences, but the critics, including the great logician Edgar Allan Poe, were publicly trying to locate the chinks in the Turk's mechanical façade.

What proved to be the death blow to Maelzel's aspirations came in 1837. A popular French magazine, *Pittoresque*, broke the story of the Turk's bogus machinery and explained how its moves were engineered by a chess expert artfully concealed inside. Now attendance at performances fell off sharply. Maelzel took his show elsewhere—to the Midwest, to New Orleans, and then to Havana, where he was a sensation. Unfortunately, a return engagement in New York and Philadelphia proved financially ruinous, and the showman returned to Havana on borrowed funds, hoping to mine the enthusiastic audiences there for all they were worth. From his last visit there, he had deduced that the friendly Cubans had not yet read of his hoax, or if they had, they didn't care.

But his 2nd Havana venture failed miserably. For one thing, the audiences were small. For another, Schlumberger contracted yellow fever and died. Depressed and penniless, Maelzel set sail for Philadelphia on July 14, 1838, aboard the *Otis*. Closeting himself in his stateroom, he drank endless bottles of cheap claret to wash away his grief. He was found dead in his berth a week later.

—B.F.

JOHN MERRICK (1863–1890). *The English Elephant Man.*

In the Mile End Road, opposite London Hospital, there was a line of small shops, including one that was vacant. Its front, except for the door, was hidden by a sheet of canvas announcing the Elephant Man was to be seen within. A crude painting depicted a nightmarish creature with the figure of a man and the characteristics of an elephant.

When I 1st called the exhibition was closed, but I was granted a private interview for a shilling. The empty shop, gray with dust, was cold and dank. It was November, 1884.

The showman pulled back a curtain, revealing a bent, blanket-covered figure crouching on a stool. "Stand up!" he called harshly. The thing arose slowly and let the blanket fall.

There stood the most disgusting specimen of humanity I have yet seen. He was a little man, naked to the waist, with an enormous misshapen head. From the brow projected a huge bony mass, like a loaf, almost covering one eye, while from the back of the head hung a bag of spongy, fungous-looking skin. The head was the circumference of his waist. Another mass of bone protruded from the mouth. The nose was a lump of flesh. From his back, hanging down to mid-thigh, were sacklike masses of flesh covered with cauliflower skin. His right arm, big and shapeless, was overgrown with the same cauliflower skin; the hand was like a fin. By contrast, his other arm was normal. From the chest hung a bag of the same repulsive flesh. The lower limbs were grossly deformed. A sickening stench arose from the fungous skin growth. From the showman I learnt the Elephant Man's name was John Merrick and he was 21 years old.

At the time I was lecturer on anatomy at the Medical College opposite. Anxious to prepare an account of the Elephant Man's abnormalities, I arranged to have him visit me at the college. To avoid being mobbed on the street he wore an unusual costume. A long black cloak hung from his shoulders to the ground. Baglike slippers hid his deformed feet. On his head he had an enormous black cap; a gray flannel curtain hung in front, with a horizontal slit so he could look out. He crossed the road in a cab, clutching my card, which ensured his immediate admission to the college. This card was to play a critical part in his life.

I made a careful examination of my visitor. He was shy and confused, and his speech was almost unintelligible because of the bony mass protruding from his mouth. I imagined he was an imbecile and luckily could not appreciate his position. The examination concluded, he left. Next day the police closed the show and the impresario took him elsewhere.

Two years passed. One day a policeman asked for me at the hospital. He told me a weird-looking creature dressed in a black cloak had turned up at Liverpool Street Station. He was unable to speak, but he had given the police my card, which had led the officer to me.

At the station Merrick seemed pleased to see me, but he was starved and exhausted. I drove him at once to the hospital, where I had him deposited on a bed and supplied with food. We decided we could not turn him out into the world again. The British public is generous; a letter to The Times asking for money for the Elephant Man brought in funds enough to maintain him indefinitely. Two empty rooms at the back of the hospital were converted into a bed-sitting room and a bathroom for him. He had now something he had never dreamed of—a home of his own for life.

I at once began to study my patient. Seeing him almost every day, I soon learned his speech so we could talk freely. He had a passion for conversation, for he had never had anyone to talk to. I found him remarkably intelligent and a voracious reader, especially of romances. In his outlook on the world, however, he was more a child than a man.

I could learn little about the Elephant Man's early days. Of his father he knew nothing. Of his mother he had some memory. Even as an infant he must have been repellent, and she had doubtless deserted him when he was very small; his earliest memories were of the workhouse. Romantic that he was, he spoke of her with pride and reverence. Most of his life had been one dull record of degradation, of being dragged from town to town, from fair to fair, like a beast in a cage. He had had no childhood. He had never experienced pleasure. His idea of happiness was to creep into the dark and hide.

For all his suffering Merrick was gentle and affectionate. I asked a friend of mine, a young, pretty widow, to call on him and she did so. As he let go her hand he bent his head to his knees and sobbed. She was the 1st woman who had ever smiled at him and shaken his hand. From this day he began to change from a hunted thing into a man.

Merrick's case attracted much attention in the papers. Everybody wanted to see him. Many ladies of note called and shook hands with him. They made his room bright with ornaments and pictures. The Queen herself came to see him many times. Little by little he grew less conscious of his unsightliness. One burning ambition of his was to go to the theater and another was to see the wonders of country life. Both of these wishes were satisfied, though special precautions were required to hide him from the public stare. With all these kindnesses, he became one of the most contented creatures I have met. "I am happy every hour of the day," he said to me. Happy as he was, however, because of his deformed mouth his face remained expressionless. He could weep but he could not smile.

In April, 1890, Merrick was found dead in bed. The method of his death was peculiar. So large and heavy was his head, he could not sleep lying down. He sat up in bed with his back supported by pillows; his knees were drawn up, and his arms clasped round his legs, while his head rested on his knees. He had often said he wished he could sleep "like other people." I think on this night he must have made the experiment. His head, when he placed it on the soft pillow, must have fallen backward, dislocating the neck. Thus it came about that his death was due to the desire that had dominated his life—the pathetic but hopeless desire to be "like other people." (As originally recounted in The Elephant Man and Other Reminiscences [1923] by Sir Frederick Treves.)

—F.D. rep.

JOSEPH MILLER (1684–1738). *Father of modern humor.*

On an evening in October, 1943, 3 professional comedians—Harry Hershfield, Joe Laurie, Jr., Ed Ford—gave a lavish New York dinner party in honor of a certain Mr. Joe Miller.

And about time. Almost all modern jokes are derived from a classic book, published over 2 centuries ago, bearing Joe Miller's name. As the late, great comedian Fred Allen once remarked: "Where would we all be without him?"

Josias or Joseph Miller was born in London just 68 years after William Shakespeare's death. Miller grew to maturity in Queen Anne's London, where Dr. Johnson, Sir Richard Steele, David Garrick also reigned. Miller decided to emulate Garrick and become an actor. At the age of 25, he appeared in his 1st play in Drury Lane. Later, he performed as the 1st Gravedigger in *Hamlet*, Trinculo in *The Tempest*, Marplot in *The Busie Body*, the latter by lady playwright Mrs. Susannah Centlivre.

Uneducated, formally or otherwise, Joe Miller was an illiterate. Unable either to read or write, Miller married his wife for only one reason—she was able to read his parts to him.

Admittedly his acting was undistinguished if not downright pedestrian, but Joe Miller was said to have had another forte: employing the double entendre, the wisecrack, and the pun to perfection. He was a tavern fly, always in debt, and most of his contemporaries never quite appreciated his one deformity—an overdeveloped funnybone. On the other hand, some sources contradict the contemporary picture of Joe Miller as a comic. They state that, like Dorothy Parker, Miller was credited with everyone else's wit. According to one historian, Joe Miller "was so exceptionally grave and taciturn that when any joke was related, his friends would father it on him."

He died August 16, 1738, leaving his wife and his children in complete poverty. In fact, he willed them only one thing—his friends. After Miller's demise, these friends attempted to raise some money for his family. They appointed one of their number, John Mottley, to collect all the stray jokes that had been variously foisted on, or originated by, Miller and have them published in a book, the proceeds to go to Mrs. Miller.

Mottley, son of a favorite of King James II, was a gambler who had resigned his job with the Government Excise Office because of unfortunate speculations. Later, during the years he caroused with Joe Miller, young Mottley had written several plays that reached the public, among them *Imperial Captive* and *The Widow Bewitched*. A month after Miller's death, Mottley began to collect Joe Miller's jokes.

The book that resulted was entitled: *Joe Miller's Jests: or, The Wits Vade-Mecum, being a collection of the most brilliant jests, the polite repartees, the most elegant bons mots, the most pleasant short stories in the English language. First carefully collected in the company, and many of them transcribed from the mouth of the facetious gentleman whose name they bear.*

The slender, 72-page volume, printed by T. Read of Fleet Street, containing 247 original quips, was sold in 1739 for one shilling a copy, went into 8 editions, and was thus secured to posterity. Most of the jokes were based on humor derived from calling one's rival an ass, on the absentmindedness of parsons, on the curse of matrimony, or on the blunders of Irishmen. Of the entire 247 original jokes, only 3 actually mentioned Joe Miller himself. One of these ¾ reads:

"There is the story of a midshipman told one night, in company with Joe Miller and myself, who said, that being once in great danger at sea, everybody was observed to be upon their knees, but one man, who being called upon to come with the rest of the hands to prayers, not I, said he, it is your business to take care of the ship, I am just a passenger."

The book sold and sold, and the number of its jokes grew and grew, until an edition issued 50 years ago contained 1,564 quips, all credited to Joe Miller.

Today, the contents of the original seem at once crude, unfunny, familiar. A typical excerpt:

"Daniel Purcel, the famous punster, calling for some pipes in a tavern, complained they were too short. The Drawer said they had no other, and those were but just come in. Ay, said Daniel, I see you have not bought them very long."

Another typical excerpt:

"A famous teacher of Arithmetic, who had long been married without being able to get his wife with child—One said to her, Madam, your husband is an excellent Arithmetician. Yes, replied she, only he can't multiply."

And a 3rd and more censorable sample:

"A little dastardly half-witted Squire, being once surprised by his rival in his mistress' chamber, of whom he was terribly afraid, desired for God's sake to be concealed, but there being no closet or bed in the room, nor indeed any place proper to hold him, but an India chest the lady put her clothes in. They locked him in there. His man, being in the same danger with himself, said, rather than fail, he could creep under the maid's petticoats. Oh, you silly dog, says his master, that's the commonest place in the house."

The entire 247 jokes represent the 1st published professional humor. They remain the foundation of all modern movie, radio, television, stage, and drawing-room stories.

To appreciate Mr. Miller's contribution fully, to realize how much his collection continues to be the comedian's Koran, note how a modern joke evolves from a basic one in his book.

In *Joe Miller's Jests* appears this story:

"A pragmatical young fellow sitting at table over against the learned John Scot, asked him what difference there was between Scot and Sot. Just the breadth of the table, answered the other."

Here, after more than 200 years, is what the joke has become:

"Once, when he was farming corn, Will Rogers found himself being relentlessly heckled by a neighbor. But Will refused to blow up. Finally the neighbor screamed at him, 'Rogers, you're not far from a fool, are you?' 'Naw,' drawled Will, 'jest the fence between us.' "

Then there's another, refined over the years, which has been revised and revived by each new generation of comedians. If Joe Miller could tell the joke, in present-day vernacular, it would go about like this:

"I was traveling on the stagecoach between Bristol and London, and a young stranger was seated beside me. I pulled out my watch at one station and compared it with the station time. The stranger leaned over and asked, 'Say, mister, would you mind telling me the time?' I didn't answer him.

"At the next station I pulled out my watch again and compared it with the time. The stranger asked the same question again and still I didn't answer. At the next station, when the same thing happened a 3rd time, the stranger said, 'Sir, I don't mind if you refuse to tell me the time, but are you deaf or what is the reason for not answering me?'

" 'Well, young man,' I said to him, 'it's this way. First you ask me the time. I tell you. Then you say it's a nice day. I agree. Then you say, "Maybe it'll rain tomorrow." And soon we get to talking, and I tell you I live in Bristol, and the next time you come around this part of the country, you stop to say hello. Then you meet my daughter, who's mighty pretty, and then you come around again, but this time it's to see her, not me. And before I know it you're telling me you love her and want to marry her —and mister, I'm telling you—I won't have any man marrying my daughter who can't afford a watch!' "

It was George Ade who insisted, "There are only 3 basic jokes, but since the mother-in-law joke is not a joke but a very serious question, there are only 2."

And the point is—both of them may be found in Joe Miller.

—I.W.

ALEXANDER SELKIRK (1676–1720). *Castaway.*

Though few will recognize him by his true name, he was the real-life prototype for the most familiar character in all fiction—Robinson Crusoe.

Church records in the tiny Scotch fishing village of Largo, County Fife, identify him as Alexander Selcraig, a hot-headed youth, perpet-

ually in trouble and at odds with the community. He was the 7th son in the Selcraig family and his mother thought him destined to a fine future. But by the time he was 19, his chief accomplishment was getting kicked out of town for beating up rivals in the middle of church services.

Alexander signed aboard a Dutch sailing vessel bound for the West Indies. He returned to Largo 6 years later and was soon in trouble again. This time he roughed up his father and several of his brothers in a family brawl. Rather than make public apology before the kirk, he left to join a band of privateers in search of gold-laden Spanish galleons in the South Seas. By now he was calling himself Selkirk, not wanting to bring further odium on the family name by having it linked with piracy.

His ship, the *Cinque Ports*, left the London docks in September, 1703. Though Selkirk would eventually see England again, the *Cinque Ports* would not. Even before they weighed anchor, he was clashing with his immediate superior, Lieut. Thomas Stradling. The *Cinque Ports* was old and overcrowded. As it lumbered toward the east coast of South America, the grumbling Selkirk emerged as the leader of a whole dissident faction within the crew. They rounded the Horn and encountered the hated Spanish off the coast of Chile. The ship survived the battles but was in need of emergency repairs.

They anchored off a rocky strip of beach known to the mapmakers as Más a Tierra, part of the Juan Fernández group. When Stradling was ready to leave again, Selkirk was not, arguing that the ship was not yet seaworthy. The rash young sailor said he would rather be put ashore on that desert island than continue in a leaky ship with an ignorant commander. Stradling was happy to oblige. At the last minute, Selkirk changed his mind. He waded into the surf, begging to be taken back. But Stradling jeered at him and sailed on. Selkirk's judgment was ultimately correct. The *Cinque Ports* waddled 1,000 mi. up the coast and ran aground off Peru. The entire crew was captured by the Spanish, tortured, and thrown into chains.

Back on Más a Tierra, there was no consolation for Selkirk. He took stock of his few possessions and spent his 1st night shivering in a tree, afraid of wild beasts. The 1st 8 months were the hardest. When he wasn't scrounging for food and fresh water, he was agonizing over his forced withdrawal from the human race. Because he would not take his eyes off the horizon to hunt for other food, he had to subsist on turtles and fish until he was sick of them.

Slowly he adjusted to his fate. He fashioned a drinking cup from a coconut shell and a knife from an iron hoop. He moved to a cave, began marking the passing days on a tree trunk, and hunted the wild goats that roamed in abundance. There were hordes of rats too, which had come ashore from passing ships. They nibbled at his feet and frustrated his efforts to build a long-term supply of food. So Selkirk domesticated cats, also left over from long-gone ships, and soon had the rat population under control.

When he could no longer hunt goats with his firelock, he learned to run them down with the acquired agility of a panther. He stitched their skins together with an old nail and some sinew until he had replaced his tattered clothing with a bizarre goat-hide costume.

A Bible had been left with his sea chest. He read its verses aloud to warm his faith and to ward off madness. He also improvised little dances with his pet cats. At length he mastered his formidable environment and made it his own private kingdom.

In January, 1709, 4 years and 4 months after Selkirk began his exile, it came to an end. Two British privateers, driven within sight of Más a Tierra by a storm, came ashore upon seeing his signal fire. Capt. Woodes Rogers described the creature they found as a shaggy man-beast dressed in goat skins and "looking wilder than the skins' 1st owners." The bug-eyed savage "seemed to speak his words by halves," Rogers noted, but eventually regained a human tongue and told his story.

Selkirk sailed with Captain Rogers and his crew and later distinguished himself in battle against the Spaniards. The erstwhile castaway was made master of a captured ship and enriched himself by £800 in captured booty. It was 3 more years before he saw England.

Selkirk was soon a celebrity. He was interviewed by a number of journalists. It was a time when a good sea story—especially a true one—was a hot item. Eventually, Selkirk's tale was picked up by an aging hack pamphleteer named Daniel Defoe. Defoe renamed Selkirk "Robinson Crusoe," and used the castaway theme to write a deathless tale of man's endurance over adversity. Today, history remembers Defoe as the father of the modern novel.

And though Robinson Crusoe earned immortality, Alexander Selkirk was less fortunate. He returned to Largo, where the townspeople soon were noticing his strange habits. In trying to adjust to civilization, Selkirk became increasingly moody and withdrawn. He finally built a small cave in the garden behind the family homestead and secluded himself there, teaching the neighborhood alley cats to do strange little dances.

Eventually Selkirk joined the Royal Navy and went to sea again. His ship was off the coast of Africa when he contracted fever and died. He was buried at sea. Back in the cave in Scotland, he left behind his rusty sea chest and a hand-fashioned coconut drinking cup. The cup was later placed in the Edinburgh Antiquarian Museum, where it was mounted on a silver pedestal.

—D.P.P.

CHARLES WATERTON (1782–1865). *English naturalist and eccentric.*

One of the truly classic English eccentrics, Charles Waterton lived a life that was filled with a constant stream of bizarre adventure, all stemming from his dedication to the study of nature. Charles was born into one of the oldest families in northern England; Shakespeare mentions the Watertons in *Richard II*. His parents were wealthy but untitled, and as the heir to the family estate, Walton Hall, Charles was free to indulge his twin penchants for high adventure and natural history.

Charles Waterton was educated as a Roman Catholic. In 1796 he was sent to Stonyhurst College, a Jesuit school, where he displayed his talent in the field of natural history. He finished his schooling in 1800, and 4 years later he decided to visit some family-owned properties in British Guiana. After managing the estates in South America until 1812, Waterton made up his mind that he would go off into the unexplored regions of the Brazilian jungle in search of the poison that Indians used in their blowguns—*wourali* or, as it is now called, *curare*. For some unexplained reason, Waterton was convinced that *wourali* was the cure for hydrophobia. It was during this and 3 subsequent trips into the jungle that Waterton performed many of the feats that guaranteed his role in history as a thoroughgoing eccentric.

In 1825 he published an account of the 4 journeys in a volume entitled *Wanderings*—which now occupies a permanent place in English literature—detailing the extraordinary dangers he faced with unflagging—if not foolhardy—courage. When a report came to him that a large python had been spotted in the vicinity of his jungle hut, he dashed off barefoot to capture it (he never wore shoes or boots in the jungle). After the natives succeeded in pinning the snake's head to the ground, Waterton threw himself upon the python's wriggling tail, and finally bound the creature's mouth with his suspenders. The safari made its way back to Waterton's hut, where they deposited the python in a large sack, closed the opening with a knotted rope, and then placed the sack in a corner of Waterton's hut to pass the night. "All night long the snake was restless and fretful," Waterton wrote, but the wanderer apparently did not object to sharing his sleeping quarters with a python.

On another occasion he was trying to capture a crocodile, but his helpers were having great difficulty in pulling the creature from the river. Finally, they got the crocodile within a few yards of the bank. "I saw he was in a state of fear and perturbation. I instantly dropped the mast, sprang up, and jumped on his back, turning half round as I vaulted, so that I gained my seat in a right position. I immediately seized his forelegs, and, by main force, twisted them on his back, where they served me for a bridle." His helpers dragged the crocodile with Waterton astride it onto the bank. "It was the 1st and last time I was ever on a cayman's back," he wrote.

On another of his trips into the South American jungle, Waterton developed a passion for having a vampire bat suck blood from his big toe. He brought one of the creatures into his quarters and purposely slept with one foot exposed. Yet despite his best efforts Waterton was frustrated in his desires. The vampire bat ignored him and instead sank its teeth into the big toe of an Indian sleeping nearby.

Waterton inherited the estate of Walton Hall in Yorkshire upon his father's death in 1806, while the wanderer was still managing the family estates in South America. When he returned to England he decided to convert Walton Hall into a sanctuary for any sort of wild animals (especially birds) that wanted to live there. Waterton brought in an ex-poacher to serve as game warden; presumably such a person would know all the tricks of the trade. No guns were allowed on Waterton's property, and he had an 8' barrier constructed around the 3-mi. circumference of the estate to keep out anything or anyone that would have preyed upon all the creatures Waterton wanted to protect.

Besides his love for animals, Walton Hall also fulfilled Waterton's other great passion, climbing. Although he set up a telescope in a room of his residence, his favorite pastime was shinning up trees to observe his winged wildlife as closely as possible. It was not unusual, especially during nesting season, to see Waterton scrambling to the top of a tall tree with great agility. He invited his guests to climb with him, and he was still clambering up trees when he was 80 years old.

As a young man Waterton had proved that his climbing ability was truly extraordinary. On a trip to Rome, taken to relax after one of his jungle journeys, he and a friend scaled their way to the top of St. Peter's. But as though that were not enough, Waterton shinned up the lightning conductor to place his gloves at the pinnacle as a token of his prowess. The unamused papal authorities ordered the gloves removed and, good Roman Catholic that he was, Waterton quickly climbed back up again to retrieve his high-flying gloves.

Waterton's home life, as expected, was far from ordinary. Although he was wealthy, he lived a Spartan existence, sleeping on the bare floor of his room with a scooped-out block of oak for a pillow. At midnight every night he arose and went—barefoot, of course—to his private chapel for prayer. After another short stretch of bare-board sleep, he got up at 4 in the morning to start his day's labors.

His labors consisted primarily of a strange sort of taxidermy. He developed a method for hardening skin so that dead creatures would look just as they did when alive—with no stuffing. Not content with preserving the animals nature had created, however, Waterton invented some of his own—composite creatures made from the parts of various species. He confounded professors of natural history with his monsters, many of which he named after prominent Protestants. Waterton's favorite creature (dubbed "the Nondescript") looked amazingly like a human being, but it was actually a South American red howler monkey.

When he ventured away from the animal sanctuary that was Walton Hall, Waterton often appeared so shabby that he was mistaken for a tramp. As a matter of fact, he seemed to have a special fondness for tramps, often showing them extraordinary generosity. He would buy new boots for any ill-shod tramp he happened to meet, and on several occasions he gave away the boots he was wearing to some unfortunate-looking soul and returned to Walton Hall in jungle fashion—barefoot.

Waterton was married in 1829 to the granddaughter of a Guiana Indian princess. His 17-year-old bride was 30 years his junior, and after their wedding (at 4 in the morning!) she accompanied the squire of Walton Hall to Paris to study stuffed birds. She died a year after the wedding, and Waterton never remarried. The remainder of his life he devoted to the preservation of wildlife at Walton Hall and to the strange adventures that he enjoyed so thoroughly. He was never seriously ill, and he baffled friends who visited him with his climbing feats and general physical dexterity well into his old age. During his 83rd year, however, he tripped while carrying a heavy log and seriously injured himself. He died shortly after the accident.

—J.L.K.

JOHN WILKES (1725–1797). *Colorful English politician.*

John Wilkes, the champion of English-American liberty, ranks high among the great lovers elected to political office. Wilkes's Irish wit and suave manner made up for his physical shortcomings—though small and squint-eyed, he was able to launch his career with an expedient marriage. "I married a woman twice my age," he wrote shortly after his wedding night. "It was a sacrifice to Plutus, not to Venus." Of course, the marriage didn't last. Once he had obtained the funds he needed, Wilkes abandoned the domestic life.

After separating from his wife, he began his dual career in earnest. First he joined the Hellfire Club—a secret fraternity which included in its membership such peccant officials as Lord Orford, Lord Sandwich, and Charles Churchill. At this time Wilkes wrote and had printed his obscene "Essay on Woman," a parody on Pope's "Essay on Man," which was to plague his political career as much as the orgies for which the Hellfire Club was infamous. Wilkes hardly slept while a member of the Hellfire Club, where wild parties with naked masked women, drinking bouts, and weird religious ceremonies were routine.

Eventually, Wilkes directed all his energies to affairs of state. Initially, he tried to get elected to Parliament. During his 1st campaign, the opposition imported a boatload of voters from another district. Wilkes promptly bribed the ship's captain to deliver his cargo to Norway. Persistent, he was. "I'd sooner vote for the devil than John Wilkes," a constituent once told him. "And what if your friend is not running?" Wilkes replied.

Finally, cleverness and bribery paid off, and in 1757, by an arrangement that cost him only $35,000 of his wife's money, John Wilkes was elected. His personal life was wild and nomadic—"the chapter of accidents," he wrote, was "the longest in the book"—but as an MP he at once proved a worthy politician. The great wit of his 1st polemics resulted in Prime Minister Lord Bute's downfall, and spurred on by his victory, enchanted by the voice of the common man, Wilkes turned his vitriolic pen against King George III himself. In issue ⚡45 of the North Briton he viciously attacked a speech of the King's and the royal sovereign immediately sought revenge.

A general warrant was issued, and Wilkes was arrested and jailed in the Tower of London. But when his case was brought to trial, the court declared that a warrant that did not name the persons to be arrested was illegal. A great victory had been won in the name of personal liberty, but the Government wasn't finished with Wilkes. With the aid of his one-time friend Lord Sandwich, evidence was gathered about Wilkes's activities in the Hellfire Club. Lord Sandwich, who invented the "sandwich" because he gambled so compulsively that he had no time to eat his meat from a plate,

spared no effort to damage Wilkes, and he gathered information about the "Essay on Woman." Both the "Essay on Woman" and Wilkes's attack on King George were declared obscene and libelous and he was banished from England. He spent 4 years in France, from whence he had the gall to advise his sovereign that all was well and that he was "engaging in amorous delights."

In 1768, Wilkes got restless and decided to cross the English Channel to face his punishment. He accepted a 2-year prison term in exchange for permission to return home, but his followers didn't, and great crowds gathered outside his prison to protest his innocence. When government troops put down a near riot—many lives were lost during this demonstration—Wilkes wrote a paper exposing the troops' brutal suppression and won still more popular support. He was elected to Parliament 3 times while in prison, the Government denying him his rightful seat, and because of his plight the lower classes were made more aware of their own disenfranchisement. His supporters grew stronger and more numerous; they rioted; there were general strikes; "Wilkes and Liberty" was shouted as a slogan and "⚡45" was scrawled on doors throughout England. There were still many who thought Wilkes would be "tremendously improved by death," but he was eventually released from jail.

Carefree as ever, Wilkes went on to draft a program of reform which included voting rights for the common man, the end of nonexistent or "rotten" boroughs, freedom of speech, and freedom of the press. The name "Wilkes" became a synonym for liberty, and the great libertine was elected lord mayor of London, went to Parliament where he advocated freedom for the American Colonies, and was chosen lord chamberlain of London. He also refused many lucrative positions in an era when there were few political vacancies due to death and none by resignation. Only in 1780, when he alienated his followers by courageously opposing the popular anti-Catholic riots led by Lord Gordon, did Wilkes lose his political power. He managed to restore order in London but his career was ruined. Although he remained in Parliament for another 10 years, he took little part in politics. But even crusty old Dr. Johnson—who had said he would rather dine with Jack Ketch, the public hangman, than with Jack Wilkes—came to admire Wilkes in later years. By the time the great libertine and libertarian died at the age of 70 in 1797, he had come to be as universally respected as he had earlier been reviled.

—R.H.

9

Disasters and Violence

Natural Disasters

The eruption of Mount Vesuvius came as a terrifying surprise to the Roman sybarites who languished in their palatial villas along the Bay of Naples. They didn't know the big mountain that rose 4,000' in back of their playground was a volcano until Pompeii and Herculaneum were buried.

When: August 24, 79 A.D.

Where: 14 mi. S.E. of Naples, Italy.

The Loss: From 20,000 to 30,000 people died by asphyxiation from carbon monoxide, or were buried alive in 2 great cities.

The Disaster: The last day of life for Pompeiians began with bustling activity. The sound of wooden-wheeled grain carts echoed through the narrow 20'-wide streets. Window shutters banged. Caccilius Jacundus, the banker, walked briskly toward the Forum. The girls at Asellinia's *thermopolia* (wine shop) prepared hot wine and spices for their 1st customers. Everywhere were loud conversations about the upcoming election and the games that were to be held that evening in the amphitheater. August 24 was no different from most other days in the resort city, but it was destined to become a nightmare of stark terror.

At 1 P.M., Vesuvius ended its 1,500 years of inactivity. The crater floor, weakened by the violent earthquake of 63 A.D., was no match for the raging pressures deep in the earth. From the volcano's mouth a mighty explosion rocketed skyward. Terrified by the sound, louder than any they had heard, Pompeiians left their shops and villas to rush into the streets, allowing their eyes to follow the gentle green slopes to the top of the mountain. A black cloud, resembling a pine tree with extended trunk, rose high into the heavens, partially blotting out the sun. Hidden within the cloak of black smoke and ash, molten rock cooled quickly and fell straight down, back into the screaming throat of Vesuvius. Four miles away, Pompeii was untouched.

With the 2nd eruption, more awesome than the 1st, darkness spread its blanket over the sky and pumice stones rained on the defenseless city. Gladiators, there for the games, and some quick-thinking natives, ran from Pompeii toward the sea. A few lived to tell about the catastrophe. But most chose to seek shelter in their homes, temples, and public baths. Singly and in groups they cowered in darkness. Pumice stones and lapilli (small fragments of lava) piled high on roofs causing many to collapse. Those inside were trapped. Stronger wooden roofs were set on fire by hot ashes. Then came poisonous carbon monoxide gas along with an oppressive odor of brimstone. In 24 hours, Pompeii and its people were buried under 30' to 50' of ash and pumice stones.

The population of Herculaneum, a city near Pompeii, watched the spectacle of Vesuvius with foreboding, and wondered of Pompeii's fate, but not for long. The volcano's tremendous heat condensed moisture on the slopes of the mountain. Soon, a river of ash and mud descended on the city of 10,000 people. There was hardly time to cry out before Herculaneum was buried beneath 60' of mud that dried hard as concrete.

Aftermath: Until the 18th century, Pompeii and Herculaneum were but vague memories. Sporadic excavations were begun in Pompeii in 1709, but serious work on Herculaneum didn't begin until 1927. Today, much of Pompeii's 160,000 acres has been uncovered, and about half of Herculaneum. Both are more popular resorts than ever. Hundreds of thousands of visitors annually crowd the narrow streets of the 2,000-year-old cities.

Tomorrow: Vesuvius has erupted several

times since 79 A.D., the last time in 1953. History could repeat itself at any moment, but until it does, Pompeii and Herculaneum are the only 2,000-year-old Roman resorts that can be visited without a time machine.

HISTORY'S BIGGEST EARTHQUAKES

To most people in the 50 States of the U.S. it is common knowledge that earthquakes occur in California. Perhaps it is less commonly known that earthquakes are not unique to California. Earthquakes also occur in other States. For about 2 months a series of the greatest earthquakes in history, with an intensity of 10, the top of the earthquake scale, struck not in California, but in a million-sq.-mi. area of the Midwestern and Eastern U.S.

When: December 16, 1811; January 23, and February 7, 1812.

Where: Missouri, Kentucky, Tennessee, Ohio, Georgia, and South Carolina.

The Loss: One death. Had these 3 big ones occurred in any large city in the 1970s, loss of life would have been 50,000 or more, and property damage would have surpassed a billion dollars.

The Disaster: Residents of New Madrid, Mo., were awakened about 2 A.M. on December 16, 1811, when the trembling earth shook them from their beds. No one had experienced an earthquake; they didn't know what was happening. Trappers and hunters had heard the old Shawnee Indian legend about the great spirit stamping his feet to shake the earth, but no white man believed it. Yet without warning, a million-sq.-mile area shook frighteningly. St. Louis, Cincinnati, and Louisville suffered falling chimneys and shattered windows.

Shocks were felt 500 mi. away at New Orleans; 600 mi. away at Detroit; and 1,100 mi. away at Boston. At least 2,600 separate shocks were counted in Louisville, Ky. The earth rose and fell to form sinks and ridges. Trees split in 2. Lake bottoms raised 15′. Streams changed directions and the Pemisco River was blown up and destroyed. The Mississippi and Ohio rivers flowed backward. In northwestern Tennessee the ground sank to form Reelfoot Lake, 5 mi. wide by 18 mi. long.

Aftermath: Geologists began the 1st serious study of earthquakes and their causes. A new department for that purpose was established at the University of St. Louis.

Tomorrow: Many newcomers to California leave after experiencing their 1st temblor to seek safety in the South and Eastern U.S. No State is exempt from earthquakes, and tomorrow the biggest in history could happen anywhere.

KRAKATOA BLOWS ITS TOP

After a half-million years of peaceful slumber, Mount Perboewaten—one of 3 volcanic cones on the uninhabited island of Krakatoa—awoke with a roar to belch steam, ash, and pumice to a height of 36,000′. Spasmodically, for the next 3 months, the supposedly extinct volcano exhibited signs of life. Then came a series of eruptions and explosions that lasted 22 hours. The whole island exploded with such force that sound waves encircled the globe.

When: August 27, 1883.

Where: On Krakatoa, the largest island among Lang, Verlaten, Polish Hat, and Krakatoa, a 4-island group in the Dutch East Indies.

The Loss: 36,417 people lost their lives; 165 villages were razed and 132 others badly damaged.

The Cause: A volcano is a hole in the earth's crust that serves as a chimney for the earth's molten center. As the core cools and the earth contracts, gas and steam are compressed under tremendous pressures (100 tons per sq. in.) that demand release. Outward through 1,800 mi. of the earth's mantle and lithosphere they fight their way along a maze of corridors toward the earth's surface. Pressure builds until magma, pumice, and ash breach the surface layers and a fiery hell explodes into the atmosphere.

The Disaster: The 1st warning of impending disaster occurred at 10:55 A.M. on Sunday, May 20, 1883. A few miles from Krakatoa, aboard the German naval corvette *Elizabeth*, Captain Hollmann noticed a billowing vapor cloud rising to an estimated height of 36,000′. From it emanated flashes of fire, detonations, and showers of sulfur-colored ash. In days the activity subsided, only to recur on June 16, and again in early July. Dutch villagers were unconcerned (there were 49 active volcanoes on Java alone). Javanese natives recalled their ancient legends of Krakatoa and prayed silently for deliverance.

Sunday morning, August 26, the sun came up in a cloudless sky. By noon the islands languished in misty vaporous heat. The lush greenness of Krakatoa shimmered in contrast to an opaque backdrop of blue. Deep in the earth, below Krakatoa, a seething, churning mass fought its way upward to freedom. The 3 plugs in Mount Rakata, Mount Danan, and Mount Perboewaten held tight.

At 1:06 P.M. the pent-up energies, held captive for centuries, pushed hard against the surface. The plugs blew. With a thunderous explosion, mushroom clouds of steam and debris shot upward 7 mi. Hundreds of thousands of people heard the eardrum-splitting blast. For an hour the clouds could be seen, then ash blacked out a 150-sq.-mi. area turning day into stygian darkness. No one could see anything for 3 days except dim flashes of light. The last telegram sent over the wires from Anjer to Batavia was at 2 P.M. Explosions continued. By 3 P.M. they were running 2 minutes apart.

The sea turned angry, black, and ominous, rising and falling 10' every 15 minutes. From every village along Sunda Strait there was an exodus of people trying to reach higher ground. Those attempting to escape by coastal roads were caught by the rising sea. A heavy rain of ash and pumice transformed everything into dark shadows. At 7:55 P.M. the whole area was shaken by a violent earthquake, followed by rain and lightning. Fear gripped Dutchmen and natives alike. The day of judgment had come. Between the rhythmic vomitings of Krakatoa, earthquake shocks crumpled buildings, and the noise of the rising winds was echoed by that of the raging sea.

The clock in the Batavia Observatory stopped at 11:32 P.M. From midnight on, lowlands near the sea were submerged by huge waves. Ships at sea rode out the confusion with little difficulty except for the total blackness and some frightened sailors. At 1 A.M., the village of Sirik, 6 mi. south of Anjer, was washed away. Telok Betong was destroyed at 1:30 A.M. Waves that followed came within 6' of refugees perched atop a 125' hill. On the decks of the *Berbice*, 15 mi. from Krakatoa, ash piled to a height of 3'.

At 6:30 A.M. a 33' wave struck Anjer and penetrated 6 mi. inland. Merak was hit about the same time. The biggest wave rushed shoreward at 7:45 A.M. It picked up the gunboat *Berouw* and deposited it more than a mile inland, 30' above sea level. All of the crew were killed. Still the eruptions continued, the earth shook, and waves from the sea assisted the grim reaper.

At 10:02 A.M., August 27, after 22 hours of eruptions, a roar that paled all others burst from Krakatoa. Three quarters of the island, 11 sq. mi. (an area almost as large as Manhattan) collapsed into the sea. The sound was heard 3,000 mi. away. The Encyclopaedia Britannica later reported, "The noise was the loudest in history." People in Texas reported that they heard what sounded like cannons.

The force of the explosion created winds that circled the globe 7 times. Outward from Krakatoa swirled a wall of water that rampaged over beaches, buried plains and villages, and clawed at hilltops to destroy everything in its path. Through the straits gigantic tidal waves escaped into the Indian Ocean to reach Cape Horn, then pushed into the Atlantic to lap at the shores of the English Channel, 11,500 mi. from Krakatoa.

At 10:32 A.M. the big killer wave hit Tjaringin, 30 mi. from Krakatoa, killing 10,000

people. When it hit the wide plains of Pepper Bay, the town of Penimbang, 10 mi. inland, was submerged. Tjeringur, Karang Antoe, Telok Betong, Beneawany, and Batavia were littered with corpses. Hundreds more were washed into the sea entangled in debris.

Krakatoa's death knell came at 10:52 A.M. when Mount Danan collapsed into the caldera 600' beneath the sea. The true death count was never known, but the most conservative estimate was 36,417 or more.

Aftermath: When it was all over and ships were dispatched to the devastated area, the *Algeeman Dagblad* reported, "The gloomiest forebodings fell short of reality." From the capital of Bantam came the message: "All gone. Plenty lives lost."

The 1st landing party on what was left of the island found not a tree, shrub, or blade of grass growing. They did find one tiny red spider spinning a web that would attract no living fly or insect.

Tomorrow: By 1923 Krakatoa was green again. In early 1928 a new island 600' long by 10' wide rose out of the sea, then disappeared. On February 3 and June 25, new explosions and eruptions were recorded. In October, 1952, a 200' cinder cone emerged from the waters. The child of Krakatoa had been born. In one year, the cone grew 300'. In 1960 the island was 1,500' wide by 3,000' long. How big will it be in the year 2000? When will Krakatoa erupt again? These are unanswerable questions.

THE GALVESTON TIDAL WAVE

For 50 years Galveston, Tex., had won countless battles with the sea. Then, right after one Labor Day, nature stopped fooling around. Hurricane-swept gulf waters sent million-ton waves hurtling shoreward. By midnight Galveston was a nightmare of devastation.

When: September 8, 1900.

Where: Galveston, Tex.

The Loss: 6,000 people died. Property damage exceeded $17 million.

The Disaster: At 10 A.M. on that fateful Saturday morning, 30,000 blasé Galvestonians went through the motions of business-as-usual. From an overcast sky a drizzling rain fell. Undaunted, late vacationers buttoned their coats to lean into the rising wind and stinging rain as they watched an angry seething surf. The weather-station barometer had fallen to 29" of mercury. Sailors aboard ships in the harbor battened down hatches and reinforced anchor and mooring lines.

By lunchtime barometers were registering 28.5". Surf watchers moved back from the tormented Gulf as wave after angry wave broke higher and higher over the jetties. Rainfall increased in intensity. The skies became darker and the damp cold of 20-mph winds penetrated the watchers' clothing, forcing them to seek shelter.

This scene had repeated itself many times, less ferociously, from 1836 when Michael B. Menard began the 1st development on Galveston Island, a narrow sandbar 25 mi. long by 2 mi. wide. Natives were familiar with seasonal storms and paid them little heed. But as Saturday wore on to 3 P.M. winds had increased to gale velocity. Joseph and Isaac Cline, weather-bureau men, knew this was no ordinary storm.

Streets in Galveston were awash with seawater. Increasingly high waves battered warehouses a block or more inland from the Gulf. Joseph Cline climbed gingerly to the top of the Levi Building. His weather instruments, a rain gauge and anemometer, had gone with the wind. He clutched a safety railing for support and looked down from his high perch to note that half of Galveston was under water.

Richard Spillane, editor of the *Galveston Tribune*, later recalled: "To go out on the streets was to court death. Cisterns, portions of buildings, telegraph poles, and walls were falling. The noise of the wind and crashing of buildings was terrifying in the extreme. The people were like rats in a trap."

By late afternoon the most hardy of the remaining surf watchers were finally getting the message and began their retreat through knee-deep water to higher ground. It was already too late to try for the mainland. Darkness slowed their progress, for the power plants were out of commission.

At 7:32 P.M. the big tidal wave hit with unleashed fury. Wind velocity was recorded at 85 mph. Everyone perished at the Old Women's Home on Roseberg Avenue. Ocean steamers were tossed over the docks into the business section. Graveyards gave up their tombstones and corpses as the ghoulish waters uncovered coffins and sent them floating about in the wreckage and out into the Gulf.

Sisters of the Ursuline Convent rescued many victims from tidewaters that rushed by their big brick building 5 blocks from the beach. The highest ground in Galveston was only 5' above sea level. Before the onslaught of the rampaging sea, houses and other buildings crumbled like cardboard playthings. The Cline home, refuge of more than 50 people, had been built to withstand the heaviest storm. But it, too, tumbled when struck by a 200'-long section of railroad trestle and track. Damaged, but still in one piece, the house floated free only to be capsized by the wind; its people were dumped into the screaming blackness.

With the coming of midnight the destructive forces of nature began to abate. Galveston had lost its biggest battle. Devastation left in the wake of the huge tidal wave was beyond description. The civilized world, learning of the catastrophe, went into a state of shock. But the story doesn't end with death, doom, and destruction.

Aftermath: Most of the people of Galveston, after a suitable time of mourning, refused to accept defeat. Though the most conservative estimates of property damage ran above $17 million, townspeople went into action. Their city was completely rebuilt. A new, higher seawall was constructed, and the entire island was raised 17'. Today, Galveston, Tex., stands as a living memorial to its early residents who refused to capitulate to an angry Mother Nature.

THE SAN FRANCISCO EARTHQUAKE

California is earthquake country. More than 1,000 mi. of its coastline follow the Great Pacific Basin where 80% of the world's earthquakes originate. The State is laced with hundreds of faults that produce a thousand or more tremors annually. Fortunately, half of them go unnoticed except by animals, birds, and the seismograph, and only 30 are capable of minor damage. A major earthquake occurs about once every 100 years to take an awesome toll of lives and property. It was a once-in-a-century quake along the San Andreas fault that pounced without warning on an unsuspecting San Francisco early one spring morning. In minutes, buildings and homes were piles of rubble. Then fires broke out to turn the devastated city into a flaming funeral pyre.

When: At 5:13 A.M. on April 18, 1906.

Where: San Francisco, Calif.

The Loss: 600 dead; 300,000 homeless. Property damage above $400 million.

The Disaster: San Franciscans slept soundly on a typical spring morning in 1906. Their storybook city by the Golden Gate snuggled comfortably in a blanket of gray mist. A cool sea breeze rippled the waters of a placid bay and lapped gently at anchored ships. Deep in the bowels of the earth, San Andreas, the granddaddy of California earthquake faults, began to grumble. Softly at 1st like muffled tympani, then crescendoing to a climactic burst of a million exploding cannons. The stomping feet of an unseen giant shook the city unmercifully. From Nob Hill to the waterfront, buildings began to crumble.

The $7-million city hall was among the 1st to go. Then the big glass dome of the Palace Hotel disintegrated in a shower of splinters. Half-awake citizens stumbled into the buckling streets to be bombarded by chunks of brick and concrete. Dazed and screaming, they sought safety, but there was none. Enrico Caruso, a towel wrapped about his famous throat, ran down Market Street gripping a picture of

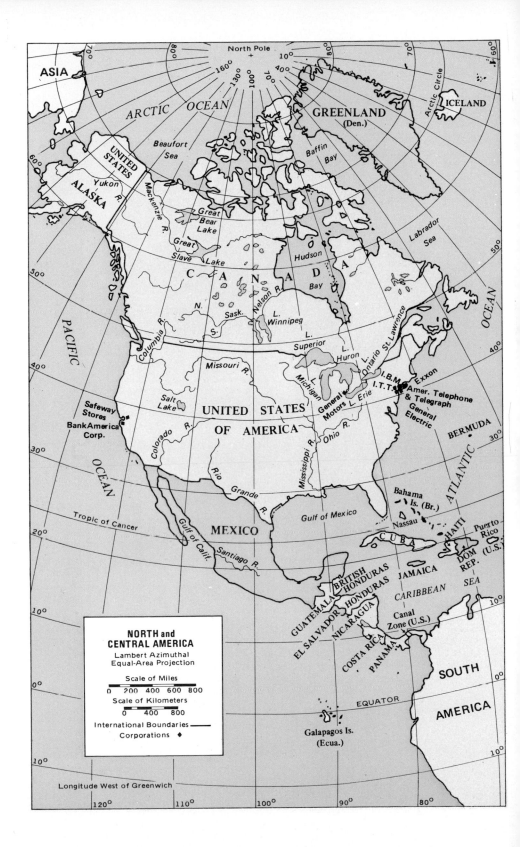

North Pole +

ASIA

ARCTIC OCEAN

GREENLAND (Den.)

ICELAND

Arctic Circle

Beaufort Sea

Baffin Bay

UNITED STATES

Yukon R.

ALASKA

Mackenzie R.

Great Bear Lake

Great Slave Lake

Labrador Sea

Hudson Bay

PACIFIC

C A N A D A

N.

Sask.

S.

Nelson R.

L. Winnipeg

OCEAN

Columbia R.

Missouri R.

L. Superior

L. Michigan

L. Huron

L. Ontario

St. Lawrence

L. Erie

I.B.M.

I.T.T.

Exxon

Amer. Telephone & Telegraph

General Electric

BERMUDA

Safeway Stores

BankAmerica Corp.

Salt Lake

Colorado R.

UNITED STATES OF AMERICA

General Motors

Ohio R.

Mississippi R.

Tropic of Cancer

Rio Grande R.

MEXICO

Gulf of Mexico

Bahama Is. (Br.)

ATLANTIC

Nassau

CUBA

HAITI

Puerto Rico (U.S.)

DOM. REP.

OCEAN

Gulf of Calif.

Santiago R.

GUATEMALA

BRITISH HONDURAS

HONDURAS

JAMAICA

CARIBBEAN

SEA

EL SALVADOR

NICARAGUA

Canal Zone (U.S.)

COSTA RICA

PANAMA

SOUTH

EQUATOR

AMERICA

Galapagos Is. (Ecua.)

NORTH and CENTRAL AMERICA

Lambert Azimuthal Equal-Area Projection

Scale of Miles

0 200 400 600 800

Scale of Kilometers

0   400   800

International Boundaries ———

Corporations ◆

Longitude West of Greenwich

120° 110° 100° 90° 80°

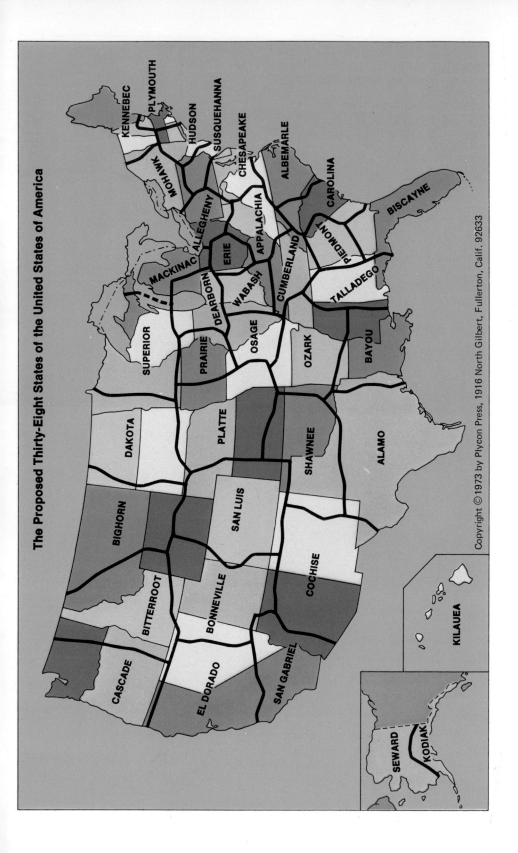

The Proposed Thirty-Eight States of the United States of America

KENNEBEC

PLYMOUTH

HUDSON

SUSQUEHANNA

CHESAPEAKE

ALBEMARLE

MOHAWK

CAROLINA

BISCAYNE

ALLEGHENY

APPALACHIA

PIEDMONT

MACKINAC

ERIE

CUMBERLAND

DEARBORN

WABASH

TALLADEGO

SUPERIOR

PRAIRIE

OSAGE

OZARK

BAYOU

DAKOTA

PLATTE

SHAWNEE

ALAMO

BIGHORN

SAN LUIS

BITTERROOT

BONNEVILLE

COCHISE

CASCADE

EL DORADO

SAN GABRIEL

KILAUEA

SEWARD

KODIAK

Copyright ©1973 by Plycon Press, 1916 North Gilbert, Fullerton, Calif. 92633

A 38-State Nation

The map (opposite) reducing the U.S. to 38 States is the creation of G. Etzel Pearcy, geography professor at California State University, Los Angeles. The new boundaries totally erase the 104 lines currently separating the 50 States. Each State's new name, chosen with the help of a poll of geography students, represents a physical or cultural aspect of the new territory. For example, Cascade (named after a major mountain range in Washington and Oregon), Cochise (named after the Apache Indian chief of Arizona), and Alamo (named after the mission in San Antonio, Tex.).

Why the need for a new map? Pearcy states that many of the early surveys that drew up our boundaries were done while the areas were scarcely populated. Thus, it was convenient to determine boundaries by using the land's physical features, such as rivers and mountain ranges, or by using a simple system of latitude and longitude. Proof of this lies in the fact that the Mississippi River borders 10 States. The practicality of old established State lines is questionable in light of America's ever-growing cities and the increasing mobility of its citizens. Metropolitan New York, for example, stretches into 2 adjacent States. Other city populations which cross State lines are Washington, D.C., St. Louis, Chicago, and Kansas City. The "straddling" of State lines causes economic and political problems. Who should pay for a rapid transit system in St. Louis? Only those citizens within the boundaries of Missouri, or *all* residents of St. Louis's metropolitan area, including those who reach over into the State of Illinois?

One of the major advantages of Pearcy's State regroupment is the money it would save taxpayers. According to the geography professor, "The screening of State budgets reveals that approximately 25% of the expenditures can be signaled as relating to fixed costs associated with the support and maintenance of the State government itself." Pearcy adds, "For example, the governors of Texas and Rhode Island do not receive salaries commensurate with the areas under their jurisdiction. Again, if the top executive in charge of the National Guard of each State would have a jeep, the cost of operation would be about the same in each instance." If 38 States replaced the current 50, Pearcy estimates the annual savings in fixed costs would be $4.6 billion, or about $100 per citizen.

When Pearcy realigned the U.S., he gave high priority to population density, location of cities, lines of transportation, land relief, and size and shape of individual States. Whenever possible, lines are located in less populated areas. In the West, the desert, semidesert, or mountainous areas provided an easy method for division. In the East, however, where areas of scarce population are harder to determine, Pearcy drew lines "trying to avoid the thicker clusters of settlement." Each major city which fell into the "straddling" category is neatly tucked within the boundaries of a new State. Pearcy tried to place a major metropolitan area in the center of each State. St. Louis is in the center of the State of Osage, Chicago is centered in the State of Dearborn. When this method proved impossible, as with coastal Los Angeles, the city is still located so as to be easily accessible from all parts of the State. In many cases, a State has 2 or more major cities within its boundaries. For example, citizens of Alamo can travel easily to Houston, Dallas/Fort Worth, and San Antonio.

The new map increases the average size of each State by about ¼. Alaska is no longer 483 times larger than Rhode Island. The panhandles of Florida, Idaho, Maryland, and Oklahoma are eliminated as "unnecessary irregularities." However, "marginal protuberances" such as the Florida peninsula and the Aleutian Island chain have remained.

Although Pearcy's study contains many logical recommendations for the regrouping of the States, he admits that additional criteria should be considered and suggests "sources of water supply, location of exploitable resources, and composition of the population might well be worthwhile factors to analyze." Also, his study does not include a selection of capitals for his States. Location and size of cities which could adequately serve as State capitals need to be determined—politically as well as geographically.

Will we one day salute a 38-State flag? An article in *Smithsonian* magazine says that the odds are slim. "To begin with, there would be so much hot air from politicians of all parties that the entire climate would be threatened. . . . The chief obstacle to such schemes is that people just don't like change."

Despite criticism, some of Pearcy's advocates are already speculating on a new look for Old Glory, and the day may come when the song titles of some familiar tunes will be changed to "Deep in the Heart of Alamo," "Carry Me Back to Old Chesapeake," "El Dorado Here I Come," and "The Cumberland Waltz."

—C.O.

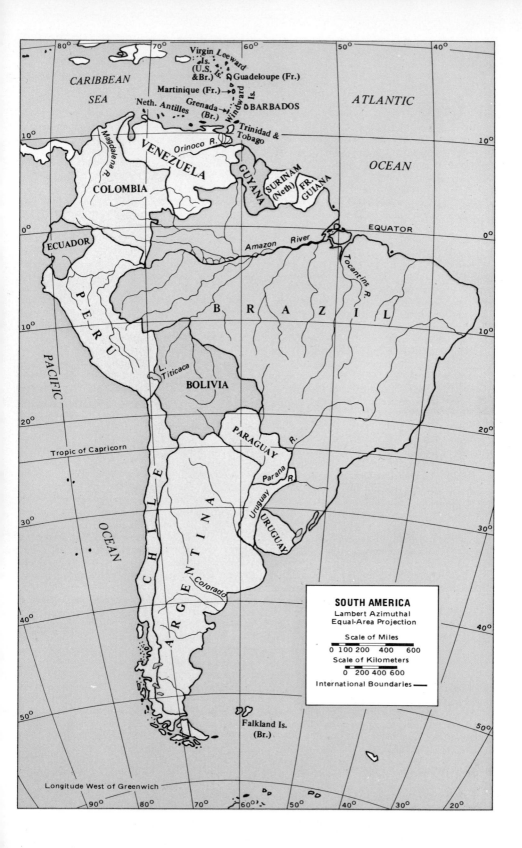

CARIBBEAN

SEA

Virgin *Leeward*
Is.
(U.S.   Guadeloupe (Fr.)
&Br.)

Martinique (Fr.) →

'Neth. Antilles   Grenada →   BARBADOS
                    (Br.)

Trinidad &
Tobago

ATLANTIC

OCEAN

Magdalena R.

VENEZUELA   Orinoco R.

COLOMBIA   GUYANA   SURINAM   FR.
                                              (Neth)   GUIANA

ECUADOR

EQUATOR

Amazon   River

Tocantins R.

P
E
R
U

B   R   A   Z   I   L

L. Titicaca

BOLIVIA

PACIFIC

PARAGUAY   R.

Parana   R.

C
H
I
L
E

Uruguay

URUGUAY

Tropic of Capricorn

OCEAN

A
R
G
E
N
T
I
N
A

Colorado

SOUTH AMERICA

Lambert Azimuthal
Equal-Area Projection

Scale of Miles

0 100 200 400   600

Scale of Kilometers

0   200 400 600

International Boundaries ▬▬▬

Falkland Is.
(Br.)

Longitude West of Greenwich

Theodore Roosevelt. Broken water and gas lines jutted into the air, assuming grotesque shapes. Sewer pipes erupted, adding an awful stench to the destruction. Everywhere fire was consuming the fallen city.

Throughout the day and night chaos reigned. Thousands tried to sleep in the parks. Others, too tired to run anymore, lay down in the path of the fire to sleep soundly. Firemen fought a losing battle with the flames. In 24 hours, San Francisco was rubble and ashes. The dead were at peace, but 300,000 homeless people wore a mask of blank despair.

Aftermath: While the city writhed in its final death throes, several babies were born in a hastily set up tent hospital in Golden Gate Park. From the ashes of destruction, a new San Francisco would rise to even greater heights. New concepts in earthquake safety would be developed, and in subsequent decades earthquake-proof buildings would be built.

Tomorrow: The complex nature of earthquakes has defied their accurate prediction, though seismologists have recently contended they are close to discovering how to pinpoint an approaching seism. Where and when will the next big one strike? Somewhere in California on some tomorrow.

THE SPANISH INFLUENZA EPIDEMIC

Without warning, the most frightening of all mass murderers, "Spanish influenza," struck a Midwestern U.S. army fort on a spring day during W.W. I. In weeks, the whole of the civilized world was busy burying its dead.

When: March, 1918.

Where: Fort Riley, Kans., then the world.

The Loss: 21,640,000 people died.

The Disaster: The previously unheard of disease 1st hit the cantonment of Camp Funston, in the 20,000 sunbaked acres of Fort Riley, and spread quickly through other military installations from coast to coast. Doctors didn't know what it was, or how to treat it. Soon the personnel of navy ships at Norfolk and Boston were out of action, their high temperatures resulting in a prognosis of pneumonia. In California, ⅓ of the prisoners at San Quentin were afflicted.

French surgeons called it *la grippe* when *les poilus*—the French "Tommies"—aching in bone and muscle, conducted their own symphony of sneezes and sniffles. Ten thousand cases of *Flanders grippe* put English Tommies out for the count. Overnight, Scotland began reporting 15 to 20 deaths a day. German doctors called it the *Blitz Katarrh* when 160,000 Berliners took to their beds. By summer, London was reporting 300 deaths a week.

Unchecked, the killer disease ravaged China and India, hopped the Pacific to zero in on Hawaii, and almost simultaneously attacked Alaska, Puerto Rico, Iceland, Norway, and the Falkland Islands. Then it struck Spain. After that, physicians dubbed it the "Spanish influenza."

This illusive harvester of death swept across the U.S., Mexico, and Canada to afflict millions and claim many hundred thousands of lives. Neither small villages nor big cities escaped. In Pennsylvania alone, a quarter-million residents were bedridden. Nowhere were there enough coffins, graves, or undertakers. Mass burials were common. Dr. Carl Holmberg, head of the Board of Health for Brockton, Mass., lamented that he was fighting a ghost. Industries were all but paralyzed, and ships at sea limped along with short crews.

Assistant Secretary of the Navy Franklin D. Roosevelt was carried ashore when the *Leviathan* docked in New York in September. Before departing from Hoboken with 3,100 troops, 200 more casualties were brought ashore to be hospitalized. On the *Leviathan's* arrival in France, 200 of its passengers were buried on foreign soil. Not a country in the world was untouched. Doctors were confounded by the disease.

A public health official in Virginia said it was caused by a tiny living poisonous plant called "the germ of influenza." Dr. Louis Dechmann of Seattle called it a negative disease, and recommended as treatment an abdomen pack of towels soaked in hot vinegar.

Churchless Sundays became the norm. Industries, businesses, and stores went on half-day work schedules. Theaters and meeting places closed their doors. Quackery throve. The marketplace became flooded with "sure cure" remedies.

From every city and hamlet suggestions poured into the War Dept. A Kansas man, Joseph Peloquin, wired: "Rinse the mouth with lime water and go to bed." Dr. Charles E. Page, a Boston physician, stated: "Influenza is caused chiefly by excessive clothing." Despite the recommendations of doctors and home-remedy specialists, the death toll mounted. Though the epidemic was of catastrophic proportions, humor was not absent. This little jingle headed the list: "I had a little bird and his name was Enza. I opened the door and in flew Enza."

By early October the flu epidemic had accomplished what the military might of Germany couldn't. Country after country had its back against the wall. In Philadelphia the death rate was 700% above normal, and rising. Military camps, in the U.S., were reporting a death every hour. Draft calls were stopped when the toll of servicemen reached 7,000. Britain reported 2,000 deaths per week. India lost a total of 12.5 million. The U.S. lost 500,000.

Only one small area in the world escaped: the tiny island of Tristan da Cunha, between Brazil and Cape Town. There was no logical explanation. Then in November, with the signing of the Armistice that marked the end of W.W. I, the epidemic ceased as suddenly as it had started. The final world death count, 21,640,000.

Aftermath: It wasn't until the 1930s and the invention of the electron microscope that the cause of influenza focused on a minute virus that resembled a cottonball. Thirty million could congregate, uncrowded, on the head of a pin.

Since that day in November of 1918, the killer virus Spanish influenza hasn't been heard from. Where did it come from and where did it go? This mystery remains unsolved.

THE JAPANESE EARTHQUAKE

In Japan, where seismographs record an earthquake every hour, the nation's attitude is one of indifference. But just before noon on a humid summer day, a giant quake transformed that indifference into demoralized panic. When the shocks were over and the smoke from resulting fires had cleared away, Tokyo and Yokohama were devastated cities.

When: At 11:58 A.M. on Saturday, September 1, 1923.

Where: Tokyo and Yokohama, Japan.

The Loss: 99,331 dead; 43,476 missing; 103,733 seriously injured; 1,500,000 homeless; 60% of Tokyo and 80% of Yokohama destroyed.

The Disaster: Office and factory workers mopped their perspiring brows and glanced often at the clock. The day was a scorcher and they waited impatiently for 12 o'clock and quitting time. Housewives fired up their hibachis to prepare lunch for their husbands and families. Inside the new earthquake-proof Imperial Hotel designed by American architect Frank Lloyd Wright, management prepared for the grand opening. The hotel rested on concrete and steel piers sunk in a 70'-thick bed of mud. This new and unproven "floating" concept of an earthquake-proof building was not acceptable to Japanese architects, who contended that unless the foundation of a building was firmly attached to solid earth it would topple with the 1st earthquake.

At 2 minutes to 12 o'clock the disastrous quake struck with the roar of a legendary dragon. Business buildings toppled, ships in the harbor were cast adrift when hawsers snapped. Thousands of people crowded into streets and narrow alleyways to be buried beneath falling debris. Onshore oil storage tanks exploded to transform the sea within the breakwater into a flaming mass.

Yellow dust clouds of crumbling buildings choked a panic-stricken populace. A hundred thousand hibachis filled with glowing charcoal were thrown about the kitchens in rice-paper homes. Tongues of flames jumped about to devour everything in reach. Sixteen-foot waves pounded beaches. Undermined bluffs tossed a commuter train and its 500 passengers into a frothy sea. Railroad tunnels collapsed to entomb hundreds more. Bridges twisting in torment gave way under the weight of people trying to escape across them.

Water and gas lines burst with the 1st shock. Three hundred and ninety-four trams overturned, their broken, twisted steel tracks rising upward grotesquely. Fire prevented rescue work. Over 40,000 people congregated in an open area only to be choked to death by dust and smoke, then consumed by the conflagration. Husbands entered the inferno searching for their families, and they, too, became trapped to suffer a fiery death. It was a day and night of terror. Food and medical supplies were gone and 9 million people were without drinking water.

When the smoke cleared away, there were 99,331 dead, 1,500,000 homeless, and 103,733 seriously injured. An additional 43,476 people were missing. Amid the rubble, the Imperial Hotel reached skyward, undamaged. The earthquake-proof design of Frank Lloyd Wright had been just that.

Aftermath: On September 2, 1923, Tokyo and Yokohama were all but leveled. From around the civilized world came offers to help, with money. Surprised Japanese officials accepted gratefully, saying: "We thought you didn't like us." In after-the-fact analysis, fire was responsible for more deaths and property damage than the earthquake.

Tomorrow: Japan accepted the catastrophe with oriental stoicism and began the massive job of rebuilding. Today, Tokyo and Yokohama are monuments to an acquired technology that promises untold future benefits to the entire world.

THE TILLAMOOK FOREST FIRE

There isn't a more terrifying conflagration than a forest fire. Whether viewed through the eyes of a vacationer, hunter, backpacker, fisherman, or lumberman, the loss in wildlife and ground cover is incomprehensible. The virgin stands of age-old Douglas fir in the Tillamook region of Oregon, fired by lightning one summer afternoon, burned out of control to consume 2 billion board feet of timber.

When: At 1 P.M. on August 14, 1933.

Where: In the Tillamook region of Oregon 60 mi. west of Portland.

The Loss: One death. 270,000 acres of

forest destroyed. Economic loss to Oregon, $200 million.

The Disaster: The forests of Tillamook were tinder-dry that August in 1933, especially in Gales Creek Canyon where a lumbering operation was in progress. It was one o'clock in the afternoon when smoke was sighted from the lookout tower high on Saddle Mountain. No one was worried. It was assumed that the lumbermen would extinguish the blaze before it got a good start, but they didn't. Regular forest crews were sent in, but the fire was out of control when they reached the canyon.

To outwit the winds of nature is backbreaking and frustrating work even for the experts, and these had plenty of help. There were fire crews, CCC (Civilian Conservation Corps) workers, and batteries of volunteers that made up an army of 3,000 men. Still, the fire was never contained. Hungry flames performed their ballet of destruction accompanied by the sound of exploding trees, louder than an artillery barrage. The heat, a quarter of a mile away from the blaze, ran to 120°, and the smoke was choking heavy.

Sparks, smoke, and wood particles rose to 8,500' to pour a normal year's supply of pollutants into the atmosphere in a few short days. State Forester Lynn Cronemiller recalled: "In all my years as Oregon's State Forester I never saw anything that even approached this burn. The most we ever succeeded in doing was to hold the line temporarily; at times we were positively overwhelmed. There was just one life lost, a CCC boy from Indiana who was killed by a falling tree. But lumber destroyed by the blaze was roughly equivalent to all the boards and planks turned out by all the sawmills in the U.S. during the entire year of 1932." No total of wildlife destroyed was ever compiled.

Aftermath: Tillamook, the worst forest fire in history, is credited with bringing about important changes in conservation methods, new educational programs beamed at prevention of forest fires, and stronger regulations of logging crews.

Tomorrow: Many innovative safety and rescue programs have since been effected, and heavy fire-fighting equipment has been developed. Tomorrow's prospects are good for fewer fires, better control, and less loss of wildlife than occurred in the out-of-control Tillamook blaze of 1933.

THE OHIO-MISSISSIPPI VALLEY FLOOD

In one month, bloated rainclouds dumped 156 billion tons of water to cause the worst flood in U.S history.

When: January, 1937.
Where: In 196 counties of the 12 States that make up the Ohio-Mississippi Valley.

The Loss: 250 people died. The tab for property damage totaled $300 million.

The Disaster: Heavy rainfall and the Ohio-Mississippi Valley just naturally go together, especially in January. The natives call it "seasonal weather." In 1937 it was a bit more than seasonal. The main valve was left turned on and it didn't stop raining all month.

When the rains began in early January of 1937, they were expected. No one gave them a thought. But 3 weeks later, with the Ohio and Mississippi rivers approaching flood stage, the rains became the chief topic of conversation. Had the downpour, in a given 10-day period, focused on Pennsylvania, the entire State would have been submerged in 4' of water. More rain fell that January in the Ohio-Mississippi Valley than at any time in recorded history.

By midnight of the 24th, "Black Sunday," the situation was critical. Land transportation was at a standstill. Martial law was declared with the mobilization of public health units, CCC (Civilian Conservation Corps), WPA (Work Projects Administration), and the military. A 12-State area was rapidly approaching national emergency status. On the 23rd, the Ohio was running above 48' at Evansville, Ind., and rising.

All along the Ohio and lower Mississippi rivers, major cities awaited the inevitable. Tent-city refugee centers sprang up everywhere. Before the flood waters abated, these centers— 1,754 of them—would care for 700,000 victims. In their records, the American Red Cross noted, "The Ohio-Mississippi Valley Flood of 1937 was, next to the World War [W.W. I.] the worst disaster in the history of the nation. In a sense, there were concentrated in one calamity as many problems as might be expected in 32 years of minor disaster activity."

January 25 saw 400 blocks in Evansville, Ind., under water. Boats were needed badly. In coordinated efforts, spearheaded by the American Red Cross, a flotilla of 7,000 boats was accumulated in 5 days, an unheard-of feat. All over the 12,700 sq. mi. of flooded area, in 196 counties, they were put to good use saving lives and property. Food, clothing, bedding, and medical supplies reached stricken areas via boats.

Hastily built kennels and corrals were put up near, or adjoining, refugee centers, for livestock, dogs, cats, and wild animals. Many thousands were saved from death. On January 26, the Ohio River was at 52.24'. Business, school, and water district activity ground to a halt. By the 29th, the last 35,000 victims, exposed to typhoid, were inoculated. Sterilized drinking water was strictly rationed. Food came into the devastated areas by rail, over repaired, but dangerous, tracks. On January 30, the Ohio River crested at 53.74'.

A flood relief chairman reported: "We got plenty of help from everywhere." The inmates of a Louisiana prison sent $63. The whole nation chipped in to contribute $25,565,680 through the American Red Cross—one of the largest donated sums for disaster victims ever collected in the U.S.

Aftermath: Though many floods have occurred in the Ohio-Mississippi Valley over the years, the magnitude of the 1937 disaster has dwarfed all others. Each year since then, hundreds of levees have been built to contain the big rivers partially. This has helped prevent another major disaster, but much remains to be done.

Tomorrow: Each winter some people in the Ohio-Mississippi Valley are evacuated from their homes, only to return in the spring to try it for another year. The inherent fighting spirit of humans cannot and will not accept defeat from any cause.

THE EASTERN SEABOARD HURRICANE

Despite modern communication networks, storm-warning broadcasts, ship-to-shore radios, and countless weather stations, hurricanes can be elusive and unpredictable. The hurricane that struck the eastern seaboard at the height of the summer season played hide-and-seek at sea for days before it came ashore to cause one of the worst disasters in the history of the U.S.

When: September 21, 1938.

Where: New York, Connecticut, Rhode Island, Massachusetts, and Vermont.

The Loss: 600 dead. An estimated 30,000 injured; 93,000 homeless; 16,000 homes and business buildings destroyed; 750,000 livestock and poultry lost; 26,000 autos and 2,500 boats ruined. Property damage above $1 billion.

The Disaster: Born as a "weak low," the 1st week in September in the Bilma Oasis of the South Central Sahara, it grew into a "circular disturbance" in the hurricane-breeding ground of the Atlantic, then seemingly vanished only to reappear on the 16th. The Brazilian ship *Alegrete* reported it in the Caribbean, 500 mi. northeast of the Leeward Islands, blowing along at 64 mph. Playing tag with ships and islands and changing directions, it missed St. Martin in the Leeward group and bypassed Miami, Fla., to ruffle Mayaguana, then kept on traveling. The storm wasn't considered serious enough to worry about. By the afternoon of the 21st, the eastern seaboard was saturated from heavy rains, catnip to a hurricane. The stage was set for a grand entrance.

The full-blown hurricane arrived in New York City and Long Island just in time to interrupt the soap opera broadcasts. Too late, weather bureaus announced the tropical storm simultaneously with its arrival. Subways were the 1st to be flooded out. Ships in the harbor doubled their moorings. At 2:30 P.M. the streets of Manhattan were targets for pieces of roofing and broken signs. A mile inland at Quogue, seawater, 2′ deep, submerged lawns and sidewalks.

On schedule, the *Bostonian*, train number 14, left Grand Central Station for New Haven, Conn. Before it reached there, all but 5 cars were derailed at Stonington. Engineer Eaton managed to get 5 cars to higher ground, saving all but 2 of his 275 passengers. New Haven's Savin Rock amusement park slid into the sea. Many people near the coast, more curious than wise, piled into family cars to head for the beaches to see what a hurricane was like. They didn't make it. Most were drowned when their cars became submerged. Lighthouses fell before the gale-force winds. Homes crumbled as if they were made of matchsticks. Boats and broken pieces of piers ended up inland in city streets. Harvard's observatory at Milton recorded 186 mph gusts. *Old Ironsides* rode out another storm safely at the Charlestown Navy Yard.

Through 5 States the hurricane rampaged. Sugar-maple orchards in Vermont were uprooted to leave bare fields. At 8 P.M. Lake Champlain resembled the stormy Atlantic. All through the night heroism, cowardice, and foolishness were part of the utter chaos that left in its wake unbelievable devastation.

Aftermath: The Treasury doors of the U.S. were opened wide by President Roosevelt, and army units were assigned to aid the storm victims. Property damage exceeded that of the San Francisco quake and the Chicago fire. There were 6,923 churches that suffered damage and many were totally destroyed. Inexplicably, Episcopal churches and synagogues were left undamaged.

Tomorrow: Along the Gulf Coast, in 1969, Hurricane Camille did as much property damage but, with more efficient warning systems, loss of life was far below the eastern seaboard tragedy.

THE ALASKA EARTHQUAKE

Anchorage, the largest city in Alaska, the 49th State, is built on unstable clay that sits astride the volcanic arc of the Great Pacific Basin, "the Circle of Fire" that begins in the North Pacific and follows around to the Kuriles and Japan. On a Good Friday evening with the temperature already at 24° and falling, and with snow transforming a good portion of Alaska's 600,000 sq. mi. into a winter wonderland, an earthquake of greater intensity than San Francisco's 1906 destroyer struck hard. Buildings crumbled, streets cracked open, the sea rose and fell creating waves of tidal height and strength to make the Alaska quake a major disaster.

When: At 5:30 P.M. on March 27, 1964.

Where: Anchorage, Alaska.

The Loss: 115 dead. Property damage $300 million.

The Disaster: Alaska is no stranger to earthquakes, but the one that hit Anchorage on Good Friday evening in 1964 was something else. In the tradition of most big earthquakes, this one struck without warning from its epicenter, 1,200' beneath Prince William Sound, 80 mi. east of Anchorage. In Valdez, "the Switzerland of America," northeast of Anchorage, a seaman was unloading the *Chena*, a 10,815-ton ship. On the dock were 3 workers and 2 children. When the quake hit, the dock, the workers, and the children disappeared.

For 500 mi. along the "volcanic arc" between Cordova and Kodiak, the earth twisted and rolled like seawater. Homes along the expensive Turnagain-by-the-sea collapsed. Downtown Anchorage buildings crumbled as though made of sand. Fourth Avenue dropped 11' and lurched sideways 14'. Fissures that measured 6' by 100' opened and closed.

Apartment buildings collapsed as did the J. C. Penney department store. Schools broke in 2 and hospitals fell. At Valdez the water drained from the harbor to rush back in successive tidal waves. At Chenega, on Prince William Sound, a 90' tidal wave demolished the town and drowned ⅓ of the population. At Crescent City, Calif., a tidal wave destroyed 56 business blocks.

Communications other than radio were out of commission. Military personnel from Fort Richardson and Elmendorf were called in. Troops patrolled downtown Anchorage. Water and gas lines were uprooted, and ruptured gasoline storage tanks poured volatile fuel into streets. Within 3 hours, and while aftershocks still shook the area, army bulldozers were at work clearing debris-piled thoroughfares, lighted by emergency-powered searchlights.

By Monday, March 30, damages were assessed. In Anchorage, 215 homes and 156 commercial buildings were destroyed, while 115 people were dead.

Aftermath: Had a quake of 8.6 intensity struck Los Angeles, New York City, or any other high-density city, the Anchorage figures would have been multiplied by thousands. Even Anchorage's death figures would have doubled had the quake struck during business and school hours. With government financing, much of Alaska was rebuilt on the same unstable ground. Six years after the disaster, the National Research Council of the National Academy of Sciences reported: "Natural disaster plans have not been developed to any degree,

nor is it clear what steps have been taken to ensure better construction practices."

Tomorrow: The council's report attempted to analyze all factors of the Alaska catastrophe, from locations of cities through economics to warning systems. To what degree this particular analysis is correct cannot be evaluated today, but according to the report, tomorrow promises the same natural disasters that have plagued the world since the beginning of time.

HURRICANE CAMILLE

To endure a hurricane is to live a lifetime in an unreal nightmarish world of indescribable terror. The initial shock dazes the mind and numbs the body; people do what they have to do. So it was along the Gulf Coast when Hurricane Camille struck with all its fury to leave a 70-mi. swath of destruction.

When: On Sunday, August 17, 1969.

Where: Along the coasts of Louisiana, Mississippi, and Alabama.

The Loss: 241 dead; 19,467 homes and 700 businesses destroyed. Property damage above $1 million.

The Disaster: When hurricane warnings are broadcast, many people leave their homes for the safety of higher ground; 150,000 did just that on August 17, 1969. Those who stayed to ride out the storm didn't know Camille's strength. Though every precaution was taken, this wasn't enough. It was dark at 7 o'clock and strong winds and rain pounded homes, then came through the walls. Electricity went off and portable generators were shorted by water. Homes began to tumble from their foundations and fall to pieces. Roofs blew off. Cargo ships snapped their moorings.

Seawater inundated homes 25' to 30' above sea level. In Gulfport, Miss., Camille seized a 600,000-gallon oil tank and hurled it 3½ mi. Telephone poles splintered like twigs. The roar of the storm resembled battlefield thunder.

Dr. Robert H. Simpson, director of the National Hurricane Center in Miami, Fla., was quoted: "In its concentrated breadth of some 70 mi., it shot winds of nearly 200 mph and raised tides as much as 30'. Along the Gulf Coast it devastated everything in its swath."

Aftermath: On the 18th, Gulfport residents returned to a scene of unbelievable wreckage strewn with the bodies of humans and animals. The Federal Government moved quickly to bring in 2,200 tons of food, mobile homes, and portable classrooms. Low-interest, long-term business loans were offered.

Tomorrow: Work began immediately on reconstruction. But what of tomorrow's hurricanes? Better warning systems and compulsory evacuation will save lives, but hurricane-proof buildings are not yet on the drawing boards.

PERUVIAN EARTHQUAKE

A one-minute-long earthquake can do as much damage as the Hiroshima atom bomb. It happened one Sunday afternoon in spring in South America. Sixty seconds of such destructive force tottered a great nation.

When: On Sunday, May 31, 1970.

Where: 15 mi. west of Chimbote, Peru.

The Loss: 70,000 dead; 800,000 homeless. Property damage estimate: billions.

The Disaster: It began with a gentle tremor to grow quickly, expending its 60-second life in monstrous destruction—the worst earthquake in the history of South America. Those who escaped from buildings were knocked off their feet. Nothing could withstand the tremendous shaking of the earth. Houses, hospitals, deluxe tourist hotels, and apartment buildings crumbled like stacks of dominoes.

Roads disappeared and dust clouds darkened the skies. Towns and cities were leveled. There was no time to escape. Huarás, Yungay, and Teófilo became rubble in seconds. An avalanche started on Mount Huascarán, a 22,205′ ice-capped peak in the Peruvian Andes; it buried Raurahirca and the remains of Yungay. Chimbote, 55 mi. west of Huascarán, resembled a bombed city; 30,000 sq. mi. were pulverized.

Aftermath: Rescue work was attempted with bare hands; no tools were available. Thousands of injured died for lack of help. The world did not know the extent of the catastrophe for 48 hours. Then help, food, and medical supplies began to arrive. But air drops from helicopters smashed on impact and whirring chopper blades started new avalanches.

Tomorrow: To offer hope for future earthquake victims is an old story. But perhaps one day soon, science will discover how to predict temblors. A prewarning system would save lives, and new methods of construction would assure earthquake-proof buildings.

CYCLONE OVER PAKISTAN

November in East Pakistan (now Bangladesh) is cyclone weather. Each year the lowlands of the Ganges delta, off the Bay of Bengal, face tropical storms that inevitably take a toll of lives and property. But not since the Yangtze River flooded Central China in 1931 had there been such a murderous storm or gruesome death count. On that fall night, 800 mi. south of the Ganges delta, winds whipped along at 150 mph, dragging in their vacuum wake a 20′ wave of water that would devastate East Pakistan.

When: November 12, 1970.

Where: East Pakistan

The Loss: Loss of life estimated at a million or more.

The Disaster: There was a full moon on November 12 and tides were at their highest when the cyclone ripped into the islands and coastline. A U.S. satellite report had been relayed to the Pakistanis, but their own meteorological system had already predicted when the storm would strike. Warnings were broadcast, but there weren't enough receiving sets; and the warnings said nothing about huge waves. Even if they had, it wouldn't have altered the outcome, as most of the areas hit were no more than a few feet above sea level. When the big waves rolled in, there was no safe place for people to retreat to; tens of thousands drowned with their doomed livestock. Those who did find temporary safety on rooftops saw the big waves approach with apprehension and were certain it was the end of the world.

Of the 26,000 residents of Manpura, only 6,500 survived. A week after the disaster, Maynard Parker of *Newsweek* reported:

> Today I flew over the worst-hit islands in the Ganges delta and everywhere the grisly sight is much the same. The bodies, blackened and bloated from the salt water, lie strewn across the landscape like big plastic dolls struck down by a petulant child. A few are sprawled in paddies and some wash in on the gentle tide, but most float face down in the canals that reach in like grasping fingers from the brown water of the Bay of Bengal. The decaying flesh fills the air with a sickening smell, attracting vultures which come to feast on the carcasses of man and beast.

Everywhere the rich rice fields were ruined. Drinking water was scarce. Food and medical supplies were not to be had. In a few days, there were outbreaks of cholera.

Aftermath: Immediately after the tragedy the U.S. pledged $10 million for relief. Communist China pledged $1.4 million. Britain dispatched her Royal Marines, a helicopter carrier, food, and medical supplies. India, too, sent money and food. Unfortunately, though there was no shortage of planes bringing in food and medical supplies, they didn't reach the people who needed them. There were too few airfields and most of these were submerged. Trucks were in abundance, but there were no roads. Much of the incoming supplies ended up on docks and in Dacca's warehouses. A high percentage found its way into the black market.

Tomorrow: Four years before the disaster, elaborate storm-warning systems were developed. Hundreds of miles of dikes were built. But they were too few and too weak. By the tomorrow after tomorrow, more precautionary measures will be in effect, but the major hope of Bengalis is that future storms will be less powerful.

THE NIGHT SAINT-JEAN-VIANNEY DISAPPEARED

The words "landslide" and "avalanche" are 2 of the most frightening in the English language; however, they usually conjure a picture of steep mountainsides. The Canadian village of Saint-Jean-Vianney sat on level ground. That's where it was on a spring night just before the earth opened up and the village disappeared.

When: Tuesday, May 4, 1971.
Where: 135 mi. north of Quebec, Canada.
The Loss: 31 dead; 38 homes gone. Property damage estimated at $1 million.
The Disaster: Saint-Jean-Vianney, a suburban community of 1,308 people supported by the nearby aluminum plant and paper mill, had its television sets tuned to the Stanley Cup hockey play-off between Montreal and Chicago. It was a typical spring night except for the dogs. Well-behaved pets they were, but on that night no amount of scolding stopped their incessant barking that drowned out the voice of the sportscaster. Booted outside, they scurried about like ants, sniffing the ground and barking even louder. Had the villagers understood dog-talk, they could have saved their lives.

What the villagers didn't know was that their community sat atop the scene of a 5-century-old landslide. At Saint-Jean-Vianney, and other locations in the province of Quebec, there lies beneath the topsoil a 100'-thick bed of unstable clay. Interlaced with pockets of sand that may become saturated with moisture, the clay can dissolve and liquefy to flow like a river.

Before the catastrophe there were signs that went unnoticed: Cracks appeared in the streets and driveways; some house foundations sank 5" to 8"; people heard thumps beneath their homes and the sound of running water; but no one gave these unusual happenings any serious thought.

It rained heavily in April and the water didn't run off, but soaked into the ground to dissolve the sand-pocked clay. On May 4 at 10:45 P.M., the liquefied earth dropped 100' to form a canyon a half mile wide. Then a river of clay flowed through the canyon, westward from Blackburn Hill toward the Saguenay River.

The lights in the village went out and television screens went black. People looked out their windows into darkness, then realized that houses, normally in view, were gone. One by one, the homes on the east side of town slid into the oozing clay. Almost at the stroke of midnight, the nightmare of terror was over: The river of flowing clay ground to a halt and

began to solidify. Exactly 38 homes had disappeared and 31 people went with them.

Aftermath: The Canadian Government declared the entire area unfit for habitation. The survivors, at no cost, were established in a new community at Arvida.

Tomorrow: The curious still visit the spot where a town disappeared. In time the yawning canyon will slowly fill with earth to blot out the telltale signs of tragedy. Tomorrow, however, another town could be built on the scene of a centuries-old landslide, and future historians could then have yet another catastrophe to record.

HURRICANE AGNES

In typical hurricane fashion, Agnes began its short but active life in a playful rather than vindictive mood. Then while growing and absorbing moisture from the saturated eastern section of the country, it turned vicious and struck southwest Virginia. In 4 days it loosed on Maryland, the District of Columbia, Pennsylvania, and New York 28.1 trillion gallons of water—enough to fill a lake 2,000' deep by 67 mi. square. Agnes was the most costly disaster in history.

When: June 21, 1972.
Where: Maryland, the District of Columbia, Pennsylvania, and New York.
The Loss: 118 people dead; 330,000 homeless; 2,400 farm buildings destroyed; 5,800 businesses devastated; 25 cities in 142 counties damaged or destroyed. Crop loss $132 million. Property damage above $3 billion.
The Disaster: By Wednesday, June 21, Agnes was approaching southwest Virginia, bloated with moisture and bent on creating havoc. It started when Agnes dumped excessive moisture into the already full James River, causing it to overflow and flood Richmond's water filtration plant. Portable filtration units were trucked in from Camp A. P. Hill to supply drinking water for 250,000 in the capital. A number of storm-battered bridges collapsed. In Alexandria, Va., a shopping center burned. Fire trucks couldn't get to it because streets were blocked with debris. In Pennsylvania, the Susquehanna River flood-crested to destroy the executive mansion of Gov. Milton Shapp.

Navy helicopters were dispatched to Pottstown, 35 mi. west of Philadelphia, to rescue victims from rooftops. Wilkes-Barre, an industrial city thought to be safe, took the brunt of the storm; its dikes didn't hold. The *Times Leader* and *Evening News* editor, Jim Lee, was quoted as saying: "We couldn't bring ourselves to believe that the river [the Susquehanna] might break through." But it did just that on June 22, pushing "safe dikes" aside like they were made of sand. In Wilkes-Barre and

Wyoming Valley, 13,000 homes were lost plus bridges and commercial buildings. Over 200,000 people were in need of rescue and relief. The heart of Wilkes-Barre became a polluted, foul-smelling lake. Wilkes College was flooded and severed electric wires started many fires that burned out of control; fire apparatus couldn't reach these.

A historic graveyard in a northern suburb gave up its caskets, sending them bobbing over floodwaters like surfboards. Looting followed the destruction of business districts and terrified rodents attacked humans. Public utilities were out of commission and manpower to do what was needed was lacking. Shock numbed the senses of survivors. It was too much, too sudden, for people to comprehend.

Aftermath: A million and a half pounds of food was air-dropped in Wyoming Valley. Clean-up work went on for months. Damage to U.S. and interstate highways ran $186 million, and to other road systems $382 million. The destruction was mind-boggling.

—F.M.W.

Man-Made Disasters

BLACK DEATH

The scourge of the 14th century, the Black Death or bubonic plague, took a far greater toll of human lives than the "plague" of Pericles, Marcus Aurelius, and the massacres of Hulagu and Tamerlane. From Central Asia the mysterious malady spread around the globe to eliminate half of mankind.

When: 1347 through 1351.

Where: Asia, Europe, Africa, Egypt, Iceland, and Greenland.

The Loss: 75 million people died.

The Disaster: Early reports of the Black Death say it entered Genoa from the Crimea on a Genoese ship; and that it began in China following a tremendous storm that caused unusual atmospheric changes. History records its origin as Central Asia. From there it spread through the civilized world. Since then medical knowledge has lifted the veil of mystery to uncover the culprit.

Black Death is endemic to rodents and transmitted to humans by the common flea. In humans the disease invades the blood, the glands under the arms and in the groin, and causes dark splotches to appear on the skin. Lack of sanitation and sound medical knowledge in the 14th century accounts for repeated epidemics of bubonic plague, cholera, and other diseases. John Richard Green (1837–1883), an English historian, had this to say: "Its ravages were fiercest in the greater towns where filthy and undrained streets afforded a constant haunt to leprosy and fever."

The island of Cyprus was 1st to succumb to the Black Death in the latter part of 1347. England was hit in early 1348. Two-thirds of the students at Oxford died. One-quarter to ½ the population of England perished. In Bristol, victims died faster than the living could bury them.

In a Latin chronicle, Carmelite friar Jean de Venette wrote of the Black Death in France: "The mortality was so great at the Hôtel-Dieu in Paris that for a long time more than 500 dead were carried daily on wagons to be buried at the cemetery of St. Innocent of Paris."

Half the population of Italy died. There were but few funeral services and even fewer single graves. Most of the dead were buried without ceremony in deep trenches, a layer of corpses, a light covering of earth, then another layer of corpses. When one trench was filled, another was dug. The plague struck in 2 forms. Pulmonary victims exhibited high fever and spitting of blood, which resulted in death within 3 days. Bubonic victims, with high temperatures, abscesses, and carbuncles, died in 5 days.

In his *Decameron*, Boccaccio wrote: "This tribulation struck such terror to the hearts of all that brother forsook brother, uncle nephew, oftentimes wife husband; nay what is yet more extraordinary and well nigh incredible, some fathers and mothers refused to visit or tend their very children as though they had not been theirs."

When the Black Death abated in 1351 at least 75 million people had perished, certainly the largest death count of any catastrophe in history.

Aftermath: Outbreaks of the Black Death, or bubonic plague, continued long after 1351, though it is believed that the domestic cat played a major role in lessening occurrences by ridding towns and villages of rodents. The disease still exists but is known by other names such as the Levant or Oriental plague, and it is no stranger to Asia Minor, Turkey, and Egypt.

Tomorrow: Twentieth-century life-styles take for granted the sanitary disposal of trash, garbage, and human waste, but should these systems cease to function for any reason, what happened in 1347 could happen again.

THE GREAT FIRE OF LONDON

The death toll from the bubonic plague that struck London in 1665 had hardly begun to taper off when a small bakeshop fire spread out of control to envelop all of London. In 4 days the great city was blackened and devastated.

When: At 1 A.M., Sunday, September 2, 1666.

Where: London, England.

The Loss: 87 churches and 13,000 homes destroyed; 100,000 left homeless.

The Cause: To pinpoint the specific cause of the London Fire in 1666 was impossible then, and even more unlikely over 300 years later. Perhaps the cleanup man, mistakenly thinking the oven coals were dead, left the firebox door open, allowing a spark to ignite an overlooked dab of baker's lard. The King's bakery, a tinderbox in Pudding Lane near the great London Bridge, was the perfect spot for the birth of a conflagration. In minutes the flames broke from the bakery to ignite adjoining buildings. By 3 A.M. the fire was out of control and raging along Fish Street by the London Bridge.

The Disaster: There was nothing to hinder the spread of the consuming flames. Fire-fighting equipment amounted to small pumps manned by from one to 3 men. At 7 A.M. on September 3, Samuel Pepys, Secretary of the Admiralty, climbed the steps to the top of the Tower of London. Flames from the buildings along the great bridge leaped hungrily into the air. All about were milling people trying to escape with no place to go but into the Thames. London's lord mayor told Pepys: "Lord! what can I do? I am spent. People will not obey me. I have been pulling down houses, but the fire overtakes us faster than we can do it."

The fire ran its unchecked course over the city and when it subsided 4 days later, only ⅓ of London was left standing. A hundred thousand people were homeless and ⅔ of the city lay in ashes.

Aftermath: No records were kept of property damage or of the number of people who perished or were injured. Hospital facilities were no better than the fire-fighting equipment, so any damage estimate would have to be reckoned in the millions of pounds sterling while the death toll would run to thousands.

THE GREAT CHICAGO FIRE

The transformation of Fort Dearborn, on the marshland near Lake Michigan, into Chicago, the Garden City of the Midwest required 68 years. A great sprawling, wooden metropolis, the city was a ready victim in the fall of 1871. It had been a hot dry summer and in the 1st week of October there were 24 fires. Approximately 300,000 people were mopping their brows wondering when the next alarm would sound. The fire that became the holocaust of the century started in the barn of Patrick and Catherine O'Leary at 137 De Koven Street,

and spread out of control to turn the largest city west of Pittsburgh into a sea of glowing ashes.

When: At 8:30 on Sunday evening, October 8, 1871.

Where: Chicago, Ill.

The Loss: 300 deaths; 17,500 buildings destroyed; 100,000 Chicagoans left homeless. Property damage of $400 million.

The Cause: With the exception of metal and stone adornments, Chicago was built entirely of wood. Five-story-high grain elevators, 4-story hotels, business buildings, homes, bridges, and raised sidewalks were all made of wood. Many of her streets were paved with pine blocks. A leading industrial city, Chicago manufactured, stored, bought, and sold inflammable goods. Almost every home had some kind of a barn that served as housing for livestock, and provided storage for wagons, sawdust and kindling for wood stoves, and coal for furnaces.

Compared with other cities in 1871, Chicago had a modern fire-alarm system: 17 horse-drawn steam fire engines, 23 hose carts, 4 hook-and-ladder wagons, 2 hose elevators, and 185 well-paid active firemen to protect 18 sq. mi. In 1870, this system had dealt successfully with 600 fires. But by Sunday, the 8th of October, Chicago firemen were tired. They had extinguished 24 fires the previous week. Two engines were in the repair shop and several of the 15 remaining engines needed maintenance work. Canvas hoses were badly worn and many were leaking. Adding to all this, a brisk wind came up off the lake early Sunday morning.

The Disaster: Chicago was primed. The night before in Farewell Hall, George Train, world traveler and lecturer, opened his address with fateful words: "This is the last public address that will be delivered within these walls!" Those who attended the lecture were still thinking about those words on Sunday, for late Saturday night 2 fires had destroyed 4 square blocks.

The O'Learys had company Sunday evening —their neighbors Daniel Sullivan and Dennis Rogers. When they left, the O'Learys retired early, about 8 o'clock. Sullivan didn't go straight home but sat down across the street in front of Thomas White's place. It was balmy and the bit of breeze was pleasantly cool.

From where Sullivan sat, O'Leary's barn was in his line of vision and at 8:30 he saw flames. Immediately he rushed across the street yelling "Fire!" Already the flames were licking at the stored hay and trapped animals. Though Sullivan worked slowly because of a wooden leg, he did manage to loose the tethered cows before the fire got too hot. There was no sign of life within the darkened O'Leary cottage.

Several people tried to turn in an alarm

before 9:00 P.M. but the alarm boxes were locked and citizens couldn't get the keys from sleepy storekeepers. Flames spread quickly to the adjoining houses of the Daltons and Lees, then on to others. By 9:30 an entire block was ablaze. By 12:30 A.M. Monday, fires had broken out in all 3 of Chicago's districts. Fanned by increasing winds, nothing could stop the hungry flames.

The sun came up Tuesday morning, October 10, on the blackened ashes of a once great city. On 73 mi. of her streets 17,500 buildings were gone. So were the lumber mills, bridges, and the $1-million courthouse. The Chicago Fire will live in memory as long as Mrs. O'Leary's legendary cow, said to have started the holocaust by kicking over a lantern.

Aftermath: Within weeks of the fire, victims had received $4,820,148.20 from individuals, businesses, other States, foreign countries, and the U.S. Government. Philadelphia reported that it had requests for relief from an astounding 14 million people who claimed to be victims of the fire. By 1871, Chicago had 6,000 new shanties, 2,000 new homes, and 500 new mansions.

THE JOHNSTOWN FLOOD

Just before her 100th birthday, Mrs. Anne Freidhoff, of Quail Valley, Calif., recalled in vivid detail what she—and her brother and 4 sisters—saw during the Johnstown flood:

> It was terrible! We were standing on our front porch watching the train below when a great wall of water came sweeping down on the town. It was rooftop high and swept away everything in its path including the train and the people. People began to scramble up the hillside to escape. Some made it, hundreds didn't. After it was all over those awful looters cut fingers and ears off dead people to get their rings and earrings.

When: At 4:10 P.M. on May 31, 1889.
Where: Johnstown, Pa.
The Loss: 2,200 lives and estimated property damage of $10 million.
The Cause: The earth-fill dam across the Conemaugh River, 14 mi. up the valley from Johnstown, was 931' wide by 272' thick at its base, and 100' high. Its rim was wide enough for a 2-track wagon road. Built by the State of Pennsylvania at a cost of $290,000, its original purpose had been to supply water for an interlocking rail and canal system between Philadelphia and Pittsburgh.

The system, completed in the late 1820s to early 1830s, was described enthusiastically by Charles Dickens, an early passenger. His only

registered complaint was the menu: Tea, coffee, bread, butter, salmon, shad, liver, steak, potatoes, pickles, ham, chops, black pudding, and sausage were served for breakfast, lunch, and dinner.

The dam began to deteriorate before Lake Conemaugh was filled. Pennsylvania spent $20,000 to repair damages caused by heavy rains in 1846. Four years later the whole system, including the unneeded dam, was sold to the Pennsylvania Railroad for $7½ million. For the next 12 years, the dam was forgotten. Then in July of 1862 a 200'-wide by 50'-high section in the dam's middle collapsed. No repairs were made.

In 1875 Congressman John Reilly bought the dam, lake, and surrounding land for $2,500, then sustained a $500 loss when he resold it to Benjamin F. Ruff in 1879. Ruff developed the property into the exclusive South Fork Fishing and Hunting Club with a wealthy nabob membership of 100 families including those of Andrew Carnegie, Andrew Mellon, Henry C. Frick, A. V. Holmes, Philander C. Knox, W. L. Dun, and John A. Harper. Each paid $2,000 to join.

The Club's manager let it be known from the beginning that the Club would brook no interference from local people, and that its owners had no intention of spending money on, what they termed, unneeded repairs on the dam. Their attitude was that the State of Pennsylvania had built the dam to last, and last it would. No thought was given to the fact that the original inadequate floodgates were badly damaged in 1862, thus destroying the only drains.

The people of the Conemaugh Valley became indifferent to any possible threat from the dam. Johnstown had been built in the early 1800s at the confluence of the Little Conemaugh and Stoneycreek rivers, and residents were well adjusted to seasonal floods that inundated the streets of Johnstown and the 1st floors of houses. Even if the dam did go out, it would raise the flood level by only a foot or 2, so it could cause no real damage.

The Disaster: In April and May of 1889, more than 40" of rain and snow fell in a 12,000-sq.-mi. area of western Pennsylvania. Watersheds of the Alleghenies were overrun with more than 5 billion tons of water, raising every creek, river, and stream above flood stage. On May 31 the entire countryside was under a blanket of ominous storm clouds. The streets of Johnstown flowed with water. Then on that memorable Friday at 3:10 P.M., the old South-fork Dam lost its 60-year battle with the elements. Filled and overflowing, the obsolete, tunnel-ridden pile of earth and stone gave way with an explosive roar. The pent-up waters of

Lake Conemaugh became a giant, 50'-high wave of destruction traveling at express-train speed down the valley—gathering mud, rocks, trees, trains, and houses as it sped along—a juggernaut of devastation.

At 4:10 P.M. the liquid avalanche attacked and killed Johnstown. To rescue drowning people was impossible. Onlookers could only watch in stunned horror while thousands disappeared. Debris and bodies piled up against the Stoneycreek Bridge. Carloads of lime and sulfur became ignited, turning the pile into a flaming crematory.

Aftermath: Though at the time, and later, hundreds of writers attempted to describe the tragedy, only the words of Johnstonian Isaac G. Reed are a fitting epitaph to express the sentiments of the survivors:

An hour of flood, a night of flame,
a week of woe without a name,
A week when sleep with hope had fled,
while misery hunted for its dead,
A week of corpses by the mile,
a long, long week without a smile,
A week whose tale no tongue can tell,
a week without a parallel!
All the horrors that hell could wish,
such was the price that was paid—for fish.

CHICAGO'S IROQUOIS THEATER FIRE

It was a raw winter day in the windy city of Chicago, the temperature a shivering 8° below zero. Prices of the bargain matinee at the "fireproof" Iroquois Theater attracted a large audience of mothers and children to see a performance of *Mr. Bluebeard,* starring young Eddie Foy. Including performers and stagehands, the plush entertainment palace that boasted 30 exits was packed with 2,400 people.

Just into the 2nd act, in a musical number called "In the Pale Moonlight," one of the bevy of high temperature carbon-arc lamps that created the illusion of moonlight, brushed against a painted canvas wing. The canvas caught fire. In seconds, other gauze drops, ropes, and props were ablaze. The heavy asbestos fire curtain was lowered to keep the flames backstage. The orchestra began to play a loud overture and comedian Eddie Foy stepped to center stage. But already 2,000 panicked people were fighting their way toward dark, unlighted exits.

When: Early afternoon on Wednesday, December 30, 1903.

Where: Chicago's famous Iroquois Theater.

The Loss: 589 people died.

The Cause: In 1903 Chicago still hadn't fully recovered from the episode of Mrs.

O'Leary's cow in 1871. Architects and builders were super cautious about fire. Stone, marble, and steel had replaced many of the wooden firetraps of the 19th century. Still, little if any thought was given to narrow dimly-lit hallways, 90° turns and inflammable decorative materials. Emergency exits were poorly marked, if at all, and no systematic inspection was made to ensure their usableness if needed. Furthermore, no one understood crowd or mob thinking, or the lack of it, in panic conditions. Safe evacuation from burning buildings was possible, but only under ideal conditions.

The Disaster: No alarm was given when the fire broke out. It didn't seem serious enough. The fire spread quickly from the canvas wing to other drops of muslin and gauze. In seconds, ropes, props, and curtains, and catwalks were ablaze. The suddenness and unexpectedness of a fire in the fireproof theater caused a lack of action. Fire extinguishers were filled with powder rather than liquid chemicals. They had insufficient pressure to reach the flaming materials. No water hoses were attached to standards.

Eddie Foy had the presence of mind to signal for the fire curtain to be lowered and the orchestra to break into an overture. These actions, along with Foy's improvised entertainment in the face of danger, saved some 600 lives. Praising Foy's actions, later, George Williams, Chicago's building commissioner, said: "It could have been a few less than that, or maybe more."

For 8 terrible minutes that seemed like hours, there was bedlam. Moving like a herd of spooked steers, people stampeded to reach exits only to find them frozen shut. Few deaths were actually caused by the fire. Smoke inhalation inspired fright, and as a result people were trampled to death. The fire was extinguished with but little damage to the theater, but the death toll that day in Chicago will long be remembered as a major tragedy.

Aftermath: When the investigation of the fire was completed, the arc-light operator was cited for criminal negligence. The tragedy itself inspired many construction changes and countless new safety regulations. Proper fire extinguishers were made mandatory; exit doors were to be kept operable; water hoses and standards were on the regular inspection list; fireproof ropes, drops, and props were a must; and design changes in all old and new buildings included wider hallways without 90° turns.

Tomorrow: For as long as man plans and builds for profit, there will be tragedies, and experience must be a patient teacher. Progress in the things that count is always the tortoise, but perhaps in time foresight, wisdom, and concern will be victorious over ignorance, greed, and apathy.

THE UNSINKABLE *Titanic*

It was on a Friday afternoon that the *Titanic*, newest luxury-liner addition to Britain's White Star Fleet, departed from Queenstown, Ireland, on her maiden voyage from Southampton to New York. It carried 1,290 passengers, a crew of 903, and 3,814 sacks of mail. There was great excitement aboard as the big ship knifed its way through the Atlantic at 23 knots, a speed certain to set a new crossing record. A few hundred miles past the halfway point, lookouts in the crow's nest sighted an iceberg less than a quarter mile away. There was no time to stop or to swerve. The muffled grinding on impact gave little indication that the unsinkable *Titanic* had been fatally wounded.

When: At 11:59 P.M. on Monday, April 15, 1912. Shortly after 2 A.M. the *Titantic* slid to its watery grave.

Where: 1,191 mi. from New York.

The Loss: 1,493 passengers and crewmen perished. The *Titanic* had cost more than $8 million.

The Cause: Even hindsight isn't infallible in trying to pinpoint the cause of a disaster. After-the-fact experts agreed that the *Titanic*'s captain, E. J. Smith, must have known of iceberg danger at least an hour before the disaster, yet there were no orders given to reduce speed. The weather was clear and cold with excellent visibility. Apparently, to achieve a record crossing was very important. The captain, passengers, and crew firmly believed the *Titanic*'s publicity, that she was unsinkable. All were afflicted with the "full speed ahead" euphoria. What could possibly happen to an unsinkable ship?

The Disaster: It was just before midnight when the iceberg was spotted dead ahead, rising 100' above the surface. Seconds later the *Titanic* rammed with a solid crunch on the portside forward, then climbed the submerged iceberg, tearing out the forward end of the ship below the waterline. The sound was so muffled that no one was frightened. After a few minutes, the more curious passengers, in a happy mood, drifted on deck to look around and reach over the bow rail to touch the iceberg. They were unaware of a 2nd danger. A fire that had broken out in the coal bunkers before leaving Southampton was still not extinguished. At 12:25 A.M., after having the damage assessed, Captain Smith ordered all persons assembled on the upper deck. With everyone in good spirits, this was accomplished in 15 minutes. Passengers were informed of what had happened and of the captain's decision to abandon ship. There was no dissension or panic until at 12:50 A.M. Chief Officer Murdock ordered: "Crews to the boats! Women and children 1st."

Cries of anguish were heard everywhere. Wives refused to leave their husbands. Crewmen began to grab women at random, shoving them forceably into lifeboats. The seriousness of the situation struck home. Husbands cooperated, literally tossing women and children into the boats. By 2 A.M. all lifeboats were on the water.

Those in the lifeboats could see that the *Titanic* had sunk 25' to 30', and her stern was out of the water. Lifeboat crews rowed furiously toward safety. A mile from the wounded liner survivors watched the *Titanic* break in 2, the forward half slipping beneath the surface. For a moment the rear half righted itself, then there was another explosion and it too began to sink in the icy waters. Survivors later reported they could hear the ship's string orchestra playing as the huge aft section disappeared.

Many ships had picked up the *Titanic*'s SOS signal: "Have struck iceberg. Badly damaged. Rush aid." The *Carpathia* arrived at the scene about 4 A.M. and took on board such shocked and dazed survivors as it could find, then headed for New York.

Harold Bride, the *Titantic*'s telegraph operator, reported that it was only by accident that the ship's radio was operational. It had gone out on Sunday, and Bride and Phillips had managed to repair it just hours before the tragedy. Other survivors reported they had heard gun shots. Several told a story about crew members who were trying to get aboard lifeboats being shot. It was also said that Captain Smith shot himself before the *Titanic* went down. Later, when surviving crew members were questioned, they gave no credence to either story. The *Carpathia*, with 700 survivors aboard, arrived in New York at 9 A.M. on April 18.

Aftermath: On July 30, 1912, the 74-page report of the Court of Inquiry, held in Scottish Hall, stated the following: "The Court, having carefully inquired into the circumstances of the above mentioned shipping casualty, finds, for the reasons appearing in the annex hereto, that the loss of said ship was due to collision with an iceberg, brought about by the excessive speed at which the ship was being navigated." Nothing was said of the fact that the *Titanic*, capable of carrying 3,500 passengers and crew, had lifeboats for a total of only 950.

THE *Lusitania*

Sixty years ago, and prior to the involvement of the U.S. in W.W. I, the *Lusitania*, a great sleek Greyhound of the seas, was torpedoed and sunk by a German submarine. The tragedy happened so quickly that escape from the mortally wounded luxury liner was all but impossible. There were few survivors and the full controversial story may never be known.

When: Shortly after 2 P.M. on May 7, 1915.

Where: 12 mi. off Old Head of Kinsale, Ireland.

The Loss: 1,198 passengers and crewmen including 128 Americans lost their lives. The 31,950-ton floating palace had cost an estimated $10 million.

The Cause: The ill-fated *Lusitania* was cursed with problems from the time Cunard directors and the British Admiralty gave their specifications to designer Leonard Peskett: It was to be the fastest ship on the seas, carry 2,000 passengers plus a crew of 800, and cruise at 24 knots. Its huge engines—capable of developing 68,000 hp—and the 4 boiler rooms containing 25 boilers, fuel storage, and complicated controls, must all be fitted below a narrow waterline beam of 88'×760', leaving space for longitudinal watertight compartments along each side. With this accomplished there was no place for fuel—the 6,600 tons of coal needed to power the *Lusitania* between Liverpool and New York.

Its watertight longitudinal compartments were transformed into coal bunkers, an expedient that would not be acceptable today. On top of this unstable powerpack, Peskett added 6 decks, making the *Lusitania* taller than any ship in use. On May 12, 1913, the giant liner went into drydock to be armed with 12 guns. On August 4, when England declared war on Germany, the *Lusitania* was registered as an armed auxiliary cruiser. German submarines were taking such a toll of British shipping that Winston Churchill ordered British ships to fly the flags of neutral countries including that of the U.S. It was alleged that he hoped the sinking of ships flying the American flag would bring the U.S. into the war.

On the fateful voyage from New York to Liverpool, the *Lusitania*'s cargo was almost entirely contraband: 1,248 cases (51 tons) of 3"-diameter shrapnel shells, 1,639 copper ingots, 76 cases of brass rods, and 4,927 boxes of .303 caliber cartridges (1,000 rounds per box) weighing over 10 tons—in all, 24 pages of manifest of which only one page was used for "clearance to sail."

The Disaster: On the morning of May 7, 1915, the *Lusitania*, heavily laden with passengers and cargo, was nearing the coast of Ireland. Capt. William Turner expected momentary contact with his navy escort ship, the *Juno*. He had not been informed that the Admiralty had canceled the escort mission on May 5. Twelve years later British Commodore Joseph Kenworthy would write in his book *The Freedom of the Seas:* "The *Lusitania*, steaming at half speed straight through the submarine cruising ground on the Irish coast, was deliberately sent."

On May 6, after several British ships had been torpedoed, Admiral Coke, at Queenstown, was forbidden to initiate retaliatory action or to send any messages via radio, but he chose to disregard orders. At 7 P.M. he sent a warning to Turner: "Submarines active off south coast of Ireland." Though Turner's orders would not allow a deviation in his course, he did reduce his speed, and warned his passengers of danger. He was still unaware there would be no navy escort. At 11:02 A.M. on the 7th, Coke sent a coded 12-word message to the tug *Hellespont* to come to Queenstown immediately. Turner intercepted this message and decided to divert the *Lusitania* to Queenstown, 25 mi. from his position 12 mi. off Old Head of Kinsale. The British Admiralty later denied that such a message was sent, but there is a certified copy of it in the Naval Station at Valentia.

At approximately 1:30 P.M. Walter Schwieger, commander of the German submarine U-20, satisfied with his toll of British shipping near Queenstown, was about to head for Germany with his last 3 torpedoes when he sighted the smoke of the *Lusitania* and changed course to intercept it. About 2:10 P.M. he fired a bow shot from 700 meters. Turner saw the torpedo approach before it struck the starboard side directly behind the bridge. There was a tremendous explosion. The great liner listed 15°. Then there was a 2nd explosion, louder than the 1st. The bridge was demolished and the big ship stopped dead, its stern out of the water. Slowly it began to nose under to starboard.

The *Lusitania* had left New York with a shortage of engine-room crewmen and able seamen. Now there weren't enough seamen to man the 48 70-passenger lifeboats. Absolute panic reigned. There was no time and nothing worked right. Launching davits were frozen. Many of the 26 collapsible canvas lifeboats, stored beneath the 22 2½-ton wooden boats, could not be lowered easily due to a 15° list. When the heavier boats were lowered, both collapsible boats and passengers were crushed against the hull. On the port side, lifeboats plunged into the sea. Now the German torpedo which had pierced the coal bunkers ignited this fuel and set off the contraband cargo. It was this 2nd explosion that sank the *Lusitania*. Within 18 minutes, the luxury liner had settled under 300' of water. Afterward only 6 scattered lifeboats could be seen floating on the ocean's surface.

Aftermath: An inquiry in London produced one cargo manifest. In the U.S. a 2nd cargo manifest was produced, and then the Cunard

Lines produced a 3rd manifest. All were different. Franklin D. Roosevelt found a 4th manifest in the papers of Woodrow Wilson. This 4th manifest, the carbon copy of the one that went down with the *Lusitania*, verified that the cargo was contraband, not innocuous.

Tomorrow: Many ships have been sunk by torpedoes since the tragedy of the *Lusitania* and more will find their way to the locker of "Davy Jones," both in war and in peace. Will the official records of tomorrow's tragedies be as fraught with controversy as the records of the *Lusitania?* This question can be answered only by those who are chosen to govern the future.

THE ST. FRANCIS DAM

In the morning hours of a March day, Dan Mathews, a maintenance man at Powerhouse 2, about a mile below the "fail-safe" St. Francis Dam, reported muddy water flowing past his station. It had rained during the night, upstream from the dam, but the muddy water seemed to be coming from beneath the massive structure itself, not over it or through the sluice gates. Chief of the Los Angeles Department of Water and Power, engineer William Mulholland, rushed from his office to investigate. After his inspection it was decided that though the situation didn't look good, there was no real cause for alarm. Twelve hours later 137,000 cubic yards of concrete tore from anchorage points and 12 billion gallons of water rushed down the valley toward 20,000 people.

When: March 13, 1928.

Where: 40 mi. north of Los Angeles, Calif.

The Lost: 450 known deaths. 700 homes destroyed. The dam had cost $1,300,000, and there were claim damages of $30 million.

The Cause: The dam, completed in May, 1926, rested on a foundation imbedded 30' in the earth. It was 175' thick at its base and tapered upward 175' above the stream bed. Had geologists been consulted, the damsite across San Francisquito Canyon would not have been chosen. But design engineers could see no problems arising from the anchoring of one side of the dam in unstable laminated rock, and the other side in rock composed of gravel and pebbles. In between these anchorage points the dam sat not upon bedrock, but upon compressed powdered rock, a substance semisoluble in water. Though built to the highest standards of the day, the dam actually relied on its sheer weight to withstand the elements and the pressures of impounded waters. In less than 2 years from its completion the modern, fail-safe St. Francis Dam collapsed.

The Disaster: The trickle of muddy water found near Powerhouse 2 on the morning of March 13 was ignored. No one in the valley was warned of impending disaster. Then 12 hours later, 1st one side of the dam, then the other, was torn from its anchorage. A wave 80' high shot from the reservoir. Pushed by the weight of 12 billion gallons of water, the wave tore huge chunks of concrete from the solid mass and propelled some pieces a mile down the valley.

It happened suddenly. And almost as suddenly, where there had been homes and people, there was a 12-mi. swath of death and destruction. Cars traveling along Highway 126 were picked up by the raging torrent and carried toward the sea. Months after the tragedy, divers along the coast were still finding the grisly remains.

Aftermath: Since the St. Francis Dam was built to supply water to the city of Los Angeles, the city assumed full responsibility for the disaster and paid death benefits and crop destruction claims totaling $30 million. Subsequent investigation into the cause of the tragedy spearheaded a movement to utilize the knowledge of geologists in the construction of dams, buildings, and bridges.

THE NEW LONDON SCHOOL EXPLOSION

It was a typical spring day at the $1-million school deep in a unique forest of 10,000 oil derricks. Until midafternoon 700 or more students and faculty members toiled at education. Then the primary grades made their exodus homeward. A few minutes later, at 3:05 P.M., the beautiful New London school exploded. Roof and walls collapsed into a pile of rubble that covered 547 students and teachers.

When: At 3:05 P.M. on Thursday, March 18, 1937.

Where: New London, Tex.

The Loss: 297 dead and 250 injured. The school had cost $1 million.

The Cause: In January, 1937, school authorities initiated an unneeded economy drive. The school's gas bill for heating was running $250 plus a month, a sum that could be saved if the school switched to the use of "free" waste-gas. Although this gas was known to have an unstable ignition point, it was being used in businesses and homes around New London. There were no ill effects and the gas cost nothing. Each school classroom had its own radiator which should have been adjusted for the burning of the waste-gas, but in their eagerness to save money the school officials did not have this done. Workmen, experienced in converting existing systems to the use of waste-gas, were not consulted. Why bother when the school janitor could make the connection with the waste-gas line just as well? It was no big thing.

The Disaster: On March 18, 1937, as on

every other school day, the primary grades were dismissed in the early afternoon. At 3:05, 10 minutes before the remainder of the students would be homeward bound, an accumulation of "raw, wet" waste-gas was ignited by a spark, perhaps from a light switch or static electricity. There was one tremendous explosion, followed by a series of smaller ones. The rumbling noise was heard for miles. In after-the-fact testimony, E. P. Schoch, University of Texas expert in the usage of combustible gases, explained that if any one of the school's main gas lines were allowed to remain open (i.e. flowing) for even half a day, the saturation point could create a potentially explosive condition.

All morning, through lunch, and into the afternoon, the airwaves around New London had been bombarded by the tiny, new radio station, located in the Piney Woods of east Texas, solely owned and operated by Ted Hudson. When the school explosion rocked the countryside, Hudson "closed the store," grabbed his portable broadcasting equipment, and lost no time covering the 12 mi. to New London.

On his arrival, the bodies of youngsters were scattered about in the debris of wood, plaster, and steel. On the spot, Hudson set up his equipment and began broadcasting: "The New London School has exploded. Children are dead. Doctors and nurses, ambulances and hearses are needed . . . coffins and strong men to dig graves." The response was immediate. Help poured into New London along with newsmen by the score, including a young broadcaster named Walter Cronkite. Into the night a grim search went on for the victims. Hospitals and mortuaries were soon filled and overflowing with the injured and dead.

Aftermath: For 3 days and nights doctors, nurses, hospital and mortuary staffs, and Ted Hudson and many like him, plus an army of other volunteers, worked round the clock. Counting from the moment the 1st victim was treated until the last body was recovered, the death toll was 297 and more than 250 had been injured.

In time, New London healed her wounds, and today the city boasts the safest, most modern school system in the nation. But the monument erected in memory of those who perished in the needless disaster will serve as a constant reminder of what Gov. James V. Allred termed the worst disaster in the history of education.

THE *Hindenburg*

Other than the storms that delayed its arrival by more than 10 hours, the flight of the zeppelin *Hindenburg*, from Frankfurt, Germany, to Lakehurst, N.J., was an uneventful routine flight. Over the years more than 32,000 passengers had flown over 100,000 mi. in Ger-

man zeppelins without a single accident. Then in the spring of 1937, on its arrival at Lakehurst, the big silver ship once again dropped its mooring lines to the ground. Navy and civilian workers grabbed them to guide the *Hindenburg* to its mooring mast.

As newsmen clicked their camera shutters and radio commentators recorded the arrival for a later broadcast, there was a puff of smoke at the zeppelin's stern, then a bigger one. The great *Hindenburg* was afire. Shortly thereafter, there was an explosion of hydrogen gas. In 34 seconds the graceful giant of the skies was a flaming funeral pyre.

When: At 7:25 P.M. on May 6, 1937.

Where: The Naval Air Station at Lakehurst, N.J.

The Loss: Fifteen passengers, 20 crewmen, and one line-handler were killed. The *Hindenburg*, last of the great zeppelins, had cost upward of $5 million.

The Cause: The real cause of the disaster may never be known, since in subsequent inquiries neither the German nor U.S. Governments were willing to consider sabotage for fear of creating an international incident. The official cause was listed as "St. Elmo's fire," though there is no other recorded case wherein St. Elmo's fire caused an explosion. Before leaving the Fatherland, both Germany's Gestapo and the S.S. had reason to believe that a bomb would be aboard the *Hindenburg*. A careful search of passengers and ship revealed no bomb, but as a precautionary measure, the 1st officer of the Luftwaffe, Col. Fritz Erdmann, plus Maj. Franz Hugo and Lieut. Klaus Hinkelbein were put aboard as passengers.

The *Hindenburg*, largest zeppelin in the world, more than 800' long, had 16 gas bags containing a total of 7,200,000 cu. ft. of explosive hydrogen gas. Its 4 V-16 diesel engines with 20' 4-bladed props developed 5,000 hp and drove the ship silently and vibrationless at a speed of 80 knots. There were sleeping compartments with baths for 50 passengers and a crew of 30, plus 1st-class dining rooms. Catwalks traversed the ship within its framework of 16 10-story-high rings and 36 longitudinal girders. Twenty-five fuel tanks carried 137,500 lbs. of fuel to give the *Hindenburg* a 10,000-mi. cruising range. Commissioned in March, 1936, the Z-129 had made 10 round trips between Germany and the U.S. The airship designed to use nonexplosive helium was filled with hydrogen gas. The only source for helium was the U.S. and the cost for more than 7 million cu. ft. would have run about $600,000. The expense was unnecessary according to the Deutsche Zeppelin-Reederei Company, operators of the Graf Zeppelin passenger lines. Hydrogen was perfectly safe when handled by experts, and who were more expert than the Germans?

The Disaster: The Z-129 or *Hindenburg* was 10 hours late on its arrival at Lakehurst, and rain, prevailing winds, and lightning prevented immediate landing. After the airship had cruised about for several hours, weather conditions changed and at 7:10 P.M. the luxury liner was 200' over the Naval Air Station. Passengers had collected their personal effects and were ready to disembark. Mooring lines were dropped. Six crewmen were at the nose ready to couple up. On the ground, 92 navy men and 139 civilians were grabbing lines to guide the Z-129 to its mooring mast. At 7:25 the mooring was just minutes from being completed. Herb Morrison of radio station WLS was recording the activity of mooring. Suddenly the commonplace became tragedy. He shouted into his microphone: 'It's burst into flames! Oh, my . . . it's burning, bursting into flames. . . . Oh, the humanity and all the passengers."

Seventy-seven hours out of Frankfurt, *something* had ignited the hydrogen gas. There was panic aboard the *Hindenburg.* Passengers broke out gondola windows to jump 100' to their death. Then there was a loud, 2nd explosion. In 34 seconds the proud queen of the air lay burning on the ground. Of those who managed to escape, badly burned, several died shortly thereafter. Of the 97 people on board, 35 died horribly.

Aftermath: The tragedy of the *Hindenburg* marked finis to an era of zeppelin travel. Airplanes were being developed, and though they carried fewer passengers and less freight, they were much faster. It was hoped that someday airplanes might even carry passengers across the ocean.

Tomorrow: The year 2000 may see what might appear as the ghost of the Z-129, but it won't be a zeppelin, nor will it be filled with gas bags. It will be a 21st-century spaceship plying its way between the star galaxies of the universe.

DEATH RODE THE BALVANO LIMITED

Not before or since the bizarre disaster aboard Italian freight train No. 8017 has such an incident occurred. Because it happened during W.W. II the details were censored, not to be published until years later. Actually, the Balvano Limited was not involved in a collision, nor was it bombed, strafed, or derailed, yet the loss of life within one tragic hour made it one of the major rail disasters of the century.

When: Shortly after 1 A.M. on March 3, 1944.

Where: Near Balvano, Italy, in the mountains inland from Salerno.

The Loss: An estimated 500 lives.

The Cause: Naples, Italy, suffered from wartime shortages and so did the railroads. First-grade coal normally used in locomotives was not available. The burning of 3rd- and 4th-grade substitutes produced a heavy volume of odorless, poisonous carbon monoxide gas, a fact that went unnoticed.

Many city dwellers—unwilling to go without butter, eggs, poultry, and dairy products—joined the increasing number of black market opportunists. They bartered with servicemen for cigarettes, candy, and gum, then exchanged these commodities for farm products that brought tremendously high prices in Naples. To reach the farmers they stole rides on freight trains that were forbidden to carry passengers. But hundreds of people rode these trains every day, another fact that went unnoticed, officially.

The Disaster: Swirling rain churned the thousands of puddles in the Salerno railroad yards and showered from the 47 cars of the Balvano Limited. Twenty of them were empties scheduled to return with civilian and military goods. It was a dark foul night just after 6 P.M. on March 2, 1944. By the time the Limited, No. 8017, reached Eboli, a few miles beyond Battipaglia, it was 7:12 P.M. and more than 100 illegal riders huddled together on open flat cars. Then came Persano and Romagnano. At each stop the number of riders increased. A 2nd locomotive was hooked on front for the 27 mountainous mi. ahead.

It was 11:40 P.M. and now No. 8017 carried 650 illegal passengers. The train chugged slowly upward another 4 mi. to stop at the small Balvano station that lay between 2 long tunnels. A downhill train was having locomotive trouble. While No. 8017 waited for the "clear track ahead" signal, half of its 47 cars were in the lower tunnel wrapped in a blanket of black coal smoke left by its 2 locomotives. Not a breath of air stirred in the tunnel for 38 minutes. Without knowing they were in danger the railroad hitchhikers, enjoying a respite from the biting rain, breathed deeply of monoxide as they fell asleep.

At 12:50 A.M. the 2 locomotives pulling No. 8017 again opened their throttles to creep slowly forward toward the uphill tunnel less than 5 mi. from the next stop at Bella-Muro. They would arrive there in 20 minutes. The terrain was steep and the route treacherous. At 1 A.M. No. 8017 entered the longest of the uphill tunnels, Galleria delle Armi, more than a mile long. Inside, the train stopped, then slipped backward, pushing the last 3 cars into the open air. The puffing locomotives continued to pour smoke and monoxide gas into the tunnel. Those who escaped death during the 38-minute layover in the 1st tunnel were less fortunate in the Galleria delle Armi.

It wasn't until 2:40 A.M., when No. 8017 was 2 hours overdue, that the stationmaster at Bella-Muro grew alarmed. But both he and the stationmaster at Balvano decided to wait rather than to walk the tracks in search of the missing train. At the scene of the disaster brakeman Giuseppe de Venuto awoke from a fitful sleep and struggled downhill for the tunnel exit. By the time he reached fresh air he knew what had happened inside the tunnel. Death rode the Balvano Limited. He must notify the authorities.

The night was severely cold, black, and wet. Venuto had no light to find his way downward over the dangerous tracks, across trestles, and through even darker tunnels. He crawled a good bit of the way. At 5:10 A.M. he reached the Balvano station, pointed back up the track, and said: "They're all dead." Then he collapsed.

Aftermath: With the arrival of civilian and military authorities at Balvano, a locomotive was detached from another train to take them uphill to the Galleria delle Armi. Along the way corpses had to be removed from the tracks. At the scene, the tunnel was strewn with bodies and the cars were filled with the dead. A U.S. Army colonel wrote in his report: "The faces of the victims were mostly peaceful. They showed no sign of suffering. Many were sitting upright or in positions they might assume while sleeping normally."

Following the disaster, the Italian Government posted guards at each tunnel. No train was allowed through unless the tunnels were clear of smoke. The 500 Balvano victims were buried in a common grave and their families were paid indemnity settlements by the Government. On All Souls' Day, November 2 each year, flowers are placed on the common grave at Balvano in memory of those who died when death rode the Balvano Limited.

EXPLOSION OF THE *Fort Stikine*

The 7,142-ton cargo vessel *Fort Stikine* left England in the month of February, 1944, carrying £2 million worth of gold bars, explosives, airplanes, and ammunition. At Karachi a part of its cargo of airplanes and ammunition was exchanged for sulfur, resin, oil, fish, and 8,700 bales of cotton. In the harbor of Bombay, the supply base for the planned Allied invasion of Japan, a fire broke out in its number 2 hold. Red flags, required to indicate explosive cargo, were not in evidence. A series of errors in judgment resulted in one of the worst disasters during W.W. II.

When: Shortly after 3:30 P.M. on April 14, 1944.

Where: In the harbor of Bombay, India.

The Loss: Incomplete death count, 1,500;

3,000 injured. 100,000 tons of Allied shipping destroyed, valued at above $1 billion.

The Cause: In April, 1944, Bombay harbor, gateway to India, was a crowded parking lot of Allied ships. Troops of many nations wandered about the city, shopping like souvenir-hungry tourists. Coolie dock workers kept one eye on the clock. At exactly 12:30 they broke for lunch. Aboard the *Belray,* seaman Roy Howard saw smoke coming from a ventilator on the *Fort Stikine.* No report was made.

Stevedores returning to the *Fort Stikine* at 1:30 found the number 2 hold filled with smoke and scrambled deckside screaming, "Fire!" The wharf-stationed fire brigade boarded the ship, but did nothing while their leader ran from the ship to phone for reinforcements. Unable to operate the dialless telephone on the wharf he set off a fire-alarm box. The time was 2:16 P.M. At 2:25 a fire station officer arrived with 2 pumps, then immediately left the ship to phone for more men and more pumps. Ten minutes later Chief Norman Coombs of the Bombay fire brigade arrived.

In the meantime, the stench of burning fish prompted the ship's captain, A. J. Naismith, to order the fish removed. With this activity going on, ordnance officer Capt. B. T. Oberst came on board with a copy of the *Fort Stikine's* stowage plan in his hand. Confronting Naismith he advised that the ship be scuttled. They were joined by dock manager Col. J. R. Sadler, who reminded them the harbor was too shallow to scuttle a cargo ship and suggested the *Fort Stikine* steam out to sea. Confused with contradictory suggestions, Naismith left the group to phone his ship's insurer for advice.

The Disaster: Explosive cargo aboard the *Fort Stikine* made it a 400'-long unmarked bomb surrounded by ships unaware of their danger. Seamen on neighboring vessels, the *Belray* and *Japalanda,* watched the activity with more boredom than interest. Firemen had pumped water into number 2 hold for about an hour when the color of the smoke suddenly changed to a yellowish-brown, the color that signifies explosives. With no further warning the ship became a thousand Roman candles followed by an explosion that rocked Bombay, left broken bodies strewn on ship decks, and killed 66 firemen and seriously wounded 83 others. In minutes there was a 2nd explosion that threw flaming metal and debris 3,000' in the air to rain death over a one-mi. circle. Fires broke out on docks, in business buildings, and in homes. The force of the 2nd explosion created a tidal wave that lifted the 5,000-ton *Japalanda* 60' in the air to drop it on dockside sheds. In hours both hospitals and mortuaries struggled to care for the injured and dead.

Aftermath: Twenty-seven ships were sunk or burned out. Docks and buildings were destroyed. The entrance to Victoria Dock and the gateway itself was fouled with the hulks of shattered ships. It required 6 months and the efforts of 10,000 men and equipment to clear the harbor of more than a million tons of debris. The toll of life was determined only by the headcount of treated victims and the dead. The unknown number of those blown to bits or cremated could have raised the official count by 1,000 or more.

The specific cause of the fire in number 2 hold was never determined. There were suspicions, but no proof of sabotage. The only facts are that the explosion and fires on that April day in Bombay harbor add up to one of the worst but least-known disasters of W.W. II.

THE JAMAICA TRAIN COLLISON

William W. Murphy, a 45-year veteran of railroading and just 4 years away from retirement, responded to the "restricted" signal on "C" tower 2 mi. before the train's 1st scheduled stop at Jamaica. With the signal's change to "approach," Murphy resumed his 30-mph speed. The next signal light on "Jay" (for Jamaica) tower showed "restricted" and again Murphy applied the air brakes. They grabbed and wouldn't release. Train 780 and its 12 cars carrying 1,000 homeward-bound passengers ground to a dead stop. Brakeman Bertram N. Biggam started to get the flares to put behind the stalled train.

Close behind on the same mainline track, train 174 with 12 cars and 1,200 passengers thundered toward Jamaica. Motorman Benjamin J. Pokorny obeyed the signal at "C" tower and brought his train to a halt. When the signal changed, he accelerated to 15 mph. In back of him, the "C" tower signal changed again to "restricted," but ahead the signal on "Jay" tower flashed "approach." Train 174 resumed full speed. Too late Pokorny saw the stopped train ahead. In his last seconds of life he pulled the brake cord.

When: At 6:26 P.M. on Wednesday, November 22—Thanksgiving Eve—1950.

Where: Near Jamaica tower at 126th Street and Hillside Avenue in the Richmond Hills district of Queens, New York City.

The Loss: 77 passengers killed; 318 injured, 14 critically.

The Cause: Neither train was equipped with an automatic-repeater signal system, an electronic device mounted in the motorman's cab. Murphy and Pokorny had to rely on signal towers spaced at intervals along their route. Normally this signal-light system worked fine, but if a signal changed after a train had passed a tower, the system didn't work at all. Pokorny

should have seen the taillights of the stalled train, if they were on. And that raised an unanswered question, for in a report by the Long Island Railroad to the Public Service Commission it was reported that within a 7-day period the taillights on 50 trains had been inoperative.

The Disaster: Passengers aboard train 780 suffered their annoyance in silence. It wouldn't be the 1st time they had arrived home late. There was no warning of danger until the headlight of train 174 bathed the last car in its blinding glare. In seconds the 2 cars were fused together. The front car of Pokorny's train telescoped the rear car of Murphy's train. Those not killed outright were overcome with fear. The trains were dark. Bedlam reigned inside the cars. People physically capable of moving couldn't because of the pileup of dead and injured bodies.

The noise of the collision was heard on 126th Street and Hillside Avenue. Soon help arrived, but it was an hour and 20 minutes before the last passenger was extricated from the bent and twisted cars. Amputations were performed on the spot and acetylene torches were used to free many trapped passengers. Priests administered last rites while doctors administered plasma. For hundreds of New Yorkers the tragedy turned Thanksgiving Day, 1950, into the blackest of black Thursdays.

Aftermath: At the conclusion of a lengthy investigation the cause of the tragedy spelled out "Pokorny." The militaristic verdict: "Disobedience of signals."

AIR COLLISION OVER NEW YORK

The 39th New York-bound passenger boarded the W.W. II-vintage 4-engine prop job, TWA Flight 266, at Port Columbus Airport just before 9 A.M. At Chicago's O'Hare International Airport the 76th New York-bound passenger boarded the DC-8 107-ton jet, United Airlines Flight 826. TWA's Constellation would fly the shorter distance at 300+ mph. UAL's DC-8 would fly the greater distance at 600+ mph. It was winter and both flights maintained radio contact with New York's Air Traffic Control. Minutes before landing the 2 flights collided 5,000' above Staten Island in one of the worst air disasters of the century.

When: At 10:34 A.M. on Friday, December 16, 1960.

Where: 5,000' above Staten Island, N.Y.

The Loss: 127 passengers and crewmen plus 6 people on the ground. Both planes were picked up in bits and pieces.

The Cause: Bad weather, poor visibility, heavy holiday air traffic, variable air speeds, frequent altitude changes, and inefficient radio communications, all contributed to the tragic collision over New York.

The Disaster: Capt. David A. Wollam, a 14,500-flying-hours veteran pointed the nose of his Constellation skyward at 9 A.M. Flight 266 was no more than airborne when the captain activated the public address system and gave his Welcome Aboard speech, telling his passengers their ETA at La Guardia Airport would be one hour and 32 minutes. They would be flying at 7,000' under Air Traffic Control Instrument flight rules.

Eleven minutes later, Flight 826 was airborne. Its captain, a 20,000-flying-hours veteran, Robert H. Sawyer, informed his passengers that they would be flying at 27,000' at 600 mph with an ETA at Idlewild Airport of one hour and 29 minutes.

An hour out of Columbus, O., New York's Air Route Traffic Control Center—ARTCC— altered Flight 266's altitude from 7,000' to 19,000' and cleared descent to 11,000' after passing over Allentown, Pa. At 10:19 A.M. Wollam advised New York that according to his instruments he was over Allentown and adjusting altitude to 11,000' as requested. New York informed Wollam that radar contact had been established.

10:12 A.M.—ARTCC to Flight 826: Captain instructed to descend to and maintain altitude of 25,000' and advised that radar service not available. Sawyer acknowledged.

10:14 A.M.—New York to Flight 826: Sawyer advised that his flight clearance limit was from Preston, N.J., to Robbinsville at 25,000'.

10:21 A.M.—Flight 826 to United's Aeronautical Radio, Inc.: Sawyer advised ARINC that his standby navigation receiver was inoperative. ARINC acknowledged but did not pass this information along to ARTCC. New York Control Center came on to instruct Sawyer to descend to 13,000'.

10:23 A.M.—Flight 826 to NYCC: "If we're going to have a delay, we would rather hold upstairs than down. We're going to need ¾ of a mile runway visibility. Do you have the weather handy?" Sawyer was advised that Kennedy Airport, Idlewild International, had 1,500' of overcast with rain, snow, and less than the desirable runway visibility. Sawyer answered: "We're starting down."

10:23 A.M.—La Guardia Airport to Flight 266: Wollam advised of measured 500' overcast, one mile visiblity, snow with wind NE at 15 knots. He was told to use runway 4 and advised that localizer beam was inoperative.

10:24 A.M.—La Guardia to Flight 266: Wollam instructed to descend from 11,000' to 9,000' and report.

10:25 A.M.—NYCC to Flight 826: Sawyer

instructed to alter his course and descend to 11,000'.

10:27 A.M.—NYCC to Flight 266: Wollam advised that radar control terminated; instructed to contact La Guardia Approach Control. LGAC instructed Wollam to maintain 9,000'.

10:28 A.M.—LGAC to Flight 266: Cleared for descent to 8,000'.

10:30 A.M.—Flight 266 to LGAC: Wollam confirmed altitude change and was instructed to maintain present heading and reduce speed for final approach course.

10:32 A.M.—Flight 266 to LGAC: Wollam reported his altitude at 6,000' and was instructed to go down to 5,000' and make a right turn to new heading of 150°.

10:33 A.M.—NYCC to Flight 826: Sawyer instructed to contact Kennedy Airport Approach Control. Sawyer acknowledged. His altimeter read 5,500'.

10:33:14—LGAC to Flight 266: Wollam instructed to descend to 1,500' and turn left to new heading of 130°. Advised that there appeared to be jet traffic at 3:00 o'clock one mile NE bound.

10:33:28—Flight 826 to KAAC: "We're approaching Preston at 5,000'." KAAC acknowledged, then gave the weather. Sawyer didn't acknowledge! Flights 266 and 826 had collided.

Flight 826 came to rest in the Park Slope section of Brooklyn, blasting a crater at Sterling Place and Seventh Ave. There were no survivors. Flight 266 fell on Miller Field, Staten Island. Five victims were extracted from the wreckage alive, only to die en route to a hospital.

Aftermath: The 2 prelanding holding patterns of Flight 266 and 826 were 10 mi. apart, but visibility was zero. Neither flight was exactly where its captain thought it to be. From "wheels up" to collision normal events turned out to be unusual, almost as though the collision over New York was predestined.

THE COLLAPSE OF WEST GATE BRIDGE

It was to be a masterpiece among bridges, and by far the largest in Australia. But from the beginning the 8-lane 8,500' West Gate Bridge, across the Yarra River in Melbourne, Australia, had more than its share of bad luck. First there was dissension among the workers that led to strikes. Then there were errors of judgment that compounded themselves until, by sheer weight of accumulation, they caused the collapse of a 393¾' span. It was one of the worst disasters in bridge-building history.

When: At 11:50 A.M. ON October 15, 1970.

Where: Melbourne, Australia.

The Loss: 35 out of 68 workers were killed. The damage was estimated at $10 million.

The Cause: From designers, prime contractors, suppliers, and engineers, West Gate's roster included the "Who's Who" of bridge building. Construction that began in 1968 like a well-oiled machine soon began to deteriorate. The big, happy, bridge-building family of more than 1,000 people broke up into small bickering groups. A workman would send out for a ham on rye without mustard. If it came back with mustard, a whole crew would stop work until the mistake was rectified. Such incidents developed into work-delaying labor strikes. In the 1st 1½ years of construction, because of poor on-site supervision, the building schedule fell 7 months behind.

Then a counterpart of the West Gate "box-girder" bridge—one under construction in Milford Haven, Wales—collapsed on June 2, 1970, killing several workmen. This news spearheaded more problems for West Gate. Unions demanded greater safety measures for workers. Contractors argued among themselves. Engineers had to recheck their mathematical equations. Workmen by the score insisted on taking unscheduled days off.

The Disaster: Construction problems, too, were pyramiding. One big headache was the almost 400'-long span between piers 10 and 11. It was decided to assemble 2 sections of the span on the ground, then hoist them into place and bolt them together. A not uncommon method of assembly, and usually successful when done with utmost care. But when the 2 sections of this particular span were brought together in August of 1970, the north half section was 4½" above the south half section.

Rather than take the sections down for correction, engineers decided to put an 8-ton weight on the high section to bring it level with the lower. On September 6 there was a major buckle. Work came to a halt, followed by a month of deliberation. Then engineers decided to unbolt the 2 sections on each side of the buckle. They theorized that the weight of the high section would cause it to lower and match the level of the lower section. Then it could be rebolted. Operation "unbolt" began at 8:30 A.M. on October 15. At 1st it appeared successful. The high section sank to within 1⅛" of the lower, but before the sections could be rebolted, the buckle became greater.

At 11:50 A.M. the huge 2-section span could tolerate no more tampering—the stresses were too great. With a terrible grinding roar, bridge, men, and equipment tumbled 160' into the river. More than half the workmen on and under the 2-section span lost their lives.

Aftermath: In the investigation that followed, only the suppliers were deemed to be blameless. Designers, contractors, and engineers were dismissed, to be replaced by counterparts who, hopefully, would complete West Gate Bridge without further mishap.

TRAIN-SCHOOL BUS COLLISION

Loaded beyond capacity, school bus number 596 detoured downhill on Gilchrest Road, in Nyack, N.Y. At the bottom it would cross the Penn Central tracks. A few minutes out of Congers, train number 2653 with 73 loaded freight cars was also heading for Gilchrest Road. Fifteen hundred feet before the crossing, the required warning blasts sounded from the diesel's air horns. The school bus maintained its speed. There was a 2nd warning blast from the train, then engineer Carpenter applied the air brakes, locking the train's wheels, but the 4,000-ton freight didn't respond. Seconds later there was a sickening crash.

When: At 7:55 A.M. on March 24, 1972.

Where: Just out of Valley Cottage near Congers, N.Y.

The Loss: Three students were killed outright and of the 46 hospital-treated victims, 2 more died. The bus had cost $8,000.

The Cause: Gilchrest Road crossing, like 2,400 others in New York State, had no gate, watchman, bell system, or flashing lights. Trees bordered Gilchrest Road right up to the crossing and though the part-time bus driver, 35-year-old Joseph Larkin, had driven this alternate route for a week, there had been no trains.

Despite the tremendous responsibility, school bus drivers are underpaid. No particular training is required, other than to pass a driving test. Because of low salary, the turnover in bus drivers is high. It invites those who are out of work temporarily, moonlighters, housewives who need part-time employment, and retirees. All of these people are probably good neighbors and excellent drivers, but they are not necessarily suited for a job that, at best, is a frustrating, nerve-racking experience.

The morning of the disaster was a normal spring day. The weather was clear and the bus had been checked for possible mechanical malfunctions. Train number 2653 was traveling at 25 mph and had sounded all required warnings. The collision shouldn't have happened, but it did.

The Disaster: The Penn Central tracks curve before the straightaway approach to the Gilchrest Road crossing. Two long warning blasts, followed by one short and then another long blast, were sounded routinely. Headed downhill on Gilchrest Road, the yellow school bus could be plainly seen from the cab window of the diesel engine. There was plenty of open space before the crossing and so 2653 thundered onward. On the side of the tracks opposite the approaching school bus, William Muccio had stopped his garbage truck to await the train's passing. He could see that the bus was not slowing down. Transfixed, he watched the distance narrow between the train and the bus. In desperation he sounded his horn. It blended with another long blast from the diesel.

From the engine cab, the engineer, brakeman, and fireman watched the yellow bus hold its speed on a collision course. The engineer hit the air brakes praying they would stop his 4,000-ton juggernaut. Inside the bus, window-seat passengers pressed their fear-ridden faces against the glass, too frightened even to cry out.

The front diesel rammed the school bus just behind its center, tearing it in 2, tossing the back half upside down off the tracks. Seats, bodies, books, and papers flew in every direction. The front half wrapped itself around the front of the engine to be pushed 1,000' down the tracks. From the kitchen window of their home, a few hundred feet from the crossing, John, Joan, and Eileen Fitzgerald saw it happen. The only words spoken were John's. He kept repeating: "My God, the bus didn't stop! The bus didn't stop."

Aftermath: An hour and 20 minutes after the tragedy 45 children and one adult were in the hospital. By noon there had been 300 X rays, 25 blood transfusions, and 17 major surgical operations. Two of those treated didn't recover. In one year, 1971, there were 906 school bus accidents in New York State alone, with 8 deaths and 402 injuries. Nationally, there were 47,000 accidents accounting for 170 deaths and 5,600 injuries. That same year, 290,000 school buses moved 20 million students per day, and each year the total increases by 500,000.

Tomorrow: By the year 2052 New York State will have warning signals at all railroad crossings. It is hoped, especially by parents, that long before that date school buses will be built 100% safer than at present, and that job-orientation and training courses will be mandatory for every school bus driver. Only well-qualified, well-paid, full-time drivers should be entrusted with the transportation of our most valuable national asset, our children.

—F.M.W.

Other Disasters: Natural and Man-Made

YEAR	KIND OR TYPE	PLACE	LOSS
79 AD	Fire	Rome, Italy	¾ of city burned.
526	Earthquake	Antioch, Syria	250,000 dead.
740–744	Bubonic Plague	Constantinople, Turkey	200,000 dead.
1228	Flood	Friesland, Holland	100,000 dead.
1290	Earthquake	Chihli, China	100,000 dead.
1545	Typhus	Cuba	250,000 dead.
1556	Earthquake	Shensi Province, China	800,000 dead.
1642	Flood	Central China	300,000 dead.
1672	Bubonic Plague	Naples, Italy	400,000 dead.
1711	Bubonic Plague	Germany & Austria	500,000 dead.
1737	Cyclone	Calcutta, India	300,000 dead.
1792	Bubonic Plague	Egypt	800,000 dead.
1831	Marine	Europe	*Lady Sherbrooke* sank. 283 dead.
1826–1837	Cholera	New Jersey	900,000 dead.
1834	Fire	London, England	Houses of Parliament burned.
1850	Marine	Margate, England	*Royal Adelaide* wrecked. 400 dead.
1855	Mine	Virginia	Coal mine exploded. 55 dead.
1856	Rail	Philadelphia, Pa.	Train wrecked. 66 dead.
1859	Marine	Irish Sea	*Royal Charter* wrecked. 450 dead.
1863–1875	Cholera	World	230,000 dead.
1865	Marine	Memphis, Tenn.	*Sultana* exploded. 1,400 dead.
1866	Fire	Quebec, Canada	2,500 buildings destroyed.
1876	Cyclone	Bakarganj, India	200,000 dead.
1877	Fire	St. John, New Brunswick, Canada	100 dead. $12,500,000 damages.
1878	Marine	The Thames, London, England	*Princess Alice.* 700 dead.
1881	Fire	Vienna, Austria	Ring Theatre. 600 dead.
1881	Typhoon	Indo-China	300,000 dead.
1883	Earthquake	Ischia, Italy	2,000 dead.
1884	Tornado	Central U.S.	800 dead.

YEAR	KIND OR TYPE	PLACE	LOSS
1884	Mine	Colorado	Coal mine exploded. 59 dead.
1887	Fire	Paris, France	Opéra Comique burned. 200 dead.
1887–1888	Flood	Honan, China	One million to 7 million dead.
1888	Blizzard	Eastern Seaboard, U.S.	400 dead.
1888	Rail	Pennsylvania	50 dead.
1891	Marine	Gibraltar	*Utopia* sank. 574 dead.
1891	Rail	Basel, Switzerland	Collision. 100 dead.
1894	Forest Fire	Hinckley, Minn.	160,000 acres burned.
1898–1908	Bubonic Plague	China & India	3 million dead.
1900	Fire	Hoboken, N.J.	300 dead. $4,500,000 damages.
1904	Marine	New York, N.Y.	*General Slocum* burned. 1,000 dead.
1907	Mine	Jacobs Creek, Pa.	Mine exploded. 239 dead.
1908	Earthquake	Sicily, Italy	100,000 dead.
1909	Hurricane	Louisiana & Mississippi	350 dead.
1909–1918	Bubonic Plague	China & India	1,335,000 dead.
1911	Flood	China	100,000 dead.
1911	Fire	New York, N.Y.	Triangle shirtwaist factory. 145 dead.
1913	Tornado	Omaha, Nebr.	100 dead.
1914	Marine	St. Lawrence River, Canada	*Pacific Empress* sank. 1,024 dead.
1915	Typhus	Serbia	150,000 dead.
1915	Marine	Chicago River, Ill.	Excursion boat *Eastland* capsized. 900 dead.
1917	Marine	Halifax, Nova Scotia, Canada	S.S. *Mont Blanc* collided with Belgian ship. Explosion started fire that burned one sq. mi. 1,400 dead.
1917–1921	Typhus	Russia	2,500,000 dead.
1920	Bubonic Plague	India	2 million dead.
1921	Cholera	India	500,000 dead.
1921	Marine	S. China Sea	*Hong Kong* wrecked. 1,000 dead.
1924	Cholera	India	300,000 dead.
1926–1930	Smallpox	India	423,000 dead.
1927	Mine	Everettville, W.Va.	Coal mine exploded. 97 dead.
1928	Flood	S. Florida	1,836 dead.
1930	Fire	Columbus, O.	Penitentiary burned. 317 dead.
1932	Earthquake	Kansu, China	70,000 dead.
1933	Earthquake	Long Beach, Calif.	115 dead.
1934	Fire	Hakodate, Japan	Fire destroyed city. 1,500 dead.
1939	Earthquake	Anatolia, Turkey	30,000 dead.
1942	Cyclone	Bengal, India	40,000 dead.
1942	Mine	Manchuria	Mine exploded. 1,549 dead.
1944	Earthquake	San Juan, Argentina	5,000 dead.
1947	Typhoon	Honshu, Japan	2,000 dead.
1947	Marine	Texas City, Tex.	S.S. *Grandcamp* exploded. Burned city. 561 dead. $67 million damages.
1948	Earthquake	Fukui, Japan	5,000 dead.
1949	Earthquake	Ecuador	6,000 dead.
1950	Earthquake	Assam, India	1,500 dead.
1951	Aircraft	Colorado	DC-6 crashed. 50 dead.
1952	Earthquake	Southern California	14 dead.
1953	Earthquake	Iran	1,000 dead.
1955	Rail	Guadalajara, Mexico	Train derailed into canyon. 300 dead.
1958	Aircraft	Kanash, U.S.S.R.	TU-104 crashed. 65 dead.
1962	Aircraft	W. Pacific Ocean	Flying Tiger Constellation disappeared. 109 lost.
1962	Avalanche	Peru, South America	3,000 dead.

YEAR	KIND OR TYPE	PLACE	LOSS
1965	Tornado	Midwest, U.S.	272 dead.
1965	Aircraft	Cairo, Egypt	Pakistan 707 crashed. 119 dead.
1967	Missile	Cape Kennedy, Fla.	Apollo 1 Spacecraft burned on pad. 3 astronauts killed.
1970	Rail	Buenos Aires, Argentina	Collision. 235 dead.
1971	Earthquake	Los Angeles, Calif.	64 dead.
1972	Aircraft	Palermo, Italy	DC-3 crashed. 115 dead.
1972	Rail	Saltillo, Mexico	Passenger train jumped tracks. 110 dead.
1972	Earthquake	Iran	5,000 dead.
1972	Flood	Rapid City, S.Dak.	225 dead.

—F.M.W.

The Murderer Who Dined Men to Death

One would be hard put to find better food for thought in the annals of crime or cooking than the story of the French murderer Père Gourier. The history of French cuisine is filled with incredible characters: Louis XIV, the Sun King, whose stomach was 3 times larger than an ordinary man's; the chef Vatel, who committed suicide when a banquet he had prepared turned out badly; the gourmand Desessart, whose stomach was so large that one gallant dueling opponent graciously drew a circle upon it which he agreed would be his only target; the anonymous cook who served Donkey's Brains à la Diplomate to Napoléon III; the far-out chef Jules Maincave, who concocted, among other delicacies, peanut butter and jelly soup. The list is endless, but no French gourmand or murderer was more incredible than Gourier—who dined men to death.

Gourier, known to history only as Father Gourier, actually murdered his many victims by wining and dining them. His technique did not involve a rare poison or, for that matter, anything illegal. No, Gourier, a rich landowner, always stayed strictly within the limits of the law. Each year he simply chose a victim and killed him at the dining table. Sometimes this took a full year, other times as little as 2 months, but Gourier managed to dispatch from 7 to 9 men before his scheme backfired.

Gourier's method was to gorge his guests with rich heavy food, not once, but at every meal, and every day for as long as it took to kill. Greed and gluttony were his accomplices. Since the meals were free, his victims happily ate as much as they could get. Money was of no importance to Gourier. The maître d'hôtel and waiters at the Brébant, Véjour, Tortoni's, the Café de Paris, and other expensive Parisian restaurants knew Gourier well. The waiters eventually discovered Gourier's taste for murder, but there was nothing they could do about it. The gourmand began to boast of his exploits. He'd suddenly appear with a new guest and a waiter would inquire about his previous night's companion. "Oh, I buried him this morning," Gourier would say. "He was nothing great. I got him in less than 2 months." His boasting led to his downfall, but not because the law caught up with him.

Gourier's end came at the hands of a certain Ameline, the 2nd assistant to the public executioner. Eugène Chavette, the son of the famous restaurateur Vachette, made an exhaustive study of the case toward the end of the 18th century, but he never determined Ameline's 1st name, or whether he was Gourier's 7th, 8th, or 9th "guest." Perhaps Gourier thought it ironic to choose a public executioner for his next victim. If so, his choice proved more ironic than he could have imagined.

In the 1st place, Ameline had an appetite even greater than Gourier's. Those who watched this trencherman swore he had hollow legs that served as reserve stomachs. Gourier feted him for one year, then another year. Ameline looked healthier than ever and hadn't gained a pound. Gourier took to feeding him only the heaviest of dishes, food that he himself had trouble digesting but which Ameline still relished at the 3rd or 4th helping.

The murderer vowed that he would kill Ameline just as he had the others, even if it required his entire fortune. But he hadn't reckoned on a 2nd factor. Ameline knew of Gourier's plans, and was ready to bite the hand that fed him. Christian Guy, in his History of French Cuisine, suggests that a waiter may have warned him, but at any rate Ameline, following a scheme of his own, periodically vanished for 2 or 3 days at a time to purge his body with castor oil and other laxatives. The excuses he made were always plausible and Gourier never suspected him.

Père Gourier's end came, thanks to the assistant public executioner, but not on the guillotine. It happened one night at Paris' most expensive restaurant, the Cadran bleu. That evening Ameline sat eating sirloin after sirloin effortlessly, while Gourier tried in vain to keep up with his guest. But the pace finally proved too much. Suddenly Gourier turned red, then white, when he was served his 14th slice of steak. Ameline, chomping on his 15th slice, laughed when Gourier threw back his head, thinking that his host was about to sneeze. But then Gourier slumped forward. Speechless, Gourier tried to pull himself up, but he failed—his eyes and mouth were about to close forever. An ironic smile remained on his lips as he toppled over his plate. The gourmand murderer must have thought it most fitting that he had got his just desserts during the main course of his last meal.

—R.H.

The Body Snatchers

Among the best-known of murderers and among the most unwise, William Burke (1792–1829) was an Irish laborer who emigrated to Scotland in 1817. There he eventually opened a used clothing store in Edinburgh and, far more importantly, rented a room from William Hare, a fellow Irishman and owner of a boardinghouse catering to vagrants and elderly pensioners. This was the era of the body snatchers or resurrectionists, those moonlighting grave robbers who supplied anatomists with bodies for dissection. Body snatchers were subject to heavy fines and deportation, but if they left the corpse's clothing behind, they could not be convicted of robbery or any serious offense. Cadavers were much in demand at the time, no questions asked, for only the relatively few bodies of men executed for murder were then legally available for the dissection table and anatomy was 1st coming into its own as a science.

It was in 1827 that Burke and his partner embarked upon their career. One of Hare's lodgers—an old man named Donald—had died owing him £4, and the landlord convinced Burke that they had stumbled upon an easy source of income. Ripping the cover off the coffin in which parish authorities had sealed Donald, the pair hid his body in a bed and filled the coffin with tanner's bark, resealing it and later selling the cadaver for £7 10s. to Dr. Robert Knox, who ran an anatomy school in Surgeon's Square. Burke and Hare soon expanded their operation. Another boarder lingered too long at death's door and they helped him through, smothering the man with a pillow and selling his body to Knox for £10.

Hare and his wife, and Burke and his mistress, Helen McDougal, proceeded to dispatch from 14 to 28 more unfortunates in similar fashion, receiving up to £14 for each body. They were careful to smother their victims, leaving no marks of violence, so that it would appear that they were merely grave robbers. Whenever the boardinghouse supply ran low, they lured victims there, usually choosing old hags, drunks, and prostitutes, whom they often plied with drink. If a candidate offered too much resistance for a pillow, Burke would pin him down while Hare smothered him, holding his hands over the victim's nose and mouth.

But the murderers got careless. First, they killed Mary Paterson, a voluptuous 18-year-old, so free with her body that it was quickly recognized by Knox's young medical students, who even preserved it before dissection as a perfect example of female pulchritude. Then they did in "Daft Jamie" Wilson, a familiar, good-natured imbecile who made his living running errands on the streets of Edinburgh. Finally, the suspicions of neighbors aroused, police caught them with the body of a missing woman named Mary Dougherty. Hare turned state's evidence at the ensuing trial, which began on Christmas Eve, he and his wife freed, and Helen McDougal was discharged for lack of evidence. Burke for some reason foolishly refused to give state's evidence. He was convicted and hanged a month later on January 28, 1829, before a crowd of some 30,000. The word the murderer contributed to the language was even heard as he stood on the scaffold in the Grassmarket, spectators exhorting the executioner with cries of "Burke him, burke him!" (i.e., don't hang but smother or strangle him to death).

The crowd wanted to "burke" Hare, too, despite his immunity, but the real brains behind the operation escaped them and is believed to have died of natural causes many years later in England where he lived under an assumed name. Throughout the trial Hare's wife had sat in court holding their baby in an attempt to win sympathy, even though the child suffered from whooping cough. Burke, who signed a post-trial confession admitting to some 16 murders, was himself dissected at Edinburgh University Medical School following his hanging, his remains viewed by tens of thousands, and for all anyone knows his skeleton might still be propped up in the corner of some classroom there. As for Dr. Knox, the crowd turned against him after the execution, threatening to destroy his school, and only police protection saved his life. Despite his protestations of innocence, he was ostracized and eventually forced to leave town.

William Burke was not the 1st person to murder for cadavers, or even to murder for this motive by suffocation; 2 female nurses, Helen Torrence and Jean Valdig, had been hanged for this crime in 1752. But with all the publicity Burke's name came to literally signify the act and figuratively to mean "stifle or hush up" in any manner, the usage perhaps strengthened a half century later by the Fenian murder of Thomas Henry Burke, undersecretary for Ireland.

It is a little ironic that Burke's name, in the form of "to burke," "burke," and "burking," should be so remembered, for Hare probably did more of the actual suffocating, his confederate's greater strength needed to hold their victims down. Burke and Hare are thought to be the inspiration for Robert Louis Stevenson's *The Body Snatchers*. As a result of their Hare "anatomy murders," existing dissection laws were modified, making it easier for anatomists to obtain bodies without resorting to illegal means.

—R.H. rep.

Murder Will Out

A selection of some of the most fascinating, gruesome, artful, bizarre, and memorable murder cases in the history of international crime.

THE MADELEINE SMITH CASE (1857)

The Murder: Murder will out? Not always. On March 23, 1857, Emile l'Angelier—vomiting and violently ill with stomach cramps—staggered home before dawn to his shabby lodgings in Glasgow, Scotland. His landlady called a doctor, who prescribed laudanum, but a few hours later Emile was dead. It was his 3rd such attack in a month. A postmortem revealed death was caused by a massive dose of arsenic—enough to kill 50 men. The murder of an obscure, 31-year-old clerk hardly merited headlines. Nevertheless, the trial of his accused murderess was one of the most sensational in the history of 19th-century British crime.

Born in England, of French extraction, Emile l'Angelier was a short, dark, self-styled ladies' man with a fatal ambition to marry above his station in life. After his death, more than 100 love letters were found in his room and in his office desk. The writer was Madeleine Smith, the beautiful 21-year-old daughter of a wealthy Glasgow architect. Her letters were both incriminating and—even more shocking to the prudish sensibilities of a Victorian society—"indecently" passionate.

The clandestine correspondence traced a romantic misalliance between an adventurous Juliet and a calculating Romeo. Emile l'Angelier met and quickly seduced Madeleine Smith in 1855, when she was only 19. Her father denounced him as a fortune hunter, and ordered his daughter to terminate the "friendship." Fiery, strong-willed, and remarkably sensual for a Victorian-bred teen-ager, Madeleine was ready to forego her inheritance at that point and marry Emile. Her lover, though, was more cautious. He obviously wanted to marry money

even more than he wanted to marry Madeleine, and wasn't above using gentle blackmail to advance his courtship. Urging Madeleine to be more persuasive in winning her parents' approval of the match, he wrote, "Think what your father would say if I sent him your letters for perusal." This was only one of many copies of letters written to Madeleine curiously preserved by Emile.

By January, 1857, Madeleine had understandably cooled toward her lover. Unbeknownst to Emile, she accepted a marriage proposal from well-to-do businessman William Minnoch, one of her father's closest friends. Then, early in February, she asked l'Angelier to return her letters and "likeness." His reply was apparently threatening, because on February 12, Madeleine wrote again begging, "Emile, for God's sake do not send my letters to Papa!" In the same letter, she denied rumors of her engagement to Minnoch. Soon thereafter, Madeleine resumed her ardent correspondence and secret meetings with the volatile Emile.

The Hunt: Madeleine's affair with Emile was common gossip and his friends, particularly spinster-confidante Mary Perry, considered her a prime suspect. So did the police. In addition to the revealing letters, Madeleine had openly purchased large quantities of arsenic on 3 separate occasions in February and March. When questioned by the Procurator-Fiscal of Glasgow, Madeleine readily admitted buying the arsenic—not to poison rats as she had told the chemists, but "for cosmetic purposes." Madeleine was equally candid in confessing she had lied to Emile about Minnoch, and that she had resumed the affair with l'Angelier only because she hoped he would then return her letters.

One of those letters, counted as key evidence against her, was delivered to l'Angelier on Saturday afternoon, March 21. In it, she wrote, "Oh beloved are you ill? Come to me sweet one. I shall wait again tomorrow night." Madeleine insisted she had written the letter on Friday, March 20. Therefore, the word "tomorrow" meant Saturday, not Sunday, the night he received a fatal dose of arsenic. She had waited all Saturday night, said Madeleine, but Emile had neither kept the date nor sent a message. Ingenious though her explanations were, Madeleine Smith was arrested on March 31 and charged with the murder of Emile l'Angelier. Her historic 9-day trial began June 30, 1857.

The Accused: Enigmatic Madeleine Smith was beautiful—with a graceful figure, fair skin, cameo-like profile, raven black hair, and intense physical vitality. During the trial, she received hundreds of marriage proposals. Her mother was an invalid and Madeleine efficiently managed the household while still in her early teens. She was keenly intelligent with a seemingly imperturbable poise, which enabled her to endure and survive the trial. If she had been born 100 years later, Madeleine would probably have been a militant feminist, perhaps even a lawyer herself. Instead she was an accused murderess, regarded at best as a flirtatious manipulator—one of the few roles available to strong-minded women in the Victorian era.

The Trial: At the trial—held in Edinburgh—Madeleine was described by an eyewitness as "wearing a brown silk dress and straw bonnet trimmed with white . . . the only unmoved, cool personage to be seen . . . Miss Smith never ceases surveying all that goes on around her, returning every stare with compound interest." Three judges—Lord Justice-Clerk Hope, and Lords Ivory and Handyside—presided over the trial. John Inglis, dean of the faculty, handled the defense and Lord Advocate James Moncrieff led the prosecution.

The most damaging testimony was given by Mary Perry. She swore Emile had told her he experienced his 1st attack after drinking a cup of cocoa prepared by Madeleine, adding, "If she [Madeleine] were to poison me, I would forgive her." The defense contended that l'Angelier was an arsenic eater and had probably killed himself deliberately, or by an accidental overdose. However, they offered no proof that he had made any arsenic purchases.

The weakest point of the prosecution's case was its utter failure to produce any evidence that Madeleine had met with l'Angelier before any one of his 3 attacks. There *was* a diary in which Emile had made notations about seeing Madeleine on one or more of those occasions; but it was ruled inadmissible on the grounds that a man might conceivably use such notes to revenge himself upon another after death.

Madeleine was never questioned directly. At that time prisoners were not allowed to go into the witness box. The verdict was Not Guilty on one count of poisoning, and Not Proven on 2 others. A verdict of Not Proven is recognized by Scottish courts, but not by English or U.S. law. Many crime buffs believe the jury was really trying to say, "We think she did it, but we can't prove it, and the cad probably deserved it anyway."

The verdict was loudly applauded by courtroom spectators, but Madeleine's counsel avoided the customary congratulatory handshake. Her parents, who never attended the trial, were equally cold. Soon after, the family actually changed its name, even though "Smith" would seem sufficiently common to guarantee anonymity in itself.

The End: Undaunted and indomitable, Madeleine moved to London in the fall of 1857, accompanied by brother Jack, the only member of the family who stood by her. There she joined poet William Morris's socialist movement, and married one of his followers. In 1909, when she was 73, the remarkable old woman emigrated to the U.S. to be near her son. She was 92, deaf, and poor when she died in 1928.

Proud, even in poverty, she had recently turned down an offer from a Hollywood studio to make a silent movie based on her life. It wasn't until 1950 that an English film was finally produced, with Ann Todd playing the title role in *Madeleine*. Unfortunately the picture failed to answer the riddle, "Did she or didn't she?"

—J.B.C. & J.Cs.

THE PROLIFIC THOMAS NEILL CREAM
(active 1878 to 1892)

The 1st Murders: In 1878, a chambermaid, Kate Gardner, was found dead behind a doctor's office in Montreal with a bottle of chloroform beside her. The police decided that she had committed suicide.

Two years later, in Chicago, Julia Faulkner died on an abortionist's operating table. The police brought a murder charge against the abortionist, but he escaped conviction.

The following year, a Miss Stack died from medicine prescribed by the same doctor that had performed the abortion on Julia Faulkner.

Soon after, the husband of the doctor's mistress, Julia Stott, died of what were 1st thought to be natural causes.

The 1st hunt: The doctor, Thomas Neill Cream, was picked up by the Chicago police in 1880 and charged with the murder of Julia Faulkner. The prosecution failed to convict him.

Cream himself offered the city a 2nd chance at prosecution. He said that Mr. Stott's death was not natural and wrote a threatening letter to the chemist who supplied Stott's medicine, accusing him of putting too much strychnine in it. He demanded that Stott's body be exhumed. It was, and when, at his trial, Julia Stott turned state's evidence against her lover, Cream was convicted of murder in the 2nd degree and sent to jail. He spent 10 years there, then was released. Soon after, his father died, leaving him a sizable estate.

The Next Murders: In 1891, Ellen Donworth, a 19-year-old prostitute in London (where Cream had moved), received a letter from a certain "H.M.D." that warned her she was about to be poisoned by Frederick Smith, of W. H. Smith and Son. Soon after, she got a 2nd letter, repeating the warning and asking her to meet the writer at the York Hotel. She did and it wasn't long before she was writhing in agony. She died on her way to the hospital, but before drawing her last breath, she said, "A tall gentleman with cross-eyes, silk hat, and bushy whiskers gave me a drink twice out of a bottle. . . . There was white stuff in it."

A week later, prostitute Matilda Clover died under similar circumstances.

On April 11, 1892, strychnine poisoning took the lives of 2 more prostitutes—Alice Marsh and Emma Shrivell. Alice died right away, but Emma lived for 6 hours after she reached the hospital. She told a Constable Crumley, who had seen the murderer leave the house, that she had entertained a doctor called Fred. She, Alice, and Fred had downed some canned salmon and beer, and Fred had given the girls 3 long pills which he said would be good for them.

The Hunt: Cream did himself in. He tried to blackmail drug firms. Posing as "A. O'Brien," he wrote a letter to the Lambeth coroner, offering to deliver Ellen Donworth's murderer for £3,000 reward. He even went so far as to print up 500 circulars reading:

. . . TO THE GUESTS OF THE METROPOLE HOTEL. I HEREBY CERTIFY TO YOU THAT THE PERSON WHO POISONED ELLEN DONWORTH ON THE 13TH DAY OF LAST OCTOBER IS TODAY IN THE EMPLOY OF THE METROPOLE HOTEL, AND YOUR LIVES ARE IN DANGER AS LONG AS YOU REMAIN IN THIS HOTEL. [signed] W. H. MURRAY

He tried to pin the crimes on a Dr. Harper, to whom he wrote threatening letters. The police identified his handwriting.

When he discovered that the police were watching him, he charged into Scotland Yard to lodge an indignant complaint. The complaint was denied. He was arrested on June 3.

The Accused: Born in Glasgow, Cream moved with his family to Canada in 1863. He was cross-eyed (particularly when excited), bald, and wore a pair of gold pince-nez. Though he acquired a degree in medicine, he made his way as a young man committing insurance company fraud, and performing as an arsonist, a petty thief, and an abortionist. In London, after serving his jail term for his U.S. and Canadian murders, he hung around with prostitutes. He affected a costume when he did so—a tall silk hat, a velvet cloak over evening clothes, a carnation, and a gold-topped walking stick. Maybe he was trying to emulate Jack the Ripper, who had won his fame 2 years before by killing prostitutes. Whatever his inspiration, he killed them too.

The Trial: One of the witnesses at Cream's trial was Lou Harvey, a prostitute to whom Cream had given some pills. She had been too smart to take them. There were other witnesses, also—people to whom Cream had bragged about his activities. The jury was out only 10 minutes before they came back with a verdict of Guilty.

The End: Thomas Neill Cream was hanged for the murder of Matilda Clover on November 5, 1892. He went to the gallows claiming alternately that he was innocent and that he was Jack the Ripper.

—A.E. & M.T.

The Peltzer Case (1882)

The Murder: Armand Peltzer was an engineer in Antwerp, Belgium, who would become renowned in the annals of true criminal escapades for having conceived the most ingenious scheme in modern history for getting away with murder.

The amorous Armand Peltzer had been smitten by the wife of another. He had fallen passionately in love with Julie Bernays, young wife of a gross and insensitive Belgian attorney named Guillaume Bernays. Peltzer determined to eliminate Bernays, thereby making Bernays's wife a widow who would be free to marry him. But in order to inherit Julie, Peltzer knew that his crime must be perfect. Thereafter, he devoted himself to inventing various means by which he might kill and survive, and eventually he became the architect of an alibi unequaled in criminal lore.

Armand Peltzer had a younger brother, Leon, who was deeply indebted to him. It was time, Armand decided, to call for repayment. Leon, after some financial indiscretions in Argentina, was living under an assumed name in New York where he worked as a linen goods salesman. Peltzer now contacted Leon, summoning him to come posthaste to a meeting in Paris. On November 1, 1881, the blond Leon boarded the passenger ship *Arizona* in New York and sailed for Europe.

The Peltzer brothers met in Paris on November 16, and Armand explained his scheme to Leon. If Leon carried out the scheme, Armand said, he would have redeemed himself and adequately paid back his long indebtedness. Leon listened closely and then readily agreed to cooperate. The basic ingredient of the plot was simple and foolproof. The crime would be committed by a person who did not exist. Therefore, after the murder, the police would have no one to look for.

Immediately, in Paris, the plot got under way. Leon changed his appearance, complexion, dress, and took on the guise of one Henry Vaughan, a millionaire preparing to establish a fleet of ships crossing from Amsterdam to Sydney. Having converted himself into the fictitious Henry Vaughan, tycoon, Leon visited Bremen, Amsterdam, Brussels, working out of the most expensive hotels, becoming known to the foremost navigation firms.

Finally, Leon wrote Guillaume Bernays—under the signature of the fictional Vaughan—explaining that British friends had recommended Bernays as an attorney who might represent the new steamship line in Brussels. Next, Leon summoned Bernays from Antwerp to Brussels to talk business, and with delight Bernays kept the appointment. Leon, now a bewhiskered and bespectacled dandy, admitted Bernays to his flat, and led him to a chair. Then, Leon drew out a noiseless pistol and shot Bernays dead through the back of the head. The murder had been neatly accomplished.

The Hunt: After the killing, Leon Peltzer burned his wig and false beard, disposed of his glasses, washed off his makeup, and departed from the flat forever. Vaughan, the murderer, vanished into thin air. A man named Leon Peltzer, recently on a visit from New York, could not be suspected. And certainly his brother, Armand Peltzer, who had been going about his business in Antwerp, could not have even the vaguest connection with the violent crime. The deed had been done by an unknown hand. The slayer was nonexistent. The perfect murder had been committed. Armand Peltzer had the slain man's wife for his own.

Only one flaw made the perfect crime imperfect, and that stemmed from human vanity. In Bâle, Switzerland, Leon Peltzer perused the newspapers daily for word of the discovery of the victim's body. When 10 days had passed without the corpse's being found, the impatient Leon, eager to see his press notices, wrote a letter to the Belgian police directing them to the body. He explained Bernays's death had been the result of a "horrible accident." He had been visiting Bernays on business, had

shown him a revolver, and somehow it had gone off by accident and killed Bernays. Frightened, the letter writer explained, and fearful because he was a foreigner, he had fled. The letter was signed "Henry Vaughan."

The Belgian police, believing Bernays's death might have been accidental, yet suspecting he might have been murdered, began an intensive investigation. They also posted a 25,000-franc reward for information leading to the apprehension of Henry Vaughan, and they circulated specimens of Vaughan's handwriting.

It was Leon's letter that unraveled the mystery. He had made one mistake. In preparing his Henry Vaughan letter, he had neglected to change or disguise his Leon-style handwriting. In the town of Verviers, a chemist saw the police photocopy specimen of Henry Vaughan's handwriting—and recognized it as belonging to Leon Peltzer. Once the police were onto Leon, the trial led swiftly to the real mastermind, Armand Peltzer, and both brothers were arrested.

The Trial: The battle between the Crown and the 5 lawyers of the defense opened in the Palais de Justice on November 27, 1882. The Crown, using 91 witnesses, showed how Armand Peltzer had directed the crime, using his brother as a puppet. Armand had guided his brother to a Parisian theatrical hairdresser for part of his disguise, had created the nonexistent shipping tycoon bearing the name Vaughan, had sent his younger brother to London to purchase the murder weapon. Throughout the long trial both Peltzers were cool, calm, and elegantly dressed, even to wearing gloves. On December 22 the case went to the jury. Despite the pleas of the defense, the jury took only a half hour to find both Peltzers guilty of murder. They were sentenced to death, but since the death penalty had been abolished in Belgium, the sentences meant life imprisonment.

The End: The Peltzers were both incarcerated in the Louvain prison. After 2 years and 4 months, Armand fell ill and died, after sharing a glass of hot wine with his younger brother. Leon lived on, learning more languages—he knew 6 in all—and spending his time as an unofficial translator for the Ministry of Justice. After 30 years behind prison walls, Leon was released on condition he live outside Belgium. Free at the age of 65, he changed his name to Albert Preitelle and moved to London. Then he moved to Ceylon, working there as a secretary for 7 years. Finally allowed to return to Brussels, he got a job with a business firm, through the help of friends. But feeling he had this job as a charity case, he decided that he didn't want to live any longer. He planned his suicide as carefully as his brother had planned the murder of Bernays. One day in 1922, when he had it all blueprinted, Leon took a train to Ostend. From there he went outside the city, jumped into the ocean, and drowned himself.

—I.W.

THE WHITECHAPEL MURDERS (1888)

The Murders: On the last day of August, 1888, Mary Ann Nichols took to the streets around Buck's Row in London's East End in an attempt to earn the fourpence she would need to rent a bed for the night. Instead of a flea-ridden cot in a doss house, however, her bed was to be a slab in the morgue, after she had been brutally disemboweled, and her throat slit from ear to ear.

While as many as 14 murders have been attributed to the Whitechapel killer who dubbed himself "Jack the Ripper," it is generally agreed that only 5 were committed by his hand: Mary Ann Nichols was the 1st, Annie Chapman the 2nd, Elizabeth Stride and Catherine Eddowes the 3rd and 4th, and Mary Jane Kelly the 5th and last. Committed within an area of about ¼ sq. mi., between August 31 and November 9, in 1888, the murders shared a number of similarities: 1) all 5 women were prostitutes; 2) all 5 had been grabbed from behind and had their throats slit; 3) there was an attempt to mutilate all of the bodies, though one attempt was thwarted; 4) every killing occurred either on the 1st or the last weekend of the month, in the early hours of the morning; 5) except for the brutal slaying of Mary Jane Kelly, all of the murders took place out-of-doors in the worst section of town; 6) in none of the cases was there evidence of sexual assault; and 7) each murder was increasingly savage as well as more audacious.

Murder in the East End was commonplace, but the Whitechapel slaughters caught and sparked the imagination of London and its newspapers. After Annie Chapman's corpse was discovered on September 8, her abdomen laid open, the intestines thrown over one shoulder, newspaper reporters began to clamor for the capture of "Leather Apron," the 1st of the many sinister sobriquets they invented under the assumption that the murderer was a slaughterman. Leather Apron, himself, fed the media's appetite for sensational news and also selected his final name on September 27, when he sent a note penned in red ink to the Central News Agency. It read in part:

Dear Boss, I keep hearing the police have caught me, but they won't fix me just yet. I have laughed when they look so clever and talk about being on the right track. . . . I am down on whores and I shan't quit ripping them till I do get buckled. . . . Grand work, the last

job was. I gave the lady no time to squeal. How can they catch me now? I love my work and want to start again. . . . The next job I do I shall clip the lady's ears off and send them to the police, just for jolly, wouldn't you?

The note was signed, "Yours truly, Jack the Ripper," and as a grisly postscript, he murdered 2 women in one night the following weekend, making off with Catherine Eddowes's left kidney.

Of the hundreds of letters which purported to be prose written by the Ripper, at least 3 are genuine: the letter mentioned above and 2 which followed the double murder of September 30. One arrived the morning after the double murders were committed, again addressed to the Central News Agency, a bloody fingerprint decorating its envelope.

I was not codding, dear Boss, when I gave you the tip. You'll hear about Saucy Jack's work tomorrow. Double event this time. Number One squealed a bit; couldn't finish straight off. Had no time to get ears for police. Jack the Ripper.

The 3rd note turned up on October 16, addressed to the head of the Whitechapel Vigilance Committee, George Lusk. It came in a cardboard box which appeared also to contain a piece of Catherine Eddowes's purloined kidney:

From Hell, Mr. Lusk, sir, I send you half the kidne I took from one woman, prasarved it for you, tother piece I fried and ate it; was very nice. I may send you the bloody knif that took it out if you only wate while longer. Catch me when you can, Mr. Lusk.

On November 9, 1888, the landlord of a small East End tenement sent his man around to evict a whore who had fallen behind in her rent. Unable to enter the locked front door, the man peeked through a broken window to discover Mary Kelly dead on her blood-soaked mattress, victim of one of the most savage mutilation murders in the history of crime. And with the murder of Mary Kelly, Jack the Ripper vanished, leaving behind a trail of blood and terror. He was never apprehended.

The Hunt: Gen. Sir Charles Warren was appointed metropolitan police commissioner in 1886, due to his ability to handle the Bantu in Griqualand West, and due also to the supposition that a military man was needed to bring to an end the increasing demonstrations by the unemployed. Sir Charles lost no time in putting his military skill to work, winning rapidly the hatred and derision of the poor and jobless.

It was Warren who was responsible for 1887's "Bloody Sunday," sending his "troops" against a large demonstration in Trafalgar Square, wounding hundreds, killing 2. It was this man who was put in charge of the Whitechapel case.

The investigation was characterized by military strategy and comic ineptitude. It confined itself almost completely to the criminal haunts found in the East End slums, as mediums, detectives in drag, and even bloodhounds were called upon to give their best. In the case of the latter, the "best" the 2 chosen dogs could give was to lose themselves promptly. In the case of the "plainclothes" policemen, one constable was beaten soundly for being a pervert, then beaten even harder for being a copper. At one point, photographs were taken of some of the murdered women's eyes because it was believed the image of the killer would be indelibly imprinted there. The results of this, too, were decidedly less than positive.

Some have suggested that the undeniable mishandling of the case was part of a deliberate cover-up. During the inquests for the various murders, many key witnesses went uncalled and allegedly Warren, himself, ordered that a piece of evidence be destroyed, after the discovery of Catherine Eddowes's body. More and more public censure was directed at the bemonocled head of Sir Charles until, on the day of the Kelly slaying, Warren was forced to turn in his resignation.

The Murderer: While the Ripper may have vanished, heated speculation as to his identity has not. In theory, the murderer has been adjudged everything from a cannibal to a cop, from a religious fanatic to a mad social reformer. Arthur Conan Doyle, creator of Sherlock Holmes, had it at one point that the murders were being committed by a psychotic midwife. Richard Baker once said: "It seems much more likely that he was a middle-aged professor with a passion for practical jokes who was no longer able to suppress his homicidal tendencies. . . . Such a theory helps to explain the one fault that can reasonably be attributed to Jack—his incorrigible long-windedness. . . .' "

Over the years, accusations have continued to be leveled at such sinister characters as Michael Ostrog, a Russian doctor purportedly sent by the Czarist Government to discredit London anarchists and demonstrators, but in November, 1970, Dr. T. E. A. Stowell ignited the flames of scandal by insinuating that the killer had been Edward, Duke of Clarence, grandson to Queen Victoria. In *Clarence* (*Was He Jack the Ripper?*), Michael Harrison claims decidedly that Edward was not the Ripper, but proposes that the murderer was a tutor of the Duke: J. K. Stephen, Cambridge man, poet, and misogynist. His evidence, like the evidence against the Duke of Clarence, is largely supposition, some of it pretty slim at that.

Speculation, rest assured, will continue.

Aftermath: By drawing sensational attention to the East End's squalor and filth, Jack the Ripper served successfully as a lever for social reform. Alone, he managed to do more in the way of exposing the plight of the poverty-stricken than all the public demonstrations of the time. "In our age of contradictions and absurdities," *Commonweal* pointed out, "a fiend-murderer may become a more effective reformer than all the honest propagandists in the world." In an open letter to the *Star*, George Bernard Shaw portrayed the Ripper as a sort of media guerrilla, who "by simply murdering and disembowelling 4 women, converted the proprietary press to an inept sort of communism."

Slum clearance began soon after the murders ceased, and residents of the area were increasingly referred to as "poor unfortunates," rather than as "scum." The Ripper set this process in motion. An editorial in *Justice*, a Social Democrat paper, summed up this line of thought with an interesting epitaph for the Ripper:

> The real criminal is the vicious bourgeois system which, based on class injustice, condemns thousands to poverty, vice, and crime.

—M.T.

The Lizzie Borden Case (1892)

The Murders: On the morning of August 4, 1892, in a quiet and most ordinary small New England town, a distraught spinster daughter found her elderly parents bludgeoned to death in their Victorian home. Andrew J. Borden, age 70, one of the leading citizens of Fall River, Mass., was a retired undertaker who had amassed $250,000 in his lifetime. He was a lean and spare man of few words, hard-working and thrifty by New England standards of the day, although somewhat obsessive and miserly by our own. He was found lying face down in a pool of blood on the black overstuffed horsehair sofa in the parlor. His face and skull were battered and crushed as if by a meat cleaver or a small hatchet. Half of his face was sliced clean off; an eye was slit from its socket and lay hanging near the crushed jaw. He had received a total of 10 blows. Upstairs in a spare bedroom lay the body of his 67-year-old wife, Abby Durfee Gray Borden. She had received 19 hatchet blows. Skull bones, hair, and face were pounded together in a bloody pulp.

The death notice in the local newspaper was quiet and unsensational. Funeral private, it read. Friends kindly omit flowers. But news of the murders spread through the community like a shock wave. People bolted their doors and avoided the streets. A grim shadow of suspicion and terror hung over the citizens of Fall River. In a hundred years' time, nothing out of the ordinary had disturbed the flow of serious commerce and Christian sobriety. But now all was changed; something unseen and unspeakable had erupted luridly in their midst.

The deceased couple left behind 2 unmarried daughters. The elder, Emma Borden, was 42 years old. She was away visiting friends at the time of the murder. The younger daughter, age 33, was Lizzie Borden. It was she who discovered the body of her father. The family maid of 3 years, an Irish immigrant girl by the name of Bridget Sullivan, was the only other person present at the house on the fateful morning.

Despite the family's considerable wealth, they lived in a déclassé section of town, in a house without gaslight or even a bathtub. They had no library and few family friends. Lizzie Borden later testified that she had exchanged no more than a few words with her father or stepmother in the last 2 years. The 4 members of the Borden family shut themselves up in their separate rooms, coming together only at mealtimes. On the morning of the 4th, the family sat down to a breakfast of 5-day-old mutton, mutton broth, rotten bananas, johnnycake, bread, cookies, and coffee. The temperature was a stifling 80° outside, yet all the windows and doors in the house were locked shut. Mr. Borden wore his usual high-necked tight collar and undertaker's black wool suit. That was the uniform he was to be buried in.

The Hunt: After the murders had been discovered and the last of the sensation-hungry crowd had faded away, one member of the Fall River police department was left on duty at the house to protect the women. Although sketches and photographs were made in the death rooms, nobody searched the basement or cellar or the daughters' bedrooms. At the time of the crime, the Bertillon fingerprinting method was considered un-American and consequently wasn't used. Chemical tests for bloodstains were still unknown. A list of Lizzie's dresses was made and then lost. A list of all the blood spatters was lost and had to be rewritten from memory. In a corner of the cellar laundry 2 days later, a policeman found a small, handleless hatchet. The break seemed to be fresh and the blade recently cleaned with ashes. He put it back. Four days after its discovery, the hatchet was retrieved by order of the chief of police. It fitted the fatal wounds exactly.

At the inquest, suspicion suddenly focused on Miss Lizzie. By her own admission, she had attempted to purchase hydrocyanic acid at a local pharmacy, to "clean a sealskin coat." The substance, several professionals testified, is fatal in small doses, absorbed readily into the nervous system, and leaves no post-mortem symptoms. It is not used as a cleaning agent. The evidence, however, was ruled out at the trial because hydrocyanic acid was not the cause of death. But the day before the murders, she had purchased a small ax. The basement of the Borden house contained a small arsenal of axes and hatchets, but this in itself was not unusual. However, it was decided to detain Miss Lizzie in the city jail and try her for murder.

The day before her imprisonment, Lizzie was observed by a friend burning a dress similar to the one she had on the day of the murders. It had paint on it, she said.

The Trial: All during the trial, Lizzie Borden sat properly attired in a blue suit, a black hat with cherry-colored ribbons, and short white gloves, as befit a gentlewoman and an heiress to a large fortune. Before the horrible events, she had been active in several church societies and taught Sunday School. Her minister sent her a fresh bouquet of flowers every day. The mayor of Fall River and all the other town notables attended the trial faithfully. Sympathy ran high for the ordeal of the middle-aged orphan.

At 1st, Lizzie testified that she was in the backyard eating pears while the crime was committed. Later a lapse of memory had her in the attic gathering lead sinkers for her fishing line. No stranger had been seen by neighbors entering or leaving the house. There were no signs of struggle or forcible entry. And yet, the defense argued, if Lizzie Borden had actually axed her parents, she would have had only 9 minutes between the completion of the crime and her discovery of it to bathe and change her bloodied clothes. She was, by all witnesses' accounts, immaculately spotless when she called for help.

One of her defense lawyers, an ex-governor of the State, summed up the argument for the defense: "Gentlemen, to find Lizzie Borden guilty you must believe that she is a fiend. Does she look it? The prisoner at the bar is a woman, and a Christian woman, the equal of your wife and mine."

The jury was out for an hour and a half. The verdict was unanimously for acquittal. Lizzie Borden, who had become somewhat of a symbol of women's rights, was tearfully embraced by throngs of well-wishers.

The End: Years later, methods used in a similar case proved that a murderer wielding an ax over his or her victim does not necessarily stand directly in the path of blood trajectory. Bloody clothes are no problem.

The new heiress enjoyed a measure of social freedom as never before. She and her sister sold their parents' home and purchased a luxurious residence in the best section of town.

After 12 years, sister Emma moved out, telling friends that her life there had become "absolutely intolerable." Lizzie stayed on by herself until her death in 1927 at the age of 66. She was worth well over a million dollars; $30,000 of it was left to the local Animal Rescue League. Her more enduring legacy was a children's jump-rope rhyme:

Lizzie Borden took an ax,
Gave her mother forty whacks;
When she saw what she had done,
Gave her father forty-one.

—S.W.

THE HAWLEY HARVEY CRIPPEN CASE (1910)

The Murder: Cora Turner Crippen, born Kunigune Mackamotzi, stage name Belle Elmore, was a flamboyant, florid woman with dark eyes, who dressed like a peacock and bedecked herself with jewelry. The last time she was seen alive was the evening of January 31, 1910, when she and her husband, mild-mannered Hawley Crippen, entertained friends, the Martinellis. The 4 of them played whist until 1:30 A.M. Mrs. Crippen stood at the top of the steps to see their guests off shortly after the end of the game.

"Don't come down, Belle," said Mrs. Martinelli. "You'll catch a cold." She caught more than a cold.

The next time any part of her was seen in public was when a piece of her stomach skin, bearing a long scar, was passed around on a soup plate at the murderer's trial at Old Bailey in London.

The Hunt: Mrs. Crippen, who fancied herself an entertainer, was not very talented, in spite of the fantastic wardrobe her husband had bought her. Nevertheless, she was active in the Music Hall Ladies' Guild, of which Mrs. Martinelli was also a member, and she had many friends. Those friends were somewhat surprised when Dr. Crippen told them, a week after the dinner party, that she had gone to California. It wasn't like her not to have talked about such a vacation. Belle was a talker.

Her friends were even more concerned when Dr. Crippen showed up only a few weeks later at a dinner dance given for the Music Hall Benevolent Fund with a female partner, a Miss Ethel Le Neve. He didn't seem the type to be fooling around while his wife was away on a vacation. Moreover, his companion was wearing a brooch which belonged to his wife.

On March 12, Miss Le Neve moved into the Crippen house. On March 24, Dr. Crippen sent Mrs. Martinelli a telegram saying that Belle had died in Los Angeles at 6 the night before. Belle's friends weren't willing to leave it at that. They wanted to know the details,

where to send flowers. Crippen then said that Belle had been cremated, and her ashes were on their way to England.

At the end of June, one of Belle's friends, who had become more and more suspicious, went to Scotland Yard and started an inquiry. Chief Inspector Walter Dew and Sgt. Arthur Mitchell went to call on Dr. Crippen at his office on July 8. Crippen immediately said that his story was not true, that his wife had left him for "a man better able to support her," possibly a comedian named Bruce Miller. Crippen had been ashamed to admit it, he confessed. He willingly took the officers to his house and showed them around. They saw nothing to arouse their suspicions and went away.

It all might have ended there, if Crippen had not lost his nerve. The day after the officials came, he went to Rotterdam with Miss Le Neve, and from there to Antwerp, where he booked passage for Quebec on the S.S. *Montrose.*

On July 11, Dew found that Crippen was missing. Suspicious, he searched the house again and found nothing. The following day, he went back once more. Again, nothing. However, on the 3rd day, Dew noticed that the bricks on the floor of the coal cellar were loose. and he began to dig in the clay under them. A few inches down, he found what later turned out to be a human body with no head, limbs, bones, or sexual features. (It was said later that Crippen threw the missing pieces overboard on the boat to Dieppe.) Shortly after, a warrant was issued for the arrest of Crippen and Miss Le Neve.

Meanwhile, aboard the S.S. *Montrose,* Le Neve had disguised herself as a boy, but not too well. The captain thought there was something strange about Mr. Robinson and his "son." They were far too affectionate with each other, and the "son's" pants seemed to be held up with safety pins. The captain sent a message to London (the 1st time wireless telegraphy was used to prevent the escape of a criminal). Dew sailed in a faster ship to Quebec, and, disguised as a pilot, boarded the S.S. *Montrose,* where he arrested Crippen for the murder of his wife.

The Accused: Crippen, an eye and ear specialist, was born in Michigan. He had bulging eyes, a straggling moustache, and thick, gold-rimmed glasses. Always, he seemed the pillar of respectability. Somewhat timid, he was dominated by his wife (who was his 2nd). She made him do domestic work, which in those days was humiliating for men. Moreover, she was unfaithful to him. Before she disappeared, she threatened to leave him and take their joint savings of £600 with her. (She did, in fact, notify the bank in December, 1909, that she was planning to do so.)

It was no wonder that Crippen had a mistress, Miss Le Neve, who worked in his office. Le Neve was the opposite of his wife—mouselike, neat, reserved, ladylike.

On January 17, 1910, Dr. Crippen ordered 5 grains of hyoscine from Messrs. Lewis and Burrows and signed for it with his own name. It was in keeping with his gentle character that he chose to use that particular drug to kill his wife. Hyoscine was used to treat meningitis and delirium tremens; as a poison, it induced a tranquilized sleep, which ended in death.

It was about 2 weeks later that Crippen did the deed.

The Trial: The trial opened at Old Bailey before Chief Justice Lord Alverstone on October 18, 1910. The prosecutor, Richard Muir, asked very damaging questions. Three days later the trial ended in a verdict of guilty. Lord Alverstone begged Crippen to "make his peace with Almighty God." Replied Crippen, "I still protest my innocence."

He remained faithful to Le Neve, and wrote a letter defending her: "In this farewell letter to the world, written as I face eternity, I say that Ethel Le Neve has loved me as few women love men, and that her innocence of any crime, save that of yielding to the dictates of her heart, is absolute. My last prayer will be that God will protect her and keep her safe from harm and allow her to join me in eternity."

Ethel stood trial; she was found innocent.

The End: Crippen died by the hangman's noose in 1910.

—A.E.

HENRI DÉSIRÉ LANDRU, THE BLUEBEARD
(active 1914 to 1919)

The Murders: "Single gentleman, aged 45, £400 per year, desires to marry homely lady of similar age and income." Ads like this, which appeared regularly in the Paris newspapers in the early 1900s, were the beginning of a series of love affairs—and the beginning of the end—for at least 9 French women.

One was a Mme. Célestine Buisson, who disappeared after going down to a Villa Ermitage in Gambais with a Monsieur Fremyet, in 1917. After some time, Mme. Buisson's sister grew concerned about her missing sister and asked the mayor of Gambais to help trace her. It might all have ended there if the mayor had not received a remarkably similar request from the sister of a Mme. Anna Collomb, who had disappeared the same way. Checking up on the owner of the villa, the mayor found that he fit the description given by both sisters, was known as M. Dupont, was bearded, and had

disappeared leaving no address. Neighbors complained about the strange black smoke that used to rise occasionally from the villa's chimney, but other than that they didn't know anything about him.

The mayor, finding the whole thing too much for him, got in touch with the authorities. They already had a file of missing women —Mme. Thérèse Laborde-Line, widow, 47; Mme. Désirée Guillin, widow, 59; Andrée Babelay, servant girl, 19; Mme. Louise Jaume, a married woman separated from her husband, 38; Mme. Anne-Marie Pascal, divorcée, 33; Mme. Marie-Thérèse Marchadier, brothel-keeper and ex-prostitute; Mme. Jeanne Cuchet, widow, about 40. But they couldn't find the elusive bearded man.

The Hunt: On April 11, 1919, Mme. Buisson's sister just happened to be walking down the Rue de Rivoli when she saw a man strolling along with a young woman. It was the bearded man who had taken her sister to the Villa Ermitage. Excited and nervous, she began to follow him. He went into a shop and ordered a white china dinner service, an act that would cost him his life. For he left his name with the shopkeeper.

The following morning, the bearded man, now Lucien Guillet, was drinking coffee with his young mistress, Fernande Segret, when a knock came at the door. When he answered it, a group of police burst in and arrested him for murder. As evidence the police took his notebook—a small black one with loose pages—in which he had carefully recorded the statistics of all his crimes. Guillet, whose real name was Henri Désiré Landru, was a meticulous book-keeper and kept an exact record of all his expenses. It was incriminating enough that the names of the missing women were penciled on the inside front cover; it was even more incriminating that train tickets to his villas (the latest one in Gambais) were recorded often as "One single, one return." The notebook told of his transactions with 283 women.

Very curious now, the police investigated his stove at Gambais. When they sifted the ashes from it, and examined the outhouse and the garden, they found hundreds of human bone fragments, some teeth, and some hooks-and-eyes.

The Accused: Henri Landru had been a sunny child who grew up to be a mercurial, intelligent adult. A sensualist, he loved roses, so much so that when the police were spading up his yard to try to find bodies, his main concern was for the flowers.

Landru was not particularly handsome. Short and frail, he had a thick red beard, a pleasing voice, excellent manners, and magnetic black eyes with long silky lashes.

At 22, he had impregnated his cousin and

later married her, becoming a loving family man, a role he played until he died.

He began his life of crime as a swindler, dealing in cars, toys, bad debts, 2nd-hand furniture. In 1900, at the age of 31, he was given a jail sentence of 3 years for cheating an aged widow over a marriage settlement. From then until his arrest for the murder of at least 9 women, he was sentenced 5 times for swindling.

When he began his career cheating women, he had no intention, it seems, of murdering them. Ladies who answered his ads were treated to a cheap dinner or 2, a little sex, lots of romance, which lasted until he got to their money—and ran. It was a time-consuming, complicated way to make a living. Often, Landru operated under several names with several appointments a day. No wonder he needed a notebook to keep it all straight. Ironically, it didn't pay much—about $250 a victim—as was later estimated.

Mme. Cuchet had been the 1st to go. Dark, curly-haired, she was a serious person with a steady job in a Paris shop. To her, Landru was M. Diard. Soon they were "in love," and he set up house with her in the summer of 1914. A few months later, she gave him 5,000 francs, probably most of her life's savings, and then he skipped. She ran into him again by chance—and it was to be the death of her. In spite of what he had done, in spite of the fact he was married, she wanted him. So he took her, and her 18-year-old son, wanting neither, to his new villa at Vernouillet. At last, sick of them, not knowing what else to do, he murdered them. After that, murder became part of his *modus operandi*.

Fernande Segret was not, and most likely never would have been, one of his victims. Fair and young, she worked in a furrier's shop. When she went to visit his villa, he bought 2 return tickets. At his trial, she said, "I have not a single reproach against him. I loved him very deeply. I was very, very happy with him."

The Trial: Fashionable women with lunch baskets and dogs flocked to the trial, fighting for seats in the courtroom. Said Landru, "If any lady would like my place, I will willingly surrender it."

That's about all he said. Throughout the trial, he refused to testify and kept saying that he was innocent. But the evidence was overwhelming—the notebook, the stove ashes, and his bank account. (When Mme. Jaume went to the villa with Landru, she took 274.60 francs. Shortly after, Landru's money supply swelled by exactly that amount. There were many such "coincidences.")

The only times he lost control were when his family was implicated. During the inquiries, his wife and son were arrested and put in jail.

His wife had impersonated 2 of the women in order to get their savings. Landru, protesting her innocence, said that the missing women were "away," that he had asked his wife to sign as a formality. His wife said, "If I have done wrong, it was unwittingly. I am a martyr and not a criminal. My misfortune has been to love my husband too well."

It took the jury an hour and a half to find Landru guilty.

The End: On February 23, 1922, Landru was executed, by guillotine. Just before the blade fell, he said, "Ah, well, it is not the 1st time that an innocent man has been condemned."

—A.E.

THE SNYDER-GRAY CASE (1927)

The Murder: The murder of Albert Snyder on March 20, 1927, in Long Island, N.Y., was a classic case of ineptitude on the part of his bungling murderers. The victim's wife, Ruth Snyder, told police an implausible story from start to finish. She and Albert had returned from a party at 2:30 A.M. that morning, said Ruth. After her husband and daughter retired, a burglar, wearing an Italian-styled moustache, entered the room and hit her on the head. Five hours later she regained consciousness and—gagged and bound—crawled to her daughter's room. Frightened, 9-year-old Lorraine alerted the neighbors, and the police arrived shortly thereafter.

They found Albert Snyder dead in the front bedroom—tied hand and foot—with a picture wire wound tightly around his neck. The right side of his head was bashed in and he had been chloroformed. A revolver was also found on the bed, and 3 live cartridges were on the floor. Although death could have resulted from any of the 3 methods, the assistant county medical examiner, Dr. Howard Neail, said Albert had actually died of asphyxia, strangled by the wire.

The Hunt: The authorities were suspicious of Ruth from the beginning. She was very loosely bound (curiously, she had asked the neighbors to leave her tied up until the police arrived); and Dr. Neail was unable to find any evidence of a blow or injury serious enough to keep her unconscious for 5 hours. Although the house had been ransacked, there was no evidence of forcible entry.

The only thing missing was money from Albert's wallet. Originally, Ruth said that the burglar or burglars—she told conflicting stories—had taken her jewels. However, after the gems were found tucked under her mattress, Ruth suddenly remembered that she had hidden them there for safety.

A search of the house yielded a bloodstained

5-lb. sash weight in a toolbox, and a bloody pillow slip in the laundry hamper. Later, insurance policies on Albert Snyder's life—totaling $90,000 in double indemnity clauses—were found in a safe-deposit box. The box was registered under Mrs. Snyder's maiden name, Ruth Brown.

Most interesting of all to Inspector Arthur Carey was a tiepin, initialed J.G., which was found on the bedroom floor. A canceled check—made out for $200 to H. Judd Gray—was discovered in Ruth's desk. Gray's name was also listed, along with 28 other men, in her address book. On the basis of this circumstantial evidence, Ruth Snyder and Judd Gray were arrested and charged with the murder of Albert Snyder. After undergoing separate interrogation—1st Ruth then Judd—they both confessed. Each blamed the other for the killing.

The Accused: On the surface, Ruth Brown Snyder was a typical suburban housewife of the jazz era. She wore her blond hair in a fashionable bob, danced and played bridge while her 44-year-old husband stayed home. In general, she acted the role of a giddy, slightly overage (32) flapper. The "real" Ruth Snyder was made of stronger—albeit not always admirable—fiber. Born in poverty, she was only 13 when she took a job as a night telephone operator so she could study shorthand and bookkeeping during the day. Ruth was ambitious, frustrated, and a voracious reader of trashy love stories, wherein Cinderella finally married the boss.

In 1915, Ruth did just that; she married her employer, Albert Snyder, an editor of *Motor Boating* magazine. However, they didn't live "happily ever after." Some of Ruth's antagonism toward the man she called "the old crab" was probably justified. For example, Albert hung a picture of his ex-fiancée, Jessie Guishard, on the wall of their 1st home, and also named his boat after her. Jessie, whom Albert described to Ruth as "the finest woman I have ever met," had been dead for 10 years.

Bored and disillusioned with her dull marriage, Ruth lived a fantasy life until June, 1925, when she met 33-year-old Judd Gray on a blind date. The timid, weak-willed Gray was a salesman for the Bien Jolie Corset Company. Their shoddy affair continued for 18 months. They usually met at the Waldorf-Astoria. Ruth would sometimes leave little Lorraine in the lobby while she and Judd enjoyed a "matinee" in his hotel room. Finally, in 1926, Albert suddenly became suspiciously accident-prone. It was never verified in court, but Judd claimed Ruth had made 7 previous attempts to drown, poison, or gas her husband.

Although both later claimed the other was the dominant partner, Judd's nickname of "Momma" or "Mommie" for Ruth would

seem to indicate that she was the real leader in their relationship. Ruth wasn't a beauty, but she exuded animal magnetism. During her trial, she received 164 marriage proposals.

The Trial: By the time of the trial (April 25, 1927) the press was calling it "The Ruth Versus Judd Case." Both prisoners had confessed and the jury had only to determine if they were guilty of "premeditated" murder. However, Ruth was now denying all. She said it was all Judd's idea. She hadn't even entered the bedroom during the killing. All she knew was that when Judd came out, he said, "I guess that's it." Judd, on the other hand, insisted that Ruth had "hypnotized" him and forced him to commit the murder by "drink, veiled threats, and intensive love." What's more, he now maintained that Ruth, not he, had tied the wire around Albert's neck, thereby causing his death.

The contemptible testimony was front-page news, both in the U.S. and Europe, for weeks. Ruth was called "the bloody blonde" and the "marble woman." Both murderers were obviously 2nd-rate monsters; and, on the basis of some of the testimony, Judd may even have been a little weak-minded. Or perhaps, subconsciously, he wanted to be caught. After he tied Ruth up and left the murder scene, he called attention to himself repeatedly. First he asked 2 men, one of them a policeman, when the next bus was due. Then he rode the bus to Jamaica and took a taxi to New York. The fare was $3.50 and Judd made a lasting negative impression on the cabby by adding a 5¢ tip.

The jury deliberated only an hour and a half. On May 9, 1927, Ruth Snyder and Judd Gray were convicted of murder.

The End: On January 22, 1928, Snyder and Gray were electrocuted at Sing Sing Prison. Just as the switch was pulled on Ruth, photographer Thomas Howard, sitting in the front row, crossed his knee and took a picture with a camera strapped to his ankle. The next morning, the *New York Daily News* devoted its entire front page to the horrifying execution shot. It is still considered one of the most famous tabloid photos in the history of yellow journalism. Thus, even in death, Ruth Snyder upstaged her paramour.

—J.B.C. & J.Cs.

THE ENIGMATIC WALLACE MURDER (1931)

The Murder: On January 19, 1931, a man named Qualtrough tried to put through a call to William Herbert Wallace at his chess club. He had trouble getting the number, and called the operator, a Miss Kelly. She later testified, "It was quite an ordinary voice. It was a man's voice. He said, 'Operator, I have pressed Button A but have not had my correspondent yet.'

I did not have any further conversation with the person in the box. I afterwards connected Anfield 1627 with Bank 3581." Wallace was not at the chess club, and Samuel Beattie, the club manager, took the call. Qualtrough left a message that Wallace should come to his house at 25 Menlove Gardens East the next night at 7:30 P.M.

Who was Qualtrough? When Wallace showed up later at the club, he said that he had never heard of him. But since Wallace was an insurance man, it might have been a business call.

The next night, Wallace went to look for Qualtrough and found that the address, 25 Menlove Gardens East, did not exist. He asked several people for advice, including a constable, but got nowhere. Alarmed, thinking a trick had been played on him, he headed for home.

He tried the key in the front door lock. It wouldn't open, which meant that the door had been bolted from the inside. Surprised, he went and tried the back door to find it locked too. He knocked twice, a signal for his wife, but no one came to the door.

His next-door neighbors, Mr. and Mrs. John Johnston, came out of their house about then, and he asked their advice. Mr. Johnston suggested that Wallace try the Johnston key in the back door. This time, Wallace was able to open the door—without the Johnston key. He went into the house, and the Johnstons saw a light go on upstairs. A minute or so later, he came out and said to them, "Come and see; she has been killed."

Lying on the floor of the little-used sitting room, face down, was Mrs. Wallace. There was a gaping 3" wound in front of her left ear. Underneath her body was a mackintosh—Wallace's mackintosh. Wallace searched the house to see if anything was missing but nothing was. Twice he put his hands to his head and sobbed. "They have finished her," he said. "Look at the brains."

It wasn't long before Constable Williams of the Liverpool City Police arrived. He questioned Wallace and searched the house, finding the main bedroom in some disorder. He found no sign of forcible entry or struggle, no murder weapon. (A charwoman, however, was to say later that an iron bar which was usually kept by the stove was missing.) Wallace, Constable Williams said, was acting in an "extraordinarily cool and calm manner."

Just before 10 P.M., Prof. J. E. W. McFall, a specialist in forensic medicine, arrived. He examined the body and said that death had taken place at 6 o'clock that evening and that she had been hit 11 times, even though the 1st blow probably killed her. He found blood and charring on the mackintosh.

The Hunt: When questioned, Wallace said that he had gotten home "possibly 5 minutes past 6" on the night of the murder. Mrs. Wallace had given him tea. He left the house about 6:45 P.M. to meet with the elusive Qualtrough. (But according to McFall, Mrs. Wallace had died at 6 P.M.)

The police looked for Qualtrough, too. They couldn't find him. Later, during the trial, a song went around the bars:

They seek him here, they seek him there
(Is he alive, do you know?)
Or in hell . . . or the Pruden-shell
That damned elusive Qualtrough.

Alan Close, a 14-year-old boy who delivered milk to the Wallaces, said he had seen Mrs. Wallace take in the milk at 6:30 that night. The paper was delivered at 6:35 P.M. The police found it spread out on the kitchen table as if someone had been reading it. A locksmith found both locks in somewhat bad condition.

On February 2, 1931, Wallace was arrested for the murder of his wife.

The Accused: William Herbert Wallace, who was apprenticed in the draper's trade at an early age, had a streak of intellectualism and adventure that belied his quiet, respectable, dull appearance. He enjoyed reading Marcus Aurelius and was interested in the Greek Stoics. He decided that in order to be a good prospective stoic, he needed to go abroad. He took jobs in India and Shanghai, where he led a singularly routine life, before returning to Manchester. There he was given a political job, which he liked very much. He met all kinds of people, including Julia Thorp, a dark-haired, pleasant woman who also had an intellectual streak. She read and spoke French, and dabbled in art and music. In 1913, 2 years later, she and Wallace were married. The marriage, according to Wallace's diaries was blissful, quiet, and without quarrels.

In August, 1914, Wallace found himself out of work so he took a job with the Prudential Assurance Company. Though he wasn't particularly gregarious, he was conscientious and his customers liked him.

He was a mild-faced man who wore glasses and had an untidy moustache. He didn't drink and smoked very little. His only recreation was chess, at which he was an average player.

The Trial: The judge at Wallace's trial was Mr. Justice Wright. E. G. Hemmerde led the prosecution. During the trial, Police Constable James Rothwell said he had seen Wallace the afternoon of the murder in Maiden Lane, and that Wallace seemed to be crying. "His face was haggard and drawn, and he was very distressed. . . . He was dabbing his eyes with his coatsleeve, and he appeared to me as if he had been crying." However, a customer of

Wallace's saw him shortly afterward and testified that he was in a fine humor. Others backed her up.

Qualtrough still hadn't been found. Was he Wallace?

Hemmerde couldn't crack Wallace, whose statements and protestations of innocence were calm and reasoned. Mr. Justice Wright said of Wallace's statements, "I have read them through very carefully, and I think it is wonderful that they are as lucid, accurate, and consistent as they are." In his address to the jury, he made it clear that the evidence against Wallace was circumstantial. But in spite of that, the verdict was guilty. The crowd in the courtroom was amazed and the public outraged. A Special Service of Intercession was held in Liverpool Cathedral. A Court of Criminal Appeal overturned the guilty verdict.

If Wallace didn't kill his wife, who did? Qualtrough, whoever he was? No one knows to this day.

The End: His innocence or guilt still undetermined, Wallace died 2 years later from cancer of the kidneys.

—A.E.

THE DE KOVEN CASE (1937)

The Murder: All young women, in murder stories, are inevitably classified as beautiful. Jean De Koven *was* beautiful. She was a professional dancer. Chaperoned by her aunt, Miss Ida Sackheim, of Brooklyn, she came to Paris on a vacation. She visited the Louvre, the Folies, the Café de la Paix. At 5:20 in the afternoon, on July 23, 1937, she returned to Le Studio Hotel on the Left Bank, after a day of sight-seeing. She changed into a blue dress and patent leather shoes. Leaving, she told the elevator man to tell her aunt she'd be back by 8 o'clock that night. "I have no time to leave her a note," she called back. "Somebody is waiting for me." As it turned out—Death was waiting for her.

When she did not return, her aunt went to the police. They laughed. They said the girl was probably having a love affair. When the 1st ransom note came, demanding $500 and warning Miss Sackheim not to go to the police ("or we will stop all negotiations and she will be taken for a ride, you know how the gangsters of *Chikago* operate"), Miss Sackheim rushed to the police again. They called it a publicity stunt this time. But 15 days later—after $240 worth of Jean De Koven's American Express traveler's checks had been cashed, with her signature miserably forged on all of them—the police knew it was not a publicity stunt.

The Hunt: M. Primborgne, a young Sûreté wizard, was assigned to the case. By this time, Jean De Koven's brother Henry had arrived from New York, and he offered a 10,000-franc reward. Governor Lehman of New York had asked the FBI to enter into the affair. But the FBI was not necessary. Primborgne, of the Sûreté, pulled off one of the most brilliant hunts in recent decades.

Shortly after Jean De Koven's disappearance, a series of bodies began turning up, all showing evidence of brutal murder—a chauffeur named Josef Cauffy, a Strasbourg cook named Jeanine Keller, a press agent named Roger Leblond, a realtor named Raymond Lesobre, a student named Fritz Frommer. Evidence convinced Primborgne that one person had murdered all of these—and Jean De Koven. Primborgne spun his web. Clues were few, but he made each one tell. There were leaves on the shoes of one corpse. The leaves were traced to Saint Cloud forest, just outside Paris. A bloodstained visiting card was found near one of the bodies. This was traced to a traveling salesman who had a nephew who had spoken of lunching with an ex-convict from Saarbrucken.

In the end, the finger pointed at Eugen Weidman, who had served 16 years for theft; who was charming and handsome; who spoke German, French, English, Portuguese. The Sûreté went to his bungalow, located outside Paris, to arrest him. He submitted, tricked them, pulled a Mauser, fired 3 times. The Sûreté men wrestled him down, slugged him unconscious with a hammer. Later, it came out, he had fired as a signal so that someone else in the house could escape.

The Accused: Weidman had killed Jean De Koven, and 5 others. Strictly for money. He was surrounded by a fantastic gang of 4 including a squeamish little man named Roger Million. Weidman regretted only Jean De Koven. "I intended just to kidnap her," he said. "I assure you, I had not thought of killing her. She told me about her life, adding that she might take some engagements to dance in important cabarets about Paris. She confessed that since she'd met me she found life more beautiful. We went for a walk in the garden, and Jean took 2 photographs of me with his camera. It was getting dark, so we went into the villa and continued to talk until 3 in the morning. Jean was drinking milk, and smoking. As she was tired, she lay down on the sofa. I was sitting near her. I needed money; I realized I would never be able to kidnap her without killing her. Suddenly I placed my hands around her neck. She stood up. She understood I was trying to strangle her. I closed my eyes, as I could not bear the sight of her lovely face. Darling Jean, how sweet she was. . . . She was gentle and unsuspecting. I enjoyed speaking English to her, which I learned in Canada. When I reached for her throat, she went down like a doll."

The Trial: Weidman's trial was a sensation and a fantasy. He turned the courthouse into a vast psychiatrist's couch. He would not look at Jean after they dug her up from under his porch (she had been well preserved in the clay), but he talked readily about himself and his crimes. French women followed the trial avidly and fell in love with him. The great French author Colette watched him and wrote for her paper, "Weidman was a romantic. He loved flowers and was cultivating roses. He also loved nature. It was not merely the necessity of the professional killer that made him choose the forests for his murders . . ."

The End: He was the last man, in France, to be guillotined in public. His execution turned into a sadistic festival, bleacherites dancing and drinking for hours before the dawn, near the great knife. He emerged from Landru's old cell bravely, and flinched only once: As he bent his head beneath the knife, he closed his eyes.

—I.W.

The Brooke-Heath Killings (1946)

The Murders: In 1946, Mrs. Margery Aimee Gardner—32 years old—had separated from her husband, set out on her own, and achieved a certain notoriety as "Ocelot Margie," after the imitation fur coat she was so fond of wearing. On the night before she died, she was dancing at the Panama Club in London with a handsome young man named Lieut. Col. Neville Heath.

Her naked corpse was discovered on June 21, 1946, in a Notting Hill (London) hotel room registered under the name of that same Lieut. Col. Heath. Many lash marks scored her body and face, and she was horribly mutilated. Mrs. Gardner's ankles were tied to the bedposts and the marks on her wrists suggested that they, too, had been bound. Suffocation was the cause of death. The murder weapon was a pillow or, more likely, her gag.

Subsequently, another victim, Doreen Marshall, was discovered in Bournemouth, at the seaside, by a woman out for a stroll with her dog. The body was covered with flies and lay in rhododendron bushes. A sharp instrument, probably a knife, was the murder weapon. She had succumbed before being severely mutilated like Mrs. Gardner. Around her body lay 27 artificial pearls from her broken necklace.

Doreen Marshall had last been seen alive in the company of Group-Capt. Rupert Brooke (a namesake of the poet), whom she had met shortly before. She had had dinner with him at his hotel, then had demanded to be taken home. "I'll be back in a half hour," the young man said to the porter. "No, in a quarter hour," Doreen had snapped.

When he returned became a question. Instead of coming in the door, he used a ladder to get back to his hotel room. (He claimed later that he did this to play a joke on the porter.)

The Hunt: Three days after the discovery of Margery Gardner's body, Police Superintendent Thomas Barratt, who was in charge of the case, received a letter. The writer of the letter was Neville Heath, who explained that while he had indeed rented the room in which Margery Gardner had met her death, he had lent Margery the key that particular night. "She had met an acquaintance with whom she felt obliged to sleep," he explained. She had asked Heath to return later and spend the rest of the night with her. When he came back to the room, the letter said, he found her dead and realized that he "was in an invidious position." Therefore, he wrote that he was going to go into hiding under an assumed name. "I have the instrument with which Mrs. Gardner was beaten and am forwarding this to you today," he wrote. "You will find my fingerprints on it, but you should find others as well." Good to his word, Heath disappeared. The murder weapon never showed up.

Three days after Doreen Marshall was reported missing, Group-Captain Brooke called the police in Bournemouth, offering information about the missing girl. Suspicious, the police determined that they had found the missing Heath—he and Brooke were one and the same. Caught, Heath asked that they get him his sports jacket, which was back at the hotel. In it was incriminating evidence—a cloak room ticket, which, the police discovered, was for a suitcase. In the suitcase were articles marked with Heath's name and a plaited leather riding whip. Also in the coat pocket was the return half of a railway ticket belonging to Doreen Marshall. In his room, they found an artificial pearl. Two days later, the girl's body was found.

The Accused: Neville George Clevely Heath was 29 years old when he was arrested. Charming and suave, he had dimples, a cupid's bow mouth, and curly hair. He had been court-martialed in 1937 for being absent without leave from the RAF. He was sent to Borstal prison in 1938 for theft, housebreaking, and fraud. He joined the Army in 1940 and was cashiered the following year for having a fake 2nd paybook, passing bad checks, and being AWOL. Shortly after, he joined the South African Army and took a wife, but divorced her in 1945. He was repeatedly brought before the courts for wearing military decorations he was not entitled to wear.

The Trial: Heath wanted to plead guilty to the murder of Margery Gardner, but his lawyer convinced him not to. His defense was insanity, and debates about insanity dominated the 3-day trial. Heath's main concern was what he would wear—he decided on a gray suit, gray shirt, and dotted blue tie.

It took the jury 59 minutes to decide on a verdict of guilty.

The End: Without appeal, Heath was executed on October 26, 1946. On his way to the scaffold, it is said, he asked the prison governor for a whiskey. "Ahhh . . ." he added crisply, "you might make that a double. . . ."

—A.E. and M.T.

Nebraska, Wyoming, and Charley Starkweather (1958)

The Murders: An absolute stillness clung to the one-story frame house where Marion Bartlett lived with his wife, Velda, and their 2 daughters. It was much too quiet behind the neatly printed note on the front door which warned: "STAY AWAY. EVERYBODY IS SICK WITH THE FLU. MISS BARTLETT," far too quiet not to rouse some neighborly curiosity and concern here in the run-down part of town, the Belmont section of Lincoln. And concern it was, late in January, 1958, that led some relatives of the family to look in and see if they couldn't be of some help.

There could be no help for the parents, each shot through the head and hidden in an outbuilding. Neither would the younger of the daughters need aid. She was dead as a result of a savage clubbing. Fourteen-year-old Caril, the offspring of her mother's 1st marriage, was nowhere to be found.

By the time that the Lincoln police had finished piecing together what had happened at the Bartlett home; by the time that the populace of Lincoln, Nebr., was beginning to feel the clammy tap of Fear's finger on its shoulder; by the time the APB had gone out for the pickup of Charles Starkweather and his girl friend Caril Fugate; by then, that duo was beginning to play a long game of chicken with the law and the Fifties' culture, whistling down Highway 77 in Charley's rebuilt '49 Ford, their only company a radio, a .38, a .22 rifle, and a .410-gauge shotgun. They were headed toward Bennet and a place to hide, on the 1st leg of the 525-mi. demolition derby in which 10 were to die.

It was an early evening in winter when the Ford got stuck traversing the muddy road to the farmhouse of Starkweather's old friend August Meyer. Impossibly stuck. When a high school couple out on a date stopped to lend a hand, Charley shot them both and took their car, also a Ford, but not as old as Charley's, and good enough to carry the couple the rest of the way to the farmhouse that Charley's

friend owned. There, ostensibly for his guns and ammunition, Charley murdered Meyer and then he decided to return to Lincoln.

C. Lauer Ward was the 48-year-old president of the Capital Steel Works, one of Lincoln's richest and most influential citizens. Nestling snugly near the heart of Lincoln's most exclusive and expensive residential area—the southeast side—was Ward's handsome, French Provincial house. He lived there with a housekeeper named Lillian and his wife, Clara, both of whom were marched to the 2nd floor, bound, gagged, and then stabbed to death, while C. Lauer was downtown in conference with Victor Anderson, the governor of Nebraska. And Charley was still there to greet Ward when he arrived home that evening, instead of the housekeeper. C. Lauer Ward didn't even have the chance to take his coat off.

Ward's black '56 Packard rode smooth. While Lincoln and the rest of the State drew closer to mass hysteria, Charley made good time drawing closer to Douglas, Wyo., some 500 mi. away. Was he getting tired of the Packard? Or did he merely realize how hot the car was? Twelve mi. out of Douglas, Charles Starkweather pulled over to the side of the road behind Merle Collison's new Buick, got out, walked over to the driver's side of the car while Caril crept into the back seat, and shot the sleeping shoe salesman 9 times in the head. The final victim.

The Hunt: It was a search for a "mad-dog killer." From the time the murders at the Bartlett house were discovered until Charles Starkweather's capture on January 30—3 days in all—Nebraska police and National Guardsmen manned hundreds of roadblocks, organized posses to cover Nebraska's back roads, and helped plan strategy with citizens' groups. The police had been given orders to shoot to kill. The governor had called on the National Guard to protect the National Bank of Commerce, on the off chance that there was some validity to the rumor that Starkweather was determined to rob it. Citizens' groups in Lincoln organized "check in" programs to help ensure safety. Parents removed their children from the schools. Doors were triple-locked. Houses blazed with lights all through the night.

Charley Starkweather was captured, finally, not by the thousands of law enforcement personnel all bent on his arrest, but by an oil company worker named Joe Sprinkle, who stumbled upon the Collison murder while intending only to help change a tire or give a lift. Instead, there was the bloody, crumpled body in the front seat. Instead, there was a kid with a rifle pointing toward him. Figuring that he "might just as well die fighting," Sprinkle rushed forward and wrestled for the gun. And as they scuffled, a deputy sheriff arrived—another accident. Caril Fugate, sobbing and screaming, "It's Starkweather! He's going to kill me . . ." made a beeline for the deputy, and Starkweather, the confusion his cover, made a bid for escape, jumping behind the wheel of the Packard and speeding off. Even at speeds of up to 110 mph, it was still a losing race. Starkweather succeeded in crashing a roadblock, continued on for some miles, only to be forced, finally, to halt when bullets shattered his windshield.

"I shot all those people in self defense," he told the deputy who had fired at his boots when Charles had declined to raise his hands, "People kept coming at me and I had to shoot. What else would you do . . . ?"

The Accused: Charles Starkweather, 3rd oldest of 7 children, was myopic, slightly bow-legged, and had a minor speech defect. He grew up poor in Lincoln, Nebr., and he died at the age of 20. He was thrown out of grade school for habitual fighting. He had acquired a reputation for being a good knife-fighter in junior high school.

He just got fired from his job as a helper on a garbage truck. He'd lean out of the cab of the truck to perfect strangers and start yelling, "Go to hell!"—Barbara Starkweather

He used to pose like James Dean. He'd stand there with a cigarette hanging out from the front of his mouth. You know, with the lips apart so the teeth would show.—LaVeta Starkweather

Even as a little kid things would build up in him 'til he'd go berserk. I don't think he would have stopped at shooting me.—Guy Starkweather

I'm sorry it had to be you, Charley, but I hope you're dead.—Michael Lydon, journalist

. . . if we'd've been left alone we wouldn't've hurt anybody.—Charles Starkweather

The Trial: Charley Starkweather was extradited back home to Nebraska for trial and that was just fine with him. ". . . Wyoming has a gas chamber and I don't like the smell of gas."

On the night of his arrest, from a cell in the tiny Douglas jail, Charley had written a letter to the world at large, but addressed it to his father: "But dad i'm not sorry for what i did cause for the 1st time me and caril had more fun, she help me a lot, but if she comes back dont hate her she had not a thing to do with the killing. all we wanted to do is get out of town." And he remained the cool and unrepentant killer through the trial, a spectator, at times, more fascinated by the strident prosecution and its no-nonsense "He's just a cold-blooded killer and nothing more!" than with his time gradually running out. As for his lawyers with their incessant prattle about a plea of insanity—Charley blocked every attempt they made to have him declared insane.

A peculiar dialogue was established during the trial between Charley and James Reinhardt, Nebraskan criminologist. Charley would describe his dreams or reminisce, Reinhardt would work toward a definitive label. His final verdict for this young man, so obviously on his way to the electric chair: "schizophrenic paranoid with an obsessive death wish."

The End: Charles Starkweather went to the electric chair on June 25, 1959. It took him 4 minutes to die.

—M.T.

Assassinations—Successful and Unsuccessful

The word "assassin" is derived from the word "hashishim," or taker of hashish. Marco Polo told of an impregnable fortress in the mountains of Persia wherein lived the Old Man of the Mountain. He was the head of a religious sect called the Ismailis (1090–1256 A.D.). When he wanted a religious or political enemy killed, the Old Man would ask for volunteers. Those persons who stepped forward were given wine drugged with hashish. While they were asleep, they were transported to a lush green valley where they were given fruit, dope, and sexual treats. After an interval they were again drugged and returned to the fortress. This was their glimpse of heaven, of eternal paradise, which was promised to them in exchange for

their total loyalty. Polo said that the Old Man would sometimes order them to jump out of high windows, simply to impress guests.

The practice of assassination has existed since time immemorial. Tens of thousands of political killings have occurred in recorded history. It is estimated that between 5,000 and 6,000 assassinations have been carried out since the end of W.W. I alone. Obviously, the majority of these were of low- or middle-level significance, but at least 70 of them were heads of state.

The Old Testament describes the slaying of King Eglon and Sisera in the 12th century B.C. Twenty of Rome's emperors were assassinated, including Julius Caesar in 44 B.C. (after a conspiracy involving over 60 persons). Cicero, the Roman orator who approved of Caesar's killing because too much power had been centralized in one man, was himself assassinated by Mark Antony's soldiers. His tongue, which had so often criticized Antony, was cut out by Antony's wife (43 B.C.).

In 12 centuries of Irish history, from 4 A.D. to 1172 A.D., 31 of 78 kings were murdered. Thomas à Becket was assassinated in Canterbury Cathedral in 1170 because he effectively challenged Henry II's move to consolidate power in the state.

Jean-Paul Marat, one of the violent leaders of the French Revolution, was stabbed to death by Charlotte Corday, who was 25 at the time (July 13, 1793). She said, "Having seen civil war on the verge of blazing out all over France, and persuaded that Marat was the principal author of this disaster, I preferred to make the sacrifice of my own life in order to save my country."

Russia, under the Czars and under the communists, had had a very heavy record of assassinations, including the murders of Paul I, Alexander II, Nicholas II, and Rasputin, as well as numerous deadly purges.

Czar Paul I of Russia (son of Catherine the Great) felt his superiority was divinely decreed. He terrorized the population, sent a large number of persons of all classes to Siberian prisons, refused subjects the right to travel abroad, and crushed any suspicion of liberal reform. On March 23, 1801, he was strangled with a scarf by a group of highly placed conspirators, with the knowledge of his son Alexander I. Paul's removal immediately improved everyone's lot. The new Czar surrounded himself with relative liberals; he organized a national education program, gave the peasants the chance to buy their own property, issued a liberal constitution for Poland, and freed the serfs of the Baltic provinces. As one writer on assassinations, Edward Hyams, put it, "The terrible sufferings and degradation of millions were somewhat relieved and a measure of hope restored." As for communist assassinations, 2 attempts were made on Lenin's life. Trotsky was killed in Mexico, presumably by one of Stalin's agents, on August 20, 1940.

King Humbert I of Italy was tyrannical to an insane degree. He treated his associates and his subjects as slaves, he enlisted in his cabinet military men who swore allegiance to him and not to Italy, and he generally turned the country into a totalitarian monarchy. He was assassinated by an avowed anarchist named Bresci on July 29, 1900. The country was saved from complete subjugation. Bresci's act was praised by Republicans and other establishment parties as a necessary and humanitarian sacrifice.

On June 28, 1914, Austrian Archduke Francis Ferdinand was killed by Gavrilo Princip, a member of a secret Serbian assassination group seeking independence for their country from the Hapsburg empire. Ferdinand was a rabid anti-Semite, and a harsh tyrant. The assassin was captured in the street as he fired his gun. (See also: Highlights of World History, Chap. 8.)

In Japan 9 Premiers have been murdered since 1860.

In the U.S. 4 Presidents have been murdered in office. Four other U.S. Presidents have been the target of unsuccessful assassination attempts: Andrew Jackson, January 30, 1835; Theodore Roosevelt, October 14, 1912; Franklin D. Roosevelt, February 15, 1933; Harry Truman, November 1, 1950.

Other significant assassinations since W.W. I. include: Rosa Luxemburg (German Socialist agitator), January 15, 1919; Emiliano Zapata (Mexican revolutionary leader), April 10, 1919; Pancho Villa (Mexican revolutionary leader), July 20, 1923; Alvaro Obregón (President of Mexico), July 17, 1928; Engelbert Dollfuss (Chancellor of Austria), July 25, 1934; Sergei Kirov (Soviet leader), December 1, 1934; Jean Darlan (French naval officer and chief of state in French Africa), December 24, 1942; Lavrenti Beria (chief of U.S.S.R. secret police), December 23, 1953; Patrice Lumumba (1st Prime Minister of the Republic of the Congo), September 15, 1960; Rafael Trujillo (dictator of Dominican Republic), May 30, 1961; Ngo Dinh Diem (president of South Vietnam), November 1, 1963; Che Guevara (Latin American revolutionary leader), October 8, 1967; Martin Luther King, Jr. (American civil rights leader), April 4, 1968.

—M.S.

FAMOUS ASSASSINATION ATTEMPTS

The Victim: ALEXANDER II, Czar of Russia.
The Date: March 1, 1881.
The Event: Sophia Perovskaya commanded the group of assassins. Armed with bombs, 4 men were deployed along the Czar's route (to and from the Winter Palace). Perovskaya stood at the site of a planned military parade. When they saw that the Czar was not going to drive over their mined street, they moved to alternate positions. The Czar's carriage was delayed, but at last it appeared. A 19-year-old student named Rysakov rushed forward and tossed a bomb. He was apprehended. The Czar alighted to determine the situation. A 2nd man charged the Czar and there was another explosion. Both the Czar and his assassin, Ignaty Grinevitsky, were mortally wounded, and died a few hours later.
The Assassins: In Russia in the late 1870s,

social unrest had reached a full boil. Alexander's grandfather Paul I, the despotic son of Catherine the Great, had been assassinated in 1801. Enforced poverty and police persecution turned the populace against the Czars' régimes, and created a revolutionary movement advocating violence against the totalitarian monarchies because no other avenues of effective dissent were available.

A mood of wrath and rebellion swept across Russia. In January of 1878, Vera Zasulich, a young typesetter for the underground paper *Land and Liberty*, shot General Trepov, the St. Petersburg chief of police, in retaliation for his severe maltreatment of a political prisoner. According to one source, Trepov was gravely wounded, but ". . . he did not die, and the trial of his would-be assassin in March was turned by her defense lawyer into a vigorous indictment of police brutality. To the surprise of everyone, Zasulich was acquitted. The Czar immediately issued an order that she be arrested again, but an enthusiastic crowd—which had formed around her in the street after her release—spirited her away from the oncoming police. She left the country and settled in Germany amidst worldwide acclaim for her heroism."

Czar Alexander II was more liberal than his predecessors. He partially "emancipated" the serfs (offering them the opportunity to purchase their own lands and to pay crushing taxes), and he promoted various feeble reforms.

The Left, however, pushed hard for basic demands: freedom for the serfs, public education, free speech, jury trials. The Left—students, pre-communists, peasants—became extremely impatient with the continuing repression of the Czars, and upped the revolutionary ante by adopting a policy of violence directed at the Government. General Mezentzev, another high officer in the St. Petersburg police, was stabbed to death in broad daylight by Sergei Kravchinsky, the editor of *Land and Liberty*, who got away and escaped into exile. Harsh police reaction escalated.

The revolutionary movement was divided on the issue of violence. The nonviolent socialists were called *Chornyi Peredel* (Black Repartition; i.e. redivision of the soil), and the militants were called *Narodnaya Volya* (The Will of the People).

In August of 1879, the leaders of the Will of the People decided to assassinate Czar Alexander. Their initial plan was to blow up the Czar's train. They split into 2 groups and, disguised as shopkeepers, rented 2 buildings along the Imperial route. They established businesses by day, and dug tunnels and mined the tracks at night.

On November 18, the Czar's train approached the 1st death trap, commanded by the respected leader Andrei Zhelyabov, born a serf and educated at the University of Odessa on a scholarship. The explosives failed to detonate here.

The back-up death trap, 24 hours down the line, was manned by Sophia Perovskaya and her comrades. According to the information they possessed, the Imperial entourage consisted of 2 trains, the 1st of which would be sent in advance to test the safety of the route; the 2nd would carry the Czar. Sophia let the 1st train go by and blew up the 2nd. The train was derailed, but no one was seriously injured. In any case, the Czar had been traveling in the 1st train.

After this setback, the revolutionaries embarked on a series of ambitious assassination attempts, including a huge bomb explosion under the dining room of the Winter Palace. All attempts were unsuccessful.

Finally, Zhelyabov and Perovskaya, now lovers, formulated the plot that eventuated in the successful March 1 tyrannicide. Their plan involved the purchase of a basement store front on Malaya Sadovaya Street, and the establishment of a bogus cheese shop. They dug a tunnel under the street and planted an explosive charge, hoping to blow up the Czar's carriage as it passed on its way to the palace. In addition, 4 bomb-carrying men were prepared to attack the Czar personally.

Immediately before the scheduled assassination, Zhelyabov was arrested. Perovskaya assumed the responsibilities of leadership. The Czar decided to travel along an alternate route, bypassing Malaya Sadovaya, and so the mined street plan had to be abandoned. A short while later, Ignaty Grinevitsky dashed out of the crowd and blew up both the Czar and himself. Apparently the revolution could now begin.

Not so. The expected uprisings failed to materialize. Numb confusion followed the assassination, and after the 6 principal conspirators were convicted and executed, their revolutionary organizations quickly deteriorated. The subsequent, ultrareactionary Government used this violent assassination to justify widespread repression of the citizenry, and the Russian revolutionary movement floundered for almost 10 years. As Edward Hyams said:

> The lesson was clear: So long as there were heirs, so long as the monarchy itself continued to exist, it was useless to assassinate Czars unless you went on to seize, demolish, and replace the whole social-political system, from the ground upwards. Most reformers failed to learn that lesson; only the Bolshevik section of the

Social Democratic movement took it to heart, and, in due course, acted on it.

—M.S.

The Victim: HENRY CLAY FRICK, chairman and strongman of the Carnegie Steel Company. Frick was an archenemy of both working people and labor unions. His company owned large coke ovens where unions were prohibited and workers lived under atrocious conditions. He was brought in by his partner Andrew Carnegie to handle the explosive conflicts that were developing at the company's largest mills in Homestead, Pa., near Pittsburgh. Upon the expiration of the prevailing contract, Frick refused flatly to recognize the union, threatening to close the mills and discharge all employees, who would then have to apply for work individually. He made good his threat. "Not a strike, but a lockout," announced Frick. The workers demanded the right to bargain collectively, and public sentiments flared up against the arbitrary manipulations of Frick. Emma Goldman described the subsequent events:

> Frick had fortified the Homestead mills, built a high fence around them. Then, in the dead of night, a barge packed with strikebreakers, under protection of heavily armed Pinkerton thugs, quietly stole up the Monongahela River. The steelmen had heard of Frick's move. They stationed themselves along the shore, determined to drive back Frick's hirelings. When the barge got within range, the Pinkertons had opened fire, without warning, killing a number of Homestead men on the shore, among them a little boy, and wounding scores of others.

It was these actions on Frick's part that resulted in the attempt on his life by the young Russian-born anarchist-intellectual Alexander Berkman.

The Date: July 23, 1892.

The Event: Berkman, an extremely gentle and sensitive man, was outraged by these murders and the exploitation of the Homestead workers. He felt moved to assassinate the industrial tyrant as a preliminary step toward the liberation of his beloved comrades. He expected to die for his act. On July 23, Berkman arrived in Homestead and managed to enter Frick's office. He described the action in his memoirs:

> For an instant the sunlight, streaming through the windows, dazzles me. I discern 2 men at the further end of the long table. . . . "Fr——," I begin. The look of terror on his face strikes me speechless. It is the dread of the conscious presence of death. "He under-

stands," it flashes through my mind. With a quick motion I draw the revolver. As I raise the weapon I see Frick clutch with both hands the arm of the chair, and attempt to rise. I aim at his head. "Perhaps he wears armor," I reflect. With a look of horror he quickly averts his face, as I pull the trigger. There is a flash, and the high-ceilinged room reverberates as with the booming of cannon. I hear a sharp, piercing cry, and see Frick on his knees, his head against the arm of the chair. I feel calm and possessed, intent upon every movement of the man. He is lying head and shoulders under the large armchair, without sound or motion. "Dead?" I wonder. I must make sure. About 25′ separate us. I take a few steps toward him, when suddenly the other man, whose presence I had quite forgotten, leaps upon me. I struggle to loosen his hold. He looks slender and small. I would not hurt him: I have no business with him. . . .

Berkman struggled further with this assailant; he fired again at Frick but the "other" man struck his hand and the shot missed. Berkman fired once more, but there was no explosion. Then he was hit from behind with a heavy object and sank to the floor.

> Confused voices ring in my ears. Painfully I strive to rise. The weight of many bodies is pressing on me. Now—it's Frick's voice! Not dead? . . . I crawl in the direction of the sound, dragging the struggling men with me. I must get the dagger from my pocket—I have it! Repeatedly I strike with it at the legs of the man near the window. I hear Frick cry out in pain—there is much shouting and stamping—my arms are pulled and twisted, and I am lifted bodily off the floor.
>
> Police, clerks, workmen in overalls, surround me. An officer pulls my head back by the hair, and my eyes meet Frick's. He stands in front of me, supported by several men. His face is ashen gray; the black beard is streaked with red, and blood is oozing from his neck. For an instant a strange feeling, as of shame, comes over me; but the next moment I am filled with anger at the sentiment, so unworthy of a revolutionist. With defiant hatred I look him full in the face. . . .

Berkman was taken away, and spent the next 14 years in prison. Frick was back on the job in a week.

The Would-Be Assassin: Alexander Berkman was born of prosperous Jewish parents in Vilna, Russia, in 1870. Russian populism surged all around him, and one of his uncles was an active revolutionary. At 12, Berkman wrote an essay denying the existence of God. He was reading revolutionary literature at 15 and was expelled from school for "precocious godlessness, dangerous tendencies, and insubordination."

Young Berkman was orphaned in 1887, and left for America 6 months later to start a new life. Upon his arrival in New York, Berkman was heavily influenced by the hanging of the unjustly convicted Haymarket martyrs just 3 months earlier. He joined anarchist groups and began his intense career of antiauthoritarian agitation. It was during this period that Berkman met Emma Goldman, with whom he was to establish a long-term partnership.

At the time of the Homestead lockout, Berkman and Goldman were living together with another couple in Worcester, Mass., where they had opened an ice-cream parlor. When news of the steelworkers' struggle arrived, Berkman jumped up. Emma wrote:

> "Homestead!" he exclaimed. "I must go to Homestead!" I flung my arms around him, crying out his name. I too would go. . . . I have never heard Sasha so eloquent. He seemed to have grown in stature. He looked strong and defiant, an inner light on his face making him beautiful, as he had never before appeared to me.

They went to Homestead, wrote a "flaming" manifesto, and returned to New York. Then the news of the Pinkertons' slaughter reached them. They were stunned. Berkman said, "Frick is the responsible factor in this crime, and he must be made to stand the consequences." Resolved to eliminate Frick, Berkman attempted unsuccessfully to produce a workable bomb. Emma went out on the streets as a prostitute to obtain money to buy Berkman a gun. She was picked up by a kindly 60-year-old gentleman who sensed her amateur status and sent her home with $10.

Alexander Berkman tried and failed to assassinate Frick. He went into prison at age 21 and came out at age 35. During his incarceration he studied and also wrote prolifically—and lost his faith in the revolutionary effectiveness of individual acts of violence. From the time of his release from prison in 1906 to his deportation in 1919, Berkman became, along with Emma Goldman, the foremost figure in American anarchism. He organized meetings and demonstrations among workers and unemployed persons. He edited *Mother Earth*, one of the best libertarian periodicals in any language. He edited Emma Goldman's many books, including her autobiography. He helped found the Ferrer Modern School, based on libertarian principles, and served there as a teacher. He made extended lecture tours against the growing W.W. I hysteria. He campaigned ceaselessly for the release of unfairly convicted political prisoners, and organized legal defense committees for convicts all over the country.

In 1916, Berkman founded *The Blast*, a San Francisco anarchist publication. In 1917 he returned to New York to agitate against the draft, for which action he was arrested and sentenced to 2 years in the Atlanta Federal Prison, 7 months of which were spent in solitary confinement for protesting the beating of fellow inmates.

Berkman and Goldman were both deported in 1919. Back in Russia, they toured the newly Leninized nation, collecting material for the official Museum of the Revolution. However, they soon became disillusioned with the authoritarian practices of the new régime, particularly the mass arrests of Russian anarchists, the destruction of Makhno's anarchist guerrilla army, and the crushing of the libertarian Kronstadt uprising in 1921. They felt that the true revolution had been betrayed. Both left Russia.

Berkman emigrated 1st to Stockholm, then to Berlin, and eventually settled in France where, lonely and exhausted, he continued to write and to organize. He published a primer of anarchist philosophy, *Now and After—The ABC of Communist Anarchism*, in 1929, and he earned a meager living by translating, editing, and occasionally ghostwriting for American and European publishers. He also received support from friends and comrades.

Growing progressively more despondent, and physically ill, Berkman finally took his own life on June 28, 1936, 3 weeks before the outbreak of the Spanish Revolution.

H. L. Mencken, the noted American journalist, wrote that Berkman was a "transparently honest man . . . a shrewder and a braver spirit than has been seen in public among us since the Civil War."

—M.S.

The Victim: WILLIAM McKINLEY, 25th President of the U.S.

The Date: September 6, 1901.

The Event: The President was shaking hands with a bustling line of well-wishers in the Temple of Music at the Pan-American Exposition in Buffalo, N.Y. Fifty soldiers and Secret Service agents roamed the premises, and although no searches were made, the crowd was carefully scrutinized. The President, flanked by his aides and several agents, wanted to shake more hands, and asked that the line be speeded up.

A 28-year-old ex-factory worker and farmhand named Leon Czolgosz moved toward McKinley and drew an Iver Johnson .32 caliber revolver from his pocket. Holding it in his right hand, he wrapped it in a large white handkerchief. He advanced toward the front of the line. A Secret Service agent touched his shoulder. Czolgosz (pronounced Chol-gots) turned slowly. "Hurt your hand?" the agent asked. Czolgosz nodded. "Maybe you better get to a first-aid station. . . ." Czolgosz shook his head and struggled to keep his voice calm. "Later," he muttered. "After I meet the President. I've been waiting a long time." Czolgosz approached McKinley and said, "Excuse my left hand, Mr. President." McKinley shook his left hand and the farmhand moved on. After several more citizens extended their greetings, Czolgosz stepped up again, standing not more than 3' from the President. Secret Service agent Samuel Ireland grabbed Czolgosz's shoulder in order to move him along quickly. Czolgosz brushed away the agent's hand and lunged forward, firing twice in rapid succession. The time was 4:07 P.M. One bullet was deflected by McKinley's breastbone, but the other bullet ripped through his stomach and lodged somewhere in his back muscles. McKinley shuddered, stiffened, stared at Czolgosz in astonishment, and collapsed into surrounding arms. He did not lose consciousness. Czolgosz was knocked to the floor and severely beaten by 8 or 9 guards. "Be easy with him boys!" McKinley is supposed to have said. Czolgosz murmured, "I done my duty." The President died 8 days later.

The Assassin: Leon Czolgosz claimed to be an anarchist. He said he didn't believe in governments, rulers, voting, religion, or marriage. Historians are quick to point out that only a week before the assassination, an anarchist periodical, *Free Society*, had published a warning against Czolgosz, denouncing him as a spy, a police agent, and a dangerous crank. Czolgosz had definitely made contact with established anarchist groups, like the Liberty Club in Cleveland, but he alienated its members due to his ignorance of libertarian literature and his indiscreet questions about violence and assassinations. It is said that Czolgosz approached the radical groups seeking conspirators for his already-formulated plans rather than for enrichment or a sense of community. He is said to have had little more than a leaflet-sized knowledge of the principles of antiauthoritarianism, and based much of his desire to be an anarchist on a newspaper clipping that described the assassination, in Italy, of King Humbert I by the self-avowed anarchist Gaetano Bresci on July 29, 1900.

However, Emma Goldman wrote in her autobiography that she protested to the editor of the *Free Society* demanding proof for the "outrageous accusation" against Czolgosz. Apparently none was forthcoming and the paper printed a retraction, admitting that a mistake had been made. Goldman recalled that Czolgosz was a conscientious student of libertarian literature and was always seeking "the right books." Most historians do not mention this and prefer to portray Czolgosz as a social failure, a low creature unable to comprehend a political philosophy or act from a positive personal idea.

Czolgosz was born in Detroit in 1873, a short time after his parents arrived from Poland. His father worked in the sewers. Young Leon was considered the best educated of the 8 Czolgosz children, and although his early life was relatively "normal," he became more and more isolated as he grew older. At 16 he was working in a bottle factory. When his family moved to Cleveland, he got a job in a wire mill where he was considered a good steady worker. He gave his savings to his family to use toward the purchase of a 51-acre farm.

In 1893, the mill workers went on strike, and this had a profound political effect on Czolgosz. He and his only friend—older brother Waldek—began to rebel against the Catholic Church which had tormented them during their childhood. In 1894, Leon met a Cleveland upholsterer named Anton Zwolinski, who was a leader of a Polish educational group in which socialism and anarchism were openly discussed. Czolgosz, although personally very remote, joined a socialist club that met above his father's grocery-saloon. He is remembered as being silent during the meetings he attended.

Leon worked fairly steadily until 1898—3 years before the assassination—when he experienced some kind of a "breakdown," the nature of which is not exactly clear. He quit his job and retired to the family farm, where he spent his time sulking, reading, and making pottery.

In 1900 Czolgosz attended a speech by the anarchist firebrand Emma Goldman. Later he sought her out at her hotel, but she was too busy to pay much attention to him. Totally alone, Czolgosz moved to West Seneca, a small town outside Buffalo, and stayed in a boardinghouse. This was before the announcement of McKinley's appearance at the Pan-American Exposition. It is not known when Czolgosz decided to kill the President, although he claimed after his capture that he had the idea only a few days before the deed was accomplished.

In a handwritten confession after the assassination, Czolgosz said that he didn't believe that "one man should have so much service and another man should have none." He complained that "McKinley was going around the country shouting about prosperity when there was no prosperity for the poor man."

Czolgosz was indicted for 1st degree murder and went on trial September 23, 1901. Two old lawyers were assigned to the case. They presented no witnesses and did not contest the unanimous medical testimony that Leon was entirely sane. Czolgosz refused to talk to the attorneys, saying that he didn't believe in courts or lawyers. He showed no interest in the proceedings, refused to take the stand, and received the verdict of guilty without the slightest emotion. The trial lasted 8 hours and 26 minutes.

On the morning of October 29, 1901, Leon Czolgosz was strapped into the electric chair at Auburn State Prison. He said, "I killed the President because he was the enemy of the good people—the good working people. I am not sorry for my crime." At 7:12 A.M., 1,800 volts of electricity charged through his body for 7 seconds, then 300 volts for 23 seconds, then 1,800 volts for 4 seconds, then back to 300 volts for 26 seconds. Contact was broken. The presiding physician ordered another 5 seconds of 1,800 volts, and Czolgosz was pronounced dead. Sulfuric acid was poured into his coffin and doctors estimated that his body would decompose in 12 hours.

Aftermath: The assassination of McKinley touched off a wave of arrests and attacks on U.S. anarchists, including Emma Goldman and Johann Most, and led to the stiff antianarchist immigration laws passed 2 years later. Czolgosz's act significantly inflamed public hostility against the cause for whose advancement he had risked everything—and lost.

—M.S.

The Victim: HUEY P. LONG, the powerful and flamboyant "Kingfish" of Louisiana politics, established a vast dynasty based simultaneously on popular social reform and increased welfare as well as on corruption and personal greed. Huey Long hated big business, but not big politics. His career attracted nationwide attention and has been the subject of a considerable number of novels, movies, and nonfiction studies. He has been called everything from a dictator to a radical. Long was a U.S. senator with presidential aspirations at the time of his death.

The Date: September 8, 1935.

The Event: The actual circumstances of Long's shooting are murky, and the written accounts are filled with contradictions. Here is the official and most generally accepted version: Long was attending a special session of the Louisiana House of Representatives in Baton Rouge. As the legislators prepared to recess, Long walked into the governor's office suite while his 5 bodyguards waited outside. Long emerged presently and hurried down one of the Capitol corridors; his bodyguards followed. From behind a recessed pillar, a 29-year-old physician named Carl Weiss approached Long. He was dressed in a white linen suit and carried a .32 caliber automatic. Without speaking, Weiss fired once, striking Huey Long in the lower right abdomen. Long cried out, "OOOOOOOhhh!" He turned, clutched his right side, and ran down the hall. Weiss was instantly disarmed, shot twice, and grappled to the marble floor. In a tornado of bullets and ricocheting shrapnel, Long's henchmen fired wildly and repeatedly, and when this was over Weiss's linen suit was dyed red from 61 large-caliber bullet wounds. After 30 hours and 44 minutes of intense medical treatment, Huey Long was also dead.

A respectable number of alternative versions have been documented, and much of the eyewitness testimony may be discounted because those who testified—Long's bodyguards and intense partisans—may themselves have killed the Kingfish in the ensuing explosion of close-range shooting. It has been proposed that Weiss perhaps punched Long in the face (Long suffered an unexplained cut on his mouth and he is alledged to have said, "That's where he hit me") and was subsequently fired upon. It has been proposed that the bodyguards—after an unclear incident—searched Weiss quickly, found the gun, and fired it. (The death bullet passed through Long and was secreted, along with all the other bullets, by the police; it is not known which bullet killed Long.) Weiss may have intended to kill Long, fired and missed; or Weiss may not have even intended to assassinate the senator. (However, apparently he *was* carrying his own .32, an uncommon practice for the doctor.)

The only eyewitnesses that testified at the coroner's inquest were Long's bodyguards and intimates, and all gave much the same overall story (the official version), although many lesser contradictions in testimony went unresolved. Two heavily documented books (*The Huey Long Murder Case*, by Hermann B. Deutsch, Doubleday; and *The Day Huey Long Was Shot*, by David H Zinman, Ivan Obolensky Pub.) posit widely varying and even opposing versions, each backed by reasonable evidence.

The Assassin: A brilliant doctor and a calm, sensitive family man, Carl Austin Weiss was born in Baton Rouge on December 18, 1905. After internships at the American Hospital in Paris and Bellevue Hospital in New York, Weiss entered into practice with his father back in Baton Rouge in 1932. He married Yvonne Pavy, daughter of Judge Benjamin

Pavy, a minor political opponent of Huey Long's.

Weiss hated Long, his parents hated Long, and his wife's family hated Long. However, Weiss's interest in politics did not manifest itself in any typical political activities. Apparently he didn't even like to talk politics. His work and his family life consumed nearly all of his energies. When not attending patients or operating, Weiss designed medical instruments. He was considered something of a "doctors' doctor," and perhaps the most highly trained young ear-nose-and-throat specialist in Louisiana.

On the day of the Long shooting, Dr. Weiss seemed entirely normal, and in fact confirmed plans to carry out an operation the following morning.

—M.S.

The Victim: ADOLF HITLER, Chancellor of Nazi Germany.

The Date: July 20, 1944.

The Event: For several years a large-scale conspiracy within the German Army had been trying to eliminate the Führer. Time bombs were placed in his plane, but they failed to explode. Three young officers, who were modeling the latest in Nazi uniforms, volunteered to carry bombs under their coats and blow themselves up in Hitler's presence. Hitler, however, departed before the bombs were set to go off. A similar plan to hide time bombs in new military packs was developed, but this, too, failed. A conspirator once showed up at a high-level conference with a bomb in his briefcase—Hitler failed to appear. Yet another suicidal attempt involved a scheme to kill the Führer in an art gallery; again, he left early and the bomb carrier hastily departed.

Adolf Hitler was not an easy target. He expected that attempts on his life would be made and took brilliant precautionary measures. During his later years, Hitler stayed out of sight as much as possible, hiding in remote fortress-headquarters. He released his traveling plans to the fewest possible functionaries, and nearly always altered them at the last minute. He arrived early, departed early, and was, as Robert Payne puts it in his biography, "rarely where people expected him to be." Hitler suspected the Army of plotting against him since the Army was the only major sector of the power structure that was not created and controlled by the Nazis themselves. The Führer constantly shifted high officers from one command to another so they would have little time to formulate any conspiracy plans. The Chancellor surrounded himself with tall sharpshooters. He wore a bulletproof vest and had 3½ lbs. of steel-plate lining under his military cap. He was a skilled marksman and always carried a revolver. Finally, the Führer possessed a special sense that warned him of impending danger and also claimed to be protected by Divine Providence.

The conspiracy to kill Hitler culminated on July 20, 1944, with a planned assassination to be followed by a vaguely coordinated coup d'état. By this time the Normandy invasion had assured Germany's defeat, but the conspirators perhaps hoped to avoid further national-suicidal mania on Hitler's part.

The time was half-past noon. Col. Claus von Stauffenberg (Klaus Phillip Schenk), chief of staff to the commander of the reserve army, arrived to meet with Hitler and 2 dozen high officers at "Wolf's Lair," the Führer's retreat headquarters in Rastenberg, East Prussia. The conference, scheduled for 1 P.M., had already begun because Hitler was to greet Mussolini at 3 o'clock. Stauffenberg, who was talking with Hitler's aides in the compound's guard bunker, sneaked into the bathroom and activated the silent acid fuse which was connected to 2 lbs. of British plastic explosive in his briefcase. He had 10 minutes.

The conference room shifted from the usual heavy concrete bunker to the *Lagebaracke*, a lighter structure with 3 open windows. Stauffenberg was disappointed because a bomb blast is considerably more lethal if contained within a tightly-enclosed area.

In spite of the altered circumstances, Stauffenberg was able to gain access to the conference room without arousing suspicion. Three minutes went by. As he entered the room, General Heusinger was expounding on the overall military situation. The small room was almost filled by a massive oak table which was supported by 2 huge oak slabs. Seated around the table were Hitler and 23 important Nazis. Additional conferees stood about the room.

Stauffenberg took his place, perhaps 5' to 6' to the right of Hitler and set his briefcase down against the inner side of one of the oak supports. Muttering about a telephone call, Stauffenberg abruptly left the room. General Heusinger's report continued. Colonel Brandt, sitting 3 chairs to Hitler's right, moved Stauffenberg's briefcase to the outer side of the oak support, probably because it was in his way. Field Marshal Keitel, one of Hitler's top aides, became concerned that Stauffenberg would not return in time to give his report and dispatched a subordinate to search for Stauffenberg. The runner returned to report that he could not locate the colonel.

As Hitler leaned across the table to look at a map, the bomb exploded. Bodies were thrown about as the walls and ceiling blasted apart. Four people were killed, several were badly hurt. The Führer suffered from shock, minor burns, and injury to the eardrums, but escaped major harm due to the protection of the heavy oak table. He recovered sufficiently to meet Mussolini 2 hours later. Stauffenberg viewed the explosion from 100 yards away, then managed to get out of the compound and onto an airplane. Assuming that he had succeeded in killing Hitler, Stauffenberg and his conspirators set into motion their plans to take over the Government.

The Would-Be Assassins: Col. Claus von Stauffenberg, who was 37, was a "liberal"—within the context of wartime Germany. He despised Hitler as early as 1936, and is said to have called him "the buffoon" and "the enemy of the world." Stauffenberg drew up a peace program which provided for a freely-elected Government, and he proposed socialist leader Julius Leber as a candidate for Minister of the Interior.

The conspiracy in which Stauffenberg was involved consisted mainly of aristocratic or high-minded military officers who held middle-rank staff positions. These officers were bound together by their class status as well as their distrust of the Nazis. Much of the motivation for their resistance was right-wing patriotism. They felt that Hitler was destroying the country, and some of them were plainly disgusted by the immorality of Hitler's actions.

A few of the principal long-term conspirators, however, were highly placed. Col.-Gen. Ludwig Beck was chief of the Army's general staff until he resigned in 1938 in protest against Hitler. Beck was formerly the effective head of the resistance against the Führer. Adm. Wilhelm Canaris was chief of Military Intelligence from 1935 to 1944. Canaris, along with his collaborators Hans von Dohnanyi (legal adviser) and Maj.-Gen. Hans Oster (chief of staff) were key organizers of the conspiracy.

Other resistance kingpins included Colonel-General Olbricht, who worked closely with Stauffenberg; Lieutenant Schlabrendorff and Major-General Tresckow, who themselves attempted unsuccessfully to bomb Hitler; and scores of other military officers and civilians who participated -in or supported the opposition.

The conspiracy against Hitler was not carried on by a group of fanatics. These men were organized and ambitious. In 1939, Winston Churchill was visited by agents of the resistance and informed of their schemes. In 1943, a conspirator met with U.S. Intelligence leader Allen Dulles to urge active contact between the Allies and the resistance. In 1944, Rommel and other important commanders were invited to join the ranks of the conspirators, or at least to support them after the coup. Rommel, however, declined as he favored the arrest and trial of Hitler rather than his assassination. Most of the generals preferred to wait for the results of the coup before committing themselves to the anti-Hitler forces.

What happened to the conspiracy after Stauffenberg's bomb failed to kill Hitler? For 2 tense hours on the afternoon of July 20, 1944, Beck, Olbricht, and the plotters in Berlin waited for the word from Wolf's Lair. No message arrived. Stauffenberg boarded his plane at 3:42 P.M. While he was in the air, Olbricht in Berlin decided to go ahead with the planned coup d'état. It was hoped that units of the reserve army would move in and surround the Berlin Administrative Center—after Hitler's death—and follow the orders of the conspirators, who would have themselves set up as the new military command.

The Führer's death was announced. Much confusion followed. Arrests were made by the conspirators, counterarrests were made by the loyalists. Stauffenberg arrived around 5 P.M. and "confirmed" Hitler's demise. New activity boiled in the War Office—the conspirators' headquarters. Phone calls announcing the coup were made to European commands and more Nazis were arrested, but already the news of the assassination was being authoritatively challenged. The reserve army units moved too slowly, and the conspirators failed to take over the propaganda ministry or the central broadcasting facilities.

At 6:45 P.M. Goebbels's broadcast to the nation gave the official confirmation that Hitler was alive. The conspirators continued their desperate telephoning but the curtain was closing. Late that night a small group of S.S. commandos shot their way into the War Office and arrested the conspirators. An instant court-martial was set up and death sentences were announced. General Beck was given the choice of suicide or arrest. He chose the former. Stauffenberg, Olbricht, and others were executed by a firing squad.

In the days and weeks that followed, Canaris, Oster, Schlabrendorff, Tresckow, and other principals were arrested and immediately or eventually executed. According to one source, 7,000 arrests were made and 2,000 death sentences were handed down by the Nazi's "people's courts." (No evidence was allowed on behalf of the defendants.)

The Führer ordered that a number of conspirators be hanged "like carcasses of meat." Accordingly, a group of unfortunates were suspended by piano wire from meat hooks at the Plotzensee barracks. Films were made of this and Hitler had them rushed to his personal projection room for viewing.

—M.S.

The Victim: MOHANDAS KARAMCHAND GANDHI was born on October 2, 1869. One of the most respected figures in modern history, Gandhi spent his life practicing and promoting nonviolent rebellion, and did more than any other single individual to free India from British rule.

The Date: January 30, 1948.

The Event: The time was 5:13 P.M., January 30, 1948. At Birla House in Delhi, Mahatma (meaning "great soul" in Sanskrit) Gandhi emerged from his quarters to conduct a prayer meeting in the gardens. Several hundred persons were present. Gandhi was weak from a long fast and was supported by a grandniece on either side. He joked with them as they walked along the covered corridor adjacent to the gardens. Gandhi climbed the brick steps leading up to the grounds and stood smiling at the crowd, which opened up to let him pass. Suddenly a man in a green pullover and a khaki jacket rushed up to Gandhi. He bowed briefly and then shot the 78-year-old pacifist 3 times—once in the abdomen and twice in the chest. Gandhi cried "*Hai Rama! Hai Rama!*" before he collapsed and died. The assassin was set upon, beaten, and dragged away.

The Assassins: Nathuram Godse was 37 when he killed Gandhi. By profession, he was the editor of a Hindu nationalist newspaper. By temperament he was reserved and polite. His father was a small-town bureaucrat who could not afford to give his son much formal education. Godse struggled for a while as a tailor, and then, at age 20, decided to devote his life to the Hindu Mahasabha, a fiercely anti-Muslim politico-religious organization that hated Gandhi for tolerating non-Hindu faiths.

Godse was the organizer of and principal participant in a dedicated if somewhat bungling assassination conspiracy that began its plotting in August, 1947. Godse decided that an armed group of assailants would have a better chance of success than a lone executioner, and he spent the next several months lining up comrades and weapons. The main conspirators were:

—*Gopal Godse*—Nathuram's younger brother.

—*Narayan Apte*—the production manager of Godse's newspaper.

—*Mandanlal Pahwa*—a young man who had seen his father and aunt murdered by a Muslim mob; considered a significant action man in the conspiracy.

—*Vishnu Karkare*—a restaurant owner and official Mahasabha representative; also Pahwa's employer.

—*Shankar Kistayya*—the youngest of the group; illiterate; functioned mainly as a carrier of illegal weapons.

—*Digambar Badge*—a bookseller and weapons-supplier.

—*Vinayak Savarkar*—an important political opponent of Gandhi's who had retired, and who would inevitably be suspected of collusion in such an affair because of his ruthless and antagonistic history. His exact relationship to the conspiracy has not been definitively established, although it is thought that he was visited at crucial points by Godse and others.

The conspiracy encountered continual setbacks in its efforts to secure serviceable weapons. Eventually, however, 2 pistols, 5 hand grenades, and 2 slabs of guncotton (explosive) were acquired. The conspirators initially tried to kill Gandhi at Birla House on January 20, 1948. They planned to set off one of the guncotton slabs during a prayer meeting, and during the resultant panic to mow Gandhi down with guns and grenades. During their last-minute preparations they suffered considerable confusion. They couldn't decide who would carry the guns and who would carry the hand grenades. They couldn't decide whether to shoot through the spaces in the thin back wall, or to move inside the garden itself. They didn't know whether to attack Gandhi from the front or the rear. They found that their guns didn't work. They even forgot to disguise themselves, until the last minute.

They arrived somewhat disheveled at the prayer meeting. After more hurried changes in plans, they took their positions around the garden. Pahwa, in full view of witnesses, detonated the mild guncotton. The expected uproar did not ensue, and the meeting continued as if nothing had happened. A woman grabbed Pahwa and he was arrested. The others slipped away.

It has been said that Pahwa revealed the names of some if not all of the conspirators by midnight of January 20. It has also been reported that he revealed nothing. In any case, Godse, Apte, Karkare, Badge, and Kistayya left town and hurried back to Bombay.

As a result of an inquiry conducted in 1967, it now seems possible that the police did in fact know the identities and intentions of at least some of the conspirators. Author Robert Payne has suggested that the police chose to "let it happen"—to allow a "permissive assassination."

Despite the alerted police, Godse was undeterred. Badge and Kistayya dropped out of the scheme and Godse dismissed his brother Gopal on the grounds that he had a wife and children. This left 3 plotters: Godse, Apte, and Karkare. Godse told them that they were best suited to carry on the work of the Mahasabha after his own capture or death, and that he himself was destined to be the actual slayer. He seemed happy and calm. On January 30, Nathuram Godse carried out his mission.

The main conspirators—8 in number—were

all arrested. Their trial was convened in Delhi on May 27, 1948, and it continued until February 10, 1949. The prosecution called 149 witnesses and all the proceedings had to be translated into several languages. Godse remained totally suave and detached during the long months of the trial. As the prosecution's version of the conspiracy gradually emerged, Savarkar—the retired political leader—continually denied any involvement and poured out elaborate legal arguments against every bit of incriminating evidence. This impressed the judge—there was no jury—and Savarkar was eventually acquitted.

On November 8, 1948, Godse took the spotlight and read to the court a 92-page handwritten statement in which he assumed full and sole responsibility for the assassination. He called Gandhi a "curse to India, a force for evil," and "a political and ethical imposter." He accused Gandhi of setting himself up as "infallible . . . the master brain guiding the civil disobedience movement." He complained of Gandhi's "egotistic pursuit of harebrained policy," and feared that because of Gandhi's actions the Muslims would take over India and Hinduism would be destroyed.

Godse blamed Gandhi for the partition of August, 1947, and said that the decision to kill him was made at that time. He cited significant Hindu legends and mythological characters to justify his use of violence, and often referred to man's subjugation to Greater Forces and Meta-Destinies, without denying his own willful act.

On February 10, 1949, Godse and Apte were sentenced to death. Savarkar was acquitted, and the remaining 5 plotters drew life terms. Godse and Apte read and wrote voluminously in jail while their appeals were being considered (and eventually rejected). On November 15, 1949, they walked to the gallows shouting, "India united!" Apte died immediately of a broken neck; Godse took 15 minutes to strangle.

—M.S.

The Victim: HARRY S TRUMAN, 33rd President of the U.S.

The Date: November 1, 1950.

The Event: While the White House was being remodeled, President Truman was making extensive use of Blair House, a 4-story Georgian mansion located across the street. The yellow brick building was set back from the Pennsylvania Avenue sidewalk by a narrow yard, a hedge, and an iron fence. A sentry box stood at each end of the façade. Ten steps led up to the front door.

President Truman was asleep in a front room on the 2nd floor. The afternoon of November 1 was warm and clear. A short distance away,

in the Harris Hotel, 2 American citizens from Puerto Rico, Oscar Collazo and Griselio Torresola, were making final preparations for their assault on the Chief Executive. Collazo, who had not fired a gun since childhood, awkwardly aimed his Walther P-38 automatic in the quiet hotel room. The 2 men set out for Blair House with 69 rounds of ammunition between them. They hoped to shoot their way inside and catch Truman in an office or a hallway.

The main door was wide open; only a flimsy screen door stood between the sidewalk and the President. The 2 Puerto Ricans separated and approached the entrance from opposite directions. Donald Birdzell, a Secret Service agent, was standing at the bottom of the front stairs. A guard (Joe Davidson) and another agent (Floyd Boring) were conversing in the east sentry booth, and a single guard (Leslie Coffelt) was stationed in the west booth.

Collazo advanced from the east. He reached Birdzell, who was facing the other way, drew his gun, and pulled the trigger. No explosion. At the sound of the click, Birdzell turned around. He saw a well-dressed Latin man holding a Walther P-38 automatic against his chest and beating it with his left hand. The gun then went off accidentally, and the bullet struck Birdzell in the leg. This was the only one of Collazo's 9 shots that hit a target. Birdzell dashed out onto Pennsylvania Avenue. Collazo, assuming that the agent was fleeing, turned and started up the 10 stairs. As Davidson and Boring opened fire from the east booth, Birdzell turned and shot from the street. Davidson and Boring were both excellent marksmen, but their line of fire was obstructed by the hedge and the iron fence. Collazo crouched on the 2nd step and returned the fire. His nose was grazed, then an ear. A bullet passed through his hat without touching him.

Simultaneously, Torresola moved in from the west. He blasted Coffelt, and downed another guard who emerged from a side door. Torresola, an experienced gunman, then turned and took out Birdzell, who was shooting at Collazo from the middle of Pennsylvania Avenue. Coffelt, fatally injured, nevertheless managed to draw a lethal bead on his assailant. He fired a final bullet into Torresola's brain. Coffelt himself died 3½ hours later. These 2 men were the only participants who did not survive the shootout. Collazo, outgunned, caught a bullet in the chest and fell face down on the sidewalk.

Twenty-seven shots were fired in less than 3 minutes. Collazo's bullet was deflected by his breastbone and he recovered. He was indicted and convicted on 3 charges: the murder of Coffelt, intent to kill the President, and assault with intent to kill 2 guards. Collazo was sentenced to be electrocuted on August 1, 1952.

The Would-Be Assassins: Oscar Collazo was 36 years old at the time of the Blair House incident; Griselio Torresola was 25. Both men were long-standing members of the Puerto Rican Nationalist party, an organization which agitated for the independence of the tiny American Territory. Neither had any record of malfeasance or violence.

Collazo was the more interesting of the 2. He was an extremely mild-mannered family man; a kind, likable, dependable citizen. He educated himself and was a voracious reader of history and literature, specializing in works about the heritage and culture of his native island. Born in Puerto Rico in 1914, Collazo automatically became an American citizen (under the Jones Act) at age 3. His father died when Oscar was a young child, and the family broke up. Oscar lived with an older brother.

He went to New York at age 17 and worked at miscellaneous unskilled jobs, such as dishwashing in the Army and Navy Club. Moving back and forth between New York and Puerto Rico, and always working, Collazo gradually became more active in the independence movement. Eventually, in New York, he settled into a position as a metal polisher. He gave English lessons to his fellow employees, and regularly went down to the docks to meet ships of Puerto Rican immigrants, whom he would orient to the alien and often hostile New York environment.

Married, divorced, and married again to one Rosa Mercado, Collazo lived in a tenement in the Bronx with his wife and her 2 daughters. He became a leader and a speaker in the nationalist movement, and maintained an active mimeograph machine in his apartment. He was a union leader in his factory and was respected by workers and management alike.

Torresola, about whom less is known, was apparently not as upstanding or accomplished as Collazo. The 2 were friends but not intimates, bound together primarily by their passion for Puerto Rican independence. Torresola arrived in New York in 1948 and lived in the Bronx on welfare with his daughter and various women. It was Torresola who procured the guns.

The U.S. Government contends, but cannot prove, that the assassination attempt of November 1, 1950, was a conspiracy timed to cause chaos and possible revolution at the exact moment that a large-scale rebellion erupted in Puerto Rico. The revolt did actually occur, but was quickly crushed by the authorities. Torresola met with the president of the Nationalist party in Puerto Rico, Harvard-educated Pedro Albizu Campos, 2 months before the Blair House shooting, and at the time of his death possessed provocative but inconclusive notes signed by Campos.

Collazo, after the incident, maintained that he and Torresola hatched the plan entirely on their own, and held no personal grudge against Truman, but simply wanted to assist their comrades who were rebelling in Puerto Rico.

His wife Rosa was arrested after the attempt but was released. Years later, in an unrelated case, she was convicted, along with 12 others, for conspiracy to overthrow the Government and sentenced to 6 years.

At his trial, Oscar Collazo spoke passionately of the economic exploitation and political manipulation perpetrated by the U.S. Government upon the people of Puerto Rico. He reminded the court of the many Puerto Ricans who were serving in Korea when they had no freedom at home. "Anything that I have done I did it for the cause of the liberty of my country, and I still insist, even to the last, that we have the right to be free. . . . I didn't come here to plead for my life. I came here to plead for the cause of the liberty of my people."

The gentle freedom-fighter, a poor shot and a lover of Swift—the English satirist—was sentenced to die. As he was escorted from the courtroom, his wife called out to him, "Goodbye, my dove!" Collazo refused his right to plead for clemency, but on July 24, only a few days before the execution date, his sentence was commuted to life imprisonment by President Truman. Collazo currently resides in the Federal Penitentiary at Leavenworth.

—M.S.

The Victim: JOHN F. KENNEDY, 35th President of the U.S.

The Date: November 22, 1963.

The Event: At 12:30 P.M., President John F. Kennedy was shot to death during a midday motorcade in Dallas, Tex. It was a tragedy that shook the nation and the world.

The presidential party had arrived at Love Field under a clearing sky. Kennedy took time to shake hands with the spectators gathered at the airport to greet him; the crowd seemed amiable and receptive to the President, who was apprehensive about this visit to Texas.

The Secret Service had been lining up the automobiles for the upcoming parade through the streets of the city. Each car was tagged with a small square of paper bearing a number which indicated the planned position of that particular car in the motorcade. Kennedy was to ride in the open 1961 Lincoln Continental limousine marked with the number "7." But the limousine was placed 2nd in line, due apparently to a mix-up.

When the parade started, the Lincoln (sans bubble-top because of Kennedy's own request to leave it off if the weather was nice) was preceded by a 1963 Ford sedan bearing Dallas Police Chief Jesse Curry and other local officials. Directly behind the presidential limousine was the Secret Service's follow-up car, a 1959 Cadillac. Although the press vehicle (usually directly in front of the President's car to facilitate photographing the President) was numbered "6," it was lined up last (14th) in the motorcade. For this reason, the photographers in that vehicle were unable to provide any footage of the assassination that was about to occur—footage that would have been of great evidential value.

The parade proceeded from Love Field through the central part of Dallas. The entourage was approaching the end of its ride to the World Trade Center, where Kennedy was to speak that day.

As the 8,000-lb. presidential vehicle lumbered off of Houston Street, making a left turn onto Elm Street, it nearly had to stop completely in negotiating the turn. The motorcade was now in Dealey Plaza.

Mr. Abraham Zapruder was stationed on Elm Street, perched atop a block of granite some 72' from the middle of the street. He was holding his 8-millimeter Bell & Howell movie camera, which was set on "telephoto" to film the President as he rode by. This film became the single most important piece of evidence in the case of the assassination of President Kennedy, as Zapruder was the only one of several photographers to capture the incident from an angle clearly showing Kennedy. He had test-shot a few frames of his secretary in his office. She was now bracing him so that he would not fall from his vantage point on the piece of stone.

First Zapruder filmed 2 motorcycles as they rolled down the street to clear the way for the President's parade. He knew that Kennedy's car would approach him at any moment. From the instant the driver of Kennedy's car, Will Greer, slowed to make the turn into Elm Street, until it disappeared beneath an overpass at the end of the street, Zapruder filmed the car.

The Zapruder film was purchased immediately after the assassination for a large amount of money by *Life* magazine, but was never released in its full form by that corporation. In 1975, *Life* returned the film to the Zapruder family. The only copies that exist officially were made for the Secret Service and the FBI. These 2 government copies are locked in the National Archives until the year 2039 by virtue of President Lyndon Johnson's Executive Order 11130. However, in 1967, New Orleans District Attorney Jim Garrison accused a Mr. Clay Shaw of being part of a conspiracy to kill President Kennedy and the FBI copy was sub-

poenaed as evidence for the ensuing trial. At that time, Garrison obtained the film, copied it, and thus became the source of the film for the many researchers and investigators who now have copies. The film is of even more importance when it is studied in the context of the official report regarding the assassination, the *Report* of the President's Commission on the Assassination of President Kennedy, also called the Warren Commission because its chairman was Chief Justice Earl Warren of the U.S. Supreme Court.

Zapruder's camera was running as the President's limousine approached him. Kennedy can be seen waving to the crowd with his right hand. Then he briefly disappears from camera view, as his vehicle moves farther down the street behind a freeway sign. When he emerges from behind the sign in the Zapruder film, his hands are rising, fists clenched, in front of his neck, his elbows pointing to either side of the street. At this moment, he has already been shot once. The 1st bullet entered the President's back approximately 5½" below his collar line.

Another shot is now fired, and the Warren Commission has contended that this 2nd bullet went wild, striking the curb near a spectator named James T. Tague. That bullet sprayed Tague's foot and cheek with chips of concrete from the curb and with fragments of lead.

The Warren Commission also stated that a 3rd bullet was fired, striking Kennedy in the head and killing him. The majority of witnesses agreed that the last shot fired hit Kennedy in the head, although there was much dispute as to the direction from which that bullet came.

It has been the position of the commission that one man, Lee Harvey Oswald, was stationed at the easternmost window on the 6th floor of the Texas School Book Depository Building, which is located on Elm Street. It has also been the official government opinion that Oswald acted alone in murdering John F. Kennedy and that there was no conspiracy of any kind behind the crime. A rifle was found on the 6th floor of the building. This 6.5-mm. bolt-action, clip-fed, 1938 Mannlicher-Carcano belonged to Oswald. Keeping in mind the Warren Commission's hypothesis that the 2nd shot went astray near Tague, and that the last bullet was the fatal shot striking the head, only one bullet is left as the cause of all other gunshot damage. Only 3 shots at most could have been fired using this rifle in the 5.6 seconds that elapsed from the last possible moment that Kennedy could have received the 1st wound (when he emerges, hit, from behind the sign in the Zapruder film), to the easily recognizable moment of the last fatal shot to the head (Kennedy reacts violently in the film at the moment of impact).

Sitting directly in front of the President in the Lincoln limousine was Gov. John B. Connally of Texas. He was sitting in one jump seat and his wife, Nellie, was in the jump seat next to him, directly in front of Mrs. Kennedy. Governor Connally was hit in the back, the bullet exiting from the right side of his chest, transiting his right wrist, and lodging in his left thigh. If the Commission is right about the number of bullets, the same bullet that struck Connally must have struck Kennedy 1st. That is to say, the bullet that hit Kennedy in the back would have had to exit from his body and go on to strike Connally.

If Oswald was firing from the 6th floor of the building, the angle of trajectory would be 17 degrees, 43 minutes, 30 seconds, in a *downward* direction. That bullet entered Kennedy's back, 5½" from his collar line—yet the only wound on the President's body, in addition to the wound in his head and the entry wound in his back, was a small slit in his throat. The Warren Commission theorized that this slit was caused by the exit of the bullet that entered Kennedy's back and continued on to hit Governor Connally. But since this bullet struck no bone in the President's body which might have deflected its angle of trajectory but exited in an *upward* direction, it seems very apparent that the single-bullet theory of the Warren Commission is a geometric impossibility.

This fact, coupled with the time element involved, suggests there was more than one gunman in Dealey Plaza that fateful day. The time lapse was determined by a frame-by-frame analysis of the Zapruder film. When Kennedy emerged from behind the sign in the film, he had already been shot. This is frame #225. When he disappeared in the film, at frame #207, he was waving to the crowd naturally. He could not have been hit at any time prior to moving behind the sign. John Connally testified that he heard the shot that hit Kennedy, turned around and looked over his right shoulder, and was then hit by a subsequent bullet. His testimony is substantiated by the Zapruder film, which shows him looking over his shoulder and then, before he can look over the other shoulder (as he claimed he was attempting to do), he is shot at a point no sooner than frame #235. Zapruder's camera operated at 18.3 frames per second. The 10 frames between the latest point Kennedy could have been hit (frame #225) and the earliest point Connally is struck (frame #235), represents a time value of .546488 seconds—just over a half second. A bullet fired from the Oswald weapon and passing through the neck of John Kennedy, as the Warren Commission claimed that this one did, would move at a speed of 1,772' to 1,779' per second according to the Warren *Report* and the FBI expert's testimony. Since it is impossible that a bullet virtually waited in midair for that half second, simple mathematics casts substantial doubt on the Commission's conclusion that one bullet caused all 7 wounds in Kennedy and Connally.

Special Agent Robert A. Frazier of the FBI testified as a firearms expert before the Warren Commission. He stated that the bolt action of the ancient Italian rifle took at least 2.3 seconds according to tests run by expert riflemen. Therefore, it is impossible that the weapon was fired twice within the half-second time slot. This means there is no possibility that Kennedy was hit by an earlier Oswald bullet at the moment of his disappearance behind the freeway sign and that a later shot hit Connally, because the time lapse between frames #207 (Kennedy's disappearance) and #235 (Connally's reaction) is only 1.5 seconds and 2.3 seconds would have been needed to fire 2 shots.

After the 1st shot, the President was leaning forward slightly, his wife aware that he'd been the victim of a bullet. She had moved closer to him and was looking at his face when a bullet struck the President in the head, exploding in a pink-red glow of blood, brain matter, and skull fragments. Terrified, Mrs. Kennedy then climbed from the seat of the limousine onto the trunk but was stopped there by Secret Service Agent Clinton J. Hill. Hill pushed Mrs. Kennedy back into the seat and shielded her body with his own as the Lincoln roared off.

None of this escaped the watchful eye of Zapruder's camera, making the Zapruder film an invaluable piece of hard evidence worthy of note in the event of conflicting conclusions by members of the Warren Commission.

It is a Newtonian law of motion that when an object is struck by a missile, that object will move in the same direction as that taken by the missile. This means that if Kennedy were hit by a gunman (presumably Oswald) situated in a window 280' behind him, his head would move forward from the impact of the bullet. The Zapruder film clearly depicts the President's head snapping BACKWARD with great violence. Applying the scientific laws governing the situation, there can be no doubt that Kennedy is reacting to a bullet fired from a position in front of the limousine. This is strong evidence that the lone assassin theory of the Commission is fallacious.

It is interesting to note that a certain area in front of the limousine at the time the fatal shot was fired was an excellent vantage point for a gunman. It is referred to by Dallas residents as the grassy knoll. At the top of this knoll, there is a wooden fence. There is a very small space between the top of that fence and the lowest foliage on the trees which line the inside of this fence. The knoll provides a spot where a gunman would be hidden from sight.

Two police officers who flanked the presidential limousine on motorcycles, Billy Martin and Robert Hargis, were so sure that the fatal shot had come from the knoll that they went directly up the embankment and peered over the fence. They saw a police officer there and, thinking the area covered, the pair left to get orders on what to do next. Minutes later pictures were taken of an officer—or a man dressed as an officer—leaving the grassy knoll area. His uniform was unlike those worn by the Dallas Police Force. His weaponry and other specifics also differed sharply from those of the officers in Dealey Plaza that day, indicating that this man was not an officer at all. This has yet to be fully investigated.

Witness Richard Carr was one of the closest observers of the fatal shot. Carr indicated that the shot came over his right shoulder or from the grassy knoll area. His testimony at the Clay Shaw proceeding in 1969 included the following exchange:

Q: As a result of the conversations with the FBI, what did you do?
A: I done as I was instructed, I shut my mouth.
Q: Were you called to testify before the Warren Commission?
A: No, sir.

It seems that the investigatory work in this case not only failed to meet the generally accepted standards for the gathering of truth, but it also served to stifle a full disclosure.

These points of evidence seem to emphasize grave inconsistencies in the official government account of the events of November 22, 1963. If, in fact, there was more than one gunman shooting at the President, as the evidence seems to indicate, there is a question as to why the plentiful clues were ignored by the Warren Commission. One member of the Commission wrote an article for *Life* magazine and also a book which supported the conclusions of the Warren *Report*—the lone-assassin single-bullet theory. This man is today the President of the U.S., Gerald R. Ford.

In determining the motives of the assassins—and those of the Warren Commission which failed to deal with the available evidence in depth, an obligation that it had to the American people—we are faced with problems. If we begin by suspecting that someone had a possible interest in having the President dead in 1963, we will find ourselves dealing with far too many people. And obviously no person or group of persons will ever admit an antipathy for the man in the face of a major investiga-

tion: *de mortuis nil nisi bonum* (of the dead say nothing but good).

Yet investigation must come about if the facts of this case are ever to be made public. And the American people have the right to a full disclosure of this situation in which it is possible that someone murdered a President of the U.S. and got away with it.

The Alleged Assassin: Lee Harvey Oswald was born on October 18, 1939, to Marguerite and Robert Oswald. In 1956, 6 days after his 17th birthday, Oswald enlisted in the U.S. Marine Corps.

In 1959, Lee Oswald was given a hardship discharge from the Marines due to a slight injury his mother had incurred. Since she was without money to pay for the medical attention she needed, Oswald was sent home to help out. After a very short stay at home, Lee Oswald decided to travel to Russia. He purchased a ticket for a luxury steamship passage, the fare far exceeding anything he or his family could have afforded.

While in the U.S.S.R., he offered State information regarding strategic military installations and codes that he had gathered while in the Marines. He requested that the Soviets employ him in a radar installation in view of his past experience; he was put to work in a transistor radio factory in Minsk. The FBI at this time ran a check through the CIA and the U.S. Embassy in Russia; Oswald was given "a clean bill."

Lee Harvey Oswald married the daughter of a Russian KGB colonel while overseas. (The Russian KGB is the equivalent of the U.S. CIA.) After 30 months in the U.S.S.R., Oswald decided to move back to the U.S. with his family. His hardship discharge from the Marines had since been changed to a dishonorable discharge. He was given a loan by the U.S. State Department and he moved to New Orleans. There he was met by a Mr. Spas T. Rankin of the China Lobby, an active CIA front. Oswald applied for a passport and, despite his questionable activities abroad, he was given his papers within 24 hours. Anyone familiar with the normal processes of obtaining a passport would realize that this was not a usual case.

By 1962, Lee Oswald had become a member of the Fair Play for Cuba Committee in New Orleans. The committee's office address was 544 Camp Street. That same office had another address as it is the corner office on the ground floor of the building. The other address is 531 Lafayette Street, and this was rented to Mr. Guy Bannister, a known conduit for money, arms, and munitions for the CIA counterinsurgency forces, still training for a 2nd invasion of Cuba, in violation of an Executive Order given by President John F. Kennedy.

Khaki-clad men could be seen frequenting the same office that was the source of "Hands Off Cuba!" literature, handed out primarily by Lee Oswald. Oswald must have been an incredibly easy man to get along with, considering his positive political convictions which differed so strongly with those of his officemates. The same could be said for Bannister and his colleagues. Or else one organization or the other was a front.

Moreover, Oswald's best friend and constant companion in New Orleans was a man named David Ferrie. Ferrie, a former Eastern Airlines pilot, was at this time a CIA operative running guns to Cuba. For a highly opinionated Marxist fanatic and communist, as the Warren Commission paints him, Oswald kept strange company just prior to the assassination of Kennedy.

In 1963, Oswald traveled to Mexico City and was met there by 2 CIA agents who were ordered by their station chief, E. Howard Hunt, to "baby-sit Oswald." He then returned to the U.S. and in mid-October began working in Dallas at the Texas School Book Depository Building, from which he allegedly shot Kennedy. He was paid $1.25 an hour. He was living on weekends with his wife in the home of Mrs. Ruth Hyde Paine. Mrs. Paine received an offer for Lee Oswald to work at a different job which would have paid about twice the money that the Depository paid him. She failed to mention this to Oswald.

The identification of Oswald in the easternmost window of the 6th floor in the Depository Building has been the source of much consternation among readers of the testimony of the witnesses. The commission's star witness, Mr. Howard Leslie Brennan, saw a man standing (according to FBI tests, an assassin from that window would have to be *kneeling* in order to perform the feat properly) in the 5th floor window. After some prodding by the Commission counsel Arlen Specter, and in fact after Specter marked the window for him, Brennan agreed it was the 6th floor. Brennan, further, identified the man in the police lineup that "most resembled" the man he saw. It is interesting to note that he could not remember later whether the others in the lineup were black or white. Also, he was not wearing his prescription glasses when he observed the man in the window. This is a typical example of the Warren Commission's "positive identifications" of Oswald in the murder of Kennedy and the later murder of Officer J. D. Tippit, for which he was also charged.

Another witness, Deputy Sheriff Roger D. Craig, observed Oswald running out of the back of the building (the commission contends that Oswald came out the front unobserved) and getting into a light-colored 1959 Rambler

station wagon. This is not dealt with in the *Report* of the President's Commission on the Assassination of President Kennedy. Craig has been the victim of many strange accidents and other misfortunes for some time now.

Accidents to witnesses are not uncommon in the case of this assassination: In the 3-year period which followed the murders of President Kennedy and Lee Oswald (who was killed by nightclub owner Jack Ruby), 18 material witnesses died—6 by gunfire, 3 in motor accidents, 2 by suicide, one from a cut throat, one from a karate chop to the neck, 3 from heart attacks, and 2 from natural causes. An actuary engaged by the *London Sunday Times* concluded that on November 22, 1963, the odds against every one of these witnesses' being dead by February, 1967, were one hundred thousand trillion to one.

All of these pieces of information lead one to think that there are too many coincidences for the case to be normal in any way. The connections between Oswald and certain U.S. governmental organizations are at least suspect. Incidentally, Attorney General Waggoner Carr found through his investigation that Oswald had an operative status with the FBI, his working number being S-172. This evidence was screened from the commission by one of its attorneys, Leon Jaworski (who, almost a decade later, was appointed Watergate special prosecutor by President Nixon).

Oswald's notebook further contained the name, address, license number, and unlisted telephone number of FBI Agent James P. Hosty. Hosty later was among the agents to aid in the investigation of the assassination.

There are 51 government files on Lee Harvey Oswald that are unavailable to the public by a May 13, 1974, Supreme Court decision, which reaffirmed the policy of the National Archives to close the documents to the American people. There can be no doubt that these documents contain information that could aid in the further investigation of Kennedy's death. Without the cooperation of the forces in control, however, the truth may never come out.
—B.C. & R.Rh.

The Victim: MALCOLM X, born Malcolm Little and died John Doe, black civil rights leader and founder of the Organization of Afro-American Unity and the Muslim Mosque, Inc.

The Date: February 21, 1965.

The Event: On this Sunday afternoon Malcolm X was to speak in the Audubon Ballroom in New York City's Manhattan district. Before he made the speech, and as he approached the lectern, he was shot and killed on the stage.

The speech was to be one of a new series of Malcolm X lectures, displaying an expanded awareness in the ideology of the man. Until a few weeks before his murder, Malcolm X had been a strict segregationalist and black supremist. His former violent preachings and strong antiwhite opinions had mellowed. He felt that the time had come for blacks and whites to coexist in peace. And specifically he felt an urgent need, as he related to his friend and biographer, Alex Haley, over the telephone the night before the assassination, to tell his followers that the Black Muslims alone were not to be blamed for such harassments as Malcolm X's house being burned February 14, 1965. Malcolm X felt the malevolent source of violence was much more powerful than the Black Muslims: larger and more political.

Malcolm X had been a member of the Black Muslims, a religious sect. He was suspended as a Muslim minister on November 23, 1963, by Elijah Muhammad. On March 8, 1964, Malcolm X broke away completely from the Black Muslims to form his own religious sect eventually, Muslim Mosque, Inc., and also the politically oriented Organization of Afro-American Unity. Tension between the Black Muslims and the OAAU simmered and grew to overt acts of violence from the time Malcolm X split from the Black Muslims until after his assassination. Immediately after the assassination of Malcolm X, the police and some of the media assumed that he was killed by Black Muslims. A Muslim mosque was burned shortly after the assassination in retaliation for the killing. To the police, the media, and the public, this vengeance against the Black Muslims supported the theory of Black Muslim responsibility for the assassination. Black Muslims could indeed have assassinated Malcolm X. However, over the years more and more evidence shows that if guilty, the Black Muslims were merely unknowing tools of a larger power structure—exactly the message in Malcolm X's aborted last speech.

Pinpointing the events of February 21, 1965, has been a futile task. News reports, eyewitness accounts, grand jury testimony, and trial testimony conflict sharply. Starting with the preparations for the lecture by the New York Police Department, the media differs on the number of uniformed police officers stationed outside the ballroom that afternoon. Reports range from a single patrolman to a special detail of 20 uniformed officers.

Malcolm X waited until about 3 P.M. and, assured that the scheduled previous speaker would not appear that day, went before the crowd with the words, "*As-salaam alaikum!* (Peace be unto you)." The room responded with "*Wa-alaikum salaam!* (And unto you be peace)." A disturbance broke out at that moment somewhere in the front audience as one man called to another, "Get your hands off my pockets—Don't be messin' with my pockets!"

Four of the 6 bodyguards with Malcolm X began to step forward. "Now brothers, be cool . . . ," Malcolm X began; and, as another diversion was created in the ballroom (a man's sock soaked in some flammable liquid and filled with matches was set ablaze in the back of the room), a male with a sawed-off shotgun moved forward to within 8' of Malcolm X and blasted buckshot through the plywood lectern and into Malcolm X's chest. Simultaneously, 2 other men advanced to the stage firing bullets into the prone body of Malcolm X.

A Malcolm X bodyguard, Charles Blackwell, saw one of the assailants flee into the ladies' lounge. This assailant escaped. Why Blackwell, a Malcolm bodyguard, didn't give chase was never brought out. One or 2 men—reports vary—fled to the stairway exit at the front of the ballroom. Reuben Francis, a Malcolm X bodyguard, who was never called to give witness as to what he saw, shot toward this exit, wounding Talmadge Hayer in the thigh. As Hayer fell outside, he was surrounded by members of the audience who began to beat him. Hayer was rescued from the crowd by 2 New York police officers, Patrolman Louis Angelos and Sgt. Alvin Aronoff, who arrested him and took him to Bellevue for treatment for his wound. (The .32-caliber bullet was not removed from Hayer's thigh until March 8, 1965.)

Immediate press accounts reported a 2nd man was beaten by the audience. This man was supposedly arrested by Patrolman Thomas Hoy. Jimmy Breslin reported in the *New York Herald Tribune*, February 22, 1965, "The other suspect was taken to the Wadsworth Avenue precinct, where the city's top policemen immediately converged and began one of the heaviest homicide investigations this city has ever seen." No further information regarding this 2nd man was made available to the press. And the press seemingly failed to follow up this fading of "the 2nd man." Ultimately, the New York police denied the arrest of a 2nd man, saying it had been a journalistic error.

Reuben Francis, the aforementioned Malcolm X bodyguard who wounded Hayer, also wounded one William Harris, 51, who was struck in the abdomen, and one William Parker, 36, who was shot in the foot. (Neither of these wounded spectators was called as a witness in the slaying trial.) Francis was indicted for shooting Hayer, jumped $10,000 bail, disappeared, and then was rearrested on February 2, 1966, in a New York Assistant District Attorney's office. On February 15, 1966, a spokesman for the District Attorney's office told *The Militant*, a weekly socialist newspaper, that "Francis had been picked up by the FBI" and was being held on $25,000 bail. On that same date "a spokesman for the

FBI denied any knowledge of Francis," according to *The Militant*. Reuben never testified and his whereabouts is unknown.

Benjamin X, the man who introduced Malcolm X to the Audubon Ballroom audience seconds before the killing, disappeared from Muslim Mosque affairs. " 'Only the police know where to find him,' one of his ex-colleagues revealed." So said the October, 1965, issue of *Ebony* magazine. No evidence is shown that even the counsels for the defense attempted to locate this Benjamin X, an ideal witness.

On February 14, 1965, Malcolm X's home had been bombed, and it was at that time members of his Muslim Mosque took over total control of Malcolm X's security system. Shortly before his death, Malcolm X had told a newsman: "I've never had a bodyguard. Your alertness is your best bodyguard." On the day of his assassination, reports had 6 bodyguards on the stage with Malcolm X. As of October, 1965, 3 of Malcolm X's former lieutenants and members of his bodyguard had vanished. Two of the 3 accused assassins of Malcolm X were Black Muslims and recognizable adversaries of his, yet they were able to pass through the security check that afternoon in the ballroom.

The Alleged Assassins: Talmadge Hayer/aka Thomas Hayer/aka Thomas Hagan, 22, was described by his lawyer as being a "closed-mouthed person." Married and the father of 2, Hayer consistently denied being a member of the Black Muslims when faced with the questionable testimony of 2 witnesses charging him as such. Hayer's brother-in-law, stepsister, and brother all testified that he was not a member of the religious sect. The prosecution was unable to prove that Hayer was or had ever been a member of the Black Muslims.

On January 21, 1966, the trial began, and on February 23, 1966, Hayer testified on his own behalf. On February 28, Hayer confessed to the assassination of Malcolm X, testifying that the other 2 defendants had nothing to do with the murder. Hayer and his 3 accomplices, whom he did not name, had been hired to carry out the assassination. He refused to say how much money he had been offered. He said that the man who hired him was not a Muslim either.

On March 11, 1965, the jury convicted the 3 defendants of the murder of Malcolm X.

Norman 3X Butler, 27, the 2nd convicted defendant, was a known and admitted Black Muslim. Not merely a member of the religious order, Butler belonged to the "Fruit of Islam," the elite Muslim security force. On the morning of the assassination, Butler had been treated by a doctor, Kenneth Seslowe of Jacobi Hospital, for superficial thrombophlebitis which resulted in his right leg's being bandaged and some oral medication prescribed.

Evidence exists that Butler was not even present in the ballroom at the time of Malcolm X's assassination. If he had been able to elude Malcolm X's security system on entering the ballroom that Sunday, and if he had indeed participated in the murder of Malcolm X, how did Butler plan on escaping from the scene of the crime while physically handicapped? Or was escape that necessary to him? Witnesses' testimony place Butler at the exit where Hayer was wounded by Reuben Francis. Could Butler have been "the 2nd man" arrested at the scene whose existence police denied?

Thomas 15X Johnson, 30, the 3rd convicted defendant, was a house painter and father of 4 children. He was a known Black Muslim. While in prison awaiting trial for the assassination of Malcolm X, and after his conviction, he strictly adhered to the sanctions of his religion down to the details of his diet.

Before the assassination, Johnson had been a companion of codefendant Butler. In fact, Johnson, Butler, and an unknown 3rd man had been arrested in January, 1965, for assault on Benjamin Brown, a Black Muslim defector.

Johnson denied being in the ballroom the afternoon of the assassination, although the prosecution placed Johnson as the man wielding the shotgun. Witnesses' testimony varies as to which of the 3—or if any of the 3—carried a shotgun.

The investigation of the assassination never established who ignited the crudely-made man's sock smoke bomb. During the trial, testimony revealed that Talmadge Hayer's fingerprint had been found on a piece of film inside the sock but no one saw who set it ablaze in the back of the room. Hayer could not have set it on fire and at the same time rushed forward to attack Malcolm X. If the fingerprint wasn't a plant, and Hayer was involved in manufacturing the smoke bomb, he would—because of the time element involved in this diversionary tactic—have needed another person to ignite it.

The 2 men who caused the verbal disorder when Malcolm X 1st walked onstage may have been the actual users of the handguns. However, this was never proved, and it leaves open the possibility that there was at least one other accomplice.

All the conflicting testimony during the trial, all the unanswered questions that remain, the lack of a complete investigation, the disappearance of key persons involved—all of this continues to cast doubts on the identity of the true killers.

B.C., S.H.Y., and R.Rh.

The Victim: ROBERT FRANCIS KENNEDY, U.S. senator from the State of New York and candidate for the Democratic nomination in the 1968 presidential election.

The Date: June 5, 1968.

The Event: There was an atmosphere of victory as Robert F. Kennedy made some short remarks to an enthusiastic crowd, consisting mainly of campaign workers, in the Ambassador Hotel in Los Angeles. Kennedy had captured 174 delegates' votes for the Democratic nomination. Everyone there was convinced that Bobby Kennedy was to be the next President.

The young New Englander (by origin) expressed thanks to his constituents, including sports heroes Don Drysdale, Rosey Grier, and Rafer Johnson. He was loudly cheered when he thanked Cesar Chavez, and then he went on to thank his staff and volunteers and voters everywhere before he left the stage in the ballroom.

Kennedy moved from the Embassy Room into the pantry area of the kitchen en route to the Colonial Room, that night's press room. His right hand was firmly grasped by Carl Uecker, the Ambassador's maître d'. Kennedy freed himself twice to shake hands, 1st with Juan Romero, and then again with Jesus Perez, employees of the hotel. Uecker regained his grasp on the senator's hand each time, and they continued through the narrow passageway, followed closely by a local armed private bodyguard.

When Sirhan B. Sirhan approached them, his small frame was unsteady, his eyes glazed. He was facing south; Uecker and RFK were facing north as they moved along. Then, before Uecker knew what was happening, Sirhan had fired his .22-caliber 8-shot Iver Johnson pistol once, and then again. When Uecker did react after the 2nd shot, he did so with fervor. With all his might, he slammed Sirhan's gun hand against the steam table to his left. Other hands reached in from all directions, grabbing portions of Sirhan's clothing and flesh. During the scuffle, Sirhan emptied his gun into the crowd, injuring 5 persons.

Rafer Johnson and Rosey Grier tackled the small dark Jordanian with more than their usual zeal, one hitting high and the other low.

"Rafer, get the gun!" someone screamed.

"GET THE FUCKING GUN!!"

As Kennedy lay on the floor mortally wounded, Juan Romero moved closer and put a rosary in Bobby's hands. Sobs, tears, and a continuing chorus of "Noooooo" eerily echoed through the hotel.

A bullet was removed from each of the 5 who had been wounded: Paul Schrade, Elizabeth Evan, Ira Goldstein, Irwin Stroll, and William Weisel. Two bullets were recovered from the counter divider of the pantry doors at the entrance. One more bullet was recovered from the door frame of the door at the back of the stage.

Three bullets had struck the senator. Two

entered in the region of one armpit, within inches of each other, and a 3rd (a fatal bullet) entered the right mastoid (i.e. the side of the head behind the right ear).

In all, 10 bullets were recovered, including those removed from the 6 victims of the shooting. Sirhan's .22 could fire only 8 shots without being reloaded. It was, of course, quite impossible for Sirhan to have reloaded his weapon and, therefore, it is apparent that another gun was also being fired that very early morning in June.

Dr. Thomas Noguchi listed the cause of death in his very complete medical report as a "gunshot wound of right mastoid, penetrating brain." In testimony, Noguchi expressed a professional opinion that the bullet was fired from a position "very, very close" to the senator. He went on to estimate that the muzzle of the gun that shot Kennedy was only "2" or 3" from the edge of the right ear." Not one witness places Sirhan any closer to Kennedy than 2' or 24", as he was firing. However, standing directly behind Kennedy was local security guard Thane Cesar who later admitted to having drawn his gun as soon as Sirhan began firing. He also concedes that his gun might have discharged but he denies having shot at Kennedy.

Further criminal research was continued in the case. A qualified criminologist, William W. Harper, reviewed the available evidence in the case and concluded that 2 different firing positions were used in the shooting and that 2 weapons had unquestionably been fired. This conclusion was based on hard evidence: comparison of a bullet removed from the abdomen of William Weisel with a bullet that lodged in the senator's neck (but which had entered near the armpit). There are no common class characteristics; the rifling marks sharply differ. That is to say, the bullets could not possibly have been fired from the same weapon. The substance of Harper's study is adhered to by several other criminologists including Drs. Herbert Leon MacDonell, Vincent P. Guinn, and Lowell Bradford. Harper unequivocally states that Kennedy was shot from a firing position entirely different from that of Sirhan B. Sirhan.

It would seem reasonable that Sirhan's gun would be test-fired to determine positively whether the Kennedy bullet or the Weisel bullet came from the Sirhan pistol. This standard police procedure, however, was not followed. Furthermore, a 2nd gun marked as evidence bore the serial number H18602, while the Sirhan gun had the serial number H53725. The police admitted that the guns had been reversed at the time of the trial, but the officials have not yet produced the Sirhan weapon so that it might be test-fired.

DeWayne Wolfer, head of the Los Angeles

Police Department Crime Laboratory at the time of the original investigation, refused to test-fire the Sirhan gun. Marshall Houts, editor of *Trauma* magazine, an in-house organ of the field of criminalistics, mentioned his "deep academic and professional concern over Wolfer's horrendous blunders" in a letter sent to Evelle J. Younger, attorney general of the State of California.

Younger was district attorney for the county of Los Angeles at the time of the Kennedy assassination and the subsequent investigation. In his former position and in his present one as attorney general, he has refused to reopen the case for any reason. Present District Attorney Joseph Busch also has refused to reopen the case or the investigation. Busch was appointed D.A. by Younger when the latter was elected attorney general.

A hearing was held on May 13, 1974, by Supervisor Baxter Ward of Los Angeles County's 5th District. The subject was the reopening of the case against Sirhan Bishara Sirhan. Drs. MacDonell, Guinn, and Bradford attended the proceedings and reiterated their professional observations. Strong support for the 2-gun theory came from these experts. Wolfer, Younger, and Busch all failed to appear.

A woman was seen with Sirhan Sirhan in the pantry area just prior to the assassination. She was wearing a polka-dot dress. This woman left before Kennedy entered through the swinging doors.

During the Kennedy speech that night, one campaign worker, Ms. Sandy Serrano, had left the room and gone onto the Embassy Room balcony to escape the smoke and heat of this evening of excitement. While she stood there, she saw a young woman in a white polka-dot dress go past her and into the building. She was accompanied by 2 other persons. Later, after the murder of Robert Kennedy, Ms. Serrano was "nearly run over" by these people as they left. The woman wearing the polka-dot dress shouted, "We shot him!," according to Serrano. She asked whom they had shot and the woman reportedly answered, "We shot Kennedy!"

The police produced a woman by the name of Cathy Fulmer, but Serrano did not identify her as the one she had seen. However, Fulmer was found dead in a motel room several days after Sirhan was convicted.

All of this evidence seems to cast substantial doubt on the government case against Sirhan as a lone assassin.

The Alleged Assassin: Sirhan Bishara Sirhan was born on March 19, 1944, in Jordan. When he was 13 years old, his parents brought him to the U.S.

The family resided in Pasadena, where Sirhan attended the local elementary, junior high, and high schools. He presented no disciplinary problems to his teachers or his parents.

Later he attended Pasadena City College, but dropped out when an illness struck his sister which resulted in her death. He had proved himself a responsible worker in the few jobs he'd had.

What might motivate the 26-year-old Jordanian to fire shots at the senator, even if his bullets never hit the mark they were intended for, might be the question that most troubles anyone looking at the facts.

According to his mother, Sirhan fell into strange company about 8 months prior to the assassination. Sirhan, with no history of any mental disorder, only then began to keep late hours in contrast to his earlier habits.

Doctors agree that if a subject cannot recall an act on some level of his conscious or unconscious mind, he may have been in some way behaviorally modified or programmed. Or he may be mentally very sick. It is doubtful that Sirhan's mental state was bad, but the possibility of behavioral modification or programming is still there since Sirhan has yet to be able to recall drawing a gun or firing it that night.

Since others could have been involved in the murder of Robert F. Kennedy, an investigation is strongly in order to determine the truth in this case once and for all.

—R.Rh. & B.C.

The Victim: DAN A. MITRIONE. Mitrione was a U.S. Government agent who was dispatched to Latin America as part of the U.S. Government's attempt to maintain totalitarian puppet-allies. He supposedly advised local officials on traffic safety, but his real job was to create sophisticated police states in order to minimize the possibility of popular rebellion against dictatorial régimes.

Dan Mitrione started as a cop in Richmond, Ind., in 1945. He became police chief in 1955 and joined the FBI in 1957. In 1960, under the State Department's International Cooperation Administration (predecessor of the Agency for International Development—AID), he went to Brazil to train police there in advanced counterinsurgency techniques. During his 7 "Public Safety" years in Brazil, the use of torture against opponents of the military régime became virtually routine. In addition, the Brazilian police, many of whom were trained by Mitrione, formed a vigilante "Death Squad" which disposed of over 100 "undesirables" without arrest or trial.

Documentation of Mitrione's activities has been compiled by a wide range of investigators, from religious groups to Hollywood film makers. NARMIC, a research/action arm of the American Friends Service Committee, reported that:

> . . . after training such a police force, Mitrione returned to the U.S. as a Latin America expert. In 1967 he trained foreign officers in the techniques of counterguerrilla warfare at the AID-Public Safety Police Academy in Washington, D.C. In July of 1969, Mitrione headed for South America again, this time to Uruguay for AID. He was the leader of a 4-man team of Public Safety advisors that trained 1,000 Uruguayan police in police management, patrolling, use of scientific and technical aids, antiguerrilla operations and border control. These trainees have in turn instructed an untold number of police in more outlying regions of the country.
>
> Mitrione himself, during his year-long stay, trained personnel in transportation techniques, established a police training facility and a radio network for Montevideo police, and set up a joint operations center of communications to facilitate cooperation between the police and the army.

To accomplish what he called "Uruguay's total penetration," Mitrione designed and initiated the following measures according to Costa-Gavras and Franco Solinas, authors of *State of Siege:*

> A network of spies and infiltrators in high schools and universities.
> Hidden cameras in terminals, etc., to photograph all persons traveling to socialist countries.
> An increase in the size of the city militia from 600 to 1,000 men.
> New gases, new .45-caliber machine guns, an increase in the use of shotguns.
> Inspection of all mail and publications coming from socialist countries.
> Inauguration of police training courses in the recruitment of informers, interrogation techniques, use of explosives, etc.

A legislative report of 7 Uruguayan senators reveals that torture is a "normal, frequent, and habitual occurrence" in police operations of Uruguay. The Rev. Louis Colonnese, director of the Latin American Division of the U.S. Catholic Conference, says that "the investigation showed many of the torture victims were students and labor leaders. . . ."

The Date: August, 1970.

The Event: In August, 1970, Dan A. Mitrione was abducted by the Tupamaros (MLN), a disciplined revolutionary underground in Uruguay. Despite near martial law, the authorities were unable to locate the kidnappers. Five days later the Tupamaros released a number of official documents that demonstrated Mitrione's police and FBI status. Many questions were asked by the Uruguayan Senate and press, and the story became a major international incident. The Tupamaros demanded that a large number of political prisoners be released in exchange for Mitrione's life. The Government refused. Mitrione was executed.

The world press distorted the events and painted a picture of a dedicated and benign do-gooder who was ruthlessly murdered by a gang of terrorist hoodlums. However, the true information began to leak out and Mitrione's death provided the world with a significant glimpse into the repressive nature of American "foreign aid."

The Assassins: The Tupamaros (MLN-*Movimiento de Liberación Nacional*) are a group of leftist urban guerrillas in Uruguay. Author John Gerassi describes their origins thus: ". . . The Tupamaros began as a militant sugarworkers' union group organized by Raul Sendic, a Socialist party official. After various unfruitful legal protest marches and demonstrations for better working conditions, one section of the group went underground and Sendic disappeared. Then, in July 1963, 'some unknown group' raided a rifle club. Shortly thereafter armed men began to hold up banks, raid the coffers of U.S. enterprises, and kidnap unpopular government or police officials. . . ."

The Tupamaros have also expropriated food from rich companies and turned it over to the poor. They have stolen police uniforms for use in their high-efficiency actions, and have taken incriminating documents from government and corporation offices. Their actions are accompanied by political explanations and programs for a democratic distribution of wealth and power.

Aftermath: Jerry Lewis and Frank Sinatra put on a show in Mitrione's memory. Newspapers all over the 2 Americas carried eulogies to this "defenseless human being" (White House characterization). The network news devoted a long segment to Mitrione's funeral. But they could not completely refute the documented evidence exploded by the Tupamaros. The people of Uruguay learned a deep and quick lesson about foreign domination, but the lesson was largely abstract for the U.S. public.

The U.S. Government sent FBI and CIA agents to Uruguay to extinguish the Tupamaros and suppress their wide popular support. Eventually, Green Beret "advisers" were brought in; meanwhile the U.S. was flying hundreds of Uruguayan police to the U.S. for training at advanced police centers.

The killing of Dan Anthony Mitrione definitely focused world attention on the role of U.S. "Public Safety Advisers," and perhaps it has encouraged a healthy political skepticism that could not have resulted from any lesser event.

—M.S.

The Victim: GEORGE C. WALLACE, the governor of Alabama, and a candidate for the Democratic nomination in the 1972 presidential election.

The Date: May 15, 1972.

The Event: On a sunny afternoon in Laurel, Md., at the Laurel Shopping Center, George Wallace delivered a campaign speech to a crowd assembled in the adjacent parking lot. After the speech, Wallace stepped from behind the bulletproof podium from which he had been speaking and moved out among the people to shake hands. A young man with short blond hair called to the governor several times. "Hey George, over here!" he shouted.

As George Wallace approached the people near the man, the blond youth suddenly fired a fusillade of shots toward Wallace, hitting him several times. The gunman, Arthur Herman Bremer, was grabbed almost immediately, and in the ensuing struggle, he emptied his weapon.

Three others were injured by Bremer's bullets. Capt. E. C. Dothard of the Alabama State Highway Patrol, who was severely wounded in the chest, survived. He was Wallace's personal security officer. Another bullet struck Secret Service agent Nicholas Zorvas in the throat, causing serious injury. The 3rd victim was a young volunteer campaign worker, Mrs. Dora Thompson, who was wounded in the knee.

As George Wallace lay on the hot pavement, his wife Cornelia emerged from the Equitable Trust Bank across the parking lot and fell weeping on her stricken husband. Minutes later, the authorities helped her from the scene, as a medical team took charge of the victims. Arthur Bremer was roughly led away by State and local police officials.

Wallace was taken to Holy Cross Hospital in nearby Silver Spring, where he was placed under the care of Dr. Joseph Schanno. Later Dr. Schanno reported that the Alabama governor had been shot at least 4 times. Two bullets were recovered during the immediate emergency operation. The medical team was able to control hemorrhaging and repair damage done to the intestine and intestinal ligaments. The thorax, or chest cavity, was also perforated by a bullet, and paralysis is still plaguing Gov.

George Wallace due to a bullet which lodged near the spinal column.

Although Wallace was running as a Democratic hopeful at the time of the assassination attempt, it was no secret that he fully intended to run for President of the U.S. as an American Independent if he was not nominated by the Democrats, as it appeared he would not be.

A poll taken one week before the final election asked potential voters whom they would have voted for had George Wallace not dropped out of the race after he was shot. The results were: Nixon, 44%; McGovern, 41%; Wallace, 15%. Wallace had been Nixon's big stumbling block. The election probably would have been sent to the House of Representatives, where Wallace would have had considerable bargaining power. As it was, almost all of Wallace's supporters shifted their votes to Richard Nixon, enabling him to win a landslide victory in November.

The Would-Be Assassin: Arthur Herman Bremer was a janitor's assistant at Story Elementary School and also a busboy at the Milwaukee Athletic Club until he quit these jobs some 18 weeks prior to the attempt on the life of Governor Wallace. Bremer had taken on these jobs when he left home soon after his 21st birthday in 1971. For the short period that he worked in 1971–1972, Bremer's records show that his total earnings were $1,611.

On September 14, 1971, Bremer purchased a 1967 Rambler for approximately $800. He rented an apartment on West Michigan Avenue in Milwaukee on October 15, 1971, for $138 per month. In January of 1971, Bremer had purchased his 1st firearm, a .38-caliber revolver.

On November 18, 1971, Bremer was arrested for the 1st time in his life. He was sitting in his car, which was parked in a "NO PARKING" zone. Next to him on the seat was some ammunition. He was approached by a police officer and upon being questioned about the boxes of bullets, he showed the officer his .38. He was originally charged with carrying a concealed weapon, but then the charge was reduced to disorderly conduct. The police department confiscated his weapon.

On January 13, 1972, Bremer bought a new gun, another .38 revolver. He had also acquired a 9-mm., 14-shot, semiautomatic Browning pistol, at some point before the assassination attempt on Wallace.

On March 1, 1972, Arthur H. Bremer began his tour along the Wallace campaign trail by attending an organizational meeting for Wallace at the Pfister Hotel in Milwaukee. On the 23rd, he appeared at the Downtowner for a $25 per plate benefit dinner for Wallace and was seen at a Wallace rally that night. He also showed up at a Humphrey rally during his pilgrimage, on April 3, 1972. On the 4th, he attended a Wallace victory party in the ballroom of the Holiday Inn Midtown.

He then began to travel out of State to political affairs; on April 7 and 8, 1972, Bremer was a guest at the exclusive Waldorf-Astoria Hotel in New York, where Hubert Humphrey was also staying. From there, he moved to the Lord Elgin in Ottawa, Canada, another aristocrat among hotels. On April 15–18, he patronized the Sheraton Motor Inn in New Carrollton, Md. On May 10, he attended a Wallace rally in Cadillac, Mich., where he sat with a neatly dressed man about 40 years old, who has remained unidentified. Bremer was next reported at a Wallace rally in Landover, Md., and then was seen back in Michigan again on May 12 and 13 at the Reid Hotel in Kalamazoo for yet another Wallace rally.

All of this traveling would seem to be far beyond the means of an unemployed janitor's assistant and former part-time busboy. It is obvious that Bremer's 18-week trip was financed by resources other than his own. It has been established that his parents did not contribute any of the money he used during his travels or spent for the guns, ammunition, clothes, and records that were found in his possession at the time of his arrest. When arrested, he claimed to be ". . . only worth about $300." It is surprising that he would have had even that much considering that a conservative estimate of his expenses while tailing Wallace is $5,000.

Artie Bremer was described time and again as a "loner." Despite that description by certain of his acquaintances and by *Life* magazine, Bremer was constantly in the company of several individuals just prior to the assassination attempt.

One of these individuals has been identified as Mr. Dennis Cassini. Before any officials could question Cassini after the murder attempt on Wallace, he was found dead of a heroin overdose, his body locked in the trunk of his automobile. The Milwaukee officials reported this incident to the Federal Bureau of Investigation. No attempt was made by the Federal authorities, then under the direction of L. Patrick Gray, to investigate this matter further.

Bremer was also seen with an older, heavyset gentleman in the waiting room of the Chesapeake and Ohio Ferry in Ludington, Mich. He was described by the attendant as having a "New Joisey brogue." Mr. Roger Gordon, a former member of the Secret Army Organization (SAO), a government intelligence agency, identified Bremer's ferry contact as a Mr. Anthony Ulasewicz, a White House operative who would become well-known in the Watergate hearings. Gordon has since left this country.

It has been reported that Charles W. Colson ordered E. Howard Hunt (both also of Watergate fame) to break into Bremer's apartment within an hour of the shooting, and plant Black Panther party newspapers and Angela Davis literature there. A small news service employee carried out the Colson assignment. Wallace was interviewed by Barbara Walters of the *Today* show. In reference to the break-in, the governor said:

> So I just wondered, if that were the case, how did anyone know where he lived within an hour after I was shot? I myself didn't know who shot me until several days later, but of course, I wouldn't know because I was in a condition not to know.

Knowledge of the suspect's identity and the location of his apartment so soon could possibly indicate prior knowledge of the incident.

All of these points could further indicate that the "loner," Arthur Herman Bremer, might well have been in collusion with some other party or parties in the attempt on the life of Gov. George C. Wallace. However, no further investigation is planned at the official level at this time.

—R.Rh. & B.C.

The FBI's All-Time Ten Most Wanted Fugitives List

REVEALING THE CHANGING PICTURE
OF VIOLENCE IN THE U.S.A.

TO BEGIN WITH: The dark side of America has long fascinated its citizens, and coupled with their penchant for rankings, what could be more natural than an all-star roster of the nation's most brutal, brilliant, and audacious criminals? Created in 1950 after discussions be-tween the late J. Edgar Hoover and the International News Service, the FBI's Ten Most Wanted list aimed at capturing the nation's most menacing desperadoes through extensive publicity. To get on the list, a fugitive's past criminal record, the nature of his deeds, and his potential threat to the community were—and still are—reviewed. Occasionally, the list has been expanded to include a particularly pressing case, such as the 1961 manhunt for a West Coast butcher-murderer, and the 1968 dragnet for James Earl Ray after the Dr. Martin Luther King assassination. And while the list can claim some of America's top public enemies, there are some, such as John Dillinger, whose activities terrorized citizens before the list's inception.

Nevertheless, an overview of the roster in the 24 years of its existence provides a curious and revealing picture of lawlessness in America. What follows is a selection of the FBI's hit parade of crime.

Most Wanted, 1950

HENRY RANDOLPH MITCHELL. *Crime:* Wanted in connection with a Florida bank robbery. *Conclusion:* Mitchell was never apprehended and the Federal warrant against him was dismissed July 18, 1958. He was the last of the original Ten Most Wanted to be removed from the list.

WILLIAM RAYMOND NESBIT. *Crime:* Wanted for a $37,000 jewel robbery and the murder of his partner, who he allegedly blew up in a powder shack with 3,500 lbs. of dynamite and 7,000 lbs. of black powder. The blast reportedly broke windows 5 mi. away. *Conclusion:* Nesbit went to prison for murder, but escaped. He holed up in a cave beside the Mississippi River in St. Paul, but was nabbed after some neighborhood boys recognized his "wanted" picture in a newspaper.

Most Wanted, 1951

ERNEST TAIT. *Crime:* Burglary. *Conclusion:* Tait was one of the few "elite" who made the Ten Most Wanted list twice. The 1st time was in 1951 after he was identified as one of 2 men involved in burglarizing an Elks lodge in New Castle, Ind. Tait was captured within 24 hours of his addition to the FBI list. He pleaded guilty to charges of 2nd-degree burglary and was sentenced to serve 2 to 5 years in prison. In 1960, Tait's name appeared a 2nd time on the FBI-list—again for burglary. He was susequently apprehended.

Most Wanted, 1952

NICK GEORGE MONTOS. *Crime:* "Little Nick" was originally put on the FBI list after he and 2 accomplices robbed an elderly man and his sister in Georgia. The search for Montos also implicated him as a key member of a Chicago-based burglary ring. The FBI listed Montos on its Most Wanted list again in 1956, after the master burglar turned escape artist and broke out of the Mississippi prison. *Conclusion:* When Montos was captured in

1954, he described himself to arresting agents as a "continental" burglar. Three months after his breakout in 1956, the FBI surrounded a motel room where Montos was holed up and forced him out with tear gas. He was eventually given additional sentences for firearms violations and the Georgia robbery.

Most Wanted, 1953

JOHN RALEIGH COOKE. *Crime:* Armed robbery. *Conclusion:* Apprehended in Detroit, telling agents it was a "relief" to be caught.

JOSEPH JAMES BRLETIC. *Crime:* Prison escape. *Conclusion:* Brletic tried to lose himself in the tiny California town of Lancaster, but was arrested there February 10 after intense media publicity when he made the Most Wanted list.

JOSEPH LEVY. *Crime:* An expert con man, Levy was wanted for bilking hundreds of victims from New England to the Mexican border. One of his favorite bad-check schemes was to buy expensive gifts for then Vice-President Richard M. Nixon, writing the check for more than the purchase and pocketing the difference. *Conclusion:* He was arrested almost at the exact moment his name was being added to the FBI list, thus giving him the all-time record for being on the list the shortest period of time.

CHESTER DAVENPORT. *Crime:* He made the FBI list after escaping from an Oklahoma prison where he was serving a sentence for cattle rustling, kidnapping, and prison escape. *Conclusion:* When Davenport was arrested, his hands were too busy for him to reach for his gun—he was milking a cow on a California farm.

Most Wanted, 1954

ALEX WHITMORE. *Crime:* Assault and robbery. *Conclusion:* A nervous Whitmore told FBI agents during his arrest in Seattle that he was "scared" and "knew it was just a matter of time" before he was picked up.

Most Wanted, 1955

GEORGE LESTER BELEW. *Crime:* Forgery, kidnapping, and prison escape. *Conclusion:* Arrested after an alert Illinois motel keeper recognized Belew's picture from an FBI handout.

Most Wanted, 1958

QUAY CLEON KILBURN. *Crime:* Prison escape, robbery, and embezzlement. *Conclusion:* Another of the select few who made the list more than once. Kilburn was captured in 1958 after being on the list less than 2 months. He again found himself a Most Wanted Fugitive in 1964 after escaping from prison, and was captured 3 months later.

Most Wanted, 1959

JOSEPH LLOYD THOMAS. *Crime:* Bank robbery, Federal parole violation. *Conclusion:* Thomas is the latest "double entry" on the FBI's list. He was 1st named in 1959 and then again put on in 1969. Agents apprehended him in 1970.

Most Wanted, 1960

JOSEPH CORBETT, JR. *Crime:* Wanted in the sensational kidnap-murder of Colorado beer baron, Adolph Coors III. *Conclusion:* Corbett led agents on a transcontinental chase that began in California, included Atlantic City, and ended in Vancouver, B.C. Corbett was convicted of murder and sentenced to life imprisonment.

STANLEY WILLIAM FITZGERALD. *Crime:* Shooting a "boozing buddy" in Truckee, Calif. *Conclusion:* His well-publicized weakness for singing sentimental Irish lullabies led to his capture. After a lusty presentation in a Colorado bar, he was quickly traced to Portland where he was apprehended.

Most Wanted, 1961

RICHARD LAURENCE MARQUETTE. *Crime:* His hatchet murder of a young Oregon woman terrorized West Coast citizens when portions of her body were found in his refrigerator and on the lawns of Portland homes. *Conclusion:* Public anxiety over the "butcher slaying" prompted the FBI to expand its list for the 1st time to more than 10 fugitives to include Marquette. Captured and brought to trial, he was found guilty of 1st-degree murder, and sentenced to a life term.

HUGH BION MORSE. *Crime:* Intent to murder his estranged wife. *Conclusion:* Friday, October 13, proved to be unlucky for Morse. On that day, a neighbor of his from St. Paul recognized Morse's picture at FBI headquarters in Washington. He was arrested minutes later and his subsequent admission to several unsolved murders led to his imprisonment for life.

Most Wanted, 1962

BOBBY RANDELL WILCOXSON and ALBERT FREDERICK NUSSBAUM. *Crime:* Wanted for murder and multiple bank robberies and bombing incidents in Washington, D.C. *Conclusion:* This pair caused one of the FBI's greatest manhunts. Nussbaum was seized early in November after a high-speed chase through rain-slicked Buffalo streets. He was craftily disguised and armed with a rifle and 2 hand grenades. Wilcoxson was arrested less than a week later after emerging from a Baltimore, Md., hideout with a girl friend. Intense media publicity and the cooperation of relatives led to their capture.

FRANCIS LAVERNE BRANNAN. *Crime:* Sought for the shotgun slaying of an elderly Illinois widow. *Conclusion:* Brannan called in desperation to the Miami FBI office for agents to "Come and get me, I'm tired of running."

WATSON YOUNG, JR. *Crime:* Young was added to the FBI list after escaping from a mental hospital and allegedly perpetrating a rape and double murder. *Conclusion:* He was known for his deep interest in funeral homes and, true to form, was arrested by Salina, Kans., police behind the wheel of a stolen funeral home ambulance, its red light flashing and siren blaring.

MICHAEL JOSEPH O'CONNOR. *Crime:* Wanted for the shooting death of an acquaintance in a tavern brawl. *Conclusion:* He was arrested 15 days after being placed on the Top Ten list. Convicted of 1st-degree murder, O'Connor was sentenced to life imprisonment.

Most Wanted, 1963

JERRY CLARENCE RUSH. *Crime:* Charged with taking over $100,000 in a Perth Amboy, N.J., bank robbery, and with escape from a Maryland prison. *Conclusion:* Rush reportedly used the bank loot for a high-living, fast-spending cross-country honeymoon. He was arrested near Miami after attempting to enter his brand-new luxury automobile. Rush was sentenced to 29 years in prison on a bank robbery conviction.

BEN GOLDEN McCOLLUM. *Crime:* Murder and robbery. *Conclusion:* Found dead in his Kentucky home after being gunned down by 2 robbers.

LEROY AMBROSIA FRAZIER. *Crime:* Escape from a Washington, D.C., prison after a long record of criminal convictions highlighted by violence. *Conclusion:* After his many crimes, Frazier went underground. His attempt to embark on another way of life in a contracting business was thwarted by publicity from a Cleveland newspaper.

HOWARD JAY BARNARD. *Crime:* Robbery. *Conclusion:* Barnard, described by the FBI as a "Houdini-like escape expert" was apprehended by Sacramento, Calif., police in 1964 after he was shot in the leg while fleeing the scene of a robbery. True to form, he was disguised in actor's makeup and fake blond hair, with cotton stuffed in his nose and mouth to distort his facial contours.

Most Wanted, 1964

GEORGE ZAVADA. *Crime:* Multiple bank robberies, including a $73,000 holdup. *Conclu-*

sion: Zavada, whose nickname "the King" so fascinated him that he had it embroidered on his underwear, was the mastermind behind a rash of California bank heists which ended when FBI agents wounded him in a gun battle. Zavada was sentenced to 46 consecutive years in prison, but he died of natural causes at Leavenworth in 1965.

JOSEPH FRANCIS BRYAN, JR. *Crime:* Multiple kidnap-murder of young boys. *Conclusion:* Two weeks after inclusion on the Ten Most Wanted list, Bryan was nabbed in New Orleans. He got a life sentence.

JESSE JAMES GILBERT. *Crime:* Charged with robbing an Alhambra, Calif., bank and killing a police officer while fleeing; prison escape. *Conclusion:* FBI agents seized him at night on a Philadelphia street corner. He was in heavy disguise and refused to admit his identity until a fingerprint check removed any doubt.

JOHN GIBSON DILLON. *Crime:* "Matt" Dillon was wanted for bail-jumping and dealing in narcotics, for which he could have received 190 years in prison. *Conclusion:* His badly decomposed body was found, wired to several hundred lbs. of weights, at the bottom of a well in a remote farm in Oklahoma. Positive identification was made by dental charts.

THOMAS HADDER. *Crime:* An accomplished escape artist, Hadder was also wanted for the killing of a Maryland police officer. *Conclusion:* FBI agents seized him as he watched a singalong in a Salvation Army Center in Oklahoma.

WILLIAM HUTTON COBLE. *Crime:* Wanted for numerous bank robberies, and escaping from a Nashville jail. *Conclusion:* A wild gun battle preceded Coble's capture by FBI agents after an attempted robbery of a Charlotte, N.C., bank. He was sentenced to 15 years in a Federal prison for robbery.

JACK CLOUSER. *Crime:* The "Florida Fox" spent more than 10 years on the FBI Most Wanted list after escaping from a mental institution in 1964, where he had been confined after being convicted of kidnapping, robbery, and assault. *Conclusion:* This former Orlando, Fla., police officer turned himself in August 22, 1974, saying he was tired of running. During his decade of eluding authorities, Clouser frequently wrote letters to law enforcement officials, and once taunted the late FBI director J. Edgar Hoover for "sleeping with a night light."

Most Wanted, 1965

EDWARD OWEN WATKINS. *Crime:* Wanted in 13 bank robberies. *Conclusion:* Watkins was captured in 1966, along with his stripteaser

bride, in Florence, Mont., after they had reportedly lived a luxurious life of eating in swank restaurants and patronizing nightclubs and gambling halls. After pleading guilty to a number of charges, he was sentenced to 2 45-year terms.

GARLAND WILLIAM DANIELS. *Crime:* A notorious bad-check artist, also wanted for violating a conditional prison release. *Conclusion:* Died of an apparent heart attack in Dallas. Identified through a fingerprint examination.

WALTER LEE PARMAN. *Crime:* A massive nationwide search was launched for Parman after he was charged in the brutal strangulation-murder of a Washington, D.C., secretary. *Conclusion:* He was traced to a Los Angeles apartment where he was living under an alias. Parman was convicted of 1st-degree murder and sentenced to life imprisonment, but later escaped.

LESLIE DOUGLAS ASHLEY. *Crime:* A mental hospital escapee charged with a brutal murder. *Conclusion:* Agents captured him in Atlanta where he was working as "Bobo the Clown" in a traveling carnival.

SAMUEL and EARL VENEY. *Crime:* This 1st brother team to be named to the list was wanted for a bloody crime spree in Baltimore. A police lieutenant was shot while investigating an armed robbery, and a police sergeant investigating the 1st shooting was found gunned down the next day. Samuel was charged in the 2nd slaying, while Earl was charged with attempting to murder the lieutenant. *Conclusion:* They were captured together at Garden City, N.Y.

WARREN CLEVELAND OSBORNE. *Crime:* Charged in the murder of a Nashville beauty shop operator. *Conclusion:* Killed in an auto crash near Mount Washington, Ky., during a high-speed chase by local officers. He was on the Most Wanted list 3 weeks.

Most Wanted, 1966

CHARLES LORIN GOVE. *Crime:* Wanted for bank robbery and prison escape. *Conclusion:* FBI agents plucked him out of a Mardi Gras crowd in New Orleans the same day his name was added to the fugitives' list.

ROBERT CLAYTON BUICK. *Crime:* Charged in a series of California bank robberies. *Conclusion:* This part-time bullfighter was apprehended 5 days after he was added to the list.

DONALD ROGERS SMELLEY. *Crime:* Armed robbery. *Conclusion:* Smelley vowed not to be taken alive. He was, however, finally seized by agents in Hollywood, Calif.

EVERETT LEROY BIGGS. *Crime:* Bank robbery and armed robbery. *Conclusion:* Biggs was taken by surprise outside his Colorado hideout.

Most Wanted, 1967

JAMES ROBERT RINGROSE. *Crime:* Wanted for passing bad checks on an international scale. *Conclusion:* Ringrose was picked up in Osaka, Japan, when he tried to cash a fraudulent check. He served a sentence in a Japanese jail before being returned to U.S. authorities. His flight of more than 7,000 mi. earns him the record for distance traveled while a fugitive.

FLORENCIO LOPEZ MATIONG and VICTOR JERALD BONO. *Crime:* They were wanted in the brutal murder of 2 U.S. Border Patrol officers who had detected the pair smuggling drugs. *Conclusion:* Both fugitives were captured at the same time after tear gas canisters were lobbed into their Los Angeles apartment hideout.

HENRY THEODORE YOUNG. *Crime:* This convicted bank robber earned the reputation of being one of the most cold-blooded prisoners at Alcatraz penitentiary. He was sought by the FBI after escaping from a minimum security prison in Washington State. *Conclusion:* Young assumed an alias and lived an unobtrusive life in Kansas City. The FBI flushed him out on a citizen's tip after the man saw Young's picture in a detective magazine. He was not prosecuted for the escape since he was serving a life sentence for murder.

ALFRED JOHNSON COOPER, JR. *Crime:* Charged with shooting a police officer, kidnapping, and fleeing prosecution for robbery. *Conclusion:* Cooper briefly enjoyed a new identity and life-style while fleeing authorities. When FBI agents captured him in Boston he was using the name Joe Brady, and had even boxed in a "Golden Gloves" tournament under that name.

Most Wanted, 1968

RUTH EISEMANN-SCHIER and GARY STEVEN KRIST. *Crime:* Sought in the bizarre kidnapping of Barbara Jane Mackle, who was found barely alive buried in a "capsule" designed to sustain her underground for a week. *Conclusion:* Eisemann-Schier, the 1st woman ever to be named as a Most Wanted fugitive, was arrested in 1969 after she had applied for a nursing service job and her fingerprints were routinely turned over to the FBI. Her alleged kidnapping accomplice, Krist, was apprehended in a crocodile-infested Florida swamp just 2 days after his addition to the list. Most of the $500,000 ransom money was found in the runabout boat Krist had abandoned. Krist was convicted of kidnapping, and sentenced to life imprisonment. Eisemann-Schier pleaded guilty to kidnapping and received a 7-year sentence.

JAMES EARL RAY. *Crime:* This reputed "loner" achieved notoriety when charged with the assassination of Dr. Martin Luther King, Jr. He became the 2nd "11th" Most Wanted fugitive. *Conclusion:* Ray, whose deed triggered some of the most violent rioting in American history, pleaded guilty to murdering Dr. King after he was captured by British authorities. News of Ray's capture, however, had to compete with bulletins concerning another assassination victim—Robert F. Kennedy, who was being buried that day. Ray twice attempted to escape from his maximum-security cell in a Tennessee prison, failing both times.

PHILLIP MORRIS JONES. *Crime:* Wanted for bank robbery in California, Florida, and Maryland. *Conclusion:* In the nearly 3 decades of the Most Wanted list's existence, he was the 1st "Jones" to be named. He surrendered to FBI agents at San Mateo, Calif.

RICHARD LEE TINGLER, JR. *Crime:* Earned the reputation of being one of the most cold-blooded killers in Ohio after he was connected to the murders of 2 teen-agers in a dairy store, and the subsequent slaying of 4 Cleveland residents, whose bodies were found buried in a neat row in a city park. *Conclusion:* Was apprehended following extensive publicity, including a description on the television program, "The FBI." Tingler was convicted of murder and sentenced to death, but because of changing attitudes regarding capital punishment, he was confined in death row at the Columbus penitentiary.

MONROE HICKSON. *Crime:* Convicted of multiple murders; wanted for prison escape. *Conclusion:* Hickson apparently died of "various diseases," according to the FBI. All but his hands and forearms had been cremated, but these remains were identified by fingerprints.

BYRON JAMES RICE. *Crime:* Charged with murdering an armored car guard. *Conclusion:* Surrendered to FBI agents in Chicago in 1972. He was subsequently sentenced to life imprisonment.

RONALD EUGENE STORCK. *Crime:* Charged with murdering 3 members of a Pennsylvania family. *Conclusion:* His was a leap-year arrest that came on February 29 in Waikiki, the 1st apprehension of a Top Tenner in Hawaii.

CHARLES LEE HERRON. *Crime:* Charged in the killing of a Nashville policeman. *Conclusion:* Herron had never been convicted for a crime previously. Although the FBI usually requires a real criminal record before placing a fugitive on the Top Ten list, the bureau made an exception in this case since Herron carried considerable amounts of inflammatory racial literature in his car.

Most Wanted, 1969

MARIE DEAN ARRINGTON. *Crime:* Sought for prison escape, when she was awaiting execution in the brutal murder of a Florida legal secretary. The victim's bullet-riddled body was also crushed when it was run over by an auto several times. *Conclusion:* The 2nd female to make the FBI's Top Ten list, Arrington was apprehended in New Orleans in 1971.

BILLIE AUSTIN BRYANT. *Crime:* It was Bryant's dubious distinction to have been the 1st fugitive responsible for the death of 2 agents since a 1934 gun battle between the FBI and Baby Face Nelson. The FBI men were shot while pursuing Bryant following a bank robbery. *Conclusion:* He was sentenced to life imprisonment for murder.

CAMERON DAVID BISHOP. *Crime:* Wanted in the alleged sabotage of 4 power transmission towers in Colorado. *Conclusion:* Bishop, who was a member of the radical Students for a Democratic Society, was the 1st so-called "revolutionary" to be placed on the list. The drift into a new area of pursuit by the FBI reflected the changing social tenor of a country whose campuses and ghettos were racked with dissent and violence. Bishop, like many extremist fugitives, disappeared into an accepting and somewhat organized underground, which provided a protection not usually afforded to the traditional FBI fugitive. On March 12, 1975, authorities apprehended Bishop in Rhode Island.

BENJAMIN HOSKINS PADDOCK. *Crime:* Prison escape. *Conclusion:* Paddock was serving a 20-year sentence for bank robbery when he escaped from the Federal Correctional Institution at La Tuna, Tex., on December 31, 1968. Paddock is still at large, and according to the FBI he is "diagnosed as psychopathic" and "reportedly has suicidal tendencies."

Most Wanted, 1970

LAWRENCE R. PLAMONDON. *Crime:* Plamondon, the "Minister of Defense" of the revolutionary White Panther party, was accused of bombing a CIA office in Ann Arbor, Mich. *Conclusion:* He was apprehended with the help of the computerized National Crime Information Center, the 1st Top Ten fugitive arrested under the system.

BERNADINE RAE DOHRN. *Crime:* Wanted for mob action, riot, and conspiracy in an alleged bombing plot in Flint, Mich., and a series of violent demonstrations in Chicago put on by the militant Weathermen faction of the SDS. *Conclusion:* Dohrn shared the Top Ten title with 15 others that year, as the list became inflated to an all-time peak with the inclusion of radical fugitives. The Government dropped the bombing indictment against her in

1973, and her name was removed from the list.

HUBERT GEROID BROWN. *Crime:* H. Rap Brown, as he was called, was a black militant who headed the Student National Coordinating Committee. He was charged with avoiding prosecution for arson and incitement to riot. *Conclusion:* He was shot and captured in New York City in 1971 during a police gun battle after an aborted holdup.

ANGELA YVONNE DAVIS. *Crime:* Wanted in connection with the murders of a judge and 3 prison inmates during an attempt to free "Soledad Brother" George Jackson in Marin County, Calif. *Conclusion:* The hunt for Davis, a self-avowed communist who was also black, beautiful, and brilliant, stirred up intense public interest. Two months after she was named as the 3rd woman on the FBI's list, Davis was taken in a New York City motel. She was acquitted by an all-white jury after a trial that lasted more than 3 months.

KARELTON LEWIS ARMSTRONG, DWIGHT ALAN ARMSTRONG, LEO FREDERICK BURT, and DAVID SYLVAN FINE. *Crime:* Sought for sabotage, destruction of government property, and conspiracy in the bombing of a University of Wisconsin building that killed a researcher and injured several others. They were all members of the radical SDS. *Conclusion:* Karelton Lewis Armstrong was captured in Toronto in 1972, but the others—including Fine, who at 18 was the youngest ever on the list—were not caught.

SUSAN EDITH SAXE and KATHERINE ANN POWER. *Crime:* Identified by the FBI as members of an unnamed revolutionary group, they were charged in the murder of a Boston police officer following a bank robbery. *Conclusion:* Three experienced criminals, whom the women allegedly helped in the bank robbery, were captured within a week, but the girls remained at large. (However, in March, 1975, Susan Saxe was arrested; Katherine Ann Power is still sought by authorities.) The fact that the Most Wanted list had grown to 16 names, prompted a *New York Times* writer to comment, "Whatever its record with ordinary criminals, the FBI isn't too hot at catching the new breed of fugitive."

Most Wanted, 1973

HERMAN BELL. *Crime:* Wanted in the killing of 2 police officers, and the robbery of a San Francisco bank. *Conclusion:* Bell, a leader of the Black Liberation Army, was taken without resistance on a New Orleans street.

Most Wanted, 1974

JOHN EDWARD COPELAND, JR. *Crime:* Rape, robbery, kidnapping. *Conclusion:* Along with an accomplice, Copeland was sought for multiple rapes, robberies, and kidnappings in California in mid-1973. Copeland's accomplice was apprehended but Copeland remains at large.

Most Wanted, 1975

BILLY DEAN ANDERSON. *Crime:* In January, 1974, a grand jury in Fentress County, Tenn., indicted Anderson for assault with intent to commit murder, attempted burglary, use of a deadly weapon in commission of a felony, and being a habitual criminal. *Conclusion:* Anderson escaped from the maximum security section of the Morgan County, Tenn., jail on August 6, 1974. Authorities are still searching for Anderson, whose criminal career spans almost 20 years.

As a side note: For all its interest in radical fugitives at the close of the stormy '60s, the FBI never added the names of those involved in the bizarre Patty Hearst kidnapping to the list. As one field agent put it, "They simply didn't qualify."

To END WITH: More than 320 fugitives have been on the list since 1950, their crimes ranging from the most brutal murders to sophisticated bank robberies. A composite of all the Top Tenners would be a 5' 9" male, weighing 167 lbs., who is 37 years old. An average fugitive would be on the list about 145 days, and his capture would take place some 960 mi.

from the scene of his crime. Most have lengthy criminal records, have served prison terms, and have been the recipient of some type of judicial leniency. Until the 1970s, when the FBI ran into heavy criticism for the preponderance of extremists on its list, the bureau apprehended an average of 15 Top Tenners each year. Between 1970 and 1973, however, only 12 were caught. The radical fugitives, who dominated the list at its peak of 16 names in 1970, were able to disappear easily into a far-flung and well-knit underground. The traditional fugitive had no such option. Aside from generating accusations that the FBI was becoming an American Gestapo, some observers argued that the expanded lists did more harm to the program than good by diluting its impact. Still, with over 300 captures to its credit, the Most Wanted list and the FBI have proven to be valuable crime-fighting tools. As for the charges of suppression, former FBI director Hoover wrote:

We are forever in the unenviable position of the policeman being assaulted by the mob. The FBI agent neither enacts the law nor judges the legality of it, but it is usually he, and he alone, who must dodge the brickbats hurled by those protesting it.

—J.B.

10

War

Famous Battles in History—Land, Sea, and Air

MARATHON, 490 B.C.

The plan of Persian King Darius called for the landing of 20,000 men on the Plain of Marathon to defeat the armies of the Greek city-states before mustering an assault against Athens itself. His strong force of infantry, cavalry, and archers achieved a beachhead and adopted defensive positions, awaiting an offensive assault by an Athenian Army of approximately 10,000, who were primarily infantrymen.

The Athenian commander, Miltiades, bided his time, felling trees and dragging them forward to narrow the open distance of one mile between the 2 armies and to establish obstacles for the Persian cavalry. Hearing that the enemy troopers had left the scene temporarily, presumably to water their horses at the springs to the north, Miltiades seized his opportunity. He discarded the conventional method of Greek phalanx attack—a slow and deliberate approach—and ordered a charge on the dead run. His men took the Persian archers completely by surprise, and their long-range arrows fell harmlessly behind the attacking Greeks. The latter closed quickly upon the hapless Persian infantry, now unprotected either by cavalry or the archers, and annihilated them. Miltiades' men, in hand-to-hand combat, armed with long spears and wearing protective bronze armor, were easily able to defeat the Persians, who had neither body armor nor adequate shields to protect themselves against the weapon thrusts of the onrushing Athenians. As the opposing forces met, the Greek flanks, where Miltiades had placed great strength, hurled back the Persian infantry and then swept inward to crush the Persian center with a pincers maneuver.

Unable to stem the Athenian charge, the Persian commander, Datis, fell back to the beach and reboarded the waiting Persian ships, hoping to sail around to the western coast of Attica and fall upon the unprotected city of Athens. Miltiades, foreseeing the Persian plan, took his men on a forced night march across the country to Athens. When the Persian fleet arrived the next morning, it found the Athenian Army poised on the high ground, ready to duplicate its victory of the day before. Dismayed, Datis abandoned his campaign and returned to Asia, leaving 6,400 dead behind him.

The victory was total for the Greeks. They lost only 192 men, who were buried on the Plain of Marathon. The burial was contrary to the usual custom in which the remains of men who had died for their country were brought to Athens for burial in the Cerameicus sepulcher. At Marathon, however, the victory was deemed so great that the slain were honored with burial on the field of battle.

—W.K.

THERMOPYLAE, 480 B.C.

In 480 B.C. Xerxes, ruler of the mighty Persian Empire, invaded Greece with over 100,000 men. He sought to avenge the Persian defeat at Marathon and to remove a developing commercial and naval competitor.

The Persian threat forced the Greek city-states to band together for the 1st time in their history. They sent an allied force north to contain the Persians. The Spartans, wishing to defend their homeland, sent a tithe of only 300 men under King Leonidas. The famous 300 formed the nucleus of the 5,000 Greeks who marched to Thermopylae.

Outnumbered, the Greeks had to rely on defensive tactics. The most easily defended location was the narrow pass at Thermopylae. Leonidas occupied it and sent 1,000 Phocaeans to defend the mountain pass on his flank. The Persians advanced rapidly through northern Greece, meeting no resistance, so the sudden appearance of a Greek Army surprised them. Xerxes halted his great army in front of the pass for 4 days.

On the 5th day, Xerxes confidently sent his Medes and Cissans forward. But the lightly armored Persian forces were no match for the heavily armored Greek hoplites. Stunned by his 1st setback, Xerxes flung wave after wave of his troops into battle. Each force was decimated by the long spears of the protected Greeks and by the savage Spartan defense. Xerxes even committed his crack troops—the Immortals. But these too were repulsed by the hoplite hedgehog of spears.

The mighty Persian Army stagnated in front of the immovable Greek wall. Xerxes was at a loss until a Greek named Malis offered to guide the Persians over a mountain pass to the Greek rear. Persian soldiers streamed along the path until they were suddenly met by the Phocaeans stationed there for just such an emergency. The Persians were dismayed at finding Greeks disputing their way but attacked them fiercely. The Phocaeans mistakenly believed they were being attacked by the whole Persian Army and withdrew to a stronger position in the hills.

The Persians were ecstatic. The path lay open and the Greeks were doomed. Leonidas ordered a retreat. With a final gesture of defense he remained behind with his Spartans to cover the retreat. Attacked from all sides, the tiny Greek force was annihilated and the road to southern Greece lay open.

—W.L.S.

ACTIUM, 31 B.C.

The fate of Europe was determined by history's decisive Battle of Actium. Had the naval forces of Antony and Cleopatra beaten those of Julius Caesar's adopted son, Octavian, then Alexandria, Egypt, would have become the capital of the Roman Empire and the non-Christian axis of European culture.

After Caesar's murder in 44 B.C. at the hands of jealous conspirators, a triumvirate was formed with Emperor Octavian governing the west, and Lepidus governing Carthagenian Africa. Antony's plum was the glamorous east—and Cleopatra. The conspirators wanted a republic governed by a people-owned Senate. Octavian and Lepidus could accept this, but Antony leaned strongly toward perpetuation of a divine emperorship. Two subsequent battles followed at Philippi where the republican army commanded by Cassius and Brutus—ringleaders of the murder conspiracy—was de-

feated. That settled the question. Rome would have an autocracy.

Octavian proceeded to incite the Senate to declare war on Cleopatra, but not on Antony. This divisive scheme didn't work. As a team, Antony and Cleopatra moved their land and naval forces to Actium, on the south side of the Gulf of Ambracia, in order to set up a fortified base. They expected to fight Octavian later, but that was in the future and they assumed that they would be ready.

On September 2, 31 B.C., the 2 navies engaged in battle. Octavian had the advantage. His ships were smaller and more maneuverable. When defeat seemed imminent, Cleopatra, for reasons known only to her, withdrew with her 60 ships, leaving Antony unsupported. Then, in a small galley, Antony recklessly abandoned his forces to follow Cleopatra. Octavian was the undisputed victor.

A year later, when Octavian invaded Egypt, Antony—led to believe that Cleopatra was dead—committed suicide. On finding out that Octavian planned a victory march through the streets of Rome displaying her as a captive, Cleopatra—very much alive—chose her lover's way out.

On returning to Rome, Octavian stepped down, turning the reins of government over to the Senate and the people. They responded by honoring him with both the title of "Augustus" and the rank of tribune for life. Octavian thus became the 1st Emperor of the Roman Empire.

—F.M.W.

TOURS, 732

In 732 a large Arab Army crossed the Pyrenees and invaded France. Commanded by the Yemenite Abd-ar-Rahman, it defeated a rebellious Moslem kingdom ruled by the Berber Othman.

Abd-ar-Rahman then pushed north, routing the forces of Eudo, Duke of Aquitaine, an ally of Othman. The vanquished Eudo was forced to seek aid from his bitter enemy, Charles Martel. Charles cooperated because the Arabs were penetrating further north, leaving plundered towns and monasteries behind them.

The Arabs advanced toward the heart of France, lured by the wealthy monasteries of St. Hilaire and St. Martin. After gutting St. Hilaire, they rode up the Roman road toward Tours. Somewhere south of the town they met Charles and his Frankish Army.

For 7 days the 2 armies sat facing each other. The Franks were waiting for additional levies, and the Arabs were trying to move their spoils to safety. Then the Arabs attacked.

With a bolstered force that totaled 30,000 men, Charles arrayed his men to receive the Arab charge. The Franks, mainly infantrymen, were heavily armored with swords, axes, javelins, and a small throwing ax called the francisca. The Arab Army totaled nearly 80,000 and was composed entirely of light cavalry. Extremely fast and mobile, the cavalry relied on the lance and sword. Because the Arabs were an offensive unit they were forced to attack the Franks or retreat south without their loot. The conquerors of Spain refused to flee before a smaller untried army, so they charged the Frankish lines.

The Franks unflinchingly received the Moslem charge, fending it off. The Arabs attacked repeatedly, searching for a weakness in the Franks' line. But the Frankish Army was like a wall against which the Arabs quickly pounded themselves to pieces.

As Arab stamina faded, the Franks counterattacked. The Arab flank was turned by an avengeful Eudo and his men from Aquitaine. Abd-ar-Rahman was killed while trying to rally his broken army. Next morning the Franks discovered the Moslem camp deserted except for abandoned plunder and the Arab dead.

Charles earned his name "The Hammer," and France never again was invaded by a Moslem Army. Although the Arabs were only raiding, a Frankish defeat at Tours would have led to greater incursions. As it happened, Abdar-Rahman's death brought on a revolt by the Berbers which destroyed Arab unity.

—W.L.S.

Hastings, 1066

When Edward the Confessor died in 1066, he left no direct heir to the throne of England. Many aspired to fill the vacancy but there were only 3 strong claimants: William of Normandy; King Harold Hardrada of Norway; and Harold Godwinson, the Earl of Wessex.

The English nobles chose Harold Godwinson, a proven general from the Welsh Wars. The 2 pretenders to the throne threatened invasion. Harold especially feared that William, the Bastard of Normandy, would dispute his rule with force, so he had the English Channel constantly patrolled by the English fleet while he prepared his army for William's invasion.

Suddenly the uneasy vigil on the Channel was interrupted by an invasion in the north of England. King Harold of Norway, at the head of his Viking warriors, routed the northern fyrdsmen and advanced on York in his attempt to win England.

Harold Godwinson was forced to relax his watch on the Channel and hurried north. By luck the English Army surprised the Vikings and in a hard battle defeated the forces of the mightiest warrior king of the north at the battle of Stamford Bridge. But just 4 days later

Harold received the worst possible news—William had landed in the south.

Harold marched his weary, depleted army toward a confrontation with this new threat, intent upon repelling William immediately. As King of England, Harold was protector of the land, and it was reported that William's army was burning and pillaging.

The Norman invader fully intended to force a decisive battle with the English Army, since his small army of 7,000 men couldn't afford to wage a drawn-out guerrilla war. The strategy succeeded: Harold played into William's hands by immediately challenging the Normans.

Confident that his magnificent infantry, weakened though it was, could gain the upper hand, Harold attacked, deploying his men in the famed "shieldwall," his fierce housecarls in the center and the southern fyrdsmen on the wings. But William was prepared. He swiftly ordered his archers forward to thin the English ranks, but the archers failed to get close enough to penetrate the thick English shields. William then committed his Breton infantry and his cavalry but these were thrown back, unable to dent the shieldwall. Then, as the Norman Army retreated in disorder, some of the English fyrdsmen broke formation to chase the enemy. This was the opening that William's cavalry needed. Wheeling around, the Normans slaughtered the unsupported fyrdsmen and launched fresh assaults on the now-weakened shieldwall. The English hung on grimly until nightfall, repulsing the enemy repeatedly. But Harold fell, killed by an arrow through the eye, and William finally won the day.

The Bastard of Normandy had earned a new title: William the Conqueror. All of England was his, after the most decisive and far-reaching battle in English history.

—W.L.S.

Constantinople, 1453

The ancient city of Constantinople, last stronghold of the ancient Roman Empire in the East, drew many conquerors over its thousand-year history. In 1453 the city was attacked by the mighty Ottoman Empire. The vast lands in the east had already fallen to the Turks, who now set their sights on the city itself.

Mohammed II, a cruel ruler but an energetic, intelligent general, commanded a force of between 80,000 and 150,000 men. His army was divided into 3 types of soldiers: the bashi-bazouks, ill-disciplined, poorly armed Turks; the Anatolian levies, recruits who were somewhat better than the bashi-bazouks; and the janissaries, soldiers who were the cream of the Turkish Army. The latter were originally Christians, taken from their parents before the age of 12 and carefully trained in the art of war. They were the finest soldiers of their time.

Mohammed also introduced something new in his siege of Constantinople—artillery. The many attempts to take the city had often failed because of its 13 mi. of thick walls. Mohammed planned 1st to blast down huge sections of the wall in order to eliminate this barrier for his infantry

To meet the Turks, Emperor Constantine XI had only 8,000 men. But these men were under the command of the resourceful Venetian, Giovanni Giustiniani. Constantine also tried to enlist aid from other Christian states, but the schism between Roman Catholic and Greek Orthodox had proved too bitter to overcome. While the rest of Christendom argued and watched, the Turks attacked Constantinople.

At 1st the battle went badly for the Turks. Their fleet could not penetrate the harbor. Breaches torn by the great siege guns were immediately patched by the valiant Roman defenders. After many attacks had been repulsed by Giustiniani, Mohammed tried to move a giant wooden tower next to the wall. Giustiniani countered by rolling barrels of gunpowder under the structure to blow it up. Giustiniani's defense proved so successful that Mohammed tried to bribe him to defect to the Turkish side.

In a last desperate assault, Mohammed sent wave after wave of expendable soldiers to attack weakened sections of the wall. But the defenders threw back each assault with pikes, crossbows, and guns, and even Mohammed's janissaries took heavy losses. Then, suddenly, Giustiniani was wounded and forced to relinquish direct command. Encouraged, the janissaries gained the advantage, and Constantine was killed while bravely trying to rally his forces. Leaderless, the city fell.

—W.L.S.

ARMADA, 1588

In 1588 Philip II of Spain sent his invincible Armada to force England back into the Catholic fold, since the execution of Mary Queen of Scots had dashed the last hope for a Catholic succession to the English throne. The Armada included 130 ships of war, 8,000 sailors and 20,000 soldiers. Its mission was to coordinate an invasion of England with the Duke of Parma's soldiers in The Netherlands.

England, ruled by Elizabeth I, had collected 180 ships to meet the Armada. The fleet was commanded by famous naval heroes—Drake, Howard, Hawkins, Raleigh, and Frobisher.

Late in July the 2 fleets met in the English Channel in a running series of battles that lasted several days. This action has often been described as a harassment conducted by tiny, skillful English ships against lumbering Spanish giants manned by incompetent sailors. This is untrue. Although the total Spanish tonnage exceeded the English fleet, the English 1st line matched the largest Spanish ships in size. In fact the English *Triumph* was the largest ship on either side.

Tactics were dictated by the strong points of the 2 opponents. The better constructed, more maneuverable English ships were armed with accurate long-range guns. The Spanish ships were loaded with short-range heavy cannon. The Spanish ships, therefore, formed a tight, defensive crescent formation, hoping to draw the English into grappling range where the Spanish could use their heavy weapons, followed by boarding soldiers. The English line refused to cooperate and pounded the Armada with their long-range guns. Great quantities of shot and powder were expended at 1st by both fleets with minimal effectiveness—the only losses suffered by either side were due to internal accidents. The English gunners constantly missed their targets, yet succeeded in keeping the Spaniards at a safe distance. Finally the English broke the Spanish crescent defense with fire ships and were able to close in on their own terms, sending many of Philip's vessels to the bottom. A changing wind allowed the Spanish remnants to escape to the north, but on the homeward journey, while rounding Scotland, they lost more ships—this time to the weather. The final tally was 51 ships lost, with over 9,000 men. The English lost little more than 100 men.

The defeat of the Armada did not immediately change the balance of power on the seas, but the path was cleared for eventual English control.

—W.L.S.

BLENHEIM, 1704

The master strategy for the French, to win the war of the Spanish Succession, called for the merger of 2 separate French armies with the army of their ally, the Elector of Bavaria. Massed in western Bavaria, at the Danube, the combined force was then to assault Emperor Leopold I's capital, Vienna. The English, Dutch, and Prussian armies, led by the Duke of Marlborough, John Churchill, thwarted the threat at the Battle of Blenheim, August 13, 1704. Churchill attacked 1st, before the 2 French armies could unite. His decision was made against the advice of his generals, who feared that a frontal attack at Blenheim, against well-entrenched positions and over swampy ground at the Nebel, could result in a Marlborough rout.

The opposing forces were almost equal.

French marshals Tallard and Marsin commanded 60,000. The duke had 56,000. But, as the attacker, he also faced far heavier losses.

For a line of defense, the French had placed heavy troop concentrations at Blenheim village and at Lutzingen, 3 mi. north. At their center, Oberglau, they allocated a light force of only 14 battalions including an Irish brigade. They reasoned, wrongly, that the swampy ground before Oberglau would act as a partial deterrent to Marlborough's advance.

Marlborough attacked palisaded Blenheim 1st, advancing under a concealing ground fog. He took heavy losses, but reinforced his position and managed to seize the low ground across the Nebel with his cavalry. The success was nearly nullified when his center, the Prussian troops commanded by the Prince of Holstein-Beck, was overrun by the Irish and mauled badly. The Irish, overconfident, allowed themselves to be cut off and were decimated by Marlborough's counterattacking cavalry. Marlborough's right flank, the cavalrymen of Prince Eugene of Savoy, faced with bad terrain over which to maneuver, charged 3 times in their sector but were nearly routed, taking huge casualties.

At 5 P.M., Marlborough massed his left flank of 8,000 cavalrymen—now across the Nebel—in 2 waves, supported by the infantry. They charged in a final effort, and Tallard's 10,000 cavalrymen, too exhausted to resist, lost their nerve and galloped from the field. Abandoned, the foot soldiers of the French center were cut down as the troopers swept through, splitting the French line in 2. Quickly, the troopers wheeled to the left and around the French barricaded inside Blenheim village. Surrounded, its defenders laid down their arms, effectively ending the battle.

Marlborough lost 5,000 killed and 8,000 wounded, mostly from Prince Eugene's difficult struggles. Tallard lost 12,000 dead and 14,000 wounded, almost half of the forces he had committed. The decisive defeat freed Germany from the French yoke. Moreover, the French permanently lost the military initiative and with it, the war.

—W.K.

POLTAVA, 1709

Hoping to establish Russia as a great Baltic power, Czar Peter the Great declared war on Sweden in August of 1700. When his soldiers met a crushing defeat at Narva, the Russian leader reorganized his men along the lines of European armies, adopting their warfare tactics, and he began to win.

In 1709, Swedish King Charles XII invaded the Ukraine with 32,000, laying siege to Poltava. He became a casualty almost at once,

when a Cossack bullet struck him in the foot. Disabled by the wound, the King was forced to turn over active command to Field Marshal Rehnsköld, but he continued to direct the strategy from his litter. The arrangement did not work.

The Swedish attack foundered, fatally handicapped by the immobility of the King. His generals, conditioned by previous campaigns to act as little more than brigade commanders, were unable to function effectively without the King's personal, on-the-spot direction. Quarreling ensued between Rehnsköld and Count Lewinhaupt, the infantry commander, and Lewinhaupt may not even have been kept fully informed of the King's orders by Rehnsköld, who disliked him personally.

In the final assault, Charles ordered his army forward in the classic pattern of attack, sending 18,000 against 44,000 well-entrenched Russians, with drums beating and bayonets fixed. His contempt for the Czar's new-found fighting ability brought about his defeat quickly as the Russians massacred his advancing troops. He lost almost 7,000 men and, with them, Sweden's domination in the Baltic. The losses of Peter the Great were less than 1,400.

The Duke of Marlborough summed up the King's performance in the battle in one short comment: "Ten years of unbroken success, and 2 hours of mismanagement."

—W.K.

QUEBEC, 1759

Engaged in a Colonial struggle with France in North America, the British decided to advance on the key French stronghold at Quebec. Many thought that the city was impregnable but General Wolfe, in a dangerous night action, sailed past the French defenses and scaled a poorly held portion of the heights with 4,500 men. In the morning the French were surprised to see a long scarlet line formed above the exposed city on the Plains of Abraham.

The French General Montcalm immediately grasped the danger of this new turn of events. The English would now be able to bring up artillery and leisurely pound Quebec into submission. Montcalm attacked, risking everything in battle.

Late in the morning, the French main body advanced in 3 groups with fixed bayonets. The British, harassed by snipers and Indians, had taken cover by lying down in the tall grass. As the French marched toward them, they rose to form a standing line. At 200 yards, the French opened fire. Encouraged by a few falling British, they rushed forward.

The British troops waited coolly until the ragged French formation was 50 yards away. Then, almost as one, they fired a terrible volley. The French were staggered. The British line marched ahead a few paces and then fired another telling volley. In 15 minutes the battle was over. Reeling from 1,400 casualties, the French fled before the attacking British.

General Wolfe was killed as his victorious army advanced toward Quebec. Montcalm died while trying to rally his broken troops. Quebec surrendered 4 days later.

—W.L.S.

Trafalgar, 1805

In ordering Adm. Pierre de Villeneuve to leave Cadiz, Spain, and bring troops to Naples, Italy, for an attack on Austria, Napoleon Bonaparte added a 2nd demand: Attack the British fleet, if seen. The order annoyed Villeneuve, who realized he would probably lose in such an encounter. He procrastinated in complying with Napoleon's demand until he learned that Adm. François Rosily was being sent as his replacement. To forestall the blot to his honor by the demotion, Villeneuve sailed for the Mediterranean. His reluctant departure, putting to sea before Rosily's arrival, solved Nelson's problem on how to entice Napoleon's fleet into battle.

On October 21, 1805, Nelson, moving sluggishly before a light wind, struck at Villeneuve's 33 ships. The British admiral split his forces into 2 parallel columns: a squadron of 15, led by Admiral Collingwood in the *Royal Sovereign*, and a smaller, slower squadron of 12, commanded by Nelson, in the *Victory*. Nelson's battle plan called for Collingwood, sailing at the head of his column, to strike 1st. Coming within range, Collingwood executed a brilliant turning maneuver, and his trailing ships followed suit, bringing their guns to bear with broadside firing. He knifed between the *Fougueux* and the 4-decker *Santa Ana*, cutting off the last 16 ships in the long French-Spanish battle line. Nelson, his ships following in single file, continued straight ahead into heavy fire. He gambled that, by steering a course directed at the lead ship in line, the enemy captains, uncertain and confused as to his intended point of contact, would crowd on sail to keep pace. Nelson's maneuver achieved the desired purpose—it widened the gap between the forward half of the French fleet and the rear ships cut off by Collingwood, and eliminated the chance that others would come about to help. Once his objective was gained, he turned sharply to starboard and closed in to engage the *Redoutable*, sailing just behind Villeneuve's flagship, the *Bucentaure*, in the center of the French battle line.

Captain Harvey, following closely in the *Temeraire*, grappled with the *Redoutable* on its other side. A 4th French ship joined the trio, locking all 4 in mortal combat. Nelson's gunners were forced to reduce the charges on their starboard cannon, to avoid shooting clear through the *Redoubtable* and into the *Temeraire*.

Twice in the 4-hour fight, Admiral Nelson ordered a cease-fire, believing the *Redoutable*, its guns momentarily silent, was about to strike its colors. He was mistaken, and the last command cost him his life. The temporary lull gave the enemy sailors time to renew the battle and permitted the sniper aloft in the *Redoutable*'s rigging an opportunity to fire the fatal musket shot that mortally wounded the admiral. Nelson, conspicuous in his admiral's frock coat with 4 stars of knighthood prominently displayed on his left breast, was only 15 yards away, an easy target for the marksman.

Over 4,000 cannon took part in the historic battle. The victory was lopsided: Villeneuve lost 18 ships, Nelson none. The tremendous engagement gave Britain control of the seas for a century, although it cost them their greatest admiral and almost 1,600 men. Of the prizes they captured all but 4 were sunk in the immediate gale that followed.

Nelson's famous flag signal, sent to the fleet for "amusement" before the ships closed for action, was verbally given to the signal officer with "confides" as the verb to follow "England." The officer requested permission to substitute, from his signal book, the signal 2-6-9 ("expects"), eliminating the need to spell out "confides." It was granted, and the message became:

253   269   863 261 471 958 220 370
England expects that every man will do his
4 27 19 24,
d u t y,

The signal also impressed Napoleon. Later, he had a similar message painted on his warships: "*La France Compte que chacun fera son devoir.*"

—W.K.

Waterloo, 1815

Napoleon, commanding only 124,000 men, hoped to defeat the Anglo-Dutch Army of 93,000, led by Wellington, and the Prussian Army of 120,000, led by Marshal Blücher, by attacking them separately before they could combine forces. The French Emperor's initial thrust was made at Charleroi, where the 2 independent allied armies, spread out across 100 mi. of Belgium, touched each other. His plan counted upon an allied withdrawal—Wellington to Ostend and Blücher back to Germany—which would further separate the allied armies.

The French right flank commander, Grouchy, was sent to attack the Prussians under General Zieten. Simultaneously, Marshal

Ney, leading Napoleon's left flank, was ordered to advance along the road to Brussels, to engage Wellington's Belgian-Dutch division. Grouchy succeeded in driving back Zieten, provoking Blücher to bring his troops forward and mass them at Sombreffe. The Prussian confidently expected to defeat Napoleon alone, and did not advise Wellington of his intention. In a bloody clash, the Prussians were sent reeling back to Wavre, 16 mi. to the north. By pure chance, they fell into a regrouping position that was roughly parallel to Wellington's own line. Napoleon, out of contact with Ney and uncertain of progress there, declined to pursue the fleeing Prussians until the next day, when Grouchy was ordered to follow them. The inexperienced field commander did so, but spread out his forces so thinly that Napoleon, later in the battle, lost Grouchy's divisions as an effective reserve when they were vitally needed.

Ney, meanwhile, had halted before taking the vital crossroads at Quatre-Bras, bluffed into stopping at Gosselies, 10 mi. south, by contact with a minor allied force under Perponcher. Both Perponcher and his superior, Baron Jean de Constant-Rebecque, ignored Wellington's 1st orders to defend Mons, some 30 mi. to the west, on the duke's mistaken belief that the French attack would come there, a compliance which would have been disastrous. Instead, they brought up reinforcements to hold Quatre-Bras. When Wellington, attending the Duchess of Richmond's ball in Brussels, learned of the clash at Quatre-Bras, he ordered his men forward to meet the French, planning for a withdrawal to a stronger position at Mont-Saint-Jean, immediately south of Waterloo.

Unaware that each had initiated a major confrontation, both Ney and Napoleon needed reserves badly. Napoleon, believing that Ney, with 50,000 men, faced only 20,000 at Quatre-Bras, gave orders for D'Erlon's division, supporting Ney's advance, to join him for the final assault on Blücher. General d'Erlon, on Ney's left wing, complied, wheeling east toward Ligny. Ney, discovering he'd lost D'Erlon, sent a messenger to bring them back. Napoleon countermanded the order, but not before D'Erlon had futilely marched all day in both directions without firing a shot.

Leaving Grouchy, Napoleon returned to Ney, to learn that the marshal was standing by while Wellington completed an orderly withdrawal to Mont-Saint-Jean. Furious, he ordered an immediate attack, but it came too late, bogged down by drenching rains that had begun, turning the fields into quagmires.

On the final day, Napoleon, after starting a diversionary feint at the Château Hougoumont, sent Ney into an all-out assault at the farm, La Haye Saint, which Wellington had fortified.

Ney's troops, the ill-fated division of D'Erlon, charged in long columns, the worst possible attacking formation that could be chosen, and they were decimated. When Wellington pulled back to the reverse side of the slope to escape the French cannonading, Ney mistook the action and ordered cavalry charges that he did not support by infantry. He lost thousands in 13 repetitive attacks on the solid British squares, riding between and around the compact defense units but unable to break them.

After day-long debilitating assaults, Napoleon finally captured La Haye Saint. He mustered his forces for a final attack on Wellington, but failed, chiefly because the duke had been warned by a French traitor of Napoleon's exact movements. The initiative was finally gained, decisively, at 8 P.M., when Zieten's Prussian troops, coming from Wavre to support Wellington, fell upon the French line and drove it back. When Napoleon's most trusted and dependable Imperial Guard also recoiled under Wellington's counterattack, the French soldiers panicked and fled. The British called for the guard to surrender, and received the short, obscene reply from its General Cambronne, "Merde!" (The Frenchman's answer is sometimes translated as "The guard dies but never surrenders.")

The dead and dying lay on the battlefield for nearly a week. The duke lost 15,000 and the Prussians, 7,000. Of 74,000 brought to Waterloo by Napoleon, over 25,000 became casualties, with another 8,000 captured. The 3 sq. mi. of rolling farmland were carpeted with almost 50,000 fallen soldiers. With the more than 40,000 casualties from Ligny and Quatre-Bras, the 2-day total reached almost 90,000 men. In the week that followed, sightseers came down from Brussels to picnic among the carnage, scavenging through the bodies for valuables. They killed the wounded who resisted the robbery.

Ironically, Grouchy—whose inexperience in field command kept Napoleon from utilizing another 33,000 men, an action that might have turned the battle in his favor—scored a useless victory over the Prussian rear guard, which he had finally caught. He defeated Thielemann's small force decisively. But his triumph came too late, after Wellington had won.

—W.K.

BALAKLAVA, 1854

In September, 1854, the Franco-British force of 56,000 men, supported by a Turkish group of 5,000, invaded the Crimea. Their objective was the capture of the Russian naval base at Sevastopol. The defense of the British base of operations, Balaklava, depended upon the control of the terrain immediately to its north. Two valleys, named South and North, respectively, ran nearly parallel to the coast, separated by the Causeway Heights, a ridge of low hills between them. Unless the Heights were controlled, the Russians could approach, sight unseen, down the North Valley and launch an attack over the Causeway Heights, coming across the South Valley to storm Balaklava.

As an advance warning, the British commander-in-chief, Lord Raglan, constructed 6 redoubts on the Heights, manned by 3,000 Turks with 9 12-lb. cannon. At the west end of the Heights and stationed in the North Valley, he posted Lord Lucan's cavalry division, comprised of Sir James Scarlett's Heavy Brigade and Lord Cardigan's Light Brigade.

The Russian attack by 25,000 men, led by Count Liprandi, came down the North Valley as expected, but it wheeled left to capture the redoubts from the Turks on the Causeway Heights. Scarlett responded in a counterattack that drove the Russians back in confusion. His fellow commander, Cardigan, chose to remain idle, although his added support would have turned the Russian withdrawal into a rout.

Lord Raglan's staff, watching from the plains, observed the Russians preparing to remove the captured Turkish cannon with them. Raglan issued an order to the Light Brigade: Advance and prevent the removal of the cannon.

He neglected to be specific. Lord Lucan, observing the action from a position on the plain, could see only the *Russian* cannon at the far end of the North Valley. Therefore he objected strenuously to the Raglan order, brought by Captain Nolan, but a long-standing feud between the 2 men prevented any clarifying discussion from taking place. Raglan's aide continued on to deliver the order to Cardigan, who also protested it in vain, pointing out that its execution meant certain disaster.

Cardigan finally complied. He led the ill-fated charge down the North Valley, taking heavy fire from Russians in positions to his left and right, on the Heights bordering the valley, and from the main Russian force to his front. Although he reached the guns he mistakenly believed he had been ordered to capture, the waiting Russian cavalry, stationed behind the guns, swept forward and drove him back with heavy losses. Of 673 men who began the charge, 113 were killed and another 134 were wounded or captured.

The Russian victory had little effect on the outcome of their campaign. Within 6 weeks, they abandoned the Causeway Heights redoubts for which the men of the Light Brigade had erroneously died.

—W.K.

SEDAN, 1870

In August, 1870, after the French Army under Marshal Bazaine was forced into the mighty fortress at Metz and besieged by the Prussians, Marshal MacMahon was ordered to effect a relief. MacMahon, told by the Emperor Napoleon III that the fall of Metz was an unacceptable defeat, hurriedly marched along the Belgian frontier toward the fortress.

The Prussian commander, Von Moltke, could hardly believe his good fortune. He abandoned his march on Paris and swung his force north to intercept MacMahon, planning to pin the luckless French Army against the political wall of the Belgian border. The 2 forces clashed north of the Argonne forest and the Prussians halted the French advance. Then the French were surprised by the Prussians at Beaumont. MacMahon was forced to pull back his force of over 100,000 into the fortress town of Sedan.

Meanwhile, Von Moltke had continued his encirclement of the French, and the situation was fast approaching the critical stage. Before MacMahon could decide on a new course of acion, he was wounded. While his successor, General Wimpffen, debated alternatives, 250,000 Prussians surrounded Sedan and the French lost all chance of escape.

Prussian artillery, commanding the heights above the town, bombarded the trapped French troops. The courageous General Margueritte led repeated cavalry charges in a valiant attempt to break out, but these all failed. Finally a flag of truce was sent from the fort. To the Germans' surprise they discovered that Napoleon III himself was in Sedan. All French forces surrendered at 4:15 P.M., September 1.

With a loss of 9,000 men, the Prussians achieved total victory, taking 100,000 prisoners and killing 17,000 Frenchmen. Superior Prussian tactics and leadership had tumbled the 2nd Empire. The war raged on for another 6 months, but Sedan was the crucial victory.

—W.L.S.

THE MARNE, 1914

The Schlieffen Plan, devised by General von Moltke's predecessor as Germany's chief of staff, called for France's conquest by a quick "Blitzkrieg" thrust through neutral Belgium, outflanking the strong French border fortifications. The westward strike was then, after capturing Paris, to swing south and east like a giant scythe to crush the main French forces from the rear in Alsace-Lorraine.

Von Moltke modified the plan, with disastrous results. He sharply limited the attack potential of his 1st and 2nd Armies—the

"Blitzkrieg" spearhead—by reassigning 5 corps for new drives on the Alsace-Lorraine and Russian fronts. His decision violated Von Schlieffen's basic strategy, which strongly advised against pursuing a simultaneous 2-front war.

In initial action, Von Kluck, the aggressive but brash 1st Army commander, had already moved his entire force north of the Marne to the Ourcq River, attacking Maunoury's 6th French Army. He continued to advance after receiving Von Moltke's orders to hold his attack on Paris in abeyance, believing that the supreme commander did not understand the real situation. But Von Kluck's extended assault opened a 25-mi. gap with Von Bülow's 2nd Army, on his left flank. When Von Moltke intercepted a radio message giving news of the separation, he sent his intelligence chief, Lieut. Col. Richard Hentsch, forward on September 8 to review the situation. Hentsch possessed oral authority to act in Von Moltke's name if necessary, since Von Moltke's headquarters were located in Luxembourg, more than 100 mi. from the front.

As Hentsch reached the 2nd Army's command post, he was informed of a night assault by D'Esperey's 5th French Army which had turned back Von Bülow's right flank. Fearing an immediate envelopment, Hentsch ordered a withdrawal, to which a weary Von Bülow readily agreed. The retreat left Von Kluck's flank highly vulnerable, although the 1st Army was itself in good position and attacking well. Hentsch arrived at 1st Army headquarters while Von Kluck was at the front, conferred with the general's chief of staff, and strongly advised a similar withdrawal. Upon Hentsch's return to Luxembourg with his full report, Von Moltke ordered a general retreat of not only the 1st and 2nd Armies, but the 3rd as well, pulling back to the Aisne.

For the French, a "miracle" at the Marne had taken place: The German threat to Paris was over. But Marshal Joffre's forces were too exhausted to follow up their great moral victory, and the German armies gained valuable time to dig in. Their primary tactics subsequently changed from rapid mobility to static entrenchment, initiating the bloody months of the next 3 years. The "fixed position" of trench warfare, protected by machine gun, barbed wire, and a new invention called the "tank," became the accepted plan for battle.

—W.K.

Air Battle of Britain, 1940

Reichsmarschall Herman Göring's aerial assault on England—given the code name, *Operation Adler* ("Eagle")—began in mid-August, to clear the way for Hitler's immediate land invasion of the British Isles. Göring's timetable called for a Royal Air Force defeat in 4 days. He commanded 3 *Luftflotten* ("Air Fleets") based in northern France, the Low Countries and Norway, with about 1,000 bombers and 800 single-engine fighters. Göring's counterpart in Britain, Air Marshal Sir Hugh Dowding, opposed the attack with almost 750 aircraft in Fighter Command of which 80% were combat-ready Spitfires and Hurricanes. In addition, the RAF also utilized 600 long-range bombers to carry out raids against Continental targets. This Bomber Command force is usually discounted in comparisons of relative battle strengths during the encounters over Kent and Sussex.

Strategically, Göring concentrated on the RAF's southeast airfields commanded by Air Vice Marshal Keith Park. Dowding responded by giving Park the option to offer only limited aircraft commitment, supported by radar, against the German airmen.

The British radar stations on the cliffs and bluffs of coastal England allowed Park to "see" incoming bombing "boxes" at substantial distances. The sophisticated early-warning system permitted great efficiency in the utilization of Fighter Command aircraft. Its flyers, guided by precise vector information on enemy strength and location, were able to strike quickly and often by surprise, without wasting valuable time and fuel on airborne defensive patrols.

Nevertheless, Göring's continual strikes, delivered throughout August, reduced Fighter Command's resistance to the point of near-collapse. It lost well over 200 veteran pilots and almost 40% of its planes. Then, on August 24, the British received an unexpected assist. Luftwaffe bombers mistakenly bombed London, and the RAF immediately countered with a raid on Berlin. The retaliation infuriated Hitler, who had promised the German people Berlin would never be touched. Hitler now concentrated his air attack on London, abandoning his original plan to destroy the RAF. The decision was a major tactical blunder which gave British Fighter Command enough time to recover.

Following the strategy change, Göring unleashed a massive daylight blow on London on September 15. The British Prime Minister, Sir Winston Churchill, visiting at Park's Group Operations Room in Uxbridge—called "the Hole" because of its location 50' underground—watched with grave concern as the battle began. Park's status blackboard, which identified the level of commitment for each fighter group, went quickly from lights on the bottom row ("Stand By") to the row 2nd from the top, which flashed red as the planes entered aerial combat. Then, one by one, the lights moved on up to the most critical row of all—the #1 line indicating that combat action had been broken off for a return to base to refuel and rearm.

All of Park's available reserves had been committed. If further incoming German planes were spotted on radar, he could not prevent wholesale annhilation of the aircraft now on the ground. As Churchill eyed the plotting markers on the large-scale map table, he discerned a slow retreat back to the east and the English Channel; the tide of battle had turned. Speaking later in Parliament, Churchill paid tribute to Fighter Command's valiant effort with a ringing: "Never in the field of human conflict was so much owed by so many to so few."

—W.K.

MIDWAY, 1942

In a 4-day showdown, from June 3 to 6, Adm. Isoroku Yamamoto lost his bid to capture Midway Island, the Central Pacific base from which he hoped to carry the war to the U.S. As an opening feint, Yamamoto sent a diversionary force north, to Dutch Harbor in the Aleutians, hoping to draw Adm. Chester Nimitz's fleet away from Midway. Nimitz, planning strategy from Pearl Harbor, was not fooled.

The Japanese bombed Midway with 108 planes flying from 4 carriers: the *Kaga*, *Akagi*, *Soryu*, and *Hiryu*. Simultaneously, 26 Midway-based aircraft struck back. The U.S. attack was ineffectual. No hits were scored and 15 planes were shot down.

The Japanese task force commander, Adm. Chuichi Nagumo, "broke the spot" twice in rapid succession, ordering planes massed on the flight decks taken below for armament changes. In response to radioed reports that a 2nd bombing strike at Midway was required, Nagumo had torpedoes removed from the planes and fragmentation bombs refitted. When news of an approaching U.S. carrier came in, minutes later, he ordered the torpedoes replaced. On each occurrence, the carrier ordnancemen, hoping to save time, violated safety procedures, storing the torpedoes and bombs near the planes instead of in the heavily armored magazines. Nagumo was caught by U.S. bombers while engaged in the 2nd rearming. He also had cleared his decks to take on the returning 1st strike, now unarmed, a decision that left him without the capability to launch defensive planes.

Steaming from Pearl Harbor, Task Force 16 (with the carrier *Yorktown*) closed to intercept Nagumo. U.S. Admirals Frank Fletcher and Raymond Spruance launched a total of 152 planes: 43 torpedo bombers (Squadrons 3, 6, and 8), 65 dive bombers, and 46 "Wildcat" fighters. Torpedo Squadron 8, striking alone

without fighter protection, lost all 15 planes. Torpedo 3's 12 planes were also annihilated. Torpedo 6 fared little better, losing 10 of 14. *Hornet*'s fighters, heading out on a calculated bearing for Nagumo which was incorrect, ran out of gas and all 30 planes were lost by ditching in the water. The *Enterprise*'s 10 "Wildcats," also low on fuel, aborted and returned to the carrier.

Nagumo's "Zero" fighters, absorbed with attacks on Torpedo 3 and by dogfighting with *Yorktown*'s 6 fighters, were drawn away from the Japanese carriers, leaving them unprotected. *Yorktown*'s 17 dive bombers, unopposed, now scored 4 direct hits on the *Kaga*, and it blew apart in massive explosions enhanced by the stockpiled—and unprotected—bombs and torpedoes in the rearming areas. The *Enterprise*'s 33 dive bombers next hit the *Akagi* and *Soryu*, causing similar explosions. Another 15 U.S. planes were shot down in this attack.

Air elements of the last Japanese carrier remaining afloat—the *Hiryu*—attacked the *Yorktown*. *Hiryu*'s bombers broke through the *Yorktown*'s defenses, inflicting fatal damage. The carrier—dead in the water and abandoned—and the destroyer *Hammann*, left to assist it, were both sunk by the Japanese submarine *I-168* the next day. The *Enterprise*'s 10 dive bombers retaliated, accompanied by 14 of *Yorktown*'s now-homeless planes, scoring 4 decisive hits on the *Hiryu*. *Hiryu*'s Capt. Tomeo Kaku, and his superior, Adm. Tamon Yamaguchi, facing the loss of their ship, committed suicide before the carrier sank.

Admiral Yamamoto, shattered by his defeat, retreated to Japanese ports after shelling Midway briefly. He had lost his 4 carriers and 13 other ships, all 275 planes, and nearly 5,000 men. Nimitz lost the *Yorktown* and *Hammann*, 91 aircraft (60% of the committed planes), and just over 300 men. But he had prevented the Japanese from moving on to attack, and perhaps capture, the Hawaiian Islands.

—W.K.

DIEN BIEN PHU, 1954

For 80 years France was involved in the governing of Indochina. During that period, the Vietnamese peasantry had lived out their lives despite foreign intervention.

The Battle of Dien Bien Phu climaxed 9 years of fighting without decisive efforts or results. The French Government was too preoccupied with other problems to be overly concerned with a war in a small Asian country far from home. French soldiers in Indochina were tired, battle weary, and had long since forgotten what they were fighting for. But the Vietminh had no such feelings or doubts. They were fighting for their homes, rice paddies, and the right to live their lives without foreign interference.

Gen. Henri Navarre, French commander in Indochina, was appointed to his command in 1953 for the sole purpose of finding a way for France to get out of an embarrassing and costly situation. Up to his takeover, French losses had exceeded 50,000 lives and $10 billion.

Because Navarre had been weaned on the logic of the Western military, he, of course, sought a purely military solution. He chose to establish a garrison in the valley of Dien Bien Phu. It would serve as a baited trap to entice the forces under Gen. Vo Nguyen Giap out into the open where they could, Navarre thought, be destroyed by the superior fighting ability of the French.

The strategy was doomed to failure. French intelligence estimates of Vietminh logistics were either misinterpreted, disbelieved, or ignored. The French concentration proved to be an easy, visible target for Vietminh mortars, whereas the garrison artillery found itself shooting blindly at invisible targets in the surrounding terrain. On May 7, the garrison fell after bloody hand-to-hand combat, and the survivors were taken prisoner.

Though the battle was relatively minor, fought with no more than 15,000 French Army regulars, mercenaries, Foreign Legionnaires, and 75 Air Force and Navy planes, it was nonetheless decisive. It heralded France's ultimate loss of her colonial empire in Asia.

—F.M.W.

Weird Weapons of the American Military, from the U.S. Camel Corps to the U.S.S. *Dolphin*

THE U.S. CAMEL CORPS

In 1848, before the 1st iron horse went West, the U.S. Army was desperately searching for a cheap, fast, efficient means of supplying its bases for the constant fight against the Indians. Also, spoils of the Mexican War had added 529,000 sq. mi. to the nation's Western wilderness and by the terms of the treaty the U.S. was responsible for the protection of settlers, towns, and travelers in what is now California, Arizona, Nevada, Utah, and the western portions of Colorado and New Mexico. About this time, Lieut. Edward Fitzgerald Beale, a friend of Kit Carson and superintendent of Indian affairs in California and Nevada, revived the idea of importing camels into the U.S. Five years later, Jefferson Davis, who was Secretary of War under President Pierce, advised the 33rd Congress, "For military purposes, for expresses, and for reconnaissances, and for transportation with troops rapidly moving across the country, the camel, it is believed, would remove an obstacle which now serves greatly to diminish the value and efficiency of our troops on the western frontier."

In 1855, through the pressure of Illinois Senator Shields, Congress voted an appropriation for $30,000 "to be expended under the War Dept. in the purchase and importation of camels."

Two men were assigned to carry through the strange experiment. One, Maj. Henry Wayne, hurried to Britain to study camels in the London Zoo. The other, David Porter, took a U.S.

Navy ship, the *Supply*, to Italy. Major Wayne and Porter met in Pisa, Italy, to watch 250 camels, owned by the Duke of Tuscany, accomplish the work of 1,000 horses. The pair then went on to Malta, Tunis, Constantinople, observing camels. The Crimean War was on, and the British were proving a single camel could carry 600 lbs. about 30 mi. a day.

The Americans acquired 3 camels in Tunis, 9 in Egypt, and 21 in Smyrna, 33 in all. And they hired Arab and Turkish camel drivers—Elias Calles, George Caralambo ("Greek George"), and Hadji Ali ("Hi Jolly"), men who knew how to handle the beasts—to accompany the cargo to the U.S. When the *Supply* arrived in Egypt, a flat-bottomed boat was used to ferry the camels aboard. The loading took 16 hours. One camel, 7'5" tall, was too large to fit into the ship—a hole had to be cut in the deck to accommodate his hump.

The journey from Egypt to Texas took 3 months. The camels proved excellent sailors. During gales they were tied down, in kneeling positions, which they didn't seem to mind at all. On May 14, 1856, the ship arrived at Indianola, Tex., a port about 120 mi. south of Galveston. When the camels were taken on land they "became excited to an almost uncontrollable degree, rearing, kicking, crying out." They were camped 60 mi. northwest of San Antonio. When the citizens of San Antonio laughed at the camels, doubting their strength, Major Wayne took this as a challenge. He assembled a crowd, brought forth one camel, made the animal kneel, hoisted 2 bales weighing together 613 lbs. on its back, and then, to convince even the worst skeptics, loaded on 2 more bales. The camel had a total of 1,256 lbs. on its back. At a signal from the major, it rose easily and walked off. The crowd went wild. The feat was considered a miracle, and the local press even ran poetry about it.

It is interesting to note that the total cost of the camel-buying spree up to 1856 was $7,331. The balance left, after the 1st draw upon the original $30,000 appropriation, was returned to Washington—setting a precedent that didn't catch on.

The arrival of a 2nd shipload of camels at Indianola on February 10, 1857, brought their number to 75.

In the months of semi-idleness at the Camp Verde caravansary before June 25, 1857, a great deal was learned about the camel. They require about as much food and water as a horse, but they drink 20 to 30 gallons at a time. They do not perspire, having a much higher body-heat tolerance than the horse or mule. When possible, they browse constantly on whatever food is available; this allows them to store energy in the form of fatty tissue. This is what their humps are composed of, and these serve as a commissary in time of famine. Ordinarily the camel will travel 3 to 4 days, covering a distance of perhaps 300 mi., under a heavy load, without food or water. Contrary to common belief, a camel's backbone is as straight as that of a horse. Their humps of pure fat will vary in size from relatively flat, after days without food, to pleasingly plump under regular feeding. The normally docile animals are capable of anger when abused and can expel their foul-smelling cuds with uncanny accuracy. On occasion 2 males will become angry enough to fight to the death. Their act of rising hind-part 1st from a kneeling position is not unique to the camel, but a characteristic of the entire ruminant (cud-chewing) family, including cattle, sheep, goats, deer, giraffes, and others.

In March, 1857, the Secretary of War ordered the formation of the 1st U.S. Army Camel Corps and appointed 35-year-old Lieut. Edward Beale, originator of the project, to command it. The animals were under fire now. Critics claimed the whole corps was a useless waste of money. Gossips whispered that Beale was using them for work on his own properties.

To answer the rumormongers, Beale decided to use the Camel Corps to open up a new supply route across the hot American desert between New Mexico and California. The journey was a minor epic, a battle against thirst, Indians, loneliness.

On the long march westward across uncharted territory the camels' surefootedness in rocky terrain, deserts, and mountains allowed them to set a pace difficult for the mules to follow. In fording rivers they were found to be strong swimmers. On seeing an approaching rider or wagon, an advance man would go forward from the caravan shouting: "The camels are coming, the camels are coming!" Invariably the encounter would be a repetition of previous near-calamities. The strange appearance of the camels, their tinkling bells and unfamiliar odor caused horses and mules to go berserk, thus adding further to the camels' unpopularity.

The camels covered the last lap, between San Bernardino and Los Angeles, 65 mi., in 8 hours. One camel, without water for 10 days, refused the drink offered him. Beale continued showing what the Camel Corps could do. At the end of the 1st year, he submitted his report to Congress. "I have tested the value of the camels, marked a new road to the Pacific, and traveled 4,000 mi. without an accident."

The Secretary of War agreed the experiment was a success. He ordered 1,000 more camels from the Middle East. But while Congress debated the request, the Civil War broke out. The project was shelved—and soon forgotten.

What happened to the original 75 camels? Beale gave 28 to the growing city of Los Angeles. They were housed on Main Street, used to transport mail and move harbor baggage up from San Pedro. In 1864 the U.S. Government auctioned the remaining camels to the highest bidder. A rancher named Sam McLeneghan bought them, sold 3 to a circus, employed the remaining 30 in a freight service between States. Gradually they were separated, and spread throughout the West. The Confederates captured several in Texas, but the mule drivers couldn't understand them and turned them loose.

There were other camels, too. Beale's success with them earlier had encouraged private companies to import them. One concern brought 32 over from China, auctioned them for $475 each in San Francisco. They were used in the Nevada salt mines, mistreated, abandoned. Another concern brought 22 camels from Tartary. These were equipped with leather shoes in order to traverse rough roads in British Columbia. But they frightened horses and were abandoned.

While most of the imported Arab drivers settled on the coast, they turned to other trades, although each of them managed to obtain or retain one camel from the original herd.

Of the imported cameleers, Elias Calles ended up in Sonora, Mexico. His son, Plutarco Calles, became President of Mexico in the early 1920s. "Greek George" served a long term with the U.S. Army and died in Montebello, Calif., in 1913. Hadji Ali, known as

"Hi Jolly," became a living legend until his death in Arizona in 1903. Once, insulted because he had not been invited to a German picnic in Los Angeles, he broke up the gathering by driving into it on a yellow cart pulled by 2 of his pet camels. In the 1930s, a monument was erected to his memory in Quartzsite, Ariz.

For years prospectors kept sighting the abandoned camels. Just 50 years ago Nevada had a law fining anyone $100 for using a camel on a public highway. In Arizona, a great red camel carrying a worn saddle on its back was seen at the turn of the century. In 1907 a prospector ran into 2 wild camels in Nevada. In April, 1934, the *Oakland Tribune* printed the following: "THE LAST AMERICAN CAMEL IS DEAD. Los Angeles—Topsy, the last camel that trekked across the desert of Ariz. and Calif. is dead. Attendants at Griffith Park destroyed her after she became crippled with paralysis in the park lot where she spent the declining years of her life." Actually, Topsy may not have been the last of the U.S. Army's camels. According to rumors, one was recently seen in the Texas desert.

The U.S. Camel Corps, which had successfully kept open communications between Texas and Colorado and had carried military loads throughout the new West, finally died of mistreatment and neglect—because it was too strange.

—F.M.W. and I.W.

THE U.S.S. DOLPHIN

Imagine a race of alien creatures, probably brighter than man. Their language is sophisticated, but its structure and logic are so different from ours that we will probably never be able to translate it. They can swim 40 knots. They can dive to depths in the water that would burst man's lungs. Imagine that these sentient creatures also love the human race and will do, for love, what humans ask of them. Then consider how man might make use of them in war.

The creatures are dolphins. The dolphin is a mammal, one of the toothed whales, which, though it lives in the ocean, breathes air and nurses its young with milk as humans do.

Dolphins *may* have already been used in war to torpedo enemy ships, blowing themselves up as they did so.

NAVY TRAINS KAMIKAZE DOLPHINS, 1973 headlines read. The stories were as sensational as the headlines. They told of secret military operations in which dolphins with explosive backpacks rammed enemy submarines, committing suicide in the process. They told of dolphins planting magnetized explosives, activated by a timing device, on the sides of enemy vessels below the water line.

The Day of the Dolphin, a movie based on this sinister rumor, related the story of Alpha and Beta, a lovable pair of dolphins who were taught to understand and speak English by a "good guy" scientist. Whereupon Beta, kidnapped by a "bad guy" government power, was equipped with a bomb backpack and sent to blow up the presidential yacht, only to be saved by the scientist and Alpha.

How true were the stories on which *Day of the Dolphin* must have been based? The Navy's official statement was, "In spite of science fiction, conjectural and sensational so-called news stories to the contrary, the Navy has never, is not, and has no plans to train any animal to injure itself in any way in connection with any alleged military mission or tactic."

Moreover, the Navy said, it would be impractical to use dolphins as suicide bombs. After all, it takes 3 months and $50,000 just to "tame" a dolphin, and far more money and time to train one. That's an extremely expensive bomb. Moreover, no matter how well trained, an explosive-carrying dolphin might miss his target. If he did, he would become a highly dangerous moving bomb. What if he were to hit a friendly pleasure boat or dock by mistake?

There were other stories. It was said that dolphins had been acting as undersea detectives and counterspies in Camranh Bay in Vietnam for over a year. Part of their job was to intercept any enemy frogmen who sneaked into the harbor, it was said. Some stories claimed that the dolphins were literally transformed into lethal weapons with switchblade knives attached to their beaks, which they would drive into enemy frogmen on a go-ahead signal from a radioman on board a ship. Such dolphins were supposedly used around Haiphong Harbor.

James Fitzgerald of Fitzgerald Laboratories, a pioneer in dolphin research, said, on the CBS television program 60 *Minutes*, that 50 to 60 enemy swimmers were indeed intercepted by Navy dolphins in Camranh Bay. He himself had trained 3 of the dolphins; the Navy, the other 3. Ray Harmon, who played the role of an enemy diver in the Navy's Anti-Swimmer Dolphin Program, told how dolphins were trained to run divers to the surface and corral them in one spot. Other reports said that dolphins were trained to tear off swimmers' face masks, regulators, and swim fins.

Responses to the stories were predictable. Letters about the Navy's inhuman treatment of these friends to humanity poured into the Office of Naval Research, naval stations, and congressional offices. People who might tolerate bad treatment of other species could not tolerate bad treatment of dolphins. For centuries, humans and dolphins have felt a kinship with each other. The Greeks even hinted at the idea that dolphins once were humans; indeed, dolphins were once land animals, but returned to the sea thousands of years ago. They could easily kill people, but they never do. There is not one recorded incident of dolphins, who kill sharks with ease, having ever killed a person. (And people have killed dolphins by the hundreds.) On the other hand, there are substantiated reports of dolphins playing with children, saving drowning swimmers, helping fishermen catch fish. Affectionate, with perpetual smiles, they evoke love in human beings, and it is unthinkable to most that they should suffer at the hands of people.

The Navy admits that it did have dolphins in Camranh Bay, but says that they were there for other reasons: to see how they responded to a new environment and to transportation over long distances. If the newspaper stories were untrue, how did they start? Picture this scene, the Navy said: A reporter, interviewing navy personnel studying and training dolphins, has been given all the "unclassified" information available—that is, all the information dealing with biological research and training for peaceful purposes. Then the reporter asks, "What about military uses?" And, since all such information is automatically secret, the navy spokesman replies, "Use your imagination." And the reporter does.

The Navy has never denied the fact that it has been studying and training dolphins for a long time—since 1961, in fact. How then did the Navy spend the millions of dollars allocated to dolphin research ($30 million by 1974)? And what did it receive in return? The spin-offs are surprising.

Submarine Skin. Max Kramer, a German scientist who came to the U.S. after W.W. II, was a pioneer in studying how the dolphin is able to swim so fast. By all superficial data, it should not be able to reach the incredible speeds it does: 40 knots (about 35 mi.) per hour. The secret, Kramer found, lies in the skin, which, because of its structure, is extremely resilient. The skin undulates as the dolphin swims, reducing turbulence and friction. Somehow the dolphin creates a vacuum around himself, which causes less friction drag. From his studies, Kramer was able to help produce a synthetic dolphin skin, lamiflo, which could be used to cover submarines, vessels, torpedoes, and superspeed aircraft, thus increasing speed.

The Dolphin's X-Ray Sonar System. Through an extremely complex sonar system, far more sophisticated than any humans have made, a dolphin, even blindfolded, can zero in on a target as small as a buckshot pellet, distinguish one metal from another, and "read" another animal's insides. The dolphin sends out thousands of tiny clicks that, put together, sound like a rusty hinge. The sound bounces off an object, then returns to the dolphin, who is able to tell how far away the object is, how big it is, and even "what" it is. In the water, sound comes from all sides so that a human would not be able to tell the direction from which sounds come. A dolphin can. Its insulated ears and the "sound windows" in its head give it a stereophonic receiving system that works on both long and short range. By unlocking the secrets of this system, the Navy hopes to improve its own sonar.

Deep Diving. Without getting the bends, a dolphin can dive to depths 3 times deeper than a human can. A human diver, even at shallow depths, must stop at underwater stages and go through pressurized "locks" to avoid getting "the bends," an illness caused by bubbles of nitrogen that collect in the tissues. A mammal, the dolphin breathes air, yet it does not get the bends. Researchers have recently discovered why. When dolphins dive, their lungs completely collapse so no exchange of gases can take place; also, at great depths they get energy from fuel stored in muscle tissue rather than from oxygen in the lungs. By studying the dolphin, we might be able to discover ways to make diving safer for human beings.

Dolphin Communication. Dr. John Lilly, an offbeat but highly qualified neurophysiologist, spent many years trying to teach dolphins to speak and understand English. In 1968, claiming partial success with his experiments, he freed his dolphins with the statement: "I felt I had no right to hold dolphins in concentration camps for my convenience." Lilly, who has experimented with LSD and has an extreme interest in other forms of awareness, feels that dolphins have a higher form of consciousness than we do and that their language and view of life are based on nonhuman, but highly intelligent, logic.

Navy personnel studied the "Margit and Peter" tapes resulting from Lilly's experiments. In these tapes a human female and a dolphin male are supposedly communicating with each other in English. One navy scientist, having heard nothing that resembles English from the dolphin on the 1st run-through of the tapes, took a glass of sherry to fortify himself and played them again. Still nothing. He claims to be fascinated with Lilly's work, but says, "I like Dr. Seuss, too."

Dr. D. Batteau, a Tufts University professor who does work for the Navy, has invented an electric "translator" that transforms human vocalizations into dolphin whistles. Using an artificial language, sailors can radio commands to dolphins working underwater.

Underwater Workers. Given all his abilities and a way of communicating with him, the

ANTI-PERSONNEL WEAPONS

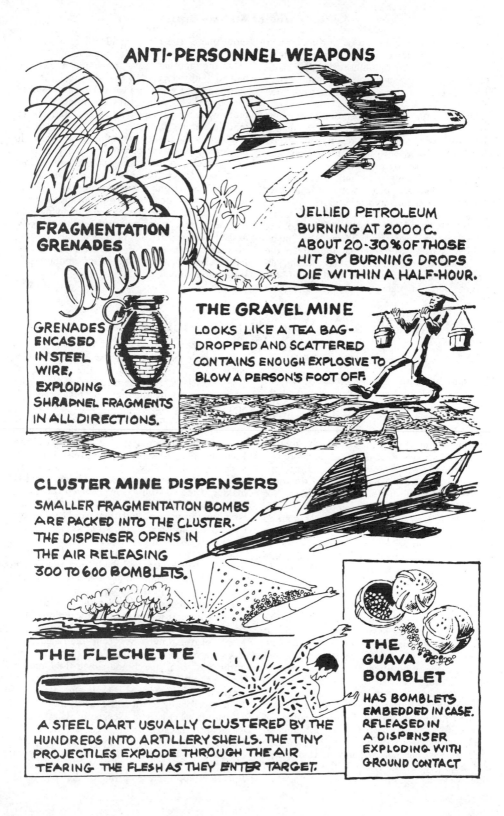

NAPALM

JELLIED PETROLEUM BURNING AT 2000 C. ABOUT 20-30% OF THOSE HIT BY BURNING DROPS DIE WITHIN A HALF-HOUR.

FRAGMENTATION GRENADES

GRENADES ENCASED IN STEEL WIRE, EXPLODING SHRAPNEL FRAGMENTS IN ALL DIRECTIONS.

THE GRAVEL MINE

LOOKS LIKE A TEA BAG-DROPPED AND SCATTERED CONTAINS ENOUGH EXPLOSIVE TO BLOW A PERSON'S FOOT OFF.

CLUSTER MINE DISPENSERS

SMALLER FRAGMENTATION BOMBS ARE PACKED INTO THE CLUSTER. THE DISPENSER OPENS IN THE AIR RELEASING 300 TO 600 BOMBLETS.

THE FLECHETTE

A STEEL DART USUALLY CLUSTERED BY THE HUNDREDS INTO ARTILLERY SHELLS. THE TINY PROJECTILES EXPLODE THROUGH THE AIR TEARING THE FLESH AS THEY ENTER TARGET.

THE GUAVA BOMBLET

HAS BOMBLETS EMBEDDED IN CASE. RELEASED IN A DISPENSER EXPLODING WITH GROUND CONTACT uses to which a dolphin can be put underwater seem infinite. Equipped with a harness containing a radio receiver, dolphins will, after training, "home" in response to an acoustic signal. Through other radio signals, commands are given.

During Navy Sealab operations, dolphins brought tools and messages to the aquanauts. They also were trained to rescue lost divers: The diver signaled with a tin cricket, and the dolphin responded by taking a line from a rescue reel and bringing it to him. The dolphins used by Sealab were able to recognize individual divers in wet suits and face masks.

In a 1972 program nicknamed "Deep Ops," pilot whales were trained to locate a lost object (missile or whatever) by following the "ping" sound of sonar. After reaching the target, the animal would press a grabber claw to the object, activating a hydrazine system in the process. That is, detached from the whale's mouthpiece, the claw would inflate a gas balloon to carry the object to the surface.

During another navy program, a dolphin named Tuffy located 7 lost missile-launching cradles valued at $4,700 each. He also matched the record of navy dives in finding "lost" dummy mines dropped off Santa Barbara Island in a mine fleet test.

There is no doubt that dolphins are valuable in peaceful military operations: They retrieve lost weapons, locate missing bombs and submarines, save frogmen who are lost or in trouble.

The Navy is pragmatic. People like Lilly are more "humanistic." Is the dolphin just another animal useful to people—a kind of living submarine, as one navy scientist put it—or is it, as Lilly claims, a truly intelligent, alien being of such a high form of consciousness that attempts by humans to use it for military purposes are immoral acts?

—A.E.

Roll Call: A Who's Who of Military Brass

GEN. AMBROSE BURNSIDE (U.S., Civil War)

On Ambrose Burnside's 1st wedding day his wife-to-be took one last look at him and responded with a resounding "No!" when the minister asked her if she took this man to be her lawful wedded husband. Whether this had anything to do with the doubtlessly abrasive whiskers Burnside wore, if indeed he wore any at the time, remains unknown to history, but the story does show how unusual situations simply "happened" to the luckless soldier. Not only did the wrong things happen, but Gen. Ambrose Everett Burnside, who later married another bride successfully, had a flair for doing the daring, innovative thing in war as well as fashion, another quality that kept his photographs in the papers and his countenance in the public's mind.

Burnside started off on the wrong foot from the moment he entered the military. After serving as a tailor's apprentice in his native Liberty, Ind., he had been appointed a cadet at West Point, graduating low in his class and excelling more in extracurricular singing and cooking than in military tactics. Following a tour with the cavalry in the West, he resigned from the Army in 1853 to set up the Bristol Rifle Works in Rhode Island, where he manufactured the breech-loading Burnside carbine of his invention. Things went badly for him, as usual, his business failing despite his new-type rifle's success, but not so badly as they would after he reentered the Army at the outbreak of the Civil War.

Burnside's expedition to the North Carolina coast in 1862, resulting in the capture of Roanoke Island, New Bern, Beaufort, and Fort Macon, won him the rank of major general and much acclaim. Yet when he took command of the Army of the Potomac later that year, he proved to be a distinct failure both as a leader and a strategist. His plan to capture Fredericksburg by crossing the river resulted in a slaughter so bloody that a special truce had to be called to bury 10,000 Union dead—making Fredericksburg long known as Burnside's Slaughter Pen. Victories would come later for the general, but they would somehow never rival his spectacular setbacks, as, for example, the much-publicized "Mud March" when Burnside marched his men out of camp near Fredericksburg and had to march them directly back again due to a heavy rainstorm that made maneuvers impossible.

Relieved of his command early in 1863, the unlucky general was next officially reprimanded by President Lincoln when, while heading the Dept. of the Ohio, he "court-martialed" ex-Congressman Clement Vallandigham for an antiwar political speech and closed the *Chicago Tribune* when that paper protested. Finally, Burnside was transferred back to the 9th Corps he had originally commanded when he enlisted (Burnside's Peripatetic Geography Class, as it was called because it traveled so widely on foot), only to face a final spectacular defeat at the battle of Petersburgh in 1864. Again it was a daring scheme that caused his downfall. Burnside approved a plan to dig a tunnel under the Confederate lines, fill it with high explosives, and attack at the moment the charges were set off. Sad to say, the tunnel was built, the attack made, and the attack repulsed. General Burnside was relieved of his command by a court of inquiry, in fact, nearly drummed out of the Army.

All of Burnside's failures hinged on "ifs." If engineers had built pontoon bridges in time for his Fredericksburg attack, he might not have been routed. If it hadn't unexpectedly rained, his "Mud March" wouldn't have come about. If he had been allowed to use the crack black troops he wanted to at Petersburgh instead of an untrained white regiment, his attack there might have been successful. Perhaps these "ifs" account for the fact that he remained so popular, for he went on to be elected as governor of Rhode Island for 3 terms, 1866–1869, and U.S. senator for 2 terms, from 1875 until his death in 1881, aged 57.

But his winning personality and patriotic spirit probably played a more important role in his political triumphs. From the constant publicity given him, the flamboyant Burnside hat that he wore in the field came to be called after the big bluff and hearty general, as were the burnside whiskers or burnsides he affected. Innovative as ever, he had chosen to wear the hair on his face in a new way, shaving his chin smooth below a full moustache and big muttonchops or sidebar whiskers. Thousands imitated him, and his burnsides, because they were only on the sides of the face, were soon called sideburns, this reversal of Burnside's name having nothing to do with his military reversals, though that might have been appropriate. The word sidebars probably also influenced the inversion, but, whatever the case, Burnside's name became one of the best known eponymous words. Though the general's whiskers have long since gone out of style, sideburns are even more popular today than they were in his time, the word now applied to any continuation of hair down the side of a man's face.

—R.H. rep.

T. E. LAWRENCE (Great Britain, W.W. I)

The film *Lawrence of Arabia* portrayed T. E. Lawrence as a fascinating, tall, romantic Robin Hood of the desert. History shows that he was 5′5½″ tall, a hopeless liar, a masochist, and a British imperialist—but no less fascinating.

The legend of Lawrence arose during W.W. I, a war that was a great disappointment to many people since it was neither the brief nor the glorious adventure they had expected. But in the midst of the prolonged slaughter there appeared a knightly Englishman leading Arabs in revolt against their Turkish masters (who

were on Germany's side). At stake was control of the Suez Canal and access to the oil which had been discovered a few years earlier.

Lawrence gained his extensive knowledge of the Middle East through his archaeological expeditions as a young man, and he was scouting the area for British Intelligence even before war broke out. When it did, he influenced the British Foreign Office to support Prince Faisal as the principal Arabian military leader. He became Faisal's chief adviser and companion, in the process assuming the robes of an Arabian prince and taking a leading role in guerrilla raids against the Turks and blowing up their railroad.

Lawrence gained his influence with the Arabs in various ways. First, he was able to immerse himself almost completely in the part of an Arab. Tom Beaumont, his machine gunner, recalled, "He was incredibly tough and made a point of doing anything the Arabs could do and doing it better. He could ride a camel faster than most of them. He could run alongside and swing into the saddle—about 9′ from the ground—while it was moving, and he could do it more easily than all the Arabs. The Arabs accepted him because of this."

Another of Lawrence's persuasive tools was gold. The British Government let him liberally distribute gold coins which captured the hearts and, at least temporarily, the loyalty of many of the nomadic tribesmen.

The Arab leaders were equally entranced by another promise Lawrence held out to them: independence once the war was over. It was a pledge Lawrence could not and did not intend to keep. As he later admitted, "I risked the fraud, on my conviction that Arab help was necessary to our cheap and speedy victory in the East, and that better we win and break our word than lose."

At the war's end, the major colonial powers began what Woodrow Wilson called "the whole disgusting scramble for the Middle East." It was revealed that, during the war, Britain and France had secretly agreed to carve up the Middle East between themselves. At the Paris Peace Conference in 1919 Lawrence held one of the more progressive views: that the British should at 1st control the Middle East, with the Arabs eventually attaining the status of a self-governing commonwealth of the British Empire. He had a deep hatred of the French and lobbied unsuccessfully to keep them out of the area altogether. In the end, Arab hopes for independence were betrayed, with Great Britain and France sharing the spoils.

In the meantime the public was being regaled by American journalist Lowell Thomas with stories of the courage and daring of Lawrence, "The Uncrowned Prince of Mecca,"

"The Deliverer of Damascus." With a lecture accompanied by films and lantern slides, Thomas appealed to the imaginations of audiences around the world and reportedly earned a million dollars doing so.

Ironically, at the time that Thomas was lauding Lawrence's strength, Lawrence was on the verge of breakdown. During the war his closest Arabian friend had evidently died of typhoid, 2 of Lawrence's brothers had been killed, and his body and spirit were nearly broken by disease, wounds, and possibly a beating and sexual attack by Turks who temporarily captured him. He staved off his collapse long enough to try to influence the results of the Paris Peace Conference—and failed. He then immersed himself in writing his version of the Arabian revolt, resulting in a book called *The Seven Pillars of Wisdom*.

Reliving his adventures while writing the manuscript proved too much for Lawrence. During the next several years he lived an aimless, confused life. Since the time he was a youngster, he had prided himself upon his endurance, calling himself "a pocket Hercules—as muscularly strong as people more than twice my size and more enduring than most." This pride now took a perverse twist and he reportedly hired a young man to beat him with a birch rod. In 1922, he enlisted in the ranks of the Royal Air Force under the assumed name of Shaw to get away from his fame, his guilt, and the need ever again to make decisions. When his identity was discovered he was thrown out and he enlisted in the Royal Tank Corps under yet a different name. But he found that existence too coarse and managed to be transferred back into the Air Force.

It was during this 2nd period in the RAF that Lawrence seemed to find peace. Although he was playing the role of a lowly aircraftsman, through his many influential friends (including Winston Churchill) he indirectly was able to bring about important reforms in the service. He also pioneered the development of high-speed launches (which he loved to drive at breakneck speeds), and helped to design, develop, and test the forerunners of the hovercraft.

In May, 1935, at age 47, and only 10 weeks after leaving the service, Lawrence suffered a fatal motorcycle accident. The evidence suggests that he swerved off the road in order to avoid hitting a young boy on a bicycle, but other stories immediately began to spread: that he had committed suicide; that he was assassinated by Germans or Arabs; even that he was done in by British leaders who feared that he would assume dictatorial powers during the war that was obviously on the horizon. Even in death Lawrence seemed larger than life. Un-

doubtedly he had brought on many of the rumors that surrounded him by seldom telling the same version of a story more than once. Charlotte Shaw, the wife of George Bernard Shaw and Lawrence's closest friend during his last decade, once exclaimed, "He is such an *infernal* liar!" Her husband, however, offered a characterization that serves as a more fitting epitaph for T. E. Lawrence: "He was not a liar. He was an actor."

—J.W.

SGT. EZRA LEE (U.S., Revolutionary War)

On the night of September 6, 1776, a rebel volunteer from Lyme, Conn., 45-year-old Sgt. Ezra Lee, riding inside the world's 1st military submarine, set out to attack Adm. Sir Richard Howe's flagship, the *Eagle*, at anchor off Staten Island, N.Y. The craft, just invented by David Bushnell, a farmer and Yale graduate, was a sailor's nightmare. Shaped like a round clam, it was 6' high and just over 7' long, with barely enough room to hold one man. To submerge, a foot spring opened a cock to let in water. For surfacing, Bushnell's design called on 2 hand pumps, to force the water ballast back out. The potential coffin carried 2 guidance instruments: a compass and a depth gauge.

Once inside the contraption, Sergeant Lee (who was probably the only noncommissioned officer ever to command an American submarine) was sealed in. He could not free himself to get out even if an emergency arose, since exterior strapping held the small entry cover secure and watertight and he had no way to reach it from within. While the submarine ran on the surface, it had 2 small tubes placed to bring in fresh air. But after submerging, Lee had only the free air within his cramped compartment upon which to rely. The supply was adequate for 30 minutes of underwater maneuvering. For motive power, designer Bushnell furnished 2 sets of windmill-shaped paddles. With a vigorous hand cranking, one paddle in each hand, Lee could manage a top speed of 3 mph. The *Turtle*, as it was quickly named, was kept in a stable position afloat by the 700 lbs. of lead used for ballast.

The ship's weaponry system was equally primitive. On deck, just behind the hatch, Lee carried an egg-shaped box loaded with 150 lbs. of gunpowder, along with a detonating apparatus and a clock timer to set the charge off. In theory, this bomb was to be placed beneath an enemy ship's bottom. To keep it in place until exploded, Lee's orders called for utilizing a long hand screw, turning the tool from within his compartment, to bore a hole into the ship's bottom. Once bored into the timber, the screw was to be left there; the box was fastened to it by a length of rope. His clock timer allowed for a maximum getaway time of 20 minutes after the device was triggered.

At almost midnight, the intrepid soldier entered his submarine and began his approach. Inside of minutes, he had lost his bearings in relation to the dimly outlined vessels of Howe's fleet, and the strong tide—outgoing, a fact no one had thought of—swept him swiftly past and far beyond the fleet, headed for open water. With frantic operation of his windmill-propulsion system, Lee managed to perspire his way back within range, 2½ hours later. Submerging, he went to work on the chosen ship's bottom. Again, he learned a fact that had been overlooked: The copper cladding over the bottom timber could not be bored by the wooden screw. The *Turtle* kept bobbing away with each turn of the screw.

By dawn, the "attack" was over. With the coming of the day, he could no longer retreat periodically to the surface to gulp in a fresh ½-hour supply of oxygen, since he would instantly be spotted. Lee began the return trip, this time assisted by the tide, which was now running shoreward. He came up to check on his position and found himself a few 100 yards off Governors Island. To his dismay, he found his approach being watched excitedly by hundreds of British soldiers running along the shore. Through his tiny windows he could see a barge being shoved into the surf, manned by a party of British Marines, coming to investigate the strange object.

With his limited speed and caught in shallow water, capture was unavoidable. Determined not to fall into enemy hands, he armed and cut the bomb loose, hoping the explosion would blow them all—including himself and the sub—to pieces. The unexpected happened. Frightened by a new floating object, the barge backed off, allowing Lee to paddle furiously away and escape. The bomb leisurely floated off. Minutes later, it exploded with a loud report that could be heard clearly by observers as far away as the Battery on the tip of Manhattan Island.

Sergeant Lee finally reached the shore, to be greeted warmly by Gen. Israel Putnam and other Colonial officers who had seen the surprising explosion. The incident did little to lessen Lee's raw courage, however. He continued his underwater attacks, but with small success. A year later he finally did succeed in drawing blood, when the curious crew of the British frigate *Cerberus* discovered and hauled in an object they thought was a wooden keg. It promptly exploded, killing 3 men and blowing a prize schooner, which the *Cerberus* had in tow, to bits. The incident caused the *Cerberus*'

captain to complain loudly about unsportsmanlike tactics.

For his pioneer exploits, Sergeant Lee received congratulations from Gen. George Washington, who then transferred the aquatic hero into the Secret Service. Later, Sergeant Lee fought in the battles of Trenton, Brandywine, Monmouth. He lived until the age of 72, dying in Lyme in 1821.

—W.K.

SGT. ANDRÉ MAGINOT (France, W.W. I)

Although André Maginot (1877–1932) had barely escaped with his life in W.W. I when severely wounded during the defense of Verdun, contaminated oysters finally caused his death from typhoid. Decorated with the Cross of the Legion of Honor and the Médaille Militaire, the former sergeant, who had enlisted as a private despite the fact that he was French Undersecretary of War in 1913, returned to government service and eventually became Minister of Defense. Determined that France would never be invaded again, he and his generals proceeded to plan and have a fortified wall built along the eastern border from Switzerland to Belgium, a wall which extended 314 km. [195 mi.] at $2 million a mile. The Maginot Line, complete with self-sufficient forts dug 7 floors deep into the earth, was meant to warn against surprise attacks from Germany into Alsace and Lorraine, but only engendered a false sense of security in France that became known as the "Maginot mentality," even though the wall was never extended to the coast.

Maginot's death spared him from seeing it easily bypassed by the Germans in W.W. II when they entered France through Belgium. The line's impregnability was never tested, but it could easily have been blasted by bombs, battered by tanks, or circumvented by paratroopers if it had been finished. The fault lay not so much with Maginot as with a war-weary country almost wanting to be lulled into a sense of false security. This the Maginot Line, like the Great Wall of China before it, readily provided.

Even now the smaller Maginot Line fortresses are being sold by the French Government. Most have been bought by those with romantic attachments to futile things, for the structures are uninhabitable white elephants with little practical use. Some of the line has already been purchased by the same Germans against whom it was built, as no French law prohibits the sale to foreigners. "It is conceivable," says one French official "that each of the fortifications could be bought by a different officer of the German General Staff."

—R.H. rep.

MAJ. VIDKUN QUISLING (Norway, W.W. II)

Of the men and women whose names have become synonyms for traitor, only Vidkun Quisling's has shed its capital letter in the dictionaries. A quisling is universally a traitorous puppet of the enemy and was one of the most quickly adopted of modern additions to the language, even inspiring the little-used verb "quisle," which means "to betray one's country." Maj. Vidkun Quisling (1887–1945) earned his rank in the Norwegian Army, having served as military attaché in Russia and Finland. An ardent fascist, he formed the National Unity party shortly after Hitler came to power in 1933, but never attracted more than a minuscule following, most Norwegians considering him mentally unbalanced. Then the Nazis invaded Norway on April 8, 1940, and the ridiculous lunatic of the Right came into power.

Quisling had met with Hitler in Berlin 3 days before, confiding strategic information to the Führer when told that Norway's occupation was imminent. The morning of the invasion he went on Nazi-controlled radio to countermand King Haakon's order for full mobilization of the Army. Haakon and his Government barely escaped to England, and Quisling, who had no official authority at all, was appointed Premier. Public reaction forced him to resign a week later, but Hitler insisted that he be reinstated the following September. Quisling had no administrative talents and proved an embarrassment to the Nazis on many occasions. Brutally suppressing all opposition, the Minister-President assumed King Haakon's chair in the palace and drove around in the bulletproof limousine presented him by Hitler. He surrounded himself with luxuries, occupying a bombproof, 46-room villa on an island near Oslo, where the walls were hung with priceless paintings from the national museum and he ate from gold dishes. So paranoid did he become that 150 bodyguards accompanied him at all times and every scrap of food he ate was sampled by someone else 1st, but this did not prevent him from becoming one of history's greatest megalomaniacs. He gave himself authority to make any document legal, issued postage stamps bearing his portrait, ordered pictures of himself hung everywhere.

Norwegians came to despise Quisling and his SS organization, the Hird, like no other countryman before him, and long before the war ended his name was a synonym for a puppet-traitor. After the Germans surrendered in Norway, he was charged with treason, theft, and murder, specifically the deaths of 1,000 Jews, whom he had ordered deported, and 100 other countrymen. Found guilty on all counts, Quisling was shot by a firing squad on October 24, 1945, Norway changing its long-standing law against capital punishment for this purpose.

—R.H. rep.

RITTMEISTER (Capt.) MANFRED FREIHERR VON RICHTHOFEN (Germany, W.W. I)

That Manfred Freiherr von Richthofen would become the highest scoring ace of W.W. I was certainly not viewed as a possibility when he began his flight training. As a matter of fact, it was seen as something of a miracle that he survived his early flight training at all. He was by no means a natural born flier. That he was brave, there was no doubt, and even his mother, when asked about his skill as a horseman, remarked, ". . . he was too brave for his own good. He would try anything, but his skill on a horse did not match his courage."

He was born into an old German family that could be traced back to at least 1543 and was uniquely devoid of military personalities. Mostly his forebears had been people of the soil, farming and raising sheep and dairy herds along the Oder River in Silesia. His father was a retired cavalry captain, but this seems to have been the extent of Manfred's military heritage. The family was moderately well off, and he was raised in an aristocratic atmosphere that put heavy emphasis on riding, hunting, and physical activity. Scholarship was not high on his list of pursuits, and if it had not been for his athletic abilities, his 2 years at the cadet school at Wahlstatt in Berlin would have been colorless. He was not considered bright by his instructors. As it turned out, it was hunter's instinct and not his education that was to work so well to his advantage when he finally mastered the mysteries of the airplane.

After 2 years at Wahlstatt, which he left in 1909, he went on to Lichterfelde for advanced studies. Von Richthofen found the atmosphere here more to his liking, and his scholarship picked up and he became interested in military history.

In 1911, at the age of 20, he joined the 1st Uhlan Regiment, a unit made up of some of the finest horsemen in the world, and although somewhat outclassed, went through the early stages of W.W. I with this group.

The traditional cavalry charge was still considered tactically feasible in 1912, but the early phases of the war demonstrated clearly that changes were taking place in warfare, and when he was blown off his horse by the explosion of a French shell that landed close by, he had had enough. When you couldn't see the man who was trying to kill you, war ceased to be fun.

Also contributing to his disenchantment with the war on the ground was the evident fact that his superiors were not particularly impressed with his abilities. He found himself moving farther to the rear, assigned finally to a position in supply. This triggered a most unmilitary letter to the commanding general requesting a transfer to the flying service, and in May, 1915, his petition was granted. He was sent to Colonge for training.

His enthusiasm grew to the point where he persuaded his pilot to give him flying lessons. They managed to borrow a dual-controlled trainer, and on days when they were not out on missions, they tried to make a pilot out of von Richthofen. They worked together for 25 hours, an extraordinarily long time in those days, before Zeumer, the instructor, decided to let the future ace of aces try landing the plane. The 1st attempt was a disaster. So was the 2nd. But Prussian perserverance being what it is, he managed to set the plane down in one piece on his 3rd try, this on Christmas Day, 1915. At last he was a pilot, at least by definition.

Single-seaters were still his goal, but still eluded him, and he had to continue as an observer. Finally, however, he was assigned to single-seaters, and in 2 weeks had destroyed 2 of them—but for the wrong side. He was transferred back to 2-seaters, but at least he was a pilot. He was flying bombing missions on the Russian Front, which satisfied some of his killer instinct as letters to his mother bear out, but he was still sportsman enough to want a quarry that would fight back.

For many months he worked on his fighter technique in borrowed Fokker single-seaters. He petitioned again for transfer to a fighter group, and was again turned down, and it was only through a stroke of luck that he met Oswald Boelcke, Germany's leading ace, who was recruiting men for his squadron. This was in August, 1916, and it was the training with this man, who has been called "the father of pursuit aviation," that turned Von Richthofen into the killing machine that he finally became.

From the outset, Boelcke was wary of Von Richthofen. He had heard of his early flying troubles, and he was also aware of the fact that Von Richthofen knew little or nothing of the mechanical side of flying. Worse, he was not inclined to learn. But to counter this, Boelcke saw in his new recruit an eagerness for the hunt, an indifference to alcohol and women, and a single-minded purpose that indicated to him that if Von Richthofen survived the 1st few missions with the new squadron, he might very well become a great fighter. It's too bad that Boelcke didn't live long enough to see what he really created. He died a few months later in a mid-air collision with one of his best friends.

The new group, Jagdstaffel 2, was to fly out of Lagnicourt, France, and Von Richthofen arrived there on September 1, 1916. There were no airplanes immediately available, and the 1st week was spent listening to "The Gospel According to Boelcke," a dissertation that Von Richthofen must have taken seriously, because he scored his 1st victory when the group went out on its initial mission on September 17. He was so excited about drawing blood that he almost crashed his new Albatross when he landed near the wreck of his victim. He got there in time to see the 2 British fliers pulled from the wreckage. One of them died while Von Richthofen watched and the other died before he could reach a field hospital. All in all, it was an exciting day for the young pilot, and to commemorate it he ordered a small silver goblet, a ritual that was to be repeated until his jeweler ran out of silver along about the 60th victory. He also made a practice of collecting souvenirs in the form of bits and pieces from the wrecks. These he sent home to his mother.

By April, 1917, he had surpassed Boelcke's record of 40 victories and became the ranking ace of the war. He was a national hero, and picture postcards of "The Red Knight" were being sold throughout Germany as a boost to a national morale that had already begun to slip. There was also evidence that the strain of the war was beginning to have an effect on Von Richthofen. He became quieter and more withdrawn. Losses in his squadron unnerved him, and he began to question his own future. The German High Command ordered him on a 6-week leave, but he got very little rest, because the leave consisted of a series of audiences with the Kaiser and other national leaders. This was not his cup of tea, and he was anxious to return to the front.

On July 6, Von Richthofen led Jagdstaffel 11 on a morning flight in search of a group of British observation planes that had been reported over the lines. This would ordinarily have been no probelm at all for the now-notorious "Red Baron," but this time he ran into a particularly tough adversary who could not be intimidated. As a result, his career was very nearly cut short. The maroon Albatross spun down, out of control, from 12,000', and only at 1,000' did Von Richthofen regain enough of his faculties to level out and make a reasonably safe landing. He had received a deep bullet wound in the head that was to keep him out of action for some time. It was a different Von Richthofen who returned to his men on July 25, 1917.

By April 20, 1918, when Von Richthofen claimed his 79th and 80th victories within 3 minutes of each other, his mood matched the gloomy weather that had kept the squadron grounded for days. On the 21st, while a mechanic was preparing his maroon triplane, he was asked to autograph a photograph. "Don't you think I'll come back?" he asked, as he complied with the request. He was also uneasy when someone took a picture of him. Boelcke had also been photographed before his last flight.

Six brightly colored Fokker triplanes took off, with Von Richthofen's maroon machine leading. In the flight was another Von Richthofen, a cousin, who was on his 1st patrol. He had been given instructions by Manfred to avoid a fight at all costs.

At about the same time a flight of Sopwith Camels was taking off from Bertangles. This was No. 209 Squadron, led by Capt. Arthur Roy Brown, who, like Von Richthofen, had a fledgling to take care of. In this case it was Wilfred R. May, a schoolmate of Brown's, and he too had been told to stay out of action.

Inevitably, these 2 groups, which had been joined by other flights, met in a furious melee. May, who could not resist getting into the fight, knocked down a triplane that was also separated from the general fight. This was very likely the younger Von Richthofen. May's guns jammed and he headed for home. His retreat was interrupted by gunfire, and he looked over his shoulder to see a maroon triplane closing on him. And right behind the triplane he saw Brown's Sopwith Camel, guns blazing. The fight had come down to about 200', and at this point, the triplane was seen to falter and glide over a low ridge, under heavy ground fire from Australian troops in the area. Von Richthofen's plane continued its glide, and made a heavy landing, demolishing the landing gear. When the Australians got to the plane, they found the pilot dead, and very shortly it was discovered that it was indeed the notorious Red Baron.

Like the man himself, this last flight has continued to be surrounded by controversy. Credit for his death has been claimed by the RAF as well as the Australians, and a good case can be made for both claimants.

So closed the career of Capt. Manfred Freiherr von Richthofen, on April 21, 1918, in his 26th year, and then also began the legend of W.W. I's Ace of Aces, The Red Knight of Germany.

—J.Ca.

Baron von Steuben (U.S., Revolutionary War)

In late February of 1778, a bulky, balding middle-aged Prussian officer, resplendent in a blue uniform gleaming with military medals, rode into Washington's camp at Valley Forge with his translator, a young Frenchman named Duponceau, 2 aides, one servant, and a greyhound. This impressive, bulbous-nosed man was introduced to General Washington as Friedrich Wilhelm Augustus Henry Ferdinand, Baron von Steuben, recommended by Benjamin Franklin and Silas Deane, who described him as a "Lieutenant-General in the King of Prussia's service."

The Baron spoke about 12 words of English, and even those caused him to turn red with embarrassment. He had been paid by the French to offer his services to Washington; he was an expert drill officer.

If a bit of harmless deception preceded Von Steuben's arrival, his presence at Valley Forge was like a breath of fresh air to Washington, whose half-naked, ill-disciplined troops could scarcely be worthy of battle against the thoroughly trained British. Steuben, as he wished to be called, was not a lieutenant-general; his rank when he was dropped from King Frederick's Army 14 years before was captain. And when he met an English friend of Benjamin Franklin's in 1777, Steuben was broke and unemployed. Aware that Congress would turn its nose up at a mere captain, having its hands full with foreign officers who all wanted high ranks in the Continental Army, Franklin became a party to this mild deception with Silas Deane and the Comte de Saint-Germain, the French War Minister. Saint-Germain knew that Steuben was the son of an accomplished Prussian officer, well educated, army-trained, and a crack drillmaster. Therefore, he, Franklin, and Deane elevated Steuben's rank for Franklin's glowing letter to Washington. But perhaps it was Steuben himself who won Washington's approval before they met at Valley Forge. In his letter to the commander-in-chief, he offered his services as a volunteer without rank simply because he wanted to help the cause of liberty. And so, with the blessings of the French War Ministry and of Franklin and Deane, the jovial baron set off for America as a volunteer, although all his expenses were paid by the French Government.

Gen. Thomas Conway was still nominally inspector-general of the Army, but Washington gave Steuben the duties of acting inspector-general without rank, pending congressional approval, to drill and train this pitifully undisciplined army.

Steuben was astonished at what he found. There was no drill manual, no book of army regulations. The ragged troops knew nothing about bayonet practice; to most, a bayonet was something to use as a spit for cooking roast beef. They were not used to instant obedience to crisp orders, as was the European way, and the officers thought drilling was beneath them.

But Steuben was a patient man; he set about writing his own manual, reducing the 21 motions considered necessary to "load firelock" to 10. This was translated into formal French by Duponceau, then to formal English, then to English the soldiers could understand. It became the "bible of the Continental Army."

It was Steuben's language barrier, however, that endeared him to the troops. In the painfully slow process of training, he would curse at them in German, sometimes bellowing at them for up to 5 minutes, red in the face, his huge hands gesturing, almost overcome with frustration over his limited English. A ripple of good-natured laughter would go through the ranks—the men liked this blustering butterball foreigner who was willing to admit his own mistakes—and Steuben, not lacking a sense of humor, would laugh with them. Then turning to Duponceau and young Benjamin Walker, he would say, "My dear Walker, my dear Duponceau, come swear in English for me."

By the end of March a new spirit was evident among the troops, despite the hardships of hunger, cold weather, and lack of clothing. From 6 in the morning until 6 at night, Steuben was out on the drill field, painstakingly putting the men through their paces, his guttural voice booming over the sound of shuffling feet. The men learned to march in column, and from that into compact masses, marching in double rank and in columns of 4. They were soon skilled in the art of bayonet combat, too. There was no doubt that their jovial Prussian teacher had turned them into a crack brigade.

Steuben was a godsend to Washington, who wrote to Congress extolling the qualities of this man who had turned the Army from a motley crew into a highly disciplined fighting force. On May 6 Washington held a reception for his officers, introducing Maj. Gen. Baron von Steuben as the new inspector-general of the U.S., by act of Congress.

On June 28, 1778, Steuben's training was put to a severe test at the Battle of Monmouth. Gen. Charles Lee had called a retreat, and Washington, flushed with anger, sent Lee to the rear for such an unwarranted breach of conduct. Gen. "Mad Anthony" Wayne leaped into the fray, urging his men to fight, to aim at the King's birds—the British officers. While Wayne was definitely the hero of Monmouth, Steuben was a hero, too. In the confusion, when one regiment faltered and started to fall back, Steuben's military discipline was put into action. Shouting hoarsely in his incomprehensible German, yet understood by his gestures, Steuben wheeled the men around with such

ease and speed that they might have been practicing on the drill field. Clearly the men were now fighting veterans, moving in coordination, firing on command, using their bayonets with deadly skill. It was the 1st time that Washington emerged victorious in a major engagement.

Again Steuben was elated when on July 16, 1779, the Light Infantry, under Gen. Anthony Wayne's command, captured from the British without need of muskets the fort at Stony Point on the Hudson River. Steuben's bayonet-trained Continentals had been taught well.

In 1781 Steuben accompanied Gen. Nathanael Greene south to Virginia to train Greene's southern army—almost to a man raw, inept recruits—and to become commander of all the Virginia troops. In time he also became President Washington's most trusted military adviser.

After the war in 1786, New York granted him 16,000 acres of land in the Mohawk Valley near Utica. But Steuben bought a country house in Manhattan on what is now East 55th Street where he opened his doors to friends and freeloaders. The kindhearted Steuben almost went bankrupt in 1790 after his so-called guests had drunk his liquor, eaten his food, and borrowed his money. Had his friends Alexander Hamilton and George Washington not come to his rescue, he might have languished penniless and forgotten. Finally, after much prodding by Washington, Congress granted him $2,500 a year for life.

Steuben never married, but adopted one of his former aides, William North. Benjamin Walker, also a former aide, was like a son to him. Both North and Walker were heirs and executors of Steuben's will when he died in November, 1794, at age 64.

A bronze statue of Steuben was erected at Lafayette Park in Washington, and another, in 1914, at Utica. Many towns have been named after him in New York, Maine, Michigan, Wisconsin, and there are Steubenvilles in both Ohio and Kentucky. On a boulder near his grave in Steuben Memorial Park, Oneida County, N.Y., is an inscription that reads, "His Services Were Indispensable to the Achievement of American Independence."

—E.J.G.

Court-Martials around the World

ADM. JOHN BYNG (1704–1757)

Britain in the early 1700s was under the political thumb of George II, the Hanoverian monarch whose principal interest was in bolstering the finances of Hanover, Germany, at the ex-

pense of England's stability. Under this regime, the Duke of Newcastle, Thomas Pelham, pampered the whims of George II and neglected the military forces of Britain.

France, out to recapture the island of Minorca previously snatched from her by the British in 1708, was occupied with outfitting 12 ships and 16,000 men under the command of Admiral la Galissonière. Though spies had informed Pelham of France's plans, no countermeasures were considered until almost too late.

Totally unprepared, a panicked English regime committed its fleet to Minorca. Under the command of Adm. John Byng, 10 undermanned warships in decaying condition sailed from Spithead on April 7, 1756. On May 20, the 2 fleets engaged in battle. Admiral Byng, outgunned and outnumbered in both ships and men, made his command decision. He abandoned the island of Minorca with its defenses of 2,800 men, under its deputy governor General Blakeney, to the French fleet, feeling that his own fleet could best be used in the protection of Gibraltar.

The Court-Martial. When word of this reached England, political forces were enraged. To save face, Pelham needed a scapegoat; Admiral Byng was tagged. Public opinion, angered by the Hanover millstone, cried out for Byng's death. He was arrested and a court-martial was held aboard H.M.S. *St. George* in Portsmouth harbor. The charge: cowardice in the face of the enemy. In the trial this charge was replaced with a substitute: "That in the battle, Byng had not done his utmost to defeat the French fleet." The sentence: Death. On March 14, 1757, Adm. John Byng was executed by a firing squad.

Significance. After Byng's execution, it became common knowledge that he had served as the scapegoat for corrupt and incompetent politicians. The only defense of the judges was they were obliged to conform to the 18th-century revisions of the Articles of War.

French dramatist Voltaire gave the best summation in his *Candide.* "Why kill the Admiral? It is because he has not killed enough other people. In England it is useful to kill an Admiral now and then—*pour encourager les autres.*"

Benedict Arnold (1741–1801)

In his early 30s, Arnold gave up his successful commercial pursuits to enter the military service of America's Revolutionary Army. He was a brilliant strategist and covered himself with battlefield glory at Ticonderoga, Quebec, and Saratoga. A national hero, Arnold was put in command of the Philadelphia area in 1778 by George Washington. Here Arnold's extravagant living and arrogant acts set in motion a series of events that led to his requesting a court-martial on December 23, 1779.

The Court-Martial. The trial took place in Norris's Tavern in Morristown, N.J. Major General Howe and his court officers were the judges. Gen. Joseph Reed and Timothy Matlack, president and secretary, respectively, of the Pennsylvania State Council, were the accusers.

Arnold was charged with issuing a military pass to Robert Shewell, a businessman of alleged Tory sympathies; of closing Philadelphia shops to the public, while buying from them for himself; of imposing menial chores on the sons of free men; and of using State wagons to transport private property.

In conducting his own eloquent defense, Arnold had the 1st 3 charges set aside. On the 4th charge, the court recommended that Arnold receive a reprimand from his commander-in-chief. Washington wrote to Arnold saying that he considered "the affair of the wagons to be imprudent and improper." This gentle wrist slap so wounded Arnold's pride, it sent him into a hell of black despair that culminated in an attempt to betray his country.

Significance. The court-martial of Benedict Arnold, inspired by rivalry and jealousy, pointed up the need for objective reform in the military court-martial system.

James Thomas Brudenell (1797–1868)

The only son of Thomas Brudenell, Earl of Cardigan, James grew up as a pampered, idolized, spoiled brat, to become, at 27, a despicable egocentric whose dream was to command his own regiment. England's 19th-century military establishment provided the perfect servant-master social order for demigod aristocrats. Into this elite of the favored highborn rode Lord Brudenell to claim, as a captain, the reputation of the most hated hero in England's history.

Contemptuous of his regimental superiors as well as his subordinates, his hatred of commoners became legend; they were animals and to be treated as such. Soon dissatisfied with the authority of a captain, Brudenell used his wealth to buy the command of the 15th King's Hussars—it cost him £40,000. Under Brudenell, the 15th was turned upside down. Officers and commoners alike were court-martialed. The intolerable treatment accorded all ranks soon inspired wholesale desertions. Then in 1833, an enraged Lieutenant Colonel Brudenell preferred charges against Captain Wathen. The charges were nonsensical and petty. In court, under cross-examination, Brudenell's testimony backfired.

The trial, discussed in London's staid *Times,* aroused public sentiment in favor of Wathen. The ensuing public outcry, plus Brudenell's testimony, turned the court against Brudenell. Not only was Wathen acquitted of all charges, but Brudenell was ousted from his command of the 15th.

Two years later a determined and ruthless Brudenell amassed the authority of his aristocratic friends and in 1834 was appointed to the command of the 11th Light Dragoons. Again *The Times* voiced the public resentment of Englishmen, but to no avail, as the power of the military closed its protective ranks.

More of a martinet than before, Brudenell had 54 officers and men of the 11th court-martialed in his 1st 6 months of command. The Light Dragoons suffered the degradations inflicted by an aristocrat gone mad. Parliament instigated an investigation into Brudenell's appointment. Pressure by the Army caused the investigation to fail and Brudenell's appointment to be upheld.

With the death of Thomas Brudenell, Lord Brudenell became not just the commander of the 11th, but also the Earl of Cardigan. Nothing could stop him now. He began to rid the 11th of all commoners in order to have a regiment of unsullied aristocrats. *The Times* printed an unsigned letter of protest against the highhandedness of the 11th's commander. The letter was attributed to a retired captain and former officer in the Dragoons, Harvy Tuckett. Lord Cardigan's seconds called on Tuckett for a written apology. It was not forthcoming. A duel was set for 5 P.M., September 12, at Wimbledon Common.

The Court-Martial. As a result of the illegal duel and Cardigan's being caught at the scene with a smoking pistol in his hand and a seriously wounded Tuckett on the ground, Cardigan was, on October 20, 1840, taken before a grand jury and remanded for trial. As a peer, he could not be tried in a common court. On February 16, 1841, he was summoned before the Lords of Parliament to answer to charges.

For once, Cardigan underestimated the power of his influential friends in high places; he expected to be hanged. Both the prosecution and defense worked together with connivance and legal trickery to have Lord Cardigan acquitted of all charges. The din of public opinion mattered not. James Thomas Brudenell, Earl of Cardigan, went on to lead the charge of the Light Brigade at Balaklava.

Significance. Despite damning testimony, public indignation, and being caught in the act, the defendant was freed. The power of England's military and aristocracy prevailed, guaranteeing the protection of one of their own. And down through the ages, the words of Alfred Lord Tennyson still resound: "Half a league, half a league/Half a league onward/All in the valley of Death/Rode the six hundred."

ALEXANDER SLIDELL MACKENZIE (1803–1848)

In 1842, the small U.S. brig, *Somers*, a training ship for naval officers under the command of Alexander Slidell Mackenzie, knifed through the choppy waters off the African coast. This was the era of wooden sailing ships, large

crews, and few officers; and together with poor food, cramped quarters, and lengthy sea duty, this caused the fear of mutiny to hang like a pall over most ships.

Mackenzie, a literary man who had written several books, disliked his job, the men who served under him, and in particular, he disliked Philip Spencer, the 18-year-old son of John C. Spencer, Secretary of War. By nature, Commander Mackenzie was a frustrated Captain Bligh, but running scared.

James W. Wales, a purser's steward, reported to Mackenzie that young Spencer had approached him with plans for a full-scale mutiny wherein Mackenzie and his officers were to be killed. On Wales's statements rested the bulk of evidence. Mackenzie and his officers were frightened. Day by day, their uncertainty fed this cancer until, in a burst of determination to prevent that which they feared, they acted. On Mackenzie's orders, Spencer, Cromwell, and Small were hanged.

The Court-Martial. When the *Somers* put into New York Harbor on December 14, 1842, a court of inquiry was called for December 28. Before completion of the inquiry and at the request of Mackenzie, a court-martial date was set for January 28, 1843, at Brooklyn. Mackenzie was charged with 3 counts of murder, 2 counts of oppression, illegal punishment, and conduct unbecoming a naval officer.

In answer to the charges, Mackenzie stated: "I admit that acting Midshipman Philip Spencer, Boatswain's Mate Samuel Cromwell, and Seaman Elisha Small, were put to death by my order, but, as under existing circumstances, this act was demanded by duty and justified by necessity, I plead not guilty to all charges."

The trial, a mere formality, presented only one side of the sordid story, for dead men cannot defend themselves. The judges were sympathetic toward Mackenzie, feeling that any commander deserved the full support of the Navy to assure discipline.

Significance. In this extremely controversial court-martial, there was no way to prove or disprove the allegations of Wales, the other officers, or Mackenzie. But the repercussions resulting forced an overhaul of naval justice. Flogging was abolished as were punishment deaths at sea. The practice of training naval officers, as on the *Somers*, gave way to the establishment of Annapolis.

Herman Melville, related to Lieutenant Gansevoort of the *Somers*, authored *Moby Dick* and other never-to-be-forgotten novels. His *Billy Budd* has preserved for all time the infamous hanging aboard the *Somers*. Over 130 years after the fact, stage plays and motion pictures are still being made, based on the testimony and court-martial of Alexander Slidell Mackenzie.

ALFRED DREYFUS (1859–1935)

For a French Jew of peasant stock, Dreyfus was a rarity. He had overcome great obstacles to become a commissioned officer on the general staff of the French military. France, in the 1890s, seethed with internal turmoil. Into this caldron of uncertainty, Martin Brucker, a spy for the statistical section of the general staff, dropped a bombshell: a letter signed with the initial "D" and stolen from the German embassy. This *bordereau* indicated a spy was operating within the elite of the general staff.

From the Minister of War, Gen. Auguste Mercier, down through the ranks, no one had the slightest notion of the spy's identity. To look among highborn French officers was unthinkable. Alfred Dreyfus would be the perfect scapegoat. He was an outsider, a Jew, and his name began with the letter "D."

The Court-Martial. On December 19, 1894, the trial began in an old gaslit palace on the rue Cherche-Midi. Present were 7 high-ranking army officers acting as judges: Gen. Charles Gonse, deputy chief of the general staff; Maj. Du Paty de Clam; Maj. Georges Picquart, observer for Auguste Mercier; Alfred Dreyfus; and his attorney, Edgar Demange. The charge: high treason. The proof: lies, hearsay, and a letter allegedly written by Dreyfus.

Picquart advised Mercier that the prosecution's evidence wouldn't hold up. Mercier became worried. The statistical section went to work. A "secret file" was produced that contained irrefutable evidence of men high in government whose names could not be mentioned because of national security. So deftly and dramatically was this handled in chambers that the decision of the judges was unanimous. Alfred Dreyfus was declared guilty and sentenced to Devil's Island for life.

Newspapers were ecstatic. Voices of the French people echoed through the streets of Paris: "Traitor, coward, death to the dirty Jew!"

After 12 years of unremitting effort by Dreyfus's wife, Lucy, his brother Mathieu, French politician Scheurer-Kestner, statesman Georges Clemenceau, author Émile Zola, and others, Dreyfus was acquitted.

Significance. The court-martial of Alfred Dreyfus demonstrated the power of the military to prosecute unjustly, and though many reforms have since been made, in the words of Clemenceau: "Military justice is to justice as military music is to music."

WILLIAM (BILLY) MITCHELL (1879–1936)

Seven days after entering the U.S. military service in 1898, Mitchell became the youngest 2nd lieutenant in the Army. An outspoken, gregarious, and respected leader of men, Major Mitchell, in 1912, transferred to the 1st U.S. military Air Force as a pilot after 2 hours of instruction from Orville Wright. In W.W. I, Brigadier General Mitchell, a staunch advocate of air power, argued often with Gen. John J. Pershing, who threatened to send him home if he didn't shut up. Mitchell also argued with his nonflying superiors in Washington, but his pleas for a large, independent air force fell on brass ears.

In 1921, with the U.S. preparing to abandon its air force experiment, Mitchell pulled out all the stops, determined to prove to the military and the American people that planes could be a greater striking force than a battleship or artillery.

In a test with 7 land-based planes carrying torpedo-shaped bombs, Mitchell led his squadron 100 mi. from land, in stormy weather, to search out, attack, and sink the unsinkable battleship *Ostfriesland*. It was all over in 21½ minutes. The Congress, Navy, and War Department referred to the incident as: "Fool Mitchell luck!"

On a tour of Hawaii and the Philippines, Mitchell reported in detail how both could be destroyed militarily. Again, no one paid any attention: no one—but the Japanese.

After the navy dirigible *Shenandoah* was destroyed in a storm over Ohio, Mitchell publicly stated: "These accidents are the result of the incompetency, the criminal negligence, and the almost treasonable administration of our national defense by the Navy and War Departments." This bombshell was heard. Mitchell's court-martial followed.

The Court-Martial. At a carefully chosen site in a small abandoned warehouse in Washington, D.C., the trial began on October 28, 1925. The charge: violations of the 96th Article of War. The proof: Mitchell's public statements. The president of the court, Gen. Charles P. Summerall, and the judges were nonflying opponents of Mitchell and of his stand for a large independent air force. Testifying for Mitchell were: Maj. Carl Spaatz; Maj. "Hap" Arnold; Maj. Gerald C. Brandt; and Eddie Rickenbacker. After 3 weeks of testimony, the prejudiced judges brought in their verdict: guilty on all counts. The sentence: 5 years' suspension from rank, command, and pay.

Significance. The trial of Billy Mitchell proved again the awesome power of the military in its court-martial system.

MUTINY ON THE *Potemkin*

It was June 13, 1905, 12 years before the Russian Revolution, but already coming events were casting their shadows. Separated from the

Black Sea fleet off Sevastopol, a single Russian cruiser, the *Potemkin*, on a gunnery exercise, bobbed gently at anchor in the waters of Tender Strait. The crew of 800 conscripted farmers suffered from harsh, inhumane treatment, hunger, and seasickness.

On deck, 2 sailors swabbed halfheartedly, their stomachs churning spasmodically with each roll of the ship. Aft, on hooks along a spar, joints of meat swayed slowly. A heavy crust of maggots gave them a most bizarre appearance. The swabbies called to their comrades, especially to Afansy Matushenko, their spokesman.

He quieted the tempers of the angry men and sent for Dr. Smirnov to inspect the meat. The doctor declared it fresh and edible. Dissatisfied, the men refused to accept his assurance. Chief Officer Giliarovsky commanded the men to disperse. Tempers flared. The crew became a mob. Captain Golikov put in one of his rare appearances, and armed seamen temporarily routed the dissenters. Golikov ordered a tarpaulin thrown over the crewmen remaining on the deck. They were to be shot.

Then Afansy Matushenko reappeared, shouting epithets inspired by the creed of a growing socialist democratic movement. A fight ensued. Captain Golikov was killed and his body thrown overboard. Mutineers took command of the *Potemkin*.

By June 17, 5 ships of the Black Sea fleet arrived from Sevastopol to quell the mutiny. One of the ships, *George the Conqueror*, joined with the *Potemkin*, and both ships escaped to Romania. There the Russian battleship, *Tchesme*, caught up with the *Potemkin* and 75 of the mutineers.

The Court-Martial. Fifty-two mutineers were sentenced to imprisonment and 3 to death. Afansy Matushenko escaped; he was never heard of again. After the trial, a bulletin was released by Russian authorities in which it was stated: "The Czar was far more impressed by the mutiny of the men of the *Potemkin* than by the disaster at Tsu Shima."

Significance. The *Potemkin* mutiny proved, as did that of the *Bounty*, that men of every nationality have a limit to their endurance. The disaster at Tsu Shima, mentioned in the Russian authorities' bulletin, referred to the Battle of the Sea of Japan in which the entire Russian fleet met destruction.

MUTINY AT WILLIAM'S HAVEN

The compulsive writhings that accompanied the death struggle of Germany's Navy, in 1917–1918, resulted from recurrent mutinies. These were encouraged by the political sharpshooting of sailors' unions, social revolutionaries, communists, and other leftist organizations that fed on the growing decay of a tottering Germany.

One of many similar incidents, it began aboard the *Prinzregent Luitpold*, at anchor in the Wilhelmshaven dockyard. Hans Becker, stoker and a leader in the sailors' union movement, was intoxicated with self-admiration, drunk with the power that allowed him to influence 1,000 less extroverted followers.

It was July 31, 1917. Six hundred dissatisfied crewmen looked forward to a promised 24-hour, duty-free watch, movies, and special food, but this was not to be. Lieutenant Hoffman announced there would be no day off, but infantry drill instead. There were angry mutterings.

Below decks, Becker told his followers: "If there are no movies tomorrow, we will go AWOL." This answer to a broken promise sparked a full-scale mutiny. The *Prinzregent Luitpold* steamed clear of the harbor to conduct an investigation. Sympathizers aboard the *Kaiserin, König Albert, Markgraf, Friedrich der Grosse, Kronprinz Wilhelm, Grosser Kurfurst, Westfalen, Rheinland, Helgoland, Ostfriesland, Posen,* and *Pillan,* rose in force. On August 5, the entire fleet steamed clear of the harbor; dissenters were imprisoned.

The Court-Martial. Those accused of lesser crimes than high treason received sentences of from 2 to 10 years in the penitentiary. In the trial for those accused of the highest crime, 3 naval officers and 3 judiciary officials acted as judges. There were 2 admirals and 5 captains among the 12 prosecutors.

Sachse, Reichpietsch, Weber, Becker, and Kobis, charged with high treason, had legal counsel and were heard separately. Stoker Petty Officer Willy Sachse was called 1st. The charge: "That said man, attached to the S.M.S. *Friedrich der Grosse* on July 15, 1917, did join in unlawful conspiracy during a state of War."

After an aggregate of 12 hours of testimony for the 5 accused, the stony-faced judges delivered their verdict: "guilty on all counts." The recommended sentence: death by a firing squad.

Admiral von Scheer, chief of the high sea fleet, exercised his right of final judgment. To Reichpietsch and Kobis, death. To Sachse, Weber, and Becker, 15 years' imprisonment for each man.

Significance. There is no short handy explanation for mutiny, nor can there be a short encapsulated sentence of a court-martial's significance. For centuries, military establishments have lived by one commandment: "Obedience or death." This irrational creed has accomplished little except to father other equally irrational creeds.

EDDIE D. SLOVIK (1920–1945)

Eddie Slovik was not a carbon copy of the proverbial clean-cut all-American boy who enters military service with bright eyes and equal amounts of uncertainty and enthusiasm. Slovik's life had been a series of frustrating events that had thrust him 1st into reform school and then into prison.

When, via the draft, he entered the service during W.W. II, he had been out of prison 2 years, was happily married, and had a reasonably good post-prison work record. But underneath this façade of normalcy, Eddie Slovik hadn't changed all that much. In training, he had told a buddy that he wouldn't fire his rifle in combat.

Fighting was heavy for the Allies in 1944 when, in August, Slovik arrived at Omaha Beach to be assigned to the "jinxed division"—"G" Company of the 109th Infantry, 28th Division. Before Slovik and other replacements arrived at Elbeuf, 5 truck hours from the Beach, the convoy ran into artillery fire and had to stop and dig in. When his unit continued on toward Elbeuf, a frightened Slovik remained in his foxhole.

For 6 weeks he stayed as "house-guest" with Canadian forces before reporting for duty with the 28th. There, he confessed to desertion, was placed under arrest, and ordered to stand ready to be court-martialed.

The Court-Martial. The confession of Private Slovik played a major role in his speedy trial. He wrote in part: "I, private Eddie D. Slovik ✳36896415 confess to the desertion of the U.S. Army . . . I turned myself over to the Canadian Provost Corps. After being with them for 6 weeks, I was turned over to American M.P. They turned me loose. I told my commanding officer my story. I said that if I had to go out there again, I'd run away. He said there was nothing he could do for me, so I ran away again AND I'LL RUN AWAY AGAIN IF I HAVE TO GO OUT THERE."

The trial, held on November 11, 1944, was one of the shortest court-martials on record, lasting only one hour and 40 minutes. Nine judges convicted Slovik for violation of the 58th Article of War: desertion to avoid hazardous duty. The sentence: to be dishonorably discharged from service, to forfeit all pay and allowances due or to become due, and to be shot to death with musketry. After a lengthy review, the sentence was upheld by Gen. Dwight D. Eisenhower. For Private Eddie D. Slovik, his lifetime of frustration came to an end before a firing squad in the snowcapped Vosges Mountains in January, 1945.

Significance. The sentence of death by a firing squad given to Eddie Slovik was the last such sentence to be carried out in the history of the U.S. military. Eddie's execution was intended as an example to discourage desertion, but men like Slovik will continue to desert a system they cannot understand.

JAMES ROBERSON (?–1954)

Since the beginning of W.W. II, more than a million servicemen have become familiar with the acronym snafu and its application to injustices within the military system. Among other things, the letters stand for "situation normal, all fouled up." The case of James Roberson is no less incredible than that of the Fort Riley, Kan., inductee who was found to be only 12 years old. They hid him in solitary for 3 months.

Young Roberson was sworn into military service in the early days of W.W. II. He was 18 years old. By the end of his enlistment, he had served with exemplary courage, earning a citation, 4 air medals, and the Distinguished Flying Cross, as a navy aerial gunner.

Then in 1947, he was honorably discharged. Out of service, Roberson was unsure of what he wanted to do. As day after lonely day passed uneventfully, he decided to reenlist in the Navy. The officer handling the reenlistment informed him that because he had not conformed to certain unexplained regulations, he would not be entitled to paid leave, travel allowance, or the usual bonus. This edict didn't set well with Roberson, and he uttered some sharp words. The officer ordered Roberson confined to quarters.

His reenlistment papers not completed, and relying on his honorable discharge, he decided to go back to Iowa and think it over. He had no sooner arrived home than he was arrested and brought to trial on charges of desertion, breaking arrest, disobeying an officer, drunkenness, and conduct prejudicial to the service.

The Court-Martial. The well-oiled wheels of military justice slipped quickly into high gear. Roberson was thwarted each time he tried to bring up his honorable discharge. In record time, he was convicted of all charges and sentenced to 4 years imprisonment. After 9 months, he was released on probation. Convinced that the Navy must know of his original discharge by now, he once more went home to Iowa.

History repeated itself. He was arrested a 2nd time and again imprisoned. His parents hired a civilian attorney who obtained a writ of habeas corpus. He was released on the orders of a Federal court judge who ruled that the Navy had no jurisdiction over James Roberson.

A climax to the Roberson affair came in 1954. In October, the U.S. Court of Claims acknowledged that Roberson had been convicted unjustly, and imprisoned illegally. For this inconvenience, he was to be awarded a cash settlement of $5,000, but for Roberson the snafu had run full circle. Young James Roberson died 2 months before the U.S. Court of Claims advised his attorney of its decision.

Significance. The questionable measures used by the military to cure disciplinary ills often trigger the side effect of snafu cases. James Roberson is only one example of such cases.

THE PRESIDIO 27

By 1968, the undeclared war in Vietnam had become the most unpopular war in the history of the U.S. Young men were running off to Canada, and other countries, to escape the draft. The use of marijuana, uppers, downers, and hard drugs, was on the rise. College students publicly burned their draft cards and participated in campus riots. Peace marches and open dissent were increasing. Singly and in groups, 18- and 19-year-olds, frightened, confused, and uncertain, became fugitives from a society they didn't understand or accept.

The stockade at San Francisco's old Presidio, built prior to W.W. I to house 56 men, was bursting with "emergency overcrowding" and held 115 prisoners. Sworn, published testimony of inmates has revealed that the once comfortable quarters were divided into small windowless cells, many with dimensions less than the army minimum of 6' by 8'. There were 5 toilets, 2 of them plugged up, and these contributed human waste to literally inches of polluted water standing on the floors of the showers. Black-painted cells were unlighted, making reading impossible. Food was both poor and in short supply. There were less than 50 drinking cups for all the prisoners.

Guards of the facility and marine guards from nearby Treasure Island allegedly dreamed up the harassing use of urine-loaded water pistols, senseless beatings, finger and testes twisting, and threats of death. On work details, these minimum-security prisoners were supervised by shotgun-armed, trigger-happy guards who often pointed their weapons at prisoners to threaten: "I'll blow your fucking heads off." This type of treatment inspired 60 suicide attempts, all denied by the Army; their word for it was "gestures."

In a work crew, Richard "Rusty" Bunch antagonized a guard by skipping away from him. "Rusty" was shot in the back for trying to escape. The date was October 11, 1968. On the morning of the 14th, 27 prisoners broke ranks to sit down on the grass, asking to speak to stockade commander Capt. Robert S. Lamont in order to express their grievances. They were arrested and charged with mutiny.

The Court-Martial. After 3 investigations, costing the Army a half-million dollars, the mutineers were tried at the Presidio, Fort Irwin, and Fort Ord, in California, and at Fort Lewis, in Washington, between January and June of 1969. Early trial sentences were for 16 years' imprisonment, but due to public outcry, later trial sentences were for 3 months. Capt. Dean Flippo, an army prosecutor, stated in the courtroom: "It is the attack on the system, not the method of the attack, that is important in determining whether there is mutiny."

Significance. More than 100,000 servicemen face trail by court-martial each year. They are confined without bail; they are not tried by a jury of their peers; they have no guarantee of impartial judges, and in 95% of the cases, the verdict is guilty. Those convicted lose all of their rights. They can and do suffer cruel and inhumane treatment during imprisonment. Some are driven insane and others resort to suicide, all in the name of discipline at all costs, for this is military justice.

THE MY LAI MASSACRE

Lieut. William L. Calley, Jr., and Charlie Company boarded helicopters for the village of My Lai in northeast South Vietnam at 7:30 A.M. on March 16, 1968. The night-before briefing of commander Capt. Ernest Medina warned of a head-on confrontation with the Viet Cong's 48th Battalion. The orders were: Kill the Viet Cong; destroy the village.

Over My Lai at 1,000', Col. Frank Barker headed the command copters. At 2,000' was Maj. Gen. Samuel Koster, commander of the American Division. At 2,500' was the commander of the 11th Infantry Brigade, Col. Oran Henderson. Photographer Ronald Haeberle and reporter Jay Roberts were to record the action of a major battle.

An hour and a half after Charlie Company landed, Chief Warrant Officer Hugh Thompson arrived over My Lai in an observation copter. What he saw was not a battle but a massacre of running, screaming old men, women, and children being machine-gunned by American soldiers. A ditch filled with moaning, squirming, and bleeding bodies was a prime target.

While Charlie Company ate lunch, surrounded by dead Vietnamese, word came down from Medina to stop the attack. Not a single enemy shot had been fired all morning, but Americans had killed more than 100 unarmed civilians, including children. After the incident, there was more than the normal amount of scuttlebutt. Colonel Henderson advised Medina there would be an investigation. Medina told his men to clam up. Then talk about My Lai petered out; there was no investigation.

Back in the U.S., 18 months later, Robert Ridenhour, a nonparticipant at My Lai but a Vietnam veteran, broke the sordid story. The chairman of the House Armed Services Committee, Congressman L. Mendel Rivers, of South Carolina, spearheaded Pentagon action. A secret investigation by the Army followed.

The Court-Martial. On November 12, 1970, at Fort Benning, Ga., Lieutenant Calley heard the charges against him: premeditated murder of 30 Orientals at a trail junction south of the village; of 70 Orientals in a ditch on the east side; and of a monk and a 10-year-old boy.

The trial received national exposure. America listened. Four long, weary months of testimony was heard. In direct and cross-examination, contradictions were frequent. At one point, in answer to a direct question, Calley said: "It was no big deal, sir." America's Commander-in-Chief publicly stated: "What appears was certainly a massacre, and under no circumstances is justified. . . . We cannot ever condone or use atrocities against civilians." Finally, 3 years from the date Charlie Company landed at My Lai, Calley's trial went to the jury. The verdict: guilty. The sentence: hard labor for life, dismissal from service, and forfeiture of all pay.

Significance. For the 1st time in history, instant communication brought the horrors of armless, legless, burned, and bombed men, women, and children into American homes in living color—not after the fact, but from on the spot. Civilians had no stomach for the carnage of war. During the Calley trial, the public was bombarded daily with recaps of conflicting testimony and contradictions. By the hundreds and thousands, citizens' letters to senators, congressmen, newspapers, and the President, stated loud and clear that they did not approve of a system of military justice that punished the bottom man on the command totem pole while judging the upper echelon as lily-white. When the verdict was in, Commander-in-Chief Nixon couldn't sleep—he intervened—saying of the Calley trial:

"Having captured the attention of the American people to the degree that it has," it required "more than the technical review" provided by the Code of Military Justice. Senator Birch Bayh made this public statement: "Reluctantly, I have concluded that the President is determined to play politics with the Calley decision and the entire My Lai tragedy." Eventually, Calley's sentence was reduced from life to 10 years. After serving ⅓ of his sentence, he was freed by a civil court in November, 1974.

—F.M.W.

Small Incidents That Started Big Wars

YEAR: 1152
WAR: War of the Whiskers
PLACE: France
OPPONENTS: France v. England
PROVOCATION: When bearded King Louis VII of France was married to Eleanor, daughter of a French duke, he received a dowry of 2 provinces in southern France. Coming home from the Crusades, King Louis VII shaved off his beard. Wife Eleanor said he was ugly without beard. He refused to grow whiskers back. Eleanor divorced him, married King Henry II of England, demanded return of her dowry of 2 provinces for new husband. King Louis would not release them. King Henry declared war to regain dowry by force.
RESULT: The war raged 301 years. Peace declared in 1453, after Battle of Rouen.

YEAR: 1325
WAR: War of the Oaken Bucket
PLACE: Italy
OPPONENTS: Independent State of Bologna v. State of Modena
PROVOCATION: Regiment of Modena soldiers invaded Bologna to steal a brown oak bucket. During the raid, Modena troops murdered several hundred Bologna citizens. Bologna mobi-

lized, went to war to recover the bucket and restore honor.
RESULT: A 12-year war, with thousands of lives lost. Modena won the battle of Zappolino, kept the bucket. Today, the *Secchia rapita* (stolen bucket) may be seen in the bell tower of the Ghirlandina, a 14th-century campanile behind the modern cathedral.

YEAR: 1704
WAR: War of the Spanish Succession; later Queen Anne's War
PLACE: Throughout Europe
OPPONENTS: France v. England; later Prussia v. Silesia
PROVOCATION: Mrs. Mashaur, Englishwoman, spilled glass of water on Marquis de Torey, Frenchman. She said it was accidental. He said it was an intentional insult. This incident stirred deeper antagonisms, power plays, and led to open war.
RESULT: A 5-year struggle ended with Peace of Utrecht. King Louis XIV of France placed one of his grandsons on Spanish Hapsburg throne.

YEAR: 1739
WAR: War of Jenkins' Ear
PLACE: Europe and Atlantic Ocean

OPPONENTS: England v. Spain

PROVOCATION: Returning from West Indies in 1731, Capt. Robert Jenkins' brig, *Rebecca*, was stopped, boarded by Spanish coast guards outside Havana. After rifling holds, the Spanish commander cut off Jenkins' ear. In London, the one-eared Jenkins protested to the King, displaying a leather case holding the ear. No action taken. Seven years later, incident was related before a House of Commons committee, and the encased ear passed around. Indignation. Headlines. Jenkins a martyr. Using his ear as an excuse (but with its real motive a takeover of the West Indies), England declared war on Spain.

RESULT: War merged with War of Austrian Succession (1740–1748), with England and Austria aligned against Spain and Prussia. Peace treaty at Aachen. Ended in a draw, with England holding mastery of seas, Spain losing almost nothing on land. Jenkins? He wound up a supervisor for the East India Company on Isle of St. Helena.

YEAR: 1840

WAR: The Opium War

PLACE: China

OPPONENTS: England v. China

PROVOCATION: The East India Company of England, suffering an adverse balance of trade with China, decided to make up its financial losses by pouring illegal opium into China for some quick profits. The Chinese imperial commissioner, Lin Tze-su, ordered all British opium destroyed. England declared war.

RESULT: British gunboats smashed Chinese fortifications. In 1842, China surrendered, was forced to give up Hong Kong (meaning "sweet stream") to the British and pay a $21 million indemnity. And the British continued to pour opium into China. In 1900, the Chinese tried to get their revenge, and were humiliated. The Boxers (actual name *Righteousness and Harmony Society*, and having nothing to do with boxing, except Chinese word for "society" sounds like "fist"), a secret organization of 40,000 patriotic militants, tried to throw foreigners out of their country. England, U.S., Germany, Russia, France, Japan sent in 16,000 troops to put down the Boxer Rebellion, and succeeded. The Chinese had to pay an indemnity running into millions of dollars (although the U.S. returned about 12 million, half of its indemnity, to China), had to give Hong Kong up to the British, and had to allow foreign nations to establish legation quarters and troops in Peking. It was not until 6 decades later that China got even. In 1965, Premier Chou En-lai, of the People's Republic of China, speaking to President Gamal Abdel Nasser, of Egypt, explained one reason for the demoralization of American troops in South Vietnam: "Some of

them are trying opium, and we are helping them. We are planting the best kinds of opium especially for the American soldiers in Vietnam. . . . Do you remember when the West imposed opium on us? They fought us with opium. And we are going to fight them with their own weapons."

YEAR: 1857

WAR: The Sepoy Mutiny

PLACE: India

OPPONENTS: England v. British Indian regiments

PROVOCATION: England's best native regiments were the Sepoys, Hindu soldiers who were Mohammedans and Brahmans. England insisted these troops use the new Enfield rifle, which had cartridges that had to be bitten off before loading. The cartridges were greased with lard (pig fat) and tallow (cow fat). Moslems were forbidden to taste lard, and Brahmans held the cow sacred. Most Indians refused to use the rifle. Some were jailed in Meerut. Their comrades mutinied, freed them, slaughtered and mutilated hundreds of English in Cawnpore, Delhi, Lucknow. *Current Day Note:* The cow is still sacred in India. "The cow is a poem of pity," said Gandhi. "Protection of the cow means protection of the whole dumb creation of God." A third of the world's cattle are in India. In Kashmir, to kill a cow even accidentally means 7 years in prison.

RESULT: England crushed the mutiny, and India came totally under the British Crown.

YEAR: 1879

WAR: War of the Fleeing Wife

PLACE: Africa

OPPONENTS: Great Britain v. Zulu Nation

PROVOCATION: Zulu Chief Sirayo's wife, Umhlana, left him. She hid in British territory. Zulu troops crossed border, kidnapped her, had her shot. England declared war over border violation.

RESULT: After initial victories, the Zulu forces were crushed by the British at Ulundi. When Zulu King Cetywayo was captured, his chiefs made peace with England.

YEAR: 1896

WAR: War of the Cricket Match

PLACE: Zanzibar

OPPONENTS: Zanzibar v. England

PROVOCATION: Adm. Sir Henry Rawson ordered the British fleet under his command into waters off Zanzibar's harbor so that his officers and sailors could disembark to watch a cricket match in which the British were to participate. This concentration of warships irked Seyid Khalid bin Bargash, the Sultan of Zanzibar. He immediately declared war, sending his lone battleship, *Glasgow*, into action. The British fleet bombarded the Sultan's palace, reduced it to rubble, killed or injured 500 of the Sultan's soldiers. When the Sultan's only battleship opened fire, the British big guns zeroed in on the vessel and sank it.

RESULT: Zanzibar sued for peace, and the Sultan escaped to become an exile in German territory. The war lasted 37 minutes, 23 seconds, the shortest war in world history.

YEAR: 1925
WAR: War of the Stray Dog
PLACE: Macedonia
OPPONENTS: Greece v. Bulgaria
PROVOCATION: Greek soldier's dog ran across border into Bulgaria. Soldier chased after his dog. Bulgarian sentry killed Greek soldier. Greek troops invaded Bulgaria, killed, wounded 48 Bulgarians. Conflict escalated.
RESULT: Emergency session of League of Nations arbitrated. Peace agreed upon. Bulgaria paid indemnity of 30 million levas.

YEAR: 1936
WAR: The Waziristan War
PLACE: Waziristan district, on the India-Afghanistan frontier
OPPONENTS: England v. Waziristan

PROVOCATION: A 16-year-old girl, Musamat Ram, against the wishes of her Hindu family, ran off with Nur Ali Shah, a Moslem school-teacher. Musamat Ram's parents objected to her lover's being a Moslem, told the police she'd been abducted. She was brought back, protesting she had become a Moslem. Her lover was sentenced to jail for 2 years. A minor Moslem tribal chief in Waziristan, the Faqir of Ipi, resenting British invasion of his land in 1919, seized upon the incident to preach *jehad*, holy war, against the British. The Faqir renamed Musamat Ram, calling her "Islam Bibi"—the Baby of Islam—and demanded vengeance for her persecution. Soon, Wiziri tribesmen were up in arms. British and Indian troops marched in. The conflict lasted 2 years, cost the British and Indians $11 million.
RESULT: The war gained neither side a victory. The British failed to catch the Faqir, who had escaped into exile. The only winner was Musamat Ram, the Baby of Islam. The Wiziri court reversed itself. She was declared a Moslem. Her lover was released from jail. They lived happily ever after.

—I.W.

An International Array of Spies

Occupational requirement: "An itching humor or kind of longing to see that which is not to be seen, to do that which ought not to be done, to know that secret which should not be known. . . ."

Three Giant Steps Backward

1480 B.C.—Joshua, ordered by Moses, led a band of 11 spies into the land of Canaan.

334 B.C.—Alexander the Great intercepted outgoing mail from his soldiers and established the earliest postal espionage system.

878 A.D.—King Alfred the Great, "pioneer of the English secret service," disguised himself as a bard (an itinerant poet-singer), wandered through the Danish military camps, and obtained sufficient information to defeat the Danes at Edington.

ACE INFILTRATORS

Here are the stories of the men and women who, through their successes and blunders, their patience and intolerance, their strengths and weaknesses, contributed to the development of the massive and sophisticated spy networks of the 20th century.

Chevalier Charles d'Eon. French. Worked for: Louis XV, 1755.

In 1755, a pretty female "reader," Lia de Beaumont, was charming the Russian court of

Czarina Elizabeth. Lia was "small and slight, with a pink and white complexion and pleasing, gentle expression." She became lady-in-waiting to the Czarina and even read to Elizabeth as she relaxed in her bath. Lia was actually Charles d'Eon, a French spy in the service of Louis XV. His mission was to prevent the signing of a military treaty between Russia and England (one promising Russian support if France attacked England's sovereign state of Hanover). The Empress heeded the advice of "Lia" and refused to sign the treaty.

Charles was an excellent female impersonator since his mother had dressed him in feminine attire at the age of 4—she would have preferred that Charles had been born a girl. Even while he was employed as a lawyer in the French finance ministry, Charles displayed a fondness for ruffles and frills. Although he was quite successful as a female agent, Charles also distinguished himself as a captain in the French Army and as an unofficial ambassador to England. At 26, he was made a chevalier. For almost a century, debates raged over Charles's "true" sex. In England, France, and throughout Europe, over $2 million was wagered on the "she-man." For 3 years, one enterprising Englishman bribed servants and resorted to window climbing in order to win his bet of $1,500—at 3–1 odds—that the chevalier was a woman. Occasionally, D'Eon was attacked, and as one historian said, "Many attempts were made to carry him off for the purpose of settling bets by a humiliating personal scrutiny." After D'Eon's death in 1810, one doctor declared that he was definitely a man, while other medical experts claimed he was a hermaphrodite.

Benedict Arnold. American. Worked for: England, Revolutionary War.

Arnold's bravery in battles in the northern Colonies and Canada gained him the rank of major general in George Washington's army. In 1778, he went to Philadelphia to take charge of American troops. Pennsylvania's supreme executive council, critical of his private behavior, referred his misconduct to Congress. When 4 of 8 charges brought against him were dropped, Arnold demanded a court-martial to vindicate himself on the remaining counts. The court-martial condemned him on only one charge—the misappropriation of army wagons. Arnold became commander of West Point but did not receive a promotion which he had expected. With the help of Maj. John André, he conspired to surrender West Point to the British for £20,000. In 1780, however, André was captured and the plot was revealed, but Arnold managed to escape. He then fought as an officer in the British Army, and after the war became a successful businessman. Arnold died, alone and forgotten, in London in 1801.

In 1973, Dr. Vincent A. Lindner, a history buff from New Jersey, brought Benedict Arnold's case before the Army Board for Correction of Military Records. Lindner claimed that insufficient evidence had convicted Arnold in the Philadelphia court-martial. The board members, however, concluded that the new evidence presented did not raise a reasonable doubt of Arnold's guilt, and they unanimously refused to clear him.

Lydia Darrah. American. Worked for: U.S., Revolutionary War.

Credited with "saving George Washington's army," Lydia Darrah, a Quaker, performed her one and only spy mission in 1777 when British General Howe and his 15,000 troops occupied Philadelphia. She eavesdropped on an officers' meeting held in her home, learned of plans for a surprise attack on the "old fox" and his army camped nearby at Whitemarsh, and delivered the information to Washington. American preparedness prevented the British from making a full-scale attack, and a disgruntled Howe returned to Philadelphia.

Nathan Hale. American. Worked for: U.S., Revolutionary War.

Former schoolteacher Nathan Hale, a captain in Washington's army, volunteered to spy on the British in New York. Dressed as a "plain young farmer," he entered enemy territory, drew maps, and recorded troop numbers. A relative of Hale's, working for the British, recognized him and betrayed him to General Howe. Hale confessed and was hanged the next day.

Carl Schulmeister. French. Worked for: France, Napoleon's campaign against Austria, 1805.

Schulmeister offered his services to the Austrians via a letter which claimed that the French, believing him to be an Austrian spy, had exiled him. He said that he was of noble Hungarian ancestry and wished to live in Austria in order to aid this country in its resistance against Napoleon. The bait worked, and Schulmeister was not only welcomed into the Austrian Army, but also became chief of intelligence. Acting as a double agent, he transmitted false information from Napoleon to the Austrians, and vital Austrian military secrets back to the Emperor. French newspapers, printed especially for Schulmeister's spy work, told the Austrians of French "unrest at home" and how Napoleon's troops in Germany were returning to quell the uprisings. Schulmeister planned an Austrian attack on the supposedly "retreating" troops of French Marshal Ney. The trap was successful, and Austria was forced to surrender. Schulmeister was "captured" by the French, "escaped," and returned to Austria to lay the foundations for Napoleon's great victory at Austerlitz. Although Schulmeister received large monetary rewards for his accomplishments in Austria and other hostile countries, he never received the one payment he desperately desired—the Legion of Honor decoration from France. Napoleon refused to "honor a spy." Schulmeister was captured after Waterloo, was ransomed for a large sum of money, and opened a tobacco stall in Strasbourg, the city in which he died in 1853.

Belle Boyd. American. Worked for: Confederate Army, Civil War.

"Femme fatale" of the Civil War, Belle Boyd captured the hearts and the minds of soldiers fighting on both Confederate and Union sides. At age 17, she killed an officer who tried to raise a U.S. flag over her home in Virginia. She crossed Union lines frequently with messages that she delivered directly to Gen. Stonewall Jackson. Although she was widely known to be a spy, her charms blinded Union forces to all suspicions. She was finally betrayed by a lover. Sent to prison, she lived like a queen, entertaining a host of admirers who brought magazines, clothing, and food delicacies. Under prisoner exchange she was returned to Richmond where she continued her espionage work. Before the war ended, she married a Union officer whom she sweet-talked into becoming a Confederate agent. Following the war, Belle Boyd, age 21, began touring the U.S. and England to give lectures on her wartime adventures. She was billed as "The Rebel Spy."

Emma Edmonds. Canadian. Worked for: Union Army, Civil War.

When Union nurse Emma Edmonds volunteered for espionage missions, she was asked to submit to a "cranial" efficiency test. After the bumps on her head were "read" by a phrenologist, who pronounced her capable of keeping secrets, she stained her body with walnut juice, donned a wig, and crossed Confederate lines posing as a young black laborer. Upon entering Yorktown, she was given an ax, shovel, and wheelbarrow, and put onto construction work on the town's fortifications. As Emma painfully labored, she sketched a map of the fort and noted the number and size of the enemy's armaments. Hiding the diagram in the bottom of a shoe, she walked it back to the Union Army. Emma completed 10 additional missions for the North, ofttimes posing as an Irish peddler woman and sometimes as a soldier. When she fell seriously ill at Vicksburg, Emma was given an honorable discharge and she returned to her New England home to write *Nurse and Spy*, an account of her life as a Union agent.

William Stieber. German. Worked for: Germany, conquest of Austria, 1866, and Franco-Prussian War, 1870.

Prince Otto von Bismarck referred to Stieber as "my king of sleuthhounds." In 1866, spy master Stieber, posing as a salesman for religious statuettes and "dirty" pictures, entered Austria and secured such an abundance of military information that Prussia was able to conquer Austria in 45 days. In 1868 Stieber went to France for 18 months, in which time he carefully studied new French military equipment, particularly their rifles and machine guns. After Napoleon III suffered a crushing defeat in the Franco-Prussian War, Stieber boasted that he had had 40,000 spies in France (10,000 is probably the more accurate estimate). In Berlin, Stieber operated a "Green House," where "people of consequence" indulged in limitless vice and perversion. The private files from the Green House were used to blackmail patrons into divulging top-secret information. In 1892, Stieber died from complications arising from arthritis. Although his service to Germany was highly acclaimed—he was called the founder of the German espionage system—his funeral provoked few tears. It is said that many attended only "to reassure themselves that the autocratic old sleuthhound was really dead."

Robert Stephenson Smyth Baden-Powell. British. Worked for: England, Boer War, 1899.

Lord Baden-Powell's favorite disguise was that of a mad butterfly enthusiast. Prior to his service in South Africa, he had dashed, net in hand, around military forts in Germany, French Tunisia, and Algeria. At the end of each "sporting" day, Baden-Powell drew pictures of his captured pets. Hidden in the sketches were accurate layouts of each fort, plus the size and location of its guns. In the Boer War, Baden-Powell was a general in the British Army, but he did find time to complete one important reconnaissance trip into the Drakenburg Mountains of South Africa. He claimed to be a newspaper correspondent "with a view to recommending the country for immigration." Wearing ragged clothing and his face enhanced by a beard (grown for the mission), he chatted freely with the Boer farmers and indulged in much "idle" gossip. The maps he drew during the trip proved to be quite valuable as they corrected numerous inaccuracies in the old maps then being used by the British military. Also an author, Baden-Powell described his tracking and scouting methods in a book, *Aids for Scouting*. Out of this book emerged the international Boy Scout movement led by its hearty advocate, Robert Baden-Powell.

Mata Hari. Dutch. Worked for: Germany, W.W. I.

Her real name was Margaretha Gertruida Zelle, and she was born in Holland in 1876. When she was 18, Gertrude left a religious school to marry a 40-year-old captain in the Dutch colonial army, Rudolf MacLeod. Some say that they met through a newspaper ad. The MacLeods lived in Java, but because her husband was an alcoholic, a wife beater, and had brutal fits in which he dragged Gertrude about by her hair, she left him and moved to Paris. She joined the chorus line of a vaudeville show but was not "cute" enough to be "discovered." Refusing to be a nobody, Gertrude established herself as Mata Hari, exotic Indian dancer, and concocted a lineage of lies to back up her story. Heavy face makeup glamorized her "regular" features, and her sensuous striptease routines more than made up for her thick waistline. According to one observer, she had "a body which lacked corporeal exaggerations and was no more exciting nude than dressed." Her expensive life-style was paid for by the Germans who commissioned her to spy on French officials and other foreign dignitaries whom she met in her "career" travels. Actually, she was highly overpaid, did very little spying, and some critics go so far as to say that she was simply an excuse for German officers to dip into the secret-service funds in order to pay for their recreation and entertainment. When she became too much of a luxury item for the German secret service, they betrayed her by mentioning her in a telegram which was "easily" decoded by the French. She was captured, tried, and sentenced. In 1917, courtesan-dancer-spy Mata Hari died before a French firing squad. She was 41.

Col. Alfred Redl. Austro-Hungarian. Worked for: Russia, W.W. I.

When the Russians learned that Col. Alfred Redl, head of the Austrian secret service, was a homosexual, they blackmailed him into committing treason against his homeland. At the beginning of W.W. I, when the Germans confiscated top-secret documents from Russian secret-service operations in Warsaw, the full extent of Redl's treachery was revealed. From 1903 to 1913, Redl was Russia's leading spy. His organization in Austria was both efficient and innovative. It was Redl who 1st used hidden cameras for surveillance, dusting powders for obtaining fingerprints, and who trained his agents in the methods of "shadowing." He had supplied Plan III, the entire Austrian invasion plan for Serbia, to the Russians, who turned it over to the Serbian military command. In addition to giving away all of his country's military secrets, he fed totally inaccurate estimates of Russia's military strength to Austrian battle strategists. Redl has been called one of history's greatest traitors, since his actions caused the slaughter of half a million of his countrymen. He was captured in Vienna after collecting his payoff money at a post office. Eventually he committed suicide.

Capt. Franz von Rintelen. German. Worked for: Germany, W.W. I.

In 1915, while the U.S. was still a neutral in W.W. I, Franz von Rintelen arrived in New York City. Posing as a businessman, he established a "front," an import-export firm, to camouflage his real purpose—to prevent ships carrying American war materials from reaching the Allied countries. He arranged for detonators to be placed on the departing ships, causing fire "accidents" to occur. Von Rintelen's aim was not to blow up the ships, causing human deaths, but to set fire to the ships' holds so that all ammunition had to be thrown overboard. His company, E. V. Gibbons, Inc., was able to obtain munitions contracts from the Allies which not only enhanced his sabotage efforts but also provided his phony company with a sizable profit. Von Rintelen's financial success enabled him to establish a new union, the Labor's National Peace Council, which was responsible for numerous strikes throughout the U.S. He was betrayed by one of his immediate superiors in the German secret service. Arrested while returning to Germany, he was kept in England until the U.S. entered the war. Then, Von Rintelen was shipped to America where he spent 4 years in prison. In 1920 he returned to Germany, found himself to be a forgotten hero, and moved to England where he died in 1949.

Mathilde Carré. French. Worked for: France and Germany, W.W. II.

One of the most beautiful and successful of the female spies was slinky, green-eyed, sensuous Mathilde Carré, nicknamed "The Cat." When France fell to the Germans, The Cat set up an espionage unit with a Polish general whom she lovingly called "Armand." They worked closely with the French resistance movement, and Mathilde traveled freely as a contact in occupied France. When arrested in 1941, she was given an ultimatum by the Germans: Become a double agent or die. From then on, The Cat worked for the enemy and led them to the doorways of over 35 key French resistance men. When tried for treason by the French in 1949, she wept hysterically as the death sentence was pronounced. It was commuted to life imprisonment, but she was released in 1954.

Klaus Fuchs. German. Worked for: Russia, W.W. II.

Although Russia fought with the Allies in W.W. II, the atomic bomb project was shared by only the U.S. and Great Britain. Klaus Fuchs, a German-born physicist, was Russia's key informant on the development of the bomb. In 1941, Fuchs, known to be a communist, was hired by the British to do nuclear research. He promptly contacted Moscow and offered his services as a spy. In 1943, he left England to become a member of the combined American-British team working on the bomb in the U.S. While working with Dr. Oppenheimer in Los Alamos, N. Mex., Fuchs was privy to all vital aspects of the bomb—design, construction, components, detonating devices. Secrets were passed by Fuchs to a Russian contact and relayed to Moscow. Defection of a cipher clerk in the Soviet embassy in Ottawa caused the disclosure of incriminating evidence against the nuclear spy ring operating in the U.S. and Canada. Eventually, this information led to the capture of Fuchs and other Russian spies—Alfred Nunn May, David Greenglass, Harry Gold, and, questionably, Julius and Ethel Rosenberg. Fuchs spent 10 years in prison, after which he continued his nuclear research in East Germany.

Banda MacLeod (Mata Hari's daughter). Dutch. Worked for: Allies, W.W. II.

Banda, a schoolteacher in Java, was a bright, personable young socialite who frequently entertained foreign diplomats, military officers, and journalists. When Japan invaded Java,

Banda's uncle, in the service of the Japanese Army, threatened to expose her as Mata Hari's daughter if she did not "use" her parties to gather information for the Japanese. Banda agreed, but actually she became a double agent. Through her trusted friend and lover, a man named Abdul (who also pretended to work for the Japanese but was a member of the Indonesian underground), Banda passed information to the Allies. Banda's work alerted the Allies to Japanese plans for the Battle of Guadalcanal, plus other major attacks in the Pacific. When the war ended, she fought for Indonesian independence from the Dutch. After independence was established under Dr. Sukarno, Banda spied for the U.S. in Communist China, where she reported on military strength and told of Russian supplies being fed into the country. In 1950, she went to North Korea, and from there she predicted the 38th Parallel invasion of South Korea. After her arrest by the communists, Banda was sentenced, without a trial, to die. She appeared before a firing squad at 5:45 A.M., the same time that Mata Hari had died many years before. (NOTE: While most historians acknowledge the existence and accomplishments of a female spy named Banda, some claim that she was not the daughter of Mata Hari. As one writer says: "If Mata Hari had been her mother, which is highly improbable, then Banda must have been 50 when she had her final adventure in espionage, whereas in most of the stories written about her, she appears as a beautiful young woman with romantic tendencies in this period of her life.")

Richard Sorge. Russian. Worked for: Russia, W.W. II.

Richard Sorge, one of the great master spies of all time, grew up in Germany and fought in the German Army in W.W. I. At the war's end, he became a communist, and he moved to Russia in 1925. Sorge established spy rings in Germany and China, but his network in Japan proved to be his greatest success. Posing as a German newspaper correspondent and Nazi party member, he was admitted to all of the elite political circles in Tokyo. In 1941 Sorge informed Moscow that Germany would invade Russia on June 22. Stalin ignored Sorge's warning, and as a result, the Russians suffered near-catastrophic losses. Chastened, Moscow leaders pressed Sorge for the answer to a crucial ques-

tion: Would Japan invade Russia? With the aid of his contact in Japan's Imperial Cabinet, Sorge conclusively answered, No. Stalin quickly ordered the 250,000 troops stationed in Siberia to return to the western front. This maneuver saved Moscow from the advancing Germans, and Sorge is credited with "changing the course of history." Sorge "supposedly" was hanged by the Japanese in 1944. Many believe, however, that he escaped and returned to Russia where he continued his work. Stalin refused to acknowledge him as a hero, probably due to Stalin's embarrassment over the successful German attack in 1941. However, the Russian people proclaimed Sorge a "Hero of the Soviet Union," named a Moscow street in his memory, and put his picture on a Russian postage stamp.

Col. Rudolf Abel. Russian. Worked for: Russia during Cold War.

Abel came to New York City in 1948, posed as a painter-photographer, and directed the Soviet spy network in the U.S. for 10 years. Although the full extent of his probings remains unknown, Abel certainly unearthed valuable information on American nuclear weapons and rocketry. A "split" nickel found by a Brooklyn newspaper boy helped the FBI capture Abel—the nickel contained a tiny piece of film with a coded message. Abel was sentenced to 30 years in prison but was exchanged in 1962 for American spy Francis Gary Powers. Abel's spy career spanned almost 30 years.

Francis Gary Powers. American. Worked for: U.S. during Cold War.

Francis Gary Powers was shot down on May 1, 1960, while flying an American U-2 jet on a spy mission over Russia. He was Russia's 1st proof that reconnaissance flights were being authorized by the U.S., and the Russian authorities used the "U-2 incident" to break up the Peace Conference in Paris. It is possible that certain U.S. military leaders deployed Powers purposely to sabotage the peace talks which Eisenhower himself acutely desired. Although he was sentenced to 3 years in jail and 7 years in a work camp, Powers was returned in a prisoner exchange for Colonel Abel. After that he lived in Los Angeles and worked as a helicopter pilot for a local radio station, giving traffic reports from atop the freeways.

—C.O.

The 8-Eyed Spy: The Family That Gave You Pearl Harbor

Millions of Americans can still recall sitting stock-still by their radios as news flashes of the Japanese surprise attack at Pearl Harbor preempted all programs on December 7, 1941.

That Day of Infamy, as President Roosevelt termed it, remains particularly memorable because it was a Sunday, a family day, making it all the more ironic that a little-known family of spies helped make the sneak attack possible.

Outwardly, the 8-eyed spy partially responsible for the ruins smoldering in "the Gibraltar of the Pacific" seemed much like any other Honolulu family. The Bernard Kühns were amiable people, had many friends on the island, and aroused absolutely no suspicion among them. Like all successful spies, they had a genius for becoming inconspicuous, having established a perfect cover. Not even a paranoid would have thought of the middle-aged man next door and his matronly wife as being secret agents, much less his beautiful teen-age daughter and his 6-year-old son. But the fact remains that the entire Kühn family—even the 6-year-old—actively spied for the Japanese, pulling off one of the greatest intelligence feats in history.

The 8-eyed spy's story, one might say, began with the alluring eyes of the Kühns's young daughter, Susie Ruth. When only a 17-year-old back in Berlin, Ruth had become the mistress of powerful Nazi Propaganda Minister Joseph Goebbels. But the club-footed Goebbels, despite his ugliness, had many ambitious women to choose from in prewar Berlin, and soon he tired of his schoolgirl mistress. One seemingly insurmountable problem presented itself, however. Young Ruth happened to be the daughter of Dr. Bernard Julius Otto Kühn, who had great influence in the Nazi party in 1935. Kühn, or Kuehn, had served as a midshipman in the German Navy during W.W. I, becoming a physician after his discharge. Embittered when his practice failed, he found it easy to blame his shortcomings on scapegoats like the Jews, and joined the Nazi party. Dr. Kühn cultivated a close friendship with Heinrich Himmler, head of the Gestapo, and himself later became a minor official of the dreaded secret police.

It wasn't easy to get rid of a girl with such connections, but the wily Goebbels finally hit on a plan. The Japanese, with whom the Nazis had close ties at the time, had requested the loan of an occidental spy to work at Pearl Harbor in the Pacific, as it was next to impossible for an Oriental to work unnoticed in an American community. It would be a kind of rent-a-spy arrangement, with the Japanese paying handsomely and picking up all the expenses. When Goebbels heard about the request, he immediately recommended Ruth Kühn and her family.

Dr. Kühn quickly accepted Goebbels's proposal, and on August 15, 1935, the Kühns landed in Honolulu. Only an elder son, Leopold, had been left behind. The family included Dr. Kühn, a pleasant scholarly man of 41; his wife, Friedel; attractive Susie Ruth; and her half-brother, Hans Joachim, sometimes called Eberhard, aged 6. Kühn bought a house

in Pearl City and a cottage in Kalama very close to the ocean—overlooking Pearl Harbor, in fact. For his cover he had a number of stories. To some he claimed to be a retired doctor with a large inheritance; to others he was a student of Hawaiian history; to still others he posed as an inventor. None of the friends who visited his well-appointed house, filled with fine paintings and sculpture, ever suspected his real profession, not even when Mrs. Kühn journeyed to Japan twice, returning the 2nd time with $16,000 that she deposited in a growing bank account. In fact, large sums were mysteriously transferred to the Kühn account over the years from a Swiss bank, until it swelled to some $100,000. But whenever there were any questions, Dr. Kühn would simply explain that he had made successful investments abroad.

In the meantime, the Kühns were collecting and transmitting secret military information on an almost unprecedented scale—each and every member of the family. By 1939 they had been instructed to obtain all intelligence possible about U.S. ships in the Pacific—especially those in Hawaii—for the Japanese were already training to implement Admiral Yamamoto's daring plan to cripple America at Pearl Harbor.

No pair of the "8-eyes" was more valuable than any other. Beautiful Ruth Kühn obtained information in several ways. At 1st she dated military personnel. An excellent dancer, tennis player, and swimmer, this gregarious, outgoing girl found it easy to extract information from her dates about their assignments, ships, or bases. When she became engaged to a young navy officer, her task was made all the simpler. But the beauty parlor she opened in Pearl Harbor turned into her most important source of valuable information. Ruth made it a policy to give her customers the best and cheapest service on the island, for they were the wives of high-ranking military personnel whose loose tongues revealed secrets that surpassed Ruth's expectations, even irritating her a bit. "They talked so much," she would later say, "that it was a relief when they left the place."

So much information leaked into the beauty parlor that Ruth's mother had to come downtown on certain days to help monitor the conversations. It was Friedel's specific job to record all intelligence that the family obtained. Frau Kühn, a heavy, bespectacled woman who looked like everybody's favorite aunt, also accompanied her husband on the "historical expeditions" he made into the mountains to further his "Hawaiian studies." She purchased and often used the 18-power binoculars with which they spied on ships in the harbor and military installations below. Sometimes Friedel and the doctor sailed his little sailboat around Pearl Harbor itself, smiling at the crews aboard

THE TRILLION DOLLAR RAT HOLE

Since 1958 the U.S. Government has spent over a trillion dollars on war budgets, not including the hundreds of billions for war-connected space flights, veterans' benefits, interest to the bankers on money borrowed for previous wars, etc.

A trillion dollars is a thousand billion, or a million million. It's quite a bit of money. And it's all gone, with not much to show for it except mutilated people and a lot of graves—a trillion dollars dropped down into a giant rat hole.

But just suppose that trillion had been spent for life instead of death, for people instead of profits. What would a thousand billion dollars have bought us?

$450 billion	Could supply a new $15,000 home or apartment for half the families in the U.S.
5 billion	Could build 2 new $30 million hospitals for each of the 16 biggest cities in the U.S., a $20 million hospital for each of 100 smaller cities, a $2 million clinic for 1,000 different small towns.
20 billion	Could be given to cancer research.
10 billion	Could be spent to cure 5 or 6 other major diseases.
20 billion	Could end the pollution in the Great Lakes.
10 billion	Could freshen up every river and stream on the continent.
20 billion	Could be used to plant a billion trees along highways, in cities, towns, and in the countryside.
20 billion	Could build 1,000 new colleges at $20 million apiece.
80 billion	Could fund 4,000,000 new scholarships a year at $2,000 per student.
10 billion	Could build 10,000 youth centers at $1 million each.
10 billion	Could revive the buffalo herds in the West and grow more grass in order to double the cattle herds and lower the price of milk and beef.
10 billion	Could make a dozen oases in the Sahara Desert.
50 billion	Could supply 50 million farm families in South America and Asia with gasoline-driven tractors.
Leaving: $285 billion	For defense and other expenses.

—Based on material by Vince Copeland

TOTAL

$1,000,000,000,000

the big ships while mentally taking notes of everything they saw.

Even little Hans Joachim was employed as a spy, probably the only bona fide or worthwhile child spy in history. Hans became an active agent before he turned 11. Frau Kühn would dress him in a sailor suit, and his father would take him for walks along the waterfront. Officers aboard the warships in port often invited the friendly "little sailor" aboard, taking him on tours of their ships and answering all the questions this "intelligent little fellow" asked about the vessels and their operations. What they didn't know was that Dr. Kühn, who wisely never came aboard, had trained the 10-year-old to ask key questions, to observe and remember anything unusual.

Little Hans was debriefed as soon as the Kühns arrived home from their walks, and his contributions, like all information the family garnered, were recorded by Frau Kühn in her fine hand. At 1st this intelligence was secretly delivered to the Japanese consul general, who forwarded it to Tokyo via couriers with diplomatic immunity. But toward the end, more elaborate precautions were taken. The Japanese master spy Takeo Yoshikawa had arrived in Honolulu to work with the Kühns. While Yoshikawa watched with binoculars from the Japanese consulate, Dr. Kühn flashed him coded messages from the attic of the Kalama cottage. Incredible as it may seem, this ancient system of lantern signals went undetected until the end.

Due to the efforts of the Kühns and Yoshikawa over the years, the Japanese knew virtually everything there was to know about Pearl Harbor by December 7, 1941. The Pearl Harbor story is American folklore today, "Remember Pearl Harbor" as famous a slogan as "Remember the Alamo" or "Remember the Maine," but the story of the spy family that helped make the surprise attack possible remains largely unknown. The Kühns's work cannot be too strongly emphasized. Five days before the attack, for example, they had transmitted to the Japanese an account describing every American ship in Hawaiian waters.

The Kühns's operation broke down only after Pearl Harbor was attacked. Busy as squirrels in their cramped attic, they were observing the results of their labor through binoculars and flashing this information to Yoshikawa in the Japanese consulate. Military intelligence, awakened from their amazing sleep by the attack, finally noticed and did something about the mysterious blinking lights emanating from the cottage, tracing them to their source and arresting the Kühns while they were still enthusiastically at work.

Dr. Kühn was tried and ordered shot as a spy, his sentence commuted to 50 years at hard labor when he volunteered valuable information about his Japanese and Nazi contacts. He was released after serving 4 years. Yoshikawa, eventually returned to Japan in exchange for an American diplomat, is today a prominent businessman in Tokyo. Frau Kühn, given a light sentence, later went back to Germany with her son, as did daughter Ruth after she served a few years in prison.

—R.H.

Military Scrapbook

THE WOLF AND THE LAMB

Once upon a time a Wolf was lapping at a spring on a hillside when, looking up, what should he see but a Lamb just beginning to drink a little lower down. "There's my supper," thought he, "if only I can find some excuse to seize it." Then he called out to the Lamb, "How dare you muddy the water from which I am drinking?"

"Nay, master, nay," said Lambikin; "if the water be muddy up there, I cannot be the cause of it, for it runs down from you to me."

"Well, then," said the Wolf, "why did you call me bad names this time last year?"

"That cannot be," said the Lamb; "I am only 6 months old."

"I don't care," snarled the Wolf; "if it was not you it was your father"; and with that he rushed upon the poor little Lamb and—

WARRA WARRA WARRA WARRA WARRA—

ate her all up. But before she died, she gasped out—

"ANY EXCUSE WILL SERVE A TYRANT."

—Aesop's *Fables*

Naturally the common people don't want war . . . but after all it is the leaders of a country who determine the policy, and it is always a simple matter to drag the people along, whether it is a democracy, or a fascist dictatorship, or a parliament, or a communist dictatorship. Voice or no voice, the people can always be brought to the bidding of the leaders. That is easy. All you have to do is to tell them they are being attacked, and denounce the pacifists for lack of patriotism and exposing the country to danger. It works the same in every country.

—Hermann Göring

11

Universe—Spaced Out

How High Is the Sky?
An Eyeful of Astronomical Facts and Figures

THE UNIVERSE AND THE SOLAR SYSTEM

So immense are the distances in the universe that astronomers have had to coin their own length units, such as the light-year, in order to cope with the problem arising out of these enormous quantities, an awkward surplus of zeroes. Each light-year—the distance traveled by light in a year—is 6 trillion mi. Yet our galaxy alone, with its billions of stars and glowing clouds of gas and dust, measures 20,000 light-years through its bulging center, and 100,000 light-years from side to side.

And this is only a small part of the universe. Outside the Milky Way galaxies are strung for billions of light-years.
—A Guide to Science. New York, Time-Life Books, 1971.

Stars in our galaxy are, on the average, 4 or 5 light-years apart. But this distance is dwarfed by the distances separating the galaxies in the vast oceans of space. The average distance between neighboring galaxies is about a million light-years. This means that the universe is mostly empty space. It has been calculated that there is 10 billion trillion times more empty space than stellar material in our galaxy. However, in the universe at large there is 10 million billion trillion times as much empty space as stellar material.
—The New Outline of Science by David Dietz. New York, Dodd, Mead and Co., 1972.

We live in the solar system, which is made up of the 9 planets, several thousands of much smaller planets or asteroids, untold millions of rocky particles or meteors, and a large number of flimsy rock-and-gas bodies called comets. In addition, some of the larger planets have moons or satellites revolving around them. The earth has one—our own moon—which is really very unimportant, and appears so glorious only because it is comparatively close to us. However, Jupiter, the largest of the planets, has no less than 12 moons.
—The Worlds Around Us by Patrick Moore. New York, Collier Books, 1956.

SIZE OF HEAVENLY BODIES IN THE SOLAR SYSTEM

The Body	Miles at Diameter
Sun	865,370
Jupiter	86,800
Saturn	71,500
Uranus	29,500
Neptune	28,000
Earth	7,926
Venus	7,610
Mars	4,140
Pluto	3,700
Mercury	3,010
Moon	2,160

EARTH

The earth spins through space like a top. It makes one complete spin or revolution every 24 hours, and this is known as a solar day. The direction of the spin is eastward. Traveling 1,100 mi. a minute, the earth takes 365¼ days to make one complete orbit around the sun, and it winds up where it started a solar year later. Annually, the earth travels 600 million mi. through space.

The distance from the earth to the sun is 93 million mi.

The earth is not round like a basketball. The earth is oblate—relatively flattened at the North and South poles—which is why the diameter at the equator is 7,926 mi. but from pole to pole only 7,900 mi.

What keeps earthlings from flying off into space as the earth spins around, and in fact what keeps earthlings alive, is gravity. Gravity acts as a magnet beneath the feet of human beings to pull them down to the earth's surface, and it is gravity that holds onto the earth's atmosphere of oxygen and other gases that earthlings breathe.

Moon

The moon, which whirls around the earth, is the earth's closest space neighbor, and the only other solar body on which human beings have walked.

The moon is only ¼ the size of the earth.

The moon's gravity is only ⅙ of that on earth. This made the U.S. astronauts, during their moon walks, ⅚ lighter than they were on earth. A person who weighed 180 lbs. on earth would weigh only 30 lbs. on the moon. Because of this weak gravity pull, champion running high jumper Dwight Stones, who leaped 7'6⅝" on earth (at Munich, West Germany, 1973) would have leaped 45'3¾" had he been on the moon.

Since the moon's gravity is too weak to capture and hold atmosphere, there is no weather at all on the moon—in fact, no wind, no sound, no life.

During a lunar day, the heat on the surface of the moon gets as hot as boiling water. But with the coming of lunar night, the temperature drops to 260°F. below zero.

It takes about 27.3 days for the moon to orbit the earth once.

No more than 59% of the moon is visible to earthlings.

From the earth, 32,000 major craters have been seen on the moon. One of the largest visible craters, Clavius, is 146 mi. in diameter. The meteorite that struck the moon and gouged out Clavius is believed to have weighed 200 billion tons.

Of all the soil brought back from the moon's surface by U.S. astronauts, the oldest proved to be around 4,600 million years of age.

Sun and Stars

The sun is 110 times larger than the earth. It would take over one million earths to fill the interior of the sun.

According to Rand McNally's Student Encyclopedia, "To get a rough picture of the size and distance of the sun in relation to the earth, think of the earth as the size of a pea. On this scale, the sun would be the size of a beach ball about 130' away."

The heat on the sun's surface is 10,000°F. Magnetic disturbances sometimes cause dark spots on the sun, and the surface then cools down to 4,500°F. The core of the sun is thought to be 27 million degrees F.

The burning of nuclear fuel is what causes the sun to shine. Inside the sun there is nuclear fusion, and during the process a small amount of matter is lost. The loss of this mass produces the sun's energy.

In producing its energy, the sun uses up about 22 quadrillion tons of hydrogen every year. Despite this, according to scientific predictions, the sun contains enough hydrogen to continue shining at its present strength for another 5 billion years.

The sun's light takes a mere 8 minutes to reach earth.

If the sun stopped shining—despite the remaining pinpricks of light from other stars—all human, animal, and plant life would freeze to death, the tropics would be as cold as the poles, and the 7 seas would turn to solid ice.

Since the sun is not solid, all parts of it do not rotate equally. The time of its rotation at its poles is 33 days, while at its equator rotation takes 25 days.

There are 100 billion stars in our galaxy. From the earth, only about 6,000 of these stars can be seen by the naked eye, and the sun is one of them.

The star nearest to earth is 4 light-years away or 25 trillion mi. distant.

Rigel, at the bottom of the star-group called Orion, is one of the brightest stars. It is 18,000 times brighter than the sun. The light from Rigel, speeding toward us at 186,272 mi. per second, takes 500 years to reach the earth. When you look skyward and spot Rigel tonight, the light you see from it started shining 20 years before Columbus set sail for the New World.

Comets and Meteors

There are said to be 2 million comets in the solar system. The most famous, Halley's Comet, was last seen when it brushed earth in May, 1910. It will next be seen by earthlings in 1986.

The most publicized comet in history, Kohoutek, was seen by earthlings in January, 1974. Ten months earlier, an astronomer, Dr. Lubos Kohoutek, 1st spotted the celebrated comet when it was still 370 million mi. from earth. At one point, the comet's head (called a coma) was 330,000 mi. in size and its tail covered 30 million mi. From outer space, the Skylab astronauts photographed it, and the *Mariner* 10 spacecraft heading toward Venus measured it. Expectations were that Kohoutek, as it came zooming into the solar system, would be "as bright as the quarter moon." But its appearance provided a disappointing view of a faint and pale phantom. However, radio astronomers were not disappointed. "They had identified," reported *National Geographic*, "2 important compounds—methyl cyanide and hydrogen cyanide—never before seen in comets, but found in the reaches of space where new stars are being born." This proved that comets were formed not in planetary orbit within our solar system but in outer space far beyond the planets. But Kohoutek will return and earthlings will have another look at it—75,000 years from now.

Sizzling hot meteors—some huge fireballs, others mere specks—bombard earth's atmosphere at the rate of one million an hour. Only about 150 meteors a year break into earth's atmosphere and survive to hit the surface of the earth. Those that make it are called meteorites. The largest meteorite ever found on earth was one that landed at Hoba West in Southwest Africa. It weighed 132,000 lbs.

—The Eds.

MERCURY

Five planets are visible to the naked eye.

Of these, Mercury, closest to the sun, is the most difficult to see. Nicholas Copernicus, who 1st recognized the sun as the center of the solar system, admitted he had never seen Mercury.

Being only $\frac{4}{10}$ of the earth's distance from the sun, Mercury appears as an evening or morning star for only a few minutes. If you have a telescope, the best time to observe this elusive planet is in the daytime.

In 1899, Giovanni Schiaparelli announced that he had studied Mercury for 17 years. From his hundreds of observations, he deduced that Mercury spun on its axis at the same rate it revolved about the sun—once every 88 days. Obviously then, the side always facing the sun must be very hot—as high as 774°F.—and the shadow side must be extremely cold—as far down as 400°F. below zero. Alas for the paper and pencil astronomer, it is not so. Just as the unsuspecting motorist has his speed clocked by radar, so radar was also used to time Mercury's spinning in 1966. The result is 58.6 days. Mercury is hot all over.

Mercury's orbit is a strange one. It appears to move a slight bit, a few miles each century. But to the careful astronomer who wants perfection or an explanation this is as if a familiar freeway had been moved a few yards overnight.

In 1847, the French astronomer Urbain J. J. Leverrier assumed the cause of the deviation was the gravity pull of a yet unknown planet, which he prematurely named Vulcan. The search for Vulcan, supposedly a planet much smaller than Mercury but closer to the sun, held the attention of astronomers for decades until Albert Einstein explained the difficulty in 1907 in his General Theory of Relativity.

VENUS

Next to the sun and moon it is Venus that is the brightest object in the sky, so bright that it can cast a shadow. In ancient cultures, Venus the evening star and Venus the morning star was not always recognized as being the same planet. To the Egyptians, it was 2 planets, and to the ancient Greeks—until Pythagoras of Samos figured the mystery out—it was Hesperos in the west, or evening, and Phosphoros, "light bearer," in the morning. In all cultures it has been identified as feminine.

The explanation for Venus's brightness is its 20-mi.-thick cloud cover that reflects ¾ of the light that strikes it. The cloud cover also accounts for the horrendous 900°F. temperature of the surface. Much as a car in a parking lot on a sunny day, or a hothouse, Venus gets heated. The radiation that does penetrate the clouds does not leave.

The cloud cover long prevented observations of its surface. At one time it was supposed that Venus was a watery planet, simply because of the clouds.

Today with the information from the American Mariners—it took *Mariner* 2 109 days to come close to Venus—and the Russian Venus probes we are more certain of our information. The atmosphere of this planet that comes nearest us—within 26 million mi.—is mostly inhospitable carbon dioxide with traces of water vapor, oxygen, poisonous hydrogen chloride, and carbon monoxide. The atmosphere bears down on the surface with a pressure 15 to 22 times what it is on earth.

The hidden surface of Venus is not smooth, as the cloud cover may have suggested, but rugged, mountainous, and arid. So Venus, the planet most like the earth in size—it is 95% of the earth's diameter—is a hostile world.

MARS

The only planet that has had an observatory established solely for its study is Mars.

During the 18th and 19th centuries, astronomers had noted the changing face of Mars. In 1881, Schiaparelli presented his maps of Mar's surface, drawn after 5 years of intensive observation. On Mars he saw many straight lines that seemed to form a complicated pattern. He called these lines *canali*, Italian for "channels." Inevitably, this was mistranslated into English as "canals." It was the conclusion of observers that there must be intelligent life on Mars seeking to conserve and distribute its scarce water by building canals from its polar ice caps to its cultivated fields.

None made so much of the idea as did Percival Lowell, a rich American aristocrat. He built the Lowell Observatory in Flagstaff, Ariz., in 1894 expressly to study Mars. Until his death in 1916, this wealthy and dedicated man had thousands of photographs taken of the planet. Detailed drawings made showed not only canals but also oases—all the features of a highly developed civilization.

Unfortunately for all the romanticists, Mars cannot sustain life. Its surface atmosphere is only 1/100 of that on earth. Although thin, and mostly carbon dioxide, it can have tremendous dust storms that last for months and cover huge portions of its pockmarked moonlike surface.

Despite its red color, apparently caused by iron oxide dust, Mars reaches a maximum of only 80°F. while at night it may cool off to a frigid 95°F. below zero. So the combination of distance—1½ times that of the earth from the sun—and its small size—its mass is a little greater than 1/10 that of the earth—makes Mars inhospitable to life. Still, the polar ice caps remain a mystery waiting for a future space probe to solve.

The planets that lie beyond Mars differ greatly from the 4 inner planets. With the exception of Pluto, which has a diameter half that of earth, they are many times earth-size but are much lighter for their size than either earth or Mars. A typical sample of Saturn would actually float on water.

JUPITER

In the solar system the largest planet is Jupiter. The mass of this giant is 2½ times the combined mass of all the rest of the solar system, not counting the sun, of course. If Jupiter were slightly larger it might have been a star generating its own light instead of being a reflector.

Like the sun, Jupiter's atmosphere is mainly hydrogen and helium with some methane and ammonia added in. Its atmosphere is strongly banded in appearance. Most remarkable is its "red spot," elliptical in shape and covering an area several times the size of the earth. It varies in color from blood red to intense pink to magenta for some as yet not understood reason. Moreover, the spot moves. At one time it was thought to be the reflection of a surface lava flow but this idea has been discarded as the temperature of this frigid giant is about

225°F. below zero, cold enough to freeze any stone.

Jupiter is definitely not a perfect sphere, being considerably flattened at its poles due to its rapid spin. It only takes 9 hours 55 minutes for this massive hulk to make one rotation. This rapid rotation also explains why such a cold planet is such a good radio emitter. Its travel around the sun is considerably slower than earth's, taking 11.86 years.

SATURN

A ball with a 45-rpm record about its middle would be recognized as a model of Saturn by practically everyone. But when Galileo, in 1610, 1st saw Saturn he thought its strange appearance was due to its being 3 spheres. It was not until 1656 that Christiaan Huygens recognized that Saturn's exotic shape was due to the presence of a very thin—perhaps only inches thick—disk.

The explanation for the disk—Saturn is the only planet so adorned—is that a one-piece moon cannot form so close to a planet. The tidal forces would be too large. As it is, Saturn has 10 satellites, the last being discovered in 1966, all beyond the outermost ring.

Saturn is much like Jupiter. Its diameter is 9.47 times earth's, it rotates in 10 hours 14 minutes, takes 29.46 years to go around the sun, has an atmosphere consisting mostly of methane, and has a temperature of 261°F. below zero.

URANUS

Uranus, the 1st planet to be beyond normal eyesight, was discovered by accident. William Herschel, in 1781, thought that he had discovered a comet. Within a few months it was realized that a new planet had been found. Until 1850, it was named Georgian, after George III, King of England.

Uranus is very unusual in that its axis of rotation is nearly parallel to the plane of its orbit. At certain times the sun is almost directly over its north pole, but the extent of warming done by the sun is affected by the fact that Uranus is 19 times farther from the sun than the earth is.

NEPTUNE

Attempts to plot Uranus' orbit failed until it was realized that an unknown planet must be pulling it out of its path. Independent calculations by Leverrier and J. C. Adams pointed to this planet's location and, in 1846, after less than one hour of searching, the new planet was found by J. Galle.

Not much is known about Neptune. It has 17.3 times more mass than earth and is 30 times as far from the sun. It has 2 moons, the 2nd not discovered until 1949.

PLUTO

The strangest, least-known, and farthest planet from earth is Pluto. Decades of searching for this planet failed until, in 1930, Clyde Tombaugh, after looking at thousands of star images, discovered the new planet while working at the Lowell Observatory. The name Pluto was chosen because the mythical Pluto's

brothers were Jupiter and Neptune and the 1st 2 letters, which form the astronomers' symbol for the planet, P and L, are the initials of Percival Lowell, the luckless founder of the observatory.

Pluto is such a small planet, has such a peculiar orbit—it actually comes closer to the sun than Neptune—that some astronomers would like to treat it as something other than a planet, perhaps a runaway moon belonging to Jupiter or Neptune.

—T.S.

The Astronomers

No one knows who the 1st astronomer was but he probably had the job of making a calendar that could be used to predict the seasons, when to plant, when to expect the annual flood. Later on he might have devised theories explaining how the sun moves.

The ancient Greeks produced a few accomplishments in astronomy although this was not one of their main interests. Anaximander (611–546 B.C.) explained the movements of the sun, moon, and planets by stating that all heavenly bodies were in the shape of wheels. Eudoxus of Cnidus (408–355 B.C.) modified this to have the planets move in concentric spheres, which was an idea that stuck around a long time. The philosopher Socrates (470–399 B.C.) had a misanthropic opinion—astronomers were good only for making calendars.

The 1st astronomer in modern terms, a collector and analyzer of data, was Hipparchus (c. 150 B.C.), who mapped the location of 1,080 stars and also classified them according to brightness in 6 categories. Hipparchus' achievement would have been lost but for Ptolemy, who worked in Alexandria from 127 to 141 A.D. Ptolemy put the data in the *Almagest* and used it to support the earth as the center of the solar system.

For 1,400 years Ptolemy's system dominated thought. It satisfied religious dogma—the earth and on it man, God's child, were the center of everything. It took a priest to upset this applecart. The Pole, Nicholas Copernicus (1473–1543), was orphaned at 10. His uncle, a bishop, raised him in the Church. Although a sideline, astronomy occupied much of his time despite the turmoil caused by the Reformation then taking place. Copernicus was able to publish 3 books on astronomy. The last, and most important, was released at his death. In it Copernicus proposed that the sun was the center of the solar system.

Copernicus' theory was not accepted readily. Not only did it dispose of man as the center of the universe, it was not much simpler than

Ptolemy's theory. It took the work of an astronomer who could not accept Copernicus' theory as true to lay the groundwork for its acceptance. Tycho Brahe (1546–1601) was arrogant, assertive, and able. As a student he argued vehemently with another over a problem in mathematics. In the resulting duel, Tycho's swordsmanship was not equal to his mathematics and he suffered the embarrassment of losing the tip of his nose. He had a replacement made of gold but things were not the same.

As premier astronomer, Tycho was able to bargain for and get the Isle of Hveen, near Copenhagen, to use as an observatory. In this Tycho installed the most accurate instruments of the time and set out to collect the most exact data ever recorded. After his patron, King Frederick II, died, Tycho was forced out by envious lords. He landed in Prague in 1597. Luckily for astronomy, his new assistant was a man named Kepler.

Johannes Kepler (1571–1630) was a strange figure. With a constantly running nose, with more interest in astrology and numerology than astronomy, he may have been the best mathematician of his times. Using Tycho's exquisite data, Kepler was able to determine that Mars—and by extension every planet—travels in an elliptical orbit—not the perfect circles that Copernicus had supposed. Kepler described the motion of the planets, saying that the speed of a planet depends on its distance from the sun—the farther away the slower it moves—without the use of computers or any mathematical aids such as logarithms.

At the same time that Kepler was making his discoveries, in Italy Galileo Galilei (1546–1642) was introducing the telescope into astronomy. Not the inventor, but the 1st user of this instrument in astronomy, Galileo was also the 1st to observe the craters of the moon, to observe that the Milky Way is made up of stars, and to observe that Jupiter has 4 moons orbiting around it. This last impressed Galileo as a miniature solar system and as proof of Copernicus' theory. Adherence to this new concept caused Galileo to get in trouble with the powerful Church. After a number of judicial hearings, he lived his last years under house arrest.

But why do the planets swing around the sun? Why don't they go spinning into space like a yo-yo with a broken string? Isaac Newton (1642–1727) provided the answer. During the plagues of 1665–1666 Newton had to return to his family farm. During this unhurried time Newton was able to discover the true nature of gravity and write laws describing its nature. Along with the development of the reflecting telescope, calculus, and theories on the behavior of light, Newton made considerable contributions to astronomy without discovering any celestial objects.

Christiaan Huygens (1629–1695) was an intellectual rival of Newton. His discoveries included the Orion Nebula in 1656, the markings on Mars, Saturn's moon Titan in 1656, and the shape of the rings of Saturn.

One of the 1st uses of Newton's theory of gravitation was in explaining comets. In the 15th and 16th centuries there had been a large number of bright comets. Comets, traditionally objects of fear, were believed to foretell earthquakes, floods, and the death of kings. Edmund Halley (1656–1742), a colleague and ally of Newton's, used the new law and established the comets of 1682, 1607, and 1531 as being the same comet. Further, he predicted that this comet would reappear in 1758, which it did. It was promptly named Halley's Comet. It last appeared in 1910. Halley was also the 1st to catalog the stars in the southern hemisphere.

William Herschel (1738–1822) discovered Uranus almost by accident, which is also the way he became an astronomer. Like his father, Herschel became a musician in the Hannover Guards in Germany. But upon being shot at a few times, and realizing musicians could be mortal, he decided to move to England to follow less martial musical pursuits. While working as a musical director, Herschel developed an interest in astronomy. Then, as now, telescopes were expensive, so he decided to make his own. His sister, Caroline, perhaps the 1st female astronomer, assisted him. Herschel became so proficient at using the telescopes he made that he was able to recognize some fuzzy spots as nebulae, stellar dust clouds. He was also able to identify many double stars.

Herschel was the 1st to attempt to measure distances to stars by scientific means—he compared the stars' brightnesses to their distances. He was off by a factor of 10 times. His other great accomplishment was to be the father of John Herschel, who became an outstanding astronomer.

Until the 20th century astronomers' attention was primarily on the solar system, with less emphasis given to outer space. After 1900, the situation reversed itself. True, astronomers like Gerald Kuiper (1905–   ) are still making discoveries—such as the satellites of Uranus and Neptune—but time, money, and instruments are increasingly devoted to the stars.

To examine distant stars, gigantic apparatus is needed. The chief provider of these instruments in the early 20th century was George E. Hale (1868–1938). An ingenious astronomer, he was the inventor of the spectroheliograph—a device that allows pictures of the sun's spectra to be taken. Hale had the ability to get generous contributions for the building of large telescopes. In 1892, he built a 40" telescope, financed by a Chicago streetcar magnate, at the Yerkes Observatory in Wisconsin. In 1904, he established the Mount Wilson Observatory in California, and by 1917 had a 60" and a 100" telescope operating. He was behind the building of the 200" telescope at Mount Palomar, Calif. These large telescopes provided the necessary tools to open up space.

The theory needed to understand the new discoveries was provided by Henrietta Leavitt (1868–1921) and Ejnar Hertzsprung (1873–1967). Leavitt, while studying the Magellanic Clouds, galaxies near our own, recognized some stars that vary in brightness in a very regular way. She was able to calculate the relationship between the star's brightness and the length of its period. If she could measure the length of the star's period, she automatically knew its brightness and had a measure of the star's and the galaxy's distance. Hertzsprung, originally a chemical engineer, determined the relationship between a star's color and brightness to find the star's size. Between the 2 astronomers a means of measuring a star's or galaxy's distance had been devised.

Harlow Shapley (1885–1972), who had started out to be a newspaper reporter but turned to astronomy, used these discoveries and his own observations of ball-like clumps of stars called globular clusters to map our galaxy.

The discovery that our galaxy is not limitless led to the discovery of galaxies beyond the Milky Way. Edwin P. Hubble (1889–1953), using the 60" and 100" telescopes at Mount Wilson, discovered not only many new galaxies but that most of them were moving away from us—we are in an expanding universe which, perhaps, began 5 billion years ago.

Sizes of these foreign galaxies were established by Walter Baade (1893–1960) working during 1942 and 1943 in war-darkened Los Angeles. Baade also discovered that there were 2 generations of stars, one old, one new. This led to the analysis of a star's evolution from birth to either death by super explosion or its transformation into a white dwarf or neutron star.

Radioastronomy gave astronomers insights unsuspected by ordinary optical telescopes. Radioastronomy was discovered accidentally by a Bell telephone engineer, Karl Jansky (1905–1950), in 1931 as he was attempting to find the causes of radio interference. Radioastronomy might have disappeared but for the interest of one amateur, Grote Reber (1911–), who built and operated his own instrument in his Illinois backyard during the '30s and '40s.

During W.W. II a Dutch astronomer, Hendrik van de Hulst (1918–), made some calculations—the only astronomy he could engage in, since The Netherlands was occupied at the time by the Germans. His calculations showed that hydrogen could emit radiation at the 21-cm. wave length. In 1951, this "song of hydrogen," as it came to be called, was discovered. Using it, Jan Oort (1900–), Dutch

galactic expert, mapped out our galaxy, producing the picture we have today of a sta. system with long, sweeping arms.

Another discovery made with the radio telescope is the presence of such familiar earth molecules as ammonia, methane, formaldehyde, and water in interstellar space. The radio telescope also led to the discovery of quasars, strong radio emitters, and pulsars, very regular radio emitters. In 1960, Allan Sandage (1926–) announced the 1st discovery of a star that acted as a radio source, a very dim object easily overlooked except for its being pinpointed by the radio telescope. Three years later, Maarten Schmidt (1929–) studied the spectrum of another quasar and recognized a tremendous, and never before realized, "red shift," the measure by which astronomers tell the speed at which galaxies and stars move. So large was the red shift that the quasar had to be the farthest object recorded up to that time.
—T.S.

Travelers in Space

The world gasped on the morning of October 4, 1957, when *Sputnik* 1 signaled the beginning of a new age. In the U.S., the gasp was anguished as the scramble began to orbit a U.S. satellite. Overnight, rocket experts, ignored since the days of Robert Goddard, became respectable, their services in high demand.

Before that autumn day, the U.S. space program had been a sporadic investigation, initially using Von Braun's German rockets, then its own developing defense arsenal to record high-altitude data. None of these rockets had entered orbit or escaped earth's gravity. *Sputnik* 2, carrying the little dog Laika, launched a month after *Sputnik* 1, increased the pressure in the U.S. Finally, *Explorer* 1 got off the ground at Cape Canaveral on January 31, 1958, and promptly discovered unsuspected layers of charged particles around the earth. These were named the Van Allen belts after the man who correctly interpreted the data.

MANNED SPACE FLIGHT

Within months, the newly organized National Aeronautics and Space Administration took over operations already begun on a 3-stage program whose goal, as set earlier by President Kennedy, was placing a man on the moon and returning him to earth safely within 10 years. The 1st phase, the Mercury program, was upstaged when the Russian Yuri Gagarin completed a full orbit of the earth on April 12, 1961, in the *Vostok* 1.

But worldwide coverage spotlighted Alan

Shepard on the 1st U.S. trip 302 mi. downrange into the Atlantic in the *Freedom* 7 on May 5, 1961. Five more Mercury flights, each one attempting a new maneuver or longer orbit time, included John Glenn's 1st orbital flight on February 20, 1962, and the final Mercury mission, a 22-orbit flight by Gordon Cooper on May 15–16, 1963. By then, the Russian cosmonaut Nikolayev had flown a 64-orbit mission in *Vostok* 3 and the only woman cosmonaut, Valentina Tereshkova, was preparing for her 48-orbit mission in June.

The Mercury and Vostok flights convinced scientists that human beings could operate their ships in a weightless environment, could conduct useful observations in space, and could come home again to tell the tale.

The next manned programs, the U.S. Gemini and the Russian Voskhod flights, proved that humans could maneuver a spaceship and dock with another vehicle and that persons could walk and work in the vacuum of space. These tasks would be necessary for landing on and leaving the moon's surface and returning to the mother ship.

Then, at Christmastime in 1968, a manned craft circled the moon. The 1st Apollo crew expressed the awe felt when looking back from deep space to the beauty of earth. For the 1st time men saw the planet as a whole and realized what they had left; how beautiful, fragile, and lonely is earth, hanging in the void. Their limited words frustrated them, but their emotion was transmitted.

Seven months later, on July 20, 1969, after a cliff-hanging, manually controlled landing with only a few seconds of fuel remaining, a quietly jubilant voice announced across a quarter-million miles, "Houston, Tranquillity Base here. The *Eagle* has landed." Man was on the moon.

Several hours later millions watched on TV that cautious "giant leap for mankind," and we all stood with Neil Armstrong on a new world.

With one exception, the rest of the Apollo flights seemed prosaic to all except the astronauts, scientists, and ground-support people involved. *Apollo 13* was the exception. An explosion on board crippled the ship far out in space. After a desperate journey around the moon and back to earth in their lunar lander, *Aquarius*, the men returned to the Apollo capsule for a hair-raising, but successful, reentry.

Apollo 17 was the last manned lunar flight, the last chapter of the lunar epic—originally politically inspired—which became the greatest engineering feat in the history of mankind.

Attention now turned to the earth-orbiting space station, Skylab, launched in 1973. Skylab restated man's adaptability wherever he may be, proving that man can work, eat, sleep, spend months in a weightless workshop high above earth's protective atmosphere, and suffer no known permanent ill effects. The 3 Skylab crews repaired damaged equipment and replaced film packets in cameras located outside their ship. They demonstrated manufacturing techniques by growing semiconductor crystals for transistors with perfection unattainable on earth, and making alloys that can't be made here because of gravity. They used the vacuum of space, impossible to achieve in our air-locked world.

They studied Comet Kohoutek and the sun, about which we understand so little. Their solar pictures were priceless long-term photographic studies above the ocean of air, which blocks much of the radiation. Then they returned to earth, telling us space wasn't so hostile—just new and unexplored, with much to give those who accept its challenge.

UNMANNED DEEP SPACE PROBES

Major unmanned probes of outer space are revealing startling information unsuspected unless directly measured. The U.S.S.R. sent off the 1st in 1959, which entered an orbit around the sun. Four U.S. attempts from 1958 to 1960 failed, until finally *Pioneer V* entered sun orbit in March, 1960. Russia's *Lunik II* and *III* had already impacted the moon and the latter had taken the 1st pictures of its backside.

The 1961–1962 Ranger Program, the soft-landing Surveyor, and the lunar orbiters sent information and pictures for use in the manned flights to come and revealed to U.S. scientists profiles of deep space radiation and meteor density.

The Mariners were launched to Venus and Mars and they, with their Russian counterparts (again 1st), sent back torrents of information negating much that was previously believed about the planets. Mars has planet-wide dust storms in its thin atmosphere and shows definite signs of water erosion. *Mariner 10* photographed Venus en route to a Mercury flyby on March 29, 1974, sending back the 1st pictures of the planet nearest the sun. The Soviet Venera probes entered Venus's clouds and telemetered data revealing an atmosphere closely resembling a description of a hurricane in hell.

Pioneer 10 traversed the rocky asteroid belt between Jupiter and Mars, to fly near Jupiter on December 3, 1973. Again surprises—the asteroid belt proved nearly empty, no hazard to navigation, and Jupiter's magnetic field was upside down and 10 times stronger than expected. On board *Pioneer 10*, now heading out of the solar system, is a little plaque engraved with 20th-century symbols. It is our 1st intentional message sent to anyone out there since Tesla fired his high-frequency spark discharges around the turn of the century. Will it be more decipherable than the "unintentional" messages sent before? Television signals escape through the same ionosphere that reflects radio waves, so Nielsen's "Top 10" are also travelers in space.

In late 1974, *Helios* left for its solar studies in orbit around the sun and *Mariner 10* passed by Mercury a 2nd time, turned on its TV cameras, and sent back more pictures.

On March 16, 1975, *Mariner 10* made its 3rd and final operational pass by Mercury, approaching within 198 mi. and sending close-up TV pictures. On this mission NASA got 3 flybys for the price of one.

Pioneer 11 swept by Jupiter on December 2, 1974, sending back the 1st Jovian polar pictures and new data on interior composition and the magnetic maelstrom surrounding the biggest planet.

UNMANNED SATELLITES

Closer to home, space is getting crowded. Somebody puts up a satellite about once a week. The Dutch are doing it, the Italians, the Chinese. Most of us take for granted the Intelsat synchronous satellite communications network. These "comsats" are parked in a stationary orbit over the equator. Intelsat IV, has communications channels exceeding all the submarine cables in existence. The UN now has on its agenda a discussion aimed at prohibiting direct television broadcasting into home receivers. The technology for doing it is available, but some countries don't want their citizens to listen to another country's broadcasts.

Weather satellites, the Nimbus and new

ESSA series, are doing more than helping the TV weatherman. Global hurricane and storm warnings save billions of dollars and many lives. One 24-hour series of weather pictures is worth 20,000 ship reports and is far cheaper. The typhoon which devastated Pakistan a few years ago was clearly seen and warnings issued, but land communication in Pakistan was too slow to alert the affected areas in time. Shipping companies route ships around storms at sea and cartographers are mapping the world with accuracy undreamed of 10 years ago.

The ERTS-I (Earth Resources Technology Satellite) is swamped by requests for data on crops, plant diseases and vigor, surface water distribution, air and water pollution, oil spills—the list is endless. A Gulf Coast shrimp fisherman said one picture was worth 20 years of sailing in his home waters.

Global navigation satellites allow ships to fix position in cloudy weather, thus saving lives and dollars by staying on course. They also help ships avoid storms. The ocean liner *Queen Elizabeth II* was one of the 1st commercial ships built to include Navsat capability. Recently an Aerosat agreement was signed for European-U.S.-Canadian air-control satellites to increase safety in the overcrowded airways.

Military satellites allow instantaneous communications and monitor troop buildup, weapons deployment, and testing. One series, the Vela Hotel, monitors the upper-atmosphere nuclear test-ban treaty. High-altitude blasts can disturb the Van Allen belt, which helps protect earth from lethal solar radiation.

Astronomical and near-earth space measurements contribute information about how solar flares disrupt communications, about the high-velocity solar wind and the shock wave formed when this wind is deflected by our magnetic shield. The Orbiting Astronomical Observatory (OAO), with its telescopes Copernicus and Uhuru, has revealed a whole chorus of radiation from the sun and stars. In late 1974, NASA received the 1st infrared astronomical data from the U.S. Air Force, exciting astronomers with the possibility of orbiting an infrared telescope. In the 1st month of operation the OAO gathered 20 times more information

than earth-based instruments had compiled in the previous 15 years.

FUTURE SPACE EXPLORATION

Where are we traveling in the future? After the 1975 Apollo-Soyuz cooperative mission inaugurates another 1st, this time in international relations, the Viking-Mars lander will be launched, complete with a life detection system. *Pioneer 11*, the other Jupiter flyby, has already been whipped around by Jupiter's gravitational field in a slingshot boost toward a look at Saturn in 1980. Venus flybys and probes are scheduled for 1978 and there possibly will be a Venus radar-mapping balloon in Venus's atmosphere in 1981–1984. A Mariner Jupiter-Saturn flyby will leave in 1977. Other missions are planned for comet and asteroid study. Every astronomer is pushing for a 1986 study of Halley's Comet. Other talking-stage projects include automatic lunar rovers, a communications satellite for exploring the backside of the moon, landers on one of Jupiter's moons, and orbiters to study Jupiter, the rings of Saturn, and Titan's atmosphere.

Spacelab, an international workshop whose crew can fly back to earth in the Space Shuttle, is under way for launch in 1980. The reusable Shuttle could supply a permanent orbiting station, and provide an earth-moon shuttle system having much lower fuel requirements than a moon rocket launched from earth. One of its tasks may be to place huge telescopes in orbit.

Talk has started about a manned lunar base operable sometime in the 1990s but no budget is now available. A solar electric-rocket propulsion system is also being developed.

Dr. Ernst Stuhlinger of Marshall Space Flight Center, when asked by a missionary why space research money wouldn't be better spent feeding hungry children, told the story of a poor people beset with plague 400 years ago. They were enraged when their local, open-handed benefactor spent some of his money supporting an experimenter who painstakingly ground lenses and built lens systems. The philanthropist refused to cut off his support

B.C.   **by johnny hart**

and the microscope was born. Later bacteria were discovered, diseases conquered, the plague suppressed.

The benefits of space exploration are already showering in from near-space satellites and probes, from space medicine and materials, from electronics and computers developed to support the space effort. Exploration of this new frontier holds more potential for the good of mankind than all the advances made in the past. Once accepted, can we ever turn back from the challenge of that unknown?

—Y.S.R.

What's Out There?

Is there intelligent life on other planets?

For a generation of Americans raised on TV shows like "Twilight Zone" and "Star Trek," the question hardly needs asking. Yet for all its current popularity, the concept of extraterrestrial intelligence (ETI) has been a long time coming. The Greeks proposed it 1st, hundreds of years before Christ, using exactly the same argument we use today—statistical probability.

ETI is only one possible type of extraterrestrial life. Life, in some form, may be scattered across space like weeds. Already, the precursors of life—organic molecules—have been detected in meteorites and interstellar dust. Planets with vegetation or animal organisms may be routine cosmic events.

For the general public, interest centers on ETI—particularly upon 3 questions: Where is it? What does it look like? Why doesn't it contact us?

First of all, you can forget about intelligent life on planets like Mars and Venus. Data from *Mariner* 9, which took 7,200 pictures of Mars in 1971, show a cold, barren surface swept by violent dust storms and blemished with enormous volcanic piles. No sign of artificial activity, such as road construction or farming, was evident. The so-called "canals" of Mars don't exist, except as natural features. Moreover, the only water on Mars is a small amount of ice in the polar cap and possibly a layer of permafrost beneath the surface. If ETI exists on the red planet, it lives in caves and taps a concealed water supply, or doesn't require water to survive. Scientists aren't betting on either possibility.

As for Venus, it's literally hot as hell. Data from 2 Soviet spacecraft that landed on Venus in the early 1970s reveal a searing 900°F. as the average surface temperature. Just as bad, the Venusian atmosphere is dense and heavy—so dense that almost no sunlight reaches the surface, and so heavy that a human being would be crushed like a beer can under a truck (if he wasn't fried 1st by the heat). In a nightmarish world like this, no scientist seriously expects ETI to exist. As astronomer Carl Sagan speculates, any organism able to survive on Venus would need leathery skin, stubby wings, and a passion for the color red

(virtually the only part of the visible light spectrum perceptible on Venus).

The 6 other planets in our solar system (besides earth) also contain environments that appear inhospitable to ETI, although discovery of lower biological forms cannot be ruled out. Jupiter, Saturn, and possibly some of their moons are regarded as possible sites for microorganisms or other forms of primitive life.

No one, of course, knows the conditions necessary for the evolution of intelligence. While it's easy to postulate weird creatures that could adapt to habitats like Venus or Jupiter, this doesn't tell us which environments are suitable for ETI and which aren't. To search for ETI, we need to make assumptions about how common it is and how long it typically survives.

Astronomers currently believe the best place to look for ETI is around stars like our own sun, which may support earthlike planets— some possibly inhabited. Since the nearest such star is 4.3 light-years away, it isn't practical to conduct the search with manned or unmanned space probes. The fastest spacecraft ever launched from earth would take 80,000 years to travel that distance. Instead, scientists are using a more promising device—the radio telescope.

It's pure speculation whether civilizations thousands of years in advance of earth use radio communications. Perhaps there are better techniques we know nothing about. Presumably, though, societies close to our own in technical development generate some form of radio energy that "leaks" into space, just as radar beams and TV signals spill out from earth. Astronomers hope to detect this energy using such monstrous machinery as the 1,000' radio dish at Arecibo, Puerto Rico. This telescope has the capability to transmit and receive signals from any similar facility in our galaxy.

It may be a long search. Radio waves vary in frequency and power. If ETI is transmitting, which frequency is it using? Is the signal strong enough to excite our receivers? How many stars should we monitor? How long should we listen? Would we be sure to recognize a signal if we picked it up?

In the summer of 1960, scientists at the National Radio Observatory in Green Bank,

W.Va., conducted a preliminary experiment, Project Ozma, to examine some of these questions. They listened for a total of 200 hours to 2 stars within 12 light-years of earth: Tau Ceti and Epsilon Eridani. They listened on a frequency of 1,420 megahertz, a natural emission frequency of hydrogen. Because of the earth's rotation, the antenna could be directed at the stars only for a certain period each day. Nothing unusual was heard. Since then, more sophisticated short-term projects have been conducted in the U.S. and the Soviet Union, none productive.

In the summer of 1971, NASA funded a 3-month study called Project Cyclops to assess the feasibility of using multiple radio telescopes to listen for ETI at distances of up to 100 light-years. The study proposed a spectacular array of at least 1,000 antennas, spread out over a 10- or 20-mi. area. No action was taken on the proposal, but it remains under discussion.

Besides leakage, once our telescopes begin listening, there are 2 other types of extraterrestrial signals we might encounter: radio beacons and interstellar messages. The 1st are signals transmitted by an advanced society to announce its presence to cultures not yet discovered; the 2nd are transmissions exchanged by societies already known to each other. The 1st, if they exist, should be easy to understand since they will likely be based on information familiar to most technological communities. Not so the 2nd, which almost certainly would be too sophisticated for us to decipher. Imagine a telegraph operator in 1840 trying to understand data transmissions from an Apollo spacecraft.

One problem plaguing the quest for ETI is our inability to estimate the average lifetime of a technological society. The longer such societies exist, the more likely they can be located (if they're using radio devices). Since the only technical society we know anything about is our own, we might gloomily suppose any civilization advanced enough to attract our attention is advanced enough to liquidate itself in a nuclear war. In fact, it may be the war that attracts our attention. If this is the case, our chances of detecting ETI may be moderately good, but the odds for contact are nil. Radio leakage from earth, which began about 1920, is now reaching star systems some 50-odd light-years away. If our nearest intelligent neighbor is no closer than 300 light-years (an entirely reasonable possibility), he's got a long wait before our signals reach him. Assuming he has the political stability to survive that wait, someday we may receive an acknowledgment—if *we* can last that long. By the same logic, if he started broadcasting 50 years ago, we need to endure another 250 years to

hear his signals and 600 more to answer those signals and receive a reply.

Some scientists have argued it may not be in our best interest for ETI to discover the radio and TV signals leaking from earth (although it's too late to prevent it). How many of us, for example, would want ETI to interpret our civilization in terms of the Rolling Stones or "Let's Make a Deal?" More seriously, what do we really know about the psychology of a society that is 100 or 500 times older than we are? Would they be benevolent, hostile, or indifferent toward us? Would they find us amusing or boring? Would it make any difference how they felt, with tens or hundreds of light-years separating our planet from theirs?

Most people assume ETI would regard earth with keen interest and actively seek to contact its inhabitants, either by radio or in person. This, however, may be a chauvinistic view. What, after all, could we offer an advanced society it doesn't already have? As the poet Archibald MacLeish reminds us, we are "a small planet of a minor star off at the edge of an inconsiderable galaxy."

Man's curiosity is limited almost exclusively to his own species. Relatively few *Homo sapiens* seek out lower forms of intelligence to study. Only in recent decades, for example, has any serious attempt been made to communicate with dolphins, one of the most intelligent creatures on earth. Worse yet, another intelligent animal, the whale, is being systematically slaughtered. If ETI has any interest in visiting earth, it may be only to survey our resources or collect specimens for a zoo.

One theory currently in vogue is that visitation occurred sometime in the earth's distant past when humans were too primitive to understand it, except as a supernatural event. Evidence of this, goes the theory, can be found in legends, artifacts, and early forms of art. It's even possible, if you accept this view, that man is an experiment of ETI, implanted on earth like rats put in a cage.

While few scientists flatly reject the idea of ancient visitation, few are rushing to take it up. The main problem is the ambiguity of archaeological evidence, which must be viewed against a backdrop of religious belief, superstition, and differences in cultural expression. The range of styles in ancient art is such that many interpretations are possible for a particular image or object. What will archaeologists think in 1,000 years when they dig up the artifacts of American society and find a Frisbee?

As for the intriguing question of what ETI looks like, prepare yourself for a shock: If we find it, it won't look like us. "The Late Late Show" notwithstanding, human beings are the peculiar result of many random evolutionary events—which are not likely to occur again in the same order under the same conditions on another planet. As Carl Sagan explains: "Start the earth over again; you won't get human beings." Ironically, then, science fiction writers who depict ETI as humanoid robots or giant gorillas suffer not from too much imagination but from too little. ETI—produced in environments not yet conceived on earth—will be stranger and more functional than these. Our fantasies, alas, fall short of reality, which is indeed more bizarre than we know.

THE GREEN BANK FORMULA

How many societies in our galaxy are capable of interstellar communication?

With only one society to talk to—our own—we can make only a crude estimate. In 1961, scientists devised an equation for this purpose, called the Green Bank Formula. It looks like this:

$$N = R_* f_p n_e f_l f_i f_c L$$

N = number of civilizations in galaxy capable of interstellar communication.

R_* = average rate at which stars develop during lifetime of galaxy.

f_p = fraction of stars with planets.

n_e = average number of planets, per star, capable of supporting life.

f_l = fraction of planets with life.

f_i = fraction of planets with intelligent life.

f_c = fraction of planets with intelligent life capable of interstellar communication.

L = average lifetime of society capable of interstellar communication.

Assigning numbers to this equation is a sobering experience. Only one quantity—R_*—is known with any certainty. All the others are rough guesses. Very rough. The worst is L, which could vary anywhere from 10 or 20 years to hundreds of *millions* of years, depending on

factors like political stability, natural catastrophes, interest in science, conquest of disease, biological longevity, and supply of food and energy.

Conservatively, scientists believe N might be roughly 1,000, assuming the average society survives in the communicative state (i.e., possesses radio communications technology) for at least 10,000 years. Surviving that long may not seem such an unlikely possibility until you consider that intelligent life on earth has existed in the communicative state for only about 40 years (directional antennas were developed in the 1930s). Since some sectors of humanity were building bombs while others were building radio telescopes, the question arises whether other societies have done the same. If so, communicative lifetimes of 10,000 years may be rare occurrences.

Taking the optimistic view, some scientists postulate that a majority of technical cultures have resolved their ideological differences and have survived for exceptionally long periods. This being so, our galaxy may contain a lot more than 1,000 societies with radio skills. Some calculations put the number at a million. Using such a figure, we find the average separation between civilizations is somewhere between 200 and 500 light-years. That's entirely too much mileage for casual conversation (even by radio), but extremely stable societies could exchange certain types of information across such distances without difficulty.

At the present time, nobody knows which estimate for N is correct—1,000 or 1,000,000. Perhaps neither is right. Everything hangs on L, the toughest piece in the puzzle. If technical societies tend to destroy themselves within a few decades of achieving radio capability, the Green Bank Formula yields the melancholy conclusion that our galaxy may contain only one example of technical intelligence —us. On the other hand, humans may be alone only in the sense that we have not yet joined the galactic community of civilizations using radio (or other means) to share scientific and other data. In time we may gain access to this communication network and in so doing learn for the 1st time how many extraterrestrial neighbors we really have.

—S.N.

Life on Other Planets: Another View

When we speculate about whether other worlds will have "life as we know it," our natural tendency is to think only of life forms that suspiciously resemble man, dogs, cats, and, at the very most, perhaps something as fantastic as a giraffe.

The fact is, however, that little is known about life-as-we-know-it. About 350,000 kinds of plants and 1.2 million species of animals have been scientifically classified. An estimated half million more life forms inhabiting this planet still await discovery and description. Between 50 million and 4 billion different kinds of living things *have* lived on this planet. Only about 1% of the classified species of living plants and ⅔₁₀ of 1% of living animals have been subjected to chemical analysis. We are shamefully ignorant.

The result of this ignorance is a biological myopia that drastically shortens our view of the dimensions of life. In order to theorize rationally about extraterrestrial life, we should take a closer look at terrestrial life. Only when we begin to perceive the diversity of life on earth can we fully appreciate the possibilities of a vastness of life beyond earth.

From greenish dust to a thriving community of living organisms—but where had the "livingness" gone and whence had it come again? The answer, or at least something approaching an answer, may be found in what happens to a much larger form of life—the lungfish—when it passes into suspended animation. Because the lungfish is larger, its body can be thoroughly examined, and more complete studies of its life history can be made. Here is a clock that can be inspected when it runs down, stops ticking, and then seemingly winds itself up again. (Perhaps someday we'll be able to do the same with the tardigrade.)

The African lungfish (*Protopterus annectans*) is known to be able to survive for 4 years out of water, in a state of profound anabiosis. Dr. Homer W. Smith, chairman of the Dept. of Physiology at the New York University School of Medicine, estimates that "if the animal has a maximal store of fat when it goes into estivation, and if it gets the breaks from nature . . . it might survive for 7 years."

When the lungfish finds itself without water, it burrows into the drying mud and secretes around its body a mucous cocoon that hardens into a tough, leathery wrapping. Virtually mummified, it breathes air through a small hole running to the surface. According to Dr. Earl S. Herald, curator of aquatic biology at the Steinhart Aquarium, San Francisco, the lungfish does not use fat, as do other animals, in estivation or hibernation. Instead, Herald says, it absorbs its own muscle tissue!

Except for the oxygen brought in from the outside world, the lungfish thus lives in an environment of its own construction, a nearly closed system (not unlike the closed-system spacecraft engineers and scientists are struggling to design). As its metabolism slows to a niggardly rate, the lungfish lives on itself. Tests have shown that lungfish in cocoons for a mere 6 months have dropped in weight from 13.2 ounces to 10.2 ounces and length from 16″ to 14⅜″. Most vertebrates, especially man, cannot tolerate much urea; the presence of as little as 10 parts per million of this toxic waste product in a vertebrate's system is usually fatal.

But the incredible lungfish's equally incredible kidney separates the urea from the water in its body over and over again. The concentration of urea builds up more and more—it has been known to go as high as 20,000 parts per million.

What keeps the lungfish alive for years in its waterless, foodless, sunless crypt? The answer seems to be a fantastic ability to conserve energy, to squeeze the last drop out of the stuff of life—to force life to feed upon life, to slow down time. Motionless, barely alive, a stinking, self-made sewer, the lungfish is nonetheless as wondrous as Keats's Grecian urn, for this thing from the dry earth is also a "foster-child of Silence and slow Time."

Eventually, the lungfish will be released from its crypt. Freshening water will come again, and it will swim once more. But there are other creatures whose entire lives are spent in environments that a student of extraterrestrial life might well call unearthly. For example, it was assumed that life could not endure the extremes of the abyssal depths of the sea—utter darkness, near-freezing temperatures, and pressure of more than 1,000 *tons* per sq. ft.

In 1951, Dr. Anton Brunn's Danish ship *Galathea II* voyaged to the Mindanao Trench, east of the Philippines, where a 34,578′ depth was found. "Before the expedition started," Brunn later recalled, "laboratory tests had suggested no life could possibly survive under pressure greater than those experienced at 25,000′ below sea level."

However, when a sample of the bottom at 33,462′ was hauled aboard the *Galathea*, Brunn found startling evidence of the life at great depths: bacteria, sea anemones, mollusks, and a minute crustacean. (One of the mollusks the *Galathea* dredged up was thought to have been extinct for 300 million years. This cap-shaped ancestor of the venerable clam was named *Neopilina galatheae* in honor of the ship. Biologists could not have been more confounded if a brontosaurus had stridden out of an unexplored jungle.)

Beyond our earth, we may encounter alien forms that are incomprehensible. These forms could be so strange and unfathomable that, as George Gaylord Simpson has said, "We might well fail to recognize them as living or might have to revise our conception of what life is." Simpson, one of the world's greatest authorities on evolution, further wrote, " 'Life as we do not know it,' if recognized at all, might have to be recognized as a 3rd fundamental kind of configuration and not, strictly speaking, as life."

We might also look around us for almost alien life here on earth—life forms whose relatively bizarre ways of life are close to the borderland of "life as we do not know it."

Energy eaters. On earth, animals feed exclusively on matter. Plants, however, "feed" (if taking in a substance can be called feeding) half on matter and half on energy in the form of sunlight converted by photosynthesis. Why not life forms that feed exclusively on energy?

Sensate plants. Several plants, the best-known being Venus's-flytrap (*Dionaea muscipula*), trap and digest insects. The existence of these plants has long delighted purveyors of imaginary monsters that imperil nubile maidens. But, from an exobiological standpoint, the plants are intriguing not merely because of *what* they do but *why* they do it. When a fly is captured in the Venus's-flytrap or when an insect drowns in the pitcherlike leaves of a pitcher plant, such as *Sarracenia purpurea*, the victim brings protein to the plant. The proteins of the digested insect may be vitally necessary to the plant because they provide the plant with nitrogen not available (or in short supply) in the soil in which it grows. Insectivorous plants are rare on earth because nitrogen is plentiful. In an environment with even a slightly different biochemical cycle, would life develop animal-eating plants in greater abundance?

Is there an intimation of higher life possibilities in the Venus's-flytrap? Most biologists would certainly say No! The Jesuit biologist-paleontologist Pierre Teilhard de Chardin was often criticized for his mystical theory that life was evolving toward an ultimate immate-rialness. But there is little mysticism in his question about plants like the Venus's-flytrap: "Is it not enough to see how certain plants trap insects to be convinced that the vegetable branch, distant as it is, is . . . subservient to the rise of consciousness?"

Sexless life forms. We tend to think of terrestrial reproduction methods as being such that animals just naturally go in 2s, as they did in entering the Ark. The many forms which manage to reproduce without the benefit of a male and female are rarely considered, being dismissed as lower life forms. Many creatures are bisexual or hermaphroditic; each individual is able to act as both a male and female. Sometimes the sex of an individual animal changes from one breeding season to another, so that a creature is a spermatozoa-producing male one season and an egg-producing female the next. Within this broad hermaphroditic framework, there are innumerable variations. At least one species of "higher" form—a vertebrate—is a complete hermaphrodite. This is a small marine fish (*Serranus subligarius*) commonly called the banded flamefish or belted sandfish. Every mature fish of this species, writes marine specialist William M. Stephens, "possesses *at the same time* functioning male and female organs. The flamefish can produce eggs and

also the sperm to fertilize them. It is literally a fish that can theoretically propagate without a mate." Although no other vertebrate is known usually to produce offspring without a mate, the existence of hermaphrodites on this planet would certainly argue for the possibility of such a form of reproduction on other planets. And this would be only the beginning. Further speculation is possible until we reach the limit of comprehension.

"Immortal" creatures. More than 4,500 years ago, around the time of the building of the Great Pyramid at Giza, a tree began to grow in what in time to come was to be called California. That tree, a towering sequoia (*Sequoia gigantea*), is still growing. Barring accident—such as being struck by lightning—it seems destined to live as long as life lasts upon this planet. Tissues of some plants seem to have a near-immortality built into them. One such tissue is the cambium of a tree, the specialized cells that form the tree's annual rings. Other cells, year after year (and, in the sequoias and some other conifers, century after century), add to the tree's height. These cells have lived as long as the tree has lived. Outer bark, limbs, and leaves have died and have been renewed; but the specialized cells of growth were in the seed when the tree was born. The sequoias and such trees as the bristlecone fir (*Abies venusta*) are outstanding examples of organisms with life-spans that appear to be indefinite. But *all* life-spans on earth are indefinitely long. Man is pushing beyond the biblical allotment of 3-score and 10. How far we can push our life-span no biologist will say; potentially we may be one with the sequoias . . .

Advanced "lower life" forms. One of the humblest of terrestrial creatures, a protozoan named *Paramecium aurelia*, looks like hardly more than a bit of protoplasm with a gullet. It would not seem possible that such a blob could learn or think. Yet, in a classic experiment, food-deprived *P. aurelia* were induced to cling to the sides of a sterile platinum wire. Previously, they had been exposed to the wire when it had been coated with food. Possibly, they had "learned" to cling to the wire. Beatrice Gelber, of the Dept. of Psychology at the University of Chicago, suggested that the *P. aurelia* were actually acting like higher animals.

In considering exotic life forms, our imagination needs stimulation, rather than restraint. Insects are so familiar to us that we lose sight of the fact that here on earth many of them are indeed exotic creatures. More than a century ago, 2 British entomologists, William Kirby and William Spence, asked what would happen if a naturalist were to announce the discovery of "an animal which 1st existed in the form of a serpent; which then penetrated into the earth, and weaving a shroud of pure silk of the finest texture, contracted itself within this covering into a body without external mouth or limbs, and resembling, more than anything else, an Egyptian mummy; and which, lastly, after remaining in this state without food and without motion . . . should at the end of that period burst its silken cerements, struggle through its earthly covering and start into day a winged bird. . . ."

They were describing, of course, the metamorphosis of a moth. Could life be more "extraterrestrial," at least in terms of our man-centered outlook on life? The moth is familiar to us only as one of the endless number of insects that, to most men's eyes, infest rather than enhance our world. But seen as a wondrous creature, the moth becomes a symbol of what extraterrestrial life *could* be.

—T.A. rep.

MESSAGE by anselm hollo

hello!

i'm one of Your molecules!

i started from Crab Nebula, but i move about. i've moved about for millions of years.

i entered Your body, perhaps as a factor in some edible vegetable, or else i passed into Your lungs as part of the air.

now, what intrigues me is this:

at what exact point, as i entered the mouth, or was absorbed by the skin, was i part of the body?

at what exact moment (later on) do i cease to be part of the body (i.e., You)?

let me know what You think.

Yrs,

The Science Fiction Observatory

—c. 150 A.D. Greek philosopher Lucian of Samosata wrote *Icaromenippus* and the *True History*, the earliest books describing voyages to other worlds. In the 1st book, Menippus took a wing of an eagle and one of a vulture and flew from Mount Olympus to the moon, which was inhabited by spirits. Having confirmed that the earth is round, he flew to the sun. But this was too bold; the gods confiscated his wings and sent him home. In the *True History*, a ship exploring the Atlantic was carried by a waterspout into the air and by winds to the moon. Its crew found the Moon-King at war with the Sun-King; which would rule the planet Jupiter! After lunar adventures with salad-wings (birds, covered with herbs), archers riding huge fleas, and people with artificial genitals, the earthmen sailed safely back.

—1532. Italian writer Ludovico Ariosto's epic poem, *Orlando Furioso*, includes a quest for "Orlando's lost wits." As everything lost on earth had gone to the moon, one Astolpho went there, too—in Elijah's fiery chariot. The moon contained rich fields, towns, lakes, rivers, unkept vows, prayers and benefits forgot, and "Orlando's lost wits," conveniently found in an urn.

—1634. Astronomer Johannes Kepler was the 1st to write space travel based on scientific knowledge gained by the newly invented telescope. He assumed the moon to consist of 2 zones, the near one burned by the sun, the far one freezing cold. There were monsters popping in and out of caves, and water, air, and vegetation with a 2-week life-span. Incorrect, but, in the light of contemporary knowledge, not illogical. As Kepler could think of no scientific way to get to the moon, he had his hero dream himself there: The title of the book is *Somnium*, Latin for "dream."

—1638. English bishop Francis Godwin published *The Man in the Moone, or, A Discourse of a Voyage Thither by Domingo Gonsales*. Sr. Gonsales was flown to the moon by a number of trained swanlike birds. He found it inhabited by a pastoral people who deported all potential criminals to the earth . . . mostly to North America! Godwin came close to describing the law of gravity, which Newton had yet to "discover."

—1657. Cyrano de Bergerac (famous as the large-nosed lover of Rostand's play) wrote *A Voyage to the Moon*, and seemed to be the 1st to employ rockets as his means of propulsion, although they were of the firecracker variety. The naked moon-men had 4 legs, musical voices, and firearms that not only shot game but cooked it! Glowworms were used for illumination; sunrays were caught and kept in transparent globes. There were also talking book-machines.

—1659. This time, in his *Voyage to the Sun*, Cyrano traveled in a "large, very light Box . . . shut tight and close . . . 6' high . . . 3' Square," and fixed up with an elaborate arrangement of hollow crystal. The sun soon exhausted the air in this crystal, and, as "Nature abhors Vacuity," he was drawn up and away, "22 Months [journey] to the great plains of Day. . . ." Here, amid "flakes of burning Snow," and intelligent human-hating birds, the story, alas, ended.

—1694. Gabriel Daniel of France issued *A Voyage to the World of Cartesius*, a voyage which did not stop at the moon, but continued onward to "the Indefinate Spaces," "the Space beyond the Universe." This may have been the 1st use of "space" in the modern sense of "outer space."

—1705. In London, the son of a Huguenot refugee, failing in the hosiery business, tried his hand at writing a story. Called *Consolidator: or, Transactions from the World in the Moon*, it failed, despite its space-traveling machine, to capture the popular imagination. The author, whose 1st name was Daniel, changed his last name from Foe to Defoe, and had subsequent success with his *Adventures of Robinson Crusoe*.

—1752. Voltaire (pseud. for François Marie Arouet)—French political scientist, satirist, and novelist—published *Micromegas*, perhaps the 1st appearance in literature of "aliens from outer space" visiting earth. These came from Saturn and from a planet in the solar system of the star Sirius, sometimes traveling by comet, sometimes by light-waves. Unlike us, with our 5 or 6 senses, the Sirian had a thousand, but the poor Saturnian had only 72.

—1816–1817. Thomas Erskine's *Armata* was probably the 1st appearance of the "twin-earth" theme in science fiction. This one was said to be attached to ours at the South Pole. Unlike earth people at that time, the people of our twin world were fearful both of technological progress and of suppressing it.

—1827. Joseph Atterley (pseud. of George Tucker) published one of the 1st U.S. cosmonaut stories, simply (if unoriginally) entitled *A Voyage to the Moon*. The space "car" was made of an anti-gravitational metal. The year before Professor Tucker published the book, one of his students at the University of Virginia was Edgar Allan Poe.

—1835. The unparalleled Edgar Allan Poe entered the area of moon voyages with *The Unparalleled Adventures of One Hans Pfall*, unquestionably influenced by Professor Tucker's book. Poe had Hans make his voyage in a balloon aided by a machine for condensing air; however, Poe's sense of the ridiculous overcame him and he never finished the "2nd part" of the story. —A.D.

—1835. In August the *New York Sun*, then a stripling journal of 4 sheets, began an exclusive series of 4 articles headlined: GREAT ASTRONOMICAL DISCOVERIES LATELY MADE BY SIR JOHN HERSCHEL AT THE CAPE OF GOOD HOPE. This series, written by Richard Adams Locke, excited New York and America for 2 months. It disclosed that Sir John Herschel, the renowned British astronomer, had invented a 7-ton telescope, with a lens 24' in diameter, capable of magnifying an object 42,000 times, so greatly that flora and fauna on the moon seemed to be only 5 mi. from the earth. Sir John, assisted by Sir David Brewster, secretly had transported the telescope to Africa, and 8 months earlier had seen lunar life as no human had seen it before.

The pair minutely observed 14 species of animal life on the moon. There were "herds of brown quadrupeds, having all the external characteristics of the bison," with hairy flaps over their eyes to protect them from extreme light; there were "gregarious" monsters, blue and swift, "the size of a goat, with a head and beard like him, and a *single horn*"; there were pelicans, cranes, bears, and "a strange amphibious creature of a spherical form, which rolled with great velocity across the pebbly beach." All of these cavorted over pyramid-shaped mountains of amethyst, among 38 species of trees, or near a lake 266 mi. long.

But the biggest sensation was saved for the final article. Sir John Herschel had seen "4 successive flocks of large winged creatures," and later observed them "walking erect toward a small wood." Adjusting his lens so that these creatures were brought but 80 yards from his eyes, he saw them clearly at last. "They averaged 4' in height, were covered, except on the face, with short and glossy copper-colored hair, and had wings composed of a thin membrane, without hair, lying snugly upon their backs, from the top of the shoulders to the calves of the legs. The face, which was of a yellowish flesh-color, was a slight improvement upon that of the large orang-utan. . . ."

These articles were so rich in detail and scientific terminology that the greater part of the public and press swallowed them whole. *The New York Times* thought the articles "probable and plausible," and felt they displayed "the most extensive and accurate knowledge of astronomy." The *New Yorker* regarded the discoveries as "of astounding interest, creating a new era in astronomy and science generally." The *Daily Advertiser* considered the series one of the most important in years. "Sir John has added a stock of knowledge to the present age that will immortalize his name and make it high on the page of science."

Locke was gratified. The daily circulation of the *Sun*, a penny newspaper, had been 2,500.

With the report of winged men 4' tall on the moon, circulation climbed to 19,000. And some of these readers, notably a club of women in Springfield, Mass., were stimulated to raise funds for sending missionaries to the moon. In pamphlet form the series of articles, entitled *Discoveries in the Moon Lately Made at the Cape of Good Hope by Sir John Herschel*, sold 60,000 copies in a month, enriching Locke and his publisher by some $25,000.

There were a few skeptics. Philip Hone, a New York resident, noted in his diary: "In sober truth, if this account is true, it is most enormously wonderful, and if it is a fable, the manner of its relation, with all of its scientific details . . . will give this ingenious history a place with 'Gulliver's Travels' and 'Robinson Crusoe.' " Edgar Allan Poe, aware that no telescope could reveal such detail even at a visual distance of 80 yards, let alone 5 mi., branded the articles as fiction. He confessed that he found few listeners, "so really eager were all to be deceived, so magical were the charms of a style that served as the vehicle of an exceedingly clumsy invention. Not one person in 10 discredited it."

When Locke at last confessed the fraud to a fellow newspaperman on the *Journal of Commerce*, who exposed him, and when Sir John Herschel, informed of Locke's stories, laughingly denied the discoveries, the truth was out, and the "Moon Hoax" was relegated to the history of entertainment rather than that of science. Locke's motive, it turned out, had been more aesthetic than commercial. Bored with the speculations and popularity of Dr. Thomas Dick of Scotland, an astronomer whose books (advocating communication with the moon through use of giant stone symbols arranged on earth) were the rage in American society, Locke had intended to ridicule Dick's pompous pronouncements. Apparently, his satire had got out of hand.

Shortly after this, Locke left the *Sun* to start a periodical of his own, the *New Era*. Later, he became editor of the *Brooklyn Eagle*, and finally a customhouse official.

—I.W. rep.

—1839. Anonymously, without so much as a pseudonym, *A Fantastical Excursion into the Planets* appeared, one of the earliest descriptions—if not the earliest description—of a trip to all the then-known planets—including a few planetoids or asteroids. All were said to be inhabited. Every prospect was pleasing, and only Mars was barren. (However, it had a flourishing mining industry.)

—1865. A young man from the French river town of Nantes ushered in an era of modern science fiction and space travel with a "practical" way of getting *From the Earth to the Moon*: Two Americans and a Frenchman were shot to the moon in a huge cylindrical "bullett" from an enormous cannon. Jules Verne, a century in advance of actual space travel, pictured even such details as the glass of water that didn't spill and the pickup at sea of the returned "capsule."

—1870. In *Round the Moon*, Verne carried the theme onward: Did his moon-rounders really see "giant ruins" on the dark side? It would now seem unlikely.

—1877. In *Hector Servadac* (named after the book's protagonist), Verne went farther than the moon, on a voyage better described by the title of one of the book's 20th-century translations, *Off on a Comet*. The comet scooped up various earthfolk and obligingly gave them a tour of the solar system before returning them all safe and sound.

—1880. It was said of Percy Greg's *Across the Zodiac* that "it is possibly the 1st interplanetary journey to be made by spaceship." (Readers familiar with the field will have noticed, however, that it was not the last.) Electricity worked the antigravity device and recycled the ship's air. Mars, the ship's destination, had an "advanced race" practicing polygamy and atheism; the Martians also had dirigibles, poison-gas guns, electric tractors, 3-D talkies, and the duodecimal system. However, they did not have resistance to a disease of earthly origin "contracted from rose-seeds," so the hero left in a hurry. But Mars had already become a favorite setting for extraterrestrial fictional adventures, ousting even the moon.

—1894. John Jacob Astor, descendant of *the* John Jacob Astor (perhaps the 1st American millionaire), published *A Journey in Other Worlds*—the other worlds being Jupiter, Saturn, and the asteroid Cassandra. Astor had the inspiration of introducing the giant prehistoric creatures of the early days of earth, despite the circumstance that they could not exist where he introduced them—a circumstance which did not deter subsequent authors from introducing them into planets equally inhospitable. Many a writer, and many a reader, dearly loves a dinosaur.

—1898. H. G. (for Herbert George) Wells, the son of a supremely unsuccessful English shopkeeper, and himself one of the 1st science fiction writers to have been a practicing scientist (he studied under Darwin's friend, Huxley), wrote *The War of the Worlds*. The worlds were the earth and Mars, and the inhabitants of Mars had "minds that are to our minds as ours are to the beasts that perish, intellects vast and cool and unsympathetic." Here, for the 1st time (and while Britain was still conquering its empire), inhabitants of another planet attempted to conquer the earth—and (almost another 1st) perished as the result of early microorganisms to which they had no resistance. *The War of the Worlds* was 40 years later to be the subject of a famous and terrifying radio dramatization produced by Orson Welles. H. G. Wells departed from the anthropomorphic tradition in making his Martians not at all humanlike in form—although he hinted that they might once have been so but were changed by evolution. In having his Martians shot to earth in giant cylinders fired by presumably giant cannons, H. G. Wells was probably influenced by Jules Verne, who had shot his earthmen to the moon in the same way. Verne, on reading Wells, is said to have exclaimed indignantly, "*Il invente!*"

—1900. *A Honeymoon in Space*, by George Griffith (pseud. for G. C. G. Jones) told about Lord Redgrave and his space yacht *Astronef*, which worked on the R-force principle. This broke gravitation up (or down) into positive and negative, just like electricity. A demonstration by the *Astronef* on earth frightened nations on the verge of war into keeping the peace; after which, Lord and Lady Redgrave left the earth in it, and for their honeymoon visited the moon, Mars, Venus, Jupiter, Callisto, Ganymede, and Saturn—certainly more interesting than Niagara Falls.

—1901. The year that Queen Victoria died, H. G. Wells, still inventing, produced his own version of the perennial and classic theme, *The First Men in the Moon*. At the 1st touch of sunlight, lunar vegetation burst out and grew rapidly before one's eyes; the interior of the moon was hollow and inhabited by rather nasty "Selenites," ruled by a Grand Lunar, who—with his writhing, bladderlike brain and shriveled insectlike limbs—was even nastier. As in *The War of the Worlds*, Wells suggested that the aliens and mankind may have been descended from once identical beings.

—1909. Garret P. Serviss, now all but forgotten but long a respected name in science fiction, published *A Columbus of Space* with the planet Venus as the new world. Edmund Stonewall's spaceship, which took him there, ran by a sort of atomic power. Venus had no canals, but its clouded surface left speculative minds free to imagine what lay beneath the clouds; in this case, everything—swamps, apemen, a villainous high priest, telepathy, a beautiful native queen, prehistoric monsters, and airplanes.

—1912. *Under the Moons of Mars* (title later changed to *A Princess of Mars*) appeared from the talented hand of someone no one had ever heard of. The book's hero, John Carter, Civil War veteran and Indian fighter, teleported himself to Mars—"a desert, dying planet"— whose atmosphere was supplied by one—and only one—air machine. Some of the Martians were green and had 6 limbs, as did many of

the Martian animals such as the thoats, which one rode, and the banths, which one hunted (and was hunted by). Some of the other Martians, however, were red, including Princess Deja Thoris, whom John Carter rescued and married. After a decorous length of time (the Martians being oviparous), the Princess laid an egg.

So, for that matter, did the book. But a few years later the author, Edgar Rice Burroughs, published *Tarzan of the Apes*, which didn't. Burroughs—a natural-born storyteller who had never taken a course in creative writing in his life—wrote a number of John Carter of Mars books, as well as several about one Carson Napier of Venus. All were good, clean action stories and great fun. In addition, they may well have contributed more popular zeal for our space program than is generally realized.

—1926. E. R. Eddison's *The Worm Ouroboros* implied that our earthly legends of witches, demons, imps, and goblins may have originated in races of that name living in another world. The book was a classic and beautiful romance of intrigue and adventure set on the planet Mercury by a British civil servant who either knew nothing of the actual physical conditions of the planet Mercury or simply didn't care. Major science fiction novels had seldom used Mercury for a background, and probably never would again.

—1927. Such writers as Donald Wandrei had already begun to combine distant time *and* distant space, as, for example, in *The Red Brain*, a story set in the remote future on a planet of the faraway star-sun Antares. It was almost the end of time, and sentient life no longer had bodies—only brains, cowering in the dust. Could the Red Brain save them? Answer: No.

—1928. Lee H. Garby and E. E. Smith (invariably described during the earlier part of his literary career as "E. E. Smith, Ph.D.") in *The Skylark of Space* produced the 1st galactic adventure story. Afterward, and without Garby, "Doc" Smith, a grain chemist somewhat unkindly (if accurately) described by author Brian Aldiss as "a doughnut-mix specialist," went on, via *The Skylark of Valeron* and other novels, to become one of the best-known, best-liked, and best- (or worst-) imitated figures in the science fiction of the '30s and '40s. He may be said to have invented "space opera" as we know it (or knew it): huge armadas charging through the interstellar darkness, galactic empires at war, vast distances, infinite sources of power, and clean-cut heroes.

—1929. Like Edgar Rice Burroughs, Otis Adelbert Kline had 3 names, and he could write like Edgar Rice Burroughs—although not exactly, of course, for Edgar Rice Burroughs has been summed up by L. Sprague De Camp as "a school of writing all to himself." By the '20s, Burroughs had created an immense audience eager for adventures on Mars and Venus involving beautiful endangered native females, horrible villainous monsters, and gallant and muscular earthmen. Burroughs, prolific as he was, could not keep up with the demand. Hence such novels as Kline's *The Planet of Peril*, which also described Venus. To many people this sort of tale constituted all they knew of science fiction.

—1930. In *The Time Machine* (1895) H. G. Wells invented the concept of time travel, but his Traveller did not leave earth. Other novels delved into our future, but it was another Englishman, Olaf Stapledon, who, in *Last and First Men*, visited mankind's far-distant future not only on earth but on Venus and Neptune as well, envisioning the most vast staggering technical and physical changes.

—1932. In *Last Men in London*, Stapledon transferred his themes from Neptune and Uranus, continuing his conjectured visions of mankind—changed even more than the Morlocks and Eloi of Wells's *Time Machine*.

—1932. Edwin Balmer and Philip Wylie collaborated on *When Worlds Collide* and its sequel, *After Worlds Collide* (1934). These are fairly well-known examples of what afterward became known as "Doomsday" and "Post-Doomsday" stories. Here the doom was caused by the entry into our solar system of 2 runaway planets named, after their discoverer, Bronson Alpha and Bronson Beta. Alpha, as predicted, collided with and destroyed the earth—but a number of earth's people meanwhile escaped to the earthlike Beta via spaceships created by a crash (in more ways than one) program.

—1937. With *Star Maker*, Stapledon extended the "twin-earth" theme to a transgalactic planet, "Other World, the most similar in all the universe to this earth."

—1938. An American radio program written by Howard Koch in the form of a news broadcast, featuring Orson Welles, and based on H. G. Wells's *War of the Worlds*, purported to describe an invasion from Mars. If Wells's English setting had been maintained, all might have been well, but as the script changed the invasion point to New Jersey, thousands of people in New Jersey, New York, and other States panicked, fled, or tied up the telephone lines demanding information and advice. No other science fiction program will ever again achieve such immediacy—and perhaps a good thing, too.

—1938. *Out of the Silent Planet*, by the great British scholar C. S. Lewis, began a trilogy of what might be called Christian science fiction books. The "silent planet" was our own earth (silent because it had fallen from Divine Grace and no longer spoke with the Voice of God), but the planet visited was Mars: a Mars that

may have lacked canals but did have water, vegetation, intelligent life, and lots of stimuli for philosophical-theological speculation. The other volumes of the trilogy were:

—1943. *Perelandra*, Lewis's name for an almost entirely watery Venus.

—1945. *That Hideous Strength*, in which scoundrels, both terrestrial and extraterrestrial, attempted to subvert and take over the earth by means of a fascist-type bureaucracy.

—1947. In *The Green Hills of Earth*, Robert A. Heinlein combined technology, tragedy, and romance, and created a future folklore. Rhysling, the Blind Singer of the Spaceways, and not yet blind, was jetman of the *Goshawk* ("the 1st [spaceship] . . . to be converted from chemical fuel to atomic power-piles . . . that did not blow up"), bound for the Jovian asteroids, as the story began. It was on this voyage that he was blinded by defective cadmium dampers in the power room: Come hell or high power, Rhysling always stuck to his post. For the rest of his life, as he moved between Luna City, Marsopolis, and Venusburg, he was a sightless deadhead, freeloading around space, singing for his suppers. On the voyage which was to return him, after so long, to the earth he could not see, another emergency exploded: A radioactive blast killed Archie Macdougal (the chief jetman) as he jawed with Rhysling in the power room and the lights went out—but blind Rhysling needed no lights to fix the breakdown and save the ship. Dying, he sang the title song of the story: "We pray for one last landing/On the globe that gave us birth;/Let us rest our eyes on fleecy skies/And the cool, green hills of earth."

—1950. Ray Bradbury was not strong on technology. Perhaps the hot breath of a rocketship would not really create a local summer in the midst of a North American winter, melt snow, make flowers bloom. But it was a lovely picture. Bradbury's Martians were an old and perhaps decadent race, seemingly without modern weaponry. The crew of one expedition from earth was, presumably, killed with the single crossbow of a jealous Martian husband. The crew of another wound up in a Martian madhouse. And did the dead, then, live again—on Mars? But the Martians, ludicrously, fatally, had no resistance to one of the mildest of earth's illnesses. Did they all die? Were those ghosts—or survivors—in the red-dry hills? What did earthfolk do with this 2nd chance at an empty world? *The Martian Chronicles* may be science fiction, they may be fantasy: They are beautiful, whatever else they may be.

—1959. *The Sirens of Titan* is the skeleton in Kurt Vonnegut's closet. His massive struggles to disassociate himself from science fiction seem vain in view of this very good book which was about, among other things, Titan (one of the moons of Saturn), Saturn itself, Mars, Mercury, and "an opportunity to see a new and interesting planet and . . . think about your native planet from a fresh and interesting point of view." If such a book is not science fiction, then neither is anything else, and the term has no meaning.

—1961. *Stranger in a Strange Land* was probably the peak novel in Robert A. Heinlein's long and infinitely influential career as writer. Part, but only a small part of the book, was set on Mars. The infinite importance of Mars to the book, most of which was set on earth, was that its protagonist, Michael Valentine Smith, was raised from infancy on Mars by Martians. It was the alien ideas and ideology of this nonhuman race, filtered through the human mind of Michael and acted out by his human body, that produced the very great effect of *Stranger*. This was one of the cult books of the counterculture, and its influence is still felt.

—1963. *Orphans of the Sky* by Robert A. Heinlein was the 1st book to tackle the still-unsolved paradox of space travel: If other solar systems lay millions of light-years away, how could humans survive the journey there? His answer was a spaceship—immense and self-operating—which was a miniature universe; it even contained farms, and had its own gravitation. With the passage of time, however, its passengers forgot that they were "in passage" and interpreted their records and textbooks as religious allegories. Arrival at a habitable planet in a universe infinitely larger than the only one they knew was an immense psychological shock, but they survived.

—1965. In *Dune*, Frank Herbert depicted the far-distant planet of Arrakis, inhabited by descendants of earthfolk. In a way, it may be described as an "ecology" novel, although certainly not propagandistic: It is simply that the one most important circumstance of life on Dune World was its exceeding lack of water; everything else—economics, sociology, war, peace, religion—derived from and depended on this perpetual and terrible scarcity. The abrupt expansion of the Sahara since the book was written makes it, in a way, horribly prophetic. (*Dune Messiah*, 1969, was its sequel.)

—1974. A technological step further than Heinlein's *Universe* is *The Dream Millennium*, by the Irish writer James White. Until we can travel faster than light, how can we successfully complete a journey to the distant stars? White's spaceship crew, male and female, were in a sort of "frozen sleep," during which they dreamed of the problems that made them leave earth; by arrival time at a habitable world they had worked them out, and could make a fresh start mentally as well as physically.

—A.D.

An Earthy Look at the American Astronauts

Few men have been as admired and glorified in recent times as the American astronauts. In the 1960s—a decade of assassinations, campus violence, and a war in a distant land—the citizenry of the U.S. was in desperate want of heroes, and the spacemen filled that need.

But the National Aeronautics and Space Administration (NASA) was not content simply to have the astronauts respected for what they were—courageous men experiencing many of the same pleasures and pains as other human beings. Instead, the astronauts were "sold" as a unique and elite cadre of supermen. It was one of the most ambitious and successful public relations campaigns in history.

From the beginning, the media treated the astronauts as exceptional individuals. In its 1st article about the original Project Mercury astronauts, *Time* said: "From a nation of 175 million they stepped forward last week: 7 men cut of the same stone as Columbus, Magellan, Daniel Boone, Orville and Wilbur Wright." *The New York Times* described them as "a group of square-jawed, trim halfbacks recruited from an All-American football team."

The astronauts told their exclusive stories in *Life*, and they presented themselves as angelic, one-dimensional characters. Walt Cunningham, crew member of *Apollo 7*, later complained, "Instead of letting us be human, they wanted us to act like Boy Scouts, live in a monastery."

Edwin "Buzz" Aldrin, Jr., the 2nd man to walk on the moon, wrote in his own book, *Return to the Earth*: "I suppose the portrayal we received in *Life* and subsequently in nearly all the media helped the space program a great deal. Unfortunately, nearly all of it had us squarely on the side of God, country, and family. To read it was to believe we were the most simon-pure guys there had ever been. This was simply not so. We may have regularly gone to church, but we also celebrated some pretty wild nights."

Yes, the astronauts were human. They were more than the "strange, plasticized, half-communicating Americans" that Norman Mailer saw in his book *Of a Fire on the Moon*.

Writing in *The New York Times*, Howard Munson declared that the astronauts, "to our relief," turned out to be not much different from the rest of us. "They cheat a little when presented with too great temptation (witness the brisk trade in postal covers that were taken to the moon and other articles that were autographed by astronauts); they get divorces from their wives [at least 6 have]; they see a psychiatrist when necessary; they get interested in freaky things like ESP, Eastern religions, poetry, one-worldism, and brotherhood."

Since the space program began, 73 pilots and scientists have been selected to be astronauts. Forty-one have sailed into space, 3 died in a fire on the test launching pad in 1967, and 5 others were killed in test flights or automobile accidents. Most of the astronauts are now retired from the NASA program.

Following are the stories of 8 of the most prominent American spacemen—their accomplishments, their human frailties, and their lives since their historic voyages. ·

Alan Shepard. On the morning of May 5, 1961, Alan Shepard soared skyward in *Freedom 7*, splashing down in the Atlantic Ocean 302 mi. from Cape Canaveral. His 15-minute suborbital flight earned him the title of "America's 1st astronaut," and he admits that it was an emotional experience that changed his life dramatically. "I was a rotten S.O.B. before I left," he said after the flight. "Now I'm just an S.O.B."

Almost 10 years later, Shepard was on the moon as part of the 3rd lunar landing mission. In between his 1st and 2nd space journeys, he had been grounded by Ménière's syndrome, an inner ear ailment which causes nausea and dizziness. After 5 years of futilely hoping that the condition would clear up by itself, Shepard underwent surgery. The operation was successful, and he was back on flight status.

Until Shepard retired from the space program in 1974, he was to some degree the leader of the other astronauts; not only did he give them guidance, he also reportedly intimidated them at times. In his book *The Making of an Ex-Astronaut*, astronaut-scientist Brian O'Leary wrote that Shepard scared him so, that O'Leary would occasionally "talk in broken sentences, turn red, and look down." O'Leary also said that "Shepard warned us to cut off all press relationships besides NASA-sanctioned ones and to give the excuse that we were in intensive training."

O'Leary provided other insights into Shepard, who was keen on monetary matters and became the 1st millionaire astronaut: "Shepard's financial concern was no great surprise, since he was vice-president and part owner of the Baytown National Bank in Houston. But it struck me as odd that our chief was a bank vice-president, yet we were explicitly prohibited to consult, to teach part-time, and to receive free gifts. I am sure he has legal justification for his outside activities, but the actual situation seemed to me to be a strange double standard."

Shepard's business interests have included banking, oil, land investments, and breeding quarter horses. Jerry Bledsoe, writing in *Esquire*, says, "Shepard and his wife live in a $150,000 white-columned mansion in an exclusive section of Houston. The children are grown and gone from home now. His friends and associates are the top crust of Texas society."

John Glenn. John Glenn, the 1st American to orbit the earth, was probably the country's most popular astronaut. He had the image of being a nonsmoker and a nondrinker. The public was told that he didn't swear, and that he went to church every Sunday. All that might be true, but he also gave NASA its share of problems.

As Glenn was about to soar into space, NASA administrator James Webb learned that Glenn had arranged to have a *Life* writer and photographer at his home with his family. According to Robert Sherrod in the *Columbia Journalism Review*, Webb was incensed for 2 reasons: "1. Vice-President Johnson was planning to call on Mrs. Glenn during the flight and would want privacy; and 2. suppose something 'unforeseeable' happened to Glenn and *Life* published photographs of the Glenn family in its agony. . . . Webb demanded that Glenn explain. Equally incensed, Glenn replied that the *Life* men were personal friends and they had a right to be in his home." Webb lodged a direct complaint with *Life*, but to no avail.

After his flight, Glenn was a national hero. He vacationed with President Kennedy, and attended untold parties. But his social activities earned the wrath of some of his fellow astronauts, leading Wally Schirra to say in a TV interview that Glenn's outside interests about eliminated him from the space program. Glenn later replied in *Esquire*, "I'm sure that there were some jealousies, but they were not expressed as such. When one guy out of a group gets all that attention, when you've worked closely together and all that, I'm sure there are some feelings back and forth."

Glenn has recently been a member of the R. C. Cola board of directors, and he owns several motels. He has made 3 attempts to get a U.S. Senate Democratic nomination in Ohio, finally winning it in 1974. He went on to win a landslide victory in the final election. Earlier, in his unsuccessful Senate bid in 1970, New York advertising executive Barry Nova was hired as Glenn's "image maker." Later, in an article in *New York*, Nova analyzed the reasons for Glenn's defeat: "John Glenn was a great astronaut and a valid national hero. He was also shallow, pedantic, and egocentric. To this day,

I don't know what he stands for; neither do the people of Ohio."

Neil Armstrong. Neil Armstrong was the 1st man to walk on the moon, despite original plans for his copilot, Edwin Aldrin, to take the 1st step. There was considerable friction between Armstrong and Aldrin in the 3 months preceding their voyage to the moon, and there was at least one preflight quarrel between the 2 astronauts.

Michael Collins, the 3rd astronaut on the *Apollo 11* journey, has verified the tension between Armstrong and Aldrin in his book *Carrying the Fire.* Collins added, "Originally, some of the early checklists were written to show a copilot 1st exit, but Neil ignored these and exercised his commander's prerogative to crawl out 1st. This had been decided in April [3 months before the landing] and Buzz's [Aldrin's] attitude took a noticeable turn in the direction of gloom and introspection thereafter. Once, he [Aldrin] tentatively approached me about the injustice of the situation."

Armstrong now lives in relative seclusion on a farm 30 mi. north of Cincinnati, O. He is a professor of engineering at the University of Cincinnati. He avoids interviews and most public appearances, and refuses to cash in on his fame. A university public relations man told *The New York Times* that he's "almost paranoiac about being used by people."

Still, Armstrong has not forgotten about his flight: "I remember on the trip home on *Apollo 11* it suddenly struck me that that tiny pea, pretty and blue, was the earth. I put up my thumb and shut one eye, and my thumb blotted out the planet earth. I didn't feel like a giant. I felt very, very small."

Edwin "Buzz" Aldrin. Probably no astronaut suffered worse aftereffects of his space flight than Edwin Aldrin, Jr., copilot on the 1st lunar landing mission. Aldrin found himself incapable of coping with the pressures of playing the hero's role in an endless stream of public appearances. He was soon on his way to having what he calls "a good old-fashioned American nervous breakdown."

Aldrin, who authored the book *Return to Earth*, had a long battle with mental depression, and eventually he received psychiatric treatment in both an Air Force and a civilian hospital.

When he and his fellow astronauts were on their postflight goodwill tours, he recalls that they were traveling with temptation because "we always took along our personal biological longings but not necessarily our wives. . . . For an astronaut, the opportunities for companionship were always available, and I guess temptation grew in proportion to supply. Some of us resisted those temptations; many resisted, then gave in. I fit the latter category."

Aldrin engaged in several extramarital affairs, and his marriage almost collapsed. Now he and his wife are reconciled and live in Hidden Hills, near Los Angeles, where he has retired from the Air Force to run a small consulting firm.

Scott Carpenter. Scott Carpenter appeared to be the most romantic of all the astronauts. He seemed to enjoy playing his guitar alone on the beach, or writing love letters to his wife, as much as soaring into space in *Aurora 7* in May 1962 on a near-repeat of John Glenn's flight.

After his only space mission, he began concentrating all his energies on undersea exploration. In 1965, he spent 30 days living in the depths of the Pacific Ocean in the Navy's *Sealab I*, but physical ailments kept him from participating in the *Sealab III* dive, in which one diver was killed.

Carpenter's marriage then collapsed, coming as a shock to those who once heard him say: "There's nothing that could part us." He founded Sea Sciences Corporation, which specialized in underwater research, and then began doing TV commercials for Standard Oil promoting its F-310 gasoline, which allegedly made car engines run cleaner. A consumer group said that the claims were false, and sued for false advertising. Subsequent tests by the California Air Resources Board indicated that F-310 caused "no significant changes in emissions" and the commercials were removed from the air.

Carpenter later told *Esquire*, "They said that I'd been bought out by big business and lied for personal gain. I resent people thinking that I would lie. . . . I learned a lot. I learned for the 1st time to distrust people in general."

In more recent years, Carpenter has remarried, has sung in public with John Stewart (formerly of the Kingston Trio), and continues his interest in the oceanic environment.

David Scott. When David Scott landed on the moon in *Apollo 15*, he was carrying 398 unauthorized envelopes in the pocket of his spacesuit. Scott had been approached prior to the flight by Horst Eiermann, a former Cape Canaveral contractor's representative. He encouraged Scott to take along these envelopes, called "postal covers" by stamp collectors. In return for the postal covers, Eiermann promised to establish $7,000 trust funds for not only Scott's children but also those of James Irwin and Alfred Worden, his fellow astronauts on the flight. Some of these unauthorized covers were sold in Germany for $1,500 apiece.

When NASA later found out about the scheme, it officially reprimanded the crew. Scott and the others returned the trust fund money, and NASA admitted its embarrassment over the astronauts who "clearly broke the verbal understanding we had against this sort of thing."

The *Apollo 15* mission was Scott's 3rd space flight. He had previously joined Neil Armstrong in *Gemini 8*, in 1966, for the 1st docking in space, and he was a crew member in the orbital flight of *Apollo 9*.

After the scandal of *Apollo 15* broke, Scott remained in the space program, but no further flights were planned for him.

The New York Times quoted Edgar Mitchell as saying that other astronauts had done similar things, but the *Apollo 15* crew were made sacrificial lambs. "The *Apollo 15* fellows were crucified," Mitchell said. "It was a political year, and NASA was headline-grabbing so as not to spoil the Boy Scott image."

James Irwin. James Irwin was with David Scott on that controversial *Apollo 15* flight. Shortly after he returned to earth, Irwin retired from the space program "to spend more time spreading the good news of Jesus Christ."

Irwin said that walking on the moon was a religious experience for him, and that he "felt the presence of God" there. Dubbing himself the "moon missionary," he began touring the Southern Baptist evangelical circuit, eventually making trips to the Holy Land and Vietnam.

In his book *To Rule the Night*, Irwin recalls his experiences on the moon. "And when we were struggling with the difficult tasks on the 1st EVA (Extra-Vehicular Activity, i.e., activi-ties away from our Lunar Module on the surface of the moon), when a key string broke and I couldn't get the station up, I prayed. Immediately, I had the answer."

Irwin, who is now president of the High Flight Foundation in Colorado Springs (a religious organization), suffered a severe heart attack recently, but still continues his spiritual activities. As for the controversial space envelopes, he contends that God "played a major part in my individual decision to refuse my share."

Edgar Mitchell. "In February, 1971, I had the privilege of walking on the moon as a member of the *Apollo 14* lunar expedition," writes Edgar Mitchell in the book *Psychic Exploration: A Challenge for Science.* "During the voyage, I made a test in extrasensory perception (ESP), attempting to send information telepathically to 4 receivers on earth."

Mitchell says that his subjects on earth got a statistically significant number of correct answers. He told *The New York Times*, "I am well aware there are those within NASA who were, and are, embarrassed by my opinions."

Considered to be the most intellectual of all the American astronauts, Mitchell resigned from the space program after his lunar flight to continue his ESP research. He is now president of the Institute of Noetic Sciences in Palo Alto, Calif., and he has a Ph.D. in astronautics and aeronautics from MIT.

—R.T.

12

Down to Earth

Some Firm Facts about Terra Firma

BIRTH OF EARTH

Our universe came into being, most cosmologists now agree, from 7 to 15 billion years ago, in an initial "big bang" explosion that's still expanding infinitely.

Our home galaxy, the Milky Way, is estimated by California Institute of Technology nuclear astrophysicist William A. Fowler to be approximately 12 billion years old. Planet earth, the sun, and all the other planets, moons, asteroids, meteoroids, and comets of our solar system are believed to be relatively young in cosmic terms—from 4.5 to 5 billion years old. Earth has a life expectancy of 12 billion years (that is, it has 7.5 billion "to go") before the sun explodes into a red giant that incinerates it.

The poetic-spiritual interpretation of earth's origin expressed in Genesis 1:2, "And the earth was without form, and void; and darkness was upon the face of the deep," received scientific affirmation from a German philosopher-scientist, Immanuel Kant, in 1755. Kant propounded that the embryo-planet had begun shaping up within a vast twirling cloud of icy stellar dust.

The present-day nebular hypothesis upholds both Kant and Genesis as to earth's dusty origin, an apparent parthenogenetic conception which took place when the embryonic solar cloud of gaseous cosmic mix began turning—including the central sun dust-cloud and its stream of outstretching planetary clouds of dust.

SIZE OF EARTH

In that earliest time, the proto-earth was 500 times heavier and 1,000 times larger than is the planet we now live upon. The heavier elements began to sink inward, while lighter elements—atmospheric hydrogen and other such —escaped into space. To this day, the phenomenon of "earth-leak" is still taking place as helium and other light gases continue to escape at the poles through gaps in the magnetic field.

The heavier elements at earth's core have achieved a condition of superfluidity whereby the combination of iron with a supposed very small increment of nickel, and perhaps cobalt also, makes for a different kind of solidity and density beyond our earth-surface standards. Earth is the heaviest planet, with an average density that's 5.5 times that of water. One terrestrial specialist once guessed that the heavy core must be made of supersolid gold, and thus the earth had "a heart of gold," but no scientist since has upheld this charmingly sentimental hypothesis.

ANATOMY OF EARTH

The proto-sun and proto-planets, twirling, compacted more and more in upon themselves. Presently the sun began to shine, the start of thermonuclear fusion. First there was a dull red glow, then presently it began to put forth the golden sunshine that makes life possible on earth. Poets extol sunlight and sunbeams, yet the fact remains that living creatures must never look directly into the face of our life-giving star lest they be quickly blinded. No wonder generations of earthlings worshiped the sun as the supreme god of humanity.

As with the sun's warming up, the pressure of heavy elements at the earth's heart set fire to similar thermonuclear fusion: Earth's center is intensely hot, alive. At the present time, scientists do not know whether earth's basal temperature is rising or cooling, or is perhaps temporarily stationary at some median point.

During the 1st 4th of earth's life, the surface of the new liquid-from-dust planet was slowly cooling and hardening, forming a viscous crust. The most ancient rocks are estimated to be 3.6 billion years old. Above the primordial earth surface stretched an atmosphere of poisonous methane and ammonia and living steam—the strange admixture out of which eventually life forms would emerge.

Eventually the surface cooled sufficiently so that the water vapor could turn liquid, and the 1st rains began to come down. "Never have there been such rains since that time," said Rachel Carson, describing the primordial downpour. "They fell continuously, day and night, days passing into months, into years, into centuries. They poured into the waiting ocean basin. . . ."

Because of this watery surface—and saltwater oceans still occupy more than 72% of earth's exterior surface—one wonders why our planet is not more appropriately called "planet water." Eighty-five percent of all "planet water's" inhabitants still live in the seas, perpetual wanderers called *plankton*. To them, "planet earth" would seem a nomenclature given by an unimportant terrestrial minority.

Now dry land was thrust up above the saltwater oceans, a massive earth-island 1st described by an American, F. B. Taylor, in 1910, and then named "Pangaea" in 1915 by an Austrian meteorologist, Alfred Lothar Wegener. In time it broke into twin-continents —Gondwana (made up of combined South America, Africa, India, Australia, and Antarctica) and Laurasia (North America, Greenland, and Eurasia). A mere 200 million years ago the 2 super-islands began to break up into today's 7 continents, a process that is still going on.

Because the continents have been wandering over earth's surface, a false expression has crept into the language of geology: "drifting continents." But the continents are made of comparatively "light" granite and merely float high upon the tops of immense plates of heavy basalt, like croutons on a thick soup. The basalt is now known to be 20 mi. thick beneath the 40-mi.-thick granite continents, and only 3 mi. thick beneath the ocean basins.

There are 6 enormous basalt plates, and numerous smaller "platelets." They are in constant slow motion, pushing against each other, and sometimes sliding beneath each other, as the Indian plate did beneath the Eurasian plate to thrust up earth's highest mountain range, the Himalayas. In 1974, FAMOUS (the French American Mid-Ocean Undersea Study) began a series of mid-Atlantic dives that proved that the North American and African plates today are being pushed apart by matter rising between them from down below, at a surface-expansion rate of a single inch per year. Geophysicist W. Jason Morgan, of Princeton University, discovered in 1971 that the movement of the plates, called "global plate tectonics," is caused by the upbubbling activity of at least 20 "pipes" of molten rock that rise from depths of 1,000 mi. or more within the earth's mantle, acting like burners on a gas stove.

Planet earth has the form of an oblate spheroid—a pear-shaped counterclockwise twirling dervish with a modest equatorial belly-bulge of 26.7 mi. *Chomolungma*, or "goddess-mother of the world," Tibetan Buddhists named the 29,028' highest mountain more familiarly called Mount Everest. Highest from sea level, that is. Hawaii's "Mount White," more familiarly called Mauna Kea, is 13,796' above sea level, but also goes down 3,280 fathoms to the floor of the Pacific Ocean, for a grand total of 33,476'. (Right alongside is "Mountain Long," or Mauna Loa, earth's *largest* mountain.) But Mount Chimborazo, in Ecuador, South America, perched right on the equator, is 20,561' high all by itself. It is also atop that 26.7-mi. terrestrial belly-bulge, and thus stretches upward or outward farther than any other height on earth.

Earth's surface comprises 196,950,000 sq. mi. Its volume is about 259,000,000,000 cu. mi. Earth's weight totals 6,588,000,000,000,000,000,000 tons. It's the heaviest of all the planets, the 5th largest, and the 3rd out from the sun. Its equatorial diameter is 7,926.68 mi. and, from pole to pole, 7,900 mi.

Each rotation about its axis requires 23 hours, 56 minutes, 4.09 seconds, and constitutes a sidereal (star) day. Rotational speed is about 17½ mi. per minute. Average speed at which earth is journeying around the sun is 18½ mi. per second. Average speed at which the entire solar system is circling within the Milky Way galaxy is 180 mi. per second. The entire Milky Way galaxy itself is meantime moving through space at 170 mi. per second.

Dr. James Van Allen in 1958 1st identified great bands of radiation, the magnetosphere, which protect life on earth from extreme solar radiation. Where they break through, near the 2 magnetic poles, the fantastic colors of the aurora borealis and the aurora australis, the "northern" and "southern" lights, make for superfireworks in the sky.

Ninety-seven percent of earth's waters are in the oceans. Another 2% are locked in the Greenland and Antarctic icecaps and in glaciers atop mountains all around the earth. This leaves only 1% of sweet, fresh waters for human plans and uses.

Water's many manifestations furnish some of earth's greatest sights. Earth's highest tides occur in Canada's Bay of Fundy, rising up to 53'. Earth's highest waterfall is Salto Angel,

3,212', 1st discovered by an American flyer, Jimmy Angel, who was searching in Venezuela for a supposed hidden treasure trove of gold. The longest river may be the Amazon, at 4,000 mi. Or is it the mid-U.S. Missouri-Mississippi. As with the Blue and White Upper Nile, who is to say which branch is the "true" river?

Rainbows, and rare moonbows, give the 7-colored spectrum across the sky, with a pot of gold at its end. Seen over water, sometimes a sunset produces a momentary "green flash."

Storms at sea are perhaps water's most fearsome manifestation. Hurricanes, floods, tornadoes are water gone mad and dangerous.

Oceans are *not* teeming with life; as much as 90% are barren, totally devoid of life, a sort of "wet desert." A 7th of earth's land surface is dry desert. The Sahara, the world's largest, is expanding southward at a fearful rate from a U.S.-sized 3.5 million sq. mi. The border nations of the Sahel, the region of West Africa that separates the desert from tropical land, are rapidly drying out, and the drought is spreading eastward toward Africa's big game preserves.

German architect/engineer Herman Sörget, during the 1930s, proposed blocking off the Congo River so as to re-create massive freshwater lakes that once existed in mid-Africa, which would then empty northward via "new" rivers across the Sahel and Sahara regions. Israeli pioneers have caused the Negev desert to rebloom. And modern Iran is reopening and reactivating ancient canals that once made this the "fertile green crescent" where human agriculture perhaps began.

In the past hundred years, nobody has heard mention of the Great American Desert, because it's been made to blossom. But in July, 1974, Lieut. Gov. John D. Vanderhoff of Colorado told a gathering of western U.S. governors, "All the easy things have been done. The current challenges we face in the West are terribly complex and terribly difficult."

One fantastic answer, calling for an investment of over $100 billion, would be the NAWAPA (North American Water and Power Alliance), which would bring vast waters southward from the Yukon River basin to provide western Canada, the U.S. and Mexico with sufficient waters far into the uncertain future.

In Saudi Arabia, Sheikh Ahmed Zaki Yamani, young minister of petroleum and minerals, is constructing conversion plants to turn Red Sea salt water into fresh water to transform the deserts of his country into a new agricultural paradise.

Earth's surface is constantly gaining weight through a steady dustfall of cosmic or micrometeoritic particles, an estimated 92,500 particles per second, some 8 billion each 24 hours, a ton or perhaps even 10 tons per day. "Shooting stars," we call these heavenly visitors when we chance to see their swift, gay splendor at night. When they encounter the earth's atmosphere, their temperature shoots upward from the −460°F. of outer space to more than 2,000°F. Raindrops *need* these dust particles to form around.

Up from earth's interior comes further building material, magma turning into lava as it wells through the mouths of volcanoes. Kilauea, on Hawaii, has been putting out steadily since 1969—producing 300,000 cubic yards of scenic lava per day.

Life on earth dwells strictly between water's boiling and freezing points. Vatnajökull, Iceland's great glacier, has a volcano, Hvannadalshnjúkur, sticking out of its south face—a dramatic confrontation between ice and fire. Yellowstone National Park has over 3,000 hot springs, fumaroles, and steam vents that geyser skyward spectacularly, indicative of the *terra infirma* state of earth's surface.

Though they're not visible, the 2 tropics, Cancer and Capricorn, are nevertheless very real, the 2 parallels of terrestrial latitude lying 23½° north and south of the equator, which mark the solstitial points of the sun's greatest annual declination north and south. Similarly, the Arctic and Antarctic Circles, demarking the frigid zones of the 2 poles, are invisible but nevertheless very real. Since the latticework of longitudinal lines had to begin *somewhere*, Greenwich, England, is earth's great zero point, and the opposite International Date Line in mid-Pacific, where all our "artificial" days begin, is very "real" though it does not, of course, exist in fact.

Earth's elliptical journey around the sun gives us our seasons, because of the tilt of earth's axis, of 23½°, with the seasons of the northern and southern hemispheres thus alternating. Its rotation gives us night and day. Earth wobbles on its axis, because of the pull of the moon. Other motions are the precession of the equinoxes, a gradual shifting wobble that takes 25,800 years to complete, and another "nodding" motion that requires only 18.6 years.

Earth's crustal variation is very slight. The top of Mount Everest is somewhat over 5 mi. high. The bottom of the greatest deep, the Marianas Trench in the Pacific, 36,198' below sea level, is somewhat over 6 mi. down. Thus the extremes above and below sea level total a mere dozen miles! An important part of every volcano's lava is water vapor from earth's interior. Meantime, by eroding limestone, water returns below ground, at the same time creating fabulous caves with glistening stalagmites and stalactites. The Carlsbad Caverns, in New Mexico, have the largest underground "chamber," the Big Room. And Mammoth Cave, Ky., is one of the earth's longest-largest: 5 sq. mi. The bottom of the Dead Sea, 1,286' below sea level, might seem to be the lowest land "surface," but there are probably deeper "dents" below the downpressing of both the Greenland and the Antarctica glaciers.

Earth's largest saltwater lake is the Caspian "Sea," 169,350 sq. mi. Largest freshwater lake is Superior, 31,820 sq. mi. When is a lake large enough to be called a sea? When does a hill become a mountain? When is an island large enough to be called a continent? The Black Hills of the Dakotas are higher than many "mountain" ranges elsewhere in the U.S.

PEOPLE ON EARTH

In the ascent of life forms on earth, man is the strangest animal yet to emerge. His difference is expressed in his most recent name, *Homo sapiens*, which implies sagacity, wisdom. The Ben Franklins and Socrateses warrant this, yet it is the Henry Fords and Thomas Edisons, descendants of *Homo habilis* (Handy Man), who have made possible human progress via sheer *invention*.

Drs. Louis and Mary Leakey uncovered skull-bits of *pre-Zinjanthropus*, or "Handy Man," in the East African Olduvai Gorge, some 1,750,000 years after man died there. Others trace the "human arrival" to much earlier dates. Several Yale scientists, after gathering fossil fragments in the foothills of India's high Himalayas, suggested that humans may have parted from their ape cousins as far back as 14 million years ago.

The Leakeys' discovery—Handy Man—had a brain that was only half the size of a modern Einstein's or Edison's. Steadily increasing brain capacity came about in man evidently because of the perpetual threat of starvation. Man needed to think and invent, or perish. The Leakeys found numerous stone tools, tapered hand axes, and vital weaponry used 2 million years ago. Adventurous Americans today often discover Indian arrowheads that a few hundred years ago served the same purpose for the Stone Age men who occupied North America before the arrival of European "discoverers."

During the 1970s and 1980s, anthropologists and paleontologists just might discover a "missing link" that carries the changeover between the animal that does not think, invent, or philosophize and the man who has learned—always the hard way—to do all these things. "Peking man," *Homo erectus*, discovered at Choukoutien, China, in 1929, was accepted as a 500,000-year-old ape-man. During W.W. II, his fossil bones disappeared, but in 1974 the Chinese Government announced that new excavations had begun to search for other pro-

genitors at Choukoutien. This is typical of modern man's worldwide interest in tracing his ancestry in the hope that he is somehow separate and unique from beasts.

The great mystery is, of course, just how man came about in the 1st place. Equally dramatic is the fact that this diminutive animal went on to improve his condition by cultivating or domesticating large numbers of plants and animals in order to serve his needs. The dog is man's devoted servant (an important arm of the early hunting pack). The horse is his dumb but obedient servant. The camel is his ever-hating drudge. The elephant, used in the Indian teak forests, is perhaps his closest animal companion. Elizabeth Mann Borgese placed these lumber-jumbos next highest in intelligence to man and said that the elephant offers a more promising approach to the study of interspecies communication than does the porpoise. The taming of wild grasses created man-dependent crops—wheat, corn, and rice —that are as much a part of the domestic scene as man's cows and chickens.

Man has spend 99% of his life-span as a hunter, a killer. He had to, in order to survive. Thus, the great early inventors of the throwing stick (for spearing animals and fish), and later the inventors of bow-and-arrow and fishline-and-hook, were major contributors to human progress. Today's "captive" population of domestic livestock lead joyless lives—caged and confined—waiting only to become chops, hamburgers, and chicken parts, or to produce milk and eggs. Americans often consider the Hindus of India—who allow "mother cow" to live without fear of the slaughterhouse—as evaders of protein reality. On the other hand, many Indians consider American hamburger-lovers as spiritual degenerates. Both are partly right. Vegetarianism is gaining widespread popularity, especially among the young.

In *Corporate Man*, Antony Jay says that "the modern corporation is a clustering of animal jealousies, status displays, hunting bands, tribal assemblies and tribal rituals . . . underneath the civilized exterior the primitive hunting band is still alive and well and living in New York, or Seattle, or Wilmington, or Poughkeepsie." The continuing military-industrial complex bears this out. Meantime, an increasing number of women have left their kitchens to join the hunting pack in the conglomerate business world.

Homo sapiens's most distinguishing early attributes were his brain and his creation of an intelligible spoken language. Archaeologists have long noted scratchings on bits of bone, rock, and ivory. In 1971, Alexander Marshack claimed that these scratchings were the 1st evidence of the mathematical abilities of man, the accountant—*Homo accomptantus*, who had

This photograph was made August 6, 1945, a few hours after the A-bomb exploded over the center of Hiroshima. It shows victims waiting to receive first aid in the southern part of the shattered city. (See: Chap. 8) *Wide World Photos.*

An advertisement for Aleister Crowley's autobiography. English-born Crowley was also author of 45 books of poetry, 15 books on the occult, as well as a mountaineer, founder of a religion, practitioner of black magic. He died in 1947 and was cremated. (See: Chap. 8)

Jean Nicot (See Ch. 8)
Drawing by Edward Sorel

Rudolph Diesel (See Ch. 8)
Drawing by Edward Sorel

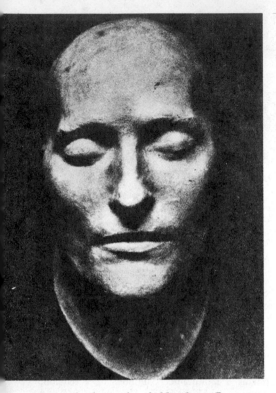

The Rosetta Stone discovered in Egypt in 1799. The inscriptions on the slab of black basalt—in Greek, hieroglyphics, and demotic writing, dating back to 196 B.C.—were deciphered by Jean-François Champollion and provided the key to the mysteries of ancient Egypt. (See: Chap. 8) *The British Museum, London.*

Plaster death mask of Napoleon Bonaparte (1769-1821) made by Dr. Francesco Antommarchi. Napoleon, a French general, first consul and Emperor of the French, was exiled to the island of St. Helena in the South Atlantic in 1815 following his defeat at Waterloo. He died of stomach cancer in 1821. The death mask can now be seen in Musée de l'armée, Paris. (See: Chap. 8) *Madame Tussaud's, Ltd.*

Mao-tse Tung and Lin Piao led the Communists who led the Chinese people in their revolution against foreign invaders and enemies within. In 1971, Lin Piao died in a plane crash soon after having been removed from a position of power. (See: Chaps. 8, 26)

In October, 1910, Dr. Hawley Crippen, an eye and ear specialist, and his mistress, Ethel Le Neve, were tried at the Old Bailey, London, for the murder of his wife. After coming under suspicion, they had tried to escape to Canada but were arrested on board ship. Dr. Crippen was hanged; Le Neve was found innocent. (See: Chap. 9) *Brown Brothers.*

Malcolm X's effectiveness as a civil rights leader was on the rise when he was assassinated in New York City on February 21, 1965. Although Malcolm himself had believed his enemies were higher placed and more political, the police put the blame on the Black Muslims. (See: Chap. 9) *U.P.I.*

WANTED

FOR

TREASON

THIS MAN is wanted for treasonous activities against the United States:

1. **Betraying the Constitution** (which he swore to uphold):
   He is turning the sovereignty of the U. S. over to the communist controlled United Nations.
   He is betraying our friends (Cuba, Katanga, Portugal) and befriending our enemies (Russia, Yugoslavia, Poland).
2. He has been WRONG on innumerable issues affecting the security of the U.S. (United Nations-Berlin wall-Missle removal-Cuba-Wheat deals-Test Ban Treaty, etc.)

3. He has been lax in enforcing Communist Registration laws.
4. He has given support and encouragement to the Communist inspired racial riots.
5. He has illegally invaded a sovereign State with federal troops.
6. He has consistently appointed Anti-Christians to Federal office: Upholds the Supreme Court in its Anti-Christian rulings. Aliens and known Communists abound in Federal offices.
7. He has been caught in fantastic LIES to the American people (including personal ones like his previous marraige and divorce).

A handbill circulated in Dallas, Tex., on November 21, 1963. Kennedy's assassination the following day has not yet been fully investigated. (See: Chap. 9)

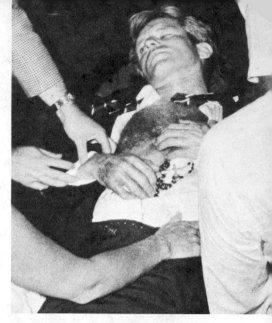

The theory that Sirhan Sirhan acted alone in killing Sen. Robert F. Kennedy in June, 1968, received a jolt when Los Angeles coroner Thomas Noguchi announced that the fatal bullets were fired from within 4″ of Kennedy. Sirhan was never closer than 2′. (See: Chap. 9) *U.P.I.*

Captain Alfred Dreyfus (walking, center), a French Jew, was court-martialed in 1894 for transmitting army secrets to Germany. Sentenced to Devil's Island for life, he was vindicated after his wife and Émile Zola spent 12 years proving he had been railroaded. (See: Chap 10) *Bibliothèque Nationale.*

begun recording the phases of the moon. According to Dr. Ralph Solecki, these Ice Age *piqûres*, were "a logical springboard leading to the more sophisticated calendars of ancient Sumer, Babylon, and Egypt." Records and archives lie beneath innumerable dust mounds in Mesopotamia—like countless clay tablets covered with cuneiform "writing"—waiting to be transcribed. Egyptian hieroglyphics, early Phoenician alphabetics, Mayan calendrical markings, await some scholar's patient translation. *Homo habilis* has never ceased to expand his spoken and written means of communication. He has invented the typewriter, telephone, telegraph, radio, TV, computer, and, most recently, the earth-girdling satellites that could take man back to the pre-Babel Tower concept of a single world language.

Man is the only spiritual animal. From his 1st days he has worshiped gods and goddesses. Originally there was an entire pantheon of nature deities—Gaea ("Mother Earth"), Poseidon/Neptune ("Father Sea"), and a strange zoo of animal omnipotences. The great animal paintings by the cave dwellers at Altamira in Spain, at Lascaux in France, and at Tassili des Adjjer in North Africa, were, as André Varagnac hailed them, "the work of some of the most gifted painters, engravers, and sculptors who ever existed." They were recorded perhaps to improve hunting, but surely they were also used for worship. We may never know this for certain. But in thousands of temples, cathedrals, and sanctuaries man has impressed his finest handiwork on stone, in paintings, and in the very design of the structures themselves.

Differences in religion have been the cause of much warfare, along with underlying and associated economic factors. Man is the only animal that consistently engages in organized warfare to kill his own kind. Modern weapons and atomic missiles make this most dangerous game a likely means of ending all life on earth.

There has been a vast increase in evangelical fervor during the 1970s, particularly to promote the concept of an "eternal" afterlife for those who have followed the precepts of a particular religion. Meantime, the exact location of a heaven somewhere within the visible universe—where all the departed souls have gone to live—makes for enchanting cosmography on the part of inventive religious interpreters. Pierre Teilhard de Chardin, for example, suggested that around us is a noösphere which clings to our own earth like the fuzz on a peach.

Man's ascendancy as ruler over the earth was accomplished as he gradually advanced from hunter to herdsman to farmer—*Homo agriculturus*. Within the Green Crescent of the Near East, man, or perhaps woman (because man

was busy hunting—in packs—wild animals in the woods), 1st learned to plant seeds and harvest crops. Today all humankind lives by a fantastic expansion of the 1st skills of these simple farmers. The plow, the combine, and the tractor obsoleted the use of mere human power and led to an age of modern agronomics.

In *The Population Bomb* (1968), Dr. Paul R. Ehrlich warned that "The battle to feed all of humanity is over. In the 1970s the world will undergo famines—hundreds of millions of people are going to starve to death in spite of any crash programs embarked upon now. At this late date nothing can prevent a substantial increase in the world death rate. . . . We must have population control at home . . . by compulsion if voluntary methods fail. We must use our political power to push other countries into programs which combine agricultural development and population control."

In 1971 the U.S. population growth rate fell below 1% for the 2nd time since 1940. Although the 1975 population of 212 million Americans represents a mere 6% of world population, Americans presently consume up to half the world's annual consumption of raw materials. A UN World Population Conference in 1974 came to the feeble "decision" that all countries *ought* to reduce their birth rates by 1985. Population growth is presently dropping in the U.S., Sweden, West Germany, Japan, Hungary, and Romania. But it continues to rise by about 2.3% annually in the underdeveloped areas, far faster than their increased production of food.

When man 1st emerged as a separate species, imminent danger of starvation was a constant menace. From the 1970s onward, this same fear is going to provide motivation for finding new ways of creating plenitude. *Homo*, the different animal who's already invented so many dramatic new ways of accomplishing wonders, is fully capable of solving this problem.

OTHER LIFE ON EARTH

In spite of all the imaginative speculations of science-fiction literature, and hopeful prognostications among scientists, the surface of earth is the only place in the entire cosmos where life is *known* to exist. And here it is possible only because of the watery environment which supports it.

Water thus *is* life and life is water. Perhaps if one could explain what water is, it would also be possible to explain life itself. Is *water* the living element, life itself, and are all the so-called living things—plankton, people, plants, pachyderms—mere peripheral capillaries on the outer fringes of the great inner flow of the planet's true *anima mundi*, the living body and spirit of "Planet Water" that pumps so endlessly and tirelessly throughout all of our world's infinite tissues and stream beds?

Life came into existence on earth possibly during the period when the earth's atmosphere was still like that of today's gaseous outer planets—a combination of ammonia and methane. In a manner explicable scientifically (and already reproduced in a laboratory), primordial simple life forms came into being. Thereafter, various necessary steps took place, making for today's "normal" living conditions. A topside layer of ozone blocked off the sun's more lethal rays. The atmosphere became filled with life-supporting oxygen. The earth's ocean basins (over a newly hardened crust of basalt) filled with salt water. The chemical content of human blood today approximates that of the ocean waters at the time when our ancestors emerged from their primordial bath-birth.

The global "biomass" of human, animal, and plant life—from microscopic one-celled jets of life to huge 100-ton blue whales (the largest creatures ever to live on earth)—collectively represents a total of 2 million million tons. Of the biomass, the human segment amounts to only one part in 10,000.

Eighty-five percent of all the planet's inhabitants still reside in the sea as perpetual wanderers, the drifting plankton. There are some 20,000 species of fish in the sea, of which less than 1/50 are used for food, oil, or fertilizer. The world catch of fish presently amounts to about 60 million metric tons, 95% caught in the northern hemisphere, of which the U.S. catch amounts to 5 million tons annually.

The size of fish populations can be fantastic. A shoal of herring, the most important food fish, may have from a half billion to 3 billion individual fish in it. However, world oceans are presently being overfished, and individual nations have been escalating their offshore territorial limits to remove foreign fishing vessels from these coastal waters.

Off the Pacific coast of South America, upwelling creates vast pastures of plankton, which nourish crabs, anchovy, and sardines. "Sharks, sailfish, bonito, and mackerel all stalk the tiny predators," Wesley Marx reported in *The Frail Ocean*. "Amid the splashing frenzy, the Eastern Tropical Pacific celebrates its fertility . . . that attracts high-seas fishing fleets and triggers one of the fiercest, most relentless battles for supremacy in man's predatory history. The object of this competition, the yellowfin tuna, ranks in the aristocracy of fishdom." A UN conference during the summer of 1974—intended to set up a meaningful "Law of the Sea"—broke up with no decisions, merely a promise to hold another indecisive talkathon the following year.

For sheer numbers of living creatures, one must turn to the microorganisms. "The microbe population on any one of us is undeniably large," Dr. Theodor Rosebury wrote in *Life on Man*, "numbering vastly more than all the people on earth. Yet they could all be packed into something hardly bigger than an ordinary soup can. They're evidently indispensable to our healthy development and well-being."

Slightly more than a million species of animals are known, and some 300,000 species of flowering plants. There are over 20,000 species of birds, of which about 1,500 fly over North America. More than 5,000 reptiles—turtles, alligators, and snakes—crawl and slither about. One, the tuatara, has been around for 200 million years, unchanged, though there are only a few left on some islands off New Zealand. Another relic of the past is the ginkgo tree, which flourished in the days of the dinosaurs (and was probably part of their diet) and which does very well in the polluted atmosphere of modern American cities. The coelacanth fish, long thought to have disappeared some 70 million years ago, was found to be still flourishing off South Africa, unchanged. The oldest "living fossil" is the lingula, a brachiopod that hasn't changed in the past half billion years.

In the beast-bird-fish or animal-vegetable differentiations, there are some anomalies. The platypus, called an aquatic mammal, breast-feeds its young but lays eggs like a bird. Also, coral, strange underwater polyps—considered holy by religious sea peoples—are both animal and vegetable in their functioning.

The merciless jungle of life-eat-life in the seas is nothing compared to the microworld of tiny creatures a mere fraction of an inch beneath the grass on any peaceful lawn. "Although the soil itself does not give birth to life, it is the incubator for the living world," Peter Farb stated in *Living Earth*. "The abundance of life to be found in the soil is staggering. The organisms vary from the submicroscopic up to the relatively gigantic earthworm." Earth's cruelest creatures turn out to be not sharks in the sea but tiny nematodes, which have more species than all other kinds of animals combined, and which pursue their prey mercilessly. Our age perhaps should be called "The Age of Nematodes," Donald E. Carr warned in *The Deadly Feast of Life*. They do at least $2 billion worth of damage to American agriculture. "It is as if we . . . were being invaded by astronomically vast colonies of malign little beings from outer space. And yet it is an ancient animal . . . perhaps eventually it will be found that anything we can do, *the nematode will be able to do better*."

The 1st trees on earth, arriving out of the sea some 300 million years ago, were giant seed ferns. Some 60 million years later, great forests of the Carboniferous Age laid down their woody deposits that changed slowly into peat, then lignite, and finally into compacted coal, our greatest fossil fuel. The largest living thing is a *Sequoia gigantea* tree, the "General Sherman," and earth's present tallest tree is a redwood, a *Sequoia sempervirens*, both ancient giants being located in California. The oldest living thing is a tiny bristlecone pine atop windswept Wheeler Peak in Nevada. It is 4,900 years old—what's left of it. (Any so-called "living tree" is in fact only 1% or even *less* "alive"; the rest is all *deadwood.*) There are 865 species of trees native to the U.S.

Earth is girdled by forests, all in imminent danger of destruction by bugs and disease, by fire, but chiefly by man. The Mayans of Yucatán cleared the jungle forests and raised great cities, the ruins of which may be viewed today. They're not unlike the great palaces and temples built where the Khmers of Cambodia cleared jungle forests for farming. Unfortunately, the soil beneath these forests, when exposed to sun and air, undergoes complex chemical changes and turns into a rocklike substance called laterite. This material makes for beautiful architecture, like the temple of Angkor Wat, but it also makes land useless for farming. Presently, the Brazilians are clearing a vast highway through tropical forests in the Amazon River basin, and one may expect a fate there similar to what overtook the land of the Mayans and the Khmers.

Useful plants are called "crops," whereas useless plants are called "weeds." Similarly, inedible wild animals are "vermin" in contrast to edible "game."

Man devours and enjoys a wide variety of vegetables, fruits, and nuts—selected primarily by taste and appearance rather than nutritive values. Poet Keats's bowl of fruit set before his sweetheart (instead of jewels or flowers or perfumes) expresses well the human epicurean enjoyment "Of candied apple, quince, and plum . . . lucent syrups, tinct with cinnamon."

Human civilization was founded on the more mundane grain crops—wheat, barley, millet. Man 1st dibbled a hole with his big toe, dropped in the seeds, swiped the hole shut, and packed it down with his heel. At Plymouth, Mass., colonists learned, when they planted Indian corn, to throw in a dead fish for fertilizer.

Earthworms are still the planet's greatest farmers. "A weight of more than 10 tons of dry earth annually passes through their bodies and is brought to the surface on each acre of land," Darwin estimated. Sir Albert Howard raised Darwin's estimate to 25 tons. Invention of the wooden plow and the horse collar (using the horse's powerful shoulders for the

1st time) added "horse power" to agriculture and to our language. Presently came mechanization—transforming farming from the primitive planting stick and the horse-drawn iron plow into industrial agronomics, with the tractor replacing the horse.

Civilization, the feeding of group-living communities of *Homo sapiens*, depends upon a sufficient food surplus. In ancient Mesopotamia, the Akkadian cosmopolitan citizenry developed a formidable human culture, primarily because they raised and stored massive cereal grain crops to feed the entire population in both good and bad times.

Humanity's basic problem—feeding everybody in good times and bad—has never changed. *The New York Times* headlined the September, 1974, opening of the UN, "Food, a Crisis for All."

In the U.S., American farmers have exceeded the accomplishments of the peasants of ancient Mesopotamia, for U.S. farmers—only 2% of the total population—feed the other 98%. One farmer, on his mammoth tractor equipped with power steering, pulls a disc plow and planter that can work as many as 12 rows of a crop at a time.

DEATH ON EARTH

Earth has been inhabited by an unbelievably diverse and ever-multiplying roster of vigorous life forms that no science-fictionist could ever have imagined. Each arrival of "new" relatives (and we must remember that all life is one close-woven family of cousins) was predicated upon planetary conditions favorable for each new species in its time, station, and comfortable adaptation to the then existing conditions on earth.

When vast changes took place, life forms were often wiped out instantaneously. Two thirds of the primitive families suddenly disappeared at the end of the Cambrian period. The greatest mass extinction took place at the end of the Permian period (midway between the Cambrian and the present), when "Nearly half the known families of animals throughout the world became extinct," as N. J. Berrill reported, in *Inherit the Earth: Man on an Aging Planet.* He said further, "Another major case of mass extinction occurred at the end of the Cretaceous period. . . . The dinosaurs large and small, the great marine reptiles, the flying reptiles, the ammonite mollusks of all sizes, and many other forms of terrestrial and marine animal life disappeared without a trace—at least 16 orders and superfamilies of living creatures."

During the 1970s or sometime in the 21st century sudden drastic earth changes could again wipe out families, most notably the one that concerns us, the family of man. If the earth warmed up suddenly, the Antarctic continental glacier would begin to melt, drowning millions of seaside residents. Changes in ocean currents take place occasionally, shifting the longtime migration patterns of massive schools of fish, with drastic effects on man's fishing industries. One great mystery of sudden mass death under freezing temperatures left mammoths, their tusks obtruding, frozen high inside a Siberian cliff. The mammoths were dug out by peasants, and scientists studied the instantly frozen giant herbivores, with bits of grass still delicately held across their palates. We don't know what massive rippling of the planet's skin might have taken place, how the sudden freezing cold was achieved, or if and when it may happen again.

Only about ⅓ of the 2,500 families of animals—whose fossilized remains have been found—are represented by living descendants. Man's descent comes from collateral lines of often secondary creatures who were somehow able to survive and adjust to changed conditions after one of nature's upsets. Meantime, man has advanced from a timid subordinate being to become a threat to the natural environment of the entire planet.

Two groups of Stone Age men presently face assimilation by their "civilized" neighbors—the bushmen of the South African Kalahari Desert and the aborigine population in Australia. Evidence seems fairly conclusive that the "more modern" Neolithic men of the later Stone Age, inventors of the bow and arrow and the wheel, most likely wiped out their earlier kin, Paleolithic man, wherever they encountered him. After all, these earlier Neanderthals had only primitive stone axes as weapons.

Among the numerous forms of animal life that have become extinct within recent times is the passenger pigeon that crowded U.S. skies a mere century and a half ago; the greak auk that furnished food and feathers to the early explorers of the North American Atlantic coast; and the heath hen that New Englanders began to "save"—too late—around 1900. Other lately departed creatures are the Eskimo curlew, the West Indian seal, the South African quagga (a desert horse), the Alaskan Steller's sea cow, the California giant grizzly bear, the Labrador duck, and the dodo bird of the Indian Ocean. Some of these, notably the dodoes, were too innocent to hide from man the hunter. Others were wiped out as humans changed the environment around them. The American bison, more usually called buffalo, were almost totally eliminated by the same kind of mass killings ("big hunts") that had eliminated the passenger pigeon. A few precariously survive.

The "future fossils" club is a large one, with a growing membership of endangered species. Organizations like the World Wildlife Fund are seeking preserves where these species may be protected from further onslaughts by human hunters. Americans are sentimental about the endangered bald eagle, our national symbol, about the last of the whooping cranes, and even the California condor, the largest land bird in America. A great effort is being made to raise and set free peregrine falcons. During the fall of 1974, a pair was set free and began dining on pigeons nearby. A mysterious phone call was placed asking, "What are you going to do about those terrible killer birds?" just before they were shot by a human hunter.

The North American timber wolf was long regarded as man's most dangerous and wiliest wilderness opponent. Today he's become an endangered species, and many of his former enemies have changed sides. James Oliver Curwood, who wrote great wilderness books in the early 1900s, put away his gun and took the side of the wolf in the 1920s.

Key deer, the kit fox, desert bighorn, sandhill cranes, and black-footed ferrets are among the many rare and endangered species in America today. Worldwide, there are such exotic creatures in trouble as the Asiatic lion, Indian tiger, Javan one-horned rhinoceros, and a genus of bird in New Zealand, the *Notornis*, that may or may not be already defunct.

Whales, earth's biggest creatures, are in special danger. Five species—the blue, humpback, gray, bowhead, and right—are now protected. But the Russians and Japanese—who still pursue sei, minke, and sperm whales—have not yet agreed to stop, though the 1974 meeting of the International Whaling Commission was the most rancorous conference in the 27 years of its existence. Citing the overwhelming vote to end whaling altogether, taken at the 1973 UN environmental conference in Stockholm, the U.S. representative pleaded for at least a 10-year moratorium. The whale is quite likely to move on soon from the "endangered" category to fossildom.

TROUBLE ON EARTH

Nature "takes the shortest way to her ends," said Emerson in summing up the immutable insistence of the land, the sea, and the air to pursue their never-ending battle with each other. Nature is neither friendly nor hostile to mankind. It is man who wishes to alter nature's ways—for example, by diking the Zuider Zee to create massive new polders of farmland below sea level; by creating high levees along the Mississippi River to prevent nature's normal springtime flooding of the great valley; or by turning the vast grasslands of the Great Plains (ground that should never have been plowed) into homestead farmland, much of which blew away during the Dust Bowl drought of 1936. Nature was not striking back, but was merely attempting to reclaim her own, taking the "shortest way," as usual.

In other words, avalanches, hurricanes, spouting volcanoes, floods, earthquakes, tsunamis, meteors from outer space, waterspouts, tornadoes, avalanches, hailstorms, and lightning bolts are not nature's angry attempt to punish man, but merely the natural forces going about their usual business.

Mankind is today building the "thousand-year problem," the new "high-level" radioactive waste from nuclear-weapons production and power plants. Presently there are 87 million gallons of the deadly stuff, and this is expected to mount up by 60 million more gallons by the year 2000. Somehow this threat-to-life material must be thrown out beyond a protective magnetosphere, but how? Nobody yet knows.

During the "good years" from 1961 to 1967, inhabitants of the sub-Sahara Sahel region (encompassing 6 of the poorest nations on earth) enjoyed relative prosperity—modest rainfalls, 1,400 new wells dug by the USAID, and moderate harvests of millet, sorghum, and peanuts. Then, in 1968, a protracted drought began. Since that time, the Sahara Desert, the earth's largest, has been moving southward by more than 30 mi. per year, wiping out all cattle and crops, and threatening the lives of millions of human inhabitants.

The change in climate in North Africa was due to an apparent expansion of polar air masses that has kept pushing the usual monsoon rains back southward beyond the Sahel. Meantime, all those wells should not have been dug since they lowered the water table and encouraged nomads to increase dangerously their herds of cattle. In the same way, during the fall of 1974, northern India experienced one of the worst droughts in many years. Some meteorologists have suggested that both dire situations may have resulted from an overall worldwide temperature drop over recent decades.

Generally, however, it is man who aggravates the dimensions of natural bad years into major disasters. The wonderful new crops of the Green Revolution demand new fertilizers and insecticides. Since these derive from petroleum products, and since oil prices have mounted astronomically, all the have-not nations are currently facing a hopeless situation. They cannot afford the new high prices for the necessary fertilizer and insecticides.

Unselfish generosity among nations has been one of the pleasanter aspects of many UN activities. But at the opening of the 29th General Assembly in September, 1974, Secretary General Waldheim called attention to the fact that rich countries have lost interest in furnishing foreign aid to poorer nations.

General Waldheim estimated that $2.3 billion was required to aid the neediest countries, where per capita yearly income is less than $400 (like Upper Volta—in the Sahel—where the yearly income is only $60), and warned the indifferent nations that "Failure to sustain international action and collective responsibility may easily put in question the survival of millions of people. Many great civilizations in history have collapsed at the very height of their achievements because they were unable to analyze their basic problems. . . . Today the civilization which is facing such a challenge is not just one small part of mankind—it is mankind as a whole."

Man's and woman's prolificacy is humanity's worst threat. Population is increasing faster than the means of adequately feeding the new "bodies." The Green Revolution has performed miracles of increased abundance. Wheat, *Triticum sativum*, feeds the Temperate Zone inhabitants of 5 continents. New high-yield hybrid wheats developed from a Japanese dwarf variety have brought an 80% increase within 24 years. Corn, *Zea mays*,—more than half of it grown in the U.S. and served to cows, pigs, and chickens—has fantastically productive new strains. Rice, *Oryza sativa*, is eaten by over half the planet's population, 90% of them inhabitants of Far Eastern nations. New high-yield rice strains are giving vastly increased harvests.

At the International Corn and Wheat Improvement Center, El Batan, Mexico, new experiments are under way in "wide crossing" of unrelated strains of wheat, barley, rye, wild grasses, and corn, in search of new superplants that will survive droughts, resist insects, and meantime yield tremendous and highly nutritive harvests. In 25 years or so, scientists hope to find the answer. Meantime, world population is expected to double by the year 2000.

Cereal manufacturers claim they can produce vegetable foods that would have the protein value of, taste like, and eliminate the need for animal "meat." More than ⅔ of the world's soybeans are produced in the U.S. The soybeans are fed to domestic animals or sold abroad for the same purpose (except for a small proportion used in Japan to make soy sauce, soybean cakes, and noodles). Yet, soybean has twice the protein content of an equivalent amount of meat or cheese and 10 times that of milk. However, people prefer to eat red meat, poultry, eggs, and milk.

Americans have recently begun to mix 44% of "textured soybean protein" with 56% ground beef for their hamburgers. The ultimate move might be to do away with the raising of livestock, and eat 100% vegetable hamburgers. The Japanese, guilty of overusing whale meat for protein, are presently experimenting with the direct use of the tiny phytoplankton from Antarctica which forms part of the whale's diet. The Russians, equally guilty of overwhaling, are also working on an edi-"krill" paste.

All energy comes from the sun, but very little of the available supply is used by the earth's photosynthetic organisms. Those in a typical freshwater lake, if assembled on the surface, would form a thick green film only ¼ of a millimeter thick. On land, the film would be thinner, and at sea infinitely more so. Thus, photosynthesis, as presently performed by nature, is a remarkably limited system.

Dr. Michael Neushul, a University of California botanist, has suggested that we will eventually convert energy from the sun—in special "light" factories—directly into food energy, thus bypassing both agricultural fields and cattle ranches, which will presumably revert to their pre-man place in the "natural" balanced ecosystems of wild nature. We may also expect to create thermonuclear fusion on earth, just as the sun does, via the miracle of laser-induced implosion. The result, scientist Edward Teller says, "will profoundly change our views on how man and matter can interact." *Homo habilis*, the inventor, is evidently about to produce numerous answers to the 1970s' needs.

The U.S. Environmental Protection Agency warned, in February, 1973, that air pollution causes 50% of the illnesses and deaths due to bronchitis, 25% of all lung cancers, 25% of all lung diseases other than bronchitis, and 10% of cardiovascular diseases. "From 60% to 85% of most city smog is caused by man's best friend, the effusive automobile," warned Robert and Leona Train Rienow in 1967.

Paris, France, began to drink an *eau nouveau* (new water) created by treating the filthy Seine waters with ozone. By 1973, ozone treatment was creating a supply of bright, clean drinking water in cities around the globe. As for purifying the lakes and seas, the Metropolitan Sanitary District of Greater Chicago is presently treating sewage sludge to turn it into liquid fertilizer, and then fertilizing strip-mined land that had previously been "as dead as the surface of the moon."

The future of humankind is fraught with countless perils, created by both nature and man. But *Homo habilis* is hard at work discovering the answers needed to survive in an always difficult world.

—H.E.F.

MAPPING THE WORLD

Nearly 500 years ago, when it was generally agreed that the earth was a sphere, mapmakers established 2 essentials. One was a standard system of meridians of longitude (from the Latin *longus*, "long") and parallels of latitude (from *latus*, "wide"), which would make it possible to pinpoint any location on the globe. The 2nd essential was a method of transferring details from a sphere to a flat map—a procedure that modern mapmakers call a "projection." Since the earth is round, it has no corners from which measurements might be made. Therefore, 2 definite measuring points are used—the North Pole and South Pole, which are the ends of the imaginary axis on which earth turns.

In mapping the earth, cartographers lay out the equator (the center line around the earth) and parallels of latitude like slices of the sphere. Each parallel is a huge circle divided into 360°. Each degree is equivalent to approximately 60 nautical miles starting at the equator (a nautical mi. measures 6,080.2′, a statute mile 5,280′). Degrees are also divided into 60 minutes, each minute equaling one nautical mi. The minute is divided into 60 seconds, making each second equal to about 101′.

The equator is at 0° latitude. Northward, the parallels from the equator are numbered from 1° to 90° (¼ of a circle) and are called "north latitude." Parallels to the south are also numbered from 1° to 90° and are referred to as "south latitude."

Parallels are not enough to pinpoint a location on the earth, so mapmakers place curved meridians (also measured in degrees, minutes, and seconds) of longitude that converge at the North and South Poles. Since the meridians cross the parallels, given the latitude and longitude of any place on earth, one can locate it exactly.

While the parallels of *latitude* begin with 0° at the equator, the 0° meridian of *longitude* used since 1884 by some 25 countries is the prime meridian on which the Greenwich Observatory is situated in London, England. (Previously, many countries used the meridians passing through their capital cities as their prime meridian.) Meridians are measured up to 180° east of Greenwich and 180° west of Greenwich. Longitude and time are inseparable. One hour is equivalent to 15° of longitude. One degree is equal to 4 minutes time-wise.

Transferring of the curved lines of the meridians and parallels to flat paper so that straight lines can be used as compass directions is done by a system generally referred to as a Mercator projection—named after Gerardus Mercator, a mathematician, geographer, and engraver who died in 1594. In his system of projection, all parallels and meridians are at right angles to each other (not curved as they would be on a globe). The converging meridians of longitude are pulled apart until they are straight and parallel. Mercator compensated by also extending the distances between parallels at an increasing rate from the equator to the poles. Lands and seas were distorted by the Mercator method, particularly in the polar regions. In straightening the meridians, Mercator produced a grid of straight lines on a map, making it of great value for accurate compass directions. Professor Edward Wright of Cambridge University improved the Mercator projection system in 1590 and this adaptation was generally accepted around 1630 and continues to serve air and sea navigators and is said to be unequaled as a navigational aid. Other types of projection are now in use, but all have some degree of distortion.

Maps of the world reveal that less than 30% of the earth is land; the rest is water. Safe navigation on water today is dependent upon a hydrographic (or nautical) chart, which shows the depths of water, positions of submarine cables, coastal landmarks, anchorages or prohibited anchorages, locations of buoys, lights or other beacons, and other information. An oceanographic chart is used to provide information about the distribution of physical and chemical properties in the sea (temperature, salinity, etc.), geology, meteorology, and marine biology.

On land, topographic maps are used by all nations to reveal the elevation of various areas. The average elevation of the U.S., except for Alaska and Hawaii, is about 2,500' above sea level. A topographic map is a detailed record of survey of a land area, with geographic positions and elevations of natural and man-made features. By means of contour lines and other symbols, topographic maps show the shape of the land—the mountains, valleys, and plains—in measurable form. They show the network of streams and rivers and other water features in their true relationship to the land, and the principal works of man in their relative size and actual position. Surprisingly, only a small portion of the earth's surface has been mapped to the degree of accuracy required today for industrial, military, scientific, and recreational purposes. (Only about 40% of the land in the U.S. is covered by topographic maps.)

Geological survey maps, using a topographic map as a base, reveal what kinds of rock exist within the borders of a country. Geologists crisscross the land, examining rock formations on its surface and making studied projections of those underground.

Geological maps are vital in determining the location, depth, and dimensions of valuable bodies of rock such as building stones or ores.

Today there is a growing use of "photogeology"—aerial and orbital (space) photography to identify and map geologic forma-

tions, certain characteristics of water, and earth faults indicating where earthquakes may occur. Long-range sensing devices in aircraft or satellites orbiting the earth can detect temperature differences in various types of rock formations. Geologic mapping plays a vital role in determining where structures are placed—and in how they are designed, built, and maintained—by analyzing the rocks and soils that surround them.

Consequent earthquakes, floods, and other disasters can make a map obsolete. Nature can cause changes in a shoreline, requiring revisions to make currently used maps accurate.

Maps reveal much to a nation about the world around it—like the little known fact that the western coast of Alaska is less than 50 mi. from the Soviet Union.

UNEXPLORED EARTH

Although they have been photographed from the air, there are still a few regions of our planet that have never been penetrated by man. These include, for example, regions of the central mountains of New Guinea, parts of the Amazon and African jungles, the Greenland ice cap, Antarctica, and northwest Siberia. They are quite remote, virtually inaccessible for close examination by man.

Although aircraft (particularly helicopters), snowmobiles, jeeps and other off-road vehicles have made many areas more accessible, methods of exploration still require the use of dog teams in Arctic regions, camels in the desert, and even shanks' mare in many areas. Mapmakers continue to be key figures in exploration today, and the modern surveyor has sophisticated equipment to enable him to measure longitude more easily than the early explorers could do it.

In the past century, many explorers were men carrying the flags of their countries with the objective of claiming the territory they discovered, particularly in the Antarctic. Today scientific work is the main goal of exploration. Much of it is done in slow stages—by examining rocks, collecting specimens found in various areas, and gradually forming a picture of life on earth in the past and the present.

In the late summer of 1974, a joint American-Mexican team of investigators found a series of major fossil beds that yielded the remains of giant tortoises, primitive horses, camels, whales, and sharks at some 18 sites in about a 350-mi. stretch between Santa Rosalia and Cabo San Lucas at the southern tip of Baja California, Mexico. Some of the remains date back 60 million years. Although the exact age of the fossil bones had not yet been determined and no human bones had been found, authorities said there was reason to believe that some of the beds will eventually turn up evidence of man. There were flakes and chips of obsidian and flint scattered throughout the sites. If these artifacts prove to be as old as the geological layers in which they were found would seem to indicate, it will strengthen the theory of scholars who claim that man entered the New World 50,000 or even 100,000 years ago. The majority view has been that migration occurred only 20,000 to 25,000 years ago. The Baja investigation was funded by the National Geographic Society.

Exploration today is concerned not only with what is where but *why* it is there. The earlier geographical aim of discovering new features of the earth's surface to include on maps is no longer the primary goal of exploration.

There is still much exploration to be done on the floors of the oceans, where progress in mapping has been slow. Long, winding valleys, steep canyons, and mountains equaling in height those on land comprise regions of the oceans and are a lure for future exploration.

Exploration under the sea is quite different from that on land. Land above the sea is characterized by the erosion of the surface from winds and rain, some of the debris spilling into the oceans. Under the sea there is a process of deposition, of filling up with the giant rubbish heaps of nature. While the world's continents have been mapped, seas charted, highest mountain peaks have been climbed, and the North and South Poles reached, man has yet to conquer the depths of the oceans. Nevertheless, the study of the oceans is picking up momentum and progress is being made—thanks to advanced techniques using new scientific equipment. There is examination of the seabed and seawaters, along with the life in them, as well as study of the feasibility of man's living underseas. Scientists predict undersea cities in the future, when the oceans will be utilized to solve some of the world's problems, such as the scarcity of food and minerals.

The past decade has seen the U.S. and Russia make vast expenditures for space research. Astronauts in orbiting spaceships, using highly scientific cameras, have been able to photograph the earth to reveal how vast, beautiful, and overpowering the sphere is in all its grandeur. Successful moon landings have inspired probes much deeper into outer space. Much has been accomplished in a few years and much lies ahead for future explorations of space—and the sea—in man's never-ending search for knowledge and adventure.

AMAZING EARTH

It has been established that the spinning earth actually does wobble on its axis at a maximum range of 72' over a 14-month period.

Scientists say the earth's north-south axis zigs and zags around the geographical North Pole in a generally circular motion—much like a spinning top beginning to lose its speed. Telescopes are continually trained on the heavens by scientists in the U.S., Russia, Japan, and Italy to determine whether there is any uniformity to this wobble and what causes it. There are varying theories: 1) some believe it's due to the melting of the polar ice caps; 2) some think it's due to the uneven land masses; and 3) others say it's because of the movements of the seas. The astronomers train their telescopes on 18 pairs of stars agreed upon by the participating nations. They know the exact time each star will cross the meridian on which the telescope is trained. Four sightings of each star are made as it crosses the meridian. Then the angular distance is measured between a pair of stars to indicate the extent to which the earth has wobbled on its axis. Since mapmakers can't make wobble maps to show the shifting of the North Pole (much too small for most scales of mapping), they adopt a "mean pole" as a base for latitude and longitude.

Most of the water in the world's great river systems ultimately derives from the glaciers of Antarctica and Greenland. Approximately ¾ of all the fresh water in the world (some 7 million cubic mi.) is stored in the form of glacial ice. This reserve is estimated to be equal to about 60 years' rainfall over the entire globe.

Mount Everest, the earth's highest peak (29,028'), located in the Himalayas, the highest of the world's mountain ranges, is so high at its summit that it penetrates the jet stream. Winds that sometimes reach 200 mph blow snow from its peak. The Himalayas—which merge with the Karakoram mountain range, the world's 2nd highest—together with the Karakoram range, boast over 500 peaks above 20,000'. North America has only one 20,000' peak (Alaska's Mount McKinley). The highest peak in Western Europe, Mont Blanc in the French Alps, rises up a mere 15,781'.

Earthquakes and volcanic eruptions are generally common in the same areas of the world. Italy, Japan, and Chile are the principal locations of both seismic and volcanic activity. The circum-Pacific belt (west coast margins of the Americas and the island archipelagoes of Asia) is the main earthquake zone, accounting for over 80% of the total energy released by earthquakes. The 2nd most active zone is the Alpine-Mediterranean-trans-Atlantic belt (North Africa, Spain, Italy, Greece, Turkey, Iran, northern India, and Burma), which accounts for 15%. This leaves only about 5% elsewhere in the world, most of it in submarine ridge areas of the Atlantic, Indian, and Arctic oceans.

END OF THE EARTH

Although there have been various religious groups predicting the end of the earth as we know it, not much attention has been focused on those theories. Geologists and scientists have made guesses as to how long the earth will last and how it might come to an end. Chan Thomas, recognized as the world's leading authority in the field of cataclysmic geology and its relationship to uniformity geology, says that a worldwide flood is a very normal part of earth's life cycle. "It has happened 300 times in the past, and will happen about 300 more times before our solar system enters the deep sleep before being reborn." He said it could happen "sometime between 30 and 500 years from now," driving the few survivors into another Stone Age like the old Stone Age of 11,500 years ago, and the new Stone Age of 6,500 years ago which followed the last 2 inundations. He explained that if Antarctica and Greenland, which contain 95% of the world's ice, were to melt it would raise the oceans all around the world up about 200'. The only way to melt them, he said, is to move them into the torrid zone. The shell of the earth, which is only about 60 mi. thick, shifts around the interior. A molten layer beneath that shell, another 60 mi. thick, serves as a lubricant for the shift. The earth's shell shows a torque—a turning or twisting force that is enough to shift the shell with the equatorial pivot points being near 0° and 180° longitude. Despite this torque the shell of the earth is not shifting. When no shift occurs the torque opposing the shift has to come from within the molten layer 60 to 120 mi. deep. When the magnetohydrodynamic energy within the earth is weakened to the extent that it no longer can supply the equal and opposite torque which prevents earth's shell from shifting to a new balance, the shell's torque will take over completely and earth's shell will shift to a new position in a fraction of one day. The icecaps would then wind up rotating equatorially and melt in tropical heat, and new icecaps will begin to form at the new poles.

There are scientific theories that the sun will burn out, but that is not expected to take place until at least 5 billion years from now. The theory is that the sun will decrease in size and cool the earth to the point that oceans will freeze, leaving the earth a sphere completely covered with ice and snow, much like Greenland today.

—J.S.

The Legend of Paper Plates

They trace their ancestry
back to the forest.
There all the family stood,
proud, bushy and strong.

Until hard times,
when from fire and drought
the patriarchs crashed.

The land was taken for taxes,
the young people cut down
and sold to the mills.

Their manhood and womanhood
was crushed, bleached

with bitter acids,
their fibres dispersed
as sawdust
among ten million offspring.

You see them at any picnic,
at ball games, at home,
and at state occasions.

They are thin and pliable.
porous and identical.
They are made to be thrown away.

JOHN HAINES

The 7 *Natural* Wonders of the World

Surrounded by a seemingly endless abundance of natural beauty, the ancients, much like ourselves, often ignored the natural world. Except possibly for the Hanging Gardens of Semiramis at Babylon, even Antipater's proverbial 7 wonders of the Alexandrian era celebrated the works of man rather than nature. Antipater's list, compiled in the 2nd century, included the Egyptian pyramids, the Olympian statue of Zeus, the temple of Artemis, the mausoleum at Halicarnassus, the Colossus at Rhodes, the lighthouse of Alexandria, and the fabled Walls of Babylon. Excluding the pyramids, not one remains today, whereas, unless they "make way for civilization," many of the natural wonders Antipater missed seeing will endure for centuries to come. In North America, especially in the western U.S., nature has been prodigal of superlatives and nowhere can this be better seen than in our great and grandiose plants, whose size and age are unequaled anywhere else on earth. These are sights every traveler should make a point to see.

When Antipater compiled his list, for example, the bristlecone pines in California's Iyno National Forest were already thousands of years old. The oldest *Pinus arista*, or "living driftwood," as the bristlecones have aptly been called, has endured for more than 4,800 years on the high windswept slopes of the White Mountains northeast of Bishop, Calif. Named "Methuselah" or "Great-granddad Pickaback," and with its birth dating back to c. 2900 B.C., this venerable bristlecone is found in the Methuselah Grove, where many of the other trees approach it in age. There is no doubt that the Methuselah Grove contains the oldest living things on earth, trees that were growing before Moses received the Ten Commandments. Amazingly, these trees still produce seed from which new trees can grow. All the bristlecones hold tenaciously to life. Gnarled, burled, and bent, the epitome of the strange beauty that comes from age and suffering, they endure at elevations up to 11,000' on an arid limestone soil totally unsuitable for most plants. Wind, fire, and ice have sculpted these trees through the ages, and so fierce is their will to live that they are sometimes found, roots mostly bared, growing almost parallel to the ground, as if praying for one more tomorrow. Most grow at the rate of only one inch in diameter every century, and although great sections of the knotted giants are dead, when bristlecones partially die, the reduced living portion stands a better chance against low precipitation and other extremes of weather.

Probably the best-known of all spectacular plants on earth is the 272.4'-tall "General Sherman," a sequoia in California's Sequoia National Park. This *Sequoia gigantea* has a 79.1' girth (at 5' above the ground), and it contains enough timber to make 35 5-room houses. From its beginnings as a minuscule seed nearly 40 centuries ago, the massive "General Sherman" has increased in weight over 250 billionfold. In combined height and girth it is by far the largest living thing on earth, a line of relatively young redwoods called the "Sentinel Trees" forming a perfect path to its base.

America is also the home of the tallest living thing. Towering above any other plant on earth is the "Howard Libbey" or "Tall Tree" redwood growing along Redwood Creek in California's Redwood National Park. A *Sequoia sempervirens* that stands 367.8' tall, the "Tall Tree" may be the tallest tree of all time, although there are unconfirmed reports that an

Australian mountain ash (*Eucalyptus regnans*) felled in 1868 reached 464'. The "Howard Libbey" was named after the president of the Arcata Redwood Company, on whose land it was located until the park was established. The "Tall Tree" can barely be seen in the Tall Trees Grove, which contains several other Brobdingnagians almost matching it in height. It is a double-formation specimen (2 trees grown together) with a dead top.

Mexico has the honor of being home to the widest living plant. Its girth far greater than even the "General Sherman" redwood, the imposing Montezuma cypress (*Taxodium mucronatum*) holding the title is found in the state of Oaxaca in Mexico and in 1949 it had a circumference of 112'–113' (at 5' above the ground). It is called the "Santa Maria del Tule" tree, after the mission near which it is located. Its only challenger was a European chestnut in Italy (c. 1770) reported as 204' in circumference, an unsubstantiated figure, while in top spread, a southern red oak in Como, Miss., takes world honors, with a 115' spread. The largest spreading plant from a single clonal growth is the wild box huckleberry (*Gaylussacia brachyera*) found in eastern Pennsylvania, which covers up to 100 acres.

As for flowering plants, the rose remains the most celebrated of flowers, and the largest living rose tree is a little-known "Lady Banksia" at Tombstone, Ariz. Located in the patio of the Rose Tree Inn Museum at 4th & Toughnut streets, an unlikely location, this "Lady Banksia" requires some 68 posts and thousands of feet of iron piping to support it. Started from a cutting imported from Scotland in 1884, it has a main trunk measuring 40" thick, stands over 9' high, and covers over 5,380 sq. ft. Its blooms would easily fill a palace ballroom. However, the world's largest flowering plant is a giant Chinese wisteria at Sierra Madre, Calif., that suggests a vast field filled with delicate flowers. Planted in 1892, today it covers almost one acre, has branches surpassing 500' in length, and weighs over 252 tons. Thirty thousand people a year come to see this fabulous plant, which is located near the Los Angeles State and County Arboretum, and which, no matter how depressing the morning headlines, never fails to display its 1½ million blossoms for a full 5 weeks each year.

To view our 7th and final natural wonder of the world, one need travel only to Arizona, where the world's largest cactus is found. Called "apartment houses of the desert" because they provide living quarters for so many bird species, the huge saguaros of the Saguaro National Monument in Arizona's small part of the Sonoran desert justly claim this title. Saguaros often reach a height of 50' before dying. The slender-ribbed plant, which sometimes lives 2 centuries, takes 75 years to develop its 1st blunt branches and years more before it weighs from 6 to 10 tons and resembles a giant candelabra or fingers afire when hit by the sun. It is a wondrous thing that thrives against great odds in the desert, supplying both food and lodging to many animals, as well as to the

Papago Indians of the region, who still harvest its fruit for cakes and syrup. During extended dry periods, the saguaro gradually uses up to a ton of stored water and decreases in girth and weight until the next rains, when it swells to its proud dimensions once again.

—R.H.

Inside the Good Earth: What's Going On under Our Feet?

The earth on which man stands has been as much a mystery to him as the heavens, and reaching its core has proved more difficult than reaching the stars. What lies within the earth? Folklore and science, ancient and modern, have tried to answer that question. One idea about the interior of the earth has endured: that it is hollow.

BELIEFS OF THE ANCIENTS: THE INNER EARTH—A HELL OR PARADISE?

The Bible refers to a pit, "the sides of the North," where the throne of God, hidden in clouds, is located.

Gilgamesh, a Sumerian and Babylonian hero, visited an ancestor in the bowels of the earth.

The Greek musician Orpheus tried to rescue his dead wife Eurydice from an underground hell.

The Buddhists believed, and still believe, that millions live in Agharta, an underground paradise ruled by the King of the World from its capital, Shamballah. Agharta was founded millions of years ago by a holy man, who, warned by the gods, sought to evade disaster by holing up in the inner earth.

It has been said that the Pharaohs of Egypt were in touch with an underworld, which could be reached through secret tunnels whose entrances were located in the pyramids.

The Incas, after being discovered by the white man, supposedly led a large number of their people, carrying much treasure, into a large tunnel that descended into the inner earth.

WHAT SCIENTISTS ONCE THOUGHT

The Eggshell Mountains. Dr. Edmund Halley, Astronomer Royal for England in the 18th century, thought that beneath its 500-mi.-thick crust, the earth was hollow. In the hollow, he said, were 3 planets.

Leonard Euler, an 18th-century mathematical genius, also thought that the earth was hollow. He maintained that it was inhabited and had a central sun.

In 1738, French mathematician Pierre Bouer, was in the Andes on a scientific expedition. While making measurements, he noticed

that the gravitational attraction of the mountains was less than would be expected from such a mass. He thought that the reason for this was the relatively light weight of granite, but, by some strange leap of logic, the French press extrapolated from his findings the idea that the mountain was hollow and inhabited. (Later scientists conjectured that lighter rock had formed on the heavy basalt mantle, like cream on milk, and that it floats there like a raft.)

WHAT DOES MODERN SCIENCE SAY?

The Earth Onion. Modern scientists have come to conclusions about the interior of the earth through seismology (the science of interpreting earthquake waves), geodetic and astronomical surveys, and subsurface heat-flow measurements. They pretty much agree on the following facts about the earth which, like an onion, is made up of layers. *The crust* is a thin skin, from 2 to 25 mi. thick, made up of granite in continental areas and of sedimentary rock layers under much of the ocean. *The mantle,* which lies beneath the crust, is composed of a basalt layer nearly 1,800 mi. thick. *The outer core* is liquid, molten because of the great internal heat. *The inner core,* still very hot (from 3,700° F. to 7,000° F.), is iron, solid because of the great pressure exerted at that depth (27,400 tons per sq. in.). To account for the earth's great weight (6 sextillion, 588 quintillion short tons), the core must be very dense.

The inside of the earth is probably still heating up from the radioactive decay of uranium, thorium, and potassium.

Fiery Ball or Dust Collector? Scientists differ on the subject of how the earth was formed. Some think that it was once a molten ball, ejected by a star, and that it is slowly cooling down. Others think that it formed from the accumulation of stellar dust and is slowly heating and expanding. Dr. K. M. Creer, a British physicist, believes he has evidence that the earth is expanding like a balloon and is now nearly twice its original size. He thinks that continents once covered the earth's entire surface. It is true that the configuration of the

eastern coast of South America could fit almost
perfectly against the western coast of Africa,
and that there is a similar fit between the
North American and Greenland coasts and
that of western Europe. Creer suggests that
when the earth was about a billion years old,
expansion caused the shell to crack open and
that the 2 sides of the crack have been drifting
apart ever since (3½ billion years). This crack
has been filled by the Atlantic Ocean.

Volcanoes. From volcanic lava, which originates a few miles to 100 mi. below the surface,
we can tell that the earth's interior is very hot
(2,000–3,000° F.), and that it contains ho-
mogenous material.

Man-made Holes in the Earth. In deep well
borings, the temperature rises about 16° F. per
thousand feet initially, but this rate decreases
as lower depths are reached.

Recently man has been attempting to pierce
the earth's crust to determine more about the
earth's origin and composition. One of the
most ambitious projects was Project Mohole,
named after the Moho discontinuity (the place
where crust and mantle meet). Through Project Mohole, a deep-sea drilling operation near
Hawaii, the U.S. hoped to reach the mantle at
a depth of 17,000′. However, the project was
canceled in 1961, when borings had reached
only 1,035′. Since then, the Russians, the
French, and the Americans have launched
other projects. One of the most recent is
FAMOUS (French-American Mid-Ocean Undersea Study), which includes deep drilling by
Global Challenger, a ship set up for that purpose. These studies have lent credence to the
theories that the oceans are shrinking and that
the continental shelves are shifting, but no evidence has been found of a hollow earth.

Modern Believers in a Hollow Earth

Concentric Spheres. In the early 1800s,
Capt. John Cleves Symmes, hero of the War
of 1812, came up with a theory that the earth
was hollow and composed of a series of concentric spheres, one contained within the other so
that they all had a common center. He had arrived at this conclusion after studying the
works of 19th-century scientists, whose theories
ranged from the idea that the earth was an oil-
covered mudball picking up dust, to one that
proposed the earth was something like a soft-
boiled egg. Symmes was an original thinker. He
rejected the laws of Newton. To back up his
hollow-earth theory, he pointed to other things
in nature that were also hollow—bones, reeds,
hair. He thought the interior of the earth
could be reached through large holes, a few
thousand miles in diameter, to be found at the
North and South Poles. In a circular he sent to
numerous prominent people, including various

heads of state, he asked for funds to finance an
expedition to one of the Poles, where, he
wrote, "We will find a warm and rich land,
stocked with thrifty vegetables and animals, if
not men, on reaching one degree northward of
latitude 82."

Before Symmes was through he had got a
good deal of backing, probably because he exuded such a fervid belief in his idea. He almost
got Congress to provide money to place "Old
Glory on those interior planets."

Symmes's Idea Takes Fire. Professor W. F.
Lyons published a book based on Symmes's
theory; however, he did not mention Symmes's
name in it. To set the record straight,
Symmes's son, in 1878, published *The Symmes
Theory of Concentric Spheres, Demonstrating
That the Earth Is Hollow, Habitable Within
and Widely Open about the Poles.* Though he
faithfully outlined his father's ideas, the son
added an embellishment of his own: that the
inhabitants of the inner earth were the Ten
Lost Tribes of Israel.

There were others besides Lyons who climbed
on Symmes's bandwagon: Cyrus Read Teed,
who founded a religion based on the hollow
earth, and William Reed, who wrote a book to
prove that there were holes at the Poles, were
2 of these disciples.

But then, in 1908, Dr. Frederick Cook
reached the North Pole. And in 1909, Admiral
Peary reached the South Pole. These expeditions should have ended forever any conjecture
about the "holes-in-the-poles" theory. They
didn't. Marshall B. Gardener, who made his
living as a maintenance man in a corset factory, wrote a book on the holes in 1913. And
the believers in the theory said that the explorers never really reached the Poles, or if they
did, they had entered the polar openings without knowing it.

The Cars of Agharta. In the 1920s, psychic
R. C. ("Doc") Andersen of Georgia, traveling with an old monk in a Stanley Steamer,
investigated the Buddhist belief in the land of
Agharta. In a Tibetan monastery, he came
across an ancient book bound in animal hide
which showed an egg-shaped device, an Aghartan car, flying over a high mountain. He also
heard that the Dalai Lama, spiritual leader of
Tibet, was supposed to be in contact with the
King of the World. In Agharta, according to
legend, the people have 2 tongues which speak
different languages, and strange animals, like
birds with teeth, exist. The Aghartans have
tremendous power: They can dry up oceans,
make trees grow, and resurrect the dead. On
the high mountains, it is said, physical evidence has been left: strange footprints in the
snow, tablets and inscriptions in Aghartan, and
wheel tracks from the cars in which the Aghartans travel.

Hitler and the Hollow Earth. Adolf Hitler, influenced by Bulwer-Lytton's science fiction novel *The Coming Race*, believed in the concept of a hollow earth. He thought humans were living on the inside surface of the sphere, which was enclosed in an infinite rock. During W.W. II, he sent a team of radar experts to spy on the British submarine fleet, using calculations based on this theory. His experts didn't find the calculations helpful but Hitler didn't stop believing. Adherents of the hollow-earth theory claim that Hitler and his closest henchmen went in a submarine to a base under the icecap at the South Pole when Germany fell.

Azerland. Search Magazine, in January, 1967, reported the discovery of an underground city, Azerland, 75 mi. west of Portland, Ore. The city reputedly has a million inhabitants, a fine harbor, and an excellent space port.

UFOs. Theodore Fitch, author of *Our Paradise inside the Earth,* believes that flying saucers originate within the earth and are piloted by small people who have discovered how to power such vehicles with "free energy." Years ahead of surface people in their culture, these beings from the inner earth are trying to prevent man from blowing up the earth, he thinks; that is why there was such a rash of UFO appearances reported after the nuclear holocaust at Hiroshima.

The Hollow Earth Society. The Hollow Earth Society is an international group with over 400 members living in more than 30 countries. Its purpose is to send an expedition to find the inside of the earth. Albert McDonald, the society's president, claims that polar explorers who have come close to finding Symmes's holes have come back with stories of warm lands with unusual animals, including that summer pest, the mosquito. He contends that people on the outer and inner surfaces of the earth are held in place by gravity centered in the shell of the planet, and that the aurora borealis and aurora australis are caused by reflections from the sun located in the inner earth.

Photographs of the Holes. Another believer in the hollow-earth theory is Ray Palmer, editor and publisher of *Flying Saucer Magazine.* In the June, 1967, issue of the magazine, he showed ESSA satellite photographs in which a dark spot appeared at the North Pole, to him proof of a hole. He believes in the vortex theory—that celestial bodies, rotating during formation, develop a hole like the one which appears in water going down a drain.

Could It Be True? If the proponents of the hollow-earth theory are right, it is necessary to reject arbitrarily all the work of earth scientists, Newton's laws, and observations of scientific polar expeditions. If the earth is hollow, how can it weigh so much? And how can we explain volcanoes and other evidences of the tremendous internal heat of the earth? So far, there is no answer.

SCIENCE FICTION

Since 1742, writers have been creating their fictions around the hollow-earth theory.

Journey to the World Underground, Baron Holberg, 1742. Nicholas Klimius falls through a cavern to find a world lit by a sun surrounded by planets. For 3 days he, too, orbits, then lands on the planet Nazar which is inhabited by trees with human heads and creeping feet. The planet is technologically somewhat advanced, with ships propelled by clockwork. Later, on another planet, Klimius finds a civilization of monkeys.

Symzonia, Captain Seaborn (pseud.), 1820. After finding bones from a huge inner-world animal, Captain Seaborn steers his ship over the rim of the world into the interior of the earth. In this world there are 2 suns and 2 moons. The utopian civilization here has developed dirigibles, flamethrowers with a range of half a mile, and ships driven by compressed air. (This work is based on Symmes's theories.)

Narrative of Arthur Gordon Pym, Edgar Allan Poe, 1833. Pym and his companion Peters meet black islanders who are exiles from Symzonia. Though they never reach the interior of the earth, they do see a white mist and a white figure rises before them, emissaries from the interior. (This work is also based on Symmes's theories. Poe tried to write 2 other stories using an inner-earth theme, but couldn't seem to get his characters down there.)

Journey to the Center of the Earth, Jules Verne, 1864. Professor Von Hardwigg, his nephew, and a native guide enter the inner world through the crater of Sneffels, an extinct volcano located in Iceland. Using a "Ruhmkorf coil" (an electric flashlight), they make their way along a 100-mi.-deep tunnel, finally reaching a mammoth underground cavern, caused as the earth cooled and formed a vacuum. In this cavern are a sky with clouds, a sea, and animal life. During their adventures, they see evidence of the evolution of plants and animals. Once they narrowly escape a herd of mastodons, guarded by a 12'-high man; they see skeletons of early man; they witness a fight to the death between giant prehistoric reptiles. (This work is based on theories about the geologic history of the earth and the evolution of living things.)

The Coming Race, Edward Bulwer-Lytton, 1871. An American descends into a deep mine, at the bottom of which lies a broad road lit by gas lamps. The road leads into a world of advanced beings, manlike in appearance, who have harnessed Vril fluid, a kind of energy, which can be conducted over 500 mi. to destroy, but can also be used for peaceful purposes. The inhabitants of this land, Vril-ya, descended into the earth during the deluge and eventually developed a utopian civilization. They plan to emerge and conquer the surface world. (This book sparked the Luminous Lodge of the Vril Society, which influenced the thinking of Adolf Hitler.)

The Goddess of Atvatabar, William Bradshaw, 1892. A group of explorers sail through the hole in the South Pole and down a vortex into an inner world to reach the continent of Atvatabar, which has a technologically advanced society. Its cavalry uses mechanical ostriches. Life is restored to dead bodies through the yearning of the souls of separated lovers which recharges a huge spiritual battery. (This book is also based on the "holes-at-the-poles" theory.)

The Land of the Changing Sun, William N. Herben, 1894. While soaring in a balloon over the North Pole, Henry Johnston and Charles Thorndyke descend and are taken into a cavern containing an underground city. Here a man-made electrical sun runs on a track, changing colors with the hours. The civilization is feudal.

Etidorpha, John Uri, 1895. The narrator, I-Am-a-Man, is taken by a blue-skinned, eyeless creature through a Kentucky cavern into a world in the inner earth. They cross a lake in a metal boat that goes 900 mph by means of an ethereal current or magnetic force. (The writer of this novel explains that the earth was formed as a sphere of energy, which spun through space collecting dust as a bubble might.)

The Great Stone of Sardis, Frank Stockton, 1897. In the ultramodern world of 1947, Roland Crewe of Sardis, N.J., invents an X-ray mechanism with which he can see through the earth. Much to his surprise, he sees a clear transparency 14 mi. down. To check it out, he invents a projectile, with which he bores down to find that the earth's core is solid diamond.

The Secret of the Earth, Charles Beale, 1899. Financed by a being from the inner world, Guthrie and Torrence Attlebridge, co-inventors of the airplane, travel north to the Pole and enter the interior of the earth. Here they find roofless houses and a city of white and gold, a paradise that was man's 1st home.

Underground Man, Gabriel Tardé, 1905. A catastrophe has driven men underground where they have founded a utopia with thermic cataracts, monocycles, electric trains, and a population whose growth is regulated by birth control.

The Smoky God, Willis George Emerson, 1908. Voyaging through an opening at the North Pole, explorer Olaf Jansen enters a world, the cradle of the human race, called Eden. It contains a central sun and is inhabited by 12' giants. Electricity operates flying cars and surcharges gorgeous fruits and vegetables. (The book is heavily footnoted with references to scientific writings that take up more space than the text.)

Symzonia: A Voyage of Discovery, J. Seymour, 1923. Albino humans speak a whistling musical language, wear snow-white garments, and are ruled by "The Best Man." (This is a satire of *Symzonia,* written over 100 years before.)

The Machine Stops, Edward M. Forster, 1928. Men living in the inner earth are ruled by a machine and can get what they want at the touch of a button.

Tarzan at the Earth's Core, Edgar Rice Burroughs, 1929–1930. Tarzan goes to Pellucidar, a world which lies on the inner surface of the earth, is lit by a central sun, and has no directions. It was 1st reached by David Innes, who bored through the earth with a mechanical prospector. Tarzan, however, gets inside through a polar hole. In Pellucidar, which is largely prehistoric, Tarzan has hair-raising adventures with reptilian beings, cavemen, and other creatures. (Burroughs wrote several other books about Pellucidar.)

The Shadow out of Time, Howard Phillips Lovecraft, 1936. A researcher's body is taken over by a member of an ancient race which dominated the earth 150 million years ago. This race was driven underground by the Great Race, a group of giant living cones which came from the transgalactic world of Yith. In the world he visits in his commandeered body, the narrator sees big airships and atomic-powered vehicles and finds out that these ancient beings have mastered time-travel and employ ESP routinely.

"Shaver Mystery," *Amazing Stories,* March, 1945. A race of malformed subhumans called "deros" (detrimental robots) inhabit underground cities. Once slaves of the Lemurians, they are in charge of what the Lemurians have left: namely, a wealth of technologically sophisticated machines. These include flying machines, projection ray machines that can project images and thoughts, tractor ray beams which can derail trains, surgical ray cannons which can perform operations or make brains boil, machines that can cause nightmares, a stim machine which causes intense sensual pleasure, and death ray machines. With these machines, the deros cause trouble on the earth, ranging from broken toes to shipwrecks. Also underground are the Titans and Atlans, forced there by intense radiation that issued from the sun some 12,000 years before; they are called "abandoneros." (Some people believe in the deros and blame all kinds of happenings on them, including stolen cars, runaway girls, and various other disasters.)

—A.E.

Animal Facts and Oddities

Male silkworm moths have such a keen sense of smell they can detect a sexy female moth 6½ mi. away.

Flying fish can stay airborne for 1,000'. Supported by air currents, they glide through the air simply because they can and they enjoy it.

Land crabs found in Cuba can run faster than a horse.

Plover birds of Egypt ride the backs of crocodiles and enter the croc's mouth to pick its teeth.

Canaries and other birds are responsible for seeding much of the wild-growing marijuana in the U.S. If harvested, the wild marijuana growing within a short distance of New York and New Jersey would make 15 million cigarettes.

Crocodiles and alligators are the only members of the reptile family that have loud voices.

Lineus longissimus is the longest worm in the world, sometimes reaching a length of 180'.

Tortoises of the Galápagos Islands can live to be 190 years of age.

Whales weighing 195 tons and mice weighing 3 ounces develop from the same size eggs.

Bee hummingbirds are so small it takes 18 of them to weigh one ounce.

Savi's white-toothed shrews, the smallest known mammals (they weigh 0.1 ounce), eat 3.33 times their own weight every day.

Hoatzin birds of South America are born with claws on their wings as well as on their feet to aid them in climbing about in trees.

Reptiles, unlike most creatures, have 2 lower jawbones that hinge to allow them to swallow food larger than their bodies.

Cobras strike and kill 10,000 people annually in India alone.

Red-eyed vireo birds have perfect pitch and will repeat their calls, note for note, 22,000 times a day without the slightest variation.

Fish have been seen at 35,000' depths where pressure can be more than 1,000 atmospheres.

Capybaras, South America's water hogs, grow to be 4.5' long and weigh up to 150 lbs. They are the world's largest rodents.

Candiru, South America's tiny parasite fish found in the Orinoco and Amazon rivers, will enter the body of a swimmer through the lower body orifices. Unless detected and removed surgically they will ultimately reach the bladder and cause death.

Ants are equipped with 5 different noses, each designed to accomplish a different task.

Gazelles drink no water. Their chemical processes extract moisture from solid food.

Brown rats double their population every 100 years and have been the mammal greatest in number, but in the 1970s they will take 2nd place to humans, who double their population every 35 years.

Whale flippers have a skeletal frame similar to man's upper arm, forearm, wrist, and fingers.

Baldheaded eagles are larger at age 2 than when fully mature.

Bonefish have tongues that can exert a crushing power of 60 lbs.

Bird species throughout the world have dwindled from 1.5 million to about 10,000 in the last 70 million years.

Reptiles are cold-blooded creatures with no built-in temperature control. They live at the mercy of their surroundings.

Swifts are the world's fastest birds. They zoom along at 200 mph.

Sharks, generally, have the reputation of eating people, but of 300 species, only the blue pointer, zambesi, tiger, mako, and hammerhead are known to eat humans. On occasion, the great white shark has also attacked and killed humans.

Russell's viper, a reptile common in India, serves human medicine by the use of its venom, an extract of which is beneficial in the treatment of hemophilia.

A human being holds the record for the longest life-span of any known mammal. At least 113 years—and maybe more.

Dingoes, wild dogs of Australia, do not bark.

Therates labiatus, the tiger beetle, exudes the fragrance of attar of roses. This attracts bees that are devoured by the beetle.

Cephalopterus ornatus, the bull bird of South America, has a voice that sounds like a cow.

Gila monsters hold reserve food supplies in their tails.

Jaguars are afraid of dogs, even little ones.

Mayfly, so named because it swarms in May, lives only 6 hours but lays eggs that require 3 years to hatch.

Some spider webs, if straightened out, would span 300 or more miles.

Meadowlarks belong to the blackbird family.

Stingarees of Australia can weigh 750 lbs. and have the most powerful venom of all fish.

Whales are the best of all animal high jumpers, often leaping more than 20' in the air.

Chameleons, tree-dwelling reptiles, change their color when emotionally aroused.

Hummingbirds have the unique ability to hover and to fly backward.

Megascolideo australis, a giant earthworm found in Australia, is ¾" in diameter and often longer than 10'.

Weaver birds of South Africa lay their eggs in communal nests that contain 100 or more separate apartments.

Piranha fish found in the waters of eastern and central South America swim and attack in schools of up to 1,000. They can strip a horse down to a skeleton in minutes, will eat their own kind, and are themselves considered a delicacy.

Snakes of all species shake their tails when emotionally aroused, but only the rattlesnake has a noisemaker.

Tiger birds of South America can imitate a tiger's voice.

Electric eels are aquatic mysteries. They can discharge bursts of 625 volts, 40 times a second.

Blue whales, the largest mammals in the world, grow to 100' in length and weigh 150 tons. They develop 600 hp and can travel long distances at 20 knots per hour.

Mound-builder birds of Australia are fully feathered when hatched and can fly immediately.

Lizards are responsible for controlling the population of insects and spiders including the black widow. They do a far more efficient job than insecticides.

Birds, proportionate to their size and weight, are 75% stronger than people.

Pandaka pygmaer, the world's smallest vertebrate, is only ⅓" long.

Sturgeon is the largest freshwater fish and can weigh 2,250 lbs.

Ostriches are the world's largest nonflying birds. They can kick like a mule, give a realistic imitation of a lion's voice, and hiss like a snake.

Sitatunga, an African antelope, has the rare ability to sleep under water.

Platypus, Australia's mystery animal, has a duck bill, otter fur, webbed feet, lays eggs, secretes a milky substance for its young, and eats its own weight in worms every day.

Storks can stand on one leg because their joints are self-locking.

Three-wattled bell birds of Costa Rica have a call that can be heard for 3 mi.

Sahara desert fish have been caught in streams that flow beneath the surface.

An Asian fish that crawls on land can live for a week out of water.

Woodpecker finches of the Galápagos Islands use cactus thorns and twigs as tools to probe holes in tree trunks and branches for edible insects.

Swordfish contribute 10 million lbs. of food annually for human consumption in the U.S.

Ostriches sometimes lay their eggs in community nests. First-hatched babies are fed the unhatched eggs.

Freshwater eels found along the Atlantic coast come from a common breeding ground in the Sargasso Sea, near Bermuda.

Reptiles purchased as pets and then flushed down toilets have been found alive and well in the sewer system of New York City.

Whale sharks reach a growth of 45' and can weigh 12 tons.

Snakes lay eggs with nonbrittle shells.

Elephants have acute hearing and can easily detect the footsteps of a mouse.

Water ouzels, birds of western North America, about the size of robins, do their hunting on underwater stream beds.

Bats are not necessarily blind. Many can see but have no night vision. Better than eyes is their sonar equipment that measures the echo of their squeaks.

Hiccup fish of Brazil swallow huge gulps of air that, when released, make a sound like a hiccup. When fully grown to 12', their hiccups can be heard for a mile.

Hornets and wasps were making paper millions of years before Egypt was born. They mix wood pulp with their saliva to form a paste that dries into stiff paper.

Elephant tusks can weigh more than 300 lbs.

Seahorses swim in an upright position, and the male carries the eggs of the female in a pouch much like that of the kangaroo. When hatching time comes, it's the male that gives birth to the baby seahorses.

Goby fish found in tropical rivers are equipped with gills and a supplementary breathing system that allows them to extract oxygen from either air or water. They prefer "walking" on land to swimming.

Archer fish in the Indo-Austroasiatic region spurt a stream of water with such accuracy they can knock down an insect 4' away.

Grunion, found in the waters of Southern California, have built-in sensors that monitor magnetic-field variations allowing them to employ split-second timing in the depositing of their eggs on shore during the months of March to August.

King salmon hatched in a tiny pool at the University of Washington were sluiced into Lake Union. Five years later they returned from the sea to Lake Union, then by special fish ladders to the tiny pool of their birth, to spawn.

A bluefin tuna caught off Nova Scotia weighed 977 lbs.

Remora fish attach themselves to a shark and are towed to a kill. There they detach themselves to feed and then reattach themselves to the shark that took them to dinner.

—F.M.W.

For further reading: Soule, Gardner. *The Mystery Monsters*. New York, Ace Books, 1965. Rood, Ronald. *Animal Champions*. New York, Grosset & Dunlap, 1969.

Unusual Animals

The Baboon Who Ran the Railroad

When James Wide lost both his legs in an accident on the Port Elizabeth main line in Africa in 1877, he thought his life as a railroad man was over. However, the railroad took care of its own and gave him a job as a signalman at the Uitenhage Tower. He lived there in a wooden shack with a garden, with his only companion—a chacma baboon he called Jack.

Jack was general housekeeper for Wide. He pumped water from the well, cleaned the house, and took care of the garden. However, it was in helping Wide run the signal tower that he was most indispensable.

In the morning, Jack would lock up the house and push Wide to work in a trolley that Wide had constructed to run on rails. For a while the baboon had help from Wide's dog, but the dog was killed by a train. After that, Jack had to do the job himself.

At the signal tower, Jack operated the levers that set signals and the tower controls that opened or closed switches on a siding as well as a human being could. In the 9 years Jack worked for the railroad and his legless master, he never made one mistake that resulted in an accident.

The Dog Who Saved 40 Lives

In the Swiss Alps, at the St. Bernard Hospice, the huge St. Bernards are not used much anymore to rescue travelers lost in the snow. People don't travel on foot now, and if anyone gets lost, helicopters come to the rescue.

The most famous of the St. Bernards of the past was named Barry. Early in the 1800s, Barry was the wonder dog of the rescue corps which set out daily from the hospice. Early in the morning, he would trot away, eagerly looking for people who had come to grief in snowdrifts or avalanches. He carried no keg of brandy around his neck. (The keg of brandy is only legend.)

After he died in 1814, Barry was stuffed and put on display. A magazine of the time reported, "For 12 years he worked and gave faithful service to the unfortunate. He saved the lives of more than 40 persons, showing an extraordinary zeal. He never had to be urged to work. If he felt a man was in danger somewhere, he ran immediately to his aid, and if he could do nothing, he returned to the convent and sought help through his barking and attitude."

The Porpoise Pilot

French Pass, a dangerous water passage through the D'Urville Islands and off the coast of New Zealand, extends from Pelorus Sound to Tasman Bay. It is a shortcut for sailors, but a risky one, with deceptive currents and jagged underwater rocks. Back on a stormy morning in 1871, the schooner *Brindle*, out of Boston bound for Sydney, approached the passage. A blue-gray porpoise began jumping up in front of the ship, as though it were bidding it welcome. Some of the sailors thought it was a young whale calf and wanted to kill it. The captain's wife talked them out of it.

The porpoise seemed to be leading the way through the channel and the ship followed it, through deep water all the way, to arrive safely on the other side. From then on, the porpoise, nicknamed Pelorus Jack, would meet and pilot every ship that came through, every ship, that is, but one. In 1903, a drunken passenger on the *Penguin* hit Jack with a bullet. Though the crew wanted to lynch the passenger, the damage was done. Jack didn't show up for 2 weeks, but then came back, apparently no worse for the experience. However, after that he would never accompany the *Penguin* again. In 1909, the *Penguin*, long considered a jinxed ship, was wrecked in the passage with great loss of life.

In April, 1912, Jack vanished, never to be seen again.

Chips, the War Dog

Chips was a sentry with the U.S. Army 3rd Infantry Division. The 1st war dog to be sent overseas in W.W. II, he arrived in Sicily in July, 1943, and accompanied his division in fighting in Africa, Italy, and other parts of Europe. It was in Germany that he performed a heroic feat. One night, he broke away from his handler and attacked a German pillbox. He actually seized one man and forced 4 more to surrender. The Army awarded him the Purple

Heart and Silver Star. Later, officials took these honors away because they were "contrary to Army policy." To make up for it, his company presented him unofficially with a battle star and campaign ribbons. Chips was discharged from the Army in 1945 and returned to his owner.

OLD ABE, EAGLE MASCOT

With red, white, and blue ribbons around his neck, Old Abe the Eagle was sworn into service in the 8th Wisconsin Regiment in April, 1861. From then on, Old Abe played his part to the hilt. It was said that as the soldiers marched, drums beating and flags flying, Old Abe flew from his perch to the metal standard holding the flag, grabbed Old Glory in his beak, and helped carry it through the streets. In a battle at Farmington, Miss., Old Abe broke his cord and flew screaming above the men. Throughout the war, Old Abe took part in 36 battles and 50 skirmishes, each time flying above the troops screaming his war cry. Once a spent bullet hit his chest, and several times his tail feathers were shot off, but he was not killed nor were any of the standard-bearers who carried him. This was strange, for the Confederates, who dreaded what they called the "Yankee Buzzard," had put a price on his head. "I would rather capture or kill that eagle than take a whole brigade," said Gen. Sterling Price, of the Confederate Army. During inspections, the eagle came to attention, and he tried to sing "Yankee Doodle" and "John Brown's Body" when the band played. After the war, he toured the country raising money (over $18,000) for wounded war veterans. His quills were used for signing State documents. He lived in a large cage in the basement of the State capitol in Wisconsin, and died from smoke from a fire which broke out there in March, 1881.

THE HORSES THAT COULD DO MATHEMATICS

With a sack tied over his head, the horse, *Muhamed*, could extract cube roots in his head, tapping out the units with one front hoof, the 10s with the other. (If the answer were 43, for instance, the horse would tap 4 times with his left foot, 3 times with his right.) And *Muhamed* was not the only genius horse in that stable in Elberfield, Germany, in the late 1800s. There were also *Kluge Hans* (*Clever Jack*) and *Zarif*. Authorities were skeptical; they were sure that the horses' feats were manipulated by their master, Karl Krall; that somehow, through gestures or other signals, he was giving them the answers. However, no one was ever able to prove any trickery. In fact, *Muhamed* performed almost as well without his master as when the master was present.

And then *Berto*, a blind stallion added to the group later, was also taught to do arithmetic. If he were blind, how could signals be sent to him? It seemed certain then that the wonder horses of Elberfield represented no hoax. In addition to being mathematical geniuses, the horses could read and tell time by the clock. Panels of scientific experts came to scoff at the horses—and left awed.

THE LOYAL JAPANESE PUPPY

Hachi went to a Tokyo railroad station to see his master off for work, as usual, one day in 1925. That evening, at 5 o'clock, he went to meet the train his master always came home on. But that night his master wasn't on it. The puppy had no way of knowing that his master had died in the city. Never giving up hope, Hachi went to the railroad station every day for the *next 10 years*—the rest of his life—and waited for the 5 o'clock train. Then, when his master didn't appear, he went sadly home. The people of Japan loved the little dog. When he died, the Government put up a statue of Hachi on the spot where he had waited and sent small replicas to all the schools in the Empire.

THE DOG WITH ESP

Jim was a black-and-white Llewellyn setter owned by Sam Van Arsdale of Sedalia, Mo. When Jim was 3½ years old, Arsdale instructed him to point out an elm tree. The setter walked over and put his paw on the trunk of one. In a similar way, the setter then identified a hickory, an oak, and a walnut tree.

In 1933, when Jim was 8 years old, he was tested by experts from the School of Education at the University of Missouri. Observers were stunned by the dog's abilities. Jim located a license plate number that he had been asked to identify in French. Then, when the command came in German, he pointed out a girl dressed in blue, a man with a black moustache, and a child with long, light-colored hair. The only explanation was that Jim, the "Wonder Dog," had ESP.

Jim had another talent, too: precognition. During his lifetime he predicted the winning horses of 6 consecutive Kentucky Derbies. In 1936, he predicted that Roosevelt would win the presidential election, even though Landon was heavily favored to win in a *Literary Digest* straw vote.

The setter was 12 years old when he died in 1937.

THE CANARY WHO SAVED A LIFE

Old Aunt Tess lived alone with her canary Bibs and her pet cat, in Hermitage,

Tenn.—against the wishes of her niece, who thought her aunt was too old to live by herself. One rainy night in 1950, the niece, as was her custom, looked over toward Aunt Tess's house to see if the lights were on. They were. That meant that Aunt Tess was all right. The niece drew the curtain. Later, as she and her husband were sitting by the fire, they heard something tapping on the window. At 1st they thought it was a branch, but the tapping went on, and then they heard an almost human cry. The niece ran to the window and drew the curtains. Aunt Tess's canary, who had been beating against the glass, fell dead on the window sill. Alarmed, the 2 drove over to Aunt Tess's house and found her lying in a pool of blood. She had fallen, striking her head as she fell. Somehow the canary had known how and where to get help, and, in the process of doing so, had lost its own life.

The Dog Who Traveled 3,000 Miles

Bobbie, a mongrel whose father was an English sheep dog, got in a fight with a big bull terrier while his master was having his car fixed. It should have been all right. Bobbie had been in fights before. But the bull terrier was part of a dog pack that chased Bobbie away from the garage. When Bobbie was at last safe, he couldn't find his way back to the garage and his master, and, though he didn't know it (at least not in the way humans do), he was far from his real home in Oregon. For when the incident happened, Bobbie's master was on a vacation, visiting relatives in Indiana.

Bobbie knew he had to get home. At 1st he made several false starts, going off in the wrong direction, and traveling in circles. Then suddenly he seemed to know where home was. He began a long trip over rivers, deserts, mountains. It was winter when he crossed the Missouri; he had to swim between cakes of ice. By the time he reached Oregon, 6 months later, his paws were raw, cut to the bone, and his legs swollen. He was emaciated. But he had found his home. His howls of happiness were so loud that people up and down the street could hear them.

How could his master be sure it was the same dog? Bobbie had a bobbed tail, several scars, and 3 missing teeth. He was easy to identify. Later, Col. E. Hofer of the Oregon Humane Society investigated Bobbie's trip and was able to find many people who had given Bobbie a temporary home during the long trek or had seen him somewhere along the way.

The Cat Who Found One Family Among Millions

Daisy, an upstate New York cat, was adopted by some summer people, whom she grew to love. However, when the summer was over they returned to New York, leaving Daisy—who was now expecting a family—behind. One month later, Daisy showed up at their apartment in the city, carrying a kitten. A few days later, she left, but she came back at the end of a week with a 2nd kitten. At the end of 5 weeks, she had made the trip 5 times and had her whole family with her in the home she had chosen for herself. How did Daisy know how to find one family among the millions in New York? What clues did she use? No one knows.

Canine World Traveler

Owney, a shaggy mongrel, was adopted by the U.S. Post Office in Albany, N.Y., after the clerks found him asleep behind some mail sacks. It wasn't long before he grew bored with his home and started traveling on the railroad mail cars. Seeing that they could do nothing about his itchy feet, Owney's owners, the mail clerks, attached a tag to his collar with a note asking other clerks in the places he visited to stamp it. Soon he was spending more time on the road than at home; he was welcome on mail cars all over the U.S. On August 19, 1895, Owney stowed away on a ship bound for Japan, where he was honored by the Mikado, then went on to China, and from there around the world. When he got home, his collar was heavy with medals from the cities where he had been. After his death, he was stuffed and put on exhibition at the Smithsonian Institution in Washington, D.C.

Jumbo, the Biggest Elephant?

Probably the largest bush elephant ever held in captivity, Jumbo was bought by the London Zoological Gardens in 1865. He was loved by the English, who took their children to ride in a howdah on his back. They also admired his great size. When he was sold to P. T. Barnum, the circus entrepreneur, in 1882, the English were extremely unhappy. Even Queen Victoria protested. But it was too late.

Jumbo was crated and sent to the U.S., where he attained fame and fortune as the biggest elephant in the world. At the age of 16, his height at the shoulder was estimated at 10′9″. One night, in 1885, after a performance, Jumbo and a baby elephant were being led across a seldom-used railroad track when an unscheduled freight train thundered around the bend. The lights and noise disoriented the huge pachyderm, and he was killed when his head was crushed between a boxcar and a flatcar.

—A.E.

13

On the Road

A Unique Tour of Unusual Historical Sites in the U.S.A.

An offbeat guided tour that, for the most part, avoids well-trodden sites and instead takes the reader on some fascinating detours to unfamiliar or long-neglected landmarks that speak a different story of America's distant past and recent past. Famous sites have been included only when we felt we could offer little-known facts about them. For the convenience of the reader, the guide has been divided into East, North, South, West, with appropriate sites to be seen in each geographic area of America the Beautiful and America the Strange.

EAST

Saratoga Battlefield, New York

Monument to a Left Leg . . . Go visit the Revolutionary War battlefield at Saratoga and ask a guide or caretaker to give you directions to the most bizarre monument built to a hero in the U.S. In a secluded spot of the park you will find the marble memorial. Sculptured in bas-relief upon the slab are a cannon, an epaulet, a wreath—and a military boot for a man's left leg. Just that. No name. On the rear of the marble slab is inscribed the following:

Erected by
John Watts de Peyster
Brev: Maj: Gen: S. N.Y.
2nd V. Pres't Saratoga Mon't Ass't'n:
In memory of
the "most brilliant soldier" of the
Continental Army
who was desperately wounded
on this spot, the sally port of
BURGOYNES "GREAT (WESTERN) REDOUBT"
7th October 1777
winning for his countrymen
the Decisive Battle of the

American Revolution
and for himself the rank of
Major General

Again, no name. Only the "most brilliant soldier" of General Washington's army.

The nameless hero who inspired the erection of this odd monument was—Benedict Arnold, one of the most infamous traitors in American history.

Yet, before attempting to deliver West Point into British hands during the American Revolution, Benedict Arnold had been a military hero. In December, 1775, the then Col. Benedict Arnold led the unsuccessful charge against Quebec, and was wounded in the left leg. At Bemis Heights, on the Saratoga battlefield, Arnold led a victorious charge against the British Redcoats, until a musket ball knocked his horse out from under him and another musket ball fractured his left thigh.

In 1779, because of his misuse of army property, Benedict Arnold was court-martialed, but he escaped with a mere reprimand from General Washington. Embittered, Arnold decided to betray his country. He requested and received command of West Point, the fort that guarded the Hudson valley. Then he made an arrangement with a former boyfriend of his wife's, British Maj. John André, to sell out the fort. Arnold demanded £20,000 if the plot worked. He is believed to have actually been paid £6,350 and been given a gift of 13,400 acres of Canadian land. But the plot failed. In September, 1780, André was captured with incriminating papers in his possession. Benedict Arnold was seated at breakfast with General Washington when a courier arrived with the news of André's capture. Arnold excused himself to speak to the courier, and never returned to the breakfast table. He escaped, crossing over to the British lines, and later he became a brigadier general in the British Army.

In 1781, Arnold took up residence in England. He became a West Indian trader. In 1790, President Washington noted in his diary that "the Traitor Arnold" was back in America visiting Detroit. Arnold was married twice, had 8 children, including 2 sons named George, one named after Washington, it was said, and the other after King George III. Arnold died in London in 1801, aged 60.

It was while Benedict Arnold was living in exile in England that Maj. Gen. John Watts de Peyster ordered the marble monument erected on the Saratoga battlefield at the spot where Arnold had been wounded in the leg. Not daring to mention a traitor's name on the monument, De Peyster built the memorial to Arnold's leg—the left leg.

While visiting the Saratoga battlefield, you might also have a look at the official 150'-high monument placed there in 1877 to celebrate the 100th anniversary of the Saratoga victory. This memorial features 4 niches, 3 of which hold statues of heroes of the battle. Horatio Gates, Philip Schuyler, and Daniel Morgan are there—but the 4th niche stands empty. It was meant for Benedict Arnold. But still, there is always the leg.

—I.W.

Frederick, Maryland

The Barbara Frietchie House . . . Here it stands, this hallowed Civil War monument to a patriotic old lady's defiance of the Southern rebels. According to John Greenleaf Whittier's classic version, a poem of 30 verses for which *Atlantic Monthly* paid him $50, the Confederate troops headed by Gen. Stonewall Jackson were marching through Frederick defiling the Stars and Stripes in September, 1862. An elderly resident, Barabara Frietchie, displayed the Stars and Stripes and cried out:

"Shoot, if you must, this old gray head,
But spare your country's flag," she said.

Impressed, General Jackson turned to his troops:

"Who touches a hair of yon gray head,
Dies like a dog! March on!" he said.

Beautiful, but unfortunately it never happened. There was a Mrs. Barbara H. Frietchie, widow of a glovemaker, living in this house when the incident was supposed to have occurred. She was bedridden at the time the Confederate troops marched by. She did not see them nor did she see General Jackson, since he did not pass her house but detoured to visit friends. Later, after the Confederates had departed and Union troops entered the city, Barbara Frietchie's niece helped her out of bed, gave her a cane and a small flag, and led her outside to wave to the Northern soldiers, several of whom paused to shake her hand.

What had really happened while the Confederates marched through was an entirely different incident, which Dr. Lewis H. Steiner, of the U.S. Sanitary Commission, included in a report to the capital: "A clergyman tells me that he saw an aged crone come out of her house as certain rebels passed by trailing the American flag in the dust. She shook her long, skinny hands at the traitors and screamed at the top of her voice, 'My curses be upon you and your officers for degrading your country's flag.'"

A number of days later, Barbara Frietchie's niece added the story of the aged crone to her aunt's adventure. Then she tried it out on C. S. Ramsburg, of Georgetown, who in turn related it to a neighbor, the famous romantic novelist Mrs. E. D. E. N. Southworth. Deciding that this was the stuff of which poetry is made, Mrs. Southworth passed the tale on to Whittier. As a result of Whittier's poem, Barbara Frietchie became a legend and her home a shrine. Mrs. Frietchie died 2½ months after the nonincident, before the poem appeared. Her quaint old house, restored in 1927, continues to attract the sentimental and the I-Am-an-American types, even though nothing eventful took place there.

—I.W.

Cooperstown, New York

The Cardiff Giant . . . One of the greatest hoaxes ever perpetrated on the American public occurred in the late 1860s. On October 16, 1869, workmen "discovered" a giant humanlike figure (10' long) on a farm outside Cardiff, N.Y. A furor was created in the neighborhood that soon spread throughout the nation. But the Cardiff Giant, as it came to be known, was not one of the great scientific discoveries of that century. Instead, it was one of the most incredible hoaxes of that or any other era.

George Hull, a tobacco farmer and cigar maker from Binghamton, N.Y., was the creator of the Cardiff Giant hoax. He was a tall man whose black hair, moustache, and black attire gave him a villainous appearance.

One night while visiting his sister in Ackley, O., Hull heard a preacher speak about biblical references to giants. That gave him the idea of making a giant manlike figure out of stone and promoting it as a petrified man.

Hull and a partner, H. B. Martin, procured a 5-ton block of gypsum and hired 2 sculptors to carve the statue. It took them 3 months, with Hull serving as their model. It finally measured

10′4½″ in height, and every small detail was considered. The giant, for example, originally had hair and a beard. But when Hull learned from geologists that hair does not petrify, he instructed the sculptors to chip away the hair and beard. ·

Once the figure was completed, Hull was still not completely satisfied. He believed that it did not look real enough, so he simulated pores of the skin by pounding large darning needles into the statue. He poured a gallon of sulfuric acid over it to give its skin a dingy, aged appearance.

The giant was then placed in a crate marked "finished marble" and it was shipped by rail to Broome County, N.Y. Hull picked it up there and, using a wagon and 4 horses, he transported it to the farm of William C. Newell, who was a party to the hoax, too. The giant was then buried in a 5′-deep grave behind Newell's barn, and there it remained for about a year.

Then on a Saturday in October, 2 unsuspecting workmen were hired to dig a well behind the barn. Shortly after they began digging, they unearthed the giant. The foot appeared 1st, and then the entire body was visible. As the story spread throughout Cardiff by word of mouth, people from miles around rushed to the farm to get a glimpse of the giant.

Immediately, newspapers started calling it the "8th Wonder of the World," and 2 days after its discovery, Newell erected a tent over the giant and began charging 50¢ for a look at it. Newell's ranch suddenly became the biggest tourist attraction in the State. The average number of visitors was between 300 and 500 daily, and on Sundays the number increased to more than 2,000.

Within a few days, Hull was already negotiating for the sale of part interest in the giant. He was determined to get as much money out of it as possible before the immense gypsum figure was discovered to be a hoax. Exactly one week after it was unearthed, Hull sold ¾ interest in the giant to 5 local businessmen for $30,000.

The new owners of the Cardiff Giant decided to move the figure to Syracuse, hoping to draw bigger audiences there. But while people rushed to view the giant, suspicions that it was all a hoax intensified. A young paleontologist at Yale, O. C. Marsh, said on November 25, 1869, that "it is of very recent origin and a decided humbug."

By December all the evidence pointed toward a hoax. With pressure mounting, George Hull confessed how the entire fraudulent plan was devised. But by then, the giant was already a phenomenon, and the public continued coming to see it in growing numbers.

The giant was moved to Albany and then to New York City for exhibition. One of the greatest hucksters of all, P. T. Barnum, tried to buy the giant from its owners. When they refused to sell, Barnum had an imitation giant made, and he began displaying it in New York City. At one time, the giants were being exhibited only 2 blocks from each other. With Barnum's salesmanship behind his version, the imitation giant was soon outdrawing the original one.

The Cardiff Giant changed ownership several times over the ensuing years, and it was displayed on and off, depending on the whims of its current owner.

Finally in 1948, 80 years after it was carved out of stone, the giant was brought to the Farmers' Museum, one of the museums administered by the New York State Historical Association in Cooperstown. It is on display there today, considered to be part of the social history of the State of New York.

—R.T.

The Smithsonian Institution, Washington, D.C.

Mystery on the Mall . . . The millions of visitors to the Smithsonian Institution on the Mall in Washington, D.C., walk into an unsolved mystery. James Smithson, an Englishman who was born in France, who never saw the U.S. and never even corresponded with anyone in this country, left a fortune to found an American establishment to be known as the Smithsonian Institution "for the increase and diffusion of knowledge among men."

No one has yet discovered the reasons for his strange action. When Smithson was born in 1765 he was christened James Lewis Macie. His mother, Mrs. Elizabeth Macie, had been widowed before the boy was born. His real father, however, was Hugh Smithson, a wealthy Briton who was later knighted as the Duke of Northumberland and who legally changed his name to Hugh Percy.

While in college, young Macie signed papers "James Smithson" and thereafter kept that name. His estate (about $500,000) was bequeathed to the U.S. and was accepted after 8 years of congressional wrangling. The Institution was founded in 1846, and today some 20 million or more people wander through its buildings every year. Smithson's body was brought to the U.S. in 1904 and rests in the castlelike red brick Smithsonian Building.

Once called "America's Attic," the modern Smithsonian is crammed with treasures and trifles, oddities, relics, and a wealth of artistic, scientific, and historical material. Smithsonian officials call the Institution "the Trustee of America's Heritage."

The Wright Brothers' 1st airplane shares

space with Lindbergh's *Spirit of St. Louis*. The original Star-Spangled Banner that waved above Fort McHenry in 1814, now tattered and torn, hangs proudly "o'er the land of the free and the home of the brave." Rockets and spacecraft are in stark contrast with the Duryea horseless carriage of 1893–1894 and a Model T Ford.

Visitors to the Museum of History and Technology smile at a statue of George Washington created by Horatio Greenough, the 1st sculpture ever commissioned by Congress, but when it was unveiled in 1841 the whole town was shocked. The statue shows a seated Washington, naked to the waist and draped in a toga. Citizens called the sculpture "the naked Washington" and complained that our 1st President looked too much like a Roman Emperor. But the figure remains.

In addition to the *Spirit of St. Louis*, the displays attracting most attention are the famous Hope diamond, the array of inaugural gowns worn by all First Ladies, the *Apollo 11* Command Module, the dinosaurs in the Natural History Museum, and the pandas at the National Zoo.

The National Zoo is part of the Smithsonian, as are the Freer Art Gallery, the National Gallery of Art, the National Collection of Fine Arts, the John F. Kennedy Center for the Performing Arts, the Renwick Gallery, and the very new Joseph H. Hirshhorn Museum and Sculpture Garden housing some 6,000 art masterpieces. In addition, a new $40 million Air and Space Museum is to open July 4, 1976, with astronaut Michael Collins as its director.

If your time is limited, try visiting the National Air and Space Museum, the Hirshhorn Museum, the National Museum of Natural History, the Museum of History and Technology, and the Freer Gallery, all of which are on the Mall and close to one another. If you have more time, stroll a few blocks to see the National Portrait Gallery, the National Collection of Fine Arts, and the Renwick Gallery, or take a bus or taxi, or drive to the National Zoo.

Summer visitors may find the Smithsonian's Folk Life Festival in progress on the Mall. Performing arts groups representing many nations entertain with native music and dancing and arts and crafts. The festival usually lasts 2 or 3 weeks, but the time may be extended for the 1976 bicentennial.

Locations: Between 7th and 14th Streets, from Independence to Constitution Avenues, are the Smithsonian Building, the Arts and Industries Building, the Air and Space Building, the Freer Gallery of Art, the National Museum of History and Technology, the Museum of Natural History, and the Hirshhorn Museum and Sculpture Garden. *Hours:* 10 A.M.

to 5:30 P.M. (Summer months: 10 A.M. to 9 P.M.) Closed Christmas Day only.

—H.E.N.

NORTH

Sauk Centre, Minnesota

Main Street . . . Today, as America digs ever so deeply into the ground of its past, the little "Main Streets" of the U.S. struggle to survive. Running water, electricity, radio and television, along with the automobile and airplane, have wiped out most of our nation's "Main Streets."

Sauk Centre, Minn., however, lives on forever, even with its modern conveniences. Buried in the heartland of the country, you can still find small-town people here, people who have a feeling for the land and those about them.

Gopher Prairie was the name Sinclair Lewis gave to his fictional town in the 1920 novel *Main Street*. He described its principal thoroughfare: "Main Street is the climax of civilization. It was not only the uninspiring, unapologetic ugliness and the rigid straightness which overwhelmed her. It was the planlessness, the flimsy temporariness of the buildings. . . . Each man had built with the most valiant disregard of all the others." In his novel, Lewis disclaimed having used the Main Street in his hometown as the prototype. The Main Street in his book, he insisted, "is the continuation of Main Streets everywhere. The story would be the same in Ohio or Montana, in Kansas or Kentucky or Illinois. . . ."

Nevertheless, Gopher Prairie in Lewis's sensational *Main Street* was based on Sauk Centre, situated 105 mi. northwest of Minneapolis off Interstate 94. A stroll down the real Main Street today reveals oversized street signs reading, "Original Main Street," and a huge banner hangs between the Montgomery Ward and Sears, Roebuck stores reading, "Visit the Sinclair Lewis Boyhood Home and Museum." While Sauk Centre takes a masochistic pride in Lewis's book, a recent survey proved few of the residents had ever read any of the author's books. Still, the high school band is called "The Main Streeters."

The 4-block business district is still lined with one- and 2-story structures. Only the Palmer House Hotel—where Lewis worked as a substitute night clerk—rises a total of 3 stories (Minniemashie House in Gopher Prairie). Main Street, and indeed all of Sauk Centre, can and should be covered on a walking tour to get the feeling and flavor which the novelist's protagonist, Carol Kennicott, got when she arrived.

The restored family home stands 3 blocks off Main Street on Sinclair Lewis Avenue. It is designated a National Historic Landmark by the National Park Service, and a merit award winner for authenticity in restoration by the American Association for State and Local History.

The Bryant Library remains as one of the landmarks of Main Street and is the temporary home of the museum, which maintains a complete collection of all Lewis's works including many foreign editions. Most of the original letters and manuscripts, however, are in the library at Yale. Numerous photographs and tapes of lectures and interviews are a part of the Byrant Library's vast collection. Memorabilia also include Lewis's death certificate, and the urn which carried his ashes from Rome to Sauk Centre.

West of the business district, a scant mile along the old Burlington Northern Railroad track, is a bridge called the Stone Arch. It was here that Lewis, as a boy, used to sneak smokes. Still visible on the bridge are the initials he carved there.

Gopher Prairie might be a state of mind, but Sauk Centre remains real, even today. Lewis wrote 22 novels, including *Arrowsmith, Babbitt, Dodsworth,* and *Elmer Gantry.* He received the Nobel Prize for literature in 1930, and died alone in a clinic outside Rome on January 10, 1951. His simple gravestone stands in the family plot in the Sauk Centre cemetery, where a brother had scattered his ashes the year after his death.

Location: The Bryant Public Library is on Main Street. *Admission:* $1 for adults, 50¢ for high school students, and 25¢ for children; fee includes tours of both the museum and Lewis's boyhood home. *Hours:* Monday through Saturday, 10 A.M. to 4 P.M.; Sundays from 1 to 5 P.M., May through Labor Day.

—J.E.J.

Rugby, North Dakota

Center of North America . . . The little town of Rugby lies about 45 mi. from the Canadian border in the north central part of North Dakota. It has a population of less than 3,000 and a typical small-town atmosphere, but there are nevertheless a few distinctive things to set it apart from thousands of other small towns across the country.

Yes, Rugby has achieved some fame that makes its townspeople proud. The U.S. Geological Survey has indicated that Rugby is the geographical center of North America. From Rugby, you would have to travel 1,500 mi. to reach the Gulf of Mexico. Turning northward from Rugby, the Arctic archipelago is 1,500 mi. away. The distance to both the Atlantic and Pacific oceans is 1,500 mi., too.

So to commemorate this central location, the people of Rugby have erected a stone cairn with a plaque reading, "Geographical Center of North America, Rugby, N.D."

The monument is actually located about a mile south of the city of Rugby, adjacent to a Texaco gasoline station. It is constructed of rocks and held together with reinforcing rods and cement. Built in pyramid style, its base is 6' square, and it stands 21' high. Volunteers from Rugby assisted Boy Scouts in erecting the landmark. Lights keep the monument in full view after dark.

Rugby is located near U.S. Highway 2, and is surrounded by a vast undeveloped land area. The early explorers errroneously called this area the Great American Desert, and despite its natural beauty, it has not yet attracted enough people to cause a population crisis. In fact, throughout the entire State of North Dakota, the population now numbers almost 100,-000 less than it did in 1930. In its Chamber of Commerce brochures and reports, Rugby emphasizes that it is "a city with room for development and expansion in almost every direction . . ." with ". . . complete facilities for new industry and economic growth."

But even if Rugby never attains the status of a big city, there is still something very appealing about a small town that has remained largely unchanged in the 90 years since it was founded. The 1st train arrived here in August, 1885, bringing English immigrants, who immediately named the new town after Rugby, England.

Today, Rugby is the Pierce County seat. Its city hall houses a museum containing Indian artifacts found in the county, as well as some Spanish-American War relics.

Each June, Rugby plays host to the North Dakota State Championship Horse Show. Horses played a major role in its early development, too. It still depends primarily on the fertile farmland for its economic survival, and takes pride in the statewide awards it has won—for example, the Community Betterment Improvement Contest trophy in 1960. No skyscrapers can yet be found in Rugby, except for the towering grain elevators that are so integral to the town's economy.

About 40 mi. north of Rugby is another unusual landmark, the International Peace Garden, a 2,339-acre site laid out by both the State of North Dakota and the Commonwealth of Canada. "As long as man shall live, these 2 nations shall not take up arms against one another," reads the dedication to the garden, which is lush with the beauty of natural greenery. Admission to the park is free, and the grounds are open year round. Picnic areas are available, as are a lodge, cabins, and camping grounds. The entire State of North Dakota has adopted the theme of the park, calling itself the Peace Garden State and heralding that fact on its automobile license plates.

Lake Metigoshe State Park is not far from the International Peace Garden, and has one of the largest, most attractive lakes in the State. It is about an hour's drive from Rugby, and many of the townsfolk fish on the lake.

Rugby was once the home of N. P. Lindberg, who is credited with having originated the slogan "Say It with Flowers." At a national florists' convention in Chicago, he said, "In North Dakota, we say it with flowers." Those words were warmly received by the convention's delegates, who soon thereafter adopted the slogan as their own.

—R.T.

Dearborn, Michigan

Greenfield Village and the Henry Ford Museum . . . You take a walk through American history when visiting Greenfield Village and the Henry Ford Museum in Dearborn, Mich. A tour of the village puts you into the workrooms of men like Thomas Alva Edison, Orville and Wilbur Wright, the studies of Noah Webster or Robert Frost, or the courtroom of a young attorney from Illinois, who signed his name A. Lincoln. Gaze into the cockpits of the trimotor airplanes used by Adm. Richard E. Byrd on his 1st historic flights over both the North and South poles.

Something for every member of the family would best describe this outstanding museum complex devoted to our history and heritage. And it is fun, too. Ride a horse-drawn carriage, the oldest operating steam train, or even an old Model T.

What makes this so different from other museums? Men like Orville Wright and Edison were among those who personally supervised the restoration of some of the historic buildings, checking to be sure everything was correct and in its place. Had it not been for the foresight of Henry Ford, a simple man who had little formal education, the world would not have a treasure house such as this today, one where we can actually step back 300 years into the past and see how our ancestors and many famous Americans lived and worked.

The Wright Brothers Bicycle Shop and home—moved from Dayton, O., piece by piece, board by board, and brick by brick—stands today as a monument to the development of aviation. A few years back, an ambitious mayor in Dayton even tried to take the museum to court to make it give the building back to Dayton because Dayton was then ready to put up some kind of Wright memorial.

Step into the former Illinois courtroom where young Abe tried some of his 1st cases as a circuit-riding attorney. This building was like

many others now preserved in the village. All of them were going to rack and ruin and were about to be destroyed when Henry Ford interceded. His crews went to work, 1st detailing and blueprinting these buildings. Each board, shelf, or piece of glass was marked and catalogued. The pieces were then shipped off to Dearborn and rechecked to be sure everything was included. Curators would pore over documents, checking out every last detail to ascertain that the materials and pieces were reassembled correctly.

Henry Ford was a man dedicated to the smallest detail, whether it be in his vast automobile empire or his real love, the collections of Greenfield Village. He arranged to move Edison's electric laboratory from Menlo Park, N.J., to Dearborn, and it was the 1st building opened, on October 29, 1929—the date coinciding with the Golden Jubilee of Edison's invention of the 1st incandescent light.

All the glass bottles, chemicals, wiring, test equipment, and every piece of the building from foundation to roof were moved. Even the trash pile outside one of the windows, where Edison and his coworkers used to throw broken test tubes and other junk, was moved to Dearborn.

During the opening dedication, a very proud Henry Ford, beaming at what had been done, asked his friend Edison, "What do you think of it?" At that, Edison replied, "It is 99½% perfect." Shocked and with a worried look on his face, Ford exclaimed, "What is wrong?" "Well, Henry," Edison drawled, "we never used to keep the place so clean."

One of the almost unnoticed buildings in Greenfield Village is a little brick shed that originally stood at 58 Bagley Avenue in what is now downtown Detroit. Henry Ford's 1st successful automobile, the "Quadricycle," was built in this shed in 1896. As basement builders of boats and other machines continue to do today, Henry Ford built the car and then found it was too big to go through the doorway. You guessed it—he had to take a sledgehammer and knock away the door and bricks to get his machine into the street.

The adjoining Henry Ford Museum is a 14-acre indoor collection encompassing some of the finest decorative arts to be found. Included are pieces of priceless Paul Revere silver, fine clocks and watches, textiles, glass, pewter, and furniture. Each section is arranged chronologically to trace the development from Pilgrim times to the 20th century. A transportation section—including 12 railroad locomotives, one weighing over 600 tons, a host of famous airplanes, and 200 restored antique automobiles—makes up part of the collection.

Bring your camera when you visit. In addition to the permanent collections, a number of outstanding special events are held annually. These include: a national Sports Car Review, the Midwest Antiques Forum, a Garden Forum, the Old Car Festival, the Muzzle-Loaders Festival, a Country Fair, an Autumn Harvest Weekend, Famous Americans Exhibit, and a special Christmas observance from early December through the holidays.

Location: A few miles from Dearborn. *Admission:* village $2.50; museum $2.50; children under 6 admitted free. *Hours:* Both the village and museum are open daily (except Thanksgiving, Christmas, and New Year's). Summer hours, mid-June through Labor Day, 9 A.M. to 6 P.M. Winter hours are 9 A.M. to 5 P.M. weekdays, and 9 A.M. to 6 P.M. weekends and holidays.

Guide maps of both the museum and village are available in several languages including Spanish, French, German, and Japanese.

—J.E.J.

Terre Haute, Indiana

Eugene V. Debs Home . . . *"While there is a lower class, I am in it; while there is a criminal element, I am of it; while there is a soul in prison, I am not free!"* Those words, spoken by Eugene Debs more than half a century ago, concisely express the philosophy of the most prominent leader of the American socialist movement. Debs crusaded uncompromisingly for the socialist cause—a crusade that turned him into both a presidential candidate and a prison convict.

Debs has been called a great social thinker by his supporters, and an agitator by his critics. His admirers have been responsible for the preservation of the Eugene V. Debs home in Terre Haute, Ind. The 2-story, unpretentious white frame house has become both a National Historic Landmark and an official Indiana State Historic Landmark.

Since the death of Debs in 1926, several other attempts have been made to establish suitable memorials to the socialist leader. Such a tribute seemed fitting for the man who was a candidate for President 5 times (1900, 1904, 1908, 1912, and 1920), and who founded industrial unionism in the U.S. But there was always opposition to such memorials for an avowed socialist. Neither Terre Haute, nor the State of Indiana, nor the Federal Government seemed to want any part of the proposal in the beginning. A professor at Indiana State University bought the Debs home in the 1940s, hoping to convince the State to assume ownership of it and convert it into a historic shrine. But when the State declined, the professor finally sold the house to a fraternity.

The Debs home changed hands several more times, and was finally purchased in 1962 by a developer who planned to turn it into an apartment building. But 2 professors and an AFL-CIO official were able to buy the house from him at the last minute. They subsequently created the Eugene V. Debs Foundation, and the home was opened to public viewing in 1965. Five of the rooms in the Debs home have been restored and furnished. And each of them is a reminder of Debs's colorful career.

Debs was born in Terre Haute in 1855, and maintained his residence there all his life. He began his political career at the age of 25 when he became city clerk, and then 5 years later, he entered the Indiana legislature.

In 1893, Debs formed the 1st industry-wide union (the American Railway Union), and became an eloquent spokesman for the labor movement. "Debs! Debs! Debs!" shouted crowds of immigrant railroaders wherever he appeared. He negotiated and fought for them, and when he refused to comply with a Federal court injunction against a strike, he was jailed for 6 months.

Debs founded the Social Democratic party in 1898, which later became the Socialist party. He was its major spokesman and prime political figure.

A pacifist, Debs made an antiwar speech in 1918 condemning W.W. I, and he was arrested and convicted in Federal court under the Espionage Law. He was sentenced to a 10-year prison term in a Federal penitentiary in Atlanta, from which he ran his 1920 presidential campaign. He received nearly a million votes in that election, running as Convict #2273.

Debs, much to his surprise, was released from prison on Christmas Day, 1921, upon orders of President Harding. "It is the Government that should ask me for a pardon," he said.

When Debs died in 1926, hundreds of dignitaries attended his funeral in Terre Haute, including Norman Thomas, who delivered the day's most moving eulogy.

The Eugene V. Debs home was the residence of Debs and his wife, Kate, from 1890 until his death. They had bought the land for $4,000 and built the house upon it. Mrs. Debs designed the home's interior, planning a fireplace in every room except the maid's room (which is now known as Debs's bedroom). Mrs. Debs's favorite color, blue, is predominant throughout the house. The home is a prime example of Midwest mid-Victorian architecture, and it contains many pieces of the original Debs furniture and art objects.

Location: 451 No. 8th Street, 3 mi. north of Interstate 70. *Admission:* Free. *Hours:* Open daily except Saturday and Monday, from 1 to 5 P.M.

—R.T.

Cincinnati, Ohio

Delta Queen Riverboat . . . In a real-life nautical version of a melodramatic movie in which the prisoner keeps getting reprieves before being led down the last mile, the venerable *Delta Queen*—the last steam-powered stern-wheel riverboat offering overnight passenger service in the U.S.—has received several stays of life by Congress, which, among other things, allowed sentiment to overcome the stringent regulations of the 1966 Safety at Sea Law.

The antique paddle-wheeler, listed in the National Register of Historic Places, received exemptions in 1966, 1968, and 1973 because the *Delta Queen*'s superstructure (made largely of wood and treated with NASA-recommended fire-retardant intumescent paint—part of more than $1 million spent in renovations including fire-safety equipment) still can't meet, and can't be altered to meet, the fireproof ocean-vessel construction standards set by the 1966 law—which calls for vessels carrying 50 or more overnight passengers to have steel superstructures.

The current reprieve is until November 1978, by which time the line will have another, more modern riverboat in service. Meanwhile, America's most famous riverboat continues to ply the Mississippi and other inland waters with its distinctive red paddle-wheel (still the original 26-ton apparatus), trying to make up in nostalgia what it lacks in modern conveniences.

Surprisingly, the 50-year-old *Delta Queen* wasn't even intended for use on the Mississippi. The 258'-long hull, made in the early 1920s on the River Clyde, in Scotland near Glasgow, was shipped to Stockton, Calif., for final assembly and overnight employment between Sacramento and San Francisco, on the Sacramento River. Accordingly, the superstructure of oak, walnut, teak, mahogany, and ironwood was completed in 1926 and commissioned for use by the California Transportation Company.

Its career in California was rather unheralded until the U.S. Navy used the boat during W.W. II to ferry troops and the wounded in and about San Francisco Bay. Decommissioned in 1947, it suffered the ignominy of being auctioned. Highest bidder for the vessel was Tom Greene, president of a Cincinnati-based line of packet steamers.

Painstakingly "crated," the *Delta Queen* was towed down the Pacific coast, through the Panama Canal, up the Gulf of Mexico to New Orleans, and then on to dry dock in Pittsburgh, where the riverboat was remodeled to the tune of close to $750,000. Thereafter, the paddle-wheeler enjoyed moderate success from 1950 to 1958, but was in financial trouble by the time Californian Richard Simonton came along to restructure the company. In 1969, the company was sold again to its present owners, Overseas National Airways.

The sturdy 4-deck riverboat has a capacity of 192 overnight passengers, and 75 officers and crew. It cruises around 35,000 mi. each year in 17 States, and to more than 110 river towns—including a colorful cross section of the Midwest and Deep South. As it does only about 8 mph, passengers have plenty of time to savor the scenery.

Cruises vary in length. In late spring and summer, the ship operates out of its home port in Cincinnati, heads up to St. Paul in late summer, and also uses New Orleans as a port of embarkation. Ports of call on the "Lower Mississippi" are New Orleans, Baton Rouge, St. Francisville, Natchez, Vicksburg, and Memphis. On the "Upper Mississippi," there is Cape Girardeau, St. Louis, Hannibal, Nauvoo, Muscatine, La Crosse, and St. Paul. Moving onto the Ohio River, the riverboat visits Cairo, Paducah, Evansville, Louisville, Madison, Marietta, Wheeling, and Pittsburgh. On the Tennessee River, the vessel goes to Kentucky Lake, the largest man-made lake in the world. Lastly, on the Illinois River, the ship cruises to the Koster Farm, Starved Rock Park, and Peoria.

Shipboard life is another reflection of the past with calliope concerts, Dixieland bands belting out old favorites from showboat days, while banjo players strum familiar rhythms. Old movies, vaudeville acts, and sing-alongs also lend a yesteryear charm. A sort of antediluvian ambiance envelops the Orleans Room at show time.

A similar mood is generated at mealtimes, which are engagingly announced by a smiling waiter who circles each deck while playing the traditional riverboat chimes. Cuisine includes such hearty and vintage repasts as Southern fried chicken, catfish, and shrimp creole. Cocktails like the "Scarlett O'Hara" and the famed mint julep are served at such watering holes as the Mark Twain Lounge.

Lectures and talks aboard the riverboat tell how the craft operates and how it navigates through the various river channels, chutes, bends, bars, reaches, as well as locks and dams. Passengers also hear about the points of interest being passed, such as parks, farms, plantations, towns, monuments, and antebellum homes. There is also literature on the ports of call, stressing the various attractions, historical and otherwise.

The crew, from the captain or master of the ship down, also enjoys relating a few tall tales, part of the riverboat's folklore, and reliving famous steamboat races in which the *Delta Queen* still participates.

Location: Home port office: 322 E. 4th Street, Cincinnati, O. *Admission:* Reservations to sail are made through travel agents or with the line itself. Visitors may arrange to board on sailing nights and other occasions by contacting the line or its agents in the various ports of call. *Hours:* The cruise schedule is in effect for the greater part of each year.

—J.A.

St. Joseph, Missouri

Pony Express Stables . . . The pony express began in St. Joseph, Mo., on April 3, 1860, when a rider and his mount departed for Sacramento, Calif.—a journey of nearly 2,000 mi. This experiment was to determine if using the central continental route could shorten the time it took to send mail to and from the West Coast, help keep California in the U.S. and on the Union side during the anticipated war between the States, and—more than incidentally—secure the lucrative mail contract from the Federal Government.

Previously, there were 2 primary mail routes to California: by ship to Panama, overland at the Isthmus of Panama, and then by ship again to San Francisco, taking overall about 22 days; and the southern U.S. overland stagecoach ride known as the Ox-Bow Route, which was operated by the Butterfield Overland Company via St. Louis, Memphis, El Paso, and Los Angeles. The central route west from the Missouri River, though 1,000 mi. shorter, was far more hazardous and hence seldom used. With the Civil War imminent, California authorities feared the 1st 2 routes were subject to interference.

On the 1st ride west, the last westbound relay rider and his horse reached Sacramento on the 10th day (April 13, 1860) and was rewarded with a reception featuring bands, top-hatted civic dignitaries, and a cheering populace. A former jockey, by the name of John Fry, is believed by some to have been the 1st rider out of St. Joseph, while others contend the honor belongs to one Alex Carlyle. (April 3, departure day, was also the date that Bob Ford shot Jesse James in St. Joseph in 1882, which prompted a local wag to suggest a municipal slogan: "St. Joseph, the city which started the pony express and stopped Jesse James.")

Despite the fact that Congress was told that daily mail service by pony express could be performed for less than $1 million—much less than the amount paid to the Butterfield line—political pressures kept the newly organized Central Overland Express Stables from the mail contract. Though financially unsuccessful, the pony express men wrote a colorful chapter in American history and proved that the central route worked, providing speeded-up service until completion of the 1st telegraph line to California put it out of business in October, 1861.

At the outset, the owners advertised in this unabashedly honest fashion:

> Wanted: Young skinny wiry fellows, not over 18. Must be expert riders willing to risk death daily. Orphans preferred. Wages $25 per week. Apply Central Overland Express.

Some 80 to 100 men (a complete roster has never been established) took on the adventurous assignments, braving hostile Indians and unknown country. They made approximately 160 complete trips across the western half of the continent in the 19 months the company functioned. (The record mail shipment was President Lincoln's 1st Inaugural Address, which took 7 days 17 hours.) The company also employed some 300–400 stock traders, stationmen, and helpers, who manned about 190 relay stations where fresh riders and horses were ready and waiting when the equestrian postman came in sight. This change of horses, and sometimes riders, was accomplished in 2 minutes or less.

Each pony express rider received a small Bible with the firm's name on it, upon which he took an oath promising good behavior, loyalty to the company, and allegiance to the U.S. and the Union.

The original stables were built in 1858 by a freighting and stagecoach entrepreneur, Ben Holladay, who became Missouri's 1st multimillionaire (though his fortune eventually crumbled). Holladay's outfit was known as Pike's Peak Stables—since much of its business was to the Colorado territory—until the company was employed by the Central Overland. With Holladay getting a piece of the action, Central Overland was begun by the firm of Russell, Majors and Waddell, with William H. Russell the guiding spirit behind the pony express concept. In the 1850s, St. Joseph was an increasingly prosperous city. Many fortunes had been made by outfitting the emigrants who used the city as a gateway to the California gold mines. With the Hannibal & St. Joseph Railroad finally reaching the growing city from the east, the city fathers fully expected St. Joseph to outstrip other Midwestern communities such as Chicago.

When the mail reached the city by train, it was transferred to the *mochilas* (the large flaps of leather with lockable pockets covering the riders' saddles). The riders began by galloping up to the ferry landing at the foot of either Jules or Francis streets, to cross over the Missouri and begin their odyssey over the plains and mountains.

The actual stables were some 125' long with a 60' frontage, covered by a shingle roof supported by heavy timbers, and with pine board walls. There were stalls for 200 horses. The stables were rebuilt in 1888 by new owners, the St. Joseph Transfer Company. The exterior, except the roof, was rebuilt with brick but the timbers and much of the other material was left intact.

The Chamber of Commerce purchased the stables in 1946 to ensure their preservation as a historic site, with a foundation created in 1950 by the M. K. Goetz Brewing Company to further this goal. Subsequently, the stables were opened to the public as a museum in 1959 and deeded the following year to the St. Joseph Museum. Exhibits tell the early history of St. Joseph, with emphasis on pony express days, and such vintage items as mail-sorting desks, advertisements for riders, saddles and *mochilas*, photographs of riders and relay stations, and other memorabilia.

Location: 914 Penn Street, St. Joseph, Mo. *Admission:* Free. *Hours:* May to mid-September, 9 A.M. to 5 P.M.; Sundays and holidays, 2 P.M. to 5 P.M. Winter months: Open only for school classes or special-interest organizations by advance request.

—J.A.

Hannibal, Missouri

Mark Twain Boyhood Home and Museum . . . Mark Twain's novels conjure up childhood memories in everyone. Twain (Samuel Clemens) was able to capture the essence of boyhood in his writing—its innocence, its humor, and its hard times—as no one else could. *The Adventures of Huckleberry Finn*, his finest novel, is probably the most influential piece of American fiction ever written.

Much of the material for Twain's books was collected while he was growing up in Hannibal, Mo., a town he described as "a little democracy . . . full of liberty, equality and 4th of July." In 1839, 4-year-old Sam Clemens moved to Hannibal with his parents. Five years later, his father built the little home which became the setting for incidents in 2 of his books, *The Adventures of Tom Sawyer* and *The Adventures of Huckleberry Finn*. The house stands today as a shrine to the great American humorist and novelist.

Hannibal, located along the Mississippi River about 100 mi. northwest of St. Louis, is now an industrial center with a population of about 19,000. As the city has expanded, the legend of Twain has grown with it, and he has been honored in every conceivable way. Hotels, restaurants, museums, parks, bridges, and shopping centers in Hannibal have all been named after the author or the characters he created.

The Mark Twain Boyhood Home was where Clemens lived until the age of 18, whereupon he left town to embark on his literary career. The house is a simple and plain white 2-story frame structure. It is now furnished with authentic period pieces from the early days in Hannibal.

Clemens's father died when Sam was 12, and the youngster lived with his mother and 4 brothers and sisters in the neat white house. His mother was a gentle and influential woman, losing her temper with young Sam only once, when he returned home after nearly drowning in Bear Creek, a forbidden swimming site.

The white board fence that borders the Mark Twain Boyhood Home is the site of a community-wide celebration each July. A nationwide competition, the National Tom Sawyer Fence Painting Contest, is held to determine the best young fence painter.

Year round, tourists are able to take some whitewash brushes and pose as if they were painting the fence. But no whitewash is actually used.

Adjoining the Clemens home is the Mark Twain Museum, where a collection of rare books, original manuscripts, furniture, clothing, and photographs is on display. The museum was dedicated in 1937.

Once you've visited the Mark Twain Boyhood Home and Museum, it would be only natural to cross the street to the Becky Thatcher House. Becky was one of the key characters in *Tom Sawyer*, and she was patterned after a real-life character, Laura Hawkins, who lived in the house across from young Clemens. That house has been preserved, too, and for Twain, it represented pure elegance.

The Thatcher house was garnished with crystal-prismed table lamps, mirrors, and mahogany candlestick holders. Today you'll find remnants in the bedroom of what attracted young Sam to Laura (Becky). A blue silk dress, a cambric nightgown, and a petticoat are all laid out neatly on the bed, and long white lisle stockings are draped on the chair.

There are other reminders of Twain throughout Hannibal, like the Pilaster House, where the Clemens family lived for a very brief period of time. It is one of the most architecturally interesting homes in town, with its wooden Greek columns which adorn the walls.

At the foot of "Cardiff Hill," where Sam and his friends played, statues of Tom Sawyer and Huck Finn have been erected. The life-size bronze figures are by Fred S. Hibbard.

The Mark Twain Cave is located 2 mi. southeast of Hannibal on Missouri Route 79. In *Tom Sawyer*, this was the cave in which

Tom and Becky Thatcher became lost and Injun Joe died. The cave is well-lit and maintains a dry, uniform 52° F. temperature.

Location: The Boyhood Home and Museum are at 208 Hill Street. *Admission:* Except for the cave, almost all other Mark Twain attractions in Hannibal are free. *Hours:* The Home and Museum are open daily (except Thanksgiving, Christmas, and New Year's) from 8 A.M. to 8 P.M. between June 1 and September 1; from September 1 to May 30, 8 A.M. to 5 P.M.

—R.T.

SOUTH AND SOUTHWEST

Dry Tortugas Islands, Florida

Fort Jefferson . . . One of America's most unusual national monuments was at one time the most dreaded prison in the country. Fort Jefferson, located on a tiny coral islet about 120 mi. west of the southern tip of Florida, had a reputation in the 19th century as the most evil of penal institutions.

Actually, Fort Jefferson was not originally built to be a prison, but instead was a military emplacement off the shores of America, designed to strengthen the nation's security. It was to be the Gibraltar of America.

Construction of Fort Jefferson began in 1846. All materials were transported from Philadelphia, 1,300 mi. away by sea. The immense structure became the largest mass of unreinforced masonry ever constructed by Americans. It is a 6-sided structure surrounding a plot of land as big as 20 football fields. The 50'-high walls are built right on the Gulf. Once the structure was completed, the Government shipped in 400 guns, which were mounted in place to "assure the country's well-being."

But Fort Jefferson, built at a cost of $1 a brick, turned out to be a fiasco. The Army discovered much too late that the water around the fort was so shallow that it would be impossible for enemy boats to travel within cannon range of the islet.

Realizing that the fort was useless for military purposes, the Government then decided to turn it into a prison. Beginning during the Civil War, therefore, it was used to house convicts.

Fort Jefferson's most famous prisoner arrived shortly after the war ended. His name was Dr. Samuel Mudd, and in a vengeful trial that went beyond the bounds of justice, he was convicted of conspiring to assassinate President Abraham Lincoln. He was sentenced to life imprisonment and was sent to Fort Jefferson in chains.

As was proved in later years, Dr. Mudd was in no way involved with the murder of President Lincoln. But through only circumstantial evidence and the hysteria of the moment, he was convicted and sentenced to spend the rest of his life in the country's most feared prison. Dr. Mudd had never seen or heard of John Wilkes Booth until about 5 hours after the assassination, when Booth and one of his coconspirators knocked on the doctor's door. Booth had broken his leg while escaping from Ford's Theater, and he desperately needed medical attention. Dr. Mudd, knowing nothing about the assassination at that time, set Booth's leg, bound it up, and convinced Booth and his friend to spend the remainder of the night recuperating at his house. Before departing the next morning, Booth paid the bill under an assumed name and fled.

When authorities learned that Booth had spent the night at Dr. Mudd's home in southern Maryland, the doctor was immediately arrested. Although the physician repeatedly asserted that he knew nothing of the plot to murder the President, the courts acted swiftly and sent him to Fort Jefferson.

When Dr. Mudd arrived at the prison in the middle of the Gulf of Mexico, it was filled not only with other convicts, but with mosquitoes as well. Carrying deadly yellow-fever germs, the flying insects attacked everyone on the island with abandon—prisoners, guards, soldiers, and officials alike. There were times when the fatal fever spread so rapidly that men were dying faster than they could be buried.

In the midst of one of the most horrifying of these epidemics, Dr. Mudd volunteered to help treat the victims of the fever. This humanitarian gesture on his part surprised some prison officials, who had previously instructed guards to give "that Lincoln murderer" the harshest of treatment while incarcerated. Dr. Mudd had been chained to the floor of his cell and badly abused by guards, but he still asked to help treat those who had been attacked by the fever. Even though he contracted the ailment himself, he survived and helped others through the ordeal.

Meanwhile, back in Washington, Dr. Mudd's wife was involved in a mission of her own: trying to secure her husband's release from prison. After 4 years, she finally succeeded in getting him "pardoned" for a crime he never committed.

Not long after Dr. Mudd departed, the rest of the prisoners left too, for the prison was closed down. Now Fort Jefferson is inhabited only by mosquitoes. In 1934, it became a national monument.

—R.T.

San Antonio, Texas

The Alamo . . . One thing is sure when you drive into downtown San Antonio, Tex. You won't miss the Alamo. Highway signs stretched across every road, bigger than those on a super-highway, guide your path.

Strangely, when at last you come upon it, there is a marked impression of its being very small. And small it is indeed, compared to almost everything else in Texas. Yet this collection of rock and stone and clay, with its fine collection of memorabilia, stands ever so tall in the eyes and hearts of its curators.

Outside the huge and heavy front doors, with their antique hinges and large handles, the City of San Antonio bustles as though there were no tomorrow. But once behind the confines of the outer door of the mission, it seems as if you have gone through the looking glass into another day.

The building and grounds abound in neatness and history. Here is a monument to the great men who fought and died for the Republic of Texas, a nation whose life span was less than 10 years. Perhaps it has been embellished even more because of a pair of legendary characters who were among the little band of troopers that held off thousands of Mexican soldiers. It was at the Alamo that Davy Crockett of Tennessee and Jim Bowie of Georgia stood their last ground, fighting to the very end.

The Alamo's story began when Mexico invited Americans to found colonies in Texas back in the 1820s, the purpose being to help fill sparsely populated, Indian-controlled areas. The newcomers got land free and in return became Mexican citizens. Having lived in the U.S., naturally they objected to trial without jury and not having a voice in government.

Gen. Antonio López de Santa Anna overthrew the constitutional Government, made himself dictator, and marched north in order to bring Texas to its knees. Crossing the Rio Grande, he attacked the Alamo, the stone-walled mission at San Antonio. A garrison of only 145 men defended this mission.

Col. William Barret Travis, a 27-year-old lawyer, served as commandant of the embattled troops. His declaration: "I shall never surrender nor retreat. I am determined to sustain myself as long as possible and die like a soldier who never forgets what is due to his honor and that of his country. Victory or Death."

The battle began on February 23, 1836. Creeping through enemy lines, a small group of reinforcements arrived on the 8th day of the siege, bringing the total strength up to 187 men. They faced attack by from 6 to 7 thousand.

On the 15th day of March the garrison was stormed. It was defended stone by stone. According to Joe, Colonel Travis's black body ser-vant and one of the 2 survivors, as reported in the *Memphis Enquirer*:

> The attack was suddenly made at 3 o'clock in the morning, after 14 days' siege. It was unexpected, as no alarm except a single voice crying out, "Col. Travis, the Mexicans are coming!" was heard from the guard on the wall; the picket guard, from whom nothing was heard, having probably been killed. Col. Travis sprang from his blanket with his sword and his gun, mounted the rampart, and seeing the enemy under the mouths of the cannon with scaling ladders, discharged his double-barreled gun down upon them; he was immediately shot, his gun falling down upon the enemy and himself within the fort. The Mexican general leading the charge mounted the walls by means of a ladder, and seeing the bleeding Travis, attempted to behead him; the dying colonel raised his sword and killed him! . . . The lady of Lieut. Dickinson was within the fort, and begged to share the honorable fate of her husband; Santa Anna, honor to his name—thrice honor to his name!—here proved himself a soldier and protected her. . . .

A Mexican version of the Alamo's fall states that the defenders, after a long night of carousing, were all drunk at the time of the attack, and offered no resistance when Santa Anna's troops walked in and slaughtered them.

After the massacre, General Santa Anna dispatched a Mexican soldier with a flag to lead the 2 survivors—Joe and the widow Dickinson—to Gen. Sam Houston's camp. The Mexican soldier also delivered a note offering the Texans peace and general amnesty if they would lay down their arms and submit to Santa Anna's Government.

At this point the people of Texas abandoned their occupations and pursuit of peace, and determined to take up arms until every Mexican east of the Rio del Norte was "exterminated."

On the 21st of April, the Texans, 600 strong under Houston, pushed close to Santa Anna's camp near a fork of the Brassos and Sabine rivers. According to military journals, General Houston addressed his troops. "Soldiers," said he, "there is the enemy, do you want to fight?" "Yes!" was the shout. "Well, then," he said, "let us eat our dinner, and then I will lead you into battle!" They obeyed the order to eat, and immediately thereafter, marched off to the attack, shouting, "Remember the Alamo!" Houston's brigade made mincemeat of the Mexican Army, captured the general, and achieved independence for Texas. When it was over,

nearly 700 Mexicans were killed and 600 prisoners were taken.

In 1845, Texas was annexed to the U.S.

Traveling to the Alamo today, you can't miss
it . . . just follow the signs.

—J.E.J. & The Eds.

Tombstone, Arizona

How does a small community isolated in the
Arizona desert ever achieve any notoriety? It's
not an easy accomplishment, but Tombstone
did it—the hard way. In 8 quick years in the
latter part of the 19th century, Tombstone
emerged from obscurity, its fame due to a
heavy dose of Western violence. Many people
died in the streets of Tombstone during that
era. Others found wealth in the silver mines,
but then quickly left town to protect their
money and their persons.

Tombstone thus returned to being a ghost
town at the turn of the century. Even today,
its population is only 1,500 (about 13,000 less
than at its peak), although many of the buildings erected in the 1880s are still standing. The
town, nevertheless, still has some vitality left in
it.

The commotion is particularly heavy during
the annual Helldorado Days celebration. For 3
days in mid-October, townspeople re-create the
notorious gunfights, hangings, and other blood-
splattering events that marred the town's beginnings. It's one horror story after another, as
visitors are "treated" to a program of events
which includes "Shooting of Marshal White,"
"Lynching of John Heath," "Cold-Blooded
Murder," "The Brisbee Massacre," and "The
Gunfight at the O. K. Corral."

That battle at the O. K. Corral was the
showdown in 1881 that left Billie Clanton and
the McLowery Brothers dead, the victims of
Virgil and Wyatt Earp and Doc Holliday. Actually, the bloodbath occurred not at the corral, but in a nearby alley. Today, fiber glass
life-size figures have been stationed in the spots
each gunslinger stood that day. Nearby, a
black-hatted dummy will challenge you to out-
draw him—at 25¢ a try.

When the tourists aren't converging on
Tombstone during Helldorado Days, the 4-mi.-
sq. town is a quiet, mellow place whose prime
appeal is its warm, dry climate, which lures
sufferers with respiratory ailments or arthritis.
The moral climate has changed there, too: For
the 1st time within memory, churches now
outnumber bars in Tombstone, 5 to 2.

There was one period recently when some
fast-talking promoters moved into Tombstone
and tried to commercialize and exploit the
small town. One promoter attempted to sell
square-inch plots of Boot Hill cemetery, but
the City Council stopped him.

More recently (and more legitimately), some
wealthy socialites from Detroit have organized
Tombstone Historic Adventures, and have restored many of the community's well-known
buildings and sites: the Wells Fargo Museum,
which contains 75,000 items from the Old
West; the Oriental Steakhouse, once a saloon
and gambling hall, which was partly owned by
Wyatt Earp in the 1880s; and the Crystal Palace, which once contained the office of town
marshal Virgil Earp.

Boot Hill, located off U.S. 80 at the north
end of town, is the burial place of (as the
name implies) those who died with their boots
on. One of the markers, resting over 3 rock-
covered graves, reads: "Tom McLowery, Frank
McLowery, Billie Clanton, 'murdered on the
streets of Tombstone.' "

Most of the other graves are unmarked, and
are the resting sites of many of the outlaws
who streamed into Tombstone in the 1880s.
There were so many killings in the town that
peace came only after President Chester A. Arthur threatened to impose martial law in the
community. Tombstone somehow survived all
its crises, earning it the motto "The town too
tough to die."

Mining production has been almost nonexistent since the turn of the century, although periodically some attempt is made to discover
new treasures. One of the Old West's richest
mines, the State of Maine Mine, was reopened
late in 1973. The Sierra Mineral Management
Corporation, which is doing the mining, leased
rights to the mine from the grandchildren of
its original owner, John Escapule, who staked
the 1st claim in 1876.

There are tours available at some of the
other, more dormant mines. Hourly tours pass
through the Goodenough Mine, which provides viewers a glimpse of how high-grade ore
was extracted. The temperature inside the
mine is a constant 53° F., so if you're planning
to take the tour, bring along a sweater or
jacket.

Editor John P. Clum's 1st column in the
Tombstone Epitaph in 1880 read: "Tombstone is a city set upon a hill, promising to vie
with ancient Rome, in a fame different in character but no less important." Although it's
debatable whether Tombstone can be compared to ancient Rome in any aspect, the
townspeople in the Arizona community seem
content with things the way they are.

—R.T.

WEST

San Jose, California

The 5½-Million-Dollar Ghosthouse . . .
Schubert had his *Unfinished Symphony*—Sarah
Winchester, her Unfinished Mansion. Between

1884, when the widow Winchester moved from Connecticut to San Jose, Calif., and 1922, when she died at the age of 83, one of the largest, weirdest, and most expensive private residences in the U.S. was "under construction." Even after 158 rooms had been built, rebuilt, and rebuilt yet again, the mansion, a $5.5-million monument to grief and guilt, was never completed. And it never will be.

In 1862, Sarah Pardee married William Wirt Winchester, whose father had manufactured the rifle that bore his name. Sarah's only child died in infancy. When her husband died of pulmonary tuberculosis in 1881, Sarah Winchester inherited his $20-million fortune, but it did not console her; she feared that the souls of the thousands of people (many of them Indians) who had been killed by Winchester rifles had cursed the fortune and would haunt her. A spiritualist medium intensified her fears and suggested that she appease the vengeful spirits by building a house that would attract the good, protective ghosts, including her husband's, but would keep the dangerous riffraff phantoms away.

Nobody knows just why she selected San Jose as the site for her wondrous house, but the millionairess' arrival in that town stirred up gossip and tall tales that persist to this day. The unvarnished truth, however, is strange enough. She began by hiring 22 carpenters, and then added a platoon of landscape gardeners who planted a 6' cypress hedge to conceal her endeavors from prying eyes; upkeep of the hedge alone required the services of 7 Japanese gardeners. During the 38 years the Widow Winchester lived there, the sound of hammers and saws never ceased. Crews of carpenters—an average of 16 men at a time, some of whom worked on the house for 20 years—labored Sundays, holidays, even Christmases, installing the 10,000 windows (some of them barred), 5 fully equipped kitchens, 13 bathrooms, 5 heating systems, 3 elevators, 48 fireplaces—all hand-carved of the finest woods—miles of secret passageways, 40 stairways (some ending in midair), and 2,000 doors, many of which opened on solid walls!

Hundreds of rooms were built and torn down again because they didn't turn out according to the architectural plan. This was not surprising, inasmuch as Mrs. Winchester herself, with no architectural training, made up the plan as she went along, sometimes sketching plans on the spot on any material handy. She depended upon her foreman to interpret her crude sketches. She *was* inventive; some of the mansion's features were decades ahead of their time. There was an intercom system connecting all the rooms. Outside window shutters could be opened and closed from the inside, by

operating cranks. The fireplaces—one room had 4!—had the 1st ashpits with hinged iron lids, and concealed wood boxes. The washtubs in the laundry had built-in washboards. Gas lights operated at the touch of a button. No expense was spared—the key to the front door, and even some of the screws, were of solid gold. The beautiful blended with the bizarre: Posts were installed upside down, chimneys stopped short of the roof, bathrooms had glass walls, some rooms had 13 windows, a greenhouse had 13 gables. Most of the stairways had 13 steps; one, though, had 44 steps and 7 turns, but rose only 9'. A huge bell tower was inaccessible except by climbing over the rooftops; it contained a smooth, unscalable well down which hung the bell rope, which could be pulled only from an underground labyrinth.

The Winchester House, officially designated a California State Historical Landmark in 1973, remains a fascinating enigma, typified by 2 cryptic messages inlaid in the stained glass windows of the mysterious Grand Ballroom, which was never completed (construction was interrupted by the earthquake of 1906, and never resumed). One inscription reads, "Wide unclasp the tables of their thoughts"; the other, "These same thoughts people this little world."

Location: 525 S. Winchester Blvd., San Jose, Calif. *Admission:* Adults: $2.50; children 6–12: $1.00; children under 6 admitted free; price includes a one-hour guided tour and admission to the Winchester Museum. *Hours:* Summer: 9 A.M. to 6 P.M. Winter: 9 A.M. to 4:30 P.M. Open every day except Christmas.
—C.E.

San Francisco, California

Alcatraz Island . . . For 30 years "the Rock" had one of the most forbidding and chilling reputations of any place on earth. Its impenetrable isolation, the near-impossibility of escape, and tales of hair-raising brutality behind the walls fed the legend. Federal prison officials did little to challenge it, reasoning that the more foreboding it sounded, the more the threat of spending the rest of their days there would deter would-be troublemakers in other jails. Adding to the mystique were Hollywood movies about life inside, with tight-lipped wardens, sadistic guards, scheming cons, and daring escapes.

Although physical mistreatment of prisoners was not allowed—in fact the food was considered the best in the Federal prison system—the harsh regime, the absence of all news of the outside world, and a tough work schedule made life far from pleasant. Adding to the sense of deprivation were the pleasure boats that daily circled the island and the bright lights of San Francisco across the bay. Because of the Code of Silence—abolished after a few years—inmates were not allowed to talk to each other under threat of a stretch in isolation, the standard and dreaded punishment for any infraction of the rules. No outside newspapers or radios were allowed, and letters and visits were restricted to imparting family news. One of the few instances of the world's intruding was when the warden posted a notice that Pearl Harbor had been bombed.

Isla de los Alcatraces (Isle of the Pelicans), as it was named by Spanish explorer Juan Manuel de Avala in 1775, sat barren and unpopulated until after the California Gold Rush, when the U.S. Army began fortifying it as a defense post for San Francisco Bay. After the need for such a fortification passed, the Army, with its fondness for uninhabitable places, used it for a military prison. Detainees included deserters who chose not to fight in the Spanish-American War, troublesome Indians, and, during and after W.W. I, conscientious objectors and the victims of Att. Gen. Mitchell Palmer's raids on political dissidents and labor agitators.

Alcatraz became a Federal prison in 1934 in response to the rising crime rate of the Depression and Prohibition years. As new Federal laws against bank robbing and kidnapping brought the "G-Men" increasingly into action, more and more of those on the "Most Wanted" list filled the country's jails and did their best to break out of them. The answer was a new escape-proof prison and Alcatraz seemed the perfect choice. James A. Johnston, a leading penologist and the 1st of 4 wardens, was dispatched to convert the island into the world's tightest cage. White-haired and soft-spoken, Johnston was nevertheless one of the toughest men on Alcatraz. It was his custom to allow prisoners to approach him from the rear, double file, as they marched from the dining hall. Only once did an inmate take advantage of that—severely beating the warden, and getting a few knocks himself from the guards—but Johnston soon returned to his post and no one laid a hand on him again.

One of the 1st and coolest escapes from Alcatraz was in 1903, during the military prison days, when 4 inmates forged themselves pardons, bribed a guard to mail them to the commander, and walked out free. Hitting the shore, 3 of them did the most likely thing. They headed for the nearest bar and soon after were picked up dead drunk. The 4th was smart enough to do his drinking farther afield and was never caught. Such stratagems had no chance in the new Alcatraz. The handpicked staff was incorruptible and in addition to the high walls, machine-gun-carrying guards, and double-locked doors, the cold waters of the bay were a further deterrent to escape. Only

George Raft, Edward G. Robinson, and John Paul Scott are known to have escaped by swimming, the 1st 2 in the movies. Scott made it in real life but was soon found, exhausted, on the shore. Of 26 would-be escapees, 8 were shot or drowned, 13 were captured, and 5 remained unaccounted for. Officials presumed them dead.

The number of prisoners was kept low— about 250 at any one time—and in its 30 years Alcatraz held a total of only a little over 1,000 men. Best-known among them were the "Big Four": Al Capone; kidnapper and bank robber Alvin Karpis (both Karpis and Capone were once listed as Public Enemy No. 1), George "Machine Gun" Kelly; and "Doc" Barker, who, in his own words, was "shot to hell" during an escape attempt. In later years both gangster Mickey Cohen and the shadowy Frank Carbo, who once controlled organized boxing, did time there. Another famous inmate, for different reasons, was Robert Stroud, "the Bird Man of Alcatraz," who was the author of highly respected scientific books on bird diseases.

When it closed in 1963, Alcatraz was crumbling, anachronistic, and the most expensive of Federal prisons, costing the taxpayer $15 a day for each inmate.

Alcatraz had sat empty for a year when a party of 5 Sioux Indians landed on the island and claimed it on the basis of a U.S. treaty with their nation which allowed Indians off the reservation to claim unused Federal land. Government officials showed no more inclination to honor that treaty than any other Indian treaty and the party soon left. In November of 1969, while San Franciscans were debating a grandiose scheme to turn the former penitentiary into a space museum and amusement center, a group of 89 men, women, and children representing 78 Indian tribes occupied the island, hoisted a blue flag bearing a red tepee and peace pipe, and prepared to make the island their home. Their manifesto said in part:

We have learned that violence breeds only more violence and we therefore have carried on our occupation of Alcatraz in a peaceful manner, hoping the Government will act accordingly. . . . Be it known, however, that we are quite serious in our demand to be given ownership of this island. . . . We are here to stay.

After 2 cold, bleak winters the number of settlers had dwindled to 15 and on June 11, 1971, Federal marshals and the Coast Guard forcibly but peacefully removed them.

From its 1st day as a Federal penitentiary, Alcatraz held an attraction for tourists, even if they could see it only through high-powered telescopes. Picture postcards of the island, with "Having Wonderful Time—Wish You Were Here" printed across them, were popular items. In the fall of 1973 Alcatraz, now part of the National Park Service's Golden Gate recreation area, was opened to the public. Visitors can see the cell blocks, visit the "deep 6" where men were held in isolation, the visiting room where, among others, Mama Capone came to see Al, and the cell where the "Bird Man" did his studying and writing. For some it is claustrophobic and oppressing; for others, walking through the Big House is the thrill of a lifetime.

Check locally for time schedules and current boat fees to the island.

—D.P.

San Simeon State Park, California

Hearst–San Simeon Estate . . . Its costs have been estimated at $20 million to $50 million, it held only a part of what was undoubtedly the largest art collection ever owned by one man, and it had a private zoo with nearly 100 species of animals. San Simeon once spread over 200,000 acres with 50 mi. of ocean front, and here, during the opulent '20s and into the Depression '30s, newspaper magnate William Randolph Hearst and his "good friend," ex-follies girl and film actress Marion Davies, entertained movie stars and statesmen, the famous and would-be famous of an era.

San Simeon also was the model for the Xanadu of Orson Welles's film *Citizen Kane* just as Hearst himself was the model for the portrait of Kane, a restless, acquisitive tycoon who died murmuring "Rosebud"—a reference to the childhood sled that symbolized all that he wanted in life but could not have.

Nearly every Friday a procession of automobiles or a private train would head north from Hollywood for a weekend at San Simeon. An ebullient Charles Chaplin was a frequent guest and Bernard Shaw dropped in during his celebrated tour of the U.S. Apparently he and Charlie did not share a weekend and history was cheated of what would have been a choice encounter. Winston Churchill and President and Mrs. Coolidge were also entertained.

During the day, visitors were free to choose for themselves among the amusements of the vast ranch. But in the evening all gathered in the appropriately named Assembly Room for the one drink per person that teetotaler Hearst allowed. Promptly at 9 P.M. he and Miss Davies led the company into the elaborate dining room where formal dress was banned and paper napkins and ketchup bottles mingled with the gold dining service. After all, this was

"the ranch" as Hearst always called it, just a simple place for the family to gather.

It had once been exactly that, Camp Hill, a family picnic spot on the San Simeon ranch Hearst inherited from his cattle baron father, along with a fortune that Hearst increased through his brand of sensational journalism. In 1919 he began to transform Camp Hill into *La Cuesta Encantada*—The Enchanted Hill. Until he died over 30 years later, Hearst continued building, rebuilding, and extending. The baroque towers atop *La Casa Grande*, the main house, replaced an earlier pair that "the Chief" didn't like, and the Neptune pool, probably the largest heated outdoor pool in the world, was enlarged twice before he was satisfied with it.

From his Gothic suite on the 3rd floor, Hearst ran his newspaper empire, supervised constant buying for his collections, and occasionally took to the airwaves to attack Roosevelt's "Raw Deal," England, and communism. While he lived and worked in baronial splendor, Hearst's own bedroom was relatively simply furnished, and was smaller than any of the estate's guest rooms.

An avid, even feverish, collector, Hearst stuffed San Simeon with his spoils, which included not only paintings, antique furnishings, and statues but entire rooms removed from European castles. His taste could most politely be called "eclectic"—embracing classical nude, medieval penitent, and Renaissance dandy.

Overseeing the vast and never-ending construction job was a diminutive and self-effacing woman named Julia Morgan, the 1st woman to earn an architecture degree from Paris's l'École des Beaux Arts. She began working with Hearst when San Simeon was still largely a dream and spent the rest of her active life turning his caprices into stone and mortar.

No practical objection stood in the way of a Hearst wish for long. When Julia Morgan pointed out his private rooms could not have the view he wanted because that view was from the roof, he ordered another story added and named it the Celestial Suite. If a grove of trees was in the way, Hearst, who could not stand to see a tree cut down, had the complete grove carefully transplanted. When he decided to install an entire set of Gothic choir stalls, to match one he already had, price was no object in tracking down and buying individual stalls from a multitude of owners. Rare animals from all over the world were brought in for his private zoo, housed not in cages but in specially enclosed acreage.

Hearst managed to outspend a personal income estimated at $15 million a year, one million going annually for his collections, and more millions allotted for the tremendous costs of building and maintaining San Simeon and other sumptuous residences. Early in W.W. II the estate was closed for a time, partly for economy, but also because Hearst thought the towers of *La Casa Grande* a likely target for Japanese submarines.

Later Hearst returned to his dream palace but it was never the same. His companies had been reorganized, reducing both his control and personal income. San Simeon was mortgaged and nearly lost but no one would foreclose on a white elephant. The zoo was given to municipal collections, although a few strays remained and their progeny can still be seen wandering the nearby hills.

Even now he continued to add to *La Casa Grande*, installing an indoor pool worthy of a Roman Emperor. Its imported Italian tiles were laid in intricate designs by imported Italian workmen. He died while making plans for the addition of another wing.

Hearst willed San Simeon to the people of California but the State was initially reluctant to take on a property that had an estimated annual upkeep of over $100,000 without the extra costs of entertaining Bernard Shaw, Winston Churchill, and half of Hollywood. When it finally opened to the public in 1958 one of the 1st guests is said to have asked, "Where is Rosebud?"

Three 2-hour tours are available to visitors at San Simeon. Tour I takes visitors through the grounds, one guesthouse, the 1st floor of the main building, and Hearst's private theater. Tour II includes the libraries and approximately 26 rooms in the upper floors of the main building. Tour III covers the last-completed section of the estate plus the garden and pool areas. It is advised that visitors begin with Tour I. You may obtain tickets up to 60 days in advance by writing: Hearst Reservation Office, Dept. of Parks and Recreation, Box 2390, Sacramento, Calif. 95811. Tickets may be purchased at the San Simeon ticket booth, but visitors should arrive early, as all tours are frequently sold out by midmorning.

Admission: Tours I and III: $4 adults, $2 children 6–18; tour II: $5 adults, $2.50 children 6–18; all tours are free to children under 6. *Hours:* 8 A.M. to 3:30 P.M. daily except Thanksgiving and Christmas.

                           —D.P.

Hawaii, Hawaiian Islands

Hawaii Volcanoes National Park . . . When Hawaii was accepted as our 50th State, not everyone in the other 49 States knew that part of our sister State included very lively volcanoes which have a habit of acting up every 3 or 4 years just to show people they are still potent. There is a town, called Volcano—named after Vulcan, the ancient Roman fire god—built on the rim of a volcano on the "Big Island" of

Hawaii (the other 3 major islands are Oahu, Maui, and Kauai). Many of the residents of Volcano are scientists who live and work around smoldering volcano walls and steam-emitting fissures in the ground.

While each of the Hawaiian Islands was basically created by volcanic action, only Hawaii has active volcanoes, with the massive Mauna Loa (13,680' high) and Kilauea Crater (4,077' high) host to this scientific community as well as being parts of the Hawaii Volcanoes National Park.

The scientists call these volcanoes "domes" because of their roundish shape; they don't have the sharp cones of a Mount Fujiyama in Japan or a Mount Vesuvius in Italy, and don't issue the fumes and burning boulders associated with violent eruptions. The reason for earth's beneficence of lesser explosiveness is that the lava here doesn't contain much gas.

Approximately 16 mi. down the mountain slope one can see the lava pools and steaming crevices of the gaping Kilauea Crater. There is a narrow ledge between this crater and the smaller Kilauea Iki, but the smaller crater—as if trying to make up for its lesser size—has been the most active recently with its fire shooting convincingly high into the sky. Mauna Kea, a few miles north, is about 100' higher than Mauna Loa, but is inactive.

The town of Volcano, characterized by ordinary houses and lawns, centers around the glowing volcano pits. Facilities located on the northwest rim of Kilauea Crater include seismographs to measure shocks and tremors of the earth, with other instruments to gauge heat and detect tilt in the earth's surface. Samples of minerals, cinders, and cooled lava are constantly under analysis.

Unlike some other areas of this planet, warnings (the seismograph's needles do a sudden dance as the earth rumbles and quivers) that the volcanoes are up to their old tricks bring people scurrying to watch the unique fireworks, while the National Park Service rangers check to make sure everyone watches from a safe vantage point.

Eruptions usually begin with a crack opening along the crater floor. Lava pours through this fissure, sometimes hurtling high into the air. Initially, these lava fountains appear to be a rather bright and intense yellow, but as the cooling lava falls back to earth it turns reddish (it's still hotter than 2,000°). If you see people with umbrellas it is because the steam, rising as clouds, sometimes condenses into water and returns as rain. There is a sort of rainbow effect then, as you see the rose and gold from the red-hot caverns diffused through the raindrops.

Fortunately, this infernolike show is contained for the most part within the crater walls, with spectators ringing the crater as if it were a natural stadium. One of the things to be careful of is a change in wind, which can blow choking fumes and cinder showers toward onlookers. The trick, of course, is to keep the wind at your back.

Not unexpectedly, the aftermath of these "safe" eruptions has people rummaging through the cinder-covered slopes for "olivines" (semi-precious stones which have a lustrous greenish-brown color) or shining black pellets called "Pele's hair" (Pele is the Hawaiian volcano goddess). Shutterbugs avidly take photographs.

Other intriguing elements of the park are Crater Rim Drive, with its views of steaming vents and odor of sulfur, and the Halemaumau Fire Pit. There are some short trails worth seeing. One 15-minute walk takes you through the Thurston Lava Tube, a 450'-long tunnel through which molten lava gushed eons ago. "Devastation Trail" has a boardwalk built over cinders which goes through about half a mile of a stark forest filled with the skeletons of ohia trees. There are also trails starting from the Sulphur Banks, where steam and gases containing sulfur issue from cracks, ultimately altering the rock and soil into opal and hard clay.

Particularly poignant, perhaps, is the "Foot-prints Trail" where barefoot Hawaiians crossed the muddy ashfalls after the 1790 explosion of Kilauea. Two other points of interest are "Tree Molds," formed by molten lava congealing around tree trunks; and the Mauna Loa Strip Road, which takes you through lava-marked terrain, said to resemble the surface of the moon more closely than any other place on earth. It is also possible to hike around the rim of Mokuaweoweo, the crater of Mauna Loa, which is some 3 mi. long, 1½ mi. wide, and 600' deep.

Volcano House, an inn perched on the rim of the Kilauea Crater, has overnight accommodations, a restaurant, and a cocktail lounge. Exhibits, relief models, and paintings tell the story of the park and its volcanoes at the Thomas Jagger Museum. A daily program features a talk by a park naturalist and a color film of recent eruptions.

Location: 30 mi. from Hilo and 96 mi. from Kailua-Kona on the Island of Hawaii. *Admission:* Both the park and museum are free. *Hours:* The park is open 7:30 A.M. to 5 P.M., Monday through Friday; 6 A.M. to 5 P.M., Saturday and Sunday. The museum is open daily, 9 A.M. to 5 P.M., with films shown hourly from 9 A.M. to 3 P.M.

—J.A.

Sightseeing in Your Own Neighborhood

Whether we pay attention to it or not, we all belong to a neighborhood of one sort or another. Some of us live in city neighborhoods, some in suburban ones, others in rural neighborhoods, such as the mountains or the high plains. What is your neighborhood? Is it a place, a group of buildings, or a collection of people? Before you get into knowing your neighborhood, look at the *Almanac's* neighborhood map, drawn up by one who lived there. As he spotted items onto the map—which he got from the local town hall—he took notes on each item and keyed these notes to the map. You can do the same for your own neighborhood.

Our sample neighborhood is a suburb, about 1½ hours from New York City. It contains 500 acres, about 200 houses, 275 apartments, and nearly 1,500 people. They are mostly young to middle-aged families with an average of slightly over 2 children per household. It can be described as a solidly middle-class neighborhood. Listed below are its parts and a description of each:

1. *Shopping Center.* People from all over this town and surrounding towns come here to shop. The land was developed and owned by a national company and the stores are leased to large chains which are not oriented to the neighborhood. Some smaller shops like the stationery and gift shops, however, are owned by neighborhood people. They like the heavy traffic which the chains bring in. The neighborhood on the whole, however, doesn't like it. Three years ago the shopping center was an orchard.

2. *Highway, U.S. Route 1.* Follows the old Boston Post Road. Four lanes of heavy traffic carry outsiders through this edge of the neighborhood as well as neighborhood residents to and from work and the many stores that line the highway strip. Two private companies have buses connecting the neighborhood to the town and the nearest city. But the service is poor and is nonexistent on Sundays or in the evenings. The very young and the old who don't drive can't get out of the neighborhood to do things. Take, for example, Mrs. Robin McKenna. You can meet her easily enough because, although she's 75 years old, you'll often find her hitchhiking along Shore Drive (4). Pick her up and she'll tell you that since the old trolley was abandoned 25 years ago, it's been harder and harder for oldsters like her to

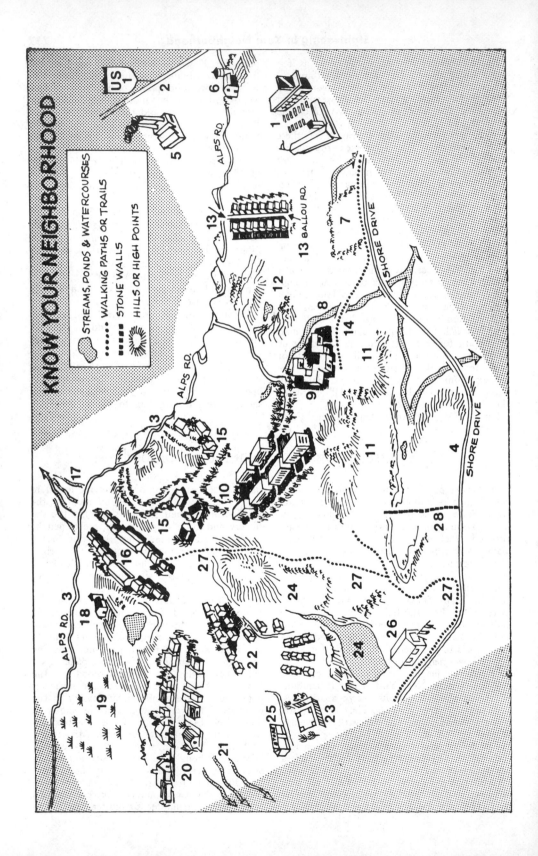

get into town. She doesn't drive, but all the large stores, doctors' offices, and meeting places are in the town or nearby city. She tells her friends to hitchhike but they're afraid. Mrs. McKenna admits that some strangers are weird, but most are friendly and all are interesting. Her regular rides get cookies from her at Christmas.

3. *Alps Road.* A feeder street for the neighborhood it bounds. It is so narrow and winding over the small hills in the neighborhood that the old farmers called it "Alps Road." Some of them live in older farmhouses along the road, but most have been squeezed out by single-family homes built over the last 10 years costing $30,000 to $40,000.

4. *Shore Drive.* Another feeder street and neighborhood divider. It is also State Highway 142 and carries outsiders through the neighborhood to the nearby shore and beaches which gave the road its name. Summer traffic is heavy and generally keeps people from crossing it to go to stores and schools in the next neighborhood. The road has mostly older, single-family houses, lived in by older couples whose children have grown up.

5. *Echlin Company.* This factory makes automobile parts. It is owned by outsiders, employs a few people from the surrounding neighborhood, and uses many inner-city blacks who commute by car from the nearby city because owning a house in the neighborhood is expensive and nearby apartments are small and lived in only by whites. But according to realtors of the area, no discrimination takes place here. Bob Gillings thinks differently. He's black, lives in the nearby city, and hasn't found a place to live in this neighborhood. "When the company moved from the city to this town, they promised the town fathers they'd bring good taxes but none of the workers. Too expensive for us to buy a house here. We can afford the rents here but we always get the 'no vacancy' sign when we ask. Heck, me and my wife are more comfortable in the city anyway."

6. *Old Colonial Farmhouse.* "For Sale." Although some of the town's famous families lived here, this home's place on the highway (2) makes its land more valuable for stores.

7. *Vacant Lot.* Owned by the owners of the shopping center next door (1), who want to build 152 apartments here. The neighborhood opposes them because apartments would bring in more traffic, especially to Shore Drive (4), alter streams through the land (8), and possibly bring in low-income residents, such as the blacks who work nearby.

8. *Streams.* These collect water from the sloping land and carry it to the nearby river. These streams are relatively unpolluted since this part of the neighborhood has been provided with sewer pipes beneath the streets to carry waste water to a plant which treats it before letting it flow out to the river. During rains, the streams here often flood the lot (7), which temporarily holds the water before it goes downstream. Buildings around these streams would make the water overflow faster and flood downstream houses. This kind of flooding already happens at the nearby apartments, where one building has been situated in the path of a stream.

9. *Apartments.* Seven buildings have 55 apartments. Developed and sold as condominiums, only about half are owner-occupied. Nonresidents own the rest as rental investments. They provide little in the way of maintenance or play facilities for those who rent from them. The renters tend to have lower incomes than the owners, are younger, and have young children. Because the owners tend not to have children living at home, they don't want to spend money on building a play lot. So the children play in the parking lots.

10. *More Apartments.* All 150 are rented to older couples or young families. The neighborhood used to be all single-family or lots. But a major developer bought the land, made a large contribution to the local political party in power, and got permission to build apartments here. Because the earth is too rocky to absorb so much sewage, the developer 1st had to put in a sewer line. The chairman of the Sewer Authority, who doesn't live in the neighborhood, is a land developer himself as well as the boss of the political party which received the contribution. So Mr. Chairman was happy to extend the sewer lines. This made the entire neighborhood suitable for apartments, and developers are madly rushing to buy up the open space.

11. *Open Space.* The play area for the apartments (10) was supposed to be here. But the developer forgot to build it. Instead he quickly sold the land and buildings to outside investors such as Dr. Robert Kelley. Dr. Kelley is a dentist who has his offices in the local town center and lives in a wealthier part of town. Many of his patients live in our sample neighborhood but they don't know that their dentist owns these apartments. Dr. Kelley doesn't want them to know.

12. *Vacant Lot.* But not for long! Another developer wants to fill in the pond with rock and dirt from the nearby hill, which he'll tear away to build 150 apartments. Mark Robbins, who lives in the apartments (9) with his mother and 2 sisters, has spotted a muskrat family living in the pond. But the developer would rather have wealthier, childless families in condominium apartments living here instead of muskrats or little boys like Mark who befriend the local wildlife.

13. *Ballou Road.* A small, single-family hous-

ing tract owned and lived in by older, working-class families. Joe Ballou lives here. He built most of the houses and named the street that he put in for them. His youngest daughter, Lisa, is still in high school, but his other children are married and live in other suburbs. Joe doesn't build houses anymore. "The market isn't so good," he says. "And besides, my wife and I are getting old enough where we'd like to enjoy life." So he and his wife have spent the last 4 winters in Florida. During the rest of the year Joe occasionally remodels bathrooms and kitchens.

14. *Footpath.* Apartment dwellers shortcut to the shopping center or bus, rather than walk along the streets, which have no sidewalks in this part of the neighborhood.

15. *Homes.* New, one-family houses worth $40,000 to $65,000. A typical owner is Bud Anderson. He is an accountant with a large firm in the city but he's planning to start his own firm soon. He and his wife Vicki send their 2 children to a private school on the other side of town rather than to the public one nearby (26) because "the quality of public schools here is poor." Streets in this section or tract have been named by the developer.

16. *Condominium Townhouses.* These townhouses have just been built on a lowland and marsh. The builder has installed a pond to collect the water that used to flow to the marsh, but this doesn't work and flooding now occurs. People who are buying the townhouses, according to the realtor, are very successful older couples. No one under the age of 18 is allowed to live here. "No burden on the schools," says the realtor. So far, families who have moved here all have 2 cars, which has added significantly to the traffic on Alps Road. The designer of these townhouses, an architect by the name of George Boswell, has won an award for his scheme. He admits, however, that they should never have been built on this land: "It was really too wet for townhouses, but if it's going to be built it may as well be designed well." Whether the well-designed buildings survive on this soggy ground, only the future will tell.

17. *Streams.* Water on this side of the neighborhood flows into a nearby tidal marsh and then into the bay.

18. *Farm.* This farmer presently raises corn for sale, vegetables for his family and friends. He also keeps some old horses and cows which graze on the fertile hillside. He has good, well-drained, upland soil which developers of nearby condominium townhouses covet. They've asked the farmer to sell, but he's holding out.

19. *Marsh.* Gradually being filled in by yet another developer, who plans 75 apartments here. His action has destroyed the marsh, forcing out ducks and other birdlife that once used

the area. But, the developer argues, now that the area is filled in, how can the town deny me permission to build here? The neighborhood wouldn't grant permission if it had its way, but it's the town's planning and zoning commission that will give permission. Its members don't live around here.

20. *Homes.* Large, newer homes on large lots. Mostly wealthy families live here with 2 to 4 children. Of course, they oppose the nearby apartments because they will reduce property values.

21. *Drain.* In this part of the neighborhood, water flows directly into the bay either through a natural stream bed or storm drains beneath the built-up areas.

22. *Old Section.* Homes in this section of the neighborhood were built on small lots and narrow streets over 50 years ago, as summer cottages for city people who wanted to be near the beach during the humid months. The houses are mostly wooden. Many have screen porches running around 3 sides. Since the soil here is quite rocky and there are no sewers, waste often flows untreated and unabsorbed by the land, directly into the bay with its beaches. The area is no longer a desirable resort spot and over the years has become a year-round neighborhood. Owners have winterized their cottages, closed in the porches, and either live here themselves or rent their places out to students during the winter.

23. *Baseball Diamond.* The only playground in the neighborhood. Because the neighborhood does not support the political party which has run the town for many years, the town doesn't build recreational facilities here. So Geno Pantani decided to take matters into his own hands. Geno moved here shortly after he married his wife Deborah. Ever since that time he's been a policeman for the local town. Now he's a sergeant. Having a lot of respect from his neighbors, he was able to get them to form a neighborhood association. He was elected their 1st president and he took as his 1st task the building of a play lot. The association put up money for the land by taxing themselves. With their own hands they filled in the marsh, then bought benches and swings 2nd-hand from the city. Now they have a small play lot and baseball diamond, a facility that is well-used by kids and their parents alike.

24. *Vacant Land.* Held by a private local foundation that administers it for the benefit of town residents. Old evergreens line the pond on one side, steep cliffs line it on the other. Many hiking trails wind their way through the area, often alongside stone walls which mark the boundaries of old farms which were here in the last century. The pond is used by neighbors for swimming in summer and for ice skating in winter. It is called Altmansburger's Pond after

the family who once owned and farmed the land. Their descendants live in houses at the end of the pond.

25. *Store.* At this corner is a local "mom-and-pop" grocery store owned by an older man and his wife who have lived next door for over 50 years. They know the neighborhood—its residents and its history. Their son was not interested in continuing the business, however, so mom and pop may close the store soon and the supermarket chain (1) will probably get their business.

26. *Public School.* Because it's on the edge of this neighborhood, the school receives 1st through 4th graders from this neighborhood and outside neighborhoods. Older children attend the town-wide middle and high schools.

27. *Footpaths.* A narrow sidewalk along the road, trodden-down dirt paths through the woods. The town built the sidewalks so nearby children could walk safely to the school. The paths were made by children wearing down the shortest route home from school.

28. *Old Stone Wall.* An old property divider dating from the 18th century. Colonial farmers here cut the trees, and then dragged stones out of the fields and piled them along the edges. Crops no longer grow here and a 2nd generation of trees has sprung up—birch, pin oak, hickory, some maple and pine trees. According to the old-timers the elms were wiped out by the Dutch elm disease.

Now that you've examined the sample neighborhood, you can start asking questions about your own neighborhood: What makes it different? What makes it a neighborhood? Is it part of a larger unit? You'll have to do a bit of legwork to answer some of these questions. But walking is the best way to get to know your neighborhood. First, get an overview, maybe by car or bus. Whether you're new or old to your neighborhood, you'll enjoy a special tour given by someone else. Many large cities offer such guided tours on foot or by bus. But if your area doesn't have one, be your own tour guide. Pretend you're a stranger and look around your neighborhood through his eyes.

Determine the shape and boundaries of the neighborhood by looking for physical obstacles. Our sample neighborhood is shaped by the major streets that cut off foot traffic. Would you ever think of walking across a 4-lane highway to borrow a cup of sugar? There are natural boundaries, too, such as rivers and hills. These characteristics often give names to the neighborhoods, such as "Riverside," "Valley Acres," or "Hollywood Hills."

Next, notice the street and road system. Generally they are the 1st things built. Houses and shops come after the roads or trolley lines have been built to link the neighborhood to the city and other neighborhoods. What are the links in your neighborhood? Some streets are laid in regular, straight lines while others, like those in the older section of our sample, follow the crooked foot and cow paths of another century. Go to the town clerk and ask how the streets were named. Some street names follow an alphabetical pattern such as Ash, Bay, Church streets. Or they may be named for States, such as Michigan Avenue in Chicago. Or they may be named for historical events or personalities. Most cities have a Madison Avenue or Washington Street. The avenues may run in one direction, the streets in another.

Traffic arteries, heavily traveled streets, are often called boulevards or highways. What happens along such arteries is different from what happens along smaller residential streets. Arteries often form commercial strips. Because they draw more traffic, stores, apartments, and factories are often located along arteries and major intersections.

Not only the homes, stores, and factories of your neighborhood feed traffic to local roads. So do outside neighborhoods. Ask yourself where your neighborhood's roads and streets begin and end. Are they carrying your neighbors' cars or outsiders'? What about buses and heavy trucks? They may be carrying goods or people to and from or through your area. Since streets, roads, and parking lots can consume as much as 50% of your neighborhood's land area, it's good to question who uses so much of your area's resources. By comparison, look to see how much of your area's land is given over to sidewalks, bicycle trails, parks, or pure open space. In our sample neighborhood, one apartment area (9, 10) provides parking for cars but no play area for children. You might also note the noise level of major streets and compare it with that of smaller ones.

Walking or bicycling not only gives you more time to look closely at your neighborhood, but also the occasional opportunity to talk to your neighbors. In addition, walking or bicycling will put your legs directly in touch with the land. In a car we tend to pay attention only to man-made features. On foot we know immediately if we're walking up the slightest hill.

The lay of the land is often hidden from us. Most neighborhoods do not have mountains or rivers in or around them. But they may have been there at one time. Unknown to most residents are the natural and artificial streams flowing under the neighborhoods. Fresh water is often obtained from these sources. Dirty water is put back. Do you know where water drains from your neighborhood? Does it settle into the ground? What if the ground is too rocky? Perhaps the waste water is carried off to a nearby river or sewage plant. These natural and man-made watercourses follow the land downhill and sometimes carve it out. Find the low points and gulleys of your neighborhood and you will find the spots where water is collecting either below or above the ground. Follow the streams. Find their sources and outflow.

If you need help, get a topographic map of the area from a local library or the U.S. Geological Survey. The map will show elevations, streams, roads, buildings, and other prominent physical features. Agricultural maps go further and tell the types of soil and vegetation. But even without the maps you can examine the earth directly: Is it sandy or rocky? Light or dark? Wet or dry? The soils of your area will often tell you its history. What was your neighborhood before it was built up? An Indian burial ground? A farm? The Back Bay neighborhood of Boston and the Marina neighborhood of San Francisco were built upon dirt hauled in to fill what was once part of a bay. Perhaps your neighborhood stands upon a sliced-off hill or a filled-in valley. If you can't find any old-timers to tell you, go to the nearest library and ask for some old maps.

A good place to go to find out about your neighborhood's soils and vegetation is the nearby park. Look at the trees and shrubs that can be grown locally and talk with other strollers. The park caretaker can certainly tell you a lot about the trees and plantings. Ask him which trees were planted and which were standing before the park was built. Ask why certain kinds of trees are popular in the area. Perhaps the evergreens were planted in your neighborhood to give privacy around the houses. Perhaps some trees have been planted to help retain sandy soil. Or still others, such as eucalyptus, might have been planted to shield crops from the wind when the neighborhood was a farm.

You may find that the land in your neighborhood once bore a forest. Was it cut for timber to build the neighborhood's buildings? Or was the forest cut to clear the land for farming? Find out which crops grew successfully in your soil and test your answer by growing them in your own backyard.

Look also at the features of the park. Statues, monuments, markers, bandshells. They may reveal some local history. Find out what cultural events take place there. There are often important neighborhood events such as parades or picnics. What was used to build the walkways or walls or fences in the park? These building materials will tell you a lot about the architecture and history of your neighborhood. The same brick that was used to pave the walkway may have been used to build your house.

What are most of the buildings in your neighborhood built of? Wood? Stucco? Concrete blocks? Very often whole neighborhoods or streets have been built at the same time and in the same style, sometimes by the same builder. Pay close attention to the shapes and styles of the buildings. Are the roofs flat or peaked? Do all houses have porches? Why?

What happens behind the building faces? How many families are in each building? Do the families who live in the buildings rent or own the property? If your neighborhood has many apartments, most likely it is a rental neighborhood, although apartments can also be owned as cooperatives or condominiums. Rental neighborhoods differ from owner-occupied neighborhoods. Renters stay for shorter periods of time than owners would. Who owns the apartments that are rented? Landlords may live in the building or they may live in a different neighborhood altogether. If outsiders, they may or may not be concerned about the neighborhood. Find out. Go to city hall, the tax office in particular, and compare the residential addresses of the property owners and the addresses of the properties they own.

How many of your neighbors work within the neighborhood? How many outsiders come to your neighborhood to work and make money? It may take some time before you're comfortable enough to ask such questions of your neighbors. If you prefer not to ask them directly, go to the main library and look up the census information for your area. The census will tell you the age of buildings, their condition, whether owned or rented. It will also tell you about the people: how many people live in the neighborhood, where they work, and how long they've lived there.

But the best way to get to know the people of your neighborhood is to get into friendly conversations with them. To do this, go to the local gathering spots and involve yourself in the activities which draw the people of the neighborhood together. Such spots include the corner market, newsstands, the local bar or the drugstore. Store proprietors are a mine of information, especially if they're native to the neighborhood. Supermarkets and chain stores, while their prices may be lower (you should find this out), are generally not as friendly. Moreover, find out if the larger stores draw shoppers from more than one neighborhood. When you find the nearest small store, get to know the owner and ask him about his shoppers. He will probably tell you that they all come from the local neighborhood and that he is devoted to them and the neighborhood.

Activities which draw people together and tighten their sense of neighborliness are such things as day-care centers, churches, schools, block parties, sports events, and politics. Canvassing for a political party or a legitimate charity provides a ready-made excuse to knock on doors and talk to your neighbors. You can find out what they think about their neighborhood and where it's going, its needs, and their goals for it. Such activities not only will tell you about a neighborhood, but they will make you a part of it.

—M.D.

If you make a map of your neighborhood, we would appreciate it if you send us a copy to: The People's Almanac, P. O. Box 49328, Los Angeles, California 90049. We will choose the best ones and use them in The People's Almanac. Winning mapmakers will be financially rewarded.

A Handy Dandy Traveler's Guide to Europe and Environs

How far is it from Moscow to Samarkand? From Cairo to Tel Aviv? What train service is available? At what time? Will the train have sleeping cars? How long is its journey?

Travel in Europe, Asia, or North Africa this year with a copy of Cook's Continental Timetable in your luggage, and you'll have those answers at your fingertips. This timetable, or "Cook's," as the British affectionately call it, is obtainable in Europe, at any office of Thomas Cook & Son, the world's largest travel agency. Or you can order a copy by airmail (ca. $4., 6–8 days delivery, from 45 Berkeley Street, London). It's not offered for public sale in the U.S.

Cook's is not just a railroad timetable. For many of Europe's seasoned tourists, it's the only practical guide to land travel on the Continent. Primarily, this 500-page, 15-oz. guide lists more than 1,500 tables which describe all principal services by rail and bus. But you'll find dozens of other tables, giving ship schedules for the English Channel crossings, for cruising in the Mediterranean or the Black Sea, and for most other navigable bodies of water in Europe and Asia. Steamer service on the Rhine and hydrofoil trips on the Danube are also regular features.

With this easy-to-use guide to work from, you can make instant changes in an itinerary, even while en route. The tables are set up with childlike simplicity. Arranged by countries, each section is preceded by a map which shows only the principal cities. Table numbers appear along straight-line connections between these cities, indicating the specific table to use.

These back-up tables are presented by Cook's in a continuous numerical sequence, for fast referral. (For users who do not speak English, information on how to interpret the tables and their symbols is also given in French and German.) All arrival or departure times are printed in the 24-hour system, which eliminates the need for A.M. or P.M. distinctions.

Are you traveling between Paris and Frankfurt, West Germany, for example? The map reference is to Table 621. A quick scan of all trains immediately points out your best choice: the crack Trans-Europe-Express train ※51, the *Goethe*. Departure is from Paris's Gare d'Est station at 0800, arriving in Frankfurt's Hofbahnhof at 1354 (1:54 P.M.). In a footnote for this table, you'll learn that the *Goethe*, although named after the famous German poet and dramatist, is a member of the French Railway system. Symbol references describe the train as being electric-hauled, with 7 cars and 230 seats, fully air-conditioned, including the 48-seat restaurant car. *Voilà*.

But, most important of all: This TEE train carries *only* passengers who hold 1st-class tickets. On many of Europe's international trains in this category, seating is almost always possible in 1st class, even without reservations. And you'll be quickly ushered off by the conductor if you hold a 2nd-class ticket, whether a surplus of empty seats exists or not.

Should you be traveling 2nd class, and prefer to remain in Paris for an additional morning of sightseeing, Cook's offers an alternative: the "D255," an express leaving Gare d'Est at one in the afternoon. Have lunch before you board it, however. This departure, according to Cook's shorthand symbols, will not couple on a restaurant car, or carry either food or drink, until after it reaches Saarbrücken, West Germany, 250 mi. away.

In the 100 years since Cook's was 1st issued (1973 was its centennial celebration), the basic coverage has gradually been extended to help solve similar problems. Are you looking for details on the amounts of foreign currencies that can be taken across national borders? Cook's has it: Hungary's limit for its forint is 400 (about $10), moving in or out of the country. Any excess sum you try to bring with you is subject to immediate confiscation during customs inspection at the border.

Do you need help in wardrobe planning? Check Cook's tabulation of monthly temperatures in 93 representative cities. In Rome, their investigators say, the *average* for early afternoon in July and August is a low of 76° and a high of 88°. That's nearly 10° warmer than the readings they give for New York City. Be prepared to wear clothing suitable for a Manhattan summer, or you'll be joining the wiser Romans who flee to the mountains for relief. If you're considering a stay in Baghdad, watch out. This sweltering capital of Iraq, Cook's points out, has midsummer averages of 93° to 110°, with sun temperatures 120° and up.

On other pages, you'll find descriptions of the monetary systems for each country, naming the paper or coin denominations being used. For a quick comparison, an equivalency in British pounds is listed. Multiply it by roughly 2½ and you have a conversion into dollars.

Signing over several hundred dollars in traveler's checks without knowing their worth in another country's currency can be unsettling. Not for Cook's customers. Are you entering Greece? Currency restrictions: 750 drachmas, taken in or out. The U.S. dollar is nearly equal to 30 drachmas. If you wish to bring along Greek currency from your present location, $25 in checks is the maximum to be cashed. If you plan to wait until arrival in Athens for large exchanges of dollars-to-drachmas, a brief glance at Cook's pages on foreign currencies is in order. Bank notes are issued only in 50, 100, 500, and 1,000 denominations. In coins, you'll be given 1-, 2-, 5-, 10-, 20-, and 30-drachma pieces. (The latter is Greece's "dollar.") With this advance tutoring, you're confidently counting in drachmas long before you reach the exchange window.

By updating monthly, Cook's keeps abreast of minor changes in local schedules. In summer months, when more trains are put on to handle the heavy influx of tourists, the tables are revised completely. Keeping its timetables current was a practice which Thomas Cook & Son followed devoutly even during the Great War of 1914–1918. Although both Allied and German armies were shelling railroad stations, rolling stock, and track into rubble, Cook's grimly kept at the updates, with a terse footnote to its patrons, that "all Services" were "subject to change or suspension without notice."

In the 1970s, the problems are less intimidating. To solve them more easily, Cook's faithful customers usually buy 2 copies. The 1st is used to plan routes, stopovers, and side excursions ahead of time. With this method, in-transit hours can be reduced and time spent in rail terminals is pared to a minimum. Specific express trains can be chosen, weeding out the "locals" that may take as much as 4 hours longer for the same distance. Well after this preplanning is finished, Cook's patrons order their traveling copy, just before the trip is to begin.

Unknown factors that could be disastrous can be avoided with this technique. Take the Moscow–Samarkand journey, for instance. Cook's gives all basic facts in its Table 877. Distance: 2,313 mi. Scheduled time: 68½ hours. Departure: Kazan station, Moscow, 2325 (11:25 P.M.). Total number of trains going through to Samarkand: 1.

Accommodations, a general note informs you, are either "Soft" or "Hard." In "Soft," the U.S.S.R.'s equivalent for 1st class in Europe, you will be booked into a large, 4-berth, couchette compartment. For certain important trains, the sleeping cars have 2-berth arrangements. In either situation, overnight trips can be embarrassing for the non-Russian since reservations are booked without regard to sex.

Riding "Hard" class is somewhat less comfortable. The choice is between a 4-bunk (not "berth") compartment, or open noncompartment coaches. Privacy is not possible.

Experienced users of Cook's will also check all footnote references and Table 877 has a real stopper. This train to Samarkand carries NO civilian traffic beyond Kuibishev, 684 mi. from Moscow. The sectional map indicates 2 other ways to reach your destination: east on the Trans-Siberian Railway (Table 878), then south at the rail junction, Novosibirsk, to cross the steppes. Or going by ship across the Caspian Sea to Krasnovodsk, western terminus for the Trans-Caspian Railroad. But again, both tables have the same footnote: forbidden to civilians, south from Novosibirsk and east of Krasnovodsk. . . .

The reason is not Samarkand itself. This Uzbek city is one of the oldest existing cities in the world, dating back over 6,000 years. In 329 B.C., Alexander the Great looted and razed the area, and was followed later by the hordes of Genghis Khan. By the 14th century, the ruthless Mongol conqueror Tamerlane chose the city to be his capital. Today, his mausoleum there is one of the most impressive monuments in Central Asia. As a tourist attraction, the city has much to offer.

Tourism by rail, however, is sharply limited to all but a select few. The entire region is cordoned off by the Soviets because of secret sites for military testing and space activities.

But why leave the Trans-Siberian train at Novosibirsk? Stay on clear to Vladivostok, 3,701 mi. and 6 days later. Enjoy the Russian tea, brewed in samovars placed in each car. Enjoy the boiled chicken and the schnitzel, or the solyanka soup. Enjoy the Romanian rice wine served daily for breakfast, along with that indescribable cereal called *Grechnivaya Kasha*.

Now *that*, say Cook's compilers—who will vouch personally for every routing the timetable has—is a trip you will always remember.

—W.K.

The Auto Show, Come See . . .

BONNIE AND CLYDE'S LAST CAR

In mid-March of 1934, Jesse Warren, a roofing contractor in Topeka, Kan., bought a new Ford for $785.92—$200 down, $585.92 to be paid by April 15. The car was a V-8, Fordor Deluxe, of a tannish-gray color which the Ford Motor Company called "Desert Sand." It bore motor number 649198 and Kansas license plates with the numbers 3-17198.

Although both Warren and his wife Ruth drove the new car, Ruth felt that it was more hers than his. It was a beautiful automobile with special equipment: fancy seat covers, bumper guards, a metal cover on the extra tire, an Arvin hot-water heater, and on the radiator cap a leaping greyhound in chrome. The windows on the new V-8s not only rolled up and down, but also slid backward almost 2" for partial ventilation. The running boards were wide and handsome; the doors, both front and back, swung outward toward the rear to open. Ford dealers said a new V-8 would get nearly 20 mi. to the gallon at 45 mph, but it could go much faster than that.

By late April the Warrens had driven 1,243 mi. and had paid the balance owed on it. On April 29, 1934, Ruth returned home from a Sunday afternoon drive. She parked the car in the driveway and left the keys in the ignition. Jesse was down the street visiting his mother.

Shortly after one o'clock Ruth's neighbors saw a man and a woman repeatedly circling the block in a Plymouth coupe. Ruth herself looked out the kitchen window once to see a cruising car; the woman in it was wearing a red dress. Later the neighbors saw the car again; this time a man was riding on the right running board. He jumped off, climbed into the Warrens' car and started it, backed out of the driveway, and sped away, following the Plymouth. The new Ford was gone, and the Warrens were not to see it until 3 months later, when, blood-soaked and riddled with bullet holes, it was famous as the automobile in which Clyde Barrow and Bonnie Parker had died.

On Monday morning a report came to the Kansas State Police that a car fitting the description of Jesse Warren's, but bearing out-of-state license plates, had been spotted near Ottawa, Kan., only 40 mi. from Topeka. It had been parked off the road behind a hedgerow; whoever was driving it had spent most of Sunday afternoon there. By Monday noon the State police found the spot behind the hedgerow. There was no car, only the tracks of new tires, cigar butts, and a pair of rose-colored ladies' panties lying on the ground—details calculated to tantalize and enrage the police.

Although law officers over the entire Midwest and Southwest stayed on the lookout for Barrow and Parker, the gray Ford dropped out of sight after it was spotted near Ottawa. Clyde, a fast and expert driver, was known to like night for traveling long distances. For this kind of driving Barrow preferred Fords. They ran at high speeds for a long time without breaking down, they got good gas mileage, and they were everywhere, a considerable advantage for someone who wanted anonymity on the highway.

By early May of 1934 law officers had narrowed their search for Bonnie and Clyde to the pine hills of north Louisiana. Frank Hamer, a famous former Texas Ranger, had been on their trail for 4 months. On hearing that Barrow had fled to the relative safety of a remote rural area, Hamer telephoned Sheriff Henderson Jordan of Bienville Parish. Sheriff Jordan verified that a mysterious gray Ford had been seen in his parish. An ambush was planned.

At midnight on Tuesday, May 22, 6 lawmen—Jordan and his deputy, Hamer and 3 more Texans—selected a spot on a country road along which Barrow often drove. They concealed their cars deep in the woods and arranged themselves to wait behind a rise on the east side of the road, rifles and automatic shotguns ready. They crouched there for hours, mosquitoes plaguing them. At last the sun rose behind them, lighting the road so that they could see anything coming a mile away. At 9:10 the gray Ford appeared, coming from the north.

Inside the car Bonnie was halfway through a bacon and tomato sandwich bought a few minutes earlier in Gibsland, a crossroads town nearby. There was a pack of cigarettes in her lap. Clyde was driving in his shirt sleeves, his shoes off. His tie was hanging over the rearview mirror. As Barrow reached the crest of the hill, the officers opened fire. Repeated volleys covered the car and its occupants. Bonnie screamed shrilly for an instant and slumped forward. Barrow's head fell backward. The car careened slowly to the left and stopped, its motor stalling. The officers scrambled over the rise of ground and onto the road, firing into the car from all directions. Then the pine woods were quiet again. Barrow and Parker were dead and bleeding inside the car. Bonnie had been hit over 50 times; Clyde, although on the side of fire, had only 27 bullet holes. The car itself had been shot 107 times; its right windows were shattered, and the front door on the driver's side looked like a sieve.

In those few moments of violence Jesse Warren's new Ford, with its leaping greyhound and its Arvin hot-water heater, had become famous. It had been driven over 7,500 mi. in the 23 days since it was stolen from the driveway in Topeka, and it now bore Arkansas license plates. Inside the trunk were some 15 other plates from States all over the Midwest, West, and South; there was also an arsenal of assorted rifles, pistols, sawed-off shotguns, and ammunition.

After inspecting the car and its contents, the lawmen took all the guns and ammunition from the trunk and put them in Jordan's car. While one of the men took a few feet of movie film, 2 others went to get the coroner in Arcadia, the parish seat. By the time the coroner arrived, a souvenir-mad mob had gathered, everyone trying to get mementos. Bits of window glass were broken off; swatches of blood-soaked clothing or upholstery were ripped away; bullets and empty shells were picked up from the road. Someone clipped a lock of Bonnie's hair, another rummaged in her purse. One man was attempting to whittle off Clyde's ear. The coroner stopped him and asked the officers to have the car towed into Arcadia so he could properly perform the autopsy.

The news of the death of Barrow and Parker was teletyped all over the U.S. Promptly, a Kansas entrepreneur, "master showman and display expert" Duke Mills, approached Jesse Warren with a plan to exhibit the car at the World's Fair in Chicago; he wanted to rent the car for $50 a week and pay Jesse a commission on the take. Warren agreed and sent Mills and a lawyer named Hall Smith to Louisiana to get the car. When the showman and the lawyer reached Arcadia, they went to Sheriff Jordan to claim the automobile. He refused to turn it over, saying he needed to keep it longer "for evidence."

In the meantime, the car had been hidden; no one in Arcadia knew where it was except Jordan, the Ford dealer Woodard, and 2 local lawyers of doubtful reputation named Wimberly and Barnette. By June, Jesse Warren had reconciled himself to having lost his car. He expressed no regret; "I've got money," he said; "Let them keep it if they want it. I can always buy another car." Ruth Warren, however, had no intention of giving up so easily. The car, she said, was theirs, and if Jesse wanted to sit back and let some red-neck sheriff do him out of a lot of money, he could, but she wasn't about to. Ruth went to Louisiana to retrieve the car.

In Arcadia she hired W. D. Goff ("Mr.

Bill" locally), an ethical and intelligent lawyer. Bill Goff took the case out of local jurisdiction and filed in Shreveport before U.S. judge Ben Dawkins, who well understood the subtlety of political connections in Bienville Parish. Ultimately Sheriff Jordan was brought before Judge Dawkins for contempt of court in refusing to surrender the automobile.

The car, hidden in a barn in Arcadia, was reluctantly turned over to Ruth Warren, who drove it, gore on the seats and brains dried on the interior, back to Shreveport, where it was loaded on a van and hauled to Topeka. Over 2 months had elapsed since Bonnie and Clyde were killed.

Mr. Warren and his family were less than eager to see the car. "We wanted," said his sister Helen later, "nothing to do with it. We thought it was horrible. There it was, parked in the driveway, just a mess. Nowadays, of course, we live in violence, but in those days it seemed incredible to us that anybody would want to look at a bloody car full of bullet holes. We thought it was awful that 2 people, 2 human beings, had been killed in it. Not Ruth; she knew exactly what to do with it." From that point on, Ruth Warren took control of the car and leased it to John R. Castle of United Shows, who exhibited it 1st at the Topeka fairgrounds. In September of 1934, Castle defaulted in paying rent; Ruth went to court again and repossessed the car. Then she rented it for $200 a month to Charles Stanley, a carnival man from Cleveland.

Between 1934 and 1940, Stanley, billing himself as "the Crime Doctor," showed the car all over the country under the sponsorship of the National Anti-Crime Association. During this time, the public had begun to pay less attention to it, primarily because there were several other cars making the rounds of fairs, each advertised as the car in which Clyde Barrow and Bonnie Parker had died. Immediately after their death, enough photographs of the car had been circulated in newspapers and magazines to allow any enterprising fellow with a 1934 Ford of the same style as the Warrens' to shoot bullet patterns in nearly perfect duplication of the originals. Some 4 or 5 fakes were being shown as the real one; people often scoffed at Stanley's exhibit as fraudulent. For this reason he was able to buy the car from Ruth Warren at a bargain $3,500. After getting the automobile, Stanley settled down to display it in an amusement park in Cincinnati. Interest in it continued to wane. By the late '40s the Crime Doctor was sick of telling youngsters who Bonnie and Clyde were. Nobody remembered them; nobody cared.

In Atlanta in 1952 a carnival showman named Ted Toddy was making a movie called *Killers All*, a documentary about notorious gangsters of the '30s. Someone suggested he try to find a famous gangster's car to accompany the movie. Toddy had heard of the automobile in Cincinnati, and since a part of his film dealt with Bonnie and Clyde and that bloody day when they were killed, he got in touch with Stanley. By November, 1952, the car had changed ownership again, this time for $14,500. Toddy exhibited his film in theaters all over the nation; the car, hauled around in a moving van, went along with it. When his film no longer interested people, Toddy went into semiretirement, and the famous Ford was stored away in a warehouse in Atlanta. While the authentic death car gathered dust, at least 5 fakes were showing up at fairs, carnivals, and shopping centers, still bringing in enough money to keep their exhibitors going.

In 1967 when Warner Brothers released the Warren Beatty-Faye Dunaway movie called *Bonnie and Clyde*, there arose a flood of new interest in the 2 desperadoes, even more than they had generated in their lifetime. Toddy again found himself the owner of a very famous car; people began asking to see it. Toddy took it out of the warehouse, cleaned it up, placed inside it 2 grotesque dummies (both wearing hats) to represent the dead killers, and went back on the road. At the same time, he began prosecuting the owner of every fraudulent Bonnie and Clyde car he encountered. The exhibitors of the fakes, however, were hard to catch. They showed their cars for 2 or 3 days and then were gone. When they were challenged by a skeptical ticket buyer, they professed vehemently that theirs alone was the real car.

Today when Toddy speaks of "the true Bonnie and Clyde Death Car," the rhetoric of an old showman comes back: "It has a magnetic appeal. I've seen people kneel before it or do the sign of the Cross. Women have walked away weeping. People come back to see it again and again, and they just stare."

By now the car has grossed over $1 million, as have its fraudulent sisters. With money like that, Clyde Barrow would never have had to rob banks.

—C.Y.R. rep.

ADOLF HITLER'S BIG CAR

In 1941, it appears, Hitler ordered 2 or more 770-K Mercedes-Benz cars equipped for his personal use. To the 20'-long chassis were added 2,000 lbs. of armor plate and bulletproof glass which, with 500 lbs. of fuel, oil, and radiator fluid, came to nearly 10,000 lbs. of weight per car. The armor plate is ½" thick while the glass is 1¼" and is said to have been tested by Hitler himself when he

shot a Lüger at it. One of the cars still bears a nicked side window.

Engines in the 770-K put out 230 hp from single-overhead-cam straight-8s but employ dual carburetors and dual ignition, 2 plugs for each cylinder, to get it. Superchargers cut in automatically if the gas pedal is floored. Nevertheless, 100 mph was probably the top speed ever reached by these Hitler cars. And even with 51-gallon gas tanks, these gas eaters get barely 3 mi. to a gallon, affording a driving range of only 150 mi. Equipped with independent front and back power brakes that surpass U.S. safety requirements, the cars could be lubricated en route by a couple of pumps on a pedal on the driver's side. Many features, such as the 4-wheel independent suspension with coil springs and hydraulic shocks, were standard equipment not only on the Hitler cars but on other contemporary models of Mercedes as well.

Two of Hitler's cars have crossed the Atlantic. The 1st was the one which Hitler presented to Field Marshal Carl Gustav Mannerheim of Finland to cement the Finno-German alliance. When the Russians attacked Finland, Mannerheim whisked his Hitler car off to neutral Sweden for safekeeping. But then the Swedish Government confiscated it, apparently for unpaid taxes, and put it up for sale. In 1948, Christopher G. Janus, managing director of Eximport Associates of Chicago, obtained it in lieu of cash for a shipment of ball bearings delivered to Sweden by his company.

Janus's car arrived in New York on June 29, 1948, and by mid-August of that year it had found a new career luring young Americans into enlisting in the U.S. Air Force. After a kickoff rally in Times Square, the car went on a nationwide tour with stops at principal recruiting centers. In a little over a year, this particular 770-K presumably enticed an endless number of men into the U.S. armed services. Reportedly it had also raised more than $100,000 for charitable causes in exhibitions throughout the U.S. Even then the car lapped up more than $2,500 for repairs, but with the handsome returns it brought for charity, no one complained.

The other Hitler car that migrated to the U.S. did so under the umbrella of the 101st Airborne Division, which had invaded Hitler's Alpine Eagle's Nest at Berchtesgaden in 1945. Information about the car's later whereabouts is sketchy. Allegedly it was, for a time, in South Africa.

In 1966, Tom Barrett, an Arizona real estate developer, bought both cars for his private collection. But by 1973, Barrett had concluded that either he had too many old cars in his Arizona collection, or not enough garage space.

He decided to unload 50 cars, including both 770-Ks, at an auction.

Until the Hitler cars went on sale, no antique car had ever brought more than $90,000. That sum was captured by Greta Garbo's Duesenberg in the fall of 1972. Within the 1st minute on the auction block, however, the initial Hitler 770-K cracked the record. It was the Mannerheim auto, and this one peaked at $153,000, falling into the hands of Earl Clark, a businessman from Lancaster, Pa. Clark wanted the car for the Lancaster, Pa. Clark park called Dutch Wonderland. The 2nd Hitler car also broke the 1972 record that day when the bidding soared to $93,000. Billy C. Tanner, an Alabama developer and George Wallace's 1964 campaign manager, bought it but he could not secure financing to complete the transaction. Consequently, he sold his option to Don Tidwell, a mobile-home manufacturer.

Next the Kruse auction people, sellers of antique and "classic" cars, put the Mannerheim 770-K back on the block, this time at its new home in the famous Dutch Wonderland Amusement Park. Earl Clark threw in some photographs, arm bands, leather-cased tool kits, and mementos valued at $15,000, and the Kruse brothers asked for an opening bid of $250,000. The bidding began at $50,000, then was raised until it reached $176,000, when the 770-K was hammered down at a new world's-record price to Robert Pass of St. Louis, Mo. In February, 1975, Pass sold the 770-K for $141,000 to A. J. Frascona, a car dealer from Wauwatosa, Wis.

—L.V.J.R.

Everybody's '57 Chevy

The 1957 Chevrolet was introduced by General Motors in late 1956, as part of their special Labor Day Sneak Preview of New Cars. The '57 Chevy sported nonfunctional tail fins and excess side trim like most American cars of that era, and it would have passed into obscurity except for the amazing popularity of the design in the years that followed. While the Chevy's competitors disappeared into the junkyards of the nation, the '57 throve, particularly the 2-door Bel-Air model. The car became a favorite of customizers in Southern California, and its popularity spread across the nation. The '57 Chevy has been almost as visible on the highways of America as the Volkswagen, particularly in California and the Midwest.

In 1965, the California Dept. of Motor Vehicles listed 35,000 '57 Chevies on the road—an astounding survival rate for an American car (although in 1957, Chevrolet enjoyed total sales of 750,000 units). No other American automobile has survived the years with equal fortitude.

However, no other American automobile, with the exception of the limited-production Studebaker Avanti, has enjoyed the unique production facilities of the '57 Chevy. There have been subsequent designs for subsequent Chevrolet model years, but the '57, unlike any other American car and contrary to American industrial practice, enjoyed a manufacturer's run of 10 years.

A dedicated group of ex-Chevrolet stylists and franchised used-car salesmen continued to turn out close to 200,000 1957 Chevrolets, focusing on the 2-door Bel-Air model, between the years 1957 and 1967, in a small auto assembly plant located outside Jacksonville, Ill.

The enthusiasts, led by ex-General Motors stylist Ardell Malowick, quit GM in mid-1957 when it was learned, to nobody's surprise, that the 1957 design was to be scrapped in favor of the longer, lower, wider '58 Chevy, which replaced the '57's peaked fins with contoured, sublimated fins.

Malowick and his associates quickly decamped and purchased their own auto assembly facilities in southern Illinois. However, Malowick was unable to finance the die molds and giant steel presses which GM and Fisher Auto Body used to construct the basic body; rather, Malowick relied on the proved European coach-building technique of pounding the body shape out by hand over wooden molds, formed from fiber-glass replicas of the real thing. In this way, some of the imperfections of Fisher's mass production were eliminated.

Malowick and associates knew that Chevrolet, which held all legal rights to the design, would not consent to the manufacture of '57 Chevies to compete with their '58s and subsequent models. Perhaps GM was aware, as Malowick now contends, that subsequent models could never compete with the '57 for purity of design. Because of legal restrictions, the post-1957 new '57 Chevies built by Malowick were sold as remarkably well-preserved used cars in car lots across the U.S.

In the sale of these cars, Molowick enjoyed the clandestine cooperation of countless used-car merchants throughout the nation who were in sympathy with his cause. Certainly, used-car dealers sought Malowick's creations with a fervor they have not displayed for any other American vehicle before or since.

Malowick was able to survive financially by his relatively high wholesale price, and a low overhead provided in part by engines and chassis pirated from Chrysler warehouses in northern Illinois (accounting partially for Chrysler's bewildering stock nose dive during and immediately after their "Forward Look" phase), and from sales to special collectors and customizers, mostly in California, who were willing to pay anything for a '57 Chevy in good condition.

By far Malowick's most successful model was, of course, the 2-door Bel Air with the metallic plum paint, many of which can be seen on the streets of most American cities today.

In 1967, Malowick was forced to close down shop because of rising costs and the rumors that General Motors was wise to his operation and was preparing legal action.

Malowick has since gone into the business of manufacturing denim boots and book bags, but he is considering another automobile operation if he can locate favorable factory conditions, possibly in Germany. There is a rumor that the giant Volkswagen Corporation, which has thought about opening a factory in the U.S., has made overtures to Malowick regarding the 1973 Buick Riviera, another classic of American design.

—M.B.

The Continuing Search for . . . Atlantis

BACKGROUND: Atlantis, that magic island with its ornate palaces and more-than-human inhabitants, has been said to lie submerged wherever there is an ocean. The idea of Atlantis has fascinated mankind ever since Plato wrote about it in 335 B.C., when he was an old man in his 70s. In the 1st Atlantean dialogue, *Timaeus,* he traced the story back through real-life people, including the scoundrel historian-politician Critias, to Solon, a statesman who supposedly heard it from an Egyptian priest about 590 B.C. According to the priest, there had existed over 8,000 years before a great Athenian nation on the Greek mainland and an empire named Atlantis on a huge island or continent. They had been rivals. When Atlantis tried to conquer the lands of the Mediterranean, the Athenians drove its armies off. Then an earthquake destroyed Athens and sank Atlantis under the sea.

In *Critias,* the companion dialogue, Plato is more explicit about the political setups of both empires and gives a detailed description of Atlantis' central city:

The palaces in the interior of the citadel were constructed in this wise: In the center was a holy temple dedicated to Cleito [Poseidon's mortal lover] and Poseidon, which remained inaccessible and was surrounded by an enclosure of gold. Here too was Poseidon's own temple, having a sort of barbaric splendor. All the outside of the temple, with the exception of the pinnacles, they covered with silver, and the pinnacles with gold. In the interior of the temple, the roof was of ivory, adorned everywhere with gold and silver and orichalcum; all the other parts of the walls and pillars and floor they lined with orichalcum. In the temple they placed statues of gold; there was the god himself standing in a chariot—the charioteer of 6 winged horses—and of such a size that he touched the roof of the building with

his head; around him there were a hundred Nereids riding on dolphins. . . .

Then, the story goes on, the Atlanteans began a moral decline, so Zeus, deciding to punish them, called the gods to a meeting. Plato's dialogue ends with an unfinished sentence: "And when he had assembled them, he spoke thus . . ."

CLUES FOR THE HUNT: Theories explaining the sinking of Atlantis, and where it might be, range from the occult to the zany to the bogus to the scientific.

When the age of exploration began in the 1500s and America had been discovered, scholars (and others) decided that Atlantis either was America or had once stood between America and Europe. Spanish historian Francisco Lopez Gomara was the 1st to say that the Atlantis story must have been based on knowledge of a New World continent. Sir Francis Bacon agreed with him. Often maps of the time showed a place called Atlantis.

If Atlantis, as an Old World continent, influenced the New World, that would explain many mysteries such as the sudden flourishing of the Mayan culture—it would not have been indigenous, but transplanted. To back up this theory, scholars began to find similarities between European and American civilizations: language, tools, customs.

In the 1800s and 1900s, Atlantis cults, many of them bizarre, were popular. Simultaneously, geologists argued about whether continents could disappear, and archaeologists did a lot of digging in places that could once have been Atlantis.

THE SEARCH: Augustus Le Plongeon was the 1st to excavate Mayan ruins in Yucatán, and from his findings, he came up with elaborate mythological theories which tied American civilization to Atlantis. His translations of Mayan manuscripts (the few left by the Spanish) told of an Atlantean queen, Moo, who, as Isis, founded Egypt. Sad-eyed and bearded, with a fierce temper, Le Plongeon and his American-born wife finally went to Brooklyn, where they wrote books putting forth such facts as that Christ spoke Mayan on the Cross—books few people believed.

Ignatious Donnelly had somewhat more solid credentials than Le Plongeon, but he was no less a wild-eyed theorizer. But who would not give some credibility to a man who spent 8 years in the U.S. House of Representatives? His book *Atlantis: The Antediluvian World,* which he wrote in 1882, went through 50 printings, the last in 1962. Many experts thought that the story of Atlantis had to be untrue because it was impossible for a continent to sink rapidly to the bottom of the sea. Donnelly did not agree. If earthquakes and volcanic eruptions can sink islands, why can't they sink continents, too? Like Le Plongeon, he made a point of similarities between Old and New World cultures and attributed them to Atlantis. He also thought that Sir Francis Bacon wrote Shakespeare's plays, and that a comet had once destroyed the earth.

Dr. Paul Schliemann had an illustrious pedigree. His grandfather was Heinrich S. Schliemann, the famous archaeologist who excavated Troy and Mycenae. Paul, however, did not have much going for him except a story. He sold the story, "How I Discovered Atlantis, the Source of All Civilizations," to the *New York American* in 1911. In it, he claimed to have been willed the secrets of Atlantis by his grandfather, who left the evidence in an old envelope of papers and an ancient owl-headed vase. One piece of evidence, which was never seen by the public, was a bronze vase inscribed "From the King Chonos of Atlantis." Currently, it is assumed that his story was a hoax.

Fragile James Churchward started his search for Atlantis with a holy source—the mysterious Caacal Tablets, which had been shown him by a Hindu priest. The tablets revealed, he said, that there were 2 sunken continents—Atlantis in the Atlantic and Mu in the Pacific—and that both had sunk when gas-filled chambers beneath them collapsed. He also claimed to have once been attacked by a flying snake.

Scottish mythologist Lewis Spence felt that Atlantis really existed 10,000 years ago and was inhabited by Cro-Magnon men.

At the turn of the century, the Krupps spent a half-million dollars of their steel fortune on an expedition to the Mato Grosso in Brazil to look for forgotten Atlantis. They found nothing.

According to most experts, it is possible that there was a kind of "Atlantis" at Tartessus (or Tarshish) in southwest Spain. Tartessus had so much silver, legend says, that the hogs ate from silver troughs and the Phoenicians, who traded there, made anchors of silver so that they could transport even more of the precious metal home. The Greeks learned of Tartessus in about 631 B.C., and it disappeared in about 500 B.C.; no one knows why. In the 1920s, Professor Adolph Schulten of Erlangen dug up the site of Tartessus, but the high water table kept him from finding much except artifacts from later civilizations.

In 1925, a retired British army officer, Percy H. Fawcett, set out for what he thought was the lost Atlantis in a remote part of Brazil. He and his party, which included his son, mysteriously disappeared. Then in 1951, the Calapalo Indians of the upper Xingú basin admitted they had killed the British explorers because the explorers had treated them badly.

Angelos Galanopoulos, a Greek scientist, thinks that Atlantis may have been Crete. Not far from Crete is a group of volcanic islands in the Aegean Sea, the remnants of a larger land mass blown up by a volcano around 1000 B.C. The theory goes that the eruption caused a tidal wave, which may have wiped out Minoan culture on Crete. Excavations on Thera, one of these islands, revealed a Minoan city dating from 1500 B.C. hidden under a blanket of volcanic material.

In 1972 the *Unesco Courier* told of the sensational find by a French diver, Dimitri Rebikoff, and an American archaeologist, Manson Valentine, off the island of Bimini. Their aerial photographs showed walls 250' long, 20' below the water surface, which were made of 25-ton, 16'-square blocks. These walls spread over an area of 38 sq. mi. Scholars from the University of Miami dated the settlement at between 7,000 and 10,000 B.C., before the building of the Egyptian pyramids. Atlantis?

In the summer of 1973, Maxine Asher, a mystic with an intense interest in Atlantis, inveigled Pepperdine University, in California, to sponsor—and give college credits for—a trip to Spain to find the fabled island. Spain was the spot, she said, because "for me vibrations are strongest there." Nearly 50 people signed up for the trip at a cost of from $2,000 to $2,800 each. Shortly after they arrived, Ms. Asher announced that on the morning of July 18, 3 divers had found a sunken city with streets and columns 14 mi. off the coast of Cádiz. In her press release, she said that the city was at least 6,000 years old and that the find was the "greatest discovery in the history of the world." The Spanish Government began an inquiry which revealed that Asher's story was a hoax. A student revealed that he had seen the press release 2 days before the historic dive had allegedly been made, and Asher disappeared. Later, reporters tracked her down to find that she was unabashedly leading another expedition, this time to Ireland, to continue the search for Atlantis.

Cultists claim that Atlanteans were really superior beings from outer space who brought civilization to primitive earth. Superscientists, the Atlanteans knew about explosives, airplanes, searchlights, and other modern inventions.

CONCLUSIONS: What were the truths in Plato's story? There *were* Greco-Perisan wars from 492–448 B.C. The little Greek island of Atalándi *was* flooded in 426, the year before Plato was born. However, chances are that his story was an allegory or a pioneer work of science fiction.

Was Mayan culture a result of Atlantean influence from the Old World? If so, then why didn't the Mayans know about the wheel, iron, and the plow? And why didn't the Old World know of tomatoes and corn until Columbus? Linguists do not feel that there are any real similarities between the Mayan language and any Old World or Oriental language.

Can a continent sink because gas-filled chambers beneath it collapse? Geologists say No. Such chambers, which would be deep underground, would be so flexible because of heat and pressure that they would never reach any size at all.

Can continents sink rapidly? Earthquakes cause only small changes in the earth's crust. If land does sink, it subsides over thousands of years. Any large areas that may have disappeared did so hundreds of thousands of years ago, long before Atlantis.

As for the idea that Atlantis was settled by aliens with a highly advanced culture, nothing was mentioned in Plato's works of any modern inventions, and none have been found in recent excavations of ancient ruins.

The name Atlantis has been used to identify ships, magazines, hotels, real estate developments, and a part of the planet Mars. And people keep digging and diving for evidence of the fabled continent everywhere. Was Atlantis real, or is it a city of the mind?

—A.E.

The Continuing Search for . . . Noah's Ark

BACKGROUND: The story of Noah's ark begins in a time when people did cruel things to each other, and God decided to destroy the world by water, but he saved one good family. Before the flood came, this family built a boat and outfitted it with humans and animals. Then, in due time, when the waters receded, the ark landed safely on a mountain. In almost all mythology, such a tale exists; with slight variations, it can be found in Muslim, Scandinavian, Polynesian, and American Indian folklore.

Upon hearing the tale, people have wondered—did it really happen? In the Western world, a lot of time and energy has gone into trying to locate Noah's famous ark, reputed to have been launched in the great deluge about 5,000 years ago. Here is an outline of how the search has been conducted through the years, and a summary of what has been learned.

CLUES FOR THE HUNT: One fact has presented little trouble, and that is what the ark looked like. All sources begin with the description in the Old Testament of the Judeo-Christian Bible. According to Genesis, God instructs Noah:

Make thee an ark of gopher wood; rooms shalt thou make in the ark, and shalt pitch it within and without with pitch. And this is the fashion which thou shalt make it of: The length of the ark shall be 300 cubits, the breadth of it 50 cubits, and the height of it 30 cubits.

A window shalt thou make to the ark, and in a cubit shalt thou finish it above; and the door of the ark shalt thou set in the side thereof; with lower, 2nd and 3rd stories shalt thou make it. . . .

Over the years research has enabled us to flesh out the Genesis meaning. Particularly helpful have been archaeological discoveries of ancient tablets and inscriptions that parallel the biblical story, most notably the Gilgamesh Tablet of Babylonia, uncovered about 1872 but written some 2 millennia before Christ and, at an estimate, one millennium after the flood. Scientists and theologians in rare agreement assume the ark to have been 450' long, 75' wide, 45' high—in other words, tall as a 3-story building and half again as long as a football field. It was divided vertically into 7 layers or stories, and horizontally into 9 sections, altogether making 63 compartments. Noah and his family along with the animals occupied the top stories, while the supplies of food and water served as ballast down below. The ship when fully loaded weighed around 100 tons with a displacement of 43,300 tons. Such a boat of pine, cedar, or cypress (gopher) and pitched with resinous bitumen would have been able to stay afloat for a year—the time required to wait for the subsiding of the flood which, according to computation, put the entire globe under 6 mi. of water.

But where did the ark land 5,000 years ago? Genesis gives no specifics other than calling the place Ararat. In the Septuagint, the Greek version of the Old Testament, "Ararat" is simply translated as "Armenia." In the ancient Assyrian language, "Urartu" is Ararat and is referred to as a broad area inclusive of what we know as Armenia. There, indeed, is a tall, eternally snow-and-ice-clad mountain rising 16,946'. Today, because of geographical shifts in national boundaries, Mount Ararat stands in northeastern Turkey at the triangle where the U.S.S.R. and Iran meet between the Black and Caspian seas.

The 1st known reference to the actual location of Noah's ark comes from Berossus, a Chaldean priest who compiled a history of Babylonia around 275 B.C. As to the ship that landed in Armenia, he is quoted by Alexander Polyhistor as saying, "Some part still remains in the mountains of the Gordyaens [Ararat] in Armenia, and some [people] get pitch from the ship by scraping it off, and use it for amulets."

After Berossus, a steady trickle of historical writers referred to the ark. In his *Jewish Antiquities*, compiled in the early centuries after Christ, Josephus says, "The Armenians call the spot the Landing-Place, and they show the relics of the ark to this day." The early Christian fathers added corroboration of a kind. Faustus of Byzantium described how a bishop of Persian origin, Jacob, went on a pilgrimage to Ararat and received a plank of the ark "from an angel." This plank, presumably, is the piece of petrified wood now preserved in a golden casket in the monastery at the foot of Ararat.

In 1670, a Dutch pilgrim-monk went to Mount Ararat in search of Noah's ark. There he met a hermit who had been inside it. The hermit's official attestation reads in full:

> I have thought it unreasonable to refuse the request of Jans Janszoon who besought me to testify in writing that he was in my cell on the holy Mount Ararat, subsequent to his climb of some 35 mi. This man cured me of serious hernia, and I am therefore greatly in his debt for the conscientious treatment he gave me. In return for his benevolence, I have presented to him a cross made of a piece of wood from the true Ark of Noah. I myself entered that Ark and with my own hands cut from the wood of one of its compartments the fragment from which that cross is made. I informed the same Jans Janszoon in considerable detail as to the actual construction of the Ark, and also gave him a piece of stone which I had personally chipped from the rock on which the Ark rests. All this I testify to be true—as

true as I am in fact alive here in my sacred hermitage.
> —Domingo Alessandro of Rome

THE SEARCH: With such sporadic, unverified reports about the ark's location, people were apparently content until the 19th century. Perhaps interest dwindled because there seemed to be no way of making certain that the stories were true; perhaps the difficulty in ascending the over 3-mi.-high Ararat was too great an obstacle. At any rate, the 1st modern ascent was made in 1829 by a German explorer, Dr. Friedrich Parrot. He discovered nothing belonging to an ark.

In 1896 at the World's Parliament of Religions, the exploit of an Indian archdeacon of the Nestorian Christian Church in Malabar, South India, was reported. "He said he had made 3 attempts to scale Mount Ararat before he succeeded. At last his toil was rewarded and he stood overwhelmed and awed as he saw the old ark there wedged in the rocks and half filled with snow and ice." The speaker added that the Indian "sincerely believed he had seen the ark and almost convinced others he had." The whole matter was greeted with some skepticism by men of the cloth, who asked jocularly if the Indian had seen "Mrs. Noah's corset hanging up in her bedroom."

Another wildly exaggerated and widely reported expedition was later discredited. It supposedly was made by a band of White Russian soldiers on the eve of the Russian Revolution; they claimed to have located the exact position of the ark. In 1930 a New Zealand archaeologist and mountain climber, Hardwicke Knight, did find some "soggy and dark" pieces of timber 9" to a foot in width at an elevation well above that of any known man-made structure and far above the timberline. Unfortunately these samples of wood did not survive the descent from their glacial protection, except as unidentifiable splinters.

In 1952, during late summer when the snows were at their thinnest, petroleum and mining engineer George Greene reconnoitered the area from a helicopter. He saw and photographed a "huge structure protruding from the ice" on a platform bordering a crevasse to the north and west of the summit at an altitude of around 16,000'. These photographs were eventually lost, and Greene, despite his enthusiasm for launching an expedition, abandoned his hopes for an official project in the face of the doubts and accusations he encountered from friends, family, and fellow scientists. However, in 1974, photographs taken by an earth-orbiting Skylab mission some 450 mi. above Ararat pinpointed a precise location for Noah's ark. The formation is at an elevation of around 14,000', in a crevasse covered with transparent ice, in the northeast quadrant of the mountain. Materials there, as revealed by the photograph and described by the Skylab crew, are "clearly foreign to anything else on the mountain and about the right size and shape to be an ark."

These 2 sets of photographs, taken in 1952 and 1974, constitute the most convincing modern evidence of the ark's existence. A French explorer, Fernand Navarra, brought back pieces of hand-tooled wood from near the summit of Mount Ararat. The samples were tested and analyzed in Bordeaux and Madrid laboratories, and validated as being no less than 3,000 years old. Navarra's book *I Found Noah's Ark* created a worldwide stir when it appeared in 1956.

The search has continued, now inspired by what is called "Ark Fever" or "Arkeology." Dr. John Montgomery, a teacher at Trinity Divinity School in Deerfield, Ill., and author of *The Quest for Noah's Ark*, has climbed Ararat twice—the south face in 1970 and the north face in 1971. Another expedition, blessed by President Nixon in 1970 and sponsored by the Denver, Colo., religious group SEARCH, was denied permission to make the ascent since the Turks justifiably consider Ararat—a highly militarized zone—of strategic importance. However, John Morris and his 12-man team, under the auspices of the Baptist research organization Institute for Creation Research, was successful in getting Turkish permission to ascend Ararat in the summer of 1972 and hopes for another ascent in 1975 or 1976.

CONCLUSIONS: There is surprising consensus as to the probable location of Noah's ark. Some of the evidence has been flimsy: Recently there was the aged Armenian who fled to America after the Turks took control of the area; he had climbed Ararat as a boy and described the ark as "absolutely petrified, just like pure stone." Other evidence—the existence of wood hewn by hand found at an improbable height, for instance—has been documented. But the passage of millennia, the 1840 volcanic eruption (which blew one side of the

mountain away, and doubtless would have exposed the "ark" to view), as well as the melting, shifting, treacherous glacier which envelops the elusive object, contribute nearly insurmountable obstacles to the determination and exploration of the site.

The task is of pressing importance to religious groups. Their interest and sponsorship has stimulated most of the recent expeditions; probably, because of Muslim-Christian antipathy, their work has been hindered by successive Turkish Governments. Ararat is traditionally and mystically considered the "cosmic mountain" connecting heaven and earth—a jumping-off point from one to the other, a ladder to God, so to speak. According to fundamentalists, the verification of the existence of Noah's ark is vital at this time. It would attest to the much-disputed veracity of the Bible, for one thing. Some even go so far as to say that it would disprove the scientific theory of evolution and reinstate the authenticity of the Old Testament version of creation.

In 1973, students in a creative writing class at Willits High School, Mendocino County, Calif., decided to see what would happen if someone were to try to build an ark today. They undertook the task of applying for the permits and permissions necessary for building and loading said ark, slyly sending out letters signed "Noah Lamechson" (Lamech was Noah's father) without mentioning the school. They received pseudo-serious replies from the Division of Highways, the Department of Fish and Game, the U.S. Coast Guard, the Bank of America, the district attorney, and others. The class published its full report on the difficulties encountered and expressed the throes of their "frustration" in a pamphlet titled "You Can't Build an Ark in Mendocino County!" Perhaps this humorous effort is an inadvertent testament to the present state of civilization. The definitive recovery of the original ark might loosen the red tape of bureaucracy in America, as well as add factual depth to biblical scholarship.

—F.B.

The Continuing Search for . . . Camelot

BACKGROUND: Probably no single story in history or legend has gripped the Western world like the haunting and thrilling tale of King Arthur and his Round Table knights. As Arthurian scholars L. Sprague and Catherine De Camp say in their book *Citadels of Mystery*, "Enough has been written about Arthur and his knights to fill a whole room in a library." In the 19th century, for instance, more than a thousand years after the "fact," there was a

veritable explosion of literature and art deepening the story of the "Stainless King" and his "Perfect Knights." Lord Tennyson in England, Mark Twain in America, Richard Wagner in Germany, all dealt with aspects of the Arthurian legend. In the 20th century writers John Erskine and T. H. White did likewise.

Central to every Arthur tale is his supposititious capital Camelot, that "rosy-red city, half as old as time." In *Idylls of the King* Tennyson described it this way:

O brother, had you known our mighty hall,
Which Merlin built for Arthur long ago!
For all the sacred mount of Camelot,
And all the dim rich city, roof by roof,
Tower after tower, spire beyond spire,
By grove, and garden-lawn, and rushing brook,
Climbs to the mighty hall that Merlin built.

More recently, and more familiarly, the Lerner and Loewe musical comedy *Camelot* consecrated the place in song:

Don't let it be forgot
That ere there was a spot
For one brief shining moment
Known as Camelot . . .
In short, there's simply not
a more congenial spot
Than happy, everaftering
Here in Camelot.

CLUES FOR THE HUNT: Tourist attractions in England boast of "Arthur's Chair," "Arthur's Table," and "Arthur's Stone." But these are actually no more than neolithic dolmens dating from prehistoric times. Was there ever a Camelot? Did Arthur ever live? Was he a man or, as some scholars suggest, a "fairy king?" These questions have plagued historians and spun a bewildering web of conjecture, hints, possibilities, proofs, and theories. There has been a centuries-old struggle between history and legend over possession of the truth.

Oddly enough, the 1st documents mentioning Arthur omit any reference to his seat or city of Camelot. Nennius, in his *History of the Britons* written in 800 A.D., describes Arthur as a *dux bellorum* or commander-in-chief of the Celtic and Briton "kinglets" fighting against the conquering Saxons. Arthur slew 940 of the enemy single-handed in one day. The next mention of Arthur comes in the *Annales Cambriae*, alternately called the Welsh Annals and the British Easter Annals, compiled c. 955 A.D. According to this record of one battle in 518 A.D., "Arthur carried the cross of our Lord Jesus Christ for 3 days and 3 nights on his shoulder, and the Britons were victors."

The Encyclopaedia Britannica, with its characteristic caution, lists 4 possible sites for the location of Camelot, and these all derive from sources written long, long after the event and are better described as literature than as history. Geoffrey of Monmouth, in his *History of the Kings of Britain* dating from 1130 to 1140, sets Arthur's court in Caerleon-on-Usk, the city of the Roman legions, where Legio II built and garrisoned his fortress in 50 A.D. to command the coastal approach to South Wales. In 1926 the National Museum of Wales began systematic exploration and excavation of the area and while they found much of historical value, they did not find Camelot.

Another document of the day, the *Welsh Triads*, as quoted by C. Henderson in his book *The Cornish Church Guide and Parochial History of Cornwall*, locates Camelot in the little town of Camelford on the Camel River in Cornwall and the site of the Battle of Camlan in 537 where Arthur was killed. Camelot itself was never found here, although certain linguistic satisfaction can be derived from connecting Camlan and "Camel," since camels are unknown in that part of the world.

By the 15th century, the location of Camelot becomes more specific. Sir Thomas Malory in his celebrated romance *Le Morte d'Arthur*, written while he was in prison in 1460 serving a term for rape and robbery, pinpoints Camelot as Winchester near the port of Southampton. His "evidence" was the existence of Arthur's tabletop, the so-called Round Table, which still hangs today in Winchester Castle. We now know that it dates only from the 12th century and is, as the De Camps put it, "a fake antique, but so old a fake as to have become a valued antiquity in its own right." Malory also blithely ignored the disparity between Arthur's "true" Round Table, which could accommodate 150 knights (and which would have to be at least 125′ in diameter), and the Winchester table, which is scarcely the size of a large dining room table.

Malory also ignored the fact that he depicted knighthood and chivalry some 6 centuries before they came into fashion and dressed his knights in armor, an anachronism of some 800 years. Sixth-century generals and soldiers were wont to smite off their ladies' heads and many, Arthur included, kept mistresses—some of whom were sisters or half sisters to their lovers. In any event Malory laid the groundwork for Tennyson, who later has Arthur say to Guinevere, "I was ever virgin save for thee," a statement as implausible in the 6th century as a miracle in a saint's life in the same period.

Malory's editor and printer, William Caxton, declined to accept Winchester as Arthur's Camelot. Instead, he placed it "in Wales, in the toune of Camelot, which dyvers now lyvyng hath seen," by which he probably meant Caerleon-on-Usk.

The 4th and last acceptable identification of Camelot with an actual place is owed to Sir John Leland, antiquary to King Henry VIII in 1542. In his *Assertion of Arthur* he places it at Queen's Camel, a village near Cadbury Castle, a large hill-fort in South Cadbury, Somerset. Leland wrote:

At the very south ende of the chirch of South-Cadbyri standith Camallate, sumtyme a famous foun or castelle, apon a very torre or hille, wunderfully enstrengtheid of nature. . . . The people can telle nothing ther but that they have hard say that Arture much resortid to Camalat. . . . Good Lorde, what and howe many most deepe Ditches are there heere? How many vallyes are there heere out of the earth delved? Againe what daungerous steepenesse? And to end in fewe wordes, truly me seemeth it is a mirackle, both in Arte and nature.

THE SEARCH: Cadbury gradually became Camelot at least in popular opinion. William Camden in 1586 reported in *Britannia* that "the local people call it Arthur's Palace." William Stukeley visited "Camalet [sic] Castle" in 1723 and drew a picture of it. But it was not until 1955 that a chance discovery of various pottery shards and pieces of glass dating from the 6th century in Cadbury Castle reawakened the possibility of scientific proof of a connection between Arthur's Camelot and Cadbury Castle. Soon after, C. A. R. Radford, leading figure in Dark Ages studies, wrote in his *The Quest for Arthur's Britain* that the collection of artifacts discovered there "provides an interesting confirmation of the traditional identification of the site as the Camelot of Arthurian legend." By 1965 some of England's most distinguished archaeologists and antiquaries revised their idea that Camelot as Cadbury was a discredited tradition. The Camelot Research Committee was formed with Dr. Radford, Sir Mortimer Wheeler, and other professionals, and Leslie Alcock, a Fellow of the Society of Antiquaries of London and of the Royal Historical Society, was appointed Director of Excavations.

Alcock and a body of some 100 workers, now certain that Cadbury was "a military site in use at the time when Arthur was a warrior," and accepting "the historical reality of Arthur and the authenticity of Camelot as working hypotheses," began 5 years of careful expert digging at Cadbury, "a steep-sided, free-standing hill with a grassy summit ridge rising above wooded flanks."

CONCLUSIONS: The results of these excavations, the most extensive ever made of any historical site in Britain, are presented in Alcock's book *Was This Camelot?* In sum, he writes, "We did not find the fabulous Camelot, nor add anything directly to historical knowledge about Arthur as a person." But the question is still wide open. Cadbury-Camelot revealed itself to be a major defensive work replete with revetments, trenches, defense lines, ramparts, and roundhouses. Unique to Britain were an iron gate-tower and a timber feasting hall 60' by 30' which *could* have been Arthur's. But aside from Arthur, the excavators found 4,000 years of history at Cadbury-Camelot. Ax-hammers, silver rings, needles, awls, wine jars, bronze knives, shields, and buckles uncovered there belonged variously to the Iron Age, the Neolithic period, the late Bronze Age of the 8th and 7th centuries B.C. There, too, was King Ethelred the Unready's mint whose silver coins of the 11th century paid the Vikings to cease their predatory raids on the Saxons. Although no silver horseshoes were found, which would have confirmed the legend that Arthur's knights make ghostly rides each night of the full moon, one huge bronze A was unearthed. Scholars say this letter was part of a temple inscription. But Arthurian romancers still believe that this stands for "Arthur" and proves, at last, there was a spot called Camelot.

—F.B.

The Continuing Search for . . . the *Santa María*

BACKGROUND: Columbus, in his flagship the *Santa María*, followed by 2 caravels, the *Niña* and the *Pinta*, reached the New World—the Bahamas island he named San Salvador—on October 12, 1492, 5 months after setting sail from the Gulf of Cádiz. The *Santa María* was the largest and most cumbersome of the flotilla, 78' in length with a beam of 26' and a draft of 7'. In addition to its complement of 2 boys and 30 seamen, it could carry around 106 tuns (barrels of wine) or 147 cubic meters of cargo.

The purpose of Columbus' voyage, simply put, was gold, and he and his men immediately set about trading with the primitive and gentle Indians found roaming naked in the mild air, as he wrote in his journal. In exchange for the little bells attached to hunting falcons, metal tips for laces used in clothing and on shoes, and wine, the Indians gave marbles, masks, and nose plugs, all of gold. Columbus cruised through the Bahamas, explored the north coast of Cuba, going deeper and deeper into the area wherever the Indians pointed their fingers indicating more gold. During the night of November 22, "without the permission or desire of the admiral" (Columbus' orders from the King and Queen of Spain read that he would be promoted in rank as soon as land was sighted), the captain of the *Pinta* set out on his own, leaving Columbus with only 2 ships.

Columbus reached what we now know as

Haiti, and which he named La Ysla Española, and was pleased with the beauty—"like springtime in Andalusia"—and the friendliness of the Taino Indians. As Christmas approached, the 2 remaining ships entertained hundreds of natives night and day, exchanging wine for fresh water . . . and more gold trinkets. Messengers from an Indian chief "some 7 leagues east" invited Columbus to visit, and Columbus—thinking he was heading for Japan—accepted. The sailing was immensely difficult, beating against the trade winds, and the ships had to make long, long tacks which turned the 7 leagues into dozens and dozens of miles. The men were exhausted both from their revels with the Indians and the tiresome sailing. On Christmas Eve, everyone fell asleep and the tragedy of the *Santa María* occurred.

Ferdinand, Columbus' son and biographer, gives Columbus' own words describing the event—an event, incidentally, he failed to report to the King and Queen on his return to Spain.

> It pleased Our Lord that at midnight, while I lay in bed, with the ship in a dead calm and the sea as peaceful as the water in a cup, all went to sleep, leaving the tiller in charge of a boy. So it happened that the swells drove the ship very gently onto one of those reefs, on which the waves broke with such a noise they could be heard a long league away. Then the boy, feeling the rudder ground and hearing the noise, gave tongue. . . .

Leaving a boy instead of a seaman at the tiller was the 1st disobedience to the admiral's orders. The 2nd was more serious. After the accident, Columbus ordered the ship's captain to take his longboat and an anchor out into deep water, so that they could heave on the cable connecting the small boat and the ship, and thus kedge the *Santa María* off the reef. Instead, the captain rushed to the *Niña* for help, and by the time he had returned with extra men, the tide had dropped. Sand had now filled around the ship and the swells, lifting and dropping the *Santa María*, burst open her seams.

After cursing the ship's captain as a wicked traitor, the superstitious Columbus was, within a matter of days, describing the wreck as "great luck" and a "heaven-sent omen." God was telling him to build a fort here for the glory of the Catholic rulers, *Los Reyes Católicos*, one which he would name La Navidad in honor of Christmas. The fort would be manned by the 39 men who could not be crowded into the small *Niña*.

The crews of the *Santa María* and *Niña*—with the help of the Taino Indians, whose canoes were large enough to accommodate 50 or 60 men—dismantled the *Santa María*, stripping it of all its timber and gear, but leaving the keel, some frames of the hull, and the bottom planking. To impress the natives, Columbus used what remained of the *Santa María* as a gunnery target, firing a cannonade of shots from the *Niña* at a distance of a few hundred yards. The fort La Navidad was built in a week. Columbus took aboard some Taino Indians, a flock of parrots, and a variety of tropical fruits to present to the Catholic rulers in Spain. Promising to pick up the men remaining in the fort the next year on his 2nd voyage, Columbus set sail to - find the missing *Pinta*—which he did—and returned home.

CLUES FOR THE HUNT: In December, 1493, Columbus returned to the area, but La Navidad had been razed by fire, all the men had been killed by hostile Indians (who had resented the white man's mania for gold and women), and everything of value had vanished. He found one of the *Santa María*'s 7 anchors in an Indian camp down the beach, a league from the site of the fort. Columbus made no attempt to look for the remains of the *Santa María*, nor did he pinpoint for posterity where the wreck actually took place.

At best Columbus' freehand maps were sketchy, with distances more vague than accurate. In modern geographical designations, we know that the *Santa María* grounded somewhere between Cap Haitien and Caracol Bay, a distance of a mere 12 mi. We further know that the ship foundered "gently and slowly," the weather was calm, and that it sat on sand, not rocks, on the protected side of a reef. But where exactly? As the late marine archaeologist Fred Dickson, Jr., wrote, "Here we have one of the most interesting, exciting, famous, and perhaps informative shipwrecks in history lying buried . . . covered with from 5′ to 10′ of sand, coral chips, and mud. Harder to find, yes. But think of the state of preservation, when we do find her."

THE SEARCH: John Frye, author of *The Search for the Santa María*, points out with a touch of bitterness that the *Santa María* is "a ship whose name is known to every schoolchild, yet few knew that the *Santa María* never returned to Spain, and still fewer knew that she had been lost on a Haitian reef." In fact, only half a dozen students of Columbus' voyages have actually visited the area in search of any telltale remains of Columbus' famous flagship, an adventure which Frye describes as "something worth doing—for itself."

In 1527 a friend of Columbus visited the spot collecting material for his *Historia de las Indias*. The natives still called the harbor Puerto Navidad, but there was no *Santa María* and no fort. In the 1780s a French topographer proposed that shoreline changes from soil erosion and shifting sands had altered locations of the past. In 1927, a young American naval officer, who started the vast sisal plantation of *La Plantation Dauphin*, and who had studied the area closely, tried to locate either the *Santa María* or where fort La Navidad had been. He failed.

The most important Columbian studies were made by the historian Samuel Eliot Morison of Harvard University. In 1939 he retraced the 4 Columbus voyages of discovery, a careful and cautious reconstruction which resulted in his prizewinning biography of Columbus, *Admiral of the Ocean Sea*. Morison, without benefit of aerial reconnaissance or underwater exploration, postulated 3 possible sites of the wreck of the *Santa María* reckoning from Columbus' times, distances, and descriptions. All 3 of his preferred locations were close to shore and within the waters protected by the 14-mi.-long barrier reef 3 mi. offshore between Cap Haitien and Caracol Point.

The search for the *Santa María* quickened in 1949 when Don J. Lungwitz, manager of *La Plantation Dauphin*, flying his plane from the plantation to the Cap Haitien airport, noticed "an oval, ship-shaped blur" on the large reef. Interest was further spurred when Edwin Link, an industrialist and amateur oceanographer, found an anchor in Cap Haitien Bay which might easily have belonged to the *Santa María*. In 1967 Fred Dickson, a treasure diver, a member of the Explorers Club of New York, and a Spanish history major at Yale University, became obsessed with the idea of finding the remains of the *Santa María*, as a "challenge for modern exploration." He set about systematically and scientifically organizing the *Santa María* Foundation, raising money, involving distinguished professors of marine geology and ocean engineering, assembling masses of technical equipment, and turning skeptics into advisers at the Smithsonian Institution.

Between 1967 and 1972 Dickson and his coworkers made 4 explorations of the reef, or coral mound. His 1st discovery 2' below the surface was of ballast stone, and the *Santa María* had carried 20 tons of this. At the 12' level they found pieces of wood, badly deteriorated but nevertheless sealed by the mud under the coral and protected from shipworms

or teredos. Then more and more uncoverings of objects—copper bolts or rods; iron rods; a nail fashioned from silver alloy in some emergency, presumably for a piece of armor; brass bolts with triangular washers or collars; and a piece of pottery. This last turned out to be the most exciting and precise find. The shard was dated by the thermoluminescent process as between 1375 and 1575 A.D. The underwater explorers defying the "wet unknown" now speculated the pottery might even have been a piece of Columbus' own dinner plate.

CONCLUSIONS: As Dickson and friends hewed and hacked away at the coral, mud, and slime of centuries, using crowbars, hoes, and picks in order to make a trench 4'–5' wide and 12" to 18" deep, they found nothing to prove that here lay the *Santa María* . . . and nothing to disprove the possibility either. "It was a trail of uncertainties," wrote John Frye, who covered the excavations for *National Fisherman* magazine. At one point Dickson, using a sophisticated electronic subbottom profiler, got signals from an area 75' southeast of the coral mound they were exploring. Seven feet under the sand, a 100'-long "thing" seemed to be buried. This appeared to the excavators to be not the *Santa María* but an earlier ship. From Africa? From China? A pre-Columbian voyage by a people heretofore unknown to have crossed oceans? At this point Vilhjalmur Stefansson's prophetic warning words were brought to the explorers' minds: "It is safer to assume that ancient men knew more than we can prove now than to discount less than perfect legends."

In 1972 Dickson died during his last expedition in quest of the *Santa María* or the "thing," which had come to assume equal importance in his adventures. He was, as Frye describes it, looking through "a curtain of frustration." The answer to the question "Was this the *Santa María?*" was always "shimmering like a mirage, sometimes taking firm shape, sometimes disappearing." With Dickson's death, interest in the *Santa María* has waned somewhat. Few today have his enthusiasm or his money-raising abilities. That he found something, however, is incontrovertible. Was it the *Santa María?*

—F.B.

The Continuing Search for . . . El Dorado, the City of Gold

BACKGROUND: Centuries before Columbus, 3 great civilizations—Inca, Aztec, and Chibcha—flourished in the New World. High in the Andes Mountains of present-day Colombia in South America and some 7,500' above sea

level, the Chibchas, specifically the Muisca tribe, ruled the isolated plateau of Bogotá, called Cundinamarca or "land of the condor." This area where the lakes looked black and the rivers ran white was protected from above by mountains and from below by surrounding jungles and savannas infested with cannibals, with Amazon women under the rule of Queen Califa (after which California may have been named), with pygmies, and—if early Spanish maps are to be believed—with men without heads.

Near Cundinamarca's capital lies Lake Guatavita. Muisca legend had it that the wife of one of the kings had drowned herself there, became the "Goddess of the Lake," and now required annual placation. At some unknown point in pre-Colombian history—the Chibchas had no written records—the custom began for the ruling King to strip naked, cover himself with resinous gums, and roll in gold dust. In a canoe, followed by his subjects, he paddled to the center of the 400' lake, threw emeralds and gold trinkets in the water and then, "in a flash of brightness," plunged into the water to wash himself. This ceremony was followed by gross festivities that included tribewide drunkenness and, according to Collier's Encyclopedia, homosexuality. For some reason—perhaps the obvious one of law and order—the ritual of the golden King and the ensuant revelries were suppressed at least by the year 1500. But the story was pretty heady stuff, even for Indians of antiquity, and news of the custom spread far and wide. When the Spaniards heard the story, they called the King *el hombre dorado* (the gilded man), which was later shortened to *El Dorado* and came to mean "golden city."

Gold, of course, meant nothing to the Indians. You could neither eat it nor buy anything with it. However, in the Americas it was abundant and so pure that it didn't need to be refined by the mercury process used for European gold. And it was considered ornamental. Indians decorated themselves with golden nose and ear plugs and breastplates, so that they would "blaze in the sun," and used sheets of beaten gold as wind chimes outside their houses.

In Europe the Spanish Kings in the late 15th and 16th centuries were nearly bankrupt. They had expelled the Jews and Moors, who had taken their gold with them. Almost as bad, when the 1st shipments of gold from Mexico began arriving in the Old World, economic stability was thrown out of balance. Still the *conquistadores*—the Spanish conquerors—as well as other Europeans, were seized with gold fever. Historian Joachim Leithauser says point-blank that gold was "the object of almost every voyage of exploration." It was at once an adventurer's incentive and his recompense.

CLUES FOR THE HUNT: In 1502, Columbus—on his 4th and last expedition to America—reached Venezuela, so named because its coast looked to him like "an odd little Venice." He had been told that there was "a

gold city 10 days from the Ganges." Since he still thought he was in India, he mistook the Orinoco River for the Ganges. Earlier, he momentarily thought he had found El Dorado in Haiti, where nuggets were the size of hen's eggs. In 1510 Balboa, already at the Pacific Ocean and not impossibly far from Cundinamarca, was contemptuously told by an Indian as he knocked a handful of ornaments out of Balboa's hand, "I can tell you of a land where they eat and drink out of golden vessels and gold is as cheap as iron is with you." Cortes, too, had been informed of this land by an Indian slave girl whom he baptized—and then used for 6 years as both translator and mistress. She had merely pointed in the direction of Bogotá.

Sebastián de Benalcázar, conqueror of Nicaragua, betrayer of Pizarro (since he preferred treasure hunting to obeying orders), governor of Ecuador in Quito, was the 1st to hear the El Dorado story from an old Indian who had actually seen one of the last ceremonies at Lake Guatavita. The year was 1536. The Indian said Cundinamarca was a mere 12 days northward. It was, however, more than that.

THE SEARCH: So much gold had already been found in the New World that no one doubted that somewhere there was a whole kingdom of gold. Expeditions approached Cundinamarca by river and by jungle. In 1530 Cortes's comrade-in-arms, Diego de Ordas, sailed up the Meta River and found some other lake instead. Benalcázar set out in 1537 only to find Hernan de Quesada already on the plateau of Bogotá. Quesada had arrived from the Caribbean coast. In 1541 Gonzalo Pizarro—younger brother of the more famous Pizarro—with a party of 200 Spaniards, 4,000 Indians, 5,000 pigs, 1,000 bloodhounds, and a herd of llamas crossed the Andes to get there. Half of his men were killed and his supplies were exhausted, but he reached El Dorado. So did the German Nicolaus Federmann. The latter came from Venezuela, where Walser, the banking firm, had originally sent him to investigate the newfound cure for syphilis made from cinchona bark or quinine water, a drink we associate more with malaria (or gin) than the pox. The journals left behind by these gold-crazed Europeans described harrowing experiences and sufferings . . . all for El Dorado.

The strongest and bravest reached the geographical El Dorado, but found no gold. The Chibchas bought their gold dust and trinkets from tribes in the lowlands. They had no mines of their own. But the search continued. As historian Walker Chapman put it: "The quest for El Dorado was an epic of human folly, really a case history in the power of man to bemuse himself with myth."

As late as 1595 Domingo de Vera, governor

of Trinidad, persuaded the Spanish King to authorize yet another overland search for El Dorado. Sir Walter Raleigh talked his way out of imprisonment in the Tower of London with his plans for an English expedition to El Dorado to be sponsored by James I. This was in 1617, and when he returned to England in 1618 without the promised cargo of limitless gold, he was beheaded.

Still the myth of El Dorado persisted. Seventeenth-century maps continued to show it, and by then it had become "the largest citie in the entyre world." Its location shifted variously, east from Colombia to the basin of the Amazon River in Brazil, to the swamp-soaked jungles of Guiana. Inevitably, after nearly a century of unfulfilled expectations, a few disbelievers appeared. The Spanish geographer De Herrera wrote sadly in 1601, "There be opinion that there is no El Dorado."

Stubbornly, 2 Franciscan lay brothers, who revived the dying faith in 1637, searched for a "Temple of the Golden Sun" on the east slope of the Andes. The Portuguese also headed in the same direction that year, starting out from Brazil. In 1714 the Dutch West India Company dispatched an army of men to see if the real El Dorado was Manoa on Lake Parima. Neither the lake nor the city existed.

The great Prussian scientist Alexander von Humboldt, beginning in 1799, scientifically and with Germanic thoroughness retraced all the steps taken by earlier seekers of El Dorado. He sailed up the Orinoco, down the Meta, and in 1801 after 45 days traveling up the Río Magdalena, he finally reached the authentic, if legendary, El Dorado—already many times discovered and revisited on the tablelands of Bogotá. Since Quesada had partly dredged Lake Guatavita and found 4,000 *pesos de oro*, Humboldt made some computations: If every year for a century 1,000 Indians dropped 5 trinkets of gold in the lake, there would be 500,000 gold pieces.

Humboldt, despite his lofty intentions of dispelling the myth, started a worldwide rage for draining the lake. The most exhaustive attempt was made in 1912 by Contractors, Ltd., of London. They shipped $150,000 worth of equipment to Colombia and lowered the level of the lake, already half dried up by a long drought. From the mud they reclaimed $10,000 worth of gold. But it had cost some $160,000. The most publicized expedition was headed by British explorer Col. Percy H. Fawcett, who disappeared in the Matto Grosso jungles of Brazil in 1925.

CONCLUSIONS: El Dorado from the beginning belonged to the category of "lost cities" and "lands of nowhere." But too many imaginations had been captured by the concept of a place with streets of gold, where gold was a contemptible commonplace instead of the supreme deity. Milton in *Paradise Lost* spoke of El Dorado. Voltaire made Candide visit there, depicting it as a never-never land where children played with golden quoits. Even Poe added his voice in an evocative passage:

> Where can it be—
> This land of Eldorado?
> Over the Mountains of Moon,
> Down the Valley of the Shadow.

Some historians suggest that the 1st explorers searching for El Dorado had been misled by the Cundinamarca legend. These scholars claim the actual El Dorado was waiting in a different form under the ground in California and in the Yukon. However, the Chibchas high in their plateau of Bogotá in the land of the condor—with its harsh, unyielding soil and its climate that is never warmer than 66° and no colder than 50°—had at the very beginning given the 1st discoverers their truest gold: the potato. It was from here that the strange tuber with its vinelike leaves and purplish flower came to the Western world. With its introduction into the diet of Europeans, famine was for a time abolished from their lives—a gift more precious than any metal.

—F.B.

A Guide to Buried Treasure in the Continental U.S.

At this moment more than $4 billion in lost treasure is scattered throughout the U.S.! That's the educated guess of an incorrigible old treasure hunter, and many of his colleagues think that that's a conservative estimate.

There's robbers' loot buried by people like Jesse James and Ma Barker "until the heat dies down," but never recovered because the robbers were shot or hung before they could retrieve it. There are incredibly rich gold mines whose owners died without revealing their locations, and which are now hidden by the camouflage provided by time. There are misers' hoards, lost caravans, and caches of pirate loot secreted from coast to coast. These bonanzas really exist, and finding one would be the fulfillment of a lifelong dream that has been shared by thousands.

No matter where one lives there's some sort of treasure lost and forgotten nearby. Getting information about this may involve spending time reading stacks of ancient newspapers to

find stories about misers who died without
revealing where they'd hidden their coins, or
legends of old silver mines in the hills that few
take seriously anymore. The public library's
card catalog will have listings of books under
"Treasure Trove" and "Treasure Hunting"
that may offer a lead—or try 910.45 in the
nonfiction shelves, if the library uses the
Dewey decimal system. Librarians are usually
glad to dig up stories about local hoards from
the "vertical file," that often overlooked collection of pamphlets and newspaper clippings.

Remember—gold, silver, jewels, and money
aren't the only valuables lying around waiting
to be discovered. Even if that old abandoned
mine doesn't have any gold left, it may have
treasures like ancient lanterns, vintage guns, or
patent medicine bottles. A single coin can
provide a grubstake that will last for years.
Anything nostalgic seems to be worth a small
fortune these days.

The most successful treasure hunters have
the heart and mind of a Sherlock Holmes but
they also carry a piece of 20th-century technology called a metal detector. Metal detectors
range from $20 toys to $1,000 examples of
sophisticated electronic wizardry. The less expensive models will find lost coins and watches
on a sandy beach, while the better ones can detect masses of metal buried deep under the
earth. A detector is a necessity for serious
treasure hunting.

World-famous treasures like the Lost Dutchman Mine in the Superstition Mountains or
Jim Bowie's lost silver mine are so well-known
that they've been searched for by untold thousands of people. Since they haven't been found
as yet, an amateur's chances of finding them
are negligible. Even relatively little-known treasures have been sought by a lot of people. But
again, anyone can be that fortunate one. All it
takes is a little more brains, a little more work,
or a little more luck.

The best clues won't be found in books
about treasure hunting—the authors of such
books keep the juiciest tidbits to themselves.
Time spent with dusty newspaper files and old
records will prove more valuable than poking
through abandoned mines and old homesteads.
That's how to find the clues—and even the
treasures—that no one else has heard of. The
clues are there, and so is the treasure.

Legal rights to treasure troves vary from
State to State and from treasure to treasure,
but there are a few general truisms. One must
have permission to search on private property.
It's a good idea to get this permission in writing and along with it, a stipulation as to how
any treasure found will be divided.

National parks and most State parks prohibit
all treasure hunting to prevent destruction of
public property. Most national forests are now
open, but rules change so it's a good idea to

check on a particular forest before searching
there. Bureau of Land Management property
generally has no restrictions.

MEXICAN GOLD: I

Montezuma's Lost Treasure Caravan

More than $10 million in gold and jewels from
the Aztec monarch's treasury was buried somewhere north of Mexico City to prevent it from
being stolen by the rapacious Spanish. Best evidence is that it's near either Taos, N. Mex., or
Kanab, U.

How It Got There. The Spanish came to the
New World to find gold, and they set about
their task with a single-mindedness that would
have made Scrooge blush. Rape, pillage, and
murder were standard business practices, despite the fact that the vast majority of the Indians they met were friendly and willing to
trade huge amounts of gold for small trinkets.

Greed completely conquered common sense,
and the Spaniards truly killed the goose that
laid the golden egg. Rather than trade peacefully for gold, they enslaved the Indians and
forced them to work their own mines, and they
stripped sacred temples of their solid gold ornaments, which they melted down into ingots
and shipped back to Spain. (Much of that
gold ended up on the ocean floor when the
galleons sank in heavy seas.) As a result the Indians revolted, hid their gold, and fled from
their conquerers.

In 1520 the Aztec ruler Montezuma learned
that Cortes and his gold-crazed troops were
heading toward his capital, which is now Mexico City. Knowing from experience that there
was no more hope of peaceful coexistence with
the Spanish than with a rabid jackal, Montezuma immediately stripped his buildings of
their gold, silver, and jewels and sent this
treasure by caravan to the north, to be buried
until the plague of Spaniards had passed.

Montezuma, unfortunately, didn't survive
this onslaught from civilized Europe. There's
no record of this treasure's ever having been
recovered, so it's likely still hidden where his
men buried it over 450 years ago. The question, of course, is "Where?"

One account says that the caravan went 275
leagues north from Mexico City, then turned
west into high mountains, where the gold
was hidden in a cave in a huge mountain canyon. There's some question of just how long a
league is, but the best guess seems to be that
the caravan ended up somewhere in the Sierra
Madres.

However, other versions say that the caravan
went much farther north, into present-day Arizona, New Mexico, or Utah. It's interesting
that some of the Pueblo Indians called their
cliff dwellings "Montezuma's castles." The
Aztec kingdom did have relations with the

Pueblo nation, but whether Montezuma's treasure was sent that far north is an open question.

Previous Searches. In the July 14, 1876, issue of the Taos, N. Mex., *Weekly New Mexican,* there's a report of a young Mexican who arrived in town to look for the treasure. Others from the town went out with him, because he seemed to have some special knowledge of where to look.

Searching among the rocks in the mountains outside town, he suddenly scrambled up a cliff ahead of the rest of the party. After a long silence he called out that he'd found a cave "filled with gold and lit into the blaze of day with precious stones." At that moment, according to the newspaper account, a powerful wind blew him off the cliff. He was dashed against the rocks below, and didn't live to tell the location of the cave. No one else has ever found a trace of it.

The town of Kanab, U., doesn't believe that the treasure is anywhere near Taos, N. Mex. Kanab came into the story in 1914, when a prospector named Freddie Crystal rode into town. He told a wealthy rancher named Oscar Robinson that he'd done a lot of research into the Montezuma legend while in Mexico, and he'd found an old book that gave him a solid clue. It seems that the book had drawings of symbols which Montezuma's men had supposedly inscribed on the rocks in a canyon near Kanab. Freddie figured he could find the treasure, if he could just come up with a grubstake.

It wasn't unusual for a businessman to outfit a prospector under an agreement to share any wealth discovered, and Robinson agreed to do just that. Crystal and his string of packhorses trailed off into the mountains, and weren't seen again for 8 years.

By 1922 the town had almost forgotten about the prospector and his tales of buried Aztec gold. It was pretty exciting when he came ambling back out of the mountains. When the people heard his story, they got even more excited. He'd found the treasure, he said, but he needed a lot of help to get it out.

Kanab just about closed up shop and migrated en masse into the mountains with Crystal. There, in a canyon on White Mountain, they found strange symbols carved into the cliffs that exactly matched those Freddie said he'd found in a book in Mexico. Nearby was a giant tunnel which had very carefully been sealed a long time ago.

The townspeople attacked that tunnel with a zeal that matched that of the original *conquistadores,* but day after day they found nothing but more rock. After 3 months everyone but Freddie had given up. Eventually he did too. He said that he was going back to Mexico to find more clues. He was never seen again.

How to Get There. Taos, N. Mex., is in northern New Mexico, about 60 mi. northeast of Santa Fe. Ask local residents to point out Taos Peak.

Kanab, U., is just north of the Arizona border, on Highway 89, about 90 mi. east of Interstate 15. Ask local residents for White Mountain, and the canyon with the symbols carved in the rocks.

MEXICAN GOLD: II

Maximilian's Millions

Emperor Maximilian of Mexico sent at least $5 million in gold, silver, and jewels out of Mexico when he learned that he was due to be deposed. His men were robbed and killed, and most of the treasure was buried in Castle Gap, Tex.

How It Got There. During the U.S. Civil War, France began to get ideas about regaining some of its lost New World empire, and as a 1st step Napoleon III placed Maximilian, the Austrian archduke, on the Mexican throne. Maximilian had delusions of grandeur, and he and his wife, Carlota, arrived with their entire Austrian fortune. They immediately used their position to amass more.

The oppressive foreign ruler was despised by the Mexican peasants, and plots for his overthrow began almost before he arrived. The Emperor at length realized that if he wanted to live to a ripe age he had best find a more agreeable climate. First, though, he wanted to get his wealth out of the country.

It's not easy to be inconspicuous when you're moving $5 million in gold and jewelry through rural Mexico, but Maximilian had a plan. He had 4 trusted aides pack all his valuables in 45 flour barrels, and sprinkle a layer of flour on top. His aides and 15 faithful peons set out in a caravan for the north, and crossed into Texas near El Paso.

The caravan had escaped the Mexican patriots, but now it had to contend with the Mexican and American bandits that roamed the lawless Texas border country. A band of former Confederate soldiers warned the travelers just how dangerous the area was, and Maximilian's men hired the soldiers on the spot as guides and guards.

A few nights later curiosity got the better of one of the guards. He had to know why a caravan of flour needed so much protection. While the rest of the camp slept he discovered the secret. Maximilian's men didn't live to see daylight.

The soldiers knew that they'd never get all that gold past the other bandits in the area, so they stuffed their saddlebags with as much as they could carry, and buried the rest. There are various versions of just how many soldiers there were, and just how they died. It's agreed, however, that some of them were soon killed by other bandits, and none lived to recover their hidden treasure.

Previous Searches. One of the men died with a doctor in attendance, and he gasped out the story of the buried millions at Castle Gap. The doctor returned to look for it many years later, but found nothing. None of the landmarks on the map drawn by the dying outlaw matched anything that he could find. Yet it's certain that Maximilian's men were escorting a fabulous treasure, and that they were killed. The treasure has never been seen again.

How to Get There. By all accounts, the treasure is still hidden somewhere around Castle Gap, high in the King Mountains north of El Paso. Ask in El Paso how to find the gap. Be prepared for hot, dry, dusty mountain country.

ROBBERS' LOOT: I

Vermont's Civil War Bank Robbery

A band of Confederate raiders robbed 3 banks in St. Albans, Vt., and buried $114,522 in gold and currency somewhere near the Canadian border.

How It Got There. On October 18, 1864, St. Albans, Vt., was a sleepy village that didn't pay much attention to all the strangers that had appeared during the previous few days. There was a war being fought and strangers were always coming and going. That war was much closer than anyone suspected.

As the afternoon wore on, the strangers began moseying over to the village green. As the town clock struck the hour of 3, they suddenly formed into 3 separate groups and converged purposefully on the 3 banks fronting the square. While some of them held the townspeople at gunpoint, the rest quickly cleaned out the banks. In minutes the task was completed, and all 22 galloped out of town.

Fourteen of the 22 were soon arrested in Canada, and St. Albans was amazed to learn that they were Confederate soldiers who had planned to use their loot to stage similar raids on other New England towns. The arrested men had some of the money with them, but $114,522 was missing. They couldn't seem to remember where it was.

The banks offered $10,000 to anyone who located the missing bundle, most of which was in gold. There were no takers.

Previous Searches. After the war, one of the soldiers came back. He didn't say much, but a local farmer secretly followed him as he wandered along the Vermont side of the Canadian border. He was obviously searching for something, but seemed confused. At length he left, empty-handed, and was never seen again.

How to Get There. St. Albans is about 20 mi. north of Burlington, Vt., near Lake Champlain. The soldier's search seems to place the treasure somewhere along the Vermont side of the border near there.

ROBBERS' LOOT: II

Mud Lake Gold

Gold bullion and money totaling $180,000—stolen from a Wells Fargo stagecoach—was thrown into Mud Lake, Ida., by escaping bandits.

How It Got There. In 1865 a stagecoach bound for Salt Lake City was attacked by the notorious Updike and Guiness gang. Four of its passengers were killed, and the driver was knocked unconscious. At least $100,000 in valuables was taken from the wealthy passengers, along with $80,000 in gold bullion from the stage's strongbox.

The driver and the surviving passengers made it to McCammon, Ida., where they told their story. A posse quickly formed, and tracked the gang to the Mud Lake area. The outlaws were trapped next to its murky waters, and they knew that they'd never escape with the heavy gold weighing them down. While the posse was still in the rocks above, it saw the robbers throw heavy sacks into the lake.

The gang made good its escape, and never returned to the area. Somehow the posse couldn't pinpoint the exact spot where they had seen the gold dumped, and there's no record that it was ever found.

Previous Searches. A treasure hunter named B. C. Nettleson and his partner Orba Duncan searched the lake for 20 years without finding a clue. Duncan continued hunting after Nettleson died, and in 1901 Duncan came up with 3 bars of solid gold which he sold in a nearby town for $25,000. He kept searching, but found nothing more.

That's all that has ever been found, according to the record, and local residents are convinced that the gold is still in the muddy bottom of the lake, or buried in lake fill.

How to Get There. Mud Lake is in east-central Idaho, in Jefferson County, about 30 mi. northwest of Idaho Falls, and about 60 mi. north of Pocatello.

ROBBERS' LOOT: III

Reno Gang Train Robbery

Gold coins, bars, and currency worth more than $80,000 were stolen from a train in Marshfield, Ind. The robbers apparently stashed it nearby, and were hung before they could retrieve it.

How It Got There. In 1868 a passenger train of the Jefferson, Madison and Indianapolis Railroad stopped for wood and water at a station in Marshfield, Ind. As the crew left the train, 5 men hidden behind a woodpile leaped out, knocked the fireman and engineer unconscious, uncoupled the passenger cars, and took off with the engine and the baggage car. The empty safes from the baggage car were found in a wooded area 20 mi. from Marshfield, but there was no sign of the contents.

A short time later 4 members of the same gang were arrested for killing 3 fellow gang members, and the good citizens of Marshfield decided that it was time the entire gang was retired. The 4 prisoners were taken to nearby New Albany for safekeeping, but that night 50 vigilantes rode into town with red bandannas on their faces and demanded to know where the loot was hidden.

With the sheriff and prison guards tied up, they dragged the gang members one by one out of their cells. They were given a choice—their money or their lives. One by one they refused to tell where the gold was buried, and one by one they were hung. The last man spit defiantly and said: "You'd hang me anyway, so why should I tell?" He was probably right.

How to Get There. Marshfield, Ind., is in Warren County, near the Illinois border in the west-central part of the State. The gold is probably somewhere in the vicinity, hidden under the rich Indiana farmland.

Robbers' Loot: IV

Jesse James's Mexican Gold

Jesse James's gang stole gold bars worth more than $1 million and buried them in the Wichita Mountains near Lawton, Okla.

How It Got There. A favorite pastime for ambitious Mexicans in the late 19th century was raising fortunes in gold to finance revolutions. During the 1870s Jesse James's gang staged a series of raids along the Mexican border with Texas, and one of these raids was at the expense of a caravan of gold bullion belonging to a Mexican insurgent general. The gang headed north into Indian Territory with its loot, and buried it in the Wichita Mountains in the present State of Oklahoma.

Previous Searches. Years later, with brother Jesse dead, Frank James bought a farm and settled down near Lawton, Okla. He made no secret of the fact that he was using the farm as a base from which to search for that gold. He'd helped bury it, but the intervening years of dodging the law had dimmed his memory. He knew that they'd left a marker of 2 pick heads and a code scratched on a bucket, but he couldn't find these clues. He was convinced that this fortune was within a few miles of the

farm, but after years of searching he had found nothing.

In the 1950s a man named Hunter Pennick dug up a brass bucket, 2 old pick heads, and an iron wedge. On the bucket was scratched an undecipherable code. Pennick dug numerous holes in all directions around his find, but discovered nothing more.

How to Get There. Lawton is located in southwestern Oklahoma, about 100 mi. from Oklahoma City. Ask local residents for the site of Frank James's old farm. Frank was sure the gold was nearby.

Obscure Caches: I

The Golden Washtub

An old prospector apparently hid a washtub half full of gold dust and nuggets worth over $1 million near Hill City, in the Black Hills of South Dakota.

How It Got There. In 1879, 2 prospectors named Shafer and Humphry picked out a claim in the Black Hills near Tigreville and began panning. They struck it rich, and worked the 20-acre claim for 2 years. One hole alone is said to have yielded 17 lbs. of gold, while another hole that was 16' by 16' in size yielded over a pound a day. They put all their dust and nuggets in a big old washtub, using a few pinches now and then to buy provisions. They agreed to split everything 50-50.

By the time that claim played out their washtub was full of gold, and Humphry decided to return to his wife and kids in Ohio. He took his half and did just that, but Shafer stayed on. A confirmed prospector, he staked out another claim farther down Newton Fork and worked it until the day he died.

Shafer had no known relatives, nor any friends. He spent his time alone working his claim, and didn't drink or use tobacco. He came into town only for provisions, and never gambled. Townspeople said that his fortune *must* have been hidden somewhere near his claim. All traces of his old cabin are gone, but old-timers remember seeing its rotting remains along the road to Deerfield. Not a single nugget has been turned up.

How to Get There. Hill City is in southwestern South Dakota, about 30 mi. southwest of Rapid City, not far from Mount Rushmore. Ask old-timers or the local librarian where Shafer's cabin was, along Newton Fork.

Obscure Caches: II

Treasure Mountain, Colorado

Gold worth anywhere from $5 million to $40 million was buried by French miners in the San Juan Mountains of southwestern Colorado in the late 18th century.

How It Got There. Tales of incredibly rich gold mines being worked by the Spanish began to drift out of the west with the French fur traders in the late 18th century. Since the French felt that they had a claim on the area themselves, they sent a party from New Orleans to find out what all the excitement was about.

The French party finally reached the San Juan Mountains in Colorado, and was amazed to find them even richer than they were rumored to be. The French set up camp and began working their 1st rich strike, without bothering to look up the Spanish.

The size of the French party and the amount of gold its members mined is in dispute, but everyone seems to agree that they buried all their gold to keep it from falling into the hands of the Spanish or the Indians.

The fields were so rich that the French changed their plans and stayed on through the 1st winter, though it got so cold and the snow was so deep that mining was impossible. They wintered in what is now Taos, N. Mex., and returned to their mines in the spring. They continued this pattern for several years, until finally trouble struck.

Trouble came in the form of Indian raids. Perhaps the Arapaho Indians began their raids because the French were friendly with the Utes, who were traditional enemies of the Arapaho. Perhaps the Spanish put them up to it because of complaints from the señoritas in Taos about the Frenchmen's "love 'em and leave 'em" ways. Perhaps it was because the Spaniards had learned just how rich the French mines were, and had decided that they didn't want anyone else making off with that much gold. Whatever the reason, the French forces were soon decimated. The survivors decided to conceal their gold and seek safety.

Some accounts claim that the French had 3 hiding places for their gold. Others say that they dug a single shaft into the bedrock of Treasure Mountain, a tunnel full of death traps. They also dug a well nearby, according to this tale, and put a map showing the gold's location in a bottle, and dropped it to the bottom of the well. Trees in the area were marked with arrows pointing to the shaft concealing the gold.

The small French party suffered more Indian attacks during their flight, and only one man—Remy Ledoux, the party's leader—survived. When he straggled into a French trading post on the Missouri River and spilled out his tale of fantastic riches in the mountains to the west, his countrymen scoffed. It was too much to believe!

Political turmoil in France made matters even more complicated. Napoleon was on his way to having himself named Emperor, and local French officials had more important things to worry about than tales of buried gold. The treasure was all but forgotten.

Previous Searches. In 1842 Remy Ledoux's grandson, who had a map which he said came from his grandfather, organized an expedition of 40 men to search for the buried gold. The map, unfortunately, wasn't drawn to scale, and all the mountains in the San Juan range looked alike to the new party. Worse, Grand-père Ledoux seems to have included false landmarks to throw off interlopers. The search party did find a fleur-de-lis scratched on a rock with an arrow underneath it, and they searched for days nearby. No luck.

Young Ledoux returned the following spring to continue his quest, but drowned in the process. His body was recovered by a William Yule, who many years later—while drinking—admitted he had Ledoux's map.

Another man—Asa Poor—obtained this map, and eventually claimed that he had deciphered an inscription in one corner. Supposedly this said: "Stand on grave at foot of mountain at 6 on a September morning, face east, where the shadow of your head falls you'll find the gold."

Although these directions seem a little strange—your shadow falls the same way whether you face east, west, or stand on your head—Poor said that he found a grave that fitted the map's description, and nearby he found a sealed shaft which seemed to be a worked-out gold mine. Snowslides and avalanches have greatly changed the mountainside, and no traces have been found of the hidden gold.

How to Get There. Treasure Mountain is located in the San Juan Mountains of southwestern Colorado, in Rio Grande County, between Summitville and Wolf Creek Pass. It's about 100 mi. east and a little north of Durango, the nearest sizable town, off Highway 160.

OBSCURE CACHES: III

Captain T.M.'s Oklahoma Treasure

A copper box full of at least $80,000 in gold coins is buried in the Kiamichi Mountains near the present community of Cloudy, Okla.

How It Got There. Captain T.M. (name unknown) and his Indian wife lived in the Seven Devils' Mountains (now the Kiamichis) around the turn of the century. Over the years the captain had hoarded $80,000 worth of gold coins, and in his old age he decided to put this in a safe place.

He put his money in a large copper box and buried it somewhere near his cabin. A few years later he died. He hadn't told his wife exactly where the box was hidden, but she had watched him whenever he went to fetch money from it. She said that he sometimes would head north and return from the east, and sometimes he'd head east and return from the north.

Unfortunately, in her old age the captain's wife couldn't seem to remember exactly where their cabin had been. Or perhaps she was exhibiting an Indian's natural reluctance to discuss gold with white men, an attitude born of long and sad experience. At any rate, she said that the cabin had stood on a low hill a half mile west of a certain rocky ledge. Local residents say that there used to be a cave near this cliff, but it's never been found.

How to Get There. Cloudy, Okla., is near the Texas-Arkansas-Oklahoma border, in Pushmataha County. Ask local residents where Captain T.M.'s old settler's cabin used to stand, or try the library's vertical file.

—C.S.

14

Communications

In the Tower of Babel: Human Languages

Language is one of the most distinctive differences between human beings and other animals. The origin of human speech, thought to have developed somewhere between Neanderthal and Cro-Magnon man, still remains a mystery. Anthropologists tell us that Neanderthal man had a pharynx too short to produce the sounds of human speech, but by 40,000 B.C. *Homo sapiens* had evolved a vocal tract with this amazing capability. Writing may be equally old. A Cro-Magnon bone, which scientists date from 30,000 B.C., has been found bearing intentional markings indicating an effort of some sort to communicate through writing.

There are now more than 3,000 languages in the world. An exact figure, however, is impossible to determine, partly because linguists tend to disagree on exactly what constitutes a language. Generally, when dialects are no longer mutually intelligible, they are considered to be separate languages. A dialect may also be considered a language if it is used in books and newspapers.

More people speak Chinese (800 million) than any other language—more than double the number speaking English (300 million), the world's 2nd most prevalent language. Hindustani, the 3rd, is spoken by 200 million people. This number includes those who speak Hindu in India and Urdu in Pakistan; the latter is derived from Hindustani but uses the Arabic alphabet.

Russian is spoken by 190 million people; Spanish by 160 million; German, Japanese, and Indochinese have 100 million speakers each; French, Arabic, Bengali, and Portuguese 75 million; and Italian approximately 55 million. More than 100 languages are spoken by over a million people each.

Chinese is not only the most widely used, but the oldest living language, dating back more than 4,000 years. Chinese writing is ideographic: that is, each character represents the object that is being described as opposed to the sounds made when the word for it is spoken. Recently the Chinese Government introduced a system to replace the 4,000 basic characters with the letters of the Roman alphabet.

The oldest known written language is Sumerian, which originated in Mesopotamia around 3,500 B.C. It was written in cuneiform script, whose symbols stand for the sounds made by syllables.

The North American Indian languages were unwritten until 1821, when a Cherokee named Sequoyah developed an alphabet of 86 phonetic symbols for his language. (See: Footnote People in U.S. History, Chap. 3.)

About half the world's population speaks a language originally derived from Indo-European, which was spoken as early as 4,000 B.C. Scholars assume it originated in the central part of the Euro-Asian continent and in a temperate climate, because the languages descending from it all have words for cold, snow, and winter, but none for tropical plants and animals such as rice, tiger, or palm. The Indo-European family includes: the Germanic languages (English, Dutch, German, and the Scandinavian tongues); the Romance languages descended from Latin (Spanish, French, Italian, and Portuguese); the Celtic group (Gaelic, Scottish, Welsh, and Breton); Greek; and the Balto-Slavic languages. There are 19 other language families including Hamito-Semitic (Aramaic, Hebrew, Berber, Coptic), Ainu (Japanese), Mongolian, Manchurian, African, and Amerindian.

Among the newest languages is New Guinea Pidgin English, which has developed into a language in less than 100 years. The term "Pidgin English" comes from a corruption of the words "business English." Found in newspapers and books in New Guinea, this language—which combines English and Portuguese with bits of German, Bengali, French, and Malaysian—has a picturesque relationship to standard English. The phrase for butter is "cow oil." Hair translates as "grass belongs head." And envelope is "pants belong letter." For the future tense the word "bimeby" is used, and the past is indicated by adding the word "finish."

The basic unit of sound into which languages are broken down is called a phoneme. The number of phonemes in human speech ranges from 11 to 67. English has between 35 and 46 phonemes, Hawaiian has 13, and Italian 26. The Japanese monkey uses 26 phonemes, various dolphins use from 7 to 19, the pig has 23, the fox 36, cows have 8, and chickens cluck in 20 different ways.

One of the most unusual sounds in human language may be found in the dialect of the South African Khoi-Khoin tribe. The language consists of harsh, staccato clicks, clacks, and kissing sounds, and is unique in that it is spoken by breathing in rather than out. These noises made by the tongue (similar to the way we say "tsk-tsk") are called the click-clack language. It sounded so much like stammering and clucking to Dutch ears that the 1st Boers in South Africa called the Khoi-Khoin "Hottentots," which word derives from the Dutch expression *hateran en tateren*, meaning to stammer and stutter.

An equally unusual means of communication is the whistle language of Kuskoy or Bird Village in Turkey. No one knows how the whistle language evolved, although it might have begun as a warning signal for Black Sea smugglers or others engaged in illegal activity. Bird Village, about 80 mi. southwest of Trabzon, takes its name from the birdlike whistling that the villagers often use in place of words. Voices don't carry far in the mountainous region, but the shrill whistles can be heard for miles, the high-pitched sounds carrying news of births and deaths, love affairs, and all the latest gossip. The whistling serves as a kind of house-to-house telegraph system. In order to get the power to "transmit," the whistler curls his tongue around his teeth so that the air is forced through his lips. No pucker is made, as in most whistling. To amplify the sound, the palm is cupped around the mouth and the whistling "words" come out with a great blast. It's said that the language is so powerful and complex that lovers can even romance each other with tender whistles from as far away as 5 mi. A similar whistling language is "spoken" by villagers in the Canary Islands, though a Kuskoyite wouldn't be understood if he whistled to someone there.

Then, of course, there are the so-called secret languages that range from Cockney rhyming slang, underworld jargon, and carny talk to the Pig Latin of schoolboys that can be traced back to the early 17th century. One of the most interesting is the female secret language developed by the women of Arawak, an island in the Lesser Antilles. This language was invented when fierce South American Caribs invaded the island before the time of Columbus, butchering and eating all the relatively peaceful Arawak male inhabitants and claiming their women. In retaliation, the women devised a separate female language based on Arawak, refusing to speak Carib and maintaining silence in the presence of all males, a revenge that was practiced for generations afterward.

Often a language has words that have different meanings in different countries. There are about 200 such words and expressions in English. In England what Americans call a cracker is a biscuit, french fries are chips, and the hood of a car is a bonnet. A misunderstanding frequently arises when an Englishman says to an American woman, "I'll knock you up," which simply means, "I'll give you a call."

Another case of confusion occasionally occurs when Iberians try to explain in English that they have a cold. Their word for that condition is *constipado*.

Languages from the same families often have words that sound the same but have different meanings. The words *die Gift* for example, can mean "poison" in German.

The migration of peoples around the globe sometimes causes the formation of hybrid languages, of which Yiddish is an interesting example. It is the official language of no country, yet is spoken by about 4 million Jews, half of whom live in the western hemisphere. Its core is medieval German, but it also contains words from ancient rabbinical Hebrew, bits and pieces of Eastern European languages, and, more recently, American English. In turn it has contributed a number of words to American English, many of which appear in the Doubleday Dictionary. Some of these are "chutzpah," meaning a lot of nerve, "schmaltz" referring to something which is overly sentimental, and "schlemiel," a real loser.

Academics have long considered the English spoken by black Americans to be simply illiterate English, but some linguists now propose that it is a true dialect, influenced to some extent by African languages, and true to a grammar of its own. Many words have made their way from African tongues into English— words like "jazz," "voodoo," "tote," "gumbo," "buckaroo," "banjo," "okra," and "juke" (box). In the African language of Wolof, widely used among the slaves brought to the 13 Colonies, there is the word "hipicat" which means a man who is very aware.

It is possible to interpret characteristics of a

people through the form and structure of their language. Some linguists say that the structure of our language actually shapes our view of the world. In that light it is perhaps interesting to note that English is the only language that uses a capital letter to indicate the 1st person singular. It is also the only western language that does not have at least 2 forms, polite and informal, of the pronoun "you."

In Siamese one shows politeness by using the word "slave" for "I."

In Arabic-speaking countries, where there has traditionally been an extreme distinction between the social roles of male and female, there is a different "you" for each sex.

In Chinese the word for "existence" is a compound of the words for "survival" and "destruction."

The English language contains more words than any other. Modern dictionaries have approximately 600,000 entries, compared with the 50,000 in Samuel Johnson's 1st English dictionary of 1755. In everyday speech only about 60,000 words are used. The most commonly used of these in order of frequency, are: the, of, and, to, a, in, that, is, I, for, as. In conversation the word "I" is used more often than any other.

People learning English as a foreign language are often confounded by the fact that pronunciation is not always reflected by the spelling of a word. There are 14 spellings for the sound "sh," and the combination of letters "ough" can be pronounced 8 different ways—as in: enough, dough, plough, borough, cough, and hiccough.

The longest word in literature appears in *The Ecclesiazusae*, by Aristophanes. It contains 170 Greek letters and written out in our alphabet has 182. The word, meaning a food preparation, is *lopadotemachoselachogaleokranioleipsanodrimhypotrimmatosilphioparaomelitokatakechymenokichlepikossyphophattoperisteralektryonoptekephalliokigklopeleiolagoiosiraiobaphetraganopterygon.*

The longest word in Webster's Third International Dictionary, 45 letters long, is pneumonoultramicroscopicsilicovolcanoconiosis," a lung disease found among miners.

The longest word in the Oxford English Dictionary, having 29 letters, is "floccinaucinihilipilification," and means deciding something is worthless.

"Antidisestablishmentarianism," with 28 letters, is the most famous long word—ask any child.

—M.N.

Toward a Universal Language

When the world was still young, according to the Bible, the Tower of Babel rose above the Plain of Shinar, and in it lived the descendants of Noah, all that were left of the world's people after the Flood. The people in the Tower spoke the same language until the Lord came to them, caused a confusion of tongues, and spread them over the earth. They could then no longer understand each other.

The world is no longer young, but its people, still plagued by a confusion of tongues, seem to have just as much difficulty understanding each other. Besides that, the world has grown smaller. A person can now circle the planet earth in 36 hours. Telstar and other communication satellites beam television programs simultaneously to earth's not-so-far corners. But how universal is reception of those programs when earth's people speak some 3,000 different languages?

Many linguists, anthropologists, and other experts feel that the answer to such lack of communication is some kind of international language. It might be an artificial language, a natural language, or a simplified version of a natural language. But the time is now.

Artificial Languages

Ludwig Zamenhof was a Jew who lived in Bialystock, Poland, a melting-pot city. In the late 1800s, young Zamenhof, still a teen-ager, often saw ill-feeling erupt among Bialystock's people, who spoke many languages—Russian, Polish, German, and Yiddish. Like many people before and after him, the boy could not help but think that some of that ill-feeling was caused by misunderstandings that arose from language difficulties. A common language, he thought, would go far to solve the problem, so he created one. It was a formidable accomplishment, even though Zamenhof was in many ways eminently qualified for such a task. His father was a language teacher. Russian, Polish, and Yiddish were spoken in the Zamenhof household. In school Zamenhof had learned even more languages: German, French, English, Latin, Greek, and Hebrew.

Zamenhof's artificial language was made up of root words from the Indo-European languages. The grammar was logical and simple, with only 16 rules to remember. The pronunciation was easy. And in its 28-letter alphabet, each letter represented only one sound. (Contrast that to English, in which the letter "c," for example, can have the sound of "s" as in "city" and "k" as in "cat," to say nothing of the number of sounds the vowels stand for.)

It was 1887 when Zamenhof completed his language. He then sent out a brochure titled

Lingvo Internacia under the name Dr. Esperanto, which meant "one who hopes" in the new language. The response to his mailing was even more than he could have hoped for. In a short time, over 1,000 people had got in touch with him and offered to learn and promote his new language, which soon took on the pen name of its inventor: Esperanto.

Probably the language became popular because it was easy to learn and use. Most Americans and Europeans understand this paragraph in Esperanto without any instruction at all: *La inteligenta persono lernas la interlingvon Esperanto rapide kaj facile. Esperanto estas la moderna, kultura lingvo por la internacia mondo. Simpla, fleksebla, praktiva solvo de la problemo de universala interkompreno, Esperanto meritas vian seriozan konsideron. Lernu la interlingvon Esperanto.*

Within a few years, Esperanto clubs had sprung up all over the world. Now several million people speak Esperanto. Over 600 schools teach it to 20,000 students a year. There are 100 journals and 7,500 books written in Esperanto, including translations of works from 65 languages. Esperanto has been used in more than 700 international conferences as well as in U.S. Army war games.

Esperanto is not the only, or even the 1st, artificial language. In the 1600s, Descartes created a language made up of numbers to represent words and ideas, and Sir Francis Bacon suggested a written system similar to Chinese ideographs. Other scholars came up with other schemes. Most, however, had little success. Their languages were rigidly logical, and very scholarly, while natural languages, used by everyone, tend to be illogical, flexible . . . and speakable. Between the time of Descartes and the present, 700 artificial languages have been created. They have included languages based on codes, on musical notes, on numbers. In one, for instance, "Honor thy father and thy mother" was written "leb2314 p2477 pf2477" and was read "lebtoreonfo peetofosensen piftofosensen."

Many experts oppose the idea of an artificial international language. Some claim that such languages will always favor one language group rather than another. Others say that we are not yet knowledgeable enough about the nature of language to be able to create one having all the factors that make up a natural language: nuances, cadences, modifications made by time. Most natural languages can be used by everybody—adults and children, scholars and blue-collar workers, young and old, doctors and dropouts. That cannot be said for any artificial language now in existence.

Other artificial languages are: Ro, Occidental, Arulo (later named Gloro), Suma, Neo, Loglan, Nordlinn, Spelin, Romanal, Nepo, Occidental (invented by Edgar de Wahl of Estonia in 1925), Novial (invented by Danish philologist Otto Jespersen in 1928), Mundolingua (invented by Julius Lott in 1890), Universal (invented by H. Molenaar in 1906), Bopal, Dil, Balta, Veltparl, Langue Bleue, Latinesce.

SIMPLIFIED LANGUAGES

"Here you have a very carefully wrought plan for an international language, capable of very wide transactions of practical business and interchange of ideas," said Winston Churchill in 1943 in a speech advocating Basic English as a world language. The grand old man, who himself used language with tremendous effectiveness and power, was talking about a simplified English system invented by linguists C. K. Ogden and I. A. Richards. Ogden and Richards had noticed that certain common words were repeated over and over again in dictionary definitions of tougher terms. It was possible, they felt, to get along with as few as 850 English words and say almost anything. With such a small vocabulary, Basic English could be mastered in less than 3 months. The system includes 18 common verbs like "come," "put," and "get." Combined with other words, these make up synonyms for a multitude of other verbs. "Make," for instance, is the basis for: make up (create), make out (discern), make a law (enact a law), make good (succeed), make eyes (flirt), and many more verb phrases. The vocabulary also includes 600 nouns and 150 adjectives, along with operational words like "of," "the," and "very."

Critics of Basic English claim that the system is too restrictive and that its synonyms are often inexact or unwieldy. Instead of "airplane" or "jet" or "helicopter," for instance, the Basic English speaker uses "winged machine for flight." Since the language was 1st devised, special classes of words, such as those needed in the sciences, have been added, bringing the real vocabulary total to nearly 8,000 words.

Attempts to create Basic French, Basic Russian, and other basic languages have also been made.

NATURAL LANGUAGES

Latin was the 1st, and perhaps the most important, universal natural language. For 1,000 years, during the Middle Ages and the Renaissance, it was used by scholars and the Roman Catholic Church throughout Europe. It still is the universal language of the Catholic Church, though services are now often conducted in the native languages of the congregations to make them more comprehensible to the ordinary person.

Today, German is considered the interna-

A Chart of Artificial Languages

Language	Inventor/Source	Characteristics
Volapük	Johann Martin Schleyer, a Roman Catholic priest, invented in 1880.	English and Latin-Romance roots, Germanic grammatical structure. Name means "world-speak." Too difficult for nonlinguists. First part of Lord's Prayer in Volapük: *O Fat obas, kel binol in süls, paisaludomöz nem olal*
Idiom Neutral	Simplified Volapük.	First part of Lord's Prayer in Idiom Neutral: *Nostr patr kel es in sieli, ke votr nom es sanktifiked.*
Esperanto	Ludwig Zamenhof, in 1887.	Probably most successful of artificial languages. Vocabulary derived from root words in Indo-European languages. Simple 16-rule grammar. A 28-letter alphabet with one sound for each letter. First part of Lord's Prayer in Esperanto: *Patro nia, kiu estas en la cielo, sankta estu via nomo.*
Ido	Descendant of Esperanto, 1907.	First part of Lord's Prayer in Ido: *Patro nia, qua esas en la cielo, tua nomo santigesez.*
Nov-Esperanto	Offshoot of Esperanto, 1925.	
Esperanto II	Another revised form of Esperanto, 1942.	
Latino Sine Flexione	Created by Giuseppe Peano, 1903.	Derived from classical Latin. First part of Lord's Prayer in Latino Sine Flexione: *Patre nostro, qui es in celos, que tuo nomine fit sanctificato.*
Interglossa	Invented by Hogben, editor of *The Loom of Language.*	Latin and Greek roots combined with Chinese syntax. "I wènt there in order to do it" reads *mi pre kine topo tendo un acte re* and translates literally "I past go place purpose a do thing."
Interlingua	Created from 1924–1951 by the International Auxiliary Language Association, an American organization.	Based on word forms in English, Italian, French, Spanish, and Portuguese. Still used in medical circles. Easy to understand, to wit: *Le Secunde Congresso Mundial de Cardiologica, que habeva loco in Washington, D.C., in septembre, 1954, adoptava interlingua como lingua secondari del summarios in su programma official.*
Monling	Relatively new international language.	Uses only monosyllabic words. Monling for "The language easiest to learn and use is obviously the best" is *ling 't top pai ken ad ploi, il klar top bon.*
Gibson Code	Invented by coast artillery officer	Uses only numerical symbols. "The boy eats the red apple" reads "5—111—409—10—5—516—2013."
Timerio	Created by mathematical-minded American in early 1900s.	A language based on numbers, each numeral representing a word or letter. It never caught on. People seemed to want a more euphonic way to say, "I love you," than "1—80—17."
Lincos	Developed by Hans Freudenthal in 1964.	A truly universal language, and perhaps the language of the future. It is composed of various scientific symbols, and is translatable into the binary code, which means it could be transmitted any place in the universe.
Solresol	Invented by Jean-François Sudre, of France, in 1827.	Author Victor Hugo and many in Europe welcomed it until 1900. The language is based on notes of the musical scale, and can be whistled, sung, or played on an instrument. Written in symbols of musical notation, it can form almost 1,200 words. But it has a difficult grammar, and its vocabulary would require a prodigious memory.

tional language of science, French the international language of diplomacy, and English the international language of trade. Because these and other natural languages are in such wide use, many linguists feel that one of them could be adopted as an international language.

On the face of it, it would seem sensible to use a language such as English for an international language. After all, only Chinese has more speakers, only French a wider distribution. In a sense, English *already* is a universal language. One-half of the world's newspapers are written in English, and ⅔ of the world's radio and television stations broadcast in English. English has a flexible structure: Meaning is determined partly by the position of the words (e.g., the man bit the dog/the dog bit the man) and partly through word parts (e.g., the "-ed" ending signals past tense in a verb). And the vocabulary is a potpourri of the world's major languages.

However, English has many drawbacks as an international language. Non-English-speaking peoples, particularly those in Asia, would view an attempt to make English a universal language as imperialistic. Moreever, English has difficult consonant combinations (desks), subtly contrasting vowel sounds (cut, caught), many words with more than one meaning (saw, can), and confusing spelling patterns (though, doe, thought, caught, caw). (Though spelling reforms have been suggested by many people, including George Bernard Shaw, not much has been done about it.)

Other languages present similar difficulties. French and Chinese have difficult sounds. Russian and German are structurally complex.

Semiofficial tongues like Pidgin English and Swahili have only limited international use. Moreover, because they are oversimplified, they sound babyish; they smack also of colonialism.

Some of the Problems

Coca-Cola has become a word in almost every language in the world. The French talk of "rocanrole" and "automation." Italians put "colcrem" on their faces and kick "futbols." Russians drive "avtomobiles" and eat "bifshteks." The Japanese eat "bituteki" with a "naifu" and "forku." English-speaking people have adopted such foreign words as: taboo, samurai, chocolate, depot, vodka, curry, and blitzkreig. The flow of words to and from languages increases as society becomes more complex, interdependent, and mobile. It would seem that a universal language would arise easily and naturally.

However, languages are more complex than their vocabularies. It is still an open question whether people shape languages or languages shape people; probably both ideas are true. Concepts in one language often cannot be translated into another. One language's rich forest of words is another's desert. The Eskimos have 12 words for "snow"; the Hawaiians lack even one word for "weather." Javanese has 10 words for "to stand" and 20 for "to sit," according to posture, attitude, and symbolism. Should all those excesses of vocabulary

so important to the cultural heritages of people be included in a universal language? If so, the vocabulary will be immense. If not, subtleties and nuances will be lost.

Languages differ, too, in how they are put together. Native Australian has 5 future tenses. In some Eskimo languages, a noun can have more than 1,000 forms. In Kwakiutl, the only way to say "The man lies ill" is "This-visible-man-near-me I-know lies-ill-on-his-side-on-the-skins-in-the-present-house-near-us." How can a universal language be one into which all kinds of language structures can be translated?

Pitch and stress and intonation differ in importance in various languages, too. They mean a great deal in English: "*You* ate Twinkies?" has a totally different meaning from "You ate *Twinkies!*" In Vietnam, however, pitch means even more. No Vietnamese is tone deaf because the same sound spoken at different pitches has entirely different meanings. It would be as if, in English, "dog" intoned in A flat meant "German shepherd" and in C sharp meant "apple." What emphasis should a universal language put on stress, pitch, and intonation . . . and how? Whom should it please?

Possible Solutions

Mario Pei, the famous linguist, believes that any language will do as a universal language, as long as it has a correspondence between spoken and written sounds. According to him, the main problem is getting it adopted and taught in elementary schools everywhere in the world.

Other experts believe that the world should be divided into major linguistic areas, in each of which one major language dominates: Hindustani in South Asia, for instance.

Margaret Mead and Rudolf Modley, anthropologists, believe that the world needs 3 languages:

1. A system of graphic symbols (glyphs) to help travelers around airports, lodging places, and so on. These should not require knowledge of any particular language. An example is the directional arrow.

2. A universal spoken language. This language should be a natural one with regular spelling; it should be non-European; it should have no religious, political, or ideological connections to speak of.

3. A written language, which can be artificial. This language should be logical and require a minimum of characters.

Whatever happens, almost everyone agrees that the time for an international language is now. The world cannot exist much longer as a kind of huge Tower of Babel.

—A.E.

Publish Your Own Book

Some writers imagine that they have only 2 options for publication: the commercial houses (McGraw-Hill, Doubleday, Harper & Row, and others of assorted shapes, sizes, and predilections) and vanity publishers (Vantage, Exposition, Dorrance, and more), which issue just about anything that an author will pay to see in print.

Writers should not depend exclusively on moneymakers to bring their creations to public notice. If writers and their friends hadn't decided throughout history to bypass the moneymakers, form "small presses," and publish their own works, the manuscripts of many classics—and best sellers—would have rotted away in basements, attics, and desk drawers.

Today this tradition of do-it-yourself publishing is too often ignored. Commercial and vanity publishers ignore the tradition because they prefer that a writer create for their profit. They are only too happy to teach a writer how to write, but seldom tell him how to publish.

But the tradition of self-publishing is ignored mainly because writers imagine that they must be commercially published in order to be proud of their work. "If my manuscript is worthwhile, why didn't a commercial house accept it?" the myth persists.

What follows is a history of some notable do-it-yourself successes, and a few flops, in England and the U.S. Other countries—particularly Russia with a vigorous *samizdat* movement under both the czars and communism—have a long history of do-it-your-selfing.

Thomas Paine's 1st self-publishing effort, *The Case of the Officers of Excise* (1772), got him fired from his exciseman job. The firing was unlucky for England. Paine left home and sailed to the American Colonies looking for work.

When Paine's next self-published tract, *Common Sense*, came off the press on January 10, 1776, not many people were thinking of independence from England. Six months later, largely because of this pamphlet, the Declaration of Independence was signed.

Paine originally thought of having his opinions published as a series of letters to the editors of Colonial newspapers, but most editors would not print the letters. At the advice of physician Benjamin Rush, Paine decided to publish his views in pamphlet form. He contracted with a printer, Robert Bell, for a 1st edition of 1,000 copies of 47 pages to be priced at 2 shillings each. Paine promised to make up any losses that Bell incurred in the printing.

Bell would receive half the profits with the other half reserved for the purchase of mittens for the Continental Army.

The 1st printing of *Common Sense* sold out in 2 weeks. Paine said that Bell had made £60 profit and demanded half of that for mittens. Bell insisted that he had made no profit and proceeded to print a 2nd, unauthorized edition. When Paine objected to the 2nd edition, Bell told him it was none of his business.

Paine enlarged the pamphlet with an appendix and an "Address to the Quakers." He paid 2 other printers to do 6,000 copies of this edition and then sold the edition to a bookseller, W. T. Bradford, for 8½ pennies per booklet, pledging the firm to sell them at no more than one shilling so that all readers could afford a copy.

Paine never made a shilling on *Common Sense*. By 1779 he was still in the hole by £39, 11 shillings for the printing of the enlarged edition, although 150,000 copies had been sold in America and others were sold in England, Ireland, France, and South America. Total sales eventually reached over 500,000 copies.

Although his 1st self-published volume in 1783 was a disaster, William Blake continued to produce and publish almost his entire life's work by himself and with the help of his wife Catherine. Like many other self-published and self-produced authors, Blake learned his production methods early, as an apprentice engraver.

When *Songs of Innocence* was finished in 1789, Blake was without funds, without credit, without a patron, and without a publisher. Blake said that his dead brother Robert revealed the solution in a dream: He should engrave his poems and drawings on copper plates. The next morning, Blake and his wife spent the last of their money on copper.

He began the process that he would use with variations for the rest of his life. Blake outlined his verse and marginal embellishments on the copper with a liquid. The remainder of the plate was then eaten away by nitric acid or other acid, leaving the raised outlines of letters and designs, like a stereotype. After a page was printed from the copperplate, he and his wife hand-colored it in imitation of the original. Blake did everything but make his own paper. He mixed his watercolors (preferring indigo, cobalt, and vermilion), applied the colors with a camel's-hair brush, and bound his books with diluted carpenter's glue. Blake said this binding was suggested to him in a dream by Joseph, the sacred carpenter.

The 1st edition of *Songs of Innocence* contained 27 engravings and was small, a mere 5" by 3", in order to save money on precious copper.

Blake was constantly hounded by poverty. Many of his prints and poems have been lost to us because he was forced to melt down engraved copper for new plates. Blake published only to his friends and patrons. He was stubborn about receiving money: If he suspected it was offered as charity and not for his work, he refused the donation.

On October 26, 1809, the *New York Evening Post* printed a notice: "DISTRESSING —Left his lodgings some time since and has not since been heard of, a small, elderly gentleman, dressed in an old black coat and cocked hat, by the name of KNICKERBOCKER."

A notice in the *Post* of November 6 reported that such a man had been seen a little above Kingsbridge by passengers on the Albany stage.

In the November 16 *Post*, "Seth Handaside," landlord of the Columbian Hotel, announced "a very curious kind of written book has been found in his room, in his own handwriting. Now I wish you to notice him, if he is alive, that if he does not return and pay off his bill for boarding and lodging, I shall have to dispose of the book to satisfy me for the same."

With this hoax, Washington Irving publicized his *History of New York* by "Diedrich Knickerbocker." Irving had the book printed in Philadelphia in order to preserve the mystery in New York. His hoax was so successful that a New York official offered to post a reward for information about Knickerbocker's whereabouts.

After the advance publicity, the 2-volume work, priced at $3, appeared in New York bookshops. Irving was acclaimed "America's 1st man of letters," and the *History* was said to be "the 1st great book of comic literature written by an American."

A self-publishing mistake occurred in 1811 when Percy Bysshe Shelley published his *Necessity of Atheism*. Although the contents outlined a position that was merely agnostic, the word "atheism" in the title was calculated to outrage.

During his 1st year at Oxford University, Shelley had the pamphlet printed by the local firm of C. W. Philips. He advertised the event in *The Oxford University and City Herald*, ballyhooing that the tract "speedily will be published, to be had of booksellers of London and Oxford."

This was at best an overstatement. No bookseller would handle the title. Undaunted, Shelley picked on the Oxford bookshop of Munday and Slatter. While the owners were out, he strewed copies of the *Necessity of Atheism* on the counters and in the window displays. He instructed the shop clerk to sell them quickly and cheaply at 6 pence each.

Shelley made his escape, but he was foiled 20 minutes later when a reverend strolled by, spotted the pamphlet in the window, summoned the proprietors, and had all copies burned in the shop's kitchen. Booksellers Munday and Slatter advised printer C. W. Philips that if he continued to print such material, harm might visit his machinery.

Shelley didn't quit. He brashly mailed his *Necessity* to bishops, his professors at Oxford, and heads of colleges. Even though he had published the tract anonymously, he made no secret of his opinions and was soon discovered to be the author. Shelley was expelled from Oxford for his self-publishing efforts.

A self-publishing flop doesn't always remain a flop. Edgar Allan Poe was not yet 20 years old when he contracted with a Boston printer to do 40 copies of *Tamerlane and Other Poems*. In 1827, Poe sank most of his meager U.S. Army private's salary into the printing of this slim volume of 406 lines of poetry by "A Bostonian" and priced at 12½¢.

Poe mailed review copies to all the proper sources but his poems were totally unreviewed. Two magazines bothered to include the title in lists of recently published books. One hundred years later a single copy of *Tamerlane* offered in a New York auction brought over $11,000.

Walt Whitman not only had some artistic know-how, he also knew how to wheel and deal. In 1855 he himself set the type for *Leaves of Grass* on the press of Andrew and James Rome in Brooklyn: 95 pages, 12 poems, somewhat under 1,000 books. He got his review copies out and attracted some notice, but he wrote the best reviews himself. In one of these reviews, Whitman described himself as "of pure American breed, large and lusty, a naive, masculine, affectionate, contemplative, sensual, imperious person."

The 1855 edition had been placed in a bookstore, but when the bookseller bothered to read the poems, he judged them morally objectionable and ordered Whitman to get them off his shelves. Whitman took his books to a shop that specialized in volumes on phrenology, the water cure, and vegetarianism. This shop, Fowlers and Wells, found little market for the poems. Whitman gave away many copies and sold the rest for pennies each to a dealer in publisher's overstock.

The next edition, 21 poems longer, did no better. Reviewers were outraged by Whitman's sexual references. Fowlers and Wells were so frightened by the thunder of the moralists that they handed the entire edition back to Whitman. Emerson himself pleaded with Whitman to delete the more racy passages, but Whitman refused.

In 1860, Whitman found his 1st commercial publisher, Thayer and Eldridge of Boston. The firm sold 4,000 copies of *Leaves of Grass* at $1.25 each and then went bankrupt.

Whitman's reputation was growing. In England, W. M. Rossetti published an unexpurgated, 28-page volume of Whitman poems in 1868, and other editions appeared on the Continent. Meanwhile, Whitman self-published 2 more editions, losing money on both.

A stroke in 1873 left Whitman in failing health, but did little to affect his entrepreneurial spirits. He recuperated at his brother's Camden, N.J., home and busied himself with writing and filling orders. He may have written the article in the *West Jersey Press* of January 26, 1876, that described him as "old, poor, and paralysed" and neglected by his ungrateful countrymen. No matter who wrote the article, Whitman sent it to Rossetti in England, and Rossetti began an international furor about the mistreatment of Whitman. Orders for *Leaves of Grass* flooded into the Camden house. With his full beard and his basket of books, Whitman became a familiar sight about town: poet, self-printer, self-publisher, and delivery boy.

In honor of the 100th birthday of the U.S., Whitman self-published his 6th edition of *Leaves of Grass* in 1876, bound in half leather and selling for $5. Because of his promotional craft and determination, his books were selling well through the world.

Gen. Henry M. Robert, a West Point graduate, was known in his time as an expert military engineer, responsible for the defenses and improvement of most of the nation's ports. Today he is remembered for his *Rules of Order*.

When Robert was assigned to San Francisco in 1867, many people of various backgrounds and customs were tumultuously converging on the city with no idea of the proper procedures for organizing and running meetings. Robert wrote a book of rules "based in its general principles upon the rules and practice of Congress, and adapted, in its details, to the use of ordinary societies."

No commercial publisher wanted his *Pocket Manual of Rules of Order for Deliberative Assemblies;* they gave the usual excuse of no market. In 1876 he placed an order with a printer for 4,000 copies of a 1st edition of 176 pages. He mailed 1,000 review copies to business leaders and clergymen. About the same time, S. C. Griggs, a Chicago commercial publisher that had previously rejected the book, agreed to distribute and the edition was gone in a few months. To date more than 2 million copies have been sold. Robert would be remembered for his riches as well as his rules if he had continued to self-publish and kept the commercial people at bay.

Mark Twain was hardly an underdog when he published *Huckleberry Finn* himself in 1885. His name was a household word. He expected to profit from the venture, but was only partly correct.

Twain formed a publishing company with his nephew, Charles L. Webster, and sold a creditable 40,000 copies of *Huckleberry Finn* by subscription in advance of publication. After publication date, Twain received an unexpected publicity break when the Concord, Mass., public library banned his novel. Twain exulted: "That will sell 25,000 copies of our book for sure!" Total sales reached over 500,000 copies.

Later he and his nephew published other books with varying success. His most important project was Grant's *Memoirs*, which sold 312,-000 sets at $9 a set. Twain gave Grant's widow a whopping 70% royalty.

Perhaps because of such generosity, Twain's self-publishing experiment ended in disaster in 1894. Twain labored 4 years on a world lecture circuit to pay off his debts.

Commercial publishers concluded that Stephen Crane's *Maggie: A Girl of the Streets* was "too grim" and morally objectionable for 1892 readers. They saw no market for a realistic novel about Crane's neighbors living in poverty on New York's Bowery. So Crane borrowed $700 from his brother and hired an uneasy printer to manufacture several hundred paperback copies. The printer was so nervous that he refused to mention his name anywhere on the book. Crane, fearing the consequences for his job as a newspaper reporter, identified the author as "Johnston Smith."

The public ignored the event. *Maggie* sold 100 copies. The rest of the edition went into the fire that warmed Crane's room through the winter of 1892. However, review copies reached the attention of Hamlin Garland and, through him, William Dean Howells, paving the way for wide acceptance of *The Red Badge of Courage* in 1895. After that success, commercial publishers were only too happy to reprint *Maggie*.

Too much "blood and guts" a commercial house said when rejecting Upton Sinclair's *The Jungle*. The author refused to compromise and, after 5 rejections, reported: "I was raging and determined to publish it myself."

Jack London contributed a manifesto calling on the socialist movement in New York to rally to the novel, which he termed "an Uncle Tom's Cabin of wage slavery. It is alive and warm. It is brutal with life. It is written of sweat and blood, and groans and tears."

Sinclair ran a prepublication subscription for *The Jungle* and, at $1.20 per copy, raised

$4,000, more money than he had earned in his 1st 5 years of writing. The novel was in type, waiting for the press to roll, when Doubleday and Page happened along in 1906 and offered to publish a simultaneous edition.

Sinclair didn't appreciate the reactionary ideas of Henry Ford. When Ford's plants were struck by the CIO in 1937 and Ford refused to bargain with the union, Sinclair reached an agreement with the union leaders and had his Hammond, Ind., printers do 200,000 copies of his novel about Ford, *The Flivver King*. Soon striking Ford workers all over the world were carrying the green paperback novel in their back pockets, much to Ford's disgust.

A dentist named Zane Grey deserves brief mention for his start in self-publishing. After moving to New York from Zanesville, O., and hanging out his shingle Dr. Grey found that tooth-drilling was too mundane a chore for his imagination. Using journals of his ancestor and well-known frontiersman Col. Eb Zane, Grey fashioned his 1st novel, *Betty Zane*. Nobody cared to publish *Betty* so he did it himself in 1904, to little success. Eight years later Harpers issued *Riders of the Purple Sage*, and Dr. Grey forgot about the tooth profession.

Carl Sandburg not only created his poems, he set them into type, rolled the presses, hand-pulled the galley proofs, and bound the books. *In Reckless Ecstasy*, Sandburg's 1st collection of poems, was manufactured by Sandburg with the help of his professor, Philip Green Wright, at Lombard College, Galesburg, Ill., in 1904. *In Reckless Ecstasy* was printed in the basement of Wright's home on a Gordon press with Caslon face type. The 50-copy, 50-page edition was bound in cardboard and held together with ribbon. A copy is now worth $500.

Certainly not every do-it-yourself published book brought adulation or cash to the author. Many books are unknown because the author lacked writing talent or had insufficient enthusiasm and endurance in proclaiming his work to the public.

Publishing-it-yourself is in the individualistic tradition of the American Dream. Although some writers may claim that the tradition is dead, that it is impossible to gain attention in competition with today's giant commercial publishers, they are wrong. The underground-press movement of the 1960s has spawned important associations, directories, and distributors. Publishing has been and remains one of our most democratic institutions.

Today, as always, if a talented author remains unpublished and unnoticed, the fault is the author's.

—B.H. rep.

Graffiti—the Handwriting on the Wall

"Why write on a wall?"
"Because it's there."

Graffiti are generally thought of as a recent phenomenon, something that appeared simultaneously with the modern bathroom. Actually, Kilroy has been here for a long time: Graffiti are one of mankind's oldest forms of communication.

The term "graffiti" derives from an Italian word meaning scribbling or scratching, and is used by archaeologists to designate the casual writings and drawings on ancient buildings. The most famous of ancient graffiti dates back to the advent of Christianity. It is a caricature of Jesus, in which he is tied to a cross but his feet rest on a horizontal board—and he has the head of a donkey. Next to him is a Christian with arms raised in adoration, and underneath is the commentary, "Alexamenos worships his god."

Since ancient documents generally record history from an aristocratic viewpoint, graffiti provide a rare record of the folk culture of antiquity. Graffiti in Pompeii were preserved almost intact when Mt. Vesuvius erupted in 79 A.D. and buried the city under volcanic ash. Pompeii's man in the street, like modern man, used walls to write humorously about politics, sex, and love:

The United fruitmen with Helvius Vestalis urge you to make Marcus Holconius Presicum duumvir with judiciary powers.

I liked a girl with a proper mat, not depilated and shorn, Then you can snug in from the cold, as an overcoat she's worn.

Serena hates Isadore.

Graffiti have been discovered in diverse places such as the Roman catacombs—"While I lived, I lived well. My play is now ended, soon yours will be. Farewell and applaud me"; the Tower of London—"While robed in the sacred vestments and administering the sacred mysteries, I was taken and held in this narrow cell"; medieval English alehouses—"Clarinda lay here/ With a young Cavalier/With her Heart full of Fear/For her Husband was near"; and frontier American outhouses—"Patrons are forbidden to leave seat while bowels are in motion." One wit wrote on the bathroom wall of a Berkeley coffeehouse: "People probably chipped these things on the walls of Egyptian bathrooms 2,000 years ago. So progress is a ball-point pen."

Contemporary graffiti can be divided into several general categories: identity, message or opinion, and art. A 4th type, dialogue graffiti, overlaps the other categories.

Identity graffiti represent an attempt by the anonymous individual to communicate and immortalize his existence by writing his name and the date, or announcing his current romance—"John and Mary"—or simply stating shyly, "I was here." This urge to leave one's mark seems as old as mankind; signatures of ancient Greek mercenaries still exist on an Egyptian sphinx and on the Great Pyramid at Giza.

The message or opinion graffitist likes to tell the world exactly what's on his mind. The bathroom wall provides a forum for uncensored communication on every possible topic. Leftist political graffiti comprise most of message graffiti, although philosophy, religion, the arts, and sex are traditional topics too:

Anarchy is against the law.

Judge Crater—please call your office.

You're never alone with schizophrenia.

Capitalism=heroin=addiction to business
Socialism=methadone=addiction to government
Anarchism=freedom.

Andy Warhol stencils.

Philadelphia is not dull—it just seems so because it is next to exciting Camden, N.J.

We are the people our parents warned us about.

Marie Montessori taut me to rite at age too.

Judas needed the money for a sick friend.

Franz Kafka is a Kvetch.

Evil spelled backwards is live.

Nietzsche is pietzsche.

I'm an atheist. I don't believe in Zeus.

Carry me back to old virginity.

Why's it all so hard?
Because that's the way it's good!

May your life be like a roll of toilet paper—long and useful.

Reality is a crutch.

Art graffiti, the most recent graffiti trend, reached its peak during the summer of 1972 in New York City, when the subway cars were furtively decorated with spray paint by ghetto adolescents with names like Taki 183, Phase-Too, and T-Rex 131. Rather than simply leaving a plain written message these graffitists embellished their names with decorative and colorful swirls, curlicues, and flourishes. Although the City of New York tried to stop the graffitists (and even went so far as to pass a law that forbade conveying unsealed cans of spray paint in public), art graffiti had prominent supporters. Pop artist Claes Oldenburg compared the decorated cars to a "big bouquet from Latin America," and Norman Mailer analyzed the graffiti explosion as a healthy outburst of the artistic urge in a repressive environment. They were not alone in this opinion; many of the graffitists have been commissioned to do murals for office buildings and for the Joffrey Ballet, and a group showing of graffiti art was held at New York's Razor Gallery.

Sometimes graffitists start talking back to each other, and a graffiti dialogue is born. One individual writes, for example, "My mother made me a homosexual," and a witty response is scrawled underneath: "Will she make me one too? How much wool does she need?"

These graffiti dialogues can develop into long-winded conversations, with several scribblers getting in on the act. In the following wall conversation, each writer has been designated by a number:

1. I have lost the equivalence of my ability to live. Please help me find my way.

2. Be like Miss Muffet. Start with your curds and your whey will follow.

3. Solipsist! Can't you tell a heavy question by the weigh?

4. Encores away, my lads?—USNA

2. Your lads are laid, your anchors weighed, and you're the fools your mothers made.—USMA

3. All of you look like targets to me.—USAF

1. See what I mean? Send out an S.O.S. and every S.O.B. within range jams the airwaves!

Graffiti dialogues often get started in response to poster advertisements. A New York subway poster for a job retraining program showed a complicated electrical unit with the question written underneath, "When this circuit learns your job, what are you going to do?" The graffiti retort: "Go on relief," "Pull out the plug," and "Become a circuit breaker." Another poster asks "Did *you* make New York dirty today?" and got the obvious comeback: "New York makes *me* dirty every day."

Synonymous with the word "graffiti" and known the world over is the notorious Kilroy. The balloon nose and mischievously prying eyes, accompanied by the announcement that "Kilroy was here," 1st appeared during W.W. II. The generally accepted theory of Kilroy's origin is that he was an infantry soldier who got tired of hearing the Air Force brag that it was always 1st on the spot. Kilroy specialized in being the 1st and only one to show up in outrageous places, like the top of the torch of the Statue of Liberty, on the packing cases of 3 elephants sent to the U.S. by the Belgian Government, and in the bathroom reserved for Truman, Stalin, and Attlee at the Potsdam Conference.

A Freudian Kilroy theory hypothesizes that Kilroy is a modern version of the ancient Oedipal legend. *Kilroy*, according to this theory, actually means "kill roi" (*roi* is the French word for king); king and father are identical, so Kilroy is an expression of the Oedipal urge to kill one's father. The accompanying urge to marry one's mother is symbolized by Kilroy's appearance in inaccessible, taboo places.

Even without psychoanalytic theories, however, Kilroy would live on, for he needs no defense or explanation. Kilroy, and graffiti in general, are simply Everyman's medium. They offer special advantages: They're free, uncensored, and available to everyone. Graffiti have been both despised and delighted in throughout history, and will undoubtedly continue to survive despite periodic janitorial cleanup and paint jobs. An anonymous scribbler in a New York bathroom summed it up:

Everything has its place, even the stupid writings in this cold john. Amen.

—S.U.

Morse Code

In 1844, S. F. B. Morse demonstrated to the U.S. Congress the feasibility of sending a message ("What hath God wrought") over a wire from Washington to Baltimore. Today there are 2 versions of Morse's original code: the General Service or International Morse Code, and the American Morse Code.

These codes have an alphabet made up of dots and dashes in various combinations which stand for individual letters. The Morse Code is so widely used that it does not qualify as a "secret" language, but it can be very mystifying to one who does not know it. It has a definite advantage over the Semaphore Code in that it can be sent in many ways—by whistle, buzzer, tapping, flags, or even by using the clenched and open hand during daylight hours. By night, lights of any kind can be used.

The flag is generally a square with a smaller square of a 2nd color in the center. White with a smaller square of red shows up well against dark backgrounds (woods, for instance) while red with a smaller square of white shows up well against light backgrounds (such as sky or a light wall).

There are 3 motions used with the flag and all start from and return to a perpendicular position in front of the sender. To make a dot, the flag is swung down to the right and brought back to position. To make a dash, the flag is swung down to the left and brought back to position. An interval is made by swinging the flag down directly in front and returning it to the original position. "Fouling" is avoided by making a figure "8" with the point of the stick

MORSE CODE

	International	American
A	·—	·—
B	—···	—···
C	—·—·	·· ·
D	—··	—··
E	·	·
F	··—·	·—·
G	——·	——·
H	····	····
I	··	··
J	·———	—·—·
K	—·—	—·—
L	·—··	— (= 5 dots)
M	——	——
N	—·	—·
O	———	· ·
P	·——·	·····
Q	——·—	··—·
R	·—·	· ··
S	···	···
T	—	—
U	··—	··—
V	···—	···—
W	·——	·——
X	—··—	·—··
Y	—·——	·· ··
Z	——··	··· ·
1	·————	·——·
2	··———	··—··
3	···——	···—·
4	····—	····—
5	·····	———
6	—····	······
7	——···	——··
8	———··	—····
9	————·	—··—
0	—————	— (= 7 dots)
period	·· ·· ··	··—·—·
comma	·—·—·—	·—·—
quotation marks	·—··—·	·—··—·
colon	———···	———·
semicolon	—·—·—·	—·—·—
question mark	··——··	··—·—·

while swinging. There are no pauses between dots and dashes, but a pause is made to indicate the completion of a letter. One interval, front, means end of word. Two intervals mean completion of sentence. Three intervals mean end of message.

To use a flashlight, use a short flash for the dot and a longer flash for the dash. There is a 3-dot pause between letters and a 5-dot pause between words. A longer pause indicates end of sentence. With a whistle, a short blast indicates a dot, a long blast a dash. The same pauses are used as with a flashlight. A lantern

is used more or less like a flag: for a dot, it is swung to the right; for a dash, to the left; and for the interval, it is moved down and up in a vertical line in front of the sender.

The 1st letters to learn are E, I, S, H (. , . . , . . . , ...) and T, M, O (–, – –, – – –), and these 7 letters can be used to form many words such as: is, it, sometimes, this, them, home, see. Accuracy is more important than speed, and speed will come with practice anyway!

—E.K.

Manual Alphabet

THE MANUAL ALPHABET was created by Abbé Charles Michel de l'Épée (1712–1789), a priest and lawyer, who established the 1st public school for the deaf in Paris. The sign language method was developed and perfected by De l'Épée's successor at the school, the Abbé Sicard (1742–1822).

The Language of Flowers
or, Say It with Flowers

African violet; white, yellow to purple; "Such worth is rare"
Apple blossom; white; "Preference"
Bachelor's button; blue; "Celibacy"
Bay leaf; green; "I change but in death"
Camelia, Japonica; white; "Reflected loveliness"

Chrysanthemum; red; "I love"
Chrysanthemum; white; "Truth"
Chrysanthemum; other colors; "Slighted love"
Clover (4-leaf); white or red; "Be mine"
Crocus; yellow or blue; "Abuse not"
Daffodil; yellow; "Regard"
Daisy; white; "Innocence"

Forget-me-not; yellow-blue; "True love"
Fuchsia; scarlet; "Fast"
Gardenia; white; "Secret untold love"
Honeysuckle; yellow; "Bonds of love"
Ivy; green; "Friendship, fidelity, marriage"
Jasmine; white; "Amiability, transports of joy, sensuality"
Leaves (dead); all colors; "Melancholy"
Lilac; purple; "First emotions of love"
Lilac; white; "Youthful innocence"
Lily; white; "Purity, sweetness"
Lily of the valley; white; "Return of happiness"
Magnolia; waxy white; "Dignity, perseverance"
Marigold; yellow; "Jealousy"
Mint; green; "Virtue"
Orange blossom; lightly orange; "Your purity equals your loveliness"
Orchid; all colors; "Beauty, magnificence"
Pansy; all colors; "Thoughts"
Peach blossom; bright pink; "I am your captive"
Petunia; all colors; "Your presence soothes me"

Poppy; white; "Sleep"
Rose; any color; "Love"
Rose; deep red; "Bashful shame"
Rose, single; pink; "Simplicity"
Rose, thornless; any color; "Early attachment"
Rose; white; "I am worthy of you"
Rose, withered; white; "Transient impressions"
Rose; yellow; "Decrease of love, jealousy"
Rosebud; white; "Girlhood, and a heart ignorant of love"
Rosemary; gray-green leaves, blue flower; "Remembrance"
Sunflower; yellow; "Haughtiness"
Tulip; red; "Declaration of love"
Tulip; yellow; "Hopeless love"
Violet; blue; "Faithfulness"
Violet; white; "Modesty"
Violet; yellow; "Rural happiness"
Zinnia; all colors; "Thoughts of absent friends"
NOTE: If you give a flower in a reversed position, meaning upside down, you also reverse the meaning.

—A.W.

Word Quiz

Try to match the words below with the men who introduced them into the language, either as inventions or as the names of characters in their writings. Score yourself: 6 correct—Good; up to 12 correct—Very Good; up to 18 correct —Superior; 19 or more correct—Super.

1. yahoo	a. Gelett Burgess
2. chortle	b. Lewis Carroll
3. ecdysiast	c. Miguel de Cervantes
4. pandemonium	d. Billie DeBeck
5. nihilism	e. Billie DeBeck
6. blurb	f. Samuel Foote
7. quixotic	g. James Hilton
8. malapropism	h. James Joyce
9. lothario	i. Edward Kasner
10. moron	j. Edward Lear
11. gargantuan	k. Samuel Lover
12. Shylock	l. H. L. Mencken
13. blatant	m. John Milton
14. ignoramus	n. Molière
15. utopian	(Jean Baptiste Poquelin)
16. runcible	o. Thomas More
17. debunk	p. François Rabelais
18. googol	q. Nicholas Rowe
19. Shangri-la	r. George Ruggle
20. heebie-jeebies	s. William Shakespeare
21. handy-andy	t. Richard Sheridan
22. panjandrum	u. Edmund Spenser
23. quark	v. Jonathan Swift
24. hotsy-totsy	w. Ivan Sergeevich Turgenev
	x. William Woodward

CORRECT ANSWERS TO WORD QUIZ

1.	v.	in *Gulliver's Travels*
2.	b.	in *Through the Looking-Glass*
3.	l.	in a letter to a stripteaser who had requested a more dignified name for her profession
4.	m.	in *Paradise Lost*
5.	w.	in *Fathers and Sons*
6.	a.	coined by the American humorist c. 1914, meaning in his words "to sound like a publisher"
7.	c.	in *Don Quixote*
8.	t.	in *The Rivals*
9.	q.	in *The Fair Penitent*
10.	n.	in *La Princesse d'Élide*
11.	p.	in *Gargantua and Pantagruel*
12.	s.	in *The Merchant of Venice*
13.	u.	in *The Faerie Queene*
14.	r.	coined, but not used in its current nonlegal sense, in *Ignoramus*, 1615
15.	o.	in *Utopia*
16.	j.	in 1871
17.	x.	in the novel *Bunk*
18.	i.	name for the figure 1 followed by 100 zeroes equal to 10^{100} suggested by Kasner's nephew while still a child
19.	g.	in *Lost Horizon*
20. d. or e.		DeBeck was a comic-strip artist
21.	k.	in the novel *Handy Andy*
22.	f.	in his plays, 1720–1777
23.	h.	applied by a physicist to particles some scientists believe to be the basis for all matter, after he spotted the word in *Finnegans Wake*
24. d. or e.		again

—R.H.

People Who Became Words

BOWDLERIZE ('bŏd-lĕ-rīz) *v.t.* To expurgate (as a book) by omitting or modifying parts considered vulgar.

"If any word or expression is of such a nature that the 1st impression it excites is an impression of obscenity, that word ought not to be spoken nor written or printed; and, if printed, it ought to be erased."—Dr. Thomas Bowdler

His inability to stand the sight of human blood and suffering forced Dr. Thomas Bowdler to abandon his medical practice in London, but this weakness apparently did not apply where vendors of words were concerned. Bowdler so thoroughly purged both Shakespeare and Gibbon that they would have screamed in pain from the bloodletting had they been alive; "to bowdlerize" became a synonym for "to radically expurgate or prudishly censor in the process."

Thomas Bowdler, the most renowned of self-appointed literary censors, was born at Ashley, near Bath, England, on July 11, 1754. After he retired from medicine, a considerable inheritance enabled him to travel about Europe, writing accounts of the Grand Tour that seem to have offended or pleased no one. Though he came from a religious family, Bowdler never earned the "Reverend Doctor" title often applied to him and his early years are conspicuous for the lack of any real accomplishments, unless one counts membership in organizations like the "Society for the Suppression of Vice." Only when he was middle-aged did he retire to the Isle of Wight and begin to sharpen his rusty scalpel on the Bard of Avon's bones. His *Family Shakespeare* was finally published in 1818. In justifying this 10-volume edition, Bowdler explained on the title page that "nothing is added to the text; but those expressions are omitted which cannot with propriety be read aloud in a family," adding later that he had also expunged "Whatever is unfit to be read by a gentleman in a company of ladies." What this really meant was that Bowdler had completely altered the characters of Hamlet, Macbeth, Falstaff, and others, and totally eliminated "objectionable" characters like Doll Tearsheet. Strangely enough, the poet Swinburne, who saw his own works bowdlerized by others, applauded the doctor many years later, writing that "no man ever did better service to Shakespeare than the man who made it possible to put him into the hands of intelligent and imaginative children."

Few writers then or now would agree with Swinburne, though *The Family Shakespeare* was a best seller and won some critical acclaim. Bowdler went on to expurgate Edward Gibbon's *The History of the Decline and Fall of the Roman Empire*, castrating that masterpiece by removing "all passages of an irreligious or immoral tendency." He firmly believed that both Shakespeare and Gibbon would have "desired nothing more ardently" than his literary vandalism and he would probably have turned his scalpel to other great authors if death had not excised him in 1825. About 10 years later Bowdler's name was 1st used as a verb, the official definition then "to expurgate by omitting or modifying words or passages considered indelicate or offensive." Today, the word more often means prudish, arbitrary, ridiculous censorship. Bowdler himself has been described as "the quivering moralist who is certain in his soul that others will be contaminated by what he himself reads with impunity."

—R.H. rep.

BOYCOTT (boi 'kot') tr.v. To abstain from using, buying, or dealing with, as a protest or means of coercion. —n. The act or an instance of boycotting.

Capt. Charles C. Boycott did not invent, propose, or practice the policy that bears his name. An impulsive but dignified, almost austere Englishman, he would surely have lived and died in obscurity had not his life—to his own misfortune—crossed that of the great Irish nationalist leader Charles Parnell. Boycotting, at that time a nameless political tactic, was one of Parnell's foremost weapons in the battle for Irish independence, and Captain Boycott was its 1st victim.

Charles Cunningham Boycott had been trained as a soldier but had resigned his commission on his marriage and had gone with his wife to farm a wild estate on Achill Island off the western coast of Ireland. Though reasonably successful in their endeavor, the Boycotts soon returned to the mainland so that the captain could accept an appointment as the earl of Erne's agent on the earl's estates at Connaught in County Mayo.

Ireland in the 1870s was an unhappy country of poverty-stricken peasants governed by absentee landlords. Yet an increasingly restive and articulate nationalistic feeling among the people was crystallizing into the Home Rule movement. Land was the crucial issue, and the people had long been united in demanding the "3 Fs"—fair rent, fixity of tenure, and freedom of sale. Under the Land Act of 1870, the tenant could become proprietor of his land, but when Boycott 1st came to County Mayo 3 years later, he found the countryside in the grip of an agricultural depression which was to continue for the next 2 decades.

In 1880, agrarian agitation took a new turn. Charles Parnell, member of Parliament and president of the Irish National Land League, had just returned from the U.S., where, as the darling of Irish-Americans from Boston to Baltimore, he had raised £70,000 for the Irish cause. Determined to take the initiative, Parnell decided on a new tactic: ostracism. Either the tenant or the landlord might be ostracized —the tenant if he attempted to buy land from which another tenant had been evicted; the landlord if he failed to accept a reduced rent fixed by the tenants themselves.

"Now what are you to do to a tenant who bids for a farm from which his neighbor has been evicted?" asked Parnell of his wildly cheering supporters in a town near Connaught on September 19, 1880. "You must show him on the roadside when you meet him, you must show him in the streets of the town, you must show him at the shop counter, you must show him in the fair and in the marketplace, and even in the house of worship, by leaving him severely alone!"

Thus it was that Lord Erne's estates, so conveniently close by, were selected as a test case. His tenants got together and fixed a new rent well below what Erne had prescribed, then offered their terms to Boycott. Now the captain's position was clear: He could not, as an agent, do anything other than uphold his employer's legal rights. He therefore refused the reduction. The tenants stood their ground, and Boycott promptly sat down and wrote out ejectments against them.

Just 3 days after Parnell's speech, a process-server attempting to deliver the ejectments was stopped by a band of hostile peasants before he reached the 1st tenant's cottage. He was forced to retreat precipitately to the captain. The next day, the peasants advanced to Boycott's house and ordered all the servants to leave, which they promptly did. Within a few hours, Captain Boycott's neat, orderly world had become a nightmare. Suddenly there were no farm laborers to gather the harvest, no stablemen to care for the horses, no cook to prepare dinner nor maid to serve it. The local shopkeepers were forbidden to serve Boycott when he entered their stores; the blacksmith was not to shoe his horse nor the laundress to wash his clothes, and even the postboy was warned against carrying Boycott's letters. "You must show him," Charles Parnell had said, "by leaving him severely alone!"

In the end, it took no less than 50 men imported from Ulster and guarded by British soldiers to harvest Lord Erne's crops on the shores of Lough Mask. As the pressure increased, Captain Boycott and his wife were forced to seek refuge for some time in a barn, where at considerable personal risk they were succored by friends from the village. The following year, the Boycotts left Ireland. Parnell was the victor in more ways than one, for in 1881 the "Magna Carta" of the Irish farmer was passed. This Land Act recognized the "3 Fs" and set up a land commission to fix a "fair rent."

One might assume that Charles Boycott would have shunned Ireland forever after, but that was not the case. He revisited it some years later while on holiday, was recognized at a public gathering in Dublin, and was generously cheered; the Irish attributed his former behavior to his army-trained sense of duty and bore him no grudge.

—N.C.S. rep.

DIESEL engine (de′zel, -sel) n. An internal-combustion engine that uses the heat of highly compressed air to ignite a spray of fuel introduced after the start of the compression stroke. Also called "diesel motor," "diesel."

Rudolph Diesel was the son of a German couple who lived in Paris until the Franco-Prussian war of 1870 forced them to flee to England. Hardly had they arrived when Rudolph's uncle in Augsburg offered to look after the boy until the war was over. At 12, Rudolph was therefore put on a train with his uncle's address on a card tied around his neck and sent via Harwich back to the Continent. Wartime delays extended the trip to 8 lonely days.

Diesel remembered this experience well when, years later, he determined that all transportation would be improved if the not-very-efficient steam engine, with its clumsy furnace, boiler, and chimney, could be replaced by something considerably more compact. The internal combustion engine existed but in an imperfect state. Diesel was working in an ice-machine factory at the time, and among his patents for the making of clear ice and the making of ice directly in a bottle ready for sale were patents for improvements on the internal combustion engine, including devices to increase compression and eliminate the ignition spark. Diesel constructed his 1st engine along these lines himself, but when he tried to start it, part of it promptly exploded and almost killed him. "The birth of an idea is the happy moment in which everything appears possible and reality has not yet entered into the problem," he noted dryly in his diary.

The experiment had proved, however, that a compression-ignition engine would work; the problem was to perfect it and to determine what fuel it would work best on. Everything from alcohol to peanut oil was tried, and experiments continued for years before diesel fuel, an inexpensive, semirefined crude oil, was arrived at. As improvements were made, it became clear that the diesel engine had greater thermal efficiency and offered greater fuel economy than any other existing engine. When in 1900 Diesel met Count von Zeppelin, the 2 men discussed the possibility of powering zeppelins with diesels. This eventually came to pass, but not until long after both inventors were dead. Oceangoing vessels started using diesels right away, however; Nansen's ship, the *Fram*, was diesel-powered when it made its Antarctica expedition in 1911.

His invention made Diesel rich and famous, and he traveled extensively. A few months before the outbreak of W.W. I, he was invited to England to attend an important congress. On the evening of September 29, 1913, he and 2 colleagues boarded the cross-channel steamer *Dresden*, dined together, and strolled up and down the deck before going to their separate cabins for the night. When the *Dresden* docked at Harwich the next morning, Diesel did not join his 2 friends on deck, nor did he answer their knock. When his stateroom was opened, they found his bed had not been slept in. The other passengers had not seen him; the crew found only his hat and overcoat by the after-rail. Ten days later, the crew of another boat fished a corpse out of the water. The pockets contained a coin purse, a medicine container, and a spectacles case, all of which Diesel's son later identified as having belonged to his father. But in accordance with prevailing custom of "finds at sea," the corpse was returned to the waves and never again recovered.

—N.C.S. rep.

GUILLOTINE (′gĭl-ĕ-tēn) n. A machine for beheading by means of a heavy blade that slides down in vertical guides.

Dr. Joseph Ignace Guillotin (1738–1814) did not invent the guillotine, did not die by the guillotine, and all his life futilely tried to detach his name from the height reducer.

The confusion began on October 10, 1789, when the eminent Parisian physician, a member of the National Assembly during the French Revolution, suggested that a "merciful" beheading device replace the clumsy sword and degrading rope then used by French executioners. Guillotin may have studied similar instruments abroad and definitely knew they existed, for the infamous "Maiden" had been used even in France during the Middle Ages and was still widely employed throughout Europe. In his speech to the French chamber Guillotin contended that hanging brought disgrace upon a criminal's family, that beheading probably felt better, being quicker and less painful at least, and that there wasn't any equality in a nobleman's being dispatched by the sword while a commoner legally had to swing by a rope for his crimes. His ideas, especially the last, gradually took hold in egalitarian France, and 2 years later the Assembly adopted decapitation as the legal means of execution for "every person condemned to death."

The specific machine accepted for the purpose was designed by Dr. Antoine Louis, secretary of the Academy of Medicine, and constructed by a German named Tobias Schmidt, who even supplied a leather bag to hold the severed heads. For some 329 francs, inclusive, the 1st Louisette or Louison, as it came to be called, was erected on the Place de Grève, and on April 22, 1792, the head of a notorious highwayman named Peletier became the 1st to plop into its basket. But Dr. Guillotin remained in the public's mind for his eloquent speech and one of many popular songs about the new machine claimed that he had invented it. Not much time passed before "la louisette" lost out to "la machine guillotine," "Madame Guillotine," and then "guillotine" itself.

The legend that Dr. Guillotin was hoist with his own petard springs from several circumstances. For one, its real designer, Dr. Louis, lost his inventive head to the guillotine during the Reign of Terror—as did thousands of victims, including, of course, the mechanically inclined Louis XVI, who is said to have recommended its oblique cutting edge as a refinement to the inventor. Secondly, Dr. Guillotin was indeed condemned to die for protecting friends suspected by Robespierre, only escaping execution by the narrowest of margins when Robespierre himself was guillotined. Finally, a Dr. J. B. V. Guillotin of Lyon had been so executed during the Terror, his name, of course, confused with the more prominent doctor's.

Many wanted to think that Guillotin became the victim of his own Frankenstein's monster—like Hugues Aubriot, the designer of the Bastille and the 1st man to be imprisoned in it—but the good doctor lived on. He lived to see Napoleon suppress the Revolution and saw the method he advocated become a symbol of needless and brutal slaughter rather than humanitarianism. But he died a full 22 years after the machine was introduced—in his own bed, peacefully, of a carbuncle on his shoulder. After his death, his children petitioned the French Government to change the name of the guillotin, but won only permission to change their own names.

—R.H. rep.

LEOTARD (lē-ĕ-tärd) n. A close-fitting garment usually with long sleeves, a high neck, and ankle-length legs worn for practice or performance by dancers, acrobats, and aerialists; also, tights.

A baby who has to be hung upside down from a trapeze bar to stop his crying would suggest to any parent a fledgling star aerialist. Such was the case with Jules Léotard, at least according to his *Memoirs*, a small volume swollen with windy conceit. At any rate, Léotard did become one of France's most famous aerialists in the 19th century, perfecting the aerial somersault, among other acrobatics, and starring in Paris and London circuses. But his name is remembered for the leotard costume he invented, which is still worn by circus performers.

That vanity played a large role as the handmaiden of his invention is witnessed by the plug the performer gave the leotard at the end of his *Memoirs*. "Do you want to be adored by the ladies?" he exhorts his male readers. "[Then] put on a more natural garb, which does not hide your best features." So far nobody earthbound has followed his advice. But the leotard in the form of leotards is more popular today than ever. Originally, the costume was a one-piece elastic garment, snug-fitting, low at the neck and sleeveless, but it became a garment covering the arms as well. Today, though no dictionary has yet noted the distinction, leotards, the plural of the word, is used for the pantyhose that little girls wear, really half-tights, and sometimes, though not as often, describes women's pantyhose.

—R.H. rep.

LYNCH ('linch) v.t. To put to death by mob action without legal sanction.

Our word for extralegal hanging definitely comes from the name of a man, but just who was the real Judge Lynch? At least a dozen men have been suggested as candidates for the dubious distinction. Scholarly opinion leans toward Virginia's William Lynch, with Virginia magistrate Charles Lynch a strong contender, but the other defendants deserve their day in court.

The earliest challenger for the title is a certain Mayor Lynch of Glasgow; according to a story from the *Pall Mall Gazette* quoted in the *New York Tribune* of January 27, 1881, Mayor Lynch flourished toward the end of the 15th century and hanged a criminal with his own hands on one occasion. Another Mayor Lynch, of England, is vaguely mentioned, and then there is Mayor James Fitzstephens Lynch of Galway, Ireland. This last Lynch is said to have sent his son to Spain about 1492 to purchase a cargo of wine. But the young man gambled away all his father's money and bought on credit, the Spanish merchant sending a representative back with him to Ireland so that he'd be sure to collect. While at sea, young Lynch killed and threw the Spaniard overboard. The elder Lynch soon discovered this crime and as town mayor sat in judgment and pronounced the death sentence on his own son. Mayor Lynch must have been insane for "justice," because when his family interceded to save the boy from hanging, he proceeded to hang him from a window of their home.

None of these accounts, if they are true, bothers to explain why the term "lynch" did not come into use until 2 centuries later, nor do the stories depict "lynchings" as we know them today. A better choice might be the

American John Lynch, a South Carolinian who followed Daniel Boone to Kentucky and was hanged as a horse thief without benefit of trial, or the Judge James Lynch who is said to have imposed brutal sentences in about 1687. But too little is known about these men. The same applies for the theory that "lynch" comes from a Lynch's Creek in South Carolina, where about 1779 a band of "Regulators" met to mete out their particular brand of "justice." One English account even makes the place Lynch Creek in North Carolina, moves the date to the Revolution, and says that here "a form of court-martial and execution was carried out on the corpse of a Tory who had already been hanged to prevent rescue."

It would be fruitless to mention all the Lynches in history who are merely alluded to as the originators of a practice that is unfortunately not yet purely historical. There are almost endless variations on tales like that of the Irishman hanged by irate neighbors or the American outlaw strung up on a tree somewhere. Either etymologists are very imaginative or the Lynches of this world have had more than their fair share of men on one or another end of a rope.

Up until fairly recently most historians gave Virginia planter and judge Charles Lynch (1736–1796) the doubtful honor of being the 1st "lyncher," or rather the 1st person to be called a "lyncher." Colonel Lynch, a militia officer who served under General Greene during the Revolution, was a leading citizen of Bedford County and his older brother John founded Lynchburg, Va. (Brother John, incidentally, has also been cited as the eponymous Lynch, complicating matters more.) It seems that the colonel had been a justice of the peace since 1766, and had taken the law into his own hands on a number of occasions. These cases usually involved Tories charged with treason, which, like all felonies, could be tried only at the courts in Williamsburg during the Revolution. Since Williamsburg was some 200 mi. away and the rude roads leading to the capital were controlled by Loyalists, Judge Lynch and 3 fellow magistrates set up a court, proper in all respects but its jurisdiction, to try treason cases. Judge Lynch became particularly famous in 1780 when he prevented local Tories from seizing ammunition stores for Cornwallis and subsequently tried them as traitors, but neither he nor the other justices ever ordered anyone hanged for the crime of treason. In fact, only in one instance—a case of proven manslaughter—was their sentence ever greater than a fine or flogging. Somehow Lynch's associate justices—James Callaway, William Preston, and Robert Adams—were never remembered for their part in the extralegal court. The colonel himself—a Quaker who had established the 1st public

church in Virginia, a former member of the House of Burgesses, and a delegate to Virginia's constitutional convention in 1776—was brought before the Virginia legislature by Tory sympathizers after the war. The assembly, however, exonerated him of any wrongdoing, terming his actions "justifiable from the imminence of the danger."

Colonel Charles Lynch's name was long accepted as the most likely source for "lynch law" and "lynch" because it was the most obvious one around. But historians began to wonder why someone who had nothing to do with extralegal hanging or mob action should be held accountable for the word. Then a Capt. William Lynch (1742–1820) was discovered. Like Charles Lynch, he was a Virginian, a militiaman, and the magistrate of an impromptu court, but his story is far more convincing. Capt. William Lynch was brought to light by Edgar Allan Poe in an editorial on "lynching" that he wrote in 1836 when he edited the *Southern Literary Messenger*. Poe claimed that the lynch law originated in 1780 when Captain Lynch and his followers organized to rid Pittsylvania County of a band of ruffians threatening the neighborhood. Poe even affixed a compact drawn up by Lynch and his men to the editorial: "Whereas, many of the inhabitants of Pittsylvania . . . have sustained great and intolerable losses by a set of lawless men . . . that . . . have hitherto escaped the civil power with impunity . . . we, the subscribers, being determined to put a stop to the uniquitous practices of those unlawful and abandoned wretches, do enter into the following association . . . upon hearing or having sufficient reason to believe, that any . . . species of villainy (has) been committed within our neighborhood, we will forthwith . . . repair immediately to the person or persons suspected . . . and if they will not desist from their evil practices, we will inflict such corporeal punishment on him or them, as to us shall seem adequate to the crime committed or the damage sustained . . . In witness whereof we have hereunto set our hands, this 22nd day of September, 1780."

There we have the 1st lynch law, down to its exact date. William Lynch's identity was further verified by Richard Venables, an old resident of the county, in the May, 1859, issue of *Harper's Magazine*. But without evidence of any actual hanging there was still room for doubt. Finally, additional proof was found in the diary of the famous surveyor Andrew Ellicott, who visited Captain Lynch in 1811 and gained his friendship. William Lynch was then living in a sparsely settled area of South Carolina called Ooleony Creek, having moved there about 10 years after he disbanded his vigilantes in 1788. Ellicott found that Lynch "possessed a strong but uncultivated mind," was "hospitable and generous to an extreme" and "a great stickler for equality and the rights of man as established by law!" The father of 12 described to him how he organized a band for the purpose of punishing crimes without the technical processes of court and police action. The same problems existed in Pittsylvania as confronted Judge Charles Lynch in Bedford County: The proper courts in the Tidewater area were too far away, too difficult to reach, and crimes of violence by both Loyalists and patriots had multiplied during the Revolution. William Lynch related how his "lynch-men," as they were called, were sworn to secrecy and loyalty to the band. On receiving information accusing someone of a crime, the accused was seized and questioned before a court of sorts. If he did not confess immediately, he was horsewhipped until he did, and efforts were made to make him involve others, who were all given the same treatment. No *legal* means were ever used by the lynch-men to establish guilt or innocence. Ellicott also mentioned the hangings that had been questioned so long. "These punishments were sometimes severe and not infrequently inflicted upon the innocent," he wrote. "Mr. Lynch informed me that he had never in any case given a note for the punishment of death; some however he acknowledged had been actually hanged." But not in the ordinary way: ". . . a horse in part became the executioner . . . the person who it was supposed ought to suffer death was placed on a horse with his hands tied behind him and a rope about his neck which was fastened to the limb of a tree over his head. In this situation the person was left and when the horse in pursuit of food or any other cause moved from his position the unfortunate person was left suspended by the neck—this was called 'aiding the civil authority.' "

At last the mystery was solved, although several major dictionaries still discredit the wrong Judge Lynch. It was not long after William Lynch and his band before vigilantes all over the country were enforcing lynch-laws and being described as lynchers. From the time when records were 1st kept in 1885 to the present there have been 4,500 to 5,000 lynchings in the U.S., though the practice is fortunately very rare today. All named after a man who did not invent the process by any means, but tried to justify it. In fact, the inscription on William Lynch's grave reads: "He followed virtue as his truest guide . . ."

—R.H. rep.

NICOTINE (nĭk ̍ĕ′tēn′) n. A poisonous alkaloid, $C_5H_4NC_4H_7NCH_3$, derived from the tobacco plant, used in medicine and as an insecticide. From *nicotiana*, any of various flowering tobacco plants of the genus *Nicotiana*, native to the Americas.

In 1559, Francis II, the 16-year-old King of France, determined that his sister, Marguerite of Valois, aged 6, should marry Don Sebastian, the King of Portugal, aged 5. To conduct the delicate negotiations, he appointed one of his ablest ministers, Jean Nicot, a notary's son of uncommon ability. Nicot was only 29, but he was a cultivated man of letters. He had begun a dictionary of the French language and had made an excellent impression on the austere Queen Catherine, mother of the young King of Portugal. Despite the abilities of the young ambassador, the negotiations failed, and the following year Francis died. However, the mission was not a complete failure. While visiting the Royal Pharmacy in Lisbon, Nicot had been given a strange plant recently brought from Florida. He cultivated it with great care, and before he left Portugal, he sent back to the queen mother, Catherine de Médicis, the 1st harvest of his tobacco plant.

It was a well-calculated gift, for Nicot had observed in Lisbon the happy effects that the "American powder" had on the general disposition of its adherents, and he also knew just how somber and bad-tempered Catherine could be. Just as he had hoped, Catherine became an enthusiastic user of what she termed the "ambassador's powder" and made it so fashionable that soon no one dared appear at court without fidgeting carelessly with his fancy box of tobacco.

Nicot also sent a small package of the powder to his friend, the Father Superior of Malta. With remarkable perspicacity, Nicot had foreseen how precious a diversion tobacco might prove to be for monks, who were endlessly occupied with songs, prayers, and responses. Nicot's friend was so zealous in spreading the use of tobacco in his order that the monks soon called it "Father Superior's powder." Nicot then returned to Paris with a whole cargo of tobacco, which proved to be a most solid foundation on which to build his fortune. It also brought him such notoriety that he became as much in fashion as the plant, which was soon referred to as nicotiana by everyone.

But fashions are fickle, and after the initial period of enthusiasm came the period of persecution. The 1st enemy was Scotland's James VI (soon to become James I of England), who fought Nicot's plant as well as papism throughout his life. Don Bartholomew of the Camara, Bishop of Granada, was offended by the discreet sneezing of his flock during his sermons. A profound theological dispute arose under Pope Urban VIII: Does a pinch of snuff savored through the nose break a fast? Pope

Innocent X even went so far as to excommunicate tobacco-users.

Tobacco divided the Sorbonne and became yet another bone of contention between the Jansenists (who were for it) and the Jesuits (who were decidedly against it). The Jesuits finally conceded that tobacco might not be forbidden fruit in itself, but only when used for the satisfaction of depraved desires; that is, only those "intentionally" defying God's command by sniffing or smoking would be excommunicated! Outside France, things were even worse. Amurat IV condemned smokers to death; the Czar ordered that their noses be cut off; the Shah Sifi simply had them impaled. In Switzerland, the Senate of Berne had "smoking" inserted with "stealing" and "killing" in the Ten Commandments.

But suddenly France discovered that a simple state tax of 2 francs per 100 lbs. of tobacco brought in approximately one million francs each year. Tobacco returned to favor, at least with the Government. Nicot was able to turn his attention back to his beloved dictionary, the oldest in the French language, which was finally printed in 1600, 6 years after his death.
—N.C.S. rep.

PANTS ('pan(t)s) n. pl. [Short for pantaloons] 1. trousers 2. chiefly Brit.: men's short underpants.

Poor St. Pantaleon, who should be hailed for his virtue and courage, is usually remembered only by men's "pants," ladies' "panties," and a word meaning sissy. St.—or San—Pantaleon, tradition tells us, came from Nicomedia in Asia Minor—his name meaning, depending on the original spelling, either "all lion" or "all compassionate." He was both of these. A Christian doctor and personal physician to Emperor Galerius Maximianus, San Pantaleon treated the poor without charge. The fame of the "Holy Moneyless One" probably inspired other jealous physicians to report him to Maximianus' co-ruler, the Emperor Diocletian, who was then busily occupied persecuting Christians. Condemned to death in 305 A.D., San Pantaleon miraculously survived 6 attempts to kill him—his hapless executioners trying liquid lead, burning, drowning, wild beasts, the wheel, and the sword before finally beheading him successfully. The Greek saint's story was a favorite one in Venice, where he became both the patron saint of doctors and a martyr especially revered by the Venetians, his name all the more popular because so many boys were baptized in his honor. Probably for this reason, and because it was comical to call a foolish character all lion, the saint's name attached itself to the buffoon in the 15th-century Italian *commedia dell'arte*. The "amorous" Pantaleon was always played by an emaciated bespectacled old man wearing slippers, one-piece, skintight breeches, and stockings that bloused out above the knees. Strolling bands of players performed variations of the comedy featuring the "seedy, needy" dotard throughout Europe and both his name and the name of the trousers he wore became "pantaloons" in England by the late 1600s. In time "pantaloons" was used as a designation for trousers in general, the word shortened to "pants" when a new style, tight-fitting from the thighs to the ankle, was introduced to America in the early 18th century. "Pants" persisted in America, ever after applied to all changes in styles, and always preferred by most Americans to the "trousers" purists have insisted upon. The word "pants" is even used for women's undergarments, though its more feminine form "panties" generally describes these.

What with the miniskirts and tights popular today, women are wearing a costume very similar in silhouette to that of the stage pantaloon of the 15th century. As for "pantywaist," a sissy or effeminate boy, it goes back to the 1890s, deriving from the name of a sleeveless underwaist that a little girl's "panties" were attached to, but which boys were sometimes made to wear. Which made the brave St. Pantaleon's humiliation as complete as theirs.
—R.H. rep.

SANDWICH ('săn(d)wĭch) n. A slice of bread covered with a filling (as of meat, cheese, fish, or various mixtures) which is usually covered with another slice of bread.

At 5 A.M. on August 6, 1762, John Montagu, 4th Earl of Sandwich, looked up from the gaming table and decided that he was hungry. The earl, an inveterate gambler in the midst of one of his famous round-the-clock sessions, wouldn't dare leave his cards for a meal and ordered his man to bring him some cold, thick-sliced roast beef between 2 pieces of toasted bread. Thus the 1st sandwich as we know it today was born.

The Romans had a similar repast called *offula* before this and it is said that the refreshment was 1st invented when, in about 100 B.C., Hillel ate bitter herb and unleavened bread as part of the Jewish Passover meal, symbolizing man's triumph over life's ills. But the modern sandwich, certainly our most convenient quick lunch or snack and possibly our main source of nourishment in this frenetic age, definitely evolves from those mighty gambling sessions, some lasting 48 hours and more, in which the industrious earl passionately participated. Those few authorities who say that the earl was at the writing table, or out on a long day's hunt and not at any table at all, only dampen a good story and are probably not correct. At any rate, the sandwich was named for Lord Sandwich and within 8 years after the above date, the term was recorded by visiting Frenchman Pierre Grosley in his *Londres* as the term for such a snack.

Gambling was only one of John Montagu's lesser vices, but the earl has as many complimentary words honoring him as any politician, another example being the beautiful Sandwich Islands (Hawaii) that Capt. James Cook named after him because he headed the British Admiralty during the American Revolution and outfitted the great explorer's ships. Lord Sandwich deserves no such glory and wasn't accorded it in his own lifetime. Sandwich became an earl when only 11, was educated at all the right schools—Eton and Cambridge—but he did very little that was right. His administration as 1st lord of the Admiralty was notoriously mismanaged, many public charges were made against him for graft, bribery, and general incompetence—and the result of the American Revolution might have been different if he hadn't been on hand to sabotage the British Navy. Lord Howe, among many officers, refused to accept a command under Sandwich, but his unpopularity dates back long before the revolt of the Colonies. After a promising start in politics, his party fell from power and the bored earl dedicated himself to a life of lechery.

In an age studded with libertines, Lord Sandwich shone brightest. Under a *nom de débauche* he became a member of the notorious Hell-Fire Club, infamous for its wild orgies and black masses, but soon fell out with his friend the great wit John Wilkes, M.P., and lord mayor of London, one of the club's founders. Wilkes had dressed a black baboon with horns and hoops and let him loose while Sandwich was invoking the devil during a black mass, the earl's embarrassment exceeding even his initial fright, when he ran out of the chapel shouting, "Spare me, gracious Devil. I am as yet but half a sinner. I have never been as wicked as I intended!" The 2 became bitter enemies, but when Sandwich sought revenge before the House of Lords by reading Wilkes's indecent "Essay on Woman," a parody (now lost) on Pope's "Essay on Man," the strategy backfired. On that same day, John Gay's *Beggar's Opera* happened to be playing in London and Sandwich became identified in the public's mind with the play's villain, the "despicable cad" who betrays the hero, his nickname remaining Jemmy Twitcher ever after.

Sandwich also knew notoriety for the 16-year-old mistress he took, Margaret or Marth Reay—a "commoner" he educated at the best schools in Paris and who bore him 5 children in the some 20 years they lived together. She was killed by a rejected suitor in 1779, making her paramour's private life a matter of public controversy just when he was having his worst troubles with the Admiralty. In 1782, the earl left the Navy when his party fell from power but the scandals associated with him plagued him the rest of his life. He died 10 years later, aged 74, an embittered man who never realized how history would honor him. Only one celebrated riposte mars his popular historical reputation. Though attributed to a number of people, the most famous political put-down in history probably made Lord Sandwich its victim. It appears that the earl had verbally attacked his archenemy Wilkes, shouting, "You, Wilkes, will either die on the gallows or from syphilis!" The great wit Wilkes simply turned, tapped his snuff-box, and looked Sandwich squarely in the eye. "That depends, my Lord," he said, matter-of-factly, "on whether I embrace your principles or your mistress."

—R.H. rep.

SILHOUETTE (sil′oo′et′) n. A representation of the outline of something, usually filled in with black or another solid color.

In 1757, when M. Étienne de Silhouette became controller-general, the economy of France was in a shambles. The Seven Years' War had just begun, and stringent economies were needed to finance it. Silhouette started his reforms with the farmers-general, whom he quite literally made bankrupt; he next subjected government officials to the same taxes that everyone else paid; finally, he severely reduced the pensions received by all courtiers, from dukes to mistresses.

The people applauded, and Silhouette, considering the court reformed, undertook to change the spending habits of Louis XV himself. Would it not be an excellent idea for the King to set an example of sacrifice for his subjects? Perhaps he might begin with the fund set aside specifically for the King's amusements? Louis reluctantly agreed, but he seemed so morose in the days following that the sympathetic Duc de Choiseul, Minister of Foreign Affairs, privately offered him funds from his department's budget so that the King might have some diversion. Louis accepted, and in time most of the courtiers found that their pensions, too, could be renewed by quiet agreements with various officials whose funds were still intact.

Budgets, moreover, are useful only when expenses are numerable. There still remained the "royal orders on the treasury," which concealed enormous expenditures, and which, since the advent of Madame de Pompadour as the royal favorite, had more than quadrupled. The all-encompassing "royal orders" included any number of irregular, unclassified expenses such as the King's losses at cards. It was a quagmire in which a far stronger man than Silhouette would have floundered.

Defeated by the weakness of the King and the wiles of the court, Silhouette instituted new taxes. To his credit, he tried to place the major burden on the rich rather than the poor. A form of income tax was established; domestics and servants in livery, horses, carriages, and luxuries were taxed; unmarried men were penalized by having to pay a triple capitation tax. To top it all off, the controller-general levied a 4 *sous*-per-*livre* sales tax on all "articles of consumption."

Silhouette suddenly found himself far and away the most unpopular man in Paris. The privileged classes were duly enraged, while the poor saw only as far as "4 *sous* per *livre*." Parliament protested vigorously; the King gave in and started granting dispensations right and left. Silhouette, desperate, suspended all government payments, thereby destroying all credit. When Silhouette left the ministry after 8 months, the country's finances were in infinitely greater disorder than when he had assumed the post of controller-general.

Silhouette was publicly loaded with derision. Breeches were made "à la Silhouette"—that is, with no pockets. A new controller-general was found, but not until the old one had become forever immortalized in the popular little shadow portraits of the day, which the people scornfully associated with the incomplete career and shadowy, unsubstantial financial policies of Étienne de Silhouette.

—N.C.S. rep.

SPOONERISM ('spü-ne-riz-em) n. A transposition of usu. initial sounds of 2 or more words (as in *tons of soil* for *sons of toil*).

The Rev. William Archibald Spooner, dean and later warden of New College, Oxford, was a learned man, but not spell woken, or well spoken, that is. "We all know what it is to have a half-warmed fish inside us," he once told an audience, meaning to say "half-formed wish." On another occasion he advised his congregation that the next hymn would be "Kinkering Congs Their Titles Take," instead of "Conquering Kings Their Titles Take," and he is said to have explained to listeners one time that "the Lord is a shoving leopard." Spooner's slips occurred both in church, where he once remarked to a lady, "Mardon me Padom, this pie is occupied, allow me to sew you to another sheet," and told a nervous bridegroom that "it is kisstomery to cuss the bride," and in his classes, where he chided one student with "You

hissed my mystery lecture," and dismissed another with "You have deliberately tasted 2 worms and can leave Oxford by the town drain!" Other mistakes attributed to him are "The cat popped on its drawers," for "the cat dropped on its paws"; "one swell foop," for "one fell swoop"; "sporn rim hectacles," for "horn rim spectacles"; "a well-boiled icicle," for "a well-oiled bicycle"; "selling smalts," for "smelling salts"; "tons of soil," for "sons of toil"; "blushing crow," for "crushing blow"; "Is the bean dizzy?" for "Is the dean busy?" and "the Assissination of Sassero," for a Roman history lecture on "the Assassination of Cicero." Spooner lived 86 years, and committed many "spoonerisms" in public, too. "When the boys come back from France, we'll have the hags flung out!" the canon told a gathering of patriots during W.W. I, and Queen Victoria once became "our queer old dean," instead of "our dear old Queen." Nobody knows how many of these spoonerisms were really made by Spooner, but they were among the many attributed to him. Spooner was an albino, his metathetical troubles probably due to nervousness and poor eyesight resulting from his condition. The scientific name for his speech affliction is "metathesis," the accidental transposition of letters or syllables in the words of a sentence, the process known long before Spooner made it so popular that his slips of the tongue and eye were widely imitated. Some of the best spoonerisms therefore aren't really spoonerisms at all, being carefully devised and far from accidental.

—R.H. rep.

UNCLE SAM (ŭn-kĕl săm) n. The U.S. Government; or the American nation or people.

Samuel Wilson, though known as jolly, genial, and generous, wasn't called Uncle Sam only because he was a friendly avuncular sort of man. The man some say was the original Uncle Sam happened to be the nephew of army contractor Elbert Anderson, who owned a store or slaughterhouse on the Hudson River in Troy, N.Y., and had a contract to supply the Army with salt pork and beef during the War of 1812.

Uncle Sam, a former bricklayer, and his uncle Ebenezer worked as army inspectors and had occasion to inspect the meat Elbert Anderson packed in barrels with the initials "E.A.-U.S." stamped on them. According to a popular version of the story, one soldier asked another what the initials U.S. (United States) meant and his companion jokingly replied that they stood for Elbert Anderson's Uncle Sam. Some respected scholars dispute the story, but no better explanation has been offered for how Uncle Sam became associated with the Army and eventually replaced the earlier Brother Jonathan as a symbol of the U.S. Government. In any case, there was a real Uncle Sam.

Samuel Wilson was born in Menotomy (now Arlington), Mass., in 1766 and died at the ripe old age of 88 in Troy, where he lies buried in the Oakwood Cemetery next to his wife Betsy. The preceding account of the origin of Uncle Sam was widely accepted during Wilson's lifetime, the major objections coming from historian Albert Matthews, who claimed that the name evolved from the initials U.S. stamped on government property, the Uncle Sam possibly being the official who saw to it that these markings were made. The term's 1st recorded use was in the *Troy Post* of September 7, 1813, which would speak well for the

Sam Wilson theory except that the story says the words derive from the initials on government wagons. Regardless of its origin, the term caught on quickly and lasted.

Uncle Sam 1st appeared in cartoons in 1830, but he was clean-shaven and wore a robe rather than trousers until Lincoln's day, when he acquired his goatee and his present attire. His costume was based on that pictured in cartoons of the comic Yankee character Maj. Jack Downing created by humorist Seba Smith, the 1st American homespun philosopher. Today Uncle Sam is best known by the ubiquitous "I Want You" posters the armed forces have used for recruiting purposes. In a recent development, Walter Botts, the model who posed for these posters, was declared ineligible for a veteran's pension—by Uncle Sam.

—R.H. rep.

Words with Character

Let's see if you know where certain words, many based on proper names, come from. All of the numbered words in the left-hand column were coined by an author listed in the alphabetized right-hand column. Can you match the name of the author with the word he

coined, as well as give the title of the author's work in which the word appeared?

If you get 4 correct, that's Fair. Anywhere between 5 and 8 correct is Very Good. Between 9 and 12 correct is Excellent. Between 13 and 16 correct—well, your name deserves to become a word.

1. stentorian	( )	a.	Karel Čapek
2. quixotic	( )	b.	Miguel de Cervantes
3. malapropism	( )	c.	Charles Dickens
4. gargantuan	( )	d.	Homer
5. scrooge	( )	e.	Ben Jonson
6. lilliputian	( )	f.	Sinclair Lewis
7. ogre	( )	g.	Molière (Jean Baptiste Poquelin)
8. lothario	( )	h.	Charles Perrault

9. Babbitt	( )	i.	Eleanor H. Porter
10. serendipity	( )	j.	François Rabelais
11. moron	( )	k.	Nicolas Rowe
12. Frankenstein	( )	l.	Mary Shelley
13. vulpine	( )	m.	Richard Sheridan
14. schlemihl	( )	n.	Jonathan Swift
15. Pollyanna	( )	o.	Adelbert von Chamisso
16. robot	( )	p.	Horace Walpole

QUIZ ANSWERS

Your answers should read: 1. (d.) from a character in *The Iliad*; 2. (b.) *Don Quixote*; 3. (m.) *The Rivals*; 4. (j.) *Gargantua*; 5. (c.) *A Christmas Carol*; 6. (n.) *Gulliver's Travels*; 7. (h.) *Contes, or Fairy Tales*; 8. (k.) *The*

Fair Penitent; 9. (f.) *Babbitt*; 10. (p.) *The Three Princes of Serendip*; 11. (g.) *La Princesse d'Élide*; 12. (l) *Frankenstein, or the Modern Prometheus*; 13. (e.) *Volpone, or the Fox*; 14. (o.) *The Wonderful World of Peter Schlemihl*; 15 (i.) *Pollyanna*; 16. (a.) *R.U.R.* (*Rossum's Universal Robots*).

—R.H.

A List of Words Commonly Misspelled

accidentally	across	among	appetite
accommodate	address	amount	approaching
accompanied	aggravate	analyze	appropriate
accumulate	aisle	apologize	approximately
achievement	almost	apparatus	arctic
acquaintance	always	apparent	argument
acquire	amateur	appearance	around

arrangement
article
ascend
assistant
athletic
attendance
audience
auxiliary
awkward
barbarous
beginning
believed
benefited
breathe
brilliant
bulletin
buried
business
buy
calendar
candidate
cemetery
certainly
changeable
chief
chosen
column
coming
comma
commemorate
committee
common
community
comparative
compelled
competition
concede
conceive
conscientious
conscious
consider
continuous
controlled
convenience
coolly
correspondence
countries
courteous
criticism
curiosity
dealt
debt
decided
decision
definite
definition
demonstration
dependent
descend
description
desirable
despair

desperate
destroy
develop
dictionary
different
difficulty
dining
disappear
disappoint
disastrous
discipline
diseases
dissatisfied
dissipation
divided
division
doctor
doesn't
doubt
during
efficiency
eighth
eligible
eliminate
embarrass
emphasize
endeavor
engine
entrance
environment
equipped
especially
exaggerated
excellent
excitement
exhausted
existence
explanation
familiar
fascinating
February
finally
foreign
forty
friend
fulfill
fundamental
generally
genius
government
grammar
grievous
guard
handsome
height
helpfulness
hindrance
hoping
humorous
hundred
hurriedly
illegible

illiterate
immediately
immigrant
inadequate
incidentally
incredible
independent
indispensable
influence
intelligence
interesting
interfere
interpreted
interrupted
irresistible
island
itself
knowledge
laboratory
laid
language
legible
leisure
library
lightning
listen
literature
livelihood
loneliness
maintenance
mathematics
maybe
meant
medicine
miniature
minimum
minute
mischievous
misspell
morale
mortgage
mysterious
naturally
necessary
nevertheless
nickel
niece
night
ninety
noisily
noticeable
nowadays
obstacle
occasionally
occurred
occurrence
off
often
omission
omitted
operate
opinion

opportunity
optimistic
original
outrageous
paid
parallel
paralyzed
parliament
particularly
partner
pastime
patience
peculiarity
perform
perhaps
permanent
permissible
perseverance
persistent
personnel
perspiration
persuade
phenomenon
physically
piece
pleasant
politics
portrayed
possession
practically
precede
predecessor
preference
preferred
prejudice
preparations
prescribe
pretense
prevalent
privilege
probably
procedure
proceed
professional
professor
prohibition
prominent
pronunciation
propaganda
propeller
psychology
pursue
puzzle
quantity
quitting
quizzes
realize
really
reasonably
received
recognize
recommend

referred	severely	supersede	until
relieve	shining	suppress	usually
religious	similar	surely	valiant
remembrance	simultaneously	surprise	valleys
repetition	sincerely	syllable	valuable
resource	sophomore	synonym	varieties
restaurant	source	temperament	vegetable
rhythm	specimen	than	vengeance
ridiculous	speech	therefore	view
sacrifice	stopping	together	vigorous
safety	strength	toward	village
satisfactory	strenuously	tragedy	villain
scarcely	stretched	transferring	whole
schedule	strictly	tremendous	wholly
secretary	studying	tries	women
seize	submit	truly	worrying
sense	subsequent	twelfth	writing
separate	succeed	undoubtedly	written
sergeant	successful	unnecessary	
serviceable	superintendent		

Sexism in Language

From the very 1st moment of her life (ignoring possible references to a male fetus), the girl-child is hidden behind the pronoun "he." Hospital instructions to new parents read: "When bathing baby, never leave him unattended." Dr. Spock, in his introduction to *Baby and Child Care*, apologizes for his constant use of the pronoun "he" to refer to all children. He reserves the pronoun "she" for the mother. (Might the 2 otherwise be confused?) In theory, "he" refers to members of either sex. In fact, hearing only the pronoun "he" to classify the students of a certain school, one little girl wondered why no girls attended. And there is the young high school girl who won an award for outstanding citizenship. The prerequisites for the award? "He must be of outstanding character . . . he must evidence excellent scholarship . . . he . . ."

Plainly, women are too often linguistically invisible, hidden in the word "man" when "human" is meant, forgotten by the word "he" when "she or he" might be more accurate. Even words that in themselves have no gender, such as "lawyer," "judge," or "president," evoke images of men unless otherwise qualified. One can only speculate about the psychic damage this invisibility has caused women who are made to feel insignificant, or absent, in the shadow of the dominant HE.

Language has asymmetrical qualities that further discriminate against women. The asymmetries include: (1) words that do not mean the same thing when applied to a woman as when applied to a man, and (2) words for which there is no equivalent for both sexes. Included in the 1st category is the word "professional."

To say of a man, "he is a professional," implies no slur. To say of a woman, "she is a professional," besmirches her honor. "Bachelor" and "spinster" do not have the same connotation. Has anyone ever looked for an available spinster? And even "widow" and "widower"—which at 1st glance appear parallel—are not always similarly used. One would be unlikely to refer to a man as Mary's widower. Many words do not even have a male equivalent. For example:

Find the Parallel Word
(an exercise in logical thinking)

Female	Male
nymphomaniac	
whore	
little old lady	
spinster	
old maid	
chick	
broad	
babe	
bird	
castrating bitch	
bitch	
the little woman	
girl (to describe females regardless of age)	

Questions

Does the parallel word mean the same as the word used for females?

Is the parallel word negative or a put-down? Does it connote status?

If you couldn't find a parallel word, why not?

What assumptions are reflected in the words in the "female" column?

(Note: In the above exercise, the bias of the Emma Willard Task Force on Education is that there really are few parallel words that have the exact connotation as the "female" word. For example, to be a "bachelor" carries status; to be a "spinster" or "old maid" doesn't. "Stud" does not have the same connotation and lack of status as "nymphomaniac" or "whore" does.)

A more subtle distinction in the way women are singled out by language is evident in the way that the same personality trait is characterized approvingly for one sex and denigrated for the other. Thus, if a man is aggressive, he is considered a go-getter, a self-starter, while a woman is considered pushy or a castrating bitch. If a woman consistently agrees with her boss, she will be thought bright; a man will be called a yes-man or an ass-licker.

Many of these discrepancies involve words that deal directly or indirectly with women's sexuality. In fact, one linguist has even made the case that "lady" is used as a euphemism for "woman," in that "woman" implies sexuality, while "lady" is desexed. Certainly, "woman" is a word that can imply the presence not only of sex, but also of power, which "lady" cannot. A lady doctor or Ladies' Lib would simply be incongruous.

Although women are used harshly by language, they are not in their own turn allowed to use harsh language. Women's language in English, at least according to stereotype, does not contain swear words. While there have been few studies of women's speech and thus no documentation of sex differences in speaking, one can make a case for a separate women's language that uses weak words like "divine," as in "a divine idea," a language imprecise, emotive, and laced with silly words. Robin Lakoff distinguished another characteristic of women's speech, the tag-form sentence: a statement of fact undercut by a final question. "We are going tomorrow, aren't we?" "This is a terrific play, isn't it?" Even when a woman is assertive, she often shows at least token or apparent passivity, as if all her assertions were only tentative. The tag-form sentence becomes a paradigm for women's paradoxical position—that is, aggression constantly balanced by passivity, real or implied. The supposed weakness inherent in women's speech may in fact be nothing more concrete than the fact that they use it. When men use women's language, they may appear effeminate. Interestingly enough, many words that accentuate hip speech, or head talk, like "groovy," "outasight," "man, like . . . ," roughly parallel in their lack of precision women's speech ("fiveish," "heavenly") and suggest further connec-

tions between politically powerless groups and feminine language.

Even more drastic examples of women's speech are found in foreign languages and cultures; there are even isolated cases of separate women's languages. The Yahi, a now-extinct Indian tribe of Upper California, had one language used by males and one used by females, each with its separate vocabulary. (For the Yahi women, this meant learning a language which they themselves never spoke—men's language.) Since women as mothers have the most contact with children, children's speech is women's language. As boys mature, they surrender this language. The fact that children share women's speech does nothing to enhance its status in the eyes of society. One wonders if some of the baby-talk quality of women's speech doesn't stem from generations of confinement with young minds and tongues.

The Women's Liberation Movement has attempted to alter the English language as it touches women. Ms. (pronounced "miz") existed before the women's movement in secretarial handbooks as the solution to the sticky problem of unknown marital status, but its use was not ensured until the publication of the most widely circulated magazine associated with the women's movement, *Ms.* The U.S. Government Printing Office, official stylemaster for government and civil-service publications has condoned the use of Ms. However, a 1973 Gallup poll found that disapproval of its use among women who knew of the term outweighed approval, 5–3. Some women say that "miz" sounds a little too much like "massa," or that the abbreviation already stands for the word "manuscript." The term's acceptance has been primarily as a written and not a verbal form of address. While "Ms." has been the most successful attempt to alter language, other attempts have included using "he/she" or a newer form "s/he" to replace "he." Replacing "men" with "people" or "persons" has become popular (almost a game or joke for some). "Jurymen" becomes "jurypeople," "postmen" becomes "postpeople," and so on. History now has an adjunct "herstory," not because the etymology of history is history (it isn't), but because "herstory" emphasizes that women have been written out of regular his-tory. And the "Madam Chairmen" of the world (a linguistic contradiction to begin with) have been deposed by hundreds of "chairpersons."

Some anthropologists claim that woman invented language. As hunters, men had small need for communication, while women, in tending crops, mothering children, and providing a stable community network, needed a complex language. If this is true, it is an unsubtle irony that language, her own creation, has turned on her to become one of the tools of her oppression. Is there a way out? There are those who would contend that as society itself becomes less sexist, so will language reflect this by becoming more egalitarian. On the other hand, since the use of language molds perceptions of reality, some hope that by changing sexist language, society may be forced to become less sexist. In Orwellian terms, societies can be manipulated by language, and Newspeak itself creates the reality in which the Ministry of Peace deals with war. What seems undebatable is that society and language are inextricably linked, and alterations to one will affect the other.

—K.C.

The Wit of Wilson Mizner

Little known to the public at large, Wilson Mizner (1876–1933) was one of the great wits of modern times. Mizner was a jack-of-all-trades: Klondike gold seeker, Florida realtor, Broadway playwright, Hollywood screenwriter, Atlantic gambler, as well as prizefight manager. Here is a capsule collection of Miznerisms.

ONE-LINERS

If you steal from one author, it's plagiarism; if you steal from many, it's research.

I respect faith, but doubt is what gets you an education.

Treat a whore like a lady and a lady like a whore.

Be nice to people on your way up because you'll meet 'em on your way down.

Life's a tough proposition, and the 1st hundred years are the hardest.

A good listener is not only popular everywhere, but after a while he gets to know something.

A drama critic is a person who surprises the playwright by informing him what he meant.

I am a stylist, and the most beautiful sentence I have ever heard is, "Have one on the house."

I've had several years in Hollywood and I still think the movie heroes are in the audience.

A fellow who is always declaring he's no fool usually has his suspicions.

Many a live wire would be a dead one except for his connections.

The gent who wakes up and finds himself a success hasn't been asleep.

Some of the greatest love affairs I've known involved one actor, unassisted.

Insanity is considered a ground for divorce, though by the very same token it's the shortest mental detour to marriage.

DESCRIPTIONS OF PEOPLE

He'd steal a hot stove and come back for the smoke.

You're a mouse studying to be a rat.

You sparkle with larceny.

TO A CONCEITED MOVIE PRODUCER: "A demitasse cup would fit over your head like a sunbonnet."

ON A COCKY MAN WHO WENT THROUGH BANKRUPTCY AND WAS COCKIER THAN EVER: "Failure has gone to his head."

ON A VERY THIN MAN: "He's a trellis for varicose veins."

ON HEAVYWEIGHT FIGHTER TOM SHARKEY WHO OWNED A SALOON WITH SWINGING DOORS: "He was so dumb that he crawled under them for 2 years before he found out they swung both ways."

TO AN ACTRESS WHO ROSE TO WEALTH AND TITLE THROUGH 5 MARRIAGES: "You're nothing but a parlayed chambermaid. You've compromised so many gentlemen that you think you're a lady."

TO A GROUP OF FRIENDS, AS A BORE TRIED TO JOIN THEM: "Gentlemen, gangrene has set in."

ON THE OWNER OF A MAJOR MOVIE STUDIO: "He's the only man I ever knew who had rubber pockets so he could steal soup."

IN GENERAL

Two signs he posted for guests when manager of the Hotel Rand, New York, 1907:

"No opium-smoking in the elevators."

"Carry out your own dead."

ON HOLLYWOOD: "It's a trip through a sewer in a glass-bottomed boat."

During a game of draw poker, his opponent took out his wallet and threw it on the table, announcing, "I call you." Mizner glanced at the wallet, pulled off his right shoe, placed it on the table, and said, "If we're playing for leather—I raise."

For a while, he was married to Myra Moor Yerkes, the 2nd richest woman in America, who owned a $2 million art collection. One day, in need of money, he took a version of *The Last Supper* off her wall and sold it. When his wife saw the empty frame, she cried out, "Bill, what happened to the masterpiece I had in the living room—*The Last Supper?*" Replied Mizner, "Some masterpiece. I got only $50 a plate."

TO A RADIO ANNOUNCER: "If you don't get off the air, I'll stop breathing it."

TO A WAITER: "Another pot of coffee, waiter, and bring it under your arm to keep it warm."

TO ANOTHER WAITER: "I've had better steaks than this for bad behavior."

Mizner once managed Stanley Ketchel, the middleweight boxing champion. In London in October, 1910, Mizner received a telephone call notifying him that a jealous rancher husband had shot and killed Ketchel. Said Mizner: "Tell them to start counting 10 over him, and he'll get up."

On his deathbed, as Mizner came out of a coma, a priest tried to comfort him. Mizner waved the priest away: "Why should I talk to you? I've just been talking to your boss."

—I.W.

You

When people use the word *you*, they mean one of 3 things:
1. the person they are talking to.

2. one, anyone, everyone.
3. me, I.

15

The Media

Behind the Front Page in the U.S.A.

THE BOSTON GLOBE

The Past. Boston is known as a bad newspaper town. In spite of that and in spite of competition from the Boston-based *Christian Science Monitor*, which is really an international newspaper, *The Boston Globe* has survived. It was almost bankrupt when Charles H. Taylor bought it in 1892. By giving the paper "mass appeal," Taylor made it relatively prosperous.

Until 1965, it was undistinguished. Then Tom Winship, who became editor at the age of 44, turned the *Globe* into a crusader, and it soon won a Pulitzer Prize for its successful campaign to block Francis X. Morrissey, a friend of Joseph P. Kennedy's, from becoming a Federal judge.

However much a crusader, the *Globe* has not been averse to protecting its own interests. In 1965, it paid scant attention to a landmark court case on the rights of consumers—this case involved one of its major advertisers, Jordan Marsh Company, a large department store.

The Present. Relatively liberal, *The Boston Globe* today is a highly respected paper with morning and evening editions (combined circulation nearly 500,000). In 1968 it backed Humphrey for President of the U.S.; in 1972, it backed McGovern. (Previously, it had not supported a presidential candidate since 1900.)

The *Globe* does not set obituaries of local people in type for eventual use because "there's sort of a feeling that it's bad luck," said Jack Driscoll, assistant to the editor. However, it doesn't mind hexing non-Bostonians; it has obituaries for 30 "outsiders" all set to go.

Scoops. In 1971, a 3 men and one women "spotlight" team from the *Globe* investigated and exposed municipal scandals in nearby Somerville; the team received a Pulitzer Prize for it.

The *Globe* was the 3rd U.S. paper (after *The New York Times* and *The Washington Post*) to publish excerpts from the Pentagon Papers.

CHICAGO TRIBUNE

The Past. Under the editorship of the flamboyant Col. Robert R. McCormick during the 1st half of this century, the *Chicago Tribune* was a colorful, biased, sometimes corrupt, brawling, crusading paper, a mirror of the city it served as well as of McCormick himself.

McCormick was paternalistic to the nth degree. Employees were given free teeth cleanings twice a year and a chest of silver when they married (provided that neither party had been divorced—an odd rule, considering that McCormick himself was married to a divorcée).

Courtly, tall, with a bristly mustache, McCormick bought his clothes in England, yet was an intense patriot. He once disapproved so much of something that happened in Rhode Island that he ordered a star torn out of the *Tribune's* big American flag. When lawyers told him that flag mutilation was an offense, he had it sewn back in. (Today, the *Tribune* still carries a sketch of an American flag on its front page, though it has dropped its former slogan "the American paper for Americans.")

The colonel was guarded by a German shepherd, and the outside door to his office was a secret panel so that visitors often could not find their way out without his help.

The early days of the *Tribune* were something like a Hollywood movie about newspapers, complete with a circulation war with Hearst's *American* during which circulation truck crews fought each other in the streets.

The *Tribune's* reputation for bias was not undeserved. During the Depression, it often used "so-called" before the names of legitimate government agencies like the National Labor

Relations Board. When, in W.W. II, other papers were reporting on German atrocities, the *Tribune* saw none. In fact, in 1946, it printed a cartoon about the Nuremberg trials and verdict showing a pedestal inscribed with the words: "German Martyrs. Nazi Criminal Convicted by a Biased Court Composed of Germany's Enemies in an Illegally Conducted Trial, upon Unlawful Evidence Illicitly Procured."

Hawkish on the Vietnam War, for a time it sent Chicago servicemen in Southeast Asia free color photographs of their families for Christmas.

In recent years, the paper has shifted politically somewhat to the middle, although it remains Republican. In 1972, it supported Richard Nixon for reelection as President, but also gave front-page coverage to McGovern's campaign. The paper's more balanced political stand came about after Clayton Kirkpatrick, a veteran newspaperman, became editor in 1969. Always influential in local politics, the paper in that year endorsed liberal Democrat candidates for congressman and city alderman.

In the early 1970s, the *Tribune* modernized its format, beefed up (and balanced) its editorial page, and initiated a new Sunday section, "Perspective," which has run articles by such divergent contributors as J. Edgar Hoover and Shirley Chisholm.

The paper has had an almost prudish view of sex. In 1969, it destroyed 1.1 million copies of its *Book World* because a review of *The Naked Ape* stated that "the human male and not the gorilla possesses the largest penis of all primates." In the recent past, the *Tribune* banned sex novels like *Candy* and *The Carpetbaggers* from its best-seller list.

The Present. The nation's 5th largest newspaper, the *Chicago Tribune* also publishes the New York *News*, and 5 Florida dailies. It also owns 5 radio stations and 4 television stations.

Though far less biased than in its early days, the paper remains basically conservative. It now pays more attention to news and views of minority groups, particularly Chicago's large black population, although it walks the line by trying to keep its conservative white Midwestern readership happy, too. It serves a wide area covering 4 States, an area the *Tribune* chauvinistically calls "Chicagoland."

The *Tribune* is also trying to attract young readers by running features planned to appeal to them and including youth-oriented comic strips. Its women's section is sympathetic to women's liberation and abortion reform.

Playing down crime and sex-scandal stories, the *Tribune* does sensationalize drug stories and crusades against drugs. For instance, it once captioned a photograph of a girl arrested for growing marijuana in her apartment with just 2 words—"Dope Suspect."

Still patriotic, the paper offers 3" by 5" American flags at a nominal price, a practice it began in 1961. Columnist Robert Wiedrich wrote, not so long ago: "Wearing Old Glory on a police uniform, a business suit, or, for that matter, on your pajamas when you kneel in prayer for this country at night is a good idea, especially in these times."

Scoops. On December 4, 1941, the *Chicago Tribune* printed in detail the war plans of the American General Staff in case of an attack on the U.S. This caused great consternation in Washington.

In a report on the Battle of Midway, it all but gave away the fact that the Navy had broken the Japanese secret code. The Government started to prosecute the paper for endangering the national security, but later dropped charges.

In 1948, the *Tribune* jumped the gun by reporting election results with a night edition headline reading DEWEY DEFEATS TRUMAN. The victorious Truman waved this edition from a train platform the next day. It was the *Tribune*'s biggest nonscoop.

Under George Bliss, the *Tribune* exposed the 1972 Cook County vote frauds (thus winning the Pulitzer Prize) and published an 8-part series on police brutality that resulted in indictments.

THE CHRISTIAN SCIENCE MONITOR

The Past. The *Christian Science Monitor* was founded in 1908 by Mary Baker Eddy, who was the originator of Christian Science, a religion based on spiritual healing and the belief that there is a higher reality above evil, pain, and sickness. The purpose of the paper, according to Mrs. Eddy, was "to injure no man, but to bless all mankind." It was not intended as a house organ for the Church.

The paper's 1st editor was Archibald McClellan, a lawyer. Its 1st managing editor was Alexander Dodds, a high-energy practical joker and fire buff. He liked fires to such a degree that he had a fire alarm signal in the newsroom and insisted that every fire had some kind of positive purpose.

In the 1st issues of the paper were stories on army tests of the Wright brothers' airplane, a series on increased yields of corn, a discussion of the Balkan crisis in the framework of political economics, and articles on truth in advertising, conservation, the invention of the hair dryer, and the development of the Pure Food and Drug Act. These stories were typical of those published by the *Monitor*; they were based on an intense interest in science, a desire to present the news thoughtfully, and the wish to deal with lasting issues. The 1st issues also included naïve jokes.

During its 1st year, the paper did place some emphasis on Christian Science news. This ended in April, 1909.

Mrs. Eddy died in 1910 and from then until the early 1920s, the *Monitor* reporters had to work within stringent limitations: a vague rule to write what some called "sweetness and light" and more specific taboos against such subjects as jazz bands and ballroom dancing.

From 1910 on, the paper published an international edition, in keeping with its world view of the news and issues. In 1917, the subtitle "An International Daily Paper" was added to the masthead.

Throughout the years, the paper has employed some colorful characters and excellent writers: Demarest Lloyd, who went on assignment in a chauffeur-driven Rolls-Royce; Roscoe Drummond; Margaret Lee Runbeck, who later became a novelist; Joseph C. Harsch; Cora Rigby, founder of the Women's National Press Club; and many others.

In 1965, the paper underwent a transformation: a new 5-column layout, different and larger type face, and the use of more photographs and artwork.

Though the paper has remained politically independent, it has supported the cause of peace, with one exception: W.W. II. It very early alienated many German Christian Scientists by warning the world against Hitler, and throughout the war it supported the Allies.

The *Monitor* came out in favor of Herbert Hoover in 1928, mainly because of his pro-Prohibition stand, and was against a 3rd term for Roosevelt because his administration had emphasized deficit spending, centralized power, and social experiment.

The Present. The *Christian Science Monitor* is one of the most respected newspapers in the world. It is noted for its thoughtful treatment of the news and careful editing. (The paper rarely runs much over 20 pages.) Like many European elite papers, it tries to put the news in perspective and analyze it. The *Monitor* has won innumerable awards for its excellent journalism.

Erwin Dain Canham, who was made editor in chief in 1964, stated in his book *Commitment to Freedom*: "The *Monitor* does not leave out news just because it is unpleasant, nor seek to throw a rosy glow over a world that is often far from rosy. To describe the *Monitor* as a 'clean' newspaper is correct but incomplete. It also strives to expose whatever needs to be uncovered in order to be removed or remedied. It seeks to put the news in a sound perspective, giving greatest emphasis to what is important and reducing the merely sensational to its place in the accurate system of values."

The paper is owned by the trustees of the Christian Science Monitor Publishing Committee; its directors are the directors of the First Church of Christ Scientist. The religion influences some of the *Monitor*'s taboos: no drug advertising, no pictures depicting smoking or drinking (though it did publish a picture of Churchill with his famous cigar), very little emphasis on medical news, no coverage of blood sports. The paper has fought against compulsory medical examinations, inoculations, and other medical procedures. It does not use the words "dead," "death," or "dying" in relation to people and accepts no paid death notices. Its phrase for death is "passed on." (There is an apocryphal story about a *Monitor* correspondent filing a story about "passed-on mules" on a W.W. I battlefield.)

No matter what its taboos, the *Monitor* is widely read by highly literate, influential people all over the world; it has daily editions in over 120 nations and a huge staff of professional journalists, with full-time correspondents stationed in several countries.

Scoops. Since the *Monitor* is an afternoon paper which stresses thoughtful presentation of the news, it claims few sensational scoops. However—

In 1910, in a *Monitor* interview, Thomas Edison predicted 3-dimensional television. The interview might be termed a long-range scoop.

On October 3, 1923, the paper published an exclusive interview with Hitler which clearly brought out the danger of his ideas. On the same page was an article by Churchill.

On May 14, 1928, it warned against the dangers of the bull market.

As early as March, 1941, the *Monitor* printed news about Hitler's plan to invade the Soviet Union, an event which took place in June of that year.

Merits. The *Monitor* is respected worldwide as a balanced, thoughtful paper which presents significant, serious news in a highly professional manner.

Demerits. The *Monitor* tends to avoid sensational news. It printed nothing about the Charles Starkweather murders, and covered the Greenlease kidnapping the day after it happened. However, it did print an item about some Chinese students who tried to kill Chou En-lai with a penknife.

THE DENVER POST

The Past. Trigger-happy, lawless, colorful, *The Denver Post* in its early days reflected the Wild West, which it more or less served with news. It was founded by a villainous bartender, Harry Tammen, and a lottery promoter, F. G. Bonfils.

Its arch-rival was *The Rocky Mountain News*, with whom it engaged in to-the-death circulation wars. During such a war, *The Rocky Mountain News* called Bonfils a rattlesnake. Bonfils sued for libel. Attorney Philip Van Cise represented the *News* and ever after that, the *Post* refused to print his name.

Such wars were economically disastrous. During one, both the *Post* and the *News* offered free gasoline as a bonus to want-ad purchasers, the gasoline being worth more than the ads. Soon all of Denver was out joy-riding on the free gasoline, the Sunday papers, both of them, went to over 100 pages, and both papers were losing money. Finally they reached a truce: the *Post* opted for morning publication, the *News* the afternoon.

The *Post* reached the height of notoriety in 1929, when it was discovered that Bonfils had suppressed information about oil operators during the Teapot Dome scandal in exchange for a large bribe. (He asked for $1 million but didn't get it.) The owner of *The Rocky Mountain News* got almost $100,000 in a similar deal. The American Association of Newspaper Editors later asked for Bonfils's expulsion from the organization.

The *Post* was isolationist. It was biased against foreigners and minorities. It was ultraconservative. From 1911 to 1946, it had no editorial page and no Washington bureau. John Gunther said that its front page looked like "a confused and bloody railway accident."

The *Post* was shameless in boosting itself and Denver. Its slogan was *"Denver Post—First in Everything,"* and every day, *in the morning*, it printed the number of minutes of sunshine residents could expect, ignoring the fact that clouds might appear in the perfect Colorado sky.

Bonfils died in 1933. *The Saturday Evening Post* wrote that a lot of people came to the funeral to see for themselves that he was really dead . . . and buried deep. He was never very popular, not even with his employees, toward whom he was paternalistic and suspicious. (He took the doors off the toilet stalls to keep staff members from stealing any stray minutes of time from their jobs.)

In 1946, Helen Bonfils, daughter of F.G., decided to revamp the *Post*. She found a new publisher, Palmer Hoyt, who had been editor and publisher of the Portland *Oregonian*. Under his leadership, the paper changed radically, going through an incredible metamorphosis to become internationalist, pro-civil rights, and antiextremist. The *Post* was one of the 1st newspapers to come out against Sen. Joseph McCarthy, who received Senate censure for his extreme anticommunist activities. It fought ultraconservative Birchers and Minutemen.

Hoyt backed Quigg Newton, a young progressive candidate for mayor against the incumbent, Ben Stapleton. Newton won. He also backed Texas financier Clint Murchison and developer William Zeckendorf in their Denver urban renewal program.

In 1960, the paper came out for Kennedy against Nixon. The last Democrat it had supported was Woodrow Wilson.

The Present. After Hoyt retired, the paper became more conservative. However, it continues to press for school appropriations, and prison and health reforms. It remains influential in State and local politics.

Still a morning daily, it serves a huge empire extending from Wyoming to New Mexico.

Scoops. On May 11, 1969, 100 lbs. of plutonium caught fire at the Rocky Flats nuclear-warhead plant owned by the Dow Chemical Company. Intense radiation spread through the building, causing over $40 million in damage. *The Denver Post*, in investigating the fire, discovered that there had been more than 200 smaller fires at the Rocky Flats plant since 1953.

THE KANSAS CITY STAR

The Past. As a young man, William Rockhill Nelson was that great American cliché—a wild scion of a highly respectable family. His father sent him away to Notre Dame to be tamed; after 2 years, Notre Dame sent him back. Following the Civil War, however, he harnessed his energy, passed the bar exam, and became a lawyer. He tried to build a cotton-growing empire in the South, but this project was a dismal failure; then he became a road builder and amassed a dazzling $200,000 worth of success. After a brief fling at politics, managing Samuel Tilden's campaign for President, he went into newspaper work. In September, 1880, he founded *The Kansas City Star*.

Kansas City was then violent, lawless, unpaved, and shoddy. Nelson set out to improve it. He ordered his reporters to dig up scandal and corruption in the city government. The *Star* attacked rigged elections, gambling and vice rings, a corrupt streetcar franchise, loan sharks, corrupt government contracting, quack doctors, and other assorted evils. Nelson considered the number of libel suits brought against the paper a positive indication that it was "doing its duty."

Standing on the line between prairie and plains, the city was hardly a garden spot. Under the *Star*'s influence it began to improve. The *Star* campaigned for parks, paved streets, tree plantings, zoning ordinances, and well-planned residential districts. These campaigns succeeded. Later when some people criticized the *Star* for its crusading, the paper sarcastically listed the streets, playgrounds, reduced carfares, "and all the other things that have . . . pretty nearly ruined the town."

Above all, Nelson wanted to build a respected newspaper that would serve the public. Like many other newspapermen of the time, he used his military title; the staff called him "Colonel." William Allen White, later the best-known country editor in the U.S., took a job with the *Star* because it was "one of the dozen best and most influential newspapers in the country." He described Nelson as "a great, hulking, 260-pounder, 6' tall, smooth-shaven, with a hard, dominating mouth . . . a mean jaw," and eyes that sometimes "squinted like the lightning of Job." He felt that Nelson had only one flaw: "His clay foot was Grover Cleveland, who could do no wrong."

Nelson refused to publish a sensational paper and would not print comics, big headlines, or "Gee whiz" stories, as his colleague Pulitzer did.

The *Star* was responsible for the arrest of notorious Frederick Bonfils, later owner of *The Denver Post*, for the operation of the Little Louisiana Lottery. Bonfils was annoyed and vengefully bought *The Kansas City Post* to fight the *Star* in 1908. By then, Kansas City saw itself as a somewhat highbrow community and would have nothing to do with Bonfils's low-down journalism. (Later, *The Kansas City Star* was one of the papers which exposed the Teapot Dome scandal, in which Bonfils was implicated for accepting a bribe.)

For a long time, the *Star* was considered a fine training ground for reporters, editors, novelists, and other writers. During the Depression, the *Star* prospered. After Nelson's heir died in the late 1920s, the paper's employees got together and bought it. By 1939, the staff was able to burn its $85 million mortgage, 2 years before it came due.

The Present. An elite paper, the *Star* is highly respected for its fairness, accuracy, and thorough coverage of the news. It is an evening paper with a daily circulation of over 315,000 and a Sunday circulation of over 400,000. It maintains its political stance—"independent but never neutral."

LOS ANGELES TIMES

The Past. When an explosion ripped through the new *Los Angeles Times* Building, immediately killing 12 people in October, 1910, the typographers' union was a logical suspect. The owner of the *Times*, Gen. Harrison Gray Otis, was a California Croesus who owned more than a million acres of ranchland in California

and Mexico and was an officer or a director in 35 California corporations. Like most tycoons of his kind, he was adamantly antiunion and had refused to allow a closed (all-union) shop at the *Times*. Competitor William Randolph Hearst offered $5,000 for information concerning the planters of the bomb, who, it appeared, had also left a 2nd bomb, which had not exploded, in Otis's home. The union denied blame, claiming the explosion was caused by a gas leak. Eventually 21 people died as a result of the bombing. Finally, 2 labor leaders were arrested, and late in their trial, as staged by Lincoln Steffens, they dramatically confessed to the crime. The bombing weakened the labor movement in the West, and the *Times* dominated journalism in Los Angeles for decades thereafter. In 1904—when the *Times* celebrated its 23rd year of publication—the *Herald-Examiner* hit the streets, but it was no real competition for Otis's paper.

Otis died in 1917, and his son-in-law, Harry Chandler, became publisher. Chandler was a New Hampshire boy who had come West, become a newspaperman, and married the boss's daughter. Chandler was responsible for some innovations in the running of the *Times*. In 1922, the paper bought a radio station, and in 1928, it became the 1st newspaper to be delivered in part by airplane.

Chandler was as conservative as his father-in-law had been. Otis had conducted a long campaign against the reform Government in Mexico. He was vengeful because he had been unable to remove the cattle from his Mexican ranch just before Díaz was overthrown. He had, from then on, pushed for any plan that would get his land, and a good chunk of Mexico, away from the reform Government. Chandler continued Otis's vendetta. Upton Sinclair, when running for governor of California in 1935, revealed that Chandler was once indicted, charged with conspiracy to send arms into Mexico, and acquitted under suspicious circumstances. Naturally after that the *Times* was violently against Sinclair, who was to lose the election. However, it was only one of several papers to call Sinclair an atheist and a socialist-communist and to print a photograph showing boxcar loads of Depression bums coming into town to celebrate Sinclair's victory. The photograph was a fake made by using extras hired from film studios. (See also: Upton Sinclair and the EPIC Campaign, Chap. 2.)

When Franklin D. Roosevelt ran for Vice-President in 1920, the *Times* said, "He adds no merit to the ticket. He is a radical of unsafe tendencies."

The paper continued its antilabor stand. It fought the establishment of a 40-hour work week, announcing in an editorial that most workers spent their spare time in "the only diversions they know—pool, poker, drinking, and petty agitation over a fancied grievance." In December, 1937, the May Company department store clerks were striking for higher pay (more than 30¢ an hour) and improved working conditions. Two *Times* headlines about the strike read ASSASSINATION OF SANTA CLAUS and MURDER OF THE SPIRIT OF CHRISTMAS. It may or may not be significant that these appeared even though the May Company was placing full-page ads in the *Times* at the time.

In 1944, Norman Chandler, Harry's son, became publisher of the *Times*. He developed the Times-Mirror Company and expanded its operations to include printing, publication of educational materials, and graphic arts. In 1960, he became president and chairman of the board of the Times-Mirror Company. His son, Otis Chandler, succeeded him as publisher of the *Times*.

Under Otis Chandler, then 33 years old, the paper underwent a miraculous transformation. The writing and editing staff was greatly improved, and its extreme bias was softened, though the paper remained Republican. Chandler himself said later, "We tended to be very conservative, and we used to bias the news—we didn't print both sides of labor-management disputes, we couldn't print much Democratic news, we were narrow in our religious coverage." Some said that *The New York Times*'s abortive effort in 1962 to start a West Coast edition panicked the *Los Angeles Times* into expansion and improvement, but Chandler denied this, saying that the changes were begun in 1959 and 75% completed by 1962. By 1965, the London *Economist* could say of the *Times* that it was the "best California newspaper. . . . a few years back it was a shoddy sheet of extreme right-wing viewpoint and with a Hollywood divorce focus for its news measurement."

Still relatively conservative, the *Times* supported Barry Goldwater for President in 1964 —with certain reservations—and Richard Nixon in 1968 and 1972. However, in 1968 and 1972, it also backed Tom Bradley, a black Democrat, against incumbent Yorty for mayor of Los Angeles. (Bradley won in 1972.)

In 1964, the paper began to publish in-depth series such as "The Press and the Courts," by Gene Blake (1964); "The View from Watts," by Jack Jones (1965); "South Koreans in Vietnam," by John Randolph (1966); "Southern California A.D. 2000," by Sterling Slappey (1966).

By 1967, with its drastic changes in format, its more balanced point of view, and greater thoughtfulness and depth, the *Times* had raised its circulation from about 525,000 in 1960 to 650,000.

The Present. The *Times* again dominates journalism in huge, rambling, 4,800-mi.-sq. Los Angeles. The 3rd largest paper in the U.S., it is the biggest and richest daily on the West Coast. The *Herald-Examiner*, constantly crippled by strikes, is currently its only competition in the city. The paper is physically huge, often running over 200 pages on Sunday; it accounts for at least 20% of the newsprint used in the 11 Western States, and it carries more advertising linage than any other daily in the country. By 1974, its circulation was over a million.

Nick Williams, the editor largely responsible for the paper's metamorphosis, now retired, says the *Times* is designed to "be a serious, opinion-leading newspaper by daily addressing itself to the issues facing Los Angeles, California, the U.S., and the world."

Today the paper emphasizes accurate coverage of the news, both domestic and foreign. Its Washington bureau has 4 times the staff it had in 1963. By 1974, there were 19 foreign correspondents in contrast to the one foreign correspondent the paper had in 1962. The *Times* maintains bureaus in all major cities of the U.S. In 1962, it began a reciprocal news service with *The Washington Post*.

Still pursuing a moderate-Republican stance, the paper's editorial pages are well balanced, with a mélange of syndicated columns. The *Times* has made it a policy not to endorse candidates for high offices such as President and governor.

It has great impact on public opinion. Ted Weegar, the assistant managing editor, wrote in the summer of 1966:

Following the Watts riots of August, 1965, the *Times* said editorially on numerous occasions that solutions to the race problem lay in the area of increased contacts with the city officials and the Negro community, and vigorous implementation of the poverty program. The *Times*'s position was not warmly received. The mayor and the chief of police were not in accord with our stand. But the paper steadfastly stuck to its viewpoint and stuck to it pretty much alone. Indeed, the newspaper found itself the only voice in the community at a time when the city desperately needed to hear from all its elements. Now, however, a year hence, other opinions are arriving at the editorial stand we took then. There has been some progress in race relations, and the road ahead is a long one, but the way was blazed by the *Times*.

The *Times*'s physical plant covers an entire city block at the Los Angeles Civic Center. With a construction cost of over $63 million, it contains the most modern equipment, including color presses and electronic data-processing machines. Its 96 press units can print up to 540,000 copies of a 64-page pamphlet in an hour.

Scoops. In 1965, the *Times* won a Pulitzer Prize for it coverage of the Watts riots.

The *Times* had the 1st exclusive interview with Alfred C. Baldwin, who was manning a listening post at the Watergate break-in. When Bureau Chief John Lawrence refused to turn the interview tapes over to the Watergate prosecutors, Judge John Sirica sentenced him to a 2½-year jail term. With Baldwin's permission, the tapes were later submitted.

NEW YORK DAILY NEWS

The Past. "Tell it to Sweeney—the Stuyvesants will take care of themselves," was Joseph Medill Patterson's motto when, in 1919, he founded the New York *Daily News*, a tabloid featuring sensational photographs and news stories concerning sex and crime. Though the tabloid was new to American journalism, Patterson had not created the idea but was copying the highly successful London *Daily Mirror*.

The paper got off to a slow start. In August, 1919, its circulation was only 26,636. However, Patterson was wealthy enough to be able to afford to wait for success. Partial heir to the great Medill-McCormick fortune, he and the flamboyant Robert R. McCormick of the *Chicago Tribune* were cousins. Patterson had socialist leanings. He had written a novel called *A Little Brother of the Rich*, in which all the wealthy people were bad guys and all the poor people were good guys. Wearing a slouch hat, with his coat collar turned up, he often went out in the streets to mingle with the common man—"the Sweeneys." Impulsive and proud, he was 6' tall with bristling hair and thin lips. His staff called him Captain Patterson. (He had been an army officer in W.W. I.)

Patterson found it hard to get people to work for him because the paper was held in such low esteem by the self-styled literati. Other publishers called the *Daily News* "the servant girl's Bible." It was described as being "by turns sobby, dirty, bloody, and glamorous," and accused of presenting the news in a way that "would appeal to the more elementary emotions of a truck driver and to the truck driver in everyone." A pioneer in yellow journalism, it aimed at the average 1920s newspaper reader, whom H. L. Mencken described as a "booby unmatchable." Twenty years before, no newspaper publisher would have been able to get away with such tactics; he would have found himself up to his neck in moral protest and lawsuits. But times and social customs were changing fast.

To catch the eye of the commuter running for the subway, *Daily News* headline writers came up with such gems as KILLER'S CAT FOUND. The gimmick worked. By 1921, the paper was successful. By 1925, circulation had jumped to over a million. The Sunday edition, which was begun in 1921, was outselling all other New York Sunday editions by 1925.

In 1924, 2 more tabloids hit the stands in New York—Hearst's *Daily Mirror* and the *Daily Graphic*, which soon acquired the nickname "Pornographic."

In 1927, all 3 papers reached a low point during their coverage of the intimate life of "Daddy" Browning and his Peaches, and the murder case involving Ruth Snyder and her corset-salesman lover. Competing fiercely, city editors approved the use of faked photographs and sent out reporters who were ruthless in the questioning of anyone who had anything to do with either case.

Then the great crash of 1929 hit the country. Patterson changed his method of operation, telling his staff, "We're off on the wrong foot. The people's major interest is no longer in the playboy, Broadway, and divorces, but in how they are going to eat, and from this time forward, we'll pay attention to the struggle for existence that is just beginning."

The *Daily News* supported Franklin Delano Roosevelt, predicting a Roosevelt victory against Alf Landon in 1936, as did the Gallup poll and the Baltimore *Sun*. All others thought that Landon would be the winner by a landslide. To show its objectivity, however, the *News* printed a "Presidential Battle Page," in which arguments on both sides were presented.

Breaking with Roosevelt over foreign policy, in 1940 the paper became isolationist and conservative, swinging like a pendulum as far as it could away from where it had begun. It has maintained its conservative stance ever since, viewing Fidel Castro as "a little communist cockroach," the UN as "a glass cigar box . . . jammed with pompous do-gooders, nervy deadbeats, moochers, saboteurs, spies, and traitors," collegiate dissenters as "kooks and kookettes, Reds, Pinks, punks, and dupes," and liberals as "bleeding hearts."

Its headlines have remained sensational and clever. When Gina Lollobrigida's performance in a film was criticized by an Italian prosecutor, the headline read CHARGES GINA/WAS OBSCENA/ ON LA SCREENA. And when, during the Profumo scandal, Mandy Rice-Davies bad-mouthed Douglas Fairbanks, Jr., the headline read QUEEN OF HEARTS CALLS DOUG A BUM.

Patterson died in 1946, but the paper is still faithful to most of his ideals, many of which seem old-fashioned to the new guard in the journalism field. As a *Daily News* employee said, reflecting on the growth in sophistication of the American public since the 1920s, "The trouble is there are fewer Sweeneys around to tell it to."

The Present. "New York's Picture Newspaper," the *Daily News* still has the highest circulation of any paper in the country. However, its circulation is falling, while *The New York Times*'s circulation is increasing.

The *Daily News* has made efforts toward improvement. It now carries at least a full page of financial news in each edition, provides more science coverage, and has toned down its page format so that the headlines are not quite so large.

Headquartered in a modern building on 42nd Street, the *Daily News* employs over 600 newsmen, over 50 photographers, and 2 pilots to fly its photographers around—a total staff of about 5,000. It also has several full-time foreign correspondents, and a respected Washington bureau.

It maintains its breezy approach and conservative attitude. It is still against communism and liberals.

The *News* puts the best picture of the day on the 1st page, without regard to who took it—a staffer or a wire service. It retouches 95% of the photographs it uses. Sometimes this causes difficulty, as when in August, 1965, it doctored up a picture of a woman boarding Frank Sinatra's yacht to look like Jacqueline Kennedy only to find that the woman was not Mrs. Kennedy after all.

The *Daily News* constantly runs promotional contests, and it sponsors events such as art shows and science fairs for high school students, the Harvest Moon Ball in Madison Square Garden (an amateur dance contest), and the New York Golden Gloves amateur boxing contest. Thousands of people write in each week with bright sayings or household hints. Thousands more order the dress patterns and needlework books which are offered for sale.

Many of the paper's by-lines are false, in keeping with a Patterson belief that readers would be disappointed if a favorite writer retired or died. Nancy Randolph, Sally Joy Brown, Elinor Ames, and Kate Cameron are not real people.

The *News* avoids printing stories about the moral turpitude of religious figures, child molesters, and homosexuals. "There's nothing sexy about an unnatural sex story," a staffer has said.

Scoops. The *Daily News* was the 1st to print a story about the resignation of Bill D. Moyers as presidential press secretary.

It keeps in close touch with the police and tends toward a law-and-order point of view. William Federici, a reporter for the *News*, once said, "I'm sure we had an awful lot to do with

defeating the civilian review board" (a proposal by Mayor Lindsay in which civilians would dominate a board investigating complaints against police). At the time the review board proposal was defeated, a *News* editorial said it freed "the world's finest metropolitan police force from the threat of hobbles and handicaps inflicted by cop-haters, Meddlesome Matties, Nervous Nellies, and Communists." *News* reporters claim that in return for the paper's friendship, the police provide exclusive tips. It was Federici's relationships with police and criminals ("guys I grew up with who turned out no good") that helped him recover the $140,000 DeLong ruby, stolen from the American Museum of Natural History in 1965.

Merits. The New York *Daily News* gives fine coverage of crimes and disasters; it has a good sports section; it provides 17 comic strips.

Its headlines and breezy style are excellent—a rarity in the field of tabloid journalism.

Demerits. The *Daily News* provides scanty coverage of world events. Frank Holeman, an editor for the paper, has said, "It isn't an important paper. . . . If Rusk wants to launch a trial balloon, he calls Scotty Reston [of *The New York Times*]. . . . If the cops knock off a cathouse on 72nd Street, they call us."

James Aronson, editor of the *National Guardian*, a left-wing weekly paper, has said that the *News* is "an obese, malevolent fishwife, screaming journalistic obscenities at more than 2 million persons a day, exhorting them to go out and kill a commie for Christ—or even just for fun."

Nat Hentoff, writer and critic, has said that the *News* "views things with stunning oversimplification, and though edited for the workingman, doesn't fight for him."

THE NEW YORK TIMES

The Past. The New York Times, 1st published in 1851, was the brainchild of journalist Henry J. Raymond and 2 financiers—George Jones and Edward B. Wesley. Then called the *New York Daily Times*, it was a 4-page paper, selling at 1¢ a copy. In its early days, the *Times* was conservative, with a high moral tone. After a period of decline from 1884 to 1896, the paper was bought by Adolph Simon Ochs, part owner of *The Chattanooga Daily Times*, who wrote to his wife at the time, "Here I am in New York ready to negotiate for the leading and most influential newspaper in America. The supreme gall of a country newspaperman burdened with debt."

Ochs revitalized the *Times*. He put more stress on news, eliminated fiction, started a weekly book section and coined the phrase "All the News That's Fit to Print," which is still included on the masthead. He also cut the price, which had risen to 3¢, back to a penny. In 3 years he more than quadrupled the circulation.

In 1935, Ochs died and his son-in-law, Arthur Hays Sulzberger, took over the paper. He, in turn, was followed by another son-in-law, Orvil E. Dryfoos, who died in 1963, when Arthur Ochs Sulzberger, the present publisher, took over.

Mildly reformist, the paper has been politically liberal for most of its life. It supported Wendell Willkie in 1940, was critical of Sen. Joseph McCarthy in the 1950s, and backed David Halberstam—who sent back pessimistic reports in his coverage of the Vietnam War—when Washington officials wanted his stories toned down.

A. M. Rosenthal, who was made managing editor in 1969, livened up the gray, somewhat monotonous layout of the *Times*, and lightened the somewhat heavy tone the paper was famous for.

The Present. The *New York Times* is the most important paper in the U.S., consistently ranking number one for editorial quality and news coverage in surveys of journalists. It is housed in an old, undistinguished building in a run-down corner of New York City, not far from seedy Times Square.

The biggest U.S. paper in total operations, it is among the top 3 in circulation, with readers in every State in the country. With *The Washington Post*, it publishes the *Herald Tribune* in Paris, and it owns radio station WQXR, educational book divisions, and interests in Canadian newsprint mills.

The *New York Times* does endeavor to print "all the news that's fit to print." Physically the paper is big; the Sunday edition usually weighs over 7 lbs. Known for its thorough coverage of the news, the *Times* prints important speeches and documents in full. (The day after it was released, the 290,000-word Warren Commission *Report* appeared in the *Times*.) James Reston, *Times* associate editor, has said, "Our primary responsibility is not . . . to the commuter reading the paper on the train. Our primary responsibility is to the historian of 50 years from now. Unique among newspapers, The *Times* is prime source material —and we must never poison the stream of history."

In addition to exhaustive news coverage, The *New York Times* provides excellent reporting on issues vital to women, on culture including rock music and other counterculture arts, religion, art, education, food, law, science. Its distinguished staff, which numbers over 1,000, includes some of the most respected newspaper people of our time: city reporter John Corry, theater critic Clive Barnes, architecture expert Ada Louise Huxtable, reporter Seymour Hersh (who 1st exposed the My Lai massacre), education editor Fred Hechinger, Pulitzer Prize winners James Reston and David Halberstam, and many others.

Moderately liberal, the "good gray *Times*" has, in the past, cooperated with the Government in suppressing politically sensitive news. For instance, the *Times* knew about U-2 flights over the U.S.S.R. months before Francis Gary Powers was shot down; it suppressed the story in "the national interest." On the other hand, it has been openly critical of the Government in its handling of the Vietnam War and China policy.

The *Times*'s only taboos are against smut and scandalmongery. It is precise in a somewhat old-fashioned way about the use of the English language on its pages. It has been known, for instance, to put quotes around the word "gas" (for gasoline) when used in headlines.

Scoops. In 1871, *Times* publisher George Jones turned down a $1 million bribe to suppress his exposé of the Boss Tweed gang.

In a rare burst of daring, the *Times* printed a story on the sinking of the *Titanic*, based on news of a distress signal from Newfoundland. The news was not confirmed until a day later.

James Reston, famous *Times* reporter, was responsible for an incredible number of scoops: the Yalta papers, the documents in the Oppenheimer case, the Eisenhower doctrine.

With *The Washington Post*, *The New York Times* printed the Pentagon Papers, and, after an attempt was made by the Government to silence the 2 papers, won a Supreme Court case on their right to publish such material.

Merits. The *Times* has a well-deserved reputation for integrity and balance in handling news coverage. American press critic John Lofton has praised it for its coverage of the Berlin crisis, for instance, and it was a crusader in its criticism of the Vietnam War. In 1971, the *Times* courageously published the highly classified Pentagon Papers.

Demerits. Some critics accuse the *Times* of dullness and overcaution. It is true that the paper has on occasion suppressed some news in "the national interest": the U-2 flights and CIA involvement in the Cuban crisis. Similarly, the *Times* did not print the 1st picture of a Buddhist monk burning himself to death, though this may have been because the editors felt such a picture was too sensational. Months later, it printed a photograph of another similar suicide.

Because the *Times* tries to print everything that's "fit to print," editing and proofreading are sometimes too hasty. Some critics feel that the paper prints too much, that it could be pared down without sacrificing accuracy.

SAN FRANCISCO CHRONICLE

The Past. In 1865, San Francisco was a theater town, and 2 young brothers, Charles and Michael De Young, decided to capitalize on that. Accordingly, they began publishing a throwaway theater program called the *San Francisco Dramatic Chronicle*. Physically unprepossessing, it was 4 pages long, the size of a sheet of letterhead. However, it carried short pieces by impressive authors such as Mark Twain and Bret Harte, as well as news of the city. It was so popular that by 1868 it became a regular newspaper selling for 2¢. It dropped the word *Dramatic* from its name.

A reform paper, the *Chronicle* fought to improve the community, exposed civic corruption, campaigned against land monopoly and the manipulations of the railroad barons.

Its reform activities made enemies for the *Chronicle* and its owners. In 1880, a verbal war in a local election broke into a gunfight. Charles De Young was so angry that he wounded the Workingmen's party candidate for mayor. The candidate's son retaliated by shooting and killing De Young.

Michael De Young was not so hotheaded. A member of the Republican National Committee for 8 years, he was active in civic and national affairs and ran the paper somewhat more conservatively.

The *Chronicle's* major competition was *The Evening Examiner*, bought by Hearst in 1880. As the city's population grew, more newspapers were founded, until there were 6 in all.

In the early 1960s, the *Chronicle* and *The Examiner* waged a circulation war, vying for the most sensational headlines and most incendiary editorials. By that time, *The Examiner* had become the most conservative Hearst paper and the *Chronicle*, long connected with the Republican establishment, was hardly liberal. The war had no ideological basis, and it fizzled to an end when the 2 papers decided to merge.

During the merger, cameraman Albert Kihn of KRON, the *Chronicle*-owned TV station, charged publicly that the station would not allow coverage of the negotiations. The *Chronicle* hired spies to snoop on Kihn, and both papers were ordered to ignore the story. It was not until the snooping was exposed in another publication that the *Chronicle* admitted to the Federal Communications Commission that it had happened.

The Present. The *Chronicle-Examiner* papers dominate San Francisco journalism but are without special distinction. They are conservatively oriented.

The *Chronicle's* obituary policy is somewhat controversial. "We catch hell for bringing up unpleasant episodes in a man's life in his obituary," Gordon Pates, the managing editor, has said, "But we feel it's part of the picture of the dead man's life."

In 1975, the *Chronicle's* circulation was 465,000. A morning paper, it has nearly 3 times as many subscribers as the evening *Examiner*. On Sunday, the publisher puts out a combined edition—the Sunday *Examiner-Chronicle*.

Scoops. The *San Francisco Chronicle* was the only San Francisco paper to put out extras upon Lincoln's assassination.

ST. LOUIS POST-DISPATCH

The Past. Joseph Pulitzer, a tall, scraggly, German-speaking immigrant from Hungary, became one of America's greatest newspaper publishers. He began his career when he founded the *St. Louis Post-Dispatch* in 1878 by merging the *Dispatch* with the *Post*, which he bought for $2,500. The *Post-Dispatch* immediately became a crusader. John A. Cockerill, whom Pulitzer hired as editor, promptly began a series of exposés: of a public utility that was extorting money from customers, gamblers ("What will the police do about it?" the *Post-Dispatch* asked innocently), a lottery racket, a horsecar monopoly, and an insurance fraud. Cockerill published a list of local tax dodgers and a list of whorehouse owners. In doing so, he and Pulitzer made enemies. Pulitzer carried a gun because of those enemies; however, on one occasion, a tomato saved him. One night in 1879 he was bringing home some tomatoes—to satisfy a craving of his pregnant wife—when he saw a suspicious character loitering near his house. Realizing that the man was waiting to jump him, Pulitzer threw a tomato at him and dashed safely into the house.

Carlotta Patti, the concert singer, sued the *Post-Dispatch* for saying that she was drunk during her performance in Leavenworth, Kans. The paper not only did not retract the story, but ran the subsequent headline, FULL AS A TICK. In the story underneath the headline, it said of Patti's attorney: "Mr. Herman is not so well provided himself that he can afford to go dancing in front of newspaper offices in war paint and feathers, and we may take a notion one of these days to set him up where the public can admire his beautiful moral proportions."

The paper stressed sensational crime reporting, which pushed sales up. Cockerill once said, "Political events do not affect our sales favorably. Next to the assassination of President Garfield, our greatest increase has been by a local hanging."

Within 3 years of its founding, the paper had 12,000 subscriptions and was making $45,000 in profits a year; by 1883, profits had risen to $85,000 annually.

The paper's most dramatic moment came

in a political fight between Cockerill and one of the city's leading lawyers. During a congressional race, Cockerill called the lawyer—who worked for Jay Gould—"a servant of the rich and corrupt." The lawyer's partner, Col. Alonzo Slayback, retaliated by calling the *Post-Dispatch* a "blackmailing sheet." The argument came to a head when Slayback, with blood in his eye, came storming up to the city room where Cockerill was chatting with a couple of his employees. Slayback drew a gun and took a shot at Cockerill. Cockerill quickly retaliated by shooting and killing Slayback. The Missouri *Republican*, which was in competition with the *Post-Dispatch*, accused Cockerill of killing Slayback in cold blood. (Cockerill was freed on a plea of self-defense, however.) Understandably, tempers rose. A group of angry citizens gathered in front of the *Post-Dispatch* Building and threatened to lynch the owner and burn the building down. Pulitzer supported Cockerill, though later he had to let him go.

Pulitzer ruled the *Post-Dispatch* from New York. He was known for his patriarchal largesse. His newsboys, for instance, got a big free Christmas dinner each year and bonuses like pocketknives and gold watches. He was also crotchety, tyrannical, and eccentric, often alienating his editors. John Dillon, his *Post-Dispatch* publisher in the early 1880s, once wrote to him: "You have a right to ask why I have sat here like a dummy . . . and blindly followed your orders. . . . In all cases in which my judgment has dissented from yours, you have been so invariably right and I so invariably wrong that you have relieved me of the necessity of thinking for myself. . . . I can say with truth that I have done for you what I have never done for anyone else in my life, in surrendering my judgment to yours without question."

Pulitzer died in 1911, and his son took over the paper. He, too, became intimately involved with it, sending memos to editors, criticizing, even writing and editing. However, he allowed his staff complete intellectual freedom, and never asked a reporter to write something that was against his personal beliefs. In 1948, the whole editorial staff save one refused to comment on the candidacy of Thomas E. Dewey, who was supported by the paper.

The *Post-Dispatch* has always made an attempt to present both sides of an issue. During the Vietnam War, for instance, it carried a column by Max Freedman, in which Freedman criticized Martin Luther King, Jr., for some remarks on the war, saying that King was in danger of "becoming the Bertrand Russell of the U.S. . . . close to putting off greatness and becoming a bore, an intruder where he has no business, and a busybody causing great mischief." On the following day, an editorial answered Freedman, calling him "petulant" and

saying his column was "among the sillier comments of the season." It further said, "Issues of war and peace in Vietnam are most definitely everybody's business, not a private preserve of self-acknowledged 'authorities,' and Dr. King's contribution is more than ordinarily welcome."

The Present. Now run by Pulitzer's grandson, Joseph Pulitzer, Jr., the *St. Louis Post-Dispatch* is a highly regarded, liberal paper, which, in spite of its claims that it clings to the center, is really leaning to the left.

The *Saturday Review* has said of it: "Its general philosophy is that its readers . . . deserve and are capable of understanding important news from any part of the world, on any subject, and of any nature. It looks on its readers as changing, and sees the frontiers of news as expanding."

It still crusades, following the precept of Pulitzer: "Never drop a big thing until you have gone to the bottom of it." Its editorial page carries a statement dating from the paper's beginning, which says that a paper is "an institution that should always fight for progress and reform, never tolerate injustice or corruption, always fight demagogues of all parties, never belong to any party, always oppose privileged classes and public plunderers, never lack sympathy with the poor, always remain devoted to the public welfare, never be satisfied with merely printing news, always be drastically independent, never be afraid to attack wrong, whether by predatory plutocracy or predatory poverty."

The *Post-Dispatch* favors improving education, housing and medical assistance, and supports trade unions, minority groups, and the UN. It covers world news thoroughly, yet pays attention to the city's problems.

In 1975, its daily circulation was 290,000, its Sunday circulation 485,000. Its physical plant covers an entire city block.

Scoops. In keeping with the sensational exposés of its early days, the *St. Louis Post-Dispatch* can take credit for several crusading scoops:

The paper was one of the journalistic heroes of the Teapot Dome scandal.

In 1927, Paul Y. Anderson exposed the State Department, which had fomented a communist scare in Mexico because American oil companies wanted an excuse to seize land there.

Anderson also exposed the Chicago police for their massacre of demonstrators during the Republic Steel Company Memorial Day rioting.

The paper exposed the Pendergast machine, the Kelly machine, the Hague machine.

Investigation by the *Post-Dispatch* caused the impeachment of Federal judge George W. English.

The *Post-Dispatch* investigated the Nixon campaign-fund story and showed that benefits were indeed received by those who contributed to this fund.

THE WALL STREET JOURNAL

The Past. In 1882, with 2 associates, newspaperman Charles Henry Dow founded Dow Jones and Company, Inc., a news agency for the financial world. Seven years later, the company published the 1st issue of *The Wall Street Journal*, which was then a mere collection of bulletins of news affecting business. In 1901, *The Wall Street Journal* was bought from Dow by Clarence Walker Barrow, a portly, friendly, hardworking newspaperman. He was a specialist in economic journalism, and he took the little financial newssheet far beyond its beginnings. Under his leadership, the *Journal* published stories to explain the facts behind statistics and formal statements so that the nonexpert could understand them.

In 1939, *The Wall Street Journal* submitted a series attacking outmoded building codes to the Pulitzer Prize board. The board returned the material, saying that "trade papers are not eligible for consideration." It outgrew its classification as a trade paper and won its 1st Pulitzer Prize in 1947. Since then, it has won several Pulitzer Prizes.

From 1940 to 1970, the paper's circulation grew from 35,000 to more than a million.

The Present. The Wall Street Journal is a special paper for people in the business and economic communities, yet it goes far beyond that designation in its treatment of the news. The *Journal* gives precedence to stock market tables and other financial news, but it also prints personality profiles, sociological background articles, and other items on the edges of the "hard" financial news.

The *Journal's* conservative editorial page is widely quoted. In 1972, Managing Editor Frederick Taylor outlawed the use of the word "reform" because, as a conservative, he believed that not all change is for the better.

The *Journal* often influences the news. On the day it ran a detailed front-page report on the depressing impact expected from the 1974 Arab oil boycott, the stock market dropped 24 points.

The *Journal* has experimented with various composition and printing innovations such as high-speed tape transmission, cold typesetting, and facsimile publication. It publishes 4 regional editions in 9 printing plants across the U.S. and runs a complex same-day delivery system. It never prints photographs, only line drawings.

Scoops. Monroe W. Karmin and Stanley Penn of *The Wall Street Journal* investigated gambling in the Bahamas, found that American gangsters had moved in, and, through their exposé, contributed to the fall of the Government there in a later election. Penn has also produced exclusives on the suspect financial dealings of Robert Vesco and Howard Hughes. In 1973, Jerry Landauer was 1st with the story that Spiro Agnew was under criminal investigation.

THE WASHINGTON POST

The Past. The Washington Post was on its last legs in 1933 when Eugene Meyer, an immigrant's son who had made a fortune in banking, bought it for $875,000. Though he poured over $6 million into it, the *Post* remained 2nd-rate and continued losing money. In 1948, Meyer turned the paper over to his son-in-law, Philip Graham. Graham was interested in profits. He bought radio and television stations, *Newsweek* magazine, and the *Washington Times-Herald*—and he kept a tight rein on spending. (One reporter remembers asking the city editor for $5 for taxi fare to cover a story under the Graham regime. He was refused on the grounds of economy and had to borrow the city editor's car. Such economies, of course, do not contribute to high-quality journalism.)

In 1963, Graham shot himself, and his widow, Katharine Graham, took over *The Washington Post*. Mrs. Graham, a tall, good-looking woman, was a reporter in San Francisco before her marriage and had worked on the editorial staff of the *Post*. She set out to make the *Post* a good newspaper. Almost immediately, she hired Ben Bradlee, a highly experienced newspaperman, as executive editor and gave him carte blanche to do whatever he had to do to improve the paper. Bradlee—gruff, witty, and shrewd—hired great reporters away from other papers by paying higher salaries and using strong persuasion. For instance, he called B. H. Bagdikian, a free-lance writer who had called the *Post* the "most irritating paper in the country," and said "Okay, you've been saying what's wrong with the *Post*, why don't you do something about it?" Unable to resist the challenge, Bagdikian joined the staff as national editor. Bradlee also hired Pulitzer Prize winners Eugene C. Patterson and Philip L. Geyelin. The latter was State Dept. correspondent for *The Wall Street Journal*. And the *Post* was on its way to becoming one of the top newspapers in the U.S.

Under Meyer, the *Post* was politically conservative. In 1938, Sen. Sherman Minton complained that 90% of the press was deliberately slanting the news to destroy the New Deal, and he named the *Post* as one of the offenders. However, the paper later became more liberal, supporting Adlai Stevenson for President in 1952 and criticizing Sen. Joseph McCarthy, the rabid anticommunist whose witch-hunts brought Senate censure.

The *Post* has fearlessly attacked presidential administrations, Republican and Democrat alike. President Eisenhower would read only the sports pages. As Vice-President, Richard Nixon would not subscribe to the *Post* because of Herblock's unflattering cartoons. President Lyndon Johnson, who did read the paper, would, through Bill Moyers, his press secretary, call Bradlee late at night to complain in colorful language about items in the *Post*. When Agnew was nominated for Vice-President, the *Post* compared it with the appointment by Roman Emperor Caligula of his horse as proconsul. (One of Agnew's associates said this was "the lowest blow he had ever received in politics.") When Haynsworth and Carswell were nominated for the Supreme Court, the *Post* came out strongly against the nominations. Many think the *Post* was partially responsible for the fact that those nominations were defeated. (A Herblock cartoon showed Judge Carswell coming up out of a garbage can.)

The Present. A reporter's paper, *The Washington Post* has a lively, competitive staff. Though there is considerable infighting among them, morale is high. (They have been known to toss a football around the newsroom in an excess of high spirits.) A national paper whose closest rival is *The New York Times*, the *Post* has a huge news-department staff, perhaps the best political staff in the country, and a fine editorial group. The *Post* and the *Times* exchange photo-transmissions of their front pages; each tries to cover the other's exclusives. With the *Los Angeles Times*, the *Post* runs an international news service for nearly 200 U.S. and over 100 foreign newspapers.

Somewhat reformist, politically independent, and leaning toward the liberal side, the *Post* serves a diverse readership: members of Congress, residents of the Virginia and Maryland suburbs, and over 100,000 slum dwellers.

Katharine Graham, the publisher of the *Post*, says about the paper: "It makes no pretense at a do-gooder's role. It is at the service of all. But the service, the journalist's role, is to offer a tough-minded appraisal of what things really look like, what's really ailing the world—and the people in it—and why. . . . The life of democracy demands above all a love of truth—precisely as tyranny alone can consistently practice the lie."

Scoops. With *The New York Times*, *The Washington Post* published, in 1971, classified Pentagon Papers on U.S. involvement in the Vietnam War, leaked by Daniel Ellsberg. The Justice Dept. obtained a restraining order against both papers, pending a ruling on permanent injunction. However, by a 6–3 vote, the U.S. Supreme Court upheld the right of the press to publish the documents under the protection of the 1st Amendment.

On February 9, 1972, Jack Anderson of the *Post* published an alleged ITT memo written by Dita Beard, who worked for ITT. The memo described the success of a plan in which ITT underwrote the costs of the Republican 1972 convention, ostensibly in exchange for the settling of an antitrust program.

It was *The Washington Post* that 1st uncovered the Watergate scandal in 1972 through the efforts of reporters Bob Woodward and Carl Bernstein.

Behind the Front Page around the World

ABC (Madrid, Spain)

The Past. ABC was founded as a weekly in 1903 by Torcuato de Tena y Alvárez-Ossorio. Two years later it was converted to a daily, the 1st in Spain, with a 3-column tabloid format.

From the beginning, ABC, "a newspaper of general information," stressed politics and literature. Its writing has always been considered the best in Spain, and many great Spanish writers and intellectuals have contributed to its pages. José Cuartero, an ABC journalist, set the tone for newspaper writing all over Spain with his precise yet expressive articles.

ABC has also included pictures, more than most European newspapers; in fact, it was the 1st in the country to use photoengravings.

The paper has always been in favor of monarchy for Spain and was taken over by the Republican Government in May, 1931, as a result of its views. In August, 1932, the Government forced the paper to suspend operations for 4 months in retaliation for its articles which urged less government censorship. Again, 4 years later, the Government intervened, occupying the building in which ABC was published and controlling the paper until Franco took over Madrid in 1939.

Like other newspapers in authoritarian countries, ABC has always suffered from repression and the editors have had to soft-pedal their stand on the monarchy. To keep the paper interesting, they have improved the quality of noncontroversial articles.

The Present. ABC is a serious paper, highly

respected throughout the world, even though its editors do not have the freedom possible in more democratic countries.

Some newspaper experts feel that the lack of freedom is so inhibiting that the paper cannot, in spite of its good points, be taken seriously. One of these is Herbert Matthews, who in his book *The Yoke and the Arrows: A Report on Spain* (1957) said: "The Spanish press is one of the greatest insults to the intelligence of the Western world. How could it be anything else under the stultifying pressure of both an obscurantist Church and a Government which uses the press as an instrument of politics and has a horror of free expression?" Concerning Spanish journalists, he said, "Talking with one is quite a different experience from reading what he has to say."

Others feel that *ABC*, operating within its limits, has been able to put before the public an amazing variety of viewpoints with subtlety and restraint. In Spain, *ABC* is an institution. It also reaches the rest of the world through its airmail edition, which was started in 1950.

A large part of its editorial space is devoted to foreign news, which comes in from *ABC* foreign correspondents and from the Spanish news agency "Efe."

THE AGE (Melbourne, Australia)

The Past. The Age was established in Melbourne in 1854 by the Cooke brothers—John and Henry. Two years later, Ebenezer Syme bought it for £2,000, and soon his brother David got into the act and took it over. It was David who "made" the paper. Fearless and liberal, a personality boy, he brought circulation from 2,000 in 1860 to 38,000 in 1879. When he died in 1908 at the age of 80, he left the paper in trust to his 5 sons.

By 1975, circulation had reached 210,000, most of it in the state of Victoria (where Melbourne is located).

The Present. Though *The Age* is somewhat a defender of tradition, it probably should be considered a liberal—but not very—newspaper. It has a world view, rather than a regional one, and considers itself "one of the world's top 7 newspapers." However, it also emphasizes its home city and the state of Victoria. Its impact on public opinion is considerable. As one newspaperman says, *The Age* "for more than half a century has frightened the life out of most politicians." Throughout the world, *The Age* is thought of as the best window into Australian thinking.

The Age's editors are conservative on social issues and avoid printing news that would offend the family reader. They claim that its readers are generally in the top 25% of the community in education and income.

Since not all the staff are university graduates when they begin working for the newspaper, some are put through a tough training program for the 1st 4 years of their employment. The new staff member is called "The Cadet" in the 1st year. He takes courses in shorthand and is enrolled at the University of Melbourne in a 3-year part-time course for which he receives a Diploma of Journalism. At the end of his apprenticeship, he is considered a trained journalist. The staff numbers over 1,000.

The Age is famous for its classified advertising; sometimes, in the Saturday edition, classified ads cover 70–80 pages. The news is written "straight," without editorial interpretation, in American rather than European style. On Thursday, the paper includes a television/radio guide; on Tuesdays and Thursdays, there is a special children's section. Physically, *The Age* has a modern lively look.

Scoops. The Age was the 1st newspaper to publish complete reports of the Prime Minister's press conferences. (*The Age* was Prime Minister Robert Menzie's favorite paper, in spite of the fact that it often attacked him.)

ASAHI SHIMBUN (Tokyo, Japan)

The Past. The journalistic world into which *Asahi Shimbun* ("Rising Sun") was born was not the most auspicious. In 1875, the Japanese Government had passed a stiff libel law and was putting editors in jail for "dangerous thoughts." Yet in 1879, Rhuhei Murayama and Noburu Kimura applied for a license to start a paper with a courageous statement: "The newspaper will be edited for easy reading, even by children, with illustrations and other devices . . . for the guidance of the common people, both men and women, young and old, in order to teach them social justice." Social justice was hardly the aim of Japan's authoritarian militaristic Government.

Kimura was soon out of the picture, replaced by Riichi Ueno. Ueno, prosaic and stable, was the perfect foil for the enterprising and effervescent Murayama, the idea man of the paper. Though *Asahi Shimbun* was begun in Osaka, Tokyo soon became its headquarters. By the turn of the century, circulation for the 2 branches was more than 150,000.

After the turn of the century, *Asahi* continually sniped at and embarrassed the traditionalist Government. In 1915, for instance, it published the 21 Demands against China at what the Government thought was the wrong time, and in 1918, it published what the Government thought was too much information about the race riots. During those years, reporters and Murayama were beaten up by right-wingers. It didn't stop them. By 1925, censorship was worse than ever. Papers were forbidden to publish anything "undermining the existing governmental and economic system." An *Asahi* historian has said: "Under the forces of totalitarian rule, restrictions on free speech were drawn tighter and tighter; the rattling of sabers became louder and louder. . . . The outward trappings of civilian control remained, but army arrogance was rampant."

In the 1930s, Japan was in the depths of a depression, as was most of the world. At *Asahi*, old Murayama, 83 years old, died; the newspaper was passed on to his adopted son and son-in-law, Nagataka Murayama. In 1936, the paper conducted a successful campaign against the military Government and its interference in civilian matters. Public opinion was against the military regime. But the young military extremists rose up with force and wrecked *Asahi*'s printing plant and editorial offices.

By 1937, there was war in China and Japan tightened control on newspapers by controlling newsprint, and slowly over the next 4 years ended any independence the Japanese press had. During W.W. II, censorship was incredibly tight, and *Asahi* did not oppose the Government. However, after the war, *Asahi*, now very left-wing, regained its freedom and attacked the postoccupation Governments viciously. Prime Minister Nobusuke Kishi, hounded out of office, said: "Violence is not only that of pistols and fists; that of the pen is more dangerous."

Gen. Douglas MacArthur stopped publication of *Asahi Shimbun* for a while because of its inflammatory stand. It accused the U.S. of breaking international law in using the A-bomb, for instance. Some even called it "red *Asahi*." However, when street demonstrations, fomented somewhat by the newspaper, got out of hand, *Asahi* called a halt.

In 1960, during the Japanese-U.S. mutual security treaty riots, *Asahi* and other newspapers were able, by their opposition, to bring down the Japanese Government and force President Eisenhower to cancel his visit to Japan.

In 1969, it opposed a trade agreement with China, and a year later berated the Sato Government for insisting on the reversion of Okinawa to Japanese sovereignty.

The Present. Asahi Shimbun has the unlikely combination of high-quality journalism and tremendous circulation (over 6 million in 1975). Its staff numbers in the thousands and it has plants in 5 cities. A hundred different editions are published every day. With over 300 bureaus in Japan and about 20 overseas, *Asahi* still subscribes to 24 different news agencies.

To get on the staff, one must be a university graduate. Only one in 80 of those who apply makes it. The qualifying examination is extremely difficult—involving a translation exercise, writing a long essay, a comprehensive test on current events, and so on. After running the gauntlet of this test successfully, the applicant then faces tough interviews with *Asahi* executives. Once on the staff, competition continues; apprentice journalists rarely get anything published, yet they keep trying. The paper has a dormitory where, every night, 500 reporters sleep over, just in case they might be needed to cover a story. And they are poorly paid, though not so poorly as other journalists who work for other papers. In compensation, *Asahi* provides bonuses and prizes.

The *Asahi* empire is huge, including radio and television broadcasting, book and magazine publishing, and other enterprises. Yet it is not a monopoly. The Japanese are newspaper readers, and *Asahi*'s competitors do very well indeed.

Asahi's headquarters are in a large 8-story triangular building near the Sukiyabashi intersection in downtown Tokyo.

Japanese, with its couple of thousand characters, presents a big production problem which *Asahi* has partially solved through modern technical innovations. It was the 1st to use telephoto transmission of handwritten copy, and in 1959–1960 it pioneered with kanji character teletype machines and facsimile radio-photo transmission of entire newspapers.

Asahi sponsors projects in exploration, science, aviation, art, music, public health, and many other fields. From 1911 to 1962, for instance, it backed Antarctic exploration and was behind the 1st airplane flight ever made in Japan (1911).

The Murayamas still own the paper and occasionally try to exert pressure in editorial matters; however, control lies, most of the time, in the hands of the board of directors, which is drawn from the paper's working staff. In 1964, tension between the owners and staff grew to such a pitch that it ended up in court. A peaceful compromise was reached.

Asahi Shimbun has been likened to an "exclusive boutique linked to a Paris couturier [which] is set amid a vast range of sound quality ware and where there is no bargain." It is a quality paper with a liberal yet moderate approach to the news and an international outlook.

Scoops. During the Boxer Rebellion in 1900, Keitaro Murai, *Asahi* correspondent, was the only Japanese journalist caught in Peking. His stories were translated and read everywhere.

In 1943, writer Seigo Nakano was arrested for criticizing Prime Minister Gen. Hideki Tojo. He later committed hara-kiri.

Excélsior (Mexico City, Mexico)

The Past. When Rafael Alducin founded *Excélsior* in 1917, he was 28 years old. It wasn't long before the paper became noted for its high-quality editorial section and its mature point of view. When Alducin died, his widow took over. She was the 1st woman in Mexico to have such an important newspaper position.

During the Depression, *Excélsior* got into serious financial trouble, but its employees bailed it out by getting together and forming a cooperative to guarantee it a source of income.

Rodrigo de Llano, "one of the giants of Mexican journalism," perhaps exerted more influence than anyone else in making the paper world-famous for quality. Under him, *Excélsior* was known as the furthest to the right of all the newspapers in Mexico. Those who were against De Llano, mostly the communists, criticized the paper as pro-U.S., pro-Franco, pro-capital, antiliberal, and often antigovernment. The year after De Llano's death in January, 1963, Gena Pastor, a Mexican columnist, commended him by saying, "In too many enterprises, the chief executive, in order to preserve a sense of importance, does not delegate responsibility . . . in order that he may maintain his prestige and superiority." De Llano provided such continuity that when he died, the paper was able to continue "on a firm foundation, a newspaper still superior."

Excélsior was the 1st paper in Mexico to install rotogravure presses and the 1st to use Ludlow machines to set headlines.

The Present. *Excélsior*, which is published in Mexico City, is read all over the country. Dr. Marvin Alisky, an authority on the Mexican press, says, ". . . one can see copies, just in by airmail, being sold rapidly at Nogales (on the U.S. border), Tijuana, Ciudad Juarez, and Nuevo Laredo. News dealers save copies for good customers as it goes quickly. . . . One finds it in the offices of government officials, teachers, business leaders, labor leaders, and also in most upper-class homes."

The paper's political stance is difficult to explain in U.S. terms. It is considered by Mexicans to be conservative and rightist as well as liberal. Since 1964, more left-wing journalists have written for *Excélsior*, and the paper has got closer to the middle of the road than it was in De Llano's day. *Excélsior*'s staff tries to combine the best of modern U.S. methods with the traditional methods of Spain.

Excélsior is technically a cooperative, but only high-ranking staff members are allowed to own shares in the company. According to De Llano, a paper like *Excélsior* "with a serious purpose, high ideals of objectivity and integrity will draw to it writers and other staff members of high quality." Still, those on the staff, like most Mexican journalists, are not very well paid. Many have to moonlight in order to make a decent living.

Excélsior is generous in presenting foreign news; it has over 25 foreign correspondents stationed in major world cities. Its interpretive articles are generally of higher quality than its news stories, which are sometimes biased. "*Foro*," an entire page open to diverse opinions, is a popular feature. "*Diorama de la Cultura*," a special supplement in the Sunday edition, contains thoughtful, well-written historical and literary essays.

Still, *Excélsior* is a family paper, and the Sunday edition also includes a 12-page comic section. Crime and small-time scandals are played down or ignored.

Le Figaro (Paris, France)

The Past. In 1826, a Parisian named Maurice Allhoy began a small witty newspaper featuring fashion, theater, manners, politics, and morals. It was the forerunner of the present-day *Figaro*. In the 1850s, Henri de Villemessant, then editor, began to buy material from writers like Rochefort, Alexandre Dumas, and Baudelaire. In the letters column, Villemessant carried on a political dialogue with his readers, becoming noted for his biting one-line answers to long-winded letters. In 1866, *Le Figaro* became a daily.

Villemessant's metaphor, in which he compares a newspaper to a department store, has been used by many journalists as a kind of philosophy of their profession. He said, "Like a well-stocked store, a newspaper should offer in its different departments, known in the profession as columns, everything that its clientele could need. It is necessary that I please serious people; it is also necessary that I am agreeable to lighthearted people or those who wish to refresh their spirits for a while." He also compared editing a newspaper to giving a dinner party at which both "harvesters and city people" had to be entertained: "Whether one likes it or not, it is necessary to give to each of my guests what suits his taste and his stomach, and, to return to my comparison of the department store, I expand my columns in order that everyone can find an ample supply of what he needs."

In 1922, the paper was bought by François Coty, the millionaire cosmetics manufacturer, who used it as a backup for a foray into politics. The paper lost much of its punch. Then in 1934 Coty died, and his ex-wife took over, immediately giving the editorship to Pierre Brisson, a highly respected journalist, and the paper's reputation began to soar.

At the beginning of W.W. II, *Le Figaro* was known as one of the best papers—if not *the* best paper—in France. When Paris fell to the Germans, Brisson took the paper to Lyons and continued to publish it under the Pétain regime. Then, forced by the Vichy Government and the Germans to say what he didn't believe, he shut the paper down. After the war, *Le Figaro* began again.

Between 1945 and 1950, circulation grew to 450,000. Conservative politically, it spoke out against communism and backed a movement to bring General de Gaulle back into power. François Mauriac, columnist and novelist, daily attacked *L'Humanité*, the leading communist paper. Usually for the U.S., *Le Figaro* represents the French bourgeoisie, not the liberals.

The paper's excellent reputation is due largely to Pierre Brisson, who died in 1964.

By 1969, Jean Prouvost, a textile manufacturer and newspaper entrepreneur, and Ferdinand Beghin, a sugar and paper industrialist, owned between them 97% of *Le Figaro's* shares. For a while, they attempted to control the paper's editorial policy. However, through an employee-ownership plan which took place later, the editors of the paper now have a deciding voice in *Le Figaro's* management.

The Present. *Le Figaro*, which has been called the "morning bible of France's upper middle class," is considered one of the best-written papers in France. Still conservative, it emphasizes domestic and foreign politics, economics, and the arts. Many of its features are hard to classify—not quite editorials, they are not exactly factual accounts or essays either.

The usual issue has a headline-heavy front page with several short articles, features, and editorial cartoons. In addition to several pages of news, the paper includes in-depth features on economics as well as on aspects of the arts. It is written by its excellent staff and several outside contributors.

Scoops. *Le Figaro* was the only French daily to cover the Jack Ruby trial and to send a reporter on President Johnson's trip to Southeast Asia in November, 1966.

HA'ARETZ (Tel Aviv, Israel)

The Past. *Ha'aretz*, whose name means "The Land," is the oldest newspaper in Israel, started in Tel Aviv in 1919 when there were only 50,000 Hebrew-speaking people in Palestine. One of its 1st journalists was Gershon Agronsky, who had been brought to the U.S. by his parents when he was a boy, joined the Jewish Correspondents' Bureau in New York, then left to enlist in the Jewish Legion of 1917. Committed to the idea of a national Jewish home in Palestine, he returned to Jerusalem after W.W. I. There he served as a one-man correspondence bureau for American and British papers and became involved in the founding of *Ha'aretz*.

In the early days, news reached the paper slowly, usually a day or so late, on the train from Cairo. In 1929, the Reuters news agency began to serve *Ha'aretz* so that the news it printed was a little less stale.

With the mass influx of people into Palestine before and after W.W. II and with the establishment of Israeli independence in 1948, the paper began to prosper.

The Present. *Ha'aretz* is one of the few quality papers in the Middle East. It bills itself as "independent liberal." Unlike other papers in Israel, most of which are controlled by labor unions, political parties, or other agencies, *Ha'aretz* is able to maintain a true independent stance. It is very difficult to predict its position on government policies; its editors decide each issue separately. Generally, however, it supports the Government on economic matters but not on issues of defense and national security. It favors better treatment of the Arabs, the conservation of natural resources, national beautification, and the separation of Church and State.

The paper is staid. Other Israeli papers are more colorful, but *Ha'aretz* will not sacrifice quality and accuracy for color. Its editorials are calm and reasoned, never premature.

Aimed at businessmen and intellectuals, *Ha'aretz* emphasizes foreign news, which it receives from its correspondents and from news agencies. Its interpretive reports on economics and parliamentary issues are carefully read and taken seriously by influential Israelis.

Ha'aretz also emphasizes literature with a Friday literary section and by printing poetry and fiction by leading Israeli writers. On Friday it relaxes its scholarly position a little by putting out an illustrated magazine which features human interest stories, fashion, sports, crime, and other popular topics.

Generally speaking, *Ha'aretz* hires reporters for their native ability rather than their academic training or newspaper experience.

JEN-MIN JIH-PAO (Peking, China)

The Past. Legend says the *Jen-min Jih-pao* ("*People's Daily*") was founded in the caves of Yenan province in 1948. In actuality, that paper was the *Liberation Daily*, later to become an important Communist party paper in Shanghai. *Jen-min Jih-pao* was born in Hopei province toward the end of the civil war, was established as the main party paper, and was moved to Peking in 1949.

The voice of Mao Tse-tung, the paper has always been considered an indicator of Chinese thinking. When the *People's Daily* showed pictures of Henry Kissinger with Chairman Mao in 1973, the Western world could be sure of a thaw in relations with Red China. During Nixon's visit to Peking that same year, Chou En-lai went off into a corner after a banquet to approve the paper's front-page layout of pictures of the Nixon trip.

However, before the thaw, the paper's coverage of Western matters was peculiar. There was no mention of the Apollo moon landing because, according to an editor, "In our view, there are a lot of more important things happening on earth."

The Present. The *People's Daily* is the official Chinese government mouthpiece, and it has been called "the ultimate voice of authority." in China. Because of the great distances and poor transportation in China, the paper is not disseminated everywhere and cannot, in some ways, be considered a national paper. However, its influence is felt everywhere.

It's circulation, like that of most communist papers, is somewhat secret. Even if it were known, the number would be deceptive, merely because each copy is often read by so many people. Issues are put in glass-enclosed boxes on city streets, and passersby stop to read. The paper is read aloud to workers in factories and on farms and over the radio. French correspondent Robert Guillain wrote: "I have seen the pedicab boy, the street sweeper, the mother of a family, stop in front of the famous paper in the public places where it is hung, and try laboriously to decipher its difficult texts. I have heard it read in public, for the benefit of college students; it comes over loudspeakers for train travelers. More often still a lecturer reads it to the illiterates who still abound among the adult population. . . ."

Only about 6 pages, the paper features long political editorials, official news releases, cultural material, articles by party leaders like Chou En-lai and Mao Tse-tung, some fiction and poetry, and political cartoons. It contains no light human-interest material, no comics, no gossip, no crime reports. Regional news is left to the provincial dailies.

Editorials are more thoughtful than timely. When asked how he would handle an assignment to produce an editorial on Chinese education, editor Chen Chun recently said, "We would send out dozens of our cadres all over the country to universities and middle schools to investigate the situation there. Then there would be an article written collectively." Such a procedure might take a month.

Headlines are often propagandistic. One such reads: HOW TO TRANSFORM ONESELF INTO BELIEVING IN THE MASSES INSTEAD OF ONESELF. Another suggests: LET'S ALL LEARN REVOLUTIONARY THEORY AND GET RID OF EXPERIMENTISM.

A People's Liberation Army soldier guards the offices of the paper, and there is little of the atmosphere of Western newspapers among the editorial staff, which numbers about 300.

The *People's Daily* has pioneered in urging the adoption of a simplified ideogram language for printed mass media and has sponsored programs requiring oral reading of the paper— in short, it has done everything to get the news to the people in spite of the high rate of illiteracy which still exists in China.

L'OSSERVATORE ROMANO (Vatican City)

The Past. The purpose of *L'Osservatore Romano,* founded in 1861, was to "refute the calumnies being launched against Rome and the Roman Pontificate, to record everything worthy of note that happened during the day in Rome, to recall the unshaken principles that are the basis of Catholicism, to instruct in the duties that people have toward their country, and to urge and promote the reverence owed to the Pontiff and Ruler." Its editors, 2 political refugees named Nicola Zanchini and Giuseppe Bastia, had considerable freedom. The official backing of the Church was kept secret.

It was not until 1890, when Pope Leo XIII decided to buy the paper, that its position became clear. The new editor reportedly said, "The Pope said to me, 'Everybody has his paper, the Holy See must also have its own. I have called upon you to take the direction of the paper. . . . Be independent of everybody; you are answerable only to me and my Secretary of State.'"

In November, 1929, *L'Osservatore Romano* moved to Vatican City (set up as a State separate from Italy) to get away from the fascists. Mussolini was then attacking the Church and suggesting social reforms that the Church was against. Count Giuseppe Della Torre, one of the paper's most famous editors, would not allow the paper to refer to Mussolini as "*Il Duce.*" When Della Torre was threatened with arrest, he retaliated by calling Hitler "anti-Christ."

In 1938, Hitler came to Rome, and the Pope went to his summer place at Castel Gandolfo to escape meeting him. Ignoring Hitler's visit, *L'Osservatore Romano* said the Pope found the air better there.

By 1939, fascists were assaulting and beating the paper's delivery men and any priests who were caught reading the paper.

Of all the Italian newspapers, only *L'Osservatore Romano* printed Allied communiqués during W.W. II. Circulation boomed. Della Torre was waylaid outside St. Peter's by fascists and escaped by the skin of his teeth.

When Rome was liberated, however, the news was carried on the last page of the paper; the front page featured a religious ceremony. A writer on Vatican affairs said, "I don't think the editor . . . intended to snub the conquerors of Rome. It was just his tactful way of reminding his readers that wars are won and lost, empires crumble, regimes rise and fall, but the Church goes on forever because her power is spiritual and not material."

In 1960, Raimondo Manzini took over as editor. He enlivened the paper considerably and doubled the staff.

The Present. L'Osservatore Romano is ultra-serious, a source of insight into Vatican thinking, and is read by people all over the world. It has influence far beyond its meager circulation. Leading churchmen and political figures read it.

Though it prints general news, its emphasis is on religious matters. What its official position with the Vatican is, no one really knows for sure. It has been called "the Vatican newspaper," "the Pope's own paper," and "the papal sword." Ignazio Weiss, an Italian journalism historian, says that it is "official" in anything it reports about the Vatican, unofficial in everything else. But the Pope is the owner, and chances are that the staff won't defy him.

The paper still carries long stories about religious ceremonies and the texts of papal speeches. It provides moral criticism of television and movies. It "regards news through the perspective of history rather than in terms of deadlines."

In 1961, John XXIII said about the paper, "We have little in comparison with other big papers, but what we have is good. . . . Our news perhaps is too dignified, too polished, too quiet; readers are not thrilled. It is a serious newspaper. . . . The emphasis is on editorials rather than on news. It doesn't want to give news, but it wants to create thought. It is not enough for it to relate events; it wants to comment on events. . . . In this paper the journal list is an interpreter, a teacher, a guide. . . . The paper appeals more to specialized people—and not to the mass of the readers. No other paper can see more, can tell more, or can give a better orientation towards educating people to truth and charity. It is the 'paper of the Pope.'"

Scoops. In the 1930s, *L'Osservatore Romano*—the only Italian newspaper free of fascist control—condemned the invasion of Finland and said it was a sign of Russia's desire to expand her territory.

It warned Italy about the seriousness of the German troops' crossing into Poland before declaring war.

PRAVDA (Moscow, U.S.S.R.)

The Past. Pravda ("Truth") began as an underground paper in St. Petersburg in 1912. Lenin was one of the founders, and he and his associates were often forced into hiding in order to continue publication.

During the Revolution, when Lenin was in Zurich trying to get back into Russia, the paper printed morale-building editorials, one of which contained the Marx-inspired words, "Proletarians of all countries, unite."

Among *Pravda's* early editors were world-famous communist leaders—Stalin, Beria, Shepilov, Molotov. Stalin said, "The press is the only instrument whereby the party can speak daily and hourly with the workers in its own language."

In 1945, David Zaslavsky, a Ukrainian called "the poor man's Shaw," was editor of the paper. He began an anti-American campaign in which he said that American freedom of the press was nothing but a capitalist string. "If the string is long . . . freedom . . . is relatively great; if short . . . negligible. Hearst, for instance, sometimes unchains his pet hoodlums . . . to freely assault the Soviet people." He further said that the Russian newsman was "free because he is immune to outside pressure . . . an official worker who gets wages but . . . does not sell himself." He also attacked Clare Boothe Luce, calling her the "political widow of Goebbels" and "full of hysterical Fascist fulminations." He said, "This honorable dame does not love us. She hates us with African, rather than American, passion."

During the Khrushchev era, Pavel A. Satyukov was editor. When that regime fell from power, Alexei Rumyantsev took over for a brief time during which he wrote editorials urging freedom of thought for intellectuals. Mikhail Zimyanin, who replaced him, took a harder line.

The Present. By American standards, *Pravda* is small, often running only 6 pages. It portrays the Soviet regime as fighting for "a scientific approach to the management of the economy, for an improvement in the farms and methods of economic construction, and for raising the level of party and state discipline and of each official's personal responsibility for his job."

It has a large circulation, somewhere around 8 million, and prints editions in 30 plants around the country. Matrices are sent by air to these plants to ensure fast delivery of the news to far-flung districts. The House of Pravda, which also prints other papers and magazines including the famous humor magazine *Krokodil*, owns schools, a Palace of Culture, and apartment houses.

The number-one paper in the Soviet Union, *Pravda* is restrained and never sensational. It is noted for its special articles on cultural subjects, science, and literature. Letters from readers—about 1,000 a day—seem to be carrying more open complaints about shoddy consumer goods, public wrongs, difficulties with bureaucracy. The masses are loyal to *Pravda*, partly because the paper often prints material written by factory workers, farmers, and soldiers.

Pravda is managed by an editorial collegium named by the presidium of the Communist party. Its editor is usually an individual high in the party. The staff is large, the majority well educated.

LA PRENSA (Buenos Aires, Argentina)

The Past. "Truth, honor, freedom, progress, civilization" were the stated goals of *La Prensa* in its 1st issue in 1869. In the years since, its editors, with the exception of those installed during the 1st Perón regime, have upheld those goals, sometimes with acts of extreme heroism admired all over the world.

The founder of the paper was Dr. José Clemente Paz. He and his son, Ezequiel P. Paz, made news the most important part of *La Prensa*, an unusual emphasis for the time. (The early Argentine press heavily featured philosophical discussions and political rhetoric) In order to remain independent *La Prensa* would not accept government subscriptions. It began an unprecedented social program through which it sponsored free medical and legal services, a library, a school of music. Herbert Matthews of *The New York Times* has said, "All the best in Argentine life was reflected in *La Prensa's* pages. It became the symbol of which the humblest Argentine was proud because he knew that wherever free journalism was respected, *La Prensa* was honored."

In 1898, Paz handed the paper over to his son, who for the next 45 years never missed a day at the office. No job was too humble 'for him—reading proofs, helping in the composing room. His creed, adopted in 1950 by the Inter-American Press Association, is a classic:

> To inform with accuracy and truth; to omit nothing that the public has a right to know; always to use an impersonal and correct style without detriment to the gravity or to the force of critical thought; to reject rumors and such statements as "it is said" or "it is asserted" in order to affirm only that about which one holds a conviction supported by proofs and documents; to consider that the omission of a news article is preferable to its erroneous or unjustifiable publication; to take care that in reporting news the writer does not allow his personal viewpoint to slip in, because to do this constitutes commentary, and the reporter or chronicler should not invade the field reserved for other sections of the daily; to remember before writing how powerful an instrument of diffusion one has at one's disposal and to bear in mind that harm caused to an official or to a private individual by false

imputation can never be entirely remedied by nobly conceded clarification or correction; to maintain a lofty calmness in polemics and not to make any statement which we might have to retract the next day; and finally, to inscribe in letters of gold in a prominent place, clearly visible about the work tables, the words of Walter Williams, distinguished North American newsman: "Nobody should write as a journalist what he cannot say as a gentleman."

Ezequiel Paz retired in 1943, and Alberto Gainza Paz, son of the founder's daughter, took over *La Prensa*. A revolution was going on which ended in the setting up of a de facto Government headed by Juan Perón. Perón immediately established a centralized office of information on official news and otherwise limited the activities of the press. Journalists had to register with the Government or be barred from working.

La Prensa, anti-Perón, did not moderate its position. On April 26, 1944, Perón suspended it for 5 days as a kind of punishment. When the paper resumed publication, Paz quoted Argentine patriot Esteban Echierria: "Equality and freedom are the principles that engender democracy."

Perón tried everything short of physical force to control *La Prensa*—he urged people to boycott it, put up posters against it, set up loudspeakers across the street from it to blast insults. *La Prensa* would not be controlled.

Then on the day the war against Japan ended in 1945, as happy people waved Allied flags, Perón's men invaded and bombed *La Prensa*. Paz was arrested and put in jail, then released.

Perón was sympathetic to the Axis (Germany, Japan, and Italy) and wanted to embarrass the U.S. with that sympathy. *La Prensa* made it difficult for him to accomplish his purpose.

In 1947, the Government demanded a huge sum for import duties on newsprint, retroactive to 1939, from *La Prensa*, with the trumped-up excuse that since *La Prensa* had printed advertising on it, it was a taxable item.

In January, 1951, the government-controlled Union of News Vendors began to pressure *La Prensa* to allow the union to handle its circulation. *La Prensa* refused, and there was violence. *La Prensa* appealed to the police, but got nowhere. Its 1,300 loyal employees kept working in spite of threats. On the night of January 26–27, Perón's men blockaded the plant. The staff of *La Prensa* decided not to abide by the blockade. The next day they marched across the plaza to the plant until armed Peronistas opened fire. One workman was killed, and 14 were wounded.

Perón took over the paper. Most of its staff left Argentina. Paz escaped in a small boat over the Río de la Plata to refuge on his mother's ranch in Uruguay. For the next 4 years, he gave Perón bad publicity all over the world.

In 1955, Perón was overthrown. On February 3, 1956, Paz returned to Argentina to take over the paper again. The 1st issue appeared as number 29,476, ignoring the years Perón had controlled the paper. From then on, it began to regain its circulation (which had dropped drastically under Perón) and its prestige.

The Present. La Prensa remains idealistic and independent, dignified yet lively. It provides excellent coverage of foreign affairs—more than most U.S. papers—and of domestic politics, economics, culture, science, and social problems.

On Sundays, 2 feature sections offer high-quality pieces on travel, history, science, art, or literature, complete with pictures.

La Prensa continues its altruistic social programs with a free medical clinic, library, and advice. In the *La Prensa* building there is a 200-seat hall in which free lectures are given.

LA STAMPA (Turin, Italy)

The Past. Over the past 100 years *La Stampa* has had a colorful history, complete with political entanglements and editorial heroism. It was founded as *Gazetta Piedmontese* in Turin in 1867. In 1895, 2 outstanding editors—Luigi Roux and Alfredo Frassati—bought it and changed its name to *La Stampa* ("The Press"). Frassati later bought out Roux. Under his direction, it became one of the leading liberal voices in Italy.

When the fascists took control in 1925, Frassati was asked to sign a fascist card. He refused. Realizing he could no longer keep the paper alive and liberal, he sold it in 1926. It reopened with a fascist staff and remained fascist until after W.W. II.

In 1948, Dr. Giulio de Benedetti, an incredibly hardworking journalist, became editor. Under him, the writing became clearer and livelier, and the physical appearance of the paper brightened. Most Italian papers were wordy, pompous, tightly packed with type. *La Stampa* was the opposite. In his 70s, De Benedetti was still working in the *La Stampa* office every day, toiling until early morning supervising minute details.

In the 1950s, *La Stampa* was bought by Fiat, the automobile company, which continues to own it to this day. Such ownership is almost a necessity in Italy, where newspaper readership and advertising are low.

The Present. Without a doubt, *La Stampa* is the most important paper in Turin and the surrounding area. It combines a strong local emphasis with national authority and prestige.

In addition to the morning edition, it puts out *Stampa Sera* ("Evening Press") in the afternoon.

La Stampa is slightly left of center, according to Frank Brutto, an authority on the Italian press. It supports government programs for domestic reform and often agrees with Italy's Socialist party on social issues. It is liberal in the Old European way—antifascist, but also anticommunist. *La Stampa*, concerned with social problems, pushes constantly for economic and social change. In spite of the fact that it is owned by Fiat, it has a great degree of editorial independence.

La Stampa, unlike most Italian papers, has a "letters from readers" column, which contains everything from letters from those wanting help to those wanting to discuss deep philosophical issues.

More than any other Italian daily, it gives space to sports news and photographs; the back page, in fact, is often devoted to large pictures.

THE TIMES (London, England)

The Past. A year after he started *The Daily Universal Register* (which became *The Times*) in 1785, John Walter was in Newgate prison serving a 16-month sentence for libeling the Duke of York. In those days, *The Times*, now staid and conservative, was something of a scandal sheet.

In 1800, John Walter II, son of the founder, took over. By then, it had become a true newspaper, which in 1804 attacked Lord Melville, Treasurer of the Navy, for incompetence. Melville was impeached, and with the impeachment, *The Times* became an authority. *The Time's* editorial writer, Edward Sterling, wrote in an article on social and political matters, "We thundered out the other day an article on social and political reform." From then on, *The Times* was known affectionately as "The Thunderer."

Thomas Barnes, one of the world's great journalists, became editor in 1819 and soon turned the paper into an important publication, doubling its circulation from 5,000 in 1815 to 10,000 in 1821. Barnes was a quiet, self-effacing individual. When he died, *The Times* mentioned his name for the 1st time in an ordinary obituary, never saying that he had any connection with the newspaper it was printed in.

John Thadeus Delane replaced Barnes. He was a strange choice—only 23 years old, a handsome Berkshire squire whose main enthusiasm was horses. He soon showed his journalistic genius. No state secret was safe from him and his reporters. His regime brought comments like Disraeli's, who said that there were 2 British ambassadors in every world capital —one representing the Queen and one representing *The Times*. In 1854, Lord John Russell wrote to Queen Victoria, "The degree of information possessed by *The Times* with regard to the most secret affairs of State is mortifying, humiliating, and incomprehensible."

In 1854, *The Times* sent out the world's 1st war correspondent—William Howard Russell—to cover the Crimean War, with the admonition "Tell the truth." Russell, moon-faced, 34 years old, did. He told about the poorly clad, half-starved British troops who weren't getting supplies. From a height, he viewed the battle at Balaklava, where he could see what was going on as plainly "as the stage and those upon it are seen from the box of a theater." In graphic detail, he described the "thin red streak topped with a line of steel" as it made its attack; then the sabers swinging among the guns of the Russians; and finally the retreat. "At 11:35 not a British soldier, except the dead and dying, was left in front of those bloody Muscovite guns." Tennyson's "The Charge of the Light Brigade" is based largely on this report.

The Times got a lot of complaints following publication of Russell's eyewitness stories and his reports about the lack of supplies. Lord Raglan, a British commander, said that Russell was giving aid and comfort to the enemy. The prince consort called him a "miserable scribbler."

Delane went to the Crimea to find out if Russell's stories were indeed true. He wrote back that the Turks were "infinitely better supplied and better appointed than the French or English."

The Times tried to get the Government to do something about the situation with no success, so the paper mounted a campaign to raise money for relief. The campaign brought £25,000 and spurred Florence Nightingale to go with 38 nurses to the Crimea.

Later, Delane made a trip to the U.S. He didn't like it. To him, Washington, D.C., was an "odious village," and Boston was a place where "nobody seems to have anything to do but lounge in and out of the hotels and gossip and drink." On October 14, 1862, Delane wrote an ill-considered editorial in which he said, "Is the name of Lincoln ultimately to be classed in the catalog of monsters, wholesale assassins and butchers of their kind?"

By 1908, *The Times* had been bought by Lord Northcliffe, who, though he saved it from ruin, meddled too much in its affairs. However, it was he who attacked the ministry for a shortage of shells which caused a British attack to fail in France in 1915. He was told by the Government that circulation of the paper would fall and he might go to jail. "Better to lose circulation than lose the war," he replied. The paper was burned on the floor of the London Stock Exchange.

In 1922, John Jacob Astor acquired the paper. It went into a decline, from which Sir William Haley, who became editor in 1952, rescued it. Before he took over, the paper was called "the Whimperer." He soon stopped that by enlivening the physical appearance and content, putting in more photographs, and writing editorials. Haley was "a curious bird, withdrawn, relentless, a latter-day Victorian, a product of self-help—he left school at 16—with a boundless appetite for work and a strong streak of puritanism that came out in his biting Profumo leader, 'It *is* a moral issue.'" (Magnus Turnstile in *The New Statesman*.)

In 1966, Lord Thomson of Fleet, a fantastically rich man, bought *The Times*, which soon merged with the *Sunday Times*. In 1970, the paper was still losing money, "fighting for its life," according to Denis Hamilton, chief executive. By 1975, however, thanks to the merger, the situation was improving.

The Present. Completely independent, *The Times* is a traditional, dignified paper and is known as the Queen of Printing House Square.

It is an establishment paper, read by leaders in government and the nobility, and 70% of those listed in Who's Who read it.

Its news coverage is thorough, more thorough even than that of *The New York Times*. "*The Times* is a record," said editor William Haley. "It has a duty, not only to its readers of today but to those of a century hence." However, *The Times* prints complete texts of speeches and documents much less often than it used to.

Stories in the paper are shorter than before, and more crisply written. A separate financial section has been added, and there is more emphasis on women's news and features.

One of the most famous features of *The Times* is its "personals" column, once placed prominently on the front page and familiarly known as The Agony Column. Author Peter Fleming was fascinated by The Agony Column, writing of it, "What strange kind of creature can it be whose wolfhound—now lost in Battersea Park—answers to the name of Effie? Why is Bingo heartbroken? And what possible use can Box A have for a horned toad?" Among other constant readers of The Agony Column were Charles Dickens, Benito Mussolini, Winston Churchill, Sherlock Holmes, and currently, the Queen of England.

An equally fascinating feature in *The Times* is the Letters to the Editor section, which, according to one commentator, is as "finely turned as antique silver," with a style of "elaborate understatement."

The Times Literary Supplement is truly international; in it books written in French, Russian, German, and Italian are reviewed as thoughtfully as those written in English. The reviews are unsigned and excellent—and poorly paid for.

Lord Thomson, who owns *The Times*, also owns nearly 40 other newspapers in the United Kingdom as well as newspapers in many foreign countries, various book publishing and educational companies, some travel companies, an airline, numerous radio and television stations, and more. He does not interfere in editorial matters at *The Times*.

Scoops. In 1856, the British Government 1st learned of Russian acceptance of peace proposals by reading *The Times*, only one example of the many times the paper scooped the Government.

The paper published the 1st British pictures, in color, of American astronauts on the moon in 1969.

DIE WELT (Hamburg, West Germany)

The Past. Die Welt ("The World") was begun during the British occupation of Germany in 1946 and in a few months had reached a circulation of nearly 500,000 in Hamburg and Essen. It was then controlled by Colonel H. B. Garland of the British Army. Hans Zehrer, a German novelist and newspaperman, was the managing director; he left because of political differences, and Rudolf Kustermeier took over.

In 1947, *Die Welt* began a Berlin edition, and by 1949, circulation had reached over one million for all 3 editions. In 1950, the British turned over control to the Germans.

In 1953, the paper was bought by Axel C. Springer, a Hamburg millionaire publisher, who had avoided the Nazi party and the Army. During the war, he had printed morale-building romantic novels for the Army. After the war, he decided to start a radio magazine. In order to do so, he had to get a printing license from British officials, who were tired of the whole procedure of listening to disgruntled German publishers. When Springer arrived, a British major asked, "And who has been persecuting you?"

"Only women," Springer replied. He got the license.

Women adore Springer. He has had 4 wives. In addition to women, he collects horses and houses—6 of them in various cities in Europe, all expensively decorated. His Hamburg mansion, for instance, is hung with ancient Chinese wall decorations.

When Springer bought *Die Welt*, for $1 million, he became the biggest publisher of newspapers and periodicals in the Federal Republic.

Die Welt was the 1st German newspaper to use telephoto, when in 1952 it began receiving wire photos from the Helsinki Olympics.

The Present. Die Welt has a large circulation—over 260,000 in 1975—and is read in over 120 countries. In addition to special issues, it routinely prints 10 editions a day. It is the only German newspaper to have an airmailed edition, printed on very thin paper.

It is a national paper. The educated German reads it *and* a local paper. Though influential in government circles, *Die Welt* does not appeal too much to youth, who feel that it is overly conservative. The London *Times* correspondent in Bonn has said that it is "conservative to the marrow, but with a strong social progressive influence."

Die Welt features clear, lively writing with many short sentences, and follows the American custom of putting the important facts in a news story 1st. An official of the newspaper says of its aims, "In the world of newspapers we want *Die Welt* to be a prestige symbol standing for intelligence and culture, for responsible thinking, initiative, and success. We want *Die Welt* to be considered as a paper of unparalleled integrity, of comprehensive, fast, and reliable news reporting, of courageous and responsible commentary. Its voice must be authoritative and disciplined, its style lively yet timely and serious and trustworthy."

Unlike many German newspapers, *Die Welt* has a light-looking layout and pleasing typography. Its major competition, *Frankfurter Allgemeine Zeitung* (FAZ) is more stolid in appearance. FAZ would probably appeal to the professor, *Die Welt* to the businessman or politician.

The paper offers a rich mix of foreign and national news, sports, science, economics, and editorials. Each day, an "extra" is included—for instance, "School and University" on Monday, "Motor" on Tuesday, "Intellectual World" on Saturday. The Sunday paper, which has an entire staff of its own, draws on the work of leading journalists and intellectuals, such as Willy Brandt.

Though Springer has a controlling interest he interferes very little in editorial matters. He has said, "Newspapers should be interested in but not take the place of politics. Newspapers must explain, illuminate, censure, or support political developments. The newspapers' task is to caution or stimulate. Newspapers are supposed to state their case, but they should never try to take the place of politics, lest they destroy politics . . . the responsibility of a publisher must follow in the traditions of Peter Zenger or Thomas Paine, in combating any threat to freedom of expression."

Scoops. Shortly after Konrad Adenauer's death in 1967, *Die Welt* published a beautifully written, definitive 32-page "tribute to Adenauer" issue.

The Day Christ Edited a Newspaper

It was one of the most unusual and dramatic experiments in the history of journalism.

It really happened, this experiment, when a hard-boiled metropolitan daily newspaper permitted a mild-mannered Congregational minister to take over as managing editor for one week. The clergyman had a theory, which he had expounded from the pulpit and in writing, that readers were not sensation-hungry, that they preferred decency and goodwill and restraint in the news reported to them. The clergyman argued that if a big-city daily were edited as Jesus Christ might have edited a paper, circulation would rise, not fall—and to this claim a newspaper publisher-editor responded by challenging the clergyman to prove it, and so one fine day in 1900 the clergyman moved in on the city desk to practice what he preached.

The clergyman was Dr. Charles M. Sheldon, renowned author of In His Steps, which became "the greatest best seller, exclusive of the Bible and Shakespeare, of all time." The newspaper, published by 37-year-old Frederick O. Popenoe, was the Topeka Capital, a leading Republican daily in Kansas. And this is the story of what took place when the Golden Rule was superimposed on the rowdy Front Page.

Dr. Charles Sheldon, the central figure in this holy journalistic crusade, was born in Wellsville, N.Y., in February of 1857. Educated at Brown University and Andover Theological Seminary (where, while still a student, he married a young Kansas woman), he was ordained as a Congregationalist minister at the age of 29. His 1st church was in Waterbury, Vt. Then, in December, 1888, he was transferred to Topeka, Kans., to become the 1st pastor of the city's new Central Congregational Church.

At once, Dr. Sheldon determined to find out how his flock lived. In the best reportorial tradition, he dressed in shabby clothes, pretended to be an out-of-work printer, and mingled with the unemployed to study job-hunting difficulties. He wound up with a job in a coal-yard bin—and a colorful Sunday sermon. Later, he divided Topeka into 7 working groups—doctors, lawyers, businessmen, railroad men, streetcar men, college students, newspapermen—and set out to live and work with each group in turn to learn its problems. With the doctors, he went into the hospitals and on their house calls for 2 weeks, and with the lawyers he went into courtrooms and visited jail cells for 2 weeks, until he learned community problems firsthand. What shocked him most profoundly was the indifference of Christians to those who were disadvantaged.

When in 1890 he noticed a dwindling number of youthful forces in his congregation, the 33-year-old Sheldon decided to abandon old-fashioned sermons and replace them with fictional serials. One chapter would be read every Sunday evening to an audience of young people, and each chapter would end on a note of suspense, in order to bring his flock back to church the following week. That summer, with the heat at 100°, Dr. Sheldon sat on his front porch scribbling what was to be his most successful novel-length serial. The story that resulted—and which he read to the younger members of his congregation, one chapter a week for 12 weeks—he called In His Steps, or What Would Jesus Do? In this story, a young minister, troubled by the modern human condition, requests his parishioners to take the following pledge: "Ask yourselves, 'What would Jesus do?'—then be guided, for this next year, by your best answer to that question." Sheldon proceeded to show the effects of this pledge on the tangled lives of a newspaper editor, an heiress, a singer, a railroad magnate, a college president.

The reading of this story filled Dr. Sheldon's pews to capacity week after week. "While it was being read, it was being published in the Chicago Advance, a religious weekly, as a serial," Dr. Sheldon recalled in 1935. "The publisher did not know the conditions of the copyright law, and he filed only one copy of the Advance each week with the department, instead of 2, which the law required. On that account the copyright was defective, and the story was thrown into the public domain." The Advance Company published In His Steps as a paperback novel in 1897, but because of the defective copyright, it was pirated throughout the world. In the next half century there were 45 translations, including versions in Russian, Welsh, Armenian, Turkish, Japanese, and Arabic. The book was said to have sold 30 million copies, the greatest single-volume best seller in history excepting only the Bible, Shakespeare, and Chairman Mao. However, no accurate figures were ever available, but even the lowest estimate of its sales—8 million, according to Frank Luther Mott, of Iowa University—is staggering. According to Twentieth Century Authors, "Dr. Sheldon received only a few hundred dollars for the work and was hard put to answer the 900 letters received every week suggesting that he should live up to the thesis of the book ('What Would

Jesus Do?') and divide his profits with those less fortunate than he."

Three years after the book was published, there were 10 different editions of it on the market, and its fame and message were known throughout the reading world. The fictional account of the newspaper editor in the book— an editor taking the pledge to conduct himself and his paper as Christ would, by ceasing to print sensational news, distortions, and liquor advertising—caused much debate in various real-life journalistic circles. At last, Frederick O. Popenoe, publisher of the *Topeka Capital*, which had a daily circulation of 11,223, confronted Dr. Sheldon and asked him, "Well, Sheldon, if we should tender you the *Capital* to make the same experiment, would you take it?" Surprised, Dr. Sheldon said, "Do you really mean it?" Popenoe replied firmly, "I do." With that, the great experiment became a reality.

The regular editor in chief of the *Topeka Capital*, J. K. Hudson, as well as his entire staff, felt strongly that no newspaper could be edited as Christ might have edited one and still be readable. Journalism professionals felt that Sheldon's theories were fresh but without "intrinsic merit." Sheldon, on the other hand, felt that a newspaper publishing mainly good news would become twice as readable and be a real asset to the community. Moreover, he felt its circulation would rise. This the veteran newspapermen doubted very much. So circulation, in the end, was to be the criterion for judging the project's success.

Between Tuesday, March 13, and Saturday, March 17, 1900, Dr. Sheldon moved into the paper's city room and took over the editor-in-chief's desk, and the entire Fourth Estate watched with curiosity. Dr. Sheldon's effort was looked upon as a news event in its own right, and 19 correspondents (including reporters from the *New York World* and the *San Francisco Examiner*, with the *Emporia Gazette* represented by William Allen White) converged upon Topeka. Meanwhile, thousands of advance subscriptions poured in for the Sheldon edition, among them one from Oom Paul Kruger, President of the Boer Republic in South Africa, then engaged in a war with Great Britain. All eyes were focused on the Topeka clergyman, and Dr. Sheldon made certain not to disappoint them.

Settled in behind the editor's desk, Dr. Sheldon tried to imagine how Christ would have acted in this role. There were practical difficulties, of course. As Dr. Sheldon recalled later, "Christ never saw an automobile, a motion picture, a railroad train, a printing press, a telephone, a sewing machine, a twine binder, a radio set, a skyscraper, a daily paper, an electric light, a printed book. He never saw a church or a Sunday school or a peace society or a republic. . . . But the inward world that Christ saw and knew is exactly the same in its loves and hates and its ambitions and passions and its heroisms, and in its pettiness and sordid scorn of goodness."

Under Dr. Sheldon's editorial guidance, all stories of scandal, vice, and crime were played down. Not omitted, but reduced to what the minister felt was their proper length. Society-page news was condensed to almost nothing. Theatrical news was dropped. For the 1st time, perhaps, in newspaper history, virtue and goodwill became hot news. Editorials were moved to the front page, and each was fully signed. Sheldon objected to the customary editorial "we" and the lack of by-line on opinions as sheer cowardice. Every front-page news story was followed by balanced editorial comment in footnotes. A great famine in India, ignored or treated casually by the competition press, was headlined by Dr. Sheldon—not only headlined but followed up by an appeal for the distant sufferers. As a result of this handling of the India famine, over $1 million in food and other relief supplies was sent to Bombay. "Sometimes, when people have asked me if the paper were not a failure as the press reports for the most part said it was," stated Dr. Sheldon, "I have replied that if it accomplished nothing more than saving several thousand children from starvation, I would always feel as if it were a success." The Sunday edition of the paper was dropped for a special Saturday night issue, which front-paged the Sermon on the Mount and featured religious stories.

At 1st the *Topeka Capital*'s hardened reporters squirmed. No smoking was permitted in the city room, no drinking—and no profanity. The business department screamed when Dr. Sheldon began to ban certain ads. "Blacklisted by Mr. Sheldon," according to John W. Ripley in *The Kansas Historical Quarterly*, "were advertisements for tobacco in all forms, patent medicines (whose ads were then bread and butter to 90% of the nation's newspapers), electric belts, Keeley Cure for Drunkenness (to Sheldon alcohol was a sin rather than a disease), bargain sales (because Sheldon did not have time to verify values), corsets (unhealthy because of their restrictive properties), and illustrations of ladies' hosiery and underwear (suggestive). Also barred were ads for theatrical and sporting events. However, small town papers cheered one particular 'thou shalt not.' A friend of the small shopkeeper, Sheldon refused to accept any advertising from the big department stores in nearby Kansas City." As a result of this policy, the *Capital* advertising department had to decline thousands of dollars in revenue.

But something else was happening. Just as the cynical staff finally got into the spirit of things, so did the general public. Readers were infected by the good fight. Circulation soared from its normal 11,223 to 362,684 copies sold daily by the end of 5 days. The Topeka presses, unable to handle the worldwide demand for copies, enlisted the presses of *The Chicago Journal*, the *Staats Zeitung* of New York, the *Westminster Gazette* of London for special editions in the U.S. and Great Britain.

When the experiment ended, and editor Hudson once again took over the reins, the final verdict remained unresolved. Critics in the newspaper world decided that the paper-edited-according-to-Christ had been too watered-down, too dull, and they suggested that the fantastic rise in circulation was merely a fluke resulting from novelty plus clever publicity. Typical of the criticisms was the one that appeared in *The New York Herald*: "A careful survey of the 1st page of the *Capital's* 1st issue under Sheldon shows an entire absence of important news of the day. Not a line about a bubonic plague at San Francisco, the dreadful tenement house fire at Newark, N.J., the wounding of 8 American soldiers in the Philippines, the advance of [General] Roberts on the Orange Free State, the death of the Italian boxer Guydo, who died as a result of a blow struck by James Jeffries in a fistic contest. None of these important news items of the day appear. . . .

"The most prominent item on the 1st page is signed by Mr. Sheldon himself and refers to the Famine in India. Another article on the 1st page refers to consumptives who flock to Colorado. . . . Another article prominent on the 1st page is a communication from Rochester, N.Y., signed by the founder of the 'Prohibition Union of Christian Men.' This article closes with the remarkable sentence, 'In the Name of Jesus Christ, the Carpenter, the liquor traffic ought to die.'"

On the other hand, there were those who contended that Sheldon had, indeed, published a new kind of newspaper which had sold because readers enjoyed seeing good news receive the same emphasis as the sordid. For this reason, they had bought copies of Sheldon's paper enthusiastically the entire week. As Dr. Sheldon concluded to one critic, "If my paper was dull, or stupid, or lacking in what the newspapermen call 'news,' it was, at least, perfectly 'clean' from Tuesday morning till Saturday night. So far as I could make it the paper had not one line in it that could not be read aloud in the family circle, or in a church prayer meeting."

Satisfied that his experiment, by his own standards, had been a success, Dr. Sheldon returned to his pulpit. He served as minister in his Topeka church, off and on, for 35 years.

However, he remained bitten by the journalistic bug, and, finally, he left his pulpit and parish to become a newsman once more. In 1920, when he was 63, he moved to New York to become editor in chief of the *Christian Herald* for 4 years. After returning to Topeka, he continued working for the *Herald* as a contributing editor. During his lifetime, he produced 35 published books. In 1946, he died in Topeka at the age of 89.

—I.W.

Advertising: Its Life and Times

EARLY DAYS OF ADVERTISING

The 1st ads were vocal; i.e. street cries used by peddlers hawking their wares. Greeks advertised by shouting announcements of the sale of cattle and slaves. Printed advertisements also developed early. A 3,000-year-old ad from Thebes calls for the recovery of a slave: ". . . For his return to the shop of Hapu the Weaver, where the best cloth is woven to your desires, a whole gold coin is offered. . . ."

In Rome, signs were pasted up proclaiming circuses and gladiator matches. Examples of poster advertising have also been found in Pompeii and Carthage.

In the Middle Ages, handbills and tacked-up notices invaded the advertising field, and they usually consisted of drawings as well as copy because few people could read. The signs advertised the goods of individual merchants. Street barkers were posted outside of shops. In Shakespeare's *A Winter's Tale*, Autolycus sings:

"Come, buy of me; come buy, come buy, buy, lads, or else your lasses cry."

The 1st newspaper appeared in England, *The Weekly Newes*, in 1622. The 1st advertisement in a newspaper is said by historian Henry Sampson to have been an ad for the return of a stolen horse.

In 1630, a Paris doctor opened a shop where you could post an ad for 3 sous; by the mid-1600s many such offices existed. This was the beginning of the centralization of advertising. These shops did not write ads or move ads out into external media like the modern advertising agency.

An ad appeared in a newspaper for Robert Turner's Dentifrice in 1661—brand names were coming into use.

During 1665, a bad year due to the plague, newspapers carried ads for preventatives and cures—Anti-Pestilential Pills, Incomparable Drink Against the Plague, The Only True Plague Water, Infallible Preventive Pills

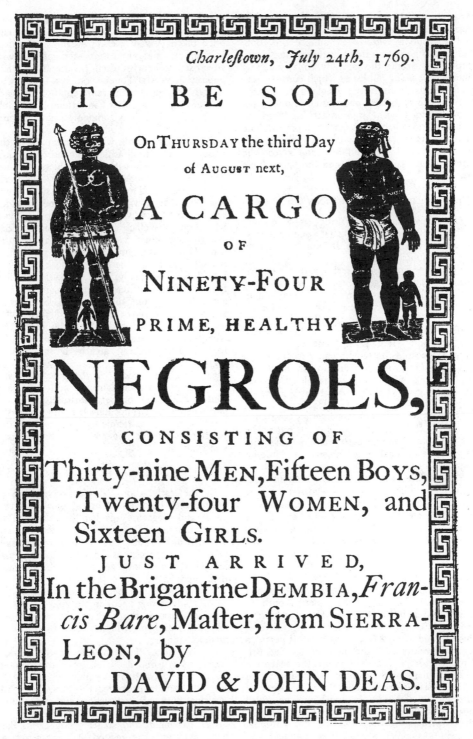

Charlestown, July 24th, 1769.

TO BE SOLD,

On THURSDAY the third Day
of AUGUST next,

A CARGO

OF

NINETY-FOUR

PRIME, HEALTHY

NEGROES,

CONSISTING OF

Thirty-nine MEN, Fifteen BOYS,
Twenty-four WOMEN, and
Sixteen GIRLS.

JUST ARRIVED,

In the Brigantine DEMBIA, *Francis Bare*, Master, from SIERRA-LEON, by

DAVID & JOHN DEAS.

Colonial businessmen made proud claims for their merchandise in this example taken from the early days of advertising. *American Antiquarian Society.*

Against the Plague, and Sovereign Cordials Against the Corruption of the Air.

The *London Gazette* announced, in 1666, that it was going to print advertisements. Newspaper ads became the rage. By 1682, shopping guides were being published which consisted entirely of ads. In the 1700s, England was glutted with pasted-up notices and posters. London became jammed with large advertising signs announcing merchants' places of business. The signs became so numerous that Charles II proclaimed, "No signs shall be hung across the streets shutting out the air and the light of the heavens."

ADVERTISING IN THE AMERICAN COLONIES

Newspapers and advertising grew up together in the Colonies. The 1st issue of the 1st successful newspaper—the *Boston News-Letter* (1704)—solicited ads.

Benjamin Franklin was the patron saint of American advertising. He was not only a writer, editor, and publisher, but an aggressive adman as well. He published the *Pennsylvania Gazette* (1st issue 1729), which carried ads for soap, books, stationery, and the 1730 almanac of Godfrey and Titan Leeds. The *Gazette* was soon to become the largest paper in the Colonies. Franklin wrote an ad for his newly invented stove which warned people that their teeth and jaws would go bad, their skin would shrivel, their eyes would fade, and assorted other woes would befall them if they continued to use old-fashioned stoves. This is cited as the 1st example of the modern technique of warning people against the dangers of "inferior brands."

Paul Revere, who made false teeth in addition to his other activities, advertised his dentures in the *Boston Gazette* in 1768.

There were 37 newspapers in the Colonies when the American Revolution began, 43 when it ended. Almost all were weeklies. Ads appeared encouraging enlistment in the Revolution.

This notice was published in 1789: "THOMAS TOUCHWOOD, GENT., proposes, on the last day of the present month, to shoot himself by subscription. His life being of no farther use to himself or his friends, he takes this method of endeavoring to turn his death to some account; and the novelty of the performance, he hopes, will merit the attention and patronage of the publick. He will perform with 2 pistols, the 1st shot to be directed through his abdomen, to which will be added another through his brain, the whole to conclude with staggering, convulsions, grinning, etc., in a manner never before publickly attempted. The doors to be opened at 8, and the exhibition to begin precisely at 9. Particular

places, for that night only, reserved for the ladies. No money to be returned, nor half-price taken. Vivant Rex et Regina. Beware of counterfeits and imposters—the person who advertises to hang himself the same night, in opposition to Mr. Touchwood, is a taylor, who intends only to give the representation of death by dancing in a collar, an attempt infinitely inferior to Mr. T.'s original and authentic performance."

Personal advertising was also rampant in the 1700s: "A tall, well-fashioned, handsome young woman, about 18 with a fine bloom in her countenance, a cast in one of her eyes, scarcely discernible; a well-turned nose, and dark-brown uncurled hair flowing about her neck, which seemed to be newly cut; walked last new years day about 3 o'clock in the afternoon, pretty fast through Long acre . . . and near the turn into Drury Lane met a young gentleman, wrapped up in a blue roccelo cloak, who she look'd at steadfastly. He believes he had formerly the pleasure of her acquaintance: If she will send a line direct to H.S. Esq., to be left at the bar of the Prince of Orange coffee house, the corner of Pall Mall, intimating where she can be spoken with, she will be informed of something greatly to her advantage. . . ."

Or this from 1790: "A young woman who has been tenderly brought up, and received a genteel Education, but left destitute of Fortune and Friends, will think herself happy could she meet a single gentleman of benevolent disposition to take her under his ONLY protection and friendship. . . ."

ADVERTISING IN THE 1800s

In the early 1800s, display advertising in printed media arrived. Whereas previous newspaper and magazine ads had been limited to short, column-sized ads, now they expanded and included illustrations. One of these was 4 pages long. Advertisers also used such devices as serial sandwich boards and giant floats to promote their products.

Volney B. Palmer became America's 1st significant advertising agent in the mid-1800s. He solicited business from advertisers, wrote copy for them, and placed the copy in a public media channel.

N. W. Ayer, currently one of the world's larger advertising agencies, was founded in 1841. By 1876, it had 20 employees.

P. T. Barnum expanded the horizons of advertising with his tantalizing and sensational promotional campaigns for Tom Thumb, the Feejee Mermaid, and singer Jenny Lind. Barnum delivered lectures on "The Science of Money-Making and the Philosophy of Humbug." In part due to his advertising and self-promotion, Barnum became an internationally famous entrepreneur.

By the later 1800s brand names took over the commercial arena. In 1871, there were 121 brand names registered at the Patent Office; by 1875, there were 1,138; by 1926, there were 69,000. Advertising became increasingly competitive.

In 1882, an electric sign was constructed and displayed by W. J. Hammer in London. The practice spread wildly. New York was soon blinking with electric signs. The public was delighted. One ad featured a chariot race made out of 20,000 light bulbs which flashed 2,500 times per minute.

Magazines became spectacular advertising vehicles. In *Harper's* of November, 1899, 135 pages of the magazine were devoted to ads and 163 to editorial matters.

Cyrus H. K. Curtis, a conservative Republican entered magazine publishing with the goal of creating a rewarding vehicle for national advertising rather than with any journalistic convictions. He was to become the country's most successful periodical publisher, with the *Ladies' Home Journal* and, later, *The Saturday Evening Post*. Curtis asked a group of national advertisers: "Do you know why we publish the *Ladies' Home Journal*? The editor thinks it is for the benefit of American women. That is an illusion, but a very proper one for him to have. But I will tell you, the real reason, the publisher's reason, is to give you people who manufacture things that American women want and buy a chance to tell them about your products."

By 1898, the *Ladies' Home Journal* had 48 pages of slick paper with color covers and illustrations as well as big-name writers. It had a circulation of 850,000. By 1900, the *Journal's* circulation reached one million. Curtis bought *The Saturday Evening Post*; it grew gradually, but acquired a huge $5 million worth of advertising revenues by 1910, with a circulation of over one million. Advertising had now become an established mass-communications form, with nationwide scope, and increasing sophistication and influence. As Joseph Seldin points out in *The Golden Fleece*, by the end of the 1800s, newspapers and magazines had become part of the U.S. marketing system with the job of "inducing mass consumption." Advertisers provided over ⅔ of magazine revenues by 1909.

Another advertising visionary was Thomas Lipton, a Scotch-Irishman who pioneered all kinds of inventive promotional tricks. According to James Wood's *Story of Advertising:* "He issued thousands of Lipton one-pound notes. They were facsimiles of those issued by Scottish banks but read across the face, '. . . Promise to pay on demand at any establishment for 15 shillings, ham, butter, and eggs as offered else-

where for One Pound Sterling.' The notes were at least a sensation. Many were redeemed at Lipton shops. More got into general circulation and were used as currency, to pay debts, or thriftily deposited in collection plates at church. Lipton fitted concave and convex mirrors in each of his shops. The one marked 'Going to Lipton's' showed people elongated and miserable; the other, marked 'Coming from Lipton's,' showed them fat and happy. He hired balloons to drop advertising telegrams. He recruited an army of 200 men, dressed them as Chinese, marched them between sandwich boards extolling his tea (Lipton's Tea). Like Barnum, he imported his own Jumbo. This Jumbo was a huge cheese he had made and shipped from Whiteborough, N.Y. For weeks in advance, Lipton advertised that it was being made, that it had been shipped, that it was on the high seas, that it had taken all the milk of 800 cows for 6 days to make it. Crowds greeted Jumbo at the docks. Gold sovereigns were hidden in the cheese. Police were called out to protect the huge crowds that swarmed on Christmas Eve when the cheese was to be cut. . . ."

A soap manufacturer, Pears, hired a famous and beautiful actress, Lily Langtry, to do a testimonial, "Since using Pears Soap, I have discarded all others." This is believed to have been the 1st such endorsement on a large scale. Pears also paid a large sum of money for a painting by artist John Millais, and started the trend of using fine art to sell products.

Ad agencies and ad agents proliferated in the 1890s. J. Walter Thompson, founder of what is now the biggest agency in America, said, "No one will ever make as much money out of advertising as I have." Independent writers or groups of writers prepared ad copy for manufacturers, and the agencies "placed" the ads. When Ayer handled the Uneeda Biscuit campaigns for the National Biscuit Company, the 1st full-service-agency approach was born. The agency took care of all aspects of the manufacturer's advertising needs from copywriting through merchandising coordination. By 1900, there were 20–25 agencies, mostly in New York.

Reform struck advertising: In 1892, Cyrus Curtis announced that the *Ladies' Home Journal* would take no patent medicine ads. The bogus potions were costing Americans millions of dollars per year, and were coming under heavy attack by commentators and consumers.

The Duryea automobile was advertised November, 1895. This is considered the 1st complete car ad.

Competitive advertising was stepped up with the introduction of the bicycle into American culture. Between 1890 and 1896, Americans spent $100 million for bicycles, produced by some 100 manufacturers. Brand name differentiation became of prime importance.

Ads for pills were projected on Nelson's Column in London by a magic lantern device in 1894.

In 1898, Sears (later of Sears, Roebuck and Co.) spent half of his operating expenses on advertising.

Ads for and by "young masseuses" were commonplace in newspapers of this period.

ADVERTISING IN THE EARLY 20TH CENTURY

In 1900, Albert D. Lasker, who became one of America's leading advertising practitioners, turned copywriting into a big business. From then on, the production of carefully researched and constructed ad copy became perhaps the central concern of advertisers. This was the beginning of the persuasive, hard-sell era. Lasker and his partner, Claude Hopkins, "researched" market areas and found out what people wanted from products. Then they advertised that their client's product offered exactly those characteristics desired.

During the 1st years of the 20th century, the Ford Motor Company produced thousands of cars, accompanied by extensive free publicity as well as carefully planned advertising. By 1928, 15 million Model Ts had been sold. A 1906 ad read: "We are making 40,000 cylinders, 10,000 engines, 40,000 wheels, 20,000 axles, 10,000 bodies, 10,000 of every part that goes into the car—think of it! For this car we buy exactly 40,000 spark plugs, 10,000 spark coils, 40,000 tires, all *exactly alike*."

During W.W. I, advertising was used effectively in Britain to marshal war energies—enlistments, conservation, etc. The same approach was used in the U.S., but not quite so successfully. Wartime references also infiltrated commercial ads, such as an ad for Cat's Paw Rubber Heels based on the slogan "Stepping On to Victory." Here is the text of a poster that was distributed by the British Government and its ad agencies: "1) Have you a Butler, Groom, Chauffeur, Gardener or Gamekeeper serving *you* who at this moment should be serving your King and Country? 2) Have you a man serving at your table who should be serving a gun? 3) Have you a man digging your garden who should be digging trenches? 4) Have you a man driving your car who should be driving a transport wagon? 5) Have you a man preserving your game who should be helping to preserve your country? A great responsibility rests on you. Will you sacrifice your personal convenience for your Country's need? Ask your men to enlist *today*."

An American W.W. I ad shows a smiling doughboy smoking a White Owl. "Did I bayonet my 1st Hun? Sure! How did it feel? It doesn't feel! There *he* is. There you are. One of you has got to go. I preferred to stay. . . .

Bullets and bayonets are the only kind of lingo a Hun can understand!"

ADVERTISING AFTER W.W. I

After W.W. I, advertising skyrocketed. In the U.S., the total advertising expenditure in 1918 was almost $1½ billion. By 1919, it was almost $2½ billion. By 1925, advertising expenditure had jumped up over $3 billion. Advertising became almost as important as industrial production itself. Americans felt giddy and strong in the '20s, and advertising sold them images of "the good life." Keeping up with the Joneses, the race for material status, became a major factor in American social relations. People were taught to seek pleasure through the acquisition of nonessential products.

Advertising and politics shook hands in 1918 when Will B. Hays, chairman of the Republican National Committee, hired superadman Albert Lasker to promote the Republican party with advertising techniques. Lasker produced propaganda in favor of the party and U.S. isolationism, and against Wilson's internationalism. Lasker himself believed that Europe was "blighted, decayed and evil." The Republicans went on to win in 1920.

Bruce Barton, an agency man, wrote a book claiming that Christ was an advertising man. He described Jesus as a business executive, and told how he had founded modern business practices and the advertising used to establish it. The book, *The Man Nobody Knows*, became a best seller. "He picked up 12 men from the bottom ranks of business and forged them into an organization that conquered the world." If Jesus had been alive, he would have been "a national advertiser," according to Barton.

Mass radio happened in the '20s. Advertisers were spending over $4 million for radio time by 1927, and $10 million by 1928. Radio ads were harsh and repetitious. Radio produced a number of changes in the advertising scene: It gave advertising a human voice with consequent emotional and dramatic appeal; it pushed advertising directly into the home; and, perhaps most important, it provided a medium where advertisers and ad agencies actually *controlled program content*—advertisers chose programs and directed them according to their own tastes. This relationship had not existed in the printed media. Additionally, radio had the effect of blurring the lines between program content and advertising messages. The foreground and the background were purposely mixed and overlapped in such a way that it was hard for the listeners to figure out when they were being solicited.

The stock market crashed on October 29, 1929. Advertising plummeted by billions of dollars from a peak of $3½ billion in 1929 to a little over $1 billion in 1933.

Advertising came under heavy attack, as did the entire economic system. Two fronts led the assault: consumer groups and the Government. The National Consumers' League, which had been formed in 1916, started in the 1930s to issue lists of manufacturers whose labor relations were reasonably humane. The publication of *Your Money's Worth*, a book by Stuart Chase and F. J. Schlink, in 1927, precipitated and exemplified the onslaught against advertising. The authors attacked not only false and misleading advertising, but the entire concept of competitive salesmanship. They formed the Consumer's Club—which became Consumer's Research, Inc., in 1929—with Schlink as president. The organization tested products and gave the results to subscribers. A split developed, and striking employees left to form their own Consumer's Union (1936), which also evaluated national products. Both groups used advertising to advance their cases, and to claim superiority over rival product-testing groups.

THE 1930S AND 1940S

More books hostile to advertising were published: *100,000,000 Guinea Pigs, Eat, Drink and Be Wary, Partners in Plunder* were among them.

Franklin D. Roosevelt, when governor of New York in 1931, told the Advertising Federation of America: "If I were starting life over again . . . I would go into the advertising business in preference to almost any other."

Bethlehem Steel opened a Public Relations Dept. in 1930; General Motors in 1931; U.S. Steel in 1936.

The U.S. Government attempted to regulate advertising to an unprecedented degree, but failed. Congress Bill S.1944 was introduced in 1933 by Sen. R. S. Copeland (although it was largely written by Rexford Guy Tugwell, a welfare liberal who was appointed an under secretary of Agriculture by FDR). The bill was a significant threat to the manufacturers and advertisers. It provided for strict controls, by the Government, of industrial quality and of advertising. It represented one of the New Deal's moves toward a "planned economy." The bill was hotly contested and finally defeated in 1934. A milder law—the Federal Food, Drug and Cosmetic Act—was passed with the approval of both advertising and industry.

In the early 1940s, the U.S. Federal Trade Commission came down hard on certain advertisers for phony claims. But in general, advertising made a comeback after the Terrible Thirties. During W.W. II, advertising advanced further. The War Advertising Council, consisting of representatives of all aspects of advertising, assisted the U.S. Government in preparing and conducting campaigns for recruitment, war bonds, and other wartime necessities. Wartime tie-ins were universal: An air-conditioner manufacturer claimed that he was sinking Japanese ships because the periscope lenses of American submarines had been made in an air-conditioned shop. Similarly, "Hitler smiles when you waste miles," from B. F. Goodrich. Or, "Idle words make busy subs. Keep it under your Stetson."

After W.W. II, television flourished and the modern superagency coalesced. Psychologists and sociologists were brought in by the advertising agencies to study human nature in relation to selling; in other words, to figure out how to manipulate people without their feeling manipulated. "Mr. Mass Motivations" himself—Dr. Ernest Dichter, president of the Institute for Motivational Research—made a statement in 1941 that typifies the developing advertising consciousness. He said that the successful ad agency "manipulates human motivations and desires and develops a need for goods with which the public has at one time been unfamiliar—perhaps even undesirous of purchasing."

THE 1950S

In the early 1950s overproduction was glutting the scene. Marketing became of equal importance with production. Hundreds of similar products were competing with each other. Millions of working-class families moved into the suburbs and became middle class, upsetting traditional class categories. The GNP jumped from $300 billion to $400 billion between 1950 and 1955. "Convenience" foods began to appear—400 million frozen pot pies were consumed in 1958. In 1957, an estimated 5,000 new grocery items were introduced. The corporate-government structure had to sell more products so it could continue to make more products and expand. An all-out effort was launched to mass-analyze the American public, broken down into Designated Market Areas. Hundreds of social scientists moved into the ad business. By 1955, McCann-Erickson had 5 psychologists on its staff.

Ernest Dichter conducted hundreds of motivation studies from his headquarters on a mountaintop overlooking the Hudson River. He commanded a staff of over 25 resident specialists, and published a monthly called *Motivations*. Dichter had a "psycho-panel" of several hundred families; he did intensive analyses of the emotional makeup of each family member, and used the families to test products and ideas on different "types."

The concept of "style" has long been used to keep people buying. Constant model changes and shifting clothes fashions do not swell up from the needs of the populace; they are deliberate contrivances. During the 1950s "planned obsolescence" was ushered in. Products were purposely made shoddily so that they would self-destruct and the customer would have to replace them. And even if people owned usable goods already, the concept of "psychological obsolescence" induced them to buy a newer item.

According to Vance Packard in *The Hidden Persuaders*, the Color Research Institute gave out an identical detergent in 3 different boxes —one yellow, one yellow and blue, and one blue. Housewives stated that the soap in the yellow box was "too strong," and in some cases it ruined their clothes. The blue box received low ratings, often leaving their clothes "dirty-looking." The 2-color box received favorable responses. Another example of research done with a view toward future psychological manipulation of the buying public.

All segments of society were considered worthy of exploitation. Clyde Miller wrote in *The Process of Persuasion*: ". . . Think of what it can mean to your firm in profits if you can condition a million or 10 million children who will grow up into adults trained to buy your product as soldiers are trained to advance when they hear the trigger words 'forward march.'"

Giveaways, contests, and quiz shows proliferated in the '50s. Quaker Oats mailed out 5 tons of dirt from the Yukon in little pouches. Three coffee companies put actual money into their packages. Dial soap gave away an oil well. Remington Rand gave away one share of every company listed in the N.Y. Stock Exchange. One contest offered a free butler service. Competition was unbounded. *The New Yorker* found 312 "finests," 281 "world's bests," and 58 "America's onlys" in its pages over a 6-month period.

In the 1950s, trading stamps proliferated. Although clearly absurd, they proved to be a perfect advertising triumph. While customers knew they were paying more in stores that gave stamps, the stamps nevertheless instilled a feeling of thriftiness. After all, the customers were getting something for "nothing" (like television), and, significantly, they were acquiring "luxury" items which they wouldn't ordinarily have bought. By 1960, there were 250–500 stamp companies. S & H was servicing 60,000 accounts and operating 600 redemption centers. One stamp company ordered 30 million catalogs printed. Housewives marched on State legislatures when they were considering outlawing trading stamps.

In the field of motivational research, the American petroleum industry found that people don't like to see pictures of gushing oil wells in ads because they resent sudden or easy wealth for others. A soup company which offered pantyhose as a premium found that people were turned off by the association of soup and feet. Then there was the Davy Crockett craze in 1955, which resulted in 300 Davy Crockett products involving $300 million.

The explosion of actual scientific advances rendered people susceptible to the designs of the admen, who used the new respect for science to sell products and introduced the Special Ingredient, the Miracle Ingredient, TCP, Activated Charcoal, Gardol, Miracle SLS, M-3, Solium, Microsheen, RX-2, WD-9, R-51, Trisilium, and others.

The confection and soft drink industry suffered a setback in the 1950s. Between 1950 and 1955, consumption of such items dropped 10%. Presumably, citizens were worried about dieting and tooth decay. (Much of the anti-sugar publicity was generated by the manufacturers of low-calorie products and toothpastes.) The industry hired Dr. Dichter. He told them that the real problem was a guilt feeling about self-indulgence on the part of the individuals in the market area. He advised them, for instance, to emphasize bite-sized pieces in order to give people a feeling that they weren't eating too much. Ultimately, the sugar industry began a campaign promoting candy as a dietary aid, suggesting that people try the "scientific nibble" of sweets to control their appetites.

Dieting became a major national issue. The consumption of low-calorie soft drinks multiplied 300 times between 1952 and 1955. The market was flooded with dietary aids, from bath salts and nonporous garments to pastes, candy, suction cups, belts, drugs. "Slim" became a significant social goal. In 1957, a congressional committee found that nearly all of the dietary products were practically worthless, and that the American public had been paying over $100 million a year for phony latter-day patent medicines. Additionally, in the area of nutrition and health, advertising oversimplified—and therefore falsified—important information. For example, in order to sell more cooking oil and modified fat products, the advertising Merlins declared that "cholesterol" was the main factor in heart disease. This was not a unanimous scientific feeling, yet it was so widely disseminated throughout the culture that it became a "fact." Much the same thing occurred with toothpastes. Several additives ranged from ammoniates to chlorophyll to antienzymes to fluoride—all of which provided inconclusive dental help. Rather than teaching people better nutritional habits and brushing techniques, the advertisers claimed that some new kind of additive would provide proper dental care.

And cigarettes, in the 1950s, didn't escape; there was a cancer scare. The manufacturers and the admen decided to push filters as an antidote to the negative publicity. Although the AMA reported that filters were nearly inconsequential, the ads promised that everything would be well. Ads began emphasizing rewards for hard work done, in place of earlier dreamy idylls and "taste/pleasure" promos. "Independent Testing Laboratories" appeared to legitimatize the universal claims that each brand was now milder, lower in tars and nicotine. When sales began to climb back up, *Printer's Ink*, an advertising trade journal, reported that "the public is approaching the smoking-health problem in adult fashion."

Another ad which exemplifies the era read: "Afraid of A-Bomb contamination? In the event of an A-Bomb attack wash contamination away with Flobar. . . ."

TELEVISION

Discussing the influence of television, Daniel Boorstin wrote: "Here at last is a supermarket of surrogate experience. Successful programming offers entertainment (under the guise of instruction), instruction (under the guise of entertainment), political persuasion (with the appeal of advertising), and advertising (with the appeal of drama)."

The low psychological and emotional intensity of much programmed television serves not only to spread acquiescence and conformity, but it represents a deliberate industry approach. Sponsors have found that if they program a show of challenging complexity or disturbing insight, the viewers will discuss it with each other as soon as the ads come on, and thus will not be able to give their full attention to the commercial announcements.

Marya Mannes commented: "The constant reminder of what is inaccessible must inevitably produce a subterranean but real discontent. . . . If we are constantly presented with what we are not, or cannot have, the dislocation deepens, contentment vanishes, and frustration reigns. Even for the substantially secure, there is always a better thing, a better way, to buy. That none of these things makes a better life may be consciously acknowledged, but still the desire lodges in the spirit. A commercial is more than an interruption; it tends to reduce news to a form of running entertainment, to smudge the edges of reality by treating death or disaster or diplomacy on the same level as household appliances or a new gasoline."

Janet Sternberg wrote ". . . The sheer impossibility of ever measuring up to the variety of selves thrust at a woman takes its toll in self-contempt. She is repeatedly exhorted by the media to assume a new persona, but of course, being human, cannot shed skins too gracefully. This repeated failure is internalized as a self-image of degradation. . . . Surrounded everywhere by images of what she should be, it becomes increasingly difficult for a woman to retain a core of self-determined identity."

Who controls television programming? This question was put to Jack Gould, television writer for *The New York Times*. "The heads of the networks as such bear final responsibility. . . . Of course, whoever has control of the dollar, the advertising program dollar, is going to make the final determination of what goes on the air in entertainment programming. It has always seemed to me very academic, the perennial controversy over whether the advertising agencies or the networks control the programming. As a practical matter and as things stand, it doesn't make any difference. So long as the sponsor can buy an individual program, so long as he can pick and choose his programs —whether the agencies conceive the programs or whether the networks conceive them—the result, in terms of program content, will be the same because both the agencies and the networks will devise the type of shows the sponsors want. . . . The real control rests with the sponsor. By the act of not purchasing certain kinds of programs the sponsor exercises a tremendous influence over television programming."

PUBLIC RELATIONS AND POLITICS

In addition to motivation research and the advent of television, the 2 most important changes that took place in advertising in the postwar era were: 1. the public relations boom; and 2. the penetration of advertising into politics.

In the U.S. during the 1950s and 1960s, public relations achieved a heady prominence. By 1960, there were up to 100,000 persons employed in public relations. The avowed goals of PR are: ". . . to take initiative in bringing about the integration of spiritual principles and material progress which, and which alone, can assure for us and our fellow man a maximum of happiness." *Fortune* magazine called PRs ". . . cheap-jack publicists, promoters, greeters, lobbyists and fixers." PR exists to convince the public of a certain item, a product, a person, a way of life, a symbol, or a corporation. Since so many nearly identical products were crowding the shelves, the advertisers began to sell "images." Corporate images, product images, and so on became at least as important as the products themselves. Content and substance gave way to engineered illusions. This practice reached its highest fruition in the wedding of politics and advertising.

Napoleon had a Bureau of Public Opinion, its function to create political trends according to the dictator's will. In the 1930s, Albert Lasker had helped sell the Republicans. Now, in the 1950s, image-building completely infiltrated the American political process, culminating in the 1956 presidential "campaign." The advertising agency of Batten, Barton, Durstine and Osborn (BBDO) handled the Eisenhower account. On retainer to the Republicans since 1952, BBDO started blocking out $2 million of TV time a year before the elections. Robert Montgomery, the actor, was brought in to supervise Ike's TV appearances, advising him on matters such as lighting, makeup, and delivery. George Murphy, actor and PR director of M-G-M, was imported to stage-manage the 1956 GOP convention. Rosser Reeves, legendary adman and creator of a large number of famous campaigns ("Can't you keep Jimmy's bike *out of the driveway?*"), conceived a saturation barrage of half-minute spots for Eisenhower which cost over $1 million a week toward the end of the election effort. One ad showed an alleged taxi driver walking his dog in the park facing the White House. He looked in awe toward the light in the White House window and said fervently, "I need you!"

Reeves, former chairman of Ted Bates and Company, created, among other things: the "Invisible Shield"; M&M's that "melt in your mouth, not in your hand"; and Minute Maid that is "better for you than oranges squeezed at home."

To quote Reeves: "I think of the man in the voting booth who hesitates between 2 levers as if he were pausing between competing tubes of toothpaste in a drugstore. The brand that has made the highest penetration on his brain will win his choice." National Republican Chairman Leonard Hall said, "You sell your candidates and your programs the way a business sells its products."

"Policies and issues are useless for election purposes," Marshall McLuhan has said of the modern political situation. What is important is the image of the candidate. Political advertising learned how to research the populace, find out what it wanted, and shape its candidate's persona based on those findings.

The Democrats, although they planned to spend over $8 million on their own campaigns, could not find a major agency to take their account in 1956. As it turned out, 37 leading agencies gave $51,000 to the Republican party and zero to the Democrats, who finally found a smaller agency to handle their account.

Since the 1950s, advertising has become essential to American politics. Virtually all candidates hired ad agencies or PR people to promote themselves, and finally, an advertising

man became one of the unelected rulers of the country: H. R. "Bob" Haldeman worked for the country's largest advertising agency before he worked for the world's most powerful political structure. Previous attempts at total national propaganda seem naïve and shortsighted. The psychosociological effects of Total Uniform Image Penetration have yet to be understood. The influence of a few central decision makers becomes hugely magnified. A small number of conservative, white, profit-oriented males, mostly between the ages of 40 and 65, control almost all of the country's most persuasive image-producing resources.

Vance Packard, in *The Hidden Persuaders*, tells of the husband and wife team of political image shapers, Clem Whitaker and Leone Baxter, who participated in over 70 winning campaigns, including those of Earl Warren and Goodwin Knight in California. They insist on complete creative control over the PR strategy. Skornia and Kitson, authors of *Problems and Controversies in TV and Radio*, described a new development called psychographics and pseudoevents. Researchers found that advertisements were becoming a substitute for the product. "Advertisers have been puzzled by the tendency of viewers and readers to pay special attention to the ads for products that they already owned. It is as if people used the ad to strengthen their impression of the product, and to get 'cued in' as to the means of relating themselves to it."

THE CONTEMPORARY ADVERTISING SCENE

The 1960s and 1970s have produced a Gross Advertising Surround. To get an idea of omnipresence, try to estimate the number of advertising images that are currently displayed in the U.S., leaving aside, if you care to, packaging that simply announces the brand name. "Every day," wrote adman Leo Bogart in 1967, "4.2 billion advertising messages pour forth from 1,754 daily newspapers, millions of others from 8,151 weeklies, and 1.4 billion more each day from 4,147 magazines and periodicals. There are 3,895 AM and 1,336 FM stations broadcasting an average of 730,000 commercials a day, and 770 television stations broadcast 100,000 commercials a day. Every day millions of people are confronted with 330,000 outdoor billboards, with 2,500,000 car cards and posters in buses, subways and commuter trains, with 51,300,000 direct mail pieces and leaflets, and with billions of display and promotion items."

An Avon ad: "Rapture is sensitive to you. . . . Rapture has beautiful hopes for you. . . ."

A Fiat ad: "Among all the wonderful Italian things America has discovered, nothing is more so than Fiat's 1100 D Sedan. That includes the wine, the women, the music, the art—even great, historic Roma. . . ."

At the beginning of the revolt in the Dominican Republic in 1965, there were 3 U.S. Information Service people in the country. By the time the U.S. military intervention was over and the revolt crushed, more than 20 official U.S. public relations workers were on the scene.

Right Guard was pushing a new Natural Scent Deodorant. One of their ads featured a long-haired young woman in wire-rimmed glasses. She spoke of how natural she was and how natural Right Guard was. "It's as if they knew what I wanted," she concluded. This ad was brought to you by BBDO, the same agency that handled Dwight Eisenhower. Gillette's $17 million, 3-month introductory campaign for Natural Scent included a big TV push and the mailing out of 20 million 10¢-off scratch 'n' sniff coupons.

Here's an example of another use of the word "natural." Lipton's new family drink mix, which "bridges the generation gap," is billed in TV commercials and on its wrapper as "100% natural flavor." The ingredients, however, are listed on the package as: "Sugar, citric acid (provides tartness), orange juice (natural flavor on corn syrup), corn sugar (aids dissolving), sodium citrate (regulates tartness), gum acacia (flavor carrier), tricalcium phosphate (aids dissolving), cellulose gum (adds body), vitamin C, orange oil (natural flavor), vegetable oil (for cloud), artificial color, BHA (preserves freshness)." Note the attempt to validate non-nutritive ingredients by forthrightly describing their effects.

This ad was withdrawn from circulation: A girl runs up in a white slip that has just been washed in the advertised soap. "Mommy, smell my slip."

How big is the modern advertising business? *Advertising Age*, the "National Magazine of Marketing," reports that "Everybody who advertised in 1972—manufacturing companies, service operations, retailers, wholesalers, distributors, associations, labor unions, schools, churches, governments, politicians, individuals placing want ads—spent an estimated $23 billion for the privilege.

"Most of this enormous total—about $13.1 billion, or 57%—was expended by national advertisers. There are, in fact, more than 17,000 such advertisers in the U.S. The hundred largest of these companies (ranging from Procter & Gamble, with an expenditure of about $275 million, to the E. & J. Gallo Winery, with an outlay of $13,300,000) invested $5.27 billion alone in advertising media last year. Thus, fewer than 1% of all of America's national advertisers accounted for 40% of all national advertising dollars. . . ."

In 1974, the 10 corporations spending the most money on advertising were:

1)	Procter & Gamble	$245,186,000
2)	General Foods	$140,930,000
3)	Bristol-Myers	$121,618,000
4)	American Home Products	$118,228,000
5)	General Motors	$115,265,000
6)	Colgate Palmolive	$ 88,273,000
7)	Lever Brothers	$ 86,550,000
8)	Sterling Drug	$ 79,757,000
9)	Sears, Roebuck	$ 79,745,000
10)	Ford Motor	$ 75,467,000

Here is an excerpt from a trade book, *What Makes Women Buy* by Janet L. Woolf:

Essentially, man's body is built for physical activity and woman's body, to bear children. In every detail, man and woman are formed and proportioned in radically different ways. Many of the facts about woman's body proportion and bone structure ultimately have an effect on designing for and selling to women. . . . Women's arms and legs are built at a slight angle, while man's are comparatively straight. It is as if women were a little knock-kneed, and "knock-elbowed" too. Woman's thigh bone inclines at a gradual angle toward the knee. This is the main reason why women are usually good dancers, yet poor runners, and awkwardly throw their legs at an angle. It also explains why women usually don't balance as well as men and are inclined to fall down more often. In a woman's arm, the bone of the upper arm or humerus is connected to the bones of the forearm at an angle—sometimes called the carrying angle. This angle makes most rotary motions, like turning the steering wheel of a car, more difficult for women. It also accounts for the stiff downward motion most women use when throwing a ball. From the selling point of view, the natural structure of a woman's arms and legs also means it handicaps her as an athlete and in doing heavy physical labor—so turns her toward more passive interests and occupations.

More from *What Makes Women Buy*:

The bone structure of their hands also influences women toward developing different interests and attitudes than men. Women's hands are proportionately smaller. And, therefore, women are usually better and quicker than most men in buttoning, handwork, assembly and inspection work which involves wrist and finger movement. Handling a baseball or a screwdriver is hard for women because of their hand proportions—tools really need to be especially designed for them. Woman's stomach and lower muscles are well developed. Correspondingly, women's lungs are not as large as men's, and her vital capacity or ability to take in oxygen is less than man's. Greater intake of oxygen gives men more fuel and more sustained energy—another reason why women tire more easily and need more frequent rest pauses than men.

In January, 1974, supercorporation ITT unveiled a $6 million ad drive to improve its image. ITT felt that its veneer of respectability had been dented by such widely publicized scandals as the undercover financing of the Republican party, the destruction of democratic governments (Chile), and lying about building bodies 12 ways. ITT introduced the corporate-image promotional scheme behind the slogan "The Best Ideas Are the Ideas That Help People."

The J. Walter Thompson advertising agency has billings of over $800 million and employs 6,000 people in 26 countries. Thompson has created advertising for the French police, "Thank you, guardians of the peace," which was ridiculed throughout the country. In 1974, the fascist Government of Chile hired J. Walter Thompson to promote a new and cleaner image of itself around the world. J. Walter Thompson also organized classes to teach corporation executives how to act when being interviewed by the press or when appearing before congressional committees.

Linda Lovelace starred in an ad for M & J Shoes, Encino, Calif., in 1973. And in the winter, the industry was hit with "Light Flu Season Disappoints Advertisers of Cold Remedies" (*Advertising Age*). It was a period of contrary events and strange bedfellows, but it was also a time of growing awareness of how the industry was harming our minority groups.

The U.S. Information Agency puts out 36 regular periodicals in 29 languages. Its purpose is to advertise and promote the Government's version of the American way of life. The Voice of America, with a budget of $50 million a year, employs 2,300 people and broadcasts 800 hours a week in 36 languages. The USIA produces more than 1,000 movies and TV shows per year which are used by more than 2,000 TV stations in 97 countries, but are not allowed to be shown in the U.S.

Paul Baran and Paul Sweezy, 2 widely respected economists, have written: "Far from being a relatively unimportant feature of the system, [advertising] has advanced to the status of one of its decisive nerve centers. In its impact on the economy, it is outranked only by militarism. In all other aspects of social existence, its all-pervasive influence is 2nd to none."

Because of large monopolies and oligopolies of industry, such as the telephone company or the oil corporations, price competition is no longer a real factor; ads become the principal way of competing in the marketplace.

Here is a memo from the advertising director of Richard Nixon's 1968 campaign, Harry Treleavan, formerly with J. Walter Thompson: "It is part of the discipline of sound advertising to put down, as briefly as possible, the advertising 'proposition'—the simplest expression of the message we want to communicate. This is not the theme or slogan; the words of the proposition may never appear in advertising; yet all advertis-

ADVERTISERS PROMOTING RACISM: A PARTIAL LISTING

Name of Advertiser	Context and/or Content of Ad	Racist Message
Granny Goose	Fat Mexican toting guns, ammunition	Mexicans=overweight, carry deadly weapons
Frito-Lay	"Frito-Bandito"	Mexicans=sneaky, thieves
Liggett & Myers	"Paco" never "feenishes" anything, not even revolution	Mexicans=too lazy to improve selves
R. J. Reynolds	Mexican bandito	Mexicans=bandits
Camel Cigarettes	"Typical" Mexican village, all sleeping or bored	Mexicans=do-nothings, irresponsible
General Motors	White, rustic man holding 3 Mexicans at gunpoint	Mexicans=should be and can be arrested by superior white man
Lark (Liggett & Myers)	Mexican house painter covered with paint	Mexicans=sloppy workers, undependable
Philco-Ford	Mexican sleeping next to TV set	Mexicans=always sleeping
Frigidaire	Mexican banditos interested in freezer	Mexicans=thieves, seeking Anglo artifacts
Arrid	Mexican bandito sprays underarm, voice says, "If it works for him, it will work for you."	Mexicans=stink the most

From: *Voices* edited by Octavio Romano. Berkeley, Calif., Quinto Sol Publications (P.O. Box 9275, Berkeley, Calif. 94709), 1973.

ing must communicate the thought of the proposition. The proposition for the Nixon for President primary advertising can be stated like this: 'There's an uneasiness in the land. A feeling that things aren't right. That we're moving in the wrong direction. That none of the solutions to our problems are working. That we're not being told the truth about what's going on. The trouble is in Washington. Fix that and we're on our way to fixing everything. . . . And of all the Republicans, the most qualified for the job by far is Richard M. Nixon. More than any other Republican candidate for the presidency, Richard Nixon will know what has to be done —and he'll know the best way to get it done. We'll all feel a whole lot better knowing he's there in Washington running things instead of somebody else.'" (*The Selling of the President*, 1968 by Joe McGinniss.)

Transit ads—small posters inside buses and subways—do $70 million of business every year. More than 70,000 mass transit vehicles carry transit advertising in 380 urban U.S. markets, and more than 40 million people are believed to ride on such vehicles every month.

Time magazine discussed the effects of image overload: ". . . After 20 years of hard-sell harangue, viewers developed a kind of filter blend up front. They did not turn off their sets; they turned off their minds. Admen refer to that phenomenon as the 'fatigue factor,' but their research departments know it by the more ominous name of CEBUS (Confirmed Exposure But Unconscious). In one recent survey, 75% of the viewers tested had no recollection of what products they had just seen demonstrated." In another study, however, a man under hypnosis recalled word-for-word a commercial he had heard 20 years earlier.

The 1970s saw the emergence of the multinational advertising agency/holding company, with offices and affiliates all over the world. The 10 largest advertising companies based on sums they spent for their clients in 1974:

1) Dentsu Advertising (Japan)	$907.7 million
2) J. Walter Thompson (U.S.)	$867.5 million
3) Young and Rubicam International (U.S.)	$750.5 million
4) McCann-Erickson (U.S.)	$703.3 million
5) Leo Burnett Co. (U.S.)	$577.7 million
6) Ted Bates (U.S.)	$565.8 million
7) Batten, Barton, Durstine and Osborn (U.S.)	$525.5 million
8) Ogilvy and Mather International (U.S.)	$523.7 million
9) Grey Advertising (U.S.)	$391.0 million
10) Doyle, Dane, Bernbach (U.S.)	$355.1 million

This ad was withdrawn from circulation: An ad for Springmaid sheets showed an Indian maiden on a mattress with her dress hiked up; next to her lay an exhausted Indian male. The ad's headline read, "A buck well spent on a Springmaid sheet."

Is there self-regulation within the advertising industry? Of course—a board, a code, designed to evaluate the industry's output. Here's an example of how it works (reported by Jerry Della Femina in *From Those Wonderful Folks Who Gave You Pearl Harbor*): A Ted Bates commercial featured a kid with a toy machine gun. He stood on a mound of dirt and massacred his "enemies." The ad was denied approval. However, the reviewers rejected it not because it showed a child with a machine gun but because they felt the ad would confuse viewers by somehow suggesting that the mound of dirt came with the gun.

An adman, Kenneth A. Longman, summarized the criticisms which have been leveled at advertising: "Advertising sells people things they neither need nor want. . . . Advertising imposes uniformity on the populace. Advertising generates senseless proliferation of a variety of goods and services. Advertising results in higher prices. Advertising is false and misleading. Most advertising is irrelevant. Most advertising exhibits bad taste—or sponsors it. Advertising is too intrusive. Advertising regulates discussion of public issues through its control of the news media."

—M.S.

Advertising Wisdom . . .

THE DOG AND THE SHADOW

It happened that a dog had got a piece of meat and was carrying it home in his mouth to eat it in peace. Now on his way home he had to cross a plank lying across a running brook. As he crossed, he looked down and saw his own shadow reflected in the water beneath. Thinking it was another dog with another piece of meat, he made up his mind to have that also. So he snapped at the shadow in the water, but as he opened his mouth the piece of meat fell out, dropped into the water and was never seen more.

"BEWARE LEST YOU LOSE THE SUBSTANCE BY GRASPING AT THE SHADOW."

—Aesop's *Fables*

THE LION AND THE STATUE

A Man and a Lion were discussing the relative strength of men and lions in general. The

Man contended that he and his fellows were stronger than lions by reason of their greater intelligence. "Come now with me," he cried, "and I will soon prove that I am right." So he took the Lion into the public gardens and showed him a statue of Hercules overcoming the Lion and tearing his mouth in 2.

"That is all very well," said the Lion, "but it proves nothing, for it was a man who made the statue."

"WE CAN EASILY REPRESENT THINGS AS WE WISH THEM TO BE."

—Aesop's *Fables*

Must Be Unseen to Be Believed:
The Tachistoscope

". . . We have reached the sad age when minds and not just houses can be broken and entered."
—*The New Yorker*

"The subconscious mind is the most delicate apparatus in the universe. It is not to be smudged, sullied or twisted in order to boost the sales of popcorn or anything else. Nothing is more difficult in the modern world than to protect the privacy of the human soul."—*Saturday Review*

"Frightening though it may appear, devices to induce subliminal stimuli mechanically are much more than mere marketing toys. They are being used commercially every day in northern America, but they do imply a certain risk of discovery and public denouncement. There are other, nonmechanically induced, subliminal techniques which are just as effective.—William Bryan Key, in *Subliminal Seduction*.

In 1957, an affable young American market researcher by the name of James Vicary set off a controversy which exploded across the country, confettied State legislatures with a barrage of new bills, and came knocking loudly at the Senate's fine oaken doors. The controversy concerned "subliminal stimuli," the means by which a person's mind can be entered and seeded with suggestions without his knowing about it. In 1957, James Vicary demonstrated the tachistoscope.

The tachistoscope, essentially, is a simple film projector with a high-speed shutter capable of flashing messages 1/3000 of a second long, at 5-second intervals. One hears about it from time to time in relation to a 6-week experiment conducted in a movie theater where, on alternate nights, the words "Drink Coca-Cola!" or "Hungry? Eat popcorn!" were flashed tachisto-

scopically—without the audience's knowledge—over the regularly scheduled features. A 60% increase in the sale of popcorn was reported for that month and a half; while Coca-Cola sales climbed about 20%. Quite a little conversation piece.

While the shutter speed of the tachistoscope can be varied—making it useful in experiments testing for attention and retention—the device has for the most part been a tool of the market researcher. One of the more interesting experiments, however, involved 2 groups of university students, and one slide of a male model in a *Playboy* advertisement. Each group would analyze the ad's model, using a scale of 1-to-5, as to how masculine he was considered.

So the 1st group was shown the slide and asked to mark down its scores. And the 2nd group was asked to watch the slide and mark down its scores. The only difference was that the 2nd time, superimposed over the slide every 5 seconds, at 1/3000 of a second, there appeared the word: "Man!" . . . "Man!" . . . "Man!"

Only one member of the 1st group used the most masculine rating of 1 in the experiment, while 26 members of the tachistoscoped group chose that evaluation. Whereas 2 members of group 1 scored the model as 2 (fairly masculine), 35 members of the 2nd group gave that same scoring. The differences between the perceptions and evaluations of the 2 groups, needless to say, were striking.

Despite the brouhaha stirred by the tachistoscope, no laws have been passed to prohibit its, or any other subliminal or subaudial technique's, use in advertising or broadcasting.

—M.T.

A Newsletter on Newsletters

A New York petroleum executive pays $490 a year for his. A part-time baggy-pants clown in San Diego spends $4 for a year's supply. An annual allotment costs a Wall Street tycoon $200, but an Iowa secretary gets by for $9.

What are they buying? Newsletters—bull's-eye distillations of hard facts, behind-the-news interpretations, and crystal-ball predictions, zeroed in on their special interests.

Whatever your interest, chances are there's a

newsletter aimed directly at you. If you don't find your subject among the 230 headings in *The Standard Directory of Newsletters'* list of nearly 5,000 publications, don't despair. Newsletters are popping up like mushrooms in one of the country's fastest-growing communications media. Soaring from a few hundred in the 1920s and 1930s to an estimated 7,000 today, they outnumber daily newspapers 4 to 1.

Some 5,000 are published by industry and organizations to keep interested readers informed. But the influential powerhouses are the 2,000 commercial newsletters published by individuals either weekly, biweekly, or monthly, and wholly supported by subscription. Rates are a few dollars a year and up—mostly up. A $200 price tag is not uncommon, and subscribers to the *10-K Transcript* business information letter part with a 10-karat $1,850 for an annual serving.

Such figures would have seemed incredible to America's 1st newsletter publisher, John Campbell, founder of *The Boston Newsletter* in 1704. But today's fragmented society of specialists is showering gold on the newsletter industry, and corporations are the biggest spenders; Xerox is reported to pay $12,000 a year for newsletters.

The media explosion was touched off in 1918 when the 1st modern newsletter, *The Whaley-Eaton American Letter*, won instant popularity and made its founders millionaires. Close on Whaley-Eaton's heels came Willard Kiplinger with the most successful entry of all. *The Kiplinger Washington Letter*, established in 1923, boasts a circulation of over 400,000 today; at $24 a reader, that's a tidy $9 million-plus per year. Kiplinger's crackling mix of fact and opinion, peppered with prophecy, is presented in a typical newsletter format—4 pages, 8½" by 11", typewritten and offset printed, and free of advertising.

These pioneers capitalized on a human peculiarity—the average person's urge to be "in the know." The ego boost of a private pipeline to inside information is the keystone of newsletter success.

But success can be elusive; newsletter mortality is high in the 1st year or 2. Some survive as they began, one-man operations with little more than a battered typewriter and a compulsion to plug a communications gap.

One of the more prosperous—and most famous—of the one-man newsletters was the *I. F. Stone Weekly*. Discontinued in 1971—much to the dismay of its 74,000 faithful followers—the *Weekly* was a pace-setting, literate examination of Washington foibles for 19 years.

"Izzy" Stone specialized in ferreting out chicanery concealed in political double-talk. "Seeking the significant detail" he called it. Happiness for Stone was scooping the big-time Washington correspondents with his exposures of bureaucratic knavery.

Stone landed a newsbeat in 1957 when he ran across deception in a U.S. Atomic Energy Commission report. AEC was fighting a nuclear-test ban, claiming that a moratorium wouldn't work because existing equipment was inadequate to detect underground tests. As "proof," AEC claimed in the report that an underground test in Nevada had not been detected beyond 230 mi.

Scurrying to the Office of the U.S. Coast and Geodetic Survey, Stone dug up information that the explosion was recorded over 3,000 mi. away. He ran the story in his newsletter, blasting the AEC falsehood, and red-faced AEC officials admitted their "misstatement." Stone's scoop won nationwide applause and scores of new subscribers.

An axiom of newsletter survival is sharp focus on a subject that will appeal to the broadest possible audience. Small wonder so many newsletters draw a bead on consumer health and safety.

Consumer Newsweek was founded in 1971 to keep readers posted on actions by government regulatory agencies. It names hazardous products banned from the market or under investigation, and passes along health tips and warnings.

A recent shocker was an item on a study by the General Accounting Office and the Food and Drug Administration revealing that 31% of chicken in stores is contaminated with salmonella. Sometimes the cause of food poisoning, salmonella was also found in smaller amounts in pork and ham. "Yet," said GAO, "Federal efforts to control the germ have been piecemeal." The study found that closer inspection was made on interstate shipments of pet turtles than on meat and poultry. Although beef was found relatively free of salmonella in the GAO checks, *Consumer Newsweek* said other tests over a wide area of the country have found beef containing large amounts of bacteria. The weekly newsletter warns consumers to cook meat and poultry as much as taste will allow and to wash hands and utensils that come in contact with the raw products.

"The Government can't assure that pesticides are safe and effective," warns another item. In a watchdog survey of the Environmental Protection Agency, GAO described tests of pesticides by EPA as inadequate. The study concludes, ". . . the number of unsafe and ineffective pesticides used by consumers could be significant." (Subscription is $15 a year. Write to 813 National Press Building, Washington, D.C. 20004.)

In the race for subscribers, no entries run harder—or for bigger purses—than newsletters in the financial field. Each publisher implies that *his* newsletter will show investors how to make money. Investment letters are usually filled with stock market tips, but a maverick in the field since 1963 is *The Contrary Investor*.

Although publisher James Fraser does devote a portion of his biweekly newsletter to evaluation of a stock, most of it is given over to his "contrary" philosophy concerning the economic scene. In one issue, *The Contrary Investor* accused large institutions of laziness in selecting their stocks. "After a while, anything that is too easy doesn't work, which is, by the way, a simply stated philosophy of Contrary Opinion Theory."

The blood pressure of many investment newsletter publishers probably exploded when James Fraser told his readers, "Letting the computer on top of your head replace automatic buy lists is healthy." Nor would stockbrokers be apt to embrace a recent pronouncement in which Fraser commented: "Wall Street is not perfect, mind you. Most investors, especially individuals . . . believe that the stock exchange community is pretty much run by a few big interests looking out for themselves. . . ." (Newsletter available at $35 per year from Box 494, Burlington, Vt. 05401.)

"The one person in 3 who has somehow managed to retain a sense of humor" is the audience aimed at by *Funny Funny World*. "Or, as Groucho Marx said, 'If you *can* find something to laugh at these days, you're not paying attention.'" Since 1971, this biweekly has been reprinting news items. For example: "*Memphis*—a man handed a lady teller in the Bank of Memphis a note which read, 'Give me all your money.' The note had been written on a withdrawal slip, but the teller calmly told the man he had not filled out the blanks properly. She told him to go over to a desk and fill it out correctly. The would-be bank robber was so unnerved that he fled. (*Memphis Press-Scimitar*)"

And anecdotes and one-liners: From Redd Foxx—"My advice is to smoke, eat, live it up a lot. Why be in a hospital dying of nothing?"

The publisher claims an advertising copywriter wrote that he enjoyed reading *Funny Funny World* because ". . . when you're stuck for an idea, it sure beats staring out the window." (Available for $35 a year from 407 Commercial St., Beverly Hills, Calif. 90210.)

Newsletters can be a significant force in publicizing social ills. *Indian Affairs* covers legislation affecting American Indians and spotlighting injustices to the 1st Americans. A recent issue describes "perhaps the most tragic aspect of American Indian life today—the wholesale abduction of children from their families." A survey in selected States showed 25–35% of Indian children taken from their families and placed in foster homes and in-

stitutions—"in most cases without due process of law. . . ." This is blamed on social workers ignorant of Indian culture and norms, who "frequently discover child-desertion, neglect, or abandonment, where none exists." (The bimonthly newsletter has a circulation of 85,000. Subscription is by membership donation of $10, students $5, to the Association of American Indian Affairs, 432 Park Ave. South, New York, N.Y. 10016.)

When the late Willard Kiplinger started *The Kiplinger Washington Letter* over half a century ago ("I just sat down one Wednesday night and wrote it"), he aimed his interpretive reporting of the Government and the economy at businessmen.

Under the helm of Austin Kiplinger, today's *Washington Letter* still offers blunt opinion: Talk of the U.S.'s becoming independent of foreign oil supplies by 1980 "is a lot of baloney." It reveals inside information: "Government keeps pretty mum" on some risky bank loans that are "in danger of going sour." And it makes predictions—Kiplinger recently devoted an entire issue to over 50 fearless forecasts for the coming decade: "Depression, a world wide bust? . . . No." Inflation, though continuing high, will be "wrestled down in the next 10 years." Gross National Product: "By 1980 . . . 2 trillions. By 1985 . . . 3 trillions." And so on for 4 pages.

An occupational hazard of newsletter prophets is the inaccurate prediction. But readers tend to remember the successes and overlook the bloopers, as long as the ratio is reasonable. On the eve of the 1948 election, one of Kiplinger's publications carried predictions of what "President" Dewey would do. Later, Kiplinger shrugged, said he had made a mistake, and went right on soothsaying. (Costs $24 a year. Write to 1729 H St., N.W., Washington, D.C. 20006.)

Some of the highest subscription rates shown in *The Standard Directory of Newsletters* appear under "Banking and Finance" (30% are over $100). Yet here is also found one of the most respected financial newsletters, free for the asking. *Monthly Economics Letter*, published by First National City Bank in New York City, has been around since 1904. Each issue offers several in-depth articles on world economy. A typical example—"The Great Depression: History Never Repeats Itself," a study of the difference between economic factors of the 1930s and today, showing that present conditions can't be measured by a '30s yardstick. (Free from Economics Department, First National City Bank, 399 Park Ave., New York, N.Y. 10022.)

"Find a need and fill it" might be the newsletter credo. New rapport with Peking? Up pops the *China Letter* to inform American businessmen of China trade possibilities. The 1974 energy crisis? In the 1st 90 days, 6 energy letters appeared on the scene. New era of newsletter growth? Of course there's a letter to cover the subject. *The Newsletter on Newsletters* was founded in 1964 to report news of the industry and give case histories of successful newsletters and newsletter management tips. A GREAT VICTORY—NEWSLETTERS ADMITTED TO CONGRESSIONAL GALLERIES, heralded a recent issue. The item tells of triumph after a 10-year battle for accreditation of newsletters in the Periodical Galleries of Congress, giving the industry a new stature in journalism.

Another item in *The Newsletter on Newsletters* applauded the results of an evaluation of 1,402 periodicals by the Periodicals Evaluation Task Force, Dept. of Defense. The study reports, ". . . in an internal communications program . . . newsletters . . . were found to have high readership, credibility, and retention characteristics. . . . They are less formal than 'slick' magazines . . . more easily directed to special groups, and usually are far more timely."

Publishers of investment and business letters derive a healthy income from private consultations with subscribers. Fees run to hundreds of dollars per hour. *The Newsletter on Newsletters* points out another lucrative source—public speaking. Publishers of newsletters on drugs, fashion, and environment are in demand as "celebrity experts" at $300 to $750 per speech. (Subscription is $29 per year. 14 E. Market St., Rhinebeck, N.Y. 12572.)

Some hardheaded readers shun the editorializing, prophesying family of newsletters. They want only solid facts and statistics on what is happening in their specialized fields. One of the most successful entries in the cold-facts arena is *Petroleum Intelligence Weekly*. Publisher Wanda Jablonski, an oilman's daughter, has piped a flow of unembellished information on the oil industry to petroleum executives since 1961. PIW's stark report that the Blank Syndicate paid x dollars a barrel in Kuwait last Tuesday would be dreary reading for many, but the industry studies it like a baseball fan poring over batting averages. (Costs $490 per year from 48 W. 48th St., New York, N.Y.)

An intellectual approach to a controversial subject is taken by *SIECUS Report*, a newsletter on sex information and education, founded in 1966. Primarily aimed at professionals (doctors, teachers, nurses, and clergy), the bimonthly is a valuable reference for parents caught in the hot debate over sex education in schools. *SIECUS* is an acronym for the Sex Information and Education Council of the U.S. In a recent issue, editor Mary Calderone, MD, restated the position of *SIECUS*: The fundamental right of freedom of sexual choice in-

volves responsibilities to self and others which require knowledge and a personal ethical code. (Subscription price to individuals, $9. To institutions, $15. 1855 Broadway, New York, N.Y. 10023.)

Dickens and Waugh, Browning and Steinbeck, Poe and Fitzgerald—newsletters cover them all. In a leisurely, scholarly style, students of literature dissect the works of their favorite authors, review the latest books about them, and report on the newest research. Newsletters in the literary field are usually quarterly, semiannual, or annual offerings. An example is the annual *Sinclair Lewis Newsletter*. Some 20 pages are filled with articles by Lewis devotees. In a recent issue, an article analyzes Lewis's *Dodsworth* in an effort to answer a recurring question: If Lewis's writing was as inept as some of his critics say, how could he ". . . attract and hold millions of readers, win both the Pulitzer and Nobel prizes, and, today, 2 decades after his death, have 10 titles in paperback?" (Subscription $1 per year [1 issue]. Write: English Dept., School of Liberal Arts and Sciences, St. Cloud State College, St. Cloud, Minn. 56301.)

About women, by women, and for women is *The Spokeswoman*. Publisher Susan Davis and editor Karen Wellisch report news of feminist achievement such as the establishment of the First Women's Bank of New York. According to *The Spokeswoman*, the bank is run primarily by women and offers a wide range of banking services tailored to women's needs. Also recorded are battles yet to be won: for example, news of action by feminist groups to gather evidence of discrimination in insurance policies. "The insurance industry," said the monthly newsletter, "is still writing policies as if the typical American family unit is a husband working and the wife staying home to take care of the kids."

A recent issue of *The Spokeswoman* tells of a protest in Indiana by women law students. They levied a charge of sexism against a State bar examination which read in part: "At a State-owned and -operated university in the Middle Western U.S., Clytemnestra Toris is the only thorn in the side of Mr. Strait Mouth, Dean of Students. Ms. (of course!) Toris, a career student, who most recently has been pursuing a graduate degree in 'Mind-Leveling,' publishes and distributes on campus and environs a newspaper 'devoted to the elimination of men.' Despite many counseling sessions, she insists on calling her publication *The Daily Dildo*. . . ." (Founded in 1971, *The Spokeswoman* is available at "$9 a year by individual check—$16 by institutional check." Write to 5464 South Shore Dr., Chicago, Ill. 60615.)

By its very nature a newsletter is a platform for the opinions of its editor. *Washington Spec-*

tator is no exception. Editor Tristram Coffin turns a baleful eye on Capitol politics and is outraged by what he sees. The result is some frank (and sometimes startling) editorializing. The *Washington Spectator* on government spending: "The Federal Government is the greatest wastrel in history. A *Los Angeles Times* series has 'uncovered $1.6 billion in major budget items of dubious value.' Samples: $189 million to build hospitals although existing institutions have a 28% vacancy rate . . . $45 million for a Selective Service System which doesn't draft anyone . . . $296 million for aid to rich school districts. . . . The Government leased a new Washington office building in April with a rent of more than $2 million a year, but 11 of the 15 floors were still vacant in early December [1974].'" (Founded in 1975, *Washington Spectator* is available at $12 a year. Semimonthly. P.O. Box 1750, Annapolis, Md. 21404.)

For those whose newsletter reading interferes with soap-opera viewing, there's a simple solution. *Daytime Serial Newsletter* gives a monthly summary of breathless happenings on a dozen daytime epics. ($8 a year, P.O. Box 6, Mountain View, Calif. 94042.) If you always wanted to run away and join a circus, you can get the latest on clowning for $4 a year from *The Specialty Showman* & *Cavalcade of*

Clowns. (7616 Lindley Ave., Suite 5, Reseda, Calif. 91335.) Or if you're under 4'10" tall, you can join the Little People of America, Inc., and receive their newsletter free. (P.O. Box 126, Owatonna, Minn. 55060.) *The Auto License Plate Collectors Association Newsletter* comes with membership in that organization. (Write P.O. Box 233, Rt. 2, Schwenksville, Pa. 19473.)

Then there's *Last Month's Newsletter* from the Procrastinator's Club of America. (They're at 1111 Broad-Locust Building, Philadelphia, Pa. 19102.) If you want to join, write them for information. There's no hurry. You can do it tomorrow . . . or the next day . . . or the next . . .

TIPS: Many newsletters have introductory trial offers at reduced rates. Check with publishers before subscribing. Consult the reference desk at your public library for *The Standard Directory of Newsletters* (Oxbridge Publishing Co., 1972). If you have an urge to start your own newsletter, read *How to Make $25,000 a Year Publishing Newsletters*, by Brian T. Sheehan (Parker Publishing Co., 1971) and *Newsletter Writing and Publishing —A Practical Guide* by Virginia Burke (Teachers College, Columbia University, 1958).

—W.H.

Tuning in on Television: From 1925 to 1975

1920s

1925—While Dr. Vladimir K. Zworykin was the father of television, the actual age of popular television began when, working independently of each other, J. L. Baird in England and C. F. Jenkins in the U.S. each developed the means to produce a blurry image on a screen. These early images were more like silhouettes, but eventually halftone pictures were created. The parts for Baird's receivers could be bought for home assembly in London for the equivalent of $32 per set.

1927—Herbert Hoover, the U.S. Secretary of Commerce, appeared on the 1st intercity television transmission from Washington, D.C., to New York.

1928—General Electric produced experimental TV programming 3 days a week over WGY-TV in Schenectady, N.Y. The 1st drama was televised live over WGY-TV in Schenectady, N.Y. Two cameras were used to telecast the performance.

1930s

1930—Felix the Cat became television's 1st "star" when he appeared in statue form on

an experimental program on NBC. The figure whirled on a turntable before the camera's eye.

1931—On a historic Tuesday night in July, CBS inaugurated the nation's 1st regular schedule of television broadcasting. New York mayor Jimmy Walker officiated at this telecast. By evening's end, George Gershwin had performed "Lisa," the Boswell Sisters had sung "Heebie-Jeebie Blues," and Kate Smith had belted out "When the Moon Comes Over the Mountain."

1932—CBS Television provided TV's 1st coverage of a presidential election. Although the network televised results well into the night, Franklin D. Roosevelt was pinpointed as the winner over Herbert Hoover early in the evening, collecting 472 electoral votes.

1937—Irvin S. Cobb, the popular American writer and humorist, spoke before an Iconoscope camera in an NBC experimental broadcast. Cobb, attired in a double-breasted suit and a crooked tie, talked about current news events.

1938—Gertrude Lawrence, the British revue and musical star, appeared with Paul McGrath in *Susan and God*, an early NBC telecast direct from the RCA Building in New York City. She was one of the theater's 1st personalities to appear on TV.

1939—Standing in front of a TV camera at the New York World's Fair, David Sarnoff of the Radio Corporation of America stated, "Now we add sight to sound." RCA's version of the commercial TV set was placed on sale—$625 for a 12-inch television screen.

—NBC provided the 1st television sportscast— the Princeton v. Columbia baseball game from Baker Field in New York City. The sole TV camera was placed so close to the baseball diamond that the cameraman spent much of the afternoon dodging foul balls.

—In an empty radio studio in New York's RCA Building, NBC-TV staged a sparring match between 2 boxers, heavyweights Lou Nova and Patsy Perroni, which was the 1st prizefight ever televised. However, 6 weeks later NBC televised the 1st real fight from Yankee Stadium before 16,738 fans when Lou Nova stopped Max Baer with a TKO in the 11th round. About 20,000 New Yorkers gathered in stores to watch the contest.

1940s

1940—The 1st color broadcast in history emanated from the CBS transmitter located atop the Chrysler Building in New York.

1941—The 1st TV commercial—an advertisement for a Bulova wristwatch—was aired over WNBT in New York. As the camera focused in for a close-up of the watch's face, an announcer read the time—10 minutes after 10 P.M. The ad cost Bulova $9.

—On the evening of December 7, just hours after the bombing of Pearl Harbor, CBS presented a 90-minute documentary about the attack and America's reaction to it. The program was TV's most impressive coverage to date of a major breaking news story. It was followed the next day by America's entry into the war.

1942—Television joined the war effort with programs like NBC's "TV Training," designed specifically for air-raid wardens in New York. CBS promoted war bonds, using guest stars like Dorothy McGuire, Jack Dempsey, and Andre Kostelanetz.

1945—Mrs. Franklin D. Roosevelt, widowed for less than one month, gave an inspiring speech when she made her TV debut on V-E Day. Wearing black and sitting poised at a desk flanked by 2 American flags, Mrs. Roosevelt spoke over NBC's television station WNBT in New York about the success of America's unified war effort.

1947—With the help of Uncle Bob Smith and Clarabell the Clown, freckle-faced marionette

Howdy Doody began entertaining the nation's children on NBC. Youngsters sitting in the Peanut Gallery participated in the show.

—TV brought wrestling into America's living rooms, and made Gorgeous George one of TV's earliest celebrities. George's peroxided blond hair was always perfectly set thanks to a permanent wave, and while he earned $70,000 a year, sportswriter Red Smith was outraged enough to say of him: "Groucho Marx is prettier, Sonny Tufts a more gifted actor, Connie Mack a better rassler and the Princeton Triangle Club has far superior female impersonators."

—The rough-and-tumble Roller Derby came to TV, saving it from financial bankruptcy. Thousands of Americans were fascinated by the fast skating and frequent brawls.

—TV news took on a serious tone when Douglas Edwards was hired as anchorman of the "CBS Evening News." In his 1st year, Edwards described major news events like the Marshall Plan proposal and the passage of the controversial Taft-Hartley Act.

—NBC telecast the World Series for the 1st time, with 4 cities—New York, Washington, Philadelphia, and Schenectady—receiving the transmission. The New York Yankees, managed by Bucky Harris, beat the Brooklyn Dodgers in 7 games.

—The durable news interview show "Meet the Press" moved from radio to TV, with Martha Roundtree as its moderator and Lawrence E. Spivak as its producer.

1948—Bill Boyd, whose motion picture career was floundering, jumped aboard a white horse and galloped into TV popularity on NBC's "Hopalong Cassidy." When Boyd sold the rights to the show several years later, he reportedly received $70 million.

—Newspaper columnist Ed Sullivan hosted one of TV's earliest variety shows, "Toast of the Town." The debut program had a budget of only $500, and guests on that 1st "really big shew" included Dean Martin and Jerry Lewis, composers Rodgers and Hammerstein, and a singing fireman named Fred Kohoman.

—Milton Berle debuted on NBC-TV, 1st emceeing 3 variety shows and then starring in his own series, "The Texaco Star Theatre." All across the nation, Tuesday night became "Milton Berle Night," and Berle eventually appeared in a record 400 shows, attired in everything from women's clothes to a Howdy Doody outfit. He earned $6,500 a week.

1949—Jackie Gleason starred as the original Chester Riley in "The Life of Riley." The series flopped and left the air, to be revived 4 years later in a popular version starring William Bendix.

—Sid Caesar and Imogene Coca, spoofing

everything from operas like *Rigoletto* to films like *From Here to Eternity*, starred in NBC's "Your Show of Shows."

—"Captain Video," a low-budget show with cardboard props and scenery, was TV's 1st science-fiction program. Although it was shoddily produced, the show gained an enormous following, with former radio actor Al Hodge as its star.

—"Kukla, Fran and Ollie" had as many adult viewers as children, all attracted by the high-voiced and big-nosed Kukla, Ollie the good-natured dragon, and Fran Allison.

—Gertrude Berg, who created and starred in the radio serial "The Goldbergs," brought the show to TV, where it was an instant hit. Cast as the lovable Jewish mother Molly Goldberg, Gertrude Berg invented Goldberg-isms like "Enter, whoever," "So who's to know?" and "If it's nobody, I'll call back."

—The Hollywood Athletic Club was the site of the 1st Annual Emmy Awards, which went practically ignored by the media. The winner of the "Outstanding Personality" award was Shirley Dinsdale and her puppet Judy Splinters.

1950s

1950—The popular radio show "Your Hit Parade" moved to NBC-TV with the hit songs of the era being sung by Snooky Lanson, Dorothy Collins, and Eileen Wilson. As each show ended, the Lucky Strike Hit Parade chorus harmonized "So long for a while . . . that's all the songs for a while. . . ."

—Groucho Marx introduced the 1st comedy show in a quiz show format, "You Bet Your Life." Bedecked in a polka-dot bow tie and with his ever present cigar, Groucho would utter one-liners and collect a $25,000-per-week salary. Not satisfied with the TV medium, Groucho said, "Intellectually, it's a joke. But unfortunately, it reflects the taste of the U.S. public."

—"It's a bird . . . it's a plane . . . it's Superman!" Those words introduced the 1st —and every subsequent—"The Adventures of Superman" show, with Clark Kent dividing his time between his heroic superhuman deeds and writing for the *Daily Planet* newspaper.

—NBC originated the 1st late-night variety-talk show, which was to change forever America's sleeping habits. The program, "Broadway Open House," aired at 11 P.M. and had 2 hosts, Jerry Lester and Morey Amsterdam.   •

—Flea catchers and shoelace threaders were the stars of "What's My Line?," where panelists tried to guess the strange occupa-tions of the show's guests. John Daly was the

host, and panelists on the 1st program were Arlene Francis, Harold Hoffman, Dr. Richard Hoffman, and Louis Untermeyer.

1951—Edward R. Murrow narrated the CBS documentary series "See It Now," featuring coverage and analysis of news events. The premiere show began with a split screen show-ing New York's Brooklyn Bridge and San Francisco's Golden Gate Bridge. As Murrow said, "For the 1st time in the history of man we are able to look out at both the Atlantic and Pacific coasts of this great country at the same time . . . no journalistic age was ever given a weapon for truth with quite the scope of this fledgling television."

—Both CBS and NBC telecast the U.S. Senate hearings on crime in America. Underworld character Frank Costello refused to allow his face to be telecast, so the cameras focused on only his hands as he answered questions from Sen. Estes Kefauver.

—Dinah Shore starred in "The Chevy Show," a 15-minute, twice-a-day program that became a weekly one-hour show in 1956. Dinah Shore, who advised her audience to "See the U.S.A. in your Chevrolet," finished each show by blowing a big kiss.

1952—Garry Moore moderated the popular "I've Got a Secret," where original panel-ists Bill Cullen, Henry Morgan, Jayne Mead-ows, and Faye Emerson tried to guess the "secrets" that contestants were hiding. Typical secrets were: "I'm understudy for the star of Broadway's biggest play" and "I'm wearing red flannel underwear beneath my evening gown."

—With Badge 714 firmly in place, Jack Webb began solving crimes for the Los Angeles Police Dept. week after week on "Dragnet." Everyone was soon humming the show's theme song, "Dum de dum dum," or saying, "Just the facts, ma'am."

—Ralph Edwards began surprising famous personalities and recounting their life stories on NBC's "This Is Your Life." The honored personality of the 1st telecast was Laura Marr Stone, a 73-year-old pioneer woman from Kansas.

—The 1st telecast of the early morning *Today* show went out to 26 NBC network stations. There was only one paid commercial on that debut airing. But its popularity grew quickly, and it wasn't long before one viewer wrote to the show asking that they please do some-thing backward since he always watched the program in his bathroom mirror while shaving.

—All 3 networks covered the 1952 presidential nominating conventions in Chicago, with 70 million Americans watching. Viewers saw the hectic events at a political confab and weren't at all surprised when an exhausted announcer said, "We're waiting for the general [Eisenhower] now. We don't know when he'll come out. And frankly, I don't care anymore."

—Adlai Stevenson preempted "I Love Lucy" to make a political speech, prompting one viewer to write to him, "I love Lucy, I like Ike, drop dead."

—Vice-presidential candidate Richard Nixon, charged with accepting illegal campaign funds, went on TV to defend himself in his so-called "Checkers" speech. Nixon declared, "Pat and I have the satisfaction that every dime that we've got is honestly ours. I should say this—that Pat doesn't have a mink coat, but she does have a respectable Republican cloth coat. . . ."

—"The Jackie Gleason Show" debuted on CBS. The rotund comedian soon had the nation rollicking with lines like "Away-y-y we go!" and characters like Reggie Van Gleason, the Poor Soul, Joe the Bartender, and eventually Ralph Kramden.

1953—"Goodyear Playhouse" presented its best TV play, *Marty*, the story of a lonely man—played by Rod Steiger—who sought comfort from a woman who was, like Marty himself, a social misfit. Paddy Chayefsky, who wrote the hour-long teleplay, later expanded his script to a full-length film, which won the Academy Award as Best Picture in 1956.

—"Person to Person" premiered on the CBS network. With Edward R. Murrow as host, viewers were able to visit the homes of famous personalities like Harry Truman, Robert Kennedy, Marlon Brando, and Jackie Robinson. Over the years, viewers were treated to Beatrice Lillie demonstrating how she put on her fur coat, the Duchess of Windsor demonstrating how she played jacks, and Michael Todd demonstrating how he kissed Elizabeth Taylor.

—Millions of American TV viewers followed the pregnancy of Lucille Ball on the "I Love Lucy" show. When Lucy actually became pregnant, the show's producers wrote her pregnancy into the program. Viewers became addicted to the show as they watched Lucy grow in size and zaniness.

—Red Skelton, a radio and film comedian, successfully switched to TV. He brought pantomime to the video tube, earning him the title of the Marcel Marceau of Television. Skelton was constantly creating new characters for himself, including Freddy the Freeloader, Clem Kadiddlehopper, Cauliflower McPugg, Willy Lump-Lump, the Drunk, and the Yokel.

1954—The Army-McCarthy hearings had TV viewers glued to their seats, as Sen. Joseph McCarthy's Senate committee probed alleged un-American activities in various government agencies. McCarthy's controversial probing techniques were finally challenged by army civilian attorney Joseph Welch, who dramatically confronted the senator with the question, "Have you no sense of decency, sir? At long last, have you no sense of decency?"

—"See It Now" presented a controversial report that discredited Sen. Joseph McCarthy's communist-searching investigation. Edward R. Murrow concluded the program by declaring: "He didn't create this situation of fear; he merely exploited it. . . . Cassius was right: 'The fault, dear Brutus, is not in our stars but in ourselves.' "

—The Academy Awards presentation was telecast for the 1st time. When the show ran overtime, William Holden was cut off the air in the middle of his acceptance speech for the Best Actor award for *Stalag 17*. Unhappy viewers had to find out in the newspapers the next day who won awards for the Best Actress—Audrey Hepburn—and Best Picture—*From Here to Eternity*. Five years later (1959), when *Gigi* won Best Picture, the last Oscar was handed out 22 minutes before the show ended and the list of credits was run 11 times to fill up the remaining time.

1955—Lawrence Welk brought his champagne music and his bubble machine to TV as a summer replacement show. "The Lawrence Welk Show" is still on the air, although many of its original cast members—Alice Lon, Dick Dale, the Lennon Sisters, Tiny Little, Jr.—have left the program.

—Children across the country learned how to spell "Mickey Mouse" when they sang along with the theme song of ABC's weekday "Mickey Mouse Club." With Mouseketeer ears perched firmly in place, millions of youngsters never missed a show.

—The 1st big-money quiz show, "The $64,000 Question," debuted on CBS with Hal March as its host. Closeted inside an isolation booth, contestants answered questions about their speciality—Dr. Joyce Brothers on prizefighting, New York cobbler Gino Prato on opera, and actor Vincent Price on art.

—When the family situation comedy "Father Knows Best" was canceled on March 27 after 6 months on the air, viewers around the country protested vehemently to CBS. The public outrage so impressed rival network NBC that it had the show on its own stations on August 31, where it remained for 3 years before switching back to CBS.

—The "Mike Wallace Interviews" show on CBS established Wallace as one of the most probing interrogators on TV. He asked questions so soul-searching that several lawsuits were filed after subjects realized just how much of themselves they had revealed. Only once over the years was Wallace truly silenced by a guest's reply. He had asked radical magazine editor Paul Krassner, "What about all those 4-letter words in your magazine?" Krassner replied, "Which ones do you mean, Mike?" Wallace was speechless.

—Mary Martin, soaring through the air with the help of some carefully camouflaged wires, starred in *Peter Pan*, the 1st network presentation of a full Broadway production. One out of every 2 Americans watched the show.

—Despite the show's title, "You'll Never Get Rich," Phil Silvers was never at a loss for get-rich-quick schemes on his CBS program. Playing Sgt. Ernest G. Bilko, Silvers ran everything from a mini-casino and a dance hall to a beauty parlor in his barracks.

—The 1st "adult" Western, "Gunsmoke," debuted on CBS, and Marshal Matt Dillon soon became an American institution.

—Judy Garland's long-awaited television debut finally occurred in her own special, titled "The Ford Star Jubilee." With her hair cropped very short and wearing a long evening gown, she sang many of the songs that had brought her fame, including "Over the Rainbow."

—Bob Keeshan, who had played Clarabell the Clown in the popular "Howdy Doody" show, debuted as Captain Kangaroo on CBS. His activities for children and his gentle manner of speech made him an early morning favorite.

—"Alfred Hitchcock Presents" appeared on CBS, offering a series of spine-tingling mysteries. Hitchcock was quoted as saying, "Television has brought murder back into the home, where it belongs."

1956—Rod Serling scripted *Requiem for a Heavyweight*, which CBS aired on "Playhouse 90" and which was a phenomenal success. It told the story of the seamier side of boxing, and starred Jack Palance and Ed Wynn.

—"The Ed Sullivan Show" played host to Elvis Presley, who made 3 appearances for an unprecedented $50,000. Presley was shown only from the waist up. Sullivan blocked out the singer's hips as they swiveled to the beat of "Hound Dog" and "Heartbreak Hotel."

1957—Robert Kennedy, a young New York lawyer, was counsel to the Senate Rackets Committee which investigated links between the underworld and unions. Kennedy's brother, John, was a member of that committee, and the siblings received national attention through televised questioning of organized-crime figures like "Tony Ducks" Corallo and "Johnny Dio" Dioguardo.

—"Perry Mason," a series based on Erle Stan-

ley Gardner's famous character, came to TV with Raymond Burr as its star. Aided by his loyal secretary, Della Street—played by Barbara Hale—Perry never lost a case.

—The children's classic, *Cinderella*, was adapted for TV by Rodgers and Hammerstein. It appeared on CBS with a cast that included Julie Andrews as Cinderella, Ilka Chase as the stepmother, and Edie Adams as the fairy godmother.

—One of television's longest-running shows, "American Bandstand," debuted on ABC in 1957. While local Philadelphia teen-agers danced the hand jive and the twist, idols Frankie Avalon and Fabian sang forgettable songs like "Bobby Sox to Stockings" and "Turn Me Loose."

—James Garner brought a new style of Western hero to the small screen as the star of "Maverick." Unlike other TV cowboys, Garner was a cowardly rogue who hated the outdoors, couldn't ride a horse, and was notoriously slow on the draw.

1958—Scandal rocked the TV game show "Twenty-One" when it was revealed that the show's producers had given some contestants the correct answers to make the show more interesting. Charles Van Doren, an English instructor at Columbia University, was one of those who had been primed with answers to the show's questions. The scandal brought big-money game shows to an end.

—Fred Astaire made his TV debut dancing with Barrie Chase on the special "An Evening with Fred Astaire."

1959—Robert Stack—with machine gun in hand—starred as Eliot Ness in the CBS show "The Untouchables," which re-created the lives of the nation's most notorious mobsters.

1960s

1960—The Leonard Bernstein concerts on CBS turned the flamboyant conductor of the New York Philharmonic into a TV celebrity. His dashing podium gestures were his most striking trait.

—TV crews filmed Nikita Khrushchev and Fidel Castro embracing each other and walking along New York's streets. Both world leaders were in the U.S. for a UN meeting.

—David Susskind, whose "Open End" interview show originated from WNTA in New York, talked with Nikita Khrushchev in an unprecedented American TV interview with the Russian Premier.

—Three years after taking over as host of "The Tonight Show," Jack Paar walked off the program after explaining to his audience that NBC censors had "unfairly" deleted one of his better jokes the previous night. Said Paar,

"There must be a better way to make a living than this." Paar, however, returned 5 weeks later.

—Possibly the most dramatic political confrontations in TV history were the debates between presidential candidates John Kennedy and Richard Nixon. In the 1st of 4 debates, Nixon looked like a heavy because of poor makeup and also lost ground by refusing to argue with Kennedy. Some political experts consider that 1st debate the turning point in the close election.

1961—The largest daytime TV audience in history watched astronaut Alan B. Shepard, Jr., soar into space for his 15-minute ride in a rocket-powered capsule. All 3 networks covered the event, beginning early in the morning in preparation for the 9:34 A.M. (EST) blast-off.

—President John Kennedy instituted the 1st live televised presidential press conferences. He displayed a keen wit and an impressive command of information.

—Jackie Gleason hosted his own quiz show, "You're in the Picture." The show's debut was so bad that the embarrassed comedian spent the entire 2nd show apologizing for the 1st one.

—Jack Paar taped 3 episodes of "The Tonight Show" in West Berlin near the East-West border, where he interviewed many soldiers of the U.S. 6th Infantry. Paar attracted high ratings as well as anger from congressmen who felt he was using the Berlin crisis for his own gain. One magazine accused Paar of nearly turning the Cold War into a hot one by endangering the delicate situation in Berlin.

1962—Jacqueline Kennedy took the nation on a personally guided tour of the White House in a 60-minute special produced by CBS and aired on all 3 networks. An estimated 80 million people saw the show.

—Johnny Carson assumed the hosting duties of "The Tonight Show" on NBC. Groucho Marx flew to New York from California to introduce Carson on his 1st show. The guests that night were Joan Crawford, Rudy Vallee, Tony Bennett, and Mel Brooks. One of Carson's early monologue jokes was, "Thank you—I'd blow you a kiss but I heard about an entertainer who did that and fell in love with his hand."

—"The Virginian," a Western based on Owen Wister's novel, debuted on NBC as the 1st 90-minute regular series.

—ABC found itself the target of considerable criticism after airing the news special "The Political Obituary of Richard Nixon." The show included an interview with Alger Hiss, who had been convicted of perjury. Some sponsors tried to cancel their contracts with the network after the show was telecast.

1963—A videotape of an opening-night Broadway play based on the Sacco-Vanzetti case was aired on TV stations owned by the Westinghouse Broadcasting Corporation. It was the 1st time a Broadway premiere had been televised.

—"The Beverly Hillbillies" jumped to the top of the TV ratings, although critics attacked it as being "insipid."

—On November 22, "As the World Turns" was interrupted on CBS by the following news bulletin delivered by Walter Cronkite: "In Dallas, Tex., 3 shots were fired at President Kennedy's motorcade in downtown Dallas. The 1st reports say that President Kennedy has been seriously wounded by this shooting." Immediately after the assassination, all TV networks canceled their regular programming for a weekend of special news programs and memorial services.

1964—Commercials seemed more interesting and creative than before, including Alka-Seltzer's "No matter what shape your stomach's in" ad, which employed quick cuts and soft sell. There were also campaign spots promoting President Lyndon Johnson created by the Doyle Dane Bernbach agency. The ads were more *against* Sen. Barry Goldwater than *for* Johnson. One of them showed a small girl picking petals from a daisy while a voice began a countdown. Then there was an atomic explosion and darkness, followed by an announcer stating: "These are the stakes—to make a world in which all God's children can live, or go into the dark."

—Daytime serials came to nighttime TV when "Peyton Place" debuted on ABC 2 nights each week.

1965—The Early Bird communications satellite led to some provocative and expensive TV programming. In the premiere one-hour Early Bird program—seen by 300 million people in Europe and the Americas—there were reports from the Dominican Republic, an appearance by Pope Paul VI at the Vatican, a statement by Martin Luther King, Jr., from Philadelphia, a shot of a heart surgery in progress in Houston, a bullfight in Spain, and 6 other events on location.

—TV's 1st black hero, Bill Cosby, costarred with Robert Culp in the adventure series "I Spy." Cosby and Culp were cast as CIA agents.

1966—When the spacecraft *Gemini 8*, with astronauts Neil Armstrong and David Scott aboard, was forced to make an emergency landing, ABC and NBC interrupted their regular programming—"Batman" and "The Virginian"—to cover the unfolding news story. The interruption caused public outrage from viewers whose favorite programs were preempted. Telephones in New York and

Los Angeles were flooded for hours with complaints.

—The wedding of Patrick Nugent and Luci Baines Johnson was televised by all 3 networks. The pompous ceremony, which was held at Washington's Roman Catholic Shrine of the Immaculate Conception, attracted protesters who were angered that the President's daughter chose to be married on the anniversary of the atomic bombing of Japan.

1967—Hal Holbrook brought Samuel Clemens to life in "Mark Twain Tonight," one of the most highly praised specials of the year.

—Chet Huntley and David Brinkley, an inseparable news team since 1956, parted for 2 weeks when Brinkley refused to cross a picket line of striking TV performers. The ratings of their nightly NBC news show dropped during Brinkley's absence.

—"Batman" reigned as one of the top-rated shows in the U.S., and capes became an "in" fashion item.

1968—"Laugh-In," a comedy show starring Dan Rowan and Dick Martin, became the nation's most popular series just weeks after its debut. These hour-long shows, each featuring about 350 zany sight gags and rapid-fire jokes, made popular such phrases as "Sock it to me!"

—TV cameras had been broadcasting election night returns of the California primary live from the Ambassador Hotel in Los Angeles. Suddenly TV watchers were told that Sen. Robert Kennedy had been shot off camera. As coverage of the tragic event continued through the night, NBC newsman John Chancellor said, "I don't know about the rest of you, but in the last few hours I seem to have lost part of my self-respect."

—Television audiences witnessed the violence on the streets of Chicago during the 1968 Democratic presidential nominating convention. Student demonstrators as well as newsmen were beaten by Chicago police in the shocking melee.

1969—William O. Johnson, Jr., in his book *Super Spectator and the Electric Lilliputians*, estimated that the average American human being will spend 9 years of his or her life watching television between the ages of 2 and 65.

—U.S. Vice-President Spiro Agnew denounced TV network news as biased and unfair. He urged the public to "register their complaints on bias through mail to the networks and phone calls to local stations." Although the subsequent letter writing and telephone campaign supported Agnew, the press itself criticized the Vice-President for trying to intimidate a medium dependent upon government licensing.

—"The Smothers Brothers Comedy Hour,"

designed to appeal to young adults, was canceled by CBS. The show had enjoyed high ratings but CBS was disturbed by the program's controversial subject material. The network finally scratched the show when the Smothers Brothers satirized U.S. senator John Pastore, who was investigating TV programming, and when guest comedian David Steinberg performed a skit about Jonah and the whale. The show's cancellation sparked numerous censorship debates. Four years later, the Smothers Brothers won a $766,300 settlement from CBS for breach of contract.

—An estimated 600 million people in 49 nations watched the live telecast of astronaut Neil Armstrong taking man's 1st step on the moon. The worldwide linkup cost $55 billion and involved about 40,000 TV technicians and other personnel.

—A hook-nosed, long-haired, ukulele-playing singer named Tiny Tim was married "live" on "The Tonight Show" before one of the largest late-night TV audiences ever. His bride, Miss Vicki, wore a $2,500 Victorian wedding gown, and Tiny Tim paraded down the aisle swinging a hand-carved walking stick. They were divorced in January, 1974.

1970s

1970—Professional football reached its greatest viewing audience on Sunday, January 11, when 70 million people watched the Super Bowl game between the Minnesota Vikings and Kansas City Chiefs from New Orleans. "How much *is* 70 million?" asked author William O. Johnson, Jr. "It is 450 times the population of Athens when Plato lived there . . . it is equal to the number of tourists who visit the Mammoth Cave over 140 years . . . it is 4 New Yorks plus 7 Chicagos plus 140 Sheboygans." As to the commercials for that game, the cost was $3,333.33⅓ per second. The Hartford Insurance Company paid $200,000 for one 60-second commercial. Incidentally, those 70 million viewers saw Kansas City whip Minnesota, 23–7.

—Diahann Carroll starred in "Julia," the 1st TV situation comedy that featured a black in the title role.

1971—Cigarette advertising on TV ended on January 1, banned by government edict because of the health hazards of smoking.

—Controversy raged when CBS presented the documentary "The Selling of the Pentagon," which dealt with the public-relations activities of the Dept. of Defense. Some government officials said that CBS had made false charges and had distorted the statements of Pentagon officials. When a House subcommittee subpoenaed CBS papers pertinent to the show, the network refused to supply them. After heated debate, the House voted not to cite

CBS for contempt, and the issue died in the Commerce Committee.

—Archie Bunker, played by Carroll O'Connor, became America's most popular bigot after CBS aired "All in the Family." Despite its immediate popularity, the show was severely attacked for its comic use of racial slurs.

—America's 3 TV networks covered President Nixon's historic trip to China. Viewers were given their 1st look at the communist nation from 18 different locations, including Peking, Shanghai, and the Great Wall of China.

1972—"The Waltons," a series about Depression-era life in rural America, debuted on CBS and became one of the nation's most popular shows.

—ABC's live coverage of the Summer Olympics in Munich brought viewers the unexpected and dramatic news sequences of the Arab terrorists' murderous attack upon Israeli athletes.

1973—Bowing to pressures, CBS granted the U. S. Catholic Conference free TV time to state their antiabortion stance after the "Maude" series aired a 2-part episode about abortion.

—The Public Broadcasting System presented the 12-part "An American Family," a documentary about the daily life of the Louds, a troubled but well-to-do California family. The show was shot over a 7-month period.

—During the spring and summer, the TV networks provided live coverage of the hearings of the Senate Select Committee on Presidential Campaign Activities—also called the Watergate hearings. The nation heard conflicting stories of the Watergate scandal, including former White House counsel John Dean's testimony that President Nixon did not "realize or appreciate at any time the implications of his involvement."

1974—TV stations throughout the country interrupted their regular programming to telecast the resignation speech of President Richard Nixon—the 1st time an American President had ever resigned. In his speech, Nixon told the nation, "I regret deeply any injuries that may have been done in the course of the events that led to this decision." The next day, as TV cameras followed citizen Nixon's return to his home in San Clemente, Gerald Ford was inaugurated as the 38th President. Ford declared, "My fellow Americans, our long national nightmare is over."

—Frank Sinatra's short-lived "retirement" officially ended with a live one-man concert at Madison Square Garden, televised as "Sinatra—The Main Event." Eleven TV cameras covered the performance, capturing the crooner and his interaction with fans.

1975—Cable television spread rapidly, allowing for better reception in isolated areas and creating a proliferation of small, independent TV stations. In Los Angeles, for example, where cable viewers have 17 stations to choose from, it is possible to see programs in 5 languages (English, Spanish, Japanese, Chinese, and Korean), as well as news reports for deaf people.

—R.T. and M.T.

Television around the World

Africa

African television has developed slowly, since much of the continent's climate is devastating to delicate equipment, its population by and large is too poor to own sets, and its nations are unable to budget for well-appointed stations. Since its beginning in 1959, in Nigeria, TV has been almost exclusively a commercial venture, but because service is basically available only in the capital cities of Africa—and to those rich enough to afford sets—revenues from advertising are minimal. Nigeria, Ethiopia, Zambia, Kenya, and Ghana all are too impoverished to produce more than 40% of their own programming, and that forces them to fall back on American importations like "Land of the Giants," "Bonanza," and "UFO." Furthermore, government censorship is so extreme in Kenya that stealing, fighting, shooting, and killing are banned from the airwaves, which limits importations there as well.

The most ambitious project in Africa at the moment is the attempt to create a nationwide educational network. A collaborative effort between UNESCO and the Ivory Coast, the program will expend $500 million over a period of about 12 years to produce primary-school-level shows domestically. The programs will reach an estimated half million children by 1976. Still, in the words of Nairobi's Morris Mwendar: "Most of us have no idea what other TV services are doing; we ought to be working with them on coproductions, trying to create television that is truly African in character."

Australia

A viewing public of about 7 million living in Adelaide, Melbourne, Brisbane, and Sydney has the choice of 4 channels when it sits down to the telly: 3 commercial stations and a government-sponsored public-service channel. With the commercial stations alone broadcasting some 17 hours every day, the overall viewing time in a city like Sydney can run to about 450 hours a week, as contrasted with a maximum of 200 hours in most European countries. Quantity, however, is not quality. Almost half of these 450 hours is spent screening imports like "I Love Lucy," "The Saint," or "Ironside," and local programming is littered with police shows and W.W. II dramas. One channel in Sydney has developed "No. 96"—a kind of "blue" soap opera concerning gangbangs, adultery, and incest as found in Sydney's Paddington district. While full frontal nudity is still taboo, even the more respectable shows are spiced up with total rear and waist-up frontal nudity. "We're not making great TV," explains one TV executive. "We are asked to produce a program that appeals to a mass market and makes money. That is what we set out to do."

CANADA

Canadian television is involved in an uphill struggle to create and maintain its identity against the barrage of U.S. programs it receives. Since 1968, Canadian channels have attempted to produce almost all of their own prime-time programming, but cable TV (subscribed to by about 25% of all Canadian homes in 1971) undermines their efforts. In the early 1970s, Canadians were devoting about 70% of their viewing time to U.S. stations, virtually ignoring their own 35 public and 60 private stations. Among Canada's most popular domestic programs, outside of ice hockey, are the *teleromans* such as "*Rue des Pignons*," about life in and around Montreal; or the variety program "*Les Beaux Dimanches*," which weekly presents an original play by a Canadian author; or Steinbeck's *Of Mice and Men*; or a ballet. Toronto's channel 79 has developed a show called "The Baby Blue Movie," which tops Friday-night ratings by screening such international fare as *The Conjugal Bed*, *Naked and Free*, or *I Am Curious* (*Yellow*).

CHINA

From 1958, when the Central People's Television Broadcasting Station opened in Peking, through the late 1960s, the development of television in China was a slow, regional business, and in 1967, with the advent of the Red Guard, it all but disappeared. Broadcasts were on the air again 3 or 4 nights a week by 1970, but there was little outside of newscasts, Peking operas, and long periods when Mao's thoughts

were flashed on the screen. While recently, with the coverage of live events such as the May Day parade or Peking's international Ping-Pong tournament, Chinese TV has been visibly advancing technically, and while "Red Flag Canal," a documentary on the struggle to build a dam in Honan province, has received acclaim from all over the world, television remains little more than an electronic newspaper in China.

EASTERN EUROPE

Television has become commonplace in Eastern European homes, with a ratio of one set to every 6 people. It is State-controlled in the U.S.S.R. satellite countries, managed by broadcasting councils made up of representatives from the trade unions, State officials, and professionals from the fields of journalism, the theater, and broadcasting. Nearly all the countries rely heavily on license fees, with a limited amount of income from advertising (usually 2 or 3 5-minute blocs are allowed between early evening shows) to fatten their budgets.

"Citizen's Forum," a series originally developed in preinvasion Czechoslovakia, is appearing all over Eastern Europe. The original Czech program devoted an hour and a half regularly to debates that pitted government ministers and experts against a studio audience, with a half-hour follow-up the next week. Time and again, a minister proved to be totally ignorant of the subject he was supposed to control: Bureaucracy was unmasked. As Jiri Pelikan, the director of Czech TV from 1963 until the Russian invasion, put it: "It was a scandal. Here were ministers revealed on television as being quite incapable of government."

ENGLAND

In November, 1936, the BBC began broadcasting Britain's 1st regular television service from the Alexandria Palace in London. There were only 100 television sets in England at the time. Since then, a commercial network has gone on the air, and the BBC itself has split into 2 separate and distinct networks. A unique system has resulted from this situation: The BBC is both competitive with the independent TV network and complementary within itself. Working together, BBC 1 and BBC 2 have created viewing fare like "Elizabeth R," "That Was the Week That Was," "Masterpiece Theatre," "Till Death Do Us Part" (the original of "All in the Family"), and many other world-renowned series. In addition, they have helped to bring playwrights like Harold Pinter and David Mercer—and directors like Ken Russell—to light. Both stations are funded out of annual license fees (about $17 for black-and-white sets, $29 for color). The average Englishman watches 3 hours of television daily.

ITV, while it is a commercial network, operates under strictly regulated conditions. A Code of Advertising Standards and Practices, for instance, provides for the review of all advertisement scripts in advance of their production, rejecting those which are judged misleading. And to make sure that its programming policy remains its own, ITV sells "spots" rather than allowing direct sponsoring of the program it airs, thus making the influence of advertisers minimal on program content.

FRANCE

France has 2 channels now, with another expected by 1976, and these networks work together producing complementary schedules: A thriller is screened on one channel, for instance, while a documentary is broadcast on the other. To deal with censorship, the French have developed the *rectangle blanc* method: the projection of a small white rectangle in one corner of the screen whenever an "adults only" program is being televised. Ideally, this method leaves censorship where it belongs: in the hands of the viewers of France's 12½ million television sets.

GERMANY

West Germany has 10 television stations, the richest public-service network in the world, with its stations gaining the bulk of their monies from limited quotas of advertising (about 20 minutes a day) and annual license fees. One of the highest-rated programs in West Germany is *"Aktenzeichen Xy . . . Ungelöst"* ("File on Xy . . . Unsolved"), an interesting experiment in audience participation broadcast live 10 times a year. During the course of each program 3 *actual* unsolved crimes are presented in dramatized form, then discussed with the detectives who worked on the case. After pictures of the criminals and/or items stolen are shown, accompanied by verbal descriptions, the viewing audience is asked to phone in any vital information that it might have pertaining to the case. Successful in terms of ratings, it has been equally successful in solving crimes. The 36 million viewers have helped solve more than 80 of the 1st 153 cases presented, and have helped the police capture 82 out of 125 suspects.

The East Germans also have a passion for thrillers. A 3-part drama called "The Lady of Genoa," however, dealt not merely with a plot to steal a painting, but tried to expose the cutthroat unscrupulousness of the international art market.

ITALY

The last major nation in Europe without a color TV system, Italy has 2 channels which, together, broadcast only about 11 hours of material each day. Within those 11 hours, 2 interesting phenomena have developed.

First, there is the rapport between the film and television industries which has provided Italian TV with film from directors like De Sica, Rossellini, Fellini, and the French director Robert Bresson.

The 2nd phenomenon is *Carosello*, a series developed in 1959, just one year after TV got its start in Italy. This 11-minute series captures more than 20 million viewers every night, and all for a bloc of 5 2½-minute commercials. Using an extremely soft sell, most of the advertisements assume the form of short playlets, followed by a brief and gentle reminder about the commodity being peddled. *Carosello* has employed world-renowned directors like Claude Lelouch and Richard Lester when advertising its products. Even Gillo Pontecorvo, of *Battle of Algiers* fame, has made a contribution. "We have managed," boasts one program executive, "to turn advertising into art."

Italy's 2 channels are a government monopoly, controlled by the nation's leading political party, the Christian Democrats, and by the Roman Catholic Church.

JAPAN

Japan, with a daily TV audience of over 31 million, has a TV system noted basically for its technical flourishes. NHK, the public-service corporation, has developed to the point where computers do most of the work. Two IBM 360 computers handle transmission for both of NHK's TV stations and its 3 radio stations as well, cutting programs in on schedule while cutting off others. And with their "Random Resources Selector," live newscasts can be managed by computer to the extent of cutting in a camera on a particular newscaster, or even handling live satellite transmissions. The latest innovation: letting the computers memorize the stations' whole film library so that any time a director wants a particular stock shot (a particular angle of a detonating A-bomb, for instance), he/she has only to press a button, rather than scan miles of videotape.

There is a slough of violence and sex on the Japanese screen, typified by samurai dramas and "hard training" programs. One quiz show, since removed from the air, penalized losing contestants by slowly snipping away their clothing with scissors. With Japan's "simultaneous" advertising (commercials that are superimposed over the program as it progresses) one doesn't have to endure the suspense of waiting through a commercial break to see the resolution of a drama.

LATIN AMERICA

Television is State-owned in only 3 of the Latin American countries—Cuba, Chile, and Colombia—with the rest of the nations operating on some sort of commercial basis. Venezuela has one government-owned station and 6 privately owned ones. Ecuador has 10 privately owned stations. Even so, it is not unusual to see the State step in. In Mexico, after the TV coverage of the student riots of 1968, the Government demanded, and received, 13% of all broadcasting time to explain its policies to the people.

The most prevalent type of program in Latin America is the *tele-novela*, essentially a soap opera. Virtually every country in Latin America bombards its TV viewers with these melodramas, most of them about poor country girls who move to the big city and suffer a series of trials and tribulations. A Buenos Aires producer has summed up the meaning of television in many neighboring countries, saying: "Novelas keep them mesmerized. For an hour or so they forget the conditions in which they live—perhaps it even stops them making revolutions."

Brazil, the land of machismo, has one female news broadcaster—Miss Universe of 1963. One of Mexico's most popular programs is *"Plaza Sesamo"*—yes, that's "Sesame Street."

MIDDLE EAST

Television in the Middle East is little more than blocks of political propaganda spaced between episodes of "Marcus Welby," "The Avengers," and "I Love Lucy," the UHF Israel squaring away against the VHF Egyptians, Jordanians, and Lebanese. In Israel, the late Ben-Gurion was opposed to television from the beginning and it is likely that the only reason the Israelis got into TV at all was as a response to telecasts immediately outside its borders, where Jordan has one station, Kuwait has one, and South Arabia has 5. During a 1973 television strike and video blackout, Israelis read Jordan's TV schedule in the Jerusalem *Post* and watched Jordan's broadcasts on their half a million sets. Local original material that has come out of the Middle East has been scant and, in many cases, it is suppressed. The Jordanians filmed an excellent drama series on the fedayeen guerrillas that was never brought to the screen. Kuwait rather sums up TV's situation in the Middle East with a show they call "Know Your Enemy," about the scene in Israel.

THE NETHERLANDS

Dutch television is probably the most democratic in the world. Any organization with over 15,000 members, all of whom have purchased an annual television license, is entitled to time on the country's 3 radio and 2 television networks. In addition, groups which do not have the 15,000-member minimum—such as the Humanists, Moral Rearmament, or the Society for Sexual Reform—are allowed occasional programs of their own. Each group granted TV time is given a proportional slice of the income from license fees, and, generously, 40% of the income from television advertising is handed over to the country's newspapers and magazines, who share it among themselves according to circulation.

SCANDINAVIA

The Norwegians had developed a concept similar to Germany's *Aktenzeichen Xy . . . Ungelöst*, which they called *Idebanken* ("The Bank of Ideas"). Essentially, the program's format was to present a problem, discuss it with a panel, then ask the viewing audience to phone in any suggestions or solutions it had. In this manner a better boat was designed for fishermen, a way was found to build simple eel traps, and a means was found for rural craftsmen to sell their products in the city. The show was scrapped in 1969, due to government pressure. It seems that the Government had decided that schools in remote areas could not be kept open. *Idebanken* had decided that they could and showed the Government how this could be done.

U.S.S.R.

Television in the U.S.S.R. is concerned with increasing socialist production the way that the U.S. has traditionally been concerned with encouraging material consumption, but in between the profiles of outstanding workers in vacuum-cleaner factories, the speeches by award-winning members of the Lenin Youth Organization, and the endless biographies of Lenin emanating from its 127 stations, the U.S.S.R. has put some fairly radical innovations to work. The U.S.S.R. was the 1st country to utilize communications satellites as integral parts of its TV networks, and the viewer is offered many fine self-help programs like "Looking After Your Eyesight," or lessons in German, engineering, chess, and television-broadcasting techniques. An interesting variation on the quiz-show concept, a show called *"Kvn,"* has 2 teams who challenge each other to do improvisations on recent news events. And with the purchase of "The Forsyte Saga" in 1969,

Russian television ceased to be the closed system that it was. The Russians worked jointly with the French to film "The Battle of Moscow," and they have imported such programs as "Casals at 88" and "Now That the Buffalo's Gone," the latter a documentary on the plight of native Americans. In 1973, the Soviet Union signed a long-term agreement with the U.S. network NBC to exchange television programs.

—M.T.

A 6-year Sampling of the Gallup Poll

Public Opinion in the U.S. in 1969

(Pollsters' questions have been paraphrased and condensed, except for those enclosed in quotation marks.)

Feb.—What should be the prison sentence for various designated crimes? Those specifying 10 years or more, by percentage figures: DOPE PEDDLING—85%; ARMED ROBBERY —60%; ARSON—53%; PASSING BAD CHECKS —16%; CAR THEFT—15%.

June—"Would you find pictures of nudes in magazines objectionable?" YES—73%; No —27%.

Aug.—Would you favor the U.S. Government's spending money to land a person on the planet Mars? OPPOSE—53%; FAVOR— 39%; No OPINION—8%.

Sept.—Have you smoked any cigarettes in the past week? YES—40%. (More men than women smoked. Persons in their 20s smoked the most.)

Sept.—"From what you have heard or read, which large city is the most interesting or different?" Ranked in order of most votes: NEW YORK CITY; SAN FRANCISCO; LOS ANGELES; WASHINGTON, D.C.; NEW ORLEANS. Also mentioned: BOSTON; CHICAGO; HONOLULU; LAS VEGAS; MIAMI.

Sept.—Do you think it is wrong or not wrong to have sexual relations before marriage? WRONG—68%; NOT WRONG—21%; NO OPINION—11%.

Dec.—For people like yourself, do you think the world will be a better place to live in 10 years from now? BETTER—39%; SAME —28%; NOT AS GOOD—27%; NO OPINION —6%.

Dec.—Did you, yourself, happen to attend church in the last 7 days? No—58%; YES —42%.

Public Opinion in the U.S. in 1970

Mar.—Is religion increasing or losing its influence in the U.S.? LOSING—75%; INCREASING—14%; NO DIFFERENCE—7%; NO OPINION—4%.

May—Asked of college students: "Would it be important to you that the person you marry be a virgin, or not so important?" NOT IMPORTANT—73%; IMPORTANT—23%; NO OPINION—4%.

Aug.—"Have you ever wished you belonged to the opposite sex?" Women: No—84%; YES —16%. Men: No—96%; YES—4%.

Sept.—Which dress lengths do you like best: skirts well above knee—the "mini"; skirts at knee; skirts well below knee—the "midi"; skirts to the floor—the "maxi"?
Women: AT THE KNEE—70%; MINI—18%; MIDI—10%; MAXI—1%; NO OPINION—1%.
Men: AT THE KNEE—51%; MINI—33%; MIDI—9%; MAXI—1%; NO OPINION—6%.

Oct.—How important is it that we try to make the UN a success?
VERY —75%; FAIRLY—12%; NOT SO—7%; NO OPINION—6%.

Public Opinion in the U.S. in 1971

Jan.—"In general, how happy would you say you are—very happy, fairly happy, or not happy?" FAIRLY—48%; VERY—43%; NOT HAPPY—6%; NO OPINION—3%.

Jan.—"Do you think violence is sometimes justified to bring about change in American society, or not?" NOT JUSTIFIED—81%; JUSTIFIED—14%; NO OPINION—5%.

Feb.—Not counting the Bible or textbooks, when did you last read a hardcover or paperback book all the way through? HAVE READ AT LEAST ONE BOOK IN PAST MONTH—26%.

Feb.—Asked of Protestants only: Did you read any part of the Bible in the last year? YES— 72%; No—28%.

Mar.—Would you prefer a 40-hour week of 4 10-hour days or 5 8-hour days? FIVE 8-HOUR DAYS—56%; FOUR 10-HOUR DAYS— 38%; No OPINION—6%.

Apr.—Asked of clergymen only: "Have you ever seriously considered leaving the religious life?" Protestant ministers: No—67%; YES —33%. Catholic priests: No—77%; YES— 23%; Jewish rabbis: No—57%; YES—43%.

June—"Do you believe that some kind of human life exists on other planets in the total universe?" YES—53%; No—47%.

June—"Do you believe in life after death?" YES—53%; No—33%; NO OPINION—14%.

Sept.—In the next few years which country— Russia or China—do you think will be a greater threat to world peace? CHINA—56%; RUSSIA—27%; NO OPINION—17%.

Oct.—"If your party nominated a generally well-qualified man for President and he happened to be a Negro, would you vote for him?" YES—70%; NO—23%; NO OPINION —7%.

PUBLIC OPINION IN THE U.S. IN 1972

Jan.—"Did you, yourself, happen to attend church in the last 7 days?" NO—60%; YES —40%.

Feb.—Asked of college students: "This card lists political positions from the far left to the far right. Considering your own political views, where would you place yourself on this scale?" MIDDLE OF THE ROAD—49%; LEFT—29%; RIGHT—12%; FAR LEFT—6%; CAN'T SAY—3%; FAR RIGHT—1%.

Apr.—"Do you think the use of marijuana should be made legal, or not?" NO—81%; YES—15%; NO OPINION—4%.

Nov.—"Do you approve or disapprove of marriage between whites and blacks?" DISAPPROVE—60%; APPROVE—29%; NO OPINION—11%

Dec.—"If you could live anywhere in the U.S. that you wanted to, would you prefer a city, suburban area, small town, or farm?" SMALL TOWN—32%; SUBURBAN—31%; FARM—23%; CITY—13%; NO OPINION—1%.

Dec.—"Are you in favor of the death penalty for persons convicted of murder?" YES—57%; NO—32%; NO OPINION—11%.

PUBLIC OPINION IN THE U.S. IN 1973

July—"If you had a son, would you like to see him go into politics as a life's work?" NO—64%; YES—23%; NO OPINION—13%.

Aug.—"Do you think it is wrong for people to have sex relations before marriage, or not?" YES, WRONG—48%; NO, NOT WRONG—43%; NO OPINION—9%.

Aug.—"How do you rate the Central Intelligence Agency?" MILDLY FAVORABLE—44%; HIGHLY FAVORABLE—23%; NO OPINION—14%; MILDLY UNFAVORABLE—12%; HIGHLY UNFAVORABLE—7%.

Aug.—"When a person has a disease that cannot be cured, do you think doctors should be allowed by law to end a person's life by some painless means if the patient and his family request it?" YES—53%; NO—40%; NO OPINION—7%.

Nov.—"On the whole, would you say that you are satisfied or dissatisfied with the honesty and standards of behavior of people in this country?" DISSATISFIED—72%; SATISFIED—22%; NO OPINION—6%.

Dec.—"Do you think the President should or should not be required to get the approval of Congress before sending U.S. armed forces into action outside the U.S.?" SHOULD—80%; SHOULD NOT—16%; NO OPINION—4%.

PUBLIC OPINION IN THE U.S. IN 1974

Mar.—"In politics, as of today, do you consider yourself a Republican, Democrat, or Independent?" DEMOCRAT—42%; REPUBLICAN —24%; INDEPENDENT—34%.

Mar.—"What is your favorite way of spending an evening?" WATCH TV—46%; READ—14%; DINING OUT—12%; HOME WITH FAMILY—10% MOVIES/THEATER—9% RESTING/RELAXING—8%; VISIT FRIENDS—8%; ENTERTAIN FRIENDS—8%; GAMES—7%; SPORTS—5%; RADIO/RECORDS—5%; DANCING—4%; SEWING—3%; HOME REPAIR—3%; CLUB/CHURCH MEETINGS—3%; OTHER—6%.

(Note: The total is more than 100% as many people mentioned more than one way of spending an evening.)

June—"Do you have occasion to use alcoholic beverages such as liquor, wine, or beer?" YES —68%; NO—32%.

July—Asked of college students: "Do you think violence is sometimes justified to bring about change in American society, or not?" NO—60%; YES—37%; NO OPINION—3%.

July—Asked of college students: "Would you favor or oppose requiring all young men to give one year of service to the nation—either in the military forces or in nonmilitary work here or abroad such as VISTA or the Peace Corps?" OPPOSE—56%; FAVOR—40%; NO OPINION—4%.

PUBLIC OPINION IN THE U.S. IN 1975

Jan.—"In the Middle East situation, are your sympathies more with Israel or more with the Arab nations?" ISRAEL—44%; ARABS—8%; NEITHER—22%; NO OPINION—26%.

INTERNATIONAL PUBLIC OPINION

These Gallup polls were based "upon a scientifically selected sample of names included in *The International Year Book and Statesman's Who's Who*, which lists the world's leading statesmen, scientists, jurists, business executives, publishers, educators, as well as leaders in other similar fields."

June, 1970—"Omitting your country, what nation of the world do you think is best governed?" The results rank the nations in this order: SWITZERLAND; GREAT BRITAIN; SWEDEN; W. GERMANY; CANADA; U.S.;

DENMARK; THE NETHERLANDS; AUSTRIA; JAPAN.

May, 1971—"What person in all of history do you admire the most?" The following are listed in order of frequency of mention: ABRAHAM LINCOLN; WINSTON CHURCHILL; MAHATMA GANDHI; WILLIAM SHAKESPEARE; SOCRATES.

These Gallup polls were taken of the international public in general.

Jan., 1971—"What is the smallest amount of money a family of 4 (husband, wife, and 2 children) needs each week to get along in this community?" Median average: U.S.— $126 wk.; W. GERMANY—$82 wk.; BRAZIL —$77 wk.; GREAT BRITAIN—$66 wk.; GREECE—$56 wk.; URUGUAY—$53 wk.; THE NETHERLANDS—$51 wk.

Mar., 1971—Asked in 9 nations of people who would like to settle in another country: "What country would you like to settle in?" Choice in Great Britain—AUSTRALIA, NEW ZEALAND; Choice in Uruguay—U.S., GERMANY; Choice in W. Germany—U.S., SWITZERLAND; Choice in Greece—U.S., GREAT BRITAIN; Choice in Finland—SWEDEN, U.S.; Choice in Brazil—U.S., ITALY; Choice in The Netherlands—AUSTRALIA, NEW ZEALAND; Choice in U.S.—AUSTRALIA, CANADA, GREAT BRITAIN, SWITZERLAND.

—The Eds.

16

The Arts—Lively and Otherwise

The 25 All-Time Box Office Champion Films

As Compiled by *Weekly Variety*

Figures as given below signify the rentals received by the distributors from the U.S.-Canada market only and omit foreign market rentals. The latter, in recent years, sometimes equal, or slightly surpass, the domestic play-off.

Film title is followed by name of director, producer, or production company; original distributor plus present distributor, if different (plus differing U.S. and Canadian distributors in case of some foreign-made films); year of release; and total rentals received to date.

The Godfather (F. F. Coppola; A. Ruddy; Par; 1972) $85,747,184

The Sound of Music (R. Wise; 20th; 1965) $83,891,000

Gone with the Wind (V. Fleming; D. Selznick; MGM; 1939) $70,179,000

The Sting (G. R. Hill; T. Bill, M. & J. Philips; Univ; 1973) $68,450,000

The Exorcist (W. Friedkin; W. P. Blatty; WB; 1973) $66,300,000

Love Story (A. Hiller; H. Minsky; Par; 1970) $50,000,000

The Birth of a Nation, released in 1915, which may have grossed as much as $50,000,000 has always been omitted because it was generally handled on a states rights and, often, under an outright cash sale; hence data are unreliable on the David Wark Griffith classic.

The Graduate (M. Nichols; L. Turman; Avco Embassy; 1968) $49,978,000

Airport (G. Seaton; R. Hunter; Univ; 1970) $45,300,000

Doctor Zhivago (D. Lean; C. Ponti; MGM; 1965) $44,390,000

Butch Cassidy and the Sundance Kid (G. R. Hill; J. Foreman; 20th; 1969) $44,000,000

The Ten Commandments (C. B. De Mille; Par; 1956) $43,000,000

The Poseidon Adventure (R. Neame; I. Allen; 20th; 1972) $42,500,000

Mary Poppins (R. Stevenson; W. Disney; BV; 1964) $42,000,000

American Graffiti (G. Lucas; F. F. Coppola; Univ; 1973) $41,200,000

M*A*S*H (R. Altman; I. Preminger; 20th; 1970) $40,500,000

Ben-Hur (W. Wyler; S. Zimbalist; MGM; 1959) $36,550,000

Fiddler on the Roof (N. Jewison; UA; 1971) $35,550,000

My Fair Lady (G. Cukor; J. L. Warner; WB; 1964) $34,000,000

Billy Jack (T. Frank; M. Solti; WB; 1971) $31,000,000

Thunderball (T. Young; Eon; UA; 1965) $28,300,000

Patton (F. Schaffner; F. McCarthy; 20th; 1970) $28,100,000

The French Connection (W. Friedkin; P. D'Antoni/Schine-Moore; 20th; 1971) $27,500,000

Funny Girl (W. Wyler; R. Stark; Col; 1968) $26,325,000

Cleopatra (J. Mankiewicz; W. Wanger; 20th; 1963) $26,000,000

Guess Who's Coming to Dinner (S. Kramer; Col; 1968) $25,500,000

From: *Variety*, January 8, 1975.

Motion Picture Academy Award-winning Films and Actors

1927–1928

Best Picture

NOMINEES: The Last Command, The Racket, Seventh Heaven, The Way of All Flesh, Wings
THE WINNER: Wings (Paramount)
DIRECTOR: William A. Wellman
PLAYERS: Clara Bow, Charles "Buddy" Rogers, Richard Arlen

Best Actor

NOMINEES: Richard Barthelmess (The Noose, The Patent Leather Kid); Charles Chaplin (The Circus); Emil Jannings (The Way of All Flesh, The Last Command)
THE WINNER: Emil Jannings

Best Actress

NOMINEES: Louise Dresser (A Ship Comes In); Janet Gaynor (Street Angel, Sunrise, Seventh Heaven); Gloria Swanson (Sadie Thompson)
THE WINNER: Janet Gaynor

Behind the Oscar

The 1st golden statuette (actually 92.5% tin) was given by the newly formed Academy of Motion Picture Arts and Sciences. It was designed by Cedric Gibbon, art director of MGM. Movie columnist Sidney Skolsky was said to have dubbed it "Oscar." The Academy Award did not originate awards in Hollywood. *Photoplay* magazine's popularity award was initiated 7 years earlier. The 1st Academy Award Ceremony was attended by 200 persons. No television audience yet. All the competing films were silent pictures. The winning picture, *Wings*, featured simulated combat actually filmed in the sky. No process shots. One player with a bit role in the film would later become famous. His name was Gary Cooper. Brooklyn-born Emil Jannings, who gained fame in Berlin, was notified in advance of his victory, so that he could pose for pictures with his statuette before leaving for Germany. The winning actress, 21-year-old Janet Gaynor, shed tears upon accepting her award from Douglas Fairbanks, president of the Academy.

1928–1929

Best Picture

NOMINEES: Alibi, The Broadway Melody, Hollywood Revue, In Old Arizona, The Patriot

THE WINNER: The Broadway Melody (MGM)
DIRECTOR: Harry Beaumont
PLAYERS: Charles King, Bessie Love, Anita Page

Best Actor

NOMINEES: Warner Baxter (In Old Arizona); George Bancroft (Thunderbolt); Paul Muni (The Valiant); Chester Morris (Alibi); Lewis Stone (The Patriot)
THE WINNER: Warner Baxter

Best Actress

NOMINEES: Ruth Chatterton (Madame X); Betty Compson (The Barker); Jeanne Eagles (The Letter); Bessie Love (The Broadway Melody); Mary Pickford (Coquette)
THE WINNER: Mary Pickford

Behind the Oscar

Silent pictures competed with pioneer sound pictures. *The Broadway Melody* had sound. Three losing nominees had sound, and one loser, *The Patriot*, was a silent. After this award, silent pictures were dead. There was local radio coverage for the 1st time. Warner Baxter, as the Cisco Kid, was a popular choice. Mary Pickford was an unpopular choice. It was generally felt Pickford couldn't act on the same stage alongside Eagles or Chatterton, but the handful of select judges who were doing the awarding gave her the Oscar for being one of the founders of the Motion Picture Academy.

1929–1930

Best Picture

NOMINEES: All Quiet on the Western Front, The Big House, Disraeli, The Divorcee, The Love Parade
THE WINNER: All Quiet on the Western Front (Universal)
DIRECTOR: Lewis Milestone
PLAYERS: Lew Ayres, William Bakewell, Slim Summerville, John Wray, Louis Wolheim

Best Actor

NOMINEES: George Arliss (Disraeli, The Green Goddess); Wallace Beery (The Big House); Maurice Chevalier (The Love Parade, The Big Pond); Ronald Colman (Bulldog Drummond, Condemned); Lawrence Tibbett (The Rogue Song)
THE WINNER: George Arliss (Disraeli)

Best Actress

NOMINEES: Norma Shearer (*The Divorcee, Their Own Desire*); Nancy Carroll (*The Devil's Holiday*); Ruth Chatterton (*Sarah and Son*); Greta Garbo (*Anna Christie, Romance*); Gloria Swanson (*The Trespasser*)
THE WINNER: Norma Shearer (*The Divorcee*)

Behind the Oscar

Garbo Talks! But not loud enough to be heard by the full Academy membership, which had taken over voting powers from a small clique of judges in a bloodless coup. Norma Shearer, bride of Irving Thalberg, who brought her to MGM and started her on the road to stardom, got the vote. Monocled George Arliss, age 70, did not attend the sell-out ceremony. Carl Laemmle, Jr.'s grimly realistic antiwar film, *All Quiet on the Western Front*, based on the Erich Maria Remarque novel, was banned in France and Germany.

1930–1931

Best Picture

NOMINEES: *Cimarron, East Lynne, The Front Page, Skippy, Trader Horn*
THE WINNER: *Cimarron* (RKO)
DIRECTOR: Wesley Ruggles
PLAYERS: Richard Dix, Irene Dunne, Estelle Taylor, William Collier, Jr., Nance O'Neill

Best Actor

NOMINEES: Lionel Barrymore (*A Free Soul*); Jackie Cooper (*Skippy*); Richard Dix (*Cimarron*); Fredric March (*The Royal Family of Broadway*); Adolphe Menjou (*The Front Page*)
THE WINNER: Lionel Barrymore

Best Actress

NOMINEES: Marie Dressler (*Min and Bill*); Marlene Dietrich (*Morocco*); Irene Dunne (*Cimarron*); Ann Harding (*Holiday*); Norma Shearer (*A Free Soul*)
THE WINNER: Marie Dressler

Behind the Oscar

The award ceremony became a national event when Vice-President Charles Curtis came in from Washington, D.C., to address the 1,800 guests. Two old pros triumphed over the glamour girls and handsome leading men. Ailing, elderly Marie Dressler won easily, as did 48-year-old Lionel Barrymore. One losing nominee, 10-year-old Jackie Cooper, snoozed through the speeches. The winning film, based on a novel by Edna Ferber, was the 1st Western to be thus honored.

1931–1932

Best Picture

NOMINEES: *Arrowsmith, Bad Girl, The Champ, Grand Hotel, Five Star Final, One Hour with You, Shanghai Express, Smiling Lieutenant*
THE WINNER: *Grand Hotel* (MGM)
DIRECTOR: Edmund Goulding
PLAYERS: Greta Garbo, John Barrymore, Joan Crawford, Wallace Beery, Lionel Barrymore

Best Actor

NOMINEES: Alfred Lunt (*The Guardsman*); Wallace Beery (*The Champ*); Fredric March (*Dr. Jekyll and Mr. Hyde*)
THE WINNER: (TIE) Wallace Beery and Fredric March

Best Actress

NOMINEES: Marie Dressler (*Emma*); Helen Hayes (*The Sin of Madelon Claudet*); Lynn Fontanne (*The Guardsman*)
THE WINNER: Helen Hayes

Behind the Oscar

The 1st of only 2 tie votes in Academy Award history. Fredric March led Wallace Beery in the balloting by one vote, and the rules (later changed) stated that if leader and runner-up were only 3 votes apart, they were both considered winners. This was unexpected, and the Academy was short one Oscar. A runner was sent out to pick up a spare one. Walt Disney made off with 2 awards. His 1st was for the creation of Mickey Mouse.

1932–1933

Best Picture

NOMINEES: *A Farewell to Arms, Forty-Second Street, I Am a Fugitive from a Chain Gang, Cavalcade, Lady for a Day, Little Women, The Private Life of Henry VIII, She Done Him Wrong, Smilin' Through, State Fair*
THE WINNER: *Cavalcade* (Fox)
DIRECTOR: Frank Lloyd
PLAYERS: Diana Wynyard, Clive Brook

Best Actor

NOMINEES: Leslie Howard (*Berkeley Square*); Charles Laughton (*The Private Life of Henry VIII*); Paul Muni (*I Am a Fugitive from a Chain Gang*)
THE WINNER: Charles Laughton

Best Actress

NOMINEES: Katharine Hepburn (*Morning Glory*); May Robson (*Lady for a Day*);

Diana Wynyard (*Cavalcade*)
THE WINNER: Katharine Hepburn

Behind the Oscar

For the 1st time—it would only happen 3 times in Academy history—both acting winners were absent from the big night. Will Rogers was MC, and he really flubbed his lines. Announcing the winning director, he spoke of his "good friend Frank"—then hesitated—and Frank Capra had started toward the stage when Rogers concluded, "Frank Lloyd, the winner." Then Will Rogers summoned 2 of the best actress nominees, Diana Wynyard and May Robson, to the stage. They came up thinking they had won in a tie, but Rogers thanked them for their performances and then announced that the winner was—Katharine Hepburn!

1934

Best Picture

NOMINEES: *The Barretts of Wimpole Street, Cleopatra, It Happened One Night, Flirtation Walk, The Gay Divorcee, Here Comes the Navy, The House of Rothschild, Imitation of Life, One Night of Love, The Thin Man, Viva Villa, The White Parade*
THE WINNER: *It Happened One Night* (Columbia)
DIRECTOR: Frank Capra
PLAYERS: Clark Gable, Claudette Colbert

Best Actor

NOMINEES: Clark Gable (*It Happened One Night*); William Powell (*The Thin Man*); Frank Morgan (*Affairs of Cellini*)
THE WINNER: Clark Gable

Best Actress

NOMINEES: Norma Shearer (*The Barretts of Wimpole Street*); Grace Moore (*One Night of Love*); Claudette Colbert (*It Happened One Night*)
THE WINNER: Claudette Colbert

Behind the Oscar

The only time a write-in vote was permitted. When nominees for best actress were made public, there was outrage that Bette Davis had not been nominated for her superb performance in *Of Human Bondage*. The Academy was inundated by calls, letters, editorials. So the Academy told its members they could vote the names on the printed ballot or write in any other name they wished. Great suspense, although nominee Claudette Colbert felt that the write-in announcement would give it to Bette Davis in a walk. But Davis came in 4th in the final voting. Colbert, certain she had no

chance, had just got on a train for N.Y. when informed of her victory. She hastened to the ceremony, grabbed her award, rushed back to the waiting train.

1935

Best Picture

NOMINEES: *Mutiny on the Bounty, Alice Adams, Broadway Melody of 1936, Captain Blood, David Copperfield, The Informer, Les Miserables, Lives of a Bengal Lancer, A Midsummer Night's Dream, Naughty Marietta, Ruggles of Red Gap, Top Hat*
THE WINNER: *Mutiny on the Bounty* (MGM)
DIRECTOR: Frank Lloyd
PLAYERS: Charles Laughton, Clark Gable, Franchot Tone

Best Actor

NOMINEES: Charles Laughton (*Mutiny on the Bounty*); Clark Gable (*Mutiny on the Bounty*); Franchot Tone (*Mutiny on the Bounty*); Victor McLaglen (*The Informer*)
THE WINNER: Victor McLaglen

Best Actress

NOMINEES: Elisabeth Bergner (*Escape Me Never*); Claudette Colbert (*Private Worlds*); Bette Davis (*Dangerous*); Katharine Hepburn (*Alice Adams*); Miriam Hopkins (*Becky Sharp*); Merle Oberon (*The Dark Angel*)
THE WINNER: Bette Davis

Behind the Oscar

Feeling guilty about not having given Bette Davis the Oscar the previous year, the membership now gave it to her for a lesser picture called *Dangerous*. Even Davis thought it was a consolation gesture and that Katharine Hepburn should have won. Davis, ever the iconoclast, upset the social crowd by coming to the posh formal event in an informal checkered dress.

1936

Best Picture

NOMINEES: *Anthony Adverse, The Great Ziegfeld, Dodsworth, Libeled Lady, Mr. Deeds Goes to Town, Romeo and Juliet, San Francisco, The Story of Louis Pasteur, A Tale of Two Cities, Three Smart Girls*
THE WINNER: *The Great Ziegfeld* (MGM)
DIRECTOR: Robert Z. Leonard
PLAYERS: William Powell, Myrna Loy, Luise Rainer

Best Actor

NOMINEES: Gary Cooper (*Mr. Deeds Goes to Town*); Paul Muni (*The Story of Louis*

Pasteur); Walter Huston (*Dodsworth*); William Powell (*My Man Godfrey*); Spencer Tracy (*San Francisco*)
THE WINNER: Paul Muni

Best Actress

NOMINEES: Irene Dunne (*Theodora Goes Wild*); Luise Rainer (*The Great Ziegfeld*); Gladys George (*Valiant Is the Word for Carrie*); Carole Lombard (*My Man Godfrey*); Norma Shearer (*Romeo and Juliet*)
THE WINNER: Luise Rainer

Behind the Oscar

A real hassle. MC George Jessel gave the wrong awards to the right winners of the newly introduced best supporting actor and actress categories. *The Great Ziegfeld* was an unpopular winner with the press, who felt its lush gaudiness had brainwashed voters. Luise Rainer's victory also came under fire, since it was felt her role in *Ziegfeld* had not been big enough. There was no dissent about Paul Muni's victory.

1937

Best Picture

NOMINEES: *The Awful Truth, The Life of Emile Zola, Captains Courageous, Dead End, The Good Earth, In Old Chicago, Lost Horizon, 100 Men and a Girl, Stage Door, A Star Is Born*
THE WINNER: *The Life of Emile Zola* (Warner Bros.)
DIRECTOR: William Dieterle
PLAYERS: Paul Muni, Gale Sondergaard, Joseph Schildkraut

Best Actor

NOMINEES: Charles Boyer (*Conquest*); Fredric March (*A Star Is Born*); Spencer Tracy (*Captains Courageous*); Robert Montgomery (*Night Must Fall*); Paul Muni (*The Life of Emile Zola*)
THE WINNER: Spencer Tracy

Best Actress

NOMINEES: Luise Rainer (*The Good Earth*); Irene Dunne (*The Awful Truth*); Greta Garbo (*Camille*); Janet Gaynor (*A Star Is Born*); Barbara Stanwyck (*Stella Dallas*)
THE WINNER: Luise Rainer

Behind the Oscar

Luise Rainer didn't think anyone could win 2 years in a row, so she stayed home with her husband, playwright Clifford Odets, the night of the ceremony. A call came to her. She had become the 1st repeat winner in Academy history. Hastily dressing, she sped to the ceremony to receive her 2nd Oscar. Apparently this jinxed her. By the following year, her career was in total eclipse.

1938

Best Picture

NOMINEES: *The Adventures of Robin Hood, Alexander's Ragtime Band, You Can't Take It with You, Boy's Town, The Citadel, Four Daughters, Grand Illusion, Jezebel, Pygmalion, Test Pilot*
THE WINNER: *You Can't Take It with You* (Columbia)
DIRECTOR: Frank Capra
PLAYERS: Jean Arthur, Lionel Barrymore, James Stewart, Edward Arnold

Best Actor

NOMINEES: Leslie Howard (*Pygmalion*); Robert Donat (*The Citadel*); James Cagney (*Angels with Dirty Faces*); Charles Boyer (*Algiers*); Spencer Tracy (*Boy's Town*)
THE WINNER: Spencer Tracy

Best Actress

NOMINEES: Fay Bainter (*White Banners*); Bette Davis (*Jezebel*); Wendy Hiller (*Pygmalion*); Norma Shearer (*Marie Antoinette*); Margaret Sullavan (*Three Comrades*)
THE WINNER: Bette Davis

Behind the Oscar

Both Tracy and Davis won for the 2nd time. Only major protest over any award came from the winner of the Best Screenplay category. This was 82-year-old George Bernard Shaw, whose scenario of *Pygmalion* had been honored with an Oscar. Roared GBS from London: "It's an insult! It's perfect nonsense. My position as a playwright is known throughout the world. To offer me an award of this sort is an insult, as if they have never heard of me before —and it's very likely they never had."

1939

Best Picture

NOMINEES: *Dark Victory, Good-bye, Mr. Chips, Love Affair, Gone with the Wind, Mr. Smith Goes to Washington, Ninotchka, Of Mice and Men, Stagecoach, The Wizard of Oz, Wuthering Heights*
THE WINNER: *Gone with the Wind* (MGM)
DIRECTOR: Victor Fleming
PLAYERS: Clark Gable, Vivien Leigh, Leslie Howard, Olivia De Havilland

Best Actor

NOMINEES: Clark Gable (*Gone with the Wind*); Laurence Olivier (*Wuthering Heights*); Mickey Rooney (*Babes in Arms*);

Robert Donat (*Good-bye, Mr. Chips*); James Stewart (*Mr. Smith Goes to Washington*)
THE WINNER: Robert Donat

Best Actress

NOMINEES: Irene Dunne (*Love Affair*); Vivien Leigh (*Gone with the Wind*); Bette Davis (*Dark Victory*); Greta Garbo (*Ninotchka*); Greer Garson (*Good-bye, Mr. Chips*)
THE WINNER: Vivien Leigh

Behind the Oscar

The voting was almost a clean sweep for *Gone with the Wind* in the major categories. The only *Wind* casualty in the landslide was favorite Clark Gable, who lost out to Robert Donat's *Mr. Chips*. Hattie McDaniel became the 1st black to carry off an Academy Award. Incidentally, as movie historian Robert Osborne reports it, "not once did anyone mention the name of Margaret Mitchell, the small woman who had simply written the book on which the victorious movie was based."

1940

Best Picture

NOMINEES: *All This and Heaven Too, Foreign Correspondent, The Grapes of Wrath, Rebecca, The Great Dictator, Kitty Foyle, The Letter, The Long Voyage Home, Our Town, The Philadelphia Story*
THE WINNER: *Rebecca* (Selznick–United Artists)
DIRECTOR: Alfred Hitchcock
PLAYERS: Laurence Olivier, Joan Fontaine

Best Actor

NOMINEES: Laurence Olivier (*Rebecca*); James Stewart (*The Philadelphia Story*); Charles Chaplin (*The Great Dictator*); Henry Fonda (*The Grapes of Wrath*); Raymond Massey (*Abe Lincoln in Illinois*)
THE WINNER: James Stewart

Best Actress

NOMINEES: Ginger Rogers (*Kitty Foyle*); Bette Davis (*The Letter*); Joan Fontaine (*Rebecca*); Katharine Hepburn (*The Philadelphia Story*); Martha Scott (*Our Town*)
THE WINNER: Ginger Rogers

Behind the Oscar

Until this year, the Academy members always knew the winners in advance. And newspapers had been pledged to release the announcement late in the evening. But when the *Los Angeles Times* broke the pledge the year before, the Academy decided that, thereafter, the winners would be kept secret, and known only when a sealed envelope was opened onstage. This was the 1st year of Price, Waterhouse and the sealed envelope. FDR addressed the gathering by radio. Walter Brennan, in taking the best supporting actor award, became the Academy's 1st 3-time winner.

1941

Best Picture

NOMINEES: *Here Comes Mr. Jordan, Citizen Kane, Blossoms in the Dust, How Green Was My Valley, Hold Back the Dawn, The Little Foxes, The Maltese Falcon, One Foot in Heaven, Sergeant York, Suspicion*
THE WINNER: *How Green Was My Valley* (20th Century-Fox)
DIRECTOR: John Ford
PLAYERS: Walter Pidgeon, Maureen O'Hara, Donald Crisp, Roddy McDowall, Anna Lee, Sara Allgood

Best Actor

NOMINEES: Cary Grant (*Penny Serenade*); Gary Cooper (*Sergeant York*); Walter Huston (*All That Money Can Buy*); Robert Montgomery (*Here Comes Mr. Jordan*); Orson Welles (*Citizen Kane*)
THE WINNER: Gary Cooper

BEST ACTRESS

NOMINEES: Bette Davis (*The Little Foxes*); Greer Garson (*Blossoms in the Dust*); Joan Fontaine (*Suspicion*); Olivia De Havilland (*Hold Back the Dawn*); Barbara Stanwyck (*Ball of Fire*)
THE WINNER: Joan Fontaine

Behind the Oscar

After being canceled because of Pearl Harbor, the Award ceremony was revived and held in February, 1942. Bette Davis, president of the Academy, wanted to open the ceremony to the public for the benefit of the Red Cross. The Academy governors turned her down. She quit her presidency. Sisters Olivia De Havilland and Joan Fontaine were both up for the best actress Oscar. Joan won. Olivia was distressed. A feud was ignited. Orson Welles' *Citizen Kane* was wiped out—voted down in best picture, best-director, best-acting categories. The Academy membership never liked one-man films, especially if the one-man was a newcomer and a genius.

1942

Best Picture

NOMINEES: *The Invaders, Mrs. Miniver, Kings Row, The Magnificent Ambersons, The Pied Piper, Pride of the Yankees, Random Hur-*

vest, Talk of the Town, Wake Island, Yankee Doodle Dandy
THE WINNER: *Mrs. Miniver* (MGM)
DIRECTOR: William Wyler
PLAYERS: Greer Garson, Walter Pidgeon

Best Actor

NOMINEES: Ronald Colman (*Random Harvest*); Gary Cooper (*Pride of the Yankees*); James Cagney (*Yankee Doodle Dandy*); Walter Pidgeon (*Mrs. Miniver*); Monty Woolley (*The Pied Piper*)
THE WINNER: James Cagney

Best Actress

NOMINEES: Bette Davis (*Now, Voyager*); Greer Garson (*Mrs. Miniver*); Katharine Hepburn (*Woman of the Year*); Rosalind Russell (*My Sister Eileen*); Teresa Wright (*Pride of the Yankees*)
THE WINNER: Greer Garson

Behind the Oscar

Wartime austerity. The gold-plated bronze Oscar was made of plaster this year. Winning for *Mrs. Miniver*, best actress Greer Garson started her acceptance speech—and couldn't stop. She rambled on for an hour, the longest speech in Academy history.

1943

Best Picture

NOMINEES: *Casablanca, For Whom the Bell Tolls, Heaven Can Wait, The Human Comedy, In Which We Serve, Madame Curie, The More the Merrier, The Ox-Bow Incident, The Song of Bernadette, Watch on the Rhine*
THE WINNER: *Casablanca* (Warner Bros.)
DIRECTOR: Michael Curtiz
PLAYERS: Humphrey Bogart, Ingrid Bergman, Paul Henreid

Best Actor

NOMINEES: Humphrey Bogart (*Casablanca*); Gary Cooper (*For Whom the Bell Tolls*); Paul Lukas (*Watch on the Rhine*); Walter Pidgeon (*Madame Curie*); Mickey Rooney (*The Human Comedy*)
THE WINNER: Paul Lukas

Best Actress

NOMINEES: Jean Arthur (*The More the Merrier*); Ingrid Bergman (*For Whom the Bell Tolls*); Joan Fontaine (*The Constant Nymph*); Jennifer Jones (*The Song of Bernadette*); Greer Garson (*Madame Curie*)
THE WINNER: Jennifer Jones

Behind the Oscar

The Academy ceremony moved from hotel banquet rooms to a theater, and the public was admitted for the 1st time.

1944

Best Picture

NOMINEES: *Double Indemnity, Gaslight, Going My Way, Since You Went Away, Wilson*
THE WINNER: *Going My Way* (Paramount)
DIRECTOR: Leo McCarey
PLAYERS: Bing Crosby

Best Actor

NOMINEES: Charles Boyer (*Gaslight*); Bing Crosby (*Going My Way*); Barry Fitzgerald (*Going My Way*); Cary Grant (*None but the Lonely Heart*); Alexander Knox (*Wilson*)
THE WINNER: Bing Crosby

Best Actress

NOMINEES: Ingrid Bergman (*Gaslight*); Claudette Colbert (*Since You Went Away*); Bette Davis (*Mr. Skeffington*); Greer Garson (*Mrs. Parkington*); Barbara Stanwyck (*Double Indemnity*)
THE WINNER: Ingrid Bergman

Behind the Oscar

Darryl F. Zanuck and 20th Century-Fox spent a fortune promoting *Wilson*, determined to have it win the best picture award. *Wilson* lost. *Going My Way* won. Zanuck was bitter. Three years later, accepting another award, he was still bitter enough to say, "This award will make up for previous disappointments."

1945

Best Picture

NOMINEES: *Anchors Aweigh, The Bells of St. Mary's, Mildred Pierce, The Lost Weekend, Spellbound*
THE WINNER: *The Lost Weekend* (Paramount)
DIRECTOR: Billy Wilder
PLAYERS: Ray Milland, Jane Wyman

Best Actor

NOMINEES: Bing Crosby (*The Bells of St. Mary's*); Gene Kelly (*Anchors Aweigh*); Ray Milland (*The Lost Weekend*); Gregory Peck (*The Keys of the Kingdom*); Cornel Wilde (*A Song to Remember*)
THE WINNER: Ray Milland

Best Actress

NOMINEES: Ingrid Bergman (*The Bells of St.*

Mary's); Joan Crawford (*Mildred Pierce*); Greer Garson (*The Valley of Decision*); Jennifer Jones (*Love Letters*); Gene Tierney (*Leave Her to Heaven*)
THE WINNER: Joan Crawford

Behind the Oscar

Joan Crawford, sick in bed with the flu, was the surprise winner—a sentimental choice—over Ingrid Bergman. Crawford accepted her Oscar and the press while propped up in her bed.

1946

Best Picture

NOMINEES: *The Best Years of Our Lives, Henry V, It's a Wonderful Life, The Razor's Edge, The Yearling*
THE WINNER: *The Best Years of Our Lives* (Samuel Goldwyn–RKO Radio)
DIRECTOR: William Wyler
PLAYERS: Myrna Loy, Fredric March, Dana Andrews, Teresa Wright, Virginia Mayo, Hoagy Carmichael

Best Actor

NOMINEES: Laurence Olivier (*Henry V*); Larry Parks (*The Jolson Story*), Fredric March (*The Best Years of Our Lives*); Gregory Peck (*The Yearling*); James Stewart (*It's a Wonderful Life*)
THE WINNER: Fredric March

Best Actress

NOMINEES: Celia Johnson (*Brief Encounter*); Jennifer Jones (*Duel in the Sun*); Olivia De Havilland (*To Each His Own*); Rosalind Russell (*Sister Kenny*); Jane Wyman (*The Yearling*)
THE WINNER: Olivia De Havilland

Behind the Oscar

When Olivia De Havilland won the best actress award, her sister, Joan Fontaine, tried to shake her hand. Olivia backed off as if confronted by a leper and cut her dead, saying, "I don't know why she does that when she knows how I feel." *The Best Years of Our Lives* beat *The Yearling* by a nose, and venerable pioneer Sam Goldwyn had his 1st accolade from the Academy. In true form, he called Hoagy Carmichael, one of the stars in his film, "Hugo" Carmichael.

1947

Best Picture

NOMINEES: *The Bishop's Wife, Crossfire, Gentleman's Agreement, Great Expectations, Miracle on 34th Street*

THE WINNER: *Gentleman's Agreement* (20th Century-Fox)
DIRECTOR: Elia Kazan
PLAYERS: Gregory Peck, Dorothy McGuire, John Garfield

Best Actor

NOMINEES: John Garfield (*Body and Soul*); Ronald Colman (*A Double Life*); William Powell (*Life with Father*); Gregory Peck (*Gentleman's Agreement*); Michael Redgrave (*Mourning Becomes Electra*)
THE WINNER: Ronald Colman

Best Actress

NOMINEES: Joan Crawford (*Possessed*); Susan Hayward (*Smash Up—The Story of a Woman*); Dorothy McGuire (*Gentleman's Agreement*); Rosalind Russell (*Mourning Becomes Electra*); Loretta Young (*The Farmer's Daughter*)
THE WINNER: Loretta Young

Behind the Oscar

The greatest longshot in Academy history came through. Before the big night, *Daily Variety* had polled a selection of the Academy's voting members and had come up with this result for the best actress: 1. Rosalind Russell; 2. Dorothy McGuire; 3. Joan Crawford; 4. Susan Hayward; 5. Loretta Young. Out of the sealed envelope came the winner—Loretta Young. Moviegoers were stunned.

1948

Best Picture

NOMINEES: *Johnny Belinda, The Red Shoes, Hamlet, The Snake Pit, Treasure of Sierra Madre*
THE WINNER: *Hamlet* (British; Universal-International)
DIRECTOR: Laurence Olivier
PLAYERS: Laurence Olivier, Jean Simmons

Best Actor

NOMINEES: Lew Ayres (*Johnny Belinda*); Montgomery Clift (*The Search*); Dan Dailey (*When My Baby Smiles at Me*); Laurence Olivier (*Hamlet*); Clifton Webb (*Sitting Pretty*)
THE WINNER: Laurence Olivier

Best Actress

NOMINEES: Ingrid Bergman (*Joan of Arc*); Olivia De Havilland (*The Snake Pit*); Irene Dunne (*I Remember Mama*); Barbara Stanwyck (*Sorry, Wrong Number*); Jane Wyman (*Johnny Belinda*)
THE WINNER: Jane Wyman

Behind the Oscar

A feisty evening. Many fans expected Olivia De Havilland to win best actress honors, but Jane Wyman took the Oscar. Few doubted that the best picture would be either *Johnny Belinda* or *The Snake Pit*—so the best picture turned out to be Laurence Olivier's *Hamlet*. Walter Wanger, furious that his film *Joan of Arc* hadn't even been nominated, was offered the consolation of a special Oscar for it—but turned it down.

1949

Best Picture

NOMINEES: *All the King's Men, Battleground, The Heiress, A Letter to Three Wives, Twelve O'Clock High*
THE WINNER: *All the King's Men* (Columbia)
DIRECTOR: Robert Rossen
PLAYERS: Broderick Crawford, Joanne Dru, John Ireland, John Derek, Mercedes McCambridge

Best Actor

NOMINEES: Broderick Crawford (*All the King's Men*); Kirk Douglas (*Champion*); Gregory Peck (*Twelve O'Clock High*); Richard Todd (*The Hasty Heart*); John Wayne (*Sands of Iwo Jima*)
THE WINNER: Broderick Crawford

Best Actress

NOMINEES: Jeanne Crain (*Pinky*); Olivia De Havilland (*The Heiress*); Susan Hayward (*My Foolish Heart*); Deborah Kerr (*Edward, My Son*); Loretta Young (*Come to the Stable*)
THE WINNER: Olivia De Havilland

Behind the Oscar

A longtime standby as a "heavy," Broderick Crawford was genuinely surprised to find himself the winner for the role of Willie Stark in *All the King's Men*. The accolade he treasured more, however, came from his mother, Helen Broderick, an established actress and uncompromising critic. She told her son, "I could find nothing wrong with your performance." The other major winner, Olivia De Havilland, was much criticized by the press for her cold acceptance speech.

1950

Best Picture

NOMINEES: *All about Eve, Born Yesterday, Father of the Bride, King Solomon's Mines, Sunset Boulevard*
THE WINNER: *All about Eve* (20th Century-Fox)
DIRECTOR: Joseph L. Mankiewicz
PLAYERS: Bette Davis, Anne Baxter, George Sanders, Celeste Holm

Best Actor

NOMINEES: Louis Calhern (*The Magnificent Yankee*); Jose Ferrer (*Cyrano de Bergerac*); William Holden (*Sunset Boulevard*); James Stewart (*Harvey*); Spencer Tracy (*Father of the Bride*)
THE WINNER: Jose Ferrer

Best Actress

NOMINEES: Anne Baxter (*All about Eve*); Bette Davis (*All about Eve*); Judy Holliday (*Born Yesterday*); Eleanor Parker (*Caged*); Gloria Swanson (*Sunset Boulevard*)
THE WINNER: Judy Holliday

Behind the Oscar

Jose Ferrer, under a cloud after the House Un-American Activities Committee investigated his alleged communist leanings, was given little chance in the best actor category—yet, in a very exciting moment, he was announced the winner. Marlene Dietrich, appearing as an award presenter, almost stole the show at the ceremony. La Dietrich wore a dress that was apparently painted on, and displayed her fabulous legs and figure to gasp-evoking perfection.

1951

Best Picture

NOMINEES: *An American in Paris, Decision before Dawn, A Place in the Sun, Quo Vadis, A Streetcar Named Desire*
THE WINNER: *An American in Paris* (MGM)
DIRECTOR: Vincente Minnelli
PLAYERS: Gene Kelly, Leslie Caron, Oscar Levant, Georges Guetary, Nina Foch

Best Actor

NOMINEES: Humphrey Bogart (*The African Queen*); Marlon Brando (*A Streetcar Named Desire*); Montgomery Clift (*A Place in the Sun*); Arthur Kennedy (*Bright Victory*); Fredric March (*Death of a Salesman*)
THE WINNER: Humphrey Bogart

Best Actress

NOMINEES: Katharine Hepburn (*The African Queen*); Vivien Leigh (*A Streetcar Named Desire*); Eleanor Parker (*Detective Story*); Shelley Winters (*A Place in the Sun*); Jane Wyman (*The Blue Veil*)
THE WINNER: Vivien Leigh

Behind the Oscar

Either *A Streetcar Named Desire* or *A Place in the Sun* was regarded as a cinch to win best picture, but a longshot, MGM's *An American in Paris* took it. There was much muttering about the number of Academy voters who worked at MGM. Marlon Brando was considered a shoo-in for best actor. But Humphrey Bogart got it. The logic of the vote: Brando was new and had time, Bogart had been too long overlooked. "Awards don't mean a thing, unless every actor plays Hamlet and then who is best is decided," said Bogart the morning after. Not exactly a turndown, for Humphrey Bogart did accept his Oscar. He didn't know it, but he set a kind of precedent that would be followed by a select few.

1952

Best Picture

NOMINEES: *High Noon, The Greatest Show on Earth, Ivanhoe, Moulin Rouge, The Quiet Man*
THE WINNER: *The Greatest Show on Earth* (Cecil B. De Mille–Paramount)
DIRECTOR: Cecil B. De Mille
PLAYERS: Betty Hutton, Cornel Wilde, Charlton Heston, Dorothy Lamour, Gloria Grahame, James Stewart

Best Actor

NOMINEES: Marlon Brando (*Viva Zapata!*); Gary Cooper (*High Noon*); Kirk Douglas (*The Bad and the Beautiful*); Jose Ferrer (*Moulin Rouge*); Alec Guinness (*The Lavendar Hill Mob*)
THE WINNER: Gary Cooper

Best Actress

NOMINEES: Shirley Booth (*Come Back, Little Sheba*); Joan Crawford (*Sudden Fear*); Bette Davis (*The Star*); Julie Harris (*The Member of the Wedding*); Susan Hayward (*With a Song in My Heart*)
THE WINNER: Shirley Booth

Behind The Oscar

This year marked the reluctant marriage between movies and television. The Academy had always turned down previous proposals from the TV networks to televise their proceedings, but this year the Academy got an offer it couldn't refuse: $100,000 persuaded them that they could live with the tube after all, especially since the major studios had been contributing less and less to the Academy's support. Without leaving their living rooms, the public was able to watch Gloria Swanson, Janet Gaynor, and Mary Pickford pass out awards.

1953

Best Picture

NOMINEES: *From Here to Eternity, Julius Caesar, The Robe, Roman Holiday, Shane*
THE WINNER: *From Here to Eternity* (Columbia)
DIRECTOR: Fred Zinnemann
PLAYERS: Burt Lancaster, Montgomery Clift, Deborah Kerr, Frank Sinatra, Donna Reed

Best Actor

NOMINEES: Marlon Brando (*Julius Caesar*); Richard Burton (*The Robe*); Montgomery Clift (*From Here to Eternity*); William Holden (*Stalag 17*); Burt Lancaster (*From Here to Eternity*)
THE WINNER: William Holden

Best Actress

NOMINEES: Leslie Caron (*Lili*); Ava Gardner (*Mogambo*); Audrey Hepburn (*Roman Holiday*); Deborah Kerr (*From Here to Eternity*); Maggie McNamara (*The Moon Is Blue*)
THE WINNER: Audrey Hepburn

Behind the Oscar

No surprises in the running this year, but some emotional highlights and some startling gaffes. TV committed most of the gaffes by cutting to commercials right in the middle of acceptance speeches, angering William Holden, one of the victims of a cutoff, and prompting him to expound backstage on a system which valued commercials over program content. Frank Sinatra received an emotional response to his winning of the Oscar for his comeback in the supporting role of Maggio in *From Here to Eternity*, a part he wanted so much that he worked for practically nothing. His gamble paid off and his near-defunct career came alive.

1954

Best Picture

NOMINEES: *The Caine Mutiny, The Country Girl, On the Waterfront, Seven Brides for Seven Brothers, Three Coins in the Fountain*
THE WINNER: *On the Waterfront* (Columbia)
DIRECTOR: Elia Kazan
PLAYERS: Marlon Brando, Karl Malden, Lee J. Cobb, Eva Marie Saint

Best Actor

NOMINEES: Humphrey Bogart (*The Caine Mutiny*); Marlon Brando (*On the Water-*

front); Bing Crosby (*The Country Girl*); James Mason (*A Star Is Born*); Dan O'Herlihy (*Adventures of Robinson Crusoe*)
THE WINNER: Marlon Brando

Best Actress

NOMINEES: Dorothy Dandridge (*Carmen Jones*); Judy Garland (*A Star Is Born*); Grace Kelly (*The Country Girl*); Audrey Hepburn (*Sabrina*); Jane Wyman (*Magnificent Obsession*)
THE WINNER: Grace Kelly

Behind the Oscar

A race between Judy Garland and Grace Kelly, Marlon Brando and Bing Crosby. Judy was in the hospital, after the birth of her son, Joey, when she heard of her loss. Brando, a 3-time loser, was gracious and humble in his acceptance speech. He later told friends he was "sure it was going to be Bing."

1955

Best Picture

NOMINEES: *Love is a Many-Splendored Thing, Marty, Mister Roberts, Picnic, The Rose Tattoo*
THE WINNER: *Marty* (Hecht-Lancaster; United Artists)
DIRECTOR: Delbert Mann
PLAYERS: Ernest Borgnine, Betsy Blair

Best Actor

NOMINEES: Ernest Borgnine (*Marty*); James Cagney (*Love Me or Leave Me*); James Dean (*East of Eden*); Frank Sinatra (*Man with the Golden Arm*); Spencer Tracy (*Bad Day at Black Rock*)
THE WINNER: Ernest Borgnine

Best Actress

NOMINEES: Susan Hayward (*I'll Cry Tomorrow*); Katharine Hepburn (*Summertime*); Jennifer Jones (*Love Is a Many-Splendored Thing*); Anna Magnani (*The Rose Tattoo*); Eleanor Parker (*Interrupted Melody*)
THE WINNER: Anna Magnani

Behind the Oscar

Jerry Lewis replaced Bob Hope as MC this year and all the winners, except for Anna Magnani, were on hand to receive their Oscars. Grace Kelly earned a chiding from Louella Parsons when she failed to acknowledge Jerry Lewis's salute to her from the industry. Grace, who was to be Princess of Monaco soon and was retiring from the screen, was there as a presenter. Miss Parsons told her readers: "It seems she might have taken a moment to thank him, give him a little kiss or something before leaving the stage so abruptly."

1956

Best Picture

NOMINEES: *Around the World in 80 Days, Friendly Persuasion, Giant, The King and I, The Ten Commandments*
THE WINNER: *Around the World in 80 Days* (Todd–United Artists)
DIRECTOR: Michael Anderson
PLAYERS: David Niven, Cantinflas, Shirley MacLaine, Robert Newton

Best Actor

NOMINEES: Yul Brynner (*The King and I*); James Dean (*Giant*); Kirk Douglas (*Lust for Life*); Rock Hudson (*Giant*); Sir Laurence Olivier (*Richard III*)
THE WINNER: Yul Brynner

Best Actress

NOMINEES: Carrol Baker (*Baby Doll*); Ingrid Bergman (*Anastasia*); Katharine Hepburn (*The Rainmaker*); Nancy Kelly (*The Bad Seed*); Deborah Kerr (*The King and I*)
THE WINNER: Ingrid Bergman

Behind the Oscar

A triumphal recognition—after 6 years of self-imposed exile—was achieved by Ingrid Bergman when the Academy presented her an Oscar for *Anastasia*. Though in Paris doing a play, Miss Bergman responded with delight: "It is the most wished-for award by all movie artists," she said, "because it comes from your co-workers." Driven from a Hollywood that castigated her for her illicit romance with Italian director Roberto Rossellini, she was honored by her peers 6 years later.

1957

Best Picture

NOMINEES: *The Bridge on the River Kwai, Peyton Place, Sayonara, Twelve Angry Men, Witness for the Prosecution*
THE WINNER: *The Bridge on the River Kwai* (Columbia)
DIRECTOR: David Lean
PLAYERS: William Holden, Alec Guinness, Jack Hawkins

Best Actor

NOMINEES: Marlon Brando (*Sayonara*); Anthony Franciosa (*A Hatful of Rain*); Alec Guinness (*The Bridge on the River Kwai*);

Charles Laughton (*Witness for the Prosecution*); Anthony Quinn (*Wild Is the Wind*)
THE WINNER: Alec Guinness

Best Actress

NOMINEES: Deborah Kerr (*Heaven Knows, Mr. Allison*); Anna Magnani (*Wild Is the Wind*); Elizabeth Taylor (*Raintree County*); Lana Turner (*Peyton Place*); Joanne Woodward (*The Three Faces of Eve*)
THE WINNER: Joanne Woodward

Behind the Oscar

Two violent deaths surrounded the Awards this year. Four days before the ceremony, a plane crash ended the life of Mike Todd and the latest marriage of Elizabeth Taylor. Elizabeth was a contender for an Oscar for *Raintree County*. Also in the running was Lana Turner for *Peyton Place*, and Lana would soon be embroiled in the scandal of her life when her boyfriend Johnny Stompanato was killed in her Beverly Hills home. Relative newcomer Joanne ·Woodward won, however, causing the one catty remark of the evening, delivered by Joan Crawford. Miss Crawford, noting that Joanne had made her own dress for the occasion, said: "Joanne Woodward is setting the cause of Hollywood glamour back 20 years by making her own clothes."

1958

Best Picture

NOMINEES: *Auntie Mame, Cat on a Hot Tin Roof, The Defiant Ones, Gigi, Separate Tables*
THE WINNER: *Gigi* (MGM)
DIRECTOR: Vincente Minnelli
PLAYERS: Leslie Caron, Maurice Chevalier, Louis Jourdan

Best Actor

NOMINEES: Tony Curtis (*The Defiant Ones*); Paul Newman (*Cat on a Hot Tin Roof*); David Niven (*Separate Tables*); Sidney Poitier (*The Defiant Ones*); Spencer Tracy (*The Old Man and the Sea*)
THE WINNER: David Niven

Best Actress

NOMINEES: Susan Hayward (*I Want to Live!*); Deborah Kerr (*Separate Tables*); Shirley MacLaine (*Some Came Running*); Rosalind Russell (*Auntie Mame*); Elizabeth Taylor (*Cat on a Hot Tin Roof*)
THE WINNER: Susan Hayward

Behind the Oscar

A big program foul-up on television. As all of the 90 participating stars were singing the grand finale of "There's No Business Like Show Business," it was discovered that the 2-hour show still had 20 minutes to go. Jerry Lewis frantically tried to improvise by some impromptu conducting, but the stars began to talk among themselves, some of them leaving, some of them bumping together in confusion, until NBC mercifully switched to a 15-minute sports filler.

1959

Best Picture

NOMINEES: *Anatomy of a Murder, Ben-Hur, The Diary of Anne Frank, The Nun's Story, Room at the Top*
THE WINNER: *Ben-Hur* (MGM)
DIRECTOR: William Wyler
PLAYERS: Charlton Heston, Jack Hawkins, Haya Harareet, Stephen Boyd

Best Actor

NOMINEES: Laurence Harvey (*Room at the Top*); Charlton Heston (*Ben-Hur*); Jack Lemmon (*Some Like It Hot*); Paul Muni (*The Last Angry Man*); James Stewart (*Anatomy of a Murder*)
THE WINNER: Charlton Heston

Best Actress

NOMINEES: Doris Day (*Pillow Talk*); Audrey Hepburn (*The Nun's Story*); Katharine Hepburn (*Suddenly, Last Summer*); Simone Signoret (*Room at the Top*); Elizabeth Taylor (*Suddenly, Last Summer*)
THE WINNER: Simone Signoret

Behind the Oscar

Not quite a grand slam, but *Ben-Hur* set an Academy record by winning 11 out of its 12 nominations. Stars stayed away from this one, still stinging from the defects of the previous year's proceedings. There was a pall on the affair from a 4-week actors' strike, plus the final pullout of studio financial support for the Academy. The prevailing studio sentiment was echoed by Paramount: "Why should Paramount support a show that sells only MGM's *Ben-Hur*?" Why, indeed?

1960

Best Picture

NOMINEES: *The Alamo, The Apartment, Elmer Gantry, Sons and Lovers, The Sundowners*

THE WINNERS: *The Apartment* (Mirisch–United Artists)
DIRECTOR: Billy Wilder
PLAYERS: Jack Lemmon, Shirley MacLaine, Fred MacMurray

Best Actor

NOMINEES: Trevor Howard (*Sons and Lovers*); Burt Lancaster (*Elmer Gantry*); Jack Lemmon (*The Apartment*); Laurence Olivier (*The Entertainer*); Spencer Tracy (*Inherit the Wind*)
THE WINNER: Burt Lancaster

Best Actress

NOMINEES: Greer Garson (*Sunrise at Campobello*); Deborah Kerr (*The Sundowners*); Shirley MacLaine (*The Apartment*); Melina Mercouri (*Never on Sunday*); Elizabeth Taylor (*Butterfield 8*)
THE WINNER: Elizabeth Taylor

Behind the Oscar

Some said Elizabeth Taylor got the Oscar out of sympathy rather than for *Butterfield 8*. The glamorous star, then married to Eddie Fisher, had almost died from a bout of pneumonia a short time before. ABC outbid NBC to televise this year's proceedings, and it was held at the Civic Auditorium in Santa Monica, creating a hue and cry from the purists who lamented that Santa Monica was *not* Hollywood.

1961

Best Picture

NOMINEES: *Fanny, The Guns of Navarone, The Hustler, Judgment at Nuremberg, West Side Story*
THE WINNER: *West Side Story* (Mirisch–United Artists)
DIRECTORS: Robert Wise, Jerome Robbins
PLAYERS: Natalie Wood, Richard Beymer, Russ Tamblyn, Rita Moreno, George Chakiris

Best Actor

NOMINEES: Charles Boyer (*Fanny*); Paul Newman (*The Hustler*); Maximilian Schell (*Judgment at Nuremberg*); Spencer Tracy (*Judgment at Nuremberg*); Stuart Whitman (*The Mark*)
THE WINNER: Maximilian Schell

Best Actress

NOMINEES: Audrey Hepburn (*Breakfast at Tiffany's*); Piper Laurie (*The Hustler*); Sophia Loren (*Two Women*); Geraldine Page (*Summer and Smoke*); Natalie Wood (*Splendor in the Grass*)
THE WINNER: Sophia Loren

Behind the Oscar

Lots of 1sts this year. The 1st time that a regular Oscar was given to an actress in a foreign-language picture (Sophia Loren for *Two Women*), the 1st double Oscar (2 directors for *West Side Story*—Jerome Robbins and Robert Wise), and George C. Scott became the 1st actor to decline an award in advance. After his nomination for best supporting actor in *The Hustler*, Scott asked that his name be removed from the polling. It wasn't, and he didn't win, but the future would tell a different tale.

1962

Best Picture

NOMINEES: *Lawrence of Arabia, The Longest Day, The Music Man, Mutiny on the Bounty, To Kill a Mockingbird*
THE WINNER: *Lawrence of Arabia* (Horizon-Columbia)
DIRECTOR: David Lean
PLAYERS: Alec Guinness, Anthony Quinn, Jack Hawkins, Jose Ferrer, Peter O'Toole

Best Actor

NOMINEES: Burt Lancaster (*Bird Man of Alcatraz*); Jack Lemmon (*Days of Wine and Roses*); Marcello Mastrioianni (*Divorce—Italian Style*); Peter O'Toole (*Lawrence of Arabia*); Gregory Peck (*To Kill a Mockingbird*)
THE WINNER: Gregory Peck

Best Actress

NOMINEES: Anne Bancroft (*The Miracle Worker*); Bette Davis (*Whatever Happened to Baby Jane?*); Katharine Hepburn (*Long Day's Journey into Night*); Geraldine Page (*Sweet Bird of Youth*); Lee Remick (*Days of Wine and Roses*)
THE WINNER: Anne Bancroft

Behind the Oscar

Smart money was on Omar Sharif and Angela Lansbury this year in the supporting categories, but both of them lost. Anne Bancroft's win wasn't that surprising considering her tour de force in *The Miracle Worker*, but there was speculation over Joan Crawford's radiant smile while accepting for Miss Bancroft. People wondered whether Joan was obviously relieved that Bette Davis, a nominee and Joan's costar in *What Happened to Baby Jane?*, lost. The relationship between these 2 powerful ladies was said to be a bit strained.

1963

Best Picture

NOMINEES: *America, America, Cleopatra, How the West Was Won, Lilies of the Field, Tom Jones*
THE WINNER: *Tom Jones* (British; United Artists–Lopert)
DIRECTOR: Tony Richardson
PLAYERS: Albert Finney, Susannah York, Hugh Griffith, Edith Evans, Joan Greenwood, Diane Cilento

Best Actor

NOMINEES: Albert Finney (*Tom Jones*); Richard Harris (*This Sporting Life*); Rex Harrison (*Cleopatra*); Paul Newman (*Hud*); Sidney Poitier (*Lilies of the Field*)
THE WINNER: Sidney Poitier

Best Actress

NOMINEES: Leslie Caron (*The L-Shaped Room*); Shirley MacLaine (*Irma La Douce*); Patricia Neal (*Hud*); Rachel Roberts (*This Sporting Life*); Natalie Wood (*Love with the Proper Stranger*)
THE WINNER: Patricia Neal

Behind the Oscar

Since Hattie McDaniel was the only black to win an Oscar before him, Sidney Poitier was aware of the importance of the occasion when he accepted his Oscar. He was practically the only winner in the acting categories who showed up. Patricia Neal, who won for *Hud*, was expecting a baby in England, and the rest of the winners were abroad also. Sammy Davis got the only laugh in a rather dull evening when he remarked upon receiving the wrong envelope: "Wait until the NAACP hears about this!"

1964

Best Picture

NOMINEES: *Becket, Dr. Strangelove or: How I Learned to Stop Worrying and Love the Bomb, Mary Poppins, My Fair Lady, Zorba the Greek*
THE WINNER: *My Fair Lady* (Warner Bros.)
DIRECTOR: George Cukor
PLAYERS: Audrey Hepburn, Rex Harrison

Best Actor

NOMINEES: Richard Burton (*Becket*); Rex Harrison (*My Fair Lady*); Peter O'Toole (*Becket*); Anthony Quinn (*Zorba the Greek*); Peter Sellers (*Dr. Strangelove . . .*)
THE WINNER: Rex Harrison

Best Actress

NOMINEES: Julie Andrews (*Mary Poppins*); Anne Bancroft (*The Pumpkin Eater*); Sophia Loren (*Marriage Italian Style*); Debbie Reynolds (*The Unsinkable Molly Brown*); Kim Stanley (*Séance on a Wet Afternoon*)
THE WINNER: Julie Andrews

Behind the Oscar

Jack Warner felt Julie Andrews lacked star quality, so he gave the role of Eliza to Audrey Hepburn. The community divided into 2 camps, pro and con, for and against the 2 ladies. There was even talk of a write-in campaign for Audrey when she was not nominated for an award. However, Hepburn showed up for the ceremony, and the camera work that night obviously played up the tension generated between the 2 ladies. Julie Andrews won her Oscar, but Hepburn's *My Fair Lady* made out awfully well, too.

1965

Best Picture

NOMINEES: *Darling, Doctor Zhivago, Ship of Fools, The Sound of Music, A Thousand Clowns*
THE WINNER: *The Sound of Music* (20th Century-Fox)
DIRECTOR: Robert Wise
PLAYERS: Julie Andrews, Christopher Plummer, Eleanor Parker

Best Actor

NOMINEES: Richard Burton (*The Spy Who Came in from the Cold*); Lee Marvin (*Cat Ballou*); Laurence Olivier (*Othello*); Rod Steiger (*The Pawnbroker*); Oskar Werner (*Ship of Fools*)
THE WINNER: Lee Marvin

Best Actress

NOMINEES: Julie Andrews (*The Sound of Music*); Julie Christie (*Darling*); Samantha Eggar (*The Collector*); Elizabeth Hartman (*A Patch of Blue*); Simone Signoret (*Ship of Fools*)
THE WINNER: Julie Christie

Behind the Oscar

Again, there was a scarcity of stars on hand. Many pictures were being made on location.

This was the 1st telecast in color, and the only star of any note appeared to be Lynda Bird Johnson, escorted by George Hamilton. The evening was not without drama, as a film bearing a message from Patricia Neal was shown. Miss Neal was recovering from a severe stroke which almost took her life, and her appearance was a moving one. A slight attempt at creating a feud between the 2 female British contenders—Julie Christie and Julie Andrews —failed completely.

1966

Best Picture

NOMINEES: Alfie, A Man for All Seasons, The Russians Are Coming, the Russians Are Coming, The Sand Pebbles, Who's Afraid of Virginia Woolf?
THE WINNER: A Man for All Seasons (Columbia)
DIRECTOR: Fred Zinnemann
PLAYERS: Wendy Hiller, Leo McKern, Robert Shaw, Orson Welles, Susannah York, Paul Scofield

Best Actor

NOMINEES: Alan Arkin (The Russians Are Coming, the Russians Are Coming); Richard Burton (Who's Afraid of Virginia Woolf?); Michael Caine (Alfie); Steve McQueen (The Sand Pebbles); Paul Scofield (A Man for All Seasons)
THE WINNER: Paul Scofield

Best Actress

NOMINEES: Anouk Aimee (A Man and a Woman); Ida Kaminska (The Shop on Main Street); Lynn Redgrave (Georgy Girl); Vanessa Redgrave (Morgan!); Elizabeth Taylor (Who's Afraid of Virginia Woolf?)
THE WINNER: Elizabeth Taylor

Behind the Oscar

The Academy was now the same age as Jack Benny. Barely 3 hours before the presentations, a strike of television technicians had been settled, so that the show could go on. Again a great number of the major acting winners failed to show. Elizabeth Taylor was informed of her win in London, but she was so angered by the fact that Richard Burton hadn't won that she refused to hold a press conference until 2 weeks later.

1967

Best Picture

NOMINEES: Bonnie and Clyde, Doctor Dolittle, The Graduate, Guess Who's Coming to Dinner, In the Heat of the Night

THE WINNER: In the Heat of the Night (Mirisch–United Artists)
DIRECTOR: Norman Jewison
PLAYERS: Sidney Poitier, Rod Steiger

Best Actor

NOMINEES: Warren Beatty (Bonnie and Clyde); Dustin Hoffman (The Graduate); Paul Newman (Cool Hand Luke); Rod Steiger (In the Heat of the Night); Spencer Tracy (Guess Who's Coming to Dinner)
THE WINNER: Rod Steiger

Best Actress

NOMINEES: Anne Bancroft (The Graduate); Faye Dunaway (Bonnie and Clyde); Dame Edith Evans (The Whisperers); Audrey Hepburn (Wait until Dark); Katharine Hepburn (Guess Who's Coming to Dinner)
THE WINNER: Katharine Hepburn

Behind the Oscar

The Academy celebrated its 40th birthday, but the occasion was a subdued one, because of the assassination of Martin Luther King a short time before the presentations. Academy President Gregory Peck accomplished what others before him had failed to do. He saw to it that 18 of the 20 acting nominees were present that night. What people expected was not that Katharine Hepburn would win again, but that Spencer Tracy might win posthumously. Mrs. Tracy was in the audience in the event that he did. But Tracy failed to win.

1968

Best Picture

NOMINEES: Funny Girl, A Lion in Winter, Oliver!, Rachel, Rachel, Romeo and Juliet
THE WINNER: Oliver! (Romulus–Columbia)
DIRECTOR: Carol Reed
PLAYERS: Ron Moody, Oliver Reed, Harry Secombe, Shani Wallis

Best Actor

NOMINEES: Alan Arkin (The Heart Is a Lonely Hunter); Alan Bates (The Fixer); Ron Moody (Oliver!); Peter O'Toole (A Lion in Winter); Cliff Robertson (Charly)
THE WINNER: Cliff Robertson

Best Actress

NOMINEES: Katharine Hepburn (A Lion in Winter); Patricia Neal (The Subject Was Roses); Vanessa Redgrave (Isadora); Barbra Streisand (Funny Girl); Joanne Woodward (Rachel, Rachel)
THE WINNERS: Katharine Hepburn AND Barbra Streisand

Behind the Oscar

Barbra Streisand tied with Katharine Hepburn this year, the 1st time 2 people got exactly the same number of votes. Some people griped over Paul Newman's slight by the Academy. Newman, in his 1st directorial effort, had been honored by the New York Film Critics as best director of the year, but he didn't even get nominated by the members of the Academy.

1969

Best Picture

NOMINEES: *Anne of the Thousand Days, Butch Cassidy and the Sundance Kid, Hello, Dolly!, Midnight Cowboy, Z*
THE WINNER: *Midnight Cowboy* (United Artists)
DIRECTOR: John Schlesinger
PLAYERS: Dustin Hoffman, Jon Voight

Best Actor

NOMINEES: Richard Burton (*Anne of the Thousand Days*); Dustin Hoffman (*Midnight Cowboy*); Peter O'Toole (*Good-bye, Mr. Chips*); Jon Voight (*Midnight Cowboy*); John Wayne (*True Grit*)
THE WINNER: John Wayne

Best Actress

NOMINEES: Genevieve Bujold (*Anne of the Thousand Days*); Jane Fonda (*They Shoot Horses, Don't They?*); Liza Minnelli (*The Sterile Cuckoo*); Jean Simmons (*The Happy Ending*); Maggie Smith (*The Prime of Miss Jean Brodie*)
THE WINNER: Maggie Smith

Behind the Oscar

It looked like 2 ends of a spectrum. The "Old Hollywood" on one side—represented by Fred Astaire, John Wayne, Cary Grant, Myrna Loy, and Bob Hope. On the other side were Jon Voight, Barbra Streisand, Elliott Gould, and Clint Eastwood. In fact, the most popular award of the evening went to the durably attractive Cary Grant—it was a special statuette commemorating his memorable performances. The audience went wild at this tribute.

1970

Best Picture

NOMINEES: *Airport, Five Easy Pieces, Love Story, M*A*S*H, Patton*
THE WINNER: *Patton* (20th Century-Fox)
DIRECTOR: Franklin J. Schaffner
PLAYERS: George C. Scott, Karl Malden

Best Actor

NOMINEES: Melvyn Douglas (*I Never Sang for My Father*); James Earl Jones (*The Great White Hope*); Jack Nicholson (*Five Easy Pieces*); Ryan O'Neal (*Love Story*); George C. Scott (*Patton*)
THE WINNER: George C. Scott

Best Actress

NOMINEES: Carrie Snodgress (*Diary of a Mad Housewife*); Jane Alexander (*The Great White Hope*); Glenda Jackson (*Women in Love*); Ali MacGraw (*Love Story*); Sarah Miles (*Ryan's Daughter*)
THE WINNER: Glenda Jackson

Behind the Oscar

George C. Scott, the reluctant dragon, who said he didn't want it, got the Oscar for *Patton*. While he wasn't present for the presentation, there is no evidence he returned the Oscar. Still, Scott maintained it was "degrading for actors to compete against one another." Karl Malden, who played Omar Bradley to Scott's Patton, agreed with Scott's right to decline but felt it could have been done more subtly. The town was again divided into 2 camps. Actually, without the controversy, it would have been a dull event. Oscar was beginning to look his age.

1971

Best Picture

NOMINEES: *A Clockwork Orange, Fiddler on the Roof, The French Connection, The Last Picture Show, Nicholas and Alexandra*
THE WINNER: *The French Connection* (20th Century-Fox)
DIRECTOR: William Friedkin
PLAYERS: Gene Hackman, Fernando Rey, Roy Scheider, Tony Lo Bianco, Marcel Bozzuffi

Best Actor

NOMINEES: Peter Finch (*Sunday, Bloody Sunday*); Gene Hackman (*The French Connection*); Walter Matthau (*Kotch*); George C. Scott (*The Hospital*); Topol (*Fiddler on the Roof*)
THE WINNER: Gene Hackman

Best Actress

NOMINEES: Julie Christie (*McCabe & Mrs. Miller*); Jane Fonda (*Klute*); Glenda Jackson (*Sunday, Bloody Sunday*); Vanessa Redgrave (*Mary, Queen of Scots*); Janet Suzman (*Nicholas and Alexandra*)
THE WINNER: Jane Fonda

Behind the Oscar

Charlie Chaplin had not been in the U.S. for 20 years, after becoming persona non grata because of both his political beliefs and his moral behavior in the intolerant fifties. All was forgiven as the fragile 83-year-old genius made his hesitant way to the podium to receive his 2nd special award for his contributions to the entertainment media. The audience of 2,900 stood and cheered and clapped for a full 4 minutes, leaving the old man tearful and moved. Seventy-five million people watched the award ceremonies on TV this night.

1972

Best Picture

NOMINEES: *Cabaret, Deliverance, The Emigrants, The Godfather, Sounder*
THE WINNER: *The Godfather* (Albert S. Ruddy –Paramount)
DIRECTOR: Francis Ford Coppola
PLAYERS: Marlon Brando, Al Pacino, James Caan, Richard Castellano, Robert Duvall, Sterling Hayden, John Marley, Richard Conte, Diane Keaton

Best Actor

NOMINEES: Marlon Brando (*The Godfather*); Michael Caine (*Sleuth*); Laurence Olivier (*Sleuth*); Peter O'Toole (*The Ruling Class*); Paul Winfield (*Sounder*)
THE WINNER: Marlon Brando

Best Actress

NOMINEES: Liza Minnelli (*Cabaret*); Diana Ross (*Lady Sings the Blues*); Maggie Smith (*Travels with My Aunt*); Cicely Tyson (*Sounder*); Liv Ullmann (*The Emigrants*)
THE WINNER: Liza Minnelli

Behind the Oscar

Marlon Brando became the 2nd actor to turn down an Oscar. A lot had happened since he won in 1954, and now Brando insisted that the American Indian did not get a fair shake in films, on TV, and on reruns. Instead, he had a starlet by the name of Maria Cruz, who called herself Sacheen Littlefeather, refuse the Oscar for him. Liza Minnelli's slight scrape on a motorcycle didn't keep her from the ceremonies and her Oscar. Diana Ross, also a contender, was criticized for running a blatant ad campaign in her attempt to win the award.

1973

Best Picture

NOMINEES: *American Graffiti, Cries and Whispers, The Exorcist, The Sting, A Touch of Class*

THE WINNER: *The Sting* (Universal–Bill/Phillips–Hill)
DIRECTOR: George Roy Hill
PLAYERS: Paul Newman, Robert Redford

Best Actor

NOMINEES: Marlon Brando (*Last Tango in Paris*); Jack Lemmon (*Save the Tiger*); Jack Nicholson (*The Last Detail*); Al Pacino (*Serpico*); Robert Redford (*The Sting*)
THE WINNER: Jack Lemmon

Best Actress

NOMINEES: Ellen Burstyn (*The Exorcist*); Glenda Jackson (*A Touch of Class*); Marsha Mason (*Cinderella Liberty*); Barbra Streisand (*The Way We Were*); Joanne Woodward (*Summer Wishes, Winter Dreams*)
THE WINNER: Glenda Jackson

Behind the Oscar

The highlight of the award ceremony came when 33-year-old Robert Opel, a Hollywood advertising man, having gained access to the backstage area with a press badge, stripped off his clothes and streaked past the footlights just as David Niven was speaking. Ad-libbed Niven as he watched the nude streaker exit, "The only way he could get a laugh was by showing his shortcomings." Wrote San Francisco columnist Terrence O'Flaherty: "There's only one trouble with streaking—the wrong people usually do it. The ones who should have removed their clothes were Cher Bono, Twiggy, and Elizabeth Taylor." For the 1st time in 22 years, Bob Hope was not on hand. Jack Lemmon bet Walter Matthau $1,000 to $500 that he wouldn't win the Oscar. He lost his bet. Enraged that his picture, *The Exorcist*, wasn't voted Best Picture, director William Friedkin refused to attend the ball celebrating the awards. By winning the award for Best Supporting Actress, 10-year-old Tatum O'Neal (*Paper Moon*)—who had once headed a juvenile ring of bicycle thieves—became the youngest winner of a full Oscar in history (Shirley Temple had been given a miniature Oscar when she was 6).

1974

Best Picture

NOMINEES: *Chinatown, The Conversation, The Godfather Part II, Lenny, The Towering Inferno*
THE WINNER: *The Godfather Part II* (Coppola Company–Paramount)
DIRECTOR: Francis Ford Coppola
PLAYERS: Al Pacino, Robert De Niro, Lee Strasberg, Michael V. Gazzo

Best Actor

NOMINEES: Art Carney (*Harry and Tonto*); Albert Finney (*Murder on the Orient Express*); Dustin Hoffman (*Lenny*); Jack Nicholson (*Chinatown*); Al Pacino (*The Godfather Part II*)
THE WINNER: Art Carney

Best Actress

NOMINEES: Ellen Burstyn (*Alice Doesn't Live Here Anymore*); Diahann Carroll (*Claudine*); Faye Dunaway (*Chinatown*); Valerie Perrine (*Lenny*); Gena Rowlands (*A Woman Under the Influence*)
THE WINNER: Ellen Burstyn

Behind the Oscar

Dustin Hoffman announced in advance that the awards were "ugly" and "grotesque," and the presentation a "beauty pageant." During the show Bob Hope said, "If Dustin Hoffman wins tonight, he's going to have a friend pick it up for him—George C. Scott." Ingrid Bergman won the Best Supporting Actress award, not for her performance in a minor role, but because of collective show business guilt (over Hollywood's ostracism of her 25 years earlier when she'd had an affair with director Roberto Rossellini). Bergman felt Valentina Cortese was more deserving of the award. Biggest flap occurred when the producer of the Best Documentary, Bert Schneider, who'd won with *Hearts and Minds*, read aloud a telegram of greetings from the head of the Vietcong delegation in Paris. Backstage, an outraged Bob Hope wrote a disclaimer, which Frank Sinatra approved and read to the divided audience.
—C.E. & The Eds.

The Super Difficult Filmlore Game

By HANK GRANT, columnist for *The Hollywood Reporter*, a motion picture and television trade daily, and commentator on films for CBS-TV.

I introduced my 1st "Filmlore Question" in my column during a dull summer month in 1969, and what I'd intended to be just a short-time feature is still running strong today.

Recently, I have been urged by readers to compile a select number of Filmlore Questions as a handy game they could have at parties, now that Charades has become old hat.

I calculatedly have selected 12 "toughie" questions, all of which got no correct answers on 1st printing and which required added clues, but you did want to become a filmlore buff, didn't you?

Answers to the following questions can be found at the end of the quiz. Frankly, if you can answer 2 of these questions correctly, you're a genius!

Questions

1. When he was 4 years old in 1918, Jackie Coogan achieved international stardom with his title role opposite Charles Chaplin in *The Kid*, but he actually had made his film debut as the title star of what previous movie?
2. What top character actor, now deceased, played a very important role for Frank Capra, who scrapped it entirely in favor of another relatively unknown actor?
3. In MGM's *The Great Ziegfeld* (1936), who played the roles of Billie Burke and Fanny Brice?
4. To date, the theatrical screen has had no less than 13 Tarzans, but can you name the 2 Tarzan movies in which 2 Tarzans appeared?
5. Can you name the movie in which Joel McCrea had his 1st speaking role?
6. Who was the only woman director Charles Chaplin had in his entire film career?
7. What Irish-born Hollywood film queen made her acting debut on the London stage with a role as a Jewish girl?
8. Can you name the late Paul Muni's 1st starring role?
9. Late soprano Grace Moore made her Hollywood film debut in what movie?
10. Can you name the well-known character actor who, within one year, played Sherlock Holmes in one movie and Dr. Watson in another?
11. D. W. Griffith made film history in 1922 with his *Orphans of the Storm*, starring Dorothy and Lillian Gish, but can you name one of 2 producers who'd previously filmed it under its original title of *The Two Orphans*?
12. What was the late Boris Karloff's monster name in the 1931 *Frankenstein* movie?

Answers to Grant's Filmlore Quiz

1. Four years before his acclaim as *The Kid*, Jackie Coogan had the starring role when he was but 16 months old in *Skinner's Baby* (Essany, 1916).
2. The late Walter Connolly was the luckless one. Frank Capra had 1st shelved Sam Jaffe's footage as the High Lama in *Lost Horizon* in favor of hiring Connolly, who'd become a top film favor-

ite at the time. But after Connolly had completed his role, Capra didn't like it and scrapped it entirely in favor of Jaffe's completed footage. Ironically, Capra had 1st signed Henry B. Walthall for the High Lama role, but Walthall died just days before production began.

3. In *The Great Ziegfeld*, Myrna Loy played the role of Billie Burke, but the role of Fanny Brice was played by Fanny Brice herself.

4. *Tarzan's New York Adventure* (1942) and *Tarzan the Magnificent* were the only Tarzan movies in which two Tarzans appeared in each. In the first, Johnny Weismuller and the very 1st Tarzan, Elmo Lincoln, who played the role of a circus roustabout, appeared. In the second movie, Gordon Scott, who was the 11th Tarzan, appeared with Jock Mahoney, who would be the 12th Tarzan.

5. Even Joel McCrea himself gave us a wrong answer till we refreshed his memory. Joel's 1st speaking role was in *Five O'Clock Girl*, starring Marion Davies (MGM, 1928). Joel played the role of Oswald the plumber, but William Randolph Hearst ordered the entire picture shelved for reasons never divulged. The movie was never released after but one preview.

6. The only woman director Chaplin ever had was Mabel Normand in one of his 1st Mack Sennett comedies. Both Sennett and Chaplin bowed to her persistence because they both loved her. Besides, she was a bigger star than Chaplin at that time.

7. Greer Garson made her acting debut in 1936, playing the role of Shirley Kaplan in the British version of the play *Street Scene*.

8. Paul Muni's 1st starring movie was *The Valiant* (Fox, 1929), which was expanded to feature length from the one-act play of the same name that previously had starred Bert Lytell in a long vaudeville tour on the Orpheum circuit.

9. We had an actual count of 67 wrong answers saying that Grace Moore had made her Hollywood film debut in her box-office smash, *One Night of Love* (Columbia, 1934), but she actually made her debut 4 years previously, playing the role of another singing star, Jenny Lind, in *A Lady's Morals* (MGM, 1930).

10. Reginald Owen played the role of Dr. Watson in *Sherlock Holmes* (Fox, 1932), and released 11 months later was his starring role as Sherlock Holmes in *A Study in Scarlet* (World-Wide, 1933). Indeed, no one has yet challenged Owen's claim to being the only actor to play both roles in separate films.

11. Pre-Griffith, Herbert Brenon produced *The Two Orphans* (Fox, 1915) with Theda Bara and Jean Sothern as his title stars, and pre-Brenon in 1911, William Selig produced it with Winifred Greenwood and Kathlyn Williams as his stars. But Griffith's *Orphans of the Storm* is the only immortal one. As recently as 1972, it was aired again and again on PBS television stations.

12. When Dr. Frankenstein brought his man-made monster to life, he impulsively named him "Adam." Some film buffs argue that the film they've seen again and again did not have this pronouncement and, indeed, Universal admits the naming was cut out of many belated releases because virtually all who'd seen the movie referred (wrongly) to Boris Karloff as "Frankenstein."

Permission of *The Hollywood Reporter* 43rd Anniversary Edition.

Stories behind Songs You Grew Up With

Auld Lang Syne   Robert Burns c. 1788

"Auld Lang Syne" has become a well-known and well-loved song in all English-speaking lands. Many people, if asked, would call it a Scottish folk song, and it is true that the melody may originally have been a folk tune. The words, however, were written by Scotland's famous poet, Robert Burns, who lived from 1759 to 1796. He wrote this particular poem about 1788, using in its 5 stanzas a goodly measure of Scottish dialect.

The title words mean, literally, "old long since" or, colloquially, "the good old days." The phrase "auld lang syne" appears at the end of each verse and in 3 of the 4 lines of the chorus, as well as in the title. Other dialect words are sometimes altered in modern versions of the song to make them more easily understood.

It is believed that the words and music 1st appeared together in published form in the *Scots Musical Museum* in 1796. The melody is also known as "The Miller's Wedding" and it was possibly in this form that Robert Burns 1st heard it. But it is a melody that is sometimes credited to composer William Shield, who used it, or something very similar to it, in his opera *Rosina*, presented at the London Covent Garden Opera House in 1783. It appeared in the overture to the opera and was played so that it imitated the sound of Scottish bagpipes.

Regardless of origin, the tune with the Burns words quickly became a famous song and before long was popular as the last song to be sung when an evening party broke up. The ritual developed that the group stood up in a circle, each one crossing his arms in front of his chest and clasping his neighbors' hands to left and right. While singing, all arms were swung forward and back in time with the music.

Still often sung at parties, picnics, around

campfires, "Auld Lang Syne" is most often sung at New Year's parties when the old year dies at midnight and the new year is ushered in.

England and Scotland both claim the song, and the U.S. has certainly adopted it as its own also.

HOME, SWEET HOME
John Howard Payne/Henry Bishop 1823

This song has, for over 150 years, embodied in words and melody what "home" means to Americans. Although no longer published separately, it is still found in community songbooks and is sung around campfires.

Controversy has swirled about the question of who wrote the words and whether Henry Bishop based the melody on a Sicilian folk song or used a totally original melody.

As to the words, it is quite certain that John Howard Payne penned the lines, now so familiar:

'Mid pleasures and palaces though we may roam
Be it ever so humble, there's no place like home . . .

Originally the song had 2 verses and a chorus. Later he wrote 2 more verses and sent them to Mrs. Joshua Bates of London.

Payne wrote his verses to be incorporated in the revision of an unsuccessful play which he turned into an opera. With music by Sir Henry Bishop, this became *Clari, the Maid of Milan,* 1st performed in London's Covent Garden Opera House on May 8, 1823. Miss Ann Maria Tree as Clari sang "Home, Sweet Home" for the 1st time on that night, and the considerable success which the opera enjoyed was credited mainly to that song.

The manuscript was sold with a group of plays to Charles Kemble, a London producer, who paid Payne £250 for the lot. Payne received no further money for the song which became very popular right away, and when it was published separately, his name did not appear on the music. It was not customary at that time to print the author's name on a song.

As to the music, Sir Henry Bishop may have adapted a Sicilian folk tune to fit Payne's words—an early edition of the song says "composed and partly founded on a Sicilian air by Henry R. Bishop"—or he may have written the tune in folk-song style to fit the story line of the opera where Clari dreams of her simple, thatch-roofed, peasant home.

"Home, Sweet Home," a rather sentimental song, quickly became the song of exiles far from home and was tremendously popular with soldiers during the Civil War. The most famous singers of the day, such as Jenny Lind and Adelina Patti, sang it in concert halls all over the world. One story goes that the famed opera star Adelina Patti did not know the song when President Abraham Lincoln requested her to sing it at the funeral service for young Willie Lincoln in 1862, and the President found a copy in a songbook for her to use.

Presumably, Payne was remembering a boyhood home when, in Paris, he wrote the words of this song. And in East Hampton, Long Island, N.Y., there is preserved what is called the "Home, Sweet Home Cottage," a small house that belonged to Payne's grandfather and where he spent some of his young years. Payne, born in New York City in 1791, spent much of his life in England and France, 1st as a rather successful actor and later as a playwright and arranger. Toward the end of his life he was named American consul in Tunis and he died there in 1852. In 1883 his remains were brought back to his native land and buried in Oak Hill Cemetery near Washington, D.C.

AMERICA Samuel Francis Smith 1831

This patriotic song has become a "semiofficial" national anthem, 2nd only to the official national anthem, "The Star-Spangled Banner," in popularity.

Most Americans know at least this 1st verse, even if they falter on the other 3:

My country, 'tis of thee,
Sweet land of liberty,
Of thee I sing:
Land where my fathers died,
Land of the pilgrims' pride,
From every mountainside,
Let freedom ring.

As was true with "The Star-Spangled Banner," the words of "America" were set to the music of an older song. In 1831 some German songbooks were turned over to Samuel Francis Smith, a young Massachusetts clergyman, with the suggestion that Smith might find some music in them which could be used either by translating the German text or by substituting new words. Smith came upon a tune he liked and wrote the verses of "America" to fit it. One story states that he wrote them at a single sitting. At any rate the song was 1st sung publicly at a children's celebration of Independence Day at the Park Street Church, Boston, on July 4th in 1831.

Only later did Smith learn that the same tune was used for the British patriotic song "God Save the King." It is not known for sure who composed the music originally. There are many conflicting stories and traditions (including the tradition that it was a beer drinker's song), and it is true that the music has been used in many countries.

The composer may have been an Englishman named Henry Carey, who lived from 1685, or thereabouts, until 1743. He is best known as the composer of "Sally in Our Alley." It is recorded that he sang a song with the words "God Save Great George Our King" to the tune we associate with "God Save the King" (and "America") at a party celebrating a British victory, Admiral Vernon's capture of Portobelo. This celebration, in 1740, was held in a tavern in Cornhill, and it was reported that Carey announced that he had written both the music and the words. The song was published in a song collection titled *Thesaurus Musicus* in 1744, giving credit to Carey as author and composer.

As "America," this is one of the few patriotic songs that did not originate in a setting of war, and its celebration of liberty and freedom continues to stir the hearts of Americans.

I WISH I WAS IN DIXIE'S LAND
(or just DIXIE)   Dan D. Emmett 1859

This song, which has come to be a kind of symbol of the South, is known and loved and sung all over the U.S. However, it was written by a Northerner to enliven the show given by Bryant's Minstrels on the New York stage.

Minstrel shows in which white men in blackface makeup did a program of song, dance, and comedy bits were popular in the mid-1800s, and Dan D. Emmett wrote many songs for such shows. He was a member of Bryant's Minstrels in 1859 when he was asked for a new "walk-around" number in which a few soloists would sing and dance at the front of the stage with the rest of the company, perhaps 6 or 8 men, at the back of the stage. "I Wish I Was in Dixie's Land" was the result, reportedly written over a single weekend. At any rate it was 1st performed at Mechanics' Hall on Broadway on April 4, 1859.

The song became a great success as time went on. Emmett sold all his rights in it to the publishing house of Firth, Pond and Company in New York City for $300. There were also editions brought out which failed to give Emmett credit as the composer.

Both North and South claimed the song, but during the Civil War it became almost a national anthem for the Confederate States, and it was given a rousing performance at the inauguration of Jefferson Davis as Confederate President. Southern sympathizers played and sang "Dixie" to embarrass and harass Northerners, especially in Washington, D.C. However, President Lincoln was very fond of the song—he'd heard it 1st in a minstrel show in Chicago in the early spring of 1860—and at the close of the Civil War, he surprised people by immediately requesting that "Dixie" be played.

There is an unsettled dispute over the origin of the word "Dixie," with 3 possibilities put forth. One story has it that "Dixie's Land" was the name given a farm in Manhattan by some slaves sent to Charleston by the farm's owner, Johann Dixie. This story is largely discredited, and the word's origin in the *dix* or $10 banknote issued in New Orleans at one time also seems improbable. The most plausible source of the term, which seems originally to have been used for Negroes and later came to mean the whole South, is the Mason-Dixon line which was the boundary between free and slave States before the Civil War.

Not only is "Dixie" a truly American song, but the lively melody has been used by serious composers wishing to give an American flavor to a piece. It was one of the tunes incorporated by the Swiss-born American composer, Ernest Bloch, in his large symphonic "rhapsody in 3 parts" entitled *America*.

BATTLE HYMN OF THE REPUBLIC
Julia Ward Howe 1861

Who has not felt a thrill at hearing those famous words: "Mine eyes have seen the glory of the coming of the Lord . . ." and "Glory, Glory, Hallelujah!"

On November 20, 1861, Julia Ward Howe and a party of friends were among some 25,000 spectators at a mammoth military review held at Bailey's Cross Roads outside of Washington. Here, President Lincoln, with members of his Cabinet and Gen. George B. McClellan, reviewed between 50,000 and 70,000 troops mobilizing to fight the Civil War. Afterwards, riding back to Washington, Mrs. Howe heard many soldiers singing the song "John Brown's Body" with its stirring march rhythm.

This melody, composed for a Sunday-school song in the South by William Steffe, had become popular with a singing group of "Tigers," members of a battalion of Massachusetts infantry. After the Harpers Ferry raid, led by John Brown in an attempt to free slaves, and the subsequent execution of Brown, one of the soldiers made up the "John Brown's Body" words. It was partly a joke because a fellow soldier was named John Brown. The song quickly spread through the Union Army.

Hearing the soldiers singing, Dr. James Freeman Clarke, a Unitarian minister, suggested to Mrs. Howe that she write some "more appropriate" words. That night she awoke, got up, and wrote the famous verses. Years later, a plaque was mounted in the Old Willard Hotel commemorating this event.

In the February, 1862, issue of the *Atlantic*

Was he/she a man or a woman? Chevalier Charles d'Eon or Lia de Beaumont? As Chevalier d'Eon (top) he was a leading French spy for King Louis XV in 1766. As Lia de Beaumont (bottom) she was a lady-in-waiting to the Russian Czarina. Over $2 million was wagered in England and Europe on the sex of the "she-man." (See: Chap. 10) *Mansell Collection.*

J. Cond. Dilin' *et Sculp.*

Capt. John Cleves Symmes, hero of the War of 1812, planned an expedition into the interior of the earth through holes at the North and South Poles. The U.S. Congress voted against supporting the venture, although there were 25 affirmative votes. This pencil sketch of Symmes was drawn by John J. Audubon. (See: Chap. 12) *New-York Historical Society.*

Astronaut Edwin E. Aldrin, Jr., 2nd man to walk on the moon, as photographed by his commander, astronaut Neil A. Armstrong, the 1st man to set foot on the moon. Aldrin was to have been 1st on the moon, but 3 months before the landing Armstrong pulled rank on him. (See: Chap. 11) *NASA.*

Atlantis, an island continent, was written about by Plato in the 4th century B.C. An earthquake was supposed to have destroyed it, plunging it beneath the sea. Many modern scientists believe it existed. This map shows the possible location of the submerged island continent. (See: Chap. 13) *Brown Brothers.*

Having seen her 1st husband drink himself to death some years earlier, Carry Nation started her crusade against alcohol in 1899. In a single year she broke up 20 saloons with her trusty hatchet. She was arrested 30 times in her life. (See: Chap. 13) *U.P.I.*

Noah's Ark, 450′ long, 75′ wide, 3 stories high, landed safely atop Mount Ararat, Turkey, 5,000 years ago. Here the dove is sent forth. The 1st modern search for the remains of the Ark began in 1829. In 1974, the earth-orbiting Skylab mission thought it had spotted the remains at a 14,000′ elevation. Engraving by Gustave Doré. (See: Chap. 13)

Clyde Barrow (of Bonnie and Clyde fame) posing with a stolen car and some of his firearms on April 17, 1933. Clyde was an expert driver who preferred Fords because they ran fast, got good gas mileage, and were a common sight on the road. (See: Chap. 13) *U.P.I.*

Eugene V. Debs, jailed for criticizing the U.S.'s prosecution of persons charged with sedition, shown in 1920 at the Atlanta Penitentiary after being notified of his 5th nomination as Socialist candidate for President of the U.S. Although in prison, Debs drew nearly a million votes against Harding. (See: Chap. 13) *Brown Brothers.*

Edgar Allan Poe, a tragic figure in American literature, married a 13-year-old girl who died of tuberculosis. Inventor of the modern detective story, known for his poems and short stories, Poe suffered poverty, alcoholism, near insanity, and died drunk in a Baltimore gutter in 1849. (See: Chap. 14) *Brown University Library.*

Percy Bysshe Shelley, whose poems *Queen Mab,* *Prometheus Unbound, The Cenci* became world famous, was a revolutionary notorious for his atheism and his vegetarian diet. He died in 1822 when his boat was caught in a storm off Viareggio, Italy. (See: Chaps. 14, 20, 26) *The Pierpont Morgan Library.*

Walt Whitman, the brilliant homosexual American poet, published *Leaves of Grass* at his own expense in 1855, and even wrote some of the favorable reviews it received. He nursed soldiers during the Civil War. He died in 1892. (See: Chap. 14) *Library of Congress.*

Samuel L. Clemens, once a Mississippi River pilot who later wrote under the name "Mark Twain," produced such hit novels as *The Adventures of Tom Sawyer* in 1876 and *The Adventures of Huckleberry Finn* in 1884. He later lost a fortune invested in a typesetting machine. (See: Chap. 14) *Culver Pictures, Inc.*

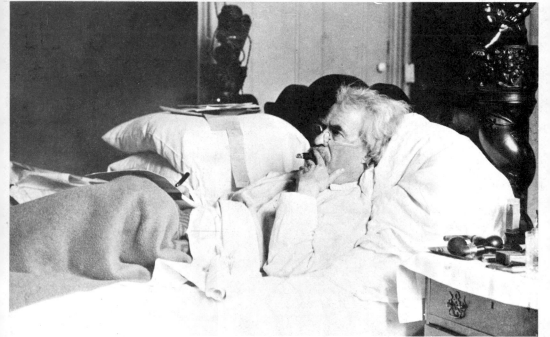

The word "boycott" entered the English language in 1880 when Capt. Charles C. Boycott, an estate manager in Ireland, ignored tenants' requests for lower rents and tried to evict them. On advice of future Prime Minister Parnell, the tenants ignored their manager and simply "boycotted" him. Crayon sketch by Sydney Prior Hall. (See: Chap. 14) *National Gallery of Ireland.*

Monthly, the verses were published anonymously, and it is said that the editor, J. T. Fields, gave them their title. Mrs. Howe was paid $5.

The song rapidly gained popularity. When President Lincoln attended the 2nd anniversary meeting of the Christian Commission in Washington in 1864, he heard Charles C. McCabe, known as the Singing Chaplain, tell of his experience in a Confederate prison during the war. He told of teaching fellow prisoners the new song, "The Battle Hymn of the Republic," and then he and a comrade began to sing it, with the audience joining in the chorus. At the close, President Lincoln called out, "Sing it again!" which they did.

A few days later McCabe attended a reception at the White House. The President recognized him and complimented him on the song. This Singing Chaplain—who eventually became a Methodist bishop—continued to perform Mrs. Howe's song, and thus helped it become known all over the land.

Julia Ward Howe was widely known and respected in her own lifetime as a writer, lecturer, and worker for the emancipation of the slaves, and she was elected as the 1st woman member of the American Academy of Arts and Letters. However, she is remembered today chiefly because she wrote these stirring words which have been called "not merely a song for the times but a hymn for the ages."

Happy Birthday to You
Mildred and Patty Hill 1893

There is one song that each American child learns, along with Mother Goose, about the time she/he turns 2: It is, of course, "Happy Birthday." But she/he probably will never discover, no matter how well educated she/he becomes, that 2 girls—2 sisters named Mildred J. and Patty S. Hill—are responsible.

At 1st, the Hills called their song "Good Morning to You!" and it was published under this title in 1893. Having gained no popularity, it was changed just a little, the words "Happy birthday" replacing "Good morning."

The rest is history. This song is a part of the personalized birthday ritual in thousands upon thousands of American homes. And as Americans have gone to live and work—and fight—in countries all around the world, this simple song has gone with them. So today the song may be heard almost anywhere.

Sweet Adeline
Richard H. Gerard/Henry Armstrong 1903

"Sweet Adeline" is a song loved and sung by generations of Americans, especially when in a mellow mood.

Although the song as it is now known dates from 1903, the melody was written by Henry Armstrong in 1896 when he was 18 years old. It did not for a time have any words, but when young Henry came from Boston to New York and went to work for Witmark, the music publishing house, he met another young man, Richard H. Gerard. He asked Gerard to write some lyrics for the tune, and the song became "You're the Flower of My Heart, Sweet Rosalie." This song went from publisher to publisher without finding a taker. Then Gerard suggested that maybe a change of title would help.

According to the story, about this time Gerard and Armstrong happened to see a poster announcing the farewell concert tour of the famed prima donna, Adelina Patti. That was it. The girl in the song would be Adeline and the title shortened to, simply, "Sweet Adeline."

In 1903 Witmark accepted and published the song. However, it still did not sell well. About a year later, The Quaker City Four, a vaudeville quartet, came to Witmark's looking for new material. They turned down song after song until they were shown "Sweet Adeline." "That's what we've been looking for," one of them said. They sang the song shortly afterward in a program given at the Victoria Theatre in New York City. It was a hit right away and soon it was being sung all over.

Barbershop quartets especially found "Sweet Adeline" a great song for the "rough and ready choral harmonization" which has always been their trademark. Today it is not only a favorite with members of The Society for the Preservation and Encouragement of Barber Shop Singing, founded in Tulsa, Okla., in 1938, but has also furnished the name for the female equivalent of the male barbershop singers, The Sweet Adelines, Inc.

"Sweet Adeline" was also used as the title of a musical comedy, written by Jerome Kern and Oscar Hammerstein II, which was made into a movie in 1929. This was not a success. However, John J. Fitzgerald—JFK's grandfather—used "Sweet Adeline" as the theme song for 2 successful campaigns that resulted in his being elected mayor of Boston.

White Christmas Irving Berlin 1942

This is one of the 3 or 4 most widely known and best loved of the 900 melodic and lyrical creations by that dean of American popular song, Irving Berlin. "White Christmas" began as part of the movie score written in Hollywood in 1942 for *Holiday Inn*. The film, produced by Paramount, starred Bing Crosby and Fred Astaire.

After being sung by Bing, the song stepped right out of the movie and became an immediate hit. It earned an Academy Award as Best Song of 1942 for its composer; it also earned him the gratitude of thousands of W.W. II Yanks fighting in the jungles and swamps of the Pacific, since it brought them a nostalgic recollection of home—with its white Christmases and Yuletide cheer and peace.

Sales figures show that since then the song has had a sheet-music sale of about 4 million. Its record sales are some 100 million copies. David Ewen says this total for a single song is without parallel in musical history.

"White Christmas" is 2nd only to "Silent Night" now as the favorite Christmas song of Americans, according to a Gallup poll. In addition to the Oscar given by the Academy of Motion Picture Arts and Sciences, its widespread popularity—a continuing popularity—was proved by its appearance on "The Hit Parade" radio (and later TV) program a record-breaking 32 times during the program's quarter-of-a-century airing.

The song also lent flavor and its music to, as well as providing the title for, the movie *White Christmas*, made some years later.

—E.S.L.

MUZAKMUZAKMUZAKMUZAKMUZAKMUZAKMUZAK

Irving Wexler, a Miami, Fla., MUZAK man, once said: "I have MUZAK in every room of my home. Twenty-four hours a day. We sleep with it on, watch TV with it on. I never allow it to be turned off because I know that music has a therapeutic effect." Others have drawn the same conclusion: Prisons and grand jury rooms, reptile houses and large department stores, beauty parlors and dentists' offices all have found MUZAK to be beneficial in some respect.

What began in 1934 as a service intended to provide—sans commercials and static—recorded medleys via telephone lines to just restaurants, the homes of the wealthy, and apartment complexes turned into a device over the years by which management could increase workers' productivity, stores and restaurants could increase consumption, and offices could reduce the amount of errors their employees made. Three factors seem to have forced this change: studies done in the late 1930s on ergonomic research (ergonomics is the study of the use of engineering methods to humanize work areas); W.W. II and its call for quick and efficient production; and the adman genius of William B. Benton.

Benton, who would later become a U.S. senator, acquired the failing MUZAK Co. in 1941 for about $100,000 and put it to work in the wartime factories playing Sousa marches and the like. The experiment worked, and a more sophisticated type of programming proved to be successful in the postwar years as well. Benton managed to turn the failing company into a moneymaking business during his years as owner, and he turned a tidy profit on his investment when he sold it to the Wrather organization in 1957.

Today, MUZAK, Inc., now a property of Teleprompter, in turn a subsidiary of ITT, has conquered the world. Eighty million people a day hear MUZAK. In the U.S., MUZAK was heard in President Nixon's Washington White House and his Key Biscayne White House. MUZAK is heard in the Pentagon. MUZAK is heard in General Motors, Texaco, Procter and Gamble, the Bronx Zoo, Bank of America, F. W. Woolworth, the Houston Astrodome, Laurel Race Track. Elsewhere in the world, MUZAK is heard in the insurance firm Lloyd's of London, in a 39-story high-rise cemetery in Rio de Janeiro, in dozens of organizations in Tokyo, in Helsinki, in Brussels, in Manila, in Madrid, in Mexico City. MUZAK is heard in Outer Space—Neil Armstrong had it piped in to him before he set foot on the moon. MUZAK earns $400 million annually.

Citing the practice of beating drums on slave ships to help speed up the rowers, and pointing to the increased production achieved by beaming music to cows and chickens, MUZAK operates on a simple principle: that effectively programmed MUZAK can stimulate certain psychological and physiological responses, such as work interest, and increased muscular activity, as well as minimize tension and reduce fatigue; that, in short, it can create an atmosphere for the worker that will promote efficiency and productivity.

According to MUZAK engineers, the average worker arrives at his job each morning in a fairly good mood, but that mood gradually dissipates until it hits a low between the hours of 10 and 11 in the morning. While morale again increases toward lunchtime, the cycle repeats itself after the midday break, becoming more intense this time, until the worker reaches absolute bottom for the day at approximately 3:30. MUZAK counters this fatigue with 15-minute segments of programmed music arranged to provide a constantly rising level of stimulation, varying inversely with the Worker Efficiency Curve. Thus, MUZAK moves from "moderate" to "bright" during the 1st work cycle, into mild and restful for the lunch period, and on into a brighter "moderate" to "bright" for the final work period. Of 105 subscribing companies, 86.4% confessed MU-ZAK "helped them in their work." As MU-ZAK's aim is to stimulate, not to entertain, its programmers shy away from vocals and tunes with an emotional identification, such as the Beatles, the Rolling Stones, or the *Internationale*.

Throughout each day, MUZAK offers 4 programs: Industrial, Office, Public Area, and Travel. The 1st 2 alternate in 15 minute segments ("We sell silence," remarked a former president of MUZAK. "Too much noise is as bad as too much silence."), and the last 2 absorb the full combined doses of the 1st 2 until 5 P.M., when Public Area MUZAK takes over completely. Programming after 5 o'clock grows progressively more upbeat and brassy as the evening draws toward a close, until by midnight the tunes are verging on the lively.

MUZAK produces a different program every day, 365 days a year.

A dean of music once described MUZAK as "pallid pap that will rot our musical teeth out," and J. B. Priestley claims that he has "had it turned off in some of the best places." In 1962, Richard Lippold challenged having MUZAK in the area when his sculpture was exhibited in Manhattan's Pan Am building, and he commissioned John Cage to design an "alternative" MUZAK program. Lippold's idea was vetoed finally by the the the Pan Am directors, one of whom explained: "The American businessman and the aesthete do not always see eye to eye." At one point, a Stuttgart whorehouse requested MUZAK's "Light Industrial Program." Whether the music was intended to increase worker efficiency or to calm down the patrons was never revealed.

—M.T.

Gallery of Painters and Their Paintings

The Painter: Leonardo da Vinci
(1452–1519)

Legends developed about Da Vinci even during his own lifetime: about his handsome face and figure, his strength, his gentleness toward animals and birds, his brilliance of mind, and the variety and scope of his talents. For Leonardo was one of the most gifted men who ever lived. He was 1st of all a painter, but he was also an architect, sculptor, engineer, and musician. He was accepted as an equal by the most learned men of his time, was friend to the rulers of Florence, Milan, and Rome, and died in the service of the King of France.

Called by the name of the little town of Vinci where he was born, Leonardo grew up in Florence. His education was modest, but in the workshop of Verrocchio, the painter and sculptor under whom he served his apprenticeship, he had an opportunity not only to learn his craft but to listen to the scholars and noblemen who came to order works of art. He tired of this after a few years and, wishing to try his hand at engineering, moved to Milan where he remained for almost 16 years. He founded a very successful atelier where he taught painting and sculpting when not busy with his blueprints and drawing board.

Leonardo traveled from one end of Italy to the other as well as into France, working on but seldom completing projects in engineering, fortification, painting, and sculpture. He was dogged by complaining letters and lawsuits for not fulfilling his contracts. In the spring

of 1506, he obtained a 3 months' leave of absence from his Florentine employer to return to Milan and work for the viceroy ruling in the name of the King of France. That initial 3-month period was extended several times until 1507, when King Louis XII personally hired Leonardo as his official court painter and engineer-in-chief. But Leonardo's restless soul could not endure the restrictions placed upon him by his official duties, and he moved to Rome, where Pope Julius II had started to work on St. Peter's. Raphael, Bramante, and Michelangelo were already present, and now Leonardo joined them.

Leonardo was 61 years old, Michelangelo only 38, and Raphael another 8 years younger. The inevitable conflict between older and younger generation took place, and Leonardo felt he was no longer wanted. When King Francis I of France offered Leonardo anything he desired if he would leave Rome and move to France to live at the royal court, Leonardo began a new life on foreign soil at an age which most of his contemporaries had failed to reach. He had already suffered a paralyzing stroke which had lamed his right arm but that meant nothing to him for he soon learned to paint with his left hand.

On May 2, 1519, he died peacefully in the arms of his benefactor, who followed his remains to the cloister of St. Florentin, where Leonardo had wished to sleep his final sleep.

The Painting: *Mona Lisa. Mona*—or *Madonna*—*Lisa* was painted from a living model, Lisa Gherardini, who would become the most looked at woman who ever lived and the subject of a portrait called the best-known painting of all time.

The real Mona Lisa was born into a large impoverished family in 15th-century Naples. When she married, in 1495, she became the 3rd wife of a wealthy Florentine merchant named Francesco del Giocondo. She began to sit for Leonardo da Vinci in 1503. His portrait of her—which took 4 years to paint and was never finished—he called *Mona Lisa.*

During the painting of the portrait, Giorgio Vasari, a gossipy art critic writing in 1568, reported: "Mona Lisa was very beautiful, and while Leonardo was drawing her portrait, he engaged people to play and sing, and jesters to keep her merry, and remove that melancholy which painting usually gives to portraits. This figure of Leonardo's has such a pleasant smile that it seemed rather divine than human."

Critics have speculated on Mona Lisa's enigmatic smile. Was the smile coquettishly directed at Da Vinci? Was the smile one of satisfaction due to the knowledge that, as the wife of a much older man, she might one day inherit his great fortune? Or was the smile due to Da Vinci's inability to handle lips? For despite his knowledge of practical anatomy he was weak in depicting the human face.

King Francis I of France paid 4,000 gold florins (equivalent of $1,470 today) for the painting of the Mona Lisa. He brought the portrait to Paris, where it eventually became the center of attraction at the Louvre.

There is some evidence that Mona Lisa was more woman than madonna. Art historian C. J. Bulliet stated: "There is a legend of a nude Mona Lisa that Leonardo made, a nude that has disappeared—and a legend of many sketches for this nude, likewise vanished—sketches made from the naked body of La Gioconda."

In 1911 a patriotic Italian, Vincenzo Peruggia, determined to return the masterpiece to its native land, stole the *Mona Lisa* by hiding the canvas under his coat, and took it back to Italy. It was recovered in 1913.

In 1962, before the painting was to be shipped to the U.S. for exhibits in Washington, D.C., and New York City, insurance appraisers put a value of $100 million on it.

THE PAINTER: TITIAN (c. 1485–1576)

The art of Titian is for lovers—for all those who delight in the beauty of the female body. Although a master of erotic suggestion, Titian was also a man who felt deeply the call of religious faith. His range was so considerable and his style so varied, that his painting pleases many different tastes.

Titian's career is a success story. A youth from the little Venetian mountain village of Pieve di Cadore, Titian filled numerable commissions. He was court painter to Charles V, a Palatine count, and a knight of the Golden Spur. His success and his example opened the way for similar aristocrats of art—Rubens, Van Dyck, Velázquez and Delacroix—and their debt to him was one of improved status as well as of inspiration.

As is often the case with great men, Titian was perfectly attuned to the time and place in which he lived. He came to Venice at an early age and studied painting with a little-known artist, Sebastiano Zuccato, and then with the brothers Gentile and Giovanni Bellini, who dominated the artistic life of Venice at the turn of the century. He became independent as a painter when he worked with Giorgione, the most fashionable and progressive artist of that day.

Titian was influenced by all his masters, as were most young painters. Though he sometimes borrowed elements from their pictures, his frank delight in the natural life around him gave his work a quality all his own. The great Emperor, Charles V, not only became his greatest patron, but also his friend and admirer. Early biographers of Titian tell with awe that Charles V honored Titian by picking up a brush he had dropped. Pietro Aretino, a poet and playwright, who was also the world's 1st gossip columnist, told us much about Titian.

"I marvel at him," wrote Aretino, "for no matter with whom he is or where he finds himself, he always maintains restraint. He will kiss a young woman, hold her in his lap and fondle her. But that's as far as it goes. He sets a good example for us all."

Titian's wife, Cecilia—a barber's daughter from his hometown village of Cadore—was a young woman who had been his housekeeper and mistress for some 5 years. Cecilia had already borne Titian 2 fine sons, Pomponio and Orazio, when in 1525, she fell seriously ill. Titian, wishing to legitimize the children, married her. The marriage was a happy one and Cecilia recovered and bore him 2 more children, both daughters. Only one of them, Lavinia, survived.

Titian died in 1576, a victim of the plague. During the last 25 years of his life, he achieved a new and extraordinary style, one which is all the more surprising in view of his great age.

THE PAINTING: *The Venus of Urbino.* Titian, who loved to paint nude red-headed women —using Titian red—with plump breasts, arms, bottoms, once stated a rule he always followed: "Never paint an old woman under any circumstances." But he was forced to break his rule when the Duchess of Urbino implored the Duke to commission Titian to paint her in the nude.

When approached with the commission, Titian was reluctant. The Duchess was not only advanced in years, but she was "vain and ugly." Then, Titian's friend, Aretino, suggested a workable compromise. According to Muriel Segal in *Painted Ladies*, "He suggested they might hire from the local brothel Titian's favorite and most seductive girl to pose for the body, sticking on a glamorized portrait of the Duchess for the head. When Her Grace saw the finished picture she was delighted, especially as it was dubbed *The Venus of Urbino*, and judged by Vasari as the most beautiful nude that Titian ever painted."

When the Duke of Urbino saw Titian's picture of his wife, he turned to Aretino and said, "If I could have had that girl's body even with my wife's head I'd have been a happier man." Aretino broke into gales of laughter, suffered a stroke, and literally died laughing.

THE PAINTER: REMBRANDT VAN RIJN (1606–1669)

Few would question the statement that Rembrandt was among the greatest painters of all time. But about his relations with friends and pupils, his behavior and character in his lifetime, there is a wide difference of opinion. Reacting against earlier romantic accounts of Rembrandt, some modern biographers have undertaken to debunk him to the point of distorting both his person and his life. Actually Rembrandt, the man and the artist, was a heroic, tragic figure of uncommon depth and intensity, a nonconformist as well as a rebel.

Rembrandt was born in Leyden, the son of a well-to-do miller. He went to grammar school and then briefly to the university. A 3-year apprenticeship to a local painter gave him his technical background, and a brief period in Amsterdam with an Italian-trained artist brought him into contact with the style of the late Renaissance. At the age of 25, Rembrandt left Leyden for Amsterdam. There he quickly achieved a career as a portrait painter, and married the wealthy Saskia van Uylenburgh, who brought him position and fortune. The young couple lived extravagantly—purchasing an expensive house with sleeping quarters and studios for pupils, as well as space for the works of art and curios that Rembrandt liked to collect. In spite of his large income, debts began to pile up. The death of 3 children in infancy, followed by that of his wife in 1642, left Rembrandt alone with a 4th child—Titus—only 9 months old. After some years, problems multiplied. His popularity with the public declined. Then his creditors seized and sold his house, putting his collection up for auction. Only the help of his loyal mistress Hendrickje Stoffels and his son Titus saved him from utter ruin. They made an arrangement by which he would nominally be an employee of their art-dealing firm, and as such, he painted his last great masterpieces. But these faithful companions died before him, and when his life came to an end in 1669, he left no property other than some old clothes and painting tools.

It was recently learned that, following the death of his wife, Saskia, another woman had appeared in Rembrandt's life. Geertge Dircks, the young widow of a trumpeter, was brought into the house to look after little Titus. For the keenly alive and passionate Rembrandt, this marked the commencement of a new love affair, which was broken off in 1649 under painful circumstances. Little is known about the role Geertge played in Rembrandt's life —save that she was his paramour and he was enamored of her. So much so that he made her a present of Saskia's ring and her other costly jewels and ornaments. It is because of these riches that we are able to learn more about the end of the story. Geertge, who departed in 1649 after violent scenes of jealousy and quarreling, started a lawsuit against Rembrandt on the grounds of broken promises of marriage. When she lost the suit Geertge sought consolation in the dissolute life of Amsterdam, giving Rembrandt the opportunity to have her shut up in a house of correction for being a prostitute.

THE PAINTING: *Syndics of the Drapers' Guild*. The group portrait of the board (or syndics) of the clothmaker's guild, also known as *De Staalmeesters*, painted 5 years before the master's death, failed to satisfy Rembrandt's clients. It was thought of as queer, and did not look as if it had been "decently posed." Allowed to gather dust for some time, it is considered today one of Rembrandt's masterpieces.

Five *staalmeesters*, of 4 different religious beliefs, gathered in brotherly unity around a table, were a typical symbol of the power of commerce and the tolerance of Amsterdam during the age of prosperity of the Dutch republic. Rembrandt had represented the regents, giving an account of the year's business, as seated before an assembly. Probably the most objectionable aspect of the portrait was that such annual gatherings for the rendering of accounts were not usual. Further, Rembrandt dramatized the scene by having his group react to someone in the audience who had just accused the board members of some failing. However, at the time of the painting,

Dutch officials were not accountable to the public.

While the aging Rembrandt had reason to be resentful toward the society of his day, there is no hint of this in the painting. With the *Syndics*, Rembrandt created his greatest monument to Dutch character. His group portrait has become the "exemplum" of good administration for generations of governors to come. The painting gained enormous popularity in the 20th century when it was adopted as an advertising label and image for Dutch Masters cigars.

THE PAINTER: FRANCISCO JOSÉ DE GOYA Y LUCIENTES (1746–1828)

When the aged Goya was in exile in France, he used to entertain his friends with tales of his wild youth. He had fled from home, he said, because of a fatal street fight. In Rome, caught in an escapade, he avoided the death penalty only through the intervention of the Spanish ambassador. One dark night in Madrid, he had been knifed in the back. None of these stories can be documented and they are possibly the romanticizing of an old man, but they show that Goya wanted to be remembered as hotheaded and impetuous, taking full part in the life around him.

Goya was born in the little village of Fuendetodos, near Saragossa, and little is known of his early training besides possible instructions by his father, José, a gilder, and an apprenticeship with José Luzán, a parish church painter. He developed his art slowly, failing twice in a competition for a scholarship to the Madrid Academy. After studying in Italy for 2 years, Goya returned to Spain and became the pupil of Francisco Bayeu and in 1773, he married his teacher's sister, Josefa. Unquestionably this connection with Bayeu helped Goya launch his painting career. Soon after, his brother-in-law persuaded Raphael Mengs, the director of the Royal Tapestry Factory in Madrid, to hire Goya. During the next 17 years, he was to paint more than 60 designs, learning to paint gay fresh colors and clear-cut lights. His art attracted royal attention and he was appointed director of the Royal Academy of Art in 1780. Later he became painter to the court.

What he thereupon did to his royal master and his master's family is one of the most scandalous incidents in the history of art. Goya, in a single portrait of King Charles and his family, did more to destroy royal prestige than all the diatribes of the journalists of the early days of the French Revolution. What makes this incident so deplorable is that neither the King and Queen nor any of their ministers seemed aware of Goya's brutal betrayal of the concept of divine right in this portrait.

Goya's reputation as a rapid painter spawned a wild story concerning the famous portrait of the Duchess of Alba. Reportedly, when the Duchess's husband was advised of the scandalous portrait, he announced that he would visit the artist to defend his honor as a Spanish grandee. But when he arrived at the studio the following day, there was his wife's picture showing the lady decently dressed. The versatile artist was supposed to have painted a 2nd portrait overnight to appease the wrath of the infuriated husband.

As he grew older, Goya became increasingly sensitive to the world in which he lived. The passions of mankind dismayed him and he was deeply shaken by the fury the Spanish War unleashed. He translated his inner turmoil into paintings—everything he had seen and done and all the thoughts that troubled him.

In 1822, when he was well past 70, he suddenly left his native land and moved to Bordeaux where, 2 years later, he died. During the last years of his life he became completely deaf, but his eyesight remained clear to the end. And what those eyes had seen, his hand had faithfully revealed on canvas.

THE PAINTING: *Nude Maja*. The identity of the *Nude Maja* has been the topic of many discussions. Theories range from Pilar Teresa Cayetana, the Duchess of Alba, to Teresita, sister of a priest. Some critics believe Goya had no model at all, but painted his "ideal" woman.

The duchess was a highly unconventional aristocrat who had posed for more than 20 pictures for her artist-lover. According to legend, she was intrigued by the Maja image —a gay lady or harlot, or both—and begged Goya to paint her in this manner. The fact that the paintings were a part of the duchess's collection at the time of her death makes this theory quite plausible.

Depicting a nude woman was unique in Spanish painting during this century and was a risk even for the well-liked and admired court painter. But Goya, a rebel by nature, concealed his deed by painting a 2nd portrait, the *Clothed Maja* which was skillfully hung in front of the nude and could be interchanged by using a mechanical device.

The Inquisition eventually learned of the painting and in 1814 ordered Goya to give his motives for creating such a portrait. The reasons he gave are not known, but presumably they were acceptable for neither the *Nude Maja* nor the *Clothed Maja* was destroyed.

After Cayetana's death, Goya sold the paintings to Manuel de Godoy, the powerful minister of Charles IV, and both paintings now hang at the Prado in Madrid.

THE PAINTER: ÉDOUARD MANET
(1832–1883)

The career of Manet was one of the most curious in the history of painting. Whereas artists like Claude Monet or Paul Gauguin were deliberate revolutionaries—and would not have had it otherwise—Manet himself was a revolutionary against his will. What he sought, and never stopped seeking, was official recognition. The day on which he was belatedly awarded the Legion of Honor, 15 months before he died, was the happiest of his life. This man, who wished for a smooth and respected career, caused the greatest scandals that any painter in the world has ever provoked. He believed his efforts would be rewarded by academic success; what he gained was the admiration and friendship of those who were most rebellious and most hostile toward the official bodies in the world of art.

Manet was born in 1832 into an upper-middle-class family in Paris. His father, a model government official, opposed an art career for his son, but when Édouard failed his examinations for the Navy, the elder Manet yielded, and in January, 1850, the young man became a pupil of Thomas Couture, at that time a very well-known painter who was considered to be "daring." However, Manet found himself in disagreement with his tutor and they soon parted company. The 1st painting he submitted to the Paris Salon, *The Absinthe Drinker*, was rejected—the 1st of many, rejections. Both subject and method of painting were said to be offending. Believing the general public would understand his work better than connoisseurs, Manet showed his paintings in a private gallery. But people were shocked, critics abusive. That year, so many paintings were refused by the Salon (Manet's among them), that Napoleon III established a *Salon des Refusés* (Salon of the rejects). Crowds came—mostly to scoff—and Manet's works were the target of the most violent insults. At the Paris World's Fair of 1867, Manet built a pavilion at his own expense in which to exhibit his works.

THE PAINTING: *Olympia*. She was a young girl named Victorine Meurand, and she had ducked into the Louvre to get out of the rain. There she bumped into Manet—and Manet's *Olympia* was born. Manet described Victorine to his Dutch wife, a piano teacher: "She is not strictly beautiful but she is like one of those macabre dwarfish demi-virgins in a Baudelaire poem." That was in 1860.

Three years later, inspired by Titian's *Venus of Urbino* and the unclothed Victorine, Manet posed her for his *Olympia*. He posed her stretched naked, reclining on the satin pillows of her bed, wearing nothing except a vivid flower in her hair, a black velvet ribbon around her throat, a gold bracelet on her arm, while an open-backed slipper graces one foot in the fashion of brothel harlots. Behind her, a black woman servant brings a client's gift of flowers. The picture was shockingly blatant.

It was not exhibited for 2 years, when it was finally submitted to the selection committee for the Salon of 1865. When the Salon opened on May 1st, visitors flocked to view the canvas, shouting, laughing, jeering, brandishing their fists and even spitting at it, and soon after the critics were also raising a storm of protest. "There she lies," roared André Gustave, "not as a pitiful whore, but as a triumphant and successful prostitute." Edgar Degas saw her and waved her off. "I look on her as on all women—as animals." In *Le Grand Journal* Amédée Cantaloube wrote, "Our eyes have never seen such a spectacle, nor one with a more cynical effect. . . . Women who are about to become mothers, and young girls, would do well to avoid this sight if they are wise." This scandal made Manet more famous. But it was not the kind of fame for which he had longed. To the public he was nothing more than a "joker," a "humbug," drawing attention to himself by any means at his disposal. The objections were, 1st of all, to the subject —which was considered indecent—but to an even greater extent to the frank manner in which the work was painted and also to the vibrant and sharply contrasted colors.

"Every painter in Paris turned up at the Manet exhibition," wrote a critic. "They all went wild with laughter."

Manet was in the habit of visiting a café in the Grande Rue des Batignolles that soon became a rendezvous for his admirers. Among them were Claude Monet, Edgar Degas, Paul Cézanne, Pierre-Auguste Renoir—and out of them came the color theories of Impressionism.

In his later years Manet finally received some public recognition. A number of his paintings were accepted for the Salon and one or 2 were even awarded medals.

THE PAINTER: VINCENT VAN GOGH
(1853–1890)

As a rule the Dutch society of the 1880s gets the full blame for Van Gogh's tragic life. But had he been born in any other clime or time, Van Gogh would have succeeded just as brilliantly in squeezing the last drop of unhappiness out of every situation into which his love for self-torture pushed him. When he had painted those landscapes and portraits and flowers that were afterward found stacked up in the garrets and basements which had played such an important part in his life, he truly had been a man "mad with color." That, combined with his obsession with the condition of the poor, the humble, and the weak, was too much for any human brain to withstand. The perfidious malice of Paul Gauguin completed Van Gogh's destruction. But if there is one fact about Vincent van Gogh that is well known, it is that he severed his left ear and gave it to a prostitute. The self-mutilation is not at all important in itself (actually, it was only an ear lobe), but it is a wildly disconcerting act and obscures the whole picture of the artist.

Van Gogh was born in Holland in 1853, the son of a vicar. Vincent was deeply religious and as a youth worked as a lay preacher among the Welsh and Belgian miners. Later he lived in Paris for 2 years and was so deeply impressed with the art of Millet that he decided to become a painter himself. A younger brother, Theo, who worked in an art dealer's shop, introduced him to Impressionist painters. Though Theo was poor himself, he gave ungrudgingly to the older Vincent and even financed his move to Arles in southern France.

In his self-chosen solitude in Arles, Vincent set down all his ideas and hopes in his letters to Theo, which read like a continuous diary. These letters, by a humble and almost self-taught artist, are among the most moving and exciting in all literature. After less than a year, Van Gogh broke down mentally. In May, 1889, he went into an asylum, but he still had lucid intervals during which he continued to paint. The agony lasted for another 14 months. In July, 1890, the 37-year-old Van Gogh committed suicide—his career as a painter had lasted but 10 years.

THE PAINTING: *The Sunflowers.* "To be sure . . . he was a man truly mad with color . . . flashes of sunlight filled his soul," wrote Paul Gauguin after he observed the many yellow sunflower studies painted by Vincent Van Gogh.

Van Gogh had invited Gauguin to share his little house of light at Arles, France, where he was convinced a new manner of painting was to be born. His yellow sunflowers played a dominant role in his experiments, unraveling the secrets of color. As he explained in a letter to his brother Theo, "Instead of trying to reproduce exactly what I have before my eyes, I use color more arbitrarily in order to express myself with more force."

Work under the sun at Arles established Van Gogh as a giant in art. But when it was over, he had only one year to live.

It is often suggested that the cynical, sarcastic Gauguin drove Vincent to his breaking point. Gauguin has written that he "felt compelled" to paint the tormented artist as he worked on the still life subject he loved so much. He showed the painting to Van Gogh, who reportedly remarked, "It is certainly I, but it's I gone mad." Shortly after, Vincent attempted to kill Gauguin with a razor.

Gauguin returned to Paris. Vincent was taken to the hospital, where it seemed doubtful that he would live, and, in the opinion of many of the townsfolk, it scarcely mattered.

THE PAINTER: PABLO PICASSO
(1881–1973)

For nearly ¾ of a century, Picasso dominated the world of art. From the days of his early youth as a classicist, through his years as a cubist and surrealist, his achievements as painter, sculptor, lithographer, and ceramist were immense and unique.

Picasso was born on October 25, 1881, in Málaga, Spain, the son of an art teacher, José Ruiz Blasco, and María Picasso López. He was known by his mother's name from the age of 20 on. At 14, he was admitted to art school in Barcelona where his adventures were a forerunner of the bohemian behavior that was to inspire headlines for decades. In 1900, he paid his 1st visit to Paris, and settled there 4 years later. During those early days in Montmartre, Picasso was a familiar figure in the cafés and bistros, but he had little artistic success. He fell in love with the beautiful Fernande Oliver, who later was to write reminiscences of their bohemian existence. Eventually he joined the circle gathered around the American expatriates Gertrude and Leo Stein and his fortunes improved. In 1907 came the 1st grand landmark in his career. That spring he invited a few friends, including the artists Henri Matisse and Georges Braque, to his studio to inspect a large painting he had been working on. It has become known as *Young Women of Avignon* (*Les Desmoiselles d'-Avignon*), and it is from this painting that some experts have dated the birth of cubism. After a period spent in designing scenery for the Ballet Russe—during which time he married his 1st wife, Olga Koklova, a dancer in the troupe—Picasso returned to Paris, where he began to paint in the neoclassic and then the surrealist style that was to occupy him until the mid-30s.

In 1936 he returned to Spain as director of the Prado Museum in Madrid. His sympathies for the Loyalist Government and his outrage at Generalissimo Francisco Franco's fascism not only caused his self-imposed exile from Spain, but also his public conversion to communism in 1944.

It was his flair for the exotic way of life that brought headlines about his personal life as well as his art and politics. Two wives, a succession of mistresses, and his children—legitimate and otherwise—provided a series of sensations for the popular press of the world. Even in death, he remained controversial. When it was learned he had bequeathed his personal collection of over 800 works of art to the Louvre in Paris, with the approval of his wife Jacqueline and his only legitimate son, Paulo, other members of the family waged a battle for their share of the master's legacy.

THE PAINTING: *Guernica*. If any one painting of the 20th century may be called the most powerful outcry of the age, that one work must be *Guernica*—painted in response to an event that took place in April, 1937.

General Francisco Franco was leading an army in revolt against the Spanish Republican Government at that time. To show the military strength he could command if he chose to do so, Franco called upon his friend Adolf Hitler to send a fleet of bombers to destroy a Spanish town. The target selected for the mission was the sleepy little city of Guernica. The armada came by one Monday afternoon and completely razed the peaceful community. Franco had proved his point. Not only were the buildings reduced to rubble, but their inhabitants were almost completely annihilated.

Picasso was outraged by such wanton obliteration of life. Commissioned to prepare a mural for the Spanish pavilion at the Paris World's Fair of 1937—with the violence wrought upon Guernica vividly in his mind—he set to work on a painting that has become an unforgettable memorial to the battered old city and its residents. The elements that make up the composition are symbolic rather than documentary and reflect a profound depth of insight into the plight of war victims everywhere. Human sensibilities are torn by the combination of poignancy and horror put together with an astonishing economy of lines. The overall mural evokes deep compassion.

The artist's death on April 8, 1973, in France, gave Spaniards cause to reflect on why he shunned his native land and whether or not he really willed *Guernica* to his country. The painting is on indefinite loan to New York's Museum of Modern Art and is purportedly the artist's gift to the Spanish people —but with one firm condition: that it will be delivered only when democracy returns to Spain.

In March, 1974, as stunned visitors looked on helplessly in the 3rd floor gallery of the museum, a vandal drew a can of spray paint from his pocket and scrawled the words "Kill Lies All" on the masterpiece. The man was seized immediately and the red lettering was removed without damage. The curator of the museum said that what saved the 25′ by 11′ painting was a heavy coat of varnish that had acted as a transparent shield.

—D.S.

She Wrote It—He Got the Credit

What do Pericle's "Funeral Oration," Homer's *Odyssey*, and St. Paul's Epistle to the Hebrews have in common? In all probability they were written by women and credited to men.

Aspasia of Miletus (See Close-Up: Aspasia, following this article) was the author of the noted "Funeral Oration" given by the great Athenian statesman Pericles at the conclusion of the war between Athens and Samos. She was perhaps the most remarkable woman of antiquity—a person of rare intellect and vision. Mighty in her use of the spoken and written word, Aspasia was the mentor of Socrates and other great men: Pericles, Phidias, Anaxagoras, Sophocles, and Euripides. Her unforgettable eulogy honored the young men of Athens who had died in battle. So eloquent and persuasive were her words that Pericles thereby strengthened the people's morale at a crucial time. He had been accused of starting the Samian War upon the entreaty of Aspasia, whose compatriots were at war with Samos. The oration temporarily silenced his enemies and saved his career.

There is no doubt that Aspasia was a powerful political influence in Athens, as well as a gifted rhetorician. The comic poets satirized her hold over Pericles. Plutarch mentions her "knowledge and skill in politics," and regards it as historical that she was reputed to be the instructor of many Athenians—including Pericles—in the art of speaking.

Praising her "goodness, wisdom, and varied accomplishments," H. J. Mozans, in *Woman in Science*, writes: "She is said to have written some of the best speeches of Pericles—among them his noted funeral oration over those who died in battle before the walls of Potidaea."

Describing her discourses as "not more brilliant than solid," Eliza Burt Gamble, in *The Sexes in Science and History*, writes: "It was believed by the most intelligent Athenians, and amongst them Socrates himself, that she composed the celebrated funeral oration pronounced by Pericles in honour of those that were slain in the Samian War."

Indeed, if Aspasia had been a man instead of a woman, the "Funeral Oration" would be credited to her as a matter of course because, in Plato's *Menexenus*, Socrates identifies her as the author, stating that she had composed "the funeral oration that Pericles pronounced." He then gives the text of one of her model funeral orations.

In his essay, *Dio*, Synesius of Cyrene (5th century A.D.) compares the model oration of Aspasia recorded in the *Menexenus* and the speech of Pericles, recorded in Thucydides. Both display Aspasia's mastery of rhetoric and interest in politics.

In both orations, we detect a viewpoint consistent with feminine authorship. In Pericles' speech, we may note the defense of culture and refinement, and the claim that an "easy and elegant way of life" is not necessarily antagonistic to bravery in war. The author consoles the younger parents of boys slain in battle by reminding them they might have more children. Widows are advised to behave decorously.

Aspasia's model oration in the *Menexenus* describes the nation as the "natural mother" of native Athenian youths slain in war. To those of alien birth, their "adopted land" is a "stepmother." The state is reminded of its responsibility to act as guardian and nurse to the wives and children of the dead. Fathers and mothers are consoled with remembrance of their children's bravery. Thus, unlike most Greek funeral orations, these 2 reveal a concern for women; Plato, a liberated philosopher, was not afraid to say that Aspasia wrote them.

Nausicaa is one of the female characters in the *Odyssey*. The English satirist Samuel Butler believed that a woman wrote the epic poem and named her the author. His theory, 1st introduced in literary journals in the 1890s, was systematically expounded in *The Authoress of the Odyssey*.

After years of benign neglect by scholars, this theory became the subject of lively speculation. In 1970 a literary symposium at the University of San Francisco was delighted by Professor Louise George Clubb's remarks that the *Odyssey* is a "woman's book"; "Penelope is very strong, very much a female heroine." In her husband's 20-year absence, she had to "manage the property, fend off a horde of suitors, and raise a son, Telemachus." Epigrammatically, Dr. Clubb added, "The *Iliad* is a story about what men do. The *Odyssey* is the sort of thing women *think* men do when they go away from home."

Richard Bentley, the 18th-century critic, commented that the "*Iliad* was written for men, and the *Odyssey* for women"—that is, from a woman's point of view. Samuel Butler sees herein a prima facie case for feminine authorship—he says that never in the history of literature has a man written a masterpiece for women.

Butler is struck by the author's realistic portrayal of women, but considers the male characters mechanical and "hopelessly wrong." Ulysses, Alcinous, Menelaus, and Nestor all seem to be alike. Women are never laughed at, and are generally given preferential treatment. As Colonel Mure comments in *Language and Literature of Ancient Greece*, "the women engross the chief share of the small stock of common sense allotted to the community."

We do not find, in the *Odyssey*, the *Iliad*'s detailed description of competitive games. Instead, there is a "preponderance of female interest" as seen in the faithful depiction of domestic life. The hand of a feminine author can perhaps be seen in the action of Telemachus' old nurse Euryclea: "She took his shirt from him, folded it carefully up, and hung it on a peg by his bed."

The author makes mistakes which a man would not fall into, such as placing a rudder at both ends of the ship, or "thinking that dry and well-seasoned timber can be cut from a growing tree." In the *Iliad*, women are few in number and importance, and they are under the protection of men. Women of the *Odyssey* direct, counsel, and protect men. Minerva is guide to Ulysses and Telemachus; Andromeda rescues Perseus. Helen is master in the house of Menelaus, of whom she can say little in praise. Queen Arête counts for more than King Alcinous; thus Nausicaa advises Ulysses: "Never mind my father but go up to my mother . . ."

Consider the scene between Ulysses and the ghost of his mother, Anticlea, in which he is told to recount his adventures *to his wife*. Wives are so much more important than husbands that, in his farewell speech to the Phaeacians, Ulysses expresses the hope that husbands will continue to please their wives and children—instead of vice versa.

To find out about the author, Butler traces many kinds of clues in the *Odyssey*. The entire locale is drawn from Sicily, the one place known to the author. She is a young unmarried woman—who else would make Ulysses say that a man can never be really happy away from his father and mother? She was of a wealthy family, for she must have had abundant leisure in order to complete her work. In fact, she was Nausicaa, a member of the household of King Alcinous and his wife Arête, who represent the author's own family.

So quite possibly Homer—at least the Homer of the *Odyssey*—was a woman, one of the many female poets of ancient Greece.

Only 3 years after publication of Butler's book, the renowned German Bible scholar Adolf von Harnack came forward with an even more provocative proposal—one with profound implications for the equality of the sexes. He claimed that Priscilla, a woman leader of the early church, was the true author of the New Testament Epistle to the Hebrews.

Scholars heaped ridicule upon Harnack, and gave his theory an unceremonious burial. However, 2 historical circumstances have converged in a "resurrection" of this theory. One is that recent archaeological discoveries on New Testament studies add to the credibility of Priscilla's authorship. Old and new evidence is set forth in *Priscilla: Author of the Epistle to the Hebrews* by Ruth Hoppin. Concurrently, the modern feminist movement has made it possible to obtain a hearing for the case. Harnack's theory is steadily gaining acceptance.

St. Paul has been given credit for The Epistle to the Hebrews, but today few scholars believe he wrote it. The "loss" of the real author's name has always been a mystery. In Hebrews, the author's grandeur of style, conversion by apostles, and ministry to former Jews conflict with what we know about Paul, who had a simple style, a conversion experience on the road to Damascus, and the commission to preach to Gentiles, not to Hebrews. However, scholars have long known the author was someone in Paul's circle, someone who found his thoughts congenial, and who worked with Timothy, Paul's right-hand man (Heb. 13:23). Next to Timothy, no one was closer to Paul than Priscilla and her husband Aquila, whom we meet in the Bible as church leaders in Rome, Corinth, and Ephesus. Paul lodged with the couple and labored with them in tentmaking and ministry. On at least one occasion they saved his life.

Priscilla was the daughter of a Roman senatorial family—the Acilii Glabriones. Recent explorations of the catacombs reinforce ancient church tradition confirming her aristocratic background. We can hereby see how she acquired the knowledge of rhetoric, literature, and philosophy so abundantly evident in the Epistle to the Hebrews.

Priscilla, who was married to a Hebrew Christian, had a long ministry at Ephesus. There, former Jews of the Essene sect were numerous. In recent decades, publication of the Dead Sea Scrolls has revealed that Hebrews was written in the context of Essene thought. Other evidence places the original destination of the letter as Ephesus. Thus, the author must have been a church leader at Ephesus who could intepret Christianity to former Jews. Priscilla meets these requirements. In fact, she and her husband tutored the learned Alexandrian Jew, Apollos. An early church writer, Chrysostom, named her the sole tutor. Revealingly, after Apollos received instruction from Priscilla, he preached on the theme that Jesus was the Messiah foretold in the Old Testament —*a subject identical with the main theme of Hebrews.*

The Epistle to the Hebrews was written from Rome (Heb. 13:24) about 65 A.D., during the Neronian persecution of Christians. Paul was in prison. We may hypothesize that Priscilla accompanied Paul and Aquila to Rome (II Tim. 4:9). One of her relatives was a former consul; perhaps she hoped his influence could free Paul. From Rome, she wrote Hebrews, pleading with her people in Ephesus to keep the faith.

Who was the eminent intellectual associate of Paul who wrote the letter—if not Priscilla? The field of possible authors is narrowed to leaders at Ephesus with a ministry to Hebrew Christians. The author's conversion (Heb. 2:3) and educational background match that of Priscilla.

How can we best account for the disappearance of the author's name and the mention of several women "Heroes of Faith" in the 11th chapter of the epistle? Harnack has given us a cogent explanation: A woman wrote it.

We have considered 3 writings of ancient times. One is a tribute to courage; one is a saga of adventure; one is inspired scripture. These writings have been inscribed in the world's consciousness by the vision, creativity, and intellect of women.

—R.Ho.

CLOSE-UP: ASPASIA

Of Aspasia's physical attractions little is known, except that her hair was golden, that her voice was silvery, and that her foot was agreeably small. It is thought that she posed for her friend Phidias when he created his *Athene of the Parthenon.* Socrates admired her eloquence. And it is said that she wrote several of Pericles' orations, notably the memorable funeral address he made at the outset of the Great Peloponnesian War.

She was born in Miletus, managed a brothel in Megara, and arrived in Athens in 450 B.C. to conduct a school for elocution and philosophy, intended principally for young ladies. It is possible that she continued to run a brothel as a sideline. At any rate, Socrates, Anaxagoras, and Euripides joined the ladies attending her classes. When Pericles, the high-domed dictator of Athens, also attended and was enchanted, Aspasia's future was made, and she forthwith withdrew from the profession of teaching to resume her role of courtesan.

It is thought that Pericles was 40 years old, and Aspasia 25, when they met. He was at the height of his popularity. He had partially democratized Greece, and ennobled its culture. He was married, keeping a courtesan from Corinth, and he had 2 adolescent sons. Now he discarded both his wife and his Corinthian to devote his full energies to his new mistress, who was already pregnant by him. Having arranged another marriage for his former wife, Pericles brought Aspasia into his house. Since she was not an Athenian citizen, he could not marry her. But he willed his fortune to their son, Pericles II, and soon neglected his followers and the council hall for her caresses.

Pericles' enemies, and even some of his supporters, resented Aspasia, and especially the part she played in political affairs. They conspired to destroy her. Led by one Hermippus, a playwright, they accused Aspasia of impiety toward their gods, and of acting as a procuress who supplied young freeborn Athenian ladies to satisfy Pericles' lust. The trial was held in 432 B.C., before a jury of 1,500 men, and Aspasia, as a foreigner, was not allowed to speak in her own defense. When Pericles realized that the evidence was going against his beloved, and that the penalty would be death, he appeared to defend her in person. Though known for his phlegmatic, judicial, aloof manner, Pericles opened his heart to the jurors. His voice quavered with emotion. He broke down and wept. And the jurors, irrationally moved, voted for acquittal.

But Aspasia's detractors were not done. Aristophanes, who detested her, held her responsible for instigating the costly Peloponnesian War. He insisted that she was still in the brothel business, that 2 high-spirited officers from Megara had kidnapped 2 of her most valued prostitutes; and that, as a result, she had urged Pericles to attack Megara. While it is more likely that Pericles had started the conflict to secure his control of the Aegean Sea, popular feeling against Aspasia mounted.

When Pericles pulled his citizenry behind the walls of Athens, hoping that his navy might be sufficient to bring about victory, misfortune struck in the form of a plague. One out of every 4 Athenian soldiers died, and Pericles lost his 2 legitimate sons. When the war ended, Pericles was accused of having bought the peace through misappropriation of funds from the public treasury. He was convicted and fined over ¼ of a million dollars. Nine years later he was back in power. One of his 1st acts was to force the legislature to legitimize his son, Pericles II, by then an Athenian general. Shortly after, Pericles was dead in his 60s. As for Aspasia, a month later she was consoling herself with a wealthy sheepdealer named Lysicles.

—I.W. rep.

Gallery of Great Performing and Creative Artists

ACTORS AND ACTRESSES—STAGE

Maude Adams (1872–1953). The most popular actress of the American theater during the early 1900s, Maude Adams attracted multitudes of fans who otherwise never entered a playhouse. This devoted following helped Maude become the highest-paid performer of her day. Working mostly in pre-income-tax times, she earned more than $1 million a year in her prime. Although an accomplished actress, it was to her personality that Maude owned her great success. She excelled in wholesome, sentimental roles that capitalized upon her heartwarming charm and joyfulness.

Maude Adams, whose real name was Maude Kiskadden, started out as a child actress, making her 1st stage appearance before she was a year old. She took her stage name from her mother, actress Annie Adams, who performed in many plays with Maude. In 1892, producer-manager Charles Frohman signed John Drew, the "1st gentleman of the stage," and selected Maude, then 20, as Drew's leading lady. She achieved Broadway fame 5 years later in James M. Barrie's *The Little Minister*, and went on to star in such other Barrie plays as *Quality Street* (1902); *Peter Pan* (1905); and *What Every Woman Knows* (1908).

Maude was a Frohman star, and Frohman demanded that his performers avoid the public eye when not on stage. He once complained when Drew strolled down Broadway saying, "If he must walk, let him walk on 5th Avenue." Frohman particularly objected to his female stars' marrying. Shy Maude, his favorite protégée, never came close to marriage. Nunlike in her personal life, on several occasions she went to live in convents. Ethel Barrymore, another Frohman star, called Maude "the original I-want-to-be-alone woman."

Although Maude appeared in plays by many authors, she scored her greatest successes in Barrie's whimsical fantasies. After Frohman's death in 1915, she produced and starred in Barrie's *A Kiss for Cinderella* from 1916 to 1918. However, in 1920, Charles Frohman, Inc., insisted that Maude could produce new Barrie plays only if she set aside her rights in the earlier ones. As she hoped to make a movie of *Peter Pan*, "the Barrie actress" refused these terms.

Maude believed that only a color film could do justice to *Peter Pan*. But lighting problems made color filming impossible at that time. Undaunted, Maude, already an expert in stage lighting, now helped scientists at General Electric develop lamps strong enough for indoor color photography. She devoted her energies, large amounts of her money, and years of her time to the project, and the lamps were ultimately developed. But while Maude was working on the lamps, she let her rights to Barrie's plays slip away. Ironically, she also lost her right to the lamps.

Maude returned to the stage for a few years

during the '30s, then became a professor of dramatic art at Stephens College in Columbia, Mo., a post she held from 1937 to 1950. She died in 1953 after a bout with pleurisy.

—N.B.

Sarah Bernhardt (1844–1923). One of the theater's greatest talents, French actress Sarah Bernhardt was also one of its most colorful personalities. Few performers ever moved audiences as Bernhardt did, or succeeded in such a wide variety of roles. None provoked more controversy. This exceedingly slender woman with a strikingly attractive face traveled with, and sometimes slept in, a coffin lined with letters from her innumerable lovers. And her entourage often included a veritable menagerie of dogs, cats, birds, turtles, monkeys, leopards, lions, and alligators. Men fought duels to the death for her, priests exhorted parishioners to shun her, and at least one woman killed herself because she couldn't get a ticket to a Bernhardt performance. Critic Jules Lemaître once said of Bernhardt, "She could enter a convent, discover the North Pole, have herself inoculated with rabies, assassinate an emperor or marry a Negro king without astonishing me."

Idolized as "the divine Sarah" by fans throughout the world, her name appeared in one publication or another every day for over 60 years. Yet her career had almost ended before it began. In 1862, after critics panned her 1st 3 stage appearances, Bernhardt—still not quite 18—tried to poison herself by drinking liquid rouge. Then, 4 years later, she almost gave up the theater to marry Prince Henri de Ligne, the father of her illegitimate child, Maurice. (Sarah had also been born out of wedlock.) But the prince's family prevented the marriage.

The temperamental actress with "the golden voice" scored her 1st notable success in 1869 in *Le Passant*. She registered still greater triumphs in *Ruy Blas* (1872); *Phèdre* (1874); *Hernani* (1877); *Fédora* (1882); *Jeanne d'Arc* (1889); and *L'Aiglon* (1900). Bernhardt grossed—and spent—$25 million, earning much of it on tours of the U.S., England, and other countries. In 1883, crowds in Copenhagen thronged about her with such enthusiasm that uninformed onlookers thought the furor signaled an overthrow of the Government.

Bernhardt's retinue of lovers was said to exceed 1,000. Many, like Edmund Rostand, were important writers and artists. Yet, with the exception of the man she married—Jacques Damala, a morphine-addicted actor—"the divine Sarah" almost never bedded with mediocre artists. She married Damala in 1882 and separated from him a year later.

Throughout her career, Bernhardt acted with such intensity that she frequently fainted at the end of a performance. In 1915, at 71, severe problems with her right leg forced her to have it amputated. After the operation, she specialized in roles that required no walking. When, in the last months of her life, a stroke made it impossible for her to leave home, Bernhardt converted her house into a motion picture set. She died of uremia in 1923, just 4 days after completing the movie *La Voyante*.

Other Bernhardt films include *Tosca* (1911); *Camille* (1912); *Queen Elizabeth* (1912); *Jeanne Dore* (1915). She also left behind gramophone records, paintings, sculptures, and a number of writings—including novels, plays, film scripts, and her autobiography, *Memories of My Life* (1907).

—N.B.

Edwin Booth (1833–1893). The greatest American actor of the 19th century, Edwin Booth was the 1st U.S-born performer to win wide acclaim in Europe. Darkly handsome and slight of build, Booth possessed a magnificent voice, a profound understanding of the characters he played, and a natural unmannered style of acting. Nat Goodwin, who burlesqued many famous persons, refused to imitate Booth, explaining, "You can't be funny exaggerating something that is not in the 1st place a little overdone . . . I couldn't be funny caricaturing perfection."

In 1846, at the age of 13, Edwin began to tour with his father, the brilliant but erratic tragedian Junius Brutus Booth. The quiet youngster had a calming influence on his eccentric father, whose flights of madness and inebriation made him a threat to his fellow performers, his career, and himself. At 16, Edwin made his stage debut in a minor part in *Richard III*, his father playing the title role. Two years later, the young actor portrayed Richard III when his father refused to go on. In the years that followed, Edwin became a star in his own right, setting a Broadway record in March, 1865, with his 100th consecutive performance as Hamlet. Other favorite roles included Richelieu, Lear, Iago, and Shylock.

Throughout his life, America's last great tragedian was afflicted with melancholia—not without reason. Mary Devlin, the woman he most loved, died of pneumonia in 1863, 2 years after he married her. Booth forever blamed himself for having been too drunk to open the telegrams which said she was dying and urged his prompt return. In 1870, Booth's only son, Edgar, died just hours after his birth. The loss led to the insanity of Edwin's 2nd wife, Mary McVicker. Then, in 1874, Edwin went bankrupt, losing the beautiful Booth Theater, which had been built to his specifications 5 years earlier.

The greatest calamity of Edwin's life was also a national tragedy. On April 14, 1865, 3 weeks after his record run in *Hamlet*, his younger brother, John Wilkes Booth, shot and killed President Abraham Lincoln in the Ford Theater in Washington, D.C. Twelve days later Booth himself was shot in a burning barn in Virginia. Desperately seeking to surpass Edwin's fame, John Wilkes had feared that chronic hoarseness would curtail his own promising acting career. The evening of the assassination he vowed, "When I leave the stage for good, I will be the most famous man in America." Grief-stricken and humiliated by his brother's mad crime, Edwin immediately retired. Ironically, a few years earlier Edwin had saved Lincoln's son Robert from being crushed by a train at Pennsylvania Railroad Station in Jersey City.

Eventually Booth rebounded from all his adversities, returned to the stage, and died in 1893 a wealthy man with many friends and admirers. A bronze statue of Edwin Thomas Booth stands in New York's Gramercy Park opposite The Players, a club for actors that he founded in 1888. The Harvard Theatre Collection in Cambridge, Mass., boasts 2 recordings Booth made in 1890.

—N.B.

Composers—Classical

Ludwig van Beethoven (1770–1827). In each of the arts, there are a few figures who loom imposingly over all others. In music, Ludwig van Beethoven is one of those, and practically every composer who lived after him has had to pay homage in one way or another to his genius.

Beethoven was born in Bonn, Germany. His family was musical and there was no doubt that the young Ludwig would receive adequate training for the profession. He showed early promise as a composer, and by 1782 had some compositions published. In 1787, he had occasion to meet and perform for Mozart. After the session, Mozart prophetically stated, "Keep your eyes on him. Someday, he will give the world something to talk about." A few years later, Beethoven moved to Vienna (where he would stay for the rest of his life) and for a year studied composition with Haydn. He was an unsatisfactory student for all his teachers in Vienna, moving one of them to remark with a great lack of perception that "he has learned nothing, and will never do anything properly."

The greatest of Beethoven's works came from a period that began about 1804. He had been in Vienna for 10 years, and had established himself as a composer and pianist of considerable repute. The compositions prior to this time reflect too many of his teachers' rules, and too much of the classic-era style that prevailed then. Beginning with the 3rd Symphony and the works that immediately followed it, Beethoven took a distinct giant step away from the past and moved into his own, establishing once and for all his identity as a truly original composer. His music was in turn both praised and castigated. Some called it the music of the future, while others considered it cacophonous and not fit to be played. Whether they liked his music or not, however, music critics generally agreed that they had a genius in their midst.

Beethoven moved easily among the nobility and aristocracy, and often times was paid greater respect than he in turn gave. But this was only in the earlier years, for as Beethoven aged, a progressive deafness (which became complete by 1820) altered his personality and behavior. In his last years, he was darkly moody and eccentric, and spent many long periods in brooding solitude.

Although Beethoven did much to change the face of music by pushing it away from the formal stylisms of the 18th century, leading it to the freer, more subjective expression of the 19th century, he actually invented no styles or forms. His media were those of Haydn and Mozart—symphonies, concerti, sonatas, string quartets, and the like. Nor did he compose as rapidly as did the 2 classic-era masters. Rather, he worked out musical ideas in his "sketchbooks," a process that sometimes took several years before the final compositional result would be produced. Thus, while less prolific than Haydn and Mozart, he eventually produced 9 symphonies, 5 piano concerti, 32 piano sonatas, 16 string quartets, an opera, a mass, and a ballet—138 opus numbers in all, plus 70 unnumbered compositions.

The symphonies are collectively the best known of Beethoven's music. The 5th has the famous 4-note motif that has come to have a variety of meanings, including "fate" and "victory." The 3rd was reputedly dedicated to Napoleon until he moved to conquer Europe; Beethoven is supposed to have ripped off the title page in anger and rededicated it to "The memory of a great man." The 6th is called the Pastoral Symphony, and is one of the 1st "program" compositions in which the music suggests an external meaning. The 9th is called the Choral Symphony, because its last movement is a magnificent choral setting for Schiller's "Ode to Joy."

By the time Beethoven composed the 9th Symphony in 1823, his deafness was a way of life. He nonetheless conducted the 1st performance of the work, hearing neither music from the performers nor accolade from the audience afterward. The soprano soloist had to take him by the arm and lead him to the front of the stage so he could *see* the response to his latest composition. Less than 3 years later, in March, 1827, a pneumonia attack was fatal, and 20,000 people attended the funeral.

Beethoven led an intense, sometimes agonizing, sometimes joyful, but always exciting and controversial life. All of this is reflected in his music. He is buried in a quiet circle in Vienna's Central Cemetery, the final resting place for all of Vienna's famous composers and musicians. As would be expected, his monument dominates all others.

—J.E.

Wolfgang Amadeus Mozart (1756–1791). Wolfgang Amadeus Mozart was one of the 1st of a long string of major composers who began as child prodigies. His father Leopold exploited the young musician's talents to the fullest. As soon as they were old enough, Leopold began showing off both Wolfgang and his sister Maria Anna in courts and castles over all of Europe. Wolfgang was only 6 when he played for the Austrian royalty at Schönbrunn Palace in Vienna. When Mozart was 8, King George III of England tested his abilities by playing all sorts of improvisational games with him. Whether or not this exploitation had any effect on the young Mozart is purely speculative; those who point to Wolfgang's early development as a composer applaud Leopold for developing the child so thoroughly and so early; those who condemn the father point to Wolfgang's early death, saying overwork ruined his health.

Composing began early; there were piano works and a symphony by 1764 when Mozart was only 8. Once the flow started, it never ceased. Nor did it vary either in quantity or quality. Mozart's early travels gave him exposure to the wide variety of music being composed in Europe, ranging from Italian operas to north German religious works to French orchestral pieces. The impressions he received were invaluable aids when he composed his later works.

As Mozart grew up, he continued both to travel and compose but the problem of making a living became an increasingly imperative one. In late 1768, he was appointed Konzertmeister to the Archbishop of Salzburg. The position brought prestige and freedom to travel, but not much money. In 1772, the archbishop died and his successor was not only unmusical but had no personal liking for Mozart. The young composer found himself eating with the servants and performing menial tasks. When he finally complained—in 1781—the archbishop had him ejected from the palace.

Mozart moved on to Vienna where he tried,

not too successfully, to make a living as a performer and composer. Soon after reaching Vienna, he met Haydn and played for him. Haydn remarked to Mozart's father that the young Mozart was the greatest composer he had ever heard, and that he possessed a "most consummate knowledge of the art of composition." The 2 composers eventually became friends and met to play chamber music. The influence they had on each other was remarkable, for it was after these meetings that they both flowered as mature, classic-era composers.

There are many stories about Mozart's compositional abilities and there is no question but that he composed with great speed. Typical of his efforts was the Symphony No. 36, the "Linz." Mozart wrote the 4-movement work, copied it, rehearsed it with the Linz court orchestra, and had it performed in a period of 4 days. The overture to *Don Giovanni* was composed *in toto*, and copied, the night before the 1st performance of the opera. Mozart's wife, Constanze, plied him with punch and told him fairy tales to keep him awake and working.

Don Giovanni was written while Mozart was in Prague, and was given a tumultuous reception by that Czech city. Prague considered Mozart as her adopted son and treated him royally whenever he visited. The Villa Bertramka, where he stayed while he wrote *Don Giovanni*, is now a national museum. When Mozart died, Prague, upon hearing of his death, went into a long period of mourning.

Vienna was not so kind. Only in Mozart's last year, did he begin to get commissions and orders for compositions there. And he quite possibly worked himself to death. His efforts to get compositions completed on time exhausted him, allowing the typhus which killed him to get a firm hold. He had 3 major works to finish—2 operas, *The Clemency of Tito* and *The Magic Flute*, and the Requiem. As he worked on the Requiem, he began to complain about his condition, claming that he had been poisoned. This led to a story that he had indeed been poisoned by Salieri, a rival composer. Constanze made the accusation and insisted for the rest of her life that it was so. While evidence has almost completely disproved the story, unfortunately, Mozart's body was never made available for examination.

He died on December 5, 1791, and the next day his funeral was held in the open air near St. Stephen's Cathedral in the center of Vienna. Only a few of his friends were present (among them, incidentally, was Salieri). No official notice of his death was taken by the city. The coffin was carried to the gate of the cemetery and handed over to the gravediggers. As was the custom in paupers' funerals, the coffin was buried in an unmarked grave with no mourners in attendance, and the location was forever lost. Later, a lovely monument to Mozart was erected in the cemetery in the circle where other famous composers of Vienna are buried.

Mozart was the complete composer; he wrote operas, symphonies, concerti, chamber works, sonatas, and songs. Many of them are played the world over. He set a level of quality in composition that only a few composers have since been able to meet.

Long after Mozart's death, an Austrian musicographer, Ludwig Köchel, catalogued all of Mozart's music, listing the compositions in chronological order. When his catalogue was published in 1862, it was such a definitive listing that it became the universal reference for all of Mozart's music. Thus, his works are listed on a program with a "K" number (K.551, for instance, is Symphony No. 41, the "Jupiter").

—J.E.

Franz Schubert (1797–1828). Of all the great Viennese masters of the time—Mozart, Haydn, and Beethoven included—only Franz Schubert was a native of the capital city of the Austrian Empire. Schubert's life, which began in poverty in 1797, ended after a brief 31 years. Yet, during that time, he composed almost 650 songs, 9 symphonies, over a dozen operas, 5 masses, and a vast amount of piano and chamber music. Some of his works now are counted among the world's favorites, but it was not that way when Schubert was alive.

The musical part of Schubert's life began when he was 11 and was accepted as a choirboy in the court chapel. His musical training, what there was of it, came at the school. The head of the school was Antonio Salieri (dean of Viennese musicians, and the same man who had been accused of poisoning Mozart), and it was he who gave the young Schubert his only real composition lessons. Schubert's stay at the school lasted for just 5 years, but Salieri continued to work with him for a few years thereafter. Even during the school period, compositions sprang from the young genius.

The 1st truly great song was "Gretchen am Spinnrade," set to words from Goethe's *Faust* and written in 1814. In the following year, Schubert composed over 150 songs, among them one of his greatest, "Erlkönig"—again to a Goethe poem. "Heidenröslein," another favorite, also came from the same year. By this time, Schubert had developed his style of song composition and was moving into the areas of opera and symphony. None of his operas ever amounted to much, but 3 of his symphonies, the 5th, 8th ("Unfinished"), and 9th ("Great") are standards for symphonic orchestras.

The Unfinished Symphony has a far less romantic tale than has often been presented. Schubert gave the 1st 2 movements of the symphony to a friend, Anselm Hüttenbrenner, in 1823, supposedly to submit to a Vienna music society as a consideration for membership. Admittance was not gained, and Hüttenbrenner never returned the score. In 1865, Johann Herbeck recovered the score and gave the 1st performance shortly thereafter. The name "Unfinished" was then applied and the stories of the symphony's creation began, none of them true.

Schubert's life was never one of wealth and comfort. He taught at his father's school after he left choir school. The pay was wretched and a few times he quit teaching in order to compose. Occasionally some friends helped out, and in later years there were a few publications. While it was not a prosperous life, it certainly was that of a *bon vivant*. Schubert had a circle of friends that spent practically every evening in one or another of Vienna's taverns. There were musicians, writers, lawyers, rich men, and poor men in the circle. They all felt a strong bond of affection for the composer, and many of the evenings were spent in someone's home listening to the playing and singing of Schubert and Johann Michael Vogl, his longtime friend. After the "Schubertiad," as such a musical evening came to be called, the young men would return to the tavern to refresh themselves and argue. It was a free life. The "Schubertiads" began in 1816 and continued until Schubert died. Many of his finest songs, among them "An die Musik," "Der Tod und das Mädchen" ("Death and the Maiden"), and "Die Forelle" ("The Trout"), were 1st heard in such sessions. The last 2 songs became bases for famous chamber works later.

The last 5 years were spent in disintegrating health. Schubert had contracted syphilis in late 1822, and the terrible disease (there being no cure in those days) slowly ate its way through his body. Still, some of the greatest works came from that time. The song cycle *Die Schöne Müllerin* (*The Pretty Miller's Daughter*) and the *Rosamunde* music were composed in 1823: "Who is Sylvia?," "Im Frühling" ("In Spring"), "Hark, Hark the Lark," and the beloved "Ave Maria" in 1825; *Die Winterreise* (*Winter Journey*) in 1827; and in the last year, 1828, "Auf dem Strom" ("On the Strand"), "Der Hirt auf dem Felsen" ("The Shepherd of the Rock"), and *Ständchen*, Schubert's beautiful and beloved *Serenade*. The disease eventually wasted his body to the point that a case of typhoid proved fatal. Schubert died in November, 1828.

Schubert as a composer lived in relative

obscurity. He met Beethoven for the 1st time, in 1827, a week before that illustrious composer died, even though both had lived in Vienna for years. Publishers generally ignored Schubert except for an occasional song or smaller work. His brother Ferdinand tried to interest publishers in the great quantity of music Schubert left behind when he died. Ferdinand met some success, but it was not until 1865 that the world began to recognize his brother's genius. Herbeck's discovery of the Unfinished Symphony was almost a turning point. After that symphony—and several other orchestral works—became familiar throughout Europe, Schubert finally gained the recognition he deserved. He is buried in the circle of famous musicians in Vienna's Central Cemetery, next to Brahms and just 2 graves away from Beethoven.

—J.E.

Richard Wagner (1813–1883). Richard Wagner was to German opera and music drama what Verdi was to Italian opera—the culmination of the nation's musical genius and an intense motivating force. When Wagner began to compose seriously, Weber had just recently died after having tentatively established a national school of German opera. Wagner also became a nationalist, this nationalism reflecting itself strongly in all his compositions; there is nothing in music more Germanic than the 4-opera cycle *Der Ring des Nibelungen* based on German mythology, or *Lohengrin* and *Parsifal*, based on old German folk tales.

Wagner was born the same year as Verdi. His father (this paternity is questionable) died when he was 6 months old, and his mother quickly married Ludwig Geyer, an actor who had been intimate with the family for some time. Geyer is now generally considered to be Wagner's true sire. He died in 1821, and Wagner's childhood and youth were at best chaotic. The year 1827 found him in Leipzig with a kindly uncle who tried to help him with his education. Wagner was largely self-taught musically up until this time. In 1828, he decided to study composition seriously. In 1831, he entered the University of Leipzig as a student.

Later, Wagner's 1st post was as director of the opera at Magdeburg. He met the actress Minna Planer there, and she became his 1st wife. (The marriage was most unhappy and drove Wagner into some spectacular affairs with other women during the next 30 years.) The couple moved to a better post in Königsberg right after their wedding in 1836.

From then on, Wagner's life was a series of climactic events, one following close upon another. He obtained a post in Riga, Latvia, which he held until 1839, when he was fired.

Because of their enormous debts and hounding creditors, he and Minna (and their dog) fled the country on a small boat bound for London. This trip was the inspiration for *The Flying Dutchman*. Next, the 2 went to Paris, where they lived in poverty as usual, while Wagner finished *Rienzi*. In 1842, they left Paris and spent the next 7 years in Dresden, during which time Wagner wrote *Tannhäuser* and *Lohengrin*. In 1849, Wagner became involved with a group of radicals and soon there was a warrant out for his arrest. He had to flee Dresden, hidden in a goods wagon and carrying a false passport. He ended up in Bordeaux, where he began a spicy affair with Jessie Laussot, the wife of a friend. The affair did not last too long, and soon Wagner and Minna were back together in Zürich. Wagner had completed the 1st 2 operas (or music dramas, as he now called them) of the *Ring*, *Das Rheingold* and *Die Walküre*, by 1856.

Wagner became romantically entangled with Mathilde Wesendonk, in 1857, the wife of another benefactor. Wagner had begun *Siegfried*, the 3rd opera in the *Ring*, while living in a cottage on the Wesendonk property in Zürich. This affair was to last for some time, even though both Minna and Mathilde's husband knew of it. Wagner and Minna separated. Minna went back to Dresden and Wagner traveled fitfully around Europe. He started *Tristan und Isolde* about this time, but his fortunes waned and by 1864, he had apparently reached the end with both creditors and friends; there was no hope left and he was faced with debtors' prison.

Then, as in fairy tales, along came the prince. This one, Ludwig II, was real, and he had taken the throne as King of Bavaria in 1864. Ludwig (alternately known as the "mad" King and the "dream" King) had a passion for Wagner's music. He had grown up in Hohenschwangau Castle surrounded by the *Lohengrin* and *Tannhäuser* legends. When Wagner set them to music, Ludwig was entranced. As soon as he had gained the throne, he summoned Wagner to Munich and gave him practically anything he wanted.

Wagner was thus able to settle in Munich, pay his bills (at the King's expense, of course), finish *Tristan und Isolde*, and begin *Die Meistersinger*. Meanwhile, the conductor Hans von Bülow had come to Munich with his wife, Cosima (Liszt's daughter), to conduct Wagner's works. Cosima and Wagner fell in love with each other and had 2 children before they could finally marry in 1870. By then Minna had died and Von Bülow had obtained a divorce.

The remainder of Wagner's life, after Cosima joined him, was one of great happiness. He, with Ludwig's assistance, built the great theater at Bayreuth where his works could be presented. He finished the *Ring* with *Die Götterdämmerung* and then wrote *Parsifal*. He died of heart disease in February, 1883.

Wagner's life and music are an integral part of his era. He was allied with Liszt and others in espousing the philosophy that music had powers of external reference, and his works, especially the *Ring*, reflected this philosophy to an almost extreme degree. His leitmotiv concept—which involved assigning a musical signature to characters, places, and even thoughts in a composition—is a manifestation of this philosophy. The belief grew and gathered in new followers. It carried into the 20th century, where it died abruptly about 1910.

An individualist and a supreme egotist, Wagner believed that because of his talent and genius, he should live like royalty. It was this belief that strained his finances until 1864, but he almost got away with it. And after Ludwig came along, he did.

—J.E.

COMPOSERS—MODERN

George Gershwin (1898–1937). One of America's most gifted composers, described as a colossus with one foot planted in Tin Pan Alley and the other in Carnegie Hall, George Gershwin was born Jacob Gershvin in Brooklyn on September 28, 1898. The family (now Gershwin) moved to New York's lower East Side, where young Jacob (now George), a late bloomer as a musician, started to study piano at the age of 13. Before that, street games and a "tough guy" image were more important to him in his milieu, but once he started, music became the guiding force of his life. Ironically, the piano that activated the latent genius's musical interest was acquired not for him but for his older brother, Ira, who later became George's lyricist. For the next 25 years George continued to take lessons, even at the zenith of his incredibly productive career.

At 15, a school dropout, he became a song-plugger, and his career was boosted by such immortals as Sigmund Romberg and Sophie Tucker. Later, as a rehearsal pianist for a Jerome Kern show, he was widely praised and encouraged by his idol, Kern himself. Through his show business and Tin Pan Alley contacts the 21-year-old Gershwin wrote his 1st Broadway musical score, for *La, La, Lucille*. Not much survived from that show, but at about the same time he dashed off "Swanee" with lyricist Irving Caesar. Written in 15 minutes, and introduced by Al Jolson, it became a smash hit. One million copies of sheet music and more than 2 million records were sold. Instant success was his.

For the next 5 seasons Gershwin wrote scores for George White's *Scandals*, which sought to supplant the *Ziegfeld Follies* as the ultimate revue on Broadway. Out of these came the standards "I'll Build a Stairway to Paradise" and "Somebody Loves Me." During this period of youthful creativity, Gershwin was experimenting with the composition of jazz as a serious musical form. Fortunately he found a kindred soul also determined to develop this genre—Paul Whiteman, who commissioned him to write a work for an all-American concert which Whiteman's orchestra would present. At Aeolian Hall in New York on February 12, 1924, *Rhapsody in Blue* was premiered to thundering critical acclaim. Now Gershwin had world fame, along with the wealth accumulated from recording royalties. Even today *Rhapsody in Blue* is one of the most widely played pieces of serious American music.

As significant as the "rhapsody" was for Gershwin's serious music, his collaboration with Ira in the same year was a partnership marked by originality, taste, and musicianship. The show was *Lady, Be Good!* and starred a youthful Fred Astaire. Thereafter almost yearly a George and Ira Gershwin musical appeared on the Broadway boards, even while George was working in the serious vein, producing the Concerto in F (1925), the vivid tone poem *An American in Paris* (1928), and the Second Rhapsody (1931).

Meanwhile the prolific brothers were making musical theater history with such gems as *Oh, Kay!* (which Gertrude Lawrence chose in 1926 for her 1st native American showcase), *Funny Face* (another Fred and Adele Astaire vehicle, in 1927), and *Girl Crazy* (which in 1930 launched 2 exciting talents, Ethel Merman and Ginger Rogers).

Gershwin's 2 masterpieces were in very different mediums: The witty, satirical *Of Thee I Sing* (1931) was the 1st musical to win a Pulitzer Prize, while the Negro folk opera *Porgy and Bess* (1935) has been called the greatest opera written by an American. *Of Thee I Sing* repeated the successful collaboration of George S. Kaufman, Morrie Ryskind, and George and Ira Gershwin that had struck pay dirt with *Strike Up the Band* (1930). *Porgy and Bess*, based on a book by DuBose Heyward, was not a success at its premiere, but later revivals on Broadway, on the road, and in foreign opera houses proved the importance and durability of this milestone in American music drama. With it Gershwin's prodigious output for Broadway ended, and he did not live to savor its success. In 1936 he and Ira moved to Hollywood and wrote exclusively for films, including 2 in which he was reunited with Fred Astaire (*Shall We Dance?* and *Damsel in Distress*, 1937). While he was working on the music for *The Goldwyn*

Follies in 1937, he was stricken with an inoperable brain tumor. He died on July 11, a man brimming with vitality, enthusiasm for life, and dynamic creativity. Gershwin's reputation today is undiminished. His songs are playable and recognizable whatever the current musical vogue; his serious works are programmed regularly by symphony orchestras, many of which have annual all-Gershwin programs.

Gershwin never married, though he was attracted by many women and did consider it. But his music was his be-all and end-all, and he was unwilling to divert any of his time to the demands of marriage. He was egocentric in his awareness of his talent and stature, but never obtrusively so, and he selflessly helped the careers of many promising newcomers (e.g., Hoagy Carmichael, Vincent Youmans). Straightforward and unassuming, he applied the same intensity to everything he undertook, whether it was sports, painting, or music.

—B.L.

Woody Guthrie (1912–1967)

I hate a song that makes you think that you're not any good. I hate a song that makes you think that you are just born to lose. Bound to lose. No good to nobody. No good for nothing. Because you are either too old or too young or too fat or too slim or too ugly or too this or too that. Songs that run you down or songs that poke fun at you on account of your bad luck or your hard traveling.

I am out to fight those kinds of songs to my very last breath of air and my last drop of blood.

I am out to sing songs that will prove to you that this is your world and that if it has hit you pretty hard and knocked you for a dozen loops, no matter how hard it's run you down and rolled over you, no matter what color, what size you are, how you are built, I am out to sing the songs that make you take pride in yourself and in your work. And the songs I sing are made up for the most part by all sorts of folks just about like you.—Woody Guthrie, quoted by Robert Shelton in booklet accompanying Woody Guthrie Library of Congress Recordings.

Woodrow Wilson Guthrie was born in Okemah, Okla., to Charles and Nora Guthrie. His sister Clara was 7 years older than he was and his brother Roy about 2 years younger than Clara. Okemah was a farming town that had had an oil boom for a few years. It had about an equal number of Indians, blacks, and whites doing their trading there.

Our family was sort of divided up into 2 sides: Mama taught us kids to sing the old songs and told us long stories about each ballad; and in her own way she told us over and over to always try and see the world from the other fellow's side. Meanwhile Papa bought us all kinds of exercising rods and stretchers, and kept piles of kids boxing and wrestling out in the front yard; and taught us never and never to allow any earthly human to scare us, bully us, or run it over us.

Woody's mother could not take the life that her husband had to lead in order to make his living—the fights and the high-pressure dealing. Her world came to look crazy, and although Woody describes her with great compassion, his sadness for her and for himself is apparent: "There was a feeling in me that I had been hunting for the bigger part of my life. A wide-open feeling that she was just like any other boy's mama." Later, when Woody's illness was diagnosed as Huntington's chorea, an incurable degenerative nerve disease, it could be seen in retrospect that this was what his mother had been afflicted with. At the time she only seemed strange.

Four of the houses Woody lived in until his teen-age years were destroyed—3 by fire. In one of the fires, his sister Clara was badly burned and died. The causes of these fires were never quite clear. Certainly the oil stoves of the time and place were dangerous. But apparently Woody felt there was the possibility that Clara might have set herself on fire or that his mother might have started the fires. At any rate, after the last fire, which occurred when he was 13, Woody's mother was sent to an insane asylum and his father moved to Pampa, Tex., where Woody's aunt treated her brother's burns and cared for him. Woody stayed with a couple of families in Okemah during this time and also began his travels on the road.

When he was 17, Woody joined his father in Pampa. During these years he tried out various possibilities. He did not know quite what he wanted to be, thinking of becoming a lawyer one day and a doctor the next.

Things was starting to stack up in my head and I just felt like I was going out of my wits if I didn't find some way of saying what I was thinking. The world didn't mean any more than a smear to me if I couldn't find ways of putting it down on something.

Woody begain painting and drawing. He paid his way during much of his travels by making signs. At the same time, he was learning to play the guitar, and he earned some money playing for local square dances.

In 1937, Woody headed out to California. According to biographer Robert Shelton, "For a time, he had a radio show for $1 a day on WKVD in Los Angeles. With Will Geer the actor and the late Cisco Houston the singer, he traveled to the migratory labor camps and helped raise some money for the workers there." On a later radio show, this one in New York City, Woody described these years:

> I've followed all kinds of big work jobs all over the country, like the oil fields, coal mines, big timber jobs, the Grand Coulee Dam, the TVA in the State of Tennessee, the harvesting of all kinds of crops like cotton, wheat, spuds, beets, and grapes and fruits and berries and vegetables. I've followed the building of the big highways like the Lincoln and the 66. And the hard rock tunnels and the WPA roads and streamlined speedways, and the building of the big ships, and the places where ferryboats land and where the subway trains and all of the other trains load up full of people, and I sang in roadhouses, hotels, messrooms, churches, union halls, saloons, and nightclubs and taverns. . . . I sing religious songs. I sing union songs. . . . I sing songs about the outlaws that the people loved and the ones the people hated. I sing any song that was made up by the people that tells a little story, a little part, of our big history of this country, yes, or that tells a part of the history of the world.

In addition to all this, Woody cut 2 records for Victor called the "Dust Bowl Ballads," joined the Merchant Marine during W.W. II (carrying a guitar bearing the words, "This Machine Kills Fascists"), was a member of the Almanac Singers with Pete Seeger, Lee Hayes, and Millard Lampell, and with them and other singers began the hootenannies of the 1940s. He was married 3 times. He suffered the death of his daughter Cathy in the late 1940s (also a death by fire). Woody was hospitalized in the early 1950s with Huntington's chorea and when he died on October 3, 1967, he was survived by 5 children and millions of people the world over to whose lives his songs such as "This Land Is Your Land," "Hard, Ain't It Hard," "Hard Traveling," and "So Long, It's Been Good to Know Yuh" had made a difference.

—J.Ta.

Scott Joplin (1868–1917). One of America's great black artists and the self-proclaimed "King of the Ragtime Composers," Joplin was born in Texarkana, Tex. Nearly everyone in his family played an instrument or sang, and young Scott became fascinated by the piano at an early age.

At 14, Scott felt that he was ready to leave home and make his fortune as a musician. He headed for Missouri and played the piano in saloons, cafés, brothels, and on the big steamboats that still sailed the Mississippi. In this era, a new type of music was developing in the Midwest. It combined elements of the black music of Africa, the Caribbean, and the southern U.S. with popular dances, band music, and the sentimental ballads of the late 19th century. Because of its tricky, syncopated rhythms, this new music was known as "ragged time" or later as "ragtime" music. Because of its association with the parlors of "sporting houses" and cheap honky-tonk saloons, and because it was developed primarily by itinerant black pianists, ragtime never became entirely respectable, which only served to increase its popularity with many Americans. Scott Joplin was to be permanently identified with this new music called ragtime.

In Sedalia, Mo., at the age of 28, Joplin faced a turning point in his career. He was persuaded by friends to study music at George Smith College, an educational institution for blacks run by the Methodist Church. Here he worked at translating the elusive rhythms of popular ragtime into formal musical notation. Meanwhile, he continued to support himself by performing on the entertainment circuit, notably at Will and Walker Williams' Maple Leaf Club, which attracted all the best musicians in the area. As a tribute to this lively institution, Joplin composed "The Maple Leaf Rag," which quickly became a favorite in Sedalia. Joplin himself was optimistic about its prospects for achieving a wider popularity. He told a friend: "'The Maple Leaf' will make me the king of ragtime composers." Nevertheless, Joplin had a difficult time in finding a publisher. Finally in 1899, he persuaded Joseph Stark, a Sedalia music dealer, to publish "The Maple Leaf Rag," and the immediate nationwide success of this piece seemed to fulfill Joplin's prediction. "The Maple Leaf" was heard everywhere, as a craze for ragtime swept America.

With the profits from his music, Joplin moved to St. Louis, retired from the ragtime performing circuit, and bought a large house in which to devote himself to composing. Joplin had developed a vision of ragtime that transcended the limits of popular music: He saw it as a unique and serious art form, as America's answer to the achievements of European composers. In 1902 he completed a fascinating ragtime ballet (*The Ragtime Dance*) and then a ragtime opera called *The Guest of*

Honor. When the music for the ballet was published it proved a dismal failure, and the opera, which never even found its way into print, has since disappeared. Joplin's wife had little sympathy for such grandiose projects, especially as their money began to run out. After the tragic death of a baby daughter, the couple separated and Joplin hit the road once again, playing the piano at familiar saloons and nightclubs.

In 1907 Joplin moved to New York where he remarried and eventually settled in Harlem. By 1910, ragtime had begun to decline in popularity, yet Joplin was hard at work writing still another ragtime opera. Joplin considered this work, *Treemonisha*, about a black woman who leads her people to freedom, to be his masterpiece. When he was unable to find a publisher he dug deep into his savings and had the vocal score printed at his own expense. Though this venture brought him no encouragement, Joplin refused to abandon the project. He worked for 3 years to orchestrate *Treemonisha*, then put together a performance to test public reaction and attract financial backing. This presentation, once again paid for out of Joplin's own pocket, took place in 1915, without orchestra or scenery. It was considered a laughable failure. The public was ready to accept a black musician as the piano player in a bawdy house, but not as a serious composer of operatic music.

During the preparations for the *Treemonisha* debacle, Joplin was under serious strain. His behavior became moody and erratic, with strong schizophrenic tendencies. After the opera disaster he suffered a total breakdown. His wife and friends were unable to help him, and he was committed to Manhattan State Hospital in the fall of 1916. Joplin never left the hospital and died there on April 1, 1917.

In recent years, Scott Joplin's music has been enjoying an astonishing revival. His rags are played frequently in concerts and recitals, and several recordings of his music have reached best-seller status. Even the long-forgotten *Treemonisha* has been performed publicly and has finally received the serious attention it deserves. For those who would like to hear the haunting, evocative sound of Joplin's music, a fine performance of some of his piano rags is available at a budget price. ("Scott Joplin Piano Rags" performed by Joshua Rifkin; Nonesuch Records H-71248.)

—M.S.M.

DANCERS

Isadora Duncan (1878–1927). A beautiful yet tragic figure, Isadora Duncan was one of the most revolutionary and controversial personalities the dance world has ever known —both on stage and offstage.

She was born Dora Angela Duncan, 4th child of Dora and Joseph Duncan in San Francisco, Calif.; her father deserted the family a few months before Isadora's arrival. Her mother supported the family by giving piano lessons and knitting. Their nomadic existence —necessary to keep distance between them and their creditors—was a difficult but happy one, for they ignored defeat. Isadora's incredible optimism in the midst of the most depressing of circumstances sustained her throughout a tumultuous life.

Isadora believed from the time she was a child that her life as an artist was destined by the gods, and that she was a mortal incarnation of Aphrodite. "I belong to the gods," she wrote. "My life is ruled by signs and portents, which I follow to my set goals."

Dancing was as natural as walking for Isadora, and when she turned 17, she decided she was ready for a professional dance career. She headed for Chicago accompanied by her mother. In order to keep from starving, Isadora took a job in a vaudeville show where she was billed as "The California Faun." Her 1st break came when she auditioned for the impresario Augustin Daly while he was in Chicago. She was immediately hired for his New York Revue.

Daly was responsible for Isadora's brief but formal ballet training. He sent her to study with a leading ballerina in New York, and then with another in London. However, Isadora was in total opposition to formal ballet, and she rebelled against its rigid set movements. Her dancing was totally free form—romantic and lyrical. Isadora challenged not only the staid direction that ballet had taken, but its costumes and musical accompaniment as well. The human form was beautiful and sacred to Isadora, and her costumes were softly draped Grecian tunics which silhouetted the body, enhancing every movement. The traditional ballet slipper was replaced by sandals or she wore no shoes at all.

The lingering Victorian attitude of the American audience was at odds with Isadora's innovations, and her costumes—or lack of them —(it was said that she once danced in Boston in the nude)—were regarded by many as "shocking and scandalous." Isadora's use of Beethoven's 7th Symphony as dance music outraged purists who felt that music should be used as its composer had intended. Sometimes, poems were read aloud during her dance. Isadora's philosophy of dance was ". . . to blend together—a poem, a melody and a dance—so that you will not listen to the music, see the dance or hear the poem, but will live in the scene and the thought that all are expressing."

Isadora was baffled by her total nonacceptance in America. She was instantly successful and widely applauded in Europe. She opened a school of dance in 1904 at Grünewald, near Berlin. It was around this time that she met and fell in love with Gordon Craig, a famous English stage designer who was also known for his revolutionary theater ideas. Isadora did not believe in marriage. She lived with Craig for a while and gave birth to their child in a little village in Holland, where she had gone to await the arrival of the baby. Deirdre was born in September of 1906. Ecstatically happy, Isadora returned to Grünewald to continue her teaching. Craig was with her occasionally, but the demands of their careers eventually separated them completely.

Isadora wanted to open another school in Paris, but she had no money and half-jokingly prayed for a millionaire to appear in her life. After a performance in Paris, Isadora received a calling card from a gentleman admirer in her dressing room. The card had come from Paris Singer, the 22nd child of Isaac Singer and an heir to his family's sewing-machine fortune. Wealthy, handsome, cultured, and charming, Singer swept Isadora off her feet. Isadora and Singer became lovers, and a child, Patrick, was born to them in May of 1910 in a beautiful villa in France.

The following 3 years were luxurious and happy ones for Isadora. Her financial worries were a thing of the past, her school in Germany was a success, and Singer wanted to finance any other school that she wanted to open. She adored her children more than anything in the world. At the age of 35, she had everything she had ever hoped for and much to look forward to.

On April 19, 1913, Deirdre and Patrick kissed their mother good-bye before going to Versailles in Singer's limousine. Minutes later, they were dead. The limousine had plunged into the Seine River when the chauffeur got out to crank the car after it had stalled. He had failed to put on the brake. Isadora wrote:

> Only twice comes that cry of the mother which one hears as without one's self—at birth and at death. . . . Why the same? Since one is the cry of supreme joy and the other of sorrow. . . . Is it not that in all the Universe there is but one great continuing Sorrow, Joy, Ecstasy, Agony—the Mother Cry of Creation.

A grieving Isadora left Singer and tried to seek relief in travel—at times contemplating suicide. While in Italy, she had an affair with a young sculptor. In an attempt to bring back her remembered joy of motherhood, she became pregnant. The child died shortly after birth. With the tragic loss of her 3 children and the emptiness of her love affairs, Isadora became totally immersed in her dancing.

In 1921, following several more love affairs, and performances and voyages all over the world—Switzerland, Greece, Paris, South America, Cuba, and North Africa—Isadora went to Russia with the intent of opening another school. The Bolsheviks had promised her support. After much red tape and many delays, Isadora found a large house and selected 50 girls as her new students. The aid promised her by the Government never materialized, and she was once again in debt.

Isadora was determined to succeed—both in her school and in her newest love affair. Her paramour was the young Russian poet Serge Essenin. Isadora was 42 years old; Essenin was 15 years younger. Essenin spoke not a word of English, and Isadora not a word of Russian. Although Isadora did not believe in marriage, she married Essenin. Perhaps it was simply for immigration purposes—to bring her new lover to the U.S. for her scheduled tour there. At any rate, their passionate relationship turned out to be stormy. His temper, frequent drunkenness, and jealousy of her notoriety—and her jealousy of his romantic wanderings—led to their eventual breakup.

In December, 1925, while in Paris, Isadora received a telegram telling her that Essenin had committed suicide. No longer was Isadora's dancing that of the joyous free spirit. Her personal tragedies now led her into dances of despair.

Nearing her 50th birthday, she went to visit friends in Nice. She was attracted by the young Italian sent to demonstrate a car she was interested in buying. During the ride the trailing end of the long, red-fringed scarf she had wrapped around her neck caught in the spokes of the rear wheel of the sports car. Her neck was broken and she died instantly—as tragic in death as in life.

—D.X.B.

Vaslav Fomich Nijinsky (1890–1950). Although Vaslav Fomich Nijinsky had a comparatively short dance career—barely 10 years—he has the reputation of being the greatest male dancer in history.

Born in Kiev, Russia, on February 28, 1890, Vaslav was the 2nd son of Fomich and Eleanora Nijinsky, Polish ballet dancers who were on tour in Russia at the time of his birth.

Nijinsky's mother had great aspirations for her son to be a dancer and she tried to enroll him at the Imperial Theater School when he was 7 years old. He was rejected because of his age but he auditioned when he reached 10 and was chosen along with 5 others from 150 applicants.

Nijinsky was a poor student scholastically but excelled in all of his dancing classes, particularly mime. In 1906, 2 years prior to his graduation from the Imperial Theater School, an unprecedented offer was made to accept him as a regular member of the Imperial Ballet. However, he turned the offer down, choosing to remain a student until his graduation at the age of 17, when he would automatically become a member.

There were few opportunities at this time for male dancers to exhibit their versatility. Nijinsky was given an occasional solo but performed mainly as a partner for the ballerinas. He took several leaves of absence from the Imperial Ballet to perform with the seasonal ballet and opera company of Serge Diaghilev, the great impresario. Michel Fokine, a brilliant young choreographer, and Anna Pavlova, the distinguished ballerina, were 2 of the company's prominent members. Nijinsky was now given the opportunity to perform roles that would demonstrate his artistic genius.

Diaghilev eventually formed a permanent company that performed the year round and he offered Nijinsky a position as his leading male dancer. The timing was perfect, as Nijinsky's disagreement with the Maryinsky Theater director over a costume he was to wear resulted in his angry resignation. Nijinsky then accepted Diaghilev's offer with great enthusiasm and began touring with the company in 1911—he would never again return to his native Russia.

Nijinsky's dynamic ability to leap effortlessly and appear to pause in midair continuously left his audiences gasping in amazement. He was a marvelous actor as well as a brilliant dancer. His favorite role was in the ballet *Petrouchka*, the story of an emotional and loving puppet who was incapable of expressing his feelings—oddly enough, very much like Nijinsky himself. When Sarah Bernhardt, the well-known actress, saw him perform *Petrouchka*, she said: "I am afraid, I am afraid, for I am watching the greatest actor in the world."

Nijinsky began choreographing new works for Diaghilev's company. His ballets *L'Après-midi d'un faune* and *Le Sacré du printemps* were revolutionary for their time and were received with bitter controversy by both the press and the audiences.

The end of Nijinsky's career came in 1917 after a dance tour of South America. During that final tour, Nijinsky suffered from acute paranoia and hired a bodyguard to protect him from his "enemies." At the completion of the tour, Nijinsky and his wife, Romola, a dancer whom he had married in 1913, settled in Switzerland. Nijinsky's mental state caused great concern. Severe disagreements with Diaghilev had totally severed their personal relationship, and his choreographic efforts had taxed his emotional stability. Lethargic, Nijinsky withdrew into himself. There were long periods of silence, and when he communicated with his wife, he spoke about God and living a simple peasant life of which dancing was no longer a part. His wife was completely bewildered by his behavior and called in a series of specialists for a diagnosis. She was told that his condition was hopeless, and in 1918 Nijinsky was forcibly removed to an asylum where he remained until his death in 1950.

—D.X.B.

Anna Pavlova (1882–1931). One of the great geniuses of the dance and the most famous ballerina of all time was born in St. Petersburg, Russia, on January 31, 1882. Anna Pavlova was the only child of an exceedingly poor family. Frail and weak because of her premature birth, she suffered throughout her childhood from one illness after another. It is astonishing that in later years this frail child showed an enormous strength and drove herself at an incredibly intense pace—giving 9 or 10 performances a week for more than 20 years.

When she was 8, Pavlova was taken by her mother to see the Imperial Ballet perform *The Sleeping Beauty*. Captivated by the enchanting ballerina and the beautiful Tchaikovsky music, she knew at that moment that her life would be dedicated to the dance. She was, however, too young at that time to be admitted to the strict Imperial Theater School which was at the Czar's court in St. Petersburg. Pavlova had to wait 2 years before undergoing the preliminary entrance examination. She was accepted—one among 7 or 8 others chosen from nearly 100 applicants.

After 7 years of arduous training under the rigid discipline of the school, Pavlova joined the Imperial Ballet at the age of 17. Her rise to the top was rapid—after only 7 years, she became the company's prima ballerina. It did not matter what Pavlova danced because of how she danced. Technique was not her only powerful asset—it was often her acting as much as her dancing that held the audience completely spellbound.

Pavlova is most famous for her interpretation of *The Dying Swan*. C. W. Beaumont, an English ballet critic who saw her perform this short 2½-minute solo in London, wrote:

> The emotion transferred was so overpowering that it seemed a mockery to applaud when the dance came to an end, our souls had soared into empyrean with the passing of the swan; only when the silence was broken could we feel that they had returned to our bodies.

This solo dance, possibly the best known in the history of ballet, was especially created for Pavlova by Michel Fokine, one of Pavlova's fellow pupils at the Imperial Theater School. He was a young choreographer, attempting a revolutionary break in the staid classical form which the ballet had retained up until that time. Fokine's ideas were not accepted by the Imperial Ballet—which appeared at the Maryinsky Theater. Pavlova was allowed to perform his works only at charity functions or, because of her status as prima ballerina, when the Maryinsky Theater was closed for vacation and she could get a leave of absence.

In 1908, Fokine's choreography caught the eye of Serge Diaghilev, who was then beginning his career as a great impresario. Diaghilev made Pavlova an offer to dance with his company as prima ballerina. She accepted but danced with Diaghilev's ballet company for only one season, leaving because of rivalry with the great male dancer, Vaslav Nijinsky. Pavlova disliked any competition and was often accused of surrounding herself with "mediocre" dancers in order to spotlight her own artistry. Because of jealousy and artistic temperament, she had many unpleasant confrontations with her male partners; and although she had her favorites, she never remained with one partner very long.

In 1908, Pavlova began her tireless life of touring by train and ship all over the world with her own company of dancers. She took ballet to the most obscure little towns she could find. For many people, it was the 1st and perhaps the last time they saw a ballet. Pavlova always studied the dances of the countries she visited, thereby constantly adding to her already extensive repertoire.

Although she traveled widely, Pavlova kept a permanent home, Ivy House, in London. She had a great love for birds of every kind, especially swans, which swam on a small lake she had designed for her London residence. She also kept flamingos, a peacock, and an aviary for the smaller birds she had collected during her travels.

By the 1920s, her career was coming to a close. Although plagued by a painful knee injury and overwork, she was driven by her desire to dance, and continued her exhausting schedule.

In January, 1931, she went to Holland to begin another tour. Upon her arrival at The Hague, she collapsed. On January 23, 1931, Pavlova, in a delirium of fever, spoke her final words: "Get my *Swan* costume ready." She died a few minutes later of pneumonia a week before her 49th birthday.

—D.X.B.

MOVIEMAKERS

Luis Buñuel (1900–   ). Born on February 22, 1900, in northeastern Spain, Buñuel was educated by Jesuits before he entered the University of Madrid at the age of 17. There he became friends with the poet and playwright Federico García Lorca and the painter Salvador Dali.

Buñuel's 1st film, *Un Chien Andalou*, financed by his mother and made in collaboration with Dali, was a 20-minute surrealist short produced in 1928. The 1st feature film he directed, *L'Age d'Or* (*The Golden Age*), was so blatantly anti-Catholic and anti-upper class that Dali later renounced the project. When the film opened in Paris, a mob attacked the theater, tore apart the seats, and destroyed an art exhibit in the lobby. All prints of *L'Age d'Or* were quickly stored in film archives and not shown to the general public again until the late 1960s.

In 1932 Buñuel made *Las Hurdes* (*Land without Bread*), a brutal documentary about an impoverished rural area. When Franco took power in Spain after the Civil War, Buñuel was banned from the country. He lived for several years in the U.S. until he was forced to resign from his job at the Museum of Modern Art in New York City when it was discovered that he had directed *L'Age d'Or*. He also worked for the U.S. Army Film Division and as a dubbing expert for Warner Brothers.

In 1947, Buñuel settled in Mexico with his wife and 2 sons and made several successful commercial films, including *Los Olvidados* (released in the U.S. as *The Young and the Damned*, 1950), a harsh portrayal of juvenile delinquents and their struggle against conventional society, and *Robinson Crusoe* (1952).

In 1960, the Spanish Government, worried about its lack of cultural achievements, absolved Buñuel and invited him to make another film in Spain, this time with their blessing. The result, *Viridiana*, so outraged the Spanish authorities that they tried to confiscate all existing prints. Happily, they failed and the film was shown at the Cannes Film Festival where it won the top prize.

Since that time Luis Buñuel has made a series of consistently controversial, but highly successful, films including *El Angel Exterminador* (*The Exterminating Angel*), *Belle de Jour*, and *The Discreet Charm of the Bourgeoisie*, which was awarded the Motion Picture Academy Award for the best foreign film in 1973. After over 45 years of filmmaking, Buñuel has vowed that he will never make another—but he has said this before.

—D.W.

Charlie Chaplin (1889–   ). From a London childhood straight out of a Dickens novel, Charlie Chaplin rose to the top of the film-world ladder and won universal popular acclaim by portraying the beloved "Little Tramp." When he left the U.S. to live in Switzerland in 1952, Chaplin had suffered the humiliation of a paternity suit and an indictment under the Mann Act, public ostracism for his political beliefs, and vitriolic attacks in the press because of his nonconformity. Earlier, however, Chaplin had been an extraordinarily popular star. People imitated the famous Chaplin walk, bought Chaplin dolls and toys, and swarmed around him when he traveled or appeared in public. Moviegoers sympathized with Chaplin's little guy whose sad but comical mannerisms were his only defense against a threatening world. By the early twenties, Chaplin's working-class audience had expanded to include intellectuals and fellow artists. Many of them—including Gertrude Stein, Winston Churchill, George Bernard Shaw, and Albert Einstein—asked to meet him. Chaplin had become known as the movie's greatest virtuoso, a reputation which has rarely been challenged.

Chaplin's inspiration for the character of the Little Tramp was a stroke of luck plus genius. In 1913 he went to work for Mack Sennett's Keystone Co. On his 2nd film, Sennett told Chaplin to find himself a costume. After rummaging in a dressing room, he appeared in baggy pants, a tight coat, a too-small hat, and too-large shoes, an outfit that came to be his trademark. As Chaplin began to improvise, the clothes made the tramp's character. He tripped over a cuspidor, turned, and tipped his hat to it. The cameramen, stagehands, and even Sennett himself began to laugh. Fortunately, movie audiences laughed too.

Chaplin's subtle style of humor soon clashed with Sennett's idea that "comedy is an excuse for the chase," and the comedian joined Essanay Co. in 1915. While there, his style matured and he began to create the refined comedies for which he is famous. In 1917 he signed a contract to do 8 films for First National for $1 million. The best of those films was The Kid (1920), in which Jackie Coogan played a foundling whom the tramp rescues from a garbage can.

The great classics of Chaplin's career were created for United Artists, the company formed by Mary Pickford, Douglas Fairbanks, D. W. Griffith, and Chaplin in 1919. In The Gold Rush (1925) the tramp is so hungry he cooks his shoe and eats the laces like spaghetti. In City Lights (1931) he avoids a traffic jam by walking in one door of a limousine and out the other, thus confusing a flower girl who thinks that he must be a millionaire. Such was Chaplin's genius that jokes grew out of the situation rather than being added "just for laughs." Even the music for City Lights was composed by Chaplin so that it would highlight rather than overpower the action on the screen.

Chaplin came under increasing attack for the "anarchistic" attitudes expressed in films such as Modern Times (1936), The Great Dictator (1940), Monsieur Verdoux (1947), and Limelight (1953). During the McCarthy period he was accused of being a fellow traveler and attacked for never becoming an American citizen. Although his films have enjoyed a recent revival in the U.S., Chaplin and his wife, Oona O'Neill, continue to live in Switzerland.

—J.R.

Sergei Eisenstein (1898–1948). It is said that Hitler's Minister of Propaganda, Goebbels, showed German filmmakers the kind of films he wanted them to produce by screening Sergei Eisenstein's masterpiece, Battleship Potemkin. Somehow the ploy failed, for whereas Eisenstein's propaganda was exuberant, explosive, revolutionary art, the German product was propaganda and nothing more. Unlike many artists, Eisenstein was commissioned to make a film by a government which he supported. Potemkin was a brilliant film in 1925; today it is still dynamic.

The son of a shipbuilder, Eisenstein chose a career in the arts over engineering or architecture. After W.W. I he worked as a designer and a director in the theater, where he developed his theory of "Soviet realism." One of his plays was staged not in a theater but in a gasworks. It was inevitable that Eisenstein would gravitate toward cinema, with its natural potential for realism.

His 1st film, Strike (1924), was so inventive and vigorous that it drew immediate attention. The 27-year-old director filmed Potemkin in 2 months. It is remarkable for its maturity and masterly use of camera techniques. Eisenstein was also a pioneer in film editing, and the film is a virtual textbook of this art. In a famous scene, a baby carriage rolls down a long flight of steps while a horrified student watches helplessly from below. The images are intercut and the action slows down, alternating the separate images into one shocking scene. So original was his style that even though it has been copied endlessly, nothing since has equaled it.

When Soviet leaders became aware of the vast technical superiority of Hollywood production, it was only natural that the titanic young film maker should be chosen to study in the U.S. Eisenstein was lured by Hollywood as doggedly as a promising high school athlete is by American universities, but the promises of complete directorial freedom and vast sums of money never materialized. He signed with Paramount, whose executives were subsequently shocked that the Russian Cecil B. De Mille could come up with ideas so devoid of popular appeal. In 6 months Eisenstein and the studio proposed and rejected 7 projects before Paramount gave him a return ticket home.

By then, Eisenstein had been called a "defector" by the U.S.S.R. and was anxious to remain in America. He undertook filming a massive folk epic about Mexico, with the financial backing of the novelist Upton Sinclair. The stocky 32-year-old director was extremely temperamental. The project expanded from its 3-month schedule into a 2-year ordeal for the novelist, whose wife had mortgaged her house to finance the picture. Sinclair accused Eisenstein of maliciously discrediting anyone who stood in his way and of trying to stay in the U.S. regardless of the cost to his friends. "The most charitable interpretation that I can place upon Eisenstein is that he is an egomaniac," Sinclair said. The project ended when Sinclair gave the editing of *Que Viva Mexico* to someone other than Eisenstein; the film was never completed. Eisenstein returned to Russia, completely dispirited, with nothing to show for 2 years' work.

After he returned to the Soviet Union, Eisenstein was a man on a leash. As a teacher in the Moscow Film Institute and while directing his later films, he was under the watchful eye of Soviet censors. Eisenstein had to apologize publicly for forgetting "those great ideas that our art is summoned to serve"—namely, socialism. He died of a heart attack in 1948 while still working on a mammoth epic, *Ivan the Terrible*. After Stalin's death in 1953, Eisenstein was once again honored in his native country.

—J.R.

Greta Garbo (1905–   ). The press followed her on trips abroad, Hollywood stars begged her to attend their parties, her lovers implored her to marry them. Still Greta Garbo remained the "mystery woman." The more she tried to evade the world's insatiable curiosity, the more the public wanted to know about the real woman behind one of the most beautiful faces of the 20th century. Born Greta Gustafsson in a Stockholm slum, she had a miserably poor childhood. Her formal education ended at the age of 14 when her father became ill and died. She 1st worked as a lady barber, then as a clerk in a large department store. The store owners noticed that she was unusually good-looking and decided to use her as a model in their catalogue and for advertising films. An extremely shy girl, it was difficult for Garbo to summon up the nerve to apply to drama school and to seek acting jobs. At last she was noticed by the director Mauritz Stiller, who featured her in *Gösta Berling's Saga* (1924).

Stiller lectured Garbo on everything—whom to see, what to wear, and how to look (she had to lose 20 lbs.). He even changed her name to Garbo—she was a willing pupil. In 1925, she was noticed by Louis B. Mayer, then director of MGM, who, while vacationing in Europe, saw her in *The Street of Sorrow*. Mayer signed a contract with Stiller, and Garbo went with him to Hollywood at a salary of $350 a week.

In her 1st few films, Garbo played a variety of roles, but primarily was cast as a seductress. Stiller was given no projects to direct and returned to Sweden, leaving Garbo to contend with Hollywood alone. At one point, she was banned from the movies for 7 months for refusing to play yet another vamp and for demanding $5,000 a week. Ultimately, the studio gave in to the glamorous star that audiences wanted to see.

The public loved to watch Garbo's gorgeous face—the long eyelashes, the deep, sad eyes, and the unsmiling lips. Alistair Cooke, the well-known essayist and newspaperman, said, "She gives you the feeling that if your imagination has to sin, it can at least congratulate itself on its impeccable taste." Her love scenes with John Gilbert, known as the screen's greatest lover, increased interest in their well-publicized affair. Although she had a number of lovers, including conductor Leopold Stokowski, Garbo never married. During the '30s, after her relationship with Gilbert broke up, she became a recluse within the movie colony. On trips she often took aliases such as "Miss Harriet Brown" and disguised herself with slouch hats and big coats.

In 1930, *Anna Christie* opened with the promotional slogan "Garbo Talks" in big letters on the marquee. While many stars lost their careers because of the introduction of sound, Garbo's vibrant, sexy voice delighted audiences. She matured before their eyes in such great roles as *Queen Christina* (1933), *Anna Karenina* (1935), and *Camille* (1937).

Garbo retired from films in 1941, never to return. It was no secret that she hated Hollywood where "it's all a terrible compromise . . . all that matters is what they call box office."

And Garbo in 1975 at the age of 70? A friend of an Almanac staffer, who dined with her in New York recently, reports: "She remains a recluse. Among her closest friends are Rod Coleman, who runs a fencing school, and his wife. Garbo adores her friends' children. Almost her entire conversation, that evening, concerned children. Her past career and movies, past or present? She discussed neither. She's very squirrelly. Collects things. She arrived with a packet of unread newspapers she meant to read. She ate like a bird. Still on health foods only. Despite her age, she still has a beautiful face, the high cheek bones still marvelous. Her voice is very low timbre, and it makes it difficult to understand what she is saying. She was almost unintelligible much of the evening. She lives in her own apartment in a New York brownstone."

—J.R.

D. W. Griffith (1875–1948). In the productions of David Wark Griffith can be found the origins or development of many basic principles of filmcraft. Cecil B. De Mille called Griffith "the master of us all."

Griffith was born in La Grange, Ky., January 23, 1875, the son of a famous Confederate colonel known as "Roaring Jake." After receiving a country school education, young Griffith acted for several years in stock companies as "Lawrence Griffith." Determined to be a playwright, he sold one play, but it was a failure. In desperation, he took an acting job at the Thomas A. Edison studio in New York, making his debut as the hero of *Rescued from an Eagle's Nest* (1907), directed by Edwin S. Porter. Within a few months, he made his directorial debut at American Biograph with *The Adventures of Dollie* (1908). Nearly 500 one-reelers of increasing excellence followed.

Porter, as early as 1903, had used close-ups as well as crosscutting between scenes of parallel action to further suspense. Griffith improved these devices and added innovations of his own. Leaving Biograph in 1913, he became director-general of the Reliance-Majestic Studios in California. During 1915–1916, he headed the Triangle-Fine Arts studios.

The Birth of a Nation (1915), his most celebrated picture, was made independently at the unprecedented cost of $100,000. Griffith directed this Civil War epic without a script, improvising freely throughout. It was the 1st movie to be shown at $2 admission prices, and it eventually grossed $50 million. This film was resented in some quarters because it depicted the Ku Klux Klan in a favorable light, but its influence upon directorial techniques was tremendous. Griffith's massive spectacle, *Intolerance* (1916)—possibly the greatest of all films—failed financially. Four stories from different periods of history were told together through intricate intercutting. Its Babylonian city was the largest set ever built.

Griffith cofounded United Artists Corp. in 1919, with his famed *Broken Blossoms* (1919) as the 1st release. More outstanding Griffith films followed, including *Way Down East* (1921) and *Orphans of the Storm* (1922). Griffith developed innumerable stars and directors including Lillian Gish, H. B. Walthall, Mae Marsh, Raoul Walsh, Erich von Stroheim, and Tod Browning.

By 1927, Griffith's concepts seemed almost Victorian. His 1st "talkie," *Abraham Lincoln* (1930), was successful; but the next, *The Struggle* (1931), was a disaster from which he never recovered. He returned briefly in 1940 as associate producer of *One Million B.C.*, but

otherwise found no employment in the film industry during the 2 decades that preceded his death on July 23, 1948.

—G.T.

Rudolph Valentino (1895–1926). To say silent-screen star Rudolph Valentino was a sex symbol is putting it mildly. Italian-born Rodolpho d'Antonguolla came to the U.S. in 1913 and after working as a gardener, a cabaret dancer/gigolo, and then a bit player in Hollywood, he zoomed to stardom under his stage name in *The Four Horsemen of the Apocalypse* (1921), which was followed by hits like *The Sheik, Blood and Sand, Monsieur Beaucaire,* and *The Son of the Sheik.* Valentino became the embodiment of romance and sex to women all over the world, his name still a synonym for a handsome lover.

Women had always been attracted to Valentino—it is said that he left Italy to escape an enraged husband—and when he came to New York he was arrested when police found him in the apartment of a woman suspected of extorting money from fun-seeking businessmen. But after his movie successes, Valentino became an object of worship to thousands of females. Women ripped his clothes off him in the streets for souvenirs, exposed their bodies to him, climbed uninvited into his bed. The crowds were unbelievable wherever he went—once when he took a stroll aboard the *Leviathan* so many women rushed to his side that the captain feared the danger of a disastrous list. The antics of individuals were even more unbelievable—one woman broke her leg climbing into his dressing room, others gladly paid his valet $20 for a vial of his used bath water. Yet despite his dark good looks, this star of stars was a timorous lover, a superstitious man who tried to bolster his sexual powers with aphrodisiacs and magic amulets, who always preferred food to women, and found his neurotic, clamorous admirers completely undesirable.

Valentino died of peritonitis caused by a bleeding ulcer when only 31 years old. Over 50,000 people, overwhelmingly women, attended his funeral in New York in 1926, and even today admirers come to mourn at his crypt in the Los Angeles cemetery where he is buried. Some 250 women have claimed publicly that the "Sheik" fathered their love children, many of whom were born years after Valentino's death.

—R.H. rep.

NOVELISTS

Honoré de Balzac (1799–1850). Honoré de Balzac, one of the supreme writers of realistic fiction, was, in his own life, a man of gross appetites and pretensions as well as of gargantuan genius and accomplishment. In his novels he could portray the heart and mind of his fellow middle-class Frenchmen with the accuracy and gusto of a Dickens or a Tolstoi, yet he pretended to be of noble birth. (The addition of the aristocratic particle "de" to his surname was strictly his own idea.) He yearned for wealth, yet when he achieved it, he squandered it and managed to be constantly in debt. In fact, he reached a point when he seemed unable to write during those infrequent periods when creditors were not yapping at his heels. He could abstain from food and drink almost to the point of starvation and then suddenly indulge himself orgiastically in all the delights of the table. A man of many love affairs, he sired 3 daughters and a son, but he took no interest in them for he found his fictional characters more real than any human being. Even his physique was one of contrasts. Balzac had a noble, leonine head and massive shoulders mounted upon spindly legs. His height was no more than 5'3". At times he would dress like a dandy, at others like a beggar. Never did Balzac approach life moderately; he always rushed in and seized it.

Born in Tours, France, Balzac was the son of a petty official and a pretty heiress. Never his mother's favorite, his childhood, including his schooldays, was miserable. He did, however, gain a great love of literature and a thorough background in the French and English novel. Against its wishes, his family agreed to support him in a Parisian garret while he wrote a tragedy based on the life of Oliver Cromwell. The only thing tragic about it was that it was wretchedly written—and his family told him so. Undaunted, Balzac turned to grinding out slightly pornographic Gothic novels. This work sustained him until he became immersed in the master-work of his life, *La Comédie Humaine*, a series of interrelated novels and stories. So prodigious was his effort that over a 20-year period he produced 97 works covering 11,000 pages. Among these are such immortal classics as *Le Père Goriot, Eugénie Grandet, La Grande Bretèche*, and the *Droll Stories*, whose raciness matches that in the milder "adult" magazine fiction today.

A typical day for Balzac was to be awakened at midnight by his servant. He dressed himself in a monk's robe and then sat at his writing table where he filled page after page of paper tinted blue so as to not ruin his eyes. When he reached a point of exhaustion, he fortified himself with countless cups of extremely strong black coffee. Not drugs or alcohol, but caffeine poisoning is believed to have hastened his death, as if even in overindulgence, Balzac was determined to be different.

However, another and more likely cause of Balzac's death may well have been love, a love that lasted for 17 years but was often impeded by circumstance and distance. In 1832 he received a fan letter from Mme. Eveline Hanska, a married Polish noblewoman who possessed great wealth. An ardent exchange of letters ensued, and 2 years later their love was finally consummated when Mme. Hanska, accompanied by her husband, met Balzac at Neuchâtel, Switzerland. She was taken aback by his ridiculous figure and eccentric appearance, while he was utterly captivated by her voluptuous form. And although she willingly took him into her bed, she was extremely reluctant to take him for life. She realized that her spendthrift lover would go through her money as quickly as he had his own, and she was not about to jeopardize her social position or her daughter's dowry. After her husband's death, Mme. Hanska stalled Balzac for 7 years, but finally yielded and married him 2 months before his death because she pitied him and realized that he had lost his health pursuing her.

Back in Paris after their marriage in the Ukraine, Balzac's condition worsened. On his deathbed he is reputed to have looked at his doctor and cried out: "Send for Bianchon!" For Balzac, his masterwork, *La Comédie Humaine*, was more real than life—Dr. Bianchon was his own fictional creation.

—J.M.

Charles Dickens (1812–1870). At times in the 19th century, vast crowds, eagerly awaiting the arrival of a ship from England, would form on the docks of New York and Philadelphia. What they were waiting for was not an exciting celebrity or a great invention, but the latest installment of a Dickens novel. Perhaps no other novelist before or since, particularly in the English-speaking world, has been able to create and sustain such popular enthusiasm. And no other novelist has received such critical acclaim at all levels, for Dickens appeals to the average reader, the child, and the intellectual alike.

There was very little indication in Dickens' early life of the success to come. His father was a minor official in the Navy Pay Office of Great Britain, who lived beyond his means and fell deeply into debt. Eventually he was sent to debtors' prison and his son Charles was forced at age 12 to take a job washing and labeling bottles in a filthy, rat-infested warehouse. So searing was this experience to Dickens that he found it extremely difficult to speak of it in later life (except through the medium of *David Copperfield*, his autobiographical novel). Dickens could never overcome the shock of his parents' apparent indifference to his fate. He wrote many years later that "I never afterwards forgot, I never shall forget, I never can forget that my mother was warm for my being sent back." And henceforth he was determined to make his life a success.

Dickens was eventually freed from the factory and sent to school by his parents. After that he served as a law clerk for a brief time. Because of his self-taught shorthand skill, he became a reporter of parliamentary debates. Everything he learned at work as well as every experience of childhood was stored up to be used in his true vocation, which was about to begin. Dickens wrote and sent a sketch to a monthly magazine, but he was so shy about it that he told no one and mailed his effort in the dead of night. So successful were his early pieces, for which he received nothing, that Dickens was asked to provide the text that was to accompany some sporting scenes. These rapidly were turned into the famous *Pickwick Papers*, an enormous hit with the public. Dickens never suffered the loss of popular acclaim.

Dickens' output was prodigious. Such novels as *Oliver Twist*, *Bleak House*, *A Tale of Two Cities*, and *A Christmas Carol* poured forth from his pen. He traveled extensively and enjoyed parties and amateur theatricals. He lent his name and abilities to such causes as prison reform and education for poor children. He never forgot his distrust of the "Establishment," whose injustices he had witnessed as a court reporter, and his experience as a lad whose only crime was being poor.

In the last years of his life Dickens had enough energy to build a 2nd career for himself. In England crowds swarmed into the theaters to hear him read such horrifying scenes as the murder of Nancy by Bill Sikes from *Oliver Twist*. In America people paid the then enormous sum of $3 just to attend one of his readings.

By Victorian standards Dickens' private life was unusual. He formed deep attachments with 2 of his wife's sisters, who had come to live in the Dickens household. The 1st was Mary Hogarth; when she died, Dickens removed a ring from her finger and kept it on his own until he himself died. Her place was taken by her sister Georgina Hogarth, who often acted as Dickens' hostess and companion in place of his dull wife. However, the truly great love of Dickens' life was Ellen Ternan, a pretty actress who was young enough to be his daughter. Dickens' wife refused to let him move out of the family home quietly, so the great defender of hearth and home and teller of Christmas stories was forced to announce their separation publicly.

When Dickens died, the whole world mourned. He was buried in the Poets' Corner of Westminster Abbey, the highest tribute England can bestow upon its writers. One of the most poignant memorials was a cartoon showing his writing desk surrounded by characters from his novels. The chair was empty.

—J.M.

Herman Melville (1819–1891). Herman Melville's life is a mystery. No one has satisfactorily explained, although many have tried, why the 32-year-old author of the monumental novel *Moby Dick* would for the next 40 years write nothing of consequence. And no one can understand why a hardy seafarer like Melville, who had experienced the delights and hardships of the South Seas both aboard ship and on shore, should spend most of his last 19 years at the humdrum job of customs inspector.

Perhaps the answer lies in Melville's early background. Descended from old American stock, Herman Melville was born in New York, the son of a prosperous dry goods importer whose business later failed. Melville's father died when Herman was only 13, and he left his family in a dire financial state. Melville was forced to make his way in the world at an early age. He was mortified at his family's loss of stature, and the remainder of his life seemed to involve a quest for security and inner peace.

After halfhearted attempts at being a bank clerk, a teacher, and a cabin boy, Melville finally shipped out to sea on a whaler bound for the South Seas. For the 1st time the world opened up to him. The beauty and the cruelty of the sea caught him forever in its spell. When his ship reached the Marquesas Islands (now part of French Polynesia), Melville and a companion jumped ship and lived among the pleasure-loving (and cannibalistic) natives. But despite his attachment to an island girl, Melville became homesick and signed on a passing whaler. This voyage did not last long, for he joined a mutiny and landed in a Tahitian jail —from which he promptly escaped. Melville renewed his wanderings among the islanders and rapidly stored up the knowledge that was to serve him so well in his books. But he still yearned for home and therefore joined the crew of another whaler as a harpooner. He left this ship in Hawaii and shortly thereafter began the last leg of his journey home by joining the crew of a U.S. naval frigate as an able-bodied seaman. When Melville arrived back in America he had everything he needed to inspire 6 years of magnificent creativity as a novelist.

In 1846, *Typee* appeared, the 1st of 2 novels based on Melville's South Seas experiences. A mixture of fact and highly colored fiction, it was greeted with enthusiasm and outrage. Missionaries were particularly offended by the negative view it presented of their activities, and in later editions Melville was forced to make deletions to soothe their injured feelings. *Omoo* followed the next year and established the author's literary reputation, which was further enhanced by the publication of *White Jacket*. This latter novel fully exposed the cruelty then extant in the U.S. Navy and was the direct cause of the elimination of flogging as a punishment.

All this artistic effort culminated in the stunning *Moby Dick*. Melville began this book as a mere retelling of old sailors' yarns about a huge albino whale named Mocha Dick or Moby Dick, but in the process he transformed it into a novel so magnificent that it defies both description and critical analysis.

After *Pierre* appeared in 1852, Melville's creative energy rapidly dried up. He was now either afraid of or tired of writing. Some poetry, a satire, and a handful of short stories were all that were left in him. His popularity dwindled until he had to publish his last works at his own expense. His brilliant short novel *Billy Budd* was not published until 33 years after his death. Financial problems pressed in upon him and domestic tragedy marred his life. One son killed himself either accidentally or deliberately, and another ran away from home. Melville repeatedly sought government employment and was greatly relieved when, in 1866, he was appointed a customs inspector in New York City, a job that he held for 19 years. When he died, only one newspaper bothered to publish an obituary. Many years passed before his true greatness was recognized.
—J.M.

Leo Tolstoi (1828–1910). Leo Tolstoi had written in his diary, "My life is some stupid and spiteful joke that someone has played on me." And now he was dying. His last words were, "This is the end . . . and it doesn't really matter." He died of pneumonia on November 20, 1910.

During his long life, Count Leo Tolstoi had been much more than the "angry young man" who turns novelist in order to change things or to better the condition of the oppressed. He was a tormented man, and his mind was plagued by the things he had done. "I put men to death," he wrote in his voluminous diary. "I fought duels to slay others, I lost at cards, wasted my substance wrung from the sweat of peasants, punished the latter cruelly, and deceived men. Lying, robbery, drunkenness, violence, murder . . . all committed by me, not one crime omitted." In other words, he had done all of the things that people expected young Russian noblemen to do, only *he* had a conscience and worried about it. These thoughts, combined with his overwhelming fear of dying, drove him to the verge of madness and suicide many times.

Leo Tolstoi, the author of what critics have called 2 great complete pictures of society, *War and Peace* and *Anna Karenina*, was born at his mother's ancestral home, Vasnaya Polyana. His parents had died by the time he was 10, and for much of the next 20 years he roamed the countryside gambling recklessly, drinking to excess, and, as he put it, "rioting with all sorts of loose women." He contracted syphilis and gonorrhea, and although his many faults (sexual and otherwise) tore at his brain, he never failed to take advantage of an opportunity to carouse when it was offered.

Tolstoi's earliest recollection was of pushing an older woman off the front porch of Vasnaya Polyana for unrequited love. He was 5 and the "older woman" was 10. This older woman grew up to be the mother of the hotheaded and quarrelsome girl named Sofia whom Tolstoi married on September 23, 1862.

Not wishing to hide anything from his new bride, Count Tolstoi promptly showed the new Countess Tolstoi his diary, which was filled to the brim with shocking confessions and the sordid details of his wild younger days. He was 34 and she was only 18, but they were married anyway. Seventeen years and 13 children later, Leo Tolstoi was so depressed that he was again seriously considering suicide, but something happened that changed his entire outlook on life.

He read the Sermon on the Mount and realized that the teachings of Christ were the key to happy living and, for Leo Tolstoi, to adopt an opinion was to act. He promptly tried to give his estate to the poor, throw his money to the peasants, and place his published works in the public domain for all the peoples of the world. His wife, who now had to support their 13 children in addition to handcopying his manuscripts (*War and Peace* was copied 7 times in its entirety), said No. But that didn't stop Tolstoi from putting on peasants' rags and working in the fields every day from sunup to sundown.

A conniving leech named Chertkov was drawn to the "new Master Tolstoi," and not only urged him to ignore his wife's pleadings but suggested that he go even further in his quest for the perfect and happy life. The solution was to give up everything to a deserving peasant . . . namely to Chertkov himself. The gullible Tolstoi drew up a new will leaving his estate to Chertkov. That was the last straw for the already enraged Countess Tolstoi. When Leo caught her foraging through his papers in search of the will, he decided to leave Russia and all of his worries behind him.

It was a cold night in October when Leo Tolstoi boarded the overcrowded, poorly heated, 3rd-class train for the Russian border. He caught pneumonia and died in a blaze of publicity one month later.

When he was 5 years old, Leo had told his

brother that he knew of a secret that would destroy all the evil in men, and this secret was buried under a little green stick near Vasnaya Polyana. His brother buried him under the little green stick near their family home.

—C.B.

PLAYWRIGHTS

Henrik Ibsen (1828–1906)

There can be no freedom 'or beauty about a home life that depends on borrowing and debt.

A Doll's House, Act I

The career of Scandinavia's great playwright was directly influenced by his unhappy childhood. In later years, he remembered only a tyrannical, embittered father, forced by business reverses to move the family to a rundown farm outside Skien, Norway. Ibsen's mother, no longer welcomed in the homes of her wealthy friends, became subject to fits of melancholy. At 16, the young Ibsen left home, apprenticed for 5 years to an apothecary in Grimstad, and 2 years later he found himself in more trouble for fathering an illegitimate son by a 28-year-old servant girl. His parents, outraged by the event, gave him such a feeling of guilt that Ibsen never wrote to them again.

Failure, for Ibsen, became a way of life. Catalina, his 1st literary attempt, was unsalable. The privately printed and unbound sheets eventually were sold as wrapping paper to a grocer. He sought admission to the university in Oslo and failed the entrance examinations. He tried a career as a journalist, without success. As a stage manager, 1st in Bergen, then in Oslo, he fared better, but lost the latter job when the theater went bankrupt. The experience was not altogether wasted. At Bergen, Ibsen's contract required him to provide one new play each year, and although none of the 5 he produced was notably received, the requirement forced him to learn the mechanics of his trade.

In 1864, Ibsen took his wife and infant son to Rome, where they spent 5 years living in poverty. He became a long-haired bohemian, complete with sideburns, a wide-brimmed hat, and a huge cloak that he threw around his short, shaggy body. Teetering on the brink of starvation, he wrote Brand, dwelling on the subject he knew best: failure on an epic scale. Six months after he submitted Brand to Danish publishers, his fortunes had changed radically. The play was hesitantly brought out in March, 1866, becoming an immediate success. With it and Peer Gynt, written in the same period, Ibsen won recognition at last. Awarded an annual stipend and the title of national poet by Norway, he dropped the bohemian appearance and became a well-dressed, neatly barbered, dignified man-of-letters in keeping with his new station.

The 1st of Ibsen's realistic dramas, The Pillars of Society (1877), dealt with hypocrisy. In A Doll's House (1879), he attacked the sacrosanct institution of marriage. The sheltered Nora Helmer commits forgery to save her unsuspecting husband. His behavior upon finding out shows Nora that, for 8 years, she has played the role of a "doll" in his eyes. She leaves Helmer so that she can be a real person. In Ghosts (1881), he continued the assault, writing of a wife and mother who had sacrificed herself to retain conventional attitudes she knows will not save her marriage.

Both plays caused him to be condemned by public and press alike, which labeled them as "immoral" and "affronts to all the decencies." In Germany, the playgoers demanded—and got —a happier ending for A Doll's House. Nora's last line was changed to "Oh, I sin before myself, but I cannot leave them!" And she stayed.

Writing in 1885, Ibsen completed The Wild Duck, a satire full of cryptical imagery and sinister implication. Following an affair he had, at age 61, with the 17-year-old Austrian girl, Emilie Bardach, Ibsen produced The Master Builder, using Emilie as the model for the play's Hilda Wangel. In 1891, he returned to Oslo to spend the remainder of his life, producing only 3 more plays. These were tragedies that dwelt on the subjects of man's miserable resignation to life, impending death, and the promise of resurrection.

In his last 15 years, Ibsen's earlier ostracism from his native land was forgotten. He was followed, photographed, and quoted at length. Ironically, he now tried to avoid the publicity and the crowds fame brought. At 72, Ibsen's life ended with the same theme of tragedy with which it had begun: He suffered a series of strokes that robbed him of even a child's ability to recite the alphabet. The 3rd stroke on May 23, 1906, killed him.

—W.K.

Molière (Jean Baptiste Poquelin) (1622–1673)

Those whose conduct gives room for talk are always the 1st to attack their neighbors.

Tartuffe, Act I

Secretly encouraged by a grandfather who loved the theater, Molière refused to follow his father as an upholsterer to the court of Louis XIV. Instead he elected to join the Béjart amateur theatrical group, then performing on a Paris tennis court. Calling themselves L'Illustre Théâtre, they opened on January 1, 1644, with young Poquelin billed as "Molière," to avoid embarrassment to his father. The offering failed. Unable to succeed in Paris, the group toured the provinces between 1646 and 1658, building a reputation as one of the most accomplished theatrical companies in France.

On October 24, 1658, returning to Paris under the patronage of Louis XIV's brother, Molière's troupe gave a performance of Pierre Corneille's tragedy, *Nicomède*. The classic lines fell flat, coming from the lips of actors accustomed to fencing vocally with Molière's jests and witticisms. Sensing the King's cold reception, Molière asked for, and was given, permission to continue with a farce that had amused the provinces, *Le Docteur amoureux* (*The Love-Sick Doctor*). The comedy relief pleased Louis, and he granted permission for them to use the Hôtel du Petit-Bourbon for future performances, sharing it jointly with an Italian company sponsored by Cardinal Mazarin. More important, *L'Illustre Théâtre* was allowed to call itself the Troupe de Monsieur, signifying a royal sponsorship. Eventually it became the ancestor of the *Comédie Française*.

Molière, as a man of multiple talents, produced many farces, comedies, ballets, and masques for the court on short notice. But he is best known for the comedies of character in which the device of caricature was used to lampoon or ridicule a vice or an affectation. One of his 1st successes, *Les Précieuses ridicules*, made fun of the absurdities in manners practiced by salons such as that of Madame de Rambouillet. In *Sganarelle* (1660), Molière reworked the medieval cuckolding theme, utilizing his gift of mimicking to play the leading role with resounding success. One year later, he presented his very popular *L'École des maris* (*The School for Husbands*), borrowing the plot from the Boccaccio and Lope de Vega versions of earlier years.

L'École's leading lady, the beautiful Armande Béjart, played her flirtatious role with such feeling that Molière took her as his wife. Too late he learned that Madeleine Béjart's younger sister had the real-life personality of a vain, cold-blooded opportunist and he found himself cast as the jealous, older, and betrayed husband. The stormy Armande mellowed somewhat in later years to justify Molière's choice.

With *L'École des femmes* (*The School for Wives*), written the year after he married, Molière championed young love and ridiculed the conventions of marriage. Two years later, in 1664, his marriage problems dampening his flair for light comedy, the dramatist turned to a more serious theme with *Le Tartuffe* (*The Hypocrite*). His attack on religious hypocrisy offended many who were deeply religious, including the King's mother, Anne of Austria. To placate her, Louis forbade a repeat performance until after she died in 1666. Molière reworked the play and put it forth again, on August 5, 1667, as *L'Imposteur*, while Louis was away at war. The play was promptly closed by Parisian mayor Lamoignon. In 1669, the ban was finally lifted to permit free performances of one of Molière's greatest triumphs.

While *Tartuffe's* fate was being disputed, Molière turned back to comedy, 1st with *L'Amour médicin* (*Love Is the Best Doctor*) in 1664, jousting with the medical profession, and in 1666 with *Le Misanthrope*, one of his greatest works. Molière himself played Alceste, the man who turns to misanthropy because of worldwide hypocrisy.

Molière's popular *Le Médicin malgré lui* (*The Doctor in Spite of Himself*), mocked the medical doctors' competence again, possibly because of the profession's inability to cure Molière's own tubercular condition, which was rapidly weakening his health. Sapped by the disease and worn by his estrangement with Armande, the victory with *Tartuffe* brought Molière respite, albeit a temporary one. Throughout 1670, and the next 2 years, he scored again, with *Le Bourgeois gentilhomme* (*The Would-Be Gentleman*), *Psyché* (a ballet of little importance except to Molière personally—it brought his beloved Armande back to him), and a last highly acclaimed comedy, *Les Femmes savantes* (*The Learned Ladies*).

In 1673, he again aimed at the ineffectual doctors with *Le Malade imaginaire*, playing the hypochondriac Argan. It was his last performance. He managed to complete the final scene despite an onstage fit of coughing blood, but died within a few hours, on February 17.

His frequent controversies with the Church produced one final, posthumous quarrel: He was denied burial in holy ground and forbidden the Extreme Unction sacrament. Only after the King's demand was the restriction lifted, with the proviso that the burial would take place quietly at night to "avoid scandal." The stipulation produced the opposite effect. In a dramatic torchlight procession that Molière would have loved, his "quiet" burial was attended by thousands of his admirers from all walks of life. They had come to pay their last respects to the greatest master of comedy that France has ever known.

—W.K.

Eugene O'Neill (1888–1953)

I find artificial light more appropriate for my work—man's light, not God's— man's feeble striving to understand himself, to exist for himself in the darkness!
Mourning Becomes Electra, Act II
(*The Haunted*)

Eugene O'Neill's decision to become a playwright came about after he was hospitalized for 5 months with tuberculosis in a sanatorium at Wallingford, Conn., in 1912. Forced to remain inactive, the ex-sailor decided to read the plays of Strindberg and Ibsen. During his long convalescence, he completed 11 one-act dramas and 2 full-length efforts. Six were eventually published as *Thirst and Other Plays*. The other 7 were destroyed.

The experiences O'Neill garnered while shipping out on freighters plying the North and South Atlantic provided the inspiration for his initial cycle of plays about the sea. *Bound East for Cardiff*, the one-act piece that 1st brought O'Neill to public attention, dealt with the last thoughts of a dying sailor. It was produced at Provincetown, on Cape Cod—so successfully that the company moved to New York City to continue as the famed Provincetown Players in Greenwich Village. In 1917, he wrote *The Long Voyage Home*, based on recollections about sailors in a London bar, and *Ile* (*Oil*), the story of a captain who, in the Melville *Moby Dick* tradition, relentlessly pursued a hunt for whales although his crew threatened to mutiny and his wife was losing her sanity. O'Neill concluded the initial series in 1918 with *The Moon of the Caribbees* (a crisis erupts on the ship *Glencairn* when women are brought aboard) and *Where the Cross Is Made* (a tale of another obsessed captain).

In 1920, O'Neill, turning his full attention to longer works, finished *Beyond the Horizon*. It ran over 100 performances and won for him the 1st of his many Pulitzer Prizes. Within the decade, he had added 2 more Pulitzers: for the tragic *Anna Christie* (1922), and *Strange Interlude* (1928), a psychological drama laced with searching soliloquies and asides.

The overriding theme of O'Neill's work was tragedy. In *Mourning Becomes Electra*, he used the classic Greek drama of Aeschylus, transposed to a post-Civil War setting. Lairnia discovers that her mother has committed adultery, and then has poisoned her husband. When Lavinia's brother Orin shoots his mother's lover, his mother commits suicide. Now Lavinia—or "Electra"—is free to be herself, but Orin's incestuous love for her drives him to suicide and Lavinia retreats into herself again. The 5-hour play, written in 13 acts, actually was subdivided into 3 units: *The Homecoming*, *The Hunted*, and *The Haunted*. O'Neill called for a formal intermission, sending the audience out for dinner.

At age 45, O'Neill surprised the theater with his one comedy about adolescence, *Ah Wilderness!* Its run of nearly 300 performances compensated for the controversies that had surrounded his other recent offerings. *All God's Chillun Got Wings*, with its theme of racial

miscegenation, provoked fears of race rioting, and this resulted in a reluctance to stage it. With *Desire Under the Elms*, he was banned in Boston and the entire cast was arrested in Los Angeles for engaging in indecent entertainment. The Nobel Prize Committee decided to view O'Neill's achievements as a whole when it awarded him the Nobel Prize for Literature in 1936.

Eugene O'Neill's creative decline came quickly, spurred by the collapse of his family life. He disappeared from public view until the appearance of *The Ice Man Cometh* in 1946. It failed in its debut, but gained some measure of success when revived in 1956 with Jason Robards, Jr., as Hickey. For its plot, O'Neill had retreated again to the scene of his youthful exploits as a seaman—the waterfront bar of Jimmy-the-Priest in New York City.

At 56, a victim of Parkinson's disease and completely unable to hold a pen—the only way he could create—O'Neill slowly gave way. After vainly trying to complete a mammoth new cycle of 11 tragedies, based on the life of an American family from Colonial days to the present, O'Neill succumbed to bronchial pneumonia, dying at 65.

His death released the restriction he had placed on the staging of *Long Day's Journey into Night*, a largely autobiographical work he'd written before 1941. Posthumously, it won for him his 4th Pulitzer Prize in 1957.

—W.K.

William Shakespeare (1564–1616)

The quality of mercy is not strain'd,
It droppeth as the gentle rain from heaven
Upon the place beneath. It is twice blessed:
It blesseth him that gives and him that takes.
The Merchant of Venice, Act IV

Of Shakespeare-the-man, the known history is scant. Traditionally, the great Bard was unhappily married, abandoned his family, and left Stratford-on-Avon to become a teacher, soldier, lawyer, or an apothecary. Further, the legends continue, he joined a traveling company of actors and went to London, or fled his birthplace to avoid arrest after stealing Sir Thomas Lacy's deer. Little or no proof exists to support any of these suppositions. There is also very slim evidence concerning either his formal education or his 1st years in London although—traditionally—he began his theater apprenticeship by holding horses outside the playhouses. The facts of baptism, marriage, parentage—and his life after 1594—are more readily established by contemporary records, including the famous will which awards his "2nd best bed with the furniture" to his wife.

Of Shakespeare-the-playwright, the picture is more extensive. The dramatist completed at least 38 plays with well over 100,000 lines of dialogue unequaled, in the history of English literature, for beauty of expression and depth of feeling. The plays' articulate command of vocabulary, coupled with his all-encompassing knowledge of persons, places, and events, has brought numerous challenges throughout the centuries concerning Shakespeare's sole right to authorship of the dramas. No conclusive evidence disallowing his claim has ever been presented.

Thirty-six of the 38 plays attributed to Shakespeare were printed in the First Folio of 1623. The canon can be roughly divided into 4 groups. In his initial works, written between 1590 and 1594, he produced the early historical plays dealing with the War of the Roses: *Henry VI*, parts 1, 2, and 3, and *Richard III*. While stilted rhetoric can be found in these 1st dramas, there was a vast improvement during the latter half of the decade with the more mature *Richard II*, *Henry IV*, and *Henry V*. With *Romeo and Juliet* and *A Midsummer Night's Dream*, he also showed the capability of handling both tragedy and comedy with the master's touch. Between 1600 and 1608, Shakespeare's experimentation in the classics with *Julius Caesar* led directly to his other 4 tragic masterpieces: *Othello*, *King Lear*, *Macbeth*, and *Hamlet*, acclaimed for their unexcelled characterizations. His "dark comedies" of the same period—*All's Well That Ends Well*, and *Measure for Measure*—were partially influenced in tone by the tragedies. Shakespeare's final efforts, between 1609 and his retirement in 1613, gave us 6 lesser dramas including the 2 generally accepted as a collaboration with John Fletcher, *Henry VIII* and *The Two Noble Kinsmen*, the latter a derivative of a Geoffrey Chaucer tale.

From 1594—when the ravages of the plague subsided and the theaters again reopened—until retirement in 1613, Shakespeare both acted and wrote for the Lord Chamberlain's Men, a London professional troupe. He shared in the profits from his plays 1st at the Globe and later at Blackfriars Theatre, enabling him to return to Stratford as a "gentleman of substance." Following his death on April 23, 1616, his remains were interred beneath the chancel of Stratford Church.

—W.K.

George Bernard Shaw (1856–1950)

> The great secret, Eliza, is not having bad manners or good manners or any other particular sort of manners, but having the same manner for all human souls: in short, behaving as if you were in Heaven, where there are no 3rd-class carriages, and one soul is as good as another.
>
> *Pygmalion*, Act V

The reading public, not the professional critic, 1st recognized the stage skills of George Bernard Shaw. Until *Plays Pleasant and Unpleasant* reached the bookstalls in 1898, Shaw was a failure as a playwright. Of 10 plays written prior to 1900, 9 were presented and nearly all failed. When the book appeared, containing 7 of the rejects, it sold extremely well. The plays were subsequently given a 2nd chance, and this time were greeted with rousing acclaim. In later years, the same book-then-stage technique was sometimes employed, with equally satisfying results.

Two of the 7 (*The Philanderer, Mrs. Warren's Profession*) dealt with "unpleasant" themes repugnant to Victorian England. But the book reviewers—public sales not withstanding—were also caustic about the "pleasant" topics (*Widowers' Houses, Arms and the Man, Candida, The Man of Destiny*, and *You Never Can Tell*), blasting them roundly. The London Times, noting that "good" actors would turn down the roles, scathingly commented that Shaw was "one who, except for the oddity of his dress and views, would never have attracted much notice."

Shaw's views on sex, marriage, and domestic bliss stemmed from his seduction, at 29, by Jenny Paterson, a wench he later described as "sexually insatiable." The amorous Jenny left a lifelong impression. Shocked into 15 years of abstinence by the unnerving experience, Shaw's later devotion for Mrs. Patrick Campbell steadfastly followed his rule that the perfect love affair was one "conducted entirely by post." His marriage to Irish heiress, Charlotte Payne-Townshend, also felt the Paterson aftershock, when Shaw spent his honeymoon in 1898 writing the antiromantic *Caesar and Cleopatra*. Two years later, in *Man and Superman*, generally regarded as one of his masterpieces, Shaw again rebelled against marriage. In the same play, he gave stage managers their greatest headache: how to stage the 3rd act, a 2-hour discourse of subjects from sex to salvation entitled "Don Juan in Hell." Nearly all elected to omit the scene as unplayable until 1951, when, staged separately, it went on a successful U.S. tour.

Of Shaw's more than 50 plays, none achieved greater unexpected success than *Pygmalion*. In it, guttersnipe Eliza is made into an elegant lady by Professor Henry Higgins when he teaches her the correct way to speak and act in society. His creation, having come to life, falls in love with her creator. Adapted for the New York stage in 1956 as *My Fair Lady*, starring Julie Andrews, the play broke Broadway records in its long run.

The play's theme was the written expression of Shaw's long-standing agitation for a new English alphabet of 42 letters, each having just one specific sound. In his will, Shaw continued the battle, leaving money in trust for research on a "Proposed British Alphabet" of at least 40 letters.

At 67, Shaw wrote *Saint Joan*, thought by many admirers to be his greatest effort. At 91, still creative, he finished *Buoyant Billions* and promptly began a new comedy, working in a one-room hut he called "The Shelter." It revolved on a swivel, to rotate with the sun. Just over 2 years later, the Methuselah of playwrights finally relinquished his deserved rank as the greatest living writer of the English language, dying at Ayot St. Lawrence, from complications following a fall, on November 2, 1950.

—W.K.

POETS

Lord Byron (1788–1824)

"The great object of life is sensation—to feel that we exist, even in pain."

George Gordon Noel Byron was born in London on January 22, 1788. As a child, his clubfoot was worsened by the treatments of quack doctors, and his unbalanced mother habitually referred to him as her "little lame brat." His father, Captain John ("Mad Jack") Byron, drank himself to death by the time the boy was 3 and also managed to squander most of his wife's fortune.

Mother and son were left to grapple not only with poverty, but with a temperamental relationship with each other that alternated between outbursts of temper and maudlin fits of affection. One evening, in the course of an argument, his mother attempted to beat Byron to death with a pair of fire tongs. Meanwhile, his nurse abused him in a more gentle manner, managing to seduce the handsome young master when he was only 9 years old.

A year later, an uncle died, making Byron the 6th Baron Byron of Rochedale. With the title came a sizable inheritance and a measure of independence. The young lord was soon shipped off to Harrow School—glad to escape both mother and nurse.

Byron was beautiful, with fierce, clear, blue-gray eyes, a fine straight nose, full lips, and a delicately chiseled chin. He had chestnut hair (which he pinned up nightly) and a fair alabaster complexion. A lifelong tendency to overweight was overcome only by starvation diets and the continuous consumption of laxatives. A little over 5'7", Byron always walked with a limp. Self-conscious, he made great efforts to overcome his physical shortcomings by excelling in sports, including boxing, fencing, riding, cricket, and swimming.

At Cambridge, Byron was an indifferent student, and in order to amuse himself he kept both a tame bear and a mistress whom he liked to dress as a boy. After graduation, he lived with his mother briefly, but soon found himself bored with their quarrels and decided to leave England. He and a friend boarded a ship for Lisbon. From there he toured Spain, riding 500 mi. on horseback to Cadiz and other cities before going on to other Mediterranean countries.

When he returned to England he had in hand the 1st 2 cantos of *Childe Harold's Pilgrimage*, a thinly veiled autobiographical account of his travels. When published, this long romantic poem caused a national sensation and established its author as a public figure. Though he received a fortune in royalty payments, Byron gave away most of the money in order to maintain his image as an aristocratic amateur. His readings—in some of London's most fashionable homes—became famous, and though his singsong voice was not entirely pleasant, it did little to distract his fans. Women chased him, adored him, and tried to possess him. One eccentric blueblood, Lady Caroline Lamb, pursued him everywhere and climaxed her passion with a scene at a masked ball in which she cut herself and fell to the ground in a pool of blood.

Byron's already dubious reputation was further undermined when rumors began to circulate concerning an incestuous relationship between the poet and his half sister. Augusta Leigh was a beauty who was said to resemble her younger half brother closely, and the 2 had come to know each other only as adults. Though he did absolutely nothing to deny the gossip, Byron became so worried over the state of his own morals that he turned to marriage. The woman he chose was the stunning Anne Isabella Milbanke, a respectable, highly educated mathematician who hoped that she could tame "the wild lord."

Yet on the wedding night Byron told her: "It is enough for me that you are my wife for me to hate you!" Shortly afterwards, she became pregnant, and his conduct toward her bordered on the insane. He tormented her by shooting off guns in her bedroom and demanded that his sister live with them, for Augusta was the only one who could calm his rages.

Lady Byron's request for a separation, following the birth of their daughter, affirmed public belief in the old stories of Byron's incest. Though his poetry was more popular than ever, he was socially ostracized. He chose to exile himself from England. Naturally, he left in truly "Byronic" style. His coach, designed after that of his hero, Napoleon, contained a bed, library, and complete dining and cooking facilities.

Travel, writing, and dissipation were easy, as the money continued to roll in. Not only was this his most creative literary period, but Byron himself estimated that he managed to involve himself with over 200 women, mostly of the lower class. In Switzerland, he spent time with the poet Shelley and his wife Mary, and resumed his love affair with Mrs. Shelley's 17-year-old stepsister. The affair resulted in a daughter, Allegra.

At the age of 31, Byron settled in Venice and began his longest affair. He was involved with the Countess Teresa Guiccioli for nearly 5 years as they traveled through Italy together. Whenever family matters demanded it, the countess would return to her husband, bringing her lover to live with them as well.

Bored with his mistress and looking for action, Byron decided to go to Greece and fight for Greek liberation from the Turkish empire. He had long before identified himself with the cause of "liberalism," once using his hereditary seat in the House of Lords to deliver a celebrated attack on industrialists and monopolies. In Missolonghi, a swampy hole of a town, he drilled troops and advanced money for building fortifications and providing medical provisions.

Yet the excesses of his life had left the would-be military hero in poor health. He became subject to convulsions and attacks of malarial fever. His face grew so swollen that he was barely recognizable. Bloodletting further weakened him, and he died at 6 P.M. on Easter in 1824, aged 36 years and 3 months.

His heart and lungs were buried in Greece, but the rest of his remains were sent to England. The authorities refused to permit his interment at Westminster Abbey.

"His misfortune is an habitual passion for excitement," Byron's wife had written. Sensationalism is the essence of his poetry. His best works—*Childe Harold, Don Juan* (unfinished), and *Manfred*—are speedy rhymed-verse narrative, vibrating with the excesses of Byron's sexual energy.

—N.H.M.

John Keats (1795–1821)

"I am a coward. I cannot bear the pain of being happy."

John Keats was born in London, in his father's livery stable, on October 31, 1795. When Keats was 9, his father died in a fall from a horse. His mother left her 4 children with their grandmother and vanished with a new husband.

Keats was of slight build, just 5' tall, delicate, with attractive features, large hazel eyes, and strawberry-blond curls. At school he refused to be bullied and "he would fight anyone, morning, noon, and night."

With the death of his grandmother when he was 15, his guardian apprenticed him to an apothecary surgeon. After 4 years he went to study in a London hospital where he received his certificate to practice medicine.

It was during lectures that he 1st attempted writing poetry, scribbling rhymes in the margins of his notes. Shortly after his graduation he decided to abandon medicine and pursue his true vocation—poetry. Through a friend he was introduced to Wordsworth and Shelley, and under their influence he published a volume of sonnets. This book sold poorly, despite favorable reviews, and Keats was disappointed but not discouraged. But when his 2nd volume, *Endymion*, was scorned by the critics he retreated to Scotland and Ireland for an extended walking tour.

He returned to England with his health badly impaired by the cold, wet weather he had encountered. He soon diagnosed his own symptoms as tuberculosis, the same disease which had claimed his mother and brother.

As his condition worsened, Keats went to live in the country with a friend. The 23-year-old poet soon fell hopelessly in love with a beautiful neighbor girl. Fanny Brawne, who was just 18, made up for her lack of interest in poetry with her devotion to the ailing poet.

Aware of the fact that he was dying, Keats felt that marriage with Fanny was impossible. In these painful circumstances he produced his best poetry, including *Ode on a Grecian Urn* and *Ode to a Nightingale*.

His condition grew steadily worse and he began to use laudanum to relieve his pain. When Shelley heard of Keats' condition, he invited the invalid to Pisa, in the hopes that the warmer Italian climate might help Keats to rally.

Although in despair over leaving Fanny, Keats headed for Italy. His correspondence with Fanny and friends in England includes some of his most beautiful writing and helped him to win a reputation, after his death, as the greatest letter writer in English literature. Keats never reached Pisa, for he died in a small room above the Spanish Steps in Rome, on February 23, 1821, at the age of 25. At his request, no name was written on his tomb, which bears only the enigmatic inscription: "Here lies one whose name was writ in water."

—N.H.M.

Edgar Allan Poe (1809–1849)

"I became insane with long intervals of horrible sanity."

On January 19, 1809, Edgar Allan Poe was born in Boston where his actor parents were performing. His father, an alcoholic, deserted his family shortly after Edgar's arrival. His mother died of consumption soon after that, and Poe was adopted by wealthy Virginia merchant John Allan and his wife.

The Allans were generous with their son and educated him at good schools in England and America. He was of medium height, with dark, rather haggard features. His piercing eyes were accented by long lashes. At the age of 17 he entered the University of Virginia but withdrew after a term, because of his excessive drinking and gambling.

The repentant young man returned home, but after repeated quarreling with his foster father, he ran away to Boston. There he spent all his money publishing his 1st volume, *Tamerlane and Other Poems*. Winning little recognition, he temporarily changed his name to "E. A. Perry" and joined the Army. After a few years he was dismissed for disobeying an order.

Penniless, and struggling desperately to overcome his need for alcohol, he took refuge with his aunt, Maria Clemm, in Baltimore. It was a productive time for him and he managed to win some popular acclaim with his short stories. Poe was 27 when he married his tubercular cousin, Virginia Clemm—who was only 13 at the time of the wedding. Mrs. Clemm became a mother to both of them. When Poe was writing, he demanded that she stay awake with him, providing him with coffee every hour until 4 or 5 in the morning. Secure in Mrs. Clemm's care, he wrote his finest metaphysical poems—including *Annabel Lee* and *The Bells*. He pasted the pages of his manuscript together to form a long scroll. He would roll it tightly, then at his dramatic readings would unroll it slowly, letting it hit the floor.

When it became apparent that Poe's gentle, plump, teen-aged wife was incurable, the poet went to pieces. He had periodically gone on drinking sprees but now he began to use opium heavily as well. Unable to hold any job, Poe moved his wife and mother-in-law to a poor cottage in Fordham, N.Y. Living in complete poverty, Virginia slept on a straw mattress. There was no money for firewood so they wrapped the sick girl in Poe's old army coat and forced Poe's cat to sleep on her chest to provide warmth. When Virginia died during the winter, Poe removed the coat from the body and wore it to the cemetery.

During the last 2 years of his life, Poe lived in dissipated and gruesome isolation. Shortly after recovering from an attempt at suicide by an overdose of opium, he went on a drinking spree and was found delirious in a Baltimore tavern. Four days later, talking to specters "that withered and loomed on the walls," he died on October 7, 1849, at the age of 40. He was buried in Baltimore.

—N.H.M.

Arthur Rimbaud (1854–1891)

"The poet makes himself a 'seer' by a long, immense and rational derangement of all the senses. All forms of love, suffering, and madness. He exhausts all poisons in himself and keeps only their quintessences."

Arthur Rimbaud, born in 1854 in Charleville, France, was the son of Vitalie and Frédéric Rimbaud. Frédéric, a soldier, left Vitalie to raise her 4 children alone. Being a religious, practical woman of peasant stock, she had plans of respectability for Arthur. A child of extreme brilliance, Arthur won all the prizes in school. He was small and shy, with a delicate complexion and marvelous blue eyes.

No direct affection was expressed in the Rimbaud home, and when Arthur found that achievement in school could not win his mother's love, he turned to other diversions for fulfillment. His friendship with Izambard, a teacher at school, was his 1st real introduction to literature. He had begun to write poetry, and under Izambard's guidance read passionately all the poets he could get his hands on. Such activity had to be hidden from his mother, a philistine in all her ways. Frustrated, and bursting with dreams of poetic beauty and greatness, he ran away to Paris. This 1st attempt was unsuccessful, for he was arrested and sent back in a few days, seething. Thus was established the pattern for the rest of his life—running away to all ends of the world but always returning to Charleville.

He wrote more and more poetry, seeking recognition; he received none, and was unable to get his work published. In 1871, at the age of 17, he wrote and enclosed poems to the Parisian poet most admired, Paul Verlaine.

Verlaine, who had published 2 books of poetry, was in part a comfortable bourgeois, a family man with a snug position as a civil servant. He was fond of sensual pleasures, however, and was more than fond of the absinthe which was to be had in any bar. After reading Rimbaud's letter, he penned a "Come, dear great soul" invitation which was to be his downfall.

Rimbaud arrived, dirty and surly, and his youth surprised the Verlaines. While Mme. Verlaine found his rude behavior disgusting, Verlaine, more softhearted than his wife and also a poet, recognized instantly the child-genius. He introduced Rimbaud to the poets of Paris, and at 1st all went well. One poet remarked, "Behold Jesus in the midst of the doctors!" Another countered, "A Satan more likely!" He was proclaimed by Hugo "a child Shakespeare!" to which Rimbaud made an acid aside about "the old dottard."

In time, Rimbaud's merciless tongue and foul habits alienated virtually all but Verlaine, who had fallen madly in love with the "devilishly seductive" boy. They became lovers. How much

Mme. Verlaine knew is unclear, but that she hated the boy there is no doubt. His philosophy of "the derangement of all the senses" succeeded only, in her eyes, in bringing her husband home in ever more cruel and drunken stupors.

Rimbaud saw in Verlaine the potential to create the poet deity he dreamed of; he wished to make him the "Son of the Sun," in a life of transcendency. Verlaine, however, lived up badly to this role of "visionary." This disappointment, added to Rimbaud's general peevishness, led to bickering, cruel jibes on Rimbaud's part, and finally violent quarrels. Perhaps impelled by emotional stress, Rimbaud continued to write poetry. Influenced by the poet Charles Baudelaire, who had recently died, and studies of alchemy and magic, he composed at this time some of the phrase-poems which were to make up the volume *Les Illuminations*.

In 1873, Verlaine and Rimbaud had their final falling out. Verlaine, in a rare show of strength, had one day left Rimbaud after one of the latter's cruelties. Rimbaud, distraught, begged him to return. Verlaine did return only to be met by a sullen Rimbaud who, in turn, threatened to leave. In the ensuing argument, Verlaine produced a pistol and shot at him, wounding him in the wrist. For this and subsequent threats he spent 2 years in prison. Rimbaud returned to Charleville to write *Un Saison en enfer* (*A Season in Hell*), at 18, his last contribution to literature. He gave up the life of the poet, for in it he had found only misery.

Rimbaud saw Verlaine once more, just after the latter's release from prison. Verlaine had turned to religion, regretted their life of debauchery, and wrote to Rimbaud, "Let us love one another in Jesus." Reported Rimbaud after their meeting: "Verlaine arrived here the other day with a rosary between his paws. . . . Three hours later he had denied his God and made the 98 wounds of our Saviour bleed afresh."

In 1878, Rimbaud left Europe, and spent most of the last 13 years of his life traveling in Africa and Egypt as a trader and merchant. He who had always despised the heat sought it out in the world's most sweltering climes. His letters home are written by another Rimbaud, still complaining, but hardworking and concerned largely with money. In the many letters from these years, there exists almost nothing of literary interest; the only books he read were concerned with science. Gone totally was the Rimbaud of the cafés and boulevards. In manner and appearance he was transformed— he was brown-skinned and strong, barely resembling the pale-skinned youth who had scandalized Paris. He referred to his previous life as merely so much foolishness. In 1891, a tumor was responsible for the amputation of a leg, and his health gradually deteriorated. In November, 1891, he died in Marseilles, at the age of 37.

> Long ago, if my memory serves me, my life was a banquet where everyone's heart was generous, and where all wines flowed. One evening, I pulled Beauty down on my knees. I found her embittered and I cursed her.
>
> —*Un Saison en enfer*

—A.W.

SCULPTORS

Alberto Giacometti (1901–1966). "It's impossible to finish," Giacometti once said, when asked why he never considered his sculptures completed. The more a sculptor tries to finish, he maintained, the more he has the feeling of starting all over again. That, very often, is what Giacometti did. After a day of sketching or painting he would destroy the day's work and begin again, not satisfied he had captured the model. It's said that for every work of his in existence 10 others were burned, torn up, or hacked to bits before they could leave his studio.

Giacometti was one of the few important 20th-century sculptors whose father had been an artist. He was born at Stampa in Italy. At 18 he studied at the École des Arts et Métiers in Geneva, then toured Italy, sketching and studying classic architecture. In 1922 he arrived at Paris and went to work for Bourdelle. Until then Giacometti had been a traditionalist who idolized the Baroque and Renaissance masters. After his service with Bourdelle he became an abstract-impressionist. But more than just his master's influence was responsible for the conversion. In his own words, Giacometti "couldn't sculpt a human head."

With his imagination running free, Giacometti became a more powerful artist. For a while he toyed with cubism. His cubist *Spoon Woman* (1926) proved a hit. But he was not the sort to be pigeonholed. As soon as biographers began to call him a cubist he ceased to be one. In the early 1930s he turned to surrealism, inspired by Dali's oils. During that decade he reigned as leader of the surrealist school of sculpture, producing such works as *The Palace at 4 A.M.* and *Woman Walking*. Gradually his figures became longer and thinner, more and more exaggerated. Finally in the early '40s he did what he loved best to do —he started all over. This time his new discovery was miniature sculpture, which he stayed with for 5 years. Then he returned to monumental proportions almost as a celebration of the war's end.

The 1950s proved one of his busiest periods. He exhibited at the Vienna Biennial in 1956, and a retrospective exhibit was staged in London by the Arts Council of Great Britain in 1955. In 1959 his works were shown as part of a major "Holder to Klee" exhibit at the same Arts Council. The last major showing of Giacometti's sculpture in his lifetime was at London's Tate Gallery in 1965. He died the following year at the age of 65.

—W.R.

Michelangelo (1475–1564). Michelangelo Buonarroti, placed by time and fate at the core of the Italian Renaissance, proved to be its most prolific and admired artist. He lived to 89 and was active more than 70 of those years; born before Da Vinci had even become famous, he survived into the Baroque era. Of the thousands of artists who flourished during his lifetime, there were few who were not influenced by him. Whenever the Renaissance style is revived, Michelangelo's works are the inspiration. They ranged from the marble *Pieta* in St. Peter's Church (Rome), his 1st important sculpture, to the plans for the church itself, to the celebrated Sistine Chapel ceiling, painted while lying supine on a scaffold.

Michelangelo was born March 6, 1475, in the small town of Caprese. His father was a minor nobleman. Turning his back on his family's demands for a more respectable career, he enrolled as an apprentice painter at the studio of Ghirlandaio in Florence. Michelangelo may have taken part in painting the frescoes of Santa Maria Novella, on which Ghirlandaio was engaged. On leaving Ghirlandaio, Michelangelo joined the Medici group of artists. It is believed Lorenzo de' Medici commissioned him to do the *Centaurs* relief now at the Bargello in Florence. In 1494, still but 19 years old, Michelangelo went to Bologna and executed carvings for the tomb of St. Dominic. By 1496 he was in Rome, where he created his famed *Bacchus* (now in the Bargello) and *Pieta*. The *Pieta* contract was drawn up on August 27, 1498. The work was probably completed in 1500. It was Michelangelo's only signed sculpture—signed, it is thought, from fear of nonrecognition.

Returning to Florence in 1501, he built the large statue of David that has become a symbol of Renaissance sculpture. It stands 18' high and is anatomically perfect. At the same time he was commissioned for other works. His reputation had spread so far that an order for a madonna came from Bruges in Flanders. But dark moments lay ahead.

In 1504 he was appointed by the Signoria of Florence to paint a battle scene for the Council Hall, in collaboration with Da Vinci. But the 2 disliked working together, there were technical problems, and it was never finished. The following year Pope Julius II hired Michelangelo to design a tomb, but it too remained undone when artist and pontiff had a falling out. Michelangelo went back to Florence; Pope Julius summoned him to return to Rome; the artist refused. For 2 years he stayed away from Rome, spending part of the time at Bologna. Pope Julius was willing to make amends. He gave Michelangelo a new task, painting decorations on the ceiling of his new Sistine Chapel. In less than 3 years it was completed, and once again Michelangelo was in favor. "Il divino" he was called by the Romans. And they meant it.

Though now hailed as a painter, he did not abandon sculpture. In fact he turned to it more and more, and to architecture. The Medici sought him out to design the Bibliotheca Laurenziana. Begun in 1524 this majestic structure was completed many years later by Ammanati. In the Medici Chapel, Michelangelo sculpted the tombs of Lorenzo and Giuliano de' Medici.

He continued working for the Medici until 1534, when he decided to settle in Rome and take papal commissions. Though perhaps not so exciting, this was more secure. Florence was a hotbed of political unrest; the Medici had been officially expelled in 1527 and a war resulted. At Rome, work still remained to be done. Thirty years after he had painted its ceiling, Michelangelo was again busy in the Sistine Chapel, adding his *Last Judgment* painting to the wall. Other works of this late period in his life include frescoes in the Cappella Paolina made at the request of Pope Paul III, and his efforts to design St. Peter's Church. He was 71 when given the position of chief architect of St. Peter's. Though he lived another 18 years, the work progressed so slowly that it was left unfinished at his death and new designs were prepared thereafter.

—W.R.

Rodin (1840–1917). While highly realistic, Rodin's work retained subtle romantic overtones. Through the medium of limited-edition bronze casting, his work is distributed today throughout the globe in far greater number than are copies of any of the Old Masters. In many ways it resembles theirs, especially in scale. Rodin thought big. He liked yards of flesh, monumental proportions. His *Thinker* owed at least something to Michelangelo's *David*.

A Parisian, Rodin was groomed as an adolescent for an art career but failed the entrance exam at the École des Beaux-Arts. So he studied under the sculptor Barye, while earning a living as a stonemason. At 24 he was employed in the studio of Carrier-Belleuse, a minor sculptor. Again he experienced defeat when his *L'Homme au nez cassé* was blackballed by the salon. For the next decade Rodin created little of importance. In 1875 he journeyed to Italy, and the trip proved a turning point in his life. Exposure to classical and baroque art, of a more vigorous sort than existed in France, brought greater realism to his style. "Michelangelo freed me from academicism," Rodin later observed. The meaning was clear: Michelangelo's works would not have pleased the academies either.

When Rodin unveiled his 1st major work, *The Age of Bronze*, in 1878, it was considered too realistic to be true. Having used life-size proportions, he was accused of taking a cast from the model's body. But critics soon saw that Rodin needed to employ no such tricks. His *Walking Man*, which followed shortly after, was well received.

In his most active decade, the 1880s, he spent 3 years in the Sèvres porcelain works and handled numerous public and private commissions. His work became a fad with Parisian society. Buyers clamored for it and were willing to pay dearly. For the Hôtel de Ville he executed a statue of D'Alembert; for the Musée des Arts Décoratifs he began work on the monumental *Gates of Hell*. Still, he accepted other commissions. In 1884 the town of Calais asked him to sculpt a monument to commemorate its liberation some 500 years earlier. This was followed in 1889 by a monument to Claude Lorraine at Nancy. Rodin was in demand across the Atlantic, too. For Buenos Aires, he built a monument to Sarmiento, completed in 1898.

It was also to the 1880s that most of Rodin's famous nonportrait, noncommemorative sculptures belong: the *Thinker*, *Fugit Amor*, the *Kiss*. All in all about 200 works of this sort issued from his studio. Many were based on drawings and engravings by William Blake, Gustav Doré, and other artists.

By the 1890s Rodin was recognized as a builder of memorials and received more and more orders for them. Probably the best known is his monument to Balzac, which at 1st was turned down by the Société des Gens de Lettres. After 1900 Rodin turned to portraits of living celebrities and did likenesses of many of the leading figures of the day: George Bernard Shaw, Baudelaire, Clemenceau, Nijinsky, and Pope Benedict XV.

In 1916, the year before his death, Rodin presented to the French nation his personal collection of his own works. A museum was built to house them, the Musée Rodin in Paris.
—W.R.

Singers—Opera

Enrico Caruso (1873–1921). Life for the most famous operatic tenor of all began at 7 Via Giovanello Agli Ottocalli in Naples, Italy, on February 25, 1873. It ended in the same city, August 2, 1921. He had gone there to recover from an infection of the lungs. In his short 48 years, Enrico—baptized Errico—Caruso became the highest paid singer in the world. So great was the demand that seats for his performances in Germany and Austria were auctioned to the highest bidder. In America, his tremendous drawing power built the Metropolitan Opera Company's box-office receipts to a staggering $100,000 per season, and made Caruso a millionaire.

Surprisingly, his American debut—on November 23, 1903, at the Met in the title role of *Rigoletto*—was unimpressive. Highly nervous with opening-night jitters, he was not in good voice, cracking on high notes. The audience was further annoyed with his distracting Italian mannerisms and an excessive use of what critics called "the Rubini sob." By the season's end, however, he had become a favorite.

Caruso began his career in 1891 when, as a promising 18-year-old, he was accepted as a pupil by Vergine. The canny voice teacher promptly signed him to a contract that Caruso had extreme difficulty in breaking 8 years later. Vergine was to receive 25% of all earnings for the 1st 5 years of *actual singing*, conditions which, in effect, snared Caruso for life. While bound by this contract, he made his official Naples debut on February 16, 1894, in *L'Amico Fritz*. In sitting for his 1st professional photograph, Caruso appeared with a bedspread draped about his shoulders—his only shirt was being laundered.

Recognition came rapidly. By 1898, he had created the tenor roles for *Adrienna Lécouvreur* and *Fedora* at Milan's Teatro Lirico. Three years later, he became a member of La Scala, where he was featured in leading roles. In 1902, his fame widened, with contracts to sing 1st with Melba at Monte Carlo and then at Covent Garden, London. The Metropolitan's manager, Heinrich Conreid, brought him to America a year later.

Caruso's success came partially from the warm affection he maintained for his fans. To those without the admission price, he passed out complimentary tickets by the thousands—and scrupulously paid for every one, a bill which often came to over $9,000 per season. The more money he earned the less it mattered for him. Hearing that his home had been robbed of nearly $500,000 in jewelry while he was singing in Cuba in August of 1920, his only concern was that his wife and child had not been hurt. "Lots of jewels will come," he said. Caruso achieved even greater rapport with the public that same August, due to a *La Bohème* performance. In singing "Rodolpho's Narrative" to Mimi, he rendered the line, ". . . your lovely eyes have robbed me of my jewels." Then he stopped, turned to the audience, and gave an expressive Italian shrug, with outspread hands, that brought down the house. In another *Bohème* performance, his comrades across the footlights were treated to the sight of Marcello struggling unsuccessfully to put on his overcoat before going out to buy medicine for a dying Mimi—the fun-loving Caruso had sewed the sleeves closed before the performance.

In his 18 years at the Met, Caruso appeared in 36 roles. He understood 7 languages, and sang in 4. Continually, he evaluated his performance, writing comments such as "great ovation" and "ultimo" on the pay vouchers he received later. An extremely talented caricaturist, he frequently did sketches of fellow performers in costume. On the practical side, remembering his early poverty, he maintained complete books on everyday expenses, and solemnly entered the cost of his marriage to Dorothy Benjamin in 1918 at $50. Intensely superstitious, he would not start trips on Tuesdays or Fridays. He sang Rhadames in *Aida*, which he introduced at the Met, a total of 64 times. By contrast, he performed in *Carmen* at San Francisco only once. Caught in the disastrous April 18, 1906, earthquake, he swore never to return, crying "Give me Vesuvius." Toward the end of his career, he ventured briefly into motion pictures, cast in the dual role of famous singer and impoverished sculptor for *My Cousin Caruso*. The reviews were so bad that his 2nd picture was never released.

With Caruso's death in 1921, the world afforded him a funeral usually reserved only for royalty. He was laid to rest at Del Pianto Cemetery in Naples, in a chapel to which the faithful pilgrimaged for years. Not until 1929, 8 years later, was his widow able to obtain permission for the lid of his coffin to be closed permanently.

—W.K.

Kirsten Flagstad (1895–1962). In her debut as *Die Walküre's* Sieglinde on February 2, 1935, Kirsten Flagstad took her place as one of the greatest Wagnerian sopranos in the 20th century. It was a role she had learned just 8 months before. Her sole previous experience with Wagner had been in Europe, singing lesser parts except for Isolde, which she knew only in Norwegian. A quick study, she had mastered Isolde within 6 weeks for a 1932 performance. Until 1935, her name was completely unknown outside of Scandinavia.

Born on July 12, 1895, in Hamar, Norway, she became familiar with Richard Wagner's operas at the age of 10. The score for *Lohengrin* was given to her for a birthday present and she learned the role of Elsa, unaware then that she would later sing it on stage. At 16, she began a program of formal voice study, making her Norwegian debut as Nuri in Eugene d'Alberts' *Tiefland* on December 12, 1913, 5 months after her 18th birthday.

Following an unsuccessful 1st marriage to Sigurd Hall in 1919—during which her only child, Else, was born—she resumed her singing career. In 1929, Norwegian lumberman Henry Johansen arranged to meet her after seeing a Flagstad performance as Elsa; they were married a year later. It was Johansen who forced Flagstad to attend the Staatsoper in Vienna, to hear *Tristan und Isolde*. The opera—her talisman in later years—nearly put her to sleep.

In 1934, the Metropolitan Opera Company, badly in need of a new Wagnerian soprano, sent director Giulio Gatti-Casazza and conductor Artur Bodanzky to St. Moritz, Switzerland. There they auditioned this widely acclaimed Norwegian singer and signed her to a one-year contract. Neither man realized then what they had accomplished until a year later, when her debut made all of America's music lovers Wagner-conscious.

Flagstad, perhaps because of her peasant shyness, insisted on near-fanatical privacy during much of her public career. She avidly read movie magazines and from them adopted the "Greta Garbo complex," wanting to be left alone. Flagstad frequently barred the doors of her dressing room to all visitors. On other occasions, she skipped out immediately after the performance, leaving critics, well-wishers, and important persons fuming. Before going on stage, she passed the time by playing countless games of solitaire, for years keeping meticulous count of the results. For good luck she adopted another ritual before the performance: Either her accompanist, Edwin McArthur, or her husband would blow cigar smoke—which she loved—in her face. Flagstad kept in touch with her admirers by personally sending out autographed photographs, and she had an alphabetical file of the people who had requested these pictures. One of Flagstad's habits brought hurt accusations that a "secretary" was signing the pictures: The signature on the pictures and the addressing on the envelopes were by the same hand. The fans were wrong. Flagstad was her own "secretary."

In 1935, following a successful series of U.S. concerts, Flagstad appeared in a joint Chicago recital with tenor Lauritz Melchior, giving an all-Wagnerian program. The evening was a failure, but it did not prevent the 2 from teaming together with resounding success for years in *Tristan und Isolde*. The association continued smoothly until April of 1937, when tactless complaints made by Flagstad about "phony promotions"—like having to be photographed with her colleagues—were passed on to Melchior. The tenor, having posed with her that same day at a railroad station in Rochester, N.Y., took exception. The famous Flagstad-Melchior feud grew from the incident, lasting through W.W. II.

With the outbreak of W.W. II hostilities, Henry Johansen returned to Norway where he became involved in lumber deals with the Nazis. His business activities led to charges of collaboration and his arrest immediately after the war, but he died in prison before he could be tried. Flagstad, torn between remaining in the U.S. during the war or joining her husband, also elected to go home. The unfortunate choice gave rise to postwar charges of collaboration against her as well. Her attempts at a U.S. comeback in the late 1940s were marred by violent anti-Flagstad demonstrations wherever she appeared. Eventually the furor died down, weakened by lack of direct evidence. She was welcomed back to the Metropolitan with *Tristan* on January 22, 1951. On that night, she was given one of the greatest ovations ever heard.

Slightly over one year later, on April 1, 1952, she gave her farewell performance in *Alcestis* and departed to live permanently in Norway. She was appointed as director of the Norwegian State Opera in February, 1953, a final refutation by fellow Norwegians of the wartime charges. Flagstad busied herself by giving recitals in the 1950s, but her health began to fail. And on December 4, 1962, she died. Ten days later she was laid to rest in a funeral that was attended by His Majesty King Olaf and other notables who had come from all corners of the world to honor the fallen Valkyrie.

—W.K.

Singers—Popular

Louis Armstrong (1900–1971). On New Year's Day, 1913, Louis Armstrong picked up a pistol in New Orleans and fired the shot that was eventually heard round the world: He was arrested, sent to reform school, and received his 1st training in music there from Captain Jones. That original bugle is still preserved in the New Orleans Waifs' Home.

At age 14, Louis formed his 1st band and worked around New Orleans until 1923, when he went to Chicago, and later he made his 1st recordings with the King Oliver band in Richmond, Ind. He married pianist Lil Hardin in 1924. They moved to New York where he joined Fletcher Henderson's band. It was Henderson who described his voice as sounding like a fish-horn. His gravelly voice became

his trademark in the 1,500-plus records he cut between 1923 and 1970.

With his trumpet he could reach F above high C with ease, a feat unheard-of in the 1920s, as were his legatos, coupled with his pure tone, continuity of phrasing, and sophisticated improvisations.

Personally, Louis was a warm, funny, gregarious, happy man whose zest for life and love of music came through in his horn, his voice, his snap-flash smile, and his unspoken-but-felt pure joy of being.

He was nicknamed Satchelmouth, for obvious physiological reasons, by an editor of the *London Melody Maker*. It was shortened to Satchmo for convenience. He was also called Pops by those who loved him. Almost everybody called him Pops.

Louis' career was constantly upwardly mobile. In New York he worked The Savoy and The Cotton Clubs, and did a Broadway revue, *Hot Chocolates*, which brought him to the attention of white audiences. He recorded "Ain't Misbehavin'," one of his 1st big records. And he also participated in one of the 1st mixed recording groups with Jack Teagarden.

In 1930 he went to Los Angeles to work Frank Sebastian's Cotton Club. The same year, he cut the 1st of many records with Lionel Hampton, "Memories of You."

In 1932, Louis went to Europe for the 1st time. He captivated audiences everywhere. In 1933, he found he could play in the upper registers with ease; those long high-note codas went over well with his audiences. In so doing, he was to influence all musicians for some time to come.

He made some unimportant movies in the late 1930s: *Skeleton in the Closet, Artists and Models, Everyday's a Holiday, Doctor Rhythm,* and *Goin' Places.* In 1943, he won the 1st *Esquire* magazine jazz poll in the trumpet and vocal categories. In January, 1944, *Esquire* held its 1st jazz concert at the Metropolitan Opera House in New York City—starring Louis, of course. He won their poll again in 1945, 1946, and 1947.

Finally, in 1947 he starred in a movie almost worthy of his talents, *New Orleans.* He also made his 1st records with Ella Fitzgerald. At the same time, his agent and longtime friend Joe Glaser suggested forming the Louis Armstrong and His All Stars Band, which reached for and brought new highs to musicians and music lovers.

Louis was an internationally traveled, musical goodwill ambassador. He toured officially for the State Department, although there were parts of Africa he refused to visit, because of their apartheid policy.

Armstrong was accepted by royalty. He was honored by U.S. presidents and foreign heads of state. He was received by the Pope. And while Carol Channing starred in the Broadway musical, *Hello, Dolly!*, it's Louis' recording in his crackling-jack voice that has made the title tune a classic.

Fellow-musician Teddy Wilson said it best years ago: "Louis is the greatest jazz musician that's ever been. He's got it all: balance, tone, harmonic sense, excitement, technical skill, and originality."

It's not easy to top perfection.

—I.S.

The Beatles: John Lennon (1940–), *Paul McCartney* (1942–), *George Harrison* (1943–), *Ringo Starr* (1940–). A washboard and banjo band thumped British skiffle tunes at Woolton Parish Church in Liverpool on June 15, 1956. Sixteen-year-old John Lennon, leader of John and the Quarrymen (and an occasional shoplifter as well as a prankish egotist), ended a set and met Paul McCartney, 14, from the nearby Liverpool Institute. Paul, who impressed John with new guitar chords, joined the band and later invited his classmate, George Harrison, 13, to meet John. All shared the American influences of Bill Haley, Elvis, the Everly Brothers, Chuck Berry, Buddy Holly, and Britain's Lonnie Donnigan—whose upbeat version of "The Rock Island Line" motivated Liverpudlian youth to form numerous skiffle bands.

The nucleus of The Beatles had come together, but drums remained a constant problem. The group evolved into Johnny and the Moondogs. Then Lennon hit upon The Beatles, inspired by Buddy Holly's group, The Crickets. Lennon had considered the names of many insects and had added the "A" for the "Beat-" pun. This was modified to The Silver Beatles, a 5-man group during the summer of 1960. The group included Stu Stucliffe, an art student and intellectual friend of Lennon's, who learned bass and affected a James Dean personality style. He left The Beatles in February, 1962, to study art, but died the following April of a brain hemorrhage. The appearance of Peter Best, son of a Liverpool nightclub owner, temporarily solved the drummer problem.

The Beatles recorded "My Bonnie" (1961) in Hamburg and came to the attention of Brian Epstein—wealthy record-store owner, army reject, and frustrated actor, who felt "like a doomed, middle-aged businessman." Epstein found The Beatles back in Liverpool at The Cavern, a popular night spot. After losing Stu, they moved Paul to bass and became a popular local Merseyside band. Epstein signed them for 25% and negotiated a contract with George Martin, record producer at Parlophone.

The Beatles had returned from Hamburg with French hair styles, down across the eyebrows. Astrid Kichener, Stu's Hamburg girl friend in 1961, hadn't liked the greasy Teddy-boy look and had recombed his hair. George, and then Paul and John, had also changed to a "Beatle haircut." Peter Best, symptomatic of his not fitting in with the band, had kept his hondo hairdo. Best was dropped by the other Beatles on the eve of their major recording contract with Parlophone, and he was replaced by Ringo Starr (Richard Starkey) from Rory Storme's group.

Quite a Liverpudlian squabble erupted between the fans of Best and of The Beatles. Later, in 1965, at the peak of Beatlemania, an album of awful "Hamburg Silver Beatle" songs was released under the caption—in tiny letters—"Peter," and—in large bold print—"Best of The Beatles." The album died a quick and deserved death.

Epstein was a perfectionist as their manager. He carefully organized The Beatles, while the boys themselves remained amused and irreverent. Hunter Davies illustrates this in his biography, *The Beatles*:

> Before they started [their 1st major recording] session, George Martin explained to them what he was trying to do. "Let me know if there's anything you don't like," said George Martin.
>
> "Well, for a start," said George Harrison, "I don't like your tie."

Their humor grew from their working-class backgrounds. John was born during a heavy Nazi air raid on Liverpool, October 9, 1940. His patriotic mother, Julia, named him John Winston Lennon. His father, an itinerant seaman raised in a Liverpool orphanage, had deserted her before the birth. His mother remarried but left John, for the most part, to be raised by Mimi, one of her 4 sisters, and Mimi's dairyman husband. John did little in school but earn a reputation as a practical joker and leading troublemaker.

Paul McCartney, by contrast, was a charming, articulate young lad. He was sexually inquisitive, won literary prizes for his essays, and conformed to his mother's expectations until she died of cancer at age 45, when Paul was 14. He simultaneously took up guitar and lost interest in school. His 1st attempts at guitar were frustrated until he realized he was left-handed, which forced him to play the guitar "upside-down."

George, the youngest of 4 children, born February 25, 1943, attended Dovedale Primary where, unknowingly, Johnny Lennon was 3 grades ahead of him. George hated school, especially what he considered the hypocrisy of the teachers. He grew into adolescence as a

Teddy-boy with long hair, flashy clothes, and blue suede shoes.

Ringo had a most anguished early childhood. His father left when he was 3. At age 6, he spent a year in the hospital for appendicitis. He was hospitalized repeatedly for pleurisy between the ages of 13 and 16. But despite his health problems he became a happy, easygoing youth, and began playing drums in his hospital ward band.

"Love Me Do" was released in 1962, reaching No. 17 on British charts; 1963 was a building year, The Beatles reaching No. 1 with 4 tunes and also appearing in concerts. Then the boyish, head-bobbing group sparked "Beatlemania," an exaggerated state of teen-age hysteria. After a $50,000 publicity campaign by U.S.-based Capitol Records, The Beatles appeared on "The Ed Sullivan Show" in February, 1964, where they nervously goofed their lyrics but were seen by 73 million viewers. According to biographer Davies, evangelist Billy Graham broke a strict rule and watched TV on the Sabbath to see The Beatles, whom he labeled a passing fad.

In March, 1964, The Beatles devastated the American market, taking the 1st 5 out of the top 10 in *Billboard*. Their songs included "Can't Buy Me Love," "Please Please Me," "She Loves You," and "I Want to Hold Your Hand"—which was the top record of the year, and eventually sold over 3 million copies. At one time, The Beatles had 12 songs on the *Billboard* hot 100, and held an incredible 9 songs in the Canadian top 10.

Beatle music displayed an unusual tonal complexity for rock; it had bright melodies, non-echo chamber recordings, and positive, romantic lyrics—a welcome relief from surfer instrumentals and the nonsense novelty tunes of the period.

Beatlemania continued due to worldwide concert tours, selected TV specials, and 2 films: *A Hard Day's Night*, which United Artists originally wanted only for the sound-track rights, but which director Richard Lester turned into a minor film classic; and *Help!*, a highly visual, but inanely plotted film.

Beatle music broke new horizons with almost every album, leading other groups into an eclectic musicland. Early recordings encompassed pop ("'Til There Was You"); rhythm and blues ("Long Tall Sally"); rock ("Please Mr. Postman"); and their unique Beatle music. Later songs included country-and-western ("Act Naturally"), and folk-rock ("You've Got to Hide Your Love Away"). Harrison mastered the sitar and explored Eastern philosophy ("Within You, Without You"). Lennon and McCartney coauthored songs of protest ("Revolution ✗9"); social comment ("Eleanor Rigby"); and stream of consciousness

("Come Together"). They stayed within the limits of the pop music tradition for "Michelle" and McCartney's "Yesterday"; advanced into avant-garde double themes ("A Day in the Life"); and introduced classical rock with George Martin's baroque piano solo recorded at a different speed ("In My Life"). Other themes included sexual satire ("Happiness Is a Warm Gun"), and psychedelic music ("Lucy in the Sky with Diamonds"). The recordings themselves became surrealistic with parts of "Rain" taped backwards. Paul wrote a song under a pseudonym, and it became Peter and Gordon's hit, "Woman."

By 1967, the group had ended its concert tours, partly because of the time needed for complex recording sessions, but mostly because they had outgrown their interdependence. Each Beatle required the freedom to reach his artistic maturity as a creative individual.

George had married Patti, a part-time model and "extra" in *Hard Day's Night*. He introduced Ravi Shankar to the West, and became a disciple of the Maharishi in India. He popularized transcendental meditation, which combined Eastern mysticism with Western materialism. Harrison has been most altruistic, promoting the Concert for Bangladesh, which earned over $20 million. His songs include such spiritual themes as "My Sweet Lord."

After a brief acting stint, John Lennon divorced his 1st wife, Cynthia, whom he had secretly married on August 23, 1962, after he learned she was pregnant with their child, Julian. Then Lennon married Yoko Ono, and they became inseparable. They formed the Plastic Ono Band and, demonstrating against the Vietnam War with a peace-in, publicly spent a month in bed together in a hotel room. They both appeared nude, front and back, on their 1st album. After unsuccessful attempts to have a child, John and Yoko found different career directions and separated in 1974. John's life-style and music have embodied social activism. He has fought a constant battle to obtain U.S. residency against authorities who hold an old British marijuana conviction against him. His songs continue to range from the bizarre to the beautiful.

Paul is the most show-biz type, giving up his old girl friend, Jane Asher, to marry Linda Eastman, an American divorcée. McCartney sued the other ex-Beatles when they hired Allen Klein to run Apple, their highly innovative but financially disastrous post-Beatle business organization. Still cherubic and insecure, Paul continues to record with wife Linda and his band, Wings. It was McCartney's 1st solo album which made the Beatle breakup overt and final. Much of his music is reminiscent of the middle-Beatle period of pop and experimental commercial songs. His individual hits include "Live and Let Die," a movie sound track, and "Band on the Run."

Sad-eyed, long-nosed Ringo has been the least active but apparently the most content Beatle until recently. He had settled down with his wife Maureen, and their children, while doing movies and pop-flavored Western songs. However, as of February, 1975, a divorce was pending.

Brian Epstein died in 1968 of an overdose, which was related to a profound depression that was caused by his losing The Beatles as clients, and by his father's death.

The Beatles were as significant sociologically as they were musically. Their songs crossed national boundaries, crystallizing youthful attitudes and pumping up England's economy —thereby earning the Order of the British Empire award from the Queen. (Lennon: "She was like a mum to us.") They symbolized a new life-style, engendering a generation which, for the 1st time in the telecommunication's world, sang together with a collective humanistic (albeit temporary) social consciousness.
—P.A.

Buddy Holly (1936–1959). From the autumn of 1957 to early 1959, singer-guitarist-composer Buddy Holly scored a succession of record hits and produced what many critics have called some of the best rock 'n' roll ever made. He was the 1st artist to go beyond the rigid, classic structure of 12 bar rock 'n' roll, and his band, The Crickets, established the tradition of the guitar-based, self-contained (writing-singing-performing) white rock group, which has since become the staple of the music industry.

Charles Hardin Holly was born on September 6, 1936, in Lubbock, Tex., where he was raised on the music of Hank Williams and Roy Acuff. At the age of 12, his father bought him a $45 Fender guitar, and within 3 years he was playing and singing his way through local radio shows and sleazy café jobs. At that time nobody suspected Holly of having the potential to be a star in the frantic new rockabilly that was emerging in those years (1954–1955). Countrified music hardly seemed the place for a shy skinny youngster with horn-rimmed glasses, crooked teeth, curly hair, and a reedy voice that sort of hiccupped from one note to another.

Despite these physical limitations, he played Lubbock's Fall Park Coliseum in the same show with Bill Haley & the Comets in the fall of 1955. Decca Records brought him to Nashville for several recording sessions, but they led nowhere. His 1st record, "Blue Days, Black Nights," came out in the summer of 1956 and didn't do well, and his 2nd release, "Modern Don Juan," also flopped. Decca lost interest.

Back in Lubbock, Holly formed The Crickets, with Holly as vocalist and lead guitarist, and 3 friends as sidemen. They drove his dad's car to Clovis, N. Mex., where Norman Petty, a composer and producer of show tunes, had his studios. And the rest, as they say in the business, is history.

Petty more or less joined the group as pianist, arranger, and cowriter. He arranged a contract by which The Crickets would record for Brunswick, and Buddy Holly, as solo artist, would sing on Coral. Ironically, both labels were subsidiaries of Decca.

The Crickets 1st great success came in 1957; it was "That'll Be the Day"—probably one of the best rocks tunes ever made. It was followed by 4 more hits over the next year and a half. Holly's solo career also prospered, as he experimented with orchestration, Latin rhythms, double-tracking, and length in his music. At the same time, Decca took advantage of his popularity by releasing some of his old Nashville tapes. Never before had a musician's work so flooded the market.

Overall, this prolific, creative output lasted less than 2 years. In late 1958 Holly married Maria Elena Santiago and settled in Greenwich Village, severing his ties with The Crickets. Then, on February 3, 1959, while on tour, he and two other singers were killed in a plane crash near Mason City, Ia., after a concert. Buddy Holly was dead at 22.

Numerous posthumous albums have revealed the full range of his music. One album contains his last experimental tapes, made in New York. Others show the influences that shaped his style: tapes of old hillbilly music, his renditions of black music, and his early attempts to copy Elvis Presley. The full development of rock, from its country-and-blues origins to an integrated musical style, can be traced more clearly in the music of Buddy Holly than in any other artist, before or since. His influence rivals that of any other rock singer except for Chuck Berry. Hardly a group today does not owe part of its style to him.

The Beatles (who took their sound and entomological name from The Crickets), The Rolling Stones, The Hollies (who named themselves after Holly), Eric Clapton, Tom Rush, The Nitty Gritty Dirt Band, Joe Cocker, The Everly Brothers, and countless other artists have done renditions of his music. Bob Dylan, an early Holly enthusiast, copied Holly's early Decca sound and made it his own, as a hearing of Holly's 1956 "Midnight Shift" will attest.

Don McLean, who has recorded at least 2 Holly numbers and eulogized him in a poignant ballad called "American Pie," told an interviewer that Holly "had a sense of rhythm which was intrinsically his own, uncopyable, and which happened to mirror the life rhythm of a whole generation." Janis Joplin was even more succinct when, shortly before her own death, she said, "Buddy Holly had soul. He'll never die."

—J.D.

Paul Robeson (1898–). Paul Robeson is a Renaissance man born too late for the actual Renaissance, and too soon for his own country's recognition of the black race.

His father was an ex-slave turned minister. His mother was a schoolteacher. Paul was the youngest of 5 children. Born in Princeton, N.J., he was an honor student at Somerville High School. Additionally, he played football, sang in the glee club, and was top man on the debating team.

It was all preparation for his 4-year scholarship in 1915 to Rutgers College in New Brunswick, N.J. His achievements there included his being named an All-American football player and becoming a 4-letter man about whom sportswriters waxed lyrical, describing him as "the colored giant" or "the dark cloud."

He went on to receive his LL.D. from Columbia University Law School, and then went through an identity crisis. He was undecided whether to be a minister, singer, actor, or lawyer. He combined all those talents when, in 1924, in addition to having accepted a position with a firm, he spent an evening in Greenwich Village singing spirituals with the famous musical arranger Lawrence Brown.

The chance get-together resulted in a series of concert tours being booked for Robeson. In 1925, he went to England to star in *Emperor Jones.* One musical followed another in the U.S. and abroad. He scored one of his greatest triumphs in 1928, when he opened in Jerome Kern's *Showboat* at the Drury Lane Theatre in London. When that powerfully pervading basso voice finished the final bars of "Ol' Man River," London was his.

By the 1930s, his repertoire included songs in 25 languages. His inquiring legalistic mind was to lead him into problems unheard of to most blacks. Robeson publicly embraced the warmth that greeted him in the U.S.S.R. He said he regarded the Soviet Union as his 2nd motherland. He also announced that he preferred living in London, because he encountered no racial prejudice there. This did not endear him to Americans who accepted him as an artist but not as a human being.

Still, Hollywood needed and wanted him. Following his stage smashes, which included *All God's Chillun Got Wings, Porgy and Bess, Black Boy, Othello, The Hairy Ape,* and *Stevedore,* he appeared in such films as *Emperor Jones, Showboat, Sanders of the River, King Solomon's Mines, Jericho, Dark Sands, Tales of Manhattan,* and *Proud Valley.*

The ambivalence continued: He was listed in *Who's Who* (primarily a British publication) but not in *Who's Who in America.* Yet it was in America that he received an honorary degree as Doctor of Humane Letters from Hamilton College.

At the height of his success, with annual earnings of over $100,000, his career came to a halt in 1949. In 1950, he was a professional politician speaking out against his own country and for the ideologies of the U.S.S.R. He had loudly endorsed and actively worked for Henry Wallace's Progressive party, and, earlier, had supported the Spanish Loyalists fighting Franco.

Even his son, Paul, Jr., born in 1927, shattered conventions: He married a white woman in 1949, long before racially integrated dinners were the thing.

Robeson moved his family to the U.S.S.R. with resultant passport difficulties. In 1952, he was awarded the Stalin Peace Prize by the Soviet Government. He was a folk hero there but ignored in his homeland.

In the 1960s, his eyesight failing and in general ill health, bureaucratic red tape was finally unraveled, and he was permitted to return to America. He was in time to see some of the changes he had agitated for before the nation was ready.

He wasn't too bitter, in print, when he was mugged on a New York street in 1965. He might secretly have considered it anticlimactic after a lifetime of far more important encounters, some of which he won, and some of which he lost.

—I.S.

Frank Sinatra (1915–). Francis Albert Sinatra of Hoboken, N.J., was perhaps the 1st successful example of the hype. A press agent, the late George Evans, "permitted" his public to discover him.

But Frankie, as his swooning fans called him (and Evans paid them to swoon as part of the package), had many riffs under his tonsils before he caused his 1st traffic jam at New York's Paramount Theater in the early '40s.

While in high school he worked on a newspaper delivery truck and had a brief transfusion of printer's ink in his veins: He got a job as a copyboy, preparatory to becoming a reporter on the *Hudson Observer.* But after graduation from David E. Rue, Jr., High School, the skinny kid found out about Bing Crosby's success. Frank had experience: He'd sung in the glee club at school.

He organized, booked, and sang in a quartet, the Hoboken Four. They auditioned for Major Bowes' Amateur Hour radio show. The group didn't make it, but Frank did, with his rendition of "Night and Day."

He did a Bowes vaudeville tour, and then became a singing M.C. and headwaiter at the Rustic Cabin roadhouse in Alpine, N.J. In those days, a "radio line" out of a supper club was almost more important than receiving a salary, because it meant exposure to millions of radio listeners. Sinatra was definitely heard —by band leader Harry James, who hired him as his vocalist in 1939 the same year Frank married Nancy Barbato.

It was at a one-nighter that a newsman asked James: "Who's that skinny little singer? He sings a great song." James replied: "Not so loud. He considers himself the greatest vocalist in the business."

He was then, and many think he is still. His last recording with the James band, "All or Nothing at All" became an all-time best seller, and remains one of the finest examples of the Sinatra intimate one-to-one style. He left James to go with Tommy Dorsey's band. Of that period, Sinatra has said: "He taught me all I know about phrasing." He recorded with the Pied Pipers, and finally became a soloist.

He was featured vocalist on *Your Hit Parade* and then became the star of his own CBS radio show, *Songs by Sinatra.* (A little girl out of Nashville was making a name for herself at the same time: Dinah Shore. The 2 still reminisce about the good old days.)

It took 5 years for Sinatra and the aforementioned George Evans to find each other. Evans hired bobby-soxers, as teen-agers were then called, at $5 per girl to fill the Paramount Theater, to faint, swoon, scream, cause a mob scene, and make page one of every newspaper in New York. Not so incidentally, Sinatra's income rose from $15 to $25,000 a week. His star ascendency rose, too: In 1943 he made his movie debut in *Higher and Higher.* In 1945, he received a special Oscar for his performance in *The House I Live In,* a short subject devoted to the theme of tolerance. In 1953 he won an Oscar for his supporting role of Maggio in *From Here to Eternity.* In the decade after *Higher and Higher,* his personal life went lower and lower. During his marriage to Nancy there were 3 children: Nancy Jr., Frank Jr., and Christina. The marriage broke up. In 1951, he married screen-star glamor-girl Ava Gardner. They divorced in 1957. He was subsequently to marry actress Mia Farrow in 1966, and divorce her in 1968.

He had frequent overpublicized altercations with newspapermen and photographers. He starred in some memorable films, however, among them *Anchors Aweigh, Till the Clouds Roll By, It Happened in Brooklyn, The Miracle of the Bells,* and *On the Town.*

But he literally begged the producer and head of Columbia Pictures, Harry Cohn, for the Maggio part in *Eternity,* offering to work for almost nothing. He got the role. After *Eternity,* he was able to diversify: He did heavy drama in *The Man with the Golden Arm* and *The Detective;* musical comedy in *Guys and Dolls;* and comedy-drama in *Von Ryan's Express.*

In 1965, his television special *Frank Sinatra: A Man and His Music* won a Peabody Award and several Emmys. In 1971, he announced his retirement in a tear-choked concert at the Los Angeles Music Center.

That retirement lasted all of 2 years. He is back at work recording, doing TV specials, and appearing at benefits.

As for his private life, even fearless newswriters hesitate to challenge the legend. He is volatile: Witness his outbursts to a newswoman in Washington, D.C., and his headlines in Australia during a 1974 tour. He is kind: Innumerable unknowns in dire need have received financial help from Sinatra. He would be the 1st to deny it. He is a political activist. He is fiercely loyal. He is a sex symbol. There are few women who would refuse a date with him. Apocryphally, he zoomed Wheaties stock sky-high years ago, when he jokingly credited the cereal for his prowess.

He is a perfectionist as an entertainer. One of a kind. Although there are times when if one closes one's eyes and listens to Frank, Jr., just possibly . . .

—I.S.

Bessie Smith (1894–1937). Bessie Smith, the "Empress of the Blues," was born in Chattanooga, Tenn. She was one of 7 children of a black Baptist part-time preacher. William Smith died shortly after her birth, leaving the family in abject poverty. Her mother and brother died when she was 8. The eldest sister supported the family with various domestic or menial jobs and the other children contributed what they could. At the ripe age of 9, the future queen of the blues made her debut on the streets of Chattanooga singing for nickels and dimes. The "Poor Man's Blues," which she recorded in 1928, recalls those early years: "Mister rich man, rich man, open up your heart and mind, Give the poor man a chance, help stop these hard, hard times/Please listen to my pleadin', cause I can't stand these hard times long,/They'll make an honest man do things that you know is wrong."

Bessie's brother Clarence had signed on as a dancer and comedian in a traveling vaudeville revue, and in 1912, when the show arrived in Chattanooga, Bessie was signed on as a dancer.

By 1922, she had established a solid reputation through the South and along the Eastern seaboard. It was the end of the war (200,000 black soldiers had fought on the European front to make the world safe for democracy), and a new spirit and morality were on the rise. Blues music began to gain in popularity. The 1st "race" record—that is, a recording made by a black performer—had been issued in 1921. The record companies originally assumed that black music would be of no interest to their white customers: Victor even went so far as to scratch the word "colored" in the recording wax.

Bessie Smith made her 1st recording in 1923. The song was "Down Hearted Blues" and it was an immediate success. Much to the surprise of Columbia, 780,000 discs were sold in less than 6 months. Company officials had once rejected that same voice as too "rough."

Shortly after her earliest recording sessions, Bessie began a triumphant southern tour, accompanied by a sizable entourage of back-up performers and stagehands, in a bright yellow-and-green railroad car with "Queen of the Blues" stenciled on its side. A large portion of her audience was to be found in small farming communities.

In the early 1920s it was difficult for black performers to be booked into white theaters. Although her recordings spread her reputation throughout the white community, her performances were officially segregated: "Command" performances were arranged at some all-white theaters, but Bessie Smith mainly played a black theater circuit. Her music contains a quality of hovering near both the heights and the depths that spoke to millions of people, sparked off near-riots at her performances, and established her with an almost legendary reputation. "I've got the world in a jug," she sang in "Down Hearted Blues, "and the stopper's in my hand."

In 1929, Bessie starred in a 2-reel short called *St. Louis Blues*, based on a song of W. C. Handy's. The plot centered around the singing of the title song, about a woman who is two-timed and driven to drink by her handsome gamblin' man. At 1st suppressed for its "bad taste," it became fairly popular between 1929 and 1932.

In September of 1929, a week after the stock market crash, Columbia released Bessie Smith's "Nobody Knows You When You're Down and Out." The record sold well, but her career was on the wane. The black community, which had always operated on a depression-level economy, was spending less money on entertainment and, for the whites, the blues seemed to lessen in popularity as they became an expression of grim reality. Austere record-company budgets necessitated that her recordings be pressed in smaller quantities than ever before, and her tours and theatrical appearances became less frequent.

On September 26, 1937, Bessie Smith was killed in an automobile accident on a Mississippi road. The controversy surrounding her death has never ended. One account has it that she bled to death on the road while waiting for medical attention. Supposedly an ambulance arrived, but its driver picked up a less seriously injured white woman 1st, then came back for Bessie. Other sources claim that Bessie Smith died in the back of an ambulance on the way to a colored hospital, after she had been refused admittance to a white hospital. Her funeral in Philadelphia was one of the most spectacular seen in that city. An estimated 10,000 mourners filed past the gold-trimmed casket as she lay in state. She was buried after a noisy, emotional ceremony in grave No. 3, range 12, lot 20, section C of the Mount Lawn Cemetery in Sharon Hill, Pa. The grave was unmarked until 1970, when a Philadelphia housewife made this fact known in a letter to the Philadelphia *Inquirer*. Two donors immediately responded with the necessary funds to erect a headstone. One was a registered nurse who, as a child, had scrubbed Bessie Smith's floors on Saturday mornings, and the other was blues singer Janis Joplin. Both said they owed an eternal debt to Miss Bessie Smith.

Columbia Records has re-released 159 of Bessie Smith's recordings as 5 double albums. ("The World's Greatest Blues Singer"—GP33, "Any Woman's Blues"—G30126, "Empty Bed Blues"—G30450, "The Empress"—G30818, "Nobody's Blues But Mine"—G31093.) For further reading: Albertson, Chris. *Bessie*. New York, Stein & Day, 1972.

—S.W.

Sideshow of Popular Offbeat Performing and Creative Artists

COMPOSER

Carrie Jacobs Bond (1862–1946). Although her songs were never directed toward Tin Pan Alley or the volatile world of musical comedy, Carrie Jacobs Bond achieved prominence as probably the 1st great American woman composer. Her name is generally forgotten today, but not her legacy: "The End of a Perfect Day" and "I Love You Truly." Even in an age touched with skepticism and with small regard for human values, the seriousness of both songs, their heartfelt sentimentality which escapes being maudlin, still is affecting.

Carrie Jacobs was born in Janesville, Wisc., of a musical family. Her grandmother was a 1st cousin of John Howard Payne, who wrote "Home, Sweet Home." As a small child, she played the piano by ear and at 9 took formal lessons. Aptitude in both painting and design were to help her in later, leaner years. Her marriage at 18 ended in divorce, but her re-marriage at 25 produced a relationship of mutual devotion. She and Dr. Frank Bond moved to Iron River, in the pine forests of northern Michigan, where several years later he lost all his money in a disastrous investment. When he died suddenly in 1895, Mrs. Bond was not only almost penniless but disabled by rheumatism and completely devoid of any practical experience but keeping house.

Fighting to sustain herself and her young son amidst poverty, the valiant widow tried running a rooming house in Chicago. She took in sewing; she painted designs on china. She continued to write songs, which she had begun originally as a mere diversion, but so dire were her straits that she penned them by candlelight on brown wrapping paper. Eventually this proved the most lucrative of her activities, as her ballads became more widely known through her performance of them at social gatherings and concerts. Though she was a gifted pianist, she had no vocal training and expressively declaimed rather than sang, much as nonsinging actors do on the stage today. Her vaudeville debut was accompanied by a chorus of boos, leaving her heartbroken, but the songs and her unique style eventually would bring her $1,000 a week and put her name in lights.

In 1901, an admirer lent Mrs. Bond enough money to publish a collection with the rather ponderous title "Seven Songs as Unpretentious as the Wild Rose." Two of them—"I Love You Truly" and "Just A-Wearyin' for You" —quickly became standards and were later issued separately. Friends helped her publicize her songs by arranging recitals. Others obtained an invitation for her to sing at the White House for President Theodore Roosevelt. She would later entertain another President, Warren G. Harding.

Henceforth Mrs. Bond devoted her life to publishing, writing words and music, and designing cover pages. A considerable variety of compositions flowed from her pen, but her masterpiece was "The End of a Perfect Day." It was the result of an uplifting moment during a Southern California motor trip in 1910, when Mrs. Bond was moved by the beauty of the flowers and the sunset. In little more than 10 years the sheet-music sale passed 5 million copies. The song was introduced as an encore at a recital in New York, then spread to concert halls, vaudeville, weddings, funerals, barrooms, and even barber shops. Echoing the love and humanity that were endangered by the outbreak of W.W. I, it was a favorite with that war's fighting men. The composer presented it often in concerts at army camps.

The close of Mrs. Bond's perfect day came in Hollywood, where she was buried with a memorial plaque inscribed with Herbert Hoover's tribute to her "heart songs that express the loves and longings, sadness and gladness of all peoples everywhere."

—B.L.

DANCERS

Josephine Baker (1906–1975). *La Revue Nègre*, the 1st American Negro troupe to play Paris, opened at the Théâtre des Champs-Élysées on the evening of September 25, 1925. The cast included Florence Mills and Sidney Bechet, but the real star turned out to be Josephine Baker, the 18-year-old daughter of an East St. Louis washerwoman. Baker sang in a chirping soprano voice, interspersing the lyrics with wordless, contrapuntal crooning; her dancing ranged from a fierce Charleston to slow, angular movements reminiscent of Egyptian tomb paintings. The Parisians, with their appetite for exotic personalities, immediately fell in love with her. They learned for the 1st time that black is beautiful, and French popular music and entertainment have never been the same since.

Baker's routines were always spectacular. For *La Revue Nègre*, she made her entrance— carried in, upside down, and doing the splits —on the shoulder of a giant. Her costume was one pink flamingo feather between the legs. The next year, her number at the Folies-Bergère was even more extravagant. A huge, flower-covered globe descended from the ceiling, stopping just above the orchestra. Slowly, the ball cracked open. Inside was Josephine, wearing nothing much except a skirt of bananas and standing on a mirror tilted slightly toward the audience. She danced and sang. Then the globe closed and, to wild applause and cheers, was hoisted back to the rafters.

Her private life, most of which she lived in public, was likewise flamboyant. She took a pet cheetah to the Paris Opéra, where the music made it so nervous that it jumped into the pit and attacked the musicians. Some days she could be seen walking swans, other days leopards, on leashes. During her 1st 2 years on the Continent, she received 40,000 fan letters, 2,000 of which proposed marriage.

Miss Baker nearly duplicated that popularity in Berlin, Barcelona, Prague, and Budapest; but ironically, she never even approached it in her own country. When she returned to New York for the *Ziegfeld Follies of 1936*, the critics didn't think much of her. Some of them believed that the singing lessons she'd been taking had destroyed her elemental charm, that she'd become too sophisticated. After the war, her revue—*Paris Sings Again*—closed in Boston not long after it opened. Though she could pack Paris music halls months on end, her appearances in even the largest American cities were always limited to just a few days.

And if living in France had allowed her to forget the bigotry in the U.S., racial hatred was thrust in her face every time she returned to her homeland. During a 1951 tour, the Stork Club dared refuse her entrance, and 3 hotels in Atlanta turned her away. (Significantly, about this time the song which usually opened her shows, "*J'ai deux amours, mon pays et Paris*," was changed to "*Paris mes amours*.") One of her later visits to this country was in 1963, to join Martin Luther King's march on Washington.

In 1956, Baker announced that her current concerts at the Paris Olympia would be her adieu. She wanted to retire to her château outside the city, and spend more time with her 12 adopted children, mostly of different nationalities and of several different colors. But her plans to turn the house into a tourist attraction failed. Money running low, she returned to the stage 3 years later. She came out of retirement to make, like Sarah Bernhardt, just one more farewell tour.

In 1973, the 67-year-old Miss Baker performed for enthusiastic audiences in New York City and Los Angeles, her 1st appearance in the U.S. since 1964. One Los Angeles reviewer wrote: "At the end of her show, Miss Baker sings 'My Way,' which was written for Frank Sinatra but is far more meaningful as she sings it. The thought comes to mind— Sinatra thinks HE's a living legend? Go sit down, Frank. You aren't even close."

In April, 1975, Miss Baker died apparently of a cerebral hemorrhage. She was 69.

—R.W.

Arthur Murray (1895–   ). Born Murray Teichman on the Lower East Side of New York City, Arthur Murray was one of 5 children born to a poor Austrian immigrant couple. He worked throughout his school days to increase the family income with any odd jobs he could find.

Murray was always shy and introverted as a child and self-conscious about his tall, lanky appearance. He wanted very much to be a part of the social activities that most of his friends enjoyed, particularly the dances, but he was afraid to socialize with girls. Finally, at the age of 14, Joe Feigenbaum, a friend of his whom he particularly admired because of his popularity with the girls, taught him his 1st dance steps.

In order to get some practice on the dance floor, Murray attended weddings in his neighborhood, where he always found willing dance partners of every size and age.

Murray won his 1st dance contest at the Grand Central Palace, a public dance hall where he later became a part-time dance teacher after graduation from high school. The 1st prize had been a silver cup, but Murray went home without anything to show for his championship dancing. His partner of the evening took it, and it eventually ended up in a pawnshop. This loss made a lasting impression on Murray, and in later years every winner in his dance contests took home a prize.

In between jobs as a dance instructor, Murray worked as a draftsman at the Brooklyn Navy Yard and as a reporter at the New Haven *Register*. Deciding to further his education, he enrolled at Georgia Tech. Murray supported himself by conducting dance parties at the Georgian Terrace Hotel, where he proved both his ability as a businessman and his excellence as a dance instructor.

Murray was inspired by a casual remark made by William Jennings Bryan one evening at the hotel: ". . . You know, I have a fine idea on how you can collect your money. Just teach 'em with the left foot and don't tell 'em what to do with the right foot until they pay up!"

Murray thought about what Bryan had said and came up with the brilliant idea of teaching simple dance steps with footprint diagrams and doing it by mail. Within a couple of years, over 500,000 dance courses were sold by mail order.

On April 24, 1925, Murray married his famous dance partner, Kathryn, whom he had met at a radio station in New Jersey. She was in the audience while he was broadcasting a dance lesson.

After their marriage, the mail-order business became less popular and the Murrays opened up a dance school offering personal instruction. Their business began to prosper, especially in 1938 and 1939 when Arthur picked 2 little-known dances, the "Lambeth Walk" and "The Big Apple," and turned them into dance crazes. They were taught at large hotel chains throughout the country, and the name "Arthur Murray" became a household word.

There are now hundreds of Arthur Murray studios all over the world, with specially trained instructors, making Arthur Murray the most successful dance instructor in history.

—D.X.B.

Salomé (1st Century A.D.) The infamous dancer, Salomé, has inspired the imaginations of many writers throughout history since her famous performance around 30 A.D. Oscar Wilde's play *Salomé* was banned in England, but the great actress Sarah Bernhardt performed it in 1894 in France. Richard Strauss wrote a well-known opera of the same name which was produced in Germany in 1905. England would not allow the opera performed in any theater until 1910, when it was staged in the honored Covent Garden. Hollywood made a film about Queen Salomé. And numismatists can even find Salomé and her husband Aristobulus on a small coin.

Salomé was the daughter of Herodias and the stepdaughter of Herod Antipas. It has been said that her well-known "dance of the 7 veils" captured the heart of Herod, and he promised to give her anything in the world she asked for. Salomé's only wish was to have John the Baptist's head on a silver platter. The gospel writers say she was influenced by her mother, who harbored a deep hatred for John.

Unnamed, Salomé danced her infamous dance in Matthew 14:6–11 in the New Testament: "But when Herod's birthday was kept, the daughter of Herodias danced before them, and pleased Herod. Whereupon he promised with an oath to give her whatsoever she would ask. And she, being before instructed of her mother, said, Give me here John Baptist's head in a charger [a platter]. And the king was sorry: nevertheless for the oath's sake, and them which sat with him at meat, he commanded it to be given her. And he sent, and beheaded John in the prison. And his head was brought in a charger, and given to the damsel: and she brought it to her mother." Unnamed, still, she danced also in Mark 6:22: "And when the daughter of the said Herodias came in, and danced, and pleased Herod and them that sat with him, the king said unto the damsel, Ask of me whatsoever thou wilt, and I will give it thee."

Nowhere in the Bible was Salomé's actual name ever mentioned—the ancient historian Josephus named her after Herod's stepdaughter —and nowhere in the Bible was her performance called the "dance of the 7 veils." Yet, though the world does not know her real name, nor know exactly what dance she performed so successfully, she has become the most famous terpsichorean in all history.

—D.X.B.

MOVIEMAKERS

Marion Davies (1898–1961). Leading lady and comedienne, best known as the protégé and companion of newspaper magnate William Randolph Hearst for nearly 35 years, Marion Davies never became a top star despite the estimated $7 million that Hearst poured into the venture.

Miss Davies left a convent school to become a chorus girl. By the age of 17, she was a dancer in the Ziegfeld Follies, where she entranced Hearst, who was then 54, married, and the ruler of a publishing empire that included 7 magazines and 10 newspapers.

Hearst set out to make her a star, hiring the best directors, drama coaches, and designers to prepare her for her film debut in *Cecilia of the Pink Roses* (1918). The following year Hearst established Cosmopolitan Pictures to produce films that would show off what he thought was her talent as a romantic heroine. *When Knighthood Was in Flower* (1922) was one of the few of these costume spectaculars that didn't lose money. *The Patsy* (1928) and *Show People* (1928) finally revealed Miss Davies' gift for light comedy and also the warmth and charm that endeared her offscreen to prop boy and star alike.

Hearst closely supervised every detail of Miss Davies' films, acting as a combination business manager, agent, drama coach, producer, and chaperone. He lavished her with gifts, such as a 14-room "bungalow" on the MGM lot, and with publicity, ordering each of his newspapers to mention her name at least once in every edition (an order not rescinded until after Hearst's death in 1951). Those who cooperated with Miss Davies also got free publicity in the Hearst publications; those who didn't—like Norma Shearer—were banished forever from their pages.

After making several sound films, despite a marked stutter, Miss Davies retired from film making in 1936. Through Hearst's generosity she had become such a wealthy woman that she was able to lend him $1 million from her personal fortune when he was in serious financial trouble.

Although they never married because Hearst's wife steadfastly refused to grant him a divorce, Miss Davies remained loyal to Hearst until his death. She married for the 1st time shortly thereafter and devoted her later years to managing her business interests.

—S.Sc.

Mickey Mouse (1928–   ). Mickey Mouse was born on a train en route to Los Angeles from New York. His early life is somewhat of a secret, and it was not until he applied for work at the Disney Studios that Mickey's film career was launched and carefully recorded. In his 1st silent film, *Plane Crazy*, he met and fell in love with his leading lady, Minnie Mouse, who also appeared in Mickey's 2nd film, *Gallopin' Gaucho*. Although he could not find financial backing for his silent movies, Mickey, confident of his talent, made a "talkie," *Steamboat Willie*. The addition of a synchronized sound track made Mickey's character come fully alive, even though his voice was rather squeaky. *Steamboat Willie* premiered in New York City where it was a box-office sensation.

Mickey's early pictures revolved around his talent as an entertainer particularly as a violinist and pianist. Not satisfied to be known only as a musician, Mickey insisted on "juicier" roles. In 1930–1931, he starred in 21 films in which he played such characters as a fire chief, soldier, hunter, cowboy, prisoner, and great lover. The studio began making color films in 1932, but Mickey, always modest and concerned with the welfare of others, continued to appear in black and white, allowing the studio to use more of its available funds to add color to the film endeavors.

By 1935 Mickey Mouse was an internationally renowned star. Germany had chosen one of his films as one of the 10 best pictures of the year (1930). Awards came in from Argentina and Cuba. Russia sent him an antique cut-glass bowl from the 1st Soviet Cinema Festival. When Mickey made his initial color film, *The Band Concert*, he received awards from the 3rd International Cinematographic Arts Exhibition in Venice and from the Brussels International Festival. Not to be outdone by foreign praise, Worcester, Mass., officially proclaimed May 12 as "Mickey Mouse Day."

Although Mickey starred in 16 pictures in 1936–1937, he was losing ground to other Disney studio stars—particularly a sailor-suited duck named Donald and a canine actor called Pluto. During the 4 years preceding W.W. II Mickey appeared in fewer films, and he sometimes took 2nd billing to Pluto. However, his popularity was reinstated with *Fantasia* (1940) for his role as "The Sorcerer's Apprentice." When war broke out, he retired to concentrate on aiding the war effort. His dedication and service were duly acknowledged—the password of the Allies on D-Day in 1944 was "Mickey Mouse." With the war ended, Mickey returned to Hollywood, but he was finding it increasingly difficult to add scope and depth to the characters he portrayed. Always the "good guy," he was not supposed to lose his temper or do anything sneaky. When he erred, critical fan mail poured into his office.

In 1955, Mickey made a smash comeback with *The Mickey Mouse Club*, a show that played 5 days a week on national television. A cast of 24 "Mouseketeers" aided him. They sang, danced and, in general, helped him make each day a glorious one—Monday was "Fun with Music Day"; Tuesday, "Guest Star Day"; Wednesday, "Anything Can Happen Day"; Thursday, "Circus Day"; and Friday was "Talent Round-Up Day."

In 1959 Mickey realized that he enjoyed public relations more than film making and agreed to become the official host for Disneyland in California and later for Walt Disney World in Florida. Currently, he is busy shaking hands, leading parades and having his picture taken with visitors to the "Magic Kingdoms."

—C.O.

NOVELISTS

Lewis Carroll (Charles Lutwidge Dodgson) (1832–1898). On July 4, 1862, 2 young English scholars took 3 little girls on a picnic. One of the men was Charles Lutwidge Dodgson, and during this outing he told a fascinating tale of a girl named Alice and what happened to her after she fell down a rabbit hole. It was not unusual for Dodgson to tell stories, for he was very fond of little girls and liked to entertain them. However, on this occasion he outdid himself and so enraptured his listeners that one of them, Alice Liddell, the model for the heroine of the story, insisted that he write it down.

That night in his room at Oxford University he worked furiously until 6 in the morning, adding incidents to flesh out the story. He illustrated the work with his own drawings and presented it to Alice, who was not the only one enchanted with the result. For Henry Kingsley, a Victorian novelist and friend of Alice's family, happened to read *Alice's Adventures Underground* and told Mrs. Liddell that he thought highly of the book and that she should urge the author to publish it.

Dodgson took this advice, but before he had his work published he very wisely decided to replace his drawings with those of the famous illustrator, John Tenniel. A more fortunate union of writer and artist could not be imagined, for in 1865 their combined efforts brought forth a book—retitled *Alice's Adventures in Wonderland*—that has become one of the most famous children's books of all time, one that appeals to child and adult alike. (A curious sidelight is that Dodgson, dissatisfied with the 1st printing, stopped the presses after 48 copies had been run off. Twenty one of these have survived and are among the rarest of rare books.) On the title page of *Alice* appeared a pen name that has become immortal—Lewis Carroll.

This cleric and mathematician chose to hide behind a pseudonym because he wished to keep his "nonsense" works separate from his mathematical and other treatises to which he attached his true name. He arrived at "Lewis Carroll" by reversing his 1st and middle names, translating them into Latin (Ludovicus Carolus), and then retranslating into English. This perfectly illustrates the playful mind of a man who delighted in puzzles, riddles, and the most elaborate word play. He has added a number of words to the English language, like "chortle" and "galumph" (a triumphant gallop), and his poems and poetic parodies have often been anthologized. *Alice's Adventures in Wonderland* and its successor, *Through the Looking-Glass and What Alice Found There*, are among the most often quoted works in the language.

Not only was Dodgson a brilliant man of letters; he was also an exceptional photographer. He was noted for his portraits of leading Victorians, and he specialized in studies of nude children, particularly girls. This latter activity caused some eyebrows to be raised, and he abruptly ceased taking pictures altogether. Some have tried to find sinister things in Dodgson's affection for little girls, but perhaps the true cause of his lifelong pursuit of preadolescent females was a lonely bachelor's need for love. He found at least one grown-up woman attractive, the actress Ellen Terry. Their relationship managed to make up in endurance what it lacked in intimacy. Perhaps, as have many of his readers, he found in his world of "nonsense" a refuge from the real world.

—J.M.

Agatha Christie (1890–). Except for Georges Simenon, Agatha Christie is the only writer of fiction whose works have sold over 300 million copies throughout the world. In the United Kingdom alone, just the paperback editions of her books sell over 1.5 million copies a year. And her singular triumphs are not confined to the world of books. Her play *The Mousetrap* has enjoyed the longest continuous run of any show at one theater. On November 25, 1952, this melodrama opened at the Ambassadors Theatre in London, and it broke the record on February 28, 1972, with its 8,000th performance. Next to Shakespeare, Agatha Christie is the 2nd most-translated English author.

These staggering achievements have been made by a generally retiring woman who gets her best ideas while eating apples in her bathtub. Agatha Christie was born in Torquay, Devon, England. Her father, Frederick Alvah Miller of New York, died when she was very young, and she was reared by her mother and educated privately. It was her mother who encouraged her writing. One day young Agatha had a cold and could not go out. Her mother suggested that she amuse herself by writing a story. Later, she studied singing in Paris but was disappointed when she realized that her voice was not of star quality. To console herself Agatha Christie wrote a novel, which she showed to a literary neighbor, and he encouraged her to continue her efforts.

From time to time she was fortunate enough to have a short story published. However, her 1st great success did not come until after her marriage to an English army officer, Archibald Christie. While he was away fighting in W.W. I, she wrote a detective novel in her free time away from her work as a volunteer nurse. After many rejections, it was finally published in 1920 under the title *The Mysterious Affair at Styles*. The book was a success, and it introduced one of the greatest fictional sleuths of all time, Hercule Poirot, a worthy successor to Sherlock Holmes. Like Holmes, Poirot relies not on gimmickry but on what he calls the "little gray cells" to solve the crime. This clever Belgian is matched by Miss Jane Marple, another Christie creation, who deftly spots murderers by drawing on her knowledge of the people in her own small English village. People are the same everywhere, she says, and it is best to suspect the worst of everyone in a murder case.

In real life Agatha Christie herself was once the subject of a mystery. She disappeared from her home in December, 1926, and a nationwide search was launched for her. An anonymous letter brought her searchers to a hotel where they found her suffering from amnesia and living under the name of the woman who was to become her husband's 2nd wife. After her divorce, she subsequently met and married Max Mallowan, an archaeologist, whom she has accompanied on his expeditions to Egypt and the Near East. These excursions have often provided backgrounds for her novels.

Now in her middle 80s, she still writes at least one novel a year, adding to a total that matches her age. Her works offer murder in pleasant surroundings. She emphasizes plot and character and eschews violence for its own sake. Among her greatest triumphs are *The Murder of Roger Ackroyd*, a tale that brilliantly defied all the canons of detective fiction, and *Ten Little Indians*, also published as *And Then There Were None*. To the public and critics alike, she remains the world's greatest mystery writer.

—J.M.

Dashiell Hammett (1894–1961). Dashiell Hammett is considered the originator of the "hard-boiled" school of detective fiction. His heroes are tough private eyes who are friends of neither the police nor the criminal, but have the respect of both. His stories and novels are so filled with violence that some critics have questioned their realism.

But Hammett's fiction was based on experiences that he himself had had while working as a Pinkerton detective for 8 years. He found being a detective exciting, a welcome change from the other occupations (newsboy, messenger boy, railroad laborer) he had tried after dropping out of school at 13. He worked on a number of famous cases, including those involving "Fatty" Arbuckle and Nicky Arnstein. He earned his 1st promotion by tracking down a man who stole a Ferris wheel.

When W.W. I began, Hammett entered the Army and was assigned to the Motor Ambulance Corps. He contracted tuberculosis, and while it ruined his health, it turned him into a writer. As he was recovering from his illness, he began writing detective stories. Many of those early short stories (and subsequently almost all of his novels) were published in *Black Mask*, a famous pulp magazine of that era.

Although having his works published in *Black Mask* was gratifying, the money he received was limited. He ate the cheapest food —sometimes none at all. Often he lived on nothing but coffee, soup, and cigarettes. All the while, he was still battling tuberculosis.

When Hammett's 1st novel, *Red Harvest*, was published in 1929, it marked the beginning of realistic, hardhitting detective fiction in America. And when he wrote *The Maltese Falcon*, he reached the zenith of both critical and public acclaim. His hero in *The Maltese Falcon* was Sam Spade, the cool and crafty private eye who solved impossible cases, guzzled booze, and bedded down with all his women.

Hammett himself soon gained renown as a ladies' man, spending much of his money entertaining women. He was an attractive man, slender and 6' tall, with streaks of gray through his dark hair and a narrow moustache.

Hammett's political views were left-wing, and he became involved in several antifascist causes. He supported the Loyalists in the Spanish Civil War.

In 1951, when he was subpoenaed to testify in a case involving 4 communists, Hammett refused to answer questions identifying the contributors to the defendants' bail-bond fund. He was held in contempt of court, sentenced to 6 months in prison and served 5 of them.

Hammett usually wrote late at night and worked into the dawn. Often when he felt he was at a crucial point in the book, he would write for 36 consecutive hours.

He often said that he had no particular admiration for his own detective novels, but that he did respect the works of Hemingway and Faulkner—the "straight" novelists.

Hammett's doctors diagnosed cancer of the lungs in November of 1960. Two months later Hammett was dead.

—R.T.

PAINTER

Grant Wood (1892–1942). He was hailed as an Iowa Moses who had come to lead American art into the Promised Land. His painting achieved fame partially because his cardboard-stiff style and his use of hard-working farm people for models was easily satirized.

A simple man, indigenous to Iowa, Wood was admired by his neighbors as perhaps no other American artist has been in his own community. Earlier he had tried to break with tradition, fleeing to Paris where he studied Impressionism. After a few unproductive years, he returned to Cedar Rapids to teach fine arts at the local high school and to attend the Art Institute. His benefactor and sponsor was the local undertaker, David Turner. Turner induced Wood to quit teaching, redecorated a loft as a home for him and his mother, bought his paintings, and managed his affairs. Cedar Rapids soon became proud of the artist in its midst. His home became a cultural center—a sort of "Greenwich Village of the Cornbelt." A commission for a stained-glass window in an American Legion post sent Wood to Munich in 1928. This trip was probably the high point of his career, for it was here he studied the work of German and Flemish painters and discovered that their precision in line technique fitted perfectly with his own needs. Wood believed that simple subjects, viewed realistically, can be beautiful. Upon his return to Iowa he attempted to paint his neighbors and his family with the same fidelity he had admired in the European masters. However, because his stained-glass window had been made in Germany, it was rejected. Success came with *American Gothic* (1930), and *Daughters of Revolution*, which Wood always called "those Tory gals."

The artist began sketching his best-known painting, *American Gothic*, as early as 1928 when he discovered the Gothic-style house while strolling in the small town of Eldon. He later learned this was a brothel. Wood's sister Nan and her dentist-friend, Dr. B. H. McKeeby, reluctantly posed for the painting after Wood assured them that they would not be recognized. Dr. McKeeby was unhappy about the painting, and for 5 years would neither admit nor deny he had been one of the models.

When the picture appeared at the Chicago Art Institute's annual exhibition in 1930, it caused a sensation and was awarded the Harris Prize. It was bought by the Art Institute for $300—a price which was fixed at the time it was entered.

When Wood was 44, he married an older woman. But success and critical acclaim had gone to the artist's head. He was unhappy until the marriage ended in divorce. Many who had previously praised his work began to criticize it. He found himself in debt again, lectured for high prices, and tried to write. Once he was freed from marriage, he staged a comeback and discovered new ways of working. He took advantage of the fact that he had nothing to lose—he determined to do the kind of work he liked and to strive for greater recognition. He looked even harder for "striking" qualities and used ever-stronger emphasis and satire. He was productive until cancer ended his life in 1942.

—D.S.

PLAYWRIGHT

Felix Lope de Vega Carpio (1563–1635)

> Some peasant girls,
> Without makeup and fancy clothes,
> Bear away our eyes
> And with them our hearts.
> *El mejor alcalde el rey*, Act I

The exact output of Spain's most prolific dramatist is unknown. He allegedly completed between 1,500 and 2,000 dramas, of which some 426 plays and 42 *autos sacramentales*, or one-act religious dramas, still survive. Lope de Vega created the mode for European drama, plotting in 3 acts with his denouement coming midway through the 3rd. Of an Asturian peasant background, he wrote for the masses with a graceful, flowing style, mostly in verse, which combined the elegant phrasing of the nobility with the crudities of the peasant. The resultant product, with its effortless rhythm, was so perfect it gave rise to the expression, *Es de Lope* ("It is Lope's"). His plays were ambitious and full of earthy passion. He created a blend of the serious with the comedic, and gave his characters—especially the women—the traits of being both shrewd and commonly wise.

Lope de Vega read Latin at 5 and translated Claudius when he was 10. When 12, he had completed his 1st 4-act play, *El verdadero amante*, and 3 years later was off to fight a war in Portugal. Next to Cervantes, who called him the *Monstruo de la Naturaleza* (the "Monster of Nature"), his reputation in Spanish literary circles was unmatched.

His dalliances, liaisons, and amours were legion. With Elena Osorio—the young married daughter of Jerónimo Velázquez, for whom he began to write plays—his affair lasted for 5 years. It ended when Velázquez sued for libel and won, forcing Lope de Vega into exile from Madrid for 10 years. Micaela de Luján—the "Lucinda" of his sonnets—coproduced 4 illegitimate children for him. However, he sired only one legitimate son, Carlos, during his 2nd marriage, which was to Juana de Guardo. Well into middle age, he continued to produce in the boudoir, having yet more progeny with the married Doña Marta de Nevares Santoya at the age of 60. She became the model for his main character in *Amarilis* in 1632, completed the year after her death. And from his experiences with Jerónima de Burgos, he wrote his best-known comedy of love intrigues, *La dama boba*.

Lope de Vega kept copious notes on his amatory and professional adventures. In 1605, when his exploits reached the ears of the Duke of Sessa, the duke became his lifelong literary patron. He, in turn, as the duke's secretary, provided consultory advice on *affairs l'amour*. In 1610, he returned to Madrid where he staged plays in the Calle de Francos until his death 25 years later. While grieving over the loss of his wife and son, he took holy orders for ordination as a priest and familiar of the Holy Inquisition in 1614. In the strangest of dichotomies, even as he wrote light comedy he presided, with cool fanaticism, over a monk's barbaric execution for heresy. And his profane writing and love affairs continued even after his union with the Church.

Of his hundreds of plays, he is well remembered for *Peribáñez*, *El mejor alcalde el rey*, and *El caballero de Olmedo*. In his most important historical play, *La bizarrías de Balisa* (1634), he dealt with the flamboyant cape-and-sword antics of the nobility. Another, *Fuente Ovejuna* (*The Sheep Well*), is extremely popular in the Soviet Union because of its proletarian theme: A young peasant girl rouses the people to kill a leader who plunders their village and attempts to rape their women. With *El niño de la guardia* and its anti-Semitic plot, he appealed to strongly-Catholic Spain. In *Pedro Carbonero*, he sought a theme that treated the Moors sympathetically.

At 72, the flames of both passion and creativity flickered and then died on August 27, 1635. His demise was perhaps aided by severe debilitation attributed to frequent religious flagellation that sometimes left the walls of his room covered with blood. His patron, the Duke of Sessa, celebrated his passing with a 9-day funeral.

—W.K.

SINGERS

Nelson Eddy (1901–1967); *Jeanette MacDonald* (1907–1965). Nelson Eddy and Jeanette MacDonald movies were box-office dynamite in the 1930s. Quaintly nostalgic today, at the height of their popularity Eddy and MacDonald were America's singing sweethearts.

Nelson Eddy was the baritone idol of the 1930s. He was born in Providence, R.I., sang in church choirs, worked as a switchboard operator, shipping clerk, and newspaper obituary writer. He was 23 when he started singing with the Philadelphia Civic Opera Company. He appeared in concerts and on radio until MGM signed him to a contract in 1931.

Jeanette MacDonald was born in Philadelphia

in 1907, and appeared in such Broadway shows as *Magic Ring*, Gershwin's *Tip Toes* in 1925, *Bubbling Over* in 1926, and *Angela* in 1928. She was signed by Ernst Lubitsch and Paramount to costar in *The Love Parade* with Maurice Chevalier in 1929. In 1935, MGM signed her to costar in films with Eddy. Their 1st was *Naughty Marietta*, followed by *Rose Marie*, *The Merry Widow*, *Maytime*, *The Girl of the Golden West*, *Sweethearts*, *New Moon*, *Bittersweet*, and *I Married An Angel*. Her other credits included *The Vagabond King* and *Monte Carlo*.

The 2 were considered a perfect team. She did venture outside their typecasting to costar with Clark Gable in *San Francisco*.

When MGM dropped Miss MacDonald's contract option in 1942, Eddy left the studio too. His subsequent credits included *The Phantom of the Opera*, *Knickerbocker Holiday*, and the voice of Willie the Whale in Walt Disney's *Make Mine Music*. His last film was *North West Frontier* with Raymond Massey.

At the height of his popularity, he was not known for his modesty. He was outspoken at all times. One notable quote which did little to endear him to his contemporaries: "I hate actresses. I have to change my phone number weekly to avoid Hollywood parties."

Sadly, in later years, he wasn't in Hollywood to refuse the parties. He was playing supper clubs with Gale Sherwood when, in 1967, he sustained a massive cerebral hemorrhage and died in Miami, Fla. He was survived by his wife Ann.

Miss MacDonald did return to MGM in 1948 to appear in *The Birds and the Bees* and *The Sun Comes Up*. After 1949, she went into semiretirement. In 1965—accompanied by her actor-husband Gene Raymond, whom she had married in 1937—Miss MacDonald went to Houston to undergo open-heart surgery performed by Dr. Michael DeBakey. Earlier that year, he had successfully performed the same operation on the Duke of Windsor. Unfortunately, Miss MacDonald suffered a fatal coronary prior to surgery, at the age of 57.

It is unfortunate that Eddy and MacDonald were so easily and so widely imitated. Their appearance in some old film clips included in MGM's tribute to nostalgia, *That's Entertainment*—released in 1974—automatically elicited some super-critical analysis. Eddy-MacDonald buffs could not care less.

—I.S.

Elvis Presley (1935–). Long sideburns, "DA" haircut, black slacks, suede shoes, sexual gyrations . . . Elvis broke upon the embryonic rock 'n' roll scene like an outlaw, receiving derogatory reviews from adult critics who tagged him "Elvis the Pelvis." Sam Phillips produced Presley's early records on the Sun label in 1954, introducing the ex-truck driver and his combination of country and western with rhythm and blues.

The new rock needed a performer to personify the new sound, and Elvis presented an absolute physical interpretation of his songs. Elvis coordinated the rhythm with twisting legs, quivering hands, and thrusting hips. His facial nuances mirrored lyrics with left lip sneers and lowered eyelids. His vocals were punctuated with breathy embellishments.

Col. Tom Parker, master promoter, signed Elvis to RCA in 1955 and developed the teen-idol image. Elvis was unique: a white man doing black music, and wiggling like the gospel preachers he had watched in Mississippi where he was born on January 8, 1935. A controversy exploded over his sensual movements. Ed Sullivan's TV show censored his appearance, showing him only from the waist up. High schools banned long sideburns, and ministers branded rock 'n' roll as evil. But youth bought the records, a stream of million-selling disks beginning with "Heartbreak Hotel" in 1956, and continuing through to 1961 with "I Can't Help Falling in Love with You." Elvis could not read music, and learned most of his songs from demo records sung by P. J. Proby and written by the team of Jerry Leiber and Mike Stroller. The Jordanaires did vocal backgrounds and his hottest hit records included: "Hound Dog"/ "Don't Be Cruel" (1956); "Blue Suede Shoes" (1956); "Love Me Tender" (1956); "Jailhouse Rock" (1957); "Hard Headed Woman" (1959); and "It's Now or Never" (1960).

Elvis's voice is a high baritone with a 2-octave range. According to Henry Pleasants in *Great American Popular Singers*, Presley's best octave is in the middle, D-flat to D-flat, weak at the bottom, and brilliant at the top.

Elvis made his 1st film in 1956, entered the Army in 1958, and withdrew from public appearances in 1961 to concentrate on 30 movies filled with fighting, dancing, driving, and bikini-clad dollies. Colonel Parker returned Elvis to the public with a 1968 TV Christmas Special to bolster faltering box-office and record sales. His comeback became complete in Las Vegas, where he attained superstar status, while his earlier peers played bar gigs or oldies-but-goodies concerts. He reestablished his recording fame with a Mac Davis song, "In the Ghetto."

Elvis Presley's personal life is kept private. His courteous, lighthearted news conferences contrast with his pugnacious, prankish activities which his payroll buddies called the "Memphis Mafia." He was deeply attached to his mother, who died in 1958. On May 1, 1967, Elvis married Priscilla Beaulieu, and Lisa Marie was born 9 months later. The marriage ended in a 1973 divorce.

Nipsey Russell, the comedian who opened Elvis's 1st show at the Sahara Tahoe, gave his explanation of the essence of the Elvis phenomenon: "Every entertainer should go to bed at night and pray he finds a Col. Tom Parker under his bed when he wakes up in the morning."

—P.A.

Kate Smith (1909–   ). If Kathryn Elizabeth Smith of Greenville, Va., had known about Weight Watchers, the world might never have known about Kate Smith. It was her considerable size, as well as her considerable voice, which made the lady a household word and favorite from the 1920s until the present. She was supposed to become a registered nurse. She never took a singing lesson in her life, and she still can't read music, but she wanted to sing.

Kate Smith has sung "God Bless America" so many times that it is now considered our country's 2nd national anthem. She introduced Bing Crosby to radio audiences on her own show. She was the 1st private citizen to get the American Red Cross Medal of Valor. In 1933, during the Depression, she was making $3,000 a week and was the highest paid woman star in radio.

Ten years later, her astute manager and friend Ted Collins had negotiated a contract that paid her $12,780 for one radio show a week. She was a favorite of soldiers in both World Wars. Although she can legally collect her Social Security, Kate keeps on singing, on records and TV specials.

It all started back in 1924 when Kathryn, whose one and only vice was always eating, asked family permission to enter the Saturday night amateur contests at the Keith Theater in Washington, D.C. She entered 3 and won all 3, a $5 gold piece for each. Finally, there was a bonus, too—a week's appearance at the theater.

Over the protests of her staunchly religious family, Kate persisted and worked the week, taking 2nd billing to comedian Eddie Dowling.

She was on her way, out of Washington to Broadway shows: *Honeymoon Lane* in 1926, *Hit the Deck* in 1929, *Flying High* in 1930. It was during that production that producer George White refused to give her time off to be with her dying father. She never forgave White. But she did meet Ted Collins that same year, a meeting which changed her entire life and made them both very rich people. When *Flying High* closed, Collins became Kate's manager and Pygmalion. In 1932, she made her 1st movie, *Hello Everybody*.

"When the Moon Comes over the Mountain" became her theme song. She accepted fat as her fate. She told one newspaperwoman that because of her size, she believed in dressing simply and being covered up. *All* of her. Even a flash of bare arm was verboten. "I want dignity, always," she insisted.

Show business gossips being what they are, for years there was talk that Kate and Collins had more than just a business arrangement. She overlooked that too. In truth, Collins was much married and had a family of his own. Kate never married.

When Collins died at 63 in 1964, Kate cut back on her own activities, but still enjoys working occasionally with some of her good pals—Perry Como and Tennessee Ernie Ford among them.

Her sign-on and sign-off lines on the radio show epitomized the simplicity and honesty that is Kate Smith: "Hello, everybody," and "Thanks for listenin'." The late President Franklin D. Roosevelt probably said it best when he presented her to Queen Elizabeth and King George VI at the White House in 1939: "Your Majesties, this is Kate Smith. This is America."

—I.S.

17

Eureka!—Science and Technology

Bolts from the Blue: Great Inventions in History

THE INVENTION: Microscope (c. 1590)
THE INVENTOR: Zacharias Janssen, Neth., and/
or Galileo Galilei, Italy

THE INVENTION: Telescope (1608)
THE INVENTOR: Hans Lippershey, Neth.
   One day in 1608 a Dutch spectacle maker named Lippershey held a lens in each hand and peered through both at once, accidentally discovering that 2 lenses placed in line would magnify an image. He mounted a lens at each end of a tube and invented the telescope.

THE INVENTION: Submarine (1620 and onward)
THE INVENTORS: J. P. Holland, Ireland; David Bushnell, U.S.; Robert Fulton, U.S.; Cornelis J. Drebbel, Neth.
   Drebbel, a Dutch inventor, is credited with building the 1st navigable submarine around 1620. It was a rowboat, carefully covered over with leather and operated by a dozen oarsmen whose oars reached the water through flexible leather closures. Drebbel figured out how to produce oxygen from saltpeter, possibly the 1st use of the gas, enabling the boat to remain underwater up to 15 hours.

THE INVENTION: Steam Engine (1698 and on)
THE INVENTORS: Thomas Savery, G.B.; Thomas Newcomen, G.B.; James Watt, G.B.

THE INVENTION: Photography (many dates; 1826 the key date)
THE INVENTORS: Johann H. Schulze, Ger.; Sir Humphry Davy, G.B.; Thomas Wedgwood, G.B.; Joseph Niepce, France; Louis Daguerre, France; et al.
   The world's 1st photograph took 8 hours to develop. Joseph Niepce, a French physicist, coated a pewter sheet with an asphalt solution, put it in an artist's camera obscura, and set it on a windowsill. In 8 hours, he had a sem-

blance of a scene on his French farm. That was in 1826.

THE INVENTION: Balloon (1783)
THE INVENTORS: Jacques E. Montgolfier and Joseph Montgolfier, France
   Hot air from a fire lifted the Montgolfier balloon at Annonay, France, in June of 1783. One story tells that the Montgolfier brothers, paper manufacturers, realized hot air's ability to float a balloon by accident. According to the legend, Jacques' wife washed a petticoat one day and hung it over a small fire to dry. The heat inflated the petticoat and caused it to rise.

THE INVENTION: Steamboat (1787 and on)
THE INVENTORS: James Rumsey, U.S.; John Fitch, U.S.; John Stevens, U.S.; Robert Fulton, U.S.; et al.

THE INVENTION: Sewing Machine (1790 and on)
THE INVENTORS: Thomas Saint, G.B.; Barthélemy Thimonnier, France; Walter Hunt, U.S.; Elias Howe, U.S.; A. B. Wilson U.S.; Isaac M. Singer, U.S.

THE INVENTION: Cotton Gin (1793)
THE INVENTOR: Eli Whitney
   Northerner Eli Whitney was tutoring at Mulberry Grove, the Georgia cotton plantation of General Nathaniel Greene's widow. Mrs. Greene urged Whitney to try to devise something to speed up the picking process. He did—in 10 days, he had constructed a toothed cylinder that grasped the lint as a brush combed out the seeds. Whitney's gin—short for engine—made cotton king in the South.

THE INVENTION: Electric Battery (1800)
THE INVENTOR: Alessandro Volta, Italy

THE INVENTION: Electric Light (1810 and on)
THE INVENTORS: Sir Humphry Davy, G.B.;
Thomas Edison, U.S.; et al.

THE INVENTION: Portland Cement (1824)
THE INVENTOR: Joseph Aspdin, G.B.

THE INVENTION: Reaper (1831)
THE INVENTOR: Cyrus H. McCormick, U.S.

THE INVENTION: Electric Generator (1831)
THE INVENTOR: Michael Faraday, G.B.

THE INVENTION: Electromagnetic Telegraph
(1837)
THE INVENTOR: Samuel F. B. Morse, U.S.

THE INVENTION: Machine Gun (1861)
THE INVENTOR: Richard J. Gatling, U.S.
   When the Civil War broke out, Gatling was
quick to see that an advantage would go to the
North (which had his allegiance even though
he'd been born in North Carolina) if its forces
had a revolving battery weapon capable of
rapid fire. He put 4 years into the effort before
he succeeded, too late for the weapon to be of
effective use in the fast-fading War between the
States.

THE INVENTION: Transatlantic Cable (1866)
THE INVENTOR: Cyrus W. Field, U.S.

THE INVENTION: Motion Pictures (1867 and
on)
THE INVENTORS: Eadweard Muybridge, G.B.;
Thomas Edison, U.S.; Louis and Auguste
Lumière, France; et al.
   Somewhere between 1867 and 1871, Eadweard Muybridge and J. D. Isaacs—to settle a
bet about whether or not a horse's hoofs could
all be off the ground at once in a race—set up
a series of cameras at trackside. Timing devices
made the camera shutters trip in sequence, one
after the other, as the horse galloped past.
Muybridge, an Englishman, performed the experiment in California. He invented a revolving
disk mechanism, called the zoopraxiscope, to
exhibit the photo sequence that showed at
least one equine foot on the ground at all times.

THE INVENTION: Typewriter (1867)
THE INVENTOR: Christopher Sholes, U.S.
   Besides Mark Twain, other early owners of
the typewriter were Henry James and Dr. Sigmund Freud.

THE INVENTION: Telephone (1876)
THE INVENTOR: Alexander Graham Bell, U.S.

THE INVENTION: Kodak Camera (1888)
THE INVENTOR: George Eastman, U.S.

THE INVENTION: X Ray (1895)
THE INVENTOR: Wilhelm Konrad von Roentgen, Ger.

The X ray was discovered by accident. Roentgen, a German physicist, began tracking down
the X ray in 1893 during his experiments with
a Crookes tube. Invented by the British physicist Sir William Crookes, the tube produced
streams of electrons, called cathode rays. Before going to lunch one day, Roentgen put the
activated tube on a book. He failed to notice
the book contained a key and rested on photographic film. When he later developed the
film, he discovered the image of the key. He
had accidentally taken the 1st X ray.

THE INVENTION: Wireless Telegraphy (1896)
THE INVENTOR: Guglielmo Marconi, Italy

THE INVENTION: Dirigible (1900)
THE INVENTOR: Ferdinand von Zeppelin, Ger.

THE INVENTION: The Airplane (1903)
THE INVENTORS: Orville and Wilbur Wright,
U.S.
   The 1st American airplane (aeroplane) was
flown by its inventors, the Wright Brothers,
December 17, 1903, on a sandy beach near
Kill Devil Hills, Kitty Hawk, N.C. The 16-hp,
chain-driven *Flyer I*, with Orville as pilot,
soared 120'—at an airspeed of 30 to 35 mph
and an altitude of 8' to 12'—in its 12-second
maiden flight. The 4th flight that day lasted
59 seconds and spanned 852'.

THE INVENTION: Radio Tube (1904)
THE INVENTORS: Sir John A. Fleming, G.B.;
Lee De Forest, U.S.; Edwin H. Armstrong, U.S.

THE INVENTION: Television (1920 and on)
THE INVENTORS: Vladimir K. Zworykin, Russia and U.S.; Philo T. Farnsworth, U.S.

THE INVENTION: Autogyro (1923)
THE INVENTOR: Juan de la Cierva, Spain

THE INVENTION: Turbojet Engine (1930)
THE INVENTOR: Sir Frank Whittle, G.B.

THE INVENTION: Radar (1935–1940)
THE INVENTORS: Sir Robert Watson-Watt,
G.B.; et al.

THE INVENTION: Xerox (1937)
THE INVENTOR: Chester Carlson, U.S.

THE INVENTION: Nylon (1938)
THE INVENTOR: Dr. Wallace H. Carothers,
U.S.

THE INVENTION: Atomic Bomb (1945)
THE INVENTORS: Enrico Fermi, Italy and
U.S.; Albert Einstein, Ger. and U.S.; J. R.
Oppenheimer, U.S.; et al.
   In 1934, physicist Enrico Fermi, who had
come to the U.S. to escape Fascism in Italy,
bombarded radioactive nuclei and achieved re-
sults he found hard to explain. He seemed to

have created elements that didn't exist naturally. Five years later, when scientists fleeing Nazi Germany brought news that the Germans had achieved nuclear fission using uranium, Fermi realized he had split the uranium atom in 1934. Certainly, for both sides, Albert Einstein's E=MC² theory had shown the way to the atom bomb.

THE INVENTION: Electronic Computer (1946)
THE INVENTORS: Dr. John W. Mauchly, U.S.; J. Presper Eckert Jr., U.S.; J. G. Brainerd, U.S.

American physicist Mauchly led a group of researchers that built the world's 1st electronic computer at the University of Pennsylvania. They called it ENIAC—electronic numerical integrator and computer. Unlike earlier computers, the work was performed by radio tubes —18,000 in total. The $400,000 brain required

a room 30' by 50'. It used 10-digit numbers and could make 5,000 additions a second and perform up to 500 multiplications a second.

THE INVENTION: Polaroid Land Camera (1947)
THE INVENTOR: Edwin H. Land, U.S.

It is said that Land 1st started thinking about the Polaroid camera when his young daughter wanted to see pictures he had just snapped of her. The idea that she would have to wait days for them to be developed upset her so that he wondered why there couldn't be a technique for snapping them and, very shortly thereafter, showing them to the subject.

THE INVENTION: The Transistor (1947)
THE INVENTORS: John Bardeen, U.S.; Walter Brattain, U.S.; William Shockley, U.S.

—N.O. & D.H.

Better Mousetraps—and Other Inventions:
Extraordinary Stories Behind Ordinary Objects
That Had to Be Invented by Someone

"If a man can write a better book, preach a better sermon, or make a better mousetrap, than his neighbor, though he builds his house in the woods, the world will make a beaten path to his door."—Attributed to Ralph Waldo Emerson, from a lecture in San Francisco, 1st published in *Borrowings*, an anthology edited by Mrs. Sarah B. Yule, Oakland, Calif., 1889.

INVENTION: Adding Machine
INVENTOR: Door Eugene Felt, U.S.; William Seward Burroughs, U.S.
YEAR: 1887–1888
HOW INVENTED: Until these 2 years, most accountants and clerks did their calculating with pencil and ledger. Said Felt, "I knew many accountants could mentally add 4 columns of figures at a time, so I decided I must beat that in designing my machines." Felt constructed the 1st key-driven adding-machine model. "It was near Thanksgiving Day of 1884, and I decided to use the holiday in construction of the wooden model. I went to the grocer's and selected a [macaroni] box." Using meat skewers for punch keys, staples for key guides, elastic bands for springs, Felt built his model with a jackknife.

He convinced his employer, Robert Tarrant, to back the invention. In 1887, they became partners in selling the Comptometer, for 15 years "the only multiple order key-driven calculator on the market."

While Felt was creating the more accurate machine, Burroughs was inventing the more marketable one. Burroughs, a mechanic's son who became a mechanic himself, applied for a patent for his Adding and Listing Machine in 1885, obtained the patent 3 years later. At the age of 28, he was vice-president of his own American Arithmometer Company, in St. Louis, Mo. In 1899, Burroughs produced 50 adding machines. However, only he and one field salesman could operate them. The salesman, says *A Computer Perspective*, "operated his so well that he refused to sell it, preferring to haul it from saloon to saloon in a wheelbarrow, betting drinks on its accuracy." Later, when Burroughs invented an automatic device that made his machine readily usable, he went to the storeroom where the original 50 were kept, took them one by one, and heaved them out the window.

INVENTION: Alarm Clock
INVENTOR: Levi Hutchins, U.S.
YEAR: 1787
HOW INVENTED: He was a 26-year-old clockmaker in Concord, N.H., a New Englander with a Yankee conscience. He believed in being at his job on time. It was his "firm rule" to awaken at 4 A.M., whatever the season. But sometimes he slept past that hour, and was distraught the rest of the day. What he wished was a device to rouse him at the exact hour he desired to be up. In past times, people had often depended upon the sun to awaken them.

But in New England, at 4 o'clock in the morning, there was no sun. Then this clockmaker looked at his shelves of clocks and was inspired. As he would write, "It was the idea of a clock that could sound an alarm that was difficult, not the execution of the idea. It was simplicity itself to arrange for the bell to sound at the predetermined hour."

He constructed a pine cabinet 29"×14", transferred the inner mechanism of one of his large brass clocks into it, inserted a pinion or gear. When "the minute hand of the clock reached and tripped the pinion" at 4 o'clock, then the "movement of the pinion set a bell in motion, and the bell made sufficient noise to awaken me almost instantly."

Hutchins lived to the age of 94. He never bothered to patent or mass-produce his alarm clock. He wasn't interested in money. He was just interested in not oversleeping. He achieved his ambition.

INVENTION: Athletic Supporter
INVENTOR: Parvo Nakacheker, Fin.
YEAR: Unknown
How INVENTED: He was a Finnish athlete "who did much of the pioneer work in developing . . . the lowly athletic supporter." To put together an athletic supporter, more commonly called a jockstrap, he "devoted much time to the study of pure anatomy and the special demands of such an item."

INVENTION: Automobile Heater
INVENTOR: Augusta M. Rogers, U.S.
YEAR: Unknown
How INVENTED: This Brooklyn lady patented a heating system not dependent on fire for the interior of automobiles. She also took out patents for an improved auto spark-arrester, a folding chair, a protective canopy to be used against mosquitoes and other insects, all this in a 4-year period.

INVENTION: Automobile Tire, Pneumatic
INVENTOR: John Dunlop, G.B.
YEAR: 1880s
How INVENTED: The Scottish veterinarian, who lived in Belfast, was constantly concerned about the accidents his son had riding his tricycle, with its metal wheels, over the rough cobblestone streets. The wheels would bump, tip the bike, send the lad sprawling. Determined to make the tricycle ride more smoothly, Dunlop got hold of rubber tubes, filled them with compressed air, fitted them on the wheels of the tricycle. Thereafter, the lad found himself "riding on air."

By 1891, the pneumatic tire was being produced by the George R. Bidwell Cycle Company, of New York City. A year later, Alexander T. Brown and George F. Stillman, of Syracuse, N.Y., patented a pneumatic automobile tire for horseless carriages. In 1895, the pneumatic tire was being manufactured by Hartford (Conn.) Rubber Works, and in that year a Duryea race car rode the tires to their 1st victory.

INVENTION: Band-Aids
INVENTOR: Many
YEAR: 1830 to 1874
How INVENTED: In a Philadelphia medical journal, 1830, Samuel D. Gross reported his use of medicated adhesive plasters for body fractures. In 1845, Dr. Horace H. Day and Dr. William H. Shecut, of Jersey City, N.J., patented an adhesive plaster painted with rubber dissolved in a solvent, which was marketed by Dr. Thomas Allcock as Allcock's Porous Plaster. In 1848, Dr. John Parker Maynard, of Dedham, Mass., announced a plaster consisting of a fluid derived from gun cotton dissolved in sulfuric ether, brushed on the skin, covered with cotton strips. In 1874, Robert W. Johnson and George J. Seabury, working in East Orange, N.J., developed a medicated adhesive plaster with a rubber base.

In 1886, Johnson left Seabury to set up his own business, Johnson & Johnson, and his Band-Aids with their rubber base hit the commercial jackpot.

INVENTION: Book Matches
INVENTOR: Joshua Pusey, U.S.
YEAR: 1892
How INVENTED: Pusey, of Lima, Pa., conceived the idea of book matches and took out a patent. More than a half century before, a friction match had been invented that was a single match. Earlier, the only friction match was one of sulfur folded inside sandpaper and quickly yanked out to ignite it. But it was Pusey who put matches in small folding books. Four years after his invention, he sold out his patent to the Diamond Match Company, of Barberton, O. The book matches did not catch on until 1896, when they finally caught fire because a brewery ordered 10 million matchbooks to use for advertising.

INVENTION: Brassiere
INVENTOR: Otto Titzling, U.S.
YEAR: 1912
How INVENTED: Titzling was born in Hamburg in 1884. He died in New York in 1942. His chance for immortality came while he was employed by an uncle making women's undergarments. In 1910, a period of heavy-boned corsets, he heard a young, aspiring opera singer, Swanhilda Olafsen, complain of discomfort and the lack of support corsets gave to her huge breasts. Inspired, he invented a chest halter to provide uplift and shapeliness for her bosom. He introduced the brassiere to the world, making and losing a fortune.

Titzling never received credit for his invention, because he had neglected to patent it. Around 1929, a Frenchman, Philippe de Brassière, a former wartime flying ace and Paris dress designer, moved to New York, took up Titzling's plain chest halters and glamorized them. Titzling sued for infringement, but lost (except for minor damages) because he had no patent. De Brassière's flair for promotion forever made his name immortal as the spurious inventor of the brassiere or bra.

INVENTION: Cash Register
INVENTOR: James J. Ritty, U.S.
YEAR: 1878
How INVENTED: Ritty owned a restaurant in Dayton, O. He felt that he suffered his greatest losses, as did other businessmen, when customers paid their bills. Too often money went from customer to the cashier's pocket. There was no fast, efficient way to record or register incoming money. How to solve the problem? One day, Ritty went on a European vacation. Aboard his transatlantic steamer, he was taken on a tour of the engine room. There he was fascinated by a device that counted the revolutions of the vessel's propeller. In a flash he had the answer to his problem. If a machine could record the turns of a propeller, then certainly there might be a machine to register customers' money paid to a cashier. The moment Ritty landed in Europe, he turned around and went back home. With the help of his brother, he built the machine he had invented in his mind. It consisted of 2 rows of keys to punch out dollars and cents, with an attached dial showing and recording the sum deposited. He named it the "Incorruptible Cashier." It was, in fact, the world's 1st cash register.

Ritty improved his machine, so that it was capable of adding up the entire day's proceeds, and then he marketed it. Sales were slow, and after 2 years he became discouraged and sold his company. Today, a single manufacturer of cash registers in the U.S. sells $300 million worth of machines a year.

INVENTION: Chewing Gum
INVENTOR: Thomas Adams, U.S.
YEAR: 1872
How INVENTED: Actually, long before chewing gum was invented as a product, the Mexican Indians gathered gum from the chicle tree, and tucked pieces in their mouths to keep their cheeks moist when they went on overland treks. Adams, a photographer on Staten Island, N.Y., got hold of a lump of Mexican gum in 1870, and experimented for 2 years trying to create a substitute for rubber. One day he stuck some of this crude gum into his mouth and began to chew it. He liked it. He tried to sell the idea of a chewing gum to a major company, was turned down, and so he began to produce and distribute it himself. Gradually enthusiasm built, and by 1890 Adams had a 6-story chewing-gum factory housing 250 employees—and the chewing-gum craze swept the nation. Upon Adams's death each of his 4 sons inherited a fortune.

INVENTION: Cylinder Lock
INVENTOR: Linus Yale, Jr., U.S.
YEAR: 1861
How INVENTED: The trouble was that while there were locks aplenty, there was not one that couldn't be easily opened with a skeleton key. Then along came Linus Yale, Jr. He lived in Salisbury, N.Y., a failed portrait painter who took up his father's business of lockmaking to survive. He decided that what the world needed was a better lock, a foolproof one that no other key but its own could open. He created the 1st pin-tumbler cylinder lock.

Preparing to move into his own factory in Stamford, Conn., Yale died on Christmas Day, 1868, before he could reap personal profits from his wonder lock. Yale's lock became "the 1st product to be mass-produced in nonidentical form."

INVENTION: Fountain Pen
INVENTOR: Lewis E. Waterman, U.S.
YEAR: 1884
How INVENTED: The 1st patent for a continuously flowing fountain pen was issued in 1830 to one D. Hyde, of Reading, Pa. But it was Waterman who constructed a practical, workable fountain pen. His own firm manufactured these earliest handmade pens, 200 being produced in 1885.

Later, Waterman developed a machine to turn out the pens en masse.

INVENTION: Ice Cream Cone
INVENTOR: Charles E. Menches, U.S., and an anonymous lady friend; Abe Doumar, U.S.
YEAR: 1904
How INVENTED: Menches was an ice cream salesman at the Louisiana Purchase Exposition, the great fair in St. Louis, Mo. Whenever Menches visited a certain lady friend, he brought a bouquet of flowers. On one occasion, for a super date, he brought flowers *and* an ice cream sandwich. Because his lady friend lacked a vase for the flowers, she took one of the sandwich layers and curled it into the form of a vase. Then she rolled the other layer to contain the ice cream itself—and the ice cream cone was born.

The other claimant for the invention was Abe Doumar, of Jersey City, N.J., who also said he had created the ice cream cone at the Louisiana Purchase Exposition. Doumar was selling souvenirs at the fair, when he overheard a vendor complain that he had run out of ice cream dishes halfway through the day. Doumar told the vendor, "Instead of selling a dish of ice cream for 5¢, why don't you make a cornucopia out of a waffle, fill it with ice cream, and sell it for 10¢?" The vendor tried it, and customers clamored for the new cones. Two years later, Doumar set up a stand on Little Coney Island, producing cones from a homemade version of a waffle iron. A year later, Doumar moved to Norfolk, Va., opened Doumar's Ice Cream Parlor, managed it until his death in 1947. Today, his sons dispense cones from the same old stand.

Not until 1924 was a machine invented to mass-produce ice cream cones. In that year, Carl R. Taylor, of Cleveland, O., patented the 1st "machine for spinning or turning a waffle" into a cone.

INVENTION: LP Record
INVENTOR: Peter Goldmark, U.S.
YEAR: 1948
How INVENTED: An employee of the Columbia Broadcasting System, Goldmark invented the 33⅓-rpm record to overcome the interruptions to music made necessary by the constant need to turn over, then change, the old 78 rpm record. He received no royalties.

He is now president of CBS laboratories in Stamford, Conn. In lieu of royalties, he receives free copies of every LP produced by Columbia. Goldmark's LP invention grossed more than $2 billion in the U.S. during 1972.

INVENTION: Margarine
INVENTOR: Hippolyte Mege-Mouries, France
YEAR: 1869
How INVENTED: Because butter was expensive and in short supply, Emperor Napoleon III, of France, sought a cheap, tasty substitute for it. Also, on the eve of the Franco-Prussian War, he needed a butter substitute that would store well on ships. The Emperor sponsored a contest, and offered a prize for the best butter substitute submitted. Mege-Mouries mixed suet fat in water heated at low temperature, and then added milk. He called the resultant product oleomargarine because he thought beef fat possessed fatty margaric acid, which it doesn't. But his nutritious, inexpensive butter substitute won the prize. It became popular in France, spread through Europe, and during a butter shortage in the U.S. during W.W. I, it caught on in the New World as well.

INVENTION: Padded Bra
INVENTOR: D. J. Kennedy, G.B.
YEAR: 1929
How INVENTED: Learning that in the 1928 Oslo, Norway, Olympics, Sweden's foremost female athlete, Lois Lung, had lost the women's 400-meter hurdle when her knee had hit one breast on the last barrier and brought her writhing to the cinder path in pain, Kennedy conceived of a protective or padded brassiere.

Kennedy's Patent No. 324,870 reads: "Breast Pads for protecting the breasts from injuries resulting from athletic sports. The garment combines 2 groups of annular [ring-shaped] rubber tubes of progressively decreasing diameters arranged in conical form and connected to each other so that when the tubes are inflated a connection of air may pass from one breast pad to the other. The 2 sets of tubes are covered with leather." Little could Kennedy know that his invention would thrive not for its use as a safety measure but for its use as the deception popularly known as falsies.

INVENTION: Parking Meter
INVENTOR: Carl C. Magee, U.S.
YEAR: 1935
How INVENTED: He was inspired to develop a curbside money collector that made urban drivers pay for their parking space and provided cities with revenue.

He found the idea difficult to sell, until Oklahoma City, Okla., agreed to install the 1st meters in July, 1935. The meters caught on immediately.

INVENTION: Pencil with Eraser
INVENTOR: Hyman L. Lipman, U.S.
YEAR: 1858
How INVENTED: Until the advent of Lipman, people used separate erasers when writing, drawing, figuring. This Philadelphian conceived the simple idea of combining pencil and eraser in one. His invention offered a pencil with a groove on top into which "a piece of prepared rubber" was glued.

He sold his patent for $100,000.

INVENTION: Refrigerator
INVENTOR: Jacob Perkins, U.S.
YEAR: 1834
How INVENTED: While Perkins invented the 1st mechanical refrigerator, and Albert T. Marshall, of Brockton, Mass., in 1899 patented a household machine with "an automatic expansion-valve for refrigerating apparatus," the prototype of the modern kitchen refrigerator was created by Georg Munters and Baltzar Carl von Platen, of Stockholm, Sweden, in 1926. The patent called for gas and water circulating a refrigerant.

The 1st actual refrigerator based on the Swedes' patent was made and sold by the Electrolux Refrigerator Sales Company, of Evansville, Ind.

INVENTION: Roller Skates
INVENTOR: Dr. James L. Plimpton, U.S.
YEAR: 1863
How INVENTED: Plimpton, of Medfield, Mass., designed the 1st skates using 4 small wheels on each skate. He made $1 million from his patent for these wooden skates. In 1866, Everett H. Barney, of Springfield,

Mass., invented and patented a metal clamp to fasten the shoes of the skater to metal roller skates.

In 1920, Barney's company was bought out by the Winchester Repeating Arms Company.

INVENTION: Safety Pin
INVENTOR: Walter Hunt, U.S.
YEAR: 1825
HOW INVENTED: Hunt, a New York Quaker, was in debt for $15. He had to find the money overnight. He tried to think of new products that were sorely needed. One thing needed was a pin that held separate articles together but did not prick the user. Musing over this problem, Hunt conceived a clasp pin with a guard covering its point. A "safe" pin.

In 3 hours, he worked out a sketch—"The distinguishing features of this invention consist in the construction of a pin made of one piece of wire or metal combining a spring, and clasp or catch, in which the point of said pin is forced, and by its own spring securely retained," explained his patent—and then he produced a tiny model, and sold it outright for $400. He never got another dime for it.

Hunt was a prolific and brilliant inventor. He also invented a repeating rifle, nail-making machine, paper collar, ice plow, dry dock, metal bullet with its own explosive charge—and, in 1832, a sewing machine (limited to sewing only a straight seam for a few inches). He suggested to his daughter she manufacture the sewing machine. When she objected that such a machine would force too many seamstresses out of work, Hunt dropped the idea and never patented it.

INVENTION: Shoelace
INVENTOR: Harvey Kennedy, G.B.
YEAR: Unknown
HOW INVENTED: We don't know. But we do know that he made $2,500,000 on the simple shoelace.

INVENTION: Soda Fountain
INVENTOR: John Matthews, U.S.
YEAR: 1832
HOW INVENTED: According to historian Stewart Holbrook, the 1st fountain "by which soda could be automatically made and dispensed" was invented by Matthews, a Massachusetts brass founder. On the other hand, Joseph N. Kane, the famous 1st facts man, credits the 1st soda fountain patent, registered in 1833, to "Jacob Ebert, of Cadiz, O., and George Dulty of Wheeling, W. Va." Kane credits the 1st ornamented fountain—white Italian marble, adorned with spread eagles—to "Gustavus D.

Dows, of Lowell, Mass., in 1858." Four years later, Dows invented "the double-stream draft arm and cock, which allowed the use of a large or small stream" of soda water.

The ice-cream soda was created by Robert M. Green, a Philadelphia soda fountain maker, who mixed ice cream with soda water and demonstrated the concoction at the Semi-Centennial Celebration in Philadelphia, in 1874. Clergymen inveighed against the frivolous act of "sucking soda" on the Sabbath, and many communities prohibited sales on Sundays. Wily druggists got around the ban by serving ice cream without soda, but with sweet syrup, on Sundays—ergo, the sundae. Another version has it: In Ithaca, N.Y., during 1897, clients of the Ithaca Hotel who quaffed their beer daily at a bar across the street found the bar closed on Sundays. They learned a new refreshment, syrup on ice cream, was being sold on Sundays at the corner drugstore. They named it—the sundae.

INVENTION: Soft Drink
INVENTOR: Joseph Priestley, G.B.
YEAR: 1767
HOW INVENTED: The British clergyman who discovered oxygen concocted the 1st glass of carbonated water. It tasted awful and could not be marketed. Forty years later, in 1807, Townsend Speakman, a Philadelphia, Pa., druggist, took Priestley's carbonated water, mixed fruit flavors with it, and turned out the world's 1st marketed soda pop, which he called Nephite Julep.

INVENTION: Toilet Paper
INVENTOR: Joseph C. Gayetty, U.S.
YEAR: 1857
HOW INVENTED: According to Joseph N. Kane, Gayetty created an "unbleached pearl-colored pure manila hemp paper" and had his name "watermarked on each sheet."

It was marketed and advertised as "Gayetty's Medicated Paper—a perfectly pure article for the toilet and for the prevention of piles." This 1st toilet paper came in 500-sheet packages, selling for 50¢.

INVENTION: Toothbrush
INVENTOR: William Addis, G.B.
YEAR: About 1770
HOW INVENTED: Incarcerated in a cell of England's Newgate Prison for provoking a riot, Addis had little to do but eat, sleep, think. He thought a good deal about some new means of making a living once his sentence was served. One morning, after washing his face, he began to clean his teeth. He cleaned his teeth as most people did in his time—he rubbed a rag against them. Going back to ancient times, this had been the ac-

cepted practice. Aristotle had advised Alexander the Great to use a rag on his teeth. George Washington's dentist had suggested a rag with some chalk on it. Now, using the same method, the imprisoned Addis considered it ineffective. By the following day, he had an idea. He saved a small bone from the meat he'd been served. He bored tiny holes in the bone, then acquired some hard bristles through his prison guard, cut them down, tied them into tufts, put glue on the ends, and wedged them into the holes in the bone. Civilization had its 1st toothbrush.

When he was released from prison, Addis went into the toothbrush-manufacturing business. His success was instantaneous.

INVENTION: Toothpaste Tube
INVENTOR: Dr. Washington Wentworth Sheffield, U.S.
YEAR: 1892
How INVENTED: Until this time, families bought porcelain jars of dental cream, dug their toothbrushes into the jars, and cleaned their teeth. Dr. Sheffield, a dentist in New London, Conn., considered the practice unhygienic and decided to do something about it. He had seen foreign foods packaged in collapsible metal tubes, and he decided to create a flexible tube container for toothpaste. No sooner said than done. Between 1892 and 1900, sales of Dr. Sheffield's Creme Dentifrice boomed. After that, Dr. Sheffield expanded operations to make tubes for dozens of other products.

INVENTION: Tranquilizer
INVENTOR: Robert Robinson, G.B.; Emil Schittler, Switz.
YEAR: 1952
How INVENTED: In 1947, the British biochemist and the Swiss pharmacologist discovered that the powdered root of a shrub from India known as sarpaganda had a quieting effect on troubled persons. They worked 5 years producing a white crystalline chemical from the shrub.

The chemical was marketed as the world's 1st tranquilizer, known as Reserpine.

INVENTION: Trouser Fly
INVENTOR: An Unknown Turk
YEAR: Before the 1700s
How INVENTED: According to Allen Edwardes: "The Turks introduced the fly to Europe between the 18th and 19th century. Its purpose was not only to facilitate urination, but also to facilitate fornication and rape."

It was a button model, which lasted until the introduction of the zipper.

INVENTION: Umbrella
INVENTOR: 6 Persons, G.B.
YEAR: 1700s
How INVENTED: The idea of umbrellas originated among the aristocracy in ancient Egypt. The modern umbrella, with ribs of steel covered by fabric, was created in the late 1700s. For their invention of the ordinary umbrella, the 6 inventors shared $10 million in profits, according to William S. Walsh. On the other hand, Joseph N. Kane has it that the 1st "umbrella is believed to have been used in Windsor, Conn., in 1740. It produced a riot of merriment and derision, the neighbors parading after the user carrying sieves balanced on broom handles."

The common umbrella inspired invention of the parachute.

INVENTION: Vacuum Cleaner
INVENTOR: John S. Thurman, U.S.
YEAR: 1899
How INVENTED: Working out of St. Louis, Mo., he obtained the basic patent for his invention of a "pneumatic carpet renovator," the modern-day, motor-driven, carpet-vacuuming machine.

INVENTION: Zipper
INVENTOR: Whitcomb L. Judson, U.S.
YEAR: 1893
How INVENTED: It was a time of lacing boots and fastening high button shoes. To remove the tedium, to speed things up, Judson was inspired to invent 2 thin metal chains that could be fastened together by pulling a slider up between them. He patented this "clasp locker or unlocker for shoes."

Judson formed the Automatic Hook and Eye Company in Meadville, Pa., in association with a friend, a promoter named Col. Lewis Walker, who thought the crude hookless fastener should not be limited to shoes but should be used to replace all buttons, eyes, hooks. In 1896, together, they put it out as the Universal Fastener. The response was poor. Judson then developed a more simplified fastener, the C-Curity which sold for 35¢ in 1910, for use not on shoes but on men's trouser flies and women's skirts. C-Curity was In-C-Cure.

Finally, Gideon Sunback, an inventive Westinghouse engineer who lived in Hoboken, N.J., joined Judson and Walker. By 1913, Sunback had invented an improved "separable fastener," one with more versatility, and 2 improvements later the Hookless No. 2 showed its 1st profit when the U.S. military ordered a great quantity of them.

And by what magic did yesterday's hookless fastener become transformed into today's zipper? An anonymous executive of the B. F.

Goodrich Co., experimenting with the hookless device, was impressed and praised it as quite a "zipper." The name zipper was immediately adopted and registered, and now we are all C-Cure.

—I.W.

Great Engineering Feats from Early Times to the Present

Man's use of practical technology predated his knowledge of the pure sciences and it was the latter that eventually led to engineering as we know it today. While it is grossly unfair to compare ancient man's efforts to improve on his surroundings with today's successes, a survey of important technological/architectural/construction/engineering progress through the ages will help us view in perspective man's advances up to the present.

298,000 B.C.   Earliest Known Houselike Dwelling
3000 B.C.   Wheeled Transportation Is Realized
2700–2200 B.C.   The Pyramids of Egypt
1800–1450 B.C.   Stonehenge—Man's 1st Celestial Observatory
1000 B.C.   The Qanats of Iran
448 B.C.   The Acropolis, Athens, Greece
300 B.C.   The Great Wall of China
313 B.C.–128 A.D.   The Roman Aqueducts
834 A.D.   The Crank Is Recognized
1000 A.D.   The Ancient City of Angkor, Cambodia
1350 A.D.   The Rope Bridge of San Luis Rey, Peru
1646 A.D.   The Taj Mahal
1725 A.D.   The 1st Successful Steam Engine
1882 A.D.   The Valveless Water Waste Preventer
1883 A.D.   The Brooklyn Bridge
1893 A.D.   The Ferris Wheel
1920 A.D.   The Panama Canal
1931 A.D.   The Empire State Building
1937–1938 A.D.   The Golden Gate Bridge and Boulder Dam
1945 A.D.   The 1st Atomic Bomb Is Detonated
1957 A.D.   Man's 1st Artificial Satellite Orbited
1969 A.D.   Manned Lunar Landing
1975 A.D.   Project Sanguine Nears Operation

298,000 B.C. (*Earliest Known Houselike Dwelling*). A Paleolithic nomadic hunting camp, uncovered by excavators preparing a new building site near Nice, France, has proved to be the earliest example yet found of man's effort to protect himself from his environment. The structures, built 300,000 years ago, were evidently made by wandering hunters who annually visited the Mediterranean shoreline. Artifacts left behind, and plant pollen found at the site, have helped archaeologists date the huts these early hunters lived in. Their oval shelters, ranging from 26' to 49' in length, and from 13' to 20' in width, were built of 3"-diameter stakes set as a palisade in the sand, braced on the outside by a ring of stones. Larger poles were set up along the hut's longer axis to support the roof. A basic feature of each hut is a centrally placed hearth, complete with windscreens built of pebbles.

3000 B.C. (*Wheeled Transportation Is Realized*). Man had lived on earth for centuries before necessity caused him to create the wheel, a device which enabled him to move heavy loads over long distances. The earliest examples of wheeled vehicles were little more than sleds with 2 attached solid wheels, but this was an enormous improvement over dragging. Early examples of these wheeled vehicles were found within a region between Lake Van in eastern Asia Minor and Lake Urmia in northern Iran, an area no more than 1,200 mi. across. This evidence indicates that these wheeled vehicles emerged more than 5,000 years ago, during the final centuries of the 4th Millennium. The remains of later vehicles, both carts and wagons, often survive as nothing more than stains in the soil, such as those found in the royal tombs at Kish and Ur, in Mesopotamia. Evidence was found during the mid-1960s in the region between the Black and Caspian seas of the U.S.S.R. that disk-wheeled vehicles flourished during the Kura-Araxes culture, beginning about 3000 B.C. Here pottery models of vehicles with well-marked, hubbed, disk wheels were found that were identical to the vehicles buried at a later date in Kish and Ur. Based on this evidence, Russia, not Mesopotamia, appears to have fostered man's tentative love affair with the wheel, a love affair that has endured throughout the ages.

2700–2200 B.C. (*The Pyramids of Egypt*). Nothing in the world has involved man's imagination and his energies more completely than the 70-odd pyramids built by the Eygptians between 2700 B.C. and 2200 B.C. The 1st pyramid was ordered built by King Joser of the 3rd Dynasty in Memphis, an area across the Nile and 12 mi. upstream from modern-day Cairo. King Joser's architect-engineer was Imhotep, who was also a physician, writer, statesman, and magician. The greatest of the pyramids was built in 2580 B.C. by King Khufu. This monument is 480' high, 748' square, and contains 2,300,000 blocks of limestone weighing 2½ tons each. Except for the Great Wall of China, it was the largest single ancient structure. The last of the pyramids of this era were built about 2200 B.C. Using only the crudest tools of wood, stone, copper, and brass, these ancient Egyptians succeeded in quarrying, moving, and raising immense slabs of limestone and granite weighing up to 30 tons apiece.

1800–1450 B.C. (*Stonehenge—Man's 1st Celestial Observatory*). This ancient monument located on Salisbury Plain in Wiltshire, England, remained a mystery to modern man until 1963, when Gerald S. Hawkins of the Smithsonian Astrophysical Observatory suggested that these monoliths were remnants of an astronomical calendar. (See also: Mysterious Happenings in History, Chap. 29.)

1000 B.C. (*The Qanats of Iran*). Three thousand years ago the ancient Persians learned how to bring water to dry valleys by using an ingenious system of underground channels—called qanats—that is still being used in modern Iran. In fact, these qanats provide 75% of the water used there today. These underground aqueducts are still hand-dug by Muqanni who sink vertical shafts to subsurface water-bearing aquifers sometimes 1,000′ deep. Precisely aligned horizontal shafts, which serve as aqueducts, connect the vertical shafts to a mouth which opens into a canal for irrigation or transportation of future drinking water. Several vertical shafts are sunk along the line to provide ventilation and a means to raise excavation materials. Dirt is piled around the entrance of each shaft to act as a retainer to prevent potentially eroding rainwater from cascading into the system, and thus destroying it. From the air, the dirt around each hole looks like a giant anthill. There are 22,000 qanat units in Iran, comprising more than 170,000 mi. of underground channels.

448 B.C. (*The Acropolis, Athens, Greece*). The epitome of European civilization is said to have been reached by the Greeks when they built their Acropolis in Athens. Acropolis—Greek for "upper city"—was the ancient term for any citadel, and the Greeks built many of them. The most famous, however, because of its majestic temples, with their perfectly proportioned shrines lifting great colonnades of gleaming marble, is located in Athens. This citadel, topping a 260′-high hill, had been used for centuries (from at least the Neolithic period some 4,000 years ago), but it was razed by the Persians in 480 B.C. By 448 B.C., Pericles, the military commander and ruler of Athens, commissioned a rebuilding of the city. The 1st new building of splendor was the Parthenon, followed by the Erechtheum, the Propylaea, the Temple of Nike (Victory), and others. Even in ruin, the beauty of the Acropolis of Athens is evident today. The buildings there stand as perhaps the pinnacles of classical symmetry and elegant beauty.

300 B.C. (*The Great Wall of China*). Extending 1,500 mi., the Great Wall of China is about 50′ high, 26′ wide at the base, and 16′ wide at the top. At one time, there were at least 40,000 watchtowers strung out along the length of this barrier. Calculations have shown that the wall was constructed of almost 400 million cubic yards of material, enough to build 120 pyramids equal in size to King Khufu's great pyramid in Egypt. This same quantity of material could be used to build a wall 6′ high around the world at the equator. Although not conceived initially as a single continuous wall, additions to the original fortifications continued until 1646 A.D., when the present version of the Great Wall was completed. During the peak of construction, every 3rd male Chinese was conscripted to labor in building it. The toll in lives due to severe weather, exhaustion, and starvation numbered in the hundreds of thousands, a high price to pay for a fortification that never really provided security.

313 B.C.–128 A.D. (*The Roman Aqueducts*). Long regarded by practicing engineers as brilliant engineering feats, the Roman aqueducts, spanning a useful life of some 440 years, are still very much in evidence today, although few, if any, continue to convey water. The Romans built over 200 aqueducts throughout their provinces, which stretched from France to Spain, and from Greece to Asia Minor. The 1st recorded aqueduct was built by the censor Appius Claudius Crassus (later Caecus) in 313 B.C. It was an underground supply approximately 10½ mi. long. The 2nd aqueduct followed 30 years later, in 283 B.C. It wasn't until 145 B.C., however, that the Marcia, the "Pride of Rome," was built. This was the 1st high-water aqueduct. Originating in the Anio Valley above Tivoli, Marcia stretched for 58 mi., but was supported by graceful Roman arches for only 6 mi. It was the widest and highest of all Roman single-tiered aqueducts. The aqueducts of the Romans often were added onto in succeeding years, so that a triple-tiered channel was the final result. The tallest of these is 160′ high and was built in 19 A.D. near Nîmes, France. When the aqueducts were at the height of their use, the Roman per capita water consumption approximated 38 gallons per day. This consumption figure is high even for today when it is compared with some European cities, but is low compared to consumption in the U.S., which is approximately 150 gallons per person per day. Although the Romans

engineered their aqueducts superbly, they were not watertight (portland cement wasn't invented until 1820 A.D.), which eventually caused them to fall into disrepair and decay. The last Roman aqueduct was built in 128 A.D. By the 6th century A.D., only a few of Rome's neglected aqueducts conveyed anything but crumbling beauty.

834 A.D. (*The Crank Is Recognized*). The crank as we know it today is a twice-bent lever or "crankshaft" used as a means of converting reciprocating motion into continuous rotary action. It was, however, unknown to the Romans, and remained unknown until around 834 A.D. when a picture of it appeared in the Utrecht Psalter, a graphic codex assembled near Reims in the Frankish kingdom under the Carolingian kings (Charlemagne was the greatest of these kings). The picture in the Psalter shows a grindstone wheel being turned by a hand crank, a familiar-enough sight today, but almost a "1st" in 834 A.D. It appears that while the Chinese of the Han Dynasty, contemporaries of the Romans, knew of the cranking device, it was reinvented in the Western world by a Frank. The 2nd known use of the crank in the West was with the hurdy-gurdy (originally a stringed musical instrument that was hand-cranked). In the history of machine design, the simple crank is 2nd in importance only to the wheel.

1000 A.D. (*The Ancient City of Angkor, Cambodia*). The largest city in the world 1,000 years after Christ was Angkor, Cambodia, discovered buried in the jungle by the French naturalist Henri Mouhout in 1858. Built to accommodate a population of over one million people (larger than the Rome of 1000 A.D.), by the Hindu Khmer Empire that reigned until approximately 1100 A.D., the city covered almost 30 sq. mi. An agricultural people, the Khmers lived chiefly on rice, and built 2 huge reservoirs to impound water for irrigating their crops. Each of these reservoirs contained over 2 billion gallons of water. Water played an important role in the lives of the residents of Angkor, as they used it not only for agriculture, sanitation, and sustenance, but also for protection. The ancient city was completely surrounded by a water-filled moat. The Khmer Empire covered all of present-day Cambodia, as well as parts of Thailand, Laos, Burma, and Vietnam. No one knows what caused this flourishing city to be abandoned to the jungle.

1350 A.D. (*The Rope Bridge of San Luis Rey*). For those who actually saw it, the hand-woven rope bridge of San Luis Rey, in Peru, was a spectacular tribute to a primitive people. While the Peruvian Incas under the great chief Roca amazed Westerners with their building feats, the bridge of San Luis Rey which crossed the Apurimac River surpassed them all. Suspended 118' above a raging river, and stretching 148' from bank to bank, the Apurimac-Chaca builders, who had no knowledge of the arch, perfected the principles of the catenary suspension bridge by reversing the arch curve. The bridge hung from rope cables, hand-twisted from the fibers of the maguey plant to "the thickness of a man's body." A unique self-tightening suspension device was used on one end of the bridge to take up the slack and keep the cables taut. The bridge was so well-built and well-maintained that it lasted over 500 years, the cables being renewed every 2 years or oftener. Not until the introduction of the wheel by the Spaniards (the Incas never did invent the wheel) did this footbridge fall into disuse. The beautiful bridge that spawned Thornton Wilder's literary masterpiece *The Bridge of San Luis Rey* collapsed and died in 1890.

1646 A.D. (*The Taj Mahal*). The "most beautifully perfect building in the world" is a phrase accorded to the Taj Mahal by all who visit it. Built in 1646 by Shah Jahan, the 5th Emperor of the Mogul Dynasty, in memory of his recently deceased wife Mumtaz-i-Mahal, the Taj Mahal was constructed by artisans gathered from all over the world. For 17 years, 20,000 or more workers labored over one of the most beautiful shrines known to man. The Taj Mahal is made of gleaming white marble, which rests on an 8-sided platform of red sandstone measuring 130' long on each side. A slender minaret 133' high stands at each corner of the platform. The building itself is 186' square, and is topped by a shining white dome 70' in diameter and 120' high.

1725 A.D. (*The 1st Successful Steam Engine*). In 1663 the Marquis of Worcester published a book entitled *Century of Inventions* in which he described an apparatus for pumping water. It was never built. In 1698, one Thomas Savery patented the marquis' idea, but the device proved only a novelty. Thomas Newcomen, meanwhile, was working on a similar but more complicated version, based on an idea by Denis Papin. Papin's idea was that if a cylinder with a fitted piston were filled with steam, and then the steam was rapidly condensed, a vacuum would result and this would allow atmospheric pressure to close the cylinder. After 10 years of experimentation, Newcomen constructed a successful working model. He sold his 1st engine to John Bate and Company of Connygree Colliery at Tipton in Staffordshire, England, where he constructed the engine in situ utilizing carpenters, blacksmiths, plumbers, and masons from the immediate area. In 1725, his engine became successfully operational, lifting 3 million lbs. of water one foot on one bushel of coal.

Within a few decades, the Industrial Revolution was born, based on improved, more efficient versions of Thomas Newcomen's engine.

1882 A.D. (*The Valveless Water Waste Preventer*). In 1882, the Metropolis Water Act, in London, England, came into being, unifying 8 separate water companies. Because the cisterns for toilets (or water closets) of the age employed only an on-off valve an enormous quantity of the city's precious water was being wasted. The responsible ministry, therefore, asked the plumbers in London to develop a positive watertight water closet system. Thomas Crapper came to the rescue with the invention of his water waste preventer, or as it later became known, Crapper's Valveless Water Preventer. His success in stemming the tide resulted in his being knighted and he became Sir Thomas Crapper. American soldiers visiting England in W.W. I were delighted with Crapper's device, which of course had his name emblazoned upon it. Returning to the U.S., doughboys delighted in describing Crapper's wonder. His name has been immortalized in American toilet slang ever since.

1883 A.D. (*The Brooklyn Bridge*). The Brooklyn Bridge—cost approximately $15 million—was described as the "8th wonder of the world" when it was completed on May 24, 1883. The longest suspension bridge of its time, spanning the East River in New York between Brooklyn and Manhattan (1,595' between towers), it was designed and initially surveyed by John A. Roebling, a famous bridge builder of the 1880s. When he died from complications resulting from a crushed foot, his son Washington A. Roebling picked up where his father left off. While inspecting the excavations for the bridge foundations, young Roebling was hit by caisson disease, a form of the bends named after the caissons used to keep out water during excavations. Crippled for life and confined to his wheelchair, Washington Roebling continued as chief engineer on the bridge and directed its construction by using field glasses from the window of his apartment located several blocks away.

1893 A.D. (*The Ferris Wheel*). In the 1889 Paris Exposition, Alexandre Gustave Eiffel achieved worldwide fame with his 1,052'-high all-steel tower that weighed 7,728 tons. It was no surprise, then, that the promoters of the 1893 World's Columbian Exposition to be held in Chicago wanted some-

thing just as attractive as Eiffel's Tower. But what could surpass that engineering marvel? George Washington Gale Ferris had the solution. He proposed constructing the largest wheel ever built, suspended in the air on 140'-high towers, designed to accommodate 36 gondolas carrying 40 passengers each. The largest wheel at that time had been constructed on the Isle of Man, and it was 72'6" in diameter. Ferris's wheel was to be 250' in diameter. To construct the axle, the Bethlehem Iron Company forged steel into a 45'6"-long, 33"-diameter cylinder weighing 56.5 tons, the largest single piece of steel forged in the U.S. up to that date. The gondolas were 24' long, 13' wide, 10' high, and weighed 13 tons apiece. It took 2 1,000-hp steam engines to turn the gigantic apparatus. Although a larger wheel was eventually constructed some 300' in diameter, in London in 1897, the Ferris wheel was unique for its time and it still retains the original builder's name.

1920 A.D. (*The Panama Canal*). President Woodrow Wilson proclaimed the official opening of the Panama Canal on July 12, 1920, after 42 frustrating years of trying to link the Atlantic and Pacific oceans. A Frenchman, Ferdinand de Lesseps, the builder of the Suez Canal, was the 1st to try to dig a canal through the Isthmus of Panama. Disease, corruption, and a lack of equipment forced De Lesseps's company into bankruptcy in 1889 after excavating 76 million cubic yards of earth. Then, on November 6, 1903, Panama and the U.S. signed the Hay-Banau-Varilla Treaty, allowing the U.S. to build the Canal, and to operate it forever. The greatest obstacle to building the Canal was disease. Col. William C. Gorgas of the U.S. Army instituted a successful campaign that all but eliminated that problem before U.S. excavation began. With disease under control, Col. George W. Goethals of the U.S. Army Corps of Engineers headed the construction team that overcame the physical obstacles: excavating the Gaillard Cut; damming the Chagres River; and constructing the 3 sets of double locks that would raise and lower the ships as they passed through the 50.72-mi.-long Canal. The main work on the Canal was completed in 1914 after removing over 211 million cubic yards of earth; expending about $380 million ($310 million for actual construction; $20 million for sanitation; $40 million paid to the original French companies; and $10 million paid to Panama for rights); and employing more than 43,400 persons (at the height of activity in 1913). Clean-up operations and minor problems, however, held off the official opening until July 12, 1920. Approximately 12,000 oceangoing vessels now pass through the Canal yearly, almost 35 a day. The record of 14,807 ship transits was set in 1968. Self-supporting, the Panama Canal charges revenues according to a ship's tonnage. The most money ever charged by the Canal for a ship's passage was $30,446 for the supertanker U.S.S. *Orion Hunter* in 1962. The smallest charge was 45¢ to swimmer Albert H. Oshiver, who swam through the locks in December, 1962. Each lock in the Canal system is 1,000' long, 110' wide, and 70' deep, allowing almost all ships but the U.S. Navy supercarriers to pass. The largest ship to sail through the Canal was the S.S. *Bremen*, with a length of 899', a beam of 101.9', a draught of 48.2', and a gross tonnage of 51,730.

1931 A.D. (*The Empire State Building*). Until December 14, 1970, the Empire State Building in New York City was the world's tallest inhabited structure, a reigning queen for almost 40 years. The tallest structure built since the construction of the Eiffel Tower, the Empire State Building proper reached a 1,250' height, while a 220' television antenna raised that height to 1,472'—over a quarter of a mile. Completed in 1931, the building contains 6,500 windows, 1,860 steps to the 102nd floor, 60 mi. of water pipes, and 10,000 tenants. Each year 1.5 million persons visit the building's 2 observatories, located on the 86th and 102nd floors. So named because New York is known as the Empire State, the famous queen is now surpassed by New York's World Trade Center Towers (with antenna 1,718'). The tallest man-made structure of all, however, is the antenna tower of television station KTHI-TV, located between Blanchard and Fargo, in North Dakota. This tower is 2,063' tall, and was constructed in 30 days at a cost of $500,000. The Empire State Building was built at a cost of $40,948,900, while the World Trade Center was completed at a cost of $650 million in 1973.

1937–1938 A.D. (*The Golden Gate Bridge and Boulder Dam*). The 1930s in the U.S. witnessed a great surge of engineering effort that resulted in the production of 2 of America's famous landmarks, both monumental engineering feats of their age: the Golden Gate Bridge spanning the entrance to San Francisco's great harbor, and Boulder Dam (now renamed Hoover Dam) that spans the Colorado River near Las Vegas, Nev.

The Golden Gate Bridge is one of the largest and most spectacular suspension bridges in the world. It spans a distance of 4,200' between towers (one of the longest spans on record), and cost $35 million when it was built by Joseph B. Strauss. It is now surpassed by the 4,260' span of the Verrazano-Narrows Bridge crossing the entrance to New York harbor. This bridge, built by Othmar H. Ammann, had cost $305 million by the time it was completed in 1964.

Boulder Dam was one of man's most imposing engineering feats, and it still ranks today as one of the world's great dams. Designed and built by the U.S. Bureau of Reclamation, the entire project cost $385 million (the dam itself cost $120 million). When completed, it was the world's highest dam (726'), the world's largest dam (4,400,000 cubic yards of concrete), and it had created one of the greatest of man-made lakes in Lake Meade, 115 mi. long and 589' deep. It can store 32,300,000 acre-feet of water, and produce 1,345 megawatts of power. It has, however, been surpassed many times in ensuing years. The current record holders are: Nurek in the U.S.S.R. at 1,017' high; Torbela in Pakistan, containing 186 million cubic yards of material; and the Grand Coulee Dam in the State of Washington, which has produced 9,771 megawatts at its peak load.

1945 A.D. (*The 1st Atomic Bomb Is Detonated*). The development of a new source of domestic energy, utilizing uranium fission, was urged by President Franklin Delano Roosevelt as early as 1939. It took the entry of the U.S. into W.W. II after the Japanese attack on Pearl Harbor, however, to give priority emphasis to using this same source of energy in a fission bomb of superlative destructive power. Advances in technology, discovery of new elements, and unheard-of international scientific cooperation had to occur on several fronts in order to create a sustained chain reaction of uranium-235 successfully. New technology was developed. Five new elements were discovered: neptunium (element No. 93); plutonium (No. 94); americium (No. 95); curium (No. 96); and berkelium (No. 97). Modern technology had done something alchemists had striven to do for centuries—transform one element into another. It has been written that "the technological gap between producing a chain reaction and using it as a large-scale power source . . . is comparable to the gap between the discovery of fire and the manufacture of a steam locomotive." Under the pressure of war, this gap was closed in 3 years. Much more had to be achieved, though, and was. At a cost of $2 billion, the 1st nuclear bomb was exploded 120 mi. southwest of Albuquerque, N. Mex., on July 16, 1945, ushering in mankind's most devastating weapon.

1957 A.D. (*Man's 1st Artificial Satellite Orbited*). Sir Isaac Newton, in his *Mathematical Principles of Natural Philosophy* (*Philosophiae naturalis principia mathematica*), published in 1687, explained the dynamics of artificial satellites, but it was 270 years before man could put Newton's theories into practice. On October 4, 1957, the U.S.S.R. successfully launched a spherical satellite weighing 183.4 lbs. that they called *Sputnik* (Russian for "fellow traveler"). Designed by Dr. Sergei Pavlovich Korolyov, the satellite elliptically orbited earth from an apogee of 588 mi. to a perigee of 142 mi. It remained in orbit approximately 92 days, and is thought to have reentered earth's atmosphere and disintegrated on January 4, 1958. (See also: Other Highlights in World History, Chap. 8.)

1969 A.D. (*Manned Lunar Landing*). Neil Alden Armstrong achieved man's greatest engineering and technological triumph of the century when he stepped from the Lunar Module *Eagle* onto the moon's Sea of Tranquility on July 21, 1969. (See also: Highlights of World History, Chap. 8.)

1975 A.D. (*Project Sanguine Nears Operation*). The world's largest electronic communication system, a U.S. Navy-planned Extremely Low Frequency (ELF) facility capable of radio-contacting submerged submarines 200' underwater, is near operational status at several sites within the U.S. after 6 years of research and development. The planned system will probably be located at only one site, but will be able to communicate instantaneously with deep-running missile-carrying submarines in case of extreme national disaster. Utilizing deeply buried cables (able to withstand nuclear attack) spread in a grid covering approximately 1,250 sq. mi., the communications network will send radio waves 2,500-mi.-long that appear in the 45 to 75 Hz frequency range. In this system, sited in specially selected rock and ground formations, the earth acts as a conductor, with the rock formations forcing the radio waves outward into the ionosphere instead of inward toward the earth's core. The saturation of the ionosphere forces some of these ELF's underwater to a considerable depth, enabling submerged submarines, carrying Polaris or Poseidon missiles, to receive and react to messages even if normal communication channels should be destroyed in a preemptive attack.

—W.W.C.

Gallery of Famous and Infamous Scientists

ARCHIMEDES (287 B.C.–212 B.C.).

Archimedes, the most celebrated mechanician of antiquity, was born in Syracuse, Sicily. He was so far in advance of his age, that his principles did not become established until the 15th century. He invented the Archimedean screw which has been applied to drainage and irrigation projects, and he also explained the theory of the lever.

He discovered what is known as the law of specific gravity, or the truth that any body weighs just as much less when held under water as the weight of the water which it crowds out of place.

Hiero, King of Syracuse, having suspected a goldsmith of putting some other metal than gold in his crown, asked Archimedes to ascertain whether it were so. Archimedes, while thinking over the matter one day, got into his bath, which chanced to be full to the brim; and he saw at once, that as much water must run over the edge of the tub as was equal to the bulk or size of his body. He then saw that if he put the crown into a vessel, and weighed the water which overflowed, and then tried a piece of pure gold equal in size to the crown in the same way, the water overflowed by the pure gold ought to equal in weight that of the crown if it also were of pure gold. He was so overjoyed at this discovery, that he ran home without waiting to put on his clothes, crying through the streets, "Eureka! Eureka!" ("I have found it! I have found it!")

He defended his native Syracuse against the Romans with great mechanical skill, inventing machines which lifted their ships out of the water, and let them drop with so much force that they sank. He also burned their ships by concentrating on them the rays of the sun with mirrors. The most celebrated of his mathematical works are those of the sphere and cylinder, which he requested should be inscribed upon his tombstone.

When Syracuse was taken, a Roman soldier entered his studio, and found him so busily at work, that he did not even know that the enemy had entered the gates. Marcellus, the Roman general, had given strict orders to his soldiers not to hurt Archimedes, and had offered a reward to whoever should bring him safe to him. The soldier ordered Archimedes to come with him; and, upon his refusing to do so, he killed him, to the grief of Marcellus, who ordered for Archimedes an honorable burial, and built a monument over his grave inscribed as he had desired.

It was Archimedes who declared that, if he could find a lever long enough, and a prop strong enough, he could, single-handed, move the world.

—S.H.K. rep.

JOHN BARTRAM (1699–1777).

Linnaeus, the father of botany, called John Bartram "the greatest natural botanist in the world," but today Bartram is largely unhonored in his own country.

Like Benjamin Franklin, his friend and benefactor, Bartram was a self-educated man. Legend has it that he decided to become a botanist late in his life, while plowing the fields on his farm outside Philadelphia. Bartram, the story goes, stopped to rest for a few moments beneath a huge oak and picked a daisy growing at the base of the tree. Plucking the petals from the flower and dissecting it, he began wondering about the mysterious processes of nature. For several days after the incident, he fought the notion of forsaking farming and devoting his life to science, but finally he could resist no more and rode into Philadelphia. There a bookseller sold him a botanical treatise in Latin and a Latin grammar with which to translate it.

The story may be apocryphal, although Bartram himself often told it, but there's little doubt that the honest plowman could barely read and write and had no knowledge of foreign languages when he made his choice. Teaching himself, reading while he wandered the countryside, his keen eye and sense of the unusual soon enabled him to secure the patronage of several Europeans, to whom he supplied New World plant specimens. It wasn't long before he was able to buy another farm on the Schuylkill in Philadelphia, which was closer to the intellectual capital of the time and where he later entertained Franklin and Washington, among other American notables.

Bartram is indisputably the 1st native American botanist and although his weak grasp of theory made it impossible for him to become one of history's great scientists, his determination and energy did indeed make him the greatest of "natural" botanists. None of Linnaeus's correspondents furnished the Swedish giant with such an abundance of original material. Bartram was the 1st in America to travel through the Colonies seeking samples for classification. His travels brought to light the spice bush and sassafras, the insectivorous plants of the South, the tulip tree, the American lotus, and the American cyclamen, to mention just a few discoveries.

It was in his mysterious valley or "great vale," what he called "my Kashmir," that Bartram made his most important finds. The uninhabited valley, 200 mi. long and set between mountain ranges, was kept secret by the botanist and for many years only he knew of the treasures that abounded in its flower-filled rifts. Today we know his vale as the Shenandoah.

Bartram's most amazing discovery was the Franklin tree (*Gordonia alatamaha*), which still continues to amaze later generations of botanists. On an autumn expedition in Georgia, he came upon the tree in full flower, its gorgeous blossoms astonishingly similar to the bloom of the tropical and oriental camellia plant. Bartram brought the tree back to his garden in Philadelphia, where he named it in honor of his friend Benjamin Franklin. But try as they have, scientists have never again been able to find the Franklin tree growing in the wild. All of the few Franklins growing in American gardens have been propagated from cuttings taken from the original tree Bartram found over 2 centuries ago.

Honors were heaped upon John Bartram in his own time, though his genius is much neglected today. A gold cup came from the founder of the British Museum, a gold medal from an Edinburgh society. Bartram also corresponded with Queen Louisa of Sweden and her brother Frederick the Great. "With him," someone has written, "Nature was a personal affair, a direct impact like weather on a bird." His life was that simple and graceful.

John Bartram died at 78, but his son William continued in his footsteps, further insuring the Bartram name a place in history with important discoveries like the flame azalea of the Blue Ridge Mountains. It is said that Bartram's death was brought on by the fear he felt at the approach of the British Army—the old man was sure that the troops would ravage his botanical garden, the 1st of its kind in America. Today the master plantsman's house and garden can be seen in Philadelphia, where his farm is now part of Fairmount Park.

—R.H.

WILLIAM HORATIO BATES (1860–1931).

William Horatio Bates exerted a vast influence on thousands of people with serious eye defects during the early 1900s with his belief that glasses were simply "eye crutches" and should be tossed away. Today his system of "eye relaxation" is generally considered to be useless and his theories unscientific quackery. He was, nevertheless, the 1st important figure in the modern cult of replacing spectacles with eye exercises for the treatment of visual defects.

Born in Newark, N.J., Bates graduated from Cornell in 1881 and received his medical degree from the College of Physicians and Surgeons in 1885. He was a clinical assistant at Manhattan Eye and Ear Hospital and attending physician at Bellevue Hospital and later at the New York Eye Infirmary. From 1886 to 1891, Bates, an eye, ear, nose, and throat specialist, taught ophthalmology at the New York Postgraduate Medical School and Hospital.

Then began a series of mysterious events. In 1902, he disappeared. Several months later, his wife learned he was working in a London hospital. When she joined him, she found him in a state of exhaustion with no memory of what had happened. Two days later, he van-

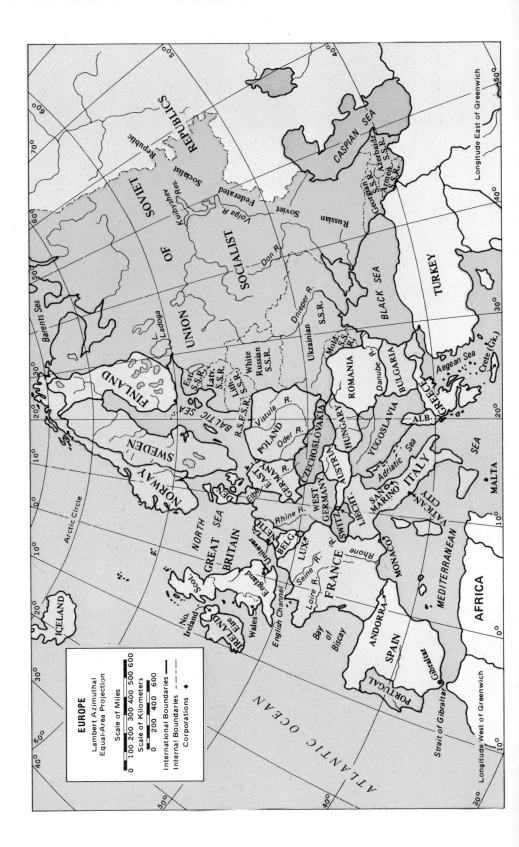

EUROPE

Lambert Azimuthal
Equal-Area Projection

Scale of Miles
0 100 200 300 400 500 600

Scale of Kilometers
0 200 400 600

International Boundaries
Internal Boundaries ---
Corporations ◆

ATLANTIC OCEAN

ICELAND

NORWAY
SWEDEN
FINLAND

Barents Sea

L. Ladoga

UNION OF SOVIET SOCIALIST REPUBLICS

Kuibyshev
Volga R.
Soviet Federated Socialist Republic

Russian
Don R.
Dnieper R.

R.S.F.S.R.
Est. S.S.R.
Latv. S.S.R.
Lith. S.S.R.
White Russian S.S.R.
Ukrainian S.S.R.
Mold. S.S.R.

CASPIAN SEA
Georgian S.S.R.
Azerbaidz. S.S.R.
Armen. S.S.R.

BALTIC SEA
POLAND
Vistula R.
Oder R.

NORTH SEA
GREAT BRITAIN
Scot.
No. Ireland
IRELAND
Eire
Wales
England
English Channel

DEN.
NETH.
BELG.
LUX.
EAST GERMANY
WEST GERMANY
CZECHOSLOVAKIA
AUSTRIA
HUNGARY
SWITZ.
LIECHT.
Elbe
Rhine R.

FRANCE
Seine R.
Loire R.
Rhône
Bay of Biscay

ANDORRA
SPAIN
PORTUGAL
Gibraltar
Strait of Gibraltar

MONACO
SAN MARINO
VATICAN CITY
ITALY

ROMANIA
Danube R.
YUGOSLAVIA
BULGARIA
ALB.
GREECE
Adriatic Sea
Aegean Sea
Crete (Gk.)
BLACK SEA
TURKEY

MEDITERRANEAN SEA
MALTA
SEA

AFRICA

Arctic Circle

Longitude West of Greenwich
Longitude East of Greenwich

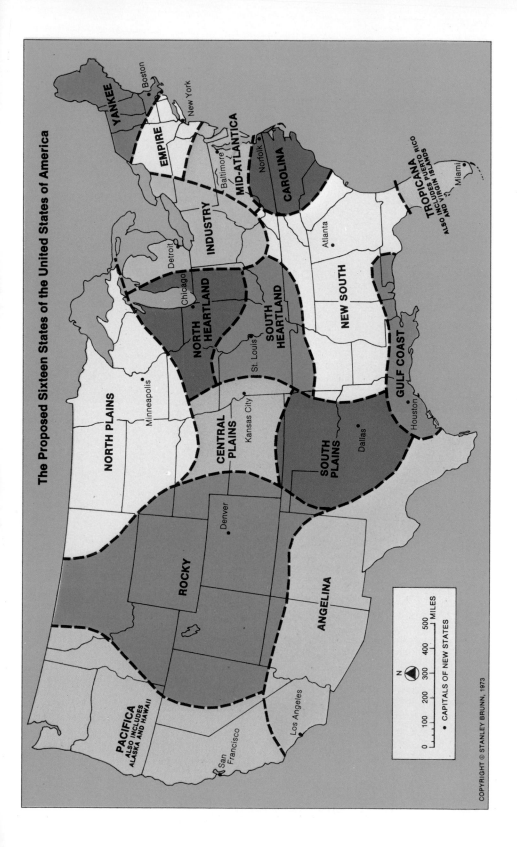

The Proposed Sixteen States of the United States of America

YANKEE
Boston
New York
EMPIRE
MID-ATLANTICA
Baltimore
Norfolk
CAROLINA
TROPICANA ALSO INCLUDES PUERTO RICO AND VIRGIN ISLANDS
Miami
INDUSTRY
Detroit
Atlanta
NEW SOUTH
Chicago
NORTH HEARTLAND
SOUTH HEARTLAND
St. Louis
GULF COAST
NORTH PLAINS
Minneapolis
Houston
CENTRAL PLAINS
Kansas City
SOUTH PLAINS
Dallas
Denver
ROCKY
ANGELINA
Los Angeles
PACIFICA ALSO INCLUDES ALASKA AND HAWAII
San Francisco

N

0 100 200 300 400 500
MILES

• CAPITALS OF NEW STATES

COPYRIGHT © STANLEY BRUNN, 1973

A 16-State Nation

Remember the Bluegrass State of Kentucky, the Buckeye State of Ohio, the Keystone State of Pennsylvania, the Sunshine State of Florida, the Hawkeye State of Iowa, the Lone Star State of Texas? Such could be the recollections of U.S. inhabitants of South Heartland, Industry, Mid-Atlantica, Tropicana, North Heartland, South Plains—in the year 2000.

Inventor of this geographical brainstorm (opposite) is Dr. Stanley D. Brunn, associate professor of geography at Michigan State University. His map divides the U.S. into 16 newly named regions, each with a designated capital. In drawing the map, Brunn separated the States "on the basis of similar economic orientation, social and cultural heritage, and political ideology." Each State is geared toward one or more metropolitan areas.

Brunn believes that the country's current political structure, based on a 50-State map, is outdated and reflects the agrarian culture and economy of the last century. He states that today's mobile and urbanized society demands a new political framework—one that efficiently meets the need for better economic and social programs. "The States as they now exist are really barriers to legislation and political progress," says Brunn.

Why should heavily populated States such as New York, California, and New Jersey have the same number of U.S. senators as North Dakota, Oklahoma, and Wyoming? Shouldn't a resident of Indiana, who lives on the outskirts of metropolitan Chicago, be concerned about Chicago's air pollution problem? If voting is a national right, why should "mobile" Americans be subjected to an array of State and local residency requirements in order to vote? How efficient is a political system with 50 versions of how to interpret laws concerning welfare payments, unemployment, education standards, marriage and divorce regulations, job equality, criminal penalties, environmental protection? Brunn answers, "With a society that is acquiring more national

than State or local awareness and orientation, and where centralized planning is more accepted, increased standardization of laws is sought."

According to Brunn, a more consolidated map will not only correct "societal inequities" but will save the taxpayers money. For example, the plan can also consolidate suburban services such as water, police and fire facilities, and school districts. If Pearcy's map of 38 States (See: 38-State Nation) claims to save $4.6 billion a year in "fixed" State costs, then Brunn's plan should save considerably more.

Changes which may lead to a new regrouping of the States are already taking place. Zip codes cross State lines in Minnesota, Wisconsin, and the Carolinas. Regional commissions, such as the one operating in Appalachia, are working to improve an area's economy, not a State's economy. The Nixon Administration's plan for city revenue sharing bypassed States' rights.

If Brunn's predictions concerning a move toward standardization of State laws does happen, some areas will lose certain "liberal advantages." Good-bye to the Nevada divorce laws, New York City's welfare payments, New Mexico's lax land development laws.

How will Americans react to losing their State identity? Brunn says, "If you come from the State of Industry, you can still say you're from Michigan. Industry will just be another label for administrative purposes. I don't think it would be that upsetting."

Brunn is the 1st to agree that his map proposal leaves many unanswered questions. How to finance the new States? How to organize political representation? What will happen to the 2 major political parties? "Realistically," he says, "I don't suppose you're going to get ¾ of the States to go along with a Constitutional convention that would put them out of business. But at least this is a plan that can set people talking and thinking about the problems."

—C.O.

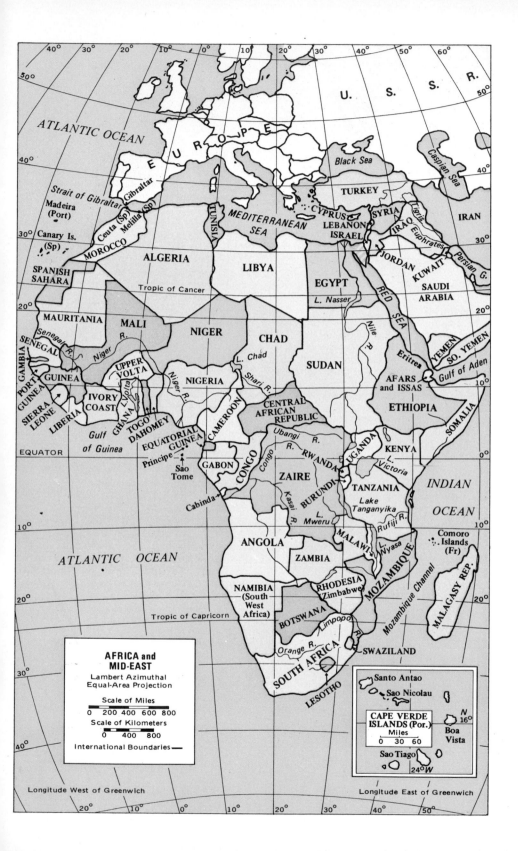

AFRICA and
MID-EAST

Lambert Azimuthal
Equal-Area Projection

Scale of Miles
0 200 400 600 800

Scale of Kilometers
0   400   800

International Boundaries ——

CAPE VERDE
ISLANDS (Por.)
Miles
0   30 60

Santo Antao
Sao Nicolau
Boa Vista
Sao Tiago
N 16°
24° W

Longitude West of Greenwich

Longitude East of Greenwich

ished again. Mrs. Bates searched for her husband throughout Europe without success. She returned to America and continued her fruitless search until she died. In 1910, a fellow occulist discovered him practicing in Grand Forks, N.Dak., where he had been for 6 years. Bates was persuaded to return to Manhattan and he served as attending physician in Harlem Hospital until 1922. In 1920, he published at his own expense a book titled *Cure of Imperfect Eyesight by Treatment without Glasses*, a "fantastic compendium," according to one Bates biographer, "of wildly exaggerated case records, unwarranted inferences, and anatomical ignorance."

Bates's Method of Eye Relaxation, as his remedy is described, is based on his theory of accommodation, a term for the focusing process which takes place within the eye when it views a new object at a greater or lesser distance. Bates believed that the cause of all refractive errors, such as nearsightedness, farsightedness, and astigmatism, was simply "strain" which was, in turn, due to an "abnormal" condition of mind." A squint or any other functional disturbance of the eye, for instance, "is simply a wrong thought and its disappearance is as quick as the thought that relaxes. If the relaxation is only momentary, the correction is momentary. When it becomes permanent, the correction is permanent."

The Bates system involves "central fixation," or learning to see without strain. The patients 1st learned to "palm" by covering both eyes with the palms of the hands and trying to think of "perfect black." When a patient was able to see a pure blackness, there was an immediate improvement of sight, Bates believed.

The patient next learned the "shift" and the "swing." By shifting, Bates meant moving the eye back and forth until one had the illusion of an object "swinging" from side to side. The shorter the shift, the greater the benefit, patients were advised.

In addition to palming, shifting, and swinging, Bates also recommended strengthening the eyes by reading under unusually adverse conditions. Patients were told that their eyes were also strengthened by looking directly at the sun for short moments so that the beneficial rays could bathe the retina, a practice which most medical authorities say may easily cause permanent retinal damage. Bates further claimed that squinting, specks in the eye, and even the twinkling of stars were all due to eye strain. While physicists generally subscribe to the idea that twinkling stars are caused by changing currents of air with different densities, Bates claimed twinkling was all in the mind. Twinkling ceases if the eyes are relieved of strain, he said.

"Not only do all errors of refraction and all functional disturbances of the eye disappear when it sees by central fixation, but many organic conditions are relieved," Bates declared. He noted that such physical conditions as glaucoma, incipient cataract, and syphilitic iritis (inflammation of the eye's iris) "have disappeared when central fixation was attained. Relief was often obtained in a few minutes and, in rare cases, this relief was permanent. Infections, as well as diseases caused by the poisons of typhoid fever, influenza, syphilis, and gonorrhea, also have been benefited by it. Even with a foreign body in the eye, there is no redness and no pain so long as central fixation is retained."

Bates taught his method to hundreds of his disciples. "Studios"—so-called because a medical degree was required to run a "clinic"—sprang up from coast to coast. Perhaps one of the best-known teachers who studied under Bates was Mrs. Margaret Darst Corbett of Los Angeles who, in 1940, successfully fought a civil suit forced on her by the organized oculists, optometrists, and ophthalmologists of Southern California for "practicing medicine and optometry without license." Witnesses ranging in age from 5 to 85 who allegedly had regained normal sight after Mrs. Corbett's lessons filled the courtroom. Some 500 persons in Los Angeles alone offered to testify for Mrs. Corbett. Her defense was simply that she was not a doctor. She was a teacher. "I normalize eyes through relaxation," Mrs. Corbett testified. "I do not diagnose or prescribe or medicate. Where there is a possibility of a pathological condition, I refer clients to their own physician for a physical examination and diagnosis. I teach that if a person has any sight at all, he can develop more, not by exercise, prodding, and urging tired eyes still further, not by use of strong glasses, but by easing and relaxing the eyes, letting them see, ceasing to force them." Mrs. Corbett, who died December 2, 1962, won her trial because she proved she enhanced poor eyesight purely through relaxation.

Bates's most distinguished converts included self-styled health authority Bernarr MacFadden and author Aldous Huxley, the victim of an early eye infection which left his corneas permanently scarred. Huxley became a believer in the Bates Method and avowed the Bates Method had greatly benefited his vision. He later (1942) wrote a book, *The Art of Seeing*, which summarized Bates's theories and included additional forms of Huxley-inspired therapy.

Bates died July 10, 1931, in New York City, but his eccentric theories and methods continued to be popular. At one time, there were more than 50 teachers in the Los Angeles area alone working with patients and teaching the Bates Method. Today, however, while there are several studios in Los Angeles and 2 in

San Francisco, there is just one in San Diego, in Kansas City, and in New York City, the latter accepting only referrals from a medical doctor.

—R.H.C.

MICHAEL FARADAY (1791–1867).

Born into extreme poverty, he had virtually no formal education and is said to have possessed a very poor memory, yet Michael Faraday became probably the world's greatest experimental genius in the physical sciences. Apprenticed to a bookbinder from an early age, Faraday applied for a job as Sir Humphry Davy's laboratory assistant in 1813, carefully preparing, illustrating, and binding notes from the great scientist's chemistry lectures and sending them to him along with his request.

Davy trained him well. As both a physicist and chemist Faraday became one of the immortals of science—discovering the principle of the electric motor, developing the 1st dynamo, formulating the laws of electrolysis, producing the 1st stainless steel, and discovering benzene and butylene, among many other brilliant accomplishments. His discovery of electromagnetic induction alone provided the basis for our modern electrified world and produced his "field concept," which in turn was the basis a century later of Einstein's revolutionary theory of relativity.

In 1824 Faraday was elected to the Royal Society, but later refused its presidency, just as he refused knighthood and many other honors offered him. The following year he became director of the laboratory of the Royal Institution, where he had begun his career as Davy's assistant. The *farad* named for the scientist is an electromagnetic unit, while a *faraday* is a unit of electricity used in electrolysis. Faraday invented the electrical terms "anode" and "cathode."

—R.H. rep.

T. D. LYSENKO (1898–).

For nearly 30 years Soviet science was headed by an uneducated, fanatical fake. This man had absolute control over a vast segment of Russia's research in genetics, biology, agriculture, and related fields.

Trofim Denisovich Lysenko was a farmer's son who attended a meeting at Leningrad in 1929. He wanted to tell of his experiments in growing winter peas to precede a cotton crop —a discovery he felt was sensational. It wasn't. The idea was old.

He was ignored by everyone except a newspaperman who saw a good story. The journalist wrote: "Lysenko gives one the feeling of a toothache. He has a dejected mien. Since he is stingy of words, all one remembers is his sullen look creeping along the earth as if he were ready to do someone in." Lysenko returned home bitter.

A year later, Lysenko's father sowed grain in winter and got a yield in the spring. When Lysenko heard of this he immediately claimed credit for the idea and said it was proof of his own agricultural "theories." He bragged loudly and incessantly. It paid off. He landed a job at the Odessa Institute of Genetics and Breeding. Since winter crops ordinarily were poor, Lysenko was put in charge of a special department to study this problem.

He refuted all established scientific theories. Mendel, Pasteur, and the rest didn't know anything. He, Lysenko, had the real answers. Even the universities, he insisted, were teaching drivel. Since Lysenko was uneducated, it was easier to scorn others than to admit he didn't know what they were talking about.

In 1935, he went to a meeting of representatives from collective farms and gave a talk, the gist of which was that those who didn't agree with his ideas were enemies of the people. He transformed his agricultural report into a political harangue. As luck would have it, Stalin himself was in the audience, and afterward he commented, "Bravo, Comrade Lysenko!" That did it. Lysenko was assumed to be a Stalin protégé. The press now called him a "genius" of the soil.

Meanwhile Lysenko had become friendly with I. I. Prezent, a man who knew all the sordid uses of public relations. Under his direction Lysenko refined the technique of charging those who ridiculed his ideas with being enemies of the proletariat. In time, many of the outstanding Russian scientists were not only removed from their positions but they were jailed or liquidated. Lysenko quickly stepped into the vacuum each time, moving ever upward—Comrade Prezent always at his side.

Soon Lysenko had a collection of followers. They were given degrees and titles and top jobs. Gradually, Lysenko and his friends controlled nearly every important position in the scientific establishment, as well as the editorial boards of newspapers and magazines.

After W.W. II, it became apparent that biology, and especially genetics, had developed tremendously elsewhere in the world. Lysenko dismissed these reports, pointing with pride to his own achievements: his prize herd of cows, bred according to his own theories; his experimental trees that would grow in barren country; and the many plans he had for future record crops of wheat, beets, and potatoes. Anyone who advocated trying new ideas taken from capitalistic countries was clearly a reactionary.

Lysenko still had Stalin's ear, and so he kept on misinforming the leader as to the state of science in the U.S.S.R. By 1950, Lysenko's cult was supreme. He had been given honors, titles, had had statues erected to him, and someone had even written a folk song about him. All this despite the fact that he had actually produced nothing extraordinary.

Just what were Lysenko's "theories?" They were evidenced in a hodgepodge of experiments without system or controls. He had truckloads of soil moved from place to place and had thousands of farmers growing a wide variety of grains in the hope of obtaining a revolutionary hybrid. An occasional result that looked promising—a new wheat for example—usually was disappointing when made into flour and baked into bread. Tastewise, it would prove a failure. Laboratory experts who ventured an opinion were ignored. After all, if it was not Lysenko's own idea, he would not receive credit for any consequent success.

When Khrushchev became the leader of the U.S.S.R., Lysenko remained a favorite. He was Khrushchev's kind of "earthy" man. Then, in 1961, science cracked the genetic code. It discovered the mechanism of protein synthesis and self-reproduction of hereditary macro-molecules. The letters "DNA" became known to everyone.

By 1962, the global press was heralding the new breakthrough. In Russia, though, it was almost impossible to publish anything about it. Finally, the small group of legitimate scientists still left found a way. They began slipping genetic articles into periodicals devoted to chemistry, physics, or mathematics. Gradually the nation's lag in biology became all too obvious. Pressure was put on authorities. Scientists asked, "Can we let the capitalistic nations get ahead of us?"

It worked. In 1962, a commission investigated the state of biologic research in the country—which meant Lysenko's empire was threatened. His superb cows, it was found, were not the result of his clever breeding techniques, but the result of secret culling. A grove of specimen trees was found to be located in a patch of moist soil, unlike the dry ground around it. Other endeavors were also exposed as contrived showpieces—ones that had cost the Government thousands of rubles.

On October 14, 1964, Khrushchev's fate—and that of his economic and agricultural policies—was determined in the Kremlin. He was out of power. And so was Lysenko. When Lysenko was dismissed as director of the Institute on Genetics, he retreated to his farm. No reference to him was made in the press. His statues were quietly removed. The folk song about him was relegated to yesterday's hit parade.

A new era began with the U.S.S.R.'s entry into the space age, and into other advanced realms of science. The fact that an ignorant fraud had controlled the U.S.S.R.'s progress in

science for 27 years is nearly forgotten now. In time people will think it was too bizarre to have happened.

But, of course, it did.

—S.Sp.

JAMES V. McCONNELL (1925–   ).

After his experiments with worms had captured the attention of scientists, James Vernon McConnell added further to his reputation as a maverick professor when he took up publishing a journal which printed parodies of scientific articles along with genuine reports of current research. To some, the serious research was funnier than the intentionally humorous articles in McConnell's journal, which he called *The Worm Runner's Digest*.

McConnell's findings regarding the nature of memory were obtained at the University of Michigan, where he joined the psychology faculty in 1956. While other experimental psychologists ran rats through mazes to study how creatures learn and remember, McConnell chose to "run" a type of flatworm called Planaria. Planarians can multiply by fission; that is, if a worm is cut in 2, the head end will survive and grow a new hind end. While the hind end will also survive and grow a new head, including the organ that serves as a brain.

Cutting up planarians became McConnell's specialty during a series of remarkable experiments. First he announced that these simple worms were capable of learning a conditioned reflex, just as dogs did in the Pavlov experiments. A healthy worm would be exposed to a bright light which was followed immediately by an electric shock. The shock would make the worm scrunch up its body. After a sufficient number of these light-and-shock treatments, most worms would contract, rear up, or otherwise react merely upon exposure to the bright light, with no shock following. In psychological evaluation, the smarter the worm the fewer the trials required to elicit this conditioned response whenever the proper stimulus—bright light—was presented. The number of shock trials needed to elicit the response to the light alone was the measure of whether the worms knew what the light meant.

A completely naïve planarian needed many shock trials before learning to scrunch when the light shone. A previously trained worm needed only a few trials; the memory returned quickly, McConnell said. Some worms never did get the hang of it.

Then Dr. McConnell reported that when he cut some trained worms and they had grown new parts, the "new" worms demonstrated that they remembered their training by quickly learning to scrunch up or writhe at the bright light. For worms whose head ends had taken part in the shock training, this seemed plausible, since if there were any memories they should reside in the brainier part of the worm. But the new worms—whose hind ends alone had been in the original training program—also showed the same recollections, so where was the seat of memory now?

The worms were cut again and the ends that had received no conditioning training were allowed to grow their missing ends. McConnell found that his new crop of worms were already conditioned to the bright light even though no part of them had ever received "training." This could be evidence of inheriting a learned bit of behavior, which was altogether contrary to reputable biology in the U.S. and even had political implications because Russian biologists had once insisted that such inherited learning was possible.

McConnell went farther—perhaps too far. Planarians are cannibals, so he diced up some of the "trained" specimens and fed the pieces to a naïve group of worms who had never undergone the light-and-shock conditioning series. After this meal, the untrained worms were naïve no more. Professor McConnell reported that they now reacted to the light as though they had received the usual conditioning, cringing at the light in anticipation of an electric shock. His conclusion: A memory, or conditioned response, had been ingested by the planarians when they ate their better-educated brethren. From 1962 to 1969 a number of scientific journals as well as popular news magazines reported difficulty in swallowing this conclusion. Other experimenters then began reporting failure in their attempts to confirm McConnell's results, and there was a flurry of running worm experiments.

McConnell's *Worm Runner's Digest* attracted so many humorous contributions that he was able to publish 2 books of them: *The Worm Re-Turns* (1965) and *Science, Sex, and Sacred Cows* (1971). More recently he has published textbooks in social psychology and general psychology, but is best known as an exemplar of the belief that one does not need to be solemn in order to be serious. McConnell was born in Oklahoma, went to college in Louisiana and Texas, and now lives in Ann Arbor, Mich.

The worm experiments showed that there is still no adequate understanding of the processes of learning and remembering, in terms of the precise, chemical and physiological events that occur. McConnell's modest proposal that memory transfer could occur through cannibalism, however, was treated with derision, and some other explanations were soon advanced by experimenters to account for the worms' behavior. The nature of the subject matter being what it was, the controversy never really raged but rather sputtered awhile and then subsided in a mixture of laughter and statistical quibbling.

—C.C.

FRANZ A. MESMER (1734–1815).

Franz Anton Mesmer doesn't entirely deserve his centuries-old reputation as a charlatan. Though he wasn't aware of the fact, Dr. Mesmer was one of the 1st to treat patients by hypnosis, and his motives generally seem to have been beyond reproach. Unaware of his hypnotic powers, the Austrian physician 1st believed that his medical successes were due to a method he had devised in which he stroked patients with magnets. Mesmer even kept a little magnet in a sack around his neck and "magnetized" everything in sight at his offices in Vienna, from the tableware to the trees in the garden. His cures for ailments ranging from gout to paralysis made him respected enough to be elected to Bavaria's Academy of Sciences, but the success of another practitioner who effected cures by manipulation alone made him abandon his magnets.

Forced to leave Austria on its account, Mesmer introduced his new "animal magnetism" to Paris in 1778. He knew that he was the "animal" involved in the process, but believed his "magnetism" to be otherworldly, not hypnotic. In any event, his spectacular method became the "in" thing, enjoying the vogue that various group therapy methods enjoy today. Mesmer made himself a fortune, prominent French figures like Lafayette, Marie Antoinette, and Montesquieu either supporting him or flocking to his lavish Place Vendôme quarters, where he conducted rituals that did cure some people. Garbed in the flowing, brightly colored robes of an astrologer and waving a magic wand, Mesmer would arrange his patients in a circle, have them join hands in the dimly lit room, and then he would pass from one to another, fixing his eyes upon, touching, and speaking to each in turn while soft music played in the background. Apparently he never did understand that the supernatural had nothing to do with his success, that his hypnotic powers accomplished this. Many reputable physicians supported his claims, but when Louis XVI appointed a scientific commission—which included Benjamin Franklin—to investigate his practice, Mesmer fell into disfavor, the investigators' report labeling him a charlatan and imposter.

A man born before his time the unknowing hypnotist died in obscurity in Switzerland in 1815, aged 81. Freud and others would profit from his work, but he would mainly be remembered as a quack occult healer. *Mesmerism* —1st named and identified by his pupil Puységur—was used for hypnotism before the latter word was coined, but today is employed mostly in the sense of to spellbind, to enthrall by some mysterious power, in fact, to sway a group or an individual by some strange animal or personal magnetism.

—R.H. rep.

J. B. RHINE (1895–   ).

Joseph Banks Rhine is given credit for making clairvoyance and telepathy respectable topics for scientific research, by virtue of his careful experiments in extrasensory perception (ESP) over a period of nearly half a century. Although only a few other psychologists agree that the existence of ESP has been proved, there is general acceptance now that the subject, to which Rhine gave the name "parapsychology," is deserving of scientific study.

Rhine was born in Pennsylvania, earned a Ph.D. degree at the University of Chicago in 1925, did postdoctoral work at Harvard, and then began teaching psychology at Duke University in Durham, N.C. His interest in parapsychology was encouraged at Duke by the eminent psychologist William McDougall. Rhine announced his early results with ESP research in 1934, at which time he was given his own parapsychology laboratory. He was successful in attracting serious students as well as grants of funds for research. Contributors for ESP research have included the Rockefeller Foundation and the U.S. Navy, among many others. After retiring from Duke University, Rhine established his own nonprofit organization, the Foundation for Research on the Nature of Man, whose activities include the Institute for Parapsychology as well as a publishing branch. Address of the foundation, which is supported by private donations, is Box 6846, College Station, Durham, N.C. 27708.

The methods, materials, and terminology adopted by Rhine became standard for the study of extrasensory perception (a name he bestowed on the subjects of clairvoyance, telepathy, and precognition). For example, his standard deck of ESP cards consists of 25 cards in all, 5 cards with 5 different designs: a star, a circle, a square, a cross, and a set of wavy lines. He even recommended that the cards be shuffled in a certain way: at least 4 dovetail shuffles followed by a cut made with a knife or thumbnail. After the cards are mixed, the experimenter holds them while the "subject" calls —guesses, some would say—the design on each card (they are out of his sight, of course). If the person has the trait Rhine calls psi (pronounced like the name Sy), he will call more hits—that is, he will name the correct design more often—than could be expected if only sheer guesswork were involved.

The card-calling experiments are Rhine's best-known work, but he also initiated research in psychokinesis (PK), which is the ability to influence the motion of physical objects by using the force of thought or will power. Rhine's experiments in psychokinesis usually involved throwing dice while "willing" certain numbers to appear—an activity often pursued in nonscientific circles. His results persuaded him that certain persons possessed a certain amount of psychic ability at certain times. Adults, children, and even animals showed psi, but their ability to repeat high-scoring runs while being observed by outsiders has been lacking.

Rhine's work has not escaped ridicule by persons who associate ESP with magic and fortune-telling, although the quality of his procedures convinced most others of his personal integrity as a scientist. Rather than admit that ESP could conceivably exist, resolute critics claim that trickery and unintentional giveaway clues will explain how some individuals made such astonishing scores that even the laws of chance could not account for the results. Unfortunately for those who wish to prove that ESP exists, the high-scoring performances continue to be very rare and unpredictable.

Rhine insists that high motivation and enthusiasm must be present in order for the psi ability to appear. He describes instances when persons whose spirit was at top level scored 25 "hits" on the unseen pack of 25 cards. As in other occult phenomena, the presence of nonbelievers during the experiment seems to reduce the likelihood of obtaining favorable results. Long and tiring sessions are also unlikely to reveal psi, whether the task is naming cards or controlling the roll of dice. Critics have said that the remarkable results Rhine obtained in the early years of his experiments were caused by excessive motivation on the part of his assistants. When better controls were used, fewer great psychic performances were reported. Both Rhine and his wife Louisa have written numerous books and articles on extrasensory perception and their work is accepted as fully legitimate psychological research, although Rhine has remarked that only this branch of psychology is asked to take elaborate measures to prevent fraud during experiments.

Since the presence of psi in a person (he is called a sensitive if he has it) is always measured, in Rhine's work, in relation to the laws of chance, the psi research compelled the nonbelievers to reflect upon how statistics are used to draw conclusions. Rhine is accused of mistaking the occasional rare chance event— which the laws of chance say will occur—for a psychical episode. His steadfast willingness to do so, however, made him the foremost authority on extrasensory perception. When public interest in telepathy, clairvoyance, precognition, and psychokinesis increased in a so-called "occult explosion" starting in the 1960s, Rhine's work showed what kind of evidence would be needed to prove that such phenomena exist.

—C.C.

NIKOLA TESLA (1856–1943).

In the little town of Smiljan in the Serbian province of Lika, then known as Croatia (Yugoslavia), a seemingly unimportant event took place—the death of a French poodle—but this was to begin a chain of events that would shape the future of the world. One day, when Nikola Tesla was 5 years old, he found his brother Dane's little black poodle dead under a bush along the side of the road. His brother accused Nikki of killing it. A short while later, Dane was found unconscious at the foot of the stone cellar steps. Dane subsequently died of his injuries. For the rest of his life, Nikki Tesla believed his parents thought he had pushed his brother.

Shortly after, Nikki overheard his mother complaining that her wrists ached from turning her eggbeater. Eager to ingratiate himself, Nikki immediately set to work seeking ways to harness the power of a nearby mountain stream to turn the cooking utensil for her. "I'm going to capture the water's power," Nikki announced confidently. When his father unthinkingly mentioned that Dane had been different from Nikki because "Dane was a genius," Nikki set out to prove he was one also. He decided at that moment that he would invent something that would startle the world. Nikki undertook experiments to harness the power of water but, when he was 9, he temporarily abandoned his work and began the study of air power. He wanted desperately to invent something that would impress grown-ups, particularly his parents.

When he was 10, Nikki entered the Real Gymnasium of Gospic, a 4-year institution similar to a combined American grammar and junior high school. He particularly enjoyed mathematics and when he 1st demonstrated his ability to supply formulas and solve equations quickly, even his teachers were amazed. He was accused of cheating and made to undergo a classroom "trial" before his parents and teachers. Despite the atmosphere of distrust and enmity, he passed with ease but he was left unhappy and confused.

Tesla's childhood was filled with eccentric schemes and experimental gadgetry; he continued his schooling at a polytechnic institution at Graz, specializing in physics and mathematics. In 1880 he finished his studies at the University of Prague. A year later, he invented an amplifer for the telephone that both magnified the sound of the voice and reduced the irrelevant sounds, or static. The finished device, his 1st invention, although never patented, was called the "telephone repeater." Today it would be described as a loudspeaker.

Within a year Tesla began development of the alternating-current theory. Tesla told his assistant: "I will produce a field of force that rotates at high speed. It will surround and embrace an armature which will require no electrical connections. The rotating field will transfer its power, without wires, through space, feeding energy by means of its lines of force to closed-circuit coils on an armature, enabling it to build up its own magnetic field that locks it into the rotating magnetic whirlwind produced by the field coils. No wires. No faulty connections. No commutator."

Tesla went to Budapest and then to Paris to find a patron or backer for his alternating-current power system. He worked for a while at Continental Edison Company of Paris. Advised that he should apply to the Edison Company in New York, Tesla, 4 years after his graduation from the University of Prague, left Paris for America.

Tesla told Thomas Edison that he had perfected—at least, in theory—an alternating-current power system. Edison, however, poohpoohed Tesla's ideas and told him that "fooling around with alternating current is just a waste of time. Nobody'll use it, ever. It's too dangerous. An alternating-current high-voltage wire gets loose and it could kill a man as quick as a bolt of lightning. Direct current is safe."

But Edison hired Tesla, and the young European did exactly what he had done for Continental Edison in Paris—he came up with a plan whereby many thousands of dollars could be saved, both in the construction and in the operation of the Edison dynamos and motors. He worked from 10 o'clock in the morning straight through to 5 o'clock in the morning the next day, 7 days a week. Tesla soon left Edison, however, and after a number of varied jobs, found backers who were willing to invest in him, and the Tesla Electric Company was formed.

Tesla's work to develop alternating current for practical application began now in earnest, and he achieved his goal. At the Chicago World's Fair of 1893 all the elaborate and painstakingly created exhibits were supplied with alternating current by the Westinghouse motors and dynamos, invented by Tesla. His equipment would later be used in the system that generated power from Niagara Falls. Tesla, now in a New York City laboratory, devoted all his time to further research.

The great scientist grew more paranoid with advancing years, a mental defect traceable to the traumas that had occurred during his youth. In 1917, informed that he was to be guest of honor at a dinner given by the American Institute of Electrical Engineers and would receive the Edison Merit of Achievement medal, Tesla refused saying, "Every time the institute awards an Edison medal, Edison is glorified more than the recipient. If I had the money to spend for such nonsense, I would gladly pay to have a Tesla medal awarded to Mr. Edison." He was prevailed upon to accept the honor, but he did not show up for the dinner. Friends found him feeding pigeons in a park behind the New York Public Library.

Tesla spent the later years of his life as a lonely, uncommunicative egotist, engrossed in thoughts and feelings that alienated him both from the world and from other people. He was unwilling to shake hands for fear of germ contamination; he was frightened by round surfaces like billiard balls and pearl necklaces; he remained intensely jealous of Edison and loved only the pigeons he fed daily. His tremendous talent was dissipated by attempts to invent death rays and devices for photographing thoughts on the retina of the eye.

In 1943, Tesla died of a heart attack. Scientific institutions throughout the world commemorated the 100th anniversary of his birth in 1956. As a final tribute, the unit of magnetic flux density in the MKS system was named *tesla* in his honor.

—R.H.C.

Immanuel Velikovsky (1895–).

Despite the ingrained human tendency to dismiss out-of-hand that which is new and different, the reaction of the scientific community to the ideas of Immanuel Velikovsky remains unprecedented in the records of modern science.

The publishing history of the man's work is a story in itself. Dr. Velikovsky's surprising theories were 1st published in early 1950, following 4 years of frustrated attempts to gain a receptive ear in established scientific circles. Public attention was drawn to his ideas through a series of popularized condensations of his manuscript in *Harper's*, *Collier's*, and *Reader's Digest*. Incensed by the popular appeal of his ideas, and by the unscientific forum to which Velikovsky had been forced to resort, several scientists collaborated in an effort to prevent publication of the manuscript. Defying this pressure, the Macmillan Company decided to go ahead, and *Worlds in Collision* went to press in February, 1950.

What followed was a modern classic case of academic demagoguery. Scientists and scholars who supported Velikovsky's thesis—and even those who simply defended his right to be heard—were shouted down. Some, like the astronomer Gordon Atwater and Macmillan editor James Putnam, were summarily dismissed from their positions. Favorable reviews of the book were killed before their publication, to be replaced by fervent attacks on "irresponsibility"

in the publishing industry. All too frequently, these attacks were written by scientists who admitted that they had not read *Worlds in Collision*, while those who had read the book grossly misrepresented the author's position and ignored or distorted his evidence. The book's publisher, Macmillan, came under such pressure from the academic community that it was forced to transfer the publication rights to Doubleday, even though at that time the book had been 20 weeks on *The New York Times* best-seller list. (Interestingly, the Britannica Book of the Year for 1950 failed to mention *Worlds in Collision* among its list of that year's best sellers.) Initial reaction culminated in a 1950 meeting of the American Association for the Advancement of Science, where a discussion was held on the subject of "Books, Civilization and Science." What came out of this discussion, as reported in *Science* magazine, was a proposal for a prepublication "theory-censoring board," its purpose being to prevent the "wrong kinds of scientific books" from being published.

Who is Immanuel Velikovsky? What had he done to provoke such an unacademic uproar in the scientific community? What had his book proposed that they found, and continue to find, so threatening?

Born in Vitebsk, Russia, in 1895, of Jewish parents, Velikovsky 1st studied in Moscow, where he graduated with full honors from Medvednikov Gymnasium. From there he studied briefly in France, traveled in Palestine, and began the study of natural science in Edinburgh, Scotland. His premedical schooling abroad was interrupted by the outbreak of W.W. I, so Velikovsky returned to Moscow. There he studied law and ancient history at the Free University and continued his medical studies at the University of Moscow. He received his medical diploma in 1921.

He spent the next few years in Berlin, where he co-founded *Scripta Universitatis*, a series of volumes containing major works by Jewish scholars of all nations, which was to become the cornerstone of the University of Jerusalem. In Berlin, he married violinist Elisha Kramer, and together they moved to Palestine, where for 15 years he practiced medicine and, after a period of psychiatric training in Vienna, psychoanalysis. Among Velikovsky's early contributions was a paper on the existence of pathological brain-wave patterns as being characteristic of epileptics.

In 1939, he interrupted his practice to travel to America, his intention being to prepare an analysis of the dreams of Sigmund Freud through the comparison of 3 historical personages who figured prominently in Freud's writings: Moses, Oedipus, and Akhenaten. It was in the course of these investigations that Velikovsky stumbled across the 1st shreds of evidence that would eventually lead him to a reappraisal and redirection of his life's energies.

Researching the biblical story of Moses, Velikovsky saw in the narrative a tale of tremendous power, of change and transformation on a huge scale. What in the events described in the Book of Exodus had actually taken place? Would they not have left their mark on other, diverse cultural histories? Inspired by this line of thought, he began to look further into the accumulated historical records of many of the world's peoples, ancient scriptural and religious writings which modern science chooses to ignore. It is the results of his extensive research into these histories that comprise the main body of *Worlds in Collision*. In this book, Velikovsky describes a series of holocausts, worldwide cataclysms which befell humanity within historical times; upheavals of such horrendous proportions that they have left their clear impression in the written and oral traditions of virtually all cultures of mankind. He further asserts that these cataclysms were not of terrestrial origin but that they resulted from a near-collision between the earth and an enormous comet. This comet, he says, originally part of the planet Jupiter, continued as a threat for nearly a thousand years, when it approached very close to the planet Mars, which in turn was shifted in its orbit and itself very nearly collided with the earth. This comet —which was feared and revered by the ancients; which passed so close to the earth that its tail deposited showers of burning oil, dust, and meteorites over most of the globe; which caused vast tidal waves, earthquakes, hurricanes, and volcanic activity, and an actual shifting of the earth's crust on its molten core as well as a reversal of the polarity of the globe; which altered the orbit of the earth around the sun and changed the lengths of the day, month, and year—this comet was to become, says Velikovsky, the morning star, "the newcomer" in Latin, the planet Venus.

These colossal events, he continues, occurred not before the dawn of civilization, but within, archaeologically speaking, recent times. The 1st holocaust which he describes (though, he says, certainly not the 1st to befall the planet), occurred only 3,000 years ago, around 1500 B.C., at the time of Exodus in the Old Testament, Prometheus in Greek mythology, and the end of the Middle Kingdom in Egyptian history. Evidence that these occurrences were indeed of worldwide proportions is found in the records of such diverse cultures as the Mayans, Sumerians, Babylonians, Chinese, Tibetans, Eskimos, American Indians, Hindus, and Lapps. The list seems almost endless. The 2nd holocaust, caused by the near-collision with Mars, occurred in 687 B.C., when, in the Bible, it is said that "the sun stood still in the sky," while, in the records of other cultures, on the opposite side of the globe, there are descriptions of a seemingly endless night.

Velikovsky's conclusions, as presented in *Worlds in Collision*, were simply irreconcilable with many of the basic assumptions in science at the time of the book's publication. It reads like a novel of speculative fiction. Were it not for the extensive use of original sources (it contains more than 4,000 footnotes) one might consider it to be the elaborate concoction of a creative paranoic. But no one can read this book without being deeply moved and troubled by it. No one has seriously suggested that this monumental work was meant as a hoax, nor has anyone doubted the sincerity with which Velikovsky presents his case.

His work is full of implications: religious, cosmological, geological, archaeological, sociological, and psychological. Yet, in those areas where scientific methods could have been applied to affirm or refute his assertions directly, very little was done during the years immediately following the publication of *Worlds in Collision*. In 1952, Velikovsky published *Ages in Chaos*, his dramatic reconstruction of the social chronology of the period between the 1st cataclysm and 687 B.C. This work, by an author already discredited in the eyes of many by the adverse publicity which surrounded his 1st book, was given little notice, although many Egyptologists have said that its assertions are well-founded, and that, if supported by archaeological evidence, it would entail a complete revamping of our ideas concerning Middle Eastern chronology. In 1955, Velikovsky published *Earth in Upheaval*, which was devoted solely to geological and archaeological evidence supporting his theses. All of these works contain challenges to modern science, questions to be reexamined, tests to be conducted. On the results of these experiments, says Velikovsky, his conclusions may stand or fall.

In the 25 years since the 1st publication of *Worlds in Collision*, many of these tests have been conducted—with very impressive results. One issue of the international quarterly *Pensée* contained an evaluation of nearly 40 predictions Velikovsky had made. Many marvel at the accuracy of these projections, yet, as Velikovsky hastens to point out, they were a "natural fallout from a single, central idea." Prof. H. H. Hess, former chairman of the space board of the National Academy of Science, commented to the doctor that while all of his predictions were made long before proof that they were right was at hand, "I do not know of any specific prediction you made that has since proven to be false." Among these correct prognoses: the extremely hot surface temperature of Venus (owing to its recent birth), the hydrocarbonaceous content of its atmosphere, and its disturbed rotation; the electromagnetic nature of solar flares; the existence of the Van

Allen radiation belt; strong remanent magnetism on the moon, evidence of its recent heating, and the presence there of carbides and aromatic hydrocarbons; and radio emissions from Jupiter.

Central to Velikovsky's thesis is his view of the solar system—he sees it not as a group of independent, electrically neutral spheres which move in an endless uniformity through a space devoid of other matter and energy but rather as a dynamic, integrated system wherein all bodies constantly affect all other bodies and any change in any part of the system must be reflected throughout. On this subject, Velikovsky engaged in an ongoing debate with Albert Einstein right up to the latter's death in 1955. Einstein, though he accepted Velikovsky's evidence of recent catastrophes, was adamant in his conviction that the heavenly bodies are neutrally charged and that space is free of electricity and magnetism. But when, just a few days before he died, Einstein learned that radio noises had been detected from Jupiter, he offered to use his influence to arrange other experiments on Velikovsky's behalf. Albert Einstein died with *Worlds in Collision* open on his desk.

Perhaps most interesting among Dr. Velikovsky's contributions is his analysis of the reaction which his work evoked from within the scientific establishment. Mankind, says he, is a victim of "collective amnesia," unable or unwilling to face its collective heritage or to recall events which occurred only a few thousand years ago. We are all familiar with the phenomenon of repression. As a psychoanalyst, Velikovsky had been trained to treat his patients gingerly, guiding them, leading them, but never telling them exactly what he believed to be at the heart of the problem. This they had to discover for themselves. But one can't put humanity on a couch and gently guide it toward a rediscovery of its repressed past. So he told it like it was, with the result that he was attacked with all the fury of a patient who has been told that he wants to kill his father and sleep with his mother.

Yet try he must. "For" says Immanuel Velikovsky, quoting from Santayana, "those who do not remember the past are condemned to live it once more."

—A.B.

Animals Used for Laboratory Research in the U.S. in 1971–1973

Rodents	45,000,000	Cats	66,195*
Frogs	15–20,000,000	Snakes	61,176
Birds	1,724,279	Lizards	51,005
Hamsters	454,986*	Swine	46,624
Rabbits	447,570*	Primates	42,298*
Guinea pigs	408,970*	Wild animals	38,169*
Dogs	195,157*	Sheep	22,961
Turtles	190,145		

Figures marked * are for 1973; all others are for 1971. Sources: Institute of Laboratory Animal Resources, and Animal and Plant Health Inspection Service.

Can Man Change the Climate?

Only in recent years have scientists come to believe that man may be able to change the climate over large regions of earth. Scientists have learned a great deal about the atmosphere over the past 2 decades. Although there are still many mysteries to be solved, the secrets of the atmosphere are surely being uncovered.

Satellites that circle the globe provide detailed pictures of cloud cover, along with measurements of radiant energy from the sun and earth. In the near future they may also provide data on temperature and humidity in the atmosphere, and perhaps even wind speed and direction.

Scientists are also discovering which factors control the general circulation of the atmosphere and what causes the circulation to change. Although many important details are still lacking, scientists have learned that the temperature difference between the equatorial and polar regions is of extreme importance. This has suggested a number of possible ways in which the circulation of the atmosphere—and, therefore, the weather and climate—can be modified.

A number of schemes have been suggested for warming the Arctic, to reduce the temperature difference between the pole and equator and change the overall circulation. The suggestion is to coat the Arctic ice with a layer of black carbon dust, which would absorb more solar heat than white snow and ice. This would probably increase Arctic temperatures and cause the ice to melt. Some scientists believe that once the ice melted, it would not return. The theory is that exposed rock, soil, and water would continue to absorb relatively large amounts of solar heat, which, in turn, would prevent snow and ice from building up in large amounts. Other scientists dispute this theory, but there is little chance it will be tried out. The enormous amount of carbon black needed—about 1.5 billion tons for a layer $\frac{4}{1000}$" thick—renders this scheme of little practical value.

Another, more feasible suggestion by Soviet engineer P. M. Barisov involves building a 60-mi.-long dam across the Bering Strait between Alaska and Siberia. He proposed pumping cold Arctic water into the Pacific Ocean. Warmer Atlantic Ocean water would then flow into the Arctic to replace it. This might lead to a small, but important, increase in Arctic temperature.

Most meteorologists agree that warming the Arctic by a small amount would change the world's overall climate and weather. Unfortunately, nobody can predict whether the change will be for the better or worse. Will deserts get more rainfall or will they become drier? Will swamps dry up or become wetter? How about the distribution of rainfall, hail, and snow in farming regions? Will a rise in sea level lead to the flooding of coastal cities? Will another Ice Age be initiated or will glaciers recede? No one know the answers to these questions for sure.

Scientists do know that weather changes seem to have global significance. Winds in one region, for example, are accompanied by opposite winds in another. If the north winds are abnormally cold and persistent in one part of the world, then south winds are abnormally warm and persistent in another part of the world. This interdependence and unity of the atmosphere means that it may not be possible to change the climate in one part of the world without producing a series of changes in other parts of the world. Tinkering with the climate

—before a more complete understanding is achieved—might well lead to catastrophe.

Before leaving the subject of changing climate, we should point out that atmospheric pollution can have an important effect on the world's climate. Perhaps the most important pollutant from this point of view is the gas carbon dioxide produced by the burning of fossil fuels. Since 1890 the amount of carbon dioxide in the air has increased about 10%. During that period of time the average worldwide temperatures increased almost 1° F. Although this may not seem like much when you are talking about a bowl of soup or tub of water, it represents an enormous amount of energy in the atmosphere. Calculations indicate that about half of that 1° F. temperature rise might be due to carbon dioxide. During the next few hundred years, the temperature increase could be as high as 2.5° F.

Carbon dioxide causes atmospheric heating because it can discriminate between the heat energy coming from sun to earth, and the heat energy leaving the earth. The essential point to remember is that heat rays coming from the sun are of short wavelength, while those leaving the earth are much longer. The sun's rays pass through the carbon dioxide gas with little absorption. But when the longer, infrared rays from the earth try to escape through the atmosphere, some of them are absorbed. They warm the air instead of passing through to outer space.

Of course, no one knows for sure whether the atmosphere's temperature will increase because of the increased carbon dioxide, or if it does, what effect it will have on climate. We do know, however, that the effect of increased carbon dioxide in the air needs further study.

—W.C.V. rep.

How Do Computers Compute?

There are 2 kinds of computers: analog and digital. Analog computers represent numbers by a physical quantity such as length, angle, or magnitude of electric voltage. The accuracy of analog computers is limited by the precision with which such physical quantities can be measured. Digital computers, on the other hand, represent numbers by separate things such as pebbles, or pulses, of electric current. A person counting on his fingers is really using the simplest of digital computers. Thus, the accuracy of a digital computer is not limited by the accuracy of measurement, but only by the number of digit-representing elements built into the machine. Digital computers are described in the following discussion because of

their great importance in the fields of science, business, and industry.

A complete understanding of how digital computers work is beyond the scope of this book, but it is possible to describe the general principles involved. When you and I do a problem in arithmetic, such as addition or multiplication, we go through several steps:

1. We write down, or store, numbers as necessary.

2. We look them up (retrieve them) as they are needed for subsequent steps.

3. We control the entire operation by performing each step in the required order.

A computer also performs the operations of storage and retrieval of information, and control of each step in the operation.

Imagine for a moment the series of operations you might follow in doing the following simple addition:

$$45$$
$$\underline{87}$$
$$132$$

Step 1
Add the 2 units figures.
$7 + 5 = 12$

Step 2
Write the units figure of the above sum as the units figure of the answer.
− −2 (answer)

A computer follows much the same routine in solving its problems, no matter how complicated they may be. The instructions are stored in the memory unit. They are "read" by the control unit, which directs the arithmetic unit to do the steps specified. The result of each step is stored in the memory unit. When a previously stored number is called for, the control unit transfers the number from the memory unit to the arithmetic unit. Thus, 3 main functions are performed: storage and retrieval of instructions and numbers, processing of numbers by arithmetic, and control of these operations by a program of instructions.

Step 3
Carry the 10s figures of the sum of step 1.
carry 1

Step 4
Add the carried figure to the two 10s figures of the problem.
$1 + 4 + 8 = 13$

Step 5
Write the units figure of the sum of step 4 as the 10s figure of the answer.
−32 (answer)

Step 6
Write the 10s figure of the sum of step 4 as the 100s figure of the answer.
132 (answer)

The required program of instructions must be available before the computation begins. When we solve a problem in arithmetic or algebra, we may not always be aware that a program has been prepared in advance. Nevertheless, stored in our memory are the rules and algorithms used to solve typical problems. If we do happen to get stuck, we merely go to a book and refresh our memory. That's where we have it over the computer. When a computer gets stuck, all it can do is seek human help!

—W.C.V. rep.

Leave On the Lights, but Turn Off the Plutonium

If sunbeams were weapons of war, we would have had solar energy centuries ago.—Sir George Porter, Nobel Laureate in Chemistry

Nuclear fission is the most dangerous method of generating electricity known to man, yet it could bring the captains of American industry enormous wealth even as it jeopardizes the safety of humanity. Through the massive production of weapons-grade nuclear materials, the civilian reactor program greatly enhances the risks of nuclear war, nuclear terrorism by fanatical groups, and nuclear-arms proliferation. In addition, the routine operation of nuclear power plants spreads throughout the world a vile spectrum of lethal poisons which can never be completely contained and which the environment cannot safely absorb. Fortunately, nuclear-fission power is as unnecessary as it is unjustified—we can meet the world's electrical needs without a single fission power plant, if we sensibly temper our energy demands.

Nuclear energy—that is, the energy inherent in the nuclei of atoms—is a broad term encompassing fission as well as fusion energy. The only kind of nuclear power generating facilities that exist today utilize fission. Fusion, a technology that might revolutionize life on earth if scientific barriers to its achievement are breached at a competitive cost, will not happen until near the end of this century, if at all.

Fission power results from the release of heat when uranium atoms, under bombardment by atomic particles known as neutrons, absorb a neutron and split into lighter elements like strontium and iodine. The splitting of the uranium atoms also releases other neutrons which repeat the process in a chain reaction. Heavier elements are also created when some of the uranium-238 atoms do not split but are transformed into plutonium-239 by the absorption of a neutron. Many elements created as a result of fission are unstable, meaning they lose energy rapidly by emitting particles. Known as radioactivity, these emissions are dangerous to living things because they can disrupt genes and tissues. Fission power is unique among all modes of energy in that no other energy technology adds comparable amounts of radiation to natural background levels. The heat released during fission is used to turn water into steam which, when directed against the blades of an electric turbine, creates electricity by the rotation of a coil within a magnetic field.

This process has mesmerized scientists, engineers, and bureaucrats primarily because of one startling fact: The fissioning of just one ounce of uranium releases about the same energy as burning 100 tons of coal. In pursuit of this dazzling energy cornucopia, many have been blinded to the problems and environmental consequences of fission.

Supporters of nuclear fission claim it is "safe, cheap, and environmentally clean," and that its risks are acceptable. They maintain that fission is a proved, available, "on-line" technology whereas alternative energies will not produce power soon enough to meet our needs. Advocates of alternative energies disagree sharply and assert that with only a small fraction of the funds now devoted to nuclear fission, safe alternative energy industries could be created within a few years, and they would yield as much energy as we will get from fission. These advocates are quick to point out how the development of the "gentle energies" has been stunted by the tremendous drain imposed by nuclear fission on U.S. energy-research funds.

The most serious problems with fission result from the fact that a single large fission plant produces as much long-lived radioactivity as the explosion of 1,000 Hiroshima atomic bombs. And it is thought that exposing people to radiation increases their risk of cancer, genetic injuries, heart disease, and many other ailments. In unborn children, radiation apparently increases the risks of birth defects and mental retardation. Yet despite this, the Atomic Energy Commission (AEC) has announced plans to license 1,000 fission plants within the next 25 years. At the end of that period, a total of 2,000 reactors may exist throughout the world (*New York Times*, July 14, 1974), producing staggering amounts of radioactivity.

The most poisonous radioactive pollutant of the many which reactors produce is plutonium. This man-made substance, which does not otherwise occur on earth, is the explosive ingredient in nuclear weapons. It is so deadly that just 3 tablespoons contain enough radioactivity to induce cancers in over half a billion people, according to Dr. John W. Gofman, M.D., Ph.D., codiscoverer of uranium-233, and now a professor of Medical Physics at the University of California. It is probably the world's most toxic substance, he says, and an infinitesimal speck—smaller than a grain of pollen—is almost certain to cause cancer if inhaled from the air or swallowed in water. Yet the

operation of 2,000 reactors will produce more than 800,000 lbs. of the stuff every year—wastes for which no disposal system exists. Instead, the plutonium must be guarded in storage sites with flawless vigilance for at least a quarter of a million years, over 125 times the length of the entire Christian era, unless a new breakthrough is made in waste technology.

The plutonium must also be kept from thieves who might divert it for terrorist purposes. Only a few lbs. of plutonium are needed to make a bomb that could obliterate cities such as San Francisco, New York, or Moscow. This destruction can be wrought with shocking ease. A secret AEC study showed that 2 physicists just out of graduate school, using literature available to the public, were able to design an atomic bomb. The supervision of plutonium is so lax currently that thousands of lbs. of plutonium and enriched uranium already are unaccounted for. The AEC *presumes* this stuff has been lost in the industrial process, but they don't know for sure. Equally unsettling are the results of a study done for the AEC and released in April, 1974, by Senator Abraham A. Ribicoff (Dem.-Conn.). The study termed current regulations to be "entirely inadequate" to protect weapons-grade materials. Yet, think how much more difficult preventing theft will become toward the end of this century when a million kilograms of plutonium are to be shipped annually among 2,000 plants throughout the world (*New York Times*, July 14, 1974).

We live in a time when virtually any country or interest group with a few trained scientists can become a nuclear power, creating an awesome risk of nuclear war or accident. Were these the only dangers of fission power, they would be grounds for abandoning it. Other problems are the unavailability of safe storage techniques for high-level nuclear wastes, the possibility of accidental catastrophic releases of radioactivity from nuclear plants, and routine radioactive emissions.

—Under routine stresses to their containers, high-level wastes seep into the environment, and critics say some have entered ground water. In their tanks, wastes are prey to saboteurs, earthquakes, wars, and accidents, any of which could release colossal amounts of radioactivity at one time.

—Safety systems protecting the public against major nuclear accidents have not even been fully tested under actual operating conditions. A reactor meltdown could cause thousands of deaths and $17 billion in damage, according to the AEC.

—The escape of only a few percent of a reactor core's radioactivity could render an area the size of California uninhabitable.

—Excluding accidents, fission plants routinely

emit radioactivity in their stack gases and waste water. According to computations by eminent scientists, the legal Federal limits for this type of radiation have been set so high that if everyone in the country were exposed to the allowable radiation limits, this would each year produce 32,000 extra cancer-plus-leukemia deaths and 150,000 to 1,500,000 extra genetic deaths. The annual cost of health care just for the genetically-induced diseases has been estimated by Nobel geneticist Joshua Lederberg at $10 billion.

It is a good thing we do not have to pay such a terrible price to meet the nation's energy needs, even though the nuclear industry is clamoring for fission. Understandably, they have been hypnotized by the prospects of gargantuan profits to be made in nuclear power—$800 billion profits from reactors alone in the next 25 years (*Business Week*, February 24, 1973). Utilities have also been hit by higher fossil-fuel prices and by the Clean Air Act's strictures against high-sulfur coal burning. So the industry is pressuring the Government and the public in a stampede toward fission power.

It has been estimated that by 1980, fission plants will provide no more than 7% of the country's total energy or about 20% of its electricity, assuming nothing is done to stop them. Thus if electrical demand could be reduced 20%, all other things being equal, nuclear fission plants could be dispensed with, even without introducing alternative technologies. Data on this point are available in a report, *The Potential for Energy Conservation*, issued by the Office of Emergency Preparedness in October, 1972. This stated that industry could, by cutting waste, reduce its energy demand not merely by 7%, but by 10 to 15% of the projected demand in 1980. At least one other estimate is even more optimistic in its projections of energy savings. So again for this, if for no other reason, the nuclear power program could be scrapped. Of course, large-scale energy conservation will imply many basic economic changes which must be weighed in abandoning fission. Some might have undesirable impacts. Similarly, in the future it may not be desirable or feasible for us to continue deriving the same proportion of our energy from fossil fuels because of economic limits to recoverable fossil-fuel reserves and the environmental damage from increased hydrocarbon combustion.

By burning trash, we could get at least 10% of our electricity. Trash is already being used as fuel at the Union Electric Company plant in St. Louis, Mo., and plans are under way in Connecticut for converting all the State's garbage to low-sulfur fuels. Other localities are following suit and for good reason: The heat

potential in the refuse from the urban population of a State like New York is so great it could produce 13 billion kilowatt hours of electricity (*New York Times*, May 22, 1974). Yet refuse combustion is only one of several practical, available, and competitive energies.

Wind power is another workable technology that can contribute energy to meet some of our needs: The "fuel" is free and nonpolluting. Civil engineering professor William E. Heronemus from the University of Massachusetts has designed a wind-power system that could be constructed off the shores of New England to produce 19 billion kilowatt-hours of electricity at a cost competitive with nuclear fission.

National Science Foundation (NSF) experts stated in December, 1972, that solar energy could ultimately "easily contribute 15–30% of the Nation's energy requirements." For far, far less than we've spent on fission, the development of this stunningly attractive and relatively pollution-free technology could be greatly accelerated. The NSF report concluded that if solar energy research were strongly supported, solar-energy "building heating could reach substantial segments of the public in a year or 2; building cooling in 5–9 years; synthetic fuels in 4–7 years; and electric power production in 9–14 years.

About a quarter of the nation's energy now is used for heating and cooling buildings. Solar energy could eventually provide 30–50% of this energy. There are no major technical barriers to this accomplishment, according to a 1973 report commissioned by the AEC. Using a specialized form of solar energy—photoelectric cells—solar energy could eventually provide 10–20% of our electricity, but technical barriers must be overcome to lower the costs of producing the cell arrays in large quantities. Direct solar energy for heating water is practical and economical, and is currently used in parts of the U.S. such as Florida, and elsewhere.

Although solar energy could soon substitute for fission, the AEC and the utilities are trying to deceive the public that solar energy is still just a gleam in the eyes of a few absent-minded scientists. Meanwhile, major oil companies—which already largely control coal, uranium, oil shale, tar sands, and gas—are buying up solar power companies so that, as Sen. James Abourezk of South Dakota says, "they can thwart solar energy development" and "eliminate interfuel competition."

Geothermal energy is yet another enormous resource that so far is relatively untapped. The hot water and steam under the Imperial Valley in California have been estimated to contain enough energy to have generated 30–90% of the U.S.'s entire electrical production in 1970. And geothermal power is no pie-in-the-sky alternative energy—it is "on-line" now. The Geyser geothermal field in Sonoma County, Calif., run by the Pacific Gas and Electric Company, generates power cheaper than the company's Humboldt Bay nuclear plant. The geothermal fields now in use generally are those close to the earth's surface and deeper reserves may be very hard to tap. The ultimate share of our power contributed by geothermal sources depends on how costly and effective this drilling will be relative to other technologies, but present indications are that it can be an important energy source.

Surely with so many alternatives available —and considering the vast quantities of energy now being wasted—there is insufficient justification for allowing irresponsible, profit-hungry industries to foist on us the huge risks and gigantic costs of nuclear-fission electricity.

—J.Be.

Meet the Meter

A quarter century from now, people will be at a loss to understand why the U.S. did not long ago adopt the metric system as the predominant standard of weights and measures. Since Great Britain finished its planned conversion to the metric system in 1975, the U.S. is virtually the only industrial country in the world which still uses nonmetric units for most practical puposes. Some of the U.S.'s nonmetric allies are Burma, Gambia, Tonga. The U.S. continues to measure length in inches, feet, yards, and miles; liquids in pints, quarts, and gallons; and dry weights in ounces and pounds, bushels and pecks. And temperature still goes by the Fahrenheit scale, on which the triple point—the temperature at which ice, liquid water, and water vapor co-exist in equilibrium—is arbitrarily set at 32° F., and the steam point—the temperature at which water boils—at 212° F. The rest of the world operates almost exclusively with a unit of length called the meter and its multiples and submultiples; with a metrically defined unit of mass, namely the gram and its multiples and submultiples; and with temperature units according to the Celsius scale (formerly called the Centigrade scale), on which the triple point corresponds to 0° C. and the steam point to 100° C.

The advantages of the metric system are impressive—so much so, in fact, that the only legal standard given for the U.S. yard is the international meter (1 yard=0.914 meter). The meter, in turn, was originally defined as a 1/10,000,000 of the distance of the earth's surface from the equator to the pole and measured as such on a platinum-iridium bar kept at the International Bureau of Weights and Measures near Paris. When sophisticated testing methods became available which showed that the bar was subject to minimal but detectable changes in length, the meter was redefined as 1 650 763.73 wavelengths in vacuum of the orange-red line of the spectrum of the element krypton-86, which is held to be invariant.

Standards for measuring mass and volume are related to units of metric length. Thus, the gram is defined as the equivalent of the weight of one cubic centimeter of water at its maximum density; that is, of water in a container which is $\frac{1}{100}$ of a meter in length, width, and height.

The metric system, like the U.S. currency, is a decimal system; all the units are related to each other by a factor of 10. Humans have used their 10 fingers to count on since the dawn of history, so the manipulation of units of 10 is almost 2nd nature. To convert from one metric unit to another, all one has to do is add easily memorized prefixes and shift the decimal point. For example, the prefix "centi" means one hundredth: $c=\frac{1}{100}=10^{-2}=0.01$. "Milli" means one thousandth: $m=\frac{1}{1000}=10^{-3}=0.001$. One millimeter is $\frac{1}{1000}$ of a meter and $\frac{1}{10}$ of a centimeter. "Kilo" means one thousand: $k=1000=10^3$. One thousand grams is one kilogram, which is approximately 2.2 lbs.; a thousand grams is also a liter in liquid measure, which corresponds roughly to one quart. Lists follow giving all the established prefixes and their equivalent values in nonmetric units; these have been prepared not only for weights and measures but for other physical quantities as well.

The nonmetric system and its shortcomings can be traced back to historical developments that took place before uniform reference standards could be established. For example, a medieval British ruler changed the Roman mile of 5,000' to 5,280' to make it conformable with the length of 8 furlongs. Another British king proclaimed that 3 kernels of grain—wheat or barley—laid end to end were the equivalent of one inch which, in turn, was $\frac{1}{12}$ the length of a human foot. As a result we have remained saddled with a complicated system of units which have no relation to one another. There are troy ounces and avoirdupois ounces and liquid ounces. A quart of water has 57.75 cubic inches, but a quart of dry measure is equivalent to 67.20

cubic inches. Pricing or cost accounting of such irregular units using our decimal currency system is an unavoidably laborious process.

The only reason for the continued use of the nonmetric system is human inertia and an unwillingness to accept change. But, contrary to popular opinion, the metric system is already so well established in the U.S. that its official adoption does not constitute the introduction of a radically new system but merely the recognition of one which is already in use in many areas. For instance, we are used to 8-, 16-, or 35-millimeter film; doctors prescribe, pharmacists fill, and nurses administer medicine in cubic centimeter units. The consumption of electricity is measured in watts and kilowatts, and the engine displacement of automobiles is now commonly given in cubic centimeters. Spurred on by General Motors, Ford, IBM, Honeywell, and scores of other large companies who have announced their orderly conversion to the metric system, subcontractors, suppliers, and machine-tool manufacturers will increasingly work to metric standards. Presumably they will produce goods in nonmetric dimensions too, for some time to come, to satisfy the replacement market. But

since that market will disappear in time, production eventually will be geared exclusively to metric standards.

There is no doubt that metrification will be universal throughout the country—whether Congress acts upon the metric conversion proposals that are before it or not. The price we pay for the dual system is much too high. It has been estimated that the U.S. loses annually between $10 and $25 billion either because customers abroad refuse to buy nonmetrically dimensioned goods or because of the waste in labor, costs, warehousing, inventory-keeping, and so on which results from dual production lines—the nonmetric one for the domestic market, and the metric one for the export market.

Inevitably there will be a certain amount of inconvenience during the transition period; but as the British experience has shown, proper planning can eliminate or at least mitigate the unsettling effects of a changeover. Signs and gauges will have to be printed to show readings in both metric and nonmetric terms. Like tourists in a foreign country who are unfamiliar with the local money units, the average person will at 1st refer frequently to conversion tables in order to translate metric

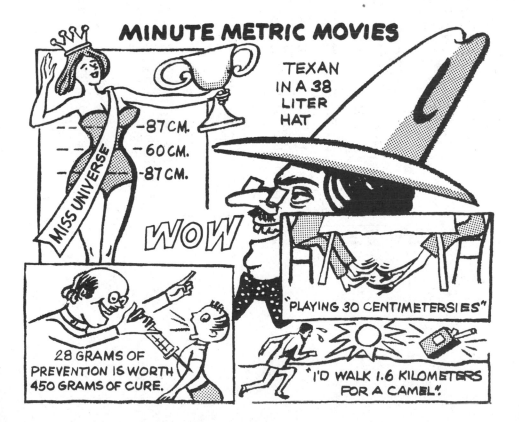

into the accustomed nonmetric terms. Several States, notably Florida and California, contemplate teacher-training programs and a revision of textbooks, so that new generations of schoolchildren are taught the metric system at the elementary school level. Those Americans who have grown up nonmetrically will have to get used to distances and speeds measured in kilometers or kilometers-per-hour instead of as mileage, to buying gas by the liter instead of the gallon, and to purchasing food by the kilogram instead of the pound.

"It's a matter of guesswork how much disorientation a person actually experiences when the dimensions of his life·change," said *Newsweek* magazine. "Does a woman feel temporarily demeaned when her hip size swells from 36 to 91, and does a motorist feel beggared by the 80 liters of gas it takes to fill up his tank? Those who have studied the matter in other countries suggest that children take to the change like a shot—a system universally based on multiples of 10 is a great deal easier and quicker to learn. But older people are likely to be thrown badly by the disorientation of familiar dimensions. When the body temperature registers as 37.5° (centigrade), is that good or bad? Just multiply by 9, divide by 5, and you'll know."

Wherever the cost of a changeover is too high, or if only trivial material is involved, the old units will probably be retained. For example, real estate is expected to remain nonmetric because it would be prohibitively expensive and endlessly complicated to rewrite old deeds or move fences to fit metric dimensions and the inchworm is not likely to become the 2.54 cm.-worm.

—D.Pe.

U.S. DEPARTMENT OF COMMERCE
NATIONAL BUREAU OF STANDARDS
WASHINGTON, D.C. 20234

NBS Letter Circular 1051
July 1973

METRIC CONVERSION FACTORS

Approximate Conversions to Metric Measures

Symbol	When You Know	Multiply by	To Find	Symbol
LENGTH				
in	inches	*2.5	centimeters	cm
ft	feet	30	centimeters	cm
yd	yards	0.9	meters	m
mi	miles	1.6	kilometers	km
AREA				
in²	square inches	6.5	square centimeters	cm²
ft²	square feet	0.09	square meters	m²
yd²	square yards	0.8	square meters	m²
mi²	square miles	2.6	square kilometers	km²
	acres	0.4	hectares	ha
MASS (weight)				
oz	ounces	28	grams	g
lb	pounds	0.45	kilograms	kg
	short tons	0.9	tonnes	t
	(2000 lb)			
VOLUME				
tsp	teaspoons	5	milliliters	ml
Tbsp	tablespoons	15	milliliters	ml
fl oz	fluid ounces	30	milliliters	ml
c	cups	0.24	liters	l
pt	pints	0.47	liters	l
qt	quarts	0.95	liters	l
gal	gallons	3.8	liters	l
ft³	cubic feet	0.03	cubic meters	m³
yd³	cubic yards	0.76	cubic meters	m³
TEMPERATURE (exact)				
°F	Fahrenheit temperature	5/9 (after subtracting 32)	Celsius temperature	°C

*1 in = 2.54 cm (exactly). For other exact conversions and more detailed tables, see NBS Misc. Publ. 286, Units of Weights and Measures, Price $2.25, SD Catalog No. C13.10: 286.

Approximate Conversions from Metric Measures

Symbol	When You Know	Multiply by	To Find	Symbol
LENGTH				
mm	millimeters	0.04	inches	in
cm	centimeters	0.4	inches	in
m	meters	3.3	feet	ft
m	meters	1.1	yards	yd
km	kilometers	0.6	miles	mi
AREA				
cm²	square centimeters	0.16	square inches	in²
m²	square meters	1.2	square yards	yd²
km²	square kilometers	0.4	square miles	mi²
ha	hectares (10,000 m²)	2.5	acres	
MASS (weight)				
g	grams	0.035	ounces	oz
kg	kilograms	2.2	pounds	lb
t	tonnes (1000 kg)	1.1	short tons	
VOLUME				
ml	milliliters	0.03	fluid ounces	fl oz
l	liters	2.1	pints	pt
l	liters	1.06	quarts	qt
l	liters	0.26	gallons	gal
m³	cubic meters	35	cubic feet	ft³
m³	cubic meters	1.3	cubic yards	yd³
TEMPERATURE (exact)				
°C	Celsius temperature	9/5 (then add 32)	Fahrenheit temperature	°F

This Letter Circular (LC1051) provides conversion factors for going from the more common customary units to metric units and vice versa. It may be reproduced freely. LC1051 is based on NBS Special Publication 365 (Revised Nov. 1972), "Metric Conversion Card", available by purchase as a wallet-size plasticized card from the U.S. Government Printing Office, Superintendent of Documents, Washington, D.C. 20402. Price 20 cents domestic postpaid, or 10 cents GPO Bookstore. Stock Number 0303-0168. Catalog No. C13.10: 365/2.   (25 percent discount on orders of 100 or more copies).

18

The Family

The Story behind Mother's Day

Date—2nd Sunday in May. *Origin*—The beginnings of this holiday may have been in the ancient spring festival known as Hilaria, dedicated to the mother goddess Cybele.

In medieval England there was a Mothering Sunday, the 4th Sunday in Lent, when children who had been away from home as apprentices returned to see their mothers, usually bringing the gift of a simnel or mothering cake, a fruit cake with almond paste, meant to be eaten on Mid-Lent Sunday.

The evolution of Mother's Day, as it exists today, began in the U.S. in 1890 when Miss Mary T. Sasseen, of Kentucky, suggested to a gathering of teachers that annual homage be paid to mothers every April 20, her own mother's birthday. Nothing came of the suggestion. In 1892, Robert K. Cummins, head of the Sunday school of the Universalist Church of Our Father in Baltimore, Md., proposed an annual memorial service on the Sunday closest to May 22, the date on which Mrs. Emily C. Pullman, mother of the church's pastor as well as mother of the inventor of the Pullman sleeping car, had died. This service was undertaken, although later the annual service was dedicated not merely to Mrs. Pullman but to all mothers worldwide. While this service was repeated for many years, it did not catch on nationally. In 1902, Fred E. Hering, of Indiana, appealed to the Fraternal Order of Eagles to support a national observance dedicated to mothers. This proposal, too, failed to excite interest.

Finally, the crusade for such a holiday achieved fulfillment through the tireless crusade of one individual. The actual creator of the modern Mother's Day observance was a 41-year-old Philadelphia woman who, ironically, had never been a mother herself. She was Anna M. Jarvis (1864–1948), who remained a spinster throughout her 84 years. Miss Jarvis was a graduate of the Female Seminary, Wheeling, W. Va. Although briefly a teacher in Grafton, W. Va., Miss Jarvis's real career was acting as caretaker to her mother, a very religious woman who taught Sunday school classes in a Methodist church for 2 decades. Miss Jarvis's total devotion to her mother—to the exclusion of marriage for herself or securing her own independence—might have offered a fascinating case-study to a Freudian psychoanalyst. When Mrs. Jarvis finally died in Philadelphia, May 9, 1905, daughter Anna Jarvis was bereft. For 2 to 3 years Miss Jarvis brooded over her loss, and about how neglectful and thoughtless most grown children were of their mothers. Miss Jarvis decided to do something about it. She conceived the idea of an international Mother's Day, a day in which all offspring paid homage to their maternal parent. With that idea, Anna Jarvis had her cause and her obsession.

On May 10, 1908, Miss Jarvis instigated simultaneous Mother's Day services in churches in Grafton, W. Va., and Philadelphia, Pa. These services were mainly held to honor her own mother. Miss Jarvis suggested the wearing of white carnations, her mother's favorite flower. Following these memorials, Miss Jarvis began a strenuous letter-writing campaign, bombarding congressmen, State governors, influential businessmen, clergymen, members of the press, with proposals that a day be set aside dedicated to mothers, both living and dead. Gradually, her hurricane of correspondence began to overcome resistance. In 1910, the governors of West Virginia, Oklahoma, and Washington proclaimed official Mother's Day holidays. Within a year, every other State in the nation had followed suit.

Encouraged, Miss Jarvis formed the Mother's Day International Association in December,

1912. In less than 2 years Miss Jarvis saw her idea become a reality. Both Houses of the U.S. Congress passed resolutions requesting the Chief Executive to proclaim such a holiday. On May 9, 1914, President Woodrow Wilson issued a proclamation directing "government officials to display the U.S. flag on all government buildings" and inviting "the people of the U.S. to display the flag at their homes or other suitable places on the 2nd Sunday in May as a public expression of our love and reverence for the mothers of our country."

The holiday quickly caught on elsewhere, and was soon being observed in Canada, Mexico, and parts of South America, as well as in Japan.

Despite her triumph, Miss Jarvis's last 3 decades of life were unhappy. She busied herself nursing a blind sister, attending Sunday school conventions, and supervising the observance of her holiday. But gradually the holiday got away from her. She lived to see what she had meant to be a religious observance slowly become a strictly commercial holiday exploited by florists, greeting-card companies, and candy manufacturers. Presently, Miss Jarvis lost her sister, then her home, and then her sight. In 1944, ailing and penniless, she was placed in a West Chester, Pa., sanitarium, there supported by friends until her death in 1948.

Minibiographies of Three Famous Mothers

Perhaps the 3 most widely known mothers in the world today are—The Virgin Mary, mother of Jesus; Mother Goose; Whistler's Mother.

The Virgin Mary (b. ca. 25 B.C.—d. after 30 A.D.)

She was cousin to John the Baptist's mother. She lived in the village of Nazareth, in Judea, where she met and married Joseph, a carpenter and a member of the house of David. According to the Eastern Church, Joseph had been married once before and brought 4 sons and several daughters to the marriage. According to some Protestants, Mary conceived these children by Joseph after the birth of Jesus. When Mary was 15, according to Justin Martyr writing in 150 A.D., "the power of God coming upon the virgin overshadowed her and caused her to conceive though she was a virgin."

The child she conceived was Jesus, and he was born in Bethlehem, and she had him circumcised after 8 days. To save Jesus from being slain by King Herod, Mary and Joseph took the child Jesus to Egypt and stayed with relatives for what may have been several years. Returning to Galilee, Mary placed Jesus in a primary school. It is conjectured that Joseph died 3 years after Jesus's bar

mitzvah. Historian Will Durant believes that, next to Jesus, Mary is the most touching figure in the New Testament, rearing her 1st-born "through all the painful joys of motherhood, proud of his youthful learning, wondering later at his doctrines and his claims, wishing to withdraw him from the exciting throng of his followers and bring him back to the healing quiet of his home . . . helplessly witnessing his crucifixion, and receiving his body into her arms . . ."

According to The Zondervan Bible Dictionary: "After the resurrection and ascension of Jesus, Mary appears in the midst of the Christian community, engaged with them in prayer . . . but without any discernible preeminence among them. This is the last notice of her in the Scripture. It is not known how or when she died."

Mother Goose or Elizabeth Foster Goose (1665– 1757)

Mother Goose, the legendary creator of fairy stories and nursery rhymes such as "Sing a Song of Sixpence," "Old King Cole," "Little Jack Horner," was known in France as far back as 1650, and she was immortalized in a French book of fairy tales, Tales of My Mother Goose, by Charles Perrault in 1697. But there was an actual American woman known by the nickname of "Mother Goose" who may have inspired a book or broadside entitled Songs for the Nursery, or Mother Goose's Melodies for Children. Allegedly, this was published (its existence remains a matter of scholarly controversy) in Boston by her printer son-in-law in 1719, just 10 years before the Perrault version appeared in English.

The woman known as the American Mother Goose was born Elizabeth Foster in Charleston, Mass., in 1665. At 27, she married a widower, Isaac Goose (formerly Vergoose), 55, of Boston. She found herself stepmother of 10 children, and she, herself, bore Goose 6 additional children, 2 of whom died in infancy. One of the surviving daughters grew up to wed a fugitive printer from England, Thomas Fleet, who established a print shop on Pudding Lane in Boston. This daughter gave birth to 7 children, and grandmother Elizabeth Goose often tended the young ones, entertaining them with fables and nursery rhymes. Some were drawn from folklore, but others possibly were her own inventions. It is said that her son-in-law, the printer Fleet, "was almost driven distracted" by his mother-in-law's singing and storytelling.

In 1719, 9 years after her husband's death, Elizabeth Goose's tales and rhymes—the ones she remembered and repeated and the ones she created—supposedly were published in a book by her son-in-law. In preparing the book, according to Vincent Starrett, Fleet "collected other rhymes, too, it is believed, from sources other than" his mother-in-law. No copy of the American Mother Goose's book has survived. Proof of its existence rests on the word of Thomas Fleet's great-grandson, John Fleet Eliot, who wrote in 1860 that "Edward A. Crowninshield, a literary gentleman [then 24 years old]" had told him "he had seen a copy of Fleet's book in the Library of the American Antiquarian Society at Worcester." The Library was never able to produce that ghost edition.

No real Mother Goose originated the well-loved stories and rhymes. But an American Mother Goose, whose own version of the age-old tales and verses may or may not have been published in 1719, did exist. This American Mother Goose died in Boston in 1757, at the age of 92, and was laid to rest in the Old Granary Burying Ground. She left an estate worth £27.

Whistler's Mother, Anna McNeill Whistler (1804–1881)

Her parents were North Carolina slaveholders, and she was raised strictly in the Episcopalian faith. At 15, she met an Indiana-born West Point cadet named George Washington Whistler, and fell in love with him. However, he married Anna's best friend the following year. In 1831, after George Whistler had been a widower for 4 years, he remarried, taking Anna McNeill as his 2nd wife. Anna inherited 3 stepchildren, but in 1834 she gave her husband their 1st of 5 children, and the 1st proved to be James McNeill Whistler, who would become the celebrated painter and do the world-renowned portrait of his mother.

Incidentally, while it was Whistler's mother who became famous, it was actually Whistler's father who was considered a genius in his time. The father, George Washington Whistler, an assistant professor of mathematics at West Point, a surveyor and engineer, constructed the 1st mile of passenger railroad track in the U.S. for the Baltimore and Ohio Railroad, invented the locomotive steam whistle (which was not named after him), surveyed part of the U.S.-Canada border, went to Russia at the request of Czar Nicholas I to build the Moscow-St. Petersburg railroad at an eventual cost of $40 million.

When the elder Whistler died in 1849, his widow, Anna, took their son James Whistler, then 15, back to Connecticut, there to resume his schooling. James became the family black sheep. He was thrown out of West Point in his 3rd year for having both an excess of demerits and poor grades, and he later quit his job with the War Department's Coast and Geodetic Survey section. In 1855, rebelling against convention, James left America to live as an expatriate abroad, mostly in Paris and London, where he became a painter. After the Civil War, Anna, a Confederate sympathizer, went to live with her son, James, in London. Hastily, her son moved his Irish model-mistress, Jo Heffernan, out of his flat, to make way for his prim, religious mother.

Although frequently at odds with his straitlaced mother, James Whistler respected her for her goodness and compassion. During her lifetime, she had devoted herself to nursing 20 members of her family and circle of friends before their deaths. James Whistler was also enchanted by his mother's face, in which he saw "grace wedded to dignity, strength enhancing sweetness." One day in 1870, when his mother was 65, James decided to paint her in his London flat. Wearing her lace bonnet and black dress, she sat in an ebony dining room chair, using a footstool because of her age, as he did his classic portrait of her. Completing it in 1871, he called it, "Arrangement in Gray and Black No. 1." The world would come to call it "Whistler's Mother."

Anna Whistler died in Hastings, England. Her artist son arranged for her burial in the Borough Cemetery. On her white gravestone was inscribed: "Blessed are they who have/not seen/And yet have believed." After the funeral, James Whistler borrowed £50 to get his mother's portrait out of hock. Later, he tried to sell the portrait in New York for $500, but there were no takers. When Degas arranged to have the painting compete in an exhibit of the French Salon, it won the 3rd-class medal, and that proved to be the turning point for Whistler. He wanted the painting to be accepted by a French museum. Through the efforts of the poet Mallarmé, and the lobbying of future Premier Clemenceau, the National Museum of the Luxembourg Palace bought the masterpiece for the equivalent of $625. Today it hangs in the Louvre. In 1934, the U.S. Postmaster issued a commemorative Mother's Day stamp bearing the painting of Whistler's mother.

How Celebrated Today—Mother's Day has been almost totally transformed into a secular holiday. The main props are flowers and gifts. The white carnation Miss Jarvis promoted, "because it typifies the beauty, truth, and fidelity of mother love," is now worn in memory of a deceased mother, while red carnations have been introduced to honor a living mother. On this day children are reminded to send their mothers bouquets of flowers, plants, boxes of candy, or to send wires or make telephone calls.

Mother's Day has received 2 severe blows in recent times. The 1st blow came from the increasing popularity of psychiatry. As H. R. Hays noted, society learned from Freud "that the innocence of childhood and the purity of women, 2 of its favorite illusions, were pure myth." The 2nd blow was administered in May, 1942, by Philip Wylie in his sensational book, *Generation of Vipers*, in which he brutally attacked the cult of mother worship and momism. Wylie said: "Megaloid momworship has got completely out of hand. . . . The machine has deprived her of social usefulness; time has stripped away her biological possibilities and poured her hide full of liquid soap; and man has sealed his own soul beneath the clamorous cordillera by handing her the checkbook and going to work in the service of her caprices. . . . The mealy look of men today is the result of momism and so is the pinched and baffled fury in the eyes of womankind."

It might be added that on March 5, 1934, a Mother-in-Law Day was added to the roster of holidays, conceived in Amarillo, Tex., by Gene Howe, publisher-editor of the Amarillo Daily News, and inspired by his desire to honor his mother-in-law, Mrs. W. F. Donald.

—I.W.

Emergency Childbirth

What to Do

1. Nature is the best helper. Childbirth is a very natural act.
2. At 1st signs of labor assign the best qualified person to remain with the mother.
3. Be calm; reassure the mother.
4. Place the mother and the attendant in the most protected place. . . .

Preparations

The mother will need a clean surface to lie on. Her bed should be so arranged that the mattress is well protected by waterproof sheeting or pads made from several thicknesses of paper covered with cloth. Cover these protective materials with a bed sheet or towels.

Supplies for emergency delivery and aftercare of mother and child should . . . consist of the following:

1. One-yard square of outing flannel, hemmed (receiving blanket).
2. Towels or sheets.
3. One or 2 diapers.
4. Four sanitary napkins (wrapped).
5. Rubber gloves.
6. Small pair of scissors or a safety razor blade with a guard on one side.
7. Pieces of white cotton tape, ½″ wide and 9″ long.
8. Roll of 3″ gauze bandage.
9. Gauze compresses, 4″×4″ size.
10. Safety pins.

The 3 Stages of Labor

Labor is the term used to described the process by which the child is expelled from the uterus and consists of contractions of the wall of the womb (uterus) which force the baby and, later, the afterbirth (placenta) from the vagina. . . .

1st Stage of Labor. The 1st stage is generally the longest and covers the period in which the small opening at the lower end of the womb gradually stretches until it is large enough to let the baby pass through. The contractions (tightening) of the uterus, which bring about this stretching . . . are 5 to 30 minutes apart and are cramplike in character.

These pains, usually beginning as an aching sensation in the small of the back, become regularly recurring cramplike pains in the lower abdomen within a short time. By placing a hand on the mother's abdomen just above the navel, tightening of the uterus may be felt as an increasing firmness or hardness. The pains disappear each time the uterus relaxes. Early pains are not very severe; they may even stop for a while and then start up again. A slight watery, bloodstained discharge from the vagina normally accompanies labor pains or occurs before the pains begin.

The mother should not attempt to push the baby down by bearing down, but should try to relax her muscles. She can do this by taking deep breaths with her mouth open during each tightening. During the 1st stage of labor, uterine contractions are involuntary and controlled. Not only is it futile for the mother to bear down, but it leads to exhaustion and may tear parts of the birth canal.

The end of this 1st stage is usually signaled by the sudden passing of a large gush of water (a pint or so). This is caused by the normal breaking of the bag of waters which surrounds the baby in the mother's womb; it cleanses and lubricates the birth canal. With some women, the bag of water breaks before labor begins or is the 1st sign of its beginning. This should not cause the mother or those helping her any concern as it usually does not affect the birth.

Preparations should be made to transport the mother to medical attention if birth is not imminent.

2nd Stage of Labor. Gradually the time between labor pains grows shorter and the pains increase in severity until they come every 2 or 3 minutes. At this point it will not be long before the baby is born. At the beginning of this stage the mother will notice a change. Instead of the tightness in the lower abdomen and pain across the back, she will feel a bearing down sensation almost as if she were having a bowel movement. This means the baby is moving down. When this happens, she should lie down and get ready for the birth of the child. The tightening and bearing down feelings will come more frequently and be harder.

If the patient has had a full meal and is

near delivering, she will often vomit. She will have an uncontrollable urge to push down, which, at this point, is permissible. However, the mother should not work too hard at it because the baby will be brought out without much straining. There will probably be more blood showing at this point; if bleeding is heavy and is pure blood, it is an extreme danger signal.

The person attending the delivery should scrub his hands thoroughly with soap and water, or wear rubber gloves. The attendant should never touch the vagina or put fingers inside. The mother should also keep her hands away from the vagina.

The very last occurrence before the child is born is referred to as crowning; the vaginal opening will bulge and the top of the child's head will actually be seen. At this time the mother should stop pushing down. She should try to breathe like a panting dog with her mouth open in order not to push the baby out too rapidly, with consequent tearing of her tissues.

The patient should be placed on her back with her knees elevated and legs separated so that the person helping her can get at the baby more easily. But the attendant helping the mother should always let the baby be born by itself. No attempt should be made to pull the baby out in any way.

Usually the baby's head appears 1st, the top of the head presenting and the face downward. Infrequently the baby will be born in a different position, sometimes buttocks 1st, occasionally foot or arm 1st. In these infrequent situations, patience without interference in the birth process is most important. The natural process is most important. The natural process of delivery, although slower, will give the child and the mother the best chance of a safe and successful birth. . . .

Usually about a minute after the head appears the mother will have another bearing down impulse; this will push the shoulders and the rest of the baby out. While supporting the head, feel around the neck to determine if the cord, which attaches the child from its navel to the placenta in the mother's womb, is wrapped around the baby's neck. If it is, try to slip it quickly over his head so that he will not strangle. If the cord is too tight, it must be cut.

As the baby is being expelled, the person helping the mother should support the baby on his or her arms so that the child will avoid contact with any blood or waste material on the bed. If there is still a membrane from the water sac over the baby's head and face at delivery, it should immediately be taken between the fingers and torn so that the water inside will run out and allow the child to breathe.

The mother sometimes has difficulty delivering the shoulders because of their width. The top shoulder is usually the 1st to present itself; slight downward pressure on the head towards the floor will help deliver the upper shoulder. . . .

Care of the Baby. After the child is born, wrap a fold of towel around his ankles to prevent slipping and hold him up by the heels with one hand, taking care that the cord is kept slack (if still attached) and there is no tension on either end. To get a good, safe grip, insert one finger between the baby's ankles. Do not swing or spank the baby. Hold him over the bed so that he cannot fall very far if he should slip from the grasp; the baby's body will be very slippery. Place the other hand under the child's forehead and bend its head back slightly so that the fluid and mucus can run out of its mouth. With a piece of gauze, wipe the mouth free of mucus and cleanse the nostrils. Pull the tongue forward by grasping it top and bottom and pulling it out to the lower lip. These operations should be done in all deliveries, whether the child breathes spontaneously or not.

The child is now on his own and should be able to start to breathe; he will usually cry within the 1st minute. At most emergency deliveries the child will cry spontaneously. If he does not cry or breathe within 2 or 3 minutes, gently compress his chest with the fingers. Spanking the buttocks or rubbing the infant's back is seldom effective. Mouth-to-mouth artificial respiration may be resorted to if other measures are not effective. Very little force should be used while blowing air into the baby's mouth; form a seal over both the baby's mouth and nose. A short puff of breath every 5 seconds is enough. As soon as the child starts to breathe or cry, artificial respiration should be stopped. . . .

Wrap the baby warmly and lay him on his left side across the mother's abdomen, beside the mother, or between her legs. Both baby and mother must be kept warm. Tears of the mother's vagina will not cause serious bleeding. There is generally no reason to cut the umbilical cord unless medical attention is considerably delayed.

3rd Stage of Labor. Usually a few minutes after the baby is born, but sometimes more than an hour, the mother will feel a brief return of the labor pains which had ceased with the birth. These are due to contractions of the uterus as it attempts to expel the afterbirth. Do not pull on the cord to hurry this process. There is no great hurry for delivery of the placenta.

If the placenta is delivered, wrap it in plastic or paper and deliver it to the doctor for examination. He must determine if any particles have been left within the mother.

Some bleeding is to be expected at this stage. A sanitary napkin can be placed in position; pressure of the thighs is sufficient to hold it in place. Keep the mother's knees raised and together while she is being transported to the hospital.

Hemorrhage after delivery can cause the mother's death at this stage. If there is profuse bleeding after the placenta is delivered, push the mother's uterus up into her abdomen by pressing the fingers immediately above the pelvis in the midline in front, and by strongly pressing down into her abdomen. This will bring her uterus up into the abdomen proper and enable grasping and holding the enlarged womb, or uterus, which will be about the size of a large grapefruit; it must contract to control the bleeding from its inside surface. To help the womb to contract, grasp it through the mother's abdominal wall just below the umbilicus (navel) and gently knead it until it becomes firm. Continue the kneading for about an hour until the uterus is firmly contracted and danger of hemorrhage is past. It may be desirable to put the baby almost immediately to the mother's breast for a minute or 2 on each side even though she will have no milk as yet. This helps the uterus contract and reduces the bleeding.

Whether or not severe hemorrhage occurs, someone should stand by the mother and occasionally massage her abdomen gently for about an hour after the afterbirth is expelled. After that, the mother should feel the rounded surface of the uterus through her abdomen and squeeze firmly but gently with her fingers. Holding onto the uterus should prevent a fatal hemorrhage.

Cleansing the Baby's Eyes

The infant's eyes should be wiped out, using separate material for each eye and wiping from the inside to the outside. Where ampules of one percent silver nitrate are available, 2 drops of the medication should be placed in the conjunctival sac, not directly on the cornea. This may be done immediately after birth or delayed until the placenta has been delivered and the mother cleaned. Where silver nitrate, one percent, is not available, note this fact on the records so that this protective procedure may be accomplished as soon as possible. This measure is essential in order to prevent the possibility of an eye defect should the mother have a gonorrheal infection, and is required by law.

Assistance under Extreme Conditions

Tying and Cutting the Cord. There should be no hurry to cut the cord. Take as much time as necessary to prepare the ties and sharp instruments.

About 5 minutes after the baby is born the umbilical cord will cease to pulsate. Tie the cord with sterile tape in 2 places, one about 4" from the baby and the other 2" farther along the cord toward the mother. Use a square knot; tighten slowly and evenly so as not to cut the cord. Do not tie the cord too tightly, as it is quite soft and may tear. Take the loose ends of the material and tie another knot on the other side. The placenta end is not as important as the end attached to the child.

Cut the cord between these 2 ties with a clean sharp instrument such as a knife, razor blade, or scissors. If the cord continues to bleed, fold it over and tie again.

A sterile dressing about 4" square should be placed over the cut end of the cord at the baby's navel and should be held in place by wrapping a "belly band" or folded diaper around the baby. If a sterile dressing is not available, no dressing or belly band should be used. Regardless of whether a dressing is applied, no solution, powder, or disinfectant of any kind should be put on the cord or navel.

If the afterbirth has not yet been expelled, the end of the umbilical cord now protruding from the vagina may be covered with a sterile dressing.

Abnormal Presentation

Breech Presentation. Occasionally the buttocks of the child presents itself 1st. Delivery is difficult since the head is the last out and must have special consideration. The attendant may help expel the baby by pressing firmly on the abdomen below the navel if all of the child's body is out except the head. No attempt should be made to pull the child out; both the mother and baby would be injured.

If the infant's buttocks and/or feet are showing, the mother can push the baby out to its navel. Making sure the infant's back is anterior (the navel toward the floor), the rescuer may pull gently on the child's ankles with one hand flat on the mother's abdomen just above the pubis, pressing down to assist the child's head into the pelvis. There is no hurry unless a hand of the baby or the cord appears outside the vagina.

In severe cases the infant may suffocate, or brain damage may occur, when the time taken to deliver the head is very long. The child can rest on the rescue man's hand, the legs straddling his arm. An air passage may then be created by inserting the index and 2nd finger of the other hand into the vaginal canal in such a way that the palm is underneath and facing the baby. Run the fingers around the baby's neck until the chin is found. At this point the 2 fingers should be run between the child's chin and the vaginal canal. As the infant's nose is reached, the rescuer should separate his fingers, placing one on each side of the baby's nose. When in this position, the attendant should push his fingers away from the infant's face, facilitating a good airway. The rescuer should keep the fingers in this position until the entire head is delivered. . . .

Protruding Cord. If a loop of the cord protrudes from the vagina before the baby is delivered, this condition must be corrected immediately since it can be very dangerous to the child. The cord will be squeezed tightly during the birth and the child will be deprived of food and oxygen.

Attempt to drop the baby away from the pelvic brim by placing the mother on her knees with the hips as high as possible and the head low. If this fails, raise the foot of the bed or stretcher while the mother is lying on her back with raised knees; this may allow the cord to reenter. Prevent protruding parts from being contaminated by wrapping in a sterile sheet or towel. Elevate the patient's buttocks as high as possible and keep her head low while transporting her.

—L.W.E. rep.

What Happened to Children of Some Famous Parents?

JOHANN SEBASTIAN BACH'S CHILDREN

Johann Bach was at the center of 7 generations of musicians, beginning with his great-grandfather Veit Bach (1555–1619). Bach, often called the Father of Modern Music, also fathered 20 children, all of whom received musical training. None had their father's genius, but 3 sons contributed significantly to the music of their day:

Wilhem Friedemann (1710–1784), the eldest son, was an outstanding organist and composer, but his personality problems affected his music adversely. He was a heavy drinker, unreliable, and hard to get along with, and never was able to break free from his father's musical influence to develop a style of his own.

Carl Philip Emanuel (1714–1788) came closest to attaining his father's musical stature. He was a brilliant harpsichordist and the greatest authority of his time on the art of playing the clavier; his "Essay on the True Art of Playing Keyboard Instruments" remains an essential source book for understanding the style and interpretation of 18th-century music.

Johann Christian (1735–1782), a fashionable and successful but relatively slight talent, was organist of the Milan cathedral. He wrote Italian operas and much orchestral, chamber, and keyboard music, but the quantity of his output exceeded its quality.

A 4th son, Johann Gottfried Bernhard (1715–1739), was an organist who got into serious financial difficulties; his father bailed him out, but soon afterward the young man died of a fever.

BENJAMIN FRANKLIN'S CHILDREN

Benjamin Franklin had 2 legitimate sons by his wife Deborah. One died at the age of 4. The other son, William (1731–1813), was with Franklin in 1752 when he flew the famous kite. William was the last royal governor of New Jersey before the Revolution; when the war broke out, he sided with the British. He was tried as a traitor and imprisoned until 1782, when he was deported to England, where he remained for the rest of his life. But in 1784, after receiving overtures toward reconciliation from his Tory son, Franklin wrote to him. "Nothing has ever hurt me so much," he confessed, "as to find myself deserted in my old age by my only son; and not only deserted, but to find him taking up arms against me in a cause wherein my good fame, fortune, and life were all at stake . . . we will endeavor, as you propose, mutually to forget what has happened." A 3rd son, acknowledged although illegitimate, was raised by Deborah Franklin.

Franklin's only daughter, Sarah (1744–?) was well known for her efforts on behalf of the rebel soldiers during the War. She married a merchant, Richard Bache, her father's successor as postmaster general, and gave Franklin 7 grandchildren, and nursed her father in his old age. His favorite grandson, Benjamin Franklin Bache, nicknamed "Lightning Rod, Jr.," was a prominent political journalist. Many of Franklin's grandsons and great-grandsons had distinguished careers.

LORD BYRON'S CHILDREN

George Gordon, Lord Byron, fathered 2 daughters, one of them illegitimate. His 1st daughter, Augusta Ada, was born in 1815 of his ill-fated marriage to Annabella Milbanke. The Byrons separated almost immediately after Ada's birth, and Byron saw very little of the girl thereafter.

Ada was 15 years old before she found out that her father was a famous poet. As she grew to adulthood, she expressed genuine fondness in her letters to him. She became an accomplished mathematician (just as her mother had been), but apparently she inherited no poetic gifts from her father. She almost bankrupted her husband when she tried to apply her mathematical techniques to racetrack betting. She died at 36, in 1852.

A case of hero worship resulted in the birth of a daughter to Claire Clairmont, who followed Byron to Switzerland and Italy. The child, born in 1817, was variously called Alba (for "Dawn"), Clara, and finally Allegra. Although never legitimized, she was supposed to receive a legacy from her father's estate. But Byron outlived her: She died of a fever in the convent where he had installed her to "get a proper Catholic upbringing," just before her 6th birthday.

Byron, who never saw his own father, was an unsatisfactory parent. His poems were his "children"; they received the love and energy no human could evoke from him.

ABRAHAM LINCOLN'S CHILDREN

Abraham and Mary Todd Lincoln had 4 boys, only one of whom survived to adulthood. Robert Todd (1843–1926) was an introvert by nature, never comfortable in the glare of publicity that surrounded him much of his life. Many thought he might have become President himself, had he ever sought the office. He was unlike his father in physique and in philosophy; he was a millionaire corporation lawyer and businessman of decidedly conservative views. Personal tragedy dogged him throughout his life: His 3 brothers died, his father was assassinated, his only son died young, and his mother's mental illness eventually forced him to institute a sanity hearing that resulted in her commitment to a sanitarium. He is said to have felt that had he accompanied his parents to Ford Theater on that fatal evening, he might have helped avert his father's assassination. Ironically, 2 years previous to the assassination, Robert had been rescued from a near accident on a train station platform by Edwin Booth, John Wilkes's brother.

ALEXANDRE DUMAS'S CHILDREN

Alexandre Dumas, père, had 3 illegitimate children, all of whom he formally acknowledged, although he married none of the mothers. The 1st and most famous was Alexandre Dumas, known forever after as Dumas, fils, to distinguish famous son from famous father. Dumas, fils, was born in 1824 to Catherine Labay, his father's current mistress; she raised the boy until he was 8, when Dumas, père, filed suit for the boy's custody and won it. Dumas, fils, grew up in various households that entertained such guests as Victor Hugo, George

Sand, Heinrich Heine, Lamartine, and Delacroix. The father was passionate and impulsive, a confirmed romantic; the son was circumspect, logical, an antiromantic in the tradition of Flaubert. But even though raised in the giant shadow of his father's huge literary successes— *The Three Musketeers, The Count of Monte Cristo*—Dumas, fils, managed to become a reputable French dramatist-writer. His major surviving work is *The Lady of the Camellias*. The son took care of his father in his last sickly days; of his father's life-style and literary style, he said to critics, "My father is a river. Anyone can foul a river."

Marie Alexandre was born in 1832 to an actress who enjoyed a short period as Dumas's favorite. Dumas saw little of this child until she was in the process of divorcing a brutal husband. She lived with her father in later years when his powers were waning, and creditors were daily callers. Marie dabbled ineffectually in painting and literature, but most of her energy went into her religion. Neither father nor daughter were any good with finances or management of any kind, and their life together was chaotic. It took Alexandre, fils, to straighten matters out.

Dumas was nearly 60 when his last child, Micaelle Clélie Cecilia, was born in 1860 to one Emilee Cordier. Dumas was inordinately fond of this child of his late years, but he died when she was 10, leaving his children a bankrupt estate.

KARL MARX'S CHILDREN

"The Father of Modern Communism" also fathered 7 children, 4 of whom survived to adulthood. His only son, Frederic Demuth (1851–1929) was illegitimate; "Freddy's" mother, Helen Demuth, was maidservant to Marx's wife. Marx never acknowledged paternity, and it was not until 12 years after his death, when Frederic Engels lay on *his* deathbed, that it was revealed—by Engels, writing on a blackboard—that "Freddy is Marx's son."

Freddy became a skilled machinist and lived a quiet, decent, not particularly happy life. Physically, he resembled his father. He was a reserved, gentle man, dedicated to socialism but not to revolution.

Jenny (1844–1883), named after her mother, was her father's favorite. She lived with her husband (a Socialist) and children in France, until she died of tuberculosis.

Laura (1846–1911) was quieter, more reliable than her 2 sisters; in this respect, she resembled her mother. She also married a French Socialist and had 3 children, all of whom died in their infancy. In her 65th year, she and her husband agreed they had nothing to live for and committed suicide.

Eleanor (1856–1898), Marx's youngest daughter, was emotionally crippled by the excessive dominance of her father's personality. "It is overmuch," she wrote, "to have Karl as my father. I do not have my own life." She did seem incapable of leading any sort of normal life, having inherited all her father's worst qualities and little of her mother's gentleness. She made political speeches, wrote some political propaganda, acted in amateur theatricals, edited her father's posthumous papers, but she lacked self-discipline, was neurotic, and most of her efforts were abortive.

During her father's lifetime, Eleanor was emotionally chained to him; after his death, she formed a similar relationship with her common-law husband, Edward Aveling. Aveling resembled her father in that he was learned, charming, brutally sarcastic, utterly unscrupulous, hot-tempered, and incapable of making a living. He. was a Marxist 2nd, an opportunist and psychotic 1st. Eleanor supported him for 15 years until, at his suggestion, she committed suicide.

The various fates of Karl Marx's progeny were so tragic that in 1898, near the end of her life, Eleanor wrote to her half brother, "I don't think you and I have been particularly bad people—and yet, dear Freddy, it really seems as though we are being punished."

PHINEAS T. BARNUM'S CHILDREN

Barnum had 4 daughters by his wife, Charity. Caroline (1833–1911) was the eldest, and his favorite. As a young woman, she traveled with him when he escorted Jenny Lind, "the Swedish Nightingale," on her American concert tour. When Caroline accompanied him to church and sang with the choir the congregation thought *she* was Jenny Lind. Caroline married a businessman and died wealthy, but never was noted for any accomplishments of her own.

Of all the children, Helen (b. 1840–?) was probably the one most like her father; she left her husband (Barnum's treasurer) and her 3 children for another man, an action described by the *New York World* as "about as sensational as anything in the Barnum family history." Her father strongly disapproved, but she blamed her passions and misfortunes on his example. "How could I help it?" she asked him. "Am I not P. T. Barnum's daughter?"

Pauline (1846–1877), Barnum's 4th daughter (the 3rd died in infancy) was a large, buxom, beautiful girl with a 1st-rate singing voice. Her father sponsored her in several touring vaudeville shows, but her budding career ended when she married a stockbroker.

Barnum's only son was illegitimate. He became a doctor; his descendants all led relatively quiet lives, and seemed rather ashamed of the "circus money" they had inherited.

JOHN D. ROCKEFELLER'S CHILDREN

"My mother and father raised but one question: Is it right, is it duty?" This was the legacy inherited (along with a huge fortune) by John D. Rockefeller, Jr. (1874–1960), the only son of America's most famous billionaire.

Awed and unquestioning, the young Rockefeller followed in his father's footsteps, faithfully filling out a daily ledger his father had taught him to use as soon as he could read and write. The boy entered every 2¢ he earned for killing flies or sharpening pencils; mending a vase netted him $1. He inculcated this habit into his 6 children, all of whom also kept ledgers.

John, Jr., had the reputation of being tight-fisted, though he always tithed 10% for charity. His one flamboyant act was a fling at speculation when he 1st entered Wall Street. He was immediately fleeced of $1 million. Deeply ashamed of having caused his father anguish, he never again undertook any transaction without consulting the elder Rockefeller (and never again did he lose money). He married Abby Aldrich, a senator's daughter, who bore him one daughter, Abby, and then 5 sons in a row: John D., III, b. 1906; Nelson Aldrich, b. 1908; Laurance Spelman, b. 1910; Winthrop, b. 1912; and David, b. 1915. Except for Winthrop, former governor of Arkansas, who died in 1969, all the senior Rockefeller's grandsons are living. John D., III, runs the Rockefeller Foundation and Lincoln Center in New York. Nelson was governor of New York and was appointed Vice-President of the U.S. in 1974. He continues to have presidential aspirations. Laurance is deeply involved in conservation and building resort hotels. David is president of Chase Manhattan Bank.

When the senior Rockefeller was 94 years old in 1933, his 59-year-old son wrote him in a letter, "I have tried to do what you would have me do. I have striven to follow in your footsteps. In all these years of striving, your own life and example have been to me the most powerful and stimulating influence."

The continuity of the Rockefeller philosophy is reflected in a statement made by Laurance, referring to his father: "It is example, not precept, which is the important influence in molding the character of the young, and my father's example was completely consistent with the precepts by which he lived."

DR. SIGMUND FREUD'S CHILDREN

Freud had 3 sons and 3 daughters, all of whom were overshadowed by his genius. He was a lenient, liberal, loving father—affectionate, but not demonstrative. His work was so demanding that the children were raised largely by their mother, Martha, but in a harmonious atmosphere.

Martin (b. 1889–   ), the eldest son, has described his childhood in Vienna around the turn of the century as idyllic. In 1957, he wrote candidly, "I have never had any ambition to rise to eminence . . . I have been quite happy and content to bask in reflected glory . . . I believe that if the son of a great and famous father wants to get anywhere in this world he must follow the advice given to Alice by the Red Queen—he will have to go twice as fast if he does not want to stop where he is. The son of a genius remains the son of a genius, and his chances of winning human approval of anything he may do hardly exist if he attempts to make any claim to a fame detached from that of his father." Martin's only claim to fame was as a devoted son; he headed his father's publishing firm, handled his father's finances and legal affairs.

Anna (1895–   ), the youngest child, was her father's favorite. By no Freudian slip, he once referred to her as "my only son, Anna." They were extremely close, their communication almost telepathic. In Freud's last years, Anna, a practicing child psychoanalyst in her own right, was her father's nurse, companion, secretary, coworker, and shield against the intrusions of the world. In 1935, during a period of illness, Freud wrote that "the one bright spot in my life is the success of Anna's work."

BENITO MUSSOLINI'S CHILDREN

Although Mussolini had 5 children by his wife, Rachele Guidi, he was a father in absentia much of the time; his son Vittorio (b. 1916–   ) stated that his father "did not belong to his family." To Mussolini, children were little more than raw material from which to create future fascists and soldiers.

Edda (b. 1910–   ), his firstborn and favorite, most resembled him in looks and personality. She was headstrong and rebellious and, even after her marriage, something of a swinger. Her father arranged her marriage to Count Galeazzo Ciano. Ciano was expected to become Il Duce's successor, but his father-in-law had him executed as a "rebel" in 1944, perhaps as a sacrificial offering to prove to Hitler his coldness and toughness. Edda fled to Switzerland with her 3 children. Commenting

on her father, she said: "There are only 2 solutions that will rehabilitate him in my eyes, to run away or to kill himself."

Vittorio became a volunteer pilot at 19; he loved W.W. II, and is said to have delighted in cruelty. When Mussolini tried to flee to Germany after his overthrow in September, 1943, Vittorio was waiting with Hitler; he had already taken refuge there. Vittorio participated in negotiations for the surrender of the Fascist hierarchy, then saved himself by going into hiding.

Bruno (1918–1941) became an air force captain and died at 23, testing a bomber.

Romano (b. 1927–   ) scarcely knew his father, but adored him nonetheless. When Mussolini's regime fell, Romano was imprisoned with his mother and sister, Anna Maria (b. 1929–   ); subsequently, he became a moderately successful jazz pianist.

A 6th child, Benito Albino (b. 1915–?) was illegitimate. His mother was Ida Dalser, whom Mussolini denounced in 1917 as "dangerous, unbalanced, and criminal." He had her interned as an enemy alien, and she spent the last 10 years of her life in a mental institution. The boy grew up under the supervision of guardians, and died during the war under mysterious circumstances—some say in an institution, like his mother; others, in naval action. His existence was not generally known until after his father's death.

CHARLES A. LINDBERGH'S CHILDREN

Four years after Charles Lindbergh made his historic flight across the Atlantic, his firstborn son, Charles, Jr., was kidnapped by Bruno Hauptmann, held for ransom, and then murdered. He was 20 months old. The tragedy transformed the elder Lindbergh's preference for privacy into a near obsession. For the next 14 years the family was to live in no permanent home. A Lindbergh child recalled a skiing trip to Switzerland that was interrupted when someone recognized his father on the slopes. The children were packed up, and the family immediately left the resort.

Lindbergh wanted a large family; Jon Morrow was born in 1932; a 3rd son, Land Morrow, was born in 1937; Anne Spencer was born in 1940; Scott was born in 1942; and a 2nd daughter, Reeve, in 1945. The family settled down in a permanent residence in Connecticut in 1946.

It was a tight-knit family, its members blessed with sound minds and healthy bodies. The children were expected to be independent, self-reliant, and responsible. Furthermore, developing worthwhile skills and striving for intellectual honesty were both strongly emphasized by the father. The children were not raised to think of themselves as the children of famous parents. (Anne Morrow Lindbergh, their mother, is a noted author in her own right; her book *Hour of Gold, Hour of Lead* deals with the tragic kidnapping of her son.) Both parents stressed principle over recognition, and integrity over fame. Though they would all inherit fortunes on their 21st birthdays, the Lindbergh children lived comfortably, but unostentatiously.

Jon, now an oceanographer and deep-sea diver, lives with his wife and children in Seattle. Land Lindbergh owns and runs a large cattle ranch in Montana. Anne Spencer married a Swiss businessman and lives in Paris with her children. The 2 youngest Lindberghs, Scott and Reeve, were educated in England and now live in the U.S. and Europe. They are both married and have children.

When Jon was a young adolescent, he often took out a lobster boat during stormy weather. When his father asked him why, Jon said the lobsters were more plentiful in stormy weather,

and that it was more of a challenge at these times. His father replied, "Good reasons, but only a fool goes against the odds consistently. They always catch up with you." The 5 Lindbergh children have remembered this advice.

—C.E.

Try this riddle on your friends

A man is driving his car when he comes upon an automobile accident. Since he is a doctor he stops to help and discovers to his horror that the injured person is his own son. He rushes his son to the hospital where the boy is taken into surgery. Another doctor enters, looks at the boy, and exclaims, "I cannot operate on him. He is my son!" How can this be?

ANSWER: The 2nd doctor is his mother. Some people will go to great lengths, such as postulating that the 1st doctor is his real father and the 2nd a stepfather, to explain this. (See also: Sexism in Language, Chap. 14.)

Kitchen Helps

ABBREVIATIONS COMMONLY USED IN COOKING

approx	approximate
bu	bushel
c	cup
doz	dozen
fl	fluid
gr	granulated
hr	hour
lb	pound
liq	liquid
min	minute
mod	moderate
oz	ounce or ounces
pd	powder
pk	peck
pt	pint
qt	quart
sq	square
sub	substitute
Tbs or T	tablespoon
tsp	teaspoon

EQUIVALENTS

Fluid Measure	Cupfuls etc.
1 oz	⅛ cup
8 oz	1 cup
10 oz	1¼ cups
12 oz	1½ cups
14 oz	1¾ cups
16 oz	2 cups
1 lb 4 oz	2½ cups
1 lb 12 oz	3½ cups

dash or pinch (as much as can be held between fingertips)	less than ⅛ teaspoon
60 drops	1 teaspoon
3 tsp	1 tablespoon or ½ oz
2 Tbs	⅛ cup or 1 fluid oz
4 Tbs	¼ cup
5 Tbs+1 tsp	⅓ cup
8 Tbs	½ cup
10 Tbs+2 tsp	⅔ cup
12 Tbs	¾ cup
14 Tbs	⅞ cup
16 Tbs	1 cup or 8 oz
1 cup	8 fluid oz or ½ pint
2 cups	1 pint (16 fluid oz) or ½ quart
4 cups or 2 pints	1 quart (32 fl oz)
4 quarts	1 gallon (128 fl oz)
8 quarts	2 gallons or 1 peck solid
4 pecks	1 bushel
16 ounces (liquid or dry)	1 pound
2 cups (liquid)	1 pound

METRIC EQUIVALENTS

5 grams	1 teaspoon
30 grams	2 Tbs
227 grams	½ pound
454 grams	1 pound
1 kilogram	2⅕ pounds
1 gill	½ cup (¼ pint)
1 liter	slightly over one quart of liquid

A Guide to Kitchen Utensils

ALUMINUM

Properties: A good heat conductor; heavier gauges cook more evenly and are longer lasting.
Cost: Moderately priced.
Use: Aluminum can be cast into a smooth, one-piece utensil which is heavy and durable. Some of these utensils are dutch ovens, griddles, pressure cookers, and skillets with lids. Or it can be rolled into various gauges for kettles, saucepans, and saucepots which are durable and fairly resistant to denting and warping. Baking pans, molds, and flour measuring cups are made of the thinner gauges.
Care: Utensils with burned-on food should be soaked before scouring. Use a fine soapy steel-wool pad for scouring, and a good sponge or dishrag for rubbing. Rinse with warm water and dry. To remove discoloration caused by alkalies, cook acid foods such as tomatoes or apples in the utensil. Vinegar, or cream of tartar, mixed with water (2 teaspoonfuls to each quart of water) can also be used.
Warped pots can be smoothed out by heating the pan, turning it upside down on a block of wood, and hammering the surface until it is level.
Controversy: Some health-conscious people believe that an excessive use of aluminum utensils releases toxic quantities of aluminum into the body. For example, according to *Best Health Articles from Prevention Magazine* by J. I. Rodale and staff, acidic ingredients such as vinegar will react to aluminum by creating a metallic taste. "Aside from the taste factor, the danger of poisoning is also present." On the other hand, in Dr. Carlton Fredricks's *Your Key to Good Health*, a Mayo Clinic physician, Dr. Russel Wilder, says that many physicians have been giving hydrated alumina or an antacid in the treatment of ulcer of the stomach and the duodenum for years and this has never aroused any suspicion of provoking stomach cancer. The amount of aluminum given by this means exceeds by many hundred times what would be derived from the cooking of foods in aluminum vessels.

BRASS (A Copper alloy—See also: COPPER.)

Properties: Although brass is very thin, it can be solid and sturdy if it is well designed and well made. Like copper it needs to be lined with tin or silver, except if it is used for teapots in which only water will be boiled.
Cost: Fairly expensive.
Use: Made into chafing dishes, kettles, saucepans, and skillets.
Care: See: COPPER.

CAST IRON

Properties: Heavy; heats slowly and evenly, and retains heat well. Excellent for browning, braising, and for making stews.
Cost: Moderate to expensive.
Use: Made into dutch ovens (which can be used on top of the stove or in the oven), broilers, griddles, muffin pans, frying pans, and skillets. These have metal or glass lids (it's nice to watch the transformation that goes on while food is cooking without lifting the lid). Waffle irons are also made of cast iron. Some cast iron utensils have rust-resistant finishes such as a porcelain-enamel coating or a nonstick lining of Teflon. Though expensive they need no seasoning and are easy to clean.
Care: A new pan needs to be washed with hot soapy water and a steel-wool pad to remove the oil that is applied at the factory to prevent rusting. Rinse and dry thoroughly. Coat the inner surface with unsalted oil and place the utensil on moderate heat until the oil appears thin. Remove and swirl the oil about, coating the bottom and sides. Now place it in a 250° oven for about 2 hours. Turn the oven off; allow the pan to remain there until the oven and the pan have cooled down; take the pan out and wipe off excess oil. It is now ready to use. Warm soapy water and a stiff brush to remove burned-on food is all that is necessary for cleaning until it is time to reseason the pan.
Acid foods such as tomatoes, vinegar, wine, or fruit juices will remove the seasoned layer, ultimately causing pitting, as will storing food or prolonged soaking. However, adding water to the utensil right after each use and allowing it to soak during the meal will certainly make cleaning the surface much easier. When rust appears, it is time to wash the pan and reseason it. To save physical energy when preparing a heavily encrusted skillet for reseasoning, place the utensil upside down in the broiler (to get a high temperature) until the burned-on food flakes off. (It may take hours, but it does work.) Allow to cool, wash, and season. Lids should be removed when the pan is not being heated to prevent moisture from forming. Water vapor causes rusting on the inside.

CLAY PRODUCTS

Properties: Heat slowly and evenly, thus retaining all the natural food flavors. Utensils vary according to quality of clay, methods of processing, and glazes used in finishes.
Clay forms include: 1. Ceramic—usually

glazed on the inside and unglazed on the outside. Higher-priced than the softer clayware.

2. Heatproof china—(See: GLASSWARE).

3. Porcelain—ovenproof china. Used for soufflé dishes, au gratin dishes, quiche dishes, etc.

4. Terra-cotta—naturally brownish-orange in color, but often glazed in various colors. It is used for surface baking, grilling, and broiling.

Be sure of where pottery was made before buying it. Some countries use a lead glaze which poses the serious danger of lead poisoning.

Cost: Cheap to expensive.

Use: Made into bean pots, casseroles, and roasting dishes (some are shaped like chickens or fish and are glazed inside and/or outside). Ideally suited for slow cooking, braising, and pot roasting.

Care: To clean, use hot water and a stiff brush. Avoid using soap or detergents on porous earthenware. To remove stains in pottery use 2 Tbs. chlorine bleach to 1 cup water. Soak 30 min., then wash. Leave pots uncovered in the open until completely dry. Unglazed pottery should never be allowed to soak.

To season, rub with a clove of garlic inside and out, and bake the pot at 375° for 6 hours. Or, after rubbing with garlic, fill the pot with water and spices such as bay leaves, peppercorns, or whatever is preferred, and simmer for about a ½ hour on top of an asbestos pad at low heat. Pour the liquid out when cool, and dry well.

In Gertrude Harris's book *Pots & Pans* she states that most clay utensils are "not affected by foods but are by sudden changes in temperature." Have the pot at room temperature before turning on the heat under it or putting it in the oven.

COPPER

Properties: An excellent heat conductor. Utensils used for cooking should be of a heavy gauge, with a tin or silver lining for safety. With use this lining will wear off and relining will be required. This should be done as soon as copper begins to show because a poisonous chemical reaction could result from contact between metal and food. Copper is often used on the bottoms of other types of metals to improve their evenness of heating.

Cost: Expensive to very expensive.

Use: Lined copper is good for utensils that are used for slow cooking, such as teakettles, saucepans (do not use for making white sauces), and baking pans (ask for those lined with nickel—it makes them sturdier). Unlined copper is used for the traditional half-globe bowl used for beating egg whites, and the preserving pan for preparing any food with a high sugar content.

Care: Before using copper as a kitchen utensil, remove the protective coating of lacquer by placing the utensil into a container of boiling water in which washing soda (different than baking soda, but also a product of Arm & Hammer) has been added. Use 1 Tbs. per quart of water. Once the lacquer has peeled off, remove the utensil, wash, rinse, and dry. Before and after use, rub unlined copper—and the outside surface of lined copper—with a cut lemon, or a vinegar and salt mixture, and allow to set for a few minutes. Wash in soapy water, rinse, and dry thoroughly. For burned-on food, soak overnight and then scour with a nylon scrub pad. Never use scouring powder or a steel-wool pad. From *Out-of the Molasses Jug* by Cindy Davis and Elizabeth Mabe (Cloudburst Press, Box 79, Bracken, British Columbia, 1974): "When copper gets badly discolored, mix up a paste of equal parts salt, flour, and vinegar. Smear it on and rub till clean. Particularly bad spots can be removed by rubbing with hot sour milk; vinegar and salt; or lemon juice and salt. Wash and dry." If commercial cleaners are used, read the instructions carefully. Tarnished copper is more efficient because dark metal absorbs heat faster.

ENAMELWARE

Properties: A poor heat conductor, but it heats up rapidly. The utensil should be labeled as to whether it is single-coated or multi-coated with enamel, a glasslike substance fused onto steel, iron or aluminum. The heavier gauges, though expensive, heat up slower but more evenly, and are more resistant to surface damage (chipping).

Cost: Cheap to expensive.

Use: Made into coffeepots, frying pans, saucepans, and saucepots. Excellent for preparing white sauces and cooking acidic foods.

Care: Scrub with a plastic scouring pad and warm soapy water to remove burned or stuck-on food. Use only wooden implements for stirring.

GLASSWARE

Properties: Absorbs and retains heat well, but heats up unevenly.

Cost: Moderately priced to expensive.

Use: Highly recommended for ovenware and the cooking of acid foods such as tomatoes, etc. There are 3 main types: 1. Heatproof for oven use only. Loaf pans, pie plates, roasting dishes (casseroles). Oven temperatures should be lowered by at least 25° as food cooks faster in glass. 2. Flameproof utensils used mainly for surface cooking, but they can also be used in the oven. Made into coffeepots, teakettles, double boilers, saucepans, skillets. (Corning Glass Company's "gourmet skillet" with a permanent handle is excellent for omelets, but food must be removed immediately as the skillet retains heat and will definitely continue cooking.) The use of an iron grid (or flame tamer) between the flame and the glassware will protect the utensil and improve its heat-conducting properties. It will not withstand sudden temperature changes. 3. Glassware used for mixing bowls, measuring cups, serving platters, and refrigerator storage dishes.

Care: Use soapy water and a plastic mesh pad to remove burned-on food. Scrub lightly because once this material is scratched it becomes more difficult to clean. Use wooden implements for mixing. Add extra water because the covers don't always fit, so there tends to be more evaporation.

Controversy: According to Adelle Davis, cooking in glassware allows the destruction of vitamin B_2 in foods due to exposure to light.

Nonstick Coating

Properties: A fluorocarbon resin bonded to aluminum and cast iron. The natural material is white, but colors are added to minimize the unsightliness of staining. This coating does not change the utensil's heating properties; it just prevents food from sticking.

Cost: Moderately priced to expensive.

Use: Teflon II, one of the most familiar trade names, is one of the more durable and scratch-resistant coatings.

Care: To clean, use soapy water and a plastic mesh pad for stuck-on food. Rinse and dry. A coat of oil is recommended before using Teflon II, or any other utensil with a nonstick coating for the first time. Use only wooden implements because it scratches easily. Discoloration is caused by overheating, which allows food and grease to penetrate the coating. Overheating also gives off sodium fluoride gas, which is potentially toxic. To remove stains boil 1 cup water, 2 Tbs. baking soda, ½ cup liquid household bleach for 5 to 10 mins. or until stain disappears. Wash thoroughly. Relining can be considered, but it could cost as much as a new pan.

Controversy: According to Adelle Davis, there are excellent preparations of lecithin available which can be sprayed or rubbed on utensils to prevent sticking; they are completely harmless and preferable to the use of Teflon.

Stainless Steel

Properties: Stainless steel must contain at least $11\frac{1}{2}\%$ chromium in order to be called stainless. Alone it does not conduct or retain heat well, so copper, aluminum, iron, carbon steel, or vanadium are added. Stainless steel utensils are easy to clean. Terms relevant to stainless steel: 1. Bottom-clad—the utensil is copperplated or aluminum is bonded to the outside bottom. 2. Two-ply—utensils have a coating of another metal on either the entire inside or the entire outside of the pan. 3. Three-ply—utensils have another metal between the inside and the outside layers of stainless steel, somewhat like a copper, aluminum, or steel "sandwich."

Cost: Moderate to expensive.

Use: Made into cookware, bakeware, implements such as spoons, knife blades, and tools.

Care: When new, give the utensil a thorough washing in soapy warm water before using. For cooking, use a medium flame to heat, then turn down. There is never a need for a high flame because of the utensil's heating properties. Overheating will sometimes turn stainless steel dark in spots. Never pour cold water into a hot thin steel pan; it will warp. To remove burned-on food, fill with water, bring to a boil, then turn off the heat and let the water remain in the utensil until it has cooled. Scrub with a nylon scrub pad in the direction of the polish lines, rinse, and dry.

Controversy: In *Let's Cook It Right*, Adelle Davis says that investigations have shown "that if even the best stainless steel utensils are scoured only once with an abrasive powder, scratch pad, or steel wool, small amounts of chromium, nickel, and other highly toxic metallic compounds dissolve into every food cooked in them thereafter. Unfortunately, food is frequently burned the 1st time such a utensil is used and the pan is quickly scoured. Some authorities believe chromium and nickel are so toxic . . . they recommend discarding any utensil which has been scoured even once. Exactly how dangerous these metals are is unknown at present, but they do appear to be considerably more toxic than aluminum."

Steel—High Carbon

Properties: Heats up quickly; does not retain temperatures. It may be coated with tin, porcelain, or enamel.

Cost: Price depends on the thickness and the method of processing.

Use: Made into bakeware, crêpe and omelet pans, saucepans, oval and regular frying pans —the best come from France and are nicely balanced (lift one!).

Care: First remove the lacquer coating that is applied at the factory by placing the utensil in boiling water for about 10 mins. Allow to cool, then scour the pan inside and out with a brush or a plastic mesh pad in the direction of the grain. Use soapy water (do not use detergents!). Rinse and dry. Pour in a Tbs. of unsalted vegetable oil, and heat until the oil appears thin. Remove from the heat and swirl the oil around so that it covers the bottom and sides. Let it stand 8 to 10 hours, or overnight. Many pans are already seasoned at the factory, but they should be washed anyway. After use, scour briskly with warm water, rinse, and dry. However, if an accumulation of food residue develops, wash the utensil thoroughly, and re-season. Do not store tightly covered because moisture trapped inside may cause rusting.

TINNED WARE

Properties: Conducts heat rapidly. It is light-weight and graded according to the quality and thickness of the base metal (usually steel, iron or copper). The heavier the coating, the better quality and more durable the utensil will be. It tends to darken with usage, but this tarnish increases the utensil's heat-absorbing qualities.

Cost: Moderate to expensive.

Use: Bread pans, pudding molds, other baking utensils, and copper utensils.

Care: To clean, use a cloth on which either baking or washing soda has been sprinkled, rub, rinse, and dry promptly. To remove burned-on food, soak the utensil with a weak solution of either baking or washing soda until the food becomes soft enough to wipe off. Care should be taken not to scratch the tin coating because exposure of base metal to moisture will cause it to rust and corrode. Food acids affect the tin coating.

WOODEN IMPLEMENTS

Properties: The best ones are made of hard-woods such as beech, boxwood, certain oaks, and rock maple. Should be a very smoothly finished raw wood, or a wood that has been coated with penetrating wood sealer. Should not be painted.

Cost: Cheap if they are domestic, and expensive if they are imported. Comparison shopping is your best guide.

Use: Many and varied uses. Some of them are: breadboards; butter molds and paddles; cheeseboards; chopping or mincing bowls with woodhandled, curved choppers to fit; cutting boards; forks; meat tenderizers; mortar and pestles; noodle boards; ravioli and cookie pattern pins; rolling pins; salad bowls; scrapers; spatulas; spoons (they do not get hot and are gentle to the utensils); and steak and fish planks.

Care: Use different boards for different foods. For example, use one board for fruits and vegetables, another board for meat, and another board for breadmaking. (The latter should always be floured.)

A wooden implement needs only a brisk rubbing with a paper towel, or a damp cloth, and an occasional rinsing with warm water. Scrub with the grain. Wipe dry immediately. Too much soaking and the use of strong detergents and abrasives will dry out natural oils and warp wood. Store in open air. To sanitize, mix 1 Tbs. of chlorine bleach per quart of cold water and pour the mixture over the board. It is important to rinse well under hot running water. Wipe with a paper towel, then dry slowly, in the sun if possible. Moldy odors (caused by being stored in a closed place) can be eliminated by sprinkling salt, and rubbing lemon, on the entire surface (this also prevents darkening). Wash with warm water, and dry with a paper towel. Again, dry in the sun if possible. Never place a wooden implement near a heater because the natural oils will dry out.

A new cutting board, or any other new wood, should be seasoned with a coat of oil overnight before using. Next day wipe off the excess oil. A wet towel between the board and the table will keep the board from slipping.

To refinish: Remove the old finish with sandpaper; apply a mixture of mineral oil and pumice to the surface with cheesecloth, or a paper towel, and rub until the wood is smooth and dry (about ½ an hour). Allow to dry for 24 hours. Wipe off the pumice dust and repeat until the board feels satisfactory. Wash and dry.

—F.C.

Recommended for the Family Reference Shelf

ENCYCLOPAEDIA BRITANNICA

"Since 1768," wrote Herman Kogan, "Britannica has served the cause of education and enlightenment in placid times and in periods of tumult. . . . In all that time its principles have withstood change . . . [especially] one basic principle—to insist on the authenticity and reliability of its contents."

Although the old 24-volume 14th edition of Britannica, which sold 3 million sets, was re-vised 41 times (with 10% of it revised annually), the authenticity and reliability of its contents came under fire. At least one critic, a student of the Britannica named Dr. Harvey Einbinder, after studying its 42,000 articles, found that 666 articles were 50 to 100 years old and had never been brought up to date. He found errors in articles on Galileo, Napoleon at Waterloo, the Old Testament, Homer, Verdi, Heat, and Vaporization.

In 1957, the board of editors undertook a

totally new version of Encyclopaedia Britannica. Today, after an expenditure of $32 million, the new Britannica has replaced the old. In 3 parts and 30 volumes, the 42 million words of the 15th edition used enough paper to circle the equator 16 times.

Exactly 4,277 contributors from 131 countries wrote material for the new 15th edition of the Britannica. Among the contributors: David Ben-Gurion on Herzl, Albert Einstein on Relativity, Norgay Tenzing on Mount Everest, Arnold Toynbee on Julius Caesar, Oswald Jacoby on Poker.

As George Steiner summed it up in *The Sunday Times* of London: "We have here an immensely stimulating, uneven, lavishly produced, and philosophically intriguing pandect of the world. . . . In essence, this new Britannica is an act of rational gaiety. . . . The phrase has been flattened to a commonplace, yet we should not forget its ancient magic: here, truly, is a 'book of life.'"

And finally it is a book of unquestionable authenticity and reliability, one recommended to all who are interested in learning. To give you some idea of the new Britannica's range and quality, we have posed a half dozen questions (all limited to biography) and then attempted to show you through brief summary and excerpt how the current Encyclopaedia Britannica has answered them.

Our Questions

1. Who was the German author who became famous for his cowboy and Indian stories about the American Wild West, although he had never set foot in the U.S.?

2. Was there a real-life Omar Khayyám?

3. What was the name of the renowned Polish pianist who was one of the signers of the Treaty of Versailles in 1919?

4. Who was the Irish dancer and courtesan who spent her last years in New York lecturing on fashion and beauty?

5. What Danzig-born German physicist invented one of the most popular instruments in medicine?

6. Who was the notorious Tichborne claimant?

Answers provided by Encyclopaedia Britannica

1. Karl May, born in Germany in 1842, died there in 1912, was the "author of travel and adventure stories for young people, dealing with desert Arabs or with American Indians in the Wild West, remarkable for the realistic detail that the author, who never traveled outside Germany, was able to achieve. A weaver's son, May was an elementary schoolteacher until arrested for theft and apparently began writing while in prison." May produced 60 books. There is a Karl May Museum in Radebeul

"containing North American Indian collections."

2. Omar Khayyám, possibly born in 1048 in Nishapur, Persia, died in 1122, was a "poet, mathematician, and astronomer, known to English-speaking readers for his *Rubaiyat* ('Quatrains') in the version published by Edward FitzGerald (1859)." The name Khayyám meant "tentmaker." He became known for a treatise he wrote in Arabic on algebra. The Sultan retained him to make astronomical observations for a reformed calendar. Omar took a pilgrimage to Mecca, often served in court predicting future events. "Omar's popularity in the West is based on his discovery by the English Victorian poet Edward FitzGerald, who freely translated many of the quatrains attributed to Omar and arranged them in a continuous elegy. . . . Some scholars have doubted that Omar wrote poetry, since his contemporaries took no notice of his verse and it was not until 2 centuries later that a few quatrains appeared under his name. A 20th-century student, Ali Dashti, concluded in *In Search of Omar Khayyám* (1971) that of the 1,000 quatrains originally attributed to Omar, 102 are authentic."

3. Ignace Paderewski, born in Russian Poland in 1860, died in New York City in 1941, was the "Polish pianist, composer, and statesman, who persuaded President Woodrow Wilson to include a paragraph on Polish independence in his famous Fourteen Points and who was prime minister of Poland in 1919. . . . He impressed most critics, notably George Bernard Shaw, as the leading pianist of his time, remarkable both for his musical culture and his mind. His personality on the concert platform, like that of Liszt, his predecessor among piano virtuosos, generated a mystical devotion. . . . His premiership was not a success. As a virtuoso, Paderewski was accustomed to flattery and he resented criticism."

4. Lola Montez, born in Ireland in 1818, died in New York in 1861, was an "adventuress and 'Spanish' dancer who achieved international notoriety through her liaison with King Louis I of Bavaria. After 5 months' study, she made a disastrous debut as a dancer in London in 1843; her striking beauty, however, brought her additional dancing engagements." Her influence over King Louis caused a furor in Bavaria, forcing her to flee and the King to abdicate. "Montez danced in America and Australia, then returned to America to lecture on fashion and feminine beauty."

5. Gabriel Daniel Fahrenheit, born in Danzig in 1686, died in The Hague in 1736, was a "German physicist who invented the alcohol thermometer (1709) and the mercury thermometer (1714) and introduced the Fahrenheit thermometric scale, which is still com-

monly used in the U.S. and Canada. He spent most of his life in The Netherlands. . . ."

6. "Tichborne claimant was the name given to a man who in 1865 claimed to be Roger Charles Tichborne, heir to a large estate in Hampshire, who had been missing at sea since 1854. After 2 marathon trials (1871 and 1874) which attracted intense public interest, the claimant was declared to be a certain Arthur Orton, a butcher's son from Wapping, a district of London." The real Tichborne was aboard a ship out of Rio de Janeiro which was lost at sea, apparently with no survivors. His mother refused to believe him dead. "In 1865 she learned through a missing-persons agency that a man claiming to be her son was working as a butcher in Wagga Wagga, Australia; she met and 'acknowledged' him in 1867, but other members of the family asserted that he was an impostor and tried to prove that he was Arthur Orton, who had jumped ship in South America in 1849." The claimant sued to win the baronetcy and inheritance. After 2 trials, he was judged to be an impostor and to have committed perjury. Orton was sent to jail in 1874. "The case received wide publicity and the claimant won a large following among the British public. Released in 1884, he died in poverty in London in 1898."

—The Eds.

TIME-LIFE BOOKS

There were, as of 1975, 15 different sets of reference books published by Time-Life Books, New York. Each set has numerous separate volumes issued periodically. Typically, one set of reference books entitled the Life Science Library has 25 volumes, with subjects ranging from The Body to Wheels. All the sets of Time-Life Books are, without exception, beautifully produced, attractively graphic, filled with lively and authoritative information. As learning tools, as well as interesting reading, all sets are highly recommended. If you wish to browse before you buy, we offer you some facts gleaned from various volumes of two sets.

From various volumes of Life Science Library

"Since the Renaissance, the world's population, overall, has doubled and redoubled. Over approximately the same period, the scientific community, by contrast, has multiplied a hundredfold each century: from a platoon counted in individuals in 1665, to a division counted in ten thousands in 1865, to an army estimated at 6 million today. This phenomenal rate of proliferation has meant that the number of scientists living at any one time has constituted 90% of the total number of scientists who lived before them. Thus we have 9 times as

many scientists now as in all previous eras put together. As a corollary, it can be reasonably estimated that 9/10 of current scientific knowledge was yet to be created when our present elder statesmen of science graduated from college in the 1920s."

Except for identical twins, who come from one egg, the chances of 2 identical human beings' being born separately from 2 different eggs are so high that the number "doesn't even have a name," and the odds against it "would have to be written as 1 followed by 9,031 zeroes." After all, "there are more than 8 million ways the 23 chromosomes of a human mother and the 23 of a father can combine."

Less than 20% of the weight of an average adult male comes from his bones. The collected bones of a 160-lb. man weigh only 29 lbs. The same amount of steel bars would weigh 4 to 5 times more.

An infant can have 300 bones in its body. An adult body consists of 206 bones. In the maturing process, no bones have been lost—they have merely fused. One out of 20 persons has an extra rib, but among those with spare ribs men lead women 3 to 1.

About 65% of the average human body consists of water.

"When the Weather Bureau 1st began using computer technology in 1955, an improvement in accuracy, 'slight but significant,' was noted almost immediately. Today 12-to-18-hour forecasts are considered 85% accurate; forecasts up to 36 hours in advance are correct about 75% of the time. Though general weather conditions for about a week in advance can be forecast with some degree of usefulness, it is still beyond the capabilities of science to make detailed predictions for more than about 3 days in advance."

Nothing is more individual than a fingerprint. The FBI has 169 million fingerprints on file, and there are "no 2 so similar that an expert cannot readily tell them apart."

A human being spends 1/3 of his or her life sleeping. Of the time spent sleeping, 1/5 of it is spent dreaming. The average person starts to have a dream about every 90 minutes, and in 8 hours of sleep, a single dream can last as long as 45 minutes.

"Tossing a coin is an exercise in probability which everyone has tried: Calling either heads or tails is a fair bet because the chance of either result is one half. No one expects a coin to fall heads once in every 2 tosses, but in a large number of tosses the results tend to even out. For a coin to fall heads 50 consecutive times, it would take a million men tossing coins 10 times a minute and 40 hours a week

—and then it would happen only once in every 9 centuries."

From various volumes of Life Nature Library

The healthiest period of a human being's life is between the ages of 5 and 15. Resistance against infectious diseases continues well into the 20s. From the 30s onward this body efficiency decreases.

"A single squirrel may hide away 20 or more bushels of food divided into many small caches, although it may not find and eat a tenth of that reserve before spring."

Among the oldest living things are the sequoia trees. They live 3,000 years or more. They owe their longevity to the thickness of their bark (which can be 2' thick), to the tannin the bark contains which fends off insects, and to their fibrous consistency that makes them almost fireproof. Only 3 things can hurt a grown sequoia: climate change, earthquakes, erosion. A sequoia is usually not fully mature until it is 300 years old.

"One large kangaroo, at a single desperate bound, is reported to have cleared a pile of timber 10½' high and 27' long."

A ruby-throated hummingbird has 940 feathers. A Plymouth Rock hen has 8,325 feathers. A whistling swan has 25,216 feathers.

"Every recorded measurement of a large mountain may be from half a dozen to a few hundred feet in error. The point is emphasized by the way the 1st 'official' height of Mount Everest was arrived at in 1852. Measurements were made from 6 places. All were different, the lowest being 28,990' and the highest 29,026'. When all 6 were averaged, the figure came to exactly 29,000'. Unwilling to publish what they thought would seem like an estimate rather than an exact figure, the surveyors arbitrarily added 2' to make the official figure, 29,002', sound better. It turned out to be 26' higher when measured by a party of Indians in 1954. Whatever its exact height, Everest is the world's highest mountain."

—The Eds.

GALE RESEARCH CO. REFERENCE BOOKS

Gale Research is one of the largest American publishers of reference books. Their thorough volumes, of great variety, are best known in public libraries, where they are usually stocked. The general reader, wishing to purchase their books, is advised to write them for their catalogue: Gale Research Co., Book Tower, Detroit, Mich. 48226. In order to acquaint you with their publications, we have selected one typical book from their list of publications and have taken sample extracts from it. This is a 455-page volume entitled, *Museum Media,*

and it fulfills a unique need. Normally, if you want to acquire a one-volume reference book on any subject—pesticides, bird decoys, kite-flying—you go to your neighborhood bookstore to buy a book published by a trade or text publisher. However, many people are unaware that among the biggest or best publishers in the U.S. are museums, galleries, art institutes. In *Museum Media*, Gale Research has listed 732 U.S. and Canadian institutions that sell books, pamphlets, catalogues, slides, film, and gives the titles and prices of what is for sale to the public. Now then, for a very brief sampling from this unusual volume:

Museum Media

Alaska National Parks and Monuments Association
334 West 5th Avenue, Suite 250
Anchorage, Alaska 99501
For Sale:
Backpacking—Rethmel, 100 pp., illus., $3.90
Field Guide to Animal Tracks—Adolph Murie, 374 pp., illus., $6.15
Mammals of Mount McKinley—Adolph Murie, 1962, 56 pp., illus., $.85

American Numismatic Society
Broadway at 155th Street
New York, N.Y. 10032
For Sale:
Barbarians on Roman Imperial Coins and Sculpture—Annalina Calo Levi, 1952, 56 pp., 17 illus., $3.50
Counterfeiting in Colonial Pennsylvania—Kenneth Scott, 1955, 168 pp., $4.00
Rare Islamic Coins—George C. Miles, 1950, 139 pp., 10 illus., $5.00

B'nai B'rith Museum
1640 Rhode Island Avenue, N.W.
Washington, D.C. 20036
For Sale:
Great Jewish Thinkers of the 20th Century—edited by A. Millgram, $2.95
Lincoln and the Jews—R. Shosteck, 1968, 16 pp., $.50
Warsaw Ghetto Uprising—77 slides with script, $10.00 rental

Canadian Film Institute
1762 Carling Avenue
Ottawa, Ont., Canada
For Sale:
Canadian Women Film-Makers: An Interim Filmography—1972, 20 pp., $1.00
The Cinema of Roman Polanski—Ivan Butler, 192 pp., 120 illus., $2.75
Horror in the Cinema—Ivan Butler, 208 pp., 65 illus., $2.75

Daughters of Utah Pioneers
300 North Main
Salt Lake City, Utah 84103
For Sale:
Brigham Young, His Twenty-Seven Wives and Families—$1.00

The Great Mormon Tabernacle—$1.00
Mormons, Their Westward Trek—$.50
Field Museum of Natural History
  Roosevelt Road at Lake Shore Drive
  Chicago, Ill. 60605
  For Sale:
  The Authentic Letters of Columbus—W. E.
  Curtis, 1895, 106 pp., 19 illus., $3.50
  The Birds of Eastern North America—C. B.
  Cory, 1899, Part 1, 142 pp., 480 illus.,
  $5.00; Part 2, 257 pp., 611 illus., $8.00
  The Civilization of the Mayas—J. Eric S.
  Thompson, 1958, 98 pp., 36 illus., one map,
  $2.00
Honolulu Academy of Arts
  900 South Beretania Street
  Honolulu, Hawaii 96814
  For Sale:
  *The Barbara Hutton Collection of Chinese
  Porcelain*—foreword by Robert P. Griffing,
  Jr., 1965, 33 pp., 36 illus., $2.50
  The Cubist Epoch—55 min. film
  Le Corbusier—55 min. film
Library of Congress
  10 First Street, S.E.
  Washington, D.C. 20540
  For Sale:
  Carl Sandburg: A Lecture—Mark Van
  Doren, 1969, 83 pp., $.50, Superintendent
  of Documents
  *A Directory of Information Resources in the
  U.S.: Federal Government*—1967, 411 pp.,
  $2.75, Superintendents of Documents
  The Giant Bible of Mainz—Dorothy Euge-
  nia Miner, 1952, 31 pp., Free
Navajo Tribal Museum
  P. O. Box 797
  Window Rock, Ariz. 86515
  For Sale:
  Bai-A-Lil-Le—Medicine Man or Witch?—
  J. Lee Correll, 1970, 57 pp., illus. and map,
  $1.00
  *Motorist Guide to the Navajo Indian Reser-
  vation*—Mary MacFarlane, 1960, 44 pp., il-
  lus. and map, $1.00
  The Story of the Navajo Treaties with Texts

in English—David M. Brugge and J. Lee
  Correll, 1971, 98 pp., $1.00
O. Henry House
  600 Lone Star Boulevard
  San Antonio, Tex. 18212
  For Sale:
  O. Henry Almanac—edited by Fritz A.
  Toepperwein, 40 pp., illus., $1.00
  The Rolling Stone—1895 newspaper, $.50
*St. Louis Medical Museum and National Mu-
seum of Medical Quackery*
  3839 Lindell Boulevard
  St. Louis, Mo. 63108
  For Sale:
  The AMA and the FDA Publication of
  "Facts on Quacks"—1968, 36 pp., 12 illus.,
  free
Uncle Tom's Cabin Museum
  R.R. #5
  Dresden, Ont., Canada
  For Sale:
  The Story of Uncle Tom—W. Chapple, 8
  pp., 2 illus., $.50
  Uncle Tom's Cabin—Harriet Beecher Stowe,
  450 pp., $3.75, paper $1.50
Washington Crossing Foundation
  Box 1976
  Washington Crossing, Pa. 18977
  For Sale:
  George Washington Crossed Here—Ann H.
  Hutton, 1948 (now in 11th edition), 72 pp.,
  5 illus., $1.25 plus postage
  How to Survive as a Prisoner of War—
  Samuel A. Newman, 1969, 183 pp., 5 illus.,
  $4.95 plus postage
  Washington Crossing the Delaware—16-mm.
  film, 28 min., color, $225 or rental fee.
Zion Historical Society
  P. O. Box 333
  Zion, Ill. 60099
  For Sale:
  *Zion City, Illinois, John Alexander Dowie's
  Theocracy*—Philip L. Cook, 1970, 20 pp.,
  illus., $1.00

                                   —The Eds.

Inside the IQ Test

A Pea under a Mattress? In a dusty London
museum in 1882, there took place an experiment reminiscent of the old fairy story about
the princess who proved her royal blood when
she complained that a tiny pea secretly placed
under a pile of mattresses disturbed her sleep.
In London, however, it was "intelligence"
rather than nobility that was being sought.
Volunteers subjected themselves to a series of
tests—judging the weights of rocks, distinguishing among high-pitched sounds, and reacting

to pinpricks. Their reward was an evaluation
of their mental abilities, which, the experimenter thought, was directly related to sensory
sensitivity.
  Though crude, this experiment was a landmark—the 1st attempt to measure intelligence
with some kind of test. Its originator was Sir
Francis Galton, a cousin of Charles Darwin.
(Experts on intelligence think Galton was
probably even brighter than his famous relative.)

Stunts? Of course, Galton's test was based on a shaky premise—that sensory sensitivity and intelligence are somehow directly related. Psychologists have since tried to devise more accurate measures of intellectual ability. It was Alfred Binet, a French psychologist, who came up with the 1st practical ones. In 1904, the Government gave him the job of culling out dull students in the schools around Paris. With Dr. Theodore Simon, Binet devised a scale with 54 multiphasic tests that would make the task easier. The Binet-Simon tests measured a fairly wide spectrum of abilities—to comprehend words, form mental images, pay attention, sustain muscular efforts, and judge distances, among others. A down-to-earth individual, Binet did not try to define exactly what intelligence was, nor did he make any wild claims for his tests, even going so far as to refer to the individual items casually as "stunts."

Simon later came up with the idea of relating age level to test performance. Other intelligence-test experts refined this idea until today IQ (Intelligence Quotient) is a score derived from a mathematical formula:

$$\frac{\text{mental age}}{\text{chronological age}} \times 100 = IQ$$

Thus, if a 10-year-old achieves a score equal to that of the average 10-year-old, his intelligence quotient is 100. If his raw score is as high as that of the average 15-year-old, then his IQ score ostensibly is 150. (In actual practice, scores are somewhat weighted.) A person scoring around 100 on an IQ test is considered average, since 100 is the mean IQ. The top 3% of the population has an IQ of over 130, the top 1% over 140.

The Stanford-Binet test in use today is a sophisticated descendant of the original series of stunts devised by Binet and Simon back in 1904. Other tests, of course, are also being used. One is the Weschler Adult Intelligence Scale, which contains more nonverbal tests—e.g. re-creating block designs or arranging items in a meaningful sequence—than does the Stanford-Binet. Another, still in the experimental stage, hopes to correlate brain-wave activity with intelligence.

What Is Intelligence? Galton, Binet, Simon and other creators of intelligence tests were trying to measure something that still has no satisfying definition. What is intelligence? Is it the ability to make judgments, to remember, to reason things out? If a person can interpret verbal analogies and see spatial relationships, does that mean he is intelligent? Many psychologists would answer, "Yes, but—"

But—what about the "idiot savant" who is severely retarded, yet has the ability to add incredibly long strings of large numbers? What about the fact that people with the same IQ

scores may excel in entirely different areas? One might be a virtual dummy in handling verbal material but perform at genius level in making designs out of blocks. A 2nd may have almost the same average in all abilities. How can these 2 minds be equated, despite their having identical scores?

But—what about other, less "intellectual" abilities? Anthropologist Carlos Casteneda states that much of our perception of the world is distorted by an agreement made long ago in our rational European heritage to perceive some things and not others. Because we perceive things according to this agreement, whether we know it or not, certain aspects of reality are filtered out. Our ability to see relationships, and thus our intelligence, is then forever skewed. Should not intelligence tests measure those abilities neglected in our culture—extrasensory perception, photographic memory, synesthesia (cross talk of the senses)?

But—what about creativity? Studies have shown that children with highly creative minds and average IQs do as well in school as high-intelligence, low-creativity children. Creative children often solve problems in highly original ways, give wrong answers for right reasons, and go off on mental tangents that show a high degree of sophistication. Are they not "thinkers" even though what they do is not presently being measured favorably on intelligence tests?

Development on a Schedule. Intelligence is not fixed and stable for life. Instead, it is constantly changing, according to what happens to the brain at various stages.

A baby's brain starts evolving before it is born. Some intellectual abilities are innate but will deteriorate if they are not developed. These include eye-hand coordination, conservation, and the ability to perceive objects as solid.

In one experiment, babies between 16 and 24 weeks old were shown 3-dimensional, non-solid images made by movie projectors. When the babies tried to touch the images, their hands went through them, and they began to cry. Somehow, the infants "knew" that things are "supposed to be" solid. Similarly, when babies saw a moving object go behind a screen, they showed signs that they expected it to come out on the other side. They "knew" that things have permanence in the real world, that they don't just disappear into thin air. Where do little babies "learn" these concepts? It seems they are either inborn or developed very early in infancy.

The brain is delicately programmed to develop certain abilities at certain ages. If something goes wrong, these abilities will be stunted or lie dormant forever. For instance, if a rat is stimulated (by petting, electric shock, or play) when it is 5 to 10 days old, it will become an explorer for life, but its ability to reason will not be influenced much. On the other hand, if it is stimulated when it is 14 days old, it will be able to solve problems better, but it will not necessarily be an explorer. Experimenters now think that stimulation releases the hormone corticosterone, which acts on the brain and sometimes causes an increase in certain kinds of intelligence.

These theories also seem to apply to human beings. Somewhere between 10 and 18 months, a child spurts ahead in his ability to think logically—if he is stimulated properly. Young children have a great capacity to perceive form, a capacity which seems to flower at ages 3 and 4 and to lessen with age. Therefore, some educators reason, why not teach children to read (a skill involving perception of form) when they are best able to discern pattern? Also, W. Ragan Callaway of the University of Toronto believes that early reading may make children brighter by exercising their brains at exactly the right time.

Which Genius Was Smarter? Dr. Catherine Cox, a psychologist, has made estimates of the IQs of famous people. Here is a sample:

Normal IQ today—100
Goethe—210
Voltaire, Newton—190
Galileo—185
Da Vinci, Descartes—180
Kant—175
Luther—170
Mozart—165
Franklin—160
Rembrandt—155
Lincoln—150
Grant—130

Who's Smart Now? What characteristics does the usual intelligent person have? Look for yourself in the following list.

1. The intelligent person is likely to be an only child or the eldest child in a family. (*Who's Who* lists more firstborns than their number in the general population justifies.) The reason for this may not be so mysterious—parents treat only children and firstborns differently.

2. The intelligent person is likely to have been breast-fed. Mothers who breast-feed children tend to be conscientious. Also, human milk contains cystine, a substance which influences learning.

3. The intelligent person is likely to sleep less. When he does sleep, his eyes move for longer periods, indicating more brain-wave activity.

4. The intelligent person is likely to be somewhat "feminine" if a boy, "masculine" if a girl. The cause? Possibly prenatal hormonal changes in the mother, some experts think.

5. The intelligent person is likely to have more surface convolutions on the cerebral cortex. A pathologist conducting an autopsy can estimate how smart his subject was by noting the number of these folds.

In essence then, intelligence tests are crude measures of something as yet inadequately defined, something highly complex, perhaps entirely chemical, and ever changing.

—A.E.

Arthur Jensen—Right or Wrong?

BERKELEY'S HITLER—WHO?

"Hitler is alive and well and spreading racist propaganda," reads a pamphlet from the Students for a Democratic Society. The "Hitler" to whom the pamphlet refers is Arthur Jensen, a respected psychologist and professor at the University of California at Berkeley. In 1969, after making a study of material in the field, he published an article in which he stated that, on the average, blacks score 15 points lower on intelligence tests than whites, Orientals, and American Indians.

This conclusion brought forth intensely hostile reactions. Some of his opponents have called for his censure by the university; others, more extreme, have wanted him hanged. When a sign appeared on his office door—saying, "Jensen must perish"—bodyguards were assigned to him, and campus police began to guard his files. Sound trucks on campus blared,

"Fight racism! Fire Jensen!" When members of the SDS broke into his classes and disrupted his lectures, he resorted to holding secret seminars for his students.

The violent, almost irrational response to Jensen's article may have come from its implied threat to the cherished American belief in the equality of all individuals and races. Many liberals and radicals believed that Jensen's "findings" would be a dangerous weapon in the hands of those who were against equal educational opportunity. Blacks might be left to stew in their own juice in the ghettoes.

Jensen says, "Research into possible genetic influence on intelligence has been academically and socially taboo. The orthodox environmental theories have been accepted because they harmonize so well with our democratic belief in human equality." When those who opposed him mentioned that his study might be misused, Jensen replied by saying, in essence, look what happens when science is made subservient to political ideology; look at the Nazis.

In May, 1969, the Society for the Psychological Study of Social Issues (SPSSI) questioned Jensen's scientific accuracy and the validity of his conclusions. It also warned that his "views may be seriously misinterpreted, particularly in their application to social policy."

To counter the SPSSI, 50 prominent academicians signed a declaration defending Jensen's right to study the relationships between heredity and human behavior and to publicize his findings. The declaration compared Jensen with men like Galileo and Einstein, who had been oppressed because of their views.

What Is the Study Really About?

Jensen's work is a study of studies—some 50 of them from 18 countries—on the relationship of genetics and education to intelligence. The results, as interpreted by Jensen, show that:

1. Blacks score 15 points lower than whites on intelligence tests. Only about 16% of blacks do better than the average white.

2. Individuals in the lower economic and social classes have lower IQs than those in the upper classes.

3. Our genes determine intelligence much more than education and environment do. Heredity is responsible for 80% of the IQ score.

Arguments Pro and Con

Can Findings about Individuals Be Extended to Racial Groups?

Anti-Jensen: While individual blacks do score lower than individual whites, this finding cannot be applied across the board to the whole black race as a genetically determined characteristic. Cultural differences, discrimination, and lack of opportunity have held blacks back and affected the development of their natural intelligence.

From time to time, other studies have "proved" racial or ethnic groups to be intellectually inferior. In 1925, for instance, a British statistician claimed that Jews were mentally inferior to the general population. (More recently, in an Israeli kibbutzim environment, the IQs of European Jewish children increased from an average of 105 to 115, and those of Oriental Jewish children from 85 to the same 115.)

Pro-Jensen: Most scientists agree that genetic influences are about twice as important as environmental factors among individuals. Biologists generally concur that a genetically conditioned characteristic that varies among individuals within a

subspecies (e.g. race) also varies genetically among different subspecies.

How Accurate and Fair Are the Tests?

Anti-Jensen: Intelligence tests now in use were created for the white middle class and therefore are culturally slanted. They do not reflect the black vocabulary or black concepts. (In reaction to this, a black psychologist has devised a vocabulary test called BITCH— "Black Intelligence Test to Counter Honkeyism"—that is based on the language of the black subculture.)

Pro-Jensen: It was on the nonverbal tests that blacks most often failed. Using material common to many cultures, the nonverbal tests measure the ability to generalize, to see differences and similarities, to perceive relationships, and solve problems. On the Wechsler intelligence tests, for instance, blacks do better on vocabularly, general information, and verbal comprehension than they do on block designs and other sections dealing with abstract, nonverbal reasoning. The opposite is true for Orientals, Mexican-Americans, American Indians, Puerto Ricans, and Arctic Eskimos.

What about Motivation?

Anti-Jensen: Blacks have been so beaten down by the discriminatory environment in which they live that they have no motivation to do well on intelligence tests.

Pro-Jensen: Why then is there little or no difference in scores which involve memory and rote learning? If blacks were really poorly motivated to take tests, wouldn't they score low on everything?

How Much Effect Does Environment Really Have on Intelligence?

Anti-Jensen: The socioeconomic conditions under which blacks live have had more effect on their intelligence than Jensen thinks. Black babies are probably born with potential mental abilities equal to whites, but never get the chance to develop those abilities. Benjamin Bloom of the University of Chicago estimates that living in a poor environment can lower an IQ as much as 20 points.

Experience changes the brain. For instance, at the University of California at Berkeley in the 1950s, researchers found evidence that problem solving changes the level of a brain enzyme important in learning and that trained brains are heavier than untrained ones. According to some physiologists, mental activity encourages the growth of myelin, a substance the brain needs in order to function.

Is it possible then that many slum children (and more slum children are black than white) are born with genetically normal brains that fail to develop because their experiences do not give them the opportunities for mental exercise? Study after study has shown that stimulation in infancy, early language experiences, and preparation for reading affect the development of intelligence. The following are just 2 of the numerous studies that show this:

1. Professor Rick Heber of the University of Wisconsin believes that many slum children are not genetically retarded. They become that way, he thinks, because they are starved for stimulation and have to live with mothers who are retarded. To prove his theory, he took black babies with an expected mean IQ of around 80 and put them in a special school every day. Social workers picked the babies up, talked to them, played with them, and taught them—at 1st on a one-to-one basis and then, as they grew up, in larger and larger groups. By the time they were 4, these children had a mean IQ of around 130. The children in the control group scored as expected—in the 80s.

2. In a New York nursery school, 3- and 4-year-olds were tutored individually for 15 minutes a day. Other children were given 15 minutes too, but that 15 minutes consisted merely of attention. The children who were tutored gained 14 IQ points in 4 months. The others gained only 2 points.

Pro-Jensen: If environment changes IQ, then why do American Indians, who live in poorer socio-economic conditions than blacks, score higher than blacks? Why haven't school busing and desegregation changed the performance of blacks on IQ tests? Why have so many compensatory education programs failed in the black ghettos? Experiments with deprived children are dramatic, but are the results lasting? Do they not represent a kind of hothouse forcing?

Who is right—Jensen or his opponents? No one really knows. The SPSSI declaration stated, "A more accurate understanding of the contribution of heredity to intelligence will be possible only when social conditions for all races are equal and when this situation has existed for several generations." That may well be so.

OTHER PROPONENTS OF JENSEN'S THEORIES

Richard Herrnstein, a Harvard psychologist, believes that:

If differences in mental abilities are inherited;

If success depends on those abilities;

If earnings and prestige depend upon success;

Then social standing (which reflects earnings and prestige) will be based, to some extent, on inherited differences. By canceling out environmental differences (giving equal opportunity), we will increase the importance of hereditary differences. Then "success" and "failure" may run in families, and we will have a class system based on intelligence.

Herrnstein's opponents say that in the future, society is likely to be more fluid in job and social structures because of the development of technology, and that success on the job will be only 25% dependent on IQ.

William Shockley of Stanford University is coinventor of the transistor and a Nobel Laureate. However, he is not a psychologist nor does he have any training in the behavioral sciences. His great interest in the findings of people like Jensen has led him to study the subject of race and genetics. He describes blacks as genetically inferior and proposes a sterilization plan under which people with low IQs would receive $1,000 for each IQ point they score below 100 if they agree to sterilization.

Shockley has been burned in effigy and has had his car sprayed with obscenities. Graffiti around Stanford read, "Sterilize Shockley."

—A.E.

Gather Around for Some Teaching Stories

A CUP OF TEA

The teacher Nan-in had a visitor who came to inquire about Zen. But instead of listening, the visitor kept talking about his own ideas.

After a while, Nan-in served tea. He poured tea into his visitor's cup until it was full, then he kept on pouring.

Finally the visitor could restrain himself no longer. "Don't you see it's full?" he said. "You can't get any more in!"

"That's true," replied Nan-in, stopping at last. "And like this cup, you are filled with your own ideas. How can you expect me to give you Zen unless you offer me an empty cup?"

MATAJURA THE SWORDSMAN

Matajura wanted to become a great swordsman, but his father said he wasn't quick enough and could never learn. So Matajura went to the famous dueller Banzo, and asked to become his pupil. "How long will it take me to become a master?" he asked. "Suppose I became your servant, to be with you every minute; how long?"

"Ten years," said Banzo.

"My father is getting old. Before 10 years

have passed I will have to return home to take care of him. Suppose I work twice as hard; how long will it take me?"

"Thirty years," said Banzo.

"How is that?" asked Matajura. "First you say 10 years. Then when I offer to work twice as hard, you say it will take 3 times as long. Let me make myself clear: I will work unceasingly: No hardship will be too much. How long will it take?"

"Seventy years," said Banzo. "A pupil in such a hurry learns slowly."

Matajura understood. Without asking for any promises in terms of time, he became Banzo's servant. He cleaned, he cooked, he washed, he gardened. He was ordered never to speak of fencing or to touch a sword. He was very sad at this; but he had given his promise to the master, and resolved to keep his word. Three years passed for Matajura as a servant.

One day while he was gardening, Banzo came up quietly behind him and gave him a terrible whack with a wooden sword. The next day, as Matajura was cooking rice, the same blow fell again. Thereafter, day in and day out, from every corner and at any moment, he was attacked by Banzo's wooden sword. He learned to live on the balls of his feet, ready to dodge at any movement. He became a body with no desires, no thoughts—only eternal readiness and quickness.

He began to learn so quickly that he brought smiles to the face of his teacher. Soon Matajura was the greatest swordsman in the land.

The Bookworm and the Boatman

Although the weather was fine and the sun was shining, it was not too hot to be comfortable. The birds were singing in the branches of the trees which grew along the margin of the river, and beneath them might be seen walking a learned scholar, book in hand.

Taking his eyes for a moment from the pages, he glanced at the cool river. It had been very hot lately, but it was better today, and as he looked he thought how inviting the river appeared. He could not swim in it, for it was infested with crocodiles, but what about a boat? "I will find a steady boatman," he said aloud, "and engage him to row me about on the broad stream for an hour or 2."

After a little searching he found the sort of boat and boatman he desired, and they were soon floating lazily upon the broad bosom of the river. After a long silence the bookworm asked, "Have you read the scriptures?"

"No, sir," was the reply.

"Then half of your life is wasted," said the scholar. "It is required of every man to know something of the teaching of the great ones,

and to meditate daily upon their sayings. It is a great pity, a very great pity indeed."

There followed a long silence, which was at last broken once more by the learned man. "Have you any knowledge of the stars, by studying which men may understand the times and seasons and the ebb and flow of the tides? Can you read them, and by their aid foretell future events?"

"No, sir," replied the boatman again.

"Then ¾ of your life has been wasted," exclaimed the scholar.

Now the boatman, happening to glance down at this moment, caught sight of a small trickle of water, which as everyone knows is often to be seen in the bottom of a boat, and is in no way a sign of danger. They were now at a great distance from the bank, and he determined to ask his passenger a question.

"Sir," said he, looking fearfully at the small pool in the boat's bottom, "I fear we are about to sink. Have you learned to swim?"

"No," said the scholarly one, "I have always relied upon the good God to preserve my poor life from danger."

"Then," said the boatman with a grin, "I am afraid the whole of your life may be wasted."

The wise one saw at once that he was being mocked, and when he had paid the oarsman he departed in silence, thinking that perhaps the fellow was right. There were other things of importance besides books and study. At any rate swimming might on occasion be more useful than reading.

As for the boatman, he too was deep in thought, for he remembered how calmly the scholar had received his statement that the boat was about to sink. "There must be something good in quiet study," thought he, "if it prepares a man to keep calm in the face of sudden dangers."

—W.E.D. rep.

Think for Yourself!

Some time ago, in the jungle, but still within easy walking of a large village, lived a hermit known as Charu. He was reputed to be a wise scholar and a very able teacher, in consequence of which many of the young men of the village, going to him 1st for advice, became in time his pupils and eventually his disciples.

Charu taught them of God and of the scriptures, telling them that He was to be found everywhere and in everything, and that nothing in the universe exists apart from Him.

He was particularly fond of speaking in praise of the simple life lived by men who chose to become hermits, away from all the noise and strife of the world.

As he taught, his disciples would sit at his

feet, dwelling upon his every word, and accepting all that he said without question.

Among them was a youth named Chakrapal, the most obedient and docile of them all. Such was his humility and modesty, that before long he began to depend entirely upon his master's word for all his actions, ceasing entirely to form any judgment for himself, and never taking a course which did not fit in with something he remembered the hermit to have said.

This frequently brought trouble upon him, as you will soon see.

The disciples were in the habit of going each day to a nearby river for a morning dip, and upon one such occasion, having bathed, they were returning together to the hermitage, when they observed a large elephant advancing towards them with great speed, his trunk raised high in the air.

The mahout, who was goading the beast on with his trident, called out to them, "Run quickly, or he may pick you up with his trunk and dash you to death!"

At this they scattered, hiding behind bushes and intending to come together again farther along the path. But Chakrapal did not run. He asked himself, "What would my wise master say about this? What would he do? Often he has said to us, 'God brings good to man, and not evil. God is in everything.' That being so, God, who is in this great elephant, will do me no harm."

Having decided that his master would have stayed his ground, trusting upon God for safety, what could he do but stay too?

The mahout, seeing him still in the path, screamed to him, "If you value your life, get out of the way!"

The animal, who had been goaded almost beyond bearing, in order to make him hurry, could not now be easily restrained, and as soon as he was within reach, picked up the unhappy disciple and waving him thrice aloft, flung him away.

But for the bushes breaking his fall, it is likely that he would have been killed upon the spot. As it was, he was dreadfully bruised.

When he failed to arrive with the others at the hermit's abode, a party set out to search for him, and finding him quite helpless, they made a litter of branches and carried him to the hermit.

After many remedies had been tried, he was sufficiently recovered to understand what they were saying to him.

"Why did you not heed the mahout's warning," they asked. "Surely he knew the creature's ways better than you possibly could."

Chakrapal paused in his moaning to reply, "Our master Charu has said that God is in all living things. Furthermore, he has taught us that God always brings good and never brings evil. I felt, therefore, that I was safe in His hands, saying that God, in the great elephant, would not bring evil to me."

Hearing this explanation, they all roared with laughter. "You foolish fellow!" exclaimed one of them at last. "Was not God in the mahout too? And did he not warn you plainly enough? What must we think of one who is foolish enough to imagine that God never speaks through man whom He has made in His own image, but chooses to speak through an enraged elephant?"

—W.E.D. rep.

Two Monks and the Beautiful Woman

An old monk and a young monk were walking through a forest when they came to a river bank and saw a beautiful young woman standing at the edge of the bank.

The woman told the monks that she was afraid to cross the river because she might slip and be carried downstream. She asked if one of the monks might help her across.

Now it so happened that these 2 monks were members of a sect which practiced celibacy and they had both taken vows never to touch a member of the opposite sex. But the old monk, sensing the extreme anxiety of the young woman, lifted her onto his back and carried her to the other side of the river.

The young woman thanked him and went on her way. The 2 monks continued on their journey, but the young monk was shocked and disturbed at having seen his older companion break his vow so nonchalantly. Finally, after 3 hours of walking and thinking, he could contain himself no longer and he burst out, "Tell me, old man, what did it feel like to break your vow of so many years? What did it feel like to allow sensuality to tempt you from your spiritual path? What did it feel like to have her smooth warm thighs wrapped around your waist, her breasts brushing against your back, her arms around your neck and her soft cheek almost one with your own? Tell me, old man, what is it like to carry such a beautiful young woman?"

The older monk remained silent for several steps and then said, "It is you who should tell me what it is like to carry such a beautiful young woman. You see I put her down 3 hours ago at the river, but you are still carrying her."

19

Love and Sexuality

Uncensored Highlights in the History of Sex in the Last 500 Years

1530—The word "syphilis" is introduced. According to travel writer Allan H. Mankoff, "It was an Italian, Girolamo Fracastoro, who originated the word 'syphilis' in a 1530 poem, 'Syphilis, sive Morbus Gallicus,' whose hero, a Greek shepherd, Syphilis, is cursed with the disease for doing the god Apollo dirty."

1665—The word "condom" 1st appeared in print. A Dr. Conton, a physician, and a Colonel Condum, of the Royal Guards, were both members of the court of loose-living King Charles II of England. While contraceptives made of sheep intestines had long been in use in the Middle East, it was Dr. Conton who popularized a male contraceptive he created from dried lamb intestines. (This device was oiled to make it flexible.) Although Dr. Conton designed the contraceptive, for reasons unknown it was probably named after Colonel Condum. One of the earliest customers for these contraceptives was that great lover, Giovanni Casanova, who purchased 12 "English caps," as he called them.

1670—The London Dancing Club was founded. According to Ned Ward, author of *The Secret History of Clubs*, its membership consisted chiefly of "bullies, libertines, and strumpets . . . any person was free to shake their rumps and exercise their members to some tune." Professional prostitutes like Oyster Moll attended and joined in wild orgiastic dancing.

1670—For leaving his wife for another woman, one John Smith of Medfield was fined £10 and sentenced to 30 lashes by a Massachusetts court.

1671—In Massachusetts, Plymouth's revised statutes fined ordinary fornicators £10, those who were engaged to each other £5.

1688—Sir Charles Sedley and his friend Buckhurst (who was the 1st man to keep Nell Gwyn, mistress of King Charles II) streaked up and down the streets of London naked. In 1663 Sedley, a flamboyant rake, had shouted profanities to a crowd as he stood naked on the balcony of the Cock Tavern in Bow Street. He was fined 2,000 marks for his behavior.

1717—Daniel Turner wrote, "The Condom being the best, if not the only preservative our libertines have found out at present, and yet by reason of its blunting the Sensation, I have heard some of them acknowledge that they often chose to risk a Clap, rather than engage *cum hastis sic clypearis*." The rakes were not using the condoms for contraceptive reasons; they cared little if the women they seduced became pregnant. However, women themselves were beginning to keep contraceptives on hand. Casanova stole a supply of them from a nun with whom he had a sexual liaison and left a poem in their place, hardly a fair exchange. Before the end of the century condoms were widely available and were being used mainly as a measure against infection.

1718—A *Treatise on the Use of Flogging*, a pornographic book on flagellation, was published. About the same time, a machine that could whip 40 persons at a time was invented. Mrs. Berkeley, an English madam, made £10,000 in 8 years from a brothel that featured flagellation.

1750—*Fanny Hill*, the famous pornographic novel, was published.

1750—In France, Marie Lajon won her case against Pierre Berle, who had kept her locked in a chastity belt.

—A.E. & The Eds.

1750—The custom of bundling became the rage in America. Courting couples would lie in the same bed partly or fully clothed, sometimes with a special bundling board between them. Often the bundling board was breached or hurdled and the couples groped in the dark for additional ways to keep warm, and that is where the controversy came in.

In his *Classical Dictionary of the Vulgar Tongue*, Grose defined bundling as "A man and woman lying on the same bed with their clothes on; an expedient practiced in America on a scarcity of beds, where, on such occasions, husbands and parents frequently permitted travelers to 'bundle' with their wives and daughters." But there was more to the practice than the scarcity of beds or the lack of heat, as Washington Irving noted in *History of New York*. Irving cited those "cunning and ingenious" Yankees who permitted young couples to bundle due to their "strict adherence to the good old pithy maxim about 'buying a pig in a poke.'" He further noted "that wherever the practice of bundling prevailed, there was an amazing number of sturdy brats born . . . without the license of the law, or the benefit of clergy . . . a long-sided, raw-boned, hardy race of whoreson whalers, woodcutters, fishermen, and peddlers; and strapping corn-fed wenches, who by their united efforts tended marvellously toward populating those notable tracts of country. . . ." On the other hand, one old gentleman, explaining the custom to his grandson late in the last century, emphasized the practicality of bundling and denied any wrongdoing on the part of the participants. "What is the use of sitting up all night and burning out fire and lights, when you could just as well get under kiver and keep warm," he said. "Why damn it, there wasn't half as many bastards then as there are now!"

In any event, bundling was with us from the beginning in America and came close to being a universal custom from 1750 to 1780, at least among "the humbler classes," those who had to economize in their use of firewood and candles. While it's true that "innocent and generous hospitality" prompted many to share their wives or daughters and never turn a cold and weary stranger away while "they could offer him even half of a bed," bundling was for the greater part confined to courting couples. No doubt its end was primarily brought about by the improved lot of the people after the Revolution, when many were able to live in larger and better heated houses. But the voices of prudes and preachers—Jonathan Edwards prominent among the latter—whispering and thundering against the custom also contributed to its downfall.

—R.H.

1752–1753—Francis Duffield and Sir Francis Dashwood started a club at Medmenham in England. In their twice yearly orgies, members engaged in Satanic games wearing white costumes.

1755—Shortly after Dr. Samuel Johnson had published his Dictionary of the English Language, a splendid British lady approached him and congratulated him on omitting all improper and coarse words from his dictionary. "Ah," replied Dr. Johnson, "so you have been looking for them, Madam?"

1757—In England, the Society for the Reformation of Manners was endorsed by King George II, who had already issued a proclamation against vice. In the 5 years the Society existed, it succeeded in getting 10,000 prosecutions, many against sexual offenders.

1776—Benjamin Franklin was unanimously selected Postmaster General of the U.S. by the Continental Congress, with the power to ban obscene matter—despite the fact that he had authored a "Letter to Young Men on the Proper Choosing of a Mistress" and the "Speech of Polly Baker" (which Jefferson loved). Both of these would later be banned by U.S. post offices as obscene.

1777—The Marquis de Sade, famous libertine from whose name came the word "sadism," was arrested in Paris, at the request of his mother, for his cruel orgiastic sexual practices. Earlier he had been accused of trying to poison women with cantharides (such as Spanish fly), and of engaging in sadism and sodomy at orgies which he staged.

1780—A list called *Covent Garden Ladies* (actually London prostitutes) was published.

1783—Louis XIV secretly married Madame de Maintenon who had been his mistress. She was 3 years older than he, placid, and no longer a great beauty, but she was comfortable. The King gave up having affairs and became almost domestic.

1786—S. G. Vogel, a German, advocated infibulation—use of a cagelike device—to prevent masturbation.

1789—In England the Proclamation Society was founded to implement the Royal Proclamation against Vice.

1792—Mary Wollstonecraft published *Rights of Women*, a treatise against the submission of females. Horace Walpole called her a "hyena in skirts."

1821—The 1st obscenity trial in the U.S. involving a book took place. Peter Holmes, publisher of *Memoirs of a Woman of Pleasure* (Cleland's *Fanny Hill*, of course), was found guilty.

1824—England's Vagrancy Act was the 1st law aimed at obscenity. The law forbade display of an obscene print or book in any street or public place.

1825—New Harmony, Ind., was founded. This community, which soon failed, mixed communism, religious free thought, and equalitarian marriage. Many other experiments like it took place in the U.S.

1826—Pope Leo XIII issued a papal bull denouncing the condom contraceptive, thundering that "it hindered the arrangement of providence."

1830s—The cancan became popular in Paris in spite of the fact that it was considered provocatively indecent. The dance, which revealed the female leg as the performers kicked, grew more and more frantic as the tempo of the music increased.

1832—Dr. Charles Knowlton, an American physician, advocated the use of such birth control devices as the sponge and condom, as well as the practices of withdrawal and douching.

1837—Victoria ascended the throne, officially beginning the Victorian Age. This was a period of sexual repression during which people in polite society called a chicken breast a bosom, banned advertisements which would reveal that ladies' underwear had legs, and put crinolines on piano legs.

1839—The Commissioner of Metropolitan Police in London estimated that there were 933 brothels and 848 houses of ill-fame in the city.

1841—The publisher of Shelley's *Queen Mab* was convicted of publishing obscene material.

1845—In Java chastity belts were still being used.

1847—Marie Duplessis died. Born to a poor peasant family, she rose to become France's most expensive and desired courtesan. At the age of 19, she had 7 gentlemen supporting and sharing her, each allotted one night of the week. Among her more notable lovers were Franz Liszt and Alexandre Dumas, *fils*. Dumas based his novel and play, *La Dame aux camélias*, on her life. The Verdi opera *La Traviata* was, in turn, inspired by the Dumas play.

1847—Chloroform was 1st used for childbirth. Church people who were against it quoted the Bible, which said children should be "brought forth in sorrow." However, Queen Victoria, who had had 6 children in such "sorrow," tried chloroform in 1853 and liked it.

1853—Sir Richard Burton, author of the *Arabian Nights*, regaled friends with the true story of a group of Englishmen who traveled to the Mideast to visit a Muslim sultan. The sultan invited his guests to join him and his wife on a camel-riding tour of the area. As the group of Englishmen watched, the Muslim sultan's wife mounted her camel, lost her balance, and tumbled back off. As she fell, her dress slipped up and her private parts were revealed to all. To the surprise of the Englishmen, the sultan was not embarrassed. On the contrary, he was pleased—because his wife had kept her face covered during her fall.

1857—The Obscene Publications Act was passed in England.

1864—Asa Mercer arranged to have a group of unmarried girls sent to Puget Sound to uplift the "bachelor element" which was "almost wholly beyond the reach of female influence and its wholesome results."

1865—Anthony Comstock, an American, began a campaign for the suppression of vice, a campaign to which men like J. P. Morgan contributed. Comstock's slogan was "Morals, not Art or Literature." He was known to have also said, "Books are feeders for brothels." He demanded that all figures in art works be clothed or at least wear fig leaves over the genitals.

1870—The 1st underarm deodorant was created.

1872—Sexologist Kraft-Ebbing coined the term "sadism."

1873—The "Comstock Act" was passed by the U.S. Congress. This stipulated that it was illegal to send obscene materials through the mails. Comstock got himself appointed special agent for the post office and claimed that in his 1st year in this job he seized 200,000 pictures and photographs, 100,000 books, more than 60,000 rubber articles (probably condoms), 5,000 decks of playing cards, and 30,000 boxes of aphrodisiacs.

1880—At the age of 73, Lady Jane Ellenborough, one of the most glamorous nymphomaniacs in history, complained of her husband, an Arabian sheik, "It is now a month and 20 days since Medjuel last slept with me! What can be the reason?" Among her countless lovers were Honoré de Balzac, King Ludwig I of Bavaria, and Ludwig's son, King Otto of Greece.

1883—Henry Varley delivered a lecture to an audience of 3,000 men on the "terrible and destructive sin of Onanism or self-abuse—a practice as common as it is hateful and injurious." He claimed that masturbation caused short stature, a contracted chest, weak lungs, and other disabilities.

1885—W. T. Stead, a London journalist, bought a 13-year-old girl for £10 and kept her in a brothel. Though he did this solely as research for a series of articles *against* prostitution, he was imprisoned.

1887—J. L. Milton in *Spermatorrhea*, which reached its 12th edition in that year, advocated the use of cages lined with spikes to prevent boys from masturbating and discussed a device which would ring a bell in the parents' room if a boy had an erection.

1888—Mark Twain published *1601*, an underground classic in pornography. Twain told a Cleveland librarian: "If there is a decent word in it, it is because I overlooked it." U.S. Secretary of State John Hay printed a secret edition of this book on the presses of the U.S. Military Academy at West Point.

1895—Oscar Wilde, the famous writer, was locked up in Reading Gaol. Accused of homosexual practices by the Marquis of Queensbury, Wilde had been brought to trial and found guilty.

1895—Freud and Breuer published *Studies in Hysteria*, a pioneer work in psychoanalysis. Freud's theories about sex and the importance of sexuality in all aspects of life had a tremendous effect on people all over the world. Until around 1910, his ideas were generally denounced by medical men and the press. Some doctors called psychoanalysis "mental masturbation" and Freud a "Viennese libertine."

1900—An American gynecologist said to a group of doctors, "I do not believe mutual pleasure in the sexual act has any particular bearing on the happiness of life." At the time, estimates of female frigidity ranged from 10% to 75% of all women.

1901—*Sexual Inversion*, by researcher Henry Havelock Ellis, was published. Based on case studies and information from a variety of sources, it was suppressed as obscene, "a filthy publication."

1904—An investigation in Paris turned up 4 manufacturers of chastity belts, which had been invented during the Crusades. A silver one with a padlock cost 50 francs.

1909—In the case of *Commonwealth of Kentucky v. Poindexter*, 2 black men who had been accused of having oral sex with each other were not convicted because there was no law on the books against such a practice. The judge immediately issued a statement against oral sex and asked that it be made illegal. Anti-oral-sex laws were then enacted in many States.

1910—In New Orleans, La., an annual guidebook for tourists gave the addresses and delineated the charms of the city's leading houses of ill-fame.

1912—Dr. Paul Ehrlich, a German, found a cure for syphilis.

1914—Margaret Sanger coined the term "birth control." Two years later, she opened the 1st birth-control clinic in the U.S. Sanger said, "A woman's body belongs to herself alone," and insisted that a woman had the right to "dispose of herself, to withhold herself, to procreate or suppress the germ of life."

1914—The U.S. Federation of Women's Clubs banned the tango and hesitation waltz as immoral.

1918—Women began to denounce the double standard, which postulated that males need not be virgins before marriage, but women must. About these women protestors, H. L. Mencken wrote: "What these virtuous beldames actually desire is not that the male be reduced to chemical purity, but that the franchise of dalliance be extended to themselves."

1920s—Charles Chaplin stunned the nation when, during a divorce trial in which he was accused of indulging in cunnilingus, he exclaimed, "But all married people do that!"

1921—U.S. movie producers hired Will H. Hays, former Postmaster General, to head an association which would establish and maintain motion picture standards. The association was originally founded to avoid censorship; however, the Hays office's arbitrary standards soon tied the industry up in knots.

1921—The renowned Hollywood comedian, Fatty Arbuckle, allegedly committed anal rape on actress Virginia Rappe, using either his penis or a Coke or champagne bottle. When she died as a result, Arbuckle faced criminal charges. He went to trial 3 times, twice got a hung jury, and the 3rd time was acquitted. But he was blackballed from films forever and died penniless.

1921—An Irish journalist after visiting the U.S.: "Unbalanced by prolonged contemplation of the tedious virtues of New England, a generation has arisen whose great illusion is that the transvaluation of all values may be effected by promiscuity."

1922—Edward Aleister Crowley's book *Diary of a Drug Fiend* was reviewed by James Douglas, who was shocked by it. The London Sunday *Express*, in that same year, exposed Crowley as a libertine, who wanted his women brought to the back door "like milk," preferred women who were exotic or deformed, and engaged in orgiastic rites.

1922—*Ulysses*, by James Joyce, was published in Paris.

1923—Adultery was made grounds for divorce in England.

1926—Dutch physician Theodor van de Velde, in his book *Ideal Marriage*, urged men to learn techniques for bringing about female orgasm. In the same year, Wilhelm Reich published *Function of the Orgasm* in which he said that failure to achieve orgasm caused mental and physical diseases. (Later Reich claimed that masturbation could combat cancer.)

1927—Judge Ben Lindsay, of Denver's juvenile court, created a worldwide sensation with a book that advocated "companionate" or trial marriages, as well as the legalization of birth control.

1928—*A Research in Marriage* by Dr. G. V. Hamilton appeared. (See: A Survey of Sex Surveys—1900–1975, Chap. 19)

1928—James J. Walker, Mayor of New York, said he had never heard of a woman who had been made pregnant by a book.

1929—Radcliffe Hall's *The Well of Loneliness*, a gentle British novel about lesbianism, was taken into court on the charge of being obscene. Judge Bushel admitted the novel had literary merit, but nevertheless ruled to censor it, stating, "I am convinced that *The Well of Loneliness* tends to debauch public morals, that its subject-matter is offensive to public decency, and that it is calculated to deprave and corrupt minds open to immoral influences. . . ." The book's publisher, Donald Friede, appealed to a 3-man appellate court, which overturned the banning and legitimatized the book.

1929—Katharine B. Davis's *Factors in the Sex Life of Twenty-Two Hundred Women* was published. (See: A Survey of Sex Surveys—1900–1975, Chap. 19.)

1930s—The invention of the latex process resulted in the manufacture of a better condom.

1931—*A Thousand Marriages*, by Dr. Robert Dickinson and Lura Beam, was published. (See: A Survey of Sex Surveys—1900–1975, Chap. 19.)

1933—*Ulysses* was cleared by a Federal judge for publication in the U.S.

1933—The Hays office would not allow motion pictures to expose the nipple on a woman's breast or the inside of her thigh.

1933—Dr. Robert Dickinson came out with *Human Sex Anatomy*, the 1st modern book by a sexologist to contain illustrations of sex positions.

1934—Henri Littière, a Parisian baker, was brought into court for making his wife wear a chastity belt. An amateur researcher into the Middle Ages, he had found such a belt in the Cluny Museum, Paris, and had had it copied by his orthopedist. It was of velvet-lined metal and was provided with 2 small openings. The judge suspended Littière's sentence and fined him 50 francs.

1936—Sulphonamide drugs were discovered and used in the treatment of gonorrhea.

1938—The New York Board of Censors banned all movies mentioning pregnancy, venereal disease, birth control, abortion, illegitimacy, prostitution, miscegenation, and divorce.

1938—*Life* magazine ran an article illustrated with still photos taken from the movie *The Birth of a Baby*, evoking great disapproval from the Comstocks. The New York district attorney arrested the publisher.

1941—From *Forbidden Words* by Robert A. Wilson:

The 1st use of modern psychology as an advertising tool occurred in 1941 when Dr. Ernest Dichter wrote a study for Pontiac explaining the sexual symbolism (headlights, pistons) of the automobile and indicating how subliminal use of this could be used to increase sales. Pontiac followed this advice, and sales skyrocketed.

1946—*God's Little Acre*, by Erskine Caldwell, was banned in St. Paul. In the same year Doubleday & Co., Inc., published Edmund Wilson's *Memoirs of Hecate County*, which contained an explicit description of a woman's genitals. A 3-judge New York court found this book obscene, and, when the case reached the Supreme Court, the vote was split, so the decision of the lower court stood.

1948—The Kinsey Report was published. (See: A Survey of Sex Surveys—1900–1975, Chap. 19.)

1950s—Oral contraceptives were tested and put on the market.

1954—The World Health Organization estimated that there were 20 million syphilitics in the world.

1957—The U.S. Supreme Court, in a historic decision, held State obscenity statutes unconstitutional and said that the reading matter of adults could not be limited in order to protect children. Justice Frankfurter called it "burning the house to roast the pig."

1959—Intrauterine devices were rediscovered and developed.

1960s—Justice William O. Douglas in *The Right of the People*: "The idea of using obscenity to bar thoughts of sex is dangerous. A person without sex thoughts is abnormal. Sex thoughts may induce sex practices that make for better marital relations. Sex thoughts that make love attractive certainly should not be outlawed."

1960—Cameraman Russ Meyer made a movie, "*The Immoral Mr. Teas*," which exposed the female breast, and though the film could not be shown in legitimate theaters, it grossed more than $1 million. (Meyer made it in less than a week at a cost of $25,000.)

1963—John D. Profumo, then British Secretary of State for War, resigned after his association with call girl Christine Keeler was made public. At the time Keeler was also sleeping with a Soviet naval attaché.

1964—The U.S. Supreme Court held *Tropic*

of Cancer not constitutionally obscene by a vote of 5 to 4.

1966—Ralph Ginzburg, publisher of *Eros* magazine, was sent to jail for 5 years for flamboyant, obscene advertising of 2 periodicals and a book.

1966—*Human Sexual Response*, by Masters and Johnson, was published. (See: A Survey of Sex Surveys—1900–1975, Chap. 19.)

1967—Great Britain legalized homosexual behavior which occurred in private between consenting adults.

1967—The World Health Organization estimated there were 30 to 50 million syphilitics in the world, an increase of at least 10 million and perhaps as much as 30 million in a period of 13 years.

1968—Abortion was legalized in Great Britain.

1968—Psychiatrist Natalie Chainess said about genital deodorants: "While fostering an overt message of a feminine 'sexy' woman, the implication of need for such a spray conveys a message of women as being dirty and smelly."

1970—Abortion was legalized in New York State.

1971—The 1st Gay Community Services Center was opened in Los Angeles.

1971—The Florida Supreme Court declared unconstitutional the law that made oral sex performed by heterosexuals a crime.

1972—Says author Robert Wilson in *Forbidden Words:*

> The current skyrocketing rise in clap and syphilis is astonishing. Gonorrhea is 29 times as common as the measles, and syphilis has killed 100 million people since 1900, or 4 times the number who died during the bubonic plague in medieval Europe.

1972—A travel guide, *Lusty Europe*, contributed to the store of human knowledge with this bit about a sight in London:

> Penis (Napoleon's). Christie's Fine Art Auctioneers (8 King Street, S.W.1) has had it. Removed from the Emperor by his confessor-priest. The catalogue described it as "a small dried-up object." "Looks like a sea-horse," said a night porter. Phone Christie's at 839-9060 if you want it. It is rather surprising that the thing was "withdrawn" (the auctioneer's own phrase) at a recent sale considering the £13,300 price and one-inch length. . . .

1973—Sexologist David Reuben recommended oral sex and estimated that 70–80% of American adults practiced it.

1973—Several American businesses bought into a German brothel chain when its owner, Kurt Kohls, put $8 million in stock up for sale. His brochure was entitled, "How to Make Money in Germany with the Oldest Profession in the World." The slogan of the brothels, run like hotels, was "Sex with Heart."

1973—The U.S. Supreme Court ruled that local laws on obscenity could supersede the Constitution.

1973—Millionaire Lord Lambton, 22-year veteran of the House of Commons in England, resigned as Defense Under-Secretary of the RAF when it became known that secret photographs of him "in flagrante" with Norma Levy, an Irish prostitute, were being offered to newspapers for $25,000. "I have behaved with credulous stupidity," admitted His Lordship. Immediately afterward, Lord Jellicoe, son of Britain's naval hero at Jutland, personal friend of Prime Minister Edward Heath and a member of his Cabinet, resigned after exposure of his "casual affairs" with ladies of the night.

1973—An aphrodisiac containing the synthetic hormone LRF was found to induce mating in rats.

1973—The U.S. Supreme Court overruled all State laws restricting a woman's right to abortion in the 1st 3 months of pregnancy.

1974—A computer program simulating a woman's monthly cycle was invented.

1974—Lavender University, a school for homosexuals, opened in San Francisco with a schedule that offered 30 classes, including Greek literature, metaphysics, and hiking.

1974—Jan Morris, formerly James Humphrey Morris, the writer who scooped the conquest of Mount Everest in 1944, wrote *Conundrum*, a book describing his/her transformation, by surgery, into a woman.

1974—Publication of the book *Lewd Foods*, in which author Robert Hendrickson recounted history's most prodigious lovers. "The French actress Mlle. Dubois, who often dined with Marshal Soubise at his naked supper parties . . . left posterity an accounting of her conquests over a 20-year period. They totaled 16,527, or over 2 a day." Messalina, Queen of Rome, and Cleopatra, Queen of Egypt, "demanded and received more than 100 men in one night . . . the *official* record holder would appear to be that anonymous . . . man cited by Dr. Kinsey who averaged 33.1 matings per week, or more than 4 times a day over a period of 30 years." Other contenders include the real-life Don Juan, a Spanish nobleman named Tenorio, who had 2,594 mistresses; the Italian poet and politician, Gabriel d'Annunzio, who boasted that 1,000 husbands hated him; the novelist Frank Harris, who seduced

2,000 women (and insured his file of their names with Lloyd's of London for $150,000; Ibn Saud, King of Saudi Arabia, who, from the age of 11 to 72, enjoyed sexual pleasure with 20,000 different women.

1975—The 1,600 gold miners working in Vatukoula, Fiji, demanded of their employers an extra 30 minutes added to their daily lunch hour to enjoy sexual pleasure. According to Reuters news service, the union secretary, Navita Raqona, stated that "a man has a sexual obligation to his wife and if he goes home exhausted at 5 P.M., he cannot fulfill it. The union wants the sex break added to the normal lunch break. After lunch and a short rest, a man is in prime mental and physical condition to meet his sexual obligations." The union requested this extra time for married men only, planning to make "alternative arrangements" for bachelors.

1975—The 1st brothel for senior citizens, in Marseilles, France, was reported. Clients' ages ranged from 60 to 77. The prostitutes charged about $10 for the service.

—A.E. & The Eds.

Dictionary of Sex Related Terms

Abortion—technically the spontaneous premature ending of a pregnancy in the 1st 12 weeks. In popular usage, the word refers to the intentional ending of pregnancy and killing of the embryo. Some people, notably members of the Roman Catholic Church, oppose abortion because they consider it to be the murder of a human being. Others say that every woman should be able to end a pregnancy if she so desires. With the growing acceptance of abortion and the obvious problems brought about by the population explosion, abortions are becoming very easy to obtain in some States. They are inexpensive compared to what they used to cost. (In California a vacuum suction abortion was about $150 in 1974.) The vacuum suction method is the most common medical technique for abortion. It is relatively safe, usually takes from 5 to 7 minutes, and is painless except for some cramping of the uterus.

Adultery—sexual intercourse between 2 people, at least one of whom is married to someone else.

Anal Intercourse—sexual intercourse by inserting the penis into the rectum (anus). Used mostly though not exclusively by homosexual men. It is said that this is a good technique to help men understand what it is like to be a woman. If done, it must be done very gently with much attention given to cleanliness. Going straight from anal intercourse to vaginal intercourse without washing the penis in between can easily lead to infection.

Aphrodisiac—according to the booklet *Herbal Aphrodisiacs* (Stone Kingdom, P.O. Box 15304, San Francisco, Calif. 94115) they are "substances which do any one of the following things: produce erections in the male, arouse sexual feeling by stimulation of the genital or nervous system, increase sensual awareness, relax inhibitions, augment physical energy, strengthen the gonads or other glands involved in sex, improve sexual health, increase the production of semen, help conquer impotence and frigidity (bearing in mind that these maladies are frequently of psychological origin), overcome sexual exhaustion, and prevent premature ejaculation." The most effective aphrodisiac is 2 people in love.

Bastard—a derogatory term referring to a child born to a woman who is not married to the father. (See also: *Illegitimate child.*) In some societies all children are considered equal and valuable and women need not be married to bear them.

Bestiality—sexual intercourse with a nonhuman animal.

Bigamy—illegal polygamy.

Birth Control—preventing pregnancy through use of a contraceptive. (See also: *Coitus Interruptus, Condom, Diaphragm, Foam, I.U.D., Pill, Rhythm Method, Spermicide, Sterilization,* and *Vasectomy.*)

Bisexuality—having sexual desire for people of both sexes.

Bondage—tying up a sexual partner to increase dramatic excitement. This technique should only be used by couples who are very familiar with each other.

Brothel—a house of prostitution.

Call Girl—a female prostitute who may be contacted by telephone when a male customer wishes her to visit him.

Castration—removal or loss of the testicles in men or the ovaries in women. Castration does not necessarily eliminate the sex drive.

Celibacy—abstention from sexual intercourse and/or living without a mate. Many religious orders practice celibacy in order to concentrate their spiritual energies better. Other people choose to experience periods of celibacy when they want to take a break from the problems and power struggles of sexual relationships.

Cervix—the narrow lower or outer end of the uterus.

Chastity—purity in thought and actions. A chaste person does not engage in illegal sexual intercourse.

Chastity Belt—a medieval device worn by women to prevent sexual intercourse, an unfortunate indicator of the relationship between men and women during certain periods. Popular history has it that a husband who was going off to war would lock his wife in a chastity belt and take the key with him, thus preventing the woman from committing adultery with anyone other than a locksmith. However, they were also used by women to prevent rape.

Circumcision—surgical removal of the foreskin from the penis. There is no conclusive evidence that this has either positive or negative effects on sexual performance and/or health.

Clap—See: *Gonorrhea*.

Clitoris—a small organ (⅕" to 1" in length) that plays a most important role in female pleasure and orgasm. Like the male penis, it is composed of a shaft and glans, and it has a similar sensitivity. It is located within the upper folds of the inner lips of the genitals, with the tip protruding from beneath a hood. When aroused, the clitoris, which is thick with nerve endings, fills with blood and becomes erect.

Cohabitation—the state of living together as a couple with or without being married.

Coitus—sexual intercourse during which the male inserts his penis into the female's vagina. The most common form of sexual intercourse, it can be done in many positions.

Coitus Interruptus—coitus in which the man withdraws his penis from the woman's vagina before ejaculation. A common form of birth control which is often ineffective because small amounts of sperm may escape before ejaculation, so that some sperm cells may make contact with the vulva and work their way inside. Another drawback is that the couple cannot let their sexual drive achieve full expression.

Conception—the formation of a potential human being. It occurs when a sperm and an ovum meet in the uterus or one of the Fallopian tubes and join to become an embryo.

Condom—a thin rubber "glove" that fits over the penis to prevent sperm from entering the vagina. This can be an effective method of birth control providing the sperm remains inside the condom, and the condom doesn't fall off when the penis relaxes after ejaculation.

Contraception—methods and materials aimed at avoiding pregnancy. (See also: *Birth Control*.)

Coprophile—someone who gains sexual satisfaction from playing with excrement.

Copulation—a sexual union. (See also: *Coitus*.)

Cuckold—a man whose wife commits adultery.

Cunnilingus—oral stimulation of the clitoris or vulva. Many women find it easier to reach orgasm this way than through coitus.

Diaphram—a shallow cup made of soft rubber which provides maximum safety when filled with spermicide before it is inserted in the vagina to cover the cervix. This device prevents sperm from entering the uterus. A good method of birth control, it has the disadvantage of discouraging spontaneity. On the other hand, it is excellent for having intercourse during a woman's period because it can hold back menstrual flow for up to 12 hours.

Dildo—an artificial penis made of plastic, rubber, or wood.

Double Standard—a moral code in which men are allowed to engage in premarital or extramarital sex, but women are not.

Ejaculation—the sudden ejection of semen from the penis. This can occur during intercourse, masturbation, or a nocturnal emission.

Embryo—medical term for a developing baby during its 1st 3 months in the mother's womb.

Erection—the swelling, hardening, and rising of the penis when it fills with blood, usually, but not always, caused by sexual excitement.

Erogenous Zones—parts of the body which become sexually stimulated when touched. These may vary from person to person and from encounter to encounter, but they usually include the external genital organs, the breasts, nipples, rectum, mouth, and certain areas of the skin such as the neck, ears, or the inside of the thighs. Potentially, the entire human body can be one big erogenous zone.

Erotic—sexually arousing or dealing with sexual love.

Eunuch—a man whose testicles have been removed. In 18th-century Europe eunuchs, or "castratos," were used to sing female parts in operas before women were allowed on the stage. The term also refers to castrated men who guard harems. Today, there are more eunuchs in India than there are Jews in Poland.

Exhibitionist—a man who gains sexual satisfaction from exposing his genitals in public.

Extramarital Intercourse—sexual intercourse with someone other than one's spouse.

Fallopian Tubes—2 tubes which carry eggs from the ovaries to the uterus. This journey takes an average of 6½ days.

Fellatio—oral contact with the penis, which sometimes leads to orgasm for the male.

Fertility—the ability to reproduce.

Fetishist—a person who is more sexually aroused by an object or a part of a person's body than by the whole person.

Fetus—medical term for an unborn baby after its 1st 3 months in the mother's womb.

Fidelity—being faithful to one's mate. Usually understood to mean abstention from extramarital intercourse.

Foam—a white, aerated material containing a spermicide. It is inserted in the vulva in front of the entrance to the cervix. Foam is best used as a supplement to other forms of birth control.

Foreplay—caresses that lead to sexual intercourse. An unfortunate term in that it implies that the caresses cannot be enjoyed for themselves, because they are merely an introduction to something bigger and better.

Foreskin—an expandable fold of skin that covers the glans of the penis. It is often removed soon after birth in a simple surgical operation called circumcision. Men with uncircumcized penises have to pay more attention to cleanliness because urine, sweat, and other secretions can get trapped under the skin.

Fornication—all sexual intercourse except that between husband and wife.

Free Love—a moral code that says it is acceptable to have sexual relationships other than those between a husband and wife, such as premarital or extramarital sex. Free love implies that it is morally proper for a couple to live together without being legally married.

French Kiss—an open-mouthed kiss which emphasizes contact between the tongues.

Frigidity—inability of a woman to enjoy lovemaking or to have an orgasm. Some women are accused of being frigid by insensitive men who use sex for their own satisfaction and do not devote any time or energy to satisfying their female partners. There are so many other reasons why a woman might not become stimulated—worry, fatigue, a clumsy partner, or just not being in the mood—that it is unwise to lump them all under the heading of frigidity. If a woman never enjoys sex, even with a partner she deeply loves, then a problem exists.

Frottage—the practice of rubbing one's genitals against another person, usually in a crowd.

Gay—See: *Homosexual.*

Genitals (*Genitalia*)—the sex organs. In a man these include the penis, scrotum, testicles, spermatic ducts, and the prostate gland. In the woman these include the vulva, consisting of the labia majora, labia minora, and clitoris; the vagina; uterus; fallopian tubes; and ovaries.

Glans—the tip or head of the penis.

Gonads—ovaries and testicles.

Gonorrhea—the most common venereal disease. In men, a severe burning while urinating develops 3 to 9 days after infection. Women may have no noticeable symptoms. The harmful microorganism *Neisseria gonorrhoeae* can enter the body during oral, anal, or genital contact. A fetus can acquire gonorrhea through the placenta.

Group Sex—sexual intercourse involving more than 2 people.

Hedonism—a moral code in which pleasure is considered to be the chief good in life.

Hermaphrodite—a person who has both male and female sex organs. An extremely rare occurrence.

Heterosexual—a person who is sexually attracted to someone of the opposite sex.

Homosexual—a person who is sexually attracted to someone of the same sex.

Hooker—a female prostitute.

Horny—having a strong physical desire for sex.

Hymen—a thin fold of mucous membrane that covers the vaginal opening. Because it is broken by the penis during the 1st sexual intercourse, there is a myth that hymenless women can't be virgins. This myth is dying, however, because the hymen can be broken in other ways as well. When the hymen breaks, there is usually a small amount of bleeding.

Illegitimate Child—the child of parents who are not married to each other. "Illegitimate" is an absurd term in that it implies that the child doesn't count or isn't the equal of other human beings.

Impotence—the inability of the male to have an erection. This happens at some time to all men, usually because of fear of putting on a bad performance or because the situation just isn't right. There are physical factors which can cause impotence, such as alcohol, diabetes, obesity, lack of protein, and some drugs. If impotence persists, one suggested remedy is the "squeeze and stuff" technique described in the pamphlet *You Can Last Longer*, published by the Multi Media Resource Center (540 Powell St., San Francisco, Calif. 94108).

Incest—sexual intercourse between close relatives such as a sister and brother or a parent and child. Incest is considered taboo because the offspring of such unions are more susceptible to hereditary diseases.

Infertility—See: *Sterility.*

Infidelity—being unfaithful to one's mate by having extramarital intercourse.

Intercourse—See: *Sexual Intercourse.*

I.U.D.—intrauterine device. (Different types are called coils, loops, and shields.) No one knows how it works, but it is very effective and has been used for centuries in primitive forms. The device is inserted into the uterus by a physician and can be removed when the woman wishes to conceive. Some women are unable to use this method of birth control as it causes much cramping and bleeding, and there is a small percentage of women who do become pregnant while wearing one. But a great many women adjust to the I.U.D. quickly and find it the most convenient birth control method available.

Kiss—to touch or caress with the lips. Kisses range from a platonic peck to passionate French kisses.

Kotex—trade name for an absorbent sanitary pad worn by women to collect the menstrual flow and discharges. There are many other brands, such as Modess.

Labia Majora—the outer lips of the vulva.

Labia Minora—the inner lips of the vulva.

Lesbian—a homosexual woman.

Machismo—a Spanish term referring to a moral code which places a high value on aggression, physical strength, and complete male dominance over women.

Male Chauvinism—a conscious or unconscious belief that men are inherently superior to women and thus deserve special privileges.

Masochism—a need to find sexual satisfaction by experiencing physical or emotional pain. (See: Sacher-Masoch, Important Persons in the History of Sex, Chap. 19.)

Masturbation—erotic self-stimulation of the genitals. Although this practice has been heavily attacked in previous centuries, it is generally accepted today as a legitimate method of gaining sexual satisfaction. Unfortunately, some people tend to rape themselves instead of making love to themselves. Masturbation has been suggested as therapy for men who experience impotence and premature ejaculation. A booklet about this for women is *Masturbation Techniques for Women Getting in Touch*, distributed by Multi Media Resource Center (340 Jones Street, Box 439, San Francisco, Calif. 94102).

Member—penis.

Menarche—the 1st menstruation.

Menopause—the time in a woman's life when menstruation occurs less frequently and then stops altogether. Menopause ends a woman's ability to conceive and can cause other changes as well. However, sex drive and sexual abilities are not affected. As one woman is quoted in *Our Bodies, Ourselves*, "Just beautiful not to have to worry about the damn periods. And no more birth control!"

Menstrual Flow—the blood, secretions, and waste which are discharged during menstruation.

Menstruation—a periodic discharge of blood, secretions, and waste from the uterus of non-pregnant women between the ages of about 12 and 47. The time from the beginning of one menstruation to the day before the beginning of the next is called a menstrual cycle. The length of this cycle differs from woman to woman, but the average is 28 days. Some women experience cramping, tenderness of the breasts, weight gain due to water retention, and other discomforts during their "period."

Minor—a person who is not legally an adult.

Miscarriage—expulsion of the fetus between the 12th and 28th week of pregnancy. A miscarriage after the 28th week is called a stillbirth.

Miscegenation—cohabitation of persons of different races. The southern part of the U.S. used to have laws against marriage between whites and blacks.

Missionary Position—sexual intercourse with the man directly atop the woman. The name was created by Polynesians who found this most common of European positions to be quite amusing.

Monogamy—marriage between one woman and one man.

Mons Veneris (Mountain of Venus)—the rounded, hairy mass of fat above the vulva which cushions the pubic bone.

Necking—to engage in kissing, fondling, and caressing. Less intense than petting.

Necrophilia—being erotically attracted to corpses and the sexual activity which may follow that attraction.

Nocturnal Emission—ejaculation of semen during sleep as a result of an erotic dream. Also known as a wet dream.

Nuclear Family—a social unit consisting of one or 2 parents and at least one child, but no one else, as opposed to an extended family in which the unit includes other relatives and in some cases nonrelatives.

Nymphomaniac—a controversial term referring to a woman who has a constant desire for sexual gratification. There are those who say the term was invented by men to describe women whose sex drive is as vigorous as the male's.

Oedipus Complex—positive sexual feelings that develop in a young child for the parent of the opposite sex and which cause the child to become jealous and hostile toward the parent of the same sex. In the case of a girl, it is called an Electra complex.

Oral Intercourse—sexual intercourse involving the mouth of one person and the genitals of another. (See: *Cunnilingus* and *Fellatio*.)

Orgasm—the climax of sexual excitement. Usually characterized by some degree of ecstasy, followed by satisfaction and relaxation. Orgasm certainly ranks as one of the best things that life has to offer, but some people become so obsessed by it that they fail to appreciate the other aspects of lovemaking. Simultaneous orgasm is nice, but not necessary. In the male, orgasm is accompanied by the ejaculation of semen.

Ovaries—2 organs about the size of unshelled almonds, located on either side and somewhat behind the uterus. They produce hormones and they produce eggs, usually one a month, which travel out through the Fallopian tubes toward the uterus.

Ovulation—the process by which a ripe egg or ovum is released from the ovaries. If the egg is not fertilized by a sperm cell, it disintegrates and is excreted, usually before menstruation.

Ovum (pl. *Ova*)—egg produced in the ovaries. The average ovum is ½₀₀ of an inch in diameter.

Paternity Suit—a legal suit filed against a man who is accused of being the father of an illegitimate child, usually in order to gain financial support for the child.

Patriarchy—a societal structure in which all important decisions are made by men and inheritance and descent are through the male line.

Pederasty—a sexual relationship between an adult man and an adolescent male.

Pedophiliac—a person who is sexually attracted only to children.

Peeping Tom—See: *Voyeur.*

Penis—the male sex organ. Comes in various shapes and sizes, but this has no bearing on sexual ability. It is made up of a long, retractable shaft and a head or glans, the underside of which is particularly sensitive to sexual stimulation. When erect, the penis can be inserted in the vagina in order to engage in coitus. The urethra opening at the end of the glans allows the release of both semen and urine. Penises have a foreskin which is often removed or circumcized.

Period—menstruation.

Petting—more intimate than necking, it usually includes caressing and fondling of a partner's genitals and other erogenous areas, but stops before coitus. Very popular among young people who are hesitant to go "all the way."

Phallus—the penis, particularly the erect penis.

Pill—a birth control pill which prevents eggs from developing. A very effective means of birth control if you don't forget to take it. One pill is taken each day for 21 or 22 days out of a 28-day cycle. Some women experience unpleasant side effects. The pill is available by prescription only because there are certain elements of risk involved for women susceptible to such things as blood clots or cancer.

Pimp—a man who finds customers for a female prostitute and usually takes a large portion of her earnings.

Placenta—the organ which unites the fetus to the mother's uterus and acts as a clearinghouse for any materials that pass between the 2. The placenta is expelled after birth.

Platonic Love—deep love and affection between 2 people without sexual desire.

Polygamy—marriage between more than 2 people. If a woman has more than one husband, it is called polyandry. If a man has more than one wife, it is called polygyny.

Pornography—a vague term pertaining to a written or visual portrayal of the sex act which is intended to provoke sexual excitement.

Premarital Intercourse—sexual intercourse before marriage.

Premature Ejaculation—occurs when a man reaches orgasm before he and his partner want him to. Basically the result of anxiety or overexcitement due to infrequent intercourse. Two possible remedies are practicing lasting a long time while masturbating, and the "squeeze" technique as described in the booklet *You Can Last Longer* or in the Masters and Johnson books. (See also: *Impotence.*)

Promiscuity—engaging in "casual" sexual intercourse without discrimination in the choice of partners. The term is often used to impose a negative judgment on someone who is having a sexual relationship with several partners.

Prophylactic—the medical term for condoms, used often as protection against venereal disease.

Prostitute—a person, either male or female, who engages in sexual intercourse for payment.

Puberty—the time in life during which the genitals become capable of reproduction. Other changes occur as well, such as the growth of body hair and breasts. After puberty comes a sometimes painful period called adolescence during which the individual is physically ready for sexual intercourse, but is denied it by cultural or religious restrictions.

Rape—sexual intercourse in which a man forces entry into a woman (or sometimes another man) without the partner's consent.

Rear Entry—sexual intercourse in which the man enters from behind. This does not necessarily mean anal intercourse.

Rhythm Method—a comparatively ineffective method of birth control, but the only one which is approved by the Roman Catholic Church. The idea is to avoid intercourse during the fertile part of the woman's cycle—just before, during, and just after ovulation.

Rubber—a condom.

Sadism—gaining sexual satisfaction by hurting others. (See: Marquis de Sade, Important Persons in the History of Sex, Chap. 19.) De Sade is described in Webster's 3rd New International Dictionary as a "Fr. soldier and pervert." There is a saying that a masochist is someone who says, "Hurt me, hurt me!" and a sadist is someone who says, "No."

Scrotum—the external pouch of skin which hangs between the male's thighs, behind the penis, and contains the testicles.

Seduce—to charm, coax, or entice someone into having sexual intercourse.

Semen—a thick white fluid consisting of sperm cells suspended in other glandular secretions. It is the semen which discharges from the penis during ejaculation. The semen from one orgasm can contain up to 500 million sperm cells.

Sexism—the belief that one sex is inherently better than the other and therefore deserves special privileges.

Sex Roles—patterns of behavior which children are forced to adopt because they belong to a certain sex. For example, boys are taught to play baseball while girls play house. Or boys are told "big boys don't cry," while girls are encouraged to "act more ladylike."

Sexual Intercourse—physical and sexual contact between 2 people; sometimes assumed to mean the union formed when a man's penis enters a woman's vagina.

Sexy—erotically stimulating.

Sin—a violation of religious law or of God's will as interpreted by church leaders. To some people it means fornication.

Sixty-Nine—simultaneous and mutual oral intercourse.

Sodomy—a confusing term because it has had many different meanings, including anal intercourse, homosexuality, and intercourse with animals.

Speculum—a plastic instrument used to separate the walls of the vagina during examination of the vagina and cervix. (See: Self-Examination for Women, Chap. 20.)

Spermatozoa (sing. *Spermatozoon*)—sperm cells. Spermatozoa are produced in the testicles and then travel through the spermatic ducts to the urethra and out through the tip of the penis. If a spermatozoon lands in a vagina, it will use its long tail to travel up toward the uterus in search of an egg to fertilize. Spermatozoa are about $1/500$ of an inch long and they may remain fertile inside a woman's body for several days.

Spermatic Ducts—2 tubes in the male which carry sperm cells from the testicles to the urethra.

Spermicide—a substance which kills sperm cells. Spermicidal creams and jellies can be inserted into the vagina prior to sexual intercourse as a means of birth control. They are more effective as a secondary method of birth control than when used alone.

Sterility—inability to have children.

Sterilization—See: *Vasectomy*.

Streetwalker—a prostitute.

Sublimation—redirecting erotic energies into nonsexual activities.

Syphilis—a common venereal disease. The 1st symptom is a chancre or painless sore which appears on the infected area (usually the genitals, but not always) between 9 and 90 days after the bacteria, *Treponema pallidum*, enters the body as a result of genital, oral, or anal contact. Fetuses can acquire syphilis through the placenta. Syphilis is a dangerous disease which, if left untreated, can lead to

heart disease, deafness, blindness, paralysis, and death.

Taboo—something which is forbidden and is considered too disturbing even to talk about. Some sexual acts, such as genital kissing and intercourse during menstruation, are losing their status as taboos, while others, such as incest, are still disapproved of by society.

Tampon—a roll of cotton or other material which is inserted into the vagina to absorb the menstrual flow.

Testes—See: *Testicles*.

Testicles—the 2 male sex glands which produce sex hormones and sperm cells. The male equivalent of a woman's ovaries, they are contained within the scrotum.

Transsexual—a person whose sex is uncertain or who considers himself or herself as belonging to the opposite sex. Some of these people have undergone sex-change operations.

Transvestite—a person who enjoys wearing the clothes of the opposite sex. A transvestite is not necessarily a homosexual.

Urethra—the canal through which urine is released. In men it runs from the bladder through the penis and is also used to carry semen out of the body. In women, the outside opening of the urethra is located between the clitoris and the opening of the vagina.

Uterus—a hollow, thick-walled muscular organ within the female body. It is located at the upper end of the vagina between the bladder and the rectum. It is here that children develop from conception to birth.

Vagina (Birth Canal)—the female sex organ extending from the vulva to the uterus. The vagina is located between the bladder, the urethra, and the rectum at a 45° angle to the ground when standing. It has 3 main functions: carrying the menstrual flow out of the body, receiving the penis during coitus, and allowing the baby to leave the mother's body during birth.

Vas Deferens—See: *Spermatic Ducts*.

Vasectomy—a sterility operation in which the male's spermatic ducts are closed off. A 100% effective means of birth control which does not affect sexual desire or ability.

Venereal Diseases—contagious diseases which are usually communicated during sexual intercourse. Ninety-nine percent of the cases of venereal disease are syphilis or gonorrhea.

Virgin—a person who has not had sexual intercourse.

Virginity—the state of being a virgin. The major problems experienced by virgins when making love for the 1st time are usually a result of high expectations, nervousness, overeagerness, and overemphasis on the event. Without these problems, 1st sex can be the dawning of a new world.

Voyeur—a person whose only sexual role is

that of watching others engage in sexual intercourse. Also known as a Peeping Tom. Many people enjoy watching a couple engaged in lovemaking, but most people would prefer to be so engaged themselves.

Vulva—the external female genitals consisting of the outer lips, the inner lips, the clitoris, and the opening of the urethra. Also, the opening between the external female genitals.

Wet Dream—an erotic dream leading to orgasm and nocturnal emission. Very common in boys approaching adolescence but lessening in frequency when they begin having sex with partners. Women also experience erotic dreams which may culminate in nocturnal orgasm.

Whore—a derogatory term for a female prostitute. Men who hate or are afraid of women, or feel inadequate about their own sexuality, often use the word for sexy or sensual women who are not actual prostitutes.

Withdrawal—See: *Coitus Interruptus*.

Womb—See: *Uterus*.

Zoophilia—erotic attraction to animals.

—D.W.

A Survey of Sex Surveys—1900–1975: Seventy-five Years of the Leading Sex Surveyors and What They Learned about Us

Survey: STUDIES IN THE PSYCHOLOGY OF SEX

Researcher: Henry Havelock Ellis (1859–1939). Born in England of middle-class parents, Ellis was both a product and a victim of the sexual repression of the Victorian era, when masturbation was referred to as "self-abuse" and said to cause impotence, blindness, and insanity, and nocturnal emissions were considered an indication of a foul venereal disease. Ellis was appalled by the damage these attitudes did to society at large and to him personally. Determined to learn more about sex for the public's sake as well as his own, he gave up his medical practice to devote his full time to sex research.

He wrote candidly in his autobiography of his own sexual difficulties. When he married, at 32, he was a virgin. Although he and his wife were passionately in love, it was a spiritual not a physical love. Both sought sexual satisfaction in extramarital affairs—and both with other women. One of Ellis's mistresses was Margaret Sanger, an early crusader for birth control. Only after his wife's death, however, was Ellis able to combine sex and love in one relationship. By this time, he was 59. Although primarily known for his studies of sex, he had a reputation as the best-read man in the world, and wrote and edited numerous books on travel, philosophy, dreams, and social concerns. The last 20 years of his life were his happiest, spent with a beloved mistress who loved him in return, and with the knowledge that Victorianism, his lifelong enemy, was being replaced (thanks in large part to his research) by a more humane attitude toward sexuality.

Topics Studied: In 7 volumes published between 1900 and 1928, Ellis presented the results of his investigations on such subjects as "The evolution of modesty," "The sexual impulse in women," "Erotic symbolism," "Sex in relation to society."

In the pages of his books, Ellis emphasized the wide range of normal human sexuality—although he also discussed such generally recognized but generally ignored variations as homosexuality, sadism, masochism, exhibitionism, voyeurism, fetishism, incest, satyriasis (male nymphomania), nymphomania, transvestism, and zoophilia.

How Done: Ellis based his studies on published case histories in the medical and psychiatric literature of his day; correspondence with readers of his early volumes; and information obtained from friends, mistresses, patients who came to him for help, and even from his wife. His approach was that of a scientific observer; it never became judgmental. "The majority of sexual perversions," he wrote, "including even those that are most repulsive, are but exaggerations of instincts and emotions that are germinal in normal human emotions."

Findings: In light of more recent sex research, Ellis's findings were accurate in many instances. He was the 1st to advance the following theories:

That sexual awareness and responses often appear in childhood.

That masturbation is common to both sexes, and its harmfulness questionable.

That girls mature physically at an earlier age than boys, but boys reach a peak of sexual activity earlier than girls.

That homosexuality and heterosexuality are not absolutes, but exist in varying degrees in different individuals.

That the absence of sexual desire among women was a Victorian myth, and that some women are more highly sexed than men, capable even of initiating sex relations.

That there are more similarities than differences in male and female orgasms.

That women, as well as men, experience orgasms during sleep—especially if the women are older and sexually experienced.

That the ability to enjoy multiple orgasms is not unusual in women.

That the causes of impotence in men and frigidity in women are usually psychological, rather than physiological.

That the 2 major causes of frigidity in women are the repression of sexuality in the formative growing-up years, and the clumsiness and ignorance of the male partner.

That monthly cyclical factors influence the degree of sexual responsiveness in women.

That many men and women remain sexually active well past middle age, and he cited the case of a woman in her 70s, recently married, "who declared that both desire and gratification were as great, if not greater, than before the menopause."

Conclusions: Ellis's writings are more literary than scientific, based as they are on a great body of sexual facts rather haphazardly collected. Basically, his theme was that the range of variation in sexual behavior *within normal limits* is immense, and that arbitrary standards cannot be applied to this area of human experience.

Public Reaction: The Psychology of Sex was intended primarily for scientific readers, but when *Sexual Inversion*, the 1st volume to be published, appeared, it was suppressed as obscene. A bookseller who had sold it was brought to trial. When the defense attorney contended that the book had scientific value, the judge called his argument "a pretence, adopted for the purpose of selling a filthy publication." The remaining volumes were published in the U.S., but even here, until 1935, they were available only to the medical profession. The work helped break the conspiracy of silence that had long stifled open discussion of sexual problems.

Survey: A RESEARCH IN MARRIAGE

Researcher: Dr. G. V. Hamilton, a Harvard graduate specializing in comparative psychology, psychiatry, and psychoanalysis, known for his previous research study of sexual behavior among apes.

Topics Studied: Dr. Hamilton wanted to know to what extent marital sex problems are caused by the institution of marriage itself, and to what extent they were caused by the individuals involved. His primary areas of investigation were (1) "Important sexual events of childhood and puberty," and (2) "Beliefs, attitudes, predicaments, and characteristic modes of performance with reference to sex and marriage."

When Done: Approx. 1928.

How Done: The data was obtained by personal "interviews" during which standardized questions typed on a card were handed, without further discussion, to the subject, who then answered orally.

Subjects Studied: One hundred married females and 100 married males. Fifty-five couples represented pairs of spouses. A considerable number were persons of outstanding intellectual and artistic achievement, most of them college graduates between 30 and 40 years of age, most of them Dr. Hamilton's patients or their friends. All were Caucasian.

Where Done: Dr. Hamilton's consulting room in New York City.

Findings and Conclusions: A higher percentage of women than men expressed dissatisfaction with their marriages—41% against 36%.

Correlating data suggested that ". . . satisfying contacts with the mother during childhood may so condition the male that when he reaches maturity only a mother type of mate will satisfy him. Thus we find that, of the 17 men who stated categorically that their wives were physically 'like' or 'very like' their mothers, 16 were rated as having expressed satisfaction with their own marriages. Of the 60 men who married women physically 'unlike' their mothers, only 21 belonged to the satisfied group." (The physical likeness or unlikeness of husband to father did not appear to be an important factor in the case of the women's appraisals of their marriages.)

Masturbation—Ninety-seven percent of the men and 75% of the women reported having masturbated at some time during their lives. Only 17 men and 42 women categorically denied having masturbated since marriage.

Attitudes toward extramarital sex: CONSERVATIVE (believe adultery is not justifiable): 15% of the men; 32% of the women. LIBERAL (middle ground): 69% of the men; 55% of the women. RADICAL (condoning adultery): 16% of the men; 13% of the women.

"Illicit" sex was admitted to by 59% of the men, 47% of the women. In addition, 29% of the men and 24% of the women had committed adultery.

The figures suggest that men who are virgins at marriage are much more likely to remain monogamous after marriage than are those who have had premarital sex experience, but that the factor of virginity at marriage is insignificant in this respect in the case of women.

Fifty-four percent of the women were rated as adequate in their capacity to experience orgasm in the sex act. "From almost every standpoint only the truly frigid woman (of whom there was but one in our group of 100 women) can afford to ignore an absent or seriously lacking orgasm capacity. Unless the sex act ends in a fully releasing, fully terminative climax in at least 20% of copulations there is likely to be trouble ahead." Dr. Hamilton's statistics also indicated that "inability to have the orgasm and more or less serious nervous symptoms occur together [in women] with significant frequency."

Thirty-six percent of the women had been able to have "normal" orgasms during the 1st year of their marriage; this number had increased to 54% at the time of their examination.

Hamilton felt that the institution of marriage fared better in his study than he had expected. Forty-eight percent of the subjects were "reasonably" satisfied with their marriages. Women were found to be more tolerant of sexual inadequacy in their husbands than the men were of sexual inadequacy in their wives. When the 200 spouses were asked, "If by some miracle you could press a button and find that you had never been married to your spouse, would you press that button?" Without qualification, 128 said No.

Public Reaction: A Research in Marriage was published in 1929 by the Medical Research Press. It was not intended for the general public. Professional reaction was respectful but the study was too limited to have a significant impact.

Survey: FACTORS IN THE SEX LIFE OF TWENTY-TWO-HUNDRED WOMEN

Researcher: Katharine B. Davis, Ph.D., a social worker, with a committee formed for this purpose by the Bureau of Social Hygiene of New York.

Topics Studied: "The sex life of normal women" from childhood past menopause. Use of contraceptives; causal factors in happiness of married life; autoerotic practices; periodicity of sexual desire; homosexuality.

When Done: Findings published in 1929 by Harper.

How Done: Questionnaires consisting of 54 questions.

Subjects Studied: Ten thousand married women, Caucasian, of above-average intelligence, education, and social position, received questionnaires by mail. One thousand responded. An additional 1,200 questionnaires were later completed by unmarried college graduates no more than 5 years out of college. Many names were obtained from women's club and alumnae organization rosters.

Where Done: Questionnaires were mailed to subjects in all parts of the U.S. Dr. Davis's committee was based in New York City.

Findings and Conclusions: Because the sampling was narrow and the questions subject to wide interpretation ("Is your marriage a happy one?"), findings were inconclusive; the questions tell more than the answers, for they reveal assumptions and attitudes that seem archaic in light of present knowledge. At the request of a prominent gynecologist, the committee tried—unsuccessfully—to establish a correlation between frequency of intercourse and sterility in later life. Contraception, euphemistically called "voluntary parenthood," was approved of in principle by 89.7%, practiced by 73.4% of the subjects. Of the 872 who claimed to have "happy" marriages, only one out of 4 worked outside the home. The researchers concluded from this that working was not conducive to marital happiness.

Ninety percent of the married women considered their husband's sex drives to be as strong as or stronger than their own; only 3.3% believed their sex drives were stronger. Masturbation was admitted to by 64.8% of the unmarried women and 40% of the married ones, but 2 out of 3 of these women considered the habit "morally degrading." Eleven percent answered Yes to the question "Have you ever had a nervous breakdown?" while another 10.4% said they had nearly reached that point.

The researchers were much concerned with the concept of "happiness," and made the correlation that the 12% of these women who denied all sex feeling or experience claimed to be the happiest. Slightly more than 50% of the single women stated they had experienced "intense emotional relations" with other women, and over 25% admitted that the relationship was carried to the point of overt homosexual expression.

Dr. Davis could not establish that homosexual relations before marriage had any effect, one way or the other, on happiness in married life. Other efforts to correlate sex histories and habits with happiness were inconclusive. Dr. Davis speculated that happiness might be more directly related to personality traits than to sex.

In an attempt to compile "an index of current feeling and thought, a reflection of the mores of today and yesterday" regarding sex, Dr. Davis included a section on "Opinions" in the single women's questionnaire.

Do you believe sex intercourse necessary for complete physical and mental health? YES: 38.7%; NO: 61.2%

Is a young man before marriage ever justified in having sex intercourse? YES: 20.9%; NO: 79%

Is a young woman before marriage ever justified in having sex intercourse? YES: 19.4%; NO: 80.5%

Is a husband ever justified in having sex intercourse with a woman or women other than his wife? YES: 24.1%; NO: 75.8%

Is a wife ever justified in having sex intercourse with a man or men other than her husband? YES: 20.7%; NO: 79.2%

Are married people justified in having intercourse except for the purpose of having children? YES: 84.6%; NO: 15.3%

Should information regarding methods for birth control be available for unmarried people? YES: 63%; NO: 36.9%
Should an abortion ever be performed? YES: 71.8%; NO: 28.1%

Survey: A THOUSAND MARRIAGES
Researchers: Robert Latou Dickinson and Lura Beam. Dr. Dickinson was a practicing gynecologist from 1882 to 1924; in a later work, *Human Sex Anatomy* (1933), he presented the 1st modern book of repute that contained illustrations of sex positions. He was one of the 1st American doctors to perform artificial insemination with sperm from a donor other than the husband. Seeking information for the treatment of infertility, he studied female response during masturbation. He was one of the 1st American gynecologists to use an electrical vibrator as a means of inducing orgasm in patients previously unable to achieve it by any other means. He also used the technique, later refined by Masters and Johnson, of observing the vaginal lining and cervix during orgasm through a phallic-shaped glass tube with a light on the end of it. His collaborator was also a gynecologist.
Topics Studied: Factual knowledge about the sexual adjustment of the subjects during marriage. Basic areas covered were: general health and circumstances and fertility of wife and husband; symptoms and diagnoses; pelvic disorders and labors; anatomical variations in internal and external genital organs and their relationships to particular sex practices; averages and extremes of sex behavior; control of conception, abstinence, and their aftermath. "The sex side of the love and marriage experience of a thousand wives."
When Done: Over the 40 years of Dr. Dickinson's practice, until the 1920s.
How Done: Physiological examinations supplemented by intensive psychological questioning covering subject's history from childhood to, in some cases, old age.
Subjects Studied: One thousand married women. The majority were Caucasian, urban, well-educated, married to professional men. Fifty percent had 1st come to the doctor for problems related to childbearing, 25% for pelvic growths and inflammations, the remainder for miscellaneous causes presumed to be of pelvic origin. Some were observed for less than a year, others for 40 years.
Where Done: Dr. Dickinson's office in New York City.
Findings: Fifty percent of the women considered their marriages sexually satisfactory. One-sixth experienced considerable persistent distress in intercourse. Eighteen of the wives had remained virgins for one or more years after marriage because neither husband nor wife knew how to perform sexual intercourse.
Average frequency of intercourse was twice a week, ranging from 16% reporting "daily or oftener" to 11% reporting "yearly or less."
Most frequent complaint—failure to reach orgasm. Duration of orgasm averaged under 15 seconds. Habitual duration of insertion: in 12%, an instant; in 40%, under 5 minutes; in 34%, 5–10 minutes; in 17%, 15–20 minutes; in 9%, 30 minutes or longer.
Of the wives who considered their marriages sexually unsatisfying, 22% were classified as frigid, 46% as suffering from dyspareunia (painful intercourse), and 22% as "maladjusted, usually with strongly worded grievance toward the husband or marriage." These women were less fertile than the "sexually adjusted" women; only 26% of them had 2 or more children, compared with 40% of the women in the other group.
A selection of 114 Jewish wives, Roman Catholic wives, and wives of Protestant ministers showed a 68% sexual maladjustment, compared with 34% in the remaining 984 cases.
Conclusions:
1. Every woman showed a capacity for sexual desire, lifelong, inconsistent and fluctuating.
2. There is an important psychosexual correlation between fertility and the degree of sexual harmony.
3. Sexual creativeness is reflected in other phases of life.
4. Sexual abstinence in marriage is ordinarily impracticable.
5. "The physical difficulty typical of the couples studied was that their common knowledge and the husband's technique were not adequate; the psychological difficulty of these couples was their inability to unify sex with the rest of life."
6. Sexual difficulties are infrequently organic (physiologically caused) in the woman. They are variants of mental and emotional behavior.
Most significantly of all, Dr. Dickinson concluded that "most of the maladjustments revealed by the study were preventable." Thirty-five years later, Masters and Johnson reached the same conclusion.
Public Reaction: Dr. Dickinson's half century of research faced continual attacks by the American Medical Association and innumerable other groups who felt his attempt to obtain an increased knowledge of the physiology of the female reproductive processes was not scientifically creditable. But his contribution outlived his critics. Writing in the *Encyclopaedia of Sex*, Dr. Albert Ellis calls Dickinson's study "The best large-scale documentation of the cause-and-effect relationships between a

Victorian upbringing and sexual frustration in adult life. . . . Nowhere else in the history of sex research are the bitter fruits of sexual Victorianism more tragically documented than in Dickinson's *A Thousand Marriages*" (published by Williams & Wilkins Co., 1931; 482 pp.).

Survey: Sexual Behavior in the Human Male

Researchers: Dr. Alfred C. Kinsey (1894–1956), together with Wardell B. Pomeroy, a psychologist; Clyde E. Martin, a statistical analyst; and Dr. Paul H. Gebhard, an anthropologist.

Dr. Kinsey was born in Hoboken, N.J., of devoutly religious, middle-class Victorian parents. He was a boy scout and achieved the rank of eagle scout. He received his B.S. degree in psychology at Bowdoin College, where he never dated, preferring to play the piano at fraternity dances. When a worried college friend confided to Kinsey that he masturbated, the 2 young men knelt (at Kinsey's suggestion) and prayed to God that the friend be given the strength to refrain from this sinful habit.

Kinsey received a Ph.D. in entymology from Harvard in 1920. During the next 20 years, he devoted himself to the study of the gall wasp, an insect which, ironically, reproduces parthenogenetically—without insemination of the female by the male. Kinsey collected, examined, and studied between 2 and 4 million gall wasps—150,000 specimens for one paper alone. From the age of 26, he was also an instructor in zoology at Indiana University, where he remained a faculty member until his death. At Indiana he met and married the 1st girl with whom he ever "went steady." The marriage produced 4 children; the family was the epitome of campus respectability.

In 1937, Indiana University launched one of the 1st college courses in sex education and marriage. As a respected biologist with conservative views and an irreproachable reputation, Kinsey was chosen to teach the course. His biographer, Dr. Pomeroy, writes: "Knowing a good deal about gall wasps but little about human sexual behavior, Dr. Kinsey went to the library to learn more. He soon discovered that no one else knew very much, either." Previously done "pioneer studies" lacked the scientific approach and scope Dr. Kinsey deemed essential. When students bombarded him with questions such as "Is masturbation harmful?" or "What effect does petting have on subsequent marital adjustment?" or "Is homosexuality abnormal?" he answered, "Neither I nor anyone else knows the answers . . . but if you, and many like you, will be willing to contribute your own sexual histories, I will be able eventually to discover enough about human sexual behavior to answer at least some of these questions." With that, he began the most extensive study of human sexual behavior as yet undertaken.

Funding was initially supplied by Kinsey himself, later by the National Research Council, Indiana University, and foundation grants. In the course of his research, Kinsey acquired one of the greatest collections of erotica ever assembled; yet he remained, according to *Time* magazine, "an almost monotonously normal human being."

Topics Studied: Questions were divided into 9 major categories:
1. Social and Economic Data
2. Marital Histories
3. Sex Education
4. Physical and Physiological Data
5. Nocturnal Sex Dreams
6. Masturbation
7. Heterosexual History
8. Homosexual History
9. Animal Contacts

When Done: Research began in 1938; findings were published in 1948.

How Done: Individual, confidential interviews lasting from 1 to 6 hours, covering from 300 to 500 questions. Records were preserved on IBM cards which were guarded "like the gold at Fort Knox." These were coded and the interpretation was never written down; Kinsey and his 3 associates spent a year memorizing the code, and were the only people alive who knew it. Even a professional cryptographer was unable to break this code.

The conduct of the interviews was in itself revolutionary, requiring unprecedented frankness. Kinsey, who had never smoked or drunk, deliberately took up both habits in moderation because he thought it would improve his rapport with his subjects. A physician colleague described his interviewing technique as "skillful beyond the imagination of those who have not experienced it . . . The subject is aware from the 1st that he is being dispassionately studied by a sincere but shrewd and extremely well-informed scientific man—well-informed in the ways of the world and of the underworld as well."

"A good interviewer," said Kinsey, "becomes very sensitive to the reactions of his subjects, immediately drops any line of inquiry which causes embarrassment, and stays with simpler matters until the subject is ready to talk in more detail."

Previous studies had used euphemisms such as "touching yourself" for masturbation, "securing a thrill from touching yourself" for orgasm achieved through masturbation, and "relations with other persons" or even "sex delinquency" for sexual intercourse. Kinsey believed that such evasive terms invited evasive answers. His questions were frank and direct, and even phrased in accordance with the vocabulary of the individual subject.

Subjects Studied: Kinsey interviewed 5,300 white males, classified as to cultural group, marital status, age (5 to 90), age at reaching puberty, educational level, occupation (from "underworld" and "day laborer" through "extremely wealthy, living primarily on income"), occupation of parent, rural-urban background, religion, geographic origin. Subjects came from every State in the U.S., but were most concentrated in the northeast. Sexual histories of non-whites were obtained, but omitted from the study because Kinsey felt the sample was insufficient.

Kinsey realized that if subjects were selected at random, many would be reluctant to answer questions on such a delicate topic; so he interviewed only volunteers, sometimes persuading 100% of the membership of a club, association, fraternity, or other group to cooperate.

Where Done: Kinsey and his associates spent time with their subjects in their homes and accompanied many of them to the homes of their friends, to theaters and concerts, to nightclubs and bars and other places of recreation. Many subjects supplemented their interviews with correspondence, sexual calendars, and diaries covering periods ranging from 6 months to more than 35 years.

Findings:

Relationship of Social Class to Sexual Behavior

1. Petting was characteristic of the upper socioeconomic class; lower levels found it "unnatural" and less acceptable for adolescents than actual intercourse, which they considered "only natural."

2. Seventy-five percent of the boys who went no further than high school had heterosexual experience—but only 42% of the boys who went to college had teen-age sexual intercourse.

3. Masturbation was condoned by upper educational levels, but considered an act against nature by lower educational levels.

4. Rate of patronizing prostitutes was 6 times higher in the lower than in the upper levels.

5. Members of upper levels, in their teens and 20s, had less extramarital intercourse.

6. Nudity was generally approved in the upper levels but considered obscene by the lower.

7. Lower levels considered premarital sex "only natural," and many in this group considered promiscuity acceptable.

Early Sexual Activity

Kinsey confirmed the findings of Havelock Ellis and others that human sexuality is clearly visible during infancy and early childhood.

He also said, "The male, in the course of his life, may change the sources of his sexual outlet, and his frequencies may vary . . . but almost never, from the time of his 1st ejaculation, is there a complete cessation of his activity until such time as old age finally stops all response."

Total Sexual Outlet

Kinsey says, "While all males must have known of the regularity of sexual activity in their own histories, the significance of the fact for the population as a whole has never been fully appreciated. The assumption that the unmarried male has only occasion outlet . . . is not in accord with facts. The total sexual outlet of the average white American male under 30 is 3.27 per week; for all white males up to age 85, the mean is 2.34 per week; 22.3% of all males fall into extreme ranges of activity; 7.6% of these average 7 or more outlets per week."

"The discussion of frequencies of total sexual outlet provides a good opportunity for understanding the futility of classifying individuals as normal or abnormal, or well adjusted or poorly adjusted, when in reality they may be nothing more than frequent or rare, or conformists or nonconformists with the socially pretended custom."

Marital Status and Sexual Outlet

For the total married population, about 85% of the male's sexual outlet comes from intercourse with the wife. Masturbation, nocturnal emissions, heterosexual contacts, and animal intercourse provide the remaining 15% of the activity. Kinsey adds, "In view of the rather high frequency of extramarital intercourse among lower social levels, it is interesting to find that the highest percentage of outlet derived from the intercourse with the wife (95.5%) is found among those persons who have not gone beyond the 12th grade in school, and the lowest percentage (61.9%) among older males who have gone to college."

Age of Adolescence and Sexual Outlet

Males who reach puberty earliest begin their sexual activity almost immediately and maintain higher frequencies in sexual activity for a matter of at least 35 or 40 years.

Exercise of the sexual capacities does not seem to impair those capacities.

In general, the boys who mature 1st are the ones who most often turn to masturbation and to premarital sociosexual contacts. They engage in both heterosexual and homosexual relations more frequently than boys who mature late.

Rural-Urban Background and Sexual Outlet

According to Kinsey, "There are few material differences between the histories of farm boys and the histories of boys raised in the city, or between adult males living in the 2 places. . . . The rural population is most distinct in having fewer sociosexual contacts (meaning premarital heterosexual petting, premarital and extramarital intercourse, and homosexual relations), and in its much higher frequencies of animal intercourse. But the city boy's interest in animal contacts as soon as they are available makes it clear that it is simply a question of opportunity which differentiates the rural and urban groups on this point."

Masturbation

Ultimately, between 92% and 97% of all males have some masturbatory experience, but it is "primarily a phenomenon of younger and unmarried groups, although it does occur in a fair number . . . of married histories. Incidence and frequency are affected by social backgrounds, and correlated with educational levels and occupational status."

The highest incidence of masturbation among single males occurs in the period between adolescence and age 15; the incidence steadily drops from that point. About half of the single population is still masturbating at 50 years of age. Among married males, the highest incidence (42.1%) occurs between 21 and 25 years of age; in the middle 50s, only 11.4% of married males masturbate.

Kinsey indicates, "There is a tremendous variation in frequency, ranging from not at all to 20 or more times per week. Masturbation is, to a certain extent, a substitute for heterosexual or homosexual intercourse; but . . . throughout the lives of many males, including married males especially of upper social levels, masturbation remains as an occasional source of outlet that is deliberately chosen for variety and for the particular sort of pleasure involved."

Nocturnal Emissions

Primarily an outlet of teen-age boys. About 83% of all males experience nocturnal emissions at some time in their lives. Over 99% of the males who go to college have nocturnal emissions at some point, but only 85% of the high school males, and only 75% of the males who never go beyond grade school experience them. There is considerable variation in frequency, from just a few in a lifetime to 2 or 3 times a night. For most males during their earlier years, nocturnal emissions are usually monthly or bimonthly.

After marriage, the percentage of males experiencing nocturnal emissions drops to below 60%, and this outlet provides only 2–6% of their total sexual activity.

The frequency of nocturnal dreams of any sort, sexual or otherwise, appears to have some correlation with the imaginative capacities of an individual.

Premarital Intercourse

Twenty-two percent of all male preadolescents attempted intercourse before marriage, chiefly between age 10 and adolescence. There was considerable variation, according to social level: Among males who went to college, 6.7% had coital experience before marriage; among those who went into high school but not beyond, about 84%; and among boys who never went beyond grade school, 98%.

At all social levels, premarital intercourse occurs much less frequently among males who are devoutly religious. It occurs *more* frequently among city boys than farm boys.

Kinsey says, "To have or not to have premarital intercourse is a more important issue for more males than any other aspect of sex. . . . Except for the 15% of the population which goes to college, most males actually accept premarital intercourse, and believe it to be a desirable part of a normal human development."

Furthermore, "The significance of premarital intercourse depends upon the success or failure with which the couple avoids an unwanted pregnancy."

Marital Intercourse

According to Kinsey, "Although marital intercourse provides the chief source of outlet for married males . . . it does not ordinarily provide more than about 85% of the total sexual outlet. . . . There is no premarital sexual activity which may not continue into marriage, although the frequencies of all these other activities are almost invariably reduced."

"The percentage of the total outlet which the married male derives from intercourse with his wife varies considerably with different social levels. For the lower level group it provides 80% of the outlet during the early years of marriage, but an increasing proportion of the outlet as the marriage continues. By 50 years of age, the lower level male is deriving 90% of his outlet from marital intercourse. On the other hand, males of the college level derive a larger proportion of their outlet (85%) from intercourse with their wives during the early years of marriage, but a smaller proportion in later years. *Not more than 62% of the upper level male's outlet is derived from marital intercourse by the age of 55.* At no time in their lives do college-bred males depend on marital intercourse to the extent that lower level males do throughout most of their marriages."

Marital intercourse, although it is the most important single source of sexual outlet, does not provide even half of the total number of orgasms experienced by the males in our American population.

Extramarital Intercourse

This was the area in which Kinsey found the greatest reluctance to answer questions. On the basis of the limited data he did collect, he suggests that about 50% of all married males have intercourse (usually sporadic) with women other than their wives at some time during their marriage. "There seems to be no question but that the human male would be promiscuous in his choice of sexual partners throughout the whole of his life if there were no social restrictions. Extramarital intercourse may occur . . . irrespective of the satisfactory or unsatisfactory nature of the sexual relations at home."

Heterosexual Prostitution

"In the U.S., the number of males who go to prostitutes is not so high as is generally believed, and the frequencies with which they go are very much lower than almost anyone has realized. . . . We find that about 69% of the total white male population ultimately has some experience with prostitutes at least once."

Homosexuality

Rather than focusing on homosexual people or homosexuality as a separate entity, Kinsey concentrated on *homosexual behavior and reactions*, and stressed the infinite gradations between complete homosexuality and complete heterosexuality. He pointed out that "The homosexual has been a significant part of human sexual activity ever since the dawn of history, primarily because it is an expression of capacities that are basic in the human animal. There are those who will contend that the immorality of homosexual behavior calls for its suppression. . . . Some have demanded that homosexuality be completely eliminated from society by a concentrated attack upon it. . . . The evidence indicates that at least ⅓ of the male population would have to be isolated from the rest of the community, if all those with *any* homosexual capacities were to be so treated. . . . At least 13% of the male population would have to be institutionalized and isolated, if all persons who were *predominately* homosexual were handled in that way."

Thirteen percent reported having been predominantly homosexual in behavior and responses for at least a 3-year period in their lives. An additional 5% reported that during at least a part of their lives, homosexual and heterosexual contacts and arousals were about equally balanced. Kinsey's figures indicated that 37% of all males experience at least one homosexual experience to the point of orgasm at some time, and that only 50% of the male population reach old age with neither a homosexual orgasm nor a homosexual arousal.

Animal Contacts

According to Kinsey, "The forces which bring individuals of the same species together in sexual relations may sometimes serve to bring individuals of different species together in the same types of sexual relations."

In the total male population, only about 8% had ever had sexual experience with animals; but among rural males of grade school level, the figure was 15%; among rural males of high school level, 20%; and in rural males of the college level, 27% had had "some animal experience to the point of orgasm." Frequencies of animal contacts varied from once or twice in a lifetime to several times a week over a period of years.

Conclusions: In every area of his study, Kinsey either found information diametrically opposed to widely held attitudes toward sexual behavior, or he uncovered situations that shouted for further examination. His documentation of the enormous variation in individual sexual activity showed the fallacy of assuming that people could be judged on the basis of any absolute norm of sexual behavior. His charts and figures indicated dramatically the great hypocrisy Americans demonstrate by preaching one kind of behavior and practicing another. Indeed, ½ of the male population was found to engage in sexual acts that were criminal offenses.

Public Reaction: Sexual Behavior in the Human Male (820 pp.), popularly known as "The Kinsey Report," was published by a medical publishing house, W. B. Saunders Co., in 1948. Although it cost $6.50, it shot immediately to the top of the best-seller lists—thanks to a deluge of free publicity (unsought by Kinsey) and denunciations. Religious and moral "leaders" pointed out that Kinsey's examinations of men's sex life altogether denied the existence of a moral factor in sexual relations. Kinsey was attacked for regarding man as merely an animal of extremely versatile sexuality, and for undermining morality by making his finds public. Other critics challenged the soundness of his methods, but the National Research Council, after investigating the various charges, found no reason to withhold its financial support from Kinsey's future research.

Sexual Behavior in the Human Male was translated into a dozen languages, and sold 275,000 copies in the U.S. Of the fortune it earned in royalties, Kinsey took not a cent for himself, but turned all profits over to his Institute of Sex Research, founded in 1947, in order to finance the continuation of his work.

Survey: SEXUAL BEHAVIOR IN THE HUMAN FEMALE

Researchers: Alfred C. Kinsey, Wardell B. Pomeroy, Clyde E. Martin, and Paul H. Gebhard.

Topics Studied: Same categories as in *Sexual Behavior in the Human Male* with an additional section comparing male and female sexual behavior.

When Done: Research began in 1938; findings were published in 1953.

How and Where Done: Techniques paralleled those used in researching the preceding work.

Subjects Studied: White females—5,940 volunteers. The sampling was comparable to that of the men, but a higher percentage of the women were urban, and their educational level was higher; 75% had attended college. Nonwhite respondents were excluded from the data in both reports because Kinsey did not trust the size or typicalness of the sample.

Findings:

Preadolescent Sexual Development

Forty-eight percent of the women reported having engaged in preadolescent sex play, primarily homosexual. One out of 4 women recalled sexual contacts before adolescence with strangers, friends, or relatives. Very little physical harm was reported from these contacts, many of which involved affection. Eighty percent of the women reported that they had been emotionally upset, but only a small portion seriously disturbed. "The current hysteria over sex offenders," said Kinsey, "may very well have serious effects on the ability of many of these children to work out sexual adjustments later in their marriages."

Premarital Intercourse

Two-thirds of the married women had experienced sexual orgasm prior to marriage, 17% of these through intercourse. Women who had not had any premarital orgasm by any means whatever tended to have less satisfactory sex lives after marriage.

Kinsey demonstrated that the human female is possessed of the capacity for sexual arousal from infancy until late in life, the beginning and end of menstruation being merely conspicuous points in a long life of sexuality. In effecting orgasm, the female engages in all the activities in which the male engages, the most frequent being masturbation, coitus, and homosexuality. Of these 3 the most effective are masturbation and homosexuality; however, the most *common* outlet is coitus.

Marital Intercourse

Incidence of orgasm varied greatly. Ten percent reported never having reached orgasm in marriage. The "average" married woman reached orgasm in 70–77% of marital intercourse.

Length of marriage	% of Marital Coitus Leading to Orgasm
In the 1st year	63%
By the 5th year	71%
By the 10th year	77%
By the 15th year	81%
By the 20th year	85%

Kinsey found that the frequency of marital intercourse declines with age—not because of the female's loss of interest, but because of the male's aging processes.

"Although we may use orgasm as a measure of the frequency of female activity," Kinsey explained, "and may emphasize the significance of orgasm as a source of physiologic outlet and of social interchange for the female, it must always be understood that we are well aware that this is not the only significant part of a satisfactory sexual relationship. This is much more true for the female than it would be for the male."

Kinsey's key finding regarding frigidity was its rarity; 9 out of 10 of the women reported having experienced orgasm by the age of 35, and an additional 8% reported having experienced sexual arousal without orgasm. This left a maximum of 2% of women who could be characterized as "frigid" in the sense of being incapable throughout their lives of experiencing either erotic arousal or orgasm. "It is probable," Kinsey concluded, "that all females are physiologically capable of responding . . . to the point of orgasm." What had commonly been termed frigidity, said Kinsey, was in reality a result of male ignorance of female anatomy—that is, inadequate stimulation.

Masturbation

Less frequent in the female (about ⅔) than in the male, but appeared to be the technique most likely to lead to orgasm; women who masturbated reported achieving orgasm in 95% of all attempts.

Petting to Orgasm

Initial source of orgasm for 24% of all women who had ever experienced orgasm. But "petting provides a great deal more than experience in orgasm. It introduces the female to the physical, psychological, and social problems involved in making emotional adjustments to other individuals, and consequently helps contribute to satisfactory marital coitus."

Nocturnal Sex Dreams

The causes and contents of women's nocturnal sex dreams are similar in cause and content to those of men, but fewer women have them. About ⅔ of the women in the sample had had dreams that were overtly sexual. For 20%, the dreams had proceeded to the point of orgasm.

Extramarital Intercourse

Twenty-five percent reported having engaged in it, the majority having been in their 30s and early 40s when it occurred. Forty was the age of maximum extramarital sexual activity.

Homosexuality

Women's homosexual relationships are less promiscuous than men's, perhaps because society is suspicious of men living together, but not of women. Twenty-eight percent of the women reported having had one or more homosexual experiences by the age of 45, compared with 50% of the men. There is evidence of more homosexual activity by women on higher educational levels.

Total Sexual Outlet

SINGLE WOMEN—Masturbation was found to be the most important source of total outlet for the unmarried females in the sample.

Coitus had been the 2nd chief source after age 20, and for those females who were still unmarried in their late 30s and 40s it was nearly as important a source of outlet as masturbation. Homosexual contacts had provided a rather important portion of the total outlet for the unmarried females in the sample between the ages of 26 and 40. Petting to orgasm had been an important source of premarital outlet for the females between 16 and 30, but had become much less important after 30.

MARRIED WOMEN—Coitus in marriage accounted for 84 to 89% of the total outlet of the married females in the sample who were between the ages of 16 and 35. After the middle 30s the importance of marital coitus had decreased. In the age group 45 to 50, only 73% of the total number of orgasms came from that source.

"Masturbation was the 2nd most important source of sexual outlet for the married females in the sample, providing between 7 to 10% of the total number of orgasms for each of the age groups between 16 and 40."

Extramarital coitus and orgasms derived in extramarital petting accounted, in various age groups, for 3 to 13% of the total outlet of the married females in the sample. This had become the 2nd most important source of outlet after age 40, providing 12% of the total orgasms in that period.

Animal contacts proved to be insignificant, relations between females and animals apparently being more myth and fable than actual practice.

Psychological Factors in Sexual Response

Apart from inherent anatomical and physiological capacity to respond to stimulus, most aspects of human sexual behavior appear to be the product of learning and conditioning. Attitudes acquired from parents, from other adults and from other children "may have considerable significance in determining [the individual's] subsequent acceptance or avoidance of particular types of sexual activity. . . . Behavior which may appear bizarre, perverse, or unthinkably unacceptable to some persons . . . may have significance for other individuals because of the way in which they have been conditioned."

"We find no reason for believing that the physiologic nature of orgasm in the female . . . is different from those of the male. But in their capacities to respond to *psychosexual* stimuli, the average female and the average male do differ." Thirty-three such psychosexual stimuli (i.e. erotic films) aroused males, whereas only 3 (movies, romantic literature, and being bitten) aroused the average female. Capacities to respond are also influenced by neural and hormonal factors, and by the menstrual cycle, the human female being *least* sensitive to stimuli at the time of ovulation, when she is most pregnable, the *most* sensitive to stimuli and arousal when she is "safest," that is, immediately before and after menstruation.

Conclusions: Sexual behavior cannot be studied without taking into account the behavioral response of the total individual, which reflects biological, psychological, and social factors. Kinsey stressed that no one person is represented by his survey figures—rather "Each person is a unique combination of the data." He emphasized the need for further research, and planned to publish additional volumes based on his data at future dates.

Public Reaction: Sexual Behavior in the Human Female (872 pp.) was published by W. B. Saunders Co. in 1953. Although this book included, in response to criticisms of the earlier volume on the male, a statement clarifying the scientific objective of the survey and defending the right of the scientist to investigate and to deliver to the public his findings, it aroused as much criticism and controversy as its predecessor. Anthropologist Ashley Montagu, one of its harshest critics, denounced Kinsey for ignoring love and motherhood, for failing to include certain segments of the population, and for dealing with people as though they were insects (referring to Kinsey's earlier studies of the gall wasp).

On the whole, the work drew more blame than praise. Psychologists emphasized that sexual behavior cannot be studied within the narrow framework of "outlet" and "incidences." Sociologists emphasized Kinsey's neglect of the role of social institutions in conditioning sexual attitudes and behavior. Others pointed out errors in sampling, collating, analyzing and evaluating this great mass of data. Some even maintained that the book would be used to justify "immoral practices."

When Kinsey died in 1956 (literally of overwork, having been warned that his heavy schedule was damaging his heart), *The New York Times* ran this editorial:

The untimely death of Dr. Alfred C. Kinsey takes from the American scene an important and valuable, as well as controversial, figure. Whatever may have been the reaction to his findings—and to the unscrupulous use of some of them—the fact remains that he was 1st, last, and always a scientist.

In the long run, it is probable that the value of his contribution to contemporary thought will lie much less in what he found out than in the method he used and his way of applying it. Any sort of scientific approach to the problems of sex is difficult because the field is so deeply overlaid with such things as moral precept, taboo, individual and group training, and long established behavior patterns. Some of these may be good in themselves, but they are no help to the scientific and empirical method of getting at the truth.

Dr. Kinsey cut through this overlay with detachment and precision. His work was conscientious and comprehensive. Naturally it will receive a serious setback with his death. Let us earnestly hope that the scientific spirit that inspired it will not be similarly impaired.

Survey: HUMAN SEXUAL RESPONSE
Researchers: William H. Masters, M.D., and Virginia E. Johnson. William Masters was born in Cleveland in 1915. As a student at the University of Rochester School of Medicine and Dentistry, he worked in the laboratory of Dr. George Washington Corner, an authority on the biology of sex. While researching the estrous cycle of the rabbit (compared with the menstrual cycle of the human female), Masters realized how much ignorance and misunderstanding still, in 1939, surrounded the *human* cycle. By the time he married in 1942, he had set his sights on research in the physiology of sex. But Dr. Corner advised him to wait until he was more mature, had achieved a reputation in an area not related to sex, and could call upon the resources of a great university medical school to support him. Accordingly, Masters trained in obstetrics and gynecology and then taught these subjects at Washington University in St. Louis. Between 1948 and 1954, he published 25 papers on hormone-replacement therapy for postmenopausal women. This was an important contribution, but was later overshadowed by his major research: the direct study of the sex act, in order to understand and treat sexual problems.

In 1954, the year after publication of the 2nd Kinsey report, Dr. Masters, at 38, launched his research. Many earlier sex surveys had involved observation of the sex act by the researcher, but their reports had always evaded the issue. Even Kinsey, whose work in this area had been more thorough than anyone's was not about to give his critics added ammunition by confessing that sexual intercourse had actually been observed at Indiana University during the 1940s. Masters frequently acknowledged his indebtedness to Kinsey, who, he said, "opened the previously closed doors of our culture to definitive investigation of human sexual response."

Virginia Johnson, 10 years younger than Masters, was referred to him by an employment agency in response to his request for "a mature woman who has a keen interest in people and who knows where babies come from." Although her academic credentials were slight, Masters hired her as a research interviewer on the basis of her intelligence, straightforwardness, probing curiosity, and deep empathy for people. Ms. Johnson, born in Springfield, Mo., had a varied background including advertising research, administrative work, business writing, and music. She was married, with 2 children. In 1964, she enrolled as a doctoral candidate in psychology at the Washington University School of Medicine. In describing their working relationship, one interviewer commented, "She was the public relations person, he the doctor. But the doctor was always in charge."

Topics Studied: How the human body responds, physiologically and anatomically, to erotic stimulation. More simply: what men and women do and why they do it, rather than what they say or even think they do.

When Done: 1953–1965.

How Done: Manual and mechanical manipulation, natural coition and, for many female study subjects, artificial coition were observed and recorded. Cardiographs and other conventional medical devices measured heart rate, blood pressure, pulse, respiratory rate, etc. Cameras were used so that responses could be studied in slow motion. The one piece of mechanical equipment that would not be considered standard in any physiology laboratory was an electrically-powered artificial phallus, made of plastic and designed for intravaginal observation and photography.

Subjects Studied: Initial subjects were prostitutes—118 females and 27 males. Later, volunteers were enlisted on the basis of their genuine concern with the sexual problems the research might solve. Some couples were referred by their physicians. Former patients of Dr. Masters brought their husbands. In all, 694 individuals, including 276 married couples, participated. Of the 142 unmarried participants, all but 44 had previously been married. The men ranged in age from 21 to 89; the women, from 18 to 78. More than 200 had gone to graduate school; another 200 had not attended college at all, and some had not finished high school. Most were Caucasian, but 11 couples were black. Thirty-four married couples were over the age of 50. The one common characteristic of the volunteers was that all were able to reach orgasm during both masturbation and coitus while under observation. Applicants who could not were eliminated. The participants experienced more than 10,000 orgasms under laboratory conditions.

Where Done: In a laboratory at the Reproductive Biology Research Foundation in St. Louis, Mo.

Findings: The research conclusively shattered these long held "phallic fallacies":

FALLACY: Women experience 2 types of orgasms, "clitoral" and "vaginal."
FACT: All orgasms in the female are physiologically the same.

FALLACY: A woman capable of experiencing multiorgasms is "oversexed" and a rarity.
FACT: All women are naturally multiorgasmic.

FALLACY: The basic causes of female failure to achieve orgasm are physiological.
FACT: The basic causes of female failure to achieve orgasm are attitudinal, "for thousands of different reasons."

FALLACY: All prostitutes are frigid.
FACT: In-depth interrogations of prostitutes revealed that the 2nd-greatest motivation for moving into or continuing in prostitution was sexual desire. (The 1st motive was economic.)

FALLACY: Nyphomania is a rare and definable disease.
FACT: Masters and Johnson's findings confirmed Kinsey's: "A nymphomaniac is a woman who has just a bit more sex tension than her partner."

FALLACY: Simultaneous orgasm is the ideal to be striven for in intercourse.
FACT: Simultaneous orgasm is a lovely thing when it happens, but to try for it deliberately would be an imposition of technique.

FALLACY: Infertility is usually the woman's fault.
FACT: "A knowledge of when to have intercourse, how to have intercourse, and how often to have intercourse could solve one out of every 8 infertility problems in this country. At least 60% of the difficulty, when the problem is unilateral, has been on the male side. It makes one think about the queens in history who were beheaded because they produced no heir to the throne." (W. Masters in a *Playboy* interview.)

FALLACY: Frequency of performance is likely to induce pregnancy.
FACT: It takes the average male 30 to 40 hours after an ejaculation to return the sperm production and seminal-fluid volume to his normal range. So if his performance during his wife's fertile period is too frequent, she is less likely to become pregnant.

FALLACY: Sexual intercourse is inadvisable during the last 3 months of pregnancy.
FACT: There is no reason not to continue sexual activity up to the very terminal states of pregnancy, providing the female partner has no pain and providing the membranes aren't ruptured and that there is no postcoital bleeding.

FALLACY: A small penis is less effective than a large one.
FACT: The difference in average erective size is much less than when the penis is flaccid. In addition, the female has the great facility of accommodating the penis regardless of size; the vagina involuntarily expands to the size sufficient for containment.

FALLACY: The male orgasm is synonymous with ejaculation.
FACT: The male orgasm is a 2-stage process. The 1st stage, identified as "a sensation of ejaculatory inevitability," lasts 2–4 seconds; the 2nd part is ejaculation. (The female orgasm, by contrast, is a one-stage process.)

FALLACY: Circumcision increases sexual responsiveness in the male.
FACT: Neurological testing revealed no clinically significant difference in sensitivity between the circumcised and uncircumcised.

FALLACY: Most impotence in the male is physiologically caused.
FACT: The chief cause of male impotence is fear of nonperformance, and can be overcome "if the male realizes that a failure because of alcohol—or the wrong person, the wrong place, or what have you—is not meaningful in terms of his masculinity, that it is not a signal for continued incapacity."

FALLACY: Basic physiological sexual responses are different in men and women.
FACT: There is no significant difference. Both men and women experienced the same response cycle in these 4 phases: excitement; plateau; orgasm; and resolution.

FALLACY: Old age and sex are mutually exclusive.
FACT: If a human male or female is in good health and has an interested partner, he or she can maintain effective sexual function into the 80-year age group.

FALLACY: Physicians are experts on the subject of sexual response.
FACT: Medical schools did not offer courses in sexual response until as recently as 1964, and then only a few schools did so. Consequently, even today many physicians share the common misconceptions, taboos, and fallacies of the general public.

Conclusions: The most far-reaching conclusion was that most sexual problems have psychological, not physiological, causes, and can be eased or eliminated.

Public Reaction: Anxious to avoid any hint of prurient interest in connection with their potentially sensational book, Masters and Johnson chose a publishing house with a conservative image: Little, Brown & Co., of Boston. When they published *Human Sexual Response* (354 pp.) in 1966, they covered it with a plain brown wrapper, directed no advertising at the general public, and released it quietly in the hope that some physicians would buy copies.

All these precautions proved futile. Even before the publication date, a prominent psychoanalyst who had somehow got wind of what was forthcoming, charged that Masters and Johnson had mechanized and dehumanized sex, that their subjects were not typical, and that they had neglected the psychological aspects of sex. A sociologist suggested that a more appropriate title would be "Sexual Body Mechanics," and expressed his dismay that some of the subjects who participated might actually have enjoyed themselves. Another critic charged that encouraging sex among the elderly was "disgusting."

This was just the beginning. Even though the text was virtually unreadable for a layman ("This maculopapular type of erythematous rash 1st appears over the epigastrium"), the book was attacked for encouraging pornography, inspiring venereal disease epidemics, unleashing a flood of bastards upon society, taking the fun out of sex, and ignoring questions of morality, decency, and human values. Thanks to all this uproar, more than 250,000 copies of the book, at $10 a copy, were sold in the U.S. It was translated into 9 foreign languages, and was dealt with in countless magazine articles.

Masters and Johnson were the 1st to admit that their findings were tentative and required further substantiation. The American Medical Association, a bastion of conservatism, lauded their investigation as "a natural and inevitable consequence of changing cultural environment." After the initial shock wore off, more commentary about the work took a positive approach, praising its scientific value. Said a London physician, writing in the *Daily Mail:* "If we are inclined to regard sexual union as something so sacrosanct that it should not be open to investigation, we should remember that a similar view was taken regarding the stars in Galileo's day."

Survey: HUMAN SEXUAL INADEQUACY
Researchers: Masters and Johnson. (Much to the surprise of even their close friends, Masters, who divorced his wife in 1972, and Johnson, who had divorced her husband in 1956, were married in 1972.)
Topics Studied: Records of couples in therapeutic treatment for sexual dysfunction.

When Done: 1959–1970.
How Done: Five years after the research that was the basis for *Human Sexual Response* was begun, a clinic was established where the researchers' findings could be utilized—used, that is, to treat couples with sexual problems. Two co-therapists, a man and a woman—either Masters and Johnson or their "2nd team"—conducted the therapy, which was based on the premise that any marital sex problem involves both partners, and therefore it is the *relationship*, not one individual, that requires treatment. One revolutionary aspect of the therapy was its emphasis on the "here-and-now," rather than the excessive probing of the past considered essential by traditional therapists.

Initially, the co-therapists alternately interview both partners and take their histories, developing an idea of the patients' philosophies and life-styles. Physical examinations and laboratory tests are made. On the 3rd day, patients and therapists discuss the findings so far. The concept of "sensate focus" is explained as "communication by touching," considered by Masters and Johnson to be the most important source of sexual stimulation. The partners are taught "sensate exercises"—massage, fondling, stroking, etc., but without specific genital stimulation. This "pleasuring" is repeated on the 4th day, this time with the genitals included. The idea is to develop a set of sensory signals between the partners. Charts and models are used to explain the anatomy of sex to the couple; a surprising number of husbands had never seen their wives' genitals.

On the 5th day, treatment of the specific problem begins. The most common of these are premature ejaculation, impotence, orgasmic dysfunction, painful intercourse, and problems relating to aging. Since each couple is different, there is no rigidly structured program. The most sensational aspect of the therapy was the use of 13 "partner surrogates"—all unmarried women, not prostitutes—to help in the treatment of 41 impotent men.

No case is considered a success until the end of an unprecedented follow-up period of 5 years.
Subjects Studied: For this survey, 790 patients were referred by psychiatrists and other counselors. Some represented both sides of a marriage (of 510 couples, 223 had dual sexual distresses, making a total of 446 patients in this category); 287 represented the "suffering" partner in a marriage; and there were 54 unmarried males and 3 single women. Most were American, some Canadian, about 12% living in St. Louis. All were middle-class and above, with 72.7% having had some higher education. More than half paid the $2,500 fee (per couple) for the treatment, which lasted 2 weeks. Others paid less, some nothing at all. Since

most patients also had travel and hotel expenses, they were obviously highly motivated.

Where Done: Begun at Washington University in St. Louis, it was moved to the Reproductive Biology Research Foundation in the same city in 1964. Sessions were conducted by the therapists at the clinic during the day, with the patients doing their "homework" at night, per the therapists' suggestions, at their homes or hotels.

Findings: The researchers measured their "failure rate," rather than their successes, anticipating criticism from conservative psychiatrists. Their overall failure rate was 20%.

Premature Ejaculation was, they found, the easiest of the male sexual inadequacies to treat. Of the 186 men treated for this problem, 97.8% responded to therapy, which incorporated use of a simple "squeeze play." (See: Impotence in Dictionary of Sex Related Terms, Chap. 19.)

Primary Impotence—that is, men who have never had an erection that lasted long enough for intercourse—was Masters' and Johnson's "disaster area." In 32 cases, the failure rate was 40.6%.

Secondary Impotence—men who failed to maintain an erection throughout intercourse more than 25% of the time—was overcome in 157 out of 213 cases, a success rate of 73.8%.

Ejaculatory Incompetence (inability to ejaculate during intercourse): 82.4% of the 17 men treated overcame the problem.

Female Orgasmic Dysfunction was successfully overcome in 80.7% of the 342 women treated for this problem.

Sexuality in the Aging: Aside from the need (in some cases) for hormone replacement, complaints were similar to those of the younger patients—but the overall failure rate was higher: one out of 3.

Conclusions: Although sex relationships are frequently distorted or used as the focus for nonsexual problems, Masters and Johnson concluded that sexual function is never destroyed, only anesthetized. The greatest cause of dysfunction, they found, is fear. When that fear is removed, nature takes its course. Most failures were attributed to irretrievably fractured marriages, excessive anxiety, or negative prior experiences with therapy.

Public Reaction: Human Sexual Inadequacy (467 pp.) was published in 1970 by Little, Brown & Co. In the 4 years since the appearance of *Human Sexual Response,* the "here-and-now" principle had become an "in" therapy, practiced by many progressive analysts; but some purists agreed with New York psychiatrist Natalie Shainess, who charged that "The efforts of Masters and Johnson have opened the door to all kinds of ill-considered research, a direct descendant being one of the research

projects done at huge cost in 1968 for the President's Commission on Obscenity and Pornography . . . 23 college students were paid to view pornography daily for a couple of hours over a 3-week period while their penises were hooked up to a contraption measuring the degree of penile expansion." Dr. Shainess blames Masters and Johnson for everything from *The Sensuous Woman* to "an alliance of industries selling sexual paraphernalia, such as vibrators, dildos, and lotions; and a variety of pornographic gold mines that include newspapers, books, films, and sex shows," even though she acknowledges that the association of their names with these industries has been without their consent. Dr. Shainess can be eloquent; the sex research team has, she said, poured a "pipeline of pornographic sewerage . . . into the vital heart of our life," and "thingified sex."

On the whole, though, professional criticism has been more respectful of the 2nd work than it was of the 1st. Masters and Johnson refuse to defend themselves on their critics' terms. "We don't want to be heroes," said Masters. "The brutal fact is that we left 99.99% of human sexual functioning unturned. We haven't scratched the surface and we're aware of it." He hopes to publish a major new report every 5 years or so, and is currently working on homosexual response and inadequacy, sexual effects of aging, and (perhaps most important of all for its preventive aspects) adolescent sexual physiology and inadequacy.

Survey: SEXUAL BEHAVIOR IN THE 1970S

Researchers: The Research Guild, Inc., an independent market-survey and behavioral-research organization, commissioned by the Playboy Foundation. Supplemented and interpreted by author Morton Hunt.

Topics Studied: Contemporary sexual behavior and attitudes in all aspects, as compared with the findings of the 1st Kinsey Report, published 25 years earlier.

When Done: 1973–1974.

How Done: Subjects completed questionnaires made up of over 1,000 items covering their backgrounds, sex education, attitudes toward sexual practices, and complete sex histories. Ten percent of the subjects were subsequently interviewed in depth—the men by Mr. Hunt, the women by his wife, author Bernice Kohn.

Subjects Studied: The sample closely paralleled the composition of adult American society. It included 982 men and 1,044 women, was approximately 90% white and 10% black. Seventy-one percent were married, 25% never married, 4% previously married but not remarried. Age, educational level, occupation, and geographical origin were roughly representative of the population as a whole.

Where Done: Information was collected in 24 U.S. cities and suburbs.

Findings: Premarital sex has become acceptable and widespread. About 75% of the single women had had intercourse before they were 25. Fifty percent of the women who married before 25 had had premarital sex, and among the younger married women, 80% had had it. The overall incidence of premarital sex among males showed a less dramatic increase than among females, but single males were found to begin their premarital coital experiences earlier. By the age of 17, nearly 75% of the noncollege males had had premarital coitus.

Extramarital sex, "at least in the eyes of those who were divorced, [was] related to the disintegration of marriage. More than 50% of the divorced males and females who had had extramarital relations say that such activities caused their separations or divorces."

Divorced persons are much more apt to be sexually active and experimental than their precursors of a generation ago. None of the divorced males were sexually inactive; they had a median of 8 intercourse partners a year. Only 9% of the divorced women were sexually inactive; the others had a median of 3.5 partners per year. Hunt contends that "much of the postmarital behavior of the divorced is aimed at the restoration of ego strength and is a preparation for renewed intimacy—when it can be found."

The double standard has been virtually abandoned, one result being the wane of prostitution, which is approximately half as widespread as it was in the '40s. Young husbands are only a little more likely, but young wives much more likely (24%) to engage in extramarital sexual activities than they were in Kinsey's day.

Oral sex is far more widely used—an average of half again as much—as it used to be. These practices are especially common today among younger men and women; more than 80% of single males and females between 25 and 34, and about 90% of married persons under 25 had practiced cunnilingus or fellatio, or both, in the past year.

Heterosexual anal intercourse is much more widely used today than formerly, although it remains primarily an experimental variation, chiefly among younger persons. Nearly 25% of all females and more than 25% of all males in the total sample had experienced anal intercourse at least once, and nearly 25% of married couples under 35 had used it at least once in the past year.

Variety of coital techniques has increased; 6% of the married men and 11% of the single men had not used the traditional "missionary position" in the past year. Nearly 75% of the married males used the female-superior position at least occasionally.

Frequency of sexual intercourse has increased for both sexes, in every age group. The median frequency for single males between 18 and 24 who were having intercourse was 33 times a year—a definite increase over Kinsey's figures. Much more remarkable is the increase among young single females: Single females between 18 and 24 who were having intercourse were doing so with a median frequency of more than once a week. The median frequency for married people 25 or younger is about 154 times a year, compared with 130 a generation ago. Increases in older groups are proportionately even larger: The median for 35- to 44-year-old married people is about 99 times a year, and for married people beyond the mid-50s, the median has risen from 26 to 49.

Rates of orgasms for females have also increased. Seventy-five percent of the younger females who were having premarital intercourse were experiencing at least some orgasms, and the median frequency of orgasm for the single females was 3 times as high as for Kinsey's females. Among married women, orgasmic regularity was found to occur in 53%. The percentage of those who only sometimes or never have orgasm has dropped from 28 to 15.

Homosexuality is more visible, but has not increased in numbers. More than half of all women and nearly half of all men *dis*agreed with the statement "Homosexuality is wrong."

Masturbation is more frequent among those between 25 and 30 in the single group (men and women) and also among the married. Since these same people are also having intercourse more frequently, Hunt feels that it reflects lessened guilt feelings rather than sexual hunger—that "young husbands and wives feel more at liberty than their counterparts of a generation ago to turn to masturbation whenever sexual frustration develops out of sexual or emotional conflict, unavoidable separation or abstinence caused by illness or other extrinsic factors."

Sex acts with animals are less common than in Kinsey's day; only 5% of the total male sample and 2% of the total female sample had ever had any kind of sexual contact with animals.

Sadomasochism: Only 3% of the married men and fewer than 1% of the married women, and 10% of the single men and 5% of the single women had ever performed sadistic sexual acts. Fewer than 1% of married men and 2% of married women, and 6% of single men and 10% of single women, have ever been on the masochistic end of a sadomasochistic transaction.

Mate swapping has been overpublicized and overestimated. Only 2% of the married males and less than 2% of the married females had ever participated in mate swapping.

Mutiple-partner sex: only 13% of the married males and 2% of the married females had ever engaged in such activity, and most of this took place before marriage. For the majority, there was only one such episode. Twenty-four percent of the single men and 7% of the single women had had multiple-partner sex, but ⅓ of the men and ½ of the women had done so only once.

Erotica: Four percent of the men and women said that pictures, drawings, movies, and prose showing or describing sexual acts either disgust them or cause a mixture of disgust and delight —yet from 50 to 90% admitted to being sexually aroused by such material.

Drugs and sex: Thirty-six percent of the women and 30% of the men stated that alcohol made intercourse more pleasurable; but 12% of the women and 27% of the men found that it made intercourse *less* pleasurable.

Twelve percent of the women and 15% of the men stated that hallucinogens made intercourse more pleasurable; 4% and 7%, respectively, say the opposite.

Forty-one percent of the women and 45% of the men stated that marijuana made intercourse more pleasurable; only 2% and 4%, respectively, reported the opposite effect.

Conclusions: "Americans are much more tolerant of the sexual ideas and acts of other persons than formerly and feel far freer to envision various previously forbidden acts as possible for themselves—and, hence, to include such acts in their own sexual repertoires."

The researchers found that "permissive attitudes about sex were more common among the young and among males than among older persons and females. Permissive attitudes generally were associated with higher education, political liberalism, white-collar status, and the absence of strong religious feelings." The age factor far overshadowed other major influences on sexual attitudes.

". . . for the past generation, a major—and permanent—reevaluation of sexual attitudes has been occurring throughout our society . . . things unseen and unheard of a generation ago or even a decade ago are now to be seen and heard on every side." Despite all this, Hunt concludes that "liberation has not cut sex loose from significant personal relationships or from the institution of marriage. . . . The great majority of people still feel that love and sex are too closely interwoven to be separable at will or for fun."

Public Reaction: Sexual Behavior in the 1970s was published in 1974 by Playboy Press. As a sign of the times it surveyed, its appearance provoked no outrage or attacks or serious challenges. By the 1970s, sex surveys had become what Havelock Ellis had hoped for at the turn of the century: respectable.

—C.E.

Gallery of Important Persons in the History of Sex

THE ORIGINAL MASOCHIST

MASOCHISM (mas′e-kiz′em) n. 1. Psychiatry. An abnormal condition in which sexual excitement and satisfaction depend largely on being subjected to abuse or physical pain, whether by oneself or by another. 2. a. The deriving of pleasure from being offended, dominated, or mistreated in some way. b. The tendency to seek such mistreatment. 3. The turning of any sort of destructive tendencies inward or upon oneself. Compare sadism.

The earliest memories of Leopold von Sacher-Masoch were of the dark and bloody tales told by his wet-nurse Handscha—tales of Ivan the Terrible, of the Black Czarina of Halicz, of Casimir III, called the Great, and his tyrannical Jewish concubine Esther—tales full of cruelty and torment, in which, more often than not, the tormentor was the dominating, lascivious female, and the tormented, the sentimental victimized male.

During Leopold's childhood his father was chief of police of Lemberg, the capital of Galicia, and he added to his son's education in violence with the tales he brought home. Leopold was 10 when the Polish landowners staged an armed revolt against the Austrian aristocracy. He was 12 in 1848, that year of revolutions, and he viewed them from the bloody streets of Prague, where his father was then posted. His imagination was stirred by the ruthless cruelties of the times, and he composed plays about the revolts and acted them out in his little puppet theater. His dreams were haunted by scenes of execution and martyrdom in which he usually found himself the prisoner of some merciless, demonic figure.

Outwardly, life was calmer after Leopold's father was transferred to Graz, in southern Austria. The Von Sacher-Masochs moved in the best society, and Leopold was their pride. The boy was granted his doctorate in law at 19 and became a lecturer in history at the university the following year. He marked his coming-of-age with the publication of *The Rebellion in Ghent under Charles V*, an excellent history grimly ignored by his academic colleagues because of its readability and because its author was known to be only 21, stagestruck, and full of wild ideas about universal freedom.

By the time he was 25, Leopold had given up both history and law for literature. He seemed to be a normal young Austrian of good family, considerable charm, and growing literary prestige. But his European sophistication hid a maelstrom of primitive emotions. His subconscious was peopled not by the educated, civilized Austrians he saw every day, but by the fierce, half-savage peasants of his Galician childhood. The mother of his vivid dreams was not the delicate, accomplished madonna-figure who presided over the elegant Graz residence, but the robust, mercilessly bullying, fear-inspiring female of the Carpathian mountains.

But it is one thing to dream and quite another to act out one's dreams in the daylight world. Leopold began to do just that. Aware that his sexual impulses were outside the norm, he set out to find the nearest possible realization of his ideal—that masterful czarina who would bully and humiliate him, who would, in fact, physically hurt him. For pain, Leopold had discovered, was the necessary prelude to pleasure.

Leopold's 1st mistress was the beautiful Anna von Kottowitz, a woman some 10 years his senior, who abandoned her husband and children to live with him, but who gradually lost interest in the whips and birches. The relationship continued for several stormy years and ended only when the new lover whom Leopold had procured for her—for he could not be entirely satisfied until she had betrayed him—turned out to be a crook. Leopold had found it necessary to write prolifically to maintain Anna in the extravagant style she demanded. He found he could write in almost any genre (except poetry, which he seems never to have attempted). He published many tales from his theatrical experience (he had done some professional acting), then a 2nd history, and finally his 1st novel. ·

He had loved Anna, but he took on Fanny Pistor, his next mistress, much as he might have hired an actress for a limited run. The contract, which both parties signed, read in part:

Herr Leopold von Sacher-Masoch gives his word of honor to Frau Pistor to become her slave and to comply unreservedly for 6 months, with every one of her desires and commands. For her part, Frau Fanny Pistor is not to extract from him the performance of any action contrary to honor . . . [she] is also to allow him to devote 6 hours a day to his professional work, and agrees never to read his correspondence or his literary compositions. . . . Frau Pistor, on her side, promises to wear furs as often as possible, especially when she is in a cruel mood. . . .

On a trip to Italy, Frau Pistor traveled 1st class as a baroness, while Leopold traveled 3rd class as her servant, and in Venice, according to formula, she managed to deceive him with another man. She proved to be exactly the despotic, brutal woman he had envisioned, and the affair was really quite a success.

Leopold's best-known book, Venus in Furs, was written at this time, and its detailed exposition of his sexual philosophy made him quite notorious. The police commissioner's son became the subject of much gossip and the object of reams of correspondence from anonymous young (and not so young) ladies. He 1st met his future wife under a lamppost on a small side street in Graz, where, heavily veiled, she had come according to agreement to recover from him a packet of compromising letters that a friend of hers had written to him. She called herself Wanda after the heroine of his latest novel, wore a long fur coat, and pretended to be very elusive. Weeks later when they were finally alone together, she went at him with a whip. Leopold was fascinated and agreed to marry her, although only at 1st in a private unwitnessed ceremony to which he came dressed in white tie and tails and she, of course, in furs.

The marriage, later formalized by a public wedding, lasted 15 years, but it was not a happy one. Wanda, like Anna before her, had not really understood what she was getting herself into. She was the daughter of a gentleman's servant and had simply wanted the socially prominent name of Von Sacher-Masoch and the presumably enviable life of an intellectual's wife. She had not realized that this particular intellectual would insist on being thrashed daily with a nail-studded whip or that he would be so persistent about her taking a lover. In spite of the fact she was pregnant a great deal of the time, her husband steadfastly continued to parade before her a succession of potential "betrayers," always optimistic that his latest find would be a success. Finally, years later, one of his candidates—a M. Armond, alias Jacques Ste. Cère, alias Jacob Rosenthal—carried her off.

Meanwhile, through it all, Leopold continued to write. Although little read now, he was a leading literary figure of his time, and the 25th anniversary of his 1st-published work was marked by a formal celebration in Graz and public ceremonies in Lemberg, Prague, and Leipzig. By then he was living with a down-to-earth young German woman named

Hulda Meister. They later married, and she loyally continued to care for him after his delicately balanced mind began to fail. Finally she had him quietly committed to an asylum after he had more than once tried to strangle her. Officially, he had died and was mourned accordingly, but actually he lived for another 10 years, during which time the German neurologist and psychiatrist Richard von Krafft-Ebing read about his career and named his particular kind of sexual aberration "masochism."

—N.C.S. rep.

The Man Who Gave Us Sadism

SADISM ('sā-dĭz-ĕm) n. 1. A sexual perversion in which gratification is obtained by the infliction of physical or mental pain on others (as upon a love object). 2. A delight in cruelty.

Physically, at least, Count Donatien Alphonse François de Sade seems to have been one of the beautiful people, a handsome little man— 5'2", eyes of blue, but oh what those 5' could do, as a masochist might describe him. Actually, various descriptions of the miniature aristocrat exist. One writer gives him "blue eyes and blond well-kept hair," another "a delicate pale face from which 2 great black eyes glared," a 3rd tells us that he was "of such startling beauty that even in his early youth all the ladies that saw him stood stock still in rapt admiration." Unfortunately, there is no authentic portrait of De Sade, but one might expect the probable descendant of the Laura made famous in Petrarch's immortal love poems 4 centuries before to present a striking appearance. In any case, this scion of high nobility was reared by his grandmother and his uncle, a literary man who prepared him for the Collège Louis le Grand, which numbered among its other notable graduates that one-man Gestapo, Maximilien de Robespierre. School was followed by considerable active service in the Army, beginning when he was only 14, and from there De Sade seems to have emerged a full-blown "fanatic of vice," the Philosopher of Vice and *professeur de crime* that Michelet and Taine called him.

When it happened, how it happened, would stymie a panel composed of Freud, Jung, Job, and the living Buddha. De Sade's upbringing was a factor, as were the licentious times in which he lived, his long years in prison, and perhaps there was even an organic problem. There is simply not enough reliable information available about De Sade—all his voluminous diaries were burned—and to try and make biography from a writer's fiction is fruitless. We know that De Sade married Renée-Pelagie de Montreuil for her money, trading

his title for her half-million-dollar dowry. The count, who always encouraged people to call him marquis, then embarked on a life of scandalous debauchery marked by habitual infidelity and sexual perversions. These included the notorious Rosa Keller affair, in which he whipped and tortured a Parisian prostitute, and what is sometimes called the Marseilles Scandal, an orgy in which he was accused of sodomy, torture, and poisoning participants with chocolate-covered bonbons containing powdered "Spanish fly." His mother-in-law, embittered about his treatment of her daughter, did her best to get him convicted on this last charge. De Sade had been in jail previously, but for the Marseilles scandal—and though the charges were ultimately proved untrue in great part— he was sentenced to death. He fled to Italy. On returning to Paris 3 years later, he found a none too comfortable jail cell waiting for him.

Though the authorities dropped the death penalty, De Sade from 1777 on would spend all but 13 of his remaining 27 years in prisons or in the lunatic asylum at Charenton. While imprisoned he began writing the novels and plays that gave his name to the language. The *120 Days of Sodom* (1785), in which 600 variations of the sex instinct are listed, *Justine, or Good Conduct Well Chastised* (1790) and *The Story of Juliette, or Vice Amply Rewarded* (1792), are among his works replete with myriad descriptions of sexual cruelty. Never able or willing to reform, De Sade died in 1814, aged 74, while still at Charenton, where he wrote and directed fashionable plays performed by the inmates, many of whom he corrupted in the process. Sometimes his insights were deep and remarkable, but his was in the main the disordered, deranged mind reflected in his life and licentious work.

"Sadism," the derivation of satisfaction or pleasure from the infliction of pain on others, can be sexual in nature or stem from a variety of motives, including frustration or feelings of inferiority. De Sade's life indicates that many such causes molded his twisted personality. His final testament read in part: "The ground over my grave should be sprinkled with acorns so that all traces of my grave shall disappear so that, as I hope, this reminder of my existence may be wiped from the memory of mankind."

—R.H. rep.

The Notorious Messalina

Probably the most notorious adultress in history was the Empress Valeria Messalina, 3rd wife of Emperor Claudius of Rome.

Her father was a chaste and stern Roman senator, and her mother was a fun-loving, sexually acrobatic lady about town. At 16, Messalina was married off to a cousin, 48-year-old Claudius, the grandson of Mark Antony.

Just 3 years later—in 41 A.D.—a band of conspirators assassinated Caligula, and the Praetorian Guard named Claudius the new Emperor. Thus, Messalina, at the age of 19, was elevated to Empress.

She had no respect for her royal husband. Although Claudius's own mother had branded him "a little monster" and relatives regarded him as a stupid oaf, Claudius was anything but a fool. During his lifetime, he wrote 20 scholarly books on Etruscan history, many learned papers on gambling, a play in Greek, and he added 3 letters to the Roman alphabet. Despite his impressive intelligence, his appearance worked against him. Tall and paunchy, he limped, stuttered, dribbled at the mouth, and was absentminded. His avocations were drinking and gambling. Unlike previous emperors and other aristocrats, he indulged in no sexual perversions. According to Gibbon, "Of the 1st 15 emperors, Claudius was the only one whose taste in love was entirely correct."

And his young wife, Messalina, had only contempt for him.

Juvenal has cruelly pictured Messalina in this period: curly, yellow hair piled high; narrow brow; large eyes set close together, thin lips. She was sensual and passionate, and she desired men in unlimited numbers. She began her scandalous career in nymphomania by enjoying a series of affairs with various palace courtiers. When she tired of them, she turned to entertainers. Desiring a handsome actor named Mnester, she ordered him to retire from the stage to become her full-time lover. Mnester refused to oblige. Messalina then hastened to the preoccupied Claudius to complain that a common actor had refused to obey an order from her. At once, Claudius commanded the actor to obey every royal order. Mnester obeyed his Emperor. Thereafter, the actor devoted himself to his mistress. In love, Messalina was wild, unrestrained, as Mnester would testify 3 years later when he was able to show the numerous scratches and scars on his body.

While Mnester was satisfactory—sufficiently so that Messalina had a bronze statue built to honor his gifts—he was not enough for his royal mistress. She began to cast about for new conquests. As Empress, she had no trouble finding them.

It was 43 A.D., and Emperor Claudius was on the march, leading Roman legions into Britain. Rome was left to Messalina, and she turned the city into her private boudoir. According to Irving Wallace, in *The Nympho and Other Maniacs:*

With a veil draped over her head, she entered taverns and alleys, searching for men. On one such excursion, filled with wine, she danced naked on a wooden platform in the Forum. Another time, she redecorated a bedroom of the palace to resemble a brothel, hung the name of Rome's most renowned prostitute on the door, then disrobed, gilded the nipples of her tiny breasts, and invited the male public to enter and be entertained at no more than the legally regulated fee. Emboldened by the heavy traffic, she challenged a particularly noted prostitute of Rome to a contest, insisting that she could entertain more men in 24 hours than her rival. Pliny the Elder tells us that she "surpassed" her rival, "for within the space of 24 hours she cohabited 25 times."

In his *Sixth Satire,* Juvenal enlarged upon Messalina's brothel victory:

There she received all comers,
Getting top price until the doors
   shut tight.
The lust, though, still raged hotly
   in her bosom.
Dirt-stained, she left the house and
   journeyed home
Exhausted, but undaunted by the sweat.
Thus smeared with lampsoot,
   she returned unfazed
To settle odors in the royal pillows.

Claudius returned from his foreign invasion still totally unaware of his wife's indiscretions. Meanwhile, Messalina continued her sexual adventures. Seeking variety, she held orgies where she forced Roman ladies to prostitute themselves with other men and women in front of their husbands. She cuckolded her husband so often that it became a joke in Rome, but by no means was her greed only sexual. One of the profligate Empress's favorite tricks was to make love to men and learn of their real estate holdings, later condemn them to death for treason, and finally confiscate their property. However, she went too far when she eliminated the freedman Polybius. Shortly afterward, when Claudius was off enjoying the mineral baths in Ostia, the venal Messalina forced her current lover, a handsome youth named Gaius Silius, to divorce his wife and marry her in a public ceremony. The couple then celebrated the ceremony by performing on the bridal bed which had been placed before the guests.

The freedman Narcissus, alarmed at Polybius' fate, took this opportunity to have Claudius informed of Messalina's treachery. Immediately, the Emperor ordered her put to death. She was either killed by sword in the gardens of Lucullus, which she had obtained by confiscation, or forced to commit suicide there with her paramour.

The evening following her death, Claudius, once more in Rome, came to dinner and was momentarily surprised that Messalina's place was empty. "Where is the Empress tonight?" he inquired.

He was told. He nodded, and returned to his wine.

—R.H. & The Eds.

The Incomparable Casanova

Frequently he ate 50 oysters for breakfast, often with a companion in his bathtub built for 2. Usually he seduced his friends' wives or daughters, sometimes 2 at a time if we are to believe him. Mostly he played the adventurer: a spy sentenced to jail and escaping over the wall, a lover dueling with an outraged husband, a gambler making several fortunes and spending them on women and wine. Always he lived by his wits. Giovanni Jacopo Casanova de Seingalt was a man of many talents: in turn, journalist, raconteur, soldier, gastronome, preacher, philosopher, violinist, alchemist, businessman, diplomat, and lover. The incomparable Casanova's guiding philosophy is expressed in a little-quoted passage found midway in his *Memoirs*: "The instants that man is compelled to give up to misfortune or suffering are so many moments stolen from his life; but he doubles his existence when he has the talent of multiplying his pleasures, no matter of what nature they may be."

So did Casanova live his life, from age 16, when expelled from a seminary in his native Venice for immoral conduct, to his death in Bohemia—where he served as a librarian for Count von Waldstein—at Dux Castle, in 1798, aged 73. In between there was more than he or any other man could write down. Casanova's famous *Memoirs* run to some 1,500,000 words, and yet they only take us through his 49th year. He 1st won fame when he was jailed as a secret agent in Venice in 1755 and escaped to France, his doubtless exaggerated account of the episode making him a romantic hero throughout Europe. The French soon appointed him head of the national lotteries, a position that made him his 1st fortune, but instead of settling down he resumed his travels. Florence expelled him; strangely enough, the Pope in Rome awarded him the order of the Golden Spur; Madrid also expelled him; from 1774 to 1782 he was a police spy for the state inquisitors of Venice. Wherever he went, never did he cease to search out new pleasures.

It's said that Casanova's famous autobiography should be trusted in the main outline as a picture of the 18th century, but not in the details, though it seems relatively tame today and the details aren't as licentious or racy as they once appeared. Casanova's elegant wit, reflected in these pages, made him the welcome guest of giants like Voltaire and Frederick the Great, but even then he was recognized as little more than a *homme à bonnes fortunes*. He is of course best remembered as a great lover, his name equaled only by Don Juan's as a synonym for the promiscuous womanizer. Women, he said, were his cuisine, and he knew or invented every trick to lure them to his banquet-bed—from ploys like his "oyster game" (he would convince a likely prospect that they should eat oysters from one another's tongues, often letting the oysters drop onto her "alabaster spheres") to poetry, music, and exaggerated accounts of his prowess in every realm. This fabled lover is a typical example of the neurotic seducer whose need to please is the very breath of life, yet he was as much a gentleman as a sensualist, a rare combination indeed.

—R.H.

The Teacher of Love

Anne de Lenclos (1616–1705), a delicately attractive French courtesan, struck an early blow for women's liberation. She was brought up by a loving father who was a struggling musician and part-time pimp. He taught her to play the harpsichord, to dance gracefully by the age of 12, to think for herself, and to quote from the essays of Montaigne. Above all, he taught her to understand the hedonistic instincts of men . . . and women.

Ninon, as she was known, developed a scathing wit and a shrewd business sense. When her parents died before she was 20, she invested a small inheritance wisely enough to give her an income for life. And soon she was besieged by a wealthy, often aristocratic clientele willing to pay her well for her sexual favors. But she was no prostitute, selecting her lovers because of their ability to return her warmth in kind. "One needs a hundred times more esprit in order to love properly than to command armies," she said, often adding, "Love without grace is like a hook without bait." She had no reluctance in enforcing her sensitive views on love. When the Comte de Choiseul was lackadaisical in bed, she dismissed him with a line from Corneille: "Oh Heaven, what a lot of virtues you make me hate!"

An abbé and a maréchal fell so strongly under her spell that each claimed the honor of having impregnated her, deciding the issue by a throw of the dice. The military man won and proudly raised their son. Even Cardinal Richelieu lusted for her body, though she preferred his mind. Ninon prevailed upon her friend and rival, Marion Delorme, to satisfy the famous cardinal, but not before he agreed to pay 50,-000 crowns.

Ninon's "business" flourished. She divided her lovers into 3 classes, "the payers, the martyrs, and the favored." The philosopher, Saint-Évremond, was a favorite, and so was the Marquis de Sévigné, who inspired the following rhapsody on love from her:

> Love! I feel thy divine fury! My trouble, my transports, everything announces thy presence. Today a new sun rises for me; everything lives, everything is animated, everything seems to speak to me of my passion, everything invites me to cherish it. . . . Since I loved you, my friends are dearer to me; I love myself more; the sounds of my theorbo and of my lute seem to me more moving, my voice more harmonious. If I want to perform a piece, passion and enthusiasm seize me; the disturbance they cause interrupts me every minute. Then a profound revery, full of delight, succeeds my transports. You are present to my eyes; I see you, I speak to you, I tell you that I love you. . . . I congratulate myself and I repent; I wish for you, and wish to fly from you; I write to you and tear up my letters. I reread yours; they seem to me now gallant, now tender, rarely passionate and always too short. I consult my mirrors, I question my women about my charms. In brief, I love you; I am mad; and I do not know what I shall become, if you do not keep your word with me this evening.

But Ninon's affair with the marquis's son seemed to have the opposite effect; by comparison to his father, the young chevalier's performance in bed was sorely lacking. He had "a soul of boiled beef," she said, "a body of damp paper, with a heart like a pumpkin fricasseed in snow."

By the time she was 40, Ninon de Lenclos had the reputation of being France's leading lady of love. "A veritable Notre Dame des Amours," said Horace Walpole years later. Ninon's intelligence perceived that "the virtue of women is the finest invention of men." In emancipating herself, she often professed that the morality of men and women was identical; that to reduce a woman to the role of a sexual object purely for the pleasure of men was to exclude her wholly from the practice of integrity of which she was completely capable. Ninon treated her clients as equals and expected from them the same consideration.

She also had the instincts of the teacher, establishing a School for Gallantry. Her pupils were young aristocrats whose mothers wanted them tutored in the more subtle arts of love. As chief lecturer, Ninon covered some basic topics: the psychology of women, the particular care of a mistress or wife, techniques of courting and seduction, and the methods of terminating an affair. Not the least was an advanced course in the physiology of sex. Her school soon became the rage of Paris. But even then the lecture course left something to be desired. In such a case, Ninon embarked with her pupil on a demonstrated program of independent study. She took him to bed to train him in the arts of foreplay and intercourse. Like Socrates, she was an amazing teacher.

Women, too, soon sought her expert advice on lovemaking. Instead of admitting them on an equal basis with her male pupils—the concept of sexual coeducation seemed beyond her—she counseled them in private. One woman asked, for example, "How large should a woman's breast be to attract a lover?" To which Ninon replied, "Large enough to fill the hand of an honest man."

And yet, her lectures on what might be called "The Treatment of a Woman" seemed to indicate that she professed the emancipation of women only in cases like her own. "It is all very well to keep food for another day," she said, "but pleasure should be taken as it comes. . . . Talk to your woman continually about herself, and seldom about yourself. Take for granted that she is a hundred times more interested in the charms of her own person than in the whole gamut of your emotions. . . . Remember, there are moments when women would rather be treated a little roughly than with too much consideration; men are often defeated because of their own clumsiness than because of a woman's virtue. . . . Should you be the one who ceases to love 1st, let the woman have the advantage of making the break and appearing cruel. . . . A woman who is through with a man will give him up for anything except another woman."

Once, tragedy struck. At 65, Ninon was pursued by her natural son, the Chevalier de Villiers. She agreed to see him only if the father kept their true relationship secret. The boy fell so deeply in love with his mother that she decided to tell him the truth, embracing him maternally. Staggering into the garden, he cried, "Mother," and killed himself with his sword.

Ninon lived to be almost 90. The fastidious voluptuary La Fare wrote what could well be her epitaph: "I never saw Ninon in her beauty; but at the age of 50, and even till she was over 60 she had lovers who adored her, and the most honorable men in France for friends. Until she was 90 she was sought by the best society of her time. She died with all her senses, and with the charms of her mind, which was the best and most lovable I have ever known in a woman."

—B.J.

THE UNFULFILLED JOHN RUSKIN

John Ruskin (1819–1900), Victorian England's foremost art critic and essayist, would have been a challenge to any psychiatrist. He was a masturbatory nympholeptic (one who suffers "a frenzy of emotion, as for something unattainable") with latent homosexual qualities. Despite sieges of manic-depression which got worse after age 50 and, eventually, delusions and the disintegration of his personality, Ruskin was also a brilliant, charming dialectician, sensitive to all forms of beauty. He wrote 37 volumes, reflecting his passion for nature, pre-Raphaelite painting, and the "moral" significance of Gothic architecture. He was an honored man in his time.

Yet his nympholepsy contained the ingredients of Victorian restraint although he eventually gave up his belief in God. His effeminate, sensitive nature was enhanced by the adulation of both parents and what he considered "a convent-bred education." The possessiveness of a well-organized mother, and her ability to strengthen the emotional bonds between them, suggests a classic Freudian oedipal relationship. When Ruskin enrolled at Oxford, his mother moved into a house near his rooms so they could have dinner together every evening. And her letters to him when he was on the continent working on an art project barely disguised the intense passions she had for her only child. As a result, he failed in his marriage and apparently remained a virgin all his life.

In 1848, Effie Gray, a pretty, middle-class English girl of 19 became his wife. He was 29. But she was shocked to discover that he had no intention of consummating their marriage on their wedding night, offering her instead an abnormal pact, which she reluctantly accepted and he later violated, to postpone intercourse for 6 years. In 1854, still a virgin, she had the marriage annulled.

Not until middle age did Ruskin finally understand his parents' pernicious effect. Accusing them of ruining his life, he gave them their emotional walking papers. "You fed me effeminately," he said, and "thwarted in me the earnest fire and passion of life!" After his father died, Ruskin said that his father had forced him to sacrifice his life in vain.

Ruskin masturbated and reproached himself with "a vice" and "a suicide committed daily." Biographers seemed to think that Ruskin's main reason for disliking the sexual woman was his realization, on marrying Effie, that they had pubic hair. Up to that time, they claimed, he had seen only female statues with bald-pated pubes.

In his teens, Ruskin manifested the 1st symptoms of nympholepsy by falling in love with the 15-year-old daughter of his father's partner in the wine business. She was a staunch Catholic who resented his "patriotic and Protestant conceit," and when he showed her a story he had written in her honor, he suffered "the rippling ecstasies of [her] derision." Yet the impossibility of possessing her "enriched her like a halo." And once when he was in Turin, he wrote his father about a girl of 10 "with her black hair over her eyes and half-naked, bare-limbed to above the knees, and beautifully limbed, lying on the sand like a snake. . . ." He added, "I don't, of course, think it proper for girls to be bare-limbed on heaps of sand, but it was picturesque if not pleasing. . . ."

As Ruskin got older he became a hard-core nympholeptic, indulging himself with the fantasy images of unattainable nymphs. And when he had a chance to teach art in a fashionable girls' school, he did so with undisguised relish. His strange relationship with beautiful, pubescent girls reached a realistic climax in the tantalizing form of Rose La Touche whose mother had asked Ruskin to give her daughter art lessons at the age of 8. The Fates were weaving "another net of love," and by the time his precocious pupil was 13, he was helplessly in love with her. And there was evidence that the mother was in love with him. Yet, the mother used his turn to atheism to oppose his desire to marry Rosie when she became 21. At 17, Rosie had led him to believe she would go against her parents' wishes and become his wife, for she seemed to love him too. But a vengeful letter from his wife, Effie, changed her mind. She wrote that her former husband could never make a woman happy because of "his peculiar nature." "He is quite unnatural and in that one thing all the rest is embraced," she said. Ruskin tried to overcome the effect of the letter, but the tragedy was compounded by Rosie's development of an intense, religious psychosis. She began to disintegrate and died at the age of 26, refusing a final visit from Ruskin because he would not swear that his love for her was 2nd to his passion for God.

Ruskin temporarily went insane, visiting spiritualists who promised to put him in touch with Rosie. He had wild visions of her, and dreams, and confused her with St. Ursula. He seemed to compensate by becoming decidedly more effeminate and called everyone "darling," which was unusual for the time. He developed the skill of being able to attract attention while appearing to shun it.

Ruskin was lecturing at Oxford. In 1883, he gave his final lecture, shocking his audience with obscene expressions and gestures, until attendants got him off the podium. And in 1889, 11 years before his death, and 32 years after he had met his lovely nymph, Rosie, he wrote of her in *Praeterita*, his personal journal: "neither tall nor short for her age; a little stiff in her way of standing. The eyes rather deep blue at the time, and fuller and softer than afterwards. Lips perfectly lovely in profile; a little too wide, and hard in edge, seen in front; the rest of her features what a fair, well-bred Irish girl's usually are; the hair perhaps, more graceful in short curl around the forehead, and softer than one sees often, in the close-bound tresses above the neck. . . ."

It was obvious that Ruskin remained a nympholeptic into old age. And perhaps his long, inarticulate moods were caused, in part, by his continued longing for his beloved nymph. He carried, always in his heart-pocket, between 2 thin slabs of gold, a letter Rosie had once written him. And when he died, an unconsummated man, a grateful nation offered a burial place in "The Poet's Corner" of Westminster Abbey close to the tomb of Tennyson, but according to his wishes, he was buried near Coniston Water where he had spent his last years.

—B.J.

The Hypnotic Rasputin

Grigori Efimovich Rasputin (1872–1916), the Siberian mystic with "the peculiar eyes," was a sexual success even by modern-day standards. As a young man in his native village of Pokrovskoye, he had joined a heretical sect called "the Flagellants" whose all night orgies of incantations, wild dances, provocative switchings, and indiscriminate copulations were practiced as sinful prerequisites of redemption.

Rasputin's name, given to him by fellow villagers, meant "the debauched one." And when he discovered that his rival, the local priest, was about to launch an investigation of his heresies, he left his young wife and farm to spread his sexual gospel elsewhere—in the woods, at 1st, then in peasant cottages where disturbed women sought him out as a savior and healer. Often he was seen in the public baths displaying his rugged body to admiring young women. When they appeared for redemption later, he urged everyone to debase themselves and "try the flesh." Then his voice would change into seductive softness as he drew closer to the prettier girls so he could caress them and fondle their breasts until they thoroughly confused sexual excitation with religious fervor. Even the husbands present didn't object since Rasputin had convinced them that intercourse with their wives was an act of redemption willed by God. Soon hordes of

peasants everywhere were throwing themselves at his feet, kissing the hemline of his black caftan, crying "Father Grigori, our Savior!"

Report of the healing powers of the bearded, unwashed holy man, with the hypnotic personality, reached into the sickroom of the Emperor's only son, Alexis, a hemophiliac. The slightest fall would cause painful blue swellings from internal hemorrhaging, and the court physicians were helpless. The Czarina had already turned to mystical men when she was desperately trying to conceive an heir to the throne. One of them, a 2nd-rate clairvoyant and former butcher's assistant, had convinced her that she was pregnant when she wasn't. For this he was banished, but not before prophesying that a new "friend" and holy man would appear to help her out.

It was November, 1905, when Rasputin was summoned to the palace by Czar Nicholas and Czarina Alexandra. Uninhibitedly, he embraced and kissed them, said a prayer over the afflicted child, soon gaining the boy's confidence with gentle strokings of his painful body and a host of Siberian fairy stories about humpbacked horses and legless riders.

The boy responded, the pains and swelling subsided, and a tearful Czarina kissed the hand of "the new friend" whom she considered heaven-sent to restore the health of her son. Whenever the internal bleeding began, Rasputin was at the bedside. Soon he achieved the political status of "Czar above Czars," since Nicholas and Alexandra sought his approval of important decisions. He actually became "a member" of the royal family.

Rasputin lost no time in consolidating this power. He set up an office-apartment and redemption center in St. Petersburg, the capital. Burgeoning petitions for political favors, which he had the power to grant, brought him huge "fees" from the rich and hopeful, while he often emptied his pockets during the same day to the poor and needy.

He kept his dining room crammed with anxious women, vying for his sexual-religious favors which he granted readily to the chosen ones in a nearby bedroom called "the holy of holies." He preferred aristocratic beauties to their peasant counterparts because "they smelled better," but he never improved his own peasant odors and continued to scoop up his food with his hands. Yet his disciples saw in him the reincarnation of Christ, sent to resolve the conflict between sexual frustration and the tenets of purity imposed by an orthodox clergy. Many found almost idyllic happiness for the 1st time in the gnarled arms of the "Holy Satyr." Some, however, were not ready for redemption and rushed from the little room in a rage, their dresses disheveled, weeping or shrieking in uncontrollable fury. Agents of the secret police, constantly on hand to protect Rasputin, removed the outraged women. Although a few preferred charges, saying that Rasputin had raped them, such accusations got no further than the desks of interested officials who didn't dare to make a move against him. Those who tried fell into disfavor with the Czar and Czarina who either ignored or disbelieved the reports of his excesses.

Many attempts were made to asassinate Rasputin as the embodiment of the Devil and a threat to the monarchy. Reactionary prelates and monarchists not only objected to his lifestyle, but to his obvious peasant populism. Iliodor, the leading priest-orator of the time, who had once befriended Rasputin, formed a conspiracy against him. Known as "the curser," he reviled the peasant monk and published false charges against him in a pamphlet called "The Holy Devil," and quoted from the Czarina's letters—which he had earlier stolen from Rasputin's desk—intimating there was a sexual relationship between the 2. This, of course, caused a national furor.

A psychotic prostitute with a religious mania was brought into the conspiracy and rehearsed as a pilgrim seeking alms from Rasputin. When he reached into a pocket for some money, she plunged a knife into his abdomen, screaming, "I have slain the anti-Christ!" But Rasputin's great strength and quickness saved his life. He prevented himself from falling and pressed a hand over his wound. After an operation in his dining room, he languished between life and death for weeks while Czar Nicholas prepared for W.W. I. Rasputin, who always opposed the monarchy's warlords, blamed himself for not being well enough to dissuade the Czar from committing Russia to the holocaust, as he had done 2 years before in convincing Nicholas to stay out of the Balkan conflict. In this sense, Rasputin was a legitimate man of peace.

As the war went from bad to worse, a dandified aristocrat, Prince Felix Yusupov, arranged a midnight party for the prelate in the basement of his castle, using his beautiful wife as bait. Yusupov fascinated Rasputin with his ability to sing gypsy songs and play the guitar. On the night of December 29–30, 1916, Rasputin, who had been warned earlier by the Minister of the Interior about a plot on his life, was enjoying himself thoroughly. He drank several glasses of poisoned wine, and ate enough cakes filled with potassium cyanide to kill a cow. Nervously, Yusupov sang the desired songs and strummed his guitar, waiting for his guest to drop dead. When he didn't, the Prince excused himself on the pretext of going upstairs to get his wife who was actually in the Crimea. Placating the other conspirators who

were becoming impatient, the Prince returned with a pistol. He shot Rasputin, who then staggered out into the courtyard where another conspirator shot him again. He was stabbed many times. Two days later his trussed-up body was found under the ice of the Neva River, one arm half-free, and his lungs filled with water. Rasputin had still been alive when submerged and he had died by drowning. He was barely 44.

Grieving peasants everywhere, and the women who loved him, mourned the death of a remarkable man, who, they believed, had been sent by God to tell the Czar the truth. "If I die," Rasputin had correctly prophesied, "the Emperor will soon lose his crown."

—B.J.

THE LOVES OF MATA HARI

One of her lovers had a typically French plan for her last-minute escape from the firing squad. Mata Hari, the most notorious spy since Delilah and the most accomplished mistress since La Pompadour, was to wear only a long fur coat on the morning of her execution. As soon as the rifles were raised, she would throw open her fur, and *certainment*, no red-blooded male would be able to fire upon her glorious body.

Actually this was not the most bizarre of the many ruses designed to save history's most celebrated spy and courtesan. As she waited calmly in her prison cell, demanding milk baths and all the luxuries she considered necessities, Mata Hari's lovers plotted incessantly. One playboy aviator volunteered to buzz St. Lazare prison and strafe his beloved's firing squad. Maître Clunet, Mata's brilliant lawyer, decided to spring a technicality on her unsuspecting jailers at the last moment—under French law no woman can be executed if pregnant, and he, her 75-year-old lover, would claim that Mata Hari was carrying his child. Most dramatic of all was the scheme conceived by Pierre de Mortissac, a nobleman who had squandered all his sizable fortune trying to win Mata Hari's love. Pierre had lifted his plan directly from the opera *Tosca*. He intended to bribe the firing squad to use blank cartridges and his lover would fall "dead" at the 1st mock volley. Late at night he and his confederates would spirit her live body from a grave dug especially shallow so that she wouldn't suffocate in her coffin.

Mata Hari, knowing all these plans and more, could afford to be confident, and she enjoyed her confinement as much as the drab surroundings permitted. Even in those final hours in prison she entertained her young doctor and the 2 incredulous nuns who watched over her. She danced her exotic nude dances, she regaled her jailers with risqué stories of her past. . . .

It was a past that has been fashionably debunked recently, for no good reason. The Dancer of the Seven Veils was in reality all that legend makes her, though even more complex a creature. Her photographs reveal a voluptuously attractive woman possessing an animal sensuality that transcends her every defect. Mata Hari knew how to "move a long, thin and proud body as Paris had never seen one moved before," the French writer Colette once observed. She was the personification of sex, but hated the men who loved her. Men paid Mata Hari with money, secrets, the lives of others, and yet she could betray them—loving what they gave, but hating what she thought they were.

Not always had Mata Hari been so. Strange as it may seem, she was an innocent, even drab Dutch housewife before becoming a spy. Behind the façade provided by the pseudonym "Mata Hari" was the rather prosaic Margaretha Geertruida Zelle. The future spy was born on August 7, 1876, in a small town in Holland, her religious parents enrolling her in a Catholic convent when she was only 14. But while on vacation in The Hague 4 years later, she met Capt. Campbell MacLeod, a handsome Scot who served in the Dutch Colonial Army. The chance meeting was to change her life. Though more than twice her age—he was over 40—this drunken roué somehow appealed to Margaretha. He married her, but even prior to taking her to Java, he revealed his essentially brutal nature. Before their 1st child was born Margaretha suffered many beatings at MacLeod's hands. He threatened her with a loaded revolver on one occasion, and he betrayed her so often with other women that she soon turned elsewhere for affection.

Nothing is recorded of Margaretha's love affairs in Java, but it is known that she studied the Vedas and other Oriental books describing the joys of sensual love, becoming adept in the ancient arts they taught. More important, those years in Java introduced her to the suggestive ritual dances that the Javanese *bayas* performed in the Buddhist temples. A new personality was already emerging as she practiced her own interpretations of these Indonesian dances. The transformation became complete when her 1st child was poisoned by a nurse holding a grudge against MacLeod. Margaretha later claimed that she strangled this servant, but, in any event, the dead child marked the emergence of a new woman. Even the birth of her daughter Banda failed to temper her hatred for MacLeod, who she felt was responsible for the death of their infant son. Deserting her husband after the family returned to Europe, she left Banda with relatives and began the career that was to make her life a legend.

No one really knows on what stage in Paris Margaretha 1st danced naked and lied to the world, saying she was born "in the south of India . . . the child of a family within the sacred caste of Brahma." But it was in about 1905, 10 years after she had sailed from the Orient, that she 1st told her audiences in soft, seductive tones that her name was Mata Hari, "the Eye of the Dawn," and that she would perform daring ritual dances never seen before outside Indian temples. Skeptical or not, editors knew good copy when they saw it and soon her stage name and photographs were a common sight in Paris newspapers. The photos of course were taken when she *began* her performances, for Mata Hari artfully shed her diaphanous coverings during each dance, the gossamer veils falling one by one until she stood almost wholly naked on the stage. The only part of herself she didn't expose was her breasts, which she always claimed her husband had disfigured in some way and she kept them covered with jeweled breastplates barely affixed to her body. Some of her dances were graceful, others frankly lewd, but all were immensely popular.

Mata Hari's exotic charms captivated the most sophisticated of cities and finally all of Europe. Men vied for her favors, and she always obliged—but never for less than $7,500 a night, she once bragged. Numbered among her countless lovers were Jules Cambron, chief of the French Ministry of Foreign Affairs, French Minister of War Messimy, the Crown Prince of Germany, Dutch Prime Minister van der Linden, the Duke of Brunswick, and Von Jagow, the Kaiser's Foreign Minister. But her favors always came high, whether she demanded cash, fabulous jewelry, or luxurious apartments on the Champs Élysées—and once her noble or millionaire lovers went broke, she abandoned them without a 2nd thought. Sex she enjoyed —so much so that she was often observed "relaxing" in Parisian brothels. But men she hated still. Except for one lover—the blinded Russian Captain Maroff, whom she pitied—men were only to be used. Mata Hari's immense vanity played a part in all this, as did her taste for the luxuries to which she'd become accustomed, but it was hatred and the cruelty it inspired that enabled her to become a spy. This cruelty was perfectly illustrated in her boast that she had killed her pony *Vichena* by thrusting a gold stiletto into its heart when one mission required that she leave France for a time. She couldn't bear the thought that anyone else would ride it.

Mata Hari became a German spy only because the Germans asked her 1st. She knew that her popularity as an entertainer was waning when the Germans recruited her between 1907 and 1910, and had the French made her a better offer, she almost certainly would have accepted it. Trained at the famous espionage school at Lorrach, she was given the code number H. 21, a series issued only to prewar agents. This number proved conclusively that she had been recruited *before* the war and did not join German intelligence later as part of a plan to deceive the Germans. During W.W. I, she performed her duties well for her employers. French intelligence suspected her activities from the beginning, even letting her join their service. But nothing could be proved at the time. It is known now that Mata Hari definitely informed the Germans of the development of the British "land ship," or tank, and that her reports on Allied plans for the offensive at Chemin des Dames prepared the Germans for that secret drive—resulting in a devastating reception that left 100,000 Allied dead and an additional 100,000 as casualties. It would require pages to list her other treacheries, the unglamorous but deadly information that her body bought. In turn, she fed the French nothing but worthless information or useless reports that were already common knowledge. No one knows the irreparable damage she did the Allied cause, since she was one spy who left no traces, but she danced for thousands, slept with hundreds, and clipped scores of Sampsons.

Mata Hari's end came when she was betrayed by the Germans themselves. Their highest paid spy, she had become a financial liability and increased French surveillance had hampered her effectiveness, so a plan to frame her was engineered by agent Capt. Walter Wilhelm Canaris, later head of the German secret service during W.W. II. She was advised to pick up a large check for her services at a neutral legation in Paris, but the Germans relayed the message with a code they knew the French had broken and she was arrested before she could cash the check.

On July 24, 1917, Mata Hari was brought before a court-martial on charges of espionage, thus becoming the most famous of the many spies tried in the hysteria of wartime France. But there is no reason to doubt that the French prosecutor was being conservative when he claimed that her activities had cost France at least 50,000 lives, the evidence indicating that at least twice that number would be a more realistic figure. The court-martial unanimously sentenced her to death. . . .

It was 4 A.M. on October 15, 1917, when Mata Hari was awakened in cell ❌ 12 at St. Lazare and prepared for the firing squad. As all the fantastic plans for her escape failed one by one, her confidence in her invincibility was shaken. Old Maître Clunet tried his maternity ploy, but when the doctor came to examine her, Mata Hari realized the futility of the scheme and refused an examination. As for the fur coat plan, its absurdity was so apparent that even Mata Hari had never considered it

more than a morale-building joke. She asked permission to write 3 last letters. One was to her daughter Banda, from whom she asked forgiveness. Ironically, the beautiful Banda would become a spy herself years later, a 2nd Mata Hari who warned an apathetic U.S. that a Communist invasion was coming in Korea and she eventually met the same fate as her mother.

But hope still prevailed as Mata Hari drank the traditional last glass of rum prescribed by law for all prisoners sentenced to death. Even as she was taken out into the chill morning to the rifle range at Vincennes, her supreme ego must have asserted itself. Mata Hari was tied to a young tree stripped of its leaves and branches. She faced her firing squad as the death warrant was read, refused a blindfold, and no witness saw any sign of fear on her face. Then this woman who had rarely been known to show any outward emotion, neither laughter nor tears, smiled toward the rifles gleaming in the early light. One likes to believe that she was sure they contained nothing but blanks, that Pierre de Mortissac's bribery had worked and all she'd have to do was play dead. It would be in character. In any case, Mata Hari stood straight up and did not flinch as Major Massard barked his terse final command. She didn't cry out when the rifles cracked and smoked. Her several lovers, watching among the witnesses—perhaps some in the firing squad itself—knew that she had died only by the crimson ropes that held her slumped body. Her playboy lover's plane did buzz the compound, but it was a futile gesture and too late by several seconds. At 5:47 the body of Mata Hari, the Eye of the Dawn, whose naked dance of death had lured so many innocents to their graves, had moved for the last time.

—R.H.

The Keeper of the Orgone

Wilhelm Reich, the "mad genius" of sex and psychiatry, alleged self-styled martyr to scientific discovery and imagination, was born on March 24, 1897, in Dobrzcynica, a part of Galicia that was then part of the Austrian empire. Until the 1930s his ideas were held in esteem within academic circles, and although he was a dissident of Freud his theories were eminently respected. Gradually, however, his thought took on more and more original direction until by the time of his death he had been almost completely rejected by the psychiatric profession as an out-and-out schizophrenic.

Reich served in the Austrian Army during W.W. I. In 1922, he received an MD from the University of Vienna. His 1st position was as assistant at the Julius Wagner-Jauregg psychiatric clinic. During 1924–1930 he conducted clinics for industrial workers in Vienna,

Berlin, and several German cities. Sometime during this period he joined the Communist party where he also attempted to be a sex counselor. When Hitler came to power, Reich emigrated to Denmark. In Copenhagen he published his *Die Massenpsychologie des Faschismus* (*The Mass Psychology of Fascism*, 1933) in which he denounced party-line communism as another form of fascism. This caused him to be expelled from the Communist party.

At the same time he was coming to be viewed with much suspicion by the orthodox psychoanalysts, especially after his book *Character Analysis*. At the conference of the International Psychoanalytic Association in Lucerne, 1934, he was officially 'shut out of that academic organization as well. Thus within a period of a few months he had been ejected by both a political and a professional organization. And now the world began closing in on him. So hostile was the Danish environment to him, that he fled to Sweden where he was also treated with suspicion and hostility.

Finally Harald Schjelderup, the Norwegian psychologist, was instrumental in securing him a teaching job at the University of Oslo. Reich worked there from 1934 to 1939. But in 1937, he fell under attack again, this time by the Norwegian press. By 1939 he had made up his mind to move to New York, where he took up psychiatric practice and lectured at the New School for Social Research until 1941.

Undoubtedly, Reich's most intriguing work has to do with the orgasm. In his *Function of the Orgasm* (1942) he says: "Orgastic potency is the capacity for surrender to the flow of biological energy without inhibition, the capacity for complete discharge of all dammed-up sexual excitation through involuntary pleasurable contractions of the body." This is to be thought of in contrast to mere ejaculative or erective potency. The key words here, one would guess, are "without inhibition."

Freud believed simply that sexual repression lay behind neurosis and carried that a step further by claiming that the actual physiological interruption of sexuality by whatever cause results in a certain neurosis. Moreover, one's entire personality is determined by his sexual characteristics. In this, of course, Reich concurred, but he felt that undischarged sexual energy itself is destructive and poisonous.

The inadequate orgasm (i.e. without spasm and brief unconsciousness) leaves surplus energy in the body that may encourage unhealthy secondary drives. Only the total orgasm releases these poisons. Reich felt that a frontal attack on the unresponsive musculature itself was the simplest way to deal with this problem and that time spent on psychoanalytic procedures designed to interpret unconscious resistances

was futile. In the early 1930s he called this muscular attack "vegetotherapy."

At the same time Reich felt that wholesale social reform was in order. Suppression of the sexual impulse in children and adolescents is the major cause of neurosis and this suppression is imposed by the rigidity of the family and the establishment. Hence he set about to overthrow the authority of all social institutions that seek to repress sexual freedom. The sexual liberation of the 1960s, then, saw in Reich an early prophet.

Even before he had failed to win over the communist and other leftist groups of Europe to his views and had moved to New York where he hoped to propagate his ideas, he had taught that the muscular rigidities adopted by the child as a resistance to punishment eventually become actual physical blocks with the result that complete orgasm is impossible and disease is inevitable. This unreleased energy, however, which he at 1st believed to be unique to living organisms, he came gradually to regard as a universal "pre-atomic" energy. He called it "orgone," a word coined from "organism" and "orgasm." This orgone is actually cosmic in scope and is reflected in both the microcosm and the macrocosm. It is, in fact the force behind the very functioning of the heavenly bodies; it extends to the depths of the universe itself and does not exclude even such phenomena as flying saucers and other mysteries. Finally, Reich saw the orgone energy to be synonymous with God and to underlie all the realities and processes of existence.

By 1945 Reich, who had left New York and taken to living in eccentric isolation in Maine, was saying that orgone energy radiates from the surface of the human body—corresponding to psychic energy—but only when the body is healthy and "unblocked." Cancer and other illnesses result when the flow is checked or inhibited. With a view to correcting this situation, Reich built what he called "orgone accumulators" or "orgone boxes," large enough for a person to sit inside. These wooden and metal-lined boxes collected life-giving rays from the superabundance of orgone energy in the cosmos and directed them at the person within the box. He sold these boxes as sexual stimulators and cures for cancer.

During the last years of his life, Reich abandoned psychiatry for what he felt were his more important discoveries in physics. In 1956, he was sentenced to 2 years' imprisonment at the Lewisburg penitentiary for disobeying a Federal court order to cease the distribution of orgone accumulators.

He died of a heart attack in 1957 on the day preceding his release. His death at such a peculiar time plus his disregard for the law in general were seized upon by some of his critics as an opportunity to accuse him of unconscious martyrdom.

But Reich had always been treated with disrespect, slander, and spite by the authoritarian establishment. In New York he had been held by the FBI at Ellis Island for several weeks in December, 1941. No reasons were ever given for that detention, but it was the beginning of the U.S. entry into W.W. II, and Reich's background was probably felt to be questionable. In 1954, the FDA seized his orgone accumulators, and many of his books and periodicals, which were subsequently burned, some of them in 1956 and the others in 1960.

In his later years Reich became obsessed with the menace of communism (which he called "red fascism") and with "emotional plague." The latter referred to the evil wrought by those who vent their frustration and sexual illness on the world, especially under the guise of fighting for some great cause. This label he eventually conferred upon anyone who opposed his ideas. He became more and more grandiose and megalomaniacal, indeed paranoic—although not entirely without reason. In 1947, the journalist Mildred E. Brady made a vicious attack on Reich in the *New Republic*. Her article was rife with distortion and slander and yet it was reprinted throughout the U.S. It was perhaps this widely quoted article, more than anything else, that inspired the FDA to move against him.

Although government psychiatrists certified that Reich was sane, it was the consensus of everyone but his staunchest followers that he was mad. Dr. Nic Waal, who wrote a sketch of Reich, said of him, "He went to pieces, partly on his own—but mostly due to other people. A human being cannot bear cruelty and loneliness in the long run."

It appears that the scientific community as well as certain hostile elements in the public at large may have done this pioneer a considerable injustice. Despite official condemnation, Food and Drug Administration scientists were obliged to admit that they found *some* evidence for the orgone. Several eminent persons, moreover, including Einstein himself, paid considerable attention to this man and his ideas. Still, no reputable scientist has ever attempted to pursue his experiments with any appreciable resolution.

—E.Re.

Rape Control Fails to Halt Increased Rape Rate

Every State in the U.S. has its own penal code definition of forcible rape from New Hampshire's new law, which defines sexual contact as "any touching of the sexual or other intimate parts of a person, including female breasts and buttocks," to older laws which define sexual contact as vaginal penetration by a male penis and/or sexual gratification involving the sex organs of one person and the mouth or anus of another. Generally the crime consists of a male engaging in sexual intercourse with a woman without her consent, and by the use of force or the threat of force.

More Awareness, but More Rapes. In 1973, thanks to the aggressive campaigning of women's groups (from the most radical Rape Crisis Centers to the conservative 11-million-member General Federation of Women's Clubs) and to realistic media coverage, the American consciousness regarding rape was raised as never before. Has this resulted in a reduction of forcible rape cases? No. The preliminary figures for 1973 from the Federal Bureau of Investigation show a 10% increase over the 46,430 rapes which the FBI Uniform Crime Report showed for 1972. Translating this into more realistic terms by recognizing that 10 rapes are committed for every one reported, America, in 1973, broke the half million mark in forcible rape.

Some observers, notably in certain law enforcement and legal defense areas, maintain that the upswing is not a genuine one; that it is accounted for by the fact that more women are now willing to report the crime than ever before. Others, while conceding the possibility of increased reports, believe that the increase is real and goes beyond the element of the reporting element per se.

Running the Horror Gamut. A woman who reports forcible rape still has to run a truly terrifying gamut of experiences beyond the rape itself—if she wants her assailant captured, tried, and convicted. If the man is a person the woman has been dating, if she bears no marks of a beating, if she has hitched a ride in a man's car, if she struck up an acquaintanceship with a man in a bar—or any one of a dozen other such circumstances—the police or the assistant district attorney will tell her she has virtually no chance of having the man convicted.

If she was raped by a stranger in her own home and beaten, cut up or otherwise severely mutilated, she may possibly stand a chance of seeing the rapist convicted. First, of course, she must be able to make a positive identification. If she wishes to see the case through to a conclusion, she must go through these steps:

1. Repeated questioning of a necessarily em-

barrassing, sometimes degrading nature by police officers and subsequent investigators; 2. In many cases, photographing of many areas of her body, sometimes her most intimate parts; 3. Examination (generally in a hospital emergency room, occasionally with police present) of her sexual organs and other parts of her body—not only to check for pregnancy or venereal disease, but to gather hard evidence in the way of semen, body hair, sperm, etc. 4. Assuming the police capture the suspect and have enough evidence to go to the D.A., the woman now must undergo even more intensive questioning by the assistant D.A. assigned to the case. He must determine how good a witness she will be, and how well she will hold up in court; 5. If the D.A. thinks he has a case, the probability is there will be a preliminary hearing to determine whether the alleged rapist should be held over for trial. The preliminary hearing is a trial in itself. The prosecutor asks his plaintiff to describe every detail of the rape to make his case. Then the defense counsel takes her through the experience all over again, on cross-examination, frequently with emphasis on her own past sex life; 6. If the defendant is held over, the trial eventually begins, probably after many continuances; which, in many cases, will be granted again and again to the defense. In the case of both the hearing and the trial, it must be remembered that there is an audience of strangers before whom the woman must repeatedly recite not only the details of the rape, but many other elements of her past and present sex life.

Chances of Conviction. And, when it's all over, what are the chances of conviction? Here's a typical record: In 1972, in the State of California, 3,439 rape arrests were made. Of these, only 753 were charged (meaning the police and D.A. thought there was a case). And of the 753, only 266 were convicted. Of those convicted, the majority were given suspended sentences, went directly on parole, or were paroled after serving brief sentences.

It *is* true that in 1974 more effective action was taken to fight rape and reduce the humiliation a victim goes through than at any other time in history. But much more needs to be done.

Some Control Efforts. Although only a beginning, some developments are worth mentioning: Four States (California, Florida, Iowa, and Michigan) passed new laws in the summer of 1974 which are expected to reduce substantially the ordeal a rape victim goes through in court; they declared introduction of the woman's past sexual history (except with the defendant) inadmissible. The California law, introduced by Sen. Alan Robbins (Dem.—No. Hollywood), added a new Section (782) to the Evidence Code as follows: ". . . Evidence of

specific instances of sexual contact of the victim involving any person other than the defendant shall be inadmissible."

Five other States (Washington, Kansas, Ohio, Nevada, and Pennsylvania) are expected to pass similar legislation by 1976.

In Massachusetts, a bill was passed requiring police departments to set up special units to investigate and prosecute rape cases. In New York, there is now a State Crime Victim's Compensation Board. Under the direction of a supervising investigator, the board deals with claims filed by rape victims who have reported the attack to the police within 48 hours of its occurrence. Rape victims may collect all uninsured hospital costs over $100, and may additionally collect for replacement of lost earnings up to $100 per week, and a total of $15,000.

On the Federal level, the rape bill introduced by Sen. Charles Mathias (Rep.—Maryland) stumbled along in the way of much such legislative effort. This bill would create a National Center for Control and Prevention of Rape, within the National Mental Health Institute, and create eligibility for nonprofit organizations for funding "for the purpose of conducting research and demonstration projects concerning the control and prevention of rape."

What such research will develop in the way of information, that previous research (going back to the 1940s and early 1950s) hasn't revealed, remains to be seen. In those years, scientists of the Kinsey Institute for Sex Research interviewed sex offenders in prisons and mental health institutions in California, Indiana, and Ohio. They published a work based on their findings, titled *Sex Offenders* in 1965. In 1971, Israeli criminologist and sociologist Menachem Amir published *Patterns in Forcible Rape*, a scholarly study of all the rape cases handled by the Philadelphia Police Department during the years 1958 through 1960. It is conceivable, however, that recent public awareness may effect greater candor from the victims and, more important, deeper insights which will result in helping men to overcome this particular compulsion.

A substantial number of other studies of rapists have been made since 1971—some elaborate, some rather primitive—but all seem to come up with the same general findings. There are, broadly speaking, 2 kinds of rapists, the criminal rapist and the psychiatric rapist. The majority of rapists are in the 15-to-24 age bracket.

Self-Protective Measures. While the research projects, law enforcement, medical and legal efforts, all work to alleviate the plight of rape victims, women themselves continue to mount increasingly aggressive and effective campaigns on all levels. An obvious 1st step is to become aware of the best ways to avoid rape. At home, these are the rules to follow:

1. Have secure locks (preferably dead bolts) on doors and windows.

2. Never open the door to a stranger. Make him identify himself, and check his identification with a phone call to the company or service he claims to, represent.

3. Never allow children to open the door. They are naturally trusting and tend to permit anyone to enter.

4. Be sure the area around your home is well-lighted.

5. Try to avoid letting strangers know you are alone. If you're a single woman living alone, don't use your 1st name on your mailbox or for your phone listing.

Away from home:

1. Never hitchhike if you can possibly avoid it. If you must, never hitchhike with a man; wait for a car with a woman driver.

2. Never pick up a stranger in a bar, or anywhere else for that matter. Certainly never go to his apartment, no matter how gentle and innocent he seems. Don't walk dark streets. If you're driving, keep your car doors locked. When you park your car, park in lighted areas. Lock your car. Before getting back in, always look into the rear-seat area 1st.

Women Strike Back. Women are taking self-defense courses in ever greater numbers. There is still a considerable difference of opinion about the advisability of a woman attempting to fight off a rapist physically. Many law enforcement people advise against it on the grounds that it may incite a rapist to greater violence; and that most women aren't strong enough to fight off the average rapist, even if they have mastered one of the martial arts.

Many women carry so-called legal weapons such as a hatpin, nail file, umbrella, aerosol cans of hairspray, whistles or other alarms. Some law enforcement people claim a woman's best defense is a loud and prolonged scream. It's also better to scream "Fire" rather than "Help."

In California, in 1974, 2 women claiming to have been raped took drastic measures—they murdered their alleged rapists. The 1st of these 2 women, 30-year-old Inez Garcia of Monterey, was convicted October 4 by a 7-woman, 5-man jury of 2nd-degree murder for shooting and killing a 30-year-old man, whom she said helped another man rape her. In that same month, 19-year-old Deborah Kantaeng of Long Beach was charged with murder in the shotgun killing of Danny Charles Allen, 21, who

Ms. Kantaeng maintains raped her. Many feminists in the Monterey and Long Beach areas, familiar with the cases, insisted that the women were being "railroaded."

Life or Death Decisions. Obviously, a woman facing a rapist is forced to make 2 very difficult decisions instantaneously: 1. *What kind of a man is the rapist?* Can he be "talked" out of the idea? Will resistance make him violent? If he is armed with gun, knife, or other weapon, of course, resistance may be out of the question anyway. 2. *What is the woman herself capable of doing in the way of effective physical resistance* . . . not only as to skill, strength and technique, but is her own emotional capacity to do violence to another, even a would-be rapist, firm enough? Could she poke both his eyes out, while pretending to caress his face—a simple technique recommended, incidentally, by some law enforcement people.

The Rape Crisis Centers. However, as stated, best estimates are that in 1973 more than ½ million women were unable to avoid rape, and over 50,000 of them reported the assaults. All of those 50,000 women went through one or more of the previously detailed difficult, frequently degrading, experiences beyond the rape itself. Many of them were helped immeasurably through these ordeals by the dedicated members of rape crisis centers, which are operating in more than 35 States across the country—

The women working in these centers—many are rape victims themselves—do not necessarily urge a rape victim to report or prosecute her case. They leave the decision solely up to the violated woman. What they do is give counsel and comfort. If the victim wishes, they sit in on police interrogations, accompany her to the hospital, and the district attorney's office. In short, their function is to help a sister through what is unquestionably one of the most degrading, humiliating experiences a woman can have, one that may leave her physically or psychologically crippled.

And they are carrying out this function with increasing effectiveness as they gain experience, and as more and more of them get funding from agencies such as the Law Enforcement Assistance Administration.

The war against rape, in short, is raging. And perhaps, in time, this vicious crime will be brought under some semblance of control.

—J.B.C. & J.Cs.

Famous Gays: Renowned Homosexuals—Past to Present

Based on lists prepared by researchers of the U.S. National Gay Task Force, supplemented by the *Almanac's* own researchers. Included among these names are celebrated persons who were both homosexual and heterosexual—in short, bisexual.

FEMALE

Sappho, Greek poet (600 B.C.)
Queen Christina, Swedish ruler (1626–1689)
Madame de Staël, French author (1766–1817)
Emily Dickinson, American poet (1830–1886)
Willa Cather, American author (1873–1947)
Gertrude Stein, American author (1874–1946)
Virginia Woolf, British author (1882–1941)
Vita Sackville-West, British author (1892–1962)

MALE

Zeno, Greek philosopher (500 B.C.)
Sophocles, Greek playwright (496?–406 B.C.)
Socrates, Greek philosopher (470?–399 B.C.)
Aristotle, Greek philosopher (384–322 B.C.)
Alexander the Great, Macedonian ruler (356–323 B.C.)
Emperor Hadrian, Roman ruler (76–138 A.D.)
Richard the Lion-Hearted, British ruler (1157–1199)
Richard II, British ruler (1367–1400)
Leonardo da Vinci, painter-scientist (1452–1519)
Benvenuto Cellini, Italian goldsmith (1500–1571)
Christopher Marlowe, British playwright (1564–1593)
King James I, British ruler (1566–1625)
John Milton, British poet (1608–1674)
Jean Baptiste Lully, French composer (1632–1687)
Frederick the Great, Prussian ruler (1712–1786)

King Gustav III, Swedish ruler (1746–1792)
Baron Alexander von Humboldt, German naturalist (1769–1859)
Lord Byron, British poet (1788–1824)
Hans Christian Andersen, Danish author (1805–1875)
Walt Whitman, American poet (1819–1892)
Samuel Butler, British author (1835–1902)
Algernon Swinburne, British poet (1837–1909)
Pëtr Ilich Tchaikovsky, Russian composer (1840–1893)
Paul Verlaine, French poet (1844–1896)
Oscar Wilde, Irish playwright (1854–1900)
Frederick Rolfe (Baron Corvo), British author (1860–1913)
André Gide, French author (1869–1951)
Marcel Proust, French author (1871–1922)
E. M. Forster, British author (1879–1970)
John Maynard Keynes, British economist (1883–1946)
Sir Harold Nicholson, British author-diplomat (1886–1968)
Capt. Ernst Roehm, German Nazi leader (1887–1934)
T. E. Lawrence, British soldier-author (1888–1935)
Jean Cocteau, French author (1889–1963)
Christopher Isherwood, British author (1904–)
Dag Hammarskjöld, Swedish secretary-general U.N. (1905–1961)
W. H. Auden, British-American poet (1907–)
Jean Genet, French playwright (1909–)
Tennessee Williams, American playwright (1911–)
Brendan Behan, Irish author (1923–1964)

The Birds and Bees—and More

The unicellular bacteria, *Trichonympha*, which lives in the intestines of wood-eating cockroaches, is completely bisexual. The sexual act is performed when the cell playing the male role enters the rear of the female through a special plasma zone and the 2 cells fuse. Which bacteria will play what sex role is determined by the number of pigment spots on each; the one with more spots becomes the female and the one with less, the male. However, in another instance of mating, the *Trichonympha* which previously played the female role may find its spots outnumbered and be forced into performing the male role.

The head and brain of the Palolo Worm (*Eunice*), which lives in coral reefs, never participate whatsoever in its own sexual life. The worm ties off its rear segments where the male and female sexual products are located. This rear end then breaks off from the worm's body and swims to the surface to join other rear ends. They all empty out their products and then die. Meanwhile, the worm's head and brain, still underwater, grow a new rear section, to repeat the process once again according to the phases of the moon.

Bedbugs (*Cimex*) achieve sexual intercourse when the male pierces a hole through the female's back by means of a spike on the front of his penis. He ejaculates into this hole, where his sperm swim around in the female's blood until they reach her ovaries. The fertilized eggs then develop into embryos which are born alive.

Male beetle mites (*Oribatei*) deposit large quantities of their spermatophores on the ground, not caring whether a female is in the area. If a female should happen along, she will pick up a few of these fungoidlike growths and deposit them in her reproductive organ. When a male and female beetle mite pass by each other, they make no signs of recognition.

Male scorpions ensure that a female will find their spermatophores. The male finds a female and grabs her by the pincers. He then ejaculates on the ground between them and pulls her forward so that her reproductive organ comes into contact with his spermatophore.

The blind garden centipede (Scutigerella) also deposits his spermatophore on the ground. The female finds the substance and takes it into her mouth, storing it in a special cheek pouch. When she lays her eggs, she places each egg in her mouth and smears it with a small amount of the stored spermatophore.

Male flatworms have a multifunctional penis. It comes out of their mouth, is equipped with spikes and poison glands, and, in addition to its sexual function, is used to catch prey.

The mite Pyemotis, which feeds on caterpillars, is sexually mature at birth. The young males remain with their mother, stinging her to suck out her bodily juices. They wait at the genital duct for a female to be born. They take no notice of their brothers, but should a sister appear, they will immediately grab her and begin to copulate.

The male honeybee's sole function seems to be to have sex once with the queen. The males, or drones, are born only from the unfertilized eggs. Females, however, are the products of fertilized eggs. Whether or not a female will grow into a sterile worker or a fertile queen is determined by the diet she receives during development. The female workers must feed the drones and, once the drones have had sex with the queen, the workers unceremoniously eject the males from the hive to die outside.

Male bearded tits, a common European bird, select their mates by pecking and plucking at a likely female. If the female tolerates a male's abuse, the 2 soon become paired and fly away from the rest of the flock. For the rest of their lives, they do not lose sight of each other for more than a moment.

Flamingos gather by the millions on East African salt lakes to perform their courtship ritual. The males congregate to one side and engage in elaborate dances. The females look on, trying to choose their mates. One by one, the females go up to the males of their choice and perform a mutual wing-stretching, bowing ritual. The pair then wades into the water where the male jumps onto the female's back, almost submerging her head, and begins to copulate.

Emperor penguins have sex only once a year for a period of 2 to 3 minutes. The female lowers herself face down on the ice, supporting herself by her beak and flippers. The male mounts her, and holding her beak in his, balances himself by his flippers. Many times, he will lose his balance and fall to the ice, only to pick himself up and mount the female once again.

Indian cobras engage in mock combat prior to copulation. They fling themselves at each other; the female struggles violently as the male attempts to place his body next to hers. Eventually, they arrange themselves with their heads and necks raised from the ground and, for an hour or more, strike at each other. The female signals her submission by laying her head on the ground, at which time the male brings one of his 2 penises into contact with her reproductive organ. Copulation lasts anywhere from 2 minutes up to a whole day.

The mating call of alligators resembles the boom of a cannon. Even alligators sometimes cannot tell the difference; fireworks displays have been known to turn on a zoo full of the animals. Females often do not eat 8 to 9 weeks prior to mating. The male, recognizing the onset of the fertility period by a scent which she emits, makes the 1st overtures. He rubs his body against hers, raises his tail out of the water, grabs her neck with his jaws, and hooks his tail about hers in order to position himself to penetrate her. Copulation usually lasts for only 3 minutes.

For many turtles, the courting period is marked by a ceremony in which the 2 stand facing each other, slowly nodding their heads up and down and from side to side for hours at a time. Eventually, the male takes the initiative and places the female's head in his mouth. Later, he sucks on her feet one at a time. The position for copulation varies among the species of turtles. Some males mount the female and steady themselves by biting her back, while others have to rear up in an almost vertical position before penetration is possible.

Octopuses mate facing each other, but their sex organs never touch. The male ejaculates onto one of his tentacles and then uses the tentacle to introduce the sperm into the female's reproductive organ.

California sea lions are voyeurs; they are stimulated by the sight of other sea lions performing sex. Oftentimes, this is the only form of sexual gratification for the younger males since the older ones jealously guard their harems. During the mating season, which lasts 2 months, the older males are expected to satisfy the sexual needs of their harem. Copulation may last an hour or longer as the pair float just below the surface of the water. Once one affair is completed, the male must hurry ashore to begin again with a new female.

Among beavers, the female initiates sexual intercourse. When she has found a suitable mate, she signals her intentions by secreting a yellowish oily substance called castoreum from a gland located between her anus and genitals. The male follows suit, and as long as he shows her the proper respect—she may have to box his ears from time to time—they will probably remain together for the rest of their lives. At mating time, the female emits a scent which stimulates the male. They glide into the water and, face to face, copulate as they swim slowly forward.

Male giraffes use their skin-covered horns only for fighting with a rival over a female. For their part, the females seem lackadaisical about sex. When prodded by a male, a female will urinate so that he may test the urine to see if she is in her oestrus (ovulating). Oftentimes a female will simply walk away during copulation, sending the unwary male plummeting to the ground.

Rhinoceroses use their brute force to test the strength of each other before mating. For hours on end, they charge one another, their 2,000 lbs. or more attaining speeds of up to 35 mph. Once the female is certain she has a worthy mate, she will instigate copulation. The male mounts her from the back and penetrates her with his 2' long penis. They continue to have sex for about an hour and a half, with the male sometimes ejaculating every 10 minutes.

Despite their size, elephants are among the most gentle lovers in the animal kingdom. Every 3 to 6 months, both males and females experience a period of musth, during which they seek out a mate. Musth is an emotional state brought on by the temporal gland, located just beneath the skin midway between the ear and the eye. The gland becomes swollen and secretes a dark strong-smelling substance which stains the lower part of the face. Once an elephant has found a suitable mate, the 2 will begin to flirt. The male offers the female food or squirts water over her back as she looks on nonchalantly. Finally, usually after a month, the female gives in and the male mounts her from the rear, gradually rising to an almost vertical position as he achieves full penetration. Afterward, the pair entwine trunks and swish their tails.

Chimpanzees are probably the most highly sexed primates. They indulge in considerable oral-genital play and mutual masturbation. Young chimps gather to watch these displays and, afterward, emulate their elders by mounting each other and giving pelvic thrusts. Female chimps seem to have an almost insatiable sex drive. During their period of oestrus, some have been observed engaging in sex more than 20 times a day.

—S.L.W.G.

20

Health and Well-Being

Some Favorite American Foods

COCA-COLA

It used to be "the real thing" when pharmacist John Styth Pemberton brewed it up in his backyard before the days of drug paranoia. The trademark "French Wine Coca—Ideal Nerve and Tonic Stimulant" was registered in 1885 for his homemade medicine which then contained the cocaine extracted from the coca plant. It is said that his assistant could "audit the composition of a batch of syrup merely by sniffing it." By the next year the wine was taken out, caffeine was added, extract of the kola nut was thrown in for flavor, and the name Coca-Cola was invented. The syrup was sold in used beer bottles and recommended for headaches and hangovers. The 1st year only 25 gallons of syrup were sold, compared to some 100 million bottles of Coke sold daily around the world in the 1970s.

Pemberton sold the business to Asa Candler, who turned it into a corporation. Although it is as symbolic of the U.S. as the American flag, Coke is now bottled in 128 foreign countries—including Bulgaria, where the 1st communist franchise was established in 1966. The company is intensely image-conscious and if you happen to print the product's name using a small c, you can count on receiving a very gentle chiding letter from Atlanta, home of the industry. Some have found the Coca-Cola company's official politeness in other situations suspect, and its image has suffered from boycotts against it on various occasions during segregation troubles in the South. Even in the northern states, boycotts occurred to protest racial discrimination in the bottling plants.

The manufacturing and bottling plants of today are quite different from the backyard brewery where Pemberton stirred his potion with an oar. Quality controls are more stringent and the secret ingredient 7X is known to only 2 or 3 people, although even the nonsecret ingredients are difficult to pin down. Coke still contains a mixture of 3 parts coca—minus the buzz—and one part cola. The kola nut contains caffeine, although much of it is removed during processing and additional caffeine is probably added. The company is not required to list caffeine on the label even though noncola beverages are subject to more complete exposure of their additives. The words "artificial coloring" may be sufficient too, though not exact. High doses of caffeine have been linked experimentally with birth defects and although the same warning pertains to coffee, the point is that parents who refuse to give their children coffee often think nothing of letting them drink great quantities of soft drinks. That is, unless they are concerned about another ingredient, sugar, which is the number-one constituent of these drinks. It is the sugar, rather than any trace of cocaine, which tends to make Coke addictive. Eight ounces of the stuff (a mere sip to most Coke drinkers) contains about 5 teaspoons of sugar. The pancreas then sends so much insulin into the blood to deal with this onslaught that the ironic result is a drastic lowering of the blood sugar level, followed by a craving for more sugar.

Phosphoric acid in Coke can upset the calcium-phosphorus balance in the body and may prevent proper absorption of iron. It also upsets the stomach. The taste of the acid is masked by the high sugar content, and the combination of sugar and acid does no good to the teeth. Since soft drinks are nonnutritive and can interfere with the appetite, protein deficiency is not uncommon among chronic cola drinkers, who can develop the same kinds of liver ailments as the chronic alcoholic.

Coca-Cola also has citrus fruit concerns in Florida. Drinks such as Hi-C are made by Coca-Cola. The migrant workers have recently complained about their inhuman living conditions and concessions have been made to provide better housing. The threat of unionism, rather than great altruism on the part of the company, was the big stimulus for making these improvements based on labor complaints.

Elsewhere in the world, Coke has a variety of reputations. In places as unlikely as Guatemala and West Africa, soft drinks have become a staple in the diet. In France there was an attempt to ban all colas in 1950 but this legislation was later repealed after much pressure. In Denmark Coca-Cola is taxed severely. But here in the U.S., the word is still out, despite the fact that Coke is nutritionally a disaster, that it is "the real thing."

PEANUT BUTTER

The peanut was probably 1st found in South America, introduced to Africa by Portuguese slave ships, and later brought to North America from Africa—again on slave ships, as it was a cheap and plentiful food source to take on transoceanic voyages. In the U.S. the peanut was originally cultivated as feed for farm animals, although today more than half of the domestic crop is used for human consumption. As early as 1964 at least 63% of the peanuts eaten by humans was in the form of peanut butter.

North American peanut butter developed independently from the peanut pastes found in Africa or South America. In the latter continent, roasted peanuts are ground and mixed with honey and cocoa. The 1st North American peanut butter was made by chopping the nuts and then beating them in a cloth sack, after the addition of salt. George Washington Carver, in his research at Tuskegee Institute, invented new improved kinds of peanut butter and, while he was at it, he used the peanut to make shampoo, ink, and linoleum.

Around the turn of the century, women made peanut butter in their homes using hand mills, small ovens, and blanchers. The American Museum of Peanut Butter History in Chicago has examples of these devices for the enthusiast to view. Today there are mechanical apparatuses to do everything from planting, cultivating, pest control, and harvesting to shelling, grading, heating, cooling, and transporting the product to the local store. During W.W. II peanuts became an important crop and, as with other industries, there was a shift to fewer but larger plants. The processing includes the stages of roasting, inspecting by high-speed color sorters, 2 millings for smooth texture, cooling, salting, and vacuum-packing.

The shelf life of peanut butter is affected by the natural oils rising to the top where exposure to light or air may cause rancidity. However, a jar of peanut butter typically lasts a year or 2 without severe spoilage, so this is a poor rationalization for adulteration. Separation can be counteracted by stirring the peanut butter or turning the jar upside down. Still manufacturers prefer to add antioxidants to prevent eventual spoilage, hydrogenated vegetable oil or corn syrup solids to prevent natural oil separation, and dextrose or sugar for both sweetening and absorption of some of the oil. There can be an undesirable reaction between the added sugar and the natural protein content of the nut though this is not very common. The heart or germ of the peanut has the most nutritive value but it is also perishable so it is removed by processors, increasing shelf life at the expense of food value. Sometimes vitamins A and C are added to enrich the product. Technically, by federal regulations which have been changed and/or overlooked many times during the past 15 years, peanut butter must be 90% peanuts. The remaining 10% is not supposed to include artificial colors, flavors, or sweeteners; chemical preservatives; or purified vitamins or minerals. The best-quality peanut butter still is the type that comes closest to being 100% peanuts, with only salt added, and is the lightest in color since long roasting (which produces an attractive darker color) decreases the thiamine content. However, color may also be affected by such secret ingredients as malt or ham which probably will not be listed on the labels.

Nutritionally, peanut butter is a good protein supplement to the diet, a fair source of calcium, iron, thiamine, riboflavin, and an excellent source of niacin. Since unadulterated peanut butter has these healthful qualities, many smaller companies are now producing the old-fashioned type of peanut butter for a health-conscious public, and other nut butters such as almond or cashew are growing in popularity as well. But beware of peanut butters which advertise themselves as old-fashioned but don't have oil separation.

SUGAR

The typical American diet piles an average of 525 lbs. of food per year into each person's digestive system and about 20% of that is sugar. Table sugar, or sucrose, accounts for a lot of this but there is also fructose from fruits, lactose from milk, maltose from malt, and a combination of fructose and glucose from honey. Glucose is the form of sugar the body utilizes for energy and this is what is meant when we speak of blood sugar. The body must break down what you feed it to get glucose or it can create its own from stores of fat. Since we can get glucose from other sources, most of us don't need the empty calories of plain sugar. Yet, although we lead less active lives than previous generations, we use more sugar than ever. The U.S. is not the worst offender so far as having a sweet tooth; England, Scotland, Ireland, and The Netherlands have an even higher per-capita intake at well over 100 lbs. per year.

Historically, sugar was known in India as early as 3000 B.C. In China "stone honey" was a delicacy, made of boiled sugarcane juice dried in the sun, sometimes with milk added. A pattern of early world competition for the spice routes soon sent table sugar westward from Southeast Asia into Europe; Islamic rule sent sugarcane cultivation into North Africa; and the slave trade in the New World is affiliated with European sugar interests in Latin America. In medieval Europe beekeeping had been important to the Church since beeswax was needed for votive candles. Honey was a byproduct. With the decline of the Church during the Reformation, the honey supply dwindled and so the changing social structure indirectly led to the more widespread use of sugar. At 1st its use was restricted to the very rich; in Italy in the 16th century, fine spun-sugar sculptures bedecked banquet tables. It was also used medicinally as a sedative. This may seem strange since sugar's main characteristic is that it is a pure energy food. However, the sedative effects probably relate to the subsequent lowering of the blood sugar level after the initial energy rush.

In the cultivation of sugarcane, weeds present a problem and, although some mechanical weeding has been developed, a great deal of it is still done by hand using a hoe. Even the harvesting is done manually in some places. Chemical fertilizers and herbicides are used (which is why organic food suppliers usually don't carry sugar). The fields are often burned prior to harvest, which is a poor way of developing rapport with the earth.

Law requires that sugar be refined before it is sold, even if that is not necessarily a virtue. The sugar juice is pressed out of the cane and is purified by heating and adding milk of lime. It is filtered, boiled, centrifuged, and crystallized. Molasses, part of the resulting residue, may be added to the sugar in varying percentages—13% for dark brown sugar while white sugar is 99.96% sucrose. For additional whitening, ash from burned beef bones is used. For powdered sugar, cornstarch is added.

Refining techniques are similar for the sugar beet which became popular in the early 19th century after sugarcane trade with the West Indies and Southeast Asia was blockaded. The Steffens process of recovering extra sucrose from molasses through 3rd or 4th boilings makes use of powdered quicklime added to diluted molasses instead of using milk of lime.

About 70% of worldwide sugar production is for domestic use and the sugar trade is based on prices negotiated between countries, biased, of course, by political relations. Although the U.S. produces most of its own sugarcane, the largest producers of cane sugar are Cuba, Brazil, and Australia, while the U.S.S.R., U.S., and France lead in beet production. There have been 3 international agreements since W.W. II to set floor and ceiling prices on sugar trade. Even when you don't buy plain sugar, it's been added to so many foods that you're probably buying it anyhow.

White sugar tends to have a negative effect on the nervous system, robs the body of B vitamins, causes tooth decay, interferes with calcium metabolism, and contributes to hardening of the arteries when used excessively. Brown, demarara, and turbinado sugar are not significantly better; "raw" sugar which is partially refined also contains 97% sucrose. Honey is a much more concentrated sweetener than sugar and so tends not to be overused as much. Other alternatives include carob molasses, carob syrup, unrefined sugarcane syrup, date sugar, palm sugar, and maple sugar. Several artificial sweeteners have been withdrawn from the market in recent years because of the infamous cyclamate furor. There is an experimental product, not yet on the market, called Aspartane—comprised of amino acids, aspartic acid, and phenylalanine—which is the creation of a contraceptive pill manufacturer. Most of us would be better off reducing our sweet craving instead of looking for artificial sources, or else developing a taste for foods with natural sweetness such as fruits, which can provide vitamins and other nutrients at the same time. Even maple syrup is sometimes adulterated since a poisonous pellet is used to kill bacteria in the tree and keep tapholes open longer. Honey is relatively pure but best in the raw and unfiltered varieties. When processed it loses vitamin F, thiamine, riboflavin, niacin, pantothenic acid, and ascorbic acid.

High blood sugar is linked with diabetes and low blood sugar with hypoglycemia. Considering the impact sugar has on our health, we should be suspicious of pro-sugar advertising and be more conscious of just how much sugar we consume.

WHITE BREAD

The most important ingredient in bread is flour and in the U.S. the most common flour is wheat, typically red winter wheat grown in the southern Great Plains States. Whole wheat bread is made from the entire grain. For white bread, however, the outer shell (bran) and kernel (germ) are removed in the milling process. The resulting flour is devitalized and then sent to commercial baking plants to undergo further adulteration. In Egypt, where bread-making is said to have begun as a profession, a baker who adulterated his bread would find himself hung by his ears to the doorpost of the bakery. Still, the history of adulterating bread is long. In the Middle Ages refined white bread was used by the Church and the surplus sold to the nobility while the poor people ate dark bread, establishing a tradition of associating white bread (also white rice, white sugar) with wealth and status.

Modern processing of wheat is one of the dubious technological advances of the Industrial Revolution. The wheat is roller-milled, which crushes the grain, thus destroying protein and vitamins. White bread need not be completely useless nutritionally, especially if eggs and butter are used, though this is rarely done with typical commercial white bread. Stone-grinding is the older method of preparation, producing coarser but more nutritious flour than the highly milled and refined white flour.

Most manufacturers remove the germ because the oils present there make rancidity possible. Vitamin E is thereby eliminated and drug companies make a healthy profit selling people back the vitamin E which has been confiscated from their bread. The removal of the germ or embryo, which is the living part of the grain, makes it difficult to claim that bread is the staff of life. The complete complex of B vitamins is found in very few foods other than liver, brewer's yeast, and wheat germ. Remove the germ, and the vitamin-deficient bread that's left does not service the heart, veins and arteries, nervous system, and digestive system. And speaking of the digestive system, manufacturers claim that they remove the bran because it is too rough for many digestive systems. Yet without such roughage we are prone toward diseases of the intestines including cancer of the colon. Since commercial concerns use chemicals to speed up the resting time of the dough, they claim that the bran wouldn't have time to soften and this is further rationale for removing it. Yet potassium bromide, which ages flour artificially, was banned in South Africa after a 1% concentration of it was found to be responsible for over 600 cases of poisoning; and chlorine dioxide, used as both a maturing agent and a bleach to make the flour whiter, is toxic.

The processed flour is sent to the baking plant. During shipment or storage it is vulnerable to absorbing odors such as paint, tobacco, solvents, and disinfectants. Shortenings added to the flour in the bread-making process include lard and beef tallow, which vary according to the cattle. Vegetable oils are usually refined, bleached, and deodorized. Fats may be hydrogenated in order to prevent oxidizing and this process in turn prevents the body from utilizing other nutrients which may be present in the bread. Chemical antioxidants are also added, the more notorious ones being BHA (butylated hydroxyanisole) and BHT (butylated hydroxytoluene). To this concoction enzymes are added—fungal proteases, amylases, and lipoxidases. Malt is a good enzymatic source and is high in vitamins and essential amino acids. However, companies usually go the other route because it is cheaper albeit nonnutritive. Soy enzymes are good and may add flavor to the extremely bland refined flour; this blandness is, of course, a reflection of the lack of nutritional substance in the 1st place.

The idea of adding vitamins and minerals to enrich white bread came in the Depression years of the 1930s when more than half the diet of city people consisted of white flour products. Even the enriched white flour—which generally has synthesized niacin, thiamine, riboflavin, and iron added back—is still missing major B vitamins and amino acids. Some protein can be found if dried or frozen eggs are used; more often the yellow tint from nitric acid serves as an egg substitute. Calcium propionate (made from the same chemicals that bring you athlete's foot remedies) retards spoilage and prolongs shelf life. Allergic reactions to this substance have been known.

Most of the large processes are handled by machine, but there are human overseers at each step along the way and some jobs, such as shaping irregular baked products, may be done entirely by hand. There is an enormous discrepancy in pay between labor and management. Women are not encouraged to enter higher positions and a 1971 manual of baking industry career opportunities says that "a professional woman should be prepared to encounter some antagonism in these fields. . . . It is most important that she have a pleasing personality, is well groomed at all times and dresses in a conservative, but fashionable manner." Considering that the baking industry ranks number one in the U.S. in the use of motor vehicles, number of plants, and number of people employed, it sets an interesting example of employment practices and of the relative values of nutrition versus profit.

The loaves are often packaged with misleading labels, then marketed. Chemical additives should be mentioned but not all are. For instance, something may have been thrown in (but not listed) to make the bread hold water so that less dough is needed per loaf. If you squeeze a loaf and it stays indented, or changes in size, beware. Not everything marked "wheat" is *whole* wheat. In Switzerland white bread is taxed and the revenue given to bakers of whole wheat bread in order to make nutritious bread available at a reasonable price. Don't hold your breath waiting for that to happen here. Just remember to buy a life-sustaining grain instead of an overrefined substance that is not of interest even to rats and insects.

EGGS

There has been a slight decrease in the popularity of eggs recently, partly because of the disappearance of breakfast as an important meal in many homes. The U.S. Dept. of Agriculture statistics show a decline in the annual per-capita use of eggs (an average of 362 in 1957 as compared to 287 in 1974). Nevertheless eggs are still big business and account for about 2.5% of total supermarket sales, or over $600 million per year.

According to some sources wild jungle fowl were domesticated about 3,000 years ago in Southeast Asia; other sources add that Columbus brought chickens with him on his 2nd trip to the western hemisphere. Today there are over 200 breeds of chickens but the most popular is the Single Comb White Leghorn, a white-egg layer. Rhode Island Red, New Hampshire Red, and Plymouth Rock hens are popular brown-egg producers.

During the late 1950s and early 1960s the egg industry took a major shift from farm flock (under 400 hens) to commercial flock (with as many as 20,000 to 100,000 hens and sometimes more). Supermarket eggs are generally from commercial flocks but it is still possible to buy farm eggs in many areas. Eggs had been primarily a corn belt industry until quite recently, when the West and Southeast became major production centers. Statistics indicate that the new commercialism means more than just keeping more chickens around for the job; it means each hen is pressed to its production capacity. One source shows a rise of individual hen activity from an average of 151 eggs per year in 1945 to 231 eggs in 1974. How do you get a hen to work 50% harder? Simple, says Science.

Methods for increasing egg production per hen are often cruel or at best they do not take into account that chickens have any affinity to nature. Genetic technology has made it possible to lower the age of sexual maturity and eliminate the winter pause. Chickens in commercial flocks usually live in windowless houses where all light, temperature, and food are automated. Only one human worker is needed to tend 20,000 hens. The typical cage is only a few feet square. Hormones may be given to increase egg production or the hens may be stimulated to produce their own hormones with artificial light. Light penetrating the hen's eye

causes the pituitary gland to secrete the egg-producing hormones. The combination of overcrowding and of light intensity frequently leads to cannibalism and other signs of social stress. In some cases cannibalism is "controlled" by debeaking (clipping the tip of the top half of the beak) the birds. Aside from losing the natural rhythms of night/day and winter/summer in regard to their body functions, commercial-flock chickens may be subjected to force-molting by having feed withheld for several days. This will result in a 2nd or 3rd laying period without the normal molt period in between. It is also common practice for the birds to be sent out for slaughter after their 1st year of laying.

There is a misunderstanding about the relationship of yolk color to nutritive value of the egg. Xanthophyll, which causes the deep yolk color, has no nutritive value itself; however, one of its natural sources is grass and so farm flocks will have seasonal changes in yolk color, while commercial flocks have such factors regulated artificially. Farm flocks lead a more natural life, getting sunlight and vitamins outdoors (in conjunction with the natural xanthophyll in their food), and they produce at a less hectic pace. It is actually the albumen, or white part of the egg, which suffers loss of nutritive quality when egg production is high, as in commercial flocks. Furthermore, the use of insecticides and other drugs in commercial flocks causes residue in both the eggs and body tissues of these chickens. Organic eggs—typically farm eggs—contain no pesticides.

Other claims are that fertile eggs have higher nutritive value than nonfertile ones and that cooked eggs are more digestible than raw. In fact, raw egg white contains a small amount of a toxic protein called avidin, which is inactivated by heat. The yolk comprises less than 1/3 of the egg but contains most of the calories, fat, iron, vitamin A, thiamine, calcium, and half of the protein and riboflavin. Studies by Everson and Souders (1957) and Hanning (1958) on the B vitamins showed that scrambled eggs had 20% less riboflavin than hard-boiled eggs but that neither method of preparation affected the available thiamine or protein. Studies on cholesterol give conflicting results, saying that while the body needs and can utilize some cholesterol, eggs do tend to raise the amount of cholesterol in the blood. Whether or not this is raised above a desirable level is debatable.

Eggs also have the properties of foaming, coagulating, emulsifying, and coloring, which make them useful in cakes, custards, meringues, mayonnaise, and other foods typical of American culinary taste. Among their nonfood uses: eggs and eggshells are used in fertilizers; fertile eggs are used in the production of the vaccines for canine distemper, mumps, and yellow fever; and egg yolks are used to preserve bull semen for artificial insemination.

MEAT

Hunting and gathering are the most primitive sources of food, followed by the development of agriculture and later by the domestication of barnyard animals. The sheep and goat were the 1st to be kept. The pig and cow represented a deeper commitment since they were fed a share of what would otherwise be human food. In many instances, animals were considered more valuable alive than dead, either as beasts of burden or for their milk, wool, etc. The Mongols sustained themselves on long journeys by drinking some of the blood of their horses, without killing the animals. Blood also appears in Irish culinary history, mixed with the milk and butter of that animal into a blood pudding. Jewish dietary law prohibits such a combination, although the taboo is based more on the milk than on the blood, stating that a lamb should not be cooked in its mother's broth. This is an example of a dietary restriction based on moralistic principles while other taboos, such as the prohibition on pork, are based on hygiene. Even today, with meat inspection, trichinosis is still a danger since no superficial inspection can detect its presence. At any rate, our meats today are more dangerous because of adulteration than because of lack of hygienic conditions. A look at the typical life of a ranch animal confirms this.

First, the pastures themselves are full of artificial pesticides and fertilizers which leave residues in the animals' flesh. That is, if they get to the pastures. Most commercial ranches these days force-feed the animals in automated feedlots using electric lights to simulate a 24-hour day. The cost factor favors a urea-carbohydrate mixture over a high protein food. Experiments have been conducted on the efficacy of including food-grade plastic, ground newspapers mixed with molasses, feathers, or treated wood. The animals' diet severely lacks vitamin A, which may be added in synthetic form, although the reason for its addition is generally economic again: It induces weight gain.

For the same reason, drugs are introduced to change the metabolism of the animal. Diethylstilbestrol, variously known as DES or stilbestrol, is a powerful sex hormone which has been known to cause loss of fertility and sex drive in the human male and early sexual maturity in females. Its use has been banned in at least 36 countries, but it is still legal in the U.S. When DES is fed to cattle an artificial marbling effect is found in the meat. In normal meat, marbling is a sign of tenderness, and in fact this fat makes such meat a better buy because extremely lean meat has a higher water content than meat which contains fat. Where marbling is the result of chemicals, however, the consumer is being duped, and at the expense of health as well as pocket.

Antibiotic drugs added to the feed produce hard, white, saturated fats instead of the normal yellow, soft, unsaturated fats and thus lead to heart disease. This tends to occur over an extended period of time rather than from a single large dose. Sodium nitrate and nitrite, which are claimed as antibotulism drugs, are really used more for their cosmetic effect in the preservation of ham, frankfurters, luncheon meats, smoked fish, and also, in many cases, beef. They cause a pinkish color. Nitrite makes the hemoglobin of our blood unable to perform its function of carrying oxygen and so it is toxic. Accidental human poisonings are known. Infants are even more susceptible to nitrites than are adults; yet many baby food manufacturers including Gerber, Beech-Nut, and Swift add nitrites to their baby foods containing meat. Worse yet, nitrites combine with other chemicals to form cancer-producing substances. In the past we could look for redness in meat as a sign of freshness but today it could be the result of chemicals.

Although it should take 3 or 4 years to produce cattle for food, modern methods make it possible to get young beef animals to markets within 12 to 18 months. Considering the unnatural lives of these animals, they can hardly be considered a good food source, but cattle ranchers find the $90-million-a-year profit accountable to drugs nourishing enough. While DES has been banned, other drugs are still acceptable from a legal, if not a health, standpoint. Tranquilizers are used to improve the appetites of the force-fed animals or to activate the hypothalamus, which controls milk production. Most beef is bred by artificial insemination and there are many experiments, reminiscent of Nazi Germany, which suggest transplanting fetuses or giving hormones to induce multiple births from the best cows. Professional foot-trimmers are used to shorten the animals' toes since they must have very restricted movements. Milk-fed veal used to be the best veal to buy but today many of these animals are kept in a state of anemia to produce the whiter flesh. Most hogs have ulcer conditions due to the processed garbage they are fed and sheep are defleeced with chemicals that interrupt cell growth.

To save the several weeks that slaughtered beef should be refrigerated and aged, processors prefer to have the animals injected with enzymes prior to slaughter to speed up aging. The enzymes from pineapple or papaya are not dangerous to humans but the overall effect is fraudulent since poor quality can be masked with such artificial tenderizing. Also, to retain artificially the redness of fresh meat, there is a practice of injecting sodium pentobarbital, an anesthetic, just prior to slaughter to delay the color changes in the muscles and thus keep them red. Perhaps a lighter shade would be preferable to this practice.

Vegetarians may avoid some of the risks of today's meat eater but they must be sure that they are getting not only sufficient protein but also vitamin B_{12}, which is supplied mostly by animal products such as eggs and cheese (and, of course, meat). Deficiencies lead to sore mouth and tongue, nervousness, neuritis, menstrual disturbances, and back pain. If in addition there is a lack of folic acid, anemia will result. However, since green vegetables supply folic acid, this is not usually the vegetarian's dilemma.

Fish present less of an adulteration problem and are a good protein source. But the pollution of oceans, lakes, and rivers makes it difficult to get pure food from these sources. Even so, things are not so bad today as they have been historically. In the Middle Ages in Europe, all street-cleaning was performed by washing everything into the nearest river.

Cooked-food counters, in existence since ancient times, have been another source of sanitary hazards. The Black Plague was largely the result of the open-air cooked-food establishments where rats bred and left their fleas and lice behind. In New York City in recent years, public television has been used to list names of restaurants with dirty kitchens. At the other extreme, Americans patronize institutional places which are totally automated.

The McDonald's hamburger chain spends about $50 million a year on advertising alone to convince Americans that they should indulge, if you can call it that, at the "golden arches." The hamburger is one of the standard items of the typical American meal purchased at such places, and it can contain almost anything. Often sodium sulfite, which destroys vitamin B, has been added to mask the smell of spoiled meat. Other cultures have also figured out palatable ways of masking undesired tastes, such as the preparation of curries in India, which originally were intended as antispoilage preparations. Today we are more likely to find that our meats are getting spoiled intentionally and that we are paying for it. Frankfurters often contain cochineal, a dye from insect scales, which produces a red color but also carries the dangerous salmonella. Worn-out pullets which are at the end of their artificial egg-laying days may be thrown into franks too. We can thank the Industrial Revolution for the railroads, canning, and preservation techniques that have led to the large-scale transportation of meat products across great distances; we should be aware that some of these advances are no blessing at all.

—P.S.

For further reading: The most authoritative books about the U.S. food industry are those distributed by Ari Publishing Co., Inc., P. O. Box 831, Westport, Conn. 06880.

"Behold, I Have Given You Every Herb Bearing Seed . . ." —Genesis 1:29

Fruits of the Earth

Apple

Afghanistan is usually credited as originating this fruit, and wild apple forests still exist there. The U.S. and France are the largest producers. Other big producers are Germany, Switzerland, Italy, and the Balkan countries. Of the U.S. crop, more than ½ is used as fresh fruit. Of the world's production ¼ goes for cider.

Two people who were instrumental in spreading apple trees in the U.S. are Jonathan Chapman, known as Johnny Appleseed, who traveled through the Midwest preaching and planting apple seeds, and Henderson Lewelling, a man who gets little mention. Lewelling is given credit for bringing grafted apple trees (as well as pear, quince, plum, and cherry trees) to Oregon from Iowa. A story is told that Lewelling sold his 1st crop of 100 apples to prospectors for $5 each, around the time of the Gold Rush. John McIntosh of Canada found the apple that bears his name.

Apple varieties that ripen during late summer are not as good for storing as the ones that ripen in late fall, which can be stored up to 9 months at temperatures slightly above freezing. Commercially, they are refrigerated with carbon dioxide added to the atmosphere to retard the natural oxidation process. Apples are also subject to spraying and waxing at harvest time. Apples that are particularly bright red and appear shiny may have been dyed and these are best peeled before eating.

Apples can be eaten raw or cooked, depending on the variety. Tart and thick-skinned varieties are better for baking.

Apricot

The "golden seed of the sun," apricots are cultivated in all of Central and Southeast Asia and in parts of southern Europe and North Africa. The Spanish missionaries brought them to California early in the 18th century and now they are also grown in Idaho, Washington, Colorado, and Utah. Spain is the world's leader in apricot production, followed by the U.S., France, Italy, Yugoslavia, Iran, and Syria.

They are ripe when they are soft and golden orange. They contain much vitamin A and potassium, and they have a high natural-sugar content. Dried apricots are an excellent source of iron, but only the unsulfured variety. The sulfur dioxide used in the process of commercial drying makes the apricot appear bright, but destroys most of the food value. Apricot kernels are eaten around the world to maintain health and it is said that they prevent cancer; however, they can be toxic if eaten in large quantities.

Avocado

Heavily cultivated in the U.S., South Africa, and Mexico. Chile, Brazil, and Australia are other big growers. Most of the U.S. crop is grown in southern Florida, Hawaii, and California. Avocados may be purchased unripe and allowed to mature. A recommended method of testing for ripeness is to place the avocado in the palm of the hand and squeeze gently. If it feels soft under the skin, it is ripe. The skin color varies with variety—some are green, others are black. Avoid soft-skinned green varieties that are turning black or have black spots. These are overripe.

Avocados provide thiamine, riboflavin, and vitamin A. They are delicious by themselves, mixed with salads, or added to cooked dishes. Try "guacamole," a Mexican recipe that blends mashed avocado with onions, tomatoes, garlic, and sometimes lemon juice (will keep it from darkening).

Banana

Native to tropical southern Asia, it was 1st established in the western hemisphere in Hispaniola, appearing in the U.S. markets in the 19th century. Chief sources of today's production are Central America, northern South America, South Africa, and the islands of the Caribbean. The U.S. is the largest importer (Americans eat an average of 18 lbs. per person a year, more than any other fresh or processed fruit). Forty percent of the people prefer green-tipped bananas, 32% prefer fully yellow bananas, 17% green but yellowing, 7% fully ripened (when there is no trace of green,

and brown spots have begun to appear), and 4% green to greenish fruit for cooking.

Ripe bananas (1% starch and 21% sugar) are easier to digest than green (22% starch and 1% sugar). Ripe, they are richer in vitamins, have a high content of ash, are low in protein and fat, and are a good source of potassium and other minerals. Bananas are not allowed to ripen fully on the plant. Bananas are often gassed in order to turn the green skin yellow to make them attractive to the consumers, when in fact, they are not ripe or fit for easy digestion. Bananas are delicious fried in butter with nuts. Plantains, related to bananas, are eaten only when cooked.

Berries

Blackberry. It is abundant in eastern North America and along the Pacific coast. The U.S. is the only place where blackberries are cultivated as a crop (about 10,000 acres). They are a good source of iron and vitamin C. In one of the battles of the Civil War, a truce was declared so that men suffering from intestinal complaints could forage openly for blackberries around the battlegrounds. *Blackberry Cordial:* Boil for 10 minutes in a pint of hot water a cupful of ripe berries, 2 cups honey, 2 or 3 cloves, and 2 sticks of cinnamon. Let cool, stir, and strain. To the liquid, add an equal amount of port wine. Dose: 1 tablespoonful in warm water as needed for diarrhea.

Blueberry. Also called "bilberry." Most of the several species in North America are gathered in large quantities in the wild. In the U.S. they are primarily cultivated in New Jersey, southwestern Michigan, and eastern North Carolina (about 20,000 acres). Elizabeth White is given credit for "taming" the blueberry. She used to offer prizes for the largest wild blueberries. The Dept. of Agriculture got interested and started crossbreeding the winners in 1909. Blueberries provide a good source of iron. Berries should be washed just before using.

Cranberry. Found in the temperate boglands of northern North America, Asia, and northern and central Europe. In the U.S. more than half of the crop is grown in Massachusetts, around Cape Cod. They are also grown in New Jersey, Wisconsin, and near the coast of Washington and Oregon. They were originally called "craneberries" because they were so popular with the cranes. They are recommended as a diuretic and the Indians used cranberries as an antidote for blood poisoning. They also cooked them with honey or maple sugar and served them with their favorite dishes.

Mulberry. About 12 or 15 varieties are native to temperate Asia and North America. Mulberry trees line the streets of many American cities including Austin, Tex., and Salt Lake City, U. The leaves of the white mulberry are fed to the silkworm in China. A very sweet delicious berry when ripe.

Raspberry. Cultivated in England, Scotland, and the U.S. (about 20,000 acres). Most of the U.S. production is on the East Coast and in Washington and Oregon. Raspberries contain vitamin C and iron. The leaves are a popular tea for menstrual cramps. *Raspberry Mousse:* 1 cup raspberries, 1 cup cream, ⅓ cup raw honey, 2 tsp. vanilla, pinch salt, 2 egg whites, stiffly beaten. Crush raspberries, whip cream, add honey, vanilla, and salt, and fold in stiffly beaten egg whites. Turn into freezer tray of refrigerator and freeze until firm, about 1 hour.

Strawberry. The U.S. leads in world production, followed by Poland, Yugoslavia, East Germany, and Italy. Strawberries are easy to grow. Spraying is not as necessary as some of the commercial growers would like us to believe. They are rich in vitamin C and provide iron and other minerals. They are said to be good for gout and scurvy.

Breadfruit

This fruit is a staple in the Pacific islands. It has a high amount of carbohydrates and is a good source of thiamine, niacin, and vitamin C. When baked, the flavor and texture are said to resemble those of potatoes. They are cooked and served with butter or eaten raw. In the South Seas, cloth is made from the tree's fibrous inner bark, the wood is used for canoes and furniture, and glue is made from the milky juice.

Cactus

The tuna or prickly cactus is grown throughout Mexico, Central America, South America, and in the southwestern States of the U.S. It is a fair source of vitamin C, phosphorus, and magnesium and is said to be a good source of organic insulin. Planting is done by breaking off a joint, letting it dry for a week, then planting it. The spines are removed by burning or agile peeling. Chilling before eating is said to enhance its flavor.

Cherry

The U.S. is the leading cherry producer, but they are a major crop in Western Europe, with West Germany, Italy, and Switzerland the leaders. Turkey, Japan, Argentina, Chile, Australia, and Canada also grow large quantities. The U.S.S.R. leads in tart cherry production with the U.S. next. Over half of the sour cherry production is used for canning and freezing. Sweet cherries are consumed fresh or canned. The fruit provides vitamin A and small amounts of calcium and phosphorus.

Coconut

Most of the world's production is on small plantations. The Philippines and Indonesia lead in producing copra (white meat of the coconut that has been dried), the most important export of the Southwest Pacific. The name comes from the Portuguese *coco* meaning grimace, because it resembles a grinning face. The coconut is a staple in many tropical areas and the tree is so useful it has inspired this South Sea proverb: "He who plants a coconut tree plants food and drink, vessels and clothing, a habitation for himself and a heritage for his children." The coconut meat is eaten raw or dried; the oil is made into soap and used for cooking. The sap of the tree is fermented to make an alcoholic beverage, the fiber from the husk of the fruit makes rope and twine, and various parts of the tree are used for building houses. Pick a coconut with lots of liquid in it when you shake it. To drink the juice, puncture one of the indented spots on the shell. To separate the meat from the shell, tap the coconut with a hammer.

Currant

Great Britain grows more black currants than any other country. In the U.S. they grow best around the Great Lakes, the Hudson River Valley, and the Rocky Mountains. The culture of the black currant has been prohibited in the northwestern U.S. because it is the host for a disease called blister rust that is destructive to the white pine. The red, white, and black varieties are eaten fresh or jellied. They contain vitamin C, calcium, phosphorus, and iron. For sore throat: Simmer, don't boil, for 10 minutes, 2 tsp. of fruit in 2 cups water, strain, and gargle, or add honey and swallow.

Date

Iraq leads in world production and Algeria and Tunisia are other large producers. In the U.S. dates are grown in Southern California and Arizona. A yearly festival is held in Indio, Calif., exhibiting the many varieties. They provide lots of sugar and minerals, are laxative and helpful to weak stomachs. For a nutritious drink, try heating 4 or 5 pitted dates slowly in a pan with a glassful of milk, until the milk becomes tan, then add vanilla.

Durian

Grown in the Philippines, Malaysia, and southern Thailand, they are seldom exported. The smell of the durian has been described as "sewagelike" or like that of a "rotten onion." According to Alfred Russell Wallace, "It has a rich butterlike custard highly flavored with almonds, but intermingled with wafts of flavor that call to mind cream cheese, onion sauce, brown sherry, and other incongruities."

Fig

Called "the poor man's food" in the Mediterranean countries. Chief producers are Italy, Portugal, Spain, Turkey, Greece, and Algeria. Smaller producers are the U.S., Mexico, Brazil, Peru, Argentina, and Australia. In the U.S. the main production is in the central valleys of California. They have a laxative effect, provide calcium and phosphorus, and dried they are high in iron. When fresh, figs should be eaten very soft; when dried they should be purchased unsulfured. Try eating a dried fig with an almond in the middle.

Grape

France, Italy, and Spain are the biggest grape producers. In the U.S. they are largely grown in California. Grapes are consumed fresh, dried for raisins, or used for wines and alcoholic distillates. They contain glucose, fructose, and some calcium, phosphorus, and vitamin A. In Europe, the "grape cure" is much renowned. It involves a diet of purely grapes or grape juice for days or weeks in order to cure chronic diseases, eliminate poisons, and cleanse the system.

Raisins. California is the largest producer of raisins; Australia ranks 2nd. Fresno County exceeds Spain in output. In Spain grapes are dried on the vine, but in California they are dipped in lye, exposed to fumes of sulfur, and dried in a tunnel dehydrator or put on trays and left in the sun for 3 to 4 hours. Then they are dried for several weeks in the shade. When dried naturally, they are high in iron and other minerals.

Grapefruit

About 90% of the world's production is in the U.S.; Florida, California, Texas, and Arizona are the largest growers. Israel, Jordan, and Brazil are also large producers. Grapefruit contains vitamin C and the pink varieties also have vitamin A. The fruit is used as an appetizer, in fruit salads, desserts, and in reducing diets. The skin and seeds are used for medicinal purposes. Buy them thick-skinned and heavy.

Guava

Grown in southern Florida and California. There are yellow and red varieties, which can be eaten fresh, or as jelly, syrup, or pudding. They are rich in vitamins A and C.

Kiwi or Chinese Gooseberry

Imported from New Zealand to the U.S.,

although some are grown in California. They contain vitamin C and should be eaten when somewhat soft.

Kumquat

Widely grown in China and cultivated throughout the subtropics as well as Southern California and Florida. The Chinese use them as a candied fruit. They are eaten fresh (the skin is also edible), preserved, or made into jams. Branches are used as Christmas decorations. Kumquats are rich in vitamin A.

Lemon

The U.S. and Italy are the chief producers of lemons, followed by Spain, Greece, Turkey, and Argentina. California, Florida, and Arizona are the largest growers in the U.S. By-products of lemons are citric acid, used in beverage manufacturing, citrate of lime, lemon oil, and pectin, which is used for making jellies and for the treatment of intestinal disorders. In Sicily, lemon oil is used in perfumes, soap, and flavoring extracts. They have a high vitamin C content. Lemons are harsh on the teeth so rinse the mouth after consumption. Buy lemons that are heavy for their size.

Lime

Mexico is the largest lime producer, followed by Egypt and the U.S. The West Indies are chief producers of lime oil. Limes contain vitamin C and have been used to prevent scurvy.

Loquat

Mostly grown in the subtropical and Mediterranean regions of China, Japan, Europe, and the U.S. (especially California). Eaten fresh or made into jam.

Mango

Grown in tropical regions such as the West Indies, Mexico, India (produces 7½ million tons a year), and the U.S. (Florida and Hawaii). They are rich in vitamins A, C, and D. Unripe, they are used for mango chutney. When ripe, mangoes are soft and *very* juicy; it has been said that the only place to eat one is in the bathtub. An overripe mango tastes like turpentine.

Melons

Native to tropical Africa, they are presently grown all over the U.S. and South America. Melons are refreshing when eaten in hot weather.

Cantaloupe or *Muskmelon.* A ripe cantaloupe has a coarse and prominent netting on the outside and a smooth stem end. It should smell sweet and yield gently to finger pressure.

Honeydew. Should be yellowish-cream in color and have a sweet smell. If it is smooth and hard, shiny, or rind is dead white or has a greenish tinge, it is not ripe.

Watermelon. A ripe watermelon sounds hollow when tapped. Look for a slightly yellowish or amber-colored underside.

Nectarine

Grown in California and Oregon. Said John Keats in 1819, "Talking of Pleasure, this moment I was writing with one hand, and with the other holding to my Mouth, a Nectarine—good God how fine. It went down soft, pulpy, slushy, oozy. . . ." They are soft and brighter in color than the peach and without fuzz. They contain lots of vitamin A. They are also eaten dried.

Olive

There are olive trees in Palestine which probably date back to the beginning of the Christian era and it was an olive branch that Noah's dove brought back to the Ark. Leading olive-producing nations of the world are those which border the Mediterranean. Fresh unprocessed olives are inedible because of their extreme bitterness. Olives are grown mainly for the production of olive oil, the highest grade of oil being called virgin, sublime, or 1st-expressed oil. This is the oil that comes out of the pulp of an olive that has been picked just after it has ripened but before it turns black. Olive oil is one of the most digestible of the edible fats.

Orange

Leading orange-producing countries are the U.S., Israel, Morocco, Spain, South Africa, Italy, Japan, India, Mexico, Brazil, and Argentina. Oranges are rich in vitamin C and provide some vitamin A. Oranges should be picked when ripe because they do not ripen or improve in quality after being picked. Unfortunately, oranges are often subjected to serious adulteration in their commercial production.

A relatively extreme example of the adulteration of oranges is described by citrus grower L. P. DeWolf in *Consumer Beware* by Beatrice Trum Hunter: "Commercial oranges are picked green. No color can be added to the green-skinned orange. First it has to be 'degreened.' This is done in what is known as the 'coloring room,' where it is shut up airtight and doused with a gas (which can cause asphyxiation). This gas destroys or removes the chlorophyll from the rind and leaves it, according to the degree of greenness, all the way from a sickly lemon color to almost white. I have seen them come out of the coloring room looking almost like peeled potatoes. While it is being gassed, the fruit is subject to artificial heat and is sometimes held in this room for 3 or 4 days. It impairs the flavor and has a tendency to hasten its deterioration and decay. After coming out of the coloring room, the fruit is washed and run through the 'color-added' machine. The color is added by passing the fruit through a vat of hot dye or else spraying it on hot while the fruit is subjected to steam heat."

Unripe oranges are not only bad-tasting but may cause serious gastric distress and digestive problems. Certain varieties of oranges, because of the climate in which they are grown, are ripe when they are green, so do not be afraid to buy a green orange, in lieu of a shiny, dyed one. Buy oranges that are firm and heavy for their size—these are the most juicy. Artificial orange drinks do not contain the nutrition found in fresh orange juice. Oranges should not be eaten by people with stomach ulcers, and because of the citric acid content, they are hard on the teeth.

Papaya

Cultivated throughout the tropical world and the warmest parts of the subtropics. The U.S. supply comes from Florida, Texas, Mexico, Hawaii, and Puerto Rico. The papaya plant produces a milky juice containing an enzyme called papain, which is noted for its meat-tenderizing qualities. It is also present in the fruit. The fruit juice is used in the preparation of various remedies for indigestion. Chester D. French, in his book *Papaya Melon of Health* (Exposition Press) tells this story:

Many years ago while cruising the jungle of Guatemala, I was seized with a severe attack of indigestion after eating ripe bananas from a naturally fallen stem of the golden fruit. I was warned by my Guatemalan friends against eating them once they had ripened on the stem of a live plant. But they were so appetizing-looking, and I was hungry. In a few minutes I was in the stages of an acute attack of indigestion. Riding a horse was a misery. I could not eat other food and suffered the whole night. Early in the morning the servant girl in a friend's house woke me with a tray of coffee and cakes. I sent her away. Food was impossible. She said to me, "One little minute, señor, and I will return with something you should eat." Presently she was back with a slice of a golden melon. "Eat of this, señor. It is a gift of the Gods to the hombre with the sad stomach," she recommended.

Believe it or not! After having eaten of this melon, my distress left me in 15 minutes. I arose and consumed a large breakfast. That was the Papaya Melon. From that day forward I could not forget such a wonderful experience. I began an intensive study of this wonderful fruit.

The papaya is also available in pulp form.

Passion Fruit and Purple Granadilla

Grows in Florida, Australia, and Hawaii and is eaten fresh, juiced, or as jam. When cut lengthwise, the pits form the shape of a cross.

Peach

The U.S. and Italy produce about half of the world's crop. In the U.S., the peach is grown in Georgia, California, Texas, Arkansas, Oklahoma, and 30 other states. Tree-ripened peaches are by far the best. They should be yellowish, soft, and fragrant; fruit picked green won't ripen. They contain vitamin A. Peaches are canned and dried. Dried, they are usually treated with sulfur dioxide, which destroys their nutritional value.

Pear

Italy is the leading producer. The U.S., China, Japan, Turkey, Argentina, Australia, and South Africa are also large producers. Many of the pear trees in Europe are in home gardens. In the U.S., Canada, and Australia, half of the commercial crop is used for canning. In France, Germany, and Switzerland large portions of their production is made into a fermented drink called "perry." A ripe pear should be soft and juicy. Unlike most fruit, pears are successfully ripened indoors. Pears are also dried.

Persimmon or Date-Plum

The oriental persimmon, called kaki, is an important and extensively grown fruit in China and Japan. It is also grown in France, Louisiana, Texas, and California. The fruit tends to be highly astringent until soft. Upon ripening it is rich in flavor and is a good source of vitamins A and C. The fruit is dried, and used in preserves, cakes, and pudding.

Pineapple

The Hawaiian Islands produce about half of the world's fresh pineapples and 60% of the world's total supply of canned pineapple products (all of the U.S. supply). Brazil, Mexico, the Philippines, Cuba, and Taiwan are other large producers. Pineapples canned in Australia, Malaysia, and South Africa are generally shipped to Great Britain. The South American and Mexican production is sold mainly to European countries.

A ripe pineapple should be yellow to golden orange, a bit soft, have a short tuft of leaves, and make a solid sound when tapped. Pineapples won't ripen or sweeten with age. A. L. Pitkanen, in his book *Tropical Fruits* (Lemon Grove, Calif., R. Prevost, 1967) says, "Only those who have traveled in the tropics know what a fresh pineapple tastes like as it comes fully ripened from the plant, very different than the usual canned pineapple which is processed not quite fully ripened."

Plum/Prune

Yugoslavia is the leading plum tree producer. Germany and the U.S. are next. California, Oregon, Idaho, and Washington are the leading plum-producing States. Šljivovica, a liqueur made from plums, is a chief product in Yugoslavia. In the U.S. it is prunes, California producing the largest amount. Prunes are made by breaking the skin of the plums and then placing the fruit in the sun to dry. This is the best way to keep plums, although they can be canned or made into preserves. They contain a high amount of potassium, some vitamin A, iron, and calcium.

Pomegranate

The plant grows wild in western Asia and northwestern India. It is cultivated in gardens from the warmer parts of the U.S. south to Chile. In Iran the pulp is made into wine. Mohammed counseled: "Eat the pomegranate for it purges the system of hatred and envy."

Rhubarb

It grows best in the cooler parts of the Temperate Zones. The fleshy, tart, and highly acid leafstalks can be eaten raw, cooked in pies, made into preserves, or used as a base for wine and aperitifs. In certain areas of the Himalayas, the leaves, which are said to contain a toxic substance, are cooked and eaten. The root has been used in China and Tibet as a cathartic. In England, the rhubarb has also been used medicinally. Persons with arthritis or rheumatism should not eat rhubarb. It should be used when the stalks are firm and crisp.

Sapodilla

Sapodilla trees grow wild in the forests of southern Mexico and northern Central Amer-

Because he felt the 4 different languages used in his native Warsaw caused human misunderstandings, Ludwig Zamenhof invented a common language in 1887. He called it Esperanto. Today, 8 million people write and speak it. (See: Chap. 14) *Stuart Kittredge.*

Taking up the challenge to publish a newspaper as Jesus Christ might have published it—playing up virtue and goodwill, playing down crime and vice—Dr. Charles Sheldon, clergyman and author of the great best seller *In His Steps*, edited the Topeka, Kans., *Capital* for 5 days in 1900. This is the front page of the 1st issue. Circulation soared from 11,223 to 362,684 copies. (See: Chap. 15)

Francisco de Goya y Lucientes, the Spanish artist, painted a nude of the Duchess of Alba. When her husband heard of the scandalous oil, he rushed to Goya's studio to avenge his honor. He found only a decently draped picture of his wife, which Goya had painted overnight. Goya died in France in 1828. (See: Chap. 16) *Biblioteca Nacional, Madrid.*

The Topeka Daily Capital.

SHELDON EDITION.　　　SHELDON EDITION.

VOL. XXII.　　　TOPEKA, KAN., TUESDAY, MARCH 13, 1900.　　　NO. 61.

Charles L. Dodgson, cleric and mathematician, published the classic *Alice's Adventures in Wonderland* in 1865 under the pen name of Lewis Carroll. A lifelong bachelor, he enjoyed a platonic love for actress Ellen Terry. (See: Chap. 16) *Gernsheim Collection, University of Texas.*

Leo Tolstoi, author of *War and Peace* and *Anna Karenina*, on his estate at Vasnaya Polyana, Russia, in 1901. Photograph was taken by American lecturer Burton Holmes, who coined the word "travelogue." The wealthy Tolstoi lived as a peasant before his death in 1910. (See: Chap. 16) *Burton Holmes, Inc.*

The French actress Sarah Bernhardt, whom Oscar Wilde called "the divine Sarah," had a career that spanned 60 years. From her stage hits, including *La Dame aux camelias* and *L'Aiglon*, she earned $25 million. She had over 1,000 lovers. Even after she had a leg amputated in 1915, she continued her stage career (See: Chap. 16) *Library of Congress.*

Agatha Christie, 84 years old in 1975, is one of the most widely read authors on earth. Her mysteries, among them *The Murder of Roger Ackroyd*, have sold over 300 million copies. Next to Shakespeare, she is the 2nd most-translated English author. (See: Chap. 16) *Paul Popper Ltd.*

The fun-loving and generous millionaire opera singer Enrico Caruso made his debut at the Metropolitan Opera House, in New York City, in 1903. In 18 years at the Met, he performed in 36 roles, singing in 4 languages. (See: Chap. 16) *Brown Brothers.*

Iowan Grant Wood's best-known painting is *American Gothic*, which he completed in 1930 and sold to the Chicago Art Institute for $300. Wood posed his sister and her dentist friend against a Gothic-style house he had discovered. He later learned this house was a brothel. (See: Chap. 16) *Art Institute of Chicago.*

Thomas A. Edison, in 1888, listening to his improved wax-cylinder phonograph, after 72 hours of continuous work on the mechanism. The most prolific successful inventor of all time, Edison was credited with 1,300 U.S. and foreign patents. (See: Chap. 17) *Edison National Historic Site.*

Except for the Great Wall of China, the Great Pyramid of Giza in Egypt is the largest single ancient structure. Constructed in 2580 B.C. by 4,000-man shifts of free citizens under the Pharaoh Khufu, it consisted of more than 2 million limestone blocks, some weighing 2½ tons. Photograph taken in 1897. (See: Chap. 17) *Burton Holmes, Inc.*

Man gets wings. The 1st U.S. airplane flight at Kitty Hawk, N.C., on December 17, 1903, flown by the brothers Orville and Wilbur Wright. The maiden flight lasted 12 seconds. (See: Chap. 17) *Mrs. Harold Miller, Aviation Hall of Fame.*

Some of the 447,570 rabbits used annually for scientific experimentation in the U.S. (See: Chap. 17) *Eli Lilly Co.*

After her mother's death in 1905, Anna Jarvis devoted herself to establishing Mother's Day, which became an official holiday in 1914. After mismanaging a $700,000 estate, Miss Jarvis died a charity case in a Pennsylvania sanitarium at the age of 84. (See: Chap. 18) *U.P.I.*

ica and they are cultivated in Florida and the West Indies. The fruit is small, round, and brown with a very sweet, yellow pulp. It has "the sweet perfumes of honey, jasmine, and lily-of-the-valley," writes Michel Étienne Descourtilz, a French botanist. The sap from the tree furnishes chicle, from which chewing gum is made.

Tamarind

Native of tropical Africa, the tamarind is now grown in Southern California, Florida, and Hawaii. The pulp is added to chutneys and curries. In the Orient the fruit is used in beverages and medicines.

Tangerine or Mandarin Orange

On the morning of the 1st frost,
The gardener plucks and presents it;
Its perfume extends to all the seats of the guest;
Spurts upon the people.

China, 5th century

The U.S., Brazil, Spain, Italy, Mexico, and Japan are the main producers of tangerines. Much of the crop grown in the U.S. is in Florida. They are rich in vitamin C. They should be purchased when heavy and deep orange. Try a tangerine with sour cream.

—A.W. & F.C.

Vegetables

Artichoke

Extensively cultivated in France, Belgium, and the Mediterranean countries, in the U.S. it grows predominantly in California (Castroville is the "artichoke heart of the world") and the South. In 15th-century Italy, the artichoke was thought to be an aphrodisiac, and for this reason it has been referred to as "dear to Venus." Artichokes are eaten steamed, boiled, stuffed, and even raw. The heart is the artichoke's most succulent feature, and can be purchased canned. To cook whole artichokes, steam them in boiling water 20 to 30 minutes. They are especially valuable for their production of levulose sugars which can be eaten by persons with diabetes. Buy your artichokes with compact green heads and tightly closed leaves. A fresh artichoke will squeak when rubbed against another one.

Asparagus

Grown extensively in France, Italy, and the U.S. Most of the U.S. production occurs in California, New Jersey, Washington, and Massachusetts. Asparagus was 1st used as a medicine, and not as a food until the 17th century. Asparagus tips are the tenderest part. Wild as-

paragus is a much loved delicacy, considered by many to be tastier than the cultivated varieties. To cook, stand them on end and steam until just tender; serve them with lemon butter or mayonnaise. Mushy asparagus is a culinary crime, and the Emperor Augustus was said to have ordered executions to be carried out "quicker than you can cook asparagus." Buy the firm, straight, thinner stalks with tightly closed tips. Asparagus contains vitamins A, C, and B, and lots of potassium. When harvesting asparagus, it is important that the knife be thrust into the ground as close to vertical as possible to avoid injuring the young shoots which are hidden in the soil.

Beet

Major beet producers are the U.S.S.R., the U.S., France, Poland, West and East Germany, Czechoslovakia, and the United Kingdom. In the U.S., they are grown commercially in 31 States. Beet greens are a good source of riboflavin, iron, and vitamins A and C. Beets can be boiled, baked, grated and added to salads, or pickled. They can also be made into a delightful borsch, a soup which is native to Russia and Poland and can be eaten hot or cold with sour cream on top. Besides the red beet, there is a yellow variety; and the beet's cousin, the white sugar beet, is used widely in the production of sugar. When buying beets, buy young, firm, smooth roots. Beet greens are delicious steamed and eaten with butter and lemon juice.

Broccoli

Grown largely in California, Arizona, New Jersey, New York, and Oregon, it contains a goodly amount of minerals and vitamins A, B, and C, and is said to be good for the digestion. A fresh head of broccoli has dark green flower clusters and tightly closed buds. To prepare it, steam whole for 8 to 10 minutes (slit the stem for faster cooking), or cut into pieces and steam for a shorter time; but be sure not to overcook it, or it will be a soggy mess. It is delicious with mayonnaise, cheese sauce, sour cream, or just butter. In Great Britain, the term broccoli refers to the cauliflower.

Brussels Sprouts

A variety of cabbage, it has been cultivated in Brussels, Belgium, since the 13th century. Much of the U.S. crop comes from northern California. It is a good source of vitamins A and C. Buy green, firm sprouts, and keep them refrigerated as they are highly perishable. Cook them briefly in a small amount of boiling water (*do not* overcook to a mush!), and serve with butter or cheese sauce. It is said that adding a walnut to the cooking pot of sprouts will cut the cabbage odor. They can also be eaten chopped raw in salads.

Cabbage

One of the most common garden vegetables in Europe, Asia, and the U.S. (mostly produced in Florida, California, Texas, New York, and Wisconsin), there are both red and green varieties. Early sailors ate cabbage to prevent scurvy, although they did not know how it did this. It has a high vitamin C content plus some vitamin A, B_1, and B_2, as well as calcium and cellulose. The latter is valuable as a laxative. Two of the most popular cabbage dishes are cole slaw and sauerkraut. Sauerkraut is white cabbage shredded and fermented in salt brine, a dish which was known to the Chinese thousands of years ago. Other favorites are sweet-and-sour cabbage, and rice dishes wrapped in cabbage leaves. Cabbage should be selected when young, crisp, and bright, the heads being heavy. It can be cooked either sliced or shredded, by steaming for about 5 minutes.

Cardoon

A tall-growing, thistlelike plant, closely allied to the artichoke. The stalk and the midrib of the young leaves are delicious cooked in boiling water and served with butter, or added to salads.

Carrot

Within the U.S. it is chiefly grown in California, Texas, and Arizona. Carrots and their juice have a very high vitamin A content and are especially good for the eyes. Buy young, firm, crisp carrots and experiment with them in your cooking—try them in soup, salad, and stew; or fried, baked, and marinated—and don't forget carrot cake!

Cauliflower

"Cauliflower is cabbage with a college education," said Mark Twain about this member of the cabbage family. These natives of Europe and West Asia are now grown in the U.S., chiefly produced in California and New York. Buy compact white heads and steam them for 4 to 10 minutes. Serve with butter or cheese sauce.

Celeriac

This large, turniplike root is a variant of celery, and is more popular in Europe than in the U.S. It is boiled and eaten alone, or served cold with oil and vinegar, or added to soups. Its flavor has been described as "celery plus celery."

Celery

Wild celery grows in swampy places in Europe and Asia. In the U.S. it is cultivated chiefly in California, Florida, and Michigan. Celery is a lot more versatile than it seems, and since it is very low in calories, many might do well to experiment with it more. To glean its full food value, it is best eaten raw. Try spreading peanut butter or cream cheese on a celery stalk for a snack. Be sure to eat the leaves too, or dry them and use them for seasoning.

Chard

Swiss chard (or seakale beet) refers to the stems and leaves of a white-rooted member of the beet family. It is popular in home gardens because it is easy to grow, but since it is highly perishable, it is difficult to ship to distant markets. The succulent stems and leaves can be cooked either separately or together. The leaves, which have a high vitamin A, B, and C content, can be steamed like spinach; and the stems, both the white and the red (ruby chard) varieties, can be cooked like asparagus, and have a nutty flavor.

Chinese Cabbage (Bok-Choi)

Largely used in Oriental cookery, in salads or stir-fried vegetable dishes. Very high vitamin content. Heads should be compact with crisp green leaves.

Collards

The large, strong-flavored leaves withstand the heat and are also raised as a source of winter greens. They are grown mainly in the southern part of the U.S. Like all greens, they are good sources of vitamin A, as well as providing some vitamin C. Collards can be steamed like spinach, and are particularly good when topped with melted cheese. In the South, they are often boiled with salt pork as a regional favorite.

Corn (Maize)

One of the most widely distributed of the world's food plants. The U.S. produces almost half of the world's total, most of it in an area called the corn belt (Iowa, parts of Illinois, Indiana, Ohio, Missouri, Kansas, Nebraska, South Dakota, and Minnesota). Brazil ranks 2nd, followed by the U.S.S.R. and Mexico. Yellow cornmeal is high in magnesium, which is needed for healthy elimination. The oil is also good for the whole body, especially the intestinal tract. Buy corn with a fresh green husk and well-filled kernels; keep refrigerated. Corn will cook in 5 minutes or even less. As soon as corn is picked the sugar starts converting into starch, so the fresher the better. Try eating young corn raw. Raw corn soup garnished with parsley is delicious. Roasted corn is good too. The dishes made from corn comprise a long list—corn chips, fritters, tortillas, corn bread, corn syrup, cornstarch, succotash, and more. The corn husks which cover the ears of corn are used to wrap tamales, and can be used for stuffing mattresses. Corncob meal may be used for cleaning furs, removing oil from metal, and for fertilizer. Cornsilk is used in smoking mixtures. Using corn as the only grain in one's diet can cause pellegra (niacin deficiency). In Mexico this disease is avoided by cooking the corn in lime water, which is a good source of niacin.

Cucumber

Grown in temperate climates all over the world, it grows wild in India. Most of our crop comes from Florida, South Carolina, and Virginia. Cucumbers are usually eaten in salads, and should be peeled because they are often waxed. They can also be baked or boiled, and served with butter. Eaten raw, they possess the enzyme erepsin which has the same powerful protein-digesting properties as the papaya. They contain vitamins C, B_1, and G, and are generally regarded as a cooling food ("cool as a cucumber") when eaten in hot climates. Ripe cucumbers and small green ones are good for pickling.

Dandelion

So often thought of as merely a weed, the dandelion has a long history of use. It grows wild all over Europe, Asia, and North America, and is now being cultivated commercially. The leaves, which have a slightly bitter taste, are very high in iron, as well as containing vitamins A and C. Some people prefer to blanch them before steaming or using them in salads. They are best eaten when young, before the plant blossoms. The root too has its uses, not only for making dandelion coffee, but also as a diuretic. The beautiful golden flowers are used to make dandelion wine, a favorite of country people.

Eggplant

The eggplant, or aubergine, as it is called in Europe, is extensively grown in eastern and southern Asia and in the U.S. Its beautiful purple color, glossy and smooth, is a familiar sight almost year round. What is not so well known is that prior to the 15th century, it was grown mainly as an ornament. People were afraid to eat it, probably because, like the tomato and the potato, it is a relative of the poisonous deadly nightshade. To select, choose a firm, shiny eggplant with a fresh green cap, and if it feels heavy for its size, all the better. If it is not to be used right away, it is better to refrigerate it. A simple and delicious way of preparing eggplant is to cook it with olive oil, and it is probably for that reason that it is extremely popular in the Mediterranean countries, where this oil is heavily used. Eggplant can be baked whole, either plain or stuffed. Many cooks like to salt this vegetable before use, and then press out any moisture. This salting and pressing is thought to cut down on the bitter taste which eggplant sometimes has. One of the most popular and well-known methods of cooking eggplant is à la Parmesan, in which the sautéed slices are layered alternately with a tomato sauce and cheese in an oven-proof dish, and then baked for about 45 minutes in a moderate oven.

Fennel

Grows wild in southern Europe and is widely cultivated throughout the U.S., Great Britain, and temperate Eurasia. Florentine fennel is particularly beloved by Italian cooks. The anise-tasting feathery leaves are a familiar sight in California, where a variety of fennel grows wild. The bulbous leaf stem of Florentine fennel can be eaten raw, like celery, or cooked in a cheese sauce. The licorice-tasting leaves can be chopped and added to salads, or used in fish soups and sauces. The seeds are used as a flavoring in Italian sausages and stuffings. Fennel is available from September to May, and it is the bulb, with a few tendrils of leaves still remaining, which is usually sold. The Greeks believed that it gave strength, courage, and long life to a man. The Romans thought it sharpened the eyesight.

Garlic

Garlic has had many properties attributed to it, and has been both glorified and reviled down through the ages. The Romans gave it to laborers to make them strong, and to soldiers to give them courage. In the Middle Ages, garlic was believed to repel vampires and werewolves, and to ward off the effects of the witch's evil eye. Its antiseptic qualities were discovered early, and eating it was thought to be a good defense against the plague. Crushed and applied to the skin, it cured insect bites and stings, and it is said that a syrup of garlic, taken internally, or as a poultice applied to the chest, helped to cure bronchial complaints. The next time you feel a cold coming on, try chewing a couple of cloves of raw garlic, but be sure to chew some raw parsley afterward—parsley is a wonderful natural breath cleaner. Garlic contains an antibiotic called allium, and also has a reputation for helping to lower the blood pressure. In fact, the list of its uses is endless. Garlic planted around the base of peach trees stops the destruction by peach borers. The bulb of garlic consists of small sections, called cloves, which are each covered by a paper-thin skin. These cloves are peeled and chopped, or pressed, for use in a wide range of dishes. It is difficult to say how much garlic is enough in cooking. Most people would undoubtedly prefer to stick to just one or 2 innocuous cloves added to Italian dishes, casseroles, etc.

Kale

Kale is a hardy plant and has always been popular in northern European countries. In fact, it is said to improve after it has been touched with frost. Among Celtic people, kale is traditionally associated with Halloween, and it is one of the ingredients of colcannon, a dish customarily eaten in Ireland on that day. Kale is a good source of vitamins A and C. The leaves should be crisp and dark bluish-green in color.

Kohlrabi

Kohlrabi is a delightful-tasting vegetable which is sometimes called the "turnip-rooted cabbage." It has a taste somewhere between that of a young turnip and the sweet stalk of cabbage. Kohlrabi is an excellent source of vitamin C, and when grated raw and added to salads, it adds a wonderful freshness. Kohlrabi can also be steamed, baked in its skin, or peeled and sautéed in oil. Boiling, however, destroys the delicate taste.

Leek

The leek is the national emblem of the Welsh; on St. David's Day, all true Welshmen wear a leek to celebrate their victory in battle over the Saxons in 640 A.D. Before that, they also wore a leek to distinguish themselves from their enemies. Leeks look like overgrown green onions, and have a milder, onion taste. They have been cultivated around the Mediterranean for at least 4,000 years. Leeks should be firm and fresh, the green part intensely green, with several inches of white toward the stem end. Leave the delicate roots on until ready to use; they help to keep the leeks fresh. Leeks are famous because of cock-a-leekie soup, the Scottish national soup, but also try them cooked in milk and served with a cheese or hollandaise sauce.

Lettuce

Of the 4 distinct types of lettuce, the most popular in the U.S. is the iceberg or crisphead variety. However, remember that the greener the leaves, the higher the vitamin A and C content. Cos or romaine is a tall, narrow type, with almost furled leaves. Butterhead lettuce is a delicate lettuce which is fairly perishable. A popular type of butterhead is Bibb, whose leaves are edged with red. The 4th type is loose-leaf, with slightly scalloped, curly leaves. All lettuce should be kept in the refrigerator and used as soon as possible. By far the most popular use is in salads, and a tip to remember is that for successful salads, the lettuce *must* be dry. If the salad is tossed while still wet, the dressing cannot adhere to the leaves, and the result is a soggy, wet mess, with all the dressing at the bottom of the bowl, a sight familiar to all of us. Another reason why salads wilt so quickly is that they are tossed with previously prepared dressing. The *oil* should be added *first*, and the salad tossed so that all surfaces are covered completely. Not only does the oil seal off oxygen which can destroy vitamins, but it also prevents salt from drawing the moisture out of the ingredients, which causes wilting immediately, especially of the lettuce leaves. When every single ingredient in the salad bowl is glistening with oil, *then* add the vinegar or lemon juice. In Europe, lettuce is popular in cookery, being braised with green peas, or made into a delicious summer soup.

Mushrooms

There are thousands of varieties of fungi, both edible and poisonous, but the mushroom which we buy today and which is available all year round is a descendant of just a single species, the common field mushroom. In the U.S., Pennsylvania is the mushroom capital. Also available, in dried form, are the big flavorsome black mushrooms from Japan; and for the gourmet, the beautiful yellow chanterelle, the honeycombed morel—and of course the highly prized truffle—are available in cans. When buying, look for the mushrooms that have opened out a little and have their gills showing. The French maintain that mushrooms improve with age (that is, the longer they are allowed to grow), and they prefer them when they have reached the almost completely flat stage, with dark brown gills, asserting that they are more flavorsome this way. Never peel or even wash commercial mushrooms—a wipe with a damp towel is all that is necessary. The versatility of mushrooms in cooking is well known, but have you ever tried a fresh mushroom soup? Unbeatable!

Raw mushrooms are also delicious, especially with a dressing of sour cream.

Mustard

The leaves, with a somewhat strong flavor, are used as greens and the seeds are used for pickling and ground to make the mustard condiment which is so popular. Mustard grows wild in California, sometimes reaching colossal heights and presenting a lovely show of yellow flowers in the spring. Use mustard greens as you would collards or kale, and try a little chopped raw in your salad. Apparently, as far back as the 17th century, a salad wasn't considered a salad in England without mustard!

Okra

Sometimes known as "ladies' fingers," okra was cultivated early in Africa, and found its way to this country via the West Indies, and possibly directly from Africa, along with shiploads of slaves. In the U.S., cultivation is limited to the hot southern States. However, the ridged pods are a familiar sight in our markets all year round. Okra is best-known as an important ingredient in the famous southern gumbos, but is also delicious parboiled and then lightly sautéed, or as fritters. If possible, choose pods under 3" long—they are then more likely to be tender. Okra supplies only a little vitamin A and C, and is correspondingly low in calories. In some countries it is used as a substitute for coffee. In the East, it is popular as a poultice to relieve pain. A perfume called ambrette is made from the musky-odored seeds. The best perfumed seeds are said to come from Martinique.

Onions

Leading onion growers are New York, Colorado, California, Texas, Michigan, and Oregon, but onions are grown in many other States as well. Mexico, Italy, and Spain are also noted for the size and quality of their onions. Varieties grown in the northern U.S. keep longer and are more pungent; the southern onions can be stored for several weeks, but not for months. There are dozens of varieties, ranging from the large yellow Spanish onions to the flat Italian red. The green and the pearl onions are not separate varieties, they are just harvested at different times. The green onions, or scallions, are harvested young when the bulbs are less than half an inch in diameter. The pearl onions are harvested later when they are one inch or bigger in diameter. Choose firm, dry onions, using the milder Bermuda or Italian red onions for salads, and don't forget to use the tops of green onions for additional vitamin A and C. In some parts of the British Isles, a raw onion is still considered a good defense against colds, and a sandwich consisting of bread, butter, and raw onion is not uncommon as a suppertime snack. Onions keep best in dry, well-ventilated storage at about 33° F. An onion placed in a newly painted room will soak up the odors.

Parsley

"The epicurean's delight," parsley is used fresh or dried. It is an excellent source of vitamins A and C (it has 3 times as much as oranges), and is rich in minerals (it has twice as much iron as spinach). In ancient Rome, sprigs of parsley were passed around during funeral orations and nibbled on by the audience.

Parsnip

This much-maligned member of the carrot family was a favorite of the Emperor Tiberius. It is a fair source of vitamins A and C. Choose smooth, medium-sized roots, if possible, and *don't* cook them in water after washing. Instead, sauté them lightly in oil or bake them. Parsnips cook very quickly, and their sweet, nutty taste is unique. Parsnip wine has been a favorite beverage in England for a long time.

Pea

Grown in parts of Asia, Europe, and North America, although in the U.S. the use of fresh and dried peas is rapidly declining while canned, and especially frozen, peas are growing in importance. The pea-canning industry is centered in Michigan, Wisconsin, Washington, New York, and New Jersey. The States with the greatest dried pea production are Washington, Idaho, Colorado, and Oregon. Pease porridge, a dish not unlike thick pea soup, was the main winter food for North European people. There are several varieties of peas to choose from, including Chinese peas or *mange-tout*, in which the peas themselves are tiny and the pods so tender that you can indeed "eat all." Cowpeas, or black-eyed peas, are technically beans, but are treated as peas and are usually sold in their dried form. Try not to overcook peas; better yet, use them raw as a delicious addition to salads. Peas are an excellent source of vitamins A and C and are said to have almost as much protein and energy value as meat.

Peppers

There are hundreds of varieties of peppers and the smallest ones are usually the hottest.

Green peppers turn red when ripe and are a very good source of vitamins C, A, and B. Spanish pepper is known as pimiento, and the mild red pepper of Hungary is called paprika. Buy firm, unblemished peppers and refrigerate until they are ready to be used. The big bell peppers can be stuffed or sliced for salads; the hotter varieties, also known as chili peppers, are used in a wide range of Mexican dishes. Be careful handling them; the substance that makes them hot can irritate the eyes if it comes into contact with them.

Potato

The potato, a member of the huge deadly nightshade family, originated in South America, where it began to be cultivated around 2500 B.C. What are sometimes called Irish potatoes are not Irish at all, but were introduced into that country in the middle of the 17th century. Potatoes quickly became the staple crop there because they were one of the few things that would grow in poor soil. However, the Irish became so dependent on the potato that when severe crop failures occurred in the 1840s, millions of Irish were forced to migrate to the U.S. Potatoes were introduced to the U.S. in 1719, and now Maine, Idaho, and California lead the field in production. Potatoes are a good source of vitamin C, iron, amino acids, protein, thiamine, vitamin G, and nicotinic acid. (Contrary to popular opinion, they are not notably high in calories —it's the butter and gravy that are fattening.) Make a habit of eating the skin; most of the vitamins and minerals lie just beneath it.

Pumpkin

Pumpkins are a member of the squash family and were a staple in the American Indian diet. They usually appear on the market in October, tapering off in November. Everyone has heard of pumpkin pie, but cream of pumpkin soup is delicious, with a fresh, delicate taste, and pumpkin bread, made with a puree of this versatile vegetable, deserves wider attention. And, as a bonus, pumpkin seeds are very good raw or roasted and salted. The pumpkin is a good source of vitamin A, and a fair source of C and energy.

Radish

There are several different varieties, and they range in shape from round to oblong; and in color from white, through pink and red, to black. They provide small amounts of vitamins A and C, and traces of minerals. Radishes are mostly eaten raw, but they can be steamed until tender, when they lose some of the piquant taste which does not appeal to everyone. Don't discard the tops—they can be steamed as a vegetable or added raw to salads.

Shallot

In looks, it resembles a small onion, except that it is divided into 2 or more cloves, like garlic. Most shallots which we see in the markets are imported, although until about 20 years ago, Louisiana produced millions of pounds. The shallot is slightly milder in taste than the onion. Store your shallots in the refrigerator in a sealed plastic bag; they should be kept cool and dry.

Spinach

Widely grown in northern Europe and the U.S. (Texas and California being the big producers), this intensely green vegetable is well known for its high iron and vitamin A and C content, and is also an important source of folic acid, one of the B vitamins. Try cooking spinach in only the water which adheres to the leaves after it is washed, or better yet, use it raw in a salad with avocado and parsley.

Squash

Extensively grown in the U.S., they were one of the staples of the American Indians, and Europeans adopted them when they arrived in the New World. There are many varieties of squash. Among the soft-skinned varieties, zucchini and pattypan or scallop are the most popular. These "summer" squashes can be sliced and sautéed, skins and all, or added to soups. The most tender of them are often eaten raw. Among the hard-skinned squashes, Hubbard is an old favorite, and acorn is also popular. These hard-skinned squashes, often called "winter" squash, are usually baked in the shell, or they can be boiled instead. They can be stored indefinitely. The soft-skinned squashes provide vitamin A, and the winter varieties are also good sources of this vitamin. Like pumpkin, squash can be used in pies and the seeds are also tasty if roasted and salted.

Tomato

The tomato originated in South America, where it still grows wild, and it is a member of the widespread deadly nightshade family. Known upon its arrival in Europe as the "love apple," and "golden apple," it was thought to have aphrodisiacal properties. Containing both vitamin A and C, it wasn't considered a food in the U.S. until the middle of the 19th century. Now its use is worldwide and its versatility is unlimited. To many people, sweet, vine-ripened tomatoes with fresh basil are an unbeatable combination.

Turnip and Rutabaga

These 2 root vegetables are closely related and are used interchangeably. Rutabagas are grown more extensively in Canada, Great Britain, and northern Europe than in the U.S. Turnips in general have white flesh and contain some vitamin C, while rutabagas, because of their yellow color, provide some vitamin A. Both have a mild sweet taste, which is at its best when the vegetables are young and are eaten raw. Turnip greens are high in vitamins A, B, and C. They can be eaten raw or cooked.

Watercress

The sprigs are a tasty and attractive addition to salads, and watercress can also be steamed as greens. In quantity, it is rich in vitamin C and minerals; and as a further bonus, it is always organically grown because it will not thrive in polluted water!

Yam and Sweet Potato

They are both members of the morning glory or *Ipomoea* family, the yam used in the U.S. not being the true tropical yam. Often our sweet potatoes are a pale yellow inside, containing much vitamin A and a good amount of C; while the yams are a deep orange, an indication of a higher amount of vitamin A. These tubers played an important part in our early history, serving as a staple for both humans and livestock. They also did their part in the survival of the South after the Civil War (where they are greatly cultivated even today), and for a century, Georgia was the leading producer. Choose small or medium-sized sweet potatoes without any visible blemish.

—J.C. & A.W.

Nuts

Almonds

The Hebrew word *shakad*, which means "vigilant" or "awakening," has been acknowledged as the source of the name "almond." Its name is mentioned in the Old Testament 73 times. The oil of the bitter almond is used for medicines. The sweet almond provides protein, iron, calcium, phosphorus, and the B vitamins. It is high in fat. The hulls are used as feed for livestock along with barley and alfalfa. Although the U.S. is one of the world's largest exporters of almonds, almost half of the almonds consumed in this country are imported from Italy.

Brazil Nuts

The Brazil nut tree reaches heights of over 150'. It is harvested for commercial use in the Amazon basin, the bulk of the work being done by low-paid migrant laborers. Brazil nuts are high in fat and contain some protein, iron, and thiamine. Two Brazil nuts have the same caloric food value as one egg.

Cashew Nut

It got its name *Anacardium* because of its heartlike shape. The actual nut is attached to the lower end of the fruit (the cashew apple). Locally, this fruit is used in beverages, jams, and jellies. After the fruit is picked (by hand), the nut is detached and sun-dried. Before the nut can be eaten, there are 2 shells and a skin that must be removed. The outer shell contains a poisonous oil that can blister the skin; it was once believed that uncooked cashew nuts were also poisonous. However, the shell oil does not in any way contaminate the raw nut. To remove this shell, and to get rid of this oil, the nuts are either placed among burning logs until the oil catches fire (the fumes of which are injurious to the eyes and skin) or put in modern roasting cylinders. Later, the inner shells are cracked open, also by hand, and the kernels heated to remove the skins. The cashew tree grows in Central and South America, the West Indies, East Africa, and India (from which the U.S. imports 64% of its supply). A delicious and nutritious drink can be made by blending 1 cup cashews, 1 quart water, 1 tbs. soy oil, 2 tbs. raw honey, and ¼ tsp. salt.

Chestnuts

There are more than 10 species of chestnut, classified by region, including the American, Chinese, Japanese, and European. The nuts of the latter 3 are exported in large quantities. In the 1920s, a blight wiped out most of the North American crop and today the U.S. imports the bulk of its chestnuts from the Mediterranean regions. Chestnuts are not to be confused with the "water chestnut," an aquatic fruit of the evening primrose. Chestnuts resemble acorns in structure. Roasted, the chestnut is a fragrant and appetizing food. Raw, it contains a certain amount of tannic acid, which may upset the stomach. In Korea, the chestnut is almost as important to the diet as the potato is in the U.S.

Filbert

Also known as the hazelnut or cobnut, the filbert is commercially grown in Turkey, Italy, Spain, and the U.S. The wild trees of the Mediterranean and the Balkans form the basis of the commercial industry. Old Chinese manuscripts indicate that the use of this nut dates back at least 5,000 years. The ancient Greeks and Romans thought filberts had medicinal qualities. The native Indians of the Pacific Northwest used the wild variety, called "chinquapin" for food. The oil from the European filbert is used in food products, perfumes, and soaps. The soft, reddish timber is used for tool handles and walking sticks. Whereas most nuts are alkaline-forming, filberts—like peanuts and walnuts—are acid-forming in the body. They are good for the teeth and gums, and when eaten in moderation, aid in normalizing the metabolism.

Macadamia Nuts

The macadamia nut is native to Australia, where it is called the Queensland nut. Most of the U.S. supply is grown and harvested in Hawaii, although there is a small industry developing in California and Florida. The supply has never been adequate for the demand. The range of distribution is limited; they are difficult to store, and are subject to mold and rancidity. The macadamia nut is high in protein, fat, and calories. It is a rich food and a good body-builder, as well as being expensive.

Pecans

Indigenous to the southern U.S., where the wild species earned its name from the Algonquin and Cree Indian words meaning "nut with hard shell to crack." There are 2 types of pecan: large ones with thin shells, and small ones with thick shells. The small ones are tastier and less expensive but harder to crack. The kernels are high in energy, easily digestible, and have a high content of potassium and vitamin B_1. The oil can be used for cooking and in salads, and it keeps well. The shells are often dyed red for commercial appeal, but of course this does nothing for the food value of the nut. The pecan shell is boiled to make a fabric dye, and the tannic acid extracted from it is used as a tanning agent for leather. Crushed shells are mixed with sand to form good rooting mediums for greenwood cuttings.

Pine Nuts

Pine nuts, also called "pignolias" and Indian nuts, supply the vast rural populations of Mexico, South America, Australia, and Europe with high protein and an easily obtainable nut food. Most of the nuts sold commercially in the U.S are imported from Italy.

Pistachio Nuts

The wild pistachio groves of Turkey, Lebanon, and Afghanistan, along with a few commercial groves in Syria and Iran, supply this country with the pistachio nut. Sicily and India are also large exporters. A large red Aleppo variety is being grown experimentally in Chico, Calif., but very few domestic groves have thus far been successful. The pistachio nut is much acclaimed for its excellent taste and high protein content. The pistachio growers sell their nuts in their natural state. The varieties vary in color from light tan shell with light green nut, to red shell with dark green nut. Most of the distributors in the U.S. roast, salt, and dye the nut and shell red, but pistachios are best eaten raw and undyed.

Walnuts

There are at least 15 species of *Juglans*. The 4 most important for their edible nuts are the Persian or English walnut, the American black walnut, the Japanese walnut, and the butternut or American white walnut. The English walnut is now imported to this country from France. It is also grown on the California coast, but the growers bleach the nuts for appearance, ruining the food value and delicate flavor. Black walnuts were important to the early native Americans as food, while Colonial Americans fed the nutmeat to their swine because it was so abundant. The black walnut is more difficult to extract than the English, yet sweeter in flavor. The Japanese walnut tree is used primarily for its wood and ornamental quality. As for the butternut, its popularity has passed with a generation. Walnut wood is among the hardest and most beautiful. Unfortunately, butternut wood is so beautiful that indiscriminate clear-cutting has greatly reduced its number. Ground walnut shells are pressed to obtain the oils, boiled to make fabric dyes, and rubbed as an abrasive to clean and polish metals. Walnut meat has a laxative effect, and it has been recommended to people with liver ailments because of its richness in minerals.

—R.Mo. & F.C.

Grains

All over the world cereals such as wheat, rice, corn, oats, barley, rye, and millet feed billions of people. Raising grains is the largest industry in the world, and bread made from grains is the most widely used food. The different grains and their varieties grow under different conditions, locations, and climates (there is a wheat harvest happening each month of the year someplace in the world). Grains have been greatly affected by modern technology, and improved methods of transportation have allowed grains to be shipped to areas which cannot grow them. However, commercial milling and processing techniques often strip the grains of their nutritional content. In their natural state grains are an important source of protein, vitamins, and minerals. There is much to be learned yet about the various grains and their value to humans and animals, though it has been established that it is important to vary the grains in one's diet.

Barley

About half of the world's crop of barley is used as livestock feed; the rest is used for human food and in malting (10%). Malted barley is used in the production of beer and other beverages (*bere* being one of barley's older names). Although barley is one of the principal crops of Africa and the Near East, its low gluten content—which results in a rather heavy bread—makes it less popular in Europe and the U.S. Barley is high in carbohydrates, with moderate quantities of protein, calcium, phosphorus, and small amounts of the B vitamins. It is easier to digest than wheat and is good for weak stomachs. Barley is great in winter soups, but try to get unhulled barley, which is not refined. Hulled barley is a good substitute for rice and potatoes when simmered for 20 minutes in water or broth. Pearl barley, which is polished, is mostly starch.

Buckwheat

A staple food in the U.S.S.R. and Poland. Other important producers are France, Canada, and the U.S. It is often used as feed for poultry and other livestock, and is an ideal crop for a field in need of revitalization. It has a single taproot which seems to extract nutrients from the soil very effectively, and farmers have a saying that if the land is too poor for anything else, it will grow buckwheat. Buckwheat is rich in vitamin E and the B complex. Buckwheat is ground into flour, which is used mainly in pancakes, and the groats are simmered to make kasha, a popular eastern European dish. It can be mixed with wheat, soybean, or barley as a cereal for breakfast.

Corn

See: Vegetable article.

Millet

It is a complete food, being high in protein (with a good balance of amino acids), rich in minerals (high in calcium and iron) and vitamins, especially riboflavin—one of the most important of the B vitamins—and lecithin. It is often given to young babies who have trouble digesting cereals. In the U.S. and Western Europe, it is grown mostly as pasture and for hay, although it is still eaten by 1/3 of the world's population, and is an important staple in much of the U.S.S.R. and other areas of Asia, and western Africa. While millet is used as birdseed, it can also serve as a delicious breakfast cereal, or as a base for many meatless dishes. Millet is usually available at a health food store as whole millet, millet grits, millet flour, and a millet mix. Unhulled millet supplies more minerals than the hulled variety.

Oats

Grown principally as livestock feed, but furfural—a solvent used in oil refining and pharmaceuticals—is also made from oat hulls. Only 5% of the total yield is grown for human consumption. Leading oat-producing countries include the U.S., the U.S.S.R., Canada, France, Poland, the United Kingdom, West Germany, Australia, and New Zealand. In the U.S., Iowa, Minnesota, and Illinois are the largest producers. Oatmeal is a good source of calcium, iron, the B vitamins, inositol, and silicon, which is necessary for the development of the muscles, brain, and nerve structure. When looking for oatmeal, try to buy steel-cut oats. These have not been submitted to the high heat necessary before oats can be rolled, and the nutrients are more likely to be intact. Oat flour is also available, which gives an unusual and delicious taste to bread.

Rice

Leading rice-producing countries include China, India, Japan, Pakistan, Indonesia, Thailand, and Burma. Other important producers are Egypt, Italy, Spain, Brazil, and the U.S. In the U.S., rice is cultivated in Arkansas, California, Florida, Louisiana, Missouri, Mississippi, and Texas. It is grown in rice paddies, or "checks" as they are known in the U.S., and is the most mechanized of all the crops, needing tractors, land planes, dikers, etc., for its cultivation. Milling removes the hull and bran layers of the kernel, making what is called white rice and stripping rice of much of its nutrients. A coating of glucose and talc is applied to give the kernel a glossy finish. Converted rice is created by treating the unmilled grain with steam, so that the B vitamins dissolve and are carried into the center. The rice is then milled and looks and tastes like white rice, but is just as vulnerable to losing its nutrients when washed. Brown rice is unrefined; only the husk has been removed. It is a source of the B vitamins, phosphorus, iron, calcium, and potassium. To cook 1 cup of brown rice, heat 2 cups of water to boiling. Add rice slowly so that the water does not stop boiling. Cover, and let simmer gently for about 20 minutes. Turn off the heat, let steam till ready to serve (10 to 15 minutes). Don't add salt to the water! Salt draws out moisture and lengthens the cooking process. Salt to taste when the rice is cooked or serve with soy sauce. Rice has much lore attached to it; in India and China it is seen as an emblem of happiness, nourishment, and fecundity. It is worth noting that for centuries the Chinese and East Indians ate unrefined brown rice and it was not until the introduction of modern milling by the British that malnutrition became widespread.

Rye

It grows in almost any kind of soil, making it an ideal crop for poor regions. It accounts for only about 1% of the world cereal crop, and is used mainly as "green" manure and in whiskey and gin distilling. Important rye-producing countries include the U.S.S.R., Poland, West Germany, Argentina, Turkey, the U.S., Spain, Hungary, France, The Netherlands, and Austria. Rye is high in carbohydrates and rich in vitamin E. Rye makes a heavy, dark bread, which is relatively chewy and filling, and which stays fresh longer than white bread. Rye can be steamed in the same way as wheat or millet to make a cereal.

Sorghum

In India, sorghum is known as *jorwar, cholum,* or *jonna;* in the West Indies as *petit mil* or Guinea corn; in China and Manchuria as *kaoliang;* and in Egypt by its Arabic name *dourra.* It contains more protein and less fat than corn. Sorghum is made into meal and flour, and sometimes the flour is mixed with that of wheat. This is done mostly in the countries where it is frequently used, such as India, northern China, and Africa. In these countries, it is the leading cereal. Sweet sorghum is grown in the U.S. mainly for fodder and the making of sorghum syrup. In China, sweet sorghum is made into spirits, while in Africa, sorghum is made into a fermented drink called *tialva.* A certain variety of sorghum is cultivated for broom corn, used in making brooms and brushes.

Wheat

Along with rice, it is one of the 2 most important grain crops in the world, and was the 1st to be cultivated. The U.S.S.R. is the leading grower, followed by the U.S. and Canada. Other large producers include Argentina, India, Turkey, Pakistan, China, Australia, France, Italy, Spain, and West Germany. Most of the wheat produced is milled into flour. Pasta is made from a variety of wheat called durum, which also gives us semolina, the name given to the hard grains which are left when the fine flour has been sieved. Bulghur is another form of wheat grown in the Near East. It cooks into a light, fluffy grain and is used in the making of the traditional dish called couscous.

Whole wheat, like other whole grains that contain the germ, is a complete protein. It contains important minerals and vitamins, particularly E and the B complex. When wheat is milled into white flour, the bran and wheat germ are lost, and what is left is mainly starch. This is what we know as white bread. The wheat germ can be used on its own as a cereal, or added to bread, cakes, and other baked goods. Keep wheat germ in the refrigerator to keep it from turning rancid. Whole wheat can be steamed unground. It may take 3 to 4 hours, but it has a delightful chewy texture. Cracked wheat cooks much more quickly and can be used as a rice substitute. Flaked wheat can be used in granola or made into a porridge. Bran, another milling by-product, can be added to bread and cereals. All wheat contains phytin, a phosphorus compound which interferes with the body's utilization of important nutrients such as calcium and iron. For this reason, some people feel that wheat products should not be eaten at all; but the value of the powerhouse of protein, vitamins, and minerals contained in whole wheat probably outweighs any disadvantage.

—J.C. & F.C.

LEGUMES

Legumes are those plants that bear their seeds in 2-valved pods, and "pulse" is the term used for the seeds of such legumes as peas, beans, and lentils. Legumes are often grown for the benefit they bring to the soil; they restore nitrogen to the earth when they are plowed under. Beans have become an important crop not only because of their protein content, but because they can be dried and saved for winter. The protein in pulses is incomplete, but since pulses can supplement one another, the body can receive a total protein by combining 2 properly chosen pulses. Beans and grains are also compatible in this way.

Alfalfa

This legume has been grown mainly as a forage crop for cattle. It is cultivated to some extent throughout the U.S., mostly in the north central and western States. It is rich in calcium, chlorine, iron, magnesium, phosphorus, silicon, and sulfur. It contains vitamins A, C, D, E, and K, the blood-clotting vitamin. It can be taken in tablet or meal form, and the leaves can be used in tea. The tiny seeds can be sprouted and added to salads.

Clover

Mostly cultivated as food for livestock, clover grows in the North Temperate Zone and is also found in South Africa and South America. The seed heads range in color from white through pink and red to purple, white being the most nutritious as a forage crop. Clover is high in protein, phosphorus, and calcium in either the fresh or dry stage. For human use, the seeds can be sprouted or used as a tea.

Fava Bean

These beans are also known as broad, horse, or Windsor beans. They are the 3rd most important beans in the world, and the principal beans in Europe. Fava beans, like all the others, are seed-propagated and grown as annuals. They consist of 21%–25% protein, 58%–64% carbohydrates, and about 1½% fat. These are the favorite beans of Near Eastern cookery, but it is interesting to note that the fava beans are potentially poisonous and can be fatal to people with an enzyme (G-6-PD) deficiency. This genetic deficiency occurs only in some families of Mediterranean origin.

French, Haricot, or Kidney Bean

This is the 2nd most important bean in the world. Brazil, China, and the U.S. produce more than half of the world's supply of kidney beans. In the U.S., California, Michigan, Idaho, and Colorado lead in the dry bean production. The kidney bean in the U.S. refers to the red to dark red ones. Pinto beans are white with brown spots and are used extensively in Mexico for *frijole* dishes. Another familiar variety is the white navy bean used for Boston baked beans. These are just a few of about 500 varieties. Dry kidney beans are very rich in protein and carbohydrates. They may be eaten as a substitute for meat. The pods of the French bean can be eaten, although they are inclined to be stringy. Green shell beans—such as stringless or snap beans, and wax beans—are a good source of energy and are rich in vitamin A. To cook dry beans, heat the water to boiling and then drop the beans in slowly so the water does not cease boiling. Don't add salt—this prolongs the cooking time. It is not actually necessary to soak dried beans overnight; if, however, you do soak them, be sure to cook the beans in the same water.

Garbanzo

Also known as chick-pea. In India, it is the most important of the pulse crops, and the green pods and tender young shoots are eaten as a vegetable. The seeds may be eaten whole or ground into a gram flour (not graham flour, which is made from wheat). Garbanzo beans can be cooked like any other, and are particularly good cold when marinated with oil and vinegar. *Huumus* is a popular Near Eastern dish, and is made by combining cooked, mashed garbanzo beans with tahini, a butter made of sesame seeds.

Lentil

Lentils have a long history of use, and some were found in an Egyptian tomb dating from 2000 B.C. It was for a pottage made of red lentils that Esau sold his birthright to Jacob. Lentils contain as much as 25% protein, and are particularly important in the diet of vegetarians. *Dhal* is a familiar and soothing accompaniment to curry; it is made from lentils which have been boiled until completely soft, and all the water has been absorbed. They are then seasoned and left to get cold and solidify, so it will be easy to slice with a knife.

Lima Bean

Remains of lima beans were found in Peru, dating from about 7000 B.C. They are grown only for their seeds, although a type called baby lima beans are also grown for their pods. They are now the main pulse crop in many areas of tropical Africa, and are grown in Burma as well. Lima beans were only one variety out of hundreds which explorers found the Indians using when they 1st came to America.

Mung Bean

Very important in India. The pods can be dried, boiled whole, or split; or else parched and ground into flour. The green pods are also eaten as a vegetable. In China, mung beans are added to green noodles and are also sprouted. In fact, these little beans are the easiest of all to sprout. Soak a handful overnight in a glass container. Next day, strain them, and cover the container with cheesecloth. Put them in a dark place and keep them slightly moist—not dry or they will shrivel, and not wet or they will mold. When sprouts are 1″ to 1½″ long (usually within 3 days), they are ready. Before they are eaten they should be exposed to the sun to manufacture chlorophyll. Seeds double their nutritive value when sprouted; and the amount of folic acid, which prevents pernicious anemia, quadruples. Use sprouts in salads, sandwiches, or in soup. They can also be sautéed very lightly in oil so they will retain their juicy, crunchy texture.

Pea

Although usually classified with other vegetables, peas are a member of the legume family. When they are dried and split for soups, etc., it is easier to think of them as pulses. Half a cup of cooked split peas provides 8 gm. of protein, but as in the case of the other legumes, this is not complete protein. Split pea soup is deservedly well known. Next time you make it, try adding 2 tsp. of caraway or dill seeds for variation.

Peanut

Peanuts are also known as groundnuts or "goobers." China, West Africa, and the U.S. are the largest commercial producers, and Suffolk, Va., is called "the Peanut Capital of the World." The nuts can be eaten raw or roasted, and are also ground into flour. A good quality oil can be extracted from them, and the shoots and leaves are also edible. Peanuts are rich in protein, minerals, and vitamins. They have more fat than heavy cream, and more food energy than sugar. Unshelled peanuts are fresher and can be roasted at home in a 400° oven for approximately 15 to 20 minutes, stirring every 5 minutes. Use 2 tsp. salt to 2 cups raw shelled peanuts. To make your own peanut butter, use an electric blender, or a seed or meat grinder. Peanut butter is made from nothing else but peanuts, with perhaps just a trace of salt, and a little peanut oil (1½ to 2 tbs. for 2 cups) if a smooth, slick consistency is desired. Add one tsp. honey if you wish. (See: Some Favorite American Foods, p. 1010.)

Soybean

The soybean is undoubtedly the king of beans, and is rapidly becoming the most important bean in the world. It was being cultivated in China before 3500 B.C., but was virtually unknown in Europe and the U.S. until 1900. There are about 30 varieties, many of them different colors, but the one we see most is yellow. Unlike other beans, soybeans are as much as 35% protein, as little as 35% carbohydrate, and 18% fat. Soybeans are the only true meat substitute in the legume family, providing *complete* protein as well as essential amino acids, calcium, and B vitamins. In fact, soybeans are being looked upon as possible saviors of the world. They are able to provide a cheap and nutritional diet for the underdeveloped countries, as well as possible meat substitutes for the wealthier countries, where it may no longer be feasible to raise livestock because of shortages of land and grain.

Soybeans are also made into flour, broken up into grits, and into a curd called "tofu," which is used extensively in Japanese and Chinese cooking. The Chinese have traditionally used very little, if any, cow's milk, making instead soy milk obtained by crushing soybeans in water. Oil made from soybeans provides linoleic acid, one of the essential fatty acids. Soybeans can be used in many ways. They can be cooked like other dried beans and then flavored with different seasonings. Soy grits, which cook much more quickly than the whole beans, can be used as a meat extender, or added to soups or other moist foods. Tofu, the soybean curd, can be cut up and added to soups or scrambled eggs; or stir-fried with vegetables, Chinese-style. Soy flour can be added in bread-making, providing extra protein and vitamins at very low cost, and can also be used to thicken soups and sauces. The versatility of this wonder bean is unlimited, but only as our natural resources become scarcer will we discover the true worth of the soybean.

—J.C.

OTHER GOODIES

Honey

Honey is made from nectar which bees gather from different plants and flowers. Nectar is changed into honey by enzyme action in the bodies of the bees, and is stored in wax cells in the hive. It is then left to ripen, and in time, it thickens because of evaporation caused by the fanning of the bees' wings. Bees produce honey for their own use, as their main source of food. Honey has been in use for thousands of years. A jar of honey, still in perfect condition, was found in an Egyptian tomb, where it was placed over 3,000 years ago. Honey contains an enzyme which prevents it from molding; therefore, it needs no preservatives. Because bees are very sensitive to pesticides, honey is fairly free from contamination; the bees, if exposed to sprays, usually die before returning to the hives.

Honey can be as much as 76% sugar, and 18% moisture. The sugar in honey, however, requires no digestive change before it is assimilated. Unfortunately, its effect on the teeth is the same as that of refined sugar, molasses, etc., in that a bacteria in the sugar breaks down into an acid which causes the calcium to erode. Honey also contains minerals, amino acids, and valuable enzymes. Look for slight cloudiness and evidence of crystallization in your honey; these signs often mean that your honey is unheated and unfiltered, and therefore retains its fine flavor. Honey is a laxative, and is also said to be good for soothing sore throats and easing hoarseness. The early Romans considered honey to have medicinal qualities, too, and felt that coriander drunk with honey was a cure for childbirth fever. A 7th-century manuscript advises the eating of honey for the bite of a mad dog or a serpent; and in the Middle Ages, warts could be removed by a poultice of honey and a yellow garden slug!

Maple Syrup

Maple syrup is made from the sap which is gathered from the sugar maple tree. This gathering—or tapping as it is called—is done in the spring during the "sugar snow," which is the last spring snow after a period of warmth. This time is chosen because it means that the warmth has started the journey of the sap from the roots, up the trunk of the tree, and to the branches. The snow halts the progress of the sap, holding it in the trunk, where it can be easily tapped. In the past, the sap was boiled out in the open, but now the liquid content is evaporated by machine until the required stage is reached. These stages are syrup, cream (from which candy is made), and the final stage, sugar. Pure maple syrup is a delicious taste treat, but one not to be overindulged in because of its high sugar content. Until about 10 years ago, maple syrup was a completely unadulterated product. Now, however, a tablet of paraformaldehyde is placed in the taphole to kill bacteria and speed up the dripping process. Traces of this tablet almost certainly find their way into the sap, but most bottles of syrup don't state whether this pellet was used or not. Avoid "maple-*flavored*" syrups completely. There may be as little as 2% maple syrup in these products, the rest being sugar and corn syrup. Look for 100% *pure*, and if possible, unadulterated maple syrup. You can still find it.

Pollen

Pollen is the male germ seed of plants and flowers, and a single grain is invisible to the naked eye. It is gathered by bees, who collect it in sacs on their back legs and take it to the hive. There it is either formed into royal jelly—which is fed exclusively to the queen and which gives her her special powers—or it is combined with honey to make bee bread, which is the food of the drones and workers. Pollen has been mentioned in the ancient writings of Egypt, China, Greece, and Russia, and experiments are presently being conducted to determine how best it can be used to help humans, since it is proving to be an amazing food. It is free from added colors, chemicals, and preservatives and is the richest source yet revealed of minerals, vitamins, and amino acids. Pollen may be as much as 13% complete protein, and in detail, it contains large quantities of vitamins A, B, C, D, E, and K; plus rutin, lecithin, amines, nuclein, guanine, xanthine, hydrocarbons, and sterol. In fact, pollen is a complete food, with a built-in life force, and the only similar food that can be compared to it is yeast. Antibiotics are present naturally, and it can be stored without loss of vitality. In medicine, its uses are only just being discovered. Cernitin, a pollen extract, has been used successfully in the treatment of influenza, urinary disorders, and measles. Tests in France prove pollen has been instrumental in curing anemia in young children and chronic constipation in adults. It helps in the recovery from shock, and as a tonic and energy restorer, it has given a new lease on life to old men. In fact, its potential appears to be unlimited. Pollen is present in varying amounts in all honeys, and it can also be purchased in powder or tablet form.

—J.C.

The Story of Dairy Products

Milk

The 1st goats were domesticated around 7000 B.C. in Iran, and cattle a little later, around 6000 B.C. in Greece. It is not certain when humans 1st started milking their domesticated animals. One of the earliest milking scenes in existence today, which shows a goat being milked, is on an Elamite seal from 2500 B.C. Milk, especially in its soured forms, as cheese, yogurt, etc., made a big difference in the life of Neolithic man, providing all-season, high-quality food that sustained him when the growing season was over, when he could no longer collect leaves and berries, and when game was scarce.

Today, the subject of milk is controversial, and not just because of the Milk Fund scandal, during which it was discovered that influential dairymen had poured money into Richard Nixon's campaign fund, in exchange for an increase in Federal milk price support. The major reason for the controversy is the large amount of artificial additives, in the form of antibiotics and other chemicals, that find their way into our daily milk, via the cow and the food she eats.

There is also the question of whether milk, *in its fresh form*, is a suitable food either for adults or, in large quantities, for children. The reason for this doubt lies in the belief that milk protein requires too many pancreatic enzymes for digestion, and therefore places a heavy demand on a possibly already overworked system. Further, milk is thought to be mucus-forming, and there are also the problems arising from lactose intolerance and allergies. Many peoples, such as the Chinese and the Maoris, traditionally do not use dairy products, and still maintain themselves in good health.

On the plus side, however, is the fact that milk is a superior source of *complete* protein, as well as of calcium and riboflavin (Vitamin B_2). It also contains smaller quantities of the other B vitamins, a small amount of vitamin C, and, usually, added vitamin D. Attention has been focused recently on the cholesterol problem, to which milk, with its animal-fat content, may contribute. However, there are tribes in Kenya who drink 9 to 14 quarts of whole milk daily, but because their diet is adequate in all other respects, their blood cholesterol is remarkably low. In other words, their balanced diets include nutrients that produce lecithin, which neutralizes the harmful effects of cholesterol. Using skim milk would appear to be the solution here, but remember that calcium, before it can be utilized, must react 1st with fat; therefore skim milk should always be drunk with meals or with a snack containing fat. Certified raw milk is best; pasteurization causes calcium to be lost, as well as the destruction of enzymes, antibodies, and hormones.

Nonfat dry milk is a good source of additional protein, vitamins, and minerals in the diet because it can be added to bread, cooked cereals, etc. However, the heating process used to dry it destroys one of the amino acids, lysine, thus making it an *incomplete* protein, and not suitable as a fresh milk substitute. The same is true of canned evaporated milk; the high heat used to process both canned and dry milk also drastically reduces the vitamin content of both. Keep your dry milk in an airtight container, in a cool place, and it will last indefinitely.

Goat's milk compares very favorably with cow's milk. Its value lies in the fact that it is more easily digested by infants, invalids, and those allergic to cow's milk. The curds are smaller and more soluble, and the fat in goat's milk is more easily assimilated.

BUTTER

Butter is churned from cream. In the old days, this was done by skimming the cream off the top of the milk and hand-churning until it separated. The particles of butter were then washed several times with water, and when it was a solid mass, it was "cut" and salt added. Nowadays butter can be made from either fresh cream or sour or "ripened" cream. Sweet butter is probably a better buy, because further additives have to be used to mask the taste and bacterial defects of the "ripened" cream. Unsalted butter is better than the salted

kind, for the same reason—a large amount of salt may be added to retard the growth of molds and yeast. Butter ranges in vitamin A content from 2,000 international units per lb. for winter butter, when the cows are fed on dry feed, all the way to 12,000 IU per lb. for summer butter, when they are out at pasture. Butter is fairly high in calories, providing about 3,200 per lb., and it does contribute to the level of cholesterol in the blood, if lecithin-producing nutrients are missing from the diet.

You can counteract this effect by using modified butter. Mix a pound of butter with a cup of one of the unsaturated oils, sunflower, safflower, or peanut oil. This way, you get butter with an excellent flavor and known essential fatty acids content. The Hunzas, renowned for their superior health, use a form of butter called "ghee," which is made by letting cream ripen at room temperature for several days until it thickens.

BUTTERMILK

Traditionally, buttermilk was the liquid left in the churn or drawn off as the butter formed. Usually, flecks of butter were left in this liquid, and the whole provided a refreshing drink. Nowadays, buttermilk is completely divorced from the business of making butter. There is a type of buttermilk on the market which is labeled "churned" but it is actually cultured and then put back into the churn, with butter added, and churned until it takes on the appearance of old-fashioned churned buttermilk. The truth is, however, that cultured buttermilk is superior even to the real churned variety. It is made from skim milk, to which lactic-acid bacteria and bits of butterfat are added, and contains more protein, calcium, and vitamin B_2. Churned buttermilk contains little calcium, because cream is a poor source of this vital mineral. Bulgarian buttermilk, sometimes available, is reputed to have special therapeutic qualities, especially for the digestive system.

It's easy to make your own buttermilk at home. Heat 3½ cups of skim milk until it is warm, but not hot, and add ½ cup of commercial buttermilk. Let stand overnight, and in the morning, your buttermilk will be thick and ready for use. For added nutrients, nonfat dry milk can be added to the milk before the buttermilk starter.

CHEESE

The average American eats a ½ ton of cheese during a lifetime. There are thousands of varieties of cheese from simple fresh cheeses like Ricotta to dessert cheeses like Brie, from heavily cooked cheeses like Swiss to uncooked cheeses like Camembert, from hard, grating cheeses like Parmesan and Romano to various kinds of adulterated "process cheese foods." Most cheeses are made from cow's milk, but some use the milk of other animals. Feta and Roquefort come from sheep's milk, Gjetöst and Gaiskäsli from goat's milk, Lapland cheese from reindeer milk, and Surati (or Panir) cheese from buffalo's milk.

Basically, cheese is made by allowing milk to ripen or sour. Then the lumpy curds are separated from the liquid whey by adding a coagulant such as rennet. The curd is then cut, heated, strained, pressed, and aged. Most commercial rennet is made from the lining of young animals' stomachs, but nonanimal rennet, such as that obtained from withania berries, is also available. It is possible to make cheese without rennet by letting the milk sour until a firm curd forms and the whey begins to separate.

Cheese is rich in protein and fat, and most cheeses contain good amounts of calcium, phosphorus, and vitamins B_2 and A.

COTTAGE CHEESE

Fermented milk foods were the standard fare of the early Egyptians and Greeks, and cottage cheese, long a popular food in Central Europe, used to be made at home in the cottages of Colonial America. Currently, consumption of cottage cheese in the U.S. has reached almost one billion lbs. annually. Uncreamed cottage cheese provides about 38 gm. of complete protein per cup, as well as calcium and some vitamins. The commercial product may, however, contain such unwanted additions as diacetyl, an artificial butter flavor, artificial dyes, as well as stabilizers and mold inhibitors.

Delicious and nutritious cottage cheese can quickly be made at home. Heat one quart of milk in a heavy utensil. Use skim milk for fewer calories. When the milk is warm (about 110°) add one tablespoon of lemon juice. Stir, keeping the heat low, until the milk curdles. Pour curdled milk into a muslin or cheesecloth bag and strain. Add salt to taste and any other flavoring you like, such as chives, parsley, or fresh basil. Seeds such as caraway or dill can be used as well, and a half cup of yogurt or sour cream can be mixed in, if you like a creamy texture. Be sure to save the whey, which contains minerals and is good for the digestive system. This whey can be drunk as is or used in bread-making, etc. If for any reason you do not want to use this whey, make your cottage cheese with rennet. In souring the milk, the lactic acid causes the calcium to be dissolved in the whey and rennet helps to prevent this loss. The procedure with rennet is pretty much the same. Add it either in liquid or tablet

form to the warmed milk, and let it stand until it sets. When firm, place it over a very low heat, or even a pan of very hot water, stirring frequently until it separates into curds.

CREAM

Cream is that part of the milk which has the highest percentage of butterfat. Whole milk usually has 4% to 5% butterfat, depending on the individual cow and on the breed. Cream has little in the way of essential fatty acids, but it does have a lot of calories, around 430 in half a cup. This compares with 170 calories in half a cup of light cream or half-and-half. However, the same amount of cream (half a cup) contains 1,900 IU of vitamin A, compared with only 500 IU, which is all half-and-half supplies.

ICE CREAM

The words "ice cream" conjure up a picture of a delicious frozen concoction of cream, milk, eggs, fresh fruit, and sugar. And so it is, if you make it yourself or buy it in a reputable health food store. But let's take a look at what you may get if you buy some ordinary ice cream, perhaps strawberry:

—The dairy products in ice cream may range from cream and milk to sweetened condensed milk to dried cheese whey. (Cheese whey? An excellent food supplement, but in ice cream?)

—50% air, beaten into ice cream with the help of cheap thickeners.

—Diethyl glycol, a chemical used as an emulsifier. It is also used in antifreeze and in paint remover, and has caused bladder stones and tumors in experimental animals.

—Propylene glycol alginate, used in germicides and in paint remover. Also used as a stabilizer in ice cream, although it was rejected for this purpose in 1942. It was OK'd for use in 1960.

—Benzyl acetate, if your ice cream is artificially flavored. This chemical is also used as a nitrate solvent.

This list gives only a small indication of the hundreds of artificial flavors, colors, smoothers, improvers, and other chemicals added to ordinary ice cream. At the moment, the law requires that on the ice cream carton, only the name (ice cream) and the flavor be printed. If the latter is artificial, this must be stated.

Even if you don't have an ice cream maker, you can still make your own, and freeze it in trays in the freezer part of the refrigerator. It takes about 2½ to 3 hours; during this time turn it in the tray, sides to middle, once or twice. Ice cream is often made in European homes this way. Of course, the method is not completely satisfactory; the ice cream can't expand and the texture isn't the same. But isn't it better than the unappetizing mass of frozen chemicals that so often passes for ice cream today?

KEFIR

Kefir originated in the Caucasus Mountains and can be made from the milk of a cow, goat, or sheep. Kefir grains cause the lactic acid and alcohol fermentation of milk that results in kefir. They are whitish or yellowish, and can be bought at health food shops. Homemade kefir can be made by placing some of these grains in warm milk and leaving the mixture overnight. In the morning, the kefir is ready, but strain it 1st, to recover the grains for further use. Refrigerate your kefir; and remember, a good kefir foams and fizzes like beer. Kefir appears to be of great benefit for old people, and in the U.S.S.R., it is one of the fermented milks used in the treatment of tuberculosis and other diseases.

KOUMISS

Koumiss is another fermented milk product, usually made from mare's milk, which originated in Russia and is still made there today in large quantities. In fact, about 230,000 horses are kept in Russia today expressly for the purpose of providing milk for koumiss. Yeast cultures are added to the milk to start fermentation, and when cow's milk is used, sugar has to be added as well because cow's milk does not contain as much lactose as mare's milk. Koumiss is a milky white liquid, slightly sour and very slightly alcoholic. It is used widely in Russian sanatoriums, where it is apparently effective in the treatment of tuberculosis. As a beverage, it is refreshing and nourishing (mare's milk is comparatively rich in vitamin C), and the slight intoxication produced by drinking quantities of it apparently never has any unpleasant consequences. Poured from glass to glass a few times, it becomes thick like whipped cream, and then tastes even better.

SOUR CREAM

Real sour or cultured cream is the result of natural lactic acid fermentation. Sometimes rennet is added to create a thicker body. Sour cream has fewer calories than mayonnaise and is used in the same way. Sometimes cream is soured by chemicals and thickened with gums; then it is not a fermented product, but the packaging does not always state this clearly.

WHEY

Whey is the liquid left over when milk has formed curds and is made into cheese. Formerly, this liquid was fed mostly to livestock, but now that methods have been found to dry it, it is being used in different ways. As noted earlier, it is often included in ice cream, and is now being added to bread and cakes, where it contributes to higher volume and better keeping qualities. Whey can also be used to make a food yeast, high in protein and vitamins, which would be of immense value to underdeveloped countries. Alcohols, vinegar, and other fermented products can be made from whey; the production of vitamin B_{12} and riboflavin from this source is also a possibility. Whey, in dried form, is available at health food stores and is a nutritive food supplement.

YOGURT

If there is such a thing as a wonder food, yogurt would surely earn that name. Popular the world over, it is known by many different names. In Armenia, it is *matzoon*, in Egypt *leben raib*. The Russians, who eat it with black bread, call it *varenetz*, and in Yugoslavia, where there are hundreds of centenarians, and where it is sold on street stands as ice cream is sold in other countries, it is known as *kisselo mleko*. Associated everywhere with long life, yogurt is nutritionally superior to ordinary milk in many ways. Perhaps yogurt and other fermented milks are the answer to the question of the suitability of milk for adults. In fact in many parts of the world, this is the only form in which milk is consumed. The protein in yogurt is partially predigested and the lactic acid has dissolved some of the calcium. Thus the protein and calcium are more easily absorbed during digestion, which is a tremendous help for sick people and babies. The bacteria in yogurt, by breaking down milk sugar into lactic acid, create an atmosphere in which gas and putrefaction cannot live. Furthermore these wonderful bacteria can synthesize the entire group of B vitamins in the intestines!

The benefits of yogurt are almost limitless. It is particularly valuable when an individual develops the fungus *Monilia albicans*. This fungus grows not only in the intestines but also in the mouth or the vagina, where it is known as thrush. If one to 3 cups of yogurt are eaten daily, this infection clears up quickly. Yogurt also aids the digestion of iron. Have you ever tried yogurt as a face mask? Its soothing astringent qualities are a help to oily skin.

Yogurt is easy to make at home; it is the "natural" pasteurization of milk. Here's a simple way to make it, if you don't have a yogurt maker. Heat fresh milk to "hand hot," about

90° to 110°. Add nonfat dry milk at this point, if you want extra nutrients. To this very warm milk, add about 3 tablespoons of yogurt (for one quart of milk). Be sure it is *real* yogurt; stir it into the milk and pour it all at once into a wide-mouthed thermos jar. Cover it tightly and let it stand overnight. Next morning, the yogurt is thick and creamy; uncap it and refrigerate it right away. If the milk isn't thickened after standing overnight, there can be several reasons. The cow may have been treated with penicillin, which destroys the bacteria and prevents the yogurt from thickening. Or the fault might lie with your starter. But chances are, you'll make delicious yogurt. Be sure to save a couple of tablespoons to start your next batch.

Where Does Milk Come From?

The milk we use is mostly cow's milk. A cow cannot start lactating until after she has calved, although there are cases of spontaneous lactation in heifers who have not produced a calf but whose pedigrees extend back for generations in high-milk-producing families.

A cow (called a heifer until she produces her 1st calf) usually calves at the age of 2 to 2½ years. The gestation takes an average of 283 days but can be as short as 265 or as long as 300 days. The newborn calf is left with his mother for the 1st 18 hours or so, and is then taken away from her. The colostrum, or 1st 3 or 4 days' milk, is necessary for the calf's survival and is unfit for human consumption. At this age, the calf learns to drink readily from a bucket.

The cow's lactation usually lasts 10 months, peaking a month or 2 after she has given birth, and declining thereafter. She is usually allowed to dry off after 10 months, so that she has a rest of 2 months before her next calf is born. The cow can breed at any time of the year and she usually has a calf at 12-month intervals. Milking is done every morning and evening, and the fact that the cow is milked mechanically or by hand, and not sucked by the calf, increases the amount of milk she eventually gives.

—J.C.

Guide to Nutrition

Protein

Use in the Body: Even a cursory list of what protein does would be too long for our purposes. In short, it regulates the myriad reactions involved in metabolism, thus keeping our bodies running, and it acts as the fuel that supplies energy. Protein builds, maintains, and repairs the body.

Deficiency May Lead to: Impairment of nonessential organs and weakening of skin, hair, and nails. Prolonged deficiency leads to atrophy and death.

Overdose May Lead to: Fluid imbalance and overworking of the entire system.

Notes: Protein is the most abundant substance in our bodies; we are 18% to 20% protein by weight. Our muscles, skin, bone, and cartilage are made up of 63% of the body's protein. Hair, nails, eyes, teeth, blood, the heart, lungs, kidneys, and nerves are all protein. This amazing substance is composed of amino acids, of which there are 22 in the body. Eight of these are considered essential, in that they are not supplied within the body and must be obtained from outside sources like plants and animals. Therefore, we need a continuous source of protein. Not only must we get all the proper proteins but we must get them simultaneously and in the right proportions. Only "complete" protein supplies these essential 8 amino acids in the desired amount and proportion.

Best Sources: Eggs and milk are the highest. Soybeans and other legumes, nuts, grains, and cereals (especially wheat germ), fish, meat (not the best of sources), and cheese, vegetables, and dried fruit.

Fats

Use in the Body: Provide energy by furnishing calories to the body, and act as carriers for the fat-soluble vitamins A, D, E, and K. Fats help make calcium available to body tissues, particularly bones, and promote normal growth and healthy blood, arteries, and nerves. They keep skin and other tissues from becoming dry and scaly. They may also be necessary for transporting and breaking down cholesterol (itself a fat). Fat deposits protect the heart, kidneys, liver, and other organs and hold them in place. A fat layer under the skin preserves heat, insulates the body against cold, and rounds out the body contours.

Deficiency May Lead to: A deficiency in fat-soluble vitamins. Also eczema, psoriasis, and other skin disorders. Extreme deficiency will retard growth.

Overdose May Lead to: Obesity and indigestion. If fats cannot be fully metabolized, they become toxic.

Notes: Fats, or lipids, are the most concentrated source of energy in the diet. They are composed of fatty acids, of which there are 2 types:

1) Saturated fats—fats that are hard at room temperature and which come primarily from animal sources.

2) Unsaturated (including polyunsaturated) fats—usually liquid at room temperature and come from vegetable sources.

Two important lipids in the diet are cholesterol (a component in most tissues) and lecithin (concentrated in the brain and nerve tissue).

Best Sources: Milk products, eggs, meat, nuts, seeds, margarine, butter, lard, and oils.

CARBOHYDRATES

Use in the Body: Provides energy for body function and activity by supplying immediate calories, thus allowing the body to use its protein for building and repairing tissues rather than energy. Carbohydrates assist in digesting and assimilating foods and help regulate protein and fat metabolism.

Deficiency May Lead to: A deficiency of vitamin E. Low energy, poor health, mental depression.

Overdose May Lead to: Tooth decay, vitamin B deficiency, indigestion, heartburn, and nausea. Excessive use may lead to diabetes, heart disease, high blood pressure, anemia, and kidney disorders. Many Americans eat too much refined sugar and starches, which creates a paradox of excess and deficiency, since these carbohydrates have no nutritional value and in fact deplete certain minerals.

Notes: There are 3 forms of carbohydrates:

1) Sugars—single (honey, fruits) and double (table sugar). Single sugars are the most easily digested. Sugars are converted to glucose, or blood sugar, for energy.

2) Starches—require long digestive action and, like sugar, are converted to glucose.

3) Cellulose—found in skins of fruits and vegetables, this carbohydrate cannot be digested and has no energy value, but it provides the roughage, or bulk, necessary to prevent constipation, regulate the bowels, and create the intestinal activity that prevents buildup of harmful bacteria in the stomach.

The U.S. is an overconsumer of carbohydrates, most of them refined. The processing of white flour and white sugar leaves these products without nutritional value. Therefore, people tend to eat more of them to satisfy their natural craving for carbohydrates. The result is a nation suffering from what one nutritionist calls "the White Plague": a high rate of diseases affecting the heart and arteries. According to reports concerning autopsies performed on American soldiers killed in Vietnam, the average young American is already a candidate for hardening of the arteries, and eventual heart attacks. The high incidence of stomach cancer in this country may be attributable to the fact that processed flour and rice do not have the roughage needed in the stomach.

Best Sources: Dehydrated fruits, unrefined wheats and cereals, legumes, nuts, potatoes (with skin) and other root vegetables, nonroot vegetables, fruits, seeds, honey, sugar. Refined sugar and starches, and the products made from them (white bread, white flour, table sugar, processed potato chips, processed rice), are not only worthless but harmful to health.

—J.D.

VITAMINS

Vitamin A

Use in the Body: Promotes healthy complexion and good eyesight. Essential to the formation of visual purple, a substance in the eye which is especially important for night vision. Protects the epithelial tissues, such as the thin skin of the mouth, nose, throat, and lungs, thereby increasing resistance to infection. Aids in growth and repair of body tissues.

Deficiency May Lead to: Inability of the eyes to adjust to darkness (night blindness). Slow growth in children, particularly of bones and teeth. Aggravation of infections in the air passages, sinuses, or lungs. Rough, dry, scaly or prematurely aged skin; diaper rash or eczema in infants. Xerosis—itching and burning of the eyes, redness of the lids, and some inflammation. Xerophthalmia—severe eye infection characterized by dry, thickened, lusterless eyeballs.

Overdose May Lead to: Fatigue, dry skin, hair loss, headaches, loss of appetite, irritability, insomnia, vitamin B deficiency.

Notes: Stored in the liver, so daily intake is not necessary. Does not dissolve in water and remains stable at normal cooking temperatures, so little is lost in cooking. However, exposure to air and sunlight can cause a serious loss of the vitamin, so vitamin-A-rich foods are best stored in the refrigerator. Excessive intake of mineral oil (such as salad dressings) causes poor absorption of A.

Best Sources: Hot red pepper, dandelion greens, dock (sorrel), kale, collard greens, cress, parsley, spinach, Swiss chard, broccoli, and other dark green vegetables. Carrots, sweet potatoes, yams, and other yellow vegetables (carrots should be juiced, blended, grated, chopped, cooked, or extremely well chewed in order to release the vitamin A). Egg yolk, whole milk and its products including butter and cheese. Apricots, mangoes, papayas, nectarines, peaches, liver, fish liver oil. Alfalfa sprouts, cantaloupe, green onions, tomatoes.

Vitamin B Complex

Use in the Body: Helps convert carbohydrates into glucose, which the body burns to produce energy. Necessary for the normal functioning of the nervous system. Essential for the maintenance of muscle tone in the gastrointestinal tract and for the health of the liver, eyes, skin, mouth, and hair.

Deficiency May Lead to: Dry, rough, scaly skin, fatigue, headache, dizziness, poor appetite, constipation and digestive disorders, nervousness and mental depression, abnormal growth.

Notes: Actually 13 separate vitamins. They dissolve in water and excess B is excreted, so it must be replaced daily. More B is required during times of stress, work, and emotional trauma. People who need extra B include alcoholics, children, pregnant women, and people who consume excessive amounts of carbohydrates. Destroyed by light, heat, sulfa drugs, oxidation, and alkalis such as baking soda. Large amounts may be lost during cooking, particularly if the cooking water is thrown away. Refining of flours and cereals removes most B vitamins. The B vitamins should be taken together in the correct proportion because that is the way the body uses them and because a large dose of one may cause a deficiency of the others.

Best Sources: Whole grains, green leafy vegetables, brewers' yeast, and organ meats.

Vitamin B₁ (Thiamine)

Use in the Body: Necessary for conversion of starches and sugars into glucose. Essential to the nervous system, heart, liver.

Deficiency May Lead to: Loss of appetite, fatigue, dull feeling, nerve pain, numbness or tingling. In severe cases, beriberi. This disease rarely occurs outside the Far East, where the main diet is white rice.

Notes: Avoid overcooking, serve foods immediately. In 1974 the average American consumed about 1.94 mgm. a day. Five hundred years ago English peasants consumed 4.2 mgm. a day.

Best Sources: Rice bran and polish (present in brown rice, but not white rice), wheat germ and bran (present in whole wheat bread, but not white bread), brewers' yeast, pork, sunflower seeds, alfalfa sprouts, raw peanuts, nuts and seeds, whole grains and beans.

Vitamin B₂ (Riboflavin)

Use in the Body: Aids in breakdown and use of carbohydrates, fats, and proteins. Necessary for maintenance of good vision and clear, healthy eyes. Also needed for cell respiration since it works with enzymes to help the cells use oxygen.

Deficiency May Lead to: Cracks at the sides of the mouth and a soreness and redness of the tongue and lips, burning and itching eyes, oversensitivity to bright light, dimness of vision, retarded growth.

Notes: Rapidly destroyed by light. If milk is left in the sun, it will lose 10% of B₂ in 30 minutes and 40% in 2 hours. Extra B₂ is needed by pregnant women, infants, and milking mothers.

Best Sources: Liver, whole milk and milk products such as buttermilk and yogurt, brewers' yeast, hot red pepper, almonds, wheat germ, wild rice, mushrooms, turnip greens.

Vitamin B₆ (Pyridoxine)

Use in the Body: Aids in breakdown and use of carbohydrates, fats, and proteins. Helps form antibodies and red blood cells. Participates in the use of energy in brain and nervous tissues and is therefore important in the regulation of the central nervous system and protection against stress. Has been used in the control of nausea and vomiting during pregnancy.

Deficiency May Lead to: Muscular weakness, nervousness, irritability, depression, mouth disorders, dermatitis, convulsions, anemia.

Notes: Need may be increased in women taking oral contraceptives.

Best Sources: Whole grains, meats, nuts, and brewers' yeast.

Vitamin B₁₂ (Cobalamin)

Use in the Body: Essential for normal functioning of all body cells, especially those of the bone marrow, gastrointestinal tract, and nervous tissue. Necessary for formation of red blood cells.

Deficiency May Lead to: Pernicious anemia. This is rare except in vegetarians who don't eat dairy products.

Notes: Primarily found in the liver. Some formation occurs in the natural bacteria within the intestine. The only vitamin which contains cobalt.

Best Sources: Meats, fish, milk and milk products, eggs, soybeans.

Biotin

Use in the Body: Assists in the formation of fatty acids and in the burning up of fatty acids and carbohydrates for body heat and energy. Also aids in the use of amino acids, folic acid, pantothenic acid, and vitamin B₁₂.

Deficiency May Lead to: Dermatitis, grayish skin color, depression, muscle pains. Rarely occurs, although it may arise if a large amount of raw egg white is consumed over a long period of time. Raw egg white contains the protein avidin, which combines with biotin in the intestines, preventing its absorption.

Notes: Unaffected by heat, but can be destroyed by exposure to air, baking soda, and strong acids. May be lost if cooking water is thrown away.

Best Sources: Organ meats, whole grains, and brewers' yeast.

Choline

Use in the Body: It is the main ingredient of lecithin, which aids in the movement of fats from the liver to the cells. Plays a part in the transmission of nerve impulses.

Notes: Not greatly affected by heat or storage, but destroyed by strong alkali. Present in all living cells, it is made by the body from the amino acid methionine, along with folic acid and vitamin B_{12}.

Best Sources: Eggs, organ meats, wheat germ and whole grains, legumes (peas, beans, lentils, peanuts), fish.

Folic Acid (Folacin)

Use in the Body: Carries carbon in the formation of heme, the iron-containing protein in hemoglobin. Aids in the formation of red blood cells and nucleic acid, which is essential for growth and reproduction. May prevent graying of hair.

Deficiency May Lead to: Anemia. Rare except during infancy or pregnancy. May occur with use of sulfa drugs, which interfere with the intestinal bacteria which produce some folic acid.

Notes: Stress, disease, and the consumption of alcohol increase the body's needs.

Best Sources: Gland meats, green, leafy vegetables, and brewers' yeast.

Inositol

Use in the Body: Along with choline, it is necessary for the formation of lecithin, which moves fats from the liver to the cells.

Best Sources: Whole grains, vegetables, nuts, citrus fruits, organ meats.

Niacin

Use in the Body: Assists in the breakdown and use of proteins, fats, and carbohydrates. Promotes good physical and mental health, maintains the health of the skin, tongue, and digestive system.

Deficiency May Lead to: Weakness, diarrhea, dermatitis, swelled tongue, irritation of the rectum, depression and irritability, and pellagra, which in advanced cases leads to delirium, hallucinations, and stupor.

Notes: Not destroyed by heat, light, or air. Most effective when used with other B vitamins.

Best Sources: Chicken and turkey (light meat contains 50% more niacin than dark meat), peanuts, organ meats, rice bran and polish,

milk and milk products, meat and fish, hot red pepper, whole grains.

PABA (Para-Aminobenzoic Acid)

Use in the Body: Enables the intestinal bacteria to produce folic acid, which, in turn, aids in producing pantothenic acid. Aids in the breakdown and use of proteins and in the formation of blood cells, especially red blood cells. May prevent graying of hair.

Deficiency May Lead to: Fatigue, irritability, depression, nervousness, headache, constipation and other digestive disorders. May result from use of sulfa drugs.

Best Sources: Organ meats and green leafy vegetables.

Pantothenic Acid

Use in the Body: Necessary for the functioning of the adrenal gland, which directly affects growth, and for the maintenance of healthy skin and nerves. Also essential for formation of cholesterol and fatty acids. Participates in the release of energy from carbohydrates, fats, and proteins and in the use of other vitamins, especially to withstand stress. May prevent graying of hair.

Deficiency May Lead to: Malfunction of the adrenal gland, irritability, dizziness, loss of appetite, stomach distress, constipation, numbness, tingling and burning sensations of the feet, increased susceptibility to infection, fatigue, breathlessness, fainting spells, depression, headaches, sleep disturbances.

Notes: Present in all living cells. More stable in a warm cooking liquid than in dry cooking. Easily destroyed by acid, such as vinegar, or alkali, such as baking soda.

Best Sources: Brewers' yeast, organ meats, legumes, eggs, whole grains.

Vitamin B_{15} (Pangamic Acid)

Use in the Body: May be effective in the treatment of hypoxia, a condition in which there is an insufficient supply of oxygen to the living cells. Research continues as to its use in treating other diseases.

Notes: Not sold as a commercial vitamin pill in the U.S.

Best Sources: Brewers' yeast and seeds.

Vitamin B_{17} (Laetrile)

Use in the Body: May prevent cancer by alleviating the nutritional deficiency which causes the disease.

Notes: Contains cyanide. Although laetrile is used to treat cancer in Europe and Mexico, its use is banned in the U.S., where research is not even allowed. This ban is currently being challenged in the courts by doctors who have openly prescribed laetrile for their patients.

Best Source: Apricot kernels (which are inside the pits).

Vitamin C (Ascorbic Acid)

Use in the Body: Primary function is to maintain collagen, a protein necessary for the formation of skin, ligaments, and bones. Helps heal wounds, form scar tissue, and mend fractures. Gives strength to blood vessels, thus preventing hemorrhaging. Aids in resisting some types of virus and bacterial infections. Aids in the absorption of iron.

Deficiency May Lead to: Bleeding, swollen or painful gums, swollen or painful joints, slow healing of wounds and fractures, tendency to bruise or bleed, lowered resistance to infection. Prolonged deficiency can lead to scurvy and finally death.

Notes: Vitamin C content of a fruit depends greatly upon how much sun it receives —the more the better. Body's need is increased by periods of stress such as anxiety, infection, injury, surgery, burns, or fatigue. Hot weather and air pollution increase the need for C, as does the use of aspirin and cigarette smoking. Most easily destroyed of all vitamins—by light, heat, air, prolonged storage, copper and iron utensils, alkali such as baking soda, and prolonged cooking. Foods containing vitamin C should be kept in the refrigerator.

Best Sources: Acerola cherries, hot and sweet peppers, guavas, kale, parsley, collard greens, turnip greens, dock (sorrel), broccoli, Brussels sprouts, persimmons, strawberries, papaya, lemons, oranges, most fruits and vegetables.

Vitamin D

Use in the Body: Regulates amount of calcium and phosphorus in the blood, thus it is necessary for bone development.

Deficiency May Lead to: Faulty development of bones and teeth, tooth cavities, rickets, tetany—muscular numbness, tingling, and spasms.

Overdose May Lead to: Excess of calcium in the blood and tissues.

Notes: Can be formed in the body when the ultraviolet rays of the sun activate a form of cholesterol in the skin, but the sun's action is inhibited by air pollution, clouds, window glass, and clothing. Primarily stored in the liver. Very stable in relation to heat, aging, and storage and relatively stable when exposed to air.

Best Sources: Sunlight, fish liver oil, egg yolks, organ meats, fortified milk and milk products, fatty fishes.

Vitamin E (Tocopherol)

Use in the Body: Prevents stored fats and vitamin A from breaking down and making harmful combinations. Unites with oxygen to protect red blood cells and keep them from rupturing. May improve the health of the circulatory system and counteract the process of aging. May play a part in increasing fertility and treating sterility. Externally, it aids the healing of burns, bruises, and wounds.

Deficiency May Lead to: Anemia in premature infants, infrequent ovulation and other problems of the reproductive organs.

Notes: Destroyed by commercial processing, cooking, storage, ultraviolet rays, iron, rancid fats and oils. Mostly stored in the muscles, fatty tissues, and liver.

Best Sources: Cold-pressed vegetable oils, margarine, wheat germ, whole grains, eggs, green leafy vegetables, organ meats, fruits, peanuts.

Vitamin K

Use in the Body: Prevents hemorrhaging, necessary for formation of prothrombin, which is necessary in blood-clotting.

Deficiency May Lead to: Increased tendency to hemorrhaging. Rare, but can result from malfunction of liver or bile duct.

Notes: Destroyed by mineral oil, alkali, alcohol, light, and rancidity. Foods should be stored in dark containers. Stable in relation to heat and cooking. Sulfa drugs and antibiotics interfere with its absorption.

Best Sources: Green leafy vegetables, alfalfa sprouts, fats, oats, wheat, rye.

—D.W.

MINERALS

Calcium

Use in the Body: Primary function is to work with phosphorus in building and maintaining bones and teeth. It also helps the blood clot, prevents the accumulation of too much acid or too much alkali in the blood, and plays a part in heartbeat regulation, nerve transmission, and muscle contractions.

Deficiency May Lead to: Tetany, a nerve disease characterized by muscle cramps and numbness and tingling in the arms and legs. Also bone malformation and general deterioration of the bones.

Notes: The most abundant mineral in the body, comprising 1½% to 2% of the weight of an adult body. Ninety-nine percent of the calcium in the body is deposited in the bones and teeth. Calcium absorption is dependent upon the presence of phosphorus and vitamins A, C, and D. Oxalic acid, found in chocolate, rhubarb, and spinach, when combined with calcium, forms a compound which may form into kidney or gall stones. Excess calcium is excreted by the body. Bedridden people often suffer calcium deficiency.

Best Sources: Whole sesame seeds, Parmesan, Swiss, and other cheeses, kelp and other seaweeds, milk and milk products, collard greens, kale, turnip greens, blackstrap molasses, almonds.

Chlorine

Use in the Body: Helps regulate the balance of acid and alkali in the blood. It is a part of hydrochloric acid, which is found in the digestive juices of the stomach.

Deficiency May Lead to: Atherosclerosis tion, weak water retention.

Notes: Excess chlorine is excreted.

Best Sources: Table salt, ripe tomatoes, celery, lettuce, kelp, spinach, salty foods.

Chromium

Use in the Body: Appears to be necessary for the metabolism of carbohydrates and improves the body's utilization of glucose. Chromium may lower the level of cholesterol in the blood.

Deficency May Lead to: Atherosclerosis (hardening of the arteries) and opacity of the cornea, which may lead to cataracts.

Notes: An essential trace element, chromium appears to be beneficial to diabetics and atherosclerotic patients. Most Americans are chromium-deficient because 60% of our diet consists of saturated fats and refined sugar and flour which deplete chromium in the body. Women taking birth-control pills need extra amounts of this mineral.

Best Sources: Brewers' yeast (especially high), nuts, grains and cereals, unrefined sugars such as honey, blackstrap molasses, shellfish, chicken, condiments and spices, meat, vegetables and fruits.

Cobalt

Use in the Body: Needed for the production of vitamin B_{12} and necessary for the normal functioning of red blood cells.

Deficiency May Lead to: Scaly skin and pernicious anemia.

Overdose May Lead to: Enlarged thyroid gland.

Notes: The smallest minimum daily requirement of any substance known to make a difference between health and disease. Little body storage.

Best Sources: Green leafy vegetables, meat, whole-grain cereals, and fruits grown in cobalt-rich soil.

Copper

Use in the Body: Aids in the formation of red blood cells and the production of hair pigment. It is present in many body-building enzymes, elastic muscle fibers, and the covering of nerve fibers.

Deficiency May Lead to: Anemia and weakening of the arteries. However, copper deficiency in humans is extremely rare.

Overdose May Lead to: Toxicity, though this is unusual because the body takes only what it needs and discards the rest. Schizophrenics are found to have high levels of copper in their blood.

Notes: An essential trace element, copper is found throughout the tissues of the body and in high concentrations in the liver, kidneys, heart, brain, and hair. Human requirements are small. The absorption of copper may be antagonized by zinc, molybdenum, and sulfur, which are contained in the best sources of copper. Women need a significant increase of copper during pregnancy and menstruation.

Best Sources: Shellfish and organ meats are especially high. Others are nuts, legumes, raisins and prunes, condiments and spices, oils such as margarine, brewers' yeast, and cereals and grains.

Fluorine

Use in the Body: Necessary for strong teeth and bones. It discourages tooth decay by reducing the growth of acid-forming bacteria and strengthens bones by assisting the deposition of calcium.

Deficiency May Lead to: Decayed teeth and softened bones, which are common in the U.S.

Overdose May Lead to: Mottling (discoloration and brittleness of young teeth), arthritis and muscular stiffness, and allergies.

Notes: An essential trace element, fluorine is concentrated in the bones and teeth in the form of compounds called fluorides. Though the body needs only a small amount of fluorine, a widespread deficiency exists in this country. The villain is the proliferation of processed carbohydrates—white sugar, white flour, and processed cereals—from which most minerals, including fluorine, are extracted.

Best Sources: Tea and seafood are the best sources, followed by fluorinated drinking water and fluoride toothpastes. Vegetables contain small amounts depending upon the water used in their cultivation.

Iodine

Use in the Body: Completes the formation of thyroxin, the thyroid hormone that controls the activity of the thyroid gland. Thyroxin in turn regulates the body's growth and development.

Deficiency May Lead to: Abnormal growth of the thyroid into a goiter. Other signs are dry hair and skin and mental and physical fatigue. Mothers with iodine-poor diets may give birth to retarded children. Although iodine deficiency is rare in civilized countries, it may result from an excessive diet of certain raw foods (such as cabbage and nuts) which interfere with the thyroid's utilization of iodine.

Overdose May Lead to: Reduction of the thyroid's synthesis of hormones.

Notes: An essential trace element, iodine is mostly converted to iodide in the body and concentrated in the 2 thyroid glands. Iodized salt generally supplies the normal adult requirement.

Best Sources: Shellfish are the best source, table salt is the most widespread. Vegetables and fruits provide varying amounts, depending on the iodine content of the soil they were grown in.

Iron

Use in the Body: Necessary for the formation of myoglobin, which transports oxygen to muscle tissue, and hemoglobin, which transports oxygen in the blood.

Deficiency May Lead to: Iron deficiency anemia (reduction of hemoglobin in the red blood cells), which in turn reduces oxygen carried in the blood to vital organs. This results in pallid skin and loss of energy.

Overdose May Lead to: The body stores iron for future use. However, alcoholism, cirrhosis of the liver, and pancreas insufficiency may result in excessive iron deposits in the liver and spleen. Excessive intake of iron leads to toxicity.

Notes: Iron is the 2nd most essential trace element in the body. It is a component of every body cell. The body stores iron primarily in the liver, spleen, blood, and bone marrow, conserving it for future use rather than absorbing it. Since vitamin C changes iron's composition and makes it easier for the body to use, the 2 should be taken together. Also, the body absorbs more iron from beans when they are eaten with meat, which also contains a good deal of iron. Additional iron is required during pregnancy, lactation, menstruation, hemorrhage, growth periods (in children), and loss of blood. Many nutritionists claim that iron deficiency anemia is fairly common in this country; at least 250,000 women have it at any given time. Iron has been beneficial in the treatment of alcoholism, leukemia, colitis (inflammation of the colon), nail disorders, scurvy, worms, peptic ulcers, and teeth and gum disorders.

Best Sources: Organ meats (especially liver), shellfish, molasses, beans, green leafy vegetables, egg yolks.

Magnesium

Use in the Body: Activates more enzymes in the body than any other mineral, acting as a primary agent in the utilization of fats, proteins, carbohydrates, and several vitamins and minerals. Magnesium aids in the formation of bones and is an important part of the fluid between cells. It is necessary for the proper function of nerves and muscles, including the heart. It may also have something to do with regulating body temperature.

Deficiency May Lead to: Heat and circulatory diseases, weakening of capillaries, nervousness and muscle excitability (twitches, spasms), chronic diarrhea, and vomiting. May occur in alcoholics, diabetics, or those suffering kidney malfunction. Sources differ widely on the frequency of magnesium deficiency, but many say that the average American is slightly deficient in his diet.

Notes: An essential bulk element, magnesium is stored in the bones in combination with calcium and phosphorus and in the red blood cells, muscles, and soft tissues. The body's need for magnesium depends on its intake of protein, phosphorus, and vitamin D, since it assists in their utilization. Calcium competes with magnesium for absorption in the body; therefore its intake requires added magnesium. The alleged American deficiency of magnesium is blamed on our diet of refined sugar and flour. Magnesium may be beneficial in treating diabetes, alcoholism, mental illness, nervousness, diarrhea, kidney malfunction, and kidney stones.

Best Sources: Nuts, beans, peanut butter, whole grains, blackstrap molasses, dairy products, green leafy vegetables, and seafood.

Manganese

Use in the Body: Manganese is an important activator for many enzymes and the production of fats and carbohydrates. It is necessary for normal skeletal development and perhaps the formation of blood. Manganese is closely related to blood sugar levels. It also maintains the reproductive processes.

Deficiency May Lead to: Abnormal body growth, stillbirths, sterility, and convulsions. However, since manganese is contained in trace amounts in most foods, deficiency in humans is practically unheard of.

Notes: An essential trace element, manganese is concentrated in the bones, liver, kidneys, pituitary gland, pancreas, and intestines. Zinc-manganese supplements are being used in the treatment of schizophrenics.

Best Sources: Nuts (especially high), tea, fruits, root vegetables, legumes, cereals and grains, green leafy vegetables, condiments and spices.

Molybdenum

Use in the Body: May be necessary for enzyme functioning.

Deficiency May Lead to: Cancer of the esophagus and digestive tract.

Overdose May Lead to: Copper deficiency. Molybdenum is toxic in large quantities.

Notes: An essential trace element, molybdenum is stored for the most part in the liver and kidneys. It is the least abundant of the essential minerals. Molybdenum is associated with the functions of vitamin E.

Best Sources: Organ meats and legumes are high. Condiments and spices, green leafy vegetables, grains and cereals.

Phosphorus

Use in the Body: Plays a part in nearly every chemical reaction in the body and performs more functions than any other mineral. Phosphorus is important for the growth, maintenance, and repair of cells, and the production of energy. It provides energy for muscle contractions and nerve impulses. It is involved in the genetic transfer of hereditary traits. Phosphorus is also an important component of phospholipids, which utilize fats and fatty acids, maintain the pH level (acidity-alkalinity) of the blood, and assist in the secretion of hormones.

Deficiency May Lead to: Stunted growth, poor quality of teeth and bones, and bone disorders. Phosphorus deficiency may result from insufficient supplies of calcium or vitamin D, both of which are needed for phosphorus absorption. Also, excess use of antacids may inhibit phosphorus absorption.

Overdose May Lead to: Since the body efficiently stores phosphorus, there is no known toxicity.

Notes: Next to calcium, phosphorus is the body's 2nd most abundant mineral, but it should be consumed in greater quantity. It functions mostly with calcium, which it needs for proper utilization; a healthy balance of calcium-phosphorus is 2:1. Phosphorus is found in every cell of the body, but 80% of it is present in the bones and teeth. It may be beneficial in the treatment of fractures, brittle bones, rickets, and teeth and gum disorders. Older people need more phosphorus because their systems generally do not absorb it too well.

Best Sources: Powdered skim milk, wheat germ, and brewers' yeast are especially high. Fish, chicken, meats, seeds, legumes, and dairy products.

Potassium

Use in the Body: Helps regulate osmosis, the pH level (acidity-alkalinity) of the blood, and the conversion of glucose to the more easily stored glycogen. Along with its partner sodium, potassium assists in the formation of muscle protein and the stimulation of nerve impulses for muscle contractions.

Deficiency May Lead to: Apathy, weakness, and poor intestinal muscle tone. Both deficiency and excess of potassium cause impaired muscular activity, slow heartbeat, and heart attack. Deficiencies may result from diarrhea, vomiting, or excessive urination.

Notes: An essential bulk element, potassium is found mainly inside the cells, where the body stores it for future use, and to a much smaller degree, in the fluids outside the cells. Potassium may be beneficial in treating hypertension, diarrhea, alcoholism, slow heartbeat, teeth and gum disorders, fever, stress, insomnia, and mononucleosis.

Best Sources: Legumes, green leafy vegetables (especially spinach), whole grains, meats, nuts, fruits, seafood, and root vegetables.

Selenium

Use in the Body: Appears to be an antioxidant that prevents oxidation of saturated fats in the blood, thus heading off such diseases as atherosclerosis. Related closely to vitamin E. May prevent certain kinds of cancer.

Deficiency May Lead to: Difficulties in handling vitamin E. Extra amounts of this vitamin may relieve selenium deficiency.

Overdose May Lead to: Toxicity. Excessive selenium may replace sulfur in tissues, resulting in brittle hair and bones.

Notes: An essential trace element, selenium is still a mystery to researchers. It may increase the incidence of dental cavities or, on the other hand, it may prevent muscular dystrophy.

Best Sources: Nuts and seafood. Also grains and cereals, green leafy vegetables, fruits, organ meats, condiments and spices, milk.

Sodium

Use in the Body: Assists with its partner potassium in the regulation of water balance, the maintenance of normal pH in the blood, and the influence of muscular activity.

Deficiency May Lead to: Is rare, because sodium chloride (salt) is present in most foods. Also, sodium is closely regulated by the body; the rate of its excretion depends on its sufficiency in the body. Vomiting, diarrhea, and excessive perspiration may deplete the body's salt.

Overdose May Lead to: Edema (swelling of the body tissues). Sodium also aggravates hypertension (high blood pressure), a widespread American disease.

Notes: An essential mineral found in the bones and the fluids surrounding cells. It generally works with potassium. Sodium is a constituent of body secretions like saliva and enzymes. Since it is lost when the body sweats, supplements are needed during hard labor on hot days. Sodium may be beneficial for the treatment of diarrhea, leg cramps, dehydration, and fever.

Best Sources: Table salt, baking powder, baking soda, green leafy vegetables, chicken, meat, dairy products, seafoods, water.

Sulfur

Use in the Body: Necessary for the formation of body tissues and the functioning of thiamine and biotin (2 B vitamins). Sulfur acts as one of the body's detoxifiers. It assists in the respiration of tissues, which builds cells and releases energy.

Deficiency May Lead to: Is rare, for sulfur is widespread in foods.

Overdose May Lead to: Toxicity, in inorganic form.

Notes: An essential element, sulfur is present in all body cells but concentrated mainly in skin, hair, and nails. It is the body's 3rd most abundant mineral (far behind calcium and phosphorus in content). A proper diet of protein supplies the body with all the sulfur it needs.

Best Sources: Meat, fish, eggs, dairy products, legumes, and nuts.

Zinc

Use in the Body: Necessary for the formation of enzymes and proteins, the respiration of body tissues (primarily the disposal of carbon dioxide), and the process of digestion. It may assist in lowering cholesterol levels. Zinc is a constituent of insulin and male sperm. It also aids in the metabolism of phosphorus.

Deficiency May Lead to: Retarded growth, anemia, and delayed sexual maturity. Deficiency is common in older people and pregnant women and, because of the American diet of refined sugar and flour, certainly not uncommon among the general population. A high intake of calcium requires a greater need for zinc; the 2 are somewhat antagonistic.

Overdose May Lead to: Loss of iron and copper from the liver.

Notes: An essential trace element, zinc is found in most tissue, especially concentrated in the prostate gland, liver, kidneys, pancreas, spermatozoa, and eyes. Zinc may be beneficial in the treatment of Hodgkin's disease, schizophrenia, leukemia, alcoholism, flesh wounds, arteriosclerosis, and sexual or growth retardation. Women on birth-control pills need extra zinc.

Best Sources: Nuts, meat, and shellfish are high. Spices and condiments, grains and cereals, legumes, egg yolks, and most other food, except refined sugar and flour and saturated fats.

WATER

Use in the Body: Necessary for all building functions in the body. Water dissolves and transports other nutrients, and thus acts as a carrier in the processes of digestion, absorption, circulation, and excretion. It also helps regulate body temperature.

Deficiency May Lead to: Dehydration.

Overdose May Lead to: Edema (swelling), usually caused by a kidney disorder rather than excessive drinking. Prolonged intake of soft water may significantly contribute to hypertension, hardening of the arteries, and apoplexy (brain hemorrhage); the presence of cadmium in soft water may be the reason.

Notes: Water, an essential constituent of all body cells, comprises over 50% of the human body. Its intake is regulated by a sensation of thirst. There are basically 3 kinds of drinking water:

1) Hard water—contains calcium, magnesium salts, and other materials.

2) Soft water—contains sodium, which has replaced the calcium and magnesium salts. Acidic and corrosive, soft water often dissolves and contains the metal of the pipes through which it passes. Often contains copper, iron, zinc, and cadmium.

3) Distilled water—pure water that has had all the minerals removed by a steam process.

Industrially polluted water has become a serious problem in this country. Most municipal drinking water has been generously laced with chlorine for purification and fluorine to help prevent tooth decay. Water may be beneficial for swollen glands, cystitis, constipation, and gallstones.

Best Sources: Spring water, tap water, milk, beverages, fruits, and vegetables.

—J.D.

Three Kings of the Kitchen

VATEL (1622?–1671)

We may live without friends; we may live without books;
But civilized men cannot live without cooks.

That was the way British poet Owen Meredith put it, but he neglected to mention that some civilized cooks could very well do without their employers. The famous French cook Vatel and his master, the notorious Prince de Condé, offer an excellent example.

Less is known of Vatel than any other great cook; not even one recipe he concocted has been passed down to posterity. Some say he was Swiss-born, baptized "Fritz Karle" Watel, but in any event, he did serve the Prince de Condé, perhaps as principal chef in that great household. Monsieur le prince, however, was a most eccentric gentleman and when Louis XIV accepted an invitation to visit his estate at Chantilly, the prince was ready to ruin himself financially in order to impress the Roi Soleil. Everything the Sun King wanted in the way of wine, women, and food was to be provided, and Louis had prodigious appetites for all.

Vatel was instructed to spare neither expense nor effort to feed the gluttonous King, and the chef drove himself to the point of nervous exhaustion in doing so. All the delicacies that could be had were fed Louis. The chef served him light refreshments in the field "in a spot carpeted with jonquils." But then—a tragedy! Vatel, who hadn't had a night's sleep for 12 days, failed to serve roasts to a few tables in the King's party during one sumptuous feast.

No doubt Monsieur le prince was furious and his chef tried all the harder to please him, though on the verge of a nervous breakdown. Finally, the breaking point came when Vatel ordered fresh fish for the King from the nearest seaport towns. Arising at 4 A.M. to check the quality of the fish that would be arriving, he found that only 2 hampers had been delivered, far too little to feed the King's party. "Is that all there is?" he asked the fishmonger, and the man replied that no more would be coming, meaning only that no more fish would be sent from *his* town. Unfortunately, Vatel misunderstood him. "I cannot survive this disgrace," he told his assistant, and he retired to his room, fixed his sword upon the door, and ran himself upon it, never more to be harried by his vexsome employer.

Ironically, 10 more loads of fish arrived from other seaports just 15 minutes after Vatel's death, and though there was talk of the chef's dedication at table the next day, the merry feasting continued unabated. As for the Prince de Condé, he grew even more eccentric with each passing year. Toward the end of his life, he announced that he, himself, was dead, and since dead men did not eat, neither would he. His doctors tricked him, telling him that dead men *do* eat, but from then until his actual demise Monsieur le prince would only dine at the table in the presence of corpses that the doctors supplied.

ANTHELME BRILLAT-SAVARIN (1755–1826)

Animals feed: man eats; only a man of wit knows how to dine.

The destiny of nations depends on the manner wherein they take their food.

A dessert course without cheese is like a beautiful woman with one eye.

The discovery of a new dish is more beneficial to humanity than the discovery of a new star.

To invite anyone implies that we charge ourselves with his happiness all the time that he is under our roof.

Probably the greatest gastronome in history, aside from the Roman Apicius (whose true identity hasn't really been established), Anthelme Brillat-Savarin, author of the above and many other well-known aphorisms on *la cuisine*, never enjoyed his great fame in his own lifetime. But he enjoyed living so much that fame was hardly necessary. A kindhearted host, an amiable guest, and a witty companion, he regarded good food and wine as the most important things in life. Once asked whether he preferred Burgundies or clarets, he replied: "Ah! Madame, that is a question I take so much pleasure in investigating that I postpone from week to week the pronouncement of a verdict."

Fame came to Brillat-Savarin with the publication of his *Le Physiologie du Goût* (*Physiology of Taste*) in 1825, a work which defies classification but belongs among the relative handful of books that never go out of fashion. He was to die the following year at the age of 71, but not before he had given the world the most trenchant discussion of food and its effects on trenchermen ever written, a masterpiece that was 30 years in the making. Appropriately enough, the greatest of French bon vivants had been born in the town of Belley—"Belley is its name and Belley is its nature," wrote Michael Stein over a century later. Becoming the town's mayor after the French Revolution, Brillat-Savarin had to flee to America during the Reign of Terror, living in Connecticut for a few years and later writing some of his most charming pages about his stay there.

Portly and gregarious, the sage of Belley remained a bachelor all his life—perhaps too devoted to both food and women ever to marry, possibly because he loved his cousin, the society beauty Madame Récamier. On returning to France, he became a familiar figure in the cafés of Paris, his little dog constantly at his side waiting patiently for an occasional tidbit. Many poked fun at him, but he seemed always to be present at the important dinners of the day, one story having him a guest of the Vicomte François René de Chateaubriand, on that evening when the succulent steak Chateaubriand was invented in the novelist's honor.

A lawyer who wrote on political economy and law, and penned a few licentious tales as well, Brillat-Savarin seems to have come from a long line of gourmets. Brillat was actually Anthelme's real name—he took on the hyphen and Savarin when his great-aunt, a discriminating diner, left him her entire fortune on the condition that he add her name to his. His sister Pierrette also loved good food. In fact, she died at the dinner table. Almost 100 at the time, her last words are among the most unusual in history: "And now, girl, bring me the dessert!"

Though Brillat-Savarin, too, was something of an eccentric—he often carried dead birds around in his pockets until they became "high" enough for gourmet cooking—his reputation did not suffer from his eccentricities. No food book has yet surpassed his bible of gastronomy, not even Prosper Montagné's classic *Larousse Gastronomique*. "Tell me what you eat and I will tell you what you are," Brillat-Savarin once declared, and the gastronomic tests in his book have been acclaimed as small masterpieces of psychological insight almost as brilliant as his discussions of food. The book might also be called the 1st diet book (in it the author offers advice on how to stay slim, but inveighs against scrawny women), and gives recipes, plus a series of dinners for various income brackets—the most extravagant including a Strasbourg *pâté de foie gras* in the shape of a bastion, truffled quail, river pike smothered in cream of crayfish, early asparagus with a special sauce, 2 dozen ortolans, and for dessert a pyramid of vanilla and rose meringues. Ironically, the immortal *Le Physiologie du Goût* had to be printed at Brillat-Savarin's expense, and when his brother later sold all rights to a publisher, he got only $120—after throwing in the author's genuine Stradivarius as well. Fortunately, today *The Physiology of Taste* is available in quality paperback from Dover Publications, 180 Varick St., New York, N.Y. 10014.

MARC-ANTOINE CARÊME (1784–1833)

Marc-Antoine Carême, "the king of cooks and the cook of Kings," as he has been called, was born in Paris, in his own words one of 25 children "of one of the poorest families in France." Some authorities claim he was a lineal descendant of a celebrated chef of Pope Leo X's; this ancestor, it is said, invented a delicious Lenten soup and the Pontiff honored him with the name Jean de Carême (Lent), which was adopted by the family. In any event, Carême worked from the time he was 7 as a kitchen scullion. Finally, accepted as an apprentice chef in his late teens, he studied under many masters—including Boucher, Laguipicre, Robert, Richaut, Bardet, Lasne, Savart, Riquert, and Robillard—until he made the subtle synthesis that marked the end of Old Regime cooking and the founding of *La Grande Cuisine Française*, classic French cooking as we still know it today.

Carême's creations reflected his considerable artistic abilities, his pastries often looking more like sculpture than the delicious desserts they were, and his supreme taste and meticulous standards—illustrated in his many books—as well as his 48-course dinners, made the French cuisine sovereign throughout Europe. Among other notables, he cooked for Talleyrand; Czar Alexander I; the future George IV of England; Lord Castlereagh; Baron Rothschild, the world's richest man; and France's Louis XVIII, who granted him the right to call himself "Carême of Paris." Yet his motto was "One master: Talleyrand. One mistress: Cooking." He was always faithful to his 1st benefactor and as a result is the one noted chef in history who was also a spy, relaying information he overheard at important dinner tables all over Europe to the French Minister of Foreign Affairs. He believed that a trencherman could only be happy living in France, but as a spy in the uniform of a master chef he sent home secret information from the St. Petersburg court, the dining rooms of the Emperor of Austria, and the House of Rothschild, among the many places which piqued the curiosity of Monsieur de Talleyrand.

Carême's culinary triumphs were far more important than his diplomatic ones, though. In his travels, he discovered and introduced to France such delicacies as caviar and Paskha, a creamy cheesecake prominent in the Russian cuisine, which the French soon adopted as the now famous *coeur à la crème*. While in England, he created a lavish pastry which he called the Apple Charlotte, after that country's Princess Charlotte, and when serving Czar Alexander, still apparently unable to forget the princess, he invented a jellied custard set in a crown of ladyfingers that he named the Charlotte Russe in her honor—a pastry still made in bakeries today. Carême's triumphs also include many gargantuan feasts. At one military fete held outside in the Champs-Élysées, he prepared and served to 10,000 guests the foodstuffs required, including: 6 cows, 75 calves, 250 sheep, 8,000 turkeys, 2,000 plump chickens, 1,000 table fowls, 1,000 partridges, 500 hams, 1,000 carp, 1,000 pike, 18,000 bottles of Macon, and 145 casks of wine.

Although most of Carême's recipes were geared to professional chefs, here is a relatively simple one for Chestnut Croquettes adapted from one of his cookbooks:

Boil chestnuts, peeling and setting aside 3–4 whole ones per serving. Mash the remaining chestnuts. Prepare a puree by combining 2 cups of mashed chestnuts, loosely packed; 2 tablespoons of melted butter; 2 tablespoons of cream; 2 eggs; adding salt and white pepper to taste. Spread the puree on a buttered plate, covering it with waxed paper, and after the puree is cool enough to mold, cover each whole chestnut with some of the mixture. Next dip each coated chestnut in beaten egg, then in fine dry bread crumbs, finally frying each in deep fat. These croquettes are particularly delicious when served with meat.

Carême's word was law to every chef worthy of the name in what was probably the world's most extraordinary culinary period. One of his recipes was a full 7 pages long and his *Pièces Montées*, made of spun sugar, ranged from harps and globes to such fantastic creations as a grotto with moss, a Chinese summerhouse, and a Venetian pavilion on a bridge. Yet, he could write, most sensibly, "It is an error for those of lesser station to try to pattern their tables after the rich. . . . Better to serve a simple meal, well prepared; and not try to cover the bourgeois table with an imitation of *les grands*." Monarch of the culinary empire, his name is today synonymous for a great chef. He died on January 12, 1833, while sampling a *quenelle* of sole prepared by a student in his cooking school. "These are good," he is supposed to have murmured critically, "but prepared too hastily. You must shake the saucepan lightly—see, like this . . ." These were his last words, for, as he lifted the saucepan, he collapsed and fell to the floor dead. Someone wrote that he had died "burnt out by the flame of his genius and the heat of his ovens." But then again he had confided to at least one person that he was destined to be appointed chief chef in paradise.

—R.H.

Leading Vegetarians

Vegetarianism appears to be as old as mankind. The Greeks called it antipreophogy, meaning anti-flesh eating. While such notables as Plato, Diogenes, and Pythagoras advocated vegetarianism in the West, in India the Buddha preached the doctrine of Ahimsa—harmlessness to all living things.

Since then many religions and other spiritual sects have advocated a vegetarian diet, either officially or unofficially. These include the Seventh-Day Adventists, the Essenes, the Hindu, Buddhist, Zoroastrian, Tao, and Jain faiths, as well as the Trappist, Benedictine, and Carthusian orders of the Roman Catholic Church, and other Christian groups such as the Rosicrucian Fellowship.

The term "vegetarian," derived from the Latin word *vegetus*, meaning "whole, sound, fresh, lively," was coined in 1842. The 1st Vegetarian Society was formed in England in 1847. In the U.S., the vegetarian movement was greatly influenced by such men as Dr. Reuben D. Mussey, the 4th president of the American Medical Association, and Rev. Sylvester Graham, of graham cracker fame. J. H. Kellogg, MD, who developed cornflakes as a prepared breakfast food, was also an enthusiastic vegetarian.

Most vegetarians give one or more of the following reasons for not eating meat:

1. TASTE PREFERENCE. They simply don't like meat.

2. HEALTH. They believe that the human body was not built to digest meat, which putrefies quickly and puts great demands on the digestive system. Many medical authorities believe that meat is high in cholesterol, which leads to heart disease. An article in the June 3, 1961, issue of the *Journal of the American Medical Association* said that, ". . . a vegetarian diet can prevent 90% of our thrombo-embolic disease and 97% of our coronary occlusions." Some also believe that animals are affected by diseases which can be passed on to humans and that meat from artificially fed animals is filled with excretory substances.

3. MORALITY. Vegetarians believe that eating dead flesh means something alive has suffered pain. Eating a dead animal brings with it all the violent energy involved in the slaughter. The meat eater consumes this violence and becomes more violent himself. How many meat eaters are willing to kill an animal, skin it, bleed it, and prepare it to be eaten? Most eaters of dead flesh not only depend on others to do the dirty work, but they also disguise the form of the food so it doesn't look like an animal and use bizarre euphemisms, such as hamburger, sausage, bologna, and frankfurter, so they won't be reminded of what they are really eating.

4. ECOLOGY AND WORLD FOOD SHORTAGE. Vegetarians claim that the protein we get from eating dead animals comes from the cereals and grains that are fed to the animals. Ninety-one percent of the corn, 77% of the soybean meal, 64% of the barley, 88% of the oats, and 99% of the grain sorghum crops used in the U.S. are fed directly to livestock animals. If these grains were fed straight to humans, much less land would be wasted and more food could be produced.

ANIMALS EATEN BY AVERAGE PERSON IN A 70-YEAR LIFETIME

SHEEP 12

CATTLE 14

CALVES 2

HOGS 23

CHICKENS 880   FISH 770 LBS.   TURKEYS 35

Today there are said to be between 3 and 4 million vegetarians in the U.S. alone.

Meat eaters often regard vegetarians as eccentrics, crackpots, freaks, but the fact remains that vegetarians have been in the mainstream of history and include some of the most familiar names in the human saga. Herewith follows a chronological list of some of the best-known or most interesting personalities, from past to present day, who practiced vegetarianism for the rest of their lives after the time they took it up, as well as those who for some shorter period in their lives were avid vegetarians.

—D.W.

PYTHAGORAS. 578–510 B.C.? Greek.

—Has been called "the founder of both science and philosophy in Europe." Traveled extensively in quest of truth, knowledge, and the meaning of life. Was a celebrated mathematician who taught the theories of geometry. Founded the 1st antiflesh society in Western civilization.

—Abstained from eating any meat, beans, or eggs. Forbade the killing of animals and even of some plant life. Ate a modest diet of bread and honey with vegetables for dessert. Was repelled by butchers and their meat shops. Did drink some wine, but preferred water.

SIR THOMAS MORE. 1478–1535. English.

—Was an undersheriff of London and speaker of the House of Commons before being named Lord Chancellor of England. Refused to approve the divorce of Henry VIII from Catherine of Aragon. Would not sign the Act of Succession which placed the King's powers over those of the Church and was imprisoned. Tried for high treason, found guilty, and was beheaded. Author of *Utopia*, a book which describes the "perfect commonwealth."

—Abolished the killing of animals in his book with the "utopian" dictate that citizens should "kill no animal in sacrifice, nor [should] they think that God has delight in blood and slaughter, who has given life to animals to the intent they should live." Spoke primarily against butchering and meat eating but also criticized those who would "waste" corn in the making of alcoholic beverages. Did drink wine.

EMANUEL SWEDENBORG. 1688–1772. Swedish.

—Gained recognition for his scientific discoveries in physics, astronomy, mineralogy, and geology. Began to have "visions" at age 57 and rejected the "mechanistic" world to devote himself to spiritual studies. Was impetus for new religious society, New Jerusalem Church, founded by his followers in 1788.

—Favored bread and butter, almonds, and cakes. Drank coffee with milk and some sweetening. Occasionally had small portions of fish and once sampled pigeon pie. Indulged in snuff-sniffing. Crusaded against meat eating because "eating the flesh of animals, considered in itself, is something profane."

PERCY BYSSHE SHELLEY. 1792–1822. English.

—Expelled from Oxford at 19. Married Harriet Westbrook, ran off to the Continent with Mary Godwin, daughter of radical author, bookseller, publisher William Godwin. Legalized his union with Mary (after 1st wife's suicide). Famed for poems like *The Cenci* and *Prometheus Unbound*, for his views on free love, revolution, atheism, for his friendship and rivalry with Lord Byron, for his life as an expatriate in Switzerland and Italy. Drowned off Viareggio, Italy, when his vessel capsized in a storm or was rammed by piratical Italian fishing boats.

—Converted to vegetarianism at 21, by friendship with 46-year-old John Frank Newton, who championed bohemianism, nudism for children, and hosted meals consisting of delicious vegetables, fruits, unbuttered breadcakes, distilled water, but sometimes allowed sparing use of butter and eggs in cooking. Attacked meat eating in his famous poem "Queen Mab," writing: "No longer now/He slays the lamb, who looks him in the face,/And horribly devours its mangled flesh." Published pamphlet *A Vindication of Natural Diet* (only 8 copies have survived) in 1813, in which he pointed out that since man has the superior ability to communicate pain, which animals do not possess, man should abstain from "the evils" of seeking "animal food." Suggested that the meat eater should "tear a living lamb with his teeth, and plunge his head into the vitals, and slake his thirst with the steaming blood," and then all men would be vegetarians. Admonished all, "Never take any substance into the stomach, that once had life." Wrote that "animal flesh is the basis not only of human disease, but of human vice as well." Promised that with a vegetarian diet, even "hereditary diseases such as consumption, gout, asthma, cancer will perish." Would not eat "muffins and crumpets with tea because they were apt to be buttered," but was indifferent to what his wife served their friends. Served mutton to one friend, Hogg, and invited another guest to enjoy "a murdered chicken." Had no real interest in food and ate absentmindedly. Occasionally fell off the wagon and was once seen by Hogg on a trip "settling down to a solitary meal of cold boiled beef."

SYLVESTER GRAHAM. 1794–1851. American.

—Introduced graham-bread—made from unbolted wheat flour. Lectured across the U.S. on dietary reform. Received strong opposition from U.S. bakers, who held a riot demonstration against him in 1847. Proposed a strict vegetable diet to prevent all forms of "intemperance."
—Based his vegetarian beliefs on what he said was scientific fact: ". . . a single lb. of rice absolutely contains more nutritious matter, than 2½ lbs. of best butcher's meat; and 3 lbs. of good wheat bread contains more than 6 lbs. of flesh; and 3 lbs. of potatoes more than 2 lbs. of flesh. . . ."

SIR ISAAC PITMAN. 1813–1897. English.

—Fired from a cloth factory for being a Swedenborgian. Established a school and taught in Bath. Became interested in phonography, a means of spelling based on phonetics or sound. Invented a system of soundhand or shorthand (at the suggestion of a publisher), and when he was 24 published Pitman's *Stenographic Soundhand*. Established a Phonetic Institute and edited a phonetic journal. Was applauded by press and business since his shorthand proved to be a timesaving boon for reporters and secretaries. Was internationally acclaimed as shorthand manuals were soon translated into dozens of languages, including Welsh, Bengali, and Japanese. Sent his brother to the U.S. in 1853 to establish a shorthand institute in Cincinnati. Twice married. Knighted 2½ years before his death.
—Was on a "piurli vejetabel deiet" because it gave him bodily health and high spirits. Ate 3 moderate meals a day, mostly fruits, did not even drink tea until later in life. Rejected alcoholic beverages and tobacco. Was vice-president of the London Vegetarian Society, and when the members honored him upon his knighthood, he wrote them that he owed "mei long kontiniud helth and pouer" to "the dietetik principelz ov yur soseieti." Wrote to *The Times* of London that "dispepsia woz karriing me tu the grave." Advised by doctors to eat animal food 3 times a day instead of once, but diet made him grow "wurz." Turned vegetarian and "graduali rekuvered mei dijestiv pouer, and hav never nown that I hav a stumik."

COUNT LEO NIKOLAEVICH TOLSTOI. 1828–1910. Russian.

—Born into a wealthy family but chose to champion the cause of the poor. Opposed war and religious intolerance. Preached a simple religious creed of brotherhood, equality, and humility. Author whose works include *War and Peace, Anna Karenina,* and the *Death of Ivan Ilyich.*
—Ate no flesh, fish, or fowl but lived mainly on vegetables, fruits, porridge, and bread. Rejected eggs, butter, and lard. Did not smoke and drank water in preference to alcoholic beverages. Said that "Vegetarianism serves as a criterion by which we know that

the pursuit of moral perfection on the part of man is genuine and sincere. . . ."

GEORGE BERNARD SHAW. 1856–1950. British.

—Converted to playwright after success as music critic and drama critic but failure as a novelist. Became socialist at 26 and one of the original founders of the Fabian Society in England (1884). Acclaimed for his social and political criticisms as found in such plays as *Candida, Man and Superman, Heartbreak House, Pygmalion,* and *Major Barbara*.
—Summed up his dietary habits by saying, "I eat 3 meals a day, and am convinced that I should be better with 2. I eat cheese, butter and eggs, but no flesh, no fowl, and no fish." Drank apple juice, barley water, and cocoa (made with water, not milk). Grew vegetables and fruits in his own garden and favored tomatoes and potatoes. Rejected meat for humanitarian reasons: "My will contains directions for my funeral, which will be followed not by mourning coaches, but by herds of oxen, sheep, swine, flocks of poultry and a small traveling aquarium of live fish, all wearing white scarves in honor of the man who perished rather than eat his fellow creatures." Belonged to the London Vegetarian Society and was severely criticized when an attack of pernicious anemia caused him to take liver injections. Replied to his critics: "Gland extracts are no more outside vegetarian diet than milk and cheese. Vegetarian diet is vital diet, vegetable diet is a different matter." When asked if his long life could be attributed to a meatless diet and abstention from stimulants, he replied, "My nearest relatives, who practiced none of these abstinences, were long-lived like myself. The Italian physician who left a big book as his testament wrote nothing in it but 'Keep your feet warm and your head cool.'"

MAHATMA GANDHI. 1869–1948. Indian.

—Studied law in London and practiced in South Africa, where he organized Hindus in discrimination protests. Returned to India, became leader of National Congress, and led movement for independence. Imprisoned in 1922 (6-year sentence) but was released due to ailing health. Organized 2 major civil disobedience movements which advocated freedom through passive resistance. Resigned from politics to doctor the sick and was renamed Mahatma ("great soul").
—Conducted an experiment of eating meat but had nightmares of goats bleeding in his stomach. Became a member of the Vegetarian Society. Ate dates, nuts, fruits, and wholemeal bread, but never more than 5 items in one meal. Said that "one should not eat to please the palate but just to keep the body going." Occasionally took small amounts of fruit juices when fasting. Would never eat eggs and refused cow's milk because it "stirred the passions." Suffered from an attack of dysentery and was advised to drink milk. Refused because of his "vow against it." Convinced by his wife to drink goat's milk (instead of cow's milk) but later regretted doing so because: "The ideal of truth requires that vows taken should be fulfilled in the letter as well as in the spirit. I have killed the soul of my vow by adhering to its outer form only, and that is what galls me."

BENITO MUSSOLINI. 1883–1945. Italian.

—Was a bricklayer, factory worker, schoolteacher, and journalist before he became Italian dictator. Founded fascism in 1919 and established it as a political party in 1921. Headed fascist march on Rome, which led to his appointment as Prime Minister. Exercised dictatorial powers for 20 years and was assassinated in 1945.
—Became a vegetarian in 1925 after an ulcer attack. Ate pasta (with butter sauce) and fruit (mainly grapes and oranges). Did occasionally eat chicken or rabbit. Liked others to recognize his "frugality" and frequently had a glass of milk placed on his desk. Returned to meat diet in 1943 on the advice of a doctor (sent to Mussolini by Hitler).

ADOLF HITLER. 1889–1945. German.

—Imprisoned in 1923 after his revolutionary tactics failed in Munich (the Beer Hall Putsch). Joined Nazi party, increased his political strength, and became Chancellor of Germany in 1933. Made himself dictator and assumed title of "Führer." Committed suicide.
—Considered himself a strict vegetarian although he was criticized for eating pigs' knuckles. Ate fresh vegetables, spinach, and spaghetti. Was especially fond of asparagus tips and artichoke hearts (in cream sauce), eggs and cauliflower (combined in various ways). Loved sweets and pastries, sometimes eating as much as 2 lbs. of chocolate a day. Consumed large amounts of eggs, which were "prepared in 101 different ways by the best chef in Germany." Had 2 menus prepared for each meal he hosted—one for the meat eaters and one for the vegetarians. Opposed to drinking and smoking. Believed that the "decadence" of civilization was in large part due to meat eating and "had its origin in the abdomen—chronic constipation, poisoning of the juices, and the results of drinking

to excess." Became vegetarian because of stomach problems. Supplemented diet (unbalanced because of large content of carbohydrates) with drugs to ward off states of depression.

SIR STAFFORD CRIPPS. 1889–1952. English.

—Practiced law and became a King's counsel at age 38. Joined Labor party, and in 1930 became solicitor general and was knighted. Considered to be a future candidate for Prime Minister but his socialistic views were met with heavy criticism. Formed the Socialist League and was expelled from Labor party. Became ambassador to Russia in 1940.
—Became a vegetarian after contracting colitis (intestinal inflammation) during W.W. I. Followed strict diet of fruit, raw vegetables, cheese, and black bread. At times, ate a boiled egg or potato. Dubbed "Christ and Carrots" by Churchill.

COMMENTS FROM OTHER VEGETARIANS

Michel de Montaigne. 1533–1592. French essayist: "For my part I have never been able to see, without displeasure, an innocent and defenseless animal, from whom we receive no offense or harm, pursued and slaughtered."

Alexander Pope. 1688–1744. English poet: "I know nothing more shocking or horrid than the prospect of . . . kitchens covered with blood, and filled with the cries of beings expiring in tortures."

John Wesley. 1703–1791. English theologian (founded Methodism): "Thanks be to God, since I gave up flesh and wine, I have been delivered from all physical ills."

Horace Greeley. 1811–1872. American journalist: "I judge that a strict vegetarian will live 10 years longer than a habitual flesh eater while suffering in the average less than ½ so much sickness."

Richard Wagner. 1813–1883. German composer: "Plant life instead of animal food is the keystone of regeneration. Jesus used bread instead of flesh and wine in place of blood at the Lord's Supper."

John Harvey Kellogg. 1852–1943. American surgeon (founder of Battle Creek Sanitorium): ". . . When one subsists entirely upon fruits, grains, and nuts, comparatively little attention need be given to the matter of combinations, as these food substances are man's most natural dietary, and mingle harmoniously together during the process of digestion."

George Arliss. 1868–1946. English actor: "Doesn't it seem probable that many of our diseases are the result of meat eating? It's an unpleasant habit . . . eating kidneys and liver and picking the bones and using blood for gravy. We shudder at the very thought of cannibals, but is there really any difference?"

Upton Sinclair. 1878–1968. American muckraker. From *The Jungle:* "At the same instant the ear was assailed by a most terrifying shriek; the visitors started in alarm, the women turned pale and shrank back. The shriek was followed by another, louder and yet more agonizing—for once started upon that journey, the hog never came back; at the top of the wheel he was shunted off upon a trolley, and went sailing down the room. And meantime another was swung up, and then another, and another, until there was a double line of them, each dangling by a foot and kicking in frenzy—and squealing. The uproar was appalling, perilous to the eardrums; one feared there was too much sound for the room to hold—that the walls must give way or the ceiling crack. There were high squeals and low squeals, grunts, and wails of agony; there would come a momentary lull, and then a fresh outburst, louder than ever, surging up to a deafening climax. It was too much for some of the visitors—the men would look at each other, laughing nervously, and the women would stand with hands clenched and the blood rushing to their faces, and the tears starting in their eyes."

POSTSCRIPT

Other philosophers who were vegetarians—Aristotle, Epicurus, Diogenes, Cicero, Socrates, Plato, Seneca, Buddha.
Part-time vegetarians include—Alfred Lord Tennyson, Jean Jacques Rousseau.
Indian statesman Jawaharlal Nehru was converted to vegetarianism by Gandhi in 1920. Later, Nehru returned to a meat diet even though it "coarsened him."
Mary Pickford (American actress) read *The Jungle* by Upton Sinclair and, from then on, never ate meat or fish.
Vegetarian Thomas Parr (Englishman buried in Westminster Abbey) lived to be 152 years old.

—C.O.

Juicy Moments in the History of Food

HIGH NOON FOR THE TOMATO: THE BITE HEARD ROUND THE REPUBLIC

Before Col. Robert Gibbon Johnson dared eat a tomato—or rather a whole basket of tomatoes —in public on September 26, 1830, the delicious "love apple" was regarded as a deadly aphrodisiac by most Americans. Thomas Jefferson and others were exceptions, but the tomato was too scarlet and shapely to please most Puritan palates and no doubt some people had been poisoned by the plant's foliage, which belongs to the deadly nightshade family and does contain dangerous alkaloids.

If any one man liberated *Lycopersicon esculentum*, and enabled us to enjoy it in the savory sauces and salads Europeans had been enjoying since they brought it back from the New World, it was the eccentric colonel from Salem, N.J. In 1808, after a trip abroad, Johnson introduced the tomato to the farmers of Salem, and each year thereafter offered a prize for the largest locally grown fruit. But the colonel was a forceful individual and wanted the tomato to be regarded as more than a mere ornamental bush. On September 26, 1830 (the exact date varies in different accounts), he announced that he would appear on the Salem courthouse steps and eat not one but an entire basket of "wolf peaches."

Public reaction in Salem was immediate. Declared Johnson's physician, Dr. James van Meeter: "The foolish colonel will foam and froth at the mouth and double over with appendicitis. All that oxalic acid! One dose and you're dead. . . . If the Wolf Peach is too ripe and warmed by the sun, he'll be exposing himself to brain fever. Should he survive, by some unlikely chance, I must remind that the skin of the *Solanum Lypcopersicum* [sic] will stick to the lining of his stomach and cause cancer. . . ." Van Meeter was there, black bag in hand, along with 2,000 other curious people from miles around, to watch Colonel Johnson commit certain suicide.

Johnson, an imposing figure dressed in his usual black suit and tricorne hat, ascended the courthouse steps at high noon as the local firemen's band played a dirgelike tune. Selecting a tomato from his basket, he held it aloft and launched into his spiel: "The time will come when this luscious, scarlet apple, rich in nourishment, a delight to the eye, a joy to the palate . . . will form the foundation of a great garden industry, and will be recognized, eaten, and enjoyed as an edible food. . . . And to help speed that enlightened day, to help dispel the tall tales, the fantastic fables that you have been hearing about the thing, to show you that it is *not* poisonous, that it will *not* strike you dead, I am going to eat one right now!"

Colonel Johnson took a big bite, and his 1st bite could be heard through the silence, and then he bit again and again and again. At least one spectator screamed or fainted with each successive chomp. As he devoured tomato after tomato, the crowd was amazed to see him still on his feet, hale and hearty. He was finally able to convince the onlookers that the tomato was safe and civilized food. Not until the entire basket was consumed did Dr. Van Meeter slink away and the band strike up a victory march and the crowd begin to cheer.

Colonel Johnson's heroic bites were to be heard around the republic, if not the world. His heroic efforts turned the tide for the tomato, which began appearing regularly in U.S. markets by 1835. But prejudices lingered, and still do. As late as 1860, the popular *Godey's Lady's Book* warned its readers that tomatoes "should always be cooked for 3 hours" before eating, and the myth yet persists that tomatoes make the blood acid.

—R.H.

The Body Owner's Manual

By Dick Gregory

Most folks go through life as though they truly believed the opening words of that old song: "I ain't got no *body!*" The average person has no idea of the *location* of the organs, glands, vessels, nerves, arteries, and other components of the body, to say nothing of a lack of knowledge of their *function*. And that internal ignorance is probably the best explanation for the kind of "food" most people shove into their bodies.

It is characteristic of the American dream for folks to work very hard to earn enough money or credit to surround themselves with pieces of machinery—a television set, a refrigerator, a dishwasher, a stereo, a clothes washer and dryer, and of course an automobile. But before they've earned a penny, Mother Nature has provided them with the finest mechanism imaginable—their own body. Yet most people appreciate this marvelous piece of equipment the least. . . .

This chapter is intended to serve as a brief Body Owner's Manual for the care, keeping, and understanding of that marvelous machine Mother Nature has given to us free of charge. Although everyone will one day have to face that "final recall" of the body machine, the length and quality of service depend upon how well the operational demands of the mechanism are understood and the care it is given.

The Filtering System

There are a number of glands in the body engaged in the filtering process, but the 2 major filters are the liver and the kidneys. In a car owner's manual, you are advised to change the filter periodically. Medical doctors sometimes offer the same advice for the body machine, calling the process of changing filters "transplants." While it is good, in fact essential, to cleanse them through proper diet, Mother Nature's filters usually carry a lifetime guarantee if treated properly.

The Liver

Everything we eat or drink is broken down and carried by the blood to the liver. In the liver, the atoms and molecules of our food are reconstructed into material which the body uses to repair, replenish, and rebuild cells and tissues.

Thus the liver is certainly one of the most important and amazing glandular organs in the entire body machine. It is the largest gland, making up about 1/40 of a person's total weight. And the liver has miraculous powers of regenerating and healing itself. Which, of course, is a blessing to most people, considering the punishment they inflict upon the liver through improper diet. If heart or brain cells are damaged and die, they cannot be replaced. But the liver, given the nourishment needed to heal itself, can remarkably "come back to life." Most abused livers need only a decent opportunity for "personal resurrection."

The liver performs a number of complex chemical functions in the body. Rearranged molecules and atoms are sent back into the bloodstream from the liver and are distributed to the other glands and parts of the body as they are needed. The by-products of the reconstruction work in the liver, along with used-up cells from other parts of the body system, are converted by the liver into bile. The

bile is collected and stored in the gall bladder and is used as needed in the digestive process and other functions of the body.

The liver is burdened with the work load of undoing the damage inflicted upon the body by improper eating and drinking habits. Poisons and narcotics which would destroy the body if left alone are passed as quickly as possible to the liver. The liver cells neutralize the poisonous components and try to convert them into harmless chemical compounds. . . . Starches, grains, meat products, and anything that has been cooked in fat give the liver a tremendous workout. Starch molecules, for example, when passing through the liver, can become lodged in the liver cells. When this happens often enough, a congestion develops which can result in cirrhosis or hardening of the liver. The liver becomes stiff as a board. The diet prepared in most kitchens may be responsible for that common phrase "room and board."

It is interesting to note that most people think of cirrhosis of the liver as a disease peculiar to heavy drinkers. While it is true that heavy drinkers are inviting this disaster, it is also quite possible for a heavy starch consumer, or a big sandwich eater, to develop cirrhosis without having had a drink of alcohol during an entire lifetime. Concentrated protein, such as meat, is also difficult for the liver to handle, and eating it runs the danger of clogging liver cells and causing inflammation. . . .

Let me offer an example, suggested by N. W. Walker in his excellent book *Become Younger*, to illustrate what most folks do to their liver every day. If a person bought a truck, and the owner's manual said the load capacity was a half ton, the new truck owner would be a fool to load up the truck with 2 or 3 tons and run it day in and day out. The truck would carry the load for a while. But one day it would break down and the owner would be running to the bank for a loan on a new truck. It's the same with the load capacity of the liver. Most folks overload its capacity every single day of their lives, 3 meals a day. And the liver handles its burdened load for a time. One day it is likely to break down.

Before the truck breaks down completely, it will slow up, the tires will give way, the springs will sag, and the frame will be pushed out of shape. And the overloaded liver will bring about the same reaction in the human body. Consider the person suffering from a "sluggish" liver—slow, lifeless movements, feet lagging, and frequently a bent frame!

The Kidneys

The other major filters are the kidneys—2 glandular organs about the size of a human fist, suspended by a ligament from the rear wall of the abdomen. Hanging loosely near the spinal column, the kidneys serve the function of filtering the water in the body as it is passed through them by the bloodstream.

The kidneys are another of Mother Nature's miracles. They are made up of more than 30 billion cells grouped into clusters of miles and miles of little filter coils. Each cluster is no larger than a speck of dust, yet contains some 15,000 cells. These tiny coils filter 4 gal. of water every day. Only 2 to 4 pt. are passed as waste through the bladder and eliminated as urine. The remaining water is recirculated by the bloodstream throughout the body system.

Every drop of liquid consumed is filtered through the kidneys. The blood is about ⅗ water, and that water content remains constant no matter how much is taken in. Excess water taken in above the 3 qts. in the blood is stored in the muscles and the liver. But it is all filtered by the kidneys.

Everyone knows what happens to water that is left standing and is not replenished by a flow of fresh, pure water. It becomes stagnant. The same thing happens in the body. It is very important to replenish the body with pure drinking water or the organic water which comes from raw fruit and vegetable juices. Pure water in the body system is the most important element in proper maintenance, with the exception of oxygen in the air.

Transmission Fluid

The bloodstream is the transmitter of food throughout the body system and at the same time the garbage collector. There are about 4 qts. of blood in constant circulation out of the 6 qts. or more in the body machine.

To appreciate the marvel of the circulating bloodstream, it might help to realize that your blood deals in more billions than the U.S. Dept. of Defense! The bloodstream is composed of some 24 or 25 billion microscopic cells. They travel so fast through the body machine, it would make the astronauts' and the NASA engineers' heads swim. Every 15 to 25 seconds, the 20 billion-plus cells travel the whole route, from head to foot, through the heart and to the lungs to get a fresh supply of oxygen and leave behind the carbonic-acid gas from the body system. Those 20 billion-plus cells make from 3,000 to 5,000 round trips through the body machine every 24 hours!

So every second of the day and night, billions of blood cells are traveling through the heart and into the breathing chambers of the lungs. And each and every one must have proper nourishment for the journey. The next time you're tempted to make a diet of pastries and coffee, stop and think if your blood cells will find it ideal fuel for the distances they must travel.

And think of the work load of the blood cells in a mere 16 cupfuls of blood.

Every cell and tissue of the body is constantly being bathed in lymph fluid. The lymph is a fluid substance made up of cells known as lymph cells; white blood cells or corpuscles, or leukocytes; and scavenger cells known as phagocytes. So completely is the body machine covered with lymph vessels for the bathing and lubricating process that if the lymph vessels were placed end to end in a straight line they would span a distance of over 100,000 mi.

The lines of the intestine, for example, are filled with lymph nodes, or knots, which continuously serve as security agents in the body to guard against the intrusion of destructive substances and liquids. Millions of other lymph security guards are located at strategic points in the body machine. For example, a specially refined lymph (cerebrospinal fluid) cushions the brain and the spinal cord against the walls of bone surrounding them. The condition of this lymph is very important in maintaining the mental and physical balance of the body machine.

Such seemingly simple acts as standing up, walking, running, and other physical movements are completely dependent upon the healthy functioning and the balanced relationship of the brain and the spinal cord. The muscles receive their impulses for physical movement from the spinal cord and the coordination comes from the brain. The ear channels are also filled with lymph. Every time the head is moved one way or the other, the lymph level changes. You can't agree or disagree without the lymph being involved! Thus the lymph is very important in keeping the physical equilibrium of the entire body machine.

The transmission fluid, the blood and the lymph, and the transmission system, the lymph and blood vessels, must be kept clean and free of clogging. Clogging, or capillary impactions, can result in such things as defective hearing, dizziness, eye trouble, unsteadiness, hemorrhoids, varicose veins, hardening of the arteries, tumors and blood clots on the brain or elsewhere in the body machine. Starches of all kinds, fried foods and other cooked fats are the great cloggers.

When functioning according to Mother Nature's design, the lymph nodes in the intestine collect fats, but they do not collect protein or carbohydrate material passing through. The collected fats are converted into a fine liquid, or emulsion, and passed into the main lymph channel in the throat and then on into the bloodstream. Mother Nature's system works very smoothly when the fats are raw, uncooked, and natural, such as in olive oil, avocado, raw nuts, and so on.

But if you throw fried foods, buttered popcorn, cooked salted nuts, or doughnuts at the lymph security agents, try as they will, they may not be able to break down the fat, since it has been converted by cooking into an inorganic product, and the fat may remain in circulation in the blood for hours, resulting in a clogging of the system. So that popcorn you eat in the movie theater may be creating a late late show in the body machine!

One further word about starches. . . . Since the starch molecule travels around the body machine in an undissolved state, unable to be used by the glands, cells and tissues of the body, the body machine tries to flush it out. If the organs designed to take care of eliminating waste become clogged, the body machine looks for other places to throw the starches out. The pores of the skin provide a perfect opening. And Mother Nature provides even for her most disobedient children. Germs thrive on starchy matter and they assist in breaking down accumulated starch molecules, forming pus, which is more easily pushed out through the pores of the skin. Instant pimples! Teen-agers with acne and pimple problems will probably be found to have heavy starch diets.

THE CARBURETOR

The lungs are made up of tiny bunches of cells similar to grapes, microscopic in size and about 400 million in number. The importance of the lungs is emphasized by the fact that the body machine can operate days, weeks, and months without food; at least days and perhaps weeks without water, but only a few minutes without air. The blood cells and corpuscles must have oxygen to burn up waste matter, break down the structure of food and liquid, and make available atoms and molecules to the cells, tissues, and glands of the body machine.

The machine takes in about a pt. of air at a time, or 20,000 pts. a day, or 2,500 gal. After each intake of air, the body lets out millions of molecules in the form of carbonic-acid gas. That's the in-and-out performance of the body machine according to Mother Nature's ideal design, with no interference in the carburetor.

When foods are eaten which produce a high degree of mucus in the system, such as cow's milk and starchy foods, the excess mucus lodges in the lungs (as well as other places in the body). The little bunches in the lungs become so tightly clogged that oxygen can't get through. The same thing happens, of course, when cigarette smoke or polluted air is inhaled. This is in addition to the nicotine content of cigarettes, which has an extremely poisonous effect upon the system. . . .

Incidentally, the "relaxing" or "soothing" effect upon the nerves cigarette smokers claim to rationalize their habit is really nothing other than a deadening or anesthetizing of the nerve centers. Death is indeed ultimate relaxation!

THE FUEL PUMP, BATTERY, SPARK PLUGS, AND OTHER PARTS

The heart is the fuel pump of the body machine, pumping oxygen through the bloodstream to various parts of the body according to their need. Since the heart is a living tissue, it must receive nourishment from the food taken into the body. However, it does not receive nourishment from the blood pumped through it, but rather from a special supply of blood coming through the coronary arteries.

The pumping action of the heart causes it to "beat." . . .

The heart beats about 100,000 to 150,000 times a day, pumping somewhere between 10,-000 and 11,000 qts. of blood throughout the body. Circulating the blood around at such a pace, the heart will pump some 45 million gal. of blood in the span of a half century. Few other fuel pumps could render that kind of service.

The rate of the heart, or the intensity of its work, depends upon the demand put upon it by other parts of the body. When an organ is called upon to do more work, it needs a greater supply of oxygen and thus the heart must work harder too. Exercising requires more oxygen, and the heart must pump it. So does eating. When the process of digestion is going on, glands and organs need greater supplies of oxygen from the heart. If the diet consists of the wrong kind of food, overloading the work of the liver and other parts of the body, the heart also feels the strain.

The action of the heart speeds up when the carbonic-acid gas content of the blood is increased. Eating an excess of carbon foods increases the carbonic-acid gas content of the blood and consequently "puts a hurtin'" on the heart. Starchy foods, cereals, and all kinds of manufactured sugar have this effect. Too much carbon food intake results in both high and low blood pressure. It is tragically amusing to hear folks talk about "having heart trouble," when, if they analyzed their diet, they would have to admit they are "giving themselves heart trouble."

The storage battery of the body machine is the nerve system. During sleep the "battery system" stores up energy to replace the vital life forces. The main distributing nerve center of the body machine is located at the base of the brain in the medulla oblongata, just above the nape of the neck. There are 2 main divisions of the battery system: the sympathetic nervous system and the central nervous system.

The sympathetic nervous system has nothing to do with a person's sympathies but rather controls the directing force coming from the brain. Breathing, the regulation of temperature and water in the body, the organs involved in eating and drinking, regulating the distribution of blood—all these functions (and many more) are affected by the sympathetic nervous system.

The central nervous system is Operation Central in the body machine. It is the network of nerves from the brain down the spinal cord, spreading throughout the body to the skin. Operation Central sends out an alarm when anything is wrong, or out of line, in the body machine. A headache, or a toothache, or any other pain, is an alarm from Operation Central, the central nervous system. And of course the purpose of the alarm is to see that the *source* and *cause* of the pain are treated.

So what treatment do most body owners give? They take an aspirin or some type of chemical "pain-killer." The result is simply to "kill" or deaden the nerve trying to do its duty. The headache, or toothache, or whatever, will disappear but the *cause* will remain unattended. It is exactly the same as the ancient custom of killing the messenger because he brought bad news to the Emperor!

Every organ, limb, and part of the body machine has 3 major nerve endings. One is in the iris of the eye. One is in the walls of the colon. One is in the sole of the feet. It is standard practice of the trained naprapath to be able to look at the eyes, the soles of the feet, or an X ray of the colon and tell exactly which parts of the body machine are in trouble. . . .

When the body machine is functioning as Mother Nature intended, the nerves and the muscles have a good working relationship. The nerves send out the impulses and the muscles get to work. They are such a team that if something is done to mess up one teammate, the other is usually directly affected.

Meat is an enemy of the muscles, which in turn makes it a potential foe of the nerves. Meat is bad for the muscles because it tempts them so. Muscles have a particular attraction to uric acid, the end product of the digestion and breaking down of protein molecules. Uric acid should be expelled through the kidneys. But because of the muscles' attraction to it, they absorb the uric acid before it can be eliminated, especially when there is an excess.

Finally the saturation point is reached. The uric acid begins to crystallize in the muscles. When the crystal-containing muscles are moved, the sharp points penetrate the covering of the nearest nerve and a sharper pain is registered. It's the 1st warning of later trouble—rheumatism, neuritis, or sciatica. Heavy meat eaters often have 7 to 12 times as much uric

acid *retained* in their system as should have been eliminated through the kidneys in the 1st place.

GAS AND THE BODY MACHINE

There is a very old joke about the roadside restaurant that had fuel pumps out front to serve the needs of passing motorists. The sign read: EAT HERE AND GET GAS. And that sign pretty well sums up the traditional American diet!

Of course, the "gas" we're talking about here is not the kind you'll find in a car owner's manual. We're talking about the natural chemical action in the body machine whereby matter is converted from a solid or a liquid into a gaseous state.

After food has passed through the stomach and the small intestine, bacteria in the body machine go to work on the residue of food as part of Mother Nature's design. The function of the friendly, helpful bacteria is to break down the residue so it can be absorbed for constructive purposes. It enters the colon from the small intestine as a liquid. The ascending colon goes to work on the liquid, taking out most of the water and the food elements the body machine will use, and sends the remaining fibrous substance on to the next sections of the colon as feces to be eliminated.

The domelike portion of the upper stomach collects the gas which develops as a result of this digestive process. And when raw natural foods are eaten, the small quantity of gas released through the work of the digestive juices can be handled quite well by the stomach.

When foods are eaten haphazardly and in the wrong combinations, like meat and potatoes, bread and butter and perhaps jam, fruit and sugar, ice cream, pie or cake, coffee and sugar, the incompatible mixtures cause a great deal of fermentation. Belching is a consequence of the consumption of canned, cooked, and processed foods.

While the fibers in raw foods *assist* the work of the intestines, the habit of eating cooked dead food causes the intestinal walls to lose their tone and degenerate over a period of time. Waste matter is not properly eliminated, and it adheres to the walls of the intestines, accumulating in the pockets of the colon.

The result is a regular gunfight or shoot-out in the body machine between the "good" bacteria and the "bad" bacteria. The "good" bacteria try to neutralize the waste matter and eliminate it. The "bad" bacteria find it very comfortable living quarters and try to get the waste matter to remain. The result of the shoot-out is an excessive amount of gas. The average restaurant meal, beginning with cocktails (alcohol is very gas-forming) and ending with coffee and sugar, is a regular showdown at the O.K. Corral.

Although a certain amount of gas in the intestines is natural and inevitable, excessive gas can cause a host of ailments, including what frequently passes for a heart attack! Gas pressure against the heart and blood vessels can send a person scampering for digitalis tablets when an enema would be more in order.

THE SEWAGE SYSTEM

This is probably the most important section of the Body Owner's Manual. It has been claimed that 9/10 of the physical disorders and diseases of body owners have their origin in the stomach and intestines. The 2 great abuses body owners inflict upon the machine Mother Nature has given them are the failure to *nourish* the organs in the body responsible for the proper elimination of waste matter and the failure to give *careful* and *immediate* attention to Mother Nature's call that waste matter must be eliminated.

First, let us trace the route of food as it leaves the plate. Food is chewed by the teeth, manipulated by the lips, tongue, and cheeks, and moistened and softened by saliva fluid. The saliva also has a chemical action on the food, and it begins the digestive process. When food is gulped or chewed very little, the digestive process is thrown out of balance from the very beginning. . . .

Food which has been chewed and insalivated in the mouth reaches the stomach through a drainpipe called the esophagus, entering at the upper opening of the stomach. Then the stomach begins its own process of digestion by secreting a fluid called the gastric juice. The gastric juice begins to dissolve and break down the mass of food so that it can be absorbed into the body. While this chemical action is going on, the fluid portion of the food and the liquids which have been consumed are being separated from the solids, absorbed through the walls of the stomach and taken by the blood to the kidneys, the skin pores, and so on. The stomach muscles are busy churning up the digested food and creating a semifluid food mass of chemically changed matter which passes into the small intestine.

The small intestine is about 1½″ in diameter, some 30′ long, and ingeniously wound around upon itself so that it occupies only a small place in the body machine compared to its length. The entire length of the small intestine is lined with a soft, velvety covering of tiny little projections known as villi. The wall is also lined with millions of glands that secrete enzymes needed for the digestion of various food elements.

In the small intestine the digestive process of breaking down food elements is completed. The enzymes secreted from the walls of the small intestine are assisted by enzymes secreted by the pancreas and bile provided by the liver. When the breakdown is completed, the digested food element is ready for absorption into the lymph system. It is picked up by the villi, which contain blood and lymph vessels.

Food that *cannot* be digested because of its nature, or *is* not digested for some other reason, is left behind in the form of waste matter, excrement, feces, or any of the more popular names. It is dumped into the large intestine, or colon, eventually to be eliminated from the body machine. The waste matter passes into the colon through a small opening known as the ileocecal valve. The valve is constructed to let the waste matter pass freely into the colon but to prevent it from getting back into the small intestine.

There are a number of reasons why food reaches the colon undigested or only partly digested. Sometimes it is not chewed well enough. Sometimes too much food has been eaten and the digestive system just couldn't handle it all. Or an imbalance or insufficient supply of digestive juices might interfere with proper digestion. And, finally, foods that are eaten together in improper combinations can greatly overtax the digestive system and end up in the colon undigested.

The colon is about 6′ long and it connects with the small intestine on the lower right side of the abdomen. It extends upward until it reaches the lower ribs, crosses over to the left side and then heads downward again. The portion on the right side going up is called the ascending colon. The portion crossing over from right to left is called the transverse colon. And the portion going down on the left side is called the descending colon. The point where the colon and the small intestine meets is called the cecum. And the other end of the colon, from which the waste matter is expelled, is called the rectum.

The colon is the great sewer of the body machine. What happens to waste matter when it reaches the colon is very, very important to the health of the entire body. When the waste matter gets to the colon, billions of bacteria invade the vegetable foods and help to disintegrate them. The undigested or partly digested part of protein—especially meat protein—undergoes putrefaction. As it putrefies in the colon, it releases some very toxic by-products. If these toxins are not neutralized and rendered harmless by the liver, or counteracted by other bacteria in the colon, they can cause great damage throughout the body.

The walls of the colon contain tiny absorbent channels which have a tendency to reabsorb the foul, putrefying, poisonous excrement back into the system. If the colon becomes clogged and if proper elimination does not take place, the whole body is poisoned. . . .

If this discussion of the effects of a clogged colon sounds a bit disturbing, it is only because it should! If a body owner becomes disturbed enough about the condition of the colon now, a great deal of trouble can be avoided later in life. And what can the concerned body owner do?

Let me answer by asking another question. What would you do with any other clogged sewer? You would flush it out, of course. You would get some Drano or Instant Plumber, or call Roto-Rooter, and go to work. Remember the colon acts just like your drain at home. When the toilet or the sink becomes clogged, all of the collected waste material backs up, and if something is not done quickly it spills over. In the same manner, a clogged colon spills toxic collected waste into the entire system. . . .

If the idea of taking enemas turns you off, think of "internal baths" as a solution. When the outside of your body machine gets dirty, you give it a bath. So if the *inside* of your body is "dirty," why not give *it* a bath? . . .

The home remedy for treating a clogged colon is the "high" enema, and it is the only "high" I recommend! (Drugs, tobacco, alcohol, and coffee "highs" have no place in my natural diet.) An enema bag is available from any drugstore. It is a "hot water bottle" equipped with a syringe, a long tube with a nozzle. This enema equipment is different from prepared and packaged enemas, so be sure to ask for an enema bag. A prepared enema will clean out only the lower part of the descending colon rather than give the entire colon a flushing.

The standard enema bag will hold about 2 qts. of water. It should be suspended from the wall at least 3' above you. Most supermarkets sell suction hooks which can be fastened to the bathroom wall, moved to any other wall, or carried when traveling.

The water used for an enema should be lukewarm. Never, never use soap, salt, bicarbonate of soda, or any other such substance in the water! It is helpful to add the strained juice of freshly squeezed lemon—one, 2, or even 3 lemons for 2 qts. of water—and a teaspoon or 2 of pure unpasteurized honey. But never add anything else. . . . It may be necessary to start with one qt. and work up to 2.

The object is to get the water well into all parts of the colon. Some people prefer a kneeling position. Others prefer to lie on the right side, with the legs doubled up toward the chest as in a fetal position. The nozzle of the syringe should be lubricated with K-Y surgical jelly. The water should be retained in the colon as long as possible.

Especially in the beginning, some discomfort may be felt. Don't be alarmed or discouraged. After a while, the feeling of discomfort will ease and more and more water will be able to be retained in the colon. As in all other new ventures, practice makes perfect in enema-taking.

Massage the abdomen gently while retaining the enema water to help loosen the impacted waste matter. Don't be surprised to find yourself hurrying back to the bathroom. I only mention it to warn you that it is not best to run off to any business or social engagements too soon after taking an enema! . . .

Laxatives, cathartics, purgatives, and the like are a different matter. A laxative does not help to restore the natural process of peristalsis in the colon. On the contrary, the laxative is actually an irritant. That's what makes a laxative a laxative. It irritates the nerves and muscles in the colon, sending them into a state of convulsions to get rid of the irritating substance. The laxative, or purgative, challenges Mother Nature rather than working along with her. It in no way helps to break down impacted waste matter or cleanse the colon. Taking a laxative is like throwing salt in the eye to produce tears to wash out a cinder! . . .

Actually, the best way to assist Mother Nature in the process of elimination in the body machine is through nutrition. . . .

The Headlights

The headlights of the body machine are the eyes. Using another analogy, the eyes are the windows to the temple. One can quickly tell the condition of the body machine by looking at the headlights. If they are dim, dull, or the color of fog lights, the body machine is in bad shape and in drastic need of immediate repair. The fuel must be changed. A diet must be provided which allows for a complete rebuilding job.

If the eyes are shiny, sparkling, and bright, it is an encouraging sign that the body machine is close to kicking on all cylinders. So as a conscientious body owner, take a good look in the mirror and see if the headlights in your own machine are on bright or dim.

Let me close with a vision and a hope for America. The Body Owner's Manual clearly suggests that the body machine is worth at least as much attention as an automobile. What is needed in this country is as many health food stores as there are filling stations

and auto repair shops. Each health station should be staffed with folks who are as well versed and trained in nutrition and the proper care of the body as good mechanics are in the care and keeping of automobiles. . . .
PERMISSION: *Dick Gregory's Natural Diet for Folks Who Eat: Cookin' with Mother Nature.* New York, Harper & Row, 1973.

Body Types

In 1940, William H. Sheldon created a system of classifying body types based on the 3 layers of cells in the developing embryo: endoderm—the inner layer, which develops into the digestive organs; mesoderm—the middle layer, which develops into the skeleton, muscles, and circulatory system; ectoderm—the outer layer, which develops into the skin, hair, nails, and nervous system.

His theory states that these layers develop differently in each person. In some people, one layer predominates, and in others the layers are more balanced. The body types are: 1. Endomorph—soft body with bulges in places. This type has strong muscles, but it is difficult to see the difference between the muscles and fat until they are squeezed. 2. Mesomorph—well-developed muscles in neck, shoulders, chest, stomach, buttocks, arms, and legs. This type has large bones and a great need for physical activity. 3. Ectomorph—thin and wiry ("a lean and hungry look"), small bones, thin chest and prominent ribs, flat stomach, and small buttocks. The arms and legs tend to be long in proportion to the body. This type has a highly developed nervous system and is usually very active.

—F.C.

Homeopathy

Homeopathy is a system of medicine formalized by Samuel Christian Hahnemann, a German physician, beginning with his medical discoveries in 1790 and his subsequent publication of several major works on the subject. The basic premise of homeopathy is "let likes be treated by likes." The homeopath treats the patient with a substance which would produce in a healthy person the same symptoms that the sick person already has. The idea is that the body naturally fights disease and that the symptoms are the manifestation of the body's attempt to throw off illness. The homeopath attempts to cooperate with the body's own cleansing procedure by helping it along and encouraging the acting out of the symptoms rather than fighting and suppressing them. Homeopathy maintains that the body is not being invaded by disease, but is producing the symptoms of disease in order to fight off the illness that is largely the result of poor diet, mental stress and anxiety, heredity, and/or environmental conditions. This is in direct contrast to allopathic medicine, which is considered orthodox today. In the eyes of homeopathy, allopathic medicine fights nature and seeks to cover up symptoms rather than let the body deal with the real problem. It also carries the risk of complications and side effects from the modern drugs it prescribes. Homeopathic drugs come from plant, animal, and mineral sources, and are given in very tiny dosages to avoid side effects and exert a subtle influence on the body. All homeopathic medicines are "proved" before use—that is, they are given to healthy people in small doses to discover the symptoms they produce. Another very important aspect of homeopathy is its belief that every person is a very individual case, and that there is no one medicine for one disease; rather, there are certain medicines which are better for certain people.

Because its views are based on entirely different principles than those of allopathic medicine, there have been fervent and largely successful attempts to suppress homeopathy. According to the homeopath, the modern patient's desire for instant relief, if only from symptoms, and his belief that disease is to be fought, has possibly been created and certainly been nurtured by medical advertising and people's ignorance of how their own bodies work.

Homeopathy grew in worldwide popularity between 1820 and 1900. Ralph Waldo Emerson and William Cullen Bryant were true believers. At its peak, in 1900, there were 22 homeopathic colleges flourishing in the U.S., and a monument to the founder, Samuel Hahnemann, was placed in Scott Circle, Washington, D.C., where it may still be seen.

In the years since, homeopathy has declined in the U.S., where it has been continually denounced as quackery by the allopathic physicians. Today, the remaining homeopathic strongholds in the U.S. and England are Philadelphia and London. Queen Elizabeth II and the Royal Family, following tradition, still have a homeopath on the Buckingham Palace medical staff. Homeopathy also remains as an alternative treatment in such countries as France, Germany, India, as well as in various nations of South America. Many well-known persons believe in homeopathy, among them Marlene Dietrich.

Young people who wish to become homeopaths in the U.S. are faced with one severe problem: In order to practice homeopathy legally, it is necessary to take a full allopathic medical school course before the student begins to study homeopathy.

—A.W.

The Bach Flower Remedies

Honeysuckle as a cure for obsession with the past? Mustard flowers for despair? Dr. Edward Bach, between 1930 and 1936, developed a healing science whereby he treated the human personality and various states of mind with the tinctures of wild flowers.

Born in England in 1886, Dr. Bach studied in London, and eventually became a prominent bacteriologist, making important discoveries in the field. After establishing a considerable practice, he became interested in homeopathy, the method of healing by which likes are treated by likes. After much devoted work and further discoveries, he began to feel that it was time to explore something he had always felt strongly—that there must be a simple, easy, and gentle type of medicine which anyone could use for self-cures, rather than depending on an elite group of physicians. He sought a medicine which would be less complicated and more effective than that provided by the common forms of medical practice.

Dr. Bach was of the mind that people were prone to a number of basic types of moods, temperaments, fears, and anxieties—12, to be exact, with a number of variations on each one. It seemed to Dr. Bach that virtually all disease was the result of a poor and distressed state of mind, and that if the state of mind were altered, and the individual took a more positive view toward himself and the world, his illness would vanish with his changed outlook. Dr. Bach's strongly developed intuitive powers and his love of nature drew him to the countryside, where his sensitivity led him to discover the remedies he sought in the wild flowers of the woods and fields. Over the years, he found 38 remedies. Among these were—

AGRIMONY for mental torture and worry concealed by a cheerful disposition.
ASPEN for vague fears and anxieties.
CERATO for self-doubt.
CHICORY for excessive self-pity.
CLEMATIS for indifference.
GENTIAN for depression and discouragement.
GORSE for hopelessness and despair.
HOLLY for hatred, envy, and jealousy.
HORNBEAM for weariness and exhaustion.
IMPATIENS for impatience and irritability.
MUSTARD for gloom and melancholia.
OLIVE for mental fatigue.
PINE for self-reproach and guilt.
ROCK ROSE for terror, panic, and extreme fright.
SWEET CHESTNUT for suicidal depression.
And there are 23 more, as well as a "rescue remedy" for severe emergencies, made up of 5 of the 38 remedies.

Most of the extracts are prepared by filling a bowl with fresh spring water and placing several handfuls of wild flowers in it, and then letting it steep for 4 hours in the hot sun. Others are prepared by simmering the flowers in water. The remedies can be taken as frequently as needed, and in combination.

Dr. Bach scandalized the medical profession of the time with his revolutionary ideas, but patients continued to flock to him and many physicians began to use the remedies, with amazing success. All manners of disease —from chronic to seemingly incurable diseases —succumbed to the flowers.

Dr. Bach himself became so sensitive toward the end of his life that even the briefest visit to the noise and crowds of the city upset him and worsened his health, so he established his headquarters in the countryside of Berkshire, England. According to Dr. Bach, when he was seeking the last of the remedies, he would become severely afflicted with the mental symptoms common to that remedy, as well as a painful physical disorder of some kind, just prior to finding the right flower. Upon taking the newly discovered remedy, his symptoms would vanish immediately.

Dr. Bach also was reported to have the power to heal patients merely by touching them, and he would sometimes develop in advance the symptoms of his patients before they came to see him. Dr. Bach was always nearly penniless. He refused to charge his patients any fees, saying that health was mankind's right. Because he was exceedingly generous, Bach never charged above the absolute minimum for the pamphlets he published about his medical discoveries. Said Dr. Bach, "I want to make it as simple as this: I am hungry, I will go and pull a lettuce from the garden for my tea. I am frightened and ill, I will take a dose of mimulus."

He died in 1936 at the age of 50, leaving behind him a few published writings on his work, and one of the most unique systems for self-healing still used today.

The 39 remedies are available by mail from:
A. Nelson & Co. Ltd. (homeopathic pharmacy)
73 Duke Street, Grosvenor Square
London, W 1M 6BY England

Books on Dr. Bach and his remedies are available through the Edward Bach Healing Centre, Sotwell, Wallingford, Berkshire, England, which also publishes a quarterly newsletter.

—A.W.

How to Stay Young

By Leroy R. "Satchel" Paige

In July, 1948, the 42-year-old Paige joined the Cleveland Indians to become the 1st black pitcher in baseball history. He won 2 of his 1st 3 games by shutouts. He was already a legend before he entered the major leagues. In the 25 years before that, hurling for barnstorming black teams and the National Negro Leagues, he pitched 3,000 games and achieved 300 shutouts and 50 no-hitters. In 1965, Paige pitched for Kansas City and became the oldest person to appear in a major-league baseball game. He was 59. He has strong ideas about staying youthful, and here are some of them:

1. Avoid fried meats which angry up the blood.
2. If your stomach disputes you, lie down and pacify it with cool thoughts.
3. Keep the juices flowing by jangling around gently as you move.
4. Go very lightly on the vices, such as carrying on in society. The social ramble ain't restful.
5. Avoid running at all times.
6. Don't look back. Something might be gaining on you.

Self-Examination for Women

At 1st, the idea of a woman examining her own vagina may seem peculiar or even physically impossible. Most women are encouraged from early childhood, subtly or directly, not to touch their own genitals. Because of this conditioning, along with the simple fact that the vagina is not so naturally accessible as the penis, women tend to masturbate much less than men. Nor do women handle their genitals when they urinate. Lacking an easy friendliness with their own bodies, young girls anxiously consult the printed instructions that come with their 1st box of tampons and many nearly give up in despair when they attempt to insert a diaphragm. Many adult women have only a vague picture of what their outer genitalia look like, and the cervix—if they know of it at all—is a mysterious organ deep inside them.

So this important area of a woman's body, felt to be far away and scarcely belonging to her, is delegated to the gynecologist. In America the gynecologist is almost always male, usu-

ally charges high fees for each visit, and rarely shares his expertise with the passive, sheet-draped, and embarrassed patient. Consequently, many women wait until a severe itch, heavy discharge, or pain signals something wrong "down there" before they go to the doctor—and by then the problem is often well-advanced.

Recently a growing number of women have recognized that they want better medical care and more information about female anatomy. These women have established more or less formal clinics all over the U.S. and in Europe at which groups of women meet to examine themselves and one another. With regular examination of the vagina and cervix by means of an instrument called a "speculum" (available free or at nominal cost from self-examination clinics), a woman can become familiar with her own unique structure and the normal changes associated with her menstrual periods. She can detect infection at the earliest possible moment, while it is still easy to treat.

Although it can be done alone, self-examination works best in a group of mutually supportive women. It is not meant to usurp the gynecologist. On the contrary, an informed and confident client will know when to see her doctor and, once there, be better able to function with her or him as a team.

How to Examine the Vagina and Cervix

You will need a plastic speculum, directional light (flashlight or gooseneck lamp), and a mirror (preferably long-handled).

Before the exam, do not douche. Douching removes vaginal secretions which are important in diagnosing a possible infection. (Some doctors advise against douching at any time since it upsets the natural balance of microorganisms in the vagina.) Do urinate. A full bladder presses against the uterus, causing discomfort during the examination.

Manipulate the sterilized speculum until you can open and close it easily.

1. Lie on a firm bed or table, supported by pillows so that you are half sitting up, with legs apart and knees bent (doctors call this the lithotomy position).

2. Using the mirror, examine the outer genitals (*labia majora* and *labia minora*—literally, large and small lips) to see that they are not tender or inflamed and are free of sores.

3. Separate the *labia* and insert the speculum —blades closed and handle pointing up —into the vagina. Press the handle sections together. This opens the blades of the speculum and spreads the vaginal walls. Push the thumbhold of the outside handle section down as far as it will go until it clicks into place.

4. Arrange the mirror and light (if possible, have a friend hold them in position) until you can see the inside of your vagina.

5. If the cervix is not visible, pull the speculum out slightly and push gently in again, aiming a little to the right or left, up or down. Keep searching gently until you find your cervix. Most cervixes are not dead-center, and you may need a little time to locate yours. Its angle will tell you whether your uterus is tilted right, left, forward, or backward.

6. Appearance of the cervix: If you have never had a child, your cervix will be one to 1½" in diameter, pink, smooth, and firm. If you have delivered one or more babies, your cervix and the cervical canal (the opening in the middle of the cervix, called the cervical "os") will be larger and possibly darker in color.

7. Appearance of the vaginal walls: The vagina should be pink and firm with ridges in it, and not sensitive to touch. Its normal secretion is clear or whitish, and will vary in quantity from woman to woman.

8. Changes during the menstrual cycle: During the 1st 2 weeks after menstruation, the healthy cervix and vagina will be pink, firm, and smooth. There may be clear mucus secreted from the cervical canal. Just before the menstrual period, the cervix may be swollen and blue with prominent veins, and the vaginal walls swollen and tender. Vaginal secretions may increase at ovulation or about one week before the period. A woman who takes the time to follow herself daily through a full month will learn the changes normal for her and later may be able to detect an early pregnancy in this way.

9. For diagnosis of infection:

Common Vaginal Infections. The following descriptions portray the typical symptoms of vaginal infections. The information is given as a rough guide to help in self-examination, but it cannot provide positive diagnosis because the symptoms of these infections vary with the individual case and with the severity of the infection. In any case, a physician should be seen if an infection is suspected. (Note: These infections are not spread strictly by sexual contact. Many women have one or more of them on several different occasions, and they may occur simultaneously in what is called a "mixed infection.")

YEAST

Discharge: White, thick, like cottage cheese.

Odor: Similar to yeast, baking bread.

Appearance: Vagina and outer genitals perhaps reddened, vagina may have white patches.

Other symptoms: Itching; maybe painful intercourse; can cause burning or painful urination.

TRICHOMONIASIS

Discharge: Frothy yellow-green; if present as mixed infection, thick and white.

Odor: Strong, unusual, unpleasant.

Appearance: May cause itching, soreness, swelling, bleeding of vagina; may cause red "strawberry" spots on cervix; possibly urinary infection as well.

Note: Trichomoniasis is passed back and forth between sexual partners, although the male usually does not have symptoms. In order to cure it, both partners must take a drug concurrently.

BACTERIAL INFECTION

Discharge: White or yellow, heavy, viscous.

Odor: Varies.

Appearance: Cloudy, puffy, pus-covered vaginal walls; may cause burning or frequent urination, lower back pain, cramps, or swollen lymph nodes.

CERVICITIS

Cervicitis is the name given to an inflammation of the cervix, which is often associated with a vaginal infection.

Urinary Tract Infection. Painful and/or frequent urination, often with burning of the urethra, indicating a growth of bacteria in the bladder or elsewhere in the urinary tract, usually associated with a vaginal infection. Drinking lots of water, especially after intercourse (which may introduce bacteria into the urethra), and urinating soon after intercourse will help prevent urinary infections, which can become chronic in many women. They are treated with oral antibiotics.

10. When you have finished, pull the speculum slightly out, then pull up the thumbhold to close the blades, and remove it from the vagina. (If you close the blades without pulling the speculum out a little, you may pinch your cervix, which will not harm you but will be uncomfortable.)
11. Observe the secretions on the speculum blades for consistency, color, and odor. Refer to the chart.
12. Wash the speculum thoroughly. To avoid transfer of infection, each woman should have her own speculum.

How to Perform a Bimanual Pelvic Examination

You will need surgical gloves and K-Y jelly, *not* vaseline.

Before the procedure, the woman to be examined should urinate, since a full bladder may make the uterus more difficult to locate.

1. The woman lies down with knees drawn up and wide enough apart to expose genitals.
2. The examiner puts on surgical glove, lubricating index and middle fingers of gloved hand.
3. The 2 lubricated fingers in a "pistol position" are inserted into the vagina.
4. Gentle exploration will locate the cervix. It feels hard, like the end of a nose. The 2 inserted fingers are placed under the cervix and held there to keep it firmly in place.
5. With the other hand, the examiner presses down on the lower abdomen. This firm external pressure should locate the uterus. Unusual uterine position, obesity, or lack of sufficient external pressure may make it difficult to find. The normal uterus is commonly the size of a lemon. Although some women may normally have a large uterus, if the uterus you are feeling is as large as an orange or a grapefruit the possibility of a tumor or pregnancy should be considered.
6. After noting the size, wiggle the uterus

gently to see that there is no pain when the attached structures are moved.
7. With hands in the same position, the examiner feels at the sides of the abdomen for the Fallopian tubes and the ovaries. When the woman feels a slight twinge, the ovaries have been located. They are almond-sized and should not be hard, enlarged, severely painful, or more painful on one side than the other. The tubes may not be felt, but if they are located they will be soft and about the thickness of a pencil. If they are hard, enlarged, or painful to the touch, something is wrong.
8. After the examination, the women may exchange roles. The examiner may want to draw a picture of what she has felt with her hands during the examination.

When You Go to the Gynecologist

1. Prepare a list of problems and questions in advance.
2. You may bring a friend, sometimes called a "patient advocate," in case you are flustered or intimidated by the doctor. She can speak for you, or remind you of questions you wish to ask.
3. Insist on a Pap test every 6 months. For this test, cells are gently scraped from the cervix with a wooden spatula and are sent to a laboratory for examination. The results are available in about a week. The cells are graded Class I, Class II, and so on, from normal cells up to a category for cancerous cells. Cervical cancer is 100% curable if found early. The test is painless. It should not be performed if you have a vaginal infection, since the infection may cause the cervical cells to appear abnormal.
4. Have a gonorrhea test every 6 months if there is any possibility you may have been exposed to it. A sample of discharge from around the cervix is taken to the laboratory for culture. This test is very important, since gonorrhea in women is usually without symptoms.
5. You can ask to watch the examination in a mirror, and you can ask questions about what you see.
6. If you don't understand the diagnosis, ask for an explanation.
7. If you are given medication, ask for the name of the drug and for a list of side effects.

Prevention

1. Cotton underwear, or no underwear, will help prevent vaginal infections by allowing air to circulate more freely to the outer vaginal area.

2. Vaginal deodorant sprays should not be used. They cause itching and swelling of vaginal tissues in some women. So can scented or colored toilet paper.

3. After using the toilet, wipe front to back. This will avoid bringing bacteria from the anus into the urethra or vagina, which can cause infection.

4. A yogurt douche will help relieve yeast infections. The yogurt bacteria crowd out the yeast organisms, and will also aid in replacing beneficial bacteria after the use of antibiotic suppositories. Eating yogurt will restore healthy bacteria in the digestive tract after taking oral antibiotics.

—E.A.G.

FOR FURTHER READING: Rothman, Lorraine. "Self-Help: Paramedic Politics." (In: *The Witch's Os*. Alleyn, Millie, Ed. Stamford, Conn., New Moon Publications, Inc., 1972.) And: Ziegler, Vicki, and Elizabeth Campbell. "Vaginal Infections." (In: *Circle One*, May, 1973.) This self-help handbook is available by mail from 409 E. Fontanero, Colorado Springs, Colo. 80907.

A Guide to Shangri-La: The Leading Longevity Sites on Earth

HUNZA

Location. Hunza is located in a remote valley some 200 mi. long but only one mi. wide. It is situated at an elevation of 8,500' and is completely enclosed by mountain peaks. These peaks soar as high as 25,550' and belong to the Karakoram Range, broadly known in the West as "the Himalayas" or the "Roof of the World." Situated in the far northeast of Pakistan, it is only a stone's throw from Pakistan-controlled Kashmir, India, Afghanistan, Soviet Russia, and China. The valley's only access is through Rawalpindi, Pakistan's new capital. From there a 45-minute plane ride takes you due north 375 mi. to Gilgit. This trip involves some of the world's most hazardous flying conditions, as the small plane must negotiate treacherous mountain passes. Although you are now only 68 mi. from Baltit, the village capital of Hunza, the rest of the trip used to require 3 days and had to be made by mule, shanks' mare, and finally—for the drop down from a height of 16,000' into the valley—by jeep. Today, the entire 68 mi. can be covered in only 3 hours on the new Karakoram Highway.

Longevity. The longevity claims made for Hunzukuts by foreign visitors vary considerably, with the highest estimate being 150 years of age. Renee Taylor writes in her book *Hunza Health Secrets for Long Life and Happiness*: "In Hunza, people manage to live to over 100 years of age in perfect mental and physical health . . . men of 90 [are] new fathers and women of 50 still conceive." Betty Lee Morales, president of the American Cancer Society and a 2-time visitor to Hunza, reported to the *Los Angeles Times* (July 16, 1973), "It's an exaggeration to say that they live to be 150 but there's no need to gild the lily. The average age is 90 when they die." Dr. Alexander Leaf, Chief of Medical Services at Massachusetts General Hospital and a professor at Harvard Medical School, has reliably reported meeting a 106-year-old man who still worked herding goats during the summer months, while "the oldest Hunzukut" was "revered" for being 110.

Dr. Leaf also has pointed out that it is "the fitness of many of the elderly rather than their age that impresses me," and he has noted that no written records of births or deaths were then kept in Hunza. According to the Mir of Hunza, out of a present population of 40,000, 6 men are over 100 years of age and many are 90 years old or more. (Before the 1st road came, there were at least 50 over the age of 100.) In America, by contrast, there are only 3 centenarians for every 100,000 people.

Living There. The handkerchief-size plots of arable land that the Hunzukuts cultivate look like staircases or terraces along the base of the mountain slope. These farms are irrigated by a system of conduits fed by the melting waters of the vast Ultar Glacier. A cluster of 6 or 7 fruit or nut trees is considered an "orchard," and a farmer may have to ascend and descend a 1,000' pathway several times a day to attend to his chores. From a distance, when the winter snows have melted, Hunza is a patchwork quilt of yellows, browns, and greens. Through its heart races the pearl-gray, murky Hunza River, whose mineral-rich water is assiduously drunk by the Hunzukuts and is called by them "our glacial milk." Whenever you raise your eyes you see the snowy *dumanis* or high peaks which are dominated by Mount Rakaposhi, one of the most stupendous mountains in the entire Karakoram Range.

The Hunzukuts believe they are the descendants of the soldiers of Alexander the Great. When Alexander's campaign against India faltered, some of his troops deserted. Taking with them their Afghani and Turkish wives, they sought the protective safety of Hunza. Certainly the Hunzukuts, with their "Mediterranean" features and fair skins, resemble no other people of Asia. Their language, Burushaski, too is unique. Hermann Berger, Sanskrit professor at the University of Munich and an authority on Himalayan languages, considers it related to Basque as spoken in the Pyrenees of southern France and Spain.

Returning travelers invariably describe Hunza as a "paradise," because of its natural, unhurried, stress-free life. Every Hunzukut, young or old, male or female, works at some form of manual labor—tilling the fields, tending livestock, gathering fruit in summer and sun-drying it against the cold, snowbound winter. Everyone goes to bed at sunset and rises at dawn. Until recently, the only electricity was in the capital, Baltit, where the Mir of Hunza used it sparingly at his palace for the benefit of foreign visitors. The Mir was also the only Hunzukut with a clock. As for the rest of the population, they told time by the movement of the sun in the sky, the shape of the moon at night, and the changing of the seasons. Even in Baltit there were no stores, no movies, no hotels, no doctors, no police, no taxes. Its people also had no "old age"—there were only "the young years," "the middle years," and "the rich years." The new road is changing all this rapidly.

For amusement, Hunzukuts play a violent form of ruleless polo, with teams performing nonstop until one side or the other has scored 9 goals. Volleyball is also popular, and you will see 70-year-old men playing alongside young boys. Each of Hunza's dozen or so villages has one flat area of ground like a village green set aside for these games, although the land in this rocky, barren, hilly, and rough valley is at a perpetual premium.

Foreign scientists in recent years have tried hard to explain the Hunzukut's health, happiness, and longevity. Probably a combination of factors is responsible. Hunza's sunshine is clear, its air is pure, its waters are mineral-rich. Farming has been entirely organic, with no artificial fertilizers or insecticides being used. The last Mir of Hunza, who ruled from 1945 to 1974 when he was deposed by the Pakistani government, called his tiny kingdom "the Land of Just Enough," adding that there is "enough of everything for each, but not enough to make anyone envious and want to take it away." By Western standards the Hunzan diet is meager. In the U.S., for instance, the average daily intake is 3,300 calories with 100 grams of protein, 157 grams of fat, and 380 grams of carbohydrate. In Hunza, according to Pakistani nutritionist Dr. S. Maqsood Ali, a Hunzukut's average caloric intake is 1,923 calories, with 50 grams of protein, 36 grams of fat, and 354 grams of carbohydrate.

Apricots—fresh in summer and sun-dried in winter—and chapatis, unbleached, unleavened, unsweetened pancakes of buckwheat, dominate the Hunzan diet. The apricot is the special soul of Hunza, because its trees are the 1st to show flowers, the earliest fruit to ripen in spring. Hunza boasts thousands of these trees, and a

man's wealth is measured by the size of his apricot orchard. (A woman cannot own land, since Hunza is a Muslim country, but a widow is entitled to the fruit of her husband's trees during her lifetime.) The seed of certain apricots yields an oil rich in polyunsaturated fatty acids and full of organic copper and iron. It is used both for cooking and as a cosmetic aid to improve the complexion. Hunza is also noted for its mulberries, which grow as big as a man's thumb and, despite their seeds, melt in the mouth. Hunza vegetables include lettuce, onions, cabbage, and carrots. These are eaten raw or, if cooked, they are set over a low fire for short periods of time, owing to the scarcity of fuel. This, of course, saves valuable minerals in the food and preserves its health-giving vitamins. Meat is eaten only a few times a year, and is considered a luxury. Goats, sheep, and yaks provide milk and butter, which are taken in limited quantities. In general, the Hunzan diet is minimal—low in animal fat, in cholesterol, in calories—a major factor, it is conjectured by many scientists, in achieving health and longevity. Additionally, Hunzukuts of necessity fast in late spring before the new harvest of grains, fruits, and vegetables comes in.

Hunza is famed and fabled for its slim, erect, graceful people who "glide rather than walk," and whose "mature men have the appearance of boys," as John H. Tobe describes them in *Hunza: Adventures in a Land of Paradise*. The Mir pointed out that in Hunza, unlike the West, "The young envy the old." As Hunzukuts passed the 100-year mark, they journeyed from their villages to the palace in Baltit to "pay their respects" to the Mir. The Mir held court each day at 10 A.M., at which time he was advised by a Council of Elders, all 20 of whom were men in their 90s or over. Whether it is diet, exercise, or the relaxed atmosphere, Hunzukuts are one of the world's healthiest people. Dr. Alexander Leaf attributes the "high degree of cardiovascular fitness as well as the general muscular tone" to physical exercise; it is necessary for the Hunzukuts to "traverse the hills on foot during the day's activities." But there is a magic and mystery as yet unsolved in Hunza, for the apricot trees, too, live to a hundred, whereas in America the average life of a fruit tree is from 25 to 30 years. Moreover, even without chemical sprays or birds, the fruits of Hunza are free of worms and insect pests.

The outside world, however, is taking its toll on Hunza. Dental caries have begun to appear among the youth, partly explained by the fact that for the 1st time Hunzukuts are importing sugar, having tired of their only sweetener—a puree of dried apricots. Goiter also has appeared now that pure white salt is being imported to replace the "impure" brownish salt, with its natural minerals including iodine and fluoride, that is found in Hunza.

Guidebook. Travelers seeking the fountain of youth—or the mixed blessings of a long life—should put Hunza on their list of places to visit. Once inaccessible both because of its remote location and the attitude of the Pakistan Government, it is now ready to cater to tourism. The visitor must get a visa to Pakistan (easy enough); then he must obtain permission from the political agent in Gilgit (available only after you arrive in Rawalpindi and pull government strings on the spot).

A modern plane whisks the visitor to Gilgit, and a new highway connects this city with Baltit, where both hotels and camping sites are available.

Interested? Better hurry. The 20th century is riding that plane and marching down that highway, along with 1,000 tourists a month. It's now or never, if you want to see the old Hunza—the original Shangri-La.

—F.B.

Transcaucasia

Location. The Soviet Union's southernmost point is dramatized—and dominated—by the Caucasus, a 750-mi.-long strip of mountains with peaks such as Mount Kazbek, the Dykh-Tau, and Mount Elbrus rising magisterially to more than 16,000′, 17,000′, and 18,000′ respectively. The Caucasian mountains run between 2 great lakes called "seas": to the west the Black; to the East, the Caspian. The region includes the Soviet Union republics of Georgia, Armenia, and Azerbaÿan. Because of its felicitous geographical location, this area—one of the world's most colorful—embraces simultaneously subtropical stretches, seacoast resorts, and Alpine villages nestling on mountainsides at altitudes of nearly 5,000′. The 1st 2 regions are bathed in year-round sunlight and are eternally green, while the latter is shaded by perpetual snow clouds.

To the east are the Mongolian republics with their Uzbek, Kirghiz, and Kazakh populations of sloe-eyed, yellow-skinned people. South of the Caucasus lie the neighboring nations of Turkey and Iran. Somewhat inadvertently the Caucasus gave its name to that division of mankind which comprises the chief race of Europe, North Africa, and Southwest Asia. The supposition was that the people of the Caucasus or "Caucasians" were racially "typical" of what we think of as Aryan.

Longevity. The total population of the area is about that of New York City—9.5 million—yet it proudly and legitimately boasts the highest number of long-lived people anywhere in the world. In fact, in the local Caucasian dialects there is no word for "elderly" or "aged," merely the Russian word which means "long-centuried." The last census, taken in 1970, revealed that 5,000 centenarians then lived in the Caucasus. Most of these were found in the Daghestan part of Azerbaijan at the Caspian end of the Caucasus, and in Abkhazia, part of Georgia at the Black Sea end of the mountains. Daghestan's population is just over a million with 70 out of every 100,000 of the population 100 years or over in age. In Abkhazia, with its half-million people, 2.58% are over 90 years old. Compare this percentage with a total 0.1% for the whole of the U.S.S.R. or 0.4% for the U.S. In a further breakdown of official figures, one out of every 300 Abkhazians is 100 years old or over. For comparison, note that in the U.S. only 3 in 100,000 reach 100 years of age.

Geriatrically, the Caucasus area is the most thoroughly and scientifically documented region in the world. Professor G. E. Pitzkhelauri, director of the Gerontology Center headquartered in Tbilisi, the capital of Georgia, helped by his assistant Dr. Deli Dzhorbenadze, has studied 15,000 people of the Caucasus, all over 80 years of age, and the 2 doctors have tested more than 700 centenarians. Many of these latter have birth certificates or baptismal records, but they have also been carefully questioned as to historical events, dates of marriage, birth of children, death of husband or wife, etc., and by arithmetical computation, the age of these very old people can be counterchecked or verified with considerable accuracy. Moreover, foreign gerontologists have frequently visited here to corroborate Russian findings.

The most spectacular recorded examples of old age or long life were those of Shirali Mislimov, who died at the age of 168 in 1973, and Tsurba, a woman who "withered away like an old tree," according to a Russian reporter witnessing her death, at the age of 160. Shirali, affectionately called "Baba"—"baby"—was born in a mountain village of Azerbaijan in 1805, a fact attested to by his internal passport. According to Dr. Abdulla I. Karayev, head of the Dept. of Physiology at Azerbaijan's Academy of Sciences and a leading Russian gerontologist, Shirali-Baba was the forebear of 5 living generations, including one great-great-great-grandchild aged 4. He continued until his death to tend an orchard he planted in 1870, and he retained vivid memories of the 1853–1856 Crimean War. He left behind a 120-year-old widow whom he had married 102 years earlier.

Tsurba, whose life facts were researched by Dr. Ramazan-Alikishi, the Daghestani gerontologist, also lived to celebrate a "double golden jubilee"—a 100th wedding anniversary. At age 140 she began to "shrink," and finally when she was 160 years old she was a mere 3' in height. She slept and died in a baby's crib.

Living There. The Caucasus has been romantically depicted in Russian literature, opera, and ballet ever since it came under Russian influence 2 centuries ago. Pushkin, Tolstoi, and Chekhov have all described its exotic charms and health-giving atmosphere. The towns of Sochi and Sukhumi on the Black Sea, and Baku, the capital of Azerbaijan on the Caspian Sea, are famous throughout Russia as resorts offering rest and pleasure. Muscovites and Leningraders vacation there regularly, with some of the more influential having their own permanent villas or, more modestly, beach houses. Many Russians make the journey for health reasons and take what is known as the "water cure" (seabathing) or the "grape cure" (a diet of nothing but luscious, sweet, Georgian grapes). The mineral waters of the Caucasus are among the finest and purest in Europe, and Borzhom, the leading brand, is exported all over Russia and even abroad. The look of these places with their wooden houses, onion-shaped domes, and natives in colorful costumes—women in brightly embroidered, circular, pleated skirts and the men in karakul hats and greatcoats with ammunition belts across the chest—has been somewhat spoiled by the huge rest houses, resembling sanatariums, built by the Government for vacationers.

To find people with genuine longevity, you have to leave these fashionable tourist centers and travel back from the sea and its crowded lowlands into the foothills and mountains of the Caucasus itself. There the terrain is excitingly rugged and the life less easy. The Abkhazians call their country "God's afterthought," meaning that God had a "good 2nd thought" when he made their hilly terrain fertile enough for them to supply the Soviet Union with much of its tobacco, tea, and citrus fruits, as well as to support the local farmers and their animals. The Daghestanis too, like the Abkhazians, are of necessity superb horsemen, since the horse is the most feasible means of climbing mountain trails to tend Alpine pastures, to herd sheep or goats, and to cross the countless Caucasian gorges over light wooden bridges.

Although the life is hard, it is curiously without inner stress and strain. One 108-year-old Abkhazian recently told the American gerontologist Dr. Alexander Leaf that the secret of his long life was: "I never had a single enemy. I read no books and have no worries." Another, a 117-year-old man, quipped when told that few Americans attain his great age, "They're too literate." Still another, a woman of 109, explained that "people don't live so long anymore because they worry more and don't do what they want."

In these Caucasian areas of great longevity, the diet consists largely of milk in the form of cheese and buttermilk; vegetables such as green onions, tomatoes, cucumbers, beans, and cabbage; meat including chicken, beef, young goat, and—in winter—pork; and fruits, particularly grapes. The long-lived people consume a surprising 1,700 to 1,900 calories a day, considerably more, according to Dr. Leaf, than for people of advanced age elsewhere in the world. Seventy percent of the calories come from vegetables, with an average of 70 to 90 gm. of protein which is largely derived from milk rather than meat. Cheese is eaten daily in the Caucasus, but it is low in fat content. The daily fat intake is around 50 gm.

Bread and potatoes, the staples of any Russian meal, are rarer in the Caucasus. Georgia is famous for its 2'-long loaves of flat, unleavened, crisply baked bread, which curl upward at one end and are served at the table while still hot. But in the hinterlands, particularly in Abkhazia, the bread substitute is *abusta*. According to Sula Benet, professor of anthropology at Hunter College in New York and author of *Abkhazia: The Long Living People of the Caucasus*, *abusta* is a patty of "cornmeal mash cooked in water without salt." It is eaten with the fingers and dipped in various sauces. Surprising, too, is the fact that food in the Caucasus is generally spicy, flavored as it is with red peppers, black pepper, garlic, and pomegranate juice.

Of the 50,000 people in Azerbaijan who are 80 or over, the majority, being Muslims, do not drink alcohol. The Abkhazians, on the other hand, drink their locally produced dry red wine, which they call "life-giving," at lunch and dinner every day. The Abkhazians, though they grow tobacco, do not as a rule smoke, while the Daghestanis do. Soviet medical authorities suggest that the Caucasian diet of buttermilk and other soured milk products, together with the numerous pickled vegetables and the wine, all combine to help destroy bacteria and "indirectly prevent the development of arteriosclerosis." Dr. Samuel Rosen of Mount Sinai Hospital of New York, during a visit to the area in 1970, credited the diet of very little saturated fat and large quantities of fruit and vegetables for the remarkably acute hearing of the aged.

In general, even at the end of their prolonged lives, these ancients have their own teeth, fairly luxuriant hair, good eyesight, erect postures, and have never known illness or sickness. They look younger than their years, and

Professor Benet, for instance, was once embarrassed in Abkhazia after making a toast to a man who looked about 70 years old. "May you live as long as Moses," she said. The man, it turned out, was already 119 and Moses had lived only to 120.

Diagnosis. Experts have countless explanations for the Caucasians' longevity. The centenarians themselves offer additional reasons. By general consensus, diet and the invigorating climate are praised as the 2 most contributory factors. Overeating is virtually unknown, and very few fat people (apart from Russian tourists) can be seen even in the seacoast towns. One centenarian attributes his long life to the fact that he bathes each morning in a cold mountain stream; another says that he has "never taken a nap in the daytime." Several others speak of the importance of a regular and active sex life. (Abkhazian men are potent even after the age of 70 and 13.6% of the women continue to menstruate beyond the age of 55.)

However, aside from the absence of hereditary "bad genes," the most telling reason for longevity here is "spiritual." These people *expect* to live a long life. Their familiar toast is, "May you live to be 300!" Dr. Leaf suggests that perhaps the U.S. is "a mortality-ridden society, programming our lives to a shorter existence." In the Caucasus there is a lifelong sense of usefulness. People there do not "retire," but continue doing daily chores of some sort until the very end. Moreover, they are granted respect as they age, and are turned to for advice. "Every day is a gift when you are over a hundred," one centenarian says, but it is a gift which is purposefully kept active within the society and its norms.

Guidebook. First you must contact Intourist, preferably through an experienced travel agency such as American Express, which will know the procedures to be followed. You must describe where you want to go, exactly, giving the specific dates of your arrival into the Soviet Union and your departure from it. Intourist will approve your visa application and handle the arrangements for your visit. Prepaid vouchers for hotel accommodations and meals will be necessary, also obtainable through Intourist.

—F.B.

VILCABAMBA, ECUADOR

Location. Ecuador, situated near the top of the map of South America, is bound by the Pacific Ocean to the west, Peru on the east and south, and Colombia to the north. Its capital city, Quito, sits just below the equator. Three hundred mi. due south from Quito lies the city of Loja, the capital of Ecuador's southernmost province. From Loja you go 30 mi. steadily upward in a southeasterly direction along a winding road to reach Vilcabamba, a valley one mi. high in altitude, one half mile in size, and with a scant population of 1,000 people.

Longevity. Vilcabamba has been studied and restudied, ever since the 1940 census revealed some astonishing facts about the long life of the valley's inhabitants. Eighteen percent of the population was over 65 years of age, as compared to 4% elsewhere in Ecuador and 9% in the U.S. Eleven percent was over 70, and 9 persons had lived to be anywhere from 100 to 130. In 1969, Dr. Miguel Salvador, president of Ecuador's Society of Cardiologists, on a government mission with 8 other doctors, thoroughly examined 628 *longevos* or extremely old people in Vilcabamba. The medical group found men of 90 still ploughing the fields side by side with younger men, women of 100 and more still gathering strands of sheep's wool or working in the local bakery, and other aged men treading the muddy ooze to make adobe, the material from which Vilcabambans build their houses. More astonishing, the Salvador mission found a total absence of serious ailments, notably heart disease. These findings have been more recently confirmed by Dr. David Davies of University College, London, and Dr. Alexander Leaf of Harvard University, both gerontologists of note. Vilcabamba has now become popularly known as the "island of immunity" or "island of health and longevity."

Living There. In the language of the Shuara Indians, who 1st inhabited the valley, *vilca* means "sacred" and *bamba* "valley." While Vilcabamba is boxed in by mountains, one peak towers like a guardian over the valley. This is 7,500'-high Mondango—literally "Altar of the Incas." The valley is crossed by 2 shallow, rushing rivers, the Vilcabamba and the Chamba. Dr. Davies describes Vilcabamba as a place of "utter tranquillity." The temperature year round never varies from 70° Fahrenheit, the wind always blows from the same direction, and each year the valley receives the same amount of sun. Because of its altitude, Vilcabamba has no snakes, spiders, mosquitoes. Instead, there is what filmmaker Gene Ayers has called "a kaleidoscopic variety of flowers, fruits, vegetables, fireflies, songbirds, and domestic animals." After the paradisiacal tone of the reports about Vilcabamba, foreigners are apt to be taken aback by the limited sanitation facilities. Ecuadoran officials have introduced modern hygiene to the area slowly, since the people have lived so long and healthily under primitive conditions. In any event

Vilcabamba's curative powers exist in a mysterious realm beyond modern notions of health standards. Albert Kramer, an American suffering from a heart ailment, simply went there to live for a year in an adobe farmhouse he rented, and he experienced what is technically known as "cardiological compensation," a spontaneous improvement in heart condition.

Sometime in the 17th century—history is dim in this part of the world—Augustine missionaries settled Vilcabamba, and the valley's only village probably looks today much as it did then. The center is the plaza with its Catholic church, garden, and fountain, around which cluster a scattering of wood and adobe huts. A few of the houses and the government office building are 2 stories in height. However, most Vilcabambans avoid the village, preferring their isolated life on the farm. Thus they escape any degree of "urban tension."

Life is meager here. Vilcabambans have a calorie intake of only 1,200 calories per day, half the number normally consumed in, say, the U.S. They eat about one oz. of meat a week. Their meals consist mainly of grain, soup, corn, yucca root, beans, potatoes, together with fruits such as oranges and bananas. The specialty of the region is *repe*, a soup of bananas and beans "laced" with white cheese, salt, and lard. The small quantity of sugar used is unrefined. The *longevos* attribute their long life to the herb teas they drink, but modern researchers discount this. Most baffling to outsiders investigating Vilcabamba is the prevalence of tobacco and alcohol. Vilcabambans, even the most aged in their hundreds, drink every day 2 to 4 cups of local rum made from unrefined sugarcane. They also smoke from 40 to 60 cigarettes daily. The tobacco is homegrown and wrapped either in maize leaves or toilet paper imported from Loja. One 104-year-old woman told Dr. Leaf that while she did not drink rum or smoke, still "I have to have my 5 cups of coffee each day." In contrast, Miguel Carpio, aged 123, said to a reporter, "I used to drink a lot, but now I take only 2 or 3 glasses a day. Every few months, though, I get the feeling to have a good drunk. So I buy a bottle with a friend and we empty it."

It is perhaps romantic to say that Vilcabambans are "contentedly involved in the business of living." Dr. Leaf more realistically describes their life as "a tedious circle of drudgery broken by religious ceremonies and an occasional fiesta." One man has been a farmer for 100 years because, as he says, "It's all I know how to do." Another man, the village carpenter, labored with the same handmade tools from 1900 until his death in the early 1970s. (He died of pneumonia contracted during a trip to the "outside world.") Each of the aged Vilcabambans has his lifelong chores—weeding fields, feeding poultry, chafing grain, grinding corn, making tiles, herding flocks, and the like. Now, while steady work habits are considered by gerontologists to be an important factor in longevity, the Vilcabambans, unlike the long-lived people of Hunza or Transcaucasia, are not cheerful about it. "Who wants to live so long?" asked 120-year-old Gabriel Sanchez of an American radio station reporter. Miguel Carpio jokingly wished he could take 15 years from his age, which would make him 107. And Hermelinda Leon, a 95-year-old woman still working in the bakery, bluntly summed up to Dr. Leaf: "Life has been hard. I would not want to live it again."

Diagnosis. Most foreign doctors credit the frugal diet and equable climate of Vilcabamba for the long lives of its inhabitants, along with their extremely quiet life. The natives sleep and awake with the passage of the sun. They remain active, have few worries, breathe the clear mountain air, and drink the sparkling fresh water from their 2 unpolluted rivers. When they do suffer from a minor ailment—there are no major ones—such as "slight asthma" or a common cold or an attack of arthritis, they go to the medicine man for a remedy of coca leaves. They also will trek 2 mi. every day to get to Sunungo, the mineral spring whose warm medicinal waters remove stiffness and pain. The village musician, Augustin Mendieta, aged 64, said he made this trip daily, in order to finger his mandolin without discomfort.

Vilcabamban longevity is a secret locked in the sacred little valley. Dr. Davies proposes that the valley should be placed under "protection" until it has been "completely investigated." Already there has been a small decline in the length of life and a slight upsurge in the appearance of disease and illness. Fewer and fewer of the local inhabitants are content with the lives of their fathers and great-grandfathers, and many of the young are moving away. Jorge Vivanco, now a journalist for *El Telegrafo*, is one of those who opted for city life. He ascribes the longevity found in his birthplace to a "lack of ambition" in the people. "No trouble, no strain. That's their secret."

Guidebook. Ecuador is a hospitable country, eager for tourists, and pleased that Vilcabamba has become a mecca for both the curious and those who need its restorative and health-giving atmosphere. There is a certain conflict between doctors who want to isolate Vilcabamba and so prevent the encroachment of deleterious civilization, and officials who see a tourist gold mine in the valley. Meanwhile, a visa to Ecuador is easily obtained. Reservations are not required, since most of the farmhouses will also take a paying guest, provided he is willing to share the austere life of the valley's inhabitants. Everything in the valley is cheap, but any luxuries you require had best be brought with you since money cannot buy what is not already there.

—F.B.

Some Famous Alcoholics

Alcoholism is a *progressive* disease which, unless arrested by total abstinence, inevitably leads to deterioration of the victim's health and ability to function. The American Medical Association's "conservative" estimate of the number of alcoholics in the U.S. today is 9 million. The disease is no respecter of age, sex, or occupation; its victims have included performers Dana Andrews*, W. C. Fields, Dick Van Dyke*, Lillian Roth, Janis Joplin, Edith Piaf, and Laurette Taylor; political figures such as senators Harold Hughes* and Russell Long*; athletes George Gipp and Jim Thorpe; and a host of writers to whose work alcoholism has often added a sad final chapter. *"Arrested" or nonpracticing alcoholics.

SINCLAIR LEWIS (1885–1951). American novelist and playwright; 1st American Nobel Prize winner in literature in 1930.

Born in Minnesota and educated at Yale, Lewis was firmly established as a major novelist by the publication of *Main Street* in 1920. Later novels brought him wealth and fame as the literary diagnostician of American values.

Lewis was a heavy drinker throughout his adult life. He preferred brandy, often consuming over a quart a day. Mark Schorer describes his pattern of ". . . complete immolation and isolation in the writing of a book, and then gregarious bouts that finally blacked out everything." James Thurber observed that with Lewis: "You couldn't always tell at 7 in the morning whether he was having his 1st drink of the day or his last one of the night." His 2nd wife, writer-lecturer Dorothy Thompson, made repeated appeals to him to do something about what she called his "pathological drinking." His drinking bouts often ended in delirium tremens and hospitalization.

During a visit to Europe in 1950, Lewis suffered a heart attack from which he never recovered; he died in Rome, at 66. He remembered his last mistress, 29-year-old Marcella Powers, in his will.

MODEST MUSORGSKI (1839–1881). Russian composer.

Musorgski was one of 5 Russian composers who tried in the last half of the 19th century to establish a "Russian National Music" movement in reaction to the traditional European school led by Tchaikovsky. Friends who collaborated with Musorgski in this effort included Rimski-Korsakov and Borodin. Musorgski is best remembered for *Night on Bald Mountain, Pictures from an Exhibition*, and his opera *Boris Godunov*.

Musorgski invariably turned to alcohol in times of stress. He drank himself to the point of physical collapse after being rejected by a lover in 1858, and after the death of his mother in 1865. Due to his chronic alcoholism, his career declined in the late 1870s, and by 1880 he was incapable of sustained musical effort. "Friends would often rescue Musorgski from some disreputable place, nearly in rags, his hair disheveled, his face swollen with alcohol," wrote a musical contemporary. His death at 42 was attributed to "alcoholic epilepsy."

EDGAR ALLAN POE (1809–1849). American poet and short-story writer; considered the father of the modern detective story.

Orphaned in early childhood, Poe was adopted and raised by a wealthy Virginia merchant. He was sent to the University of Virginia, but was promptly expelled for drinking and gambling. Later, he was admitted to West Point, but, after just 7 months, drunkenness and indebtedness caused him to be dismissed from the Academy and he was disowned by his foster father.

A college classmate wrote: "Poe's passion for strong drink was as marked and as peculiar as that for cards . . . without a sip or a smack of the mouth he would seize a full glass and send it home at a single gulp." He was slight of build and sickly, subject to flights of fancy and fits of depression. His low tolerance for alcohol was described thus by his biographer, Hervey Allan: "The effect upon Poe of even a small quantity was all out of usual proportion. He seems to have been so sensitively organized that a dram . . . was sufficient to make his actions and conversation unusual. One glass was literally too much; 2 or 3 were disastrous; and a continued round reduced him to a caricature of himself."

Poe, at 27, married Virginia Clemm, who was 13 years old and tubercular at the time; when she died in 1847, Poe, in his anguish and despite failing health, sought relief in alcohol and drugs. He died after a drinking bout, while stuffing ballot boxes during a Baltimore election, at the age of 40.

JOHN BARRYMORE (1882–1942). American stage and screen actor.

John Barrymore was literally "born" to the theater. His father was a successful actor, and John, his brother Lionel, and their sister Ethel were raised by a grandmother who operated a popular theater in Philadelphia. When Lionel and Ethel chose acting careers, it was almost inevitable that John would join what was to become known as the "royal family of the theater."

"Acting, romance, and drinking occupied John Barrymore about equally," wrote Hollis Alpert in *The Barrymores*. John was remarkably successful at all 3: For a decade he was America's preeminent actor, setting standards of performance that some critics say have never been equaled; he was married and divorced 4 times, the 4th marriage, at 53, to a girl of 19; and he lived and died a chronic alcoholic. Gene Fowler, in his biography of Barrymore, estimates that ". . . in 40 years he consumed 640 barrels of hard liquor."

John's career began to decline in 1934 when he appeared on a movie set ". . . in so dazed and drunken a condition that he was unable to remember any of the words of his new script." Failing memory and failing health plagued him the rest of his life. His last years were spent performing roles that parodied his former greatness—when he was not in the hospital, or on extravagant trips aboard his yacht in a futile search for a "cure" for his alcoholism. He made an enormous amount of money in his lifetime, but after his death in 1942, his effects were sold at auction to satisfy his creditors.

EUGENE O'NEILL (1888–1953). American playwright, Nobel Prize winner in 1936.

Eugene O'Neill was the son of a well-known actor. He earned an early reputation as a heavy drinker, was suspended from Princeton for throwing a beer bottle through a window in college president Woodrow Wilson's house during a party, and spent the next few years in an almost successful attempt to drink himself to death. He was a habitué of Jimmy the Priest's, a Manhattan saloon later used as the setting for his play *The Iceman Cometh*, which examined the despair and delusions of alcoholism. His favorite drink, according to a contemporary, was "Benedictine by the tumblerful." He contracted tuberculosis and, while in a sanitorium, began to write.

His early plays were successful, but O'Neill was drinking heavily during the time they were produced. A theatrical colleague commented, ". . . he went on drinking bouts that lasted 2 or 3 weeks, so bad that his friends never knew if they would be able to pull him through."

O'Neill quit drinking abruptly at the age of 37. He volunteered to participate in a pre-Kinsey study of human sexuality, and the psychiatrist who conducted the study offered free therapy sessions as payment for O'Neill's services. During these sessions, the doctor told O'Neill that he drank to bury his oedipal problems. O'Neill thereupon stopped drinking for the remainder of his 65-year life.

PAUL VERLAINE (1844–1896). French poet.

His moral conduct earned him the title "the Deplorable Verlaine," while his poetry established the school of Symbolism in French literature.

Raised and educated in Paris, Verlaine began publishing poems and mingling in advanced literary circles while in his early 20s. Among his acquaintances were Victor Hugo, Anatole France, and Theodore de Banville. He had published several books of verse by the time he was 26.

Verlaine's fondness for absinthe had taken him well down the path of alcoholism by the time he married 17-year-old Mathilde Maute. A year after this marriage, Verlaine abandoned his wife and infant son to travel with the 17-year-old poet Rimbaud. Their homosexual association lasted some 18 months until Verlaine, in a fit of anger, shot and slightly wounded Rimbaud. Verlaine was sentenced to 2 years in prison.

By 1875, his drinking had increased and his poetry production had declined. As his talent diminished, however, his literary reputation, based upon his earlier work, grew. He was able to support himself by lecturing on the poetic doctrine of Symbolism. Meanwhile, he was living in an ever increasing alcoholic squalor. He was looked after, when not in hospitals, by 2 elderly prostitutes. He died at the age of 51.

HART CRANE (1899–1932). American poet.

Hart Crane was the unhappy offspring of incompatible parents and he left home before finishing school. By the time he was 20—and had a job he thoroughly hated in a drugstore in Akron, O.—his poetry had begun to appear in "little" literary magazines. He left the drugstore and traveled extensively during his early 20s. "Travel," as described in his published letters, apparently meant finding a variety of places in which to get drunk. He was, however, producing poetry which received critical acclaim.

His work came to the attention of Otto Kahn, a wealthy banker and patron of the arts, who gave the 26-year-old Crane an endowment on which to live while writing poetry. Crane moved to Mexico and produced 2 volumes of poetry, *White Buildings* and *The Bridge*. His drinking, however, progressed, and he was a confirmed, hopeless alcoholic at the age of 33.

"The story of his life," wrote Brom Weber, "is a record which vibrates with an explosive terror . . . elated, wretched, violent, Rabelaisian."

Crane committed suicide at 33 by jumping overboard, while returning by ship to the U.S. from Cuba.

GEN. ULYSSES S. GRANT (1822–1885). Commanding general of Union forces in the Civil War, 18th President of the U.S.

Abraham Lincoln, when informed that General Grant drank whiskey while serving in the field during the Civil War, is said to have quipped: "Find out the name of the brand so I can give it to my other generals."

That Grant was a drinking man is well documented, but it is questionable whether the term "alcoholic" accurately applies to him. On one occasion, however, his fondness for whiskey interrupted his military career. Ten years after his graduation from West Point, and after distinguished service in the Mexican War, Captain Grant was stationed at Fort Vancouver, an isolated outpost in Oregon. He was separated from his new wife and a son he had never seen, and in his loneliness he took to excessive drinking. His tippling came to the attention of a superior officer, who demanded that he resign his commission. He was relieved of duty on May 1, 1854.

Grant returned to uniform in 1861 when Lincoln called for Union volunteers. Grant served with such distinction that he soon rose to the rank of general, and in 1864 was put in command of all the Union armies. There was still criticism of his drinking, but President Lincoln let the general's military performance speak for itself.

Grant emerged from the war a national hero and was nominated for the Presidency in 1868. Elected, he served 2 terms and, though he was an unwilling and unpolished politician, he was a popular President. He died of throat cancer at the age of 63.

JACK LONDON (1876–1916). American novelist and short-story writer.

He was an illegitimate child, raised in poverty by a stepfather, with the Oakland waterfront as his playground. He went to work on a boat at 14, later shipped out as a seal hunter, and traveled the world as an able seaman. *The Call of the Wild*, published when he was 27, established him as a writer.

At the peak of his success, London often boasted to friends about his early drinking exploits. He began drinking, he claimed, at the age of 5 when he would sample the beer he was required to carry in a pail from a neighborhood saloon to his stepfather. As a sailor at 14, he said, he could outdrink his older shipmates. He drank heavily throughout his life, preferring whiskey, reaching and passing the quart-a-day mark.

London wrote a book titled *John Barleycorn, or Alcoholic Memoirs* 3 years before his death. In it, he discussed his lifelong addiction to alcohol. At the conclusion of the book, he stated: "I intend to continue to drink, but more skillfully, more discreetly." His consumption of whiskey, however, subsequently increased.

At 40, Jack London was the best-paid, best-known popular writer in the world; he had money, success, a secluded retreat in northern California, and a devoted wife. At 40, Jack London committed suicide with an intentional overdose of drugs.

O. HENRY (1862–1910). William Sydney Porter, who wrote under the pseudonym of O. Henry, was an American short-story writer whose "surprise" endings set a trend in short fiction.

He was the son of a North Carolina doctor. As a young man, he worked as a ranch hand and then as a teller in a Texas bank. While employed at the bank he was accused of embezzlement, and fled to Honduras. In 1897 he returned to Texas and was arrested, convicted, and sentenced to 5 years imprisonment. Throughout the years following his release from prison until his death at 48, he drank heavily and supported himself with his highly salable stories, which were much in demand by the magazines of the day.

"O. Henry had to be guarded and *made* to write," observed Upton Sinclair. "He could not write anything bad, it seemed, but it was agony for him to write at all." Magazine editors would send assistants to sober him up, watch over him, and compel him to meet publishing deadlines. His last years were spent roaming the streets of New York, drinking heavily and writing sporadically, but writing incomparably well.

DYLAN THOMAS (1914–1953). Welsh poet.

Dylan Thomas was born in Wales, worked briefly as a journalist, and after W.W. II devoted his full energies to poetry, receiving worldwide acclaim. A critical review of his work stated: ". . . with imagery that derives both from the ages-old, peaceful fishing villages of his home and the world of 20th-century man, his work has a force and vitality that has affected the whole world of letters."

Thomas made 4 lecture tours of the U.S., attracting wide attention for his brilliant dramatic readings and for his legendary self-destructive drinking bouts. "His tour was a fantasy of missed appearances, muddled appointments, drunken binges, boorish behavior—and beauty," wrote Upton Sinclair.

John Brinnin, who chronicled Thomas's tours in *Dylan Thomas in America*, said of his 1st trip: "The purest lyrical poet of the 20th century . . . here he was, sadly crumpled in drunken exhaustion, black-tongued and tipsy . . . unable to think for himself, to face himself, or to face for what they were, the insatiable attentions that could only destroy him."

Doctors told Thomas that to continue to drink was to die, but he drank on. "Do not go gentle into that good night," he wrote. "Rage, rage against the dying of the light." He died suddenly of acute alcoholism in the midst of his 1953 U.S. lecture tour, at the age of 39.

F. SCOTT FITZGERALD (1896–1940). American novelist and short-story writer.

Scott Fitzgerald's early novels and numerous short stories, plus his own self-indulgent lifestyle, made him the personification of the Roaring Twenties, a generation of "flaming youth." He was born in St. Paul to a prosperous family, attended Princeton, and served in the Army during W.W. I. The publication of *This Side of Paradise* when he was 24 brought him instant fame and the money to enjoy it. His marriage to Zelda Sayre the same year was hailed as "the romance of the century," and their extravagant escapades amid fashionable society in the U.S. and in Europe enhanced his reputation. Fitzgerald's alcoholism contributed to his image in the 1920s and to his downfall in the 1930s. "He was committing suicide on the installment plan," wrote Sara Mayfield. ". . . if Scott took more than 3 cocktails, he was off on a spree that left him shot for a week."

As Fitzgerald's drinking continued, his productivity began to decrease, his health failed, and his financial problems accumulated. Zelda suffered an emotional breakdown in 1930, and was in and out of various mental hospitals for the rest of her life. Fitzgerald went through his publicly confessed crack-up, that period when "in a real dark night of the soul it is always 3 o'clock in the morning, day after day." He spent his last years in Hollywood, receiving some comfort from his mistress Sheilah Graham, working off and on as a screenwriter, producing numerous magazine stories, and writing his unfinished novel, *The Last Tycoon,* which was published after his death. He died of a heart attack at the age of 44.

HORACE LIVERIGHT (1886–1933). American publisher, theatrical producer, and filmmaker.

Liveright founded a publishing firm in New York in 1918 which published the work of many little-known authors who were later to emerge as the American literary giants of the '20s and '30s. He also founded the Modern Library series, and was a vigorous crusader against the strict literary censorship of the period. In the mid-'20s, he produced several successful plays.

"He loaned courage and money to many fumbling talents," wrote Ben Hecht. "There was in New York no more popular and exciting figure than Liveright. Beauty, success, and admiration attended him like a faithful retinue, and hundreds of hangers-on were proud to boast of his friendship."

Progressive alcoholism, however, took its toll, and during a period spent in Hollywood in the late '20s, Hecht observed that Liveright ". . . seemed to do nothing but drink himself into nightly comas."

Liveright returned to New York and dropped from public sight. When he died late in 1933, he was bankrupt and deeply in debt. Six people attended his funeral.

WILLIAM SEABROOK (1886–1945). American author.

William Seabrook was a successful writer of 1st person travel and adventure books until alcoholism slowed his active life. He lived for 2 years among the Arabs, and also with the natives of Haiti, and among cannibals in Africa, writing books about his experiences. He was educated in Switzerland, served in the French Army in W.W. I, and worked as a reporter for *The New York Times* before turning to free-lance writing.

Seabrook had himself committed to an insane asylum in the mid-'30s in the hope of curing himself of alcoholism. The book *Asylum* chronicled that experience. In it he says: "I had been begging, pleading, demanding toward the last, to be locked up . . . shut up . . . chained up . . . where I couldn't get out and where I couldn't get my hands on a bottle. I had become a confirmed, habitual drunk, without any of the stock alibis or excuses." He spent 7 months in the asylum and, when released, thought himself cured.

In his autobiography, *No Hiding Place,* published 7 years later, he confessed that he had been unable to free himself of the compulsion to drink. He took his own life with an overdose of sleeping pills at the age of 59.

—C.E.

Upton Sinclair, in his book *The Cup of Fury*, mentioned other well-known persons he regarded as alcoholics or problem drinkers. In each case, according to Sinclair, the individual's drinking was sufficiently serious to affect his work, talent, or career adversely.

King Edward VIII of England, later Duke of Windsor
Douglas Fairbanks, Sr., actor
George Sterling, poet
Stephen Crane, novelist
Finley Peter Dunne, magazine publisher, writer
Eugene V. Debs, presidential candidate
Isadora Duncan, dancer
Edna St. Vincent Millay, poet
Maxwell Bodenheim, poet, novelist
Sherwood Anderson, writer
Theodore Dreiser, novelist
Klaus Mann, writer
Donald McLean, diplomat (defected to U.S.S.R. in 1951)
Ambrose Bierce, writer
Joaquin Miller, poet

Rube Waddell, baseball pitcher
Bugs Raymond, baseball pitcher
Harry Greb, prizefighter
Mickey Walker, prizefighter
Jimmy Slattery, prizefighter
George Gipp, football player
Willie Ritola, long-distance track star
George Travers, golfer
Jim Thorpe, football and baseball player, track star
Grover Cleveland Alexander, baseball pitcher
John L. Sullivan, prizefighter
Fred Herreshoff, golfer
Rollie Hemsley, baseball catcher
Walter Hagen, golfer
Tony Galento, prizefighter
Tommy Armour, golfer

A Synoptic History of the Promotion and Prohibition of Drugs

c. 5000 B.C. The Sumerians use opium, suggested by the fact that they have an ideogram for it which has been translated as HUL, meaning "joy" or "rejoicing."

c. 3500 B.C. Earliest historical record of the production of alcohol, the description of a brewery in an Egyptian papyrus.

c. 300 B.C. Theophrastus (371–287 B.C.), posed origin of the use of tea in China.

c. 2500 B.C. Earliest historical evidence of the eating of poppy seeds among the Lake Dwellers of Switzerland.

c. 2000 B.C. Earliest record of prohibitionist teaching, by an Egyptian priest, who writes to his pupil: "I, thy superior, forbid thee to go to the taverns. Thou art degraded like the beasts."

c. 350 B.C. Proverbs 31:6–7: "Give strong drink to him who is perishing, and wine to those in bitter distress; let them drink and forget their poverty, and remember their misery no more."

c. 300 B.C. Theophrastus (371–287 B.C.). Greek naturalist and philosopher, records what has remained as the earliest undisputed reference to the use of the poppy juice.

c. 250 B.C. Psalms 104:14–15: "Thou dost cause grass to grow for the cattle, and plants for man to cultivate, that he may bring forth food from the earth, and wine to gladden the heart of man."

350 A.D. Earliest written mention of tea, in a Chinese dictionary.

4th century St. John Chrysostom (345–407), bishop of Constantinople: "I hear man cry, 'Would there be no wine! O folly! O madness!' Is it wine that causes this abuse? No. For if you say, 'Would there be no wine!' because of drunkenness, then you must say, going on by degrees, 'Would there were no night!' because of the thieves, 'Would there were no light!' because of the informers, and 'Would there were no women!' because of adultery."

c. 450 Babylonian Talmud: "Wine is at the head of all medicines; where wine is lacking, drugs are necessary."

c. 1000 Opium is widely used in China and the Far East.

1229 The ecclesiastic authorities of Toulouse declare: "We also forbid the laity to possess any of the books of the Old or New Testament . . . that any should have these books translated into the vulgar tongue we strictly forbid."

1382 John Wycliffe completes his translation of the Bible into English.

1493 The use of tobacco is introduced into Europe by Columbus and his crew returning from America.

c. 1500 According to J. D. Rolleston, a British medical historian, a medieval Russian cure for drunkenness consisted "in taking a piece of pork, putting it secretly into a Jew's bed for 9 days, and then giving it to the drunkard in a pulverized form, who will turn away from drinking as a Jew would from pork."

c. 1525 Paracelsus (1490–1541) introduces laudanum, or tincture of opium, into the practice of medicine.

1526 Six thousand copies of Tyndale's English Bible are printed at Worms and smuggled into England.

1529 Charles V (1500–1558), Holy Roman Emperor and ruler of The Netherlands, decrees that the "reading, purchasing, or possessing any proscribed books, or any New Testaments prohibited by the theologians of Louvain" are crimes, the punishments for which are that "the men be beheaded, the women buried alive, and the relapsed burned."

1536 William Tyndale, translator of the New Testament and the Pentateuch, is burned at the stake as a heretic, at Vilvorde Castle, near Brussels.

1559 Valdes's Spanish Index, decreeing the prohibition of all religious literature in the language of the people, is published. The penalty for possessing prohibited books is death.

1600 Shakespeare: "Falstaff . . . If I had a thousand sons, the/1st human principle I would teach them should/be, to foreswear thin potations and to addict themselves to sack." ("Sack," a term now obsolete, referred to a type of wine.)

17th century The prince of the petty state of Waldeck pays 10 thalers to anyone who denounces a coffee drinker.

17th century In Russia, Czar Michael Federovitch executes anyone on whom tobacco is found. "Czar Alexei Mikhailovitch rules that anyone caught with tobacco should be tortured until he gives up the name of the supplier."

1601 The Spanish Dominican Alonso Giroi demands the complete prohibition of all religious books in the people's language.

1613 John Rolfe, the husband of the Indian princess Pocahontas, sends the 1st shipment of Virginia tobacco from Jamestown to England.

c. 1650 The use of tobacco is prohibited in Bavaria, Saxony, and Zurich, but the prohibitions are ineffective. Sultan Murad IV of the Ottoman Empire decrees the death penalty for smoking tobacco: "Wherever the Sultan went on his travels or on a military expedition his halting-places were always distinguished by a terrible increase in the number of executions. Even on the battlefield he was fond of surprising men in the act of smoking, when he would punish them by beheading, hanging, quartering, or crushing their hands and feet. . . . Nevertheless, in

spite of all the horrors of this persecution . . . the passion for smoking still persisted."

1680 Thomas Sydenham (1624–1680): "Among the remedies which it has pleased the Almighty God to give to man to relieve his sufferings, none is so universal and so efficacious as opium."

1690 The "Act for the Encouraging of the Distillation of Brandy and Spirits from Corn" is enacted in England.

1691 In Luneberg, Germany, the penalty for smoking (tobacco) is death.

1717 Liquor licenses in Middlesex, England, are granted only to those who "would take oaths of allegiance and of belief in the King's supremacy over the Church."

1736 The Gin Act (England) is enacted with the avowed objects of making spirits "come so dear to the consumer that the poor will not be able to launch out into an excessive use of them." This effort results in general lawbreaking and fails to halt the steady rise in the consumption of even legally produced and sold liquor.

1745 The magistrates of one London division demand that "publicans and wine-merchants should swear that they anathematized the doctrine of Transubstantiation."

1762 Thomas Dover, an English physician, introduces his prescription for a "diaphoretic powder," which he recommends mainly for the treatment of gout. Soon named "Dover's powder," this compound becomes one of the most widely used opium preparations during the next 150 years.

1770 Women in New England organize boycotts against tea imported from Britain; some of these associations call themselves "Daughters of Liberty," their members pledging themselves not to drink tea until after the Revenue Act is repealed. They also popularize various tea substitutes such as brews of raspberry, sage, and birch leaves— the most popular of which, made from the 4-leaved loosestrife, is called "Liberty Tea."

1773 To protest [British tea policies], a band of Bostonians, dressed as Mohawk Indians, boards 3 British ships in Boston Harbor and throws overboard 342 chests of tea (December 16, 1773). This episode leads to the passage of the Coercive Acts (1774) by the British Parliament, which in turn leads to the assembly of the 1st Continental Congress (September 5, 1774) and to the War of Independence and the birth of the U.S. as a nation.

1785 Benjamin Rush publishes his *Inquiry into the Effects of Ardent Spirits on the Human Body and Mind*; in it, he calls the intemperate use of distilled spirits a "disease," and estimates the annual rate of death due to alcoholism in the U.S. as "not less than

4,000 people" in a population then of less than 4 million.

1789 The 1st American temperance society is formed in Litchfield, Conn.

1790 Benjamin Rush persuades his associates at the Philadelphia College of Physicians to send an appeal to Congress to "impose such heavy duties upon all distilled spirits as shall be effective to restrain their intemperate use in the country."

1792 The 1st prohibitory laws against opium in China are promulgated. The punishment decreed for keepers of opium shops is strangulation.

1794 The Whiskey Rebellion, a protest by farmers in western Pennsylvania against a Federal tax on liquor, breaks out and is put down by overwhelming force sent into the area by George Washington.

1797 Samuel Taylor Coleridge writes "Kubla Khan" while under the influence of opium.

1800 Napoleon's army, returning from Egypt, introduces cannabis (hashish, marijuana) into France. Avant-garde artists and writers in Paris develop their own cannabis ritual, leading, in 1844, to the establishment of Le Club des Haschischins.

1801 On Jefferson's recommendation, the Federal duty on liquor is abolished.

1804 Thomas Trotter, an Edinburgh physician, publishes *An Essay, Medical, Philosophical, and Chemical, on Drunkenness and Its Effects on the Human Body*: "In medical language, I consider drunkenness, strictly speaking, to be a disease, produced by a remote cause, and giving birth to actions and movements in the living body that disorder the functions of health. . . . The habit of drunkenness is a disease of the mind."

1805 Friedrich Wilhelm Adam Sertürner, a German chemist, isolates and describes morphine.

1822 Thomas De Quincey's *Confessions of an English Opium Eater* is published. He notes that the opium habit, like any other habit, must be learned: "Making allowance for constitutional differences, I should say that in less than 120 days no habit of opium-eating could be formed strong enough to call for any extraordinary self-conquest in renouncing it, and even suddenly renouncing it. On Saturday you are an opium-eater, on Sunday no longer such."

1826 The American Society for the Promotion of Temperance is founded in Boston. By 1833, there are 6,000 local temperance societies, with more than one million members.

1839–1842 The First Opium War. The British force upon China the trade in opium, a trade the Chinese had declared illegal.

1840 Benjamin Parsons, an English clergyman, declares: ". . . alcohol stands preeminent as a destroyer. . . . I never knew a person become insane who was not in the habit of taking a portion of alcohol every day." Parsons lists 42 distinct diseases caused by alcohol, among them inflammation of the brain, scrofula, mania, dropsy, nephritis, and gout.

1841 Dr. Jacques Joseph Moreau uses hashish in treating mental patients at the Bicêtre.

1842 Abraham Lincoln: "In my judgment, such of us as have never fallen victims, have been spared more from the absence of appetite, than from any mental or moral superiority over those who have. Indeed, I believe, if we take habitual drunkards as a class, their heads and their hearts will bear an advantageous comparison with those of any other class."

1844 Cocaine is isolated in pure form.

1845 A law prohibiting the public sale of liquor is enacted in New York State. It is repealed in 1847.

1847 The American Medical Association is founded.

1852 Susan B. Anthony establishes the Woman's State Temperance Society of New York, the 1st such society formed by and for women. Many of the early feminists, such as Elizabeth Cady Stanton, Lucretia Mott, and Abby Kelly, are also ardent prohibitionists.

1852 The American Pharmaceutical Association is founded. The association's 1856 constitution lists one of its goals as: "To as much as possible restrict the dispensing and sale of medicines to regularly educated druggists and apothecaries."

1856 The Second Opium War. The British, with help from the French, extend their powers to distribute opium in China.

1862 Internal Revenue Act enacted, imposing a license fee of $20 on retail liquor dealers, and a tax of $1 a barrel on beer and 20¢ a gallon on spirits.

1864 Adolf von Baeyer, a 29-year-old assistant of Friedrich August Kekule (the discoverer of the molecular structure of benzene) in Ghent, synthesizes barbituric acid, the 1st barbiturate.

1868 Dr. George Wood, professor of the theory and practice of medicine at the University of Pennsylvania, president of the American Philosophical Society, and the author of a leading American text, *Treatise on Therapeutics*, describes the pharmacological effect of opium as follows: "A sensation of fullness is felt in the head, soon followed by a universal feeling of delicious ease and comfort, with an elevation and expansion of the whole moral and intellectual nature, which is, I think, the most characteristic of its effects . . . the intellectual and imaginative faculties are raised to the highest point compatible with individual capacity. . . . It seems to make the individual, for the time, a better and greater man. . . . The hallucinations, the delirious imaginations of alcoholic intoxication, are, in general, quite wanting. Along with this emotional and intellectual elevation, there is also increased muscular energy; and the capacity to act, and to bear fatigue, is greatly augmented."

1869 The Prohibition party is formed. Gerrit Smith, twice Abolitionist candidate for President, and associate of John Brown, and a crusading prohibitionist, declares: "Our involuntary slaves are set free, but our millions of voluntary slaves still clang their chains. The lot of the literal slave, of him whom others have enslaved, is indeed a hard one; nevertheless, it is a paradise compared with the lot of him who enslaves himself—especially of him who has enslaved himself to alcohol."

1874 The Woman's Christian Temperance Union is founded in Cleveland. In 1883, Frances Willard, a leader of the WCTU forms the World's Woman's Christian Temperance Union.

1882 The 1st law in the U.S., and in the world, making "temperance education" a part of the required course in public schools is enacted. In 1886, Congress makes such education mandatory in the District of Columbia, and in territorial, military, and naval schools. By 1900, all the States have similar laws.

1882 The Personal Liberty League of the U.S. is founded to oppose the increasing momentum of movements for compulsory abstinence from alcohol.

1883 Dr. Theodor Aschenbrandt, a German army physician, secures a supply of pure cocaine from the pharmaceutical firm of Merck, issues it to Bavarian soldiers during their maneuvers, and reports on the beneficial effects of the drug in increasing the soldiers' ability to endure fatigue.

1884 Sigmund Freud treats his depression with cocaine, and reports feeling "exhilaration and lasting euphoria, which in no way differs from the normal euphoria of the healthy person. . . . You perceive an increase in self-control and possess more vitality and capacity for work. . . . In other words, you are simply more normal, and it is soon hard to believe that you are under the influence of any drug."

1884 Laws are enacted to make antialcohol teaching compulsory in public schools in New York State. The following year similar laws are passed in Pennsylvania, with other States soon following suit.

1885 The Report of the Royal Commission

on Opium concludes that opium is more like the Westerner's liquor than a substance to be feared and abhorred.

1889 The Johns Hopkins Hospital, in Baltimore, Md., is opened. One of its world-famous founders, Dr. William Stewart Halsted, is a morphine addict. He continues to use morphine in large doses throughout a phenomenally successful surgical career lasting until his death in 1922.

1894 The Report of the Indian Hemp Drug Commission, running to over 3,000 pages in 7 volumes, is published. This inquiry, commissioned by the British Government, concludes: "There is no evidence of any weight regarding the mental and moral injuries from the moderate use of these drugs. . . . Moderation does not lead to excess in hemp any more than it does in alcohol. Regular, moderate use of ganja or bhang produces the same effects as moderate and regular doses of whiskey." The commission's proposal to tax bhang is never put into effect, in part, perhaps, because one of the commissioners, an Indian, cautions that Muslim law and Hindu custom forbid "taxing anything that gives pleasure to the poor."

1894 Norman Kerr, an English physician and president of the British Society for the Study of Inebriety, declares: "Drunkenness has generally been regarded as . . . a sin, a vice, or a crime. . . . [But] there is now a consensus of intelligent opinion that habitual and periodic drunkenness is often either a symptom or a sequel of disease considered as one of a group of nervous affections. . . . The victim can no more resist [alcohol] than a man with ague can resist shivering."

1898 Diacetylmorphine (heroin) is synthesized in Germany. It is widely lauded as a "safe preparation free from addiction-forming properties."

1900 In an address to the Ecumenical Missionary Conference, Rev. Wilbur F. Crafts declares: "No Christian celebration of the completion of 19 Christian centuries has yet been arranged. Could there be a fitter one than the general adoption, by separate and joint action of the great nations of the world, of the new policy of civilization, in which Great Britain is leading, the policy of prohibition for native races, in the interest of commerce as well as conscience, since the liquor traffic among child races, even more manifestly than in civilized lands, injures all other trades by producing poverty, disease, and death. Our object, more profoundly viewed, is to create a more favorable environment for the child races that civilized nations are essaying to civilize and Christianize."

1900 James R. L. Daly, writing in the *Boston*

Medical and Surgical Journal, declares: "It [heroin] possesses many advantages over morphine. . . . It is not hypnotic; there is no danger of acquiring the habit. . . ."

1901 The Senate adopts a resolution, introduced by Henry Cabot Lodge, to forbid the sale by American traders of opium and alcohol "to aboriginal tribes and uncivilized races." These provisions are later extended to include "uncivilized elements in America itself and in its territories, such as Indians, Alaskans, the inhabitants of Hawaii, railroad workers, and immigrants at ports of entry."

1901 In Colorado, a bill is introduced, but is defeated, making not only morphine and cocaine but also "malt, vinous and spiritous liquors" available only on a physician's prescription.

1902 The Committee on the Acquirement of the Drug Habit of the American Pharmaceutical Association declares: "If the Chinaman cannot get along without his 'dope,' we can get along without him."

1902 George E. Petey, writing in the *Alabama Medical Journal*, observes: "Many articles have appeared in the medical literature during the last 2 years lauding this new agent. . . . When we consider the fact that heroin is a morphine derivative . . . it does not seem reasonable that such a claim could be well founded. It is strange that such a claim should mislead anyone or that there should be found among the members of our profession those who would reiterate and accentuate it without 1st subjecting it to the most critical tests, but such is the fact."

1903 The composition of Coca-Cola is changed, caffeine replacing the cocaine it contained until this time.

1904 Charles Lyman, president of the International Reform Bureau, petitions the President of the U.S. "to induce Great Britain to release China from the enforced opium traffic. . . . We need not recall in detail that China prohibited the sale of opium, except as a medicine, until the sale was forced upon that country by Great Britain in the Opium War of 1840."

1905 Sen. Henry W. Blair, in a letter to Rev. Wilbur F. Crafts, superintendent of the International Reform Bureau: "The temperance movement must include all poisonous substances which create or excite unnatural appetite, and international prohibition is the goal."

1906 The 1st Pure Food and Drug Act becomes law; until its enactment, it was possible to buy, in stores or by mail order, medicines containing morphine, cocaine, or heroin, and without their being so labeled.

1909 The U.S. prohibits the importation of smoking opium.

1910 Dr. Hamilton Wright, considered by some the father of U.S. antinarcotics laws, reports that American contractors give cocaine to their Negro employees to get more work out of them.

1912 A writer in *Century* magazine proclaims: "The relation of tobacco, especially in the form of cigarettes, and alcohol and opium is a very close one. . . . Morphine is the legitimate consequence of alcohol, and alcohol is the legitimate consequence of tobacco. Cigarettes, drink, opium, is the logical and regular series." And a physician warns: "[There is] no energy more destructive of soul, mind, and body, or more subversive of good morals, than the cigarette. The fight against the cigarette is a fight for civilization."

1912 The 1st international Opium Convention meets at The Hague, and recommends various measures for the international control of the trade in opium. Subsequent Opium Conventions are held in 1913 and 1914.

1912 Phenobarbital is introduced into therapeutics under the trade name of Luminal.

1913 The 16th Amendment, creating the legal authority for a Federal income tax, is enacted. Between 1870 and 1915, the tax on liquor provides from ½ to ⅔ of the whole of the internal revenue of the U.S., amounting, after the turn of the century, to about $200 million annually. The 16th Amendment thus makes possible, just 6 years later, the 18th Amendment.

1914 The Harrison Narcotic Act is enacted, controlling the sale of opium and opium derivatives.

1914 Congressman Richard P. Hobson of Alabama, urging a prohibition amendment to the Constitution, asserts: "Liquor will actually make a brute out of a Negro, causing him to commit unnatural crimes. The effect is the same on the white man, though the white man being further evolved it takes a longer time to reduce him to the same level." Negro leaders join the crusade against alcohol.

1916 The *Pharmacopoeia of the United States* drops whiskey and brandy from its list of drugs. Four years later, American physicians begin prescribing these "drugs" in quantities never before prescribed by doctors.

1917 The president of the American Medical Association endorses national prohibition. The House of Delegates of the association passes a resolution stating: "Resolved, The American Medical Association opposes the use of alcohol as a beverage; and be it further Resolved, That the use of alcohol as a therapeutic agent should be discouraged." By 1928, physicians make an estimated $40 million annually by writing prescriptions for whiskey.

1918 The Anti-Saloon League calls the "liquor traffic" "un-American, pro-German, crime-producing, food-wasting, youth-corrupting, home-wrecking, [and] treasonable."

1919 The 18th [Prohibition] Amendment is added to the U.S. Constitution. It is repealed in 1933.

1920 The U.S. Dept. of Agriculture publishes a pamphlet urging Americans to grow cannabis (marijuana) as a profitable undertaking.

1920–1933 The use of alcohol is prohibited in the U.S. In 1932 alone, approximately 45,000 persons receive jail sentences for alcohol offenses. During the 1st 11 years of the Volstead Act, 17,972 persons are appointed to the Prohibition Bureau, 11,982 are terminated "without prejudice," and 1,604 are dismissed for bribery, extortion, theft, falsification of records, conspiracy, forgery, and perjury.

1921 The U.S. Treasury Dept. issues regulations outlining the treatment of addiction permitted under the Harrison Act. In Syracuse, N.Y., the narcotics clinic doctors report curing 90% of their addicts.

1921 Thomas S. Blair, MD, chief of the Bureau of Drug Control of the Pennsylvania Dept. of Health, publishes a paper in the *Journal of the American Medical Association* in which he characterizes the Indian peyote religion a "habit indulgence in certain cactaceous plants," calls the belief simply a "superstition" and those who sell peyote "dope vendors," and urges the passage of a bill in Congress that would prohibit the use of peyote among the Indian tribes of the Southwest. He concludes with this revealing plea for abolition: "The great difficulty in suppressing this habit among the Indians arises from the fact that the commercial interests involved in the peyote traffic are strongly entrenched, and they exploit the Indian. . . . Added to this is the superstition of the Indian who believes in the Peyote Church. As soon as an effort is made to suppress peyote, the cry is raised that it is unconstitutional to do so and is an invasion of religious liberty. Suppose the Negroes of the South had a Cocaine Church!"

1921 Cigarettes are illegal in 14 States, and 92 anticigarette bills are pending in 28 States. Young women are expelled from college for smoking cigarettes.

1921 The Council of the American Medical Association refuses to confirm the association's 1917 resolution on alcohol. In the 1st 6 months after the enactment of the Volstead Act, more than 15,000 physicians and 57,000 druggists and drug manufactures

apply for licenses to prescribe and sell liquor.

1921 Alfred C. Prentice, MD, a member of the Committee on Narcotic Drugs of the American Medical Association, declares: "Public opinion regarding the vice of drug addiction has been deliberately and consistently corrupted through propaganda in both the medical and lay press. . . . The shallow pretense that drug addiction is a 'disease' . . . has been asserted and urged in volumes of 'literature' by self-styled 'specialists.' "

1924 The manufacture of heroin is prohibited in the U.S.

1925 Robert A. Schless: "I believe that most drug addiction today is due directly to the Harrison Anti-Narcotic Act, which forbids the sale of narcotics without a physician's prescription. . . . Addicts who are broke act as agents provocateurs for the peddlers, being rewarded by gifts of heroin or credit for supplies. The Harrison Act made the drug peddler, and the drug peddler makes drug addicts."

1928 In a nationwide radio broadcast entitled "The Struggle of Mankind Against Its Deadliest Foe," celebrating the 2nd annual Narcotic Education Week, Richmond P. Hobson, prohibition crusader and antinarcotics propagandist, declares: "Suppose it were announced that there were more than a million lepers among our people. Think what a shock the announcement would produce! Yet drug addiction is far more incurable than leprosy, far more tragic to its victims, and is spreading like a moral and physical scourge. . . . Most of the daylight robberies, daring holdups, cruel murders, and similar crimes of violence are now known to be committed chiefly by drug addicts, who constitute the primary cause of our alarming crime wave. Drug addiction is more communicable and less curable than leprosy. . . . Upon the issue hangs the perpetuation of civilization, the destiny of the world, and the future of the human race."

1928 It is estimated that in Germany one out of every hundred physicians is a morphine addict, consuming 0.1 grain of the alkaloid or more per day.

1929 About one gal. of denatured industrial alcohol in 10 is diverted into bootleg liquor. About 40 Americans per million die each year from drinking illegal alcohol, mainly as a result of methyl (wood) alcohol poisoning.

1930 The Federal Bureau of Narcotics is formed. Many of its agents, including its 1st commissioner, Harry J. Anslinger, are former prohibition agents.

1936 The Pan-American Coffee Bureau is organized at the 1st Pan-American Coffee Conference, in Bogotá, Colombia. A principal objective of the bureau is "to formulate a cooperative effort for the promotion of increase in per-capita consumption of coffee in the U.S. through the creation of a fund to conduct an educational and advertising campaign." During the 1st 4-year period from the start of the bureau's advertising (1938 to 1941), U.S. coffee consumption increases approximately 20%, while it takes 24 years (1914 to 1937) for another similar increase to occur.

1937 Shortly before the passage of the Marijuana Tax Act, Commissioner Harry J. Anslinger writes: "How many murders, suicides, robberies, criminal assaults, holdups, burglaries, and deeds of maniacal insanity it [marijuana] causes each year, especially among the young, can only be conjectured."

1937 The Marijuana Tax Act is enacted.

1938 Since the enactment of the Harrison Act in 1914, 25,000 physicians have been arraigned on narcotics charges, and 3,000 served penitentiary sentences.

1938 Dr. Albert Hofmann, a chemist at Sandoz Laboratories in Basle, Switzerland, synthesizes LSD. Five years later he inadvertently ingests a small amount of it, and reports its effects on himself.

1941 Generalissimo Chiang Kai-shek orders the complete suppression of the poppy; laws are enacted providing the death penalty for anyone guilty of cultivating the poppy, manufacturing opium, or offering it for sale.

1943 Col. J. M. Phalen, editor of the *Military Surgeon*, declares in an editorial entitled "The Marijuana Bugaboo": "The smoking of the leaves, flowers, and seeds of Cannabis sativa is no more harmful than the smoking of tobacco. . . . It is hoped that no witch hunt will be instituted in the military service over a problem that does not exist."

1946 According to some estimates, there are 40 million opium smokers in China.

1949 Ludwig von Mises, leading modern free-market economist and social philosopher: "Opium and morphine are certainly dangerous, habit-forming drugs. But once the principle is admitted that it is the duty of government to protect the individual against his own foolishness, no serious objections can be advanced against further encroachments. A good case could be made out in favor of the prohibition of alcohol and nicotine. And why limit the government's benevolent providence to the protection of the individual's body only? Is not the harm a man can inflict on his mind and soul even more disastrous than any bodily evils? Why not prevent him from reading bad books and seeing bad plays, from looking at bad paintings and statues and from hearing bad music? The mischief done by bad ideologies, surely, is much more pernicious, both for the individual and for the whole society, than that done by narcotic drugs."

1951 According to UN estimates, there are approximately 200 million marijuana users in the world, the major places of use being India, Egypt, North Africa, Mexico, and the U.S.

1951 Twenty thousand lbs. of opium, 300 lbs. of heroin, and various opium-smoking devices are publicly burned in Canton, China. Thirty-seven opium addicts are executed in the southwest of China.

1954 Four fifths of the French people questioned about wine assert that wine is "good for one's health," and ¼ hold that it is "indispensable." It is estimated that ⅓ of the electorate in France receives all or part of its income from the production or sale of alcoholic beverages; and that there is one outlet for the sale of alcohol for every 45 inhabitants.

1955 The Präsidium des Deutschen Ärztetages declares: "Treatment of the drug addict should be effected in the closed sector of a psychiatric institution. Ambulatory treatment is useless and in conflict, moreover, with principles of medical ethics." This view is quoted approvingly, as representative of the opinion of "most of the authors recommending commitment to an institution," by the World Health Organization in 1962.

1955 The Shah of Iran prohibits the cultivation and use of opium, used in the country for thousands of years; the prohibition creates a flourishing illicit market in opium. In 1969 the prohibition is lifted, opium growing is resumed under state inspection, and more than 110,000 persons receive opium from physicians and pharmacies as "registered addicts."

1956 The [U.S.] Narcotic Drug Control Act is enacted; it provides the death penalty, if recommended by the jury, for the sale of heroin to a person under 18 by one over 18.

1958 Ten percent of the arable land in Italy is under viticulture; 2 million people earn their living wholly or partly from the production or sale of wine.

1961 The UN's "Single Convention on Narcotic Drugs of 10 March 1961" is ratified. Among the obligations of the signatory states are the following: "Art. 42. Known users of drugs and persons charged with an offense under this Law may be committed by examining magistrate to a nursing home. . . . Rules shall be also laid down for the treatment in such nursing homes of unconvicted drug addicts and dangerous alcoholics."

1962 Supreme Court Justice William O. Douglas declares: "The addict is under compulsion not capable of management without outside help. . . . If addicts can be punished for their addiction, then the insane can also be punished for their insanity. Each has a disease and each must be treated as a sick person."

1963 Mrs. Jean Nidetch, a formerly overweight housewife, incorporates Weight Watchers, an organization of diet clubs. By 1968, approximately 750,000 persons join Weight Watchers.

1963 Tobacco sales total $8.08 billion, of which $3.3 billion go to Federal, State, and local governments in excise taxes. A news release from the tobacco industry proudly states: "Tobacco products pass across sales counters more frequently than anything else —except money."

1964 The British Medical Association, in a Memorandum of Evidence to the Standing Medical Advisory Committee's Special Subcommittee on Alcoholism, declares: "We feel that in some very bad cases, compulsory detention in hospital offers the only hope of successful treatment. . . . We believe that some alcoholics would welcome compulsory removal and detention in hospital until treatment is completed."

1964 An editorial in *The New York Times* calls attention to the fact that "the Government continues to be the tobacco industry's biggest booster. The Dept. of Agriculture lost $16 million in supporting the price of tobacco in the last fiscal year, and stands to lose even more because it has just raised the subsidy that tobacco growers will get on their 1964 crop. At the same time, the Food for Peace program is getting rid of surplus stocks of tobacco abroad."

1966 Sen. Warren G. Magnuson makes public a program, sponsored by the Agriculture Dept. to subsidize "attempts to increase cigarette consumption abroad. . . . The Dept. is paying Warner Brothers $106,000 to insert scenes designed to stimulate cigarette smoking in a travelogue for distribution in 8 countries, and is also spending $210,000 to subsidize cigarette commercials in Japan, Thailand, and Austria." An Agriculture Dept. spokesman corroborates that "the 2 programs were prepared under a congressional authorization to expand overseas markets for U.S. farm commodities."

1966 C. W. Sandman, Jr., chairman of the New Jersey Narcotic Drug Study Commission, declares that LSD is "the greatest threat facing the country today . . . more dangerous than the Vietnam War."

1967 New York State's Narcotics Addiction Control Program goes into effect. It is estimated to cost $400 million in 3 years, and is hailed by Governor Rockefeller as "the start of an unending war. . . ." Under the new law, judges are empowered to commit addicts for compulsory treatment for up to 5 years.

1967 The tobacco industry in the U.S. spends an estimated $250 million on advertising smoking.

1968 The U.S. tobacco industry has gross sales of $8 billion. Americans smoke 544 billion cigarettes.

1968 Canadians buy almost 3 billion aspirin tablets and approximately 56 million standard doses of amphetamines. About 556 million standard doses of barbiturates are also produced or imported for consumption in Canada.

1968 Six to 7% of all prescriptions written under the British National Health Service are for barbiturates; it is estimated that about 500,000 Britons are regular users.

1968 Abram Hoffer, MD, and Humphry Osmond, MD, claim that "strong evidence supporting the use of LSD in a treatment program for alcoholism comes from all parts of the world. It is one of the brightest hopes for the victims of a long-neglected, little-understood disease."

1968 Brooklyn councilman Julius S. Moskowitz charges that the work of New York City's Addiction Services Agency, under its retiring commissioner, Dr. Efren Ramirez, was a "fraud," and that "not a single addict has been cured."

1969 The legal alcoholic beverage industry in the U.S. has a gross sale of $12 billion—more than is spent on education, medical care, and religion combined. Americans consume approximately 650 million gal. of distilled spirits, 100 million barrels and 6 billion cans of beer, 200 million gal. of wine, 100 million gal. of moonshine (illegal whiskey), and an unknown amount of homemade wine and beer.

1969 The world production of tobacco is 4.6 million metric tons, with the U.S., U.S.S.R., China, and Brazil as the leading producers; of wine, 275 million hectoliters, with Italy, France, and Spain as the leading producers; of beer, 595 million hectoliters, with the U.S., Germany, and the U.S.S.R. as the leading producers; of cigarettes, 2,500 billion, with the U.S., U.S.S.R., and Japan as the leading producers.

1969 U.S. production and value of some medicinal chemicals: barbiturates: 800,000 lbs., $2.5 million; aspirin (exclusive of salicylic acid): 37 million lbs., value "withheld to avoid disclosing figures for individual producers"; salicylic acid: 13 million lbs., $13 million; tranquilizers: 1.5 million lbs., $7 million.

1969 A report issued by the UN Food and Agriculture Organization discloses that, despite warnings about the deleterious effects of smoking on health, the consumption of cigarettes throughout the world is growing at the annual rate of 70 billion cigarettes. The U.S. exports tobacco leaf to 113 countries; tobacco accounts for ⅓ of all Greek exports, and ⅕ of the Turkish exports.

1969 The parents of 6,000 secondary-school pupils in Clifton, N.J., are sent letters by the Board of Education asking permission to conduct saliva tests on 'their children to determine whether or not they use marijuana.

1970 New York State assemblyman Alfred D. Lerner introduces a bill to ban the sale of candy cigarettes in New York State, "to deglamorize smoking in the eyes of children."

1970 Dr. Alan F. Guttmacher, president of Planned Parenthood-World Population, declares that the pill is "a prophylaxis against one of the gravest sociomedical illnesses—unwanted pregnancy."

1970 Dr. Albert Szent-Györgyi, Nobel Laureate in Medicine and Physiology, in reply to being asked what he would do if he were 20 today: "I would share with my classmates rejection of the whole world as it is—all of it. Is there any point in studying and work? Fornication—at least that is something good. What else is there to do? Fornicate and take drugs against this terrible strain of idiots who govern the world."

1970 Per-capita cigarette smoking increases, "from 3,993 for each smoker in 1969, to 5,030 for each one in 1970."

1970 Tobacco consumption is increasing rapidly in Russia: "In 1960, Soviet retail stores sold $1.5 billion rubles of tobacco products. By 1968, the figure had risen to $2.5 billion, more than a 50% rise."

1970 Having passed both houses of Congress by unanimous votes, the Comprehensive Alcohol Abuse and Alcoholism Prevention, Treatment, and Rehabilitation Act of 1970 is signed into law by President Nixon.

1970 According to a release of the U.S. Dept. of Health, Education, and Welfare, "An estimated 1.3 billion prescriptions were filled in 1970, at a consumer cost of $5.6 billion. Of these, 17%, or 214 million, were for psychotherapeutic drugs (antianxiety agents, antidepressants, antipsychotics, stimulants, hypnotics, and sedatives)."

1970 Henry Nargeolet, chief of the Central Service of Pharmacy and Drugs of the French Ministry of Public Health and Social Security, declares, after the French National Assembly adopts a new antidrug bill, that drug addiction will henceforth be considered as a contagious disease in France, as are alcoholism and venereal disease.

1970 The world production of tobacco is 4.7 million metric tons; of wine, 300 million hectoliters; of beer, 630 million hectoliters; of cigarettes, 2,600 billion.

1971 President Nixon declares that "America's Public Enemy No. 1 is drug abuse." In a message to Congress, the President calls for the creation of a Special Action Office of Drug Abuse Prevention.

1971 New York City mayor John Lindsay testifies before a House subcommittee that "with intensive research it should be feasible to develop an inoculation against heroin which would be administered to youngsters in the same way as vaccines against smallpox, polio, measles . . . and only a Federal scientific task force approaching the scale proposed for cancer research can bring the sort of breakthrough we need."

1971 A survey of smoking habits and economics by the *Sunday Telegraph* (London) reveals that: in Spain, tobacco is a state monopoly, with annual gross income last year at $210 million; in Italy, it is also a state monopoly, with profits at $1.3 billion or 8% of the total tax revenue; in Switzerland, government revenue from tobacco taxes was $60 million, or 5% of the total; in Norway, it was $70 million, or 3% of the total; and in Sweden, it was $350 million, or 2% of the total tax revenue.

1971 On June 30, 1971, President Cevdet Sunay of Turkey decrees that all poppy cultivation and opium production will be forbidden beginning in the fall of 1972.

1971 John N. Mitchell, Attorney General of the U.S., declares: "I refer to the fact, acknowledged now by all professionals in the field, that alcoholism as such is not a legal problem—it is a health problem. More especially, simple drunkenness per se should not be handled as an offense subject to the processes of justice. It should be handled as an illness, subject to medical treatment. . . . [We] know that it does little good to remove alcoholism from the purview of the law if you do not substitute a full-dress medical treatment—not only a detoxification process, but a thoroughgoing program aimed at recovery from the illness of alcoholism. Again, the program must include the closest cooperation and communication, starting at the top level, between the public health officials and law-enforcement officials. The police must have an understanding that their role continues—not in an arresting capacity, but in one of helping subjects in the designated health centers, voluntarily if possible, involuntarily if necessary."

1972 Myles J. Ambrose, Special Assistant Attorney General of the U.S.; "As of 1960, the Bureau of Narcotics estimated that we had somewhere in the neighborhood of 55,000 heroin addicts . . . they estimate now the figure to be 560,000 addicts."

1972 The Bureau of Narcotic and Dangerous Drugs proposes restricting the use of barbiturates on the ground that they "are more dangerous than heroin."

1972 The House votes 366 to 0 to authorize "a $1 billion, 3-year Federal attack on drug abuse."

1972 At the Bronx House of Correction, out of a total of 780 inmates, approximately 400 are given tranquilizers such as Valium, Elavil, Thorazine, and Librium. " 'I think they [the inmates] would be doing better without some of the medication,' said Capt. Robert Brown, a correction officer. He said that in a way the medications made his job harder . . . rather than becoming calm, he said, an inmate who had become addicted to his medication 'will do anything when he can't get it.' "

1972 On December 23, Reuters reports: "The Italian Government has approved a law under which drug addicts would be treated as sick people rather than criminals. A government statement said that under the new law . . . an addict would face minimal penalties and none at all if he agreed to submit to medical treatment."

1972 In England, the pharmacy cost of heroin is $.04 per grain (60 mg.), or $.00067 per mg. In the U.S., the street price is $30 to $90 per grain, or $.50 to $1.50 per mg.

1972 President Nixon calls "drug abuse the nation's Public Enemy No. 1," and proposes Federal spending of $600 million for fiscal 1973 "to battle the drug problem from poppy-grower to pusher."

1973 According to *Barron's*, the weekly financial newspaper, health care is the largest industry in the U.S. In fiscal 1973, Americans will spend $90 billion on health care, compared with $76.4 billion for defense. Only 32% of the total bill is paid for directly, 30% coming from insurance companies, and 38% from the Government.

1973 A nationwide Gallup poll reveals that 67% of the adults interviewed "support the proposal of New York governor Nelson Rockefeller that all sellers of hard drugs be given life imprisonment without the possibility of parole." Among the typical comments cited by Gallup: "The seller of drugs is not human . . . therefore he should be removed from society."

1973 Myles J. Ambrose, Special Attorney General in charge of the Office for Drug Abuse, defending the methods used by his agents in apprehending alleged drug abusers: "Drug people are the very vermin of humanity. . . . Occasionally we must adopt their dress and tactics."

1973 "Citing opposition from 'misguided softliners,' " Governor Rockefeller signs into law "the toughest antidrug program in the nation." He also requests the legislature "to provide funds to nearly double the State's narcotics treatment facilities. . . . The new law calls for mandatory minimum jail terms for drug pushers and possessors but will allow parole under lifetime supervision."

1973 Michael R. Sonnenreich, executive director of the National Commission on Marijuana and Drug Abuse, declares: "About 4 years ago we spent a total of $66.4 million for the entire Federal effort in the drug abuse area. . . . This year we have spent $796.3 million, and the budget estimates that have been submitted indicate that we will exceed the $1 billion mark. When we do so, we become, for want of a better term, a drug abuse industrial complex."

—T.Sz. rep.

21

Human Behavior—and Daily Life

Studying the Strange People of Nacirema

The anthropologist has become so familiar with the diversity of ways in which different peoples behave in similar situations that he is not apt to be surprised by even the most exotic customs. In fact, if all of the logically possible combinations of behavior have not been found somewhere in the world, he is apt to suspect that they must be present in some yet undescribed tribe. This point has, in fact, been expressed with respect to clan organization by Murdock. In this light, the magical beliefs and practices of the Nacirema present such unusual aspects that it seems desirable to describe them as an example of the extremes to which human behavior can go.

Professor Linton 1st brought the ritual of the Nacirema to the attention of anthropologists 20 years ago, but the culture of this people is still very poorly understood. They are a North American group living in the territory between the Canadian Cree, the Yaqui and Tarahumare of Mexico, and the Carib and Arawak of the Antilles. Little is known of their origin, although tradition states that they came from the east. According to Nacirema mythology, their nation was originated by a culture hero, Notgnihsaw, who is otherwise known for 2 great feats of strength—the throwing of a piece of wampum across the river Pa-To-Mac and the chopping down of a cherry tree in which the Spirit of Truth resided.

Nacirema culture is characterized by a highly developed market economy that has evolved in a rich natural habitat. While much of the people's time is devoted to economic pursuits, a large part of the fruits of these labors and a considerable portion of the day are spent in ritual activity. The focus of this activity is the human body, the appearance and health of which loom as a dominant concern in the ethos of the people. While such a concern is certainly not unusual, its ceremonial aspects and associated philosophy are unique.

The fundamental belief underlying the whole system appears to be that the human body is ugly and that its natural tendency is to debility and disease. Incarcerated in such a body, man's only hope is to avert these characteristics through the use of the powerful influences of ritual and ceremony. Every household has one or more shrines devoted to this purpose. The more powerful individuals in the society have several shrines in their houses and, in fact, the opulence of a house is often referred to in terms of the number of such ritual centers it possesses. Most houses are of wattle and daub construction, but the shrine rooms of the more wealthy are walled with stone. Poorer families imitate the rich by applying pottery plaques to their shrine walls.

While each family has at least one such shrine, the rituals associated with it are not family ceremonies but are private and secret. The rites are normally only discussed with children, and then only during the period when they are being initiated into these mysteries. I was able, however, to establish sufficient rapport with the natives to examine these shrines and to have the rituals described to me.

The focal point of the shrine is a box or chest which is built into the wall. In this chest are kept the many charms and magical potions without which no native believes he could live. These preparations are secured from a variety of specialized practitioners. The most powerful of these are the medicine men, whose assistance must be rewarded with substantial gifts. However, the medicine men do not provide the curative potions for their clients, but decide what the ingredients should be and then write them down in an ancient and secret language. This writing is understood only by the medicine men and by the herbalists who, for another gift, provide the required charm.

The charm is not disposed of after it has served its purpose, but is placed in the charm-box of the household shrine. As these magical materials are specific for certain ills, and the real or imagined maladies of the people are many, the charm-box is usually full to over-flowing. The magical packets are so numerous that people forget what their purposes were and fear to use them again. While the natives are very vague on this point, we can only assume that the idea in retaining all the old magical materials is that their presence in the charm-box, before which the body rituals are conducted, will in some way protect the worshiper.

Beneath the charm-box is a small font. Each day every member of the family, in succession, enters the shrine room, bows his head before the charm-box, mingles different sorts of holy water in the font, and proceeds with a brief rite of ablution. The holy waters are secured from the Water Temple of the community, where the priests conduct elaborate ceremonies to make the liquid ritually pure.

In the hierarchy of magical practitioners, and below the medicine men in prestige, are specialists whose designation is best translated "holy-mouth-men." The Nacirema have an almost pathological horror of and fascination with the mouth, the condition of which is believed to have a supernatural influence on all social relationships. Were it not for the rituals of the mouth, they believe that their teeth would fall out, their gums bleed, their jaws shrink, their friends desert them, and their lovers reject them. They also believe that a strong relationship exists between oral and moral characteristics. For example, there is a ritual ablution of the mouth for children which is supposed to improve their moral fiber.

The daily body ritual performed by everyone includes a mouth-rite. Despite the fact that these people are so punctilious about care of the mouth, this rite involves a practice which strikes the uninitiated stranger as revolting. It was reported to me that the ritual consists of inserting a small bundle of hog hairs into the mouth, along with certain magical powders, and then moving the bundle in a highly formalized series of gestures.

In addition to the private mouth-rite, the people seek out a holy-mouth-man once or twice a year. These practitioners have an impressive set of paraphernalia, consisting of a variety of augers, awls, probes, and prods. The use of these objects in the exorcism of the evils of the mouth involves almost unbelievable ritual torture of the client. The holy-mouth-man opens the client's mouth and, using the above mentioned tools, enlarges any holes which decay may have created in the teeth. Magical materials are put into these holes. If there are no naturally occurring holes in the teeth, large sections of one or more teeth are gouged out so that the supernatural substance can be applied. In the client's view, the purpose of these ministrations is to arrest decay and to draw friends. The extremely sacred and traditional character of the rite is evident in the fact that the natives return to the holy-mouth-men year after year, despite the fact that their teeth continue to decay.

It is to be hoped that, when a thorough study of the Nacirema is made, there will be careful inquiry into the personality structure of these people. One has but to watch the gleam in the eye of a holy-mouth-man, as he jabs an awl into an exposed nerve, to suspect that a certain amount of sadism is involved. If this can be established, a very interesting pattern emerges, for most of the population shows definite masochistic tendencies. It was to these that Professor Linton referred in discussing a distinctive part of the daily body ritual which is performed only by men. This part of the rite involves scraping and lacerating the surface of the face with a sharp instrument. Special women's rites are performed only 4 times during each lunar month, but what they lack in frequency is made up in barbarity. As part of this ceremony, women bake their heads in small ovens for about an hour. The theoretically interesting point is that what seems to be a preponderantly masochistic people have developed sadistic specialists.

The medicine men have an imposing temple, or *latipso*, in every community of any size. The more elaborate ceremonies required to treat very sick patients can only be performed at this temple. These ceremonies involve not only the thaumaturge but a permanent group of vestal maidens who move sedately about the temple chambers in distinctive costume and head-dress.

The *latipsoh* ceremonies are so harsh that it is phenomenal that a fair proportion of the really sick natives who enter the temple ever recover. Small children whose indoctrination is still incomplete have been known to resist attempts to take them to the temple because "that is where you go to die." Despite this fact, sick adults are not only willing but eager to undergo the protracted ritual purification, if they can afford to do so. No matter how ill the supplicant or how grave the emergency, the guardians of many temples will not admit a client if he cannot give a rich gift to the custodian. Even after one has gained admission and survived the ceremonies, the guardians will not permit the neophyte to leave until he makes still another gift.

The supplicant entering the temple is 1st

stripped of all his or her clothes. In everyday life the Nacirema avoids exposure of his body and its natural functions. Bathing and excretory acts are performed only in the secrecy of the household shrine, where they are ritualized as part of the body-rites. Psychological shock results from the fact that body secrecy is suddenly lost upon entry into the *latipsoh*. A man whose own wife has never seen him in an excretory act suddenly finds himself naked and assisted by a vestal maiden while he performs his natural functions into a sacred vessel. This sort of ceremonial treatment is necessitated by the fact that the excreta are used by a diviner to ascertain the course and nature of the client's sickness. Female clients, on the other hand, find their naked bodies are subjected to the scrutiny, manipulation and prodding of the medicine men.

Few supplicants in the temple are well enough to do anything but lie on their hard beds. The daily ceremonies, like the rites of the holy-mouth-men, involve discomfort and torture. With ritual precision, the vestals awaken their miserable charges each dawn and roll them about on their beds of pain while performing ablutions, in the formal movements of which the maidens are highly trained. At other times they insert magic wands in the supplicant's mouth or force him to eat substances which are supposed to be healing. From time to time the medicine men come to their clients and jab magically treated needles into their flesh. The fact that these temple ceremonies may not cure, and may even kill the neophyte, in no way decreases the people's faith in the medicine men.

There remains one other kind of practitioner, known as a "listener." This witch doctor has the power to exorcise the devils that lodge in the heads of people who have been bewitched. The Nacirema believe that parents bewitch their own children. Mothers are particularly suspected of putting a curse on children while teaching them the secret body rituals. The counter-magic of the witch doctor is unusual in its lack of ritual. The patient simply tells the "listener" all his troubles and fears, beginning with the earliest difficulties he can remember. The memory displayed by the Nacirema in these exorcism sessions is truly remarkable. It is not uncommon for the patient to bemoan the rejection he felt upon being weaned as a babe, and a few individuals even see their troubles going back to the traumatic effects of their own birth.

In conclusion, mention must be made of certain practices which have their base in native aesthetics but which depend upon the pervasive aversion to the natural body and its functions. There are ritual fasts to make fat people thin and ceremonial feasts to make thin people fat. Still other rites are used to make women's breasts larger if they are small, and smaller if they are large. General dissatisfaction with breast shape is symbolized in the fact that the ideal form is virtually outside the range of human variation. A few women afflicted with almost inhuman hypermammary development are so idolized that they make a handsome living by simply going from village to village and permitting the natives to stare at them for a fee.

Reference has already been made to the fact that excretory functions are ritualized, routinized, and relegated to secrecy. Natural reproductive functions are similarly distorted. Intercourse is taboo as a topic and scheduled as an act. Efforts are made to avoid pregnancy by the use of magical materials or by limiting intercourse to certain phases of the moon. Conception is actually very infrequent. When pregnant, women dress so as to hide their condition. Parturition takes place in secret, without friends or relatives to assist, and the majority of women do not nurse their infants.

Our review of the ritual life of the Nacirema has certainly shown them to be a magic-ridden people. It is hard to understand how they have managed to exist so long under the burdens which they have imposed upon themselves. But even such exotic customs as these take on real meaning when they are viewed with the insight provided by Malinowski when he wrote:

> Looking from far and above, from our high places of safety in the developed civilization, it is easy to see all the crudity and irrelevance of magic. But without its power and guidance early man could not have mastered his practical difficulties as he has done, nor could man have advanced to the higher stages of civilization.
>
> —H.M. Rep.

P.S. Now spell Nacirema backwards. And read the article again. . . .

—The Eds.

Human Behavior Experiments

Human behavior can be cruel, irrational, and brutal; it can also be kind, warm, compassionate. Why do people act the way they do? Why do some people hate and willingly harm others with no apparent cause? What are the forces that control us? Are they social pressures, inner conflicts, or chemicals rampaging through our bodies? Psychologists construct situations in their experiments with these questions in mind. The answers they discover range from surprising to downright terrifying. The 5 experiments discussed here are a selection of the typical problems researchers focus on, but their conclusions have excited much controversy and even questions about the morality of the research itself.

ON BEING SANE IN INSANE PLACES

In an experiment later written up as "On Being Sane in Insane Places," D. L. Rosenhan, of Stanford University, and 8 associates (3 women, 5 men) voluntarily entered 12 mental institutions. They complained to staff psychiatrists of hearing voices which said "hollow," "empty," or "thud." They reported no other symptoms. The "patients" were chosen for the experiment on the basis of being normal everyday people and they represented a wide range of occupations, from housewife to artist to pediatrician. After being admitted to the hospitals, all pseudo-patients told the staff that their symptoms had disappeared, and all acted normally. In trials in 12 different hospitals, it took pseudo-patients between 7 to 52 days to be released. In almost all cases, they were discharged with diagnoses of "schizophrenia in remission"; not once were they discharged as being sane.

Upon reading these astounding facts, one might assume that the experiments were conducted in hospitals chosen for inadequate or incompetent staff or overcrowding. This was not the case. Most of the hospitals tested were funded by the local, State, or Federal Government, and several were considered excellent. They varied as to newness and number of staff, though one well-staffed, expensive, and modern hospital was included in the test. Results were no different there.

Once the pseudo-patients were in the mental hospitals, they observed many enlightening facts about what happens to a person when people think he is crazy. They found that patients were considered less than human and were treated as though they were invisible. Often they would address staff with simple questions such as asking when a given doctor would be in, and they would be totally ignored, with the staff member walking straight past them, or would receive a curt non-reply like "Hello, how do you feel today?" There was little privacy or activity allowed the patients, but when disorders arose from these stultifying conditions they were attributed to the patient's "disease." Many pseudo-patients took notes of their observations, 1st secretly and then openly when they found that nobody cared. One nurse, commenting on her patient's "psychosis," mentioned his "compulsive note-taking behavior." Another pseudo-patient overheard a staff psychiatrist complaining about patients "oral acquisitiveness" in lining up in the cafeteria lounge a half hour before lunch. The good doctor overlooked the fact that in the hospital there was nothing else to do. Treatment was minimal. Drugs replaced a doctor's time. All pseudo-patients combined were given 2,100 pills, which they, like many real patients, discarded.

An interesting sidelight to the experiment was the fact that although not one psychiatrist, nurse, or attendant suspected the hoax, 35 patients of the 118 residing in admittance wards with the experimenters suspected they were faking. "You're not crazy, you're some journalist (or professor) checking up on conditions here," was heard over and over again.

To verify these disturbing findings, the researchers notified a leading teaching hospital that in a given 3-month period, one or 2 pseudo-patients would attempt to gain admission to their hospital. The hospital staff was well-acquainted with the experiment. Of 193 patients admitted during the 3-month period, 41 were alleged to be pseudo-patients by staff members, including 23 by psychiatrists with the greatest amount of training. Actually, not one pseudo-patient presented himself during that period.

Dr. Rosenhan was forced to conclude that insanity is very poorly defined and that the label of insanity, once applied, is far less a product of a person's behavior or characteristics than of the context in which a person is encountered.

THE MOCK PRISON

A 2nd experiment, conducted by Dr. Philip G. Zimbardo, of Stanford University, Calif., tested a slightly different aspect of roles and the effect they have on people's behavior. In his experiment, unlike Rosenhan's, no one was duped. All participants were fully informed of the nature and details of the experiment. Even so, the results were so extreme that the experiment had to be terminated after 6 days of the 14 days originally scheduled.

The Zimbardo experiment involved setting up a mock prison and assigning volunteers to be either prisoners or guards. The prison was set up in the Stanford psychology building. Volunteers were chosen from among male students in the Palo Alto area after carefully screening them for any psychological or physical problems. They were then randomly assigned to be prisoners or guards. Zimbardo himself served as superintendent.

Prisoners were subjected to strict discipline.

The moment they entered the mock prison, their personal belongings were taken away, they were given loose smocks to wear, and they were assigned to bare cells. They received stocking caps to wear over their hair to simulate the shaved heads of real prisoners. They had to ask permission to write letters, smoke, or go to the bathroom, and were deprived of showers, windows, and outdoor exercise.

Those assigned to be guards were depersonalized as well. They wore identical khaki uniforms and silver reflector sunglasses. Their only instructions were to maintain law and order, and to do so they were issued billy clubs, whistles, and handcuffs.

The 2nd morning the prisoners staged a riot. The guards responded by hosing them with chilling carbon dioxide and stripping them. The guards also devised a "good prisoner cell" with special privileges, to divide and confuse the inmates.

As time went on, guards became more domineering and abusive and began devising degrading, tedious tasks for the prisoners. The prisoners responded by becoming meek and passive after their initial defiance. They became nonsupportive of each other and, in post-experimental interviews, were overwhelmingly deprecative of fellow prisoners.

Despite the fact that all the participants knew they were merely acting in an experiment, all took their roles quite seriously. Guards pressured one another to use their power to abuse the prisoners, often to the point of cruelty. The occasional kind guard was looked upon as a sissy, and never once in the experiment did a kind guard try to restrain even the most sadistic guard or remind him that they were just part of an experiment.

The prisoners also took their parts quite seriously. One had to be released the 3rd day for severe depression; another developed a psychosomatic rash over most of his body. A total of 5 had been released by the 6th day, at which time the experiment was terminated because of the severity of the participants' reactions. At the outset, Zimbardo had feared that 2 weeks would prove too short a time to simulate real prison conditions; he found that 6 days were more than enough. He demonstrated in a short time how vulnerable people are to assigned roles and to acting as they think they are supposed to act, even in direct conflict with how they feel inwardly. He also verified certain suspicions about the American prison system. The experiment leads one to pause and consider the more subtle consequences of roles that are less consciously assumed, and which one takes on for a longer time. Zimbardo also explicitly points to the "prisons" of racism and sexism in which we all reside.

TEACHER EXPECTATIONS AND STUDENT LEARNING

The 1st 2 experiments showed how people fit themselves and others into preconceived roles. In another experiment, Robert Rosenthal and Lenore Jacobson explored how innocent subjects are affected by another person's expectations of them, and how expectations change the interactions between any 2 people. They chose to conduct their research in an unnamed elementary school, in the San Francisco area. The entire student body was given an intelligence test. Teachers were told the test would reveal which children were about to "bloom," that is, go through a learning spurt. Children designated "late bloomers" were actually picked at random from all levels of intelligence. Teachers did not change their methods or materials for teaching these exceptional pupils, yet at the end of the year, when the test was administered again, 1st and 2nd graders who had been chosen at the time of the 1st test had gained twice the number of IQ points as other children.

In grades 3 to 6 the difference in IQ gain was much less dramatic. The experimenters theorize that the younger children were both more malleable and had less established reputations so that teachers were open to new ideas about their abilities. But how can one explain the great difference in IQ gain between the special group and their peers? The experimenters cite another experiment in which 2 identical groups of rats were designated as fast and slow learners and then given to laboratory assistants to be taught a maze. The rats that the assistants expected to be smarter did in fact perform better. These results at 1st seem incredible since the rats were truly identical in intelligence. But when the lab workers were questioned, it turned out that they had been more patient with the "fast" learners, had led them through more trials, and had treated them more kindly. The same phenomenon happened with the specially designated students. They performed better because they were given more attention. Teachers challenged them more because they expected more from them, and gave more positive reinforcement for each success. Behavior and achievement really can be affected by another's expectations.

EUPHORIA, ANGER, AND BODY CHEMISTRY

Many psychologists maintain that while environment and one's associates are important influences on behavior, body chemistry is the all-important factor in behavior. Stanley Schachter and Jerome E. Singer, of Columbia University and Pennsylvania State University, set out to discover to what degree behavior can be changed by altering a person's body chemistry.

Their subjects were told they were about to participate in an experiment which would test the effect of a chemical called epinephrine on vision. They were given an injection of epinephrine, which is actually another name for adrenaline. Some of the subjects were injected with a placebo to form a control group for comparison. All were told that the drug would take 15 or so minutes to enter their bloodstream sufficiently for the vision tests. In the meantime, a situation was set up to test their receptivity to 2 emotions, euphoria and anger.

In the euphoria situation, an actor, introduced as another subject, remained in the room with the 1st subject. They were left with a good supply of paper, pencils, and rubber bands and told they could doodle and generally amuse themselves until the drug had taken effect. The actor then began playing with the paper and rubber bands, making paper airplanes, playing a mock basketball game with balls of paper, and so on. The actor invited the subject to join in, and the subject was rated according to how he responded to this suggestion.

In the 2nd or anger experiment, both the subject and the actor were asked to fill out a long, personal, and often embarrassing questionnaire while waiting for the drug to take effect. The actor began by complaining about the 1st few questions and worked himself up into a fury over the later embarrassing ones. Subjects were rated according to how angry they got after 1st observing the actor and then having to answer the same questions.

One further factor was involved. One third of the subjects in the 1st experiment were told that the drug often would cause a more rapid heartbeat and pulse—the real side effects of adrenaline. Another 3rd were told to expect such side effects as numbness and itching, which do not actually occur in conjunction with adrenaline. The 3rd group was told nothing at all.

In the euphoria experiment, the subjects who had been misinformed reacted the most, followed by the ones who had been told nothing of side effects. Finally came those who had been correctly informed about what to expect and those who had been given the placebo. In the anger experiment, no subjects were misinformed, but those who were told nothing about side effects became considerably angrier than those who had been told what to expect or those who had been given a placebo.

The experimenters concluded that given unexplained physiological arousal, a person will experience heightened reaction to his surroundings. When given the correct explanation for the feeling of arousal, the individual is unlikely to respond as strongly to external stimuli. A person will feel more "centered." A person with wrong information as to an aroused state responds much the same as an uninformed person, since he is expecting other symptoms. Finally, given the same external stimuli, a person will react to these stimuli to a greater degree the more that he or she is physiologically aroused. One can see from this experiment that physiological factors are important in determining to what degree a person is susceptible to his or her surroundings (including its social pressures), but the experiment does not attempt to explain why some people release adrenaline spontaneously in certain situations, while others do not.

We are left with the same question: What makes some individuals victims of social roles and expectations to a greater degree than others? The final experiment discussed here touches on this question.

OBEDIENCE TO AUTHORITY

The 5th experiment is Stanley Milgram's remarkable work on obedience to authority. Part of it was staged at Yale University, and part in a warehouse in Bridgeport, Conn. Later, the experiment was repeated in 50 places because nobody would believe it.

This experiment deals with the specific situation of conflict between an experimenter's instructions and a subjects conscience. As in all the other experiments discussed so far, it deals with the degree to which an individual is willing or is forced by some part of his or her internal makeup to submit to an arbitrary outside definition of who he or she is.

The experiment was set up as a learning trial. Two subjects entered the laboratory together. One was actually an actor. They were told that they were to participate in a test of memory in which one of them would be the teacher and the other the pupil. The situation was rigged so that the actor always got the role of pupil and the real subject became the teacher. The experimenter then explained the procedure. The teacher was to read off word pairs which the pupil was to memorize. Then the teacher was to repeat the 1st part of each pair and several alternatives for the 2nd part. If the pupil answered incorrectly, the teacher was to administer an electric shock to the pupil. With each wrong answer, the voltage of the shock would be increased. Though the upper levels of shock could be painful, the experimenter carefully explained, they could not cause permanent tissue damage. The ostensible purpose of the experiment was to determine the effect of punishment on memory and learning ability.

The experiment then proceeded. At lower to middle shock levels, the actor expressed pain and asked to be released from the rest of the experiment. In many trials, the actor spoke of being afraid to participate because he had a bad heart, and at middle levels of shock complained that his heart was bothering him. At upper levels of shock the actor screamed in agony and pleaded with the "teacher" to stop and finally, at the highest levels, was silent, after saying he would no longer cooperate. Since the actor was out of sight in the next room, many subjects feared that he had been killed.

Most "teachers" protested and argued with the experimenter about inflicting pain, but most went on with the shocks when the experimenter refused to budge from the position that "the experiment must go on," and "the experiment requires that you continue." Fully 65% of the teachers went on to administer the highest level of shock despite the agonized protests of the actor-victim. Even when the teachers believed the victim to have heart disease, it made no difference in their obedience.

In variations of the experiment, Milgram found that the closer the victim was to the teacher, physically, the greater was the number of disobedient teachers. When administration of the shock involved actually pushing the pupil's hand down on the shock plate, only 30% of the teachers obeyed (still an astounding figure). Also, most teachers would "cheat" when given a chance, such as when the experimenter left the room, by giving the minimum shock to the actor. This fact seemed to indicate that teachers in the tests were not inherently vicious, merely obedient. Further, in a variation in which the experimenter received the shocks, not a single subject proceeded after the experimenter's initial protests and requests that the experiment be terminated, despite the fact that he had agreed to see it through to the end. Clearly it was the authority figure rather than any sense of scientific requirement that was being obeyed.

The implications of Milgram's work are frightening. Few people are able to stand up for what they know is right even when challenged by a self-appointed authority with no ability to enforce his instructions. Few people weigh the words of another person just like themselves as heavily as those of a person they believe to be somehow "above" them. Most individuals ignore the dictates of their own conscience when pressured by a "superior's" expectation of a given behavior or response.

Milgram notes that most of the obedient subjects displayed a high degree of tension characterized by flushing, sweating, increased heartbeat, and other signs of physiological arousal. Those who were quickest to refuse to continue administering shocks remained the most placid. These individuals were "centered" like those given accurate explanations of the side effects of epinephrine in Schachter's work. They experienced little tension and their bodies reflected their emotional calm. Why were these individuals so centered when many others experienced such painful conflict? Milgram attributes obedience to the hierarchical structure in the blood of the human race, to the tendency to shift responsibility for an action from the person who performs it to the highest member of a hierarchy who is involved in it, and to social influences that encourage one to conform. He doesn't explain why 35% of the subjects were able to overcome all these factors and say No.

Few people would correctly predict the results of this experiment. Even fewer would predict that they would find themselves in the obedient majority, yet it has been repeated many times with the same results each time. Each person must ponder these results, and must watch out for situations in which one evades personal responsibility for one's actions. Many of Milgram's obedient subjects, like many Nazi war criminals at the Nuremberg war crime trials or the participants in the My Lai massacre, claimed to be innocent, saying "I was only following my orders." The answer to the question of where each person would stand in a conflict between authority and conscience is present, unnoticed and tragic, in our normal behavior, in everyday life.

—D.Ru.

Seven Common Superstitions

SNEEZING

If you are in the presence of someone who sneezes, protect him from danger by saying, "God bless you," or *"Gesundheit."* Other acceptable blessings are "Long may you live," or "May you enjoy good health."

Origin. Ancient man believed that his breath was also his soul or "essence of life." When God made man, he "breathed into his nostrils the breath of life." A rapid departure of that breath—a sneeze—is the same as expelling life from one's body. Also, it leaves a vacuum in the head which evil spirits can enter. Roman citizens feared sneezing when a plague hit their city during the reign of Pope Gregory the Great. Since they regarded the sneeze as a sure sign of approaching sickness, Pope Gregory instituted the use of the phrase "God bless you" to shield sneezers from any ill effects.

Getting out of Bed on the "Right" Side

To arise from the left side of the bed will put you in a sour mood and will subject your entire day to misfortune. Get up from the right and step 1st on your right foot. If you err, walk backwards until you have returned to bed and can begin again.

Origin. The Romans thought the left side to be the "evil one." A citizen entered a friend's home with his right foot forward. Some wealthy families even hired a "footman" to insure proper entry of all guests. The English word sinister (meaning wicked or evil) is derived from the Latin word meaning "left side."

Breaking a Mirror

This will bring you 7 years of bad luck or might cause the death of someone in the family. If a mirror is broken, remove it from the house and, if possible, bury it in the ground (to counteract the evil consequences).

Origin. Before the invention of mirrors, man gazed at his reflection, his "other self," in pools, ponds, and lakes. If the image was distorted, it was a mark of impending disaster. The "unbreakable" metal mirrors of the early Egyptians and Greeks were valued items because of their magical properties. After glass mirrors were introduced, it was the Romans who tagged the broken mirror a sign of bad luck. The length of the prescribed misfortune, 7 years, came from the Roman belief that man's body was physically rejuvenated every 7 years, and he became, in effect, a new man.

Spilling Salt

If you fall victim to this dilemma, simply take a pinch of salt and toss it over your left shoulder, "right into the Devil's face."

Origin. Salt was once a rare and costly commodity. As such, it was economic waste to spill any. Also, salt is a purifier, a preservative, and it symbolizes the good and lasting qualities of life. It was mixed into the foods used in the religious ceremonies of both the Greeks and Romans. One source of this superstition is Leonardo da Vinci's painting of the Last Supper—the betrayer Judas has accidentally spilled salt onto the table.

Walking under Ladders

If you walk under a ladder, the wrath of the gods will be upon you. Should you forget and do so, quickly cross your fingers or make a wish.

Origin. A ladder leaning against a wall forms a triangle with the wall and the ground. This triangle signifies the Holy Trinity and to enter into the sacred enclosed area is a punishable offense. Also, crossing through this forbidden zone may weaken the powers of the gods and unleash the powers of evil spirits.

Encountering a Black Cat

Avoid the paths of black cats. If one crosses your route, return home.

Origin. The Egyptians worshiped the cat and punished anyone who dared to kill one. In the Middle Ages, however, the black cat was linked to witches and Satan. Since it was believed that a witch had the power to transform herself into a cat, it was thought likely that a cat who crossed one's path was a witch in disguise.

Opening Umbrellas Indoors

Umbrellas are to be used only outdoors. Failure to adhere to this dictate will bring about the "righteous anger of the sun."

Origin. Umbrellas were used in the East as early as the 11th century b.c. Members of the political and religious hierarchy used them not only as a protective measure against the hot sun rays, but also as a device to ward off any spirits who might do them harm. Because of the umbrella's sacred relationship to the sun, it is wrong to open it in the shade.

Three Vital Good Luck Charms: From Whence Did They Come?

Four-leaf clover. When Adam and Eve were evicted from the Garden of Eden, Eve snatched a 4-leaf clover (which were plentiful in the Garden) as a remembrance of her days in Paradise. Also, the rarity of the plant (at one time) contributed to its value, although seeds which grow only 4-leaf clovers are now available. One old saying on the luck of the clover: "One leaf for fame,/One leaf for wealth,/And one leaf for a faithful lover,/And one leaf to bring glorious health,/Are all in a 4-leaf clover."

Horseshoe. Three theories: 1. St. Dunstan, a blacksmith by trade, encountered the Devil at his door. The Devil wanted to be "shoed." Dunstan, recognizing the "evil one," tied him up and went to work, inflicting great pain on his customer. The Devil screamed for mercy, and Dunstan released him—but only after the Devil promised never to enter a home protected by a horseshoe. 2. Witches rode broomsticks because they were deathly afraid of horses. Hence, a horseshoe is a good protective charm against witches. 3. Horseshoes are made of iron, a good-luck metal, and are crescent-shaped like the moon which is a sign of prosperity.

Rabbit's foot. Early man was puzzled by the rabbit: at the rabbit's cleverness while hunting, its ability to burrow underground, its meetings with other rabbits on moonlit evenings. Man was particularly impressed by the animal's swiftness, which was due to its powerful hind legs. The rabbit became a sign of good fortune, and its hind foot became a treasured amulet.

Nine Rules of Superstitious Etiquette

1. *Do not* take any risks or attempt any new enterprise on Friday the 13th. Historically, Friday is a day of calamity. Jesus died on Friday. Eve tempted Adam with the apple on Friday, and the biblical Flood began on that fatal day. The number 13 is catastrophic. It represents the number of men present at the Last Supper. The Greek philosophers and mathematicians scorned it as an "imperfect" number. In Norse mythology, there were 12 gods present when Loki, spirit of evil and dissension, stormed a banquet hall (making him the 13th guest) and killed Balder, hero and most revered of all the gods.
2. *Do* hang a horseshoe with its prongs pointed upward—so the good luck does not "run out."
3. *Do not* light 3 cigarettes with one match. Although 3 is usually a lucky number, it represents the Holy Trinity, and one should be careful of its use. The Orthodox Church, at one time, forbade any layman to light the 3 altar candles with one taper, although a priest was permitted to do so. In the Boer War, British soldiers conserved matches by using one to light 3 cigarettes. The long illumination from the match gave the enemy time to zero in on the soldiers, and the 3rd man was often a perfect target.
4. *Do* wear clothing inside out. It is an excellent disguise to keep Death from recognizing you and singling you out as its victim.
5. *Do not* get married in May. The Romans honored their dead in that month, and it is a very unlucky time for lovers.
6. *Do* knock on wood (3 times) after mentioning good luck. The religious significance of wood comes from the Crucifixion of Jesus on the Cross. Also, man was once in awe of lightning bolts which struck the forests, and he believed that the god of lightning resided in an oak tree. To knock on wood insures that your good luck will continue.
7. *Do not* cross knives on the dinner table. It symbolizes the crossing of daggers and swords in dueling matches. Also, their magical iron composition has the power to bring on an argument.
8. *Do* enter and exit from the same door when visiting a friend's house. If you leave for a while and then return—sit down outside the door and count to 10 before your 2nd entrance.
9. *Do not* trip before you start out a new day or before you begin a new adventure. It is a bad omen for you and your associates. To counteract the stumbling, turn around 3 times and say, "I turn myself 3 times about and thus I put bad luck to rout."

The Superstitious: A Baker's Dozen

Hitler favored the number 7 (he planned major military battles on the 7th of the month) and had the Nazi swastika designed to resemble an ancient Buddhist symbol representing, among other things, the wheel of life.

Cornelius Vanderbilt had the legs of his bed placed in dishes of salt—to ward off attacks from evil spirits.

Somerset Maugham had the "evil eye" symbol carved into his fireplace mantel and had it stamped on his stationery and books.

Napoleon Bonaparte feared cats (ailurophobia) and the number 13.

Winston Churchill petted black cats to obtain good luck.

Al Jolson always wore old clothes to open a new show.

Mary Queen of Scots (according to some) had her fortune told by a deck of cards before her death and was dealt a hand full of spades.

Admiral Lord Nelson tacked a horseshoe to the mainmast of his ship.

Samuel Pepys, English diarist, wote, "Now I am at a loss to know whether it be my hare's foot which is my preservative against wind, for I never had a fit of collique since I wore it."

Samuel Johnson, English author, never entered a house with his left foot 1st because it "brought down evil on the inmates."

Charles Stewart Parnell, Irish Nationalist leader, never signed a legislative bill that contained 13 clauses. He would not sign until a 14th was added.

President Harry S Truman displayed a horseshoe over the door of his office in the White House.

Shakespeare wrote, "For many men that stumble at the threshold/Are well foretold that danger lurks therein."

—C.O.

For further reading

Maple, Eric. *Superstition and the Superstitious.* New York: A. S. Barnes and Co., 1972. Explores and explains a multitude of superstitions, including those surrounding house and garden, work and travel, recreation and entertainment, body and clothes.

Batchelor, Julie Forsyth, and De Lys, Claudia. *Superstitious? Here's Why!* New York: Harcourt, Brace & World, Inc., 1954. Covers everything from charms, hiccuping, and black cats to umbrellas, warts, and "crossing your heart."

Find Your Phobia

You, too, can, may, probably *do* have a phobia. There are by official estimate thousands of them on the scene today—specific phobias such as the fear of nude men and women, ugly people, beautiful people, long hair, short hair, good deeds, bad deeds, and life after death. The little fears range from the fear of oneself (*monophobia*) to the fear of everyone else (*anthrophobia*), and psychiatrists say they've already scientifically labeled over 700 of the redoubtable dreads—although they've just started counting.

We have plenty of *vestiophobes*, people with an aversion to wearing clothing, around today, and there are even a few nonstreakers left who suffer from the fear of not wearing clothes. Among sexual phobias, or hang-ups, we can report *gynephobia*, the fear of women, its companion *androphobia*, the fear of men, as well as *pornophobia*, the fear of prostitutes, and *gamophobia*, the fear of marriage. Then, too, almost everyone has some form of *zoophobia*, the fear of other animals, ranging from the fear of dogs to the fear of cats and rats. But there are also *botanophobes*, who dislike plants, and even *anthophobes*, who fear just flowers. *Acrophobia*, the fear of heights, is also high on the list, as is *claustrophobia*—the dread of closed or of narrow places. The fear of thunder has 4 names, *astraphobia*, *keraunophobia*, *ceraunophobia* and *tonitrophobia*. The number of names for this very reasonable fear of sudden disastrous explosions is almost matched in our time by the number of names for the fear of being alone—*autophobia*, *eremophobia*, and *monophobia*.

It could be that The Bomb, which has by now leveled the collective subconscious, is responsible for the whole phobia explosion. There is even a specific phobia for this called *nucleomitiphobia*. Of the 700 newly catalogued and very odd phobias, Bomb-related fears certainly make up a large percentage. One is *logizomechanophobia*, the fear of computers computing, and machines (or politicians) machinating; another has to be *nyctophobia*, the fear of impending darkness; and then there is plain old *thanatophobia*, the dread of death or doomsday. Maybe The Bomb even explains fears like *optophobia*, the fear of opening one's eyes.

But how can anyone generalize about fears when there are such specific ones around as *arachibutyrophobia*, the fear of getting peanut butter stuck in the roof of the mouth? Actually, at least 14 million adult Americans suffer from unreasonable fears of one kind or another says Dr. Leslie Solyom, assistant professor of psychiatry at Montreal's McGill University. "Phobias can strike anyone," he notes, "and not all phobia victims are timid, shy, retiring persons." Most of these phobias spring from an unpleasant childhood experience, often reactivated by something "unrelated to the phobia itself, such as a bad marriage or an unpleasant job." Dr. Solyom has treated some really kinky cases, including a cabdriver who had to change jobs because he feared red lights; a housewife who wouldn't go to church because she feared she would shout obscenities in the midst of the service; and an insurance agent who quit his job because he was afraid of being contaminated by germs, hardly touched anything, and washed his hands 32 times daily.

Some psychiatrists believe that phobias develop as a defense against anxiety. The anxiety, instead of remaining diffuse, is displaced onto a concrete object and is thus reduced. Generally the person afflicted is aware of the unreasonableness of his fear but is unable to control it. There are several major fallacies about phobias that should be corrected. First, it should be understood that otherwise healthy people can have phobias. Second, phobias are not signs of severe mental disorders but are, rather, signs of neurotic conflicts. Third, severe fear and death *do not* result from phobias. And finally, the best way to deal with phobias is not to force the person to live with them. Desensitization of the individual to the phobic situation is the best treatment.

Fortunately, there have been recent advances in treating phobic patients. British doctors are desensitizing patients to their abnormal fears by injection of a barbiturate anesthetic, their method consisting of deliberately provoking an anxiety by having the patient imagine himself in the situation he fears. As his anxiety builds up, he is given an intravenous injection of the anesthetic agent, the idea being to break the bond between stimulus and response—the patient learning to associate previously feared situations with relaxation and tranquility.

In Hillside Medical Center—the Jewish Hospital in Long Island, N.Y.—extensive work is being done with phobic patients. Dr. Charlotte Zitrin, a director of the hospital's program, calls it a process of "densensitization in the imagination." Teaching a patient not to fear dogs unreasonably involves this process, she says. "If the patient is afraid of dogs, we tell him, 'Imagine you are across the street and half a block away from a small gentle dog on a leash.' Gradually we bring the dog closer to sniff at the patient's feet. Then we make it a larger dog. Then one not on a leash. Then we instruct the patient to go out to see a friend who has a dog or go to a pet shop and examine a dog. This works."

Many clinics throughout the country are trying to help phobic patients with radical departures from traditional treatment methods. Dr. Manuel D. Zane of White Plains Hospital, N.Y., for example, contends that the why is not the important question in phobia cases. "Don't try not to have a fearful reaction, because it will come," he tells his patients. "Try to learn to deal with the fear when it happens. The most important thing is to learn not to panic over getting panicked." Such behavioral therapy is also practiced by a national organization of "nervous and ex-mental patients" called Recovery, Inc., based in Chicago, which abounds with slogans like "The situation is distressing but not dangerous," "Don't think in extremes —life is neither a disaster nor a picnic," and "There is no limit to the amount of discomfort you can bear." Another psychiatrist goes so far as to treat patients with contamination fears by having them sniff and dab samples of their own urine, and still another therapist, Dr. Herbert Fensterheim, has developed a "relaxation machine" to help treat phobic patients at his New York hospital clinic.

Behavioral therapy doesn't get at the root reason for a phobia. In fact, it dismisses the underlying reason as irrelevant and is interested only in eliminating or modifying the fear. At any rate, it has proved less costly, far less time-consuming, and much more successful for phobia patients than conventional psychoanalysis. Just ask the man behaviorists have cured of fear of his own handwriting; the man who once feared 101 of 102 phobias on the Long Island Jewish Hospital's "Fear Inventory" —he omitted only the fear of being raped; the woman who once showered every half hour for fear of body odor; or the man who so gravely feared heart attacks that he often ran to his doctor's office, racing up 3 flights of stairs to get there.

At any rate, even though we've learned how to treat phobias successfully, nobody has yet discovered just what a phobia is or exactly what causes a phobia. There may even be a certain survival value in being phobic or paranoid today. Whatever the case, you can get a good case of *ergophobia*, the fear of work, just trying to keep up with the phobias circulating presently. About the only phobics that haven't turned up are politicians suffering from *verbophobia*, an aversion to words—though many have had *sophophobia*, the fear of learning, especially from past mistakes.

In short, we can only conclude that the best you can do today is hope you don't develop *iatrophobia*, the fear of doctors, so you can still be cured when you develop the phobia of your choice—cured, that is, if your friendly neighborhood psychiatrist doesn't develop the fear of phobic patients. Or it might be advisable for everyone to contract *phobophobia*, or *pantophobia*, both shorthand for the fear of fears.

—R.H.

A Plethora of Phobias

Acrophobia—*fear of heights*
Aerophobia—*fear of high objects or heights*
Agoraphobia—*fear of open places*
Ailurophobia—*fear of cats*
Algophobia—*fear of pain*
Androphobia—*fear of men*
Anthophobia—*fear of flowers*
Apiphobia—*fear of bees*
Anthrophobia—*fear of people*
Arachibutyrophobia—*fear of peanut butter sticking to the roof of the mouth*
Astraphobia—*fear of storms, lightning, thunder*
Autophobia—*fear of being alone*
Baccilophobia—*fear of microbes*
Ballistophobia—*fear of bullets*
Bathophobia—*fear of depth*
Belonephobia—*fear of pins and needles*
Botanophobia—*fear of plants*
Ceraunophobia—*fear of thunder*
Chromophobia—*fear of certain colors*
Claustrophobia—*fear of enclosed places*
Clinophobia—*fear of beds*
Decidophobia—*fear of making decisions*
Domatophobia—*fear of being confined in a house*
Entomophobia—*fear of insects*
Eremophobia—*fear of being alone*
Ergophobia—*fear of work*
Gephydrophobia—*fear of crossing bridges*
Gynephobia—*fear of women*
Hematophobia—*fear of blood*
Hydrophobia—*fear of water*
Iatrophobia—*fear of doctors*
Keraunophobia—*fear of thunder*
Monophobia—*fear of being alone*
Mysophobia—*fear of germs or contamination*
Necrophobia—*fear of dead bodies*
Nosophobia—*fear of disease*
Nucleomitiphobia—*fear of nuclear bombs*
Nyctophobia—*fear of night*
Ochlophobia—*fear of crowds*
Ombrophobia—*fear of rain*
Optophobia—*fear of opening one's eyes*

Pantophobia—*fear of fears*
Pathophobia—*fear of disease*
Peccatophobia—*fear of sinning*
Pediphobia—*fear of children or dolls*
Phobophobia—*fear of one's own fears*
Ponophobia—*fear of work*
Psychrophobia—*fear of cold*
Pyrophobia—*fear of fire*
Sitophobia—*fear of food*
Sophophobia—*fear of learning*
Stenophobia—*fear of open places*
Syphilophobia—*fear of syphilis*
Taphephobia—*fear of being buried alive*

Technophobia—*fear of technology*
Thalassophobia—*fear of the ocean*
Thanatophobia—*fear of death*
Tonitrophobia—*fear of thunder*
Topophobia—*fear of performing (i.e., stage fright)*
Trichophobia—*fear of hair*
Tropophobia—*fear of moving or making changes*
Verbophobia—*fear of words*
Vestiophobia—*fear of clothing*
Xenophobia—*fear of strangers*
Zoophobia—*fear of animals*

Teaching Stories on Human Behavior

THE MAN AND HIS TWO WIVES

In the old days, when men were allowed to have many wives a middle-aged Man had one Wife that was old and one that was young; each loved him very much, and desired to see him like herself. Now the Man's hair was turning gray, which the young Wife did not like, as it made him look too old for her husband. So every night she used to comb his hair and pick out the white ones. But the elder Wife saw her husband growing gray with pleasure, for she did not like to be mistaken for his mother. So every morning she used to arrange his hair and pick out as many of the black ones as she could. The consequence was the Man soon found himself entirely bald.

"PLEASE ALL, AND YOU WILL PLEASE NONE."
—Aesop's *Fables*

THE LAMB'S ADVICE TO MEN

How delightful it is to wake up one morning to find that winter is over and that the warm spring air is fanning one's cheek!

It was upon such a morning that a lamb, happy and grateful for the delicious, sweet grass of the field in which he was feeding, spied 2 men afar off. After a time, they entered the field, and as they drew nearer, he was able to hear what they were saying.

He soon gathered that each of them considered himself to be possessed of not a little wisdom. Many were the topics which they discussed, and their manner of speaking made it quite evident that each valued his own opinion very highly indeed.

"Man is the cream of creation," declared one. "Just think, my friend; man has speech and a language with which he is able to express his thoughts."

"True," said the other. "When a noble idea is born within the mind of a man, he is in a position to make it known to others. He can draw the attention of his friends to things of beauty, and thus delight their souls."

"He can describe all the wonderful scenes which he has witnessed to those who have been unable to travel and see for themselves," continued the 1st.

"By means of speech men may band themselves together to carry out their common desires. They may also settle their disputes by explanation rather than by force," rejoined the 2nd.

"I offer continual praise to God that He has granted me this good gift of speech, by which I never cease to pour out the very best of advice to all round me," concluded the one who had 1st spoken.

They both turned their heads very slowly toward the lamb, who had been walking silently by their side. They could hardly believe their ears, for the lamb was talking to them. Here was something new to pass on to their friends!

"Sirs," began the lamb, "you believe that men alone possess the power of speech, but in that you are mistaken. Just consider. Would the birds be justified in saying that man has no knowledge of music because he does not sing their songs, and in their manner?

"Again, you have ideas. You build towns and cities. You make houses in which to live. Ugly chimneys pour out smoke where once were trees and flowers. And then you use your gift of speech to describe the beauty which you saw before you began to spoil it.

"Banding together, you set your mind upon a thing, and feel obliged to quarrel with those whose idea is not yours and who are banded against you.

"Even though you meet to talk things over, in your heart you mean to have your own way, and so you come to strife in the end.

"You have laws because you do not believe that all will be just, and judges to punish those who break them. People are bound by oath. Policemen are appointed to keep you in order.

"Why is this?

"Do any other creatures in the whole world make themselves so troublesome? Do other creatures band themselves together and go into other lands to kill others by thousands? Surely not! It is man, and man alone, who does these things.

"Until you can dismiss the policeman and the judge, and learn to expect justice as the reward of love, instead of banding yourselves together to enforce it, do not boast of being the cream of creation.

"Take a lesson from the sheep, for we have much better ways. We eat, we feed, we sleep together. Neither is greater or less than another, and so we have nothing to quarrel over.

"Do not make so much of the ants and bees, who are clever little creatures it is true, but who bite and sting, causing discomfort and often killing one another.

"Rather take your example from sheep and lambs, who are hated by none."

Surely this lamb gave the wise ones much to think about.

—W.E.D. rep.

22

Honors

The Nobel Prize Awards

Listings of the laureates are based on the official *Nobelstiftelsens Kalender*, published annually by the Nobel Foundation, Stockholm. The new feature, "Behind the Award," is exclusive and based on firsthand private interviews with the Nobel Prize judges and officials, with Scandinavian journalists who have covered the awards for many years, and with Nobel Prize winners around the world.

Alfred Bernhard Nobel, a shy, unhappy Swedish bachelor, invented dynamite, and became one of the richest men in the world. To ease his conscience after inventing the deadly explosive—and because he did not believe in leaving his millions to relatives ("inherited wealth is a misfortune which merely serves to dull man's faculties")—Nobel decided to leave his fortune to reward "those persons who shall have contributed most materially to the benefit of mankind during the year immediately preceding." With this reward in mind, Alfred Nobel, seated in the Swedish Club of Paris, on November 27, 1895, in the presence of 4 witnesses, writing on a torn half sheet of paper, signed a brief homemade will establishing the Nobel Prizes. Two weeks later Nobel was dead.

The Nobel Foundation, at Sturegatan 14 in Stockholm, run by a board of 6 members whose chairman is appointed by the Government, administers Nobel's will and oversees the investment of his money. Nobel left behind $9 million to be invested "in safe securities . . . the interest accruing from which shall be annually awarded in prizes." The prizewinning money, now worth $37 million, comes from interest on investments in Swedish real estate, bonds, railroad securities; in Danish, Japanese, Dutch, French, West German securities; and in American Wall Street common stocks, which are handled by Brittingham, Inc., of Wilmington, Del.

The 5 original awards—in the fields of literature, physics, chemistry, medicine, peace—are voted upon by 4 organizations, 3 in Stockholm and one in Oslo. The Swedish Academy of Science votes for the annual winners in physics and chemistry. The Caroline Institute, Sweden's leading hospital, has its staff of 45 physicians and instructors decide the medicine prize. The Swedish Academy, consisting of 18 writers, votes the award in literature. Because Nobel wanted to draw neighboring Norway closer to Sweden, he arranged for the peace prize to be given by a Nobel Committee of 5 prominent Norwegians appointed by the Storting, Norway's governing body. In 1968, a 6th award was established by the Central Bank of Sweden —a yearly prize in economics to be voted upon by members of the Swedish Academy of Science.

Annually, on December 10, the anniversary of Nobel's death, in Stockholm and in Oslo, each prizewinner receives a gold medal, illuminated diploma, and an envelope containing a cash pledge of anywhere from $30,000 to $125,-000—tax-free for American winners.

Generally, prizes have gone to the foremost creative persons in each field. Yet numerous awards have reflected the prejudices and politics of the Scandinavian judges. The Swedish Nobel Prize institutions have been consistently anti-Russian in the science and literature awards, contemptuously anti-American in the literature awards, persistently pro-German in science (until Germany lost W.W. II), and always pro-Scandinavian in every category.

Herewith the winners from 1901 to 1974:

LITERATURE

1901 René F. A. Sully-Prudhomme (1839–1907), French. Work: *Stanzas and Poems. Behind the Award*—This initial prize should have gone to Leo Tolstoi, but one of the 18 literary judges, Dr. Carl David af Wirsen, a poet and critic, denounced Tolstoi behind closed doors for advocating anarchism, for holding eccentric religious beliefs, and for having said cash prizes were harmful to artists. The majority of other judges, who were anti-Russia, agreed with Wirsen, and passed over Tolstoi. Recently, a modern judge, Dr. Anders Osterling, apologized in private, saying, "Prudhomme got the 1st Nobel Prize because of the conservative makeup of the Academy at that time, because of Swedish nationalism, because politics made the committeemen purposely avoid Tolstoi." . . . Émile Zola, the 1st to be nominated for the 1st award, was also voted down by the judges because he was "too daring"—and Nobel had not liked his novels.

1902 Theodor Mommsen (1817–1903), German. Work: *History of Rome*.
Behind the Award—Herbert Spencer, the British philosopher who died the next year, was the runner-up. The great Tolstoi was voted down again. Tolstoi said he did not mind, "because it saved me from the painful necessity of dealing in some way with money —generally regarded as very necessary and useful, but which I regard as the source of every kind of evil." Tolstoi lived until 1910, and was ignored in 9 consecutive Nobel votes.

1903 Björnstjerne Björnson (1832–1910), Norwegian. Work: *Sunny Hill; Beyond Human Power*.
Behind the Award—In his lifetime, Nobel admired Björnson's work, so the judges were guided by his hand from the grave. In this vote they rejected Henrik Ibsen because his writings were "too realistic" and not full of idealism.

1904 Frédéric Mistral (1830–1914), French. Work: *Mireio*.
Behind the Award—Mistral would have won it all by himself, according to unpublished notes on a history of the Academy made by a Swedish judge, "but before the final decision was made, his narrative in verse, *Mireio*, happened to be published in a decidedly inferior Swedish translation which, unfortunately, had been made by a member of the Academy, and the final voting resulted in an unhappy compromise which split the prize."
José Echegaray (1832–1916), Spanish. Work: *Great Go-Between*.
Behind the Award—This Spanish dramatist won while Thomas Hardy and Joseph Conrad were ignored. In fact, Hardy was passed over in every vote until his death in 1928, and Conrad in every vote until he died in 1924.

1905 Henryk Sienkiewicz (1846–1916), Polish. Work: *Quo Vadis*.

1906 Giosuè Carducci (1835–1907), Italian.

Work: *Barbarian Odes*.
Behind the Award—Anders Osterling, former Secretary of the Swedish Academy, said Carducci "is one of the few prizewinners who have been chosen unanimously." To elect him unanimously, the Nobel judges passed over Mark Twain, Rainer Maria Rilke, George Meredith, and Henry James. While Carducci, an antiromantic poet and politician, was admired in Italy (and Sweden), he never acquired international renown.

1907 Rudyard Kipling (1856–1936), British. Work: *Jungle Book; Captains Courageous*.
Behind the Award—The nominees for this one included Algernon Swinburne and Georg Brandes, but Kipling won as "the result of a compromise." Chosen at 42, he remains the youngest literature winner. As one Nobel judge told us, "We do not like to honor young men, because if they are too young, they may retrogress. Sinclair Lewis is a case in point." Stockholm was in mourning for King Oscar's death when Kipling arrived for his award. He wrote, "We reached the city, snow-white under sun, to find all the world in evening dress, the official mourning which is curiously impressive. Next afternoon, the prizewinners were taken to be presented to the new King . . . They said that the last words of the old King had been, 'Don't let them shut the theatres for me.' So Stockholm that night went soberly about her pleasures, all dumbed down under the snow."

1908 Rudolf C. Eucken (1846–1926), German. Work: *Meaning and Value of Life*.
Behind the Award—Crotchety senior judge Wirsen wanted Swinburne, lesser judges wanted Selma Lagerlöf, so another compromise was reached. Secretary Osterling admitted that Eucken was "unquestionably one of the Academy's weakest selections," and Donald Fleming, writing in *Atlantic*, labeled it "a scandalous choice." As for Eucken, the great unread, he taught philosophy at Basle, Jena, Cambridge, and is not even listed in *Twentieth Century Authors*.

1909 Selma Lagerlöf (1858–1940), Swedish. Work: *Story of Gösta Berling*.
Behind the Award—She was elected over Wirsen's vigorous opposition. He equated her work with "artificiality" and "unreality" and regarded her as one of "the fads of the day." Former Swedish Prime Minister Hjalmar Hammarskjöld, one of the judges, said of Miss Lagerlöf, after she too became a judge, "She writes idiotically, but she votes quite intelligently." For the 9th time Sweden's leading dramatist, August Strindberg, was not even nominated. Judge Sven Hedin hated Strindberg for ridiculing him, and judge Carl David af Wirsen regarded Strindberg as "old-fashioned," and other judges frowned on

Strindberg's drinking, 3 divorces, and belief in black magic.

1910 Paul J. L. Heyse (1830–1914), German. Work: *Novellen*.
Behind the Award—Said judge Wirsen, "Germany has not had a greater literary genius since Goethe." No further comment.

1911 Maurice Maeterlinck, (1862–1949). Belgian. Work: *Blue Bird*.
Behind the Award—Said Secretary Osterling in *Nobel, the Man and His Prizes:* "The only occasion on which Strindberg came near being officially considered. He was, in fact, proposed by the future Archbishop of Sweden, Nathan Soderblom, later on a member of the Academy, but the nomination came a few weeks too late, and instead of being laid aside for consideration the next year, as was by then the custom, it was returned at the sponsor's own request, and was never submitted by him again. . . . It seemed futile to submit Strindberg's name to a panel made up as the Academy was in those years. He died, moreover, only a month before Wirsen, who had been his sworn opponent ever since he had been bitterly satirized in Strindberg's book *The New Kingdom*." The winner, Maeterlinck, an ex-attorney and beekeeper, was able to curse in Flemish and lived out of wedlock with French actress Georgette Leblanc. He wound up in Los Angeles, one more exile from Hitler's terror.

1912 Gerhart Hauptmann (1862–1946), German. Work: *The Weavers*.

1913 Rabindranath Tagore (1861–1941), Indian. Work: *Collected Poems and Plays*.
Behind the Award—This almost unknown Indian got the award mainly because of the enthusiasm of one Nobel Prize judge, an Orientalist and fellow poet, Verner von Heidenstam, and one unnamed Swedish professor who knew Bengali. The committee was preparing to give the award to the French literary historian Émile Faguet, when von Heidenstam read Tagore's only collection of poetry in English (translated by Tagore himself) and told his colleagues, "I cannot recall having seen for decades anything comparable in lyric poetry." The body of judges then decided to read Tagore, but alas, he had not been translated into Swedish. So his work was turned over to a Swedish professor who could read Bengali. The professor became so enthusiastic that he insisted the judges learn Bengali so they might read Tagore in the original. Recalled Dr. Osterling, "He gave me a language book on Bengali, but the alphabet was so long, so complex, I gave it up and waited for the professor's Swedish translations to come through." The professor's translations clinched the medal for the man called

the Bengal Shelley. Tagore was knighted by the British King, gave up his knighthood in protest over British repression in India. He composed 3,000 songs, took up oil painting at 68, and wrote 100,000 lines of poetry—against Milton's 18,000. He was the 1st non-European to receive the literary prize.

1914 No Award
Behind the No Award—The Swedish judges all had the award lined up for Carl Spitteler, a Swiss jack-of-all-writing whom Nietzsche admired and had recommended for the job of critic on a Munich paper and whom Romain Rolland called "the greatest German poet since Goethe." But then came Sarajevo, and the award was shelved, not to be dusted off for Spitteler until 6 more years had passed.

1915 Romain Rolland (1866–1944), French. Work: *Jean-Christophe*.
Behind the Award—Rolland got the prize not for his novels but for his pacifism. Before the voting began, the Spanish author Perez Galdos was backed by a majority of judges and considered a shoo-in. Then, the great Rolland. caught in Switzerland by the advent of World War I, denounced the war, in fact all wars, and was savagely attacked in both France and Germany. When Anatole France was asked why he had not joined Rolland in speaking out against the conflict, France said, "I was afraid." But hear this— 6 years later when Anatole France's enemies declared his Nobel Prize was illegal because he had not been properly nominated for it by a member of the French Academy, it was proved he had been recommended by one member—Romain Rolland. Anyway, the Swedish judges, although not moved by Rolland's epic *Jean-Christophe*, were moved by his courageous pacifism, which conformed to Nobel's ideals, and they switched their final votes to him.

1916 Verner von Heidenstam (1859–1940), Swedish. Work: *Nya Dikter*.

1917 Karl A. Gjellerup (1857–1919), Danish. Work: *Golden Bough*.
Henrik Pontoppidan (1857–1943), Danish. Work: *Kingdom of the Dead*.
Behind the Award—Gjellerup was a Danish atheist who took up Buddhism, a German wife and residence. Pontoppidan was a patrician Danish recluse. Both were also writers. They won the prize while Bertolt Brecht, Maxim Gorki, Paul Valéry, Sean O'Casey were alive and at their peak.

1918 No Award

1919 Carl F. G. Spitteler (1845–1924), Swiss. Work: *Prometheus and Epimetheus*.
Behind the Award—Spitteler was elected over Marcel Proust.

1920 Knut Hamsun (1859–1952), Norwegian. Work: *Hunger; Growth of the Soil.*
Behind the Award—In dissent against Hamsun, judge Per Hallstrom had stated: "For the most part he has exerted an anarchic influence, and the idealistic tendency which the Nobel Prize is intended to encourage he has probably never recognized as even legitimate." Hamsun, who had been a dairyhand in Dakota, a streetcar conductor in Chicago, a fisherman in Newfoundland, was dead broke when he won the prize. He was also very proud. Bowing before King Gustav as he received the award, he suddenly blurted, "Of course, I do not need this money! I have more than this at home!" The night of the ceremony, Hamsun got roaring drunk. He pulled the whiskers of one Nobel judge. He sidled up to another, the dignified Selma Lagerlöf, and snapped his fingers against her new corset, exclaiming, "Y'know, sounds like a bell buoy!" Smashed out of his mind, he tried to share his Nobel money with 2 Swedish friends who were judges. When they refused his offer, he tried to give his money and diploma to his hotel room steward, but was again refused, and Hamsun wound up "by forgetting them in the elevator, where they were found the next morning." Pro-German, because his books sold well in that country, Hamsun welcomed the Nazis when they invaded Norway in April, 1940. He wrote articles backing Quisling, the Norwegian traitor, and he considered Hitler a "fatherly type." Yet, taken to Berlin in 1943 to meet Hitler, he proceeded to bawl out *Der Führer* for his "mistakes and errors," which made Hitler furious. When Norway was liberated, 86-year-old Hamsun was arrested, confined in an old people's home, and his property was confiscated. Sad story.

1921 Anatole France (1844–1924), French. Work: *Crime of Sylvestre Bonnard; Penguin Island.*
Behind the Award—A debate raged over France's lack of idealism. Judge Harald Hjarne argued that for France's "dainty hothouse . . . the *idealistic* literature prize of Alfred Nobel was not intended." He favored Galsworthy. Judge Henrik Schuck pitched for France, insisting the author was not the kind of cynic "who with indifference has watched justice and humanitarianism trampled underfoot." The 77-year-old France came for his award shivering under 3 overcoats, sat through the ceremony sound asleep and snoring softly.

1922 Jacinto Benavente y Martínez (1866–1954), Spanish. Work: *Bonds of Interest.*
Behind the Award—James Joyce, who had published *Ulysses* the year before, should have been the winner. A minister of Ireland proposed to nominate him, but Joyce told the minister it would cost him his job. In 1946, when Dr. Sven Hedin, a Swedish literary judge, was asked if James Joyce had ever been considered, Hedin looked puzzled and said, "Joyce? Who is he?"

1923 William Butler Yeats (1865–1939), Irish. Work: *Collected Poems of W. B. Yeats.*
Behind the Award—Secretary Erik Axel Karlfeldt urged his fellow judges to give the award to Thomas Hardy because of the "discontent and disappointment" in England over Hardy's constant omission, and because "Yeats, who is much younger, may be considered later." But Hardy's pessimism and fatalism counted against him. Of all the prizewinners who passed before King Gustav, the monarch liked Yeats the most "because he had the manners of a courtier." (King Gustav, who bestowed Nobel Prizes for 70 years, was so nearsighted he once presented a Nobel Prize to his own secretary by mistake.)

1924 Wladyslaw S. Reymont (1867–1925), Polish. Work: *The Peasants.*
Behind the Award—Guglielmo Ferrero, author of *Roman History*, was a strong contender. But the older judges considered him wanting in scholarship. The choice shifted to 2 Polish authors, Reymont and Stefan Zeromski. The people of Poland wanted Zeromski. The judges, naturally, gave the award to Reymont.

1925 George Bernard Shaw (1856–1950), British. Work: *Androcles and the Lion; Pygmalion.*
Behind the Award—Receiving the award at the age of 69, with his great successes behind him, G.B.S. wanted to turn the prize down but was finally persuaded to accept it. He told the Nobel judges, "The money is a lifebelt thrown to a swimmer who has already reached the shore in safety!"

1926 Grazia Deledda (1875–1936), Italian. Work: *The Mother.*
Behind the Award—The judges secretly decided to give the prize to someone of Italian citizenship. The favorite was Gabriele D'Annunzio. Next choice was Guglielmo Ferrero, a professor of history. Third choice was Grazia Deledda, little-known but admired by Mussolini. In the debate, Ferrero was dropped as being a minor historian. A wrangle ensued over D'Annunzio. His private life was considered too fantastic, too immoral—his numerous mistresses, his affair with actress Eleonora Duse, his adventure as dictator of Fiume—and at last he was voted down. And that left Deledda the winner.

1927 Henri Bergson (1859–1941), French. Work: *Creative Evolution.*

1928 Sigrid Undset (1882–1949), Norwegian. Work: *Kristin Lavransdatter.*

1929 Thomas Mann (1875–1955), German. Work: *Buddenbrooks.*

Behind the Award—The award was given for a novel, *Buddenbrooks*, which he had published 28 years earlier, with no mention of *The Magic Mountain*, published 5 years earlier. Mann lost part of his $46,229 prize to the Nazis, presented part to a German author's league, used the rest to go to Palestine to research *Joseph and His Brothers*. He was embarrassed by the publicity. "It is an unnerving experience to have come publicly into the possession of a sum of money, as much as any industrialist puts away every year and no notice taken of it, and suddenly to be stared in the face by all the wretchedness of the world."

1930 Sinclair Lewis (1885–1951), American. Work: *Main Street; Babbitt; Arrowsmith.*

Behind the Award—Lewis's publisher, Alfred Harcourt, lobbied for this award. The judges were split on Lewis. Half felt his writing was erratic, uneven. The rest felt his work was important. At last he was voted the prize because it was agreed that to continue to ignore American writers would be scandalous. In fact, Theodore Dreiser proved to be the runner-up. In Stockholm, Lewis gave a brilliant speech attacking the U.S. genteel literary establishment, saying, "American professors like their literature clear, cold, pure, and very dead."

1931 Erik A. Karlfeldt (1846–1931), Swedish. Work: *Dalecarlian Frescoes in Rhyme.*

Behind the Award—Karlfeldt was a poet and librarian, secretary of the Swedish Academy, and a friend of all the judges. He had turned down the prize once. This time, because he needed the money, he agreed to accept it. Karlfeldt won over Maxim Gorki of Russia, among others, despite the fact that he died 6 months before the voting. The judges ignored the rules in order to honor him posthumously and give security to his widow and daughters.

1932 John Galsworthy (1867–1933), British. Work: *The Forsyte Saga.*

Behind the Award—The popular favorite was muckraker Upton Sinclair, who had been nominated by an international petition signed by 770 prominent persons including Bertrand Russell, Harold Laski, Edwin Markham, Albert Einstein—but in the final voting he was defeated.

1933 Ivan A. Bunin (1870–1953), French. Work: *Gentleman from San Francisco; Well of Days.*

Behind the Award—Bunin was the only Russian to win the prize 1st 33 years of the awards. Actually he was an anticommunist expatriate who had not seen Russia in 15 years. A minor novelist who had translated *Hiawatha* into Russian, Bunin lived in a Paris attic. Explained the secretary of the Swedish Academy privately, "We voted for Bunin to pay off our consciences on Chekhov and Tolstoi."

1934 Luigi Pirandello (1867–1936), Italian. Work: *Six Characters in Search of an Author.*

Behind the Award—Said Malcolm Cowley, "The Italian Ambassador in Stockholm had to engage in backstairs intrigue to keep the prize from going to Benedetto Croce, the one Italian who clearly deserved it. Pirandello, the successful candidate, was a politically harmless man on whom the dictator [Mussolini] could rely." So the fascist-hating Croce was passed over, and Pirandello won the $41,318.

1935 No Award

1936 Eugene O'Neill (1888–1953), American. Work: *Anna Christie; Mourning Becomes Electra.*

Behind the Award—Since the medicine prize judges did not regard Dr. Sigmund Freud as eligible, Freud was nominated for the literary prize in 1936 by Thomas Mann and Romain Rolland. Learning of this, Freud wrote Arnold Zweig, "Don't let yourself get worked up over the Nobel chimera. It is only too certain that I shall not get any Nobel Prize. Psychoanalysis has several good enemies among the authorities on whom the bestowal depends. . . ." Freud was right. His enemies voted him down.

1937 Roger Martin du Gard (1881–1958), French. Work: *The Thibaults.*

1938 Pearl S. Buck (1892–1973), American. Work: *The Good Earth; The Mother.*

Behind the Award—Dr. Sven Hedin, a Nobel judge who was an old China hand and whose publisher in America was Pearl Buck's husband, enjoyed the Chinese background in Buck's books and convinced another judge, Selma Lagerlöf, to side with him. The remaining 16 judges, who for the most part opposed this award, were led by Dr. Anders Osterling. Said Osterling, "I felt she did not deserve the prize and I fought her. She'd done a few good things, but most of her work was mediocre." Hedin and Lagerlöf, because of their seniority, won over the others after a long debate. When notified, Pearl Buck graciously announced that Theodore Dreiser was more deserving of the honor.

1939 Frans E. Sillanpää (1888–1964), Finnish. Work: *Meek Heritage.*

Behind the Award—Sillanpää, "the most widely unknown author on earth," according to Nobel biographer Herta Pauli, was an impoverished giant who'd married his housekeeper and had 7 children by her. He got the $35,000 prize because one of the Nobel judges, 81-year-old Selma Lagerlöf, angered by Russia's invasion of Finland (she had turned her own Nobel gold medal over to the Finns to be melted down), badgered the weaker judges into taking a symbolic stand against Soviet aggression. Ignored in the intense politicking were 2 superior authors, F. Scott Fitzgerald and Virginia Woolf, who became ineligible in the next year and the year after because of their premature deaths.

1940   No Award
1941   No Award
1942   No Award
1943   No Award
1944   Johannes V. Jensen (1873–1950), Danish. Work: *The Long Journey.*
Behind the Award—The literary judges preferred Jensen, a fellow Scandinavian, to H. G. Wells, Willa Cather, and W. Somerset Maugham, the latter of whom they privately regarded as "too popular and undistinguished."
1945   Gabriela Mistral (1889–1957), Chilean. Work: *Havoc.*
Behind the Award—Politics. Her poems were unknown in Sweden or to the judges save one. The dark horse nominees were Jules Romains, Benedetto Croce, Hermann Hesse. But, as judge Sven Hedin explained, "because one of our judges, Hjalmar Gullberg, a poet, fell in love with Mistral's verse, and translated all of it into Swedish to convince us, he single-handed swayed our entire vote."
1946   Hermann Hesse (1877–1962), Swiss. Work: *Steppenwolf; Demian.*
Behind the Award—He was nominated by his friend Thomas Mann. Since German-born Hesse's best novel was published 19 years before this award, Swedish newspapers questioned it. The Swedish Academy judges explained they voted for Hesse because he was "one of those who 1st eluded German suppression of free opinion." They did not explain that the German suppression Hesse eluded was not Hitler's—but the Kaiser's in 1912. They also did not explain that Academy secretary Hallstrom did not feel Hesse's novels would have been approved by Nobel "unless the inventor of dynamite had wanted to glorify an instinct for evil"—but once Hesse turned from novels to poetry, a prize to him could be justified.
1947   André Gide (1869–1951), French. Work: *The Immoralist; The Counterfeiters.*
Behind the Award—Off and on for 20 years, Gide was runner-up in the secret balloting. The judges respected him but were troubled about his self-confessed homosexuality. Finally, although one liberal judge switched his vote to denounce Gide on moral grounds, the conservative majority changed its mind and elected him a Nobel laureate.

1948   T. S. Eliot (1888–1965), British. Work: *The Waste Land.*
1949   William Faulkner (1897–1962), American. Work: *The Sound and the Fury; Sanctuary.*
Behind the Award—Robert Coughlan, in his biography of Faulkner, wrote that a week after learning of his Nobel award, Faulkner went on his annual hunting expedition with friends, started drinking heavily, and was in an alcoholic stupor until the week before he was to leave for Stockholm. His friends were worried, but suddenly Faulkner stopped drinking, remained cold sober throughout the ceremony, and delivered one of the great acceptance speeches in Nobel Prize history.
1950   Bertrand A. Russell (1872–1970), British. Work: *Human Knowledge.*
1951   Pär F. Lagerkvist (1891–1974), Swedish. Work: *Barabbas.*
1952   François Mauriac (1885–1970), French. Work: *Thérèse.*
1953   Winston Churchill (1874–1965), British. Work: *Second World War Series.*
Behind the Award—Despite protests from literary purists that Churchill was more a politico than an author, the judges stood firm. They insisted rightly that he was an author in the tradition of Burke and Disraeli. They pointed to his reportage from India and the Sudan, his biography of Marlborough, his epic history of W.W. II, his public speeches ("How many flashing phrases . . . have been imprinted in our consciousness!").
1954   Ernest Hemingway (1899–1961), American. Work: *The Old Man and the Sea; A Farewell to Arms.*
Behind the Award—A Nobel Prize judge said: "He had been put to a vote several times before, and once he was very, very close to winning. Our conservatism had kept the award from him." But finally, it was not high regard for Hemingway (Albert Camus and Concha Espina were favored over him) but high regard for one of their own that determined the 1959 award. The senior judge, Per Hallstrom, was about to retire, and Hallstrom was a Hemingway fan who loved *The Old Man and the Sea.* So the judges voted the award to Hemingway because they wished it to be considered, in the words of one of them, "a gesture of courtesy toward the dean of the Academy, who at that time was nearly 90 years old."
1955   Halldór K. Laxness (1902–). Icelander. Work: *Independent People.*
1956   Juan Rámon Jiménez (1881–1958) Spanish Work: *Platero and I.*
1957   Albert Camus (1913–1960), French Work: *The Plague; The Stranger.*

1958 Boris L. Pasternak (1890–1960), Russian. Work: *Dr. Zhivago.*

Behind the Award—Pasternak's writings were anticommunist, and this gave the judges a chance to thumb their noses at the Soviet Union. Pasternak said he would "joyfully" accept the award. But then *Pravda* raged that this "reactionary bourgeois award" had not been given to a novelist and poet but rather to a "lampooner who had blackened the socialist revolution" and who was now a member of the "archreactionary fraternity." Sadly, Pasternak was forced to reject the award. "This refusal," said the Nobel Committee, "does not affect the validity of the prize, and even though it could not be presented, Pasternak retains his position in the line of prizewinners."

1959 Salvatore Quasímodo (1901–1968), Italian. Work: *Incomparable Earth.*

Behind the Award—Although he was not mentioned in a single standard English or American biographical dictionary of writers before he was voted a Nobel laureate, the selection of the Sicily-born poet caused no fuss. What did cause a fuss was that he checked into Stockholm's Grand Hotel for the ceremony with a woman who was not his wife.

1960 Saint-John Perse (1887–), French. Work: *Chronique.*

1961 Ivo Andrič (1892–), Yugoslavian. Work: *The Bridge on the Drina.*

1962 John Steinbeck (1902–1968), American. Work: *The Grapes of Wrath; Of Mice and Men.*

Behind the Award—*The Times* of London editorialized, "Mr. John Steinbeck's disarming doubts about his own merit are, perhaps, shared by many. . . . It is becoming difficult to take seriously the standards of judgment of an international literary prize which overlooks or deliberately ignores the claims of such writers as Valéry, Malraux or Brecht, preferring to honor the accomplishments . . . of Pearl Buck and Quasimodo."

1963 Giorgos Seferis (1900–), Greek. Work: *The Thrush; Log Book III.*

1964 Jean-Paul Sartre (1905–), French. Work: *Nausea; No Exit.*

Behind the Award—Sartre flatly rejected the prize award and the check for $53,000. He is the only laureate ever to turn down the prize of his own free will. In declining, Sartre stated, "It is not the same thing if I sign Jean-Paul Sartre or if I sign Jean-Paul Sartre, Nobel Prize winner. A writer must refuse to allow himself to be transformed into an institution, even if it takes place in the most honorable form." The Nobel Academy's only official comment: "The laureate let it be known that he did not wish to accept the prize, but the fact of his declining this distinction naturally in no way modifies the validity of the award."

1965 Mikhail A. Sholokhov (1905–), Russian. Work: *And Quiet Flows the Don.*

Behind the Award—The 1st pro-Soviet writer-citizen to be honored by the Swedish judges. There is no clue to the turnabout of the Academy except in the remark of one judge: "Convinced communist though he is, Sholokhov abstains from all political comment." In 1974, a Russian émigré publishing house in Paris brought out a scholarly study, with a foreword by Aleksandr Solzhenitsyn, which challenged Sholokhov's authorship of *And Quiet Flows the Don.* According to the exposé, an anti-Bolshevik White Russian officer, Fedor D. Krukov, wrote the book before dying of typhus in 1920. Somehow, the exposé claimed, the 21-year-old Sholokhov got hold of the manuscript, tacked on a new ending, and published it under his own name when he was 23.

1966 Samuel Y. Agnon (1888–1970), Israeli. Work: *The Bridal Canopy; A Guest for the Night.*

Nelly Sachs (1891–1970), Swedish. Work: *Collected Poems.*

1967 Miguel Angel Asturias (1899–1974). Guatemalan. Work: *Men of Corn; Mulata.*

1968 Yasunari Kawabata (1899–1972), Japanese. Work: *Snow Country; Thousand Cranes.*

Behind the Award—Among the nominees in this particular year were Chairman Mao Tsetung, Gunter Grass, Alberto Moravia, Robert Graves, Lawrence Durrell. Yet, none was seriously considered because, as *The People's Almanac* learned exclusively, the Swedish Academy had secretly determined that the 1968 award should go to a Japanese writer. A Swedish official was flown to Tokyo to scout the field. The leading Japanese writers —Mishima, Abe, Oe, Tanizaki—were passed over for the lesser-known Kawabata, who was considered a safer choice. In April, 1972, Kawabata put a gas hose in his mouth and committed suicide.

1969 Samuel Beckett (1906–), Irish. Work: *Waiting for Godot.*

Behind the Award—Among those voted upon, besides Beckett, were Eugène Ionesco, Vladimir Nabokov, André Malraux, Leopold Senghor, President of Senegal. Beckett, one-time secretary to James Joyce and an avant-garde author, was able to get the $72,800 prize only because the Swedish Academy had been infused by some younger blood and had become more liberal.

1970 Aleksandr I. Solzhenitsyn (1918–), Russian. Work: *The Cancer Ward; One Day in the Life of Ivan Denisovich.*

Behind the Award—The winner, whose anti-Stalinist novels are banned in his homeland, was nominated by François Mauriac, among others. The Soviet Union accused the Swedish judges of "anti-Soviet motives" in crowning a novelist who was banned by Russian authorities. The Soviet Union was right. The award was political as well as literary. Solzhenitsyn declined a trip to Stockholm, fearful that he might not be allowed back in Russia to be with his 2nd wife and children. He suggested that the ceremony be held in Moscow's Swedish Embassy. Swedish Premier Olof Palme chickened out on this, feeling such a ceremony might be interpreted as a political manifestation against the Soviet Union. In 1973, Solzhenitsyn told the foreign press that his life had been threatened by the KGB (Soviet Security Police). In February, 1974, after publishing in Paris *The Gulag Archipelago*, an exposé of Stalinist repression and terror, Solzhenitsyn was arrested, then deported from Russia. He now lives in exile in Norway. He finally received his Nobel Prize in Stockholm on December 10, 1974.

1971 Pablo Neruda (1904–1973), Chilean. Work: *The Poetry of Neruda*.

Behind the Award—Ricardo Reyes adopted the pen name of Pablo Neruda (from a Czech writer who had died in 1891) because his laborer-father disapproved of poetry. Neruda became a Loyalist during the Spanish Civil War. Spain's great poet, Federico García Lorca, who was killed or murdered in that war, called him "A real man who knows that the reed and the swallow are more immortal than the hard cheek of a statue." Neruda wrote 7,000 pages of poetry in his lifetime. In one of his best-known radical poems, "The United Fruit Co.," he wrote: "Jehovah divided his universe:/Anaconda, Ford Motors,/Coca-Cola Inc., and similar entities:/the most succulent item of all,/The United Fruit Company Incorporated." In 1953, he won the Stalin Peace Prize and praised Stalin; in 1963, disenchanted, he said of Stalin, "This cruel man stopped life." In 1970, he started to run as communist candidate for President of Chile, then withdrew. When Salvador Allende became President, he appointed Neruda Ambassador to France. This appointment, as well as the fact that his closest rival for the Nobel Prize, Patrick White, received poor reviews on his latest book, won the $88,000 award for Neruda, whom the Swedes called "the poet of violated human dignity." Noting that in the previous 10 years 3 other diplomats had become laureates, Neruda welcomed the latest "Nobel old age pension for diplomats."

1972 Heinrich Böll (1917–), German. Work: *Billiards at 9:30; Group Portrait with Lady*.

Behind the Award—Drafted into the Wehrmacht, he was wounded 3 times. A Catholic, he refused to pay Church taxes as a protest against "the fiscalization of faith." A leftist democrat, he is also published in East Germany. When a housewife boxed the ears of Chancellor Kiesinger, because of his Nazi past, Böll outraged the nation by sending her flowers. He was the 1st German inside Germany to get the Nobel Prize since Mann won it in 1929 (Hesse and Sachs got it while in exile). Many believe Böll got the award "to defuse East-West political tensions." Notified of his $100,000 prize while visiting Athens, Böll announced he would give part of it to assist jailed writers and their families around the world, and then defended writers in Greece who were political prisoners. He believes future Nobel winners "should be" the South American Garcia Marquez, the Russian Vladimir Maximoff, the Englishman Graham Greene, the Americans "possibly Mailer, Bellow, Salinger."

1973 Patrick White (1912–), Australian. Work: *The Tree of Man; Voss*.

Behind the Award—He topped Graham Greene, André Malraux, Vladimir Nabokov to win the $121,000 prize. He won for introducing "a new continent into literature . . . for the 1st time [he] has given the continent of Australia a voice that carries across the world." Freely translated this means the Swedish Academy was once more playing it safe after recent controversies and playing its game of geographical distribution by giving Australia its 1st literary award. White, graduate of the RAF, student at Cambridge, music and dog lover, is a tight-lipped loner. About his body of work, he's said, "The books are more important than words."

1974 Eyvind Johnson (1900–), Swedish. Work: *The Novel About Olav*.

Harry E. Martinson (1904–), Swedish. Work: *The Road; The Days of His Grace*.

Behind the Award—Two Nobel judges were made winners by Nobel judges. Both were virtually unknown outside their native Sweden. Wrote Professor Sven Delblanc, of Uppsala University, in the Stockholm *Expressen*: "The choice reflects a lack of judgment by the Academy . . . this can only too easily be interpreted as corruption through comraderie. Mutual admiration is one thing, but this smells almost like embezzlement." Among nominees who did not get the prize were Graham Greene, Vladimir Nabokov, Saul Bellow.

—I.W.

PHYSICS

1901 Wilhelm C. Roentgen (1845–1923), German. Work: The discovery of X rays.
Behind the Award—Roentgen was chosen by a relatively large majority of the Nobel Prize Physics Committee to receive the 1st prize. It was a good choice, one that has withstood the test of time. Roentgen was the 1st human being to see inside the human body through the magic of X rays. His discovery was not without controversy. The newspapers expressed fear that X rays would allow men to see women naked beneath their clothes, and the New Jersey legislature forbade the use of the X ray in opera glasses.

1902 Hendrik A. Lorentz (1853–1928), Dutch.
Pieter Zeeman (1865–1943), Dutch. Work: Research into the effects of magnetism upon radiation.

1903 Antoine H. Becquerel (1852–1908), French.
Pierre Curie (1859–1906), French.
Marie S. Curie (1867–1934), French. (b. Poland). Work: Study of the radiation phenomena, which were discovered by Becquerel.
Behind the Award—"The only human being ever to win 2 Nobel Prizes was Madame Marie Curie," said the director of the Nobel Foundation when Mme. Curie won the Nobel Prize in chemistry in 1911. (Since then, others have won 2 prizes, but it is still rare.) Mme. Curie put in a modern bathroom and changed the wallpaper in their Paris house with part of the prize money.

1904 John W. S. Rayleigh (1842–1919), British. Work: The discovery of argon.

1905 Philipp E. A. von Lenard (1862–1947), German (b. Hungary). Work: The cathode-ray experiments.
Behind the Award—Von Lenard was one of the men who kept Einstein from getting the Nobel Prize in the early days. An anti-Semite, he claimed that Einstein's theory of relativity was useless, not proven, not even a discovery. When Einstein did get the prize in 1921, Von Lenard wrote a blistering letter to the Swedish Academy of Science in protest.

1906 Joseph J. Thompson (1856–1940), British. Work: Research into the ways in which gases conduct electricity.

1907 Albert A. Michelson (1852–1931), American (b. Germany). Work: Making optical measuring instruments and investigating spectroscopic and meteorological phenomena.
Behind the Award—The only American citizen to be given the physics prize in the 1st 20 years was Michelson, and what helped him was that he was born in Germany.

1908 Gabriel Lippmann (1845–1921), French (b. Luxembourg). Work: Development of color photography.
Behind the Award—Lippmann ended his Nobel lecture with, "Perhaps progress will continue. Life is short and progress is slow."

1909 Guglielmo Marconi (1874–1937), Italian.
Carl F. Braun (1850–1918), German. Work: Developing the wireless telegraph.
Behind the Award—In his Nobel lecture, Marconi said that he had never had formal university training in physics or electrical engineering. However, he did attend a course of physics lectures at Leghorn.

1910 Johannes D. van der Waals (1837–1923), Dutch. Work: The mathematical relations between gases and liquids.

1911 Wilhelm Wien (1864–1928), German. Work: Discovering laws concerning the radiation of heat.
Behind the Award—Thomas A. Edison, who was seriously being considered for the prize, renounced it in advance so that a person who needed it more might get it.

1912 Niles G. Dalén (1869–1937), Swedish. Work: Inventing gas regulators for acetylene buoys, beacons, and railway lights.

1913 Heike Kamerlingh Onnes (1853–1926), Dutch. Work: Low-temperature experiments which led to helium liquefaction.

1914 Max von Laue (1879–1960), German. Work: Using crystals to diffract X rays.

1915 William H. Bragg (1862–1942), British.
W. Lawrence Bragg (1890–1971), British. Work: Using X rays to determine the structure of crystals.

1916 No Award

1917 Charles G. Barkla (1877–1944), British. Work: Discovering X-ray radiation of elements.

1918 Max K. E. L. Planck (1858–1947), German. Work: Formulating the quantum theory.

1919 Johannes Stark (1874–1957), German. Work: Discovering the splitting of spectral lines in an electrical field.

1920 Charles E. Guillaume (1861–1938), French (b. Switzerland). Work: Discoveries relating to alloys.

1921 Albert Einstein (1879–1955), American (b. Germany). Work: General contributions to theoretical physics, especially for discovering the law of photoelectric effect.
Behind the Award—Einstein should have got the prize 7 years earlier for his general theory of relativity. But from Germany, a former Nobel Prize winner in physics, Philipp von Lenard, an anti-Semite and a follower of

Hitler, lobbied against Einstein. Because Von Lenard hated Einstein as a Jew, he convinced the Swedish Academy of Science that Einstein's theory of relativity was not a discovery, had not been proven, and was of no benefit to mankind. So in every vote after 1916, the judges ignored Einstein. But at last Einstein's fame became so great that the judges gave him a consolation prize for a minor discovery.

1922 Niels H. D. Bohr (1885–1962), Danish. Work: Research into atomic structure and radiation.

1923 Robert A. Millikan (1868–1953), American. Work: Studies of electrons of the photoelectric effect.
Behind the Award—Millikan, who did not go to Sweden until the year after he won the award, said that the Swedes gave him 2 medals—"One was solid gold, to put in the vault for safekeeping. The other was a brass replica, just to keep around the house to show people."

1924 Karl M. G. Siegbahn (1886–), Swedish. Work: Work in X-ray spectroscopy.

1925 James Franck (1882–1964), German.
Gustav Hertz (1887–), German. Work: Discoveries of laws relating to electrons.

1926 Jean B. Perrin (1870–1942), French. Work: Research on the discontinuous structure of matter and the discovery of sedimentation equilibrium.

1927 Arthur H. Compton (1892–1962), American. Work: Discovering the Compton effect, which has to do with the change in the wavelength of X rays when they collide with electrons.
Charles T. R. Wilson (1869–1959), British. Work: Discovery of the cloud chamber, a way of tracking electrically charged particles.

1928 Owen W. Richardson (1879–1959), British. Work: Research into electron emission from heated bodies.

1929 Louis-Victor de Broglie (1892–), French. Work: Discovery of the wave nature of electrons.

1930 Chandrasekhara V. Raman (1888–1970), Indian. Work: Research into light diffusion.
Behind the Award—During the awarding of the prize, Raman, from the University of Calcutta, sat on the platform listening to a speech about himself and "could not keep back" his tears.

1931 No Award

1932 Werner Heisenberg (1901–), German. Work: Making up a quantum mechanics, and new discoveries about hydrogen.
Behind the Award—Heisenberg once said that Nobel records are kept secret so that the judges can evaluate the candidate's personal behavior in addition to his scientific work. Heading the list of personal crimes, which can take a candidate out of the running, is publicity seeking.

1933 Erwin Schrödinger (1887–1961), Austrian.
Paul A. M. Dirac (1902–), British. Work: The development of certain facets of atomic theory.

1934 No Award

1935 James Chadwick (1891–1974), British. Work: Discovering the neutron.
Behind the Award—A neutron is so tiny it would take 10 trillion of them to cover an inch. They can smash into atoms, Chadwick said, "the way a wooden toothpick can penetrate a magnetic field where a steel pin cannot."

1936 Victor F. Hess (1883–1964), American (b. Austria). Work: Discovery of cosmic radiation.
Carl D. Anderson (1905–), American. Work: Discovering the positron.

1937 Clinton J. Davisson (1881–1958), American.
George P. Thomson (1892–), British. Work: Discovering how crystals diffract electrons.
Behind the Award—When Davisson, a struggling father of 4, found out he had to pay his own way to Sweden to collect the prize, he went to the bank to borrow the money to do so. He then used part of his prize check to repay the bank. A decade later a reporter asked him if the Nobel money had affected him, and he answered, "Outwardly, we live as before. But below the decks, there is a serenity which previously was lacking and which wealth alone can bring."

1938 Enrico Fermi (1901–1954), American (b. Italy). Work: Research on radioactive elements.

1939 Ernest O. Lawrence (1901–1958), American. Work: The invention of the cyclotron.
Behind the Award—Lawrence was nominated in 1938, but lost the prize to Fermi. His invention, the cyclotron, "spirals atomic bullets up to tremendous speeds by repeated electrical pushes." The year before he received the award, a San Francisco Fair promoter wanted to borrow the cyclotron for an exhibition of atom smashing. When Lawrence mentioned that loose neutrons could break out and sterilize the spectators, the promoter changed his mind.

1940 No Award
1941 No Award
1942 No Award
1943 Otto Stern (1888–1969), American (b. Germany). Work: Research into the

magnetic properties of atoms and discovery of the proton's magnetic moment.

1944 Isidor Isaac Rabi (1898–), American (b. Austria). Work: Discovery relating to magnetic properties of atomic nuclei.

Behind the Award—A developer of the hydrogen bomb, Rabi was later a science adviser to NATO.

1945 Wolfgang Pauli (1900–1958), American (b. Austria). Work: Discovering the exclusion principle in atomic theory.

1946 Percy Williams Bridgman (1882–1961), American. Work: Work in high-pressure physics.

1947 Edward V. Appleton (1892–1965), British. Work: Research into the physics of the upper atmosphere.

1948 Patrick M. S. Blackett (1897–1974), British. Work: Improving the Wilson cloud-chamber method and other discoveries relating to nuclear physics and cosmic rays.

Behind the Award—A few weeks before he received the award, Blackett published a book in which he said Russia had the right to turn down the U.S. plan for international atomic control. He said the arrangement favored the U.S. over Russia. After he won the prize, the British Foreign Office told the United Nations that it disowned Blackett, and, in effect, that Blackett's opinions were his own and did not represent those of the British Government.

1949 Hideki Yukawa (1907–), Japanese. Work: Theories about the existence of mesons.

1950 Cecil F. Powell (1903–1969), British. Work: Using photography to track particles in nuclear processes.

1951 John D. Cockcroft (1897–1967), British.

Ernest T. S. Walton (1903–), Irish. Work: Research into transmuting atom nuclei with artificially accelerated atomic particles.

1952 Felix Bloch (1905–), American (b. Switzerland).

Edward M. Purcell (1912–), American. Work: Development of a method of measuring magnetic fields of atomic nuclei.

1953 Frits Zernike (1888–1966), Dutch. Work: Invention of the phase-contrast microscope.

1954 Max Born (1882–1970), British (b. Germany). Work: Research in quantum mechanics and nuclear physics.

Walter Bothe (1891–1957), German. Work: Developing the coincidence method of measuring time.

1955 Willis E. Lamb, Jr. (1913–), American. Work: Research into the structure of the hydrogen spectrum.

Polykarp Kusch (1911–), American

(b. Germany). Work: Measuring the electromagnetic properties of the electron.

1956 John Bardeen (1908–), American.

Walter H. Brattain (1902–), American.

William B. Shockley (1910–), American (b. England). Work: Developing the transistor.

Behind the Award—Bardeen heard the news about the award on the radio as he was making scrambled eggs. "He dropped the pan," his daughter said. Shockley, one of the other prizewinners, left Bell Laboratories shortly after he received the award and started his own company. This enterprise failed, partly because of friction between Shockley and his assistants. Shockley admitted he was not a good administrator. In 1963, he took an endowed chair as professor of engineering science at Stanford University and 2 years later began to talk about his views on heredity. These views, in which he has advocated voluntary sterilization of those with low IQs, have caused great controversy, partly because he based them on studies in which blacks were reported to score lower than whites on intelligence tests. Radicals and liberals have opposed his stand bitterly.

1957 Tsung-Dao Lee (1926–), American (b. China).

Chen Ning Yang (1922–), American (b. China). Work: Disproving the law of parity conservation in nuclear physics.

Behind the Award—Yang and Lee won their prize shortly after they had made their discovery. A Western acupuncturist, Dr. Nguy, gen Van Nghi of Marseilles, said in a book that the 2 scientists based their work on the theory and laws of yin and yang, guiding principles of Chinese philosophy.

1958 Pavel A. Cherenkov (1904–), Russian.

Ilya M. Frank (1908–), Russian.

Igor Y. Tamm (1895–1971), Russian. Work: Discovery of the Cherenkov effect.

1959 Emilio G. Segrè (1905–), American (b. Italy).

Owen Chamberlain (1920–), American. Work: Discovering the antiproton.

Behind the Award—In 1972, Oreste Piccioni, a physics professor at the University of California, San Diego, brought a $125,000 suit against Chamberlain and Segrè, claiming that he had been responsible for originating the research that won them the prize. He said that he was not allowed to join the staff at the Berkeley laboratory where the 2 worked because of security regulations. (He was not a citizen and had been associated with Socialist causes in Italy.)

Therefore, he went to Segrè and Chamberlain with his idea, asking them to perform the experiment. They did, he said, and they won the prize for it. When asked why he had waited so long to bring suit, he said that when he brought up the matter earlier, they had promised him favors in exchange for his silence. Though other scientists have complained that the prize has been given unfairly, this was the 1st civil court case over a Nobel Prize.

1960 Donald A. Glaser (1926–), American. Work: Invention of a bubble chamber for the study of subatomic particles.

1961 Robert Hofstadter (1915–), American. Work: Investigating atomic nuclei and researching the structure of nucleons.

Rudolf L. Mössbauer (1929–), German. Work: Finding a method of producing and measuring recoil-free gamma rays.

1962 Lev D. Landau (1908–1968), Russian. Work: Studies on condensed gases.

Behind the Award—Rumor had it that Edward Teller, creator of the hydrogen bomb, was being considered for the award in 1962. He never did get a Nobel Prize.

1963 Eugene P. Wigner (1902–), American (b. Hungary).

Maria Goeppert-Mayer (1906–), American (b. Poland).

J. Hans D. Jensen (1907–), German. Work: Contributing to nuclear and theoretical physics.

1964 Charles H. Townes (1915–), American.

Nikolai G. Basov (1922–), Russian.

Aleksandr M. Prochorov (1916–), Russian. Work: Fundamental research in quantum electronics.

Behind the Award—The academic world was astounded when Townes shared the prize with 2 unknown Russians, who had published nothing beyond crudely duplicating notes. However, they had, with primitive instruments, discovered the maser-laser principle; Townes had discovered the same principle using far more sophisticated equipment. Professor Erik Rudberg, chairman of the Physics Prize Committee, stated that findings with primitive instruments should be rewarded just as much as findings discovered by "button pushing on expensive instruments."

1965 Richard P. Feynman (1918–), American.

Julian S. Schwinger (1918–), American.

Sin-itiro Tomonaga (1906–), Japanese. Work: Research in quantum electrodynamics.

Behind the Award—When Feynman won the prize, a student put his picture over the face of Christ in a plaque of *The Last Supper*. Feynman is an iconoclast and a natural showman, perhaps the only writer to include a picture of himself beating drums in a college physics text. He describes his work in terms of playing chess with a Martian: "If you don't know the rules and you see only parts of the board, how do you know how to play? If you know all the rules, can you tell what's in the Martian's mind when he moves the pieces in a certain way? The biggest mystery of physics is where the laws are known, but we don't know exactly what's going on. We don't know the strategy in the middle game. . . ." Feynman once asked an editor of the *Almanac*, "Do the Nobel committees really investigate the personal lives of winners before giving the award?" He was told, "Yes, they certainly do." Amused, Feynman said, "Well, that finally explains something that's puzzled me. I made my prizewinning discovery in 1949, but I was not honored for it until 1965. Now I can see it was my personal life that kept me from getting the award those many years—until the Nobel committee finally saw I had settled down with my 3rd wife and I now had a child, and that I had become the model of a family man."

1966 Alfred Kastler (1902–), French. Work: Discovering and developing optical methods for studying Herzian resonances in atoms.

1967 Hans A. Bethe (1906–), American (b. Germany). Work: Contributing to the theory of nuclear reaction and discovering energy production of the stars.

Behind the Award—When Bethe got the award, he was asked what dangers such an honor might hold. "Well, I think that the main danger is that from now on I may feel I can only do important work," he said.

1968 Luis W. Alvarez (1911–), American. Work: Studies in the physics of subatomic particles and the development of techniques for detecting them.

Behind the Award—Alvarez commanded a large team which came up with the research that won Alvarez the prize. Probably for the 1st time, the Nobel judges recognized the importance of a researcher's ability to administrate, organize, and coordinate a team of people to get the answers to a difficult problem. An associate remarked of Alvarez, "He's a bit of a swashbuckler with great imagination and unusual ideas such as [exploring] the pyramid of Khafre to find hidden chambers." Alvarez also designed the 1st bad-weather landing system for planes (he's an enthusiastic pilot), floated spark chambers to the upper atmosphere to observe high-energy physics, and developed an indoor golf trainer with a photoelectric cell to keep track of the head of the golf club while the golfer swings. One of his golf trainers was given to former President Dwight D. Eisenhower.

1969 Murray Gell-Mann (1929–), American. Work: Research into the interactions of elementary particles, including the theoretical model that he calls "the Eight-fold Way."
Behind the Award—Fond of literary allusions, round-faced, bespectacled Murray Gell-Mann chose the name "the Eight-fold Way" from Buddhism: "This is the noble truth that leads to cessation of pain. This is the noble Eight-fold way—right views, right intentions, right speech, right action. . . ." Gell-Mann got into physics very casually. When filling out an application form, he had to put down his future occupation. He wanted to be an archaeologist (he still pursues it as a hobby), but his father said there was no money in that and suggested engineering. Gell-Mann hated engineering, so he put down physics. Gell-Mann is awed by the simplicity of his discoveries. "Why should an aesthetic criterion be successful so often? Is it just that it satisfies physicists? I think there is only one answer —nature is inherently beautiful," he says.

1970 Louis Néel (1904–), French.
Hannes Alfvén (1908–), Swedish. Work: Research into ferromagnetism and antiferromagnetism as well as basic work in magnetohydrodynamics.

1971 Dennis Gabor (1900–), British (b. Hungary). Work: Inventor of holography.
Behind the Award—A refugee from Hitler's Germany, Gabor invented holography, a method of taking 3-dimensional photographs using laser beams. He 1st got the idea when watching a tennis match at Rugby in 1947, when he wondered if different 3-dimensional images of play from various parts of the court could be filmed. He set out to find a way to do it and, years later, was successful. He named his invention "holography" from the Greek words for *whole* and *image*. The viewer of a holographic image can look around objects to see other objects at 1st hidden. Holography is now an important industry with applications in component testing and the storing of computer data. It may eventually be the basis for 3-dimensional television and movies. With 100 patents to his credit, Gabor said upon winning the prize, "I feel that I am very, very lucky. Every Nobel winner is lucky, but I'm extra lucky. Most people get the prize for one thing they spent a long life in science to accomplish. I'm an outsider. I worked in industrial laboratories most of my life, and industrial workers rarely get

Nobel prizes. What I did was not pure science. I consider it an invention."

1972 John Bardeen (1908–), American. Leon N. Cooper (1920–), American. John R. Schrieffer (1929–), American. Work: Discovery of a theory explaining superconductivity, the property of supercold metals to lose their electrical resistance.
Behind the Award—Bardeen was one of the few people to win a Nobel Prize twice. He shared the prize for physics in 1956. (The other 2 people to win the prize 2 times were Marie Curie and Linus Pauling.) The idea for the discovery 1st came to Schrieffer while he was riding the New York subway. Work was completed in January, 1957. On the day it was done, a colleague of Bardeen's met him in the hall. He reports the meeting: "It seemed we must have stood there for 5 minutes without him saying a word. Finally he said, 'Well, we've solved the problem of superconductivity.' It was the most enormous news I had ever heard. He just had to tell someone, but he couldn't get started." Students, who once called the shy professor "Smiling Jack," now call him "Whispering John." The morning that he won the prize, Bardeen was unable to open his electronically controlled garage door, a device made possible by the work for which he had won the prize in 1956. Cooper, the 3rd member of the team, is called the "Swinging Scientist" because of his mod clothes and his love of art and French cooking. The discovery, called the BCS theory from their initials, may make it possible for electricity to be transmitted for long distances without any power loss.

1973 Ivar Giaever (1930–), American (b. Norway).
Leo Esaki (1926–), American (b. Japan). Work: Research in miniature electronics.
Brian David Josephson (1941–), British. Work: Research regarding semiconductors and superconductors.
Behind the Award—The prize this year was $122,000. Esaki, on winning it, said, "Americans think an American Esaki won the award. On the other hand, the Japanese think a Japanese Esaki won it, and that's fine with me because science is international and the Nobel Prize is international."

1974 Antony Hewish (1924–), English. Work: Invention of new uses of small radio-telescopes.
Martin Ryle (1918–), English. Work: Discovery of pulsars in outer space.
Behind the Award—The 1st Nobel Prize ever given to astronomers. Aware of radio signals or pulses from afar, Dr. Hewish

thought they might be coming from intelligent life outside the solar system. He finally concluded, according to *The New York Times*, they "were coming from relatively small celestial objects that were spinning. A spinning source of radio waves will give the impression when viewed from one point of turning off and on repeatedly." Dr. Ryle's radiotelescopes "had extended man's view of the universe far beyond the limits of light telescopes . . . it is now possible to 'see' objects in the universe several billion light-years away. A light-year is about 3.6 trillion mi."

—A.E.

CHEMISTRY

1901 Jacobus H. van't Hoff (1852–1911), Dutch. Work: Discovered laws of chemical dynamics and osmotic pressure.
Behind the Award—For the 1st few years, the Academy's problem was not to whom to give the prize, but in what order. Clearly, there were many who were deserving. Van't Hoff, in 1874, had founded the new branch of stereochemistry and, if the prize had then existed, would have won it easily. But his 1874 achievements were, by 1901, ineligible under Alfred Nobel's standards for the award. Van't Hoff had, however, continued his brilliant work in the fields of chemical reaction and osmosis. Of 20 proposals submitted by nominators for the 1901 consideration, Van't Hoff's name was the choice on 11, an obvious mandate for the Academy to follow.
1902 Emil H. Fischer (1852–1919), German. Work: Synthesized sugars and purines.
1903 Svante A. Arrhenius (1859–1927), Swedish. Work: Developed theory of electrolytic dissociation.
Behind the Award—Arrhenius received nominations for both the chemistry and the physics prizes. In each category, he was obviously the 1st choice by the majority of the proposers, raising the unique question of which prize to give him. The Committee for Chemistry offered a compromise: award Arrhenius half of each prize. The Academy debated the issue long and hard. Unlike King Solomon, it could find no way to split the Swede's theory into 2 equal halves that would please both physicists and chemists. Tempers rose on the Committee for Physics, which had no intention of allowing its sister committee to award half of its own prize. Rebuffed, the Chemistry Committee, by a 3–2 vote, elected to set back the decision on Arrhenius for a year. In the end, after a chemist quietly mentioned that the procrastination might damage Arrhenius' standing

among world scientists, the Academy voided the year's delay and selected him for the current prize.
1904 William Ramsay (1852–1916), British. Work: Discovered the gaseous, indifferent elements of helium, argon, neon, krypton, and xenon.
1905 Adolf von Baeyer (1835–1917), German. Work: Researches on organic dyestuffs and hydroaromatic compounds.
1906 Henri Moissan (1852–1907), French. Work: Isolated the element fluorine, and developed the electric furnace.
Behind the Award—The name of Frenchman Marcelin Berthelot had been suggested nearly every year, to honor his rank as one of the founders of 19th-century thermochemistry. He had, in fact, won Britain's Davy Medal, awarded by the Royal Society. But the Academy's 1906 nominees included another Frenchman, 25 years younger, whose accomplishments were more current: Moissan. The case for Mendeleev, discoverer of the periodic table, had been seriously damaged when one member of the Chemistry Committee eloquently pointed out that Mendeleev's work had been derived from that of Cannizzaro. To honor Mendeleev, he noted, without also crediting Cannizzaro would be unfair. Put to the vote in the chemistry section of the Academy, Mendeleev was scrapped and Moissan squeaked by on a split decision, 5–4. Berthelot's age had been a consideration in passing him over. Ironically, both Berthelot and Moissan died in the following year.
1907 Eduard Buchner (1860–1917), German. Work: Discovered cell-free fermentation.
1908 Ernest Rutherford (1871–1937), British. Work: Investigated the artificial disintegration of the elements and the chemistry of radioactive substances.
Behind the Award—The groundwork of Rutherford's research in radioactivity revolutionized scientific thinking in both the physics and chemistry disciplines. But his nomination again brought the Arrhenius dilemma of 1903 to the surface: for physics? Or chemistry? There was a strong backing for Gabriel Lippmann in physics, for his photographic method to reproduce colors by an interference technique. Yet Rutherford could not be overlooked. He had earned a reputation as one of the greatest scientists of all time. The 2 committees met to review the work for which he had been nominated, and unanimously decided that it could be rated as of greater importance to future chemical research than to the field of physics. They ignored the fact that Rutherford's experimentation to determine the nature of alpha

radiation employed techniques ordinarily those of a physicist, not a chemist. His concept of the atom, later developed more fully by Niels Bohr, laid the foundation for studies in nuclear physics. The device used for counting the alpha particles, codeveloped with H. Geiger, was basically a physicist's tool. Nevertheless, the vote was cast to honor the New Zealand-born director of the physical laboratory at the University of Manchester, England, in chemistry instead.

1909 Wilhelm Ostwald (1853–1931), German. Work: Redefined catalysis and the conditions for chemical equilibrium and velocities in chemical reactions.

Behind the Award—Both Van't Hoff and Arrhenius received their just recognition by the Academy almost with the inception of the prizes. A 3rd great scientist, Ostwald, who was also responsible for the rapid rise of the new discipline, physical chemistry, had to wait. Of the 3 men, Ostwald's published works gave greater impetus to universal acceptance of physical chemistry theories, but Nobel rules forbid an award as a general recognition of overall excellence. When his definitive discoveries in catalysis and the related researches were made public, the German could no longer be shunted aside, having qualified without reservation. Moreover, the Academy could once again turn to physical chemistry for its winner without being accused of favoritism toward it, since in the years intervening since 1903, other branches of chemistry had been acknowledged.

1910 Otto Wallach (1847–1931), German. Work: Pioneered research into the field of alicyclic substances.

1911 Marie S. Curie (1867–1934), French (b. Poland). Work: Discovered the elements of radium and polonium, isolated the element radium, and studied its compounds.

Behind the Award—Pierre and Marie Curie shared the 1903 prize in Physics with Becquerel for their work on radiation phenomena. In 1898, the French couple, working laboriously with pitchblende—only one gram of radium salts could be obtained from 8 tons of pitchblende—reported their discovery of the new elements radium and polonium. It remained for Arrhenius to declare, as one of her nominators, that Madame Curie's discovery of radium ranked as the "most important during the last century of chemical research." Technically, the 1903 Physics Prize award presented a possible obstacle for the selection of Curie again, since radium had been discovered during the experimentation leading to the earlier honor. Fortunately, the committee noted and took advantage of a specificity: the discovery of radium, per se, had not yet been the subject for an award. Had Pierre Curie not been killed in a street accident in 1906, he, too, would have been named as a prize recipient. Madame Curie's selection for a 2nd prize was not equaled, in any category, until Dr. Linus Pauling received 1st the Chemistry Prize in 1954 and then the Peace Prize in 1962.

1912 Victor Grignard (1871–1935), French. Work: Discovered the so-called Grignard reagent.

Paul Sabatier (1854–1941), French. Work: Developed a method for hydrogenating organic compounds in the presence of finely divided metals.

Behind the Award—Grignard protested the decision made by the Nobel committee, saying the award should have been split between Sabatier and his colleague, the Abbé Jean-Baptiste Senderens. He added further to the committee's embarrassment when he suggested that a 2nd prize then be given, to himself and his teacher, Barbier.

1913 Alfred Werner (1866–1919), Swiss (b. Germany). Work: Promulgated new theories on atom linkages in molecules.

Behind the Award—Werner's theories were attacked, and charges were leveled that his prizewinning work had been incomplete. Ten years later, G. N. Lewis, a codiscoverer with Harold Urey of heavy water in 1932, defended the Swiss's ingenious deductions with his own pioneer work on chemical valence, saying, "While some of his theoretical conclusions have not proved convincing, he marshaled in a masterful manner a great array of facts which showed the incongruities into which chemists had been led by the existing structural formulae of inorganic chemistry."

1914 Theodore W. Richards (1868–1929), American. Work: Determined exact atomic weights for a great number of elements.

Behind the Award—For the 1st time, the Academy acknowledged a non-European with the choice of Harvard professor Richards. The selection compensated partially for the ignoring of his compatriot, Josiah W. Gibbs, Yale professor of mathematical physics at the turn of the century. Gibbs's work in thermodynamics unquestionably qualified him for nomination, along with Jacobus van't Hoff and Emil Fischer, for one of the 1st awards. Had he lived beyond 1903, Gibbs would have been a certain winner.

1915 Richard M. Willstätter (1872–1942), German. Work: Researches on coloring matter in the vegetable kingdom, especially on chlorophyll.

1916 No Award

1917 No Award

1918 Fritz Haber (1868–1934), German.

Work: Invented the process of synthesizing ammonia from nitrogen and hydrogen.

Behind the Award—Haber's early experiments, for which he was awarded the prize, found that temperatures of about 500° centigrade and pressures of about 200 atmospheres were optimum for producing ammonia, using powdered osmium or uranium as a catalyst. In later mass production, manufacturers learned, to their initial sorrow, that Haber's use of carbon steel for the reaction chamber was dangerous. At high temperature and under great pressure, hydrogen decarburized and penetrated into the red-hot iron. The chamber became very brittle and subject to explosive cracking, on the order of an enormous hand grenade. Frequent explosions occurred before a revised chamber design, contributed by Carl Bosch, solved the problem. Haber, however, had been awarded the honor for his method, now used by nearly the entire world, with Carl Bosch's adaptation, for the production of nitrogen fertilizers.

1919 No Award

1920 Walther H. Nernst (1864–1941), German. Work: For his thermochemical researches.

1921 Frederick Soddy (1877–1956), British. Work: Researched radioactive substances and isotopes.

1922 Francis W. Aston (1877–1945), British. Work: Discovered, by using the mass spectrograph, isotopes of many nonradioactive elements, and verified the whole-number rule.

Behind the Award—In 1815, William Prout originally proposed a whole-number rule which assumed that all elements were simply multiples of the atomic weight of hydrogen. The Academy noted that Prout's hypothesis of a "primordial" atom had been on the right track, except that science had found that the atomic building block consisted of a positively-charged nucleus with a varying number of negatively-charged electrons revolving around it. In his acceptance speech, Aston warned that future research workers should beware of releasing the energy of the atom, fearing that it might prove uncontrollable. He speculated that all of the earth's hydrogen "might be transformed at once and the success of the experiment published at large to the universe as a new star." Research scientists at Alamogordo, N.M., in 1945, proved that he was wrong, although they were not absolutely certain until the 1st atomic bomb had been experimentally exploded.

1923 Fritz Pregl (1869–1930), Austrian. Work: Invented a method for organic microanalysis.

Behind the Award—Although 23 Germans have won the prize, Pregl is the only one ever to win for Austria. Prior to 1930, Nobel committee members leaned heavily toward the Germans, awarding them nearly half of the total prizes. Since W.W. II, the emphasis has been overwhelmingly on Great Britain or the U.S. with these 2 nations producing almost 60% of the winners. While some critics may now accuse the committee of bias *toward* the U.S. or Britain, as supposedly was done in the early years with the German selections, the most probable explanation for the skewed Anglo-U.S. concentration may be better research facilities and greater financial grants. No one, however, can ever accuse the committee of bias toward their own countrymen—only 4 Swedes have ever been accorded the honor in chemistry, the last being in 1948.

1924 No Award

1925 Richard A. Zsigmondy (1865–1929), German (b. Austria). Work: Clarified the nature of colloidal solutions.

1926 Theodor Svedberg (1884–1971), Swedish. Work: Research on colloidal systems.

Behind the Award—When the Academy awarded Svedberg the prize for the experimental results in the field of colloidal chemistry, it could easily have given him a 2nd award for his invention, the ultra-centrifuge. Developed primarily to assist him in his work at the University of Uppsala, Sweden, the tool is now a primary aid in the investigation of substances of high molecular weights, and is particularly valuable for studies with the giant protein molecules.

1927 Heinrich O. Wieland (1877–1957), German. Work: Researched bile acids and analogous substances.

1928 Adolf O. R. Windaus (1876–1959), German. Work: Research on the sterols and their relation to the vitamins.

Behind the Award—Having chosen Heinrich Wieland in 1927 for his researches in the bile acids, the committee in the following year voted for recognition of Windaus's closely related work with sterols. Windaus, in fact, had discovered that the sterols and the bile acids studied by Wieland came from the same parent substance. The committee's decision was justified. The studies with sterols led the expatriate German, director of the chemical laboratories at the University of Göttingen since 1915, into vitamin D research and the discovery of vitamin D_3, the main antirachitic component of vitamin D.

1929 Arthur Harden (1865–1940), British. Hans von Euler-Chelpin (1873–1964), Swedish (b. Germany). Work: Investigated the fermentation of sugar and of fermentative enzymes.

1930 Hans Fischer (1881–1945), German. Work: Synthesized hemin and researched both hemin and chlorophyll.

Behind the Award—According to Alfred Nobel's will, the prizes were to be awarded ". . . to those persons who shall contribute most materially to benefiting mankind during the year immediately preceding." Fischer is one of the few laureates who have met the qualification literally, having completed his work on hemin synthesis during 1929. Both a medical doctor and a research chemist, he confirmed that hemin—the coloring matter in blood—and chlorophyll—the substance giving green plants their color—can be derived from the same porphyrin.

1931 Carl Bosch (1874–1940), German.
Friedrich Bergius (1884–1949), German. Work: Invented and developed chemical high-pressure methods.

Behind the Award—The Haber-Bosch method for synthetic production of ammonia is now in use almost everywhere in the world, to manufacture nitrogen fertilizers. The annual total amount is calculated in millions of tons.

1932 Irving Langmuir (1881–1957), American. Work: Discovered fundamental properties of absorbed films and investigated surface chemistry.

1933 No Award

1934 Harold C. Urey (1893–), American. Work: Discovered heavy hydrogen, or deuterium.

Behind the Award—Working from Aston's isotope researches, Urey announced the discovery of heavy hydrogen in 1931 during his work at Columbia University. The Nobel committee gave Urey full credit, but the chemist set the record straight during his Nobel Prize acceptance speech in Stockholm. He described the valued assistance he received from his research associate, Dr. G. M. Murphy, during the studies. Inadvertently, the award to Urey helped the U.S. to win the war against Japan in 1945. The eminent recognition he had received brought him into the "Manhattan Project," the U.S. military program set up for the development of the atomic bomb. As head of the gaseous-diffusion program for uranium separation, Urey's fame attracted the scientific talent which produced the nuclear bomb that forced the Japanese surrender.

1935 Frédéric Joliet-Curie (1900–1958), French.
Irène Joliet-Curie (1897–1956), French. Work: Synthesized new radioactive elements.

Behind the Award—Irène Joliet-Curie, the daughter of Nobel Prize winners Pierre and Marie Curie, became director at the Curie Laboratory of the Radium Institute, Paris, succeeding her mother in 1932. The research for which she was jointly awarded the 1935 prize eventually killed her. In 1956, she died from leukemia caused by overexposure to the radioactive materials used in the experiments. Her husband, Frédéric Joliet-Curie, became head of the French atomic energy commission in 1946. Four years later, the uproar caused by his avowed dedication to the French Communist party forced his resignation.

1936 Peter J. W. Debye (1884–1966), American (b. Holland). Work: Studied molecular structure by investigations on dipole moments and on diffraction of X rays and electrons in gases.

1937 Walter N. Haworth (1883–1950), British. Work: Researched carbohydrates and vitamin C.
Paul Karrer (1889–1971), Swiss (b. Russia). Work: Researched carotinoids, flavins, and vitamins A and B.

1938 Richard Kuhn (1900–1967), Austrian. Work: Researched carotinoids and vitamins.

Behind the Award—Kuhn was forbidden by Hitler to accept the award. (See also: 1939.)

1939 Adolf F. J. Butenandt (1903–), German. Work: Studied the chemistry of sex hormones, isolated and named the male sex hormone, androsterone.
Leopold Ružicka (1887–), Swiss (b. Yugoslavia). Work: Researches on polymethylenes and higher terpenes.

Behind the Award—The Swiss professor from Zurich appeared in Stockholm for the December ceremonies. The German, Butenandt, formally notified the Academy that, in accordance with the German national policy established by Adolf Hitler, he would not accept the award. Ten months later, on October 1, the prize money reverted to the general Nobel Foundation fund when Butenandt did not appear to claim it. In 1948, after the Third Reich had been defeated in W.W. II, both Butenandt and Richard Kuhn, the chemistry winner for 1938 who had also declined his award, wrote to the Academy, expressing regret for their refusals, made under threat of violence. The Academy by then could do nothing about the forfeited prize money, but, by special decree, it awarded the 2 Germans their diplomas and gold medals in July, 1949.

1940 No Award

1941 No Award

1942 No Award

1943 Georg von Hevesy (1885–1966), Hungarian. Work: Used isotopes as tracer elements in researches on chemical processes.

1944 Otto Hahn (1879–1968), German. Work: Discovered the fissionability of uranium and other heavy atomic nuclei elements.

Behind the Award—The $34,000 prize was awarded to Hahn while he was being held in military custody by the U.S. Army from 1944 to 1946. Otto Hahn had continued his experiments under Hitler and in April, 1946, after his release by the U.S., he became the president of Kaiser Wilhelm Gesellschaft, the highest scientific position in postwar Germany. Because his inability to claim his prize money within the one-year rule had not been of his own choosing, the King of Sweden interceded on his behalf and the requirement was waived. The neutral Swedes overlooked his Nazi associations in favor of his great contribution to science. Insisted one Nobel judge: "Dr. Hahn is the true father of the atomic bomb. He discovered it long before the Americans, and he alone deserved the recognition and the prize."

1945 Artturi I. Virtanen (1895–1973), Finnish. Work: Researches and inventions in agricultural chemistry, and especially in the area of fodder preservation.

1946 James B. Sumner (1887–1955), American. Work: Discovered that enzymes can be crystallized.

John H. Northrup (1891–), American.

Wendell M. Stanley (1904–1971), American. Work: Prepared enzymes and virus proteins in a pure form.

1947 Robert Robinson (1886–1975), British. Work: Researches on certain vegetable products, particularly alkaloids.

1948 Arne W. K. Tiselius (1902–1971), Swedish. Work: Discovered new methods of separating and detecting colloids and the serum proteins.

1949 William F. Giauque (1895–), American (b. Canada). Work: Studied the behavior of substances at extremely low temperatures.

1950 Otto P. H. Diels (1876–1954), German.

Kurt Alder (1902–1958), German. Work: Developed the diene synthesis.

1951 Edwin M. McMillan (1907–), American.

Glenn T. Seaborg (1912–), American. Work: Discoveries in the field of the transuranium elements.

1952 Archer J. P. Martin (1910–), British. Richard L. M. Synge (1914–), British. Work: Discovered partition chromatography.

1953 Hermann Staudinger (1881–1965), German. Work: Discoveries in the chemistry of macromolecular substances.

1954 Linus C. Pauling (1901–), American. Work: Researches into the nature of the chemical valence bond and its application to complex substances.

Behind the Award—Pauling used basic theories of quantum mechanics to propound his explanation of the valence forces binding the molecule together. Long a vehement critic of nuclear tests that sought improved ways to blow the atom apart—the antithesis of his lifelong work—he wrote *No More War!* in 1958 to support his beliefs. The Nobel committee awarded him the 1962 Peace Prize for his contributions to world peace, the 1st man in the history of the prizes to be given 2 awards. (See also: Physics, 1972).

1955 Vincent du Vigneaud (1901–), American. Work: Researches on sulfur compounds, the pituitary hormones, and the 1st synthesis of a polypeptide hormone.

1956 Cyril N. Hinshelwood (1897–1967), British.

Nikolai N. Semenov (1896–), Russian. Work: Performed parallel but independent studies on the mechanism of chemical reactions.

Behind the Award—The investigations which brought the U.S.S.R. its sole Chemistry Prize, shared with Hinshelwood, were in the specialized branch of chemistry called reaction kinetics. Only twice before (in 1901 and 1909) had the Academy given awards in this field. The 2 scientists, working independently in Leningrad and in Oxford, learned that a great many chemical processes are the result of a chain of reaction as the molecules recombine. Semenov's early work began with experimental studies on explosions. Hinshelwood considered problems of a wider scope.

1957 Alexander R. Todd (1907–), British. Work: Studied the nucleotides and the nucleotidic coenzymes.

1958 Frederick Sanger (1918–), British. Work: Isolated and identified the amino acid components of the insulin molecule.

1959 Jaroslav Heyrovský (1890–1967), Czech. Work: Invented and developed the polarographic method of analysis.

1960 Willard F. Libby (1908–), American. Work: Developed the "atomic time clock" for determining geologic age by measuring the amount of carbon 14 in organic substances.

Behind the Award—With the death of any living thing, the carbon atoms inside its tissues begin to decay at a rate that can be predicted. Libby created the carbon 14 clock, a Geiger-counter device which recorded how much carbon had been lost by an object since its life ended. By figuring the amount of loss, Libby could tell how much time had passed since the object's death. Thus, Libby's time clock could date ancient bones, wood, papyrus as far back as 60,000 years. This discovery proved the Dead Sea Scrolls were authentic and the Piltdown man was a hoax.

1961 Melvin Calvin (1911–), American. Work: Established the chemical reactions which occur during photosynthesis.

1962 Max F. Perutz (1914–), British (b. Austria).

John C. Kendrew (1917–), British. Work: Discovered the molecular structure of myoglobin and hemoglobin.

1963 Karl Ziegler (1898–), German. Giulio Natta (1903–), Italian. Work: Changed simple hydrocarbons into complex molecular compounds.

1964 Dorothy C. Hodgkin (1910–), British. Work: Determined the structure for biochemical substances such as penicillin and vitamin B_{12}.

Behind the Award—Except for the Curies, Mrs. Hodgkin is the only woman to win the Chemistry Prize. Her brilliant analysis of vitamin B_{12}'s structure was ranked as a crowning triumph in the history of X-ray crystallography.

1965 Robert B. Woodward (1917–), American. Work: Developed techniques for the syntheses of involved organic compounds, specifically chlorophyll and sterols.

Behind the Award—Woodward's achievements in synthesis are legion, ranging from quinine, cholesterol, cortisone, to strychnine. His successes with complex substances previously given up on by other scientists led his nominators to remark, "He has shown that almost no synthesis is impossible."

1966 Robert S. Mulliken (1896–), American. Work: Performed fundamental work on chemical bonds and the electronic structure of the molecule by the molecular orbital method.

1967 Manfred Eigen (1927–), German. Ronald G. W. Norrish (1897–), British.

George Porter (1920–), British. Work: Researches on the extremely fast chemical reactions caused by disturbing equilibrium by micro-energy pulsations.

1968 Lars Onsager (1903–), American. Work: Discovered the reciprocal relations which exist between voltage and temperature that fundamentally affect the thermodynamics of irreversible processes such as in living cells.

Behind the Award—The U.S. swept all 3 science categories for the 1st time since 1946. Onsager was honored for the work he published in 1931, when he was only 28. His findings, now called "the reciprocity relations of Onsager," were so far ahead of their time 37 years ago that few scientists understood them. Today, Onsager's hypothesis is universally accepted as the 4th Law of Thermodynamics.

1969 Derek H. R. Barton (1918–), British.

Odd Hassel (1897–), Norwegian. Work: Performed independent researches on conformation analysis, the reaction by certain compounds when their 3-dimensional molecular shape is known.

1970 Luis F. Leloir (1906–), Argentinian (b. France). Work: Discovered the sugar nucleotides and their effect on the biosyntheses of carbohydrates.

Behind the Award—Leloir left Buenos Aires in 1943 to escape the unsettling conditions caused by political turmoil. After working in St. Louis, Mo., with Carl and Gerty Cori, themselves Nobel laureates for 1947 in Physiology and Medicine, he returned to Argentina to head a modern research laboratory placed at his disposal. The nominations that recommended him pointed out that the real test for a discovery's importance lies in the new research it opens up and the secondary discoveries which follow. In the extensive work which has developed with sugar nucleotides since the award, it has been Leloir, however, who has made all the most important discoveries. Actually, he could have been chosen for the prize in Physiology and Medicine just as easily. His sugar nucleotide research may produce a cure for diabetes.

1971 Gerhard Herzberg (1904–), Canadian. Work: Researches into the structure of the molecule, and especially the free radicals.

Behind the Award—The 1st Canadian ever to win the prize, Herzberg was lecturing in the Soviet Union when informed. Initially, he was told he had won the Physics Prize, a natural mistake for the Russians to make since Herzberg had been director of the division of pure physics for the National Research Council of Canada since 1948. Told that he had been the sole winner in his category, the vegetarian widower who climbs mountains for relaxation clapped his hands together gleefully and laughed.

1972 Christian B. Anfinsen (1916–), American.

Stanford Moore (1913–), American. William H. Stein (1911–), American. Work: Pioneered studies in enzymes.

1973 Geoffrey Wilkinson (1921–), British. Ernst Fischer (1918–), German. Work: Researches on the organometallic "sandwich" compounds.

Behind the Award—The Academy, mindful of past charges that their selections had crossed category boundaries on occasion, announced that this year's prize was "in chemistry for chemists." Working independently, the 23rd German and the 19th British chemist to win Nobel Prizes since 1901 studied methods by which organic and metallic compounds can combine. The pioneers in the field of transition metal chemistry initiated experiments that may have found a way to eliminate lead in gasoline, ultimately reducing the automobile exhaust pollution problem that is causing smog in the world's largest cities. Wilkinson, beginning the work for which he was honored in the early 1950s at Harvard, was dismissed there in 1955 "because they thought they could do without me." He now heads one of the top inorganic research groups in the world, based at the Imperial College of Science and Technology, University of London. The prize which he shared was, because of astute investment by the Nobel Foundation, worth approximately $125,000, a 275% increase since 1953.

1974 Paul J. Flory (1910–), American. Work: For researches in polymer chemistry.

—W.K.

Physiology and Medicine

1901 Emil A. von Behring (1854–1917), German. Work: Treatment of diseases, especially diphtheria, through use of antitoxins.
Behind the Award—Also considered for the prize in 1901 were Joseph Lister, who introduced antiseptics to the operating room, and Robert Koch, pioneer in bacteriology.

1902 Ronald Ross (1857–1932), British. Work: Research into the transmission of malaria by the mosquito.
Behind the Award—A young military surgeon, Ross was able to prove what other scientists had suspected—that a certain type of mosquito spread malaria. At the time, Ross was working in India. His plans for doing research with human beings were stymied by the natives, who wanted nothing to do with inoculation. So he switched to studying birds, and was able to prove that the *Culex* mosquito was the culprit in transmission of bird malaria. His discovery spurred mosquito control through such methods as swamp drainage.

1903 Niels R. Finsen (1860–1904), Danish. Work: Use of concentrated light rays to treat skin diseases, especially *lupus vulgaris* (skin tuberculosis).
Behind the Award—Watching a cat sunning itself in the street gave Niels Finsen the idea that light rays had healing properties. During his lifetime, he treated over 2,000 people, including himself, using this therapy. When he received the prize, he was in a wheelchair, doomed to die within the year. He tried to give his prize money to his smallpox institute, but his friends persuaded him to keep half

for his family. They matched his gift to the institute to make up the difference.

1904 Ivan P. Pavlov (1849–1936), Russian. Work: Study of gastric juice secretions in the digestive system.
Behind the Award—Pavlov, the only Russian to win a Nobel Prize under the Czars, was the man who, in his famous experiment where he induced dogs to salivate at a non-food stimulus, discovered conditioned reflexes. This discovery had tremendous impact on the development of psychology. However, Pavlov did not receive the award for this epoch-making experiment, but for other work he did on the physiology of digestion.

1905 Robert Koch (1843–1910), German. Work: Discovery of the bacillus which causes tuberculosis.
Behind the Award—The biggest fiasco in Nobel history. Koch was on his way to discovering a serum, tuberculin, to combat tuberculosis. Kaiser Wilhelm II got Koch nominated for the Nobel Prize. Impressed, the Nobel judges gave Koch the prize for tuberculin. Six months later, Koch's cure began to kill. The serum proved imperfect, and the Nobel medicine judges were condemned as fools.

1906 Camillo Golgi (c. 1843–1925), Italy. Santiago Ramón y Cajal (1852–1934), Spain. Work: Research on the nervous system and the distribution of cells.

1907 Charles L. A. Laveran (1845–1922), France. Work: Study of disease caused by protozoa.

1908 Paul Ehrlich (1845–1915), German. Elie Metchnikoff (1845–1916), French (b. Russia). Work: Introduction of quantitative methods and other work on immunology.
Behind the Award—The Nobel committee had some doubts about awarding the prize to Ehrlich because of criticism of his "side-chain theory." However, they gave it to him anyway. Ehrlich felt that certain disease organisms had an affinity for specific body organs; he created modern clinical hematology; he discovered that the tubercle bacillus is acid-fast. One of his greatest achievements was the production of preparation 606, an arsenic compound called salvarsan, that cured syphilis. Kaiser Wilhelm II was very pleased with Ehrlich for winning the award. He was so pleased that he invited Ehrlich to an audience, during which he suggested that the scientist find a cure for cancer. (The Kaiser was worried about cancer in his family.) When Ehrlich refused to make any promises about a cancer cure, the Kaiser ended the audience.

1909 Emil Theodor Kocher (1841–1917), Swiss. Work: Work on the thyroid gland.

1910 Albrecht Kossell (1853–1927), German. Work: Study of cell chemistry.

1911 Allvar Gullstrand (1862–1930), Swedish. Work: Research on the refraction of light through the eye (ocular dioptrics).

1912 Alexis Carrel (1873–1944), American (b. France). Work: Development of surgical techniques—vascular suture and transplantation of blood vessels and organs.

Behind the Award—A letter from a Washington, D.C., physician: "I spoke with one of the Nobel Prize committee, who was active at the time [and] the name of Dr. Harvey Cushing came up for selection in the field of medicine. The Swedish doctor told me that after it became apparent that the Nobel Prize was awarded to Dr. Alexis Carrel for a work which was subsequently demonstrated not to be his in origin, the Nobel Prize committee in medicine simply and flatly decided that never again would the prize be awarded a surgeon. The prize was denied to Dr. Cushing on this basis alone."

1913 Charles R. Richet (1850–1935), French. Work: Research on anaphylaxis (allergies).

Behind the Award—It was by accident that Richet discovered the effects of prolonged exposure in allergic reactions. In 1898, he was trying to find the toxic dose of poison from a sea anemone, by testing an extract made from anemone tentacles on dogs. To the survivors of the 1st round of tests he gave smaller doses than he had the 1st time. All of them got sick, much to his surprise, and one died, even though the dose was one he considered below lethal level. He reached the conclusion that this "induced sensitization" was partially caused by changes in the body brought about by the 1st dose. This led to research in allergy and the realization that it can be due to exposure to anything in the environment—strawberries, cat hair, house dust, or one's spouse.

1914 Robert Bárány (1876–1936), Austrian. Work: Study of the inner ear.

1915 No Award
1916 No Award
1917 No Award

Behind the No Award—The award was suspended during W.W. I. In 1917, however, Ross G. Harrison was recommended for the prize for his work in tissue culture, but of course could not receive it. Later, he was again mentioned for a prize, but the committee decided then that his discovery was "too old," and, on 2nd thought, not important enough. Many scientists disagree with that assessment.

1918 No Award

1919 Jules J. P. V. Bordet (1870–1961), Belgian. Work: Discoveries in immunology.

Behind the Award—Bordet, like Harrison, had been considered for some time by the committee. Had he not had several powerful supporters, he might have been passed over as Harrison was.

1920 Schack August S. Krogh (1874–1949), Danish. Work: Discovery of how blood-capillary action is regulated.

1921 No Award

1922 Archibald V. Hill (1886–   ), English. Work: Discoveries concerning heat production through muscular activity.

Otto F. Meyerhof (1894–1951), American (b. Germany). Work: Finding the correlation between the lactic acid and oxygen in the muscles.

1923 Frederick G. Banting (1891–1941), Canadian.

John J. R. Macleod (1876–1935), Canadian. Work: Discovery of insulin.

Behind the Award—There was a big feud when these 2 shared the prize. Banting said that when he made his discovery, Macleod had not even been in the laboratory. Therefore, Banting gave half his prize money to another doctor who had been present in the laboratory. Macleod, who had participated in earlier research, countered by giving half of his winnings to someone who had worked with him.

1924 Willem Einthoven (1860–1927), Dutch. Work: Invention of the electrocardiograph.

Behind the Award—The committee was somewhat reluctant to award a prize in Medicine and Physiology to an inventor. They thought he might more logically receive the prize in Physics. However, Einthoven proved himself worthy by showing the valuable results of the electrocardiogram's clinical use.

1925 No Award

1926 Johannes A. G. Fibiger (1867–1928), Danish. Work: Cancer research.

Behind the Award—Another goof by the committee. The conclusions Fibiger drew from his research were all wrong. Twice burned, the committee was very cautious after this. It wasn't until 1966 that it made another award for cancer research, even though there were several breakthroughs during the interval.

1927 Julius Wagner-Jauregg (1857–1940), Austrian. Work: Discovery of the use of malaria to combat paralysis.

1928 Charles J. H. Nicolle (1866–1936), French. Work: Research on typhus.

1929 Christiaan Eijkman (1858–1930), Dutch. Work: Discovery of Vitamin B.

Frederick G. Hopkins (1861–1947), English. Work: Discovery of vitamin A.

1930 Karl Landsteiner (1868–1943), American (b. Austria). Work: Discovering human blood groups.

Behind the Award—In discovering human blood groups, Landsteiner revolutionized blood transfusion and influenced serology and immunochemistry. Later, he and A. S. Weiner discovered the Rh factor, which can cause fatal blood incompatibility in newborns.

1931 Otto H. Warberg (1883–1970), German. Work: Discovery of certain aspects of the respiratory enzyme.

1932 Edgar D. Adrian (1889–), English.
Charles S. Sherrington (1857–1952), English. Work: Research on the nervous system, particularly the function of neurons.

Behind the Award—Previous to winning the award in 1932, Sherrington had received 134 nominations, beginning in 1902. If he hadn't lived so long, he might never have received the prize. His greatest discovery—his magisterial concept of the "integrative action of the nervous system"—was not mentioned in his citation.

1933 Thomas H. Morgan (1866–1945), American. Work: Discovery of the function of chromosomes in heredity.

1934 George R. Minot (1885–1950), American.
William P. Murphy (1892–), American.
George H. Whipple (1878–), American. Work: Discovery that liver extract increases formation of red blood cells.

1935 Hans Spemann (1869–1941), German. Work: Research in the development of the embryo.

Behind the Award—At the time Spemann received the award, German scientists were fleeing the Hitler regime in droves.

1936 Henry H. Dale (1875–1968), English.
Otto Loewi (1873–1961), American (b. Germany). Work: Discoveries relating to nerve impulses.

1937 Albert von Szent-Györgyi (1893–), American (b. Hungary). Work: Research in metabolism and vitamins.

1938 Corneille J. F. Heymans (1892–1968), Belgian. Work: Discovery of how the carotid sinus affects respiration rate.

1939 Gerhard Domagk (1895–1964), German. Work: Discovery of the 1st sulfa drug.

Behind the Award—W.W. II started before the prize was awarded to Domagk, who was a German. Even so, the majority of the professors at the Caroline Institute wanted to give it to him for his discovery of the 1st "miracle drug," which saved so many lives during the war. However, the Kultur Ministerium in Berlin sent a telegram to the Swedish Foreign Office, saying that the award wasn't wanted. The Nobel committee gave

the prize to Domagk anyway. Domagk tried to find out what the German Government wanted to do, but without success. He wrote the Nobel committee thanking them, adding that he had to await his Government's decision before he could accept. He was asked to send a copy of his letter to the German Ministry for Foreign Affairs. Shortly after, he was arrested and taken at gunpoint to police headquarters, where he was treated roughly and interrogated by an SS officer. He was released, then arrested again, and forced to turn down the prize. Since this was the 1st time the prize had been declined, the committee had to make a decision about what to do in such cases. They decided they would return the prize money to the general fund if it were not collected before October 1 of the following year. After the war, Domagk wanted to accept the prize, but it was too late. However, he was invited to the 1947 Nobel Festival, where his achievements were praised and he was given a diploma and gold medal, but no money.

1940 No Award
1941 No Award
1942 No Award
1943 Henrik Dam (1895–), Danish. Work: Discovery of vitamin K.
Edward A. Doisy (1893–), American, Work: Discovery of chemical nature of vitamin K.

1944 E. Joseph Erlanger (1874–1965), American.
Herbert S. Gasser (1888–1963), American. Work: Research in functions of single nerve fibers.

1945 Alexander Fleming (1881–1955), British.
Howard W. Florey (1898–1968), British.
Ernst B. Chain (1906–), British (b. Germany). Work: Discovery of penicillin and its ability to cure certain diseases.

Behind the Award—Experimenting with staphylococcal germs in 1928, Sir Alexander Fleming found a blue-green mold on one of his culture plates that was close to an open window. The germs in the culture were dead. Fleming, in his publication of the results of the experiments, wrote one paragraph on the idea that the mold might be a disease-fighter. Ten years later, Florey and Chain extracted a small amount of the active principal from the mold. To test it out, they gave 8 mice a dose of streptococci, then, according to Florey, "We sat up through the night injecting penicillin every 3 hours into the 4 mice. I must confess that it was one of the more exciting moments when we found in the morning that all the untreated mice were dead and all the penicillin-treated ones alive." Penicillin saved the lives of countless wounded soldiers in 1942. It soon was lauded as a miracle drug. It was true that it could cure blood poisoning, bone infections, pneumonia, and gonorrhea. Fleming predicted that it would one day be used in toothpaste and lipsticks. Of course, because of its side effects and the fact that it becomes less effective with repeated use, his prediction has not come true. The 1st potent strain of penicillin in the U.S. was developed from mold found on a rotten cantaloupe in a Peoria, Ill., market. The discoverers of the usefulness of penicillin made very little money from it. When Dr. Chain heard that they had won the prize, he said, "Is it true? Are you sure? After all, no one in our group has ever received a penny out of penicillin."

1946 Hermann Joseph Muller (1890–1967), American. Work: Discovery of genetic effects of X-ray irradiation.
Behind the Award—A controversial figure, Muller was extremely energetic and had a good sense of humor. He liked to say that the evolutionary history of his hair had been from brown to gray to bald. The discovery for which he received the prize had to do with genetic mutation, a process that concerned him all his life. The atom bomb greatly alarmed him; he felt it could have adverse genetic effects on future generations. In 1955, with 8 other scientists including Einstein, he signed a paper appealing to all countries to give up war because the hydrogen bomb threatened the "continued existence of mankind." He also wanted to freeze the sperm of gifted people for use in the future, a desire that brought upon his head the wrath of the Catholic Church. According to *The Catholic World*, such ideas would turn the world into an animal farm.

1947 Carl F. Cori (1896–), American (b. Czechoslovakia).
Gerty T. Cori (1896–1957), American (b. Czechoslovakia). Work: Study of carbohydrate metabolism and enzymes.
Bernardo A. Houssay (1887–1971), Argentine. Work: Discovering the function of a hormone produced by the pituitary gland in the metabolism of sugar.
Behind the Award—Houssay was the 1st South American scientist to win a Nobel Prize. The year before he received it, dictator Juan Perón had him fired from the University of Buenos Aires because he had signed a petition favoring "democracy and American solidarity." Perón had the newspapers attack the Swedes, saying they had "political ends in mind" in giving the prize to Houssay. Perón called Houssay "the gland detective who could have done research more useful on tuberculosis and syphilis."

1948 Paul H. Müller (1899–1965), Swiss. Work: Discovery that DDT could kill insects.
Behind the Award—A DDT substance was described as early as 1874. However, Paul Müller, who was not a medical man, found out almost 70 years later that it killed insects. He was then working with the Colorado beetle. Since DDT is a contact poison, the beetle larvae were paralyzed even though they hadn't consumed it. After Müller's discovery, the insecticide was used to control a Naples typhus epidemic in 1944. Though DDT has saved millions of lives, it has become controversial for several reasons. It leads to ecological imbalances. It can be carried far from the point at which it is 1st used. It takes a long time to degrade, so that all animals and humans now have some DDT in their tissues.

1949 Walter R. Hess (1881–), Swiss. Work: Research into how parts of the brain control body organs.
Egas Moniz (1874–1955), Portuguese. Work: Discovery of the value of prefrontal lobotomy for certain mental diseases.
Behind the Award—When Moniz 1st introduced prefrontal lobotomy, a surgical severing of nerve fibers which relaxes tension and relieves depression in the mentally disturbed, it was hailed as a great step in medicine. However, it wasn't long before the honeymoon was over. Reports said that the operation turned people into human vegetables, dulled their consciences, cut away their souls. After that, prefrontal lobotomy was not much used. Today, behavior change through much more delicate surgery has regained some favor, through such operations remain controversial.

1950 Philip S. Hench (1896–1965), American.
Edward C. Kendall (1886–1972), American.
Taedus Reichstein (1897–), Swiss (b. Poland). Work: Hormone research, including the discovery of cortisone.

1951 Max Theiler (1899–), American (b. South Africa). Work: Development of a vaccine for yellow fever.
Behind the Award—In developing his vaccine (17D virus), Theiler injected some into himself and his coworkers. He survived, but 6 other researchers got sick and died. During W.W. II, an estimated 59 million servicemen going to the tropics were protected by the vaccine, perfected in 1937.

1952 Selman A. Waksman (1888–), American (b. Russia). Work: Discovering streptomycin, used in treating tuberculosis.

1953 Fritz A. Lipmann (1899–), American (b. Germany).

Hans A. Krebs (1900–), British (b. Germany). Work: Biochemical studies on the metabolism of cells, including the discovery of coenzyme A.

1954 John F. Enders (1897–), American.
Thomas H. Weller (1915–), American.
Frederick C. Robbins (1916–) American. Work: Finding better ways of detecting polio viruses in tissue cultures.

Behind the Award—Neither Albert Sabin nor Jonas Salk, both of whom developed an effective polio vaccine, received a Nobel Prize.

1955 Axel Hugo Theorell (1903–), Swedish. Work: Discoveries concerning oxidation enzymes.

1956 Dickinson W. Richards, Jr. (1895–), American.
André F. Cournand (1895–), American (b. France).
Werner Forssmann (1904–), German. Work: Developing a technique for inserting a catheter through a vein to reach the heart.

1957 Daniel Bovet (1907–), Italian (b. Switzerland). Work: The development of drugs for relaxing muscles.

1958 George W. Beadle (1903–), American.
Edward L. Tatum (1909–), American.
Joshua Lederberg (1925–), American. Work: Discovery of the fact that genes carry hereditary traits.

1959 Severo Ochoa (1905–), American (b. Spain).
Arthur Kornberg (1918–), American. Work: Synthesis of ribonucleic acid (RNA) and deoxyribonucleic acid (DNA).

1960 F. Macfarlane Burnet (1899–), Australian.
Peter B. Medawar (1915–), British (b. Brazil). Work: Discovering acquired immunity, which enables an organism to accept foreign tissues.

1961 Georg von Békèsy (1899–), American (b. Hungary). Work: Studies of the inner ear.

Behind the Award—The prize this year was $48,300. Georg Békèsy, the man who won it, had only honorary medical degrees. He would never be allowed to treat a patient. It was through his work as a telephone engineer that he began his studies of the inner ear, particularly the cochlea (a spiral canal in the inner ear). He built models, and he put a hole in the head of a corpse and then, using strobe lighting, he watched the effect of sound waves on the cochlea, which is linked to the eardrum by 3 tiny bones. His findings have given ear specialists new methods of diagnosing deafness.

1962 Francis H. C. Crick (1916–), English.
James D. Watson (1928–), American.
Maurice H. F. Wilkins (1916–), British. Work: Studies of the molecular structure of deoxyribonucleic acid (DNA) and its ability to transfer information.

1963 Alan L. Hodgkin (1914–), English.
Andrew F. Huxley (1917–), English.
John C. Eccles (1903–), Australian. Work: Studies of nerve cells and their electrochemical exchanges.

1964 Konrad E. Bloch (1912–), American (b. Germany).
Feodor Lynen (1911–), German. Work: Research relating to cholesterol metabolism.

1965 François Jacob (1920–), French.
André M. Lwoff (1902–), French.
Jacques L. Monod (1910–), French. Work: Discovery of body cell processes that have to do with genetic control of enzymes and virus synthesis.

Behind the Award—These 3 men shared the 1st Nobel Prize in science given to any Frenchman in 30 years. Before they received it, they had been fighting, without much luck, to take over the administrative council of the Pasteur Institute from mossback politicians. The council had refused to raise salaries to the level of those at the Sorbonne, were stalling on construction of a molecular biology building, and would not accept help from the French Government. After they received the prize, the 3 men used a press conference to lambaste the French establishment for the inadequate research conditions in their country. They had been back from Stockholm only 3 weeks before they were able to get control of the institute. "We've gone from zero to the condition of movie stars," one of them said.

1966 Charles B. Huggins (1901–), American (b. Canada). Work: Treatment of prostate-gland cancer with hormones.
Francis P. Rous (1879–1970), American. Work: Discovery of a cancer virus.

Behind the Award—This was the 1st prize awarded for cancer research since the Fibiger disaster in 1926. Rous was being commended for work he had done 56 years before. Then he showed that malignant connective-tissue tumors in chickens could be transferred to healthy ones. (The tumor is known today as Rous's sarcoma virus, RSV.) When researchers were unable to transfer rat and mouse tumors in the same way, they were skeptical of Rous's findings.

1967 Halden Keffer Hartine (1903–), American.
George Wald (1906–), American.
Ragnar A. Granit (1900–), Swedish

(b. Finland). Work: Discoveries about the chemical and physiological processes of the eye.

1968 Robert W. Holley (1922–), American.

H. Gobind Khorana (c. 1922–), American (b. India).

Marshall W. Nirenberg (1927–), American. Work: Discovery relating to the function of enzymes in cells in genetic development.

Behind the Award—A. Hugo Theorell, who won the prize in 1955, said that Holley, Khorana, and Nirenberg had broken the genetic code, which gave man the power to control the physical and perhaps mental makeup of future generations artificially. The 3 men, relatively young, shared a prize of $70,000. A close associate said that Nirenberg was a true genius because he did one thing very well but had trouble driving cars and had been seen to trip over his feet. Nirenberg, who had great concern about the possibly detrimental uses of the discovery, more or less dropped out of sight soon after receiving the award and suffering the attendant publicity. Holley had been a member of the Salk Institute team that 1st synthesized penicillin. Khorana, who was born in Raipur, India, was watching a sunset when told he had been selected for the prize. "I find it difficult to think," he said in a press interview. "I work all the time, but then I guess we all do."

1969 Max Delbrück (1906–), American (b. Germany).

Alfred D. Hershey (1908–), American.

Salvador E. Luria (1912–), American (b. Italy). Work: Discoveries about genetic structure of viruses.

Behind the Award—When Delbrück found out at 5 A.M. that he had been chosen for the prize, he took a tranquilizer, then played the piano. He and Hershey and Luria were being rewarded for work they had done 25 years before, work that proved to be a model for studying ways viruses attack cells. They did their work separately, but were in communication with each other.

1970 Bernard Katz (1911–), British.

Ulf von Euler (1905–), Swedish.

Julius Axelrod (1912–), American. Work: Discoveries about nerve fiber substances.

Behind the Award—When Axelrod arrived at the dentist one November morning, the dentist told him, "Julie, you've won the Nobel Prize!" Because the dentist was a great kidder, Axelrod did not believe him. Later, with cotton in his mouth, he received a telephone call from a radio station wanting his

reaction. Only then did he believe the news. Chief of pharmacology at the National Institute for Mental Health, Axelrod had had a tough time early in his career. Born on the Lower East Side of New York City, he failed to gain admission to medical school because of the Jewish quota. One of his 1st research papers was turned down by *Nature*, a British journal. To celebrate the Nobel Prize, his colleagues threw a champagne party for him, in spite of government regulations, at which he said, "Now I'm going to send out all my lousy papers to be published—I've got a notebook full of them." Von Euler, the 3rd Swede to win the medicine prize, also had a champagne party, his at the Royal Caroline Institute. Katz, when told the news, was so sleepy he had to take a cold shower before he could comprehend what had happened.

1971 Earl W. Sutherland, Jr. (1915–1974), American. Work: Discoveries concerning the action of hormones.

Behind the Award—Sutherland was the 1st prizewinner in a decade to be the only recipient. Professor Rolf Luft of the Nobel award committee said, "Very seldom can a discovery today be credited to a single person." Sutherland had got interested in medical research when reading Paul de Kruif's book *Microbe Hunters* as a teen-ager in Burlingame, Kans. After being notified of the award, he entertained reporters while watching the World Series in his gold pajamas and, as an enthusiastic sport fisherman, he said, "It will probably be too cold to go fishing in Sweden in December." He was humble about his discoveries, saying, "I chiefly sit back at my desk and pat my assistants on the back, telling them, 'Why don't we try this or why don't we try that?'" He gave special credit to his assistant researcher, Jim Davis, who had been with him for 20 years at the time. His discoveries may help in the treatment of diabetes, manic-depressive psychosis, and cancer.

1972 Gerald M. Edelman (1929–), American.

Rodney R. Porter (1917–), British. Work: Learning the exact chemical structure of an antibody.

1973 Karl Ritter von Frisch (1887–), Austrian.

Konrad Lorenz (1904–), Austrian.

Nikolaas Tinbergen (1907–), Dutch. Work: Research on behavioral patterns.

Behind the Award—These 3 men are the most eminent founders of a new science called ethology, which gets its name from the Greek word for habit or manner and which is concerned with animal behavior. Von Frisch studies insects; his most famous work was deciphering the language of the bees, including the complex dance they do to tell one another where pollen can be found. Lorenz started by studying jackdaws in his parents' attic, then went on to geese, primates, and other animals. He demonstrated "imprinting" by being in the right place at the right time to become the "mother" of a group of baby geese. The author of *On Aggression*, Lorenz has applied his findings to the behavior of human beings, which has made him somewhat controversial, especially among behavioral psychologists. Tinbergen's brother Jan won the Nobel Economics Prize in 1969. Lorenz and Von Frisch had been considered for the prize before, but had been turned down because their work, it was felt, did not apply directly to human beings.

1974 Albert Claude (1899–), American (b. Luxembourg).

Christian Rene de Duve (1917–), Belgian (b. England).

George Emil Palade (1912–), American (b. Romania). Work: Creation of modern cell biology.

—A.E.

PEACE

1901 Jean H. Dunant (1828–1910), Swiss. Work: Founded International Red Cross.

Frédéric Passy (1822–1912), French. Work: Founded 1st French peace organization.

Behind the Award—Typically, there was controversy over this 1st peace prize. Some felt that Nobel had not intended the prize to be awarded to more than one person. Others, among them Nobel's former secretary, felt that Dunant, founder of the International Red Cross, should not have received the prize. And there were those who felt that, if he got any prize at all, it should have been the one for medicine.

1902 Elie Ducommun (1833–1906), Swiss. Charles A. Gobat (1843–1914), Swiss. Work: Both led the Bureau International Permanent de la Paix.

1903 William R. Cremer (1828–1908), British. Work: Founded Workmen's Peace Association.

1904 Institute of International Law. Work: Codified international law.

Behind the Award—This was the 1st prize to be awarded to an organization rather than an individual. The institute was a private group of politicians and jurists who wanted to investigate the principles of international law. They were not complete pacifists. In the introduction to the institute's *Handbook of the Rules and Observances of Warfare* was this statement: "War occupies a considerable place in the pages of history, and it is not rea-

sonable to suppose that man will be capable of breaking away from it so soon, despite the protests it arouses and the disgust it inspires. For it proves to be the only possible solution to the conflicts which jeopardize the existence, the freedom, and the vital interests of nations. But a gradual raising of accepted standards and morals should be reflected in the way war is conducted. . . ."

1905 Bertha von Suttner (1843–1914), Austrian. Work: Led peace movements.

Behind the Award—Pure nepotism. Bertha Kinsky had been Alfred Nobel's secretary before marrying an Austrian named Von Suttner. She expected to win the 1st one. She didn't. Finally, a witness to Nobel's will and a Nobel nephew put pressure on the Norwegian judges, and Bertha got the 5th Peace Prize.

1906 Theodore Roosevelt (1858–1919), American. Work: Arbitrated end of Russo-Japanese War.

Behind the Award—The winner was the same Teddy Roosevelt who had said, "No triumph of peace is quite so great as the supreme triumph of war!" The vote was pure politics. Newly independent Norway needed the support of the U.S. The Scandinavian press said the judges had made a "laughingstock" of themselves.

1907 Ernesto T. Moneta (1833–1918), Italian. Work: Founded peace societies and wrote a 3-volume work on peace.

Louis Renault (1843–1918), French. Work: Worked on behalf of peace at The Hague and other international conferences.

Behind the Award—During the revolution of 1848, Moneta, then 15 years old, fought with his 60-year-old father at the barricades of Milan. Like many pacifists of his time, he did not believe in nonviolence in the face of aggression.

1908 Fredrik Bajer (1837–1922), Danish. Work: President of International Peace Bureau, Bern.

Klas P. Arnoldson (1844–1916), Swedish. Work: Worked toward Norwegian-Swedish union.

Behind the Award—Swedish conservatives were infuriated that Arnoldson was given the Peace Prize, because the journalist-pacifist had backed Norway when, 3 years before, it had broken away from Sweden to become independent. A Stockholm paper said that Norway had insulted their country and "dishonored every Swedish man who takes pride in his national honor."

1909 August M. F. Beernaert (1829–1912), Belgian. Work: Arbitration.

Paul H. Benjamin d'Estournelles de Constant (1852–1924), French. Work: Fought for European union.

1910 Permanent International Peace Bureau. Work: Pacifist activities.

1911 Tobias M. C. Asser (1838–1913), Dutch. Work: International law.

Alfred H. Fried (1844–1921), Austrian. Work: Founded peace publications.

1912 Elihu Root (1845–1937), American. Work: Pan-American relationships.

Behind the Award—A Norwegian editor called Root "an outstanding militarist, eager for conquest." It was true that during his tenure as Secretary of War, he followed American imperialist policy to some extent. However, he was in favor of Pan-American friendship, and he solved problems concerning Japanese-American relations.

1913 Henri La Fontaine (1854–1943), Belgian. Work: Pacifist publications.

1914–1916 No award because of W.W. I

1917 International Red Cross. Work: Implemented Geneva Convention; war relief.

1918 No Award

1919 Woodrow Wilson (1856–1924), American. Work: Helped to set up the League of Nations.

Behind the Award—Although he had participated in W.W. I to "make the world safe for democracy," President Wilson was an ardent pacifist whose efforts for the establishment of the League were praised by many. Later, however, the tide turned, and people began to see him as an ivory-tower ex-teacher who had been led down the garden path by wily European politicians like Clemenceau and Lloyd George, as the European nations made secret treaties that defeated the purpose of the League.

1920 Léon V. A. Bourgeois (1851–1925), French. Work: Involved with League of Nations.

1921 Karl Hjalmar Branting (1860–1925), Swedish.

Christian L. Lange (1869–1938), Norwegian. Work: Contributed to League of Nations.

Behind the Award—Prime Minister Branting was the 3rd head of a nation to win the prize.

1922 Fridtjof Nansen (1861–1930), Norwegian. Work: Helped prisoners of war and refugees.

Behind the Award—The famous Arctic explorer and relief worker, put in charge of the return of prisoners of war in 1920, performed miracles. By September, 1921, he had sent home nearly 400,000 prisoners all for only £400,000. As Commissioner for Refugees for the League of Nations, he issued an identity card (the "Nansen passport"), approved by 52 governments, which helped the refugees find homes and work in new countries. Dan-

ish writer Jens M. Jensen said of him, "The Nobel Peace Prize has in the course of the years been given to many different sorts of men. It has surely never been awarded to anyone who in such a short time has carried out such far-reaching *practical* peace work as Nansen."

1923 No Award

1924 No Award

1925 J. Austen Chamberlain (1863–1937), British. Work: Locarno Pact.

Charles G. Dawes (1865–1951), American. Work: Dawes Plan (German reparations).

1926 Aristide Briand (1862–1932), French.

Gustav Stresemann (1878–1929), German. Work: Locarno Pact.

Behind the Award—A Norwegian writer, A. O. Norman, had this to say of the 1925 and 1926 Peace Prize winners: "Austen Chamberlain, who resembles his father, the imperialist, in everything but intelligence, Stresemann, who would willingly belong to the German Nationalists if he were not too canny and Briand, who can belong to anything at all, if he believes that France and himself stand to win by it." The 3 were involved in a conference in Locarno with representatives of 4 other countries to set boundaries and relations in regard to war. The Locarno Pact, the culmination of that conference, was, according to bourgeois radical and socialist groups, the result of power politics. At the time, the Weimar Republic was secretly rearming.

1927 Ferdinand E. Buisson (1841–1932), French. Work: Pacifist activities.

Ludwig Quidde (1858–1941), German. Work: Worked against secret military training; pacifist writings.

1928 No Award

1929 Frank B. Kellogg (1856–1937), American. Work: Briand-Kellogg Pact of 1928.

1930 Nathan Söderblom (1866–1931), Swedish. Work: World brotherhood through the Church.

Behind the Award—Those who didn't know that Söderblom had been a personal friend of Nobel's were puzzled at his being chosen for the prize. When Nobel was dying, Söderblom, then a young pastor, visited him often. He spoke at Nobel's funeral services. Later, Söderblom gained more importance: He became an archbishop and pacifist of some renown, and was once received in the White House by Calvin Coolidge.

1931 Jane Addams (1860–1935), American. Work: Founded women's peace organization; lectured.

Nicholas Murray Butler (1862–1947), American. Work: Pacifist organizing and negotiating.

Behind the Award—Butler, president of Columbia University, was in early years in favor of American military policy and had fired several professors because they were pacifists. However, he later established and ran the Carnegie Endowment for International Peace. A friend of the Kaiser's, he couldn't believe that this man, who had seemed to him to be a fellow pacifist, would start W.W. I. Jane Addams, a practical idealist who started Hull House, gave her Nobel Peace Prize money, $15,755, to the Women's International League for Peace and Freedom. She was about to go under ether for an operation at Johns Hopkins Hospital when she 1st heard she had won the prize.

1932 No Award

1933 Norman Angell (c. 1872–1967), British. Work: Wrote pacifist literature.

1934 Arthur Henderson (1863–1935), British. Work: Disarmament.

1935 Carl von Ossietzky (1889–1938), German. Work: Founded antiwar organizations.

Behind the Award—The most courageous prize ever awarded. Ossietzky, a newspaper editor and dedicated pacifist, exposed Germany's secret rearmament and told Hitler, "Soldiers are murderers!" Hitler threw him into the Papenburg concentration camp. He was nominated for the Peace Prize by Switzerland's National Assembly, the Norwegian Labor Party, Albert Einstein, Romain Rolland, and Thomas Mann. He was opposed in Norway by Quisling and Knut Hamsun, and in Germany by Goering, who influenced the Nobel family to say that a prize to Ossietzky was not "in conformity with the founder's intentions." Nevertheless, Norway's 5 judges voted him the $39,303 Peace Prize. As a result, Hitler banned the Nobel Prizes and when the Nazis invaded Norway, they arrested the Nobel judges. Ossietzky, suffering tuberculosis, died a Nazi prisoner.

1936 Carlos Saavedra Lamas (1880–1959), Argentinian. Work: Presided over the League of Nations, and in Buenos Aires helped end the long Chaco War.

1937 Edgar A. R. Cecil 1864–1958), British. Work: Active in the League of Nations.
Behind the Award—Secretary of State Cordell Hull as well as the Foreign Minister of Cuba nominated President Franklin D. Roosevelt, but he was voted down.

1938 Nansen International Office for Refugees. Work: Relief for refugees.
Behind the Award—Franklin Delano Roosevelt nominated Cordell Hull for his work in lowering trade barriers.

1939 No Award
Behind the No Award—Roosevelt again nominated Cordell Hull, this time for his

work in formulating the Good Neighbor Policy.

1940 No Award
1941 No Award
1942 No Award
1943 No Award
1944 International Red Cross. Work: Humanitarian efforts on behalf of prisoners and Jews in W.W. II.

1945 Cordell Hull (1871–1955), American. Work: Good Neighbor Policy.
Behind the Award—At last, Cordell Hull won the Peace Prize. Right after W.W. II began, he started to work on the foundations of the United Nations and managed to talk Roosevelt and Churchill into using it, rather than regional agreements, to settle issues created by the war. However, when it came time to set up the United Nations, he was too ill to participate.

1946 John R. Mott (1865–1955), American. Work: Methodist pacifist.
      Emily Balch (1867–1961), American. Work: Quaker pacifist.
Behind the Award—Finland had nominated 77-year-old Madame Alexandra Killontoy of Russia, the world's 1st female ambassador, friend of Stalin, author of *Free Love*, who had mediated the end of the Finnish-Russian War. When she was defeated for the Peace Prize, the Russians were furious.

1947 Friends Service Council (Great Britain). American Friends Service Committee (U.S.). Work: Pacifism and relief work.
Behind the Award—When Henry J. Cadbury, chairman of the American Friends Service Committee, came to Oslo to accept the prize, he refused the hotel room that had been reserved for him, saying, "We find it possible to cancel the rooms reserved for us at a very stylish hotel and to live in a private house, thus conforming to the simplicity of our Quaker tradition." The suit he wore to the Nobel dinner came from a pile of second-hand clothing destined to be sent to refugees overseas. His group decided to use the prize money "in an effort to improve Russian-American relations."

1948 No Award

1949 John Boyd Orr (1880–1971), British. Work: Founded Food and Agriculture Organization.
Behind the Award—Up for the award were Eleanor Roosevelt, Eva and Juan Perón, Drew Pearson, the International Red Cross, and CARE.

1950 Ralph J. Bunche (1904–1971), American. Work: Settled Arab-Israeli dispute.
Behind the Award—At the last minute, Bunche was called in to pinch-hit for Count Folke Bernadotte, who was murdered by an Israeli terrorist, to negotiate a truce in the

Palestine dispute. He performed admirably. It was he who suggested that the Security Council order the Jews and Arabs to end hostilities and complete the armistice settlement, a bold stroke that worked. Bunche was the 1st black to win a Peace Prize.

1951 Léon Jouhaux (1879–1954), French. Work: Disarmament; improving world working conditions.

1952 Albert Schweitzer (1875–1965), French. Work: Humanitarian activities.

Behind the Award—The great musician-doctor-humanitarian went into the depths of French Equatorial Africa to Lambarene, where he built a hospital for the natives and cured them of their diseases—leprosy, malaria, sleeping sickness, dysentery. To raise money, he went back to Europe and gave organ recitals. He felt that progress must be based on some ethical principle or it would mean the end of civilization. His ethical principle was respect for life—all life.

1953 George C. Marshall (1880–1959), American. Work: Framed the Marshall Plan.

Behind the Award—A soldier, Chief of the U.S. General Staff of W.W. II, Marshall was never a member of a peace organization. In his Nobel lecture, he said, "There has been considerable comment over the awarding of the Nobel Peace Prize to a soldier. I am afraid this does not seem as remarkable to me as it quite evidently appears to others. . . . The cost of war in human lives is constantly spread before me, written neatly in many ledgers whose columns are gravestones. I am deeply moved to find some means or method of avoiding another calamity of war."

1954 Office of the U.N. High Commissioner for Refugees. Work: Relief for refugees.

1955 No Award

1956 No Award

1957 Lester B. Pearson (1897–1972), Canadian. Work: Solution of Mideast crisis.

1958 Father Georges H. Pire (1910–1969), Belgian. Work: Relief for refugees.

Behind the Award—Some critics of the prize wondered if refugee work really contributed to world peace. Father Pire was active in the French resistance in W.W. II and set up a camp to care for several hundred French children after the war.

1959 Philip J. Noel-Baker (1889–), British. Work: Disarmament.

1960 Albert J. Luthuli (1899–1967), South African. Work: Nonviolent resistance.

Behind the Award—The 1st African black to win an award, Luthuli, a Zulu chief, practiced Gandhi's principle of nonviolence. (Gandhi never did receive a Peace Prize, a glaring oversight.) When Luthuli was notified that he had won the prize, the apartheid Government, which had already restricted his movement, was reluctant to let him go to Norway to accept it. In the end, they granted him a travel permit and allowed him to stay in Oslo for a week.

1961 Dag Hammarskjöld (1905–1961), Swedish. Work: Secretary-General of the United Nations.

Behind the Award—Hammarskjöld was nominated by Dr. Ralph Bunche and Adlai Stevenson. Before the voting, he was killed in an airplane crash in Africa. Despite Nobel's insistence that the prize go to living persons, for the 2nd time in Nobel history an award was made posthumously.

1962 Linus C. Pauling (1901–), American. Work: Advocated banning nuclear tests.

Behind the Award—Said *Life* magazine, "An extraordinary insult to America. . . . However distinguished as a chemist, the eccentric Dr. Pauling and his weird politics never have been taken seriously by American opinion. Why should a committee of 5 Norwegians be so taken in, or so rude?"

1963 International Red Cross.

League of Red Cross Societies. Work: Relief work with refugees.

1964 Martin Luther King, Jr. (1929–1968), American. Work: Nonviolent resistance; civil rights.

Behind the Award—King was the youngest person ever to receive the peace award. It was felt that the Nobel committee wanted to give moral support to the equal rights movement. In his speech at the award ceremony, King said that the award had been given to him to recognize the fact that "nonviolence is the answer to the crucial political and moral question of our time—the need for men to overcome oppression and violence without resorting to violence and oppression."

1965 UN Children's Fund (UNICEF). Work: War and peace help to children.

Behind the Award—Begun in 1946 to aid children suffering from the effects of W.W. II, this organization expanded its activities to support children in developing countries, to give help to mothers and children, to direct campaigns against epidemics, to improve nutrition, and to help out in catastrophes. Its work is limited to countries whose governments ask for help and are willing to contribute equally with UNICEF. So far, government contributions have been *double* those of UNICEF.

1966 No Award

1967 No Award

1968 Rene Cassin (1887–), French. Work: Wrote declaration of human rights for United Nations.

1969 International Labor Organization. Work: Reformed world working conditions.

1970 Norman E. Borlaug (1914–), American. Work: Developed high-yield wheat.

Behind the Award—A leader in the "Green Revolution," Borlaug, an agricultural geneticist, developed in Mexico strains of disease-resistant, high-yield hybrid grain. Use of such grains improves living conditions in developing countries. He was working in the fields when news of the award reached him. "Our green miracle," he said, had brought the award to a "dirty-handed scientist." He believes that, as important as the "Green Revolution" is, it will only delay world famine unless something is done about population explosion. He planned to invest his $78,400 award in an experimental agricultural station.

1971 Willy Brandt (1914–), German. Work: Efforts at East-West détente.

Behind the Award—A unanimous choice of the committee, Brandt was himself a little uneasy over winning the prize, for he felt his work was not yet done. He is the illegitimate child of a cleaning woman in Lübeck, somewhat expressionless, honest, roughhewn. When the 300 deputies in the Bundestag gave him a standing ovation after the award was announced, a rare smile crossed his face.

1972 No Award

1973 Le Duc Tho (1911–), North Vietnamese.

Henry Kissinger (1923–), American (b. Germany). Work: Negotiated the Vietnam cease-fire agreement.

Behind the Award—Probably the most controversial recent award. For the 1st time in the history of the Nobel Prize, committee members (2 of them) resigned in protest because they disagreed with the committee's choice. Le Duc Tho refused the prize because he felt "peace was not yet really established in South Vietnam" and probably too because he felt he had been the victor and did not want to share the prize equally with a representative of the vanquished. The West German press made the ironic suggestion that the 1974 Peace Prize might go to Golda Meir and Anwar Sadat. *The New York Times* called it the "war prize." *Le Monde*, of Paris, labeled it a "masquerade." A Saigon government spokesman said that giving the award to Tho was like "nominating a whore as honorary chairman of the PTA." In general, those in the know were surprised at the award. Scandinavian nations were against American bombing of North Vietnam the December before, when Olof Palme, Sweden's Premier, compared the bombing to "the Nazi massacres of W.W. II." This angered President Nixon so much that he refused to receive the new Swedish ambassador to the U.S.

1974 Eisaku Sato (1901–1975), Japanese.

Sean MacBride (1904–), Irish. Work: Efforts for human rights and limitation of nuclear weapons.

Behind the Award—There were 50 nominees this year, including Richard M. Nixon again. The award to Sato was a shoddy political affair. Vegetarian Sato, Prime Minister of Japan from 1964 to 1972, was indicted for taking $56,000 in bribes in 1954 and was accused by his wife of beating her and going out with geishas. A 14-month lobbying effort on behalf of Sato was mounted by millionaire construction tycoon Morinoskuka Kajima, who got Japan's former UN delegate, Toshikazu Kase, to visit 10 nations to pressure the Nobel Peace Committee, as well as plead with 5 Norwegian judges, and who privately printed a 224-page book, *In Quest of Peace and Freedom*, a collection of Sato's speeches translated into English (which 2 Kissinger aides flew to Tokyo to proofread) for the Norwegian Nobel judges. Said a member of Japan's Parliament: "It's just a bad joke. The prestige of the Nobel Prize has surely dropped." The Oslo *Dagbladet*, which regarded Sato as a mere politician, called the award "close to a scandal." The other Peace Prize winner, Sean MacBride, Foreign Minister of Ireland and champion of the liberation of Namibia from South African rule, served in the Irish Republican Army for 8 years and became its chief of staff.

—A.E.

Economic Science

1969 Ragnar Frisch (1895–1972), Norwegian.

Jan Tinbergen (1903–), Dutch. Work: For development of econometrics—the application of mathematical and statistical methods to economic problems.

Behind the Award—The only prize not mentioned in Alfred Nobel's will, this one was instituted in 1968 by the Central Bank of Sweden to celebrate the bank's 300th anniversary. While the annual cash prize came from the bank, the winners were voted by the Swedish Royal Academy of Science.

1970 Paul Anthony Samuelson (1915–), American. Work: For creating new scientific analysis to be used in economic theories.

1971 Simon Kuznets (1901–), American. Work: For inventing the concept of Gross National Product.

Behind the Award—First winner who was never a government economic adviser. This Russian-born retired Harvard professor von the $86,400 prize over a field of 200 nominees.

1972 Kenneth J. Arrow (1921–), American. John R. Hicks (1904–). British. Work:

For their pioneering contributions to general economic equilibrium theory and welfare theory.

Behind the Award—The pair shared a $98,-100 award. Arrow said he needed his part of the money for personal security; Hicks said he would donate his half to the library of the London School of Economics. Arrow was also well known for his Impossibility Theorem, which mathematically proved "there is not, and in principle cannot be, any perfect form of government."

1973 Wassily Leontief (1906–), American. Work: For devising the input-output formula that shows how changes in one economic sector affect performance in other sectors.

Behind the Award—He conceived his award-winning theory while a student at the University of Leningrad. As the 3rd American economics laureate to have emigrated from Russia, Leontief joked, "Do you think there should be an antitrust investigation?" A liberal who was sympathetic to the student uprisings at Harvard, Leontief once suggested that New York City's garbage problem could be solved by levying high taxes on bottles, plastic wrappings, other disposable commodities.

1974 Gunnar Myrdal (1899–), Swedish. Friedrich A. von Hayek (1899–), Austrian. Work: For their pioneering work in the theory of money and economic fluctuations.

Behind the Award—Wrote Dr. Paul A. Samuelson, 1970 economics winner, of this award in *The New York Times*: "In no sense has their work been joint. Indeed, their policy conclusions, if followed literally, would be at loggerheads and self-canceling. . . . It is often charged that such award-granting committees are influenced by political beliefs, so that a 'liberal' like Jan Tinbergen of The Netherlands stands a better chance than a free-market 'conservative' like Milton Friedman. This may explain the coupling together of the interventionist do-gooder Dr. Myrdal with the unreconstructed Dr. von Hayek, who argued . . . that mild piecemeal reforms lead inevitably to the totalitarian hell of Hitler and Stalin."

—I.W.

International Lenin Prize for Strengthening Peace Among Peoples

Who: Established on June 23, 1925. Originally named after Vladimir Ilich Ulyanov, whose pseudonym was N. Lenin (the N. stood for no name, was merely an initial), leader of the Russian Revolution in 1917, and ruler of Russia until his death in 1924. From 1935 to 1956 the award was called the Stalin Peace Prize, after Lenin's successor, Iosif Vissarionovich Dzhugashvili, who went by the name of Joseph Stalin. After Stalin's death in March, 1953, his successor, Nikita Khrushchev, began the process of de-Stalinization. Stalin's name was removed from the gold medal. And once more the peace award was named after Lenin.

What: There are 2 sets of Lenin Prizes. One set is domestic and includes 50 awards which are given to Soviet citizens for achievements in art, literature, science, and engineering. For example, Galina Ulanova, the Soviet ballerina, has won one of these $50,000 internal awards 4 times. On the other hand the Lenin Peace Prize honors citizens of any nation in the world who have made contributions in "promotion of peace among nations."

When: The prizes are usually announced on April 22, Lenin's birthday. The award is supposed to be made annually, but lately it has been given every 2nd or 3rd year for peace efforts made in the previous year.

Where: Headquarters: Moscow, U.S.S.R.

Prize: A Soviet encyclopedia says, "The award consists of 100,000 rubles, a diploma, and a gold medal engraved with Lenin's bust." In fact, the cash prize is much less, and the amount given varies from award to award. In 1963, each winner received 10,000 rubles or $11,000. In 1967, each winner received 25,000 rubles or $27,750. Recipients of the award are invited to attend a ceremony in Moscow and give an address.

Eligible: Anyone, anywhere, who has contributed to the Soviet version of peace. In theory, Russian citizens are also eligible but they are rarely given this award. Winners are usually communists, those sympathetic to communism or to Russia, or simply leftists more tuned in to the aims of the U.S.S.R. than to those of capitalist countries. There are supposed to be 10 recipients annually, but since 1960 the Lenin Peace Prize has been bestowed on no more than 7 persons in a single year.

Judges: There is a special award committee controlled by the Presidium of the Supreme Soviet of the U.S.S.R.

Award Winners:

1960 Cyrus S. Eaton, U.S. Industrialist.
     Dr. Sukarno, Indonesia. President 1949–1965

Laurent Casanova, France.

Aziz Sharif, Iraq.

1961 Dr. Fidel Castro, Cuba. Prime Minister. ("Whose entire life is dedicated to the struggle for freedom and independence.")

Sekou Toure, Guinea. President.

Mrs. Rameshwari Nehru, India. Pacifist.

Mikhail Sadoveanu, Romania. Author.

Antoine Georges Tanet, Lebanon. Architect.

Ostap Dkluski, Poland. Founder of World Peace Council. Communist leader.

William Morrow, Australia. Labor leader.

1962 Pablo Picasso, France. Artist. (He went to Moscow to accept award 4 years later.)

Kwame Nkrumah, Ghana. President 1951–1966.

Istvan Dobi, Hungary. President.

Faiz Ahmad Faiz, Pakistan. Poet.

Olga Poblet de Espinosa, Chile. University professor.

1963 Ahmed Ben Bella, Algeria. President 1963–1965. Overthrown. President of government-in-exile in Moscow. ("Ardent champion of peaceful coexistence.")

Modibo Keita, Mali. President of government-in-exile in Moscow. (For his work in the anticolonial movement.)

1965 Jamsaranglin Sambu, Mongolia. Parliament leader.

Miriam Vire-Tuominen, Finland. Member of World Council of Peace.

J. P. Courtis, Nigeria. National leader.

Giacomo Manzù, Italy. Sculptor. ("An outstanding representative of realistic directions in art.")

Miguel Angel Asturias, Guatemala. Author.

1967 The Rev. Dr. Martin Niemöller, West Germany. Evangelical pastor.

Rockwell Kent, U.S. Artist. (Accepting award in Moscow, Kent condemned his native U.S. for a "most criminal, cruel, and unjust war in Vietnam.")

Abram Fischer, South Africa. Communist lawyer. (In jail for sabotage, 1966, the year of his citation.)

David Alfaro Siqueiros, Mexico. Artist. (Died in 1974.)

Ivan Malek, Czechoslovakia. Scientist.

Herbert Warnke, East Germany. Labor leader.

1968 No Award.

1969 No Award.

1970 Dr. Linus Pauling, U.S. Scientist. (Given for "activity in defense of peace.")

1971 No Award.

1973 James Aldridge, Australia. Author. (Award given in Soviet Embassy, London, "for his outstanding struggle for the preservation of peace." Award $14,500.)

Leonid I. Brezhnev, U.S.S.R. Soviet party general secretary.

Salvador Allende, Chile. President. (Overthrown 1973 and was murdered.) Trade union leader.

1974 Luis Corvalan, Chile. Communist leader. Presently in jail.

Jeanne Martin Sisse, Guinea. Politician.

Raymond Goor, Belgium. Clergyman.

—The Eds.

The International Jerusalem Prize

Who: Established by the Municipality of Jerusalem, Israel, and the Jerusalem International Book Fair, in 1963.

What: Given to the author who, in his works, has made outstanding contributions to the concept of freedom of the individual in society.

When: Every 2 years, usually in April.

Where: Headquarters: The Jerusalem International Book Fair, P. O. Box 1508, Jerusalem, Israel.

Prize: $2,000. The winner is invited to accept the prize in Jerusalem, and to give a speech of acceptance at the opening of the Book Fair at Binyanei Haooma.

Eligible: Any author, without bar as to race, color, or creed.

Judges: A committee of 3 judges, all distinguished Israeli men of letters, nominated to serve by the mayor of Jerusalem, currently Teddy Kollek. A different committee is nominated for each new biennial award.

Award Winners:

1963 Bertrand Russell, England. Author, philosopher.

1965 Max Frisch, Germany. Novelist.

1967 André Schwarz-Bart, France. Novelist.

1969 Ignazio Silone, Italy. Novelist.

1971 Jorge Luis Borges, Argentina. Novelist.

1973 Eugene Ionesco, France. Playwright.

1975 Simone de Beauvoir, France. Author.

—The Eds.

The Templeton Foundation Prize for Progress in Religion

Who: John Templeton, a retired U.S. investment counselor, established an award in 1973 "to do for religion what Alfred Nobel did for science and literature."

What: "Established to call attention to and provide recognition of ideas, insights, actions, accomplishments which have been or may be instrumental in widening or deepening man's knowledge and love of God."

When: Given annually in April.

Where: Headquarters: Templeton Foundation, Inc., P. O. Box 408, Englewood, N.J. 07631. European Office: 2 Bristow Park, Upper Malone Road, Belfast BT9 6th, North Ireland.

Prize: $97,600 or £40,000 "awarded each year at a celebration in honor of the recipient."

Eligible: "Nominations will be sought from a wide constituency that will include all the major religions of the world. Official organizations will be invited to submit nominations, and leaders of the theological and religious institutions will be contacted for nominations. . . . The judges will consider a nominee's contribution to the knowledge and love of God made during his entire career. Qualities sought in awarding the Prize will be freshness, creativity, innovation and effectiveness. Such contribution may involve a study, or a life, or the inspiration of a new movement or thrust in religion, or a religious institution."

Judges: A panel of 9 judges representative of the world's major faiths. A central committee screens annual nominations, with finalists submitted to the panel of judges.

The current Templeton Prize judges are: Her Majesty Fabiola, Roman Catholic, Queen of the Belgians; Professor Suniti Kumar Chatterji, Hindu, National Professor of India in the Humanities; Sir Muhammad Zafrulla Khan, Islamic scholar, former president of the International Court of Justice at The Hague; The Rev. Dr. James McCord, Protestant, president of Princeton Theological Seminary, U.S.; Sir Alan Mocatta, Jewish, judge of the Queen's Bench Division of the High Court, England; The Lord Abbot Kosho Ohtani, Buddhist, patriarch of the Shin Sects, Japan; The Rev. Dr. Norman Vincent Peale, Protestant, minister of Marble Collegiate Church, U.S.; Her Serene Highness Princess Poon Pismai Diskul, Buddhist, president of the World Fellowship of Buddhists; The Rt. Rev. Robin Woods, Anglican, Bishop of Worcester, England.

Award Winners:

1973　Mother Teresa, Yugoslavia. For her work in ministering to the ailing and poor in the slums of Calcutta, India. For establishing an order of nuns that helps the needy in South America, Tanzania, Jordan, Ceylon, Australia, Northern Ireland.

1974　Brother Roger, prior of the Taize Community in France. For establishing in Taize a nondenominational group of brothers dedicated to bringing about a visible unity among Christians. For his Council of Youth, conceived in 1970, whose worldwide membership consists of thousands of young adults.

1975　Dr. Sarvepalli Radhakrishnan, former professor of Eastern religion and ethics at Oxford, 1st Indian to be elected a Fellow of the British Academy, former president of India. For his lifelong efforts which "led to a rediscovery of God" and for his "special contribution to modern Hinduism."

　　　　　　　　　　　　　　　　—I.W.

23

All in Sport

What Was the Greatest Baseball Team in the Last Half Century?

Whenever baseball fans meet, one question always arises and one argument always ensues—which of the great baseball teams was the greatest in modern times?

There can never be a definitive answer, because all of the players were subject to human frailties upon occasion, because the teams were at their peaks in different years or even eras, and because the rules, the ball, and the size of the parks have changed. Still, in these days of technological advances, an almost definitive answer may be found, and in 1970 the National Broadcasting System sought to find such an answer.

In 1970, NBC set out to obtain a consensus of opinion on the 8 best baseball teams of the last 50 years. First, a panel of experts selected 2 teams—the 1951 New York Giants and the 1969 New York Mets—as candidates. To choose 6 additional teams, NBC held a national popularity poll among baseball fans. More than 7,000 fans submitted their choices in writing. Then the panel of experts—Joe DiMaggio, Ted Williams, Willie Mays, Stan Musial, major league public relations director Joe Reichler, NBC telecaster Curt Gowdy—screened the fans' 40 favorite teams to pick 6 more of the greatest ones.

The teams selected to join the 1951 New York Giants and 1969 New York Mets were the following: the 1927 New York Yankees; the 1929 Philadelphia Athletics; the 1955 Brooklyn Dodgers; the 1942 St. Louis Cardinals; the 1961 New York Yankees; the 1963 Los Angeles Dodgers.

Among other teams that ranked high in the balloting, but could not be included in the tournament, were the 1931 and 1934 St. Louis Cardinals; the 1936 New York Yankees; the 1954 Cleveland Indians; the 1957 Milwaukee Braves; the 1960 Pittsburgh Pirates; the 1966

and 1969 Baltimore Orioles; the 1967 Boston Red Sox; and the 1968 Detroit Tigers.

Once the 8 best teams had been selected, their complete records were fed into a computer by Computer Research in Sports, Inc., of Princeton, N.J. Then the 8 teams were paired off, and their scientifically computerized records were pitted against one another. The winners of the 1st 4 games met in 2 semifinal computerized matches, and the 2 finalists met in the big championship game.

What emerged, finally, was a scientific answer to the persisting question—which was the best baseball team in the world between 1920 and 1970?

Now, through special permission of NBC Sports, New York, *The People's Almanac* is reproducing the complete results of this All-Great Baseball Tournament.

But 1st, a look at the players on the 8 top teams—

The tournament was studded with outstanding baseball names. The 1927 Yankees easily led the field in votes garnered. That was the "Murderers Row" team of Babe Ruth, Lou Gehrig, Bob Meusel, Tony Lazzeri, and the year Ruth hit 60 home runs.

The Yankees of 1961 captured the imagination of the sports world as Roger Maris and Mickey Mantle made their assault on Ruth's home-run record.

The 1955 Dodgers were the 1st of a long list of Brooklyn pennant winners to capture a World Series crown. And they did it against their archrivals, the New York Yankees. Jackie Robinson, Roy Campanella, Duke Snider, Pee Wee Reese, Gil Hodges, and Don Newcombe led that club.

Another Dodger team was prominently mentioned in the balloting, but this group had a different look and a different home. The 1963 Los Angeles Dodgers had such standouts as

25-game-winner Sandy Koufax, 19-game-winner Don Drysdale, Tommy Davis (the league's leading batter for the 2nd straight year), Maury Wills, and Frank Howard.

The 1929 Athletics boasted Hall of Fame's Jimmy Foxx, Lefty Grove, Al Simmons, and Mickey Cochrane. Simmons led the league with 157 runs batted in, and Grove posted a league leading, earned-run average of 2.81 as Philadelphia won 104 games.

The 1942 Cardinals registered a 106–48 won-lost slate and had the National League's 2nd and 3rd leading hitters in Enos Slaughter and Stan Musial. Mort Cooper was the top mounds-man with a 22–7 record.

Now, Play Ball!

1st Opening Game

1969 N.Y. METS NIP 1951 N.Y. GIANTS 4–3 IN 10TH INNING IN OPENER OF COMPUTERIZED TOURNEY

COMPUTER PARK—Tommy Agee's 10th inning double scored Bud Harrelson with the winning run as the 1969 New York Mets defeated the 1951 New York Giants, 4–3, in the opening game of a computerized tournament viewed by an estimated 5,500,000 on the NBC television network.

Agee's game-winning hit in the 10th followed walks to Harrelson and Tom Seaver, the winning pitcher, and came at the expense of loser George Spencer, last of 3 Giant pitchers. Spencer came on in the 10th in relief of Larry Jansen. Sal Maglie, the starting pitcher for the '51 Giants, worked 6 innings and was touched for 3 runs and 7 hits.

Willie Mays, the rookie centerfielder, solved Seaver for a 2-run homer in the 2nd inning to give the '51 Giants a shortlived lead. But after scoring a run in the 3rd, the Mets moved out front on Wayne Garrett's 2-run triple off Maglie.

The Giants tied it up in the 7th on a triple by Bobby Thomson and Eddie Stanky's single, one of 3 hits the 2nd baseman had off Seaver.

The box score follows:

1st Round—1st Game

1951 New York Giants	AB	R	H	RBI
Stanky 2B	4	0	3	1
Dark SS	5	0	0	0
Mueller RF	5	0	0	0
Irvin LF	4	0	0	0
Lockman 1B	4	0	1	0
Thomson 3B	3	2	1	0
Mays CF	4	1	2	2
Westrum C	4	0	0	0
Maglie P	1	0	0	0
Thompson PH	1	0	0	0
Jansen P	0	0	0	0
Rigney PH	1	0	0	0
Spencer P	0	0	0	0
Totals	36	3	7	3

1969 New York Mets	AB	R	H	RBI
Agee CF	4	2	2	1
Garrett 3B	5	0	2	2
Jones LF	5	0	2	1
Shamsky RF	5	0	1	0
Boswell 2B	4	0	1	0
Kranepool 1B	5	0	1	0
Grote C	5	0	0	0
Harrelson SS	3	1	2	0
Seaver P	3	1	2	0
Totals	39	4	13	4

1951	New York Giants	020	000	100	0–3
1969	New York Mets	001	002	000	1–4

None out when winning run scored

1951 New York Giants	IP	H	R	ER	BB	SO
Maglie	6	7	3	3	4	5
Jansen	3	5	0	0	0	2
Spencer (L.0–1)	0*	1	1	1	2	0

1969 New York Mets	IP	H	R	ER	BB	SO
Seaver (W.1–0)	10	7	3	2	3	6

* Pitched to 3 batters in 10th.

E.-Lockman, Kranepool. DP.-Mets, 2. LOB-Giants, 6 Mets, 13. 2B.-Stanky, Agee. 3B.-Garrett, Thomson, Kranepool. HR. Mays (1) SH.-Seaver. T.-0:00:15. A-1.

2nd Opening Game

BERRA'S SINGLE IN 7TH GIVES 1961 N.Y. YANKEES 9–8 WIN OVER 1929 PHILADELPHIA A'S

COMPUTER PARK—Yogi Berra's lone hit, a 2-run single in the 7th inning, earned the 1961 New York Yankees an uphill 9–8 victory over the 1929 Philadelphia Athletics in the 2nd game of the computerized tournament.

Berra's game-winning blow was one of a total of 26 hits made by the power-laden line-ups of the Yankees and Athletics. This surprising barrage of base hits was put together by the computer at the expense of 2 of the game's quality pitchers, the Yankees' Whitey Ford and the Athletics' Lefty Grove. It included no less than 5 home runs. Clete Boyer hit 2, and Mickey Mantle, Elston Howard one each for the Yankees. Jimmy Dykes, the 3rd baseman for the A's, belted a grand slam in the 3rd inning to move Philadelphia out front, 5–1.

The Yankees got those 4 runs back in the 4th on Max Bishop's error, Elston Howard's double, Bill Skowron's single and Boyer's home run. Both teams then pecked away in more moderate fashion with the A's leading, 8–7, until Yogi singled home the winning runs in the 7th after the Yankees had loaded the bases on Roger Maris's walk and 2 Philadelphia errors.

As usual, Clyde the Computer didn't dally. It took him just 15 seconds to spew out the complete 9-innings, play-by-play, once the necessary statistics were ingested.

The box score follows:

1st Round—2nd Game

1961 N.Y. Yankees	AB	R	H	RBI
Richardson 2B	5	0	1	0
Kubek SS	5	0	1	0
Maris RF	3	1	0	0
Mantle CF	5	3	1	1
Howard C	4	2	2	2
Berra LF	5	0	1	2
Skowron 1B	5	1	1	1
Boyer 3B	5	2	3	3
Ford P	2	0	0	0
Lopez PH	1	0	0	0
Arroyo P	0	0	0	0
Totals	40	9	10	9

1929 Phila. Athletics	AB	R	H	RBI
Bishop 2B	5	2	3	0
Haas CF	4	1	1	0
Cochrane C	6	0	2	2
Simmons LF	5	1	3	1
Foxx 1B	5	1	2	0
Miller RF	3	2	1	0
Dykes 3B	5	1	2	5
Boley SS	4	0	1	0
Grove P	4	0	1	0
Hale PH	1	0	0	0
Totals	42	8	16	0

1961 New York Yankees	010	411	200-9
1929 Philadelphia Athletics	104	021	000-8

1961 New York Yankees	IP	H	R	ER	BB	SO
Ford (W.1–0)	7	14	8	8	5	1
Arroyo	2	2	0	0	0	0

1929 Philadelphia Athletics	IP	H	R	ER	BB	SO
Grove (L.0–1)	9	10	9	6	4	5

E.-Richardson, Bishop 2, Grove. DP.-Yankees 1. LOB-Yankees 8, Athletics 13. 2B-Bishop, Boley, Howard, Miller, Dykes, Kubek. 3B-Richardson. HR.-Howard, Dykes, Boyer 2, Mantle. SB.-Simmons, Maris. SH.-Haas. T.-0:00:15.

3rd Opening Game

1927 N.Y. YANKEES DEFEAT 1963 L.A. DODGERS

COMPUTER PARK—Held to one run in 8 innings, the 1927 New York Yankees erupted for 4 runs at the expense of Sandy Koufax in the 9th inning to defeat the 1963 Los Angeles Dodgers, 5–1, in the 3rd game of the computerized baseball tournament.

The 4-run cluster by the '27 Yankees snapped a 1–1 tie and a pitching duel between Koufax and the Yankees' Hall of Famer Waite Hoyt.

Lou Gehrig started the rally off Koufax in the 9th with a double. A single by Tony Lazzeri, followed by triples by Joe Dugan and Earle Combs topped off the scoring.

Babe Ruth earned the Yankees a 1–0 lead in the 1st inning by solving Koufax for a home run. The Dodgers nicked Hoyt for the equalizer in the 5th on a home run by, of all people, Sandy Koufax.

The box score follows:

1st Round—3rd Game

1927 N.Y. Yankees	AB	R	H	RBI
Combs CF	5	0	2	2
Koenig SS	5	0	0	0
Ruth RF	3	1	1	1
Gehrig 1B	3	1	1	0
Meusel LF	4	0	0	0
Lazzeri 2B	4	1	1	1
Dugan 3B	4	1	1	1
Collins C	3	1	1	0
Hoyt P	4	0	1	0
Totals	35	5	8	5

1963 L. A. Dodgers	AB	R	H	RBI
Gilliam 2B	4	0	1	0
Wills SS	4	0	0	0
W. Davis CF	4	0	0	0
T. Davis LF	4	0	1	0
Fairly 1B	4	0	2	0
Howard RF	4	0	1	0
Roseboro C	4	0	0	0
McMullen 3B	4	0	1	0
Koufax P	3	1	1	1
Moon PH	1	0	0	0
Totals	36	1	7	1

1927 New York Yankees	100	000	004–5
1963 Los Angeles Dodgers	000	010	000–1

1927 New York Yankees	IP	H	R	ER	BB	SO
Hoyt (W. 1–0)	9	7	1	1	0	3

1963 Los Angeles Dodgers	IP	H	R	ER	BB	SO
Koufax (L. 0–1)	9	8	5	5	3	6

E.-Lazzeri, Dugan. LOB-Yankees 6, Dodgers 7. 2B-Gehrig. 3B.-Dugan, Combs. HR.-Ruth, Koufax. SB.-Ruth, McMullen. T.-0:00:15

4th Opening Game

JOHNNY HOPP'S SINGLE SENDS STAN MUSIAL HOME WITH WINNING RUN AS 1942 CARDINALS BEAT 1955 DODGERS

COMPUTER PARK—Johnny Hopp singled home Stan Musial with the winning run in the 8th inning as the 1942 St. Louis Cardinals defeated the 1955 Brooklyn Dodgers, 3–2, in the

4th game of the computerized baseball tournament.

Hopp's game-winning hit came after Musial singled with 2 out and advanced to 3rd on Walker Cooper's double. Cooper had doubled in the 7th and scored the Cards 2nd run of the game on another Hopp single.

Cardinal righthander Mort Cooper went all the way for the victory, scattering 7 hits. Both Dodger runs were the result of homers. Roy Campanella belted one leading off the 4th and Gil Hodges connected with 2 down in the 8th.

The Cardinals posted their 1st run off loser Don Newcombe in the 6th when Terry Moore singled and scored on Enos Slaughter's double.

The box score for the 1942 Cardinals—1955 Dodgers game follows:

1st Round—4th Game

1955	Brooklyn Dodgers	AB	R	H	RBI
	Gilliam 2B	4	0	1	0
	Reese SS	5	0	0	0
	Snider CF	3	0	0	0
	Campanella C	4	1	2	1
	Furillo RF	3	0	1	0
	Hodges 1B	3	1	1	1
	Robinson 3B	4	0	0	0
	Amoros LF	4	0	0	0
	Newcombe P	3	0	1	0
	Zimmer PH	1	0	1	0
	Totals	34	2	7	2

1942	St. Louis Cardinals	AB	R	H	RBI
	Brown 2B	4	0	0	0
	Moore CF	4	1	1	0
	Slaughter RF	4	0	1	1
	Musial LF	3	1	1	0
	W. Cooper C	4	1	2	0
	Hopp 1B	4	0	2	2
	Kurowski 3B	4	0	0	0
	Marion SS	3	0	1	0
	M. Cooper P	3	0	0	0
	Totals	33	3	8	3

1955	Brooklyn Dodgers	000	100	010—2
1942	St. Louis Cardinals	000	001	11X—3

1955	Brooklyn Dodgers	IP	H	R	ER	BB	SO
	Newcombe (L.0—1)	8	8	3	3	1	2

1942	St. Louis Cardinals	IP	H	R	ER	BB	SO
	M. Cooper (W.0—1)	9	7	2	2	3	4

E.-Reese, Hopp. LOB.-Dodgers 9, Cardinals 7. 2B.-Slaughter, Newcombe, W. Cooper 2. HR.-Campanella, Hodges. SB.-Gilliam. S.-Hodges. T.0:00:15.

1st Semifinal Game

'61 N.Y. YANKS BEAT '69 N.Y. METS

COMPUTER PARK—The 1961 New York Yankees advanced to the finals of NBC's computer baseball tournament when they pushed across a run in the 9th inning to defeat the 1969 New York Mets, 2–1.

The Yankees scored the winning run after Yogi Berra opened the 9th with a single and was forced at 2nd by Bill Skowron. Skowron moved to 2nd on Clete Boyer's infield out and tallied on winning pitcher Whitey Ford's run-scoring single.

The Mets got on the scoreboard in the 2nd inning. Ron Swoboda singled, stole 2nd and came in on Jerry Grote's RBI single. The Yankees evened it on Roger Maris' leadoff homer in the 4th.

Ford went all the way to pick up his 2nd victory in the computer series. The Yankee lefthander allowed 8 hits, fanned 4 and walked 2. Tom Seaver permitted only 6 hits but absorbed the loss.

The box score follows:

1st Game—Semifinal Round

1969	New York Mets	AB	R	H	RBI
	Agee CF	4	0	2	0
	Harrelson SS	4	0	1	0
	Jones LF	4	0	1	0
	Clendenon 1B	4	0	0	0
	Swoboda RF	3	1	1	0
	Charles 3B	3	0	0	0
	Grote C	4	0	2	1
	Weis SS	4	0	1	0
	Seaver P	3	0	0	0
	Totals	33	1	8	1

1961	New York Yankees	AB	R	H	RBI
	Richardson 2B	3	0	0	0
	Kubek SS	3	0	0	0
	Maris RF	3	1	1	1
	Mantle CF	4	0	0	0
	Howard, C	4	0	1	0
	Berra LF	4	0	2	0
	Skowron 1B	4	1	0	0
	Boyer 3B	3	0	1	0
	Ford P	2	0	1	1
	Totals	30	2	6	2

1969	New York Mets	010	000	000—1
1961	New York Yankees	000	100	001—2

Two out when winning run scored

1969	New York Mets	IP	H	R	ER	BB	SO
	Seaver (L. 1—1)	8⅔	6	2	2	5	6

1961	New York Yankees	IP	H	R	ER	BB	SO
	Ford (W.2—0)	9	8	1	1	2	4

LOB—Mets 8, Yankees 8

DP-Yankees 1. 2B-Berra. 3B-Swoboda. HR-Maris. SB-Swoboda. S-Boyer. T.-0:00:15.

2nd Semifinal Game

THE BABE SLAMS 2 IN OVERCOMING 1942 CARDINALS

COMPUTER PARK—The 1927 Yankees, powered along on a 2-homer salvo by Babe Ruth, scored 3 runs in the 8th inning to eliminate the 1942 St. Louis Cardinals, 6–4, in the last game of the computerized semifinal round. The victory earned the 1927 Yanks the right to meet the 1961 Yankees in the title game.

Ruth's pair of home runs accounted for 3 runs, all at the expense of Mort Cooper, the starting and losing pitcher for the 1942 Redbirds. The Babe smacked a 2-run homer in the 5th and then came through again at long range with a solo clout leading off the 8th.

Enos Slaughter and Stan Musial, who each stroked 3 hits, paced the 8-hit attack for the Cardinals off winning pitcher Waite Hoyt. It was the 2nd tournament triumph for Hoyt.

The box score follows:

2nd Game—Semifinal Round

1942 St. Louis Cardinals	AB	R	H	RBI
Brown 2B	5	0	1	0
Moore CF	3	1	0	0
Slaughter RF	4	2	3	1
Musial LF	4	1	3	1
W. Cooper C	4	0	1	2
Hopp 1B	4	0	0	0
Kurowski 3B	3	0	0	0
Marion SS	4	0	0	0
M. Cooper P	3	0	0	0
H. Walker PH	1	0	0	0
Totals	35	4	8	4

1927 New York Yankees	AB	R	H	RBI
Combs CF	4	0	3	0
Koenig SS	3	1	1	1
Ruth RF	4	2	2	3
Gehrig 1B	2	0	0	0
Meusel LF	3	1	0	0
Lazzeri 2B	4	1	2	1
Dugan 3B	4	0	1	0
Collins C	4	1	2	1
Hoyt P	4	0	0	0
Totals	32	6	11	6

1942 St. Louis Cardinals	000	200	020—4
1927 New York Yankees	000	030	03X—6

1942 St. Louis Cardinals	IP	H	R	ER	BB	SO
M. Cooper	8	11	6	6	3	3

1927 New York Yankees	IP	H	R	ER	BB	SO
Hoyt	9	8	4	4	2	1

LOB—Cardinals 6; Yankees 7.

E-Kurowski. 2B-Slaughter, Musial, W. Cooper, Lazzeri. HR-Ruth (2). SB-Collins, Marion. S. Koenig. T-0:00:15

Final Championship Game

1927 YANKEES TRIUMPH OVER 1961 YANKEES IN ALL-TIME BASEBALL TOURNAMENT

COMPUTER PARK Lou Gehrig's 2-out home run off Whitey Ford in the 10th inning earned the 1927 New York Yankees a 5–3 victory over the 1961 New York Yankees to win the final round of NBC's Computer Baseball Tournament.

Gehrig's 2-run blast broke up a 3–3 pitching duel between Ford and Hall-of-Fame righthander Waite Hoyt.

Roger Maris, who smacked a record 61 homers in 1961, hit 2 home runs off Hoyt to account for 2 of the 1961 Yankees' 3 runs. Babe Ruth connected for a 2-run homer for the 1927 Yankees in the 1st inning.

The box score follows:

Final Round

1961 Yankees	AB	R	H	RBI
Richardson 2B	5	0	1	1
Kubek SS	5	0	1	0
Maris RF	5	2	2	2
Mantle CF	4	0	1	0
Howard C	5	0	1	0
Berra LF	4	0	0	0
Skowron 1B	3	0	1	0
Boyer 3B	4	1	1	0
Ford P	4	0	1	0
Totals	39	3	9	3

1927 Yankees	AB	R	H	RBI
Combs CF	4	1	0	0
Koenig SS	5	1	2	0
Ruth RF	5	2	3	2
Gehrig 1B	5	1	1	2
Meusel LF	4	0	1	1
Lazzeri 2B	3	0	2	0
Dugan 3B	4	0	0	0
Collins C	4	0	1	0
Hoyt P	4	0	0	0
Totals	38	5	10	5

1961 New York Yankees	111	000	000	0—3
1927 New York Yankees	200	001	000	2—5

1961 New York Yankees	IP	H	R	ER	BB	SO
Ford	9⅔	10	5	5	2	0

1927 New York Yankees	IP	H	R	ER	BB	SO
Hoyt	10	9	3	3	3	5

LOB—'61 Yankees 8; '27 Yankees 6.

E-Boyer, 2B-Kubek, Meusel. HR-Maris 2, Ruth, Gehrig. T-0:00:15.

—The Eds.

The Little League World Series

Little League Baseball originated in Williamsport, Pa., in 1939 with the formation of 3 teams. Today the program is worldwide, providing girls and boys from 8 to 18 with a well-planned and supervised sports activity.

Having roots in some 31 countries, the program involves slightly more than 9,000 leagues and 2½ to 3 million youngsters. Thousands of adult volunteers are instrumental in guiding the program and helping to formulate policy.

As the Little League program grew, its value to the youth of this nation was recognized and eventually the Congress of the U.S. deemed it proper to grant a Federal Charter—the only such sports program to have this distinction.

Numerous other youth baseball programs have emulated Little League, copying its format and rules. Throughout its history Little League has adhered to the original concepts of discipline, sportsmanship, and safety.

The list of Little League volunteers reads like a Who's Who listing. The names of young men who have moved through Little League to successful futures is even more impressive.

In addition to providing a soundly organized program for America's youth, Little League has been a leader in promoting safety features essential to any sound effort. Many of the features developed by Little League have found their way to other areas of the sports world, including the adult professional level.

Little League, with its softball and baseball programs for girls and boys, is healthy and growing through the dedication and efforts of men, women, and youngsters around the world.

1947—1st Little League World Series

After some 8 years of slow growth, beginning in 1939, the 1st official Little League Tournament was held at what was then known as the Max M. Brown Memorial Park. The site in Williamsport, Pa., since has become known as the Original Little League Field.

In the 1st tournament, 11 teams were entered for a total of 10 games. A 12th team, Montgomery, had to bow out at the last moment. All but one of the teams was from Pennsylvania and most of those were from, or close to, the Williamsport area. The "outsider" was Hammonton Little League of New Jersey. Pennsylvania teams entered in the tournament came from Lock Haven, Montoursville, Perry Jersey Shore, Williamsport (Lincoln Little League, Maynard Midget League, Brandon Little League, and Sunday School Little League), and Milton (Milton Midgets).

The championship game saw Maynard Midget League of Williamsport go against Lock Haven Little League. The 2,500 fans attending saw a total of 23 runs scored as Maynard defeated the neighboring city, 16–7. Tony Ingersoll, Maynard 3rd baseman, batted 1,000 for the day, going 4 for 4. Jack Losch, centerfielder for the winners, later starred at the University of Miami and with the Green Bay Packers.

1948—2nd Little League World Series

The popularity of the Little League World Series spread rapidly following the success of the 1st tournament in 1947.

Moving to a more manageable 8-team tournament from the initial 12 teams, the series gained a greater national flavor with 5 States other than Pennsylvania entered. Teams participating were from Middletown, Conn.; St. Petersburg, Fla.; Hammonton, N.J.; Corning, N.Y.; and Alexandria, Va. Pennsylvania entries represented Lock Haven, Harrisburg, and Williamsport-Loyalsock.

In the final game of the tournament Lock Haven, making its 2nd bid for the Little League title in as many years, had to come from behind to down the youngsters from St. Petersburg, Fla., 6–5.

St. Petersburg opened the game with 3 runs in the 1st inning. Lock Haven came back with one run in the 1st, 2 in the 2nd, and a big 3-run 4th inning to take a 6–3 lead.

The challengers picked up one run in the 5th, ending the inning with the bases loaded. In the last inning St. Petersburg pulled to within one run of Lock Haven, 6–5. With the tying run on 3rd base and 2 out, Larry Lytle, Lock Haven centerfielder, made a running catch of a line drive shot to end the game and clinch the victory.

Joey Cardamone, Lock Haven catcher, won the hearts and cheers of the fans with his display of sportsmanship throughout the game. As each opposing player crossed home plate after hitting a home run, Joey stepped up, smiling, to shake the player's hand.

The consolation game was won by Hammonton, N.J., 10–1 over Williamsport-Loyalsock.

1949—3rd Little League World Series

New steel bleachers, the result of a $7,500 community fund-raising effort, greeted the thousands of fans attending the 3rd annual Little League National Tournament, August

24–27, 1949, at the original Little League field on West 4th Street, Williamsport.

Eight teams were entered in the tournament from the 400 Little Leagues then operating in 25 States. To commemorate this 3rd tournament, Williamsport officials issued a special cachet to be used on all mail going from the city.

Lock Haven Little League, defending its 1948 championship, went down to defeat, 3–0, in the Series opener against Pensacola (Fla.) Little League. The Florida team went on to reach the final game where it was defeated by Hammonton, N.J., 5–0 before more than 10,000 fans.

Hammonton was making its 3rd appearance in Little League tournament play and was the consolation winner in 1948. Joey DiGiacomo, a left-hander, gave up one hit, struck out 14 and walked 2 in gaining the victory.

Bridgeport (Conn.) Little League won the consolation game, 12–1 over Corning, N.Y. Other teams participating in the 1949 tournament were Lafayette, Ind.; Canton, O.; and North Charleston, S.C.

1950—4TH LITTLE LEAGUE WORLD SERIES

This midcentury year saw the official incorporation of Little League Baseball in order to better manage the needs of a growing concern.

It also saw the State of Texas lay claim to the Little League title as Houston Little League defeated Bridgeport, Conn., 2–1 before approximately 9,000 fans.

For the 1st time since the Series began there was only one team (Punxsutawney Little League) representing Pennsylvania.

The strength of the Houston team lay in the ability of Billy Martin, 12, who pitched 2 no-hitters enroute to the championship game. In the final tilt Martin gave up just one hit, a single.

The Series also saw young Gordon Andrews, the St. Petersburg, Fla., pitcher, strike out 21 batters for a new tournament record. But St. Petersburg was eliminated by Kankakee, Ill., who went on to win the consolation game, downing Hagerstown, Md., 1–0.

Clinton, S.C., and Westerly, R.I., also fielded teams in this 4th Series.

National interest in the World Series was evident with 6 motion picture companies covering the final game—Paramount News, News of the Day, Warner-Pathé, Universal, Telenews, and 20th Century-Fox Movietone. The game was also covered live by NBC radio and on a rebroadcast by NBC television.

1951—5TH LITTLE LEAGUE WORLD SERIES

The 1951 Little League World Series was opened officially when Hall of Famer Cy Young threw out the 1st ball. It was the 2nd straight year that saw Little League teams from Texas (North Austin Little League) and Connecticut (Stamford Little League) hooked up in a duel for the championship.

However, the youngsters from the Nutmeg State were determined to wear the crown home, and that they did, defeating the Texans 3–0 before one of the largest crowds yet to witness a Little League Series contest—well over 10,000 were estimated in attendance.

The big gun for Connecticut was Andy Wasil, a right-handed fast baller, who fanned 16 and allowed only 3 scattered hits. In addition Wasil powered a 2-run homer over the right centerfield fence to aid his team's cause.

The consolation game saw Fairmont, W. Va., defeat San Bernardino, Calif., 5–4. Other teams in the tournament included Potter-McKean, Pa.; Pensacola, Fla.; Portland, Me.; and Chicago, Ill.

It was announced that 766 leagues were affiliated with Little League in 1951 and the program was being played in 35 States and 5 foreign countries.

1952—6TH LITTLE LEAGUE WORLD SERIES

Foreign flavor was introduced into the Little League World Series in 1952 as Montreal Little League, from Quebec, Canada, became one of the participants.

Tabbed by many veteran Little Leaguers as one of the most exciting games played in the Series, the final game saw the Pennsylvania entry, Monongahela Little League, go out in front of Norwalk, Conn., by one run in the 2nd inning. They added another in the top of the 3rd.

Norwalk came back to cut the lead to one run by scoring in the bottom of the 3rd and they tied the game 2–2 in the 4th.

The Pennsylvania lads then regained the lead with a booming home run by Richard Sacane, shortstop, in the top of the 5th.

Trailing by one run and at bat for the final time, Norwalk sent its smallest player, Harry Brown, to pinch hit. He drew a walk and immediately stole 2nd base. The next batter grounded out and then Brown raced home on a long single by Ralph DiMagilo, to tie the game. When the throw-in took a bad hop, DiMagilo went on to 2nd base. On the next pitch he stole 3rd and was in position to score.

Monongahela, seeing disaster about to strike, decided to change pitchers; but the relief pitcher zoomed in a high pitch that went over the catcher's head while DiMagilo raced in with the winning run as Norwalk won it 4–3.

The consolation game was won by Hackensack, N.J., 2–0 over San Diego, Calif. Teams eliminated earlier in the Series were Little

Rock, Ark.; Whiting, Ind.; Montreal, Canada; and Mooresville, N.C.

1953—7TH LITTLE LEAGUE WORLD SERIES

The 1953 World Series was one that generated a great deal of interest, because of the high caliber of the teams participating. It was termed by many as one of the best matched tournaments since the Series began.

The week-long eliminations saw the final game pitting the determined South Side Little League of Birmingham, Ala., against a good, strong team from Schenectady, N.Y. The outcome? The lads from Dixie won the flag, 1–0.

The hero of the day was diminutive Joe Sims, a left-handed pitcher, who his teammates claimed "could throw a baseball through the hole in a candy lifesaver." Sims, employing a huge wad of bubble gum, displayed iron nerves as he guided his team to victory.

The lone tally of the afternoon came in the 1st inning on a pair of walks given up by Schenectady starting pitcher, Stevie Buchheim, and a single to left field by Dick DeRoberts, Alabama centerfielder, which scored Bruce Gordon. The Southern region representative went out in front to stay.

Front Royal, Va., won the consolation game 3–0 over Camp Hill, Pa. Teams from North Newton, Mass.; Little Rock, Ark.; Vancouver, B.C.; and Joliet, Ill., also took part in Series play.

1954—8TH LITTLE LEAGUE WORLD SERIES

Bouncing back from a 1–0 defeat at the hands of Alabama in 1953, Schenectady (N.Y.) Little League powered its way to a 7–5 victory over Colton (Calif.) Little League to claim the coveted crown.

Sparked by a homerun blast by pitcher Bill Masucci in the 1st frame with one man on base, Schenectady went on to add 3 more runs in the 2nd inning and build a commanding lead.

Masucci, a right-hander, gave up only 4 hits in posting the win. However, 2 of those hits accounted for 4 of Colton's 5 runs.

Colton did not get on the scoreboard until the 3rd inning when Ken Hubbs homered. The Californians pulled to within one run of the New York club in the 5th inning when Norm Housley drilled a 3-run shot over the leftfield wall, making the score 5–4.

In the home half of the inning New York added 2 insurance runs making it 7–4 going into the top of the 6th.

With one out, Colton put 2 men on by virtue of walks. On the strength of John Doty's sharp single to right field, Clarence Brumm scooted home with the 5th California run. But, Masucci bore down and sealed the victory by

setting down the last 2 batters via the strike-out route. (An excellent book, *Destiny's Darlings* by Martin Ralbovsky—New York: Hawthorn, 1974—tells the story of the 1954 Schenectady champions and what became of the team members in the 20 years that followed their victory.)

The consolation game was won by Masontown, Pa., with a 7–1 victory over Melrose Park, Ill., in 9 innings of play. Teams participating in preliminary contests included Hampton, Va.; Galveston, Tex.; Lakeland, Fla.; and Needham, Mass.

1955—9TH LITTLE LEAGUE WORLD SERIES

This year saw the 1st extra-inning championship game as the Morrisville (Pa.) Little Leaguers battled Delaware Township Little League of New Jersey to a 3–3 tie at the end of 6 innings of regulation play.

The end came in storybook fashion in the bottom of the 7th inning when the Morrisville catcher, Richie Cominski, poled a solo blast into the leftfield bleachers to ice the victory for the Keystone State representatives.

Earlier, in a see-saw duel, New Jersey had scored in the 1st, 2nd, and 4th innings. Morrisville tallied in the 1st, with 2 runs, and tied it in the 4th on Harry Foulke's homerun.

Herb Harrison, the Jersey pitcher, struck out 13 batters before being forced to leave the mound because of the Little League rule limiting pitchers to 6 innings.

The consolation game, won by Auburn, Ala., 1–0 over Winchester, Mass., also went into the 7th inning before being decided. Earlier games had eliminated leagues from Hamtramck, Mich.; Glen Falls, N.Y.; Alexandria, La.; and San Diego, Calif.

1956—10TH LITTLE LEAGUE WORLD SERIES

This year marked the arrival of the 1st former Little Leaguer in the Major League Baseball ranks as Joey Jay joined the Milwaukee Braves.

As for the championship, Roswell, N.M., won the title game, 3–1, downing Delaware Township, N.J., who finished as runnerup for the 2nd year in a row. New Jersey had taken the lead, 1–0 in the 4th inning with a blast over the centerfield fence by Henry (Sweet Pea) Singleton. Play was tight with each team getting just 2 hits. Both teams played errorless ball.

Tom Jordan, the New Mexico right-handed pitcher, gave his father an unforgettable birthday present as he struck out 14 batters to equal the then existing record. He was also cast into the hero's role with his game-winning 3-run homer in the 4th inning.

The consolation game was won by Winchester, Mass., 2–1, over Colton, Calif.

Other teams participating in the Series included Eastchester, N.Y.; Hamtramck, Mich.; Auburn, Ala.; and Upper Darby, Pa.

1957—11TH LITTLE LEAGUE WORLD SERIES

As Little League Baseball moved into the 11th annual World Series a new era was dawning, an era of foreign competition and a complete realignment of geographical areas covered by the growing program. As a result, only 4 teams were in the '57 Series.

Arriving to compete in the tournament were the Monterrey (Mexico) Little Leaguers—a team of mighty mites who immediately became the "darlings" of the Series.

Riding on the strong pitching arm of Angel Macias, the poised, pint-sized youngsters from south of the border proved they could play baseball to the point of perfection as they shut out a big La Mesa, Calif., team, 4–0 for the Little League crown.

Chewing gum with a vengeance, Angel proceeded to twirl the 1st perfect game for the title. The ambidextrous youngster, who not only pitched and batted from either side of the plate, had his right-hand fastball and curve working to perfection. He faced the minimum 18 batters, striking out 11. His teammates, playing smoothly behind him, never permitted a ball out of the infield.

Monterrey scored all 4 runs in the 5th inning in a rally that saw 9 Mexican batters stride to the plate. Although Lew Riley, the California pitcher, tried hard to stem the tide, it definitely was Monterrey's day.

In the consolation game, Bridgeport, Conn., defeated Escanaba, Mich., 4–3.

1958—12TH LITTLE LEAGUE WORLD SERIES

From the 4 teams in 1957, the tournament had been expanded to 7. The entries were highlighted by the news that once again a team from Monterrey would be a strong contender.

The report proved true as the youngsters from Mexico breezed to a 10–1 victory over Kankakee, Ill., to capture the title for the 2nd year in a row.

The outcome of the final game of the classic was never in doubt as the lads from south of the border opened the scoring in the 1st inning and beat a constant staccato on home plate for 5 frames. The only run of the 6th inning was the lone score chalked up by Illinois.

Six of the Monterrey runs were home runs by Andres Galvan, Manuel Mora, Hugo Lozano, and Juan Castro. Hector Torres was almost the perfect pitcher for the Monterrey team, holding the Illinois boys hitless for 4 innings.

The consolation game was won by Gadsden, Ala., by virtue of its 2–0 win over Darien, Conn., in 9 innings of play.

Other teams participating in the Series were Valleyfield, Quebec, Canada; Honolulu, Hawaii; and Portland, Oreg.

1959—13TH LITTLE LEAGUE WORLD SERIES

Although the setting had changed to the new stadium in South Williamsport, the trappings were much the same. In fact, the winner of the 13th annual World Series was the Hamtramck (Mich.) Little League which was making its 3rd bid to cop the crown, as Art Deras led his Hamtramck teammates to a 12–0 victory over Auburn (Calif.) Little League.

Deras, who had turned in 10 no-hit ballgames in season play, struck out 14 batters and walked only 2 in his 3-hit effort. He further aided his team's cause with a 3-run homer in the 5th inning—his 33rd of the season.

Bobby Sunada, an American-born Japanese right-hander, suffered his 1st defeat in 3 years of Little League pitching with the California team.

Auburn opened the game with a single by Phil Olrich and a line shot down 3rd by Sunada giving rise to high hopes for the California rooters. The West Coast lads failed to muster a scoring punch, however, and never threatened again.

The consolation game was won by Schenectady, N.Y., 1–0 over Oahu, Hawaii. Teams from Valleyfield, Quebec, Canada; San Juan, Puerto Rico; and Gadsden, Ala., contested the early games.

1960—14TH LITTLE LEAGUE WORLD SERIES

The Little League World Championship came back to its home State this year, as Levittown, Pa., blanked the Fort Worth (Tex.) Little Leaguers, 5–0 before approximately 15,000 fans—the largest crowd yet to witness the classic.

While the sweltering crowd cheered, Levittown pitcher Joe Mormello kept his fastball sizzling as he notched the 3rd no-hit, no-run game in Series history. Mormello fanned 16 batters and gave up 2 walks in going the 6 full innings.

The Texans had men on base in the 4th and 6th innings, but failed to score.

Mormello opened the scoring for his club with a homerun blast in the 1st frame with teammate Jim Gardner on base.

Jim Williams, the Fort Worth pitcher, ran into big trouble as Levittown unloaded the big guns in the 3rd inning. Julian Kalkstein led off with a homer; Gardner singled and Mormello walked; Joe Fioravanti lined out. The

Fort Worth manager made a pitching change with Dave Hooper moving to the mound.

Jim Grauel greeted Hooper with a double which tallied the final 2 runs for the Keystoners. The Series was broadcast by ABC-TV to 126 affiliated stations across the country.

The consolation game was won by Lakewood, Calif., who defeated Monterrey, Mexico, in a thriller, 4–3. Other teams participating in the Series made an international roster—Pearl Harbor, Hawaii; New Boston, O.; West Berlin, Germany; and Toronto, Ontario, Canada.

1961—15TH LITTLE LEAGUE WORLD SERIES

El Cajon Little League of California rode a mighty homerun blast in the final inning to a 4–2 win over the stunned El Campo Little League of Texas to lock up the 1961 title.

Playing before more than 16,000 perspiring fans, it appeared for a time that the cherished crown was headed for the Lone Star State.

California took the lead in the 2nd inning when Mike Salvatore, El Cajon pitcher, was hit by a pitch, stole 2nd, went to 3rd on a wild pitch, and then came home on a single by teammate Carl Buffo.

In the 4th frame El Campo came up with its 1st run when, with the bases loaded and with the Texans anxious to score, Bill Shutt bunted and Salvatore's throw to his catcher, Roger Cargin, went astray.

One out later, Phil Winfield crossed the plate on a passed ball to put the Lone Star State ahead, 2–1.

It was in the 6th inning that the California bats began to explode. Mickey Alasantro singled. Todd Lieber followed with a one-bagger and the California fans began to smell a rally. Salvatore took 2 pitches for a 2–0 count and then unloaded a 200′ screamer over the fence to save the day for the West Coast.

In the consolation game, Monterrey, Mexico, rode to a 4–0 victory over Hilo, Hawaii. Eliminated earlier in Series play were teams from Levittown, Pa.; Montreal, Quebec, Canada; Terre Haute, Ind.; and Pirmasens, Germany.

1962—16TH LITTLE LEAGUE WORLD SERIES

The 1962 championship game saw San Jose Little League of California shut out the midwestern representative, Kankakee, Ill., 3–0.

Much of the credit for the California victory must go to the biggest Little Leaguer ever to take the Series field—Ted Campbell, who at 12 years of age stood 6′ 1″ tall and tipped the scales at 210 lbs. His pitching was something to behold.

Campbell twirled a no-hitter and issued just one walk in going the distance.

As the more than 20,000 fans watched, San Jose tallied 2 runs in the 4th inning as a result of errors by the Kankakee battery.

The 3rd and final tally came in the 5th inning as Vaughn Takaha, California shortstop, poled a homerun over the centerfield wall.

Credit must also go to Dan Brewster, Kankakee pitcher, who allowed only 3 hits and one walk.

This was the 2nd successive year that California claimed the Little League flag. For Kankakee, it was the 3rd time in Little League Series play. Each time they finished in 2nd place.

Doing play-by-play commentary was Jackie Robinson.

The consolation game was won by Pitman, N.J., over Monterrey, Mexico, 8–5. Competition leading up to the final playoffs had been vigorous between teams from Del Rio, Tex.; Stoney Creek, Ontario, Canada; Vienne, France; and Kunitachi, Japan (the 1st all-Japanese team to compete in the World Series).

1963—17TH LITTLE LEAGUE WORLD SERIES

California maintained its domination of the World Series, as Granada Hills Little League claimed the crown nipping the Eastern Regional representative, Stratford, Conn., 2–1 in an extra-inning affair. This was only the 2nd extra-inning championship game since the Series began.

Utilizing the curveball pitching of Dave Sehnem and the slugging of Ken Kinsman, Granada Hills took the lead in the 4th inning with a booming homerun off Stratford pitcher Johnny Slosar.

Connecticut, however, came back in the top of the 5th to tie it at 1–1 when Harold Smith garnered a single, moved to 3rd, and scored on a passed ball.

With the score tied at the end of the regulation 6 innings, the title game moved into extra innings. In the home half of the 7th Kinsman lined a single to center, Fred Seibly grounded to the pitcher, and Kinsman was out on the force at 2nd. On the double play attempt, the throw to 1st went wild and Seibly took 2nd. He then scored when Jimmy (Nails) Walker hit a short looper behind 1st base. The play at the plate was high and Granada Hills had a 2–1 victory.

The number of teams in the Series was cut to 7 when the team from Tokyo, Japan, was withdrawn at the last moment by action of the Japanese Government. Teams remaining in the competition included Houston, Tex.; Valleyfield, Quebec, Canada; and Monterrey, Mexico. In the consolation game, Duluth, Minn., defeated Izmir, Turkey, 3–1.

1964—18TH LITTLE LEAGUE WORLD SERIES

The growth and interest in Little League Baseball was evidenced in the more than 20,000 fans who jammed the stands and terraces surrounding the Howard J. Lamade Memorial field to watch Staten Island, N.Y. shut out Monterrey, Mexico, 4–0 for the Series title.

Danny Yaccarino posted a no-hitter and poled a homerun to pace his club to the win. The youngster missed notching a perfect game when he issued a walk in the final inning.

The right-hander sounded the victory charge in the opening stanza with a homer over the rightfield fence. The classy New Yorkers added a 2nd run in the 2nd inning when Greg Klee singled and moved to 2nd on a throwing error. He came home on an error when the ball was dropped on a tag play along the 3rd base line.

Staten Island posted the final 2 runs in the 4th. Klee again singled, moved to 2nd on a bunt by Ed Codnig, and scored on a fielder's choice. Godnig came in on a single by Bob Nugent to make it 4–0.

Yaccarino held the Mexican lads to 3 easy fly balls to the outfield and several easily handled infield grounders.

The consolation game was won by Mobile, Ala., 3–2 over Tachikawa City, Japan. Other cities sending teams to the Series included Bartlesville, Okla.; La Puente, Calif.; Valleyfield, Quebec, Canada; and Wiesbaden, Germany.

All 8 teams journeyed to New York City where the Staten Island youngsters · were treated to a ticker-tape parade. All teams visited the World's Fair and were guests of the *New York Daily News* during their 3-day stay.

1965—19TH LITTLE LEAGUE WORLD SERIES

The Little League flag remained in the East as Windsor Locks, Conn., turned back Stoney Creek, Canada, 3–1 in the 19th annual Little League World Series that was played before more than 20,000 enthusiastic fans.

It was Dale Misiek's 2-run homer and the clutch pitching of Mike Rocha that kept the title from the 1st Canadian team to reach the championship bracket.

The youngsters from Canada went into the lead in the 1st inning when Jeff Dalton, who had drawn a walk off Roche, moved around the bases and eventually scored on a passed ball. Canada managed to put men on base in every inning but could not score.

In the 4th frame the Connecticut bats exploded when Frank Aniello opened with a single and advanced to 2nd on a wild pitch. Misiek then put his 180 lbs. into a towering drive that sailed over the centerfield fence

giving Windsor Locks a 2–1 lead. The attack continued with one out when Ed Holmes singled up the middle and took 2nd on another wild pitch. Steve Scheerer cracked a sharp single to short left field to score Holmes, and Connecticut had all it needed on the scoreboard.

In the consolation game Waco, Tex., downed Jeffersonville, Ind., 5–1. Teams from Maracaibo, Venezuela; Phoenix, Ariz.; Tokyo, Japan; and Rota, Spain, also proved their competitive spirit in Series play.

1966—20TH LITTLE LEAGUE WORLD SERIES

For the 1st time since 1950 a Texas Little League team won the World Series as the Houston Little Leaguers rode roughshod over the Little Leaguers of West New York, N.J., 8–2 before some 21,000 excited fans.

West New York jumped into a 2-run lead in the 1st inning and held on for 2½ innings.

However, in the 3rd inning the Texas uprising began and even a thunderstorm couldn't stop it.

With 2 Texans on base, the game was delayed some 43 minutes due to a heavy rain. When it resumed, Mark Harding banged out a single to load the bases. Steve Reeves punched a long single to score Tom Herrick and Byron Boyne. Harding then came in to tally on a fielder's choice play. The inning ended 3–2, Houston.

Texas added 3 more runs in the 4th when Ray Plumb homered, Herrick was hit by a pitch; Schneider moved Herrick to 2nd with a single. Herrick was retired at 3rd on Boyne's single, Harding reached 1st on an error, and Reeves doubled home Schneider and Boyne to make the score 6–2, Houston.

Two more insurance runs were added by Texas in the 5th as Raymer doubled and Dave McCaleb homered.

The consolation game was won by Sacramento, Calif., 6–0 over Wakayama, Japan. Preliminary contests were well fought by teams from Windsor, Ontario, Canada; Monterrey, Mexico; Kankakee, Ill.; and Rhein-Main, Germany.

1967—21ST LITTLE LEAGUE WORLD SERIES

History was made as the Little Leaguers from West Tokyo, Japan, parlayed classy fielding, timely hitting, and strong pitching to defeat Chicago Little League, 4–1 in the 21st annual World Series.

Despite a morning-long rain, 17,000 fans turned out to watch Masahiro Miyahara toss a 3-hitter enroute to victory.

West Tokyo got its 1st run when centerfielder Kenichi Tsuchiya belted a 220' homer.

The Pacific visitors then clinched the Series flag in the 5th inning with 3 more runs as Seiichi Hayashi walked, Tsuchiya singled, and Takeshi Shiono drove in Hayashi with a single. Tsuchiya later scored on a wild throw by Ken Snyder. Shiono added the final run as he crossed home plate on a single by Miyahara.

Rich O'Leary broke the ice for Chicago in the 5th with a single. Snyder followed in similar fashion. Tom Calabrese punched a grounder up the middle and O'Leary came around to score. Miyahara had seen enough, so he then locked the door on the midwest hopefuls.

The consolation game was won by Newtown-Edgemont, Pa., who edged Linares, Mexico, 2–1. Good sportsmanship was the hallmark of other teams participating in the Series—Fast Trail, British Columbia, Canada; Tampa, Fla.; Rota, Spain; and Northridge, Calif.

1968—22ND LITTLE LEAGUE WORLD SERIES

When the dust had settled on the 22nd annual Little League World Series, the very polite and very well-trained youngsters from Japan had chalked up their 2nd consecutive championship by edging Virginia, 1–0 before a crowd estimated at 25,000.

The Little Leaguers from Wakayama, Japan, capitalized on 2 errors in the 4th inning to post an unearned run. Hideaki Higashide, the Japanese pitcher, then tied the Richmond, Va., batters in knots to preserve the win.

Wakayama's run developed when with one out, Takauki Nishide walked. Tim Reid, a fine catcher with a strong arm, tried to pick off Nishide at 1st. Reid's throw went into right field and the alert Nishide motored to 3rd.

The throw-in was fielded by Roger Miller who slipped and fell as the ball rolled away. Nishide, who had paused at 3rd, broke for home. It looked like Miller could still make the play at the plate, but Reid was given another error when he dropped Miller's throw and the run scored.

Richmond, which showed plenty of power in winning its 1st 2 Series games, just couldn't cope with Higashide's curve ball.

The consolation game was won by Santa Ana, Calif., with a 1–0 victory over Sherbrooke-Lennoxville, Quebec, Canada. Other teams sharing the excitement of Series play included Chinandega, Nicaragua; Terre Haute, Ind.; Hagerstown, Md.; and Wiesbaden, Germany.

1969—23RD LITTLE LEAGUE WORLD SERIES

Hopes of returning the Little League crown to U.S. soil were dashed in this Series that saw a new entry, Taiwan, blank Santa Clara, Calif., Little League, 5–0 before an estimated 27,000–30,000 fans.

The Little Leaguers from Taipei, Taiwan, proved to the many fans that they could play baseball. When the game ended, many said it was the best team ever to play in the World Series.

The California lads tried gamely in the 1st and 3rd innings when they had men on 1st and 2nd and 1st and 3rd respectively. Each time they failed to furnish the scoring punch. They never threatened again.

In a hectic 2nd inning Taiwan capitalized on 3 hits, 2 passed balls, 2 stolen bases, a walk, and a wild pitch to post a 2-run lead.

They added 2 more runs in the 4th inning when they combined 2 hits with 3 Santa Clara errors to pad their score.

For the 1st time the consolation game ended in a "no contest" by agreement of both teams after 9 innings of play with the score tied 1–1 between Elyria, O., and West Tampa, Fla. The game was called in order that the championship game could begin on time.

Yankee great Mickey Mantle, was the sportscaster of the day for ABC-Television. The championship game was broadcast to Nationalist China where it was heard in the wee hours of the morning.

Other teams participating in the series included Newberry, Pa.; Wiesbaden, Germany; Mayaguez, Puerto Rico; and Valleyfield, Quebec, Canada.

1970—24TH LITTLE LEAGUE WORLD SERIES

After a drought of 3 years, the Little League title came back home this year in a championship game that pitted Wayne, N.J., against Campbell, Calif. The Garden State lads won it, shutting out California, 2–0.

However, it wasn't the big bats of the Jersey Little Leaguers as expected, but the great defensive plays executed in the field and a big 2-out, 2-run double by little Dave Shaver that won the game as some 30,000 fans cheered.

Wayne threatened in the 1st inning and then bunched 3 hits together in the 2nd to get the needed runs on the scoreboard.

Ron Webb singled to short centerfield and moved to 2nd on Bill Lee's bunt. Bob Houghton pinch-hit for Tom Olsen and beat out a chopper as Webb rambled over to 3rd.

Mike Fantau took a called ball and Houghton steamed to 2nd; the stage was set. Fantau struck out, however, and that put little Shaver in the limelight. The youngster stepped in and lined a double to centerfield where it bounced past Kevin Linnane, enabling Webb and Houghton to scamper home with the 2 big runs.

California managed to get men on base in each inning but the 6th, but the tight defensive play of the fired-up Wayne Little Leaguers shut the door each time.

In the consolation tilt, Chinandega, Nicaragua, blanked Highland, Ind., 3–0. Other teams participating were Chiayi, Taiwan; Nashville, Tenn.; Wiesbaden, Germany; and Valleyfield, Quebec, Canada.

1971—25TH LITTLE LEAGUE WORLD SERIES

In an overtime thriller, the Tainan Little League from Taiwan exploded for 9 runs in the 9th inning to down Gary, Ind., 12–3 and thus return the Little League flag to the Far East.

As some 32,000 fans watched, the 2 teams battled to a 3–3 tie at the end of the regulation 6 innings. Then in the top of the 9th, Tainan cracked the game wide open, garnering 9 runs to demolish the Gary contingent, the 1st all-Negro squad in Series history.

Led by Lloyd McClendon, Gary's ace moundsman, the Indiana representatives jumped to a 3–0 lead in the 1st inning when with 2 men on base McClendon unloaded his 5th Series homer into the centerfield crowd.

The Far East champions notched one run in the 3rd and 2 in the 4th to lock up the game at 3–3.

The Tainan barrage began in the top of the 9th and wound up with 6 hits, 4 walks, 2 bunts, one sacrifice fly, and one wild pitch as the Gary squad appeared to fold.

The hero for the Pacific Little League was Chin-Mu Hsu who set a strikeout record of 22 for the Series.

The consolation game went to Wahiawa, Hawaii, 3–1 over Madrid, Spain. Other teams participating in the Series included Caguas, Puerto Rico; Brockville, Ontario, Canada; Augusta, Me.; and Lexington, Ky.

1972—26TH LITTLE LEAGUE WORLD SERIES

The Far East continued its dominance in Little League Baseball, winning its 5th World Series in the last 6 years as Taipei, Taiwan, captured the flag with a 6–0 shutout over Hammond, Ind.

Taipei, which allowed only one run in 18 innings of series play got 4-hit pitching from Chen Chih-Shun and power hitting from Lin Hsiang-Jui. John Davis, a left-hander, tried in vain to silence the Taipei batters. Lin tagged Davis for a home run in the 2nd.

George Leonakis relieved Davis in the 3rd and the Far East youngsters promptly scored 3 runs on 3 hits and 4 errors as the Indiana defense fell apart before the 30,000 fans.

Mike Rozgeny got 2 of his team's 4 hits. Chen struck out 12 and did not issue a walk.

Once again the title game was beamed back to Taiwan, where national interest was high.

In the consolation game, Pearl City, Hawaii, and San Juan, Puerto Rico, battled to a 5–5 tie over the regulation distance. The game was called due to a noon curfew established to assure time for the title game.

Other teams making the trip to the stadium included Madrid, Spain; New York City, N.Y.; Vienna, Va.; and Windsor, Ontario, Canada. All 8 teams concluded the series with a 3-day tour of Washington, D.C.

1973—27TH LITTLE LEAGUE WORLD SERIES

Getting their 3rd straight no-hitter—2nd in a row by pitcher Huang Ching-hui—and their usual explosive run-scoring attack, Taiwan's Far East champions rolled to their 3rd straight Little League World Series championship by downing the Tucson (Ariz.) Little Leaguers, 12–0.

Ailing Mike Fimbers, a southpaw with a sharp curveball and change-up, managed to hold the Far East champs at bay until the 4th inning when Fimbers, who had an attack of asthma, ran into trouble. The Taiwanese found the combination and quickly picked up 3 runs before the inning ended.

Fimbers was replaced by Mike Martinez who ran into a buzz saw as Taiwan tallied 5 runs in the 5th and added 4 more in the 6th.

Only 2 Arizona players reached base—Tony Bravo on Huang's only walk in the 1st and Martinez on an error. Huang whiffed 16 of the 19 men to face him.

Tainan City set 5 batting records. Their 12 homers in 3 games, and their 57 runs in 3 games broke the old Series record of 34 set in 1962. The other marks were set in earlier games.

In the consolation game, Tampa, Fla., downed Birmingham, Mich., 2–1 in 7 innings. Earlier battles were also hard-fought by teams from Bitburg Air Force Base, Germany; Whalley, British Columbia, Canada; Colonie, N.Y.; and Monterrey, Mexico.

1974—28TH LITTLE LEAGUE WORLD SERIES

Playing in methodical fashion, the Far East Leaguers from Kao Hsiung rolled over all opposition to claim Taiwan's 4th straight World Series flag before more than 30,000 fans attending the annual classic. Victim of the Kao Hsiung onslaught was Red Bluff, Calif., 12–1.

The victory also gave Taiwan all 3 Little League world titles this year. Earlier, Taiwan captured the Senior Little League title at Gary, Ind., and the Big League title at Fort Lauderdale, Fla.

The hard-hitting Taiwanese rapped out a total of 13 hits including 4 homers as they scored 5 runs in the 1st, one in the 2nd, one in the 3rd, 2 in the 4th, and 3 in the 5th.

Key man for the champions was Lin Wen-Hsiung, who had 2 home runs and 2 singles for the day's work. He struck out 15 men, gave up 2 hits and walked one.

The only bright spot for the California Little Leaguers was a home run shot by Greg Shoff in the 5th inning.

All the games involving the Far Eastern team were beamed back to Taiwan via 3 television networks. This meant the Taiwanese followers back home were watching the game at 3 A.M.

The consolation game was won by Maracaibo, Venezuela, 2–0 over Tallmadge, O.

The Series was capped off with the usual 3-day Washington, D.C., tour. A special treat developed when newly named President Gerald R. Ford met the entire Little League group in the White House and spent some 23 minutes with them for pictures and conversation.

Other contenders in Series play were teams from New Haven, Conn.; Athens, Greece; Esquimalt, British Columbia, Canada; and Jackson, Tenn.

Following the 1974 tournament, non-U.S. teams were banned from further competition in the Little League "World" Series because officials declared that the Taiwanese put too much emphasis on baseball, thus taking the fun out of the sport.

—G.G.

The All-Time Heavyweight Championship of the World

One night in 1967, 3 men locked themselves into a small room over a savings and loan office in Miami, and proceeded to record on tape one of the most unusual boxing matches in the history of the sport. By the time the evening had ended, 2 prizefighting immortals had fought 13 bloody rounds for the All-Time Heavyweight Championship of the World.

The fight was the climax of 15 elimination bouts among the greats of heavyweight boxing, from John L. Sullivan through Joe Louis to Muhammad Ali, and it had been created entirely in the flickering innards of a National Cash Register Model 315 computer.

The human brains behind this electronic diversion belonged to Murry Woroner, a Miami promoter and radio-TV producer, and Henry Meyer II, head of a computer firm. Broadcast nationwide to some 380 radio stations, their tournament became a roaring success. On the evening of December 18, more than 16 million Americans abandoned television and leaned into radio sets for the final match. The real Dempsey and Marciano listened to their epic battle at a radio station in Los Angeles, where a large room had been converted to a simulated gymnasium, complete with ring and punching bags.

Radio advertising receipts for the tournament were estimated at more than $3 million.

Ring experts questioned whether a computer, fed a set of human variables, could predict a fair outcome to a fight between men of different eras, styles, and abilities. If so, they reasoned, why go to the trouble of staging sporting events at all?

But Murry Woroner, a fight fan himself, saw infinite possibilities in the idea. He felt that modern electronics could resolve any sporting argument, including the one over which fighter was the all-time best.

Woroner began by gathering a small group of boxing experts, including Nat Fleischer, editor of *The Ring* magazine, and Hank Kaplan, past president of the World Boxing Historians Association, who owned one of the most complete libraries of information on the subject. With their help, Woroner created a rating sheet that broke the skill of boxing down into 58 "factors." These factors included such things as speed, hardness of punch, accuracy, prior injuries, susceptibility to cuts, courage, ability to defend, and killer instinct. He sent the sheet to 250 boxing experts and writers and asked them to rate the fighters. Using this information, he reduced the field to 16 contenders:

> Jack Dempsey v. Jim Corbett
> John L. Sullivan v. Jim Braddock
> Bob Fitzsimmons v. Jack Sharkey
> Jim Jeffries v. Joe Walcott
> Joe Louis v. Jess Willard
> Max Baer v. Jack Johnson
> Rocky Marciano v. Gene Tunney
> Muhammad Ali v. Max Schmeling

Next Woroner and Guy LeBow, the veteran ring announcer hired to recreate the bouts, began to do some original research of their own. They dug through yellowed newspapers and magazines. They dredged up ancient round-by-round accounts of fights long forgotten. They sought out motion picture films of every bout that had ever had a lens opened upon it, including one classic that was shot by Thomas A. Edison. They interviewed each man that still lived except Gene Tunney, who refused them. They asked every question they could devise:

What pattern of punches did the fighter prefer? At what pace and rhythm did he like to move? What hurt him the most? Where did he cut most easily?

Out of this chaos they distilled a punch-by-punch story of each fighter's bouts for his 5 best years. This information was to be put into the computer along with each man's reactions in varying situations, so that the machine could predict a most probable response to any given event.

Finally, Woroner and LeBow deposited their mountain of data at the feet of their computer man, Henry Meyer. He isolated himself in a Miami hotel room and began to design a program. Using frequent conferences with expert Hank Kaplan and periodic trips to NCR headquarters in Dayton, Meyer slowly condensed thousands of random facts into the kind of tiny magnetic impulses that turn a computer on.

The NCR-315, which held some 160,000 "memory" positions, used more than 2,000 variables to make 60 million calculations over 18 months. Realizing the impossibility of programming a fighter's personal feelings, attitudes, or frame of mind, Meyer worked out probability formulae based on the opinions of ring experts that were their best guesses about how a boxer would fight in top shape in his prime. The final program had some surprising subtleties. Meyer even built in a deterioration factor so that the fighters lost a tiny bit of energy on each punch. Certain other factors, such as speed, were modified depending on the corresponding factor of the opposing fighter. Of all the variables listed, Meyer found that the most important was raw courage.

Next the program was tested on the computer. Meyer began to play games with it, running hundreds of simulated bouts through the circuits and producing rooms full of printout sheets covered with the round-by-round details and the final result of each fight: KO, TKO, or decision.

Ready for broadcast, Woroner, LeBow, and sound engineer Frank Linale got together in Woroner's tiny studio in Miami under conditions of tight security. These 3 men were to be the only ones who knew the outcome until it was announced on the air.

Now LeBow's considerable talent came into play. The computer program lacked one vital element: It listed the punches thrown in each round but it did not list them in sequence. In their final script, Woroner and LeBow could rearrange and dramatize the punches, throwing in a clinch here and a missed haymaker there if they desired.

Linale's contribution was the realistic ring sound he laid onto the track behind LeBow's voice. He had taped actual fight crowds in Miami, capturing the grunts and moans, pops and whistles, boos and roars—even the shuffle and creak of leather on leather, the thunk when a fighter was hit. What came out was

exciting enough to raise a sweat on the in-the-flesh fighters, who cheered themselves on along with millions of other listeners. The finished tapes were to be shipped to bank vaults or security safes at Western Union for delivery to participating stations shortly before air time.

Thus the elimination bouts began. The 1st-round eliminations saw the following results:

> Dempsey over Corbett (KO, 7)
> Sullivan over Braddock (D)
> Louis over Willard (KO, 15)
> Fitzsimmons over Sharkey (D)
> Baer over Johnson (D)
> Marciano over Tunney (D)
> Jeffries over Walcott (KO, 10)
> Ali over Schmeling (D)

Boxing aficionados had frowned at the Marciano-Tunney pairing. Matching 2 potential all time winners in the 1st round seemed premature and unfair. Experts suspected a bug in the program when the masterful boxer Tunney was awarded only one round and lost the decision to the unpolished slugger from Massachusetts. Nevertheless, Tunney, who had defeated Dempsey twice to take and hold the crown, was out in the 1st round.

Others, including Nat Fleischer, had rated Jack Johnson as the greatest heavyweight of all time. But the 1st black to hold the crown was outpointed by underdog Max Baer, whose computer program had him flooring Johnson 3 times. It was the biggest upset of the tournament.

Dempsey pounded James Corbett into submission in 7. It was a quick curtain for "Gentleman Jim," the boxer who linked bare knuckles to the glove era. In the days when a round was ended only by a knockdown or dragdown, Corbett 1st gained prominence by going 61 rounds with the great black heavyweight Pete Jackson and had astonished the elite by giving a sparring exhibition in full dress—white tie and tails—with John L. Sullivan. A scientific boxer and ring strategist, Corbett cut Sullivan to shreds when they met for the championship.

Quarter Finals
Dempsey over Sullivan (KO, 7)
Louis over Fitzsimmons (TKO, 10)
Marciano over Baer (TKO, 13)
Jeffries over Ali (D)

The Great John L. had made it through the 1st elimination with a decision over James J. Braddock, but fell to the meat grinder, Jack Dempsey, in the quarter finals. The computer allowed the old bare-knuckle champ to get in a couple of good licks in the 3rd and 6th rounds, but Dempsey's windmill fists ended it in round 7.

Muhammad Ali, the most contemporary of

the group, also fell in the 2nd go-round. He was outpointed by Jim Jeffries, an attacker and a hitter with a good defense, who had KO'd Jersey Joe Walcott in the 1st round pairings. A strong, well-proportioned fighter, Jeffries fought at around 220 lbs. He had got his early training as a sparring partner for Jim Corbett. Utilizing the much imitated "Jeffries Crouch," he KO'd Bob Fitzsimmons for the title in 1899, retired for awhile, then tried a comeback and was decked by Jack Johnson in 1910. A man of fierce determination, it may have been Jeffries' staying power and strong finishes that convinced the computer he could catch the darting Ali. Muhammad received severe punishment to the body in the 9th and took a count.

Semifinals
Dempsey v. Louis
Marciano v. Jeffries

In the "Dream Match" of the mythical tournament, Jack Dempsey weighed in at 191 and Joe Louis, the Brown Bomber, at 200. Both fighters had come up from hard times: Dempsey as a brawling, street-fighting kid who rode the rods looking for matches, and Louis as the 7th child of pickers in the cotton fields of Alabama. At 23, Joe became the youngest man ever to win the crown and defended his title successfully 25 times.

Dempsey had announced his retirement after failing in his attempt to regain the title from Tunney in 1927. The Colorado slugger stalked his opponent like a tiger, with dark-jowled scowls and leaping, slashing attacks. Tunney had beaten him with strong legs and superior boxing skill. But in Louis, Dempsey faced a paralyzing puncher whose killer instinct matched his own. Louis could be hit, however. That had been proved even by such minor lights as Two-Ton Tony Galento, the garrulous barrel, who brought out a winging left hook that stunned Joe in the 1st round of their title fight and dropped him with another in the 3rd. Buddy Baer had knocked Louis out of the ring and even Tami Mauriello had bounced him off the ropes with a right to the chin. Both of these surprises caught Joe in round one and he went on to wipe the canvas with his unfortunate attacker. Perhaps it was the data that Dempsey was a master at following up when he had an opponent hurt that swung the computer in Jack's favor.

In a bloody, free-swinging affair, Dempsey was down twice but had Louis on the canvas 4 times to win a unanimous decision. The NCR-315 gave Jack 9 rounds, Joe 4, and called 2 even. Dempsey carried the fight to Louis in the early going and weathered a late rally by the Bomber.

When Rocky Marciano TKO'd Jim Jeffries in the 14th round of their semifinal, the climactic program was plugged in. It would be Dempsey v. Marciano and forget about boxing skill. This was a meeting of 2 sluggers, 2 drivers, 2 steel-knuckled killers who moved in only one direction in a ring: straight ahead. And they seemed evenly matched.

But Rocco Francis Marchegiano must have had at least one small edge in the blinking eye of the computer: He had never lost a professional fight. Beginning in 1947, Rocky fought 49 times and won every bout, 43 by knockouts. Eleven of those knockouts came in the 1st round. He had cooled the great Joe Louis in the 8th round of their match in 1951 and had KO'd Jersey Joe Walcott in the 13th to take the title in 1952. He defended the crown 6 times and retired from boxing undefeated. Dempsey had lost twice to Tunney and had been knocked out of the ring by Luis Angel Firpo in one of the bloodiest battles in ring history. But Firpo did not know how to take advantage of Dempsey's momentary blur and was floored 9 times in the 1st 2 rounds before Jack's right hand finally took him out.

That was the match-up as Woroner and LeBow rolled the tape in the small Miami recording studio. Woroner, doing color and interviews, stated that the winner would receive a gold and diamond championship belt, valued at $10,000. LeBow characterized the final conflict as the meeting of an undefeated fighter with an indomitable will to win against a steel-jawed slasher of animal cunning and ferocity. Referee Ruby Goldstein was announced, the fighters were introduced, and the bell rang for Round 1.

Round 1: Dempsey took the 1st stanza on crowding body shots and quick counters that brought some blood to Rocky's mouth as the round ended. (Round: Dempsey)

Round 2: Dempsey continued to work on Marciano's body with hooking rights under the heart. Rocky got in a rip to the mid-section but took a hard left-right combination that had him grabbing for a clinch. A straight right to the head by Dempsey and Marciano was bleeding again, this time from the nose. Rocky ignored it and the 2 fighters got into a toe-to-toe street brawl, connecting furiously with little attempt at defense. A right to the head made Dempsey stumble but Jack landed more and Rocky was bleeding badly as the round ended. (Round: Dempsey)

Round 3: Marciano opened up on Dempsey's head with combinations and floored the Mauler with an explosive right. After the mandatory 8 count, Dempsey moved in close to nullify Marciano's brutal attack and scored with a solid left as they parted. Again, they squared up and traded head shots, neither man willing to give an inch. (Round: Marciano)

Round 4: The fighters took turns snapping necks in this round, demonstrating their ability to take punishment. (Round: even)

Round 5: The pace began to tell. Marciano shook Dempsey with hooks to the head and the Mauler countered with a right under the heart that got to Rocky. Marciano demonstrated his nonstop punching technique, flailing away with both hands at Dempsey's chest and head. Dempsey concentrated on Marciano's body in the exchange. (Round: even)

Round 6: Dempsey mounted a fierce attack scoring with a left to the body and right to the head, but received a hard left to the mouth and a jolting uppercut by Marciano. Rocky went into a deep crouch, bobbing and weaving, and Dempsey followed suit. Jack whipped both fists to the body and was straightened up by Rocky's right. Dempsey's weaving, jerking motion made Rocky miss and Jack got in a good left before the round ended. (Round: even)

Round 7: Dempsey dominated the 7th with quick, explosive combinations fired from his weaving crouch. A left to the mouth slowed Rocky and a series of lefts and rights to the head jolted him. (Round: Dempsey)

Round 8: Marciano came back strong making Dempsey miss and shocking him with body smashes. Rocky tied Jack up and scored with both hands after the break. Then Jack missed a left over the head and Rocky leaped in with a left and right to the jaw and Dempsey went down. He took a 9 count sitting in the middle of the ring then leaped up and challenged the Brockton Blockbuster toe-to-toe, both men pumping hooks at each other as fast as their arms would move. (Round: Marciano)

Round 9: Rocky dominated the tiring Dempsey almost completely in this round. Dempsey, trying to rush in after a break, received jolting hooks under the heart and a left to the head that drove him back. A left hook to the mouth, a straight right smash, and another vicious left, and Dempsey went down for the 3rd time. Up at 9, he was checked by Referee Goldstein, then flew back at Marciano, giving as much as he received as the round concluded. (Round: Marciano)

Round 10: Rocky landed good combinations to the head and received straight lefts to chin and body. The fighters' faces were lumped and pulpy from the punishment received. Marciano whipped an explosive right to the body and followed with a left to the chin and a brutal right uppercut that put Dempsey down a 4th time. Jack got up more slowly this time and weathered Rocky's attack until the bell. (Round: Marciano)

Round 11: Dempsey found his 2nd wind and took the fight to Marciano, sidestepping Rock's attack and shooting lefts that brought a flow of blood from Marciano's nose. Dempsey ripped another left hook and Marciano went into a bob and weave, blood streaming from his face. The fighters exchanged good body shots and Dempsey landed a slashing left and right at the bell. (Round: even)

Round 12: After having absorbed brutal punishment all through the fight, Dempsey seemed to take charge of the battered Marciano in this round. Marciano, always bulling forward, was staggered with 2 exploding shots to the mouth. A Dempsey hook to the head had Rocky hanging on. Dempsey rushed to the kill, scoring with a left, but Rocky managed to tie him up. Jack broke and swung a left-right-left to Rock's jaw. But the Brockton Blockbuster would not go down. He took everything Jack could throw and survived the round. (Round: Dempsey)

Round 13: Dempsey charged in for the kill but Rocky had revived and met him with a left hook to the head. Dempsey was stunned and on the defensive as Rocky whipped a flashing left and right to the mouth. Dempsey threw a left hook but Marciano countered with a head-rattling right to the point of the chin and Dempsey went down again. After a mandatory 8 count, Jack rose to his feet and tried to fight back but Marciano was too strong, too determined. The Rock charged like a wild animal, smashing body blows and straightening Dempsey up with rights. Dempsey had to fight furiously to ward off the charging Rocky's flurry of rights and lefts to the head. Rocky continued to batter through Dempsey's defenses. Another buzz saw of brutal combinations to the head and jaw put the Manassa Mauler down and out.

Winner: Marciano, by a KO at 2:28 of the 13th round. Dempsey had been floored 6 times, Marciano none.

Aftermath: As the real Marciano accepted the $10,000 belt in Los Angeles, he paid tribute to his transistorized rival. "He was always my idol. I copied everything from him," said Rocky. Dempsey just shrugged and said "It's only a computer."

"All we've really done is start more arguments," Murry Woroner admitted.

—M.H.

The Super Fight: Muhammad Ali v. Rocky Marciano

Rocky Marciano accepted the title of All-Time Computerized Heavyweight Champion of the World with modesty. But Muhammad Ali, eliminated in the quarterfinals of the make-believe tournament, did not greet the outcome with aplomb. He filed suit against promoter Murry Woroner for $1 million, claiming his electronic defeat by Jim Jeffries had defamed him.

The suit eventually was settled in court for $1. And it gave Woroner another idea. If 16 million people would listen to a computerized bout staged for radio, how many would pay to watch one on television? The Miami producer queried Marciano and Ali: How would they like to act out a bout for the camera, based on a computer-written script, and show the world who might win a Super Fight between 2 living undefeated ex-champions? They would like it very much, they said, especially when Woroner explained that he planned to beam the fight into more than 1,000 theaters worldwide, via closed-circuit television, and that the gate could top $5 million. Marciano announced he would take a flat fee for his stint; Ali asked for a cut of the profits.

Once again the NCR-315 computer was fed 129 variables on each boxer; once again it began to whir, blink and spew out round-by-round results of an imaginary conflict. Before the computer had reached its decision, the fighters were ready to do their thing for the cameras.

In the summer of 1969, Woroner sealed off a television studio in an out-of-the-way district of North Miami Beach and put 4 camera crews to work filming Rocky and Muhammad throwing leather.

Rocky had lost 50 lbs. and donned a toupee for the match. Ali was in good shape, despite a layoff. Under Woroner's direction, they sparred for the equivalent of 70 rounds, acting out every possible situation for the film editors to use when matching scenes to the computer's script. So that no one would know the outcome prior to the televised bout, Woroner filmed 7 different endings for the fight: each boxer winning by a KO, a TKO, or a decision, plus a draw.

As the fighters simulated reality, the few privileged onlookers speculated about which man might have won a real fight, if they could have met in their primes. Both were undefeated in professional boxing: Marciano's record was 49-0-0 with 43 KOs, Ali's was 29-0-0 with 24 KOs. Marciano gave up height and weight to the Louisville Hummingbird. The 5'10½"

Marciano fought at 184 lbs., the 6'3" Ali at 211. And Ali had the reach on Rocky by more than a foot. Muhammad's arms stretched 82" and the Brockton Blockbuster's only 68".

The styles of the 2 men couldn't have been more disparate. Rocky described his: "I'd get low, making myself a smaller target, a tougher man to hit on the chin. My game was to always bob and weave and never let myself be maneuvered out in the middle of the ring."

Rocky was always on the attack, always driving forward with short, brutal chops to the arms, body, and head of his opponent. He would try for the quick kill—opening fast and attempting to hurt his man as early as he could.

"I think if I could corner [Ali]," Rocky said, "I would knock him out."

But a butterfly is difficult to corner. "My main motive when I enter the ring is to hit and not be hit," Muhammad said, commenting on his philosophy of fisticuffs. He claimed that his left jab had been timed at 400ths of a second and that his dancing feet had kept him far from harm's way. "In all my fights, pro and amateur, I never remember being cut, scratched or marked," he said.

Everyone agreed that if it went to a decision, the winner would have to be Ali. But Rocky could very well take it with a KO.

And so the 2 heavyweights began prancing about the ring, as the cameras hummed. Even though they were supposed to pull their punches, some blood flowed.

"I think it was Marciano who threw the 1st real punch," Woroner said later. They had been fooling around when Marciano suddenly let one go to the midsection. Ali followed with a shot to the head. But the fighters respected each other and apologized for these slips. Afterward, Ali commented that Marciano had surprised him. At 45, the Blockbuster was herding the agile younger man into the corners, as he had in the days of his prime.

Marciano called Ali "the fastest man on wheels," after the filming.

In January, 1970, the fight was televised. An estimated million fans paid $5 each for the privilege of watching it in America and some 15 million more queued up in England, Australia, and Mexico.

The Fight

In the opening rounds, Ali had it all his way. While the Rock plowed stolidly in, missing hooks, the Butterfly flitted and flirted, snapping jabs that brought blood to Marciano's face. Ali also threw a lot of body punches, unusual for him.

But in the 10th round, Rocky's patience paid off. He finally cornered Ali and cut him down. The Louisville Lightfoot was up immediately and darting quickly. He continued to pepper the stalking Rocky and was winning on points when Marciano rallied. With blood streaming from simulated cuts, Rocky put the big finish on the film by knocking Ali out at 57 seconds into the 13th round. It was the same round in which he had bounced Jersey Joe Walcott to take the heavyweight title in another come-from-behind finish, and the same round in which he had KO'd Jack Dempsey to win the mythical All-Time Computerized Heavyweight Championship.

Muhammad, who had watched the bout in a theater, said, "That computer must have been made in Alabama."

"That was no Ali, I knew," said his trainer.

Rocky Marciano never learned that he had won the Super Fight. Three weeks after filming was completed, he was killed in a plane crash.

—M.H.

The All-Time Middleweight Championship of the World

Spurred by the success of his All-Time Heavyweight Boxing Tournament, staged via computer in 1967, Promoter Murry Woroner came back the following year with an All-Time Middleweight elimination that promised to answer some intriguing questions.

How good was Stanley Ketchel, the "Michigan Assassin," who had been called the greatest middleweight of all time? Who was Norman Selby, the mysterious persona behind the legend called "Kid McCoy"? What would the computer make of Marcel Cerdan, the Tiger of Casablanca, or Sugar Ray Robinson, the only man to win the middleweight title 5 times? Could Harry Greb take Tony Zale?

Sensing a winner, the Ford Motor Co. bought the series for some 500 radio stations, paying $500,000 for the privilege. Twelve one-minute commercials were guaranteed for each fight and a nationwide "Pick the Winners" contest was set up for the listeners, with a grand prize for the national winner.

The boxers nominated for the eliminations were selected through a poll of sports experts and paired by 3 men with impeccable ring credentials, Nat Fleischer, editor of *The Ring* magazine, and Chris and Angelo Dundee, well-known managers and trainers.

As in the heavyweight tournament, punch-by-punch data on all fights from their 5 best years were fed into an NCR-315 computer, along with a rating on each of 129 variables such as speed, courage, agility, killer instinct, and ability to give and take various punches. Fight results were printed out by the computer and the round-by-round action re-created by ring announcer Guy LeBow, with authentic sound effects simulating an actual broadcast.

The Preliminaries
Carmen Basilio v. Marcel Cerdan
Emile Griffith v. Kid McCoy
Gene Fullmer v. Stanley Ketchel
Tiger Flowers v. Rocky Graziano

Jack "Nonpareil" Dempsey v. Sugar Ray Robinson
Bob Fitzsimmons v. Jake LaMotta
Mickey Walker v. Dick Tiger
Harry Greb v. Tony Zale

BASILIO-CERDAN

Background: Carmen Basilio won the middleweight championship from Sugar Ray Robinson in 1957 in a 15-round split decision, then lost it back to him in 1958. He had previously won the welterweight title twice. A tough, unorthodox slammer, Basilio would wade in weaving and throwing leather, willing to take 20 punches to get in one bomb that could end it all.

Marcel Cerdan, French boxing legend, KO'd the supposedly unbeatable Tony Zale in 1948 to win the middleweight title, but a dislocated shoulder forced him to surrender it to Jake LaMotta in 1949. Cerdan, who lost only 4 of 113 professional bouts, was killed in a plane crash on his way back to the U.S. for a rematch with LaMotta.

The Fight: Cerdan's speed and clever, whirlwind style made Basilio miss in the 2nd round. Cerdan floored him in the 3rd and Basilio counterattacked, putting the Frenchman down twice. A right to the head and left to the jaw took Basilio out in Round 4.

Winner: Cerdan, KO 4.

GRIFFITH-McCOY

Background: Born in the Virgin Islands, Emile Griffith came to New York and began a boxing career that gave him the welterweight championship 3 times and the middleweight crown twice between 1961 and 1968. In one of the tragedies of the era, Benny (Kid) Paret died of cerebral injuries following his KO loss to Griffith in '61, a bout that gave Emile the welterweight championship.

The flamboyant turn-of-the-century boxer Kid McCoy, who inspired the saying "The Real McCoy," was actually a mild-mannered Indiana farm boy named Norman Selby. "Kid McCoy" was born in the minds of newspapermen, one of the earliest examples of the synthetic creation of a "celebrity." Norman Selby, a handsome, somewhat tubercular-looking chap, had lightning feet and hands and he won fights. Because he lacked the lumpy muscles, hairy torso, and flattened nose that stereotyped the boxer in the public's imagination, a legend was created: Kid McCoy, a sensitive, milk-skinned pretty boy, who could fight because he had run away from home at 13 and had battled his way through the most ferocious hobo jungles in the country, learning the basics of survival as he went. Supposedly he had mastered every trick in the book, and this included his infamous "corkscrew punch," a left hook that he would twist as it landed in order to cut the skin.

Unfortunately, Norman Selby attempted to live up to the legend. After 10 marriages and a career as a championship fighter, restaurateur to the stars and motion picture actor, in the 1920s Selby was convicted of manslaughter in the death of a girl friend and for that and other offenses was sentenced to 48 years in prison.

The fight: In his bout with the tough Griffith, McCoy gave almost as much as he got. He danced and jabbed, landed the corkscrew and had Griffith bleeding at both eyes. But Emile came back strong in the final 2 rounds to win a close decision.

Winner: Griffith, D.

FULLMER-KETCHEL

Background: Gene Fullmer, the Utah strongboy, was an all around athlete who held the middleweight championship twice. A dock brawler, he charged like a football guard, whirling both fists. His bulling style enabled him to beat Ray Robinson for the title with a decision in 1957. Robinson KO'd him in a rematch. He had given a brutal beating to Kid Paret weeks before the Paret-Griffith fight and many felt that Paret's fatal injuries actually were received in the Fullmer bout.

Stanley Ketchel was a 2-fisted wildman of the 1903–1910 era. He began boxing when he was 16 and his short but fascinating career ended when he was shot by a jealous husband at the age of 24. In that time, he won 49 fights, 46 by a KO, and lost 4. One of Ketchel's managers described his training regimen: He went to look for the fighter and found him in bed smoking opium, with a blonde on one side and a brunette on the other.

Ketchel had the gall in 1909 to challenge the giant Jack Johnson, who outweighed the little Assassin by 25 lbs. for the bout. Johnson had agreed to let Ketchel stay the limit and was toying with him until the 12th, when Stanley decided to smoke. He exploded a right under Johnson's ear and the big heavyweight went down. Some say that Johnson faked the knockdown for a laugh. But there was nothing humorous about his mood when he bounced up. Jack laid Ketchel out with a murderous right to the mouth that broke off all of Stanley's front teeth at the gums.

The fight: Gene Fullmer was no match for the Michigan swinger. Ketchel dropped a bomb on Fullmer that put him down for 9 in the 5th round, had him on the canvas again in the 6th and beat him senseless in the 7th, when Referee Ruby Goldstein stopped the fight.

Winner: Ketchel, TKO 7.

FLOWERS-GRAZIANO

Background: Tiger Flowers fought just after W.W. I. A clever boxing southpaw, Flowers lacked a real power punch and suffered from a fragile jaw. In 1924, he won 36 straight bouts. He took the middleweight title from Harry Greb in 1926 in a 15-round decision. The Georgia Deacon died after minor eye surgery in 1927, at the age of 32.

Rocky Graziano was a fighter of the punching bag school. Like his buddy from New York's Lower East Side, Jake LaMotta, he was willing to take a pounding in order to give one. His vicious battles with Tony Zale, in which they traded the middleweight crown in 1946–1948, are still mentioned with awe. Graziano and LaMotta both went into show business after retirement from the ring and Graziano's life story was enacted by Paul Newman in the film *Somebody Up There Likes Me.*

The Fight: Graziano's raw power was too much for Flowers. Rocky took everything the Tiger could throw and then KO'd him in the 11th.

Winner: Graziano, KO 11.

JACK "NONPAREIL" DEMPSEY-ROBINSON

Background: The Nonpareil (not related to heavyweight champ Jack Dempsey) won the middleweight title in 1884 and lost it 7 years later to Ruby Bob Fitzsimmons, suffering 13 knockdowns in the fight. The Nonpareil was fast and durable but no match for Fitzsimmons, who later won the heavyweight crown.

Sugar Ray Robinson has been called "pound for pound the greatest fighter of his era." He held the middleweight title 5 different times and the welterweight title once. At one point in 1951, the brilliant boxing-ring general had won 93 bouts in a row. Out of 202 fights, he won

175 and failed to finish only once. That occured on a sultry night in New York when Ray had challenged light-heavyweight champion Joey Maxim for his title. The heat at Yankee Stadium was so intense that Ray could not answer the bell for the 14th round and the fight went to Maxim on a technical KO, the only KO to mar the Sugarman's record.

The fight: Dempsey began the bout confidently, in his standup style, counteracting Robinson's flicking lefts and strong right crosses. But Ray took control in the 4th and dominated the rest of the fight. In the 7th he had the Nonpareil hanging on after a rocking right and in the 11th, following hard body shots, Robinson brought Dempsey's hands down with a blast to the midsection, then followed with a whiplash right to the head. Dempsey was virtually out on his feet when the referee stopped the bout.

Winner: Robinson, TKO 11.

FITZSIMMONS-LAMOTTA

Background: Described by one opponent as a "bald kangaroo," Ruby Robert Fitzsimmons was a curious-looking fellow. He carried the chest and shoulders of a heavyweight on the spindly legs of a lightweight. This gave him the unusual combination of fast footwork and a hard punch and helped him win world championships in the middleweight, light heavyweight and heavyweight divisions. Born in England, raised in New Zealand, Ruby Bob began his fistic rise in the U.S. One of his most famous bouts was staged in the Wild West when he beat Irishman Pete Maher—with some help from Judge Roy Bean, who convinced a party of Texas Rangers not to stop the bout, and Bat Masterson, who guarded the entrance. Fitzsimmons's famous "solar plexus" punch helped him take the heavyweight crown from Gentleman Jim Corbett in 1897.

Jake LaMotta, fighter and comedian, was the 1st man ever to defeat Sugar Ray Robinson professionally. He won a decision in 1943. Jake stopped Marcel Cerdan for the middleweight championship in 1949, then lost the title to Robinson in 1951. Later, LaMotta said that he had fought Sugar Ray so many times that he had begun to fear diabetes. A back-alley brawler who dragged himself up from the New York slums, LaMotta was renowned for staying on his feet no matter what hit him.

The fight: It took 14 rounds of blacksmith blows from Fitzsimmons to knock the "immovable object" down in this bout, one of the wildest in the tournament. Both fighters landed steadily, Ruby Bob with long, looping bombs and LaMotta with short triphammers from a crouch. LaMotta refused to clinch, pushed Fitz

around the ring and cut his eye in the 9th. But Bob took over by the 14th and had Jake down twice for counts of 9. Needing a KO to win, LaMotta roared back in the 15th but Fitz held on for the decision.

Winner: Fitzsimmons, D.

WALKER-TIGER

Background: Mickey Walker, "The Toy Bulldog," learned how to fight from the tough itinerants who hung around the freight yard that he lived near as a kid in New Jersey. He loved to take on the big guys and always bragged about his decision over Bearcat Wright, the 280 lb. giant who outweighed Mickey by 120 lbs. Walker also fought to a draw with Jack Sharkey, who won the heavyweight crown a few months later. "The Toy Bulldog" won the welterweight championship in 1922 and the middleweight prize in 1926, with a decision over Tiger Flowers.

Dick Tiger of Nigeria won the British middleweight title in 1958 and the world title in '62 by defeating Gene Fullmer. In 1966, he moved up to light heavyweight and took the title on a close decision over Jose Torres. In 1967 he squeaked past Torres in a rematch to hold the championship. An aggressive, crouching style marked this clever counterpuncher.

The fight: Mickey Walker's strength and speed held up under the hardest shots Dick Tiger could throw. By the 7th, Walker was bleeding from around both eyes but managed to hurt Tiger in the 8th with a barrage of left hooks and long rights. In the early going of the 9th, Walker flattened the tired Tiger for the count.

Winner: Walker, KO 9.

GREB-ZALE

Background: Henry Greb was one of the greats in his division. He came on like a windmill, flailing both fists incessantly at his opponent. He was smart and fast and his ring mastery enabled him to be the only fighter ever to defeat Gene Tunney. The victory gave him the vacant light-heavyweight title but he lost it to Tunney in 1923. It wasn't too long before he grabbed the middleweight championship from Johnny Wilson. He held it until 1926.

Tony Zale, a tough steelworker from Gary, Ind., took the middle title in 1941. He loved to mix it up and proved it in an incredible series of bouts with Rocky Graziano. A durable, aggressive body puncher, Zale retired after losing his title to Marcel Cerdan and never fought again.

The fight: Greb outpointed Zale in every

round. He stunned him in the 7th, after Zale had opened a gash over his eye, and continued his 2-fisted, whirling attack into the 14th round. At the opening bell, he charged out and floored Zale with a right. Tony got up once but was flattened immediately.

Winner: Greb, KO 14.

Quarter Finals

Cerdan v. Griffith
Ketchel v. Graziano
Robinson v. Fitzsimmons
Walker v. Greb

Cerdan-Griffith: Marcel Cerdan had Emile Griffith on the canvas in the 6th and 10th rounds as he dominated the fight. Referee Ruby Goldstein stopped it in the 10th, giving Cerdan a TKO.

Winner: Cerdan, TKO 10.

Ketchel-Graziano: Stanley Ketchel bounced Rocky Graziano for an 8 count in round one but Rocky bulled back to survive 4 more vicious knockdowns before finally failing to rise in the 11th. The fight was a free-swinging one; Ketchel was decked by the clubbing fists of Graziano twice in the 8th and once in the 10th. But the Michigan Assassin prevailed.

Winner: Ketchel, KO 11.

Robinson-Fitzsimmons: Midway through the 1st round, Sugar Ray Robinson flashed a blinding right to open a cut above Bob Fitzsimmons's eye. He continued to work on the eye in round 2 and had Ruby Bob bleeding so freely in the 3rd that the Referee awarded a TKO to Robinson.

Winner: Robinson, TKO 3.

Walker-Greb: In one of the most exciting matches of the mythical tourney, Mickey Walker edged a 15-round decision over Harry Greb on a score of 146–144. It was Walker's power punching v. Greb's hitting and footwork. Greb cut Walker in round 4 and the final rounds were toe-to-toe. But there were no knockdowns.

Winner: Walker, D.

Semifinals
Cerdan v. Ketchel
Robinson v. Walker

Cerdan-Ketchel: In 12 bloody rounds, Marcel Cerdan was floored 5 times and Stan Ketchel

twice before the Michigan Mauler finally put the Ferocious Frenchman down for the big sleep at 2:08 of the 12th round. Cerdan was decked in the 7th, twice in the 9th, and twice in the 12th.

Winner: Ketchel, KO 12.

Robinson-Walker: The arms of Sugar Ray Robinson were a bit too long for the Toy Bulldog. Robinson set himself up for the all-time finals by outpointing Walker 145–141 in a close one.

Winner: Robinson, D.

Finals
Sugar Ray Robinson v. Stanley Ketchel

Background: It was a duel made in promoters' heaven. Ray Robinson, the angelic boxing master, v. Stan Ketchel, the demonic fury, who fought as if every round put his life on the line. Ketchel had become a ring legend in 8 years. Robinson fought everybody and beat the greatest during a 25-year career.

Sugar Ray had an assortment of punches that would rival a soda fountain. Ketchel was as tough as homemade iron. Robinson's flickering feet and hands kept him in control of a fight. It was said that Ketchel could stop any man on any given evening. What would the computer have to say about it?

The fight: The real Sugar Ray Robinson listened to his computer image on the radio and said: "I kept ducking and blocking, feinting and moving. . . . I felt every punch."

His transistorized alter ego felt one especially in the 1st round when Ketchel surprised him with a right to the head. Robinson, down for one of the few times in his life, knew that he was in a fight.

Ketchel moved in to work on the body and Robinson used his reach to punish the little battler to the head. Robinson drew blood in the 3rd and kept it flowing. In the final rounds, knowing he needed a knockout to win, Ketchel unleashed a brutal attack, but Robinson's long arms and clever combinations kept him at bay. The officials gave the mythical all-time championship to Sugar Ray 147 to 139. Even though Robinson tilted the electrons in his favor in every round except the 1st and 8th, he never had Ketchel off his feet.

Winner and All-Time Middleweight Champion: Sugar Ray Robinson, D.

—M.H.

Your Form Sheet: Entries in the Greatest Horse Race of Modern Times—Pick the Winner

Horse—Count Fleet   Jockey—Johnny Longden

Triple Crown winner of 1943, Count Fleet belongs to one of the most distinguished equine families. His sire, Reigh Count, won the 1929 Derby. His son, Count Turf, took the Derby in 1951, and his grandson, Lucky Debonair took it in 1965. Among his other offspring were Counterpoint, 1951 Horse of the Year, and the 1951 Filly Champion, Kiss Me Kate.

Count Fleet showed early talent, winning the Two Year Old Championship in 1942. "Old Zeke" was leading money winner of 1943, as well as Three Year Old Champion/Horse of the Year. Coming down the stretch of the 1943 Belmont Count Fleet injured his leg. Jockey John Longden eased him to an easy victory; but he had to be retired at stud.

British-born John Longden rode until he was 59. He started 32,000 races and won over 6,000. He was leading winner in 1947–1949, and a member of both the Jockey and Racing Halls of Fame. Longden became a successful trainer, too, winning both a Derby and Preakness with Majestic Prince in 1969.

—M.Le.

Horse—Exterminator   Jockey—Albert Johnson

Exterminator's skin clung tight to a gangly frame, and his ribs stuck out. He was nicknamed "Slim" and "Old Bones." His career started as companion to the top horse in his stable, Sun Briar. When Sun Briar was scratched, Exterminator became an afterthought entry in the 1918 Derby. Going off as a 30–1 longshot, Exterminator won running away. The awkward looking chestnut gelding went on to win a U.S. record of 34 stakes.

Nothing fazed Exterminator. His 100 starts between 1918 and 1923 saw him travel from Mexico to Canada and back again. He had 10 different trainers and won for all of them. He ran all distances in any kind of weather and under almost unbelievable handicaps. Thirty-five times he carried over 130 lbs., several times as much as 140. Exterminator ran in the money 84 times, with an even 50 victories. He won the Pimlico Cup 3 times in a row and so dominated the Saratoga Cup, winning it 4 times, that in 1921 no one would enter against him. It was one of only 16 walk-overs in modern U.S. racing history.

Albert Johnson was just coming into his own in the early 1920s. In 1922, atop Morrich, he took the Derby, and repeated in 1926 on Bubbling Over. He also recorded back-to-back wins in the Belmont, in 1925 on American Flag, and 1926 on Crusader.

Horse—Man o' War   Jockey—Clarence Kummer

Man o' War is the acknowledged standard of thoroughbred excellence. He was the odds-on favorite in every race he ran, from his 3–5 maiden effort to as high as 1–200. Thousands filled the tracks just to watch him run.

Averaging a 9½-length margin of victory, he dominated racing through 1919 and 1920. Rival owners had to be cajoled into racing against him, and he often faced only one or 2 other horses. In the Lawrence Realization, though Clarence Kummer made every effort to hold him back, Man o' War won by 150 lengths! His sole loss, the 1919 Sanford Memorial, has the ring of fiction to it. Running in mud, he was upset by a horse named Upset.

Man o' War closed his racing career with a match race victory over Sir Barton, 1919 Triple Crown winner, and retired to stud. Among his sons, Clyde Van Dusen won the 1929 Derby, and War Admiral the Triple Crown in 1937. Man o' War was a popular tourist attraction. Over half a million people visited him before his death in 1947.

Clarence Kummer was 1st Man o' War's exercise boy, and later his regular jockey. He had already won the 1919 Jockey Club Gold Cup on Purchase, a feat Man o' War duplicated. In 1925 he took his 2nd Preakness aboard Coventry, and in 1928 his 2nd Belmont Stakes on Vito.

Horse—War Admiral
Jockey—Charlie Kurtsinger

Despite being a Triple Crown winner and Horse of the Year in 1937, there is no doubt that War Admiral is most famous for one race he lost!

"The Bay Dancer" was born to success. Smaller than his sire, Man o' War, but with the same spirit and perfect conformation, War Admiral was favored in every race he ran. He took the Derby at 3–5 and went on to sweep all his races in 1937. Winning the Belmont, he broke the track record for the mile and a half.

But War Admiral had to share the limelight with another great horse, Seabiscuit. Finally, a match race was arranged at Pimlico, in November, 1938. Over 40,000 fans installed War Admiral as the 1–4 favorite. The race was close down the stretch, with Seabiscuit maintaining a slim lead throughout. War Admiral made a final attempt to overtake the leader, and failed. This race stands with *Man o' War-Sir Barton* (1920) and *Nashua-Swaps* (1955) as one of the 3 classic matches of all time.

Charlie Kurtsinger was in the twilight of a successful career when he rode *War Admiral*. He had already won a Derby, 2 Belmonts, a Preakness and 2 Jockey Club Gold Cups. Kurtsinger took a severe spill in the 1938 Travers. He expressed his willingness to return to riding, but only if he could stay with *War Admiral*. When the horse's owners decided otherwise, Charlie Kurtsinger retired.

Horse—Nashua   Jockey—Eddie Arcaro

Nashua, the pride of Kentucky, was the culmination of the art and science of thoroughbred racing. His breeding was impeccable; his sire, *Nasrullah*, produced among others *Bold Ruler*. *Nashua* was trained by the legendary Sunny Jim Fitzsimmons and was ridden by Eddie Arcaro. The result was 22 wins in 30 starts.

Nashua was named Two Year Old Champion in 1954 and Three Year Old Champion/Horse of the Year in 1955. Although he lost the Derby to *Swaps*, *Nashua* came back to defeat his rival in a classic match race. He was retired to stud in 1956, the 1st horse to be syndicated for over $1 million.

George Edward Arcaro is one of only 2 men to win 5 Kentucky Derbies. In all, Arcaro won 17 Triple Crown races and 2 Triple Crowns (on *Whirlaway*, 1941, and *Citation*, 1948.) Yet, he lost 250 races in a row before ever riding a winner.

Eddie was leading money winner 3 times. When he retired, in 1962, he had won 549 stakes races and over $30 million, both records.

Horse—Citation   Jockey—Steve Brooks

Citation was in many ways a transitional horse. He ended one era and began another. When he won the Triple Crown in 1948, it brought to a close an amazing 10-year span that saw 5 horses do the same. The next winner was *Secretariat*, in 1973. At the same time he was the 1st-ever equine millionaire earner. Yet purses have so increased that *Citation* is only 11th on the all-time money-winners list.

The big chestnut colt was the star of Calumet Farms' stable. When he won the Derby as a 5–4 favorite, his stablemate *Coaltown* placed 2nd. *Citation* was in the money in 44 of 45 starts, winning 32. He was Two Year Old Champion of 1947, and Horse of the Year in 1948.

Steve Brooks was given the chance to ride *Citation* in this race when the horse's regular rider, Eddie Arcaro, was assigned to *Nashua*. Winner of over 4,000 races, Brooks was elected to the Jockey Hall of Fame in 1962, and the Racing Hall of Fame in 1963. He was top

money winner of 1949, when he brought home a 16–1 shot, *Ponder*, in the Kentucky Derby.

Horse—Tom Fool   Jockey—Ted Atkinson

1953's Horse of the Year, *Tom Fool*, is perhaps better known for his achievements as a sire than as a racer. Syndicated for $1,750,000, *Tom Fool* repaid his backers with such progeny as *Tim Tam*, the 1958 Derby Winner, and the great *Buckpasser*. In all he sired over 30 stakes winners.

Of course, *Tom Fool* was no mean runner himself. He started 7 times in 1951, winning 5 and placing in the others. As a result he was named Two Year Old Champion. In 1952 he was lightly raced due to poor health; but he came back in 1953 to win 10 of 10 stakes events. *Tom Fool* was the 2nd of only 3 horses to win the Metropolitan, Suburban and Brooklyn Handicaps, the so-called N.Y. Handicap Triple Crown. He won 21 of 30 career starts.

A member of both the Racing Hall of Fame and the Jockey's Hall of Fame, Ted Atkinson brought in over 3,700 winners in his 21-year career. Known as the "Slasher" for the way he used his whip, Atkinson was top winner in both 1944 and 1946. He took ⅔ of the Triple Crown—the Preakness and Belmont—aboard *Capot* in 1949. In 1947 he won over $1 million.

A bad back forced Ted to retire in 1959, but he went on to a career as a track official.

Horse—Kelso   Jockey—Ismael Valenzuela

The early 1960s belonged to *Kelso*. The big gelding, with 39 victories in 83 starts, was named Horse of the Year a record 5 times between 1960 and 1964. *Kelso*'s racing earned him almost $2 million, another all-time record.

Kelso seemed to get better with age. He had placed 2nd 3 times in a row in the Washington, D.C., International before winning it in 1964, at 7 years old. In the final 5 months of his career he broke or tied 3 U.S. records; for a mile and an eighth on turf, 2 mi. on dirt, and a mile and a half on turf.

Ismael Valenzuela shared many of *Kelso*'s triumphs. He was aboard for the 3 frustrating 2nds in the International, and had the satisfaction of riding the winner in 1964. One of the top riders of the 1960s, Valenzuela drew such mounts as *Bold Ruler*, whom he guided to a victory in the 1957 Preakness, and *Tim Tam*, winner of the 1958 Derby.

Horse—Buckpasser   Jockey—Braulio Baeza

Ogden Phipps' *Buckpasser* ruled racing in 1965–1967. In 1965 he was Champion Two Year Old. In 1966 he was Horse of the Year, emulating his sire, *Tom Fool*, and in 1967 Best Older Horse. He ran in the money 30 of 31 times, 25 times 1st.

Buckpasser, known for blazing speed in the stretch, set the World's Record for the mile at Arlington Park in 1966. He was leading money winner for 2 straight years (1965, 1966) and was syndicated for stud for a then record $4,-800,000.

Panama-born Braulio Baeza was the leading money winner in racing in 1965–1968. In 1967 Bacza's come-from-behind tactics brought him 256 wins and a record $3,088,888 in purses. In 1961 he took the Derby on *Sherluck,* a 65–1 outsider. He repeated in 1963 with *Chateaugay,* at 10–1.

Horse—Equipoise   Jockey—Ray Workman

Running during the Depression years, *Equipoise* never got the acknowledgement he deserved. Yet the "Chocolate Soldier" was one of the gamest of thoroughbreds.

"He couldn't bear the thought of another horse's passing him," said his owner, Sonny Whitney. "He was disqualified several times for biting the neck of a horse that tried."

Equipoise showed courage early. He stumbled at the start of the 1930 Pimlico Futurity, losing 20 lengths to the leaders. Yet he came back to defeat 2 fine horses, *Mate* and *Twenty Grand.* *Equipoise* went to the gate 51 times and came back a winner 29. He was leading sire of 1942, when his son *Shut Out* took the Derby and Belmont.

Ray "Sonny" Workman was one of the most efficient jockeys of his era. He had the best winning percentage in the country in 1930, 1933 and 1935. Between 1936 and 1940 he rode 1,152 winners in only 5,751 attempts. Workman won the 1928 Preakness on *Victorian* and the 1935 Hopeful Stakes on *Red Rain.* He was elected to the Jockey's Hall of Fame and the Racing Hall of Fame.

Horse—Swaps   Jockey—Willie Shoemaker

California breeding was taken lightly in racing circles—before *Swaps.* The chestnut colt came East in 1955 to take the Derby from favored *Nashua. Swaps* won 19 of 25 starts in 1955 and 1956, setting 2 world's records in the process. Forced out of competition by a broken leg, *Swaps* was nursed in a special sling. When he regained his health he was retired to stud. *Swaps'* son *Chateaugay* won the 1963 Derby.

Nineteen-year-old Willie Shoemaker came into his own as a premier jockey in 1950, when he broke a 44-year record by riding 388 winners. The "Shoe" was leading money winner 10 times and leading rider 5. In 1953 he rode 458 winners. Still active, Willie is currently the winningest rider of all time, surpassing Johnny Longden. He has racked up well over 6,500 wins. Despite Shoemaker's great success, one of his more memorable moments came in 1956, when he *lost* the Derby on *Gallant Man* be-cause he simply misjudged where the finish line was.

Horse—Native Dancer   Jockey—Eric Guerin

Native Dancer was the 1st 4-legged TV star. Born in 1950, his career coincided with the development of television. His unique appearance and exciting racing style combined to make him popular with millions who had never followed racing before.

In 1952 *Native Dancer* went 9 for 9, and was named Two Year Old Champion/Horse of the Year. Nicknamed the "Gray Ghost" for his color, *Native Dancer* always put on a good show. His natural style was to lay back off the pace and then come from behind to win by huge margins.

Going into the 1953 Derby, *Native Dancer* had won 11 of 11; but he finished 2nd to *Dark Star.* It was his only loss in 22 races. *Native Dancer* holds the world's record at 6½ furlongs.

Native Dancer has sired 2 Derby winners, *Dancer's Image* and *Kauai King.*

Eric Guerin owns 4 Triple Crown victories. *Native Dancer* gave him a Preakness and Belmont in 1953. He had already won the 1947 Derby on *Jet Pilot* and took another Belmont in 1954 on *High Gun.* In 1944 Guerin participated in a racing oddity. He was one of 3 winning jockeys in a triple dead heat during the Carter Handicap.

"THE GREATEST HORSE RACE OF MODERN TIMES"

The announcer's voice droned on in a familiar monotone, as thousands of race fans strained to hear the words:

"They're off! *Buckpasser* is going to the front, *Citation* is 2nd . . . *Man o' War* is 3rd . . ."

But the drumming hooves existed only in the listeners' minds. The horses were illusion. The track that thousands "watched" was deserted.

The race at Gulfstream Park in Florida, which matched the greatest horses of all time, was the product of a computer. It was being broadcast as a promotional gimmick by a Miami radio station, whose call letters stood for "Wonderful Isle of Dreams."

Staged in 1968, radio station WIOD's "Race of the Century" compared the records of the premier runners of our time electronically, in an attempt to answer an age-old question: Which was the greatest horse of all? Was it *Man o' War,* the fabled "Big Red," who lost only one race in his career? What about *Citation, Count Fleet* and *War Admiral,* all winners of the Triple Crown—the Kentucky Derby, Preakness, and Belmont Stakes? How would the computer sort out the incredible histories of such champions as *Native Dancer, Kelso, Exterminator, Equipoise?* Could any of these animals run last?

The Super Race began when radio station representatives asked a group of sportswriters and broadcasters to pick a field of the greatest horses in American track history. Their concensus:

Horse	Owner
Count Fleet	Mrs. John D. Hertz
Exterminator	W. S. Kilmer
Man o' War	Glen Riddle Farm
War Admiral	Samuel D. Riddle
Nashua	Belair Stud
Citation	Calumet Farm
Tom Fool	Greentree Stable
Kelso	Bohemia Stable
Buckpasser	Ogden Phipps
Equipoise	H. P. Whitney
Swaps	R. C. Ellsworth
Native Dancer	A. G. Vanderbilt

A computer at the University of Liverpool in England was used to determine horse-by-horse positions. The criteria fed into the machine emphasized class of competition, weight-carrying ability and the overall records of each horse. Less importance was given to speed records, margins of victory, and total earnings. Digesting all of these facts, the computer printed out the entire race, showing margins between horses at 5-second intervals.

Juggling the qualifications in their own minds, racing experts came up with varying predictions about which champion could not possibly be beaten. Max Hirsch, dean of American trainers, who had seen all 12 horses in action, took *Man o' War*, with *Count Fleet* 2nd and *Buckpasser* 3rd. Louis Feustel, *Man o' War*'s trainer, agreed.

"I'd have to fear *Buckpasser* a little, and maybe *Citation*," he said. "But *Man o' War* was the greatest. Even when he was walking or jogging, he wanted to get there 1st."

"Big Red" set 5 world records as a 3-year-old and lost only one time in his 21-race career. Hirsch always felt that it was because his horse, *Donnacona*, accidentally blocked the great champion in a 1919 race at Saratoga, allowing *Man o' War* to be upset by *Upset*.

Each horse was to carry 126 lbs. for the simulated race, which was to go a mile-and-a-quarter.

Count Fleet got the inside pole position, with jockey Johnny Longden up. Next came *Exterminator*, with Albert Johnson; *Man o' War*, Clarence Kummer; *War Admiral*, Charley Kurtsinger; *Nashua*, Eddie Arcaro; *Citation*, Steve Brooks; *Tom Fool*, Ted Atkinson; *Kelso*,

Ismael Valenzuela; *Buckpasser*, Braulio Baeza; *Equipoise*, Sonny Workman; *Swaps*, Willie Shoemaker; and finally *Native Dancer*, under Eric Guerin.

The illusory gates clanged open and announcer Joe Tanenbaum began to read the race over the public address system and the radio.

THE RACE

Buckpasser broke to the front, followed by *Citation* and *Man o' War*. At the quarter, *Buckpasser, Citation, Man o' War*, and *Swaps* were bunched in that order, with barely a head separating one horse from the next. *Kelso* was 5th by a length, *Equipoise* 6th by half a length, followed by *War Admiral, Exterminator, Count Fleet, Nashua, Native Dancer*, and *Tom Fool*.

At the half mile, *Buckpasser* had taken control and led *Citation* by 2 lengths. *Man o' War* had not made his move and was 3rd by half a length. *Kelso* was 4th by a length and *Exterminator* had moved into 5th. *Swaps* was 6th and *Count Fleet* was 7th but beginning to fade badly. By the three-quarter mile mark, the *Count* had dropped back to 11th, leading only *Native Dancer*.

At one mile, *Buckpasser* had been challenged for the lead and passed by *Citation*, who now led by half a length. But *Man o' War* was coming up full throttle and trailed *Buckpasser* by only a head. *Kelso* was 4th by 2 lengths over *Exterminator*. *Swaps*, running 6th, had opened a huge gap between himself and *Nashua* who had moved up. *Count Fleet, Equipoise*, and *Native Dancer* brought up the rear.

The ghost of "Big Red" thundered into the stretch and passed *Buckpasser*. Now he trailed *Citation* by half a length and was moving up. The race became a duel between these 2 champions as *Buckpasser* faded to 3rd by a length.

By the 70-yard post, *Man o' War* had fought to within a jaw of *Citation* and this powerful animal who always wanted to be 1st had his eye on the finish line, dead ahead.

Now *Citation*, under tremendous pressure, showed his blood by stretching to the limit to inch ahead of the challenger. He flashed under the wire a bare neck ahead of *Man o' War* to win the Greatest Horse Race of All Time in 2:00 and start one of the greatest arguments of the year among surprised handicappers. *Buckpasser* held on for 3rd, by a length and a half; *Exterminator* had surged ahead of *Kelso* to come in 4th by 1½, and *Kelso* was trailed by *Swaps* and *Nashua*. (See chart.)

In an informal poll of the same people who had chosen the entries, it was found that some 40% had picked *Man o' War* to win. In a contest for the general public, sponsored by WIOD, more than half of the 11,000 participants chose "Big Red."

One writer had it figured close: He picked *Citation, Tom Fool,* and *Buckpasser,* with a time of 2:00⅓.

A handicapper who felt *Man o' War* should have run all of the competition off the track suggested that the way the factors were weighted for the computer had shifted the favor to *Citation,* who had more than twice as many races to his credit.

Even though no betting was allowed, the odds had been posted by the Aqueduct pressbox oddsmaker. *Citation* would have paid handsomely at 12–1. *Buckpasser* came in at 10–1 and *Man o' War* got the favorite's role, at a mere 2–1 payoff.

—M.H.

The World Cup

History of Soccer

The 1st soccer player was probably a prehistoric figure. Somewhere, somehow, at the close of a day of hunting he found a strange amusement in watching a roughly round object, perhaps a tangled bundle of weeds, roll where he kicked it. This sportive Everyman has never died. As an ancient Greek or Roman, he devised simple rules for this game. As an Eskimo, he used a leather ball filled with moss. As a Polynesian native, he kicked a football made of bamboo fibers. His present incarnation is in the thousands who play, and the millions all over the world who watch soccer games. For a few weeks every 4 years, these people turn their eyes toward the event which determines who will be the world soccer champions. That event is the World Cup competition, the most widely viewed sport event on earth.

The sport played at the World Cup is formally known as association football, and its principal center of development was England. Although several times outlawed in that country because the monarchs felt it took interest away from the military sport of archery, it stubbornly and steadily grew in popularity. By the early 19th century, several variations of the game were being played at the prestigious public schools of Eton, Harrow, and Rugby. At 1st, kicking was the only allowed method of propelling the ball, but a variation also permitting the ball to be carried was introduced by Rugby in 1823.

Eventually, it became apparent that some uniformity of rules would be necessary if the game was to be played competitively. In 1863, a number of the clubs devoted to the kicking game banded together as the London Football Association and adopted a set of uniform rules. This was the beginning of association football, later referred to as "assoc.," which was further corrupted into the term "soccer." Groups devoted to the ball-carrying game organized themselves into the Rugby Football Union in 1871, adopting the rules then in use at Rugby School, and that game has henceforth been known as rugby football.

Soccer in the U.S.

The 1st year that a football-like game was recorded as having been played in the U.S. was 1609. In Colonial days, it was not an uncommon sight to see youths practicing kicking an inflated bladder on the village greens or in the fields. The sport attained collegiate recognition in the 1830s, being played at Princeton, Harvard, and Yale. It became such a rough-and-tumble game that it was temporarily banned at the latter 2 institutions. In 1876, the aforementioned colleges, plus Rutgers and Columbia, formed the American Intercollegiate Football Association and adopted the Rugby rules, making American football a carrying as well as a kicking game. In the century or so since, the rules have continually changed, blending soccer and rugby rules, and adding strictly American features as well. The result is a sport that has over-shadowed U.S. participation in soccer and, with a couple of exceptions, American teams have fared poorly at the World Cup competitions in which they have participated.

RULES OF THE GAME

The international rules of soccer are as follows: The playing field has a length of a minimum of 100 yards and a maximum of 130 yards. The width is from 50 to 100 yards. The field markings are the end lines ("goal lines"); the side lines ("touchlines"); a halfway line; and on each end of the field, rectangular penalty and goal areas. In the middle of each of the goal lines are set 2 goal posts, 8 yards apart, spanned by a crossbar 8' off the ground and backed by a net.

The purpose of the game is to make more goals than the opposing team. A goal is scored when the ball passes between the goal posts under the crossbar as a result of being kicked or propelled by the head of a team member ("headed").

The spherical ball used is a minimum of 27" and a maximum of 28" in circumference.

There are 11 men on each of the 2 teams. Except for the goalkeeper, they may roam the field. The defensive players are the left fullback, right fullback, and the center halfback, left halfback, and right halfback. There are 5 forwards: outside right, inside right, center, inside left, and outside left.

A referee, assisted by 2 linesmen, controls the game.

The game is made up of 45-minute halves. There is a one-minute interval between halves, at which time the teams reverse their positions on the field.

Immediately prior to the game, the team captains flip a coin, with the winner having the option of a choice of goals or kickoff. The game starts with a place kick from the center of the field by the center forward. Usually he kicks it to one of his nearby team members to the left or right.

Kicking, heading, and blocking the ball with the body are the techniques used to manipulate the ball. There are a few circumstances under which the use of the hands is also allowed: If the ball is propelled across a touchline, a player on the opposing team throws it back onto the field. Also, the goalkeeper may handle the ball when it comes into his penalty area. He is permitted to carry the ball 4 steps and throw or kick it to a teammate.

The short kick used by the players to advance the ball while running, keeping it under control, is called the "dribble." The long kick to another player or out of bounds is also used. Tripping, pushing or holding are prohibited. Blocking and other types of body contact are forbidden. The exception is when such contact accidentally occurs in the process of trying to play the ball. When infractions

occur, the opposing team is allowed a free direct or indirect kick, depending upon the violation. In the indirect kick, the ball must be touched by someone other than the kicker before a goal can be scored.

Soccer's only complicated rule states that an offensive player is offside if he is nearer the goal line than is the ball at the moment his teammate starts to pass the ball to him, unless there are at least 2 defending players (the goalkeeper and one other) between him and the goal line. This rule does not apply if he receives the ball after it has been touched by a member of the defending team, or if he receives the ball directly from a goal kick, a corner kick, a throw-in, or from the referee dropping the ball into play. The offside infraction is called only when the player who is offside actually participates in the play.

Soccer's relatively simple rules have helped to make it a universally understood and appreciated game. But not until the World Cup competition began did soccer achieve the status attributed to it by English author Anthony Burgess: "the only international language, apart from sex."

HISTORY OF THE WORLD CUP

Before the World Cup tournament was established, the Olympic Games presented the prime opportunity for soccer teams from all nations to compete. But as Henry Delauney (one of the Frenchmen who conceived of the World Cup) noted, there was a problem with the Olympics' demand for only amateur players. Those nations which funneled their best players into professional teams were at a disadvantage because they had to send men not good enough for the professional leagues.

The other World Cup pioneer was another Frenchman, Jules Rimet, who was President of the French Football Federation from 1919 to 1949, and President of the Federation Internationale des Football Associations (FIFA) from 1920 to 1954. It was at the 1st FIFA meeting in 1904 that the organization declared that it had the right to establish a world championship soccer competition. But the idea was not to become a reality until 26 years later. In the interim, it was discussed at length in FIFA meetings. Finally, in 1928, Delauney's resolution that a World Cup be established was passed. The Cup was named after Delauney's fellow crusader, Rimet.

Five nations volunteered to host the 1st international competition to take place in 1930: Italy, Sweden, Spain, Holland, and Uruguay. Normally, a European site would have been natural, but Uruguay had carried the Olympic soccer championship in 1924 and 1928. In its enthusiasm, that country offered to build a new stadium in central Montevideo, and to pay all of the traveling and hotel expenses of the visiting teams. These incentives overshadowed what the Europeans were prepared to provide and they withdrew. Thus the stage was set for the 1st World Cup competition.

THE WORLD CUP CHAMPIONSHIPS

1930

Uruguay's enthusiasm at being chosen the host nation for the 1st World Cup soon turned to bitterness. Only a few months before the games were to convene, not one European nation had decided to enter. Citing the difficulty of what in those days was a 3-week journey, and the hardships of salary loss to the amateur players who would have to abandon their jobs, the European teams decided to sit this one out. It was only through cajolery and threats that the games eventually took on a truly international flavor. In Romania, King Carol personally picked the team members and pressured their employers to give them time off. Belgium, Yugoslavia, and France also decided to enter the competition. England had left FIFA several years before and so did not participate, but the U.S. entered a team made up mostly of British and Scottish professionals. In the absence of the competition that England, Scotland, and Austria would have provided, Uruguay was the definite favorite.

The competition began with 4 qualifying pools, with the winner in each pool going on to the semifinals. Argentina triumphed over Chile, France, and Mexico in the Pool I games. In the match between Argentina and France, the referee inadvertently blew the whistle to signal the end of the game 6 minutes before time had actually run out. Mounted police had to be brought onto the field to restore order.

The Pool II games began with an upset. Yugoslavia beat Brazil 2–1, and went on to qualify by also beating Bolivia. Not surprisingly, Uruguay triumphed in Pool III, 2–1 over Peru and 4–0 over Romania. The Pool IV victors were the Americans, who decisively beat Belgium and Paraguay.

The U.S. was less successful in the semifinals, totally falling apart in the 2nd half of their game with Argentina, which they lost 6–1. Three of the 6 goals were shot during the last 9 minutes of the game.

The Uruguay-Yugoslavia match began with a shocker—a goal by Seculic of Yugoslavia only 4 minutes into the game. But the tide soon turned and the final score was 6–1, Uruguay's favor.

The final was between Argentina and Uruguay. The game was played to a crowd of 90,000, with thousands more assembled outside the stadium. Arriving Argentinians were searched for weapons and soldiers with fixed bayonets kept the crowd moving.

Pablo Dorado, Uruguay's right-winger, scored the 1st goal some 12 minutes into the game, but his Argentinian counterpart soon evened the score. Argentina's Stabile, a master of fine ball control, stunned the Uruguayans with another goal shortly before the half.

The 2nd half saw Uruguay's Pedro Cea follow a brilliant dribble with a goal that again evened the score. The host team regained its confidence and secured the win with a goal from Santos Iriarte, the young outside-left, and another by Castro only seconds before the end. The final score was Uruguay 4, Argentina 2. Jules Rimet handed the golden 50,000-franc cup to the dazed Uruguayan team captain.

In Uruguay, the following day was declared a national holiday; in Argentina an angry mob pelted the Uruguayan embassy with stones. The World Cup was on its way.

1934

The 1934 games convened in Italy. In the grip of fascism, the nation wanted to win as a symbol of national strength. The Uruguayan victors of 1930 failed to participate, partly because they still resented the absence of the major European teams at the previous championship, and partly because they were in the throes of a players' strike. The favorites were the Italians, managed by the authoritarian, discipline-conscious Vittorio Pozzo, and the Austrian "Wunderteam" led by manager Hugo Meisl, the other giant of European football between the wars.

The format consisted of a series of qualifying games followed by a knock-out competition with 16 teams in the 1st round. The winners went on to a 2nd round, which found Italy victorious over Spain, Austria over Hungary, Germany over Sweden, and Czechoslovakia over Switzerland.

In the semifinals, the Italians battled the Austrians. A downpour transformed the field into a muddy plain that particularly confounded the precise playing style of the Austrians. Italy had a goal 18 minutes into the game, and Austria did not even have its 1st shot at the goal until the game was almost over. In the final minute, Austrian Zischek penetrated the Italian defense and headed toward the shot that could have tied up the game. But his shot was wide and Italy's place in the final was assured.

The other semifinal game featured Czechoslovakia contesting the Germans. The audience included a sportily-dressed Mussolini. The solid Aryans clung to their "W" formation, looking wooden compared to the smaller but sprightly Czechs. The latter scored on a long attack by right-winger Junek, his kick deflected but transformed into a goal by Nejedly. However, in the 2nd half, Czech goalkeeper Planicka inexplicably stood motionless as a long kick by Germany's Noack shot by him to tie up the game. Then the Czechs rallied and gained 2 more to assure their participation in the final.

In the final, the Czechs' speed and agility was pitted against the power and endurance of the Italians. Although the stands were not as full and the atmosphere not as riotous as in Montevideo 4 years earlier, both teams were in good form and keyed for victory.

The Czechoslovakian team made the 1st move with a long kick by Puc, which turned into a goal when the Italian goalkeeper was a split-second too slow. Not until 8 minutes from the scheduled end did Italy manage to tie it up with a curving kick that amazed even Orsi, the kicker. The game went into extra time. After 97 minutes of play, Schiavio of Italy made another goal, bouncing the Czechs and cinching the World Cup for the nation that had been so determined to win.

1938

France hosted the games in 1938, and the troubles of the world were reflected in the microcosm of the World Cup: Spain could send no team because it was in the middle of its civil war; the best players on the Austrian team had been annexed by the Germans; squabbling and hurt pride kept Uruguay and Argentina from participating; and England still failed to join the competition. This left the Hungarians and Czechs as the teams most likely to dethrone the Italian defenders.

The competition reverted to 2 rounds leading to the semifinals. The 2nd round found the Italians defeating their French hosts 3–1, with center-forward Piola the master of the field. The Cubans were destroyed by the Swedes, 8–1 with 4 by Gustav Wetterstroem, the "bombadier of Norkopping." Hungary shut out Switzerland, 2–0. The Brazil-Czechoslovakia match looked like a battlefield. There were several serious injuries, 3 expulsions, and a 1–1 score even after extra time. For the replay the Brazilians substituted 9 new players, the Czechs 6, and the much more placid game ended in a 2–1 win for Brazil.

Brazil met Italy in the semifinals. Undone by the sin of pride, the Brazilians reserved 2 of their best players for the final they were never to reach. Colaussi made the 1st point for Italy, Meazza the 2nd, ripping and losing

his shorts in the process. Brazil's Romeo scored its lone goal late in the game. Italy was victorious 2–1. The other semifinal match saw Hungary melt down Sweden's "team of steel." Sweden's Nyberg scored its only point a mere 35 seconds into the game, but it was downhill from there to the final score of 5–1.

The final got off to a quick start. After 6 minutes, Serantoni of Italy got the ball to Biavati who transported it almost the length of the field. It went from Meazza to Colaussi to goal. Within seconds, Titkos of Hungary evened the score. Another quarter of an hour into the game, Piola gave Italy the advantage and they retained control of the game thereafter. Hungary found one more point, but Italy smashed in 2 others for a final score of Italy 4, Hungary 2. It was the last World Cup for 12 years; the world had other scores to settle.

1950

In 1950, World Cup co-founder Jules Rimet got the World Cup out from under his bed, where he had hidden it during the war. In honor of hosting the 1st competition since 1938, Brazil erected the largest stadium in the world in Rio de Janeiro. It was designed to hold 200,000 people but unfortunately not even the help of the army was able to ensure its completion by the time the crowds arrived.

Brazil, relatively untouched by the war, had raised its skill and its enthusiasm to new heights. Argentina once again withdrew in a huff, as did Czechoslovakia, Turkey, and France. Hungary and Russia were behind the Iron Curtain; Austria felt that its team wasn't ready; and Germany was barred as an aftermath of the war. But England, which had joined FIFA—the international football association—in 1946, was participating for the 1st time. Even so, a mere 13 teams vied for the honors.

Italy would have been a strong contender but for the 1949 air crash which killed 8 of the members of the national team. At the outset, England was highly considered, as was the Brazilian team, which was accompanied by a coach determined to instill his team with a new sense of discipline.

The competition went back to a pool system. The most dramatic game was England's match against the U.S. The American team was not the underdog—it was whatever comes "under" the underdog. And indeed, in the 1st half, the English dominated the play even though they did not manage a point. Then the U.S.'s Bahr shot, the English goalkeeper seemed ready to intercept routinely, but Gaetjens headed it out of his reach and into the goal. During the entire 2nd half the American defense held, and the upstart Colonial team had the slim but sweet victory of a 1–0 score.

The initial rounds led to a final pool, a format never used again. The competitors in the final pool were Uruguay, Brazil, Spain, and Sweden. Brazil, using a style which permitted individual virtuosity in the context of teamwork, crunched the tired Spaniards 6–1, and the Swedes 7–1. This gave them 4 points in the final pool match (2 per win). The Cup would go to the team with the most points.

The Uruguay team experienced unexpected difficulty with the hard-fighting Spaniards and had to work very hard to salvage a tie, which gave them one pool point. They were more fortunate in being able to reverse Sweden's halftime lead to a final 3–2 win. The game between Spain and Sweden went well for the latter. Two of the Spanish players bickered on the field, adding to the team's confusion and Sweden's 3–1 victory. Now Uruguay, with 3 pool points, was the runner-up, and the final game—not officially a "final"—was between the confident Brazil and the hopeful Uruguay.

Brazil had good reason to be confident. They had honed to a fine edge the art of alternating short passes with long, angled, passing kicks. The Uruguayans, casual but determined, rose to the challenge with a flexible defense characterized by several spectacular saves. The Brazilians went instantly on the attack. Zizinho, Jair, and Ademir led the brutal advances that penetrated the Uruguayan defense; but repeatedly, Andrade and Valera intercepted and the goalkeeper worked minor miracles defending the goal. Their successful defense inspired the Uruguayans to launch their own offense, but they were thwarted by Brazil's goalkeeper, Barbosa. A couple of minutes into the 2nd half, Brazil scored at last, pulling the Uruguayan defense this way and that until Frianca was able to boot the ball in for the 1st goal of the game. Uruguay responded by stepping up its own attack. On the 3rd try, Perez was successful; it was a shot that Barbosa could only reach with his fingertips. Uruguay scored again 20 minutes later, its all-out effort resulting in a final score of 2–1. Valera, the hero of the match summarized the strategy this way: ". . . We succeeded in erecting a cage from which the Brazilian forwards were rarely able to escape. . . . Our plan was to see that every Brazilian forward must beat at least 2 defenders before being able to shoot." After 20 years, Uruguay was on top again.

1954

In 1954, West Germany was readmitted to the World Cup and Scotland competed for the 1st time. Uruguay was considered a strong contender, with 5 players who had participated

in the spectacular 1950 final game again representing their country. But the new favorite was Hungary, which had twice soundly defeated the English during the preceding year.

The elimination scheme adopted for the tournament, held that year in Switzerland, was complex. One game in the quarter-finals has become immortal in its shame. Known as "The Battle of Berne," it pitted Brazil against Hungary. The 1st half witnessed a series of fouls; in the 2nd half, the situation degenerated to fistfights and kicking. The game ended with a score of Hungary 4, Brazil 2, but the violence went on. Allegedly, Ferenc Puskas, an injured Hungarian team member watching from the sidelines, hit the Brazilian Pinheiro in the face with a bottle. Thereupon the Brazilians invaded the Hungarian dressing room where further mayhem ensued. As British soccer star Bobby Moore recalled, "It should have been one of the greatest soccer exhibitions of all time. Instead these 2 nations disgraced the showpiece of the world."

The other quarter-final games ended as follows: Germany 2, Yugoslavia 0; Austria 7, Switzerland 5; and Uruguay 4, England 2.

A great downpour of rain greeted the semifinal match between Hungary and Uruguay, but it failed to dampen the skill of either team. The 1st Hungarian goal came from Kocsis to Czibor, past a gallant lunge by Uruguay's Maspoli. It was soon joined by another, headed in by Hidegkuti. Uruguay rallied close to the end with 2 goals. Hohberg was responsible for both, and after the 2nd he was so heartily congratulated by his team that they accidentally knocked him out and he had to be revived with smelling salts. The game went into extra time, during which Hungary made 2 more goals, for a victory of 4–2.

In the other semifinal game, Austria lost to the Germans, 6–1. The Austrian goalkeeper, Walter Zehman, appeared unsure of what game was being played and what he should do about it. Time and time again, the Germans came at him from one side or the other, sometimes from the center, and time and time again in the 2nd half the ball invaded the net. However, the German success was not entirely due to Austrian weakness; the Germans played a powerful, accurate, and manipulative game. They went from underdog to final contender.

The final set West Germany against Hungary. The Hungarian core consisted of Puskas, Kocsis, Hidegkuti, and Bozsik. Greatest of these greats was Ferenc Puskas, the team captain and an army major. As was true in several of the communist countries, the Hungarian Army inducted the best players, made them soldiers, and had them play for the army team. It was a technique guaranteed to produce good player selection, discipline, and teamwork, if not always good morale.

Puskas had been injured in a foul by a German in an earlier match. Although his ankle had not quite healed, he decided to play. Once again it rained as the Hungarians mounted a strong attack 6 minutes into the game, culminating in the 1st point, flowing from Puskas's formidable left foot. It was shortly followed up by another from Czibor. Such a start would be enough to demoralize most opponents, but the Germans came back strongly and within a few minutes Morlock had put them on the board, and Helmut Rahn equalized the score.

The 2nd half began with an insidious Hungarian assault, headed by Puskas. But both of his credible shots were deflected by German goalkeeper Turek, and a header by Kocsis bounced off the bar.

The German drive came next, culminating in a goal by Rahn who advanced, stopped, and kicked the ball past a desperate Grosics. The score was Germany 3, Hungary 2. It had become clear that Puskas, for all his valiant efforts, was not in top form: his injured ankle made him a slower, more plodding player when speed and flexibility were at a premium. He nearly evened the score with a goal, but while his team rejoiced, the referee had other thoughts—Puskas had been offsides. The final effort by Hungary's Czibor was also to no avail, his clear, powerful kick deflected by the acrobatic Turek. For the 1st time, the Germans had made their mark at the World Cup.

1958

The 1958 competition held in Sweden was the scene of the World Cup debut of the Russian team and of Pelé, the Brazilian whose name became almost synonymous with soccer. It also signaled the beginnings of the "4-2-4" system, introduced by Brazil. Of it, English soccer authority Brian Glanville wrote, "The 4-2-4 system solved the old Brazilian problem of pivotal covering in defense by simply putting the left-half alongside the center-half. . . . Two players foraged and passed in midfield, while 2 wingers and 2 central strikers stayed in attack." Sounding a cautionary note he added, "If you had the extraordinary talent at your command that the Brazilians had, it was a marvelous system. If not, it would present as many difficulties as it solved. . . ."

In the quarter-finals the Swedes failed to make any headway against the Russians in the 1st half, but then Kurt Hamrin cut loose. On his 3rd try he headed it in, and minutes later another goal made it 2–0 for Sweden. The Germans, thanks to their persistent star Helmut Rahn, bettered the hapless Yugo-

slavs, 1–0. Brazil triumphed over Wales with the same score. The point, after 66 minutes of the Welch rebuffing Brazilian attacks, was by Pelé, who called it the most important point he ever scored. The injured and tired Irish failed to stand up to France's 2nd-half onslaught, losing 4–0.

The semifinal game between Sweden and West Germany nearly failed to take place because the president of the German Football Association threatened to withdraw his team unless the Swedes stopped refusing to seat some of the German fans. The fans were seated. German Hans Schaefer scored Germany's point. In a play resulting in the tie point, Sweden's Liedholm brought the ball under control with his hand before dribbling it. That's how most observers called it, but not the referee, so there was no penalty. Several fouls marred the remainder of the game, in which Swedish aggressiveness compensated for lack of speed. The final score: Sweden 3, West Germany 1.

In the other semifinal game, Brazil had its way with France. It was a field day for Pelé, who scored 3 of Brazil's 5. The French garnered 2.

Thus the final pitted Sweden against Brazil. Sweden took the lead within 4 minutes, with a play by Liedholm. For the 1st time in this World Cup, Brazil found itself behind—but not for long. Garrincha dribbled the ball with crazy, swerving precision and set it up for Vavá to score; a combination that was successfully repeated about 20 minutes later. In the 2nd half, Pelé came to the fore with a goal and the Brazilian team commenced to swarm over the field like ants: very speedy and tightly organized ants. Zagolo made it 4 for Brazil. Sweden managed a 2nd goal, this time by Simmonson, but Pelé soon nailed down victory with Brazil's 5th and final point. The 4-2-4 system, the brilliance of Vavá and the 17-year-old Pelé, the amazing teamwork—all had paid off by putting the gold cup in the hands of Brazil.

1962

When bidding to host the World Cup in 1962, Chile had just suffered one of her disastrous earthquakes. The president of the Chilean Football Federation plaintively summed up the essence of Chile's bid: "We must have the World Cup because we have nothing." And so the World Cup was awarded and Chile erected 2 new stadia and raced to be ready for the hordes of players and fans.

Violence marred several of the early games, notably that of Italy against Chile. The atmosphere had been inflamed by Italian journalists' criticism of the backwardness of Chile, while Chileans resented Italy's recruitment of South American players. In the quarter-finals, Brazil's Garrincha assured their victory over England, 3–1, and moved out of the shadow of the absent, injured Pelé. Yugoslavia conquered Germany 1–0, a triumph of versatility over caution. The Chileans found Russia's great goalkeeper Yachine inexplicably slow, failing to intercept a ball kicked from 35 yards. The home team prevailed, 2–1. Czechoslovakia beat Hungary 1–0, saved by their goalkeeper Schroiff even though their defense at times resembled Swiss cheese. Scherer scored Czechoslovakia's one point.

The semifinals matched, or mismatched, Chile with Brazil. Garrincha was a one-man Brazilian army, kicking in the 1st goal, heading in a 2nd. Chile responded with one, but within a few minutes Vavá made it 3 for Brazil. Chile had another on penalty, a point matched by Vavá. In the last 10 minutes, the game deteriorated. Garrincha was kicked by Rojas and sent off for responding likewise. As he headed off the field, a spectator let fly with a bottle to the back of Garrincha's head, gashing it. Then Landa, a Chilean, was also expelled. It was an unfortunate but perhaps understandable conclusion to a game that saw Chile defeated 4–2 in front of fans who had dared to hope that in addition to hosting the World Cup they could keep it.

The other semifinal match featured a tight Czechoslovakian defense which thwarted Yugoslavia's attacks. Additionally, the Czechs found Yugoslavia's weakness on the wings and exploited it. Their 2–1 lead turned to a 3–1 final score when Scherer responded to a penalty. It was an upset that sent the Czechs into a final against Brazil.

The Brazilians were favored, but the Czech semifinal upset raised some doubts. At first it was uncertain whether the reprimanded Garrincha would be allowed to participate. He was permitted to play, but turned out to play less than his usual starring role in Brazil's win.

The Czechs lost little time making their 1st goal, putting the Brazilians in the one-down position. Amarildo quickly evened the score after advancing to the goal along the left goal line. The Czech performance continued to be more than credible, but well into the 2nd half Amarildo faked out his man, passed to Zito, and watched Brazil take the lead. Brazil's 3rd point underscored the fact that Czech goalkeeper Schroiff was in poor form: A high kick from Santos was touched by Schroiff, but he evidently had the sun in his eyes. He dropped the ball and Vavá booted it in. For the 2nd time in a row, this time with Amarildo as the man of the hour, Brazil took the Cup.

1966

In 1966, the World Cup competition finally came home to England, the country where soccer was formally invented. England almost lost the World Cup, literally. It was stolen from a Westminster shop window where it had been on display. It was unearthed in a garbage pile by a dog named Pickles. If anyone had been regarding the trophy with blasphemous awe, this little incident must have put the prize back in a more realistic perspective.

After the opening rounds came the quarter-finals, again on a knockout basis. England met a surly Argentina, angered by earlier calls by English referees. Fouls were rife and finally Rattin was sent off. Even with only 10 men the Argentinians showed their strength, particularly in midfield; and England scored only one goal, a header by Hurst. The game was over 1–0, but the action was not. Argentina's players started pummeling the referee, who was rescued by policemen, and in general created mayhem. Ramsey, the Englishmen's manager, sniffed, "Our best football will come against the team which comes out to play football, and not to act as animals."

The Uruguay v. Germany match was not any more peaceful. Two Uruguayans were expelled from the game, paving the way for the Germans to rule the field and close the game with a 4–0 advantage.

Meanwhile, Russia's greater power allowed them to bulldoze a 2–1 victory over skillful Hungary. The obscure North Korean team had got as far as the quarter-finals and was dazzling the crowds by scoring 3 quick goals against Portugal. Eusebio of Portugal turned out to be the savior, responsible for 4 goals, 2 of them on penalties. José Augusto made it 5 for Portugal against North Korea's 3.

The semifinal match between Germany and Russia should have been a cinch for Germany once Russia's Chislenko was sent off for kicking Germany's Held. But German caution stubbornly prevailed and the Russians managed a goal of their own to Germany's 2.

England met Portugal in their semifinal game. England played well, better than in any of their previous games at this competition, highlighted by Bobby Charlton's deft control of the ball. It was a tribute to Portugal that the final score was only 2–1 for England.

England was overjoyed at participating in a final on her own territory, and was optimistic as well. After all, in over a half century of play the English had won every match they had played against Germany. Their morale was so high that they were undaunted when Germany's Haller scored the 1st point after 13 minutes, upon having England's Wilson head it right in front of him. England answered with a penalty kick (upon a foul of Bobby Moore) that was parlayed into a point with a header by Hurst. English goalkeeper Banks withstood 2 strong attacks by the Germans, and the half found the score still tied 1–1.

Each team had obviously figured out the strengths and weaknesses of the other, and most of the 2nd half was a stalemate. Then, with about 12 minutes left, Peters and Weber dueled for the ball; Peters won, and made it 2 for England. The desperate Germans became more daring in their pursuit, giving England another chance which it failed to complete. With only a minute left, Charlton fouled Held. The free kick was worked into a goal by Weber and the game went into extra time.

The English had more strength left than the Germans. Geoff Hurst dispatched a ball which struck the bottom of the bar and bounced down. It was a disputed goal, but the referee judged that it had indeed crossed the line. Again Germany sacrificed defense in favor of an unsuccessful attack, and England's Hurst took advantage of that fact to become the 1st player in the history of the World Cup Final to score 3 points. The game was over, England 4, Germany 2.

1970

In 1970, strong lobbying characterized the competition among potential hosts. Mexico and Argentina were the strongest contenders and Mexico won. Given the Mexican summer heat and the respiratory difficulties common at 7,000', it was a decision many of the players, especially the Europeans, bitterly resented. The highlight of the qualifying games was the contest of champions, England against Brazil. Team manager Alf Ramsey's 1966 reference to Argentine players as "animals" had festered into Latin hatred of England. Now, on the eve of the match, Mexicans surrounded the English players' hotel and kept up a night-long din to deny the English their rest. The English struggled valiantly in the match, fighting the 98° heat and the Brazilians. Ludicrously, this match like many others started at noon, putting the demands of European television above the comfort and health of the players. The game featured an admirable defense which contained Pelé, but ultimately let the Brazilians score the single point.

In the quarter-finals, the delirious fans urged on the home team, Mexico, against Italy. But Italy's Riva, dominating the 2nd half, scored

2 of his team's 4. Mexico was unable to muster more than one. The Uruguay-Russia match was closer, ending 1–0 in favor of the Soviet Union. The Brazil-Peru confrontation was characterized by risk-taking on both sides, but Brazil's confident coordination was reflected in the score: Brazil 4, Peru 2. Finally, England —minus their star goalkeeper Gordon Banks —tired 1st and in overtime gave up their game to West Germany, 3–2.

A game between Brazil and Uruguay was the 1st part of the semifinal competition. The underdog Uruguayans made a startling 1st goal, shot by Cubilla at an extreme angle. It took Brazil some time to equalize with Clodoaldo parlaying Tostado's pass into a goal. The Uruguayans were playing rough, more so in the 2nd half when Brazil began to take control. Tostado fed Jairzinho for Brazil's 2nd, and a Pelé-Rivelino combination made it 3. The final score stood at Brazil 3, Uruguay 1.

The other semifinal pitted Italy against West Germany. The Germans began the match slowly, roused not so much by a goal by Italy's Boninsegna, but by the fact that the Italians then turned cautious. This gave Germany the opportunity to dominate the midfield and launch repeated attacks. Even so, it took time for Germany to tie up the game. It was in extra time that the game turned into, as a columnist put it, a "basketball" tourney. A foul on Franz Beckenbaur put his arm in a sling and gave Italy the edge. Caution thrown to the wind, both sides frantically scored. The game which had started so placidly ended with 4 for Italy, 3 for West Germany.

In the final, Brazil's defense was admittedly not the best, but their magnificent offense was. Understandably, the Italians, while proud of their defense, were nervous going in. Pelé gave them cause by making an awesome leap which beat out the Italian defense and headed in the 1st goal. The Italians were able to respond when an error by Clodoaldo sent goalkeeper Felix scrambling out of the goal area in a futile effort to regain control of the ball. Instead, Boninsegna passed him by and shot into an empty goal. But the Italians failed to press their attack. In the 2nd half, Brazil's Gerson let fly a low, successful kick. A 3rd Brazilian point was earned by Jairzinho on a pass from Pelé. And a 4th goal was forthcoming just minutes before the end, Jairzinho to Pelé to Carlos Alberto. The 4–1 victory was Brazil's 3rd, and so the Cup went to them. The daring attacks, the willingness to allow artistry within the framework of a solid team, had won a decisive victory over the trend toward defensive, workmanlike, and often boring soccer.

1974

West Germany, many times a bridesmaid and once before the bride, hosted the 1974 competition. Seen by an estimated 600 million television viewers, the 1974 World Cup more than ever captured the attention of the globe. According to *Time* magazine, factories in Rio de Janeiro shut down; Italy's attempts to find a viable government were interrupted as 3 leaders left meetings to watch a game; and in Zaire, Africa, bus drivers left their buses when the Zaire Leopards had their match.

The elimination games were more placid than expected. The style known as total football, characterized by rushes by the entire team, was absent after having been popularized by West Germany and Holland. Also absent was representation by the U.S. and England, whose teams lost out in the elimination matches.

Eight nations fought it out for places in the semifinals: East Germany, Yugoslavia, Argentina, Sweden, Brazil, The Netherlands, West Germany, and Poland. The last 4 triumphed and went on.

The West Germany-Poland semifinal took place on a playing field reduced to a morass by rain. Accurate passing was almost impossible, and yet the action was smooth and featured a series of dazzling attacks. Wingers Gadocha and Lato pierced Germany's defense, keeping goalkeeper Maier frantically busy in the 1st half, making 3 saves. Maier's Polish counterpart, Jan Tomaszewski put in an equally brilliant performance, particularly in his 2nd-half deflection of Hoeness's penalty kick. Finally, a quarter of an hour from the end, German Gerd Muller tunneled his way in, faked out Tomaszewski, and assured Germany's place in the final.

Holland's semifinal battle with Brazil was unfortunately reminiscent in its roughness of 1954s "Battle of Berne." Brazil was minus superstar Pelé, who retired from international competition after helping Brazil win the last Cup. The Brazilians substituted ferocity for finesse, and by the end of the half, 3 of their players had been warned for dangerous play. Shortly before the end, fullback Luis Pereira tackled Neeskens and was sent off. Neeskens made the 1st Dutch goal, the 2nd came from Johan Cruyff, considered by many to be the world's best soccer player. Cruyff shrugged off Brazil's brawling tactics, saying, "The technical way of beating us was gone. All they had left was the physical way." But even the physical way yielded no results, and the Flying Dutchmen were on their way to the final.

The Dutchmen went into the final with some of the wind out of their sails as a result of the brutal Brazilian bout. Nonetheless, the Dutch team took the early advantage with a successful penalty kick after Cruyff had been tripped in the penalty area. For the next half hour they dominated the field, but the impetus passed to the Germans after they tied the score, also on a penalty kick. Gerd Muller struck with another German goal minutes before half-time, making it 2–1. The 2nd half saw the Dutchmen make repeated assaults, following up high passes from the center and wings, but German goalkeeper Maier and his defenders successfully beat back the attacks. The whistle blew and the hosts had won their World Cup.

—J.W.

Big Moments in Sports History

1874: THE GREAT INTERNATIONAL RIFLE MATCH

No event in the sporting world has excited more general attention than the Grand International Rifle Match at Creedmoor, Long Island, between the American and Irish teams, said *Harper's Weekly* in 1874 when the 2 countries shot it out for the championship of the world before an unruly crowd of 8,000 cheering people. Since early morn on September 26, the day of the Grand Match, coaches, tallyhos, hacks, and high-wheeled bikes choked the roads leading from New York to Creedmoor, site of America's 1st rifle range. The L.I. railroad ran special trains jammed with spectators. Across the country telegraph offices stood by ready to flash shot-by-shot reports of the daylong match.

The year before, Ireland had won the rifle championship of the British Isles. Maj. Arthur B. Leech, captain of the Irish team, then challenged America for the world title. Col. George W. Wingate, one of the founders of the recently formed (1871) National Rifle Association of America, in accepting the challenge, yielded to Ireland's terms of a long-range match, at distances of 800, 900, and 1,000 yards. This was conceding a lot, for none of the Americans had ever fired beyond 600 yards. Ironically, the finest long-range shots the world had ever seen were right in America—the professional buffalo hunters on the western plains—but they were more interested in bagging hides at $50 each than in a rifle match.

The untested team selected by Colonel Wingate to do the shooting was: Maj. Henry Fulton, G. W. Yale, Col. John Bodine, Lt. Col. H. A. Gildersleeve, L. L. Hepburn, and Gen. T. S. Dakin. The terms of the match: 15 rounds per man at each of the 3 distances; .44 caliber rifles of 10 lbs. maximum weight firing identical loads of black powder; the Americans to use breechloaders of U.S. manufacture, the Irish to fire their own muzzleloaders (considered more accurate); telescopic sights were barred; standard English targets, measuring 12′×6′. The square bull's-eye (4 points) was 3′×3′; the "center" (3 points) was 6′×6′, with a 2′ space on each side called an "outer" (2 points).

The veteran Irish team, experts at long-range, were the odds-on favorites as they took position in front of the huge roped-off throng at exactly 10:30 A.M. It was a hot, dry day. Captain Walker, Ireland's lead-off man, took his place between the red flags that marked the firing point, got down on his stomach and squinted at the target. A strange sight greeted the captain's eye. The target seemed to dance in the shimmering heat waves, a phenomenon unknown in cloudy Ireland. No marker rose up when he fired. It was a clean miss. Behind him came groans mixed with thunderous cheers. Colonel Wingate ran in front of the spectators and appealed to them to quiet down.

America's 1st man was Major Fulton, a 28-year-old Civil War veteran. Lying on his back with his feet toward the target, he rested the barrel of his Remington on his legs—a position which enabled him to keep his luxurious blond beard out of the dust—and squeezed the trigger for a bull's-eye. (Of the 12 men who shot that day, 5 used the feetfirst position; 7 the headfirst stomach-down stance. Comparative scores later showed that the feet-first men averaged 157 points against 154 for the conventional shooters.)

When the 800-yard stage was over, America led 326–317 and both teams retired to a large tent for a lunch complete with speeches and toasts.

At the 900-yard stage Ireland figured to overcome America's 9-point lead. Cheers resounded from the crowd when the marker at the target rose to indicate a bull's-eye as Ireland's J. K. Milner got off his 1st shot. But a murmur of disappointment soon followed when the umpire decreed that the bull's-eye must go for zero. Poor Milner had hit the wrong target. But then the Irish got a couple of breaks. The 1st one came when Dakin of the American team touched off a shot which fell far short of the target. The miss was caused by a defective load. Then clouds obscured the sun, giving the Irish the filtered light to which they were accustomed on their native sod. Firing accurately at 900 yards, they cut America's lead to 7 points.

Now for the final 1,000-yard stage, Ireland's best distance. It was neck and neck all the way and when the Irish finished, the score stood 931–913 in their favor. But the match was not yet over. Major Fulton and Colonel Bodine still had 3 shots each to fire. Both had been shooting well but Fulton, feeling the pressure, could not find the bull's-eye and rang up 3 "centers." Now came Colonel Bodine, America's anchor man. If he did no better than Fulton the score would be tied.

Carefully sighting the target, the colonel scored one bull's-eye, then another. Ireland now led by one point and only one shot remained. If Bodine hit the target America would win, since the minimum score was 2 points. If he missed, Ireland would win. It was then that the crowd broke through the ropes and lined up on either side of the colonel's firing point, almost as far as the target. The elderly Bodine called for a bottle of ginger beer to steady his nerves but as he opened it the bottle broke and a piece of glass cut deeply into his trigger hand. Bleeding profusely, he wrapped his hand in a handkerchief and waited until the crowd quieted down. The colonel remained calm. Slowly he got on his stomach, sighted the rifle and inhaled deeply, then let half out. At last came the shot and the *spat* of the bullet on the iron target.

"He's on!" the crowd roared and the white disk rose to signal a 4-point bull's-eye. America had won, 934 to 931, and the rifle championship of the world was theirs.

—J.Du. rep.

1889: The Last Bareknuckle Prizefight

Everyone knew that no man could stand up to John L. Sullivan and swap punches with him. A devastating 2-handed hitter, Sullivan had toured the country taking on all comers and had offered $1,000 to anyone who could stay 4 rounds. Drunk or sober, he had flattened 59 men in a row. Only a few were able to survive the 1st round, none the 4th. His only weakness was his fondness for the bottle—he used to drink bourbon out of steins—and for this reason his perfectly trained opponent, Jake Kilrain of Baltimore, was given an even chance to outlast him in a finish fight.

Kilrain was not a slugger but he could go distance and he was a good wrestler, which was useful in bareknuckle fighting, where a fall could be almost as punishing as a knockdown blow. "Sullivan was no wrestler," said the *New York World* the day of the fight (July 8, 1889) and added with journalistic candor unknown today: "According to the history of all such drunkards as he, his legs ought to fail him after 20 minutes of fighting."

When the men came to scratch at 10 A.M. at Richburg, Miss., before a crowd of 3,000 fans, most of whom had come by train from New Orleans to the secret ring site (bare fist fighting was illegal in all 38 States), the thermometer registered 100° in the shade. It was a test between 2 champions for $10,000 a side, winner take all. Sullivan, resplendent in green breeches and flesh-colored stockings, was champion by popular acclaim; Kilrain, by decree of Richard K. Fox, publisher of the *Police Gazette*, who ignored Sullivan's claim and awarded the *Gazette*'s championship belt to his opponent. "I would not put Fox's belt around the neck of a bulldog," snorted the great John L.

From the start Kilrain pursued his battle plan by avoiding all toe-to-toe slugging and by sidestepping the rushes of the ever-advancing Sullivan. These tactics drove Sullivan into a fury. "Why don't you fight? You're supposed to be the champ, ain't you?" bawled Sullivan in the 4th round, which lasted over 15 minutes. (Under the rules a round ended only when a man went down and could, therefore, last a few seconds or several minutes.) In the 7th round, as the men clinched, Kilrain hooked to the head and brought a flow of blood from John L.'s ear. "First blood, Kilrain," announced referee John Fitzpatrick and there was an exchange of bills among the sports. (Betting was always brisk on 1st blood and 1st knockdown.) Sullivan scored the 1st clean knockdown in the next round. As the fight wore on, both men were soaked in blood, their backs scorched crimson by the burning sun. There was no decisive turning point in the battle but after the 30th round it was evident that Sullivan was getting to his man. Jake was tiring, not Sullivan, who was now scoring all the knockdowns and most of the falls. But Kilrain kept on coming to scratch round after round although his eyes were glassy and his head rolled loosely on his shoulders as if his neck were broken. In the 75th round a doctor said to Kilrain's seconds, "If you keep sending him out there, he'll die." That was enough. They tossed in the sponge and the fight was over.

The last bareknuckle fight in ring history had lasted 2 hours and 16 minutes. A new era of padded gloves and 3-minute rounds under the modern Queensberry rules soon replaced the old barefisted brawlers. Sullivan lost his crown to Jim Corbett in a glove fight 3 years later. As for Kilrain, who was so near

death at the end of the fight, he lived to be a pallbearer at Sullivan's funeral in 1918 and did not die until 1937 when he was 78.

—J.Du. rep.

1931: THE ALL-TIME CHAMPIONSHIP BRIDGE MATCH

Contract bridge, from its quiet beginnings around 1926, had by 1931 become a national rage. It seems likely that the Big Depression was partly responsible. People had no money to spend on other diversions and a deck of cards didn't cost much, so practically everybody played contract.

Into this situation stepped a lean, suave, quick-witted super-irritant named Ely Culbertson. He was then 40 years old, son of a Russian mother and an American father, and possessed of a manner which some people thought charming but which led others to cast their eyes about in search of blunt instruments. His life in America, up to this time, had been that of an obscure professional card player who haunted the bridge clubs in New York City, sometimes prospering, sometimes broke and in debt. He was certainly one of the ablest card tacticians in the country and his handsome wife, Josephine, was considered to be the best player of her sex.

By 1930 the contract fad was approaching the proportions of a plague, and growing week by week. Culbertson saw the potential, realizing that if he played his cards right, he might very well reap both fame and fortune out of the new national obsession.

In the spring of 1930, a British bridge expert published a statement to the effect that American bridge players were a sad lot of blokes. Culbertson promptly issued a sassy challenge. He would bring a team of 4 to London and play 300 duplicate boards against a British team. The challenge was accepted and now Culbertson had to raise money to get himself and his team to England. He began taking orders for his 1st book on bridge, not a line of which had been written. He got the money, dictated the text of his book right up to the hour of sailing, and then took off with Mrs. Culbertson and 2 young men who could play the Culbertson system—Theodore Lightner and Waldemar von Zedtwitz. The arrival of these brash, unknown Americans created a big stir not only in England but on the Continent. The English bridge writers treated them with great condescension and laughed at them in print. Following which the Culbertson team proceeded to clobber the English, winning the match by nearly 5,000 points.

Ely and Jo Culbertson came home famous. Culbertson's Blue Book had been published during the play of the match in London and now was selling furiously all over the U.S. The name Culbertson was fast becoming almost a synonym for contract bridge and, of course, this didn't set well in certain quarters. As the Culbertson system grew and prospered, the book sales and prestige of the old established masters, such as Milton Work, Whitehead and Lenz, declined.

Culbertson began to needle these older men. He wrote about them and he talked about them on the radio. He charged that they were trying to ruin his reputation through a whispering campaign, calling him a dissolute gigolo and a "suspicious Russian." Eventually, he drove them to the wall, and they turned to fight.

A dozen of the old masters joined forces in an organization called Bridge Headquarters. Their stated purpose was to "standardize" the game, and they sponsored a method of play which they called the Official System. They went through the motions of inviting Culbertson into the group, but he simply threw back his head and cackled at them. He picked out Sidney S. Lenz as the best card player in the group and challenged Lenz to a match of 150 rubbers, Lenz to choose his own partner. Culbertson would bet $5,000 against $1,000 that he and his wife, playing the Culbertson System, would beat Lenz and his partner, hewing to the Official System.

The old guard had to put up or shut up, and finally Lenz accepted the challenge.

Between the time when the rules were agreed upon and the match got under way, the nation's press discovered that it had something special on its hands. In the week prior to December 7, 1931, 24 special cables were laid into the Culbertson apartment in the Hotel Chatham, where the 1st half of the contest was to be staged. A large press room, complete with rows of typewriters and telegraph keys, was established down the hall from the Culbertson drawing room to make reporters comfortable.

Sidney Lenz was then 58, an amateur magician, a Ping-Pong champion, a superb bridge player and a wealthy man. He chose as his partner Oswald Jacoby, a handsome young fellow with dark hair and the build of a fullback, member of the championship bridge team called The Four Horsemen.

On the night the match started, there was classic confusion in the various rooms and corridors of the hotel. The place swarmed with reporters and cameramen and society people and celebrities. Chosen to referee the contest was Lieut. Alfred M. Gruenther, a 32-year-old chemistry instructor at West Point. Everyone was most polite and after 2 rubbers, Lenz and Jacoby were 1,715 points ahead.

The card table was at one end of the Cul-

bertson drawing room. Across the center of the room stood high folding screens and there were 6 cracks, each about an inch wide, through which the reporters and favored guests could watch the contest. There was a chair at each crack and the rule said that no reporter or guest could look through a crack more than 15 minutes at a time, and it was required that everyone walk on tiptoe. Signs ordering "Complete Silence!" hung throughout the apartment, and on the door where the 2 Culbertson children were abed was a sign saying, "Quiet! Little Children Asleep and Dreaming."

Those who were present every night for 5 weeks might well have become bored with the proceedings if it hadn't been for Culbertson. He needed no press agent. He was consistently late getting to the card table and this infuriated Sidney Lenz, a man of little patience. Culbertson went into long periods of meditation before bidding or before playing a card, and Lenz soon grew bitter about the entire proceedings.

At the end of the 27th rubber, Lenz was ahead by more than 7,000 points but on December 15, Culbertson took the lead for the 1st time. He never relinquished it after that and each evening as he arrived (late) at the table, he'd smile sweetly at Lenz and in his rich Russian accent he'd say, "Well, Sidney, have you changed your system yet?"

Public interest in the contest reached such a pitch that one evening Jack Curley, the wrestling impresario, arrived at the Chatham demanding the right to switch the play to Madison Square Garden. He proposed that the players should occupy a glass cage and the audience follow the play on huge electrical scoreboards. He insisted that a fortune could be made from such an arrangement. "A fortune for you," said Culbertson, "but I'm interested only in making a fortune for myself."

The public got immense satisfaction out of the knowledge that these great stars of the game were frequently guilty of bonehead plays. On December 28, Jacoby quit after a loud dispute with Lenz. Late in that evening's session, Lenz suddenly turned on Jacoby.

"Why do you make such rotten bids?" he demanded.

Jacoby stared at him and didn't answer. Culbertson smiled and said, "Shall we play another rubber?"

"Not with me, you don't!" snapped Jacoby, rising to his feet.

Referee Gruenther intervened, saying that the rules required another rubber. Jacoby sat down again.

The next evening Lenz had a new partner, a rotund former Navy officer, Comdr. Winfield Liggett, Jr. Commander Liggett agreed to play as his old friend's partner but told the press that the contest was proving nothing at all about the relative merits of the bidding systems.

The 2nd half of the match was played at the Waldorf-Astoria in quarters provided by Lenz. It all came to an end on the night of January 8, with the Culbertsons victors by 8,980 points. After the last card had dropped, Lenz stood up and shook hands with Mrs. Culbertson. Culbertson walked over to join in the felicitations, but Lenz turned his back on him. Lieu-tenant Gruenther went back to West Point to pursue a career that would eventuate in his becoming Supreme Allied Commander in Europe.

Contract bridge, of course, is not what it was in those frenzied days, but it remains one of the most popular of our indoor sports and Culbertson rated as one of its top authorities until his death in January, 1956. Three years before he died, he attended Lenz's 80th birthday and the 2 men shook hands.

—H.A.S. rep.

Money and Sports: A History of the Marriage

The 1st professional baseball team was "owned" by the players themselves, and embodied a kind of players' control over when, where, and how they should play, as well as how profits should be shared. At the time, most other baseball players also liked the idea of this arrangement. It took more than ⅓ of a century to convince most of them that anyone else should "own" their labor or their contracts. (The basketball players took even longer.) And even in our enlightened era, many are still not convinced.

Prior to 1876, when the National League was formed, professional baseball players often moved around between whichever teams would pay them the most money, or they formed their own teams. But the capitalists who formed the new league had other ideas. They had the money for sports fields, promotion, and players' salaries, but they insisted that players sign contracts containing what was known as a reserve clause, giving their "owners" the right to reserve their services, and exclude them from playing for other league teams. This infuriated the players, but since these owners seemed to be the only ones around able to borrow the money to bankroll such a large-scale operation (and since a good many players earned big money "fringe benefits" by fixing games) most grudgingly took their pay packets and played the game.

In 1882, however, the American Association was formed. Although the new league also had what the players called a slave system—whereby owners doled out among themselves monopolistic rights for contracting certain players—at least now players could choose between the 2 leagues. This meant owners had to compete for them. But this free competition lasted only one year. The owners of the 2 leagues finally decided among themselves that monopoly was best for all of them, and they agreed not to hire each other's players. So the players were right back where they started.

In 1884, just 8 years after the National League was founded, its monopolistic ways of doing business were put to a stern test. Realtor Henry V. Lucas declared that the reserve rule "reserves all that is good for the owners." Since it was time to do something about the player's "bondage," he formed a new Union League. Naturally, the threat of free competition did not endear itself to the monopolists or their friends in the press. It was all-out war. But, as its finances plunged deeper and deeper into the red, the Union League collapsed after only one year. As part of the price of peace and profit, Lucas himself was admitted to the National League as owner of the St. Louis franchise. Monopoly was still intact.

Smashing the Players' League

The owners had a good thing going, until they started pushing the players too hard. As the 1880s ended they were trying to establish a sort of productivity scale for players, whereby each man would be graded on his playing from A to E, with salaries ranging in grades from $2,500 down to $1,500. In effect, this would have taken away the player's right to negotiate his salary with the only boss he was allowed to work for. Full-scale rebellion broke out. Under the leadership of their union, the National Brotherhood of Professional Players, the athletes set up their own league. The National League was decimated. Even by paying huge salaries, it could hold so few of its players that it had to fill almost every position with rookies. It became known as the sand-lot league. The American Association found itself in a similar position. The Players' League promptly managed to attract more fans than either of the old leagues. Not surprisingly, other capitalists, including those who owned the newspapers, did not like the idea of workers deserting a business and setting up their own. So the new league found it impossible to raise money. It could not get bank loans. More often than not, its games received no press coverage. . . . Without financial backing from the banks, the players found it hard to stand up to cutthroat competition. In a year this most popular of the 3 leagues, comprised of almost all the top players, had folded. The American Association (which used to refer to the NL as "the rich man's league") went down shortly thereafter. The players had been beaten back. The rule of monopoly continued. . . .

Who Controls Sports?

Throughout the sports industry, as in every other industry under capitalism, control is exercised, not by the consumers (fans), nor by the producers (players), but by the owners of capital. It is they who decide whether or not to stage their spectacles and when, where, and how to do so. Ownership gives them the power to dictate the complete development or non-development of the industry, the very life and working conditions of those (players) whose labor they buy, and the nature of the product they produce. And the basis of their decisions is 1st and foremost, personal profit. In this, sports owners are just like other capitalists (although some of them may, incidentally, be big sports fans on the side). However their loyalty to their capital will always surpass their loyalty to the team. If it did not they might quickly find themselves out of business. And there is a lot of money involved.

Indeed, the 1st thing we notice about the sports industry is that it is very expensive to become an owner. When the 1st professional baseball league was formed in 1871 the entrance fee for a team was just $10. Five years later, when the National League was formed, the price of a franchise was just $100 plus players' salaries. By the mid-1960s, CBS had bought the New York Yankees for $15 million and later the Vancouver Canucks hockey team was purchased for $6 million. At these prices a situation is rapidly being created in which only corporations of substantial size, or syndicates of their executives, can raise the capital to buy a team. Under these conditions, a professional sports operation becomes little more than a cog in a giant corporate empire (or syndicate of interlocking directorates) and is run in the same way as the rest of the enterprise. "There's not much need, really, to document football's place in the great American free-enterprise system," wrote a columnist in the Toronto *Telegram's Weekend Magazine.* "All pro sports are run as efficiently, cold-bloodedly and greedily as any other big business with a lust for a buck." As elsewhere in the "game" of capitalist big business, we find boards of directors dictating from the top to their production managers who dictate to supervisors (coaches) dictating to workers (players). And the latter have been reduced to little more than pawns in a giant corporate machine concerned much more with profit than "play". . . .

Monopoly Ownership

One reason an aspiring sports magnate is willing to pay millions of dollars for a team is that the possession of a league franchise puts him in a monopolistic position in marketing his product in a particular city and hiring the players who will produce the product. The toleration by the dominant elements in society of such monopolistic agreements in restraint of a free-player market as the reserve and option clauses written into all major-league contracts reflects the usefulness of the sports industry in providing a profitable investment channel for their surplus capital, and even more importantly, for furthering the sort of competitive, work-hard, be-disciplined, produce-more, consume-more ideology our capitalists find so attractive. The laws governing sports, including especially the 1922 Supreme Court decision exempting baseball from the antitrust laws, arise out of both the economics of this capitalist industry and the place of sports production, including ideological indoctrination, in this society generally. Thus, the sports industry provides a graphic illustration of how, when the economic situation in a major industry violates the laws of capitalist society (in this case, the antitrust laws), the laws are reinterpreted to agree with the economic "realities" and not the other way around. . . .

—P.H. rep.

The Crossword Puzzle

Newspaperman Arthur Wynne created the 1st crossword puzzle which appeared in a publication in the U.S. An Englishman born in Liverpool, editor Wynne placed the puzzle in the December 21, 1913, "Fun" page of the Sunday supplement to the New York *World.*

Did the idea of the crossword puzzle spring full-blown into Wynne's mind? Well, no—editor Wynne wanted something bright and new as a steady space filler. He had a vague recollection of a puzzle he'd once seen in the London *Graphic.* So the 1st American crossword puzzle was born.

This puzzle was an instant if modest success

The World's First Crossword Puzzle (1913)

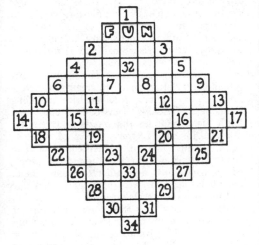

Solution:

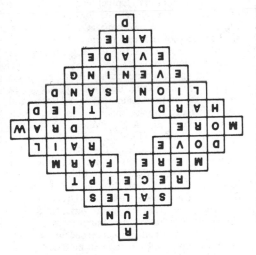

Fill in the squares of the puzzle so that the words spelled by the letters agree with these definitions:

2-3.   What bargain hunters enjoy.
4-5.   A written acknowledgment.
6-7.   Such and nothing more.
10-11. A bird.
14-15. Opposed to less.
18-19. What this puzzle is.
22-23. An animal of prey.
26-27. The close of a day.
28-29. Elude.
30-31. The plural of is.
8-9.   To cultivate.
12-13. A bar of wood or iron.
16-17. What artists learn to do.
20-21. Fastened.
24-25. Found on the seashore.
10-18. The fiber of the gomuti palm.
6-22.   What we all should be.
4-26.   A daydream.
2-11.   A talon.
19-28. A pigeon.
F-7.   Part of your head.
23-30. A river in Russia.
1-32.   To govern.
33-34. An aromatic plant.
N-8.   A fist.
24-31. To agree with.
3-12.   Part of a ship.
20-29. One.
5-27.   Exchanging.
9-25.   To sink in mud.
13-21. A boy.

with the readers of the *World*. It was diamond-shaped and some of the clues were: A written acknowledgment (7 letters) (Ans: receipt); the fiber of the gomuti palm (3 letters) (Ans: doh); to sink in mud (5 letters) (Ans: mired).

Wynne made other puzzles and is also given credit for the 1st insertion of black squares in the spaces between the letters. Although he deserves this credit, crosswords of many shapes and kinds had appeared before 1913 in 19th-century English periodicals for children. The mid-Victorian puzzles were derived from the "word square," a group of words arranged so the letters read .alike vertically and horizontally. According to Margaret Petherbridge Farrar and Prosper Buranelli, the *World's* puzzle experts in the 1920s, "A magical relation was thought to exist between the words in a word square." Such squares had a cabalistic force in the minds of the readers.

In 1913, English adults paid little attention to the American revival of the crossword puzzle; but when this interest became a positive craze in the 1920s, English enthusiasm grew. Soon almost all daily papers in the U.S. and Great Britain had crossword features. Not only that, but *les mots croisés* appeared in France, and puzzles sprang up in most other languages except for those which do not lend themselves to vertical and horizontal word arrangement by letter, such as Chinese.

There are national differences in the style of crosswords. According to Margaret Petherbridge Farrar, former puzzle editor of *The New York Times*, the British style uses many unkeyed letters with no cross clues, eliminates most short words, and features difficult definitions. In the U.S., conservative rules usually call for symmetrical patterns, no more than ⅙ of the squares black, allover interlock of words, no cutoff segments or unkeyed letters. Quality of the puzzle is judged by the ingenuity of word combinations and skill in selection of definitions or clues.

The golden age of the crossword puzzle was during the 1920s in the U.S. when many fads swept the country—from goldfish swallowing to making bathtub gin. As *Publishers Weekly* reports, "The crossword puzzle was America's favorite licit indoor activity in the days before television."

Interest in working crossword puzzles was intense, and when the puzzles began to appear in book form in 1924, one became an outstanding best seller. The 1st of these, the *Crossword Puzzle Book*, appeared under the imprint of the Plaza Publishing Company and it turned Simon and Schuster into a top publishing firm. Amazingly, the publishers did not want their names on the book because they were not sure it would be a success.

Popular interest in the 1920s is shown by aids which were marketed to help puzzle-solvers. One was a crossword "finder," an indicator with a series of movable alphabets on paper strips which were supposed to aid in forming proper letter arrangements before they were written in the squares. The device allowed the trial of test words, "saving erasures and changes on the puzzle chart. The indicator, which can be carried in the pocket, does not require a pencil for marking and its construction permits as ready operation as a small adding machine." (*Popular Mechanics*, March, 1925.)

The main interest among fans in the 1920s was in the puzzle as an aid to language development. The literary intelligentsia including Franklin P. Adams, Heywood Broun, and Ruth Hale, took up the puzzle and fed this interest. In *The Literary Digest* of June 6, 1925, Arthur Maurice, former editor of *The Bookman*, claimed to have found 40 words which had grown unfamiliar through general mental laziness but were now resurrected due to the crossword puzzle craze.

Maurice said, "It is the subtle restoration of these words, a direct result of the crossword puzzle, that is galvanizing casual talk into a new and healthy flexibility. A cathedral, for example, is no longer a blur of vague images. The picture has cleared with the rescued understanding of 'apse' and 'nave.'"

Another reason for the extraordinary success of crossword puzzles according to Columbia University professors of psychology H. E. Jones and Prescott Leeky, was the low cost of working them and, the professors added, "The puzzles appeal to the sex instinct in that they supply a new reason for social gatherings, of young particularly."

In the 1920s, as now, there were 2 schools of puzzle solution fans: those who grimly armed themselves with dictionaries, gazetteers, and classical Latin phrase books, and free souls "who'd sooner die in the flames than consult a reference book." (*Publishers Weekly*.)

Among feats recorded: The fastest time for completing the London *Times* crossword is 3 minutes, 45 seconds. This record was set by Roy Dean, age 43, of Bromley, Kent, in the BBX "Today" radio studio on December 19, 1970. On the other hand, in May, 1966, *The Times* received an announcement from a Fijian woman that she had just succeeded in completing their crossword No. 673 from the April 4, 1932, issue.

The world's largest published crossword puzzle, with 3,185 clues across and 3,149 down, was constructed by Robert M. Stilgenbauer of Los Angeles. It took 11 years of his spare time between May 15, 1938, and publication in 1949 for him to do this.

The interests of the modern fan have grown much more diverse than his fellow enthusiast's were in the 1920s. Variations on the puzzle include abstruse definitions, Double-Crostics, puns and anagrams, and theme puzzles (such as music or sports), the latter difficult and a challenge to one's knowledge of the given theme.

Over 30 general-circulation crossword puzzle magazines appear on the newsstands today. The main publishers are Harle, Charlton, and Dell. A few of these magazines, such as *All-Star Fill-Ins* by Harle, have a circulation of over half a million.

A study of newer puzzles shows a current trend to the "Hide-a-Word" or identify-type of puzzle. Definitions are not required in this type, only spotting the words in the letter diagram. The speciality magazines feature more varieties of puzzles than the daily newspapers, which usually cling to symmetrical patterns with blacked-out squares. There are cryptograms and many patterns not using numbers in the magazines.

Among the themes for puzzles in a recent issue of *Top-Notch Fill-in Puzzles* are "Vice and Virtue" (Clues: odium, strife, greed) and "Economically Speaking" (Clues: income, system, value).

Reference aids for the modern fan who approaches his puzzles as a treasure trove to be unlocked include 2 crossword puzzle dictionaries: Andrew Swanfeldt's *Crossword Puzzle Dictionary* (2nd ed., Crowell), has 568 pages and 53,000 entries with 200,000 equivalents; Frank Eaton Newton's *The Perma Crossword Puzzle and Word Game Dictionary* (Permabooks), has 191 pages and places its emphasis on difficult words. The Simon & Schuster Series 100 of its *Crossword Puzzle Book*, edited by Margaret Petherbridge Farrar, contains material of historical interest to fans.

Sophisticated fans like *New York* magazine's "The World's Most Challenging Crossword," which requires wit and reasoning rather than dictionary work.

There is one national club, The National Puzzler's League (2301 Tower Drive, Austin, Tex. 78703), founded in 1883. This is for hobbyists interested in word puzzles; its monthly publication, *The Enigma*, is edited by Mr. and Mrs. J. H. Petroski.

The magazine, *Top-Notch Fill-In Puzzles*, a Harle Publication, lists a number of contests which might interest puzzle fans. These include the Aries Puzzle Contests (P. O. Box C-710, Scottsdale, Ariz. 85252), and Aquarius Contests (7551 Melrose Ave. Dept. 9097, Los Angeles, Calif. 90046). See current issues of this magazine for entry blanks.

—M.J.M.

Sports Immortals

THE THREE-FOOT-HIGH HITTER

You could count on the knuckles of one thumb the number of midgets who have appeared in major league ball games. His surname was Gaedel, his given name Edward, he was 26 years old, and he was born on June 25, 1925, in Chicago, Ill., of 2 midgets. All that, however, is relatively unimportant. In short, the vital statistic is that Eddie Gaedel was 43" small, though the tallest short story in baseball history.

When St. Louis Brown's owner Bill Veeck brought Edward Gaedel up to the majors on August 19, 1951, there were those who thought he was just another Veeck stunt. They were right. The baseball career of William L. (for Lunacy as one writer put it) Veeck, Jr., was built on gimmicks that increased attendance, and the midget, though he might have looked like an hors d'oeuvre, was the main course of that kinky career.

It was beautiful. A midget. A brownie for the Browns. An anatomic bomb. After locating Gaedel in Chicago, Veeck and his confederates trained the midget, who knew nothing about baseball except that you hit the ball with the bat and ran like you were escaping the Valley of the Jolly Green Giant. Young Gaedel had been a stunt man and vaudeville entertainer. His past, however, wasn't important when one considered that it would be as easy for a pitcher to throw through the eye of a needle as enter the kingdom of his 1½' strike zone.

All Veeck had to do, he thought, was teach his midget how to crouch and point him in the direction of 1st base. The imp's imp was signed to a standard contract making him one of baseball's better paid players at $100 a day —although he was hired for only one day and waived the 30-day notice clause. Veeck also took out a $1 million insurance policy protecting himself against "sudden death or sudden growth," which when canceled (short rate?) would come to just $1.50 for one day. The insurance policy may have indicated Veeck's apprehension at the prospect of his miniature man driving for the fences, because Gaedel grew overconfident, swinging from the heels as his practice sessions progressed.

On the day of the big game not even the scorecard reading "⅛ Gaedel," which has since become a collector's item, aroused the slightest suspicion. Neither did the Browns arouse any suspicion, running true to form and losing the 1st game of the doubleheader. There was much Veeckian celebration between games, including a band featuring Satchel Paige on the drums at home plate, but no one suspected anything, not even a nervous Eddie, ready to resign, was stuffed inside a 7' birthday cake and rolled out onto the infield grass. "Ladies and gentlemen, as a special birthday present to manager Zack Taylor," the PA announcer explained, "the management is presenting him with a brand-new Brownie!" Up popped Veeck's midget, from a cake that cost more than he did, but still no one caught on.

In the last half of the 1st inning, though, everyone understood. "For the Browns," came the grating announcement over the loudspeaker, "number-one-eighth, Eddie Gaedel, batting for Saucier." Instant happiness came to everyone connected with the Browns except center-fielder Frank Saucier, the only man in baseball history ever taken out for a midget pinch hitter. Gaedel, lustily waving 3 bats, approached the plate. "This can't be," umpire Ed Hurley said, pulling off his mask and getting down on his knees to examine Gaedel closely. But it was. Zack Taylor came trotting out with the midget's contract, a time-stamped telegram to American League headquarters, and a copy of the Browns active list proving that there was room on the roster for the midget. Hurley had to motion number ⅛ into the batter's box.

The Tiger's Bobby Cain had thought Gaedel was just another Veeck gag. When he realized he would have to pitch to the mini-hitter his mouth opened wide and he just gawked for a moment before walking halfway to the plate to confer with Detroit catcher Bob Swift, who was laughing so hard he nearly fell over. "Let's go," Gaedel squeaked. "Throw it in there, fat, and I'll moider it." He was slightly more than twice as tall as his 17" bat, but the right-handed runt considered himself a threat. Veeck got a little nervous. Would his midget swing for the fences? He remembered that Gaedel had once asked him how tall Wee Willie Keeler was.

When Bob Swift regained his composure, and Cain accepted his fate, they discussed how they would pitch to the pixie. There was no precedent in baseball history, but they *had* to decide to pitch him low. After a delay of some 15 minutes in all, Gaedel inched up to the plate. Swift sat down on both knees behind the midget. Hurley rubbed his eyes. Cain was ready to pitch to the shrunken strike zone.

But Gaedel didn't go into his crouch! The midget's sad eyes changed, and supreme confidence usurped his being. Assuming a classic stance like a dinghy of the Yankee Clipper, feet spread wide, bat high, he stared at the confines of Sportsmen's Park. What fantasies he must have had. The resounding crack of the bat, a long, long drive, the concussive deafening roar of the crowd as the ball soared over the center-field roof and he himself was trotting around the bases tipping his cap. . . . And that would be only the beginning. . . . What did Wee Willie Keeler, what did Rizzuto have that the human proton, the protean pygmy didn't have. . . . As for Veeck, he was thinking, "I should have brought a gun up here. I'll kill him, I'll kill him if he doesn't get on base!"

Cain, however, ruined all Gaedel's grandiose plans and spared him possible assassination. Cain simply had no control, none at all. He lobbed in 4 pitches, but the midget got nothing to swing at. The 1st 2 were about head high, but Cain couldn't come down. The only man in the history of big league baseball ever to walk a midget! Cain was so hysterical he could just about reach his hysterical battery mate. Gaedel never got a chance to gain immortality with a mighty Ruthian blast, for ball 3 and ball 4 were so high they wouldn't have been strikes on Wilt Chamberlain.

With a barely perceptible look of scorn on his face, the midget took his pass and trotted down to 1st base. There he held one foot on the bag while waiting for pinch-runner Jim Delsing, the only man ever to pinch-run for a midget. Then he slapped Delsing on the rump, shook hands with the 1st-base coach, bowed to the crowd, and cut across the infield to the Browns' dugout behind 3rd. He took a long time to get there, waving and bowing, thoroughly enjoying his moment upon the stage.

According to Veeck's plans, the Browns were to beat the Tigers 1–0 in the 2nd game of the doubleheader, his midget representing the winning run, but the lowly Browns couldn't have won with Snow White and the Seven Dwarfs; despite the best laid plans of midgets and maestros, St. Louis was shortchanged 6–2. The following day, in the words of one reporter, the American League president Will Harridge "turned thumbs down on Tom Thumb." Harridge had tried to outlaw the midget while plate umpire Hurley was examining his papers, but Veeck had refused to answer the phone and had shut off the office teletype. Soon the league leader passed a new rule requiring all player contracts to be approved by the president. Veeck, for his part, termed this decision "unfair to the little man."

As for Eddie Gaedel, the midget never played in another ball game. After his sententious farewell speech ("Now that someone has finally taken a step to help us short guys, Harridge is ruining my baseball career."), he hung up his spikes. Veeck got him many bookings on the basis of his sole sterling performance, including one baseball date at Comisky Park, where he landed at 2nd base with 3 other midgets disguised as Martians, "captured" Nellie Fox and Luis Aparicio, and informed the crowd over the public address sytem that his little people were going to help Veeck's White Sox. About a year after this, on June 18, 1961, Eddie Gaedel died, at age 36, a month before another great competitor, Ty Cobb. Veeck writes in his autobiography that *The New York Times* gave Eddie a front page obituary, an honor usually reserved for statesmen and Nobel Prize winners, but in reality it was just one of the 7,500 deaths the *Times* reported that year, and was on page 12. It was unusual only in that Gaedel rated 3 stars in the *Times Index*, indicating an unexplained violent death. His body had been found in the bedroom of his apartment on Chicago's South Side, and an inquest was ordered when police noted bruises on his face and body. The *Times* did acknowledge, however, that Eddie Gaedel was the only midget ever to play in the major leagues, and no midget, it is certain, will again step up to bat in a big league baseball game. In fact, Eddie was probably the 1st and last Lilliputian to reign in the entire Brobdingnagian world of professional sports.

—R.H.

THE PEDESTRIAN

Edward Payson Weston, America's greatest and most durable walker, 1st came into prominence as the result of an election bet made with a friend. The terms were that the loser would walk from Boston to Washington in 10 consecutive days, arriving in time to see the Inauguration of the new President on March 4, 1861. Weston, who had bet against Lincoln, began his payoff trek at Boston's State House at one o'clock, February 22, which gave him 10 days to hike the 478 mi. to the Capitol. Accompanied by a cortege of buggies, the 22-year-old pedestrian, who stood 5'7" and weighed 130 lbs., walked the 1st 5 mi. in 47 minutes and then settled down to a steady 3¼-mph pace.

At every town throngs waited for him and cheered him on. In one village he was kissed by a bevy of ladies who requested that the kisses be relayed to the President. A more serious delay took place outside of Leicester, Mass., where he encountered foot-deep snows and fell down several times. But he kept plodding on, through Worcester, Hartford, New Haven, and arrived in New York the morning of February 27.

Weston followed no set routine. Sometimes, after a catnap on a kitchen table in a farmhouse, he would start his walking day at midnight. Often he snatched sleep alongside the road. His longest snooze, in a Trenton tavern, was less than 6 hours. Once a day he managed to sit down to a solid meal but most of the time he ate on the walk, munching sandwiches and doughnuts offered by villagers as he trudged by. Always a purist, Weston refused to ride on the new steam elevator to his upstairs room in the Continental Hotel, Philadelphia. "I will not alter my mode of travel," said Weston and walked to his room. Two days later, after an all-night walk, he reached Baltimore, ate breakfast, and then started out in a driving rain over muddy roads on the final lap. He made the Capitol on March 4 just as the clock struck 5, too late to see Lincoln sworn in but not too late for the Inauguration Ball, which he had enough strength to attend that night.

Weston literally walked for peanuts on that 1st trip. In accordance with the terms of the bet, all he got—besides fame—was a bag of peanuts for his pains.

He never again walked for peanuts. He walked for money, competing against professionals in 6-day, go-as-you-please tests (walk or run at any time) and in cross-country walks against time with prize money at stake. He was not unbeatable on the indoor track, where he was limited to a mere 6 days, but in 1879 he won the Astley Belt, emblematic of world supremacy, by besting "Blower" Brown, the pride of Britain, on a London track. In that match the American covered 550 mi. in the 6 days and won a $2,500 side bet from Sir John Astley himself, donor of the belt.

But it was over the long haul in open country, with a fat wager as the goal, that the humble Weston was at his best. Going it alone at distances of 1,000 mi. or more, he could keep up such a relentless pace that it was necessary to provide relays of fresh horses for the referees and timekeepers. On cross-country tours he wore a short jacket, tight-fitting knee breeches, stout brogans with red tops, a silk derby and buff gloves. He always carried a light walking stick to fend off hostile dogs.

In this snappy garb Weston took off from Portland, Me., on October 29, 1867, and headed for Chicago with $10,000 riding on him. To win the bet (the stake was supplied by his backers), Weston had to cover the distance (1,237½ mi.) in 26 days. Accompanied by 6 men in carriages to see that he was propelled solely by his red-topped brogans, the tireless pedestrian got so far ahead of schedule that he found time to stop and address crowds along the way, attend church services, and still finish with time to spare. The Great Pedestrian Feat, as it was called in newspapers throughout the land, made him overnight a figure of national prominence.

Weston kept on walking and walking, here and abroad, almost to the end of his long life. In 1907 at the age of 68, he repeated his Portland-Chicago performance, covering a route

19 mi. longer and bettering his record made 40 years before by 29 hours. Two years later, in celebration of his 70th birthday, he walked from New York to San Francisco in 104 days and 7 hours, a distance of 3,895 mi. The next year he walked back over a different route, covering 3,600 mi. in 76 days, 23 hours and 10 minutes. And the indefatigable Weston, still trim and wiry, was not yet through. In 1913, at the age of 74, he hiked from New York to Minneapolis, a distance of 1,546 mi. in 51 days.

That was Weston's last big walk. An ironic fate awaited the man who saw Lincoln in 1861. In 1927, while walking in a Brooklyn street, he was struck by an auto and suffered such severe injuries that he was confined to a wheelchair for the last 2 years of his life. He died, age 90, in 1929.

—J.Du. rep.

First to Swim the Channel

On the morning of August 25, 1875, Capt. Matthew Webb of Dawley, Shropshire, 27-year-old master of an English sailing vessel, woke up in a Calais hotel to find himself famous. The day before he had done the impossible: He had swum the English Channel, the 1st person in history to do so. While he slept that night the world heard all about him—how he had plunged off the Admiralty Pier at Dover and had battled current and high seas for 21¾ hours over a 50-mi. zigzag course to reach the sands at Calais.

Days of glory awaited the Shropshire lad. At Dover, where a huge throng welcomed him upon his return, the mayor of the city said, "In the future history of the world I don't believe that any such feat will be performed by anyone else." [The mayor of Dover was wrong. The feat would be duplicated and improved upon many times in the years that followed. But still, Matthew Webb was the 1st. Actually, he wasn't really the 1st. Three months earlier, Paul Boyton, U.S., had swum the Channel successfully in 23 hours, 30 minutes—but *he* wore a life jacket, whereas Webb went it alone. Today, a century later, Webb's time has been cut better than in half. Present record holder: Lieut. Richard Davis Hart, U.S. Army, swam the Channel from England to France on August 21, 1972, in 9 hours, 44 minutes.]

Webb became a national hero. Crowds mobbed him wherever he went. Thousands flocked to see the stocky 5'8" blond captain cleave the waters with the powerful stroke that had conquered the Channel. (Webb used the breaststroke, the crawl being then unknown. At the rate of 25 to 27 strokes a minute, he swam low in the water, with mouth and nose under, blowing porpoiselike as his head emerged.)

Acclaimed as the world's greatest swimmer, Webb toured English resort beaches giving swimming exhibitions and staging feats of endurance. A couple of years of this, however, and interest in him began to slacken. He became more and more of a stunt man and would pick up a few purses by betting that he could stay in the water for a certain number of hours. Once at Scarborough he won £400 by swimming about for 74 continuous hours.

In 1881, accompanied by his bride, he moved to the U.S. to bolster his diminishing fortune, but little money came in. In the summer of 1883, his manager Fred Kyle got him booked at Nantasket Beach, Mass., to give daily exhibitions of swimming. The captain was now no longer the shining Shropshire lad who had brought fame to England 8 years before. At 35 he weighed 200 lbs., and his closely cropped hair was thin on top. With him at Nantasket, where he was no great attraction, lived his wife and their 2 small children.

What was needed, Manager Kyle thought, was another big one like the Channel swim— something that no man had ever tried before. Like the Niagara River rapids below the falls, for instance—perhaps the angriest stretch of water on earth. If Webb could get through them he would again have done the impossible, and there would be a fortune in it.

At the foot of Niagara Falls there is a huge circular gorge of constantly boiling water. The Niagara River empties out of the gorge and is relatively quiet for a brief stretch. Then, about 2 mi. below the falls, it gathers momentum as the walls of the river close in. Through this ever-narrowing funnel a tremendous volume of water, wild for want of room, reaches a pace of nearly 30 mph and throws the surface into a series of great billows that break up to 30' high. These are the Whirlpool Rapids, some ¾ mi. in length, and below them is the Whirlpool itself, a giant disk of foaming eddies and furiously revolving water.

On June 10, 1883, the captain came to Niagara Falls to examine the rapids. Attired in a pearl-colored derby and gray frock coat, he drove along the river on the Canadian side and surveyed the rapids from the heights above. Then he walked down to the water's edge for a closer view. A few minutes' study seemed to satisfy him. "A rum bit of water," was his only comment.

Six weeks later they were back in Niagara Falls determined to stage the event. During an interview with the press, the captain outlined his plan. He would, he said, dive into the river and let the current take him down toward the rapids. He would try to stay in the middle, away from the rocks along the river's edge. "When the water gets very bad I will go under the surface and remain beneath until I am compelled to come up for breath. . . . When I get through I will try to land on the Canadian side, but if the current is too swift I will keep on down to Lewiston [5 mi. below] on the American side."

As the hour approached, some 500 spectators had gathered on the suspension bridge down-river, upon the cliffs on either side, and along the river's edge. There was but one comment from the crowd: "If he goes in he'll never come out alive." No one knew this better than John McCloy, a veteran ferryman who had rowed back and forth across the calmer parts of the river for years. As McCloy rowed Captain Webb slowly downstream to his starting point, he asked his passenger if he had a family and how much money he had left from the Channel swim. "Most of it is gone," Webb answered. "Well," said McCloy, "if I was you I'd go ashore and keep the rest." There was no reply and the 2 men went on in silence, as far down as the ferryman dared take the skiff.

Far below on the suspension bridge, where the 1st wild water began, the crowd saw the captain stand up in the boat and plunge into the middle of the river. He came to the surface and with slow sweeping strokes went straight ahead toward the bridge. For several minutes he swam through smooth green water, gathering speed as he went, then hurtled like a startled salmon under the bridge and, a moment later, came to the 1st huge wave of the rapids. Instantly he vanished, but in another second he was thrust to the surface. For 100 yards or more the crowd caught glimpses of him as he was tossed wildly from crest to crest. Again he was engulfed and for more than 200 yards no one saw him, until suddenly he shot upward and spun crazily about, nearly erect above the water. Dead or alive, none could say. Then a rushing mountain of water closed over him, and he was seen no more. Less than 4 minutes had elapsed from the time he hit the 1st wave until his final disappearance.

Kyle left for Nantasket to comfort the captain's wife. Four days later searchers found the body near Lewiston. It was face downward in the water, the arms and legs extended as though in the act of taking a breaststroke. Later an examination by 3 doctors revealed that there were no bones broken and no injuries sufficient to cause death; nor had Captain Webb been drowned. Their verdict was that life had been pressed out of him by the force of the water and that "no living body can, or ever will, pass through the rapids alive."

Today in Oakwood Cemetery, Niagara Falls, "by brooks too broad for leaping" lies the grave of the Shropshire lad. "And the name died before the man." So run the lines of the poet A. E. Housman, another Shropshire lad.

—J. Du. rep.

CRADLE GENIUS WITH A CUE

Just around the turn of the century a seemingly bizarre bit of billiard matchmaking sent a 12-year-old boy to play Al Taylor, then about 30, and one of the country's best balkline players. It was agreed that little Willie Hoppe would be allowed to climb on the table to make his shots. At the outset of the match, which was held at the luxurious American Billiard Academy in Chicago, Taylor was very jovial. He patted Willie on the head and promised to buy him ice cream if he won. And Willie did win, 300 to 207. Taylor burst into a rage, slamming his cue across his knee. After buying ice cream for his conqueror, he gave up billiards and went to Colorado to take up mining.

The victory over Taylor made Willie nationally famous as "The Boy Wonder," a name he always detested but which ironically persisted, not only after his hair grew thin and gray, but even after his retirement from tournament billiards in 1952. The match with Taylor, however, was just another milestone in an implausible childhood and youth.

Six years before, Willie and Frank Hoppe had invaded the poolroom of their father's Commercial Hotel in Cornwall-on-the-Hudson, N.Y. They were attracted by the sharp click of billiard balls and the fast quips of traveling salesmen who met there to play and kibitz. Willie was 6, Frank 8. Their father, a good player, watched at 1st as they dragged soap-boxes up to the table and stood on them to imitate the shots they had seen. But he soon took over the boys' instruction, drilling them several hours each morning. For Mr. Hoppe had fixed on an idea: He was determined to see his tykes trim the visiting drummers.

Impressed (and embarrassed) when the little Hoppes made them look like so many jelly-fingered beginners, the patrons of the Commercial persuaded Papa Hoppe to take his boys to Professor Daly's billiard academy in New York. In an exhibition there Frank and Willie did so well that they stayed for 2 weeks at the invitation of the professor, who had noted how they pleased the crowds in his establishment. At the end of the engagement Mr. Hoppe reached a decision. He summoned his wife, billed Frank and Willie as "The Boy Wonders" and put his show on the road.

The boys barnstormed through the small towns of the country. Pool hall proprietors paid from $1 to $25 for an exhibition. Their fortunes were uncertain. Sometimes Mama had to pawn her diamond to get the family out of town. When Willie was 12, Frank quit the act, determined to study stenography. (He returned to Cornwall and died there in the late '30s after teaching billiards in Chicago.) But Willie stuck with it. He soon became enough of an attraction in himself. He improved his situation by mastering the more difficult balkline billiards, at which Americans Jake Schaefer and George Slosson, and Frenchman Maurice (The Lion) Vignaux, were making handsome incomes. After his balkline victory over Taylor, Willie prospered.

At 16, William toured with Jake Schaefer. But when, 2 years later, he challenged Slosson, who had dethroned Schaefer for the 18.2 championship, Slosson sneered that he would not play an unknown.

Soon thereafter, Willie made a reputation which no one could ignore. (Slosson did meet and lose to him the following year.) He went to Paris to play Vignaux for the world's 18.1 title.

The night of January 15, 1906, some 3,000 Frenchmen crowded into the lavish ballroom of the Grand Hotel to watch the old Lion defeat this challenger who looked like a lad at his 1st formal dance. The white-maned Vignaux had majestic bearing and a gift for dramatic flourish. He seemed like an eminent professor about to squelch a college freshman. But plump, round-faced Willie, his hair plastered and parted in the middle, was quite calm. He bent over the table like a laboratory scientist, prepared to capitalize on every error Vignaux made. Whenever Vignaux missed, he yielded the table with an elaborately sardonic bow. Willie, not realizing its effect on the Lion's blood pressure, would give him a moonfaced grin and return to work. While the audience booed his cold efficiency, Hoppe scored repeated high runs and won the title, 500–323. He returned to New York to be met by a great crowd and a brass band playing "The Yankee Doodle Boy"; he was the champion of the world—and still only 18 years old.

—M.M.W. rep.

A Gallery of Sports Greats

Auto Racing

Mario Andretti

Mario Andretti, one of the world's most versatile racing drivers, has been successful as a driver with sprint cars, modified stocks, Formula One cars, and the Indianapolis-type cars on racing surfaces ranging from dirt tracks to paved ovals.

His record of achievements since joining USAC in 1964 includes 34 victories—17 on paved ovals, 9 on paved-road courses, and 7 on dirt tracks and the Pikes Peak Hill Climb. He won the Indianapolis 500-mi. race in 1969.

Born in Italy, Andretti resides in Nazareth, Pa. He drove his 1st race in 1953, only 13 years after he was born. It was a Formula Junior at Ancona, Italy. He began racing modified stock cars when he was 18, later moving to sprint cars and midgets.

He was named Rookie of the Year at Indianapolis in 1965, finishing 3rd in the race. The same year he captured the national driving championship.

Andretti set qualifying speed records at Indianapolis in 1966, but went out of the race early due to engine trouble. He again won the national driving title. He finished 2nd among USAC drivers in 1967 and 1968, but regained the driving championship in 1969.

His victories include the Daytona 500 (the biggest stock car race), a couple of Formula One Grand Prix races, and 3 international endurance races (including the Sebring 12-Hour sports car). He held the world's closed-course speed record of 214.158 mph until broken by A. J. Foyt in 1974.

Juan Manuel Fangio

Juan Manuel Fangio has been called by some authorities the greatest race driver of all time. Eight years after the Federal Internationale de l'Automobile began to count points and name a world champion driver, he won 5 times.

The son of an Italian immigrant, he was born in Argentina in 1911. He went to work at the age of 11 as a grease monkey in a garage to help the family. He became a mechanic in his late teens and was soon riding as a mechanic in a stock car race.

Fangio became enthused about racing and started saving his money to own his own race car, a Ford Model T. His family was against racing, but he secretly took part in a few races and moved up to a Ford V-8 special.

Fangio then began racing Chevrolet coupes and a special Chevrolet-based single-seater. By 1949 he had won enough races to become famous throughout Argentina.

He won 5 of 11 Argentina Gran Premio races, where he competed against the best drivers of Europe.

One of his greatest triumphs was winning the Nurburgring race, the Grosse Preis of

Germany, by 3 seconds. Driving a Mercedes, he beat the Ferrari team of Mike Hawthorn, Peter Collins, and Luigi Musso by daring driving as he broke lap records.

Fangio's Grand Prix world champion driving titles were in 1951, 1954, 1955, 1956, and 1957.

A. J. Foyt

A. J. Foyt, one of America's greatest race-car drivers, is the 1st man ever to win 4 500-mi. national championship races. Winner of the Indianapolis 500 3 times, he captured the Schaefer 500 at Pocono, Pa., in 1973.

Born in 1935, the Houston, Tex., driver started racing in 1953 in his hometown with a midget built by his father, Tony. Foyt ran his 1st USAC race in a midget in 1956.

Foyt has won 5 national driving championship titles (1960, '61, '63, '64, '67). He has won 45 national championship races, 13 more than the nearest driver, Mario Andretti.

In 39 races in his 1st 4 years of national championship driving, he finished in the top 4 on 15 occasions and was in the top 11 (where points are awarded) 28 times.

He captured his 1st Indianapolis 500 in 1961 with a record speed of 139.130 mph. He won his 2nd Indy 500 in 1964, again with a record speed, 147.350. He won 9 other championship races that year and became the 1st 4-time national driving champion. When Foyt won the 1967 Indy 500 with a record speed of 151.207, he joined Louis Meyer, Wilbur Shaw, and Mauri Rose as the only 3-time winners.

Foyt teamed with Dan Gurney in 1967 to win the famed 24 Hours of Le Mans race.

Foyt has also won USAC championships in dirt, stock, and sprint divisions. He is a respected competitor in midget races, which he has mostly limited himself to in recent years.

Foyt set a world closed-course speed record, 217.854 mph, on August 3, 1974, at Talladega, Ala., at the Alabama International Motor Speedway.

Stirling Moss

Many experts rate Stirling Moss as the greatest racing driver of all time. In 466 races, including Grand Prix, rallies, sprints, and record-breaking attempts, he won 194 times. No other driver comes close to that number.

Moss, born in England in 1929, was virtually born into racing. His father, a highly successful dental surgeon who had been a race driver (including 2 runs at Indianapolis), taught Stirling how to drive at a very young age when he could barely reach the control pedals. He started training for a driving career by stripping

a $45 Austin to lighten it and driving it around neighborhood fields.

After wearing out the Austin, he switched to a BMW briefly and then in 1948 to a Cooper, which he used to win 8 races in 9 starts. He surprised the racing world by driving the Cooper, then considered a crazy racing contraption, to 3rd place in his 1st race on the Continent, a Formula 2 event at Garda, where he met European aces with their Ferraris and Maseratis. He was on his way to a great sports-car driving career.

After winning his 1st British championship, he was offered a Maserati by the factory. In the Monza race, he was leading the Ferrari and Mercedes teams and appeared on the way to victory when his car broke down. Signed the following year by Mercedes as their No. 2 driver (behind Juan Manuel Fangio), he finished in several races 2nd behind the famed driver. He did manage to win the British Grand Prix ahead of Fangio. Moss returned to Maserati when Mercedes withdrew from racing, and he beat Fangio at Monte Carlo and Monza.

Moss was seriously injured in a race crash in 1962, ending a competitive career that saw him become champion of Great Britain 10 times and one of the world's best-known sports figures.

Jackie Stewart

Jackie Stewart is generally recognized as the most successful Grand Prix race driver in history.

When he retired from competition in October, 1973, he had won 27 Grand Prix victories, topping the record 25 that had been set by Jim Clark, who lost his life in a 1968 crash.

Born in 1939 in Dumbarton, Scotland, Stewart has lived for several years in Begnins, Switzerland. He was 34 years old when he retired from active competition, announcing his retirement 2 weeks after his withdrawal from the U.S. Grand Prix at Watkins Glen, N.Y., following the crash that claimed the life of François Cevert, his teammate on the Tyrrell-Ford team.

Driving his 1st Formula One race in 1961, Stewart 1st attracted international recognition in 1965 when he won his 1st Formula One victory, the Italian Grand Prix. He finished that year 3rd in the world standings.

He captured the 1st of his 3 world championships in 1969 when he won 6 of the 11 scheduled races. His other world titles came in 1971 and 1973.

Stewart, who stands only 5'4" tall, had a great season in his final year of competition. He won the Grand Prix of South Africa, Belgium, Monaco, The Netherlands, and Germany. He finished 1973 with 71 points, topping the 1972 world champion, Brazil's Emerson Fittipaldi, who collected 55 points.

Stewart won more than a million dollars during his racing career.

—J.S.

BASKETBALL

Kareem Abdul-Jabbar

The exploits of Kareem Abdul-Jabbar (born Ferdinand Lewis Alcindor) leave no room for conjecture. Ever since bursting onto the national scene at New York City's Power Memorial High School, he has been magnificent.

A 7'2", 225-lb. center, Jabbar has withstood inordinate pressure. He was a 3-time All-American prep while losing only once in 117 games. Proportionate feats were expected once he enrolled at UCLA to play for John Wooden. UCLA's successful recruiting effort was aided by the work of 2 famous alumni, Dr. Ralph Bunche and Jackie Robinson.

He didn't disappoint them. He was the major factor in the Bruins' 88–2 3-year record (1967–1969) which produced 3 national championships and a 47-game winning streak. In unprecedented fashion, Abdul-Jabbar was selected MVP in all 3 NCAA championship tournaments.

A history major with an IQ of 131, he set collegiate marks for career field-goal percentage (.639) and season (.667). In 3 years, he averaged 26.4 points and 15.5 rebounds.

Due largely to his dominance, the dunk shot was banned after his sophomore year. As a result, he developed a greater variety of shots, enhancing his development as a pro. He stirred controversy by participating in the boycott, by blacks, of the 1968 Olympics.

Following college he signed with the Milwaukee Bucks, with a contract calling for nearly $1½ million. He was the NBA's most celebrated newcomer since Chamberlain, and responded by earning the title of "Rookie of the Year."

The following season, Milwaukee won the league title and Abdul-Jabbar earned the Podoloff Cup. He repeated as Podoloff Cup winner in 1972 and again in 1974. Abdul-Jabbar captured scoring titles in 1971 (31.7) and 1972 (34.8). He has been selected for the NBA All-Star game in each of his 5 seasons. He is unstoppable close to the basket, and uses the dunk, jumper, and hook with great effectiveness.

Abdul-Jabbar (born April 16, 1947) adopted the Islamic faith in 1968 and took his present name in 1971. Many other black athletes have since followed suit.

Abdul-Jabbar, aloof and introspective, is proud of his West Indian heritage. He is devoted to his wife and small daughter, and continually strives to improve himself on and off the court. He has said: "I'll always have pressure, because I set high standards for myself. It's important. You've got to grow."

Wilt Chamberlain

Awesome in size, strength, and athletic prowess, Wilt Chamberlain has experienced an unparalleled basketball career. He was the game's most devastating force and, almost befittingly in the turbulent times he dominated, its most controversial subject.

Chamberlain (born August 21, 1936) attended Overbrook High School in Philadelphia, then Kansas University. At Kansas U., he scored 52 points in his varsity debut against Northwestern. In 2 varsity seasons (1957–1958) he averaged 29.9 points and 18.3 rebounds.

The Jayhawks lost to North Carolina (by one point) in the 1957 NCAA finals, and that game has haunted Wilt ever since. It gave birth to his image as a "loser."

Professionally, he played with the Harlem Globetrotters (1959), bypassing his senior year at Kansas U.; Philadelphia-San Francisco Warriors (1960–1964); Philadelphia 76ers (1965–1968); Los Angeles Lakers (1969–1973). He was drafted originally as a 1st round territorial choice of the Warriors.

His playing statistics are staggering. He averaged 50.4 points in 1962, abetted by a record 100-point game against the New York Knicks. He was the 1st pro to amass 30,000 career points and shoot 70% from the field (72.7). He grabbed 55 rebounds in one game and owns the all-time standard of 23,924. He was unstoppable in close, actually scaring people with his ferocious dunk shots.

Chamberlain was scoring champion 7 straight years (1960–1966); All-Pro 1st team 7 times; and MVP on 4 occasions. He has been compensated nicely—his $3 million, 5-year contract with the Lakers was the highest ever paid a pro athlete.

Along the way, though, he acquired many critics. Many seemed to overlook the fact that he *did* play on NBA title teams in 1967 and 1972. Coaches couldn't relate to him. He was a pitiable foul-shooter, and didn't react well under pressure; he angered blacks by not speaking out on important issues; he embraced Richard Nixon in a brief political honeymoon; but he throve anyway.

A 7'2", 275-pounder, Chamberlain prefers "Big Dipper" and dislikes "Stilt" among his sundry nicknames. His autobiography, *Wilt; Just like Any Other 7-Foot Black Millionaire Who Lives next Door*, was candid but not critically acclaimed. In it he revealed a huge sexual appetite.

When not on the road, he lives in a sumptuous 22-room mansion in the Santa Monica Mountains overlooking Los Angeles.

Bob Cousy

Bob Cousy used sleight of hand to wend his way to basketball immortality. He quarterbacked the Boston Celtics to 6 NBA titles (1957, 1959–1963) after a notable career at Holy Cross. Driven by a powerful ego, he wouldn't argue the point if you called him the greatest guard who ever lived.

Born August 9, 1928, to French parents on Manhattan's Upper East Side, Cousy took up basketball seriously following a family move to St. Albans in the borough of Queens. He was outstanding at Andrew Jackson High School but received only 2 scholarship offers—from Holy Cross and Boston College.

He was a substitute on the Crusaders' 1947 national championship team. Cousy and Holy Cross coach Doggie Julian had a personality clash after Bob's sophomore year and Julian resigned. Cousy finished his collegiate career in 1950, winning consensus All-America honors. He left a playing record of 99–19.

Boston coach Red Auerbach considered the 6'1" playmaker too small for the pros but was forced to accept him after drawing Cousy's name from a hat in a player pool with Philadelphia and New York. It didn't take Auerbach long to change his mind about Cousy.

"Cooz," as he was called, played in the 1st of 13 All-Star games in 1951, his rookie year. In 924 regular-season games, he averaged 18.4 points and was assist champion 6 times. The all-time assist leader, until surpassed by Oscar Robertson, he was the Podoloff Cup (MVP) recipient in 1957.

Cousy was capable of every conceivable ball-handling trick. His behind-the-back dribbling and passing drove the Boston Garden crowds to bedlam. Opponents were usually exhausted, and not amused. He was the model for every fancy-Dan in the country.

He coached Boston College from 1964–1969, compiling a 117–54 record and making 3 NIT appearances. He returned to the NBA as player-coach of the Cincinnati Royals in 1970. The Royals became the Kansas City-Omaha Kings after that season, and Cousy devoted himself solely to coaching. While with the Kings, he developed superstar guard Nate Archibald. He resigned suddenly in 1973.

Robertson, Jerry West, and Walt Frazier would be extraordinary competition for Cousy as basketball's all-time premier guard. Greatest or not, he still ranks as the game's creative genius.

Nat Holman

Five years after James Naismith invented the game, Nat Holman was born February 1, 1896, on Manhattan's Lower East Side. At the age of 8, Holman played for the 1st time—his ball was a sack stuffed with rags.

Later, at Commerce High School in New York, Holman opted for versatility by starring in 4 sports. Pro baseball beckoned—by way of an offer from the Cincinnati Reds—but it was refused. Basketball then became the *idée fixe* of his life.

While studying physical education at New York's Savage School, he began playing for money. He would eventually play for teams in Newark, Bridgeport, Syracuse, New York, Germantown, and Chicago, but was immortalized as the driving genius of the original Celtics.

Holman and Dutch Leonard joined the Celtics in 1921. In the ensuing years, the team won 720 of 795 games. The Furey brothers ran the Celtics and gave Holman what is believed to be the sport's 1st long-term, lucrative contract.

Holman was to basketball what Jack Dempsey, Red Grange, and Babe Ruth were to their respective games—its golden boy of the Roaring 20s, the Golden Age of Sports. He was innovative, fast, cocksure, and remarkably talented. He pioneered double-figure scoring, often producing half the Celtics' points, and took pro-basketball out of its Stone Age by giving it respectability.

The original "Mr. Basketball" retired from competition in 1930 to devote full time to his head coaching duties at City College of New York, a position he had taken in 1920. In 1950, CCNY, whose best players were lured without scholarships from the sidewalks and slums of New York City, scored an unprecedented "grand slam" by winning both the NIT and NCAA tournaments.

As it turned out, however, 4 players from that team were later found guilty of shaving points. This was life's cruelest blow to Holman, a man of unquestionable integrity. Later, all 4 overcame the scandal's stigma and achieved success in the business world.

As 35-year CCNY coach (1920–1952, 1955–1956, 1959–1960), Holman's record was a lofty 423–190. His achievements won him wide acceptance. For many years he has been president of U.S. Committee, Sports for Israel.

George Mikan

Though bulky, slow, and nearsighted, George Mikan was the 1st big man (6'10", 250 lbs.) to exert a dominating influence on the game. He also engineered, with the Minneapolis Lakers, pro sports' 1st dynasty.

Born June 18, 1924, in Joliet, Ill., he had very little basketball background when he enrolled at De Paul University in 1942. But with the encouragement of coach Ray Meyer, Mikan developed quickly. He scored in double figures as a freshman, then was All-American his sophomore season (1944). Two more All-American years followed. He was national scoring champion both seasons and collegiate Player of the Year. De Paul won the NIT crown in 1945 with Mikan scoring 120 points, 53 in one game.

Mikan, along with Oklahoma State's 7′ Bob Kurland, and 6′11″ Don Otten of Bowling Green, forced the NCAA to ban goal-tending in 1945. "Big Number 99" and Kurland met in 5 heralded match-ups, with the former winning 3.

In 1947, Mikan signed with the National League Chicago American Gears. His contract —$60,000 for 5 years—was the best of the era, but paltry by today's standards.

When he switched to the Basketball Association of America (BAA), later to become the NBA, the Lakers were off for the races. John Kundla's team captured world championships in 1949–1950, 1952–1954. Mikan and forwards Jim Pollard (the "Kangaroo Kid") and rugged Vern Mikkelsen formed an unbeatable front line.

In 520 pro games, Mikan averaged 22.6 points. He led the league in scoring 3 times, and played in the NBA's 1st 4 All-Star games. He was All-Pro 6 times before retiring at the end of the 1956 season.

He had to wear thick glasses to correct his vision, and was forced to overcome numerous injuries. He broke his leg, nose, arch, both feet, 4 fingers, and received cuts and scratches that accounted for 166 stitches. Because of his omnipresence in the middle, the NBA widened the foul lane from 6′ to 12′; but Mikan went right on overpowering people.

He was commissioner of the ABA from 1968–1969, and in that service introduced the red-white-blue ball. He is now a lawyer and travel agency owner in Minneapolis.

Mikan has received almost every conceivable basketball honor. He is a member of the Citizens Savings Hall of Fame and Naismith Hall of Fame. He was named AP Player of the First Half Century (Hank Luisetti was 2nd), and the NBA chose him for its Silver Anniversary Team.

Bill Russell

The Boston Celtics dominated basketball for over a decade and the primary reason was a lean, bearded wonder named Bill Russell. A tireless and implacable worker, Russell was the game's foremost defensive genius and its noblest warrior.

He was born February 12, 1934, in Monroe, La., but moved to Detroit, and then on to Oakland during his boyhood. He had to share uniforms with another player on the McClymonds High School junior varsity as a sophomore, but 2 years later was starting center and a good one.

At San Francisco University, the 6′9″ Russell and guard K. C. Jones led the Dons to 60 straight wins, a record not surpassed until 1972 by UCLA. USF won national championships in 1955–1956. Russell claimed a gold medal in the 1956 Olympic Games at Melbourne.

The Celtics launched their dynasty in 1956 by acquiring the draft rights to Russell from the St. Louis Hawks in exchange for Ed Macauley and Cliff Hagan. In Russell's 13 seasons (1956–1969), Boston won 11 NBA championships. Only in 1958 and 1967 were the Celtics denied. Russell was player-coach in 1967–1969.

During his career, he took 21,721 rebounds and led the league 4 times. He corralled 51 rebounds in one game, 49 twice. He was All-Pro 1st team 3 times, league MVP 5 times, and participated in 12 All-Star games. He also set a multitude of play-off records.

His duels with Wilt Chamberlain will be talked about as long as the game is played. Their rivalry turned bitter in later years, and neither would utter a kind word about the other.

Russell also grew more outspoken. He championed black causes and racial harmony. He exuded warmth and possessed an infectious, high-pitched cackle, but refused to sign autographs, considering it too impersonal.

After retiring, he became a commentator for ABC sports, and a lecturer on college campuses. He returned to the NBA in 1973 as coach and general manager of the Seattle SuperSonics. Seattle owner Sam Schulman, Russell said, made him an offer he couldn't refuse.

Russell was a unanimous choice for the NBA Silver Anniversary Team. He is a member of the Citizens Savings Hall of Fame and its All-Time All-America Team.

—R.M.

GOLF

Patty Berg

Patty Berg, one of America's pioneer professional women golf players, is recognized as one of the sport's all-time greats.

Born in Minneapolis, Minn., in 1918, she was runner-up in the U.S. Amateur when only 17. Second again in 1937, she won the title in 1938. Turning professional in 1940, she was the 1st president of the Ladies Professional Golf Association, which she helped form in 1948.

She has won 83 events in her career, 41 since

the LPGA was formed. She won 3 Vare trophies for low-scoring average, in 1953, 1955 and 1956. In 1952 she shot a record one-round 64, which stood until broken by Mickey Wright's 62 in 1964.

Miss Berg was leading money winner on the professional tour 3 times, and is one of the all-time high money winners. She won the U.S. Open Championship in 1946, and was the 1st to make a hole in one in that event, in 1959, at Churchill Valley Country Club. She was named Associated Press Woman Athlete of the Year 3 times, and she was elected to the LPGA Hall of Fame in 1951.

Since recovering from surgery in 1970, she has played a limited schedule on the professional tour, but remains the chief ambassador for women's golf. Her activities include clinics, speeches, promotions, committee work, public relations, and teaching golf in her residence area of Fort Myers, Fla., particularly to youngsters.

Walter Hagen

Walter Hagen was not only one of the foremost all-time great players but the golf world's leading showman in his day. He is credited with opening doors in country clubs for tour pros and gaining respect and prestige for professionals.

Hagen's tournament career, which spanned 1914 to 1940, saw him win 5 PGA Championships and 4 British Opens. He won the U.S. Open twice. As the game's most colorful player during that period, he journeyed to many places. He played in approximately 1,500 exhibition golf matches in the U.S., Canada and foreign countries and about 200 open tournaments. Affectionately known as The Haig, he was notorious for being late at tee time or any appointment, loved parties (even before a crucial match), dressed well and rode in a chauffeured limousine. He was always expected to do the unexpected.

His good times during his golf days did not deter his impressive play. He won 60 open tournaments and his winning of 11 major titles was 2nd only to Bobby Jones's 13 until equaled by Jack Nicklaus in 1972.

Hagen, who left school at the age of 12 to become a full-time caddie at a club in his hometown, Rochester, N.Y., turned professional at the age of 18. He won his 1st U.S. Open at the age of 21. He became golf's 1st millionaire. He won the 1st $1,000 prize ever offered for a pro event when he won the Panama Exposition tournament in San Francisco in 1915 and later he defeated Bobby Jones in a 72-hole match in Florida, earning $6,800, the largest sum ever won by a golfer for one match. He received a salary of $30,000 per year as president of the Pasadena Golf Club in St. Petersburg, Fla., in 1924 and 1925—an unheard-of salary in those days.

Hagen, who was born in Rochester, N.Y., in 1892, died in 1969.

Ben Hogan

No list of all-time great golfers would be complete without the name of Ben Hogan, who compiled an impressive record in professional golf during the decades of the 1940s and 1950s.

Born in Dublin, Tex., in 1912, he started playing golf as a youngster swinging left-handed. He soon switched to the right side, turning professional when he was still in his teens. He did not achieve national recognition until he was 28 years old, in 1940, when he won 4 tournaments after curing a bad hook by hitting countless practice balls.

His career interrupted by military service during W.W. II, he returned to pro golf and won the 1st of his 9 major championships in 1946 when he captured the national PGA title and finished runner-up in the Masters. He won 12 other tournaments that year, and continued his winning ways in 1947 and 1948, capturing 18 titles.

In 1949, after winning the Bing Crosby Invitational and the Long Beach Open, he was involved in a near-fatal accident when his car, in which his wife was a passenger, collided with a bus on a Texas highway. He suffered a fractured shoulder, rib, pelvis and ankle, developing a blood clot which threatened to reach his heart and required surgery. He won his fight for life, had to learn to walk all over again, and few believed he would ever play golf again. Working out regularly and rebuilding his strength, the determined Hogan made a comeback in the professional ranks 10 months later. It was quite dramatic—for he tied Sam Snead with a score of 280, including 3 successive 69s, in the Los Angeles Open. Snead won in the playoff. His comeback story was told in the motion picture *Follow the Sun*, with Glenn Ford in the starring role.

He proved his comeback was for real by winning both the U.S. Open and the Masters in 1951 and 1953. He added to his laurels by winning the British Open in 1953, shooting a 68 in the final round.

Bobby Jones

Robert Tyre Jones, better known as Bobby Jones, is considered one of golf's truly immortal players. Jones, who never turned professional, dominated major tournaments during the decade of the 1920s, climaxing his play with his famous "Grand Slam" in 1930—victories in the U.S. Open, British Open, U.S. Amateur, and British Amateur.

He retired from active competition at the end of that year, although only 28 years old, an age when most professionals are just beginning to win major championships. In his 15-year career, he amassed 21 wins, 13 of them major championships—a record that stood until 1973, when it was equaled by Jack Nicklaus. Jones won 4 U.S. Opens, 5 U.S. Amateurs, 3 British Opens, and one British Amateur. In the 8 years preceding his retirement from tournament competition, he won 62% of the national championships he entered.

Jones, who was born in Atlanta, Ga., in 1902, began playing golf as a child and became an accomplished player early, competing in the 1916 U.S. Amateur when he was only 14 years old. He had already won the Georgia Amateur that year. After winning the Southern Amateur in 1917, 1920, and 1922, he won his 1st major championship, the U.S. Open, in 1923 by beating Bobby Cruickshank by 2 strokes in a play-off. Runner-up in the U.S. Open the next 2 years, he won the titles again in 1926, 1929, and 1930. He was runner-up in the Open one other time and tied for 2nd once. In 8 out of 9 successive U.S. Opens, Jones won 4 and was runner-up in 4. It was in an era when golf had several great professional and amateur stars.

He competed in only a few tournaments each year, playing an average of about 3 months out of the 12 in competition, but he did play fun matches with his father and friends at his home club in Atlanta, taking time out from his law practice. He helped Cliff Roberts launch the Masters in Augusta in 1934.

He became ill with a spinal ailment in the late '40s, and later was confined to a wheelchair. He died December 18, 1971, at the age of 69.

Jack Nicklaus

Jack Nicklaus has won more major titles and more money than any other golfer in the history of the sport. He is bracketed with Bobby Jones and Ben Hogan as golf's top 3 all-time great stars.

Born in Columbus, O., in 1940, he began playing golf when he was only 10 years old and won the Ohio Open at the age of 16 and the U.S. Amateur at 19. He finished 2nd in the U.S. Open when he was 20. He turned professional after winning his 2nd U.S. Amateur title in 1961.

In 1962, in his 1st full year on the pro tour, he defeated Arnold Palmer in a play-off to win the U.S. Open. He won 2 other tournaments that year and finished 3rd in the money standings. He won the Masters the following year, at the age of 23, and added the PGA

Championship and Tournament of Champions the same year.

Nicklaus, who plays a limited schedule of 18 to 25 tournaments a year, concentrates his attention on major events. He has won 14 major titles, breaking the record of 13 set by Bobby Jones in 1930. In addition, he has captured the Tournament of Champions title 5 times.

Winner of over 50 professional titles, Nicklaus trails only Sam Snead, Ben Hogan, Arnold Palmer, and Byron Nelson in total victories. Nicklaus was the 1st player to top the $2 million mark in earnings. He has won the money title 6 times, was runner-up 3 times and 3rd twice. His 4th place finish in 1970 was his lowest position. He was PGA Player of the Year in 1967 and 1972.

Nicklaus is noted for his long, booming drives off the tee, but admits that several tour pros hit the ball farther than he does. His accuracy, putting ability, and smart thinking give him the edge. He has stubby hands with short fingers, causing him to use an interlocking grip instead of the conventional overlapping one.

Arnold Palmer

Arnold Palmer's charisma, which has drawn a legion of fans called "Arnie's Army," has made him history's most publicized golfer and he is credited with building the PGA tour from a $2 million a year prize in 1960 to $7 million in 1969. Because of his impact on the sport, he was named "Athlete of the Decade" for the 1960s in a nationwide poll of sportswriters and broadcasters.

Born in Latrobe, Pa., in 1929, he learned golf from his father, a club professional. After attending Wake Forest College and spending 2 years in the Coast Guard, he won the 1954 U.S. Amateur title and turned professional the following year when he was 25 years old. After finishing 32nd and 19th in the money standings in 1955 and 1956, respectively, he became the 5th leading money winner in 1957 and continued in the top 10 every year through 1971. He was the leading money winner 4 times, runner-up 3 times and 3rd twice during that period.

Palmer, who has won 80 tour titles, became golf's 1st million-dollar winner. He won more than $100,000 a season for 8 years, his highest earning being $209,603 in 1971.

He won his 1st major title in 1958, capturing the Masters. He won another Masters championship and added the U.S. Open in 1960. He won the British Open in 1961, his 3rd Masters title in 1962, and his 4th Masters in 1964. He was runner-up 3 times for the PGA Championship and won 3 Tournament of Champions titles. He was twice named PGA Player of the Year, in 1960 and 1962. He was a member of the 1961, 1965, 1967 and 1971 Ryder Cup teams.

When not playing on the pro tour, Palmer is involved in vast business enterprises, including a club-manufacturing company, sports clothes, golf carts, golf courses, a chain of franchised pitch-and-putt courses, driving ranges, franchised dry-cleaning establishments, and golf instructional materials.

Gene Sarazen

Born in New York in 1902, Gene Sarazen began playing golf while a caddie at the age of 9 and went on to win the U.S. Open at the age of 20 and the national PGA title at 21. One of a handful of men to win the 4 major titles open to professionals, he captured 2 U.S. Opens, 3 PGA Championships, a Masters, and a British Open.

The son of Italian parents of average means, Sarazen (born Saraceni) dropped out of grade school to help support the family and soon turned to professional golf. Because his fingers were too short for him to grip the club in an overlapping grip with comfort, the stocky Sarazen used an interlocking grip with the left thumb around the shaft. His strong arms and wrists made up for his short physical stature.

Sarazen is credited with launching the use of the sand wedge in the early 1930s after experimenting with the club in his garage, and he became a master at employing it. He was particularly noted for his prowess in short play. While he was not long off the tee, he was usually quite accurate. He was known as one of the fastest players on the tour, hitting quickly and walking briskly.

Sarazen provided what few fans followed the pro tour in the '20s and '30s with some dramatic come-from-behind charges. One came when he fired a 68 in the final round of the 1922 U.S. Open to win the title. He took only 100 strokes in the final 28 holes to repeat as U.S. Open champion in 1932. In the 1935 Masters, after trailing Craig Wood by 3 shots, he made a double eagle by holing a 220-yard shot, forced a play-off, and defeated Wood the next day.

Harry Vardon

Harry Vardon achieved greatness on the golf courses of both England and the U.S. and his form was widely copied by many players.

Vardon, who was born in Grouville, Isle of Jersey, England, in 1870, is generally credited with inventing the overlapping grip, now commonly referred to as the "Vardon grip." He began employing the grip in the 1890s, although J. H. Taylor, another famous English player of the same era, reportedly had started using the grip even earlier. Vardon evolved his own version of the overlapping grip and it became universally adopted by golfers in his day. It has been in use ever since, with some slight modifications or exceptions, and is still considered the best way to hold a club.

He won 6 British Opens (a record), finished runner-up 4 times and in the top 5 on 6 other occasions. He was in the top 5 16 times in a span of 21 years. He won the British PGA in 1912. He toured the U.S. on several occasions, winning the U.S. Open in 1900. He tied for 1st and lost the play-off in 1913 and tied for 2nd in 1920 when he was 50 years old.

He was noted for his great fairway wood play and his graceful and smooth swing with all clubs. He was able to achieve distance without undue exertion of power, and employed lighter clubs than were commonly used with the gutta-percha ball of the 1890s, and later with the rubber ball, neither of which came close to attaining the distance of today's balls. His perfect timing inspired many players to copy his form.

Vardon used a big pivot in his swing, much more than other players did then. At the top of his swing, only the toes of his left foot remained in contact with the ground. He had a wide arc and maintained full control of the plane of the swing, sweeping through the ball very cleanly as he hit off the sand tees used in those days.

Glenna Collett Vare

Glenna Collett (Mrs. Edwin H. Vare) is generally recognized as the greatest female amateur player the U.S. ever produced.

Born in New Haven, Conn., in 1903, she took up golf at the age of 4 and became a pupil of Alex Smith, a 2-time winner of the U.S. Open. She won the U.S. Women's Championship a record 6 times, finishing runner-up twice and a semifinalist twice in a span of 14 years. She captured the North and South and the Eastern title 6 times each, while dominating women's amateur play during the 1920s.

Glenna won the French Amateur, and was runner-up twice in the British Amateur, losing to the famed Joyce Wethered, the incomparable British star, and Diana Fishwick, respectively, in 1929 and 1930. During her prime she was considered 2nd only to Miss Wethered among the best women players of the world.

Glenna's game developed rapidly in her teens and she was able to win her 1st national title at the age of 19 in 1922. At the age of 54 her game was still good enough to capture the Rhode Island title. The Vare trophy, awarded by the Ladies Professional Golf Association each year for lowest stroke average, is named in her honor.

Joyce Wethered

Joyce Wethered, a famous British amateur player, is recognized as the greatest female golfer in history.

Born in 1901, she began competing in tournaments at the age of 19 and remained virtually unbeatable for a decade before giving up championship play and settling down as Lady Heathcoat-Amory. She won the English Ladies championship 5 successive years, beginning in 1920. She won 4 of 6 British women's championships, finishing runner-up once and semifinalist once.

Her early successes were enough to satisfy her competitive desires and she retired from active tournament play in 1925, but she returned to play in the 1929 British women's championships at St. Andrew's and defeated Glenna Collett in the final. She again retired from the championship scene. After leaving championship play, she limited her tournament play to foursomes at Worplesdon, which she won 8 times in 15 years.

Miss Wethered was known for her deep concentration while playing a match, so much so that sometimes she was unaware she had holed the winning putt and that the match was over. She was very seldom seen practicing and was noted for being oblivious to her opponents' presence.

In her book, published in 1933, she wrote: "If I could only bring myself to forget the excitement and importance of the match I was playing in, then I gave myself an infinitely better chance of reproducing my best form."

Mickey Wright

Mickey Wright is generally named with Babe Didrikson Zaharias and Joyce Wethered as among the all-time greats in women's golf.

Born in San Diego, Calif., in 1935, Miss Wright joined the professional tour in 1956 and has won 82 tournaments, a record for the LPGA. She also holds the record for the most victories in one year (14 in 1963), widest margin (12 strokes), most birdies in one round (9, shared with Joanne Carner), and she held the record for 9 holes (30) until it was broken by Marlene Hagge's 29 in 1970.

Miss Wright won the Vare Trophy for low-scoring average 5 straight times, 1960–1964, and was leading money winner 4 straight times, 1961–1964. One of her best seasons was 1966 when she won 7 tournaments and earned over $40,000. She ranks behind only Kathy Whitworth in all-time record earnings.

She has won 4 U.S. Opens and 4 LPGA titles, the only player to win both in the same year, 1958 and 1961. Although playing a limited tournament schedule in recent years, she

won the prestigious Colgate-Dinah Shore in 1973 while participating in only 8 events that year. When she sank a 25' birdie putt on the final hole of the Colgate-Dinah Shore in 1973, she did it with a putter she has been using exclusively for 18 years, a rarity in golf circles. That putt gave her the largest 1st prize in the history of professional golf at that time— $25,000.

Named Associated Press Woman Athlete of the Year in 1963 and 1964, she was elected to the LPGA Hall of Fame in 1964.

—J.S.

HOCKEY

H. A. H. (Hobey) Baker

His real name was Hobart Amery Hare Baker, but everyone called him Hobey. His name is almost legend in U.S. college hockey history.

Born in Wissahickon, Pa., in 1892, he learned early in life how to skate effortlessly and to handle a hockey stick. He was recognized as a master craftsman with a stick. Hockey writers reported that once the puck touched his stick, he never had to look down again.

Entering Princeton University in 1910, he excelled not only in hockey but also in football, golf, track, swimming, and gymnastics, serving as captain of the hockey team in his final 2 years. As a rover, he was a one-man team called "Baker and 6 other players." As captain of the Princeton football team, he drop-kicked a 43-yd. field goal to tie a game with Yale. Princeton later honored Hobey Baker by naming its ice rink after him.

When he graduated from Princeton, Hobey joined the St. Nicholas hockey team. He helped his team win the Ross Cup, beating the Montreal Stars. Hobey was one of the few hockey stars not born in Canada.

He joined the Lafayette Esquadrille, a flying unit, during W.W. I. A survivor of the war, he was later killed in a crash while testing a new plane.

Baker was elected to the Hall of Fame in 1945.

Gordon (Gordie) Howe

No list of great hockey players would be complete without the name of Gordon Howe, who spent 25 glorious seasons with the Detroit Red Wings. Howe holds the record for the most goals (786), the most points in a career (1,809), and the most career assists (1,023).

Howe was born in 1928 at Floral, Sask., and played his last amateur season with the Saskatoon Lions juveniles and then played one year of minor pro with Omaha of the U.S. League before joining Detroit in the 1946–1947 season.

Gordie was known as one of the game's best all-around players, combining the arts of shooting, scoring, stickhandling, and all other hockey skills. He displayed an ability to shoot with equal dexterity from either side and had an effortless skating style. He was rough and tough, but never a bully.

Howe may well be ranked the game's greatest player of all time. Bobby Orr, Boston's great defenseman, thinks so, and so does Bobby Hull, another Hall of Famer.

Howe established many records. He played the most seasons (25), most regular-season games (1,687), won the most Hart Memorial Trophies as the NHL's most valuable player (6), most Art Ross Trophies as league scoring champion (6), in addition to the most career goals, points, and assists. He was also named to the most NHL All-Star teams (21–12 times to the 1st team, 9 to the 2nd).

Howe's last season with Detroit was 1970–1971. He was elected to the Hall of Fame in 1972.

H. W. (Howie) Morenz

Howard William Morenz was a runaway leader in a 1950 Canadian Press poll to select the outstanding hockey player of the half century.

Born in Mitchell, Ont., in 1902, Morenz began his hockey career at nearby Stratford. He joined the Montreal Canadiens for the 1923–1924 season.

A colorful player, he became a great box-office attraction for the Canadiens because of his reckless speed and his headlong rushes. U.S. sportswriters called him "the Babe Ruth of Hockey." He also earned other nicknames such as the "Stratford Streak," "Canadien Comet," "Hurtling Habitant," and the "Mitchell Meteor."

Morenz, who played with the Canadiens for 11 seasons, was noted for his great stickhandling ability and a snapping shot. He was traded to Chicago and then went to the New York Rangers midway through the 1935–1936 season and came back to the Canadiens for the 1936–1937 season. He broke his leg in a game on January 28, 1937, and it led to his death on March 8, 1937.

Morenz scored 270 goals during his career and won the Hart Trophy 3 times: 1927–1928, 1930–1931, and 1931–1932.

In the 1928–1929 season he scored 40 goals in 44 games and in 1924–1925 he tallied 30 goals in 30 games. He was twice NHL scoring champion.

He was named to the 1st All-Star team twice and once to the 2nd. He was elected to the Hall of Fame in 1945.

Bobby Orr

Bobby Orr quickly achieved superstar status in the National Hockey League. He was a "rookie of the year" in 1967–1968 and had 4 consecutive 100-or-more-point seasons from 1969–1970 to 1972–1973, a rare feat. In the 1970–1971 season, he assisted on 102 goals to set a record.

Born 160 mi. north of Toronto, in Parry Sound, where youngsters begin skating at a very young age, he learned how to handle a stick efficiently enough to play organized hockey as a Minor Squirt at the age of 6. He went through the age brackets of Peewees and Bantams and began attracting attention of NHL talent scouts when he was 12. He was signed by the Boston Bruins when he was 14 to play Junior A hockey.

Playing against boys 4 and 5 years older, he was an immediate success. At age 16, *Mac-Lean's* magazine, a Canadian periodical, said of him: "He is a swift, powerful skater with instant acceleration, instinctive anticipation, a quick accurate shot, remarkable composure, and unrelenting ambition. . . ."

When he played his last year as a junior for the Oshawa Generals in the Ontario Hockey Association, ads in the local newspaper advised: "See Boston's $1 million Prospect, Bobby Orr!" When Orr joined Boston, manager Milton Schmidt said he would not trade him for $2 million. Leighton Emms, who managed Boston in Orr's rookie year, had earlier said he would not trade Orr even-up for the whole Toronto team.

E. W. (Eddie) Shore

Eddie Shore brought the National Hockey League a caliber of rough and tough hockey from 1926 to 1940 that perhaps may never be equaled. He was without doubt one of the best and most durable players in NHL history.

Born in Ft. Qu'Appelle, Sask., in 1902, he quickly moved up through the amateur ranks and joined the Boston Bruins as a defenseman in 1926–1927 in the NHL. He typified the rough-and-tumble aspects of the game like no other player. He was particularly talented in taking up the offense and setting up plays. He literally knocked down any opponent in his way, thus involving himself in fistic battles and penalties.

He became the sport's leading drawing card at a time when hockey was making a bid as a big-time sport in the U.S. He not only hit harder than any defenseman, but he could skate faster than most forwards. He became one of the most hated players, but of course was beloved by another segment of players and fans.

Shore remained with the Bruins for 13 years,

scoring 105 goals and adding 179 assists. He is the only defenseman to win the Hart Trophy 4 times—1932–1933, 1934–1935, 1935–1936, and 1937–1938. He was voted 7 times to the NHL's 1st All-Star team and once to the 2nd team. He was a member of 2 Stanley Cup winning teams, 1928–1929 and 1938–1939. He finished his career with the New York Americans in the 1939–1940 season.

Sportswriters recall that Shore antagonized fans, fought opponents and stirred more controversy than any other player with the possible exception of Maurice "The Rocket" Richard. Shore was elected to the Hall of Fame in 1945.

—J.S.

TENNIS

Maureen Connolly

This petite teen-ager was one of the greatest women's singles players in tennis history. She won 9 major world titles before she was 20. When she was 18 she became the 1st female to score a Grand Slam.

Maureen "Little Mo" Connolly was born in San Diego, Calif., and wasted no time. By the age of 16 she had learned enough to win the U.S. singles title at Forest Hills. Startled tennis fans began comparing her to Helen Wills Moody. Seldom had they seen such a hard forehand, such concentrated drive in one so young.

The following year, the 17-year-old Maureen charged Wimbledon and won the all-English crown by defeating Louise Brough 7–5, 6–3. In 1953, she repeated at Wimbledon, added the French and Australian baubles to her jewel box and came to Forest Hills with an opportunity to become the 1st woman and the 1st player since Don Budge to achieve a Grand Slam. It took less than 45 minutes of speedy footwork and long ground-strokes for Little Mo to finish Doris Hart 6–2, 6–4.

After her 3rd Wimbledon victory in 1954, tragedy struck. Indulging in her 2nd love, riding, she was injured when her frightened horse ran into a truck. Her leg was broken and she was unable to defend her U.S. title that year.

It proved to be the end of her playing career. In about 4 years of blistering tennis, Maureen had won both the U.S. and Wimbledon titles 3 times, the Australian singles and doubles once, the French singles twice, doubles and mixed doubles once, the Italian singles once, the U.S. clay court singles twice and doubles once, and had won 9 out of 9 in Wrightman Cup play. She was ranked best in the world from 1952 to 1954 and was voted Woman Athlete of the Year by the AP 3 years running.

Maureen Connolly died prematurely in 1969.

Billie Jean King

When she was just a kid, she dropped softball and began looking for a more ladylike sport. Billie Jean King (then Moffitt) loved to run and hit things. So she began whunking tennis balls on the public courts of Long Beach, Calif., where she discovered another favorite pastime: charging the net.

She began tournament play in 1958: By 1959 she was 16 and good enough to meet Wimbledon star Maria Bueno in the Eastern Grass Court championships. Reaching the finals of the national 18-and-under tourney in 1960 she lost to Karen Hantze but picked up a doubles partner. She and Miss Hantze became the youngest team to take the Wimbledon doubles, in 1961.

Finally, in 1966, she won her 1st Wimbledon singles title and followed up in 1967 with major triumphs in all fields. She fought to titles in the singles, doubles, and mixed doubles for a Wimbledon triple sweep. It was the 1st for a woman since Doris Hart in 1951.

Billie Jean returned to America and added the U.S. national singles laurel to her wreath, defeating Ann Jones 11–9, 6–4 to return the title to her country for the 1st time since 1961. As frosting, she added the doubles and mixed doubles championships and became the 1st double triple-sweep winner since Alice Marble in 1939.

Ms. King won Wimbledon again in 1968, 1972 and 1973. As the dividing lines between amateur and professional became dimmer, she led a minor revolt against USLTA rules and lost her eligibility.

The U.S. national tournament became the U.S. Open in 1970, and had been available to pros as well as amateurs since 1968. Billie Jean regained her status and won the singles title in 1971 and 1972.

It was in September, 1973, that 29-year-old Ms. King gained her greatest celebrity when she accepted the challenge of 55-year-old Bobby Riggs in what was billed as the Battle of the Sexes and a showdown match between a Women's Libber and a Male Chauvinist. Riggs, who had been USLTA singles champion in 1939 and 1941 and earlier in 1973 the conqueror of Margaret Court Smith 6–2, 6–1, was the solid favorite. But when they collided in the Houston Astrodome and on national TV for $100,000, "Ms." King mercilessly crushed Riggs 6–4, 6–3, 6–3.

In 1974 she became player-coach of the Philadelphia Freedoms in the World Team Tennis League, an experiment in matching pro tennis teams the way pro baseball and football teams are matched.

Karel Kozeluh

In the early days of the game, the amateurs had all of the great tournaments—Wimbledon, Forest Hills, Davis Cup—and so they got the international glory. But there were great professional players who had never spent a day as an amateur, and Karel Kozeluh was one of them.

Kozzie was an all-around athlete in his country, Czechoslovakia. He excelled at soccer and the resultant leg power made him an incredible baseline player in tennis. He became the acknowledged iron man of defensive play.

Some of the top amateurs in the late '20s and early '30s who took Kozeluh on for a "workout" got far more than that. One was Bill Tilden, who was best in the world at the time. Kozzie thought he could beat the master and one day he got the opportunity. Tilden wanted to sharpen his game and asked Kozzie to play a 5-set match. It was the King of Attack against the Sultan of Defense.

In a textbook demonstration of ground strokes and court tactics, Kozeluh took a 5–2 lead in the 1st set. Then Tilden stopped the match and ordered Karel to serve to his backhand for the rest of the session. Kozzie's opinions of this were never officially recorded.

In 1931, Kozeluh got another chance. He met Tilden in Big Bill's professional debut in New York. Tilden's booming drives kept the Czech fighting from backcourt and despite some fantastic recoveries, Kozzie dropped the match 6–4, 6–2, 6–4.

The year 1929 had been a pinnacle for Kozeluh: He won the U.S. Professional Tennis Association singles championship and teamed with Vincent Richards to take the doubles title. He swept to singles victories again in 1932 and 1937.

René Lacoste

Until 1927, the Davis Cup had been won only by the U.S., Australia, and Great Britain. In that year it was captured for the 1st time by a non-English speaking nation, France. And the turning point came when a 23-year-old newcomer stood up to the acknowledged master of the game and beat him.

René Lacoste had played in the U.S. championships as early as 1923 but had not left an indelible impression. In the interim, however, he had written a book. Like a major-league pitcher in baseball, Lacoste's "book" was about his opponents—their strengths, their weaknesses, and how to play on them.

Next to Bill Tilden's name he had written the admonition to keep the ball in the center when going to the net. He knew enough to avoid the vicious Tilden backhand.

When Lacoste met Tilden in Davis Cup play at the Germantown Cricket Club in Philadelphia in 1927, the U.S. was leading 2–1. Tilden was in top form and seemed unbeatable. But Lacoste was a stone wall.

Everything that Big Bill could fire at the Frenchman came methodically back, as though the American were hitting balls against the side of a building. Gradually, Tilden's powers diminished. Lacoste, parrying every shot like a tennis machine, won the match 6–3, 4–6, 6–3, 6–2. His victory turned the tide and the Frenchmen took the silver cup home with them.

This ended America's domination of the Cup and began a French reign that saw Lacoste and his fellow "Musketeers," Henri Cochet, Jean Borotra, and Toto Brugnon, conquer the Cup *and* Wimbledon for 6 straight years and take the U.S. title for 3.

Rod Laver

From an anthill court in Queensland to immortality at Forest Hills: Rod Laver, a small Australian powerhouse, could blast a tennis ball so hard that it would literally knock the racket out of his opponent's hand.

In 1962, he became the 2nd man in history to win the Grand Slam—Wimbledon, Australia, France, and the U.S.—in one year. It hadn't been done since Don Budge did it in 1938, the year Laver was born.

He began playing at 13 on a dirt court that his father had laid out for him. At 18, on his 1st trip to the U.S., he won the junior championship. In 1961, after several tries, Rod the Rocket took Wimbledon, using his left-handed power and wrist-whipping spinners to flatten Chuck McKinley in 55 minutes, 6–3, 6–1, 6–4.

It was but a prelude to 1962. He took Wimbledon again, won the Australian and French titles and came to Forest Hills with a great chance at the Grand Slam. He reached the finals and faced his Davis Cup teammate Roy Emerson, who had beaten him the year before. But Laver would not be stopped. He won 6–2, 6–4, 5–7, 6–4.

The 1962 Grand Slam was accomplished against amateurs. By 1969, the championships had been opened to pros and the best players in the world were Rod's competition. He battled past John Newcombe in a stirring match to win the Wimbledon title for the 4th time. Again, he took the Australian and French crowns. Once more he visited Forest Hills, this time with a $16,000 1st prize at stake and he reached the finals with a 2nd Grand Slam (and 1st Open Grand Slam) within his reach.

His opponent was fellow Australian Tony Roche. Rain had softened the court and the footing was unsure. But Laver triumphed 7–9,

6–1, 6–2, 6–2. He was acknowledged as the greatest tennis player alive.

In 1971, Laver achieved the seemingly impossible feat of winning 13 straight matches against the cream of the world's pros in the Tennis Champions Classic. His total prize money for that year was a record $292,717.

Suzanne Lenglen

It is said that her father placed a handkerchief on the court and gave her 5 francs every time she hit it. There is no doubt that Papa Charles was· the guiding hand behind the remarkable career of France's queen of tennis, Suzanne Lenglen. His training and regimen worked well. His daughter became one of the greatest women players of all time.

Suzanne was playing tournament tennis at 12 and won the world hard court championship at 15. She was 20 in 1919 when she met and defeated 7-time winner Mrs. Lambert Chambers in the Wimbledon singles. From then until 1926, she was beaten only once, and then by default.

Suzanne was a ballerina with a tennis racket. Volatile and dramatic, she combined the movements of a dancer with the strokes and tactics of tennis and she never made a mistake. She revolutionized tennis dress for women and was worshiped almost as a cult figure. Opposing players considered it a crowning achievement if they scored a point against her; to win a game was akin to a miracle.

In the women's singles at Wimbledon in 1925, going after her 6th title, she lost only 5 games in the 5 matches she played.

Her only low point came in 1921. Playing the American champion Molla Mallory in the 2nd round of the U.S. championships, something went wrong. Ms. Mallory took the 1st set 6–2 and was leading in the 2nd when Ms. Lenglen left the court, coughing and crying. She defaulted because of illness, her only loss during amateur play.

In the Match of the Century, Suzanne met and defeated the American champion Helen Wills in 1926. The same year, she turned professional and went on a tour of the U.S., Cuba, and Mexico.

Maurice McLoughlin

At the turn of the century, tennis was a rather soft game played politely on rich people's lawns. Maurice McLoughlin, the California Comet, changed all that. He removed the sissy label and converted the game from defensive to offensive. He took tennis from the aristocracy and, through his power and personality, gave it to the people as a spectator sport.

A Northern Californian, McLoughlin split the tennis world asunder with his new, forceful style. First he would cannonade his "American Twist" service, which curved left and bounced right, then he would follow it to the net to put away the return with a smashing drive. This tireless, dynamic approach pushed him to the top quickly.

In 1913 he took the national title for the 2nd year and helped the American Davis Cup team drop the British. In 1914, even though Australia eliminated the U.S. in the Davis Cup challenge round, McLoughlin defeated the famed Norman Brookes in straight sets, including one of the most sensational ever played, 17–15.

It was McLoughlin's slingshot service against Brookes's superior ground strokes. Brookes almost had his breakthrough at 40–0 in the 18th game, but McLoughlin bore down on his service hummer, aced 3 out of 5, then came in behind an American Twister and chopped Brookes's return for the final point.

Brookes continued gamely, but this set all but finished the match. McLoughlin won the next 2, 6–3, 6–3.

Australia still won the series, 3–2, but this one match may have done more for the game than any before it, because it made people realize that tennis could be an exciting game to watch as well as to play.

Helen Wills Moody

Everyone thought it was to be the 1st of many classic matches when the Princess, Helen Wills, at last faced the Queen, Suzanne Lenglen, of France. But the Fates intervened and this historic 1926 match between 2 of the greatest women players in the history of tennis turned out to be the only time they ever met.

Helen Wills was 15 and in pigtails when she gave her 1st intimations of greatness. Born in Berkeley, Calif., she attended the University of California. Years of hard work, excellent coaching and competing against men players gave her unusual power, pinpoint control, unexcelled timing and tempo. Her classic beauty, her slim grace, her white visor and imperturbable features all became famous trademarks.

Helen reached the U.S. finals in 1922, when she was 16. She won the national championships 7 times, the 1st in 1923 when she was 17, the last in 1931. She helped her doubles team win in 1922, 1924–1925, and 1928. She was the Olympic singles and doubles champion in 1924. In 1927 she took the 1st of 8 Wimbledon titles in singles play.

Between 1927 and 1933, "Little Miss Poker Face" went undefeated and, amazingly, did not lose a set from 1927 until her Wimbledon match in 1933.

The word "sadism" comes from the Marquis de Sade, a delicate, blue-eyed author, 5'2" in height. His participation in the Marseilles Scandal, an orgy which included sodomy, torture, poisoning, brought him the death penalty, later commuted to confinement in a lunatic asylum. (See: Chap. 19) *The Bettmann Archive.*

Gertrude Stein, an innovative Pennsylvania writer, became a renowned expatriate after settling in Paris. Her friends included celebrities ranging from Hemingway to Picasso. One of her most successful books was *The Autobiography of Alice B. Toklas* in 1933. (See: Chap. 19) *Sophia Smith Collection, Smith College.*

Dutch-born Mata Hari, who studied the Vedas in Java, became a renowned dancer in Paris in 1905, where she often performed in the nude. She entertained countless lovers, was said to charge them a minimum of $7,500 a night. The highest-paid German spy in W.W. I, she was shot by a firing squad for costing France 50,000 lives. (See: Chap. 19) *Brown Brothers.*

Grigori Rasputin, a Russian holy man and healer, was summoned by the Czarina Alexandra in 1905 to cure her afflicted son. Rasputin succeeded, and soon was a power behind the throne. His sexual excesses were legend. (See: Chap. 19) *Culver Pictures, Inc.*

Dr. Alfred C. Kinsey, a staid Indiana University biologist, selected to teach a course in sex education, found little information available. Kinsey was inspired to launch his famous series of sex surveys. The 1st, published as *Sexual Behavior of the Human Male* in 1948, caused a sexual revolution. (See: Chap. 19) *News Bureau, Indiana University.*

The patron saint of orchards, John Chapman, better known as Johnny Appleseed, traveled from the east coast of the U.S. as far west as Fort Wayne, Ind., where he died and is buried. (See: Chap. 20) *Indiana Dept. of Commerce.*

The immortal Sultan of Swat, George Herman "Babe" Ruth, booms one out of the park. The only baseball player ever to hit 50 or more home runs 4 times, 40 or more home runs 13 times, 2 home runs in a game 73 times. His lifetime total of 714 home runs was finally exceeded by Hank Aaron in 1974. (See: Chap. 23) *Brown Brothers.*

The last bare-knuckle prizefight in history pitted the boozing, invincible John L. Sullivan against the well-trained Jake Kilrain for the heavyweight championship. They met at a secret site in Richburg, Miss., on July 8, 1889. Fighting in 100° heat, Sullivan won by a TKO in the 75th round. This photo was taken in the 7th round as they clinched. (Sullivan at ʟ.) (See: Chap. 23) *U.P.I.*

Perhaps the greatest of Olympic pictures. Dorando Petri, a middle-aged Italian candymaker, finishing the 1908 marathon in London's Olympic Stadium. Dorando fell 5 times before the finish. British officials helped him to his feet and across the finish line. Dorando was disqualified and the victory given to Johnny Hayes of the U.S. (See: Chap. 23) *Radio Times Hulton Picture Library*.

Voted by sportswriters the greatest all-around athlete of the last half century in 1950, Jim Thorpe, an Indian, was an All-American football hero and a track and field star in the 1912 Olympics. He even played major league baseball between 1913 and 1919, batting .327 one season. (See: Chap. 23) *Jim Thorpe.*

Paavo Nurmi, the Flying Finn, scoring one of his 4 long-distance track victories at the 1924 Olympics in Paris. He was pursued constantly by his teammate, Ville Ritola, who finished 2nd to him in 3 events. (See: Chap. 23) *Brown Brothers.*

Pelé is the greatest soccer player in the history of association football. Only 5'8" and weighing 160 lbs., he led Brazil's national team to 3 World Cup championships. Here, Pelé (R) is helping his team defeat Guadalajara, Mexico. (See: Chap. 23) *U.P.I.*

In 1969, Rocky Marciano (L), 1952 heavyweight champion, and Muhammad Ali, the 1964 and 1974 champion, fought a mock title fight in a TV studio. A computer spewed out the winner. Who won? (See: Chap. 23) W*oroner Films, Inc.*

White supremacists were chagrined when Jack Johnson defeated Tommy Burns in 1908 to become the 1st black heavyweight boxing champion. For over 6 years he beat the best boxers the white race had to offer, including Jim Jeffries. At age 37, he was KO'd by Jess Willard on April 5, 1915. (See: Chap. 23)

SAN FRANCISCO CHRONICLE, TUESDAY, JULY 5, 1910.

JACK LONDON SEES TRAGEDY IN THE DEFEAT OF WHITE CHAMPION

WHITE MAN OUTCLASSED BY NEGRO, WHO SHOWED NO YELLOW

Johnson a Veritable Fighting Machine Who Won as He Pleased

By JACK LONDON.

JOHNSON SAYS THAT IT WAS NO EASIER THAN HE EXPECTED

By JACK JOHNSON.

INCIDENTS OF DAY AT RENO PRECEDING THE BIG BATTLE

Great Quantities of Jeffries Money Force Down the Odds

The only woman in the world who was considered better than Helen Wills was Suzanne Lenglen, the French legend who had never been defeated in her own country, who had won the Wimbledon singles title 6 times and had been enthroned as international champion. A match that could have filled the Coliseum was staged at the tiny Carlton Club in Cannes in 1926, amid near-riots and fainting bodies. The French veteran worked carefully in the 1st set, overcame a 1–2 deficit and won it 6–3. Helen took the 1st 3 games of the 2nd set and Suzanne gasped to the sidelines for cognac. She evened the match, and then Helen went to 5–4. Suzanne, benefiting from a bad call, pushed it to 6–5 but Helen fought gamely to even it at 6–6. Helen brought the final 2 games to deuce but Suzanne was too clever for her. She took the set and the match 8–6 and promptly fainted. Shortly thereafter, Ms. Lenglen turned pro and the girls never met again.

In 1933 it looked as though the reign of the new Helen Wills Moody had finally ended when she defaulted to Helen Jacobs in the 3rd set of the finals at Forest Hills, saying a back injury made it impossible to continue. But in 1935, in a thrillingly close one, she came back to defeat Ms. Jacobs at Wimbledon 6–3, 3–6, 7–5. She won the Wimbledon title for the last time in 1938, once more playing against Helen Jacobs.

William T. Tilden II

Was he the greatest tennis player of all time? From 1920 to 1926, Big Bill Tilden dominated world tennis. A master of court tactics with a flair for the dramatic, he often would allow an opponent a large lead, then battle back from the edge of defeat to destroy him. He combined an overpowering forehand and backhand, a rifle-shot serve and a mastery of spin to defeat the best the game had to offer.

William Tatem Tilden II was born in 1893 in Philadelphia, Pa., and attended the University of Pennsylvania. He began to play tennis at the age of 5 and won his 1st tournament at 8. But it was not until he was 27 that he claimed international attention by taking the Wimbledon singles in 1920.

Later that year he advanced to the American finals at Forest Hills and faced William "Little Bill" Johnston. Johnston had concentrated on Tilden's backhand to beat him the previous year. All winter, Tilden had worked indoors improving the stroke. The effort paid off. He took Johnston after 5 epic sets, 6–1, 1–6, 7–5, 5–7, 6–3, and from then until 1926 he conquered the greats of the game, helped the U.S. to dominate Davis Cup play and reigned as national singles champion. In 1926, he was beaten for the 1st time in 7 years

in the U.S. championship by Henri Cochet of France, 6–8, 6–1, 6–3, 1–6, 8–6. The following year, Frenchman René Lacoste triumphed over Big Bill in the USLTA final at Forest Hills 11–9, 6–3, 11–9.

But Tilden was far from through. In 1929, he came back to win the U.S. title for a 7th time. In 1930, he took Wimbledon for the 3rd time. He turned pro in 1931 and thrilled spectators for many more years. Tilden died in 1953, at the age of 60.

—M.H.

TRACK AND FIELD

Roger Bannister

He called it ". . . rather like Everest. A challenge to the human spirit . . . that seemed to defy all attempts to break it."

By 1954, several men had taken up the challenge of the 4-minute mi. The Swedes' Gunder Hagg and Arne Andersson came within 1.4 and 1.6 seconds of the Everest of distance records. Roger Bannister decided that he would be the 1st to conquer it. Born in 1929 in Harlow, England, Bannister was a medical student and a self-coached runner.

On May 6, 1954, at Oxford University, he knew that conditions were far from ideal—the wind was at near-gale force and would slow him by one second per lap. But time was short—other runners were after the historic mark. It would be Bannister's 1st race in 8 months, but he was at a psychological peak. Should he make a try for it?

The race was scheduled for 6 o'clock. At 5:15, it rained. The wind came in gusts. But as the runners lined up for the start, the wind began to drop. Bannister decided to go for broke.

The plan was for former Oxford teammates Chris Brasher and Chris Chataway to pace Bannister and drive him to the fastest possible lap times. Brasher took the lead and paced Roger to a 57.5 1st lap. Shortly after the 1:58.2 half mile, Chataway went into the lead. At ¾, the time was 3:00.5 and Bannister knew that somehow he had to run the last lap in 59 seconds.

At the top of the backstretch he passed Chataway and his entire world became the 200 or so yards of land dead ahead. He burst the tape and collapsed, near unconsciousness. Then the announcer read the time: "3 minutes . . ." The rest was lost in the roar of the crowd.

Bannister had run the mile in 3:59.4. Waves of worldwide publicity followed the epic race. Then, on June 21, Australian John Landy ran a 3:57.9 to shatter the new record set by Bannister.

It was a setup. On August 7, the 2 runners met in the Mile of the Century in Vancouver, B.C. BOTH men broke 4 minutes as Bannister won the duel at 3:58.8 to Landy's 3:59.6.

Fanny Blankers-Koen

She has been called the greatest all-around female track and field performer in history. In between training and competing in the high jump, long jump, 100-m. and 200-m. sprints and 80-m. hurdles, she somehow found time to marry and have 2 children.

Fanny Blankers-Koen was born in 1918 in Amsterdam. By the time she reached the 1948 Olympic Games in London, she was a slim matron of 30 who had broken world records in the high jump and long jump. But since Olympic performers are limited to 3 individual events, she chose to enter the 100-m. and 200-m. sprints and the 80-m. hurdles.

For starters, Mrs. Blankers-Koen blazed to an 11.9 100-m. for her 1st gold medal. Then she won the hurdles prize at 11.2. This brought her 2 distinctions: It was the 1st double victory for a woman since Babe Didrikson Zaharias in 1932—and it set a new world record for women. She continued with another gold medal for her 24.4 200-m. run, then anchored the Dutch 400-m. relay team to 1st place to become the only female winner of 4 gold medals in Olympic history.

At various times, this amazing woman held world records in the 100-yd., 100-m., 220-yd., 80-m. hurdles, high jump, and pentathlon. In European championships, she totaled 5 gold medals.

Her all-time best times and distances: 100-yd. (10.8), 100-m. (11.5), 220-yd. (24.2), 80-m. hurdles (11.0), long jump (20'6"), high jump (5'7¼"), pentathlon (4,692 pts.).

Paavo Nurmi

As a boy he made deliveries by pushing a heavy cart up a steep hill. As a man, his legs found lighter work. They carried him to 20 world records during 12 years of competition. He had been called the greatest middle-distance runner of all time and the premier athlete of sport's Golden Age.

Paavo Nurmi was born in Turku, Finland, in 1897. He set his goals early and pursued them with grim determination and a grueling regimen. To develop an even pace, he bounded along behind trolley cars. To be sure that his pacing was true, he raced with a stopwatch in his hand.

It worked. Paavo broke every record in the book from 1500-m. to 10,000-m.; he shattered every mark from one to 6 mi.; and he claimed the one-hour distance mark by running 11 mi.,

1,648 yds. in 60 minutes, a record that stood for 17 years.

In 1931, moving 2 mi. in less than 9 minutes was considered a feat that no human could achieve without a bicycle. Running on boards in Madison Square Garden, Nurmi became the 1st to cover the distance under 9:00. His time: 8:59.5.

He set 6 world marks in the 3 Olympics from 1920 to 1928 and 3 of those championships came within 48 hours. At Paris in 1924, 27 years old and at his peak, the long-legged, big-chested Finn ran 6 races in 6 days. He won the 1500-m. in 3:53.6 and within 1½ hours came back to win the 5000-m. in 14:31.2, both world marks. Two days later, in blistering heat, he captured the cross-country title.

The Flying Finn was finally beaten in 1932, by bureaucracy. While he wanted to end his career with a victory in the Olympic marathon in Los Angeles, Nurmi was barred from competition and suspended from the amateur ranks because he allegedly had made a small profit on an expense account.

Jesse Owens

He ran and jumped 25 years ahead of his time. The records he set in the Olympic Games of 1936 held up for 2 decades or more. In one meet in college competition, he broke 5 world records and tied a 6th—all in about one hour flat.

Jesse Owens was born in 1913 in Danville, Ala., the son of a sharecropper. While attending East Technical High School in Cleveland, O., he ran the 100-m. in 10.3, the 100-yd. dash in 9.4 (an American high school record not equaled until 1954) and the 220-yd. dash in 20.7.

He reached the zenith of his career in Berlin at the 1936 Olympics. Adolf Hitler had declared that the new Olympic Stadium was to become a temple to Aryan supremacy. Over 110,000 spectators gathered to witness the triumph of the "new Reich." Then Jesse Owens went into action. He broke the Olympic record in the semifinals of the 100-m. at 10.2, a mark later disallowed because of wind. In the following days he won the 100-m., tying the Olympic and World's records at 10.3; set a new Olympic record in the long jump at 26'5¼"; broke the Olympic and World records in the 200-m. on a turn with 20.7; and helped the 400-m. relay team set an Olympic and world record with 39.8.

But this remarkable athlete's greatest day on a track had probably come a year earlier, on May 25, 1935, when as a sophomore he represented Ohio State in a championship meet against Michigan in Ann Arbor. Owens tied the world's record for the 100-yd. at 9.4 and set new world's records in the long jump, at 26'8¼"; the 220-yd. low hurdles, straight, at 22.6; and the 220-yd., straight, at 20.3. Under a new rule, Jesse's 220-yd. marks were also accepted as world's records for the 200-m. dash and hurdles. So in one hour or so that day, Jesse Owens broke 5 world's records and tied a 6th.

Jim Thorpe

In 1913 the Amateur Athletic Union (AAU) deprived Big Jim Thorpe of his amateur status and returned his 1912 Olympic records and trophies to Stockholm. He had played baseball for money in 1909–1910 and this made him a professional athlete, they said.

After decades of entreaty, the AAU restored Jim Thorpe's amateur standing in 1973, 20 years after his death. This historic move paved the way for the return of the prizes the great Indian athlete had won 60 years before.

Born in 1888 near Indian Territory in what is now Oklahoma, James Francis Thorpe was a member of the Sac and Fox tribe. In 1904 he enrolled at the Carlisle Indian School in Pennsylvania and by 1912 had achieved status as a superstar for his accomplishments in football and track.

Jim was not a one-man track squad, despite popular myth. Coach Pop Warner's team was small but talented. Against Lafayette, however, Jim led a 7-man squad to victory by winning 6 of the 7 events he entered.

It was only natural that he should enter the decathlon, pentathlon, high jump, and long jump in the 1912 Stockholm Olympic Games. He won the decathlon and pentathlon with shocking ease; he finished 4th in the high jump and 7th in the long jump.

His Marks:

Pentathlon: First: 200-m. (22.9); long jump (23'2¼"); discus (116'8¼"); 1500-m. (4:44.8). Third: javelin (153'2¾").

Decathlon: First: 1500-m. (4:40.1); 110-m. high hurdles (15.6); high jump (6'1½"); shot put (42'3¼"). Third: long jump (22'3¼"); discus (121'3¾"); tie for pole vault (10'7¾"); tie for 100-m. dash (11.2). Fourth: 400-m. (52.2); javelin (149'11").

Stella Walsh

She probably ran longer than any woman in history. This Polish marvel began her track career in 1930 and was still going strong in 1953 at the age of 42.

Born in Poland in 1911, raised in the U.S., Stella Walsh competed for Poland in the 1932 and 1936 Olympic Games. In Los Angeles, she won the 100-m. dash in 11.9 and

in Berlin was 2nd in the event to Helen Stephens.

Stella took her 1st U.S. AAU championships in 1930. She was just 19 when she had triumphed in the 100-yd. and 220-yd. sprints and the long jump.

In 1933, she lined up for a 60-m. dash that was to make history. She broke the tape in 7.3, a new world's record. She lowered the world standard in the 100-m. to 11.7 in 1934 and lowered it again, to 11.6, in Berlin in 1937. She set the 220-m. record in 1935, with a 23.6, and the 220-yd. record in the same year in Cleveland, with a 24.3.

It would be fair to say that after 18 years of competition, a sprinter's legs might be a bit sprung. But Stella Walsh astounded the world in 1948 by once more winning the AAU titles in the 100-yd., 220-yd., and long jump events. She was 37 years old.

At the end of a long and brilliant career, Stella could lean back and count some 40 U.S. championships and world records.

Mildred Didrikson Zaharias

She could stand at home plate and bounce a baseball off the left field wall on the fly. She mastered tennis, bowling, and basketball with incredible ease. She won more than 50 major golf tournaments, including 3 women's national opens.

Mildred "Babe" Didrikson Zaharias also was one of the finest track and field performers of all time. This Texan, born in Beaumont in 1914, was named the greatest woman athlete of the 1st half of the 20th century by the AP.

She gained her 1st national attention at an AAU meet in 1930 in Dallas by winning the baseball throw and the javelin. Her 2nd place in the long jump was good enough to top a world record.

In 1931 she continued her record-breaking performance in the Jersey City AAU meet. She threw a baseball 296' to set a world record and won the 80-m. hurdles and the long jump.

This turned out to be just a warm-up for the 1932 Olympics in Los Angeles. She was proficient in the javelin, shot put, high jump, long jump, and hurdles, but she decided to enter the last 3 events. Babe threw the javelin 143'4" for a new Olympic and world record. She whizzed over the 80-m. hurdles in 11.7, another Olympic and world record. And she did the same to the high jump but was disqualified for "diving" over the bar and finished in 2nd place.

The reigning figure in women's track and field for a decade, she later became a world champion golfer. In one of the greatest comebacks in sports history, Babe recovered from a cancer operation in 1953 and won the 1954 women's national open. She succumbed to the disease in 1956.

Emil Zatopek

He trained so hard that competition itself became a lark. He slogged along for miles through the rain in heavy soldier's boots; he increased his distance gradually until he was running more than 13 mi. a day. He pushed his body beyond its limits and continued to push. He turned into a running machine.

Emil Zatopek was born in 1922 in Northern Moravia, a part of Czechoslovakia. He began a running career in 1941 that brought him 18 world records, the last set in 1955. He was almost unbeatable at 10,000-m. but during his career he mastered every distance from 800-m. up to the marathon.

His achievements are legend. From 1948 to 1954, he was undefeated in 38 races over 10,000-m. Between 1949 and 1955, he set 18 world records between 5000-m. and 30,000-m. Zatopek was the 1st man to run more than 20 km. in an hour—he ran 12 mi., 810 yds. in 1951—and he was a 4-time Olympic champion and 3-time European champion in the 5000-m., 10,000-m., and marathon.

His greatest triumph may have been in the '52 Helsinki Olympics. He proved himself superior to the great Finns Kolehmainen and Nurmi when he breezed to victory in the 5000-m. (14:06.6), 10,000-m. (29:17.0), and then went on to take the marathon.

The final lap of the 5000-m. was a chiller. Four men fought for the lead. Zatopek was challenged in the backstretch by the Englishman Chris Chataway. Around the final bend, Zatopek ran with furious intensity, almost as if his life depended on winning. The unfortunate Chataway tripped and fell but Emil still had to run the bell lap in 58.1 to stave off Alain Mimoun of France.

Some of Zatopek's world marks: 5000-m. (13:57.2), 10,000-m. (28:54.2), 20,000-m. (59:51.6), 25,000-m. (1 hr. 16:36.4), 30,000-m. (1 hr. 35:23.8), 6 mi. (27:59.2), 10 mi. (48:12.0), 15 mi. (1 hr. 14:01.0).

—M.H.

A Short Selection from the Baseball Hall of Fame

With Inscriptions from Plaques Honoring Elected

TYRUS R. COBB (1886–1961)
Detroit, Philadelphia, A.L. 1905–1928.
"Led American League in batting 12 times and created or equaled more major league records than any other player. Retired with 4,191 major league hits."
GEORGE H. (BABE) RUTH (1895–1948)
Boston, New York, A.L.; Boston, N.L. 1915–1935.
"Greatest drawing card in history of baseball. Holder of many home run and other batting records. Gathered 714 home runs in addition to 15 in World Series."
WALTER P. JOHNSON (1887–1946)
Washington, 1907–1927.
"Conceded to be fastest ball pitcher in history of game. Won 414 games with losing team behind him. Many years holder of strike out and shut out records."
CHRISTY MATHEWSON (1880–1925)
New York, N.L. 1900–1916; Cincinnati, N.L. 1916.
"Greatest of all the great pitchers in the 20th century's 1st quarter. Pitched 3 shutouts in 1905 World Series. First pitcher of the century ever to win 30 games in 3 successive years. Won 37 games in 1908. 'Matty was master of them all.' "
HONUS WAGNER (1874–1955)

Louisville, N.L. 1897–1899; Pittsburgh, N.L. 1900–1917.
"The greatest shortstop in baseball history. . . . Known to fame as 'Honus,' 'Hans,' and 'The Flying Dutchman.' Retired in 1917, having scored more runs, made more hits, and stolen more bases than any other player in the history of his league."
NAPOLEON (LARRY) LAJOIE (1875–1959)
Philadelphia (N) 1896–1900; Philadelphia (A) 1901; Cleveland (A) 1902–1914; Philadelphia (A) 1915–1916.
"Great hitter and most graceful and effective 2nd-baseman of his era. Managed Cleveland 4 years. League batting champion 1901–03–04."
TRISTRAM (TRIS) SPEAKER (1888–1958)
Boston (A) 1909–1915; Cleveland (A) 1916–1926; Washington (A) 1927; Philadelphia (A) 1928.
"Greatest centerfielder of his day. Lifetime major league batting average of .344. Manager in 1920 when Cleveland won its 1st pennant and world championship."
DENTON (CY) YOUNG (1867–1955)
Cleveland (N) 1890–1898; St. Louis (N) 1899–1900; Boston (A) 1901–1908; Cleveland (A) 1909–1911; Boston (N) 1911.
"Only pitcher in 1st 100 years of baseball to win 500 games. Among his 511 victories were 3 no-hit shutouts. Pitched perfect game May

5, 1904, no opposing batsman reaching 1st base."

GROVER CLEVELAND ALEXANDER (1887–1950)
"Great N.L. pitcher for 2 decades with Phillies, Cubs, and Cardinals starting in 1911. Won 1926 World Championship for Cardinals by striking out Lazzeri with bases full in final crisis at Yankee Stadium."

EDWARD T. COLLINS (1887–1951)
Philadelphia-Chicago; Philadelphia, A.L. 1906–1930.
"Famed as batsman, base runner and second baseman and also as field captain. Batted .333 during major league career, 2nd only to Ty Cobb in modern base stealing. Made 3,313 hits in 2,826 games."

HENRY L. GEHRIG (1903–1941)
New York Yankees, 1923–1939.
"Holder of more than a score of Major and American League records, including that of playing 2,130 consecutive games. When he retired in 1939, he had a lifetime batting average of 340."

WILLIE KEELER (1872–1923)
"Hit 'em where they ain't!"
"Baseball's greatest place-hitter; best bunter. Big league career 1892 to 1910 with N.Y. Giants, Baltimore Orioles, Brooklyn Superbas, N.Y. Highlanders. National League batting champion '97–'98."

GEORGE H. SISLER (1893–1973)
St. Louis-Washington, A.L.; Boston, N.L. 1915–1930.
"Holds 2 American League records, making 257 hits in 1920 and batting .419 in 1922. Retired with Major League average of .341. Credited with being one of best 2 fielding 1st basemen in history of game."

ROGERS HORNSBY (1896–1963)
"National League batting champion 7 years —1920 to 1925; 1928. Lifetime batting average .358 highest in National League history. Hit .424 in 1924, 20th-century Major League record. Manager 1926 World Champions St. Louis Cardinals. Most Valuable Player 1925 and 1929."

JOSHUA (JOSH) GIBSON (1911–1947)
Negro Leagues 1930–1946
"Considered greatest slugger in Negro Baseball Leagues. Power-hitting catcher who hit almost 800 home runs in League and independent baseball during his 17-year career. Credited with having been Negro National League Batting Champion in 1936–38–42–45."

A Short Selection from the American Bowling Congress Hall of Fame

DONALD JAMES (BOSCO) CARTER
Miami, Fla.

Carter became the 1st star to win a "grand slam" of bowling's match game titles when he won the All-Star, World's Invitational, PBA National championship, and the 1961 ABC Masters. In 1970 he was voted the "greatest bowler in history" in a poll of veteran writers by Bowling magazine. Carter bowled with some of bowling's most famous teams, starting with the Hermann Undertakers of St. Louis and Ziern Antiques before joining Pfeiffers of Detroit. He bowled 266, 253, 235 in Budweiser's record 3858 series in 1958. In ABC tournament competition, he has a 22-year average of 201 and was a member of 3 championship teams. He has a 337-game average of 208 in Masters play. His 20 championships include 6 Professional Bowlers Association titles. He has 5 800 series; the highest is 824. He has 13 sanctioned 300 games and 5 sanctioned 299 games. Leg and knee ailments have limited his tournament play in recent years. Carter was the 1st president of the Professional Bowlers Association.

EDWARD P. (NED) DAY   Milwaukee, Wis.

One of the game's great stylists, Day was one of the 1st to make extensive exhibition and match game tours. He was also one of the 1st to perform in film shorts produced by Pete Smith in Hollywood. He was noted as a great instructor. A member of the champion Heil Products team in Milwaukee, he later bowled more than a decade with top Chicago teams. He was a member of the Falstaff team that captured the 1956 ABC tournament championship. He was 1st in all events in the 1948 ABC. He won 10 other tournament titles, including the 1943 Petersen Classic. After going into virtual retirement in the late 1950s, he won the nationally televised Championship Bowling tournament filmed in Toledo in 1959.

EDWARD ANTHONY LUBANSKI
Detroit, Mich.

Lubanski became the 2nd man to win 3 ABC titles in one tournament when he bowled with the champion Pfeiffer team in 1959, and also won singles and all events. He has the highest lifetime ABC tournament average ever compiled, 204 for 25 years. Formerly a pitcher in the St. Louis Browns' farm system, he won 23 games for Wausau in the Wisconsin State League in 1947, a record that stood until the circuit folded in 1953. Quitting baseball at the age of 21, he joined Ed (Sarge) Easter (then 67 years old) as the youngest-oldest duo ever crowned national doubles champions. For many years Lubanski was one of the few top stars still using a 2-finger ball. He won the Central States and Michigan State all events and 7 other titles, most of them in the Midwest. He bowled 2 800 series and 11 sanctioned 300 games.

ENRICO (HANK) MARINO
Los Angeles, Calif.

Born in Palermo, Sicily, he came to Chicago with his parents when he was 11 years old. He became a star in Chicago before moving to Milwaukee in 1930, where he operated a bowling establishment until retiring in 1965. He also operated the Llo-de-Mar bowling center in Santa Monica, Calif., for several years with Ned Day and movie comedian Harold Lloyd. He was elected "bowler of the half century" in 1951. Known for his concentration and ability to solve lane conditions, he bowled 11 sanctioned 300 games and 5 800 series, including an 833. He appeared in the ABC tournament 57 years in a row, winning the 1916 doubles. He won the 1925 Petersen Fall Classic and Bowling Proprietors Association individual match title in 1935.

ANDREW VARIPAPA   Hempstead, N.Y.

Varipapa, a leading instructor and exhibition bowler, was one of the 1st bowlers to make nationwide tours. An expert trick-shot artist,

he starred in the 1st bowling film short, *Strikes and Spares*, in 1934, and later made many other such films. His trick shots have often overshadowed his competitive bowling, but he has an impressive list of achievements in tournaments. He won the 1946–1947 national All-Star at the age of 55 and won it again the following year, the 1st bowler to repeat as All-Star champion. He broke the Phillies Jackpot on national television in 1959 to win $6,000 for 9 strikes in a row. When at the age of 78 he developed a painful wrist and arm ailment that prevented his bowling right-handed, he took up bowling left-handed and within 18 months was averaging 180. Although he has bowled numerous perfect games in exhibitions, he has had only one sanctioned 300.

RICHARD ANTHONY WEBER   St. Louis, Mo.

Weber has the distinction of being the leading tournament moneywinner of all time, amassing a total of more than $500,000 during 20 years of topflight play on the Professional Bowlers Association tour. He has won more PBA titles—24—than anyone else. His career in big-time bowling was launched in 1955 when the St. Louis Budweisers signed him while he was employed as a struggling postal clerk in Indianapolis. He proved an immediate success as anchorman of the famous lineup that included Don Carter, Ray Bluth, Pat Patterson, Tom Hennessey, and Whitey Harris. Weber bowled 258, 258, 259 in Budweisers' record 3858 series in 1958. He was a member of the Carter Gloves team that won the 1962 ABC Classic team title. He is known for his ability to adjust or correct his delivery at the foul line.

A Short Selection from the Women's International Bowling Congress Hall of Fame

MARION LADEWIG   Grand Rapids, Mich.

Winner of 2 WIBC tournament all-events championships, in 1950 and 1955, one team title in 1950, and one doubles crown in 1955, she was named the national's Woman Bowler of the Year 9 times. She won 8 national All-Star titles and 4 World Invitationals, including both championships in 1963. She was runner-up in the 1962 WIBC Queens tournament. She had a league average of 204 in 1952–1953. The only woman in the Grand Rapids sports Hall of Fame, she was named Michigan's "woman athlete of all time" and is a member of the State's athletic Hall of

Fame, the only bowler and 1st woman accorded the honor.

MERLE MATTHEWS
Huntington Beach, Calif.

She won 3 WIBC tournament championships —the 1948 doubles and 1962 and 1963 team. She captured the 1948 national All-Star and was a member of 4 California State team titlists, 2 all events, one singles and one doubles. She possesses 11 Los Angeles team championships, 3 all events, one singles and one doubles. Named Southern California Woman Bowler of the Year in 1950 and 1958, she was the 1st woman to be selected for the Southern California bowling Hall of Fame.

BEVERLY ORTNER　　Tucson, Ariz.

She rolled the 1st WIBC sanctioned 800 3-game series, 818, on games of 267, 264, and 287. She averaged 206 in 1967–1968, 205 in 2 leagues during 1968–1969, bowled a 300 game and 22 other 3-game series above 700. Winner of several State and local championships in her native Iowa, she was a member of the 1969 WIBC team champions.

—J.S.

A Short Selection from the College Football Hall of Fame

SAMUEL BAUGH　　Texas Christian

Slingin' Sammy Baugh owned one of the great passing arms of all time. Spinning 30 and 40 passes a game, he gained almost 2 mi. through the air for the Horned Frogs and passed them to 2 Bowl triumphs during his 3 varsity seasons.

CHARLES BEDNARIK　　Pennsylvania

In 1969, a panel of football experts named Chuck Bednarik the greatest center of all time. Entering Penn after 30 combat missions as an aerial gunner in W.W. II, Chuck eschewed specialization and went both ways—offensive center and defensive linebacker. His Quakers had an undefeated season in 1947 and won 24 of 27 while he played.

ALBERT BOOTH　　Yale

"Little Boy Blue" may have been the most exciting of them all. In a storybook upset, Albie came off the bench in the 2nd quarter of Yale's duel with the Red Cagle-led Army team in 1929 and put on a show that Old Blues still brag about. Calling all the plays, he ran for 2 quick touchdowns and kicked the PATs that overcame Army's 13–0 lead. Then he caught a punt and threaded his way through every soldier on the field—70 yds. for the game-winning TD. He was only a sophomore.

JAMES CROWLEY, ELMER F. LAYDEN, HARRY STUHLDREHER, DON C. MILLER　　Notre Dame

Sportswriter Grantland Rice christened them the Four Horsemen. Not one of them weighed more than 170 lbs., but each could run and pass and they worked their tricky shifts, multiple exchanges, spins and laterals with the versatility of acrobats. In their final game together and one of their greatest, the Four Horsemen, behind the Seven Mules, met Stanford in the 1925 Rose Bowl for the national championship. The Indians' Ernie Nevers put on a powerful display but had 2 flat passes intercepted by Layden and run back for touchdowns. The Mules stopped Nevers inches short of the goal in the 4th quarter on a still-disputed call and Notre Dame went on to win 27–10.

GEORGE GIPP　　Notre Dame

Perhaps George Gipp's greatest day in football came after his death, even though he had many during his fantastic playing career. In 1928, a weak Irish team was being stopped by Army. During halftime, Knute Rockne told the team that Gipp had made 2 deathbed requests: to join the Catholic faith and that when the odds were going against the team and all seemed lost, for Rockne to ask them to "win one for the Gipper." This was the game, Rockne said. Notre Dame won 12–6.

OTTO GRAHAM　　Northwestern

In 1942, Otto set a Big Ten passing record with 89 completions in 182 tries and in 1943 he almost singlehandedly whipped Wisconsin by scoring 4 touchdowns, passing to a 5th and kicking 3 PATs. He scored on a run of 97 yards to help the College All Stars beat the Washington Redskins 27–7 in his final collegiate appearance.

HAROLD E. (RED) GRANGE　　Illinois

On October 18, 1924, halfback Red Grange became known as the Galloping Ghost when he raced for 4 touchdowns in 12 minutes in the opening quarter of a game against Michigan. He made the 4 touchdowns the 1st 4 times he handled the ball, returning 2 kickoffs 95 and 67 yds., a punt 56 yards and bursting through scrimmage for a 44-yd. romp. Taken out, he returned in the 4th quarter, ran 12 yds. for his 5th TD and passed 18 yds. for his last one. The orange 77 that adorned his jersey was retired after his final game.

THOMAS D. HARMON　　Michigan

Old Number 98 was a superstar comparable to Red Grange. He averaged just less than 6 yds. per carry in his 3 years at Ann Arbor, led the nation in rushing *and* passing in 1939 and 1940. As tailback in Fritz Crisler's tricky single wing, Harmon specialized in spectacular long runs and in one game against California he scored on jaunts of 94, 86, 80 and 72 yds.

W. W. (PUDGE) HEFFELFINGER   Yale

Pudge was named to football's 1st All American team in 1889 and didn't put down his cleats until 50 years later. He is everyone's guard on every all-time team. He used a unique stand-up style and was the 1st guard to pull out of the line to lead interference on end runs. As a freshman against Princeton in the championship game, Heff broke up the inexorable Tiger wedge play by balling himself up and hurling himself through the air at the apex man.

WILBUR F. (FATS) HENRY
Washington & Jefferson

It is believed that Fats Henry may have blocked more punts than any man in history. The chunky tackle actually took a punt off the kicker's foot and ran it for a TD in one game. As a punter, his deep, arcing kicks pushed rivals back to their own goals time after time.

WILLIAM M. HESTON   Michigan

Michigan never lost a game while Willie Heston played for them in 1902–1904. The swift halfback led the Fielding (Hurry Up) Yost-coached Wolverines to 43 wins and one tie and spearheaded an offense so potent it earned the title "point-a-minute." Heston scored 93 touchdowns in his college career; one of the most famous was a naked reverse that broke open the 1902 Rose Bowl game against Stanford, which Michigan went on to win 49–0.

ALVIN (BO) MCMILLIN   Centre College

Tiny, unknown Centre College, of Danville, Ky., faced invincible Harvard in 1921. With the game deadlocked in the 3rd period, the quarterback of Centre's Praying Colonels, Bo McMillin, unleashed a 32-yard reverse run that brought down Harvard 6–0, a feat which an AP poll voted "the biggest upset of a half century."

HAROLD (BRICK) MULLER   California

A prime mover of Andy Smith's "Wonder Team" of 1920, end Brick Muller led his mates to a victory over the undefeated and untied Ohio State squad in the 1921 Rose Bowl and helped establish West Coast football when he took a lateral and heaved a celebrated 53-yard touchdown pass that broke the Buckeyes' back. He was the 1st player from the Far West to make the All American team (1921–1922).

BRONKO NAGURSKI   Minnesota

He has been called the strongest man who ever played the game. A devastating fullback, some say he was even better at tackle, which he also played for the Gophers. He led the 1934 Minnesota team to 8 straight wins and helped them run up 270 points to 38 for their opponents.

ERNEST A. NEVERS   Stanford

Stanford had not beaten California in 8 tries when Ernie Nevers led the Indians onto the field in 1925. The big fullback handled the ball on every play except 3 and Stanford upset the Bears in the Big Game 27–14.

PATRICK J. O'DEA   Wisconsin

The kicking feats of this legendary Human Kangaroo seem like something out of a Walt Disney movie. A rugby trickster from Australia, Pat O'Dea could curve an 85-yd. punt and drop it in your hat. He recorded a punt of 110 yds., with the wind. He could drop-kick 50 yds. straight through the uprights and boom 60-yd. kicks from a dead run. Against Minnesota in 1899, he caught a punt, dodged a flying tackle and punted the ball back, straight through the goal posts 60 yds. away. The trick broke the Gophers' spirit.

ARTHUR POE   Princeton

Arthur Poe was the most renowned of a famous football family—the Poes of Princeton—and a grandnephew of the poet, Edgar Allan Poe. The 150-lb. end ruined Yale in 1898 when he picked up a fumble and scooted 95 yds. for the only score of the game and destroyed Eli hopes again in 1899 by drop-kicking a last-gasp field goal to give the Tigers a squeaky 11–10 win. It was the 1st drop kick he had ever attempted.

JAMES THORPE   Carlisle Indian School

Named the greatest male athlete of the 1st 50 years of the century, Jim Thorpe played many great games for the tiny Carlisle Indian School in Pennsylvania in the 1908, 1911–1912 seasons. Against Dickinson, he racked up 17 points in 17 minutes. In one of his most memorable games, crippled though he was by a badly sprained ankle, Thorpe played almost the entire game against hated rival Harvard in 1911 and booted 4 field goals with the injured leg, one a 48-yarder, in leading Carlisle to an 18–15 victory.

—M.H.

History of the Olympic Games

THE ANCIENT GREEK GAMES

On the west coast of Greece, 10 mi. from the sea, rises a broad, fertile plain. High mountains covered with pine, oak, and olive trees surround the plain. Where the Alpheus, and its northern tributary, the Cladeus, flow together in the valley lies Olympia, the site of many ancient religious ceremonies. The Temple of Hera, goddess of the seasons, was probably the oldest place of worship at Olympia. The most famous site was Altis, the sacred grove of Zeus, in the center of Olympia.

The origin of the Greek games held at Olympia is steeped in myth, but it seems certain that some form of athletic contest took place for centuries before their recorded beginning date of 776 B.C. One myth suggests that Zeus and Kronos fought for possession of the earth in the mountains surrounding Olympus. When Zeus was the victor, celebration games were held below in the valley. Pindar the poet tells the legend of Pelops, who won the hand of Hippodamia as his bride on the site of Olympia. According to legend, King Oenomaus, father of Hippodamia, had decreed that no suitor would be allowed to marry his daughter unless he could escape with her in a chariot. Oenomaus had succeeded in overtaking 13 previous suitors, and, by the terms of the race, they were slain by his poisoned spear. Using guile, however, Pelops convinced Oenomaus's charioteer to remove the axle pins from his master's vehicle, causing the king to die when his chariot crashed. Pelops instituted the Olympic games in honor of his victory.

In a later account, Iphetus, King of Elis, and Lycurgus, the Spartan lawgiver, wished to bring peace to the war-torn Peloponnesus. Iphetus consulted the oracle at Delphi, and was told that Zeus was angered because the games had been so long neglected. Thereafter, around 820 B.C., the games were supposed to have been restored, and the names of Iphetus and Lycurgus inscribed on a bronze discus which, according to a record of the 2nd century, A.D., hung in the Temple of Hera.

The 1st recorded game took place in 776 B.C. with one event, a one-stade (the length of the stadium) race. Coeroebus, a cook for the local town of Elis, won the race. Thereafter, for nearly 1,200 years, Olympic contests were held every 4 years at the site.

Men came from all over Greece to compete. Foot races of one stade, 2 stades, and 12 or 24 stades, were run. The javelin, discus, boxing, and wrestling events were added later. Many altars, shrines, temples, baths, and several gymnasiums were built for the athletes to worship and train in. The stadium held 45,000 spectators, and later a hippodrome was built for chariot races.

Two of the contests deserve special mention. The pentathlon was a 5-round elimination event including the broad jump, javelin, foot race, discus, and wrestling. Aristotle (who was scornful of the one-sided development of the boxers and wrestlers) offered high praise to the beautifully proportioned physiques of the pentathlon athletes. The Greek idea of manly beauty was embodied in their athletes. Physical perfection, according to one source, was an ideal to be sought after, even more than friendship.

The pancratium was a quite different contest: a fight-to-the-finish battle combining boxing and wrestling. Only eye-gouging and biting were prohibited. A winner was proclaimed when either of the contestants lay unconscious or one held up his hand in defeat. Any infractions of the rules were punished by fines, disqualification, banishment, or a whack by a stout stick. The judges (one in the beginning and later up to 10) were, by all accounts, fair and impartial.

The original inspiration behind the games seems to have been religious, although other historians believe that they were intended to keep soldiers in practice for war. Others think they were always largely secular. Until the last 400 years of the ancient games, all of the contestants had to take an oath that they were freeborn Greek citizens, and that they (and their close relatives) were under no suspicion of criminal offense or sacrilege. Athletes participated in a ritual with priests at the beginning of the games, sacrificing a pig to Zeus and a black ram to Pelops.

For the period surrounding the duration of the games (one day in early years, up to 5 days in later games) a one-month truce was declared throughout Greece where no fighting was permitted among the city-states. Everyone who wished to attend the games was guaranteed safe passage. Evidently, the truce was strictly enforced, especially around Olympia. Spectators and contestants were required to leave off their armaments before entering the games. The period of truce, unfortunately, has not been preserved in the modern revival of the games.

Married women were not allowed to compete or watch. Virgins, however, participated in a separate series of games which, according to legend, Hippodamia began in gratitude to Hera for her marriage to Pelops; these games were probably older than the actual Olympic games. If a woman appeared as a spectator at the Olympic games, the penalty was to be thrown off a nearby cliff. One woman, Pherenice of Rhodes, from an illustrious family of Olympic victors, braved the games. Her son, Pisidores, had been training with his father for a boxing event, but at her husband's death, Pherenice oversaw his training. On the day of the contest, she disguised herself as a trainer and eagerly watched her son's struggle. When he won, she rushed out to embrace him, and her robe slipped, exposing her as a woman. Because she came from a great athletic family, the judge spared her life—provided she didn't show up again. Later, women were allowed to be spectators, to enter chariots in the races, and, eventually, to compete in the chariot races.

Olympic contestants were required to train very diligently. They ate very little in the morning—fermented bread, or cheese, and water—and trained all day without rest. The evening meal, however, was substantial—6½ lbs. of meat was an ordinary meal for some of the he-men athletes. Milo of Croton in the 6th century B.C. was the greatest Olympic victor. He won the wrestling crown 6 times and was never defeated. He was equally well-known for his eating and his tricks. A typical meal for Milo included 7 lbs. of meat, 7 lbs. of bread, and 4–5 quarts of wine. Milo supposedly consumed a whole 4-year-old bull one day at Olympia. One of Milo's feats was to hold a pomegranate in his hand so tightly that no one could open his fist, yet so gently not one drop of juice was squeezed from the fruit. He would also tie cords around his forehead and hold his breath until his veins popped out, bursting the cords. Another of Milo's tricks was his undoing. Wandering in the forest, he noticed a tree had been cut with an ax. Wedges of wood had been placed in the cuts, and Milo attempted to widen the cuts with his bare hands. Unfortunately, his hands got stuck in the tree and there he stayed, until a pack of hungry wolves devoured him.

The inhabitants of the hometown of an Olympic victor would break a hole in their defensive wall when the athlete returned. The rationale behind this ritual was that with such a famous champion in the town, there was no need for fortification against the enemy. Poems were written to the victors, statues made of them (some of which went permanently on display at Olympia), vase paintings depicted their contests, and their exploits were sung by choirs of youths. They were sometimes worshiped after death like minor gods. Losers, however, were greeted by scorn. Cheaters were considered to have offended Zeus, and fared even worse.

They were fined and the money went to build "Zanes" or statues of Zeus near the stadium which bore the name of the offender and his offense—warnings to future athletes.

The Olympic Games reached their height in the 5th–4th centuries B.C., and their decline coincided with the decline of Greek supremacy and the rise of the Roman Empire. Aristophanes observed that Greek youths were no longer interested in their sports—they had deserted the gymnasiums, were pale-faced and narrow-chested. The large cities began to hire professional athletes, many of whom were not native Greeks but swiftly nationalized to comply with the rules. One of the most outrageous farces took place when the Roman Emperor Nero arrived at the games in 66 A.D. with 5,000 bodyguards and hangers-on. He entered several events and invented some others on the spot. During the chariot race, Nero lost his mount, but his rivals stopped the race until he got back on. Needless to say, Nero was pronounced victor of all the events he entered.

In 388 A.D., the 291st Olympiad took place with the last recorded victor being Prince Varastades, later King of Armenia, who won the boxing event. Six years later, Emperor Theodosius I, a Christian, abolished the games because they were a pagan spectacle. Barbarians looted the site, earthquakes and fire destroyed some buildings, and Theodosious II ordered the rest of the temples leveled. Finally, the Cladeus River changed course and covered the valley with silt. Few would hear about Olympia and her games for 1,500 years.

THE 1ST MODERN OLYMPICS, ATHENS, GREECE, 1896

Attempts were made to revive the Olympics in Athens in 1859 and 1870. These games were well attended but it was the initiative of a young Frenchman, Baron Pierre de Coubertin (smarting at his country's defeat by Prussia in 1870 because the French had gone soft), which created the modern Olympics. Interested in physical education and scornful of its absence in French schools, the baron visited the Olympic site and his interest grew, culminating in the suggestion, at a meeting of the Athletic Sports Union in Paris, that the ancient Olympic games be revived. In 1894, 13 countries met to plan the 1st modern Olympiad; all agreed upon Athens in 1896.

The Greek Government was short on money, but a private donation of $184,000 from a wealthy Greek merchant, George Averoff, helped rebuild the stadium. Track and field events were considered to be the heart of the games and inspired the most interest. Greece had the largest number of competitors, but was without a track or field winner going into the marathon finale.

The marathon race of about 25 mi. had not been part of the ancient games, but it was added, at a Frenchman's suggestion, to commemorate the run by the soldier-Olympic star Pheidippides between Marathon and Athens to announce the Athenian victory over the Persians. His message was brief: "Rejoice, we conquer." Then he dropped dead.

The Greeks had expected to win the discus, a classic event. Robert Garrett had been unable to obtain a regular discus at Princeton, but practiced with one fashioned by a friend. In Athens, a friendly Greek lent him a real discus and Garrett found, to his delight, that the disk was much lighter and more aerodynamically sound than his homemade one.

To the dismay of the Greeks, Garrett won the discus throw. A local writer, however, took pains to point out that the 2 Greek favorites had thrown with much better form.

The host nation desperately wanted a marathon winner. George Averoff, who had financed the stadium, offered 100,000 drachmas and his daughter's hand in marriage to any Greek who won the race. A barber and tailor offered to shave and clothe a Greek winner for life and the owner of a chocolate factory promised 2,000 lbs. of chocolate.

Spiridon Loues, a water carrier and devoutly religious man, prepared for the race by praying for 2 nights and fasting the day before. Greek spectators were disappointed when a Frenchman—and later Edwin Flack, an Australian representing the London Athletic Club—took the lead. Undaunted, Loues kept his pace steady; some claim he even stopped to drink wine, but considering what spirits would have done to his stomach, that's highly unlikely.

Midway in the race an American, Arthur Blake, was leading, but he had never trained for such a long race and soon collapsed. Loues took the lead. As their countryman entered the stadium, the Greek crowd went wild. Women tore off jewels to throw at his feet. Greek Princes Constantine and George ran down from their seats and accompanied Loues on his last lap to the finish line.

Since he was married, Spiridon did not take up the nuptial offer, but some say he did accept 365 free meals and free shoe polishing for life. He was given a field, thereafter called "the Field of Marathon." King George I of Greece told Loues he could have anything he wanted. The only thing the water carrier would accept was a cart and horse, so he wouldn't have to run after his mule any longer. Later, when life was hard, Loues wished he had asked for more.

After the games, King George gave a breakfast party for all the Olympic participants.

PARIS, FRANCE, 1900

The next Olympics were held as a sidelight to the French International Exposition in Paris. French politicians got control and almost ruined the games. Some of the events were scheduled for Sunday and many of the best U.S. athletes from Princeton, Pennsylvania, and Syracuse, with their Puritan heritage, refused to compete on the Sabbath. Europeans were amazed at this attitude; to them, Sunday was the perfect day for sporting divertissements. Americans nevertheless took 17 of the 23 track and field events, with sprinter Alvin Kraenzlein and jumper Ray Ewry collecting 7 gold medals between them. The French outscored other nations, although team victories have always been unofficial. The International Olympic Committee (IOC) frowns on keeping team scores.

The field at the Bois de Boulogne, in Paris, was ideal for picnics but no place to run a race because there was no cinder track. The best throws by discus and hammer competitors landed in a grove of picturesque trees. Michel Theato, a French bread delivery man, won the marathon; some suspected he knew the road so well from his deliveries that he took a few shortcuts.

St. LOUIS, MO., U.S., 1904

The 3rd Olympics in 1904 was also staged with a world's fair: the St. Louis Exposition. Interest centered again on the marathon. Felix Carvajal, a Cuban postman, raised money for passage by running around Havana's public square, but in New Orleans, the story goes, he lost his funds in a dice game. He worked and hitchhiked his way to St. Louis where a group of U.S. weightlifters, amused and touched by his plight, shared their food and lodging with the small Cuban. Carvajal went to the marathon starting line in trousers, long-sleeved shirt, and street shoes; but an American, concerned about the August heat, clipped off his sleeves and pants legs.

Fred Lorz, an American, was the early marathon leader but his pace forced him to the sidelines by the halfway mark. He waved at passing runners and accepted a lift in a truck which soon overtook the competitors. About 5 mi. from the finish, the vehicle broke down and Lorz, now rested, decided to jog to keep his muscles loose. When he arrived at the stadium the crowd cheered. Lorz decided to play along with the hoax, which ended just before presentation of the cup when he confessed that he had ridden part of the way. Only fellow runners' support that they knew he was playing a joke saved Lorz from lifetime suspension.

The St. Louis heat finished off many contestants. Thomas Hicks, of Boston, reached the stadium near collapse but his trainers administered a strychnine shot (then not illegal) and he became the winner. Carvajal, who led once, had stopped to pick and eat some green apples, suffered cramps, and lay down awhile but still came in 4th.

Few European countries could afford to send athletes all the way to St. Louis, so only 10 foreign countries were represented in the games. U.S. athletes dominated. Pygmies and Kaffirs from Africa, Moros and Igorots from the Philippines, and American Indians competed in a series of events, including a mud fight and pole climb, called "Anthropology Day."

The Greeks had been clamoring to have the games in Athens rather than at different sites. De Coubertin, despairing of the poorly attended French games and American-dominated St. Louis games, suggested separate events at Athens. The Greeks welcomed the idea and staged them, but only once, in 1906. For the 1st time, an official U.S. Olympic Committee selected an American team whose members, while at sea, suffered several major injuries in rough waters.

Remembering Robert Garrett's unstylish victory of 1896, the Greeks had 2 discus events —freestyle and Greek style—but Werner Jarvinen won the latter, the 1st of many Finnish victories over the years. Greek tradesmen again offered lifetime services for a native-born marathon winner, but Canadian William Sherring, only 115 lbs., won the race.

Austrian weightlifter Josef Steinbach was accused of being a professional and was so jeered when going against the Greek champion that he left the arena. While the Greek was being honored as 2-hand winner, Steinbach came back and, with exaggerated ease, raised the weight, barely lifted by the Greek, over his head 3 times. The next day, he won the one-hand lifting competition before a subdued audience.

The question of amateur v. professional athletes has plagued Olympic committees, athletes, and sports enthusiasts since the games' ancient origins. De Coubertin insisted, and was supported by others on the original committee, that the Olympics be free of professionalism and commercialism. Rules require competitors to sign a statement that they have never been paid for playing or coaching sports, and do not intend to become professionals. Avery Brundage, longtime U.S. Olympic official, espoused strict amateurism in the face of criticism that the costs of constant training, necessary to win at the Olympics, means that athletes must find some kind of subsidy—whether state-paid token jobs, as in the Soviet Union, or athletic scholarships, as in the U.S. By the spirit, if not by the law, very few Olympic competitors could technically qualify as amateurs since there are time limits on the amount of training, and limitations on gifts.

Another philosophical issue is team scoring and its inherent nationalism. The IOC has always tried to keep nationalism to a minimum in favor of individual achievement. Team scoring is unofficial, not sanctioned by the IOC. But teams, spectators, and the press (and sometimes even officials) encourage nationalism. Major powers have often used the success of their Olympic athletes as fuel for their rivalries.

LONDON, ENGLAND, 1908

The 1908 Olympics were originally awarded to Rome, but because the Italian Government was not financially able to stage them, they were transferred to London. The track and stadium were well prepared and, despite steady rain, huge crowds came to see what was by now a world event. From the beginning there was friction between participants and British officials. In the opening parade, the British neglected to provide American and Swedish flags; and the Finns, under Russian rule, refused to carry the Russian flag. Some top Irish athletes quit, refusing to represent Great Britain. British officials and judges seemed to take a chauvinistic interest in their athletes and a hard line against U.S. athletes, some of whom were of Irish descent.

British-American antagonism came to a head in the 400-m. run. Three Americans and one Briton, Wyndham Halswelle, were the finalists. In the last 100 yards of a close race, U.S. runner J. C. Carpenter took a wide turn into Halswelle's lane and opened up, leaving Halswelle behind. British judges called a foul, disqualified Carpenter, and ruled a rerun among the other 3. Feelings ran so high that the American team almost quit and the 2 U.S. runners refused to run again. Halswelle won in Olympic history's only walkover.

The climax event was the traditional marathon race, which provided another controversy. There were 28 runners who were to run from Windsor Castle 26 mi. to the Olympic stadium, then, before King Edward VII, the Royal Family, and frenzied thousands, to circle the last 385 yards inside the stadium. (The 26 mi., 385 yards standardized the distance for all future Olympics.) The betting favorite was Tom Longboat, an Indian from Canada. The sentimental favorite was Dorando Petri, a wispy middle-aged moustached Italian candy-maker. The U.S. entries included Johnny Hayes, an Irishman who worked for Bloomingdale's Department Store when he wasn't running, Louis Tewanima, who had

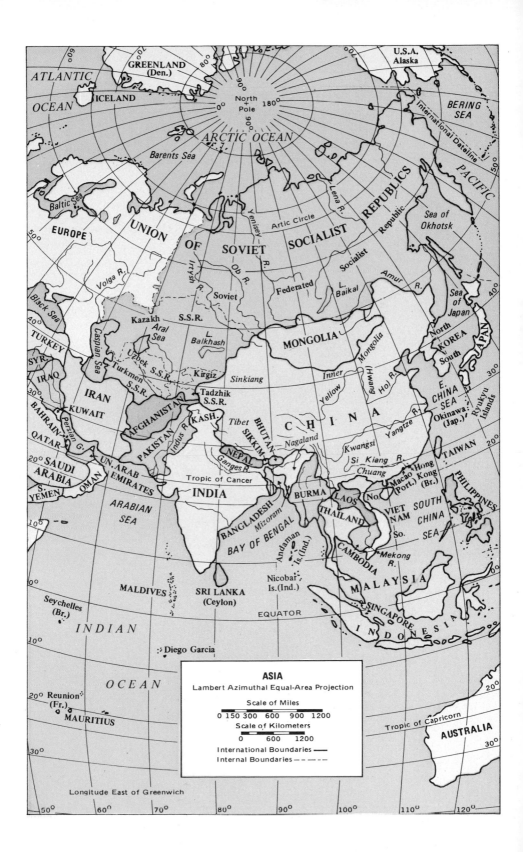

ATLANTIC
OCEAN
ICELAND

GREENLAND
(Den.)

North
Pole
180°

ARCTIC OCEAN

U.S.A.
Alaska

BERING
SEA

International Dateline

PACIFIC

Barents Sea

Baltic Sea

EUROPE

UNION

OF

Volga R.

Irtysh R.

SOVIET

Yenisey

Artic Circle

SOCIALIST

Lena R.

REPUBLICS

Republic

Sea of
Okhotsk

Ob R.

Soviet

Federated

L.
Baikal

Socialist

Amur R.

Sea
of
Japan

Black Sea

Caspian Sea

TURKEY

SYR.

IRAQ

IRAN

Kazakh

Aral
Sea

L.
Balkhash

MONGOLIA

Mongolia

North
KOREA

JAPAN

S.S.R.

Uzbek S.S.R.

Turkmen
S.S.R.

Kirgiz

Sinkiang

Inner

Yellow

Hol R. (Hwang)

South

E.
CHINA
SEA

Ryukyu
Islands

BAHRAIN

KUWAIT

Persian G.

Tadzhik
S.S.R.

Yellow

Yangtze R.

Okinawa
(Jap.)

QATAR

AFGHANISTAN

KASH.

Tibet

BHUTAN

C H I N A

Kwangsi

Yangtze

TAIWAN

SAUDI
ARABIA

UN. ARAB
EMIRATES

PAKISTAN

Indus R.

NEPAL

SIKKIM

Nagaland

Si Kiang R.

Macao Hong
(Port.) Kong
(Br.)

PHILIPPINES

S.
YEMEN

OMAN

Ganges R.

Tropic of Cancer

INDIA

BANGLADESH

BURMA

No.

LAOS

VIET
NAM

SOUTH
CHINA

ARABIAN
SEA

Mizoram

THAILAND

So.

SEA

Andaman
Is.(Ind.)

CAMBODIA

Mekong
R.

MALAYSIA

Seychelles
(Br.)

MALDIVES

BAY OF BENGAL

Nicobar
Is.(Ind.)

SRI LANKA
(Ceylon)

EQUATOR

SINGAPORE

INDONESIA

INDIAN

Diego Garcia

OCEAN

Reunion
(Fr.)

MAURITIUS

Tropic of Capricorn

AUSTRALIA

ASIA

Lambert Azimuthal Equal-Area Projection

Scale of Miles

0 150 300 600 900 1200

Scale of Kilometers

0 600 1200

International Boundaries ⎯⎯⎯

Internal Boundaries ⎯ ⎯ ⎯

Longitude East of Greenwich

MAP
Showing Course of the
TRUELOVE RIVER

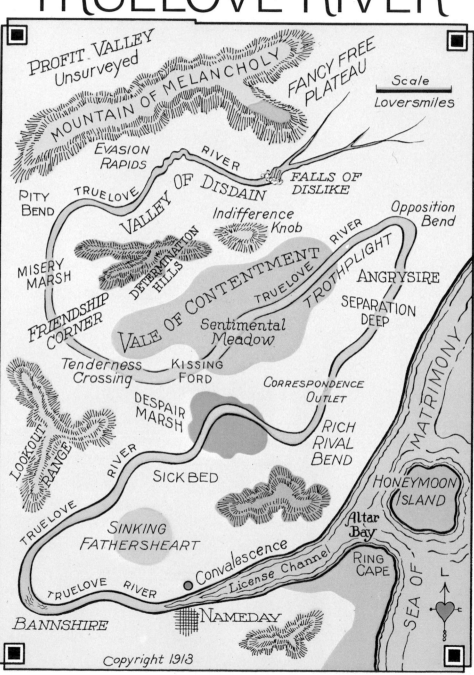

PROFIT VALLEY
Unsurveyed

MOUNTAIN OF MELANCHOLY

FANCY FREE PLATEAU

Scale
Loversmiles

EVASION RAPIDS

RIVER

FALLS OF DISLIKE

PITY BEND

TRUELOVE

VALLEY OF DISDAIN

Indifference Knob

Opposition Bend

MISERY MARSH

DETERMINATION HILLS

VALE OF CONTENTMENT

TRUELOVE RIVER

TROTHPLIGHT

ANGRYSIRE

SEPARATION DEEP

FRIENDSHIP CORNER

Sentimental Meadow

Tenderness Crossing

KISSING FORD

CORRESPONDENCE OUTLET

RICH RIVAL BEND

MATRIMONY

DESPAIR MARSH

Lookout RANGE

RIVER

SICK BED

HONEYMOON ISLAND

TRUELOVE

SINKING FATHERSHEART

Altar Bay

RING CAPE

Convalescence

License Channel

SEA OF

TRUELOVE RIVER

BANNSHIRE

NAMEDAY

Copyright 1913

PUZZLE
THE SECOND EXPEDITION OF THE VESSEL PINTA

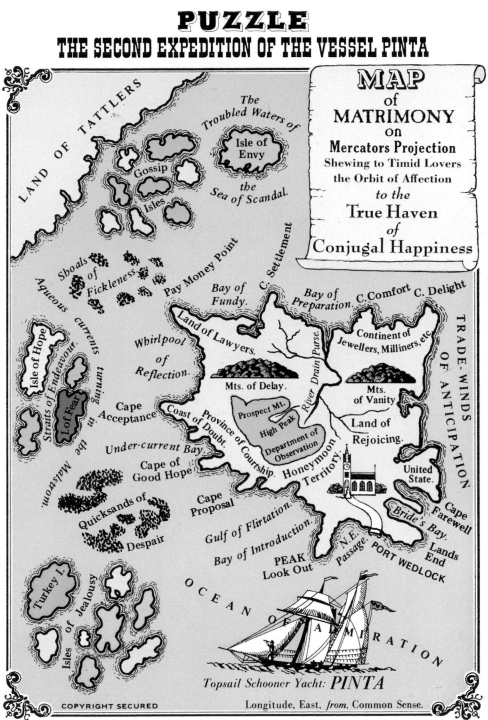

MAP of MATRIMONY on Mercators Projection Shewing to Timid Lovers the Orbit of Affection to the True Haven of Conjugal Happiness

Topsail Schooner Yacht: *PINTA*

Longitude, East, *from*, Common Sense.

If the Candidate for **Port Wedlock** now starting from Peak Look-out on board the Vessel Pinta, wishes to be as successful in the navigation of unknown waters as the memorable Hero of the First Expedition proved to be, he can spell out a safe channel by using nine of the initials of the most dangerous obstacles in the Ocean of Admiration and be enabled to arrive safely to join the Bride now awaiting him to lead her to the Altar.

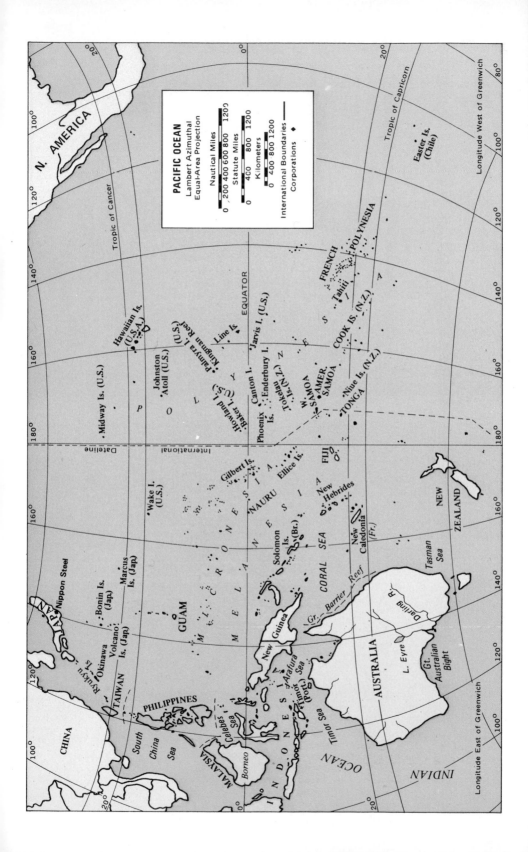

been a roommate of Jim Thorpe's at Carlisle, and a youngster named Forshaw.

Two hours and 50 minutes after the race began, the leading runner appeared in the stadium. He was the frail, dark-haired Italian, Dorando. The audience greeted him with a mighty roar. But it is doubtful if Dorando heard. He had punished himself terribly. He was out on his feet. He started on the last 385 yards amid a great demonstration. Two-thirds of the way around he staggered, collapsed. Four British officials lifted him. He plodded forward. Fifteen yards from the finish he fainted. The officials again lifted him, dragged him across the line. The spectators cheered him as the Olympic victor. Minutes later Johnny Hayes of Bloomingdale's bounced briskly into the stadium, circled it, and finished firmly on his feet. The Americans cheered *him* as the victor. Then came the official announcement. Dorando 1st. Hayes 2nd.

After a protest by Coach Mike Murphy of the U.S., and a bitter argument, Dorando was disqualified and the Olympic medal was awarded to Hayes.

In defeat, Dorando became an international hero. Especially in America, where the cult of the underdog was invoked, Dorando became a household name. In New York there was a Dorando craze. Everyone, it seemed, wanted to see the Great Almost.

So, in December, 1908, he was brought, by promoters, to New York. He was greeted, by press and sport fans, as a conquering hero. Irving Berlin wrote a song, *Run, Run, You Son of a Gun, Dorando*. Willie Hammerstein contracted Dorando to appear on the stage of his topical vaudeville house, the Victoria, at Broadway and 42nd. On the same stage Hammerstein was presenting Jack Johnson, cartoonists Rube Goldberg and Bud Fisher, Sober Sue ("You Can't Make Her Laugh— $1,000 If You Can!"), and the film *The Great Train Robbery*. Daily, Dorando appeared on the Victoria stage. According to one account, "Dorando could not speak a word of English. He simply appeared, in a misfit suit of foreign clothes, gawky and ill at ease, while Loney Haskell went into his lecture."

To see Dorando on the stage, in the streets, in the press, was not enough. New York wanted to see him run. So Dorando turned professional, and met Tom Longboat in a special match race in the old Madison Square Garden. It was a sellout. Longboat set a fast pace from the opening gun, then Dorando stepped in front. With the tape a half mile away, Longboat caught Dorando. They matched it stride for stride, but Dorando couldn't make it. He broke, wobbled, fell unconscious from exhaustion. Longboat was the winner. Three weeks later, in Buffalo, Dorando ran against Longboat again. This time he permitted Longboat to get far out in front, then set out to catch him. After 18 mi., Dorando fell to his knees in defeat.

He returned to New York, found the big town was too busy for him. He went home to Italy, richer, to receive a belated hero's welcome. After a few years he drifted into obscurity, only to be resurrected by Mussolini. He was given a pension to discover marathon runners who would win for a new Italy. He worked with Boyd Comstock, the University of Southern California pole-vaulter, who was a coach under *Il Duce*. He bought a hotel in San Remo, slept in a room papered with photographs of himself and 1908–1909 clippings from New York papers, and became Italy's foremost sport legend.

STOCKHOLM, SWEDEN, 1912

The tactful, friendly, and fair handling of the events by the Swedes in Stockholm did much to dispel the enmity created 4 years earlier by the British. For the 1st time, an electrical timing device, public address system, and photo-finish camera were used.

The hero of these games was Jim Thorpe, the half Sac-Fox Indian, half Irish athlete from Carlisle Indian School, who had led his football team to victories over Ivy League colleges, Syracuse, Navy, and Nebraska, and been almost a one man track team, winning 6 events in a victory over previously undefeated Lafayette.

There was no question that Bright Path (Thorpe's Indian name) would train for the Olympics; the question was, for which events? He decided on the pentathlon and decathlon, the 5- and 10-event competitions. During the sea voyage, while other athletes ran daily on a cork track on deck, Thorpe dozed in a deck chair. A *New York Evening Mail* reporter asked him, "What are you doing— thinking about your uncle Sitting Bull?" "No," Thorpe replied, "I'm practicing the broad jump. I've just jumped 23'8"." At Stockholm, it was no different. There Thorpe lay in a hammock and dozed.

Mike Murphy, U.S. Olympic coach, complained to Thorpe's Carlisle coach, Glenn (Pop) Warner: "I've seen some queer birds in my day, but your Indian beats all. I don't see him do anything—except sleep!" "Don't worry, Mike," said Warner. "All those 2-for-a-nickel events you've got lined up for Thorpe won't bother him. He's in shape. What with football, lacrosse, baseball, and track back at school, how could he be out of shape? This sleeping is the best training ever—for Jim."

Thorpe was the easy victor in both his chosen events, scoring twice as many points as his nearest pentathlon rival and breezing to the decathlon title. Legend has it that King Gustav V asked for an official visit to congratulate Thorpe, but the Indian claimed he was engaged in weight lifting and begged not to be disturbed. What he was lifting was tankards of Swedish beer. Gustav did meet Thorpe, finally, to present a bronze bust of himself for the decathlon win, and a jeweled Viking ship model for his pentathlon victory.

Later, a Boston newspaper disclosed that Jim had played semipro baseball in 1909. Thorpe admitted accepting a small amount, pleading that at the time he had been ignorant that this would endanger his amateur status. The IOC, however, felt the infraction to be significant and reclaimed Jim's 2 gold medals, and awarded them to the 2nd-place finishers. Thorpe's records were struck from the Olympic books.

Thorpe later played pro football, as well as 8 seasons with the New York Giants baseball team. In 1950, an Associated Press poll of sportswriters named Thorpe the "greatest male athlete" of the 1st half of the century.

Hannes Kolehmainen, "the Flying Finn," won gold medals in the 5,000-m., 10,000-m., and cross-country events of 1912. A brother competed in the 10,000-m. and marathon. The marathon was won by K. K. McArthur, South Africa, ahead of Lewis Tewanima, one of Thorpe's Carlisle teammates. The race was marred by a fatality when Portugal's Lazaro collapsed after 19 mi. and died the next day.

There were 57 women competitors in these games.

In the 800-m. race, 4 U.S. finalists plotted against their main threat, fast-finishing Hans Braun of Germany. Teen-ager Ted Meredith agreed to force the early pace to wear Braun out and allow one of his teammates to win; but Meredith did not fade, and instead won the gold medal, as 3 Americans broke the world record ahead of Braun.

Surprise shot-put victor was Pat McDonald, a policeman who directed traffic at Times Square, well-known for stopping traffic to escort ladies across the street. The shot-put favorite, 2-time champion Ralph Rose, lost (legend has it) because the event was held in the morning and Rose's trainer had great difficulty getting him out of bed.

ANTWERP, BELGIUM, 1920

No Olympics were held in 1916, due to the war. In 1920, the defeated nations—Germany, Austria, Bulgaria, Hungary, and Turkey—were not invited. Russia also did not compete—not again until 1952. The American team sailed on the *Princess Matoika*, which had returned U.S. war dead and reeked of formaldehyde. Accommodations were cramped, the athletes sleeping in hammocks deep within the ship. Food was scarce. The only cheerful notes were struck on ukeleles by Duke Kahanamoku and his fellow Hawaiian swimmers, appropriate music for a shipboard romance between Dick Landon of Yale (later a gold-medal high jumper) and diver Alice Lord. Accommodations were no better in Antwerp. When hop-skip-and-jump champion Dan Ahearn's request for a bed instead of a small cot was denied, he sought a hotel room and was thrown off the team for insubordination. Many teammates refused to compete and, despite a fiery speech by Ahearn against capitalistic and aristocratic oppression, he was reinstated and peace was restored.

Although Americans won the unofficial team title, Finland's athletes provided many highlights. This was the Olympic debut of Paavo Nurmi, the Phantom Finn, who at 12 had quit school in order to work following his father's death; at 15 had begun to train after hearing about Hannes Kolehmainen's Olympic victories of 1912. Legend has it that he practiced by racing a mail train through his town.

Paavo's face never showed emotion. One reporter called him "a mechanical Frankenstein, created to annihilate time." He wore a stopwatch and consulted it at the beginning of each lap, to keep his predetermined pace, not caring where other competitors were on the track. His heart beat only 40 times a minute; his favorite food was oatmeal.

Nurmi led most of the 5,000-m. at Antwerp, but was overtaken by Jacques Guillemot, a French veteran who had been badly gassed in the war. The next day, the 2 met in the 3,000-m. race and the tables were turned. Nurmi won a 2nd gold medal and the Finns took 1sts in the discus, javelin, shot-put, hop-step-and-jump, pentathlon, and marathon, Kolehmainen repeating. The U.S. and Finland tied in track and field gold medals.

The American star was Charlie Paddock, "the world's fastest human," with a flying-leap finish in the dashes which was spectacular and disconcerting to rivals.

Navy won 8-oar crew competition and Jack Kelly, a Philadelphia bricklayer, triumphed in single scull rowing and, with his cousin, won the doubles, too. Denied entry in England's Diamond Sculls—"a gentleman's event"—because he worked with his hands, Kelly lived to see his son, John Kelly, Jr., win that event twice, and see his daughter, Grace, give up a film career to marry Prince Rainier III of Monaco.

1ST WINTER OLYMPICS, CHAMONIX, FRANCE, 1924

The 1st Winter Olympics proved successful. Thorlief Haug's 3 gold medals in skiing led Norway's overall victory. Finland's speed skater, Clas Thunberg, took 2 gold medals, and Sweden made a strong showing in figure skating.

PARIS, FRANCE, 1924

The U.S. team members sailed off in a good ship this time and were lodged, upon arrival, at a princely estate, Rocquecourt. They were heroes of a neighboring village after helping put out a local fire.

The Finns again challenged the U.S. in track and field, winning 10 gold medals to the Americans' 12. Paavo Nurmi, with 4 victories, was the star, pursued this time by a countryman, Ville "Willie" Ritola, who ran 7 races in 7 days, winning 2 gold medals and being 2nd to Nurmi 3 times. On July 10, Nurmi won the 1,500- and 5,000-m. events with little more than an hour of rest between races. Albin Stenroos, 40, onetime wrestler, won the marathon.

The Americans were dominant in swimming as Johnny Weissmuller won at 400-m., anchored a winning 800-m. relay team, and defeated Kahanamoku, 2-time champ in the 100-m. freestyle. The Yale crew won 8-oar rowing with Benjamin Spock (later a renowned baby doctor and war protestor) in the 7th seat.

Tennis, a regular Olympic event since 1896, had its last stand. To amateur tennis champions, Wimbledon and Forest Hills meant much more than the Olympics. Bill Tilden, the sport's great star of the '20s, never competed in the Olympics. Ironically, the 1924 games attracted 2 of the best: Helen Wills and Vincent Richards. The U.S. swept all 5 titles.

WINTER OLYMPICS, ST. MORITZ, SWITZERLAND, 1928

The 2nd Winter Olympics saw Norway win the championship again with 6½ 1sts in skiing, speed skating, and figure skating. Sonja Henie, who had made her 1st appearance (as Norwegian champion at the age of 10), in 1924, finishing last, had thereafter practiced ballet and skating 7 hours a day and won the world title in 1927 at 14. She took her 1st gold medal at the 1928 Olympics. Sonja transformed figure skating into an art, adapting Anna Pavlova's "Dying Swan" sequence from *Swan Lake*. After gold medal performances in the 1932 and 1936 Olympics, Sonja retired at the ripe age of 23 to become a professional and make many witless but popular movies. She became the 3rd-biggest box-office draw, behind Shirley Temple and Clark Gable, amassing more wealth than any sports figure has ever done—$47.5 million.

AMSTERDAM, THE NETHERLANDS, 1928

Some said the American track and field athletes were overcoached, overfed, and overconfident. Aboard the U.S.S. *President Roosevelt*, they quickly consumed their allotment of ice cream, some overindulged in a cracker-eating contest, and they dallied away time gambling on Monte Carlo nights. They used play money and when the ship docked, one fellow threw his poker winnings overboard; dockside youngsters, thinking this a new level of tourist extravagance, dove into the water to retrieve the "money."

Except for Percy Williams, a surprising 19-year-old from Vancouver, who won the dashes, the Americans were disappointing. Canadian men and women gave outstanding performances. The Finns, as usual, won all running events over 800-m., Nurmi defending his 10,000-m. title, again finishing ahead of Ritola. However, Willie beat Nurmi at 5,000-m. Some believed Paavo let Willie win, although the latter was strong at this distance and won by a good margin.

For the 1st time in Olympics' history, the U.S. lost the 400-m. hurdles. An Englishman, David George Cecil Brownlow, Lord Burghley, was the victor.

French athletes, refused entry to a practice field where the German team was working out, were outraged—especially when it almost was repeated by the belligerent gatekeeper the next day. Dutch authorities ironed things out just in time.

The marathon was won by an Algerian auto-factory worker, El Ouafi (or "Waffle" as he was to be called), a vegetarian who drank only water and milk. Ouafi was so far behind early in the race that officials thought he had lost his way. A Chilean won 2nd place and was so overjoyed he draped himself in a Chilean flag, then waltzed around the stadium.

Johnny Weissmuller won 2 more gold medals in swimming, Japan scored its 1st victory (hop-skip-and-jump), the University of California took rowing honors, and Uruguay won a 2nd straight soccer championship.

WINTER OLYMPICS, LAKE PLACID, N.Y., U.S., 1932

Seventeen countries entered teams, and while Scandinavians dominated skiing and Canadians triumphed in ice hockey, the Americans swept the medals sweepstakes, mainly because Europeans were not familiar with American rules in speed skating and some other events. Americans even won twice in bobsledding. Eddie Egan, Olympic lightweight boxing champion of 1920, won a bobsled event to become the 1st person to win in both summer and winter games.

Los Angeles, Calif., U.S., 1932

A long-discussed idea came to reality: an Olympic Village of 550 cottages was constructed on 250 acres in a Los Angeles suburb. Male athletes stayed in the village; women in a hotel. The complex included an open-air theater where athletes could see films of the previous day's events. But there were many complaints: political and racial disturbances, fears that training secrets would be stolen, and intrusions into the peace and quiet by the American public. According to Zack Farmer, grizzled ex-cowboy millionaire who organized the 1932 Olympics:

> They said Americans are known as the most undisciplined goddam people in the whole world. Oh, we got privacy for those athletes, all right. We fenced it all in and put cowboys out on riding the fences. Those Europeans used to love to watch those cowboys lassoing any SOB who tried to climb over the fence.

Under Farmer's guidance, the Olympics made a $1,300 profit . . . in a Depression year!

Brazil had no money to spend on its athletes, but 69 of them embarked from Brazil on a naval boat carrying 50,000 bags of coffee. They were to stop in ports along the way and sell the coffee to raise funds, but there were few buyers. When the boat reached Los Angeles, 45 athletes didn't even have the $1-per-head landing charge; sadly, they waved goodbye to the lucky 24 and set off to sell their beans and return home.

Paavo Nurmi was forced out of the games when the IOC decided he was really a professional and had accepted too much "expense money" on a German tour.

By this time, women were coming into their own in Olympic competition, and Mildred "Babe" Didrikson was the premier performer. She started training in 1928 when her father, a Norwegian immigrant, read stories of the Olympics. She played basketball in high school and after graduating, a Dallas insurance company offered her a $75-per-month job as a clerk; a place on the company basketball team went with the job. She was All-American in basketball and won the Women's AAU track championship in Dallas.

At the 1932 National AAU finals in Chicago, the Olympic qualifying event, Babe Didrikson was the sole representative of her team and entered 8 of the 10 events. Babe ran herself ragged that afternoon. At the end, she had won 5 events and 30 points; the 22-woman Illinois Women's Athletic Club was 2nd with 22 points.

Opening day of the '32 Olympics in Los Angeles was a thrill for the Babe, although she was uncomfortable in the regulation white stockings which U.S. women had to wear. She never wore stockings. She threw the javelin 143'4", an Olympic and world record. She then broke the world record in the 80-m. hurdles for another gold medal. In the high jump, she was up against her nemesis, Jean Shirley, whom she had tied in the AAU meet. Both cleared 5'5¼", but officials ruled Babe had dived over the pole instead of jumping feet 1st (a rule later changed). She was disappointed with the silver medal.

After the Olympics, Babe turned professional and took up golf, becoming the greatest woman golfer. She was chosen Woman Athlete of the Year 5 times and Greatest Female Athlete of the half century in an AP poll.

American women took all track and field events at Los Angeles except for the victories of Stella Walasiewicz who, although living in the U.S., ran for her native Poland in 1932 and 1936. Stella Walsh, as she was known in the U.S., was not as brilliant as Babe Didrikson, but she was almost as versatile and more durable in championship competition. She won 40 U.S. and world titles, competing until well after the age of 40.

Eddie Tolan, U.S., won 2 gold medals in the sprints. Janusz Kusocinski, Poland, surprisingly beat the Finns in the 10,000-m. Japanese men and U.S. women dominated swimming. The 400-m. freestyle title went to Buster Crabbe, who became a competitor with Weissmuller for the Tarzan role.

The most colorful participant was probably the Italian cyclist, Attillo Pavesi, who set out on the 2½-hour, 100-km. race well fortified. He carried a bowl of soup and a bucket of water on his handlebars, 12 bananas, buns, sandwiches, and spaghetti in a bib tied around his shoulders, and 2 spare tires around his neck.

Winter Olympics, Garmisch-Partenkirchen, Germany, 1936

The 4th Winter Olympics were held near Munich, amid an enormous number of Nazi military groups, which worried many Americans. Sonja Henie took her 3rd and last figure-skating title; Karl Shafer, Austria, also repeated in men's skating. Miss Henie was one of Hitler's favorites. Norway's Iva Ballangund won 3 gold and one silver medal in speed skating. Teammate Birger Ruud won his 2nd Olympic ski-jumping title and the downhill race. Ruud's 2 brothers, Sigmund and Asbjørn, were also famous ski-jumpers and all 3 were later put in concentration camps for refusing to turn "quisling"—the term derived from Maj. Vidkun Quisling, the Norwegian who collaborated with the Germans in 1940. (See: Roll Call, Chap. 10.)

BERLIN, GERMANY, 1936

A great furor developed in the U.S. over whether the U.S. should participate in the 11th Olympics in Berlin because of the Nazi Government. Avery Brundage, then president of the U.S. Olympic Committee, insisted that the plight of Jews in Germany was of no concern to sportsmen.

Nazi youth at 1st opposed holding the Olympic games. Perhaps the fact that German athletes had not done so well in the 1932 games was behind the German nonparticipation movement. Hitler, however, overcame the opposition and decided to make the games a showcase for Nazism. A huge Olympic Village was built at enormous cost.

The question of discrimination against Jews came to a head when 2 U.S. athletes, Martin Glickman and Sam Stoller, were not permitted to run in the 400-m. relay, being replaced by Jesse Owens and Ralph Metcalfe, excellent black runners. It has been suggested that the reason was that Germany and Italy had shown faster teams than expected. Although the black runners were undoubtedly a bit faster than the American Jews, the tactics used to remove them were questionable. To this day, some believe that Brundage and Dean Cromwell, an assistant coach, made a decision to bow to Nazi pressure to remove the Jewish athletes. Since Owens and the "black auxiliaries" (as one German paper slightingly referred to them) had already won several gold medals, some speculated that U.S. officials thought it would be less embarrassing to the Nazis if blacks, rather than Jews, won the race. It was a painful situation for Glickman and Stoller, the only Jews on the U.S. team and the only Americans who went home without competing in an event.

Jesse Owens was the undisputed star of the 1936 Olympics. He was a beautiful runner with satin-smooth style—a born sprinter. At Ohio State, in a Big Ten Conference meet, he had broken world records in the 100- and 220-yd. dashes and broad jump and tied the 200-m. hurdles mark, all within an hour. Owens was the only track and field competitor to win more than one gold medal at Berlin—he won 4—the 100 in world-record time, the 200, the 400-relay anchor, and the broad jump, with a world mark of 26'5" plus that stood for 24 years.

In the jumping event, Owens was called for fouls in the semifinals and had only one jump left. Lutz Long, a friendly German jumper, advised him to jump from the rear of the board to be safe. Owens did and got into the finals, where he beat the German on his last effort. Long hugged him in admiration, but Hitler—eager to congratulate Long—shunned Owens. Long became a pilot and died in the 1st week of W.W. II; years later Owens, returning to Germany, met Long's widow and son.

Black U.S. athletes won every flat race to 800-m., outscoring all other nations, as well as their own teammates.

The Germans reinstituted the ancient Greek lighting of the torch at the shrine of Zeus at Olympia; then it was carried, relay-style, nearly 2,000 mi. across 7 countries.

Aboard ship, American swim star Eleanor Holms, a 1932 winner, now married, was suspended from the team for drinking champagne, partying and gambling, but made the best of her stay in Berlin:

> It was a *fantastic* Olympics, spectacular! I had such *fun*. You know, athletes don't think much about the politics of it all. . . . Göring was fun. He had a good personality, lots of chuckling. And so did the little one with the clubfoot [Josef Goebbels]. Göring gave me a sterling silver swastika. I had a mold made of it, and I put a diamond Star of David in the middle of it.

Hendrika Mastenbrock, a 17-year-old Dutch woman, won 3 gold medals in swimming.

According to *All That Glitters Is Not Gold* by William O. Johnson, Jr., Dr. Paul Martin of Lausanne, Switzerland, who competed in 5 Olympics as a runner, has related the most amazing story of the '36 games:

> The Olympic athlete in Berlin was elevated to a godlike creature. We were the gods of the stadium. The Germans had even reserved a sort of heavenly forest near the Olympic Village for those gods. And there the prettiest handpicked maidens would offer themselves to the athletes—especially to the good Aryan types. Olympic babies born out of such encounters were cared for by the state. There was every indication that this Woods of Love was a matter of state policy by the Nazis. . . .
> It was interesting that before submitting to the Olympic god of her choice, the girl would request her partner's

Olympic badge. In case of pregnancy, the girl would give this information to the state or Red Cross maternities to prove the Olympic origins of her baby. Then the state would pay for the whole works.

12TH AND 13TH OLYMPICS

The 1940 Olympics was awarded to Tokyo, but due to military involvement with China, Japan did not hold them. The 13th games were to be held in Helsinki, but W.W. II precluded this.

WINTER GAMES, ST. MORITZ, SWITZERLAND, 1948

Germany, Italy, and Japan, the defeated nations in W.W. II, were not invited. These games were marred by fighting, especially between 2 hockey teams vying to represent the U.S. and among the Ligue Internationale Sur Glace, the U.S. Olympic Committee, and the IOC. At 1st, both hockey teams were ruled ineligible, then the American Hockey Association team was permitted to play, but the IOC said it could not receive medals. That proved academic: As expected, Canada won again.

Gretchen Fraser won the slalom and the 1st-ever U.S. medal in skiing. Dick Button, at 18, won men's figure skating.

LONDON, ENGLAND, 1948

England was still on postwar rationing, and the nation did not put on a great spectacle such as last seen in Berlin in 1936. The IOC ruled the new state of Israel could not compete because it was not yet a member of the IOC; this decision averted an Arab walkout. Despite low-key advance publicity, opening ceremonies were impressive with Household Cavalry, Grenadiers, and Highland Scots likened to a DeMille Technicolor opus. Spectators were treated to 3 "superstars."

Czechoslovakia's Emil Zatopek, who trained wearing boots in bad weather and "ran like a man who had been stabbed in the heart," captivated track fans by dueling the favored Viljo Hcino, Finland's record-holder, in the 10,000-m. Hcino could not keep it up, and quit. Zatopek put on a show of speed to become the 1st Czech gold winner in the Olympics.

Robert Mathias, youngest American trackman at 17, bested the world's strongmen to win the decathlon, finishing the last events— the javelin and 1,500-m.—in a rainy, fogdarkened, muddy Wembley stadium. All of his main rivals had finished before sunset, but as he capped 12 hours of competition, spec-

tators and athletes were lighting matches to find their way around. Asked what he would do to celebrate, Mathias said, "Start shaving, I guess."

Also amazing was Fanny Blankers-Koen of The Netherlands, the "Flying Housewife" or "Marvelous Mama." She became the 1st woman to win 4 gold medals in the dashes, hurdles, and a relay. Rules limited women to 4 events; at the time, she held world records in the broad and high jumps.

At Torbay, where yachting events were held, Dane Paul Elvestrom began a string of victories in 4 consecutive Olympics.

After disqualifying the U.S. relay team for an incorrect baton pass, officials reversed themselves when they viewed the official films of the event.

The U.S. swept all the men's swimming events.

WINTER GAMES, OSLO, NORWAY, 1952

Hjalmar Andersen, Norwegian truck driver, won 3 distance speed-skating events. Norwegians also won 3 ski events and the team title. Andrea Mead Lawrence, of Vermont, took gold medals in both giant and regular slaloms. Canada won ice hockey for the 6th time in 7 Olympics. Dick Button retained his figure-skating title and performed a complicated triple-spin jump for the 1st time.

HELSINKI, FINLAND, 1952

Avery Brundage, known as "Slavery Bondage" because of his emphasis on keeping the games as purely amateur as De Coubertin had desired, was elected president of the International Olympic Committee shortly before the games opened.

At the opening ceremonies, Paavo Nurmi carried the Olympic torch into the stadium, lit one torch, and Hannes Kolehmainen, triple winner of 1912, bounded to the top of the stadium to light a 2nd Olympic torch. Ceremonies were disrupted by a woman in flowing robes who appeared to be part of the spectacle until she grabbed the microphone; she was a German student "peacenik."

The Russians entered a team after an absence of 40 years—confident that millions spent on sports programs would pay off in championships and propaganda. They housed athletes not at Olympic Village, but at their Porkkala Naval Base in Finland, where a huge banner portrait of Stalin hung. The Hungarians, not to be outdone, put up an even larger picture of Stalin.

When Horace Ashenfelter, an FBI agent, was the surprise winner over the Russian record holder in the steeplechase, writers had fun: "Communist Trails FBI Man." Russian men did well at Helsinki; their women even better.

Biggest hero of 1952 was Emil Zatopek, the thin Czech who appeared to run in apparent agony. He swept the distance events—the 5,000- and 10,000-m. runs (ahead of a French Algerian, Alain Mimoun, both times). Also, remarkably, he won the marathon, a race he had never run before. Emil called it "a very boring race." Before the race, Emil had asked advice of Britain's Jim Peters, the world's best marathon runner. Then:

> After 16 mi., he turned to Peters and said, "We go a little faster, yes?" Peters went faster but there was the Czecho-slovak shadow, trotting alongside and saying with a grin, "Don't we go faster?" The psychological effect was shattering. Peters did not even finish the race and Zatopek went on to win in an Olympic record.

In 1948, Zatopek had courted his future wife, Dana, by playing catch with her with a jave-lin. In '52, Dana Ingrova Zatopek set a world javelin record. The press called them "Czech and double Czech."

Bob Mathias, at 21 a 4-time U.S. decathlon champion and fullback at Stanford, repeated his decathlon victory, this time with ease, smashing the point record set by Glenn Morris in 1936.

Pole-vaulter Bob Richards, known as "the vaulting vicar" because he was a preacher, and shot-putter Parry O'Brien, a repeat champion, were both extremely popular with the Russians.

In unofficial team scoring, the Russians led the U.S. going into the final day. Then 5 U.S. boxers won gold medals to overtake the Soviets. Best among them was a 16-year-old mid-dleweight from Brooklyn, Floyd Patterson.

WINTER GAMES, CORTINA D'AMPEZZO, ITALY, 1956

Popular hero of these games was Toni Sailer, 20-year-old Austrian from the village of Kitz-bühel, who drank a mixture of milk, sugar, and honey at breakfast for extra strength, and wine at lunch and dinner for relaxation. After Anderl Molterer, "The White Blitz from Kitz," covered the 1.7-mi. giant slalom in a best time of 3 minutes 6.3 seconds, Sailer, "The Younger Blitz from Kitz," bettered that by 6 seconds. Sailer also won the special 2-run slalom over treacherous conditions which took a toll of 28 skiers. He went on to appear as a romantic lead in a German film, and make a big-selling record.

The Russians, who had shunned the 1952 Winter games, brought out the most powerful team, winning 6 gold medals and 121 points. Evgeni Grishin, a Moscow engraver who had competed as a cyclist at Helsinki, won 2 speed-skating events. Ice hockey had never been played in Russia before W.W. II, but the Soviets took 1st, with the U.S. 2nd, and Canada 3rd. Hayes Alan Jenkins and Tenley Albright won figure-skating titles.

MELBOURNE, AUSTRALIA, 1956

Tensions grew out of world events before the November games. In the Midwest, Israel, aided by Great Britain and France, marched into the Gaza Strip; in Europe, Russian tanks rolled into Budapest to crush the Hungarian revolt. At the time, 17 Hungarian athletes were en route to Australia aboard a Soviet steamship; the rest of the team, assembled in Czechoslovakia awaiting a flight to Melbourne, considered returning home to fight. But the border was sealed, so, reluctantly, fearing for families and friends, the Hungarians decided to compete. The British team helped provide clothes, pocket money, and even spikes and swimming trunks. Afterward, 45 Hungarians chose to remain in the West, including dis-tance running ace Laszlo Tabori.

Egypt, Lebanon, and Iraq withdrew, pro-testing the Israeli invasion. Spain, Switzerland, and The Netherlands withdrew because of Russia's rape of Hungary. The Red Chinese quit because Olympic officials had mistakenly raised the Nationalist Chinese flag over their camp.

Although East and West Germany partici-pated as a single team, the cold war was a major influence. A Russian journal later charged that Russian athletes had been under constant pressures of corruption by agents of the U.S. which, it said, "did its utmost to force upon Soviet athletes an acquaintance with young women."

The Australians proved excellent hosts, sup-plying "superbeds" for the tallest athletes and abundant turkey for Americans on Thanks-giving. Due to Australia's quarantine laws, for the 1st time the IOC allowed an event (the equestrian events in Stockholm) to be held apart from the main games.

Australians were extremely sports-minded, and they had much to cheer about: Betty Cuthbert won 3 gold medals in sprint events and Aussie swimmers were superb. Murray Rose, 17-year-old vegetarian who ate seaweed jelly for pep, set Olympic freestyle records at 400- and 1,500-m.

The scoreboard stated that "Classification by points on a national basis is not recog-nized," but everyone watched how the Amer-icans and Russians were stacking up against each other. The most obvious rivalry was between U.S. and Russian schoolteachers Harold Connolly of Boston and Mikhail Krivonosov of Minsk, who had taken turns breaking the hammer-throw record that year. The Russian was favored and led until the 5th of 6 throws, when Connolly let go a winning heave.

Connolly escorted Czech discus-thrower Olga Fikotova, a gold medal winner, around Olympic Village and their romance, continued by mail after the games, made headlines when Connolly went to Prague and asked permission of the Czech President to marry Olga and bring her to the U.S. "No force in the world will be able to separate me forever from the girl I love with all my heart and soul," was Connolly's statement. After some delay (the Czechs did not want to lose a champion) and with help from the U.S. State Department, they were married in Prague with Zatopek as best man. Both Connollys were on future U.S. Olympic teams, Harold through 1968 and Olga through 1972.

The Russians piled up huge scores in gymnastics as Larisa Latynina won 4 gold medals and 2 others; and Viktor Churakin 3 golds and 2 others. They won 5 Greco-Roman wrestling titles. Vladimir Kuts won the 2 major distance running events.

The Hungarians gained minor revenge over the Soviets in a bitterly fought semifinal water polo match after a Russian butted a Hungarian, drawing blood. The Hungarians gathered at one end of the pool, apparently to plot retaliation, but the Russians decided to leave the pool and forfeit the match. One observer said they were lucky to get out of the pool alive.

India won 7 straight Olympic field hockey matches, the longest run in a team event.

In platform diving, everyone thought Gary Tobian, U.S., was the best diver—everyone except judges from Russia and Hungary who consistently rated him poorly. Even Mexico's Juan Capilla, the winner, thought Tobian deserved the title

WINTER OLYMPICS, SQUAW VALLEY, CALIF., U.S., 1960

Speed skaters Lydia Skoblikova, a 21-year-old blonde, and Yevgeny Grishin paced the Soviet Union to the unofficial title by a landslide. Carol Heiss and David Jenkins (younger brother of '56 champion Hayes Alan Jenkins) won figure-skating titles for the U.S.

The U.S. hockey team amazingly defeated Canada, and then Russia for the championship after the Russian captain, in a dressing-room visit during an early-round game, gestured that the players should inhale oxygen.

A new event, the biathlon, was added; it combines cross-country skiing and marksmanship over a 20-km. course. One 2-minute penalty is added for each miss.

Walt Disney headed the pageantry committee for the Squaw Valley games, which were highly successful despite European skepticism before the games.

ROME, ITALY, 1960

The Roman Olympic Organizing Committee made a deal with the Association of Roman Thieves not to engage in street thefts, and during the games, complaints of pickpocketing, purse-snatching, and holdups were at a low. International goodwill was high since Soviet and U.S. athletes had come to know one another, having competed in each other's country.

The decathlon boiled down to a duel between close friends, Rafer Johnson, U.S., and Yang Chuan-kwang, Formosa, both students at UCLA. Yang beat Johnson in all 6 running events, but Johnson was so much better in the field events that he was ahead when they started the last event, the 1,500-m. run. Yang needed to win by at least 10 seconds, as he had often done before. Johnson doggedly stayed close. Yang won by only 1.2 seconds and Johnson set a new Olympic decathlon mark, 8,392 points, 58 more than Yang. Johnson, after a brief movie career, went to work for the U.S. People-to-People Foundation.

American track efforts were disappointing, but Don Bragg vaulted 15'5⅛", well above the old record:

All I ever really wanted to be was Tarzan. It was my dream and my obsession. . . . I knew Hollywood would believe I was Tarzan if I had that medal. All my life, I was emulating Johnny Weissmuller—he's the guy. I was constantly swinging on trees. I built up my forearms that way.

New Zealand's Peter Snell and Aussie Herb Elliott starred in middle-distance events.

Sisters Tamara and Irina Press led Russian women to 6 track and field victories. Sprinter Wilma Rudolph, from Tennessee, won 3 gold medals—the 1st American woman to achieve this. She had been crippled and confined to bed for 4 years as a child.

Italy had prepared a unique setting for certain events. The mossy Basilica of Maxentius, a 3rd-century public assembly hall, was refurbished for the wrestlers. Gymnasts swung and spun in the Baths of Caracalla, where wealthy Romans had taken steam baths 1,500 years earlier. Part of the marathon was run on the Appian Way, where Caesar's legions had once trod. The winner was Abebe Bikila, an Ethiopian running in his bare feet.

Among the boxing champions was Cassius Marcellus Clay, flashy 18-year-old light heavyweight, who took hundreds of snapshots of people of all nationalities with his Brownie camera. Clay soon turned professional and became the youngest heavyweight champion ever.

The Soviets dominated gymnastics (Boris Shakhlin and Larisa Latynina gathered 13 medals in all) just as the U.S. dominated swimming.

The Germans ended U.S. dominance (since W.W. I) in 8-oar rowing with revolutionary tulip-shaped oars, an extremely high stroke and a seating change—the 4th and 5th oarsmen on the starboard side.

Russia's overall victory margin, 807½ to 564½ for the U.S., was nearly twice that of 1956. More than 100 TV companies presented the games to a massive international audience. In the heat of Rome's summer, a British cyclist died after taking a stimulant.

WINTER GAMES, INNSBRUCK, AUSTRIA, 1964

Siberian schoolteachers (Lydia Skoblikova, the 1st athlete, male or female, to win 4 gold medals in the Winter Olympics; and Claudia Boyarski, a cross-country skier) paced Russia to 11 gold medals in 34 events. Skoblikova won all 4 speed-skating events from 500- to 3,000-m. An English toboggan competitor and an Australian downhill skier were fatalities.

TOKYO, JAPAN, 1964

Unheralded Billy Mills, a Marine and part Sioux Indian, staged a strong finish and won the 10,000-m. run, a feat never before achieved by an American. (Lewis Tewanima, also an Indian, had finished 2nd in 1912.) In all distances over 1,500-m., it was said, Americans preferred to drive. But 4 days later, Bob Schul ran away with the 5,000-m. title.

Americans won so many track and field titles that the Japanese played an abbreviated version of the "Star-Spangled Banner." One fan, an MGM musician, didn't like that and, seating himself below the torch, finished the anthem on his trumpet.

Al Oerter, U.S. discus star, won his 3rd games title, with a record 200', just 5 days after suffering torn rib cartilages. Lee Calhoun and Glenn Davis repeated their 100- and 400-m. hurdle wins of 1960.

Ethiopian palace guard Abebe Bikila, this time wearing shoes, repeated his marathon victory of 1960. Later, in 1968, after dropping out with an ankle injury, he met with a tragic auto accident which left his legs paralyzed:

It was the will of God that I won the Olympics, and it was the will of God that I met with my accident. I was overjoyed when I won the marathon twice. But I accepted those victories as I accept this tragedy. . . . I have to accept both circumstances as facts of life and live happily.

Tamara Press again won the shot put and added the discus title; her sister Irina won the pentathlon, a new event for women. The Soviet defending discus champion was so distressed to finish 5th that, in the tradition of female Olympians, she had her hair cut off.

Americans won 14 gold medals in 36 track and field events, and 16 firsts in 22 swimming events. Don Schollander, U.S., and Dawn Fraser, Australia, were the standout swimmers, Dawn winning her 3rd Olympic 100-m. freestyle.

Basketball, for the 4th straight time, came down to a battle between the U.S. and Russia. Princeton's Bill Bradley and Lucious Jackson led the Yanks to a 73–59 victory.

Russian Vyacheslav Ivanov became a 3-time single-scull champion. Gymnast Larisa Latynina boosted her 3-Olympic medal haul to 17 —including 9 gold medals.

New Zealanders were so elated at Peter Snell's victory in the 800- and 1,500-m. runs that they broke into a dance during the closing parade.

This was the last time women could compete without a "sex test." Sprinter Ewa Klobukowska of Poland, 3rd in the 100-m., was later found to have an irregular chromosome count and failed the "sex test" before the European Cup meet.

Tokyo spent a great deal of money on the games and the Japanese hoped for one gold medal in track, but their favorite finished 3rd and suffered so much from his defeat that 2 years later he committed hara-kiri. The Japanese did win 3 out of 4 judo medals, but the giant Dutchman, Anton Geesink, won the coveted open class.

WINTER OLYMPICS, GRENOBLE, FRANCE, 1968

Jean-Claude Killy equaled Toni Sailer's feat by winning the slalom, giant slalom, and downhill, and he was referred to as "immortal," "grand," "cute," and "legendary." A furor developed around charges that Killy flashed the brand name on his skis as often as possible when photographed. Henceforth, skiers were required to put tape over brand names on skis to guard against commercialism.

American skiers had a rough time: Eight of

the 14 team members suffered training or race mishaps.

Norwegians won the most gold medals, 14. Sweden's Toini Gustaffson won 2 golds in women's cross-country skiing. Italy's Eugenio Monti, coming out of retirement at 40, won the single bobsled title and was pressed into service as pilot for Italy's 4-man sled, which was victorious, too.

Luge, the sport of sledding down an icy chute feet 1st, had a scandal when judges and jury decided 2 East German women had illegally heated sled runners.

MEXICO CITY, MEXICO, 1968

The IOC bowed to international pressure, and limited the amount of time a team could train at Mexico City where altitude (7,500') would be a problem for endurance runners. Russia's invasion of Czechoslavakia was of concern at the time. Vera Calaska—who married teammate Josef Odlozil amid wild enthusiasm at the city's cathedral—won 4 gold medals in gymnastics which she presented to 4 political leaders who had attempted to achieve Czech independence. Earlier, in her homeland, she had been forced into hiding when Russian tanks advanced, and she had practiced for the Olympics in cellars.

Hundreds of students had been killed by police in Mexico City during a demonstration a few weeks before the games.

On the victory stand, U.S. black sprinters Tommie Smith and John Carlos, 1st and 3rd in the 200-m., bowed their heads and raised black-gloved, clenched fists during the U.S. National Anthem. According to Carlos:

> Tommie and I were just telling them that black people and minority people were tired of what was taking place in the U.S. and all over the world. We were telling them about roaches and rats and diseases that plague the poor. . . . I don't think we were very successful. The press and TV blew it all out of proportion.

They were denounced, expelled from Olympic Village, their visas canceled, and they were ordered out of Mexico.

The U.S. won 95 medals, and its swimmers accounted for 23 of the 40 gold, plus 15 silver and 20 bronze. Nearest rival was Russia, with 69 medals (21 gold).

Kenya's runners, used to high altitudes, won 3 gold medals, 4 silver ones, and a bronze; the 1,500-m. favorite, Jim Ryun of Kansas, was edged by Kipchoge Keino.

An 18-year-old California swimmer, Mark Spitz, brashly predicted that he would win a record 6 gold medals, but did not win any.

Americans generally suffered from "Montezuma's Revenge," spending a good deal of time in the restrooms. A Mexican swimmer became a national hero with his surprise victory.

A 3-day equestrian endurance test outside Mexico City in rain and mud resulted in the death of 7 horses. A Frenchman and the British team were winners. Grand Prix jumping in the capital was an esthetic affair. Bill Steinkraus, 43-year-old book editor, in his 5th try won the 1st gold medal for the U.S. in this event. Marion Coakes of Great Britain became the 1st woman to win a medal in this event, riding a pony of nondescript breeding.

Dick Fosbury executed his backward "Fosbury Flip" at 7'4½" to win the high jump.

The small Kenyan track team was given a Homeric welcome upon its return to Kenya. In addition to Keino, they boasted champions in the steeplechase, and the 10,000-m., and silver medals for a relay.

WINTER OLYMPICS, SAPPORO, JAPAN, 1972

These games made an antihero of Avery Brundage, IOC president, who arrived with a list of 40 alleged professionals among the skiers and single-handedly got the expulsion of Austria's Karl Schranz, the premier skier. The U.S.S.R. triumphed in ice hockey and matched East Germany with the most gold medals; the Germans dominated the luge, and had success in the biathlon and figure-skating. A Russian duo, reportedly not on speaking terms, won the pairs figure skating. Dutchman Ard Schenk was a sensation with 3 speedskating victories, obliterating the 10,000-m. record.

A Swiss woman, 17-year-old Marie Terese Nadig, took the downhill over favored Austrian Anne Marie Proell, and beat her again in the giant slalom.

The Japanese, who had never won a gold medal in the Winter Olympics, had trained hard for the ski jump and were rewarded with a sweep of the 70-m. jump.

Dianne Holum and Anne Henning, both of Northbrook, Ill., split 4 medals in "speedo skato," as the Japanese called it.

MUNICH, GERMANY, 1972

Despite the great effort that went into these Olympics—the novel stadium architecture, a parklike setting, and construction of a subway system—death and tragedy befell the peaceful, plastic Munich Olympics. Eight Arab guerrillas (of the Black September Movement) invaded the Israeli athletes' dormitory and held hostages before TV cameras, while demanding release of 200 Arabs in Israeli jails. Israel refused and before the tragedy ended, 11 Israeli athletes, 5 Arabs, and a German policeman, were dead. Three terrorists were apprehended (later to be released to meet demands of terrorists who seized a plane). German security precautions and judgment were criticized. Many wanted to stop the games, but Avery Brundage insisted that they continue. Some Dutch and Norwegian athletes went home.

Up to that point, the Munich games had been a success. Kip Keino, Kenya, won the steeplechase. Finn Lasse Viren fell down in the 10,000-m., but got up to win the event.

U.S. athletes generally fared poorly, with the great exception of Mark Spitz, who exceeded his prophecy of 4 years earlier. Spitz won 7 gold medals in swimming—a feat which seemed impossible. Immediately, according to certain critical reporters, Spitz began to auction himself off for post-Olympic jobs.

Rick De Mont was stripped of a gold medal for swimming under the influence of a stimulant, although he had reported his use of the drug for an asthma condition and no one had told him this was not permitted.

Black Americans Vince Matthews and Wayne Collete were accused of an undignified performance on the victory stand after the 400-m. run: talking, jiving, and looking away from the U.S. flag. The IOC immediately banned them from future Olympics, over protests by the U.S. Committee and some athletes. "If I looked cynical or disgusted," said Matthews, "it was partly because of what I had to go through to get here."

Olga Connolly, who had become a U.S. citizen by marriage, was chosen to carry the U.S. flag in the opening ceremony, but did not dip the flag when passing in front of foreign heads of state. She took her moment to argue for world peace, unity, and love; she was politely but firmly told this was not the time or place. After the Israeli deaths, she was not permitted to hold meetings in the Village. She threw the discus badly: "Something had to give, and the athlete in me died."

1976 OLYMPICS: MONTREAL, CANADA, AND INNSBRUCK, AUSTRIA

After the 1972 Olympics, Avery Brundage stepped down and Lord Michael Killanin, of Ireland, was elected president of the IOC. Los Angeles fought long and hard to get the 1976 Olympics, hoping to stage a super extravaganza to coincide with the American Bicentennial. The Committee, however, chose Montreal; critics said that Brundage, piqued by lack of U.S. recognition for his work, influenced this decision.

The Winter games were awarded to Denver, but Coloradans, concerned about ecology and finances, voted down the necessary bond issue. Consequently, the 1976 Winter Olympics will be held at Innsbruck, Austria.

—J.L.

FOR FURTHER READING:
Johnson, Jr., William O., *All That Glitters Is Not Gold.* New York: Putnam, 1972.
Coote, James, *A Picture History of the Olympics.* New York: Macmillan, 1972.

An Encyclopedia of Sports Oddities

ARCHERY

Ann Butz is the only archer to capture the Las Vegas, Detroit, and National championships; these tournaments make up archery's Triple Crown.

The distance record for the handbow is held by Sultan Selim III. In 1798, the Sultan shot an arrow 972 yards 2⅔ inches. Even modern science has not been able to change the archer's tools enough to help moderns surpass this century-old mark.

The 17th-century Japanese archer Wada Daihachi fired 8,133 arrows down the 384' Royal Hall in a 24-hour period, an average of 5 shots per minute. In Daihachi's day, Japanese archers used 8' longbows, considered the largest longbows in history.

Archery may hold the distinction of being the world's oldest sport; its history stretches back 20,000 years.

AUTOMOBILE RACING

A. J. Foyt, Dan Gurney, and 2 Volkswagens pulled off one of auto racing's most outrageous and successful stunts. In 1964, during the Nassau Speed Week, a Grand Prix for VWs was held. The 2 drivers devised a strategy for winning the 100-mi. race. As the race began, Gurney came up behind Foyt and began pushing him with his own high-powered bug. After 7 laps, Gurney had pushed Foyt around at such high speeds that they had passed every other car in the race. The 2 drivers kept the tandem positioning until they were within ¼ mi. of the finish line; then Gurney passed Foyt and came in for the winner's checkered flag. Gurney was disqualified because his car was not a regulation production VW, and that gave the $1,000 prize to the 2nd-place finisher, Foyt. Actually Foyt's car had been one of the slowest entries.

During the 1971 Indy 500, A. J. Foyt's 9-second fuel stop on the 14th lap set a standing record for the fastest pit stop in an official race.

In 1894, the 1st major auto race was held on a course between Paris and Rouen, France. The steam-driven car which won the race had a top speed of about 11 mph.

The citizens of Beisdorf, Germany, endured an afternoon of sports cars whizzing through their town which was on the course of a cross-country race, but when the noisy autos were still speeding through at 4 A.M. the villagers decided they had had enough. They blocked the street with logs. As successive cars came to a screeching halt in front of the barrier the townspeople rushed toward the vehicles and pulled the keys from their ignitions. After a dozen cars were incapacitated, the race was halted and rerouted.

The most rugged test of cars and drivers is the East African Safari which winds through Nairobi, Kenya, Uganda, and Tanganyika, over 3,100 mi. of rocky, steep, and treacherous roads. Drivers have had to rebuild bridges to get across this arduous course. In its 20-year history, there have only been 3 occasions when more than half the starters finished the race. One year, a mere 7 of the original 84 cars crossed the finish line.

The Cortina Run is only 400 yards long, but considering the conditions of the race, that is about all any human can safely tackle. The Cortina offers competition in "auto-bobbing," a daredevil blend of auto racing and bobsledding. The competitors are all national champions or winners of major auto-racing events.

BASEBALL

Harriet Smith of the Hollywood Girls pitched 200 games in one season, in 1931, and threw 83 innings in one week.

A record commonly thought to be held by Bob Feller and Nolan Ryan is really held by Mark Koenig, 2nd baseman for the New York Yankees. In establishing the record for the fastest pitch, both Feller and Koenig were measured by the same U.S. Army machine. Feller's fastest pitch was measured at 98.6 mph; Koenig was measured 16 years earlier at 127 mph. (Koenig's record is rarely recognized.)

The one-inning stolen-base record by a team was set by Washington (AL) in 1915, and tied by Philadelphia (NL) in 1919. Each team stole 8 bases in one inning.

Duke Farrell, catcher, once threw out 8 men trying to steal during the course of a single game.

The all-time record for stolen bases in one season was set by Jimmy Johnston of the San Francisco Seals (CL) in 1913. Johnston stole 124 bases during the 201-game season. In 1974, Lou Brock of the St. Louis Cardinals (NL) stole 118 bases in a 154-game season.

Arthur Leonard, who played with Boston (NL) in 1876, made 8 errors in one game.

The record for most errors in a game by one team is 12, held jointly by Detroit (AL) and Chicago (AL). Detroit mishandled the ball 12 times in a game v. Chicago, May, 1901, and Chicago tied the record in a game against Detroit, May, 1903.

A line drive travels 100 yards in 4 seconds flat. A fly to the outfield travels 98 yards in 4.3 seconds.

A record for catching a baseball was made in 1931 by Joe Sprinz of San Francisco (PCL). He caught a ball dropped out of a blimp 800' above the ground; besides breaking into the record books, Sprinz also broke his jaw as a result of the ball's velocity.

Leonard Ballard, who pitched in the Northwestern League during the 1914 season, tossed 74 consecutive innings without giving up a base on balls.

Pitching for East Rowan High, Salisbury, N.C., Phil Robbins threw a no-hitter in which he struck out 19 and picked off a player who'd gained a walk; the only other out of the 7-inning game was a pop foul to the catcher. His opponents, Monroe High, failed to hit a ball into fair territory.

The old Philadelphia Athletics baseball team scored 261 runs in one day. In a double-header on October 20, 1865, they defeated Williamsport 101-to-8, and followed up by crushing Danville 160-to-11.

Babe Ruth once clouted 125 home runs in one hour. In February, 1927, before an exhibition game at Wrigley Field, Los Angeles, the Babe stood at the plate for one hour while 6 different pitchers hurled at him, and he banged out 2 home runs every minute.

In the 1880s, there was a major league pitcher named Hugh Daly. His 5-year career saw a no-hitter and a game in which he struck out 16 men during a time when 4 strikes were required to get a strikeout. Hugh Daly had only one arm.

In a 1940 game between Jersey City and Montreal, a Jersey hitter laid down a slow rolling bunt which crept along the 3rd base line while 2 runners scored. The Montreal 3rd baseman, Bert Haas, waited as long as possible for the ball to roll foul. Finally, he saw that it would stay fair by an inch or so, and the runs would count. Haas lay down on the ground and blew at the ball with all his might; his breath pushed the ball foul and the umpires ruled in his favor. The runs didn't count.

Lindy Chappoten, a pitcher in the class D Sooner State League, was traded by the Shawnee Hawks to the Texarkana Bears of the Big State League. In return for the young Cuban pitcher, the Hawks received 20 uniforms. Shortly after, Chappoten won 20 games—one per uniform.

BASKETBALL

Perhaps the most dominating team in professional sports history was the Original Celtics of the old American Basketball League. One year they won 90% of their 150-game season. They were disbanded in 1928.

A basketball attendance record was set in Olympic Stadium, West Berlin, where 75,000 fans showed up to watch the Harlem Globetrotters in 1951.

St. Thomas College set a record for quick field goals in a losing effort against Albright College. St. Thomas scored 4 field goals in only 16 seconds.

The Puerto Ricans are enthusiastic basketball fans. In 1938, the citizens of the U.S. Territory held a 3-week national celebration to commemorate the 25th anniversary of basketball's introduction to the island.

In a basketball game in the 1974 regional boys' tournament in Sweden, 13-year-old Mats Wermelin scored 272 points to lead his team to victory. Final score: 272–0.

One of the most commonly asked questions about basketball is: Who was the tallest basketball player in the history of the game? Vasily Akhatyev of the Soviet Union was 7'7.3" tall.

Bob Lanier of Detroit (NBA) has the largest foot in professional basketball; he wears a size 22 shoe.

Holding the record for the most personal fouls committed in one season is Bailey Howell, Baltimore (NBA). During the 1964–1965 season, Howell was charged with 345 personal fouls.

Boone Trail High School and Angier High, both of North Carolina, hold the record for most overtimes in a single game. The 2 teams played 13 extra frames before Boone Trail could pull out a 56–54 victory.

Larry Breer of Kipp High, Kans., performed one of the most heroic feats in high school sports history. In a game against Aurora High, all of Breer's teammates fouled out of the game. Since there were only 5 males enrolled at Kipp that year, Breer had to go it alone against Aurora for the final 3 minutes of the game. The score remained tied at 49–49 for 2 minutes 45 seconds, as Breer held Aurora scoreless. Then with only 15 seconds left in the game, Aurora finally scored and beat Kipp High, and Larry Breer, 51–49.

The players of Towns County High of Clayton, Ga., grew so angry at the officials that they shot at the opposition's basket until they had scored 56 points for the other team. Towns County lost the game 129–41.

BICYCLE RACING

Tsugunobu Mitsuishi of Tokyo, Japan, set the slow cycling record by staying stationary for 5 hours 25 minutes. This phenomenal record, set in 1965, seems to have discouraged competition in the sport.

Old-time 6-day bicycle champion Bobby Walthour, broke his left collarbone 18 times, and his right collarbone 28 times in competition. During his career, he amassed 46 stitches on his legs, and 69 stitches over his face and head. Also, Walthour endured 32 fractured ribs, 8 broken fingers, and a broken thumb. He was considered fatally injured 6 times and twice pronounced dead—but lived on.

At an 1898 6-day "Go as You Please" race in Madison Square Garden, Charlie Miller pedaled 2,093.4 mi. So many of his rivals were hospitalized for exhaustion that public fury just about put an end to the 6-day bicycle races.

The record for the highest speed on a bicycle was set by Frenchman Jose Meiffret. On July 19, 1962, at Freiburg, West Germany, Meiffret pedaled at a rate of 127.243 mph. Meiffret was 50 years old when he set the mark.

Sheila Young of Detroit was the 1st woman from the U.S. ever to win a world cycling title. In fact, her 1973 victory in San Sebastian, Spain, was the 1st cycling championship won by any U.S. entry since 1912. Six months earlier, 23-year-old Miss Young had captured the world title in the 500-m. speed ice skating event at Strömsund, Sweden. She was the 1st person ever to win in world championship competition in both sports. Originally, Miss Young took up cycling to condition her body for ice skating. Her brother, Rodger, was a cyclist on the 1972 U.S. Olympic team in Munich.

BILLIARDS

The span of time over which Willie Hoppe won championship matches stretched from 1901, when he was only 14 years old, to 1952. Hoppe dominated the sport for half a century.

In the 1920s, Henry Lewis had a run of 46 using his nose instead of a cue stick.

"Old Style Play," or 4-ball carom billiards, died out in 1880 because Jacob Schaefer, Sr., dominated the sport to such a degree that it became impossible to find opponents for him.

Captain Mingaud, a political prisoner in Paris during the 1790s, was the 1st man to round off a cue tip. He requested a longer stay in prison to perfect his skill at billiards; by the time he consented to leave, he was the greatest trick-shot artist in the world.

The fastest 300-point billiard match on record was played in 1905—and took only 35 minutes to play.

Players in championship games walk from one to 3 mi. while circling the table, and moving from the table to their chairs.

George Henry Sutton, of Toledo, O., had no hands—yet won a national billiard championship, and once made a consecutive run of 3,000 balls.

During a title match held on September 1, 1865, a fly landed on the ball that Louis Fox was aiming at. The distraction snapped Fox's concentration and he missed the shot; his opponent then ran the table and won the match. Two days later, Fox's body was discovered floating in a river where he'd apparently drowned himself.

Prof. Harvey C. Lehman, of Ohio University, Athens, spent several years researching the peak performance ages of athletes in various fields. Using over 10,000 players as subjects, Lehman discovered that billiards champions have the highest average age of any sport considered. The peak age of a billiards master is 34.35; the average age of the people who set records in billiards is 35.67.

Bowling

In the 47 nations where bowling is popular there are an estimated 60 million bowlers.

The game of 9 pins was established by the German religious leader Martin Luther.

Tokyo World Lanes Bowling Center is the largest bowling hall in the world. The Japanese establishment has 252 lanes.

In a game at Coral City Lanes, Miami, Fla., Pat Crowe faced 5 consecutive 8–10 splits. Mr. Crowe is the husband of Alberta Crowe, president of the Women's International Bowling Congress.

A doubles team competing in a 1955 ABC tournament had a combined age of 165 years. Joseph Lehnbeutter was 82, and his partner, Jerry Ameling, was 83.

Art Morin of Taunton, Mass., made 22 spares in 30 frames; he failed to get even one strike and ended with a 3-game score of 465.

Don McCune of Munster, Ind., won only 2 tournaments during his 1st 10 years as a pro. In his 11th year, 1973, McCune won 6 tournaments and tied Billy Hardwick's PBA record for the most victories in one season.

Boxing

Jack Dempsey's 8- to 10-in. punches traveled at an estimated 135 mph.

For a brief period, there was a sport in Kiev, U.S.S.R., called face slapping. The initial contest set an unequaled endurance record. In 1931, Wasyl Bezbordny and Michalko Goniusz slapped (open hand) each other's bloody faces for 30 hours. The contest was halted by spectators because neither man would be the 1st to quit.

In a boxing match at Hot Spring, S. Dak., on December 26, 1902, Oscar Nelson and Christy Williams knocked each other down a record 47 times. Nelson hit the canvas 5 times, and Williams 42.

The longest match with gloves and 3-minute rounds took place in New Orleans on April 6, 1893. Andy Bowen battled with Jack Burke for 110 rounds. Finally the 2 badly mauled fighters refused to go on and the bout was called "no contest."

Al Couture knocked out Ralph Walton in 10½ seconds. Walton was still adjusting his mouthpiece when Couture flew across the ring and caught him with the knockout punch. This took place in Lewiston, Me., on September 24, 1946.

The longest bareknuckle fight on record occurred in Melbourne, Australia, on October 19, 1856. James Kelly and Jack Smith fought for 6 hours 15 minutes.

During John McNeill's tenure as deputy boxing commissioner of New York, 1924–1936, he saw 30,000 fights and 75,000 rounds of boxing.

Onetime light heavyweight champion, Battling Levinsky fought 58 hours in one year. In a single week he fought 6 different men.

Between August 10, 1938, and November 29, 1948, Hal Bagwell of Gloucester, England, fought 183 consecutive bouts without a defeat and only 5 draws.

Joe Grim, 150-lb. fighter from Philadelphia, sustained 20 years of being hit by men like Jack Johnston and Bob Fitzsimmons without being knocked out once. Grim, who actually had no offense and whose only defense was his incredible ability to absorb punches, was billed as the man who couldn't be knocked out, and he became one of the biggest draws in boxing. Finally, in 1920, he was KO'd by Sailor Burke.

Jim Mace, the English champion, and Joe Coburn, onetime U.S. titleholder, fought a bareknuckles bout in New Orleans in 1870. The fight was billed as the fight of the century, but when the actual contest was held it went 3 hours 48 minutes and neither man struck a blow.

Mace holds the record for the longest career of any professional fighter in history. He was in the ring for 35 years.

Only one fighter has ever been knighted. Sir Dan Donnelly, champion of Ireland around 1815, received the singular honor.

Between 1905 and 1918, Abe "The Newsboy" Hollandersky fought 1,309 boxing matches and 387 wrestling matches.

Jack Dempsey fought only 138 minutes as world champion. During that time he made $2,137,000—or $15,000 per minute.

During his 18-year career as a boxer, James J. "Gentleman Jim" Corbett never had a black eye or a bloody nose.

Terry McGovern, holder of the bantam and featherweight crown, and a man who defeated the lightweight champion, was a "has been" before his 22nd birthday.

CHESS

Robert Wyler, of Glendale, Calif., has played as many as 1,000 games at a time through the mail.

During W.W. II, RAF POWs frequently used chess games with German guards to distract their captors and help comrades escape.

Some chess masters insist that they will not play unless smoking is banned from the room. Not infrequently this tactic is intended to torture opponents who are chronic smokers. If it affects their game adversely, so much the better.

The 1st U.S. champion, Paul Morphy, had such great powers of recall that he was able to recite the text of the civil code of Louisiana from memory; he passed the bar exam in that State at age 19. When he was 21, he became the youngest world champion of chess and retired 3 years later due to lack of competition.

A match between Dr. Munro MacLennan and Lawrence Grant began at Aberdeen University, Scotland, on November 24, 1926, and is still being played. The contestants make one move each time they correspond.

FOOTBALL

Quarterback Bob Waterfield, of the Cleveland-Los Angeles Rams, threw a football 60' at a record speed of 68.18 mph.

In 1893, T. L. Bayne coached both sides of a game between Tulane and Louisiana State. This 1st Tulane coach also built the goalposts, umpired, managed ticket sales, chose the field, and picked the school colors. Bayne was gifted with a green umbrella for his services.

In 1923, the Rutgers kickoff man, Homer Hazel, scored a touchdown against Villanova only 8 seconds after the game clock began. His kickoff went into the end zone where a Villanova player fumbled the ball; Hazel, who ran the 100-yard dash in 10 seconds flat, raced down field and smothered the ball while it was still in play in the end zone.

Tom Dempsey, of the New Orleans Saints, holds the record for the longest field goal in NFL history: 63 yards against Detroit on November 8, 1970. Dempsey has only half a foot and only a stump of a right arm.

The longest undefeated streak in football is held by Washington University. From 1907 to 1917, in 63 games, their record was 59 wins and 4 ties.

The high school team of Hugo, Colo., once had a 3-game stretch in which they scored 386 points, and held their opponents to 6 points.

The greatest number of points scored in a single game by a single player (collegiate) was 100 by Leo Schlick of St. Viator, in 1916. Schlick scored 12 touchdowns in one afternoon.

The most fumbles by a pro team during a season was 56 by the 1938 Chicago Bears.

In contrast, the record for fewest fumbles over a season is held by the 1959 Cleveland Browns, who fumbled only 8 times.

The game was between Evanston High School and Green River High School in Wyoming. Green River quarterback Phil Summers said to the referee: "Haven't we got a 5-yard penalty on this?" Then he took the ball from his center and began stepping off the yardage. But he didn't stop until he had reached the end zone 71 yards later. This touchdown provided the margin of victory, 20–13. Green River coach, Jerry McMillan, said Summers had pestered him all season to try the play. "I didn't think it would work," he admitted.

The 1969 Oakland Raiders were penalized 1,274 yards during the season, a professional record.

The New York Giants of 1927 allowed only 3 touchdowns and 20 points all season.

After a 72–0 defeat at the hands of Bucknell College, the Ohio Wesleyan coach, Jack Fouts, was asked what had happened. "We just weren't up for this one," he conceded.

The 1st time the "hidden ball" trick was used occurred in a 1903 game between Harvard and Carlisle. Carlisle was leading 40–0 and coach "Pop" Warner remembered a practice session when one of his players had shoved the ball under another player's shirt. The stunt hit Warner as comedy more than strategy, so he used it against hapless Harvard as a finishing touch to the humorously one-sided game.

A halfback for the University of Washington, J. Haines, scored all the points on both sides during a game against the University of Southern California. On December 7, 1935, Haines ran for a 25-yard touchdown; earlier in the game he'd been hit for a safety by the Trojans. The final score was Washington 6, USC 2.

GOLF

The oldest golfing club in the world is the Honorable Company of Edinburgh Golfers, which came into being in March, 1744.

The Yale golf course is laid out so that a player going 18 holes covers one city and 3 towns: New Haven, Woodbridge, Orange, and West Haven—all in Connecticut.

In August, 1913, playing on the Old Course at Herne Bay, England, a 182-lb. Englishman, Edward Bliss—aged 50 and with a 12 handicap—hit the longest drive in golf history: 445 yards. In the years since, Craig Wood hit one 15 yards short of that, and Jack Nicklaus's best was 100 yards short.

Even though Joyce Wethered's drive struck a swallow over the fairway in 1927, she still managed to break par by getting 2 birdies on one hole.

Art Wall, Jr., holds the record for most

holes-in-one during a career. Wall had 37 aces during his 31-year professional career.

The fastest golf drive on record is 120 mph by Gene Sarazen. Since the U.S. Golf Association permits manufacturers to produce a golf ball with a top limit of 250' per second, this record is not an absolute.

John J. Humm, an amateur champion from Long Island, N.Y., once shot a 34 on a 9-hole course using only a No. 3 iron. The following day on the same course, using all 14 clubs, he could manage only a 40.

On the shores of the Dead Sea, the Sodom and Gomorrah Golfing Society golf course was 1,250' below sea level, the lowest course in the world. Since 1948, when the clubhouse was stricken by fire, the course has been inoperable.

Richard Carroll, of New York, won 2 tourneys on the same day. One was the Westchester Recreation Tourney at the Mohansic Club, York Town Heights, and the other was the Peekskill Elks Tourney at the Briar Hall Country Club. His scores were 73 and 71 respectively.

Dave Tuch celebrated his 50th birthday with friend Sam Force by playing one round of golf at Governors Island, N.Y.; then a round at the Jackson Park Club in Chicago, Ill.; then a final round for the day at the Virginia Country Club in Long Beach, Calif.

The Eldorado Golf Club in California has 15 courses, more than any other club in the world.

Jack Robinson scored 2 holes-in-one on the Haydock Park Course, London, within 4 days. Robinson had only one arm.

When Dow Finsterwald shot a double eagle in the St. Petersburg Open, he defied odds set by the *Professional Golfer Magazine* of 1.5 million to one. He accomplished the feat on a par 5, 501-yard hole.

HARNESS RACING

Goldsmith Maid is considered the greatest trotting horse that ever lived. *Maid*, as she was originally named, was the 1st foal of *Alexander's Abdallah* and a mare who pulled the cart of a New Jersey hat peddler. Her 1st owner, John B. Decker, failed to tame the high-strung *Maid* and she became a farm animal.

The only human to have any rapport with the young mare was a black youth who worked for Decker. On Christmas Eve, 1863, the young farmhand, known only as Sam, used the 6-year-old *Maid* to elope with his girl friend. Sam was amazed by *Maid*'s speed and tried to tell Decker, but the owner ignored his employee's entreaties. Determined to prove *Maid*'s ability, Sam took her out nights and successfully raced her against all comers —using his prize money to provide comforts for his new bride.

Eventually, Decker sold *Maid* to "Jersey Bill" Thompson. The new owner was able to make a harness horse of her, and finally she began to race professionally. She was now 8 years old. Thompson quickly sold her to Alden Goldsmith, who changed her name to *Goldsmith Maid*, made money with her, and then 4 years later, in 1869, sold her to Budd Doble and Barney Jackman. These 2 men owned *Goldsmith Maid* for 2 years. They had paid Goldsmith $15,000 for her and she earned $100,000 for them.

When *Goldsmith Maid* was 14, Doble and Jackman sold her to Harry N. Smith for $32,000. Smith had purchased *Goldsmith Maid* with the intention of retiring her to breed. One day he noticed that she still seemed to have some speed. He quickly put her back in a harness and on the track. Over the next 6 years, she won another $100,000.

During her career she won $364,200, which stood as a record for decades. From 1871 to 1874 she was undefeated, and she was beaten only once in 1875. She tied her own best time when she was 18 years old, won her final race when she was 20 years old, and died of pneumonia when she was 28.

HOCKEY

The fastest recorded skater is Bobby Hull (Chicago, NHL) who has been timed at 29.7 mph.

The Stanley Cup represents the world championship in professional hockey. The 1st cup was given in 1893—then worth about $49—by Canada's Governor-General, Lord Stanley. The Montreal Canadiens have been the most frequent winners of the Cup, taking it 18 times from the year 1916 to the present. Since the National Hockey Association took over presentation of the Cup in 1910, $6,000 has been spent altering the trophy.

The record for the greatest number of team goals scored in the shortest time was established by the Pittsburgh Penguins in a contest against the St. Louis Blues on November 22, 1972. The Penguins racked up a smashing 5 goals in a mere 2 minutes 7 seconds.

The dubious distinction of achieving the most penalties in a single game belongs to Jim Dorey, of the Toronto Maple Leafs, in a clash with the Pittsburgh Penguins on October 16, 1968. Dorey was whistled down 9 times and wound up with 48 minutes in the bad box.

Eddie Shore, of the Boston Bruins, was perhaps the roughest player in hockey history. Besides the numerous fractured bones he suffered, Shore also had 19 scars on his scalp, and cuts and gashes over his entire body which it had taken 600 stitches to repair.

Joseph Henri Maurice Richard, of the Montreal Canadiens, became the highest scorer in NHL history by driving his 325th goal into the net in 1952; the scoring puck was awarded as a souvenir to Queen Elizabeth II of England. By the time Richard wound up his career in 1960, he had tallied 626 goals.

Howie Young, famous for rough play and his consistent record as the league's leader in penalty time, was once arrested for fighting with a Detroit policeman in a restaurant. The officer, Joseph Curto, explained that Young had stolen part of his breakfast.

Mervin Dutton was wounded by an exploding shrapnel shell during W.W. I. He lay for one hour in a pool of his own blood. When the stretcher bearers finally got him, they managed to move only a few yards before another shell came their way. They dropped the stretcher and dove for cover. The shell exploded a dozen feet from Dutton's already mangled body and filled him with 48 fragments of metal.

The next day, when the doctors told Dutton his life probably depended on having his leg amputated, he refused. He told them he played hockey and couldn't spare the leg. His leg was hoisted to a 30° angle and remained there for 14 months. Finally he recovered, played professional hockey, and eventually served a term as president of the National Hockey League.

HORSE RACING

The skeleton of the oldest known horse is estimated to be 45 million years old.

In 1831, Squire George Osbaldeston rode 200 mi. in 8 hours 39 minutes. Osbaldeston used 20 horses. His speed/distance record still stands.

History's greatest breeder was Darius of Persia (522–485 B.C.), who had more than 50,000 brood mares. Darius's horses were half the size of today's.

Kincsem, a Hungarian mare, was unbeaten in 54 races (1877–1880) and holds the world's record for best win-lose percentage.

The 1st public racetrack was built in 1174 and named the Smithfield Track of London.

The owners of the speedstar, Alsab, made one of the finest deals in history. The horse they bought for $700 earned $350,015 during its career.

On December 29, 1945, the record for the slowest time for a winning horse was set by Never Mind II. During a 2-mi. steeplechase, Never Mind II refused the 4th jump and his rider gave up and returned to the paddock. Then the rider was told that all the other horses had fallen or been disqualified. Immediately he "raced" Never Mind II back to the field and finished in 11 minutes 28 seconds (normal time is around 4 minutes).

Foaled in 1888, Logan ran 388 races—a record number of starts—and won 76.

Kingston made 74 starts and never finished out of the money.

Rubio, a retired racehorse who had been pulling a farm plow for 3 years, won the 1908 Grand National Steeplechase in England. With 66–1 odds against him, Rubio netted his owner, Major F. Douglas-Pennant, a prize sum of $12,000.

The Tetrarch, called by many Englishmen the fastest horse of all time, was so swift that he couldn't control his legs. His hind hooves cut and bruised the fetlocks and shins of his front legs. At the end of his 2-year-old season in 1913, during which he was undefeated, The Tetrarch had to retire because his legs were so badly damaged.

Jockey Eddie Arcaro rode 250 losers before he finally won his 1st race. After that, for most of his 31 years in the saddle, he seemed never to stop winning. Before his retirement in 1961, Arcaro won 4,779 races, including 5 victories in the Kentucky Derby, 6 in the Preakness Stakes, and 6 in the Belmont Stakes. He rode Whirlaway and Citation to Triple Crown championships, and guided the inimitable Kelso to numerous victories.

In 1904, Moifaa was being shipped from Australia to England to compete in the Grand National Steeplechase when the ship was wrecked. The thoroughbred, given up for dead by owners and crew, swam to an island where he was found by fishermen. They returned Moifaa to his trainer in time to be reconditioned, to enter the big race, and to win it against 25–1 odds.

Jockey Levi Barlingume, rode until 1932 when, at age 80, he fell and broke his leg at Stafford, Kans., thus ending the longest recorded career of any jockey.

A 40–1 longshot, Nickel Coin, won the Grand National Steeplechase in 1951 after being trained on a diet of duck eggs and beer.

Kitchner was the lightest winning jockey in history. He weighed in at 49 lbs. when he rode Red Deer, winner of the 1844 Chester Cup in England. It is said that Kitchner weighed only 40 lbs. in 1840.

Over a period of 3 days in October, 1933, Gordon Richards rode 12 straight winners. He accomplished the feat in England.

Every thoroughbred race horse in the world is a descendant of one of 3 horses which were imported to England in the 18th century: Byerly Turk, Darley Arabian, or Godolphin Barb.

In order to make the required weight for a race, jockey Alfred Johnson lost 14 lbs. in one day.

Steve Donoghue rode 108 consecutive losers, yet also won 3 consecutive English Derbys.

The 1929 Grand National Steeplechase had 66 starters, the record for the most horses participating in one race.

Mountain Climbing

The Matterhorn—Zermatt, Switzerland—was not scaled until July 14, 1865, when Edward Whymper climbed the 14,782′ peak. Since then, Herman Schaller, a guide, has climbed the Matterhorn 233 times.

A mountaineer who had a wooden leg climbed Mont Blanc, as well as 5 mountains over 13,000′.

Mountaineer Christopher Timms, of New Zealand, survived the longest recorded fall in history. On December 7, 1966, Timms slid down an ice face of Mt. Elie de Beaumont, 7,500′, into a crevasse. His companion was killed, but Timms came out of the fall with only a concussion, cuts, and bruises.

Rowing and Yachting

The record for speed rowing is held by James Paddon of Australia, who rowed a mile in 5 minutes in 1924.

Mrs. Lottie Schoemmell holds the woman's rowing freshwater and saltwater speed records. Recorded June 12, 1927, covering the 30 mi. between Long Beach and Catalina, Calif., her saltwater mark is 11 hours 29 minutes. In freshwater, Mrs. Schoemmell rowed 32 mi. in 7 hours 48 minutes. The latter mark was accomplished August 19, 1927, Lake Champlain, N.Y.

King George V owned the most successful racing yacht in history. His craft, *Britannia*, 1893–1935, won 231 races in 625 starts.

The largest private sailing yacht in history was the *Sea Cloud*, owned by Mrs. Marjorie Merriweather Post-Close-Hutton-Davies-May. The craft was 350′ long and had 30 sails.

In 1884, Tanneguy DeWogan built a boat out of compressed paper. The Parisian traveled 2,500 mi. in the craft without a single leak.

Shooting

The record for the most birds shot by one man in a lifetime is attributed to the 2nd Marquess of Ripon (1867–1923). He bagged 556,000 birds, 241,000 of which were pheasants. On the morning of September 22, 1923, he shot 52 birds, then himself fell dead on a grouse moor.

The 1937, .30 caliber, M 1903, Standard U.S. Army Ordinance Dept. rifle had a muzzle velocity of 4,840 mph.

W. F. Carver, sharpshooter in the 1890s, shot at 63,625 wooden balls which were tossed before him for 6 days and nights. Carver hit 58,819.

Ed McGivern shot a .45 5 times from 15′ into an area with a diameter of 1.1875″. He accomplished this rapid-fire feat twice on August 20, 1932, at the Lead Club Range, S. Dak.

The stag with the most numerous antler points, 33 (plus 29), was shot by King Fredrick I of Prussia in 1696.

During the 1964 deer-hunting season, hunters caused $500,000 worth of damage to the community of Cody, Wyo. The figure includes money lost due to the killing of livestock, cutting of fences, contamination of water, litter, destruction of property, and gates left open that allowed livestock to escape.

On November 13, 1955, J. J. Fénykövi of Hungary shot the largest animal ever slain by a big-game hunter. Forty-eight miles from Macusso, Angola, he killed a 24,000-lb. bull African elephant (*Loxodonta africana*). The kill required 16 large-caliber shells.

Near Fairbanks, Alaska, Allen Dale Murphy killed 2 2,000-lb. buffalo in one day, and he used only 2 bullets. At the time, Murphy was 8 years old.

Skating

The longest regularly held race on ice is the *Elfstedentocht*. The race, held in The Netherlands, is 124 mi., 483 yds. long. Jeen van den Berg holds the speed record for the race: 7 hours 35 minutes, set on February 3, 1954.

Joseph Arenault, of Prince Edward Island, won his last speed skating trophy when he was 93 years old.

Mark Koch skated 313.5 mi. in 50 hours 26 minutes, at Greenville Community Rink in Pennsylvania on February 14, 1971. This is the longest skating marathon on record.

Skiing

The highest altitude ever skied was recorded by Yuichiro Miura of Japan. On May 6, 1970, he skied 1.6 mi. down Mt. Everest starting from an elevation of 26,200′. He reached a peak speed of 93.6 mph.

Skis were used in warfare for the 1st time at the Battle of Oslo in 1200 A.D. King Sverre of Sweden initiated their use against Norway.

On January 8, 1949, at Salisbury, Conn., the Salisbury Hill skiing record was broken 21 times. This is said to be the greatest number of times a record in any sport has been surpassed in one day.

The Weissfluhjoch-Kublis Parsenn course, near Davos, Switzerland, is the longest downhill run in the world—9 mi.

On August 25, 1955, Ralph Miller, U.S., set the speed skiing record at 109.14 mph. The record was set on the slopes of the Garganta Schuss, Portillo, Chile. The slope has a 62° lean.

Manfred Wold of East Germany holds the world's record for the longest ski jump, 541.3′, set March 23, 1969, at Planica, Yugoslavia.

Soccer

Constantine Fatouros, a Greek soccer referee, had to disguise himself as a Catholic priest to escape an angry crowd at a match on the island of Chios. Unfortunately, he was discovered before his ship could leave for Athens, but he suffered only a barrage of flying fruit.

The largest crowd ever to attend a soccer match was 199,854 spectators at the World Cup final in Rio de Janeiro, Brazil, on July 16, 1950. The game pitted Brazil against Uruguay. Uruguay won the match, 2–1.

On March 8, 1961, Colin Jones headed a soccer ball 3,412 times in 34 minutes 8 seconds at Queensferry, near Chester, England. Jones set this record for heading when he was 15 years old.

Soccer teams in Kenya frequently retain medicine men to stand by the field mumbling incantations and casting spells because many of the players depend on witchcraft for luck and confidence. A ball is occasionally taken out of play because a team claims it has been bewitched.

Dave Lovatt of Derby, England, was fined 10 shillings for smiling at a referee during a game.

Sir Stanley Matthews, who played over 80 international games for England, played in a major contest on his 50th birthday.

A London clerk, Charlie Cooper, made a 70¢ bet in a soccer pool and won $630,375. His regular job paid $28 per week.

The record for winnings in a soccer pool was set March 24, 1965, when Geoffrey Liddiard, London, won $886,258. His original bet had been 52¢.

Surfing

The largest wave ever ridden by a surfer is purported to have been 50' high. The wave hit Minole, Hawaii, on April 3, 1868. The surfer, Holua, rode the wave only to save himself from being crushed by it.

The longest surfing rides in the world are those at Matanchen Bay near San Blas, Nayarite, Mexico. Proficient surfers can take the waves as far as 5,700'.

Swimming and Diving

Alex Wickham, of the Solomon Islands, set a high dive record of 205'9"—the height of a 20-story building—in 1918. Gamblers at the site of the dive, an Australian cliff, offered 5-to-1 odds that he would not make the dive, and 10-to-1 that if he did dive he wouldn't live. Wickham lost consciousness before he hit the water, but survived. His bathing suit was torn off by the force of the landing, and his entire body was black and blue for several weeks.

The Orthlieb Pool in Casablanca, Morocco, is the largest swimming pool in the world. It measures 1,574' long and 246' wide, or 8.9 acres in size. The Orthlieb is filled with saltwater.

The speed record for "ice" swimming was set by Wilhelm Simons of Berlin, Germany, on February 3, 1968. In the 35.6° water of the river Riessersee, Simons swam 30 meters in 43.7 seconds. He was 69 years old.

When Zoe Ann Olsen of Oakland, Calif., defended her National Diving championship in 1949 at Seattle, Wash., she had her arm and right hand in a cast.

In 1930, Johnny Pearce, 17, of Zebulan, N.C., swam 2½ mi. with a lighted pipe in his mouth.

During a 22-mi. swim from Catalina Island to San Pedro, Calif., Issac Papke was accompanied for 12 hours 45 minutes by a 30' whale. The whale got very close to Papke but never touched him. Afterward, Papke said that he enjoyed the company but worried because "whales can swallow people."

Tennis

Rodger Taylor, Great Britain, and Wieslaw Gasiorek, Poland, played 126 games in a 1966 King's Cup match. They fought to a draw.

In a San Francisco tennis match, Howard Kinsey and Mrs. R. Roark volleyed a ball for 78 minutes, hitting it 2,001 times. They stopped only because Kinsey, former Davis Cup contestant, had to give a lesson.

The fastest serve was measured at 154 mph in June, 1963. Michael Sangster, Great Britain, made the serve.

In Australia in 1925, Lum Pao-Hwa, of China, played 764 games in one week.

The oldest surviving tennis court in Great Britain is the Royal Tennis Court at Hampton Court Palace. It was built by King Henry VIII in 1529.

Track and Field

The late Bill Robinson, professional tap dancer, holds the backward running record in the 50-yard, 75-yard, and 100-yard races. His times were 6 seconds, 8.2 seconds, and 13.2 seconds, respectively.

The record for the 3-legged race is held by Lawson Robertson, coach of the University of Pennsylvania and the U.S. Olympic track team, and Harry Hillman, coach at Dartmouth. On April 24, 1909, they ran a 3-legged 100 yards in 11 seconds flat.

John A. Finn, of Brooklyn, N.Y., set the 100-yard In-Sack record at 14.2 seconds on April 20, 1941.

Perhaps the greatest all-round American athlete next to Jim Thorpe was R. P. Williams, a New

Englander whose feats never reached most record books. In 1905, at Milford, he did a running broad jump of 25'; in 1905, at New London, holding weights, he did a standing broad jump of 15' 4"; in 1905, in New London, holding weights, he did a standing back jump of 13' 3"; in May 1906, at Winthrop, on an accurately measured track and timed by 5 watches, he ran the 100-yard dash in 9 seconds flat. Not in the record books because, alas, he was a professional, and in those days you had to be lily-white.

Noah Young ran a mile in 8 minutes 30 seconds carrying a 150-lb. man on his back. Young weighed 198 lbs. He made the run on April 12, 1915, at Melbourne, Australia.

Anton Haislan won $2,000 at a Paris exhibition for being the "most durable pedestrian." He walked 15,000 mi. over a period of 22 months; during the walk, he pushed a special perambulator containing his wife and daughter.

The Tutsi tribesmen in Central Africa often high-jump over 8'.

Wrestling

Japan's Osamu Watanabe set a record when he won the featherweight wrestling title in the 1964 Olympics. It was his 186th consecutive win and left him still undefeated in official contests.

In a match in Providence, R.I., Stanley Pinto entangled himself in the ropes and lost the event after he forced his own shoulders to the mat for 3 seconds.

William J. "Happy Humphrey" Cobb was the heaviest professional wrestler in history, weighing in at 802 lbs. Later, Cobb lost 570 lbs. in 3 years to get down to 232.

William Muldoon and Clarence Whistler wrestled in New York in 1880 for 9 hours 35 minutes straight without a fall. The contest was called a draw.

During the 1912 Olympic games in Stockholm, Max Klein of Russia and Alfred Asikainen of Finland engaged in a middleweight grappling contest that lasted nearly 11 hours.

Animal Athletes

The cheetah is generally considered the fastest of land animals with sprint speeds of approximately 70 mph. The barracuda is the fastest of fish and can attain speeds of over 60 mph. The fastest animal on earth is the North American duck hawk which has been timed at 200 mph. This bird normally cruises at 65 mph. Two other birds, the merganser and the Tibetan swift, are also purported to have a top speed of 200 mph. The racing pigeon has the most stamina at high speeds. In 1932, a pigeon owned by L. F. Curtis, of Chestnut Hills, Mass., was timed at an average speed of 67 mph over a 600-mi. course.

The longest flight by a homing pigeon was recorded between April 8 and June 1, 1845. A pigeon owned by the 1st Duke of Wellington flew from the tip of the Ichabo Islands, West Africa, to Nine Elms, London, England; a distance of 5,400 mi. It is suspected that the pigeon actually flew 7,000 mi. because it would have circumvented the Sahara Desert. The bird fell dead one mi. from its loft.

A racing pigeon owned by E. S. Peterson flew 803 mi. in 24 hours to win a 1941 San Antonio Racing Club event.

The beaked chaetodon, a fish which inhabits the various rivers emptying into the East Indian and Polynesian seas, uses his long snout like a gun to shoot insects above the water. Tiny drops of water are the hunting fish's ammunition.

In Canton, China, a fighting cricket called Genghis Khan won fights with as much as $90,000 at stake.

Betta fish will fight each other to the death in battles lasting as long as 6 hours.

The record long-distance swim by a fish was recorded at the Taronga Park aquarium in Sydney, Australia, between the years 1934 and 1939, during which time a gray nurse shark, Skipper IV, swam continually, covering an estimated 105,000 mi. Actually Skipper IV never gave up, but the coming of W.W. II took away her audience.

A Chesapeake-Labrador dog named Curly traveled 650 mi. from Billings to Alexander, N.D., between December 1 and December 23, 1948. After arriving in Alexander, Curly slept for 72 hours, then decided to leave and went back to Billings.

Miscellaneous Sports Oddities

Ted Terry rode his bull, Ohadi, from Ketchum, Ida., to Times Square, New York. He began the trip in July 1937, and arrived in New York City on August 11, 1940.

Anton Lewis of Brockton, Mass., set the record for bar-chinning when he chinned himself 78 times in April, 1913. This event took place in England.

In May, 1966, Stephen Williams, of Altrincham Grammar School, England, set a tiddledywinks speed record by potting 24 winks from 18" in 21.8 seconds.

The wealthy citizens of Mexico City play a game called frontenis which is a cross between jai alai, squash, and handball. The courts, which are found only in the private homes of the Mexico City aristocracy, are 38 yds. long, 10 yds. wide, and have walls 9 yds. high. The racquet resembles a tennis racquet with tougher strings to bat the hard rubber ball (the size of a tennis ball and very heavy). The game is fast and exciting, and sports promoters have tried unsuccessfully to make the sport public. The problem is that all of the players are wealthy and prefer to keep the game exclusively among the rich of Mexico; no amount of money can induce them to turn professional.

The international wheelchair games have entrants from 35 nations who can choose from 36 areas of competition.

In Wales there is a sport called "purring" in which 2 men face each other with their hands on each other's shoulders, then begin kicking each other in the shins with the reinforced toes of heavy shoes. The 1st man to let go of his opponent's shoulders is the loser.

In 1900, Johann Huslinger walked from Vienna to Paris, 871 mi., on his hands. At 10 hours a day, the journey took Huslinger 55 days.

John H. Schueter of Watertown, Wis., is suspected to be the world's champion cigar smoker. He smoked 24 cigars a day, 438,000 in his lifetime (approximate value $50,000), and lived until he was 81.

Perry Greene of Maine was considered the greatest wielder of the 11-lb. wood-chopping ax. The sport is to sharpen an 11-lb. ax until a man can literally shave with the tool, then hold it with one hand above one's face and lower it toward the nose. The slightest slip would split the contestant's face. Greene did this daily. Not one man in 10,000 can touch his nose with the 11-lb. ax.

—J.F. and the Eds.

24

Lists—1 to 10 (or More)

20 Illegitimate Children

1. Guillaume Apollinaire. Poet.
2. Sarah Bernhardt. Actress.
3. Giovanni Boccaccio. Author.
4. Cesare Borgia. Catholic cardinal.
5. Aleksandr Borodin. Composer.
6. Pope Clement VII. Spiritual head of the Catholic Church.
7. Leonardo da Vinci. Artist.
8. Josephine de Beauharnais. Napoleon's wife.
9. Frederick Douglass. Abolitionist.
10. Alexandre Dumas, *fils*. Novelist and playwright.
11. Desiderius Erasmus. Scholar and author.
12. Alexander Hamilton. U.S. Secretary of the Treasury.
13. Jenny Lind. Singer.
14. Marilyn Monroe. Actress.
15. Bernardo O'Higgins. Dictator.
16. Francisco Pizarro. Conqueror of Peru.
17. James Smithson. Chemist and inceptor of Smithsonian Institution.
18. August Strindberg. Playwright.
19. Richard Wagner. Composer.
20. William the Conqueror. First Norman ruler.

20 Celebrities Who've Been Psychoanalyzed

1. Marlon Brando. Actor.
2. Jim Brosnan. Baseball player.
3. Sid Caesar. Comedian.
4. Patty Duke. Actress.
5. Bud Freeman. Jazz saxophonist.
6. Ben Gazzara. Actor.
7. Graham Greene. Novelist.
8. Margie Hart. Stripteaser.
9. Moss Hart. Playwright.
10. Hermann Hesse. Novelist.
11. Ken Heyman. Photographer.
12. William Inge. Playwright.
13. Josh Logan. Director.
14. Claudia McNeil. Actress.
15. Tony Randall. Actor.
16. The Rev. Harry B. Scholefield. Unitarian minister.
17. Rod Steiger. Actor.
18. Vivian Vance. Actress.
19. Tennessee Williams. Playwright.
20. Natalie Wood, Actress.

The Most Loved Person in History

During 1974, visitors to Madame Tussaud's world-renowned wax museum in London (founded in Paris in 1770, moved to London in 1802) were handed questionnaires that asked, "Who is your favorite hero or heroine of all time?" Results of the poll are as follows:

1. Jesus Christ
2. Winston Churchill
3. John F. Kennedy
4. Joan of Arc
5. Moshe Dayan

Postscript: Of the nearly 250 wax figures in the Madame Tussaud exhibition, the favorite of visitors in 1974 proved to be Pablo Picasso, followed in order of preference by Agatha Christie, John F. Kennedy, Winston Churchill, and Mahatma Gandhi.

The Most Hated Person in History

During 1974, visitors to Madame Tussaud's internationally famous wax museum in London were handed questionnaires that asked, "What person do you most hate and fear?" Results of the poll are as follows:

1. Richard M. Nixon
2. Adolf Hitler
3. Jack the Ripper
4. Moshe Dayan
5. Abdul Salam Muammar el-Qaddafi

Postscript: "LONDON, August 9 (UPI) Richard M. Nixon's figure was removed from the hall of world statesmen at Madame Tussaud's wax museum today and was placed in storage."

The 9 Breeds of Dog That Bite the Most

According to a 27-year study of dogs in the New York City area made by Dr. Robert Oleson, of the U.S. Public Health Service, these are the 9 dogs most apt to take a nibble out of a human being. They are, in the order of their aggressiveness:

1. German shepherd
2. Chow chow
3. Poodle
4. Italian bulldog
5. Fox terrier
6. Mixed chow chow
7. Airedale
8. Pekingese
9. Mixed German shepherd

Some Crime Statistics

Before his death in 1972, J. Edgar Hoover, longtime Director of the FBI, concluded a 5-year study based on the police records in 2,400 U.S. cities.

1. Most probable months for burglaries are December, January, and February.
2. Most probable night for burglaries is Saturday night.

3. Most burglaries occur between 6 P.M. and 2 A.M.
4. Most assaults, rapes, and murders take place in July and August.
5. Most murders happen on a weekend.
6. Most murders occur between 6 P.M. and 6 A.M., most often at night.

11 People Who Disappeared and Were Never Found

1. Charles Ross. Child heir. (In 1874.)
2. Dorothy Harriet Arnold. Socialite. (In 1910.)
3. Ambrose Bierce. Author. (In 1913.)
4. Colonel P. H. Fawcett. Explorer (In 1925.)
5. Joseph F. Crater. Judge. (In 1930.)
6. Amelia Earhart. Aviator. (In 1937.)
7. Glenn Miller. Musician. (In 1944.)
8. Martin Bormann. Nazi leader. (In 1945.)
9. Paula Weldon. College student. (In 1946.)
10. Richard Covin Cox. West Point cadet. (In 1950.)
11. Michael Rockefeller. Anthropologist. (In 1961.)

Some Leading Best-Selling or Distributed Books

1. The Bible (1800–1950)
   1½ billion copies
2. *Quotations from the Works of Mao Tse-tung*
   800 million copies
3. *The Truth That Leads to Eternal Life*, Jehovah's Witnesses (1968)
   65 million copies
4. *American Spelling Book* by Webster (1783)
   50–100 million copies
5. *A Message to Garcia* by Hubbard (1899)
   50 million copies
6. *In His Steps* by Sheldon (1897)
   30 million copies
7. *The Common Sense Book of Baby Child Care* by Spock (1946)
   24 million copies
8. *The Guinness Book of World Records*
   24 million copies
9. *Valley of the Dolls* by Susann
   17 million copies
10. *American Red Cross First Aid Book*
    16 million copies
11. *Infant Care*, U.S. Government (1914)
    15 million copies
12. *Your Federal Income Tax*, U.S. Government
    14 million copies

Most Common Last Names in U.S.

1. Smith
2. Johnson
3. Williams
4. Jones
5. Brown
6. Miller
7. Davis
8. Anderson
9. Wilson
10. Thompson

Some Most Married People in History

1. King Mongut of Siam (and of *The King and I*)
   9,000 wives and concubines*
2. King Solomon of the Old Testament
   700 wives*
3. Queen Kahena of the Berbers
   400 husbands*
4. August the Strong of Saxony
   365 wives*
5. Theresa Vaughan of England
   61 husbands
6. Ibn Saud of Saudi Arabia
   35 wives*
7. Brigham Young of Salt Lake City, U.S.
   27 wives*
8. Glynn de Moss Wolfe of the U.S.
   19 wives
9. Beverly N. Avery of the U.S.
   14 husbands
10. Calamity Jane of the U.S.
    12 husbands
11. Tommy Manville of the U.S.
    11 wives
12. Kid McCoy of the U.S.
    10 wives
13. Pancho Villa of Mexico
    9 wives
14. Marie MacDonald of the U.S.
    8 husbands
15. Artie Shaw of the U.S.
    8 wives

*denotes polygamist

Famous Left-Handed People

1. Harpo Marx. Harpist, stage and screen comedian.
2. Charlie Chaplin. Screen actor, director, musician, artist.
3. Judy Garland. Actress, singer.
4. Leonardo da Vinci. Artist, writer, inventor.
5. Paul McCartney. Composer, musician, singer.
6. Jack the Ripper. Murderer.

7. Babe Ruth. Baseball player.
8. Harry S Truman. Politician, U.S. President.
9. Betty Grable. Screen actress.
10. George II of England. King.
11. Cole Porter. Composer.

12. Kim Novak. Screen actress.
13. Mandy Rice-Davies. Ex-call girl.
14. Ronald Searle. Satirical cartoonist.
15. Rex Harrison. Screen actor.
16. Gerald Ford. U.S. President.

15 Renowned Redheads

1. Lucille Ball. Screen, TV comedienne.
2. Lizzie Borden. Alleged murderess.
3. General George A. Custer. Military leader.
4. Emily Dickinson. Poet.
5. Harold "Red" Grange. Football hero.
6. Judas Iscariot. Biblical informer.
7. Thomas Jefferson. U.S. President.
8. Rod Laver. Tennis champion.

9. Sinclair Lewis. Author.
10. Walter Reuther. Labor union leader.
11. Margaret Sanger. Feminist, birth control advocate.
12. George Bernard Shaw. Playwright.
13. Svetlana Stalin. Dictator's daughter.
14. Mark Twain. Author.
15. Martin Van Buren. U.S. President.

10 Largest Countries (by Area)

		Area in miles	Area in kilometers	% of world land area
1.	U.S.S.R.	8,650,000	22,400,000	14.9
2.	Canada	3,851,809	9,976,139	6.7
3.	China	3,691,500	9,560,900	6.4
4.	U.S.	3,615,122	9,363,123	6.4
5.	Brazil	3,286,488	8,512,004	5.7
6.	Australia	2,967,909	7,686,849	5.1
7.	India	1,261,810	3,268,900	2.0
8.	Argentina	1,072,763	2,778,456	1.9
9.	Sudan	967,491	2,505,805	1.7
10.	Algeria	896,588	2,332,164	1.6

10 Most Populous Countries

1800

1. China — 295,273,000
2. India — 131,000,000
3. Russia — 33,000,000
4. France — 27,349,000
5. Germany — 24,833,000
6. Turkey — 20,912,000
7. Vietnam — 17,000,000
8. Japan — 15,000,000
9. Italy — 14,134,000
10. Indonesia — 13,476,000

1850

1. China — 429,931,000
2. India — 203,415,000
3. Russia — 64,903,000
4. France — 35,783,000
5. Japan — 33,111,000
6. Germany — 29,800,000
7. Turkey — 26,636,000
8. Italy — 25,017,000
9. U.S. — 23,192,000
10. U.K. — 20,817,000

1900

1. China — 372,563,000
2. India — 283,870,000
3. Russia — 116,238,000
4. U.S. — 75,995,000
5. Germany — 56,367,000
6. Japan — 43,756,000
7. France — 38,962,000
8. Indonesia — 37,694,000
9. U.K. — 37,000,000
10. Italy — 33,172,000

1930

1. China — 438,933,000
2. India — 338,061,000
3. U.S.S.R. — 147,028,000

4. U.S.	122,775,000	3. U.S.S.R.	208,827,000
5. Germany	65,218,000	4. U.S.	180,698,000
6. Japan	64,450,000	5. Indonesia	97,069,000
7. Indonesia	60,727,000	6. Pakistan	93,832,000
8. U.K.	46,052,000	7. Japan	93,419,000
9. France	41,835,000	8. Brazil	70,992,000
10. Italy	40,310,000	9. West Germany	56,175,000
		10. U.K.	52,709,000

1950

SOURCE: *The World in Figures.* By Victor Showers. N.Y., John Wiley & Sons, 1973.

1. China	582,603,000
2. India	357,303,000
3. U.S.S.R.	170,557,000

Latest

4. U.S.	151,132,000	1. China	900,000,000
5. Japan	83,419,000	2. India	600,000,000
6. Indonesia	77,271,000	3. U.S.S.R.	255,000,000
7. Pakistan	75,842,000	4. U.S.	212,000,000
8. Brazil	51,989,000	5. Indonesia	135,000,000
9. U.K.	50,225,000	6. Japan	112,000,000
10. West Germany	49,843,000	7. Brazil	108,000,000
		8. Bangladesh	80,000,000
1960		9. Pakistan	65,000,000
1. China	646,530,000	10. Nigeria	63,500,000
2. India	435,512,000		—The Eds.

15 Oldest Cities

1. Gaziantep, Turkey	3650 B.C.?		8. Luxor, Egypt	before 2160 B.C.
2. Jerusalem, Israel	3000 B.C.?		10. Shaohing, China	2000 B.C.?
2. Kirkuk, Iraq	3000 B.C.?		11. Lisbon, Portugal	2000 B.C.?
2. Zurich, Switzerland	3000 B.C.?		11. Porto, Portugal	2000 B.C.?
5. Konya, Turkey	2600 B.C.?		13. Loyang, China	1900 B.C.?
6. Giza, Egypt	before 2568 B.C.		14. Amman, Jordan	17th century B.C.?
7. Sian, China	2205 B.C.?		14. Ankara, Turkey	17th century B.C.?
8. Asyut, Egypt	before 2160 B.C.			

15 Most Populous Cities
(Including Adjacent Suburban Areas)

1800			*1850*	
1. Canton, China	1,500,000		1. London, England	2,362,000
2. Hangchow, China	1,000,000		2. Soochow, China	2,000,000
2. Kingtehchen, China	1,000,000		3. Peking, China	1,649,000
2. Nanking, China	1,000,000		4. Canton, China	1,236,000
2. Tokyo, Japan	1,000,000		5. Paris, France	1,227,000
6. London, England	865,000		6. Changchow, China	1,000,000
7. Peking, China	700,000		6. Kingtehchen, China	1,000,000
8. Istanbul, Turkey	598,000		6. Sian, China	1,000,000
9. Paris, France	548,000		6. Siangtan, China	1,000,000
10. Kyoto, Japan	530,000		10. Wuhan, China	996,000
11. Naples, Italy	331,000		11. Istanbul, Turkey	900,000
12. Patna, India	312,000		12. Calcutta, India	795,000
13. Isfahan, Iran	300,000		13. Hangchow, China	700,000
13. Lucknow, India	300,000		14. Bombay, India	644,000
13. Madras, India	300,000		15. Foochow, China	600,000

1900

1. London, England	6,581,000
2. New York, U.S.	3,437,000
3. Paris, France	2,714,000
4. Berlin, Germany	1,889,000
5. Chicago, U.S.	1,699,000
6. Vienna, Austria	1,675,000
7. Wuhan, China	1,500,000
8. Tokyo, Japan	1,440,000
9. Philadelphia, U.S.	1,294,000
10. St. Petersburg, Russia	1,265,000
11. Constantinople, Turkey	1,125,000
12. Moscow, Russia	1,039,000
13. Sian, China	1,000,000
14. Calcutta, India	949,000
15. Canton, China	900,000

1930

1. London, England	8,216,000
2. New York, U.S.	6,930,000
3. Tokyo, Japan	4,971,000
4. Berlin, Germany	4,243,000
5. Chicago, U.S.	3,376,000
6. Shanghai, China	3,259,000
7. Paris, France	2,891,000
8. Osaka, Japan	2,454,000
9. Buenos Aires, Argentina	2,034,000
10. Moscow, U.S.S.R.	2,026,000
11. Philadelphia, U.S.	1,951,000
12. Vienna, Austria	1,875,000
13. Leningrad, U.S.S.R.	1,614,000
14. Detroit, U.S.	1,569,000
15. Peking, China	1,565,000

1950

1. New York, U.S.	12,296,000
2. London, England	8,348,000
3. Paris, France	6,436,000
4. Tokyo, Japan	6,277,000
5. Shanghai, China	6,204,000
6. Chicago, U.S.	4,921,000

7. Buenos Aires, Argentina	4,722,000
8. Calcutta, India	4,578,000
9. Moscow, U.S.S.R.	4,137,000
10. Los Angeles, U.S.	3,997,000
11. Berlin, Germany	3,336,000
12. Leningrad, U.S.S.R.	3,191,000
13. Mexico City, Mexico	3,050,000
14. Bombay, India	2,839,000
15. Peking, China	2,768,000

1960

1. New York, U.S.	14,115,000
2. Tokyo, Japan	9,124,000
3. London, England	8,172,000
4. Paris, France	7,369,000
5. Shanghai, China	6,977,000
6. Buenos Aires, Argentina	6,739,000
7. Los Angeles, U.S.	6,489,000
8. Chicago, U.S.	5,962,000
9. Moscow, U.S.S.R.	5,046,000
10. Mexico City, Mexico	4,871,000
11. Calcutta, India	4,405,000
12. Bombay, India	4,152,000
13. Peking, China	4,148,000
14. São Paulo, Brazil	3,825,000
15. Philadelphia, U.S.	3,635,000

Latest

1. New York, U.S.	16,207,000
2. Tokyo, Japan	11,324,000
3. Shanghai, China	11,000,000
4. Peking, China	10,000,000
5. Paris, France	9,251,000
6. Mexico City, Mexico	8,590,000
7. Buenos Aires, Argentina	8,353,000
8. Los Angeles, U.S.	8,351,000
9. Osaka, Japan	7,839,000
10. São Paulo, Brazil	7,693,000
11. London, England	7,418,000
12. Moscow, U.S.S.R.	7,300,000
13. Chicago, U.S.	7,049,000
14. Calcutta, India	7,031,000
15. Bombay, India	5,971,000

10 Highest Cities

	Elevation	
	feet	meters
1. Lhasa, Tibet, China	12,002	3658
2. La Paz, Bolivia	11,910	3630
3. Cuzco, Peru	11,152	3399
4. Sucre, Bolivia	9,331	2844
5. Quito, Ecuador	9,249	2819
6. Toluca, Mexico	8,793	2680
7. Bogotá, Colombia	8,675	2644
8. Cochabamba, Bolivia	8,390	2557
9. Addis Ababa, Ethiopia	7,900	2408
10. Asmara, Ethiopia	7,789	2374

10 Highest Buildings

	Year completed	HEIGHT feet	HEIGHT meters
1. Sears Tower Chicago, Ill., U.S.	1974	1450	442
2. World Trade Center New York, N.Y., U.S.	1972	1350**	411**
3. Empire State New York, N.Y., U.S.	1931	1250	381
4. Standard Oil (Indiana) Chicago, Ill., U.S.	1971	1136	346
5. John Hancock Center Chicago, Ill., U.S.	1967	1107	337
6. Chrysler New York, N.Y., U.S.	1930	1046	319
7. Eiffel Tower Paris, France	1889	984	300
8. 60 Wall Tower New York, N.Y., U.S.	1934	950	290
9. Dallas Tower Dallas, Tex., U.S.	UC*	913	278
10. Bank of Manhattan New York, N.Y., U.S.	1930	900	274

*under construction
**2 buildings of equal height

10 Countries with Highest Life Expectancies

	men	women	avg.
1. Sweden, Europe	71.8	76.5	74.2
2. The Netherlands, Europe	71.0	76.4	73.7
3. Iceland, North Atlantic	70.8	76.2	73.5
3. Norway, Europe	71.0	76.0	73.5
5. Denmark, Europe	70.6	75.4	73.0
6. Ryukyu Islands, West Pacific	68.9	75.6	72.3
7. Canada, North America	68.7	75.2	72.0
8. France, Europe	68.0	75.5	71.7
8. Japan, Asia	69.0	74.3	71.7
10. U.K., Europe	68.5	74.7	71.6

10 Countries with Lowest Life Expectancies

	men	women	avg.
1. Guinea, Africa	26.0	28.0	27.0
2. Upper Volta, Africa	32.1	31.1	31.6
3. Chad, Africa	29.0	35.0	32.0
4. Angola, Africa			33.5
4. Guinea-Bissau, Africa			33.5
6. Central African Republic, Africa	33.0	36.0	34.5
7. Gabon, Africa	25.0	45.0	35.0
7. Togo, Africa	31.6	38.5	35.0
9. Burundi, Africa	35.0	38.5	36.7
10. Nigeria, Africa	37.2	36.7	36.9

10 Hottest Cities

	Average Temperature	
	(° F)	(° C)
1. Timbuktu, Mali	84.7	29.3
1. Tirunelveli, Tamil Nadu, India	84.7	29.3
3. Khartoum, Sudan	84.6	29.2
3. Omdurman, Sudan	84.6	29.2
5. Madurai, Tamil Nadu, India	84.0	28.9
5. Niamey, Niger	84.0	28.9
7. Aden, Southern Yemen	83.9	28.8
8. Tiruchirapalli, Tamil Nadu, India	83.8	28.8
9. Madras, Tamil Nadu, India	83.5	28.6
9. Ouagadougou, Upper Volta	83.5	28.6

10 Coldest Cities

	Average Temperature	
	(° F)	(° C)
1. Ulan-Bator, Mongolia	24.8	−4.0
2. Chita, U.S.S.R.	27.1	−2.7
3. Bratsk, U.S.S.R.	28.0	−2.2
4. Ulan-Ude, U.S.S.R.	28.9	−1.7
5. Angarsk, U.S.S.R.	29.7	−1.3
6. Irkutsk, U.S.S.R.	30.0	−1.1
7. Komsomolsk-na-Amure, U.S.S.R.	30.7	−0.7
8. Tomsk, U.S.S.R.	30.9	−0.6
9. Kemerovo, U.S.S.R.	31.3	−0.4
10. Novosibirsk, U.S.S.R.	31.8	−0.1

10 Longest Rivers

			LENGTH	
	Outflow and Location		mi.	km.
1. Nile	Mediterranean Sea, Egypt		4,160	6,690
2. Amazon	Atlantic Ocean, Amapa-Para, Brazil		4,080	6,570
3. Mississippi-Missouri	Gulf of Mexico, Louisiana, U.S.		3,740	6,020
4. Yangtze	East China Sea, Kiangsu, China		3,720	5,980
5. Yenisey	Yenisey Gulf in Kara Sea, Russia, U.S.S.R.		3,650	5,870
6. Amur	Tatar Strait, U.S.S.R.		3,590	5,780
7. Ob-Irtysh	Gulf of Ob in Kara Sea, U.S.S.R.		3,360	5,410
8. Plata-Paraná	Atlantic Ocean, Argentina-Uruguay		3,030	4,880
9. Yellow (Hwang)	Yellow Sea, Shantung, China		3,010	4,840
10. Congo (Zaire)	Atlantic Ocean, Angola-Zaire		2,880	4,630

10 Nations with Greatest Percentage of Population in Active Armed Forces—1972

1. Guinea-Bissau   4.55
2. Laos   3.96
3. Taiwan   3.71
4. Mongolia   3.57
5. North Korea   3.12
6. Jordan   3.01
7. South Vietnam   2.80
8. Albania   2.49
9. Israel   2.45
10. Portugal   2.34

Lack of an active armed forces by no means suggests that a nation has no defenses or that it lacks violence. For example, Costa Rica, with a population of 2,000,000 has 3,000 police, 1,200 Civil Guardsmen and a number of private armies controlled by political parties and

10 Nations with Least Percentage of Population in Active Armed Forces—1972

1. Costa Rica   0
2. Iceland   0
3. Malta   0
4. Bangladesh   .0004
5. Malawi   .03
6. The Gambia   .04
7. Burundi   .06
8. Chad   .06
9. Niger   .06
10. Upper Volta   .06

wealthy landowners. Since 1950, Costa Rica has received about $2 million in military assistance from the U.S.

SOURCE: *The Almanac of World Military Power* by Col. T. N. Dupuy and Col. Wendell Blanchard. New York, R. R. Bowker, 1972.

13 Countries with Highest Birth Rates
(Number of live births per thousand of population)

1. Swaziland, Africa   52.3
2. Niger, Africa   52.2
3. Rwanda, Africa   51.8
4. Dahomey, Africa   50.9
4. Togo, Africa   50.9
6. Bangladesh, Asia   50.6
7. Afghanistan, Asia   50.5
8. Angola, Africa   50.1
8. São Tomé and Príncipe, Africa   50.1
10. Liberia, Africa   50.0
10. Saudi Arabia, Asia   50.0
10. South Yemen, Asia   50.0
10. North Yemen, Asia   50.0

11 Countries with Highest Death Rates
(Number of deaths per thousand of population)

1. Angola, Africa   30.2
2. Guinea-Bissau, Africa   29.9
3. Upper Volta, Africa   29.1
4. Mali, Africa   26.6
5. Afghanistan, Asia   26.5
6. Dahomey, Africa   25.5
6. Togo, Africa   25.5
8. Portuguese Timor, Asia   25.4
9. Burundi, Africa   25.2
10. Central African Republic, Africa   25.1
10. Guinea, Africa   25.1

What's in a Name?

PERFORMERS

Celebrated Names (*and Their Real Names*)

Allen, Woody
  (*Allen Stewart Konigsberg*)
Astaire, Fred
  (*Frederick Austerlitz*)

Bacall, Lauren
  (*Betty Perske*)
Ball, Lucille
  (*Dianne Belmont*)
Bara, Theda
  (*Theodosia Goodman*)

Benny, Jack
　(*Benny Kubelsky*)
Bernhardt, Sarah
　(*Rosine Bernard*)
Burton, Richard
　(*Richard Jenkins*)
Callas, Maria
　(*Cecilia S. A. M. Kalogeropoulos*)
Cantor, Eddie
　(*Izzie Itskowitz*)
Cliburn, Van
　(*Harvey Lavan*)
Colbert, Claudette
　(*Lily Chauchoin*)
Crosby, Bing
　(*Harry Crosby*)
Curtis, Tony
　(*Bernie Schwartz*)
Davies, Marion
　(*Marion Douras*)
Day, Doris
　(*Doris Kapelhoff*)
Dietrich, Marlene
　(*Magdalene von Losch*)
Faye, Alice
　(*Ann Leppert*)
Fields, W. C.
　(*Claude William Dukenfield*)
Foxx, Redd
　(*John Elroy Sanford*)
Garbo, Greta
　(*Greta Gustaffson*)
Gardner, Ava
　(*Lucy Johnson*)
Garland, Judy
　(*Frances Gumm*)
Goddard, Paulette
　(*Pauline Levy*)
Goulet, Robert
　(*Stanley Applebaum*)
Grant, Cary
　(*Archibald Leach*)
Hayworth, Rita
　(*Margarita Cansino*)
Karloff, Boris
　(*William Henry Pratt*)
Lamarr, Hedy
　(*Hedwig Kiesler*)
Lewis, Jerry
　(*Joseph Levitch*)
Loren, Sophia
　(*Sofia Scicolone*)
Martin, Dean
　(*Dino Crocetti*)
Mistinguett
　(*Jeanne Bourgeois*)
Monroe, Marilyn
　(*Norma Jean Baker*)
Muni, Paul
　(*Muni Weisenfreund*)

Negri, Pola
　(*Appolina Chapulez*)
Pickford, Mary
　(*Gladys Smith*)
Robinson, Edward G.
　(*Emmanuel Goldberg*)
Rogers, Roy
　(*Leonard Slye*)
Shaw, Artie
　(*Arthur Arshawsky*)
Wayne, John
　(*Marion Morrison*)

OTHER PEOPLE

Celebrated Names (*and Their Real Names*)

Arden, Elizabeth
　(*Florence N. Graham*)
Billy the Kid
　(*Henry McCarty*)
Calamity Jane
　(*Martha Jane Burke*)
Carroll, Lewis
　(*Rev. C. L. Dodgson*)
Conrad, Joseph
　(*Teodor J. K. Korzeniowski*)
Diamond, "Legs"
　(*John T. Nolan*)
Father Divine
　(*George Baker*)
Ford, Gerald R.
　(*Leslie L. King, Jr.*)
France, Anatole
　(*Anatole Thibault*)
Gorki, Maxim
　(*A. Max Peshkov*)
Graziano, Rocky
　(*Tom Barbelo*)
Henry, O.
　(*William Sidney Porter*)
Hitler, Adolf
　(*Adolf Schicklgruber*)
Houdini, Harry
　(*Ehrich Weiss*)
Lenin, Nikolai
　(*Vladimir Ilich Ulyanov*)
Loti, Pierre
　(*Julien Viaud*)
Marciano, Rocky
　(*Rocco Marchegiano*)
Maurois, André
　(*Émile Herzog*)
McCoy, Kid
　(*Norman Selby*)
Molière
　(*Jean Baptiste Poquelin*)
Orwell, George
　(*Eric Arthur Blair*)
Robinson, Sugar Ray
　(*Walker Smith*)

Rohmer, Sax
  (*Arthur S. Ward*)
Saki
  (*Hector Hugh Munro*)
Schultz, Dutch
  (*Arthur Flegenheimer*)
Stalin, Joseph
  (*Iosif V. Dzhugashvili*)
Stendahl
  (*Marie Henri Beyle*)
Tintoretto
  (*Jacopo Robusti*)

Trotsky, Leon
  (*Lev D. Bronstein*)
Twain, Mark
  (*Samuel Clemens*)
Voltaire
  (*François Marie Arouet*)
Walcott, Jersey Joe
  (*Arnold Raymond Cream*)
West, Rebecca
  (*Cecily Isabel Fairfield*)

The People Who Never Were—Yet Live Today

SUPERMAN; ALSO, CLARK KENT, KAL-EL
(b. 1938–)

Born Kal-El, son of the scientist Jor-El and his wife, Lara, of the doomed planet Krypton. Jor-El predicted the planet-devouring Kryptonian explosion for years in the Kryptonian Senate, but no one would listen. Finally, in desperation, he constructed a one-man rocket ship to save his infant son Kal-El. The rocket escaped fiery destruction by scant seconds as Krypton was consumed by an atomic fire that also claimed the lives of Superman's parents.

The rocket landed near Smallville, Ill., where the infant Kal-El was found and adopted by John and Martha Kent. His foster parents soon discovered that their new son had amazing powers, including the power of flight, super strength, heightened sensory perception, great speed, and invulnerability. Fortunately for young Clark and the world at large, the Kents recognized that there was both a potential for good and a potential for evil in their son's abilities. Wisely, they instilled in him a strong moral obligation to aid people all over the world. Their contribution cannot be overstated. It was due to the Kents' encouragement that Clark 1st became Superboy, using a costume constructed from materials found in the crashed Kryptonian spaceship.

Several explanations have been offered for Superman's amazing abilities, but it is generally considered that he owes his powers to the difference between Krypton's original red sun and the earth's yellow sun. All survivors of the planet Krypton, including Clark's cousin Linda (Supergirl) Lee and the citizens of the miniature city Kandor (shrunk and placed in a bottle by the evil genius Braniac), have super powers when exposed to the earth's sun.

After Clark graduated from Smallville High, he went to work as a reporter for the Metropolis *Daily Planet*, under the direction of editor Perry White. Superman discovered that he could use his "mild-mannered" reporter's guise to further his personal cause of achieving world justice. Of course, there have been countless attempts to discover Superman's real identity.

Eventually, the *Daily Planet* was taken over by a giant conglomerate, Galaxy Communications, headed by the mysterious Morgan Edge. Edge switched Kent from his job on the newspaper to Galaxy Broadcasting, where Kent has established himself as a perceptive and resourceful reporter on the network's evening news program.

Superman, as Clark Kent, has dated many girls, but he has had few lasting relationships over the years. He continues to see Lana Lang, a high school chum, fellow reporter Lois Lane, and the mermaid Lori, inhabitant of an underseas city on Atlantis. He remains one of the more eligible bachelors in the U.S. His personal wealth, mostly contained in his Arctic Fortress of Solitude, is beyond reckoning.

Although Clark Kent has taken part in this country's wars as Superman, he maintains a strictly nonpartisan stance in his super activities, preferring to deal with criminals of both human and alien descent. Great heroes attract great villains. Superman has been plagued by his archenemy Lex Luthor, a boyhood genius who might have devoted his prodigious scientific talents to the good of mankind had not the enthusiastic Superboy caused an accident which left Luthor bald. Luthor traditionally pursues 2 goals: world domination and the destruction of Superman.

Superman has also dealt with the fiendish Braniac, a computer who successfully masqueraded for many years as a green human being. Superman has also confronted Mr. Mxyztplk, the Imp from the Fifth Dimension, who can be returned to his home only by being tricked into pronouncing his own name backwards.

For many years, Superman was plagued by chunks of kryptonite, radioactive remnants of his home planet, which had the power to weaken and possibly kill him. Kryptonite's various forms, of which green was the most deadly and the most common, complicated Superman's life until a freak accident in 1970 at a secret government testing laboratory in New Mexico rendered all kryptonite harmless.

Superman has had some difficulty lately with villains utilizing magic, the one force that can consistently overpower him. He has also evidenced a heightened social awareness, intervening in racial and class problems where the old Superman would ne'er have trodden.

He resides at 344 Clinton Ave. in Metropolis, but since this is also the address of Clark Kent, Superman's residence is a secret divulged only to a select few. Those interested in contacting him are urged to write the *Daily Planet*.

—M.B.

Wonder Woman; also, Princess Diana of Paradise Isle, Diana Prince
(b.?–)

Little is known of Wonder Woman's early existence on Paradise Isle because the island is still uncharted and was discovered only by chance during W.W. II.

The circumstances surrounding her birth are shrouded in mystery. While the legend of her being sculpted by her mother is a quaint parable, modern scientists now feel that she was more likely a product of parthenogenesis, i.e., virgin birth. Whatever the true circumstances, she was born to Queen Hippolyte who was then, and still is, the ruler of Paradise Island.

This island is inhabited entirely by women. The women are said to wear bracelets that make their bodies bulletproof and act as reminders of the slavery in store for women if they submit to men. The island's women also possess the gift of Eternal Life as long as they stay on Paradise Isle. But the Queen's daughter, Princess Diana, was to follow a different destiny.

During W.W. II when Diana was barely out of her teens, Capt. Steven Trevor, U.S. Army Intelligence Service, crash-landed his plane off the coast of the island. Princess Diana rescued Trevor from drowning and fell in love with the handsome pilot. During his recovery he told her about the Nazis and the threat they posed to democracy. Even though her country was ruled by a Queen, Princess Diana had no doubts about the value of democracy and felt it her duty to go to America with Steven to try to change, "a world torn by the hatreds of wars of men."

Though Princess Diana had to give up Eternal Life when she left the island, she was able to take with her to America some very valuable aids: an invisible plane able to travel at 3,000 mph and possessing the power to transcend time and space; a magic golden lasso that could compel obedience nonviolently; and, of course, her bracelets that made her body bulletproof.

Upon taking up residence in the U.S., Princess Diana disguised herself as American Diana Prince, and worked at various jobs as a secretary and nurse. She called upon her patroness, the goddess Diana, protector of women and wild animals, to help protect her adopted country from foreign powers. Diana became so involved in this fight that she soon traded her skirt for a costume patterned after the American flag with an eagle emblazoned on her bosom. She became known as Wonder Woman.

In her early years in America, Wonder Woman was frequently spotted doing good and conquering her country's enemies using force tempered by love and justice. Whenever possible, Wonder Woman tried to convert her enemies and often employed her telepathic and "magical" female powers to do so. She took an active role in protecting women from sadistic and evil men and, aided by a band of college girls, sought to teach women to become more independent and self-respecting.

As the years went on, Wonder Woman became immersed in the male-oriented society of the '50s that found previously strong-willed women (who had worked in munitions factories and had run local governments) again relegated to household tasks by the men who returned from the war. This switch in society's attitude caused Wonder Woman great distress and she too changed, giving up her plane, magic lasso, and bracelets, which were the by-products of a feminine technology.

Now Wonder Woman, or Diana Prince, became a mere mortal who tried to outdress reporter Brenda Starr and took orders from a mysterious mastermind named "I Ching." Diana still had adventures, but in them she used karate instead of superhuman powers. And she remained an easy prey for any attractive man, including the ever-present Capt. Steve Trevor.

—C.M.

Sherlock Holmes (b. 1853?–d.   )

Not much is known of the early life of Sherlock Holmes, genius of detection, who, in his deerstalker cap and inverness coat, solved criminal cases that even Scotland Yard could not crack. Through clues in books published by his "Boswell," Dr. John H. Watson, most biographers have come to the conclusion that he was probably born in 1853. Though Holmes was related to the Vernets, Parisian artists, his ancestors were mostly country squires. He had a brother Mycroft, 7 years older than he, who, behind the scenes, ran the British Government.

Probably in 1871, Holmes went to a university (whether Cambridge or Oxford is not known). He was a loner, choosing to spend his time in solitary analytical thought, forming the theoretical bases of his extraordinary methods of detection. During this time, an incident in which a bull terrier bit him on the ankle brought about a friendship with a certain Victor Trevor, which in turn hurled Holmes into his 1st case, "The Gloria Scott," involving the decoding of a mysterious message about flypapers and hen pheasants. His success in this case suggested to him that he might devote his life to the detection and prevention of crime.

It was in 1881 that Holmes met Watson, then recuperating from a war wound. Holmes's description of Watson reveals his tremendous powers of observation: "Here is a gentleman of a medical type but with the air of a military man. Clearly an army doctor, then. He has just come from the tropics, and his face is dark, and that is not the natural tint of his skin, for his wrists are fair. He has undergone hardship and sickness, as his haggard face says clearly. His left arm has been injured. He holds it in a stiff and unnatural manner. Where in the tropics could an English army doctor have seen such hardship and got his arm wounded? Clearly in Afghanistan."

By the time he met Watson, Holmes was already in the detective business. The 2 almost immediately saw the possibilities in a relationship between them and soon set up housekeeping at 221B Baker Street.

They made a truly odd couple. Watson objected to Holmes's strange habits: keeping his cigars in a coal scuttle and his tobacco in a Persian slipper, impaling his correspondence to the mantelpiece with a jackknife, and, most serious, sniffing cocaine (3 doses a day by 1887), a habit which Watson probably weaned him from eventually.

Though Watson did set up a medical practice from time to time, he found his true vocation as general factotum and chronicler of Holmes's career in detection.

A Study in Scarlet was the 1st book Watson published. Holmes didn't think much of it, telling his friend, "Honestly, I cannot congratulate you on it. Detection is, or ought to be, an exact science, and should be treated in the same cold and unemotional manner. You have attempted to tinge it with romanticism, which produces much the same effect as if you worked a love story or elopement into the 5th proposition of Euclid." In spite of this bucket of cold water, Watson continued to write stories, some 60 of them, about Holmes's cases,

each as "romantic" as the 1st. The cases involved a number of strange items and happenings: the worm unknown to science, the giant Sumatran rat that haunted the good ship Matilda, the Sussex vampire, the opal tiara, the singular affair of the aluminum crutch, the blue carbuncle, the speckled band, the redheaded league.

The most famous master criminal with whom Holmes dealt was the dastardly Professor Moriarty, who was, in Holmes's words, "a genius, a philosopher, an abstract thinker," with a "brain of the 1st order." Moriarty's operation was huge, a criminal network that covered Europe. After Moriarty tried to murder Holmes and burn the rooms at Baker Street, Holmes went in pursuit of him. They met in a death struggle on the Reichenbach precipice, where, it is said, the redoubtable Holmes wrestled the master criminal over the edge of the cliff to fall to his death below. There is some controversy about what happened next to Holmes, for he disappeared for 2 years. He himself claimed that he went on a long journey under the name of Sigerson: to Tibet where he met the head lama, to Persia, to Khartoum, ending up in Paris where he conducted some research into coal-tar derivatives. (There are those who believe that Holmes in actuality had amnesia during this period.)

After that, he resumed his career, and Watson resumed writing books about it. The good doctor delighted in telling of Holmes's disguises: a plumber, a loafer, an old salt, a drunken groom, an old woman, a priest, a crippled bookseller. He delighted also in telling about the great detective's uncanny ability to extract from the smallest piece of evidence a whole story of crime. (It is no accident that Holmes was the author of a little known classic monograph on over 100 varieties of tobacco ash.) For some reason, the 2 men quarreled in 1896, and Holmes was left without his Boswell for a period of time. It had happened before that Watson had left the scene (usually to get married), but this was the 1st time the 2 had had a falling out.

They made up, and the 2 stayed together until Holmes's retirement, in 1912, to a small farm upon the South Downs, overlooking the Channel, where he took up beekeeping. So engrossed was he in this retirement hobby that he wrote a book about it: A Practical Handbook of Bee Culture, with Some Observations upon the Segregation of the Queen.

Holmes came out of retirement once to break a W.W. I master-spy ring which was threatening the security of the British Empire.

The circumstances of his death are uncertain. The late W. S. Baring-Gould claims that Holmes died at the age of 103, just after sunset, with the word "Irene" on his lips. (Irene

Adler, glamorous adventuress, may have been The Woman in Holmes's life.)

E. V. Knox said that Holmes died at the age of 98 from a sting by one of his bees, possibly an Italian queen.

There are equally conflicting versions of the death of Watson.

—A.E.

"Uncle" Scrooge McDuck (b. 1860s–   )

Born in Scotland, son of a Glasgow miner. As a youth, he earned money shining shoes and gathering and selling firewood. In 1879–1880, he left Scotland and moved to the U.S., where his uncle was a riverboat captain on the Mississippi. He traveled across the country until he ran out of money in Montana, failed as a prospector, then hired on as a cowboy in 1882. He staked a land claim, built a shack, and mined for copper. The mine boomed and Scrooge was able to return to Scotland as a wealthy duck in 1884.

He traveled widely and his lust for money led him to Africa where he found and developed the Star of the World diamond mine and became a millionaire. He left the mine to be run by employees and continued his travels. Scrooge traded pearls in Indochina, bought and sold yaks in Tibet, and financed a network of salesmen in the Gobi desert. In 1898, he heard about the Alaska gold rush and crossed the Bering Strait. He worked hard, saved his money, and met *the* woman of his life—Glittering Goldie, the Star of the North. Eventually Scrooge tired of mosquitoes, mud, and ice, so he moved to town and opened a bank and general store. By 1902, he had made his 1st billion.

After more travels Scrooge found his home for life. On the site of Old Ft. Duckburg on the Tulebug River, he staked a claim to 10 acres and built a wooden money bin. It was in this period that Scrooge remarked:

No man is poor who can do what he likes to do once in a while
And I like to dive around in my money like a porpoise
And burrow through it like a gopher . . .
And toss it up, and let it hit me on the head.

He financed a chemical gas factory, a smelter, and other industries. By 1910 his business was a colossus and the city of Duckburg was growing. The challenge was gone so Scrooge hit the road again.

He sold rain hats in Arabia, lawn mowers in the Sahara, and started a salt business in Egypt before being forced out by the political situation. He discovered a diamond mine in the Congo and in 1916 he prospected for emeralds in South America. Scrooge returned to New York in 1921 and hit the stock market—he bought RCA for 5¢ a share and sold it for $538 a share in 1929. Staunchly conservative during the Roosevelt years, his industrial business was tripled by W.W. II. By the late 1940s he possessed 3 cubic acres of money. His health declined because his pores became clogged with gold dust and minerals from his habit of swimming in his money. He also became addicted to Amazonian Nutmeg Tea. In his later years, he became nasty and greedy and obsessed with protecting his fortune, particularly from the Beagle Boys, a family of thieves who made 20 attempts to get Scrooge's money. Because of his lower-class origins, Scrooge had an intense need for social acceptance by the traditionally wealthy of the duck world.

In his old age, he was driven by the need to prove himself as good as ever through making such deals as selling the people of tropical Indochina an enormous stove used for heating aircraft hangars. Uncle Scrooge McDuck is believed to be alive today although his whereabouts is unknown. His fortune, said to exceed that of J. Paul Getty, is estimated at $1 multiplijillion, 9 obsquatumatillian, 623.62.

—D.W.

(Scrooge's adventures have been admirably chronicled by his Boswell, Carl Barks, a former dishwasher, miner, sailor, and lumberman who went to work in the Disney studios during the '40s. Barks 1st undertook the illumination of the crusty capitalist's life with the book *Only a Poor Old Man*, in *Uncle Scrooge* №1 (1951). This is generally believed to be the 1st authorized chapter in the great duck's biography.

Through the years, no other artist or writer has come close to Barks in continuously and creatively presenting Scrooge's life or homespun philosophy. Barks has also collaborated extensively on the adventures of Donald Duck. See "Interview with Donald Duck" by Dave Wagner, *Radical America*, Vol. 7, No. 1. This also contains much information on Scrooge. Barks is now retired and lives in Goleta, Calif., where he paints in oils. His various oils depicting Scrooge amid his wealth are considered to be the finest visual presentations of the reclusive tycoon, since no photographs exist.

—M.B.

Sources: Walt Disney Studio Archives, Burbank, Calif.

For further reading: *Informal Biography of Scrooge McDuck* by Jack Chalker. Baltimore, Md.: Mirage Press, n.d. (P. O. Box 7687, Baltimore, Md. 21207).

Tarzan of the Apes (b. 1888–   )

Tarzan of the Apes, also called Tarzan the Terrible and Son of God, was born in a cottage made of packing crates and mud on the shores of Africa on November 22, 1888. His real name was John Clayton, and he was the son of Lord Greystoke and his delicate wife Alice who, not long before his birth, were marooned on those wild shores by savage mutineers. Had it not been for this disaster, the young lord might have been born in an English castle.

His mother, shocked into vague madness by an encounter with a 350-lb. ape (which she bravely shot and killed), died a year after his birth. Clayton, heartbroken, then wrote in his diary, "My little son is crying for nourishment —Alice, Alice, what shall I do?" Though Clayton was not to know it, help for the baby did come, and from unexpected quarters. It wasn't long after that that Kerchak, king of the apes, and his troop went on a rampage, entered the cabin (Clayton had carelessly left the door open), and killed the grief-stricken husband and father. Had it not been for Kala, mate of Tublat, who was mourning the loss of a baby, little John Clayton might have been killed too. However, Kala grabbed him to her bosom and adopted him as her own.

Thus began the strange, fantastic story of Tarzan, boy of the jungle, who grew up as an ape child. For the next 19 years, he led an almost idyllic life, swinging through the trees (but not on vines, as Hollywood would have it), playing tricks on his foster father, and growing up to be an athletic miracle. At the age of 10, he was as strong as a man of 30. At 19, he had, according to his biographer, Edgar Rice Burroughs, "the grace of a Greek god" and "the thews of a bull."

However healthy the life, it had done little for his intellectual development. That he did for himself. Visiting the cabin where he was born, he found books in which were what he called "little bugs." With his natural mental endowments, it wasn't long before he was able to decipher those little bugs and read English, using a children's illustrated alphabet and a dictionary. It was inevitable, however, that the child of the jungle, self-taught, would have holes in his education.

Tarzan was somewhat lonely, for as he grew he surpassed the apes in intellectual achievement. He made friends with Tantor the elephant (later with Sheeta, the leopard), but this did not end his yearning to be with his own kind: the men he had seen in his father's books.

In his teen-age years, a tribe of cannibals did settle nearby. However, they earned Tarzan's eternal enmity, for it was a cannibal who killed Tarzan's mother Kala with a poisoned arrow. He, in turn, killed the assassin and, hungry, almost ate a piece of the dead warrior. Something stopped him. (Burroughs says it was a hereditary repulsion toward cannibalism; how-

ever, Burroughs maintained a somewhat romantic Victorian view toward Tarzan, attributing to him feelings he could not possibly have had. For instance, Burroughs claimed Tarzan's love for Kala was that of a young English schoolboy.)

In 1908, Tarzan met Jane Porter, who by sheer coincidence was marooned on that same shore. She was 19, with long yellow hair and blue-gray eyes, a fit match for the bronzed, gray-eyed young god. Jane was accompanied by her addlepated old father, his companion (equally eccentric), her maid, and, believe it or not, Tarzan's 2nd cousin, Lord Greystoke (who unwittingly was holding the title that rightfully belonged to Tarzan).

Tarzan and Jane fell in love, of course, pledging that love in a woodland bower where Tarzan did "what no red-blooded man needs lessons in doing. He took his woman in his arms and smothered her upturned panting lips with kisses." He did no more. In spite of the fact he had been brought up by animals, he had somehow, through a kind of hereditary understanding, developed a full-blown sense of Victorian sexual morality.

Through a series of misadventures involving the cannibals, some pirates, buried gold, and abductions, Tarzan and Jane were separated. She sailed back to her native U.S. He, with a new-found friend, a Frenchman, followed her there.

It was several months later that Jane, living on a farm in Wisconsin and facing marriage for financial reasons to a cold-hearted villain, saw a 4-cylinder French touring car drive up. Who should step out of it but Tarzan. In short order he saved her from the villain and a forest fire, only to have to renounce his true love. (She, in a weak moment, had agreed to marry Tarzan's 2nd cousin.) Two years later, Tarzan had his heart's desire and married Jane. In the interim, however, he had some spine-tingling adventures: a duel, a fight with bandit Arabs, a brief fling with a countess. (Though his heart always belonged to Jane, Tarzan was wildly attractive to women, including the beautiful Russian countess and the queen of La, a lost Atlantis in the heart of Africa. He wasn't always able to fight them off, though what did take place would hardly shock anyone today.) He also learned to drink absinthe and smoke cigarettes.

During the rest of his life, Tarzan lived either at his English country estate (he got his title at last) or his African estate and, when he grew bored with both, traveled the world. Though outwardly urbane, he never did shake off his jungle childhood. (Once, on the green lawn of Westerfalcon Hall, he found and ate an earthworm, a treat for an ape, much to Jane's horror.)

During his lifetime, Tarzan had 2 sons, one

adopted, which, along with his wife, he was always rescuing from horrible fates. He conducted a running battle with the dastardly Rokoff and sundry other villains: the River Devil, the Lion Man, a Minunian scientist who shrank him to the height of 18", and the monster Numa, a celestial lion that threatened to eat up the moon. (Biographers other than Burroughs doubt the truth of this story.) In W.W. I, he lassoed a bomber. In W.W. II, he joined the RAF and flew planes over Burma, China, and Japan. (He was also in the Foreign Legion.) Though most of his adventures were in Africa, where he visited such little known places as the Great Thorn Forest, he also traveled throughout the world, including Hollywood, where movie-makers made fortunes chronicling his life and those of his sons.

There is no record of what happened to Tarzan after 1946. There are those who think he still lives, pushing 90 years of age, though he dropped out of sight so long ago. May he swing through the trees forever!

—A.E.

The Lone Ranger (b. 1850–)

The Lone Ranger's career in law enforcement began in Texas a few years after the Civil War. Following a family tradition, he joined the Texas Rangers to assist in maintaining law and order along the Rio Grande. His brother, Daniel Reid, was then a captain in the organization.

The Ranger's personal vendetta against injustice in the Old West is traceable back to a fight between a 6-man Ranger detachment and the members of the notorious "Hole-in-the Wall" Butch Cavendish gang. With Captain Reid in command, the small group of Rangers had been ambushed in a narrow ravine with high walls, called Bryant's Gap. In the shoot-out that followed, Captain Reid and 4 other Rangers were killed. The last man, Reid's younger brother, was badly hit and left by Cavendish to die.

Ranger Reid finally regained consciousness, days later. He found himself being cared for, in a cave, by the Indian Tonto. During his recovery, Ranger Reid learned that he was the only survivor from the massacre. You are the "lone Ranger" left alive, Tonto told him, and the anonymous name was the one by which he was known for the rest of his career.

Together, the Lone Ranger and Tonto buried the 5 men who had fallen. To fool the Cavendish gang, should it return, they created a 6th —a dummy—grave for Reid. Knowing that he would be marked for instant death if he reappeared openly, the Lone Ranger assumed a disguise: an eye mask made from his late brother's black vest, cloth that once had been

honored by having the silver star of the law pinned to it.

In the years that followed, the Lone Ranger and Tonto ranged relentlessly across 7 Western States in their common crusade against the forces of Evil. They rested only to get new supplies and make an occasional visit to the hidden silver mine which Reid and his brother Daniel had discovered. In their long absences, the mine was managed by an elderly, retired Ranger named Jim, who took only enough silver for his personal needs. During these reunions, the Lone Ranger also recast a new supply of silver bullets, the trademark he used to spread panic among the outlaws.

The selection of the precious metal for the bullets was deliberate. Its value constantly reminded the Lone Ranger of the high cost of human life, and of the necessity to take it only when he had no other choice. For that reason, he shot to kill only when there was no alternative.

The Masked Rider of the Plains often traveled in disguise. He took off his black mask to assume roles as a bearded prospector, a drawling cowboy, or a hundred other occupations common to the frontier. When he had to, he could even adopt the appearance of a Mexican, complete with sombrero and accent. While wearing these disguises, he never openly lied to curious people who wondered about the newcomer in their midst. Their questions were deftly parried with answers which encouraged a wrong conclusion to be made. Cowboys, for example, who were "sure" he must have punched cattle with them along the Chisholm Trail, were told that it "might" have been true. No one, whether it be passengers on a train, who—seeing him firmly issuing orders— believed he was a railroad detective, or town citizens, who—noticing his impressive arrival— mistook him for an Eastern banker, ever forced him to cross the line separating truth from falsity.

In appearance, the Lone Ranger was a commanding figure, standing just over 6' tall and weighing about 190 lbs. His speech, possibly reflecting his early years in Detroit, was of a distinctly formal, Eastern style. An intensely dedicated man, he rarely smiled, and his clear, piercing blue eyes demanded instant respect from utter strangers. His voice was deep and rich, or—when it had to be—stern and commanding.

During the Lone Ranger's early pursuit of Butch Cavendish—a foe who was to plague him again and again—the Masked Rider's horse was killed. Badly in need of another, he heard of the legendary white stallion of Wild Horse Valley. Traveling there with Tonto on *Scout*, he found the animal locked in mighty combat with a huge buffalo. The stallion, its sides dripping red with blood, was in danger of losing its life until the Ranger's silver bullets intervened. The 2 men remained there to nurse the wounded stallion back to health. They were rewarded for their efforts when the horse, after 1st bolting for the freedom of Wild Horse Valley to resume its former life, stopped and returned to its saviors.

The stallion's flanks shone like silver in the dazzling sun, Tonto said—and "Silver" it was named, the great horse with the thundering hooves and the speed of light. In future missions, the Lone Ranger and his new-found friend, shod with shoes of silver from the Reid mine, departed the scene where Justice had been done with a ringing "Hi-Yo, Silver, Awa-a-way!"

The Lone Ranger's adventures were almost without limit. He saved cowboys caught in the rampages of flood waters. He recovered stolen maps that located valuable mines, and "found" deeds that kept loans from being foreclosed. He defeated attempts by crooked town bankers to acquire illicit wealth. He rescued the hapless from hundreds of predicaments. In the course of his exploits, he met many famous men including General Custer and President Grant. For one period, lasting well over a year, he fought the Black Arrow syndicate, a group whose ultimate goal was the takeover of the U.S. Government. One by one, he met and captured the members of the band, working his way up to the secret leader himself, the acting governor of a Western State.

Throughout his career, the Lone Ranger gave full credit to the help of his faithful companion, Tonto. In their initial meeting in the cave, the Ranger had learned that he and the tall Indian had been boyhood friends. Tonto then had called him "Kemo Sabay," a native term for "Faithful Friend." It was Tonto, he told others, who gave him the name "Lone Ranger," and who christened the great white stallion "Silver." And he attributed his ability to ride rapidly in pursuit of outlaws to Tonto's talent as a tracker. It always guided him in the right direction, with the reliable Indian riding alongside.

Years after the Ranger's one-man crusade began, he found the son of his long-dead brother, Daniel. The boy had been cared for, after being saved in a wagon train massacre, by old Grandma Frisbie. Upon her death, young Daniel Reid, Jr., became the Lone Ranger's responsibility. Daniel spent part of the year at an Eastern school, and the remainder with his uncle and Tonto, learning the historical heritage of the Golden West.

One of the last captures officially credited to the Lone Ranger was the dispersal of the Ace Perigon Gang. During this encounter, he was recognized by a former Texas Ranger friend, Martin, who was then a member of the gang. Martin, at the cost of his own life, helped the Lone Ranger escape and bring the gang to justice. As he lay dying, Martin made the Lone Ranger promise to carry on his fight against Evil, and to train someone else to take his place, when he finally joined Martin and the others in the Great Roundup in the Sky. The Lone Ranger promised Martin that someone would always be ready to meet the challengers of Evil, whether it be Daniel Reid, Jr., or another.

There is no death date given for the "Lone Ranger." He lives.

—W.K.

Some 9-Day Wonders—on the 10th Day

Certain celebrities dominated the news briefly in their time and then disappeared from the headlines. What happened to them?

Headline—1926: GERTRUDE EDERLE

At the Peak: At 7:09 on the morning of August 6, 1926, Gertrude Ederle—"Trudy" to her friends—dived into the choppy waters at Cap Gris Nez, in France, to attempt what no woman had ever done before her: the crossing of the English Channel. Nineteen and confident, she was determined not only to cross the 35-mi.-wide Channel, but to do it in record time. The *New York Daily News* and the *Chicago Tribune*, evidently sharing her confidence, were backing her attempt, and noted reporter Westbrook Pegler, assigned to ghostwrite Trudy's account of the crossing for the *Tribune*, followed alongside her in a small boat, accompanied by his wife and Gertrude's trainer, Thomas Burgess. Optimism was the prevailing mood.

Not that it would be a breeze. She had attempted the Channel once before, in 1925, and had failed, as had countless other swimmers, both male and female. On this trip, waves and winds buffeted her so mercilessly that after she'd been in the water 12 hours, Burgess was moved to beg her to come out. Trudy looked up and without missing a stroke asked, "What for?" At 9:40 that evening, she clambered out of the water onto the beach at Kingsdown, England, where a British immigration officer wryly asked for her passport. It had taken her 14 hours and 31 minutes to swim the Channel, the best time ever recorded by man or woman.

Back in the States, Trudy, the daughter of a Manhattan delicatessen owner, was hailed as a heroine and feted with a ticker-tape parade in New York City. She went on tour for 2 years and her income from endorsements, public appearances, and a 1927 movie called *Swim, Girl, Swim,* earned her $2,000 a week, most of which she donated to the Woman's Swimming Association, which had sponsored her 1st try at crossing the Channel.

While on tour, Trudy realized that her hearing had been impaired by her 14½-hour odyssey, and she was forced to curtail her engagements. At the age of 21 she suffered a nervous breakdown, and in 1933, while visiting friends in Hempstead, Long Island, she fell, suffering a fractured pelvis and an injured spine. She was in a cast for 4 years.

As the 1930s waned, Trudy recovered, and made a comeback at Billy Rose's Aquacade at the 1939 New York World's Fair.

And Today: Gertrude Ederle shares a house with an old friend in Flushing, N.Y., where she has lived since the mid-1930s. Her hearing now so badly impaired that she wears a hearing aid and must read lips, Trudy at 67 teaches swimming to youngsters at the Lexington School for the Deaf in Manhattan.

"I proved women's lib 45 years ago," she said in 1971. "People said women couldn't swim the Channel, but I proved they could."

—B.F.

Headline—1929: Roy Riegels

At the Peak: Roy Riegels was a better-than-competent defensive lineman for the University of California's championship football team and had been elected captain by his teammates toward the end of the 1928 season. But history remembers him only as the man who blew the 1929 Rose Bowl for his team on New Year's Day by carrying the ball 70 yards in the wrong direction. It was a blunder of epic proportions, for it provided opposing Georgia Tech with the winning edge in a game that gridiron pundits had said would determine which team was the best in college football.

Seventy-two thousand people were on hand at Pasadena, cheering wildly as the Tech quarterback, Stumpy Thomason, fumbled on his own 36-yard line midway through the 2nd quarter. A mad scramble ensued, and Riegels, a lineman who rarely had the opportunity of getting his hands on the ball, grabbed the pigskin and started running.

At this point, a confused Riegels apparently lost his bearings in the blur of uniforms, spun around, and reversed field. A few startled Tech players made a stab at tackling him, but

then thought better of it and let Riegels dig his own grave. Galloping off into the sunlight toward his own goal line, he evidently had no idea that he was in error; a lone California teammate, Ben Lom, renowned for his speed, chased after Riegels, screaming, "No, Roy, no —not that way!" but his pleas were drowned out in the roar of the crowd.

Lom caught up with Riegels on the California 10-yard line and dragged him to a halt on the 2; at that point he got the bewildered ballcarrier to turn around momentarily, in the hope of blocking for him and gaining back some of the lost yardage, but Tech was already there and they hit Riegels with all they had, stopping him cold on the one-yard line. Dejected beyond words, Riegels sat on the ground. His teammates tried their best to console him.

On the next play, kicker Lom dropped back into the end zone to punt, but the kick was blocked and Tech scored a 2-point safety. Tech went on to win 8–7.

Riegels took a sound drubbing in the nation's press for many days to come ("BLUNDER DEFEATS CALIFORNIA: CAPTAIN ELECT RUNS 69½ YARDS TO WRONG GOAL," was the headline on the story the *Chicago Daily Tribune* ran the next day), and his name became a household word. He had asked to leave the game after the mishap, but at the urging of his teammates, he returned in the 2nd half. In the wake of the disaster, California coach Nibs Price said that Riegels was his smartest player, and "It was an accident that might have happened to anyone."

And Today: After he graduated, Riegels became a teacher and coached high school football in California. He served in the U.S. Air Force during W.W. II and later worked in the agriculture field. Today he is owner of the Roy Riegels Chemical Company, Woodland, Calif.

"All the times I've run across or heard people saying 'wrong way,' even though they weren't referring to me, I immediately turned around to see if they were speaking about me," Riegels said not long ago. "I still don't understand how I did it."

—B.F.

Headline—1934: The Dionne Quintuplets

At the Peak: The birth of 5 identical daughters to Elzire Dionne on a small farm in the backwoods of northern Ontario on the bleak morning of May 28, 1934, made instant headlines throughout the world and was universally hailed as a miracle of human fertility.

Nonetheless, Elzire and her husband Oliva were more depressed than exhilarated. They already were supporting 4 children on a monthly income of barely $100 and were not sure how they would manage to pay the delivery fees for the Quints, much less feed them.

Trading on the fame of their new offspring was one solution. Within 48 hours of the birth, representatives of the Chicago World's Fair had telephoned Oliva Dionne, inviting him to place the infants on exhibit at the fair in return for 23% of the gate receipts. Confused, depressed, and in desperate need of cash, Dionne agreed at once.

But the contract was quickly aborted when Dr. Allan Dafoe, the Quints' physician, stepped in, insisting that the girls were still much too small and frail to be moved. The Canadian Prime Minister, ostensibly outraged by the prospect of vaudeville tours and film contracts for infants barely old enough to open their eyes, also interceded and made the quintuplets wards of the state, establishing a trust fund of $1 million for them. In the meantime, they were to be raised not by their parents, but by Dafoe and a round-the-clock staff of nurses and nuns in a specially built, 9-room nursery on the Dionne farm. The parents and their 4 older children were to remain in the old farmhouse, segregated from the Quints.

For 7 years the girls lived a goldfish-bowl existence. Five million tourists came to gawk at them through one-way windows, and a miniature empire of souvenir shops, motels, gas stations, quick-food stands, and bus lines sprouted up in the fertile soil surrounding the Dionne farm. Dafoe grew rich on product endorsements and book royalties, and the Canadian Government took in some $4 million in gasoline taxes. In 1941, after years of legal struggles, Elzire and Oliva Dionne regained from Dafoe the custody of their daughters and North America's "number one peep show" drew to a close. But the Quints remained in enforced isolation behind a barbed-wire fence surrounding a new, heavily guarded residence that had been built on the Dionne farm. Their privacy abused and their freedom denied them, the girls were treated harshly by their parents and deprived of the $30,000 a year due them from movie appearances and endorsements. Later, the girls were to write retrospectively that they had had "a painfully unhappy childhood."

And Today: The years since they faded from the public eye have not been kind to the Dionne quintuplets. Émilie, who had been living at a nuns' rest home in the Laurentians, suffocated in 1954 during an epileptic seizure. Marie died 16 years later in squalid obscurity in a Montreal apartment. The most troubled of the quintuplets, she had sought happiness as a nun but had failed to find it. On the road to emotional security, she had married a civil servant, Florian Houle, in 1959. But Marie,

who bore 2 children, was haunted by several miscarriages, and the frequent work-related absences of her husband strained their marriage. She had been separated from Houle and living alone for several years when she died of malnutrition on February 27, 1970.

The 3 surviving sisters—Yvonne, Cécile, and Annette—live today in St. Bruno, a suburb of Montreal. Yvonne, who is unmarried, teaches in a kindergarten there. With Cécile, she came to Montreal in the early 1950s to attend nursing school, and it was during that time that Cécile met Philippe Langlois. A courtship ensued that was, for the oversheltered Cécile, eye-opening and breathlessly romantic. The 2 were married in 1957. Financial problems subsequently beset the Langlois family, and their only child, a daughter, died in infancy. In 1974, on the eve of her 40th birthday, a chastened Cécile, separated from her husband, moved to St. Bruno to join her 2 sisters. Annette, who also had married in 1957, was already divorced.

The Dionne sisters are intensely private women who live inconspicuously but comfortably on the income from a $250,000 trust fund. Still troubled by memories of their childhood, they rarely see their parents, who continue to live on the farm at Callander and have yet to see all their grandchildren. Says one friend, the women "are not on good terms with their parents, and I don't believe the relationship will get warmer. But they are closer and happier now than ever before. They have their own lives now."

—B.F.

Headline—1937: SIMONE SIMON

At the Peak: 1937. The kittenish dark lady of the screen tiptoed out of the dressing rooms of Darryl F. Zanuck's celluloid factory and took her place in the sunbaked movie lots of Hollywood—for a brief period of time. The year before, "Europe's Sweetheart" had come from a well-earned artistic film success in France to Twentieth Century-Fox. The directors, with whom she constantly quarreled, had accorded her 2 minor roles, in *Under Two Flags* and *Girl's Dormitory.* She lost the female lead in the 1st film to Claudette Colbert; commentators now say that had she held onto it, the part would have guaranteed her stardom in the U.S. A minor part in the 2nd film, alongside Ruth Chatterton and Herbert Marshall, deluged Fox studios with fan mail for the French spitfire. Simone had played a school girl in love with her headmaster, and had rescued a nondescript movie from the oblivion it likely deserved. In 1937, she found herself billed with Jimmy Stewart and Gale Sondergaard (later famous as "the Spider Woman") in *Seventh*

Heaven, a remake of a silent classic—highly thought of at the time but now relegated to the Late Late Show.

The following year, Simone was embroiled in a suit with her private secretary, who had passed over $10,000 in checks by forging Simone's signature. In retaliation, the secretary testified in court that her boss had circulated gold-plated keys to her home among choice paramours. The only man whose name was besmirched in print during this brouhaha was George Gershwin. She returned briefly to France, where she successfully co-starred with Jean Gabin in Jean Renoir's *The Human Beast*. Hollywood chanced her again, in *All That Money Can Buy* (the film version of Stephen Vincent Benét's *The Devil and Daniel Webster*), but she is probably best remembered as the austere wraith of the 2 "Cat People" horror films of the early 1940s, well-loved by monster fans.

And Today: Simone Simon's stage successes in Paris were short-lived. The French press, as ours, has forgotten her redundant name. A New York movie buff has said that she is retired, somewhere in France.

—W.F.R.

Headline—1938: Hedy Lamarr

At the Peak: The 1938 film *Algiers* was memorable for several reasons. There was a fine performance by Charles Boyer who uttered the famous line, "Come with me to the Casbah"—and it introduced Americans to Hedy Lamarr, a young woman of extraordinary beauty, and one of the important screen stars to emerge during the late 1930s.

Born in Vienna as Hedwig Kiesler, she had been appearing in European pictures, usually in bit parts, since she was a teen-ager. Her one starring role had been in *Ecstasy*, an arty Czech film which showed her floating on her back in a pond and frolicking through some woods—all in the nude. A few years after that, she met Louis B. Mayer in London. Though struck by her appearance, Mayer was aware of the Lolita-like image *Ecstasy* had given Miss Kiesler. Never a man to buy a scandal knowingly, he was reluctant to offer her a contract. But he finally capitulated and, now known as Hedy Lamarr, she came to the U.S.

After *Algiers*, Lamarr appeared in one mediocre film after another. Her ability to reject good scripts—like *Casablanca* and *Gaslight*—and pick the forgettable ones—*Experiment Perilous* and *Ziegfeld Girl*—was phenomenal. Nevertheless, because of her overwhelming beauty, she managed to prolong her career until the end of the war. As had Garbo before her, Lamarr projected a mysterious sensuality,

and it was an attractive alternative to the open-faced "cuties" typified by Betty Grable.

Her last film of any importance was released in 1950. She played opposite Victor Mature in Cecil B. DeMille's *Samson and Delilah*. Despite the critics' bad-mouthing, it was the biggest box-office success of the year, and there was immediate talk of a comeback. But it remained mostly talk and, for the next 15 years, her only press consisted of short notices that she was either getting married or divorced, both of which she did quite frequently.

And Today: In January, 1966, she made headlines once more. She was arrested in the parking lot of a Los Angeles department store. Allegedly, she hadn't paid for some items that were in her shopping bag. The next day, looking chic, she held a press conference and denied the charge, saying she had enough money to buy whatever she wanted. But when reporters visited her Beverly Hills home—from which the bank was trying to evict her—they found it badly in need of repairs. Newspaper stories mentioned windows that were broken and without drapes. A partially completed swimming pool in the back yard was, so the reports said, empty except for some mud and a discarded Christmas tree. A 10-year-old Lincoln was parked in the driveway, the initials "H.L." pasted on its dashboard in Blue Chip stamps. Eventually a jury found Miss Lamarr innocent. Not long after, she moved to New York, where she still lives.

The next year her autobiography, *Ecstasy and Me*, was published. It was subtitled *My Life as a Woman*, since it wasn't much more than an account of one exotic sex adventure after another. The book's 2 introductions, one by a psychologist and the other by a doctor, rather breathlessly recommended it as a document of certain medical interest. Reviewers were undecided as to whether the narrative was fictionalized fact or factualized fiction. It really didn't matter—the public's interest in Hedwig had long since waned.

—R.W.

Headline—1938: Magda Lupescu

At the Peak: 1938. She was the mistress of the mountebank King Carol II of Romania who had just declared himself not merely a monarch but a dictator. Magda did much of his hatchet work, seeing to the bloody purges of Hitler's pistol-happy minions running amok in this politically volatile country. When German hobnailed boots and tank treads completely overran Romania in 1940, driving Magda and Carol out forever, Magda Lupescu contented herself with jet-setting on 3 continents.

She was born Elena Wolff in 1896, to a

Jewish family in a little town called Hertza. The village is in Bessarabia, a district once part of Romania but now within the boundaries of the Soviet Union. Her father changed the family name to Lupescu—a natural Latinization of the original "wolf" derivative— probably because the country was rabidly anti-Semitic even before the Nazis overran the entire continent. Married briefly to an artilleryman in W.W. I, she divorced him just after the Armistice. Somehow she managed to meet Prince Carol, son of the aging King Ferdinand I. Just when and how this happened is not really clear. Certainly Carol was an infamous womanizer until he came across her, probably in 1923. Quite obviously she stole his heart away for good and all.

While consorting with the wily Jewess from Hertza, Carol was still married to Zizi Lambrino, daughter of a Romanian general. King Ferdinand annulled this marriage in 1925, after the birth of Carol's son Mircea. Carol then married Princess Helen of Greece. But his continuing affair with the young woman the caustic Romanian press had dubbed "Magda" was by now discussed openly. When Ferdinand died in 1927, Carol was prevented from succeeding him because of his relationship with Magda Lupescu, and the scandalous pair was exiled. Carol's 4-year-old son Michael was crowned in the traditional European fashion and a regency was appointed to run the country in the boy's name. Carol and Magda set up housekeeping on the Riviera. Princess Helen got her divorce in 1928.

In the meanwhile, the National Peasant party, a leftist but crypto-fascist organization, took control of Romania and made Iuliu Maniu the new Prime Minister. Maniu recalled Carol to Romania late in 1930 as King Carol II, subject to certain conditions. He was to be a constitutional monarch guided entirely by Maniu. And he was to sever all ties with Magda Lupescu. Carol ignored these conditions, and Magda returned to Bucharest. For this reason, Carol was never actually crowned. Maniu, himself an authoritarian, denounced Carol's arrogant policies and at 1st won support by playing on Magda's Jewishness and the couple's immorality. Ultimately, he resigned in protest.

The country, ravaged by the worldwide Depression of the '30s, was rife with racist-nationalist factionalism, political assassination, and street terror. The Iron Guard, a fanatically fascist, anti-Semitic, and pro-German party, grew every year in strength. In 1938, Carol set up his diabolical National Renaissance Front, over which he ruled as absolute dictator, styling himself a "national savior" seeking "rebirth" in a new "corporate state." Magda Lupescu headed, in those bleak days, a corrupt

coterie engineered to counter the Nazi goon-squad tactics of the Iron Guard by using the same thuggish street tactics, including murder. The press—what was left of it—referred to her as "the she-wolf" or "the Lupescu"—a sound like spitting. When Carol's Prime Minister, Armand Calinescu, was shot down in cold blood in September, 1939, the pair knew their rule was near an end. They fled westward in 1940, just ahead of Hitler.

And Today: Since Carol died in Portugal in 1953, that country has been Magda's retreat. Now known as Princess Elena, she resides in Estoril, presumably living on the millions Carol took with him from Romania. She travels a great deal, but the Portuguese Government admits—somewhat sheepishly—that she still calls Estoril home.

—W.F.R.

Headline—1939: DOUGLAS CORRIGAN

At the Peak: Douglas Corrigan had a passion for sweets as well as for flying, and when he took off in his ancient Curtis Robin J-6 monoplane from New York's Floyd Bennett Airfield on the foggy morning of July 17, 1938, he had laid in a supply of fig bars along with the 320 gallons of fuel and 16 gallons of oil he carried with him. The 31-year-old pilot and airplane-mechanic was on his way back to the West Coast, he told the airport manager that morning; the day before he had arrived in New York from Long Beach, Calif., after setting a new nonstop transcontinental speed record by making the trip in less than 28 hours—and this in a battered craft he had picked up at an auction for $900 6 years earlier. The plane had failed safety inspections and was devoid of radio, safety devices, and beam finder.

Laden with extra gas tanks that blocked his view, Corrigan's plane taxied precariously for 3,200' along the east-west runway and was airborne at 5:17 A.M. And then, mysteriously, the plane swept round in a wide arc and headed out over the Atlantic. Ground crew and hangers-on at the airport stopped what they were doing and stared in disbelief as it continued going in the wrong direction.

Corrigan flew through an impenetrable fog for 24 hours, presumably convinced that he was California-bound. When he emerged from the murk some 24 hours later, he was flying over water, not over the arid plains of the Southwest. He was, in fact, headed in the general direction of Ireland. When he put down at Dublin's Baldonnel Airport, he blithely informed officials there that he had "accidentally" flown the wrong way.

Corrigan chalked up his navigational miscue to the fog, a faulty compass, and the lack of a radio. "My intention was to go down the coast and get around the mountains in Pennsylvania," he has explained. "I took off over Jamaica Bay, right where Kennedy Airport is now, and when I made my turn to come from east to west, I was in the fog." He realized his "mistake" when he looked down over Ireland, and noticed that "all the houses were made of stones, the roofs were grass, and the streets were cobblestones."

Corrigan returned to the States immediately and was accorded a hero's welcome, perhaps for having provided some mirth and excitement during the dreariest years of the nation's history. He was showered with requests for interviews and product endorsements, received a ticker-tape parade in New York City, and was congratulated publicly by the U.S. Ambassador to Great Britain, Joseph P. Kennedy. In 1939, Corrigan played himself in *The Flying Irishman*, a cinematization of his misadventure. All told, his new-found fame earned the $50-a-week pilot-mechanic over $75,000.

Corrigan tested bombers for the Government during W.W. II and also flew in the U.S. Army Ferry Command. In 1946 he ran for the U.S. Senate on the Prohibition ticket, after which he worked as a commercial pilot—this time for a small California airline. In 1950, he bought a 20-acre orange grove in Santa Ana, Calif., settling down there with his 3 sons and his wife Elizabeth, who died in 1966.

And Today: He lives in comfortable obscurity in the same house he's occupied since 1950, although the grove was sold in 1969. Corrigan enjoys an easy life these days. "We have enough to live on, so I guess I won't have to work any more," he says. Not long ago, he was asked—once again—if he had really meant to fly to California. "Sure," he answered. Then he added, "Well, at least I've told that story so many times that I believe it myself now."

—B.F.

Headline—1942: KARL DOENITZ

At the Peak: 1942. That year, as vice-admiral and commander of the German U-boat fleet, he was responsible for torpedoing 6,266,-000 tons of Allied shipping to the bottom of the Atlantic. From the start of his swashbuckling career as the sea warrior extraordinaire of the 20th century, Karl Doenitz was pitted against formidable odds, facing both the greater numbers of the enemy and the political machinery of the Third Reich. Ironically, the zenith of his career was reached as Nazi Germany was blown to gravel by the pincer action of the Allied advance into the heart of Hitler's empire, Doenitz succeeded Hitler as

Führer, but his reign lasted little more than a week.

He was born in 1891, and joined the German Navy as a very young man. During W.W. I his crew was interned in Turkey, at what was then Constantinople, after a historic sea battle involving the German warships *Breslau* and *Goeben*. Restless amid the sultry Turkish shore life, young Doenitz requested transfer to the submarine service after his release. He had his way, was promoted to 1st lieutenant and given command of the U-25. Later, as skipper of the dreaded U-63, he was captured in a skirmish off the island of Malta when he was forced to surface. That was in 1918, and he spent the last months of the war in a British prison camp.

Karl Doenitz's acquaintance with Grand Admiral Erich Raeder in the postwar years was to etch his name indelibly in history. It was Raeder who convinced him of the efficacy of remaining a naval man, despite the Versailles Treaty's stricture that Germany was to have no Navy. As the Nazis ascended to frightful power in Europe, Doenitz worked secretly, under the protection of Hermann Göring, Otto Schniewind, and others in the Hitler inner circle, to reconstruct an invincible German Navy. Distrustful of the combat punch of surface vessels, Doenitz foresaw victory in the coming war at sea by shrewd submarine action. Despite the Versailles Treaty and peacetime RAF air espionage, Doenitz—overseeing every aspect, from fabrication to undersea field test—managed to create a brand-new Navy. In 1937, in fact, when Doenitz was commander of the 1st Submarine Flotilla, he put to sea as the sole passenger of the U-37. Snooping around the British coast near Portland, Doenitz was again forced to surface by British depth charges. He was allowed to return to Berlin after some apologetic bowing and scraping.

The German Navy entered the next war with a fleet of U-boats trained in the now-famous, "wolf-pack" tactics (*Rudelsystem*) and shielded from the highly boasted British ASDIC (Anti-Submarine Defense Investigation Committee) sonic detection—all due to Karl Doenitz, then flag officer of U-boats. By then he had set up a liaison system between subs and planes. Up until improved Allied technology was put in use around 1944, the Nazis were practically undisputed masters of the high seas.

Unfortunately for Doenitz, he grew more unpopular at home as he advanced in rank and military power. Joseph Goebbels disliked him from the beginning for his friendship with Pastor Martin Niemöller, once a U-boat commander, but by then merely a jailed clergyman. Doenitz fell out of favor with Grand Admiral Raeder for complaining that the Gestapo was harassing submarine personnel. Doenitz had always been accused of being too democratic in the Navy, of promoting a friendly esprit between officers and sailors to prevent mutiny. Nonetheless he rose to the rank of grand admiral in 1943, and was headquartered in Kiel with a portrait over his desk of Grand Admiral Alfred von Tirpitz, 1st advocate of total U-boat action in W.W. I. By the end of hostilities in 1945, Doenitz had sunk 15 million Allied tons.

Before Hitler's death, he named Doenitz to succeed him. But the Third Reich fell within days, and Doenitz was tried and convicted with other Nazi war criminals at Nuremburg. He served 10 years in Spandau Prison.

And Today: The German Embassy reports that Karl Doenitz lives on quite a small pension in a tiny house in the vicinity of Hamburg. He is 84 years old and so enfeebled that he is unable to receive visitors.

—W.F.R.

Headline—1963: CHRISTINE KEELER

At the Peak: In 1963, London's tabloid *News of the World* paid her £23,000 for the serialization of her life story, and a Danish filmmaker has since produced a movie about her *sub rosa* exploits among the British upper crust. Christine Keeler, whatever her ultimate intent may have been, caused the toppling of the Tory Government of that year and outrageously endangered the national security of her country—and possibly that of others as well. Here is a hindsight look at what is sure to go down in the history of this century as the Profumo Affair.

Born in Middlesex in 1942, Christine grew up in a converted railway car with her mother and stepfather, Ted Huish. Earning her keep as a babysitter, she seems to have chosen prostitution as a profession when still a teen-ager. After being seduced and impregnated by a GI, she headed for the big town at age 16. For perhaps a year she worked as a waitress in London, then was hired as a showgirl in a club. She was apparently moonlighting as a prostitute at the time because she soon got involved with a wealthy Arab who frequented the club. He in turn introduced Christine to the man who was to change her life—Dr. Stephen Ward, osteopath.

Ward fingered the spines of only the wealthy and titled. His sidelines were sketching portraits of such celebrities as Sophia Loren and Prince Philip and pimping for lords, tycoons, and spies. Ward found it expedient to employ the red-light services of both Christine and her blond, pixie-faced roommate, Marylin ("Mandy") Rice-Davies, then 16 years old.

Ward was a good friend of the playboy Viscount Astor, and had penetrated Astor's "Cliveden set" by offering it his whores and related product lines. At a party in Cliveden in 1961 Ward (who had his own cottage there) introduced Christine, naked in a swimming pool, to Lord John Dennis Profumo, War Minister of the Government. Profumo was married to actress Valerie Hobson, who had appeared in such films as *Great Expectations* and *The Bride of Frankenstein.*

What followed was an affair of some duration between Christine and Profumo, conducted at Ward's flat in Wimpole Mews. Whether the lord knew or not, Christine was often frolicking on the same premises with Evgeny "Honeybear" Ivanov, naval attaché to the Russian Embassy and a known spy. After receiving security warnings, Profumo ended the meetings with Christine, but already dark hints of his indiscretions were in the London dog sheets. Possibly to avoid exposing both Ward and Profumo, Christine took up with some West Indian blues musicians and drug users. One of the crew, a Jamaican named Johnnie Edgecombe, grew jealous of her telephone clientele. One night when Christine was visiting Mandy Rice-Davies at Ward's flat (Mandy was still in Ward's harem), Edgecombe showed up and started shooting wildly through the door. When he was brought to trial, Christine was a key witness. But she had fled to Spain, allegedly using money supplied by Profumo.

Now, all hell broke loose. On March 22, 1963, Profumo denied that he had ever been to bed with Christine Keeler. But a London paper was in possession of a letter he had written to Christine. It was addressed to "Darling," and seemed to contradict his testimony. Stephen Ward then sent a letter to Prime Minister Macmillan's private secretary, and the contents became known to the House of Commons. A full investigation by British MI-5 intelligence showed that "Honeybear" Ivanov had asked Christine to find out from Profumo when nuclear warheads would be delivered to West Germany. The purpose was to forestall a U.S.-U.S.S.R. showdown over the Cuban missile crisis. By the time of the trial, Ivanov had been recalled to Moscow, where he was committed to a mental institution. (He has not been heard of since.)

By the summer of 1963, the Profumo affair was café and bar talk the world over. Profumo confessed to having had an affair and resigned in early June. Within days, Ward was stopped in his white Jaguar and arrested by Scotland Yard. Released on a bail equivalent to $8,400, Ward was ordered to stand trial on 8 counts, the charges ranging from running a brothel to arranging for abortions. The trial itself, in July and August, was a kind of Rabelaisian

Miss Universe pageant, with a parade of vivacious hookers taking the stand and swapping stories of 2-way mirrors, bacchanales with whips and marijuana, and even mention of a naked, masked, male "host" whose real identity was too sensitive for the world to know. The stars of the extravaganza were Vickie Barrett (née Janet Barker), Mandy Rice-Davies, and Christine Keeler. Christine herself told how Ward had dubbed her a "modeling assistant" for the purpose of luring shopgirls into his call-girl cotillion. Ward enjoyed sticking his tongue out at the press during the trial, but committed suicide just as the jury was instructed to hand in a verdict.

Christine's personal life was further exposed in the Old Bailey by conflicting accounts of her affair with Jamaican jazz singer Aloysius "Lucky" Gordon. In a sober state, Christine testified that Gordon had beaten her up in April, after her return from Spain. Gordon retorted that all he got from her in return for marijuana was VD. In a drunken tape-recorded confession, Christine finally admitted that Gordon was not guilty of the assault charge, and he was released. In December, 1963, Christine was sentenced to 9 months for perjury and conspiracy to obstruct justice. "All I want," she said tearfully after the court adjourned, "is for everyone to let me be a normal girl again." But by then she had purchased a Georgian house, valued at that time at $39,000, after selling her spicy story to the press.

And Today: Christine's name has rarely been in the press the last several years. It is known that she married engineer James Levermore and bore his son Jimmy. Levermore later filed for divorce on the grounds of desertion. In the late '6os, Christine seems to have taken up with such bohemian Londoners as Penelope Tree and Marianne Faithfull. A Washington reporter for the *London Observer* said that he spoke with Christine Keeler in 1973, when she was settling into a new flat in Chelsea—but he suspects she has moved since.

—W.F.R.

Headline—1968: ALEXANDER DUBCEK

At the Peak: In January, 1968, he ascended to the position of 1st Secretary of the Central Committee of Czechoslovakia's Communist party. This maneuver made him the kingpin of that troubled country's Government. The months that followed have been recorded in recent history as Prague's "springtime of freedom." Dubcek set the party apparatus in motion to make sweeping reforms. His outlook was viewed by political commentators the world over as humane and democratic. The intelligentsia and the workers hailed him as a liberator who made every effort to do away with the iron-fisted bureaucracy and political repression so characteristic of Communist-controlled nations.

Dubcek had worked his way up through the rank and file of Eastern European Communism. Born in the Slovak village of Uhrovec on November 27, 1921, he was raised in the Soviet Union and attended school there. His father, Stephan Dubcek, was a cabinetmaker who had emigrated to the U.S. before W.W. I, only to return to Europe a few months before his son's birth and become one of the 1st members of the Czechoslovak Communist party. Young Alexander joined the party at 18. His family returned from Russia to their native land just before W.W. II. During that conflict, Dubcek was a partisan guerrilla. When hostilities ceased in 1945, he found work in a yeast factory, despite the general treatment of partisans as heroes. Dubcek, in fact, had been wounded twice in combat.

But when the Soviets took over Czechoslovakia in 1949, Dubcek entered political life as an *apparatchik*, or "petty bureaucrat." In 1953, he was named chief secretary of the Regional Committee of Slovakia in Banska Bystrica. It was a high-level post which Dubcek filled until 1955. Eugen Loebl, a political exile and economist who knew Dubcek well, has remarked that "Only men who actively supported Stalinism in Czechoslovakia remained in office during those years. In order to advance his career Dubcek approved the purge trials of the 1950s and helped to organize public opinion in favor of them."

Viewed by the party as a promising young turk, Dubcek was sent to the Higher Party School in Moscow in 1955, where he was put through close scrutiny and testing until 1958. That year he was sent home to become chief secretary of the Regional Committee of the Communist party in Bratislava—the city he would come to call home. Within 2 years he was a member of the Presidium and was also the industrial secretary of the Central Committee of the Communist party, with headquarters in Prague. As head of all industry in the country, Dubcek became the right-hand man of Antonin Novotny, then the pro-Stalinist President of Czechoslovakia. Novotny saw to it that Dubcek would share the spoils of the Khrushchev "liberalization" era and appointed Dubcek the 1st secretary of the Slovak party in 1963. Dubcek, allegedly on the advice of a known Soviet agent named Vasil Bilak, took advantage of ethnic polarities in his politically confused country. In January, 1968, he replaced Novotny as 1st secretary and President.

The "springtime of freedom" in Czechoslovakia was short-lived. In August, 1968, the Soviet Army invaded with its tanks and curfews. In April, 1969, Dubcek was forced to step down, surrendering the Presidency to Dr. Gustav Husak, an old enemy.

And Today: Alexander Dubcek is a victim of what *Life* magazine crassly called "socialist downward mobility." From April to October, 1969, he served as chairman of the National Assembly. In January, 1970, he was named Ambassador to Turkey, only to be recalled in June of that year and ousted from the party. In the late spring of 1971, it was discovered that he managed a garage for the Bratislava parks department and he was photographed commuting on city trains with his fellow "comrades." In the fall of 1972, Dubcek was reportedly working at a desk job and wearing a green uniform at the Regional Forestry Administration. At that time he lived with his family in Bratislava on Mouse Street—perhaps an apt name. Recently, the Czechoslovak Embassy in Washington confirmed that Alexander Dubcek still labored as a clerk in Bratislava. However, during 1975, Dubcek began to openly criticize the Czech Government. Fearing a resurgence of support for Dubcek and his democratic ideals, the Government launched a strong propaganda campaign against him and told him that he was free to leave the country forever.

—·W.F.R.

25

The People's Directory

The People's Directory

Do you want help? Do you want friends? Do you want new interests?

It's all here in the White Pages.

Do you want to collect buttons? Do you want to save a compulsive gambler? Do you want to go upward and onward with Horatio Alger? Do you want to protest against pay toilets? Do you want to meet fellow crossword-puzzle freaks? Do you want to save the world from The Bomb? Do you want to know more about the *Titanic*? Do you want to learn how to do nothing?

Just consult this special directory prepared exclusively for you by the editors of *The People's Almanac*. The editors have communicated directly with each of the organizations listed to be certain that the material is firsthand, complete, accurate, and up-to-date. Feel free to write to any of these organizations—serious or crazy—and rub elbows with the likes of John Wayne, Carol Doda, Nelson Rockefeller, Soupy Sales, Bing Crosby, Joan Baez. If any listing here is not what it purports to be, or if you have new listings to suggest, feel free to write the editors of *The People's Almanac*, P.O. Box 49328, Los Angeles, Calif. 90049.

A

Aaron Burr Association, Tremont, Inca Road, Linden, Va. 22642
. . . Founded in 1946 "as a patriotic and educational organization interested in the life and career of Col. Aaron Burr, who served as the Vice-President of the U.S. from 1801 to 1805." Supports historical research and proper determination and interpretation of historical facts. Protests against the use of derogatory terms in any description of Col. Aaron Burr and advocates that he was "intelligent, learned, brave, adventurous, ambitious, forceful, just, straightforward, outspoken, compassionate, considerate, etc." Annual dues are $7.50 and this includes a subscription to *The Chronicle of ABA*. Among the members are descendants of the Burr family in America.

Amnesty International of the U.S.A., Inc., 200 W. 72nd St., Room 64, New York, N.Y. 10023
. . . Founded in 1966. Works for the release of Prisoners of Conscience and opposes the death penalty and "the torture, cruel, inhuman, or otherwise degrading treatment of anyone imprisoned, detained, or restricted in violation of the provisions of the Universal Declaration of Human Rights." Is an affiliate of Amnesty International which has 1,100 groups in 31 countries. Has advisory status with the UN, UNESCO, the Council of Europe, the Organization of African Unity, and the Organization of American States. Each group "adopts" 3 Prisoners of Conscience "selected from countries balanced geographically and politically to ensure neutrality." Publishes a variety of books, pamphlets, and reports. Cost of membership is $10 for students, $15 for nonstudents, and $20 for couples. Members and patrons have included Erich Fromm, Pablo Casals, the Archbishop of Canterbury, Ramsey Clark, Joan Baez, William Buckley, Jr., Sen. Jacob Javits, Frank Mankiewicz. 5,000 members, 80 chapters.

Anti-Vivisection Society, American, 1903 Chestnut St., Philadelphia, Pa. 19103
. . . Founded in 1883 for the prevention of cruelty to animals and "to promote the educational, charitable, and humane work of the society." Dues are $2 per year or $25 for a life membership. Publishes the *A-V*. 12,000 members.

Atheist Association, Box 2832, San Diego, Calif. 92112
. . . Founded in 1925. States that "God is a myth, religion is a fraud, the clergy are selfish deceivers," and that "the nearest thing to a god the Atheists have is the regard for Truth, and our doctrine is human happiness." Asks for $5 membership fee "to help expose the gigantic fraud of religion, to help make these deceivers pay taxes on their $10 billion annual income, on their $400 billion in property." Celebrates the birthdays of Thomas Paine and Robert Ingersoll. Publishes *The Atheist*. 200 members.

Autograph Collector's Club, Universal, 1211 Avenue I, Brooklyn, N.Y. 11230
. . . Founded in 1965 "to advance the interest of autograph collectors and popularize the art and study of autograph collecting." Publishes *The Pen and Quill*, and supplies members with a *Glossary of Autographic Terminology* which provides basic and essential information for both novices and professional collectors. Holds annual auction with stamp- and coin-collecting organizations. Cost is $6 for U.S.A. members, $10 for foreign members. 455 members.

B

Barber Shop Quartet Singing in America, Inc., The Society for the Preservation and Encouragement of, 6315 3rd Ave., Kenosha, Wis. 53141
. . . Founded in 1938. Purpose: "To preserve and encourage the barbershop style of singing; to sing in harmony and to live in harmony with your fellowmen. The society has one goal toward which it is constantly striving, and that is to 'Keep America Singing' with 'Songs of Service.'" Holds annual local, district, State, national, and international contests in quartet and chorus singing. Welcomes into its membership adult males, "young and old, from every walk of life who get satisfaction from being a central part of a chord of music whether it originates from the heart or from a musical arrangement." Publishes bimonthly magazine, *The Harmonizer*. Dues are $18 per year. Offers records and tapes for sale. Members have included Bing Crosby, James Gregory, and William Hanna. 35,000 members, 750 chapters.

Bottle Clubs, The Federation of Historical, % Gene Bradberry, 4098 Faxon Ave., Memphis, Tenn. 38122
. . . Founded in 1969 "to promote, foster, and encourage all activities toward the betterment of bottle collecting." Club membership is $10 per year. *The Federation Jour-*

nal is published twice a year and a monthly newsletter is issued to each member. Regional meetings are held twice a year. In 1976 the 1st bottle exposition will be held in St. Louis with the support and backing of Anheuser Busch, Corning Glass, and others. 2,500 members, 123 chapters.

Bullfighting, The International Council Against, % Alfred Weirs, 1 Littledale, Lanes End, Darenth, Kent, England
. . . Founded in 1960 "to end bullfighting —internationally." Membership is £1 per year and includes a subscription to their newsletters. Sponsors an annual meeting in London.

Button Society, National, Box 116, Lamoni, Ia. 50140
. . . Founded in 1938 "to promote educational exhibits, to encourage research, to publish and disseminate information among its members, and to preserve for future generations all that is beautiful and historical in buttons." Annual dues are $5. Publishes bimonthly, *The National Button Bulletin*. Sponsors State meetings and an annual convention. Prepares various books and pamphlets. 2,234 members, 29 chapters.

C

Checks Anonymous, The New Life Group of, P.O. Box 81248, Nebraska Penal and Correctional Complex, Lincoln, Nebr. 68501
. . . Founded in 1963 by the inmates of the Nebraska Penal and Correctional Complex "to provide for the rehabilitation and recovery of convicted habitual check writers and also for the payment and restitution to their victims." Provides the public with information to help prevent the passing of bad checks. Publishes the *C.A. Monthly*. Dues are 75¢ a month. Holds "Bad Check Writing Symposiums" throughout the State of Nebraska at the request of chambers of commerce, bankers' associations, credit bureaus, and law enforcement agencies.

Circus Fans' Association of America, P.O. Box 605, Aurora, Ill. 60507
. . . Founded in 1926 for "grown-up kids who once carried water for the elephants or wanted to—and who still continue to do so on an advanced scale." Helps "to preserve and perpetuate the circus and to bring to the public a true understanding and appreciation of the educational and recreational value of the circus." Aids circus museums across the country, works against unfavorable circus legislation, gathers advance information for circus agents, helps with contracts and licenses. Publishes a bimonthly magazine, *The White Tops*. 2,000 members.

Clowns of America, 2715 E. Fayette St., Baltimore, Md. 21224

. . . Founded in 1968. Intends "to teach and educate and act as a gathering place for the serious-minded amateur, semiprofessional, and professional clown . . . and to learn about an art misunderstood for many generations." Dues are $7 and all members receive a membership certificate and card, a copy of the constitution and bylaws, plus 12 issues of the official publication, *Calliope*, which includes articles written by members and information on props, makeup, costuming, clown's tips, and tricks. Sponsors National Clown Week, August 1–7. 3,200 members.

Comic Art Fans and Collectors, Academy of, P.O. Box 7499, North End Station, Detroit, Mich. 48202

. . . Founded in 1961 "to promote interest in and the preservation of American comic books." Distributes, for purchase only, microfilm reels of over 100 rare comic books and a 4-volume reference book, *The Who's Who of American Comic Books*. No membership fee. 2,500 members, 20 chapters.

Common Cause, 2030 M St. NW, Washington, D.C. 20036

. . . Founded in 1970 as a citizens' lobby to revitalize self-government at the Federal, State, and local levels. States that "through extensive lobbying efforts in the public interest, we are giving the ordinary citizen the great strength he needs in a society where government is supposed to 'derive its just powers from the consent of the governed.'" Membership cost is $15 per year; $7 for those under the age of 26. Issues a *Report from Washington* 10 times a year. The member-elected governing board convenes 3 times a year and meetings are open to all members and to the public. 330,000 members. Local steering committees function in all 50 States and in more than 325 congressional districts.

Consumer's Education and Protective Association, 6048 Ogontz Ave., Philadelphia, Pa. 19141

. . . Founded in 1966 "to protect consumers against fraud, illegal fees and charges, deceptive advertising, packaging, and labeling." Investigates consumers' complaints and negotiates with merchants to settle disputes. If necessary, engages in peaceful, educational picketing. Claims to have saved hundreds of homes from sheriff's sales and to have secured refunds of hundreds of thousands of dollars for victims of consumer fraud. Conducts consumer education programs and strives to combat the rising cost of living. Initiation fee is $3 and monthly dues are $2. A year's subscription to their newspaper, *Consumer's Voice*, is $3. 25 chapters in 10 States.

Count Dracula Society, 334 W. 54th St., Los Angeles, Calif. 90037

. . . Founded in 1962 for the "serious study of horror films and Gothic literature." Student membership is $7. Nonstudent is $10. Sponsors annual Mrs. Ann Radcliffe Awards for best in horror in cinema, literature, and television. Has honored Vincent Price, Peter Lorre, Lon Chaney, Jr., Alfred Hitchcock, Rod Serling, Ray Bradbury, Boris Karloff, plus many others. Holds film conferences, film seminars, and other related activities. Publishes *The Count Dracula Quarterly*. 700 members, 5 chapters.

D

Ding-a-Ling Club, National, P.O. Box 248, Melrose Park, Ill. 60161

. . . Founded in 1971 "to promote the idea that a ding-a-ling is a wonderful, loving, intelligent, friendly, and the most desirable kind of person to know . . . a real bell-ringer!" Dues are $3 a year and new members receive a membership card, button, and bumper sticker. Publishes a monthly newsletter, *Pealings*, which promotes "less wiles, more smiles; less tears, more cheers; less shove, more love." Sponsors an annual National Ding-a-Ling Day on December 12. 600 members.

Dowsers, Inc., The American Society of, 957 Norwood Ave., Schenectady, N.Y. 12303

. . . Founded in 1961 "to increase recognition of the value of dowsing, to improve the quality of dowsing practices, to interest people in finding out if they can dowse, to study the dowsing process." Claims that "everyone is born" with the capacity to dowse, that children up to the age of 15 or 16 "are almost universally sensitive," and that "in any group of 25 adults between 2 and 5 will obtain the dowsing reaction immediately when properly instructed." Dues are $6 per year. Publishes a quarterly, *The American Dowser*, and sponsors an annual convention. 1,200 members, 9 chapters.

E

Exotique Dancers' League, % Jennie Lee, 755 N. Pacific Ave., San Pedro Harbor, Calif. 90731

. . . Founded in 1955 "to improve the art and image of striptease." Only professional strippers or exotic dancers may join, and cost for a lifetime membership is $2. Publishes *EDL Bulletin* and *American Guild of Variety Artists Newspaper*. Sponsors contests for "Top 10 Best Undressed," "Miss Striptease America," "Miss New Comer," "Miss Noveltease," and winners receive the

Fanny Award. Members have included Carol Doda, Babette Bardo, Tempest Storm, Rita Atlanta, and Gypsy Rose Lee was an honorary member. Chooses Man of the Year, and past recipients include actors Mike Connors and Tony Curtis, plus NBC-TV's Bullwinkle J. Moose. 750 members, 6 chapters.

Expectant Fathers' Day Association, P.O. Box 1414, Hollywood, Fla. 33022
. . . Founded in 1942 "to aid in honoring the forgotten man—the expectant father." Celebrates annual Expectant Fathers' Day in September, when special events are held in honor of expectant fathers. Not a membership organization.

Experiment in International Living, Brattleboro, Vt. 05301
. . . Founded in 1932 "for the purpose of furthering international brotherhood and peace on a person-to-person level through cross-cultural living experiences among people everywhere." Is a nonprofit organization recognized by the U.S. Office of Education. Has a wide range of programs for high school and college students, graduate students, teachers, and young professionals. Cost of programs varies according to format, country, and other considerations. Publishes a quarterly newsletter *Odyssey*, and numerous catalogs, brochures, and reports. There are over 50,000 Experiment alumni, and national offices are located in more than 40 countries.

F

Fiddlers' Association, American Old-Time, 6141 Morrill Ave., Lincoln, Nebr. 68507
. . . Founded in 1965 "to preserve and promote the art and skill of old-time fiddling and its related arts and skills." Annual dues are $5. Publishes *American Fiddlers' News*, which gives up-to-date information on fiddling contests, records, music, books, and on fiddling news around the world. 5,000 members.

Flat Earth Research Society, International, P.O. Box 2533, Lancaster, Calif. 93534
. . . Founded in 1800. Aims "to establish as a fact that this earth is flat and plane and that it does not spin and whirl 1,000 mi. an hour and to expose modern astronomical science as a fraud, myth, a false religion." Claims that the society's factual proof that the earth is flat has been ignored because "it's a thing that can't be explained" and that to disprove the round-earth theory "would bring down the government, would bring down education—it would bring down everything." Dues are $5 per year and include a subscription to *Flat Earth News*. 100 members, 2 chapters.

Fortean Organization, The International, P.O. Box 367, Arlington, Va. 22210
. . . Founded in 1965 and derives its name from American writer Charles Fort (1874–1932) "who demonstrated that we live in a wild, weird, wonderful world." Investigates the borderlands of science and considers open-mindedly "UFOs, sea and lake monsters, falls of blood, psychic phenomena, abominable snowmen, poltergeists, phantom planets, unidentified submarine objects, and the entire spectrum of the mysterious and unknown. . . ." Invites all "adventurous spirits" to join for $6 a year, which includes a subscription to their quarterly, *The INFO Journal*. Holds annual convention in August. 1,500 members, 4 chapters.

Freedom of Information Center, P.O. Box 858, Columbia, Mo. 65201
. . . Founded in 1958 by the School of Journalism at the University of Missouri, "to report and comment on actions by the government, society, and the media that affect the acquisition, presentation, and dissemination of information." Acts as a "national clearinghouse of information, immediately at hand, on problems of the flow of information, on the debates these problems occasion, and on the solutions, defeats, and victories that come in the unending struggle of the individual to be informed of the purposes of his government and of nongovernmental organizations that manipulate information in ways they believe to be in his interest." Membership is $25 annually. Issues 2 monthly reports, a bimonthly *Digest*, and offers numerous publications for sale. 1,200 members.

Friends of Animals, Inc., 11 W. 60th St., New York, N.Y. 10023
. . . Founded in 1957 as "a humane conservation organization dedicated to regaining ecological balance through preservation of wildlife's territory and elimination of human brutality to animals." Claims that "America has an annual surplus crop of 25 million unwanted cats and dogs—who will die of hunger, disease, or exposure" and that "only a few 'lucky' ones will be humanely destroyed in the death chambers of animal shelters." Membership dues are $10 annually. Publishes *Actionline*. 50,000 members.

Friends of the Earth, 529 Commercial St., San Francisco, Calif. 94111
. . . Founded in 1969 "to restore and preserve the Earth's resources through a lobbying and educational program aimed at improving public awareness and achievement of better environmental legislation." Annual dues are $7.50 for students, $15 for nonstudents. Monthly publication is *Not Man Apart*.

Members have included Candice Bergen, Paul Ehrlich, Karl Menninger, George Plimpton, and Pete Seeger. 20,000 members.

Friends of Micronesia, 2390 Parker St., No. 11, Berkeley, Calif. 94704
. . . Founded in 1970 to "increase public awareness and develop support for the Micronesian people." Issues a quarterly newspaper and various other publications. Dues are $5 per year. Holds an International Conference in Micronesia. 3,000 members, 14 chapters.

Frisbee Association, International, P.O. Box 4578, North Hollywood, Calif. 91607
. . . Founded in 1967 to honor the game of Frisbee (a plastic saucer-shaped disk which game players throw back and forth). Aims "to serve as the focal point of worldwide Frisbee communications, to encourage self-improvement in Frisbee skills, to sanction competitions, to promote rapport among all Frisbee enthusiasts." Has a proficiency rating system which certifies each member as a novice, an amateur, an expert, or a master. Lifetime membership costs $1, and a subscription to the *IFA Newsletter,* published quarterly, is $2 a year. Holds an annual tournament. Members have included Prime Minister Pierre Trudeau of Canada, actor Richard Burton, and astronaut Neil Armstrong. 66,000 members, 37 chapters.

G

Gamblers Anonymous, P.O. Box 17173, Los Angeles, Calif. 90017
. . . Founded in 1957 as "a self-help fellowship designed to help the compulsive gambler to control his gambling problem." No dues or fees. Members attend regular meetings and GA sponsors 3 conventions a year. Publishes a monthly bulletin. 6,500 members, 350 chapters.

Good Bears of the World, Hawaiian Den, P.O. Box 8236, Honolulu, Hawaii 96815 (International Headquarters: Berne, Switzerland)
. . . Chartered in 1973 in Berne, Switzerland, "to promote goodwill, to encourage affection toward children, especially ailing children, and to engage and participate in all activities exercised by other corporations in promoting the realization of the objects of this association." Forms local groups, called dens, which distribute teddy bears to lonely and sick children in hospitals and other institutions. Plans to expand its humanitarian efforts into research, education, and related fields. Celebrates Good Bear Day on October 27, the birthday of Theodore Roosevelt, after whom the teddy bear is named. Publishes a newsletter, *Bear Tracks.* 500 members, 7 chapters.

H

Horatio Alger Society, % Carl T. Hartmann, 4907 Allison Dr., Lansing, Mich. 48910
. . . Purpose is "to further the philosophy of Horation Alger, Jr., and to encourage the spirit of strive and succeed that for half a century guided Alger's undaunted heroes—lads whose struggles epitomized the Great American Dream and flamed hero ideals in countless millions of young Americans." A free copy of monthly publication, *Newsboy,* will be sent to those interested in joining. Cost of membership is $5 annually. 218 members, 7 chapters.

Horror Films and Science Fiction Films, Academy of, 334 W. 54th St., Los Angeles, Calif. 90037
. . . Founded in 1972 to present awards for the best horror film and best science fiction film of the year. Membership is by invitation only and details can be obtained by writing to the above address. Sponsors an annual theater presentation in Hollywood. Patrons include noted film actors, directors, writers, and producers. 200 members.

I

Insurance Consumers' Union/Policyholders Protective Association, P.O. Box 3232, Jekyll Island, Ga. 31520
. . . Founded in 1971 "to compel insurance companies to pay just claims and treat consumers fairly." Founder and chairman John Gregg, a former insurance agent, says: "What we are doing is using the collective muscle power of many thousands of little people to offset the economic imbalance between the individual policyholder and his multibillion-dollar insurance company adversary." Voluntary contributions, suggested at a minimum of $15 per year, qualifies one for membership. Distributes 2 books, *The Health Insurance Racket and How to Beat It* and *Policyholders' Guidebook on Insurance Collecting* (both authored by John Gregg). 4,000 members, divisions in 14 States.

J

Jim Smith Society, 2016 Milltown, Camp Hill, Pa. 17011
. . . Founded in 1969. The *Jim Smith Society Newsletter* states that "membership is not open to any Smith . . . just Jims." Members must possess "vision, imagination, and spirit." Quarterly newsletter gives information on Jim Smiths everywhere. A $5 membership fee entitles one to a member-

ship certificate and card, 2 Jim Smith wooden nickels, 4 issues of the newsletter, and "surprise features." Sponsors an annual Fun Festival. Plans for 1976 include a pilgrimage to Philadelphia and possibly York, Pa., for ceremonies at the grave of James Smith, signer of the Declaration of Independence. 475 members.

Jogging Association, National, 1910 K St. NW, Suite 202, Washington, D.C. 20006
. . . Founded in 1968 "to promote preventative medicine through exercise, fitness, and health-book sales, motivational materials." A $10 initiation fee is required to join and renewal dues are $8 a year. Publishes a newsletter, *The Jogger.* Sponsors an annual National Jogging Day. Members have included Richard M. Nixon, Strom Thurmond, Stuart Udall, and Neil Armstrong. 6,200 members, 50 chapters.

Juggler's Association, International, 45 1st Ave., 5-K, New York, N.Y. 10003
. . . Founded in 1947 "to further the art of juggling; to render assistance to fellow jugglers." Cost of membership is $7 for the 1st year; $6 thereafter. Publishes a monthly newsletter. Holds annual world juggling championships. 225 members.

K

Kitefliers' Association, International, 321 E. 48th St., New York N.Y. 10017
. . . Founded in 1948 "to encourage kite flying as an amateur sport." Publishes *The Young Sportsman's Guide to Kite Flying* and *The Complete Book of Kites and Kite Flying,* and occasional newsletters. Sponsors annual Ben Franklin Flyoff on January 17 (Franklin's birthday) in Sarasota, Fla., an annual Flyoff in New York's Central Park and every 10 years holds a Flyoff in India on the lawn of the Hunting Palace of the Maharajah of Bharatpur. No fees or dues. Send a self-addressed stamped envelope for membership card. Prominent members have included the Maharajah of Bharatpur, some members of the Kennedy family, former NYC mayor John Lindsay, Vice-President Nelson Rockefeller, and Sen. Jacob Javits. 25,000 members, 2 chapters

L

La Leche League International, Inc., 9616 Minneapolis Ave., Franklin Park, Ill. 60131
. . . Founded in 1956 "to help mothers who wish to breast-feed their infants." Dues are $8 per year and include a subscription to a bimonthly publication. Holds an international conference every 3 years. Sponsors

workshops, seminars, and lectures on childbirth and breast-feeding. Members have included Princess Grace of Monaco, Natalie Wood, and Susan St. James. 80,000 members, 1,800 chapters.

Legal In-Service Project Reservists' Committee, 355 Boylston St., Boston, Mass. 02135
. . . Founded in 1969 "to inform and counsel service people of their legal rights, to expose and organize against corruption within the military (such as racism, sexism, individual harassment, recruiting practices), and to fight militarism and imperialism." No membership dues but a voluntary contribution entitles members to a subscription to their newsletter, *Redline.* 2,700 members.

Liars Club, Burlington, Burlington, Wis. 53105
. . . Founded around 1930. According to founder and 1st president Otis Hulett, "We're probably the only honest men on the face of the earth. You see, everybody is a bit of a liar, but we are the only ones who admit it." Each year approximately 97,000 worldwide liars submit letters to the club in the hope of winning the title of World Champion Liar. "Sometimes," says Hulett, "we figure we've seen the last of some stories. But they come back and haunt us year in year out—like the one about the man who had one bullet left in his gun, and 2 bears acomin' at him. So he shot his gun at a knife which cut the bullet in 2. And each half killed a bear."

M

Marijuana Laws, National Organization for the Reform of, 2317 M St. NW, Washington, D.C. 20037
. . . Founded in 1970 as a "nonprofit public interest lobby working for the elimination of criminal penalties for smoking marijuana." Does not encourage or advocate the use of marijuana but feels that "unjust laws, like the current marijuana laws, do irreparable harm to our entire legal system." Cost for joining is $10 for students and the military, $15 for all others. Publishes a newsletter, *The Leaflet.* Members have included Ramsey Clark and Dr. Benjamin Spock. 20,000 members, 50 chapters.

Marxist Studies, American Institute for, 20 E. 30th St., New York, N.Y. 10016
. . . Founded in 1964. Is a nonprofit, educational, research, and bibliographical institute "to help foster Marxist scholarship in the U.S.; to help produce a dialogue among Marxist and non-Marxist scholars." Members represent varied philosophic outlooks but all "are agreed as to the significance of the Marxist and all believe that only through

the fullest and most cordial discussion and intellectual intercourse can the cause of science and of reason be served." No membership dues. Subscription to the bi-monthly newsletter *AIMS* is $4, which lists current publications available through the institute. 3,600 members.

Mayflower Descendants, General Society of, P.O. Box 297, Plymouth, Mass. 02360
. . . Founded in 1897 "to perpetuate the memory of our Pilgrim Fathers, to maintain and defend the principle of civil and re-ligious liberty as set forth in the Compact of the *Mayflower*, to cherish and maintain the ideals and institutions of American free-dom." Publishes original material in regard to the Pilgrims. Preserves and marks his-torical spots made memorable by the Pilgrims. Applicants for membership "must be of bona fide descent from one of the 23 families on the *Mayflower* who are presently known to have descendants." Publishes the *Mayflower Index* and *The Mayflower Quar-terly*. Fees differ according to which branch of the 50 State societies you join. Members have included President Taft, astronaut Alan Shepard, Nelson and Winthrop Rockefel-ler, Grandma Moses, Bing Crosby, and Edie Adams. 16,000 members.

Millard Fillmore Society, 43 N. Madison Ave., Spring Valley, N.Y. 10977
. . . Founded in 1963 "to perpetuate the memory of the 13th President, holding his actions as exemplary examples of inconsis-tency." Members point out that Fillmore, "the most forgotten President of the U.S.," was "the 1st to establish the White House Library, the 1st to have a bathtub, an iron cookstove, and a stepmother." Sponsors an annual birthday party for Fillmore on Janu-ary 7 and a national essay contest. Topic: "What would America be today had there been no Millard Fillmore?"—cash prizes are awarded to winners. Holds a yearly Millard Fillmore Day at Shea Stadium to raise funds so that institutionalized children can attend a New York Mets baseball game. A donation to the society entitles one to mem-bership. Will soon publish a magazine, *Milestones with Millard*. 15 chapters.

Monopoly Association, United States, 1866 City National Bldg., Detroit, Mich. 48226
. . . Founded in 1963 for enthusiastic players of Monopoly, the real-estate trading game distributed by Parker Brothers, Inc. Initia-tion fee is $7, with annual renewal dues of $6. Holds an annual tournament in October. Publishes *Tourney Notes*. 450 members.

Mothers-in-Law Club International, Inc., 699 Park Lane, Cedarhurst, Long Island, N.Y. 11516

. . . Founded in 1971 "to provide aid to every family throughout the country and world and to dispel the hackneyed concept of the mother-in-law myth." Dues are $10 per year. Issues a newsletter. Holds monthly meetings.

Mothers of Twins Clubs, Inc., National Or-ganization of, % Mrs. Thomas Meyer, 5402 Amberwood Lane, Rockville, Md. 20853
. . . Founded in 1960 "to broaden the un-derstanding of those aspects of child develop-ment and rearing which relate especially to twins, through interchange of information between parents, educators, doctors, and others with a direct interest and appropriate experience." Application fee is $5, dues are $20, plus an annual 25¢ membership fee. Publishes *MOTC's Notebook*, the official newsletter which reports the latest news on research projects, plus other articles of in-terest to mothers of twins. 9,000 members, 225 chapters.

N

Name Society, American, State University College, Potsdam, N.Y. 13676
. . . Founded in 1951 "for the study of the etymology, origin, meaning, and applica-tion of all categories of names—geographical, scientific, personal, commercial, popular—and the dissemination of the results of such study." Membership dues are $10 per year. Publishes a quarterly, *Names*. 900 mem-bers.

National Nothing Foundation, 300-56 Plum St., Capitola, Calif. 95010
. . . Founded in 1973 "to protest the pro-liferation of special days and weeks by pro-viding Americans with one 24-hour period when they can just sit—without celebrating or honoring anything." Founder Harold Coffin was selected as Chairman of NNF "Because nothing is something he does better than anybody else." National Nothing Day is celebrated worldwide every year on Janu-ary 16. "The only regret of the negative thinkers in the Nothing Foundation is that in order to combat the proliferation of spe-cial days they were forced to create an addi-tional special day." An expression of interest in the foundation's purposes qualifies one for membership. Total number of members is unknown. Publishes nothing. Holds no meetings or conventions.

Ninety-Nines, Inc., P.O. Box 59964, Okla-homa City, Okla. 73159
. . . Founded in 1929 by Amelia Earhart. Purpose is "to provide a close relationship among women pilots and to unite them in any movement that may be for their bene-

fit or for that of aviation in general." Assists aerospace education groups such as the Civil Air Patrol, Civil Defense, National Aerospace Education Council, and National Intercollegiate Flying Association. Sponsors variety of air races. Membership is by invitation only and is limited to women possessing active pilots licenses. Husbands of Ninety-Nines, called 49½ers, are strong supporters of the group's activities. 4,300 members, 141 chapters.

Non-Parents, National Organization for, 8 Sudbrook Lane, Baltimore, Md. 21208
. . . Founded in 1972 as "a population organization and a personal rights organization which supports the emergence of child-free life-styles in the hope of achieving a better and more spacious and humane world for ourselves, and for the children of tomorrow." Works to change both economic and social discrimination against non-parents. Dues are $10 per year and membership is open to both parents and non-parents who "share the philosophy that those who elect to remain child-free must be accorded respect and equitable treatment, as well as recognition of their significant contribution to society." Members have included Hugh Downs, Jim Bouton, Shirley MacLaine, Anthony Newley, and Alvin Toffler. 2,000 members, 30 chapters.

North American Trail Complex, 307 S. Highland, P.O. Box 805, Bloomington, Ind. 47401
. . . Founded in 1971 "to develop a vast network of hiking trails, interconnecting all regions of the continent, to encourage expeditionary and nomadic interests." Dues, which are $7 per year, include a subscription to a periodic newsletter, the Echo, and entitle members to a 20% discount on guide maps. Needs "volunteer scouts"—no experience required—to explore and take notes on sections of the trail study routes to help evaluate their desirability and conditions. 5,000 members.

P

Parents Without Partners, Inc., 7910 Woodmont Ave., Suite 1000, Washington, D.C. 20014
. . . Founded in 1957. An international organization of single parents—widowed, divorced, separated, or never married—"who have come together for mutual help so that our single-parent homes can better provide a happy family environment in which to bring up our children." Membership cost is $6.50 per year. Publishes The Single Parent magazine, which features articles on such topics as child-rearing, income taxes, remarriage, psychological problems and adjustments, plus many others. Individual chapters sponsor lectures, discussion groups, newsletters, recreational and social activities. 90,-000 members, 746 chapters.

Pay Toilets in America, Committee to End, 1326 Amherst Place, Dayton, O. 45406
. . . Founded in 1970. Purpose is to eliminate pay toilets in the U.S. through legislation and public pressure. Ira Gessel, founder and 1st president of CEPTIA, states, "When a man's or woman's natural body functions are restricted because he or she doesn't have a piece of change, there is no true freedom." Membership cost is 25¢ and entitles you to a subscription to their publication, Free Toilet Paper. Sponsors annual Thomas Crapper Memorial Award which is given to "the person who has made an outstanding contribution to the cause of CEPTIA and free toilets." 1,500 members, 7 chapters.

Political Items Collectors, American, % Donald Coney, 66 Golf St., Newington, Conn. 06111
. . . Founded in 1945 "to encourage the collection, preservation, and study of political Americana." APIC follows the paths of political candidates, and its quarterly publication, The Keynoter, contains feature articles on candidates, parties, and campaigns. A Committee on Ethics "alerts the membership to the output of fake items (brummagem) and the organization strives to curb the production and distribution of such items, denouncing all fake items." Collectibles include buttons, jewelry, sheet music, tokens, medals, badges, ribbons, posters, canes, ballots, handbills, and other novelty items. Cost is $8 annually. 2,000 members, 35 chapters.

Popular Culture Association, University Hall, Bowling Green University, Bowling Green, O. 43403
. . . Founded in 1969 "to encourage the academic study of our popular culture, i.e. the media and mass communication." Cost is $7.50 for students, $15 for nonstudents. Publishes Journal of Popular Culture and Popular Culture Newsletter. 2,000 members, 8 chapters.

Procrastinators' Club of America, Inc., 1111 Broad-Locust Bldg., Philadelphia, Pa. 19102
. . . Founded in 1956 "to promote the fine art of procrastination to nonprocrastinators, to make known the benefits of putting things off until later, to honor those people who have performed exceptional acts of procrastination, and to have fun." Publishes Last Month's Newsletter. Sponsors National Procrastination Week, the 1st week in

March. Has protested against the War of 1812, attempted to get the founders of the Liberty Bell to fix the crack, and has traveled to Spain to raise money for 3 ships with which to discover America. Holds irregular and late meetings. Membership cost is $5 per year. 1,900 members, 3 chapters.

Prospector's and Treasure Hunter's Guild, 210 Exanimo Bldg., Segundo, Colo. 81070
. . . Founded in 1971. "Provides information on technical developments in the fields of prospecting, small mining, and treasure hunting." An initiation of $1 plus $5 annual dues entitles new members to a membership diploma and card, decal, technical bulletins, and discounts on equipment. The guild participates in conventions such as the Oklahoma City Treasure Show, the annual convention of the Prospector's Club of Southern California, and the West Coast Prospector's Olympics. Members have included adventurer/author Karl von Mueller, treasure hunter Rus Hendricks, and movie star John Wayne. 3,500 members.

Pussycat League, Inc., 255 W. 84th St., New York, N.Y. 10024
. . . Founded in 1969 "to answer militant feminism and to promote American femininity." Dues are $7 per year. Publishes a monthly newsletter, *Adam's Rib.* 1,500 members, 7 chapters.

Puzzlers' League, National, c/o Mary J. Youngquist, Editor, 299 McCall Road, Rochester, N.Y. 14616
. . . Founded in 1883. Devoted to the fun of word puzzling, "a pastime which will give you more pleasure, for less expense, than any other hobby under the sun." Membership is $5 per year and includes a subscription to the monthly publication *The Enigma,* the "battleground where members entertain each other, where the constructors challenge the solvers, and where wit and humor are the order of the day." Approximately 75% of the word puzzles appearing in *The Enigma* can be solved with the help of a dictionary, a thesaurus, and a book of synonyms and antonyms. 200 members.

R

Ragtime Society, Inc., P.O. Box 520, Weston, Ontario, Canada
. . . Founded in 1962 "to find and preserve classical ragtime music and to pursue such other activities as will serve to maintain and develop interest in this music and the music related thereto." Dues are $5 per year and include a subscription to the bimonthly publication *The Ragtimer.* Offers record albums, sheet music, and books for sale. Holds an annual convention in Toronto. 500 members.

Retired Persons, American Association of, 1909 K St. NW, Washington, D.C. 20006
. . . Founded in 1958 "to help its membership achieve retirement lives of dignity, independence, and purpose." Sponsors consumer education, tax aid, and health education programs. Publishes *Modern Maturity* and *Dynamic Maturity,* plus the *AARP News Bulletin.* Applicants must be 55 years old or older. Dues are $2 a year (includes spouse). 6 million members, 1,700 chapters.

Richard III Society, Inc., c/o Mrs. Linda McLatchie, 9 Weld St., Apt. 48, Framingham, Mass. 01701
. . . Founded in U.S. in 1960, in U.K. in 1920. Purpose is "to assess history of 15th century in light of recent research and establish the truth about Richard III in the face of Tudor and Shakespeare myth." Publishes a quarterly, *Ricardian,* and a bimonthly, *Register.* Membership is $6 for individuals, $10 for couples. 350 members in U.S., 1,500 worldwide.

Right to Keep and Bear Arms, Citizens Committee for, 3214-A, West McGraw, Suite 7, Seattle, Wash. 98199
. . . Founded in 1971 "to defend the 2nd Amendment to the U.S. Constitution." Annual dues are $15. Publishes a monthly newsletter, *Point Blank,* and distributes a book, *Our Vanishing Freedom,* about the right to bear arms. 23,000 members.

S

Sane/A Citizen's Organization for a Sane World, 318 Massachusetts Ave. NE, Washington, D.C. 20002
. . . Founded in 1957 "to educate the American public about the nuclear-arms race, disarmament, and the military budget and to encourage citizen participation in national policy matters affecting war and peace issues." Publishes newsletter *Sane World* plus numerous pamphlets and reports. Annual dues are $15 per person, $5 for senior citizens, $3 for students. Encourages active member participation in community activities. Past recipients of Sane's annual Eleanor Roosevelt Peace Award have been George McGovern, Eugene McCarthy, Dr. Benjamin Spock, Daniel Ellsberg, and Andrei Sakharov. Offers, for sale, a 30-minute slide show entitled "Guns or Butter? Uncle Sam's Military Tapeworm," narrated by Paul Newman. 25,000 members.

Separationists, Society of, P.O. Box 2117, Austin, Tex. 78767

. . . Believes that "the individual taxpayer who does not care to participate in organized religion . . . should not be forced to endure an additional tax burden through any programming, planning, or legislation by members of the governing bodies, either local, State, or national." Claims that the "Federal Government under various programs of assistance is spending $26 million a day in direct cash grants for religious purposes and that this does not count the money they receive indirectly by being free from all taxation." Membership is $12 per year. Publishes a monthly newsletter plus various pamphlets and reports. One of the original founders of SOS is Madalyn Murray O'Hair, whose efforts resulted in the Supreme Court decision to remove Bible reading and prayer recitation from the public schools. 35,000 members, 16 State organizations.

Separation of Church and State, Americans United for, 8120 Fenton St., Silver Spring, Md. 20910
. . . Founded in 1948 "to defend and maintain religious liberty in the U.S. by the dissemination of knowledge concerning the constitutional principle of separation of church and state." Membership cost is $10 per year. Publishes a periodical, *Church and State.* Holds many regional and State meetings and one national meeting every year. Members have included former Sen. Sam J. Ervin and Bishop Edward C. Carroll. 100,000 members, 10 chapters.

Servas Committee, Inc., United States, P.O. Box 790, Old Chelsea Station, New York, N.Y. 10011
. . . Founded in 1948 as "an international cooperative system of hosts and travelers established to help build world peace, goodwill, and understanding by providing opportunities for deeper, more personal contacts among peoples and diverse cultures and backgrounds." Has branches in 50 countries on 6 continents. Annual registration fee is $3. Publishes committee newsletter. 2,000 members.

Shackamaxon Society, Inc., P.O. Box 1777, Philadelphia, Pa. 19107
. . . Founded in 1967. Is a nonprofit corporation of young Philadelphians "dedicated to creative programs which make Philadelphia history come alive." Fee for active members is "a pound of flesh," and associate members pay $25 per year. Sponsors annual W. C. Fields Day, Philadelphia-New York Hoagie Competition, and Celebration of the Troop Withdrawal from Old Fort Mifflin in 1777. Holds periodic Revolutionary War reenactments at Old Fort Mifflin, complete with musket and cannon fire. Publishes a variety of booklets and pamphlets. 100 members.

Signers of the Declaration of Independence, Descendants of the, 1300 Locust St., Philadelphia, Pa. 19107
. . . Founded in 1907 "to keep alive the importance of our Declaration of Independence and promote the ideals our signers fought and many actually gave their lives for." To join, applicants must show documented proof of lineal descendancy. Holds annual meeting at Independence Hall. A $5 enrollment fee is required, $8 annual dues for adults, $2 for junior members. Publishes *The Signer's Bulletin.* 850 members, 4 chapters.

Small Castle Owners of Great Britain and Ireland, Ancient and Honourable Order of, Exhibitors Bldg., Grand Rapids, Mich. 49502
. . . Founded in 1966 "to band together owners of original and authentic castles in order to interchange thoughts on mutual problems." No membership dues but applicants must "own authentic castle—one which was originally built as a fortification and must have much of the defensive architecture still in existence." Issues membership certificates and cards.

Spiritual Healers, National Federation of, Shortacres, Church Hill, Loughton, Essex 1G10 1LG, England
. . . Founded in 1954 "for the due promotion and encouragement of the study and practice of the art and science of spiritual healing—all forms of healing of the sick in body, mind, or spirit, by means of the laying on of hands, or by either prayer or meditation, whether or not in the actual presence of the patient." Has affiliated associations throughout Britain and in Australia, Canada, New Zealand, and South Africa. Full membership is open to healers who can "furnish proof of their bona fides and satisfy the membership committee of their integrity and suitability as federation members." Associate membership is open to all who wish to support the work of the federation. Sponsors national and international conferences, teaching schools, and lectures. Publishes monthly magazine, *Spiritual Healer.* 90,000 members, 12 chapters.

Survivors of Surgery, 3526 N. Oketo Ave., Chicago, Ill. 60634
. . . Celebrates SOS Day, May 8, "in recognition of the beautiful, brave champions of the human race who were bold enough to undergo surgery and survived." States that SOS is "a glorious tribute to the indomitable spirit and willpower of mankind to continue its attempt to survive."

T

Telephone Users' Association, Inc., 816 National Press Bldg., Washington, D.C. 20004
. . . Founded in 1963 as a nonprofit organization "to represent consumer interests in communication fields, particularly telephonic, in court proceedings (rate cases), and in other ways." Publishes a booklet, "How to Save Money on Your Telephone Bills." Not a member organization.

Thoreau Society, Inc., State University College, Genesee, N.Y. 14454
. . . Founded in 1941 as "an informal organization of students and followers of the life and writings of Henry David Thoreau." Publishes quarterly, *Thoreau Society Bulletin*, which tells of the activities of members, prints unpublished Thoreau writings, tells of Thoreau's significance today, and includes reprints of rare Thoreauviana. Sponsors annual convention on the Saturday nearest July 12, in Concord, Mass. Membership is $2 per year or $50 for life membership. 1,000 members.

Titanic Historical Society, Inc., P.O. Box 53, Indian Orchard, Mass. 01051
. . . Founded in 1963, "to investigate and perpetuate the history and memory of the R.M.S. *Titanic* and its sister ships, *Olympic* and *Britannic*." Cost for joining is $7 per year, and members receive a membership certificate and card plus 4 issues of the publication, *Titanic Commutator*. Researches the possibility of salvaging the lost liner and is involved with reprinting *Titanic* books published in 1912. Members include survivors of the *Titanic*. 450 members.

Turtles International, Ltd., 4900 South Karlov Ave., Chicago, Ill. 60632
. . . Founded in 1972. Dedicated to "a better world through humor," and strives to "upgrade the cultural levels of conversation." States that turtlism is "basically sticking your neck out, having fun a lot, promoting friendship, and all the while keeping clean thoughts." Is a charitable organization which donates all proceeds to hospitals for crippled children and homes for mentally retarded children. As the Earl of Turtledom says, "A Turtle is a person who knows that a sense of humor is the pole that adds balance to our steps as we walk the tightrope of life." Lifetime membership is $1. Sponsors a variety of special events during "International Turtle Awareness Week." Offers a number of official turtle accessories for sale: flying turtle pins, bumper stickers, jacket patches, turtle power T-shirts, and a 45 rpm record of the turtle song as recorded by "ole"

lonesome George Gobel. Members have included Chicago Mayor Richard Daley, Howard Hughes, Johnny Carson, and 50 astronauts. There are more than 5 million card-carrying Turtles in the world today.

U

Unicorns, Ltd. Conglomerate, c/o W. T. Rabe, Lake Superior State College, Sault Ste. Marie, Mich. 49783
. . . The conglomerate, "in the traditional American concept, includes a wide range of activities with varied interests." The affiliate agencies listed below require no membership fees or dues. Membership cards are issued upon request, but please send a self-addressed stamped envelope. For other prominent organizations included in Unicorns, Ltd., write to the above address.

UNICORN HUNTERS—Founded in 1969 and "dedicated to the proposition that every man has a unicorn which he is predestined to hunt. It is not necessary that he actually find or slay this unicorn, merely that he diligently seek it." Official publication is *The Woods-Runner*. Sponsors annually, "Snowman Burning Rite to Mark End of Winter, Beginning of Spring," "Shakespeare's Birthday Party," and "Unicorn Hunting Season" (licenses and hunting guides are issued). Members have included newsman Harry Reasoner and Soupy Sales. Well over 3,000 members.

THE NEW ORIGINAL DANCING CUCKOOS—Founded in 1963 "to preserve the spirit of Laurel and Hardy, enjoy their films, confuse the laity." Sponsors annual Mae Bush Banquet at which time the Fine Mess Awards is given to "a public figure who has distinguished himself in the spirit of Laurel and Hardy." Members have included Orson Bean and Dick Van Dyke.

STONE SKIPPING AND GERPLUNKING CLUB OF MACKINAC ISLAND—Founded in 1969 "to encourage development of the sport of stone skipping." Publishes annual newsletter, *The Boulder*. Sponsors International Stone Skipping Tournament every year—current world record is 18 skips established in 1936 (prior to formal competition). 1,500 members.

V

Voluntary Sterilization, Inc., Association for, 708 3rd Ave., New York, N.Y. 10017
. . . Founded in 1937 "to make voluntary sterilization available to all consenting adults without regard to marital status, parenthood, or any other nonmedical criteria." Acts as a

clearinghouse for all material on voluntary sterilization. Supports educational, research, and service programs. Assists those seeking sterilization by referring them to one of the organization's 1,900 cooperating physicians, by referring those for whom sterilization is deemed inadvisable to appropriate agencies, and by informing those of limited financial means of the possibilities of obtaining the operation through city or county health departments and clinics. Cost of membership is $10. Publishes *AVS News* 3 times a year. Sponsors an international project "to foster, stimulate, and support voluntary sterilization activities in various types of health programs all over the world." Members have included Dr. Paul R. Ehrlich, Arthur Godfrey, and Shirley MacLaine. 20,000 members.

W

Wild Horse Organized Assistance, Inc., P.O. Box 555, Reno, Nev. 89504
. . . Founded in 1971 by Velma B. ("Wild Horse Annie") Johnston "to provide care and protection for wild free-roaming horses and burros, and to take whatever steps necessary for the protection and survival of endangered wild horse and burro foals." Conducts field studies, distributes educational material, and provides scholarships for research. Publishes a news bulletin twice a year. Membership is $2 for juniors (under 18), $5 for adults, and $15 for families. Members have included Amanda Blake (Miss Kitty of *Gunsmoke* fame) and Albert G. Miller (writer of the television series *Fury*, a story about a boy and his horse). 10,000 members.
Wildlife, Defenders of, 2000 N St. NW, Washington, D.C. 20036
. . . Founded in 1925 for "the preservation of all forms of wildlife." Publishes *Defenders of Wildlife News*. Membership cost is $5. 40,000 members.
Wizard of Oz Club, The International, c/o Fred M. Meyer, 220 N. 11th St., Escanaba, Mich. 49829
. . . Founded in 1957 "to promote reading, collecting, and enjoyment of the work of L. Frank Baum and his associates and successors in Oz." Publishes a magazine, *The Baum Bugle*, which tells how to recognize 1st editions of Baum books, contains short stories and other writings by Baum, and features Oz music, advertising, and comic strips. Issues, once a year, *Oziana* which contains stories, poems, and artwork by club members. Distributes *Oz Trading Post* where members list Baum and Oz materials for sale or trade. Sponsors annual conven-

tions for the Merrylanders, the Gillikins, the Ozmopolitans, the Munchkins, the Quadlings, the Winkies—of Oz. Cost for joining is $2.50 a year. 1,100 members.
Woman's Own Name, Center for a, 261 Kimberly, Barrington, Ill. 60010
. . . Founded in 1973. Its purpose is "to eliminate discrimination against women who choose to determine their own names despite their marital status, and to educate the public through the collecting, compiling, and distributing of information and materials relating to the names issue." Issues a 56-page booklet, "For Women Who Wish to Determine Their Own Names After Marriage," which covers the basic aspects of names law, children's names, common law and court procedures for name change, historical viewpoints on the issue, comments from persons who have visited the center, and quotations from authorities in the field. Has established an international network comprised of 200 individuals, agencies, and attorneys who provide information and/or support to persons on a local basis.
World Future Society, P.O. Box 30369, Bethesda Branch, Washington, D.C. 20014
. . . Founded in 1966 as a "nonprofit, independent association of scientists, scholars, government officials, businessmen, and others interested in possible social and technological developments during the coming years." Acts as a clearinghouse or forum for forecasts and other ideas about the future. Membership is open to all interested in the future. Annual dues are $10 and include a subscription to the bimonthly journal *The Futurist*. Offers members reduced prices on books, a speakers' bureau, a placement service, the right to participate in local groups, invitations to the periodic general assemblies, and other programs of the society. About 12% of membership is outside the U.S. 15,000 members, 72 chapters.

Z

Zero Automobile Growth, Committee for, P.O. Box 44666, Indianapolis, Ind. 46204
. . . Founded in 1973 "to ring the bell on the automobile, to alert the American people to the full scope of the auto problem, and to educate them to the kind of life-style a society can achieve that does not depend on automobiles." States that "zero auto growth does not mean the end of the automobile, but it is the 1st step in building a more balanced and flexible transportation network for the nation." Membership dues are $2 for students, $5 for nonstudents. Distributes periodic leaflets. Holds an annual "Lemon Day Anti-Car Rally." 130 members, 5 chapters.

Zero Population Growth, Inc., 1346. Connecticut Ave. NW, Washington, D.C. 20036 . . . Founded in 1968 by Dr. Paul R. Ehrlich, ZPG's goals are "stabilization of U.S. population size, followed by reduction to a more reasonable level; stabilization of energy and resource consumption; land use planning." Membership is $15 per year, $8 for students. Fee includes subscription to a newsletter, *National Reporter,* and a quarterly journal, *Equilibrium.* 15,000 members, 200 chapters.

—C.O.

FOR FURTHER READING: *Encyclopedia of Associations.* Edited by Margaret Fisk. Detroit, Mich., Gale Research Co., 1975.

26

Keeping the Faith: Religion

Major World Religions

ANIMISM

Derived from the Latin word *animus*, meaning "spirit," Animism is the belief that all beings, objects, and natural phenomena have souls. Animism is considered by many to be the original religion and is still widespread today, particularly in Africa, South America, and parts of Asia. Indeed, traces of Animism can be found in many of the "advanced" religions of the modern world.

Beliefs and forms of worship vary widely from place to place and tribe to tribe.

JUDAISM

The religion of the Jewish people, Judaism is the oldest of the monotheistic (one god) religions, and both Christianity and Islam are based upon its principal beliefs. The words "Judaism" and "Jew" are derived from "Judah," the ancient Jewish kingdom of southern Palestine.

Judaism was founded by Abraham, who made an agreement with God that he and his offspring would spread the doctrine that there was only one God. In return, God promised Abraham the land of Canaan (Israel) for his descendants.

The Jews 1st came into being as a nation in the 13th century B.C. when the prophet Moses led the Jews out of Egypt, where they had been slaves, and into the land of Canaan. Since that time Judaism has had to struggle to survive. The Jews were kept captive by the Babylonians from 586 B.C. to 537 B.C. and in 70 A.D. Jerusalem was destroyed by the Roman Army and the Jews were either massacred or dispersed. In modern times the Jews have suffered much the same treatment at the hands of the Russians in the late 1800s and early 1900s and the Germans in the 1930s and 1940s. But in 1948 the nation of Israel was reestablished.

Today there are close to 15 million Jews in the world, ¾ of whom live in the U.S., Israel, and the U.S.S.R.

The basic beliefs of Judaism are a love of learning (in ancient times, on the 1st day of school, children were fed honey cakes in the shapes of the letters of the alphabet so that they would associate learning with sweetness); the worship of God out of love, not out of fear; and the performing of heartfelt good deeds without concern about rewards.

Judaism is based upon 2 fundamental texts: the Bible (which in Judaism means the Old Testament) and the Talmud, a compendium of laws, traditions, poetry, anecdotes, biographies, and prophecies of the ancient Jews.

HINDUISM

The word "Hinduism" is derived from "Hindu," the Old Persian name for India, and it describes the religious as well as the social practices and beliefs that the Indian people have developed over more than 50 centuries.

One of the distinguishing elements of Hinduism is the caste system. Historically, India has 4 major castes or divisions of society, each created from a different part of Brahma, an Infinite Being, who pervades all reality. On top are the Brahmans, who originated from Brahma's face and are the caste of priests and intellectuals. The 2nd caste, the Kshatriyas, were created out of Brahma's arms. They are the rulers and men of war and have the same privileges as the Brahmans. The 3rd group, the Vaisyas, sprang from Brahma's thighs. They are farmers, artisans and merchants. The Sudras were made from his feet and it is their duty to serve the 3 castes above them. Far beneath the 4 castes are the pariahs or "untouchables." Mahatma Gandhi renamed the pariahs Harijans, or "Children of God."

Although a person is bound to his caste for life, he is not bound to it through eternity. Hindus believe that after the individual dies, the soul takes up a new life. Whether it will be better or worse than the previous one depends upon karma, which in Sanskrit means "work" or "action." The doctrine of karma has its counterpart in the Judeo-Christian religions, expressed in the biblical saying "Whatsoever a man soweth, that shall he also reap."

Hinduism is rich in sacred scriptures such as: 1. the *Vedas*, which date back to c. 2500 B.C. and include the *Upanishads* ("secret doctrine"), which provide the basis for modern philosophic Hinduism; and 2. the *Mahabharata*, which includes the *Bhagavad-Gita*, or "Song of the Lord," a dramatic poem which discusses the questions of killing, salvation, and attachment.

Three deities dominate popular Hinduism: Brahma the Creator, Vishnu the Preserver, and Siva (Shiva) the Destroyer. Other popular gods are Kali, goddess of death, wife of Siva; Krishna, god of love, an incarnation of Vishnu; and Lakshmi, who brings good fortune.

Today there are over 500 million Hindus subscribing to a great number of sects and schools. Of great influence in the West are the various schools of Yoga ("union" in Sanskrit). Based on the *Sutras* of Patanjali (2nd century B.C.), Yoga has as its goal the freeing of the individual from illusion and achieving union with Brahma.

ZOROASTRIANISM

A religion of ancient Persia, Zoroastrianism still exists on a limited scale in India and Iran. It was founded by Zoroaster (Zarathustra in Persian), who, at the age of 30, began to have a series of revelations which inspired him to preach the new faith. After he converted the King, Vishtaspa, the religion grew rapidly, becoming the state religion of Persia in 226 A.D. Eventually, it was eclipsed by the rise of Islam and today there are fewer than 200,000 practicing Zoroastrians.

TAOISM

According to Chinese tradition, the founder of Taoism was Lao-tze ("old master" or "old philosopher" in Chinese), who is said to have lived in the 6th century B.C., in Honan Province. His name at birth was Li Erh, and he served as an astrologer or librarian in the court of the Chou dynasty. Tradition relates that he had a meeting with Confucius, whom he criticized for his egotism and pride.

The main text of Taoism is the *Tao-te-Ching*, a beautifully simple book allegedly written by Lao-tze. It teaches that peace can be found only in the cultivation of optimism, humility, passivity, and inner calm. The simple, natural life is the ideal one, the wise person seeks to conform to the slow, gentle rhythm of the universe.

Modern Taoism has strayed far from the teachings of Lao-tze, having accumulated an elaborate array of gods and rituals. Because the communists officially banned Taoism when they came to power in China in 1949, it is difficult to estimate how many followers the religion has today. Some say 30 million, others say 55 million.

BUDDHISM

Buddhism is both an ethical philosophy and a religion, deriving from the teaching of Gautama Buddha. Buddha, in Sanskrit, means "the enlightened one" and the title was 1st given to an Indian philosopher named Siddhartha (c. 563–483 B.C.), whose family name was Gautama. Born at the foot of the Himalayas in Lumbini in southern Nepal, Buddha was the son of a rajah of the Sakya clan and a member of the 2nd Hindu caste, the Kshatriyas (warriors and rulers). It had been prophesied he would be a universal teacher or a universal ruler. To keep him from becoming a teacher, his father tried to shield him from experiences that would reveal the misery of the world to him. Nonetheless, at 29, in the royal park, Buddha chanced to see a dead body, a sick man, an old man, and a yellow-robed monk with a begging bowl. The 1st 3 revealed the misery of the world to him, while the peace of the beggar suggested a suitable goal for his life. Leaving his wife, his child, and his princely inheritance behind, he became a wandering hermit in search of enlightenment.

For years Buddha sought but did not find. Finally he seated himself under a wild fig tree and resolved not to get up before he understood the cause of human misery. For 49 days he stayed there, holding out against the temptations of the Wicked One, Mara. Finally, he achieved nirvana, or enlightenment, after he realized all suffering is the result of desire, and the transcendence of desire would cause suffering to cease. For the rest of his life he preached this new gospel, dying at the age of 80.

Buddha taught a way of life which he called the Middle Path because it avoids the extremes of self-denial and self-indulgence. The aim of Buddhism is to achieve nirvana, which in Sanskrit means "blowing out." In nirvana, desire, passion and the ego are extinguished and the individual achieves the end of suffering—the serenity of utter extinction.

Buddhism, in its original form, is a democratic do-it-yourself religion in which salvation can be achieved directly without using intermediaries such as gods and priests. But, like so many religions, as it spread, Buddhism became more and more like those it replaced and Buddha, who was an atheist, was worshiped as a god surrounded by other gods and served by an elaborate structure of monastic orders, priesthoods, temples, and ritual.

The 2 main schools of Buddhism are Hinayana ("the lesser vehicle") and Mahayana ("the greater vehicle"). Hinayana—or Theravada ("the doctrine of the elders"), as it is also known—emphasizes that each individual is responsible for his or her own salvation. It is dominant in Burma, Cambodia, Thailand, and Ceylon.

Mahayana lays stress on universal salvation, saying that all beings are tied together. It established itself firmly in China and spread to Korea and Japan, producing a diversity of sects including Nichiren, Lamaism, and Zen.

Nichiren is a native Japanese phenomenon. Founded by Nichiren (1222–1282) in an age when Japan was ruled by feudal lords, it adapted Buddhism to the Bushido warrior cult by teaching that the state and religion should be a unity. Lamaism, the religion of Tibet and neighboring regions, blended Mahayanist teaching with native demon worship and the erotic practices of tantrism.

Zen Buddhism was brought to China from southern India in the 6th century by the philosopher Bodhidharma. Stressing self-reliance and meditation, Zen seeks to substitute intuitive awareness for intellect and logic. It is intended to train the mind to jump beyond the limits of thought, to leap from thinking to knowing.

Today there are almost 250 million Buddhists in the world, almost all of whom live in Asia.

CHRISTIANITY

Jesus Christ (c. 4 B.C.–29 A.D.) is considered to be the inspiration for Christianity, although the word "Christian" was not used in his lifetime. The primary source of information about him is the New Testament—in particular the Gospels of Matthew, Mark, Luke, and John, and the Acts of the Apostles. Bible archaeology has revealed no indisputable evidence of his existence, but early non-Christian historians such as Suetonius, Tacitus, and Josephus refer to him in their discussions of the then new Christian movement. His name was actually Joshua, which means "Jehovah is salvation" in Hebrew; Jesus is the Greek for Joshua. Christ is from a Greek word meaning "anointed one"; it is a translation of the Hebrew word "Messiah."

Born in Bethlehem, in Judea, Jesus was the son of a carpenter, Joseph, and his wife, Mary. According to the New Testament, his birth was foretold to his mother by the archangel Gabriel and was attended by miracles. Jesus was 30 when he was baptized by John the Baptist and took up his religious mission. For 3 years he preached a doctrine of charity, brotherly love, and repentance, with a promise of salvation to believers. During his ministry, he is said to have performed numerous miracles. His claim that he was the Son of God and the Savior of the Jews foretold by the Hebrew prophets brought him into conflict with the leaders of the Jewish people. Accused of sedition and other crimes against the state, he was tried by Pontius Pilate, the Roman procurator of Judea, and sentenced to death by crucifixion. His followers reported that he rose from the dead on the 3rd day and appeared to them before ascending to heaven. (See also: Highlights of World History, Chap. 8.)

From a small sect at 1st limited to Palestinian Jews, Christianity spread throughout the Roman world. Because they refused to worship the Roman Emperor as a god, Christians were persecuted for nearly 300 years. With the conversion of the Emperor Constantine to Christianity in 312, the Christian sect was granted recognition and freedom to practice its beliefs openly. As its membership grew, the Church was torn by theological controversies. When a variety of differences arose between the Church of Rome and the patriarchate of Constantinople, the Pope excommunicated the Patriarch (1054); the Eastern Orthodox churches date their origin from that event. Five hundred years later, the Protestant Reformation, an attempt to reform the Roman Church, led to a further division and the formation, eventually, of over 250 Protestant sects, more than 200 of which are represented in the U.S.

In the 19th century, attempts were made in England and the U.S. to bring the Protestant churches of the world together. These attempts culminated in the ecumenical movement of the present century, which aims ultimately to reunite all Christian churches. The World Council of Churches, organized in Amsterdam in 1948, created a world fellowship of over 260 Orthodox and Protestant denominations with over 400 million members, who act together in matters of common interest. Although not a member, the Roman Catholic Church cooperates in some activities.

Christianity today has over one billion adherents.

Roman Catholicism

Roman Catholicism, which recognizes the Bishop of Rome, or Pope, as its head, is the largest of the branches of Christendom. Its early history is identical with the early history of Christianity. Over the centuries the Church acquired vast amounts of land and wealth in the various countries of Europe, arousing the envy of various rulers and governments. A 900-year struggle began when kings and emperors claimed the right to a voice in the appointment of bishops, and the Popes opposed them with the threat of excommunication.

During the Renaissance, the Church gained a widespread reputation for extravagance, corruption, and failure to practice what it preached. Throughout Europe, a sweeping theological revolution got under way which resulted in the birth of the Protestant churches. Later centuries saw a continuous weakening of the power of the Church until 1929 when Benito Mussolini made peace with the Church, established Roman Catholicism as the state religion of Italy, and gave Vatican City to the Pope as his domain.

Roman Catholics believe that theirs is the only true religion. A faithful Catholic is one who accepts the teachings of Christ as revealed in the Bible, the laws of the Church, and the encyclicals of the Popes (according to the doctrine of papal infallibility of 1870, the Pope is never in error in matters of faith and morals when he speaks as the head of the Church). Roman Catholics believe in the Trinity, holding that there is only one God in 3 persons, the Father, the Son, and the Holy Ghost, who are distinct from and equal to each other. According to the doctrine of original sin, when Adam disobeyed God in the Garden of Eden, all of his descendants shared in his sin. Christ was placed on earth to redeem mankind by sacrificing himself on the Cross. According to a papal bull (official declaration) of 1950, Mary, mother of Christ, was taken up bodily into heaven.

Catholics hold that the soul is immortal. At death, each man and woman will be sent to heaven or hell, depending on which they have earned by their deeds during life and their obedience to the laws of God; before entering heaven, many souls must spend some time in purgatory until they have been made pure. Christ is to come to earth a 2nd time, whereupon all humans will be resurrected bodily and Christ will sit in judgment upon them.

The Roman Catholic Church has over 550 million members, including 48 million in the U.S.

Coptic Church

A theological controversy in the 5th century led to the creation of the Coptic Church, the native Christian church of Egypt. The Catholic Church held that Christ had 2 natures, human and divine. The Copts maintained that Christ had only a single divine nature. Labeled as heretics by the Church of Rome, they went their own way. Members of the Coptic Church number about one million and constitute about 60% of all Christians in Egypt.

Eastern Orthodoxy

The Eastern Orthodox churches, or Eastern communion, came into existence as the result of a lengthy series of theological, political, and cultural differences with the Church of Rome. The Byzantine Church, the branch of the Catholic Church presided over by the Patriarch of Constantinople, had disagreed strongly with the Popes on the use of icons; Rome favored the use of images in worship, while Constantinople opposed them (and still does, in the form of statues). Under Pope Nicholas I, in the 9th century, Rome asserted its claim to sovereignty over the entire Church, but the Patriarch insisted he and the heads of its other main divisions—the Patriarchs of Syria, Antioch, and Jerusalem—had jurisdiction in their own territory. But perhaps the greatest source of irritation to the Byzantines was that the Pope had crowned Charlemagne Emperor of the West in 800 while the traditional Roman Emperor still reigned in Constantinople. In the 11th century the disagreements between East and West broke out with redoubled bitterness, and Pope Leo IX excommunicated the Patriarch, Michael Caerularius, in 1054. The breach widened still further in 1204 when the Crusaders took Constantinople, sacked the Cathedral of St. Sophia, confiscated church buildings, and tried to convert the Orthodox to the Roman faith.

Eastern Orthodox churches are bound together by a belief in the Trinity, the human and divine nature of Christ, and other dogmas established by the 1st 7 councils of the Church, held between 325 A.D. and 787 A.D. However, the Eastern communion does not accept more recent Catholic dogmas such as the infallibility of the Pope and the Immaculate Conception, although it reveres Mary as the mother of Christ. In contrast to Roman Catholics, who hold that the Holy Ghost proceeds from God and Christ, the Orthodox believe it proceeds from God alone. Other Orthodox doctrines not subscribed to by Catholics are that Christ is the sole head of the Church, and that its authority resides within its members, "the totality of the people of God." Salvation is regarded as possible only through the Church, good works, and belief in Christ. Heaven and hell are considered real places.

The Eastern communion includes, besides the patriarchates of Constantinople, Jerusalem, Antioch, and Alexandria (all of which are quite small in membership), the national churches of Greece, Russia, Romania, Cyprus, Yugoslavia, Albania, Bulgaria, Georgia, and Czechoslovakia. American adherents number about 4 million, the largest group being Greek Orthodox. World membership in Eastern Orthodox churches is estimated to be about 100 million.

Lutheranism

Lutheranism, the largest branch of the Protestant Church, grew out of the teachings of Martin Luther (1483–1546), a German priest. First an ascetic Catholic monk and then a professor of theology, he became convinced, by the study of the Scriptures, that salvation was obtained through the grace of God and not through the mediation of the priesthood. This principle conflicted with the fundamental Church practice of the sale of indulgences, which entitled the purchaser to forgiveness of sins. Luther attacked this custom in his 95 Theses (1517), and when he failed to withdraw his charges, he was excommunicated (1521). (See also: Highlights of World History, Chap. 8.)

From the start, Luther and his followers were in conflict with Rome and its adherents. This helped to produce an armed conflict: From 1618 to 1648 Catholic and Protestant princes grappled in a religious and territorial struggle known as the Thirty Years' War, which devastated Germany.

The term "Lutheran" was 1st used as an expression of reproach in a papal bull; Luther himself favored "Evangelical" as a name for his Church.

The basic Lutheran principle is "justification by faith"—that man's faith in God, rather than man's good works, will bring about his salvation. If people have faith in Christ, repent their sins, study the Scriptures, and receive the sacraments, Lutherans assert, their hearts will be altered and they will live the true Christian life. Lutherans regard the Bible as their sole guide; although they employ ordained ministers, they believe that every person is a priest and can approach God directly. They accept the Trinity and the virgin birth of Christ.

About 80 million persons are Lutherans today. Lutheranism is the religion of half the people of Germany. In Iceland, Finland, Norway, and Sweden it is the established Church and receives support from the state. In the U.S., membership is over 8 million.

Anglicanism

Anglicanism is a Protestant branch of Christianity with churches throughout the world that have the same form of worship as the Church of England. American adherents call their church the Episcopal or Protestant Episcopal Church. The term "Anglicanism" comes from the Latin word for "English"; "Episcopal" comes from *episkopos*, a Greek word meaning "bishops."

Anglicanism began in England after Henry VIII (1497–1547) declared that the King, not the Pope, was the supreme head of the English Church. Although Henry took this step because he wanted to annul his marriage to Catherine of Aragon and the Pope had refused the annulment, the break with Rome came as the climax to over 100 years of protest by Englishmen against the authority of the Pope and the heavy financial burden of supporting the Church. The Archbishop of Canterbury was made the head of the Church of England, which prepared its own prayer book and statement of doctrine (the 39 Articles). Anglicanism was introduced into America in Jamestown, Va., in 1607 and many of the Founding Fathers of the U.S. were Episcopalians. Sometimes called the "bridge Church," Anglicanism agrees with Roman Catholicism on most issues, but like other Protestant groups, Anglicans reject the authority of the Popes. They believe that the Bible represents the final statement of life and religion, but it is not always to be interpreted literally. In general, Episcopalians do not believe in a physical heaven or hell and hold that God, after the Last Judgment, will re-create man with a "spiritual body"; however, members differ in their beliefs to some degree.

Anglicanism has some 65 million members throughout the world; in the U.S. it has over 3 million.

Presbyterianism

Presbyterianism was inspired by the teachings of the Swiss Protestant reformer John Calvin (1509–1564), who started a movement that spread to France, Germany, and other parts of Europe. On the Continent, the Reformed Church came into being in response to his message. The fiery John Knox (1505?–1572), a friend of Calvin's, brought his doctrines to Scotland. When Puritanism took power in 17th-century England, the Presbyterians were the largest faction within it.

Presbyterianism was 1st introduced to America by the Dutch Reformed in New Amsterdam and by the English Puritans in New England. Large numbers of Scottish immigrants spread the faith throughout the Colonies; by the time of the Revolution, Presbyterians were an important element in America.

The Westminster Confession (1645–1647), the most famous statement of English Calvinism, is the basis of the Presbyterian creed. Presbyterians believe that the Scriptures are "the only infallible rule of faith and practice."

They also believe in the Trinity and the existence of heaven and hell. A once important Calvinist tenet, predestination (holding that God, not the individual, determines the individual's fate) is no longer emphasized. Church rule is democratic. The individual church is governed by the "session," consisting of a "teaching elder" (an ordained minister) and "ruling elders" (members elected from the congregation). The world membership of the Presbyterian Church has been estimated at 40 million, including over 4 million members in the U.S. In Scotland, Presbyterianism is the established religion.

Baptists

The largest non-Catholic Christian group in the U.S., the Baptists hold that only believers (not infants) may be baptized and that baptism must be administered by immersion (rather than by sprinkling).

The Baptist Church has no recognized founder. Some Baptists trace its development directly from John the Baptist, others from the Anabaptists of 16th-century Europe. Early Baptists were split into 2 groups: the General Baptists, who believed that Christ died for all people, and the Particular Baptists, who held the Calvinist doctrine that Christ died only for the elect. In 1608 a group of English Puritans, seeking to escape persecution, settled in Amsterdam and founded the 1st Baptist church. In 1611 members of this congregation returned to England and established the 1st Baptist church there. In the U.S. the 1st Baptist church was established by Roger Williams at Providence, R.I., in 1639, after he was banished from the Massachusetts Bay Colony.

Baptists hold that the Bible is the supreme authority in every matter of faith. Many Baptists are fundamentalists: They accept the Bible as literal truth. Many believe that heaven and hell are real places and that there will be a physical resurrection of the dead on the Day of Judgment. In general, they believe in the Trinity and the virgin birth of Christ and hold that one is saved by faith in Christ and by the grace of God.

About 4/5 of the 35 million Baptists in the world live in the U.S.

Methodism

Methodism was born in England out of the teachings of an Anglican clergyman, John Wesley (1703–1791). The word "Methodism" was originally applied in derision because of the methodical way Wesley and his associates studied and performed their religious duties.

Wesley underwent a profound religious experience in London in 1738: "I felt I did trust in Christ, Christ alone, for salvation," he wrote in his *Journal*. Setting out as an evangelical preacher, stressing conversion and holiness in place of the formalism of the Church of England, he sought to breathe new life into the Episcopalian faith. Although he always considered himself a loyal Anglican, he was often forbidden to preach in Anglican churches, and by the end of the 18th century his movement had its own flourishing societies in Great Britain and the young U.S. By 1850 the Methodists were the largest Protestant group in the U.S.

Although Methodists accept the Trinity and practice baptism and communion, they hold that individual love of God and individual religious experience mean more than formal doctrine. Salvation is achieved by a life of holiness, repentance, and faith, and is available to everyone. Most believe in judgment after death, in which the morally good will be rewarded and the wicked punished.

In 1972, a study made by the Corporate Information Center of the National Council of Churches on the stockholdings of churches in corporations working on military contracts revealed that the United Methodist Church owned over $59 million worth. The United Presbyterian Church was a close 2nd, but all major Protestant denominations were on the list. "Ethical and moral concerns have not been expressed through the investment policies and responsibilities of the Church," the report declared, pointing out that Protestant groups were assisting in the manufacture and use of weapons of mass human and environmental destruction. However, the report did not imply that the Churches were hypocritical in their investment policies.

Worldwide, Methodists now number about 16 million adults, including over 13 million in the U.S.

Latter-Day Saints (Mormons)

The Church of Jesus Christ of Latter-Day Saints, whose members are generally known as Mormons, was founded in the U.S. in 1830 at Fayetteville, N.Y. Its headquarters today are in Salt Lake City, U.

Two men played outstanding roles in the founding and development of Mormonism: Joseph Smith (1805–1844) and Brigham Young (1801–1877).

Smith, son of a poor New England farmer, declared in 1827 that a vision had led him to dig up golden plates covered with sacred writings. Translated by him, they were published as the *Book of Mormon*. As a result of other revelations, he affirmed that he had been chosen as a priest and was to found a new religion. Believers flocked to him, but the hostility of neighbors repeatedly forced him and his followers in the new movement to travel onward—1st to Ohio, then to Missouri and Illinois. In 1844, after introducing polygamy, he and his brother were murdered by a mob. (See also: U.S.A.—Year by Year, Chap. 4.)

Brigham Young, a New York painter and glazier, was selected to head the Mormons after Smith's death. Under his leadership the Mormons trekked West in 1846–1847, settling in Salt Lake City. With Young in command, the Church flourished, and when Utah was made a Federal Territory he was appointed its 1st governor. Young, who continued to promote polygamy among the Mormons, had 27 wives.

Mormons believe in a purposeful universe in which humans have been placed to make themselves more like God by faith and works. They hold that God was once a man, and men, too, may become gods. They believe in the Trinity as 3 distinct personages and they practice baptism. Missionary work is emphasized, and abstinence from coffee, tea, and alcohol is considered important.

The Mormon Church has a membership of close to 4 million, about 80% of whom live in the U.S.

Jehovah's Witnesses

Although Jehovah's Witnesses has fewer members than many other Christian sects, energetic proselytizing has made it extremely well known.

The movement was founded by Charles Taze Russell (1852–1916), a Congregationalist haberdasher from Allegheny, Pa. At 1st his followers were known as Russellites, but in 1931 the name was changed to Jehovah's Witnesses.

The Witnesses believe that Christ became the King of heaven in 1914 and cast out Satan, thus beginning great troubles on earth which will climax in the Battle of Armageddon and the destruction of Satan. They believe that exactly 144,000 people will go to heaven, but that the rest of humanity will live in a paradise on earth. Jehovah's Witnesses believe that theirs is the only true faith and the only way to salvation. They refuse to salute flags or participate in wars between nations.

Today the sect has close to 2 million members, all of whom are considered ministers. Twenty-five percent of the Witnesses are Americans.

Christian Science

Christian Science is a system of spiritual healing and a religion based on the principles taught by Mary Baker Eddy (1821–1910), who, while suffering from an injury in 1866, experienced a remarkable recovery which she declared came about after reading how Jesus healed in the Gospel of St. Matthew. In 1875

she published *Science and Health with Key to the Scriptures* and 4 years later, she founded the Church of Christ, Scientist.

According to Eddy, belief in the truths of the Bible makes it possible to heal the sicknesses of the body. God is spirit, and humans created in His image are also spirit; matter does not exist, nor illness, except as an illusion; a person can overcome sickness if faith is strong enough. What others call "death," Christian Science refers to as "only an incident in the dream of mortality."

The Church does not release membership figures.

United Church of Christ

The United Church of Christ, one of America's newer Protestant groups, came into being in 1957 when the Evangelical and Reformed Church united with the General Council of the Congregational Churches of the U.S.

The 1st of these organizations was itself created by a previous union (1934) between the Reformed Church in the U.S. and the Evangelical Synod of North America. Each of these groups had its roots in European Protestantism; their beliefs were carried to the American Colonies by immigrants from Switzerland and the German states.

By contrast, the General Council of the Congregational Churches of the U.S. was rooted in Congregationalism. This faith began in 16th-century England, where it was known as a Separatist movement because its members wanted to break away from the Church of England, for they were strongly opposed to bishops and presbyteries. After exile in Holland, a small group, called the Pilgrims, migrated to America, establishing their 1st church in the New World at Plymouth, Mass., in 1620. Congregationalism became the established religion in some of the Colonies. Always active in education, it founded Harvard, Yale, and many other colleges.

The 2 million members of the United Church of Christ are free to interpret God's word in their own way, so worship varies with the individual church.

SHINTOISM

The native religion of Japan, Shintoism developed out of primitive worship of ancestors and natural forces, but it has been influenced by Confucianism and Buddhism. The word "Shinto," which is Chinese (*shin tao*), means "the way of the gods."

After Buddhism became established in Japan it overshadowed Shintoism for centuries. In 1868, however, the Emperor Meiji seized power from the shogun and revived Shintoism. It was made the state religion and it was taught in the schools. Since Shintoism emphasized the divine origin of the Emperor's family, the military lords of Japan strongly promoted it, using it to justify their expansionist policies. After the surrender of Japan in 1945, Gen. Douglas MacArthur disestablished Shintoism as a state religion. The Emperor, renouncing his claims to divinity, declared that the throne depended on the people's confidence and affection, not divine right.

Today there are about 65 million followers of Shintoism, many of whom are also practicing Buddhists. Shintoism places great emphasis on physical and mental purity.

ISLAM

The word "Islam" means "submission" (i.e., to the will of God) in Arabic, and the followers of Islam are known as Muslims or Moslems (from the Arabic for "those who submit").

Mohammed (c. 570–632), prophet and founder of Islam, was born in Mecca (located in Saudi Arabia), where he passed his youth as a shepherd and trader. At 24 he married his employer, Khadija, a rich widow 15 years older than he was. He was a well-to-do merchant of 40 when he had a vision in which the archangel Gabriel revealed to him he had been selected to be the prophet and teacher of the worship of one god, Allah; at the time his people worshiped idols and animistic spirits. Other revelations followed, which were later set down in the Qur'an (Koran), the sacred book of Islam. Preaching the new faith, Mohammed began to gather followers, but at the same time he aroused hostility in Mecca, where an ancient black stone called the Kaaba was worshiped. In 622, to escape a plot to murder him, Mohammed fled to Yathrib (now called Medina). The Islamic era is dated from the year of his flight, called the "hegira."

In 630 Mohammed led his followers against Mecca, which surrendered to him; battles and treaties with other cities and tribes made him supreme in Arabia.

Mohammed preached a holy war against nonbelievers and his followers made it a reality. Within 100 years after the prophet's death, Egypt and Syria were Muslim countries and the faith had penetrated as far as Algeria and Tunis. Over the centuries the teachings of Islam have spread far and wide and today it is the leading religion in more than 20 countries. At present a religious revival is taking place in the Middle East. The victory of Israel over the Arab forces in 1967 was taken by many Muslims as a punishment from Allah for their failure to heed his prophets, and large numbers turned back to the Orthodox religion in their trouble. Arab victories in the 1973 war led

them to believe they had won back Allah's favor.

Muslims express their belief in one god in the official confession of faith, the Shahada: "La ilaha illa Allah, wa Muhammadun rasulu Allu" ("There is no god but Allah, and Mohammed is his messenger"). All-powerful and gracious, Allah rewards the good and punishes the sinful.

Islam has 28 prophets, most of whom are familiar from the Old and New Testaments: They include Adam, Abraham (the 1st Muslim), Noah, Jacob, Moses, David, Solomon, Elijah, Jesus (who did not die on the Cross but was lifted up to heaven by Allah), and John the Baptist. Another is Alexander the Great. All of these prophets prepared the way for the final prophet, Mohammed. Muslims believe that each of the prophets brought revelations from Allah but man turned away from them, so God sent other prophets to repeat His message. Differences between the beliefs expressed in the Bible and the Koran are said to be due to errors in the Bible text.

To be a Muslim in good standing, one must obey "the Five Pillars of Islam": 1. Repeat the confession of faith every day. 2. Pray 5 times a day—at dawn, noon, in the middle of the afternoon, at dusk, and after dark. The faithful must pray facing the Sacred Mosque at Mecca. Bowing the head to the ground acknowledges the greatness of Allah. 3. Give alms. The believer is obliged to contribute a prescribed amount, traditionally a 40th part of his income. 4. Fast. This is compulsory all through the daylight hours of the month of Ramadan, the 9th month of the Muslim calendar, which commemorates the 1st revelation of the Koran. (Abstinence from sex is part of the fast.) 5. Make a pilgrimage to Mecca at least once, if health and finances permit. While there, the believer must walk around the Sacred Mosque 7 times and kiss the Kaaba Stone.

Of the 530 million people who are presently believers in Islam, only one out of 4 is Arabic.

A completely American offshoot of Islam is the black nationalist movement known as the Black Muslims which was founded in Detroit in 1930 by Wali Farad, who was known to his followers as "the Savior" or "the Great Mahdi." An anti-integrationist movement, the Black Muslims identify themselves with an ancient lost tribe of Muslims, the Shabazz. Members take Mohammedan names in place of Western ones and are required to give up vices such as overeating, drinking, using narcotics, and fornication, which their leaders say were foisted on blacks by their white masters. Women are taught homemaking and are expected to obey their husbands.

After Farad disappeared in 1934, he was succeeded by his disciple Elijah Muhammad. With the help of an outstanding preacher named Malcolm X, who was assassinated in 1965 (See: Assassinations, Chap. 9), membership swelled to 100,000.

SCIENTISM

The word "science" comes from the Latin word *sciens*, which means "knowing." Followers of scientism are called "scientists," a term which was 1st used by William Whewell in 1840. The study of science began as a hobby among Greek intellectuals. For centuries those who acquired scientific knowledge kept it secret and although this practice is less common today, there are still many scientists who believe that their knowledge would be misused if it were spread to noninitiates. From a small sect, scientism has risen to the heights of respectability and its basic principles are taught to schoolchildren throughout the world.

Scientists believe that the order of the universe can be determined by systematic study and analysis. They believe that theirs is the only true path and that other paths are "mere superstitions." Over the years scientism has split into over 1,200 different sects or "fields," each with its own sacred texts.

It is estimated that the worldwide scientific community has over 3 million members, although the number of believers is much greater.

MAOISM

Maoism (or "Mao Tse-tung Thought," as it is known in China) is an outgrowth of Marxism-Leninism which was brought to China from the Soviet Union in the 1920s. Its founder, Mao Tse-tung (1893–   ), aligned himself with the poor peasants of China and gained control of the Chinese Communist party in 1935. By the time the People's Republic of China was established in 1949, Mao was the acknowledged hero and leader of the revolution and the new Government.

Pictures of Mao are prominent throughout China and everyone in the country who can read reads *Quotations from the Works of Chairman Mao Tse-tung*, the main text of Maoism and the 2nd most widely distributed book in the world. Dedicated Maoists refer to this book whenever problems arise. They claim that it always provides the proper inspirational quotation.

The main tenets of Maoism are faith in the Communist party, faith in the masses, and transcendence of personal desires in order to serve the people as a whole.

It is estimated that there are 800 million Maoists in China alone, although they don't all agree on practical interpretations of the scripture.

—F.D. and D.W.

Prophets of the Word: Successful Preachers and Evangelists

JOHN WESLEY (1703–1791)

History remembers John Wesley as the founder of the Methodist Church. But he was also the spiritual begetter of modern evangelism.

Wesley left the churches to preach in the streets and in the fields. He discarded predestination and held out, to all people, the possibility of individual salvation through faith alone. He bypassed the wealthy and comfortable to inflame the masses with visions of a loving God blind to social distinctions.

It was pretty heady stuff. England in the 18th century was at a low ebb, spiritually and morally. Crime and lawlessness were rampant. Government was corrupt. Gambling flourished, and people at every social level were becoming chronic gin guzzlers. The Church itself was sterile and decadent, typified by the fox-hunting parson and absentee rector.

John Wesley came upon the scene like an August cloudburst. He declared that "⁹⁄₁₀ of the men in England have no more religion than horses," and that the clergy "are the pests of the Christian world, the grand nuisance of mankind, a stink in the nostrils of God."

Wesley knew what he was talking about. His family had produced many ministers for the Church of England. His father was the scholarly rector of Epworth parish. Keeping to family tradition, John entered Christ Church, Oxford, to study for holy orders.

At Oxford he led a small student group in regular devotions and frequent communion. Some students derisively tagged Wesley and his friends "the Holy Club." Others nicknamed them "Methodists," because of their strict discipline, or method, while pursuing the Christian life.

After his ordination, John Wesley headed for the Georgia Colony in America. His mission was to minister to the settlers and Indians. He also hoped a stint in the wilderness would help him sort out his own confused religious beliefs. On the boat going over he saw a group of German Moravians face a harrowing mid-ocean storm with impressive inner calm. It was the sort of spiritual peace Wesley longed for. Later, he borrowed much of the simple solemnity of the Moravians' personalized God for his own budding theology.

Georgia was a disaster for Wesley. He alienated the Indians with his starchy high churchmanship. And he lost credibility with the settlers by getting into an awkward romantic entanglement with the niece of the chief magistrate of Savannah.

Back in Europe, he visited Moravian societies in Holland and northern Germany. Then he returned to England, planning to promote a religious awakening through the group dynamics of small "band-societies." He found that church after church was closed to him. The established clergy was unwilling to provide a forum for Wesley's gospel of salvation by faith alone, or for his pungently radical notions of democratic Christianity.

So he took to the byways and the hedges to, in his words, "promote vital, practical religion, and by the grace of God, to beget, preserve, and increase the life of God in the souls of men."

Wesley's remarkable itinerancy spanned the next 50 years. In that time, he traveled some 250,000 mi., mostly afoot or on horseback. He preached 4 or 5 times daily—between 40,000 and 50,000 sermons in all. He endured the hostility of landlords and country squires—who were often in cahoots with the local clergy. Sometimes there was violence. Mobs were unleashed against him. As biographer John Langley Hall describes it: "When struck by a stone he would wipe the blood from his face and continue preaching. Church bells were rung to drown his voice, he was pelted with stink bombs, and on one occasion a man was even bribed to shout, 'Fresh salmon!' as a tasteful temptation to desert him."

Born of the industrial revolution, Methodism as preached by John Wesley was primarily a religion for the poor. Wesley skirted the large cathedral cities, concentrating on the small factory towns of industrializing England. He made the poor feel important, as important as the rich. As Hall records, "the poor were amazed to find a man speaking in a cultured Oxford voice who was actually interested in whether they even had a soul!"

When Wesley died, something very much like a rebirth of morality was going on in Britain. There were vast improvements in education, medicine, and prison reform, all of which Wesley had agitated for. Slavery would be abolished within a few years of his death, another cause he had long championed. Lines dividing upper and lower classes were dimming, and religious life was exciting and progressive once again.

Wesley left behind more than 600 lay preachers to carry on his work, and nearly 200,000 converted Methodists. Though he was loyal to the Mother Church to the very end, Methodists withdrew entirely from the Church of England soon after he was gone. In America, the Methodist movement fell on especially fertile ground.

It was an American President, Woodrow Wilson, who said more than 100 years after Wesley's death: "The Church was dead and Wesley awakened it; the gospel was shrunken into formulas and Wesley flung it fresh upon the air once more in the speech of common men."

—D.P.P.

FATHER DYER (1812–1901)

The circuit-riding frontier preacher is as authentic a figure of the pioneer West as the gunslinger or the cowboy. And John Lewis Dyer, known to history as Father Dyer—the Snowshoe Itinerant—probably comes closest to matching folk myth with actual deeds.

Dyer had passed 49 rather undistinguished years when he left the comforts of Minnesota in the spring of 1861 and followed the gold rush to Pikes Peak. He set out with his carpetbag, Bible, Methodist hymnal, and $14.75 and ended up walking most of the 1,000 mi. to Buckskin Joe, a raw boom-camp located on the Continental Divide. For the next 29 incredible years, Father Dyer trekked up and down the spine of the Colorado Rockies, in all extremes of temperature, preaching burning hell in every home, barn, saloon, mining site, and fancy house that would have him, clear to the Mexican border.

After his death, the State of Colorado enshrined his likeness in stained glass beneath a gold-leafed dome of the State capitol. In life he was accustomed to far less posh surroundings. When he was 6, he hired out as a farmhand working for whiskey wages. After a man-sized drunk in a flax field at age 9, he swore off the stuff for life. Dyer fought in the Black Hawk War as a young man and later farmed and worked the Wisconsin lead mines.

His 1st wife died, leaving him to raise their 5 children alone. A disastrous 2nd marriage ended as soon as John Lewis learned his bride had neglected to terminate an earlier union, making the earnest miner a party to bigamy.

The burden of sin weighed heavily. One day, deep in a mine shaft, Dyer felt he was suffocating. Then he heard the voice of his redeemer. He laid down his pick and shovel and walked out of the mine to a new life proselytizing for the Lord.

The sturdy Methodist had already preached his way well into middle age when he joined a caravan West, hoping to see his son, who had left the previous year. He rode until his horse gave out in Omaha. Then he walked another 750 mi. to Buckskin Joe, shrinking his gaunt frame from 192 to 163 lbs.

"I found that a man at 49, getting fat, could walk, work, and preach off all the fat," he recounted later in his autobiography.

Father Dyer was to continue hiking the Rocky Mountain wilderness and preaching wherever he found listeners until he was 79. He saw many lesser men come West attempting to emulate his mission, but all fell far short.

He made his pastoral rounds to the rough mining camps 3 times a week and 3 more times each Sunday. He traveled the steep, dangerous terrain by horse or mule when conditions would permit it. When they didn't, he dismounted and continued on foot. When the snow deepened, he hand-fashioned 2 11' Norwegian-style skis, which he called "snowshoes." He kept right on going.

Once Dyer was forced to shovel snow for 3½ days in order to travel as many miles. He soon became a legend, crossing the Continental Divide twice a day on his rude, oversized "snowshoes."

Typically, Dyer would enter a mining camp and blow his tin horn to call the miners to worship. If no one came he would go to wherever the largest number of souls had gathered. That sometimes meant preaching in some unlikely places.

He thought nothing of walking into a barroom and bellowing: "Would you boys all put up your whiskey and stack your chips for a half hour while we preach a bit of sermon?" According to legend the preacher was never thrown out.

But he was frequently heckled. And Father Dyer—big, rawboned, and tough as old moose hide—was not above stopping a sermon long enough to thrash an apology out of some disorderly miner.

Out on the circuit he slept where darkness overtook him: in a teepee, pueblo, or lineshack, on the ground or in a snowbank. He never carried a gun, but armed with only a penknife and his 2 meaty fists, he was considered a formidable target for wild animals or wild men.

Since Father Dyer rarely made enough money from preaching to survive, he supplemented his meager income by working as a deputy assessor, carpenter, newspaper peddler, gold prospector, and mail carrier. He ferried gold dust over 13,400' Mosquito Pass between Buckskin Joe and Cache Creek for a percentage of what he delivered.

On one such journey he neared the crest of the divide and saw the swirling outlines of a killer blizzard headed straight for him. Loaded down with mail sacks and gold dust, he was nearly blown over a precipice and almost smothered in several feet of snow. Dyer managed to cling to the path on the ridge and shouted into the black howling wind: "O God, into Thy hands I commit my soul, my life, my all; my faith looks up to Thee." With that he let go, his skis breaking trail on an even course.

Hunching into icy blasts, he whistled down the steep slopes to the canyon floor. The missionary's feet were badly frozen. He lost all of his toenails and much of the skin on his feet. But he was back on the pass inside of 3 weeks.

With his clothes threadbare, his plug hat patched with antelope skin, and his shoes half-soled with rawhide, Dyer was the inspiration for many a legend. Some mythmakers have him shouting Scriptures and howling hymns while barreling down snowy grades, his booming voice bouncing off snowy cliffs and peaks all the way down.

Dyer swore that he once came down a steep precipice above Lake Jefferson with such momentum that his skis caught fire from friction with the snow. He supposedly tramped out onto the frozen lake and allowed his skis to melt down into the ice until the smoldering wood was extinguished.

Father Dyer preached his last sermon on July 22, 1890. By then his majestic mountain chain was no longer a wilderness. When he died in Denver at almost 90, the wilds he helped conquer were already a fast-fading memory.

—D.P.P.

D. L. MOODY (1837–1899)

The big, full-bearded figure of Dwight Lyman Moody straddles the 19th century as a flesh-and-blood link joining the camp-meeting Calvinism of the early frontier with the business efficiency of the modern revival.

Moody was of a generation of farm boys who went to the big city at a time of extravagant possibilities for a young man of grit and energy. Like his contemporaries—McCormick, Armour, Morgan—his was the gospel according to Horatio Alger. He shared their convictions and world view and adapted their techniques to the business of saving souls.

Yet, his biographers agree: Moody's most imminent qualities were his sincerity, broad humanity, and plain-dealing sense of doing God's work. It would be for later men and women to drown out the sermon with the clang of the cash register.

Young D.L. (he hated his 1st 2 names and never used them) seemed bound for anything but glory in the early days near Northfield, Mass. His father drank much, worked little, and died when D.L. was only 4. The widow and 9 children faced a grim world with little more than creditors to keep them company. Moody stopped his formal education at 10 and hired out as a farmhand. But he hated farming as much as he had hated schooling. At 17 he made the inevitable trek to Boston, where a maternal uncle agreed to teach him the retail shoe business. A condition of his employment was that the country nephew would shun the city evils and straightaway join the Congregational Church (the Moodys had been nominal Unitarians back in Northfield).

In the next 2 years the country bumpkin became a super shoe salesman, pledged his life to Christ from the back of a shoe store, and set out for Chicago, where there were fortunes to be made.

In the lush, ravenous atmosphere of Chicago in the 1850s Moody's life diverged on 2 tracks. By selling shoes, collecting debts, and speculating in land, he was soon on his way toward his ambition of earning $100,000. He onced loaned a man $100 at 17% interest *a day!*

But his life as a churchman was growing, too. Though unordained and undereducated, D. L. Moody began a remarkable ministry as an itinerant Sabbath school worker among the poor and derelict in Chicago's seamier neighborhoods. He stalked the red-light districts and shantytowns, pockets filled with sugar candy for recruiting dead-end kids into his ragtag Sunday school class. In what he later called "the severest struggle of my life," Moody turned away from business, gave his money to charity, and began a fevered search for God's "lost lambs" in the emergent urban jungle.

For all his exposure to the cruelties of modern industrial life, Moody never was a social reformer. The horrors of the day only convinced him more of the need for individual submission to Jesus. Later, during the Civil War, as a missionary at the front, Moody would move among the wounded soldiers asking each: "Are you a Christian?" It is said that if he found a man already "saved," Moody would move on, searching for those who needed to be kept alive until they could be converted. Harvesting souls for Christ was Moody's mission. Life's bitter blows—whether a shell-maimed soldier or a family marred by the factory—would take care of themselves once conversion had occurred.

After 12 years in Chicago Moody had his own church and a thriving Sunday school and had become the driving force behind the city's Young Men's Christian Association. He had tamed his country tongue to become a commanding preacher whose plain but forceful speaking style captivated large audiences. Other ministers heard of his drawing power and invited the lay minister to speak at churches all over Chicago. D. L. Moody had become an evangelist.

In 1870, at a YMCA convention in Indianapolis, Moody 1st heard Ira D. Sankey, a sweet-voiced psalm-singer who, from Monday to Friday, was a Federal tax collector. Moody approached him, brushing aside conventional introduction: "Where do you live?" he asked.

"Are you married? What is your business?" Sankey barely had a chance to answer when the big, bearded evangelist said abruptly, "You'll have to give that up. I have been looking for you for 8 years. I want you to come to Chicago and help me in my work."

The collaboration between the 2 men was to breathe new life into the traditional revival. Moody's sermons were perfectly suited to his audience. His people were late-19th-century Americans, born to the farm but struggling for survival in an industrial world unforseen by their small-town moral teachers. In his rich homey style he would tell the aged Bible tales with a familiarity and simplicity that was irresistible to his flock. The prodigal son, receiving Moody's treatment, became nothing more than a farm boy lured to the wicked city now returning with head bowed. Moody would conclude and Sankey would sing meltingly, "Come home, O prodigal child." The worshipers were helpless before an appeal so tailored to their extravagantly sentimental era.

His preaching was barren of literary allusion because he believed literature was "useless." He shunned poetry in his sermons because he couldn't memorize the lines. He could never recite the Lord's Prayer without a text.

But Moody's impact was enormous. He introduced into evangelism the techniques of post-Civil War capitalism, using advertising, public relations, and business organization to promote the Word of God. By turning his parishioners away from the social strife of the day to the disposition of their souls, he froze in time a large segment of American Protestantism.

In 1873 Moody and Sankey swept Victorian Britain with an evangelistic crusade witnessed by millions. Returning to the U.S., they held a triumphal 4-month revival in the New York Hippodrome, where the evangelist and the hymn singer attracted an estimated 11,000 nightly.

For the next 8 years they swelled crowds from Boston to San Francisco. At one meeting in Philadelphia the audience included President Grant, a Supreme Court justice, the governor of Pennsylvania, and several congressmen and senators.

Moody founded the Bible Institute of Chicago (now the Moody Bible Institute), which earned a reputation as "the West Point of Christian work." Returning to the scene of his poor and undistinguished youth, he founded the Northfield Seminary for girls in 1879 and the Mount Hermon School for boys 2 years later.

D.L. spent his last years away from the evangelistic trail, with the exception of a huge revival under a circus tent at the Chicago

World's Fair. He died peacefully in his bed, at Northfield, 9 days before the birth of the 20th century.

—D.P.P.

BILLY SUNDAY (1862–1935)

Billy Sunday liked to call himself "a rube of the rubes," and a "hayseed of the hayseeds." But his *New York Times* obituary was more accurate in describing him as the greatest high-pressure, mass-conversion Christian evangelist America or the world has ever known.

He was a professional baseball player turned preacher. His flamboyant, highly theatrical performances effectively banished all restraint and solemnity from the revival service. He became the master symbol of ragtime religion in the age of ballyhoo.

Billy's father, the senior William A. Sunday, died of pneumonia in a Union Army camp one month after the birth of his namesake. Following other family tragedies, young Sunday was raised in orphanages and by foster parents. He worked his way through public school as a stableboy, errand runner, hotel worker, farmhand, fireman, and undertaker's helper. In the small-town games that passed for organized sport he proved himself a natural athlete.

While playing with a local baseball team he was "discovered" by Pop Anson, manager of the Chicago Whitestockings. Sunday was a poor batter but a capable outfielder. He held the record for stolen bases until it was broken by Ty Cobb in 1915. As a player for National League teams in Chicago, Philadelphia, and Pittsburgh, his moral character was presumably on a par with that of his fast-living handlebar-moustachioed colleagues.

Then one day, sitting drunk with his teammates on a curbside in Chicago, Billy heard the strains of a familiar gospel tune being played by a tiny band across the street. He stood up and told his buddies: "I'm through. I am going to Jesus Christ. We've come to a parting of the ways."

He renounced his sinful habits and became a lay worker for the Chicago YMCA, though he continued to play baseball for another 5 years. Sunday might have spent his life doing humble chores for the Y but for a fortuitous meeting with J. Wilbur Chapman, a popular evangelist. Chapman needed an advance man and Billy was available.

Two years later, Chapman was ready to return to a settled church in Indiana. Billy was left flat. Nevertheless, he had learned the revival business from poster plastering to tent raising. So when ministers in Garner, Ia., asked him to fill in for Chapman, Billy dusted off his old Y speech on "Earnestness in Christian Life" and answered the call.

Gradually, Billy shed the decorum of his mentor and began to punctuate his sermons with the gyrations, gymnastics, and rapid-fire street epithets that would make him a preaching sensation. During a sermon he would skip, run, leap, and fall down on the stage in endless imitations of drunkards, society women, liberal clergymen, and moral backsliders. He would pound the pulpit, jump up on the pulpit, break furniture, and stamp his feet, perspiration spinning from his grimacing face. Then, crouching and weaving, with his coat and vest stripped away, Billy would shadowbox with "the Devil." One of his best-remembered acts was to slide into "home plate" like a sinner trying to slide into heaven, only to be called "out" by God the umpire.

His farm-belt audiences listened slack-jawed to this spokesman for the Lord denounce a "red-nosed, buttermilk-eyed, beetle-browed, peanut-brained, stall-fed, old saloonkeeper"; or report that David "socked Goliath in the coco between the lamps and he went down for the count." But when Sunday called for declarations for Christ the corn-fed sinners jammed the sawdust-strewn aisles and stumbled by the dozen to the front of the tabernacle. It became known as "hitting the sawdust trail," and it was Sunday's personal trademark of success. Conventional clergymen would criticize him for turning worship into vaudeville, but they couldn't deny his results.

Sunday was as much a social critic as gospel preacher. His condemnations of booze, modernism, foreigners, socialism, and high fashion were pure fire. With America's entry into W.W. I he turned his verbal guns on the Kaiser and draft dodgers. He prayed that the German leader would "go to hell with the rest of them," and asked God to "strike down in his tracks" any man who failed to do his duty. A revival scheduled in a particular town often shrewdly coincided with a threatened labor strike or the appearance of a prohibitionist candidate on the local ballot.

Sunday peaked in 1917 with a New York City revival that netted 98,264 conversions. He was now a millionaire thanks to numerous "free-will offerings" which went directly to his earthly support.

After New York there was nowhere to go but down. The war had destroyed America's rural naïveté, leaving behind a world too weary for holy wars protecting the Sabbath and the purity of American womanhood. The 18th Amendment stole much of his prohibitionist thunder. Almost overnight, Billy Sunday was painfully out of date. Americans—at least in the cities —were being willingly seduced by the Jazz Age and were in no mood for reforming themselves or their neighbors.

Sunday fully developed D. L. Moody's use

of business techniques to advertise and conduct revivals. He produced tens of thousands of conversions at a time of growing preoccupation with worldly pleasures. But with war's end he became an instant anachronism in a world revolutionized by the radio and the automobile.

He spent his last 15 years tent-preaching in the same back-country farm towns where his ministry had begun.

—D.P.P.

FATHER DIVINE (c. 1864–1965)

His followers often chanted "He is God, he is God, he is God, God, God!" The women among them wore sweaters with a "V" for "virgin," and, slightly modified, a popular tune of the period serenaded him with the words "I can't give you anything but love, Father. . . ." The bald, paunchy little man—he was 5'2"—wore $500 silk suits, was chauffeured about in a Duesenberg, or flew with his army of secretaries in a private plane. The "Heavens" established by his disciples (some 20 million of them, he claimed) made him rich, but he owned next to nothing in his own name. He didn't even have a bank account. He fed, clothed and housed the poor of all races at his missions, helped Fiorello La Guardia and Franklin Roosevelt get elected by lending his support, and consoled thousands searching for some faith to hold onto during the Great Depression. Yet husbands sued him, claiming that their wives frolicked in his heavenly boudoir, "The Sun Dial," and one domestic-relations judge denounced him from the bench as a methodical home-wrecker. To some, Father Divine was a saint or folk hero, to others a black Elmer Gantry or P. T. Barnum. Whichever the case, he was a genuine American phenomenon.

Father Divine claimed that he'd arrived on earth intact in a puff of smoke at "about the time of Abraham" to spread a creed of peace, communal living, celibacy, honesty, and racial equality. More likely he was born on Hutchinson's Island, Ga., anywhere from 1864 to 1877, his real name probably being George Baker. As the son of a Georgia sharecropper and former slave, there were few opportunities open to him, and from childhood on he worked at odd jobs, even preaching in Sunday schools, until he became a disciple of Sam Morris, a Negro who promoted the idea that he was "Father Jehovah." He then joined a group called "Live Ever, Die Never." These cults formed the basis for his own movement and he was soon promoting himself along similar lines, much to the annoyance of Georgia officials. He was tried as a public nuisance, booked as "John Doe, alias God," and given the choice of confinement in a mental institution or leaving the State.

With a few adherents, Father Divine opted for the 2nd alternative and headed north, where he settled in Harlem in 1915 and began persuading thousands of followers that he was God. His logic and language often were not of this world. "God is not only personified and materialized," he once said. "He is repersonified and rematerialized. He rematerialized and He rematerializes. He rematerialates and He is rematerializatable. He repersonificates and He repersonificatizes." Such indescribable tortuosities, and others such as "repersonifiably metaphysicalizationally" were probably uttered both to impress and confuse his followers and thus convince them of his divine origins. Though not so intended, they can be viewed as the ultimate satire on the semantics of the hucksterism that has pervaded American life before and after him.

Father Divine began building the financial base for his empire by putting his followers "out to work in the service," which meant placing them in jobs from which his movement received a kickback. Soon he was able to open his 1st "Heaven," a communal dwelling which he established in 1919 at Sayville, Long Island. But it was the philosophy and organization of the Kingdom of Peace movement that made it so popular—and so well endowed. For example, Father Divine preached that those who joined his kingdom entered a new life, and that they could never die while they believed in him. In fact, no one associated with him ever did die— for as soon as someone came down with an illness likely to be fatal, he'd be turned out of Heaven and dropped in a nearby flat, thus enabling the preacher to say truthfully, "No one dies in My House."

The Heavens also provided rooms for as little as $5 a week, meals at about 35¢ (5¢ during the Depression), and indigent followers ate and slept free. The spiritual observances accompanying this mass cooperative or primitive communism were based on the Last Supper, and while there were songs and impromptu sermons, there were no formal services. Disciples rich and poor, black and white, male and female, ate from a banquet table often laden with as many as 50 different dishes. In accord with Father Divine's teachings, they adopted names like Positive Love, Miss Charity, and Holy Quietness, discarding their family names.

Father Divine preached purity of the body and mind, which included sexual abstinence, and he forbade his followers to drink, smoke, swear, use cosmetics, go to the movies, or accept gifts or tips. "Peace" became the standard greeting and farewell of all members because "Hello" began with a swear word. Despite its shortcomings, the Kingdom attracted millions who wanted peace, who wanted to believe that life was wonderful and that they could be virtuous, honest, reliable, and clean. The movement gained a worldwide membership, attracting even millionaires (one man left Father Divine an estate worth $10 million), and the Heavens eventually numbered 75 or more. All were united behind the motto "Father Will Provide."

Father did indeed provide. Money poured into the Heavens for the preacher and his disciples. In fact, they once toted over $500,-000 in rumpled bills, stuffed into old Gladstones and purses, to a Philadelphia bank. As for his divinity, he never really denied it and banners on the walls of all the movement's missions and houses read "Father Divine Is God." The legend of his extraterrestrial connections grew when a judge who sentenced him to jail on a disorderly conduct charge dropped dead a few days later. "I hated to do it," said Father Divine from his cell. But later he would claim that he had had a hand in dropping the 1st atomic bomb on Hiroshima. "I am the author and finisher of atomic energy," he said. "I have harnessed it." There was much truth in his only lengthy public statement on his divinity: "I don't have to say I'm God, and I don't have to say I'm not God. I said there are thousands of people who call me God. Millions of them. And there are millions of them call me the Devil, and I don't say I am God, and I don't say I am the Devil. But I produce God and shake the earth with it."

The preacher nonpareil, the minister of the malapropism could be just as evasive about sex —which he thoroughly enjoyed, even though he denied its pleasures to his disciples. It's said that when he seemed to be violating his own tenets, he'd explain to his partner of the night: "I am bringing your desire to the surface so that I can eliminate it." His policy of segregating even married couples at his Heavens led to much speculation and one of his confidential lady "secretaries" revealed the line he invariably used at the moment of seduction—"Mary wasn't a virgin." he would whisper.

In 1946 Father Divine married his "Sweet Angel," a 22-year-old white Canadian previously named Edna Rose Kitchings, who became Mother Divine. He explained at the time that he had transferred the spirit of his 1st wife, a Negro, into the person of his 2nd—stressing that they were one and the same. Then he added that after his "bodily disappearance" from earth, his spirit would be possessed by the new Mother Divine.

Father Divine lived with his "Spotless Virgin Bride" until his death in 1965, when he was anywhere from 88 to over 100 years old. His movement's worth at the time was estimated at more than $10 million. Eighteen secretaries were at his side to record his last words. When the doelike eyes in his round cherubic face were finally closed, Mother Divine announced that there would be no period of mourning but instead an extensive period of sumptuous feasting. Father, she explained, wouldn't have wanted it any other way—and who could have known better than she.

—R.H.

EVANGELINE BOOTH (1865–1950)

Even in her 80s, Evangeline Booth still had the spunk and energy of the young English beauty who made her father's London-based Salvation Army an American institution.

Today the Army claims 27,000 officers and cadets in 91 different countries. Its charitable works for the poor, the derelict, and the spiritually lost are world-famous. The Salvation Army is more than street-corner bands and Christmas bell ringers. It is a multimillion-dollar organization operating a far-flung network of hospitals, welfare missions, homes for unwed mothers, employment agencies, and family-counseling clinics.

But on Christmas morning, 1865, it was no more than an idea forming in the mind of an unconventional Methodist minister named William Booth. That same morning his wife gave birth to the couple's 8th child, a girl.

Catherine Booth had just read *Uncle Tom's Cabin* and wanted to name her baby Little Eva. Booth demurred and wrote Evelyne on the birth certificate. Years later, in the U.S., Evelyne would be persuaded by Frances Willard, founder of the Woman's Christian Temperance Union, to adopt the name Evangeline as more dignified, befitting the commander of Salvationist forces in America.

Though all the Booth children accepted their father's vision of a paramilitary Christian movement, Evangeline threw herself into the cause at an early age with characteristic gusto. The Booths preferred street corners to indoor churches, and popular musical instruments like banjos, tambourines, and drums to organs, in their drive to reach the lower depths of London society.

The Salvation Army was a controversial late arrival in Victorian England. Violence and abuse dogged the steps of its "soldiers." Like her colleagues, Evangeline weathered harassment from street toughs, bullying saloonkeepers, and unsympathetic civil authorities.

At 15 she was a sergeant selling the Army paper *War Cry* in the slums of East London. In her early 20s she was a captain and a compelling skid-row evangelist. But she feared she was still not reaching deep enough into the city's underworld. So Evangeline Booth dressed in rags and became a flower girl on the steps in

Piccadilly Circus, ministering incognito to alcoholics, beggars, and prostitutes.

She became commander of the London detachment and her father's favorite troubleshooter. Once a splinter group in the U.S., led by her brother Ballington Booth, sought to lure American Salvationists away from their London affiliate and into a rival group called Volunteers of America. When Evangeline arrived in New York, the doors to Army headquarters on 14th Street had been locked against her. Undaunted, she mounted the fire escape and climbed through a rear window. The dissidents hissed and booed until she literally wrapped herself in an available American flag and challenged: "Hiss that, if you dare." In the stunned silence she played her concertina and sang "Over Jordan without Fearing." Ballington's rebellion was quelled.

On another occasion the resourceful "hallelujah lassie" lowered herself down a tin mine in an ore bucket and overwhelmed the miners, singing "Nearer, My God, to Thee" while suspended in darkness.

She was assigned by headquarters to Canada in 1894. Sensing the drift of the times, she soon followed the sourdough migration to the vice-ridden boomtowns of the Yukon. There she set up soup kitchens, medical clinics, and makeshift wilderness chapels. One night, on the banks of the Yukon River, she preached to 25,000 miners and converted a notorious Yukon outlaw known as Soapy Smith. Smith told Evangeline he would go straight, but he was killed by vigilantes before he could prove that he meant it.

When Evangeline was named commander for the U.S., her life's mission began to unfold. In the years from 1904 to 1934 she changed her citizenship, boosted the number of Army missions in America from 696 to 4,500, and was able to turn over to her successor $35 million in the bank and $48 million in accumulated Army property.

Just prior to the American entry into W.W. I she organized the campaign for gathering and sterilizing linen for bandages. After 1917, she sent hundreds of her "lassies" to the front, where they served hot coffee and doughnuts in the trenches, cared for the wounded and dying, and helped homesick American farm boys compose letters to send back home. The battlefield courage and compassion of Evangeline's girls became famous. At the 10-year anniversary of the Armistice she prayed at the Arc de Triomphe and was escorted to a special memorial celebration by Gen. John J. Pershing and Field Marshal Ferdinand Foch.

In 1934 she was elected chief of the worldwide Salvation Army. Returning to the U.S., she was greeted in New York by Mayor Fiorello La Guardia and a ticker-tape parade.

Until her death in 1950, Evangeline remained remarkably active in the administration of her father's ambitious undertaking. Every year on her birthday she gave spirited interviews to reporters, and every year she thrilled her public by taking her favorite saddle horse for a brisk cross-country gallop.

—D.P.P.

AIMEE SEMPLE MCPHERSON (1890–1944)

From the Wesley brothers in the 1750s down to Billy Graham in the 1970s, Americans have always loved their evangelists. Yet no revivalist in our history has been more enthusiastically loved—or more thoroughly disgraced—than Aimee Semple McPherson, who became a national institution in the 1920s.

Though she was ultimately to make millions through her preaching, Aimee's career got off to a shaky start. In 1907, while a farm girl of 17, she married an itinerant preacher named Robert Semple who took her to China and died shortly thereafter, leaving his young wife pregnant and destitute. After the birth of her daughter, Aimee found her way back to the U.S., where she married Harold McPherson, who fathered her 2nd child, a son, but restlessness soon overcame her. Packing up her mother, 2 children, and a large tent, she set out in a battered car for a career as a traveling revivalist.

Her 1st great success came in Southern California, which provided fertile ground for her ecstatic, optimistic rendering of the gospel. In 1921, while Sister Aimee was speaking at an outdoor rally in San Diego, an inspired old woman rose from her wheelchair and tottered toward the podium. She was followed by hundreds of other cripples, as hysteria swept the arena. Overnight, Aimee Semple McPherson developed a national reputation as a faith healer. Nevertheless, Sister Aimee remained modest about her miracles. "I am not a healer," she said. "Jesus is the healer. I am only the little office girl who opens the door and says 'Come in.'"

Soon Sister Aimee had raised enough money to open the Angelus Temple near downtown Los Angeles, which was to serve as a permanent base for her activities. This building, which cost $1,500,000 to build (a handsome sum in 1923), was topped by a huge rotating lighted cross which could be seen for a distance of 50 mi. There was also a powerful in-house broadcasting station which sent the message of Sister Aimee's "Foursquare Gospel" around the world. A special "Miracle Room" displayed stacks of crutches, wheelchairs and braces left over from faith cures. The main temple provided seats for 5,000 of the faithful, and Sister

Aimee was able to attract a full house nearly every time she preached.

Instead of the familiar fire and brimstone of traditional evangelists, Sister Aimee stressed a gentler brand of salvation which emphasized the pleasures of heaven rather than the torments of hell. Her dramatic stage presence and her beautiful golden hair added powerfully to her appeal. There was always a good deal of show-business pageantry in Aimee's services. In her "Throw Out the Lifeline" number, a dozen maidens clad in white clung desperately to a storm-lashed Rock of Ages, while special-effects men labored mightily to create thunder, lightning and wind. Just when all seemed lost, out jumped Sister Aimee in an admiral's uniform to order a squad of lady sailors to the rescue. They tossed out the blessed lifeline, while the male chorus, dressed as coastguardmen, swept the mechanical waves with searchlights. The virgins were saved, trumpets blared and the congregation cheered while the American flag waved triumphantly over all.

Unfortunately, no one was available to rescue Sister Aimee when she herself needed it most. After reaching her peak in 1925, she was soon to suffer a spectacular fall from grace. In mid-May of 1926, Aimee drove to a hotel facing the Pacific Ocean, changed to a swimsuit, and then sat on the beach, working on a sermon. Her secretary left for a short while, and when she returned Sister Aimee had disappeared. The supposition was that the great revivalist had gone out for a swim, suffered a cramp or some other difficulty, and drowned.

Thousands of the faithful camped along the sands while boats patrolled offshore, searching for a clue. One grief-stricken girl actually committed suicide. A young man jumped into the water, shouting, "I'm going after her," and drowned. A professional diver died of exhaustion.

Meanwhile, both police and newsmen scoured the West for some clue to Sister Aimee's fate. For a month, every lead brought authorities to a dead end. Then, on the 31st day, a ransom note was delivered to the Angelus Temple. It stated that Sister Aimee had been kidnapped, and would be released in exchange for $500,000.

The following day—at one o'clock in the morning, to be exact—Sister Aimee suddenly turned up in the Mexican border town of Agua Prieta. She confirmed that she had been abducted from the beach, held prisoner in a remote desert shack, and had finally escaped through a window and stumbled for miles across burning desert sands to safety.

The police were suspicious. She showed no evidences of captivity or flight. Her dress was neat, her pale skin untouched by the desert sun. Reporters, equally suspicious, began chasing clues. It quickly became obvious that Sister Aimee, who had been divorced by her husband a few years before, had been having an affair with one Kenneth Ormiston, the operator of her radio station. Coincidentally, her lover had disappeared from sight the very same day that Aimee had vanished from the California beach.

When the Los Angeles district attorney launched a formal investigation, conclusive evidence was found to show that during the time of her alleged captivity, Sister Aimee and her married lover, Ormiston, had indeed been seen together in several hotels and at a seaside cottage. The district attorney was about to start criminal proceedings against Aimee when her friend William Randolph Hearst, the publishing tycoon, intervened on her behalf and got the charges dropped.

When the facts were eventually made public, Sister Aimee's popular appeal fell off dramatically. The great evangelist now appeared to be a "woman with a past." Nevertheless, Aimee struggled to continue her career and regain her former image. Love came again to Aimee at the age of 40, but 2 days after her marriage to roly-poly Dave Hutton, he was sued by another female for breach of promise. Aimee fainted, fell, and hit her head on some flagstones, and after her recovery the couple was divorced.

Through all these troubles, a sizable number of the Foursquare faithful stood by Sister Aimee; her services at the Angelus Temple continued to provide one of the best shows in town. Her popularity, though greatly diminished, continued into the 1940s.

On a September evening in 1944, Sister Aimee spoke to an enthusiastic crowd in Oakland, California. The next morning she was found unconscious in her hotel room and died soon afterward. Then came sad news. The coroner's verdict was that Sister Aimee had died from an overdose of sleeping pills.

—M.S.M

CHARLES E. COUGHLIN (1891–   )

Charles E. Coughlin was 35 when he took to the airwaves for the 1st time, in 1926. A chain-smoking parish priest who presided over the Shrine of the Little Flower, a small wooden church in Royal Oak, Mich., he called his sermons "The Golden Hour," and hoped they would bring new members to his tiny pastorate.

They did. He received 8 letters after that 1st broadcast, and another radio appearance some weeks later brought in 100. Within a decade Coughlin became known outside his pastorate and he began peppering his homilies on Christianity and the virtuous life with vitriolic pronouncements on the state of the economy and the shortcomings of prominent statesmen, including Presidents Hoover and Roosevelt. By the early 1930s his strident, rasping brogue was heard every Sunday at 4 P.M. by over 30 million Depression-weary Americans, who wrote him 10,000 letters a day. In later years, his mail was to reach as high as a million letters a week, and he hired 4 secretaries and 106 assistants to handle it.

Coughlin's speeches were the essence of street-corner rabble-rousing, and they were mired in hate, bigotry, and economic and political ignorance, but they fed on the anger and anxiety of a nation with 15 million unemployed. A national poll in 1934 showed the "Radio Priest" to be 2nd in power and national popularity only to FDR, his archenemy, whom he referred to variously as "the great liar and betrayer" and "the scab President." Some 1,250,000 of Coughlin's supporters deluged CBS with letters of protest in 1936 when the network tried to tame one of his more vindictive broadcasts—an attack on the Versailles Treaty.

With fellow demagogues Francis Townsend and Gerald L. K. Smith, Coughlin formed the Union party in 1936, and unsuccessfully backed Congressman William Lemke for the Presidency. Soon after, NBC and CBS dropped his broadcasts, but an angered—and resourceful—Coughlin was able to sell his services to a mini-network of 47 independent radio stations throughout the nation, and his influence remained powerful. In a speech emanating from the studios of station WJR in Detroit, Coughlin claimed that 56 of the 59 members of the Soviet Communist party's Central Committee were Jews and that it was Jewish money that had started the Russian Revolution. And since Jews and communists were one and the same, he declared, the Jews were getting just what they deserved at the hands of Hitler. He said this in 1938.

A storm of controversy followed this broadcast, and a few of the stations in the radio empire he had assembled canceled his contract. Otherwise, his power remained unabated. In 1940, Coughlin was forced off the airwaves altogether by his Church superiors, but he continued to hold forth from his pulpit in Michigan. The Federal Government ordered him to discontinue his magazine *Social Justice* with the outbreak of W.W. II.

In 1966 Coughlin retired to his home in Royal Oak. He was distressed by the "atheistic teachings" of the Black Panthers, and the "sanctified murder" of legalized abortion. He was especially disturbed by the activities of radical priests like the Berrigans. "They're always talking about the rights of man," he said, "never the rights of God. It has become fashionable for priests to be activists." But then he added, almost as an afterthought, "I guess I was a pioneer."

—B.F.

CARL McINTIRE (1906–)

The Rev. Carl McIntire has been fulminating against the 20th century for nearly 40 years, earning for himself a special place in the hearts of right-wingers everywhere.

Over the years he has fought communists, Catholics, "apostate" Christians, the American civil-rights movement, existentialism, the 1970 census, gun registration, and the Rev. Billy Graham, to name but a few.

Reverend McIntire received worldwide attention in the early 1970s while enthusiastically boosting the cause of the Vietnam War. Later he made news when he ran afoul of the U.S. Federal Communications Commission's "fairness doctrine" for broadcasters. Defeat in the latter case lost him about half the 600 stations that once carried his 20th Century Reformation Hour. Tax problems and legal disputes surrounding McIntire properties in New Jersey and Florida have also clouded the feisty pastor's influence.

But Carl McIntire has lost before. And losing a fight has never dulled his taste for combat. At 69 he is still the undisputed dean of the far-right radio preachers.

His ultraconservatism emerged even when he was a young man. While attending Princeton Theological Seminary in the 1920s, he came under the influence of fundamentalist theologian J. Gresham Machen. When Professor Machen spurned "modernist" trends at Princeton and founded the breakaway Westminster Seminary in Chestnut Hill, Pa., McIntire was one of the young turk reactionaries who went along.

Carl McIntire was ordained in the Presbyterian Church in 1931 but he was ousted 4 years later when the Church's ideological rift flared into open warfare. An ecclesiastical court found McIntire, and other young Machenites, guilty of "causing dissension and strife" and "seriously undermining the peace of the Church."

An unfrocked McIntire repaired to his Bible Presbyterian Church in Collingswood, N.J. There he shaped the nucleus for a whole splinter-group denomination. In 1941 he merged with other renegade Protestant fundamentalists to form the American Council of Christian Churches as a right-wing alternative to the National Council of Churches. Six years later he similarly established the International Council of Christian Churches to harass the "communist-infiltrated" World Council of Churches.

He began a career of turning up at NCC meetings and at those of other ecumenical groups with his band of placard-waving bitter-enders. He once stood in the snow for 4 consecutive nights in Berlin to protest a World Congress of Evangelism, which he called "a monstrosity of ecumenicalism."

Protest has always been McIntire's thing. He gave particular attention in the 1950s and 1960s to any perceived weakening of U.S. cold-war resolve. A delegation of Russian churchmen, or a visiting Soviet official, could frequently expect a greeting from the New Jersey firebrand and his true believers.

When the Nixon Administration began dabbling in "Ping-Pong diplomacy," McIntire responded by flying to Taiwan to recruit an all-Christian, anticommunist table-tennis team. He brought his players to the U.S. and demanded they receive the same White House courtesies shown to the visiting Red Chinese team. As usual, McIntire was ignored.

Angered, he took his Taiwan team across the street from the White House and set up a protest Ping-Pong tournament within view of the Oval Office. To drive home his point, McIntire and an aide engaged in a free-swinging Ping-Pong match while their table was paraded meaningfully down Pennsylvania Avenue.

But it was the Vietnam War, at its lowest ebb in public support, that gave the fiery radio preacher his greatest opportunity for public demonstration. From 1969 to 1972 he organized a series of "Victory in Vietnam" marches in Washington, D.C. On a few occasions he was able to muster several thousand hawkish die-hards to the nation's capital. He briefly booked South Vietnamese Vice-President Nguyen Cao Ky to one of his pro-war pep rallies. However, horrified State Dept. diplomats quickly convinced Ky that his appearance at a McIntire rally would do the war effort no good.

Generally the Vietnam victory marches were pitiful flops. When the turnout fell far short of his projections, McIntire fumed that his followers had been kept away by inclement weather or "fear of hippies."

McIntire's sorties into public affairs are launched from his headquarters in Collingswood, N.J. There, in addition to his church and the offices of the Twentieth Century Reformation Center, he maintains a broadcasting studio, bookstore, mail room, computer center, high school, and offices of the International Council of Christian Churches.

In 1963 he purchased a hotel and other buildings in the declining resort town of Cape May, N.J., and turned them into a vacation spa and Bible conference center for his followers. He established Shelton College nearby, teaching a 4-year course in McIntire-style orthodoxy.

In Cape Canaveral, Fla., after space business fell off and real estate values declined, McIntire moved in with plans for a multimillion-dollar "Gateway to the Stars" Bible center with regular bus service to Cape May. He bought the old Cape Canaveral Hilton and renamed it the Freedom Center Hotel and installed a scale model of the original Temple of Jerusalem he picked up at the Canadian Expo.

Then came the setbacks. In 1969 the American Council of Christian Churches dropped its founding father from the executive board because his antics were giving less flamboyant fundamentalists a bad name. The New Jersey Board of Higher Education withdrew accreditation from Shelton College. The city of Cape May slapped 6 tax liens against buildings on the college grounds. In Florida, McIntire faced losing the options on his Cape Canaveral property and found his Gateway to the Stars hopelessly embroiled in a court dispute.

But the most damaging blow, by far, was delivered by the Federal Communications Commission when it revoked the broadcast license for his radio station WXUR in Media, Pa. McIntire had consistently refused to allow dissenting views on his station, the Government charged, thus violating the fairness doctrine.

The doughty preacher cried "government censorship" and purchased a W.W. II vintage Navy minesweeper equipped with a 10,000-watt radio transmitter. With the words "Radio Free America" emblazoned on the ship's side, McIntire chugged out to sea from Cape May planning to broadcast his radio message from beyond the 3-mi. U.S. territorial limit. But the 1st day's broadcast cut in on several land-based stations and brought a permanent injunction against Radio Free America from a Federal court.

McIntire came ashore, at least temporarily bent to the government's will. But conservative congressman John Rarick of Louisiana introduced legislation in the House of Representatives to restore WXUR's license, and powerful senators like Sam Ervin of North Carolina and William Proxmire of Wisconsin began questioning the fairness of the fairness doctrine in light of the McIntire case.

Meanwhile, the indefatigable fundamentalist was openly discussing plans for going to sea again—this time on a ship of foreign registry, one not subject to the dictates of an American court.

—D.P.P.

BILLY GRAHAM (1918–   )

He's Numero Uno . . . Mr. Christian . . . year after year on the Gallup Poll of "Most Admired Americans." He's been friend and spiritual adviser to 5 American Presidents and caller on crowned heads and Prime Ministers. He's big business, and a self-proclaimed "citizen of heaven." He's the Moses of Middle America, a media-oriented John the Baptist for the electronic age. He's the Rev. William Franklin Graham, Jr., a man the world calls Billy.

As a boy on his father's dairy farm deep in the Southern Bible Belt he was better known as "the fastest milker in Mecklenburg County"; later he was known as the best Fuller Brush salesman in all North Carolina. Billy is still the supersalesman: earnest, confident, and fiercely convinced he is selling the best product in the whole world.

The Grahams were no-nonsense Reformed Presbyterians. Their idea of a good time was a family outing to a tent revival. Mrs. Graham quietly prayed that her son would grow up to do the Lord's work. But young Billy Frank was impressed by nothing so much as baseball. Then, at age 16, a fire-breathing evangelist named Mordecai Ham passed through town, leaving a born-again Billy in his wake.

The next year Billy entered Bob Jones Bible College, but left after one semester, feeling stifled by Jones's brand of ultrafundamentalism. Resuming his studies at the Florida Bible Institute in Tampa, he tried out his 1st sermons on local congregations and earned the nickname "the preaching windmill" for all his arm-flailing efforts.

In 1939, as an ordained Baptist minister, he headed for Wheaton College in Illinois, where he won a B.A. degree in anthropology and a wife, the former Ruth McCue Bell, a missionary's daughter. Graham tried pastoring in a small town in Illinois, and later ran a complex of Bible training schools in Minneapolis.

But he was restless. He became a barnstorming evangelist with the Youth for Christ organization and got his big break in Los Angeles in 1949. Shortly after opening an 8-week tent revival he found newspaper reporters teeming through his canvas cathedral. Billy was told he had been "kissed" by William Randolph Hearst and that the autocratic newspaper baron had ordered his editors across the country to "puff Graham."

Warmed by the glow of the mass media, Billy outdid himself. In 8 weeks the wavy-haired blue-eyed country crusader claimed 3,000 converts including a local gangster, a war hero, a down-and-out former Olympics champion, and an alcoholic radio cowboy. It made terrific copy.

The Luce publications on the East Coast picked up the refrain, saying Graham heralded "a great spiritual awakening" in mid-century America. Billy's rallies became huge successes, swelled by thousands aching for a glimpse of evangelism's new rising star.

Though Graham's message may not be modern, his methods certainly are. In the 1950s the ambitious young preacher developed a natural instinct for utilizing modern organization and publicity, the mass media, packaging, and charisma. He was both a product and an expression of an exceedingly image-conscious decade.

On his way up, Graham was careful to nurture the Protestant Church establishment. He never competes with the regular churches. In fact, he coordinates his crusades to boost local church membership. Critics within the ecclesiastical family have taken issue with Graham's fundamentalism and the escapism of his sentimental Christianity. But in the evangelism business, nothing succeeds—or mutes criticism —quite like success.

Old-time evangelists staged city-wide campaigns. Graham takes on countries, whole continents, and global "strategic areas." He has led crusades to Africa, Australia, Canada, the Caribbean, England, France, Holland, India, Japan, Korea, South America, New Zealand, Switzerland, and even Iceland.

During an early trip to England, he indelicately suggested that socialism had done more harm to Her Majesty's kingdom than all the bombs of the Nazi blitz. Englishmen were outraged. Fleet Street demanded his deportation as an undesirable alien. His Great Britain crusade was nearly scuttled by the remark. But Graham apologized in person before the House of Commons, then went on to explain the purpose of his ministry. He finished with more gained than lost.

He never would indulge in such gaucherie today. Twenty years have made him an institution, the established figurehead of mid-American spiritual life. He no longer wears Kelly-green suits and hand-painted ties. He no longer peppers his sermons with attacks on the UN and U.S. Supreme Court. Success has toned down Graham's theology, too. He doesn't draw vivid verbal pictures of a literal hell anymore, nor claim that heaven is precisely 1,600 mi. from earth in each direction. Nevertheless, he is still a fundamentalist (though an enlightened one, they say), stating his belief in "personal devils" and maintaining that 27 signs foreshadowing the end already have been observed.

Graham now is imminently respectable. Blessing the Holiday Inns and the status quo, he has become the balm of the Silent Majority and proof text of the political establishment.

Nothing has done so much for Billy Graham's stature as his much-publicized familiarity with every American President since Harry Truman. Though the intensity of the relationships has varied (he felt closest to Nixon, least so with Truman), each President has recognized a certain 2-way benefit in associating with the preacher.

Graham makes Presidents feel good about themselves. As unofficial symbol of civil religion in a nation that professes church-state separation, he imparts goodness and justification to presidential acts. Lyndon Johnson possessed a Southerner's taste for good preacher talk, but it didn't hurt that Graham also quietly and uncomplainingly stood by Johnson at a time when the Texan's Vietnam policies were drawing the moral condemnation of most of the rest of the world.

But the handsome evangelist's obvious political assets were most effectively exploited by the Nixon Administration. Graham and the self-made man from Orange County shared similar backgrounds and almost identical views on the issues. They were friends long before Richard Nixon became President. Each time Nixon ran for office, Billy went to elaborate lengths to profess impartiality. Yet somehow, he always managed to convey his preference in terms that were clear enough.

Graham's immense popularity below the Mason-Dixon line made him a key player in Nixon's 1968 "Southern strategy." And the preacher was among the President-to-be's closest advisers the night Spiro Agnew was served up to the American people from a Miami hotel room (although it should be noted that Graham favored Sen. Mark Hatfield of Oregon for his track record as an active Christian and for the balance he would bring to the GOP ticket).

On Inauguration Day, 1969, Graham delivered the opening prayer, giving thanks that "in Thy sovereignty Thou hast permitted Richard Nixon to lead us at this momentous hour of our history." Billy became a familiar fixture of the 1st Nixon term, along with moon astronauts and White House guards in their unforgettable comic-opera get-ups.

Less than 3 weeks after 4 students were shot to death at Kent State, President Nixon chose to relate to students by appearing at a Billy Graham rally at the conservative University of Tennessee. While the President and the preacher spoke of the need to obey authority, 47 protesting students were arrested for disturbing a "religious" assembly, and a football all-American threatened to stomp any hippie who dared touch the flag.

Months later, Graham hit the peak of his career as defacto high priest of civil religion speaking at "Honor America Day," a political "nonpolitical" rally he organized with Nixon chums Bob Hope and J. Willard Marriott. Facing thousands of flag-waving patriots and a half-dozen television camera crews, Graham stood on the steps of the Lincoln Memorial and summoned his audience to honor the nation and its institutions, to shun extremism, and to embrace "the American dream."

When the floods of Watergate broke, Billy steadfastly refused to cast a stone at his old friend. But when the seamy language of the White House transcripts found public print, Graham allowed as how reading the presidential conversations was "a profoundly disturbing and disappointing experience," though he had "no intention of forsaking him now."

Billy was conspicuously absent at the White House during the yearlong death throes of the Nixon Presidency.

Even without the glamour of presidents and kings, Graham is big business in his own right. The Billy Graham Evangelical Association operates on a $20 million annual budget, with headquarters in Minneapolis and branch offices in Paris, London, Frankfurt, Sydney, Buenos Aires, Atlanta, and Burbank, Calif. About ⅓ of the budget goes for radio and television time. Each year 3 crusades are filmed and then shown in prime time on a syndicated basis. Graham's weekly radio program, "The Hour of Decision," is heard on 900 stations. Another $7 million or so goes to publish *Decision* magazine, which has a circulation of 3.5 million in 5 languages. His Evangelical Association also owns World Wide Pictures, making and distributing movies, and Grayson Company, which publishes his writings.

At the Minneapolis headquarters a bank of computers gobbles up 10 mi. of 18″ paper every month. His mail room, working in 3 shifts, sends out 8 million pieces of mail a year. Incoming mail averages 50,000 letters a week, and, like a well-run political campaign office, each is answered with one of 40 form responses, depending upon the spiritual or moral issue raised.

The Graham association figures its man has faced some 50 million people at his rallies over the years. And it calculates that somewhere between 3.5% and 4.5% of that number have made decisions for Christ.

Billy Graham does things in a big way. He had his own pavilion at the New York World's Fair. When the Cunard Lines put the *Queen Mary* up for sale, Graham offered to buy it, seeing the *Queen*'s potential as a floating conference center. Such a man, with financial resources in 8 figures, is bound to have his critics. But those looking for a latter-day Elmer Gantry have come away disappointed.

Graham takes an annual salary of $24,500 from the Billy Graham Evangelical Association. It is his total income. He has no truck with blessing pacts or freewill offerings or the other time-honored gimmicks of the evangelism trade. Donations go into the association, crusades are carefully audited, and royalties from his movies and books go into a trust fund for the Graham children.

In fact, the Reverend Billy frustrates all kinds of would-be critics. Reporters who meet him invariably describe a warm, engaging man, absolutely sincere and well informed. Whatever one thinks of his world view, or his role as sanctifier of presidential politics, it is nearly impossible not to admire the smoothness with which he runs his vast organization and the gracefulness with which he avoids all controversy.

Graham has succeeded beyond the wildest dreams of other evangelists—past and present. Though his roots are in Southern fundamentalism, he has built upon this foundation and adapted his views as the social and political climate in America has changed. In so doing, he has won access to centers of power and influence never imagined by his predecessors.

Presidents come and go, but Billy Graham, his grip firm upon the subconscious yearnings of the middle-American psyche, goes on and on.

—D.P.P.

ORAL ROBERTS (1918–)

For 30 years, Granville Oral Roberts has weathered the fickle fortunes of faith healing to become one of the best-known charismatic religious leaders in the U.S.

Gone is the backwoods miracle man who left his Pentecostal audiences rolling in the dust and babbling in tongues. Today it is a vastly sanitized Oral Roberts reaching millions of Americans through prime-time television. His quarterly TV crusades skillfully blend cosmetic Christianity and popular music, exuding all the emotional dynamism of the Lawrence Welk show.

The son of a poor Oklahoma dirt farmer, Roberts heads a multimillion-dollar worldwide evangelistic enterprise. A Bible college dropout, he is president of his own university—a showplace around Tulsa. Though an awkward boy in his youth, with a pronounced speech defect, Oral Roberts today is 2nd only to Billy Graham in mass appeal—and his influence is increasing.

Surely, something very much like a miracle must have happened somewhere along the way.

Roberts makes it clear in his half-dozen separate autobiographies that his life has been chock full of miracles; and that his career has turned on direct spoken orders from God.

His books recount how he was cured of tuberculosis by divine intervention at age 17. Within weeks of full recovery the adolescent Roberts was ordained in the Pentecostal Holiness Church to become a traveling gospel preacher. Eleven years on the circuit brought

an older—but still destitute—Roberts and his young family to Enid, Okla., where he accepted a settled pastorate for $55 a week.

In 1946 the young Oklahoma preacher could plainly see that his colleagues who performed miracles were far more popular than the non-healing clergy. At that moment, God told Brother Oral to go forth and heal the sick and cast out demons. An early autobiography tells how—much to his surprise—he found he had the power to restore a man's badly crushed foot merely by touching it.

Roberts moved to Tulsa, where he substituted one week for Steve Pringle, a popular tent revivalist. On his 2nd night police arrested a man for firing a revolver at the tent from across the street. Though no motive was ever determined, the incident brought the fledgling healer a windfall of free publicity.

A year later he was broadcasting over 2 radio stations, urging his listeners to find their "point of contact" with the Lord by laying hands on their home radio receivers. He incorporated as Healing Waters, Inc., in 1948.

Roberts' name-recognition soared after he placed his public career in the able hands of L. E. "Pete" White, who would later promote Billy James Hargis out of obscurity as well. Soon national news media were "discovering" this darkly handsome young man who was filling a 10,000-seat auditorium nightly in Atlanta, Ga. In 1955, Healing Waters, Inc., took in $3 million. A staff of 287 helped with audits and bookkeeping and sales of books, tracts, films, and "Jesus Heals!" lapel pins.

Made prosperous at last by "love offerings" and royalties from his books, Roberts could now indulge himself as a gentleman-farmer. He bought a 280-acre ranch near Tulsa, where he pastured purebred cattle and hangared his 12-passenger airplane. In Tulsa he built the 7-story Abundant Life Building as headquarters for the Oral Roberts Evangelistic Association, Inc., successor to Healing Waters.

Then, in the late '50s, public reaction set in against the practitioners of faith healing. The Rev. Jack Coe, 2nd only to Roberts in the field, was jailed in Florida for practicing medicine without a license. In Detroit a diabetic woman attended a Roberts revival, then threw away her insulin, believing herself cured. She was dead in 3 days. Faith cures were denounced by the national Presbyterian and Lutheran churches and the American Medical Association—among others.

With his unerring sense of timing, Roberts withdrew from active public healing and concentrated on building Oral Roberts University near Tulsa. In 1966 he withdrew his televised healing programs from all 115 stations. A year later he gave orders to strike the last of his huge canvas tents.

In April, 1968, still another divine inspiration made his rise to respectability complete: He left the Pentecostal faith and joined a Methodist church. The storm that followed cut deeply into his popular standing as well as his financial support. Roberts turned inward and later emerged with a new theory he called "Seed-Faith," which could help anyone through times of adversity.

He wrote a book about Seed-Faith that outsold all his earlier works. The money started flowing again. Soon he was back on television—this time with star-studded spectaculars that appeal to middle-class Americans in a way his televised tent meetings never could.

In the turbulence of the late '60s and early '70s, many Americans looked to mysticism and antirationalism for answers, giving new currency to religious leaders like Oral Roberts. With renewed popular interest in what is now called psychic healing, paranormal cures, and ESP, Roberts's star shines brighter than ever.

—D.P.P.

BILLY JAMES HARGIS (1925–   )

"Kill a Commie for Christ" may have been a macabre put-on devised by the New Left of the 1960s, but one could almost believe it a serious rallying cry to the banner of Billy James Hargis.

As founder and leader of the Christian Crusade, the rotund Oklahoma evangelist struggles against the dark forces of World communism in all its many forms. In Hargis's view that includes the UN, the National Council of Churches, rock 'n' roll, the *Playboy* philosophy, long hair, modern art, mental health programs, sex education, and national magazines like *Time* and *The Saturday Evening Post*. Since Hargis mentally divides all human endeavor into 2 camps—either pro-Christian or procommunist—he necessarily enlarges the enemy's influence mightily.

The Christian Crusade, with headquarters in Tulsa, Okla., operates a multi-million-dollar complex of religious and educational institutions, including 2 youth camps and an agency offering guided tours of the Holy Land, Greece, and Rhodesia. The Crusade's far-right message is spread through books, pamphlets, a magazine and weekly newsletter, and taped radio broadcasts aired over more than 100 stations. Most of its tax-exempt income is drawn from direct mail solicitations sent regularly to a computer list of 200,000.

The Crusade's founder was born in Texarkana, Tex. Hargis was apparently raised hardpan dirt poor and filled with a rural fundamentalism as angry and tempestuous as an Oklahoma dust storm. As a lad of 10, the future firebrand evangelist promised his life to the Lord if He would see his mother through a serious operation. The Lord kept His end of the bargain, and Billy James kept his.

After high school Hargis entered unaccredited Ozark Bible College in Bentonville, Ark. The fact that he left after little more than a year didn't stop him from being ordained in the Rose Hill Christian Church at age 18. He pastored small rural congregations in Missouri and Oklahoma for awhile. Then he found his true calling—the one that would make him rich and famous—the fight against "godless Communism."

"I'd rather win souls to Christ than fight Communism, any day," he explains, "but a man has to do what God calls him to do. . . ."

Hargis earned his spurs with the far right in the early '50s, working with the Rev. Carl McIntire on "Project Bible Balloon." Hargis supervised the launching of thousands of gas-filled balloons that were subsequently floated across the Eastern European frontiers and into Russian satellite countries. Each balloon carried a selected Bible verse translated into 7 languages, intended to "succor the spiritually starved captives of Communism."

A few years later Hargis was quoted as an expert on communism in an official U.S. Air Force manual for noncommissioned officers. The Tulsa crusader used the opportunity to denounce the "treasons" of the National Council of Churches. The NCC bitterly complained to the Pentagon and Reverend Hargis found himself back in the salubrious glow of national publicity.

Though his politics are at very least "exotic," in relation to the American mainstream, he counts a number of congressmen, governors, and several high-ranking military men among his supporters.

The Hargis mind-set is described in reports from his 11th annual conference of the Christian Crusade, held in Tulsa in 1969. Alabama Governor George C. Wallace appeared and praised the delegates for their work "against subversive elements." Retired Brig. Gen. Clyde G. Watts announced that there are "one or more Communist cells in every major educational institution in the U.S." And longtime Hargis intimate retired Maj. Gen. Edwin Walker flatly stated that President Nixon was "financing revolutionists at home" while "tripping around like a fairy in Asia."

Reverend Hargis, a graduate of the "bawl and jump" school of Southern evangelism, has done well for himself in the rarefied atmosphere of the fringe right. In 1965 the Christian Crusade Cathedral was built in Tulsa for ¾ of a million dollars. It houses a chapel, administrative offices, publishing and broadcasting facilities, an auditorium, and a museum of Christian art and artifacts. Later, data processing equipment, a bookstore, and library were added.

Meanwhile, Reverend Hargis has traded in the $40,000 home he said was "a shack by U.S. standards." In 1971 the *Oklahoma Journal* reported that the Church of the Christian Crusade had purchased a hilltop home for the Hargis family in Tulsa's "Executive Estates." The new homestead had been listed for $500,-000 but was probably sold to the preacher at a somewhat lower price. Its exterior is white marble. It contains 11,000' of floor space, including a heated indoor swimming pool, a 40' game room, an 85' sun deck, a fallout shelter, and 90 telephone outlets.

Billy James Hargis has "arrived," at last.

—D.P.P.

REVEREND IKE (1935–   )

Successful evangelists have a problem with money. While they regularly draw greenback gushers from the faithful, most of them strive to give at least the appearance of personal humility.

Not the Reverend Ike. Not with his showy homes in New York and Hollywood, 2 Rolls-Royces, 2 Mercedes, a Bentley, drawers full of jewelry, and a Liberace-style wardrobe that reportedly costs his followers $1,000 a week. But then the Rev. Dr. Frederick J. Eikerenkoetter II (who graciously shortens it to Reverend Ike) is not trying for any humility awards. Far from being an embarrassing side effect of his flamboyant ministry, the money that rolls in is the whole point.

From his rhinestone-speckled lapels to his platform patent leathers, Ike is the virtual embodiment of his own theme: that regardless of what you may have heard, conspicuous consumption is truly next to godliness. Forget about meekness and repentance, he counsels his mostly black middle-class audiences, "When you kneel down to pray, you put yourself in a good position to get a kick in the behind."

That kind of talk, along with his garish style, has taken the handsome mulatto evangelist from the drab world of black storefront churches in New York and Boston to popularity and glittering success on a national scale. The son of a South Carolina Baptist minister of Dutch-Indonesian extraction, the Reverend Ike is today America's top-rated black radio preacher, beaming a 15-minute message of positive money-lust and instant divinity over some 80 stations.

When he made the switch from fundamentalism to the worldly pleasures in 1965, he invented the "Blessing Plan." The plan is simplicity itself: Give whatever you can afford to Reverend Ike, and it will be returned—with interest—to those who possess sufficient faith.

"Pledge at least $100!" he begins. "Borrow it if necessary. People borrow for the doctor and the lawyer and they save for the undertaker but rob God! DON'T LET THIS BE YOU. Send an extra offering. And believe for EXTRA blessings." To make it even easier, Ike allows for blessings on the installment plan, either by the month or by the week.

One year after his conversion to Mammon, the fruits of the Blessing Plan enabled Eikerenkoetter to buy a $600,000 movie theater on a full city block in the Washington Heights area of Manhattan. The plan also provided him the wherewithal to pour $1 million into remodeling the theater as the United Palace, with a 5,000-seat auditorium, offices for his United Christian Evangelistic Association, and headquarters for the Science of Life Institute.

In the late 1960s Reverend Ike took to the road. In Los Angeles he announced that "the *lack* of money is the true root of all evil." In Houston he told a crowd of 5,000, "I can love the Lord a lot better when I've got money in my pocket. Bless money. Money is God in action!"

The *Miami News* described Ike passing the plate at the Miami Beach Convention Hall saying: "All of you who can give $100 come up to the front of the altar . . . and those of you who can't give $100, take out $50 and bring it up . . . and if you haven't got that then take out a 10 or a 5. . . . No change please. . . . Hold those bills high, I want everyone to see your faith."

In San Francisco he booked the Cow Palace for one night at $25,000. One observer remarked that Reverend Ike's money pitch would make the late Sister Aimee seem shy and his healing demonstrations make Oral Roberts look dignified. Back in New York he packed Madison Square Garden, instructing 20,000 wide-eyed worshipers: "Don't wait for your pie in the sky, by and by. Say I want my pie right *now*—and I want it with ice cream on top!"

If to some Reverend Ike appears blasphemous and radical, he means no threat to established institutions. On the contrary, with his scorn of black militants, gamblers, and pushers and his distaste for the world of welfare, he could be someone's ideal symbol of black capitalism in the religion business.

In that role he stands in the spotlights of his United Palace Auditorium, the personification of everything his followers want to be—successful, good-looking, prosperous, and wildly pleased with himself. And to his altar they will likely continue to come, clutching tightly their eager offerings.

—D.P.P.

MARJOE GORTNER (1943–   )

Marjoe Gortner was not the 1st person to turn religion into a con game. But he was the 1st to expose himself, and all the tawdry tricks of his trade, in a feature-length movie.

His cinematic confessional, released in mid-1972, was a momentary *cause célèbre* of the new film journalism. But in the larger tradition of American Protestant revivalism, Marjoe will probably be best remembered for his scandalizing departure from the salvation circuit.

His early ministry was bizarre enough. His parents were California evangelists who knew from the beginning they had a potential preaching superstar on their hands. They named their infant son Marjoe: a contraction of Mary and Joseph. At 3 he was ordained in the Church of the Old Time Faith, in Long Beach. At 4½ he performed his 1st marriage, causing a legal flap and eventually a change in California law to require marrying ministers to be at least 21.

According to the filmed self-exposé, Marjoe's parents relentlessly drove him toward even more garish success. For the next 10 years he was carried around to independent Pentecostal churches and tent meetings throughout the South and Midwest. On stage he was a costumed, blue-eyed, pipe-voiced marionette animated by divine inspiration—or so his rapt country audiences fervently believed. Backstage he was a small, frightened boy, carefully coached by parents who sometimes held his head under water to discipline him to learn his lines.

At 14 he ran away and was taken in by an older woman who became both substitute mother and his mistress. She gave him a home while he attended high school in Santa Cruz and worked as a boardwalk hawker, auctioneer, and small-time rock musician. At San Jose State College he was baptized in civil rights, the youth revolution, and psychedelics.

He resolved to return to preaching. This time, however, he would sermonize on the God within. The fabulous Marjoe would return to his vulnerable backwoods Christians, using the pulpit to turn them on to social change and the new consciousness of the late 1960s.

It was a colossal bust. The faithful sat unmoved beneath the canvas tent. Crowds dwindled. Host pastors asked: "When are you going to preach of the blood, Marjoe? When are you gonna preach on the *fire?*" Frustrated by the flop of his radical revivals, Marjoe grimly decided to give them the show they wanted.

Calculating the effect of his body and voice on the emotions, he would strut, leap, and twitch himself into religious frenzy. Frankly copying the hand-on-hip swagger of Rolling Stone singer Mick Jagger, Marjoe thrilled worshipers, many of whom no doubt believed rock 'n' roll to be the work of the devil. As a hip Elmer Gantry, he was the soul of hypocrisy. Hard-earned dollars were heaped on the stage. Brother Marjoe, beaming with heavenly grace, raked them in.

Four and a half years later he wanted out. He also wanted to be a movie star. He achieved both desires by starring in an 83-minute cinema verité exposé of himself and his racket. In 1972–1973 *Marjoe*, the movie, played to tens of thousands of Americans, most of whom would never dream of attending a revival. Fundamentalist preachers said the man who had deceived them was obviously controlled by Satan. Sophisticates pointed out that they had said all along that such people are usually charlatans.

As for Marjoe, he began to wonder about the long-term value of being the newest centerpiece at chic Eastern parties; he wondered, too, whether his fledgling career as an actor would ever get him away from roles that typecast him as a wayward clergyman.

—D.P.P.

Super Bible Statistics

Do you know how many verses, words, letters there are in the Old and New Testaments combined? Do you know the longest and the shortest verses in the Bible? Do you know how many times the word "Lord" appears in the Bible?

You might not know to this day except for the persistence and industry of an eccentric British Bible scholar and theologian named Dr. Thomas Hartwell Horne, who determined to find the answers to these questions for himself

and for posterity. Born in London in October, 1780, educated at Christ's Hospital School, Dr. Horne became a barrister's clerk. He yearned to be an author, and at the age of 20 he published *A Brief View of the Necessity and Truth of the Christian Revelation*. More books followed, but to support himself, Dr. Horne took a position in the British Museum as assistant librarian of printed books. His main work was that of bibliographer. Although his body served the British Museum, his heart was elsewhere.

In a London filled with romantics and rebels like Byron, Keats, Coleridge, Dr. Horne gave his full devotion to the Holy Bible. Eager to popularize the good book, Dr. Horne decided to build on paper a tree filled with fascinating biblical lore. But to acquire the information he needed, the obsessed religious scholar realized that he would have to follow John's dictum—search the Scriptures—dissect the King James Version of the Bible as no man in history had done before him.

Quietly, Dr. Thomas Hartwell Horne set out on his long and lonely statistical journey. The Bible was his domain and for 17 years he combed every inch of it. For 3 of those years, toiling in his spare time night after night, Dr. Horne counted the words—and the letters in those words—of every verse in the Old Testament, the New Testament, the Apocrypha. The fruits of his monomania appeared in his book *Introduction to the Study of the Scriptures*, which was happily completed well before his death in January, 1862.

Herewith some of the Bible statistics produced by Dr. Thomas Hartwell Horne:

	Old Testament	New Testament	Total
Books	39	27	66
Chapters	929	260	1,189
Verses	23,214	7,959	31,173
Words	593,493	181,253	774,746
Letters	2,728,100	838,380	3,566,480

The Apocrypha

Books	14
Chapters	183
Verses	6,031
Words	125,185
Letters	1,063,876

Now, within the shape of a typographical tree, Dr. Horne summed up his findings, and then added some mindboggling information about the Bible:

The longest chapter or its equivalent is the 119th Psalm; the shortest is the 117th Psalm. The 117th is also the midpoint of the Bible [by word count].

The middle verse of the Bible is the 8th verse of the 118th Psalm.

The longest name is in the 8th chapter of Isaiah. [Ed.: Maher-shalal-hash-baz, 2nd son of Isaiah.]

The word "and" occurs 46,277 times; the word "Lord" 1,855 times.

The 37th chapter of Isaiah and the 19th chapter of II Kings are alike.

The longest verse is the 9th verse of the 8th chapter of Esther; the shortest verse is the 35th of the 11th chapter of John. [Ed.: Longest verse is 90 words, describes Persian Empire; shortest verse is 2 words, "Jesus wept."]

The finest piece of reading is the 26th chapter of Acts.

The name of God is not mentioned in the Book of Esther. It contains knowledge, wisdom, holiness, and love.

Dr. Horne may have been the 1st, but he certainly was not the last to attempt a statistical breakdown of the Bible. According to William S. Walsh, in his *Handy-Book of Literary Curiosities*, 1892, an anonymous "religious enthusiast . . . produced this astonishing monument of misapplied industry" (the countdown differing slightly from Dr. Horne's):

The words of the Bible contain 3,586,589 letters.

The word "and" occurs 46,227 times, the word "reverend" but once, "girl" but once, in 3rd chapter and 3rd verse of Joel; the words "everlasting fire" but twice, and "everlasting punishment" but once.

The 21st verse of the 7th chapter of Ezra contains all the letters in the English alphabet, except the letter J.

The 8th, 15th, 21st, and 31st verses of the 107th Psalm are alike.

Each verse of the 136th Psalm ends alike.

The anonymous statistician tallied 773,692 words in the King James version of the Bible as compared with Dr. Horne's 774,746 words. The discrepancy may be due to counting a hyphenated word variously as one word or 2.

While the anonymous statistician found 3,586,589 letters in the King James Version as against Dr. Horne's 3,566,480, 2 other number freaks, counting independently, came up with 3,586,489 letters and 3,567,180 letters respectively.

—I.W.

Holy Places in the World

JERUSALEM

Jerusalem, meaning "foundation of peace," is the cradle of 3 great historic religions. Sacred to Jews, Christians, and Muslims, this world center of monotheism has been a holy city for 35 to 40 centuries. Its geographical features are also religious symbols and help explain its spiritual preeminence. At an elevation of 2,500', it is a city set on a hill, a place to which one ascends. Many ancient peoples thought of mountains as holy and there they built their altars. Set apart by its inland location, away from major trade routes, Jerusalem developed an intense spiritual preoccupation.

In Old Testament times, Jerusalem stood in the center of a web of sacred places, where altars to Yahweh had been built. Later, its own temple was the center of Hebrew worship from the time of King David—who made Jerusalem the nation's capital c. 1000 B.C.—to 70 A.D., when it was destroyed by the Roman legions under Titus. To worship in the temple, Jews made an annual pilgrimage at Passover. This is the city of Israel's Kings, prophets, and religious leaders; the site of the crucifixion, resurrection, and ascension of Christ, as well as Mohammed's ascent into heaven. Under the name of Zion, the city is the object of Jewish messianic hope, and symbolizes heaven to Christians.

Enclosed by ancient walls, the Old City sector is visited by pilgrims of all faiths. Muslims, who in common with Jews revere the Holy Land for its patriarchs and prophets, consider Jerusalem a chief shrine after Mecca and Medina. The elegant 7th-century Dome of the Rock (Mosque of Omar), said to be built on the site of Mohammed's ascension, almost compares in sanctity with the Kaaba in Mecca. Of the great Temple of Herod, only a portion of the western wall was left exposed. From the 5th century to modern times, except for 1948 to 1967, Palestinian Jews have prayed at this Wailing Wall daily and have gathered there to recite the lamentations of Jeremiah on the anniversary of the temple's destruction. The southern wall is now being excavated.

Among the many Christian sites in Jerusalem, the Church of the Holy Sepulchre, today marking the tomb of Christ, and the Via Dolorosa, where Jesus is said to have carried his Cross, are most notable.

In 135 A.D. Hadrian demolished Jerusalem and then rebuilt it as a pagan shrine, in retaliation for the Jewish revolt led by Bar Kochbar. Hadrian considered Christianity a Jewish sect. He tried to obliterate the sites of the crucifixion and resurrection by covering them with concrete. Then he erected a statue of Jupiter over Calvary and he built a temple to Venus over the site of the tomb. Of course, the statues served instead as obvious markers, drawing Christian pilgrims like a magnet for almost 2 centuries.

MECCA

Any place people seek as a particular or unique goal is called a "mecca." The city that gave us this word is Mecca, the holiest city of Islam, and the birthplace of Mohammed, founder and prophet of the Islam faith. Islam, sometimes called Mohammedanism, dates from 622 A.D., the year of Mohammed's hegira, or flight from Mecca, which he later returned to and conquered.

Now one of Saudi Arabia's 2 federal capitals, Mecca has long been an international marketplace where commerce and religion converge. Religious festivals in and around the city once attracted idol-worshiping pilgrims and traders in incense and other commodities. Today Mecca draws an immense number of Muslims —1,200,000 during the April, 1965, hajj (pilgrimage) and often more than 15 million annually. The faithful, both men and women, are required to make a pilgrimage or hajj at least once during their lifetime, and if they die on the way they are considered martyrs. It is not unusual for martyrdoms to occur; in 1974, 460 Indonesian pilgrims—more than 1% of the total—died en route to Mecca. Lacking warm clothing, many succumbed to the severe Saudi Arabian winter. Alarmed by the death toll, the pilgrimage affairs director appealed to relatives to accompany aged pilgrims. Some pilgrims have spent 3 years walking from Asia to the Holy City.

In the courtyard of the great mosque, El Haram, is the central shrine of Islam, a cube-shaped granite temple draped in black camel's-hair veiling, called the Kaaba. Formerly a repository for idols, the 50'-square Kaaba is now a place of prayer. In the southeast corner of the building is the Kaaba stone, or black stone of Abraham, presumably given him by the angel Gabriel. Pilgrims are required to kiss the stone, now worn hollow by centuries of this ritual and held together by a wide silver band. Outside is the Zamzam, a holy well supposedly used by Hagar, the mother of Abraham's son, Ishmael, founder of the Arab people. Pilgrims must walk around the Kaaba 7 times, an old pagan ritual. The sevenfold circuit is known as *tawaf*. Then they walk a sevenfold course between the sacred hills of Safa and Marwah, in memory of Hagar. Upon completion of all rituals, the honorary title *hajj* (pilgrim) is conferred upon a Muslim.

For about 530 million Muslims, Mecca is their spiritual home, the city they face when they pray, wherever they may be.

ROME

Rome is one of the world's oldest cities. Once it was a hilly, marshy agricultural town no one had ever heard of except for its Latin settlers. Its primitive religion, a form of animism, or spirit worship, was distinctively ceremonial, marking the seasons of the year and the major events of life with elaborate rites. These became the ceremonies of state in later times and influenced the Christian festivals and the Church calendar.

It was inevitable that Rome should become the main center of Christianity. In contrast to provincial Jerusalem, so lofty and inaccessible, where the new faith emerged, Rome was the center of a vast network of roads. By the 1st century, all sorts of foreign cults had found acceptance in Rome, where they merged with indigenous gods and ceremonies. People were dissatisfied with religion and philosophy. Disenchantment with Emperor worship and the vain formality of state religion fanned the flames of mystical cults from Greece and the Orient, especially worship of the sun-god Mithras, a Persian. import. The way was paved for the vigorous new faith with its sincere promise of personal salvation.

For 15 centuries Roman Catholicism was the primary religion and cultural impetus of Western Europe, and today it claims over 550 million adherents, nearly $\frac{1}{4}$ of the world's population. Rome is the see of the Pope, who resides in Vatican City, an independent papal state within city boundaries, since February 1929. A see is the jurisdictional area of a bishop, and the Pope is the Bishop of Rome, which became the Holy See c. 42 A.D. The death of early apostles Paul and Peter in Rome—which is well attested to—and aid, both financial and pastoral, given to churches in other cities, tended to make the Roman bishop preeminent. As Rome's political power declined, Roman bishops assumed temporal as well as religious leadership.

Rome draws hundreds of thousands of religious pilgrims and other visitors annually. They are shown the Colosseum, where Christians were thrown to the lions; the Monastery of the Three Fountains, on the site of Paul's martyrdom; and numerous historic churches. The Vatican is open to visitors all year. Within it is the Sistine Chapel, private chapel of the Pope, built in the 15th century for Pope Sixtus IV, after whom it is named. Impressive beyond measure is many-domed St. Peter's Basilica. A prior edifice, built by Constantine and consecrated in 326 A.D., was revered for almost 1,200 years. Pope Julius II (1503–1513) had it razed to make way for the present structure, which took 120 years to build. Today St. Peter's is the largest church in the world and attracts more than 10 million visitors every year. Visiting priests are honored to celebrate mass at one of its many altars, and parents seek a head start in life for their children by having them baptized there.

Still a focal point of world travel, Rome is a place consecrated by the blood of martyrs, a long history of spiritual travail, and the prayers of the faithful.

LHASA

Like Mecca, Lhasa (meaning "God's house"), is a national center of trade, the capital of a region (the Tibet Autonomous Region of China) and a sacred city. Founded in the 5th century as a Buddhist fortress, Lhasa was known to Westerners as the Forbidden City because of its remote location and insularity. Behind its high walls, which were demolished in the 18th century, religion throve. Lhasa was a spiritual center even before Buddhism was brought to Tibet in 642 A.D. Until recently, the city was the center of Lamaism, a religion derived from Buddhism by Padmasambhava, a Buddhist monk from India who established the 1st Lamaic order about 770.

"Lama" means "superior one" and refers to the monks, who are also called lamas. Until the Chinese repression of religion in the 1960s, nearly $\frac{1}{5}$ of the population of Lhasa resided in lamaseries. There were 15,000 monks in Drepung and Sera, the 2 great monasteries adjacent to Lhasa. These monks were of the strict Yellow Hat sect, so-called because of the yellow hats they wore. The common people honored their gods daily with incense and prayer flags, and they chanted a prayer which was carved on rocks and tallied on prayer wheels. Even banners and streamers proclaimed this ritual chant, om mani padme hum ("o lotus jewel, amen").

Like the Kaaba of Mecca, the Jokang (cathedral) was the central shrine to which Lhasa owed its sanctity. Numerous small chapels housed statues and relics within a 3-storied building, and a gilded life-size statue of the Buddha as a young prince stood in its inmost shrine. Other temples and monasteries surrounded the city, of which the majestic Potala Palace of the Dalai Lama was the most impressive. A 6-mi.-long, circular pilgrim's path enclosed an area westward to Kundeling monastery. Around this path the devout walked every day. Some pilgrims placed their bodies on the ground, measuring their length, the entire distance. In February or March thousands of monks from near and far and an influx of pilgrims passed through the chorten (shrine) at the city entrance for Losar, the New Year Feast. The Monlam Chenmo, or Great Prayer, began on the 3rd day of the New Year, ushering in 3 weeks of continual prayer meetings, at which the gods were beseeched for happiness and prosperity.

Under communist control, Lhasa has been modernized, increasing in size and population. But the great cathedrals and monasteries have been desecrated, and the practice of religion is suppressed.

Varanasi (Benares)

Many cities are indebted to nearby rivers—pulsating channels of trade and commerce, life-sustaining sources of water for crops. One city, Varanasi (formerly Benares), capital of India's Uttar Pradesh State, owes its distinctive life to the sacredness of the Ganges River, upon whose north bank it stands. The Hindu's veneration of the Ganges, or Ganga, as they call it, has roots deep in their religious consciousness. To them, the river personifies a mother, cherished as both human and divine, exalted as a symbol of purity, viewed as the giver of salvation.

In fact, the word "Hindu" is derived from the name of a river. In the 6th century B.C., Persian invaders applied the word to people living near the Indus River, which is the "Sindhu" River in Sanskrit. As the Rig Veda, oldest of Hindu sacred writings, testifies, water was venerated from the earliest times by the agricultural Vedic Hindus. Eventually, Ganga came to be the most sacred of the sacred rivers. Ritual bathing in its waters is considered even more effective at one of the ancient holy places such as Varanasi, on prescribed days during the Mela ("festival"). However, the Hindu who bathes in the Ganga even once, no matter where or when, is virtually assured of salvation.

Today as in the past the water of the Ganga is used by pilgrims for washing, cooking, and drinking. They consider it clean although it is used for disposal of human bones and ashes, as well as the dead bodies of people and animals. Every year about one million pilgrims visit Varanasi, to bathe in the Ganga from numerous ghats, the bathing places with steps that line the river's crescent-shaped, stone-lined bank. Around the sacred areas of the city is the Panchkosi Road, a 50-mi. circuit every Hindu aspires to walk. According to their religion, if they die in Varanasi they will be released from the endless cycle of rebirths. They come to a city of great antiquity, a city of prehistoric origins and a center of religion and philosophy by the 2nd millennium B.C. Devout Hindus believe the city has always existed. In the 7th century A.D., Benares had nearly 100 temples dedicated to the Hindu god Siva. Records of pilgrimages date from this time.

Now the city has over 1,500 temples, most of them built in the last 200 years following a long period of Muslim invasion. Popular with foreign tourists is Durga Temple, with its swarms of monkeys in nearby trees, but the principal Hindu shrine is the Golden Temple. At nearby Sarnath is a deer park where Buddha preached a sermon (c. 6th century B.C.).

Varanasi combines sanctity and learning. Scholars are attracted to Hindu University, the center of Sanskrit studies, just as pilgrims crowd into the holy city all year round.

Machu Picchu (Vilcapampa)

On July 24, 1911, a dauntless American archaeologist named Hiram Bingham made an incomparable discovery on the summit of a precipice over a foaming river. In a search for the last Inca capital, he found the Lost City of the Incas, now called Machu Picchu ("old mountain"), but once known as Vilcapampa, a center of sun worship. He saw a breathtaking array of temples, palaces, plazas, and numerous stairways—a city of white granite structures of unsurpassed beauty, made with matchless skill. In the distance were hundreds of stone-faced terraces where crops had been grown to feed the inhabitants of this magnificent stone sanctuary. These included Incan Emperors and nobles, Priests of the Sun, and Chosen Women, or Virgins of the Sun, a corps of female assistants trained from childhood and chosen for their beauty. Authorized visitors to the sacred precincts had to undergo purification rites and remove their sandals as a sign of humility; unauthorized visitors were excluded physically by walls and psychologically by the threat of death.

This is where the last Incan Emperors found refuge from Spanish conquistadors in the 16th century. This is where the 1st Inca, Manco the Great (c. 1200) built a memorial temple with 3 great windows facing the rising sun. Other buildings on the site are the Principal Temple and the Semicircular Temple, revered for the royal burial place underneath it. Its gently sloping, curved outer wall was a model for the famous Temple of the Sun in Cuzco. Above all, the Incas had to placate the sun-god, though lesser homage was paid to moon, stars, thunder, and lightning. High in the Andes Mountains, on the Peruvian plateau, the rarefied atmosphere does not retain the heat of the sun, and nights were bitter cold. There was no guarantee the sun would return from its annual journey northward, and fear was acute at the time of their winter solstice on June 21 or 22. Only the priests could stop its flight. This they did by roping a huge gold disk, representing the sun, to a stone pillar called the Intihuatama, "the place to which the sun is tied," or colloquially, "hitching post of the sun." The Spaniards used to destroy these structures, but never reached the one at Machu Picchu, which stands intact. We can imagine the ceremonial processions of the priests and Chosen Women up the white granite stairways to Intihuatama Hill, where the priests extended their hands to the rising sun and threw kisses to it as an act of reverence.

When the Inca dynasty ended in 1572, the

city was gradually abandoned, and it remained hidden from view due to its unique location. Machu Picchu is today a holy place, where tourists arrive by train, then take a bus up 5-mi.-long Hiram Bingham Highway, to look upon a marvelous sight. Surrounded by dizzy slopes, they sense the height and depth of creation. Gazing upon the vast panorama and eerie quietude of Machu Picchu, they thrill to the mystery of the past.

LALIBELA (ancient ROHA)

In the wilds of northern Ethiopia, in Wallo Province, there is a small town named for Lalibela, a pious Christian monarch of the 12th century. According to local legend, he is responsible for the town's amazing rock-hewn churches, 11 in all, built by divine command and with the aid of angels. There is scarcely any other explanation for the incredible complex of shrines carved in the solid pink rock encircled by trenches. In a maze of tunnels and galleries, 4 of these buildings are literally monolithic, hewn from single chunks of rock freed by digging deep trenches around each of them.

Largest of this group is the Church of the World's Redeemer, which is 109′ long by c. 75′ wide, and it is set 35′ deep in the rock so that its roof is level with the ground. Inside are 5 arched aisles. Emanuel's Church imitates the ancient "sandwich wall" style, alternating layers of wood and stone. Painted, flowerlike designs on the ceilings are a feature of the Church of St. Mary's, and its cruciform shape distin-

guishes the elegant Church of St. George. Every one of Lalibela's churches is still in daily use. They are served by 1,000 Coptic priests, since the Orthodox Church of Ethiopia is closely related to the Egyptian Coptic Church.

In 1966, Princess Hirut Desta organized the Ethiopian Committee for the Restoration and Preservation of the Churches of Lalibela. An international team worked 4 years to repair the ravages of 8 centuries and reveal the original contours of the holy city.

Lalibela is known as the "New Jerusalem," with its population of 9,000, which is tripled by throngs of pilgrims during major religious holidays. Beating drums, shaking rattles, chanting voices mark these occasions when visitors cram the sunken courtyards of the underground churches, or shop and exchange gossip. Brightly garbed *debteras*, a lay religious order unique to Ethiopia, perform ritual dances.

There are 14,000 churches in Ethiopia, with clergy numbering a quarter of a million. It all started c. 330 A.D. when King Ezana of Aksum, capital of early rulers, was converted to Christianity by Bishop Frumentius. Ethiopian Christians have clung to their faith though isolated from the West by surrounding Muslim states. In the 16th century, Muslim invaders destroyed hundreds of medieval churches, which were later rebuilt, but they could not tear down those carved out of the mountain. The rock-hewn sanctuaries of Lalibela, with their unique architectural charm, symbolize a nation's enduring faith.

—R.Ho.

Modern Atheists/Agnostics of the Western World

"An atheist is a man who has no invisible means of support."—John Buchan (1875–1940) Scottish writer and historian

> Poems are made by fools like me,
> But only God can make a tree,
> And only God who makes the tree
> Also makes the fools like me.
> But only fools like me, you see,
> Can make a god, who makes a tree.
> —E. Y. Harburg

Atheist—one who "denies" the existence of God.

Agnostic—one who "doubts" the existence of God.

Questioning the existence of a god or gods reaches back to the days of Socrates. The following philosophers, reformers, rationalists, skeptics, and freethinkers spoke out on this complex and highly controversial issue.

ATHEISTS

MICHEL DE MONTAIGNE (1533–1592)

His Person: French essayist and wit. His political views have been described as anywhere from extremely reactionary to libertarian. Saint-Beuve commented that Montaigne was a good Catholic, only he was not a Christian. This stoic-skeptic-epicurean followed a critical method that questioned everything and left the finding of answers to the lesser intellects.

His Belief: "O senseless man, who cannot possibly make a worm and yet will make Gods by the dozens!"

MARQUIS DE SADE (1740–1814)

His Person: Nicknamed the "grand marquis" by fashionable Paris, described as "that frenzied pornographer" by Desmond McCarthy. Wrote *Justine*, which Rousseau warned would damn any girl who read but a single page. Spent a total of 27 years in the prisons or asylums of the Monarchy, the Republic, the Terror, and the Empire, and was hailed by Apollinaire as "the freest spirit that has ever lived." Described himself: "Imperious, choleric, irascible, extreme in everything, with a dissolute imagination . . . atheistic to the point of fanaticism." Attempted one escape from the Bastille. Failing that, he scattered leaflets and called out through an improvised megaphone, urging the populace to storm that prison. Freed by the Revolution of 1790. Imprisoned by the Revolution of 1801. Has been claimed as a precursor to Freud, the surrealists, Baudelaire, the existentialists, Nietzsche, and Stirner. Wrote: *Justine, Juliette, Philosophy in the Bedroom.* The word "sadism" is based on his name.

His Belief: ". . . Anything beyond the limits and grasp of the human mind is either illusion or futility; and because your god having to be one or the other of the 2, in the 1st instance I should be mad to believe in him, and in the 2nd a fool."

ARTHUR SCHOPENHAUER (1788–1860)

His Person: German philosopher who was the 1st avowed atheist. Kant's critique of the proofs of God had a profound influence on him at the start of his career: "When the stench of a corpse fills my nostrils I become indignant." The coexistence of divine freedom with human freedom was impossible. Nothing was left of God but His "mortal remains." Developed his thesis that the world is Idea, organized and directed by the Will. Obsessed by many phobias and fears, he always slept with loaded pistols at hand.

His Belief: "Theism [belief in God] is incompatible with the responsibility of a moral being because in theism responsibility always falls back on the Creator of that being. . . . If our will is free it is also original being, and vice versa."

MIKAIL BAKUNIN (1814–1876)

His Person: A revolutionist and "apostle of universal destruction," he demanded the complete annihilation of the prevailing social and political order. Celebrated the biblical Satan as the 1st revolutionary. Was condemned to life imprisonment in Germany, extradited to Austria, and later given over to the Russian Czar, who imprisoned him for many years. Following his release, he faced exile to Siberia and promptly escaped to London. Wrote: *God and the State.*

His Belief: "Even if God existed it would be necessary to abolish him."

KARL MARX (1818–1883)

His Person: German philosopher and revolutionary theorist. Descended from a line of rabbis, brought up as a Lutheran. Wanted to teach but turned to a journalism career when his reputation as a dangerous thinker barred him from joining any school faculties. Wished to transform society by eliminating hierarchical class divisions. His ideal society would be based on genuinely productive and voluntary work, rather than on "alienated" labor. The worker would no longer be "related to the product of his labor as to an alien, hostile, powerful, and independent object." Wrote: *Communist Manifesto, Das Kapital.*

His Belief: "The proofs of the existence of God are nothing but proofs for the existence of the essentially human self-consciousness. . . . Man is the supreme being for man. . . . Atheism and communism . . . are but the 1st real coming-to-be, the realization become real for man, of man's essence."

AMBROSE BIERCE (1842–1914?)

His Person: American writer of short stories, fables, and epigrams. Pursued career as freelance journalist and newspaper columnist, serving on staff of *San Francisco Sunday Examiner.* His *Examiner* columns reviled organized religion, big business, and the human race in general. Known for his bitter and sarcastic wit. Disappeared into the wilderness of Mexico, and was never heard of again. It is said that he intended to join Pancho Villa's revolutionary forces. Wrote: *The Devil's Dictionary, An Occurrence at Owl Creek Bridge.*

His Belief: "If there is a God—a proposition that the wise are neither concerned to deny nor hot to affirm—nothing is more obvious than that for some purpose known only to himself he has ordered all the arrangements of this world utterly regardless of the temporal needs of man. This earth is about the worst that a malevolent ingenuity, an unquickened apathy, or an extreme incapacity could have devised."

FRIEDRICH NIETZSCHE (1844–1900)

His Person: German philosopher and writer credited with phrase "God is Dead" and the doctrine of "nihilism." Plagued throughout life with attacks of dizziness, headaches, and numerous physical ailments. Resolved that only man's "will to live" could make him free. Aimed to make a godless existence endurable and meaningful. Became a professor at age 24. Son of a Lutheran minister. Died insane. Wrote: *Thus Spoke Zarathustra, The Joyful Wisdom, The Anti-Christ.*

His Belief: "In fact, we philosophers and 'free spirits' feel ourselves irradiated as by a new dawn by the report that the 'old God is dead'; our hearts overflow with gratitude, astonishment, presentiment, and expectation."

"You say you believe in the necessity of religion. Be sincere! You believe in the necessity of the police."

JOHANN MOST (1846–1906)

His Person: A Russian anarchist, he was repeatedly jailed for writing subversive pamphlets and newspaper articles. Escaped from Russia to Germany after being imprisoned for 16 months for his essay praising the nihilists. Then forced to flee Germany for England, where he discovered the English penal system. Spent his last years in America, where he served more prison terms for "seditious writings" and "criminal anarchy." Also received the dubious honor of being publicly whipped by anarchist Emma Goldman.

His Belief: "God is merely a specter, fabricated by designing scoundrels, through which mankind is tyrannized and kept in constant dread. But the phantom instantly dissolves when examined under the glass of sober reflection."

GEORGE SANTAYANA (1863–1952)

His Person: American-Spanish philosopher, critic, poet, teacher. Believed in a world of ideas, called "essences"—all that was, that is, that will be, and that *never* will be. Thought that religion was "a product of the imagination" and that knowledge is "faith in the unknowable." Brought up on fairy tales, romantic adventures of the past, and imbued with the ideals of Plato, Aristotle, and Spinoza. Was sympathetic to God believers: called the story of the Virgin Mary the "fairest flower of poesy," called Christianity "poetically true." Has been described as an "ancient poet writing a commentary on the modern world." Died in a convent in Rome. Wrote: *The Last Puritan, The Life of Reason, Lucifer: A Theological Tragedy.*

His Belief: "My atheism, like that of Spinoza, is true piety toward the universe and denies only gods fashioned by men in their own image, to be servants of their human interests."

MAXIM GORKI (1868–1936)

His Person: Russian novelist and playwright. He was born into the lower classes, the son of an upholsterer. Picked junk from the city dumps to earn his keep as a child. Enjoyed sudden literary fame and success after years of anonymity and poverty. Devoted almost all of his considerable literary income to the revolutionary movement, in which he was a leading figure. Awarded the prized Order of Lenin. Wrote: *The Lower Depths.*

His Belief: "This 'search for God' business must be forbidden for a time—it is a perfectly useless occupation."

NIKOLAI LENIN (1870–1924)

His Person: Bolshevik ideologist, leader of the Russian Revolution of 1917, and founding father of the Soviet Republic. The son of a schoolteacher. When he was 17, his brother was hanged for taking part in an unsuccessful assassination plot against the Czar. Received a law degree at St. Petersburg University, then became involved with revolutionary groups. Exiled to Siberia for 3 years. After years of revolutionary agitation and exile, he returned to Russia and was made chairman of the Council of People's Commissars, appointed by the November, 1917, 2nd All-Russian Congress of Soviets. He remained head of state until his death. His embalmed body, preserved in a mausoleum on Moscow's Red Square, is an object of pilgrimage.

His belief: "God-making is the worst way of spitting in one's own face."

ALFRED JARRY (1873–1907)

His Person: French writer, poet, playwright, illogician, and founder of "pataphysics," the science of "laws governing exceptions." Went about Paris wearing a cyclist's costume and carrying pistols, practiced the consumption of alcohol as a transcendent discipline, and lived in a dark, monkish cell on the third and a half floor of an apartment building. One of his fictional characters insisted: "God—or myself—created all possible worlds, they coexist, but men can hardly glimpse even one." Wrote: *Ubu Roi.*

His Belief: "If souls are independent, man is God."

ROBERT FROST (1874–1963)

His Person: Four-time Pulitzer Prize winner for excellence in poetry, he is perhaps the best-loved of American poets. Was invited to read at the Inauguration of President John Kennedy. Was the unofficial poet laureate of this country.

His Belief: "I turned to speak to God/About the world's despair;/But to make bad matters worse/I found God wasn't there."

ANDRÉ BRETON (1896–1966)

His Person: Poet and critic, founder and principal theorist of the surrealist movement.

Was concerned with abolishing the separation between art and daily social reality. Experimented with techniques of automatism (allowing the unconscious mind to find expression through uncontrolled or uncensored images) and dream research. Was interested in the revolutionary movements of his time and attempted to develop an aesthetics and a politics that would integrate the theories of both Marx and Freud. Wrote: *Manifestos of Surrealism, Nadja, Surrealism and Painting.*

His Belief: "Everything that is doddering, squint-eyed, infamous, sullying, and grotesque is contained for me in this single word: God."

ANDRÉ MALRAUX (1901–   )

His Person: French man of letters and *homme d'état.* As a youth was existentialist and Marxist activist. Fought in Spanish Civil War on the side of the Loyalists and in the French resistance during W.W. II. Served as Minister of Information on General de Gaulle's staff. Was France's Minister of Culture in De Gaulle's last administration. Author of several novels. Wrote: *Man's Fate, Man's Hope, Anti-Memoirs.*

His Belief: "To the absurd myths of God and an immortal soul, the modern world in its radical impotence has only succeeded in opposing the ridiculous myths of science and progress."

JEAN-PAUL SARTRE (1905–   )

His Person: French philosopher who contends that if God really exists, then man's freedom is mere illusion. Believes that without a God, individuals are free to create meaning and values for their lives. Considers Descartes to be the "classical champion of freedom." Wrote: *Being and Nothingness, Existentialism and Humanism.*

His Belief: "Thus the passion of man is the reverse of that of Christ, for man loses himself as man in order that God may be born. But the idea of God is contradictory and we lose ourselves in vain. Man is a useless passion."

MADALYN MURRAY O'HAIR (1919–   )

Her Person: The American who triggered the 1963 Supreme Court decision which eliminated prayer in the public schools. Has called herself the "most hated woman in the U.S." Calls for the total separation of church and state. Believes churches should be compelled to pay taxes (on property, income, etc.).

Her Belief: "I want to be able to walk down any street in America and not see a cross or a sign of religion. I won't stop till the Pope—or

whoever the highest religious authority is—says that atheists have a right to breathe in this world."

JOHN LENNON (1940–   )

His Person: Liverpool-born rock 'n' roll superstar and songwriter; former member of the Beatles, who, at the height of their fame, said they were "bigger than Jesus."

His Belief: "God is a concept by which we measure our pain."

AGNOSTICS

DAVID HUME (1711–1776)

His Person: British philosopher who believed that all knowledge results from sense experience. Thought that the existence of God was an unproved hypothesis. However, he spoke out against the atheists of his time and was criticized for his conflicting opinions. Argued against the possibility of miracles. Wrote: *Dialogues Concerning Natural Religion, Natural History of Religion.*

His Belief: "A miracle is a violation of the laws of nature. . . ."

CHARLES DARWIN (1809–1882)

His Person: British naturalist who proposed that man evolved from a process of "natural selection" and shared a common ancestry with monkeys. Studied to be both a doctor and a minister. Signed on as a naturalist for a 5-year scientific voyage aboard the government vessel *Beagle*—considered the trip to be "the 1st real training or education" of his mind. Daydreamed that ancient manuscripts or letters would one day be discovered and would prove what was written in the Gospels. Married to a deeply religious woman who had some of Darwin's comments on religion omitted from an early edition of his *Autobiography.* Wrote: *Origin of Species, Descent of Man.*

His Belief: "The mystery of the beginning of all things is insoluble by us, and I for one must be content to remain an Agnostic."

ROBERT G. INGERSOLL (1833–1899)

His Person: Prominent American lawyer and lecturer who spoke out on religion, politics, and education. Friend of Andrew Carnegie, Walt Whitman, Mark Twain. Attorney general of Ilinois. Inspired by Thomas Paine's fight for political and religious freedom. Colonel in Civil War. Lectures include: "The Gods," "The Liberty of Man, Woman, and Child," "What We Must Do to Be Saved."

His Belief: "I feel as though I could exist without God just as well as he could exist without me. And I also feel that if there must be an orthodox God in heaven I am in favor of electing him ourselves."

CLARENCE DARROW (1857–1938)

His Person: American criminal lawyer, lecturer-debater, writer, and humanitarian. Became internationally famous as the defense attorney in the Scopes evolution case in Dayton, Tenn., which challenged the constitutionality of the then existing antievolution law. Fought for an awareness and tolerance of man's conflicting beliefs and advocated a "philosophy of mechanism" which insisted that there must be a cause for every antisocial act, and once that cause was found and either removed or eliminated, the victim of the cause could be made well and whole again. Campaigned against poverty, capital punishment, and all injustices he believed to be "intolerant" and destructive to mankind. Called an "atheist," and "anarchist" by some; called a "most religious man," "one of the few true Christians" by others. Wrote: *Crime: Its Cause and Its Treatment, Infidels and Heretics.*

His Belief: "I do not consider it an insult, but rather a compliment to be called an agnostic. I do not pretend to know where many ignorant men are sure—that is all that agnosticism means."

HENRY LOUIS MENCKEN (1880–1956)

His Person: American editor, essayist, author, and—above all—a newspaper man. Began career as cub reporter (age 19) on *Baltimore Morning Herald*—became editor in 6 years. Worked for *Baltimore Sun* for great part of his career. Possessed a "superb gift for communications" which won him notoriety as one of America's "most colorful and influential public figures." Fought for limitation of governmental powers, and believed in free speech "up to the last limits of the unendurable." Fought against paternalisms (communism, Nazism, etc.). Declared enemy of puritanism. Persuaded Clarence Darrow to become defense lawyer in Scopes evolution trial. Has been called the "Sage of Baltimore," "our greatest practicing literary journalist," "the private secretary of God Almighty," and "an 18-karat, 23-jeweled, 33rd-degree, bred-in-the-bone and dyed-in-the-wool moron." Wrote: *In Defense of Women, The American Language, Prejudices, Treatise on the Gods.*

His Belief: "As for religion, I am quite devoid of it. The act of worship, as carried on by Christians, seems to me to be debasing rather than ennobling. It involves groveling before a Being, who, if He really exists, deserves to be denounced instead of respected."

BERTRAND RUSSELL (1872–1970)

His Person: British philosopher who contributed to the fields of mathematical logic, education, religion, and politics. Lost Labor party's support when he stood for Parliament in England and a Fellowship at Trinity College because of religious beliefs. Lost a teaching position in the U.S. because of his agnosticism and his "alleged advocacy and practice of sexual immorality" (case was tried by a Roman Catholic judge). Nobel Prize winner. From staunch Presbyterian background. Imprisoned while campaigning for nuclear disarmament. Established Bertrand Russell Peace Foundation. Wrote: *The History of Western Philosophy, On Education, Marriage and Morals, Why I Am Not a Christian, Which Way to Peace?*

His Belief: "The whole conception of God is a conception derived from the ancient Oriental despotisms. It is a conception quite unworthy of free man. . . . A good world needs knowledge, kindliness, and courage; it does not need a regretful hankering after the past or a fettering of the free intelligence by the words uttered long ago by ignorant men."

CRITICS ''IN GOOD FAITH''

Although the following considered themselves believers in God, their inquiries into the existence of God and the value of religion led to contemporary forms of atheism.

RENÉ DESCARTES (1596–1650)

His Person: French. Generally hailed as the founder of modern philosophy. Contributed to the science of mathematics by formulating concepts for relating mathematics to reality, mind to matter. Originator of the phrase "I think, therefore I am." Wrote a book which suggested that man lived on an "earth in motion" but did not publish it because of persecution of others who had promoted "revolutionary theories" (i.e., Galileo). Believed himself to be a convinced Catholic. Wrote: *Discourse on Method, Principles of Philosophy.*

His Belief: "I must inquire whether there is a God as soon as the occasion presents itself; and if I find that there is a God, I must also inquire whether He may be a deceiver; for without a knowledge of these 2 truths I do not see that I can ever be certain of anything."

IMMANUEL KANT (1724–1804)

His Person: German philosopher whose critique of the proofs of God contributed to later forms of atheism. Began his writing career as a scientist with treatises on fire, wind, anthropology, and natural history. Attempted in his religious dialogues to demolish the old Cartesian arguments and reestablish the idea of God on newer grounds. As the impetus for a moral act, the desire to please God was for Kant "a servile and pathological urge." Wanted to lead religion back to a question of ethics. Man and God, he said, exist on an equal footing. Wrote: *Critique of Pure Reason.*

His Belief: "The concept of a supreme being is in many respects a very useful idea; but just because it is a mere idea, it is altogether incapable by itself alone of enlarging our knowledge of what exists . . . we can no more extend our stock of theoretical insight by mere ideas, than a merchant can better his position by adding a few noughts to his cash account."

G. W. F. HEGEL (1770–1831)

His Person: German philosopher and teacher whose beliefs revolved around "the systematic method of developing the absolute spirit" in all phases of life. Began study for the ministry but preferred study of philosophy. Fought to overcome opposing viewpoints presented by religion and philosophy, but also presented "one of the most influential sources of contemporary atheism." Wrote: *The Phenomenology of the Spirit, The Philosophy of Right.*

His Belief: "Without the world God is not God."

FËDOR MIKHAILOVICH DOSTOEVSKI (1821–1881)

His Person: Russian novelist, who plumbed the psychological depths of the atheism of his day, and insisted that atheistic thought sprang from a hatred of the world as it is. The possibility of leading a meaningful life without God preoccupied much of his life and work. Met with a Fourierist study group as a young man and was imprisoned for subversive activity. Sen-

tenced to death, he was suddenly pardoned while standing in front of the scaffold. Did 4 years of hard labor, where the only book he was allowed to read was the Bible. Prolific and much-acclaimed literary output. Was hailed at his death as a true patriot, Christian, and humanitarian. Wrote: *The Possessed, Crime and Punishment, The Brothers Karamazov.*

His Belief: "To recognize that there's no God without recognizing at the same time that you yourself have become God makes no sense."

OF INTEREST

THOMAS PAINE (1737–1809)

An American hero by all standards save one, Thomas Paine became a target for abuse after publication of his religious beliefs in *The Age of Reason*, 1794. Although Paine insisted that he believed in God, his criticism of religion and of the Bible led many to label him an atheist, a "hater of Christ," "a man steeped in sin." However, he has also been called a "profoundly religious man," a man of "religious fervor, strength, and devotion."

His Person: Believed in a God of moral truth, not a God of mystery and obscurity. Disbelieved the doctrine of the virgin birth. Did not look upon the Bible as the word of God. Called a "filthy little atheist" by Theodore Roosevelt. Was 1st to name country the "United States of America." Was 1st to propose American independence. Advocated justice for women. Urged purchase of the Louisiana Territory. Son of Quaker parents. Wrote: *Common Sense, The American Crisis, The Rights of Man.*

His Belief: "The only idea man can affix to the name of God is that of a 1st cause of all things."

—C.O. and S.W.

A Ticket to the Oberammergau Passion Play

Oberammergau is a Teutonic "Little Jerusalem" perched in the Bavarian Alps of southern Germany. The village spills out on a single flat flood plain, in a valley at the source of the Ammer River. The village name means a "pasture in the upper Ammer Valley." Today it also connotes *the* Passion Play. There is an Unterammergau just 5 mi. downstream to the north, but nobody has heard of it because it does not relive Christ's last days in Jerusalem every 10 years. Access to both villages is by train up the Ammer Valley, or by motorcar south from Germany's 1972 Summer Oympics city of Mu-

nich toward her 1936 Winter Olympics city of Garmisch-Partenkirchen. Turn west just before arriving in Garmisch.

When Oberammergau, a village of nearly 6,000 people, last staged the Passion Play in 1970, more than half a million people from all over the world made the pilgrimage to sit among the ageless mountains—Mount Kofel being the most famous—for 6½ hours on hard seats, empathizing with the suffering and death of Christ. The actors are always amateurs. So are the producers. Farmers, shopgirls, and in particular wood-carvers—truly the mainstay occupation of the Oberammergauers—have made the Passion Play one of the world's most successful box-office hits.

Most tickets are sold with 2 nights' lodging included, creating a scheduling avalanche which a rented computer tries to cope with. Forty traffic controllers are on the site to direct the 8,000 buses and 100,000 cars that arrive in a typical summer. Some tickets are sold through travel agents, a few of whom have been known to go bankrupt when they thought they had Passion Play tickets for their tours and then did not.

In 1970, more than a million, twice as many as attended, had to be turned away. The lucky ones who get tickets and can attend usually spend 2 nights in Oberammergau: the 1st to prepare themselves by a medieval vigil for witnessing one of the 98 scheduled performances, and the 2nd to recover from the mystical experience. In 1970 these pilgrims left more than $10 million behind.

Oberammergauers do not stage the play to make money for themselves, however. No individual makes any great personal profit. For instance, in 1960, the highest-paid performers (they spurn use of the words "actor" and "actress") received only $1,875 for 6 months of part-time work preparing the performance and 6 months of full-time work presenting it. Profits are split 4 ways, one quarter for the next play, one quarter for the church, one quarter for the performers, and one quarter for improving the accommodations for the pilgrims' 2 nights in the village. Treating the play essentially as a religious service, the community has steadfastly refused to allow it to be recorded, filmed, or televised, and has not even permitted the cast to go on tour.

Since the German economy was desperately depressed after W.W. I, the promised 1920 production was delayed until 1922. In that year Oberammergau received a dazzling offer from an American film company for rights to the play. In silent defiance, the performers sheared their locks and shaved their faces the night after the last scheduled performance.

The origin of the Oberammergau Passion Play goes back to a 1633 promise which, unlike more modern pledges, is still being honored. In that year, Europe was ravaged by a plague that spread like a prairie fire, fanned by the winds of the Thirty Years' War (1618–1648). The ghastly deaths caused by the plague were temporarily warded off by Oberammergauers who barricaded their mountain entrances and exits. But then a villager named Karl Schisler, who had been working some distance away from Oberammergau, got homesick and slipped past guards back into the village. In no time, 100 villagers were infected and died in agony, and

the terrified living turned to God for protection: If He would spare them, they would enact the last days of Christ on earth every 10 years "from now until the end of time." In 1633 the village elders joined hands in the local church to swear this solemn vow. Today they still join the cast and visitors each morning a performance is given to celebrate a mass.

Until 1800, the Oberammergau performances were largely private. In that year, however, Napoleon's troops shelled the town and several famous Austrian Army commanders attended the play while defending Oberammergau. In 1840, princes, princesses, and dignitaries from all over Europe flocked to Oberammergau, arriving, according to one report, "on foot, often without shoes and stockings, in a long procession, praying loud and devoutly; in the eyes of the people the visit to this play serves a holy purpose, they look upon the way there as a pilgrimage undertaken to save their souls."

Artists, churchmen, royalty, and statesmen showed up in 1850 but the masses did not arrive until 1860, when the 1st railroad was completed from Munich to Starnberg. The year 1870 witnessed fewer performances (due apparently to the outbreak of the Franco-Prussian War in July, 1870) but more illustrious guests —counts, countesses, and archdukes, as well as composers and archbishops. In 1871, repeat performances attracted King Edward VII of England and King Ludwig II of Bavaria. The latter was even then building his Linderhof and Neuschwanstein castles in the nearby Alps, partly with the help of workers from Oberammergau.

The influx of the famous increased vastly in 1880. Most noteworthy was the Prussian Crown Prince Friedrich Wilhelm, who temporarily ascended the throne as Emperor of Germany in 1888, then died shortly thereafter. By 1890, European royalty came as a matter of course while American celebrities made their debut, among the 1st of these being Thomas Edison. The 1900 performance attracted Sweden's King Oskar II, America's John D. Rockefeller, France's Alexandre Eiffel who built the Tower, and Germany's Count Zeppelin who constructed airships.

Perhaps the most famous 1930 visitor was Henry Ford, who presented that year's Christus, Alois Lang, with a motorcar in appreciation for his acting talents. Lang accepted the certificate entitling him to his choice at a Munich car dealer. William Randolph Hearst made it in 1934, as did a chief of the Blackhead Indians, arrayed in native finery and carrying a calumet (a ceremonial pipe), which he presented to the same Christus, Alois Lang. Hitler also arrived, escorted by a dozen cars, to take the seat he had booked under an assumed name. This same Führer issued an order in 1943 that would have converted the theater into an airplane parts factory, but the villagers successfully refused to comply with the order.

There has always been decided antagonism felt by the Jews toward this most Christian of all Christian art-worship services. In 1970, the 36th performance in the festival's 336-year history, the controversy erupted again. It swirled this time in a new religious awareness that followed the 2nd Vatican Council. The American Jewish Committee released a critique which was supported by 7 Christian scholars, alleging that the 1970 script still "reveals the sin of anti-Semitism," in spite of superficial alterations. Jewish groups demanded that Munich's Julius Cardinal Dopfner boycott the opening because of the text, but he attended anyway only to declare at the opening mass: "We are all agreed that the text today needs a new version."

Actually, the 1970 version was supposed to have a totally new script. Stephan Schaller, a modern-day Benedictine from Ettal, wrote one after laborious consultation with Jewish groups and after reconciling the play with the spirit of the 2nd Vatican Council. But Oberammergau's 26-man play committee rejected it as too bland. Now still another special committee is at work making revisions for the 1980 performances.

While anti-Semitism persists in the play, it reached its most painful pitch in the 1930s. In 1934, Oberammergau scheduled a special performance to commemorate the 300-year anniversary of the Passion Play. This time a new plague was on hand to harass the villagers—Nazism. In an effort to make his Bavarian subjects look like Aryans rather than Jews while playing their biblical roles, Hitler appointed his Bavarian State Minister, Esser, High Commissioner for Tourist Traffic and ordered him to preside over the Passion Play committee. But the villagers refused to modify their makeup and costumes, though they paraded agreeably, regularly "heiling" Hitler.

During August, 1934, the audience paid tribute to Field Marshal von Hindenburg on the occasion of his death and to Hitler when he attended a performance. Hitler was inspired only by the character of Pilate, whom history

records as a brutal Roman governor, but whom Hitler exalted by commenting: "There he stands like a firm rock in the middle of the whole muck and mire of Jewry."

Since Pilate was the only redeeming feature of the play in official Nazi eyes, it was not surprising in 1940 that Nazism said no to the Oberammergauers. Officials characterized the play as sentimental drivel that would divert manpower and energy from the struggle for world conquest. But by 1950, the Nazi plague too had abated.

Wood-carvers and seamstresses are both indigenous to Oberammergau. The more than 500 carvers comprise the basic "between-plays" industry of the community, while the local seamstresses produce and maintain approximately 1,000 costumes in the Passion Play wardrobe. Six seamstresses begin work at least a year before each performance, making new costumes and altering old ones. Likewise, the village choir and orchestra are always busy rehearsing, and often carry off prizes from district music festivals.

The most famous portrayers of Christ over the years have been Josef Mayr, 1870–1890; Anton Lang, 1900, 1910, and 1922; Alois Lang, 1930 and 1934; and Helmut Fischer, 1970. At present, some 1,700 villagers are involved in any one production, and therefore individuals are not singled out for acclaim. Distinguished or not, the Christ impersonator must memorize 7,000 words and be onstage 5 hours for each performance in a role that demands at least stamina, if not always talent.

Presented originally in front of the church, the play has been performed on the Passion Meadow since 1830. Several theaters preceded the present one, which was built in 1900 and seats 5,200. Arrangements in the theater are such that the audience sits under cover while the stage remains open to the sky. The Alpine backdrop lends beauty, grandeur, and sometimes sound effects when thunderstorms break over the mountains between 4 and 4:30 P.M. during the crucifixion. When the play ends about 5:15 P.M., there is no applause, only a musical presentation of the Apostles' Creed.

—L.V.J.R.

American Saints and Potential Saints

Achieving canonization is usually a long and rigorous process. Being a worker for the Catholic faith is not enough. A "fame of sanctity" must be present, one great enough to induce the local bishop to introduce the candidate's "cause." The candidate must also be possessed of "heroic virtue." After his or her writings and actions are judged to be without "defect in

faith or morals," the candidate may be declared "Venerable."

In the case of nonmartyrs (there need be none for martyrs), 4 miracles are sought. When 2 are discovered, the candidate is beatified and is then called "Blessed." After 2 more miracles, the candidate is declared a Saint by the Pope, which affirms that the candidate is now in heaven, and is worthy of devotions from and imitation by all of the faithful.

The canonization ceremony is held in Rome, at St. Peter's Basilica, at a cost to the Saint's backers of $10,000. This fee provides for the use of the church, the Vatican's Swiss Guard, and the Holy See's choir.

Bl. Sebastian de Aparicio (1502–1600)

Cause. He began his religious life late, receiving his friar's habit at the age of 72, in the convent of San Francisco at Mexico City.

He was assigned the dreary task of procuring the daily bread from the local convents, but accepted it joyfully. He spent the last years of his life working miracles—an almost unheard-of power since most miracles attributable to saints occur after they have died.

Devil's Advocate. Regardless of his miraculous powers, he was married twice. While he claimed these unions were unconsummated, there is no proof of his claim.

Nomination. So widespread was his fame that the Bishop of Puebla, Diego Romano, felt urged to initiate the canonization process before Sebastian de Aparicio died.

Present Stage. He was beatified in 1789. The time lapse since beatification seems to indicate a bias against his 2 marriages, and despite the claim of miracles, there have only been 2 since his death, and thus he probably never will be declared a Saint.

The 116 American Martyrs (d. 1542–1731)

Cause. The list includes Father Juan de Padilla, a Franciscan, and the 1st Catholic killed for Christ in the U.S. The martyrs were killed mostly by Indians, but also by frontiersmen, throughout the South and the Southwest, and represent various religious orders, laymen and clergy included.

Devil's Advocate. Because of the number involved, and the time lapse since their deaths, it will be difficult to verify that all were killed for religious reasons only, and thus, all of them cannot be elevated to Sainthood.

Nomination. The list was compiled under the direction of Bishop Gannon of Erie, and sent to the Congregation of Rites by the late Archbishop of Philadelphia, Cardinal Dougherty.

Present Stage. The cause has been recognized by the American bishops as a legitimate one, and as such, "should be promoted by all American Catholics."

St. Philip of Jesus (1571–1592)

Cause. Born in Mexico, St. Philip left the Franciscans to become a merchant. He later repented and rejoined the order in the Philippines. He volunteered for missionary work in Japan and was martyred at Nagasaki.

Devil's Advocate. He left the order and the Kingdom of God to seek riches. While his repentance was strong, and his martyrdom tragic (he was crucified), this indiscretion cannot be overlooked.

Nomination. The Franciscans were his main promoters.

Present Stage. He was canonized in 1862, and has become the patron saint of Mexico City.

Marie of the Incarnation (1599–1672)

Cause. Soon after her husband's death, she began receiving revelations concerning the Incarnation, the Sacred Heart, and the Trinity. Leaving her 12-year-old son in the care of her sister, she entered a monastery.

While there, she wrote *Relation of 1633,* which, with *Relation of 1654* (written in Canada), provides a history of her mystical life. Later, in 1639, she set sail for Canada, becoming the 1st woman missionary to the New World.

Devil's Advocate. Though she may have been a woman of sanctity, God obviously has not chosen to work miracles through her.

Nomination. Her cause was introduced in 1893.

Present Stage. She was declared "Venerable" by Pope Pius X on July 19, 1911.

Bl. Marguerite Bourgeoys (1620–1700)

Cause. After several unsuccessful attempts to enter the cloister, she set sail for Canada. While there, she opened the 1st school in Montreal, and also established schools and missions for the Indians and a training school for the poor.

As the scope of her work grew, other women were recruited. The group later melded into a new kind of religious community, one not bound to the cloister, but free to go about—one dressed not in religious habits, but in the costume of the poor. The Church was not too happy with her independent group, but later recognized it, naming it the Sisters of the Congregation of Notre Dame.

Devil's Advocate. Like many others who have been beatified but not canonized, she lacks the required number of miracles. Miracles for canonization must occur *after* beatification, and, in her case, there have not been any.

Nomination. She was beatified in 1950 by Pope Pius XII. In paying her tribute, he said, "Her influence is still being felt . . . as foundress of a Congregation of secular women, she realized the dream cherished for France by Saint Francis de Sales."

Present Stage. As with many others, only the lack of miracles is stopping her from being declared a Saint.

The North American Martyrs—
St. Isaac Jogues et al. (d. 1642–1649)

Cause. Daniel, Brebeuf, Lalemant, Garnier, and Chabanel were massacred within the confines of Canada, while Goupil, LaLande, and Jogues were martyred near Auriesville, N.Y. Jogues's fellow missionaries knew that he desired the grace of martyrdom, so when the news of his murder by the Indians reached them in Quebec, they celebrated a Mass of Thanksgiving rather than one of Requiem.

The *Relation* says of the murders of Brebeuf and Lalemant:

> Before their deaths, both their hearts were torn out through openings made in their chests; these barbarians feasted on their warm blood. While still full of life, pieces of their thighs, calves, and arms were removed by the butchers, who roasted them on coals and ate them in their sight.

Devil's Advocate. Did they indeed die for the faith? Were they killed because of it? Incontrovertible proof of this must be presented.

Nomination. Their cause was promoted vigorously, but it wasn't formally introduced by the Jesuit hierarchies of North America until 1912.

Present Stage. Beatified in 1925, they were canonized on June 29, 1930. Annually, hundreds of thousands of pilgrims visit the 2 sanctuaries erected in their honor. One, the Shrine of Our Lady of Martyrs, is in Auriesville, N.Y., and was built by the Jesuits in 1884. The other is in Midland, Ont.

Kateri Tekakwitha (1656–1680)

Cause. Born in Auriesville, N.Y., the resting-place of the North American Martyrs, she fled to a Christian village because of native opposition to her devotion to Christ.

There, at the age of 21, she received her 1st Holy Communion. She lived a life of austerity and charity, and did something unheard-of—she made a private vow of chastity—an exceptional act, as an Indian woman's survival depended upon getting a husband. Her death at the age of 24 was an inspiration to the Indian community and was followed by an outbreak of religious fervor among them.

Devil's Advocate. Her sanctity may be unquestioned, but she lacks the necessary number of miracles.

Nomination. A collection of biographical data written by Jesuit missionaries in the years following her death provided the documentation for her cause, which was introduced in Rome in 1932. The Tekakwitha League, located at Auriesville, and one of her prime promoters, publishes a quarterly and directs other activities to disseminate knowledge of her.

Present Stage. As a tribute to her, the 1st instance of the liturgical use of the vernacular which was *sanctioned* by the Roman Catholic Church was in the church of the Indian village where her bones lie. The people sing the responses to the Mass in Iroquois, and the inscriptions on the Stations of the Cross are in the same language.

Recently, Kateri Tekakwitha was declared "Venerable."

Bl. Marie Marguerite d'Youville
(1701–1771)

Cause. After her husband's death, she became the Lady of Charity in her parish, helping the sick and the poor. Later, she and 3 companions made a profession of service to the needy, often taking the destitute into their communal home.

The residents, wary of her because she had had a thieving husband, stoned and insulted D'Youville and her companions, often publicly refusing them Holy Communion. But she continued her charitable ways, buying farms to support the needy and teaching catechism to the farmers' children. She founded the Order of the Grey Nuns, inaugurated closed retreats for women, began the 1st home for foundlings in North America, and opened hospital wards for wounded soldiers.

Devil's Advocate. Her inability to exert any positive influence on her husband—who was despised equally in France and Canada for defrauding both Indians and merchants—casts her in an unfavorable light. Also, since 1959, there have been no further miracles attributed to her.

Nomination. She was declared "Venerable" in 1890 and was beatified in 1959.

Present Stage. No additional miracles have been attributed to her, but if some arise, her chances for Sainthood will be bettered.

Father Junípero Serra (1713–1784)

Cause. Originally a missionary in Mexico, after the Spanish exiled the Jesuits Serra was appointed president of the Franciscans' California missions. While there, he founded 9 missions, including the ones at San Diego, San Francisco, and Santa Clara.

As a crusader for better treatment of the Indians, he became embroiled in several conflicts with the military. He petitioned a list of grievances entitled *Memorial*, but did most of the reforming on his own, baptizing and confirming thousands, as well as introducing agriculture and domestic animals.

Devil's Advocate. Weak though they were, he had associations with the military, as well as having been Commissary of the Holy Office of the Inquisition.

Nomination. In 1934, at the request of the Bishop of Monterey-Fresno and of the Franciscan provincial of the Province of Santa Barbara, the process of beatification was opened.

Present Stage. Though Serra is probably the most famous of the Franciscan missionaries to America, and as a tribute to him, his statue is now in the Hall of Fame in the Capitol at Washington, D.C., interest in his cause appears to have waned. The compilation of historical data has not even been completed yet, let alone the investigation into possible miracles. However, Father Litz, of the Bishop Neumann Shrine in Philadelphia, considers him "an excellent candidate."

St. André Grasset de Saint-Sauveur (1758–1792)

Cause. A secular priest and one of the Martyrs of Paris, a group of 191 men massacred in various Parisian prisons during the French Revolution. Born in Canada, he moved to France and was soon imprisoned by one of the antireligious cliques for refusal to support by oath the Civil Constitutions of the Clergy.

Devil's Advocate. It has to be decided whether the Paris Martyrs died for purely political reasons or for their refusal to submit to the civil authorities because it meant surrendering their religious independence.

Nomination. St. André Grasset de Saint-Sauveur and his 190 contemporaries were canonized by Pope Pius XI on October 17, 1926.

Present Stage. Although he died in France, St. André Grasset was the 1st Canadian (martyr or nonmartyr) to be declared a Saint.

Magin Catala (1761–1830)

Cause. Born in Spain, he worked with the Franciscans in Mexico and California. Though he suffered from severe inflammatory rheumatism, he did not allow it to deter him from his work. He visited the sick, preaching in both Indian languages and in Spanish. Despite his poor health, he was an ascetic of sorts, wearing the heavy and confining clothes of his order, and existing on a diet of corn gruel and milk.

Devil's Advocate. Although he had the powers of miracle and prophecy while alive, no miracles have been attributed to him since his death. Also, his fame for working miracles while he was alive may well deter the Church from canonization, because of the papal decree that no candidate shall have a "public cult."

Nomination. In 1884, Archbishop J. S. Alemany of San Francisco instituted the process of beatification.

Present Stage. Because of the time lapse since the introduction of this cause, there is doubt as to whether he will ever be declared a Saint.

Bl. Rose Philippine Duchesne (1769–1852)

Cause. As a French missionary to the U.S., she opened a school in St. Charles, Mo., the 1st free school west of the Mississippi for Catholic and non-Catholic children. While in Missouri, she operated a free parish school, a small orphanage, a school for Indian girls, as well as a novitiate for the order she founded, the U.S. branch of the Society of the Sacred Heart.

She didn't fully realize her dream of doing missionary work among the Indians until the age of 72. Despite her age, her help was appreciated. As one nun put it, "If she cannot work, she will forward the work of the mission by her prayers." She had a special place in her heart for the Indians, especially the Potawatomi, who felt the same way about her, giving her the name Quah-kah-ka-num-ad, "Woman who prays always."

Devil's Advocate. As with many others, she has been unable to produce more miracles since her beatification.

Nomination. She was beatified on May 12, 1940.

Present Stage. Definitely one of the most admired Catholics in America, her cause is still being actively promoted. The search goes on for miracles. Only 2 more, and she will be declared a Saint.

St. Elizabeth Bayley Seton (1774–1821)

Cause. Of wealthy Colonial stock and a distinguished family background, her decision to convert after she was left a widow with 5 children was met with derision and opposition by her Episcopal family and friends. But, aided by her faith, she soon adopted a religious habit and received the title "Mother."

In 1809, she, along with her novitiates, moved to Emmitsburg, Md., founding the American Sisters of Charity. While there she laid the foundation of the American parochial school system, introducing the 1st completely free parochial school, including a free lunch. She visited the sick and poor of the neighborhood, converting many, principally Negroes. She and her sisters also founded orphanages in Philadelphia and New York City.

Nomination. She was proposed for sainthood in the 1880s, declared "Venerable" in 1959, and beatified in 1963. Celebrating her beatification, the late Francis Cardinal Spellman declared: "She was not a mystical person in an unattainable niche. She battled against odds in the trials of life with American stamina and cheerfulness; she worked and succeeded with American efficiency." In the decade that followed, only one factor kept her from being canonized. Usually, 4 miracles are required for Sainthood, and Mother Seton had only 2.

Present Stage. At last, Pope Paul VI waived the requirement of 4 miracles, and announced satisfaction with one of the miracles attributed to Mother Seton. This miracle occurred in 1963 when a New York construction worker, near death from a form of meningitis, prayed to her, touched his body with one of her relics, and recovered his health. On September 14, 1975, Mother Seton became the 1st native-born American to be canonized as a saint. (Mother Cabrini, canonized in 1946, was a naturalized American who had been born in Italy.)

FELIX DE ANDREIS (1778–1820)

Cause. When the religious houses in Rome were suppressed, he went "underground," preaching 4 or 5 times a day. So valued was his work, that only with the personal permission of Pope Pius VII was he allowed to leave for missionary work in the U.S.

He taught theology in Bardstown, Ky., and later when the mission moved to St. Louis, Mo., he became the 1st superior of the Congregation of the Mission (Lazarists) in the U.S.

Devil's Advocate. There seems to be no "heroic virtue," except for his "underground" speeches to the theology students in Rome.

Nomination. The process was begun in 1900, and the information was forwarded to Rome in 1902.

Present Stage. No word has been heard from Rome since the data was submitted in 1902, so it appears, once again, a cause has just faded away.

JEAN MATHIAS PIERRE LORAS (1792–1858)

Cause. Emigrating from France, he was appointed the 1st bishop of the newly created see of Dubuque, Ia. When the Government resettled the Indians outside of Iowa, he conceived a plan to people Iowa with newly arrived Irish and German immigrants.

With grants from mission-aid societies, he built churches, as well as bought land for future parishes. He also established a diocesan college to train native clergy, a cathedral boy's school, a cathedral girl's school, and Mount St. Bernard Seminary. He loved the new land of America so much that he turned down a prestigious bishopric in France to remain in America.

Devil's Advocate. While there seem to be no major problems, the historical data must be collected and forwarded to Rome for evaluation.

Nomination. His cause was introduced in 1937.

Present Stage. Though Bishop Loras appears to have an excellent case, the process is not moving quickly at all. Apparently, the compilation of historical data has not even been completed.

FREDERIC BARAGA (1797–1868)

Cause. Through a missionary society, he realized his dream of working among the American Indians. He worked with the Ottawas and Chippewas of Upper Michigan, transforming dilapidated missions into model Christian communities. But his work was not limited only to the Indians. The development of copper mines in the area attracted white settlers, which extended his labors and his territory.

To aid in the advancement of the faith, he went directly to the people. Even his letters to the individual parishes were in the native tongue. His grammar books and dictionaries were the 1st published in the Chippewa and Ottawa languages, and are still being used as an aid in the study of linguistics.

Devil's Advocate. The claims that have been made on behalf of this candidate need careful evaluation, and of course proof of miracles must be forthcoming.

Nomination. His cause was introduced in 1933.

Present Stage. A complete study of his life has been made, including his time in Yugoslavia where he was a parish priest. One of his promoters, Father Wolfe, has forwarded the historical data to Rome. There is much public interest in Baraga, according to Father Litz.

MOTHER THEODORE GUERIN (1798–1856)

Cause. She entered a convent in France, and was busy teaching mathematics when an appeal came from the Bishop of Vincennes, Ind., for missionaries.

Upon her arrival, she opened an academy for girls, the 1st in Indiana. She also established the motherhouse for her new order, the Sisters of Providence of St. Mary's-of-the-Woods, as well as setting up 10 other schools.

Devil's Advocate. There has been no verification of her "heroic virtue" and no onset of miracles.

Nomination. Her cause was introduced in 1940 by Bishop Francis S. Chaland.

Present Stage. The latest word is that her writings have been declared to be "without defect in faith or morals." The consensus is that she will soon be declared "Venerable."

St. Anthony Mary Claret (1807–1870)

Cause. One of Spain's most popular preachers, he founded a congregation of preachers called the Sons of the Immaculate Heart. As Archbishop of Santiago, Cuba, he reformed the seminary and clergy there. He made extensive visitations to the outlying districts, curtailing the widespread concubinage and illegitimacy.

Believing that favorable material conditions were essential for a good Christian family life, he introduced sound farming methods and credit unions to the poor. He later returned to Spain as Queen Isabella's confessor, and while there founded societies to publish and distribute free Catholic literature.

Devil's Advocate. St. Anthony Mary Claret may have been a true Christian. However, unlike many of his contemporaries who desired to remain missionaries, he accepted the highly visible and political post as Queen Isabella's confessor.

Nomination. He was beatified by Pius XI on February 25, 1934.

Present Stage. He was declared a Saint by Pius XII on May 7, 1950.

Bl. John Nepomucene Neumann (1811–1860)

Cause. He enjoyed being a missionary of sorts among the German immigrants of Maryland, Virginia, and Ohio, avoiding an appointment as bishop until he saw that he could do more that way. As Bishop of Philadelphia, he placed the Redemptorists (the Congregation of the Most Holy Redeemer), of which he was a member, at the forefront of the parochial school movement.

During his bishopric, over 80 churches were constructed in the diocese. He became fluent in 12 languages so he could preach to the swelling masses of immigrants. He heard the confessions of the Irish in Gaelic, and translated religious texts for the Germans.

He introduced 6 teaching orders into the diocese, established the 1st parochial school to serve a black neighborhood, and founded the religious order, the Sisters of the Third Order of St. Francis of Glen Riddle.

Devil's Advocate. Bishop Neumann's cause lacks the necessary number of miracles.

Nomination. His cause was introduced in 1897, and he was declared "Venerable" 14 years later by Benedict XV. In 1963, he became the 1st American bishop to be beatified.

Present Stage. Father Litz said that 24 cases of possible miracles have been forwarded to

Rome. When asked about possible Sainthood, he said, "The Lord only knows. Only through Him do the Saints work miracles. It is impossible to predict with exactness when anyone will be declared a Saint unless their cause has progressed to that stage."

Francis Xavier Seelos (1819–1867)

Cause. In 1843, he emigrated from Bavaria to America to join the Redemptorists. He served in Baltimore for several years, until being transferred to Pittsburgh, where Father Neumann became his spiritual leader.

Later, he became prefect of students and rector of the Redemptorists' seminary in Cumberland, Md. Desiring to do missionary work, he personally pleaded with Pope Pius IX to ward off his appointment as Bishop of Pittsburgh. He spent the last years of his life traveling with the Redemptorist missionaries.

Devil's Advocate. There seem to be some problems ascertaining the complete sanctity of either his writings or his life.

Nomination. His cause was introduced in 1912. The historical data was presented, but it was judged incomplete, and rejected.

Present Stage. A new biography of Seelos, *The Happy Ascetic,* has been presented to Rome. It is supposed to have remedied the defects of the previous one, and a decision on it is expected soon.

St. Francis Xavier Cabrini (1850–1917)

Cause. At the age of 12, Mother Cabrini took a private vow of virginity, which at the age of 18 became a permanent one. She, with members of the Missionary Sisters of the Sacred Heart (an order she founded), left Italy for New York in 1889.

In New York, she worked among the Italian immigrants, establishing orphanages, schools, adult classes teaching Christian doctrine, and Columbus Hospital.

She also traveled throughout the U.S. and in South America and Europe, founding convents, schools, orphanages, and hospitals.

Nomination. An informative hearing was begun by Cardinal George Mundelein in 1928. Her cause was introduced by Pope Pius IX in 1931. She was declared "Venerable" 2 years later, and was beatified in 1938. The rule of canon law that 50 years must elapse before canonization was waived in her honor. She was canonized in 1946, less than 30 years after her death. Pope Pius XII, in paying her tribute, said that "because of the will of God, she accomplished what seemed beyond the strength of a woman."

Present Stage. Canonized as of 1946.

JAN CIEPLAK (1857–1926)

Cause. He was a professor at the Catholic Academy in St. Petersburg until the Russian Revolution in 1917. He was appointed Archbishop of Achrida, but soon fell into disfavor during the Russian Civil War. In 1923, he was arrested as a counterrevolutionary for refusing to give the Church's treasures to the State and was sentenced to death, but through the intervention of the Holy See and the U.S. and British Governments, his sentence was commuted.

In 1925, he paid a 3-month visit to one of his benefactors, the U.S. During that period, he visited 375 parishes and 800 institutions in 25 dioceses. He died in Passaic, N.J., as he was preparing to serve in a new post as an archbishop in Poland.

Devil's Advocate. While there were no problems with his writings, there are difficulties verifying the total sanctity of his actions.

Nomination. His cause was introduced in 1952.

Present Stage. In 1960, his writings were declared to be "above reproach in faith or morals," and when a decision is reached on his "heroic virtue," he should be declared "Venerable."

MOTHER KATHERINE DREXEL (1858–1955)

Cause. Born into a wealthy family, the granddaughter of Francis Martin Drexel, founder of a Philadelphia banking house, she outlived all her relatives, inheriting the family fortune. She made a pilgrimage to Rome and spoke to the Pope of the virtual abandonment of the Negroes and Indians in America. He answered her, saying, "Why not become a missionary yourself, my child?"

She did, founding the Sisters of the Blessed Sacrament for Indians and Colored People. With her inheritance she built and maintained missions for the Southern Negroes and the Indians of the Southwest, established Xavier University in New Orleans, La., and set up 49 foundations throughout the Northeast.

Devil's Advocate. Though she sought to make up for it later, her rich, sheltered life as a child, including being educated at home by private governesses, is a stumbling block to her canonization.

Nomination. The drive for her canonization is moving smoothly. Father Litz, who is also handling Bishop Neumann's cause, said that the latest word is that her writings have been declared to be "without fault in faith or morals."

Present Stage. Because of the decision on her writings, the next step—the declaring of Mother Drexel as being heroic in virtue, thus winning for her the title of "Venerable"—is "on its way," according to Father Litz.

Other Americans Who Are Being Considered or Whose Causes May Soon Be Introduced

ARCHBISHOP JOHN CARROLL (1735–1815). First U.S. bishop, and staunch defender of Colonial independence.

FATHER ISAAC THOMAS HECKER (1819–1888). Writer, publisher, and founder of the Paulists.

MOTHER MARIA MADDELENA BENTIVOGLIO (1824–1905). Foundress of the U.S. Branch of the Poor Clares.

MOTHER ALPHONSA LATHROP (1851–1926). Founder of the Servants of Relief for Incurable Cancer.

FATHER THOMAS AUGUSTINE JUDGE (1868–1933). Founder of the Trinitarians.

FATHER EDWARD FLANAGAN (1886–1948). Founder of Boys' Town, Nebr., and a great believer in the saying that "there's no such thing as a bad boy."

SISTER MIRIAM THERESA DEMJANOVICH (1901–1927). Member of the Sisters of Charity of St. Elizabeth. The diocesan investigation has been completed, and the information has been forwarded to Rome.

—M.Ho.

"In the Beginning . . .": Stories of Creation

AFRICAN (EFIK-IBIBIO)

Many years ago the sun and the water were great friends, and both lived on the earth together. The sun very often used to visit the water, but the water never returned his visits. At last the sun asked the water why it was that he never came to see him in his house. The water replied that the sun's house was not big enough, and that if he came with his people he would drive the sun out.

The water then said, "If you wish me to visit you, you must build a very large compound; but I warn you that it will have to be a tremendous place, as my people are very numerous and take up a lot of room."

The sun promised to build a very big compound, and soon afterward he returned home to his wife, the moon, who greeted him with a broad smile when he opened the door. The sun told the moon what he had promised the water, and the next day he commenced building a huge compound in which to entertain his friend.

When it was completed, he asked the water to come and visit him the next day.

When the water arrived, he called out to the sun and asked him whether it would be safe for him to enter, and the sun answered, "Yes, come in, my friend."

The water then began to flow in, accompanied by the fish and all the water animals.

Very soon the water was knee-deep, so he asked the sun if it was still safe, and the sun again said, "Yes," so more water came in.

When the water was level with the top of a man's head, the water said to the sun, "Do you want more of my people to come?"

The sun and the moon both answered, "Yes," not knowing any better, so the water flowed in, until the sun and moon had to perch themselves on the top of the roof.

Again the water addressed the sun, but, receiving the same answer, and more of his people rushing in, the water very soon overflowed the top of the roof, and the sun and the moon were forced to go up into the sky, where they have remained ever since.

(Permission: *African Folktales and Sculpture.* By James Johnson Sweeney and Paul Radin. New York, Bollingen Foundation, 1952. Reprinted by permission of Princeton University Press.

BIBLICAL—OLD TESTAMENT

In the beginning God created the heavens and the earth. The earth was without form and void, and darkness was upon the face of the deep; and the Spirit of God was moving over the face of the waters.

And God said, "Let there be light"; and there was light. And God saw that the light was good; and God separated the light from the darkness. God called the light Day, and the darkness he called Night. And there was evening and there was morning, one day.

And God said, "Let there be a firmament in the midst of the waters, and let it separate the waters from the waters." And God made the firmament and separated the waters which were under the firmament from the waters which were above the firmament. And it was so. And God called the firmament Heaven. And there was evening and there was morning, a 2nd day.

And God said, "Let the waters under the heavens be gathered together into one place, and let the dry land appear." And it was so. God called the dry land Earth, and the waters that were gathered together he called Seas. And God saw that it was good. And God said, "Let the earth put forth vegetation, plants yielding seed, and fruit trees bearing fruit in which is their seed, each according to its kind,

upon the earth." And it was so. The earth brought forth vegetation, plants yielding seed according to their own kinds, and trees bearing fruit in which is their seed, each according to its kind. And God saw that it was good. And there was evening and there was morning, a 3rd day.

And God said, "Let there be lights in the firmament of the heavens to separate the day from the night; and let them be for signs and for seasons and for days and years, and let them be lights in the firmament of the heavens to give light upon the earth." And it was so. And God made the 2 great lights, the greater light to rule the day, and the lesser light to rule the night; he made the stars also. And God set them in the firmament of the heavens to give light upon the earth, to rule over the day and over the night, and to separate the light from the darkness. And God saw that it was good. And there was evening and there was morning, a 4th day.

And God said, "Let the waters bring forth swarms of living creatures, and let birds fly above the earth across the firmament of the heavens. So God created the great sea monsters and every living creature that moves, with which the waters swarm, according to their kinds, and every winged bird according to its kind. And God saw that it was good. And God blessed them, saying, "Be fruitful and multiply and fill the waters in the seas, and let birds multiply on the earth." And there was evening and there was morning, a 5th day.

And God said, "Let the earth bring forth living creatures according to their kinds; cattle and creeping things and beasts of the earth according to their kinds." And it was so. And God made the beasts of the earth according to their kinds and the cattle according to their kinds, and everything that creeps upon the ground according to its kind. And God saw that it was good.

Then God said, "Let us make man in our image, after our likeness; and let them have dominion over the fish of the sea, and over the birds of the air, and over the cattle, and over all the earth, and over every creeping thing that creeps upon the earth." So God created man in his own image, in the image of God he created him; male and female he created them. And God blessed them, and God said to them, "Be fruitful and multiply and fill the earth and subdue it; and have dominion over the fish of the sea and over the birds of the air and over every living thing that moves upon the earth." And God said, "Behold, I have given you every plant yielding seed which is upon the face of all the earth, and every tree with seed in its fruit; you shall have them for food. And to every beast of the earth, and to every bird of the air, and to everything that creeps on the earth, everything that has the breath of life, I have given every green plant for food." And it was so. And God saw everything that he had made, and behold, it was very good. And there was evening and there was morning, a 6th day.

Thus the heavens and the earth were finished, and all the host of them. And on the 7th day God finished his work which he had done, and he rested on the 7th day from all his work which he had done. So God blessed the 7th day and hallowed it, because on it God rested from all his work which he had done in creation.

(Permission: *The Holy Bible*, Revised Standard Version, 1946. Reprinted by permission of the National Council of the Churches of Christ.)

CHINESE

Before heaven and earth had taken form all was vague and amorphous. Therefore it was called the Great Beginning. The Great Beginning produced emptiness and emptiness produced the universe. The universe produced material-force which had limits. That which was clear and light drifted up to become heaven, while that which was heavy and turbid solidified to become earth. It was very easy for the pure, fine material to come together but extremely difficult for the heavy, turbid material to 1st solidify. Therefore heaven was completed 1st and earth assumed shape after. The combined essences of heaven and earth became the yin and yang, the concentrated essences of the yin and yang became the 4 seasons, and the scattered essences of the 4 seasons became the myriad creatures of the world. After a long time the hot force of the accumulated yang produced fire and the essence of the fire force became the sun; the cold force of the accumulated yin became water and the essence of the water force became the moon. The essence of the excess force of the sun and moon became the stars and planets. Heaven received the sun, moon, and stars while earth received water and soil. . . .

When heaven and earth were joined in emptiness and all was unwrought simplicity, then without having been created, things came into being. This was the Great Oneness. All things issued from this oneness but all became different, being divided into the various species of fish, birds, and beasts. . . . Therefore while a thing moves it is called living, and when it dies it is said to be exhausted. All are creatures. They are not the uncreated creator of things, for the creator of things is not among things. If we examine the Great Beginning of antiquity we find that man was born out of nonbeing to assume form in being. Having form, he is governed by things. But he who can return to that from which he was born and become as though

formless is called a "true man." The true man is he who has never become separated from the Great Oneness. [From *Huai-nan Tzu*.]

EGYPTIAN

Before the land of Egypt rose out of the waters at the beginning of the world, Ra the Shining One came into being. He was all-powerful, and the secret of his power lay in his Name which was hidden from all the world. Having this power, he had only to name a thing, and that thing too came into being.

"I am Khepera at the dawn, and Ra at noon, and Tum in the evening," he said—and as he said it, behold, he was the sun rising in the east, passing across the sky and setting in the west. And this was the 1st day of the world.

When he named Shu, the wind blew. The rain fell when he named Tefnut the spitter. After this he spoke the name of Geb, and the earth rose above the waters of the sea. He cried, "Nut!"—and that goddess was the arch of the sky stretching over the earth with her feet on one horizon and her hands on the other. Then he named Hapi, and the sacred River Nile flowed through Egypt to make it fruitful.

Then Ra went on to name all the things on earth, which grew into being at his words. Last of all he spoke the words for "Man" and "Woman," and soon there were people dwelling throughout the land of Egypt.

After this Ra himself took on the shape of a man and became the 1st Pharaoh of Egypt. For thousands of years he reigned over the land, and there was peace and plenty . . . and ever afterwards the Egyptians spoke of the good things "which happened in the time of Ra."

At last, however, even Ra grew old: for it was decreed that no man should live for ever, and he had made himself a man to rule over Egypt. . . .

Presently . . . Apophis (the Dragon of Evil) entered into the souls of the people of Egypt and many of them rebelled against Ra and did evil in his sight, worshiping the Dragon of Darkness instead of the Eye of Day.

Ra perceived these things and the plots which the evil among men were preparing against his divine majesty. Then he spoke to his attendants, saying, "Gather together the high gods who are my court. Summon Shu and Tefnut, bid Geb and Nut hasten to the council hall—send even for Nun, the spirit of the waters out of which I arose at the beginning of the world. Gather them secretly; let not the evil among men know that I am aware of their doings. . . ."

When all were gathered Nun spoke for them, saying, "Life, health, strength be to you, Ra, Pharaoh of Egypt, maker of all things! Speak to us so that we may hear your divine will."

Then Ra answered, "Nun, eldest of all things, and all ye gods whom I have called into being—look upon mankind, whom also I made at a glance of my all-seeing Eye, naming them in the beginning that they might appear upon the earth and multiply to be my servants in life and in death. See, they have plotted against me, they have done evil things—the wicked among them gather even now in Upper Egypt to work further ill in my sight. Tell me, shall I slay them all with a burning glance of my Eye?"

Nun answered, speaking for all the gods: "Ra, greater than I out of whom you came in the beginning; you who are mightier than all the gods you have created—if you send forth the burning glance of your Eye to slay mankind, it will turn all the land of Egypt into a desert. Therefore make a power that will smite men and women only; send out that which will burn the evil but not harm the good."

Then answered Ra, "I will not send forth the burning glance of my Eye. Instead I will send Sekhmet against mankind!"

As he spoke the name, Sekhmet leapt into being, in form as a mighty lioness of gigantic size. Away she sped into Upper Egypt, and slaughtered and devoured mankind until the Nile ran red with blood and the earth beside it became a great red marsh.

Before long the most wicked among men had been slain by Sekhmet, and the rest prayed to Ra for mercy. And Ra wished to spare them, for he had no desire to slay all of mankind and leave himself the ruler of a desolate earth with no human beings to serve him.

But, having tasted blood, Sekhmet would not cease from her hunting. Day by day she stalked through the land of Egypt slaying all whom she met; and night by night she hid herself among the rocks on the edge of the desert, waiting for the sun to rise so that she might hunt once more.

Then said Ra, "Sekhmet cannot be stayed except by a trick. If I can deceive her and save mankind from her sharp teeth and from her claws, I will give her greater power yet over them so that her heart shall rejoice and she shall not feel that honor has been taken from her."

So Ra summoned before him swift and speedy messengers and commanded them, saying, "Run like the shadow of a body—swifter and more silently than the body itself—to the island of Elephantine that lies in the Nile below the First Cataract. Bring me the red ocher that is found there alone—bring it with speed."

Away sped the messengers through the darkness and returned to Heliopolis, the city of Ra, bearing loads of the red ocher of Elephantine. There, by Ra's command, all the priestesses of the Temple of the Sun and all the maidservants of the royal court were set to crushing barley and making beer. Seven thousand jars did they make and, by the command of Ra, they mingled the red ocher of Elephantine with it so that it gleamed in the moonlight red as blood.

"Now," said Ra, "carry this upstream to protect mankind. Carry it to where Sekhmet means to slaughter men when day returns, and pour it out upon the earth as a trap for her."

Day dawned and Sekhmet came out into the sunlight from her lair among the rocks and looked about her, seeking whom she might devour. She saw no living thing. But, in the place where yesterday she had slain many men, she saw that the fields were covered to the depth of 3 hands' breadths with what seemed to be blood.

Sekhmet saw and laughed with a laugh like the roar of a hungry lioness. Thinking that it was the blood she had shed upon the previous day, she stooped and drank greedily. Again and again she drank, until the strength of the beer mounted to her brain and she could neither hunt nor kill.

As the day drew to its close she came reeling down to Heliopolis, where Ra awaited her—and when the sun touched the horizon she had not slain a single man or woman since the evening before.

"You come in peace, sweet one," said Ra, "peace be with you and a new name. No longer are you Sekhmet the Slayer: you are Hathor the Lady of Love. Yet your power over mankind shall be greater even than it was—for the passion of love shall be stronger than the passion of hate, and all shall know love, and all shall be your victims." . . .

So mankind was saved by Ra, and given both a new delight and a new pain.

(Permission: *Tales of Ancient Egypt*. By Roger Lancelyn Green. London, The Bodley Head, 1970.)

GREEK

First of all, the Void came into being, next broad-bosomed Earth, the solid and eternal home of all, and Eros [Desire] the most beautiful of the immortal gods, who in every man and every god softens the sinews and overpowers the prudent purpose of the mind. Out of Void came Darkness and black Night, and out of Night came Light and Day, her children conceived after union in love with Darkness. Earth 1st produced starry Sky, equal in size with herself, to cover her on all sides. Next she produced the tall mountains, the pleasant haunts of the gods, and also gave birth to the barren waters, sea with its raging surges—all this without the passion of love. Thereafter she lay with Sky and gave birth to Ocean with its deep current, Coeus and Crius and Hyperion and Iapetus; Thea and Rhea and Themis [Law] and Mnemosyne (Memory); also golden-crowned Phoebe and lovely Tethys. After these came cunning Cronus, the youngest and boldest of her children; and he grew to hate the father who had begotten him.

Earth also gave birth to the violent Cyclopes —Thunderer, Lightner, and bold Flash—who made and gave to Zeus the thunder and the lightning bolt. They were like the gods in all respects except that a single eye stood in the middle of their foreheads, and their strength and power and skill were in their hands.

There were also born to Earth and Sky 3 more children, big, strong, and horrible, Cottus and Briareus and Gyes. This unruly brood had a hundred monstrous hands sprouting from their shoulders, and 50 heads on top of their shoulders growing from their sturdy bodies. They had monstrous strength to match their huge size. . . .

Of all the children born of Earth and Sky these were the boldest, and their father hated them from the beginning. As each of them was about to be born, Sky would not let them reach the light of day; instead he hid them all away in the bowels of Mother Earth. Sky took pleasure in doing this evil thing. In spite of her enormous size, Earth felt the strain within her and groaned. Finally she thought of an evil and cunning stratagem. She instantly produced a new metal, gray steel, and made a huge sickle. Then she laid the matter before her children; the anguish in her heart made her speak boldly: "My children, you have a savage father; if you will listen to me, we may be able to take vengeance for his evil outrage: he was the one who started using violence."

This was what she said; but all the children were gripped by fear, and not one of them spoke a word. Then great Cronus, the cunning trickster, took courage and answered his good mother with these words: "Mother, I am willing to undertake and carry through your plan. I have no respect for our infamous father, since he was the one who started using violence."

This was what he said, and enormous Earth was very pleased. She hid him in ambush and put in his hands the sickle with jagged teeth, and instructed him fully in her plot. Huge Sky came drawing night behind him and desiring to make love; he lay on top of earth stretched all over her. Then from his ambush his son reached out with his left hand and with his right took the huge sickle with its long jagged teeth and quickly sheared the organs from his own father and threw them away, backward over his shoulder. But that was not the end of them. The drops of blood that spurted from them were all taken in by Mother Earth, and

in the course of the revolving years she gave birth to the powerful Erinyes [Spirits of Vengeance] and the huge Giants with shining armor and long spears. As for the organs themselves, for a long time they drifted round the sea just as they were when Cronus cut them off with the steel edge and threw them from the land into the waves of the ocean; then white foam issued from the divine flesh, and in the foam a girl began to grow. First she came near the holy Cythera, then reached Cyprus, the land surrounded by sea. There she stepped out, a goddess, tender and beautiful, and round her slender feet the green grass shot up. She is called Aphrodite by gods and men, because she came near to Cythera, and the Cyprian, because she was born in watery Cyprus. Eros [Desire] and beautiful Passion were her attendants both at her birth and at her 1st going to join the family of the gods. The rights and privileges assigned to her from the beginning and recognized by men and gods are these: to preside over the whispers and smiles and tricks which girls employ, and the sweet delight and tenderness of love.

Great Father Sky called his children the Titans, because of his feud with them. He said that they blindly had tightened the noose and had done a savage thing for which they would have to pay in time to come. . . .

Night gave birth to hateful Destruction and the black Specter and Death; she also bore Sleep and the race of Dreams—all these the dark goddess Night bore without sleeping with any male. Next she gave birth to Blame and painful Grief, and also the Fates and the pitiless Specters of Vengeance: It is these goddesses who keep account of the transgressions of men, then Deceit and Love and accursed Old Age and stubborn Strife.

Hateful Strife gave birth to painful Distress and Distraction and Famine and tearful Sorrow; also Wars and Battles and Murders and Slaughters; also Feuds and Lying Words and Angry Words; also Lawlessness and Madness— 2 sisters that go together—and the Oath, which, sworn with willful falsehood, brings utter destruction on men.

(Permission: *Hesiod's Theogony.* Translated by Norman O. Brown. New York, The Liberal Arts Press, Division of the Bobbs-Merrill Co., 1953.)

GYPSY

In Gypsy mythology, God baked the 1st men and women in an oven. Some, however, were kept too long in the oven and they turned out dark: the black race. The 2nd time God opened the oven door too soon and the baking was not quite ready: the white race. The 3rd time God produced images baked properly to the right color: the Indians, ancestors of the Gypsies.

(Permission: *Dictionary of Gypsy Life and Lore*. By H. E. Wedeck. New York, Philosophical Library, Inc., 1973.)

HINDU

In the beginning was Self (Atman) alone, in the shape of a person. He, looking round, saw nothing but his Self. He 1st said, "This is I"; therefore he became "I" by name. Therefore even now, if a man is asked, he 1st says, "This is I," and then pronounces the other name which he may have. And because before all this he (the Self) burnt down all evils, therefore he was a person (purusha). Verily he who knows this burns down everyone who tries to be before him. He feared, and therefore anyone who is lonely fears. He thought, "As there is nothing but myself, why should I fear?" Then his fear passed away. For what should he have feared? Verily fear arises from a second only. But he felt no delight. Therefore a man who is lonely feels no delight. He wished for a second. He was as large as man and wife together. He then made this, his Self, to fall in 2, (pat) [the word "pat" means 2] and thence arose husband (pat) and wife (patni). Therefore Yagnavalkya said, "We 2 are thus (each of us) like half a shell." Therefore the void which was there is filled by the wife. He embraced her and men were born. She thought, "How can he embrace me after having produced me from himself? I shall hide myself." She then became a cow, the other became a bull and embraced her, and hence cows were born. The one became a mare, and the other a stallion, the one a male ass, and the other a female ass. He embraced her, and hence one-hoofed animals were born. The one became a she-goat the other a he-goat; the one became a ewe, the other a ram. He embraced her, and hence goats and sheep were born. And thus he created everything that exists in pairs, down to the ants.

(Permission: *Brihadaranyaka Upanishad*. Translated by F. Max Müller.)

MAYAN

This is the account of how all was in suspense, all calm, in silence, all motionless, still, and the expanse of the sky was empty.

This is the 1st account, the 1st narrative. There was neither man, nor animal, birds, fishes, crabs, trees, stones, caves, ravines, grasses, nor forests: There was only the sky.

There was nothing brought together, nothing which could make a noise, nor anything which might move, or tremble, or could make noise in the sky.

There was nothing standing; only the calm water, the placid sea, alone and tranquil. Nothing existed.

There was only immobility and silence in the darkness, in the night. Only the Creator, the Maker, Tepeu, Gucumatz, the Forefathers, were in the water surrounded with light. They were hidden under green and blue feathers, and were therefore called Gucumatz. By nature they were great sages and great thinkers. In this manner the sky existed and also the Heart of Heaven, which is the name of God and thus He is called.

Then came the word. Tepeu and Gucumatz came together in the darkness, in the night, and Tepeu and Gucumatz talked together. They talked then, discussing and deliberating; they agreed, they united their words and their thoughts.

Then while they meditated, it became clear to them that when dawn would break, man must appear. Then they planned the creation, and the growth of the trees and the thickets and the birth of life and the creation of man. Thus it was arranged in the darkness and in the night by the heart of Heaven who is called Huracan.

The 1st is called Caculha Huracan. The second is Chipi-Caculha. The 3rd is Raxa-Caculha. And these 3 are the Heart of Heaven.

Then Tepeu and Gucumatz came together; then they conferred about life and light, what they would do so that there would be light and dawn, who it would be who would provide food and sustenance.

Thus let it be done. Let the emptiness be filled! Let the water recede and make a void, let the earth appear and become solid; let it be done. Thus they spoke. Let there be light, let there be dawn in the sky and on the earth! There shall be neither glory nor grandeur in our creation and formation until the human being is made, man is formed. So they spoke.

Then the earth was created by them. So it was, in truth, that they created the earth. Earth! they said, and instantly it was made.

Like the mist, like a cloud, and like a cloud of dust was the creation, when the mountains appeared from the water; and instantly the mountains grew.

Only by a miracle, only by magic art were the mountains and valleys formed; and instantly the groves of cypresses and pines put forth shoots together on the surface of the earth.

And thus Gucumatz was filled with joy, and exclaimed: "Your coming has been fruitful, Heart of Heaven; and you, Huracan, and you, Chipa-Caculha, Raxa-Caculha!"

"Our work, our creation shall be finished," they answered.

First the earth was formed, the mountains

and the valleys; the currents of water were divided, the rivulets were running freely between the hills, and the water was separated when the high mountains appeared.

Thus was the earth created, when it was formed by the Heart of Heaven, the Heart of Earth, as they are called who 1st made it fruitful, when the sky was in suspense, and the earth was submerged in the water.

So it was that they made perfect the work, when they did it after thinking and meditating upon it.

(Permission: *Popol Vuh: The Sacred Book of the Ancient Quiche Maya.* Translated from the original text by Adrián Recinos. Norman, Okla., University of Oklahoma Press, 1950.)

NAVAJO

The 1st world was inhabited by insects and insectlike people. It was such an unpleasant place that all of the insects made themselves wings and flew to the sky to look for a new home. Finally they found a crack in the sky and emerged into the 2nd world.

The 2nd world was a blue world of birds who strongly resented the invasion of the insect people. There was constant fighting, and at last the insect people followed the voice of the blue wind to the 3rd world.

The 3rd world, or yellow world, began to look more like the world we now know, and people and animals began to look more like they do now. There were 4 mountains in this land, one in each direction, and the mountain people began to teach First Man and First Woman how to plant corn and how to build homes. They also warned everyone not to bother the water monster.

But the coyote did not heed the warnings. He went to the home of the water monster and kidnapped his 2 children.

Suddenly the oceans rose and the land began to flood. All of the people and animals gathered on top of the highest mountain. The people planted a giant reed on top of the mountain and climbed up inside it. Finally after 4 days of climbing the giant reed, they reached the 4th world.

This 4th world was even more beautiful than those before, and here were other people and other kinds of animals. Here First Man and First Woman learned more about growing corn and the proper roles of the sexes.

But the coyote still had the children of the water monster, and First People were horrified to find the waters of their new world suddenly rising. Again they planted a reed and began to climb, but this time they could not reach all the way. Nor could they find a hole. So the yellow hawk tried to scratch a hole in the dome. The heron and the buzzard also helped,

but the locust was the one who finally succeeded in getting through. Then the spider spun a rope so that everyone could climb up through the hole.

The new world was only a small island, so the ants were 1st, carrying the soil of the 4th world. The other people followed, carrying seeds of corn and other treasures from the 4th world.

The people had not even gotten settled in the 5th world when the waters there started rising. This time First Man and First Woman decided that someone must have offended the water monster. They searched everyone, and of course, found his children with the coyote. They took them to the lake and put them in a small boat. The waters went down immediately and floods have never again destroyed man's world.

(Permission: *Myths and Modern Man.* By Barbara Stanford and Gene Stanford. New York, Simon and Schuster, Inc., Washington Square Division, 1972.)

NORSE

In the very beginning of time . . . there was no Earth as we know it now: there was only Ginnungagap, the Yawning Void. In this moved strange mists which at length drew apart leaving an even deeper Gap, with Muspelheim, the Land of Fire, to the south of it, and Nifelheim, the Land of Mist, to the north of it. . . .

Deep down in Ginnungagap lay the Well of Life, Hvergelmir, from which flowed rivers which the cruel breath of the north froze into grinding blocks of ice.

As the ages passed, the grinding ice piled up mysteriously above the Well of Life and became Ymir, the greatest of all Giants, father of the terrible Frost Giants, and of all the Giant kin.

Ymir grew into life, and with him appeared the magic cow Audumla whose milk was his food. And very soon the ice of Ymir broke off in small pieces and each became a Rime Giant —a father of witches and warlocks, of ogres and trolls.

Audumla herself needed food, and she licked the ice about her and found in it the salt of life that welled up from Hvergelmir.

On the 1st day that she licked the ice there came forth in the evening the hair of a man; the 2nd day she licked, and in the evening there was a man's head showing; and by the ending of the 3rd day the whole man was there.

He was the 1st of the Æsir, and his name was Buri; he was tall and strong, and very fair to see. His son was called Borr, and this Borr

married the giantess Bestla, and they were the
mother and father of the Æsir who planted
the World Tree, Yggdrasill, and made the
Earth.

Borr had 3 sons called Odin, Vili, and Ve,
and of these Odin, the Allfather, was the
greatest and the most noble.

They fought against Ymir the great Ice Giant, and slew him, and the icy water gushed
from his wounds and drowned most of the
Rime Giants, except for one who was named
Bergelmir. He was wise and clever, and for this
reason Odin spared him.

For Bergelmir built himself a boat with a
roof, and took shelter in it with his wife and
children so that they escaped being drowned in
the flood.

But Odin and his brothers thrust the dead
Ymir down into the void of Ginnungagap and
made of his body the world we live in. His ice-
blood became the sea and the rivers; his flesh
became the dry land and his bones the mountains, while the gravel and stones were his
teeth.

Odin and his children set the sea in a ring
round about the earth, and the World Tree,
the Ash Yggdrasill, grew up to hold it in place,
to overshadow it with its mighty branches, and
to support the sky which was the ice-blue skull-
top of Ymir. . . .

When Odin had set the stars in their courses
and had lit the earth with the Sun and Moon,
he turned back to the new world which he had
made. Already the Giants and other creatures
of evil were stirring against him, so he took
more of the bones of Ymir and spread the
mountains as a wall against Giantland, or Jo-
tunheim. Then he turned back to the land
made for men, which he called Midgard or
Middle Earth, and began to make it fruitful
and fair to see.

Out of Ymir's curly hair he formed the trees,
from his eyebrows the grass and flowers, and he
set clouds to float in the sky above and sprinkle
the Earth with gentle showers.

Then for the making of Mankind, the Allfather Odin took an ash tree and an elder upon
the seashore and fashioned from them Ask and
Embla, the 1st Man and the 1st Woman. Odin
gave them souls, and his brother Vili gave them
the power of thought and feeling, while Ve
gave them speech, hearing, and sight.

From these 2 came children enough to people Midgard: But sin and sorrow overtook
them, for the Giants and other creatures of
evil took on the shapes of men and women, and
married with them, despite all that Odin could
do.

(Permission: *Myths of the Norsemen*. By
Roger Lancelyn Green. London, Penguin Books
Ltd., 1960.)

SCIENTIFIC

At some very early date, 10 or 20 billion years
ago, the universe was in apparent chaos. Everything that there was, was squeezed into a su-
per-dense kernel, a hot and hectic nuclear
cloud, shapeless and unformed. All the matter
of the universe was there, in a broken-up state
of protons, neutrons, and electrons, independent from one another but very closely packed.
The temperature was one trillion degrees, and
this primal kernel was finally so dense, so hot,
and so highly charged that it exploded.

The explosion sent all the particles of matter
in the universe flying. The universe had begun
to expand.

During the 1st 100 seconds of this explosive
expansion, the pieces of matter remained separate, while the universe began to cool. Before 5
minutes had gone by, the temperature dropped
to one billion degrees.

With this cooling and expanding, protons
and neutrons began to combine, forming simple nuclei. Very soon after, electrons hooked
up with these nuclei, and the simple atoms
came into being.

After half an hour, all of the atomic elements of the universe had been formed. The
universe continued to cool, and gradually the
temperature fell to 40 million degrees. The 1st
day.

Time passed. The larger products of the explosion of the universe remained gaseous, as
large clouds thinly distributed in space. But in
certain parts of these clouds, the molecules exerted enough mutual gravitational attraction to
start condensation in various places. Smaller
and denser clouds formed, gradually pulling together into tighter and tighter masses. Within
these condensing clouds, some gases began random whirling motions, which grew more and
more rotational, flattening and tightening the
clouds further.

Then, about 5 billion years ago, one of these
whirling clouds became so condensed that matter began to be heavily concentrated in its center, forming into a large lump. This central
lump, an emerging star, was surrounded by a
miscellany of debris from the universal explosion. The debris included concentrations of
matter which were smaller than the star and
these cooling streams around the star fell
loosely under its gravitational control, rotating
as they condensed.

The new star was our sun. As it condensed,
its internal nuclear fires got hotter and began
to glow, so that "then there was light."

Some of the secondary bodies circling the
sun were engulfed by it because their orbits
were too elliptical. Others were captured by
larger secondary bodies and incorporated into

them. But some of them fell into orbits which were safely circular, well spaced from their neighbors, and of a proper size to continue. They were the protoplanets of our solar system.

The powerful radiant energy of the sun now began to clean up the solar system, sending all the free gases from the system into space, and driving away the gases which surrounded the protoplanets. A mixed array of infant planets survived. The farthest planets were less affected by the sun's energy, and remained large and gassy. But the gassy shells of the closer bodies were driven off completely, leaving small and solid planets revolving around the sun.

Among these inner planets which have circled the sun for the last 4 or 5 billion years is our earth. In its early days the earth had a crust of molten rock and an atmosphere of hot gases. Large quantities of hydrogen, helium, and other gases escaped the atmosphere altogether, leaving a hot aqueous vapor around the planet. The moist vapor formed a sort of hot-water envelope over the earth.

Meanwhile, at the core of the planet, carbon was forming into carbides, the most stable of the carbon compounds at high temperatures. In addition to large quantities of carbides, the earth's core contained nitrides, which had resulted from combining nitrogen molecules in the great heat.

Then, the material at the center of the earth erupted, sending carbides and nitrides to the surface of the planet. Rising into the steamy atmosphere, the chemicals combined with water, to enter the hot, moist envelope in solution. Carbides with water formed simple hydrocarbons; nitrides in water produced ammonia.

The earth's atmosphere was now teeming with organic chemicals. But the young planet was still cooling, causing the atmosphere to become more and more condensed. Finally, it began to rain. Torrents of hot rain fell upon the earth, filling the basins on the earth's surface, forming new, hot oceans. The hot oceans, holding a great variety of organic compounds in solution, overflowed.

In time, the carbon compounds in the oceans gradually united into long carbon chains. Nitrogen compounds combined to form large and complicated molecules. By accretion the molecules grew larger and larger, and they began to exhibit colloidal properties.

A colloidal suspension is one in which finely divided particles of a substance are suspended in a gaseous, liquid, or solid medium. The new and complex globules in the oceans were mostly solutions of various salts and carbohydrates in water, with small particles suspended in these solutions. The colloidal particles collected in masses, separated by a layer of water adhering to their surfaces.

One important colloidal substance, called protoplasm, is made up of about 75% water with salts, proteins, carbohydrates, and fats present in solution. This solution also contains complex organic constituents held in suspension. These are separated by a layer of water. "Protoplasm" means "1st form," and it is the physicochemical basis of all things which are said to be alive.

The globules now filling the hot oceans absorbed more and more molecules and gradually formed membranes around themselves. Some of these membranes possessed the property of selective permeability, admitting certain substances and excluding others, thus enabling the globules to maintain a constant chemical composition. Those primitive globules, which happened, by chance, to develop selectively permeable membranes, continued to grow.

Of the globules which did develop efficient methods of growth, some could not stop. They reached greater and greater volumes, until the membranes could no longer contain their oversized masses. But some of these giant globules happened, by accident, to possess the ability to separate, breaking up into smaller units which were supportable. Thus, they not only grew, but managed, by reproduction, to survive their own growth.

These successful globules continued their growth and reproduction, occasionally united with one another, initiating innumerable variations, as different combinations arose and perished. More and more complex and wonderful forms emerged: primitive, living cells.

The process of natural selection had begun. As variations arose by chance, some tended toward the preservation of the individual, others toward its destruction. Those variations, however slight, which were in any degree profitable to the individual cell in its complex relations to other cells and to the external environment tended toward its preservation, and only those cells which happened to possess the most profitable variations survived. In this way, nature improved upon her products; simple living cells became more sophisticated and their characteristics became more diverse.

Plant and animal cells of a similar type began to unite into colonies. Reproduction continued. Offspring tended to inherit the advantages that their parents had exhibited, and in the billions of young colonies produced, the number of offspring was increasing geometrically.

Competition arose among the increasing numbers of living things. Food, space, water, and air were in demand. The slightest advantages helped to determine which animals and which plants would survive to pass on new characteristics to their offspring and which would simply perish.

The time was about 2,000 million years ago, and the earth was in its Archeozoic, or "primitive life," stages. All life was concentrated in the salt seas, in the forms of simple one-celled animals and plants. Extensive volcanic activity and mountain-building was going on, and there was no life outside the warm oceans.

Eight hundred million years passed, and the earth entered the Proterozoic, or "1st life," era. Invertebrate phyla evolved, becoming more and more varied from one another. After another 650 million years, the earth entered the Paleozoic era, the era of "ancient life," in which extremely diverse products of evolutionary development were abundant.

At the beginning of the Paleozoic era, around 550 million years ago, the earth's climate was uniformly mild and the continents were submerged beneath wide, shallow, salt seas. There was no life except in the salt water, but there it was teeming. On the ocean floor, corals fastened themselves and found food in the water which they had learned to filter. There were nautiloids, like squids on conch shells, and crinoids, which look like flowers but are really animals. Most numerous were the trilobites, looking like scarabs with shield-shaped heads and many legs, and the brachiopods, somewhat like clams. The largest animals at this time were the 6' eurypterids, or sea scorpions, with their powerful crunching claws.

The 1st period of the Paleozoic era, the Cambrian period, lasted for 105 million years. In the next period, the Ordovician, which lasted another 70 million years, the invertebrates reached the peak of their dominance, the brachiopods were abundant, and the trilobites and nautiloids had reached their climax. It was then, in the Ordovician period, that a new creature emerged, different from the rest in one important aspect: It had bones.

These boned animals were the ostracoderms —primitive, jawless fishes. Not only did the jawless fishes have an outer covering of bone, but they had developed something new—a living, growing skeleton, giving inner support. The vertebrates had arrived.

The jawless fishes had small, simple brains connected to the spinal column. Some of them had eyes, other had eyes and nostrils for smelling. They were good swimmers and as time went on the more advanced jawless fishes left the ocean to become the early colonists of freshwater streams.

The Ordovician period was followed by the Silurian period, in which invertebrates were highly developed, jawless fishes were abundant, and jawed fishes began to appear. The next period, the Devonian, which began some 330

million years ago, was the Age of Fishes. All classes of fishes flourished, including an early bony fish called Cheirolepis. This new jawed fish was the earliest creature on earth to exhibit lungs.

The Mississippian period, begun about 280 million years ago, saw the great move of animals out of the water and into the swamps. At this time the climate was warm and moist and the lowland on the continents had grown up in lush vegetation with giant clubmosses and ferns up to 60' tall. Dying plants decayed in the swamps, and peat, which later turned to coal, was being produced.

Scorpions, spiders, and insects had made their way to the swamps. Soon after, lobe-finned fishes developed a means of living on land. Their stalked fins developing into legs with toes, their lungs strengthening, and their unpaired fins disappearing , the lobe-finned fishes had become the world's 1st amphibians, well adapted to land life.

The amphibians continued to evolve through the Pennsylvanian period, along with the dominant giant clubmosses. At the end of this period, a new form emerged. Swamps were drying up, and survival depended upon thicker skin, better lungs, and stronger legs. These advantages were given to the 1st of earth's reptiles.

The Paleozoic era ended with the Permian period, which began 230 million years ago. With the uplift of mountains, variable climates arose—from hot, dry deserts to cold, barren regions. In the milder, moist regions, amphibians continued, but in other areas, the reptiles dominated. They had conquered the dry land, pushed into every possible new environment under the pressure of their growing population. In the Permian period, thousands of new reptile species evolved.

The Age of Reptiles began a new era 200 million years ago: the Mesozoic era. The mountains, reduced by rivers and glaciers, washed into the seas. The earth's climate was uniformly warm and tropical. The Triassic period, which began the era, saw the height of reptile dominance. It was at the end of this period that the reptile's successor made his 1st appearance. With a change in the skull, which provided more room for chewing and for better teeth, and with an improvement in the limbs to allow them to swing back and forth underneath the body, a few reptiles were beginning to take the 1st steps toward the evolution of the mammal.

The 1st mammals did appear, few in number and primitive in form, in the Jurassic period. They were warm-blooded, had a diaphragm, a coat of hair, and suckled their young. At this time, too, the 1st birds appeared.

The last period of the Mesozoic era, the

Cretaceous period, began with the continued dominance of highly specialized reptiles, but ended with their mass extinction. Mountain-building created such a drastic change in climate, from warm to cold, that most reptiles simply perished. But the various reptiles-turned-mammal survived. They were of 2 types, the marsupials and the placental mammals. The latter, a line of insectivores which had developed a uterus and a placenta and an umbilical cord connecting the mother to the embryo, gave rise to all the living placental mammals in the world.

The earth is now in the Cenozoic, or "recent life," era. This began only 70 million years ago and has become the Age of Mammals. The 1st primates and the 1st rodents appeared in the Paleocene period. The early primate exhibited an opposite thumb, larger brains, a bony eye socket, and keener vision, but had a poorer sense of smell than its ancestors.

In the Eocene period, other mammal types appeared, with the even- and odd-toed hoofed mammals, advanced carnivores, and lemurs and tarsiers. The lemurs and tarsiers both had grasping hands, flat nails, and an enlarged cerebrum. The eye was by far the dominant sense organ.

From the tarsioids came the New World and the Old World monkeys, with their forward-pointing nostrils, opposable thumbs, and considerably enlarged brains.

From the Old World monkeys came the 1st apes, which had lost their tails, increased their brain size, and developed a better balance of the head on the spinal column.

Time passed. Periods came and went, and through them all—the Oligocene period, the Miocene period, the Pliocene period—the primates continued to develop. The climate changed. Mountains were pushed higher. Open grasslands replaced the forests in the temperate zones, and the forests were restricted to the tropics.

Then, about one million years ago, the Pleistocene period began. It was to become the Age of Man.

At this time, the earth went through some extreme climatic changes. The temperature dropped—only a few degrees, but it was sufficient to wipe out a great number of species and to plunge the world into long and cold winters. The shortened, cooler summers were not enough to melt all the snows of previous winters, and year by year ice accumulated. Four times in the last million years sheets of ice up to one mi. thick have pushed southward, covering large land areas beneath frozen glaciers. The smaller monkeys took to the restricted tropical jungles; only the larger, heavier apes were able to bear the cold.

Early in the Pleistocene period, a primitive ape-man appeared, called *Australopithecus*. He had differentiated hands and feet, smaller teeth and no fangs, and a fully upright posture. These characteristics distinguished him from the other apes, but with his larger brain he was distinguishing himself in other ways. This ape-man learned to use primitive tools and to organize in groups of cooperative hunters. This new intelligence worked; the ape-man survived.

The skull of the ape-man's descendants continued to grow. From a capacity of 600 cubic cm., it reached one of 1,000 cubic cm. With this improvement, the new creature learned to use fire and stone tools, and, in time, language was invented. Man had arrived in the world in a new improved form: *Homo erectus*, or *Pithecanthropus*.

Competition within the species had not ended, though. There was still a struggle to survive, and intelligence, now a well established advantage in the world of natural selection, became a deciding factor. Those animals that were able to make the best use of tools, or to hunt most efficiently, lived and multiplied. Their offspring tended to have larger and larger skulls, until skull capacity reached 1,400 cubic cm. This happened about 10,000 years ago. The newly evolved animal became agricultural and produced works of art. He developed civilizations and learned to control his environment. This animal is considered the latest earthly creation of the expanding universe: modern man.

—R.C.

The Golden Rule

Christianity: Therefore all things whatsoever ye would that men should do to you, do ye even so to them: for this is the law of the prophets.

Matthew, 7:12

Judaism: What is hateful to you, do not to your fellowmen. That is the entire Law; all the rest is commentary.

Talmud, Shabbat, 31a

Brahmanism: This is the sum of duty; do naught unto others which would cause you pain if done to you.

Mahabharata, 5, 1517

Buddhism: Hurt not others in ways that you yourself would find hurtful.

Udana-Varga, 5, 18

Confucianism: Surely it is the maxim of lov-
ing-kindness: Do not unto others that you
would not have them do unto you.

Analects, 15, 23

Taoism: Regard your neighbor's gain as your
own gain and your neighbor's loss as your
own loss.

T'ai Shang Kan Ying P'ien

Zoroastrianism: That nature alone is good
which refrains from doing unto another
whatsoever is not good for itself.

Dadistan-i-dinik, 94, 5

Islam: No one of you is a believer until he desires for his brother that which he desires
for himself.

Sunnah

A Dissenter's View: Do not do unto others as
you would that they should do unto you.
Their tastes may not be the same.

George Bernard Shaw, 1903

27

Passing On—the Final Trip

The Choice

One day God asked the 1st human couple, who then lived in heaven, what kind of death they wanted—that of the moon or that of the banana. The couple wondered what the difference was, so God explained: The banana puts forth shoots that take its place and the moon itself comes back to life.

The couple considered for a long time before they made their choice. If they chose to be childless, they would avoid death for themselves, but they would also be very lonely and would be forced to do all of the work by themselves and would not have anyone to work and strive for.

So they asked God for children, well aware of the consequences of their choice. And their request was granted.

Since that time, each human has spent only a short time on this earth.

—A legend from Madagascar

Famous Last Words

Walt Whitman said, "Last words are not samples of the best, which involve vitality at its full, and balance, and perfect control and scope. But they are valuable beyond measure to confirm and endorse the varied train, facts, theories and faith of the whole preceding life."

Karl Marx, however, had a different opinion. Michael Hastings—in *Tussy Is Me*, his biographical novel about Eleanor Marx, the youngest daughter of Karl Marx—relates a conversation which took place between Marx and his housekeeper, Helen, on the day that Marx died:

"Tell me your last words, Karl—I'll write them down."

"You can hardly spell your own name!"

"Your last word to all mankind, Mohr—?"

"I haven't got one—"

"Your dying breath, Mohr; so I can put it in all those big fat books—like, 'words on their deathbeds the great men said'—come along Karl—think!"

"Go on, get out—last words are for fools who haven't said enough."

Fortunately, not everyone agreed with Karl Marx. . . .

The Last Words of
ADAMS, JOHN QUINCY (1767–1848), American President

"This is the last of earth! I am content."

ALLEN, ETHAN (1738–1789), American Revolutionary soldier

In answer to his doctor, who said, "General, I fear the angels are waiting for you": "Waiting, are they? Waiting, are they? Well—let 'em wait!"

ANDRÉ, JOHN (1751–1780), English officer

On the scaffold: "It will be but a momentary pang."

ARCHIMEDES (287?–212 B.C.), Greek mathematician

To a Roman soldier: "Stand away, fellow, from my diagram."

ARNOLD, BENEDICT (1741–1801), American traitor

Referring to his Continental uniform: "Let me die in the old uniform in which I fought my battles for freedom. May God forgive me for putting on any other."

BEECHER, HENRY WARD (1813–1887), American clergyman

"Now comes the mystery."

BISMARCK, OTTO EDUARD LEOPOLD VON (1815–1898), Prussian statesman

"I do not want a lying official epitaph. Write on my tomb that I was the faithful servant of my master, the Emperor William, King of Prussia."

BONAPARTE, NAPOLEON (1769–1821), French Emperor

"France! Army! Head of the army! Josephine!"

BOOTH, JOHN WILKES (1838–1865), Lincoln's assassin

"Tell my mother—I died—for my country. I thought I did for the best. Useless! Useless!"

BUDDHA (563?–483? B.C.), Indian philosopher

"Beloved, that which causes life, causes also decay and death. Never forget this; let your minds be filled with this truth. I called you to make it known to you."

BYRON, GEORGE GORDON (1788–1824), English poet

"Now I shall go to sleep."

CAESAR, JULIUS (100–44 B.C.), Roman statesman

"Thou, too, Brutus, my son!"

CARLYLE, THOMAS (1795–1881), Scottish historian

"So this is Death—well—"

COLUMBUS, CHRISTOPHER (1451–1506), Italian explorer

"Into Thy hands, O Lord, I commend my spirit."

CONFUCIUS (551–479 B.C.), Chinese philosopher

"No intelligent Monarch arises; there is not one in the kingdom that will make me his master. My time has come to die."

CRANE, HART (1899–1932), American poet

As he jumped overboard to commit suicide: "Good-bye, everybody!"

CROMWELL, OLIVER (1599–1658), English statesman

"My desire is to make what haste I may to be gone."

DARWIN, CHARLES (1809–1882), English naturalist

"I am not the least afraid to die."

EARHART, AMELIA (1898–1937), American aviatrix

In a letter to her husband before her last flight: "Please know that I am quite aware of the hazards. I want to do it because I want to do it. Women must try to do things as men have tried. When they fail, their failure must be but a challenge to others."

EDISON, THOMAS (1847–1931), American inventor

In a coma: "It is very beautiful over there."

FRANKLIN, BENJAMIN (1706–1790), American scientist and philosopher

To his daughter when she asked him to change his position in bed: "A dying man can do nothing easy."

GAINSBOROUGH, THOMAS (1727–1788), English painter

"We are all going to heaven, and Van Dyck is of the party."

GOETHE, JOHANN WOLFGANG VON (1749–1832), German poet

"More light!"

HARRIS, JOEL CHANDLER (1848–1908), American writer and creator of "Uncle Remus"

"I am about the extent of a tenth of a gnat's eyebrow better."

HOUSMAN, ALFRED EDWARD (1859–1936), English poet

After his doctor told him a "dirty" story: "Yes, that's a good one, and tomorrow I shall be telling it again on the Golden Floor."

HOUSTON, SAM (1793–1863), American general

"Texas—Texas—Margaret—"

IRVING, WASHINGTON (1783–1859), American author

"Well, I must arrange my pillows for another weary night! When will this end?"

JACKSON, THOMAS "STONEWALL" (1824–1863), American Confederate general

"Let us go over the river, and sit in the shade of the trees."

KIDD, CAPTAIN WILLIAM (1645?–1701), Scottish pirate

Before being hanged: "This is a very fickle and faithless generation."

LAFAYETTE, MARQUIS DE (1757–1834), French soldier and statesman

"What do you expect? Life is like the flame of a lamp; when there is no more oil—zest! It goes out, and it is all over."

LOUIS XIV (1638–1715), French King

To his servants: "Why do you weep? Did you think I was immortal?"

MARIE ANTOINETTE (1755–1793), French Queen

To the executioner, after she stepped on his foot: "Monsieur, I beg your pardon."

MATHER, COTTON (1663–1728), American clergyman

"Is this dying? Is this all? Is this what I feared when I prayed against a hard death? Oh, I can bear this! I can bear it!"

MORE, SIR THOMAS (1478–1535), English statesman

To the executioner: "Pluck up thy spirits, man, and be not afraid to do thine office: My neck is very short; take heed, therefore, thou strike not awry, for saving of thine honesty."

NELSON, LORD HORATIO (1758–1805), English naval commander

"Thank God I have done my duty."

POE, EDGAR ALLAN (1809–1849), American writer

"Lord help my poor soul."

ROOSEVELT, FRANKLIN DELANO (1882–1945), American President

"I have a terrific headache."

ROOSEVELT, THEODORE (1858–1919), American President

"Please put out the lights."

ROUSSEAU, JEAN JACQUES (1712–1778), French philosopher

"I go to see the sun for the last time."

SHAW, GEORGE BERNARD (1856–1950), English playwright

To his nurse: "Sister, you're trying to keep me alive as an old curiosity, but I'm done, I'm finished, I'm going to die."

SOCRATES (470?–399 B.C.), Greek philosopher

"Crito, I owe a cock to Asclepius; will you remember to pay the debt?"

THOREAU, HENRY DAVID (1817–1862), American writer

"Moose. Indian."

WASHINGTON, GEORGE (1732–1799), American President

"Doctor, I die hard, but I am not afraid to go."

ZIEGFELD, FLORENZ (1867–1932), American theatrical producer

In a delirium: "Curtain! Fast music! Lights! Ready for the last finale! Great! The show looks good. The show looks good."

—C.O.

Rest in Peace

A Collection of Bizarre Gravestone Epitaphs

In an Edinburgh, Scotland, cemetery

Beneath this stone a lump of clay
Lies Uncle Peter Dan'els
Who early in the month of May
Took off his winter flannels

Thomas Stagg's epitaph in St. Giles Churchyard, London

That is all

In a Thurmont, Md., cemetery

> Here lies an Atheist
> All dressed up
> And no place to go

In a Larne, Ireland, cemetery, epitaph of a man who had been hanged

> Rab McBeth
> Who died for the want
> of another breath
> 1791–1823

Gravedigger Robert Phillip's epitaph, Kingsbridge, England, cemetery

> Here I lie at the Chancel door;
> Here I lie because I am poor;
> The farther in the more you pay;
> Here I lie as warm as they.

In a London cemetery

> Ann Mann
> Here lies Ann Mann,
> Who lived an old maid
> But died an old Mann
> Dec. 8, 1767

In a Ribbesford, England, cemetery

> Anna Wallace
> The children of Israel wanted bread
> And the Lord sent them manna,
> Old clerk Wallace wanted a wife,
> And the Devil sent him Anna.

In the Pawtucket, R.I., Oak Grove Cemetery, epitaph on a huge boulder over the grave

> William P. Rothwell, M.D.
> 1866–1939
> This is on me.
> R.

In the Winterborn Steepleton Cemetery, Dorsetshire, England

> Here lies the body
> Of Margaret Bent
> She kicked up her heels
> And away she went

In the Boot Hill Cemetery, Tombstone, Ariz.

> Here lies
> Lester Moore
> Four slugs
> From a forty-four
> No Les
> No More

Prof. S. B. McCracken's epitaph in an Elkhart, Ind., cemetery

> School is out
> Teacher
> Has gone home

In a Ruidoso, N.M., cemetery

> Here lies
> Johnny Yeast
> Pardon me
> For not rising

In a Charleston, S.C., cemetery

> Reader, I've left this world, in which
> I had a world to do;
> Sweating and fretting to get rich:
> Just such a fool as you.

In a Cripple Creek, Colo., cemetery

> He called
> Bill Smith
> A liar

Atheist Arthur Haine's epitaph in a Vancouver, Wash., cemetery

> Haine
> haint

In a Savannah, Ga., cemetery

> Here lies old Rastus Sominy
> Died a-eating hominy
> In 1859 anno domini

An infant's epitaph in a Plymouth, Mass., cemetery

> Since I have been so quickly done for
> I wonder what I was begun for.

In a Uniontown, Pa., cemetery

> Here lies the body
> of Jonathan Blake
> Stepped on the gas
> Instead of the brake

In the Barlinine Cemetery, Glasgow, Scotland

> Here beneath this stone we lie
> Back to back my wife and I
> And when the angels trump shall trill
> If she gets up then I'll lie still!

An attorney's epitaph in Willwood Cemetery, Rockford, Ill.

> Goembel
> John E.
> 1867–1946
> "The defense rests"

In a Stowe, Vt., cemetery

> I was somebody.
> Who, is no business
> of yours.

Written by a widow on her adulterous husband's gravestone in an Atlanta, Ga., cemetery

> Gone, but not forgiven

In a Silver City, Nev., cemetery

> Here lays Butch,
> We planted him raw.
> He was quick on the trigger
> But slow on the draw.

An old maid's epitaph in a Scranton, Pa., cemetery

> No hits, no runs, no heirs.

A widow wrote this epitaph in a Vermont cemetery

> Sacred to the memory of
> my husband John Barnes
> who died January 3, 1803
>
> His comely young widow, aged 23, has many qualifications of a good wife, and yearns to be comforted.

Arthur C. Homans's epitaph in a Cleveland, O., cemetery

> Once I wasn't
> Then I was
> Now I ain't again.

A lawyer's epitaph in England

> Sir John Strange
> Here lies an honest lawyer,
> And that is Strange.

In a Georgia cemetery

> "I told you I was sick!"

John Penny's epitaph in the Wimborne, England, cemetery

> Reader if cash thou art
> In want of any
> Dig 4 feet deep
> And thou wilt find a Penny

In the East Dalhousie Cemetery, Nova Scotia

> Here lies
> Ezekial Aikle
> Age 102
> The Good
> Die Young

In a Waynesville, N.C., cemetery

> Effie Jean Robinson
> 1897–1922
> Come blooming youths, as you pass by
> And on these lines do cast an eye
> As you are now, so once was I;
> As I am now, so must you be;
> Prepare for death and follow me.

To which someone, who saw this, added

> To follow you
> I am not content
> How do I know
> Which way you went

—The Eds.

FOR FURTHER READING: *Over Their Dead Bodies* by Thomas C. Mann and Janet Greene. Brattleboro, Vt., Stephen Greene Press, 1962. *Grave Humor* by Alonzo C. Hall. Charlotte, N.C., McNally of Charlotte, 1961.

Death: Do-It-Yourself

Some Well-Known Suicides

"Many die too late, and some die too early. The maxim: die at the right time still sounds foreign to us."—Friedrich Nietzsche

An average of 70 people a day, nearly 26,000 a year, kill themselves in the U.S. Worldwide, the number of known suicides reaches about 1,000 per day. The number of attempted suicides is 10 times greater than the number of those that succeed.

Every era, every society, has been troubled and perplexed by man's deliberate decision to end his life. Suicide knows no boundaries. It cuts across the spectrum of human life without regard for age, sex, race, nationality, or status.

Following are capsule accounts of some prominent—and some less prominent—men and women who have chosen suicide as the only alternative to their "dilemma of living."

WOLFE TONE (1763–1798)

Life: Irish revolutionist Wolfe Tone was the founder of the United Irishmen, a political group whose purpose was to reform the Irish Parliament—then a stronghold of Protestant aristocrats—so that Irishmen, regardless of their status or religion, could be admitted. The peaceful movement, also called the "brother-hood of affection," turned reactionary after war between Great Britain and France broke out in 1793. Political pressure caused Tone to emigrate to America. Subsequently, he went to France to seek military aid and convinced the French Government to dispatch a naval expedition to invade Ireland. The mission would have succeeded, but the fleet, when close to the Irish shore, was hit by a storm and could not land. Tone said that "England had not had such an escape since the Armada."

Death: Captured at sea while commandeering a French ship, Tone was brought to trial in Dublin. He confessed his crimes and asked that he be allowed a soldier's death before a firing squad. The request was denied and he was sentenced to be hanged. Refusing to submit to such an "indignity," Tone cut his throat with a razor.

MERIWETHER LEWIS (1774–1809)

Life: Explorer and former governor of the Louisiana Territory, Meriwether Lewis stands as one of American history's great adventurers. President Thomas Jefferson noted that Lewis was "remarkable even in infancy for enterprise, boldness, and discretion." Governor at 33, Lewis found the office a difficult one because of the feuds between the territory's officials and political parties. Financial problems plagued Lewis, due in part to his "land speculation" investments in the new territory. Anxiety over his financial state was increased when the U.S. Government questioned the validity of his public expenditures for the territory.

Death: On his way to Washington to defend his use of government funds, Lewis stopped overnight at a log cabin in Tennessee. There he shot himself twice. He died at the age of 35. Although the majority of historians agree that Lewis's death was a suicide, a few historians say that the evidence supporting such a claim is not only inconclusive, but suggests that Lewis was murdered.

JAMES A. HARDEN-HICKEY (1854–1898)

Life: Self-proclaimed King of the island of Trinidad, Baron James A. Harden-Hickey startled the world in 1893 when he announced his plans to "found a nation" on this island which he insisted was "an independent state." Of Irish and French descent, enamoured as a child by the glamour of the French court, married to a Standard Oil heiress, Harden-Hickey proposed to set up a kingdom on Trinidad, with himself as its military dictator. (The is-

land, about 60 sq. mi., was 700 mi. off the Brazilian coast in the South Atlantic Ocean; it was not the larger British West Indian island of Trinidad, off the coast of Venezuela.) Believing in the feasibility of his plan, Harden-Hickey bought a schooner, had postage stamps printed, and proudly wore a homemade crown. Great Britain seized Trinidad in 1895 and a year later surrendered it to Brazil. Baron James A. Harden-Hickey became a "King without a country."

Death: Harden-Hickey believed that suicide was "a privilege," a theory which he developed in his book *Euthanasia: The Aesthetics of Suicide.* He wrote: "We must shake off this fond desire of life and learn that it is of little consequence when we suffer; that it is of greater moment to live well than to live long, and that oftentimes it is living well not to live long." When the battle for possession of Trinidad was lost, Harden-Hickey planned to invade England in order to save his honor. He asked his wealthy father-in-law for money to do so and was turned down. He also tried to raise funds by selling his ranch in Mexico, but that too failed. Feeling depressed and deserted, he decided to kill himself. Although in his book he had suggested 88 poisons and 51 instruments that could be used for self-destruction, many of them exotic, Harden-Hickey committed suicide with a routine drug—he took an overdose of morphine.

JACK LONDON (1876–1916)

Life: American writer and great outdoorsman, Jack London is best known for his books *The Call of the Wild, The Sea Wolf,* and *White Fang.* His search for the realities in life and death extended throughout his career. A sailor, oyster pirate, hobo, gold prospector, factory hand, and war correspondent, London embodied his experiences and philosophies in 51 books written over a span of 16 years. His books have been translated into more than a dozen languages, and his "passionate affirmation of life, his faith in the ultimate perfectibility, through struggle, of man and society" remains internationally popular.

Death: Although he suffered from digestive ailments, uremia, rheumatism, and insomnia, London rejected the advice of his doctors. The effects of too much alcohol coupled with a poor diet resulted in severe illness and pain. At age 40, he took a lethal dose of "morphine sulphate with atropine sulphate."

CAPTAIN LAWRENCE OATES (1880–1912)

Life: British explorer Lawrence Oates was a member of an expedition into the Antarctic which was led by Captain R. F. Scott in

1910. The South Pole was successfully reached in 1912, but it was on the return trip that Oates committed what most historians refer to as a "heroic" suicide.

Death: Bad weather, lack of food, and sickness delayed the expedition during its return trip. Oates's feet froze and he became partly crippled. Believing that his condition would weaken the chance of survival for the others, he deliberately left the shelter one night and walked to his death in a sub-zero Antarctic blizzard.

IVAR KREUGER (1880–1932)

Life: Swedish industrialist and "Match King" Ivar Kreuger was the world's most brilliant thief, forger, gambler, and swindler. Although he supplied 65% of the world's matches from his factories located in 34 countries, Kreuger's dream was "to control every match produced on the face of the earth." He loaned vast sums of money to 15 different countries (including France, Spain, Poland, Greece, Hungary, and Yugoslavia) in exchange for monopolistic control of the match industry. His generous state loans gained for him the reputation of "Savior of Europe" and "Savior of the World." Obsessed with the continuous growth of his empire, Kreuger purchased everything from gold mines, forests, and railways to telephone companies, film companies, and banks. Unwavering faith in his own "superior" intellect, cleverness, and manipulative talents propelled Kreuger into the role of world financier and statesman. The Wall Street crash of 1929 forced Kreuger into financial collapse.

Death: Kreuger forged signatures on loan papers, faked financial records, created imaginary banks to hold imaginary money, and was engaged in innumerable other fraudulent business transactions. The economic crisis following 1929 left Kreuger facing bankruptcy and criminal exposure. All attempts to restructure his holdings failed, and on March 12, 1932, he shot himself. As one historian of the Kreuger legend said, "Financial genius or gifted rogue, superman or imposter, sane or mad, he cannot readily be reduced to human dimensions."

ADOLF HITLER (1889–1945)

Life: As German head of state, Hitler thought himself to be a Messiah whose goal was to "redeem the German people and reshape Europe." As a youth, he failed in his attempts to become an artist, an architect, a Benedictine abbot. He joined the Army, then was so devastated by Germany's defeat in W.W. I that he suffered from "hysterical blindness and mutism." While recuperating in the hospital,

he had a "vision" that he would lead Germany out of bondage. The postwar German Army commissioned Hitler to teach political philosophy to the soldiers. His rise to Chancellor of Germany took him 12 years. A master of persuasive techniques, he said that he "learned the use of terror from the Communists, the use of slogans from the Catholic Church, and the use of propaganda from the democracies." He ordered the massacre of 6 million Jews, but worried about "the most humane way to cook lobsters."

Death: At the time of his death, Hitler may have been suffering from brain damage. Also, he took numerous vitamins and medications, including weight-reducing pills, sleeping pills, and other drugs. Faced with defeat in W.W. II, he elected to kill himself. He and his then-mistress, Eva Braun, retired to the air-raid shelter of the Chancellery in Berlin where he swallowed cyanide capsules. Hitler had ordered his new bride to shoot him, in case the poison was not effective. Although the cyanide was adequate, Eva Braun shot him in the left temple and then poisoned herself.

PRINCE FUMIMARO KONOYE (1891–1945)

Life: Former Premier and Foreign Minister of Japan, Konoye argued against war in the months preceding the Japanese invasion of Pearl Harbor. Following the Japanese surrender which ended W.W. II, Konoye considered suicide out of fear that he would be listed as a war criminal. For a few months he waited, hoping that his antiwar sentiments would be considered. Also, there had been some speculation that he would be chosen to write a new constitution for Japan. Finally, his name did appear on the list of war criminals issued by General Douglas MacArthur in December, 1945. Konoye was informed that he would be taken prisoner in 24 hours.

Death: Konoye hosted a dinner party for his friends on the same day that he received news of his pending capture. Following the party, he went to his bedroom and took poison.

JAMES VINCENT FORRESTAL (1892–1949)

Life: Appointed as the 1st U.S. Secretary of Defense by President Franklin D. Roosevelt, Forrestal was also a member of the National Security Council, National Security Resources Board, and the Hoover Commission. As Undersecretary and Secretary of the Navy, he had reorganized the U.S. Navy and built it into one of the world's largest military forces. One of the most important and influential government officials, Forrestal fought against communism, advocated military control over the atomic bomb, and opposed establishment of the nation of Israel. A loner, estranged from his family and with few close friends, he dedicated himself to his job, working 18 to 20 hours a day.

Death: Forrestal resigned as Secretary of Defense in 1949 and shortly afterward was awarded the Distinguished Service Medal by President Truman. Five days after receiving the award, he was admitted to Bethesda Naval Hospital for what was termed "occupational fatigue." Approximately a month and a half later, he jumped from the 16th floor of the hospital.

VLADIMIR MAYAKOVSKI (1893–1930)

Life: Russian poet and playwright, spokesman for the Revolution, Mayakovski was imprisoned several times for his outspoken social and political criticism. After the Revolution, he tried to create "an art that will pull the republic out of the mud." His poems include "150 Million" and "A Cloud in Trousers"; his plays include *The Bedbug* and *The Bathhouse.*

Death: Mayakovski believed that his political philosophy was ruining the quality of his work. Distressed by personal strife and by criticism from his literary adversaries, he shot himself. The note he left behind said, "I don't recommend it for others." Boris Pasternak wrote of Mayakovski's suicide, "It seems to me that Mayakovski shot himself out of pride, because he condemned something in himself, or close to him, to which his self respect could not submit."

CESARE PAVESE (1908–1950)

Life: Italian novelist and poet, Pavese's works include *Carcere, Bella Estate,* and *La Casa in Collina.* Pavese's father died when he was 6. His mother was a stern disciplinarian who showed little warmth and affection. His life and his works sought to offset his disillusionment with politics, morality, love, and to mitigate his loneliness. Some believe that his death was caused by an unhappy love affair with an American actress. Upon hearing of his death, the actress commented, "I didn't know he was such a famous writer."

Death: One month before his death, Pavese received the Strega Prize, Italy's major literary award. His last diary entry read, "The thing most feared in secret always happens. . . . All it needs is a little courage. The more the pain grows clear and definite, the more the instinct for life asserts itself and the thought of suicide recedes. It seemed easy when I thought of it. Weak women have done it. It needs humility not pride. I am sickened by all this. No words. Action. I shall write no more." He then took an overdose of sleeping pills.

MARILYN MONROE (1926–1962)

Life: American actress and sex symbol, Marilyn Monroe appeared in such films as *All About Eve, Gentlemen Prefer Blondes, How to Marry a Millionaire, Some Like It Hot,* and *The Misfits.* Born in Los Angeles, her childhood and adolescent years were marked by confusion and discord. Her mother, suffering from paranoid schizophrenia, was unable to care for her, and Marilyn Monroe's family life was limited to what was provided by the different foster families with whom she stayed. At one time, she lived in an orphanage. Her career began as a pinup model, then advanced to bit parts in films. Eventually, she became celebrated as a dramatic actress and comedienne.

Death: After a Hollywood studio broke her contract, Marilyn withdrew from public life to reassess her career as well as her private life. An unhappy love affair and possible pregnancy added to the problems she already faced. Her dependency on barbiturates grew, and it was an overdose of these which finally claimed her life. Some question whether or not her death was a suicide, but a "psychological autopsy" done in Los Angeles revealed "not only her suicidal state of mind prior to her death but also the fact that she had made several attempts at suicide previously."

SYLVIA PLATH (1932–1963)

Life: American writer who was 1st published when she was 8, Sylvia Plath had a career filled with honors, scholarships, and awards. Although at Smith College she was named "outstanding teacher," she gave up the academic life to become a free-lance writer. Her poems and short stories were published in leading magazines. She wrote a novel, *The Bell Jar,* and books of poetry, *The Colossus* and *Ariel.* An account of her early life as recounted in *The Bell Jar* describes her nervous breakdown, her attempted suicide, and her hospitalization in a mental institution. In the last pages of *The Bell Jar,* she said, "How did I know that someday—at college, in Europe, somewhere, anywhere—the bell jar, with its stifling distortion wouldn't descend again."

Death: Many of Sylvia Plath's poems revolved around a death theme. Friends believe this was a result of the death of her father when she was a child. She wrote, "Dying is an art, like everything else. I do it exceptionally well. I do it so it feels like hell. I do it so it feels real. I guess you could say I've a call." After several unsuccessful suicide attempts, Sylvia Plath ended her life. She locked herself in the kitchen, sealed off the doors and windows, and breathed gas fumes from the oven.

OTHER SUICIDES

ARMSTRONG, EDWIN H. (1890–1954). American inventor of regenerative circuit for radio. Jumped from 13th floor of apartment building.

BOULANGER, GEORGES (1837–1891). French general. Shot himself due to grief over death of his mistress.

CAMPBELL, WILLIAM W. (1862–1938). American astronomer. Jumped from 3rd floor of apartment building.

CAROTHERS, WALLACE H. (1896–1937). American chemist who led development of synthetic fibers. Drank poison mixed in lemon juice.

CASTLEREAGH, VISCOUNT (1769–1822). British statesman. Cut his throat.

CATO THE YOUNGER (95–46 B.C.). Roman Stoic philosopher. Fell on his sword.

CHATTERTON, THOMAS (1752–1770). British poet. Swallowed arsenic.

CLEOPATRA (69–30 B.C.). Queen of Egypt. Chose death from the bite of an asp (according to legend).

CRANE, HART (1899–1932). American poet. Jumped overboard from a boat in Caribbean.

CREECH, THOMAS (1659–1700). British classical scholar. Hanged himself.

DEMOSTHENES (385–322 B.C.). Greek orator

and statesman. Took poison to escape being captured by Macedonians.

EASTMAN, GEORGE (1854–1932). American inventor of Kodak camera. Shot himself.

ESENIN, SERGEI (1895–1925). Russian poet. Cut his wrists, then hanged himself.

FADEYEV, ALEXANDER (1901–1956). Russian novelist. Shot himself while in a state of mental depression.

HANNIBAL (247–183 B.C.). Carthaginian general. Took poison to evade capture by Romans.

HEMINGWAY, ERNEST (1899–1961). American writer. Shot himself.

HIMMLER, HEINRICH (1900–1945). Hitler's chief of police. Poisoned himself.

KAMMERER, PAUL (1880–1926). Austrian biologist. Shot himself.

LEY, ROBERT (1890–1945). German Nazi leader. Strangled himself with a towel (while awaiting trial as a war criminal).

NERVAL, GÉRARD DE (1808–1855). French writer. Hanged himself with an apron string.

PONIATOWSKI, PRINCE JOSEPH ANTON (1763–1813). Polish general. Drowned himself by plunging his horse into river.

TELEKI, COUNT PAUL (1879–1941). Hungarian statesman. Shot himself in temple with revolver.

WOOLF, VIRGINIA (1882–1941). British novelist. Drowned herself.

—C.O.

Good-bye, Cruel World, or: Notes on the Suicide Note . . .

I wish to be buried in Uniondale Cemetery #4, facing Marshall Ave., so that I may be able to see the fair weather friends and thank them for the sarcastic and hateful remarks.

I would like my sister Frances to have the piano that you have in your apartment. Do this or I will haunt you.

The suicide note, like suicide itself, can run the gamut from clear lucidity to complete concealment of the reason behind it. Suicidologists have described these last messages as cries for help, acts of cultural breakthrough necessary to the suicide's "success," and as artifacts of the most deadly of art forms, the ultimate in pregraveyard graffiti.

Practicality often runs hand in hand with a final desire to tie up the loose ends before departure. In Britain a workman, about to hang himself in an abandoned house, chalked his final words on the wall outside.

Sorry about this. There's a corpse in here. Inform police.

The famous inventor and industrialist George Eastman laid out pencil, paper, and revolver, and was equally terse.

To my friends:
    My work is done. Why wait?

            G.E.

And briefer still. An empty house. Everything is quiet. The note, carefully placed on the table for the police to find, answers all.

Why suicide?
Why not?

Only recently has the suicide note been recognized as a valid research tool, useful in discovering the causes and possible means of prevention of suicide. In the past 15 years, suicide notes have been examined for their syntactical and graphological characteristics, their semantic similarities, and the organizations of thought by such noted scientists in the field as Schneidman and Farberow, J. Jacobs, C. J. Frederick, and Lester and Lester. Osgood and Walker, in a 1959 study, by comparing genuine suicide notes with spurious ones, concluded that, generally, suicide notes are: 1. prone to stereotyping; 2. less reliant on adjectives and adverbs; 3. more reliant on terms of endearment and words denoting certainty ("always," for instance, or "never"); and 4. identifiable by their handwriting when examined by graphologists. Approximately one suicide in 5 leaves such a note.

One 45-year-old laborer 1st left precise instructions before making his final political comment.

> My small estate I bequeath to my mother;
> my body to the nearest accredited medical school;
> my soul and heart to all the girls;
>
> and my brain to Harry Truman.

Notes are found in many forms. A few have been printed with lipstick on a mirror. Others are typed cleanly. Some are scrawled hurriedly with chalk, pencil, stick—often whatever comes to hand easily is used. Even blood if a gory suicide has had time to linger and realizes he's forgotten the obligatory note.

Does suicide reduce itself to a question of personal success or failure? Not really. For one 50-year-old Hollywood actor, the road back to the top was too long and too hard to travel.

> I tried so hard
> to make a comeback.

(Exit, Act III)

But on the other hand, Ralph Barton, a successful satiric writer in 1931, wrote that he was doing it because he was fed up with inventing devices ". . . for getting through 24 hours of every day. . . ." He added that his remains should be left to "any medical school that fancies them, or soap can be made of them. In them I haven't the slightest interest except that I want them to cause as little bother as possible."

Nor is making money the key to a happy life. A prominent banker once left a note consisting of a long list of instructions, including: "Sorry to be a nuisance this way. Call [and he named his choice of undertakers]."

Many suicide notes simply describe the sensations of the approaching death, such as the note left by a British physician who had taken a slow-acting poison: "Waiting. Feeling very happy. First time I ever felt without worry, as if I were free. My heart must be strong. It won't give up. . . . Pulse running well. Feel fine—when will it be over?"

And a note written by a man who had sent halfway around the world for his suicide weapon, a black widow spider, reported: "I feel the effects now. The room is going around and around. I can barely see what I'm writing. Maybe it is the end. Who knows? I don't care. It is very pleasant. Yes. No."

A former soldier described the effects as he succumbed to carbon monoxide, writing: "Terrific smell of gas fumes . . . It would be 6:34 civilian time. . . . Eyes smart a bit. . . . Afraid somebody will come by now. . . . This is slow. 6:36 P.M. . . . Engine sounds smooth. Faculties temporarily sharpened. . . . No particular desire to get out. . . . Seems to be getting the better of me fast. . . . It's been just 15 minutes now. . . . Seems to be terrific pressure 1st . . . going . . . go . . . go. . . ."

One woman left 3 notes: "There is nothing mysterious about this," read the 1st. "I'm doing this of my free will." The 2nd read: "I am taking whiskey. It makes it easier." And the 3rd added: "It's harder than I thought."

Suicide notes have been a mainstay of the theater, the novel, the film. In his diaries Dostoevski speaks of being obsessed by the note of a 17-year-old girl:

> I am undertaking a long journey. If I should not succeed, let people gather to celebrate my resurrection with a bottle of Cliquot. If I should succeed, I ask that I be interred only after I am altogether dead, since it is particularly disagreeable to awake in a coffin in the earth. It is not *chic!*

And suicide itself has had a long association with poets and artists and writers, as well as movie stars and actors. The Russian poet Sergei Esenin wrote a final poem in his own blood before hanging himself.

Three surrealists had notes prepared months or even years before their deaths. Jacques Rigaut had already written "Suicide is a vocation" before he shot himself. Jacques Vache, who took his own life (and that of a friend) with an overdose of opium, had penned:

> I shall die when I want to die, and then I shall die with someone else. To die alone is boring; I should prefer to die with one of my best friends.

And René Crevel, called the most beautiful of surrealists, before gassing himself, had written:

> Is it true . . . that one commits suicide for love, for fear, for syphilis? It is not

true. . . . Suicide is a means of selection. Those men commit suicide who reject the quasi-universal cowardice of struggling against a certain spiritual sensation so intense that it must be taken, until further notice, as a sensation of truth. Only this sensation permits the acceptance of the most obviously just and definitive of solutions: suicide.

Eighteenth-century poet Eustach Budgell threw himself into the river, leaving behind the note:

What Cato did and Addison approved
Cannot be wrong

Sylvia Plath left a simple line asking that her doctor be notified, and actress Carol Landis left a letter to her mother. Van Gogh left a message in the media he knew best, when he painted the frightening canvas *Cornfield with Crows*. And before drowning herself, Virginia Woolf wrote to her husband:

I have a feeling I shall go mad. I cannot go on any longer in these terrible times.

I hear voices and cannot concentrate on my work. I have fought against it but cannot fight any longer. I owe all my happiness to you but cannot go on and spoil your life.

The wife of Dante Gabriel Rossetti wrote simply:

My life is so miserable I wish for no more of it.

Some suicides phrase their notes in the form of newspaper obituaries, referring to themselves in the 3rd person. Many of these are printed verbatim in the obituary columns. Others leave behind notes reading only "I'm sorry" or "No comment."
"Th-th-th-that's all, folks!" wrote a San Francisco dishwasher, using the tag line from the Bugs Bunny cartoons. And then he hung himself.

—M.T. & W.K.

Where There's a Will (There's an Insight into the Deceased)

In those days was Hezekiah sick unto death. And Isaiah the prophet the son of Amoz came unto him, and said unto him, Thus saith the Lord, Set thine house in order: for thou shalt die, and not live.

Isa. 38:1

There is no legal obligation to make a will. It is perfectly acceptable to die "intestate," i.e., without leaving a will. The law, in all States, provides for equitable distribution of one's property to the heirs, if any. In some cases, if no heirs can be found, the estate will be gathered into the public coffers for the benefit of all.

The purpose of a will, however, is to allow the deceased to express one final wish for the disposition of his worldly goods. The right is available for anyone with the desire to make the legal declaration. Normally, the intent is written, valid when attested to by a certain number of witnesses. But it can be oral as well, so long as the spoken words represent the true desires of the individual involved, free of the elements of fraud, undue influence, or coercion.

The practice of leaving a will has been in use since people 1st began to acquire property. The following are some of the more interesting bequests, the last testaments made by personalities of the past.

THE PAST

Nek'ure   Egyptian Pharaoh's son
Died: c. 2601 B.C.

Last Will: Provided for the disposition of 14 towns, 2 estates; distributed to his wife, 3 children, and an unknown female. Carved on his tomb, the will is the oldest known to exist. Its opening words pointed out that King Khafre's son had made the decisions about his property "while living upon his 2 feet and not ailing in any respect."

Aristotle   Greek philosopher   Died: 322 B.C.

Last Will: Left 3 executors to handle his affairs until his chosen son-in-law, Nicanor, came of age. If Nicanor died prior to the time when Aristotle's daughter was old enough to marry him, Theophrastus was named as the 2nd choice. If Herpylis married—and the executors were commanded to see that she did not disgrace Aristotle's name by her choice—she was given permission to use the ancestral home at Stagyra, suitably furnished by the executors.

Virgil   Roman poet   Died: 19 B.C.

Last Will: Asked that his *Aeneid* be burned with his death, a request he later canceled. Virgil gave ¼ of his property to Emperor Augustus, the percentage which Romans considered advisable if the remaining assets were to be distributed in accordance with the deceased's wishes. It insured the Emperor's support of the will.

William the Conqueror   British King   Died: 1087

Last Will: Distributed large sums of money, dictating the names and amounts to his secretaries. Some beneficiaries: his 3rd son, King Henry I, £5,000, in silver; the Nantes clergymen, a sum to repay them for burning the town.

Petrarch   Italian poet   Died: 1374

Last Will: Remembering the chill of an Italian winter, the poet left 200 gold florins to Boccaccio, to buy a robe that would stave off the cold.

Christopher Columbus   Spanish mariner   Died: 1506

Last Will: The discoverer of America directed that, among a list of his obligations, payment of one half mark in silver be made to "a Jew who lived at the entrance to the ghetto in Lisbon, or to another one who may be named by a priest." Speculation that he ordered the payment because he himself was Jewish has been further fanned by scholars who point out that his use of contemporary Jewish expressions and viewpoints indicates a firsthand study of Jewish literature.

Henry VIII   British King   Died: 1547

Last Will: The much-married monarch humbly noted, in a last testament of just under 7,000 words, that he would not have objected if his cadaver had been buried "in any place accustomed for Christian folke." However, he went on, "because we would be lothe in the reputation of the people to do injurie to the dignitie which we unworthilie are called unto," a better choice would be at Windsor, "midwaye betweene the Stalles and the high aulter." By his side, he wanted Queen Jane Seymour, mother of his son, Edward VI, indicating that Jane, of his 6 wives, was his favorite.

François Rabelais   French author   Died: 1553

Last Will: Opened in Paris, the entire will read: "I have nothing. I owe much. The rest I leave to the poor."

William Shakespeare   British playwright   Died: 1616

Last Will: Shakespeare left considerable real estate holdings in and near Stratford to his 2 daughters, Susanna and Judith, making cer-

tain exceptions. Lesser bequests were made to friends, and to the family. The will was that of a typical country squire, but its content puzzles historians. Shakespeare mentioned his wife only with the curious bequest, "I give unto my Wiffe my 2nd-best bed with the furniture." This was written into the will as a scribbled interlineation. And he omitted all mention whatsoever of his literary works. The omission contributed to the controversy that "William Shackspeare"—as he signed the will —did not author the Elizabethan dramas.

John Donne   British poet   Died: 1631

Last Will: The greatest of the metaphysical poets, Donne left £500 to maintain his mother, and a 54-line poem entitled "The Will." "Any man's *death* diminishes *me*," he wrote earlier in his *Devotions*, "because I am involved in *Mankind*; And therefore never send to know for whom the *bell* tolls; It tolls for *thee.*"

Cardinal de Richelieu   French prelate and statesman   Died: 1642

Last Will: The powerful minister of King Louis XIII left 1.5 million livres to his monarch, all of his considerable gold and silver to one favorite niece, and favored other nephews and nieces equally well. He pointedly excepted the Duchesse d'Enghien, who incurred his ire with her marriage. The cardinal's books were given to one nephew provided that a cleaner was hired, for 400 livres yearly, to sweep the library out daily and to wipe the books as often as necessary.

Eleanor Gwyn   British actress   Died: 1687

Last Will: Nell Gwyn, or "E.G.," as she signed her "Last Request," made her will one month before her death. Addressed to the duke of Albans, one of the 2 illegitimate sons she had had as the mistress of Charles II, she itemized 14 requests, including a wish to be buried in the chancel of St. Martin's-in-the-fields, London. She also asked the duke to set aside £100 for geting debtors out of prison and another £20 annually "for the releasing of poore Debtors out of prison every Christmas Day."

Samuel Pepys   British diarist and public official   Died: 1703

Last Will: In a 12-page will, buttressed later by a 2-page codicil, Pepys noted that he had arrived at "the 69th year of age" and was making his will "with all humility and thankfulness and with a satisfaction inexpressible," a state of mind that would have surprised his contemporaries. He gave his valuable library, along with the famous diary he had written in cipher, to John Jackson, his nephew.

Peter The Great Russian Czar Died: 1725

Last Will: Advising his ministers to keep Russia continually at war for the good of the nation, Peter wrote out a complete plan of strategy for a Russian conquest of Europe.

David Garrick British actor Died: 1779

Last Will: The bequest gave Mrs. Garrick several options. She could elect to accept £1,000 outright, another £5,000 within 12 months, and £1,500 as an annual annuity. But the generous provisions were contingent upon several thought-provoking conditions. She had to continue to live in their chief place of residence at Hampton. She could not move permanently outside of England. And she had to give up her right to the income from her £10,000 dower settlement. If she did not agree—and he gave her 3 months to furnish a reply, in writing, to his executors—the alternative was to accept £1,000 annually, with all other legacies being canceled. To the British Museum, Garrick gave his collection of old English plays.

Samuel Johnson British author Died: 1784

Last Will: To God, Johnson bequeathed ". . . a Soul polluted with many sins but I hope purified by Repentance." After making certain small gifts to others, he gave the bulk of his estate, totaling £2,300 in the form of an annual annuity for "Francis Barber, my Man Servant, a Negro." Dr. Johnson's library was sold for £250, and his Litchfield house was given to relatives.

Benjamin Franklin American statesman Died: 1790

Last Will: Reminding his Tory son, William, of his activities during the Revolutionary War, a bitter Franklin left him "all my books and papers which he has in his possession, and all debts standing against him on my account books," provided his executors did not demand repayment. To General George Washington, he gave his "crabtree walking-stick, with gold head curiously wrought in the form of a cap of liberty," an item which eventually passed into the safekeeping of the U.S. Government. Franklin's original gift of £2,000 for loans, bearing interest, to "married apprentices of upright behaviour," generated millions of dollars for subsequent charitable projects.

George Washington American President Died: 1799

Last Will: The $600,000 estate was given to his wife, Martha. He delayed the freedom of his slaves until after her death, stating, "To emancipate them during her life, would, tho earnestly wished by me, be attended with such insuperable difficulties on account of their intermixture by marriages with the dower negroes, as to excite the most painful sensations, if not disagreeable consequences from the latter, while both descriptions are in the occupancy of the same proprietor." To his mulatto slave, William Lee, he gave immediate freedom. Lee became famous after Washington's death, and was "buried" 5 times—in North Carolina, Arkansas, Missouri, and twice in New York. Each interment was faithfully recorded as the demise of the original William.

Patrick Henry American patriot and politician Died: 1799

Last Will: Henry's famous declaration, "Give me liberty or give me death," was taken to heart by his widow, Dorothea. He 1st provided for her generously, but then—if she were to remarry—he cut her off without a cent, or "no more of my estate than she can recover by Law." She voted for freedom of choice and married his cousin, Judge Winston.

Horatio Nelson British admiral Died: 1805

Last Will: Writing to his countrymen while his flagship closed to do battle with the French at the battle of Trafalgar, Nelson detailed the services which his mistress, Lady Hamilton, had performed for England. He bequeathed her as ". . . a legacy to my King and country; that they will give her an ample provision to maintain her rank in life." Both the King and the admiralty ignored the gift.

Marquis de Sade French writer Died: 1814

Last Will: The man whose name has been immortalized by the word "sadism" recorded his deep gratitude to Madame Quesnet. He gave her 80,000 livres since "during the Reign of Terror, she saved me from the revolutionary blade all too surely suspended over my head." The marquis insisted that his corpse be kept in an open coffin in the death chamber for a full 48 hours, "at the end of which period the said coffin shall be nailed shut." Only then, after he was found to be definitely dead, was he to be buried in the woods at Malmaison.

**Gouverneur Morris   American statesman
Died: 1816**

Last Will: Married late in life to the young and vivacious Ann Randolph, the Revolutionary War politician willed her a substantial income. Mindful and appreciative of the many happy moments she had given him, Morris added a provision that, should she decide to marry again, her income would be doubled.

Paul Revere   American patriot   Died: 1818

Last Will: Revere "sold" his thriving copper-manufacturing business to his son, Joseph Warren, giving him 4 years to pay off its appraised value through mortgages naming Revere's other children and grandchildren as beneficiaries. The provision allowed an equal distribution of the equity. Joseph fared better than Frank, Revere's grandson who had changed his name to Francis Lincoln. Frank was cut off with $1.

Caroline of Brunswick   British Queen   Died: 1821

Last Will: Married to King George IV, who had unsuccessfully accused her of infidelity in seeking to have their marriage dissolved, she added a codicil to her will that called for a plaque to be attached to her coffin. It gave the vital statistics and added her indignant response to his charge: She was billed as "The Outraged Queen of England."

**Napoleon Bonaparte   French soldier and Emperor
Died: 1821**

Last Will: In a testament written 21 days days before his demise, Napoleon wrote, "I die prematurely, assassinated by the English oligarchy." He "left" bequests that totaled 6 million francs, although he had no funds for the purpose. Among them, he "gave" 10,000 francs to Cantillon, the French officer whose unsuccessful attempt to assassinate Wellington had caused the Iron Duke to write his own will. It was the exiled Napoleon's opinion that Cantillon "had as much right to assassinate that oligarchist, as the latter had to send me to perish upon the rock of St. Helena."

James Smithson   British landlord   Died: 1829

Last Will: Alienated from England because of his illegitimate birth as the son of the 1st duke of Northumberland, Smithson gave $500,000 to the U.S. to found "an establishment for the increase and diffusion of knowledge among men." It became the Smithsonian Institution of Washington, D.C. The grant was valid only if his nephew died without children, legitimate or illegitimate.

Sarah Siddons   British actress   Died: 1831

Last Will: During her lifetime, Siddons set up a trust fund of £5,500 to provide for her companion, Martha Wilkinson. The balance of her estate was divided into 3 equal shares, bequeathed to her daughter Cecelia, her son George, and the widow of her deceased son Henry. Jointly, to George and Cecelia, Siddons also gave her most prized possessions: "my inkstand made of the mulberry tree planted by the immortal Shakespear and also the gloves which were worn by him—." They had been given to her by David Garrick, actor and manager of the Drury Lane Theatre.

Jeremy Bentham   British philosopher   Died: 1832

Last Will: The entire estate was given to London Hospital, provided that Bentham's preserved remains were permitted to preside over its board meetings. All terms of the will were conscientiously followed. His body was turned over to Dr. Southward Smith, who performed the complete dissection and the anatomical lecture, for public and medical student alike, that Bentham had stipulated. The bones were reassembled into a skeleton topped by a wax mask cast from the philosopher's expressionless face. The likeness was outfitted in Bentham's clothes and placed within a glass-fronted mahogany case, sitting upright in an armchair. For 92 years, the wax apparition was present, although duly noted as "not voting," at the meetings.

**John Jacob Astor   American merchant
Died: 1848**

Last Will: Nearly all of Astor's estate, valued at $150 million and perhaps the largest in the world at the time, went to his son, William Backhouse. Another $30,000, given to Alexander Hamilton, reverted when Hamilton was killed by Aaron Burr in 1804, before the will was probated. He also gave $100,000 to the Astor Library with the condition that the income from the invested money be used to buy additional books. This reference library became a part of the giant N.Y. Public Library.

**Robert Louis Stevenson   British novelist
Died: 1894**

Last Will: Requested that he be buried at the top of Mount Vaea, Samoa, "under the wide and starry sky" he had described in his "Requiem."

J. M. W. Turner   British painter   Died: 1851

Last Will: After making small legacies and giving his paintings to the nation, Turner left the rest ". . . for the support of 'poor and decayed' legitimate male artists born in England and of English parents." His relatives fought the will, claiming the £140,000 at issue, and won. The artists received nothing.

Duke of Wellington   British soldier   Died: 1852

Last Will: Shaken by an attempted assassination attempt, the Iron Duke, in 1818, wrote out a will in Paris. Arthur Wellesley listed assets of approximately £199,700, including £130,000 in exchequer bills he "believed" were being held by a Mr. Coutts.

Heinrich Heine   German poet   Died: 1856

Last Will: Leaving his entire estate to his wife, provided she would marry again, Heine explained his reason for the condition with Teutonic bluntness. "Because," his will read, "then there will be at least one man to regret my death."

Samuel Houston   American frontier hero and statesman   Died: 1863

Last Will: The Texan expressed firm rules regarding the education of his sons. They were to devote no time to the abstract sciences, concentrating on a thorough study of the Holy Scriptures, geography, history, and the English language. In other subjects he was equally emphatic: "I wish my sons early taught an utter contempt for novels and light reading."

Abraham Lincoln   American President Died: 1865

Last Will: Lincoln left no will, the only U.S. President to die intestate, a circumstance precipitated by his assassination. His net worth of $110,295 was awarded to his wife and 2 sons. The U.S. Congress, with strict observance of accounting rules, paid his salary only to the day of death.

Charles Dickens   British novelist   Died: 1870

Last Will: Leaving just less than £80,000, Charles John Huffham Dickens—as his will named him—noted that he had paid to his wife, from whom he was separated, £600 annually while assuming all expenses for the family. Later, he asked that those who came to his funeral "wear no scarf, cloak, black bow, long hatband, or other such revolting absurdity."

Brigham Young   Mormon Church leader Died: 1877

Last Will: Young's will, accounting for $2.5 million in cash and real estate, provided for a distribution to 17 wives and 48 children. His dependents were carefully divided into 3 "classes": wives with children, wives without children, and children of deceased wives. No mention was made of women who had been "sealed" to the polygamous leader by Mormon Church rituals. Young defined, for purposes of the will's coverage, the term "wife."

Karl Marx   German radical leader   Died: 1883

Last Will: The founder of communism had accumulated no personal wealth, leaving a scant £250.

Jefferson Davis   President of the Southern Confederacy   Died: 1889

Last Will: Left 3 plantations. One to his wife, one each to Mary Ellis and Mary Dorsey.

Phineas T. Barnum   American showman Died: 1891

Last Will: With no sons to inherit his fortune, the master showman offered his grandson, Clinton H. Seeley, $25,000 if "he shall habitually use the name of Barnum, either as Clinton Barnum Seeley, or C. Barnum Seeley, or Barnum Seeley in his name, so that the name Barnum shall always be known as his name." Clinton readily agreed, accepting Barnum's 2nd choice. The Barnum estate totaled $4.1 million. In retaliation for his daughter Helen's notorious conduct, Barnum revoked the earlier, generous provisions he had made for her and instead gave her some western property he considered to be worthless, in return for a "quit claim" on his estate. The Denver, Colo., land proved to have valuable mineral deposits which made Helen wealthier than all the other Barnum heirs put together.

Alfred Nobel   Swedish chemist and inventor Died: 1896

Last Will: The inventor of dynamite and nitroglycerin directed that his property be sold for cash, with the proceeds to be invested in safe securities that produced income. From the income accruing annually, prizes were to be awarded ". . . to those persons who shall contribute most materially to benefiting mankind during the year immediately preceding." The money was to be divided into 5 equal shares and given for the most important discovery or invention in physics, physiology or medicine, chemistry, literature, or in the cause of universal peace. Nobel directed that all prizes except the one for peace be awarded by the Swedish Academy of Science. The latter prize was to be determined by a committee of 5 who had been elected by Norway's Storting. Although Nobel's prizes were to be given with "no consideration whatever . . . paid to the nationality of the candidates, that is to say, that the most deserving be awarded the prize, whether he or she be a Scandanavian or not . . . ," the selection of winners has sometimes been challenged, with critics claiming that Nobel's directive has been violated.

Since 1900

Cecil Rhodes British statesman and empire builder Died: 1902

Last Will: In his 1st 5 wills Rhodes repeatedly called for a ". . . Secret Society, the true aim and object whereof shall be the extension of British rule throughout the world," and, eventually, "the ultimate recovery of the United States of America." In his 6th and last will he created the Rhodes Scholarships, limiting the eligible applicants to Anglo-Saxons who came from Great Britain, the U.S., or Germany.

Mary Baker Eddy Founder of Christian Science religion Died: 1910

Last Will: In previous gifts Mrs. Eddy gave her son, George W. Glover, $245,000 and her adopted son, Ebenezer J. Foster, $45,000. Her will left an estate of at least $2 million to the Mother Church of Boston, the parent church of Christian Science. Her sons contested the will without success. Eddy also left $10,000 to each of her grandchildren, and $100,000 to be set up as a trust fund for the education of Christian Science practitioners.

Florence Nightingale British nurse Died: 1910

Last Will: The founder of modern nursing left £36,128. She refused burial in Westminster Abbey and gave her body "for dissection or postmortem examination for the purpose of Medical Science." The provision was ignored. She was buried at East Wellow, among her ancestors.

Margaret Nothe Philadelphia housewife Died: 1913

Last Will: On one page of her handwritten book of kitchen recipes, under the title "Chili Sauce Without Working," Mrs. Nothe wrote the delicious will that was accepted by the probate court:

> 4 quarts of ripe tomatoes, 4 small onions, 4 green peppers, 2 teacups of sugar, 2 quarts of cider vinegar, 2 ounces ground allspice, 2 ounces cloves, 2 ounces cinnamon, 12 teaspoons salt. Chop tomatoes, onions and peppers fine, add the rest mixed together and bottle cold. Measure tomatoes when peeled. In case I die before my husband I leave everything to him.

J. P. Morgan American financier Died: 1913

Last Will: The male members of the family (one son, 2 sons-in-law) were willed $5 million outright. The distaff side (wife, 3 daughters) were left a total of $10 million, in trust, with the power to will the principal. Morgan's 3 sisters were not provided for, not from lack of affection, but because "the property which they already have makes the same seem unnecessary." His art treasures were given to his son, with the advice that they be placed on permanent display "for the instruction and pleasure of the American people." Morgan also gave each employee of J. P. Morgan and Co. a year's salary.

Anthony Comstock American morals crusader Died: 1915

Last Will: The small estate of the "soldier of righteousness" included 2 insurance policies, valued at $3,000 each, his stamp collection, and the painting showing General Sheridan at Cedar Creek.

Andrew Carnegie American industrialist and philanthropist Died: 1919

Last Will: After selling out to J. P. Morgan for $400 million in 1900, Carnegie devoted the balance of his life to giving away his fortune. He felt that, after one's family's needs were provided for, the wealth which remained was to be held only as a public trust, ". . . to be administered for the benefit of the community." Carnegie built 2,509 free libraries in following this philosophy, spending over $56 million. Before his death, he had managed to give away over $308 million.

Mrs. Frederick Cook British drapery manufacturer's widow Died: 1925

Last Will: The longest will ever recorded, Mrs. Cook's final testament had 95,940 words on 1,066 pages, bound into 4 volumes. She left $100,000 to be distributed, along with instructions to burn her diary.

Charles Millar Canadian lawyer Died: 1927

Last Will: Having neither dependent nor near-relative at hand, Millar bequeathed his considerable fortune "to the Mother who has given birth in Toronto to the greatest number of children" during the 10 years which followed his death. The fertility clause sent Canadian wives into a bedroom competition that the newspapers called the Stork Derby. The will was contested bitterly for 12 years, with claims that the clause provoked "immorality," but to no avail. On May 30, 1938, the $568,000 estate was distributed to 4 mothers who had produced 9 children within the specified time span. One winner immediately announced her solid support of birth control in the future.

Thomas Alva Edison   American inventor
Died: 1931

Last Will: Left most of $12 million to his 2nd wife's children. William, his son by his 1st wife, challenged the codicil, executed when Edison was 84, charging undue influence. He claimed the codicil cut his bequest from an annual income of $650,000 to $130,000.

T. E. Lawrence   British adventurer   Died: 1935

Last Will: A legend in his lifetime, "Lawrence of Arabia"—who died of injuries received in a motorcycle accident—left £100 to each of his 2 executors, along with his only copy of Shelley's poems.

Basil Zaharoff   International financier and munitions king   Died: 1936

Last Will: The "mystery man of Europe" was reported to have accumulated a fortune of £100 million during an armament career in which he was accused of promoting warfare for personal profit. His will, naming his 2 daughters as his heirs, showed the sum as a mere £1 million.

John D. Rockefeller   American oilman and philanthropist   Died: 1937

Last Will: After assets were transferred to the Rockefeller Foundation, the residual estate of $25 million was left in trust primarily to Mrs. Margaret Strong de Cuevas, his granddaughter, and her descendants. Rockefeller did so, to the exclusion of his other grandchildren, because they had already been provided for "when the time came that I felt it wise to place upon my children the responsibility of owning and administering substantial sums." By that time, Margaret's mother, Bessie, had died, thus necessitating this separate trust.

Adolf Hitler   German dictator   Died: 1945

Last Will: Mentioning that he and Eva Braun were marrying and then choosing to die "to escape the shame of overthrow or capitulation," the dictator wanted it clearly understood that his painting collection "bought by me during the years" had always been intended to establish a picture gallery in his hometown, Linz.

Conrad Cantzen   American actor   Died: 1945

Last Will: Remembering his "at liberty" days when he was down on his luck, Cantzen left $226,608.34 to establish a shoe fund ". . . for the people who can't buy shoes, even if they are not paid-up members of Equity. Many times I have been on my uppers, and the thinner the soles of my shoes were, the less courage I had to face the managers in looking for a job." The bequest dumbfounded Broadway, since Cantzen's panhandling along Broadway in his last years had indicated he was penniless. Today, any professional actor who qualifies can "do the shoe bit," beginning with a visit to the offices of Actors Equity in New York City.

Franklin Delano Roosevelt   American President   Died: 1945

Last Will: Left approximately $1.1 million, held in joint trust by his son, James, Basil O'Connor, and Henry Hackett, for the benefit of his widow and their children. From the income of the trust, Mrs. Roosevelt was to pay a sum up to $1,000 annually for the living expenses of Marguerite (Missy) Le Hand, Roosevelt's personal secretary since his years as governor of New York.

W. C. Fields   American comedian   Died: 1946

Last Will: The portion of his estate that could be located was worth $700,000. Because of his secretiveness, and his desire to have cash available wherever he was in the world, Fields had opened some 200 bank accounts under fictitious names and he kept no record of the deposits or the banks. His safe-deposit box in a Berlin bank contained $50,000, deposited under another name, but this was lost when Berlin was bombed in W.W. II. His executors were able to find 45 of these bank accounts, but the remaining deposits—estimated at $600,000—were never found. Although he once said, "Anybody who hates children and dogs can't be all bad," Fields left instructions that there be established the "W. C. Fields College for orphan white boys and girls, where no religion of any sort is to be preached. Harmony is the purpose of this thought." He bequeathed to his wife, Harriet, $10,000, and to his son, Claude, $10,000. He left his mistress, Carlotta Monti, $25,000, plus his dictionary, 2 bottles of perfume, and a Cadillac. He left his brothers and sisters, and 9 friends, small sums, as well as his possessions ranging from file cabinets to 2 fly catchers.

Henry Ford   American industrialist   Died: 1947

Last Will: Ford's worth amounted to $600 million, primarily as stock in the Ford Motor Co. Having previously provided for his wife, he gave all the Class "A" nonvoting stock of the Ford Motor Co. to the Ford Foundation.

The Class "B" voting stock was divided into 5 equal shares, for his son, Edsel, and his 4 grandchildren.

George Orwell   British novelist   Died: 1950

Last Will: Requested that his grave be marked with his real name, Eric Arthur Blair. Left £9,909.

George Bernard Shaw   British playwright
Died: 1950

Last Will: The socialist author left a capitalist estate of $1,028,252. Reaffirming his belief in creative evolution rather than in any specific church creed, he asked that memorials to him that took "the form of a cross or any other instrument of torture or symbol of blood sacrifice" be omitted. His ashes were to be sprinkled at Ayot St. Lawrence. "Personally," he wrote in his final instructions, "I prefer the garden to the cloister." Shaw, after making numerous small bequests, left the bulk of his sizable fortune for the development of a British alphabet having 40 letters. The request was contested in court by the British Museum, charging that the conditions imposed were too vague. Seven years later, a compromise was accepted, with only a £500 prize being offered in a competition to select a letter design. The 4 winners who split the award were also asked to continue their studies in the search for a replacement to Dr. Johnson's alphabet.

Albert Einstein   American physicist   Died: 1955

Last Will: After disposition of an estate of $65,000, Einstein left his manuscripts and royalties to Hebrew University, and his beloved violin to his grandson.

Lord Redesdale   British nobleman   Died: 1958

Last Will: Left $361,000 to be shared by all of his daughters except Jessica. An avid foe of communism for his entire life, Redesdale never forgave his daughter for naming a Redesdale grandson "Lenin."

Clark Gable   American movie actor   Died: 1960

Last Will: Gave his 1st wife, Josephine Dillon, title to the North Hollywood home at 12746 Landale, and all the rest to his last wife, Kathleen.

Ernest Hemingway   American writer   Died: 1961

Last Will: Written in 1955 at Finca Vigia, Cuba, his will gave his wife, Mary, sole control and omitted any provision for the children, stating he had "complete confidence" she would provide for them according to written instructions he had given her.

Marilyn Monroe   American movie actress
Died: 1962

Last Will: Left over $1 million, although the estate was later declared insolvent. She set up $100,000 in trust to provide $5,000 annually for her mother's care, gave $25,000 to close friends, and bequeathed her personal effects to her acting mentor, Lee Strasberg. To her psychiatrist, Dr. Marianne Kris, she willed the balance of the trust, after her mother's death, for her use in psychiatric work.

Pope John XXIII   Head of Roman Catholic Church
Died: 1963

Last Will: Reaffirmed his faith and his gratitude for the honors given to him by the Church. He expressed 2 earthly wishes: that his own family attend his burial service, and, in a codicil, that the Lateran Palace transformation, into the Holy See of the Roman Vicarate, be completed.

John F. Kennedy   American President   Died: 1963

Last Will: To save huge death and inheritance taxes, Kennedy placed his $10 million estate in trusts. After minor bequests, including the sum of $25,000 and household effects to his wife, Jacqueline, he divided the remainder into 2 equal shares as trust funds for Jacqueline and the 2 children, John and Caroline. The trustees were also empowered to pay to Jacqueline, out of the trust principal, whatever sums were necessary to "enable her to maintain the standard of living to which she is accustomed," up to 10% annually of the trust's total principal.

Jawaharlal Nehru   Prime Minister of India
Died: 1964

Last Will: Following his cremation, Nehru asked that a handful of his ashes be scattered in the Ganges River. He took care to explain that his request bore no religious significance, noting, ". . . the Ganges has been to me a symbol and a memory of the past of India, running into the present, and flowing on to the great ocean of the future." To insure that no portion of his remaining ashes were preserved, he directed that they be disposed of by carrying them aloft ". . . in an airplane and scattered from that height over the fields where the peasants of India toil."

Winston Churchill   British Prime Minister
Died: 1965

Last Will: The great wartime leader of Britain in the 1940s left a simple will disposing of

£304,044, primarily to Lady Churchill. He asked that he be buried at Bladon, near Woodstock, with his parents.

Karl Tausch German businessman Died: 1967

Last Will: Herr Tausch, of Langen, in the province of Hesse, wrote the shortest will ever conceived: "*Vse zene.*" The Czech words meant "All to wife."

Drew Pearson American columnist Died: 1969

Last Will: As Pearson's stepson, Tyler Abell, recalled it, ". . . the son of a bitch had written 7 wills," spaced out over 31 years. They were scribbled on blank paper, hotel stationery, and Western Union forms during Pearson's travels. Only the 1st, attested to in Iowa, was legally acceptable. His estate, valued at over $2 million, left Abell life insurance worth $5,000, with the bulk of the fortune going to Pearson's 2nd wife, Luvie. The lawyers ultimately shared: Some $130,000 went for legal fees to fight cases brought by people named in subsequent wills. The IRS grabbed about $300,000 for taxes. Another $45,000 was paid to settle 2 major libel suits still pending in 1969. Eventually, Pearson's daughter, Mrs. Ellen Arnold, named in a holographic will drawn up in Kentucky in 1962, reached a compromise with Luvie. Mrs. Arnold received title to a 160-acre Potomac farm worth about $500,000.

The legal will gave his former partner, Robert S. Allen, the index files for Pearson's "Washington Merry-Go-Round" column, although later wills bequeathed them to Allen's successor, Jack Anderson. Allen dropped his claim in return for $4,000. Pearson died wealthy but cash-poor—he had also been forced into the lecture circuit to refurbish an overdrawn bank account.

Aleksandr Kerenski Russian revolutionist Died: 1970

Last Will: The head of Russia's provisional government between the 1st Russian Revolution of April, 1917, and the Bolshevik Revolution in the following October left approximately $30,000 to his son, Oleg. A 2nd son, Gleb, was not mentioned.

Marjorie Merriweather Post Breakfast-food heiress Died: 1973

Last Will: Left most of her $150 million fortune to her 3 daughters. Her Texas real-estate holdings included nearly all of 2 counties. The base for the fortune came from the cereal products promoted as Postum, Post Toasties, and Grape Nuts. Mrs. Post bequeathed sums as great as $50,000 to some of her loyal retainers.

—W.K.

Afterlife and Reincarnation

It may seem that conflicting ideas about what happens after death are relatively unimportant, that our knowledge and understanding of how a people *lives* is what matters. A closer look shows that, among many cultures, the way of life cannot be understood except in terms of the culture's ideas of an afterlife. Often it is these ideas which mold the entire culture.

Beliefs about the afterlife vary tremendously, and those of one group, though closely resembling those of another, may yet have subtle variations which are very significant and worthy of much elucidation. However, just about all are combinations of the ideas that an afterlife is:

First—1. Total oblivion. 2. Somewhere else. 3. Here.
Second—A. Physical. B. Nonphysical, solely spiritual.
Third—i. Automatically the same for everyone. ii. Pleasant. iii. Unpleasant, according to a judgment which will come after death. iv. An opportunity for further progress.

By arbitrarily categorizing the various concepts in this way we can, for example, describe the Christian idea of a soul's going on to a heaven or hell as 2Bii/iii. However, there are many Christians who believe that they will have a new physical body in the afterlife, and this would be 2Aii/iii. On the other hand, some Christians believe in reincarnation, which would probably be shown as 3Aiv.

This system is one of the ways in which we can attempt to put into order the multitudinous variety of beliefs that people have held as to what will happen to them after death.

1Ai—*complete oblivion for everyone.* The belief that all awareness is totally and permanently snuffed out when the body dies is held by modern materialists, whether they be humanists, atheists, or communists. At their best such believers have demonstrated a high degree of selflessness and ethical behavior, but this credo may at times contribute to a feeling of purposelessness which may lead to antisocial behavior. It may also lead to a disregard for the value of human life and individuality. (This A is included here because most subscribers to 1 do not believe that man has any nonphysical nature.)

1 Bi—*oblivion, though with spiritual involvement, for all*. The differentiation between physical oblivion and spiritual oblivion may seem a fine distinction, but a form of spiritual oblivion is the closest description of the belief of early cultures that one's spirit did go on to *somewhere*, but that it was a somewhere of almost nothingness. The early Jews called this somewhere Sheol, and it was, apparently, a desolate place:

". . . in Sheol, for which you are bound, there is neither dying nor thinking, neither understanding nor wisdom." (Eccles. 9:10) The Mesopotamians held a similar point of view, as did the early Greeks, whose spirits occupied Hades, a dreary place where they could only chirp meaninglessly like birds. Hades had much in common with the underworld of the shamanistic cultures of many "primitive" peoples, and included a provision that properly qualified "heroes," like the shamans, might rescue a soul and return it to life.

So, if the underworld is a place that can be actually visited, we have already blended into category 2, in which the afterlife is somewhere else.

2 Ai—*a physical existence somewhere else for everyone*. The early Celts believed that life went on much as usual in some other location, and so did many American Indian tribes, but in many such cultures one had to earn the right to enter, which indicated some form of judgment.

2 Aii/iii—*a physical existence somewhere else, pleasant for some, unpleasant for others*. Norse warriors were spurred to valor by the belief that if they died fighting courageously they would enter Valhalla, a place of constant feasting and other pleasures which, in its northern fashion, much resembled the gardens of delight complete with dancing houris which were promised to the valiant soldiers of Islam. (About those who did not get to partake of these rewards we are less clear; probably Hades or its equivalent was the only other place to go. Indeed, going back to the Egyptians of 2000 B.C. we find that they weren't clear either, for anyone not qualified to unite with the sun-god would *either* be annihilated (1) *or* go to hell (*iii*) *or* enter the underworld of nothingness (B).) As their thinking became too sophisticated to accept Hades for everyone, the Greeks began to look forward to the Elysian fields, but only if they had been initiated into the Orphic mysteries. It was this idea of qualifying for some form of "heaven" that led to the concept of a judgment for all, an idea that began to appear in Jewish writing after the exile to Babylon. The Jews had probably been exposed to Zoroastrian thought during the exile,

and the Zoroastrian faith was based on the idea of a duality, including a heaven and a hell. The Christian and Muslim faiths inherited the heaven and hell concept when they developed from Judaism (the Muslim garden of delights being a separate reward reserved for warriors).

Judgment is not always based on how one has lived. In Melanesia the decision may depend on whether the proper rituals have been performed by surviving relatives, and indeed the spirit's whole future depends upon its survivors. If they remember it in the appropriate rituals, and call on it for advice, the spirit will continue to exist in the land of the dead. If the rituals are not performed, or if the spirit is forgotten by the living, it ceases to exist (1). Such concepts explain the emphasis on ancestor worship in many cultures, for it is only by rituals to indicate that they remember their ancestors that people can help them to stay in existence.

2 Bii/iii—*a heaven or hell for the spirit*. In many cases there is not much difference between those beliefs which expect a future physical body and those which hold out for an entirely nonphysical afterlife. In Christianity, adherents to both ideas may attend the same church, either unaware or uncaring of the difference between them. Some of those holding to a solely spiritual future feel that ultimately they will become a part of a greater whole, will blend in, so to speak, with God. This is a more Eastern idea. However, apart from the Christians who believe in the immediate saving grace of Christ, most accept that the average man or woman is not yet worthy to blend with or be a companion to the Ultimate. This problem is overcome in a variety of ways.

2 Biv—*the soul has an opportunity to develop further*. Some Christians feel that, except for those who are beyond saving, they will go to purgatory. There they will be purged of their sins before moving on up to heaven. Spiritualists (who may or may not also be Christian) expect a variety of nonphysical planes, through which they will work their way upward toward the Ultimate, gradually developing and improving themselves as they go. The lower of these planes can also interact with the living (3), which forms the whole basis of spiritualism and mediumship. Occasionally a spirit will be so involved with earthly things that he will be unable or unwilling to start on this upward journey, and will remain earthbound—the spiritualist explanation for ghosts.

3 Bi—*the spirit remains here*. To some cultures ghosts are a permanent fact of life. The dead, though no longer visible, remain active participants in community activities, to be consulted, fed, included in rituals, and propitiated at every turn. Some tribes in South America regard all such spirits as hostile, and the en-

tire life of every individual is directed toward trying to propitiate or fend off the attack of a host of malign, though invisible, beings. The result is a rigid, ritualized, and fear-pervaded existence offering little opportunity for mental or spiritual development since any changes in the status quo might infuriate the spirits even more.

In Africa the spirits are usually more reasonable, becoming angry only when given cause. Frequently they are believed to stay in spirit form for only a time, after which they will again be reincarnated. The belief is also held by some shamanistic cults, and young children may be routinely examined for birthmarks or other signs which might indicate who they were in their last lifetime.

3—*a future life on earth*. Reincarnation cannot really be categorized, since just about every category in our table applies to it. It involves both the physical (A) and the spiritual (B), its rules apply to all (*i*) in most systems, it may be pleasant or unpleasant according to how one has lived previously (*ii/iii*), and it does present an opportunity for further advancement (*iv*).

One cannot generalize about reincarnationist doctrines, for they vary widely. Basically, they involve the idea that a soul, or spirit, survives bodily death and, either immediately or after a sojourn in some spiritual plane, returns to inhabit another human body. (The idea that humans may return as animals is properly known as metempsychosis and is rejected by most Western reincarnationists and many from the East, too.) The idea is that, since we are not yet worthy to be reunited with God or to attain whatever is our ultimate goal, we return time and again to work on our faults and develop our strengths. The doctrine of karma, or "as you sow so shall ye reap," usually accompanies reincarnation. Often misconstrued as a form of punishment, karma, properly understood and much simplified, is a teaching tool through which· when we do right things, things go right for us; when we do wrong things, things go wrong, until we have learned from our mistakes. The learning is often subconscious, so that, though we do not remember what mistakes we may have made in a previous life, our subconscious does remember, which is what matters.

Not all schools of thought recognize a specific soul personality that continues. Rather than seeing reincarnation as an opportunity for individual development, some see it as a continuing process for humankind as a whole. Perhaps an analogy would be that of an ocean which is destined to raise its temperature slowly. Many drops may in some way separate from it and be heated. They return to the ocean to warm it a little, and more drops

separate out to gain heat. These 2nd drops may contain some of the same atoms of water that were in the 1st drops, yet they are not the same drops. Nonetheless, the overall temperature of the ocean slowly rises, just as humankind's "group soul" slowly evolves as each soul separates from it to incarnate here, and then returns, hopefully slightly improved, after death. Future incarnations may involve elements of previous souls, but not the total individual soul personality. At the other extreme from this is the very personal theory that all those with whom we are closely involved are souls with whom we have had contact in previous lives.

Reincarnation has been attacked from many points of view. Some say that it leads to apathy —that if you see a person dying in the street you will say, "Oh, it's his karma," and let him lie there. It is true that the rigid Indian caste system was a product of early reincarnationist thought which maintained that it was your karma to be born into a certain position in life, and that you could not change this. Every religion has its positive and its negative aspects (Christianity had its Inquisition), and this cannot be denied. However, the enlightened reincarnationist holds that helping the dying person may earn positive karma, that there may even be a karmic debt involved, and so he helps. Some believe that this would involve the same soul: i.e., "A" needs help, and "B" gives it because, whether they are aware of it or not, either "A" helped "B" in a previous life or "B" harmed "A." "B" now has a chance to cancel the debt. A less personal credo holds that karmic debts are to humankind as a whole, and an act of kindness may cancel a debt even though it is not to the individual involved in the original debt.

Skeptics say that reincarnation is wishful thinking on the part of those who don't like to face the prospect of death. However, for many people reincarnation is *not* desired, because the aim is to perfect oneself beyond the need for further earth lives. There is also a growing quantity of scientifically researched material suggesting that reincarnation may be more than wishful thinking. Ian Stevenson of the University of Virginia at Charlottesville has a huge collection of cases in which people have claimed to remember previous lives. In many cases a young child has given sufficient information to enable its family to find the family to which the child says it used to belong. There are cases in which Stevenson could find no way that the child could have gained information about the "previous family," and yet he or she gave a great deal of information later found to be accurate and specific to that family. The claim that these people are possessed by the spirits of the previous individuals is sometimes countered by actual physical evidence, such as birth-marks that exactly resemble scars or death wounds of the previous personality.

It is well known that reincarnation is accepted by most Hindus and Buddhists (though not all), but in fact just about every society has some sects which believe in reincarnation. The Egyptians and the Greeks both adopted the idea as their religious ideas developed, though it was never universally accepted in Greece. The Druids would even lend money with the understanding that it would be repaid in a future incarnation. Algonquin Indians, Australian aborigines, and many African tribes include reincarnation in their beliefs, despite the common Western idea that the concept originated in Asia. Among the Jews, the Essenes and Pharisees accepted the idea, which continued to be popular among European Jews until at least medieval times. The Druses, a Muslim sect, not only believe in reincarnation but regard memories of past lives as commonplace, though until recently they were forbidden to discuss the memories outside their own people.

Many modern reincarnationists are Christians who find no dichotomy in the 2 belief systems. It is known that reincarnation was a common belief at the time of Jesus, and many feel that the fact that he did not speak against it indicates an acceptance of the belief. St. Augustine, though he obediently followed the church line against rebirth, was a great ad-mirer of Plato and Plotinus, both reincarnationist thinkers, and some scholars feel that there are hints at rebirth in some of his writing. Origen, a church father considered to be 2nd only to Augustine in his influence on the early growth of the Church, openly espoused reincarnation. Some Christians believe that Christ's forgiveness involves the removal of negative karma for people who are "saved." Thus the "wheel of life" (as the constant cycle of rebirths is called) is broken and they will not have to return again, though others will.

Reincarnation would explain the many apparent injustices in the world and, contrary to what is believed by the uninitiated, should not cause a fatalistic "That's my karma, there's nothing I can do about it" attitude. Rather, it gives a sense of total self-responsibility. There are no "outs," no excuses, no *they* who can be blamed for our difficulties and failures. Rather, our present is created from what we did in our past, and our future is being formed right now by how we handle our present. It is the *present* which is important to the sincere reincarnationist. To be always fussing about what we *were*, peasant or potentate, priest or princess, is like a high-schooler worrying about the work he did in elementary school. It is not yesterday's lessons that should be on our minds but today's, for they are all that we can learn today.

—D.R.

Vampires

"To die, to be really dead, that must be really glorious. . . . There are far worse things awaiting man than death. . . ."—
Count Dracula, in Bram Stoker's *Dracula*

Vampire legends have developed independently in many cultures of the world, and all of these tales have the same fundamental characteristics. Such tales have been recorded in Greece, Rome, England, Ireland, Russia, Hungary, Czechoslovakia, Romania, and Bulgaria. Cases of suspected vampirism have been reported even in the 20th century.

Vampires by tradition leave their graves at night and return to them before the light of day. Their active hours are spent sucking blood from the necks of their mesmerized victims. Vampirism supposedly occurs in an epidemic form, which throws a village into an uproar. Often when the grave of an alleged vampire is dug up, he is reported to have had fresh blood in his veins. A typical description says, ". . . they found him as though he were in a trance, gently breathing, his eyes wide open and glaring horribly. . . . His mouth was all slobbered and stained with fresh blood." In Romania these beings are often referred to as the "Moroi" or the "undead."

According to tradition, to kill a vampire, it is necessary to run a stake through its heart or to behead it, and then one must burn the corpse. (However, in 1823 England outlawed the practice of driving stakes through the hearts of suicides, although suicides were thought to be potential vampires.)

The most reliable method of fending off vampires is to keep some garlic around. Naturally, anyone who shows a marked aversion to garlic is suspect. If the situation seems particularly dangerous, it is wise to rub the hearth, all keyholes, and any domestic animals with garlic juice. It has been said that a cross also provides protection.

The explanations for vampirism are many. It is often said that candidates for becoming full-fledged vampires are: suicides, anyone under a curse, illegitimates, the excommunicated, the 7th son of a 7th son, those born with teeth or a caul, and—most especially—those who have been bitten by a vampire.

Some occultists offer a tentative explanation of this phenomenon. They say that the physical body is not the only body which a person possesses—he also possesses what is known as an "astral" body, which exists on a different plane. When a person dies, his astral body will eventually leave his physical body. However, in certain cases, this astral body is trapped within his physical body at the time of death. When this occurs, the astral body will see to it that the basic life fluid, blood, is made available to the corporeal body through vampirism.

Also worth mentioning is the common everyday occurrence we have all experienced: being around someone who seems to sap our energy and leaves us feeling tired. This might be explained as a mild case of what could be called vampirism.

The story that a vampire can assume the form of a bat is due to the existence of the "vampire bat," an actual species of bat which is found in Mexico. This bat thrives on blood, which it obtains by piercing its victim's flesh with its 2 sharp front teeth. This bat primarily attacks cattle.

Count Dracula, the most famous vampire in history, was created by novelist Bram Stoker, in 1897. This vile creature was named after a historical figure, who, though not an actual vampire, was surely as bloodthirsty as his fictional counterpart. Dracula's prototype was Prince Vlad Tepes, known to the peasants of Wallachia and Transylvania (located in 15th-century Hungary, which is now part of Romania), as Vlad "The Impaler," owing to his favorite practice of impaling his live victims upon stakes. At a time when the Turks and Romanians were engaged in vigorous battle, Vlad Tepes's victims included not merely his enemies, but countless numbers of his own countrymen and countrywomen, and even members of his own court, who had made the grave mistake of offending him in some way. A most gruesome account describes how "certain envoys of the sultan had come to greet the prince officially, and they refused to take off their turbans. Vlad Tepes, who was hypersensitive about any slight to his vanity, speedily ordered the turbans of the Turkish envoys to be nailed to their heads. The Turks agonized within a pool of blood at the very foot of the throne."

Impalement, even though Vlad's favorite form of torture, was not his only amusement. Boiling alive, decapitation, scalping, skinning, and general maiming were commonly included among his pastimes.

The nickname "Dracula," meaning "son of devil" or "son of Dragon," was given the prince because his father, also named Vlad, was called Dracul, or "devil." The words "devil" and "vampire" are interchangeable in many languages. Thus the association of Dracula with vampirism.

When Bram Stoker decided to write a novel about a vampire, a subject which had always fascinated him, he chose the faraway region of Transylvania as the site for his novel. Stoker carefully researched the exploits of Vlad Tepes and learned that the ruins of the real-life "Castle Dracula" were located in the same area. In addition, Stoker familiarized himself thoroughly with the peasants' vampire tales in that part of Europe, although he did not actually visit Transylvania.

Throughout vampire legend, there is a preponderance of male vampires. However, there is the infamous and grisly tale of one Elizabeth Báthory who, while not actually a vampiress, showed a marked proclivity for fresh blood. Elizabeth was born in 1560 in Hungary, and married Count Ferencz Nadasy. Her manservant, Thorko, introduced her to certain black arts. Aided by her nurse, Ilona Joo, Elizabeth began torturing servant girls at her castle. When her husband died in 1600, Elizabeth was free to exercise her whims without restraint. According to vampire buffs Raymond T. McNally and Radu Florescu:

> Elizabeth was afraid of becoming old and losing her beauty. One day a maid accidentally pulled her hair while combing it. Elizabeth instinctively slapped the girl, so hard that she drew blood which spurted onto her own hand. It immediately seemed to Elizabeth as if her skin in this area took on the freshness of that of her young maid. Blood! Here was the key to an eternally beautiful skin texture. The countess then summoned Thorko and another accomplice, Johannes. They stripped the maid, cut her, and drained her blood into a huge vat. Elizabeth bathed in it to beautify her entire body.

Over the next 10 years, Elizabeth and her accomplices tortured and killed at least 50 young girls. But then a potential victim escaped and reported what was happening. A band of soldiers, sent to examine the castle, discovered evidence that supported the girl's story. All of Elizabeth's henchmen were tried and executed. Elizabeth—because of the entreaties of her cousin, who was the Prime Minister—was spared. Confined to her room, she died 4 years later.

No piece of fiction has so richly portrayed vampirism as Stoker's novel, except perhaps for *Carmilla*, by Sheridan Le Fanu. There have, however, been several classic films produced on the subject. The 1st of these, made in 1922, was a silent entitled *Nosferatu*, directed by F. W. Murnau. In 1931 came the famous *Dracula*, with Bela Lugosi, who had previously played the same role in a stage production. The film was directed by Tod Browning. In 1932 *Vampyr*, directed by Carl Dreyer, was freely adapted from the vampire story *Carmilla*.

Since then, there have been many vampire films—a deluge of them, in fact—with only a precious few doing justice to the tradition of horror surrounding vampirism. Two of the noteworthy exceptions are *The Horror of Drac-* ula (1958), directed by Terence Fisher and starring Christopher Lee, and Roman Polanski's *The Fearless Vampire Killers* (1967), a satire starring Polanski and his late wife, Sharon Tate.

—A.W.

FOR FURTHER READING: *In Search of Dracula* by Raymond T. McNally and Radu Florescu. Greenwich, Conn., New York Graphic Society, 1972. The most readable and comprehensive of the many Dracula books which have been published in the past few years.

28

The Curiosity Shop

The Most Odd, Unusual, Strange, Unique, Incredible, Amazing, Uncommon, Unheard of, Fantastic Facts in the World

An Exclusive from *The People's Almanac*

"There are more things in heaven and earth, Horatio, than are dreamt of in your philosophy." So spoke Shakespeare's Hamlet. History has proved this true. Ever since human beings began to keep written records, certain connoisseurs of the incredible have noted those bizarre people, places, things which most of their fellows could not imagine in their wildest fancies. In the last half century, the oddity hunter has become a respected and widely followed specialist.

The People's Almanac decided to seek out the foremost of modern-day oddity hunters and to poll them on what they, themselves, considered the most astonishing and diverse facts they had uncovered in their researches. Herewith, from material dug up over many decades by these curators of the curious, the 5 to 12 favorite odd facts selected by each one or with the assistance of the *Almanac* editors . . .

NORRIS AND ROSS MCWHIRTER'S 10 BEST ODDITIES

The fabulous McWhirter twins, Norris and Ross—both graduated from Oxford and served in the British Navy, both worked for the BBC as TV commentators, both married and had 2 children—have succeeded Robert Ripley as the leading curators of the unbelievable. They conceived and wrote the *Guinness Book of World Records*, a phenomenon of the publishing world that had sold millions of copies in successive editions. Instead of picking their own favorite oddities, the McWhirters suggested several of their "entries which people seem to enjoy" most, and invited the *Almanac* editors to make the remainder of the selections.

1. *The Greatest Welfare Swindle.* "The greatest welfare swindle yet worked was that of the gypsy Anthony Moreno on the French Social Security in Marseilles. By forging birth certificates and school registration forms, he invented 197 fictitious families and 3,000 children on which he claimed benefits from 1960 to mid-1968. Moreno, nicknamed *El Chorro* ('the fountain'), was last reported free of extradition worries and living in luxury in his native Spain having absquatulated with an estimated $6,440,000."

2. *The Worst Woman Golfer.* "A woman player in the qualifying round of the Shawnee Invitational for Ladies at Shawnee-on-Delaware, Pa., in c. 1912, took 166 strokes for the 130-yard 16th hole. Her tee shot went into the Binniekill River and the ball floated. She put out in a boat with her exemplary, but statistically minded, husband at the oars. She eventually beached the ball 1½ mi. downstream, but was not yet out of the woods. She had to play through one on the home stretch."

3. *The Record Human Cannonball.* "The record distance for firing a human from a cannon is 175' in the case of Emanuel Zacchini in the Ringling Bros. and Barnum & Bailey Circus in 1940. His muzzle velocity was 145 mph. On his retirement the management was fortunate in finding that his daughter-in-law, Florinda, was of the same caliber."

4. *The Greatest Miser in History.* "An estate of $95 million was left by the notorious miser Henrietta (Hetty) Howland Green (née Robinson) (1835–1916). She had a balance of over $31,400,000 in one bank alone. She was so mean that her son had to have his leg amputated because of the delays in finding a *free*

medical clinic. She herself lived off cold oat-meal because she was too mean to heat it, and died of apoplexy in an argument over the virtues of skimmed milk."

5. *The Most and Least Drinkers.* "The freest alcohol drinkers are the white popula-tion of South Africa, with 2.05 U.S. gallons of proof alcohol per person per year, and the most abstemious are the people of Belgium with ⅛ of a U.S. gallon per person. It was esti-mated in 1969 that 13% of all males between 20 and 55 years of age in France were suffer-ing from alcoholism. In the U.S. in 1972, con-sumption of distilled spirits reached an all-time high of 1.9 gallons per person, due, it is said, to increased usage of gin and vodka."

6. *The Most Hanging Attempts.* "The only man in Britain to survive 3 attempts to hang him was John Lee at Exeter Gaol, Devonshire, England, on February 23, 1885. Lee had been found guilty of murdering, on November 15, 1884, Emma Ann Whitehead Keyse of Bab-bacombe, who had employed him as a foot-man. The attempts, in which the executioner, James Berry, failed 3 times to get the trap open, occupied about 7 minutes. Sir William Harcourt, the Home Secretary, commuted the sentence to life imprisonment. After release, Lee emigrated to the U.S. in 1917, was mar-ried and lived until 1933."

7. *The Longest Survival on a Raft.* "The longest recorded survival alone on a raft is 133 days (4½ months) by 2nd Steward Poon Lim (born, Hong Kong) of the U.K. Merchant Navy, whose ship, the S.S. *Ben Lomond*, was torpedoed in the Atlantic 750 mi. off the Azores at 11:45 A.M. on November 23, 1942. He was picked up by a Brazilian fishing boat off Salinas, Brazil, on April 5, 1943, and was able to walk ashore. In July, 1943, he was awarded the British Empire Medal."

8. *The Most Successful Complainer.* "Ralph Charell, a New York network television execu-tive, claims to have been successful in collect-ing for every misadventure that has damaged him. His total receipts in settlement for such complaints as poor telephone and car rental service, gas and electric overcharges, failure to deliver on time, imperfect goods, improper in-stallation, landlord disputes, and the like, have come to $75,591.22 as of July 24, 1973—and he is still complaining!"

9. *The Upside Down Record.* "The longest period of time for which a modern painting has hung upside down in a public gallery un-noticed is 47 days. This occurred to *Le Bateau*, by Henri Émile Benoît Matisse (1869–1954) of France, in the Museum of Modern Art, New York City, between October 18 and De-cember 4, 1961. In this time 116,000 people had passed through the gallery."

10. *The Longest Prison Sentences.* "The

longest recorded prison sentences were ones of 7,109 years, awarded to 2 confidence trick-sters in Iran (formerly Persia) on June 15, 1969. The duration of sentences are propor-tional to the amount of the defalcations in-volved. A sentence of 384,912 years was de-manded at the prosecution of Gabriel March Grandos, 22, at Palma de Mallorca, Spain, on March 11, 1972, for failing to deliver 42,768 letters.

"Richard Honeck was sentenced to life im-prisonment in the U.S. in 1899, after having murdered his former schoolteacher. It was re-ported in November, 1963, that Honeck, then aged 84, who was in Menard Penitentiary, Chester, Ill., was due to be paroled after 64 years in prison, during which time he had re-ceived one letter (a 4-line note from his brother in 1904) and 2 visitors, a friend in 1904 and a newspaper reporter in 1963. He was released on December 20, 1963.

"Juan Corona, a Mexican-American, was sentenced to 25 consecutive life terms for mur-dering 25 migrant farm workers he had hired, killed, and buried in 1970–1971 near Feather River, Yuba City, Calif., on February 5, 1973, at Fairfield, Calif."

JOSEPH NATHAN KANE'S 12 BEST ODDITIES

Joseph Nathan Kane, a noted research histo-rian, published the 1st edition of his renowned reference book, *Famous First Facts*, in 1933. Four decades of original research since then have brought many additional obscure items to light, featured in later editions of his book as well as in his own syndicated newspaper col-umn.

1. *A Parachute Wedding.* The site of the 1st parachute wedding was the World's Fair, New York City, on August 25, 1940. "Reverend Homer Tomlinson of the Church of God, Ja-maica, Long Island, N.Y., performed the mar-riage ceremony for Arno Rudolphi and Ann Hayward. The minister, the married couple, the best man, the maid of honor and 4 musi-cians were all suspended in parachutes."

2. *The Origin of Circus Tights.* "Tights (circus) are believed to have been introduced in 1828 by Nelson Hower, a bareback rider in the Buckley and Wicks Show, as the re-sult of a mishap. The performers wore short jackets, knee breeches and stockings, but How-er's costume failed to arrive and he appeared for the show in his long knit underwear."

3. *The 1st Glass Dress.* In 1893, a dress of spun glass was made for Georgia Cayven from 12 yds. of glass cloth (at $25 a yard). The manufacturer was the E. D. Libbey Glass Com-pany, Toledo, O., who exhibited it at the World's Columbian Exposition, Chicago, Ill.

"The cloth was made into a dress for her, but was not practical for wearing purposes."

4. *Over Niagara Falls in a Ball.* "The 1st person to go over Niagara Falls in a rubber ball was Jean Lussier who made the descent July 4, 1928, in a ball of his own construction weighing 750 lbs. and costing $1,485. It was equipped with oxygen tanks and reinforced with cushions. It was set adrift from a launch and went over the Horseshoe Falls."

5. *Honoring an Insect.* The citizens of Enterprise, Ala., dedicated the 1st monument to an insect on December 11, 1919, "in profound appreciation of the Boll Weevil and what it has done as the herald of prosperity." Because of the destruction that the weevils caused, farmers were forced to diversify their crops, resulting in a tripling of their income over the best cotton years.

6. *Mail through the Snow.* "The 1st international dog sled mail left Lewiston, Me., on December 20, 1928, in charge of Alden William Pulsifer, postmaster of Minot, Me., and arrived January 14, 1929, at Montreal, Canada. A regular 8' mushing sled weighing 200 lbs. was pulled by 6 blackhead Eskimo dogs. They averaged 9 mph. . . . The mail pouch contained 385 letters which were placed in government-stamped canceled envelopes. The trip was not an official one. The sled returned to Lewiston on February 2nd, passing through 4 States and provinces and 118 cities, covering 600 mi. of which 90% was barren of snow."

7. *Packaging Rattlesnake Meat.* George Kenneth End of Arcadia, Fla., packed the 1st rattlesnake meat in March, 1931. "On April 9, 1931, canned rattlesnake meat was served at a dinner to American Legionnaires at the Hillsboro Hotel, Tampa, Fla. End founded and became president of the Floridian Products Corporation which made its 1st sale of canned rattlesnake May 22, 1931."

8. *The 1st Presidential Car Ride.* Theodore Roosevelt was the 1st President to ride in an automobile. Accompanied by Col. Jacob Lyman Greene, he rode in a purple-lined Columbia Electric Victoria on August 22, 1902, through the streets of Hartford, Conn. The presidential car was followed by 20 carriages in a tour of Hartford.

9. *The Flea Circus.* "The 1st flea circus was an 'Extraordinary Exhibition of the Industrious Fleas' at 187 Broadway, New York City, which opened January, 1835. Admission was 50¢ and performances were given from 11 A.M. to 3 P.M. . . . A cold spell forced the exhibit to close to enable the exhibitor 'to fill up the vacancies that grim death had made.' It was reopened January 20, 1835, for one week."

10. *The Church on Water.* In 1843, the world's 1st floating church was constructed. The Floating Church of Our Savior was moored in the East River at the foot of Pike Street in New York City. "The church was organized by the Young Men's Church Missionary Society, an auxiliary of the City Mission Society. The society dissolved in 1844 and deeded the church to the Protestant Episcopal Church Missionary Society for Seamen in the City and Port of New York which emanated from it. The 1st clergyman was the Rev. Benjamin Clarke Cutler Parker, who was called by the title of 'missionary,' rather than clergyman. In 1906 the corporate title was changed to Seaman's Church Institute of New York."

11. *Artificial Snow.* "The 1st artificial snow from a natural cloud was produced November 13, 1946, by Vincent Joseph Schaefer of the General Electric Company who flew in an airplane over Mt. Greylock, Mass. He dispensed small dry-ice pellets over a tract about 3 mi. long from a height of about 14,000'. Snow fell an estimated 3,000' but because of the dry condition of the atmosphere beneath the cloud, it evaporated before reaching the ground. Previously, he produced snow in a cold chamber on July 12, 1946."

12. *The 1st News Photographs.* Mathew Brady of New York City, with the permission of Abraham Lincoln and the U.S. Secret Service, traveled with the Union Army. He took over 7,000 photos, 2,000 of which the Government bought for $25,000. They were the 1st news photographs of distinction. Brady had his own studio, Brady's Daguerrean Miniature Gallery, which he opened in 1844 at Broadway and Fulton streets in New York.

R. BRASCH'S 9 BEST ODDITIES

Rabbi Dr. R. Brasch, an Australian scholar in theology, history, philosophy, as well as a linguist, an author, broadcaster, lecturer, has gained world renown for his books, *How Did It Begin?*, *How Did Sports Begin?*, *How Did Sex Begin?*

1. *Why Is the Color Blue Used for Boys and Pink for Girls?* Since babies look alike, it was long ago decided to identify their sexes through use of different colors. In ancient times, it was believed that evil spirits menaced the well-being of infants. It was also believed that evil spirits were allergic to certain colors, especially to blue. According to Dr. Brasch: "It was considered that the association of blue with the heavenly sky rendered satanic forces powerless and drove them away. Even in our own time Arabs in the Middle East continue to paint the doors of their homes blue to frighten away demons. Thus, the display of blue on a young child was not merely an adornment but a necessary precaution."

On the other hand, since female babies

were considered inferior, it was felt they required no special color to protect them. In later times, parents became very much -conscious of the neglect of girls and introduced for them the new "pink" look.

2. *Why Did the Best Man Originally Accompany the Bride and Not the Groom?* At the beginning of history, the best man attended a wedding heavily armed. His duty was to stay with the bride and protect her against other men who might capture her for their own purposes.

Warriors who wanted a bride of their own would "set out with their companions—to wrest the bride from her original groom. . . . It was for this reason, too, that Scandinavians used to hold their weddings under the cover of night. Behind the High Altar of one of the Swedish churches, so it was said, were kept lances with sockets for torches. These served the Best Men in their hazardous task, as weapons and sources of illumination, to detect and repel possible abductors."

As the centuries passed, and the danger of the bride's being kidnapped decreased, only then did the best man escort the groom, while the bridesmaids accompanied the bride.

3. *What Was the Origin of the Halo?* Surprisingly, the halo is both pagan and un-Christian in origin. Many centuries before Christ, natives decorated their heads with a crown of feathers. "They did so to symbolize their relationship with the sun-god: their own 'halo' of feathers representing the circle of light that distinguished the shining divinity in the sky. Indeed, people came to believe that by adopting such a 'nimbus' men turned into a kind of sun themselves and into a divine being."

Later in history, the Roman emperors who began to think of themselves as divine beings wore a crown in public to imitate the sphere of light from the sun.

The need to preserve art objects also added to the development of the halo. "Statues were kept not in museums but in the open. Therefore they were subject to deterioration through various causes. To protect them from the droppings of birds, the rain and the snow, a circular plate—either of wood or brass—was fixed upon their heads!"

4. *Why Does a Person Join His Hands When Praying?* The joining of hands during prayer does not have a religious derivation. It is not even mentioned in the Bible, nor did it become part of the Christian tradition until the 9th century. Until that time, in both Hebrew and Christian worship, the most common posture of prayer involved the spreading of arms and hands toward heaven.

The joining of hands "leads back to men's early desire to subjugate each other and developed out of the shackling of hands of prisoners!

"Though the handcuffs eventually disappeared, the joining of hands remained as a symbol of man's servitude and submission and his inability (or even lack of inclination) to grasp a weapon."

Christianity adopted "the gesture representing shackled hands as a sign of man's total obedience to divine power."

5. *What Is the Origin of the Expression "To Peg Out"?* The phrase "to peg out" owes its origin to the game of croquet. In the early part of the 20th century, 2 sticks (officially called "pegs") were introduced into the game, and a player had to strike them while making the winning stroke.

"Then, in 1922, to make the game more difficult, one of the pegs was removed from the play and the other moved into the center, a practice claimed 1st to have been introduced in Australia. The winning hit had to touch the peg. The game was finished, and one 'pegged out.' The term was then transferred (so croquet lovers assert) from their lawn to life. When the 'game' is over, you 'peg out.' "

6. *Why Is the Diameter of the Golf Cup 4¼ Inches?* The diameter of the golf cup evolved purely by chance. "Two golfers on the St. Andrews links found that one hole was so badly worn that they could not use it. Much of its sand had been removed by previous players for building tees. Anxious to repair the damage and continue their game, they looked around and discovered nearby part of an old drainpipe. They inserted this in the hole. It was the 1st 'cup,' and because it happened to measure 4¼" across, all cups are now that size."

7. *What Made the British Make Male Homosexuality a Punishable Offense but Not Lesbianism?* The basis of the British acceptance of lesbianism has a historical origin dating back to the Greek philosopher Parmenides (c. 450 B.C.), who believed that female homosexuality was a natural behavior. Many theories were presented over the centuries to justify lesbianism, including heredity, glandular imbalance, and a lack of opportunity to meet and socialize with the opposite sex.

"While still in modern times male homosexuality has been the cause of much abhorrence, public outcry, and numerous prosecutions, lesbianism, through the ages, has been tolerated and very rarely proscribed by law. Indeed, its very omission in British legislation, it has been claimed, was due to a queen's whim (or ignorance). When an Act of Parliament was about to be passed and duly presented for signature to Queen Victoria, she had been greatly upset that her own sex was suspected of practicing the abominable vice of homosexuality. In protest, she had struck out the passage concerning women. It has never been restored."

8. *Why Does X Stand for a Kiss?* There are several theories of why X has come to represent a kiss. One hypothesis looks at the mathematical meaning of X, where it can signify zero or "(an) infinity (of delight)." It can also "multiply" love and joy.

"However, the prosaic explanation of this romantic sign may be twofold. Originally it represented the formalized, stylized pictures of 2 mouths × touching each other—X. But then, a little more complicated, the kiss entered the cross by a chain of events and really owes everything to men's lack of education.

"Early illiterates signed documents with a cross. They did so for an obvious reason. A cross was so simple to draw, and yet, being also a sacred symbol, implied the promise of truth. But to solemnly confirm further the veracity of what had been endorsed thus, the writer kissed his 'signature,' as he was accustomed to do with the holy book. And that is how, finally, by its very association, the cross came to be identified with a kiss."

9. *What Is the Origin of the White Floral Buttonhole Worn by the Bridegroom?* "In Anglo-Saxon times, men accompanying the groom fastened their, then still buttonless, jackets with a ribbon which they pulled through holes in the lapels. The knot they tied, they were convinced, not only secured their garment around the neck but, much more significantly, would act as a love charm: tying magically together the groom and the bride."

Even though modern jackets have buttons, thus eliminating the need for ribbons, the buttonhole has nevertheless been preserved. "The white flower now pinned into it by the male members of the bridal party takes the place of the original loveknot, adding to its own fertility spell."

BRAD STEIGER'S 7 BEST ODDITIES

Brad Steiger has published more than 40 books and innumerable articles on paranormal subjects. His best-known works include *Mysteries of Time and Space*, *The Psychic Feats of Olof Jonsson*, and *Revelation: The Divine Fear*.

1. *The Mysterious 3¢ Piece.* "In Autumn of 1956, just a few weeks after our marriage, my wife was walking across the bedroom floor of our apartment when she suddenly complained that something was in her shoe, and shook out not a pebble nor a bead, but an 1852 silver 3¢ piece."

2. *The Ancient Sandal Prints.* In Antelope Springs, U., in 1968, fossilized sandal prints were discovered. "One print had a squashed trilobite embedded in it. According to paleontology, this would indicate that someone was walking about in sandals more than 500 million years before man is supposed to have evolved."

3. *The Aged Stones.* "Off the Atlantic Coast of the U.S. are over 50 sites composed of megalithic blocks of stone at least 10,000 years old." There is speculation that these blocks may be remnants of the lost continent of Atlantis.

4. *The Half-Million-Year-Old "Spark Plug."* An object was found in the Cosco Mountains of California which had a striking resemblance to an everyday spark plug. "According to a geologist who viewed the encrustation of fossil shells that enveloped it, the object would have to be at least 500,000 years old."

5. *The Unexplained TV Image.* "The image of a hand was photographed as it appeared on the screen of a television set on Christmas Eve, 1968. One catch, however; the set was unplugged at the time."

6. *The Grand Canyon Mystery.* "A man was photographed leaning over the brim of the Grand Canyon—7 years before he actually visited the site. The camera he would buy in 1955 is clearly visible in the film exposed in 1948."

7. *A Visit to a UFO.* In 1968, a patient in a Honolulu hospital was confined to his bed, with pins through his tibiae and femurs. Although he could not move, he informed a hospital orderly that he would leave the hospital for an hour that evening to visit friends on a UFO. "At bed check that evening the patient was found to have disappeared, *leaving the metal traction pins on his bed*. Military policemen made an extensive search of the hospital and the surrounding grounds but failed to produce any trace of the supposedly immobile man. When next the patient's room was checked, he was once again lying in traction, the pins back in place. He explained that he had been with his otherworldly friends, just as he had told the young orderly he would be."

GEORGE LAYCOCK'S 6 BEST ODDITIES

George Laycock, who holds a degree in wildlife management from Ohio State University, has published more than a dozen books on natural history and conservation. From 3 of these books—*Autumn of the Eagle*, *The Alien Animals*, and particularly *Strange Monsters & Great Searches*—all of which emphasize a naturalist's view of the unusual in human experience with animals, Laycock and the editors have selected half a dozen of the strangest true tales.

1. *The Prehistoric Fish That Lives Today.* "Millions of years before [giant dinosaurs ruled the earth], no vertebrate animals at all yet lived on land. All life was in the sea, and fishes were evolving from lower creatures. One step in this rise of animals has long drawn the attention of scientists. This is the mystery of how creatures of the seas finally came out onto land to live. Which of the fish fathered the land dwellers? What manner of creature ventured from those ancient seas millions of years ago to wander among the giant ferns and primitive plants?"

It was believed by many that the Coelacanth "gave rise to land creatures." Hundreds of fossils of this prehistoric fish were extant in museums. "It possessed, most interestingly of all perhaps, strange stumps connecting its fins to its body. These short stumps reminded scientists of beginning legs. . . ." With these fins the Coelacanth could not only swim, but walk the ocean floor and wade onto shore.

"When scientists discussed Coelacanths they spoke of them in the past tense. All evidence pointed toward a story that ended millions of years ago. Saber-toothed tigers were gone. Mammoths were gone. Dinosaurs were gone. . . . The Coelacanth, according to the records of the rocks, had lived 200 million years before the dinosaurs. . . . But they had started on their downward trail at least 100 million years ago. The youngest fossil remains of them were judged to be 70 million years old. No wonder scientists spoke of the Coelacanth as history. Any creature that has been gone for 70 million years is extinct indeed."

In December, 1938, the captain and crew of a trawler fishing off the southeast coast of Africa saw an unbelievable fish 250' below the surface of the Indian Ocean. It swam, but it also walked the ocean floor. The trawler's crew netted it and brought it aboard. They had seen nothing like it before. "Steel blue in color, the monster fish had large scales, weighed 125 lbs., and was 5' long. The crew members soon found that the fish was still alive. If they put a hand close to its gaping jaws, it grabbed for them with those snapping sharp teeth. It lived 4 more hours."

The captain took the creature to a local museum curator. Unable to identify it, she summoned Prof. J. L. B. Smith, an expert at the Albany Museum 25 mi. west of Grahamstown, South Africa. When Professor Smith saw the fish, he was stunned. "He felt as if he had stepped into a time capsule and been whisked back through the history of the earth 10 million years, 20 million, 70 million. Before him was the remains of a true Coelacanth. Only days before it had been alive. . . ."

Among the scientists of the world, the news caused a sensation. "This set in motion one of the most heartbreaking searches in all the world of natural history." Professor Smith was determined to find another Coelacanth, "one that was whole so specialists could study its organs and structure part by part. What facts such a specimen might reveal!" Professor Smith deduced how the fish had survived since prehistory, and where it might be found. Because of its slowness, "the Coelacanth must live in deep waters. Deep waters, rough rocky ledges, places where strong currents sweep food fish past those menacing jaws. That was not the kind of place where a trawl net could work, and it was not the kind of habitat found where the trawler had taken the strange fish."

Professor Smith prepared a circular, with a drawing of the fish, a £100 reward for the finder of the elusive creature, and a warning. "If you have the good fortune to catch or find one, do not cut or clean it in any way but get it whole at once to cold storage." Thousands of these circulars were distributed.

Fourteen years later, a fisherman, Ahmed Hussein, working 200 yds. off the shore, near the Comoro Islands in the Indian Ocean, hauled in a weird monster fish. Trying to sell it at the market, he was shown by a friend the yellowing circular offering a reward. Professor Smith was notified. In a special plane supplied by the Government, Professor Smith arrived. He unwrapped the fish. He stared at it. He recalled his emotions later. "I'm not ashamed to say that I wept. It was a Coelacanth." The odd fish that brought animal life to land had been found. "In the world of science, the Coelacanth has been hailed as the greatest biological discovery of the century."

2. *The Champion Eagle Bander.* Charles L. Broley, the "eagle man," made a major contribution to man's understanding of the bald eagle. By profession, Broley was a bank manager in Manitoba. But when he retired in 1938, and sought a hobby to occupy his time, he turned to birdwatching. Before long, his interest was focused on eagles, and he spent much of his time scaling trees in search of them.

"He would swing, spiderlike, on a web of fragile ropes, 100' above the earth, until he could secure a death grip on a jungle of sticks and heave himself into a nest of protesting— and sometimes threatening—birds."

Broley became concerned with the bald eagle after learning how land developers and irresponsible gunners had been driving them from their nesting trees. "The Florida eagles, prior to 1939, were also giving up a large share of their annual egg production to oologists, that band of incurable kleptomaniacs who took thousands of eggs from the nests of wild birds and kept them in carefully labeled storage cases."

There was also the unsolved mystery of why a sizable segment of the Florida eagle population would vanish from the State during the summer. No one knew where it went, or why it returned each fall.

A professional conservationist, Richard H. Pough, issued Broley 4 eagle bands and a banding permit. "Try banding some nestlings," Pough suggested. And then he quickly added, "Find a boy to do your climbing." Shinnying up trees was not an advisable pastime for retired bankers so far as Pough was concerned.

Traveling south to Tampa, Broley decided to do his own climbing, and he set out to design his own climbing equipment. "Next he began building a rope ladder with 2 long pieces of rope, between which he fitted 12″ sections of wood as steps."

But Broley had severe problems securing this ladder in nesting trees. He used weights and pulleys for a while. "Later refinements of this system included a slingshot, which Broley handled with uncanny accuracy, and a fisherman's large casting reel to keep the line from tangling."

Once the ladder was in place and Broley had climbed to the top, he encountered his most serious problem. "No man is welcomed to the home of an eagle." Nevertheless, Broley would actually climb into the nest, grab the reluctant bird's left wing, hold it down with his knee, and then grope for its left foot to attach the aluminum band.

"The 1st year Broley banded 44 eagles, more than had ever been banded before in all of Florida. Broley began to get occasional returns from his banded eagles, and from surprisingly distant points. More than ⅓ of the recovered bands were taken from eagles 1,000 mi. or more up the eastern seaboard from their home nests."

Broley continued banding eagles for 12 years. He did all his banding in Florida, and spent his summers in Ontario where he "trained" for the work ahead of him. "When I could chin myself 18 times without pausing, I figured I was ready to climb again," he said.

Broley never fell from a tree nor was he ever injured by an eagle. During his remarkable retirement career, "he banded more than 1,200 eagles. His eagle work ended with the 1958 season. He had searched as diligently as ever along the same 100 mi. of coast where a short time ago he had banded as many as 150 eagles a year. But at the end of the season he had located only one young bald eagle on which to place a band."

In the spring of 1959, Broley died, "not by falling 100′ from the top of a longleaf pine tree, but while fighting a brush fire near his home in Canada."

3. *The Acclimatizers.* As he looked around the city of Cincinnati in 1872, Andrew Erkenbrecher was depressed by the fact that he did not see the "wonderful little songbirds that had brightened the days of his youth back in Germany. Being a man of action, Erkenbrecher promptly embarked on a bold plan to correct this oversight. He would bring to Cincinnati the songbirds of Europe—and thus render this city on the banks of the Ohio a little more bearable for human beings."

Erkenbrecher, who had come from Germany at age 15 and had amassed a large fortune, arranged to import a large shipment of European birds to the U.S., never thinking of the immense problems that might be involved in the project. He announced that he would spend $5,000 to bring these birds to Cincinnati, adding, "It may be expected that the ennobling influence of the song of birds will be felt by the inhabitants."

Actually, over a 2-year period, Erkenbrecher spent $9,000 buying and transporting his songbirds, at an average of about $4.50 per pair. Four thousand birds were imported, including the robin redbreast, the wagtail, the skylark, the starling, the dunnock, the blackbird, the goldfinch, the nightingale, the song thrush, the great tit, the dutch tit, the Hungarian thrush, the missel thrush, the crossbill, the siskin, the dipper, the corncrake, and even some house sparrows.

"To acclimatize these imports to Cincinnati conditions, the Cincinnati Acclimatization Society housed them in the garret of a towering old mansion standing in a part of the city known as Burnet Woods. Then, on a morning in May, Erkenbrecher and some of his bird-loving associates released the immigrants from their lengthy captivity."

There was considerable excitement as the birds flew into the warm blue skies that day. But gradually, the birds began to disappear. "For all the fine intentions of this and similar acclimatization societies across this land and others, failure greeted their efforts more often than success."

The ironic thing is that there were many birds already native to Cincinnati of which Erkenbrecher was apparently unaware. In the early 1800s, John J. Audubon had worked in Cincinnati and he was impressed with the variety of bird life in the Ohio River Valley. More than 300 species had been recorded, including songbirds like wood thrushes, orioles, low-breasted chats, and warblers.

Still Erkenbrecher insisted on importing the European birds, all for nought. In its 1884 bulletin, the Cincinnati Society of Natural History listed the birds that he had brought to America, and added, "While we deem the above facts of sufficient ornithological importance to merit a record in permanent form, and cannot but admire the sentiment which promoted the introduction of these birds, we may properly at some time express the opinion that the general principle is, zoologically speaking, a wrong one. . . ."

4. *An Octopus to Remember.* Some years ago, early-morning strollers on the beach at St. Augustine, Fla., came upon a strange form that remains a center of controversy even today. The shapeless mass, which apparently had washed ashore during the night, had no head by the time it reached the sand, and its legs were only stumps. Some strollers thought it might be a dead elephant, but it was apparently a sea creature. Everyone agreed that they had never seen anything like it before.

"One of the 1st scientists to study it and venture an opinion on its identity, according to F. G. Wood writing in *Natural History* magazine, was Prof. A. E. Verrill of Yale University. The professor was known worldwide as an authority on giant squid of the ocean depths. But what Professor Verrill suggested about the monster lying lifeless on the St. Augustine beach sounded farfetched. He thought at 1st that it might be a giant octopus.

"But the more he thought about this the more unlikely the whole idea seemed. Finally he declared publicly that he had changed his opinion."

Verrill's change of mind was understandable, since no giant octopus is recorded in science. There are 140 different species of octopi, and the largest one is often said to be *Octopus dofleini* of the North Pacific, which has an arm span of about 20'. But even this biggest of known species is much smaller than the creature found on the Florida beach that morning.

For over 2 months, the monster lay there on the sand, decaying with time. "Samples of it were taken and shipped off to the Smithsonian Institution and the museum at Yale University. . . . Once or twice the creature was moved. One time an investigating scientist using a dozen men and block and tackle, stretched it out the better to measure it. The remaining parts measured 21' long, and weighed an estimated 6 tons. As the creature continued to weather in the tropic air the hide grew so tough that an ax would not penetrate its 3"-thick skin, but would instead simply bounce off."

Decades after the creature was found, scientists still speculated on what it might be. Dr. Joseph F. Gennaro, Jr., a biologist, wrote in *Natural History* how he compared microscope slides of the creature's tissue with samples of both octopus and giant squid. He concluded that the "monster" washed ashore was the largest octopus ever to be measured. The arms of the creature were eventually judged to have once measured 100'. "From the tip of one tentacle to the tip of an opposing one it could have stretched across 200' of ocean."

Still, authorities continue to debate whether the monster really was a giant octopus. Dr. Gilbert L. Voss, an expert on cephalopods at the Rosensteil School of Marine and Atmospheric Science, University of Miami, doubts that it was. He notes that the soft body of an octopus decays quickly when exposed to the sun and wind. But the St. Augustine monster turned tough instead, leading Dr. Voss to conclude that it might have been the remains of a whale or a shark.

"In a sense, it is too bad that the men of science do not solemnly agree that the creature was indeed a giant octopus. Without such a monster the depths of the sea lose some of their mystery. One might like to know that down there somewhere there really is an octopus with a 200' reach, providing, of course, one did not come face to face with it."

5. *Feathered Monsters.* When explorers of the 15th, 16th, and 17th centuries embarked on voyages for new lands and continents, they often found wild animals and birds which were unknown in their own homeland. When Portuguese sailors landed on the island of Mauritius in 1507, they found one of the strangest beasts of all—the dodo—which "looked as if it had been designed by a prankster playing a joke on naturalists."

The dodo, which weighed about 50 lbs., had a somewhat round-shaped body perched upon short, yellow legs. "Its wings were small; they would not begin to lift that great weight from the ground. Its tiny tail was a curled plume, standing up like a little feather duster. The bird's head was dominated by its bill, 9" long, thick, and hooked on the end. Unlike the crow or jay, this bird seemed slow-witted, not very bright at all. This shortcoming was hidden behind a comical look on its face."

The poor dodo stumbled clumsily when it moved through the forest, with its undercarriage dragging on the ground. He was easy to capture, and since he weighed 3 times as much as a turkey, it was thought that he'd provide a bit of fresh meat for hungry sailors. But the bird was difficult to chew; the longer it simmered in the boiling pot, the tougher it became.

Since the dodo was too heavy to propel himself into flight, his wings were used primarily for fighting. "As they rushed upon each other, the pounding of their wings against the flesh of their neighbors resounded through the forest like claps of thunder."

In 1599, when Comdr. Jacob Van Neck landed on Mauritius, he decided to bring a dodo back to Europe with him. "The ponderous bird, fat and unbelievable, soon became a favorite wherever it was displayed."

But when Mauritius, located near Madagascar, was colonized by Holland in 1644, the dodo's fate was sealed. With the colonist came "hogs, dogs, cats, and people, all of which would consume dodos and their young or eggs . . . [the dodo] is believed to have become extinct about 1681. . . ."

Once the dumb and ugly dodo was gone, there was little evidence that it had ever existed at all. A few European artists had painted pictures of it, but there was only one stuffed dodo which ended up in a museum in Oxford, England.

"There, when the staff was cleaning up the place one day, someone noticed the old stuffed dodo. What a ratty-looking specimen it was! The feathers were broken, rough, and out of place. Its general run-down appearance was enough to make a tidy museum staff feel shame and chagrin."

The museum director, after examining the tired specimen, ordered his staff, "Take the bird out and dispose of it." The last known dodo was burned to ashes, but somehow its head and one leg were saved before it was fed to the flames.

In 1865, in a muddy swamp on Mauritius, a collection of preserved dodo bones was uncovered. "From these spare parts museum workers assembled skeletons of the bird. These became the foundations for restorations, or man-made dodos. Today, you may see in a museum what appears to be a preserved dodo, but it will be only the work of a clever taxidermist who has assembled a counterfeit model of one of the most remarkable big birds that the world ever knew."

6. *The Abominable Snowman.* In the massive Himalayas, above the 13,000' elevation, the snow is so heavy and the wind blows so cold that it seems unlikely that any living creature could ever inhabit the area. But there is an ever-increasing number of stories to refute that theory.

"Col. L. A. Waddel was exploring the slopes of Mt. Everest, the world's highest peak, in 1887. When he came down he reported unidentified footprints. Three years later another climber reported having seen the prints again. This time they were at an elevation of 18,500'. The tracks led uphill and vanished among the boulders. Russian soldiers reported shooting and killing such a creature in their mountain country in 1925."

The stories have continued through the years. In 1942, a Polish soldier fleeing from a Russian prison camp via the Himalayas encountered 2 manlike creatures 100 yards from him. "He estimated them to be 8' high and said they had massive arms, square heads, and were covered with thick coats of brown fur."

Tibetan tribesmen believe these bizarre creatures have lived there for centuries. They have names for them—the most popular is "Yeti." But the strange beings are more commonly known as "Abominable Snowmen."

There is continuing speculation over what these creatures really are. "Maybe giant bears. Some insisted and even said they belonged to the species *Ursus arctos isabellinus.* But the Abominable Snowman, as proved by his footprints, walks on 2 feet. Bears can walk on 2 feet but do not do so for more than a few steps. They are definitely not known to go leaping about snowfields on their hind feet.

"Others claim that the mysterious tracks in the snow were left by a langur monkey. But these creatures are too small, and besides, they, too, walk on all 4 feet."

Italian explorer A. N. Tombazi encountered the Abominable Snowman while climbing the Himalayas in 1925. He later wrote, "Unquestionably, the figure in outline was exactly upright, and stopping occasionally to uproot some dwarf rhododendrons. It showed dark against the snow and wore no clothing."

Tombazi as well as some subsequent explorers have sighted footprints of the creature. Eric Shipton spotted tracks in 1936 and again in 1951, and photographed them the 2nd time. The foot that he photographed had 4 toes, so it couldn't have been that of a bear.

Two Norwegians are said to have come upon 2 sets of tracks in 1948. They followed them and came upon a pair of "Yeti."

"But what the Norwegians are said to have done next was not exactly the approved way of capturing an Abominable Snowman; they tried to lasso it. This effort failed and we are spared details of why or how. The Norwegians came down the mountain and reported that the Abominable Snowman looks a lot like a large ape."

From the many reported sightings of the Snowmen, a composite portrait can be made. The feet are at least 12"–14" long, and are quite broad. Their hair is long and brownish, and hangs over their eyes. "Their heads are said to be pointed on top and their eyes are deeply sunken and reddish. Their light-colored faces are without hair, we are told, and not at all pretty, except perhaps to another Yeti. They do not have a tail. The feet, like most of the body, are covered with hair."

The dream of some explorers is to capture a Yeti, but no one can quite agree on what one would do with it after it was seized. "Although these may be primitive manlike creatures, as some seriously believe, we have every reason to suspect that they want no part of our cherished civilization. As we look about us, this is sometimes understandable."

SANDERS, GIRLING, DAVIES, AND SANDERS' 10 BEST ODDITIES

Deidre Sanders, Dick Girling, Derek Davies, and Rick Sanders, collaborated to produce one of the top odd-fact books published in Great Britain. It was entitled *Would You Believe It?*, "Useless information you can't afford to be without," and it appeared in 1973.

1. "There was once a Society for the Prevention of People Being Buried Alive, and a number of devices were patented to help further the members' aims. The simplest of these was an ordinary electric bell, by means of which anyone who woke up down below could raise the alarm. A more cynical device was a coffin fitted with nails which, when driven home, punctured capsules of poison gas."

2. "Guards at the jail at Alamos in Mexico have to serve out the sentences of any prisoners who escape while they are on duty."

3. "You share your birthday with at least 9 million others."

4. "Organized crime in the U.S. represents 1/10 of the national income."

5. "New Yorkers drink 2 million cups of coffee every 20 minutes."

6. "Cecil Rhodes [British South African who made a fortune in the Kimberley diamond mines and died in 1902, providing for the Rhodes Scholarships] left large sums of money in his 1st will to the cause of subverting the U.S. and bringing it back to its rightful place in the British Empire."

7. "The lives of 70% of the world's population are unviolated by newspapers, radio, television, or telephone."

8. "Among the personal effects left in King Farouk's palace after his flight from Egypt [after a military revolution in 1952] were: a number of pocket radiation counters, each inscribed 'Measure nuclear energy yourself'; a vast collection of American comic books; 6 bedside telephones; 50 walking sticks; 75 pairs of binoculars; 1,000 ties, many with 5" monograms; a series of photographs of copulating elephants; one of the largest stamp collections in the world; and a $20 double eagle which had disappeared some years previously from the museum of the Philadelphia Mint."

9. "If you subtract 40 from the number of times a cricket chirps in a minute, divide by 4 and add 50 to the result, you have the temperature Fahrenheit."

10. "Only 7 men have ever known the formula for Coca-Cola. Today only 2 men are in on the secret, and they take the precaution of never traveling in the same aircraft. The company's advertising budget is believed to

have totaled by now more than $35 million—roughly equivalent to the cost of providing one free bottle to every family in the world. During W.W. II, American servicemen swallowed 10 million bottles of Coke a day. Now 90 million are drunk every day in 158 countries."

THOMAS R. HENRY'S 10 BEST ODDITIES

Thomas R. Henry, a leading science writer and Pulitzer Prize winner, published *The Strangest Things in the World* (Public Affairs Press, Washington, D.C., 1958), a compendium of nature's paradoxes, curiosities, contradictions.

1. *A Spider 9' Long.* " 'With other classes of animals, and even with plants, man feels a certain kinship—but spiders are not of his world. Their strange habits, ethics, and psychology seem to belong to some other planet where conditions are more monstrous, more active, more insane, more atrocious, more infernal than on our own. Frightfulness and ruthlessness appear a part of their nature and we stand appalled when it dawns upon us that they are far better armed and equipped for their life work than we for ours.'

"Thus writes Dr. W. E. Stafford, U.S. Department of Agriculture naturalist. There probably is quite general agreement with his sentiments. One chills at the picture of some other planet where spiders and their kind, who have evolved minds equal to that of humans, are the dominant animals.

"Once gigantic spiderlike creatures ruled this world. They were as big as lions or gorillas. Their realm was the earth of the Silurian geological era of 350 million years ago—a time of warm, quiet seas which, especially in the northern hemisphere, covered large areas that now are dry land. These creatures were the euripterids, or sea scorpions, whose nearest extant relatives are the horseshoe crabs with sky-blue blood that are common along the Atlantic coast of the U.S., and the venom-fanged land scorpions. They exceeded in size all living invertebrate animals.

"Many were 5' to 6' long; one was 9' long. Presumably they were free-swimming, predacious creatures with massive, crushing jaws. Their chief prey, it is believed, were the much smaller, crablike trilobites with whom they shared a common ancestry. These were shelled animals, the imprints of whose hard shells in mud (which later became rock) are among the most ancient records of animal life on this planet. The trilobites were creatures who crawled on shallow sea bottoms. Their only defense was to roll themselves in balls. They appear to have been the dominant form of life for at least 100 million years."

2. *The Flower That Grows through Solid Ice.* "A plant that drills through several inches

of solid ice to bloom in early spring is the blue moonwort of the Swiss Alps. It belongs to the primrose family. In autumn it develops thick, leathery leaves. These lie flat on the ground, expectant of the snow and ice sheet that may cover them to a depth of several feet.

"When spring arrives and the hot sun melts most of the snow and some of the ice, water trickles down to the rootlets and arouses growth in the sleeping plant. Internal combustion ensues with the floral tissues. The resulting heat melts the ice about the uprising flower buds and the stem pushes its way upward. More water flows to the roots and finally the plant tunnels a passage to the air and sunshine. . . . It undergoes the usual transformations, is fertilized by early bees, and forms many hundreds of wonderful blue flower groups which look as if they were beds over a thick layer of transparent ice. The leaves are now no longer thick and fleshy, but thin and papery. They yield up their carbon compounds as fuel to melt a tunnel through the ice and for the production of buds and blossoms on a flower stem above the ice mantle."

3. *Forests That Eat Meat.* "Relic groves of the great meat-eating forests of 150 million years ago still thrive on the floors of deep, warm seas.

"These are made up of plant-animals—predacious trees with red blood and hearts—the crinoids. There are about 700 extant, compared to more than a thousand extinct, species. For a hundred million years they were among the ocean's dominant life forms. Fossil crinoids, or 'stone lilies,' make up great marble beds in both America and Europe. In 1934 the Smithsonian Johnson expedition dredged 19 species, including 2 not hitherto known to science, from the bottom of the great Puerto Rico Deep.

"The crinoids are highly developed animals, although they look like plants. They can by no means be considered as a form of life on the dividing line of the animal and vegetable worlds. Rather they are animals which have taken on the superficial appearance of plants. They are very highly specialized animals—so much so that there are few places in the world where they can survive in great numbers.

"In life they usually are brilliantly colored. Judging from those that are found on the sea bottoms today, one of the ancient meat-eating forests must have presented a very colorful spectacle of red, green, purple, and yellow 'blossoms.'

"Most of them live in deep water. There are free-moving varieties as well as those that are fixed to the bottom with stems like plants. Until recent years few were recovered in good condition because of the tendency of one of these plant-animals to break itself to pieces when agitated. When brought up from the bottom to the deck of a ship the crinoid would proceed to break off the featherlike arms which make up the blossoms. This was its natural defense reaction in the depths. Its way of escape when one of its arms was seized by a fish was to break it off. Then it could grow another quite easily. As a matter of fact, this is the way the crinoid grows—one of the most wasteful processes of growth in nature. It breaks off one arm and grows 2 instead; but it cannot increase the number of its arms without discarding an old one.

"Another difficulty is that the gorgeous colors of the meat-eating flowers are fast only in salt water. They fade rapidly in air, fresh water, or alcohol so that there can be only a fleeting impression of the true coloration."

4. *Where Trees Are Square.* "A few miles north of the Panama Canal Zone is 'the valley of square trees.' This is the only known place in the world where trees have rectangular trunks. They are members of the cottonwood family. Saplings of these trees now are being grown at the University of Florida to find out if they retain their squareness in a different environment. It is believed, however, that the shape is probably due to some unknown but purely local condition. That the cause is deepseated is indicated by the fact that the tree rings, each representing a year's growth, also are square."

5. *The Special Language of Bees.* "Study of bee language now has advanced to differentiation of bee dialects. Some years ago Dr. Karl von Fritsch of the University of Munich established the fact that bees actually possessed a means by which they could communicate with each other and without which the remarkable organization within the swarm would have been nearly inexplicable. Their language consists primarily of signs like that of deaf and dumb persons. Dr. von Fritsch reached the point where he could get some idea of what the bees were talking about and even predict their behavior from their conversation.

"Recently Dr. von Fritsch has found that different varieties have quite different languages, perhaps as far apart as French and German; one variety cannot tell what another is discussing. He has gone one step further—to the discovery that the insects probably talk also in sounds that are inaudible to the human ear. The audible buzzing is not a means of communication.

" 'There are indications,' he says in a report to the Rockefeller Foundation, 'that sounds, probably in the supersonic range, play a role in their communications.

" 'Physiologically it would be interesting to know how they judge distance. Their dances indicate with remarkable exactness the distance between the hive and the feeding place. How do they adjust themselves to the changing positions of the sun when they use it as a compass? Apparently they have an excellent memory for time, for they seem to know that the sun at a certain time will occupy a certain place in the heavens.' "

6. *Meet a Real Mermaid.* "The prototypes of the mermaids of legend are among the least known of all animals to naturalists because of their underwater habitat and their secretive habits. They are the manatees of the Caribbean region and the dugongs of the Indian Ocean. They constitute the only remaining species of the serenia, or moon creatures, distant relatives of the elephant. Both have a somewhat human facial appearance. They feed standing upright in the water, their flippers held out before them like arms. Sometimes the females hold their calves in these flippers. Seen from a distance, they have a curiously human appearance, which may account for the many reports of mermaids and mermen.

"This is especially true of the dugong—a creature of the open sea, with a white, almost hairless body. It is extremely secretive and has almost never been captured alive. When one is washed ashore or caught in a fisher's net it causes superstitious fear among the natives. The manatees are not so human in appearance and are much better known.

"The creatures seldom make their appearance above water in daylight. They prefer to graze in the moonlight, and this has added to their humanlike appearance which has given rise to the mermaid legends.

"One of the few persons to study the animal at close range, O. W. Barrett, an American explorer, tells us the following concerning the manatee:

" 'The animal still is fairly common in most freshwater bayous, lagoons, and rivers along the east coast of Nicaragua. . . .

" 'Families consisting of a bull, a cow, and one or 2 calves usually . . . merge into a herd of from 10 to 50 or more individuals living in a certain stretch of river, concentrating during the day and scattering at night. They generally graze at night, although a few individuals may be seen feeding in broad daylight. The body is held nearly vertical while grazing. The head is held well out of water, while the armlike flippers poke the grass toward the mouth. The noise made by the flapping of the huge upper lip and the crunching of the large teeth can be heard distinctly 200 yards or more away. The sound is much like that of horses grazing in a pasture. Adult manatees appear to average somewhere between 9' and 10' in length. Some—old females, presumably—may reach 12'.'

"A much more seclusive animal is the true mermaid of legend—the dugong of the open ocean. Unlike the manatee, it is a creature of the sea and seldom ventures into the freshwater rivers and lagoons. Few naturalists ever have actually seen one of the creatures. Mrs. Barrett's 1st acquaintance with the creature came in Mozambique, when some native fishermen caught in their net what they described as a 'white porpoise.' They were terrified and gladly presented their catch to an Italian blacksmith. This man crudely embalmed the animal, placed it in a rough coffin and freighted it to Johannesburg, where he rented a showroom and made a fortune exhibiting 'the only genuine mermaid—half fish, half human.' "

7. *A Crocodile with Life after Death.* "There is an animal that can bite—it might even slash off a man's arm—after it is dead. Alive it is relatively inoffensive. Being killed makes it positively mad.

"Its uncanny ability to bite half an hour or more after its neck has been broken is a major risk for followers of one of the most adventurous of professions—the jungle crocodile hunters. Their story is a saga paralleling that of the Antarctic whalers who 1st told of Moby Dick. One of the most expert of them is Dr. Fred Medem, Smithsonian collaborator and professor of zoology at the University of Bogotá. He has twice been bitten painfully by 'dead' reptiles.

"The animal is the caiman, smaller than either alligator or crocodile and probably more closely related to the former. Its hide, like that of its 2 fellow crocodilians, is valuable for leather and during the past few years it has been pursued close to extinction by professional hunters in Colombian and Brazilian jungles and lagoons. Dr. Medem is an eminent zoologist. He doesn't believe, of course, that any animal that is completely dead can bite off a man's arm, but he is hard put to explain what he himself has experienced. He thinks that part of the caiman's nervous system which activates its snout and mouth is somehow disconnected from the rest and does not die at the same time. Thus the dead reptile has no consciousness when it bites. It is a reflex action of one small segment of the nervous system that somehow is not completely dead."

8. *The Insect That Is Born Pregnant.* "Among nature's weirdest tricks is the strange phenomenon known as merokinosis, reported for a single family of almost microscopic insects. The little creatures are fathers and mothers before they are born. They are a species of mite which infests grass. They belong to a family which, almost alone among insects, gives birth to living young.

"Nearly all insects are egg layers. The eggs, usually deposited in enormous numbers, hatch outside the body of the mother. Then the individuals go through a series of metamorphoses—nymph, larva, and the like—before reaching their own reproductive maturity.

"These grass mites, however, are born fully adult animals. A sack on the body of the female swells until it is about 500 times the original body size. It is filled with eggs and a nutritive fluid. Within this sack the eggs hatch and the new generation passes through all the ordinary stages of insect metamorphosis. Finally, when they are fully mature, the mother dies, the sack breaks, and the host of new mites emerges.

"It was long thought that the mites were striking examples of parthenogenesis, or asexual reproduction. Females isolated as soon as they were born gave birth to large numbers of young. Parthenogenesis is not uncommon among the lower animals. Invariably however, except in this one case, all the offspring are of one sex. The supposedly virgin birth families of the mites contain both males and females in various proportions."

9. *The Plant That Strikes Men Dumb.* "A plant cultivated in the gardens of the Venezuelan National University at Caracas might well be a boon to pestered husbands and harassed mothers.

"It is described under the popular Spanish name of *planta del mudo*. It looks like sugarcane. According to the probably exaggerated claims, anybody who chews the stem is stricken dumb for at least 48 hours, presumably due to some paralyzing effect on some part of the vocal apparatus. It is not known whether anybody has tried to extract the marvelous talk-stopping principle.

"American botanists are unable to identify the plant. They explain, however, that the northern portion of South America long has been known as the world's greatest storehouse of plants with strange physiological effects. There is one, for example, alleged to grow hair on bald heads, another which makes everything look red."

10. *The Suicide Marches of Lemmings.* "Mass death marches of lemmings long have intrigued biologists and psychologists.

"The Lapland lemming is a short-tailed animal, related to the meadow mouse, that looks like a miniature rabbit. Through the sub-Arctic winter it lives completely buried under snow through which it burrows in search of mosses and lichens.

"It is extremely prolific; females produce 2 litters of from 4 to 6 offspring every year. The numbers soon become far too great to subsist on the sparse supply [of food] available in the Scandinavian mountains.

"Then, irregularly in periods of from 5 to 10 years, occurs one of the weirdest phenomena of animal life. Acting apparently on a common, subconscious, simultaneous impulse, the entire lemming population starts a mass migration out of the mountains to the lowlands. The animals proceed in a straight line, a few feet apart, each usually tracing a shallow furrow in the soil. They are a devouring scourge, stripping the earth of all vegetation in their path. Their progress seems irresistible. No obstacle stops them. If they come across a man they glide between his legs. If they meet with a haystack they gnaw through it. If a rock stands in their way they go around it in a semicircle and then resume the straight line of their march. When they come to a lake, river, or arm of the sea they swim directly across, vast numbers being drowned on the way. If they encounter a boat they climb over it, so as not to be diverted from a straight line. Curiously, they seem to avoid human habitations. They resist fiercely all efforts to stop them. They will bite a stick or hand, crying and barking like little dogs. Multitudes are destroyed every mile of the way. When the migrating horde reaches the sea it moves straight on—to inevitable destruction.

"A few linger behind and eventually make their way back to the mountain habitat. Numbers are so reduced that they are seldom observed. Then a new generation starts and builds up for the next migration."

WILLIAM IVERSEN'S 10 BEST ODDITIES

William Iversen, an executive editor at Fawcett Publications wrote *O the Times! O the Manners!* with the subtitle, "Being the lively and true histories of money, shaves and haircuts, bathing, toasts and toasting, swearing, dancing" (New York: William Morrow and Co., 1965).

1. *Price for a Girl: 3 Cows and a Bull.* "Like most primitive peoples, the cattle-keeping Africans originally had but 2 uses for money: to pay a debt of 'blood money' to the relatives of one's victims and to purchase wives. A girl in the medium-price range went for 3 cows and a bull, though most fathers were open to any reasonable deal and prices were scaled to the year and model. Since no clear distinctions were made between women and cattle, a man who preferred girls to cows could invest his wealth in wives and count himself fairly successful when he had between 6 and 10. As late as January, 1964, in fact, a Masai chief who was impressed with actress Carroll Baker's efforts to understand tribal ways offered to buy the blond movie star for 150 cows, 200 goats and sheep, and $750 in cash —a princely price considering that Masai maidens were currently valued at only $200 and 12 cows."

2. *Biggest Money in the World.* "The Pacific is the home of the biggest money in the world —the Great Stone Money of the Island of Yap. The larger denominations of this cumbersome currency stand 12′ high, weigh over a ton, and are cut in the shape of huge millstones. A hole in the center permits the native Yappers to trundle the smaller pieces of change around by means of stout wooden axles, but the really big money is kept on display outside the houses of the original owners. Title to a stone may be transferred by means of an inscription, and physical possession is not essential to ownership. One family traded for years on the hidden value of a huge wheel that had sunk into the sea while being transported from a Palau stone quarry 400 mi. away."

3. *The Squaw on the Indian Penny.* "The U.S. Mint's outlay for models' fees has been practically nil. Legend has it that when the eagle was selected as our national emblem the Philadelphia Mint adopted a live specimen named Peter, who posed for several early coins before he got tangled up in the Mint's machinery. Peter died as a result of his injuries, but he retained his Civil Service status through the thoughtfulness of fellow employees who had the bald bird stuffed.

"Though the Mint was not on a 1st-name basis with the bison who posed for the buffalo nickel, the Indian was long thought to be a chap named Two Guns Whitecalf. According to designer James Earle Fraser, however, the portrait was a composite of 3 other braves—Irontail, Two Moons, and a taciturn type with long braids who never did give his name.

"The Indian on the old penny was a pale-faced squaw named Sarah Longacre, daughter of a Mint official, while the Lincoln, Washington, Jefferson, Franklin, Roosevelt, and Kennedy coins were all done from portraits. When designer John Sinnock added his initials to the Roosevelt dime in 1946, word spread among the benighted that the tiny 'J.S.' stood for Joseph Stalin and was the work of subversives boring from within the Mint."

4. *William Became the Conqueror because of Haircuts.* "As a result of Paul's aversion to long hair, the clergy of the Roman Church had been tonsured since the 7th century. The shaved heads of monk and priest were so familiar a sight at the time of the Norman invasion of England that one of King Harold's spies, assigned to make a count of William's troops, mistook the close-cropped Normans for an army of priests sent to 'chant masses.' The erroneous intelligence, relayed to the English monarch, led to such a fatal misjudgment of Norman strength that William became the Conqueror."

5. *Why Men Walk on the Outside of a Woman.* "In 16th-century England, the habit of emptying chamber pots out of upper-story windows into the gutter made a city stroll so hazardous that gentlemen gallantly took the side nearest the curb when walking with their ladies—a position they have assumed ever since, without quite knowing why."

6. *Pompadour Used Perfume instead of Water.* "While French Kings and courtesans possessed baths of considerable splendor, bathing was extremely occasional and wariness of water continued into the 18th century, when the arts of powdering and perfuming reached their apogee. The Marquise de Pompadour spent an estimated £1 million a year on fragrances, and it was rumored that Du Barry secreted scented pads about her person in order to seduce Louis XV. Most people were quite content with their own natural aroma, however. When an outspoken lady friend told Samuel Johnson that he 'smelled,' the gamy and garrulous doctor had no quarrel with the intent of her statement but expressed great concern over her misuse of verbs. 'You *smell*,' he corrected; 'I *stink*.' "

7. *Origin of the Turkish Bath.* "Aristocratic British travelers, in the 18th century, were becoming more and more beguiled by the pleasures of the Islamic baths, or *hammams*. Their accounts glowed with poetic enthusiasm. 'It was ecstatic enjoyment, it was Elysium, nothing seemed wanting to perfect bliss,' one freshly bathed adventurer rhapsodized. Lady Mary Wortley Montagu (whose grimy hands were considered remarkable even by the French) attended a wedding reception at 'one of the finest baths in Constantinople,' where the young bridesmaids 'appeared without other ornament or covering than their own long hair braided with pearl or ribbon. . . . 'Tis not easy to represent to you the beauty of the sight,' she concluded, 'most of them being well proportioned and white skinned; all of them perfectly smooth and polished by frequent use of bathing. . . .'

"When Victoria took the throne in 1837, Windsor Castle was plagued with 53 overflowing cesspools. There were no baths at all in Buckingham Palace at the time of her coronation, and those of her subjects who thought such matters important made do with portable hip baths that had to be filled by hand. Reformers raised their voices against this deplorable lag in basic hygiene. 'We must have a standard of cleanliness as well as of truth,' David Urquhart pleaded. 'We must look for one tested by long experience and fixed from ancient days—this is The Bath.'

"The Bath, as Urquhart saw it, was nothing less than the complete Islamic treatment, with its emphasis upon cleansing the pores from within by means of perspiration as well as from without by means of soap and water. It was

Urquhart who named it the 'Turkish Bath,' and it was he who led the fight for the building of 2 large public baths in London—fitted, of course, with private cubicles_where proper Victorians could sweat in seemly solitude."

8. *The Day General Washington Cussed like a Trooper.* "In an earlier order issued by John Adams, naval officers were authorized to punish swearing sailors 'by causing them to wear a wooden collar or some shameful badge,' but such orders were generally ignored by American officers trained in the great British tradition of 'damn' and 'hell.' Washington's own conversation was reputed to be amply spiced with both of these gentlemanly oaths, though he seldom indulged in the hard profanity used in patriot ranks. According to the earwitness account of Gen. Charles Scott, however, Washington swore one day at Monmouth 'until the leaves shook on trees. Charming, delightful! Never have I enjoyed such swearing before or since. Sir, on that day, he swore like an angel from heaven.' "

9. *The Dance of Death.* "Legend has it that until quite recently the elders of Gaua, in the New Hebrides, came to the dance armed with bows and arrows and shot to kill any dancer who weakened the magic potency of the dance by so much as a single mistake. Under such exacting demands, dancing tended to become the full-time career of a professional caste, as it did in India, where temple dancers have traditionally dedicated their lives to the worship of dancing gods."

10. *A Dance That Speaks for Itself.* "Though divided into 4 regional types, all Indian dances developed from the same ancient source, and their every step and gesture is codified in the pages of the *Natya Sastra*—a book which is believed to contain the dance secrets of the gods. 'When the neck is moved backward and forward like the movement of a she-pigeon's neck, it is called *Prakampita*. Usage: To denote "You and I," folk-dancing, swinging, inarticulate murmurings and the sound uttered by a woman at the time of conjugal embrace.' The hand held in one position conveys no less than 30 possible meanings, including 'short man,' 'the massage of wrestlers,' 'holding the breasts of women,' 'saying "It is proper" ' and 'the flapping of elephant ears.' When the dancer's 3rd finger is doubled under the thumb, it may be construed as 'flower,' 'screw pine,' 'the union of man and woman,' or 'rubbing down a horse.'

"Over countless centuries, the Indian dance has perfected 39 such significant hand gestures and 45 eloquent eye movements, in addition to a numerous variety of postures, gaits, steps, jumps, and psychic conditions. All serve the purpose of storytelling dance dramas whose influence has spread through Asia to the islands of the South Seas, where the myths and legends told by a hula dancer's hands form a graceful counterpoint to her swaying hips and undulating torso. To the untutored eye of the mainland American, the story elements of the Hawaiian hula are considerably less interesting than the febrile footnotes of the dancer's pelvis, which speaks the same international language of *l'amour* that grandfather learned at carnival peep shows under the spangle-tossing tutelage of some itinerant Little Egypt."

JOHN GODWIN'S 5 BEST ODDITIES

John Godwin, an Australian who is now a resident of San Francisco, Calif., and who has authored 11 books, published *This Baffling World* (New York: Hart Publishing Co., 1968), "A documented account of the greatest puzzlements of all time—unexplained natural phenomena, historical happenings that still mystify, and people of extraordinary talents which defy comprehension," a work which became a best seller. Godwin has selected "my most baffling mysteries."

1. *The Firewalkers.* "On 3 continents and in 9 different countries I have watched men walk slowly through the length of pits filled with live coals, glowing embers or red-hot rocks. I checked their feet both before and after the ceremony and never discovered either a form of skin protection or even a trace of a blister. In Tahiti I threw a handkerchief into the pit and watched it turn to white ash in a flicker. But the natives who stalked across *both* ways gave no sign of discomfort, although the heat generated was such that none of the spectators could approach within 10 yards without getting their faces singed."

2. *The Ultimate Murder Mystery.* "On New Year's Day, 1963, 2 bodies were found in a lovers' lane by the Lane Cove River in Sydney, Australia. They belonged to Dr. Stanley Bogle, the country's top research physicist, and his girl friend. Both were partially undressed, but covered with newspapers. Since then the combined efforts of local police, the FBI, and Interpol have been unable to discover: (a) How they were killed; (b) Why they were killed; (c) Who killed them. This is the only case in the annals of criminology where *all* 3 of these salient questions have remained unanswered."

3. *She Sees without Eyes.* "For the past 8 years a Russian woman named Rosa Kuleshova has been giving demonstrations of eyeless sight at the Moscow Academy of Science. She is blindfolded by a lab assistant. Onlookers like myself check the bandages. Then, holding her 3rd and 4th right-hand fingers above the paper, she proceeds to read out whatever is placed

before her; fluently and without hesitation. This phenomenon is called 'dermo-optics' but to date no one—not even Rosa herself—has been able to fathom the physiological process involved."

4. *Who Were the Amazons?* "Ancient Greek, Persian, and Median chroniclers have given detailed descriptions of a female warrior state in Asia Minor. These reports, from a score of unconnected sources, tally so extensively that they could not have been figments of imagination. From them we know about Amazonian battle tactics, dress, art, and government, including the names of their queens. With the Roman era these accounts ceased—as if the Amazons had evaporated. Did this supposedly powerful nation really exist? And if so, what happened to extinguish it with barely a trace?"

5. *Miracle in Brooklyn.* "From 1865 until her death in 1910, Mollie Fancher was confined to her bed in a room in Brooklyn, N.Y. She was permanently paralyzed, completely blind, and able to use only one hand. During that period she developed psychic abilities that stunned panels of doctors. She 'read' books and newspapers held beyond her possible range of vision. She could invariably tell who rang the doorbell. If she didn't know their names she would give graphic descriptions of them. She harbored 5 distinct personalities, speaking in different languages, 2 of them in fluent French and Spanish of which the ordinary Mollie couldn't pronounce a word. She gave accounts of street accidents several blocks away —at the moment they were happening! No rational explanation of even one of her abilities has ever been advanced."

DOROTHY ROSE BLUMBERG'S 5 BEST ODDITIES

Dorothy Rose Blumberg, a Phi Beta Kappa with a Master's Degree from Columbia University, gained renown in oddity circles in 1969 with the publication of her fascinating book, *Whose What?* Her work was subtitled, "A reference book for all the strange expressions that have entered the American language."

1. *Aristotle's Lantern.* "The name applied to the bony mouth structure of sea urchins (*Echinoderma*), 1st described by the Greek philosopher Aristotle (384–322 B.C.) in his great work on natural history, the *Historia Animalium*.

"Echinoderm means prickle skinned, an appropriate term for the unlovely sea creature that looks like an oversized chestnut burr. Legless, living mouth downward on the ocean floor, the sea urchin depends for food on whatever is swept its way by the lowest currents. It belongs to the same family as the starfish, and

when dissected, shows the same 5-branched configuration. An outer skin covers a thin, globular shell divided into 5 sections. The prickles are attached to the shell by a ball-and-socket joint, and are used primarily for protection, sometimes for locomotion, occasionally for urging bits of food toward the mouth.

> The urchin has 5 hollow teeth inside [observed Aristotle], and in the middle of these teeth a fleshy substance serving the office of a tongue. . . . The mouth-apparatus of the urchin is continuous from one end to the other, but to outward appearance it is not so, but looks like a horn lantern with the panes of horn left out.

"Aristotle came upon the little creature during a 2-year sojourn on the island of Lesbos. The philosopher, then some 40 years old, had left Plato's Academy in Athens and was engaged in a series of investigations into 'these beings that are the work of nature,' the 1st time anyone had systematically gone about sorting, taking apart (hardly dissecting, as we know it), identifying, and classifying. With the large number of facts thus assembled, he reasoned, it would then be possible to search out common attributes, to generalize, to discover the universals embodied in the particulars.

"There is scarcely a field of classical learning to which Aristotle did not make a unique contribution. Logic and metaphysics, ethics and aesthetics, physics, astronomy, and the nature of dreams, he studied them all, and his writings continually reflect the enthusiasm and delight with which he examined his world. 'In all nature there is something of the marvelous,' he wrote in *De Partibus Animalium.* '. . . we should study every kind of animal without hesitation, knowing that in all of them there is something natural and beautiful.' Even the legless sea urchin."

2. *Balaam's Ass.* "The animal who reproached her master, the Gentile prophet Balaam, when he beat her unjustly.

"After wandering 40 years in the wilderness, the Children of Israel were camped on the plains of Moab. They had already defeated 2 Palestinian kings; Balak, King of Moab, feared he would be the 3rd. He therefore ordered the seer Balaam to go and curse the Israelites that they might be overcome in battle.

"Balaam at 1st demurred, having been warned by the Lord in a dream that he must not carry out the King's command. But after an even more peremptory message brought by Balak's couriers, Balaam saddled his ass and set out with the King's men although he knew he would be able to speak only such words as God put into his mouth.

"On the way an angel, invisible to the little company, took his stand in the middle of the road. Only the ass saw the angel and so turned aside into a field, whereupon Balaam struck her a great blow with his stick. The ass returned to the road, but a bit farther on, the angel once more bestrode the path and the ass moved aside and was again beaten. A 3rd time the angel stood before them, so that they could not pass at all. The ass folded her legs and lay down, nor would she move though Balaam rained blows upon her.

"Suddenly the animal raised her head, opened her mouth, and spoke. 'What have I done to thee, that thou hast struck me 3 times?' 'Why,' said Balaam, 'thou has made sport of me. And if my stick had been a sword I would have slain thee.' 'But have I not served thee faithfully to this very day? Have I ever failed thee?' And Balaam had to answer, No.

"At that moment the prophet's eyes were opened, and he too saw the angel standing with drawn sword. Fearful and contrite, Balaam offered to abandon his mission, but he was told to proceed. When he finally climbed a hill above Moab and looked down upon the hosts of Israel, not curses but a blessing issued from his lips and a prophecy of victory for the sons of Jacob.

"The Book of Numbers, which contains the story of Balaam, is part of the Hexateuch (the 5 books of Moses plus Joshua). These books are a combination of 2 versions, one written about the 10th or 9th century B.C., the other somewhat later. They are differentiated by the fact that the earlier one uses the term *Jahweh* to name the Deity, and hence is referred to as the J version; the other, the E version, uses *Elohim*. While there is a difference on a number of details in the Balaam story, the versions agree on one point of particular interest: that it is possible for a man to be a true prophet and yet not be a Hebrew.

"Talking animals are quite common throughout folklore. In the Bible, however, the only other instance is the serpent in the Garden of Eden."

3. *Kepler's Dream.* "A treatise in the form of a fable written by the astronomer Johannes Kepler (1571–1630) and published posthumously, describing how the movements of the heavenly bodies would look to an inhabitant of the moon and including a 'moon geography.'

"When Johannes Kepler was admitted to the University of Tübingen in 1589 as a student of theology, one of his teachers was Magister Michael Maestlin, professor of mathematics and astronomy. Although the rest of the faculty, citing holy writ, held with Ptolemy that the universe revolves around the earth, Maestlin was a confirmed believer in the heliocentric theory announced less than a half century earlier by Copernicus. In his public lectures, Maestlin taught Ptolemy, but to a select and intimate circle, of which young Kepler was one, he expounded on the structure of the universe as Copernicus had laid it out.

"Later, Kepler began to jot down some thoughts as to how the motions of the stars and planets including the earth would look to someone living on the moon. For a time these thoughts remained notes only, but his interest was revived when he encountered Plutarch's *On the Face of the Moon's Disk.* The idea then began to take shape of writing a detailed description of the moon in fanciful form. In the summer of 1609, when he was living in Prague under appointment as imperial mathematician, he discussed his plan with a learned friend, Wackher von Wackenfels, and thereupon sat down and composed his *Somnium seu Astronomia Lunari—A Dream or Astronomy of the Moon.*

"The end product was a remarkable blend of scientific fact and imaginative fantasy. In it Kepler dreams of himself as a youth living in Thule with his mother, a gentle soul conversant with wise and friendly spirits who often convey her to distant lands or bring her news of other far places. One such place is Levania. In the course of describing the inhabitants, plants, and animals of this imaginary land, Kepler sets down the actual results of his own many years of astronomical observations. In contrast to the fanciful 'geography' drawn from Plutarch, Kepler presents with great accuracy the phenomena exhibited by the sun, the earth, and the other planets as they would appear from the moon. These include the alternation of day and night, heat and cold and the seasons, and the paths of the planets. It was Kepler who 1st determined that the planetary orbits were elliptical rather than circular. All this, as he put it, was 'to make an argument for the motion of the earth taking the moon as an example.' To the body of the work he later added numerous notes, astronomical, physical and geographic, which greatly enhanced its scientific value; and he finished it off with his own Latin translation from the Greek of Plutarch's 'moon geography.'

"Although the *Dream* was not published during Kepler's lifetime, a number of sketches of it were made which passed from hand to hand among astronomers and other scientists and intellectuals, who found it provocative and exciting. No one, therefore, was prepared for a turn of events which caused the document to have near fatal consequences.

"Witch-hunting reached a peak in Germany in the early 1600s. In the spring of 1615 one of those accused was Kepler's mother, then living in Leonberg in the duchy of Württemberg.

"Kepler, who was working as court mathematician in Linz, heard nothing of this until almost the end of the year. He at once dispatched a furious letter to the councilor of Leonberg, lashing out at the attempt to persecute and bring to the rack a defenseless old woman and stating his intention of fighting all charges until they were wiped out.

"The letter put a stop to whispered accusations against Kepler, but it had no effect on the court action against his mother, an action which dragged on for the next 5 years.

"A hearing was finally held in May, 1618. The proceedings continued sporadically for 2 more years, while a case of witchcraft was constructed out of the most fantastic testimony, from some 30 or 40 witnesses. In July, 1620, the order went out to arrest 'the Kepler woman' and if she did not confess, to bring her to torture.

"Kepler in Linz was informed of the crisis by his sister Margarete. He immediately wrote to the Duke of Württemberg, declaring that, since he was eternally obligated to his mother by divine and natural rights, he would attend the trial and take an active part in the proceedings himself. This he did, even to writing most of the concluding statement.

"His mother continued her sturdy defiance both during the trial and after she was returned to prison. Loaded with chains, brought into the torture chamber itself and made to look upon the horrible instruments, she still did not break. 'Do with me what you will,' she declared. 'I have nothing to admit.'

"Finally, the Duke decreed that the terror Frau Kepler had undergone during her 14 months imprisonment had invalidated the 'evidence,' and on October 4, 1621, she was released."

4. *Roget's Thesaurus*. "A collection of English words and phrases arranged according to the ideas they express, rather than in alphabetical order, published in 1852 by the English physician and lecturer Peter Mark Roget (1779–1869), and offered 'to facilitate the expression of ideas and to assist in literary composition.'

"As Roget noted in the introduction to the 1st edition of the *Thesaurus*, his was not the 1st attempt at such a compilation. The earliest, dating from about the 10th century, is the *Amera Cosha*, or *Vocabulary of the Sanskrit Language* (a translation was published in 1808), somewhat confused but 'exhibiting a remarkable effort at analysis at so remote a period of Indian literature.' A more orderly classification, in Roget's opinion, was to be found in the 17th-century work of Bishop John Wilkins, *An Essay towards a Real Char-*

acter and a Philosophical Language; but the schema of symbols that accompanied it was too complicated and artificial to be useful. The same criticism applied to an anonymous French work that appeared in 1797.

"In his own system Roget took the classifications of natural history as his guiding principle. Words were divided into categories in the same way that plants and animals had been divided into families. As genus branched off into related but differing species, so the meanings of words shaded into other meanings related but not the same. A particular innovation was the inclusion of phrases synonymous with single words for which no individual or one-word synonyms existed.

"This ambitious work, which might have been a lifetime project for another man, was merely the capstone of Roget's long and versatile career. He was born in London of a Swiss father and an English mother. A graduate of Edinburgh Medical School at 19, he spent the next 40 years tutoring, practicing medicine, and lecturing, 1st on animal physiology, then on the theory and practice of medicine. He was one of the founders of the Manchester Medical School and the 1st to hold the Fullerian professorship of physiology at the Royal Institution. He wrote treatises on electricity, galvanism, and electromagnetism; he tried to make a calculating machine; he devised a successful slide rule for performing mathematical operations of involution (raising a number to any power) and evolution (extracting any root of a number); and besides designing a pocket chessboard, found the 1st complete solution to the knight's move—to start on a given square, to visit every square once only, and to end on a given square of a different color."

5. *Robert's Rules of Order*. "A manual of parliamentary procedure, 1st published in 1876, written by Brig. Gen. Henry Martyn Robert (1837–1923) of Robertville, S.C.

"'Where there is no law, but each man does what is right in his own eyes, there is the least of liberty,' wrote General Robert. His famous *Rules* were intended to provide a maximum of liberty within a necessary framework of order. The son of a minister, Robert had graduated from the U.S. Military Academy at 20 (he was an acting assistant professor during his senior year), and, after serving all through the Civil War on the Union side, returned to the Academy (1865–1867) to take charge of the department of military engineering. His experience and talents in that field were later put to use when he took part in designing a sea wall 17' high and 7½ mi. long to protect Galveston from Gulf floods, and a 2 mi. causeway (finished in 1909) to connect that island city with the Texas mainland.

"The 1st edition of the *Rules of Order* was

a modest one, 4,000 copies 'enough to last 2 years,' Robert estimated. That should be ample time, he felt, to test the efficiency of the manual and to produce criticism useful for a revised edition. In 1893 a revised edition appeared, and another in 1915; the 75th-anniversary printing that came out in 1951 is based on the 1915 plates.

"As a guide to the best use of his manual, Robert appended a study outline. Suggesting that classes be formed among an organization's members, he recommended that the simplest rules be learned 1st, and added that it is better to know how to find a correct ruling than to worry about memorizing it."

The *Almanac* Anthology

YES, VIRGINIA, THERE IS A SANTA CLAUS

Until you were 7 or 8 years old, you knew there was a Santa Claus. Then, before another Christmas, some cynic told you otherwise, stunned you with adult reality, insisted you face the fact that Santa was a make-believe, a myth, a wish, no more. The moment of terrible truth. You wavered, trying to cling to the past before being torn into the grown-up world.

One bleak autumn day in 1897, a little New York girl named Virginia O'Hanlon came up against this disillusionment. In desperation, she went to her father for the final word. Her father, Dr. Philip F. O'Hanlon, consulting surgeon to the N.Y. Police Department, was too wise to tackle the question alone. As Virginia recalled the search for truth 36 years later:

"Quite naturally I believed in Santa Claus, for he had never disappointed me. But when less fortunate little boys and girls said there wasn't any Santa Claus, I was filled with doubts. I asked my father, and he was a little evasive on the subject.

"It was a habit in our family that whenever any doubts came up as to how to pronounce a word or some question of historical fact was in doubt, we wrote to the Question and Answer column in *The Sun*. Father would always say, 'If you see it in *The Sun*, it's so,' and that settled the matter.

" 'Well, I'm just going to write *The Sun* and find out the real truth,' I said to father.

"He said, 'Go ahead, Virginia. I'm sure *The Sun* will give you the right answer, as it always does.' "

And so Virginia sat down and wrote her parents' favorite newspaper.

Her letter found its way into the hands of a veteran editor, Francis P. Church. Son of a Baptist minister, Church had covered the Civil War for *The New York Times* and had worked on *The New York Sun* for 20 years, more recently as an anonymous editorial writer. Church, a sardonic man, had for his personal motto, "Endeavor to clear your mind of cant." When controversial subjects had to be tackled on the editorial page, especially those dealing with theology, the assignments were usually given to Church.

Now, he had in his hands a little girl's letter on a most controversial matter, and he was burdened with the responsibility of answering it.

"Is there a Santa Claus?" the childish scrawl in the letter asked. At once, Church knew that there was no avoiding the question. He must answer, and he must answer truthfully. And so he turned to his desk, and he began to write his young correspondent, and what he wrote was to become one of the most memorable editorials in newspaper history.

Editorial Page, New York Sun, 1897

We take pleasure in answering thus prominently the communication below, expressing at the same time our great gratification that its faithful author is numbered among the friends of *The Sun*:

Dear Editor—

I am 8 years old. Some of my little friends say there is no Santa Claus. Papa says, "If you see it in *The Sun*, it's so." Please tell me the truth, is there a Santa Claus?

VIRGINIA O'HANLON

Virginia, your little friends are wrong. They have been affected by the skepticism of a skeptical age. They do not believe except they see. They think that nothing can be which is not comprehensible by their little minds. All minds, Virginia, whether they be men's or children's, are little. In this great universe of ours, man is a mere insect, an ant, in his intellect as compared with the boundless world about him, as measured by the intelligence capable of grasping the whole of truth and knowledge.

Yes, Virginia, there is a Santa Claus. He exists as certainly as love and generosity and devotion exist, and you know that they abound and give to your life its highest beauty and joy. Alas! how dreary would be the world if there were no Santa Claus! It would be as dreary as if there were no Virginias. There would be no childlike faith then, no poetry, no romance to make tolerable this existence. We should have no enjoyment, except in sense and sight. The external light with which childhood fills the world would be extinguished.

Not believe in Santa Claus! You might as well not believe in fairies. You might get your papa to hire men to watch in all the chimneys on Christmas eve to catch Santa Claus, but even if you did not see Santa Claus coming down, what would that prove? Nobody sees Santa Claus, but that is no sign that there is no Santa Claus. The most real things in the world are those that neither children nor men can see. Did you ever see fairies dancing on the lawn? Of course not, but that's no proof that they are not there. Nobody can conceive or imagine all the wonders there are unseen and unseeable in the world.

You tear apart the baby's rattle and see what makes the noise inside, but there is a veil covering the unseen world which not the strongest man, nor even the united strength of all the strongest men that ever lived could tear apart. Only faith, poetry, love, romance, can push aside that curtain and view and picture the supernal beauty and glory beyond. Is it all real? Ah, Virginia, in all this world there is nothing else real and abiding.

No Santa Claus! Thank God! he lives and lives forever. A thousand years from now, Virginia, nay 10 times 10,000 years from now, he will continue to make glad the heart of childhood.

Aftermath

Francis P. Church's editorial was an immediate sensation, and became one of the most famous ever written anywhere in the world. *The New York Sun* published it annually before Christmas (uncredited to Church) until 1949, when the paper went out of business. Shortly after the editorial appeared, Church married, had no children, and died in April, 1906.

As for the little girl, Virginia O'Hanlon, she grew up to get a Bachelor of Arts degree from Hunter College at the age of 21, obtained her Master's from Columbia the following year, and in 1912 became a teacher, later a principal, in the New York City school system. She married, became Virginia Douglas, and had offspring of her own. After 47 years as an educator, she retired, and during all those years she received a steady stream of mail about her Santa Claus letter. She replied to all correspondents by sending them an attractive printed copy of the Church editorial.

Virginia O'Hanlon Douglas died on May 13, 1971, at the age of 81, in a nursing home in Valatie, N.Y.

—I.W.

Logan's Lament

For many years, one branch remained on the centuries-old elm; but several summers ago, time took its toll—the Logan Elm in Circleville, O., one of the nation's most famous landmarks, finally died.

It was under this old elm tree that John Logan, a leader of the Mingo Tribe, made his eloquent plea for peace between his tribesmen and the settlers in 1774—Logan's Lament—a speech which for generations was memorized and recited in schoolrooms throughout the U.S.

Logan's real story is more tragic than either his lament or legend ever tells. One night in April, 1774, while he was away on a hunting trip, a band of men broke into his cabin, brutally massacring his family. The following morning, upon arriving home, Logan found the bodies of all the relatives he thought he had in the world. He swore to avenge them.

Three generations had been destroyed in as many minutes. Half-white himself, his father captured as a child and raised by the Cayugas, John Logan, or Tahgahjute, had been known as a friendly man much respected by the Shawnee tribe into which he had married, but now blind hate overcame him. Swearing revenge against the white man, Logan sent a declaration of hostilities to Virginia's Governor Dunmore—attributing the mass killing to a drunken band led by militia captain Michael Cresap—and when the Shawnee chief, Cornstalk, supported Logan's declaration in 1774, there resulted the bloody uprising known as Lord Dunmore's War. Tribes went on the warpath throughout the Ohio Valley, and before militiamen finally overpowered the Indians at Point Pleasant, hundreds of lives were lost on both sides. Both settlers and Indians had been brutally massacred.

Logan was through with war then, had had his revenge, yet so intense was his sorrow that he refused to meet with Governor Dunmore in a council of peace. Cornstalk, speaking for all the Shawnee, accepted Dunmore's proposal, but John Logan would not sit with his enemies. Instead, he wrote Dunmore a letter that would go down in history.

Logan's Lament

I appeal to any white man to say if ever he entered Logan's cabin hungry and he gave him not meat; if ever he came cold and naked, and he clothed him not. During the course of the last long and bloody war, Logan remained idle in his cabin, an advocate for peace. Such was my love for the whites that my country-men pointed as they passed and said "Logan is the friend of the White Man." I had even thought to live with you but for the injury of one man—Colonel [sic] Cresap who last Spring in cold blood and unprovoked, murdered all the relations of Logan, not sparing even my women and children. There runs not a drop of my blood in the veins of any living creature. This called on me for revenge. I have sought it. I have killed many. I have fully glutted my vengeance. For my country I rejoice at the beams of peace. But do not harbor a thought that mine is the joy of fear. Logan never felt fear. He will not turn on his heel to save his life. Who is there to mourn for Logan? Not one.

Aftermath

Logan's Lament was reprinted in newspapers and schoolbooks throughout the U.S., often without the correct historical background, and his words became part of the folklore of many States, although he really read the letter from under the elm in what is now Logan's State Park in Circleville.

But Logan's story may have been even more tragic than his words reveal—for, at least according to one version, the Indian discovered that his family had not been murdered by white men. It is said that Logan learned that a band of Indians had really massacred his family and realized that his revenge had no meaning at all, that he had injured those innocent of any crime against him. His death 6 years later was the supreme irony. In 1780, after a drunken quarrel, Logan attacked another Indian and was killed by him. The other man turned out to be a nephew unknown to Logan—the last of his once large family.

—R.H.

The Most Beautiful Last Will and Testament Ever Written

When a person sits down with his or her attorney to prepare a last will and testament, one would expect the document produced by this meeting to be legalistic, dry, morbid. Certainly, one would not expect inspired prose verging on poetry.

Yet when Williston Fish, an attorney in Chicago, Ill., sat down in 1897 to draft a will for one Charles Lounsbury, what Fish produced as a testament proved to be sheer prose poetry.

In its time, Lounsbury's will was printed and reprinted around the world. To generations of attorneys, it became a classic.

However, if a will is defined as "a written instrument legally executed by which a man makes disposition of his estate to take effect after his death," then the Lounsbury will was no legal will at all. It was, in fact, a literary article. There was only an attorney-business-man, and part-time author, in Chicago named Williston Fish who created the fictional will as a literary effort.

Williston Fish was born on January 15, 1858, in Berlin Heights, O., the eldest son in a family of 8 children. Self-taught in Greek and Latin, he briefly attended Oberlin College, then won appointment in 1877 to the U.S. Military Academy at West Point. In 1881, the year of his graduation, he married, and subsequently had 3 children. He remained in the Army for 6 years, studying law on the side. After resigning from the Army, he was admitted to the Illinois Bar in 1887, then chose to enter into a business career. But his heart was always in writing, and he published at least 3 books and 500 articles, stories, poems for periodicals.

In 1897, he hit upon the idea of a perfect will and upon a wealthy, nonexistent client named Charles Lounsbury.

As Fish recalled it later: "The name, Charles Lounsbury, of the divisor in the will, is a name in my family of 3 generations ago —back in York State where the real owner of it was a big, strong, all-around good kind of a man. I had an uncle, a lawyer, in Cleveland named after him, Charles Lounsbury Fish, who was a most burly and affectionate giant himself and who took delight in keeping the original Charles Lounsbury's memory green. He used to tell us of his feats of strength. . . . His brain, my uncle always added, was equal to his brawn, and he had a way of winning friends and admirers as easy and comprehensive as taking a census. So I took the name of Charles Lounsbury to add strength and goodwill to my story."

The will that Williston Fish had written found its way into print for the 1st time the year after it was created. It appeared in *Harper's Weekly* on September 3, 1898. It was picked up and reprinted widely. But in recent years, it has been forgotten.

A Last Will

He was stronger and cleverer, no doubt, than other men, and in many broad lines of business he had grown rich, until his wealth exceeded exaggeration. One morning, in his office, he directed a request to his confidential lawyer to come to him in the afternoon—he intended to have his will drawn. A will is a solemn matter, even with men whose life is given up to business and who are by habit mindful of the future. After giving this direction he took up no other matter, but sat at his desk alone and in silence.

It was a day when summer was 1st new. The pale leaves upon the trees were starting forth upon the yet unbending branches. The grass in the parks had a freshness in its green like the freshness of the blue in the sky and of the yellow of the sun—a freshness to make one wish that life might renew its youth. The clear breezes from the south wantoned about, and then were still, as if loath to go finally away. Half idly, half thoughtfully, the rich man wrote upon the white paper before him, beginning what he wrote with capital letters, such as he had not made since, as a boy in school, he had taken pride in his skill with the pen:

The 1st portrait of Sherlock Holmes, master detective, drawn by Sidney Paget. Holmes's wizardry was made public in 1887 by author A. Conan Doyle, and in 60 stories the eccentric detective solved cases involving the hound of the Baskervilles, the blue carbuncle, the redheaded league. (See: Chap. 24) *Westminster Public Libraries.*

Anton Lang, the most famous portrayer of Jesus Christ, in the Oberammergau Passion Play staged in southern Germany. The play, which originated in 1633, has never been filmed, televised, or gone on tour. Lang, who once received a new car as a gift from Henry Ford for his performance, had to memorize 7,000 words and be onstage for 5 hours in his role. (See: Chap. 26) *Burton Holmes, Inc.*

In the only known photograph taken with one of his 27 multiple wives, Brigham Young, Prophet of the Mormon Church and advocate of polygamy, posed with Margaret Pierce, his 17th wife, in Nauvoo, Ill., in 1846. (See: Chap. 26) *Irving Wallace.*

Sister Aimee Semple McPherson's theatrical style made her one of the U.S.'s favorite evangelists. But in 1926 she disappeared mysteriously and the ensuing sex scandal permanently clouded her image. (See: Chap. 26) *U.P.I.*

Founded in the 5th century, Lhasa ("God's House"), the Forbidden City, is the capital of Tibet and onetime residence of the Dalai Lama. It was a holy city until the Chinese Communists took over and suppressed religion. This photograph of Lhasa was taken in 1896. (See: Chap. 26) *Burton Holmes, Inc.*

The Great Buddha at Kamakura, Japan. Siddhartha Gautama, who became known as the Buddha, preached that enlightenment can be reached by the individual without the use of gods, priests, and idols. However, after his death, his followers saw fit to build thousands of idols of him all across Asia. (See: Chap. 26) *David S. Strickler from Monkmeyer.*

Walking with a Staff by Shen Chou (1427-1509). A Taoist view of a man out walking. (See: Chap. 26)

A memorable gravestone epitaph, an ode to the Wild West, which still may be seen in Boot Hill cemetery, Tombstone, Ariz. (See: Chap. 27)

Max Schreck as the vampire Count Orlock in F. W. Murnau's 1922 film classic *Nosferatu*. (See: Chap. 27)

On May 30, 1966, Tranh Quang, a Buddhist nun, burned herself to death in Hue, South Vietnam. She used self-immolation as a means of making a political and spiritual statement; most suicides have a different motivation. (See: Chap. 27) *U.P.I.*

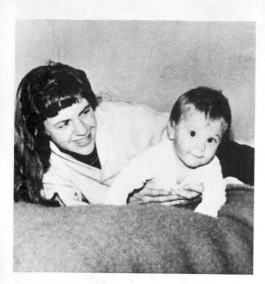

Sylvia Plath, born in 1932, gained renown for her novel *The Bell Jar* and her books of poetry. Shown here in a happy domestic mood, she committed suicide in 1963. (See: Chap. 27) *Sophia Smith Collection, Smith College.*

Comedian W. C. Fields as Queen Victoria, painted in 1940 by John Decker, known for his many portraits of film stars. A major liquor company wanted to use this painting in its ads with the caption, "W. C. Fields says, 'Fit for a Queen!'" but Fields refused permission. (See: Chap. 27) *John Decker.*

In May, 1828, a strange illiterate from nowhere, 17-year-old Kaspar Hauser, appeared in Nuremberg carrying an anonymous letter of introduction. He had no knowledge of time, food, fire, had lived in a 7' by 4' dark cell all his life. Known as the Mystery Man of Europe, he was stabbed to death in December, 1833. (See: Chap. 29) *Germanisches Nationalmuseum.*

In 1669, a mysterious prisoner was jailed in France by order of King Louis XIV. He was known as "the man in the iron mask." Actually, his mask was not iron but black velvet stiffened with whalebone. In prison 34 years, he was not identified even after his death. Who was he? Drawing by Vierle. (See: Chap. 29) *Historical Pictures Service.*

IN THE NAME OF GOD, AMEN

I, CHARLES LOUNSBURY, being of sound and disposing mind and memory (he lingered on the word memory), do now make and publish this my last will and testament, in order, as justly as I may, to distribute my interests in the world among succeeding men.

And 1st, that part of my interests which is known among men and recognized in the sheep-bound volumes of the law as my property, being inconsiderable and of none-account, I make no account of in this my will.

My right to live, it being but a life estate, is not at my disposal, but these things expected, all else in the world I now proceed to devise and bequeath.

Item—And 1st, I give to good fathers and mothers, but in trust for their children, nevertheless, all good little words of praise and all quaint pet names, and I charge said parents to use them justly but generously as the needs of their children shall require.

Item—I leave to children exclusively, but only for the life of their childhood, all and every the dandelions of the fields and the daisies thereof, with the right to play among them freely, according to the custom of children, warning them at the same time against the thistles. And I devise to children the yellow shores of creeks and the golden sands beneath the waters thereof, with the dragon-flies that skim the surface of said waters, and the odors of the willows that dip into said waters, and the white clouds that float high over the giant trees.

And I leave to children the long, long days to be merry in, in a thousand ways, and the Night and the Moon and the train of the Milky Way to wonder at, but subject, nevertheless, to the rights hereinafter given to lovers; and I give to each child the right to choose a star that shall be his, and I direct that the child's father shall tell him the name of it, in order that the child shall always remember the name of that star after he has learned and forgotten astronomy.

Item—I devise to boys jointly all the useful idle fields and commons where ball may be played, and all snow-clad hills where one may coast, and all streams and ponds where one may skate, to have and to hold the same for the period of their boyhood. And all meadows, with the clover blooms and butterflies thereof; and all woods, with their appurtenances of squirrels and whirring birds and echoes and strange noises; and all distant places which may be visited, together with the adventures there found, I do give to said boys to be theirs. And I give to said boys each his own place at the fireside at night, with all pictures that may be seen in the burning wood or coal, to enjoy without let or hindrance and without any incumbrance of cares.

Item—To lovers I devise their imaginary world, with whatever they may need, as the stars of the sky, the red, red roses by the wall, the snow of the hawthorn, the sweet strains of music, or aught else they may desire to figure to each other the lastingness and beauty of their love.

Item—To young men jointly, being joined in a brave, mad crowd, I devise and bequeath all boisterous, inspiring sports of rivalry. I give to them the disdain of weakness and undaunted confidence in their own strength. Though they are rude and rough, I leave to them alone the power of making lasting friendships and of possessing companions and to them exclusively I shall give all merry songs and brave choruses to sing, with smooth voices to troll them forth.

Item—And to those who are no longer children or youths or lovers I leave Memory, and I leave to them the volumes of the poems of Burns and Shakespeare, and of other poets, if there are others, to the end that they may live the old days over again freely and fully, without tithe or diminution; and to those who are no longer children or youths or lovers I leave, too, the knowledge of what a rare, rare world it is.

Aftermath

Speaking of the numerous reprintings of "A Last Will," Fish wrote good-naturedly: "Whenever a newspaper did not have at hand what it really wanted . . . it would run in this piece of mine. In return for the free use of the piece, the paper, not to be outdone in liberality, would generally correct and change it. . . . Some writers can boast that their works have been translated into all foreign languages, but when I look pathetically about for some little boast, I can only say that this one of my pieces has been translated into all the idiot tongues of English."

Although a lawyer, Williston Fish devoted 35 years of his life working as a realtor and as an executive in many railroad companies. He retired in 1923, concentrated fully on his writing career, and died in Western Springs, Ill., on December 19, 1939, at the age of 81.
—I.W.

THE BEST TRIBUTE TO MAN'S BEST FRIEND

On that fall day in 1870 when country lawyer George Graham Vest stood up in Judge Foster Wright's courtroom in Warrensburg, Mo., to defend a dog, few present could have imagined that what they were about to hear would become the most memorable tribute in modern history to man's best friend.

But 1st, the series of events that brought George Graham Vest into the courtroom as counsel on behalf of a dog's good name.

The canine in question was not an unknown mongrel. He was a foxhound named Old Drum, and around Johnson County he was held in high regard for his speed and dependability. Old Drum's proud owner was Charles Burden.

One summer's morning in 1870, Old Drum was found dead from a bullet wound on or near the property of Leonidas Hornsby, who was one of Burden's neighbors. Investigating the untimely death of his hunter, the distressed Burden decided that circumstantial evidence clearly indicated Hornsby had killed the dog.

Seeking some kind of redress for his loss, Burden went to the Justice of Peace Court in Warrensburg to file suit. Informed that $150 was the maximum amount for which he could sue in this kind of case, Burden immediately filed against Hornsby for that sum.

The case of Burden v. Hornsby was tried, and after a verdict was given for Hornsby, it was appealed, and then appealed again, until it reached the State Circuit Court for final judgment.

On the day of the last trial—a jury trial—Judge Wright presided. Considering that the issue was the value of one foxhound, a formidable array of legal talent had been assembled. Appearing upon behalf of the defendant, Hornsby, were 2 attorneys who would one day become national figures. One was Francis Cockrell, who would later be elected to the U.S. Senate from Missouri, and the other was Thomas Crittenden, who would later become governor of Missouri. Appearing on behalf of Charles Burden and the deceased Old Drum was Col. Wells Blodgett, a well-known local attorney.

As the court convened, Colonel Blodgett felt the odds were against his client and his client's dog. The opposition had more manpower. The opposing lawyers had bigger reputations than his own. Even worse, Cockrell and Crittenden knew every member of the jury personally. The opposition exuded confidence.

Then, quite by accident, Colonel Blodgett learned that the only attorney in the area equal to the opposition in forensic skill happened to be in the courthouse that very afternoon. This was George Graham Vest, a onetime senator in the Confederacy who, 8 years hence, would be elected to the U.S. Senate from Missouri and serve in the Senate as one of its leading debaters from 1879 to 1903. Vest, who practiced in nearby Sedalia, happened to be visiting the courthouse on another legal matter. Colonel Blodgett went to Vest at once and implored him to come aboard as special counsel. Apparently because the elements in the case appealed to him, or perhaps because he was a dog fancier, Vest consented to assist in the case.

Judge Wright had a crowded calendar, and he did not get to Burden v. Hornsby until late in the afternoon. Determined to get the case to the jury that very day, Judge Wright re-cessed the court for supper, and announced that the pleading would begin in the evening.

That night, when the court was called to order, the kerosene lamps revealed a gallery thick with people. Not an empty seat could be found. The word had gone out that George Graham Vest had joined Colonel Blodgett against Cockrell and Crittenden, and a real donnybrook was in the offing.

Judge Wright's gavel rapped, and Burden v. Hornsby, with the ghost of Old Drum in the wings, was under way.

Colonel Blodgett spoke 1st. No record exists of the effectiveness of his appeal to the jury.

Then it was the turn of the defendant's lawyers. Thomas Crittenden addressed the jury, followed by Francis Cockrell. Both spoke flippantly of the monetary worth of Burden's property loss, and they "said it was ridiculous to make so much ado about a dog of small value."

Confidently, they concluded their pleas, not realizing that they had given George Graham Vest exactly the opening he wanted.

Vest was on his feet for the final argument. The courtroom was hushed as he fixed his attention on the jurors. He was not interested in the evidence previously presented. He was not interested in the legalisms surrounding a $150 property loss. He was interested in only one thing. A man's beloved pet and companion, a dog, had been maligned.

Vest began to speak, addressing himself only to the subject of dogs and to all the Old Drums in history.

Even years after, when he had become governor of Missouri, Crittenden could not forget Vest's speech. Remembering it, he said:

"I have often heard him, but never had I heard from his lips, nor from the lips of any other man, so graceful, so impetuous and so eloquent a speech as this before the jury in that dog case. He seemed to recall from history all the instances where dogs had displayed intelligence and fidelity to man. He quoted more lines of history and poetry about dogs than I had supposed had been written. He capped the monument he had erected by quoting from the Bible about the dog which soothed the sores of the beggar Lazarus as he sat at the rich man's gate, and by giving Motley's graphic description of how the fidelity of a dog kept William of Orange from falling into the hands of the Duke of Alva.

"It was as perfect a piece of oratory as was ever heard from pulpit or bar. Court, jury, lawyers, and audience were entranced. I looked at the jury and saw all were in tears. The foreman wept like one who had just lost his dearest friend. The victory for the other side was complete. I said to Cockrell that we were defeated; that the dog, though dead, had won, and that we had better get out of the court-house with our client or we would be hanged."

When Vest had finished, the jury was so mesmerized that it returned a unanimous judgment of $550 in damages instead of $150 for Charles Burden—actually, for Old Drum. When Judge Wright collected his wits, he reduced the judgment to the Court's legal limit of $150.

While no record was kept of the last half of George Graham Vest's tribute to a dog, the 1st portion has fortunately been preserved. It was this speech that originated the saying, "A man's best friend is his dog."

George Graham Vest speaking

"Gentlemen of the jury, the best friend a man has in this world may turn against him and become his enemy. His son or daughter whom he has reared with loving care may prove ungrateful. Those who are nearest and dearest to us—those whom we trust with our happiness and good name—may become traitors in their faith. The money that a man has he may lose. It flies away from him, perhaps when he needs it most. A man's reputation may be sacrificed in a moment of ill-considered action. The people who are prone to fall on their knees to do us honor when success is with us may be the 1st to throw the stone of malice when failure settles its cloud upon our heads. The one absolute, unselfish friend that man can have in this selfish world—the one that never proves ungrateful or treacherous—is his dog.

"Gentlemen of the jury, a man's dog stands by him in prosperity and poverty, in health and sickness. He will sleep on the cold ground, where the wintry winds blow, and the snow drives fiercely, if only he can be near his master's side. He will kiss the hand that has no food to offer; he will lick the wounds and sores that come in encounter with the roughness of the world. He guards the sleep of his pauper master as if he were a prince. When all other friends desert, he remains. When riches take wings and reputation falls to pieces, he is as constant in his love as the sun in its journey through the heavens.

"If fortune drives the master forth an outcast in the world, friendless and homeless, the faithful dog asks no higher privilege than that of accompanying him to guard against danger, to fight against his enemies. And when the last scene of all comes, and death takes the master in its embrace, and his body is laid away in the cold ground, no matter if all other friends pursue their way, there by his graveside will the noble dog be found, his head between his paws, his eyes sad but open in alert watchfulness, faithful and true even to death."

—I.W.

29

The Unknown and Mysterious

A Chronology of Mysterious Happenings in History

The Event: THE BUILDING OF THE CHEOPS PYRAMID
When: About 2650 B.C.
Where: Egypt
The Mystery: The stones in the pyramid built by Cheops are put together so accurately you can't get a piece of paper between them. The pyramid itself weighs at least 6 million tons. Traditional history tells us that it was erected during the 22 years of Cheops's reign by 4,000 stonemasons and 100,000 workers, who each year spent 3 months dragging the stones into position. The mystery? Some of the stones weigh as much as 5 tons. How could humans, working with primitive machines available at the time, lift those stones? How were the 100,000 workers fed? How were the stonemasons able to shape the stones with such precision?

The entrance to the "chamber of the King," where Cheops was supposedly entombed, was plugged with a piece of granite larger than the corridor. The Arabs found it when they entered the tomb for the 1st time in the 9th century. Inside the tomb they found no body or tools, only a box of red granite. The mystery? The granite plug, because it was larger than the corridor, had to be placed there during the building. How could grave robbers get in, then? What was the box for?

The height of the pyramid is 148.20 m., a measure directly related to the distance from the earth to the sun—148,208,000 km. (This distance was not calculated so precisely until 1860 A.D.) The pyramid is oriented to the cardinal directions with an error of only 4° 35′. (Tycho Brahe, the great 16th-century astronomer, made an error of 18° when placing the Uranienborg Observatory.) The mystery? If the pyramid was built not as a tomb but as an astronomical monument, how were the Egyptians able to make such accurate measurements?

Possible Solutions: All kinds of people—from archaeologists to mystics—have theories about the pyramids.

How was it built? Some say that the stones were floated up the Nile on rafts, then put in place with wooden rollers.

To float a 5-ton stone, a raft would have to displace 5 tons of water. There is no evidence that the Egyptians had such monster rafts.

Others say that it was built by the superior superrace of Atlantis. Still others say it was built by beings from outer space. Morris K. Jessup, astrophysicist and UFO buff, says, "Levitation is the only feasible answer. I believe that this lifting machine was a spaceship, probably of vast proportions; that it brought colonists to various parts of the earth . . . that it supplied the heavy lift power for erecting great stone works; and that it was suddenly destroyed or taken away. Such a hypothesis would underwrite all the movements of stone over which archaeologists and engineers have pondered."

What was the pyramid built for? In the olden days, there were those who believed that the philosophers' stone, a power capable of transforming base metal into gold, was hidden inside the pyramid.

In the late 1800s, Charles Piazzi Smith, an astronomer, wrote a 600-page book in which, among other things, he claimed to have discovered a universal unit of measurement—the "pyramid inch." The "discovery" was grist for the mill of a group of believers between 1890 and 1935. They thought the pyramid revealed through the pyramid inch the history and future of the race from a Christian point of view and was, in fact, a "Bible in stone."

Each corridor, each room, had a meaning. The measurement used in building the pyramids was the royal cubit, which approximated in length the human forearm.

Some people think the pyramid was a giant grain elevator, but there is not much evidence to back up this theory.

In 1960, a fertilizer salesman named Reinhold Schmidt claimed that he was picked up by a UFO and taken to the inside of a pyramid where he saw hidden chambers and the cross on which Christ died. He also saw 32 pamphlets, written in English in black ink, which told the history and future of the human race. He is, however, the only person to claim such an experience.

There are those who think that Thoth, the Egyptian god, was in reality a spaceman, who had the pyramids built to hide cosmic secrets.

What's inside the pyramid? In 1969, Dr. Walter Alvarez, a Nobel Prize winner, led a group of American scientists in setting up cosmic ray detectors around it. In this way, he thought, they could discover where the hidden chambers, if any, were. (The rays would pass through empty space more quickly than through solid stone.) A strange thing happened—the readings for one day were not the same as the readings for another. Dr. Amr Gohed, who was in charge of the IBM 1130 computer facility the research team used, said of the readings, "It defies all known laws of science and electronics. Either the geometry of the pyramid is in substantial error, which would affect our readings, or there is a mystery which is beyond explanation—call it what you will, occultism, the curse of the Pharaohs, sorcery, or magic—there is some influence that defies the laws of science at work in the pyramid."

The Event: THE DEATH OF THE MAN IN THE IRON MASK
When: November 19, 1703
Where: The Bastille, Paris, France
The Mystery: Who was the "man in the iron mask," whose identity aroused the curiosity of all Europe for decades after his imprisonment by Louis XIV? The facts are these:

By order of the King, a mysterious prisoner was jailed in 1669 at Pignerol, in a cell with windows protected by iron bars and a basketwork grille. He had not been tried or sentenced. His jailer, from then until the prisoner's death 34 years later, was M. de Saint-Mars, an under officer of the musketeers, a subordinate of D'Artagnan, later immortalized by novelist Alexandre Dumas. Saint-Mars's job was to keep the prisoner from being recognized or communicating with anyone.

In 1681, the prisoner was moved to Exiles. In 1687, he was moved again, this time to the prison at Île Sainte-Marguerite in the Bay of Cannes. To make sure he would remain unidentified, Saint-Mars took the prisoner there in a sedan chair covered with waxed cloth.

Sometime during his stay at Île Sainte-Marguerite, the prisoner wrote something, probably desperate, with a steel fork on a silver plate. He threw it out the window to land on the beach, where it was picked up by a fisherman. When the fisherman brought it to the prison, Saint-Mars asked him if he could read. "No," the fisherman replied, and Saint-Mars said, "It is lucky for you, for it would have been necessary to put you to death if you could."

In 1698, Saint-Mars took the prisoner to the Bastille. On the journey, tradition has it, Saint-Mars stopped at his Château of Palteau, near Villeneuve, and ate his dinner with 2 pistols beside his plate, facing the masked prisoner. (This story gives the 1st reference to a mask, which was not made of iron as legend has it, but of black velvet stiffened with whalebone.)

In 1703, the prisoner died. In his journals, Étienne du Jonca, the King's lieutenant at the Bastille, wrote, "On the same day, 19 November, 1703, the unknown prisoner, always masked with a mask of black velvet, whom M. de Saint-Mars, the governor, brought with him on coming from the Île Sainte-Marguerite, whom he had kept for a long time, the which happening a little ill yesterday on coming from mass, he died today, about 10 o'clock at night, without having had a serious illness. . . . And this unknown prisoner, kept here for so long, was buried on Tuesday at 4 o'clock P.M., 20 November in the graveyard of St. Paul, our parish. . . ." In the church register, it was recorded that the prisoner's name was Marchioly. (The name was probably a false clue.)

Who had the masked prisoner been? The King would not tell, nor would his advisers, and they were the only ones who knew. M. de Chamillart, one of those advisers, was asked to tell the secret on his deathbed; he refused.

Louis XV, who also knew, said, "If he were still alive, I would give him his freedom." Later Louis said, "No one has yet told the truth and all conjectures are false."

Possible Solutions: The mistress of the previous minister said the prisoner was a son of Anne of Austria, the wife of Louis XIII, fathered illegitimately by the English Duke of Buckingham. He had been put in jail, she stated, because he looked so much like Louis XIV.

There were other rumors that maintained the prisoner had royal blood. Andrew Lang, 19th-century mystic, said the prisoner was the eldest natural son of King Charles II of Eng-

land, a rogue and master hoaxer who had incurred the anger of the King of France. It
was rumored, too, that the prisoner was really
Louis XIV himself, kept in prison while his
illegitimate half brother occupied the throne.
While in prison, the rumor continued, he
married and had a son, who was taken to
Corsica and given the name *de buona parte*
("of good family") and became the grandfather of Napoleon.

Until 1869, the most credible theory was
that the man in the iron mask was an envoy
of the Duke of Mantua, one Mattioli, who had
double-crossed the King of France. This was
discredited by a letter written by Saint-Mars in
1681, which showed that Mattioli had been
out of his custody for 13 years.

Evidence from state papers unearthed after
the French Revolution and other sources now
tells us that the man was probably a valet (confidential secretary) named Eustache Dauger,
whose father had been captain of Cardinal
Richelieu's musketeers and was probably
known at court. Eustache was the black sheep
of the family, dishonorably discharged from
the army, disinherited by his mother for un-
stated reasons, accused of the murder of a
drunken page on the staircase of the Royal
Palace.

Why was he imprisoned, though, if indeed
he was the man in the "iron" mask? Rumor
has it that he might have been illegitimate
royalty, or was used as the King's double on a
secret mission, or impersonated the King.
But no one knows for sure, or probably ever
will.

The Event: THE MOVING OF THE COFFINS
OF BARBADOS
When: 1807–1820
Where: Barbados, the West Indies, in the
parish of Christ Church at Oistin's Bay
The Mystery: On a coral shelf 100′ above
sea level stands the beautiful cemetery of Christ
Church, where people of wealth in Barbados
put up family vaults. The vault of the Barbados coffins mystery is built partly above and
partly below ground. The top section is made
of large coral blocks cemented together, the
roof is arched, and the walls slope inward a bit.
It was built in 1742 for the body of Col.
Thomas Elliott, who was instead buried at
sea.

In July, 1807, the 1st body, that of Mrs.
Thomasina Goddard, in its plain wooden coffin, was put on the highest shelf of the vault.

Then the Chase family, notorious for insanity, suicide, and murder, entered the picture. The head of the family, a man with a
vicious temper, was so cruel to his slaves that
they had threatened his life.

On February 22, 1808, the Chase baby,

Mary, died, probably killed by her father in
a fit of rage. Her body, in its heavy metal coffin, was put in the vault.

Only a few months later, eccentric Dorcas,
the family teen-ager, starved herself to death in
a locked cabin in the garden. Her body was
taken to the vault. When they reached the
outside door, 2 blacks opened it and, followed
by pallbearers carrying the coffin, proceeded
down the stone steps. Light came only from
burning torches. The inner door to the vault
was opened and all shouted in fear. Mary
Chase's coffin stood on its head in the opposite corner from where it had been put.

The mourners righted Mary Chase's coffin
and put Dorcas down next to her sister. A
month later, Colonel Chase killed himself. His
body was placed in the vault also.

Eight years later, a child related to the
Chases died and was carried to the vault. By
this time, the hinges had rusted. It took 2
blacks to open the door. When they did, they
stared in terror. Mrs. Goddard's coffin, as
usual, was in its place, but the Chases' coffins
littered the floor. Strange, because each
weighed about 500 lbs. and needed 4 men to
move it.

A month later, a woman who was putting
flowers on a grave heard a "loud cracking
noise" and the "sound of someone moaning"
in the vault. Her horse began foaming at the
mouth in terror and later had to be treated
by a veterinarian. The Sunday after, several
horses tied outside the church broke away in
fear and galloped down the hill to die in the
sea.

The vault was becoming infamous. The next
funeral, this time for one Samuel Brewster,
drew a large crowd of more than 1,000 people, some from Cuba and Haiti. During a wild
storm, the lead coffin was carried by 4 black
slaves to the vault, where the same bone-chill-
ing scene lay before their eyes—coffins, standing on end, were strewn about the interior.

At this point, the governor of the island,
Lord Combermere, became involved. He personally attended the next funeral, that of Mrs.
Thomasina Clarke, daughter of Thomasina
Goddard, whose coffin had always remained
on the shelf where it had been put. Combermere inspected the vault, sounded for a
subterranean passage (there was none), and
ordered the workmen to replace the upended
coffins before bringing in the new one. Then
he had the floor covered with fine sand and
had a new lock put on the door. Finally, the
door was sealed with a coating of cement.
Combermere and others stuck their signet rings
in it while it was still wet, making permanent
impressions.

On April 18, 1820, a sunny day, Combermere opened the vault for the last time. The

cement on the door had not been disturbed. After masons broke through it, they were prevented from opening the door more than half an inch by something leaning against it. When they forced the door open, a heavy object fell down the interior steps with a crash—it was a coffin, of course. As they entered the vault, the masons saw a bony arm, that of Dorcas Chase, sticking out through a hole in the side of the coffin. All the other coffins, including that of Mrs. Goddard, were scattered around the vault in complete disorder. Combermere gave up. He had the dead removed elsewhere for burial.

Possible Solutions: Researchers from the London Science Museum and the Society of Psychical Research investigated the mystery of the Barbados coffins but came up with no answers.

It seems unlikely that the coffins were disturbed by earth movements because the vault was located on a bed of coral. There was no underground passage and no entry to the vault except through the front door. Governor Combermere, in his final sealing of the vault, had eliminated any possibility that someone had entered the vault secretly. Jewelry which was placed in the vault was left undisturbed, so it is unlikely that the coffins were being disturbed by grave robbers. Nevertheless, the Elliott vault was abandoned as a final resting place for the Barbados dead.

The Event: THE APPEARANCE OF KASPAR HAUSER

When: May 26, 1828

Where: Nuremberg, Germany

The Mystery: The boy, when Georg Weichman the shoemaker found him, was in a bad way. He seemed to be either drunk or crazy, and he certainly was exhausted. He had with him a letter addressed to the "Captain of the 4th Squadron of the 6th Regiment of Cavalry in Nuremberg." Not knowing what else to do with the boy, Weichman took him to the captain's house.

Once there, all the boy could say was, "I want to be a soldier as my father was." Since he seemed to be hungry, he was offered meat, bread, and beer. Inexplicably, he ate only the bread and then drank some water. His feet were swollen, as if he had walked a long way, and his eyes squinted against the light, as if he were used to being in a dark place. He seemed to be about 17 years old.

The captain took him to the police station. There the youth repeated the sentence about wanting to be a soldier and on a piece of paper he wrote the name "Kaspar Hauser."

The letter he had given the shoemaker was supposedly from a day laborer. Its contents were brief: Kaspar had been left at his house in 1812. He did not know his own origins. The note ended with a plea that the boy be allowed to join the army. Kaspar now produced a 2nd note, which seemed to be from his mother. Written in Latin, it said that she was too poor to take care of Kaspar and that his father was dead.

Those who later described Kaspar Hauser as he appeared at this time varied widely in their accounts of what he was like. Some, probably the more romantic, said that he stumbled like a baby, had no depth perception, and often sat staring into space. Supposedly he could see the stars even during the day. Noise and light bothered him. Whenever he heard a clock strike, he leaped in alarm as if he had never heard such a sound before. He was frightened of thunderstorms and moonlight but loved snow. When he saw a lighted candle, he put his finger in the flame, but then cried out in surprise at the pain. Kaspar called all humans "boy" and all animals "horse." His sense of color was limited, and he had no conception of money. Was Kaspar retarded or had he been kept in a limited environment for so long that he lacked experience with common things?

The boy was put in the care of a professor, who taught him German. When he became fluent enough to explain himself he said that all his life he had been kept in a cell 6' to 7' long, 4' wide, and 5' high, with a dirt floor and 2 closed windows. He had slept on a straw bed and had been given only bread and water. His only toy had been a wooden horse.

Kaspar was finally put in the care of an Englishman, Lord Stanhope, who was interested in finding the boy's relatives. Stanhope theorized that the young man was related in some way to the ducal family of Baden. Also concerned was German criminologist Anselm von Feuerbach, who believed Kaspar was of royal blood.

Shortly after Kaspar was adopted by Stanhope, he was attacked in a cellar by a man disguised in blackface. Then on December 14, 1833, Kaspar went for a walk in the park at the invitation of a man who told him the gardener wanted him to see a new artesian well. Accepting the invitation was a fatal mistake. Kaspar was found in the park, stabbed dangerously near the heart but not yet dead. There were no footprints found in the snow but his, and there was no sign of a weapon. The boy lived for only 3 days. An autopsy showed that he had a large liver, which—along with his deformed legs—substantiated his story that he had spent a great part of his life in a cell. His wound, however, had not been self-inflicted—before he died, Kaspar said, "I didn't do it myself." Then, he added cryptically, "Many cats are the sure death of a mouse."

After his death, there was great interest in the identity of the boy. Books were written about him, but who he was has never been established with certainty.

Possible Solutions: Many believe that Kaspar Hauser was the legitimate son of Duke Karl Frederick of Baden, and that the boy was smuggled out of the castle by the morganatic wife of the duke's grandfather so that he could not succeed to the throne. A dead peasant baby, so the story goes, was put in his place. Kaspar Hauser did resemble the Baden family. The grand duke, however, later threw open all the family archives to refute the story and no evidence was found to support it.

Some people thought that Kaspar was Hungarian, mainly because he seemed to understand words spoken in that language. No evidence ever appeared to support such a theory. Rumor had it, too, that he was the illegitimate child of the daughter of an innkeeper and a priest.

One rather farfetched theory says that Kaspar Hauser was the victim of an experiment by extraterrestrial beings who brainwashed him and transformed his personality, giving him false memories. The beings then placed him on earth in order to study human behavior. Proponents of this theory like to quote Feuerbach, who said, "Kaspar Hauser was not of this world. He was brought to us, but he came from another planet, perhaps from another universe entirely."

Kaspar Hauser is buried in Ansbach cemetery. His tombstone reads: "Hic jacet CASPARUS HAUSER, Aenigma Sui Temporis, Ignota Nativitas, Occulta Mors, MDCCCXXXIII." (Here lies Kaspar Hauser, an enigma of his time, of unknown birth, of peculiar death, 1833.)

The Event: THE DEVIL'S FOOTPRINTS
When: February 8, 1855
Where: Towns in south Devonshire, England (Topsham, Lympstone, Exmouth, Teignmouth, Dawlish)
The Mystery: The snow fell heavily the night of February 8 in Devonshire. The following morning, a baker in Topsham stood in the doorway of his shop. To his amazement, he saw prints, all in a single line, which came to within a yard of his shop, then turned to the right until they reached a 5' brick wall and *continued on the top of the wall.* The prints were also seen by others on the tops of houses, in enclosed courtyards, in open fields, over hayricks, over 14' walls, over a 2-mi. estuary. The track looked like a small horseshoe, which measured from 1½" to 2" across and about 4" long. The steps were 8" apart, *in a single line.* In order for one creature to have made all the marks that appeared that

morning, it would have had to cover 60 mi. in 13 hours, at an average speed of 9 strides *per second.*

When the tracks came to a wall, then continued on the top of the wall, the snow was not displaced as it would have been had an animal made a leap. In places, it appeared that the snow had been removed, not pressed down; in others, it seemed that the tracks were branded into the snow.

A letter from an eyewitness said, "It was quite inexplicable that the animal, considering the scale of the foot, should leave, in single file, one print only, and as had already been observed, with intervals exactly preserved as if the prints had been made by a drill or any other mechanical frame. . . . A scientific friend informed me of his having traced the same prints across a field up to a haystack. The surface of the stack was wholly free from marks of any kind, but on the opposite side of the stack, in a direction exactly corresponding with the tracks thus traced, the prints began again."

Needless to say, the people of Devonshire were frightened out of their wits and were afraid to go outside at night. The newspapers, even those in London, carried stories about the event. The *Illustrated London News* printed an item from a correspondent in Heidelberg which said that a Polish doctor of medicine had seen similar tracks on a sand hill in Russian Poland, near the border of Galacia. The inhabitants there attributed the tracks to supernatural influences.

The Reverend Mr. Musgrave, in a sermon, suggested that the tracks might be those of a kangaroo. What other animal, he asked could jump like that?

Whatever, the tracks were never seen again.

Possible Solutions: As mentioned, the Reverend Mr. Musgrave thought the tracks might have been made by a kangaroo. There were some kangaroos in a private zoo nearby. However, they hadn't got out the night of the snowfall. Moreover, a kangaroo does not make single-line tracks, but paired, 4-toed impressions, several yards, rather than 8", apart.

Some thought the tracks were made by walking birds. Birds don't wear horseshoes, though. Still others thought the tracks might have been made by otters, rats, polecats, frogs, or badgers. A rabbit, they argued, moves in leaps, and its 4 feet together leave a mark in the shape of a horseshoe. But identifiable rabbit tracks were made that night, and they didn't look anything like the mysterious prints. And while a rat can run up a wall, it would leave traces. There were no such marks. Besides, rat tracks that had been left that night also differed from the mystery tracks.

Professor Richard Owen, famous for his identification of the leg bone of the extinct New Zealand moa, had a novel theory. He thought the tracks were made by a badger, which moved in such a way that the fore and hind foot had got blended. He failed to explain why the tracks were not in a double line and how the badger's flat foot turned into a horseshoe.

The truth was, no one could explain it. No known creature makes regular footprints in a regular line. A biped may hop on one foot for a little while, but not for 60 mi. When galloping, the animal may leave prints that seem to be in a single line, but when one examines the prints, one sees separate feet. And what quadruped could gallop at the same pace for such a long time?

And why were such footprints never seen again?

It was the devil, said some of the people in Devonshire, and perhaps their explanation is as acceptable as any.

NOTE: In 1953 and 1954, sea creatures were found on Canvey Island, England. They looked somewhat like a pig, had gills but no scales, and had 2 short legs ending in feet on which the toes were arranged in the shape of a "U." Could one of these creatures have made the devil's footprints?

The Event: THE FINDING OF THE PREHISTORIC CUBE
When: 1885
Where: Austria
The Mystery: In coal beds belonging to the Tertiary period (12 to 70 million years ago), there was found a metal cube, made of iron, carbon, and a little bit of nickel. Many experts think it could have been made only by human hands. *But there were no people then, and certainly no technology.*

Embedded in the coal, the cube measured 2½" by 1⅘", weighed 28 oz., and had an incision that ran around it horizontally.

Discovered by a Dr. Gurlt, the cube created a minor sensation. Articles about it appeared in *Nature*, the British scientific magazine, in November, 1886, and in *L'Astronomie*, published in Paris, in 1887.

The cube was put in the Salzburg Museum. A few years ago, the Russian journalist G. N. Ostroumov decided to investigate the story of the cube. Officials at the Salzburg Museum said it was lost, probably sometime before W.W. II. The file for the period in which the cube was found was also missing. Ostroumov published articles saying the whole thing was a hoax.

Possible Solutions: There are experts who think the cube was a meteorite. However, if it had come from space, the cube would not have retained its form but would have assumed an irregular shape during its fiery descent through the earth's atmosphere.

Other people think the cube is from an earlier terrestrial civilization that was highly technological but which was wiped out by a natural disaster.

Could some intelligence from another planet have planted it here? If so, why? Some postulate that it might have been a data collector. If this were so, it might have stored a record of earth events, and perhaps—say those who believe this theory—the intelligence that planted the cube also retrieved it from the Salzburg Museum.

Perfect shapes do occur in nature. However, the cube did not have enough sulfur to be made of pyrite, the natural mineral that sometimes occurs in geometric shapes. Still, the idea that the shape did develop naturally cannot be entirely discounted. Very old cylindrical objects have turned out to be parts of petrified trees.

NOTE: Similar items that have been found are:

—A fossil screw with perfect spiral formation was found inside a rock from the so-called "Abbey Gallery" in Treasure City, Nev. "The stratum in which it was found is extremely old," experts say.

—Objects resembling bullets have been found in the bones of prehistoric animals.

—Perfect glass lenses, metal nails, chains, and batteries—all far older than the technology of the time they date back to—have been discovered.

The explanations? Take your pick: hoaxes, alien beings, or early, technologically advanced civilizations that disappeared leaving only traces are just some of the possibilities.

The Event: THE DISAPPEARANCE OF THE CREW OF THE *Mary Celeste*
When: November, 1872
Where: The Atlantic Ocean
The Mystery: On December 4, 1872, the *Dei Gratia*, a British brig skippered by Capt. David Read Morehouse, was somewhere between New York and Gibraltar when its crew spotted a ship moving in a strange and erratic manner. The ship's jib and foremost staysail were set, and it was sailing on a starboard tack. When the crew of the *Dei Gratia* hailed it, there was no answer.

The captain ordered mate Oliver Deveau to row over and find out what was going on. This small boarding crew identified the ship as the *Mary Celeste*, which had been docked in New York at the same time as the *Dei Gratia*. When they went aboard, *there was no one there.*

While accounts vary, they agree on certain things. In the cabin, all 6 windows were battened up with wood planking and canvas. Chests of clothes were dry, and razors were not rusty—obviously the ship had not been swamped. A vial of sewing machine oil stood upright by a reel of cotton thread, which would lead one to believe that there had been no heavy seas. There was plenty of food and water—enough for months—on board. On a slate in the mate's cabin was the message "Fanny, my dear wife . . ." Water lay on the floor of the ship's galley, and the scuttle hatch was off.

One of the pumps was drawn to let the sounding rod down. There was some damage —a clock was spoiled by water, the compass in the binnacle was broken, there were gashes on the rail, the rigging was torn. The lifeboats, if any, were gone. It looked as though those aboard had left in a great hurry. A woman's clothes and a child's toys lay about, and an impression the size of a child's body was on the captain's bed.

Morehouse ordered Deveau and 2 others to take the *Mary Celeste* to Gibraltar, where she was put in custody of the British Vice-Admiralty Court as a derelict and an investigation was begun. Morehouse wanted to claim her as salvage.

The inquiry lasted for weeks. It was established that the last entry in the logbook on November 24 gave a latitude of 56° N. and a longitude of 27° 20' W. On board had been the captain, Benjamin Briggs, a straitlaced New Englander; his wife; his baby daughter; and a crew of 7. New evidence provoked questions. Was there a bloodstained hatchet buried in the mast? Had the rails been intentionally slashed? Where were the ship's bills of lading and its manifest? What happened during the 10 days between her abandonment and her discovery by the *Dei Gratia*? Was an Italian sword found? How were the lifeboats, if any, launched?

The court gave a judgment for salvage of £1,700 to the *Dei Gratia*, and gave the *Mary Celeste* back to her owners, but it offered no satisfactory explanation of what had happened to the derelict.

Possible Solutions:

1. The crew of the *Dei Gratia* murdered everyone aboard the *Mary Celeste* for the salvage money. (If so, it was a less profitable venture than they had expected it to be.)

2. The crew of the *Mary Celeste* found water in the bilge, misinterpreted its importance, and abandoned the ship in panic. (If so, the captain, who was both level-headed and competent, was probably already dead of a heart attack or other illness at the time.)

3. The *Mary Celeste* was becalmed and run down by pirates, who boarded her and murdered everyone. (There was no evidence of pirates in that area at the time, however.)

4. Everyone on board died of plague. (What happened to the bodies?)

5. The ship was attacked by a giant squid.

6. Somehow the captain's wife had been killed, and the grieving captain had jumped overboard. The crew got drunk and, following a series of bloody fights, left the ship in groups. After the dead were buried at sea, the others sought land using the lifeboats.

7. In *Strand Magazine*, published in London in 1913, an Oxford M.A., Howard Luforth, gave this version, incredible as it may seem: A platform had been built by the crew from which they could observe the captain and his mate swim in a race around the ship. The 2 swimmers were eaten by a shark and the platform collapsed, dumping the crew in the sea.

8. The ship's cargo of alcohol had exploded. (There was no evidence of fire or explosion reported by the *Dei Gratia* boarding crew.)

9. A submarine had taken the captain and crew off the ship, carried them to the bottom of the ocean, then transferred them to a UFO which flew them into outer space.

10. One member of the crew was a homicidal maniac, who killed everyone on board and then committed suicide. (What happened to the bodies was not explained.)

11. According to spiritualists at a séance, Captain Briggs had found a newly arisen Atlantis, where he went ashore. Everyone left the ship to admire the meadows and marble houses on the marvelous island, whereupon the island sank again, drowning them all.

NOTE: Whatever the true cause, those on the *Mary Celeste* were never found. There is a painting of the *Mary Celeste* in the museum of the township of Aulec, New Brunswick. There is also, according to John Godwin in *This Baffling World*, a *Mary Celeste* museum. He says: "In New York City, at 45 Wall Street, a small museum dedicated to the mystery of the *Mary Celeste* is maintained by the Atlantic Mutual Insurance Company. The *Mary Celeste* Room simulates an underwriter's office of bygone days. Among the memorabilia is a 35" model of the ship, authentic in every detail. A lap desk, which originally belonged to the ship's master, stands exactly as it appeared when the vessel was boarded by the crew of the *Dei Gratia*."

The Event: THE DISAPPEARANCE OF DAVID LANG

When: September 23, 1880

Where: A farm about 12 mi. from Gallatin, Tenn.

The Mystery: David Lang's 2 children, George, 8, and Sarah, 11, were playing in the yard with a wooden wagon pulled by wooden horses when Lang and his wife came out of the vine-covered brick house. Lang probably talked to the children about the toy, which he had bought for them in Nashville that morning. Then he began to walk across the pasture, which was burned brown by a dry spell. At this time, Judge August Peck and Lang's brother-in-law came driving up the lane in a buggy. The judge saw Lang in the field and was just going to shout to him when it happened. *Lang vanished from the earth.* One minute he was standing in an open field, on which there was short grass but no trees, stones, or fences. The next minute he was simply gone.

Mrs. Lang and the 2 men went to the spot where Lang had disappeared, thinking that he might have fallen into a crack in the earth. But they found no such crack. Mrs. Lang became hysterical and was led, screaming, into the house. Someone rang a huge bell, which brought the neighbors to help. Soon scores of people were searching the field and nearby land, but to no avail.

A surveyor and geologist who examined the field later found limestone bedrock just a few feet underground. There was no fracture in this bedrock.

For a month the search went on. Curiosity seekers came to gawk. All the Lang servants except the cook quit in fear.

A year later, the grass where Lang had disappeared had grown high and thick in a circle 20' in diameter. Not one of the farm animals would graze there, and it seemed free of insects. It was as though an ominous presence hovered over that piece of ground.

One day in early August, 1881, Sarah and George approached the green circle of high grass. Sarah called out, "Father, are you anywhere around?" There was no answer, but she repeated the question 4 times. They were about to walk away when they heard a faint cry for help, a cry that came out of nowhere. Quickly the children ran and got their mother, who returned with them to the spot and called as they had done. *Her husband answered.* For several days, the family returned, and each day when they called, the answering voice became fainter, until finally there was no response at all.

Possible Solutions: Lang, like many other people who have strangely disappeared, went into the 4th dimension—or so some people think. Others feel that he may have been picked up by a UFO invisible to the human eye.

The Event: ALBERT OSTMAN IS CARRIED AWAY BY A SASQUATCH
When: 1924

Where: Canada, the mainland just opposite Vancouver Island

The Mystery: Albert Ostman, a Scandinavian lumberjack, chose a wild area at the head of Toba Inlet on the Powell River for a combination vacation-prospecting trip. Somewhere near, there was a lost gold mine he wanted to find. From an old Indian he hired to take him up the fjord, he 1st heard of the giant Sasquatch, a name which means "wild men of the woods." These creatures, hairy though they were, seemed human, and resembled the yeti of the Himalayas.

With him Ostman had food supplies for 3 weeks, a rifle, a sleeping bag, and other basic equipment. As soon as he was well started on his way, he dismissed the Indian. He found a good place to spend the 1st night, where he made a bed of branches and hung his supplies on a pole, high above the ground. In the morning, when he found that his things had been disturbed, he thought a porcupine might have done it. When the same thing happened the 2nd night, he realized it could not have been a porcupine. Whatever it was had not touched the salt, which porcupines always take 1st. The 3rd evening, intending to stay awake all night, he did not undress, but took off his boots and put them in the bottom of his sleeping bag. Half asleep, he suddenly felt himself being picked up. Still in the sleeping bag, he was thrown over something and carried along. For perhaps 30 mi. he was jounced about in the confining sack. Then he was dropped to the ground. It was still dark. He heard voices, but he recognized no words. When he finally worked his way out of the sleeping bag, he looked up and saw 4 giant creatures, standing like humans on 2 legs. Somewhat whimsically, he said, "What do you chaps want with me?"

It was a Sasquatch family—a mother and father and 2 children, one male and one female. When Ostman described them later, he called the father and mother the "old man" and the "old woman." The "old man," who was between 7' and 8' tall, was obviously the one who had carried him through the woods. The Sasquatch father was gesturing and explaining his trip in some kind of speech, while the "old woman" objected.

At daybreak, Ostman saw where he was—in a natural bowl high in the mountains with only one way to get out. He was trapped. At 1st he was too exhausted to try to make a break. He bided his time, while he checked over his supplies. Although much had been brought along, several things were missing, including his prunes and matches. However, his snuff was still there.

For 7 days, the lumberjack was held prisoner. During that time, the young male offered him grass and sweet roots to eat. This youth and the "old man" developed a liking for snuff, which proved to be the instrument of Ostman's escape. When, on the 7th day, Ostman offered snuff to the "old man," the "old man" ingested all that was left. His eyes began to roll, and he charged off to the spring for water. Ostman headed for the opening in the encircling mountain walls and freedom.

He camped out the 1st night and finally emerged from the woods near a logging operation. He did not tell his story for many years because he thought, and rightly so, that no one would believe it. When he finally did tell it, he gave detailed descriptions of the Sasquatch. The male, he said, was barrel-chested with long forearms, short fingers, a hairy body, and a 2"-long penis. The female, over 7' tall, had a wide pelvis and drooping breasts. They were herbivores, eating evergreen tips, grasses, roots, and ferns.

Possible Solutions: Was Ostman making up the story? Many experts, including Ivan Sanderson, world-famous zoologist, think not.

Do Sasquatch exist? Those who think so talk about the 100 or more sightings of Sasquatch since 1920, the photographs of footprints, and the 3 films which have been made. The footprints, which could not have been made by a "machine," are exactly the kind a huge humanoid would make.

The films are another story. One made by Roger Patterson, a Sasquatch believer, shows a "female" with suspiciously slim hips and an overly human walk. There are those who think this film is a hoax, and that its central male character is also a human dressed up in an "ape" costume.

People who do not think Sasquatch exist ask some hard-to-answer questions: Why hasn't one been captured? Why haven't the pilots in fire-prevention helicopters spotted the huge creatures? How can the Sasquatch possibly gather enough herbaceous material in those relatively barren woods to feed themselves?

If the Sasquatch do exist, what are they? Anthropologists will tell you that they are a lost tribe of Indians living a primitive existence in the American Northwest. Believers in visitations by extraterrestrial beings will tell you that they are homunculi raised elsewhere and put on earth for experimental reasons. Others will tell you that they are a new species of orangutan.

NOTE: In Willow Creek, Calif. there is a huge redwood statue of a Sasquatch (or Bigfoot) in the middle of town, and each year the townspeople hold a carnival called "Bigfoot Daze." There are footprints in the sidewalks (a kind of primitive Grauman's Chinese Theater), and Bigfoot ashtrays and rings are for sale in all the gift shops.

The Event: THE LOCH NESS MONSTER RAISES ITS UGLY HEAD
When: 1933
Where: Loch Ness, Scotland
The Mystery: Loch Ness is a huge lake, 750' deep, twice the depth of the North Sea. It is 24 mi. long and varies in width from one to 3 mi. For 1,500 years, people have been seeing a monster in it. Long ago on St. Columbia's Day, legend has it, people saw a "very odd-looking beastie, something like a huge frog, only it isn't a frog."

In 1933, several people saw the monster. One was a patrolman in Inverness-shire, who described it as a series of humps above the water preceded by a long thin neck on which there was a small snakelike head. Its skin was gray-black. On May 22, John Mackay, who ran the hotel at Drunnadrochit, saw it, too. The water frothed as it vanished, he said.

Two months later to the day, a couple from London saw the monster cross the road. Its size astounded them—its body was 5' high and as wide as the road. It moved like a big snail in a sequence of jerks. Later, when shown a picture of a plesiosaurus marine reptile, the man said the monster looked like it.

During the early 1930s, several photographs were taken of the monster. Sir Edward Mountain, who lived near the lake, arranged for people with binoculars to watch the lake for appearances of the monster. The vigil paid off. A few weeks later, he was even able to take a movie of it.

Since W.W. II, the monster has been taken very seriously. In October, 1954, the passengers on a bus driving by the lake were able to observe the monster for 10 minutes as it surfaced not more than 100 yards away.

In December, 1954, a fishing boat was crossing the lake when its echo-sounder began to chart something swimming at a depth of 540'. It was recorded as a creature with a small head on a long neck, 8 short legs, and a 15' tail. It measured about 50' in length. Experts who analyzed the chart said it was a living thing.

Four years later, the British Broadcasting Company, attempting to produce a program about the monster, recorded an object on the echo-sounder that moved 12' deeper, then disappeared at 60'. Two days after, 4 men riding by on a bus saw humps emerging in the same spot; there was a big wash as the humps submerged.

Since then, various scientific teams have investigated the monster. In 1973–1974, Japanese scientists using deep-water equipment began a major study.

Possible Solutions: There seems to be little doubt that there is something big living in Loch Ness. What manner of creature is another matter.

Lt. Comdr. T. R. Gould, an expert on sea serpents, felt the creature was a huge newt, perhaps a leftover from prehistoric times, which had been trapped in the lake. Others, including Dr. Maurice Burton, think that it is some kind of otherwise extinct reptile, possibly a plesiosaur.

It is possible, experts believe, that the monster divides its time between the lake and the ocean, going from one to the other through an underground water route. It might seek the lake at breeding season or to escape predators in the sea.

The Event: A GREEK SHEPHERD MIRACULOUSLY HEALS A LAMB WITH BROKEN LEGS
When: 1941
Where: Athens, Greece
The Mystery: Athanasios Contogcorgc, shepherd, 1st healed a child's crooked legs when he was 28 years old. (Before that, he had confined himself to animals.) Word spread, and he was soon seeing close to 60 patients a day. Known as "Vlahos" (Greek for "shepherd"), he acquired an international reputation and treated statesmen and millionaires, including King Paul of Greece, who broke his foot in a skiing accident, and Haile Selassie of Ethiopia, who suffered a sciatica attack when visiting Greece. At one time, he was treating both the American and British Ambassadors.

But he was not an MD, and it wasn't long before the medical establishment attacked him as a fraud and brought a case against him in an Athens court.

When the judge asked him why he had healing powers, he said he didn't know. "But you do *profess* to heal, do you not?" a doctor asked.

"I do heal," answered the shepherd.

He was then asked if he had a medical certificate from a university or had other permission to practice medicine. Before he could answer, a doctor jumped up and said, "The man cannot even read or write. He is illiterate. How could he have any kind of legal certificate to practice medicine? The man is a charlatan and must be stopped from practicing his black magic and deluding the hill people."

Then the shepherd, obviously hurt, said, "If the doctors in the courtroom can do what I am about to do, I will stop my healing."

The doctors were not happy with that statement, saying the shepherd was probably going to perform some showy trick. However, the judge told the shepherd to proceed.

The shepherd went to the back of the courtroom, untied a lamb that had been tethered there, patted it, then broke its legs. The people in the room could hear its legs snap. The doctors, asked to examine the lamb, could not

deny that the creature's legs, sticking out at bizarre angles, were indeed broken.

Without any theatrics, the shepherd then put the lamb on the floor and set its bones in place, whereupon the lamb got up and began to run around the courtroom. The doctors, upon examining it, were astounded.

"Now, my friends," said the shepherd, "which one among you will do the same?"

He won his case.

Possible Solutions: Who knows what causes healing hands? The shepherd said, "The power of God goes through my hands." Believers would agree.

The Event: THE STRANGE DISAPPEARANCE OF FLIGHT 19
When: December 5, 1945
Where: The Bermuda Triangle, off the coast of Florida
The Mystery: Flight 19 should have been routine. It was a normal training flight from the Naval Air Station at Fort Lauderdale, Fla.—5 TBM Avengers, torpedo bombers equipped with excellent navigational and radio equipment. One plane had a crew of 2; the others had 3 men each. Their planned course was a triangle—160 mi. east, 40 mi. north, then southwest back to the base.

At 2:02, the 1st plane took off, and soon they were all flying in formation at a speed of 200 mph.

The 1st sign of trouble came 1½ hours later. By that time, they should have returned to base. Instead, there was a weird radio message from the flight commander, "Calling tower. This is an emergency. . . . We seem to be off course. . . . We cannot see land . . . (REPEAT) . . . We cannot see land." When asked for their position, he said, "We are not sure of our position. We can't be sure of just where we are. We seem to be lost." Then, when told to head due west, he radioed, "We do not know which way is west. Everything is wrong . . . strange. We can't be sure of any direction. Even the ocean doesn't look as it should."

Fifteen minutes later, personnel in the control tower heard the men on the planes talking back and forth. Then the flight commander did something extremely unusual—he turned control over to one of his men.

At 4:25, the last message came, "Not certain where we are . . . about 225 mi. northeast of base. . . . Looks like we are—"

A Martin flying boat with a crew of 13 men took off to begin a search for the missing planes. Five minutes later, it vanished. Six planes were now inexplicably lost.

All night long, Coast Guard planes searched, and in the morning, an aircraft carrier sent up more planes. Before night, there were 21 ships, 300 planes, and 12 land-based parties looking for the missing Flight 19 and the Martin flying boat. But there was no trace of them, not even an oil slick.

Adding to the mystery were several unanswered questions: Why was there no SOS from Flight 19? Why was there no debris? Why hadn't the Martin flying boat simply landed on the water? What happened to the Martin's emergency radio equipment? The naval inquiry board that investigated the disappearances said, "We are not able to even make a good guess as to what happened."

Since then, both planes and ships have continued to vanish in the Bermuda Triangle, the area bounded by Florida, Bermuda, Puerto Rico, and Jamaica. (In Europe, the area is called both the Magic Rhombus and the Triangle of Death.)

In 1965–1966, the National Bureau of Standards studied the coastline along the edge of the Triangle, using special microphones and instruments to pick up ultrasonic noise. They did hear some strange whispering sounds, but technicians could not identify them.

In 1967, the Navy spent over $5 million searching the ocean floors with research submarines but found nothing.

Possible Solutions: Perhaps it is simply coincidence that so many ships and planes have vanished in the Bermuda Triangle. Since the area is heavily traveled, statistically speaking, accidents are more likely to take place there.

On the other hand, some scientists think that some parts of the ocean may periodically produce chemical compounds which could affect humans to the extent that they lose their sense of direction. Researchers at the Max Planck Institute in Germany, for instance, have detected high concentrations of nitrous oxide (laughing gas) near Iceland. They think it possible that the oceans may go through chemical phases; during one of these phases, catabolism—chemical reactions related to organic decomposition—may occur.

Perhaps the Bermuda Triangle is one of several so-called "vile vortices," spaced evenly around the world. These areas are characterized by magnetic and gravitational anomalies, which may be caused by their bowlike shapes. Maybe the planes fell *up.*

Or, could it be that alien beings in underwater bases captured the planes and ships (or at least their crews)? Or was it UFOs from outer space, which came through magnetic or gravitational "holes" in the sky?

Finally, did the ships and planes and the people on them pass into the 4th dimension through a kind of gap in time?

If so, are they now in a parallel universe?

We may never know the answer.

The Event: A WOMAN DIES IN FLAMES
When: July 2, 1951
Where: St. Petersburg, Fla.

The Mystery: The last people to see Mary Reeser alive were her friend Mrs. P. M. Carpenter and her son Richard Reeser, who dropped by to see her the night of July 1. Mrs. Reeser, 67, was ready for bed in a rayon nightgown, bedroom slippers, and a housecoat.

The next morning, a Western Union boy who had come to deliver a telegram to Mrs. Reeser got no answer to his knock. He sought the help of Mrs. Carpenter, who, when she tried Mrs. Reeser's door, found the brass doorknob too hot to touch. Alarmed, she asked some nearby workmen to help her get in.

The inside of the room was extremely hot, even though the windows were open. Near one of the windows was a pile of charred wood which had once been a chair and a shrunken skull and some bits of bone which had once been Mrs. Reeser. A small table and a floor lamp had burned, too; the wall was coated with soot starting 3'–4' above the floor. A base plug in the wall had melted, which, according to a clock that had stopped, caused a short-circuit at 4:20 A.M. The heat had been so terrific that some pink candles on another table had melted and run out of their holders.

Experts estimated that it would have taken a fire burning at a temperature of 3,000° to destroy Mrs. Reeser's 170-lb. body and the chair so completely. Where had the fire come from? There had been no lightning that night. Why hadn't the whole room burned? Wilton Korgman, an anthropologist, said, "Never have I seen a skull so shrunken nor a body so completely consumed by heat. This is contrary to normal experience, and I regard it as the most amazing thing I have ever seen."

Possible Solutions: Lightning? There wasn't any that night. Explosives or chemicals? None were present. An electrical fire? The melting wall plug had blown the fuses before the fire began. Months later, baffled police attributed the impossible fire to "a neglected cigarette."

The Event: A UFO LANDS IN WEST VIRGINIA
When: September, 1952
Where: Flatwoods, W.Va.

The Mystery: In streams of fire, the round thing wobbled down to earth, then dropped out of sight behind the trees. Eddie May, 13, and his brother Fred, 12, ran to tell their mother what they had seen. A skeptical Mrs. May went outside and saw a red pulsating light glowing on the hillside. Alarmed, she sent the 2 boys to get help, and they soon returned with Gene Lemon, a young National Guardsman.

Lemon was armed with only a flashlight as

he led the Mays and 3 other children up the hill. It was the perfect setting for a UFO landing—a misty, eerie night on a brush-covered hill. Lemon, one of the boys, and the May dog were about 50' ahead of the rest of the group, when they saw the red, glowing thing and smelled something sulfurous. They stopped at a gateway in an old broken-down fence to look at the object, which seemed about 6' high and 25' in diameter. Soon the others arrived on the scene, and everyone stared in awe.

Then the Mays' dog began to growl, as something moved in the trees near them. Suddenly a figure came into view. It was a 10'-tall being wearing a helmet. Its body (or suit) was of a dark silky material. Inside the helmet was a round red "face" with 2 eyes that reflected the light. It was not walking but somehow sliding over the ground.

Meanwhile, there was a hissing sound and the smell of sulfur. The dog fled in fear, followed closely by the terrified humans. They phoned the sheriff from Sutton, a nearby town, only to find that he and his deputy were out checking a story about a crashed plane. (There was no crashed plane.) The news of the UFO spread fast. Within a half hour, a large group of people had assembled, including Lee Stewart, Jr., editor of the Braxton paper. Mrs. May was in a state of hysteria, her children in shock.

Lemon, the editor Stewart, and some others went back up the hill. By then, however, the thing was gone, but the sulfur smell still hung in the air, and there were skid marks in the bushes.

Possible Solutions: Explanations of what UFOs may be range from the scientific to the mystical.

Professor Françoise le Lionnais believes they are a collective illusion. Astronomer Paul Muller says they may be lens-shaped clouds. Dr. Herman Oberth, a famed German rocket expert, said in 1955 that he believed UFOs came from outer space somewhere. But a few weeks later—now working for the U.S., under top security, at the Redstone Arsenal in Alabama —he no longer made such statements.

In 1955, too, Gen. Douglas MacArthur said, "The nations of the world will be forced to unite . . . for the next war will be an interplanetary war." And a Washington UFO study dated March, 1965, reported, "The U.S.A. has to admit it has no explanation for at least 633 sightings clearly made in detail and by people in full possession of their faculties. What is certain is that these things were not test balloons in the sky; neither were they light-refraction phenomena, or stars, aircraft, missiles, or flying objects of man-made or known physical origin."

Many believe that long before the 1st appearance of humans, the earth was visited by aliens in "flying saucers." UFOs, they say, brought civilization. For proof, they cite cave paintings and other primitive art forms which seem to depict alien beings in helmets and round flying objects. They talk of strange sightings in the sky recorded in the time of Cicero, and indecipherable languages found in South America, and pyramids built of stones impossible to lift, and Ezekiel's wheel. Perhaps the incident at Flatwoods was merely an inspection visit by aliens to see what earthlings were up to now.

—A.E.

An Atlas to Enigmatic Lands:
A Guided Tour to Places on the Earth
Which Remain Confounding and Mystifying

The Place: NAZCA
Location: The Peruvian desert, 15° south latitude, between 73° and 75° west longitude.
The Enigma: From the air above the Nazca desert, one sees the ground come alive with huge outlines of geometric figures and spiders, birds, fish, llamas, condors, snakes, 6-petaled flowers, and haloed gods. Some of the figures are longer than 2 football fields; some of the lines are 40 mi. long. It is estimated that the pattern has been there for 700 to 1,500 years. Drawn on the ground, by exposing the light yellow soil which lies under the dark surface of

the ground, the lines have remained because there is little rain and erosion there.

At the end of the plateau are statues, buildings, and carvings. One is an 80'-high double rock which seems to represent a human head, but contains drawings of at least 14 heads which show, symbolically, 4 races of man. An Inca, Tupac Yupanqui, says of the carvings: "The white men from the stars created them . . . created them in their likeness, in the likeness of the strangers living in the 4 quarters of the world. . . ."

Many of the carvings can be seen only at a certain time—an hour of the day, a time of year—when light hits them at a special angle. Daniel Ruzo, a Peruvian explorer, took a photograph of a bas-relief carved on a hill which showed an old man's face. The *negative* of the photograph depicted a *young* man. Some of the statues and carvings show animals not indigenous to South America—tortoises, African lions, and camels, for instance.

The enigmas? Who did the lines and the carvings? How did they do them?

Some Explanations: Dr. Maria Reiche, a German astronomer, spent 20 years charting the lines of Nazca from a high ladder. She has correlated her findings with positions of the sun, moon, and stars, and feels that the lines represent a huge "desert calendar," the South American version of Stonehenge.

Those who believe that alien beings from outer space have been visiting the earth for thousands of years think that the lines were either made, or ordered to be made, by extraterrestrials. An aerotrain flying just above the ground might, they feel, have inhaled the surface dirt to expose the patterns.

Professor J. Alden Mason, curator emeritus of the University of Pennsylvania, believes that the lines were made following a smaller model.

Who made the lines? It was not the Incas, the Indians say, but another race before them. The triangles and trapezoids of the lines bear no relation to more recent Inca roads.

Today: Those who want to see the lines can get to the area by going 1st to Lima, then flying in a small plane to either Paracas or Nazca. The Pan-American Highway that goes from Lima to Valparaiso passes through the lines. However, to appreciate them, they should be seen from the air, perhaps from a chartered plane.

The Place: STONEHENGE
Location: England, the Salisbury Plain, 8 mi. north of Salisbury, 2 mi. west of Amesbury.
The Enigma: Stonehenge, that huge monument of prehistoric men, stands a broken, ancient mystery on an English plain. Who built it? How did they build it? Why did they build it?

Constructed of huge blocks of sandstone (sarsen stone) hauled from great distances, it was probably begun in 2200 B.C., with later generations adding to it. The Heel Stone, which was part of the original construction, is a huge boulder in its natural state, 16' high and 8' thick, brought from 24 mi. away. In later centuries, giant bluestones from Pembrokeshire's Prescelly Mountains, 135 mi. away in Wales, were added. After Stonehenge was rebuilt about 1600 B.C., it was an arrangement of concentric circles of bluestone pillars, topped with lintels joined by a mortise-and-tenon joint, and surrounded by an outer circle of 56

regularly spaced, small circular pits called the Aubrey Holes.

Some Explanations: In 1140, Geoffrey of Monmouth, in his *History of the Kings of Britain,* said Aurelius Ambrosius built Stonehenge by bringing the "Dance of Giants" from Ireland. Inigo Jones, the 17th-century architect, thought it was a Roman temple.

John Aubrey, who stole precious relics and wrote a gossipy book about Shakespeare and others called *Brief Lives,* attributed Stonehenge to the Druids. This was a popular theory until archaeologists proved that it was built before the Druids arrived in England.

It was a British professor of astronomy, Gerald S. Hawkins, who, in 1963, came up with the theory popularly accepted today—that Stonehenge was a giant stone calendar and observatory. He was attached to an experimental missile base nearby when he became interested in Stonehenge and thought that its arrangement might have something to do with movements of the heavenly bodies. When a person stands in the center of the Stonehenge circle, specific stars, or the sun, or the moon, appear over certain stones in such a way and so often that it cannot be pure coincidence. Hawkins fed his calculations into a computer, and the computer said he was right. The most significant cycle occurs every 18.6 years at Stonehenge, when the moon rises in midwinter over a certain stone.

How did the ancients transport the stones? Probably by water on rafts and by land on sledges. Estimates of how long it took to build Stonehenge differ. The most extreme estimate is that it was built over a time span of 9 centuries, or 30 generations.

Today: Each year the members of the Most Ancient Order of Druids go to Stonehenge to perform rites which they say date back to Atlantis. There is, however, no proof that the Druids were even connected with Stonehenge at all since the site was probably in ruins and abandoned by 300 B.C. Historically and chronologically, Stonehenge and the Druids are from different eras.

The Place: THE LOST COLONY OF ROANOKE
Location: Roanoke Island, N.C.
The Enigma: In 1584, 2 English sea captains financed by Sir Walter Raleigh discovered Roanoke Island. A year later, Raleigh sent 7 ships under the command of Sir Richard Grenville to colonize the island. In 1587 more colonists, led by Governor John White, settled on Roanoke. But because added supplies were needed to survive the bitter winter ahead, White returned to England. The British war with Spain delayed White, and it was not until 3 years later that he returned with supplies for the 121 settlers of Roanoke, who had included his wife,

daughter, and granddaughter (Virginia Dare, the 1st white child born in the New World).

Approaching Roanoke in July, 1590, the sailors on White's ship alerted the colonists "with a trumpet a Call, and afterwardes many familiar English tunes of Songs, and called to them friendly." But the Roanoke colonists did not rush to greet the ship, not one human figure was visible on shore, and the silence was ominous. When the sailors landed and entered the village, they found it mysteriously deserted. No sign of the 121 colonists existed. The entire population had vanished. The fort and homes still stood intact. There were no bodies, no signs of destruction, no indication of battle. It had been agreed that an inscribed cross would be left as a signal of distress if the settlers had to leave in haste, but no such mark was found. The only clue to the fate of the "Lost Colony" was the word "CROATAN" carved in the bark of a tree near the gate of the fort, and the letters "CRO" carved on another tree stripped of bark. What had happened to the colonists?

Some Explanations: Although it was generally assumed that the colonists were overwhelmed by hostile Indians, no evidence remained of such violence. Many other theories have been advanced. According to one, the colonists abandoned Roanoke to move to Croatan Island. There, they constructed a ship to take them to some more civilized outpost but perished at sea soon after sailing. According to another theory, Spanish seamen, eager to wipe out English claims to America, invaded Roanoke, took the colonists captive, and massacred them.

But the most intriguing and credible theory of all is that the colonists, fearing either the elements or an attack by a savage nomadic Indian tribe, took refuge with the friendly Croatan Indians who lived nearby, and eventually intermarried with and were assimilated by these Croatans. In 1719, over a century after the disappearance of the colonists, when white hunters came to Robeson—or Robinson—County, N.C., just 100 mi. inland from Roanoke, they found a tribe of unusual Indians whose skins were light and who spoke English. A 1790 census of the Robinson County Indians revealed that 54 of the 95 family names were those of the lost colonists.

Today: Wrote Edwin C. Hill in 1934: "In Robinson County, N.C., live some 12,000 Indians known as the Robinson County Indians. They are a fine and handsome people. Some have blue eyes. Some have gray eyes. They speak only the English language. They use phrases of speech that have scarcely been heard since the days of Shakespeare. . . . If tradition holds any truth, they are the descendants of the lost colonists of Roanoke." Or so it seems. It is unlikely we shall ever know the truth about the fate of the "Lost Colony."

The life of Roanoke is re-created annually at the Waterside Theater, Roanoke Island, Manteo, N.C. There, between June 21 and August 31, an outdoor historical drama is staged by 150 performers. Admission prices range from $1.50 to $3.50. The play, billed as *The Lost Colony—The Greatest Disappearing Act Ever to Appear in America*, enjoyed its 35th season in 1975.

The Place: EASTER ISLAND (Rapa Nui)

Location: The Pacific Ocean, 2,500 mi. west of Chile.

The Enigma: When the Dutch navigator Jaakob Roggeveen discovered Easter Island in 1722, he found huge stone statues there. He probably wondered who carved them and why. Had he known how many statues there were— over 100 completed and 150 half finished— and had he been able to comprehend the magnitude of the task, he would have been even more astounded than he was.

Easter Island is tiny—35 mi. in circumference—and far from any other land. It is volcanic and somewhat barren, with very few trees, plenty of insects, and almost no animal population but rats, and its native inhabitants.

The statues, with their ruthless expressions and gigantic size, dominate the island. Some are as high as a 3-story house and weigh over 60 tons. They represent Caucasian males with long ears, large eyes, jutting chins, and little legs. Although they have some decorations around their stomachs, they are otherwise naked. All were carved so symmetrically that when they were erected, they had perfect balance.

Pierre Loti, the French writer, came to the island in 1870. He described the statues: "What race did they represent with their turned-up noses and their thin lips thrust forward in an expression of disdain or mockery? They have no eyes, only deep cavities under their large, noble foreheads, yet they seem to be looking and thinking. . . ."

Some of the statues are now toppled and broken. Most had topknots made from red stone once, but all these have long since fallen off.

Construction on the statues stopped suddenly sometime in the 1600s. Some statues are half-carved from the volcanic rock and the carvers' tools lie scattered about.

Some Explanations: What humans did the statues represent? Obviously not Polynesians, yet who would have visited the island before Roggeveen except Polynesians? (Captain Cook, they say, found red-haired and blond white people on many of the islands. How did they get there?)

According to the islanders' legend, the "long ears"—led by a chief named Hoto-Matua—came to the island in 475 A.D., after a voyage of 120 days from a place in the east. Many years after, the "short ears" (Polynesians?) came and were enslaved by the "long ears," who made them work on the statues. Sometime in the 1600s, the "short ears" got fed up with their enslavement and killed all the "long ears" but one, who had many descendants.

It was Thor Heyerdahl, the Norwegian ethnologist, who in 1947 came up with a reasonable explanation of where those "long ears" originated. Similarities in the names of gods, in plants (notably the sweet potato), and in the arts led him to believe that the "long ears" came from South America, perhaps what is now Peru. To prove that men could have sailed by raft to Easter Island, he built a raft of balsa wood, the *Kon-Tiki*, and sailed across the Pacific to an atoll 4,000 mi. west of Peru.

But who were those white men? Scandinavians? Men from Atlantis or Lemuria or outer space? The mystery remains.

Today: The statues still stand on Easter Island.

The Place: OAK ISLAND
Location: Mahone Bay, Nova Scotia
The Enigma: Evidence of buried treasure was found on Oak Island in 1795. Since then, people have been digging for that treasure almost constantly, but no one has managed to unearth it, even though its location is known exactly.

The original discoverers of the treasure were 3 young woodsmen who were canoeing out on the bay. They saw live oaks, which were not indigenous to the area, growing on one of the islands and went over to investigate. On shore, they found a heavy ring bolt, the kind used to moor ships, and, in a clearing, there was a giant oak tree, covered with marks and figures. One of its branches had been cut off 4' from the trunk. Under it was a depression. The men began to dig immediately, not knowing they were beginning a monumental task that would take months. Ten feet below the surface of the ground, they uncovered an oak platform. There was another platform at 20', another at 30'. Realizing that digging any farther would involve more resources than they had, they gave up. However, others soon took up the search for the treasure in what became known as the "Money Pit."

In 1849, a syndicate decided to drill into the site to see what lay below the previous diggings. At 98', the drill hit oak, and under the oak, judging by the shreds of gold that clung to the drill, part of the treasure. At that point, seawater surged into the hole from an underground chamber which was somehow connected to the ocean.

Since then, many people have, with no success, tried to get to the treasure, which lies 170' deep in the earth and is elaborately guarded by tunnels, tides, and wooden platforms. One of the diggers was the young Franklin Roosevelt. More than $1.5 million has been spent on excavations to date.

Some Explanations: Gilbert Heddon, an American, investigated the possibility that the treasure was buried by Captain Kidd. In a book, he found a chart of the island on which Kidd was supposed to have hidden his treasure. It was remarkably like Oak Island. But when Heddon hunted up the book's author, he learned that the island on Kidd's map was in the South Seas.

Why did the people who buried the treasure do it so elaborately? And how did they do it? Obviously it took a tremendous amount of manpower and time. How did they expect to retrieve the treasure? One theory is that the gold belonged to the French fortress at Louisbourg and was buried on Oak Island by men from its garrison, who would have had the time and manpower for such a project.

Other theories, which are weaker, trace the treasure to Marie Antoinette and to a Spanish galleon.

Today: Digging is still going on at Oak Island.

The Place: THE OREGON VORTEX
Location: Near Sardine Creek, about 19 mi. from Medford, Ore.
The Enigma: The Oregon Vortex is a spot about 165' in diameter in which gravity appears to play strange tricks. Roughly in its center is an old wooden shed, once an assay office for a gold mining company—now called the House of Mystery. People who enter the building find themselves leaning at an angle of about 10° toward the center of the 165' circle. A 28-lb. ball hangs *at an angle* from a chain hung on a beam in the shack.

Other weird things happen in the vortex. Cigarette smoke makes spirals. If an empty glass jar is placed on a board sloping uphill, toward the center of the circle, the jar will roll uphill. Compasses don't work in the vortex. A light meter will register different readings within and outside it. Birds won't go within its limits. Trees growing inside it have limbs that droop and lean toward magnetic north, and visitors entering the area assume a posture that inclines toward magnetic north. If 2 men of equal height stand a short distance apart, and are viewed by a 3rd observer, one will seem to be taller than the other. According to a guide: "As another person retreats from you toward the south, he becomes taller. This is contrary to the laws of perspective, and must be seen to be believed."

Some Explanations: Some scientists argue that the vortex does not defy the laws of nature. One skeptic, Herbert B. Nichols, former natural science editor of *The Christian Science Monitor*, took a carpenter's level, a light meter, and a plumb bob with him when he visited the site. Nichols claimed that there were no supernatural forces at work in the vortex and that visitors were mere victims of optical illusion.

However, promoters of the "House of Mystery" continue to dispute the optical-illusion theory. They claim that instruments placed outside the vortex have proved that. The steel ball *does* hang at an angle.

Today: If you wish, try to solve the phenomenon yourself. The House of Mystery is open to tourists from March 1 to October 15; summer hours are 8 A.M. to 6 P.M. Address: 4303 Sardine Creek Road, Gold Hill, Ore. 97525.

The Place: THE LASCAUX CAVE PAINTINGS
Location: Montignac, the Dordogne, France
The Enigma: Called the Sistine Chapel of Prehistory, the caves at Lascaux contain paintings which were made 15,000–20,000 years ago. The ancient people who made them were far more sophisticated than one might suppose. Unlike civilizations which came later, they had a feeling for perspective (which was not rediscovered until almost the 15th century) and used shadows and highlights expertly. Their painting materials were yellow ocher and lipstick-shaped sticks of manganese and ferric oxide. To make these, they had to extract materials from the ground, purify them, pound them to powder, and mix them with grease—a complex procedure for primitive human beings. They built scaffolds to reach high up on the cave walls. Why did they make these paintings? Why did their sophistication show nowhere else in their lives?

Some Explanations: Jacques Boucher de Perthes, who 1st recognized the importance of the cave paintings, worked from 1828–1859 to get people to appreciate them. However, it was difficult to date the paintings, and without knowing for sure how old they were, it was hard to realize their full worth. Henri Breuil, who studied the caves at the turn of the century, often crawling on his stomach or swimming in icy water to do so, made invaluable sketches of the paintings.

Most experts thought the cave paintings represented "hunting magic" or records of kills. Andrew Leroi-Gourhan, an ethnologist working in the late 1940s, disputed this. He statistically studied 72 groups of cave pictures in 66 European caves, and found that certain animals nearly always appeared in the center roof compositions; that male and female figures also appeared in certain places nearly all the time. The paintings represent a great symbolic idea of some kind, he felt.

Today: The cave is closed to the public.

The Place: ZIMBABWE
Location: 17 mi. southeast of Fort Victoria, Rhodesia
The Enigma: In 1871, young geologist Karl Mauch asked a trader, Adam Renders, how to get to the nearest ruins. The trader was happy to supply the information. On Mauch's way there, he was captured by natives, but later he was rescued. Ultimately, he reached his destination—Zimbabwe.

Zimbabwe consists of an elliptical temple with walls 740' around, 34' high, 10' wide at the top, and it is surrounded by stone walls. Three hundred feet above, there is another building built into the rock, and this has stone steps leading up to it. There is a cave nearby. Someone speaking in the cave can be heard in the elliptical building.

Who built Zimbabwe?

Some Explanations: Is Zimbabwe in the Land of Ophir from whence came King Solomon's gold? After all, the area is famous for its ancient mines, which, it is estimated, produced 650 tons of gold.

Did Queen Hatshepsut of Egypt know about Zimbabwe? There is some archaeological evidence—a hieroglyphic here and there, drawings which seem to depict Egyptians—that would lead one to believe she might have.

Did the ancient Israelites or the Egyptians build the mysterious city? Or the Phoenicians, who were known to travel extensively?

Ancient Chinese coins have been found on the beaches of East Africa. Did the Chinese build it?

Today: Modern archaeologists think that Zimbabwe is not ancient, but was begun in the 15th century, probably by native Africans who may have migrated from the area later. The Bantus, who live there now, have no legends about the city at all.

From 1946–1962, Roger Summers, curator of the National Museum at Bulawayo, and Keith R. Robinson, chief inspector of monuments, excavated Zimbabwe. They were assisted by architectural expert Anthony Whitty. Their excavation revealed that the site was occupied by people using iron, and living in huts, before the 4th century B.C. In the 11th century, newcomers started building walls. In 1450, the mouments were added.

—A.E.

Queen Victoria's Saucerman

The "Jumping Man" made his official debut in 1837, the same year that 18-year-old Victoria ascended to the throne of England. He terrorized the English countryside for almost 70 years, suddenly appearing from nowhere and vanishing just as rapidly with 30'-high leaps that carried him from sight. His fantastic jumps led the London *Morning Post* to remark on October 19, 1929, that he was ". . . clearly no ordinary mortal, if indeed, he were of this world at all."

Miss Jane Alsop, a 25-year-old London girl, was the apparition's 1st recorded victim. She had heard a violent ringing of the bell on the gate in front of her house, which was situated near the London docks. When she opened her front door, a tall stranger was standing on the stoop. Exactly what happened next remained unclear, but Jane later testified to police that she had thrust a lighted candle toward her visitor, peering intently to see whether his face was familiar. With a roar, the creature had stumbled back, throwing off a long cloak wrapped about it. The sight she saw left her petrified.

The man's body was covered by a tight-fitting garment which resembled a slick, stark-white, oilskin jumpsuit. His head was completely enclosed by a globular object which was fastened to the collar of his tunic. His encased arms terminated in sharp, metallic claws. Inside the transparent globe, Miss Alsop could see 2 eyes which glared at her with a white fury.

Before she could slam the door, the creature leaped upon her, blazing a blue-white ray of flames through an opening in the front of the head-covering globe. As he knocked her to the ground, her screams brought her sister running, and the sudden presence of the 2nd woman sent the assailant bounding off into the night.

The attack was reported to the Lambeth police, who skeptically took down the information. The story carried more credence a few days later, when a young butcher came forward and related a similar incident which had occurred just a few days before.

His 2 sisters had come to visit with him that night. Shortly after they had left, he had heard loud screaming and had rushed out to see his sister Margaret staggering away from a nearby alley. He had then run into the dark street to find his other sister, Lucy, lying on the cobblestone pavement, moaning. When the 2 girls had recovered, their story paralleled Jane Alsop's to a baffling degree. Again, when

startled by a scream, the creature had turned and, to the girls' utter astonishment, jumped—sailing cleanly over the brick wall adjacent to the alley. The jump was impossibly high for a human to make, they said, and the young butcher, fearing he'd be laughed at, had kept silent. Who, he asked, would believe a leap of over 14'?

The "Jumping Man," as the newspapers called him, dropped from sight after the Alsop attack, and nothing further was noted until 1845. Then new reports began to come in, this time from the Ealing and Hanwell districts of London. Another weird figure had been seen, leaping with shrieks and groans over hedges and walls. This time a man believed to be the phantom was actually caught and the scare abated for the moment. But it developed that the apparition had simply left London for the countryside. Accounts during the 1860s and 1870s were filed from Warwickshire, Lancashire, Lincolnshire, Surrey, Worcestershire, and Middlesex counties, telling of a fantastic creature which was being encountered on dark but moonlit nights. It came soaring over the high hedge on one side of a country road, landing noiselessly in the roadbed to confront a startled villager. Then, with another tremendous bound, it sprang up and over the hedge on the far side, to disappear without a trace. The frightened countryfolk made no attempt to catch the specter but instead raced to bar their doors. Nothing human, they said, could take such gigantic hops—only the devil himself.

Superstition and nonsense, said the police, until the "Jumping Man" put on a performance which was hard to refute. At a British army post near Aldershot in the summer of 1877, 2 sentries on duty at a powder-magazine gate were alerted by a harsh and grating noise, as if a heavy metal object had just landed on the entrance road. One Private John Regan, said the army report, stepped forward and peered down the road, but saw nothing except the other sentry at his post some 30' away. Regan concluded that it must have been his imagination. But as he turned to resume his watch, a cold and icy breath fanned his cheek. Private Regan screamed and jumped back, dropping his rifle. In the same instant, the other sentry came on the run. As the 2 soldiers stood there, huddled together, a large and dark shape passed overhead and landed without a sound a short distance away. In the dim light, a strangely glowing figure straightened up and stood quietly, a queer "shining" bubble on its shoulders.

The sentry still armed shouted a hasty challenge and immediately afterward fired. The bullet had no effect. Instead, the figure bounded toward and over the 2 men, belching out a stream of blue flame directly at Regan's face. Regan stooped to pick up his rifle and both men fired a number of shots, again with no visible effect. Finally, in complete panic, they ran from their posts.

The Army's report on the court-martial included in precise detail the same description Jane Alsop had given some 40 years before. A tall, thin creature. Tight-fitting white suit, with a slight phosphorescent glow, clinging to the body. A glasslike bubble over the head. Luminous, reddish eyes like burning coals. Blue flames coming from the mouth aperture. An attack only after a scream had occurred. Fantastic jumps. And prompt disappearance without a trace.

One puzzling new question had been added, however. How could both soldiers—one, a crack shot—have missed at such point-blank range?

In October, 4 months later, the townspeople of Newport asked themselves the same question. The "Jumping Man" was spotted on the thatched roof of a cottage near the edge of town. Eyewitnesses swore that it stood there for some time, watching and listening intently with its huge ears, which seemed to taper to a point. A crowd gathered and moved to surround the cottage. Then one man screamed an order to rush in. The sudden shout startled the visitor, and it bounded over the heads of the mob, reappearing moments afterward on top of Newport's old Roman arch. Another townsman with a gun took careful aim and fired, but was dumbfounded to see the creature still standing there, unhurt. Then, after it had looked down on the crowd for a few minutes more, the manlike figure hopped away with 20'-high leaps, the sight of which left the mob speechless. They caught up with it again as it stopped on a high wall and more shots were fired but, as before, the thing bounded off. There was only one answer: Bullets could not harm this strange phantom.

In the decades that followed, the "Jumping Man" was reported again and again. Strangely enough, now the apparition never harmed anyone, and it rapidly disappeared when it realized it had been seen.

In September, 1904, the creature made its last-reported appearance, this one in the older section of Liverpool. For more than 10 minutes, hundreds of spectators watched its antics in broad daylight. The "Jumping Man" bounded up and down William Henry St., then leaped easily from Stitt St. over a row of terraced houses onto Haigh St. Those who rushed around the corner saw it briefly as the creature made its final mighty leap which carried the white-suited shape back across the slate roofs toward Salisbury St. And with this dramatic, almost joyful performance, the stranger seemingly vanished for good.

The question of what the thing was has never been answered. Man it was not—no human yet has achieved an 8'-high jump in the earth's gravity, much less the 30-footers measured and credited to the "Jumping Man." Animals, trained or wild, have also been ruled out—the phantom was definitely humanoid.

Its garments, described many times throughout almost a full century of sightings, bore a striking resemblance to the space suit worn by astronaut Neil Armstrong as he stepped to the surface of the moon in July, 1969. Its huge leaps were duplicated by other astronauts in the early 1970s as they bounded about on this barren satellite having a gravitational pull only ⅙ that of the earth. And the creature itself seems to have existed by breathing a gaseous substance which, when exhaled, combined with oxygen to produce the bluish-white but harmless flame.

The physical evidence points inescapably to one fantastic but completely plausible conclusion. The "Jumping Man" of Queen Victoria's England may have come from outer space—a being sent from beyond our solar system to observe the strange life-forms found on the planet we call earth.

—W.K.

The Adventure—of Adventures

On a hot summer's afternoon in August of 1901, 2 respectable English schoolteachers, Annie Moberly and Eleanor Jourdain, decided to visit Versailles on a sight-seeing expedition. They had never been there before. After looking in on the Palace of Versailles, they started to walk toward the Petit Trianon—and sud-denly, without realizing it, they walked backward in time. They crossed a garden that did not exist in 1901 but which had existed in 1789. They saw and spoke to people who had been dead for more than a century. Their incredible psychic adventure, fully supported by years of research, created a sensation when it was announced in 1911. It was debated by scientists, scholars, philosophers, and it has been debated ever since.

Annie Moberly was the daughter of an Oxford don who became the Bishop of Salisbury in England. Annie was the 10th of 15 children. She was well educated, honorable, religious, imaginative. She became a teacher and was appointed the 1st principal of St. Hugh's College, a small school for girls, in Oxford.

Eleanor Jourdain was also the daughter of a parson and the 1st of 10 children. Although descended from a Huguenot family, she was thoroughly British. She was introspective and prim, yet fanciful and independent as well. She published 7 weighty textbooks, one on symbolism in Dante. She, too, set out to teach, held several positions, ran a school of her own, and after her psychic adventure was to become vice-principal of St. Hugh's College under the older Annie Moberly.

In 1901, Eleanor Jourdain, eager to learn French, had moved to Paris temporarily, where she was sustaining herself by tutoring English children in that city. Annie Moberly, who at that time knew Miss Jourdain only slightly, came over to Paris to enjoy a short vacation and to offer Miss Jourdain the post of vice-principal at St. Hugh's. The 2 teachers became good friends and began taking trips outside Paris. Neither had ever been to Versailles, and they decided to go by train to visit its historic palace and beautiful grounds.

On August 10, 1901, Annie Moberly, age 55, and Eleanor Jourdain, age 38, with Baedeker guidebook in hand, arrived at Versailles, toured the palace, and then rested before taking a sight-seeing stroll through the gardens. At last, enjoying the lively wind and overcast sky after a week of hot weather, they started their walk. Their destination was the Petit Trianon, a small private château at the far end of the grounds, which King Louis XVI had presented to his wife, Queen Marie Antoinette, for her personal use.

Trying to find the Petit Trianon, Moberly and Jourdain missed a right turn, kept going straight ahead, began wandering aimlessly— and thus, as they would later claim, they took leave of the 20th century and reentered the 18th century.

From what they reconstructed afterward, here is what they saw and here is what they encountered:

Moberly, alone, saw a woman shaking a white cloth out of the window of a building. Jourdain, alone, saw some old-fashioned farm implements including a plow, lying on the grass. They both viewed 2 men wearing what appeared to be masquerade costumes—small tricornered hats and long grayish-green coats —and thought them to be gardeners. They

asked these men the way to the Petit Trianon, and one man answered mechanically that they must continue ahead. Then, off to the right, Jourdain, alone, saw a cottage, with a woman passing a jug to a young girl standing in the open doorway.

Jourdain remembered later how she felt as they had plodded onward. "I began to feel as though I were walking in my sleep; the heavy dreaminess was oppressive." Finally, they reached the edge of a wood, where they could see a man seated near the steps of a garden kiosk, its columns topped by a round roof. Moberly also recalled her reactions: "Everything suddenly looked unnatural, therefore unpleasant; even the trees behind the building seemed to have become flat and lifeless, *like a wood worked in tapestry.* There were no effects of light and shade and no wind stirred the trees. It was all intensely still."

The 2 ladies had a closer glimpse of the man near the steps, and they were frightened. He was swarthy, pockmarked, and he wore a large hat and heavy black cloak. "The man's face was most repulsive—its expression odious," Moberly recalled. About to hasten away, the 2 women saw a younger man who apparently had come from behind some rocks that hid the path. He was handsome, his hairstyle resembling "an old picture," and his face was flushed. He spoke to them eagerly in oddly accented French, trying to divert them from the path they had taken. They finally understood that he was giving them directions to the Petit Trianon.

Following the young man's directions, Moberly and Jourdain took another path to their right, crossed an attractive rustic bridge spanning a tiny ravine, skirted a narrow meadow, and at last came upon the Petit Trianon. On the lawn before the Trianon they stopped, and Annie Moberly watched an aristocratic lady— wearing a large white hat, and an old-fashioned long-waisted green bodice above a full short skirt—sitting and sketching the scenery. She was rather pretty, although not young, and she stared at Moberly. Then a uniformed official emerged from the Petit Trianon to escort the English ladies through the château before sending them away.

Annie Moberly and Eleanor Jourdain left the palace grounds and took a carriage to the Hôtel des Réservoirs in Versailles to have tea, before returning to Miss Jourdain's apartment in Paris. Neither of them mentioned to the other the visit to Versailles, at least not until a week later when Miss Moberly was recording impressions of her visit to France. As Miss Moberly came to the afternoon at Versailles, she began to feel a strange, dreamy, unnatural oppression. She stopped writing and turned to Miss Jourdain and asked, "Do you think that

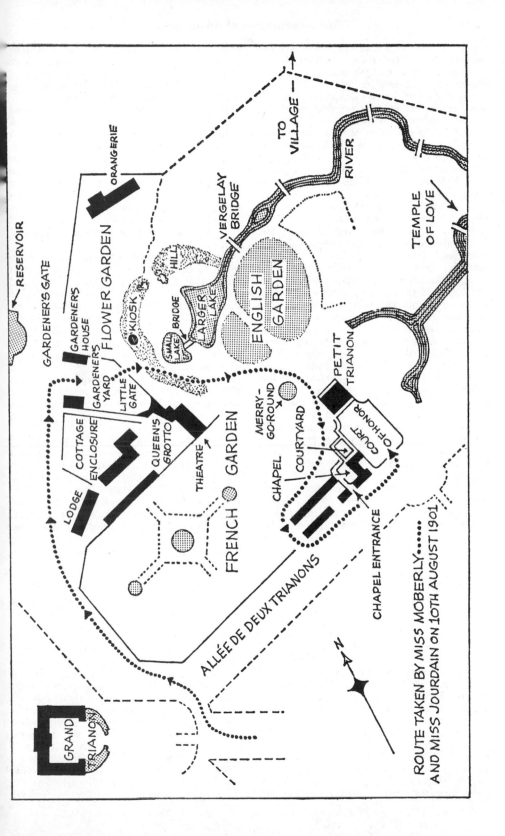

RESERVOIR

GARDENER'S GATE

GARDENER'S HOUSE

FLOWER GARDEN

ORANGERIE

TO VILLAGE

HILL

KIOSK

SMALL LAKE

BRIDGE

LARGER LAKE

VERGELAY BRIDGE

RIVER

ENGLISH GARDEN

TEMPLE OF LOVE

GARDENER'S YARD

LITTLE GATE

LODGE

COTTAGE

ENCLOSURE

QUEEN'S GROTTO

THEATRE

FRENCH GARDEN

MERRY-GO-ROUND

CHAPEL

COURTYARD

PETIT TRIANON

COURT OF HONOR

CHAPEL ENTRANCE

GRAND TRIANON

ALLÉE DE DEUX TRIANONS

N

ROUTE TAKEN BY MISS MOBERLY••••••
AND MISS JOURDAIN ON 10TH AUGUST 1901

the Petit Trianon is haunted?" Miss Jourdain nodded firmly. "Yes, I do." And for the 1st time, each woman told the other how eerie an experience it had been for her.

Three months later, when Annie Moberly was back in Oxford, Miss Jourdain came from Paris to be her house guest. Obsessively, they resumed their discussion of that afternoon at Versailles—the atmosphere, the haunting quality of that day, the unusual attire the people wore—and how it became apparent that while they had both seen certain things, each of them had seen something the other had not seen—or had been unable to see. Jourdain, alone, had seen the plow on the grass and the woman and girl in the cottage doorway. Moberly, alone, had seen the aristocratic lady sketching before the Petit Trianon. In those moments, both women perceived that something unusual, indeed something very unusual, had happened to them at Versailles—they had, inexplicably, stumbled backward through time into another age. They vowed to keep their experience secret, while each wrote up a separate and detailed account of the adventure, and both agreed to do thorough research on the history of Versailles and the Petit Trianon.

For 9 years, Moberly and Jourdain did their detective work—digging into every archive available that had information on the background of Versailles. The 2 ladies visited Versailles again and again (finding it as it really was in the 1900s, and only once experiencing another slipping-back into the past). When they had completed their sleuthing, they had learned that their afternoon in Versailles in 1901 had actually been an afternoon in 1789, the very day when the mobs of the French Revolution were about to close in on Versailles. The 2 "gardeners" in greenish coats the women had met in 1901 were actually 2 Swiss Guardsmen on duty that day. The girl in the cottage doorway was named Marion and she had lived with her mother on the palace grounds. The repulsive man in the black cloak seated near the kiosk steps was the Comte de Vaudreuil, a Creole friend of the Queen of France. And, most exciting of all for Moberly and Jourdain, they discovered—from a portrait done by Wertmüller, and from the journal of Madame Éloffe, the Queen's dressmaker (who had made her mistress 2 green bodices and several short white skirts for that summer of 1789)—that they had come upon Queen Marie Antoinette herself as she sat sketching before her château.

The only sight Moberly and Jourdain did not identify was the rustic bridge spanning the ravine that they had to cross to reach the Trianon. The earliest map they could find— one that Contant de la Motte had copied in 1783 from the original plan for Marie An-

toinette's garden (which had been drawn by her architect Mique but had subsequently been lost)—had not shown the rustic bridge or ravine. But no matter. Moberly and Jourdain were satisfied. They already had enough.

In 1911, Moberly and Jourdain published their findings pseudonymously in a little book entitled *An Adventure*. The book itself was a sensation, although critics did not take it seriously. Worst of all, the London Society for Psychical Research, which collected facts on psychic experiences and had such prestigious members as Henri Bergson, John Ruskin, Lewis Carroll, Lord Tennyson, rejected the adventure of the schoolteachers and announced that the experience was built on "the weakness of human memory."

Defensively, Moberly and Jourdain began to reveal to friends, to faculty members, to their pupils, that they were the ones who had had the adventure at Versailles. The families of their students were appalled. Faculty members were skeptical, and conflict grew. And generally, throughout England and France, the 2 schoolteachers were ridiculed by the majority of scholars, historians, and experts in psychic phenomena. The 2 women were regarded as romancers or hysterics—and the things they claimed to have seen were regarded as no more authentic than the rustic bridge and the ravine that they·had been unable to prove had ever existed at Versailles.

But in the end, Moberly and Jourdain scored a stunning triumph. True—in 1901 there was no rustic bridge and no ravine, even though the women swore they had crossed such a bridge. True—De la Motte's map of the gardens, done in 1783, showed neither the bridge nor the ravine. But suddenly, one day in 1912, Moberly and Jourdain learned that the long-lost original map of the gardens drawn by Marie Antoinette's architect Mique had been found—had been discovered, charred and crumpled, stuffed inside an old chimney in a house at Montmorency. And Mique's original map was legible—and lo, it showed the ravine and the rustic bridge over it, which De la Motte had sloppily failed to copy down. Moberly and Jourdain were vindicated—and they published news of the great find in a 3rd edition of *An Adventure* issued in 1924—an edition which, for the 1st time, bore their real names as the authors, for they were no longer ashamed but now were proud of their book.

How many other human beings had ever— since man has existed on earth—made such a journey as this one, backward and backward through the time barrier into the distant past —and had returned with word of it?

Miss Jourdain died in 1924 at the age of 61. Miss Moberly died in 1937 at the age of 91.

—I.W.

Psychic Phenomena

INTRODUCTION

First a few definitions. Basically, psychic phenomena refer to events that cannot be explained by presently accepted laws of physics or psychology. A useful shorthand term is *psi*. The scientific study of psi is called parapsychology or psychical research. The former is the more modern term, but in the articles that follow we have used the 2 interchangeably.

The range of phenomena called psychic is huge. We have telepathy and clairvoyance, precognition and psychokinesis, dowsings, hauntings, séances, mediumships, astral projections, auras, psychic healings, and "the survival question," which refers to the search for proof of life after death. These forms of psi are all interrelated. For example, auras are usually seen only by clairvoyants; they seem to change during psychic healing, and may be a visual form of the force used in psychokinesis; what they represent may also be involved in astral projection and perhaps even in the survival question. Categorizing psi is obviously not easy, but the phenomena are usually broken down into 3 main types: ESP, extrasensory perception, which involves information coming to the individual *from* the environment; PK, psychokinesis, mind over matter, or the effect of the individual's mind *on* his environment; and the survival question. Just about every aspect of psi fits into one or more of these 3 categories.

Psychic phenomena are, of course, controversial. Do such matters really exist? Is it all imagination, coincidence, and fraud? What *has* been proved by the parapsychologist and what has not?

To begin with, it must be admitted that a large percentage of the experiences reported as psychic adventures probably are not. We are a suggestible species, and the will to believe is strong. On the other hand, there are scientists who feel that total acceptance of psi will upset many of the theories of science, and their determination *not* to believe in psi is just as strong, and just as foolish, as is the overly credulous approach. In fact it is the old science that would have been upset by psi. The new physics of relativity, subatomic particles, and quantum mechanics is fazed very little by the concept of a consciousness that can span time and space, or cause the heap of atoms in a compass needle to move. (The atoms that constitute a compass needle, or anything else, are all moving anyway; it's just a matter of getting them all to move in the same direction at the same time.)

However, most psychic phenomena are still controversial. In recent years the world of psi has been electrified by the young Israeli Uri Geller. He seems to be able to bend keys, spoons, and other objects by gently rubbing them. He seems to have caused objects to dematerialize and rematerialize elsewhere. He seems to be telepathic. But there are doubts. Many of his feats can be duplicated by stage magicians—which is not to say that he does not do them psychically, just that he *might* not. He is almost too eager to display his talents, to persuade others that they are real. Geller has convinced many fine scientists that he is genuine, and many others that he is a fraud. At the time of this writing, the jury is still out.

Again, spiritualists are excited by the Raudive tapes, recordings made in silence yet which appear to contain scattered words, messages, voices from, it is alleged, the spirit world. The controversy between believers and nonbelievers rages bitterly.

These are the dramatics. Seldom publicized are the handful of scientists who devote themselves to making sure that some research is properly conducted in spite of the lack of funds and time (most parapsychologists have full-time jobs in other fields). Representative of this caliber of research is the Parapsychological Association, an international body of qualified investigators. In 1969 the PA was, after several previous rebuffs, accepted as an affiliate of the American Association for the Advancement of Science (AAAS). A major breakthrough for the PA, this acceptance indicated that the AAAS considered the methods used in parapsychology to be based on proper scientific principles.

Nearly 90 years before this event the 1st scientific group, the Society for Psychical Research, was formed in England in 1882, headed by famous scholars and scientists of their time, among them F. W. H. Myers, William Crookes, and Henry Sidgwick. Psychical research has come a long way since then; researchers believe there is now sufficient proof that some form of ESP and PK does exist—but they are often divided as to exactly what form and in which instances. Accusations of sloppy experimentation and outright fraud are still made, sometimes with good reason. Nevertheless, when all the chaff has been winnowed out, we are still left with something. Elusive though they may be, it seems almost impossible that psychic phenomena are a total illusion.

In the articles which follow we will, for the most part, deal with the various subjects from the point of view of those who work with them. Obviously people do not work on something unless they believe it exists. However, there is still doubt in some quarters about the reality of psychic phenomena, in spite of much spontaneous and experimental evidence.

Though psi and science are now firmly linked by parapsychology, psi retains its other, older connections. Psychical researchers, who read the life stories of the saints or of the gurus, recognize many proclaimed miracles as being similar to events that they have sought, and sometimes found, in the laboratory. Psi seems often to be a side effect of spiritual discipline, something that happens naturally when one has purged oneself of ego. Yet all spiritual teachers are emphatic that psychic gifts are not to be sought for themselves; for the most part, in fact, they must be put aside, ignored, lest they distract the disciple from his spiritual path.

Again, there is a close connection between psi and the occult, so close, in fact, that many people find it hard to separate the 2. Occultists believe that their path will enable them to develop and use psi at will, that ESP and PK may be used in both white and black witchcraft, for example. Let us examine this further. Occult rituals use candles, altars, and geometric designs; however, to designate psi as occult would be as foolish as saying that all candles or all geometric designs are occult. Rather, it should be understood that the forces, powers, faculties, or whatever are used

to produce psi seem to be neutral. If they exist and can be harnessed, they can be used to heal or to hurt, to comfort or to terrify. Like atomic power or electricity, they are of themselves neither good nor bad; their effect depends on the orientation and intentions of the person using them.

—D.R.

FOR FURTHER READING

The Imprisoned Splendor by Raynor C. Johnson. Wheaton, Ill., Quest Book, 1971; 1st published in 1953. Johnson is rather biased toward the "psychic aether" explanation of psi, but whether he is right or wrong, the book remains an excellent introduction to psychic phenomena.

The Medium, the Mystic, and the Physicist by Lawrence LeShan. New York, Viking Press, 1974. LeShan uses his extensive contacts with one of this century's finest mediums to compare the experiences and theories of mediumship, mysticism, and physics, and concludes that all are actually saying the same thing. Essential reading for anyone interested in theories about how and why psi works.

Human Personality and Its Survival of Bodily Death by F. W. H. Myers. New Hyde Park, N.Y., University Books, 1961. One of *the* basic source books of psi. A parapsychologist once wrote that it sometimes seems that everything modern researchers have discovered is just a footnote to Myers and his survey of various aspects of psychic phenomena. The depth and breadth of his insight are incredible. Though 1st written in 2 volumes in 1901, this work has been abridged and the one-volume version is easier to read and adequate for all but the most dedicated student.

Tuning in on ESP

INTRODUCING ESP

Extrasensory perception can be defined as having knowledge of something without using the 5 "normal" senses or using logical deduction. In other words, when you "just know" something and there is no way for you to have obtained that information, ESP is one explanation.

The startling dream that turns out to be true; the feeling of "I am sure something is wrong," and it is; the time you put your hand on the phone to call someone, and it rings because that person unexpectedly decided to call you—all these things lead to the feeling that there must be some explanation beyond coincidence. Furthermore, there must be some aspect of human beings which we have not yet identified, some link between us and our uni-

verse which remains a question mark. The attempt to clarify the how and the why of these unknowns is a major part of the psychical researcher's work.

In earlier, more superstitious days it was not deemed prudent to ask too many questions about such "supernatural" gifts as the soothsayers seemed to have, but in the 18th century, when mesmerism was all the rage, it was discovered that mesmerized subjects could sometimes describe a distant scene or answer questions before they were spoken aloud. Interest in ESP grew throughout the 19th century and the early part of the 20th, but the man who really brought the subject to the attention of the American public was J. B. Rhine, then of Duke University. Dr. Rhine started work at Duke in 1927 and published his 1st book on the parapsychological work done there in 1934. Statistics and specially designed cards had been used previously in psychical research, but Rhine and his associates brought the statistical approach to ESP to a level that was pronounced acceptable by the American Institute of Mathematical Statistics (See: Dr. Rhine, Famous and Infamous Scientists, Chap. 17). In spite of a storm of controversy, more and more reputable scientists have been attracted to the study of ESP over the years, and parapsychology is now taught for credit in a number of American colleges.

ESP is a complicated subject for a number of reasons. It is usually considered to divide itself into 3 types, each of which will be discussed in more detail later. One is telepathy, or the perception of what is in the mind of someone else; another is clairvoyance, the perception of objects or events currently happening; and the 3rd is precognition, the perception of future events. This classification leaves out retrocognition, or awareness of past events. Psychic sensitives are frequently unable to tell whether their impressions relate to the past or the future, so perhaps retrocognition and precognition should be categorized together as "out-of-time-cognition," but since retrocognition is not commonly investigated, for the moment the term precognition continues to stand.

It is not easy to differentiate between telepathy, clairvoyance, and precognition. A famous example of ESP is that of Emanuel Swedenborg, a brilliant Swedish scientist of the 18th century who, while in Gothenburg, described the course of a fire near his home in Stockholm, 300 mi. away. This is generally accepted as a case of clairvoyance, but it is equally possible that he was getting the information from the mind of someone who was watching the fire, perhaps a relative or neighbor. Or he could have been using precognition by "reading" the message that was to be delivered to him later; this described the course of the fire. The same problem in parapsychology causes many experiments to be grouped together as "general ESP" rather than being put in a specific category. For this type of test, the term GESP is used.

There are many variables which seem to affect ESP. The relationship between the people involved is very important. Many family members have experienced a rapport which appears to be telepathic, but they learn that this can be spoiled by emotional differences. The same thing occurs in the laboratory. A good relationship between the person being tested (the subject) and the experimenters and anyone else involved is vital. Without this, the subject cannot relax, and relaxation has a strong link with significant ESP scores.

Because ESP seems to work at a subconscious level it is not fully controllable, and tests are being conducted to find out what helps it and what hinders it. Caffeine seems to be effective in producing higher scores, and sodium amytal has reduced scores to the chance level in some tests. Apart from this, results of research with drugs and with alcohol have so far been confusing, some pointing one way and some another. One's personality and attitude toward ESP may also play a part. Extroverts and believers in ESP usually have higher scores than do introverts and skeptics.

Recent research suggests that harder ESP tasks are often more likely to achieve success than comparatively easy ones. It seems that, faced with a simple test such as picking one symbol out of a choice of 5, the mind attempts to analyze intellectually which is right, rather than use ESP. However, when faced with an almost infinite number of possibilities from which to choose, the mind more or less throws up its hands in horror and quits. This leads to the quiescent, relaxed state of mind in which ESP is most successful. In one test, 2 separate subjects were given the geographical coordinates of a place unknown to them or to the experimenters and told to describe what was at that location. Their descriptions of an island—the location of a mountain, docks, and the orientation of an airstrip—all fit the tiny speck of an island in the Indian Ocean which was the target. One even mentioned correctly that the language spoken there was French.

This test highlights another strange thing about ESP, which is that distance seems to make very little difference to its success.

Because of all the variables and complications involved, the problem of designing a repeatable experiment in parapsychology has not yet been overcome. In most branches of science an experiment designed by one researcher can be repeated by another, and very similar results will be obtained by both. There are so many variables affecting ESP that this has not yet been done in parapsychology. The best hope in this direction seems to be in the use of small animals instead of people as subjects. Presumably they are less moody. It is important that a repeatable experiment be perfected, because most branches of science regard ESP as unproved, and possibly nonexistent. They are therefore not willing to cooperate in finding out exactly what it is and how it works. A repeatable experiment will help to overcome their opposition.

TELEPATHY

Early studies of spontaneous ESP cases looked only for the explanation of telepathy. If someone "knew" something and could have obtained it from another person's thoughts, that was telepathy. If what they knew was at that time unknown to anyone else, then it was dismissed as coincidence, for clairvoyance was inconceivable. The early research was mainly with "spontaneous" cases—events that just happened unexpectedly to people. ("I *knew* you were going to say that." "I didn't know that was what you were hoping I'd do, but something just *made* me do it.") Among spontaneous cases telepathy seems to be the commonest form of ESP, so the telepathy-oriented approach is understandable. Yet under experimental conditions telepathy is extremely difficult to isolate.

If I look at a card and you try to "read my mind" you may get the symbol by telepathy, but you may also "read" the card itself, by clairvoyance. Even if I *imagine* a card, so that there is no physical card on which you can focus clairvoyantly, after the test I still have to write down what I visualized so that the scores can be totaled. So perhaps what you pictured was a precognition of what I would write down later. Experiments for "pure telepathy" have been designed, and have given highly significant results, but they are complicated and not common.

Among the most intriguing recent studies of telepathy have been those at the Dream Laboratory of the Maimonides Medical Center in Brooklyn. Here, while each volunteer slept, an agent tried to influence his or her dreams by concentrating on a randomly chosen art print. The dreamer was connected to an EEG machine in another room, so that the experimenters would know when he was dreaming. As soon as each dream finished they woke the subject and asked him to describe his dream. Some subjects achieved more success than others, but overall the results were very significant.

One subject reported a dream involving "a storm . . . an aspect of grandeur . . . almost a biblical scene of some sort . . . direction was important . . . a feeling of New Mexico . . . a lot of mountains . . . almost as though . . . another civilization." The target picture that night was *Zapatistas*, which depicts Mexican-Indians following a revolutionary leader, some on foot, some mounted, against a background of clouds and mountains. This type of "hit" certainly makes one wonder where some of our dreams come from. For a while this research was supported by a grant from the National Institute of Mental Health, but this is no longer the case. The psychological and sociological study of behavior, and particularly such phenomena as mass hysteria and mobs, might benefit from a greater understanding of telepathy. Other questions, such as whether our unspoken thoughts and emotions may subtly influence others, add emphasis to the concept

of mankind as a united brotherhood rather than a confusion of isolated units.

CLAIRVOYANCE

This is the form of ESP in which one becomes aware of objects or events. Literally, the word means "clear seeing" and applies to those who "see" psychically—their impressions take the form of pictures. Others may receive their psychic impressions in the form of spoken words or messages that only they hear, and this is properly called clairaudience. Those who get a "feeling" that comes in neither words nor pictures have clairsentience. However, for most purposes the 3 are lumped together and called clairvoyance.

The experiment mentioned earlier in which the subject described a place of which he knew only the longitude and latitude appears to be a clear case of long-distance clairvoyance. Yet, where distance is involved, one always has to wonder whether astral projection is involved. Did the subjects perhaps project to the correct location in order to describe it? Some experimenters are now using the term "remote viewing" so that there is no need for them to clarify whether they are referring to clairvoyance or to astral projection.

Almost certainly Edgar Cayce, a simple Kentuckian who died in 1945, was clairvoyant. While in a trance, Cayce (pronounced Kaycee) would be given the name and address of someone he had never met or heard of. He would promptly describe their physical and emotional condition, often in medical terms unknown to Cayce in his conscious state, and suggest the proper treatment. When followed, his treatment almost always worked. In many cases medicines were mentioned which neither the awakened Cayce nor the patient could identify. Sometimes much research was necessary before they could be found. In one case the patient, unable to find what Cayce had prescribed for him, had Cayce dictate the formula while in trance. Later it was discovered that the medicine had been made in France some 50 years previously. When the patient at last contacted the son of the original manufacturer, the formula he was given was the exact duplicate of that received from Cayce.

The use of clairvoyance for diagnosis is one of the most promising practical applications of ESP. Some clairvoyants diagnose by seeing the patient's aura. Others can get a clear picture of what is actually wrong by "tuning in" to the patient. Sometimes they will even feel the sensations from which the patient is suffering.

In the research laboratory, clairvoyance is an easy form of ESP to test, though the term GESP is often used to indicate that telepathy and precognition have not been completely ruled out. Subjects may be asked to guess at ESP cards showing symbols such as a square, circle, or star, or at similar symbols written down and sealed in envelopes. Pictures of persons, places, or scenes are also used, and make more interesting targets.

Probably the most outstanding experimental clairvoyant of recent times is Pavel Stepanek, a Czechoslovakian who has been tested both in his home country and in America. Most psychic sensitives seem to lose their ability after being subjected to lengthy laboratory testing, but Stepanek's talent has survived more than 10 years of research.

A very simple form of clairvoyance is that known as psychometry, or "token object reading." The clairvoyant holds an object or photograph, and from it seems to get impressions of its history and the people to whom it has belonged. The difficulty of reducing this type of experiment to statistics and of calculating the chance probability of any answer's being right or wrong makes it unpopular in the laboratory, but for the would-be clairvoyant it is an interesting way to start practicing.

PRECOGNITION

Precognition is the seeing of the future by ESP. Its history goes way back beyond the times of the biblical prophets. The dreams that Joseph interpreted were prophetic; they gave warning of what was to come. So did the ancient oracles. The future is an uncertainty fraught with worry, and if there is any chance that man can peer through its curtains he will try to do so. There is much disagreement as to whether the many forms of divination of the future have merit in themselves, or whether they are just ways for the sensitive to focus his mind and get himself into a state wherein his precognitive abilities will work. Most people accept the idea that the crystal ball is such a focus, and that tea leaves and many other devices probably serve the same purpose.

The responsibility of having precognitive ability is very serious. The issuance of a prophecy can cause it to be fulfilled. If someone is told he will die in a year's time, or that a relationship will break up, he may give up his home, stop trying to fight his illness, or abandon the relationship. Yet, though the psychic must be careful of how he words his predictions, he must not, in many instances, remain silent. There were at least 34 precognitions of the tragic Aberfan coal-tip disaster in which 144 people were killed, but no action was taken to avert the tragedy. The sinking of the *Titanic* and the assassination of President Kennedy were foreseen by many people. Many of those who had experienced precognition did try to give warning. Those who did not speak out now regret it bitterly, wondering whether, had they added their voices to those who did speak, tragedy might have been prevented.

The Central Premonitions Registry (P. O. Box 482, Times Square Station, New York, N.Y. 10036) was set up both to resolve this problem and to research the accuracy of predictions. It does not handle personal forecasts, but only those of general and national interest.

In the laboratory there are many ways of testing for precognition. A subject may be asked to predict the order of a pack of cards *after* it has been shuffled (but he may use psychokinesis to influence the shuffle so that the cards will fall as he has predicted).

A more interesting format is the so-called "chair test." Before a meeting starts, a chair somewhere in the room is picked at random, and a psychic sensitive is asked to describe the person who will sit in it at the meeting. A scoring system is used to calculate the number of points of correspondence between the circumstances of the person who actually does sit in the chair and the sensitive's prediction.

One experiment which has been successfully repeated by several researchers involves mice or gerbils. The animal is put in a cage divided into 2 halves by a barrier low enough to be jumped over quite easily. The floor on both sides is wired to give a very mild electric shock. The shocks are given randomly on the 2 sides, and if the animal moves to the opposite side to avoid the shock just *before* it is given, this is shown as a precognitive "hit" by the automatic equipment monitoring the experiment. The average score is about 8% above a baseline established by observing the animal's movements from side to side with no electric shocks being given.

The Maimonides Dream Laboratory experiments mentioned under Telepathy were also adapted to precognition. The dreamer was told to dream of an experience that he would have the following day. After his dreams were recorded by one experimenter, another experimenter, who did not know what the dreams were, used a random-selection system to pick an art print, and designed an environment around the theme of the print. Later in the day the dreamer was taken into that environment. For example, when the print showed a scene of snow and ice, all the furniture in the room was covered with white sheets, a fan blew cold air at the subject, and the experimenters dropped ice cubes down the back of his neck. His dreams had in several respects corresponded to the theme of coldness and snow. In one series of such tests, 8 nights of dreams resulted in 5 dreams directly matching the target (judged by independent judges), and 2 corresponded quite closely—a strong indication of the reality of precognition.

Such indications raise major philosophical problems. If we can see the future, does it mean that the future already exists? Can it be changed? What does this do to the concept of free will? Such are the questions that must be faced if it is eventually proved beyond a doubt that all forms of ESP are a fact. Some parapsychologists feel strongly that this has already been proved. Others believe that they will have to produce the "repeatable" experiment to become acceptable in the eyes of most scientists. Even then there will be hesitation on the part of some people. Many of humankind's ideas will have to change if ESP is to be

integrated into our concepts of reality, and resistance to change is basic to human nature.

FOR FURTHER READING

The ESP Reader, edited by D. C. Knight. New York, Grosset & Dunlap, 1969. One of the best introductions to the world of ESP, this anthology presents highlights from most of the better-known cases in a style that is both literate and easy to read.

Dream Telepathy by Montague Ullman and Stanley Krippner with Alan Vaughan. New York, Macmillan, 1973. Written by the experimenters and one of their subjects, this is a fine account of the experimental work at Maimonides Dream Laboratory. Background material and a roundup of other ESP dream cases are valuable additions.

Astral Projection

Occult lore says that man has an astral (nonmaterial) body as well as a physical body. Though the 2 usually coexist in the same space, under certain conditions they may separate, with consciousness accompanying the astral body. In addition, the consciousness alone can leave the physical body. Either of these happenings is called astral projection (AP) or an out-of-the-body experience (OBE).

Many cases of AP have been reported, and the subject cannot be dismissed offhand as a psychological aberration, for in general the reports support each other strongly, having many things in common. With or without the astral body, the consciousness presumably can penetrate solid objects; physical ills disappear; and to reach another place, one has only to think of being there. A "silver cord" is frequently said to link the astral and physical, and if this is broken death will result. However, this cord is supposed to be infinitely stretchable so it does not confine one distance-wise.

The literature of parapsychology is packed with intriguing AP tales, from collections of anecdotes by Sidgwick, Crookall, Smith, and Green to firsthand accounts by such legendary astral projectors as Sylvan Muldoon, Oliver Fox, "Yram," and, more recently, businessman Robert Monroe.

For the most part these many experiences can be divided into 4 types. In the 1st 2 the projector remains earthbound. Often he will attempt to get corroboration of his experience by visiting friends. Typically he will call to them, tap them on the shoulder, or even try to move physical objects to draw attention to himself, but he will fail because the astral body is invisible to most people. Sometimes, however, the friends will later confirm his

account of what was happening to them at the time of his "visit."

The 2nd or reciprocal type of earthbound astral trip is rarer. In it the astral body *is* seen by others, and these cases immeasurably strengthen the case for AP. Two of the best-known OBE anecdotes which fit into this category are the following:

One evening in 1881, S. H. Beard, an Englishman, was reading about astral projection and decided to try an astral visit to his fiancée, Miss L. S. Verity. To the surprise of all concerned, not only did he succeed, but she, maidenly modest in her bedroom, saw and recognized him, and told her younger sister of the experience.

In 1863, businessman S. R. Wilmot of Connecticut was sailing from Liverpool to New York. He shared a stateroom with another gentleman. One night he "saw" his wife (who was in America) beside his bunk and (oh, scandal!) the other gentleman saw her too. In fact the next morning he was quite outspoken about such unseemly goings-on! To Wilmot's amazement, when his wife met him she told him how she had seemed to visit him one night, and asked in surprise if the stateroom was really arranged in a certain way—which was not how she had pictured it before his trip. She gave a perfect description of Wilmot's actual room.

Even stranger are the projections involving dimensions of existence other than this one. Some seem wonderful, some terrifying, some just different, and the visitor is often guided by indescribable but kindly "guardians." The 4th type evolves from this—but the projector is given a choice of not returning to his body. This is commonest when the individual is near death, as described by Dr. John C. Lilly in *The Center of the Cyclone*. His guides told him he could go through a door, and so die, or return to his pain-wracked body to continue his work on earth.

OBEs most often occur during severe illness, injury or fatigue, under anesthesia or drugs, and during childhood. Under hypnosis someone may be told to leave his body and obtain certain information, but even if he gets the information we cannot know if he actually projected, or if he used clairvoyance to get the target material. This problem complicates scientific attempts to prove objectively that OBEs do occur.

How does one project at will? A strong desire to be elsewhere helps. Freedom from distraction and complete physical relaxation seem important (though occasionally a physical body continues some routine activity during an AP). From here on, opinions vary, every expert recommending the way that works best for him. Favorite suggestions are simply to imagine oneself floating upward, which is usually what happens in an unplanned projection, or to visualize the astral body floating above one, and then, by an effort of will, project the consciousness into it.

Many people believe that astral projection during sleep is normal, though unremembered, and that floating or falling dreams can be converted to true OBEs by programming the mind beforehand.

There are other methods, but the question arises as to whether universal AP is desirable. Some people have experienced pain on returning to the body. Others have felt themselves trapped in other dimensions, a terrifying experience. (However, those who reported this trouble did in fact get back somehow, or they would not be able to tell of it.)

Another problem is that of ethics. If everyone could glide through closed doors at will, no "invasion of privacy" law would be enforceable, and as for Peeping Toms. . . . Supposing Victorian Miss Verity had been nude when Mr. Beard popped into her bedroom? Obviously the need for self-policing would be great.

All this may seem farfetched, but belief in OBEs is more common than might be supposed. In a 1952 survey at Duke University, 155 students were asked if they had ever seen their physical bodies from a viewpoint completely outside the body, and 30% said they had. This feeling is sometimes explained by psychologists as a hallucination of the body image. However, cases where the astral visitor is seen by others, or where he gets evidential information, rebut this.

Recently, research on OBEs has spurted, motivated by a desire to prove the possibility of survival after death. If a nonphysical consciousness can exist away from the body, this lends support to the belief that some form of consciousness can continue without the body after physical death. Organizations interested in this type of research include the American Society for Psychical Research, the Psychical Research Foundation, and the Division of Parapsychology at the University of Virginia in Charlottesville.

FOR FURTHER READING
Journeys Out of the Body by Robert A. Monroe. New York, Doubleday, 1971. A fascinating 1st-person account of this hardheaded businessman's experiences—1st involuntary, later at will—of many types of astral projection.

The Enigma of Out-of-Body Travel by Susy Smith. New York, Garret/Helix, 1965. Cited by the American Society for Psychical Research as the most useful book for an overall view of OBEs, this contains historical accounts, modern anecdotes, and well-informed discussion of the implications of astral projection.

How's Your Aura Today?

The aura is a band of colored light said to surround the human body, and about which numerous claims are made. Many psychics say they can see it clairvoyantly, and that from a person's aura they can get impressions about that individual's personality, talents, ailments, future tendencies, past activities, and even, so they say, his past lives. One of the highest compliments such a psychic can give is to tell a person that he or she has a beautiful aura. On the other hand, many people have been embarrassed to hear that their auras are covered with red sparks or spots, which reveal anger or irritation to a psychic no matter how perfectly one may be controlling one's external reactions.

Attempts have been made to interpret the aura on the basis of its color, and though no system is universally accepted, there is considerable correspondence between different codes. Sky blue has always been considered the color of serenity, and green that of balance. Yellow indicates intellectual activity, and violet shows spiritual advancement. Clear colors are generally "good," while muddy colors indicate undesirable states of mind or spirit. Thus, a clear red indicates vigor and good physical health, but a dark or murky red may show anger, lust, or other uncontrolled "earthy" emotions. Some occultists feel there are several auras, relating to various aspects of the physical, mental, emotional, and spiritual, all superimposed upon each other but extending from the body for different distances.

For centuries all this has been a matter provoking amused contempt from skeptics who have denied the existence of anything resembling an aura, let alone the possibility that it might give information not readily available in other ways. However, recently developed photographic techniques confirm that human beings (and indeed every living thing, both animal and vegetable) is surrounded by a glowing, pulsing aura whose shape and colors can be a guide to physical, mental, and emotional states. It has even been shown that the aura may indicate the onset of illness before the sufferer becomes aware of any symptoms, and in this way it can "foretell the future."

The aura is captured on film by placing the subject in an electrical field while he is photographed. This is usually known as Kirlian photography because the complex technique was developed by Russian researchers Semyon and Valentina Kirlian. Several similar methods of photographing the aura have also been developed by Western scientists, and some startling discoveries have been made.

For example, Dr. Thelma Moss of UCLA photographed the fingertips of one volunteer at intervals while he resolutely got drunk. The early pictures show the blue and white aura which is considered normal, but as his alcohol level rose, his aura became steadily pinker, brighter, and larger until he was, to quote Dr. Moss, "all lit up." A similar effect is frequently obtained when drugs are being used. Emotional factors such as a broken engagement may bring about a smaller aura, as will faintness or fatigue. Other physical ills often show as unevenness in aura shape, or as splotches of a different or darker color.

More recent research in Kirlian photography indicates that variations of color and corona size may be due to ultraviolet sparks from the equipment onto the back or front (or both) of the film. If this should prove to be the case the condition of the individual photographed would be quite irrelevant to Kirlian photography, and the phenomena would therefore have no connection with any form of aura.

Long before the Kirlians (who made their discovery more or less by accident), scientists had worked to demonstrate the existence of the human aura. Nineteenth-century physicist Karl von Reichenbach claimed to have discovered a force field which he called "odyle," but it was visible only to clairvoyants, and science discredited him. During this century

Wilhelm Reich suffered the same fate after naming a similar force "orgone." Both men asserted that the force also emanated from inanimate objects, and this is confirmed by Kirlian photographs showing a steady, nonpulsing corona around nonliving objects such as coins and rings.

Researchers trying to use Kirlian photography for medical diagnosis look over their shoulders for the ghost of British physician Walter Kilner. Early in this century Kilner claimed that anyone could see the aura, and use it in diagnosis, with the aid of a dicyanin-dyed screen placed between viewer and patient. He felt that certain variations in the aura indicated specific conditions, including epilepsy, malignancy, and pregnancy. His work, later confirmed by biologist Oscar Bagnall, seemed to herald a medical breakthrough, but was not widely popularized. In actual fact not everyone can see auras through a dicyanin-dyed screen, and modern experimenters suspect that both Kilner and Bagnall may themselves have been a little clairvoyant.

Another doctor, Shafica Karagulla, works with clairvoyants who can diagnose illness by seeing auras. She has taken them into hospital waiting rooms to make notes on randomly selected patients, and when compared with medical diagnoses the psychic readings have been startlingly accurate.

Professor Harold Burr of the Yale University School of Medicine studied an auralike electrodynamic field which surrounds every living thing and which he called the Life or L-field. During his 40 years of research Burr made some mind-blowing discoveries. The L-field of an unfertilized salamander egg, for instance, indicates where the animal's head and nervous system will be located *after* fertilization and development. Burr even suggested that the L-field *dictates* where they will be, that it is a kind of blueprint of the developing life, and that all living things have such a blueprint, which actually guides their growth. His inference was that this form of aura not only mirrors what the individual *is*, but also guides what it becomes!

So far there is no agreement as to whether these discoveries concern one and the same aura, or several completely different phenomena. Psychics claim that just about every color can be seen in the aura, and believe that white occurs only rarely, in very spiritual individuals. However, Kirlian photography shows mainly blue and white auras for nearly everyone. Many clairvoyants say the aura they see is a spiritual, nonphysical thing, whereas the Kirlian aura is believed to involve emissions of cold electrons or gases from the body, and so has a physical source. Burr's L-field can be measured by a voltmeter so it, too, is physical, but it is not yet clear whether this is what is photographed by the Kirlian technique. Future research may be able to bring together the varied findings of Reichenbach, Reich, Burr, the Kirlians, Thelma Moss, and others so that we may find out more about the fascinating but elusive human aura.

Spiritualism and Séances

Spiritualism is based on 2 beliefs: that there is a life after death, and that some individuals, called mediums, can communicate with the spirits of those who have "crossed over."

Historically, spiritualism's 1st major impact on the world was with the "Rochester rappings." In 1848 the Fox family, of Hydesville, N.Y., was plagued by noises in their newly rented house. Daughter Kate, snapping her fingers, found that the raps would repeat the number of snaps with apparent intelligence. A code was developed, and soon crowds were gathering, for it seemed that the raps could give all manner of information. The rappings continued to follow Kate and her sister Maggie when they moved elsewhere. The girls always insisted that the rappings were caused by the spirits of the dead.

In fact the Fox sisters were not the 1st to claim communication with spirits. Shamans and witch doctors have exhibited mediumistic talents since man 1st felt the need for religion, and many religious groups have believed their leaders to be guided by spirits. However, it was the Fox sisters who were at the right time and place, sociologically and psychologically, to gain international attention.

In 1849, nearby Rochester saw the 1st public demonstration of spiritualism. Small spiritualist circles sprang up in and around the city, spread across the country, and invaded Europe. By 1855 spiritualism claimed over 2 million adherents.

At 1st American scientists dismissed spiritualism as a fad, but in England both society and science embraced it immediately. It is said that even Queen Victoria took part in a table-tilting circle, and most of the major events of spiritualism's history took place in Europe.

By this time the spirits had progressed far beyond mere rappings, though they often announced their presence by banging or by tilting a table. Typically, a séance started with hymn singing and a Bible reading to attract the higher-minded spirits. The medium would then go into a trance. Most experienced mediums had a regular "control"—one particular spirit who would pass on messages from other spirits. Some mediums simply informed their sitters that so-and-so sent a message to Mrs. X saying such-and-such. Others would apparently have their bodies taken over by the control or by other spirits, who would then converse directly with the sitters. In smaller circles the Ouija board became popular, as did automatic writing.

The phase of spiritualism most open to charges of fraud was physical mediumship. Usually the sitters held hands around a table, so that, in theory, everyone was checking on the whereabouts of everyone else. Often the medium was tied to her chair, with researchers holding her hands and feet, yet even then strange things happened. Objects levitated, musical instruments played, messages appeared on previously clean slates, perfumes or dancing lights filled the air, hands caressed the sitters. Sometimes there were apports—the unexplained appearance of objects that had not been seen in the locked room at the start of the séance.

The highest symbol of mediumship was to be able to cause the spirits to materialize. For this the medium retired to a cabinet, in which he or she could concentrate his other energies and produce ectoplasm, a whitish, foamy substance alleged to be secreted by the medium's body. It was of ectoplasm that the spirits formed their visible bodies (though occasionally investigators found them to consist of cheesecloth draped over the very material body of the medium himself). Harm to the materialized spirit was said to cause harm to the medium, so touching the materialization or introducing strong light into the room was normally forbidden, except for an occasional photograph. Obviously this left plenty of room for fraud during a séance, and all the tricks of the magician's trade were discovered at one time or another in the supposedly demure séance room. At the same time, much happened that could not be explained.

D. D. Home was one of the greatest mediums of the time. Though American by upbringing, he went to Europe in 1855 and was accepted into high society. His exploits included a levitation during which, 3 men swore, he floated out of one window and into another. His image was somewhat tarnished by a rather sordid court case, but his ability as a medium was not in question. His immense popularity caused him to be scrutinized by believer and skeptic alike, but Home was never caught in any attempt at fraud.

Eusapia Palladino presented a very different picture. An Italian peasant who deliberately rebuffed all of society's efforts to refine her, she would cheat whenever the opportunity presented itself. However, some of her phenomena occurred under circumstances that seemed to rule out chicanery. Once during a séance a 15½-lb. melon was moved from a chair behind her to the séance table in front of her. Observers stated that it had no stalk which could have been grasped, and that she was controlled by them at all times. Eusapia had her ups and downs, doing best in Europe, where she was perhaps most at home, and less well in England (1895) and America (1909). Critics feel that her admitted deceptions invalidated all her work; others believe that they may have augmented what was in fact a genuine gift.

Though the golden age of physical mediumship was soon over, other forms continued, and the messages kept coming. Perhaps most astonishing of all were the cross-correspondences, in which several widely separated mediums received different messages, all purporting to come from a few recently deceased physical researchers. They were like pieces of a puzzle—no one piece making sense alone, but becoming clearer and more relevant when considered with the rest.

Another type of puzzle concerns the identity of the "control." Is it truly a spirit from the beyond communicating directly? Is the contact perhaps not direct, but via telepathic links with the medium? This would explain why information received is often nearly correct, yet slightly "bent." Might the control be simply a subordinate personality of the medium, brought forth under trance as subordinates are brought forth by hypnotism in other multiple-person-

ality cases? Trance states seem to increase ESP, and much of the phenomena occurring at a séance could be explained by ESP and PK (psychokinesis) without recourse to spirits. In this space age, some controls profess to be extraterrestrial beings—is this another possibility? Or is the true explanation still unguessed?

Unlike many other mediums, Eileen Garrett willingly cooperated with scientists to discover what really happened when her controls took over, but even at her death in 1970 Mrs. Garrett remained uncertain where the truth lay.

There have been many other great mediums, and even more of varying reputation, but most mediums now regard spiritualism solely as a religion and are unwilling to subject it to the scrutiny of the scientist. For their part, parapsychologists usually prefer not to get involved in the religious atmosphere of a typical séance. Thus, though spiritualism was responsible for much of the early interest in psychical research, and historically the 2 are intertwined, they now go their separate ways, each, one suspects, rather glad to be free of the other.

(The subject of séances cannot be left without a word of caution. When one opens oneself to control, in trance or by using the Ouija board or automatic writing, one is taking a risk. The movie *The Exorcist* depicted an "entity" contacting a child through her games with the Ouija board, appearing pleasant at 1st but later becoming diabolical. Students of the subject claim that this is not an isolated incident. Whether the control is by a spirit entity or part of one's own subconscious, there is still danger. If spirits exist they can be evil as well as good, and Freud made it clear that there are corners of the subconscious that we would certainly not wish to have control us.)

Ghosts and Hauntings

"Do I believe in ghosts? No—but I'm afraid of them"—Marquise du Deffand, 1697–1780
The popular image of a ghost is of an insubstantial, whitish form floating through an ancient castle accompanied by terrifying moans, groans, and the clanking of chains. It is, of course, the spirit of some long-dead individual, the whole thing is extremely frightening, and sometimes the ghost portends death or tragedy.

Yet every year *Fate*, a major magazine concerned with the unexplained, receives between 100 and 200 very happy reports of experiences in which it appears that loved ones—people and animals—have in some way returned after death.

What are these apparitions that arouse such varied emotions? Perhaps the clearest under-

standing can be gained by looking at a number of different, yet typical, sightings.

Most interesting is the ghost with a purpose, like Mr. F.G.'s fair-haired sister, who appeared briefly to him in 1876. A salesman, he was far from home, but this sighting sent him posthaste to tell his parents about the incident. As he described his sister, he mentioned a scratch on her face, upon which his mother burst into tears and explained that while attending to the body after her daughter's death she had accidentally made just such a scratch and then carefully hidden it with makeup so that no one else knew of its existence. Thus the ghost provided comforting evidence of survival after death, *and* succeeded in prompting F.G. to visit his parents. His mother died shortly afterward, and he might not otherwise have seen her alive again.

Another type of sighting is one in which a dying person seems to see dead relatives and friends waiting to welcome him. This may be mere hallucination (like many other ghost tales), but if he names someone who is believed to be living, but that person is later discovered to have died before the "sighting," then the case becomes more interesting. In one case, a dying woman, Mrs. Blank, said that she saw and heard a young girl who had spent "the happiest week of her life" singing with the Blank daughters some 6 years previously. Mrs. Blank said that this apparition was singing, with others, to welcome her to heaven. There was no reason for her or her family to believe the girl was dead, but it was later discovered that the girl had died 11 days before she was "seen and heard" by the dying Mrs. Blank.

Not all ghosts are so purposeful. Often referred to as "haunts" are cases where one figure is seen to do the same thing time after time. Haunts may be seen by many people, and they usually seem unaware of the living. Equally pointless are the cases in which the noises of past battles are heard, though nothing is seen. Investigation may show that the noises duplicate exactly the progress of the battle concerned, even though the people who hear them have no historical knowledge of what happened. A 1942 Allied Forces landing near Dieppe seems to have been "heard" on the same date in 1951 by 2 English ladies staying in a hotel near where the landing took place, and other similar cases have been reported.

It has been suggested that these haunts are not related to surviving entities at all, but are the result of a sort of vibration, absorbed by the locale as a result of very intense emotions at the time the original act (or battle) took place. An alternative explanation may be retrocognition in which one sees or hears the past psychically, by ESP.

Spiritualists believe that many ghosts are spirits who are bound to earth by strong emotional ties or a refusal to accept the fact that they have died. Some mediums specialize in "rescuing" such entities by persuading them that their place is on other planes, not on earth.

The word "poltergeist" refers to a boisterous ghost, and this is a different matter. A typical poltergeist case has objects flying around, bottles falling over, screw-top lids coming loose. Usually no one is harmed (although there are exceptions), but the events are frightening to any family that has to endure them. Occasionally showers of stones will rain onto and into a house. More horrifying is the "fire poltergeist," in which flammable objects keep bursting into flame for no apparent reason, but these cases are rare and are unlikely to be investigated while occurring. Some people believe these, and perhaps all poltergeist phenomena, are cases of possession by evil or demonic spirits.

However, investigators have managed to get to the scene of a number of "normal" poltergeist cases, and most of them think it unlikely that a ghost or spirit is responsible for the flying objects. Experience shows that poltergeists usually afflict groups within which there is considerable tension. The "center" of the activity is often a child or adolescent, although elderly centers have been reported. The person feels frustrated and inwardly angry, and these feelings seem to find expression through psychokinesis—mind over matter. When angry, it is normal to want to throw things, but usually we restrain ourselves. It is believed that the person central to poltergeist events actually *does* throw things—not physically, but by mentally causing objects to move. PK, like ESP, works subconsciously, so that even the person concerned is rarely aware of what he or she is doing.

Usually, as time goes by, tensions fade, and the phenomena gradually cease. However, poltergeists attract a lot of attention, and sometimes the people involved enjoy the attention so much that they use trickery to keep the activity going. A competent investigator usually discovers this, but he then has to decide whether all the events were hoaxes, or whether some of the original phenomena were genuine. Some cases have been very thoroughly observed and investigated, and it is clear that not all are due to trickery.

Similarly, many accounts of encounters with apparitions seem to be neither fraud nor psychological hallucination. Therefore, though we still have no clear understanding of just what a ghost is, there must be ghosts!

Psychokinesis

Otherwise known as PK, psychokinesis is the influencing or moving of physical objects by, for want of a better term, willpower. In other words, PK is mind over matter. If the gambler can really affect the fall of dice by concentrating, then he is using PK. In the realm of psi, PK is the other side of the coin from ESP, for whereas with ESP something is coming into the mind from the outside, with PK something is going from the mind to affect part of the environment, most often, though not always, by affecting the movement of inanimate objects.

The 1st major attempt to prove or disprove the existence of PK was made by Dr. J. B. Rhine and his associates in the 1930s, with a long series of experiments to see whether PK could affect the fall of dice. At 1st subjects attempted to make the dice fall with a specific face upward. Later dice fell down a chute while subjects tried to will them to fall toward the left or the right at the bottom. The results of some of these experiments were positive, since they would have occurred by chance only once in many thousands of repetitions—strong evidence that PK was in action. Since then, various machines have been developed to ensure that PK experiments are even more rigidly controlled, and many different types of targets have been used. Ingo Swann, an artist and psychic, has attempted to change the temperature inside sealed, insulated containers, with highly significant results. Subjects have also tried either to speed or slow the motion of various forms of pendulum—again with, in some cases, great success.

Even more exciting are reports of PK experiments with Nelya Kulagina, a middle-aged Russian woman. Russian films have shown her apparently causing metal cylinders, matches, a matchbox, cigarettes, compass needles, and even the compass itself, to move—always without touching them, and sometimes when they were under a Plexiglas cover. Kulagina has known untouched objects to fall from shelves in her apartment when she was angry, occurrences reminiscent of poltergeist phenomena which are probably also due to PK.

In thoughtography (or psychophotography) there are changes in photographic emulsion which create unexpected pictures or other unexplainable effects. The only apparent explanation is that either fraud or PK is involved.

The best-known thoughtographer at the present time is Ted Serios, whose exploits with both thoughtography and alcohol have made him a legend in the world of psi. At his best, Serios has produced Polaroid pictures of buildings and faces, as well as innumerable blurs, smudges, and all-black and all-white photographs which seem unexplainable. His informal and often inebriated way of working has brought him—and Jule Eisenbud, who has researched his abilities—considerable criticism. Several stage magicians have claimed to be able to reproduce his effects by sleight of hand, but to date none has done so under the controlled conditions that have, at times, been used for Serios. On the other hand, Serios' validity has not yet been proved beyond all doubt.

Members of the Veilleux family of Maine also seem to have a talent for psychic photography which is currently under investigation. However, their ability seems more allied with "spirit photography" (alleged photos of and by the spirits of the dead), which may or may not involve the use of PK, than it does with thoughtography, which almost certainly involves PK.

It has been suggested that many of the phenomena observed at séances may involve PK instead of spirits. For example, and assuming there is no trickery, a trumpet can be made to float through the air by the medium's use of PK as well as by spirits lifting the trumpet. Both spiritualist and PK theories have their adherents, but final proof favoring one side or the other is still lacking.

More positive proof has been obtained in connection with "psychic healing," which probably involves the use of PK. In 1961, Dr. Bernard Grad of McGill University had a healer work on a group of mice daily. Each mouse had a small skin wound, and at the end of 14 days the wounds had healed significantly more than those of a control group of mice, wounded at the same time and kept in identical conditions but not given healing sessions.

Sister Justa Smith, then of Rosary Hill College, Buffalo, N.Y., had the same healer direct his power to sealed tubes containing an enzyme. The activity of the enzyme was speeded up as much as it would have been had the tubes been subjected to an electromagnetic force of 13,000 gauss. (The earth's magnetic field is only 0.5 gauss.)

From these and other experiments it is apparent that healers do affect things in some way, so PK may be potentially beneficial. However, it also has potentially terrifying connotations. This is explained well in *The World of Ted Serios* by Jule Eisenbud. Eisenbud, a psychiatrist, hypothesizes that PK was so natural to primeval man that he could not differentiate between what he had caused to happen and what happened by accident. So if Ug and Og had an argument and Ug was subsequently crushed by a falling boulder, everyone would assume that Og had used PK to cause the boulder to fall. Thus every accident caused guilt feelings, and it became preferable to deny the PK ability completely and blame "the spirit of the boulder." This was the start of pantheism.

A belief in PK as a powerful force could give us the same problems today, creating ever increasing guilt feelings whenever someone we had momentarily "cursed" came to grief. However, PK experiments usually involve small objects. There is no evidence that we can control large leaping boulders, so our enemies are probably safe.

In any event, we do not yet have a final verdict on the existence of PK. Research statistics point to its reality, but the nagging doubts of the skeptics have not yet been completely eliminated.

Humans have long known that their physical environment can have an effect on their minds. It is awe-inspiring to consider that perhaps the mind, unaided by muscle, can have an effect on the environment. It would, however, be only fair.

Dowsing and Dowsers

When a person walks across a field with just a stick in his hand, and by the movements of that stick detects minerals buried far below, he is dowsing. There are few virtuosos at this ancient art, but many people can achieve occasional success. Usually a forked stick is used, one fork held in either hand, but sometimes a single straight twig is preferred. If the stick turns in the hand, this indicates the presence of minerals below. Hazel and peach twigs are the traditional favorites, though other fruit or nut woods have their advocates. In today's society, however, 2 L-shaped lengths of coat hanger or copper wire are often easier to come by than a peach tree, and these seem to do the job just as well.

In England and America dowsers have searched mainly for water (hence the expression "water witching") but early European miners dowsed to detect metals. A few people were even able to track down criminals with the rod, but this led to widespread abuses, so the Inquisition condemned this form of dowsing, while approving it for finding water. The subject has always been controversial: Some sects believed the rod was moved by the devil, and Martin Luther stated that dowsing violated the 1st commandment. Not many agree with this today, but we still have no certain explanation of the dowser's successes.

For instance, what can we make of John Mullins, a famous English dowser? Wealthy Sir Henry Harben had spent over £1,000 (in the last century, and pre-inflation) on professional geological advice and on well-drilling based on that advice. His estate remained short of water. Finally, Sir Henry sent for Mullins, who promptly indicated locations for 5 wells, giving the depths at which water would be found. In all cases he was correct. Many similar tales are told of him and of his contemporary, William S. Lawrence, both of whom "outguessed" experienced geologists on a number of occasions.

The same thing happened in Saratoga Springs, where fortunes were made and lost by men trying to find mineral water. The large companies involved in the search often used several dowsers independently to confirm one another's findings before expensive well-digging was begun.

The popular image of a dowser has him striding across the countryside, rod in hand, but this is not always the case. Two of the best-known dowsers have worked successfully while sitting comfortably at a table, dowsing with a pendulum suspended over a map of the area concerned. Henry Gross of Maine, probably America's best-publicized dowser, frequently used this method, as did Britain's Evelyn Penrose. Miss Penrose perhaps brought dowsing full circle in that she dowsed as much for metals as for water. She found metals, oil, and water for the Government of British Columbia, and worked for tough-minded businessmen located in the U.S., England, and Australia. An interesting point about her dowsing was that she described different physical sensations according to which metal she was seeking. Silver, she said, itched, while tin gave her a feeling of exhilaration.

While dowsing has brought fertility to previously arid farmland and financial success to miners, it is also credited with saving lives. In Vietnam, American forces made good use of the L-shaped coat-hanger dowsing rod to detect mines and other booby traps. Most of the men did not profess to know how or why the rods turned to give them warning—they were just glad that they did!

Perhaps prompted by the news reports from Vietnam, the U.S. Dept. of the Interior and Utah State University conducted a dowsing research project in which over 150 people were asked to place wooden blocks wherever they got a dowsing reaction along a certain course. Each subject walked separately, not knowing where his predecessors had placed their blocks, yet there was a strong tendency for the blocks to be grouped in specific locations. These locations also tended to be where the earth's magnetic field changed abruptly. Such changes may be caused by water below the ground, so in this sense the experiment's results may help explain dowsing. However, magnetic-field changes are not necessarily due to water, and Professor Duane Chadwick, who conducted the experiment, emphasizes that since no wells were dug, there is no proof that any of the places chosen by several subjects would actually yield water.

One explanation put forward is that the

dowsing rod may serve as a sort of "amplifer" of ESP impulses. This is supported by the fact that Dutch psychic M. B. Dykshoorn often uses a divining rod to supplement his clairvoyance. Perhaps the dowser receives information by ESP, and, though he is unaware of it, his muscles react just enough to move the rod. Some believe the dowser perceives the water itself; others say he senses the change in the magnetic field. Since the 5 senses do not perceive magnetism, the latter would still be a form of ESP, but with a rather more physical tie-in.

Another theory is that different substances give off specific vibrations to which a dowser is physically sensitive, making his muscles twitch so that, unconsciously, he turns the rod. The study of the effects of different substances and their vibration is termed radiesthesia, and its proponents consider it a science that can be used in medical diagnosis.

Yet another theory maintains that the rod itself is affected by the substances being dowsed. Most dowsers sincerely try to hold the rod still, yet it moves anyway. Unwilling to accept the unconscious muscle-movement theory, some are convinced that the rod moves of its own volition. In 1530 Georgius Agricola commented that if this were the case the rod would move for everyone, which it does not with any degree of accuracy. Nearly everyone can get *some* dowsing reaction, whether right or wrong (of Chadwick's more than 150 subjects, only one got no reaction at all), but few can approach Evelyn Penrose's purported 80% success rate. An even higher rate of 93% "hits" was reported for American John Shelley, former president of the American Society of Dowsers, based in Schenectady, N.Y.

Skeptics dismiss the whole subject as a sham. They say that a dowser's successes are due to an understanding of geology, a surveying of the lie of the land, vegetation, and so on. The record of the many dowsers who have repeatedly succeeded where geologists have failed suggests that this is not the whole story.

—D.R.

30

Survival in the Belly of the Monster

The Man Who Survived the Belly of the Monster

"Then the men feared the Lord exceedingly; and offered a sacrifice unto the Lord, and made vows. Now the Lord had prepared a great fish to swallow up Jonah. And Jonah was in the belly of the fish 3 days and 3 nights . . . And the Lord spake unto the fish, and it vomited out Jonah upon the dry land."

—Jonah 1:16–17; 2:10

In February, 1891, the ship *Star of the East* was off the Falkland Islands when the crew spotted an 80' sperm whale. Two rowboats filled with crewmen were launched to capture the monster. Closing in, one harpooner let go his weapon and shafted the whale, which lashed out, almost overturning the boats. Returning to the ship with their dead whale, the crewmen realized one sailor, James Bartley, was missing. It was decided he had been tossed overboard in the fight and had drowned.

Six hours later the crewmen began removing the blubber from the dead beast. By midnight the task was still unfinished, and the sailors went to bed. In the morning, they resumed their job. Then the unexpected happened. According to M. de Parville, editor of the *Journal des Débats*, writing in Paris in 1914, "Suddenly the sailors were startled by something in the stomach which gave spasmodic signs of life. Inside was found the missing sailor, James Bartley, doubled up and unconscious. He was placed on deck and treated to a bath of seawater which soon revived him, but his mind was not clear and he was placed in the captain's quarters." Recovering, Bartley recalled being hit by the whale's tail and that he had been "encompassed by great darkness, and he felt he was slipping along a smooth passage that seemed to move and carry him forward. His hands came in contact with a yielding, slimy substance, which seemed to shrink from his touch. He could easily breathe, but the heat was terrible. It seemed to open the pores of his skin and draw out his vitality. The next he remembered he was in the captain's cabin."

Except for the fact that his face, neck, hands had been bleached white, Bartley—like Jonah—survived the belly of the monster.

Today, we are all in the belly of the monster, and the monster is everywhere, in hostile environments inside and outside the city, in the system, in government, in business, in technology, in routine. Survival is up to each of us, individually or working together, but the *Almanac* would like to offer a few hints to help all Bartleys emerge from the belly safely. . . .

—I.W.

Growing Food in the City

Remember the energy crisis? The meat shortage? Now some experts are predicting worldwide famine in the next decade. Already it is reality in much of the world. In the U.S., artificial shortages have been contrived to raise prices. Much of the food that is available is of poor quality because of mass farming techniques. Growing your own food makes more and more sense. Only by controlling every step —from the preparation of the soil to the preparation of a meal—can you be sure your food is free of chemicals damaging to both your health and the taste of your produce, and only by growing your own can you protect yourself from shortages, either real or contrived. Besides, it's rewarding, easy, and fun.

Most seeds will grow almost anywhere if given half a chance. Even a one-room basement apartment can be made into a little farm, and a house with a backyard can provide a good proportion of a family's food needs. You can grow cucumbers in a hanging pot, tomatoes in a bushel basket by a sunny window, or herbs on a windowsill. But even if you have only a dark cupboard, you can grow a crop of sprouts.

SPROUTS

Sprouts are the easiest "crop" to grow, and the one that requires the least space. Any edible seed that produces a nonpoisonous plant (tomato and potato leaves and stalks are poisonous) can be sprouted. Usable seeds include grains, legumes, nuts, and vegetables. A sprout is a seed in the beginning stages of germination which would go on to produce a whole new plant if it were not eaten. The sprouting process releases nutrients stored in the seed for the dormant plant embryo. Sprouts contain high concentrations of vital minerals, vitamins, and proteins needed for sustaining life in any living organism, be it a plant or a human being. They are an excellent food.

The basic process for producing sprouts is simple. Soak seeds for 6 to 12 hours, drain, then place in a well-ventilated container in a dark, warm place. An acceptable container is a wide-mouthed jar covered with cheesecloth or nylon netting secured by a rubber band or string. The seeds should be rinsed and drained 2 to 4 times daily. Seeds can also be successfully sprouted between layers of moistened paper towels lying on a draining rack placed in a glass or metal pan. They should be sprinkled lightly twice daily and the upper layer of paper towels should be resoaked and squeezed out before it is replaced. No matter what method is used, sprouting seeds should be kept moist but not wet, and in a dark place. When they are ready, which takes between 2 and 5 days, they should be drained thoroughly and refrigerated. Leafy sprouts should be left out in the light for a few hours to increase the vitamin content before they are refrigerated.

Perhaps the most popular sprout is that which is germinated from the mung bean. These are the long crunchy sprouts used in Chinese cooking. Easy to sprout, they are ready in 3 to 5 days and can be added to just about any dish you can think of. Another versatile and highly nutritious sprout grows from the tiny alfalfa seed. The sprouts are ready in 2 to 4 days and can be used raw in salads and sandwiches instead of lettuce. They are also

good cooked. After you have sprouted these 2 almost foolproof seeds, try something a little more exotic. Always be sure to use "seed-quality" rather than "food-quality" seeds; the latter are sometimes dead and won't sprout. Also make sure you use only untreated sprouts to avoid the poisons which are sometimes added to seeds to reduce field planting losses. Your best bet is to buy seeds for sprouting at a reliable health food store.

YOGURT

A 2nd item which can be produced in a cupboard farm is yogurt. Yogurt is a milk product created by the propagation of bacteria cultures. Basically, if you place a tablespoon of yogurt in a glass of milk, the bacteria reproduce and spread through the milk, and within 6 to 12 hours, transform it all into yogurt. But if you try this unrefined method, the mixture probably won't "yog" correctly, because yogurt cultures are very delicate and particular. They insist upon a controlled environment. The milk which is to be cultured must be free of bacteria that might compete with the yogurt bacteria. Therefore milk to be used to make yogurt must either be boiled, be made from sterile powdered milk, or be a combination of the 2. If it is boiled, it must then be cooled until it is lukewarm to the touch, lest the yogurt bacteria be killed by the high heat. The milk and yogurt mixture (approximately one tablespoon of yogurt to 2 cups of milk) should be placed in a covered glass or clay bowl in a warm place. An oven which has been preheated to 200° and then turned off would be fine, or the top of the stove above the pilot. The yogurt should be ready in 6 to 12 hours. If it isn't, either the heat wasn't consistent or the original boiled milk wasn't cooled down enough. Try the process again. If your luck is really bad, try adding a half teaspoon of unflavored gelatin dissolved in a small amount of warm water.

After the yogurt is ready, it should be stored in the refrigerator. A new batch should be made every 4 or 5 days to keep the culture active and the flavor good. After you've got the hang of making it, you can experiment with the differences between whole and nonfat milk, powdered milk made with cold or warm water, and so on. All these factors influence the taste and texture of the yogurt.

One last note: Don't try to make yogurt the same day you bake bread. It won't work. Yogurt cultures abhor competition, and yeast in the air seems to make them roll over and go to sleep. It's usually easiest to make yogurt right before you go to bed, so that the cultures can work when they're least likely to be disturbed. Unless your house has no heat and you live in a cold climate, it probably won't get too cold in your kitchen.

CITY GARDENS

Survival in the city would be pretty tough on a diet of yogurt and sprouts, though you'd probably stay healthy for a while. Anyone willing to take a little more time can grow lots of fruit and vegetables. The 1st thing to consider is where you can plant your seeds. Can you plant on the roof, do you have some yard area, or is there a vacant lot in the neighborhood that you and interested friends could turn into a garden? Or are you restricted to indoor space? If the latter is the case, you will have to custom-fit containers to the space available and to the space needed by each plant's root system. If you have never had a garden before, it may be necessary to do some research on the needs of various plants. For example, while spinach or lettuce can be grown in a medium-sized flowerpot, tomatoes or corn require a bushel basket. If you know what a mature plant looks like, you can safely assume that the root system will be proportionate, and can make a fairly good educated guess as to minimum acceptable container size. Indoor gardens sometimes require artificial lighting—plants need 14 to 16 hours of light a day. If your windows don't provide enough daylight, a "grow" light or combination of incandescent and fluorescent lighting will be close enough to natural sunlight to satisfy your plants. If you have outdoor space, light is no problem if you choose a sunny spot and plant rows north and south for even distribution of sunlight. However, if your space is on a slope, the rows should be planted along the slope to prevent erosion and to facilitate watering. Seeds can either be planted directly in the ground or kept in pots outdoors. The 2nd option allows you to bring your plants indoors to lengthen the growing season artificially.

The 1st step in laying out a garden is preparing the soil. Plants like a good fertile soil with a neutral pH. If you are planting outdoors, have your soil analyzed for acidity. If it's too acidic (pH 0–5) you can add ground limestone, crushed marble, or bone meal, all of which are alkaline, when you dig in your compost. If you are planting indoors you can use neutral potting soil from a local nursery. This should be mixed with equal parts of peat, construction (not sea) sand, and compost. The peat holds water, the sand keeps the soil from packing, and the compost provides necessary nutrients and beneficial bacteria which break the nutrients down into forms usable by plants. If you don't have compost ready by the time you begin to plant, buy some fertilizer at a garden shop, but begin your own compost pile

anyway. You'll need more later in the growing season.

COMPOST

Compost is the richest fertilizer that exists, and is composed of decayed organic matter. You can make your own by combining a 6" layer of "green matter" (leaves, grass, and decomposable kitchen scraps) with 2" layers of manure and earth. Water should be added to moisten, but not soak, each layer. The sequence of layers should be repeated until the compost reaches a height of 3' to 4'. When it reaches the desired height it should be turned every 2 weeks. It should be hot, which indicates the presence of bacterial action—that is, decay. If it doesn't heat up, you need more nitrogen. Add chicken manure for a layer or 2 or bone meal or blood meal, all high in nitrogen. If the compost smells, add ground limestone. Your fully decayed compost will be ready to dig into your garden in 2 to 3 months. You will be providing the best food for your plants while simultaneously enriching the soil and helping to alleviate the garbage problem.

Where do you keep a compost heap? If you have outdoor space you can dig a pit, build an above-ground wood frame for it, or simply pile it up in a heap. Cover your pit, frame, or heap with heavy plastic or burlap bags. Backyard heaps should not include meat scraps, as these attract neighborhood animals. If you have no outdoor space, get a plastic garbage can and punch some holes around the sides a few inches from the bottom. Proceed with layers as outlined above. Make sure you use well-aged manure to avoid an odor problem.

PLANTING

Now you're ready to plant. You can start plants from seeds or you can plant seedlings. If you are efficient and live in a climate with a long growing season, it's best to start just about every variety of plant from seed. This means you probably should begin indoors before the frost-free date. Tomato plants, for example, should be started about 6 weeks before you intend to put them in the ground. The easiest way to start plants is in peat pots or cardboard egg cartons, both of which can be placed directly in the soil, which will help ease transplant shock. Before you put the seed into the ground, you can soak it overnight in "manure tea," a mixture of warm water and a spoon of aged manure. This soaking will speed up the germination process.

When seedlings get so big their leaves touch one another, it's time to thin them. Using scissors, cut off every other seedling at ground level. The remaining plants will have enough room for their roots to get much stronger. Make sure at this point that you don't hurt the young seedlings by drowning them. They are still quite delicate. If they seem to be growing too tall and are spindly, they may be reaching for light. Make sure they're close to a bright window. Or their soil may be too rich, causing them to "speed." Try starting over with a blander soil. Another reason plants grow tall and skinny is that their pots are too small for adequate development of their root systems. It's time to transplant.

When the seedlings are a few inches high, they can be placed in bigger pots or in the ground. If you live in a cold climate but your plants are getting too big to keep inside, you might consider building them a cold frame. This is a miniature greenhouse dug a few inches into the ground and rising about a foot above it. You can use wood or cinder block for the walls and glass or plastic for the roof. If possible, build walls lower on the south side. The sloping top will provide more sun. Matured compost should be dug into the soil of the cold frame and your seedlings can be planted when they are 6" to 8" tall. If the soil is so frozen you can't dig into it, lay down a layer of gravel for drainage before you put in the compost and plants.

Now, for those who stayed indoors: It's time to think about your plants' final homes. Choose large enough pots to accommodate mature plants. No matter what sort of container you use, drainage is crucial. For most containers the easiest way to assure drainage is to cover the bottom with a layer of gravel. Then add your potting soil-sand-peat-compost mixture. It is good practice to plant more seedlings in a pot than it will ultimately be able to hold and then snip off the weakest ones.

Back to cold-frame people. As soon as the ground in your yard is well thawed, dig some compost into the soil and then add some earthworms to dig air tunnels and break down minerals. Let it all sit a week before you plant your seedlings. When you plant, make sure you leave adequate space between plants as indicated on the seed package. Weed the garden every few days. As plants get bigger they will become less vulnerable to weeds. When the plants get about a foot high, you can "mulch" —that is, cover the ground around the plants with a 2" to 3" layer of organic matter which will conserve moisture and discourage weeds. Good materials for mulch are hay, grass, or hosed-off seaweed. Each of these materials adds nutrients to the soil, and each breaks down at a different speed. Grass clippings will need to be replaced more frequently than hay. Once you have mulched your garden, weeding will no longer be necessary.

If you think insects will be a problem, and

they almost always are, take some simple precautionary measures. Plant garlic and chives throughout your garden. Plant a marigold hedge. Some gardeners claim these plants fend off insects. You can also order praying mantis or ladybugs for specific infestations. These beneficial insects will gobble up the undesirables.

If something went wrong and your seedlings didn't make it through transplanting, you can buy seedlings at a nursery and still have enough time left to harvest in the fall. Certain plants are more temperamental than others and their seedlings are more likely to fail, but it's fun to try everything, with one exception. If you wish to plant fruit trees (and minature ones can even be grown in a pot inside and yield plenty of fruit), start with a young tree. Fruit seeds may produce an attractive plant, but seldom will such plants bear good fruit.

HYDROPONICS

If space is really limited, a city gardener may find it worthwhile to investigate "hydroponics," literally "water-culture." Plants grown by this method are fed nutrients in a solution form they absorb directly. Soil is therefore not necessary for nutritive value. Hydroponics involves one of 3 methods: water-, gravel-, or sand-culture. In water-culture, plants are grown in tanks, are supported by corks, and must be fed a precise, perfected solution. In gravel-culture, plants are placed in a coarse gravel base and are fed from the bottom, using a pump mechanism to keep water and air moving. The simplest and most practical method is sand-culture, in which plants are placed in supportive building sand and fed from above. A wick mechanism can be arranged to provide even feeding—in which one end of the wick is placed in the food solution and the other lies on top of the sand. By adjusting the thickness of the wick, you can regulate the flow of the solution. Mixtures for making these solutions can be purchased in garden stores. They are usually made from fish emulsions and are added to water.

CHICKENS AND RABBITS

The city dweller does not have to subsist on totally vegetarian fare. Small animals can be raised in screened-in cages on a roof or in a backyard. Chickens can be raised for both meat and eggs, and can subsist on a diet of garden insects and the discarded outside leaves of leafy vegetables. Rabbits can also be raised for their meat. They reproduce very rapidly and—like chickens—love Swiss chard. If you wish to raise animals for meat, you will have to learn to butcher them, but this is perhaps the only honest way to be a carnivore.

PRESERVING FOODS

No matter what method you use to grow food or where you grow it, you can enjoy the fruits of your labors all year long. Indoor plants are not limited to any particular season. In addition, food grown in the summer can be preserved by several methods. These include canning, freezing, drying, curing, and outdoor storage. Freezing is perhaps the simplest. Foods to be frozen are blanched (briefly plunged in boiling water), then quickly cooled in cold water, then placed in moisture-proof plastic freezing dishes and frozen. They will keep for a long time this way. However, if you use this method, you are dependent on the electric supply and will live in perpetual fear of a power failure. Canning, preserving, and drying allow you to be more self-reliant.

In canning and preserving, fruits and vegetables are prepared according to recipes often using sugar or vinegar as preservatives. Before foods are canned, the spores of potentially harmful bacteria must be killed by cooking at high temperatures. Low-acid foods are more prone to the most dangerous of these bacteria, the one which causes botulism, than are high-acid foods. For this reason, it is safer to can pickled string beans, for example, than string beans in water. Anyone who wishes to try his or her hand at canning should use a good cookbook written expressly for the purpose and should follow all directions meticulously. The later stages of canning preservation, in which the food is placed in sterile jars and sealed, are as important and hazardous as the early ones. But if one is conscientious and careful, canning can be exciting and rewarding.

Drying involves heating foods at temperatures of 150° to 200° for 12 or more hours until the moisture is completely removed. Foods will then last for up to 4 months. Drying can be accomplished in the sun in certain areas, or in an oven set at low heat with the door left ajar. Food is set in the sun or in the oven spread out on cloth-covered wood trays. When you wish to use the dried food, simply cook it in water. Unfortunately, many of the vitamins in dried foods are dissipated either in the drying procedure or during storage. Another disadvantage of drying is that it is extremely time-consuming. It does have the advantage of shrinking food so that it may be preferred to canning if storage space is minimal.

When your harvest is over and your food "put by" for winter, one small task remains: preparing your garden for the next year. Simply turn over the dead stems and vines of your plants together with some compost. You will be helping along the natural process by which death nurtures new life. If you are lucky, the next spring you will find familiar-looking plants sprouting out of the ground all by themselves.
—D.Ru.

Trees Speak a Secret Language

If you are hiking in the wilderness and become lost you can find the right direction by using the trees for guides. The Indians of North America used this technique when the sun or stars were not visible. Examine several trees—their foliage, the way the tops are leaning, their bark, and the moss growing on them—and they will indicate to you which direction to go.

You need to observe 3 or 4 trees for directional purposes. It is essential that you choose trees growing in an exposed place. Check each tree for the side that has the most leaves and branches growing on it. One side of each tree should appear to have distinctly more foliage. In the northern hemisphere this will be the south side of the tree. Now look closely at the top of the tree. The tops of trees almost always lean to the south or southeast. The bark is duller and darker on the north side. If you see a tree stump, it also can help you find your way. Check the ring pattern. The tree rings will be thicker on the side to the north and thinner on the southern side. In areas with heavy precipitation, trees will have moss and lichen growing on them, and this is another indication of direction. The moss or lichen *generally* grows on the north side of trees in North America. It will appear as a short velvety covering ranging from green or brown to a dull gray.

You may wonder why the trees grow in this manner. Sunlight produces foliage. The southern side of a tree usually gets more direct sunlight and therefore it produces larger branches with more leaves. Because the branches on the southern side are reaching for more sunlight, the tendency is for them to grow horizontally, away from the trunk. The northern side of a tree will usually have a more upward growth of branches. Moss grows on the northern side because moisture is retained longer here.

There is one other thing to remember about cold areas of North America. Deciduous trees grow on the warmer, south-facing slopes. This is because in the northern hemisphere, the southern slopes of the hills receive the most direct rays from the sun.
—N.N.

Wilderness Survival

EQUIPMENT

Whether you go into unfamiliar territory for a day or a month, you should always go prepared. Remember that much of our wilderness country was preserved in its natural state because the terrain was too forbidding and its life-sustaining resources too few to support civilization. It can, at times, still prove to be a hostile environment.

Below is a "minimum equipment" list with some explanation of the parts.

1. Compass. Be sure you know how to use it.

2. Maps. USGS topographic survey maps are best, but if you can get more up-to-date trail maps, take them too. The more maps the better; discrepancies between them can alert you to possible hazards.

3. Wooden matches. Keep them in a waterproof case, or waterproof the matchheads by repeated dunking in melted paraffin.

4. Knife. The basic tool. A must.

5. Food. Some concentrated foods such as beef jerky, bee pollen, chia seeds, dried fruit and nut mixtures can keep you going for a long time.

6. Water in a canteen. You never know for sure if you'll find good water. The maps can be wrong.

7. Emergency shelter such as a rain poncho or a tarp. Space blankets are compact and lightweight. Modern foil and plastic creations are excellent emergency equipment, although they won't take heavy use.

8. Ditty bag. Various small extras such as first-aid equipment (adhesive tape, gauze, antiseptic, bandages, a snake-bite kit); fishing gear (hooks, line, sinkers); a small, extra compass; twine or cord; and perhaps a candle. Parachute cord is a nylon rope that is strong enough (550-lb. test) to hold your weight; 50' compress into a compact bundle.

9. Extra clothes. Your head, hands, and feet are the "radiators" of your body. If they are warm, you'll be warm, so extra dry socks, gloves, and a wool stocking cap can be valuable for their light weight. A light wool sweater is also useful. Wool is the only fabric that insulates when wet. When dry, it is one of the best insulating fabrics since it (unlike nylon) breathes and allows perspiration to escape.

TRAIL SIGNS

	ROCK	BUNCHED GRASS	BROKEN BRANCH	TREE TRUN
TRAIL GOES RIGHT				*BLAZE
TRAIL GOES LEFT				
THIS IS THE TRAIL				
THIS IS NOT THE TRAIL				

* BLAZES HURT TREES BUT YOU SHOULD KNOW HOW TO READ THEM IF ALREADY THERE

Lost!

In cases of low visibility, or when you are without compass and map, and you can't backtrack easily, sit down and think. Have a bite to eat. Think about where the trail should be or was and figure out which direction you came from. Then go back if you're 100% sure. If uncertain, tie a flag visible from all directions to a tree or some high point, and walk a circle around the flag, moving as far away as you can while still keeping the flag in sight as you look for the trail. If you don't find the trail, seriously consider making camp; don't rush off haphazardly. If you have to, find shelter. Mark your path with piles of rocks, tied bunches of grass, or twigs. (See: Trail Signs illustration.)

After you find shelter, start exploring the area carefully, being mindful not to lose sight of your camp, as you look for familiar territory or roads. Look for roads in the distance, on the sides of hills, or across meadows. They are generally straighter than any natural phenomenon. Climb a tree! Look for lights at night. If you find some, mark the direction on the ground, and look for rooftops or other signs of habitation in the morning. Sniff the air! You may be able to detect smoke from a camp or habitation. Note the wind direction and mark your trail so you can find your way back if you lose the scent. Don't try moving cross-country at night. Even a full moon can throw tricky shadows and make footing difficult, hiding pitfalls, etc. The exception: When in the hot desert, it is sometimes better to move at night to conserve water and avoid heat prostration.

When choosing shelter for the night, look for a spot that won't be flooded and is protected from the wind on as many sides as possible. Wind direction commonly shifts during the course of a night. Always put twice as much insulation under you as over you. With a little padding, a shallow hip and shoulder hole will increase comfort. On cold nights, don't pick valley bottoms or hollows; cold air will collect there. In some areas a lean-to with a fire in front is one of the easiest shelters to construct from natural materials. (See: Lean-to illustration.)

Rescue

Do not expect to be rescued. Even when someone figures you're lost and sends out a party, rescue is far from certain. Signing up at park headquarters or trail heads is a good idea, but this doesn't guarantee being found. People have died in the Yosemite Valley area while waiting several days for rescue from the cliffs.

What this means is that if you can get yourself out, do so; but if one of your party is injured, or for some other reason you can't move far, you have to work hard to get help to reach you. Build a bright fire at night and a smoky fire by day. Clear an area visible from the air and lay out a message with rocks or brush. Use bright colors, shiny metal, or flashing mirrors to signal aircraft.

—The Eds.

LEAN-TO

People's Psychiatry Sheet:
Handling Psychiatric Emergencies

You and your friends can handle many psychiatric emergencies. The crucial elements are trying instead of drawing back, and trusting your own intuition. This sheet is meant as a simple guide, saying no more than common sense, but legitimizing people's efforts to help their sisters and brothers in trouble. Experience is, of course, the best teacher of all.

1. The 1st thing to do is LISTEN. Don't be in a hurry to give advice. LISTEN 1st; try to understand what's happening, what the person is feeling. Get into the person's FRAME OF REFERENCE.

Look for a "handle" to their situation. Try to figure out what's oppressing them, what's making them feel the way they feel. Once you've done that, you can start looking for options, for a way out of the dilemma.

2. You need to be CALM. If you can't be calm, find someone else who can be. As you listen, try to be accepting; don't start laying your trip on them. If they feel something, they have a reason for feeling it; respect their integrity. If you're calm and listening, you can start responding to them, which will help clarify the situation.

3. Understand how people's SELF-ESTEEM can be shot to pieces by crassness, inappropriate humor, or a casual air. Most people in emotional distress are feeling empty and helpless. Try not to make them feel worse about themselves. Look for the genuine assets in them, and in their situation. Try to restore their self-confidence.

4. Follow your hunches and your feelings: They're almost always right. Get in touch with what you feel, then think about it. If you feel sad, chances are the other person feels sad. If you feel scared, chances are the other person is scared too. If you feel angry, chances are the other person is angry too, or manipulating you. If you feel confused, chances are the other person feels confused too. Go ahead and say things like "I'm really confused by what you say," or "You must really feel horrible about all that." Use feelings, not ideas, as your main guide.

5. Don't be ashamed of being ignorant or feeling helpless. The other person probably feels the same way. Therapy is a human act, not some mysterious mumbo jumbo: Ask questions if you're ignorant; admit it if you feel helpless. Don't pretend to know what you don't. (That's mystifying to the other person.)

6. Let the other person tell you in his own way what's wrong. Don't make him follow *your* rules. Don't get him to "act out his feelings" or do things you learned in some groovy encounter group. This isn't fun and games: If you're trying to help a sister or brother through a trying time, you'd better accept the responsibility that goes with that.

7. People become disturbed in different ways. Some are horribly depressed; some in a state of panic; some violent; some confused and irrational; some incomprehensible. Almost everyone in an emotional crisis is terrified of LOSING CONTROL. They want to feel some kind of support, some kind of protection. Try to give them that.

Try to talk in as quiet a place as possible; if you can see them again, let them know that, and do it. If you can help them deal with their problem without losing control (and humiliating themselves), you are doing good work. (At some future time they may want to relax their control: but they'll do it some place that is protective.)

8. In the same line of thought, if you feel they are out of control, or that they are too much for you to deal with, don't pretend you can do what you can't do. Decide on bringing someone with more experience to see them, or think about a hospital.

Many people are horrified of mental hospitals. You and your friends should know which hospitals in your area are good and which are atrocious; which shrinks are sympathetic and which are absolute pigs.

If a friend is too disturbed for you to handle, get him to someone who can help him calm down or to a hospital. It's foolish to take chances with people's lives, especially if they are dangerous to themselves or others.

Don't get hung up on the rhetoric of we-should-all-be-able-to-take-care-of-one-another. Sometimes we simply can't. Then it's good to know what your options are.

9. Tell people what you're doing. Don't mystify them. Don't make phone calls behind their backs, or agree with them when you're planning something else. No matter how flipped out someone is, there's always a part of him that's aware of reality: Speak to that part, and he'll respond.

10. If you start feeling bored, try to focus in on the problem. That's where you should be anyway. What's going on? How can you help? How can they help themselves? Do they need a hospital? a shrink? medication? (Al-

though medicines are grossly abused, sometimes they're useful: especially if they can keep a sister or brother out of the hospital.) What is the real problem, and what are their options?

11. A word about DEPRESSIONS . . . Life in this oppressive society is filled with insults, painful experiences, and real losses. Not only is our SELF-ESTEEM smashed time and again. We also have to endure separations from people close to us—friends who leave, who die, who are killed, who go to jail, etc. There's a natural healing over after such a loss, but it takes time.

Don't expect people not to feel these human feelings. Help them integrate their experience and feelings into themselves.

Often, DE-pression is a cover for OP-pression. If there's no "real" loss going on, look for the oppression that's making the other persons feel like shit. Help them understand that it's not "in their heads" but in the real world that such oppression exists.

Help them get in touch with others who share their oppression. Agree with them they're not bad or crazy. Help them get angry if they deserve to get angry.

12. A word about PARANOIA . . . Paranoia, as radical therapist Claude Steiner has said, is a state of "heightened awareness." Paranoid feelings are almost always justified, at least in part. Don't argue with them; try to see where they're true and what that means for them.

This society makes all of us suspicious, mistrustful, manipulated: "paranoid." Help the paranoid person recognize the truth of his paranoia, and then help him to stop being immobilized or destroyed by his awareness.

13. A word about VIOLENT people . . . Violent people are often very frightened, and can be calmed down if you protect them and treat them as people, not monsters. Sometimes, though, people are just out of touch. Don't try to be a hero and endanger yourself and others. Do what you can without being foolhardy. Talk straight to someone who's violent; be reasonable, not threatening.

14. We all need to share experience in handling common psychiatric problems. You and your friends can build a list of halfway houses, decent hospitals, and other therapy resources. If you deal with these problems yourself, you can encourage others to do the same.

15. It's important to remember that the roles of therapist and patient are interchangeable. You may be helping someone today and being helped tomorrow. That's the way it should be. Our common task is developing our skills, so we can help and strengthen one another and the movement for social change.

—M.Gl. rep.

Your First-Aid Kit

Accidents are the most common cause of death after the 1st year of life and throughout the years of childhood and early adulthood; thereafter, they remain one of the leading causes. Emergency situations cut across all dividing lines. Everyone is a potential victim. It is important to be aware of this.

BE PREPARED

1. Become familiar with first-aid procedures and techniques beforehand. For openers, take the very inexpensive first-aid course offered by the American Red Cross in your area.

All members of a household which has a potential problem—due to heart disease, epilepsy, a pregnancy, high danger of snakebites, small children susceptible to poisoning—should go over together the available literature on their specific condition. Do not trust a single source of information. Rather, shop around among the different sources until you arrive at a thorough understanding of the condition and its possible complications. Many doctors, hospitals, medical centers, State medical associations, and the American Red Cross put out

excellent pamphlets on various medical emergencies and health conditions; avail yourself of these free, informative publications.

2. Equip your household and traveling "unit" (whether a backpack, VW bug, or a complete camper) with a first-aid kit and at least one comprehensive first-aid book. (See: FOR FURTHER READING, at end of article)

The first-aid kit should be well-stocked, appropriate both to the number and the state of health of the people to be serviced, as well as to the place(s) in which it will be used. Obviously, a wilderness expedition will have to consider many situations not relevant to an urban residence, and a factory must anticipate emergencies different from those expected in a preschool play group.

3. Practice safety about the house, yard, and when driving. Use foresight, consideration, and responsibility in your everyday dealings with your environment. Discuss first-aid prevention and what to do in various emergencies with your household. Let each member of the family study a particular emergency, and have each one conduct drills for the entire family. Take

care to prevent small children from developing morbid fears.

4. Live a healthy life. You might be helped by meditation or some other form of centering. If you eat healthy, well-chosen foods and can combine physical exercise, rest, and interesting mental activity, your chances of recovering from a serious injury are greatly increased.

5. If you have any special health problems, it is wise to wear a Medic Alert tag or carry an explanatory card. The identification should pinpoint your problem, tell which drugs are helpful or harmful to you, and give your blood type. The Medic Alert Foundation International of Turlock, California 95380 (phone 1-209-634-4917), sells pendants or bracelets with the above information. It also maintains a central file with detailed information on each member. This information is available to a first-aider or a physician 24 hours a day, and requires only a collect phone call.

BLEEDING

If the bleeding is profuse, it is of the utmost importance to control it immediately. A person can survive a limited period of heavy bleeding.

There are 2 kinds of bleeding: 1. bleeding from a vein, which oozes out in a smooth stream; this type of bleeding can normally be controlled with direct pressure; 2. bleeding from an artery, which spouts out intermittently in a pulsating fashion; this type of bleeding may require a tourniquet, although 2 other methods of control should be tried 1st.

Treatment

1. Cover the whole wound with sterile gauze, a clean piece of cloth or clothing, or—in a dire emergency—with your hand.
2. Press firmly over the wound with your palm until the bleeding stops. If an arm or leg is involved, raise it and then press firmly.
3. Apply additional layers of cloth on top of the original ones and secure them firmly (but not tightly enough to block circulation). If blood saturates this dressing, do not remove it; simply add more layers on top of it.
4. If bleeding cannot be controlled by pressing directly on the wound, and if the blood comes from an arm or leg, then apply pressure to the supply artery. *For the arm:* Hold the arm up with one hand around the wrist. Press as hard as you can with all 4 fingers of the other hand on the inner arm (midway between the armpit and elbow, and midway between the topside and the underside of the arm). *For the leg:* Make a tight fist and press as hard as you can with it on the side of the groin, just above the inside of the thigh. This method of applying pressure will slow

down the bleeding in the extremity below the point of pressure. Another person, if available, should continue direct pressure over the wound.

5. If the bleeding cannot be controlled by either of these methods and if it is so rapid that the person's life is in danger, then *apply a tourniquet.* Use only on an arm or leg.

How to apply a tourniquet:

a) Place the tourniquet between the bleeding wound and the heart.
b) Use any material such as rubber tubing, a belt, tie, strip of cloth, stockings.
c) Wrap the material tightly around the limb and tie a half, open knot.
d) Lay a strong, short piece of wood or similar item horizontally over the half knot, and tie a full, closed knot over the stick to secure it in place.
e) Twist the stick around in a circle to tighten the tourniquet. Keep twisting until it stops the bleeding. It should be tight enough to block the circulation.
f) Fix the stick in the tightened position with a bandage and tape, or with the loose end of the tourniquet, or any other device.

NOTE: Use a tourniquet ONLY if a severe, life-threatening hemorrhage exists and blood loss cannot be controlled by pressure at the nearest pressure points or by other means. The tourniquet technique is a LAST-RESORT decision in which you have decided to risk loss of the limb to save the patient's life. Once applied, it should NOT be loosened; if blood clotting has occurred, loosening may permit a clot to be released into the patient's system, with potentially fatal results. After a tourniquet is in place, the attention of a doctor is an absolute must. Put the initials, TNT (for "tourniquet"), on the patient's forehead, using blood, lipstick, etc. Somewhere, in written form (note attached to shirt collar or other highly visible location), indicate the *exact* minute for tourniquet application (9:53 P.M., etc.) to warn the doctor. Tourniquet removal in 10–15 minutes (much emergency-room care is less than 10 minutes away) may not effect the chances of saving the limb; beyond 30 minutes, amputation is almost a foregone conclusion.

6. If the wound goes deep into the head, neck, chest, or abdomen, see below under Special Deep Wounds.
7. Treat the person for shock.
8. Carefully take the patient in a prone position to a doctor for cleansing of the wound, stitching, possible tetanus shot, etc.
9. If a part of the body is severed, do not put the severed part in any fluid. Instead, place it in a clean piece of cloth or in a clean empty

container for the doctor. If possible, alert the physician or hospital in advance of your arrival as to the nature of the wound, so that they can make necessary preparations.

Special Deep Wounds

When wounds go deep into the head, neck, chest, or abdomen, it is particularly important that no additional harm be done to the victim (through some careless form of handling or transportation) before medical care is available.

Treatment

1. Stop the bleeding and protect from contamination as given under Bleeding.
2. Except in head wounds, ease any breathing difficulty by gently propping up the head and shoulders with pillows. If the difficulty is severe or breathing has stopped, apply artificial respiration. (See: Breathing Difficulty or Stoppage.)
3. If there is a head wound, keep the victim lying flat without a pillow.
4. If there is a chest wound, do not remove any object stuck in the chest. Do immediately bandage the wound (or around the wound) snugly and thoroughly to prevent dangerous entrance and exit of air, preferably using sterile gauze and adhesive tape.
5. Do not move the affected parts at all, if possible. Summon an ambulance immediately. However, if medical assistance will be delayed, transport the victim carefully and in a supported, prone position to the nearest medical help.
6. Do not give food or liquid, as the victim will probably have surgery.
7. Treat for shock.

Breathing Difficulty or Stoppage

Whenever a person of any age has stopped breathing (regardless of the reason), start artificial respiration *immediately*. Quick action is of utmost importance: One can survive a lack of oxygen for only 3 to 5 minutes. Get anyone who has severe difficulty in breathing to a hospital for oxygen immediately. If necessary, administer artificial respiration also.

Treatment

How to administer mouth-to-mouth or mouth-to-nose breathing (artificial respiration).

1. Lay the victim down on his back and quickly wipe out any foreign matter in the mouth with your finger.
2. If available, place pillow or rolled-up blanket under the victim's shoulders.
3. Tilt the victim's head back as far as it will go. Pull or push the jaw so that it juts out.

4. *If the victim is an adult,* cover his mouth tightly with your mouth, pinch his nostrils shut, and blow vigorously into his mouth. *If the victim is a child,* place your mouth over his mouth *and* nose, making a relatively leakproof seal, and blow gently.
5. Remove your mouth from the victim. This will permit you to inhale, and it will allow air to exhale from the victim's mouth. Listen for that exhalation.
6. Keep up a steady rhythm of inhaling and exhaling. For an adult, blow vigorously 12 to 15 times a minute; for a child, blow gently about 20 times a minute.
7. If, after the 1st few blows, air is not going into the victim's lungs, recheck the position of the head and jaw. If they are not properly placed, the tongue tends to block the air passageway. If they are placed properly and air still does not go through, then quickly check for foreign matter in the throat.

To remove foreign matter *in a child,* suspend him momentarily by the ankles (or doubled over at the waist with hands and head hanging downward) and slap sharply 2 or 3 times between the shoulder blades. Hopefully, this will dislodge the obstruction.

To remove foreign matter *in an adult,* quickly turn the victim on his side and slap him sharply several times between the shoulder blades. Then, once again, sweep your fingers through the victim's mouth to remove any foreign matter. Reposition the victim and resume artificial respiration.

8. If the patient vomits, quickly turn him on his side and wipe out his mouth. Then reposition him and begin again. (If desired, one may cover the victim's mouth or nose with a handkerchief when applying artificial respiration.)
9. Continue your efforts until the patient revives or *for at least 4 hours,* as people have revived after appearing lifeless for that long.
10. When the victim revives, keep him quiet until he's breathing regularly. Cover him and treat for shock.
11. During the recovery period, the victim should be in the care of a doctor since complications may develop.

This technique applies even in drowning cases. Do not bother trying 1st to remove water from a drowning victim; begin artificial respiration immediately.

Most victims recover within 15 minutes after beginning artificial respiration, but it may take much longer as mentioned above. In some cases, the use of a resuscitator may be necessary in addition to artificial respiration; have someone else send for this assistance at the earliest possible moment.

Choking Due to Foreign Object in Throat

1. First, have the victim try to cough out the object on his own.

2. Reassure him, as he may be panicky.

3. If that doesn't work, follow the procedure above for removing foreign matter from the throat. (See also: Breathing Difficulty or Stoppage, *Treatment* #7, paragraphs 2 and 3.)

4. If the object does not fall out, rush the victim to a hospital.

5. If the victim has severe difficulty breathing, apply artificial respiration. (The object is probably lodged in the windpipe.)

Broken Bones, Joint Injuries, Sprains

If you are untrained, it is safest to treat apparent joint injuries and sprains as if they were broken bones. This is because it is often difficult to determine whether a bone is actually damaged in an area that appears to be only bruised or strained. Even physicians require X rays to confirm the site and nature of such damage.

The elderly and persons afflicted with certain diseases are more likely to suffer fractures (broken bones) in a fall because of the brittleness of the bones due to a lack of calcium and other minerals important to the skeletal system.

Symptoms

Pain, swelling, bruising, or deformity over the injured area; loss of power or movement of a limb; grating when the ends of the bone rub together; unnatural mobility of the area. Also, no symptoms may be apparent, but the nature of the accident will indicate that bones could have been broken.

Treatment

1. First, treat any bleeding from the injury, as well as any breathing difficulty.

2. Do not allow the person to place weight on the injured area.

3. Treat for shock.

4. Do not try to move the patient yourself. This is particularly important in fractures (or suspected fractures) of the neck, spine, and hip.

5. Get medical help or, if necessary, proper instructions on moving the patient. If the patient must be moved, apply splints and/or some other form of support that prevents movement of the damaged bones. Unlike many other injuries, one normally has more time to consider the proper handling of broken bones; it is important in preventing future deformity of the bone to immobilize it properly at the time of the accident.

6. Cold compresses (cold, wet cloths) may be applied gently to the injury while waiting for medical assistance.

Recovery

While recovering from a properly bandaged or plastered broken bone, the following measures will aid the healing:

1. Move the surrounding extremities and joints to ensure good circulation and minimize wasting of muscles. For instance, exercise the fingers of an arm set in a cast.

2. With doctor's approval, bathe daily in hot and cold water or apply compresses to areas such as the wrist and ankle (if they're not set in plaster). Water therapy increases the circulation to the bone.

3. During the period of healing, be sure to supply a nutritious diet, including foods containing calcium. Restrict sugar intake since it inhibits calcium absorption.

4. Comfrey, traditionally called "knitbone," is an effective and natural healer for broken bones. It is available in tablet, root, and leaf form.

Burns

1. If the burn is a 3rd-degree burn (charred skin), seek medical attention immediately.

2. For 1st-degree burns, apply cold water or submerge in cold water. Apply dry dressing if desirable. For 2nd-degree burns, place burned part in cold water (*not* ice water—you can induce shock) until pain is reduced. Apply clean cloths wrung out in ice water, blot gently dry. Apply sterile gauze or clean cloth as desired to protect.

3. If clothing sticks to the skin, cut around it, but do not try to separate the burned cloth from the burn itself.

4. Do not use antiseptics, ointments, home remedies, or sprays on severe burns. Call a doctor. Keep arms and legs elevated if affected by burns.

5. Do not break blisters, although they may break on their own.

6. In more serious burns, treat for shock. In cases of shock, intravenous plasma may be needed. Therefore, if possible, have someone phone ahead to alert the hospital staff.

Electrical Shock

In today's world of electrical appliances, everyone should be familiar with current flow and possible electrical mishaps. One is most likely to be electrocuted by touching household appliances or other electrical equipment with wet hands, or when standing on a wet floor, or when simultaneously touching grounded metal objects, or when handling faulty equipment (such as frayed cords and overloaded extension cords). Bathrooms are particularly high-risk areas.

Treatment

1. Do not touch the victim with your bare hands or you may be shocked yourself.
2. Pull or push the victim off the live wire with a wooden stick (without sap) or a cane or any other nonconductor of electricity, such as rubber, leather, or a lot of dry cloth. If possible, use insulated gloves. Make sure you are standing on a dry surface and that your body and clothes are dry.
3. Throw the breaker or remove an old-style fuse. If the problem involves high tension wires, your own risk is great. Unless you're willing to place yourself in danger, phone the power company 1st to get the power turned off.
4. If the victim is not breathing or is having severe difficulty in breathing, apply artificial respiration. (See: Breathing Difficulty or Stoppage.) Continue, if necessary, for at least 4 hours.
5. If the victim suffers from heart failure, a trained person should apply external heart massage.
6. Treat for shock.
7. If a doctor or ambulance cannot be summoned quickly, and transportation is necessary, check first for internal injuries and broken bones.

Poisoning

Poisoning is the 3rd most common cause of accidental death to children. Each year, over 500,000 children swallow poisonous household products. Some 100,000 of these poisonings are due to common aspirin. Almost always, the poisonings are preceded by a period of tensions and irritations in the household so that the person in charge is too tired or worried to take the usual precautions.

There are some 250,000 potential poisons you can buy in your neighborhood stores. Many of these are not labeled as poisons, nor are they generally recognized as poisons because they are not meant to be ingested at all (i.e., perfumes) or are not meant to be ingested by children (i.e., "pep" pills). Crawlers and toddlers are the most susceptible to poisonings because of their newfound mobility, their insatiable curiosity, and their irresistible oral urges.

The Federal Government operates some 550 Poison Control Centers throughout the country. Obtain the phone number of the one nearest to you beforehand—particularly if there are small children in your household—and post it in your house along with a complete, authoritative, and easy-to-read poison chart. And most important, practice poison prevention. Don't forget that houseplants and outdoor plants can be poisonous and even fatal; the American Red Cross puts out an excellent information sheet on poisonous plants.

Treatment

The treatment varies according to the nature of the poisoning. One must act quickly in any kind of poisoning to stop the absorption of the poison into the system. Treatment is discussed under these categories: *Swallowed Poisons, Skin Contamination, Eye Contamination,* and *Inhaled Poisonous Fumes or Smoke.*

Swallowed Poisons

1. If available, follow the direction for antidote on the label of the poison container.
2. If not available, then immediately dilute the poison with a glass of milk or water or both. (This applies to both corrosive and noncorrosive poisons.)
3. After this, determine quickly whether the poison is corrosive or noncorrosive so that you can know whether to induce vomiting. If you cannot determine this from the following list, immediately call your nearest Poison Control Center or hospital.

Corrosive Poisons

Acids (strong)
Ammonia
Benzine
Bleach
Carbolic acid disinfectants
Cleaning fluid
Corn and wart remover
Disinfectant
Drain cleaner
Furniture polish
Gasoline
Grease remover
Gun cleaner
Lighter fluid
Lye
Lysol
Kerosene
Metal cleaner
Oven cleaner
Oxalic acid
Paintbrush cleaner
Paint thinner
Petroleum
Sulfuric acid

Toilet bowl cleaner
Turpentine
Typewriter cleaner
Washing soda
Wood preservatives

Noncorrosive Poisons

Alcohol
Analgesic
Aspirin
Beer
Bufferin
Empirin
Heart medicine
Hormones
Iron pills and syrup
Laxatives
Paregoric
Pep pills
Reducing medicine
Sleeping pills
Soap
Tranquilizers
Vitamins
Wax

4. Do not induce vomiting if:
a. the patient is unconscious;
b. the patient is in convulsions;
c. the patient has ingested a corrosive poison or has a severe burning sensation in his or her mouth (which indicates corrosive poisoning).

5. *If the poison is corrosive,* call your nearest Poison Control Center or emergency hospital quickly for further instructions.

6. *If the poison is noncorrosive,* induce vomiting. The best way is to give one tablespoon (for a child) of syrup of ipecac. Then follow with a glass of milk or water.

If you don't have syrup of ipecac, then put 2 tablespoons of salt in a glass of water. For a child aged 1–5, give 1–2 cups; beyond 5 years give as much as 4 cups.

Or put the blunt end of a spoon at the back end of his throat while holding him face down on your lap.

7. When vomiting begins, keep the patient face down with his head lower than his hips (across your lap) to prevent the vomit from entering his lungs.

8. After the patient's vomiting is over, call the nearest Poison Control Center or emergency hospital.

9. If the patient doesn't vomit by any of these means in 15 minutes, take him immediately to the nearest Poison Control Center or emergency hospital.

10. Treat for shock.

11. Save the poison container, the intact label, and any remaining poison to take to the doctor; if none is available, then bring in some of the vomit for examination.

Skin Contamination

1. Drench skin with running water. Continue this for 10 minutes.

2. Remove any affected clothing simultaneously with the drenching.

3. Cover the area loosely with a clean cloth.

4. Do not apply ointments, greases, powders, etc., and do not give alcohol.

5. Treat for shock and call a doctor.

6. Take the container, intact label, and any remaining poison to the doctor.

Eye Contamination

Speed is of the essence here too.

1. Pry the eyelids apart and *gently* pour or run moderately warm water over the eyeball. Continue for 5 minutes.

2. Do not use any chemicals in the eye as it may cause further damage.

3. Seek medical assistance immediately.

Inhaled Poisonous Fumes or Smoke

1. Immediately carry patient into fresh air; do not let him walk as it uses up too much oxygen.

2. Loosen all tight clothing, including undergarments.

3. If breathing has stopped or is irregular, then apply artificial respiration *immediately.* (See: Breathing Difficulty or Stoppage.) Continue until patient has recovered or is pronounced dead by a doctor.

4. If patient is convulsing, keep him in bed in a semidark room; avoid jarring or noise.

5. Treat for shock and summon medical aid.

SHOCK

When in a state of shock, the patient may not have sufficient blood pumped through the body and his tissues may not get enough oxygen. If not promptly treated, the victim's heart will get weaker and begin to fail. If a person remains in shock too long, death could result even though the injury suffered may not be fatal in itself. This is especially true of the aged and the weak.

In any serious injury, it is important to treat the victim promptly for shock (along with any other treatment required). The more serious the injury, the greater the danger from shock. *Treat for shock even though the victim exhibits few or no signs of shock.* An accident victim may suddenly collapse after 1st seeming normal and alert. The treatment is quite simple and cannot do any harm if not needed.

Symptoms

Pale, cold, and clammy skin; shallow and irregular breathing; weak and rapid pulse; dilated pupils; possibly beads of perspiration; a feeling of weakness and thirst; or none of these.

Treatment

1. Have the patient lie down flat. (This places less demand on the body than sitting or standing.) In case of vomiting, turn the head to one side so the vomit will go outside of the patient's mouth.

2. If there are no head or chest injuries or any difficulty in breathing, then raise the lower part of the body 8"–12". If the victim complains of pain over this, then discontinue this.

3. Loosen any tight clothing, particularly about·the neck.

4. Keep the victim warm (to prevent loss of body heat) but avoid sweating.

5. Speak soothingly and reassuringly to the patient. Give him a feeling of confidence in you and in his own recovery. Speak calmly and matter-of-factly about what you are doing as you begin to do it. This will help to orient him. But do not disturb the patient with unnecessary questioning, movement, noise, or hubbub.

6. Gentle stroking of the head (if it is not injured) or light, rhythmical massaging elsewhere is very soothing. Holding the hands or feet in a warm, reassuring way can help to bring a person back.

7. Do not give water if the victim is unconscious or nauseated. Also, do not give water if medical care will arrive within 30 minutes. If medical care will be delayed longer than this, then give only small sips and not enough to cause nausea.

8. Do not give any alcohol.

9. If necessary to transport patient, have him in a prone position.

Just as proper diet plays an indispensable role in prevention and treatment of disease and minor disorders, so does it nurture the body back to health after sustaining an accidental injury. The following measures are particularly beneficial:

1. Try to avoid devitalizing and hard-to-digest foods during the period of healing following an accident. Specifically, avoid sugar, white flour products, fatty meat and heavy starches; foods containing toxic additives; and overcooked, overprocessed foods. Include a high proportion of fresh fruits and vegetables in the diet and, if possible, fresh juices without additives.

2. Short, partial fasts of 2 or 3 days, using fruit and vegetables juices (without additives and preferably fresh) are often beneficial. When breaking the fast, reintroduce food gradually into the diet, and keep it light at 1st.

3. During times of stress, the body may need more than the nutrients supplied by the food we take. During these times, one may benefit from natural food supplements. One of the old time medicinal herbs is comfrey, long used as a natural blood purifier and a remedy for healing wounds. Vitamin C is also helpful in healing wounds and in respiratory conditions, and the vitamin B complex is useful in building up general resistance.

—P.Ba.

FOR FURTHER READING:
Standard First Aid and Personal Safety by The American Red Cross, 1st edition. New York, Doubleday, 1973.
New Ways in First Aid by Dr. Joel Hartley. New York, Hart Publishing Co., 1971.

Recharging Yourself through Meditation

There are almost as many definitions of meditation as there are people meditating. It has been described as a 4th state of consciousness (neither waking, sleeping, nor dreaming); as a way to recharge one's inner batteries; as a state of passive awareness, of "no mind." Some teachers regard meditation as the complement to prayer: "Prayer is when you talk to God; meditation is when you listen to God." Meditation teaches the conscious mind to be still. The mind must learn to be still and listen, whether it listens to God, to the subconscious, or to an outside influence. Which of these one listens to depends on one's point of view and on which of the many forms of meditation one is attempting.

Contemplative meditation is a preliminary exercise for beginners in which one stares at an object, trying to focus the entire consciousness on it and on nothing else. In meditation "with seed," also known as concentrative meditation, one *mentally* focuses the mind on a visualized object, phrase, or part of the body. Meditation *without* seed is far more difficult, for here nothing is visualized; the mind becomes, or tries to become, a blank. There is·also "open" meditation, in which one tries to be totally aware of one's environment, the sounds, the sensations (roughness of a sweater on an arm, weight of one's body pressing down on a chair, etc.). The reverse of this is meditation involving total sensory withdrawal, tuning out the environment. Mantra meditation involves the continuous repetition of a sound. (Transcendental meditation is one version.) Although we think of a meditator as sitting motionless, there is moving meditation too. The renowned whirling dervishes of the Sufis are actually meditating as they whirl. Tai Chi Ch'Uan, an oriental discipline now becoming popular in the West, combines slow physical movements with the mental techniques of meditation.

Why do people meditate? Why leave a busy schedule to sit silently, spending valuable time apparently doing nothing? Isn't this a flight from the world? Couldn't we spend our time more constructively? Doesn't it foster anti-intellectualism? Doesn't such passivity make us mentally flabby, unable to face reality let alone try to change and improve it?

Opponents of meditation ask these questions and then answer them affirmatively themselves. Most who have had experience in meditation disagree. The latter will tell you that with meditation they are calmer, more able to cope with problems. Far from withdrawing from life, they meet it more exuberantly, are able to think more clearly about what should be done to improve it, and have more energy to do what needs doing. Yet until recently all this was subjective. We could not tell if people were really benefiting from meditation, or if it was just the brief rest from routine that made them feel so good.

With the explosion of Western interest in meditation came, inevitably, the scientists. They moved meditation into the laboratory, measured it, tested it, computerized it, and they found that the meditators were right. Meditation really did things for its advocates.

They *were* more relaxed. Galvanic skin response, which is higher when you are relaxed, has been known to quadruple during meditation, whereas it only doubles during a full night's sleep. Meditators have lower anxiety levels, so they become more tolerant. Their reaction times are faster, and their senses seem to be more alert. Oxygen consumption goes below sleep levels; the heartbeat and entire metabolism seem to slow during meditation. There is also evidence that meditation increases ESP scores and, perhaps most significant of all, it has helped drug users to get off drugs.

Of course these tests cannot be said to be typical of *all* meditators, or of all types of meditation. Some produce results very different from others. When a clicking sound is repeated near us, most people react sharply the 1st few times, then adapt to it by "tuning it out." In one test Zen meditators, who generally practice the awareness-of-environment type of meditation, did not adapt to the sound at all. They continued to react to each click as they did to the 1st. On the other hand, yoga meditators, given the same test, did not even react to the 1st click, presumably because much yoga meditation involves turning inward and tuning out the senses.

Much has been made of the connection between meditation and the alpha waves of the brain. Experienced meditators can usually emit strong alpha waves, and alpha from some parts of the brain does seem to evoke feelings of peace. However, some practitioners of Kriya yoga, who meditate on visions of deities, have been found to emit very fast beta waves, rather than the expected slower alpha. Thus not all meditation involves alpha, and it is certain that not all alpha waves involve meditation, so much research remains to be done in this area.

Exactly why meditation has the effects it does is not known for certain. It is suspected that in Western society people have become overintellectualized. The conscious mind rarely stops ticking, let alone pauses to try to commune with the subconscious. In meditation it is trained to quiet down, to tune out all external and internal noise. Then it can become aware of what is coming from the subconscious, enabling conscious and subconscious to work together in closer harmony, with less internal friction and consequently less stress. Beginning meditators, once they have mastered the basic techniques, may find themselves overwhelmed with long-forgotten memories, often very emotional ones. Obviously this can be deeply disturbing, and those who stop meditating because of this may report that meditation is harmful or frightening. However, when these experiences have been worked through and accepted into consciousness (as in psychoanalysis), the meditations become very peaceful. Patience is the key.

Another effect of meditation is to de-automatize the meditator. We all know that we become used to things. If we were perceiving the sky, a tree, a loved one's face for the 1st time, we would be full of wonder, but we are used to them, so our senses become jaded; we are automatized. The form of meditation that tunes out the senses helps us to de-automatize. While we meditate we are unaware of any sensory input. Then, meditation over, we reawaken to a world in which, hopefully, "all things are made new." The awareness-of-environment type of meditation helps us not to automatize at all, as with the Zen Buddhists who did not automatize to the clicks.

It is also possible that by tuning out all normal stimuli we may be better able to sense weaker "signals." (The stars are always in the sky, but in the presence of the "everyday" sun we cannot sense them.) These signals may be from God (mediation is, after all, recommended by all major religions), or from the environment in the form of ESP, or perhaps from other sources, but they must surely help us to be more aware of our universe, and so of ourselves.

Meditation techniques abound. Some may be helpful, others just a distraction. No one technique is essential, but here are a few that have been found useful. Some people achieve very satisfying meditative states without any of them.

The spine should be straight. The lotus and other cross-legged positions are good, but you can just as well sit in a straight-backed chair, feet on the ground, hands on knees. Concentrative or contemplative meditations are best for beginners. Either stare at or visualize an object, perhaps one of spiritual significance, perhaps one that is just beautiful. An uplifting or soothing phrase will do. Or observe your breathing. Whatever, focus your whole attention on it;

there is nothing else in the universe. . . . Thoughts will come and go. Let them go; let them float by like fluffy clouds that cannot really ruffle the clear blue of the sky beyond. Let them go, and return to your focus. Relax, be comfortable. Be still. At 1st, try for no longer than 10 minutes, preferably twice a day, preferably in the same place, preferably not just after a meal. Later you can meditate longer —20 to 30 minutes is ideal. Unsupervised meditation for over an hour at a time can lead to problems and for most people is unnecessarily time consuming. Meditation is beautiful, but it is a means to a more fulfilling life; it should not be an end in itself. Peace.

—D.R.

The Wisdom of a Fox

A fox once lived with his family in a cave in the hillside. One day a tiger came round that way, and hearing him prowling round, the fox's wife became very anxious, for she knew that her young cubs were in danger of being devoured.

"Do not be alarmed," said her husband. "Whenever the tiger comes within hearing I will say, 'What are the babies crying for?' and you will answer, 'They are asking for tiger's flesh.'"

Presently the tiger came along, and this is what he heard: "What are the babies crying for, my dear?" "Why, they are asking for tiger's flesh; we must find a tiger."

The tiger ran for his life, and at some distance met a wolf. "Why are you running so

fast?" asked the wolf, whereupon the tiger told him what he had heard. "Do not be so foolish," said the wolf. "Return with me and we may both be sure of a good meal; but in order that you may not leave me in the lurch, let us tie our tails together."

This being done they returned, but the wily fox was quite equal to the occasion.

"What are the babies crying for?" asked he. "For tiger's flesh," answered his trembling wife. "They need not wait long," said her husband, "for I have sent a wolf to fetch a tiger for us."

Hearing this, the tiger fled faster than ever, dragging the wolf, by whom he thought he had been betrayed, upon the ground behind him.

Thus the fox by his wit had saved his family.

—W.E.D. rep.

A Psychological Tip

Whenever you are called upon to make up
  your mind
And you are hampered by not having any,
The best way to solve the dilemma, you'll find
Is simply by spinning a penny.

No—not so that chance shall decide the affair
While you're passively standing there moping
But the moment the penny is up in the air
You suddenly know what you're hoping.

—P.He. rep.

CALENDARS—1776 to 2000

DIRECTIONS FOR USE

Look for year you want in the index at left. The number opposite each year is the number of the calendar to use for that year.

1974-1978 Calendars are indicated for ready reference.

INDEX

1776... 9	1801... 5	1826... 1	1851... 4	1876...14
1777... 4	1802... 6	1827... 2	1852...12	1877... 2
1778... 5	1803... 7	1828...10	1853... 7	1878... 3
1779... 6	1804... 8	1829... 5	1854... 1	1879... 4
1780...14	1805... 3	1830... 6	1855... 2	1880...12
1781... 2	1806... 4	1831... 7	1856...10	1881... 7
1782... 3	1807... 5	1832... 8	1857... 5	1882... 1
1783... 4	1808...13	1833... 3	1858... 6	1883... 2
1784...12	1809... 1	1834... 4	1859... 7	1884...10
1785... 7	1810... 2	1835... 5	1860... 8	1885... 5
1786... 1	1811... 3	1836...13	1861... 3	1886... 6
1787... 2	1812...11	1837... 1	1862... 4	1887... 7
1788...10	1813... 6	1838... 2	1863... 5	1888... 8
1789... 5	1814... 7	1839... 3	1864...13	1889... 3
1790... 6	1815... 1	1840...11	1865... 1	1890... 4
1791... 7	1816... 9	1841... 6	1866... 2	1891... 5
1792... 8	1817... 4	1842... 7	1867... 3	1892...13
1793... 3	1818... 5	1843... 1	1868...11	1893... 1
1794... 4	1819... 6	1844... 9	1869... 6	1894... 2
1795... 5	1820...14	1845... 4	1870... 7	1895... 3
1796...13	1821... 2	1846... 5	1871... 1	1896...11
1797... 1	1822... 3	1847... 6	1872... 9	1897... 6
1798... 2	1823... 4	1848...14	1873... 4	1898... 7
1799... 3	1824...12	1849... 2	1874... 5	1899... 1
1800... 4	1825... 7	1850... 3	1875... 6	1900... 2

1901... 3	1926... 6	1951... 2	1976...12
1902... 4	1927... 7	1952...10	1977... 7
1903... 5	1928... 8	1953... 5	1978... 1
1904...13	1929... 3	1954... 6	1979... 2
1905... 1	1930... 4	1955... 7	1980...10
1906... 2	1931... 5	1956...13	1981... 5
1907... 3	1932...13	1957... 1	1982... 6
1908...11	1933... 7	1958... 2	1983... 7
1909... 6	1934... 2	1959... 3	1984... 8
1910... 7	1935... 3	1960...11	1985... 3
1911... 1	1936...11	1961... 6	1986... 4
1912... 9	1937... 6	1962... 7	1987... 5
1913... 4	1938... 7	1963... 1	1988...13
1914... 5	1939... 1	1964... 9	1989... 1
1915... 6	1940... 9	1965... 4	1990... 2
1916...14	1941... 4	1966... 5	1991... 3
1917... 2	1942... 5	1967... 6	1992...11
1918... 3	1943... 6	1968...14	1993... 6
1919... 4	1944...14	1969... 2	1994... 7
1920...12	1945... 2	1970... 3	1995... 1
1921... 7	1946... 3	1971... 4	1996... 9
1922... 1	1947... 4	1972...12	1997... 4
1923... 2	1948...12	1973... 2	1998... 5
1924...10	1949... 7	1974... 5	1999... 6
1925... 5	1950... 1	1975... 6	2000...14

7

1977

JANUARY

S	M	T	W	T	F	S
						1
2	3	4	5	6	7	8
9	10	11	12	13	14	15
16	17	18	19	20	21	22
23	24	25	26	27	28	29
30	31					

FEBRUARY

S	M	T	W	T	F	S
		1	2	3	4	5
6	7	8	9	10	11	12
13	14	15	16	17	18	19
20	21	22	23	24	25	26
27	28					

MARCH

S	M	T	W	T	F	S
		1	2	3	4	5
6	7	8	9	10	11	12
13	14	15	16	17	18	19
20	21	22	23	24	25	26
27	28	29	30	31		

APRIL

S	M	T	W	T	F	S
					1	2
3	4	5	6	7	8	9
10	11	12	13	14	15	16
17	18	19	20	21	22	23
24	25	26	27	28	29	30

MAY

S	M	T	W	T	F	S
1	2	3	4	5	6	7
8	9	10	11	12	13	14
15	16	17	18	19	20	21
22	23	24	25	26	27	28
29	30	31				

JUNE

S	M	T	W	T	F	S
			1	2	3	4
5	6	7	8	9	10	11
12	13	14	15	16	17	18
19	20	21	22	23	24	25
26	27	28	29	30		

JULY

S	M	T	W	T	F	S
					1	2
3	4	5	6	7	8	9
10	11	12	13	14	15	16
17	18	19	20	21	22	23
24	25	26	27	28	29	30
31						

AUGUST

S	M	T	W	T	F	S
	1	2	3	4	5	6
7	8	9	10	11	12	13
14	15	16	17	18	19	20
21	22	23	24	25	26	27
28	29	30	31			

SEPTEMBER

S	M	T	W	T	F	S
				1	2	3
4	5	6	7	8	9	10
11	12	13	14	15	16	17
18	19	20	21	22	23	24
25	26	27	28	29	30	

OCTOBER

S	M	T	W	T	F	S
						1
2	3	4	5	6	7	8
9	10	11	12	13	14	15
16	17	18	19	20	21	22
23	24	25	26	27	28	29
30	31					

NOVEMBER

S	M	T	W	T	F	S
		1	2	3	4	5
6	7	8	9	10	11	12
13	14	15	16	17	18	19
20	21	22	23	24	25	26
27	28	29	30			

DECEMBER

S	M	T	W	T	F	S
				1	2	3
4	5	6	7	8	9	10
11	12	13	14	15	16	17
18	19	20	21	22	23	24
25	26	27	28	29	30	31

8

JANUARY

S	M	T	W	T	F	S
1	2	3	4	5	6	7
8	9	10	11	12	13	14
15	16	17	18	19	20	21
22	23	24	25	26	27	28
29	30	31				

FEBRUARY

S	M	T	W	T	F	S
			1	2	3	4
5	6	7	8	9	10	11
12	13	14	15	16	17	18
19	20	21	22	23	24	25
26	27	28	29			

MARCH

S	M	T	W	T	F	S
				1	2	3
4	5	6	7	8	9	10
11	12	13	14	15	16	17
18	19	20	21	22	23	24
25	26	27	28	29	30	31

APRIL

S	M	T	W	T	F	S
1	2	3	4	5	6	7
8	9	10	11	12	13	14
15	16	17	18	19	20	21
22	23	24	25	26	27	28
29	30					

MAY

S	M	T	W	T	F	S
		1	2	3	4	5
6	7	8	9	10	11	12
13	14	15	16	17	18	19
20	21	22	23	24	25	26
27	28	29	30	31		

JUNE

S	M	T	W	T	F	S
					1	2
3	4	5	6	7	8	9
10	11	12	13	14	15	16
17	18	19	20	21	22	23
24	25	26	27	28	29	30

JULY

S	M	T	W	T	F	S
1	2	3	4	5	6	7
8	9	10	11	12	13	14
15	16	17	18	19	20	21
22	23	24	25	26	27	28
29	30	31				

AUGUST

S	M	T	W	T	F	S
			1	2	3	4
5	6	7	8	9	10	11
12	13	14	15	16	17	18
19	20	21	22	23	24	25
26	27	28	29	30	31	

SEPTEMBER

S	M	T	W	T	F	S
						1
2	3	4	5	6	7	8
9	10	11	12	13	14	15
16	17	18	19	20	21	22
23	24	25	26	27	28	29
30						

OCTOBER

S	M	T	W	T	F	S
	1	2	3	4	5	6
7	8	9	10	11	12	13
14	15	16	17	18	19	20
21	22	23	24	25	26	27
28	29	30	31			

NOVEMBER

S	M	T	W	T	F	S
				1	2	3
4	5	6	7	8	9	10
11	12	13	14	15	16	17
18	19	20	21	22	23	24
25	26	27	28	29	30	

DECEMBER

S	M	T	W	T	F	S
						1
2	3	4	5	6	7	8
9	10	11	12	13	14	15
16	17	18	19	20	21	22
23	24	25	26	27	28	29
30	31					

9

JANUARY

S	M	T	W	T	F	S
	1	2	3	4	5	6
7	8	9	10	11	12	13
14	15	16	17	18	19	20
21	22	23	24	25	26	27
28	29	30	31			

FEBRUARY

S	M	T	W	T	F	S
				1	2	3
4	5	6	7	8	9	10
11	12	13	14	15	16	17
18	19	20	21	22	23	24
25	26	27	28	29		

MARCH

S	M	T	W	T	F	S
					1	2
3	4	5	6	7	8	9
10	11	12	13	14	15	16
17	18	19	20	21	22	23
24	25	26	27	28	29	30
31						

APRIL

S	M	T	W	T	F	S
	1	2	3	4	5	6
7	8	9	10	11	12	13
14	15	16	17	18	19	20
21	22	23	24	25	26	27
28	29	30				

MAY

S	M	T	W	T	F	S
			1	2	3	4
5	6	7	8	9	10	11
12	13	14	15	16	17	18
19	20	21	22	23	24	25
26	27	28	29	30	31	

JUNE

S	M	T	W	T	F	S
						1
2	3	4	5	6	7	8
9	10	11	12	13	14	15
16	17	18	19	20	21	22
23	24	25	26	27	28	29
30						

JULY

S	M	T	W	T	F	S
	1	2	3	4	5	6
7	8	9	10	11	12	13
14	15	16	17	18	19	20
21	22	23	24	25	26	27
28	29	30	31			

AUGUST

S	M	T	W	T	F	S
				1	2	3
4	5	6	7	8	9	10
11	12	13	14	15	16	17
18	19	20	21	22	23	24
25	26	27	28	29	30	31

SEPTEMBER

S	M	T	W	T	F	S
1	2	3	4	5	6	7
8	9	10	11	12	13	14
15	16	17	18	19	20	21
22	23	24	25	26	27	28
29	30					

OCTOBER

S	M	T	W	T	F	S
		1	2	3	4	5
6	7	8	9	10	11	12
13	14	15	16	17	18	19
20	21	22	23	24	25	26
27	28	29	30	31		

NOVEMBER

S	M	T	W	T	F	S
					1	2
3	4	5	6	7	8	9
10	11	12	13	14	15	16
17	18	19	20	21	22	23
24	25	26	27	28	29	30

DECEMBER

S	M	T	W	T	F	S
1	2	3	4	5	6	7
8	9	10	11	12	13	14
15	16	17	18	19	20	21
22	23	24	25	26	27	28
29	30	31				

10

JANUARY

S	M	T	W	T	F	S
		1	2	3	4	5
6	7	8	9	10	11	12
13	14	15	16	17	18	19
20	21	22	23	24	25	26
27	28	29	30	31		

FEBRUARY

S	M	T	W	T	F	S
					1	2
3	4	5	6	7	8	9
10	11	12	13	14	15	16
17	18	19	20	21	22	23
24	25	26	27	28	29	

MARCH

S	M	T	W	T	F	S
						1
2	3	4	5	6	7	8
9	10	11	12	13	14	15
16	17	18	19	20	21	22
23	24	25	26	27	28	29
30	31					

APRIL

S	M	T	W	T	F	S
		1	2	3	4	5
6	7	8	9	10	11	12
13	14	15	16	17	18	19
20	21	22	23	24	25	26
27	28	29	30			

MAY

S	M	T	W	T	F	S
				1	2	3
4	5	6	7	8	9	10
11	12	13	14	15	16	17
18	19	20	21	22	23	24
25	26	27	28	29	30	31

JUNE

S	M	T	W	T	F	S
1	2	3	4	5	6	7
8	9	10	11	12	13	14
15	16	17	18	19	20	21
22	23	24	25	26	27	28
29	30					

JULY

S	M	T	W	T	F	S
		1	2	3	4	5
6	7	8	9	10	11	12
13	14	15	16	17	18	19
20	21	22	23	24	25	26
27	28	29	30	31		

AUGUST

S	M	T	W	T	F	S
					1	2
3	4	5	6	7	8	9
10	11	12	13	14	15	16
17	18	19	20	21	22	23
24	25	26	27	28	29	30
31						

SEPTEMBER

S	M	T	W	T	F	S
	1	2	3	4	5	6
7	8	9	10	11	12	13
14	15	16	17	18	19	20
21	22	23	24	25	26	27
28	29	30				

OCTOBER

S	M	T	W	T	F	S
			1	2	3	4
5	6	7	8	9	10	11
12	13	14	15	16	17	18
19	20	21	22	23	24	25
26	27	28	29	30	31	

NOVEMBER

S	M	T	W	T	F	S
						1
2	3	4	5	6	7	8
9	10	11	12	13	14	15
16	17	18	19	20	21	22
23	24	25	26	27	28	29
30						

DECEMBER

S	M	T	W	T	F	S
	1	2	3	4	5	6
7	8	9	10	11	12	13
14	15	16	17	18	19	20
21	22	23	24	25	26	27
28	29	30	31			

11

JANUARY

S	M	T	W	T	F	S
			1	2	3	4
5	6	7	8	9	10	11
12	13	14	15	16	17	18
19	20	21	22	23	24	25
26	27	28	29	30	31	

FEBRUARY

S	M	T	W	T	F	S
						1
2	3	4	5	6	7	8
9	10	11	12	13	14	15
16	17	18	19	20	21	22
23	24	25	26	27	28	29

MARCH

S	M	T	W	T	F	S
1	2	3	4	5	6	7
8	9	10	11	12	13	14
15	16	17	18	19	20	21
22	23	24	25	26	27	28
29	30	31				

APRIL

S	M	T	W	T	F	S
			1	2	3	4
5	6	7	8	9	10	11
12	13	14	15	16	17	18
19	20	21	22	23	24	25
26	27	28	29	30		

MAY

S	M	T	W	T	F	S
					1	2
3	4	5	6	7	8	9
10	11	12	13	14	15	16
17	18	19	20	21	22	23
24	25	26	27	28	29	30
31						

JUNE

S	M	T	W	T	F	S
	1	2	3	4	5	6
7	8	9	10	11	12	13
14	15	16	17	18	19	20
21	22	23	24	25	26	27
28	29	30				

JULY

S	M	T	W	T	F	S
			1	2	3	4
5	6	7	8	9	10	11
12	13	14	15	16	17	18
19	20	21	22	23	24	25
26	27	28	29	30	31	

AUGUST

S	M	T	W	T	F	S
						1
2	3	4	5	6	7	8
9	10	11	12	13	14	15
16	17	18	19	20	21	22
23	24	25	26	27	28	29
30	31					

SEPTEMBER

S	M	T	W	T	F	S
		1	2	3	4	5
6	7	8	9	10	11	12
13	14	15	16	17	18	19
20	21	22	23	24	25	26
27	28	29	30			

OCTOBER

S	M	T	W	T	F	S
				1	2	3
4	5	6	7	8	9	10
11	12	13	14	15	16	17
18	19	20	21	22	23	24
25	26	27	28	29	30	31

NOVEMBER

S	M	T	W	T	F	S
1	2	3	4	5	6	7
8	9	10	11	12	13	14
15	16	17	18	19	20	21
22	23	24	25	26	27	28
29	30					

DECEMBER

S	M	T	W	T	F	S
		1	2	3	4	5
6	7	8	9	10	11	12
13	14	15	16	17	18	19
20	21	22	23	24	25	26
27	28	29	30	31		

12

1976

JANUARY

S	M	T	W	T	F	S
				1	2	3
4	5	6	7	8	9	10
11	12	13	14	15	16	17
18	19	20	21	22	23	24
25	26	27	28	29	30	31

FEBRUARY

S	M	T	W	T	F	S
1	2	3	4	5	6	7
8	9	10	11	12	13	14
15	16	17	18	19	20	21
22	23	24	25	26	27	28
29						

MARCH

S	M	T	W	T	F	S
	1	2	3	4	5	6
7	8	9	10	11	12	13
14	15	16	17	18	19	20
21	22	23	24	25	26	27
28	29	30	31			

APRIL

S	M	T	W	T	F	S
				1	2	3
4	5	6	7	8	9	10
11	12	13	14	15	16	17
18	19	20	21	22	23	24
25	26	27	28	29	30	

MAY

S	M	T	W	T	F	S
						1
2	3	4	5	6	7	8
9	10	11	12	13	14	15
16	17	18	19	20	21	22
23	24	25	26	27	28	29
30	31					

JUNE

S	M	T	W	T	F	S
		1	2	3	4	5
6	7	8	9	10	11	12
13	14	15	16	17	18	19
20	21	22	23	24	25	26
27	28	29	30			

JULY

S	M	T	W	T	F	S
				1	2	3
4	5	6	7	8	9	10
11	12	13	14	15	16	17
18	19	20	21	22	23	24
25	26	27	28	29	30	31

AUGUST

S	M	T	W	T	F	S
1	2	3	4	5	6	7
8	9	10	11	12	13	14
15	16	17	18	19	20	21
22	23	24	25	26	27	28
29	30	31				

SEPTEMBER

S	M	T	W	T	F	S
			1	2	3	4
5	6	7	8	9	10	11
12	13	14	15	16	17	18
19	20	21	22	23	24	25
26	27	28	29	30		

OCTOBER

S	M	T	W	T	F	S
					1	2
3	4	5	6	7	8	9
10	11	12	13	14	15	16
17	18	19	20	21	22	23
24	25	26	27	28	29	30
31						

NOVEMBER

S	M	T	W	T	F	S
	1	2	3	4	5	6
7	8	9	10	11	12	13
14	15	16	17	18	19	20
21	22	23	24	25	26	27
28	29	30				

DECEMBER

S	M	T	W	T	F	S
			1	2	3	4
5	6	7	8	9	10	11
12	13	14	15	16	17	18
19	20	21	22	23	24	25
26	27	28	29	30	31	

13

JANUARY

S	M	T	W	T	F	S
					1	2
3	4	5	6	7	8	9
10	11	12	13	14	15	16
17	18	19	20	21	22	23
24	25	26	27	28	29	30
31						

FEBRUARY

S	M	T	W	T	F	S
	1	2	3	4	5	6
7	8	9	10	11	12	13
14	15	16	17	18	19	20
21	22	23	24	25	26	27
28	29					

MARCH

S	M	T	W	T	F	S
		1	2	3	4	5
6	7	8	9	10	11	12
13	14	15	16	17	18	19
20	21	22	23	24	25	26
27	28	29	30	31		

APRIL

S	M	T	W	T	F	S
					1	2
3	4	5	6	7	8	9
10	11	12	13	14	15	16
17	18	19	20	21	22	23
24	25	26	27	28	29	30

MAY

S	M	T	W	T	F	S
1	2	3	4	5	6	7
8	9	10	11	12	13	14
15	16	17	18	19	20	21
22	23	24	25	26	27	28
29	30	31				

JUNE

S	M	T	W	T	F	S
			1	2	3	4
5	6	7	8	9	10	11
12	13	14	15	16	17	18
19	20	21	22	23	24	25
26	27	28	29	30		

JULY

S	M	T	W	T	F	S
					1	2
3	4	5	6	7	8	9
10	11	12	13	14	15	16
17	18	19	20	21	22	23
24	25	26	27	28	29	30
31						

AUGUST

S	M	T	W	T	F	S
	1	2	3	4	5	6
7	8	9	10	11	12	13
14	15	16	17	18	19	20
21	22	23	24	25	26	27
28	29	30	31			

SEPTEMBER

S	M	T	W	T	F	S
				1	2	3
4	5	6	7	8	9	10
11	12	13	14	15	16	17
18	19	20	21	22	23	24
25	26	27	28	29	30	

OCTOBER

S	M	T	W	T	F	S
						1
2	3	4	5	6	7	8
9	10	11	12	13	14	15
16	17	18	19	20	21	22
23	24	25	26	27	28	29
30	31					

NOVEMBER

S	M	T	W	T	F	S
		1	2	3	4	5
6	7	8	9	10	11	12
13	14	15	16	17	18	19
20	21	22	23	24	25	26
27	28	29	30			

DECEMBER

S	M	T	W	T	F	S
				1	2	3
4	5	6	7	8	9	10
11	12	13	14	15	16	17
18	19	20	21	22	23	24
25	26	27	28	29	30	31

14

JANUARY

S	M	T	W	T	F	S
						1
2	3	4	5	6	7	8
9	10	11	12	13	14	15
16	17	18	19	20	21	22
23	24	25	26	27	28	29
30	31					

FEBRUARY

S	M	T	W	T	F	S
		1	2	3	4	5
6	7	8	9	10	11	12
13	14	15	16	17	18	19
20	21	22	23	24	25	26
27	28	29				

MARCH

S	M	T	W	T	F	S
			1	2	3	4
5	6	7	8	9	10	11
12	13	14	15	16	17	18
19	20	21	22	23	24	25
26	27	28	29	30	31	

APRIL

S	M	T	W	T	F	S
						1
2	3	4	5	6	7	8
9	10	11	12	13	14	15
16	17	18	19	20	21	22
23	24	25	26	27	28	29
30						

MAY

S	M	T	W	T	F	S
	1	2	3	4	5	6
7	8	9	10	11	12	13
14	15	16	17	18	19	20
21	22	23	24	25	26	27
28	29	30	31			

JUNE

S	M	T	W	T	F	S
				1	2	3
4	5	6	7	8	9	10
11	12	13	14	15	16	17
18	19	20	21	22	23	24
25	26	27	28	29	30	

JULY

S	M	T	W	T	F	S
						1
2	3	4	5	6	7	8
9	10	11	12	13	14	15
16	17	18	19	20	21	22
23	24	25	26	27	28	29
30	31					

AUGUST

S	M	T	W	T	F	S
		1	2	3	4	5
6	7	8	9	10	11	12
13	14	15	16	17	18	19
20	21	22	23	24	25	26
27	28	29	30	31		

SEPTEMBER

S	M	T	W	T	F	S
					1	2
3	4	5	6	7	8	9
10	11	12	13	14	15	16
17	18	19	20	21	22	23
24	25	26	27	28	29	30

OCTOBER

S	M	T	W	T	F	S
1	2	3	4	5	6	7
8	9	10	11	12	13	14
15	16	17	18	19	20	21
22	23	24	25	26	27	28
29	30	31				

NOVEMBER

S	M	T	W	T	F	S
			1	2	3	4
5	6	7	8	9	10	11
12	13	14	15	16	17	18
19	20	21	22	23	24	25
26	27	28	29	30		

DECEMBER

S	M	T	W	T	F	S
					1	2
3	4	5	6	7	8	9
10	11	12	13	14	15	16
17	18	19	20	21	22	23
24	25	26	27	28	29	30
31						

31

Utopia

Leading Theoretical Utopias throughout History

Name of Utopia: THE REPUBLIC
Who Created: Plato (427?–347 B.C.). He was 23 when the Peloponnesian War between Sparta and Athens came to an end, leaving Athens, where he lived, in a state of political and economic depletion.
Described in: The Republic (c. 370 B.C.).
Population: 5,040—the number conveniently addressed by an orator.
Political and Social Structure: a meritocracy having:
—Guardians, or rulers. Chosen on the basis of good stock, physique, mind, and education. Main virtue is wisdom. The rule of the guardians is justified to themselves as well as others on the basis of the "noble" or "medicinal" falsehood that God put gold in them while he put silver in the auxiliaries and iron and copper into the workers.
—Auxiliaries, or warriors. Made up of young guardians not yet ready to be rulers and others from the guardian class who have a violent, rather than philosophical, nature. Main virtue is valor.
—Workers. Farmers and artisans.
—Slaves.
Property and Distribution of Goods: Guardians and auxiliaries share houses, meals, and various goods in common. Each receives a fixed yearly stipend that provides for no luxuries. Not allowed to possess or even be near gold or silver. "We shall tell them that they have the divine metals always in their hearts." The working and merchant classes are left to work things out for themselves. "They will easily find for themselves most of the legislation required."
Production: Manual work is thought of as narrowing and the mechanical arts as servile. Economy based on agriculture and artisanship.
Family/Marriage/Sex: A community of spouses and children for the guardians and auxiliaries. "No one is to know his own child,

nor any child his parent." Only the "best" of both sexes are to be brought together to have children, and if the "worst" have children, these children are to be "put out of sight in secrecy and mystery." There are certain ages for childbearing, and if children are born other than in this prime period, they are "disposed of." Children born outside of wedlock are declared "unauthorized and unholy." Love, as opposed to mere sex, takes place between men but in a temperate manner so that a lover might kiss or embrace his beloved as a son, but "never be suspected of going beyond this."
Place of Women: In the guardian class, at least, men and women share in the same education, in child care, in guardianship of other citizens, and in war.
Education and Culture: Children are brought up in a state nursery. They are taken to war as observers to "have their taste of blood like puppies." As they grow up they learn gymnastics, military training, music, the intellectual and aesthetic disciplines, and finally the mathematical sciences and dialectic, "the power of seeing things as a whole." The best, at the age of 35, are selected to command in war and in the practical activities of life, and at the age of 50 become full-fledged rulers.
   The arts must conform to ethical standards. Music and poetry are especially subversive and so must conform to special esthetic rules and portray only "the image of the 'good.'"

Name of Utopia: UTOPIA (Derived from the Greek, meaning "Nowhere.")
Who Created: Sir Thomas More (1478–1535). Scholar. Friend of Erasmus. Wrote during the enclosure movement.
Described in: Utopia (1516).
Population: Each city has roughly 100,000 inhabitants. Fifty-four cities.
Physical Layout: Crescent-shaped island.

Cities are no closer to each other than 24 mi., no farther than a day's walk. The capital city, Amaurot, is square in shape, 2 mi. to a side. Houses are uniform and contiguous, each with a garden in back. Blocks vie with each other in the fruitfulness and beauty of their gardens.

Political and Social Structure: Basis is the family. Each year every 30 families elect a magistrate, called a Syphogrant. Over every 10 Syphogrants is a Tranibor. All the Syphogrants, numbering 200, elect a Prince of the city from a list of 4 candidates named by the people. There is an island-wide council every year.

Property and Distribution of Goods: No private property or money. Every month there is a combination festival and free exchange of goods between city and country. Within the city there are 4 marketplaces where the families bring the goods they've produced. These goods are transferred to storehouses where the father of each family picks up what his family needs. In addition, a great council meets yearly at Amaurot to examine the production of the regions and apportion regional surpluses to those regions which may suffer a scarcity, "so that the whole island is, as it were, one family." Gold is devalued by being used for chamberpots, and for chains on slaves; pearls and diamonds are given to children as toys. Meals are taken in common at farmhouses or at block-wide halls. Houses are open to visitors and are changed by lot every 10 years.

Production: Integration of agriculture and industry. Everyone does agricultural work for 2 years; then, some stay in the country while others go back and forth between city and country. Each farmstead is composed of a "family" of 40 people. Many eggs are hatched in incubatorlike buildings (an anticipation on More's part). Everyone learns a trade which is passed down within the family. There are 6 hours of labor per day.

Family/Marriage/Sex: Each household is an industrial as well as a domestic unit. A city household may consist of 10 to 16 members ruled by master and mistress. Great obedience and respect is accorded older members. A bride and bridegroom may see each other naked before marriage so that neither is saddled with a deformed spouse. However, premarital sex is punished.

Place of Women: Patriarchal. Women serve main meals. Husbands have the power to chastise their wives. But women are not barred from the priesthood.

Education and Culture: The crowning pleasure is considered to be cultivation of the mind. A general belief in God but toleration for all creeds.

Crime and Punishment: It is a serious crime to travel without a passport from the Prince.

Name of Utopia: ABBEY OF THÉLÈME
Who Created: François Rabelais (1494–1553). French satirist. A typical Renaissance man, with an encyclopedic knowledge, a love of literature, a hatred for scholastic doctrines, and a contempt for monastic life.
Described in: Gargantua (1534), Book I.
Physical Layout: A hexagonal-shaped château with 6 towers, surrounded by a forest. No wall about *this* convent. The Abbey contains large apartments, libraries, art galleries, a riding court, theater, pool, tennis courts, orchards, parks, an archery range, and a Garden of Pleasure.
Political and Social Structure: The Abbey is inhabited by an aristocracy based on intelligence and knowledge. The women have to be "faire, well featur'd, and of sweet disposition" and the men "comely, personable, and well-conditioned." No king or prince, no laws or politics. Only one rule: "Do as thou wilt."
Property and Distribution of Goods: A rich patron supplies everything desired.
Family/Sex/Marriage: The "Jollie Friars and Nuns" can marry if they wish and either leave or remain at the Abbey. Also, while at the Abbey one can take a mistress.
Place of Women: Generally equal, although men and women excel at different skills—men at riding and weaponry, women at sewing.
Daily Life: "All their life was spent . . . at their own free will and pleasure," which meant eating, drinking, playing, walking in the fields, hawking, hunting, singing and, if they wished, labor. "There should be neither Clock nor Dial . . . the greatest losse of time, that I know, is to count the hours—what good comes of it?"

Name of Utopia: CHRISTIANOPOLIS
Who Created: Johann Valentin Andreä (1586–1654). Humanist scholar, traveler, social reformer, and Lutheran preacher.
Described in: Christianopolis (c. 1618).
Population: 400.
Physical Layout: Square-shaped city, 700' on a side, located on an island. Well-fortified with 4 towers and a wall. Two rows of buildings, plus a government building and storehouses. All buildings are 3 stories, with public balconies leading to them. Plenty of fresh air and ventilation. A system of zoning separates the food-supply area, drill and exercise area, and public area from industrial areas.
Political and Social Structure: "A republic of workers, living in equality, desiring peace and renouncing riches." Citizens meet in guild halls to "act on sacred as well as civil matters." Twenty-four councilmen-at-large and a triumvirate of Minister, Judge, and Director of Learning.
Property and Distribution of Goods: The only

money is in the republic's treasury. Houses are publicly owned and allocated along with furniture. Meals are private, but food is obtained from public storehouses.

Production: Industrial areas divided into: 1. agriculture and animal husbandry; 2. food shops and light industry; and 3. heavy industry (metallurgy, glass, earthenware). "The men are not driven to a work with which they are unfamiliar, like pack animals to their task, but they have been trained before in an accurate knowledge of scientific matters. . . . Their artisans are almost entirely educated men." Every week each workman receives out of a common stock what is necessary for his work, "For the whole city is, as it were, one common workshop." A special group makes sure there is sufficient stock for what is to be produced. If there is sufficient stock, "the workmen are permitted to indulge and give free play to their inventive genius." Their labors "seem to benefit rather than harm their physical bodies." Working hours are few, so that the rougher trades do not create rough men.

Family/Marriage/Sex: Nuclear family. Lack of chastity is severely punished. The purpose of marriage is reproduction. Even married people "may not injure or weaken themselves by too frequent intercourse."

Place of Women: Share college education with men, but they can't vote and they have the special functions of cloth work and housework. "No woman is ashamed of her household duties, nor does she tire of attending the wants of her husband."

Education and Culture: After the age of 6, the children move to a community-run school where the teachers are respected members of the community and not "the dregs of human society nor such as are useless for other occupations." The students learn all intellectual disciplines as well as a trade. Neither letters nor work is such "that one man, if given enough time, cannot master both." Within his centers of learning Andreä has invented (a century and a half before the British Museum) the 1st museums. "Instruction enters altogether more easily through the eyes than through the ears."

Crime and Punishment: The judges "punish most severely those misdeeds which are directed straight against God, less severely those which injure men, and lightest of all those who harm property." The death sentence is rare.

Name of Utopia: THE COMMONWEALTH

Who Created: Gerrard Winstanley (1609–1652). Leader of the Diggers, possibly founder of the Quakers. In response to the enclosure movement, which was depriving more and more people of land, this small group, numbering about 20 or 30, began sowing crops on private land. They were promptly thrown off the land by the authorities and persecuted.

Described in: The Law of Freedom in a Platform (1652).

Political and Social Structure: No kings, no arbitrary controls. Law rules everything, its source being "the spirit of universal righteousness" and a sense of "common preservation," or mutual aid. The law is administered by a host of officers: peacemakers, overseers, soldiers, taskmasters (prison wardens), executioners, and judges. A parliament 1st abolishes the old monarchical laws and then enacts new "more easy laws."

Property and Distribution of Goods: No money or wages. Personal goods and houses are privately owned, but the means of production are held in common. Goods are fetched from free stores and shops according to the needs of families.

Production: Basically agricultural, but there are also many trades. Parliament gives out orders for the planting and reaping of the commonwealth's land.

Family/Marriage/Sex: Private, nuclear family headed by the father. The father trains his children and does *not* spare the rod. Anyone may marry whomever he or she loves, irrespective of birth. If a man gets a woman pregnant, he must marry her. Rape incurs the death penalty.

Place of Women: The men are definitely in charge.

Education and Culture: Every child is educated in a trade and in book learning by his father and by officers. There is no special group of scholars, since scholars tend to be idle. Continuing adult education takes place in church on the Sabbath, when the laws are read and there is discussion and instruction in historical and scientific subjects.

Crime and Punishment: Whipping, slavery, and death are the common penalties. The death penalty is given to anyone who espouses religion and, at the same time, seeks to possess land privately.

Name of Utopia: HARMONY

Who Created: Charles Fourier (1772–1837). As a child, Fourier noticed "the contrast which exists between commerce and truth." Shocked, he naïvely began to take the merchants aside and "tell them what was being done to them." This earned him a hard spanking. Later, against his will, he was apprenticed to a cloth merchant and embarked on a career in commerce. "I lost the best years of my life in the workshops of deceit." He wrote voluminously and made many attempts to attract a benefactor who would finance his utopian scheme. He approached Napoleon, the Czar, the Duke of Bedford, the U.S. Congress, Chateaubriand, and Lady Byron, among others. He would wait in his lodgings every day at noon in case his "candidate" should appear. But none came. He spent most of his life alone, his books were ridiculed, and only late in life did he attract some disciples.

Described in: Théorie des quatre mouvements (1808). *Traité de l'association domestique agricole* (1822). *Le Nouveau Monde industriel* (1829–1830).

Population: 1,620 in each Phalanstery.

Physical Layout: In the center of a territory, or Phalanx, is the Phalanstery, or palace, consisting of 3 wings; one for noisy industry and noisy children, one for quiet activity, and one for banquet halls and grand salons. At opposite ends of the Phalanstery are 2 temples, one for music, gymnastics, and poetry, the other for celebrating man's unity with the universe. On the summit is an observatory, telegraph, and signal tower.

Political and Social Structure: A complex hierarchical arrangement but no coercive measures. For example, the declarations of the supreme industrial council, composed of high-ranking officers from each work group, are not binding, but the wishes of the work groups do not differ from those of the council, whose opinion is held in high esteem. Each Phalanx is governed by a "regency," or council composed of those contributing the most capital and knowledge. The general intent is not the abolition of classes, but class harmony.

Property and Distribution of Goods: The concept of private property is retained, but everyone is guaranteed a minimum income. Production is "associated," or cooperative. Each shares in the total profit on the basis of his contributions of capital, labor, and talent. There is commercial exchange between Phalanxes.

Production: Economy based on agriculture supplemented by "necessary" industries. A system of "attractive labor" connects people with the jobs most appropriate to their "passional types." People form work groups, or "series," being drawn together by personal affinity and common predisposition to particular types of work. Eventually, every Harmonian tries 40 or more occupations. He moves from work group to work group, finding friends everywhere and passion and gaiety in work. Workshops are clean and elegant. Dirty work is done by "Little Hordes" of young boys naturally attracted to filth. Great public projects are undertaken by "industrial armies" made up of industrial athletes.

Family/Marriage/Sex: In Harmony, marriage naturally disappears. Love being a "compound passion," monogamy is rare. Social institutions are charged with making sure that no one capable of love is ever frustrated in his or her desires. First, everyone receives a "sexual minimum." Erotic saints administer to the less appealing of the community. Beyond this, everyone can pursue his or her desires in an open manner. A place is made for every so-called perversion. Only "inauthenticity"—not adhering to the rules of the game one has freely chosen—is punishable. There is no limit to the games one can choose; some even choose chastity or fidelity, at least for a time. A Court of Love decides whether people are playing according to the rules, and its officials organize festivals and orgies, keep records of each individual's sexual proclivities, and match like with like. Persons with rare manias meet at international conventions.

Education and Culture: Common education creates a common culture among rich and poor, which eliminates class differences. Every child participates in the opera so as to gain an understanding of unity. A combination of parental support—largely ignored—and the reprimands and jeers of peer groups spurs the child's development.

Name of Utopia: ICARIA

Who Created: Étienne Cabet (1788–1856). Born of a French working-class family. Received a good education, became a lawyer, and was made attorney general of Corsica by Louis Philippe. Fell into disgrace because he thought he could impose his counsels on the King. Persecuted for an article he wrote. Exiled to England, he wrote his utopia, which became very popular with the French working class. Played an active part in the Paris revolution of 1848. Finally, he came to America with a group of followers to start a new nation. This attempt failed and he died disillusioned.

Described in: Voyage en Icarie (1840).

Physical Layout: Isolated from the rest of the world by mountains and rivers. Divided into 100 provinces, each province divided into 10 communes. The capital is Icaria, which is built in the shape of a perfect circle. A river, altered to run straight, flows into the center of the city where it divides to form a round island on which is a public square and the main public building. By the building is a terrace with an "immense" column surmounted by a "colossal" statue. All streets run straight. Symmetry is the rule. There are thousands of "street cars" (drawn by horses). Sidewalks are covered by glass canopies.

Political and Social Structure: A "democratic republic," but with a strong state apparatus. The entire population is organized into popular assemblies which refer matters they can't handle to a legislature consisting of 2,000 recallable deputies, and to an executive branch composed of a President and 15 ministers.

The population is also divided into 15 committees, each under the guidance of a committee of experts. The committees of experts have the real power over everyday concerns. There are supposed to be no classes, but there is a bureaucracy of experts.

Property and Distribution of Goods: All personal property and means of production form "a single social Capital." The distribution of goods is determined by law according to the principle of equality. The state makes means of production available, collects goods in storehouses, and dispenses goods to each family.

Production: "All must exercise a trade and work the same number of hours." There is an attempt to reduce hours and render work agreeable and without danger. Extensive use of machinery. Every vocation is considered equally respectable. Public distinction for especially productive workers. Militarylike order and discipline.

Family/Marriage/Sex: Six-month courtship. Education and public opinion—not law—encourage conjugal fidelity.

Place of Women: Like the men, they have trades, but retire earlier (at 50 instead of 65). Given attention and respect. Yet, they are expected to prepare meals.

Education and Culture: Aims at forming "good workers, good parents, good citizens, and true men." Rigid censorship controls artistic production.

Daily Life: Everything is regulated by law. For example, "no one can eat anything which the Republic does not approve." A committee determines number of meals, mealtimes, number of courses, ingredients of food, and the daily menu. Another committee determines every aspect of daily attire. There is a uniform for every "condition" (age, sex, marital status, etc.) and every occasion.

Name of Utopia: UNITED STATES OF AMERICA (in the year 2000)

Who Created: Edward Bellamy (1850–1898). New Englander. His utopian novel won enthusiasm and brought converts to socialism.

Described in: Looking Backward (1888).

Political and Social Structure: A single syndicate represents the people, and it is "to be conducted in the common interest for the common profit . . . the nation [is to be] organized as one great business corporation . . . the final monopoly." As such, it competes with other countries organized in the same way. This supercorporation, modeled on the military, is a gigantic hierarchy based on merit and accomplishment. At the head is the President, commander-in-chief of the "industrial army." Under him are the 10 major generals of the 10 industrial departments and under them the generals of the various trades. Fi-

nally, within each trade we find lieutenants, captains, colonels, foremen, and superintendents. A gerontocracy: The President is elected, but only those over 45 (retirement age) can vote.

Property and Distribution of Goods: Guaranteed annual income of $4,000 (in 1887 dollars). Each citizen receives a yearly credit card for this amount and can spend it as he wishes. He can retire at 33, on half-income, if he chooses. Sample shops display all purchasable goods, even in small towns. When an order is taken, it is sent to a central warehouse which dispatches the goods to the buyer's home by pneumatic tube. Service labor can be hired from the state. If someone wants to publish a book, he can pay for it out of his "credit" account and receive royalties. A group can start a magazine or newspaper by guaranteeing the support of an editor out of its members' own "credit" accounts. No wages, trade, or money per se.

Production: Everyone between 21 and 45 is a state employee. For 3 years each person works where the state determines he is needed. After that he may study the trade of his choosing in a national school. More arduous and less attractive work is made acceptable by its having shorter hours. Even though there are no wages, the factories have piecework in order to gauge individual merit for the annual regrading of the labor army. Consumer petitions play a part in determining what is produced.

Family/Marriage/Sex: Candor, restraint, and absence of artificiality are the rule. Marriage is not compromised by obligations to parents.

Daily Life: After 45, one lives a leisurely existence that includes travel, special vocations, hobbies, attending sports events. Or if one wishes, one can stay home and have music and sermons piped in (an anticipation of the radio).

Name of Utopia: NOWHERE. England is the locale of the narrative, but "Nowhere" is the world at large in the 21st century.

Who Created: William Morris (1834–1896). Born of an English bourgeois family and educated at Oxford. Interested in medieval art, he 1st had someone build him a medieval-style house, then developed an interest in rediscovering and preserving the old medieval arts and handicrafts. He made a business out of this and learned "the theory and to some extent the practice" of weaving, dyeing, and textile printing. His designs are complex and luxurious. He invented the Morris chair. He became a socialist because he felt that "art cannot have a real life and growth under the present system of commercialism and profit-mongering."

Described in: News from Nowhere (1891).

Population: The same as that of England at the end of the 19th century, but spread out.

Physical Layout: "Exquisitely beautiful" architecture expressing a "generosity and abundance of life." A few old buildings are maintained; the old Parliament buildings are, significantly, used as a storehouse for dung.

Political and Social Structure: No national government. Federation of autonomous communes. Local organs of direct democracy fashioned after the medieval Mote. Great care is taken to allow the minority to express itself. Formally, a narrow majority vote is not a winning one, but the minority usually bows to the will of the majority without being coerced. In personal matters everyone does as he pleases. No class distinctions.

Property and Distribution of Goods: No private property or wages. Goods are distributed freely in stores that are often tended by children. To the children, storekeeping is something of a game which also teaches them about the various goods, where products come from and how they are made. Households are private, but visitors are welcome. People refer to one another as "neighbor."

Production: Machinery is used when doing the work by hand would be irksome, but otherwise all production is handcrafted. People work at their own pleasure and for the pleasure they receive from making useful and especially beautiful objects. Work "is a pleasure which we are afraid of losing, not a pain . . . instead of avoiding work, everybody seeks it." Idleness is considered a disease. A new source of energy (anticipating electricity) allows for decentralization of industry.

Family/Marriage/Sex: People often fall in and out of love and contract or end a marriage. There are no divorce courts since there is no property settlement to be disputed, and enforcing a contract that involves passion or sentiment is considered absurd. "We do not deceive ourselves, indeed, or believe we can get rid of all the trouble which besets the dealings between the sexes but we are not so mad as to pile up degradation on that unhappiness by engaging in sordid squabbles about livelihood and position, and the power of tyrannizing over the children."

Place of Women: Neither men nor women tyrannize their mates. Women do "what they can do best, and what they like best," which includes waiting on the men (the justification given is that men are incompetent housekeepers).

Education and Culture: No schools. Formal education is thought of as a concomitant of poverty and the need to cram all learning into a short period. People may best learn by picking up books and acquiring information in their own way when they are so inclined. The formal Christian religion has been replaced by a "living" religion that embraces humanity.

Crime and Punishment: No prisons. People couldn't be happy "if they knew that their neighbors were shut up in a prison." There are no habitual criminals, only the occasional committing of errors. Even murder is not punished, but the violent transgressor atones to the family of the person murdered.

—R.R.

Name of Utopia: PALA

Who Created: Aldous Huxley (1894–1963).

Described in: Island, a novel published the year before his death. Thirty years before the publication of *Island,* Huxley described another utopia in his classic novel *Brave New World.*

Population: The population of Pala is over one million, though an exact figure is never given.

Political and Social Structure: Constitutional monarchy. The position of the Raja, or monarch, is hereditary. The duties of the Cabinet, House of Representatives, and Privy Council are not clearly explained in the novel beyond saying that Pala is a federation of self-governing units—geographical, professional, and economic—that these 3 branches of government oversee. The social structure of Pala is built around the blending of science and religion. The religion is Mahayana Buddhism, which teaches that everything from food to sex can be a road to enlightenment and liberation. Science on the island is dedicated to practical tasks like improving crop yields and devising psychological methods for reducing aggressive personalities. An essential part of life on Pala is the mescalinelike drug Moksha, which produces mystical visions allowing islanders to achieve ultimate consciousness.

Property and Distribution of Goods: Cooperative community. The islanders grow rice, vegetables, fruit, and poultry. They live very simply, managing to provide for most of their own needs and importing as little as possible from the outside world. Competition has been eliminated, and the community has passed from a system of mutual aid in a village community to streamlined cooperative credit unions. Population is controlled so that there are never more people than goods, and so that everyone on the island enjoys plenty.

Production: All members of the community work and enjoy their opportunity to do so, for work, like food and sex, is considered another road to enlightenment. Members of the community are permitted to change jobs at their own discretion, both to prevent boredom and to permit a greater wealth of experience. Along with the island's agricultural production, there are 2 potteries and a furniture factory. All other materials are imported, but because Pala is not a consuming community these commodities are sparse.

Family/Marriage/Sex: While the attitudes of the islanders toward marriage are rather traditional, their attitudes toward sex and the family are not. Everyone on the island belongs to a Mutual Adoption Club (MAC). The MAC consists of from 15 to 25 assorted couples, made up of newlyweds, couples with growing children, and grandparents. Along with blood relations, everyone has deputy mothers and fathers, aunts and uncles, and so on. This allows children freedom from their parents, and parents from their children. Islanders practice a yoga of love similar to the male continence practiced at the Oneida colony in America (Huxley uses Oneida to describe sexual behavior on his island), and this system is called Maithuna. Sexual liberation exists without sexual jealousy. Artificial insemination is widely practiced by the islanders so that families have a variety of types. Children are limited to 3 per family, though most islanders stop at 2.

Place of Women: Though women hold a variety of posts on Pala and take their place beside men in all activities, the islanders consider men superior to women.

Education and Culture: Children on Pala receive 2 kinds of education concurrently. The 1st begins with the taking of Moksha, so that "they might experience their transcendental unity with all other sentient beings." At the same time they learn in their psychology and physiology classes that "each individual has his or her own constitutional uniqueness." One of the more interesting features of Pala's educational program is its search for children with special gifts. The most intriguing of these gifts is the susceptibility to hypnosis, called on the island somnambulism. Somnambulists can distort time, making one minute the subjective equivalent of 30. During a period of somnambulism, tremendous amounts of intellectual ground can be covered.

Why the Experiment Failed: Pala is invaded by a militaristic neighbor anxious to obtain Pala's rich oil resources, and the utopia collapses.

Name of Utopia: SHANGRI-LA
Who Created: James Hilton (1900–1954).
Described in: Lost Horizon, published in 1933. The novel, generally neglected at the time of its 1st publication, was awarded the Hawthornden Prize, and soon became a classic. Two films based on the novel have been made, and the 1st, directed by Frank Capra, is highly regarded.
Population: Fifty lamas reside in the lamasery

that overlooks the valley where a village of nearly 1,000 Tibetans live.

Physical Layout: Shangri-La is located in a valley, surrounded by mountains, in an unexplored and nearly inaccessible region of Tibet. The utopia of the lamasery has been in existence for nearly 200 years.

Political and Social Structure: A theocracy. The lamasery and village are ruled by the High Lama, a godlike figure to all in Shangri-La. The High Lama, a French priest named Perrault, 1st arrived in Shangri-La in 1734, at the age of 53, to build a Christian monastery. Because of the air, and his development of an unnamed drug, the priest has lived for another 200 years during which time he has converted Shangri-La into a utopia where civilization might be saved from the peril of some future holocaust. Under the direction of the High Lama are 50 lamas who, like the High Lama, were lost European travelers. They spend their time in pursuit of knowledge and the arts. The political and social structure of the community is built around the word moderation, and moderation is practiced in all things—from government to love.

Property and Distribution of Goods: While the distribution of property and goods is never discussed, a rather vivid picture of the lamasery, and the valley that supports it, is provided. The valley contains a rich, fertile area 12 mi. long, and 5 mi. wide, on which a wide variety of crops is grown. There is also a rich gold deposit that provides the currency with which the lamasery buys goods not provided for in the valley. These goods are brought by native bearers who, though they never see the pass through the mountains that leads to Shangri-La, do know of a spot nearby where they are met by the village's inhabitants. Things like automobiles have never found their way to Shangri-La, but modern bathroom fixtures have. The villagers, who believe the High Lama to be a representative of God, provide for his, and the other lamas', welfare.

Production: All work is done by the Tibetan villagers, while the lamas pursue their more aesthetic ends.

Family/Marriage/Sex: Hilton offers no description of family, marriage, or sex in the village except to say that they exist, and that good manners, consideration, and moderation are the key to all 3 institutions. There are no marriages, or families in the lamasery—though love, or at least a highly platonic form of it, exists there. The one woman member of the lamasery that the novel introduces, Lo-Tsen, is described as having had many men love her, though that love has never been physically consummated. At the novel's end, however, she leaves the lamasery because of her love for someone.

Place of Women: There is at least one woman, Lo-Tsen, already at the lamasery studying to be a lama, and another is brought to Shangri-La during the course of the novel. However, their roles are never clearly defined, though it might be surmised they enjoy the same rights and privileges as men.

Education and Culture: The lamasery is dedicated to preserving and providing a home for the cultures of the East and West. To that end, the lamasery boasts a library in ex-cess of 30,000 volumes, including Plato in Greek, Newton in English, and Nietzsche in German. New volumes are delivered periodically. The same attention paid to literature is paid to the other arts in Shangri-La, and as a result there is no sense—be it sight, hearing, or taste—that is not pleased by the environment. A former student of Chopin's, for example, resided at the lamasery and often played not only the well-known pieces of his teacher, but a large number of Chopin's unpublished works as well.

—D.C.

Attempted Utopias

Name of Utopia: HARMONY SOCIETY

Founder: George Rapp (1757–1847). Rapp was a Lutheran minister who, after a split with church authorities in his native Germany, brought his followers to America to prepare for the 2nd coming of Christ, an event that Rapp believed to be imminent.

Where and When: Though Rapp's split with the church occurred in 1787, he did not bring his followers to America until 1804. The 1st settlement, called Harmony, was established in Butler County, Pa., and was such a success that Rapp feared his followers might grow idle. To prevent this, in 1814 he moved the settlement farther west to 24,000 acres of land near the Wabash River in Indiana.

Ten years later, Rapp decided to take his followers back to Pennsylvania. He sold Harmony to the English social reformer Robert Owen, who renamed the site "New Harmony" and used it to continue communal experiments he had begun in England. Rapp returned to Pennsylvania and began the town of Economy (now Ambridge), northwest of Pittsburgh, which flourished until the end of the century. New Harmony attracted about 900 settlers, but conflicts of class and culture quickly arose. The community, which ran through 5 constitutions within a year, split into 4 separate communities and disbanded after 2 years.

Population: 839 men, women, and children came with Rapp from the city of Würtemberg, Germany.

Political and Social Structure: In the Harmony Society, George Rapp was thought to be the representative of God, and all power in the Society was held by Rapp, who was called Father by his followers. There remain photographs of footprints in limestone rock that Rapp claimed were the footprints of the angel Gabriel, from whom he received instructions.

Property and Distribution of Goods: Before joining the Society, members were expected to sign the Articles of Association. This charter, and the 9 subsequent, similar ones, asked all joining members to relinquish their property, real and personal, to "Father Rapp and associates" for the benefit of the community. In return, the agreement promised, Father Rapp and associates would take new members into the community and allow them to attend all religious services and to receive all religious instruction. Father Rapp also promised that he would provide all the necessities of life, "meat, drink, clothing, etc., and indeed not only during their healthful days, but also if any of them got sick or otherwise infirm and unable to work." Because Father Rapp and his followers believed the 2nd coming imminent they worked laboriously to prepare a fortune to give the Lord upon his return so that they might rule with him.

Family/Marriage/Sex: In 1807 the Harmonists adopted one of their more interesting customs, that of celibacy, which they practiced throughout their history. They believed that celibacy would encourage men to put the community ahead of the family, would lead to maximum productivity by preventing distractions of the flesh, and would ease the community's burden by keeping the society childless. A rumor developed that Father Rapp's son, John, died as a result of being castrated for sexual indulgences, and that the castration was performed by his father, but this rumor has never been proved.

Place of Women: Because they were not burdened with the childbearing and -raising, women were expected to work alongside the men in community work. One visitor to New Harmony wrote that its women seemed "intentionally disfigured and made as ugly as it is possible for art to make them, having their hair combed straight up, and a little skullcap, or black crepe bandage across the crown and tied under the chin." The visitor went on to say that he didn't think it would be difficult to observe the custom of celibacy.

Education and Culture: Religious education was considered important, and this was Father Rapp's province. There was little concern given to formal training, though the town did boast a schoolmaster and a rather high literacy rate.

Why the Experiment Ended: The Harmonists, despite great financial success, ceased functioning at the turn of the century, nearly 100 years after their formation. One of the 2 most widely accepted reasons for this dissolution was that after the death of Father Rapp the Society lacked the strong leadership it needed. The other was the rule of celibacy, for though the community had material wealth, it had few members. (Note: An extensive program of restoration has been completed at Economy. Visitors may now see it —14th & Church Sts., Ambridge, Pa. 15003 —as its members did at the zenith of its career.)

—D.C.

Name of Utopia: NASHOBA

Founder: Frances Wright was born in 1795 to a prosperous Scots family. She 1st became known for her essays on morality. Upon staying in New Harmony, she was converted to the ideals of communitarianism.

Where and When: Founded in 1826. While at New Harmony, Wright began thinking of communal associations as a way to cope with the problem of slavery. She created a plan that she felt would solve the difficulty: Settle slaves in village cooperatives where they could learn skills for survival and self-reliance—"schools of industry" where their excess earnings would be set aside to pay for their freedom and for passage to Africa. She founded Nashoba with 15 blacks and several whites, near Memphis, Tenn., on 2,000 acres of land. The community lasted 4 years.

Political and Social Structure: Despite egalitarian ideals, whites were firmly in control. Wright appointed a group of trustees, all white, to act as overseers when she was away. Blacks were considered to need more education before they could be socially responsible.

Property and Distribution of Goods: All labor was done cooperatively, survival needs taken out of a common pool, tools of production treated as if they were communal property. Private property existed only in personal effects.

Family/Marriage/Sex: Wright felt that the emancipation of humanity meant "desire unleashed and fulfilled," that the nuclear family should be abolished along with religion, private property, and black slavery. In Nashoba blacks and whites slept together, the only sexual restraints being lack of mutual desire.

Place of Women: Wright thought marriage a master-slave relationship with women as slaves. "In wedded life the woman sacrifices her independence and becomes part of the property of her husband . . . this inflicts a crushing penalty on the woman and brands with infamy the offspring of love." At Nashoba, women were in all ways equal to men.

Why the Experiment Ended: News of the experiment leaked out, creating a scandal in the area. But the main problems were economic: Not enough was being produced to pay for upkeep, much less pay off debts. In desperation, they attempted to replace the cooperative society with one based on small individual private property and individual income from productive labor. When it became clear that this too would not succeed financially, the land was sold. In 1830 the blacks were taken to Haiti and given their freedom.

— J. Cu.

Name of Utopia: BROOK FARM

Founder: George Ripley (1802–1880). After embracing the ideals of transcendentalism, George Ripley, a Unitarian minister, began Brook Farm in the hope of creating an ideal civilization where the labor and social machinery needed for existence might be reduced to a minimum to permit maximum time for spiritual and mental development.

The need for financial aid and reform, and the influence of F.M.C. Fourier's doctrines, as advocated by Arthur Brisbane and Horace Greeley, prompted Ripley to convert Brook Farm into a Fourierist phalanx 3 years after its inception.

Where and When: On a tract of land purchased by Ripley about 10 mi. from Boston in West Roxbury, Mass. The experiment lasted from 1841 to 1847.

Population: Brook Farm, which began with a scant 20 members, had nearly 200 inhabitants at the time of its collapse.

Political and Social Structure: Brook Farm was formally organized with the signing of articles of association and the formation of a joint-stock company. Members paid for their board by laboring on the farm, though income for the community was derived from the school, which came to be considered among the finest of the day.

George Ripley served as the community's manager, overseeing both the school and the farm. There was, however, a minimal amount of political and social structure at Brook Farm because transcendentalist Ripley and his followers believed that a person's power resided within, and that the individual, not God or the external environment, had the power to create a better world.

As a result, Brook Farm, more than any

other utopian experiment in American history, gained the respect of the nation's intellectuals. Nathaniel Hawthorne became one of its charter members, and later wrote a novel, *The Blithedale Romance*, based on his experience at the farm. Visitors included Henry James, Ralph Waldo Emerson, and Margaret Fuller, all of whom came away impressed with Ripley's experiment.

In 1844 the structure of Brook Farm changed radically with the adoption of Fourierism by Ripley. The community became centralized through the organization of phalansteries, which banded together individuals into specialized production groups called series. The once highly individualistic cooperative became a community cooperative with the formation of, for example, the cattle series, the education series, and the amusement series.

Property and Distribution of Goods: From the beginning Brook Farm was a cooperative, not a communistic, colony. Arising out of its transcendental philosophy came the belief that the individual had a right to private property. Hence, it did not attack, as did many other communal experiments, private ownership, the organized state, the church, or the family. To this end the articles of association declared that "real estate purchased by the Association in pursuance of these articles shall be made to the Trustees, their successors in office or survivors as joint tenants, and not as tenants in common."

Family/Marriage/Sex: "Any married couple with their children may live together, eat together, and have a paramount right to each other." This statement stood as the published consensus of the community's members in regard to the family during the commune's transcendental period. As with all things, decisions were left to the individuals involved. While the divorce rate was high, there seems to have been very little sexual scandal at Brook Farm, another reason it was unique among utopias.

Even when the farm converted to Fourier's philosophy it inserted in the introduction of its new constitution a statement to the effect that it would make no revolutionary changes in respect to marriage.

Place of Women: While the women at Brook Farm held no important offices in the community, feminism was a favorite subject of its inhabitants. Feminist Margaret Fuller was a frequent visitor and lecturer. One group of women began manufacturing collars, capes, and caps, an industry they hoped would serve the purpose of "the elevation of women to independence, and an acknowledged equality with men." Men often helped with chores traditionally thought to be women's work, but this was due to the fact that the men greatly outnumbered the women.

Education and Culture: The Brook Farm School was among the finest and most progressive of its time. It introduced the kindergarten long before that name was known in America, and, more important, anticipated the philosophy of John Dewey by stressing experience as a means of learning. During the school's 6-year college preparatory course, students studied traditional subjects like mathematics and philosophy (both taught by Ripley), but they also devoted 3 years to agricultural areas, attempting, as was the school's aim, to combine the theoretical and the practical.

Why the Experiment Ended: Brook Farm hoped to solve a number of its problems, mostly financial, by converting itself into a Fourier phalanx. The change brought a number of new residents, but it was soon obvious that the spirit that had made Brook Farm was gone. In late 1847 the phalanstery, the structure that was to be the center of the community, was destroyed soon after completion. The community never survived this loss and in a few months disbanded.

Name of Utopia: FOURIER PHALANX MOVEMENT

Founder: Charles Fourier (1772–1837). Though he never left France, the writings and teaching of the eccentric Charles Fourier served as the inspiration for more than 40 communal experiments in the U.S. during the 1840s.

Disillusioned because his family had lost its fortune during the French Revolution, Fourier set out to create a society in which revolution would not exist. In his 6 volumes, *Le Nouveau Monde industriel et sociétaire*, Fourier suggested that the evils of mankind could be corrected only by reorganizing society into scientifically organized communities called phalanxes.

The phalanx was to be set up as a joint-stock company, with members sharing in the proceeds of their industry according to their investment, skills, and labor. Once the success of this venture had been demonstrated, Fourier believed the world would follow suit and become a universal joint-stock company, sharing the benefits of its labor.

Fourier suggested that it would take more than 30,000 years for the entire world to convert to his social philosophy. He predicted a number of stages, called periods, before Harmony, the period in which the whole world would live in 2,985,984 phalanxes, the number necessary to contain the earth's population. His collected works describe that world in great detail. Men would have tails with eyes, the sea would lose its salt content and turn to lemonade, and wild beasts would become docile. He even described a theory of immortality that contained details of transmigration.

Before a single one of his phalanxes was

built Fourier died, in his simple room, in Paris.

Albert Brisbane (1809–1890) carried on. Brisbane, an American, had studied in Europe with Hegel, Goethe, and Fourier. He returned to America in 1840, convinced that Fourier's philosophy was the solution to the problems inherent in the coming industrial revolution. He wrote *The Social Destiny of Man*, in which he explained Fourier's principles to an American audience.

Horace Greeley, editor of the *New York Tribune*, quickly became a convert and offered Brisbane space in his paper to explain his ideas. The national depression of the 1830s made the country receptive, and response to Brisbane's series of articles was tremendous. In August of 1843 hundreds of delegates met in Rochester, N.Y., and a drive was begun to organize phalanxes. The following April a national convention was held in New York City; George Ripley, founder of Brook Farm, was elected president, and Brisbane and Greeley vice-presidents, of an association dedicated to putting Fourier's plan into operation.

Where and When: Without real consideration for the exactness Fourier suggested, phalanxes quickly sprang up in Massachusetts, New York, Pennsylvania, New Jersey, Ohio, Illinois, Indiana, Wisconsin, Michigan, Iowa, and even Texas. Most of these experiments did not survive their 1st year, a few lasted for 3, and only one, the North American Phalanx, in Red Bank, N.J., lasted for more than a decade. By 1850 the movement was dead. However, no utopia begun in America after the introduction of Fourierism escaped the influence of its philosophy.

Political and Social Structure: In his collected works Fourier described 60 "malevolent characteristics" that had transformed the world into a "sink of corruption." To correct this situation Fourier proposed the phalanx, where society could be reorganized so that every man, woman, and child could be ascribed a place on the social scale in accordance with their worth.

The phalanx was to be organized so that it held 1,620 members, who were to reside in a phalanstery, a 6-story building with a long body and 2 wings. In front of the building there was to be a parade ground and, on the inside of the 3-sided building, inner courtyards were to be constructed. The phalanstery was to stand on a 3-sq.-mi. tract of land, and was to contain apartments for members, general purpose rooms, and a dining room. The apartments were to be rented at various prices, depending on size and accommodations.

Once at the phalanx, spontaneous associations of people, called groups, would form to do particular tasks. These groups would con-

tain 7 people, 2 at each extreme and 3 in the center in respect to attitudes toward the work engaged in at the phalanx. Five groups would constitute a series, which, like the group, would have 2 wings and a center. Each series would be involved in specific work areas—for example, a garden series, an education series, and so on, until these series united to form a phalanx. Individuals eventually would belong to 30 or 40 groups, so as to fulfill themselves.

Property and Distribution of Goods: The phalanx would be set up like a joint-stock company, though it was not necessary for stockholders to be members, or members stockholders. The phalanx would keep accounts for members, charging for room, board, and general expenses, and giving credit, at a fixed rate, for work done at the phalanx.

Fourier's phalanx was not to be communistic; he firmly believed in capitalism and in the profit motive; in fact, he hoped that the phalanxes would operate at a profit. These profits were to be divided among members and stockholders in the following way: $5/12$ to laborers, $4/12$ to capital (the phalanx's stockholders), and $3/12$ to the talented (writers and artists). As part of his economic plan he hoped to provide incentive for members to work harder by having the phalanstery provide both humble and sumptuous apartments, meals, and clothes. Those that produced more would earn more and thereby be able to afford more.

Family/Marriage/Sex: Though highly critical of family life in the present social structure, Fourier avoided being too specific about family life in the future. He did claim that before the phalanx could succeed, a change in traditional sentiments toward marriage would be necessary. One-third of the membership would need to remain celibate, and the remaining members would be permitted only a few children.

Fourier felt that the family concentrated all its affections within its own boundaries, and neglected those on the outside. He claimed that "the life of married households, or couples, is unsociality reduced to its lowest form," and that "civilized love, in marriage, is, at the end of a few months, or perhaps the 2nd day, often nothing but pure brutality, chance coupling, induced by the domestic tie . . ." and that ";individuals, considered separately, seek nothing but to escape the sweet household." While families were to retain their individuality and live in separate apartments when 1st entering the phalanx, Fourier felt that the associative life would end family exclusiveness.

While most of Fourier's followers in America played down his attitudes toward marriage because of their fears that Americans would react violently, Albert Brisbane, in his column in the

Tribune, attacked the institution constantly. Debate was stirred, and charges of free love, being leveled against most of the utopian experiments of the day, were also directed at the Fourierists, though they were largely unfounded.

Place of Women: As was the case with most of the utopian experiments of the 19th century, the Fourierists had their ardent feminists. The most notable among them was Margaret Fuller, author of *Women in the Nineteenth Century.* Horace Greeley, though he rejected a number of the book's premises, published it to the general acclaim of the Fourierists. In her book Fuller demonstrated how marriage had enslaved women, and encouraged them to rise up, en masse, and demand their human rights.

The North American Phalanx, most successful of the Fourier experiments, took the lead in this respect. Not only did women receive equal pay and job opportunity, but they were permitted to take an active part in policy-making. One visitor remarked, "All the women . . . have the right to speak in public assemblies, but none avail themselves of the right but they who have talent for it, or have something good to say."

Education: Education and culture were the work of the education series and the culture series on the phalanx. Fourier had some definite advice on how children should be handled by each. It was his belief that children belonged to a neuter sex, that they were devoid of familial and sexual love. He thought it best that they remain in that state for as long as possible; hence, their education should prevent them from forming any traditional family ties. He was also strongly opposed to any form of sex education, and he went so far as to say that even biblical stories involving sex should not be taught.

As part of their education children were to work in the phalanx, and in a capacity that they would enjoy. Since all children love to play in dirt, Fourier reasoned, that is what they should do in the phalanx.

Why the Experiment Ended: Of the nearly 50 phalanxes that began, and failed, in the 1840s, not one came even close to following the philosophy of Fourier. Proper capital was seldom raised as phalanxes rushed to organize. Membership was another problem. Fourier had suggested 1,620, but not a single phalanx waited for that many people to begin their experiment. As a result of insufficient funds and membership, inadequate phalansteries were built; instead of castlelike accommodations, many were living in huts.

Of these ill-fated attempts, Albert Brisbane said, "Not one of them had the tenth, nor the twentieth part of the means and resources —pecuniary and scientific—necessary to carry out the organization [Fourier] proposed. In a word, no trial, no approach to a trial of Fourier's theory has been made. I do not say that his theory is true, or would succeed, if fairly tried. I simply affirm that no trial of it has been made; so that it is unjust to speak of it, as if it had been tested."

As the years passed Brisbane became more and more disillusioned, until he finally said of the man he had once compared to Christ, "If ever a man deserved to be hanged for intellectual rashness and violence, it is Fourier."

Name of Utopia: MODERN TIMES

Founder: Josiah Warren (1799–1874). Warren, an inventor and manufacturer of considerable success, devised a lard-burning lamp that proved less costly than tallow, as well as a process by which sunburned bricks could be manufactured from lime and gravel. He believed that the wealth he had gained could be significant only if shared by many, and as a result joined Robert Owen's community at New Harmony. When that failed he blamed it on the suppression of individuality, and said that it was wrong for men to readjust to society. "Man seeks freedom as the magnet seeks the pole or water its level, and society can have no peace until every member is free."

Where and When: In 1847, after the collapse of New Harmony, Warren established his 1st commune, Equity, in Tuscarawas County, O., but the area proved uninhabitable, and many of his followers developed diseases, particularly malaria. In 1851 Warren purchased between 700 and 800 acres in "the Garden of New York, the center of Long Island," and moved his followers there. He called the new community "Modern Times."

Political and Social Structure: Warren based the political and social structure of his commune on 2 principles, "Individual Sovereignty" and "Equitable Commerce." Individual sovereignty meant a community without government, laws, institutions, rules, organizations, or regulations, except those an individual might wish to make for himself. Equitable commerce meant that, in exchange for goods, an individual could issue a promissory labor note, thereby allowing him to establish the rate of exchange for his own labor.

All of this meant that Modern Times was an experiment in communal anarchy, and though Warren and his chief disciple, Stephen Pearl Andrews, never used that word to describe their community they did say, "We protest against all laws which interfere with individual rights. . . . We believe in perfect liberty of will and action—hence we are liberals. We have not compacts with each other save the compact of human happiness, and we hold that every man and every woman has a perfect and inalienable right to do and perform . . . as he or she may choose now and hereafter."

Life at Modern Times was described thus by one visitor: "Broad avenues, tree-shaded streets, pretty cottages, surrounded by strawberry beds and well-tilled gardens, formed the outward appearance of Modern Times. The occupants were honest, industrious, and had learned to mind their own business, while readily cooperating with their neighbors for mutual advantage. They were free from sectarian dissensions, courts of law, policemen, jails, rum shops, prostitutes and crime. No one acquired wealth save by his own industry."

Property and Distribution of Goods: Land was offered in Modern Times at $22 an acre, the cost to Warren. Once bought, it was the individual's responsibility to protect and preserve what he or she had; to have done otherwise would have been in violation of Warren's concept of individual sovereignty. Goods were obtained through the principle of equitable commerce, so that whatever one attained was done through private initiative and labor.

Family/Marriage/Sex: Adin Ballou, founder of the Hopedale commune, wrote of 2 adulterers whom he expelled and who went to Modern Times, "they undoubtedly found congenial companionship, and unbridled liberty to carry their doctrines out to the farthest limit, with no one to question or reproach them, or say them nay."

The community's lack of rules, and Warren's refusal to question couples as part of his doctrine of individual sovereignty gave Modern Times the reputation for being a haven for free love. But just as Warren had refused to question unmarried couples, he refused to question the sanctity of a marriage. "We don't steal anything, not our neighbor's ox, nor his wife, nor his niece, nor his daughter, nor his sister; that would be interfering with the sovereignty of the individual. But if we can make a fair compact—an amicable agreement, where all parties will be rendered happy —who shall, or should complain?"

Place of Women: In Warren's community women enjoyed the same status and standards as men, as Warren's philosophy applied equally to them. They were permitted to set the price for their own labor, and they enjoyed sexual freedom without censure. In all, Warren's concept of individual sovereignty accorded women rights and privileges they did not have in the outside world.

Why the Experiment Ended: In order to purchase products they could not produce the members of Modern Times were forced to sell certain of their products outside their community. When the panic of 1857 occurred, their rather limited industries could not survive and the community, beset by financial woes, was forced to fold.

Name of Utopia: ONEIDA
Founder: John Humphrey Noyes (1811–1886). Noyes was part of a movement called Perfectionism which he explained by comparing it with 2 of the great issues of the day, slavery and temperance: "As the doctrine of temperance is total abstinence from alcoholic drinks, and the doctrine of antislavery is immediate abolition of human bondage, so the doctrine of Perfectionism is immediate and total cessation from sin." He believed the most effective means to achieve this cessation from sin was through communal, communistic living.

Where and When: In 1835, Noyes began an Adult Bible School in Putney, Vt., where, as he described it, "the school advanced from a community of faith, to a community of property, to a community of households, to a community of affections." By late 1847, Noyes's New England neighbors were sufficiently scandalized by the "community of affections" to cause an investigation to be launched. Charges of adultery were brought against Noyes and some of his followers, who jumped bail and fled to Oneida, N.Y., where in 1848 they began their communal experiment in earnest. They remained there until 1879, when the experiment ended.

Political and Social Structure: Noyes's followers believed him to be "the permanent medium of the spirit of Christ" and as such he enjoyed dictatorial power in Oneida. According to Noyes's interpretation of the New Testament the church of the 1st century practiced communism, and he felt that if people were to achieve perfection they would again have to live in a communist community. As a result, members of the community owned nothing privately; everything was shared communally.

The community's activities were organized into 48 departments, which were supervised by 21 committees, all of which Noyes controlled. One of the community's more interesting social functions, and central features, was the practice of holding criticism sessions. Usually presided over by Noyes, these sessions were meant to check abuses in the practice of complex marriage.

Property and Distribution of Goods: All property and goods were commonly owned, and shared. In fact, one house, called the Mansion House, served as the main living quarters for Oneida members. The structure was 60' long, 35' wide, 3 stories high, contained a habitable garret, and 3 large basement rooms. The 1st floor held the kitchen and dining room, the 2nd an all-purpose room, and the remainder of the house was divided into small bedrooms and sitting rooms.

The community was self-supporting, largely because one of its members had invented an animal trap, considered the finest of its kind at that time, and gave the proceeds to the community. This freed Oneida from the economic hardships that many other communal experiments faced, and permitted it the luxury of pursuing its religious goals.

Family/Marriage/Sex: What made Oneida one of the most revolutionary Utopias in history was the Oneidan practice of complex marriage. Complex marriage meant that every male in the community was married to every female, and vice versa. This is not to be confused with the practice of free love, an experiment conducted at a number of Utopian communities, or with Mormonism, where only men were allowed the luxury of several partners. Complex marriage was different for a number of reasons, and Noyes was responsible for all of them.

First, unlike the free love communities, Noyes carefully supervised and controlled the sexual activity of his followers. His supervision went so far, in fact, that the Oneidans actually conducted eugenic experiments, the 1st ever tried on humans.

Noyes developed the philosophy because he felt the monogamous family bred selfishness, and if the experiment in "Bible Communism" was to be a success, monogamy would have to be abolished—hence, the complex marriage. He explained this to his followers by saying that the Second Coming had occurred, in 70 A.D., and that it was no longer necessary for men to live according to the moral laws which govern them in a state of sin, but that they should be free to enjoy the "liberty of the Gospel."

Place of Women: Though Noyes believed women inferior to men, he did feel that they should be spared the agonies of childbirth (possibly because his own wife suffered 4 stillbirths in 6 years), and that birth control should be practiced. To this end he developed the theory of male continence. This meant that male control of ejaculation became a form of worship in the community, making the female's orgasm the primary concern of every sexual encounter.

The older, "more perfect" men introduced virgins into the system of complex marriage at the age of 13. It was believed that these young women might better learn and enjoy sexual relations with the more experienced men; by the same token, young virgin men were introduced into the system by older, more experienced women. The Oneidans felt that this system would also provide a source of sexual partners for the older, perhaps less sexually desirable in the community.

Education and Culture: Children were placed in a laboratory nursery where they could be raised in accordance with Noyes's ideas of Perfectionism. Three men and 15 women cared for them, in a rather traditional manner considering the surroundings. Mothers were permitted to visit their children for only 2 hours a week, and were warned against forming strong attachments.

Why the Experiment Ended: What began as an internal squabble over Noyes's autocratic rule ended with his being charged with statutory rape because of his practice of introducing underage girls into the complex marriage of the community. Noyes was forced to flee to Canada, and without his guiding presence in the community it was only a question of time before the experiment failed. A year after his departure the communistic system was dropped, and the community incorporated itself.

Name of Utopia: FERRER COLONY AND MODERN SCHOOL
Founder: Twenty-two anarchists founded the Francisco Ferrer Association as a cultural center and evening school, then added an experimental day school, and finally it became an experimental community. The association was named for Francisco Ferrer, a radical who built a network of anticlerical schools in Spain, and who was executed after an uprising in Barcelona in 1909.

The experiment was different, and remarkable, because it managed to bring together newly arrived eastern European Jews with native-born, college-educated Anglo-Saxons at a time in America's history when such contact was rare.

Harry Kelly, Joseph Cohen, and Leonard Abbott, 3 men heavily involved in the radical causes of their day, were among the association's most influential members during its formation. Elizabeth and Alexis Ferm, who came to the community to serve as co-principals of the school in 1920, became its dominant members.

Where and When: The Francisco Ferrer Association was begun in New York City on June 12, 1910. The Ferrer Modern School followed 16 months later, on October 13, 1911. Finally, because of an upsurge in police harassment and violence from other anarchists, the association purchased a 140-acre tract of land near New Brunswick, N.J., in Stelton, and began the Ferrer Colony on May 16, 1915. It remained an ongoing venture until the early 1950s.

Political and Social Structure: The association was never doctrinaire. The ethos of the Ferrers leaned toward extreme radicalism and as a result they supported a number of protest movements while in New York. In keeping with their anarchist philosophy there was no declaration of principles at the colony. In fact, members had decided that the colony would continue only for as long as members chose to stay and work together.

Among the community's most enduring and successful traditions were lecture and discussion groups. Among the lecturers that came to the Ferrer Center were Clarence Darrow, Margaret Sanger, and Lincoln Steffens. No communal policy was set without benefit of communal discussion and democratic vote. Unlike former communal experiments, at the Ferrer Center no single individual set standards or policy.

Property and Distributon of Goods: Land for the colony was purchased at Stelton, N.J., for $100 an acre and then resold to individual colonists for $150. This allowed 9 acres to be set aside for the school, around which the community was to be built.

People were poor and in the beginning supplies were difficult to obtain. But as the community developed, a sense of camaraderie grew as neighbors helped one another to farm or build homes. By 1922 nearly 90 houses, the colony's peak number, had been built.

One of the great differences between the Ferrer Colony and other communal experiments was that many of its members did not live at the colony, but visited from New York City on weekends and holidays. Also, unlike other experiments, many of those who lived at the colony would commute by train to New York, where they worked.

Family/Marriage/Sex: Because of its anarchist philosophy the Ferrers did nothing to intrude on human relationships, whether those relationships were sanctioned by marriage, or not. As a result the Ferrer colony, like most utopian colonies, gained the reputation of being a haven for free love.

Two other facts about the colony deserve notice. First, Margaret Sanger, the great advocate of birth control, was a frequent lecturer and visitor at the colony. Second, there were a considerable number of marriages between Jews and gentiles at Ferrer, an uncommon custom at the turn of the century.

Place of Women: Though a goodly number of lecture and discussion groups devoted themselves to the problems of women, there was no organized movement at the colony concerned with women's rights.

Education and Culture: The chief purpose of the Ferrers had always been to provide working-class children with a libertarian education. They hoped to initiate lives of free self-expression and to nurture a collective social commitment.

During the school's 1st decade, in New York and then at Stelton, it experienced great difficulty in finding a principal who could provide the leadership necessary for such an education. It wasn't until 1920, at Stelton, that the problem was solved with the arrival of Elizabeth and Alexis Ferm. In a short time they transformed the Modern School into the most progressive educational experience in America during the 1920s.

Because of their aversion to intellectual abstraction they converted the newly completed educational building's 4 classrooms into craft and manual training areas. The assembly hall became a kindergarten area, leaving only the library for academic work. The curriculum soon centered around printing, weaving, art, music, carpentry, nature study, and outdoor experiences, all activities for which materials could easily be found. The only time that attendance was required was at morning assembly. The Ferms were so effective that on one occasion, a teachers' holiday, the children, rather than miss school, took over the entire operation for 3 weeks.

Why the Experiment Ended: Bowing to the growing influence of the Ferms, a number of the colony's leaders, Kelly and Cohen among them, had left Stelton by the end of the 1st decade, taking with them much of the community's driving force.

The 1940s, and the war, brought on new problems. The Army purchased the property adjoining the settlement, and the community suddenly found itself the victim of theft, vandalism, and rape. Many of the colonists sold their property and moved to Miami and Los Angeles.

Finally, and most important, was the fact that few of the families were sending their children to the school in the late '40s and early '50s. As they became more and more middle class, so did their children, and the assimilation of the onetime anarchists into the American mainstream became unavoidable.

Name of Utopia: SPANISH ANARCHIST COLLECTIVES

Founder: The collectives were begun by the workers of Spain during the Spanish Civil War. Franco had declared war on the legally elected Popular Front government in Madrid. The country was without effective central leadership, and the workers and peasants created their own institutions to administer the cities and farms of Republican Spain (that area not controlled by Franco's military forces), and established a militia to fight the Francista forces.

Because of the war, the socioeconomic experiment of these workers and peasants has gone largely unnoticed until recently.

Where and When: The experiment took place in Spain during the Spanish Civil War, from 1933 to 1936.

Population: Estimates vary on how many people were involved in the collectives, but they do range as high as 8 million, and as low as 3 million. The extensiveness of the experiment can be judged by the fact that there were approximately 1,700 agrarian collectives, and nearly 80% of the industry in republican-held areas was involved.

Political and Social Structure: The anarchist collectives must be divided into 2 parts: the industrial and the rural.

INDUSTRIAL. Factories were taken over by workers, who then elected managers, both technical and administrative. These managers were subject to recall at any time, and no decisions were made that did not involve the workers. Problems beyond the capacity of a single plant were handled by local economic councils.

Among the best of these collectives was one in operation in Barcelona, Spain's largest city at the time. In order to feed the population, the food unions, together with restaurant and hotel workers, opened communal dining rooms in each of the city's neighborhoods, where as many as 120,000 people were fed daily. Wholesale food establishments were then created, and these establishments organized themselves as the Food Workers Industrial Union. The workers became their own bosses, fixed their own wages, and the system, which embraced all of Catalonia, was coordinated by 500 workers.

RURAL. The communal traditions of Spain's agrarian life were rather solid, and collectivism came naturally. Expropriated lands were turned over to peasant syndicates, and these syndicates organized the 1st collectives, pooling not only their land, but animals, tools, grain, fertilizer, and harvested crops as well.

The Regional Federation of Levant, for example, was an agrarian federation embracing 5 provinces, with a population of 1,650,000, and contained 78% of the nation's most fertile land. The number of collectives in the federation rose from 340 in 1937, to 900 by the end of 1938, with 40% of the population living on them.

All of the collectives, both industrial and agrarian, were organized by the CNT—the National Confederation of Workers Associations. Small farmers who did not want to join a collective were called "individualists," and were permitted to continue working their lands as long as they did not hire wage laborers.

Property and Distribution of Goods: The collectives offered an alternative to both state and private capitalism, communism, and socialism by being the workers' economic collectives, without private property, or elitist governments. The custodian of these collectives was the CNT, though even they could not do as they pleased without the consent of the workers, which was obtained through conventions or congresses.

The collectives were an attempt to organize the populace on the basis of mutual aid and solidarity; all the finances of the collectivized plants, industries, and unions were deposited in the Central Labor Bank of Barcelona. The bank acted as a clearinghouse for the collectives, channeling funds from the more successful to the less successful. This monetary support was not necessarily given as actual cash. Rather it consisted of commodities whenever possible. This was one of the more interesting features of the collectives. They either abolished or drastically curtailed the use of the country's official currency, preferring to issue their own "money" in the form of vouchers, coupons, tokens, ration books, and certificates. The chief objective of all these methods of distribution was to allot material necessities to every person according to his needs.

Place of Women: One of the more important achievements of the collectives was the acceptance of the right of women—regardless of their occupation or function—to a livelihood. In half of the collectives, women earned the same amount as men; in the others, on the premise that they did not live alone, they received less.

Education and Culture: Before the Civil War, illiteracy was nearly 70% in most of rural Spain, but the collectives in these areas—by organizing one or 2 free schools per collective, and having the teachers' unions provide teachers—almost succeeded in wiping out illiteracy.

So that education could be truly universal, schools were open to children until they reached the age of 14 or 15. This also guaranteed that parents would not send their children out to work sooner.

Why the Experiment Ended: When the Nationalists, under General Francisco Franco, won the Civil War, the collectives, despite their considerable success, were forced to close down. It ended one of the most successful—and inspiring—utopian experiments ever conceived. (The only English-language book on the subject is *The Anarchist Collectives* edited by Sam Dolgoff, and published in 1974 by Free Life Editions, 41 Union Square West, New York, N.Y. 10003.)

—D.C.

Captain Mission's Unique Pirate Utopia

This is a true story of a fugitive who wanted to establish a better society to live in—and who tried to create such a society in the early 1700s.

François Mission was born in Provence, France. At the age of 16—tall, strong, handsome—he went to sea. He matured into a contradiction—a combined "man of action and dreamer." A brilliant fencer, he was also a thinker. His social philosophy, although crude and strange, was democratic and "the deepest passion in his life was love of man." But even as he loved his neighbor, he was forced, as part of his profession, to kill his neighbor. Once, after boarding an enemy vessel, and disposing of a half-dozen ferocious Moors, he was remorseful, and when his ship, the *Victoire*, docked in Italy, he sought solace by hurrying straightaway to a Catholic Church and the confessional.

By chance, the Italian priest who heard Mission's confession was also a young, restless, somewhat radical dreamer. His name was Père Caraccioli, and Mission's confession of his seafaring adventures and sins so stimulated and intrigued the good father, that he promptly discarded his cassock and went to sea with his visitor.

Together, the 2 young men spent weeks discussing the troubles of the world and brewing their own utopian remedies. Then, suddenly, the *Victoire* became locked in battle with a Dutch ship. An enemy cannonball killed the *Victoire*'s captain, and the 2nd-in-command hurried to run up the flag of surrender. François Mission would not have it. He decked his superior, took over command, and above the roar of conflict he exhorted his fellows to rally and, in the end, to win.

After the battle, there was indecision. Mission and Caraccioli conferred. Then the ex-priest confronted the men, and he said, "You, François, and you, my friends, have often spoken idly of wanting to be not subjects to a king but free citizens in a better world, in which liberty and equality of rights prevail. You have wished for an ideal Republic. Then here it is, the Republic of the *Victoire*!"

Thus began one of the most unique episodes in history. The ship, *Victoire*, was renamed *The Republic of the Sea*, and placed under the leadership of Captain Mission. The members of the crew, 200 able-bodied Frenchmen, plus 35 sick and wounded, became socialized pirates.

Never before had Cartagena, or the Spanish Main, or the West Indies, known buccaneers such as these. Instead of the white skull and crossbones on the traditional black field—the Jolly Roger—they hoisted a pure white flag embroidered with the motto "For God and Liberty." On shipboard they divided all money and all belongings, and dwelt in physical equality. Profanity and intoxication were forbidden, and anyone found guilty of either outrage was "tied to the grating and severely whipped."

On every possible occasion, Captain Mission exercised his belief in equality and liberty. Capturing a Dutch boat, he freed all the black slaves and made them citizens of his amphibious democracy. His raids on shipping were as bloodless as possible, performed with great sensitivity and good manners, and were continued only to obtain food, arms, supplies, and voluntary citizens. From the 1st Dutch ship, Captain Mission, using verbal persuasion only, won 11 volunteers for his floating utopia. From the 2nd prize, an England merchantman, Mission lured 30 British converts.

At last, when his company and his riches had grown excessively large, and his dreams had inflated with them, Captain Mission realized that he must anchor his utopia. He remembered a warm, friendly, hidden island, with a broad expanse of white beach and deep harbor. He sailed for it. It was a small island in the Comoro group, between Madagascar and the east coast of Africa. Here Captain Mission and his followers built a bustling pirate paradise. After the miniature amphitheater was constructed—according to Capt. Charles Johnson, a contemporary historian writing in 1726—Mission rose and spoke:

"Here comes into being today the Republic of Libertatia. You, my people, are the Liberi. We dedicate ourselves to the spread of liberty, and the love of liberty, toleration, and the love of humanity under whatever faith and whatever skin. May our fortune equal the greatness of our hope!"

Captain Mission decided that his Libertatia must have democracy and popular law. To this end, the pirates and colonists were divided into groups of 10, and each group elected one of its number as a representative to the Central Assembly. In the newly constructed State House, the representatives elected Captain Mission their 1st lord conservator for a term of 3 years. He, in turn, chose Thomas Tew, of Salem, his admiral, heading a 3-ship fleet, and the ex-priest, Caraccioli, his Secretary of State. Thus, a Frenchman, an American, and an Italian ruled a polyglot citizenry over 2 centuries before the formation of the UN.

The experiment, the Tom Thumb nation,

flourished. A printing press with its fonts of type was captured in a raid, and a newspaper was born. All money went into a common state treasury. Neither walls nor hedges were permitted to divide neighbors' homes from one another. And, since the colonists were of many nationalities and spoke French, English, Portuguese, and Dutch, a new official language, a kind of Esperanto, was invented and taught.

Mission and his aides married native royalty, but his subjects complained about the lack of enough women for all. Mission realized that to perpetuate his Perfect State he must find additional mates in order to supply everyone. He led his Navy on a special raid, intercepted a vessel Mecca-bound, kidnapped 100 choice females, brought them back to utopia, and presented them to their waiting grooms.

In the end, while discontent from within was at a minimum, danger from without grew. Portuguese ships tried to enter and crush Mission's colony, and were repulsed. Then neighboring tribes, fearing Mission might grow too powerful and subsequently overwhelm them, united and struck at him. Mission was caught off guard, but he and his people fought back. The pirates cut down wave after wave of Africans, but the sheer numbers finally engulfed the Liberi, and at last, beaten, they withdrew to their ships. From the safety of the main decks, they watched their utopia being pillaged and burned. Then they sailed away. Captain Mission's spirit was broken, and mere weeks later, when a hurricane demolished his vessels, he went down, almost gladly, with his ship.

—I.W.

The Almanac's Exclusive Symposium on Utopia

The *Almanac* editors polled a number of persons, well known in their respective fields, on their individual ideas about utopia. Each was asked, "Give us your personal version of utopia" and each was asked 9 questions.

The following persons responded to the *Almanac* poll:

BUCKMINSTER FULLER, JR., designer, inventor, philosopher, father of the geodesic dome and author of *Spaceship Earth* and other books.

MONTY HALL, television producer and host of *Let's Make a Deal*.

JILL JOHNSTON, author of *Lesbian Nation* and a staff member of *The Village Voice*.

EARTHA KITT, singer and entertainer.

JOHN LENNON, singer-composer and formerly a member of the Beatles.

DESMOND MORRIS, author of *The Naked Ape* and other books.

DR. BENJAMIN SPOCK, author of the all-time best seller, *The Common Sense Book of Baby and Child Care*.

IRVING WALLACE, author of *The Word* and other books.

DAVID WALLECHINSKY, author of *Chico's Organic Gardening and Natural Living* and other books.

Their answers follow.

1. *What would the physical environment of your utopia be like?*

FULLER: As near perfect as possible. Technology would provide a high standard of living for all. Man would have as much control over his environment as possible—controlled climate, for example. There would be no nations, no borders, no government as we now know it, no wars, no fierce competition. Everyone would be a world citizen, a born student of life and nature, a comprehensivist, uninhibited, benevolent, appreciative of himself and others.

HALL: Tall trees, birds singing, shimmering lakes—quiet—a blend of flora and fauna. Temperature ever in the 70s, with the water temperature in the 80s, and in the 20s in the mountains that surround the area.

JOHNSTON: Silky and transparent.

KITT: All mechanical devices to be run by the energy of the sun.

LENNON: Typical.

MORRIS: In utopia there would be no questionnaires.

SPOCK: Much less industry, no trash, no pollution.

WALLACE: A small country divided into rural communities, each with a limited shopping center and gathering places for relaxation, talk, recreation. Like Venice, no vehicles permitted.

WALLECHINSKY: The cities would look more like the countryside. Streets would be lined with fruit trees and each block would have a vegetable garden, tended by senior citizens and children.

2. *What family structures would exist?*

FULLER: The basic family structure would remain intact but it would not be so insular. Since people would interact freely without inhibitions, their children would be exposed to many diverse individuals and spend much time away from the family without difficulty. The roles of husband and wife would be limitless, without personal strictures. Members of the family—individuals in general—would no longer "belong" to each other.

HALL: Mothers, fathers, grandparents, grandchildren. Two children to a family, living close to each other.

JOHNSTON: Compatible gangs.

KITT: Two children per family. Every family should have a place to grow food.

LENNON: Any.

MORRIS: It is impossible to detail the features of utopia as requested because the essential utopian quality is diversity, variability, and unpredictability. If I can tell you what kind of weather, families, crimes, government, etc., there would be, then already that is a utopia I want to escape from.

SPOCK: Essentially the same as now, but with less tension. More diffusion with the neighborhood.

WALLACE: Couples, the married and unmarried treated equally under law. All community children raised as brothers and sisters. Limitations on family size.

WALLECHINSKY: Any and all.

3. *How would the government be organized?*

FULLER: What government?

HALL: Kibbutz style as in Israel. Everyone doing what he does best, and no need to receive rewards greater than the next.

JOHNSTON: By sparrows and patient bulls.

KITT: Have suggestion boxes placed every 20 or so blocks to get people's opinions freely in regard to their gripes and desires. Nonopinionated officers should be put in office to carry them out.

LENNON: Toss a coin.

SPOCK: Most governmental functions such as police, schools, health facilities *and industry* divided into small neighborhood units controlled by the workers and citizens of neighborhood.

WALLACE: Country would be ruled by a council, selected not by election but by tests as to fitness. Everyone would be taught government, and everyone would be eligible for the ruling council. Term of the council might be 2 years.

WALLECHINSKY: Regional councils made up of recallable delegates from neighborhoods and work places would carry out decisions made at mass meetings and by general assemblies. Delegates from regional councils could gather for further coordination. On every level, the people on top would have no authority to make decisions, only to carry them out.

4. *How would work and goods be divided?*

FULLER: Naturally, since cooperation and efficient technology will have replaced competition and low-yield production, there will be enough wealth and goods for all to have a high standard of living. Since automation will have eliminated a good many jobs, especially the unpleasant ones, work will no longer be a drudgery or a necessity. Everyone will spend most of his time doing what interests him, and in this way the interests of a few will supply the world's technology.

HALL: According to one's abilities and one's needs.

JOHNSTON: By straw and wishbone. Or: Just enough.

KITT: According to need not greed—reward those with greater incentive by allowing those persons who create work for others to pay less taxes. No one should have to pay more than 5% taxes. Food should be measured out so no one gets more than he needs. This would eliminate greed and fat people. Respected doctors would decide the proper amounts.

LENNON: Color of eyes.

SPOCK: Wages would be much more equal than now. People would select their own work.

WALLACE: All necessary goods and services—from basic foods and housing and clothes to medical help—would be state-owned or people-controlled. Private enterprise could exist only for luxuries and extras. Everyone would be educated or trained for some kind of occupation of his choice, and everyone would work a minimum amount of time. There would also be a minimum guaranteed wage for every living adult, and a maximum set on what anyone could earn and keep.

WALLECHINSKY: An office, factory, farm, or store would be run by a general assembly of all workers who would decide policy and elect managers and administrators, who would be recallable at any time. Each establishment would send delegates to industry-wide regional assemblies in order to coordinate production and distribution.

5. *How would education take place?*

FULLER: Individually, when possible. Television would be used on a large scale. Children would begin learning when they were ready to learn and be treated at all times as intelligent beings who need to explore and discover. They would be taught how the world works 1st hand. And their education would be comprehensive, not specialistic. The large school buildings that obsess today's society would be obsolete.

HALL: Equal opportunity for all. Gifted ones then directed to specialized training for the benefit of society.

JOHNSTON: By imitation (as usual).

LENNON: Slowly.

SPOCK: In a great variety of wildly experimental schools and colleges run by students, faculty, and in the case of elementary schools, by parents.

WALLACE: Everyone would attend free schools for 16 years. Everyone would be educated and then trained in something that interests him. Teaching would be one of the best paying professions.

WALLECHINSKY: All voluntary. Schools would be run by teachers, students and parents. Most instruction would take place outside of classrooms and campuses. Sex education would begin with practical experience in which older women teach young boys and older men teach young girls.

6. *What crimes would there be, and how would they be punished?*

FULLER: Murder would perhaps be the only real crime, and it would be rare in a world without frustration. Robbery would be pointless in a world of universal wealth; greed would be mere extravagance.

HALL: Don't know what crimes, but the perpetrators would have to earn their way back into society by doing work assigned.

JOHNSTON: Crimes of persuasion punishable by detection.

KITT: There will always be crime, so punishment should be the severest. This would eliminate crime no matter who commits it. The needs of criminals should be studied. A man may steal a loaf of bread because of hunger, but if food is equally measured for all, there would be no crime.

LENNON: Plenty. Somehow.

SPOCK: Most criminality would be eliminated by giving all parents security and seeing that all children are given love and enjoyable schooling. Prisons should be staffed for rehabilitation.

WALLACE: There could be no crimes resulting from poverty or inequality. There would inevitably be crimes created by psychological ills, tempers, passions, and other human frailties. Judges and jurors would be trained for their jobs. No capital punishment, no jails. There would be understanding rehabilitation centers.

WALLECHINSKY: Murder, rape, and economic exploitation; punishment would be service to the community as well as a severe tongue-lashing by anybody who was so moved. Hardcore repeaters would be forced to watch Richard Nixon's Checkers speech over and over for 12 hours a day.

7. *What would be YOUR role in this society?*

FULLER: I would be 1st of all a consumer, enjoying life to its fullest. Like everyone else, I would be a world citizen, learning, traveling, creating and contributing, if possible, to the world's knowledge.

HALL: To perform whatever I do best: entertain, govern, mediate.

JOHNSTON: Transparent.

KITT: As a woman, I always feel like a mother to all. I would be a protector and guide.

LENNON: Heavenly.

WALLACE: I'd like to improve it. Also, I'd like to write about it.

WALLECHINSKY: I would like to dabble in everything and have a good time.

8. *Why isn't life like this now?*

FULLER: We are basically ignorant, still governed by old reflexes. We are capable of generating the plenty needed to give every person on earth a high standard of living, yet our competitive systems keep this standard in the hands of a few. Technologically, our old political, religious, and economic systems are obsolete, yet we cling to them. Our whole system of "rationality" needs revision.

HALL: Too many people with too many differences fighting for their just place in the sun —but always at the expense of someone else.

JOHNSTON: It is.

KITT: We have been so caught up in material things that we have allowed real love to die. A tight family unity should be exercised on a personal level and in society at large.

LENNON: Isn't it?

SPOCK: Industry is unable to see anything beyond profits, and government is the servant of industry.

WALLACE: The power of private enterprise and state tyranny makes it impossible at present. The worship of individual leaders makes it impossible. Above all, the education and goals given people make it impossible.

WALLECHINSKY: Too many people want to get ahead of everyone else and too few people realize that we are all in this together and might as well learn the joys of cooperation.

9. *Any other comments?*

HALL: There'll never be a utopia until all differences are submerged—all are treated equally—all love each other. But you said utopia, didn't you, and not any existing country we now know!

KITT: When a person works hard to obtain a fair share of "the pie," he should be rewarded instead of punished by high taxes which make him become a thief to reward himself.

LENNON: No.

MORRIS: The real world in which I live is already sufficiently curious, rebellious, eccentric, and evolving to give me my utopia right here and now. By spending half my time in a sleepy Mediterranean village and half in a busy British city, I literally get the best of both worlds. My crime would be not to recognize that I already live in a utopian state; and my greatest punishment would be to be confined in the classic conception of a utopia, where nothing ever goes wrong and everyone is permanently, boringly happy.

WALLACE: As you know, "utopia" means "nowhere." Utopia can exist nowhere for everyone because it is a personal, subjective idea or dream for each individual. What may be utopia for me may be hell for you. The best we can do is compromise to get along with our fellow humans, and strive for a better world free of tyranny, injustice, war, and want.

WALLECHINSKY: It's not worth it unless it's fun.

32

By the People, for the People

America Speaks

Although there are over 200 million people in the U.S., only a privileged few are allowed to express their ideas and feelings to a mass audience. The editors of *The People's Almanac* believe that the unheard Americans deserve a forum. We believe that there is a truer U.S. than the one which is portrayed on the television set—a U.S. with greater depth and greater diversity than may at 1st seem apparent. We also believe that the best way to learn about the real America is to listen to the words of its people.

MIKE LEFEVRE, steelworker, Cicero, Ill.

"You can't take pride anymore. You remember when a guy could point to a house he built, how many logs he stacked. He built it and he was proud of it. . . .

"It's hard to take pride in a bridge you're never gonna cross, in a door you're never gonna open. You're mass-producing things and you never see the end result of it. . . .

"Pyramids, Empire State Building—these things just don't happen. There's hard work behind it. I would like to see a building, say, the Empire State, I would like to see on one side of it a foot-wide strip from top to bottom with the name of every bricklayer, the name of every electrician, with all the names. So when a guy walked by, he could take his son and say, 'See, that's me over there on the 45th floor. I put the steel beam in.' " (From: *Working* by Studs Terkel. New York, Pantheon Bks., 1974.)

WYOMING WILSON,
vending machine factory worker,
Cincinnati, O.

"I worked in the restaurant for a long time. The man who owned it and his wife were hill-billies too, so I didn't have too much trouble there. I was making a dollar an hour. Some days I'd get good tips and other days I didn't do so good. . . .

"While I was working in the restaurant . . . there was this guy come in there and he was drunk. He ordered ham and eggs. He ate about half the eggs and then he just laid his face right down in the plate, right in the eggs. I went over to him and I said, 'You better get your face up out of those eggs.' Well, he raised up and looked at me, then he reached over and pinched me. So I hit him over the head with a ketchup bottle. I never did have too much trouble when I worked in the restaurant." (From: *Hillbilly Women* by Kathy Kahn. Garden City, N.Y., Doubleday, 1973.)

JAMEY McDONALD, convict, San Diego, Calif.

"I ended up in the joint because I wanted to keep up with the Joneses. All my life . . . I'm only 30 years old, been in since I've been 18. I started off with the Georgia chain gang. I ran away with a girl to get married, and we stopped at a motel. Now this may sound funny, but I didn't have no thought of stealing. I went down to get a Coke and when I came back my wife said to me (we'd only been married a few hours), 'When we get home to Philadelphia, we won't have no television in the apartment. If we take this, they won't even know it.'

"I *did* take it, you know. I'm not going to say she *made* me take it, but I *did* take it, and I ended up getting 3 years for that. I knew it was wrong, but when I pulled in to the motel, the sign said, 'Free TV.' I told the judge this and he laughed; then he sentenced me to 3 years." (From: *Paroled but Not Free* by Erickson, Crow, Zurcher, and Connett. New York, Behavioral Publications, 1973.)

RODNEY S., high school student,
New York City, N.Y.

8:30 P.M. "I was sent up to bed. I am not sleepy at all. The lights are on in my room, in the hall, and in the bathroom. I smell my brother's cough medicine. I hear my mother and father talking. As I go upstairs, I can feel the wooden banister under my hands."

8:45 P.M. "I'm washing up. The water feels warm against my face. I can see myself in the mirror as I wash. I soon hear my mother and brother coming upstairs."

9:00 P.M. "My brother has a fairy tale book and he thinks he is really reading it. (He can't, because he is only 6 years old.) The lights are off in the bathroom, and in my mother's and father's room. I'm still doing my English homework and my parents are still talking downstairs."

9:12 P.M. "I have just started yawning. My brother is crying because my father had to speak to him. I can hear the noise of the heaters in the house giving more steam. I can't explain the sound very well, except that it is the same as when a television set messes up. My eyes are starting to get watery."

9:17 P.M. "I'm climbing into my bed. As I get into the top bunk, my brother is kneeling in the lower bunk singing the 'Star-Spangled Banner,' saying the Pledge of Allegiance, and singing 'America the Beautiful.'"

9:30 P.M. "I start feeling as though I don't ever want to get out of bed. My eyes are starting to get heavy. I still hear my brother talking to himself. The lights are still on in the bathroom and in my parents' room. The heaters are still making their noises."

9:40 P.M. "My brother is now falling asleep, talking to himself."

9:50 P.M. "My father comes upstairs. The light is off in my room. My brother looks at the darkness and asks me, is it morning? The heaters stop making their crazy sounds. The house is quiet, everything is getting blurry. The last thing I remember is my hand hanging over the side of the bed and my brother playing with it." (From: *The Me Nobody Knows* edited by Stephen M. Joseph. New York, Discus, 1969.)

ERIKA TAYLOR,
lives on a 70-acre farm in Oregon
in a semi-commune with her husband

"I went to California in 1966 after I graduated from high school. My parents moved out there, and I went too. It was just when all that good stuff was happening. There was just the most incredible energy. I'd come from the Main Line in Philadephia, really posh, egotisti-

cal, money-oriented scene, where our social stuff was based around drinking. . . . I had said, 'Oh, marijuana, what's that all about? I'll never smoke grass.' And then my younger sister turned me on. I went out with her and her friends and we started getting stoned, and then the next week we took acid. A month later I moved away from home and lived up on this mountain, which was just about a half hour away from where my parents lived. It was up in the redwoods. There was a little log cabin up there. It was the 1st commune that I ever lived in. A bunch of really nice people. . . . The beginning of that whole scene was really good. You'd go into a park and people would turn you on and smile, and you could just hold a stranger's hand and walk along and talk, and just feel really at ease. Then a lot of hard drugs started showing up, a lot of speed, and that naturally changed a lot." (From: *Good Times* by Peter Joseph. New York, Morrow Paperbacks, 1974.)

RUTH NELSON, systems analyst

"I enjoy working in the field of data processing for many reasons; one is that the work is done by individuals. I've heard many programmers express the feeling of satisfaction they get from doing a job entirely by themselves rather than with a committee. They identify with the system they use in working with their particular type of computer.

"Another thing I like about programming is that you always know when you've made a mistake, because when you do, the system won't come out right. Then you're able to keep on trying until you finally get it perfect. There are no maybes, only wrong or right. There may be many different ways of approaching a problem, but only one that will come out exactly right. I get great satisfaction from having done something correctly." (From: *Saturday's Child* by Suzanne Seed. Chicago, J. Philip O'Hara, 1973.)

GENEVA, East Bronx, New York City, N.Y.

"I want to get out of this neighborhood. It's too filthy around here to raise children, and like sometimes you see people on the street eating out of garbage cans. Like the other day I see this man. He didn't look like a bum, you know, but it looked like candy he was taking out of the garbage cans and everything. So it was my last 50¢, but I gave it to him. I said, 'Don't eat out of garbage cans.' And he said, 'Thank you,' and walked away. It doesn't matter to me that it was my last 50¢, but it makes me sad and mad for him eating out of the garbage can." (From: *The Block* by Herb Goro. New York, Vintage Books, 1970.)

BILL DUNN, Skid Row resident,
Philadelphia, Pa.

"What I remember most is that when I got older, maybe 14 or 15, I used to go down to the Row a lot. I'd find an excuse to walk through there on my way into town or something. Partly curiosity, but mostly the rumor that my father was there. I guess it was my age as much as anything. I was looking, like all kids that age, I guess, for parts of myself, for searching out roots—for that part of my lost father in me. I didn't tell anyone about it. It took me a long time—walking the Row, asking around.

"Finally I found him. He was standing outside a bar, leaning a little uncertainly against the glass, squinting into the sun. He didn't look much like the old photographs my mother had kept, his hair was matted, he was filthy and unshaven. When I told him who I was he just stared at me. His mouth dropped open a little, and then his hands moved up shaking and slowly covering his face. I just said 'Why?' But he didn't say anything. He just pushed me away and staggered into the bar. I'll never forget that. He didn't say anything." (From: *Skid Row and Its Alternatives* by Blumberg, Shipley, and Shandler. Philadelphia, Temple University Press, 1973.)

JOSEPH PLECK, teacher, Ann Arbor, Mich.

"There was a dodge-ball game we played regularly, which had 2 forms. In the 1st form, there were 2 teams, and the idea was to throw the ball at people on the other team. If you hit them, they were out, but if they caught the ball you threw at them, then you were out—the game going on until everyone on one team was out. In the 2nd form, sometimes called 'bombardment,' or 'German' dodge-ball, the principle was the same, except that there were no teams, only individuals. With several balls going in a class of 30, the energy level could get quite high. I was never much good at throwing the ball with any force or accuracy, but I got to be very good at dodging, so my basic strategy was to avoid being hit. But the problem was that I often ended up as one of the last 2 people in the game. Then the other person would keep throwing the ball at me until I was so worn down and exhausted that I would finally be hit, with the whole class watching this gladiatorial contest. This got to be extremely painful, both because I always lost and also because it showed everyone else that I couldn't really throw the ball. I soon learned to let myself get hit about halfway through the game. I learned several things in this game: I learned to be hyper-alert to attacks from other

men, and good at dodging them; I also learned that it is extremely important to avoid being conspicuous in the male war of all-against-all." (From: "My Male Sex Role—and Ours," *Win*, April 11, 1974.)

KENNETH RUTH, police officer,
formerly with the 1st Air Cavalry Division

"First of all we go into the village and ask people who they think are Viet Cong. So we were given 2 people that we were told were Viet Cong. What we do, is we took these 2 guys out in the field and we strung one of 'em up in a tree by his arms, tied his hands behind him, and then hung him in the tree. Now what we did to this man when we strung him up is that he was stripped of all his clothes, and then they tied a string around his testicles and a man backed up about 10' and told him what would happen if he didn't answer any questions the way they saw fit. Now all we had to go by was that we were told that he was a suspect by other villagers. Now the other villagers weren't going to point out themselves, and somebody had to be pointed out.

"So they'd ask a guy a question: 'Do you know of any enemy units in this area?' and if he said, 'No,' the guy that was holding that string would just yank on it as hard as he could about 10 times, and this guy would be just flying all over the place in pain. And this is what they used—I mean anybody's just going to say anything in a situation like this to get answers out of him. And then when they were done, when the guy was just limp and hanging there, the South Vietnamese indigenous troops, who worked with the Special Forces, went up there and then to get kicks, would run their knife through his ear and carve little superficial wounds on his body, not deep ones, but just you know, trickle it down his body to make fun of the guy. We took a guy to the other end of the village, and we didn't do this, all we did was burn his penis with a cigarette to get answers out of him. I'm sure people understand what that would be like if it was done to yourself or to your children.

"This is just one of the things I saw. I could just go on all day. All of us could. . . . It isn't just Lieutenant Calley." (From: *The Winter Soldier Investigation* by the Vietnam Veterans Against the War. Boston, Beacon Press, 1972.)

FRED ROSEN, househusband, Rifton, N.Y.

"Running my high school half mile, I notice that coming to the final turn I'm still side by side with the great Clark High School half miler (whose name I still remember: Kanapacik!) and to this day, 14 years later, that moment is engraved on my memory. . . . And the locker room after track meets, the great comradery, throwing soap, snapping towels. . . . And, like the moment on the far turn, I still remember a great summer camp slide into 3rd, a basket from the corner in the Police Boys Club. . . . But clearest of all is the pop fly I dropped in a junior high school game letting in the winning run; nobody on my team would talk to me for days. . . . And 18 years later I still think to myself, 'Why didn't I put my arm up to shade the sun? . . . Why didn't I just try to catch the ball instead of trying for a Willie Mays basket catch?' And not only do I still think it, but I agonize over it." (From: "Confessions of a Straightman," *Win*, April 11, 1974.)

FRANK, drug seller, Berkeley, Calif.

"I was driving on the Nimitz Freeway at around 2 o'clock in the afternoon one day, completely stoned on acid, when a cop pulled me over to the side. I was really freaked out and was sure I was going to get busted, so I rolled up all the windows of my car and refused to even let the cop speak to me. This made the cop so mad that he started screaming for me to roll down the window, he cursed and yelled for about 3 minutes when all of a sudden I rolled down the window and said in a very cool voice, 'I'll have 2 hamburgers and an order of fries.' This remark, instead of infuriating him, actually made him laugh and he told me he was at 1st going to give me a speeding ticket but decided to let me off with a warning instead." (From: *America in Legend* by Richard M. Dorson. New York, Pantheon Books, 1973.)

MAGGIE MAE HORTON,
civil rights organizer,
Fayette County, Tenn.

"Law and order. We got the best laws in Tennessee. I don't think they got no better in Washington. But we don't go by 'em. We don't enforce 'em. I don't fight the law, I fight the white crackers and the white churchgoin' people. We don't only have a problem with our law enforcement, we have a problem with our best citizens—both black and white. . . . That's the biggest problem we have here—of gettin' involved. . . .

"Even the ministers, they wanta stay outa this. They say, 'We gonna stay here and pray till Shiloh come.' Hell, Shiloh here. Anytime a white man can beat you up and do what he want—come to your house, kick you outside— Shiloh hasn't got here? To me, I ain't waitin'. Jesus ain't doin' nothin' for me. He give me my hands and knowledge to do it. All I need is just give me the strength and I'll do the thing myself. That's what we gonna work forward to —trying to get peoples to quit waitin' for God to come do somethin' for 'em. You know, we ain't afraid as we used to be, but we have a custom of what have been taught us all our lives, that God gonna feed you. We don't have enough knowledge to know that it's already picked. All we have to do is get up and get it." (From: *Our Portion of Hell* by Robert Hamburger. New York, Links Books, 1973.)

MARY LOWE, Camden, Ala.

"I worked in Tuscaloosa as a waitress. I've been through integration. Folks down here have a fit if colored folks come in to eat. But I've served them. I know what's going to happen. I've got nothing against colored people. And I'll tell you what—they don't give you as much trouble as white people do. And they tip better. . . .

"When we moved to Camden 5 years ago, all the wives of the men who worked on the dam project used to wear our short shorts to town. And these local women raised a ruckus about it. People around here just didn't wear shorts.

"They went down to the courthouse and tried to get a petition to keep us from wearing our short shorts to town. So we wore them shorter and shorter and shorter. Camden's a small country town, and they're used to going around fully dressed. They're old-fashioned. But now people are used to short shorts. When we moved in, the old people were afraid. Now they're used to us. . . .

"I'd hate to leave this town. I've met so many good folks here. It's true a few people run this county. They've lived here all their lives, and for generations before that their families have been here. But I'd still love to stay. And we will, if my husband can get a job at the paper mill." (From: *Down Home* by Bob Adelman. New York, Quadrangle, 1974.)

JACOB SLOTNIK, tailor, age 81,
Worcester, Mass.

"That's how my life is. Sometimes—lonesome in the house—during the week I don't mind, I go to the store. But Sunday—and now I can't work how I used to—arthritis, sometimes I can't keep the thimble there—but I can't stay home, you know, I get crazy. Lots of people, they get 65, they give up—walk about like dead people—thank God I got a trade, I don't have to go to my children and ask them for a few dollars. That's lucky. And down in the store the customers come, we talk a little, this one comes and that one, I see people, the day goes by. . . ." (From: *Manscapes* by Colin Henfrey. Boston, Gambit, 1973.)

THECLA R., child, aged 3 years 7 months, New Haven, Conn.

"Once there was a little girl. She ate too many raisins. She got sick. The doctor had to come. And they had to stick a needle in her. She cried. Then he had to listen to her heart. And then he had to give her some pills. Then he had to go home to his little girl. Then she had to eat lunch. Then she got better. Then she could have someone to play with. Then that child that was playing with her slept for the night. Then she had to eat her breakfast with her daddy and mommy. Then she had to go to school." (From: *Children Tell Stories* by Pitcher and Prelinger. New York, International Universities Press, 1963.)

WILLIE ELMA JAMES, maid, St. Louis, Mo.

"We didn't have any milk and we didn't have any money and my husband said, 'I just can't let these children starve.' Nobody wanted any steps washed or anything. When he left home, he knew we didn't have any milk. So he took a half a gallon of milk off somebody's step and brought it home for the children; that's the 1st time I'd ever known him to take anything. Later on when he got a job he went out there to try to pay the people, and they told him no. Said they didn't feel bad long as they knew that some hungry child had some milk." (From: *The Workers* by Kenneth Lasson. New York, Bantam Books, 1971.)

BEN BLACK ELK, son of Sioux chief, Black Elk, S.D.

". . . many schools for Indian children make them ashamed they are Indians. . . . The schools forget these are Indian children. They don't recognize them as Indians, but treat them as though they were white children. . . . This makes for failure, because it makes for confusion. And when the Indian history and the Indian culture is ignored, it makes our children ashamed they are Indians. I started to school when I was 7 years old. I couldn't speak a word of English. I had long hair that hung to my waist, and it was in 4 braids. When I made progress in school a braid was cut off to mark my progress. . . ." (From: *I Have Spoken*, compiled by Virginia Irving Armstrong. Chicago, The Swallow Press, 1971.)

LISA MAH, worker in the Chinatown Neighborhood Arts Program, San Francisco, Calif.

"We wanted to be known as that nice Chinese family upstairs or down the street, you know, whom you wouldn't ever want to hurt in any way. My family was very aware that they were embattled Chinese in a white district, that they had spent many years finding that place to live, and that at any moment they could be asked to leave. And somehow a quality I sensed out of all this, about being Chinese, was a vulnerability. At any moment you could be thrown out. So you had to watch your step and you had to be very clever, you had to placate, you had to maneuver. And no matter what happened you did not get openly angry, because if you did, you would have lost your dignity. No matter what they did you had to be stronger than they, you had to outlast them." (From: *Longtime Californ'* by Victor G. and Brett De Bary Nee. New York, Pantheon, 1973.)

PAT O., student, Boston, Mass.

"I guess I always wanted to get married when I was a little girl and still do. Then, in the 5th grade, I wanted to be a teacher because I really liked that teacher; she always thought up new projects for us. I even remember kindergarten. We were allowed only 2 turns on the swings and I wanted it all the time. The 1st grade was more interesting—we colored pigs. In the 2nd grade, there was a lot of drawing. I did a dog with his tail wagging and the teacher got mad and said, 'You're not supposed to draw what you can't see.' But I had it pretty good. She let me get up and tell the class stories I had made up." (From: *Personal and Vocational Interplay in Identity Building* by Jeannette G. Friend. Boston, Brandon, 1973.)

BERNADETTE CLOSYNSKI, housewife, Conn.

"I've been married 22 years and marriage between my husband and me is a 50–50 proposition. Neither one of us makes a decision without consulting the other and this is the way I think a marriage should be. We've had a very happy, successful marriage. We very seldom argue. My husband has a hobby of fishing, so I have adopted his hobby. He and I go out in his boat, we go out on the river and we sit there for hours on end. We say a few words to each other, discuss a few problems at home—once in a while if I'm not catching the fish and he should hook one, he hands the rod to me so I can reel it in. . . .

"This is a happy marriage too because I let him think he is the boss and he knows that I let him think he is the boss. But then if he wants to do something I will go along with it." (From: *Couplings and Groupings* by Megan Terry. New York, Discus, 1972.)

BABE SECOLI,
checker at a supermarket for 30 years

"I don't have to look at the keys on my register. I'm like the secretary that knows her typewriter. The touch. My hand fits. The number 9 is my big middle finger. The thumb is number one, 2 and 3 and up. The side of my hand uses the bar for the total and all that.

"I use my 3 fingers—my thumb, my index finger, and my middle finger. The right hand. And my left hand is on the groceries. They put down their groceries. I got my hips pushin' on the button and it rolls around on the counter. When I feel I have enough groceries in front of me, I let go of my hip. I'm just movin' the hips, the hand, and the register, the hips, the hand, and the register. . . . (As she demonstrates, her hands and hips move in the manner of an Oriental dancer.) You just keep goin' one, 2, one, 2. If you've got that rhythm, you're a fast checker. . . .

"I'm a checker and I'm very proud of it. There's some, they say, 'A checker—ugh!' To me, it's like somebody being a teacher or a lawyer. I'm not ashamed that I wear a uniform and nurse's shoes and that I got varicose veins. I'm makin' an honest living. Whoever looks down on me, they're lower than I am." (From: *Working* by Studs Terkel. New York, Pantheon Books, 1974.)

MARY WILLS, waitress, Silver Springs, Md.

"One of the nice things about being a waitress—the responsibility is not yours. If it's wrong it don't fall on your shoulders, it's the person that told you to do it. So if someone tells me to stand on my head in that dining room, I'm going to do it, and then if somebody comes along and says that I shouldn't have done that, I can say. 'Well, there's the lady that told me to do it. It's not my responsibility.'" (From: *The Workers* by Kenneth Lasson. New York, Bantam Books, 1971.)

SHARON ATKINS, receptionist, Midwestern U.S.

"I changed my opinion of receptionists because now I'm one. It wasn't the dumb broad at the front desk who took telephone messages. She had to be something else because I thought I was something else. I was fine until there was a press party. We were having a fairly intelligent conversation. Then they asked me what I did. When I told them, they turned around to find other people with name tags. I wasn't worth bothering with. I wasn't being rejected because of what I had said or the way I talked, but simply because of my function. . . .

"You come in at 9, you open the door, you look at the piece of machinery, you plug in the headpiece. That's how my day begins. You tremble when you hear the 1st ring. After that, it's sort of downhill. . . .

"I never answer the phone at home. It carries over. The way I talk to people on the phone has changed. Even when my mother calls, I don't talk to her very long. I want to see people to talk to them. But now, when I see them, I talk to them like I was talking on the telephone. It isn't a conscious process. I don't know what's happened." (From: *Working* by Studs Terkel. New York, Pantheon Books, 1974.)

L.P., high school student, New York City, N.Y.

"The only true time I feel at peace is when I am asleep. Because I have no fear and no needs. I think sleep is the most closest thing to death so death must be even more peaceful. But you know what I very rarely feel like going to sleep. And when I do feel like going to sleep I don't feel like waking up. When I wake up I be very mad because I still feel sleepy but I can't go back to sleep.

"And another time I feel at peace is when I am home looking at TV with no one else home but me and my mother. But don't let no one knock on the door or the phone ring. Because someone will ask me to come down and I become very disturbed. I bet I know what is going on in your mind this boy is sick in his head. But I bet you feel like this at times." (From: *The Me Nobody Knows* edited by Stephen M. Joseph. New York, Discus, 1969.)

PAMELA WARDWELL, housewife,
New York City, N.Y.

"I sit outside on our stoop, enjoying the baking sun, and my son plays through the iron fence with the 2 little girls who live in the old brownstone apartment house down the block. They are sweet children. Annie, the older sister, is about 5, Linny perhaps 3; they have pretty, delicate faces, always dirty, round, blue eyes, uncombed straw-blond hair, and are usually dressed in ill-assorted checks and plaids. Annie tells me long stories, sitting beside me on the steps, or shows me the treasures she carries with her in a tiny plastic pocketbook. Linny stands by with a grubby thumb in her mouth and indicates her wants (a gum ball, her shoe tied) with urgent, wordless noises. Today they are alone on the sidewalk and my son, who is not allowed to play beyond our fence, is trying to climb the bars. I hear him ask, 'Where's your Mommy?' and Annie reply, 'We don't have a Mommy. Don't you know our Mommy died?' My heart sinks. Where I come from, the safe suburbs, children's mothers don't die." (From: *Voices of Brooklyn* edited by Sol Yurick. Chicago, American Library Assn., 1973.)

KATHERINE TILLER, miner's wife, Trammel, Va.

"When we were living in Ragland, W.Va. where John had a job for a while, we had to pay for our water. We had been cut off work about 3 months, and one day we hadn't paid our water bill for that month. This man came up to the door and he wanted $2.50 or he was going to cut off the water. I begged him, I told him just as soon as we got our paycheck we'd pay him. He just said no, and he cut it off.

"I got so mad. I got wild. My whole body got numb. It affected my hands and my eyes and it lasted a long time. I must have been about 6 months pregnant at the time. I kind of date my trouble with the baby back to that time. That's why he was born premature, why he wasn't strong enough, why he couldn't make it.

"He was such a beautiful baby, such a fat little baby, with bright red hair. And we took him home. The next morning, the baby began to make strange little noises and bring his little arms up in the air and his little mouth would draw up. When Mama saw him she said to take him back to the hospital. So we took him back. I knew then the baby wasn't going to make it. And he didn't. His lungs collapsed.

"I was so hurt. He was like a ray of sunshine to the family. Our oldest boys, Johnny and Mark, they'd even named him after a Cincinnati baseball player, a black man named George Crow. But of course, we called him Kevin. He was such a lovely baby, after he was born John felt like everything was going to be just fine from then on. Then to have him snatched away like that. . . . We didn't have any money. And people that says money don't matter is dead wrong, 'cause when you don't have it, it does matter." (From: *Hillbilly Women* by Kathy Kahn. Garden City, N.Y., Doubleday, 1973.)

ROBERTO ACUNA, farmworker, Arizona and California

"According to Mom, I was born on a cotton sack out in the fields, 'cause she had no money to go to the hospital. When I was a child, we used to migrate from California to Arizona and back and forth. The things I saw shaped my life. I remember when we used to go out and pick carrots and onions, the whole family. We tried to scratch a livin' out of the ground. I saw my parents cry out in despair, even though we had the whole family working. . . .

"Being a migrant, it tears the family apart. You get in debt. You leave the area penniless. The children are the ones hurt the most. They go to school 3 months in one place and then on to another. No sooner do they make friends, they are uprooted again. Right here, your childhood is taken away. So when they grow up, they're looking for this childhood they have lost.

"I wanted to be accepted. It must have been in 6th grade. It was just before the Fourth of July. They were trying out students for this patriotic play. I wanted to do Abe Lincoln, so I learned the Gettysburg Address inside and out. I'd be out in the fields pickin' the crops and I'd be memorizin'. I was the only one who didn't have to read the part, 'cause I learned it. The part was given to a girl who was a grower's daughter. She had to read it out of a book, but they said she had better diction. I was very disappointed. I quit about 8th grade. . . .

"When people have melons or cucumber or carrots or lettuce, they don't know how they got on their table and the consequences to the people who picked it. If I had enough money, I would take busloads of people out to the fields and into the labor camps. Then they'd know how that fine salad got on their table." (From: *Working* by Studs Terkel. New York, Pantheon Books, 1974.)

3RD-GRADERS, Vermont, in answer to the question "What troubles you about being a child?"

I don't like school
Im to small
Hereing my mother and Father yell.
I wouldn't have to go to school.
older kids push around.
My biggest sister hollers at me
They don't let you stay home alone.
I would like to be stronger
I get blame on evey thing.
You cannot do anything you want.

they don't take me wait then.
an older brother
Daddy and Mother said that you can not do that you are to small.
growup beat us.
We can't do what we want.
to do my arithmetic
There is only one thing that bothers me. I can't voat.
The only thing that I dont like about being a child is that you cant do what you want.
(From: *What Bothers Us About Grownups* edited by Russel Hamilton and Stephanie Green. Brattleboro, Vt., Stephen Greene Press, 1971.)

HARPMAN JAMESON,
civil rights organizer,
Fayette County, Tenn.

"When I was growin' up I was always around a good number of whites. All my neighbors around in the country houses was white. Whites was never a strange person to me. Mosta my playmates was white. One old playmate is in business in Fayette County now. When we was growin' up every birthday cake he got my grandmother cooked it. And when she cooked his cake she brought me a slice of his cake. And when she cooked mine she carried him a slice of mine. This particular fellow, he don't speak to me today. And I haven't done no more to him than I have to you—only registered and stood up like a man. We used to trade birthday cakes. Now he won't even speak. I go in his store maybe, to buy a part—the dealership he's in, I use that brand on my car. And I go in his place to buy a part now. He'll say, 'Yes, what can I do for you?' And I tell him what I want. He never acts like he ever saw me before or that he know me at all. And my grandmother cooked these cakes until he went off to college. We live in the same neighborhood, we vote in the same precinct, but we haven't spoke since I registered to vote."
(From: *Our Portion of Hell* by Robert Hamburger. New York, Links Books, 1973.)

RICHARD LEVY, Brooklyn native

"It was against the law to park at Plum Beach after midnight. Before midnight you can do whatever you want. . . .
"Most guys seldom even got their girl to Plum Beach in the 1st place. After all, a girl didn't want to get a bad reputation. One of my favorite lines was, 'I think my rear left tire is flat, before we get a blow-out we'd better pull over and check it out.' This said just as we passed the Ocean Parkway, the one before Plum Beach. A few other favorites were, 'I'm

getting sleepy (yawn), let's pull over for a few moments,' or 'I have to make an important phone call . . . it'll just take a second . . . I'll pull over in this place . . . there's a telephone booth here.' (It had been out of order since my older brother used to park here in the late '40s.) Boy, just once I would have loved to have said, 'We're going to park, and I'm going to rip your panties off.' Very often, though, when the moment of truth came I chickened out and sped past the damn place, rationalizing that I wouldn't have gotten anything anyway. And even if we did park, there were still hassles.
"All the girls wore these hard, pointy brassieres. They had hooks in the back that seemed welded together (by the girls' fathers, no doubt). And the metal-ribbed girdles they wore were always camouflaged by at least 2 crinolines. How anyone ever got laid, I'll never know." (From: *Voices of Brooklyn* edited by Sol Yurick. Chicago, American Library Assn., 1973.)

ULF S., child, aged 2 years 10 months,
New Haven, Conn.

"I hurt my leg and I tell my mommy. I got a scratch and she put Band-Aid on it. And I put Band-Aid on my hand. And I went on a good truck ride. I fall down in the truck, and the car run over me. And I hurt myself in the street, and it was a bone. I got in the truck and the man shut the door so I won't fall out the truck. And then I bumped my head in the truck. Then I ride in the airplane and go to my grandpa." (From: *Children Tell Stories* by Pitcher and Prelinger. New York, International Universities Press, 1963.)

TERRY WHITMORE,
ex-Marine, deserter, now living in Sweden

"I had a strong hunch I was on my way to Nam. But I couldn't tell my mother that. 'Mama, I'm going back there, probably I need a little more training. Probably I'll have to learn to say "kill" a few more times, and then everything will be all right.' She said, 'Son, you're going to Vietnam.' I said, 'No, no, just going back for more training. . . .'
"When we got back to Lejeune the guys laid it on us. They said, 'I guess you know you're going to Hot Nam.' I was for the war then. I was scared but I didn't want to show it, and I said, 'O.K., let me go over there and kill a couple of gooks. . . .'
"Some guy had stepped on a booby trap and they were calling for evacuation—for a helicopter to take him. So we had to set up a ring—for the helicopter to land—to guard the helicopter. I just happened to be standing

alongside the officer when the radio man said, 'Look, sir, we got children rounded up. What do you want us to do with them?' The guy says, 'Goddam it, marine, you know what to do with them. Kill the bastards. If you ain't got the goddam balls to kill them, marine, I'll come down there and kill the motherfuckers myself.' The marine said, 'Yes, sir,' and hung up the phone. About 2 or 3 minutes later I heard a lot of automatic fire—and a lot of children's screaming. I heard babies crying. I heard children screaming their fucking lungs out. I heard 'em. And that got next to me. I heard a machine gun go off. You know a machine gun when you hear it. There were a lot of children. It lasted only 20 or 30 seconds. We didn't, they didn't get all the children, though. 'Cause the next day we went into some other hamlets. And I saw a little girl. It really bugged me—I knew her parents had been killed. She had her little brother with her. It

had to be her little brother. She was carrying him. She was just standing there—like 'What is going on?' She saw us tear the hamlet apart. . . This little girl is standing there looking at us. She don't know what to say. As we walk by she's just looking at us. Her little brother is crying, but she's just looking at us, sort of puzzled. Sort of in a daze. She was about 5 or 6 years old. The baby was less than a year old. We left her under the tree. I don't know—I'm scared to say—but I think they killed that kid. I left. I didn't want to see it. I knew some guy was going to come along and shoot her while I was standing there—and I couldn't stand to see that. So I left. I'm sure some guy killed her.

"That was the only huge massacre I was in." (From: *Conversations with Americans* by Mark Lane. New York, Simon & Schuster, 1970.)

—D.W.

Invitation to the Reader

We hope that you have found *The People's Almanac* to be of interest and value, and we hope that your minds and emotions have been stimulated. But now, if we have our wish, it is your turn to stimulate us to help make the 2nd edition of *The People's Almanac* much better and even more comprehensive than the 1st.

If there is any subject you missed that you would like to read about in the next *Almanac*, tell us what it is and we will try to include it. If you or your friends have written something that you think belongs in a future *Almanac*, please send us a copy. Our address is:

The People's Almanac
P.O. Box 49328
Los Angeles, Calif. 90049

We will pay for anything we publish. If you want your material returned, please include a stamped, self-addressed envelope with your submission.

Further, if you have a specialty, an observation, an experience, an unusual or inside bit of knowledge, please let us know about it. If you have books to recommend, recipes or household hints to share, utopias to discuss, or general knowledge to pass on, please write us

about it—and through us let people everywhere be informed and entertained.

As to the present *Almanac*, if there is anything in it that confused you, please ask us to explain. We shall be happy to do so. If you have found any facts that are wrong or discovered any major omissions, please let us know. We will eagerly correct the errors or fill in what is missing in editions to follow. Too, we will be interested to know what you liked most in *The People's Almanac*, as well as what you disliked most.

Above all, we visualize this as a participatory *Almanac*, one in which people will involve themselves by collaborating to make it the perfect reference book to be read for pleasure. We hope the pages in editions-to-come will reflect your interests as well as our own. It is only through airing and sharing ideas that new solutions can be found to deal with the many problems of modern society. So let us know what you have learned to this point in your lives, and together we can try to transform our dreams into reality.

DAVID WALLECHINSKY
IRVING WALLACE

Index

Aaron, Hank, 258
Aaron Burr Association, 1249
Abbey of Thélème, 526; utopia, 1419
ABC (Madrid), 787
Abdul-Jabbar, Kareem, 1180
Abel, Rudolf, 650
A-bomb, 237; aftereffects of, 508; development of, 508; 1st used, 507
Abominable Snowman, 1348
Abu Dhabi, 481
Acropolis, 917
Across the Zodiac, 670
Actium, battle of, 616
Actors and actresses, 862
Acuna, Roberto, 1444
Adams, Abigail Smith, 261
Adams, John, 261
Adams, John (mutineer), 516
Adams, John Quincy, 263
Adams, Maude, 862
Adding machine, 1st, 910
Adelman, Bob, 1441
Aden, *see* Southern Yemen
Adenauer, Konrad, 393
Adler, Bill, 51
Adventure, An, 1384
Adventures in Living Plants, 68
Advertising: accounts, largest, 809; history of, 800; subliminal, 812; TV, 807; TV commercials, 32; in the U.S., 32
Aesop's *Fables,* 811
Afars and Issas, 471
Afghanistan, 360
Africa, German East, 458
African creation myth, 1304
Afrikaner nationalists, 450
Afro-American Unity, Organization of, 601
Afterlife and Reincarnation, 1334
After Worlds Collide, 672
Age, The (Melbourne), 788
Ages in Chaos, 930
Agnes (hurricane), 553
Agnew, Spiro, 324; resignation of, 257, 258
Agnostics, modern, 1294
Agony Column, The, 796
Air Collisions, New York, 564
Air-conditioning, 1st, 174
Aircraft disasters, 561, 565
Airplane, 1st, 909
Ajman, 481
Akeret, Robert U., 65
Alamo, the, 165, 710
Alarm clock, 1st, 910
Alaska, purchase of, 187
Alaskan Earthquake of 1964, 550
Albania, 360
Alcatraz Island, 713

Alcindor, Ferdinand ("Lew"), 1180
Alcoholics, famous, 1071
Aldrin, Edwin ("Buzz"), 510, 673, 675; *quoted,* 511, 512
Alexander the Great, 512
Alexander II, assassination of, 587
Alexandra of Russia, 998
Alfalfa, 1030
Alger, Horatio, Jr., 187, 1253
Algeria, 361
Algerine Constitution, 169
All-American football team, 1st, 200
Allen, Chris, 68
Allen, Ethan, 132
Allende, Salvador, 257, 376, 408
"Almighty Dollar, The," 166, 340
Almonds, 1027
Alphabet, Amerind, 107; invention of, 483; manual, 758
Alpha waves, 1414
Alternating current, 1st, 928
Altgeld, John P., 44
Aluminum, sources of, 415
Amendment, 24th, 248; 25th, 252; 26th, 256
"America," 849; composition of, 162
America, discovery of, 513; naming of, 493
America Gets Its Name, 493
America in Legend, 1441
American Colonization Society, 158, 422
American Connection, 71
American Express card, 341
American National Red Cross, 196
American Oil, 388
American Telephone & Telegraph, *see* AT&T
American Traveller, The, 159
America Speaks, 1438
Amerind alphabet, 107
Amin, Idi, 463
Amistad incident, 167; mutiny, 523
Amnesty International, 1249
Ampo security pact, 417
Anarchists, 72
Andaman Islands, 404
Anderson, Jack, 408, 787
Anderson, R. C. ("Doc"), 692
Andersonville prison camp, 186
Andorra, 471
Andreä, Johann V., 1419
Andreis, Felix de, 1302
Andretti, Mario, 1178
Anegad, 481
Angel, Jimmy, 466
Angle Falls, 466
Angkor, 918
Anglicanism, 1266
Angola, 362
Angostura Bitters, 461

Anguilla, 475
Animal athletes, 1222
Animal Facts and Oddities, 695
Animal magnetism, 926
Animals, facts about, 1006; laboratory use of, 931; unusual, 697
Animism, 1262
Ankole, 462
Anna O., *see* O., Anna
Antietam, battle of, 182
Antigua, 475
Antiques, 352
Antiques, selling, 351
Antiques Journal, The, 352
Antique Trader, The, 352
Antitrust suits, ITT, 408
Anti-Vivisection Society, 1249
Antiwar demonstrations, 252, 255, 256
Anzio, battle of, 233
Aparicio, Sebastian de, 1299
Apartheid, 450
Apollo II, 510
Apple, 1015
Apricot, 1016
Aqueducts, Roman, 917
Arab-Israeli War of 1967, 418
Arab Mind, 55
Arab oil embargo, 257, 258
Arango, Doroteo, *see* Villa, Francisco
Ararat, 732
Arbuckle, Fatty, 967
Archaeology, 67
Archery oddities, 1213
Archimedes, 921
Architecture, religious, 67
Ardennes, battle of, 236
Arellano, López, 399
Argentina, 363
Ariosto, Lodovico, 668
Aristotle, last will, 1326
Aristotle's Lantern, 1355
Ark, Noah's, 731
"Arkansas toothpicks," 164
Armada, defeat of the, 618
Arm & Hammer baking soda, 353
Armata, 669
Armenia, 451
Armstrong, Henry, 851
Armstrong, Louis, 892
Armstrong, Neil, 255, 510, 661, 675; *quoted*, 511, 512
Armstrong, Virginia, 1442
Arnold, Benedict, 132; court-martial of, 638; memorial to, 700; spy, 647
Arouet, François, *see* Voltaire
Arrowroot, sources of, 482
Art, Chinese, 74; erotic, 74
Arthur, Chester A., 271
Arthur, King of England, 733
Arthur, Nell Herndon, 271
Artichoke, 1021
Artificial insemination, 1st U.S., 187
Artificial respiration, 1409
Arts, The, 830
Aruba, 477
Asahi Shimbun (Tokyo), 788
Ashmun, Jehudi, 158
Asparagus, 1021
Aspasia of Miletus, 859, 861
Asphalt, sources of, 461

Assad, Hafez, 457
Assassinations, 52, 126, 186, 228, 242, 253, 256, 258, 270, 272, 288, 310, 460, 472, 504, 533; Adolf Hitler, 593; Alexander II, 587; Dan Mitrione, 605; George C. Wallace, 607; Harry S Truman, 596; Henry Frick, 589; Huey Long, 592; John F. Kennedy, 597; Malcolm X, 601; Mohandas Gandhi, 595; predictions of, 1, 2, 5, 6, 7, 10, 16, 17; Robert F. Kennedy, 603; William McKinley, 590
Assassinations—Successful and Unsuccessful, 586
Associated Press, start of, 174
Astor, John Jacob (author), 670
Astor, John Jacob, last will, 1329
Astral projection, 1390
Astronauts, earthy look at, 673; 1st female, 247, 660; U.S., 673
Astronomers, biographies of, 658; early, 658; 1st female, 659
Astronomical hoaxes, 669
Astronomy, facts and figures, 654
Atheist Association, 1250
Atheists, modern, 1291
Athletes, animal, 1222
Athletic supporter, 1st, 911
Atkins, Sharon, 1443
Atlantic Charter, 231
Atlantis, search for, 729
Atlantis: The Antediluvian World, 730
Atom bomb, 1st, 909, 920
AT&T, 362
Atterley, Joseph, *pseud.*, 669
Attic and Junkyard, 345
Attica State Prison riot, 256
Attucks, Crispus, ·129
Aubergine, 1023
Augustin I of Mexico, 427
"Auld Lang Syne," 848
Aunt Jemima pancake mix, 353
Auras, 1391
Australia, 364
Austria, 365
Authors, female, 859
Autobahn, 393
Autograph Collector's Club, 1250
Autographs, selling, 350; valuable, 349
Autogyro, 1st, 909
Automobile, classic models, 728
Automobile, 1st U.S., 148
Automobile, unusual, 725
Automobile heaters, 1st, 911
Automobile tires, 1st, 911
Auto racing greats, 1178; oddities, 1213
Autosuggestion, 525
Avocado, 1016
Avon: bottles, valuable, 348; products, 353
Awami League, 366
Awards, Oscars, 831
Ayub Khan, Mohammad, 437
Azerbaijan, 451
"Azerland," 693

Baade, Walter, 659
Baath party, 457
Baboon who ran a railroad, 697
Baby Ruth, 355
Bach, Edward, 1061
Bach flower remedies, 1061
Bach's children, 945

Bacon, Delia, 85
Bacon, Roger, 513
Bacon-Shakespeare controversy, 85
Baden-Powell, Robert, spy, 648
Bahamas, 471
Bahrain, 471
Bahutu, 446
Baker, George, *see* Father Divine
Baker, Hobart ("Hobey"), 1186
Baker, Josephine, 899
Baker-General of the U.S., 139
Baker Island, 479
Baker's chocolate, 353
Bakunin, Mikail, 1292
Balaguer, Joaquín, 384
Balaklava, battle of, 621
Balfour Declaration, 412
Ball, Ian M., 517
Ball, John, 513
Ball, Lucille, 819
Balloon, 1st, 908
Balloonists, 140
Balmer, Edwin, 672
Balvano Limited Disaster, 562
Balzac, Honoré de, 877
Banana, 1016
Banda, H. Kamuza, 424
Band-Aids, 1st, 911
Bandaranaike, Sirimavo, 454
Bangladesh, 365; cyclones, 552
BankAmericard, 342, 367; Corporation, 366
Bank of Italy, 367
Bank robberies, Civil War, 742
Banks, selling, 350
Banks, toy, 346
Banned books, 91
Bannister, Roger, 1191
Baptist Church, 1267
Baraga, Frederic, 1302
Barbados, 471; coffins, 1366
Barber Shop Quartet, Inc., 1250
Barbie doll, 355
Barbier, Charles, 521
Barbuda, 475
Barley, 1029
Barnard, Christiaan, 516
Barnum, H. L., 94
Barnum, Phineas T., 109, 702; last will, 1330
Barnum's children, 947
Barrow, Clyde, 725
Barrymore, John, 1072
Bartley, James, 1399
Barton, Bruce, 804
Barton, Clara, 196
Bartram, John, 921
Baseball, computer match, 1131; invention of, 172; Little League, 1136
Baseball cards, selling, 351
Baseball Hall of Fame, 1194
Baseball oddities, 1214
Baseball players, shortest, 1173
Baseballs, source of, 398
Baseball teams, greatest, 1131
Basic English, 749
Basilio, Carmen, *quoted,* 59
Basketball, invention of, 202
Basketball greats, 1180
Basketball oddities, 1215
Bass, Charlotte A., 127
Bastille, fall of, 514

Basutoland, *see* Lesotho
Bataan Death March, 232
Bates, William H., 921
Bathory, Elizabeth, 1338
Battalino, Christoper ("Battling"), *quoted,* 59
Battery, 1st electric, 908
"Battle Hymn of the Republic," 850
Battles, famous, 615; *see also* specific battle
Batutsi, 446
Batwa, 446
Baudouin I, 368
Baugh, Samuel ("Sammy"), 1197
Bay of Pigs, 245, 314
Beadle Dime Novels, 180
Beagle, HMS, 500
Beale, Charles, 694
Beale, Edward Fitzgerald, 625
Beam, Lura, 979
Bean, dried, 1031
Bean sprout, 1031
Beard, Dita, 408
Beatles, The, 248, 395, 893
Beaumont, Lia de, 646
Beauties & the Beasts, 62
Bechuanaland, *see* Botswana
Beckford, William, 519
Beecher, Henry Ward, 192
Beecher-Tilton Case, 192
Bee pollen, 1033
Bees, language of, 1350
Beet, 1021
Beethoven, Ludwig van, 535, 864
Beetleboarder (vocation), 344
Behavior, human, *see* Human behavior
Behavior modification, 1089
Behn, Herman, 407
Behn, Sosthenes, 407
Belgian Congo, *see* Zaire
Belgium, 367
Belize, 471
Bell, Alexander Graham, 362
Bell, Daniel, 18
Bellamy, Edward, 199, 1422
Belleau Wood, battle of, 220
Belly dancer (vocation), 344
Belorussia, 451
Benares, *see* Varanasi
Bendix, William, 817
Bentham, Jeremy, last will, 1329
Benton, William B., 852
Berg, Patty, 1182
Bergerac, Cyrano de, 668
"Berkeley Mafia," 405
Berkeley Psychic Institute, 11
Berkman, Alexander, 590; *quoted,* 589, 590
Berle, Milton, 817
Berlin, Irving, 851
Berlin Wall, building of, 245
Bermuda, 472
Bermuda Triangle, 1373
Bernays, Guillaume, 573
Bernhardt, Sarah, 863
Berries, 1016
Bessent, Malcolm, 1
Best from Books, 51
Best-selling books, 1226
Better Mousetraps, 910
Beurdeley, Michel, 74
Bhumipol Adulyadej, 459
Bhutan, 368

Biafra, 434
Biathlon, 1st, 1210
Bible, Authorized Version, 497
Bible, early translations, 496
Bible, 1st in German, 495
Bible, Gutenberg, 513
Bible, King James Version, 496
Bible, New Testament, 12
Bible statistics, 1286
Biblical creation story, 1305
Bicycle racing oddities, 1215
Bierce, Ambrose, 1292
Bifocals, invention of, 141
Billiard players, greatest, 1177
Billiards oddities, 1215
Bill of Rights, adoption, 143
Bilson, Thomas, 497
Binet-Simon IQ test, 958
Bingham, Hiram, 1290
Biographies of U.S. heroes, 72
Biology for children, 68
Birch, Harvey, 93
Bird, Robert Montgomery, 166
Birds and Bees, 1006
Birdseye, Clarence, 353
Birds Eye frozen foods, 353, 464
Birendra Bir Bikram Shah Dev, 431
Birth, see Childbirth
"Birth control" (term), 967
Birth rates, highest, 1232
Birthright of Man, 60
Bismarck, Otto von, 392
Black Bart, see Bolton, Charles
Blackberry, 1016
Blackberry cordial, recipe for, 1016
Black Death, 554
Black Elk, Ben, 1442
"Black Friday" (1869), 189
Black Hand, 504
Black mass, 526
Black Muslims, 602, 1269
Black Panthers, 254
"Black Power," 251
Blacks, IQ of, 959
Black September terrorists, 424
Blake, William, 752
Blankers-Koen, Fanny, 1192
Blavatsky, Helena P., 16
Bleeding, treatment for, 1408
Blenheim, battle of, 618
Bligh, William, 516
Blishen, Edward, 64
Block, The, 1439
Bloomer, Amelia, 87
Bloomers, origin of, 87
Blow, Henry, 178
"Bluebeard," see Landru, Henri
Blueberry, 1016
Blumberg, Dorothy, oddities from, 1355
Bly, Nellie, 88, 200
Bobbs-Merrill books, 408
Boccaccio, Giovanni, quoted, 554
Body Owner's Manual, 1053
Body snatchers, 570
Body types, 1060
Boer War, spies in, 648
Bokassa, Jean-Bedel, 375
Bok-Choi, 1022
Bolívar, Simón, 384, 466, 514
Bolivia, 368

Bolshevik party, 515
Bolton, Charles E., 89
Bolts from the Blue, 908
Bonaire, 477
Bonaparte, Napoleon, see Napoleon I
Bond, Carrie Jacobs, 898
Bond, Julian, 250
Bone injuries, treating, 1410
Bonin Islands, 478
Bonner, James, 18
Bonnie and Clyde's Last Car, 725
Book matches, 1st, 911
Book of Survival, 62
Books, best sellers, 1226; selling, 351; valuable, 348
Booth, Edwin, 863
Booth, Evangeline, 1276
Booth, John Wilkes, 288
Boot Hill cemetery, 712
Bordaberry, Juan María, 465
Borden, Lizzie, 576
Borneo, North, see Sabah
Boston Globe, The, 775
Boston Massacre, 129
Boston Tea Party, 131
Boston Women's Health Book Collective, 60
Botswana, 472
Bottle Clubs Federation, 1250
Bottles, Avon, 348
Bougainville, 438
Boulder Dam, 920
Boulding, Kenneth E., 28
Bounty mutineers, descendants of, 516
Bourguiba, Habib, 461
Bourgeoys, Marguerite, 1299
Bousbir (brothel), 430
Bowditch, Nathaniel, 147
Bowdler, Thomas, 760
Bowie knife, invention of, 164
Bowling Hall of Fame, 1195; Women's, 1196
Bowling oddities, 1216
Boxing, 58; bareknuckle, 1166; computer matches, 1144, 1148, 1149; oddities, 1216
Boycott, Charles C., 761
Boyd, Belle, 647
Boyle, W. A. ("Tony"), 255
"Boy Orator," 273
Bradbury, Ray, 672
Bradshaw, William, 694
Brady, James Buchanan ("Diamond Jim"), 90
Brady, Mathew, 181
Brahan Seer, see Odhar, C.
Brahe, Tycho, 658
Braille, Louis, 520
Brasch, R., oddities from, 1342
Brassiere, 1st, 911
Brassiere, 1st padded, 913
Brazil, 369
Brazil nuts, 1027
Bread, white, 1011
Breadfruit, 1017
Brehm, Marie Caroline, 127
Bremer, Arthur Herman, 607
Brennan, D. G., 19
Breton, André, 1293
Breuer, Josef, 502; quoted, 503
Bridge failures, Australia, 565
Bridge match of 1931, 1167
Bridges, Brooklyn, 919; Golden Gate, 920; San Luis Rey, 918

Bright, Greg, 64
Brill, Abraham A., 45
Brillat-Savarin, Anthelme, 1046
Brisbane, Albert, 1428
Bristlecone pines, oldest, 690
British Guiana, *see* Guyana
British Honduras, *see* Belize
Britton, Nan, 275
Broccoli, 1021
Brodie, Steve, 199
Brodie, William, "Deacon," 521
Broederbond (secret society), 450
Broley, Charles L., 1345
Bronstein, Lev, *see* Trotsky, Léon
Bronstein, Yette, 128
Brook Farm, 168, 1426
Brooklyn Bridge, 919
Brothels, largest, 430
Browder, Sue, 71
Brown, Edmund ("Pat"), 322
Brown, Hubert ("Rap"), 613
Brown, John, 179
Brown, Phyllis, 334
Brown, Robert W., 359
Broz, Josip, 468
Brudenell, James, court-martial of, 638
Brunei, 472
Brunn, Stanley D., following 992
Brussels sprout, 1021
Bryan, William Jennings, 273
Bubar, David, 1
Bubble gum, 356
Bubonic plague, 554
Buchanan, James, 268
Buckets, valuable, 347
Buckpasser, 1154
Buckwheat, 1029
Buddha, *see* Gautama Buddha
Buddhism, 1263
Buena Vista, battle of, 173
Buganda, 462
"Bugging," *see* Electronic eavesdropping
Buildings, highest, 1230; tallest U.S., 920
Bulgaria, 370
Bullfighting, Council against, 1250
Bulwer-Lytton, *see* Lytton
Bundling, 965
Bundy, McGeorge, 28
Bunker Hill, battle of, 133
Buñuel, Luis, 874
Bunyoro, 462
Burden, Charles, 1362
Burden v. *Hornsby*, 1362
Buried treasure, 1378
Buried treasure, U.S., 739
Burke, Martha Jane ("Calamity Jane"), 99
Burke, William, 570
"Burking," 571
Burma, 371
Burma-Shave road signs, 54
Burns, Robert, 848
Burns, treatment of, 1410
Burnside, Ambrose, 630
"Burnside's Slaughter," 630
Burr, Aaron, 1249
Burroughs, Edgar Rice, 671, 694
Burroughs, William S., 910
Burton Holmes, Inc., 100
Burundi, 371
Bushnell, David, 632

Butler, Benjamin F., 197
Butter, 1034
Butterfield, Alexander, 257
Buttermilk, 1034
Button Society, 1250
Butts, Alfred Mosher, 356
B.V.D. underwear, 356
Byng, John, court-martial of, 637
Byron, George Gordon, 885
Byron's children, 945
By the People, for the People, 1438
Byzantine Church, 1265

Cabbage, 1022; Chinese, 1022
Cabet, Étienne, 1421
Cabinda, *see* Angola
Cabrini, Frances, St., 1303
Cactus, edible, 1017
Cadbury Castle ("Camelot"), 734
CADPIN, 428
Caesar, Sid, 817
Caetano, Marcello, 442
Caiaphus, 490
Calamity Jane, *see* Burke, Martha
Calcium, 1041
Calendars, 1776 to 2000, 1416
Califa, Amazon queen, 738
California Lands, 367
Calley, William L., Jr., court-martial of, 643
Calvin, John, 1266
Calvinism, 1266
Cambodia, 372
Camel cigarettes, 353
Camel Corps, U.S., 625
"Camelot," JFK's, 315
Camelot, search for, 733
Cameras, 354; 1st Kodak, 909; 1st Polaroid, 910
Cameroon, 373
Camille (hurricane), 551
Campaign buttons, selling, 351
Campbell's soup twins, 356
Campobello, 296
Canada, 373
Canary who saved a life, 698
Cantaloupe, 1018
Canton Island, 479
Cantzen, Conrad, last will, 1332
Capet, Hugues, 389
Cape Verde Islands, 472
Caramanlis, Constantinos, 396
Carbohydrates, 1038
Carbonated drinks, 1st, 914
Card dealer (vocation), 344
Cardiff Giant, 701
Cardoon, 1022
Carême, Marc-Antoine, 1047
Carl XVI of Sweden, 455
Carlos IV of Spain, 528
Carlson, Grace, 127
Carmichael, Stokeley, 251
Carmilla, 1338
Carnegie, Andrew, last will, 1331
Carnival barker (vocation), 344
Carol II of Romania, 1243
Caroline Islands, 477
Caroline of Brunswick, last will, 1329
Carpenter, Scott, 675
Carré, Mathilde, 649
Carroll, Lewis, *see* Dodgson, C.

Carrot, 1022
Carson, Rachel, 246
Carte Blanche card, 341
Carthage, *see* Tunisia
Caruso, Enrico, 890
Carver, George Washington, 1010
Casanova, Giovanni, 995
Casey at the Bat, 200
"Casey Jones," 210
Cashew nuts, 4117
Cashless Society, The, 342
Cash register, 1st, 912
Caste system (India), 402
Castle Owners club, 1258
Castro, Fidel, 381
Catala, Magin, 1301
Catalogs, valuable, 346
Cathay, 513
Catholic Inquisition, 513
Catholicism, Roman, 1264
Cats, 74
Cat who found its family, 699
Cauliflower, 1022
Cavendish, Richard, 71
Cave paintings, 1379
Cayce, Edgar, 17
Ceausescu, Nicolae, 444
Celebrities, psychoanalyzed, 1224; real names of, 1232
Celeriac, 1022
Celery, 1022
Cement, 1st Portland, 909
Censorship in the U.S., 91
Census, history of, 78
Census Bureau, U.S., 78
Central African Republic, 375
Ceuta and Melilla, 472
Ceylon, *see* Sri Lanka
Chaco War, 439
Chad, 375
Chamberlain, Wilt, 1180
Chambers, Whittaker, 238, 319
Champollion, Jean-François, 514
Chancellorsville, battle of, 183
Chandler, Harry, 779
Chandler, Norman, 780
Chandler, Otis, 780
Chang Fu-Jui, 74
Chang Kuo-t'ao, 506
Channel Islands, 394
Channel swim, 1st, 1176, 1244
Chaplin, Charles ("Charlie"), 241, 874
Chappaquiddick—Kennedy-Kopechne accident, 255
Chard, 1022
Charlemagne, 389; crowning of, 513
Charles II of France, 513
Charlotte Temple, 144
Charms, lucky, 1092
Chase Manhattan Bank, 391
"Checkers" speech, 241, 320, 329
Checks Anonymous, 1250
Cheek, Joel, 355
Cheese, 1034
Cheese, cottage, 1035
Chefs, famous, 1045
Cheiro, *see* Hamon, Louis
Cheops, Great Pyramid of, 11, 1364
Cherokee alphabet, 107
Cherry, 1017

Chessman, Caryl, 244
Chess oddities, 1217
Chess players, mechanical, 535
Chestnuts, 1027
Chevrolet, Louis, 354
Chevrolet automobiles, 354; the 1957 classic, 728
Chevron Gas, 388
Chewing gum, 1st, 912
Chiang Ching-kuo, 458
Chiang Kai-shek, 458, 506
"Chicago 8," 42
Chicago Fire, 555
"Chicago Seven," 255
Chicago Tribune, 775
Chichi-shima Island, 478
Chickamauga, battle of, 183
Chickens, raising, 1402
Chico's Organic Gardening and Natural Living, 1435
Childbirth, emergency, 942
Child labor, U.S., 98
Children, illegitimate, 1224
Children of famous parents, 945
Children's crusade, U.S., 98
Children Tell Stories, 1442, 1445
Chile, 376
Chimney sweep (vocation), 343
China, 377; Great Wall of, 917; model citizen in, 56; Republic of, *see* Taiwan
China, selling, 350
China Letter, 815
Chinese creation myth, 1306
Chinese Erotic Art, 74
Chinese Exclusion Act, 196
Chinese riots of 1871, 190
Chlorine, 1042
Choking, treatment for, 1410
Chotiner, Murray, 320, 324
Chou En-lai, 377; *quoted,* 507
Christian, Fletcher, 516
Christian, Tom, 518
Christian Crusade, 358, 1284
Christianity, 1264
Christianopolis, 1419
Christian Science Church, 1268
Christian Science Monitor, 776
Christie, Agatha, 903
Christmas Island, 478
Christmas tree farmer (vocation), 344
Chromium, 1042
Chrysler, Walter, 391
Chubbuck, Chris, 258
Church, Francis P., 1358
Church, James A., 353
Church architecture, 67
Churchill, John, 618
Churchill, Winston, 455
Churchill, Winston, last will, 1333
Church of Christ, Scientist, 1268
Church of England, 1266
Church of Jesus Christ of Latter-Day Saints, 121, 1267
Church of Scientology, 356, 358
Cieplak, Jan, 1304
Cinque, "Field Marshall," 258
Cinque (mutineer), 523
Cinque Ports, 539
CIO, formation of, 228
Circus Fans' Association, 1250

Citadels of Mystery, 733
Citation, 1154
Cities, coolest, 1231
Cities, highest, 1229
Cities, largest ancient, 918
Cities, most populous, 1228
Cities, oldest, 1228
Cities, warmest, 1231
Citizen Kane, 715
City vegetable gardens, 1401
Civil Rights Acts of 1964, 248
Clairvoyance, 1388
Claret, Anthony, St., 1303
Clari, the Maid of Milan, 849
Clarke, Arthur C., 19
Clark University (Mass.), 45
Claudius I, 994
Clay, Cassius, abolitionist, 170
Cleland, John, 524
Clemens, Samuel, 754; boyhood home, 709
Cleopatra, 1963 film, 247
Cleveland, Frances Folsom, 271
Cleveland, Grover, 271
Climate, man-made changes in, 931
Clocks, selling, 350; valuable, 349
Closynski, Bernadette, 1442
Clover, 1030
Cloves, sources of, 459
Clown (vocation), 343
Clowns of America, 1251
Coates, Robert, 524
Cobalt, 1042
Cobb, Tyrus ("Ty"), 1194
Coca-Cola, 354, 1009, 1349
Cochrane, Elizabeth, *see* Bly, Nellie
Coco, Imogene, 817
Cocoa, sources of, 393
Coconut, 1017
Cody, William ("Buffalo Bill"), 99
Coelacanth, 1345
Coffee, sources of, 380
Coffins, "moving," 1366
Coins, selling, 351; valuable, 346
Coin's Financial School, 204
"Cold War," 306
Collards, 1022
Collazo, Oscar, 597
Collectibles, selling, 350; valuable, 345
Collectives, Spanish, 1432
Collectors' magazines, 352
Collector's News, 352
Collector's Weekly, 352
Collett, Glenna, 1185
Collins, Michael, 510, 675
Collins, Ted, 907
Colombia, 379
Colonía Dublan, 122
Colonía Juárez, 122
Colt revolver, 1st, 163
Columbia, 511
Columbus, Bartholomew, 398
Columbus, Christopher, 384, 399, 443, 493, 513,
  735; last will, 1327
Columbus of Space, A, 671
COMECON, 445
Comets and meteors, facts about, 655
Comic Book Fans, 1251
Comic books, selling, 351; valuable, 347
Comic strips, early, 206, 213
Coming Race, The, 693

Committee for Industrial Organization, *see*
  CIO
Common Cause, 1251
Common Sense, 134; publishing of, 752
Common Sense Book of Baby and Child Care,
  1435
Commonwealth, The (utopia), 1420.
Communication, electronic, 921
Communications, 746
Communion wafers, recipe, 61
Communism, 1270; in the U.S., 239
Communist Manifesto, 498; *quoted,* 499
Comoro Islands, 472
Composers, classical, 864; modern, 868; offbeat,
  898
Compost, making, 1401
Compromise of 1850, 174
Computer, 1st, 910
Computer matches, baseball, 1131; boxing, 1144,
  1148, 1149; horse races, 1153
Computers, 932; 1st U.S., 237
Comstock, Anthony, 91; last will, 1331
Concentration camps, Nazi, 236
Confederate Descendants in Mexico, 120
Congo, 380
Congregational Churches, 1268
Congress of Vienna, 476
Conigliano, Emmanuele, 527
Connolly, Maureen, 1188
Connally, John B., 599
Consolidator, 669
Constantinople, battle of, 617
Constitutional Convention, 141
Consumer credit counseling, 342
Consumer Newsweek, 813
Consumer's Education Assn., 1251
Continental Bakeries, 408
Contogeorge, Athanasios, 1373
Contraceptive pills, 1st, 244
Contraceptives, 964; oral, 968
Contrary Investor, The, 814
Conversations with Americans, 1446
Cook, Mrs., last will, 1331
Cook, James, Captain, 481
Cook Islands, 472
Cooks, famous, 1045
Cook's Continental Timetable, 723
Coolidge, Calvin, 275
Coolidge, Grace Goodhue, 275
Cooper, Gordon, 660
Cooper, James Fenimore, 92
Coors, Adolph, murder of, 610
Copernicus, Nicholas, 658; theory of, 514
Copper, 1042; sources of, 438
Coptic Church, 1265
Copywriting, development of, 804
Coral Sea, battle of, 232
Cork, sources of, 442
Corn, 1022
Corrigan, Douglas, 1244
Corvair, safety of, 392
Cosa Nostra, *see* Mafia
Così Fan Tutte, 527
Cosmographiae introductio, 493
Costa Rica, 380
Cottage cheese, 1035
Cotton gin, 144; 1st, 908
Coué, Émile, 525
Coughlin, Charles (Father), 1278
Count Dracula Society, 1251

Countries, largest, 1227; most populous, 1227
Country Music Encyclopedia, 63
Couplings and Groupings, 1443
Court-Martials around the World, 637
Cousy, Robert, 1180
Coverdale, Miles, 496
Cowpens, battle of, 138
Cox, Archibald, 257
Cox, Patricia ("Tricia") Nixon, 321
Coxey's Army, 205
Cozzini, Georgia, 127
Cranberry, 1016
Crane, Clarence A., 355
Crane, Hart, 1072
Crane, Stephen, 754
Crank, 1st use of, 918
Crapper, Thomas, 919
"Craps," origin of term, 153
Cream, 1035; sour, 1036
Cream, Thomas Neill, 572
Creation myths, 1304
Credit cards, 341; cost of, 341; history of, 341
Credit Jungle, The, 342
Crete, 396
Crime, organized, 62
Crimean War, 796
Crime in the U.S., 62, 239
Crime statistics, 1225
Crippen, Hawley Harvey, 578
Cripps, Stafford, 1052
Criswell, Jeron King, 2
Critias, 729
Crosby, Enoch, 92
Crosby, Harry L. ("Bing"), 1233
Crossword puzzles, history of, 1170
Crowell, Joan, 68
Crowley, Aleister, 526
Crusades, the, 491
Crusoe, Robinson, 539
Crystal, Freddie, 741
Cuba, 381; blockade of, 247
Cuban Revolution, 243
Cube, prehistoric, 1369
Cucumber, 1023
Culbertson, Ely, 1167
Culbertson, Josephine, 1167
Culebra, island of, 443
Curaçao, 477
Curiosity Shop, 1340
Currant, 1017
Currier & Ives prints, selling, 351; valuable, 349
Curve of Binding Energy, 69
Cycles, 55
Cyclones, Bangladesh, 552; Pakistan, 552
Cylinder lock, 1st, 912
Cyprus, 462, 472
Cyrenaica, 423
Czechoslovakia, 382
Czolgosz, Leon, 591

Dacia, *see* Romania
Dahomey, 382
Dáil Cireann, 411
Daily News (New York), 781
Dairy products, directory of, 1033
Dalepa, Raimundo, *quoted,* 431
Dam, Boulder, 920
Dams, failure of, 560
Dancers, 871; offbeat, 899
Dancing Cuckoos club, 1259

Dandelion, 1023
Danger, Eric P., 57
Daniel, Gabriel, 669
Daniel, Margaret Truman, 303
Daredevils, U.S., 161
Darrah, Lydia, 647
Darrow, Clarence, 1295
Darvall, Denise Ann, 516
Darwin, Charles, 500, 1294; *quoted,* 501
Dassin, Jules, 396
Date, 1017
Daud, Sadar Mohammed, 360
Davies, Marion, 715, 901
Davis, Angela Yvonne, 613
Davis, Jefferson, last will, 1330
Davis, Katharine B., 978
Dawes, William, 115
Dawn Man, 101
Dawn Woman, 101
Daylight Saving Time, 1st, 220
Daytime Serial Newsletter, 816
D-day, 234, 515
"Dead man's hand," 99
Dean, John, 256
"Dearos," 96
Death: Do-It-Yourself, 1320
Death rates, highest, 1232
Debs, Eugene V., home of, 706
DeCarlo, Charles, 20
Decatur, Stephen, Sr., 146
Declaration of Independence, 134
Declaration of Independence, Descendants of
  Signers, 1258
"Deep Ops," 630
Deep-sea life, 666
Defoe, Daniel, 540, 669
De Freeze, Donald ("Cinque"), 258
DeFreeze, Donald D., 523
De Koven, Jean, 583
Delane, John Thadeus, 795
DeLouise, Joseph, 4
Delta Queen, riverboat, 707
Democratic Convention of 1968, 254
Dempsey, Jack, *quoted,* 58
Dempsey v. Marciano, 1146
Denmark, 383
Denver Post, The, 777
Depression of the 1830s, 1428
Depressions, 1st U.S., 166
Dervishes, whirling, 462
Descartes, René, 1295
"Detente" with Russia, 327
Devil's footprints, 1368
Devil's Island, 473
Dewey, Edward R., 55
Dewey, Thomas E., 305
DEW System, ITT control of, 408
Diamonds, sources of, 449, 450
Díaz, Porfirio, 122
Dickens, Charles, 878; last will, 1330
Dickinson, Angie, 311
Dickinson, Robert L., 979
Dictionaries, 1st U.S., 149, 160
Dictionary of Sex Terms, 970
Didius Julianus, 533
Didrikson, Babe, *see* Zaharias
Diego Garcia, 473
Dienbienphu, battle of, 624
Diesel, Rudolph, 762
Diet of Worms, 495

Digby, Robert, 119
"Digby Chicken," 119
Diners Club card, 341
Ding-a-Ling Club, 1251
Dio Cassius, *quoted*, 534
Dionne Quintuplets, 1241
Directory, The People's, 1249
Dirigible, 1st, 909
Disappearances, 1370, 1373, 1376
Disasters, aircraft, 561, 565; Man-Made, 554;
    marine, 558, 563, 565; Natural, 543; rail, 562,
    564, 566; school bus, 566; table of, 567
Disasters and Violence, 543
Disney items, valuable, 348
Distant Early Warning System, *see* DEW
Divine, Father, *see* Father Divine
Diving oddities, 1221
Dix, Dorothea, 168
"Dixie," 850
Dixon, Jeane, 4
Dr. Scholl's foot aids, 355
Doctors' Mob of 1788, 117
Documents, selling, 350
Dodecanese Islands, 396
Dodge, Mary Mapes, 432
Dodgson, Charles, 902
Dodo bird, 477, 1347
Doenitz, Karl, 1245
Dogs, biting breeds, 1225
Dogs, tributes to, 1361
Dog who saved 40 lives, 697
Dog who was a sentry, 697
Dog who was a world traveler, 699
Dog who went 3,000 miles, 699
Dog with ESP, 698
Dohrn, Bernadine Rae, 613
Dole, Sanford B., 204
Dollar, shrinking value of, 340
Dollar bill, U.S., 340
Dolls, selling, 350
Dolphins, use of in war, 627
Dominica, 482
Donner party, 172
Dominican Republic, 384
Don Giovanni, 527
Donne, John, last will, 1327
Donnelly, Ignatius, 730
Donner party, 172
"Don't give up the ship," 153
Doolin, Dennis J., 56
Dorado, *see* El Dorado
Dorr, Thomas, 168, 169
Dorson, Richard M., 1441
Dostoevski, Fëdor, 1296
Douglas, Helen Gahagan, 319
Douglas, Stephen, 285
Douglas, William O., 335
Down Home, 1441
Down to Earth, 677
Dowsers, Inc., 1251
Dowsing, 1397
Doyle, Arthur Conan, 1235
Dracula, 1338; castle of, 445
Dracula Society, 1251
Draft dodgers, W.W. I, 220
Draft riots of 1863, 183
Drayton, Grace Gebbie, 356
Dream Millennium, The, 673
Dreams, anthology of, 74; of famous people, 74
Dred Scott decision, 177

Dressmaking, 61
Drexel, Katherine, 1304
Dreyfus, Alfred, court-martial of, 640
Dror, Yehezkel, 29
Droughts, African, 427
Drug industry, ethics of, 59, 71
Drugs chronology of, 1075; mind-altering, 250
"Dry guillotine," 473
Dubai, 481
Dubble Bubble gum, 356
Dubcek, Alexander, 1247
DuBois, W. E. B., 211
Duchamp, Marcel, 216
Duchesne, Rose Phillipine, 1301
"Duchess, The," 275
Dugong, 1351
Dumas, Alexandre, 1365
Dumas's children, 946
Dunbar, Paul Lawrence, 211
Duncan, Isadora, 871
Dune, 673
Dune Messiah, 673
Dunleavy, Francis J., 407
Dunn, Bill, 1440
Du Pont family, 391
Durant, William C., 354, 391
Durian, 1017
Dutch Guiana, *see* Surinam
Duvalier, François ("Papa Doc"), 398
Duvalier, Jean-Claude ("Baby Doc"), 398
Dwellings, 1st, 916
Dyer, John Lewis, 1271
Dying Swan, The, 873

Eagle, 511
Eagle banding, 1345
Eagleton, Thomas, 257, 326
Eagle who was a mascot, 698
Earth, facts about, 654, 677; history of, 1311;
    interior of, 691
Earth in Upheaval, 930
Earthquakes, Alaska, 550; biggest, 544; Japan,
    548; Peru, 552; San Francisco, 546
Easter Island, 376, 478, 1377
Eastern Orthodox churches, 1265
Eastern Seaboard Hurricane, 550
East Germany, 392
Eastman, George, 199, 354
Eavesdropping, electronic, 359
Echeverría, Luis, 429
Ecology, preservation of, 246
Economy (utopia), 1425
Ecuador, 384
Eddison, E. R., 671
Eddy, Mary Baker, 776, 1268; last will, 1331
Eddy, Nelson, 905
Ederle, Gertrude, 1240
Edison, Thomas Alva, 120; last will, 1332
Edmonds, Emma, 648
Edmunds Act of 1872, 121
Education, 64
Edwards, Ralph, 818
Efik-Ibibio creation myth, 1304
Eggplant, 1023
Eggs, 1013
Egypt, 385
Egyptian creation myth, 1306
Ehrlich, Paul R., 20, 1261
Ehrlichman, John D., 257, 259
"Eight-Eyed Spy," 650

Eight-hour day, fight for, 40
Eikerenkoetter, Frederick, 1285
Einstein, Albert, 514; last will, 1333
Eire, 411
Eisemann-Schier, Ruth, 612
Eisenhower, David, 325
Eisenhower, Dwight D. ("Ike"), 276
Eisenhower, Julie Nixon, 321
Eisenhower, Mamie Doud, 276
Eisenstein, Sergei, 875
El Dorado, search for, 737
Electrical shock, handling, 1410
Electric battery, 1st, 908
Electric generator, 1st, 909
Electric light, 1st, 909
Electrocution, 1st nonhuman, 131; 1st U.S., 201
Electronic eavesdropping, 359
Eletronic Invasion, The, 359
Electronic money transfer, 343
Elephant Man, 536
Elephant who was the biggest, 699
Elijah Muhammad, 602
Elizabeth II of England, 396
Ellice Islands, 474
Ellis, Henry Havelock, 976
Ellsberg, Daniel, 256, 257
El Salvador, 386
Emancipation Proclamation, 182, 289
Emeralds, sources of, 380
Emergency childbirth, 942
Emerson, Ralph Waldo, 86; *quoted,* 493
Emerson, Willis George, 694
Emmett, Dan D., 850
Empire State Building, 920
Enco Gas, 388
Encyclopaedia Britannica, 953
Encyclopedia of the Unexplained, 71
Enderbury Island, 479
End Poverty in California, *see* EPIC Campaign
"Enemies List," Nixon's, 256, 358
Energy, alternate sources of, 935; problem, 933
Engel, George, 41, 44; *quoted,* 43, 44
Engels, Friedrich, 498
Engineering feats, 916; table of, 916
English, Basic, 749
English Channel swim, 1st, 1176, 1240
Enigmatic lands, 1375
Enjay Gas, 388
Enola Gay, 507
Enovid, 244
Eon, Charles d', 646
EPIC Campaign, 48
Epidemics, influenza, 547
Epirus, 396
Episcopal Church, 1266
Epitaphs, 1318
Epizootic of 1872, 191
Epstein, Brian, 893
Equatorial Guinea, 473
Equity (utopia), 1429
"Era of Good Feelings," 263
Erasers, 1st, 913
Erikson, Leif, 436
Eritrea, 387
Eritrean Liberation Front, 388
Erskine, Thomas, 669
Escort, male (vocation), 345
ESP, 676, 927, 1386
Esperanto, 749
Espionage Act, passage of, 220

"Essay on Man," 542
"Essay on Woman," 542
Essenin, Serge, 872
Esso Gas, 388
Estonia, 451
Ethiopia, 387
ETI, 663
Etidorpha, 694
Eugenic experiments, human, 1431
Europe, Allied invasion, 515
Evangelists, 1270
Evans, Oliver, 148
Excélsior (Mexico City), 789
Exercise, 70
Exiles, U.S., 112, 118
Exodus from Egypt, 512
Exotique Dancers' League, 1251
Expectant Fathers' Day Association, 1252
Experiment in International Living, 1252
Explosions, *Fort Stikine,* 563; *Hindenburg,* 561;
  New London School, 560
Extrasensory perception, *see* ESP
Extraterrestrial intelligence, *see* ETI
Extraterrestrial life forms, 663
Exxon, 388
Eyadéma, Étienne, 460
Eye Relaxation (Bates'), 922
Eyesight, abnormal, 59

Facts, odd and unusual, 1340
Fahrenheit, Gabriel D., 954
"Fair Deal" program, 306
Fairfax, Sally, 279, 280
Faith healing, 1283, 1373
Falange, The, 453
Falla, 301
False teeth, Washington's, 280
Family, The, 939
Family Reference Shelf, 953
Famines, African, 427
Famous First Facts, oddities from, 1341
Famous people, most hated, 1225
Fancher, Mollie, 1355
Fancher Train massacre, 178
Fangio, Juan Manuel, 1178
Fanny Hill, 524
Fantastical Excursion into the Planets, A, 670
Fantasy broker (vocation), 345
Faraday, Michael, 924
Farewell America, 52
Farquhar, John, 520
Father Divine, 1275
Fats, 1037
Fava bean, 1031
FBI's 10-Most-Wanted List, 608
Federal Reserve notes, 340
Feinberg, Gerald, 21
Feminists, 53, 72
Fennel, 1023
Ferdinand, *see* Francis Ferdinand
Ferenczi, Sandor, 45
Ferm, Alexis, 1431, 1432
Ferm, Elizabeth, 1431, 1432
Ferrer Colony, 1431
Ferrer Modern School, 1431
Ferrie, David, 601
Ferris wheel, 919
Fetishism, 74
Fezzan, 423
Fiddlers' Association, 1252

Fielden, Samuel, 41, 44
Field events oddities, 1221
Fields, William C., last will, 1332
Fig, 1018
Figaro, Le (Paris), 790
Fiji, 473
Filberts, 1027
Fillmore, Abigail Powers, 267
Fillmore, Millard, 267, 1255
Filmlore Game, 847
Films, biggest earners, 830
FinanceAmerica Corporation, 367
Finder of the unusual (vocation), 345
Finding your way when lost, 1403, 1405
Finland, 389
Firearms, selling, 351
Fires, Chicago of 1871, 555; forest, *see* Forest
  fires; Iroquois Theater, 557; London of 1666,
  554; unusual, 1374
First-aid, 1407
First 1st President, 261
First Men in the Moon, The, 671
Fischer, Adolph, 41, 43, 44; *quoted,* 43, 44
Fish, Williston, 1360
Fission, nuclear, 933
FitzGerald, Edward, 954
Fitzgerald, F. Scott, 1074
Fitzgerald, John ("Honey Fitz"), 95, 310
Flagellation, 964
Flagstad, Kirsten, 891
Flat Earth Society, 1252
Flea Market Quarterly, 352
Flight 19, disappearance of, 1373
Flint, Charles R., 406
Floods, 549; Johnstown, 556; St. Francis Dam,
  560
Florence, 413
Flower "language," 758
Flower remedies, 1061
Flowers, largest, 426
"Flu," *see* Influenza
Fluoridation of water, 1st U.S., 236
Fluorine, 1042
Fokine, Michel, 873
Folk art, selling, 351; valuable, 347
Fonthill, 519
Food, growing your own, 1399
Foods, U.S. favorites, 1009
Football, 1st All-American team, 200;
  oddities, 1217
Football Hall of Fame, 1197
Foot binding, 74
Foot boxing, 459
Footnote People in U.S. History, 85
Footnote People in World History, 518
Footprints, the devil's, 1368
Ford, Betty Bloomer, 334
Ford, Gerald Rudolph, Jr., 328, 333;
  President, 259; Vice-President, 257
Ford, Henry, 215, 216, 218; last will, 1332;
  museum of, 705
Ford's "Peace Ship," 218
Forest fire lookout (vocation), 344
Forest fires, Tillamook, 548
Forgery and forgers, 531
Forrest, Nathan, 184
Forrestal, James, 1322
Forster, Edward M., 694
Fort Dix Stockade, 68
Fortean Organization, 1252

Fort Jefferson, 710
Fort Stikine Explosion, 563
Fort Sumter, attack on, 180
Fort Ticonderoga, attack on, 132
Fountain pen, 1st, 912
Fourier, Charles, 1420, 1427
Fourier phalanx movement, 1426, 1427
"Fourteen Points," 220
Fox sisters, 1393
Foy, Eddie, 557
Foyt, A. J., 1179
France, 389
Francisco Ferrer Assn., 1431
Francis Ferdinand of Austria, 504
Franco, Francisco, 453
Franklin, Benjamin, 130; last will, 1328
Franklin's children, 945
Frederick Barbarossa, 492
Fredericksburg, battle of, 182, 630
Freedom, 356, 358
Freedom of Information Center, 1252
"Freedom Riders," 245
Freedom, 660
Freeman, Orville, 21
Free Speech Movement, Berkeley, 249
FRELIMO, 430
French Guiana, 473
French Revolution, 144, 514
Freud, Sigmund, 45, 503
Freud-Jung split, cause of, 48
Freud's children, 948
Freud Visits America, 45
Frick, Henry Clay, 203; assassination
  attempt, 589
Friend, Jeanette G., 1442
Friendly Islands, *see* Tonga
Friends of Animals, 1252
Friends of the Earth, 1252
Friends of Micronesia, 1253
Frisbee Association, 1253
Fritchie, Barbara, house of, 701
Fromm, Erich, *quoted,* 34
From the Earth to the Moon, 670
Front de Libération Québec, 374
Front Page in the U.S., 775
Frost, Robert, 314, 1293
Frozen foods, 1st U.S., 353
Fruits, directory of, 1015
Fuchs, Klaus, 509, 649
Fugate, Caril, 585
Fugitives, radical, 613; *see* FBI's 10-Most-
  Wanted List
Fujairah, 481
Fuller, Alfred C., 356
Fuller, Buckminster, Jr., 1435
Fuller, Margaret, 1429
Fuller Brush man, 356
Fulton, Robert, 149
Function of the Orgasm, 1002
Funny Funny World, 814
Fust, Johann, 513

Gable, Clark, last will, 1333
Gabon, 473
Gaedel, Edward, 1173
Gagarin, Yuri, 245, 660
Gairy, Eric M., 474
Galápagos Islands, 385, 500
Gale Research Co., 956
Galileo, 658

Gallery of Painters, 853
Gallery of Performers, 862
Gallery of Scientists, 921
Gallup Poll, sampling of, 827
Galveston Tidal Wave, 545
Gambia, The, 473
Gambler's Anonymous, 1253
Gandhi, Mohandas K. ("Mahatma"), 403, 1051; assassination of, 595
Garbanzo beans, 1031
Garbo, Greta, 876
Garby, Lee H., 671
García, Kjell Laugerud, 397
Gardens, city, 1401
Garfield, James A., 126, 270
Garfield, Lucretia Rudolph, 270
Gargantua, Bk.I, 1419
Garlic, 1023
Garrick, David, last will, 1328
Garrison, Jim, 598
Gary, Joseph Eaton, 42; *quoted,* 44
Gas rationing, W.W. II, 232
Gat, narcotic shrub, 468
Gates of Horn and Ivory, 74
Gatling, Richard J. 182
Gautama Buddha, 1263
Gays, *see* Homosexuals
Gehrig, Henry L. ("Lou"), 1195
Geneen, Harold Sydney, 407
General Electric, 390
General Motors, 391
"General Sherman" (tree), 690
Generator, 1st electric, 909
Georgia (U.S.S.R.), 451
Gerard, Richard H., 851
German East Africa, 458
Germany, 392
Geronimo, 197
Gershwin, George, 868
Gettysburg, battle of, 183
Gettysburg Address, 184
Ghana, 393
Ghosts, 1394
Giacometti, Alberto, 888
Giannini, Amadeo Peter, 367
"G.I. Bill of Rights," 235
Gibraltar, 474
Gibson Code, 750
Gilbert and Ellice Islands, 474
Gillette, King C., 354
Ginzburg, Ralph, 968
Giscard d'Estaing, Valéry, 390
Glass, selling, 350
Gleason, Jackie, 817, 819
Glenn, John, 246, 660, 674
Goddess of Atvatabar, 694
Godfrey of Bouillon, 492
Godoy, Manuel de, 528
Godse, Nathuram, 595
Godwin, Francis, 668
Godwin, John, oddities from, 1354
Godwin, Paul M. B., 56
Goethals, George W., 919
Gogh, Vincent van, 857
Golan Heights, 457
Golden Gate Bridge, 920
Golden Rule, versions of, 1314
"Golden washtub," 743
Goldman, Emma, 72, 590, 591; arrest of, 590; *quoted,* 590, 591

Golfers, worst, 1340
Golf greats, 1182
Golf oddities, 1217
Good Bears of the World, 1253
Good-bye, Cruel World, 1324
Good Cook, A, 61
Good luck charms, 1092
Good Soldier: Schweik, 382
Good Times, 1439
Goodyear, Charles, 167
Goose, Elizabeth Foster, 940
Gopher Prairie, 703
Gordon, Charles ("Chinese"), 455
Gordon, Theodore J., 22
Göring, Hermann, *quoted,* 653
Gorki, Maxim, 1293
Goro, Herb, 1439
Gortner, Marjoe, 1286
Gourier, "Père," 569
Gourmands, 90, 569
Gowon, Yakubu, 434
Goya y Lucientes, Francisco, 856
Graffiti, 755
Graham, Katherine, 786
Graham, Sylvester, 1050
Graham, William ("Billy"), 1280
Grains, directory of, 1028
Granadilla, 1020
Grange, Harold ("Red"), 1197
Grant, Ellen ("Nellie"), 269
Grant, Hank, 847
Grant, Julia Dent, 269
Grant, Ulysses S., 269, 1073
Grape, 1018
Grapefruit, 1018
Grasset, André, St., 1301
Gravity, discovery of, 514
Gray, H. Judd, 580
Great Britain, 394; German rocket attacks on, 235
Great Fire of London, 554
Great Plains, history of, 53
Great Pyramid of Cheops, 11
Great Stone of Sardis, 694
Great Train Robbery, 211
Great Wall of China, 917
Greco, El, 59
Greece, 396, 462
Greek creation myth, 1307
Greeley, Horace, 1428
Green, Stephanie, 1445
"Greenbacks," 340
Greenbank, Anthony, 62
Green Bank Formula, 665
Greenfield Village, 705
Green Hills of Earth, The, 672
Greenland, 436, 474
Greg, Percy, 670
Greg Bright's Maze Book, 64
Gregory, Dick, 1053
Grenada, 474
Grey, Zane, 755
Greyhound bus, 354
Greystoke, Lord, *see* Tarzan
Grier, Roosevelt ("Rosey"), 604
Griffin, Al, 342
Griffith, David W., 877
Griffith, George, *pseud.,* 671
Grimaldi, House of, 477
Guadalcanal, battle of, 232

Guadeloupe, 474
Guam, 474
Guano, sources of, 477
Guatemala, 396
Guava, 1018
Guerin, Theodore (Mother), 1302
Guernica, 859
Guess, George, *see* Sequoyah
Guevara, Ernesto ("Che"), 369
Guillotine, Joseph I., 762
Guinea, 397
Guinea-Bissau, 475
Guinness Book of World Records, oddities from, 1340
Gulf of Tonkin Resolution, 249
Gunderson, Genevieve, 127
Gunpowder, invention of, 513
Gutenberg Bible, 513
Guthrie, Woody, 869
Guyana, 475
Gwin, William M., 120
Gwyn, Nell, last will, 1327
Gypsies, 445
Gypsy creation myth, 1308

Ha'aretz (Tel Aviv), 791
Habyalimana, Juvenal, 445
Hachiya, Michihiko, *quoted,* 509
Haden-Guest, Anthony, 56
Hafez, E. S. E., 22
Hagen, Walter, 1183
Hahnemann, Samuel, 1060
Haines, John, 689
Hair care, 69
Haiti, 398
Haldeman, Harry R. (Bob), 257, 259
Hale, Edward Everett, 112
Hale, George E., 659
Hale, Nathan, 647
Hale, Sarah J., 160
Hall, Granville Stanley, 45
Hall, Monty, 1435
Hall of Fame, baseball, 1194; bowling, 1195, 1196; football, 1197
Halo, origin of, 1343
Hamburger, Robert, 1441, 1445
Hamburgerology, 56
Hamburger University, 56
Hamilton, Gilbert V. T., 977
Hamilton, Russel, 1445
Hammett, Dashiell, 903
Hammurabi's code of laws, 512
Hamon, Louis, 16
Hanks, Nancy, *see* Lincoln
Hannibal, Mo., 709
Hanson, John, 261
Hans Pfall, Adventures of, 669
"Happy Birthday," 851
Hard Day's Night, 894
Harden-Hickey, James, 1321
Harding, Florence Kling, 275
Harding, Warren G., 126, 275
Hare, William, 570
Hargis, Billy James, 358, 1284
Hargreaves, Robert, 70
Harmon, Thomas ("Tom"), 1197
Harmony (utopia), 1420
Harmony Society, 1425
Harness racing oddities, 1218
Harpers Ferry, attack on, 179

Harris, Mary ("Mother Jones"), 97
Harrison, Benjamin, 272
Harrison, Caroline Scott, 272
Harrison, George, 893
Harrison, William Henry, 265
Hartford Convention, 151
Hartford Life Insurance, 408
Hašek, Jaroslav, 382
Hassan II, 430
Hastings, battle of, 617
Hated people, 1225
Hauntings, 1394
Hauser, Kaspar, 1367
Hawaii, annexation of, 207; Republic of, 204
Hawaii Volcanoes National Park, 716
Hawkins, Gerald S., 1376
Hawthorne, Nathaniel, 86
Hayakawa, Samuel Ichiye, 254
Hayden, Tom, 255
Hayes, Lucy Webb, 270
Hayes, Rutherford B., 270
Haymarket Affair, 40
Haywood, Big Bill, 212, 213
Hazelnuts, 1027
Health and Well Being, 1009
Hearst, Patricia, 258, 614
Hearst, Randolph, 258
Hearst, William Randolph, 715, 901
Heart transplants, 1st, 516
Heaters, 1st automobile, 911
Heath, Neville, 584
Heavyweight champion, all-time, 1144, 1148
Hebrews, Epistle to the, 860
Hector Servadac, 670
Hegel, Georg W. F., 1296
Heine, Heinrich, last will, 1330
Heinlein, Robert A., 672, 673
Heinz, Henry J., 188, 354
Heinz 57 varieties, 354
Heller, Peter, 58
Hellfire Club, 542
Helmer, Olaf, 22
Hemings, Sally, 262
Hemingway, Ernest, last will, 1333
Hendrickson, Robert A., 342
Henfrey, Colin, 1442
Henrietta Maria of England, 530
Henry, Albert, 472
Henry, O., *see* Porter, William S.
Henry, Patrick, last will, 1328
Henry, Thomas, oddities from, 1349
Henry VIII, 1266
Henry VIII, last will, 1327
Henry Ford Museum, 705
Hepburn, James, *pseud.,* 52
Herben, William N., 694
Herbert, Frank, 673
Herculaneum, 543
Hermaphrodites, vertebrate, 667
"Hermitage, The," 264
Herodianus, 533
Herodotus, *quoted,* 484
Heroes, favorite, 1224
Hero in America, The, 72
Heroines, favorite, 1224
Hersch, Jeanne, 60
Herschel, Caroline, 659
Herschel, John, 669
Herschel, William, 659
Hertzsprung, Ejnar, 659

Herzl, Theodore, 412
Hessians in the U.S., 123
Heth, Joice, 165
Hickok, James Butler ("Wild Bill"), 444
Hicks, John, Jr., 117
Hidalgo y Costilla, Miguel, 428
"Hidden ball" play, 1st, 1217
Hidden Persuaders, 806
Hieroglyphics, Egyptian, 483
Hill, Brian, 74
Hill, Mildred, 851
Hill, Patty, 851
Hillard, E. B., 57
Hillbilly Women, 1438, 1444
Hilton, James, 1424
Hindenburg Explosion, 561
Hindu creation myth, 1308
Hinduism, 1262
Hirohito of Japan, 416
Hiroshima, bombing of, 237, 306, 507
Hirshfield, Leo, 356
Hispaniola, 384, 398
Hiss, Alger, 238, 319
Historical sites, U.S., 700
History, worldwide, 483
History Book—People's Edition, 115
History Was Buried, 67
Hitler, Adolf, 392, 1051, 1322; assassination
    attempt, 593; cars of, 727; emergence of, 515;
    last will, 1332
Hoaxes, 701; astronomical, 669; Atlantis
    discovery, 730
Hobbies, 352
Ho Chi Minh, 467
Ho Chi Minh Trail, 421
Hockey greats, 1186
Hockey oddities, 1218
Hofer, J. L., 70
Hoffa, James, 251
Hoffman, Abbie, 255
Hogan, Ben, 1183
Holberg, Baron, 693
Hollow-earth fiction, 693
Hollow Earth Society, 693
Hollow-earth theory, 692
Holly, Buddy, 895
Holman, Nat, 1181
Holmes, Burton, 99
Holmes, Sherlock, biography, 1235
Holt, Michael, 74
Holy places, 1287
Home, Daniel Dunglas, 529
"Home, Sweet Home," 849
Homeopathy, 1060
Homer, 512
Homestead Act of 1862, 182
Homestead strike, 203, 589
Homosexuals, famous, 1005
Homo Zinjanthropus, 458
Honduras, 399
Honey, 1032
Honeydew, 1019
"Honey Fitz," *see* Fitzgerald, John F.
Honeymoon in Space, 671
Hong Kong, 399
Honors, 1098
Hoover, Herbert C., 276
Hoover, J. Edgar, 608
Hoover, Lou Henry, 276
Hoppe, William, 1177

Horatio Alger Society, 1253
Horne, Thomas Hartwell, 1286
Horror Films, Academy of, 1253
Horse races, computerized, 1153
Horse racing oddities, 1219
Horses that could do math, 698
Horse thieves, 1st female, 167
Horton, Maggie Mae, 1441
"Hot line," installation of, 247
Houdin, Jean Eugène Robert, 58
Houses, unusual, 712, 715
Houston, Samuel, last will, 1330
"Howard Libbey" (tree), 690
Howe, Gordon ("Gordie"), 1186
Howe, Julia Ward, 850
How High Is the Sky?, 654
Howland Island, 479
How to Stay Young, 1062
How to Use Color to Sell, 57
Hoxha, Enver, 361
Hubble, Edwin P., 659
Hudson, Jeffery, 530
Hudson Institute, 23
Hughes, Emmet John, 29
Hughes, Irene, 5
"Hughes Loan, The," 322
Huks (*Hukbalahap* guerrillas), 441
Hull, George, 701
Human behavior, 1085
Human behavior experiments, 1087
Human rights, 60
Humans, 1st, 512
Humber, Thomas, 65
Humble Gas, 388
Humboldt, Alexander von, 739
Hume, David, 1294
Humorists, 537, 773
Hungary, 400
Hunt, E. Howard, 256
Hunza, 1065
Hurd, Frank J., 61
Hurd, Rosaline, 61
Hurricane Agnes, 553; Camille, 551
Hurricanes, 550
Husak, Gustav, 382
Hussein Ibn Talal, 418
Huxley, Aldous, 1423
Huygens, Christiaan, 659
"Hyde, Mr.," *see* Brodie, William
Hyde Park, 295
Hyderabad, 401
Hydroponics, 1402
Hypnotism, 1st use of, 926

IBM, 406
Ibsen, Henrik, 881
Icaria (utopia), 1421
Icaromenippus, 668
Ice cream, 1035
Ice cream cone, 1st, 912
Iceland, 436, 475
I-Ching, 526
Idiom Neutral, 750
Ido, 750
Idylls of the King, quoted, 734
I Have Spoken, 1442
Ike, Reverend, *see* Reverend Ike
Iliad, 512
Illegitimate children, 1224
Illustrated Book of World Records, 51

Impeachments, U.S., 188, 189, 193
Incas, Lost City of the, 1290
Income tax, U.S., 356
In Dahomey, 211
India, 401
Indian Affairs, 814
Indian relics, selling, 350
Indian Wars, Modoc, 192
Indonesia, 404
Industrial Workers of the World, *see* IWW
Influenza epidemics, 547
Ingersoll, Robert G., 1294
In His Steps, 798
Inquisition, beginning of, 513
Insane asylums, U.S., 168
Insanity experiments, 1088
Insectivorous plants, 667
Inside the Census Bureau, 78
Inside the Good Earth, 691
Insurance Consumers' Protective Assn., 1253
Insurance policies, unusual, 352
Insurrections, U.S., 157, 162
Integral Yoga Hatha, 60
Intelligence quotient, *see* IQ
Interglossa, 750
Interlingua, 750
Internal Revenue Service, 356
International Business Machines, *see* IBM
International Jerusalem Prize, 1129
International Lenin Prize, 1128
International Red Cross, 456
International Telephone & Telegraph, *see* ITT
Interpol, 37; Nazis in, 37; recent exposés of, 39
Interpretation of Dreams, 45
In This Corner, 58
Inventions, 908, 910; *see also* by item
Inventions Necessity Is Not the Mother Of, 64
Invitation to the Reader, 1446
Iodine, 1042
IQ tests, 957, 959
Iran, 409
Iraq, 410
Ireland, 411; Northern, 1885, 411
Ireland, Samuel, 531
Ireland, William Henry, 531
Ireson, Benjamin, 150
Iridology, 66; chart, 66
Iron, 1043
"Iron curtain," 1st use of term, 238
Iroquois Theater Fire, 557
Irrigation systems, 1st, 917
IRS, *see* Internal Revenue Service
Irving, Washington, 150, 753
Irwin, James, 676
Islam (religion), 1269
Island, 1423
Isla Vista bank burning, 367
Isle of Man, 394, 436
Israel, 412; U.S. recognition of, 238
Issas, 471
Italy, 413
ITT, 407, 852; in Chile, 408; military contracts,
   408; scandal, 787; DEW System, 408
Iturbide, Agustín de, 158, 427
Iversen, William, oddities from, 1352
Ivory Coast, 414
Ivory soap, 354
Iwo Jima Island, 478
IWW, 212

Jackson, Andrew, 264
Jackson, Rachel Donelson, 264
"Jack the Ripper," 575
Jacobson, Lenore, 1089
Jacoby, Oswald, 1168
Jagger, Mick, 395
Jamaica, 415
Jamaica Train Collision, 564
James, Jesse, 108, 743
James, William, 47
James, Willie Elma, 1442
James gang, lost loot of, 743
Jameson, Harpman, 1445
James I of England, 496; *quoted,* 498
Jansky, Karl, 660
Jantsch, Erich, 23
Japan, 416; bombing of, 417; occupation of,
   237, 417
Japanese Earthquake of 1923, 548
Jarry, Alfred, 1293
Jarvis, Anna M., 939
Jarvis Island, 479
Java, 404
Jaworski, Leon, 601
"Jay's Treaty," 282
Jeanne d'Arc, *see* Joan of Arc
Jefferson, Thomas, 262
Jehovah's Witnesses, 1268
"Jekyll, Dr.," *see* Brodie, William
Jenks, Jacquetta A. M., *pseud.,* 519
Jen-min Jih-pao (Peking), 791
Jenness, Linda, 128
Jensen, Ann, 6
Jensen, Arthur, 959
Jensen, Bernard, 66
Jensen, Ellen L., 128
Jerome, Jerome K., *quoted,* 74
Jerusalem, holy site, 1287
Jerusalem Prize, International, 1129
Jesus, 1264; *Capital* "editor," 798; crucifixion of,
   490; ministry of, 489
Jevtic, Borijove, *quoted,* 505
Jewelry, selling, 351
Jews in public office, 1st U.S., 132
Jim Smith Society, 1253
Joan Anglicus, 518
Joan of Arc, 513
Joe Miller's Jests, 538; *quoted,* 538
Jogging Association, 1254
John of England, 513
John XXIII (Pope), last will, 1333
Johnson, Andrew, 269
Johnson, Claudia ("Lady Bird") Taylor, 277
Johnson, Laurence A., 73
Johnson, Lyndon B., 277
Johnson, Rafer, 604
Johnson, Samuel, last will, 1328
Johnson, Virginia E., 986, 988
Johnston, Jill, 1435
Johnston Island, 478
Johnstown Flood, 556
Joke books, 537
Jonahs, recent, 1399
John VIII, *see* Joan Anglicus
John of England, *see* Joan Anglicus
Jonathan, Leabua, 422
Jones, Ernest, 45, 46, 503
Jones, G. C. G., 671
Jones, John Paul, 137
Jones, Robert ("Bobby"), 1183

Jones, Stacy V., 64
Jonsson, Olof, 7
Joplin, Scott, 870
Jordan, 418
Joseph, Peter, 1439
Joseph, Stephen M., 1439, 1443
Josephus, *quoted*, 732
Jost Van Dyke, 481
Jourdain, Eleanor, 1381
Journey in Other Worlds, 670
Journey to the Center of the Earth, 693
Journey to the World Underground, 693
Juan Fernández Islands, 376
Juárez, Benito Pablo, 120
Judaism, 1262
Juggler's Association, 1254
Juliana of The Netherlands, 431
Jumbo, largest elephant, 699
"Jumping Man, The," 1380
Junagadh, 401
Jung, Carl Gustav, 45
Jupiter, planet, 657

Kaaba, 447
"Kabouters," 432
Kahn, Herman, 23
Kahn, Kathy, 1438, 1444
Kaiser, Henry J., 367
Kale, 1024
Kamikaze pilots, 236
Kane, Joseph Nathan, 1341
Kansas City Star, The, 778
Kant, Immanuel, 1295
Kapital, Das, 499
Karl Marx: His Life and Thought, 51
Kashmir, 402
Kaunda, Kenneth, 470
Kazakh, 451
Keats, John, 886
Keeler, Christine, 1246
Keeping the Faith, 1262
Kefauver, Estes, 239
Kefir, 1036
Kemmler, William, 201
Kendall, Lace, 58
Kennedy, Caroline, 311
Kennedy, Edward, 255
Kennedy, Edward ("Ted"), 97
Kennedy, Jacqueline Bouvier, 311
Kennedy, John F., 52, 97, 126, 309; assassination of, 597; last will, 1333; *quoted*, 127
Kennedy, John Fitzgerald ("John-John"), 311
Kennedy, Joseph P., 97, 310
Kennedy, Joseph P., Jr., 310
Kennedy, Patrick ("P.J."), 97
Kennedy, Robert, 62, 97, 253; assassination of, 603
Kennedy, Rose, 97
Kennedy-Nixon TV debates, 244, 313, 322
Kent, Clark, *see* Superman
Kent State shooting, 255
Kentucky Derby, 1st, 193
Kenya, 418
Kenyatta, Jomo, 418
Kepler, Johannes, 658, 668, 1355
Kerenski, Aleksandr, 515; last will, 1334
Ketchel v. Robinson, 1152
Khalifa, Al-, family, 471
Khartoum, fall of, 455
Khmer Empire, 918

Khmer Rouge, 372
Kiamichi Mountains treasure, 744
Kidnapping for ransom, U.S., 192
Kidnappings, Mackle Case, 612; recent Mexican, 429
Kidney bean, 1031
Kilimanjaro, Mount, 458
Killy, Jean-Claude, 1211
Kilrain, Jake, 1166
Kilroy graffiti, 757
Kim Il Sung, 419
King, Alberta Williams, 258
King, Billie Jean, 1188
King, Leslie L., *see* Ford, Gerald R.
King, Martin Luther, Jr., 253
King-Hele, Desmond, 24
Kingman Reef, 479
Kings of the Kitchen, 1045
King Solomon's mines, 444
Kinmen, 458
Kinsey, Alfred C., 980, 983
Kiplinger Washington Letter, 814
Kirghiz, 451
Kirlian photography, 1392
Kissinger, Henry, 326, 431; *quoted*, 477
Kitchener, Horatio, 455
Kitchen Helps, 949
Kitchen utensils, guide to, 950
Kitefliers' Association, 1254
Kitt, Eartha, 1435
Kiwi, 1018
"Kiwis," 433
KKK, *see* Ku Klux Klan
Kleenex, 356
Kleindienst, Richard, 254
Kline, Otis Adalbert, 71
KMT, *see* Kuomintang
Knickerbocker, Diedrich, *pseud.*, 150
Knowles, Joe, 100
Kodak camera, 354; 1st, 909
Kohlrabi, 1024
Konoye, Fumimaro, 1322
Kopechne, Mary Jo, 255
Korea, 419
Korean War, 306; casualties in, 242; start of, 240
Koumiss, 1036
Kozeluh, Karel, 1189
Krakatoa, 405; eruption of, 544
Kremer, Gerhard, *see* Mercator
Kreuger, Ivar, 1322
Krist, Gary Steven, 612
Kublai Khan, 513
Kühn, Ruth, 651
Kühn family, spies, 651
Ku Klux Klan, 1st, 187
Kumquat, 1018
Kunstler, William, 255
Kuomintang (KMT), 457
Kurtz, Edwin B., Jr., 68
Kuwait, 475
Kwangsi Chuang, 379

Labor organizers, U.S., 97
Lacoste, René, 1189
"Lady Banksia" (rose), 690
La Leche League, 1254
Lalibela, holy site, 1291
Lamarr, Hedy, 1243
Lamizana, Sangoule, 464

Land of the Changing Sun, 694
Landru, Henri Désiré, 579
Landslides, Saint-Jean-Vianney, 553
Lane, Harriet, 268
Lane, Mark, 1446
Lang, Alois, 1297, 1298
Lang, Anton, 1298
Lang, David, 1370
Language of flowers, 758
Languages, artificial, 748; basic, 749; human, 746; international, 751; sign, 758; universal, 748; unusual, 747
Lansing, Robert, 294
Lao Dong party, 467
Laos, 420
Lao-tze, 1263
Lascaux cave paintings, 1379
Lasson, Kenneth, 1442, 1443
Last and First Men, 672
Last Men in London, 672
Last Men of the Revolution, 57
Last West, 53
Last Wills, 1326
Last wills, most beautiful, 1360
Last words, famous, 1316
Latino Sine Flexione, 750
Latvia, 451
Laver, Rod, 1189
Law of Freedom in a Platform, 1420
Lawrence, James, 153
Lawrence, Thomas Edward, 631; last will, 1332
Lawrence of Arabia (film), 631
Laycock, George, oddities from, 1344
LBJ Ranch, 277
League of Nations, 294
Leakey, Louis S. B., 458
Learning experiments, 1089
Leavitt, Henrietta, 659
Lebanon, 421
Ledoux, Remy, 744
Lee, Ann ("Mother"), 131
Lee, Ezra, 632
Lee, Mary, 69
Leek, 1024
Leeward Islands, 475
Le Fanu, Sheridan, 1338
LeFevre, Mike, 1438
Left-handed people, famous, 1226
Legal In-Service Committee, 1254
Léger, Jules, 374
Legumes, directory of, 1030
LeHand, Marguerite "Missy" 296
Leigh, Augusta, 885
Lemmings, suicide of, 1352
Lemon, 1018
"Lemonade Lucie," 270
Lenclos, Anne de, 995
Lend-Lease Bill of 1941, 230
Le Neve, Ethel, 578
Lenglen, Suzanne, 1190
Lenin, Nikolai, 515, 1293
Lenin Peace Prize, 1128
Lennon, John, 893, 1294, 1435
Lentil, 1031
Lenz, Sidney S., 1168
León, Ponce de, 443
Leonard, Jon N., 70
Leotard, Jules, 763
Le Plongeon, Augustus, 729

Lesbian Nation, 1435
Lesotho, 422
Lesseps, Ferdinand de, 919
Lettuce, 1024
Lever Brothers, 463
Leverhulme Trust, 463
Levy, Richard, 1445
Lewis, Clive Staples, 672
Lewis, Diehl, 61
Lewis, Meriwether, 1321
Lewis, Sinclair, 703, 1071
Lexington, battle of, 116
Leyte Gulf, battle of, 236
Lhasa, holy site, 1289
Liars Club, 1254
Liberia, 422; U.S. blacks in, 158
Libertatia, Republic of, 1434
Liber Trigrammaton, 526
Libya, 423
Liddy, Gordon, 338
Liechtenstein, 475
Life Cycle Book of Cats, 74
Life expectancy, highest and lowest, 1230
Life forms, unfamiliar, 666
Life of George Washington, 113
Life on other planets, 663
Life on Other Planets: Another View, 665
Life Savers, 355
Liggett, Winfield, Jr., 1168
Lima bean, 1031
Lime, 1018
Lincoln, Abraham, 112, 126, 184, 284; last will, 1330; *quoted,* 177
Lincoln, Mary Todd, 285
Lincoln, Nancy Hanks, 289
Lincoln, Robert Todd, 285
Lincoln, Willie, 285
Lincoln-Douglas debates, 286
Lincoln's children, 946
Lincoln's "Dream," 185, 291
Lincos, 750
Lind, Jenny, 175
Lindbergh's children, 948
"Lindenwald," 264
Line Islands, 478
Lingg, Louis, 41, 44; *quoted,* 43
Linn, Bill, 7
Lipton, Thomas J., 463
Lists, 1224
Lithuania, 451
Little, Malcolm, *see* Malcolm X
"Little Boy," *see* Hiroshima
Little League World Series, 1136
Live Longer Now, 70
Lively arts, 830
Liveright, Horace, 1074
Living My Life, 72
Livingstone, David, 470
Lloyd's of London, 352
Loch Ness monster, 1372
Locke, Richard Adams, 669
Locks, 1st cylinder, 912; valuable, 349
Lockwood, Belva Ann, 128
Lodge, Henry Cabot, 313
Logan, John, 1359
Logan's Lament, 1359
Loh, May, 61
Lollipops, 356
London, Jack, 1073, 1321
London Fire of 1666, 554

Lone Ranger, biography, 1239
Long, Huey P., assassination of, 228, 592
Longevity, 70
Longevity sites, 1065
Longfellow, Henry Wadsworth, 115
Long March, the, 506
Longtime Californ', 1442
Lon Nol, 372
Looking Backward, 199, 1422
Loquat, 1018
Loras, Jean Mathias, 1302
Los Alamos, N. Mex., 508
Los Alamos Primer, 69
Los Angeles Times, 779
L'Osservatore, see Osservatore
Lost Cause, The, 121
Lost Colony of Roanoke, 1376
Lost Horizon, 1424
Louisiana Territory, purchase of, 148
Lounsbury, Charles, 1360
L'Ouverture, Toussaint, *see*
　Toussaint L'Ouverture
Louwage, Florent E., 38
Love and Sexuality, 964
Lovecraft, Howard Phillips, 694
Lowe, Mary, 1441
LSD, 250
Lucien of Samosata, 668
Ludlow Massacre (1914), 97
Ludlow War, 217
Ludwick, Christopher, 124, 139
Lumumba, Patrice, 470
Lunar landing, *see* Moon walk
Lungfish, African, 666
Lupescu, Magda, 1243
Lusitania, sinking of, 558
Luther, Martin, 494, 1266; *quoted,* 495
Lutheranism, 1266
Luther's 95 Theses, 494
Luxembourg, 476
Lynch, origin of word, 763
Lynch, William, 763
Lynn, Edwin C., 67
Lysenko, Trofim D., 924
Lytton, Edward Bulwer, 693

Macadamia nuts, 1028
Macao (Macau), 476
MacArthur, Douglas, 306
McCarthy, Joseph, 239, 307
McCartney, Paul, 893
McClintic, Richard, 7
McConnell, D. H., 353
McConnell, James V., 925
McCormick, Robert R., 775
McDonald, Jamey, 1438
McDonald, Jeanette, 905
McDuck, Scrooge, biography, 1237
Macedonia, 396
McGovern, George, 326
McHale, John, 25
Machine gun, 1st, 909; invention of, 182
Machine Stops, The, 694
Machu Picchu, holy site, 1290
McIntire, Carl, 1279
McKee, Russell, 53
Mackenzie, Alexander, court-martial of, 639
McKinley, Ida Saxton, 272
McKinley, William, 126, 272; assassination of,
　590

Mackle, Barbara Jane, 612
McLellan, David, 51
Macleod, Banda, 649
McLoughlin, Maurice, 1190
McPhee, John, 69
McPherson, Aimee Semple, 1277
McWhirter, Norris, 1340
McWhirter, Ross, 1340
Madagascar, *see* Malagasy Republic
Madison, Dolley Todd, 263
Madison, James, 262
Maelzel, John Nepomuk, 161, 534
Mafia—Menace or Myth, 35
Magic, 71
Magicians, 58
Maginot, André, 633
Maginot Line, 633
Magna Carta, 513
Magnesium, 1043
Magowan, Robert A., 446
Magruder, Jeb Stuart, 257
Mah, Lisa, 1442
Main Street, 703
Make Your Own Musical Instruments, 65
Making a living, ways of, 343
Making of a Model Citizen in China, 56
"Malachy Papal Prophecies," 12
Malagasy Republic, 424
Malawi, 424
Malaya, Federation of, 425
Malaysia, 425
Malcolm X, assassination of, 601
Maldives, 476
Mali, 426
Malory, Thomas, 734
Malowick, Ardell, 728
Malraux, André, 1294
Malta, 476
Man, early, 680
Manchukuo, 416
Mandarin orange, 1021
Mandell, Muriel, 65
Mandino, Og, 55
Manet, Édouard, 857
Manganese, 1043
Mango, 1018
"Manifest destiny," term 1st used, 171
Man in the Iron Mask, 1365
Man in the Moon, 668
Man-Made Disasters, 554
Mann Act, passage of, 216
Man Nobody Knows, 804
Man o' War, 1153
Man's best friend, 1361
Manscapes, 1442
Manuscripts, selling, 350
"Man without a Country," 112
Maoism, 1270
Mao Tse-tung, 377, 506, 1270; *quoted,* 507
Maple syrup, 1033
Mapmaking, 686
Mapping the World, 686
Mapping your neighborhood, 717
Maps, selling, 351
Marathon, battle of, 615
Marciano v. Dempsey, 1146
Marciano v. Muhammad Ali, 1148
Marcos, Ferdinand, 440
Marcus Island, 478

Mardian, Robert C., 259
Margarine, 1st, 913
Margrethe II of Denmark, 383
Maria Louisa of Spain, 528
Mariana Islands, 477
Marie de' Medici of France, 530
Marie of the Incarnation, 1299
Marijuana, 250; sources of, 416
Marijuana Laws Organization, 1254
Marine disasters, 558, 563, 565
Marine insurance, *see* Lloyd's of London
Marjoe, 1286
Marlborough, *see* Churchill
Marlowe, Harriet, Lady, *pseud.,* 519
Marne, battle of the, 622
Marriage of Figaro, The, 527
Marriages, most numerous, 1226
Mars, planet, 656
Marshall, Thomas Riley, 294
Marshall, Thurgood, 252
Marshall Islands, 477
Marshall Plan, 306
Martian Chronicles, The, 672
Martin, Victoria, *see* Woodhull
Martinique, 476
Martinsburg strike, 195
Martyrs, Canadian, 1300; 116 U.S., 1299; of
    Paris, 1301
Marx, Groucho, 818
Marx, Karl, 498, 1292; last will, 1330
Marxist Studies Institute, 1254
Marx's children, 946
Mary Celeste, mystery of, 1369
Mary the Virgin, 940
Masai tribe, 459
Más a Tierra, 539
Masochism, origin of word, 991
Massacres, 424; Mexico City of 1968, 428
Master Charge, 342
Masters, William H., 986, 988
Masters of Magic, 58
Mata Hari, 648, 999
Matoaka, *see* Pocahontas
Matsu, 458
Mau Mau, 419
Mauritania, 426
Mauritius, 476
Maury, Matthew F., 120
Maxmilian of Mexico, 120
Maximilian's lost treasure, 741
Maxwell House coffee, 355
May, Karl, 954
Mayakovski, Vladimir, 1323
Mayan creation myth, 1309
Mayflower Descendants Society, 1255
Mayle, Peter, 67
Mazes, 64
Mead, Margaret, 25
Meat, 1014
Mecca, 447; holy site, 1288
Medal of Honor, 1st, 182
Media, The, 775
Meditation, uses of, 1413
Mediums, 1393
Medved, Michael S., 48
Melilla, *see* Ceuta and Melilla
Melons, 1018
Melville, Herman, 879
Memoirs of a Coxcomb, 524

Mencken, Henry Louis, 1295; *quoted,* 590
Men from Interpol, 37
Me Nobody Knows, The, 1439, 1443
Mental institutions, U.S., 1088
Mercator, Gerardus, following 266; Projection,
    following 266
Mercedes-Benz, Hitler's, 727
Mercer, Lucy Page, 296
Merchandising, U.S., 73
Mercouri, Melina, 396
Mercury, planet, 656
Meredith, James, 246, 251
Merlis, Edward A., 32
Mermaids, prototype for, 1351
Merrick, John, 536
Mesmer, Franz A., 926
Mesmerism, 926
Messalina, Valeria, 993
Messick, Hank, 35, 62
Meteors, facts about, 655
Methodist Church, 1267, 1270
Metric conversion table, 938
Metric system, 936
Mexican War, 428
Mexico, 427; Confederates Descendants in, 120;
    Mormons in, 121
Meyers, Ethel Johnson, 8
Michelangelo, 889
Mickey Mouse, 901
Mickey Mouse Club, 819
Micombero, Michel, 372
Micromegas, 669
Micronesia, 477
Microscope, 1st, 908
Middleweight champion, all-time, 1149
Midgets, 109, 530, 1173
"Midnight Ride of Paul Revere," 116
Midnight Ride of William Dawes, 115
Midway, battle of, 232, 624
Midway Islands, 478
Mikan, George, 1181
Milburn, Anna, 128
Milgram, Stanley, 1090
Military leaders, biographies of, 630
Military weapons, U.S., 625
Milk, 1033
Millar, Charles, last will, 1331
Millard Fillmore Society, 1255
Miller, Joseph ("Joe"), 537
Millet, 1029
Minerals, directory of, 1041
Minerva, Republic of, 481
Misers, greatest, 1340
Missing persons, 1225
Mission, François, 1434
Misspelled words, common, 769
Mitchell, Charlene, 128
Mitchell, Edgar, 676
Mitchell, John, 259
Mitchell, Maria, astronomer, 173
Mitchell, William ("Billy"), court-martial of,
    640
Mitrione, Dan A., assassination of, 605
Mizner, Wilson, 773
Mizoram, 403
Moberly, Annie, 1381
Mobile Bay, battle of, 185
Mobil Oil, 388
Mobutu, Joseph D., 469
Mobutu Sese Seko, 469

Mocha coffee, sources of, 468
Model T Ford, 1st, 215
Modern Times (utopia), 1429
Modoc Indian War, 192
Mohammad Ahmed ibn Abdullah, 455
Mohammad Reza Pahlavi, 409
Mohammed, 1269
"Mohole," 692
Molas, 438
Moldavia, 444, 451
Molière, 881
Molina, Arturo, 387
Molly Maguires, 193
Molybdenum, 1043
Monaco, 477
Mona Lisa, 853
Money, largest, 1353
Mongolia, 429; Inner, 379
Monitor, 181
Monk, Maria, 165
Monling, 750
Monopoly Association, 1255
Monroe, James, 263
Monroe, Marilyn, 62, 311, 1323; last will, 1333
Monroe Doctrine, 158
Montagu, John, *see* Sandwich, Lord
Montaigne, Michel de, 1291
Monte Carlo, 477
Montez, Lola, 954
Montezuma cypress, widest, 690
Montezuma's lost treasure, 740
Montgomery, John, 733
Montgomery Ward catalogs, 346
Montserrat, 475
Monument to a left leg, 700
Moody, Dwight Lyman, 1272
Moody, Helen Wills, 1190
Moon, facts about, 655
Moonshiner (vocation), 344
Moon walk, 1st, 255, 510, 661, 675, 921; TV coverage of, 822
Moore, Clement C., 528
More, Thomas, 1049, 1418
Morenz, Howard ("Howie"), 1187
Morgan, John Pierpont, last will, 1331
Morgan, Julia (architect), 715
Morgan Guaranty Trust, 391
Morgan horse, lineage of, 142
Mormon Church, 1267
Mormon Polygamists in Mexico, 121
Morocco, 429
Morrill Act of 1862, 121
Morris, Desmond, 1435
Morris, Gouverneur, last will, 1329
Morris, William, 1422
Morse, Samuel Finley Breese, 170
Morse Code, 757
Morte d'Arthur, 734
Morton, Joy, 355
Morton salt, 355
Moses, 512
Moss, Stirling, 1179
Moss, Thelma, 1392
Most, Johann, 1293
Mother Earth, periodical, 590
Mother Goose, 940
Mothers, 3 famous, 940
Mother's Day, 941
Mothers-in-Law Club, 1255
Mothers of Twins Clubs, 1255

Motion Picture Academy awards, 831
Motion pictures, early, 211; 1st, 909
Mountain climbing oddities, 1220
Mount Pelée, 476
Mount Sinai, 512
"Mount Vernon," 278
Moviemakers, 874; offbeat, 901
Mozambique, 430
Mozart, Wolfgang Amadeus, 527, 865
"Muckrakers," era of the, 211
Mud-bathing, 445
Mudd, Samuel, 710
Mud Lake gold, 742
"Mud March," 630
Muhammad Ali v. Marciano, 1148
Mulberry, 1016
Mung bean, 1031
Murderers, Extraordinary, 569, 571
Murders, Brooke-Heath Case, 584; Coors Case, 610; De Koven Case, 583; Dr. Crippen Case, 578; Henri Landru Case, 579; Lizzie Borden Case, 576; M. Smith Case, 571; Peltzer Case, 573; Snyder-Gray Case, 580; Starkweather Case, 585; Thomas Cream Case, 572; Whitechapel Case, 575; William Wallace Case, 581
Murder Will Out, 571
Murray, Arthur, 900
Murrow, Edward R., 818, 819
Museum Media, 956
Museums, sale items of, 956
Mushroom, 1024
Musical instruments, making, 65
Muslim Mosque, Inc., 601
Muslims, 1269
Musorgski, Modest, 1071
Mussolini, Benito, 1051; last days, 234
Mussolini's children, 948
Mustard, 1025
Mutinies, *Potemkin* revolt, 640; Wilhelmshaven revolt, 641
MUZAK, Inc., 852
Mwambutsa, Ntare V., 372
My Lai massacre, 253, 643
Mysterious happenings, chronology of, 1364
Mysterious places, 1375

N, Dr., 9
NAACP, incorporation of, 215
"Nacirema," people of, 1085
Nadasy, Ferencz, 1338
Nader, Ralph, 59, 250, 392; *quoted*, 343
Nagaland, 403
Naismith, James A., 202
Naked Ape, The, 1435
Names, common last, 1226; unusual, 71
Name Society, 1255
Namibia, 477
Naming the baby, 71
Napoleon I, last will, 1329; Russian retreat, 514
Napoleon III, 120
Narrative of Arthur Gordon Pym, 693
NASA, 660
Nash, Charles, 391
Nashoba (utopia), 1426
Nasser, Gamal Abdel, 386
Nation, Carry Moore, 102
National Aeronautics and Space Administration, *see* NASA

National Association for the Advancement of Colored People, *see* NAACP
National debt, U.S., 164
National Nothing Foundation, 1255
Nations, armed forces of, 1232; largest, 1227; most populous, 1227
Nations of the world, 360
Natural Disasters, 543
Natural foods, 61
Natural Hair Care Comix, 69
Natural selection, 500
Nauru, 477
Nausicaa, 860
Navajo creation myth, 1310
Nazca (Peru), 1375
Nectarine, 1019
Nee, Brett, 1442
Nee, Victor G., 1442
Neebe, Oscar, 41; *quoted,* 43
Nehru, Jawaharlal, 402; last will, 1333
Neighborhoods, mapping your, 717
Nek'ure, last will, 1326
Nelson, Horatio, 620
Nelson, Horatio, last will, 1328
Nelson, Ruth, 1439
Nelson, William Rockhill, 778
Nepal, 431
Neptune, planet, 657
Netherlands, The, 431
Netherlands Antilles, 477
Neumann, John Nepomucene, 1303
Never on Sunday, 396
Nevis, 475
New Age Baby Name Book, 71
New American Practical Navigator, 147
New Caledonia, 478
New Deal, 299, 300
Newell, William C., 702
New Harmony (utopia), 1425
New Hebrides, 478
New London School Explosion, 560
News from Nowhere, 1422
Newsletters, 812
Newspapers, U.S., 775; worldwide, 787
Newton, Huey, 254
Newton, Isaac, 514, 659
New York Times, The, 782
New Zealand, 432
Ngouabi, Marien, 380
Nguema, Francisco Macias, 473
Nicaragua, 433
Nicholas of Russia, 998
Nicklaus, Jack, 1184
Nick of the Woods, 166
Nicobar Islands, 404
Nicot, Jean, 765
Nicotine, origin of word, 765
Nietzsche, Friedrich, 1292
Niger, 433
Nigeria, 434
Nightingale, Florence, last will, 1331
"Night writing," 521
Nijinsky, Vaslav, 872
Nimeiry, Gaafer al-, 454
Nine-day wonders, 1240
Ninety-Five Theses, 494
Ninety-Nines, Inc., 1255
Niños Héroes, Los, 308
Nippon, *see* Japan
Nippon Steel, 435

Niue Island, 478
Nixon, Donald, 322
Nixon, Frank, 328
Nixon, Hannah, 328, 329
Nixon, Julie, *see* Eisenhower
Nixon, "Pat," *see* Nixon, Thelma
Nixon, Richard Milhous, 317; pardon, 259, 328; resignation, 259, 328; resignation speech, 823
Nixon, Thelma C. ("Pat") Ryan, 320
Nixon, Tricia, *see* Cox
Nixon-Kennedy TV debates, 244, 313, 322
"Noah Lamechson," 733
Noah's Ark, search for, 731
Nobel, Alfred, 1098
Nobel, Alfred, last will, 1330
Nobel Prize, chemistry, 1111; economic science, 1127; literature, 1098; peace, 1123; physics, 1106; physiology and medicine, 1117
Nobel Prizes, 1098
Noguchi, Thomas, 604
Non-Parents Organization, 1256
Norse creation myth, 1310
North American Phalanx, 1429
North American Trail Complex, 1256
North Briton, №45, 542
Northern Rhodesia, *see* Zambia
Northern Yemen, 468
North Pole, discovery of, 215
North Vietnam, 467
Norway, 435
Nostalgia, selling, 350
Nostradamus, *see* Nostredame
Nostredame, Michel de, 13
Nothe, Margaret, last will, 1331
Nouveau Monde industriel, 1427
Nova Scotia, Tory Descendants in, 118
Novaye, Baron de, 15
Novelists, 877; offbeat, 902
Nov-Esperanto, 750
Nowhere (utopia), 1422
Noxzema, 356
Noyes, John Humphrey, 1430
Nuclear bomb, 69, 237; 1st used, 507
Nuclear fission, 933
Nude Descending a Staircase, 216
Nude Maja, The, 856
Nuremberg War Crimes Trial, 515
Nurmi, Paavo, 1192
Nursing homes, 59
Nutrition, 61; guide to, 1037
Nuts, directory of, 1027
Nyerere, Julius, 458
Nylon, 1st, 909
Nylon stockings, 1st, 230

O., Anna, 502
Oak Island treasure, 1378
Oates, Lawrence, 1321
Oats, 1029
Obedience experiment, 1090
Oberammergau play, 1296
Obscenity trials, 1st U.S., 965
Occult, the, 526
Occultism, 71
Occupations, unusual, 343
Ochs, Adolph Simon, 782
Ocussi-Ambeno, 481
Oddity hunters, 1340
Odhar, Coinneach, 15

Odyssey, 860
Office of Price Administration, *see* OPA
Off on a Comet, 670
O'Hair, Madalyn Murray, 1294
O'Hanlon, Virginia, 1358
Ohio-Mississippi Valley Flood, 549
Oil embargo, 257, 258
O.K. Corral, gunfight at, 712
Okinawa Island, 417
Okra, 1025
Olav V of Norway, 436
Old Age, the Last Segregation, 59
Old Drum (dog), 1361
"Old Glory," origin of term, 162
Olduvai Gorge, 458
Olive, 1019
Olive oil, sources of, 462
Olympia, 857
Olympic Games, 1st Winter, 1205; history of,
   1199; modern, 1200; Munich massacre, 424,
   1212
Olympics massacre of 1972, 424, 1212
Olympio, Sylvanus, 460
Oman, 478
Omar Khayyám, 954
O'Morgain, Malachy, 12
Onassis, Jacqueline, *see* Kennedy, Jacqueline
Oneida (utopia), 1430
O'Neill, Eugene, 882, 1072
Onion, 1025
Ono, Yoko, 894
On the Road, 700
Oort, Jan, 660
OPA, establishment of, 230
OPEC, 448
Opera singers, *see* Singers
"Operation Barbarossa," 515
"Operation Bootstrap," 443
"Operation Overlord," 515
Ophir, land of, 444, 1379
Opium, sources of, 460, 462; Wars, 400, 645
Optical illusions, 1378
Opus Dei, 453
Orange, 1019
Oregon vortex, 1378
Organization of Petroleum Exporting Countries,
   see OPEC
Orgies, 542; sexual, 526
Orgone, 1002
Origin of Species, 500
Orkney Islands, 394
Orlando Furioso, 668
Orleans, siege of, 513
Orphans of the Sky, 673
Orr, Bobby, 1187
Orwell, George, last will, 1333
Oscar II, 218
Oscar winners, 831
Osservatore Romano, L' (Vatican City), 792
Ostman, Albert, 1371
Oswald, Lee Harvey, 598, 600
Other Side of the Looking Glass, 1
Otis, Harrison Gray, 779
Otto, Herbert A., 29
Ould Daddah, Moktar, 426
Our Bodies, Ourselves, 60
Our Portion of Hell, 1441, 1445
Outcault, R. F., 206
Outlaws, U.S., 89, 108
Out of the Silent Planet, 672

Over the Counter . . . , 73
Owen, Robert, 1425
Owens, Jesse, 1192, 1207

Pacific Islands, misc., 478
Packard, Vance, 806
Padded bra, 1st, 913
Paderewski, Ignace, 954
Padilla, Juan de, 1299
Pahlavi, *see* Mohammad Reza Pahlavi
Paige, Leroy ("Satchel"), 1062
Paine, Ruth Hyde, 601
Paine, Thomas, 752, 1296
Painters, gallery of, 853; offbeat, 904
Paintings, selling, 351
Pakistan, 436; Cyclone, 552
Pala (utopia), 1423
Palestinian Resistance, 418
Palmer, Arnold, 1184
Palmyra, 479
Panama, 437
Panama Canal, 437, 919
Panharmonicon, 535
Panic of 1857, 178; of 1873, 192; of 1907, 214
Pantaloons, origin of word, 766
Papaya, 1019
Paper Plates, Legend of, 689
Papissa Joanna, 518
Pappenheim, Bertha, *see* O., Anna
Papua New Guinea, 438
Paradise Program, 56
Paraguay, 439
Paramecium aurelia, 667
Parapsychology, 71, 927
Parents without Partners, 1256
Paris Commune of 1871, 514
Park Chung Hee, 420
Parker, Bonnie, 725
Parkhurst, Charles H., 103
Parking meter, 1st, 913
Paroled but Not Free, 1438
Parsley, 1025
Parsnip, 1025
Parsons, Albert, 41, 44; *quoted,* 43, 44
Passing on, 1316
Passion fruit, 1020
Passion Play, 1296
Patai, Raphael, 55
"Pataphysics," 1293
Patch, Sam, 161
Patent, definition of, 82; 1st U.S., 143; how to
   get, 82, 85
Patent System, chronology, 84; U.S., 82
Pathet Lao, 421
Patriarca, Raymond L. S., 35
Patternless Fashions, 61
Patterson, Joseph Medill, 781
Pavese, Cesare, 1323
Pavlova, Anna, 873
Payne, John Howard, 849
"Payola," 244
Pay Toilets Committee, 1256
Pea, 1025; dried, 1031
Peace Corps, creation of, 245
Peach, 1020
Peanuts, 1032
Peanut butter, 1010
Peanut industry, 448
Pear, 1020
Pearcy, G. Etzel, following 546

Pearl Harbor, 231, 299, 650
Pearson, Drew, last will, 1334
Peary, Robert, 215
Peasants' Revolt, 513
Pecans, 1028
Pekkanen, John, 71
Peltzer, Armand, 573
Peltzer, Leon, 573
Pelvic examination, 1064
Pemba, 458
Pemberton, John S., 354
Pencil with eraser, 1st, 913
Pendergast, Thomas Joseph ("Big Tom"), 302
Penrose, Evelyn, 1397
Pension plans, 227
Pentagon Papers, 256, 257
People's Almanac address, 1446
People's Daily (Peking), 791
People's Directory, 1249
People Who Became Words, 760
People who disappeared, 1225
Peppers, 1025
Pepys, Samuel, last will, 1327
Perelandra, 672
Perelman, Suzanne, 69
Pericles, 861; Age of, 485; Funeral Oration, 487, 859
Perkins, Josephine Amelia, 167
Perón, Eva ("Evita"), 363
Perón, Isabel Martinez de, 363
Perón, Juan, 363
Perpetual calendar, 1416
Perry, Oliver Hazard, 153
Persia, *see* Iran
Persimmon, 1020
Personal and Vocational Interplay in Identity Building, 1442
Pertinax, 533
Peru, 439
Peruvian Earthquake, 552
Peter the Great, last will, 1328
Peters, Arno, following 266; Projection, following 266
Petersburg, battle of, 185
Petrarch, last will, 1327
Petroleum Intelligence Weekly, 815
Phaedo, *quoted,* 488
Phalanx movement (utopia), 1426, 1427
Philip of Jesus, St., 1299
Philippines, 440
Phobias, description of, 1094; dictionary of, 1095
Phoenician alphabet, 483, 484
Phoenix Islands, 478
Phonograph records, 1st LP, 913; selling, 350
Phosphorus, 1044
Photoanalysis, 65
Photography, 1st, 908
Phrenology in the U.S., 163
Physiology of Taste, 1046
Picasso, Pablo, 858
Picture writing, 483
Piedras Verdes Valley, 121
Pierce, Franklin, 267
Pierce, Jane Appleton, 268
Pilate, Pontius, 490
Pillars of Hercules, 474
Pimpaneau, Jacques, 74
Pineapple, 1020
Pine nuts, 1028

Pistachio nuts, 1028
Pitcairn: Children of Mutiny, 517
Pitcairn Island, 516
Pitman, Isaac, 1050
PK, *see* Psychokinesis
Plague, bubonic, 554
Plain Speaking, 328
Planaria, 925
Planet of Peril, The, 672
Planting hints, 1401
Plath, Sylvia, 1323
Plato, 1418; *quoted,* 488, 729
Playwrights, 881; offbeat, 905
Pleck, Joseph, 1440
Pliny the Elder, *quoted,* 484
Plugging in and Shedding Light—Special Articles, 31
Plum, 1020
"Plumbers, The," 256
Plunkitt, George Washington, 104
Plutarch, *quoted,* 485, 486
Pluto, planet, 658
Pocahontas, 105
Poe, Edgar Allan, 669, 693, 753, 886, 1071
Poets, 885
Poisoning, treatment for, 1411
Poisons, table of, 1411
Poland, 441
Poland Bill of 1874, 121
Polaroid camera, 1st, 910
Politburo, 452
Political ephemera, valuable, 347
Political Items Collectors, 1256
Polk, James Knox, 266
Polk, Sarah Childress, 266
Pollen, edible, 1033
Polls, Gallup, 827
Poll tax, U.S., 172
Polo, Marco, 513
Poltava, battle of, 619
Poltergeists, 1395
Polynesia, French, 479
Pomegranate, 1020
Pompeii, 543
Ponte, Lorenzo da, 527
Pontius Pilate, *see* Pilate, Pontius
Pony Express, 180; stables, 708
Pool, Ithiel De Sola, 26
Pope, Alexander, 542
Popular Culture Assn., 1256
Population, U.S., *see* U.S. Population
Poquelin, Jean Baptiste, *see* Molière
Pornography, 524; in the U.S., 91
Porpoise who was a pilot, 697
Porter, David, 625
Porter, W. Sydney, 1073
Portland cement, 1st, 909
Portugal, 442
Post, Marjorie Merriweather, last will, 1334
Post, Wright, 117
Posters, valuable, 346
Post Office, U.S., 161
Potassium, 1044
Potato, 1026
Potemkin mutiny, 640
Pots and pans, guide to, 950
Potsdam Agreement, 419
Powell, Adam Clayton, 251
Powell, John Wesley, 188
Power, Katherine Ann, 613

Powers, Gary Francis, 244, 650
Practical Navigator, New American, 147
Pravda (Moscow), 793
Preachers, 1270
Precognition, 1389
Predictions by Modern Scientists, 18; by Others, 28; by Psychics of the Past, 11; by Present-Day Psychics, 1
Prehistoric cube, 1369
Preholda, Robert, 26
Prensa, La (Buenos Aires), 794
Presbyterianism, 1266
Preserving food, 1403
Presidents of the U.S., *see* specific President
Presidio 27, court-martial of, 643
Presley, Elvis, 906
Price fixing by U.S. firms, 245
Princess of Mars, A, 671
Princip, Gavrilo, 504
Príncipe, 480
Printing, invention of, 513
Prints, valuable, 349
Priscilla (N.T. disciple), 860
Prison camps, 68
Prison experiment, mock, 1088
Prison, Alcatraz, 713
Prison sentences, longest, 1341
Pritikin, N., 70
Prizefighting, *see* Boxing
Prizes, 1098
Procrastinators' Club, 1256
Procter, Harley, 354
Product names, American, 353
Profiles in Courage, 311
Profumo, John D., 968, 1246
Project Sanguine, 921
"Prometheus Project," 21
Prophets, 1270
Prospector's Guild, 1257
Proteins, 1037
Protestantism, 494
Prune, 1020
Psychiatric emergencies, handling of, 1406
Psychic healing, 1396
Psychic phenomena, 1385
Psychics, 529, 1355
Psychoanalysis, beginning of, 502; development of, 45
Psychoanalyzed celebrities, 1224
Psychokinesis (PK), 927, 1395
Psychophotography, 1396
P. T. Barnum Was Right, 32
Ptolemy, 658
Ptolemy's *Geography,* 493
Public opinion, international, 828; in the U.S., 827
Public relations, 807
Publishing your own book, 752
Pueblo incident, 253
Puerto Rico, 443
Pulitzer, Joseph, 784
Pullman, George Mortimer, 178
Pumpkin, 1026
Punt, Land of, 449
Puppy who was loyal, 698
Pure Food and Drug Act, 212
Pussycat League, Inc., 1257
Puzzlers' League, 1257
Puzzles, crossword, 1170
"Pyramid inch," 11, 1364

Pyramidology, 11
Pyramids, Egyptian, 916, 1364
Pythagoras, 1049

Qaddafi, Muammar el, 423
Qanats, Iranian, 917
Qatar, 479
Quantrill, William C., 183
Quebec, battle of, 619
Quemoy, *see* Kinmen
Quest for Noah's Ark, 733
Quintuplets, Dionne, 1241
"Quisling," origin of term, 634
Quisling, Vidkun, 634

Rabbits, raising, 1402
Rabelais, François, 1419; last will, 1327
Race horses, greatest, 1153
Races, auto, 1213; bicycle, 1215; harness, 1218; horse, 1219
Racing, auto, 1178
Radar, 1st, 909
Radiation sickness, 508
Radical fugitives, 613
Radio telescopes, use of, 663
Radio tube, 1st, 909
Radish, 1026
Raffles, Thomas Stamford, 449
Rafflesia, largest flower, 426
"Ragged Dick" series, 187
Ragtime, 870
Ragtime Society, Inc., 1257
Rail disasters, 562, 564, 566; Italy, 562; New Jersey, 566
Rainier III of Monaco, 477
Raisin, 1018
Rall, Gottleib, 124
Ramanantsoa, Gabriel, 424
Rape, 1003
Rapp, George, 1425
Ras al-Khaimah, 481
Raspberry, 1017; mousse, recipe for, 1017
Rasputin, Grigori, 998
Ray, James Earl, 612
Reagan, Ronald, 258
Reaper, 1st, 909
Reber, Grote, 660
Rebozo, Charles ("Bebe"), 324
"Red Baron, The," 635
"Red Brain, The," 671
Red Cross, American National, 196; International, 456
Redesdale, Lord, last will, 1333
Redheads, famous, 1227
Redl, Alfred, 649
Redonda, 475
Redwoods, tallest, 690
Reed, Ed, 109
Reeser, Mary, 1374
Reeves, John, 9
Reference books for the home, 953
Reformers, social, 168; U.S., 97, 104
Refrigerator, 1st, 913
Regio Aromatica, 450
Reich, Wilhelm, 1001
Reichstag fire of 1933, 515
Reincarnation, 1334
Relativity, theory of, 514
Religions, major, 1262
Religious critics, 1295

Religious skeptics, 1291
Religious wars, Irish, 412
Rembrandt, see Rijn, R. van
"Remember the *Maine*," 208
Reno gang train robbery, 742
Reporters, 1st female, 88
Republic, The, 1418
Republic of the Sea, 1434
Research Guild, Inc., 989
Respiration, artificial, 1409
Retired Persons Assn., 1257
"Retirement" communities, 1st, 244
Return to Earth, 675
Réunion Island, 479
Revelle, Roger, 26
Revere, Paul, last will, 1329
"Reverend Ike," 1285
Reynolds, Richard Joshua, 353
Rhee, Syngman, 420
Rhine, Joseph Banks, 927, 1396
Rhine, Louisa, 927
Rhodes, Cecil, 444, 470; last will, 1331
Rhodesia, 443; Northern, see Zambia
Rhubarb, 1020
Rice, 1029
Rice-Davies, Mandy, 1246
Richard the Lion-Hearted, 492
Richard II of England, 513
Richard III Society, 1257
Richardson, Elliot, 257
Richelieu, Duc de, last will, 1327
Richthofen, Manfred von, 634
Ridley, Charles Price, 56
Ridout, Ronald, 74
Riedesel, Friedrich von, 125
Riegals, Roy, 1241
Rifle Match of 1874, 1164
Right to Bear Arms group, 1257
Rijn, Rembrandt van, 855
Rimbaud, Arthur, 887
Rintelen, Franz von, 649
Riots, Anti-Chinese of 1871, 190; Attica State
    Prison, 256; 1863 draft riots, 183; 1st U.S.,
    117; Race riots of 1943, 233; Race riots of
    1966, 251; Race riots of 1967, 252; Race riot
    of 1968, 254; summer of 1964, 249; Watts
    riot of 1965, 250
Ripley, George, 1426, 1428
Rivers, longest, 1231
Roanoke Colony, 1376
Robbers' loot, 742
Robbins, Shawn, 10
Roberson, James, court-martial of, 642
Robert, Henry Martyn, 1357
Roberts, Oral, 1283
Robert's *Rules of Order,* 754
Robeson, Paul, 896
"Robinson Crusoe," see Crusoe
Robinson v. Ketchel, 1152
Rockefeller, John D., 388; last will, 1332
Rockefeller, Michael, 405
Rockefeller, Nelson, Vice-President, 259
Rockefeller's children, 947
Rodin, François, 889
Roebling, John A., 919
Roerich, Nicholas K., 17
Roget's *Thesaurus,* 1357
Roha, see Lalibela
Rolfe, John, 106
Rolfe, Rebecca, see Pocahontas

Rolle, Andrew, 121
Roller Derby, 1st, 817
Roller skates, 1st, 913
Rolling Stones, 395
Rom, see Gypsies
Roman aqueducts, 917
Roman Catholicism, 1264
Romania, 444
Rome, 413; holy site, 1288
Romney, George, 123
Roosevelt, Eleanor Roosevelt, 296
Roosevelt, Elliott, 296
Roosevelt, Franklin D., 126, 295; last will, 1332
Roosevelt, Theodore, 273
Rosen, Fred, 1440
Rosenhan, D. L., 1088
Rosenkowitz sextuplets, 258
Rosenthal, Robert, 1089
Rose tree, 690
Rosetta stone, 483, 514
Ross, Charley, 192
Rostand, Jean, 27
"Rough Riders," 209, 273
Round Table, Knights of the, 733
Round the Moon, 670
"Roving" as an exercise, 70
Rowing oddities, 1220
Rowsome, Frank, Jr., 54
Rowson, Susanna, 144
Royadis, Emmanuel, 518
Royall, Anne, 264
Rubin, Jerry, 255
Ruby, Jack, 601
Rugby, N. Dak., 704
Rules of Order, 1357
Ruskin, John, 997
Russell, Bertrand, 1295
Russell, William, 1182
Russell, William Howard, 796
Russian Revolution, 515
Russo, Anthony, 256, 257
Russo-Japanese War, 416
Rutabaga, 1027
Ruth, George ("Babe"), 1194
Ruth, Kenneth, 1440
Rutt, Chris L., 353
Rwanda, 445
Rye, 1030
Ryukyu Islands, 417

Saba, 477
Sabah (North Borneo), 426
Sacco-Vanzetti case, 224
Sacher-Masoch, Leopold von, 991
Sade, Donatien de, 993, 1291; last will, 1328
Sadism, origin of word, 993
Safety pin, 1st, 914
Safety razor, 354
Safeway Stores, 446
Sagamore Hill, 273
Saguaros, largest, 690
St. Christopher, 475
St. Croix, 481
St. Eustatius, 477
St. Francis Dam, failure of, 560
Saint-Jean-Vianney, disappearance of, 553
St. John, 481
St. Kitts, 475
St. Louis Post-Dispatch, 784
St. Lucia, 482

St. Maarten, 477
Saints, U.S., 1298
St. Thomas, 481
St. Vincent, 482
Saladin, Sultan of Egypt, 492
Salazar, Antonio de Oliveira, 442
Salomé, 900
Salvador, Francis, 132
Salvation Army, 1276
Samizdat, 453
Samoa, American, 479; Western, 479
Sampson, Deborah, 139
San Blas Islands, 438
Sandage, Allan, 660
Sandburg, Carl, 755
Sandwich, Lord, 542, 766
Sandwich, origin of word, 766
Sane World Organization, 1257
San Francisco Chronicle, 784
San Francisco Earthquake, 546
San Juan Bautista, 443
San Juan Hill, 209
Sankey, Ira D., 1273
San Luis Rey, Bridge of, 918
San Marino, 479
San Simeon State Park, 715
Santa Claus, 1358
Santa Maria, search for, 735
"Santa Maria del Tule" (tree), 690
Santayana, George, 1293
São Tomé and Príncipe, 480
Sapodilla, 1020
Sarajevo, 504
Saratoga, battle of, 136; battlefield, 700
Sarazen, Gene, 1185
Sartre, Jean-Paul, 1294
Sasquatch, the, 1371
Satchidananda, Swami, 60
Satellites, 1st unmanned, 920; military, 662;
    unmanned, 661
"Saturday Night Massacre," 257
Saturday's Child, 1439
Saturn, planet, 657
Saudi Arabia, 447
Sauk Centre, 703
Saxe, Susan Edith, 613
Scarification, practice of, 383
Schacter, Stanley, 1089
Schipper, Kristofer, 74
Schliemann, Paul, 730
Schlumburger, William, 535
Schmidt, Maarten, 660
Schoeffer, Peter, 513
Scholl, William, 355
Scholl's foot aids, 355
School bus disaster, 566
School for Gallantry, 996
School of the Americas, 438
School That I'd Like, The, 64
Schopenhauer, Arthur, 1292
Schubert, Franz, 866
Schulmeister, Carl, 647
Schulz, Charles M., 31
Schwab, Michael, 41, 43, 44
Science and Technology, 908
Science fiction, chronological list of, 668; films,
    1253; hollow-earth theme, 693
Science Fiction Observatory, 668
Science for children, 68
Science . . . of Iridology, 66

Scientism (belief), 1270
Scientists, gallery of, 921
Scientist's creation theory, 1311
Scientology, see Church of Scientology
Scotch tape, 355
Scotland, 395
Scott, David, 675
Scott, Dred, 177
Scrabble, 356
Scrapbooks, valuable, 347
Sculptors, 888
Seaborn, Captain, pseud., 693
Seabrook, William, 1074
Seale, Bobby, 255
Séances, 1393; Lincoln's, 290
Sears, Roebuck catalogs, 346
Secoli, Babe, 1443
Secret of the Earth, 694
Sedan, battle of, 622
Seed, Suzanne, 1439
Seelos, Francis Xavier, 1303
Segretti, Donald, 256
Selassie, Haile, 387
Selcraig, Alexander, see Selkirk
Selenium, 1044
Self-examination for women, 1062
Self-publishing, 752
Selkirk, Alexander, 539
Selma-Montgomery march, 249
Senegal, 448
Separationists' Society, 1257
Separation of Church and State group, 1258
Sepoy Mutiny, 645
Septimius Severus, see Severus
Sequoias, largest, 690
Sequoyah, 107
Serios, Ted, 1396
Serra, Junipero, 1300
Servas Committee, Inc., 1258
Serviceman's Readjustment Act of 1944, 235
Serviss, Garret P., 671
Seton, Elizabeth, St., 1301
7 Natural Wonders, 689
Seven Pillars of Wisdom, 632
Severus, Lucius Septimius, 534
"Seward's Folly," 187
Sewing, 61
Sewing machine, 1st, 908
Sex, history of, 964
Sex education, 67
Sexism in Language, 771
Sex related terms, 970
Sex surveys, 976
Sextuplets born, 258
Seychelles, 480
Seymour, J., 694
Shackamaxon Society, Inc., 1258
Shadow out of Time, The, 694
Shainess, Natalie, 33
Shakers, attacks on in U.S., 155; founding of, 131
Shakespeare, William, 85, 883; last will, 1327;
    plays, spurious, 532; signatures, spurious, 531
Shallot, 1026
Shangri-La, 1424; guide to, 1065
Shapley, Harlow, 659
Sharjah, 481
"Shaver Mystery," 694
Shaw, Clay, 598
Shaw, George Bernard, 884, 1051; last will, 1333
"Shawnee Prophet," 110

Shaykh al-, family, 447
Sheldon, Charles M., 798
Sheldon, William H., 1060
Shelley, Percy Bysshe, 753, 1049
Shepard, Alan, 660, 674
Shepherd (vocation), 343
Sheraton hotels, 408
Sherman Anti-Trust Act, 200
Shestack, Melvin, 63
Shetland Islands, 394
She Wrote It, 859
Shiloh, battle of, 181
Shintoism, 1268
Shipton, Mother, *see* Sonthiel
Shirley, Myra Belle, 108
Shock, treatment for, 1410, 1412
Shockley, William, 961
Shoelace, 1st, 914
Shooting matches, 1164
Shooting oddities, 1220
Shore, Dinah, 818
Shore, Eddie W., 1187
Shot heard round the world, 132
Siddik, Abbe, 376
Siddons, Sarah, last will, 1329
SIECUS Report, 815
Sierra Leone, 448
Sightseeing in Your Own Neighborhood, 717
Sightseeing in the U.S., offbeat, 61
Signal Gas, 388
Sign language, 758
Sihanouk, Norodom, 372
Sikkim, 402, 404; *see also* India
"Silent Cal," 275
Silent Spring, 246
Silhouette, Étienne de, 767
Silverware, selling, 351
Simon, Simone, 1242
Sinatra, Frank, 896
Sinclair, Upton, 48, 754; *quoted,* 1052
Sinclair Lewis Newsletter, 815
Singapore, 449
Singer, Jerome E., 1089
Singers, offbeat, 905; operatic, 890; popular, 892
Sinkiang, 379
Sino-Japanese War, 416
Sioux War, 2nd, 194
Sirens of Titan, The, 672
Sirhan, Sirhan Bishara, 604
"Sit-ins," 244
Sitting Bull, death of, 202
Six Crises, 322, 323
16-State Nation, following 922
Skating oddities, 1220
Skelton, Red, 819
Skid Row and Its Alternatives, 1440
Skiing oddities, 1220
"Skipper Ireson's Ride," 150
Skylab, 661
Skylark of Space, The, 671
Skylark of Valeron, 671
SLA, 258
Slotnik, Jacob, 1441
Slovik, Eddie D., court-martial of, 642
Small Castle Owners club, 1258
Smaller than Baltimore, 471
Smith, Bessie, 897
Smith, E. E., 671
Smith, George, 356
Smith, Gerrit, 87

Smith, John, Captain, 105
Smith, Joseph, 1267; death of, 170
Smith, Kate, 907
Smith, Madeleine, 571
Smith, Miles, 497
Smith, Samuel Francis, 849
Smith Brothers cough drops, 355
Smithson, James, 702; last will, 1329
Smithsonian Institution, 702
Smoky God, The, 694
SNCC, 251
Snoopy (biography), 31
"Snowshoe Itinerant," 1271
Snyder, Ruth Brown, 580
Sobhuza II of Swaziland, 480
Soccer, history of, 1157; oddities, 1221; World Cup chronology, 1157
Social Destiny of Man, 1428
Socrates, death of, 488
Soda fountain, 1st U.S., 164, 914
"Soda pop," 1st, 914
Sodium, 1044
Soft drink, 1st, 914
Solar energy, 935
Solar system, 654
Solomon Islands, British, 480
Solresol, 750
Solzhenitsyn, Aleksandr, 456
Somalia (Somali Republic), 449
Somare, Michael, 438
Somnium, 668
Somoza Debayle, Anastasio, 433
Songs, stories behind, 848
Sonthiel, Ursula, 12
Sorge, Richard, 650
Sorghum, 1030
Souls of Black Folks, 211
Sour cream, 1036
South Africa, 450
South America, freeing of, 514
Southern Yemen, 468
South Vietnam, 467
South-West Africa, *see* Namibia
Southworth, E.D.E.N., Mrs., 701
Souvanna Phouma, 421
Soviet Union, *see* U.S.S.R.
Soybean, 1032
Space age, beginning of, 515
Space exploration, future, 662
Space flight, 1st, 245; 1st by female, 247; 1st on TV, 821; 1st U.S., 246; manned, 660
Space probes, unmanned, 661
Spaceship Earth, 1435
Space stations, 1st, 661
Spain, 453
Spanish-American War, 207, 441, 443
Spanish anarchist collectives, 1433
Spanish Civil War, 453
Spanish Influenza Epidemic, 547
Spanish Sahara, 480
Spartacus, 370; slave revolt, 512
Specialty Showman, 816
Species, extinct, 683
Spies, August, 40, 44; *quoted,* 41, 42, 44
Spies, female, 647, 648, 649, 651; 1st U.S., 93; international, 646
Spinach, 1026
Spinning Wheel, The, 352
Spirit of St. Louis, 224
Spiritual Healers group, 1258

Spiritualism, 1393
Spock, Benjamin, 1435
Spokeswoman, 815
Spooner, William A., 768
Spoonerism, origin of word, 768
Sports, 1131; money and, 1169; oddities, 1213; oddities, miscellaneous, 1222
Springer, Axel C., 797
Sprouts, growing, 1400
Sputnik, 1st, 921
Sputnik I, 515
Spy, The, 93
Squash, 1026
Sri Lanka, 454
Stagecoach robberies, 89
Stalingrad, 515
Stampa, La (Turin), 795
Stamps, selling, 351; valuable, 347
Standard Oil, 388; exposé of, 211
Stanford-Binet IQ test, 958
Stanley, Henry Morton, 470
Stanton, Elizabeth Cady, 52
Stapeldon, Olaf, 672
Starkweather, Charles, 585
Star Maker, 672
Starr, Belle, 108
Starr, Ringo, 893
Stars, facts about, 655
Statue of Liberty, 197
Stauffenberg, Claus von, 593
Steamboat, 1st, 908; 1st U.S., 149
Steam engine, 1st, 908, 918
Steiger, Brad, oddities from, 1344
Stephen of Blois, *quoted,* 492
Sterilization association, 1259
Steuben, Friedrich von, 636
Stevenson, Robert Louis, 521; last will, 1329
Stewart, Jackie, 1179
Stieber, William, 648
Stockton, Frank, 694
Stoker, Bram, 445, 1338
Stonehenge, 917, 1376
Stone Skipping Club, 1259
Storekeeping in the U.S., 73
Stover, Lloyd V., 27
Stowe, Harriet Beecher, 175
Stowe, Mary L., 127
Stranger in a Strange Land, 673
Stratton, Charles S., 109
Strawberry, 1017
"Streaking," 1st, 964
Street vendor (vocation), 344
Strikes, Auto workers', of 1937, 391; Auto workers', of 1972, 256; Cloakmakers', of 1890, 201; 1st general, 195; 1st U.S., 149; Miners', of 1891, 202; Miners', of 1892, 203; Miners', of 1914, 217; Railroad, of 1886, 198; Railroad, of 1894, 205; Steelworkers', of 1892, 203; Students', of 1968, 254; Students', of 1969, 254; Teachers', of 1968, 254; Textile workers', of 1912, 216; Textile workers', of 1929, 225; United Mine Workers', of 1894, 205
Strikes of 1934, 227; of 1937, 228
Student Non-Violent Coordinating Committee, *see* SNCC
Stroessner, Alfredo, 439
Suarez, Hugo Banzer, 369
Subliminal advertising, 812
Submarine, 1st, 908; 1st U.S., 632
Subways, 1st U.S., 189

Sudan, 454
Suez Canal, 385
Sugar, 1010; sources of, 381, 471
Suharto, T. N. J., 405
Suicide notes, 1324
Suicides, 1st on TV, 258; list of, 1320, 1324
Sukarno, Achmed, 404; *quoted,* 405
Sulfur, 1045
Sullivan, Ed, 817
Sullivan, John L., 1166
Sulzberger, Arthur Ochs, 783
Sun and stars, facts about, 655
Sun City, Ariz., creation of, 244
Sunday, William ("Billy"), 1274
Sunflowers, 858
Superman, biography, 1234
Superpower, 70
Supersonic flight, 1st, 238
Superstitions, common, 1091
Surfing oddities, 1221
Surinam, 480
Survival, 62; equipment, 1404; in the city, 1399; techniques, 101
Surviving in the wild, 1403, 1404
Survivors, 1399
Survivors of American History in Foreign Lands, 118
Survivors of American History in the U.S.A., 123
Survivors of Surgery club, 1258
Suspended animation, 666
Swaziland, 480
Sweden, 455
Swedenborg, Emanuel, 1049
"Sweet Adeline," 96, 851
Sweet potato, 1027
Swimming oddities, 1221
Swindles, greatest, 1340
Swiss chard, 1022
Switzerland, 456; exiles in, 456
Syllabaries, Amerind, 107
Symbionese Liberation Army, *see* SLA
Symmes, John Cleves, 692
Symposium on Utopia, 1435
Symzonia, 693
Symzonia: A Voyage of Discovery, 694
Syndics of the Drapers' Guild, The, 855
Syria, 456
Syrup, maple, 1033

Tachen Islands, 458
Tachistoscope, 812
Tadzhik, 451
Taft, Nellie Herron, 274
Taft, William Howard, 273
Taiwan, 457
Taj Mahal, 918
Tamarind, 1021
Tammany Hall, 103, 104
Tammany Society, start of, 141
Tanganyika, 458
Tangerine, 1021
"Tania," 258
Tanzania, 458
Taoism, 1263
"Taps" bugle call, origin, 182
Tar and feathering, "recipe" for, 129
Tarbell, Ida, 211
Tardé, Gabriel, 694
Tarzan, biography, 1237

Tarzan at the Earth's Core, 694
Tarzan of the Apes, 671
Tausch, Karl, last will, 1334
Taylor, Erika, 1439
Taylor, Isaac, *quoted,* 485
Taylor, Margaret Mackall, 267
Taylor, Theodore B., 69
Taylor, Zachary, 173, 266
Teaching Stories, 961
Teaching stories, 1097, 1415
Tecumseh, 110
Tekakwitha, Kateri, 1300
Telegraph, 1st, 170, 909
Telepathy, 1387
Telephone, 1st, 909
Telephone Users' Assn., 1259
Telescope, 1st, 908
Television, 1st, 909; *see also* TV
Temperance crusaders, 87, 102
Templeton Foundation Prize, 1130
Ten Commandments, 512
Tennessee Valley Authority, *see* TVA
Tennis greats, 1188
Tennis oddities, 1221
Tennyson, Alfred, *quoted,* 734
Tenskwautawa, 110
Tereshkova, Valentina, 247, 660
Terkel, Studs, 1438, 1443, 1444
Terra firma, *see* Earth
Terrestrial life, unfamiliar, 2970
Terry, Megan, 1443
Tesla, Nikola, 928
Tet Offensive, 253
Tetzel, Johann, 495
Thailand, 459
Thanksgiving Day, U.S., 160
Thayer, Ernest Lawrence, 200
Thélème, Abbey of, 526, 1419
Théorie des quatre mouvements, 1421
Thermopylae, battle of, 615
Thessaly, 396
38-State Nation, following 546
This Hideous Strength, 672
Thomas, Bill, 61
Thomas, Dylan, 1073
Thoreau, Henry D., 172
Thoreau Society, 1259
Thorpe, James ("Jim"), 1193, 1198
Thoughtography, 1396
Thrace, 396
Thucydides, *quoted,* 487
Thumb, Tom, 109
Tibbets, Paul, Jr., 507
Tibet, 378
Tichborne, Roger C., 955
Tidal waves, 545, 546
Tilden, William T., II, 1191
Tillamook Forest Fire, 548
Tiller, Katherine, 1444
Tilton, Theodore, 192
Timaeus, 729
Time-Life Books, 955
Time Machine, The, 672
Times, The (London), 795
Timetables, Cook's, 723
Time travel, 1381
Timor, Portuguese, 481
"Tippecanoe and Tyler Too," 266
Tippit, J. D., 601
Tired Dragons, 67

Tires, 1st automobile, 911
Titanic, sinking of, 558
Titanic Society, 1259
Titian, 854
Tito, Marshal, *see* Broz, Josip
Tobacco, 1st French use of, 765
Tobago, 460
Togo, 460
Toilet paper, 1st, 914
Toilets, 1st, 919
Tokelau Islands, 478
"Tokyo Rose," 239
Tolstoi, Leo, 16, 880, 1050
Tomato, 1026; history of, 1053
Tombstone, Ariz., 712
Tone, Wolfe, 1320
Tonga, 481
Tools, selling, 351
Toothbrush, 1st, 914
Toothpaste tube, 1st, 915
Tootsie Roll, 356
Topeka Capital, 798
Toro, 462
Torresola, Griselio, 597
Torrijos, Omar, 437
Tortola, 481
Tory Descendants in Nova Scotia, 118
Touré, Ahmed Sekou, 397
Tourniquets, use of, 1408
Tour of U.S. historical sites, 700
Tours, battle of, 616
Toussaint L'Ouverture, Pierre Dominique, 398, 399
Townsend, Claire, 59
Townsend Plan, 227
Toys, valuable, 349
Track and field greats, 1191
Track and field oddities, 1221
Trademark, definition of, 82; how to get, 83, 85
Trademarks, American, 353
Trafalgar, battle of, 620
Train robberies, Reno gang, 742
Tranquilizer, 1st, 915
TransAmerica Corporation, 367
Transatlantic cable, 1st, 909
Transcaucasia, 1067
Transistor, 1st, 910
Transjordan, 418
Transylvania, 444
Traore, Moussa, 426
Travel and Leisure, 341
Traveler's Guide to Europe, 723
Travelers in Space, 660
Travelogue, 1st, 99
Travels of Marco Polo, 513
Treasure, buried, 1378; *see also* Buried Treasure
Treasure Hunter's Guild, 1257
Treasure Mountain gold, 743
Treaty of Ghent, 154
Treaty of Westphalia, 456
Tree, largest, 690; oldest, 690; tallest, 690; widest, 690
Trenton, battle of, 124
Treves, Frederick, 537
Trevor-Roper, Patrick, 59
"Tricky Dick," 319
Trinidad and Tobago, 460
Tripolitania, 423
Tripping in America, 61
Tri-State Trader, 352

Trojan War, 512
Trotsky, Léon, 515
Trouser fly, 1st, 915
Trucial States, *see* United Arab Emirates
Truman, Bess Wallace, 302
Truman, Harry S, 302; assassination attempt, 596
Truman, Margaret, *see* Daniel
Tshombe, Moise, 470
Tucker, George, 669
Tunisia, 461
Tupamaro guerrillas, 465, 606
Turbojet engine, 1st, 909
Turk (chess player), 535
Turkey, 462
Turkmen, 451
Turner, James, last will, 1329
Turner, Nat, 162
Turnip, 1027
Turtle, 1st U.S. submarine, 632
Turtles International, 1259
Tutankhamen, tomb of, 222
TV, African, 823; Australian, 823; British, 824; Canadian, 824; Chinese, 824; Dutch, 826; Eastern Europe, 824; father of, 816; French, 825; German, 825; Italian, 825; Japanese, 825; Latin American, 826; Middle East, 826; Scandinavian, 826; U.S.S.R., 826; years 1925 to 1975, 816
TVA, 299
TV around the world, 823
TV commercials, 32
TV in The Netherlands, 432
Twain, Mark, 186
Twain, Mark, *see also* Clemens, Samuel
Tweed, "Boss," *see* Tweed, William M.
Tweed, William M., trial of, 189
Tyler, John, 265
Tyler, Julia Gardiner, 266
Tyler, Letitia Christian, 266
Tyler, Wat, 513
Typewriter, 1st, 909
Typhoid Mary, 212

UAW, recognition of, 228
UFOs, 693, 1374
Uganda, 462
Ukraine, 451
Umbrella, 1st, 915
Umm al-Qaiwain, 481
UN, founding of, 515; 1st session of, 238
"Uncle Sam," *see* Wilson, Samuel
Uncle Tom's Cabin, 175
Underground Man, 694
Underground presses, U.S.S.R, 453
Underground Railroad, 166
Under the Moons of Mars, 671
UNESCO, 456
UNICEF, 456
Unicorn Hunters, 1259
Unicorns, Ltd., 1259
Unidentified Flying Objects, *see* UFOs
Unilever Group, 463
United Arab Emirates, 481
United Automobile workers, *see* UAW
United Brands Co., 399, 415
United Church of Christ, 1268
United Nations Educational, Scientific and Cultural Organization, *see* UNESCO
United Nations International Children's

Emergency Fund, *see* UNICEF
United States of America, *see* U.S.
Universe—Spaced Out, 654
Unknown and Mysterious, 1364
Upper Volta, 464
Uranus, planet, 657
Uri, John, 694
Urinary infections, 1064
Uruguay, 465
U.S., description of, 70, 1085; economic statistics, 79; geographical center, 704; how created, 464; public opinion in, 827; quiz about, 76; travel in, 70; 2000 A.D. (utopia), 1422
U.S.A., The Presidency, 261; Red, White and True, 76; Year by Year, 129
U.S. Camel Corps, 625
U.S. Census Bureau, 78
U.S. Government in Action, 79
U.S. heroes, biographies, 72
U.S. history, Great Plains, 53
U.S. Patent System Today, 82
U.S. Population, 1770, 129; 1780, 138; 1790, 143; 1800, 146; 1810, 150; 1820, 156; 1830, 161; 1840, 167; 1850, 174; 1860, 180; 1870, 189; 1880, 195; 1890, 200; 1900, 209; 1910, 215; 1920, 221; 1930, 226; 1940, 229; 1950, 239; 1960, 244
U.S. Presidents, "1st woman," 293; *see also* specific President
U.S. prison, Alcatraz, 713
U.S.S. *Dolphin,* 627
U.S.S.R, 451; industrialization of, 453; invasion of, by Hitler, 515; religion in, 452; repression in, 452; underground press in, 453; women in, 452
U.S. Trust Territory of the Pacific Islands, *see* Micronesia
Utopia, 1418
Utopia, symposium on, 1435
Utopias, attempted, 168, 1425; fictional, 1418; pirate, 1434
"U-2 incident," 650
Uzbek, 451

Vacuum cleaner, 1st, 915
Vaginal infections, 1063
Valentino, Rudolph, 877
Vallandigham, Clement L., 112
Vampires, 445, 1337
Van Buren, Martin, 264
Vanderbilt, Cornelius, 194
Varanasi, holy site, 1290
Vardon, Harry, 1185
Vare, Glenna Collett, 1185
Vatel (chef), 1045
Vathek, 519
Vatican City, 481
Vaughan, Alan, 10
Vecelli, Tiziano, *see* Titian
Veeck, William L., 1173
Vega, Lope de, 905
Vegetables, directory of, 1021
Vegetarianism, 1048
Vegetarians, famous, 1048
Velikovsky, Immanuel, 929
Venezuela, 466
Venice, 413
Venus, planet, 656
Venus of Urbino, 854
Verlaine, Paul, 1072

Verne, Jules, 670, 693
Versailles, map of, 1383; time travel to, 1381
Verse by the Side of the Road, 54
Vesco, Robert, 381
Vesey, Denmark, 157
Vespucci, Amerigo, 493; *quoted,* 494
Vespucius, Americus, *see* Vespucci
Vest, George Graham, 1361
Vesuvius, eruption of, 543
Viet Minh, 466
Vietnam, 466
Vietnam Moratorium Day, 255
Vietnam War, 327
Vilcabamba, 1069
Vilcapampa, *see* Machu Picchu
Villa, Francisco "Pancho," 122, 218
Village Voice; The, 1435
Vinci, Leonardo da, 853
"Vinland," 436
Virgil, last will, 1326
Virgin Gorda, 481
Virginia whiskey cake, recipe for, 145
Virgin Islands, 481
Visual abnormalities, 59
Vitamins, directory of, 1038
Vivisection, anti, 1249
Vlad Tepes, 445, 1338
Vocations, unusual, 343
Voices of Brooklyn, 1444, 1445
Volapük, 750
Volcanoes, 543, 544; Hawaii, 716; *see also* Mount Pelée
Volcano Islands, 478
Voltaire, 669
Voluntary Sterilization, Inc., 1259
Vonnegut, Kurt, Jr., 672
Vortigern, 532
Vostok I, 660
Voyage en Icarie, 1421
Voyage to the Moon (1657), 668
Voyage to the Moon (1827), 669
Voyage to the Sun, 669
Voyage to the World of Cartesius, 669
Vulcanization of rubber, 167

Wagner, Richard, 867
Wake Island, 478
Waldseemüller, Martin, 493
Wales, 395
Walkers, professional, 1175
Wallace, Alfred Russel, 501
Wallace, George C., 256; assassination attempts, 607
Wallace, Irving, 45, 1435, 1446
Wallace, William Herbert, 581
Wallachia, 444
Wallechinsky, David, 1435, 1446
Wall Street Journal, The, 786
Walnuts, 1028
Walsh, Stella, 1193
Wanderings, 540
Wandrei, Donald, 671
War, 615; shortest in history, 646; Waziristan, 646
War correspondents, 1st, 796
Ward, Stephen, 1246
Wardwell, Pamela, 1443
War of the Cricket Match, 645
War of the Fleeing Wife, 645
War of Jenkins' Ear, 644

War of the Oaken Bucket, 644
War of the Spanish Succession, 644
War of the Stray Dog, 646
War of the Triple Alliance, 439
War of the Whiskers, 644
War of the Worlds, 670, 672
Warren, Charles, 575
Warren, Earl, 319, 305
Warren, Josiah, 1429
Warren, Lavinia, 110
Warren, Lingan A., 446
Warren *Report,* 598
Wars started by small incidents, 644
Washington, George, 113, 278; last will, 1328
Washington, Martha Dandridge, 279
Washington Post, The, 257, 786
Washington's "Farewell Address," 145
Washington Spectator, 815
Washkansky, Louis, 516
Watauga Association, 130
Watel, Fritz, *see* Vatel
Water, body's need for, 1045
Water closets, 1st, 919
Watercress, 1027
"Watergate," 257, 258, 327, 787
Waterloo, battle of, 620
Watermelon, 1019
Waterton, Charles, 540
Water witching, 1397
Watson, T. J., Sr., 406, 407
"Waxhaws, The," 264
Wayne, Henry, 625
Waziristan War, 646
WCTU, 102; founding of, 192
Weapons, weird, 625
Weather, *see* Climate
Weathermen, (radical group), 613
Webb, Del, 244
Webb, Jack, 818
Webb, Matthew, 1176
Webster, Noah, 140, 149, 160
Wecter, Dixon, 72
Weems, Mason Locke, 113
Weidman, Eugen, 583
Weiss, Carl, 592
Weiss, Myra Tanner, 127
Welch, Ola-Florence, 320
Welk, Lawrence, 819
Welles, Orson, 671, 715
Wellington, Duke of, last will, 1330
Wells, Herbert George, 670, 671, 672
Welt, Die (Hamburg), 797
Wesley, John, 1270
Western Samoa, *see* Samoa
West Gate Bridge Collapse, 565
West Germany, 392
Westminster Confession, 1266
Weston, Edward Payson, 1175
"Wetbacks," 428
Wethered, Joyce, 1186
What Bothers Us about Grownups, 1445
What Do You Know about the U.S.?, 76
What's Out There?, 663
Wheat, 1030
"Wheatland," 268
Wheeled vehicles, 1st, 916
Wheeler, Margaret, 67
When Worlds Collide, 672
"Where Did I Come From?," 67
Whey, 1036

Whirling dervishes, 462
Whiskey Rebellion, 144, 281
Whistler, Anna McNeill, 941
Whistler, James, 941
Whistler's Mother, 941
White, James, 673
Whitechapel Murders, 575
"White Christmas," 851
Whitman, Walt, 753
Whitmore, Terry, 1445
Whitney, Eli, 144
Whittier, John Greenleaf, 150, 701
Who's Who of Military Brass, 630
Why England Slept, 310
Wickman, Carl Eric, 354
Wilde, Oscar, 196
Wild Horse Assistance, 1260
Wildlife Defenders, 1260
Wilhelmshaven mutiny, 641
Wilkes, John, 541
"Wilkes and Liberty," 542
William the Conqueror, last will, 1327
Williams, Nick, 780
Wills, famous, 1326; most beautiful, 1360
Wills, Mary, 1443
Wilson, Edith Bolling, 274, 293
Wilson, Samuel, 768
Wilson, Woodrow, 274, 293
Wilson, Wyoming, 1438
Winchester, Sarah, 712
Winchester House, 712
Windward Islands, 482
Winstanley, Gerrard, 1420
Winter Soldier Investigation, 1440
Withholding Tax Act, 233
Wit of Wilson Mizner, 773
Wittenberg, 494
Wizard of Oz Club, 1260
"Wobblies," 212
Wollstonecraft, Mary, 514
Woman's Bible, 52
Woman's liberation, 53, 72
Woman's Own Name Center, 1260
Woman's rights convention, 1st, 174
Women's Christian Temperance Union, *see* WCTU
Women's rights, 514
Wonders of the World, 7 Natural, 689
Wonder Woman, biography, 1235
Wood, Grant, 904
Wood, Robert E., 65
Woodcraft, 101
Woodhull, Victoria C., 128
Woodstock rock concert, 255
Word, The, 1435
Word origins, 759, 760, 769
Words, longest, 748
Words Commonly Misspelled, 769
Workers, The, 1442, 1443
Working, 1438, 1443, 1444
Works Progress Administration, *see* WPA
World Future Society, 1260
World History, 483
World Nations, 360
World records, 51
Worlds in Collision, 929

World's Columbian Exposition, 204
World through Blunted Sight, 59
Worm Ouroboros, The, 671
Would You Believe It?, oddities from, 1349
Wounded Knee, occupation of, 257
Wounded Knee Massacre, 202
Wounds, treatment of, 1409
WPA, 299
Wrestling oddities, 1222
Wright, Frances, 1426
Wright, Mickey, 1186
Wyatt, James, 519
Wycliffe, John, 496
Wylie, Philip, 672
Wynne, Arthur, 1170

Xerox, 1st, 909
X ray, 1st, 909

Yachting oddities, 1220
Yale, Linus, 912
Yalta Conference, 299, 300
Yam, 1027
Yameogo, Maurice, 465
Yankees (N.Y.), 1135
"Yellow Kid," 206
Yemen, 467
Yeti, 1348
Yezo, Ann Marie, 127
Yi King, see I-Ching
YMCA, 1st U.S., 175
Yoga, 60
Yogurt, 1036; preparing, 1400
Yòshikawa, Takeo, 653
"You Can't Build an Ark in Mendocino County," 733
Young, Brigham, 1268; last will, 1330
Young, Vaughn, 37
Younger, Cole, 108
Young Men's Christian Association, *see* YMCA
Youville, Marie M., d', 1300
Yugoslavia, 468
Yurick, Sol, 1444, 1445

Zaharias, Mildred ("Babe"), 1193
Zaharoff, Basil, last will, 1332
Zaire, 469
Zambia, 470
Zamenhof, Ludwig, 748
Zanzibar, 458
Zapata, Emiliano, 428
Zapruder, Abraham, 598
Zapruder film, 598
Zatopek, Emil, 1194
Zelle, Margaretha G., *see* Mata Hari
Zero Auto Growth group, 1260
Zero Factor, 126
Zero Population Growth, Inc., 1261
Zimbabwe, *see* Rhodesia
Zimbabwe temple, 1379
Zimbardo, Philip G., 1088
"Zimmerman Note," 219
Zinc, 1045
Zion, *see* Israel
Zipper, 1st, 915
Zoroastrianism, 1263

Update

Various last-minute happenings are here appended to keep *The People's Almanac* as accurate and timely as possible.

Chapter 4   U.S.A.—Year by Year

1975. MAY 12. A U.S. container ship, the S.S. *Mayagüez,* was seized by Cambodians 7 mi. from the Wai Islands in the Gulf of Siam. The Cambodians, who had fired upon or captured 25 other ships and fishing boats in the same area 10 days before this, were probably trying to lay claim to the islands. Although previous Cambodian governments had announced a 12-mi. limit to their territorial waters, the U.S. now considered anything beyond 3 mi. from shore to be international waters. Because the U.S. had recently and ignominiously retreated from Cambodia and Vietnam, President Ford very likely wanted to show the world the U.S. still had military clout. Immediately, President Ford ordered the Pentagon to launch a retaliatory attack. On May 14, U.S. planes sank 3 Cambodian gunboats. At 7:07 P.M. of that day, the Cambodian radio announced that the captive ship would be released. At about the same time, U.S. Marines invaded Tang Island and boarded the deserted *Mayagüez.* As American pilots bombed mainland Cambodia, a boat carrying the 39 released members of the *Mayagüez* crew approached the U.S. destroyer *Wilson.* At 11:08 P.M., President Ford learned that the crew members were safe. Thirty-five minutes later, U.S. pilots bombed the mainland again. When the fighting finally ended, 38 American lives had been sacrificed to liberate the 39 *Mayagüez* crew members. President Ford's popularity rose 11% in the public opinion polls.

MAY 17. The U.S. Coast Guard boarded the Polish trawler *Kalmar* and forced it to shore in San Francisco for straying 2 mi. within the U.S.'s 12-mi. limit. The ship and crew were held under armed guard until the Polish Government paid a $350,000 fine to the U.S.

Chapter 7   World Nations and People

MALAGASY REPUBLIC. On February 5, 1975, President Ramanantsoa was overthrown by Col. Riciard Ratsimandrava. Six days later, the colonel was assassinated. Despite a very active political year, the most dominant force in the Malagasy Republic is still a highland elite group known as "the 48 families."

MOZAMBIQUE. When Mozambique became independent of Portuguese political control on June 25, 1975, the man who assumed the office of President was Samora Moises Machel, a 41-year-old ex-guerrilla soldier from a peasant family.

NIGERIA. While traveling outside the country, the nation's leader, Gen. Yokubu Gowon, was overthrown by a military coup on July 29, 1975, but most of the people in Nigeria were unaffected by this change of government.

CAPE VERDE ISLANDS. Cape Verde became independent on July 5, 1975, but the ruling Party for Independence of Guinea-Bissau and Cape Verde has plans to unite the two areas into a single nation. There are more Cape Verdeans living abroad than there are in Cape Verde, including about 250,000 dwelling in the United States.

COMORO ISLANDS. On August 3, 1975, President Abdallah was deposed by a group wanting closer ties to France. The coup occurred 2 days after Abdallah had ordered French police forces and government officials to leave the islands as soon as possible.

Chapter 11   Universe—Spaced Out   Travelers in Space

On July 17, 1975, at 12:09 P.M. (EDT) the twain finally met when the U.S. Apollo and the Soviet Union Soyuz spaceships touched one another 140 mi. above the Atlantic Ocean. The linkup of the 2 ships took place through use of a connecting docking module. Two orbits of the earth later, the 3 American astronauts and 2 Russian cosmonauts were shaking hands, exchanging gifts (the American present was Conway Twitty's recording in Russian of his country-western song "Hello Darlin' "), and sitting down to lunch.

Chapter 14   Communications   In the Tower of Babel

According to revised 1975 estimates, the 10 major languages of the world and the number of speakers for each are: Chinese—800 million; English—300 million; Spanish—200 million; Russian—190 million; Hindi—180 million; Bengali—120 million; Arabic—115 million; and Portuguese, German, and Japanese—100 million each.

Chapter 16   The Arts—Lively and Otherwise
The 25 All-Time Box Office Champion Films

Jaws (Spielberg/Zanuck-Brown/Univ. 1975) $80,000,000.

Chapter 19   Love and Sexuality
Uncensored Highlights in the History of Sex

1975—City officials in Vienna, Austria, banned married women from becoming prostitutes. Only single or divorced women could legally practice prostitution, according to the new edict.

Chapter 20   Health and Well-Being   Leading Vegetarians

Some well-known vegetarians of today include film and TV performers Cloris Leachman, Dennis Weaver, and James Coburn; author Will Durant; violinist Yehudi Menuhin; musician George Harrison; and basketball players Bill Walton and Neal Walk.

Chapter 22   Honors   The Nobel Prize Awards

PHYSICS. 1974. *Behind the Award*—On March 21, 1975, speaking in Montreal, noted British astronomer Sir Fred Hoyle stated that the 1974 Nobel physics award given to Antony Hewish, of Cambridge University, for his discovery of pulsars in outer space, was a mistake, that the real discovery had been made by Hewish's assistant, Jocelyn Bell Burnell, who went unrecognized. Hewish, admitting he was "angry" about Hoyle's allegation, called it "untrue." Embarrassed, Mrs. Burnell said Hoyle had "drastically exaggerated the situation."

Chapter 23   All in Sport   Golf

On August 10, 1975, golfer Jack Nicklaus won the PGA championship. It was his 16th major tournament victory, and a world's record.

Chapter 26   Keeping the Faith: Religion   Prophets of the Word

The Rev. Carl McIntire announced plans for a new attraction in Cape Canaveral. As a display piece, he brought in 40 Vietnamese refugees to live in a simulated Vietnamese village "like our boys went into during the war."

Chapter 27   Passing On—the Final Trip   Where There's a Will

JAMES KIDD, Arizona Hermit and Miner; Died: 1956
Last Will: Kidd disappeared in 1949, and was declared dead in 1956. Seven years later, his handwritten will was discovered accidentally. The will stated, "After my funeral expenses have been paid and $100 given to some preacher of the Gospel to say farewell at my grave, sell all my property [which amounted to over $275,000] and have this balance money go in a research for some scientific proof of a soul of a human body which leaves at death." From around the world, 137 petitions came from persons and organizations seeking Kidd's legacy. His money was finally awarded to The American Society for Psychical Research of New York City in 1971. The Society concentrated its effort on recording the deathbed experiences of people in the United States and India. The group's final report, filed in June, 1975, said that dying might be one of the most exciting experiences of life, one of "incredible freedom, harmony and wholeness." But the Society was unable to produce what Kidd most desired: a photograph of the soul leaving the human body.

Chapter 29   The Unknown and Mysterious   Astral Projection

On June 3, 1975, Robert Antoszczyk, who taught yoga at the YMCA in Ann Arbor, Mich., was found dead after experimenting with astral projection. He had been alone in his room. The coroner's report attributed his death to an overdose of cocaine, but his friends and family firmly stated that Antoszczyk did not take drugs. One theory is that he had entered into such a deep trance that his heart slowed to the point where it no longer sent enough blood to his brain to sustain life.